D0765469

SECOND EDITION

THE INTERNATIONAL MOTOR RACING GUIDE

A Complete Reference from Formula One to NASCAR

PETER HIGHAM

DAVID BULL PUBLISHING

Library of Congress Control Number: 2002105027

ISBN: 1 893618 20 X

David Bull Publishing, logo, and colophon are trademarks of David Bull Publishing, Inc.

Book and cover design: Tom Morgan, Blue Design, Portland, Maine

Printed in the United States

10 9 8 7 6 5 4 3 2 1

David Bull Publishing
4250 East Camelback Road
Suite K150
Phoenix, AZ 85018

602-852-9500

602-852-9503 (fax)

www.bullpublishing.com

CONTENTS

3

Introduction

1951 Consalvo Sanesi suffers the rain which prematurely stopped the 1951 International Trophy at Silverstone.

In the years since the first edition of the International Motor Racing Guide appeared, I've sometimes been asked why I chose to write a reference book of such scope. Why not concentrate on a particular series like Formula 1, NASCAR or IndyCar racing?

The most obvious answer is that there are already plenty of good books that limit themselves to a single series. But more importantly, I believe that a full appreciation of any type of racing requires a wider perspective. Even if you follow only one series closely, it helps to understand what's happened elsewhere in the motorsports world. To a fan solely obsessed by the Formula 1 World Championship, for example, Juan Pablo Montoya's career so far amounts to little more than two promising seasons. But within the broader context of the IMRG, the true fan can review the Montoya story in its entirety—from his successful foundation in the F3000 and CART championships and his remarkable 2000 win at the Indy 500.

Montoya is the most recent example of a versatile driver who has excelled in more than one major international category. Others to have succeeded in more than one category include some of the greatest names in racing history: Mario Andretti, Jim Clark, A.J. Foyt, Dan Gurney, Jacky Ickx, Nigel Mansell, Stirling Moss, Tazio Nuvolari, and Jacques Villeneuve to name a few. The IMRG puts the world of international motor racing in context, and provides everything you need to know about the careers of motor racing's greatest and not so great drivers, the circuits where they raced, and all major events and championships past and present.

That said, the IMRG does have some boundaries. I've limited myself to four-wheeled vehicles and circuit racing. Both motorcycle racing and rallying are distinct disciplines and separate books would be required to do these sports justice.

The need for a comprehensive guide to motor racing first occurred to me more than twenty years ago. Having just graduated from university, I spent the year travelling Europe, attending as many Grands Prix as I could before my funds ran out. For me, the events of that season would summon up the widest range of emotions imaginable. There was the bitter disappointment of the San Marino GP, boycotted by the Formula One Constructors' Association in a squabble over weight rules. There was the disbelieving horror

of Zolder, where I watched from the corner as Gilles Villeneuve crashed in practice for the Belgian GP. And there was the jubilation of seeing my hero Elio de Angelis win in Austria, among the closest finishes in Grand Prix history.

That season also sparked my desire to learn as much as possible about all types of motor racing. In fact, you might say that the original inspiration for the IMRG came from the late Jim Crawford, who was favoured to win the 1982 British F1 Championship. I had read in *Autosport* that Crawford had previously done a couple of Grands Prix and I wanted to know more. I bought the *Marlboro Guide to Grand Prix Racing*, assuming I had found a complete reference source comparable to those covering other sports. Unfortunately, I soon found that it only published details on drivers who had scored Grand Prix points. I was frustrated first by Crawford's omission, and then by the book's lack of depth and concentration on one element of the sport. And so the search for an all-encompassing reference book to the sport began. That search ended when I decided to write my own book, one that covers all aspects of a driver's career in every international racing category from F3 on up.

In addition to the drivers, I've also charted the changing shape of the world's leading circuits in the Racing Around the World section. It's impressive to watch a driver round Monte Carlo's Tabac corner and remember all the stars who have treaded that same stretch of pavement since 1929. The same is true for other hallowed sections of track, such as Turn 1 at Indy or Daytona, Spa's Eau Rouge, or the pits straight at Le Mans. Details of national champions and major race winners complete the story. No other source book reflects the complete and rich traditions of the world's most intriguing sport. The IMRG chronicles the heroes of all forms of international motor racing and the venues where they plied their trade.

As much as motor racing is about tradition, it also is about change: changes in speed, technology, teams, drivers, and locations. Inevitably, looking back over the sport's history reminds us that life is in a constant state of flux. The same weekend in 1982 that Gilles died in Belgium a young Ayrton Senna was emerging in the supporting Formula Ford 2000 Championship as a star of the future. Since then

Senna too has come and gone in a spectacular career cut short by tragedy.

But even in the face of such devastating losses, the sport itself always seems to come back stronger than ever. When I finished the first edition of the IMRG in 1994, Michael Schumacher had just captured his first championship. Since then the German has gone on to equal Juan Manuel Fangio's record five World Championship victories. In the United States, NASCAR's Winston Cup has become more popular than ever despite losing its greatest star, Dale Earnhardt, at Daytona in 2001.

Who can say where we'll be by the time I start thinking about a third edition? Until then, I hope this book will add to your enjoyment of the sport and will help chart the arrival of the sport's next star.

Acknowledgements

Updating this book has been an enjoyable and rewarding task, and I have received vital information and help from various individuals and organisations. As with the first edition I am indebted to the staff and correspondents of Haymarket Magazines' various motor racing titles for their knowledge and help.

Also, special thanks to Beth Agan at the Indy Racing League, Simon Arron, Jaimes Baker, Mark Braddel, Patricia Brault, Peter Burroughs, Lito Calvalcanti, Joao Cunca at forix.com, Donald Davidson at the Indianapolis Motor Speedway, Pierre Deshormes at Chimay, Fiona Fallon, Laurence Foster, Peter Foubister, Ian France, Andy Hallbery, David Hayhoe and the Grand Prix Database, Henry Hope-Frost, Tim Jackson of Renault UK, Matt James, Bruce Jones, Gordon Kirby, Ben Martin, Carl McKellar at Grovewood PR, Wolfgang Neumayer at formel3guide.com, Chris Nixon, Martin Nott, Peter Nygaard, Mark Piedade, John Pulford at Brooklands Motor Museum, Fabio Ravaioli, Nigel Roebuck, Tony Schulp, Paul and Betty Sheldon of the Formula One Register, Marcus Simmons, Damien Smith, Quentin Spurring, Jiro Takahashi, Steven Tee, Johnny Tingle, Tege Tornvall, Gary Watkins, Antonio Watson, Mike Weston, Tim Wright, and John Zimmermann for answering specific and less specific questions. Also many thanks to the photographers of LAT Photographic past and present for the images.

I have been very fortunate for the faith and enthusiasm of David Bull, and for the skill of his team—especially James Penhune, Anna Gilbert, and Tom Morgan—in turning a raw manuscript into the finished article. Thanks also to Angela Barosso and Rachel Bernstein. No one understands taking an idea to the printed page better than my father Adrian, and his help—from taking me to my first race to proofreading yet again—has been vital. It would be impossible to write a single word without the complete support and understanding of my extended and immediate family. Especially to Francoise, Luc, and Joe—thank you for making this possible.

2000 Michael Schumacher scored Ferrari's first drivers' World Championship since 1979 and started an era of domination for the team.

Abbreviations

Race results

The top 6 results published in the F1, and in subsequent categories, include the following information: position, driver, car, laps completed, time (for cars on the lead lap)/reason for retirement. The following details are given when only a list of race winners is given in the championship sections: date, race title, circuit, winner, nationality, car and speed in miles per hour.

Nationality/Grands Prix

A . . . . .Austria	DR Dominican Republic	INT . . . . . .International	PA . . . . .Panama	SK . . . . .Slovakia
AND . . . . .Andorra	DZ . . . . .Algeria	IRL . . . . .Ireland	PAC . . . . . . .Pacific GP	SLO . . . . .Slovenia
ARM . . . . .Armenia	E . . . . .Spain	IS . . . . .Iceland	PE . . . . .Peru	SU . . . . . .Soviet Union
AUS . . . . .Australia	EAK . . . . .Kenya	J . . . . .Japan	PES . . . . .Pescara GP	SWA . . . . .Namibia
B . . . . .Belgium	EC . . . . .Ecuador	JAM . . . . .Jamaica	PL . . . . .Poland	SYR . . . . .Syria
BG . . . . .Bulgaria	ES . . . . .El Salvador	KWT . . . . .Kuwait	PRC . . . . .China	T . . . . .Thailand
BLR . . . . . . .Belarus	ET . . . . .Egypt	LAR . . . . .Libya	PY . . . . .Paraguay	TN . . . . .Tunisia
BR . . . . .Brazil	ETH . . . . .Ethiopia	LB . . .Long Beach GP	QA . . . . .Qatar	TR . . . . .Turkey
C . . . . .Cuba	EU . . . . .European GP	LR . . . . .Latvia	R . . . . .Russia	TW . . . . .Taiwan
CDN . . . . .Canada	EW . . . . .Estonia	LT . . . . .Lithuania	RA . . . . . . .Argentina	UAE . . . . . .United Arab
CH . . . . . .Switzerland	F . . . . .France	LUX . . . . .Luxembourg	RCH . . . . .Chile	Emirates
CI . . . . .Ivory Coast	FL . . . . . . .Liechtenstein	LV . . . . . .Las Vegas GP	RI . . . . .Indonesia	USA . . .United States of
CL . . . . .Sri Lanka	GB . . . . .Britain	MA . . . . .Morocco	RL . . . . .Lebanon	America
CO . . . . .Colombia	GCA . . . . . .Guatemala	MAC . . . . .Macau	RO . . . . .Romania	YU . . . . .Yugoslavia
CR . . . . . . .Costa Rica	GR . . . . .Greece	MAL . . . . . . .Malaysia	ROK . . . . .Korea	YV . . . . .Venezuela
CS . . . .Czechoslovakia	GRG . . . . .Georgia	MC . . . . .Monaco	ROU . . . . . . .Uruguay	Z . . . . .Zambia
CUR . . . . .Curacao	H . . . . .Hungary	MEX . . . . .Mexico	RP . .Philippine Islands	ZA . . . . . .South Africa
CY . . . . .Cyprus	HK . . . . . . .Hong Kong	MOC . . . . .Mozambique	RSM . . . . .San Marino	ZWE . . . . . .Zimbabwe
D . . . . .Germany	HKJ . . . . .Jordan	N . . . . .Norway	RSR . . . . . . .Rhodesia	
DAL . . . . . . .Dallas GP	HR . . . . .Croatia	NIC . . . . . .Nicaragua	S . . . . .Sweden	
DDR . . . .East Germany	I . . . . .Italy	NL . . . . .Holland	SA . . . . . .Saudi Arabia	
DET . . . . . . .Detroit GP	IL . . . . .Israel	NZ . . . . .New Zealand	SF . . . . .Finland	
DK . . . . .Denmark	IND . . . . .India	P . . . . .Portugal	SGP . . . . . . .Singapore	

Race Results

Number . . . . .Finishing position (eg 1 equals first)	n/a . . . . .not available
= . . . . .Dead heat	NC . . . . .Not classified. Running at finish but completed
DNP . . . . .Practised but did not participate in qualifying	insufficient distance to be classified as
DNQ . . . . .Did not qualify	finishing the race
DNS . . . . .Qualified but did not start	R . . . . .Retired
NPQ . . . . .Did not pre-qualify	F . . . . .Fastest race lap
DSQ . . . . .Disqualified from the final race result	
F2 . . . . .Competed in a concurrent F2 race, not eligible	
to be classified in race result	

F1 Drivers' Records Charts

Q . . . . . .Qualifying position
R . . . . . .Race result
NT . . . . .No time recorded in qualifying
F . . . . . . .Fastest lap

Race Formulae/Governing Bodies

2.5l	2.5-litre Tasman Cup formula	Can-Am	Canadian-American Challenge	FIA	Federation Internationale de l'Automobile	(h)	Handicap race
Atlantic	Formula Atlantic					IRL	Indy Racing League
Brabham	Formula Brabham	CSI	Commission	FISA	Federation Internationale de Sport Automobile	INT	International Championship
AAA	Automobile Association of America		Sportive Internationale			NASCAR	NASCAR Winston Cup
ACO	Automobile Club de l'Ouest	Cyc	Cyclecar	FL	Formula Libre (no or limited rules)	Pacific	Formula Pacific
		E	European Championship			SC	Sports Cars
ACF	Automobile Club de France	F1	Formula 1	FOCA	Formula One Constructors' Association	TC	Touring Cars
		F2	Formula 2			USAC	United States Automobile Club
BARC	British Automobile Racing Club	F3	Formula 3	G8	Group 8	V	Voiturette
		F3000	Formula 3000	GP	Grand Prix (prior to F1)	W	World Championship
CART	Championship Auto Racing Teams	F5000	Formula 5000	GT	Grand Touring		

F1 World Championship

1983 The Ferraris of Patrick Tambay and Rene Arnoux lead at the start of the 1983 German Grand Prix.

The Formula 1 World Championship has been the dominant series in world motorsports since it was inaugurated in 1950. The governing body, the Commission Sportive Internationale (CSI), introduced the first rules to be called Formula 1 in 1947, although the history of the sport's premier single-seater category stretches back to the earliest days of the century with the Gordon Bennett Trophy and the first Grand Prix in 1906.

Races for the new championship were originally centred on Europe's finest circuits, although the Indianapolis 500 was officially a round for the first decade. By the end of the fifties events in Argentina and a true United States Grand Prix had been added.

The new decade saw British and Commonwealth drivers and teams move to the fore to compete with Ferrari. New races in Mexico and South Africa confirmed the spread of the formula's popularity. By the end of the sixties, teams replaced the national colours of Italian red, British Racing Green, or French blue with liveries derived from commercial sponsors.

Increased sponsorship and the wide availability of the Ford Cosworth DFV engine in the early seventies led to more private teams, especially from British constructors. These years also saw increasing television coverage add to the awareness and popularity of the series. As the seventies drew to a close, the numerous British teams belonging to the Formula One Constructors' Association (FOCA) sought a more equitable share of the sport's increasing revenues. FOCA, under the leadership of March founder Max Mosley and Brabham team owner Bernie Ecclestone, threatened a breakaway championship if the governing Federation Internationale de Sport Automobile (FISA) and the major motor manufacturers and their teams (Renault, Alfa Romeo, and Ferrari) did not compromise.

Eventually, the resulting agreement saw Ecclestone take control of Formula 1's commercial affairs. When Mosley was elected President of FISA's parent organisation, the Federation Internationale de l'Automobile (FIA), the coup was complete. Under their direction, the last two decades have seen Grand Prix racing grow into a true world sport producing undreamt-of income from commercial activity and television rights. Ecclestone remains the most influential person in maintaining Grand Prix racing's pre-eminence.

F1 has struggled in the United States, where successful events at Watkins Glen and Long Beach were eventually replaced by American championships due to increasing costs to the promoters. The reintroduction of the United States Grand Prix at the Indianapolis Motor Speedway in 2000 has promised to give the series a successful and permanent home in the world's largest market. With races now added in Asia (Japan, Malaysia), Oceania (Australia), and Eastern Europe (Hungary), today the World Championship truly lives up to its title.

Rules

1950-51	4500cc normally aspirated and 1500cc super charged maximum engine capacity
1952-53	World Championship races were for Formula 2 as there were not enough competitive F1 cars at the time. 2000cc normally aspirated and 500cc super charged maximum engine capacity
1954-57	2500cc normally aspirated and 750cc super charged maximum engine capacity
1958-60	Maximum engine capacity unchanged, commercial fuel compulsory
1961-65	1300cc minimum and 1500cc maximum engine capacity. No supercharged engines. Commercial fuel remained compulsory. 450kg minimum dry weight. Oil could not be replaced during the race. Roll-over bar compulsory. Bodywork not allowed to enclose the wheels
1966-68	3000cc normally aspirated and 1500cc super charged or turbocharged maximum engine capacity. 500kg minimum dry weight
1969-71	Maximum engine capacity unchanged. 530kg minimum dry weight
1972	Maximum engine capacity unchanged. Maximum of 12 cylinders. 550kg minimum dry weight
1973-82	Maximum engine capacity unchanged. 575kg minimum dry weight
1983-85	Maximum engine capacity unchanged. 575kg minimum dry weight. Flat underside to the car mandatory
1986	1500c supercharged or turbocharged maximum engine capacity. 575kg minimum dry weight
1987-88	3500cc normally aspirated and 1500cc super charged or turbocharged maximum engine capacity
1989-94	3500cc normally aspirated maximum engine capacity
1994	Maximum engine capacity unchanged. Revised aerodynamic and airbox rules introduced during season to improve safety. Underside of car had a 10mm stepped flat bottom from German GP. All electronic driver aids banned
1995-97	3000cc normally aspirated maximum engine capacity. Additional 50mm stepped flat bottom. Smaller front and rear wings
1998-99	Maximum engine capacity unchanged. Car narrowed by 20cm. Grooved tyres mandatory
2000	Maximum engine capacity unchanged. Engines restricted to a maximum of 10 cylinders
2001- to date	Maximum engine capacity unchanged. Electronic driver aids such as traction control reintroduced from 2001 Spanish GP

Qualifying

1996- 2002	Drivers had to qualify within 107% of the pole position time

WORLD CHAMPIONS

year	DRIVERS' CHAMPIONSHIP driver	nat	car	CONSTRUCTORS' CUP constructor
1950	Giuseppe Farina	I	Alfa Romeo 158/Alfa Romeo 159	-
1951	Juan Manuel Fangio	RA	Alfa Romeo 159	-
1952	Alberto Ascari	I	Ferrari 500	-
1953	Alberto Ascari	I	Ferrari 500	-
1954	Juan Manuel Fangio	RA	Maserati 250F/Mercedes-Benz W196	-
1955	Juan Manuel Fangio	RA	Mercedes-Benz W196	-
1956	Juan Manuel Fangio	RA	Lancia-Ferrari D50	-
1957	Juan Manuel Fangio	RA	Maserati 250F	-
1958	Mike Hawthorn	GB	Ferrari Dino 246	Vanwall
1959	Jack Brabham	AUS	Cooper T51-Climax	Cooper-Climax
1960	Jack Brabham	AUS	Cooper T53-Climax	Cooper-Climax
1961	Phil Hill	USA	Ferrari Dino 156	Ferrari
1962	Graham Hill	GB	BRM P57	BRM
1963	Jim Clark	GB	Lotus 25-Climax	Lotus-Climax
1964	John Surtees	GB	Ferrari 158	Ferrari
1965	Jim Clark	GB	Lotus 33-Climax	Lotus-Climax
1966	Jack Brabham	AUS	Brabham BT19-Repco/Brabham BT20-Repco	Brabham-Repco
1967	Denny Hulme	NZ	Brabham BT20-Repco/Brabham BT24-Repco	Brabham-Repco
1968	Graham Hill	GB	Lotus 49-Ford/Lotus 49B-Ford	Lotus-Ford
1969	Jackie Stewart	GB	Matra MS10-Ford/Matra MS80-Ford	Matra-Ford
1970	Jochen Rindt	A	Lotus 49C-Ford/Lotus 72-Ford	Lotus-Ford
1971	Jackie Stewart	GB	Tyrrell 001-Ford/Tyrrell 003-Ford	Tyrrell-Ford
1972	Emerson Fittipaldi	BR	Lotus 72-Ford	Lotus-Ford
1973	Jackie Stewart	GB	Tyrrell 005-Ford/Tyrrell 006-Ford	Lotus-Ford
1974	Emerson Fittipaldi	BR	McLaren M23-Ford	McLaren-Ford
1975	Niki Lauda	A	Ferrari 312T	Ferrari
1976	James Hunt	GB	McLaren M23-Ford	Ferrari
1977	Niki Lauda	A	Ferrari 312T2	Ferrari
1978	Mario Andretti	USA	Lotus 78-Ford/Lotus 79-Ford	Lotus-Ford
1979	Jody Scheckter	ZA	Ferrari 312T3/Ferrari 312T4	Ferrari
1980	Alan Jones	AUS	Williams FW07B-Ford	Williams-Ford
1981	Nelson Piquet	BR	Brabham BT49C-Ford	Williams-Ford
1982	Keke Rosberg	SF	Williams FW07C-Ford/Williams FW08-Ford	Ferrari
1983	Nelson Piquet	BR	Brabham BT52-BMW/Brabham BT52B-BMW	Ferrari
1984	Niki Lauda	A	McLaren MP4/2-TAG	McLaren-TAG
1985	Alain Prost	F	McLaren MP4/2B-TAG	McLaren-TAG
1986	Alain Prost	F	McLaren MP4/2C-TAG	Williams-Honda
1987	Nelson Piquet	BR	Williams FW11B-Honda	Williams-Honda
1988	Ayrton Senna	BR	McLaren MP4/4-Honda	McLaren-Honda
1989	Alain Prost	F	McLaren MP4/5-Honda	McLaren-Honda
1990	Ayrton Senna	BR	McLaren MP4/5B-Honda	McLaren-Honda
1991	Ayrton Senna	BR	McLaren MP4/6-Honda	McLaren-Honda
1992	Nigel Mansell	GB	Williams FW14B-Renault	Williams-Renault
1993	Alain Prost	F	Williams FW15C-Renault	Williams-Renault
1994	Michael Schumacher	D	Benetton B194-Ford	Williams-Renault
1995	Michael Schumacher	D	Benetton B195-Renault	Benetton-Renault
1996	Damon Hill	GB	Williams FW18-Renault	Williams-Renault
1997	Jacques Villeneuve	CDN	Williams FW19-Renault	Williams-Renault
1998	Mika Hakkinen	SF	McLaren MP4/13-Mercedes-Benz	McLaren-Mercedes-Benz
1999	Mika Hakkinen	SF	McLaren MP4/14-Mercedes-Benz	Ferrari
2000	Michael Schumacher	D	Ferrari F1-2000	Ferrari
2001	Michael Schumacher	D	Ferrari F2001	Ferrari
2002	Michael Schumacher	D	Ferrari F2001/Ferrari F2002	Ferrari

Race distances

1950-57	Over 300 km or 3 hours
1958-65	Minimum between 300 and 500 km or 2 hours
1966-70	Minimum between 300 and 400 km
1971- to date	Maximum of 325 km

Points

1950-57 8-6-4-3-2 points awarded to the top five finishers, plus 1 extra point awarded for fastest lap. Drivers were allowed to share cars, the points being divided accordingly

1958-59 8-6-4-3-2 points awarded to the top five finishers, plus 1 extra point awarded for fastest lap.
No shared drives allowed

1960 8-6-4-3-2-1 points awarded to the top six finishers, no extra point for fastest lap

1961-90 9-6-4-3-2-1 points awarded to the top six finishers

1991-2002 10-6-4-3-2-1 points awarded to the top six finishers

What is a Grand Prix start?

Those who question whether Alain Prost started 199 or 200 Grands Prix are in fact asking when a driver should be credited with starting a race.

Various sources have various definitions, resulting in minor but annoying discrepancies in the number of events competed in by de la Rosa, Laffite, Jarier, and the aforementioned Prost, to name but a few. For the record, I have credited a driver with a start based on the following definition:

A driver who was on the grid (or in the pits prior to making a delayed entrance) when the original signal to start was given, or who joined at any subsequent restart.

Thus, if a driver was eliminated in a start line shunt that stopped the event and prevented him from taking the restart, he is still credited with starting that Grand Prix. This means that Mike Thackwell (who was prevented from taking the restart of the Canadian GP in 1980 when his teammate requisitioned his undamaged Tyrrell) did start, and is therefore the youngest driver to have participated in a World Championship Grand Prix. Also, this definition means that Niki Lauda did start at the Nurburgring in 1976, albeit with near-fatal consequences.

Organisers added a concurrent Formula 2 race to enlarge the field in the 1958 Moroccan and the 1957-58, 1966-67, and 1969 German Grands Prix. Although the F2 drivers were not eligible to be *classified* in the overall results, they have always been credited as starting the Grand Prix.

The only exception to this definition relates to cars being specifically used to make a Grand Prix movie. Some drivers, most notably Phil Hill while filming Frankenheimer's *Grand Prix*, have appeared in races complete with bulky cameras to record the action. But they were never truly in the race, and have never been recorded as competing.

Finally, if a driver fails to complete the parade lap, he has not started the event, as he has not taken the signal to start. Thus, when Alain Prost crashed into the barriers on the way to taking his place on the grid for the 1991 San Marino GP, he did not register a Grand Prix start—hence the confusion over his record.

Indianapolis 500

The Indy 500 was officially a round of the Formula 1 World Championship from 1950 to 1960. Its inclusion in the series had little impact other than to confuse fans and record keepers. Of the European drivers, only Alberto Ascari raced at the Brickyard, and he failed to finish the 1952 race. Conversely, the race's winner, Troy Ruttman, went on to compete unsuccessfully in the 1958 French GP.

Although these were exceptions rather than the rule, the top six results of the Indy 500 and year-end championship positions of the relevant drivers are recorded from these years in order to provide the full championship story. However, in order to avoid distorting the Grand Prix records, I have omitted details of these races from the drivers' summary at the conclusion of each year, as well as from my analysis of F1's overall and manufacturer records and the F1 sections within the drivers' A-Z index.

Shared Drives

From the early years of Grand Prix racing the car was more important than the driver. Often when a team's fastest driver was delayed or retired from a race, its second driver would be called into the pits and replaced by his faster colleague. For the first eight years of the championship, drivers who shared a car that finished in the leading positions shared the points, but from 1958 points were only awarded to drivers who completed an event solo. If a driver was thus classified twice in a race in two different cars, the better result is recorded in the drivers' performance table unless he has been classified twice within the top six in that event, or if it was achieved in different types of car—in these cases both are published.

1950

The works Alfa Romeos of Giuseppe Farina and Juan Manuel Fangio dominated the inaugural drivers' World Championship. Each scored three Grand Prix wins, with Farina clinching the title at the final race. Veteran Italian Luigi Fagioli completed a championship clean-sweep for the marque, finishing second on four occasions.

They relied again on the supercharged 158 "Alfetta," a pre-war voiturette, or Formula 2 car, which had been virtually unbeatable since World War II. A modified version, dubbed 159, was introduced for Farina at the Italian GP. But the search for ever-increasing performance from the Alfa's engine resulted in poor fuel efficiency. To take advantage of the additional pit stops this required, Ferrari decided to build a 4.5-litre normally aspirated engine. Although slightly less powerful in theory, this engine would also use less fuel. The potential of Ferrari's plan was confirmed by Raymond Sommer's performance at Spa, when his slow but reliable Lago-Talbot briefly snatched the lead during the Alfa Romeo pit stops.

The new Ferrari 375 appeared in its final form at Monza, where Alberto Ascari finished second in Dorino Serafini's car after his own car had retired. Alfa Romeo would face a serious challenge in 1951.

BRITISH AND EUROPEAN GRAND PRIX

13 May 1950. Silverstone. 70 laps of a 2.889-mile circuit = 202.202 miles. Warm, dry and sunny. World Championship round 1

1	Giuseppe Farina	Alfa Romeo 158	70	2h13m23.6
2	Luigi Fagioli	Alfa Romeo 158	70	2h13m26.2
3	Reg Parnell	Alfa Romeo 158	70	2h14m15.6
4	Yves Giraud-Cabantous	Lago-Talbot T26C-DA	68	
5	Louis Rosier	Lago-Talbot T26C	68	
6	Bob Gerard	ERA B-type	67	

Winner's average speed: 90.950 mph. Starting grid front row: Farina, 1m50.8 (pole), Fagioli, 1m51.0, Fangio, 1m51.0 and Parnell, 1m52.2. Fastest lap: Farina, 1m50.6. Leaders: Farina, laps 1-9, 16-37, 39-70; Fagioli, 10-14, 38; Fangio, 15

GRAND PRIX DE MONACO

21 May 1950. Monte Carlo. 100 laps of a 1.976-mile circuit = 197.600 miles. Cool, dry and sunny. World Championship round 2

1	Juan Manuel Fangio	Alfa Romeo 158	100	3h13m18.7
2	Alberto Ascari	Ferrari 125	99	
3	Louis Chiron	Maserati 4CLT/48	98	
4	Raymond Sommer	Ferrari 125	97	

1950 DRIVERS' RECORDS

(excluding Indianapolis 500)

driver	car	GB Q	GB R	MC Q	MC R	CH Q	CH R	B Q	B R	F Q	F R	I Q	I R
Alberto Ascari	Ferrari 125	-	-	7	2	5	R	-	-	-	-	-	-
	Ferrari 275	-	-	-	-	-	-	7	5	NT	DNS	-	-
	Ferrari 375	-	-	-	-	-	-	-	-	-	-	2	2
Clemente Biondetti	Ferrari 166I-Jaguar	-	-	-	-	-	-	-	-	-	-	25	R
"B Bira"	Maserati 4CLT/48	5	R	14	5	8	4	-	-	-	-	15	R
Felice Bonetto	Maserati 4CLT/50-Milano	NT	DNS	-	-	12	5	-	-	11	R	23	DNS
Antonio Branca	Maserati 4CL	-	-	-	-	17	11	13	10	-	-	-	-
Eugene Chaboud	Lago-Talbot T26C	-	-	-	-	-	-	11	R	10	DNS	-	-
	Lago-Talbot T26C-DA	-	-	-	-	-	-	-	-	NT	5	-	-
Louis Chiron	Maserati 4CLT/48	11	R	8	3	16	9	-	-	14	R	19	R
Johnny Claes	Lago-Talbot T26C	21	11	18	7	14	10	NT	8	15	R	22	R
Gianfranco Comotti	Maserati 4CLT/50-Milano	-	-	-	-	-	-	-	-	-	-	26	R
Geoffrey Crossley	Alta GP	17	R	-	-	-	-	12	9	-	-	-	-
Philippe Etancelin	Lago-Talbot T26C	14	8	4	R	6	R	-	-	-	-	16	5
	Lago-Talbot T26C-DA	-	-	-	-	-	-	6	R	4	5	-	-
Luigi Fagioli	Alfa Romeo 158	2	2	5	R	3	2	3	2	3	2	5	3
Juan Manuel Fangio	Alfa Romeo 158	3	R	1	1F	1	R	2	1	1	1F	1	RF
Giuseppe Farina	Alfa Romeo 158	1	1F	2	R	2	1F	1	4F	2	7	-	-
	Alfa Romeo 159	-	-	-	-	-	-	-	-	-	-	3	1
Joe Fry	Maserati 4CL	20	10	-	-	-	-	-	-	-	-	-	-
Bob Gerard	ERA B-type	13	6	-	-	-	-	-	-	-	-	-	-
	ERA A-type	-	-	15	6	-	-	-	-	-	-	-	-
Yves Giraud-Cabantous	Lago-Talbot T26C-DA	6	4	-	-	7	R	9	R	5	8	-	-
Jose Froilan Gonzalez	Maserati 4CLT/48	-	-	3	R	-	-	-	-	8	R	-	-
Emanuel de Graffenried	Maserati 4CLT/48	8	R	11	R	11	6	-	-	-	-	17	6
David Hampshire	Maserati 4CLT/48	16	9	-	-	-	-	-	-	18	R	-	-
Cuth Harrison	ERA C-type	15	7	13	R	-	-	-	-	-	-	21	R
Leslie Johnson	ERA E-type	12	R	-	-	-	-	-	-	-	-	-	-
Joe Kelly	Alta GP	19	NC	-	-	-	-	-	-	-	-	-	-
"Pierre Levegh"	Lago-Talbot T26C	-	-	-	-	-	-	10	7	9	R	20	R
Henri Louveau	Lago-Talbot T26C-GS	-	-	-	-	-	-	-	-	-	-	14	R
Guy Mairesse	Lago-Talbot T26C	-	-	-	-	-	-	-	-	-	-	11	R
Robert Manzon	Simca-Gordini 15	-	-	16	R	-	-	-	-	13	4	10	R
Eugene Martin	Lago-Talbot T26C-DA	7	R	-	-	9	R	-	-	-	-	-	-
David Murray	Maserati 4CLT/48	18	R	-	-	-	-	-	-	-	-	24	R
Nello Pagani	Maserati 4CLT/48	-	-	-	-	15	7	-	-	-	-	-	-
Reg Parnell	Alfa Romeo 158	4	3	-	-	-	-	-	-	-	-	-	-
	Maserati 4CLT/48	-	-	-	-	-	-	-	-	12	R	-	-
Alfredo Pian	Maserati 4CLT/48	-	-	NT	DNS	-	-	-	-	-	-	-	-
Paul Pietsch	Maserati 4CLT/48	-	-	-	-	-	-	-	-	-	-	27	R
Charles Pozzi	Lago-Talbot T26C	-	-	-	-	-	-	-	-	16	6	-	-
Franco Rol	Maserati 4CLT/48	-	-	17	R	-	-	-	-	7	R	9	R
Tony Rolt	ERA E-type	NT	R	-	-	-	-	-	-	-	-	-	-
Louis Rosier	Lago-Talbot T26C	9	5	10	R	-	-	-	-	NT	6	13	4
	Lago-Talbot T26C-DA	-	-	-	-	10	3	8	3	6	R	-	-
Consalvo Sanesi	Alfa Romeo 158	-	-	-	-	-	-	-	-	-	-	4	R
Harry Schell	Cooper T12-JAP	-	-	NT	R	-	-	-	-	-	-	-	-
	Lago-Talbot T26C	-	-	-	-	18	8	-	-	-	-	-	-
Dorino Serafini	Ferrari 375	-	-	-	-	-	-	-	-	-	-	6	2
Brian Shawe-Taylor	Maserati 4CL	NT	10	-	-	-	-	-	-	-	-	-	-
Raymond Sommer	Ferrari 125	-	-	9	4	-	-	-	-	-	-	-	-
	Ferrari 166/F2/50	-	-	-	-	13	R	-	-	-	-	-	-
	Lago-Talbot T26C	-	-	-	-	-	-	5	R	-	-	8	R
	Lago-Talbot T26C-GS	-	-	-	-	-	-	-	-	17	R	-	-
Piero Taruffi	Alfa Romeo 158	-	-	-	-	-	-	-	-	-	-	7	R
Maurice Trintignant	Simca-Gordini 15	-	-	12	R	-	-	-	-	-	-	12	R
Luigi Villoresi	Ferrari 125	-	-	6	R	4	R	4	6	-	-	-	-
	Ferrari 275	-	-	-	-	-	-	-	-	NT	DNS	-	-
Peter Walker	ERA E-type	10	R	-	-	-	-	-	-	-	-	-	-
Peter Whitehead	Ferrari 125	-	-	NT	DNS	-	-	-	-	19	3	18	7

SHARED DRIVES - British GP: Joe Fry/Brian Shawe-Taylor (Maserati 4CL) 10; Peter Walker/Tony Rolt (ERA E-type) R. French GP: Philippe Etancelin/Eugene Chaboud (Lago-Talbot T26C-DA) 5; Charles Pozzi/Louis Rosier (Lago-Talbot T26C) 6. Italian GP: Dorino Serafini/Alberto Ascari (Ferrari 375) 2; Piero Taruffi/Juan Manuel Fangio (Alfa Romeo 158) R

1950 FINAL CHAMPIONSHIP POSITIONS

Drivers								
1	Giuseppe Farina	30	8	"B Bira"	5		Robert Manzon	3
2	Juan Manuel Fangio	27	9=	Louis Chiron	4		Dorino Serafini	3
3	Luigi Fagioli	24 [28]*		Reg Parnell	4		Raymond Sommer	3
4	Louis Rosier	13		Mauri Rose	4	19	Felice Bonetto	2
5	Alberto Ascari	11		Peter Whitehead	4	20=	Tony Bettenhausen	1
6	Johnnie Parsons	9	13=	Philippe Etancelin	3		Eugene Chaboud	1
7	Bill Holland	6		Yves Giraud-Cabantous	3		Joie Chitwood	1
				Cecil Green	3		*Best four results count	

5	"B Bira"	Maserati 4CLT/48	95
6	Bob Gerard	ERA A-type	94

Winner's average speed: 61.331 mph. Starting grid front row: Fangio, 1m50.2 (pole), Farina, 1m52.8 and Gonzalez, 1m53.7. Fastest lap: Fangio, 1m51.0. Leaders: Fangio, laps 1-100

INDIANAPOLIS 500

30 May 1950. Indianapolis. 138 laps of a 2.500-mile circuit = 345.000 miles. Race scheduled for 200 laps but stopped due to rain. Warm and dry at the start, heavy rain later. World Championship round 3

1	Johnnie Parsons	Kurtis-Offenhauser	138	2h46m55.97
2	Bill Holland	Deidt-Offenhauser	137	
3	Mauri Rose	Deidt-Offenhauser	137	
4	Cecil Green	Kurtis KK3000-Offenhauser	137	
5	Joie Chitwood/			
	Tony Bettenhausen	Kurtis KK2000-Offenhauser	136	
6	Lee Wallard	Moore-Offenhauser	136	

Winner's average speed: 124.002 mph. Starting grid front row: Walt Faulkner (Kurtis KK2000-Offenhauser), 134.343 mph (pole), Fred Agabashian (Kurtis KK3000-Offenhauser), 132.792 mph and Rose, 132.319 mph. Fastest lap in the lead: Parsons, time n/a. Leaders: Rose, laps 1-9, 33, 105-109; Parsons, 10-32, 34-104, 118-138; Holland, 110-117

GRAND PRIX DE SUISSE

4 June 1950. Bremgarten. 42 laps of a 4.524-mile circuit = 190.008 miles. Warm, dry and sunny. World Championship round 4

1	Giuseppe Farina	Alfa Romeo 158	42	2h02m53.7
2	Luigi Fagioli	Alfa Romeo 158	42	2h02m54.1
3	Louis Rosier	Lago-Talbot T26C-DA	41	
4	"B Bira"	Maserati 4CLT/48	40	
5	Felice Bonetto	Maserati 4CLT/50-Milano	40	
6	Emanuel de Graffenried	Maserati 4CLT/48	40	

Winner's average speed: 92.766 mph. Starting grid front row: Fangio, 2m42.1 (pole), Farina, 2m42.8 and Fagioli, 2m45.2. Fastest lap: Farina, 2m41.6. Leaders: Fangio, laps 1-6, 21-22; Farina, 7-20, 24-42; Fagioli, 23

GRAND PRIX DE BELGIQUE

18 June 1950. Spa-Francorchamps. 35 laps of an 8.774-mile circuit = 307.090 miles. Warm, dry and sunny. World Championship round 5

1	Juan Manuel Fangio	Alfa Romeo 158	35	2h47m26
2	Luigi Fagioli	Alfa Romeo 158	35	2h47m40
3	Louis Rosier	Lago-Talbot T26C-DA	35	2h49m45
4	Giuseppe Farina	Alfa Romeo 158	35	2h51m31
5	Alberto Ascari	Ferrari 275	34	
6	Luigi Villoresi	Ferrari 125	33	

Winner's average speed: 110.046 mph. Starting grid front row: Farina, 4m37 (pole), Fangio, 4m37 and Fagioli, 4m41. Fastest lap: Farina, 4m34.1. Leaders: Fangio, laps 1-6, 20-35; Farina, 7-11, 18-19; Fagioli, 12; Sommer, 13-17

GRAND PRIX DE L'AUTOMOBILE CLUB DE FRANCE

2 July 1950. Reims. 64 laps of a 4.856-mile circuit = 310.784 miles. Hot, dry and sunny. World Championship round 6

1	Juan Manuel Fangio	Alfa Romeo 158	64	2h57m52.8
2	Luigi Fagioli	Alfa Romeo 158	64	2h58m18.5
3	Peter Whitehead	Ferrari 125	61	
4	Robert Manzon	Simca-Gordini 15	61	

5	Philippe Etancelin/		
	Eugene Chaboud	Lago-Talbot T26C-DA	59
6	Charles Pozzi/		
	Louis Rosier	Lago-Talbot T26C	56

Winner's average speed: 104.829 mph. Starting grid front row: Fangio, 2m30.6 (pole), Farina, 2m32.5 and Fagioli, 2m34.7. Fastest lap: Fangio, 2m35.6. Leaders: Farina, laps 1-16; Fangio, 17-64

GRAN PREMIO D'ITALIA

3 September 1950. Monza. 80 laps of a 3.915-mile circuit = 313.200 miles. Warm, dry and sunny, turning overcast. World Championship round 7

1	Giuseppe Farina	Alfa Romeo 159	80	2h51m17.4
2	Dorino Serafini/			
	Alberto Ascari	Ferrari 375	80	2h52m36.0
3	Luigi Fagioli	Alfa Romeo 158	80	2h52m53.0
4	Louis Rosier	Lago-Talbot T26C	75	
5	Philippe Etancelin	Lago-Talbot T26C	75	
6	Emanuel de Graffenried	Maserati 4CLT/48	72	

Winner's average speed: 109.709 mph. Starting grid front row: Fangio, 1m58.6 (pole), Ascari, 1m58.8, Farina, 2m00.2 and Sanesi, 2m00.4. Fastest lap: Fangio, 2m00.0. Leaders: Farina, laps 1-13, 16-80; Ascari, 14-15

1951 Juan Manuel Fangio celebrates victory at the Spanish Grand Prix to clinch his first world title.

1951

Juan Manuel Fangio was the quickest Alfa Romeo driver by 1951, invariably qualifying ahead of Giuseppe Farina. Fangio's three Grand Prix victories (one of which was shared with Luigi Fagioli) were enough to win the 1951 World Championship. But the Alfa Romeo 159's engine was now so highly developed that it only achieved 1.6 mpg, requiring two or more fuel stops to complete a Grand Prix.

A strong challenge had been expected from Ferrari, but it was not until the second half of the season that it fully materialised. Jose Froilan Gonzalez, the "Pampas Bull," scored Ferrari's first Grand Prix win at Silverstone, with team leader Alberto Ascari winning the subsequent German and Italian races.

These were the first defeats inflicted on Alfa Romeo

in five years, and they brought the Ferrari drivers into championship contention. But their incorrect tyre choice for the final Grand Prix in Spain handed Fangio victory and his first crown. With their rivals gaining in competitiveness, Alfa Romeo decided to withdraw from Grand Prix racing rather than build the totally new car it would need to stay ahead. The marque would not return to Grand Prix racing until 1979.

A much-vaunted new challenger from Britain, the supercharged V16 BRM, appeared for its home Grand Prix. It was the most advanced car of the time, and should have been able to compete with the Italians. Although Reg Parnell finished fifth at Silverstone, it was a disappointment, and the team rarely mounted a concerted challenge. Their failure, combined with Alfa's withdrawal, led to Formula 1 being abandoned for the following season.

GRAND PRIX DE SUISSE

27 May 1951. Bremgarten. 42 laps of a 4.524-mile circuit = 190.008 miles. Heavy rain. World Championship round 1

1	Juan Manuel Fangio	Alfa Romeo 159	42	2h07m53.64
2	Piero Taruffi	Ferrari 375	42	2h08m48.88
3	Giuseppe Farina	Alfa Romeo 159	42	2h09m12.95
4	Consalvo Sanesi	Alfa Romeo 159	41	
5	Emanuel de Graffenried	Alfa Romeo 159	40	
6	Alberto Ascari	Ferrari 375	40	

Winner's average speed: 89.140 mph. Starting grid front row: Fangio, 2m35.9 (pole), Farina, 2m37.8 and Villoresi, 2m39.3. Fastest lap: Fangio, 2m51.1. Leaders: Fangio, laps 1-23, 29-42; Farina, 24-28

INDIANAPOLIS 500

30 May 1951. Indianapolis. 200 laps of a 2.500-mile circuit = 500.000 miles. Hot, dry and sunny. World Championship round 2

1	Lee Wallard	Kurtis-Offenhauser	200	3h57m38.05
2	Mike Nazaruk	Kurtis-Offenhauser	200	3h59m25.31
3	Jack McGrath/ Manuel Ayulo	Kurtis KK3000-Offenhauser	200	4h00m29.42
4	Andy Linden	Sherman-Offenhauser	200	4h02m18.06
5	Bobby Ball	Schroeder-Offenhauser	200	4h02m30.27
6	Henry Banks	Moore-Offenhauser	200	4h03m18.02

Winner's average speed: 126.244 mph. Starting grid front row: Nalon, 136.498 mph (pole), Wallard, 135.039 mph and McGrath, 134.303 mph. Fastest lap in the lead: Wallard, 1m07.26. Leaders: Wallard, laps 1, 5-6, 17-59, 82-200; McGrath, 2-3, 7-16; Green, 4, 78-81; Davies, 60-77

GRAND PRIX DE BELGIQUE

17 June 1951. Spa-Francorchamps. 36 laps of an 8.774-mile circuit = 315.864 miles. Warm, dry and sunny. World Championship round 3

1	Giuseppe Farina	Alfa Romeo 159	36	2h45m46.2
2	Alberto Ascari	Ferrari 375	36	2h48m37.2
3	Luigi Villoresi	Ferrari 375	36	2h50m08.1
4	Louis Rosier	Lago-Talbot T26C-DA	34	
5	Yves Giraud-Cabantous	Lago-Talbot T26C	34	
6	Andre Pilette	Lago-Talbot T26C	33	

Winner's average speed: 114.326 mph. Starting grid front row: Fangio,

4m25 (pole), Farina, 4m28 and Villoresi, 4m29. Fastest lap: Fangio, 4m22.1. Leaders: Villoresi, laps 1-2; Farina, 3-14, 16-36; Fangio, 15

GRAND PRIX DE L'AUTOMOBILE CLUB DE FRANCE ET D'EUROPE

1 July 1951. Reims. 77 laps of a 4.856-mile circuit = 373.912 miles. Hot, dry and sunny. World Championship round 4

1	Luigi Fagioli/ Juan Manuel Fangio	Alfa Romeo 159	77	3h22m11.0
2	Jose Froilan Gonzalez/ Alberto Ascari	Ferrari 375	77	3h23m09.2
3	Luigi Villoresi	Ferrari 375	74	
4	Reg Parnell	Ferrari 375	73	
5	Giuseppe Farina	Alfa Romeo 159	73	
6	Louis Chiron	Lago-Talbot T26C	71	

Winner's average speed: 110.962 mph. Starting grid front row: Fangio, 2m25.7 (pole), Farina, 2m27.4 and Ascari, 2m28.1. Fastest lap: Fangio, 2m27.8. Leaders: Ascari, laps 1-8, 45-50#; Fangio, 9, 51-77*; Farina, 10-44 (#in Gonzalez's car; *in Fagioli's car)

BRITISH GRAND PRIX

14 July 1951. Silverstone. 90 laps of a 2.889-mile circuit = 259.974 miles. Warm, dry and sunny. World Championship round 5

1	Jose Froilan Gonzalez	Ferrari 375	90	2h42m18.2
2	Juan Manuel Fangio	Alfa Romeo 159	90	2h43m09.2
3	Luigi Villoresi	Ferrari 375	88	
4	Felice Bonetto	Alfa Romeo 159	87	
5	Reg Parnell	BRM P15	85	
6	Consalvo Sanesi	Alfa Romeo 159	84	

Winner's average speed: 96.107 mph. Starting grid front row: Gonzalez, 1m43.4 (pole), Fangio, 1m44.4, Farina, 1m45.0 and Ascari, 1m45.4. Fastest lap: Farina, 1m44.0. Leaders: Bonetto, lap 1; Gonzalez, laps 2-9, 39-47, 49-90; Fangio, 10-38, 48

GROSSER PREIS VON DEUTSCHLAND

29 July 1951. Nurburgring. 20 laps of a 14.167-mile circuit = 283.340 miles. Warm, dry and sunny. World Championship round 6

1	Alberto Ascari	Ferrari 375	20	3h23m03.3
2	Juan Manuel Fangio	Alfa Romeo 159	20	3h23m33.8
3	Jose Froilan Gonzalez	Ferrari 375	20	3h27m42.3
4	Luigi Villoresi	Ferrari 375	20	3h28m53.5
5	Piero Taruffi	Ferrari 375	20	3h30m52.4
6	Rudolf Fischer	Ferrari 212	19	

Winner's average speed: 83.723 mph. Starting grid front row: Ascari, 9m55.8 (pole), Gonzalez, 9m57.5, Fangio, 9m59.0 and Farina, 10m01.0. Fastest lap: Fangio, 9m55.8. Leaders: Fangio, laps 1-4, 11-14; Ascari, 5-9, 15-20; Gonzalez, 10

GRAN PREMIO D'ITALIA

16 September 1951. Monza. 80 laps of a 3.915-mile circuit = 313.200 miles. Hot, dry and sunny. World Championship round 7

1	Alberto Ascari	Ferrari 375	80	2h42m39.3
2	Jose Froilan Gonzalez	Ferrari 375	80	2h43m23.9
3	Felice Bonetto/ Giuseppe Farina	Alfa Romeo 159	79	
4	Luigi Villoresi	Ferrari 375	79	
5	Piero Taruffi	Ferrari 375	78	
6	Andre Simon	Simca-Gordini 15	74	

1951 FINAL CHAMPIONSHIP POSITIONS

	Drivers								
1	Juan Manuel Fangio	31 (37)*	8	Felice Bonetto	7	15=	Manuel Ayulo	2
2	Alberto Ascari	25 (28)*	9	Mike Nazaruk	6		Bobby Ball	2
3	Jose Froilan Gonzalez	24 (27)*	10	Reg Parnell	5		Yves Giraud-Cabantous	2
4	Giuseppe Farina	19 (22)*	11	Luigi Fagioli	4		Emanuel de Graffenried	2
5	Luigi Villoresi	15 (18)*	12=	Andy Linden	3		Jack McGrath	2
6	Piero Taruffi	10		Louis Rosier	3		*Best four results count	
7	Lee Wallard	9		Consalvo Sanesi	3			

1951 DRIVERS' RECORDS

(excluding Indianapolis 500)

driver	car	CH Q	CH R	B Q	B R	F Q	F R	GB Q	GB R	D Q	D R	I Q	I R	E Q	E R
George Abecassis	HWM 51-Alta	20	R	-	-	-	-	-	-	-	-	-	-	-	-
Alberto Ascari	Ferrari 375	7	6	4	2	3	2	4	R	1	1	3	1	1	4
"B Bira"	Maserati 4CLT/48-OSCA	-	-	-	-	-	-	-	-	-	-	-	-	19	R
Felice Bonetto	Alfa Romeo 159	-	-	-	-	-	-	7	4	10	R	7	3	8	5
Antonio Branca	Maserati 4CLT/48	-	-	-	-	-	-	-	-	17	R	-	-	-	-
Eugene Chaboud	Lago-Talbot T26C-GS	-	-	-	-	14	8	-	-	-	-	-	-	-	-
Louis Chiron	Maserati 4CLT/48	19	7	-	-	-	-	-	-	-	-	-	-	-	-
	Lago-Talbot T26C	-	-	9	R	8	6	13	R	-	-	17	R	12	R
	Lago-Talbot T26C-DA	-	-	-	-	-	-	-	-	13	R	-	-	-	-
Johnny Claes	Lago-Talbot T26C-DA	18	13	11	7	12	R	14	13	18	11	21	R	15	R
Philippe Etancelin	Lago-Talbot T26C-DA	12	10	10	R	10	R	-	-	21	R	-	-	13	8
Luigi Fagioli	Alfa Romeo 159	-	-	-	-	7	1	-	-	-	-	-	-	-	-
Juan Manuel Fangio	Alfa Romeo 159	1	1F	1	9F	1	1F	2	2	3	2F	1	R	2	1F
Giuseppe Farina	Alfa Romeo 159	2	3	2	1	2	5	3	RF	4	R	2	3F	4	3
Rudolf Fischer	Ferrari 212	10	11	-	-	-	-	-	-	8	6	NT	DNS	-	-
Philip Fotheringham-Parker	Maserati 4CL	-	-	-	-	-	-	16	R	-	-	-	-	-	-
Bob Gerard	ERA B-type	-	-	-	-	-	-	10	11	-	-	-	-	-	-
Yves Giraud-Cabantous	Lago-Talbot T26C	15	R	8	5	11	7	-	-	11	R	14	8	14	R
Chico Godia-Sales	Maserati 4CLT/48	-	-	-	-	-	-	-	-	-	-	-	-	17	10
Jose Froilan Gonzalez	Lago-Talbot T26C-GS	13	R	-	-	-	-	-	-	-	-	-	-	-	-
	Ferrari 375	-	-	-	-	6	2	1	1	2	3	4	2	3	2
Aldo Gordini	Simca-Gordini 11	-	-	-	-	17	R	-	-	-	-	-	-	-	-
Emanuel de Graffenried	Alfa Romeo 159	5	5	-	-	-	-	-	-	-	-	9	R	6	6
	Maserati 4CLT/48	-	-	-	-	16	R	-	-	16	R	-	-	-	-
Georges Grignard	Lago-Talbot T26C-DA	-	-	-	-	-	-	-	-	-	-	-	-	16	R
Duncan Hamilton	Lago-Talbot T26C	-	-	-	-	-	-	11	12	20	R	-	-	-	-
Peter Hirt	Veritas Meteor	16	R	-	-	-	-	-	-	-	-	-	-	-	-
John James	Maserati 4CLT/48	-	-	-	-	-	-	17	R	-	-	-	-	-	-
Juan Jover	Maserati 4CLT/48	-	-	-	-	-	-	-	-	-	-	-	-	18	DNS
Joe Kelly	Alta GP	-	-	-	-	-	-	18	NC	-	-	-	-	-	-
Chico Landi	Ferrari 375	-	-	-	-	-	-	-	-	-	-	16	R	-	-
"Pierre Levegh"	Lago-Talbot T26C	-	-	13	8	-	-	-	-	19	9	20	R	-	-
Henri Louveau	Lago-Talbot T26C	11	R	-	-	-	-	-	-	-	-	-	-	-	-
Guy Mairesse	Lago-Talbot T26C	21	14	-	-	19	9	-	-	-	-	-	-	-	-
Robert Manzon	Simca-Gordini 15	-	-	-	-	23	R	-	-	9	7	13	R	9	9
Onofre Marimon	Maserati 4CLT/50-Milano	-	-	-	-	15	R	-	-	-	-	-	-	-	-
Stirling Moss	HWM 51-Alta	14	8	-	-	-	-	-	-	-	-	-	-	-	-
David Murray	Maserati 4CLT/48	-	-	-	-	-	-	15	R	NT	DNS	-	-	-	-
Reg Parnell	Ferrari 375	-	-	-	-	9	4	-	-	-	-	-	-	-	-
	BRM P15	-	-	-	-	-	-	NT	5	-	-	8	DNS	-	-
Paul Pietsch	Alfa Romeo 159	-	-	-	-	-	-	-	-	7	R	-	-	-	-
Andre Pilette	Lago-Talbot T26C	-	-	12	6	-	-	-	-	-	-	-	-	-	-
Ken Richardson	BRM P15	-	-	-	-	-	-	-	-	-	-	10	DNS	-	-
Franco Rol	OSCA 4500G	-	-	-	-	-	-	-	-	-	-	18	9	-	-
Louis Rosier	Lago-Talbot T26C-DA	8	9	7	4	13	R	9	10	15	8	15	7	20	7
Consalvo Sanesi	Alfa Romeo 159	4	4	6	R	5	10	6	6	-	-	-	-	-	-
Harry Schell	Maserati 4CLT/48	17	12	-	-	22	R	-	-	-	-	-	-	-	-
Brian Shawe-Taylor	ERA B-type	-	-	-	-	-	-	12	8	-	-	-	-	-	-
Andre Simon	Simca-Gordini 15	-	-	-	-	21	R	-	-	12	R	11	6	10	R
Jacques Swaters	Lago-Talbot T26C	-	-	-	-	-	-	-	-	22	10	22	R	-	-
Piero Taruffi	Ferrari 375	6	2	5	R	-	-	-	-	6	5	6	5	7	R
Maurice Trintignant	Simca-Gordini 15	-	-	-	-	18	R	-	-	14	R	12	R	11	R
Luigi Villoresi	Ferrari 375	3	R	3	3	4	3	5	3	5	4	5	4	5	R
Peter Walker	BRM P15	-	-	-	-	-	-	NT	7	-	-	-	-	-	-
Peter Whitehead	Ferrari 125	9	R	-	-	20	R	-	-	-	-	19	R	-	-
	Ferrari 375	-	-	-	-	-	-	8	9	-	-	-	-	-	-

SHARED DRIVES - French GP: Luigi Fagioli/Juan Manuel Fangio (Alfa Romeo 159) 1; Jose Froilan Gonzalez/Alberto Ascari (Ferrari 375) 2; Juan Manuel Fangio/Luigi Fagioli (Alfa Romeo 159) 11. Italian GP: Felice Bonetto/Giuseppe Farina (Alfa Romeo 159) 3

Winner's average speed: 115.533 mph. Starting grid front row: Fangio, 1m53.2 (pole), Farina, 1m53.9, Ascari, 1m55.1 and Gonzalez, 1m55.9. Fastest lap: Farina, 1m56.5. Leaders: Fangio, laps 1-3, 8-13; Ascari, 4-7, 14-80

GRAN PREMIO DE ESPANA

28 October 1951. Pedralbes. 70 laps of a 3.925-mile circuit = 274.750 miles. World Championship round 8

1	Juan Manuel Fangio	Alfa Romeo 159	70	2h46m54.10
2	Jose Froilan Gonzalez	Ferrari 375	70	2h47m48.38
3	Giuseppe Farina	Alfa Romeo 159	70	2h48m39.64
4	Alberto Ascari	Ferrari 375	68	
5	Felice Bonetto	Alfa Romeo 159	68	
6	Emanuel de Graffenried	Alfa Romeo 159	66	

Winner's average speed: 98.771 mph. Starting grid front row: Ascari, 2m10.59 (pole), Fangio, 2m12.27, Gonzalez, 2m14.01 and Farina, 2m14.94. Fastest lap: Fangio, 2m16.93. Leaders: Ascari, laps 1-3; Fangio, 4-70

1952

Having clinched a second successive championship in 1951, Alfa Romeo withdrew from Grand Prix racing rather than build the new car they would need to beat Ferrari in 1952. This left the disappointing BRM project as the only factory concern other than Ferrari in Formula 1. When the British team did not appear in Turin for the Valentino Grand Prix, the first non-championship event of the year, World Championship promoters switched their races for the next two years to Formula 2 rather than suffer a season with just one competitive marque. Although these years proved to be a walkover for Ferrari, the category benefited from the promise of additional teams, including Maserati, Gordini, HWM, ERA, Connaught, and Cooper.

Ferrari team leader Alberto Ascari decided to miss the opening round of the championship in Switzerland to race unsuccessfully at Indianapolis instead. In his absence teammate Piero Taruffi won, but thereafter Ascari was unstoppable and remained unbeaten until July 1953.

Maserati introduced the new A6GCM and signed reigning World Champion Juan Manuel Fangio to lead its attack. But Fangio would be sidelined for a year after breaking his neck in a crash in a pre-season non-championship race at Monza. Still, Maserati became increasingly competitive when a modified engine was introduced towards the end of the season, and Jose Froilan Gonzalez showed its promise by leading for thirty-six laps in Italy.

Also in 1952, new stars emerged from England: Mike Hawthorn had a number of fine performances in his private Cooper-Bristol, and Stirling Moss made his debut for HWM at Bremgarten.

GRAND PRIX DE SUISSE

18 May 1952. Bremgarten. 62 laps of a 4.524-mile circuit = 280.488 miles. Warm and dry. World Championship round 1

1	Piero Taruffi	Ferrari 500	62	3h01m46.1
2	Rudolf Fischer	Ferrari 500	62	3h04m23.3
3	Jean Behra	Gordini 16	61	
4	Ken Wharton	Frazer-Nash FN48-Bristol	60	
5	Alan Brown	Cooper T20-Bristol	59	
6	Emanuel de Graffenried	Maserati 4CLT/48-Plate	58	

Winner's average speed: 92.586 mph. Starting grid front row: Farina, 2m47.5 (pole), Taruffi, 2m50.1 and Manzon, 2m52.1. Fastest lap: Taruffi, 2m49.1. Leaders: Farina, laps 1-16; Taruffi, 17-62

INDIANAPOLIS 500

30 May 1952. Indianapolis. 200 laps of a 2.500-mile circuit = 500.000 miles. Warm, dry and sunny. World Championship round 2

1	Troy Ruttman	Kuzma-Offenhauser	200	3h52m41.88
2	Jim Rathmann	Kurtis KK3000-Offenhauser	200	3h56m44.24
3	Sam Hanks	Kurtis KK3000-Offenhauser	200	3h58m53.48
4	Duane Carter	Lesovsky-Offenhauser	200	3h59m30.21
5	Art Cross	Kurtis KK4000-Offenhauser	200	4h01m22.08
6	Jimmy Bryan	Kurtis KK3000-Offenhauser	200	4h02m06.23

Winner's average speed: 128.922 mph. Starting grid front row: Fred Agabashian (Kurtis-Cummins), 138.010 mph (pole), Andy Linden (Kurtis KK4000-Offenhauser), 137.002 mph and Jack McGrath (Kurtis KK3000-Offenhauser), 136.664 mph. Fastest lap in the lead: Bill Vukovich (Kurtis KK500A-Offenhauser), 1m06.60. Leaders: McGrath, laps 1-6; Vukovich, 7-11, 13-61, 83-134, 148-191; Ruttman, 12, 62-82, 135-147, 192-200

GRAND PRIX DE BELGIQUE ET D'EUROPE

22 June 1952. Spa-Francorchamps. 36 laps of an 8.774-mile circuit = 315.864 miles. Heavy rain. World Championship round 3

1	Alberto Ascari	Ferrari 500	36	3h03m46.3
2	Giuseppe Farina	Ferrari 500	36	3h05m41.5
3	Robert Manzon	Gordini 16	36	3h08m14.7
4	Mike Hawthorn	Cooper T20-Bristol	35	
5	Paul Frere	HWM 51/52-Alta	34	
6	Alan Brown	Cooper T20-Bristol	34	

Winner's average speed: 103.127 mph. Starting grid front row: Ascari, 4m37 (pole), Farina, 4m40 and Taruffi, 4m46. Fastest lap: Ascari, 4m54. Leaders: Behra, lap 1; Ascari, laps 2-36

GRAND PRIX DE L'AUTOMOBILE CLUB DE FRANCE

6 July 1952. Rouen-les-Essarts. 76 laps of a 3.169-mile circuit = 240.844 miles. Race scheduled for 3 hours. Overcast and dry at the start, rain later. World Championship round 4

1	Alberto Ascari	Ferrari 500	76	3h00m00.0
2	Giuseppe Farina	Ferrari 500	76	
3	Piero Taruffi	Ferrari 500	75	
4	Robert Manzon	Gordini 16	74	
5	Maurice Trintignant	Simca-Gordini 15	72	
6	Peter Collins	HWM 52-Alta	70	

Winner's average speed: 80.281 mph. Starting grid front row: Ascari, 2m14.8 (pole), Farina, 2m16.2 and Taruffi, 2m17.1. Fastest lap: Ascari, 2m17.3. Leaders: Ascari, laps 1-76

BRITISH GRAND PRIX

19 July 1952. Silverstone. 85 laps of a 2.927-mile circuit = 248.795 miles. Overcast and dry. World Championship round 5

1	Alberto Ascari	Ferrari 500	85	2h44m11.0
2	Piero Taruffi	Ferrari 500	84	
3	Mike Hawthorn	Cooper T20-Bristol	83	
4	Dennis Poore	Connaught A-Lea-Francis	83	
5	Eric Thompson	Connaught A-Lea-Francis	82	
6	Giuseppe Farina	Ferrari 500	82	

Winner's average speed: 90.921 mph. Starting grid front row: Farina, 1m50 (pole), Ascari, 1m50, Taruffi, 1m53 and Manzon, 1m55. Fastest lap: Ascari, 1m52. Leaders: Ascari, laps 1-85

GROSSER PREIS VON DEUTSCHLAND

3 August 1952. Nurburgring. 18 laps of a 14.167-mile circuit = 255.006 miles. Warm, dry and sunny. World Championship round 6

1	Alberto Ascari	Ferrari 500	18	3h06m13.3
2	Giuseppe Farina	Ferrari 500	18	3h06m27.4
3	Rudolf Fischer	Ferrari 500	18	3h13m23.4
4	Piero Taruffi	Ferrari 500	17	
5	Jean Behra	Gordini 16	17	
6	Roger Laurent	Ferrari 500	16	

Winner's average speed: 82.162 mph. Starting grid front row: Ascari, 10m04.4 (pole), Farina, 10m07.3, Trintignant, 10m19.1 and Manzon, 10m25.3. Fastest lap: Ascari, 10m05.1. Leaders: Ascari, laps 1-18

Formula 1

(excluding Indianapolis 500)

driver	car	CH Q	CH R	B Q	B R	F Q	F R	GB Q	GB R	D Q	D R	NL Q	NL R	I Q	I R
George Abecassis	HWM 52-Alta	10	R	-	-	-	-	-	-	-	-	-	-	-	-
Alberto Ascari	Ferrari 500	-	-	1	1F	1	1F	2	1F	1	1F	1	1F	1	1F
Bill Aston	Aston NB41-Butterworth	-	-	-	-	-	-	30	DNS	NT	R	-	-	31	DNQ
Marcel Balsa	BMW Special	-	-	-	-	-	-	-	-	NT	R	-	-	-	-
Elie Bayol	OSCA 20	-	-	-	-	-	-	-	-	-	-	-	-	10	R
Gunther Bechem	BMW Eigenbau	-	-	-	-	-	-	-	-	NT	R	-	-	-	-
Jean Behra	Gordini 16	7	3	5	R	4	7	-	-	NT	5	6	R	11	R
Gino Bianco	Maserati A6GCM	-	-	-	-	-	-	28	18	NT	R	12	R	24	R
"B Bira"	Simca-Gordini 15	11	R	18	10	-	-	-	-	-	-	-	-	-	-
	Gordini 16	-	-	-	-	8	R	10	11	-	-	-	-	-	-
Felice Bonetto	Maserati A6GCM	-	-	-	-	-	-	-	-	NT	DSQ	-	-	13	5
Eric Brandon	Cooper T20-Bristol	17	8	12	9	-	-	18	20	-	-	-	-	20	13
Alan Brown	Cooper T20-Bristol	15	5	9	6	-	-	13	22	-	-	-	-	21	15
Adolf Brudes	Veritas RS-BMW	-	-	-	-	-	-	-	-	NT	R	-	-	-	-
Heitel Cantoni	Maserati A6GCM	-	-	-	-	-	-	27	R	NT	R	-	-	23	11
Piero Carini	Ferrari 166/F2	-	-	-	-	19	R	-	-	NT	R	-	-	-	-
Johnny Claes	Simca-Gordini 16S	-	-	19	8	-	-	-	-	-	-	-	-	-	-
	Simca-Gordini 15	-	-	-	-	20	R	23	15	-	-	-	-	NT	DNQ
	HWM 52-Alta	-	-	-	-	-	-	-	-	NT	R	-	-	-	-
Peter Collins	HWM 52-Alta	6	R	11	R	7	6	14	R	NT	DNS	-	-	28	DNQ
Gianfranco Comotti	Ferrari 166/F2	-	-	-	-	18	12	-	-	-	-	-	-	-	-
Alberto Crespo	Maserati 4CLT/48-Plate	-	-	-	-	-	-	-	-	-	-	-	-	26	DNQ
Tony Crook	Frazer-Nash 421-BMW	-	-	-	-	-	-	25	21	-	-	-	-	-	-
Ken Downing	Connaught A-Lea-Francis	-	-	-	-	-	-	5	9	-	-	13	R	-	-
Piero Dusio	Cisitalia D46-BPM	-	-	-	-	-	-	-	-	-	-	-	-	NT	DNQ
Philippe Etancelin	Maserati A6GCM	-	-	-	-	16	8	-	-	-	-	-	-	-	-
Giuseppe Farina	Ferrari 500	1	R	2	2	2	2	1	6	2	2	2	2	3	4
Ludwig Fischer	AFM 1-BMW	-	-	-	-	-	-	-	-	NT	DNS	-	-	-	-
Rudolf Fischer	Ferrari 500	5	2	-	-	-	-	15	14	6	3	-	-	14	R
	Ferrari 212	-	-	-	-	17	11	-	-	-	-	-	-	-	-
Jan Flinterman	Maserati A6GCM	-	-	-	-	-	-	-	-	-	-	15	9	-	-
Paul Frere	HWM 51/52-Alta	-	-	8	5	-	-	-	-	NT	R	-	-	-	-
	Simca-Gordini 15	-	-	-	-	-	-	-	-	-	-	11	R	-	-
Tony Gaze	HWM 52-Alta	-	-	16	15	-	-	-	-	-	-	-	-	-	-
	HWM 51/52-Alta	-	-	-	-	-	-	26	R	NT	R	-	-	30	DNQ
Yves Giraud-Cabantous	HWM 52-Alta	-	-	-	-	10	10	-	-	-	-	-	-	-	-
Jose Froilan Gonzalez	Maserati A6GCM	-	-	-	-	-	-	-	-	-	-	-	-	5	2F
Emanuel de Graffenried	Maserati 4CLT/48-Plate	8	6	-	-	11	R	NT	19	-	-	-	-	27	DNQ
Duncan Hamilton	HWM 51/52-Alta	-	-	-	-	-	-	11	R	-	-	-	-	-	-
	HWM 52-Alta	-	-	-	-	-	-	-	-	-	-	10	7	-	-
Mike Hawthorn	Cooper T20-Bristol	-	-	6	4	15	R	7	3	-	-	3	4	12	NC
Willi Heeks	AFM 8-BMW	-	-	-	-	-	-	-	-	NT	R	-	-	-	-
Theo Helfrich	Veritas RS-BMW	-	-	-	-	-	-	-	-	NT	R	-	-	-	-
Peter Hirt	Ferrari 212	19	7	-	-	NT	11	24	R	-	-	-	-	-	-
Hans Klenk	Veritas Meteor	-	-	-	-	-	-	-	-	NT	R	-	-	-	-
Ernst Klodwig	Heck-BMW	-	-	-	-	-	-	-	-	NT	R	-	-	-	-
Willi Krakau	AFM 7-BMW	-	-	-	-	-	-	-	-	NT	DNS	-	-	-	-
Rudolf Krause	Greifzu-BMW	-	-	-	-	-	-	-	-	NT	R	-	-	-	-
Chico Landi	Maserati A6GCM	-	-	-	-	-	-	-	-	-	-	16	9	18	8
Roger Laurent	HWM 52-Alta	-	-	20	12	-	-	-	-	-	-	-	-	-	-
	Ferrari 500	-	-	-	-	-	-	-	-	NT	6	-	-	-	-
Arthur Legat	Veritas Meteor	-	-	21	13	-	-	-	-	-	-	-	-	-	-
Dries van der Lof	HWM 52-Alta	-	-	-	-	-	-	-	-	-	-	14	NC	-	-
Lance Macklin	HWM 52-Alta	12	R	14	11	14	9	29	13	-	-	9	8	32	DNQ
Robert Manzon	Gordini 16	3	R	4	3	5	4	4	R	4	R	8	5	7	14
Kenneth McAlpine	Connaught A-Lea-Francis	-	-	-	-	-	-	17	16	-	-	-	-	22	R
Harry Merkel	BMW Eigenbau	-	-	-	-	-	-	-	-	NT	DNS	-	-	-	-
Robin Montgomerie-Charrington															
	Aston NB41-Butterworth	-	-	15	R	-	-	-	-	-	-	-	-	-	-
Stirling Moss	HWM 52-Alta	9	R	-	-	-	-	-	-	-	-	-	-	-	-
	ERA G-type-Bristol	-	-	10	R	-	-	16	R	-	-	NT	R	-	-
	Connaught A-Lea-Francis	-	-	-	-	-	-	-	-	-	-	-	-	9	R
David Murray	Cooper T20-Bristol	-	-	-	-	-	-	22	R	-	-	-	-	-	-
Helmut Niedermayr	AFM 6-BMW	-	-	-	-	-	-	-	-	NT	R	-	-	-	-
Robert O'Brien	Simca-Gordini 15	-	-	22	14	-	-	-	-	-	-	-	-	-	-

driver	car	CH		B		F		GB		D		NL		I	
		Q	R	Q	R	Q	R	Q	R	Q	R	Q	R	Q	R
Reg Parnell	Cooper T20-Bristol	-	-	-	-	-	-	6	7	-	-	-	-	-	-
Josef Peters	Veritas RS-BMW	-	-	-	-	-	-	-	-	NT	R	-	-	-	-
Paul Pietsch	Veritas Meteor	-	-	-	-	-	-	-	-	7	R	-	-	-	-
Dennis Poore	Connaught A-Lea-Francis	-	-	-	-	-	-	8	4	-	-	-	-	19	12
Fritz Riess	Veritas RS-BMW	-	-	-	-	-	-	-	-	NT	7	-	-	-	-
Franco Rol	Maserati A6GCM	-	-	-	-	-	-	-	-	-	-	-	-	16	R
Louis Rosier	Ferrari 500	NT	R	17	R	9	R	-	-	-	-	-	-	17	10
Roy Salvadori	Ferrari 500	-	-	-	-	-	-	19	8	-	-	-	-	-	-
Harry Schell	Maserati 4CLT/48-Plate	18	R	-	-	12	R	NT	17	-	-	-	-	-	-
Rudolf Schoeller	Ferrari 212	-	-	-	-	-	-	-	-	NT	R	-	-	-	-
Andre Simon	Ferrari 500	4	R	-	-	-	-	-	-	-	-	-	-	8	6
Hans Stuck	AFM-Kuchen	14	R	-	-	-	-	-	-	-	-	-	-	-	-
	Ferrari 212	-	-	-	-	-	-	-	-	-	-	-	-	33	DNQ
Piero Taruffi	Ferrari 500	2	1F	3	R	3	3	3	2	5	4	-	-	6	7
Max de Terra	Simca-Gordini 11	NT	R	-	-	-	-	-	-	-	-	-	-	-	-
Eric Thompson	Connaught A-Lea-Francis	-	-	-	-	-	-	9	5	-	-	-	-	-	-
Charles de Tornaco	Ferrari 500	-	-	13	7	-	-	-	-	-	-	17	R	25	DNQ
Maurice Trintignant	Ferrari 166/F2	NT	DNS	-	-	-	-	-	-	-	-	-	-	-	-
	Simca-Gordini 15	-	-	-	-	6	5	-	-	-	-	-	-	-	-
	Gordini 16	-	-	-	-	-	-	21	R	3	R	5	6	4	R
Toni Ulmen	Veritas Meteor	16	R	-	-	-	-	-	-	-	-	-	-	-	-
	Veritas Meteor-BMW	-	-	-	-	-	-	-	-	NT	R	-	-	-	-
Luigi Villoresi	Ferrari 500	-	-	-	-	-	-	-	-	-	-	4	3	2	3
Ken Wharton	Frazer-Nash FN48-Bristol	13	4	7	R	-	-	-	-	-	-	-	-	-	-
	Frazer-Nash 421-Bristol	-	-	-	-	-	-	-	-	-	-	7	R	-	-
	Cooper T20-Bristol	-	-	-	-	-	-	-	-	-	-	-	-	15	9
Graham Whitehead	Alta F2	-	-	-	-	-	-	12	12	-	-	-	-	-	-
Peter Whitehead	Alta F2	-	-	-	-	13	R	-	-	-	-	-	-	-	-
	Ferrari 125/F2	-	-	-	-	-	-	20	10	-	-	-	-	29	DNQ

SHARED DRIVES - Swiss GP: Andre Simon/Giuseppe Farina (Ferrari 500) R. French GP: Rudolf Fischer/Peter Hirt (Ferrari 212) 11; Emanuel de Graffenried/Harry Schell (Maserati 4CLT/48-Plate) R. Dutch GP: Chico Landi/Jan Flinterman (Maserati A6GCM) 9

1952 FINAL CHAMPIONSHIP POSITIONS

	Drivers							
1	Alberto Ascari	36 (53.5)*		Luigi Villoresi	8	16=	Felice Bonetto	2
2	Giuseppe Farina	24 (27)*	9	Jose Froilan Gonzalez	6.5		Alan Brown	2
3	Piero Taruffi	22	10=	Jean Behra	6		Art Cross	2
4=	Rudolf Fischer	10		Jim Rathmann	6		Paul Frere	2
	Mike Hawthorn	10	12	Sam Hanks	4		Eric Thompson	2
6	Robert Manzon	9	13=	Duane Carter	3		Maurice Trintignant	2
7=	Troy Ruttman	8		Dennis Poore	3	22	Bill Vukovich	1
				Ken Wharton	3		*Best four results count	

GROTE PRIJS VAN NEDERLAND

17 August 1952. Zandvoort. 90 laps of a 2.605-mile circuit = 234.450 miles. Cool, overcast and wet. World Championship round 7

1	Alberto Ascari	Ferrari 500	90	2h53m28.5
2	Giuseppe Farina	Ferrari 500	90	2h54m08.6
3	Luigi Villoresi	Ferrari 500	90	2h55m02.9
4	Mike Hawthorn	Cooper T20-Bristol	88	
5	Robert Manzon	Gordini 16	87	
6	Maurice Trintignant	Gordini 16	87	

Winner's average speed: 81.089 mph. Starting grid front row: Ascari, 1m46.5 (pole), Farina, 1m48.6 and Hawthorn, 1m51.6. Fastest lap: Ascari, 1m49.8. Leaders: Ascari, laps 1-90

GRAN PREMIO D'ITALIA

7 September 1952. Monza. 80 laps of a 3.915-mile circuit = 313.200 miles. Warm, dry and sunny. World Championship round 8

1	Alberto Ascari	Ferrari 500	80	2h50m45.6
2	Jose Froilan Gonzalez	Maserati A6GCM	80	2h51m47.4
3	Luigi Villoresi	Ferrari 500	80	2h52m49.8
4	Giuseppe Farina	Ferrari 500	80	2h52m57.0
5	Felice Bonetto	Maserati A6GCM	79	
6	Andre Simon	Ferrari 500	79	

Winner's average speed: 110.049 mph. Starting grid front row: Ascari, 2m05.7 (pole), Villoresi, 2m06.6, Farina, 2m07.0 and Trintignant, 2m07.2. Fastest lap: Ascari and Gonzalez, 2m06.1. Leaders: Gonzalez, laps 1-36; Ascari, 37-80

1953

Alberto Ascari remained the man to beat in the second and final year of Formula 2, winning the first three Grands Prix of the season. He was finally beaten into fourth position in the dramatic French Grand Prix, ending a record run of nine successive victories stretching back to the 1952 Belgian GP. At Reims, his new team-mate Mike Hawthorn recorded his first Grand Prix win by overtaking Juan Manuel Fangio at the last corner after a breathtaking wheel-to-wheel dice for the lead. Ascari won two more races on the way to retaining the championship, while Giuseppe Farina also won for the

Formula 1

1953 DRIVERS' RECORDS

(excluding Indianapolis 500)

driver	car	RA		NL		B		F		GB		D		CH		I	
		Q	R	Q	R	Q	R	Q	R	Q	R	Q	R	Q	R	Q	R
Kurt Adolff	Ferrari 166C	-	-	-	-	-	-	-	-	-	-	27	R	-	-	-	-
Alberto Ascari	Ferrari 500	1	1F	1	1	2	1	1	4F	1	1F	1	8F	2	1F	1	R
John Barber	Cooper T23-Bristol	16	8	-	-	-	-	-	-	-	-	-	-	-	-	-	-
Edgar Barth	EMW-BMW	-	-	-	-	-	-	-	-	-	-	24	R	-	-	-	-
Erwin Bauer	Veritas RS	-	-	-	-	-	-	-	-	-	-	33	R	-	-	-	-
Elie Bayol	OSCA 20	-	-	-	-	-	-	15	R	-	-	-	-	NT	DNS	13	R
Gunther Bechem	AFM 2-BMW	-	-	-	-	-	-	-	-	-	-	30	R	-	-	-	-
Jean Behra	Gordini 16	11	6	-	-	14	R	NT	10	22	R	9	R	12	R	-	-
Georges Berger	Simca-Gordini 15	-	-	-	-	20	R	-	-	-	-	-	-	-	-	-	-
"B Bira"	Connaught A-Lea-Francis	-	-	-	-	-	-	11	R	19	7	15	R	-	-	-	-
	Maserati A6SSG	-	-	-	-	-	-	-	-	-	-	-	-	-	-	23	11
Pablo Birger	Simca-Gordini 15	14	R	-	-	-	-	-	-	-	-	-	-	-	-	-	-
Felice Bonetto	Maserati A6GCM	15	R	-	-	-	-	-	-	-	-	-	-	-	-	-	-
	Maserati A6SSG	-	-	13	3	-	-	2	R	16	6	7	4	10	4	7	R
Alan Brown	Cooper T20-Bristol	12	9	-	-	-	-	-	-	-	-	17	R	-	-	-	-
	Cooper T23-Bristol	-	-	-	-	-	-	-	-	21	R	-	-	-	-	24	12
Piero Carini	Ferrari 553	-	-	-	-	-	-	-	-	-	-	-	-	-	-	20	R
Louis Chiron	OSCA 20	-	-	-	-	-	-	NT	NC	NT	DNS	-	-	NT	DNS	25	10
Johnny Claes	Connaught A-Lea-Francis	-	-	17	NC	-	-	21	12	-	-	25	R	-	-	30	R
	Maserati A6SSG	-	-	-	-	10	R	-	-	-	-	-	-	-	-	-	-
Peter Collins	HWM 53-Alta	-	-	16	8	16	R	17	13	23	R	-	-	-	-	-	-
Tony Crook	Cooper T24-Alta	-	-	-	-	-	-	-	-	25	R	-	-	-	-	-	-
Jack Fairman	HWM 52/53-Alta	-	-	-	-	-	-	-	-	27	R	-	-	-	-	-	-
	Connaught A-Lea-Francis	-	-	-	-	-	-	-	-	-	-	-	-	-	-	22	NC
Juan Manuel Fangio	Maserati A6GCM	2	R	-	-	-	-	-	-	-	-	-	-	-	-	-	-
	Maserati A6SSG	-	-	2	R	1	R	4	2F	4	2	2	2	1	4	2	1F
Giuseppe Farina	Ferrari 500	4	R	3	2	4	R	6	5	5	3	3	1	3	2	3	2
John Fitch	HWM 52/53-Alta	-	-	-	-	-	-	-	-	-	-	-	-	-	-	26	R
Theo Fitzau	AFM 7-BMW	-	-	-	-	-	-	-	-	-	-	21	R	-	-	-	-
Paul Frere	HWM 53-Alta	-	-	-	-	11	10	-	-	-	-	-	-	16	R	-	-
Oscar Galvez	Maserati A6GCM	9	5	-	-	-	-	-	-	-	-	-	-	-	-	-	-
Bob Gerard	Cooper T23-Bristol	-	-	-	-	-	-	12	11	18	R	-	-	-	-	-	-
Yves Giraud-Cabantous	HWM 53-Alta	-	-	-	-	-	-	18	14	-	-	-	-	-	-	28	15
Helmut Glockler	Cooper T23-Bristol	-	-	-	-	-	-	-	-	-	-	NT	DNS	-	-	-	-
Jose Froilan Gonzalez	Maserati A6GCM	5	3	-	-	-	-	-	-	-	-	-	-	-	-	-	-
	Maserati A6SSG	-	-	5	3	3	RF	5	3	2	4F	-	-	-	-	-	-
Emanuel de Graffenried	Maserati A6SSG	-	-	7	5	9	4	9	7	26	R	11	5	8	R	9	R
Duncan Hamilton	HWM 53-Alta	-	-	-	-	-	-	-	-	17	R	-	-	-	-	-	-
Mike Hawthorn	Ferrari 500	6	4	6	4	7	6	7	1	3	5	4	3	7	3	6	4
Willi Heeks	Veritas Meteor	-	-	-	-	-	-	-	-	-	-	18	R	-	-	-	-
Theo Helfrich	Veritas RS	-	-	-	-	-	-	-	-	-	-	28	12	-	-	-	-
Hans Herrmann	Veritas Meteor	-	-	-	-	-	-	-	-	-	-	14	9	-	-	-	-
Peter Hirt	Ferrari 500	-	-	-	-	-	-	-	-	-	-	-	-	17	R	-	-
Oswald Karch	Veritas RS	-	-	-	-	-	-	-	-	-	-	34	R	-	-	-	-
Ernst Klodwig	Heck-BMW	-	-	-	-	-	-	-	-	-	-	32	15	-	-	-	-
Rudolf Krause	BMW Eigenbau	-	-	-	-	-	-	-	-	-	-	26	14	-	-	-	-
Chico Landi	Maserati A6SSG	-	-	-	-	-	-	-	-	-	-	-	-	20	R	21	R
Hermann Lang	Maserati A6SSG	-	-	-	-	-	-	-	-	-	-	-	-	11	5	-	-
Arthur Legat	Veritas Meteor	-	-	-	-	19	R	-	-	-	-	-	-	-	-	-	-
Ernst Loof	Veritas Meteor	-	-	-	-	-	-	-	-	-	-	31	R	-	-	-	-
Lance Macklin	HWM 53-Alta	-	-	15	R	17	R	16	R	12	R	-	-	15	R	27	R
Umberto Maglioli	Ferrari 553	-	-	-	-	-	-	-	-	-	-	-	-	-	-	11	8
Sergio Mantovani	Maserati A6SSG	-	-	-	-	-	-	-	-	-	-	-	-	-	-	12	7
Robert Manzon	Gordini 16	8	R	-	-	-	-	-	-	-	-	-	-	-	-	-	-
Onofre Marimon	Maserati A6SSG	-	-	-	-	6	3	8	9	7	R	8	R	5	R	-	-
	Maserati A6GCM	-	-	-	-	-	-	-	-	-	-	-	-	-	-	4	R
Kenneth McAlpine	Connaught A-Lea-Francis	-	-	14	R	-	-	-	-	13	R	16	13	-	-	18	NC
Carlos Menditeguy	Gordini 16	10	R	-	-	-	-	-	-	-	-	-	-	-	-	-	-
Roberto Mieres	Gordini 16	-	-	19	R	-	-	24	R	-	-	-	-	-	-	16	6
Stirling Moss	Connaught A-Lea-Francis	-	-	9	9	-	-	-	-	-	-	-	-	-	-	-	-
	Cooper T24-Alta	-	-	-	-	-	-	-	-	13	R	12	6	-	-	10	13
Luigi Musso	Maserati A6SSG	-	-	-	-	-	-	-	-	-	-	-	-	-	-	NT	7
Rodney Nuckey	Cooper T23-Bristol	-	-	-	-	-	-	-	-	-	-	20	11	-	-	-	-
Andre Pilette	Connaught A-Lea-Francis	-	-	-	-	18	11	-	-	-	-	-	-	-	-	-	-
Tony Rolt	Connaught A-Lea-Francis	-	-	-	-	-	-	-	-	10	R	-	-	-	-	-	-

driver	car	RA Q	RA R	NL Q	NL R	B Q	B R	F Q	F R	GB Q	GB R	D Q	D R	CH Q	CH R	I Q	I R
Louis Rosier	Ferrari 500	-	-	8	7	13	8	10	8	24	10	22	10	14	R	17	16
Roy Salvadori	Connaught A-Lea-Francis	-	-	11	R	-	-	19	R	28	R	13	R	-	-	14	R
Harry Schell	Gordini 16	NT	7	10	R	12	7	20	R	9	R	10	R	-	-	15	9
Albert Scherrer	HWM 53-Alta	-	-	-	-	-	-	-	-	-	-	-	-	18	8	-	-
Adolfo Schwelm Cruz	Cooper T20-Bristol	13	R	-	-	-	-	-	-	-	-	-	-	-	-	-	-
Wolfgang Seidel	Veritas RS	-	-	-	-	-	-	-	-	-	-	29	16	-	-	-	-
Ian Stewart	Connaught A-Lea-Francis	-	-	-	-	-	-	-	-	20	R	-	-	-	-	-	-
Jimmy Stewart	Cooper T20-Bristol	-	-	-	-	-	-	-	-	15	R	-	-	-	-	-	-
Hans Stuck	AFM 4-Kuchen	-	-	-	-	-	-	-	-	-	-	23	R	-	-	29	14
Jacques Swaters	Ferrari 500	-	-	-	-	NT	DNS	-	-	-	-	19	7	13	R	-	-
Max de Terra	Ferrari 166C	-	-	-	-	-	-	-	-	-	-	-	-	19	9	-	-
Charles de Tornaco	Ferrari 500	-	-	-	-	NT	DNS	-	-	-	-	-	-	-	-	-	-
Maurice Trintignant	Gordini 16	7	7	12	6	8	5	23	R	8	R	5	R	4	R	8	5
Luigi Villoresi	Ferrari 500	3	2	4	RF	5	2	3	6	6	R	6	8	6	6	5	3
Fred Wacker	Gordini 16	-	-	NT	DNS	15	9	-	-	-	-	-	-	NT	DNS	-	-
Ken Wharton	Cooper T23-Bristol	-	-	18	R	-	-	14	R	11	8	-	-	9	7	19	NC
Peter Whitehead	Cooper T24-Alta	-	-	-	-	-	-	14	9	-	-	-	-	-	-	-	-

SHARED DRIVES - Argentinian GP: Maurice Trintignant/Harry Schell (Gordini 16) 7. Dutch GP: Felice Bonetto/Jose Froilan Gonzalez (Maserati A6SSG) 3. Belgian GP: Johnny Claes/Juan Manuel Fangio (Maserati A6SSG) R. German GP: Alberto Ascari/Luigi Villoresi (Ferrari 500) 8; Luigi Villoresi/Alberto Ascari (Ferrari 500) R. Swiss GP: Juan Manuel Fangio/Felice Bonetto (Maserati A6SSG) 4; Felice Bonetto/Juan Manuel Fangio (Maserati A6SSG) R. Italian GP: Sergio Mantovani/Luigi Musso (Maserati A6SSG) 7

team in Germany.

At the season's last race at Monza, Maserati was still looking for its first win. The Italian GP proved to be a classic slipstreaming battle, with Ascari, Farina, Fangio, and Onofre Marimon (Fangio's protégé and teammate) battling for the lead. Marimon was delayed in the pits on lap 46, but the fight for the lead continued until the very last corner of the race. Farina challenged Ferrari teammate Ascari, who spun, colliding with Marimon's lapped car in the process (Ascari was not classified as a finisher as he did not cross the line after the winner). Farina took to the grass in avoidance, allowing Fangio through to score Maserati's maiden Grand Prix victory. This was the only World Championship F2 race not won by Ferrari.

The championship featured its first Grand Prix outside Europe when it opened in Buenos Aires. Although Fangio failed to finish, local stars Gonzalez and Oscar Galvez (after whom the circuit would later be renamed) did finish in the points behind the dominant Ferraris.

GRAN PREMIO DE LA REPUBLICA ARGENTINA

18 January 1953. Buenos Aires. 97 laps of a 2.431-mile circuit = 235.807 miles. Race scheduled for 3 hours. Hot, dry and sunny. World Championship round 1

1 Alberto Ascari	Ferrari 500	97	3h01m04.6
2 Luigi Villoresi	Ferrari 500	96	
3 Jose Froilan Gonzalez	Maserati A6GCM	96	
4 Mike Hawthorn	Ferrari 500	96	
5 Oscar Galvez	Maserati A6GCM	96	
6 Jean Behra	Gordini 16	94	

Winner's average speed: 78.135 mph. Starting grid front row: Ascari, 1m55.4 (pole), Fangio, 1m56.1, Villoresi, 1m56.5 and Farina, 1m57.1. Fastest lap: Ascari, 1m48.4. Leaders: Ascari, laps 1-97

INDIANAPOLIS 500

30 May 1953. Indianapolis. 200 laps of a 2.500-mile circuit = 500.000 miles. Very hot, dry and sunny. World Championship round 2

1 Bill Vukovich	Kurtis KK500A-Offenhauser	200	3h53m01.69
2 Art Cross	Kurtis KK4000-Offenhauser	200	3h56m32.56
3 Sam Hanks/ Duane Carter	Kurtis KK4000-Offenhauser	200	3h57m13.24
4 Fred Agabashian/ Paul Russo	Kurtis KK500B-Offenhauser	200	3h57m40.91
5 Jack McGrath	Kurtis KK4000-Offenhauser	200	4h00m51.33
6 Jimmy Daywalt	Kurtis KK3000-Offenhauser	200	4h01m11.88

Winner's average speed: 128.740 mph. Starting grid front row: Vukovich, 138.392 mph (pole), Agabashian, 137.546 mph and McGrath, 136.602 mph. Fastest lap in the lead: Vukovich, 1m06.24. Leaders: Vukovich, laps 1-48, 54-200; Agabashian, 49; Jim Rathmann (Kurtis KK500B-Offenhauser), 50; Hanks, 51-53

GROTE PRIJS VAN NEDERLAND

7 June 1953. Zandvoort. 90 laps of a 2.605-mile circuit = 234.450 miles. Warm, dry and sunny. World Championship round 3

1 Alberto Ascari	Ferrari 500	90	2h53m35.8
2 Giuseppe Farina	Ferrari 500	90	2h53m46.2
3 Felice Bonetto/ Jose Froilan Gonzalez	Maserati A6SSG	89	
4 Mike Hawthorn	Ferrari 500	89	
5 Emanuel de Graffenried	Maserati A6SSG	88	
6 Maurice Trintignant	Gordini 16	87	

Winner's average speed: 81.033 mph. Starting grid front row: Ascari, 1m51.1 (pole), Fangio, 1m52.7 and Farina, 1m53.0. Fastest lap: Villoresi, 1m52.8. Leaders: Ascari, laps 1-90

GRAND PRIX DE BELGIQUE

21 June 1953. Spa-Francorchamps. 36 laps of an 8.774-mile circuit = 315.864 miles. Hot, dry and sunny. World Championship round 4

1 Alberto Ascari	Ferrari 500	36	2h48m30.3
2 Luigi Villoresi	Ferrari 500	36	2h51m18.5
3 Onofre Marimon	Maserati A6SSG	35	
4 Emanuel de Graffenried	Maserati A6SSG	35	
5 Maurice Trintignant	Gordini 16	35	
6 Mike Hawthorn	Ferrari 500	35	

Winner's average speed: 112.470 mph. Starting grid front row: Fangio, 4m30 (pole), Ascari, 4m32 and Gonzalez 4m32. Fastest lap: Gonzalez, 4m34. Leaders: Gonzalez, laps 1-11; Fangio, 12-13; Ascari, 14-36

GRAND PRIX DE L'AUTOMOBILE CLUB DE FRANCE

5 July 1953. Reims. 60 laps of a 5.187-mile circuit = 311.220 miles. Hot, dry and sunny. World Championship round 5

1953 FINAL CHAMPIONSHIP POSITIONS

Drivers								
1	Alberto Ascari	34.5 (47)*	7	Bill Vukovich	9		Oscar Galvez	2
2	Juan Manuel Fangio	27.5 (29)*	8	Emanuel de Graffenried	7		Sam Hanks	2
3	Giuseppe Farina	26 (32)*	9	Felice Bonetto	6.5		Hermann Lang	2
4	Mike Hawthorn	19 (27)*	10	Art Cross	6		Jack McGrath	2
5	Luigi Villoresi	17	11=	Onofre Marimon	4	18=	Fred Agabashian	1.5
6	Jose Froilan Gonzalez	13.5 (14.5)*		Maurice Trintignant	4		Paul Russo	1.5
			13=	Duane Carter	2		*Best four results count	

1	Mike Hawthorn	Ferrari 500	60	2h44m18.6
2	Juan Manuel Fangio	Maserati A6SSG	60	2h44m19.6
3	Jose Froilan Gonzalez	Maserati A6SSG	60	2h44m20.0
4	Alberto Ascari	Ferrari 500	60	2h44m23.2
5	Giuseppe Farina	Ferrari 500	60	2h45m26.2
6	Luigi Villoresi	Ferrari 500	60	2h45m34.5

Winner's average speed: 113.646 mph. Starting grid front row: Ascari, 2m41.2 (pole), Bonetto, 2m41.5 and Villoresi, 2m41.9. Fastest lap: Fangio and Ascari, 2m41.1. Leaders: Gonzalez, laps 1-29; Fangio, 30-31, 35-36, 39-41, 45-47, 49-53, 55-56; Hawthorn, 32-34, 37-38, 42-44, 48, 54, 57-60

1	Alberto Ascari	Ferrari 500	65	3h01m34.40
2	Giuseppe Farina	Ferrari 500	65	3h02m47.33
3	Mike Hawthorn	Ferrari 500	65	3h03m10.36
4	Juan Manuel Fangio/			
	Felice Bonetto	Maserati A6SSG	64	
5	Hermann Lang	Maserati A6SSG	62	
6	Luigi Villoresi	Ferrari 500	62	

Winner's average speed: 97.171 mph. Starting grid front row: Fangio, 2m40.1 (pole), Ascari, 2m40.7 and Farina, 2m42.6. Fastest lap: Ascari, 2m41.3. Leaders: Ascari, laps 1-40, 54-65; Farina, 41-53

BRITISH GRAND PRIX

18 July 1953. Silverstone. 90 laps of a 2.927-mile circuit = 263.430 miles. Overcast with occasional rain. World Championship round 6

1	Alberto Ascari	Ferrari 500	90	2h50m00.0
2	Juan Manuel Fangio	Maserati A6SSG	90	2h51m00.0
3	Giuseppe Farina	Ferrari 500	88	
4	Jose Froilan Gonzalez	Maserati A6SSG	88	
5	Mike Hawthorn	Ferrari 500	87	
6	Felice Bonetto	Maserati A6SSG	82	

Winner's average speed: 92.975 mph. Starting grid front row: Ascari, 1m48 (pole), Gonzalez, 1m49, Hawthorn, 1m49 and Fangio, 1m50. Fastest lap: Ascari and Gonzalez, 1m50. Leaders: Ascari, laps 1-90

GRAN PREMIO D'ITALIA

13 September 1953. Monza. 80 laps of a 3.915-mile circuit = 313.200 miles. Warm, dry and sunny. World Championship round 9

1	Juan Manuel Fangio	Maserati A6SSG	80	2h49m45.9
2	Giuseppe Farina	Ferrari 500	80	2h49m47.3
3	Luigi Villoresi	Ferrari 500	79	
4	Mike Hawthorn	Ferrari 500	79	
5	Maurice Trintignant	Gordini 16	79	
6	Roberto Mieres	Gordini 16	77	

Winner's average speed: 110.694 mph. Starting grid front row: Ascari, 2m02.7 (pole), Fangio, 2m03.2 and Farina, 2m03.9. Fastest lap: Fangio, 2m04.6. Leaders: Ascari, laps 1-6, 9, 11-24, 29-33, 36-40, 42-45, 47-49, 53-79; Fangio, 7-8, 11, 25, 27-28, 34-35, 41, 50-52, 80; Farina, 10, 12-13, 26, 46

1953 Juan Manuel Fangio disputes the lead with Giuseppe Farina, Alberto Ascari and Onofre Marimon at Monza.

GROSSER PREIS VON DEUTSCHLAND

2 August 1953. Nurburgring. 18 laps of a 14.167-mile circuit = 255.006 miles. Warm, dry and sunny. World Championship round 7

1	Giuseppe Farina	Ferrari 500	18	3h02m25.0
2	Juan Manuel Fangio	Maserati A6SSG	18	3h03m29.0
3	Mike Hawthorn	Ferrari 500	18	3h04m08.6
4	Felice Bonetto	Maserati A6SSG	18	3h11m13.6
5	Emanuel de Graffenried	Maserati A6SSG	17	
6	Stirling Moss	Cooper T24-Alta	17	

Winner's average speed: 83.876 mph. Starting grid front row: Ascari, 9m59.8 (pole), Fangio, 10m03.7, Farina, 10m04.1 and Hawthorn, 10m12.6. Fastest lap: Ascari, 9m56.0. Leaders: Ascari, laps 1-4; Hawthorn, 5-7; Farina, 8-18

GRAND PRIX DE SUISSE

23 August 1953. Bremgarten. 65 laps of a 4.524-mile circuit = 294.060 miles. Warm, dry and sunny. World Championship round 8

1954

The new 2.5-litre Formula 1 attracted new manufacturers Mercedes-Benz, renowned for their pre-war successes, and Lancia to the championship. Juan Manuel Fangio signed to lead Mercedes, while Alberto Ascari moved from Ferrari to Lancia.

Neither new marque was ready for the opening rounds in Argentina and Belgium, where Fangio won in guest appearances for the works Maserati team. This coincided with the first appearance of Maserati's classic racing car—the Gioacchino Colombo-designed 250F. But when the streamlined Mercedes-Benz W196 made its debut at Reims, it proved to be in a class of its own, taking design and construction to a new level. Fangio and teammate Karl Kling lapped the field in a dominant display.

With Lancia still delayed (forcing Ascari into a Maserati, as well) Mercedes appeared unbeatable. At Silverstone, however, the W196's all-enveloping bodywork made it difficult even for Fangio to judge the wide-open corners, and he could only finish fourth in a car dented from hitting the oil drums that marked the course. Jose Froilan Gonzalez repeated his 1951 win for Ferrari, but despite this, the team was unable to satisfactorily develop their new F1 cars throughout the season.

Now equipped with conventional open-wheel bodywork, Fangio won the German, Swiss, and Italian GPs

1954 DRIVERS' RECORDS

(excluding Indianapolis 500)

driver	car	RA Q	RA R	B Q	B R	F Q	F R	GB Q	GB R	D Q	D R	CH Q	CH R	I Q	I R	E Q	E R
Alberto Ascari	Maserati 250F	-	-	-	-	3	R	NT	RF	-	-	-	-	-	-	-	-
	Ferrari 625 (555)	-	-	-	-	-	-	-	-	-	-	-	-	2	R	-	-
	Lancia D50	-	-	-	-	-	-	-	-	-	-	-	-	-	-	1	RF
Elie Bayol	Gordini 16	15	5	-	-	-	-	-	-	-	-	-	-	-	-	-	-
Don Beauman	Connaught A-Lea-Francis	-	-	-	-	-	-	17	11	-	-	-	-	-	-	-	-
Jean Behra	Gordini 16	17	R	7	R	NT	6	5	RF	9	10	14	R	12	R	18	R
Georges Berger	Gordini 16	-	-	-	-	NT	R	-	-	-	-	-	-	-	-	-	-
"B Bira"	Maserati 250F	10	7	13	6	6	4	10	R	19	R	-	-	-	-	15	9
Eric Brandon	Cooper T23-Bristol	-	-	-	-	-	-	25	R	-	-	-	-	-	-	-	-
Alan Brown	Cooper T23-Bristol	-	-	-	-	-	-	26	DNS	-	-	-	-	-	-	-	-
Clemar Bucci	Gordini 16	-	-	-	-	-	-	13	R	16	R	10	R	17	R	-	-
Peter Collins	Vanwall Special	-	-	-	-	-	-	11	R	-	-	-	-	16	7	NT	DNS
Jorge Daponte	Maserati 250F	18	R	-	-	-	-	-	-	-	-	-	-	19	11	-	-
Juan Manuel Fangio	Maserati 250F	3	1	1	1F	-	-	-	-	-	-	-	-	-	-	-	-
	Mercedes-Benz W196	-	-	-	-	1	1	1	4F	1	1	2	1F	1	1	2	3
Giuseppe Farina	Ferrari 625	1	2	-	-	-	-	-	-	-	-	-	-	-	-	-	-
	Ferrari 553 Squalo	-	-	3	R	-	-	-	-	-	-	-	-	-	-	-	-
Ron Flockhart	Maserati 250F	-	-	-	-	-	-	NT	R	-	-	-	-	-	-	-	-
Paul Frere	Gordini 16	-	-	10	R	NT	7	-	-	6	R	-	-	-	-	-	-
Bob Gerard	Cooper T23-Bristol	-	-	-	-	-	-	18	10	-	-	-	-	-	-	-	-
Chico Godia-Sales	Maserati 250F	-	-	-	-	-	-	-	-	-	-	-	-	-	-	13	6
Jose Froilan Gonzalez	Ferrari 625	2	3F	NT	4	-	-	-	-	-	-	-	-	NT	3	-	-
	Ferrari 553 Squalo	-	-	2	R	4	R	-	-	-	-	-	-	5	RF	-	-
	Ferrari 625 (555)	-	-	-	-	-	-	2	1F	-	-	-	-	-	-	-	-
	Ferrari 625 (735/555)	-	-	-	-	-	-	-	-	5	2	1	2	-	-	-	-
Horace Gould	Cooper T23-Bristol	-	-	-	-	-	-	20	15	-	-	-	-	-	-	-	-
Emanuel de Graffenried	Maserati 250F	13	8	NT	R*	-	-	-	-	-	-	-	-	-	-	21	R
Mike Hawthorn	Ferrari 625	4	DSQ	5	4	-	-	-	-	-	-	-	-	-	-	-	-
	Ferrari 553 Squalo	-	-	-	-	8	R	-	-	-	-	-	-	-	-	3	1
	Ferrari 625 (555)	-	-	-	-	-	-	3	2F	-	-	-	-	7	2	-	-
	Ferrari 625 (735/555)	-	-	-	-	-	-	-	-	2	2	6	R	-	-	-	-
Theo Helfrich	Klenk Meteor-BMW	-	-	-	-	-	-	-	-	21	R	-	-	-	-	-	-
Hans Herrmann	Mercedes-Benz W196	-	-	-	-	7	RF	-	-	4	R	7	3	8	4	9	R
Karl Kling	Mercedes-Benz W196	-	-	-	-	2	2	6	7	NT	4F	5	R	4	R	12	5
Hermann Lang	Mercedes-Benz W196	-	-	-	-	-	-	-	-	11	R	-	-	-	-	-	-
Roger Loyer	Gordini 16	16	R	-	-	-	-	-	-	-	-	-	-	-	-	-	-
Lance Macklin	HWM 54-Alta	-	-	-	-	15	R	-	-	-	-	-	-	-	-	-	-
Umberto Maglioli	Ferrari 625	12	9	-	-	-	-	-	-	-	-	-	-	13	3	-	-
	Ferrari 553 Squalo	-	-	-	-	-	-	-	-	-	-	11	7	-	-	-	-
Sergio Mantovani	Maserati 250F	-	-	11	7	NT	DNS	-	-	15	5	9	5	9	9	10	R
Robert Manzon	Ferrari 625	-	-	-	-	12	3	15	R	12	9	-	-	15	R	17	R
	Ferrari 553 Squalo	-	-	-	-	-	-	-	-	-	-	22	DNS	-	-	-	-
Onofre Marimon	Maserati 250F	6	R	4	R	5	R	NT	3F	8	DNS	-	-	-	-	-	-
Leslie Marr	Connaught A-Lea-Francis	-	-	-	-	-	-	22	13	-	-	-	-	-	-	-	-
Carlos Menditeguy	Maserati 250F	9	DNS	-	-	-	-	-	-	-	-	-	-	-	-	-	-
Roberto Mieres	Maserati 250F	8	R	12	R	11	R	NT	6	17	R	12	4	10	R	11	4
Stirling Moss	Maserati 250F	-	-	9	3	-	-	4	RF	3	R	3	R	3	10	6	R
Luigi Musso	Maserati 250F	7	DNS	-	-	-	-	-	-	-	-	-	-	14	R	7	2
Reg Parnell	Ferrari 625	-	-	-	-	-	-	14	R	-	-	-	-	-	-	-	-
Andre Pilette	Gordini 16	-	-	8	5	-	-	12	9	20	R	-	-	-	-	-	-
Jacques Pollet	Gordini 16	-	-	-	-	NT	R	-	-	-	-	-	-	-	-	16	R
John Riseley-Prichard	Connaught A-Lea-Francis	-	-	-	-	-	-	21	R	-	-	-	-	-	-	-	-
Giovanni de Riu	Maserati 250F	-	-	-	-	-	-	-	-	-	-	-	-	21	DNS	-	-
Louis Rosier	Ferrari 625	14	R	-	-	13	R	30	R	18	8	-	-	-	-	-	-
	Maserati 250F	-	-	-	-	-	-	-	-	-	-	-	-	20	8	20	7
Roy Salvadori	Maserati 250F	-	-	-	-	10	R	7	R	-	-	-	-	-	-	-	-
Harry Schell	Maserati 250F	11	6	-	-	NT	R	16	12	14	7	13	R	-	-	4	R
Jacques Swaters	Ferrari 625	-	-	14	R	-	-	-	-	-	-	-	-	16	8	19	R
Piero Taruffi	Ferrari 625	-	-	-	-	-	-	-	-	13	6	-	-	-	-	-	-
Leslie Thorne	Connaught A-Lea-Francis	-	-	-	-	-	-	23	14	-	-	-	-	-	-	-	-
Maurice Trintignant	Ferrari 625	5	4	6	2	9	R	-	-	7	3	-	-	-	-	-	-
	Ferrari 625 (555)	-	-	-	-	-	-	8	5	-	-	-	-	11	5	-	-
	Ferrari 625 (735/555)	-	-	-	-	-	-	-	-	-	-	4	R	-	-	-	-
	Ferrari 553 Squalo	-	-	-	-	-	-	-	-	-	-	-	-	-	-	8	R

* Camera car, not competing in the Grand Prix.

driver	car	RA		B		F		GB		D		CH		I		E	
		Q	R	Q	R	Q	R	Q	R	Q	R	Q	R	Q	R	Q	R
Luigi Villoresi	Maserati 250F	-	-	-	-	14	5	NT	R	10	DNS	-	-	6	R	-	-
	Lancia D50	-	-	-	-	-	-	-	-	-	-	-	-	-	-	5	R
Ottorino Volonterio	Maserati 250F	-	-	-	-	-	-	-	-	-	-	-	-	-	-	NT	R
Fred Wacker	Gordini 16	-	-	-	-	-	-	-	-	-	-	15	R	18	6	-	-
Ken Wharton	Maserati 250F	-	-	-	-	16	R	9	8	NT	DNS	8	6	-	-	14	8
Peter Whitehead	Cooper T24-Alta	-	-	-	-	-	-	24	R	-	-	-	-	-	-	-	-
Bill Whitehouse	Connaught A-Lea-Francis	-	-	-	-	-	-	19	R	-	-	-	-	-	-	-	-

SHARED DRIVES - Belgian GP: Mike Hawthorn/Jose Froilan Gonzalez (Ferrari 625) 4. British GP: "B Bira"/Ron Flockhart (Maserati 250F) R; Luigi Villoresi/Alberto Ascari (Maserati 250F) R. German GP: Jose Froilan Gonzalez/Mike Hawthorn (Ferrari 625 (735/555)) 2. Italian GP: Umberto Maglioli/Jose Froilan Gonzalez (Ferrari 625) 3. Spanish GP: Emanuel de Graffenried/Ottorino Volonterio (Maserati 250F) R.

1954 FINAL CHAMPIONSHIP POSITIONS

Drivers							
1 Juan Manuel Fangio	42 (57.14)*		Roberto Mieres	6		Mike Nazaruk	2
2 Jose Froilan Gonzalez	25.14 (26.64)*		Luigi Musso	6		Andre Pilette	2
		12	Jack McGrath	5		Luigi Villoresi	2
3 Mike Hawthorn	24.64	13=	Onofre Marimon	4.14	23=	Duane Carter	1.5
4 Maurice Trintignant	17		Stirling Moss	4.14		Troy Ruttman	1.5
5 Karl Kling	12	15=	Sergio Mantovani	4	25	Alberto Ascari	1.14
6= Hans Herrmann	8		Robert Manzon	4	26	Jean Behra	0.14
Bill Vukovich	8	17	"B Bira"	3	*Best five results count		
8= Jimmy Bryan	6	18=	Elie Bayol	2			
Giuseppe Farina	6		Umberto Maglioli	2			

to secure his second World Championship. It is the only time a driver has won the title representing more than one marque. Sadly, Fangio's win at the Nurburgring was marred by the death in practice of his friend Onofre Marimon.

The Lancia D50 finally appeared at the last race of the year in Spain. Ascari put it on pole, led in the early laps, and set fastest race lap before clutch problems intervened, but its promise was evident. Mike Hawthorn benefited from Lancia's unreliability to win in the Squalo Ferrari.

GRAN PREMIO DE LA REPUBLICA ARGENTINA

17 January 1954. Buenos Aires. 87 laps of a 2.431-mile circuit = 211.497 miles. Race scheduled for 3 hours. Dry and overcast at the start, heavy rain later. World Championship round 1

1	Juan Manuel Fangio	Maserati 250F	87	3h00m55.8
2	Giuseppe Farina	Ferrari 625	87	3h02m14.8
3	Jose Froilan Gonzalez	Ferrari 625	87	3h02m56.8
4	Maurice Trintignant	Ferrari 625	86	
5	Elie Bayol	Gordini 16 (54)	85	
6	Harry Schell	Maserati 250F	84	

Winner's average speed: 70.137 mph. Starting grid front row: Farina, 1m44.8 (pole), Gonzalez, 1m44.9, Fangio, 1m45.6 and Hawthorn, 1m47.0. Fastest lap: Gonzalez, 1m48.2. Leaders: Farina, laps 1-14; Gonzalez, 15-32, ?-?; Hawthorn, 33-34; Fangio, 35-?, ?-87 (Gonzalez led during a heavy rain storm - exact laps not recorded)

INDIANAPOLIS 500

31 May 1954. Indianapolis. 200 laps of a 2.500-mile circuit = 500.000 miles. Very hot, dry and sunny. World Championship round 2

1	Bill Vukovich	Kurtis KK500A-Offenhauser	200	3h49m17.27
2	Jimmy Bryan	Kuzma-Offenhauser	200	3h50m27.26
3	Jack McGrath	Kurtis KK500C-Offenhauser	200	3h50m36.97
4	Troy Ruttman/ Duane Carter	Kurtis KK500A-Offenhauser	200	3h52m09.90
5	Mike Nazaruk	Kurtis KK500C-Offenhauser	200	3h52m41.85
6	Fred Agabashian	Kurtis KK500C-Offenhauser	200	3h53m04.83

Winner's average speed: 130.840 mph. Starting grid front row: McGrath, 141.033 mph (pole), Jimmy Daywalt (Kurtis KK500C-Offenhauser), 139.789 mph and Bryan, 139.665 mph. Fastest lap in the lead: McGrath, 1m04.04. Leaders: McGrath, laps 1-44, 89-91; Daywalt, 45-50, 55, 60; Art Cross (Kurtis KK4000-Offenhauser), 51-54, 56-59; Vukovich, 61, 92-129, 150-200; Sam Hanks (Kurtis KK4000-Offenhauser), 62; Bryan, 63-88, 130-149

GRAND PRIX DE BELGIQUE

20 June 1954. Spa-Francorchamps. 36 laps of an 8.774-mile circuit = 315.864 miles. Warm, dry and sunny. World Championship round 3

1	Juan Manuel Fangio	Maserati 250F	36	2h44m42.4
2	Maurice Trintignant	Ferrari 625	36	2h45m06.6
3	Stirling Moss	Maserati 250F	35	
4	Mike Hawthorn/ Jose Froilan Gonzalez	Ferrari 625	35	
5	Andre Pilette	Gordini 16 (54)	35	
6	"B Bira"	Maserati 250F	35	

Winner's average speed: 115.064 mph. Starting grid front row: Fangio, 4m22.1 (pole), Gonzalez, 4m23.6 and Farina, 4m26.0. Fastest lap: Fangio, 4m25.5. Leaders: Farina, laps 1-2, 11-13; Fangio, 3-10, 14-36

GRAND PRIX DE L'AUTOMOBILE CLUB DE FRANCE

4 July 1954. Reims. 61 laps of a 5.187-mile circuit = 316.407 miles. Overcast and dry at the start, rain later. World Championship round 4

1	Juan Manuel Fangio	Mercedes-Benz W196	61	2h42m47.9
2	Karl Kling	Mercedes-Benz W196	61	2h42m48.0
3	Robert Manzon	Ferrari 625	60	
4	"B Bira"	Maserati 250F	60	
5	Luigi Villoresi	Maserati 250F	58	
6	Jean Behra	Gordini 16 (54)	56	

Winner's average speed: 106.613 mph. Starting grid front row: Fangio, 2m29.4 (pole), Kling, 2m30.4 and Ascari, 2m30.5. Fastest lap: Herrmann, 2m32.9. Leaders: Kling, laps 1-2, 29-33, 38, 54-57, 60; Fangio, 3-28, 34-37, 39-53, 58-59, 61

BRITISH GRAND PRIX

17 July 1954. Silverstone. 90 laps of a 2.927-mile circuit = 263.430 miles. Cold and wet. World Championship round 5

1	Jose Froilan Gonzalez	Ferrari 625 (555)	90	2h56m14
2	Mike Hawthorn	Ferrari 625 (555)	90	2h57m24
3	Onofre Marimon	Maserati 250F	89	
4	Juan Manuel Fangio	Mercedes-Benz W196	89	
5	Maurice Trintignant	Ferrari 625 (555)	87	

| 6 | Roberto Mieres | Maserati 250F | 87 | |

Winner's average speed: 89.687 mph. Starting grid front row: Fangio, 1m45 (pole), Gonzalez, 1m46, Hawthorn, 1m46 and Moss, 1m47. Fastest lap: Ascari, Behra, Fangio, Gonzalez, Hawthorn, Marimon and Moss, all 1m50. Leaders: Gonzalez, laps 1-90

GROSSER PREIS VON DEUTSCHLAND UND EUROPA

1 August 1954. Nurburgring. 22 laps of a 14.167-mile circuit = 311.674 miles. Warm, dry and sunny. World Championship round 6

1	Juan Manuel Fangio	Mercedes-Benz W196	22	3h45m45.8
2	Jose Froilan Gonzalez/			
	Mike Hawthorn	Ferrari 625 (735/555)	22	3h47m22.3
3	Maurice Trintignant	Ferrari 625	22	3h50m54.4
4	Karl Kling	Mercedes-Benz W196	22	3h51m52.3
5	Sergio Mantovani	Maserati 250F	22	3h54m36.3
6	Piero Taruffi	Ferrari 625	21	

Winner's average speed: 82.832 mph. Starting grid front row: Fangio, 9m50.1 (pole), Hawthorn, 9m53.3 and Moss, 10m00.7. Fastest lap: Kling, 9m55.1. Leaders: Fangio, laps 1-14, 17-22; Kling, 15-16

GRAND PRIX DE SUISSE

22 August 1954. Bremgarten. 66 laps of a 4.524-mile circuit = 298.584 miles. Damp and dull at the start, drying. World Championship round 7

1	Juan Manuel Fangio	Mercedes-Benz W196	66	3h00m34.5
2	Jose Froilan Gonzalez	Ferrari 625 (735/555)	66	3h01m32.3
3	Hans Herrmann	Mercedes-Benz W196	65	
4	Roberto Mieres	Maserati 250F	64	
5	Sergio Mantovani	Maserati 250F	64	
6	Ken Wharton	Maserati 250F	64	

Winner's average speed: 99.211 mph. Starting grid front row: Gonzalez, 2m39.5 (pole), Fangio, 2m39.7 and Moss, 2m41.4. Fastest lap: Fangio, 2m39.7. Leaders: Fangio, laps 1-66

GRAN PREMIO D'ITALIA

5 September 1954. Monza. 80 laps of a 3.915-mile circuit = 313.200 miles. Warm, dry and sunny. World Championship round 8

1	Juan Manuel Fangio	Mercedes-Benz W196	80	2h47m47.9
2	Mike Hawthorn	Ferrari 625 (555)	79	
3	Umberto Maglioli/			
	Jose Froilan Gonzalez	Ferrari 625	78	
4	Hans Herrmann	Mercedes-Benz W196	77	
5	Maurice Trintignant	Ferrari 625 (555)	75	
6	Fred Wacker	Gordini 16 (54)	75	

Winner's average speed: 111.992 mph. Starting grid front row: Fangio, 1m59.0 (pole), Ascari, 1m59.2 and Moss, 1m59.3. Fastest lap: Gonzalez, 2m00.8. Leaders: Kling, laps 1-3; Fangio, 4-5, 23, 68-80; Ascari, 6-22, 24-44, 46-48; Moss, 45, 49-67

GRAN PREMIO DE ESPANA

24 October 1954. Pedralbes. 80 laps of a 3.936-mile circuit = 314.880 miles. Warm, dry and sunny. World Championship round 9

1	Mike Hawthorn	Ferrari 553 Squalo	80	3h13m52.1
2	Luigi Musso	Maserati 250F	80	3h15m05.3
3	Juan Manuel Fangio	Mercedes-Benz W196	79	
4	Roberto Mieres	Maserati 250F	79	
5	Karl Kling	Mercedes-Benz W196	79	
6	Chico Godia-Sales	Maserati 250F	76	

Winner's average speed: 97.452 mph. Starting grid front row: Ascari, 2m18.1 (pole), Fangio, 2m19.1, Hawthorn, 2m20.6 and Schell, 2m20.6. Fastest lap: Ascari, 2m20.4. Leaders: Schell, laps 1-2, 10, 13, 15-17, 19, 21, 23; Ascari, 3-9; Trintignant, 11-12, 14, 18, 20; Hawthorn, 22, 24-80

1955

The 1955 season was dominated by two tragedies, one of which brought the very existence of the sport into question. First, Alberto Ascari survived crashing his Lancia into the harbour at Monaco only to die four days later testing a sports car at Monza. But what followed was the worst accident ever to afflict motor racing. Although it did not occur in a Grand Prix, its repercussions were felt in all branches of the sport. During the Le Mans 24-hour race, a collision on the pit straight launched the Mercedes of "Pierre Levegh" (a pseudonym for Pierre Bouillon) into the crowd; it burst into flames, killing "Levegh" and over 80 spectators. The French, German, Swiss, and Spanish GPs were all cancelled, and only the British and Italian races were held after the disaster.

The Le Mans accident led to the withdrawal of Mercedes from racing at the end of the year. An enduring consequence of the accident is that motor racing remains outlawed in Switzerland to this day. Lancia immediately pulled out of Grand Prix racing following the death of Ascari; its cars and designer Vittorio Jano were re-employed by Ferrari. Ferrari's 4-cylinder engine had become obsolete since the F2 years, and increasing debts prevented the company from developing a new unit. The V8 Lancia-Ferrari D50 presented a ready-made solution and would eventually return Ferrari to full competitiveness.

Juan Manuel Fangio won all but two rounds for Mercedes to successfully defend his drivers' title. These included a home victory in Buenos Aires, in which he drove without relief while most of his competitors suffered from heat exhaustion in possibly the hottest weather ever experienced for a World Championship Grand Prix. New Mercedes recruit Stirling Moss scored his first Grand Prix victory at Aintree. Fangio shadowed him across the line, with Karl Kling and Piero Taruffi completing a 1-2-3-4 for the team.

Mercedes' only defeat came at Monaco, which had been restored to the World Championship calendar for the first time since 1950. Maurice Trintignant recorded a first victory after Fangio, Moss, Ascari, and Roberto Mieres had all retired ahead of him.

Tony Brooks won the non-championship Syracuse Grand Prix for Connaught—the first continental Grand Prix win for a British car since the twenties.

GRAN PREMIO DE LA REPUBLICA ARGENTINA

16 January 1955. Buenos Aires. 96 laps of a 2.431-mile circuit = 233.376 miles. Race scheduled for 3 hours. Extreme heat, dry and sunny. World Championship round 1

1	Juan Manuel Fangio	Mercedes-Benz W196	96	3h00m38.6
2	Jose Froilan Gonzalez/			
	Maurice Trintignant/			
	Giuseppe Farina	Ferrari 625 (555)	96	3h02m08.2
3	Giuseppe Farina/			
	Umberto Maglioli/			
	Maurice Trintignant	Ferrari 625 (555)	94	
4	Hans Herrmann/			
	Karl Kling/			
	Stirling Moss	Mercedes-Benz W196	94	
5	Roberto Mieres	Maserati 250F	91	
6	Harry Schell/			
	Jean Behra	Maserati 250F	88	

Winner's average speed: 77.515 mph. Starting grid front row: Gonzalez, 1m43.1 (pole), Ascari, 1m43.2, Fangio, 1m43.6 and Behra, 1m43.8. Fastest lap: Fangio, 1m48.3. Leaders: Fangio, laps 1-2, 26-34, 43-96; Ascari, 3-5, 11-21; Gonzalez, 6-10, 22-25; Schell, 35-40; Mieres, 41-42

Formula 1

1955 DRIVERS' RECORDS

(excluding Indianapolis 500)

driver	car	RA Q	RA R	MC Q	MC R	B Q	B R	NL Q	NL R	GB Q	GB R	I Q	I R
Alberto Ascari	Lancia D50	2	R	2	R	-	-	-	-	-	-	-	-
Elie Bayol	Gordini 16	15	R	16	R	-	-	-	-	-	-	-	-
Jean Behra	Maserati 250F	4	6	5	3	5	5	6	6	3	R	6	4
Pablo Birger	Gordini 16	9	R	-	-	-	-	-	-	-	-	-	-
Jack Brabham	Cooper T40-Bristol	-	-	-	-	-	-	-	-	25	R	-	-
Clemar Bucci	Maserati 250F	20	R	-	-	-	-	-	-	-	-	-	-
Eugenio Castellotti	Lancia D50	12	R	4	2	1	R	-	-	-	-	-	-
	Ferrari 555 Supersqualo	-	-	-	-	-	-	9	5	-	-	4	3
	Ferrari 625 (555)	-	-	-	-	-	-	-	-	10	6	-	-
Louis Chiron	Lancia D50	-	-	19	6	-	-	-	-	-	-	-	-
Johnny Claes	Maserati 250F	-	-	-	-	NT	DNS	-	-	-	-	-	-
	Ferrari 625	-	-	-	-	-	-	16	11	-	-	-	-
Peter Collins	Maserati 250F	-	-	-	-	-	-	-	-	24	R	11	R
Jack Fairman	Connaught B-Alta	-	-	-	-	-	-	-	-	21	DNS	-	-
Juan Manuel Fangio	Mercedes-Benz W196	3	1F	1	RF	2	1F	1	1	2	2	1	1
Giuseppe Farina	Ferrari 625 (555)	5	2+3	14	4	-	-	-	-	-	-	-	-
	Ferrari 555 Supersqualo	-	-	-	-	4	3	-	-	-	-	-	-
	Lancia-Ferrari D50	-	-	-	-	-	-	-	-	-	-	5	DNS
John Fitch	Maserati 250F	-	-	-	-	-	-	-	-	-	-	20	9
Paul Frere	Ferrari 555 Supersqualo	-	-	NT	8	8	4	-	-	-	-	-	-
Jose Froilan Gonzalez	Ferrari 625 (555)	1	2	-	-	-	-	-	-	-	-	-	-
Horace Gould	Maserati 250F	-	-	-	-	-	-	15	R	22	R	21	R
Mike Hawthorn	Vanwall VW1	-	-	12	R	9	R	-	-	-	-	-	-
	Ferrari 555 Supersqualo	-	-	-	-	-	-	5	7	-	-	14	R
	Ferrari 625 (555)	-	-	-	-	-	-	-	-	12	6	-	-
Hans Herrmann	Mercedes-Benz W196	10	4	-	-	-	-	-	-	-	-	-	-
Jesus Iglesias	Gordini 16	17	R	-	-	-	-	-	-	-	-	-	-
Karl Kling	Mercedes-Benz W196	6	4	-	-	6	R	3	R	4	3	3	R
Jean Lucas	Gordini 32	-	-	-	-	-	-	-	-	-	-	22	R
Lance Macklin	Maserati 250F	-	-	21	DNQ	-	-	-	-	16	8	-	-
Umberto Maglioli	Ferrari 625 (555)	NT	3	-	-	-	-	-	-	-	-	-	-
	Ferrari 555 Supersqualo	-	-	-	-	-	-	-	-	-	-	12	6
Sergio Mantovani	Maserati 250F	19	7	-	-	-	-	-	-	-	-	-	-
Robert Manzon	Gordini 16	-	-	13	R	-	-	11	R	11	R	-	-
Leslie Marr	Connaught B-Alta	-	-	-	-	-	-	-	-	19	R	-	-
Kenneth McAlpine	Connaught B-Alta	-	-	-	-	-	-	-	-	17	R	-	-
Carlos Menditeguy	Maserati 250F	13	R	-	-	-	-	-	-	-	-	16	5
Roberto Mieres	Maserati 250F	16	5	6	R	13	5	7	4F	6	R	7	7
Stirling Moss	Mercedes-Benz W196	8	4	3	9	3	2	2	1	1	1F	2	RF
Luigi Musso	Maserati 250F	18	7	8	R	7	7	4	3	9	5	10	R
Cesare Perdisa	Maserati 250F	-	-	11	3	11	8	-	-	-	-	-	-
Luigi Piotti	Maserati 4CLT/48-Anzani	-	-	-	-	-	-	-	-	-	-	NT	DNS
Jacques Pollet	Gordini 16	-	-	20	7	-	-	12	10	-	-	19	R
Tony Rolt	Connaught B-Alta	-	-	-	-	-	-	-	-	14	R	-	-
Louis Rosier	Maserati 250F	-	-	17	R	12	9	13	9	-	-	-	-
Roy Salvadori	Maserati 250F	-	-	-	-	-	-	-	-	20	R	-	-
Harry Schell	Maserati 250F	7	6	-	-	-	-	-	-	-	-	-	-
	Ferrari 555 Supersqualo	-	-	18	R	-	-	-	-	-	-	-	-
	Vanwall VW2	-	-	-	-	-	-	-	-	7	R	13	R
	Vanwall VW3	-	-	-	-	-	-	-	-	NT	9	-	-
Hermano da Silva Ramos	Gordini 16	-	-	-	-	-	-	14	8	18	R	18	R
Andre Simon	Mercedes-Benz W196	-	-	10	R	-	-	-	-	-	-	-	-
	Maserati 250F	-	-	-	-	-	-	-	-	8	R	-	-
Mike Sparken	Gordini 16	-	-	-	-	-	-	-	-	23	7	-	-
Piero Taruffi	Ferrari 555 Supersqualo	-	-	15	8	-	-	-	-	-	-	-	-
	Mercedes-Benz W196	-	-	-	-	-	-	-	-	5	4	9	2
Maurice Trintignant	Ferrari 625 (555)	14	2+3	9	1	-	-	-	-	13	R	-	-
	Ferrari 555 Supersqualo	-	-	-	-	10	6	8	R	-	-	15	8
Alberto Uria	Maserati 250F	21	R	-	-	-	-	-	-	-	-	-	-
Luigi Villoresi	Lancia D50	11	R	7	5	-	-	-	-	-	-	-	-
	Lancia-Ferrari D50	-	-	-	-	-	-	-	-	-	-	8	DNS
Peter Walker	Maserati 250F	-	-	-	-	-	-	10	R	-	-	-	-
	Connaught B-Alta	-	-	-	-	-	-	-	-	NT	R	-	-
Ken Wharton	Vanwall VW3	-	-	-	-	-	-	-	-	15	9	-	-
	Vanwall VW4	-	-	-	-	-	-	-	-	-	-	17	R
Ted Whiteaway	HWM 54-Alta	-	-	22	DNQ	-	-	-	-	-	-	-	-

SHARED DRIVES - Argentinian GP: Jose Froilan Gonzalez/Maurice Trintignant/Giuseppe Farina (Ferrari 625 (555)) 2; Giuseppe Farina/Umberto Maglioli/Maurice Trintignant (Ferrari 625 (555)) 3; Hans Herrmann/Karl Kling/Stirling Moss (Mercedes-Benz W196) 4; Harry Schell/Jean Behra (Maserati 250F) 6; Luigi Musso/Sergio Mantovani/Harry Schell (Maserati 250F) 7; Clemar Bucci/Harry Schell/Carlos Menditeguy (Maserati 250F) R; Sergio Mantovani/Luigi Musso/Jean Behra (Maserati 250F) R; Eugenio Castellotti/Luigi Villoresi (Lancia D50) R. Monaco GP: Jean Behra/Cesare Perdisa (Maserati 250F) 3; Piero Taruffi/Paul Frere (Ferrari 555 Supersqualo) 8. Belgian GP: Roberto Mieres/Jean Behra (Maserati 250F) 5; Cesare Perdisa/Jean Behra (Maserati 250F) R. British GP: Mike Hawthorn/Eugenio Castellotti (Ferrari 625 (555)) 6; Ken Wharton/Harry Schell (Vanwall VW3) 9; Tony Rolt/Peter Walker (Connaught B-Alta) R

1955 FINAL CHAMPIONSHIP POSITIONS

Drivers								
1	Juan Manuel Fangio	40 (41)*	9=	Jean Behra	6		Carlos Menditeguy	2
2	Stirling Moss	23		Luigi Musso	6		Cesare Perdisa	2
3	Eugenio Castellotti	12	11	Karl Kling	5		Luigi Villoresi	2
4	Maurice Trintignant	11.33	12	Jimmy Davies	4	21	Umberto Maglioli	1.33
5	Giuseppe Farina	10.33	13=	Tony Bettenhausen	3	22=	Walt Faulkner	1
6	Piero Taruffi	9		Paul Frere	3		Hans Herrmann	1
7	Bob Sweikert	8		Paul Russo	3		Bill Homeier	1
8	Roberto Mieres	7		Johnny Thomson	3		Bill Vukovich	1
			17=	Jose Froilan Gonzalez	2		*Best five results count	

GRAND PRIX DE MONACO ET D'EUROPE

22 May 1955. Monte Carlo. 100 laps of a 1.954-mile circuit = 195.400 miles. Hot, dry and sunny. World Championship round 2

1	Maurice Trintignant	Ferrari 625 (555)	100	2h58m09.8
2	Eugenio Castellotti	Lancia D50	100	2h58m30.0
3	Jean Behra/			
	Cesare Perdisa	Maserati 250F	99	
4	Giuseppe Farina	Ferrari 625 (555)	99	
5	Luigi Villoresi	Lancia D50	99	
6	Louis Chiron	Lancia D50	95	

Winner's average speed: 65.805 mph. Starting grid front row: Fangio, 1m41.1 (pole), Ascari, 1m41.1 and Moss, 1m41.2. Fastest lap: Fangio, 1m42.4. Leaders: Fangio, laps 1-49; Moss, 50-80; Trintignant, 81-100

INDIANAPOLIS 500

30 May 1955. Indianapolis. 200 laps of a 2.500-mile circuit = 500 miles. Windy and dry. World Championship round 3

1	Bob Sweikert	Kurtis KK500D-Offenhauser	200	3h53m59.53
2	Tony Bettenhausen/			
	Paul Russo	Kurtis KK500C-Offenhauser	200	3h56m43.11
3	Jimmy Davies	Kurtis KK500B-Offenhauser	200	3h57m31.89
4	Johnny Thomson	Kuzma-Offenhauser	200	3h57m38.44
5	Walt Faulkner/			
	Bill Homeier	Kurtis KK500C-Offenhauser	200	3h59m16.66
6	Andy Linden	Kurtis KK4000-Offenhauser	200	3h59m57.47

Winner's average speed: 128.209 mph. Starting grid front row: Jerry Hoyt (Stevens-Offenhauser), 140.045 mph (pole), Bettenhausen, 139.985 mph and Jack McGrath (Kurtis KK500C-Offenhauser), 142.580 mph. Fastest lap in the lead: Bill Vukovich (Kurtis KK500C-Offenhauser), 1m03.67. Leaders: McGrath, laps 1-3, 15, 25-26; Vukovich, 4-14, 16-24, 27-56; Jimmy Bryan (Kuzma-Offenhauser), 57, 59-88; Sweikert, 58, 89-132, 160-200; Art Cross (Kurtis KK500D-Offenhauser), 133-156; Don Freeland (Phillips-Offenhauser), 157-159

GRAND PRIX DE BELGIQUE

5 June 1955. Spa-Francorchamps. 36 laps of an 8.774-mile circuit = 315.864 miles. Warm, dry and sunny. World Championship round 4

1	Juan Manuel Fangio	Mercedes-Benz W196	36	2h39m29.0
2	Stirling Moss	Mercedes-Benz W196	36	2h39m37.1
3	Giuseppe Farina	Ferrari 555 Supersqualo	36	2h41m09.5
4	Paul Frere	Ferrari 555 Supersqualo	36	2h42m54.5
5	Roberto Mieres/			
	Jean Behra	Maserati 250F	35	
6	Maurice Trintignant	Ferrari 555 Supersqualo	35	

Winner's average speed: 118.833 mph. Starting grid front row: Castellotti, 4m18.1 (pole), Fangio, 4m18.6 and Moss, 4m19.2. Fastest lap: Fangio, 4m20.6. Leaders: Fangio, laps 1-36

GROTE PRIJS VAN NEDERLAND

19 June 1955. Zandvoort. 100 laps of a 2.605-mile circuit = 260.500 miles. Cool, dry and overcast at the start, light rain later. World Championship round 5

1	Juan Manuel Fangio	Mercedes-Benz W196	100	2h54m23.8
2	Stirling Moss	Mercedes-Benz W196	100	2h54m24.1
3	Luigi Musso	Maserati 250F	100	2h55m20.9
4	Roberto Mieres	Maserati 250F	99	
5	Eugenio Castellotti	Ferrari 555 Supersqualo	97	
6	Jean Behra	Maserati 250F	97	

Winner's average speed: 89.623 mph. Starting grid front row: Fangio, 1m40.0 (pole), Moss, 1m40.4 and Kling, 1m41.1. Fastest lap: Mieres, 1m40.9. Leaders: Fangio, laps 1-100

BRITISH GRAND PRIX

16 July 1955. Aintree. 90 laps of a 3.000-mile circuit = 270.000 miles. Hot, dry and sunny. World Championship round 6

1	Stirling Moss	Mercedes-Benz W196	90	3h07m21.2
2	Juan Manuel Fangio	Mercedes-Benz W196	90	3h07m21.4
3	Karl Kling	Mercedes-Benz W196	90	3h08m33.0
4	Piero Taruffi	Mercedes-Benz W196	89	
5	Luigi Musso	Maserati 250F	89	
6	Mike Hawthorn/			
	Eugenio Castellotti	Ferrari 625 (555)	87	

Winner's average speed: 86.468 mph. Starting grid front row: Moss, 2m00.4 (pole), Fangio, 2m00.6 and Behra, 2m01.4. Fastest lap: Moss, 2m00.4. Leaders: Fangio, laps 1-2, 18-25; Moss, 3-17, 26-90

GRAN PREMIO D'ITALIA

11 September 1955. Monza. 50 laps of a 6.214-mile circuit = 310.685 miles. Warm, dry and sunny. World Championship round 7

1	Juan Manuel Fangio	Mercedes-Benz W196	50	2h25m04.4
2	Piero Taruffi	Mercedes-Benz W196	50	2h25m05.1
3	Eugenio Castellotti	Ferrari 555 Supersqualo	50	2h25m50.6
4	Jean Behra	Maserati 250F	50	2h29m01.9
5	Carlos Menditeguy	Maserati 250F	49	
6	Umberto Maglioli	Ferrari 555 Supersqualo	49	

Winner's average speed: 128.494 mph. Starting grid front row: Fangio, 2m46.5 (pole), Moss, 2m46.8 and Kling, 2m48.3. Fastest lap: Moss, 2m46.9. Leaders: Fangio, laps 1-7, 9-50; Moss, 8

1956

The withdrawal of Mercedes-Benz at the end of the 1955 season triggered a changing of the F1 order for 1956. Juan Manuel Fangio and Stirling Moss signed for Ferrari

1956 DRIVERS' RECORDS

(excluding Indianapolis 500)

driver	car	RA Q	RA R	MC Q	MC R	B Q	B R	F Q	F R	GB Q	GB R	D Q	D R	I Q	I R
Elie Bayol	Gordini 32	-	-	11	6	-	-	-	-	-	-	-	-	-	-
Jean Behra	Maserati 250F	4	2	4	3	4	7	7	3	13	3	8	3	5	R
Jo Bonnier	Maserati 250F	-	-	-	-	-	-	-	-	-	-	-	-	NT	R
Jack Brabham	Maserati 250F	-	-	-	-	-	-	-	-	28	R	-	-	-	-
Tony Brooks	BRM P25	-	-	13	DNS	-	-	-	-	9	R	-	-	-	-
Eugenio Castellotti	Lancia-Ferrari D50	2	R	3	4	5	R	2	2	8	10	3	R	2	8
Colin Chapman	Vanwall VW3	-	-	-	-	-	-	5*	DNS	-	-	-	-	-	-
Louis Chiron	Maserati 250F	-	-	NT	DNQ	-	-	-	-	-	-	-	-	-	-
Peter Collins	Ferrari 555 Supersqualo	9	R	-	-	-	-	-	-	-	-	-	-	-	-
	Lancia-Ferrari D50	-	-	9	2	3	1	3	1	4	2	2	R	7	2
Paul Emery	Emeryson Mk1-Alta	-	-	-	-	-	-	-	-	23	R	-	-	-	-
Jack Fairman	Connaught B-Alta	-	-	-	-	-	-	-	-	21	4	-	-	16	5
Juan Manuel Fangio	Lancia-Ferrari D50	1	1F	1	2+4F	1	R	1	4F	2	1	1	1F	1	2
Ron Flockhart	BRM P25	-	-	-	-	-	-	-	-	17	R	-	-	-	-
	Connaught B-Alta	-	-	-	-	-	-	-	-	-	-	-	-	24	3
Paul Frere	Lancia-Ferrari D50	-	-	-	-	8	2	-	-	-	-	-	-	-	-
Olivier Gendebien	Lancia-Ferrari D50	10	5	-	-	-	-	11	R	-	-	-	-	-	-
Bob Gerard	Cooper T23-Bristol	-	-	-	-	-	-	-	-	22	11	-	-	-	-
Gerino Gerini	Maserati 250F	NT	4	-	-	-	-	-	-	-	-	-	-	17	10
Chico Godia-Sales	Maserati 250F	-	-	-	-	14	R	17	7	25	8	16	4	18	4
Jose Froilan Gonzalez	Maserati 250F	5	R	-	-	-	-	-	-	-	-	-	-	-	-
	Vanwall VW1	-	-	-	-	-	-	-	-	6	R	-	-	-	-
Oscar Gonzalez	Maserati 250F	NT	6	-	-	-	-	-	-	-	-	-	-	-	-
Horace Gould	Maserati 250F	-	-	16	8	15	R	-	-	14	5	13	R	-	-
Emanuel de Graffenried	Maserati 250F	-	-	-	-	-	-	-	-	-	-	-	-	19	7
Bruce Halford	Maserati 250F	-	-	-	-	-	-	-	-	20	R	11	DSQ	22	R
Mike Hawthorn	Maserati 250F	8	3	-	-	13	DNS	-	-	-	-	-	-	-	-
	BRM P25	-	-	10	DNS	-	-	-	-	3	R	-	-	-	-
	Vanwall VW2	-	-	-	-	-	-	6	10	-	-	-	-	-	-
Chico Landi	Maserati 250F	11	4	-	-	-	-	-	-	-	-	-	-	-	-
Les Leston	Connaught B-Alta	-	-	-	-	-	-	-	-	-	-	-	-	20	R
Umberto Maglioli	Maserati 250F	-	-	-	-	-	-	-	-	24	R	7	R	13	R
Robert Manzon	Gordini 16	-	-	12	R	-	-	-	-	-	-	-	-	-	-
	Gordini 32	-	-	-	-	-	-	15	9	18	9	15	R	23	R
Carlos Menditeguy	Maserati 250F	6	R	-	-	-	-	-	-	-	-	-	-	-	-
Andre Milhoux	Gordini 32	-	-	-	-	-	-	-	-	22	R	-	-	-	-
Stirling Moss	Maserati 250F	7	R	2	1	2	3F	8	5	1	RF	4	2	6	1F
Luigi Musso	Lancia-Ferrari D50	3	1	8	R	-	-	-	-	-	-	5	R	3	R
Cesare Perdisa	Maserati 250F	-	-	7	7	9	3	13	5	15	7	6	DNS	-	-
Andre Pilette	Gordini 32	-	-	NT	6	-	-	-	-	-	-	18	DNS	-	-
	Lancia-Ferrari D50	-	-	-	-	16	6	-	-	-	-	-	-	-	-
	Gordini 16	-	-	-	-	-	-	19	11	-	-	-	-	-	-
Luigi Piotti	Maserati 250F	12	R	-	-	-	-	-	-	-	-	19	R	15	6
Alfonso de Portago	Lancia-Ferrari D50	-	-	-	-	-	-	9	R	12	2	10	R	9	R
Louis Rosier	Maserati 250F	-	-	15	R	10	8	12	6	27	R	14	5	-	-
Roy Salvadori	Maserati 250F	-	-	-	-	-	-	-	-	7	R	9	R	14	11
Giorgio Scarlatti	Ferrari 500	-	-	17	DNQ	-	-	-	-	-	-	17	R	-	-
Harry Schell	Vanwall VW1	-	-	5	R	6	4	4	R	-	-	-	-	-	-
	Vanwall VW2	-	-	-	-	-	-	NT	10	5	R	-	-	10	R
	Maserati 250F	-	-	-	-	-	-	-	-	-	-	12	R	-	-
Archie Scott-Brown	Connaught B-Alta	-	-	-	-	-	-	-	-	10	R	-	-	-	-
Piero Scotti	Connaught B-Alta	-	-	-	-	12	R	-	-	-	-	-	-	-	-
Hermano da Silva Ramos	Gordini 16	-	-	14	5	-	-	-	-	-	-	-	-	-	-
	Gordini 32	-	-	-	-	-	-	14	8	26	R	-	-	21	R
Andre Simon	Maserati 250F	-	-	-	-	-	-	20	R	-	-	-	-	-	-
	Gordini 16	-	-	-	-	-	-	-	-	-	-	-	-	25	9
Piero Taruffi	Maserati 250F	-	-	-	-	-	-	16	R	-	-	-	-	-	-
	Vanwall VW1	-	-	-	-	-	-	-	-	-	-	-	-	4	R
Desmond Titterington	Connaught B-Alta	-	-	-	-	-	-	-	-	11	R	-	-	-	-
Maurice Trintignant	Vanwall VW2	-	-	6	R	7	R	-	-	-	-	-	-	-	-
	Bugatti T251	-	-	-	-	-	-	18	DNS	-	-	-	-	-	-
	Vanwall VW4	-	-	-	-	-	-	-	-	16	R	-	-	11	R
Wolfgang von Trips	Lancia-Ferrari D50	-	-	-	-	-	-	-	-	-	-	-	-	12	DNS
Alberto Uria	Maserati 250F	NT	6	-	-	-	-	-	-	-	-	-	-	-	-
Luigi Villoresi	Maserati 250F	-	-	-	-	11	5	10	R	19	6	21	R	8	R

driver	car	RA		MC		B		F		GB		D		I	
		Q	R	Q	R	Q	R	Q	R	Q	R	Q	R	Q	R
Ottorino Volonterio	Maserati 250F	-	-	-	-	-	-	-	-	-	-	20	NC	-	-

*Qualifying time set by Harry Schell. SHARED DRIVES - Argentinian GP: Luigi Musso/Juan Manuel Fangio (Lancia-Ferrari D50) 1; Chico Landi/Gerino Gerini (Maserati 250F) 4; Alberto Uria/Oscar Gonzalez (Maserati 250F) 6; Juan Manuel Fangio/Luigi Musso (Lancia-Ferrari D50) R. Monaco GP: Peter Collins/Juan Manuel Fangio (Lancia-Ferrari D50) 2; Juan Manuel Fangio/Eugenio Castellotti (Lancia-Ferrari D50) 4; Elie Bayol/Andre Pilette (Gordini 32) 6. Belgian GP: Cesare Perdisa/Stirling Moss (Maserati 250F) 3. French GP: Cesare Perdisa/Stirling Moss (Maserati 250F) 5; Mike Hawthorn/Harry Schell (Vanwall VW2) 10. British GP: Alfonso de Portago/Peter Collins (Lancia-Ferrari D50) 2; Eugenio Castellotti/Alfonso de Portago (Lancia-Ferrari D50) 10. German GP: Alfonso de Portago/Peter Collins (Lancia-Ferrari D50) R; Luigi Musso/Eugenio Castellotti (Lancia-Ferrari D50) R. Italian GP: Peter Collins/Juan Manuel Fangio (Lancia-Ferrari D50) 2; Juan Manuel Fangio/Eugenio Castellotti (Lancia-Ferrari D50) 8; Umberto Maglioli/Jean Behra (Maserati 250F) R; Luigi Villoresi/Jo Bonnier (Maserati 250F) R

1956 FINAL CHAMPIONSHIP POSITIONS

Drivers								
1	Juan Manuel Fangio	30 (34.5)*	10	Jack Fairman	5	Horace Gould	2
2	Stirling Moss	27 (28)*	11=	Ron Flockhart	4	Dick Rathmann	2
3	Peter Collins	25		Don Freeland	4	Louis Rosier	2
4	Jean Behra	22		Mike Hawthorn	4	Hermano da Silva Ramos	2
5	Pat Flaherty	8		Luigi Musso	4	Luigi Villoresi	2
6	Eugenio Castellotti	7.5	15=	Johnnie Parsons	3	25= Gerino Gerini	1.5
7=	Paul Frere	6		Cesare Perdisa	3	Chico Landi	1.5
	Chico Godia-Sales	6		Alfonso de Portago	3	27 Paul Russo	1
	Sam Hanks	6	19=	Harry Schell	3	*Best five results count	
				Olivier Gendebien	2		

and Maserati, respectively. BRM, now owned by the Owen Racing Organisation, returned with Mike Hawthorn as lead driver, while Bugatti made a one-off, final, and unsuccessful appearance at the French GP.

Although Fangio and Moss again finished first and second in the championship, consecutive wins in Belgium and France by Peter Collins, Fangio's Lancia-Ferrari teammate, almost gave the young Englishman the title. A win in the season's last race at Monza would have made Collins champion if Fangio failed to score points. But with 13 laps to go, Collins, then running a close second to Moss's Maserati, gave his car to Fangio, who had retired earlier. The Argentinian took second place and his third successive World Championship. The season also saw Luigi Musso record his first win when he shared a car with Fangio in Argentina.

Of the British challengers, Vanwall and BRM both showed increasing promise—particularly in qualifying for the French and British GPs and in the early laps at Silverstone, when Hawthorn led for BRM. Results, however, were not forthcoming, and the best finish for a British car was Ron Flockhart's third in Italy for Connaught.

And after the tragedies of the previous year, Formula 1 thankfully enjoyed a season without fatalities.

GRAN PREMIO DE LA REPUBLICA ARGENTINA

22 January 1956. Buenos Aires. 98 laps of a 2.431-mile circuit = 238.238 miles. Race scheduled for 3 hours. Warm, dry and overcast. World Championship round 1

1	Luigi Musso/			
	Juan Manuel Fangio	Lancia-Ferrari D50	98	3h00m03.7
2	Jean Behra	Maserati 250F	98	3h00m28.1
3	Mike Hawthorn	Maserati 250F	96	
4	Chico Landi/			
	Gerino Gerini	Maserati 250F	92	
5	Olivier Gendebien	Lancia-Ferrari D50	91	
6	Alberto Uria/			
	Oscar Gonzalez	Maserati 250F	88	

Winner's average speed: 79.385 mph. Starting grid front row: Fangio, 1m42.5 (pole), Castellotti, 1m44.7, Musso, 1m44.7 and Behra, 1m45.1. Fastest lap: Fangio, 1m45.3. Leaders: Gonzalez, laps 1-3; Menditeguy, 4-42; Moss, 43-66; Fangio, 67-98* (*in Musso's car)

1956 Race winner Stirling Moss splits the successful Lancia-Ferraris of Juan Manuel Fangio and Peter Collins at Monza.

GRAND PRIX DE MONACO

13 May 1956. Monte Carlo. 100 laps of a 1.954-mile circuit = 195.400 miles. Warm, dry and sunny. World Championship round 2

1	Stirling Moss	Maserati 250F	100	3h00m32.9
2	Peter Collins/			
	Juan Manuel Fangio	Lancia-Ferrari D50	100	3h00m39.0
3	Jean Behra	Maserati 250F	99	
4	Juan Manuel Fangio/			
	Eugenio Castellotti	Lancia-Ferrari D50	94	
5	Hermano da			
	Silva Ramos	Gordini 16 (54)	93	
6	Elie Bayol/			
	Andre Pilette	Gordini 32	88	

Winner's average speed: 64.936 mph. Starting grid front row: Fangio, 1m44.0 (pole), Moss, 1m44.6 and Castellotti, 1m44.9. Fastest lap: Fangio, 1m44.4. Leaders: Moss, laps 1-100

INDIANAPOLIS 500

30 May 1956. Indianapolis. 200 laps of a 2.500-mile circuit = 500.000 miles. Warm, dry and overcast. World Championship round 3

1 Pat Flaherty	Watson-Offenhauser	200	3h53m28.84
2 Sam Hanks	Kurtis KK500C-Offenhauser	200	3h53m49.30
3 Don Freeland	Phillips-Offenhauser	200	3h54m59.07
4 Johnnie Parsons	Kuzma-Offenhauser	200	3h56m54.48
5 Dick Rathmann	Kurtis KK500C-Offenhauser	200	3h57m50.65
6 Bob Sweikert	Kuzma-Offenhauser	200	3h59m03.83

Winner's average speed: 128.490 mph. Starting grid front row: Flaherty, 145.596 mph (pole), Jim Rathmann (Kurtis KK500C-Offenhauser), 145.120 mph and Pat O'Connor (Kurtis KK500D-Offenhauser), 144.980 mph. Fastest lap in the lead: Paul Russo (Kurtis KK500F-Offenhauser), 1m02.32. Leaders: J Rathmann, laps 1-3; O'Connor, 4-10, 22-40, 42-44, 46-55; Russo, 11-21; Flaherty, 41, 45, 76-200; Parsons, 56-71; Freeland, 72-75

GRAND PRIX DE BELGIQUE

3 June 1956. Spa-Francorchamps. 36 laps of an 8.774-mile circuit = 315.864 miles. Wet and overcast, drying later. World Championship round 4

1 Peter Collins	Lancia-Ferrari D50	36	2h40m00.3
2 Paul Frere	Lancia-Ferrari D50	36	2h41m51.6
3 Cesare Perdisa/			
Stirling Moss	Maserati 250F	36	2h43m16.9
4 Harry Schell	Vanwall VW1	35	
5 Luigi Villoresi	Maserati 250F	34	
6 Andre Pilette	Lancia-Ferrari D50	33	

Winner's average speed: 118.445 mph. Starting grid front row: Fangio, 4m09.8 (pole), Moss, 4m14.7 and Collins, 4m15.3. Fastest lap: Moss, 4m14.7. Leaders: Moss, laps 1-4; Fangio, 5-23; Collins, 24-36

GRAND PRIX DE L'AUTOMOBILE CLUB DE FRANCE

1 July 1956. Reims. 61 laps of a 5.187-mile circuit = 316.407 miles. Warm, dry and overcast. World Championship round 5

1 Peter Collins	Lancia-Ferrari D50	61	2h34m23.4
2 Eugenio Castellotti	Lancia-Ferrari D50	61	2h34m23.7
3 Jean Behra	Maserati 250F	61	2h35m53.3
4 Juan Manuel Fangio	Lancia-Ferrari D50	61	2h35m58.5
5 Cesare Perdisa/			
Stirling Moss	Maserati 250F	59	
6 Louis Rosier	Maserati 250F	58	

Winner's average speed: 122.964 mph. Starting grid front row: Fangio, 2m23.3 (pole), Castellotti, 2m24.6 and Collins, 2m24.9. Fastest lap: Fangio, 2m25.8. Leaders: Collins, laps 1, 47-48, 50-61; Castellotti, 2-3, 39-46, 49; Fangio, 4-38

BRITISH GRAND PRIX

14 July 1956. Silverstone. 101 laps of a 2.927-mile circuit = 295.627 miles. Warm, dry and overcast. World Championship round 6

1 Juan Manuel Fangio	Lancia-Ferrari D50	101	2h59m47.0
2 Alfonso de Portago/			
Peter Collins	Lancia-Ferrari D50	100	
3 Jean Behra	Maserati 250F	99	
4 Jack Fairman	Connaught B-Alta	98	
5 Horace Gould	Maserati 250F	97	
6 Luigi Villoresi	Maserati 250F	96	

Winner's average speed: 98.661 mph. Starting grid front row: Moss, 1m41 (pole), Fangio, 1m42, Hawthorn, 1m43 and Collins, 1m43. Fastest lap: Moss, 1m43.2. Leaders: Hawthorn, laps 1-15; Moss, 16-68; Fangio, 69-101

GROSSER PREIS VON DEUTSCHLAND

5 August 1956. Nurburgring. 22 laps of a 14.167-mile circuit = 311.674 miles. War, dry and sunny. World Championship round 7

1 Juan Manuel Fangio	Lancia-Ferrari D50	22	3h38m43.7
2 Stirling Moss	Maserati 250F	22	3h39m30.1
3 Jean Behra	Maserati 250F	22	3h46m22.0
4 Chico Godia-Sales	Maserati 250F	20	

5 Louis Rosier	Maserati 250F	19	

No other finishers. Bruce Halford (Maserati 250F) finished 4th on the road but was disqualified for receiving outside assistance and subsequently ignoring black flag. Winner's average speed: 85.496 mph. Starting grid front row: Fangio, 9m51.2 (pole), Collins, 9m51.5, Castellotti, 9m54.4 and Moss, 10m03.4. Fastest lap: Fangio, 9m41.6. Leaders: Fangio, laps 1-22

GRAN PREMIO D'ITALIA E EUROPA

2 September 1956. Monza. 50 laps of a 6.214-mile circuit = 310.685 miles. Warm with rain showers. World Championship round 8

1 Stirling Moss	Maserati 250F	50	2h23m41.3
2 Peter Collins/			
Juan Manuel Fangio	Lancia-Ferrari D50	50	2h23m47.0
3 Ron Flockhart	Connaught B-Alta	49	
4 Chico Godia-Sales	Maserati 250F	49	
5 Jack Fairman	Connaught B-Alta	47	
6 Luigi Piotti	Maserati 250F	47	

Winner's average speed: 129.733 mph. Starting grid front row: Fangio, 2m42.6 (pole), Castellotti, 2m43.4 and Musso, 2m43.7. Fastest lap: Moss, 2m45.5. Leaders: Castellotti, laps 1-4; Moss, 5-10, 12-45, 48-50; Schell, 11; Musso, 46-47

1957

Juan Manuel Fangio moved to Maserati for his final full season of Grand Prix racing. The 250F was modified, but although work had begun on a new V12 engine, the new unit was only used once and driven by Jean Behra. Mike Hawthorn replaced the "maestro" at Ferrari, and Stirling Moss moved to Tony Vandervell's improving Vanwall team.

Fangio started with a hat trick of Grand Prix wins before Vanwall came good at Aintree. Having retired his own car, Moss took over from an ill Tony Brooks to record the first win for a British car in a World Championship Grand Prix.

The following race at the Nurburgring proved the ideal stage for one of Fangio's greatest drives, which would also secure him his fifth world title. Delayed by a lengthy pit stop, the Argentinian rejoined almost a minute behind the Lancia-Ferraris of Hawthorn and Peter Collins. Fangio repeatedly beat the old lap record as he closed in on the leaders during the last ten 14-mile laps. On the penultimate lap he passed both Ferraris, and although Hawthorn fought back, the champion was not to be denied victory.

Stirling Moss rounded off the season with two further wins for Vanwall. The first of these was at Pescara on the longest circuit ever used in the World Championship. The race had been elevated to championship status due to the cancellation of the Belgian, Dutch, and Spanish Grands Prix.

John Cooper's team offered a glimpse of the future by fielding rear-engine cars in which Jack Brabham showed promise, and Roy Salvadori finished fifth in Britain.

Moss had finished second to Fangio in the final championship standings for a third successive season. With the Argentinian not contesting the whole 1958 championship, Moss would start as favourite to win his first World Championship.

GRAN PREMIO DE LA REPUBLICA ARGENTINA

13 January 1957. Buenos Aires. 100 laps of a 2.431-mile circuit = 243.100 miles. Race scheduled for 3 hours. Hot, dry and sunny. World Championship round 1

1957 DRIVERS' RECORDS

(excluding Indianapolis 500)

driver	car	RA Q	RA R	MC Q	MC R	F Q	F R	GB Q	GB R	D Q	D R	PES Q	PES R	I Q	I R
Edgar Barth	Porsche 550RS	-	-	-	-	-	-	-	-	NT	F2	-	-	-	-
Carel Godin de Beaufort	Porsche 550RS	-	-	-	-	-	-	-	-	NT	F2	-	-	-	-
Jean Behra	Maserati 250F	3	2	-	-	2	6	2	R	3	6	4	R	-	-
	Maserati 250F (V12)	-	-	-	-	-	-	-	-	-	-	-	-	5	R
Jo Bonnier	Maserati 250F	13	7	-	-	-	-	17	R	-	-	9	R	13	R
Jack Brabham	Cooper T43-Climax	-	-	13	6	13	7	13	R	NT	F2	16	7	-	-
Tony Brooks	Vanwall VW7	-	-	4	2	-	-	-	-	-	-	6	R	-	-
	Vanwall VW4	-	-	-	-	-	-	3	1	-	-	-	-	-	-
	Vanwall VW1	-	-	-	-	-	-	NT	R	5	9	-	-	-	-
	Vanwall VW6	-	-	-	-	-	-	-	-	-	-	-	-	3	7F
Ivor Bueb	Connaught B-Alta	-	-	16	R	-	-	-	-	-	-	-	-	-	-
	Maserati 250F	-	-	-	-	-	-	19	8	-	-	-	-	-	-
Eugenio Castellotti	Lancia-Ferrari D50	4	R	-	-	-	-	-	-	-	-	-	-	-	-
Peter Collins	Lancia-Ferrari D50	5	6	2	R	5	3	8	4	4	3	-	-	7	R
Paul England	Cooper T41-Climax	-	-	-	-	-	-	-	-	NT	F2	-	-	-	-
Jack Fairman	BRM P25	-	-	-	-	-	-	16	R	-	-	-	-	-	-
Juan Manuel Fangio	Maserati 250F	2	1	1	1F	1	1	4	R	1	1F	1	2	4	2
Ron Flockhart	BRM P25	-	-	11	R	11	R	-	-	-	-	-	-	-	-
Bob Gerard	Cooper T43-Bristol	-	-	-	-	-	-	18	6	-	-	-	-	-	-
Dick Gibson	Cooper T43-Climax	-	-	-	-	-	-	-	-	NT	F2	-	-	-	-
Chico Godia-Sales	Maserati 250F	-	-	-	-	-	-	-	-	16	R	12	R	15	9
Jose Froilan Gonzalez	Lancia-Ferrari D50	10	5	-	-	-	-	-	-	-	-	-	-	-	-
Horace Gould	Maserati 250F	-	-	12	R	14	R	15	DNS	15	R	11	R	18	10
Masten Gregory	Maserati 250F	-	-	10	3	-	-	-	-	10	8	7	4	11	4
Bruce Halford	Maserati 250F	-	-	-	-	-	-	-	-	13	11	14	R	14	R
Mike Hawthorn	Lancia-Ferrari D50	7	R	5	R	7	4	5	3	2	2	-	-	10	6
Hans Herrmann	Maserati 250F	-	-	18	DNQ	-	-	-	-	11	R	-	-	-	-
Les Leston	Cooper T43-Climax	-	-	21	DNQ	-	-	-	-	-	-	-	-	-	-
	BRM P25	-	-	-	-	-	-	12	R	-	-	-	-	-	-
Stuart Lewis-Evans	Connaught B-Alta	-	-	14	4	-	-	-	-	-	-	-	-	-	-
	Vanwall VW4	-	-	-	-	10	R	-	-	9	R	-	-	-	-
	Vanwall VW5	-	-	-	-	-	-	6	7	-	-	-	-	-	-
	Vanwall VW1	-	-	-	-	-	-	-	-	-	-	8	5	-	-
	Vanwall VW7	-	-	-	-	-	-	-	-	-	-	-	-	1	R
Mike MacDowel	Cooper T43-Climax	-	-	-	-	15	7	-	-	-	-	-	-	-	-
Herbert MacKay-Fraser	BRM P25	-	-	-	-	12	R	-	-	-	-	-	-	-	-
Umberto Maglioli	Porsche 550RS	-	-	-	-	-	-	-	-	NT	F2	-	-	-	-
Tony Marsh	Cooper T43-Climax	-	-	-	-	-	-	-	-	NT	F2	-	-	-	-
Carlos Menditeguy	Maserati 250F	8	3	7	R	9	R	11	R	-	-	-	-	-	-
Stirling Moss	Maserati 250F	1	8F	-	-	-	-	-	-	-	-	-	-	-	-
	Vanwall VW3	-	-	3	R	-	-	-	-	-	-	-	-	-	-
	Vanwall VW1	-	-	-	-	-	-	1	R	-	-	-	-	-	-
	Vanwall VW4	-	-	-	-	-	-	NT	1F	-	-	-	-	-	-
	Vanwall VW5	-	-	-	-	-	-	-	-	7	5	2	1F	2	1
Luigi Musso	Lancia-Ferrari D50	6	R	-	-	3	2F	10	2	8	4	3	R	9	8
Brian Naylor	Cooper T43-Climax	-	-	-	-	-	-	-	-	NT	F2	-	-	-	-
Cesare Perdisa	Lancia-Ferrari D50	11	6	-	-	-	-	-	-	-	-	-	-	-	-
Luigi Piotti	Maserati 250F	14	10	20	DNQ	-	-	-	-	-	-	13	R	17	R
Alfonso de Portago	Lancia-Ferrari D50	NT	5	-	-	-	-	-	-	-	-	-	-	-	-
Roy Salvadori	BRM P25	-	-	17	DNQ	-	-	-	-	-	-	-	-	-	-
	Vanwall VW1	-	-	-	-	6	R	-	-	-	-	-	-	-	-
	Cooper T43-Climax	-	-	-	-	-	-	14	5	NT	F2	15	R	-	-
Giorgio Scarlatti	Maserati 250F	-	-	15	R	-	-	-	-	12	10	10	6	12	5
Harry Schell	Maserati 250F	9	4	8	R	4	5	7	R	6	7	5	3	6	5
Andre Simon	Maserati 250F	-	-	19	DNQ	-	-	-	-	-	-	-	-	16	11
Alessandro de Tomaso	Ferrari 625	12	9	-	-	-	-	-	-	-	-	-	-	-	-
Maurice Trintignant	Lancia-Ferrari D50	-	-	6	5	8	R	9	4	-	-	-	-	-	-
Wolfgang von Trips	Lancia-Ferrari D50	NT	6	9	R	-	-	-	-	-	-	-	-	8	3
Ottorino Volonterio	Maserati 250F	-	-	-	-	-	-	-	-	-	-	-	-	NT	11

SHARED DRIVES - Argentinian GP: Jose Froilan Gonzalez/Alfonso de Portago (Lancia-Ferrari D50) 5; Cesare Perdisa/Peter Collins/Wolfgang von Trips (Lancia-Ferrari D50) 6. Monaco GP: Wolfgang von Trips/Mike Hawthorn (Lancia-Ferrari D50) R; Giorgio Scarlatti/Harry Schell (Maserati 250F) R. French GP: Mike McDowell/Jack Brabham (Cooper T43-Climax) 7. British GP: Tony Brooks/Stirling Moss (Vanwall VW4) 1; Maurice Trintignant/Peter Collins (Lancia-Ferrari D50) 4; Stirling Moss/Tony Brooks (Vanwall VW1) R. Italian GP: Giorgio Scarlatti/Harry Schell (Maserati 250F) 5; Andre Simon/Ottorino Volonterio (Maserati 250F) 11

1957 FINAL CHAMPIONSHIP POSITIONS

Drivers						
1 Juan Manuel Fangio	40 (46)*	8= Peter Collins	8	Wolfgang von Trips	4
2 Stirling Moss	25	Sam Hanks	8	17 Paul Russo	3
3 Luigi Musso	16	10 Jim Rathmann	7	18=Andy Linden	2
4 Mike Hawthorn	13	11 Jean Behra	6	Roy Salvadori	2
5 Tony Brooks	11	12=Stuart Lewis-Evans	5	20=Jose Froilan Gonzalez	1
6= Masten Gregory	10	Maurice Trintignant	5	Alfonso de Portago	1
Harry Schell	10	14=Jimmy Bryan	4	Giorgio Scarlatti	1
		Carlos Menditeguy	4	*Best five results count

1 Juan Manuel Fangio	Maserati 250F	100	3h00m55.9
2 Jean Behra	Maserati 250F	100	3h01m14.2
3 Carlos Menditeguy	Maserati 250F	99	
4 Harry Schell	Maserati 250F	98	
5 Jose Froilan Gonzalez/			
Alfonso de Portago	Lancia-Ferrari D50	98	
6 Cesare Perdisa/Peter Collins/			
Wolfgang von Trips	Lancia-Ferrari D50	98	

Winner's average speed: 80.616 mph. Starting grid front row: Moss, 1m42.6 (pole), Fangio, 1m43.7, Behra, 1m44.0 and Castellotti, 1m44.2. Fastest lap: Moss, 1m44.7. Leaders: Behra, laps 1-2, 9-12, 81, 84; Castellotti, 3-8; Collins, 13-25; Fangio, 26-80, 82-83, 85-100

1957 Juan Manuel Fangio included victory at Rouen in his fifth and final World Championship victory.

GRAND PRIX DE MONACO

19 May 1957. Monte Carlo. 105 laps of a 1.954-mile circuit = 205.170 miles. Warm, dry and sunny. World Championship round 2

1 Juan Manuel Fangio	Maserati 250F	105	3h10m12.8
2 Tony Brooks	Vanwall VW7	105	3h10m38.0
3 Masten Gregory	Maserati 250F	103	
4 Stuart Lewis-Evans	Connaught B-Alta	102	
5 Maurice Trintignant	Lancia-Ferrari D50	100	
6 Jack Brabham	Cooper T43-Climax	100	

Winner's average speed: 64.718 mph. Starting grid front row: Fangio, 1m42.7 (pole), Collins, 1m43.3 and Moss, 1m43.6. Fastest lap: Fangio, 1m45.6. Leaders: Moss, laps 1-4; Fangio, 5-105

INDIANAPOLIS 500

30 May 1957. Indianapolis. 200 laps of a 2.500-mile circuit = 500.000 miles. Warm, dry and overcast. World Championship round 3

1 Sam Hanks	Epperly-Offenhauser	200	3h41m14.25
2 Jim Rathmann	Epperly-Offenhauser	200	3h41m35.75
3 Jimmy Bryan	Kuzma-Offenhauser	200	3h43m28.25
4 Paul Russo	Kurtis KK500F-Novi	200	3h44m11.10
5 Andy Linden	Kurtis KK500G-Offenhauser	200	3h44m28.55
6 Johnny Boyd	Kurtis KK500G-Offenhauser	200	3h45m49.55

Winner's average speed: 135.601 mph. Starting grid front row: Pat O'Connor (Kurtis KK500G-Offenhauser), 143.948 mph (pole), Eddie Sachs (Kuzma-Offenhauser), 143.822 mph and Troy Ruttman (Watson-Offenhauser), 142.772 mph. Fastest lap in the lead: J Rathmann, 1m02.75.

Leaders: O'Connor, laps 1-4, 7-9; Ruttman, 5-6, 10-11; Russo, 12-35; Hanks, 36-48, 54-110, 135-200; Johnny Thomson (Kuzma-Offenhauser), 49-53; J Rathmann, 111-134

GRAND PRIX DE L'AUTOMOBILE CLUB DE FRANCE

7 July 1957. Rouen-les-Essarts. 77 laps of a 4.065-mile circuit = 313.005 miles. Very hot, dry and sunny. World Championship round 4

1 Juan Manuel Fangio	Maserati 250F	77	3h07m46.4
2 Luigi Musso	Lancia-Ferrari D50	77	3h08m37.2
3 Peter Collins	Lancia-Ferrari D50	77	3h09m52.4
4 Mike Hawthorn	Lancia-Ferrari D50	76	
5 Harry Schell	Maserati 250F	70	
6 Jean Behra	Maserati 250F	69	

Some reports switch Schell and Behra's finishing positions. Winner's average speed: 100.016 mph. Starting grid front row: Fangio, 2m21.5 (pole), Behra, 2m22.6 and Musso, 2m22.7. Fastest lap: Musso, 2m22.5. Leaders: Musso, laps 1-3; Fangio, 4-77

BRITISH AND EUROPEAN GRAND PRIX

20 July 1957. Aintree. 90 laps of a 3.000-mile circuit = 270.000 miles. Warm, dry and overcast. World Championship round 5

1 Tony Brooks/			
Stirling Moss	Vanwall VW4	90	3h06m37.8
2 Luigi Musso	Lancia-Ferrari D50	90	3h07m03.4
3 Mike Hawthorn	Lancia-Ferrari D50	90	3h07m20.6
4 Maurice Trintignant/			
Peter Collins*	Lancia-Ferrari D50	88	
5 Roy Salvadori	Cooper T43-Climax	85	
6 Bob Gerard	Cooper T43-Bristol	82	

Collins drove the car for insufficient laps (3) to score points; Trintignant scored all 3 points. Winner's average speed: 86.803 mph. Starting grid front row: Moss, 2m00.2 (pole), Behra, 2m00.4 and Brooks, 2m00.4. Fastest lap: Moss, 1m59.2. Leaders: Moss, laps 1-22, 70-90; Behra, 23-69 (*in Brooks' car)

GROSSER PREIS VON DEUTSCHLAND

4 August 1957. Nurburgring. 22 laps of a 14.167-mile circuit = 311.674 miles. Hot, dry and sunny. World Championship round 6

1 Juan Manuel Fangio	Maserati 250F	22	3h30m38.3
2 Mike Hawthorn	Lancia-Ferrari D50	22	3h30m41.9
3 Peter Collins	Lancia-Ferrari D50	22	3h31m13.9
4 Luigi Musso	Lancia-Ferrari D50	22	3h34m15.9
5 Stirling Moss	Vanwall VW5	22	3h35m15.8
6 Jean Behra	Maserati 250F	22	3h35m16.8

Winner's average speed: 88.780 mph. Starting grid front row: Fangio, 9m25.6 (pole), Hawthorn, 9m28.4, Behra, 9m30.5 and Collins, 9m34.7. Fastest lap: Fangio, 9m17.4. Leaders: Hawthorn, laps 1-2, 15-20; Fangio, 3-11, 21-22; Collins, 12-14

GRAN PREMIO DI PESCARA

18 August 1957. Pescara. 18 laps of a 16.032-mile circuit = 288.576 miles. Very hot, dry and sunny. World Championship round 7

1 Stirling Moss	Vanwall VW5	18	2h59m22.7
2 Juan Manuel Fangio	Maserati 250F	18	3h02m36.6
3 Harry Schell	Maserati 250F	18	3h06m09.5
4 Masten Gregory	Maserati 250F	18	3h07m39.2
5 Stuart Lewis-Evans	Vanwall VW1	17	

6 Giorgio Scarlatti   Maserati 250F   17
Winner's average speed: 96.525 mph. Starting grid front row: Fangio,
9m44.6 (pole), Moss, 9m54.7 and Musso, 10m00.0. Fastest lap: Moss,
9m44.6. Leaders: Musso, lap 1; Moss, laps 2-18

GRAN PREMIO D'ITALIA

**8 September 1957. Monza. 87 laps of a 3.573-mile circuit = 310.851
miles. Hot, dry and sunny. World Championship round 8**

1	Stirling Moss	Vanwall VW5	87	2h35m03.9
2	Juan Manuel Fangio	Maserati 250F	87	2h35m45.1
3	Wolfgang von Trips	Lancia-Ferrari D50	85	
4	Masten Gregory	Maserati 250F	84	
5	Giorgio Scarlatti/			
	Harry Schell	Maserati 250F	84	
6	Mike Hawthorn	Lancia-Ferrari D50	83	

Winner's average speed: 120.279 mph. Starting grid front row: Lewis-
Evans, 1m42.4 (pole), Moss, 1m42.7, Brooks, 1m42.9 and Fangio, 1m43.1.
Fastest lap: Brooks, 1m43.7. Leaders: Moss, laps 1-3, 5, 11, 21-87; Behra,
4, 6; Fangio, 7-10; Brooks, 12-15; Lewis-Evans, 16-20

1958

Formula 1's governing body, the CSI, announced a number of changes for the new season. Races were limited to 300 km or two hours; points would now only be awarded to drivers who drove the complete distance and did not share their car; and commercial fuel was made obligatory. Aviation fuel, which was also permissible, became standard.

This season is often regarded as one of the more unjust World Championship results. Although Stirling Moss won four races for Vanwall, he was denied the championship once again in a final-round decider in Casablanca. Countryman Mike Hawthorn only won once, but snatched the title by a single point, and immediately announced his retirement from the sport. Sadly, Hawthorn would die in a road accident outside Guildford within months of his greatest triumph.

Vanwall and BRM both missed the start of the season while struggling to make their engines competitive using the commercial aviation fuel stipulated in the new rules. While waiting for Vanwall, Moss won in Argentina in a Rob Walker-entered Cooper-Climax, surprising the Ferrari team by not stopping to refuel. Maurice Trintignant also won for the team in Monte Carlo, confirming the promise of these nimble rear-engine cars.

But with Vanwall ready to race, the season developed into a battle between the British Racing Green cars of Moss and Tony Brooks and the Ferraris of Hawthorn and Peter Collins. At mid-season the Italian marque dominated, with Hawthorn winning in France (where Fangio finished fourth in his final Grand Prix), followed by Collins' win in Britain. It was to be his final victory: two weeks later the flamboyant Collins was fatally injured in a crash at the Nurburgring's Pflanzgarten corner during the German GP. Teammate Luigi Musso and Vanwall's Stuart Lewis-Evans also lost their lives after accidents during the French and Moroccan GPs, respectively.

Vanwall won the final four Grands Prix to secure the inaugural constructors' title, but Hawthorn had done just enough to become Britain's first World Champion—albeit for Ferrari.

GRAN PREMIO DE LA REPUBLICA ARGENTINA

**19 January 1958. Buenos Aires. 80 laps of a 2.431-mile circuit = 194.480
miles. Warm, dry and sunny. World Championship round 1**

1	Stirling Moss	Cooper T43-Climax	80	2h19m33.7
2	Luigi Musso	Ferrari Dino 246	80	2h19m36.4
3	Mike Hawthorn	Ferrari Dino 246	80	2h19m46.3
4	Juan Manuel Fangio	Maserati 250F	80	2h20m26.7
5	Jean Behra	Maserati 250F	78	
6	Harry Schell	Maserati 250F	77	

Winner's average speed: 83.610 mph. Starting grid front row: Fangio,
1m42.0 (pole), Hawthorn, 1m42.6, Collins, 1m42.6 and Behra, 1m42.7.
Fastest lap: Fangio, 1m41.8. Leaders: Behra, lap 1; Hawthorn, laps 2-9;
Fangio, 10-34; Moss, 35-80

GRAND PRIX DE MONACO

**18 May 1958. Monte Carlo. 100 laps of a 1.954-mile circuit = 195.400
miles. Hot, dry and sunny. World Championship round 2**

1	Maurice Trintignant	Cooper T45-Climax	100	2h52m27.9
2	Luigi Musso	Ferrari Dino 246	100	2h52m48.2
3	Peter Collins	Ferrari Dino 246	100	2h53m06.7
4	Jack Brabham	Cooper T45-Climax	97	
5	Harry Schell	BRM P25 (58)	91	
6	Cliff Allison	Lotus 12-Climax	87	

Winner's average speed: 67.979 mph. Starting grid front row: Brooks,
1m39.8 (pole), Behra, 1m40.8 and Brabham, 1m41.0. Fastest lap:
Hawthorn, 1m40.6. Leaders: Behra, laps 1-27; Hawthorn, 28-32, 39-47;
Moss, 33-38; Trintignant, 48-100

GROTE PRIJS VAN NEDERLAND

**25 May 1958. Zandvoort. 75 laps of a 2.605-mile circuit = 195.375 miles.
Windy, dry and overcast. World Championship round 3**

1	Stirling Moss	Vanwall VW10	75	2h04m49.2
2	Harry Schell	BRM P25 (58)	75	2h05m37.1
3	Jean Behra	BRM P25 (58)	75	2h06m31.5
4	Roy Salvadori	Cooper T45-Climax	74	
5	Mike Hawthorn	Ferrari Dino 246	74	
6	Cliff Allison	Lotus 12-Climax	73	

Winner's average speed: 93.915 mph. Starting grid front row: Lewis-
Evans, 1m37.1 (pole), Moss, 1m38.0 and Brooks, 1m38.1. Fastest lap:
Moss, 1m37.6. Leaders: Moss, laps 1-75

INDIANAPOLIS 500

**30 May 1958. Indianapolis. 200 laps of a 2.500-mile circuit = 500.000
miles. Warm, dry and sunny. World Championship round 4**

1	Jimmy Bryan	Epperly-Offenhauser	200	3h44m13.80
2	George Amick	Epperly-Offenhauser	200	3h44m41.45
3	Johnny Boyd	Kurtis KK500G-Offenhauser	200	3h45m23.75
4	Tony Bettenhausen	Epperly-Offenhauser	200	3h45m45.60
5	Jim Rathmann	Epperly-Offenhauser	200	3h45m49.45
6	Jimmy Reece	Watson-Offenhauser	200	3h46m30.75

Winner's average speed: 133.791 mph. Starting grid front row: Dick
Rathmann (Watson-Offenhauser), 145.974 mph (pole), Ed Elisian
(Watson-Offenhauser), 145.926 mph and Reece, 145.513 mph.
Fastest lap in the lead: Bettenhausen, 1m02.37. Leaders: Bryan,
laps 1-18, 26, 31, 47-48, 50-52, 66-104, 126-200; Bettenhausen, 19-
20, 22-25, 35, 49, 53-65, 105-107; Eddie Sachs (Kuzma-Offenhauser),
21; Amick, 27-30, 32-34, 36-46; Boyd, 108-125

GRAND PRIX DE BELGIQUE ET D'EUROPE

**15 June 1958. Spa-Francorchamps. 24 laps of a 8.761-mile circuit =
210.264 miles. Very hot, dry and sunny. World Championship round 5**

1	Tony Brooks	Vanwall VW5	24	1h37m06.3
2	Mike Hawthorn	Ferrari Dino 246	24	1h37m27.0
3	Stuart Lewis-Evans	Vanwall VW4	24	1h40m07.2
4	Cliff Allison	Lotus 12-Climax	24	1h41m21.8
5	Harry Schell	BRM P25 (58)	23	
6	Olivier Gendebien	Ferrari Dino 246	23	

Winner's average speed: 129.920 mph. Starting grid front row: Hawthorn,
3m57.1 (pole), Musso, 3m57.5 and Moss, 3m57.6. Fastest lap: Hawthorn,
3m58.3. Leaders: Brooks, laps 1, 3, 5-24; Collins, 2, 4

Formula 1

1958 DRIVERS' RECORDS

(excluding Indianapolis 500)

driver	car	RA Q	RA R	MC Q	MC R	NL Q	NL R	B Q	B R	F Q	F R	GB Q	GB R	D Q	D R	P Q	P R	I Q	I R	MA Q	MA R
Cliff Allison	Lotus 12-Climax	-	-	13	6	11	6	13	4	20	R	5	R	-	-	-	-	16	7	16	10
	Lotus 16-Climax	-	-	-	-	-	-	-	-	-	-	-	-	13	5	-	-	-	-	-	-
	Maserati 250F	-	-	-	-	-	-	-	-	-	-	-	-	-	-	13	R	-	-	-	-
Edgar Barth	Porsche RSK	-	-	-	-	-	-	-	-	-	-	-	-	NT	F2	-	-	-	-	-	-
Carel Godin de Beaufort	Porsche RSK	-	-	-	-	17	11	-	-	-	-	-	-	-	-	-	-	-	-	-	-
	Porsche 550RS	-	-	-	-	-	-	-	-	-	-	-	-	NT	F2	-	-	-	-	-	-
Jean Behra	Maserati 250F	4	5	-	-	-	-	-	-	-	-	-	-	-	-	-	-	-	-	-	-
	BRM P25	-	-	2	R	4	3	10	R	9	R	8	R	9	R	4	4	8	R	4	R
Jo Bonnier	Maserati 250F	-	-	16	R	15	10	14	9	16	8	13	R	11	R	14	R	-	-	-	-
	BRM P25	-	-	-	-	-	-	-	-	-	-	-	-	-	-	-	-	10	R	8	4
Jack Brabham	Cooper T45-Climax	-	-	3	4	5	8	8	R	12	6	10	6	NT	F2	8	7	15	R	NT	F2
Tommy Bridger	Cooper T45-Climax	-	-	-	-	-	-	-	-	-	-	-	-	-	-	-	-	-	-	NT	F2
Tony Brooks	Vanwall VW10	-	-	1	R	-	-	-	-	-	-	-	-	-	-	-	-	-	-	7	R
	Vanwall VW7	-	-	-	-	3	R	-	-	-	-	-	-	-	-	-	-	-	-	-	-
	Vanwall VW5	-	-	-	-	-	-	5	1	5	R	9	7	-	-	5	R	2	1	-	-
	Vanwall VW9	-	-	-	-	-	-	-	-	NT	R	-	-	-	-	-	-	-	-	-	-
	Vanwall VW4	-	-	-	-	-	-	-	-	-	-	-	-	2	1	-	-	-	-	-	-
Ivor Bueb	Connaught B-Alta	-	-	-	-	-	-	-	-	-	-	17	R	-	-	-	-	-	-	-	-
	Lotus 12-Climax	-	-	-	-	-	-	-	-	-	-	-	-	NT	F2	-	-	-	-	-	-
Ian Burgess	Cooper T45-Climax	-	-	-	-	-	-	-	-	-	-	16	R	-	-	-	-	-	-	-	-
	Cooper T43-Climax	-	-	-	-	-	-	-	-	-	-	-	-	NT	F2	-	-	-	-	-	-
Giulio Cabianca	OSCA	-	-	25	DNQ	-	-	-	-	-	-	-	-	-	-	-	-	-	-	-	-
	Maserati 250F	-	-	-	-	-	-	-	-	-	-	-	-	-	-	-	-	20	R	-	-
Robert la Caze	Cooper T45-Climax	-	-	-	-	-	-	-	-	-	-	-	-	-	-	-	-	-	-	NT	F2
Peter Collins	Ferrari Dino 246	3	R	9	3	10	R	4	R	4	5	6	1	4	R	-	-	-	-	-	-
Bernie Ecclestone	Connaught B-Alta	-	-	-	-	-	-	-	-	-	-	21	DNS	-	-	-	-	-	-	-	-
Paul Emery	Connaught B-Alta	-	-	23	DNQ	-	-	-	-	-	-	-	-	-	-	-	-	-	-	-	-
Jack Fairman	Connaught B-Alta	-	-	-	-	-	-	-	-	-	-	19	R	-	-	-	-	-	-	-	-
	Cooper T45-Climax	-	-	-	-	-	-	-	-	-	-	-	-	-	-	-	-	-	-	11	8
Juan Manuel Fangio	Maserati 250F	1	4F	-	-	-	-	-	-	8	4	-	-	-	-	-	-	-	-	-	-
Maria Teresa de Filippis	Maserati 250F	-	-	22	DNQ	-	-	19	10	-	-	-	-	-	-	15	R	21	R	-	-
Ron Flockhart	BRM P25	-	-	NT	DNQ	-	-	-	-	-	-	-	-	-	-	-	-	-	-	15	R
	Cooper T43-Climax	-	-	17	DNQ	-	-	-	-	-	-	-	-	-	-	-	-	-	-	-	-
Olivier Gendebien	Ferrari Dino 246	-	-	-	-	-	-	-	-	6	6	-	-	-	-	-	-	5	R	6	R
Gerino Gerini	Maserati 250F	-	-	20	DNQ	-	-	-	-	15	9	18	R	-	-	-	-	19	R	17	11
Dick Gibson	Cooper T43-Climax	-	-	-	-	-	-	-	-	-	-	-	-	NT	F2	-	-	-	-	-	-
Chico Godia-Sales	Maserati 250F	9	8	18	DNQ	-	-	18	R	11*	R	-	-	-	-	-	-	-	-	-	-
Christian Goethals	Cooper T43-Climax	-	-	-	-	-	-	-	-	-	-	-	-	NT	F2	-	-	-	-	-	-
Horace Gould	Maserati 250F	10	9	27	DNQ	-	-	-	-	-	-	-	-	-	-	-	-	-	-	-	-
Masten Gregory	Maserati 250F	-	-	-	-	14	R	9	R	-	-	-	-	-	-	-	-	11	4	13	6
Andre Guelfi	Cooper T45-Climax	-	-	-	-	-	-	-	-	-	-	-	-	-	-	-	-	-	-	NT	F2
Mike Hawthorn	Ferrari Dino 246	2	3	6	RF	6	5	1	2F	1	1F	4	2F	1	R	2	2F	3	2	1	2
Hans Herrmann	Maserati 250F	-	-	-	-	-	-	-	-	-	-	-	-	12	R	-	-	18	R	18	9
Graham Hill	Lotus 12-Climax	-	-	15	R	13	R	15	R	-	-	-	-	-	-	-	-	-	-	-	-
	Lotus 16-Climax	-	-	-	-	-	-	-	-	19	R	14	R	NT	F2	12	R	12	6	12	12
Phil Hill	Maserati 250F	-	-	-	-	-	-	-	-	13	7	-	-	-	-	-	-	-	-	-	-
	Ferrari Dino 156	-	-	-	-	-	-	-	-	-	-	-	-	NT	F2	-	-	-	-	-	-
	Ferrari Dino 246	-	-	-	-	-	-	-	-	-	-	-	-	-	-	-	-	7	3F	5	3
Ken Kavanagh	Maserati 250F	-	-	19	DNQ	-	-	20	DNS	-	-	-	-	-	-	-	-	-	-	-	-
Bruce Kessler	Connaught B-Alta	-	-	21	DNQ	-	-	-	-	-	-	-	-	-	-	-	-	-	-	-	-
Stuart Lewis-Evans	Vanwall VW5	-	-	7	R	1	R	-	-	-	-	-	-	-	-	-	-	-	-	-	-
	Vanwall VW4	-	-	-	-	-	-	-	-	12	3	-	-	-	-	-	-	-	-	3	R
	Vanwall VW9	-	-	-	-	-	-	-	-	10	R	7	4	-	-	-	-	-	-	-	-
	Vanwall VW6	-	-	-	-	-	-	-	-	-	-	-	-	-	-	3	3	4	R	-	-
Tony Marsh	Cooper T45-Climax	-	-	-	-	-	-	-	-	-	-	-	-	NT	F2	-	-	-	-	-	-
Bruce McLaren	Cooper T45-Climax	-	-	-	-	-	-	-	-	-	-	-	-	NT	F2	-	-	-	-	NT	F2
Carlos Menditeguy	Maserati 250F	6	7	-	-	-	-	-	-	-	-	-	-	-	-	-	-	-	-	-	-
Stirling Moss	Cooper T43-Climax	7	1	-	-	-	-	-	-	-	-	-	-	-	-	-	-	-	-	-	-
	Vanwall VW7	-	-	8	R	-	-	-	-	-	-	-	-	-	-	-	-	-	-	-	-
	Vanwall VW10	-	-	-	-	2	1F	3	R	6	2	1	R	3	RF	1	1	1	R	-	-
	Vanwall VW5	-	-	-	-	-	-	-	-	-	-	-	-	-	-	-	-	-	-	2	1F
Luigi Musso	Ferrari Dino 246	5	2	10	2	12	7	2	R	2	R	-	-	-	-	-	-	-	-	-	-
Brian Naylor	Cooper T45-Climax	-	-	-	-	-	-	-	-	-	-	-	-	NT	F2	-	-	-	-	-	-
Francois Picard	Cooper T43-Climax	-	-	-	-	-	-	-	-	-	-	-	-	-	-	-	-	-	-	NT	F2
Luigi Piotti	OSCA	-	-	26	DNQ	-	-	-	-	-	-	-	-	-	-	-	-	-	-	-	-
Troy Ruttman	Maserati 250F	-	-	-	-	-	-	-	-	18	10	-	-	26	DNS	-	-	-	-	-	-

driver	car	RA		MC		NL		B		F		GB		D		P		I		MA	
		Q	R	Q	R	Q	R	Q	R	Q	R	Q	R	Q	R	Q	R	Q	R
Roy Salvadori	Cooper T45-Climax	-	-	4	R	9	4	11	8	14	11	3	3	6	2	11	9	14	5	14	7
Giorgio Scarlatti	Maserati 250F	-	-	14	R	16	R	-	-	-	-	-	-	-	-	-	-	-	-	-	-
Harry Schell	Maserati 250F	8	6	-	-	-	-	-	-	-	-	-	-	-	-	-	-	-	-	-	-
	BRM P25	-	-	11	5	7	2	5	3	3	R	2	5	8	R	7	6	9	R	10	5
Wolfgang Seidel	Maserati 250F	-	-	-	-	-	-	17	R	-	-	-	-	-	-	-	-	19	R	-	-
	Cooper T43-Climax	-	-	-	-	-	-	-	-	-	-	-	-	NT	F2	-	-	-	-	-	-
Carroll Shelby	Maserati 250F	-	-	-	-	-	-	17	R	15	9	-	-	-	-	10	R	17	4	-	-
Alan Stacey	Lotus 16-Climax	-	-	-	-	-	-	-	-	-	-	20	R	-	-	-	-	-	-	-	-
Andre Testut	Maserati 250F	-	-	24	DNQ	-	-	-	-	-	-	-	-	-	-	-	-	-	-	-	-
Maurice Trintignant	Cooper T45-Climax	-	-	5	1	8	9	-	-	-	-	-	-	7	3	9	8	13	R	9	R
	Maserati 250F	-	-	-	-	-	-	16	7	-	-	-	-	-	-	-	-	-	-	-	-
	BRM P25	-	-	-	-	-	-	-	-	7	R	-	-	-	-	-	-	-	-	-	-
	Cooper T43-Climax	-	-	-	-	-	-	-	-	-	-	12	8	-	-	-	-	-	-	-	-
Wolfgang von Trips	Ferrari Dino 246	-	-	12	R	-	-	-	-	NT	3	11	R	5	4	6	5	6	R	-	-

*Qualifying time set by Juan Manuel Fangio. SHARED DRIVES - French GP: Stuart Lewis-Evans/Tony Brooks (Vanwall VW9) R. Italian GP: Masten Gregory/Carroll Shelby (Maserati 250F) 4

1958 FINAL CHAMPIONSHIP POSITIONS

Drivers

							Manufacturers		
1	Mike Hawthorn	42 (49)*	13	Jimmy Bryan	8		1	Vanwall	48 (57)*
2	Stirling Moss	41	14	Juan Manuel Fangio	7		2	Ferrari	40 (57)*
3	Tony Brooks	24	15	George Amick	6		3	Cooper-Climax	31
4	Roy Salvadori	15	16=	Tony Bettenhausen	4		4	BRM	18
5=	Peter Collins	14		Johnny Boyd	4		5	Maserati	6
	Harry Schell	14	18=	Cliff Allison	3		6	Lotus-Climax	3
7=	Luigi Musso	12		Jo Bonnier	3				
	Maurice Trintignant	12		Jack Brabham	3		*Best six results count. No points awarded		
9	Stuart Lewis-Evans	11	21	Jim Rathmann	2		for Indianapolis 500, points only awarded to		
10=	Jean Behra	9	*Best six results count				first car to finish for each manufacturer		
	Phil Hill	9							
	Wolfgang von Trips	9							

GRAND PRIX DE L'AUTOMOBILE CLUB DE FRANCE

6 July 1958. Reims. 50 laps of a 5.187-mile circuit = 259.350 miles. Warm, dry and sunny. World Championship round 6

1	Mike Hawthorn	Ferrari Dino 246	50	2h03m21.3
2	Stirling Moss	Vanwall VW10	50	2h03m45.9
3	Wolfgang von Trips	Ferrari Dino 246	50	2h04m21.0
4	Juan Manuel Fangio	Maserati 250F	50	2h05m51.9
5	Peter Collins	Ferrari Dino 246	50	2h08m46.2
6	Jack Brabham	Cooper T45-Climax	49	

Winner's average speed: 126.148 mph. Starting grid front row: Hawthorn, 2m21.7 (pole), Musso, 2m22.4 and Schell, 2m23.1. Fastest lap: Hawthorn, 2m24.9. Leaders: Hawthorn, laps 1-50

BRITISH GRAND PRIX

19 July 1958. Silverstone. 75 laps of a 2.927-mile circuit = 219.525 miles. Warm, dry and sunny. World Championship round 7

1	Peter Collins	Ferrari Dino 246	75	2h09m04.2
2	Mike Hawthorn	Ferrari Dino 246	75	2h09m28.4
3	Roy Salvadori	Cooper T45-Climax	75	2h09m54.8
4	Stuart Lewis-Evans	Vanwall VW9	75	2h09m55.0
5	Harry Schell	BRM P25 (58)	75	2h10m19.0
6	Jack Brabham	Cooper T45-Climax	75	2h10m27.4

Winner's average speed: 102.049 mph. Starting grid front row: Moss, 1m39.4 (pole), Schell, 1m39.8, Salvadori, 1m40.0 and Hawthorn, 1m40.4. Fastest lap: Hawthorn, 1m40.8. Leaders: Collins, laps 1-75

GROSSER PREIS VON DEUTSCHLAND

3 August 1958. Nurburgring. 15 laps of a 14.167-mile circuit = 212.505 miles. Warm, dry and overcast. World Championship round 8

1	Tony Brooks	Vanwall VW4	15	2h21m15.0
2	Roy Salvadori	Cooper T45-Climax	15	2h24m44.7
3	Maurice Trintignant	Cooper T45-Climax	15	2h26m26.2
4	Wolfgang von Trips	Ferrari Dino 246	15	2h27m31.3
5	Cliff Allison*	Lotus 16-Climax	13	

*Allison finished 10th on the road behind cars in the concurrent F2 race, he was not awarded points. No other F1 finishers. Winner's average speed: 90.268 mph. Starting grid front row: Hawthorn, 9m14.0 (pole), Brooks, 9m15.0, Moss, 9m19.1 and Collins, 9m21.9. Fastest lap: Moss, 9m09.2. Leaders: Moss, laps 1-3; Hawthorn, 4; Collins, 5-10; Brooks, 11-15.

GRANDE PREMIO DE PORTUGAL

24 August 1958. Oporto. 50 laps of a 4.603-mile circuit = 230.150 miles. Damp and overcast at the start, drying. World Championship round 9

1	Stirling Moss	Vanwall VW10	50	2h11m27.80
2	Mike Hawthorn	Ferrari Dino 246	50	2h16m40.55
3	Stuart Lewis-Evans	Vanwall VW6	49	
4	Jean Behra	BRM P25 (58)	49	
5	Wolfgang von Trips	Ferrari Dino 246	49	
6	Harry Schell	BRM P25 (58)	49	

Winner's average speed: 105.041 mph. Starting grid front row: Moss, 2m34.21 (pole), Hawthorn, 2m34.26 and Lewis-Evans, 2m34.60. Fastest lap: Hawthorn, 2m32.37. Leaders: Moss, laps 1, 8-50; Hawthorn, 2-7

GRAN PREMIO D'ITALIA

7 September 1958. Monza. 70 laps of a 3.573-mile circuit = 250.110 miles. Hot, dry and sunny. World Championship round 10

1	Tony Brooks	Vanwall VW5	70	2h03m47.8
2	Mike Hawthorn	Ferrari Dino 246	70	2h04m12.0
3	Phil Hill	Ferrari Dino 246	70	2h04m16.1
4*	Masten Gregory/ Carroll Shelby	Maserati 250F	69	

| 5 | Roy Salvadori | Cooper T45-Climax | 62 |
| 6 | Graham Hill | Lotus 16-Climax | 62 |

*No points awarded to drivers of shared cars. Winner's average speed: 121.220 mph. Starting grid front row: Moss, 1m40.5 (pole), Brooks, 1m41.4, Hawthorn, 1m41.8 and Lewis-Evans, 1m42.4. Fastest lap: P Hill, 1m42.9. Leaders: P Hill, laps 1-4, 35-37; Hawthorn, 5-6, 9, 15-34, 38-60; Moss, 7-8, 10-14; Brooks, 61-70

GRAND PRIX DU MAROC

19 October 1958. Ain Diab. 53 laps of a 4.724-mile circuit = 250.372 miles. Warm, dry and sunny. World Championship round 11

1	Stirling Moss	Vanwall VW5	53	2h09m15.0
2	Mike Hawthorn	Ferrari Dino 246	53	2h10m39.8
3	Phil Hill	Ferrari Dino 246	53	2h10m40.6
4	Jo Bonnier	BRM P25 (58)	53	2h11m01.8
5	Harry Schell	BRM P25 (58)	53	2h11m48.8
6	Masten Gregory	Maserati 250F	52	

Winner's average speed: 116.227 mph. Starting grid front row: Hawthorn, 2m23.1 (pole), Moss, 2m23.2 and Lewis-Evans, 2m23.7. Fastest lap: Moss, 2m22.5. Leaders: Moss, laps 1-53

1959

Tony Vandervell shocked the motor racing world by announcing that reigning constructors' champions Vanwall would not compete in 1959 due to his ill health. Together with Mike Hawthorn's retirement and subsequent death in a road accident, this meant neither champion would defend his crown. Instead, Cooper came to the fore as Britain's leading team and Ferrari's main challenger. The team won five of the eight races, the manufacturers' title, and a first drivers' championship for Jack Brabham.

With the Argentinian GP cancelled, the season opened at Monaco with Brabham's first win. Three weeks later at Zandvoort, and nine years after BRM made its highly publicised debut, the marque finally won a Grand Prix. Jo Bonnier started from pole and benefited when the gearbox on Stirling Moss's Rob Walker Cooper broke in the closing laps.

The old-fashioned front-engine Ferrari Dino 246s won easily at Reims, but a strike in Italy forced the team to miss the British GP, and Brabham triumphed again. The German GP had been moved to Avus, but the meeting was marred by tragedy. Jean Behra was killed on the fearsome banked North Curve during the supporting sports car race. In the Grand Prix, Ferrari again dominated, with Tony Brooks leading Dan Gurney (impressive in his second race) and Phil Hill to a 1-2-3 finish.

Moss made it a three-way championship finale by winning the next two Grands Prix. The decider was the first F1 race in the United States, held at Florida's Sebring airfield. Moss and fellow contender Brooks both retired early, confirming Brabham as champion. The Australian ran out of fuel in the closing laps, allowing 22-year-old teammate Bruce McLaren to become the youngest ever winner of a Grand Prix. The exhausted Brabham pushed his car across the line to finish fourth.

GRAND PRIX DE MONACO

10 May 1959. Monte Carlo. 100 laps of a 1.954-mile circuit = 195.400 miles. Hot, dry and sunny. World Championship round 1

1	Jack Brabham	Cooper T51-Climax	100	2h55m51.3
2	Tony Brooks	Ferrari Dino 246	100	2h56m11.7
3	Maurice Trintignant	Cooper T51-Climax	98	
4	Phil Hill	Ferrari Dino 246	97	

| 5 | Bruce McLaren | Cooper T51-Climax | 96 | |
| 6 | Roy Salvadori | Cooper T45-Maserati | 83 | transmission |

Winner's average speed: 66.669 mph. Starting grid front row: Moss, 1m39.6 (pole), Behra, 1m40.0 and Brabham, 1m40.1. Fastest lap: Brabham, 1m40.4. Leaders: Behra, laps 1-21; Moss, 22-81; Brabham, 82-100

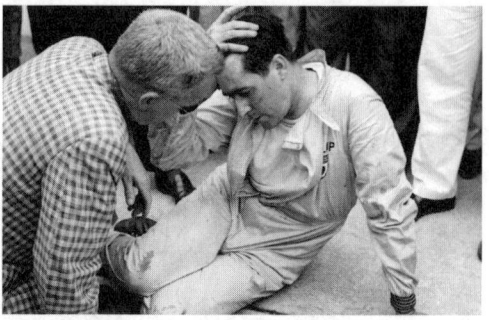

1959 Jack Brabham collapses after pushing his car across the line and clinching the championship at Sebring.

INDIANAPOLIS 500

30 May 1959. Indianapolis. 200 laps of a 2.500-mile circuit = 500.000 miles. Warm, dry and overcast. World Championship round 2

1	Rodger Ward	Watson-Offenhauser	200	3h40m49.20
2	Jim Rathmann	Watson-Offenhauser	200	3h41m12.47
3	Johnny Thomson	Lesovsky-Offenhauser	200	3h41m39.85
4	Tony Bettenhausen	Epperly-Offenhauser	200	3h42m36.25
5	Paul Goldsmith	Epperly-Offenhauser	200	3h42m55.60
6	Johnny Boyd	Epperly-Offenhauser	200	3h44m06.23

Winner's average speed: 135.857 mph. Starting grid front row: Thomson, 145.908 mph (pole), Eddie Sachs (Kuzma-Offenhauser), 145.425 mph and J Rathmann, 144.433 mph. Fastest lap in the lead: Thomson, 1m01.89. Leaders: Thomson, laps 1-4, 49-84; Ward, 5-12, 14-16, 46-48, 85-200; J Rathmann, 13, 17-30, 32-33, 41-42; Pat Flaherty (Watson-Offenhauser), 31, 34-40, 43-45

GROTE PRIJS VAN NEDERLAND

31 May 1959. Zandvoort. 75 laps of a 2.605-mile circuit = 195.375 miles. Warm, dry and sunny. World Championship round 3

1	Jo Bonnier	BRM P25 (59)	75	2h05m26.8
2	Jack Brabham	Cooper T51-Climax	75	2h05m41.0
3	Masten Gregory	Cooper T51-Climax	75	2h06m49.8
4	Innes Ireland	Lotus 16-Climax	74	
5	Jean Behra	Ferrari Dino 246	74	
6	Phil Hill	Ferrari Dino 246	73	

Winner's average speed: 93.446 mph. Starting grid front row: Bonnier, 1m36.0 (pole), Brabham, 1m36.0 and Moss 1m36.2. Fastest lap: Moss, 1m36.6. Leaders: Bonnier, laps 1, 12-29, 34-59, 63-75; Gregory, 2-11; Brabham, 30-33; Moss, 60-62

GRAND PRIX DE L'AUTOMOBILE CLUB DE FRANCE ET D'EUROPE

5 July 1959. Reims. 50 laps of a 5.187-mile circuit = 259.350 miles. Very hot, dry and sunny. World Championship round 4

1	Tony Brooks	Ferrari Dino 246	50	2h01m26.5
2	Phil Hill	Ferrari Dino 246	50	2h01m54.0
3	Jack Brabham	Cooper T51-Climax	50	2h03m04.2
4	Olivier Gendebien	Ferrari Dino 246	50	2h03m14.0
5	Bruce McLaren	Cooper T45-Climax	50	2h03m14.2
6	Ron Flockhart	BRM P25 (59)	50	2h03m32.2

Winner's average speed: 128.136 mph. Starting grid front row: Brooks, 2m19.4 (pole), Brabham, 2m19.7 and P Hill, 2m19.8. Fastest lap: Moss, 2m22.8. Leaders: Brooks, laps 1-50

1959 DRIVERS' RECORDS

(excluding Indianapolis 500)

driver	car	MC Q	MC R	NL Q	NL R	F Q	F R	GB Q	GB R	D Q	D R	P Q	P R	I Q	I R	USA Q	USA R
Cliff Allison	Ferrari Dino 156	15	R	-	-	-	-	-	-	-	-	-	-	-	-	-	-
	Ferrari Dino 246	-	-	NT	9	-	-	-	-	14	R	-	-	8	5	7	R
Peter Ashdown	Cooper T45-Climax	-	-	-	-	-	-	23	12	-	-	-	-	-	-	-	-
Astrubel Bayardo	Maserati 250F	-	-	-	-	NT	DNQ	-	-	-	-	-	-	-	-	-	-
Carel Godin de Beaufort	Porsche RSK	-	-	14	10	-	-	-	-	-	-	-	-	-	-	-	-
	Maserati 250F	-	-	-	-	20	9	-	-	-	-	-	-	-	-	-	-
Jean Behra	Ferrari Dino 246	2	R	4	5	5	R	-	-	-	-	-	-	-	-	-	-
	Behra-Porsche	-	-	-	-	-	-	-	-	NT	DNS	-	-	-	-	-	-
Lucien Bianchi	Cooper T51-Climax	19	DNQ	-	-	-	-	-	-	-	-	-	-	-	-	-	-
Harry Blanchard	Porsche RSK	-	-	-	-	-	-	-	-	-	-	-	-	-	-	16	7
Jo Bonnier	BRM P25	7	R	1	1	6	R	10	R	7	5	5	R	11	8	-	-
Jack Brabham	Cooper T51-Climax	3	1F	2	2	2	3	1	1	4	R	2	R	-	-	2	4
	Cooper T45-Climax	-	-	-	-	-	-	-	-	-	-	-	-	3	3	-	-
Chris Bristow	Cooper T51-Borgward	-	-	-	-	-	-	16	10	-	-	-	-	-	-	-	-
Tony Brooks	Ferrari Dino 246	4	2	8	R	1	1	-	-	1	1F	10	9	2	R	4	3
	Vanwall VW5	-	-	-	-	-	-	17	R	-	-	-	-	-	-	-	-
Ivor Bueb	Cooper T51-Climax	17	DNQ	-	-	-	-	-	-	-	-	-	-	-	-	-	-
	Cooper T51-Borgward	-	-	-	-	-	-	18	13	-	-	-	-	-	-	-	-
Ian Burgess	Cooper T51-Maserati	-	-	-	-	19	R	13	R	15	6	-	-	16	14	-	-
Giulio Cabianca	Maserati 250F	-	-	-	-	-	-	-	-	-	-	-	-	21	15	-	-
Mario Araujo de Cabral	Cooper T51-Maserati	-	-	-	-	-	-	-	-	-	-	14	10	-	-	-	-
Phil Cade	Maserati 250F	-	-	-	-	-	-	-	-	-	-	-	-	-	-	18	DNS
Alain de Chagny	Cooper T51-Climax	20	DNQ	-	-	-	-	-	-	-	-	-	-	-	-	-	-
George Constantine	Cooper T45-Climax	-	-	-	-	-	-	-	-	-	-	-	-	-	-	15	R
Colin Davis	Cooper T51-Maserati	-	-	-	-	17	R	-	-	-	-	-	-	18	11	-	-
Jack Fairman	Cooper T43-Climax	-	-	-	-	-	-	15	R	-	-	-	-	-	-	-	-
	Cooper T45-Maserati	-	-	-	-	-	-	-	-	-	-	-	-	20	R	-	-
Maria Teresa de Filippis	Behra-Porsche	21	DNQ	-	-	-	-	-	-	-	-	-	-	-	-	-	-
Ron Flockhart	BRM P25	10	R	-	-	13	6	11	R	-	-	11	7	15	13	-	-
Olivier Gendebien	Ferrari Dino 246	-	-	-	-	11	4	-	-	-	-	-	-	6	6	-	-
Keith Greene	Cooper T43-Climax	-	-	-	-	-	-	NT	DNQ	-	-	-	-	-	-	-	-
Masten Gregory	Cooper T45-Climax	11	R	-	-	-	-	-	-	-	-	-	-	-	-	-	-
	Cooper T51-Climax	-	-	7	3	7	R	5	7	5	R	3	2	-	-	-	-
Dan Gurney	Ferrari Dino 246	-	-	-	-	12	R	-	-	3	2	6	3	4	4	-	-
Bruce Halford	Lotus 16-Climax	16	R	-	-	-	-	-	-	-	-	-	-	-	-	-	-
Hans Herrmann	Cooper T51-Maserati	-	-	-	-	-	-	19	R	-	-	-	-	-	-	-	-
	BRM P25	-	-	-	-	-	-	-	-	11	R	-	-	-	-	-	-
Graham Hill	Lotus 16-Climax	14	R	5	7	14	R	9	9	10	R	15	R	10	R	-	-
Phil Hill	Ferrari Dino 246	5	4	12	6	3	2	-	-	6	3	7	R	5	2F	8	R
Innes Ireland	Lotus 16-Climax	-	-	9	4	15	R	-	-	13	R	16	R	14	R	9	5
Pete Lovely	Lotus 16-Climax	22	DNQ	-	-	-	-	-	-	-	-	-	-	-	-	-	-
"Jean Lucienbonnet"	Cooper T45-Climax	23	DNQ	-	-	-	-	-	-	-	-	-	-	-	-	-	-
Bruce McLaren	Cooper T51-Climax	13	5	-	-	-	-	-	-	-	-	-	-	9	R	-	-
	Cooper T45-Climax	-	-	-	-	10	5	8	3F	9	R	8	R	-	-	10	1
Bill Moss	Cooper T51-Climax	-	-	-	-	-	-	NT	DNQ	-	-	-	-	-	-	-	-
Stirling Moss	Cooper T51-Climax	1	R	3	RF	-	-	-	-	2	R	1	1F	1	1	1	R
	BRM P25	-	-	-	-	4	RF	7	2F	-	-	-	-	-	-	-	-
Brian Naylor	JBW-Maserati	-	-	-	-	-	-	14	R	-	-	-	-	-	-	-	-
Fritz d'Orey	Maserati 250F	-	-	-	-	18	10	20	R	-	-	-	-	-	-	-	-
	Tec-Mec F415-Maserati	-	-	-	-	-	-	-	-	-	-	-	-	-	-	17	R
Michael Parkes	Fry-Climax	-	-	-	-	-	-	NT	DNQ	-	-	-	-	-	-	-	-
Tim Parnell	Cooper T45-Climax	-	-	-	-	-	-	NT	DNQ	-	-	-	-	-	-	-	-
David Piper	Lotus 16-Climax	-	-	-	-	-	-	22	R	-	-	-	-	-	-	-	-
Bob Said	Connaught C-Alta	-	-	-	-	-	-	-	-	-	-	-	-	-	-	13	R
Roy Salvadori	Cooper T45-Maserati	8	6	-	-	16	R	-	-	-	-	-	-	-	-	11	R
	Aston Martin DBR4/250	-	-	13	R	-	-	2	6	-	-	12	6	17	R	-	-
Giorgio Scarlatti	Maserati 250F	18	DNQ	-	-	21	8	-	-	-	-	-	-	-	-	-	-
	Cooper T51-Climax	-	-	-	-	-	-	-	-	-	-	-	-	12	12	-	-
Harry Schell	BRM P25	9	R	6	R	9	7	3	4	8	7	9	5	7	7	-	-
	Cooper T51-Climax	-	-	-	-	-	-	-	-	-	-	-	-	-	-	3	R
Carroll Shelby	Aston Martin DBR4/250	-	-	10	R	-	-	6	R	-	-	13	8	19	10	-	-
Alan Stacey	Lotus 16-Climax	-	-	-	-	-	-	12	8	-	-	-	-	-	-	12	R
Henry Taylor	Cooper T51-Climax	-	-	-	-	-	-	21	11	-	-	-	-	-	-	-	-
Mike Taylor	Cooper T45-Climax	-	-	-	-	-	-	24	R	-	-	-	-	-	-	-	-
Trevor Taylor	Cooper T51-Climax	-	-	-	-	-	-	NT	DNQ	-	-	-	-	-	-	-	-

driver	car	MC		NL		F		GB		D		P		I		USA	
		Q	R	Q	R	Q	R	Q	R	Q	R	Q	R	Q	R	Q	R
Andre Testut	Maserati 250F	24	DNQ	-	-	-	-	-	-	-	-	-	-	-	-	-	-
Alessandro de Tomaso	Cooper T43-OSCA	-	-	-	-	-	-	-	-	-	-	-	-	-	-	14	R
Maurice Trintignant	Cooper T51-Climax	6	3	11	8	8	11	4	5	12	4	4	4	13	9	5	2F
Wolfgang von Trips	Porsche 718	12	R	-	-	-	-	-	-	NT	DNS	-	-	-	-	-	-
	Ferrari Dino 246	-	-	-	-	-	-	-	-	-	-	-	-	-	-	6	6
Rodger Ward	Kurtis-Offenhauser	-	-	-	-	-	-	-	-	-	-	-	-	-	-	19	R

1959 FINAL CHAMPIONSHIP POSITIONS

Drivers

1	Jack Brabham	31 (34)*
2	Tony Brooks	27
3	Stirling Moss	25.5
4	Phil Hill	20
5	Maurice Trintignant	19
6	Bruce McLaren	16.5
7	Dan Gurney	13
8=	Jo Bonnier	10
	Masten Gregory	10
10	Rodger Ward	8
11	Jim Rathmann	6
12=	Innes Ireland	5
	Harry Schell	5
	Johnny Thomson	5
15=	Tony Bettenhausen	3
	Olivier Gendebien	3
17=	Cliff Allison	2
	Jean Behra	2
	Paul Goldsmith	2

*Best five results count

Manufacturers

1	Cooper-Climax	40 (53)*
2	Ferrari	32 (38)*
3	BRM	18
4	Lotus-Climax	5

*Best five results count. No points awarded for Indianapolis 500, points only awarded to first car to finish for each manufacturer

BRITISH GRAND PRIX

18 July 1959. Aintree. 75 laps of a 3.000-mile circuit = 225.000 miles. Warm, dry and sunny. World Championship round 5

1	Jack Brabham	Cooper T51-Climax	75	2h30m11.6
2	Stirling Moss	BRM P25 (58)	75	2h30m33.8
3	Bruce McLaren	Cooper T45-Climax	75	2h30m34.0
4	Harry Schell	BRM P25 (59)	74	
5	Maurice Trintignant	Cooper T51-Climax	74	
6	Roy Salvadori	Aston Martin DBR4/250	74	

Winner's average speed: 89.884 mph. Starting grid front row: Brabham, 1m58.0 (pole), Salvadori, 1m58.0 and Schell, 1m59.2. Fastest lap: Moss and McLaren, 1m57.0. Leaders: Brabham, laps 1-75

GROSSER PREIS VON DEUTSCHLAND

2 August 1959. Avus. Aggregate two 30-lap heats. 60 laps of a 5.157-mile circuit = 309.420 miles. Warm, dry and overcast. World Championship round 6

1	Tony Brooks	Ferrari Dino 246	60	2h09m31.6
2	Dan Gurney	Ferrari Dino 246	60	2h09m33.2
3	Phil Hill	Ferrari Dino 246	60	2h10m36.7
4	Maurice Trintignant	Cooper T51-Climax	59	
5	Jo Bonnier	BRM P25 (59)	58	
6	Ian Burgess	Cooper T51-Maserati	56	

Winner's average speed: 143.331 mph. Starting grid front row: Brooks, 2m05.9 (pole), Moss, 2m06.8, Gurney, 2m07.2 and Brabham, 2m07.4. Fastest qualifier: Allison, 2m05.8, reserve driver so started from the back. Fastest lap: Brooks, 2m04.5. Leaders: Heat 1: Brooks, laps 1-2, 5-13, 15, 18-22, 24-30; Gregory, 3-4, 23; Gurney, 14, 16-17. Heat 2: P Hill, laps 1, 6, 8-9, 15, 18-19; Brooks, 2-5, 7, 10, 12, 16-17, 22-30; Gurney, 11, 13-14, 20-21. Heat 2 overall lead: Brooks, all bar Gurney, 11, 13-14, 20-21

GRANDE PREMIO DE PORTUGAL

23 August 1959. Monsanto. 62 laps of a 3.380-mile circuit = 209.560 miles. Hot, dry and sunny. World Championship round 7

1	Stirling Moss	Cooper T51-Climax	62	2h11m55.41
2	Masten Gregory	Cooper T51-Climax	61	
3	Dan Gurney	Ferrari Dino 246	61	
4	Maurice Trintignant	Cooper T51-Climax	60	
5	Harry Schell	BRM P25 (59)	59	
6	Roy Salvadori	Aston Martin DBR4/250	59	

Winner's average speed: 95.310 mph. Starting grid front row: Moss, 2m02.89 (pole), Brabham, 2m04.95 and Gregory, 2m06.33. Fastest lap: Moss, 2m05.07. Leaders: Moss, laps 1-62

GRAN PREMIO D'ITALIA

13 September 1959. Monza. 72 laps of a 3.573-mile circuit = 257.256 miles. Warm, dry and sunny. World Championship round 8

1	Stirling Moss	Cooper T51-Climax	72	2h04m05.4
2	Phil Hill	Ferrari Dino 246	72	2h04m52.1
3	Jack Brabham	Cooper T45-Climax	72	2h05m17.9
4	Dan Gurney	Ferrari Dino 246	72	2h05m25.0
5	Cliff Allison	Ferrari Dino 246	71	
6	Olivier Gendebien	Ferrari Dino 246	71	

Winner's average speed: 124.388 mph. Starting grid front row: Moss, 1m39.7 (pole), Brooks, 1m39.8 and Brabham, 1m40.2. Fastest lap: P Hill, 1m40.4. Leaders: Moss, laps 1, 4, 15, 33-72; P Hill, 2-3, 5-14, 16-32

UNITED STATES GRAND PRIX

12 December 1959. Sebring. 42 laps of a 5.200-mile circuit = 218.400 miles. Warm, dry and sunny. World Championship round 9

1	Bruce McLaren	Cooper T45-Climax	42	2h12m35.7
2	Maurice Trintignant	Cooper T51-Climax	42	2h12m36.3
3	Tony Brooks	Ferrari Dino 246	42	2h15m36.6
4	Jack Brabham	Cooper T51-Climax	42	2h17m33.0
5	Innes Ireland	Lotus 16-Climax	39	
6	Wolfgang von Trips	Ferrari Dino 246	38	

Winner's average speed: 98.827 mph. Starting grid front row: Moss, 3m00.0 (pole), Brabham, 3m03.0 and Schell, 3m05.2. Fastest lap: Trintignant, 3m05.0. Leaders: Moss, laps 1-5; Brabham, 6-41; McLaren, 42

1960

Cooper's victorious 1959 campaign clearly showed that rear-engine cars were the future for F1 design. Moving the engine behind the driver saved weight, centralized mass, and improved aerodynamics. Even Ferrari experimented with the rear-engine 246P.

Bruce McLaren and Cooper followed their 1959 Sebring victory by winning the opening round at Buenos Aires, where Innes Ireland demonstrated the promise of the new rear-engine Lotus 18 by leading the opening lap before spinning. Impressed, Stirling Moss and team owner Rob Walker replaced their Cooper with a new Lotus and promptly won at Monaco.

Jack Brabham triumphed at the Dutch GP for Cooper (where Jim Clark made his Championship debut), before the F1 teams travelled to Spa for what would be a tragic Belgian Grand Prix. In practice, Stirling Moss suffered serious leg, back, and facial injuries after crashing at Burneville, and Mike Taylor broke his collarbone in a separate incident. Worse was to come, however: Chris Bristow and Alan Stacey were both killed in separate accidents during the race. Brabham won again, but like Michael Schumacher's victory at Imola in 1994 when Ayrton Senna lost his life, the result meant little. This came barely a month after Harry Schell had died testing at Silverstone.

Three more successive victories secured Brabham's second World Championship win for Cooper. Then the organisers of the penultimate round at Monza decided to use the banking, which prompted a boycott by the British teams and a 1-2-3 for Ferrari. Phil Hill's victory in the venerable Dino 246 was the last for a front-engine car. The season ended with the United States GP at California's Riverside circuit. With the title already lost, Ferrari skipped the race to concentrate on preparing for the new 1.5-litre formula, and Moss won in only his second race since returning from injury.

The final year of the existing formula was also the last time the Indy 500 officially counted towards the World Championship.

1960 Stirling Moss' private Lotus 18 won at Monaco but a serious accident at Spa meant the title remained elusive.

GRAN PREMIO DE LA REPUBLICA ARGENTINA

7 February 1960. Buenos Aires. 80 laps of a 2.431-mile circuit = 194.480 miles. Very hot, dry and sunny. World Championship round 1

1 Bruce McLaren	Cooper T45-Climax	80	2h17m49.5
2 Cliff Allison	Ferrari Dino 246	80	2h18m15.8
3* Maurice Trintignant/			
Stirling Moss	Cooper T51-Climax	80	2h18m26.4
4 Carlos Menditeguy	Cooper T51-Maserati	80	2h18m42.8
5 Wolfgang von Trips	Ferrari Dino 246	79	
6 Innes Ireland	Lotus 18-Climax	79	

*No points awarded to drivers of shared cars. Winner's average speed: 84.664 mph. Starting grid front row: Moss, 1m36.9 (pole), Ireland, 1m38.5, G Hill, 1m38.9 and Bonnier, 1m38.9. Fastest lap: Moss, 1m38.9. Leaders: Ireland, lap 1; Bonnier, laps 2-15, 21-36, 41-67; Moss, 16-20, 37-40; McLaren, 68-80

GRAND PRIX DE MONACO

29 May 1960. Monte Carlo. 100 laps of a 1.954-mile circuit = 195.400 miles. Dry at the start, rain later. World Championship round 2

1 Stirling Moss	Lotus 18-Climax	100	2h53m45.5
2 Bruce McLaren	Cooper T53-Climax	100	2h54m37.6
3 Phil Hill	Ferrari Dino 246	100	2h54m47.4
4 Tony Brooks	Cooper T51-Climax	99	
5 Jo Bonnier	BRM P48	83	
6 Richie Ginther	Ferrari Dino 246P	70	

Winner's average speed: 67.473 mph. Starting grid front row: Moss, 1m36.3 (pole), Brabham, 1m37.3 and Brooks, 1m37.7. Fastest lap: McLaren, 1m36.2. Leaders: Bonnier, laps 1-16, 61-67; Moss, 17-33, 41-60, 68-100; Brabham, 34-40

INDIANAPOLIS 500

30 May 1960. Indianapolis. 200 laps of a 2.500-mile circuit = 500.000 miles. Warm, dry and overcast. World Championship round 3

1 Jim Rathmann	Watson-Offenhauser	200	3h36m11.36
2 Rodger Ward	Watson-Offenhauser	200	3h36m24.03
3 Paul Goldsmith	Epperly-Offenhauser	200	3h39m18.58
4 Don Branson	Phillips-Offenhauser	200	3h39m19.28
5 Johnny Thomson	Lesovsky-Offenhauser	200	3h39m22.65
6 Eddie Johnson	Trevis-Offenhauser	200	3h40m21.88

Winner's average speed: 138.767 mph. Starting grid front row: Eddie Sachs (Ewing-Offenhauser), 146.592 mph (pole), J Rathmann, 146.371

mph and Ward, 145.560 mph. Fastest lap: in the lead: J Rathmann, 1m01.59. Leaders: Ward, laps 1, 4-18, 38-41, 123-127, 142-146, 148-151, 163-169, 171-177, 183-189, 194-196; Sachs, 2-3, 42-51, 57-61, 70-72, 75; Troy Ruttman (Watson-Offenhauser), 19-24, 52-56; J Rathmann, 25-37, 62-69, 73-74, 76-85, 96-122, 128-141, 147, 152-162, 170, 178-182, 190-193, 197-200; Thomson, 86-95

GROTE PRIJS VAN NEDERLAND

6 June 1960. Zandvoort. 75 laps of a 2.605-mile circuit = 195.375 miles. Warm, dry and sunny. World Championship round 4

1 Jack Brabham	Cooper T53-Climax	75	2h01m47.2
2 Innes Ireland	Lotus 18-Climax	75	2h02m11.2
3 Graham Hill	BRM P48	75	2h02m43.8
4 Stirling Moss	Lotus 18-Climax	75	2h02m44.9
5 Wolfgang von Trips	Ferrari Dino 246	74	
6 Richie Ginther	Ferrari Dino 246	74	

Winner's average speed: 96.254 mph. Starting grid front row: Moss, 1m33.2 (pole), Brabham, 1m33.4 and Ireland, 1m33.9. Fastest lap: Moss, 1m33.8. Leaders: Brabham, laps 1-75

GRAND PRIX DE BELGIQUE

19 June 1960. Spa-Francorchamps. 36 laps of an 8.761-mile circuit = 315.396 miles. Warm, dry and sunny. World Championship round 5

1 Jack Brabham	Cooper T53-Climax	36	2h21m37.3
2 Bruce McLaren	Cooper T53-Climax	36	2h22m40.6
3 Olivier Gendebien	Cooper T51-Climax	35	
4 Phil Hill	Ferrari Dino 246	35	
5 Jim Clark	Lotus 18-Climax	34	
6 Lucien Bianchi	Cooper T45-Climax	28	

Winner's average speed: 133.622 mph. Starting grid front row: Brabham, 3m50.0 (pole), Brooks, 3m52.5 and P Hill, 3m53.3. Fastest lap: Brabham, P Hill and Ireland, 3m51.9. Leaders: Brabham, laps 1-36

GRAND PRIX DE L'AUTOMOBILE CLUB DE FRANCE

3 July 1960. Reims. 50 laps of a 5.187-mile circuit = 259.350 miles. Warm, dry and overcast. World Championship round 6

1 Jack Brabham	Cooper T53-Climax	50	1h57m24.9
2 Olivier Gendebien	Cooper T51-Climax	50	1h58m13.2
3 Bruce McLaren	Cooper T53-Climax	50	1h58m16.8
4 Henry Taylor	Cooper T51-Climax	49	
5 Jim Clark	Lotus 18-Climax	49	
6 Ron Flockhart	Lotus 18-Climax	49	

Winner's average speed: 132.530 mph. Starting grid front row: Brabham, 2m16.8 (pole), P Hill, 2m18.2 and G Hill, 2m18.4. Fastest lap: Brabham, 2m17.5. Leaders: Brabham, laps 1-3, 5, 7, 9-10, 12, 14, 18-50; P Hill, 4, 6, 8, 11, 13, 15-17

BRITISH GRAND PRIX

16 July 1960. Silverstone. 77 laps of a 2.927-mile circuit = 225.379 miles. Warm, dry and overcast. World Championship round 7

1 Jack Brabham	Cooper T53-Climax	77	2h04m24.6

Formula 1

1960 DRIVERS' RECORDS

(excluding Indianapolis 500)

driver	car	RA		MC		NL		B		F		GB		P		I		USA	
		Q	R	Q	R	Q	R	Q	R	Q	R	Q	R	Q	R	Q	R	Q	R
Cliff Allison	Ferrari Dino 246	7	2	18	DNQ	-	-	-	-	-	-	-	-	-	-	-	-	-	-
Edgar Barth	Porsche 718	-	-	-	-	-	-	-	-	-	-	-	-	-	-	12	7	-	-
Carel Godin de Beaufort	Cooper T51-Climax	-	-	-	-	21	8	-	-	-	-	-	-	-	-	-	-	-	-
Lucien Bianchi	Cooper T45-Climax	-	-	-	-	-	-	15	6	15	R	17	R	-	-	-	-	-	-
Jo Bonnier	BRM P25	4	7	-	-	-	-	-	-	-	-	-	-	-	-	-	-	-	-
	BRM P48	-	-	5	5	4	R	7	R	10	R	4	R	13	R	-	-	4	5
Roberto Bonomi	Cooper T51-Maserati	17	11	-	-	-	-	-	-	-	-	-	-	-	-	-	-	-	-
Jack Brabham	Cooper T51-Climax	10	R	-	-	-	-	-	-	-	-	-	-	-	-	-	-	-	-
	Cooper T53-Climax	-	-	2	DSQ	2	1	1	1F	1	1F	1	1	3	1	-	-	2	4F
Chris Bristow	Cooper T51-Climax	-	-	4	R	7	R	9	R	-	-	-	-	-	-	-	-	-	-
Tony Brooks	Cooper T51-Climax	-	-	3	4	10	R	2	R	-	-	9	5	12	5	-	-	9	R
	Vanwall VW11	-	-	-	-	-	-	-	-	14	R	-	-	-	-	-	-	-	-
Ian Burgess	Cooper T51-Maserati	-	-	24	DNQ	-	-	-	-	22	10	20	R	-	-	-	-	23	R
Giulio Cabianca	Cooper T51-Ferrari	-	-	-	-	-	-	-	-	-	-	-	-	-	-	4	4	-	-
Mario Araujo de Cabral	Cooper T51-Maserati	-	-	-	-	-	-	-	-	-	-	-	-	15	R	-	-	-	-
Ettore Chimeri	Maserati 250F	21	R	-	-	-	-	-	-	-	-	-	-	-	-	-	-	-	-
Jim Clark	Lotus 18-Climax	-	-	-	-	11	R	10	5	12	5	8	16	8	3	-	-	5	16
Antonio Creus	Maserati 250F	22	R	-	-	-	-	-	-	-	-	-	-	-	-	-	-	-	-
Chuck Daigh	Scarab	-	-	21	DNQ	16	DNS	18	R	23	DNS	-	-	-	-	-	-	18	10
	Cooper T51-Climax	-	-	-	-	-	-	-	-	-	-	19	R	-	-	-	-	-	-
Bob Drake	Maserati 250F	-	-	-	-	-	-	-	-	-	-	-	-	-	-	-	-	22	13
Piero Drogo	Cooper T43-Climax	-	-	-	-	-	-	-	-	-	-	-	-	-	-	15	8	-	-
Nasif Estefano	Maserati 250F	20	14	-	-	-	-	-	-	-	-	-	-	-	-	-	-	-	-
Jack Fairman	Cooper T51-Climax	-	-	-	-	-	-	-	-	-	-	15	R	-	-	-	-	-	-
Ron Flockhart	Lotus 18-Climax	-	-	-	-	-	-	-	-	8	6	-	-	-	-	-	-	-	-
	Cooper T51-Climax	-	-	-	-	-	-	-	-	-	-	-	-	-	-	-	-	21	R
Fred Gamble	Behra-Porsche	-	-	-	-	-	-	-	-	-	-	-	-	-	-	14	10	-	-
Olivier Gendebien	Cooper T51-Climax	-	-	-	-	-	-	5	3	11	2	12	9	14	7	-	-	8	12
Richie Ginther	Ferrari Dino 246P	-	-	9	6	-	-	-	-	-	-	-	-	-	-	-	-	-	-
	Ferrari Dino 246	-	-	-	-	12	6	-	-	-	-	-	-	-	-	2	2	-	-
	Scarab	-	-	-	-	-	-	-	-	20	DNS	-	-	-	-	-	-	-	-
Jose Froilan Gonzalez	Ferrari Dino 246	11	10	-	-	-	-	-	-	-	-	-	-	-	-	-	-	-	-
Horace Gould	Maserati 250F	-	-	-	-	-	-	-	-	-	-	-	-	-	-	NT	DNS	-	-
Keith Greene	Cooper T45-Maserati	-	-	-	-	-	-	-	-	-	-	22	R	-	-	-	-	-	-
Masten Gregory	Behra-Porsche	16	12	-	-	-	-	-	-	-	-	-	-	-	-	-	-	-	-
	Cooper T51-Maserati	-	-	20	DNQ	17	DNS	-	-	17	9	14	14	11	R	-	-	-	-
Dan Gurney	BRM P48	-	-	14	NC	6	R	12	R	7	R	6	10	2	R	-	-	3	R
Bruce Halford	Cooper T45-Climax	-	-	17	DNQ	-	-	-	-	-	-	-	-	-	-	-	-	-	-
	Cooper T51-Climax	-	-	-	-	-	-	-	-	16	8	-	-	-	-	-	-	-	-
Jim Hall	Lotus 18-Climax	-	-	-	-	-	-	-	-	-	-	-	-	-	-	-	-	12	7
Hans Herrmann	Porsche 718	-	-	-	-	-	-	-	-	-	-	-	-	10	6	-	-	-	-
Graham Hill	BRM P25	3	R	-	-	-	-	-	-	-	-	-	-	-	-	-	-	-	-
	BRM P48	-	-	6	7	5	3	6	R	3	R	2	RF	5	R	-	-	11	R
Phil Hill	Ferrari Dino 246	6	8	10	3	13	R	4	4F	2	12	10	7	10	R	1	1F	-	-
	Cooper T51-Climax	-	-	-	-	-	-	-	-	-	-	-	-	-	-	-	-	13	6
Innes Ireland	Lotus 18-Climax	2	6	7	9	3	2	8	RF	4	7	5	3	7	6	-	-	7	2
Alberto Rodriguez Larreta	Lotus 16-Climax	15	9	-	-	-	-	-	-	-	-	-	-	-	-	-	-	-	-
Pete Lovely	Cooper T51-Ferrari (625LM)	-	-	-	-	-	-	-	-	-	-	-	-	-	-	-	-	20	11
Willy Mairesse	Ferrari Dino 246	-	-	-	-	-	-	13	R	5	R	-	-	-	-	3	3	-	-
Bruce McLaren	Cooper T45-Climax	13	1	-	-	-	-	-	-	-	-	-	-	-	-	-	-	-	-
	Cooper T53-Climax	-	-	11	2F	9	R	14	2	9	3	3	4	6	2	-	-	10	3
Carlos Menditeguy	Cooper T51-Maserati	12	4	-	-	-	-	-	-	-	-	-	-	-	-	-	-	-	-
Stirling Moss	Cooper T51-Climax	1	3F	-	-	-	-	-	-	-	-	-	-	-	-	-	-	-	-
	Lotus 18-Climax	-	-	1	1	1	4F	3	DNS	-	-	-	-	4	DSQ	-	-	1	1
Gino Munaron	Maserati 250F	19	13	-	-	-	-	-	-	-	-	-	-	-	-	-	-	-	-
	Cooper T51-Ferrari	-	-	-	-	-	-	-	-	19	R	NT	15	-	-	8	R	-	-
Brian Naylor	JBW-Maserati	-	-	19	DNQ	-	-	-	-	-	-	18	13	-	-	7	R	17	R
Arthur Owen	Cooper T45-Climax	-	-	-	-	-	-	-	-	-	-	-	-	-	-	11	R	-	-
David Piper	Lotus 16-Climax	-	-	-	-	-	-	-	-	21	DNS	24	12	-	-	-	-	-	-
Lance Reventlow	Scarab	-	-	23	DNQ	20	DNS	16	R	-	-	-	-	-	-	-	-	-	-
	Cooper T51-Climax	-	-	-	-	-	-	-	-	-	-	23	DNS	-	-	-	-	-	-
Roy Salvadori	Cooper T51-Climax	-	-	12	R	-	-	-	-	-	-	-	-	-	-	-	-	15	8
	Aston Martin DBR4/250	-	-	-	-	18	DNS	-	-	-	-	-	-	-	-	-	-	-	-
	Aston Martin DBR5/250	-	-	-	-	-	-	-	-	-	-	13	R	-	-	-	-	-	-

driver	car	RA Q	RA R	MC Q	MC R	NL Q	NL R	B Q	B R	F Q	F R	GB Q	GB R	P Q	P R	I Q	I R	USA Q	USA R
Giorgio Scarlatti	Maserati 250F	18	R	-	-	-	-	-	-	-	-	-	-	-	-	-	-	-	-
	Cooper T51-Ferrari	-	-	22	DNQ	-	-	-	-	-	-	-	-	-	-	-	-	-	-
	Cooper T51-Maserati	-	-	-	-	-	-	-	-	-	-	-	-	-	-	5	R	-	-
Harry Schell	Cooper T51-Climax	9	R	-	-	-	-	-	-	-	-	-	-	-	-	-	-	-	-
Wolfgang Seidel	Cooper T45-Climax	-	-	-	-	-	-	-	-	-	-	-	-	-	-	13	9	-	-
Alan Stacey	Lotus 16-Climax	14	R	-	-	-	-	-	-	-	-	-	-	-	-	-	-	-	-
	Lotus 18-Climax	-	-	-	-	13	R	8	R	17	R	-	-	-	-	-	-	-	-
John Surtees	Lotus 18-Climax	-	-	15	R	-	-	-	-	-	-	11	2	1	RF	-	-	6	R
Henry Taylor	Cooper T51-Climax	-	-	-	-	-	-	14	7	13	4	16	8	NT	DNS	-	-	14	14
Mike Taylor	Lotus 18-Climax	-	-	-	-	-	-	-	-	19	DNS	-	-	-	-	-	-	-	-
Alfonso Thiele	Cooper T51-Maserati	-	-	-	-	-	-	-	-	-	-	-	-	-	-	9	R	-	-
Maurice Trintignant	Cooper T51-Climax	8	3	-	-	-	-	-	-	-	-	-	-	-	-	-	-	-	-
	Cooper T51-Maserati	-	-	-	-	16	R	19	R	-	-	18	R	-	-	-	-	19	15
	Aston Martin DBR5/250	-	-	-	-	-	-	-	-	-	-	21	11	-	-	-	-	-	-
Wolfgang von Trips	Ferrari Dino 246	5	5	8	8	15	5	11	R	6	11	7	6	9	4	-	-	-	-
	Ferrari Dino 156P	-	-	-	-	-	-	-	-	-	-	-	-	-	-	6	5	-	-
	Cooper T51-Maserati	-	-	-	-	-	-	-	-	-	-	-	-	-	-	-	-	16	9
Vic Wilson	Cooper T43-Climax	-	-	-	-	-	-	-	-	-	-	-	-	-	-	16	R	-	-

SHARED DRIVES - Argentinian GP: Maurice Trintignant/Stirling Moss (Cooper T51-Climax) 3

1960 FINAL CHAMPIONSHIP POSITIONS

Drivers

1	Jack Brabham	43
2	Bruce McLaren	34 (37)*
3	Stirling Moss	19
4	Innes Ireland	18
5	Phil Hill	16
6=	Olivier Gendebien	10
	Wolfgang von Trips	10
8=	Jim Clark	8
	Richie Ginther	8
	Jim Rathmann	8
11	Tony Brooks	7
12=	Cliff Allison	6
	John Surtees	6
	Rodger Ward	6

15=	Jo Bonnier	4
	Paul Goldsmith	4
	Graham Hill	4
	Willy Mairesse	4
19=	Don Branson	3
	Giulio Cabianca	3
	Carlos Menditeguy	3
	Henry Taylor	3
23	Johnny Thomson	2
24=	Lucien Bianchi	1
	Ron Flockhart	1
	Hans Herrmann	1
	Eddie Johnson	1

*Best six results count

Manufacturers

1	Cooper-Climax	48 (58)*
2	Lotus-Climax	34 (37)*
3	Ferrari	26 (27)*
4	BRM	8
5=	Cooper-Maserati	3
	Cooper-Ferrari	3

*Best six results count. No points awarded for Indianapolis 500, points only awarded to first car to finish for each manufacturer

2	John Surtees	Lotus 18-Climax	77	2h05m14.2
3	Innes Ireland	Lotus 18-Climax	77	2h05m54.2
4	Bruce McLaren	Cooper T53-Climax	76	
5	Tony Brooks	Cooper T51-Climax	76	
6	Wolfgang von Trips	Ferrari Dino 246	75	

Winner's average speed: 108.695 mph. Starting grid front row: Brabham, 1m34.6 (pole), G Hill, 1m35.6, McLaren, 1m36.0 and Bonnier, 1m36.2. Fastest lap: G Hill, 1m34.4. Leaders: Brabham, laps 1-54, 72-77; G Hill, 55-71

GRANDE PREMIO DE PORTUGAL

14 August 1960. Oporto. 55 laps of a 4.602-mile circuit = 253.110 miles. Hot, dry and sunny. World Championship round 8

1	Jack Brabham	Cooper T53-Climax	55	2h19m00.03
2	Bruce McLaren	Cooper T53-Climax	55	2h19m58.00
3	Jim Clark	Lotus 18-Climax	55	2h20m53.26
4	Wolfgang von Trips	Ferrari Dino 246	55	2h20m58.84
5	Tony Brooks	Cooper T51-Climax	49	
6	Innes Ireland	Lotus 18-Climax	48	

Stirling Moss (Lotus 18-Climax) finished 5th on the road but was disqualified for driving in the wrong direction after a spin. Winner's average speed: 109.256 mph. Starting grid front row: Surtees, 2m25.56 (pole), Gurney, 2m25.63 and Brabham, 2m26.05. Fastest lap: Surtees, 2m27.53. Leaders: Gurney, laps 1-10; Surtees, 11-35; Brabham, 36-55

GRAN PREMIO D'ITALIA E EUROPA

4 September 1960. Monza. 50 laps of a 6.214-mile circuit = 310.700 miles. Warm, dry and overcast. World Championship round 9

1	Phil Hill	Ferrari Dino 246	50	2h21m09.2

2	Richie Ginther	Ferrari Dino 246	50	2h23m36.8
3	Willy Mairesse	Ferrari Dino 246	49	
4	Giulio Cabianca	Cooper T51-Ferrari	48	
5	Wolfgang von Trips	Ferrari Dino 156P	48	
6	Hans Herrmann	Porsche 718*	47	

*Porsche ineligible for manufacturers' points as they entered an F2 car. Winner's average speed: 132.069 mph. Starting grid front row: P Hill, 2m41.4 (pole), Ginther, 2m43.3 and Mairesse, 2m43.9. Fastest lap: P Hill, 2m43.6. Leaders: Ginther, laps 1-16, 18-25; P Hill, 17, 26-50

UNITED STATES GRAND PRIX

20 November 1960. Riverside. 75 laps of a 3.275-mile circuit = 245.625 miles. Warm, dry and sunny. World Championship round 10

1	Stirling Moss	Lotus 18-Climax	75	2h28m52.2
2	Innes Ireland	Lotus 18-Climax	75	2h29m30.2
3	Bruce McLaren	Cooper T53-Climax	75	2h30m14.2
4	Jack Brabham	Cooper T53-Climax	74	
5	Jo Bonnier	BRM P48	74	
6	Phil Hill	Cooper T51-Climax	74	

Winner's average speed: 98.996 mph. Starting grid front row: Moss, 1m54.4 (pole), Brabham, 1m55.0 and Gurney, 1m55.2. Fastest lap: Brabham, 1m56.2. Leaders: Brabham, laps 1-4; Moss, 5-75

1961

The new 1.5-litre engine formula was introduced in 1961, much to the annoyance of the British teams, who had hoped to continue with the 1960 rules. Despite being

Formula 1

1961 DRIVERS' RECORDS

driver	car	MC		NL		B		F		GB		D		I		USA	
		Q	R	Q	R	Q	R	Q	R	Q	R	Q	R	Q	R	Q	R
Cliff Allison	Lotus 18-Climax	15	8	-	-	-	-	-	-	-	-	-	-	-	-	-	-
	Lotus 18/21-Climax	-	-	-	-	NT	DNQ	-	-	-	-	-	-	-	-	-	-
Gerry Ashmore	Lotus 18-Climax	-	-	-	-	-	-	-	-	26	R	25	16	25	R	-	-
Giancarlo Baghetti	Ferrari Dino 156	-	-	-	-	-	-	12	1	19	R	-	-	6	RF	-	-
Lorenzo Bandini	Cooper T53-Maserati	-	-	-	-	17	R	-	-	21	12	19	R	21	8	-	-
Carel Godin de Beaufort	Porsche 718	-	-	15	14	14	11	17	R	18	16	17	14	15	7	-	-
Lucien Bianchi	Emeryson Mk2-Maserati	20	DNQ	-	-	-	-	-	-	-	-	-	-	-	-	-	-
	Lotus 18-Climax	-	-	-	-	21	R	-	-	-	-	-	-	-	-	-	-
	Lotus 18/21-Climax	-	-	-	-	-	-	19	R	30	R	-	-	-	-	-	-
Jo Bonnier	Porsche 787	9	12	11	11	-	-	-	-	-	-	-	-	-	-	-	-
	Porsche 718	-	-	-	-	9	7	13	7	3	5	4	R	8	R	10	6
Jack Brabham	Cooper T55-Climax	17	R	7	6	11	R	14	R	9	4	-	-	-	-	-	-
	Cooper T58-Climax	-	-	-	-	-	-	-	-	-	-	2	R	10	R	1	RF
Tony Brooks	BRM P48/57-Climax	8	13	8	9	7	13	11	R	6	9F	9	R	13	5	6	3
Ian Burgess	Lotus 18-Climax	-	-	17	DNQ	24	DNQ	24	14	25	14	-	-	-	-	-	-
	Cooper T53-Climax	-	-	-	-	-	-	-	-	-	-	24	12	-	-	-	-
Roberto Bussinello	De Tomaso F1/004-Alfa	-	-	-	-	-	-	-	-	-	-	-	-	24	R	-	-
Jim Clark	Lotus 21-Climax	3	10	10	3F	16	12	5	3	8	R	8	4	7	R	5	7
Bernard Collomb	Cooper T53-Climax	-	-	-	-	-	-	21	R	-	-	26	R	-	-	-	-
Jack Fairman	Ferguson P99-Climax	-	-	-	-	-	-	-	-	20	DSQ	-	-	-	-	-	-
	Cooper T45-Climax	-	-	-	-	-	-	-	-	-	-	-	-	26	R	-	-
Olivier Gendebien	Emeryson Mk2-Maserati	21	DNQ	-	-	-	-	-	-	-	-	-	-	-	-	-	-
	Ferrari Dino 156	-	-	-	-	3	4	-	-	-	-	-	-	-	-	-	-
	Lotus 18/21-Climax	-	-	-	-	-	-	-	-	-	-	-	-	-	-	15	11
Richie Ginther	Ferrari Dino 156	2	2F	3	5	5	3F	3	15	2	3	14	8	3	R	-	-
Keith Greene	Gilby-Climax	-	-	-	-	-	-	-	-	23	15	-	-	-	-	-	-
Masten Gregory	Cooper T53-Climax	19	DNQ	16	DNQ	12	10	16	12	16	11	-	-	-	-	-	-
	Lotus 18/21-Climax	-	-	-	-	-	-	-	-	-	-	-	-	17	R	11	11
Dan Gurney	Porsche 718	11	5	-	-	10	6	9	2	12	7	7	7	12	2	7	2
	Porsche 787	-	-	6	10	-	-	-	-	-	-	-	-	-	-	-	-
Jim Hall	Lotus 18/21-Climax	-	-	-	-	-	-	-	-	-	-	-	-	-	-	18	R
Walt Hansgen	Cooper T53-Climax	-	-	-	-	-	-	-	-	-	-	-	-	-	-	14	R
Hans Herrmann	Porsche 718	13	9	12	15	-	-	-	-	-	-	11	13	-	-	-	-
Graham Hill	BRM P48/57-Climax	4	R	5	8	6	R	6	6	11	R	6	R	5	R	2	5
Phil Hill	Ferrari Dino 156	5	3	1	2	1	1	1	9F	1	2	1	3F	4	1	-	-
Innes Ireland	Lotus 21-Climax	10	DNS	-	-	18	R	10	4	7	10	16	R	-	-	8	1
	Lotus 18/21-Climax	-	-	-	-	-	-	-	-	-	-	-	-	9	R	-	-
Jackie Lewis	Cooper T53-Climax	-	-	-	-	13	9	18	R	15	R	18	9	16	4	-	-
Roberto Lippi	De Tomaso F1/002-OSCA	-	-	-	-	-	-	-	-	-	-	-	-	32	R	-	-
Tony Maggs	Lotus 18-Climax	-	-	-	-	-	-	-	-	24	13	22	11	-	-	-	-
Willy Mairesse	Lotus 18-Climax	-	-	-	-	20	R	-	-	-	-	-	-	-	-	-	-
	Lotus 21-Climax	-	-	-	-	-	-	20	R	-	-	-	-	-	-	-	-
	Ferrari Dino 156	-	-	-	-	-	-	-	-	-	-	13	R	-	-	-	-
Tony Marsh	Lotus 18-Climax	-	-	-	-	22	DNQ	-	-	27	R	20	15	-	-	-	-
Michel May	Lotus 18-Climax	14	R	-	-	-	-	22	11	-	-	27	DNQ	-	-	-	-
Bruce McLaren	Cooper T55-Climax	7	6	13	12	15	R	8	5	14	8	12	6	14	3	4	4
Stirling Moss	Lotus 18-Climax	1	1F	4	4	-	-	-	-	-	-	-	-	-	-	-	-
	Lotus 18/21-Climax	-	-	-	-	8	8	4	R	5	R	3	1	-	-	3	R
	Ferguson P99-Climax	-	-	-	-	-	-	-	-	NT	DSQ	-	-	-	-	-	-
	Lotus 21-Climax	-	-	-	-	-	-	-	-	-	-	-	-	11	R	-	-
Massimo Natili	Cooper T51-Maserati	-	-	-	-	-	-	-	-	28	R	-	-	-	-	-	-
Brian Naylor	JBW 1960-Climax	-	-	-	-	-	-	-	-	-	-	-	-	31	R	-	-
Tim Parnell	Lotus 18-Climax	-	-	-	-	-	-	-	-	29	R	-	-	27	10	-	-
Roger Penske	Cooper T53-Climax	-	-	-	-	-	-	-	-	-	-	-	-	-	-	16	8
Andre Pilette	Emeryson Mk2-Climax	-	-	-	-	-	-	-	-	-	-	-	-	33	DNQ	-	-
Renato Pirocchi	Cooper T51-Maserati	-	-	-	-	-	-	-	-	-	-	-	-	29	12	-	-
Ricardo Rodriguez	Ferrari Dino 156	-	-	-	-	-	-	-	-	-	-	-	-	2	R	-	-
Lloyd Ruby	Lotus 18-Climax	-	-	-	-	-	-	-	-	-	-	-	-	-	-	19	R
Peter Ryan	Lotus 18/21-Climax	-	-	-	-	-	-	-	-	-	-	-	-	-	-	13	9
Roy Salvadori	Cooper T53-Climax	-	-	-	-	15	8	13	6	15	10	18	6	12	R	-	-
Giorgio Scarlatti	De Tomaso F1/001-OSCA	-	-	-	-	-	-	26	R	-	-	-	-	-	-	-	-
Wolfgang Seidel	Lotus 18-Climax	-	-	-	-	23	DNQ	-	-	22	17	23	R	28	R	-	-
Hap Sharp	Cooper T53-Climax	-	-	-	-	-	-	-	-	-	-	-	-	-	-	17	10
Gaetano Starrabba	Lotus 18-Maserati	-	-	-	-	-	-	-	-	-	-	-	-	30	R	-	-
John Surtees	Cooper T53-Climax	12	11	9	7	4	5	7	R	10	R	10	5	19	R	9	R

driver	car	MC		NL		B		F		GB		D		I		USA	
		Q	R	Q	R	Q	R	Q	R	Q	R	Q	R	Q	R	Q	R
Henry Taylor	Lotus 18-Climax	18	DNQ	-	-	-	-	-	-	-	-	-	-	-	-	-	-
	Lotus 18/21-Climax	-	-	-	-	-	-	25	10	17	R	-	-	23	11	-	-
Trevor Taylor	Lotus 18-Climax	-	-	14	13	-	-	-	-	-	-	-	-	-	-	-	-
Maurice Trintignant	Cooper T51-Maserati	16	7	-	-	19	R	23	13	-	-	21	R	22	9	-	-
Wolfgang von Trips	Ferrari Dino 156	6	4	2	1	2	2	2	R	4	1	5	2	1	R	-	-
Nino Vaccarella	De Tomaso F1/003-Alfa	-	-	-	-	-	-	-	-	-	-	-	-	20	R	-	-

SHARED DRIVES - British GP: Jack Fairman/Stirling Moss (Ferguson P99-Climax) DSQ. United States GP: Olivier Gendebien/Masten Gregory (Lotus 18/21-Climax) 11

1961 FINAL CHAMPIONSHIP POSITIONS

Drivers

1	Phil Hill	34 (38)*
2	Wolfgang von Trips	33
3=	Dan Gurney	21
	Stirling Moss	21
5	Richie Ginther	16
6	Innes Ireland	12
7=	Jim Clark	11
	Bruce McLaren	11
9	Giancarlo Baghetti	9
10	Tony Brooks	6
11=	Jack Brabham	4
	John Surtees	4
13=	Jo Bonnier	3
	Olivier Gendebien	3
	Graham Hill	3
	Jackie Lewis	3
17	Roy Salvadori	2

*Best five results count

Manufacturers

1	Ferrari	40 (52)*
2	Lotus-Climax	32
3	Porsche	22 (23)*
4	Cooper-Climax	14 (18)*
5	BRM-Climax	7

*Best five results count. Points only awarded to first car to finish for each manufacturer

informed of the change over two years earlier, they struggled to find suitable engines for the start of the season. Consequently, they had to make do with underpowered 4-cylinder units while purpose-built V8s from Coventry Climax and BRM were being made ready. Ferrari would start the year as overwhelming title favourites, having prepared for the new formula and introduced the purposeful V6-powered "shark-nose" 156.

At the season's first race at Monaco, Richie Ginther led the early laps for the Italians, but Stirling Moss conjured up his greatest drive to pass and hold off the Ferraris to win for Rob Walker and Lotus. It was a temporary triumph, however, with the Italian marque winning the next four events. Even when the works cars of von Trips, Ginther, and Phil Hill were delayed in France, debutant Giancarlo Baghetti won in a private entry after a slipstreaming duel with Dan Gurney's Porsche. Baghetti is the only driver to win his first Grand Prix since the championship started in 1950.

A correct tyre choice in the wet/dry German GP gave Moss a second win, but it was the Ferraris of Wolfgang von Trips and Phil Hill which led the championship before the penultimate round at Monza. Von Trips led Hill 2-1 in victories and by eight points in the championship. Early in the race, however, von Trips collided with Jim Clark's Lotus approaching Parabolica, which launched the Ferrari into the crowd, killing the German and fourteen spectators.

The Italian tragedy gave the title to Hill, but Ferrari elected to miss the final race in America. Innes Ireland spun early at Watkins Glen, but recovered to score Team Lotus's first Grand Prix win. The marque's previous successes had come courtesy of Stirling Moss and Rob Walker Racing.

GRAND PRIX DE MONACO

14 May 1961. Monte Carlo. 100 laps of a 1.954-mile circuit = 195.400 miles. Warm, dry and hazy. World Championship round 1

1	Stirling Moss	Lotus 18-Climax	100	2h45m50.1
2	Richie Ginther	Ferrari Dino 156	100	2h45m53.7
3	Phil Hill	Ferrari Dino 156	100	2h46m31.4
4	Wolfgang von Trips	Ferrari Dino 156	98	electrics
5	Dan Gurney	Porsche 718	98	
6	Bruce McLaren	Cooper T55-Climax	95	

Winner's average speed: 70.697 mph. Starting grid front row: Moss, 1m39.1 (pole), Ginther, 1m39.3 and Clark, 1m39.6. Fastest lap: Ginther and Moss, 1m36.3. Leaders: Ginther, laps 1-13; Moss, 14-100

GROTE PRIJS VAN NEDERLAND

22 May 1961. Zandvoort. 75 laps of a 2.605-mile circuit = 195.375 miles. Windy, dry and sunny. World Championship round 2

1	Wolfgang von Trips	Ferrari Dino 156	75	2h01m52.1
2	Phil Hill	Ferrari Dino 156	75	2h01m53.0
3	Jim Clark	Lotus 21-Climax	75	2h02m05.2
4	Stirling Moss	Lotus 18-Climax	75	2h02m14.3
5	Richie Ginther	Ferrari Dino 156	75	2h02m14.4
6	Jack Brabham	Cooper T55-Climax	75	2h03m12.2

Winner's average speed: 96.190 mph. Starting grid front row: P Hill, 1m35.7 (pole), von Trips, 1m35.7 and Ginther, 1m35.9. Fastest lap: Clark, 1m35.5. Leaders: von Trips, laps 1-75

GRAND PRIX DE BELGIQUE

18 June 1961. Spa-Francorchamps. 30 laps of an 8.761-mile circuit = 262.830 miles. Warm, dry and overcast. World Championship round 3

1	Phil Hill	Ferrari Dino 156	30	2h03m03.8
2	Wolfgang von Trips	Ferrari Dino 156	30	2h03m04.5
3	Richie Ginther	Ferrari Dino 156	30	2h03m23.3
4	Olivier Gendebien	Ferrari Dino 156	30	2h03m49.4
5	John Surtees	Cooper T53-Climax	30	2h04m30.6
6	Dan Gurney	Porsche 718	30	2h04m34.8

Winner's average speed: 128.144 mph. Starting grid front row: P Hill, 3m59.3 (pole), von Trips, 4m00.1 and Gendebien, 4m03.0. Fastest lap: Ginther, 3m59.8. Leaders: P Hill, laps 1, 3-5, 8, 11-13, 15, 17-18, 21-23, 25-30; Gendebien, 2, 6-7; von Trips, 9-10, 14, 16, 19-20, 24

GRAND PRIX DE L'AUTOMOBILE CLUB DE FRANCE

2 July 1961. Reims. 52 laps of a 5.187-mile circuit = 269.724 miles. Very hot, dry and sunny. World Championship round 4

1	Giancarlo Baghetti	Ferrari Dino 156	52	2h14m17.5

2	Dan Gurney	Porsche 718	52	2h14m17.6
3	Jim Clark	Lotus 21-Climax	52	2h15m18.6
4	Innes Ireland	Lotus 21-Climax	52	2h15m27.6
5	Bruce McLaren	Cooper T55-Climax	52	2h15m59.3
6	Graham Hill	BRM P48/57-Climax	52	2h15m59.4

Winner's average speed: 120.510 mph. Starting grid front row: P Hill, 2m24.9 (pole), von Trips, 2m26.4 and Ginther, 2m26.8. Fastest lap: P Hill, 2m27.1. Leaders: P Hill, laps 1-12, 18-37; von Trips, 13-17; Ginther, 38-40; Baghetti, 41-43, 45, 47, 50, 52; Bonnier, 44; Gurney, 46, 48-49, 51

BRITISH GRAND PRIX

15 July 1961. Aintree. 75 laps of a 3.000-mile circuit = 225.000 miles. Cool, wet and overcast at the start, drying later. World Championship round 5

1	Wolfgang von Trips	Ferrari Dino 156	75	2h40m53.6
2	Phil Hill	Ferrari Dino 156	75	2h41m39.6
3	Richie Ginther	Ferrari Dino 156	75	2h41m40.4
4	Jack Brabham	Cooper T55-Climax	75	2h42m02.2
5	Jo Bonnier	Porsche 718	75	2h42m09.8
6	Roy Salvadori	Cooper T53-Climax	75	2h42m19.8

Winner's average speed: 83.907 mph. Starting grid front row: P Hill, 1m58.8 (pole), Ginther, 1m58.8 and Bonnier, 1m58.8. Fastest lap: Brooks, 1m57.8. Leaders: P Hill, laps 1-6; von Trips, 7-75

GROSSER PREIS VON DEUTSCHLAND UND EUROPA

6 August 1961. Nurburgring. 15 laps of a 14.167-mile circuit = 212.505 miles. Showers. World Championship round 6

1	Stirling Moss	Lotus 18/21-Climax	15	2h18m12.4
2	Wolfgang von Trips	Ferrari Dino 156	15	2h18m33.8
3	Phil Hill	Ferrari Dino 156	15	2h18m34.9
4	Jim Clark	Lotus 21-Climax	15	2h19m29.5
5	John Surtees	Cooper T53-Climax	15	2h20m05.5
6	Bruce McLaren	Cooper T55-Climax	15	2h20m53.8

Winner's average speed: 92.255 mph. Starting grid front row: P Hill, 8m55.2 (pole), Brabham, 9m01.4, Moss, 9m01.7 and Bonnier, 9m04.8. Fastest lap: P Hill, 8m57.8. Leaders: Moss, laps 1-15

GRAN PREMIO D'ITALIA

10 September 1961. Monza. 43 laps of a 6.214-mile circuit = 267.189 miles. Very hot, dry and sunny. World Championship round 7

1	Phil Hill	Ferrari Dino 156	43	2h03m13.0
2	Dan Gurney	Porsche 718	43	2h03m44.2
3	Bruce McLaren	Cooper T55-Climax	43	2h05m41.4
4	Jackie Lewis	Cooper T53-Climax	43	2h05m53.4
5	Tony Brooks	BRM P48/57-Climax	43	2h05m53.5
6	Roy Salvadori	Cooper T53-Climax	42	

Winner's average speed: 130.107 mph. Starting grid front row: von Trips, 2m46.3 (pole) and R Rodriguez, 2m46.4. Fastest lap: Baghetti, 2m48.4. Leaders: P Hill, laps 1-3, 5, 7, 10, 14-43; Ginther, 4, 6, 8-9, 11-13

UNITED STATES GRAND PRIX

8 October 1961. Watkins Glen. 100 laps of a 2.350-mile circuit = 235.000 miles. Warm, dry and sunny. World Championship round 8

1	Innes Ireland	Lotus 21-Climax	100	2h13m45.8
2	Dan Gurney	Porsche 718	100	2h13m50.1
3	Tony Brooks	BRM P48/57-Climax	100	2h14m33.6
4	Bruce McLaren	Cooper T55-Climax	100	2h14m43.8
5	Graham Hill	BRM P48/57-Climax	99	
6	Jo Bonnier	Porsche 718	98	

Winner's average speed: 105.410 mph. Starting grid front row: Brabham, 1m17.0 (pole) and G Hill, 1m18.1. Fastest lap: Brabham, 1m18.2. Leaders: Moss, laps 1-5, 16, 24-25, 34-35, 39-58; Brabham, 6-15, 17-23, 26-33, 36-38; Ireland, 59-100

1962

Having dominated the first year of the 1.5-litre formula, Ferrari was rocked by the departure of team manager Romolo Tavoni and several of his engineering staff. The Italian marque's advantage was diminished further as V8 engines from BRM and Climax were now widely available for their British rivals.

When Stirling Moss was seriously injured at Goodwood before the championship began, he announced his immediate retirement from international motor racing. In his absence, Grand Prix racing was a two-way fight between a new generation of British drivers: Graham Hill, now with BRM, and Jim Clark of Lotus.

The season opened at Zandvoort, where Clark gave the sensational new Lotus 25 its debut. The car featured revolutionary monocoque chassis construction, which was lighter and more rigid than the conventional tubular space-frame. However, early teething troubles cost Clark vital points, and clutch problems hampered his first two races.

Hill won in Holland, beating the conventional works Lotus 24 of Trevor Taylor, but lost to Bruce McLaren in the final laps of the Monaco GP. It all came right for Clark at the Belgian GP, where he scored his first Grand Prix victory. Dan Gurney made up for his narrow defeat in the 1961 French GP by winning this year's event at Rouen—the only victory for Porsche as a Grand Prix car constructor.

Another Clark win at Aintree was followed by the best race of the year at Nurburgring. The first three cars, led by Hill, were separated by less than five seconds at the finish, while Clark, who had stalled at the start, stormed through the field to finish fourth.

A win apiece for the two championship protagonists at Monza and Watkins Glen set up a tense finale at the new South African GP at East London. Clark led Hill off the line and opened a convincing lead. He appeared to have won both the race and the title, until failing oil pressure forced him to retire, giving Graham Hill his first World Championship.

GROTE PRIJS VAN NEDERLAND EUROPA

20 May 1962. Zandvoort. 80 laps of a 2.605-mile circuit = 208.400 miles. Warm, dry and sunny. World Championship round 1

1	Graham Hill	BRM P57	80	2h11m02.1
2	Trevor Taylor	Lotus 24-Climax	80	2h11m29.3
3	Phil Hill	Ferrari Dino 156	80	2h12m23.2
4	Giancarlo Baghetti	Ferrari Dino 156	79	
5	Tony Maggs	Cooper T55-Climax	78	
6	Carel Godin de Beaufort	Porsche 718	76	

Winner's average speed: 95.425 mph. Starting grid front row: Surtees, 1m32.5 (pole), G Hill, 1m32.6 and Clark, 1m33.2. Fastest lap: McLaren, 1m34.4. Leaders: Clark, laps 1-11; G Hill, 12-54, 56-80, P Hill, 55

GRAND PRIX DE MONACO

3 June 1962. Monte Carlo. 100 laps of a 1.954-mile circuit = 195.400 miles. Dry and overcast. World Championship round 2

1	Bruce McLaren	Cooper T60-Climax	100	2h46m29.7
2	Phil Hill	Ferrari Dino 156	100	2h46m31.0
3	Lorenzo Bandini	Ferrari Dino 156	100	2h47m53.8
4	John Surtees	Lola Mk4-Climax	99	
5	Jo Bonnier	Porsche 718	93	
6	Graham Hill	BRM P57	92	engine

Winner's average speed: 70.417 mph. Starting grid front row: Clark, 1m35.4 (pole), G Hill, 1m35.8 and McLaren, 1m36.4. Fastest lap: Clark, 1m35.5. Leaders: McLaren, laps 1-6, 93-100; G Hill, 7-92

GRAND PRIX DE BELGIQUE

17 June 1962. Spa-Francorchamps. 32 laps of an 8.761-mile circuit = 280.352 miles. Warm, dry and sunny. World Championship round 3

1961-1962

1962 DRIVERS' RECORDS

driver	car	NL		MC		B		F		GB		D		I		USA		ZA	
		Q	R	Q	R	Q	R	Q	R	Q	R	Q	R	Q	R	Q	R	Q	R
Gerry Ashmore	Lotus 18/21-Climax	-	-	-	-	-	-	-	-	-	-	-	-	24	DNQ	-	-	-	-
Giancarlo Baghetti	Ferrari Dino 156	12	4	-	-	14	R	-	-	-	-	13	10	18	5	-	-	-	-
Lorenzo Bandini	Ferrari Dino 156	-	-	10	3	-	-	-	-	-	-	18	R	17	8	-	-	-	-
Carel Godin de Beaufort	Porsche 718	14	6	21	DNQ	13	7	17	6	17	14	8	13	20	10	14	R	16	11
Lucien Bianchi	Lotus 18/21-Climax	-	-	-	-	-	-	18	9	-	-	-	-	-	-	-	-	-	-
	ENB 1962-Maserati	-	-	-	-	-	-	-	-	-	-	25	16	-	-	-	-	-	-
Jo Bonnier	Porsche 804	13	7	-	-	-	-	9	R	7	R	6	7	9	6	9	13	-	-
	Porsche 718	-	-	16	5	-	-	-	-	-	-	-	-	-	-	-	-	-	-
Jack Brabham	Lotus 24-Climax	4	R	6	8	15	6	4	R	9	5	-	-	-	-	-	-	-	-
	Brabham BT3-Climax	-	-	-	-	-	-	-	-	-	-	24	R	-	-	5	4	3	4
Ian Burgess	Cooper T59-Climax	-	-	-	-	-	-	-	-	16	12	16	11	25	DNQ	-	-	-	-
John Campbell-Jones	Lotus 18-Climax	-	-	-	-	19	11	-	-	-	-	-	-	-	-	-	-	-	-
Jay Chamberlain	Lotus 18-Climax	-	-	-	-	-	-	-	-	20	15	29	DNQ	29	DNQ	-	-	-	-
Jim Clark	Lotus 25-Climax	3	9	1	RF	12	1F	1	R	1	1F	3	4	1	R	1	1F	1	RF
Bernard Collomb	Cooper T53-Climax	-	-	-	-	-	-	-	-	-	-	22	R	-	-	-	-	-	-
Nasif Estefano	De Tomaso F1/801	-	-	-	-	-	-	-	-	-	-	-	-	30	DNQ	-	-	-	-
Richie Ginther	BRM P48/57	7	R	13	R	-	-	-	-	-	-	-	-	-	-	-	-	-	-
	BRM P57	-	-	-	-	9	R	10	3	8	13	7	8	3	2	2	R	7	7
Keith Greene	Gilby-BRM	-	-	-	-	-	-	-	-	-	-	19	R	23	DNQ	-	-	-	-
Masten Gregory	Lotus 18/21-Climax	16	R	-	-	-	-	-	-	-	-	-	-	-	-	-	-	-	-
	Lotus 24-BRM	-	-	20	DNQ	8	R	7	R	-	-	-	-	6	12	7	6	-	-
	Lotus 24-Climax	-	-	-	-	-	-	-	-	14	7	-	-	-	-	-	-	-	-
Dan Gurney	Porsche 804	8	R	5	R	-	-	6	1	6	9	1	3	7	13	4	5	-	-
	Lotus 24-BRM	-	-	-	-	20	DNS	-	-	-	-	-	-	-	-	-	-	-	-
Jim Hall	Lotus 21-Climax	-	-	-	-	-	-	-	-	-	-	-	-	-	-	18	DNS	-	-
Mike Harris	Cooper T53-Alfa Romeo	-	-	-	-	-	-	-	-	-	-	-	-	-	-	-	-	15	R
Graham Hill	BRM P57	2	1	2	6	1	2	2	9F	5	4	2	1F	2	1F	3	2	2	1
Phil Hill	Ferrari Dino 156	9	3	9	2	4	3	-	-	12	R	12	R	15	11	-	-	-	-
Innes Ireland	Lotus 24-Climax	6	R	8	R	5	R	8	R	3	16	-	-	5	R	16	8	4	5
Bruce Johnstone	BRM P48/57	-	-	-	-	-	-	-	-	-	-	-	-	-	-	-	-	NT	9
Neville Lederle	Lotus 21-Climax	-	-	-	-	-	-	-	-	-	-	-	-	-	-	-	-	10	6
Jackie Lewis	Cooper T53-Climax	19	8	-	-	-	-	16	R	15	10	21	R	-	-	-	-	-	-
	BRM P48/57	-	-	19	DNQ	-	-	-	-	-	-	-	-	-	-	-	-	-	-
Roberto Lippi	De Tomaso F1/002-OSCA	-	-	-	-	-	-	-	-	-	-	-	-	28	DNQ	-	-	-	-
John Love	Cooper T55-Climax	-	-	-	-	-	-	-	-	-	-	-	-	-	-	-	-	12	8
Tony Maggs	Cooper T55-Climax	15	5	17	R	-	-	-	-	-	-	23	9	-	-	-	-	-	-
	Cooper T60-Climax	-	-	-	-	10	R	11	2	13	6	-	-	12	7	10	7	6	3
Willy Mairesse	Ferrari Dino 156	-	-	4	7	6	R	-	-	-	-	-	-	10	4	-	-	-	-
Timmy Mayer	Cooper T53-Climax	-	-	-	-	-	-	-	-	-	-	-	-	-	-	12	R	-	-
Bruce McLaren	Cooper T60-Climax	5	RF	3	1	2	R	3	4	4	3	5	5	4	3	6	3	8	2
Roger Penske	Lotus 24-Climax	-	-	-	-	-	-	-	-	-	-	-	-	-	-	13	9	-	-
Ernest Pieterse	Lotus 21-Climax	-	-	-	-	-	-	-	-	-	-	-	-	-	-	-	-	13	10
Ben Pon	Porsche 787	18	R	-	-	-	-	-	-	-	-	-	-	-	-	-	-	-	-
Ernesto Prinoth	Lotus 18-Climax	-	-	-	-	-	-	-	-	-	-	-	-	27	DNQ	-	-	-	-
Ricardo Rodriguez	Ferrari Dino 156	11	R	15	DNS	7	4	-	-	-	-	10	6	11	14	-	-	-	-
Roy Salvadori	Lola Mk4-Climax	17	R	12	R	-	-	14	R	11	R	9	R	13	R	11	DNS	11	R
Heinz Schiller	Lotus 24-BRM	-	-	-	-	-	-	-	-	-	-	20	R	-	-	-	-	-	-
Rob Schroeder	Lotus 24-Climax	-	-	-	-	-	-	-	-	-	-	-	-	-	-	17	10	-	-
Wolfgang Seidel	Emeryson Mk2-Climax	20	10	-	-	-	-	-	-	-	-	-	-	-	-	-	-	-	-
	Lotus 24-BRM	-	-	-	-	-	-	-	-	-	-	21	R	28	DNQ	-	-	-	-
Gunther Seiffert	Lotus 24-BRM	-	-	-	-	-	-	-	-	-	-	30	DNQ	-	-	-	-	-	-
Doug Serrurier	LDS Mk1-Alfa Romeo	-	-	-	-	-	-	-	-	-	-	-	-	-	-	-	-	14	R
Tony Settember	Emeryson Mk2-Climax	-	-	-	-	-	-	-	-	19	11	-	-	21	R	-	-	-	-
Hap Sharp	Cooper T53-Climax	-	-	-	-	-	-	-	-	-	-	-	-	-	-	15	11	-	-
Tony Shelly	Lotus 18/21-Climax	-	-	-	-	-	-	-	-	18	R	27	DNQ	-	-	-	-	-	-
	Lotus 24-BRM	-	-	-	-	-	-	-	-	-	-	-	-	22	DNQ	-	-	-	-
Jo Siffert	Lotus 21-Climax	-	-	18	DNQ	17	10	-	-	-	-	17	12	-	-	-	-	-	-
	Lotus 24-BRM	-	-	-	-	-	-	15	R	-	-	-	-	26	DNQ	-	-	-	-
John Surtees	Lola Mk4-Climax	1	R	11	4	11	5	5	5	2	2	4	2	-	-	20	R	5	R
	Lola Mk4A-Climax	-	-	-	-	-	-	-	-	-	-	-	-	8	R	-	-	-	-
Trevor Taylor	Lotus 24-Climax	10	2	14	R	3	R	-	-	10	8	26	R	-	-	-	-	-	-
	Lotus 25-Climax	-	-	-	-	-	-	12	8	-	-	-	-	16	R	8	12	9	R
Maurice Trintignant	Lotus 24-Climax	-	-	7	R	16	8	13	7	-	-	11	R	19	R	19	R	-	-

Formula 1

driver	car	NL Q	NL R	MC Q	MC R	B Q	B R	F Q	F R	GB Q	GB R	D Q	D R	I Q	I R	USA Q	USA R	ZA Q	ZA R
Nino Vaccarella	Lotus 18/21-Climax	-	-	22	DNQ	-													
	Porsche 718											15	15						
	Lotus 24-Climax													14	9				
Heini Walter	Porsche 718											14	14						

1962 FINAL CHAMPIONSHIP POSITIONS

Drivers

1	Graham Hill	42 (52)*
2	Jim Clark	30
3	Bruce McLaren	27 (32)*
4	John Surtees	19
5	Dan Gurney	15
6	Phil Hill	14
7	Tony Maggs	13
8	Richie Ginther	10
9	Jack Brabham	9
10	Trevor Taylor	6
11	Giancarlo Baghetti	5
12=	Lorenzo Bandini	4
	Ricardo Rodriguez	4
14=	Jo Bonnier	3
	Willy Mairesse	3
16=	Carel Godin de Beaufort	2
	Innes Ireland	2
18=	Masten Gregory	1
	Neville Lederle	1

*Best five results count

Manufacturers

1	BRM	42 (56)*
2	Lotus-Climax	36 (38)*
3	Cooper-Climax	29 (37)*
4	Lola-Climax	19
5=	Ferrari	18
	Porsche	18 (19)*
7	Brabham-Climax	6
8	Lotus-BRM	1

*Best five results count. Points only awarded to first car to finish for each manufacturer

---

1	Jim Clark	Lotus 25-Climax	32	2h07m32.3
2	Graham Hill	BRM P57	32	2h08m16.4
3	Phil Hill	Ferrari Dino 156	32	2h09m38.8
4	Ricardo Rodriguez	Ferrari Dino 156	32	2h09m38.9
5	John Surtees	Lola Mk4-Climax	31	
6	Jack Brabham	Lotus 24-Climax	30	

Winner's average speed: 131.891 mph. Starting grid front row: G Hill, 3m57.0 (pole), McLaren, 3m58.8 and T Taylor, 3m59.3. Fastest lap: Clark, 3m55.6. Leaders: G Hill, lap 1; T Taylor, laps 2-3, 5, 8; Mairesse, 4, 6-7; Clark, 9-32

GRAND PRIX DE L'AUTOMOBILE CLUB DE FRANCE

8 July 1962. Rouen-les-Essarts. 54 laps of a 4.065-mile circuit = 219.510 miles. Warm, dry and sunny. World Championship round 4

1	Dan Gurney	Porsche 804	54	2h07m35.5
2	Tony Maggs	Cooper T60-Climax	53	
3	Richie Ginther	BRM P57	52	
4	Bruce McLaren	Cooper T60-Climax	51	
5	John Surtees	Lola Mk4-Climax	51	
6	Carel Godin de Beaufort	Porsche 718	51	

Winner's average speed: 103.225 mph. Starting grid front row: Clark, 2m14.8 (pole), G Hill, 2m15.0 and McLaren, 2m15.4. Fastest lap: G Hill, 2m16.9. Leaders: G Hill, laps 1-29, 33-41; Clark, 30-32; Gurney, 42-54

BRITISH GRAND PRIX

21 July 1962. Aintree. 75 laps of a 3.000-mile circuit = 225.000 miles. Warm, dry and sunny. World Championship round 5

1	Jim Clark	Lotus 25-Climax	75	2h26m20.8
2	John Surtees	Lola Mk4-Climax	75	2h27m10.0
3	Bruce McLaren	Cooper T60-Climax	75	2h28m05.6
4	Graham Hill	BRM P57	75	2h28m17.6
5	Jack Brabham	Lotus 24-Climax	74	
6	Tony Maggs	Cooper T60-Climax	74	

Winner's average speed: 92.247 mph. Starting grid front row: Clark, 1m53.6 (pole), Surtees, 1m54.2 and Ireland, 1m54.4. Fastest lap: Clark, 1m55.0. Leaders: Clark, laps 1-75

GROSSER PREIS VON DEUTSCHLAND

5 August 1962. Nurburgring. 15 laps of a 14.167-mile circuit = 212.505 miles. Heavy rain. World Championship round 6

1	Graham Hill	BRM P57	15	2h38m45.3
2	John Surtees	Lola Mk4-Climax	15	2h38m47.8
3	Dan Gurney	Porsche 804	15	2h38m49.7
4	Jim Clark	Lotus 25-Climax	15	2h39m27.4
5	Bruce McLaren	Cooper T60-Climax	15	2h40m04.9
6	Ricardo Rodriguez	Ferrari Dino 156	15	2h40m09.1

Winner's average speed: 80.314 mph. Starting grid front row: Gurney, 8m47.2 (pole), G Hill, 8m50.2, Clark, 8m51.2 and Surtees, 8m57.5. Fastest lap: G Hill, 10m12.2. Leaders: Gurney, laps 1-2; G Hill, 3-15

GRAN PREMIO D'ITALIA

16 September 1962. Monza. 86 laps of a 3.573-mile circuit = 307.278 miles. Dry and overcast at the start, light rain later. World Championship round 7

1	Graham Hill	BRM P57	86	2h29m08.4
2	Richie Ginther	BRM P57	86	2h29m38.2
3	Bruce McLaren	Cooper T60-Climax	86	2h30m06.2
4	Willy Mairesse	Ferrari Dino 156	86	2h30m06.6
5	Giancarlo Baghetti	Ferrari Dino 156	86	2h30m39.7
6	Jo Bonnier	Porsche 804	85	

Winner's average speed: 123.620 mph. Starting grid front row: Clark, 1m40.35 (pole) and G Hill, 1m40.38. Fastest lap: G Hill, 1m42.3. Leaders: G Hill, laps 1-86

UNITED STATES GRAND PRIX

7 October 1962. Watkins Glen. 100 laps of a 2.350-mile circuit = 235.000 miles. Dry and overcast. World Championship round 8

1	Jim Clark	Lotus 25-Climax	100	2h07m13.0
2	Graham Hill	BRM P57	100	2h07m22.2
3	Bruce McLaren	Cooper T60-Climax	99	
4	Jack Brabham	Brabham BT3-Climax	99	
5	Dan Gurney	Porsche 804	99	
6	Masten Gregory	Lotus 24-BRM	99	

Winner's average speed: 110.835 mph. Starting grid front row: Clark, 1m15.8 (pole) and Ginther, 1m16.6. Fastest lap: Clark, 1m15.0. Leaders: Clark, laps 1-11, 19-100; G Hill, 12-18

SOUTH AFRICAN GRAND PRIX

29 December 1962. East London. 82 laps of a 2.436-mile circuit = 199.752 miles. Dry and windy. World Championship round 9

1	Graham Hill	BRM P57	82	2h08m03.3
2	Bruce McLaren	Cooper T60-Climax	82	2h08m53.1
3	Tony Maggs	Cooper T60-Climax	82	2h08m53.6
4	Jack Brabham	Brabham BT3-Climax	82	2h08m57.1
5	Innes Ireland	Lotus 24-Climax	81	
6	Neville Lederle	Lotus 21-Climax	78	

Winner's average speed: 93.594 mph. Starting grid front row: Clark, 1m29.3 (pole) and G Hill, 1m29.6. Fastest lap: Clark, 1m31.0. Leaders: Clark, laps 1-61; G Hill, 62-82

1963

Having come so close to the title twelve months earlier, Jim Clark and the Lotus 25 totally dominated 1963. He won seven races, and only lost the remaining three due to mechanical failures. Both Ferrari and BRM had built semi-monocoque cars to challenge the Lotus, but neither proved a match.

Ferrari attempted to end their losing streak since September 1961 by signing John Surtees to lead their challenge. BRM retained World Champion Graham Hill while former Ferrari drivers Phil Hill and Giancarlo Baghetti moved to the new and chaotic ATS team. Dan Gurney joined Jack Brabham's team after Porsche withdrew from F1 racing and he made a strong impression, but he was unable to win a Grand Prix. In the opening round Clark retired (although he was still classified as a finisher), leaving Graham Hill to record the first of his five wins around the streets of Monaco.

Clark won the next four races to take command of the championship. The run ended when engine problems slowed him at the Nurburgring, allowing Surtees past to score his first win for Ferrari. The Italian GP followed, and once again the organisers wanted to use Monza's combined road and banked course. But the banking was abandoned after initial practice when some teams protested that these corners were too bumpy and dangerous. Clark duly triumphed in the race to clinch his first championship.

Graham Hill won the United States GP after electrical problems left Clark on the grid. The Scotsman then charged through the field to finish third and won again in Mexico. The final race of the year in South Africa gave the irrepressible Clark his seventh victory, a record for wins in a single season that lasted until the championship was expanded to sixteen races. With England's Hill and Surtees the only other winners, British drivers won every race in 1963.

1963 Jim Clark and team owner Colin Chapman celebrate a first World Championship at Monza.

GRAND PRIX DE MONACO ET D'EUROPE

26 May 1963. Monte Carlo. 100 laps of a 1.954-mile circuit = 195.400 miles. Warm, dry and sunny. World Championship round 1

1	Graham Hill	BRM P57	100	2h41m49.7
2	Richie Ginther	BRM P57	100	2h41m54.3
3	Bruce McLaren	Cooper T66-Climax	100	2h42m02.5
4	John Surtees	Ferrari Dino 156	100	2h42m03.8
5	Tony Maggs	Cooper T66-Climax	98	
6	Trevor Taylor	Lotus 25-Climax	98	

Winner's average speed: 72.447 mph. Starting grid front row: Clark, 1m34.3 (pole) and G Hill, 1m35.0. Fastest lap: Surtees, 1m34.5. Leaders: G Hill, laps 1-17, 79-100; Clark, 18-78

GRAND PRIX DE BELGIQUE

9 June 1963. Spa-Francorchamps. 32 laps of an 8.761-mile circuit = 280.352 miles. Wet and overcast. World Championship round 2

1	Jim Clark	Lotus 25-Climax	32	2h27m47.6
2	Bruce McLaren	Cooper T66-Climax	32	2h32m41.6
3	Dan Gurney	Brabham BT7-Climax	31	
4	Richie Ginther	BRM P57	31	
5	Jo Bonnier	Cooper T60-Climax	30	
6	Carel Godin de Beaufort	Porsche 718	30	

Winner's average speed: 113.815 mph. Starting grid front row: G Hill, 3m54.1 (pole), Gurney, 3m55.0 and Mairesse, 3m55.3. Fastest lap: Clark, 3m58.1. Leaders: Clark, laps 1-32

GROTE PRIJS VAN NEDERLAND

23 June 1963. Zandvoort. 80 laps of a 2.605-mile circuit = 208.400 miles. Warm, dry and sunny. World Championship round 3

1	Jim Clark	Lotus 25-Climax	80	2h08m13.07
2	Dan Gurney	Brabham BT7-Climax	79	
3	John Surtees	Ferrari Dino 156	79	
4	Innes Ireland	BRP 1-BRM	79	
5	Richie Ginther	BRM P57	79	
6	Ludovico Scarfiotti	Ferrari Dino 156	78	

Winner's average speed: 97.522 mph. Starting grid front row: Clark, 1m31.6 (pole), G Hill, 1m32.2 and McLaren, 1m32.3. Fastest lap: Clark, 1m33.7. Leaders: Clark, laps 1-80

GRAND PRIX DE L'AUTOMOBILE CLUB DE FRANCE

30 June 1963. Reims. 53 laps of a 5.187-mile circuit = 274.911 miles. Occasional rain. World Championship round 4

1	Jim Clark	Lotus 25-Climax	53	2h10m54.3
2	Tony Maggs	Cooper T66-Climax	53	2h11m59.2
3	Graham Hill	BRM P61	53	2h13m08.2*
4	Jack Brabham	Brabham BT7-Climax	53	2h13m09.5
5	Dan Gurney	Brabham BT7-Climax	53	2h13m27.7
6	Jo Siffert	Lotus 24-BRM	52	

*Hill penalised 1 minute for being pushed at start, no points awarded. Winner's average speed: 126.005 mph. Starting grid front row: Clark, 2m20.2 (pole), G Hill, 2m20.9 and Gurney, 2m21.7. Fastest lap: Clark, 2m21.6. Leaders: Clark, laps 1-53

BRITISH GRAND PRIX

20 July 1963. Silverstone. 82 laps of a 2.927-mile circuit = 240.014 miles. Warm, dry and sunny. World Championship round 5

1	Jim Clark	Lotus 25-Climax	82	2h14m09.6
2	John Surtees	Ferrari Dino 156	82	2h14m35.4
3	Graham Hill	BRM P57	82	2h14m47.2
4	Richie Ginther	BRM P57	81	
5	Lorenzo Bandini	BRM P57	81	
6	Jim Hall	Lotus 24-BRM	80	

Winner's average speed: 107.341 mph. Starting grid front row: Clark, 1m34.4 (pole), Gurney, 1m34.6, G Hill, 1m34.8 and Brabham, 1m35.0. Fastest lap: Surtees, 1m36.0. Leaders: Brabham, laps 1-3; Clark, 4-82

GROSSER PREIS VON DEUTSCHLAND

4 August 1963. Nurburgring. 15 laps of a 14.167-mile circuit = 212.505 miles. Warm, dry and sunny. World Championship round 6

1	John Surtees	Ferrari Dino 156	15	2h13m06.8
2	Jim Clark	Lotus 25-Climax	15	2h14m24.3
3	Richie Ginther	BRM P57	15	2h15m51.7
4	Gerhard Mitter	Porsche 718	15	2h21m18.3
5	Jim Hall	Lotus 24-BRM	14	
6	Jo Bonnier	Cooper T66-Climax	14	

Winner's average speed: 95.785 mph. Starting grid front row: Clark, 8m45.8 (pole), Surtees, 8m46.7, Bandini, 8m54.3 and G Hill, 8m57.2.

Formula 1

1963 DRIVERS' RECORDS

driver	car	MC Q	MC R	B Q	B R	NL Q	NL R	F Q	F R	GB Q	GB R	D Q	D R	I Q	I R	USA Q	USA R	MEX Q	MEX R	ZA Q	ZA R
Chris Amon	Lola Mk4A-Climax	15	DNS	15	R	12	R	17	7	14	7	14	R	15	DNS	-	-	-	-	-	-
	Lotus 24-BRM	-	-	-	-	-	-	-	-	-	-	-	-	-	-	-	-	19	R	-	-
Bob Anderson	Lola Mk4-Climax	-	-	-	-	-	-	-	-	16	12	-	-	19	12	-	-	-	-	-	-
Peter Arundell	Lotus 25-Climax	-	-	-	-	-	-	16	DNS	-	-	-	-	-	-	-	-	-	-	-	-
Giancarlo Baghetti	ATS 100	-	-	20	R	15	R	-	-	-	-	-	-	21	15	20	R	21	R	-	-
Lorenzo Bandini	BRM P57	-	-	-	-	-	-	21	10	8	5	3	R	-	-	-	-	-	-	-	-
	Ferrari Dino 156	-	-	-	-	-	-	-	-	-	-	-	-	6	R	9	5	7	R	5	5
Carel Godin de Beaufort	Porsche 718	-	-	18	6	19	9	-	-	21	10	17	R	25	DNQ	19	6	18	10	20	10
Lucien Bianchi	Lola Mk4-Climax	-	-	16	R	-	-	-	-	-	-	-	-	-	-	-	-	-	-	-	-
Trevor Blokdyk	Cooper T51-Maserati	-	-	-	-	-	-	-	-	-	-	-	-	-	-	-	-	-	-	19	12
Jo Bonnier	Cooper T60-Climax	11	7	13	5	8	11	11	NC	-	-	-	-	-	-	-	-	-	-	-	-
	Cooper T66-Climax	-	-	-	-	-	-	-	-	12	R	12	6	11	7	12	8	8	5	11	6
Jack Brabham	Lotus 25-Climax	16	9	-	-	-	-	-	-	-	-	-	-	-	-	-	-	-	-	-	-
	Brabham BT3-Climax	-	-	6	R	-	-	-	-	-	-	-	-	7	5	-	-	-	-	-	-
	Brabham BT7-Climax	-	-	-	-	4	R	5	4	4	R	8	7	-	-	5	4	10	2	2	13
Tino Brambilla	Cooper T53-Maserati	-	-	-	-	-	-	-	-	-	-	-	-	26	DNQ	-	-	-	-	-	-
Peter Broeker	Stebro 4-Ford	-	-	-	-	-	-	-	-	-	-	-	-	-	-	21	7	-	-	-	-
Ian Burgess	Scirocco 02-BRM	-	-	-	-	-	-	-	-	20	R	19	R	-	-	-	-	-	-	-	-
Mario Araujo de Cabral	Cooper T60-Climax	-	-	-	-	-	-	-	-	-	-	20	R	22	DNQ	-	-	-	-	-	-
John Campbell-Jones	Lola Mk4-Climax	-	-	-	-	-	-	-	-	23	13	-	-	-	-	-	-	-	-	-	-
Jim Clark	Lotus 25-Climax	1	8	8	1F	1	1F	1	1F	1	1	1	2	3	1F	2	3F	1	1F	1	1
Bernard Collomb	Lotus 24-Climax	17	DNQ	-	-	-	-	-	-	-	-	-	-	21	10	-	-	-	-	-	-
Frank Dochnal	Cooper T53-Climax	-	-	-	-	-	-	-	-	-	-	-	-	-	-	NT	DNS	-	-	-	-
Paddy Driver	Lotus 24-BRM	-	-	-	-	-	-	-	-	-	-	-	-	-	-	-	-	-	-	21	DNS
Nasif Estefano	De Tomaso F1/801	-	-	-	-	-	-	-	-	NT	DNP	-	-	-	-	-	-	-	-	-	-
Richie Ginther	BRM P57	4	2	9	4	6	5	12	R	9	4	6	3	4	2	4	2	5	3	7	R
Masten Gregory	Lotus 24-BRM	-	-	-	-	-	-	19	R	22	11	-	-	12	R	-	-	-	-	-	-
	Lola Mk4A-Climax	-	-	-	-	-	-	-	-	-	-	-	-	-	-	8	R	14	R	-	-
Dan Gurney	Brabham BT7-Climax	6	R	2	3	14	2	3	5	2	R	13	R	5	14	6	R	4	6	3	2F
Mike Hailwood	Lotus 24-Climax	-	-	-	-	-	-	-	-	17	8	-	-	-	-	-	-	-	-	-	-
	Lola Mk4A-Climax	-	-	-	-	-	-	-	-	-	-	-	-	-	-	18	10	-	-	-	-
Jim Hall	Lotus 24-BRM	13	R	12	R	18	8	18	11	13	6	16	5	17	8	16	10	15	8	-	-
Graham Hill	BRM P57	2	1	1	R	2	R	-	-	3	3	4	R	-	-	1	1	3	4	6	3
	BRM P61	-	-	-	-	-	-	2	3	-	-	-	-	2	16	-	-	-	-	-	-
Phil Hill	ATS 100	-	-	17	R	13	R	-	-	-	-	-	-	14	11	15	R	17	R	-	-
	Lotus 24-BRM	-	-	-	-	-	-	14	NC	-	-	-	-	-	-	-	-	-	-	-	-
Innes Ireland	Lotus 24-BRM	5	R	-	-	-	-	-	-	-	-	11	R	-	-	-	-	-	-	-	-
	BRP 1-BRM	-	-	7	R	7	4	9	9	11	R	-	-	10	4	-	-	-	-	-	-
Piet de Klerk	Alfa Special	-	-	-	-	-	-	-	-	-	-	-	-	-	-	-	-	-	-	16	R
Kurt Kuhnke	Lotus 18-Borgward	-	-	-	-	-	-	-	-	-	-	26	DNQ	-	-	-	-	-	-	-	-
Roberto Lippi	De Tomaso F1/002-Ferrari	-	-	-	-	-	-	-	-	-	-	-	-	28	DNQ	-	-	-	-	-	-
John Love	Cooper T55-Climax	-	-	-	-	-	-	-	-	-	-	-	-	-	-	-	-	-	-	13	9
Tony Maggs	Cooper T66-Climax	10	5	4	7	9	8	2	7	9	10	13	6	10	R	13	R	10	7	-	-
Willy Mairesse	Ferrari Dino 156	7	R	3	R	-	-	-	-	-	-	7	R	-	-	-	-	-	-	-	-
Bruce McLaren	Cooper T66-Climax	8	3	5	2	3	R	6	12	6	R	5	R	8	3	11	11	6	R	9	4
Gerhard Mitter	Porsche 718	-	-	-	-	-	-	16	R	-	-	15	4	-	-	-	-	-	-	-	-
Brausch Niemann	Lotus 22-Ford	-	-	-	-	-	-	-	-	-	-	-	-	-	-	-	-	-	-	15	14
Tim Parnell	Lotus 18/21-Climax	-	-	-	-	-	-	-	-	-	-	25	DNQ	-	-	-	-	-	-	-	-
Ernest Pieterse	Lotus 21-Climax	-	-	-	-	-	-	-	-	-	-	-	-	-	-	-	-	-	-	12	R
Andre Pilette	Lotus 18/21-Climax	-	-	-	-	-	-	-	-	-	-	23	DNQ	27	DNQ	-	-	-	-	-	-
David Prophet	Brabham BT6-Ford	-	-	-	-	-	-	-	-	-	-	-	-	-	-	-	-	-	-	14	R
Ian Raby	Gilby-BRM	-	-	-	-	-	-	-	-	19	R	24	DNQ	23	DNQ	-	-	-	-	-	-
Pedro Rodriguez	Lotus 25-Climax	-	-	-	-	-	-	-	-	-	-	-	-	-	-	13	R	20	R	-	-
Ludovico Scarfiotti	Ferrari Dino 156	-	-	-	-	11	6	13	DNS	-	-	-	-	-	-	-	-	-	-	-	-
Doug Serrurier	LDS Mk1-Alfa Romeo	-	-	-	-	-	-	-	-	-	-	-	-	-	-	-	-	-	-	18	11
Tony Settember	Scirocco 01-BRM	-	-	19	8	-	-	20	R	18	R	22	R	24	DNQ	-	-	-	-	-	-
Hap Sharp	Lotus 24-BRM	-	-	-	-	-	-	-	-	-	-	-	-	-	-	18	R	16	7	-	-
Jo Siffert	Lotus 24-BRM	12	R	14	R	17	7	10	6	15	R	9	9	16	R	14	R	9	9	-	-
Moises Solana	BRM P57	-	-	-	-	-	-	-	-	-	-	-	-	-	-	-	-	11	11	-	-
Mike Spence	Lotus 25-Climax	-	-	-	-	-	-	-	-	-	-	-	-	9	13	-	-	-	-	-	-
John Surtees	Ferrari Dino 156	3	4F	10	R	5	3	4	R	5	2F	2	1F	1	R	3	9	2	DSQ	4	R
Trevor Taylor	Lotus 25-Climax	9	6	11	R	10	10	7	13	10	R	18	8	-	-	7	R	12	R	8	8
Sam Tingle	LDS Mk1-Alfa Romeo	-	-	-	-	-	-	-	-	-	-	-	-	-	-	-	-	-	-	17	R

driver	car	MC		B		NL		F		GB		D		I		USA		MEX		ZA	
		Q	R	Q	R	Q	R	Q	R	Q	R	Q	R	Q	R	Q	R	Q	R	Q	R
Maurice Trintignant	Lola Mk4A-Climax	14	R	-	-	-	-	-	-	-	-	-	-	-	-	-	-	-	-	-	-
	Lotus 24-Climax	-	-	-	-	-	-	15	8	-	-	-	-	-	-	-	-	-	-	-	-
	BRM P57	-	-	-	-	-	-	-	-	-	-	-	-	20	9	-	-	-	-	-	-
Rodger Ward	Lotus 24-BRM	-	-	-	-	-	-	-	-	-	-	-	-	-	-	17	R	-	-	-	-

1963 FINAL CHAMPIONSHIP POSITIONS

Drivers

1	Jim Clark	54 (73)*
2=	Richie Ginther	29 (34)*
	Graham Hill	29
4	John Surtees	22
5	Dan Gurney	19
6	Bruce McLaren	17
7	Jack Brabham	14
8	Tony Maggs	9
9=	Lorenzo Bandini	6
	Jo Bonnier	6
	Innes Ireland	6

12=	Jim Hall	3
	Gerhard Mitter	3
14	Carel Godin de Beaufort	2
15=	Ludovico Scarfiotti	1
	Jo Siffert	1
	Trevor Taylor	1

*Best six results count

Manufacturers

1	Lotus-Climax	54 (74)*
2	BRM	36 (45)*
3	Brabham-Climax	28 (30)*
4	Ferrari	26
5	Cooper-Climax	25 (26)*
6	BRP-BRM	6
7	Porsche	5
8	Lotus-BRM	4

*Best six results count. Points only awarded to first car to finish for each manufacturer

Fastest lap: Surtees, 8m47.0. Leaders: Ginther, lap 1; Surtees, laps 2-3, 5-15; Clark, 4

GRAN PREMIO D'ITALIA

8 September 1963. Monza. 86 laps of a 3.573-mile circuit = 307.278 miles. Warm, dry and sunny. World Championship round 7

1	Jim Clark	Lotus 25-Climax	86	2h24m19.6
2	Richie Ginther	BRM P57	86	2h25m54.6
3	Bruce McLaren	Cooper T66-Climax	85	
4	Innes Ireland	BRP 1-BRM	84	engine
5	Jack Brabham	Brabham BT3-Climax	84	
6	Tony Maggs	Cooper T66-Climax	84	

Winner's average speed: 127.743 mph. Starting grid front row: Surtees, 1m37.3 (pole) and G Hill, 1m38.5. Fastest lap: Clark, 1m38.9. Leaders: G Hill, laps 1-3, 24-26, 29-30, 32, 34-35, 37, 39-41; Surtees, 4-16; Clark, 17-23, 28, 36, 42-45, 48-51, 53-54, 56-86; Gurney, 27, 31, 33, 38, 46-47, 52, 55

UNITED STATES GRAND PRIX

6 October 1963. Watkins Glen. 110 laps of a 2.350-mile circuit = 258.500 miles. Hot, dry and sunny. World Championship round 8

1	Graham Hill	BRM P57	110	2h19m22.1
2	Richie Ginther	BRM P57	110	2h19m56.4
3	Jim Clark	Lotus 25-Climax	109	
4	Jack Brabham	Brabham BT7-Climax	108	
5	Lorenzo Bandini	Ferrari Dino 156	106	
6	Carel Godin de Beaufort	Porsche 718	99	

Winner's average speed: 111.288 mph. Starting grid front row: G Hill, 1m13.4 (pole) and Clark, 1m13.5. Fastest lap: Clark, 1m14.5. Leaders: G Hill, laps 1-6, 32, 35, 83-110; Surtees, 7-31, 33-34, 36-82

GRAN PREMIO DE MEXICO

27 October 1963. Mexico City. 65 laps of a 3.107-mile circuit = 201.955 miles. Dry and overcast. World Championship round 9

1	Jim Clark	Lotus 25-Climax	65	2h09m52.1
2	Jack Brabham	Brabham BT7-Climax	65	2h11m33.2
3	Richie Ginther	BRM P57	65	2h11m46.8
4	Graham Hill	BRM P57	64	
5	Jo Bonnier	Cooper T66-Climax	62	
6	Dan Gurney	Brabham BT7-Climax	62	

Winner's average speed: 93.305 mph. Starting grid front row: Clark, 1m58.8 (pole) and Surtees, 2m00.5. Fastest lap: Clark, 1m58.1. Leaders: Clark, laps 1-65

SOUTH AFRICAN GRAND PRIX

28 December 1963. East London. 85 laps of a 2.436-mile circuit = 207.060 miles. Hot, dry and windy. World Championship round 10

1	Jim Clark	Lotus 25-Climax	85	2h10m36.9
2	Dan Gurney	Brabham BT7-Climax	85	2h11m43.7
3	Graham Hill	BRM P57	84	
4	Bruce McLaren	Cooper T66-Climax	84	
5	Lorenzo Bandini	Ferrari Dino 156	84	
6	Jo Bonnier	Cooper T66-Climax	83	

Winner's average speed: 95.116 mph. Starting grid front row: Clark, 1m28.9 (pole), Brabham, 1m29.0 and Gurney, 1m29.1. Fastest lap: Gurney, 1m29.1. Leaders: Clark, laps 1-85

1964

John Surtees, already a seven-times motorcycle World Champion in the 350cc and 500cc classes, became the only man to win world titles both on two and four wheels when he won the 1964 F1 World Championship. And he secured the drivers' title after an epic three-way title decider in Mexico City more reminiscent of a far-fetched Hollywood script.

The year started with a battle between the previous season's Championship protagonists. BRM built their first full-monocoque chassis and Graham Hill and Richie Ginther enjoyed a 1-2 victory in the opening Monaco GP. Jim Clark and Lotus then imposed themselves on the season with three successive wins. These included a bizarre finish at Spa where Clark ran out of fuel after crossing the line unaware that rivals Hill and Dan Gurney had also run dry and that he was the winner. Gurney did win for the Brabham team both in France and at the Mexican finale.

However, by the second half of the season Ferrari had come to the fore, Surtees winning in Germany and in Italy after a battle with Gurney. In between, teammate Lorenzo Bandini scored his only Grand Prix victory in a race of attrition on the bumpy Zeltweg circuit in Austria. Sadly, practice for the German Grand Prix had been marred by an accident that befell popular privateer Count de Beaufort, who would later succumb to his injuries.

1964 DRIVERS' RECORDS

driver	car	MC		NL		B		F		GB		D		A		I		USA		MEX	
		Q	R	Q	R	Q	R	Q	R	Q	R	Q	R	Q	R	Q	R	Q	R	Q	R
Chris Amon	Lotus 25-BRM	18	DNQ	13	5	11	R	14	10	11	R	9	11	-	-	-	-	11	R	12	R
	Lotus 25-Climax	-	-	-	-	-	-	-	-	-	-	-	-	17	R	-	-	-	-	-	-
Bob Anderson	Brabham BT11-Climax	12	7	11	6	19	DNS	15	12	7	7	15	R	14	3	14	11	-	-	-	-
Peter Arundell	Lotus 25-Climax	6	3	6	3	4	9	4	4	-	-	-	-	-	-	-	-	-	-	-	-
Richard Attwood	BRM P67	-	-	-	-	-	-	-	-	24	DNS	-	-	-	-	-	-	-	-	-	-
Giancarlo Baghetti	BRM P57	-	-	16	10	17	8	-	-	21	12	21	R	15	7	15	8	-	-	-	-
Lorenzo Bandini	Ferrari Dino 156	7	10	-	-	-	-	-	-	8	5	4	3	7	1	-	-	-	-	-	-
	Ferrari 158	-	-	10	R	9	R	8	9	-	-	-	-	-	-	7	3	-	-	-	-
	Ferrari 1512	-	-	-	-	-	-	-	-	-	-	-	-	-	-	-	-	8	R	3	3
Edgar Barth	Cooper T66-Climax	-	-	-	-	-	-	-	-	-	-	20	R	-	-	-	-	-	-	-	-
Carel Godin de Beaufort	Porsche 718	-	-	17	R	-	-	-	-	-	-	23	DNS	-	-	-	-	-	-	-	-
Jo Bonnier	Cooper T66-Climax	11	5	-	-	-	-	-	-	-	-	-	-	-	-	-	-	-	-	-	-
	Brabham BT11-BRM	-	-	12	9	14	R	-	-	9	R	12	R	-	-	-	-	-	-	-	-
	Brabham BT7-Climax	-	-	-	-	-	-	-	-	-	-	-	-	10	6	12	12	9	R	8	R
Jack Brabham	Brabham BT7-Climax	2	R	7	R	3	3	5	3F	4	4	6	12	-	-	-	-	-	-	-	-
	Brabham BT11-Climax	-	-	-	-	-	-	-	-	-	-	-	-	6	9	11	14	7	R	7	R
Ronnie Bucknum	Honda RA271	-	-	-	-	-	-	-	-	-	-	22	13	-	-	10	R	14	R	-	-
Mario Araujo de Cabral	ATS 100	-	-	-	-	-	-	-	-	-	-	-	-	-	-	19	R	-	-	-	-
Jim Clark	Lotus 25-Climax	1	4	2	1F	6	1	1	R	1	1F	-	-	-	-	4	R	1	R	-	-
	Lotus 33-Climax	-	-	-	-	-	-	-	-	-	-	2	R	3	R	-	-	NT	7F	1	5F
Bernard Collomb	Lotus 24-Climax	20	DNQ	-	-	-	-	-	-	-	-	-	-	-	-	-	-	-	-	-	-
Frank Gardner	Brabham BT10-Ford	-	-	-	-	-	-	-	-	19	R	-	-	-	-	-	-	-	-	-	-
Richie Ginther	BRM P261	8	2	8	11	8	4	9	5	14	8	11	7	5	2	9	4	13	4	11	8
Mike Hailwood	Lotus 25-BRM	16	6	14	12	-	-	13	8	12	R	13	R	18	8	17	R	16	8	17	R
Walt Hansgen	Lotus 33-Climax	-	-	-	-	-	-	-	-	-	-	-	-	-	-	-	-	17	5	-	-
Graham Hill	BRM P261	3	1F	3	4	2	5	6	2	2	2	5	2	1	R	3	R	4	1	6	11
Phil Hill	Cooper T73-Climax	9	9	9	8	15	R	10	7	15	6	8	R	-	-	-	-	19	R	15	9
	Cooper T66-Climax	-	-	-	-	-	-	-	-	-	-	-	-	20	R	-	-	-	-	-	-
Innes Ireland	Lotus 24-BRM	15	DNS	-	-	-	-	-	-	-	-	-	-	-	-	-	-	-	-	-	-
	BRP 1-BRM	-	-	-	-	-	-	16	10	11	R	-	-	-	-	-	-	-	-	-	-
	BRP 2-BRM	-	-	-	-	-	-	-	-	10	10	-	-	11	5	13	5	10	R	16	12
John Love	Cooper T73-Climax	-	-	-	-	-	-	-	-	-	-	-	-	-	-	24	DNQ	-	-	-	-
Tony Maggs	BRM P57	-	-	15	DNS	18	DNS	-	-	23	R	16	6	19	4	-	-	-	-	-	-
Bruce McLaren	Cooper T66-Climax	10	R	-	-	-	-	-	-	-	-	-	-	-	-	-	-	-	-	-	-
	Cooper T73-Climax	-	-	5	7	7	2	6	6	7	R	7	R	9	R	5	2	5	R	10	7
Gerhard Mitter	Lotus 25-Climax	-	-	-	-	-	-	-	-	-	-	19	9	-	-	-	-	-	-	-	-
Andre Pilette	Scirocco 02-Climax	-	-	-	-	20	R	-	-	24	DNQ	-	-	-	-	-	-	-	-	-	-
Ian Raby	Brabham BT3-BRM	-	-	-	-	-	-	-	-	17	R	-	-	-	-	25	DNQ	-	-	-	-
Peter Revson	Lotus 24-BRM	19	DNQ	-	-	10	DSQ	-	-	22	R	18	14	-	-	18	13	-	-	-	-
	Lotus 25-BRM	-	-	-	-	-	-	16	DNS	-	-	-	-	-	-	-	-	-	-	-	-
Jochen Rindt	Brabham BT11-BRM	-	-	-	-	-	-	-	-	-	-	-	-	13	R	-	-	-	-	-	-
Pedro Rodriguez	Ferrari Dino 156	-	-	-	-	-	-	-	-	-	-	-	-	-	-	-	-	-	-	9	6
Jean-Claude Rudaz	Cooper T60-Climax	-	-	-	-	-	-	-	-	-	-	-	-	-	-	20	DNS	-	-	-	-
"Geki" Russo	Brabham BT11-BRM	-	-	-	-	-	-	-	-	-	-	-	-	-	-	23	DNQ	-	-	-	-
Ludovico Scarfiotti	Ferrari Dino 156	-	-	-	-	-	-	-	-	-	-	-	-	-	-	16	9	-	-	-	-
Hap Sharp	Brabham BT11-BRM	-	-	-	-	-	-	-	-	-	-	-	-	-	-	-	-	18	NC	19	13
Jo Siffert	Lotus 24-BRM	17	8	-	-	-	-	-	-	-	-	-	-	-	-	-	-	-	-	-	-
	Brabham BT11-BRM	-	-	18	13	13	R	18	R	16	11	10	4	12	R	6	7	12	3	13	R
Moises Solana	Lotus 33-Climax	-	-	-	-	-	-	-	-	-	-	-	-	-	-	-	-	-	-	14	10
Mike Spence	Lotus 25-Climax	-	-	-	-	-	-	-	-	13	9	-	-	-	-	-	-	NT	R	5	4
	Lotus 33-Climax	-	-	-	-	-	-	-	-	-	-	17	8	8	8	8	6	6	7	-	-
John Surtees	Ferrari 158	4	R	4	2	5	R	3	R	5	3	1	1F	2	R	1	1F	2	2	4	2
John Taylor	Cooper T71/73-Ford	-	-	-	-	-	-	-	-	20	14	-	-	-	-	-	-	-	-	-	-
Trevor Taylor	BRP 1-BRM	14	R	-	-	-	-	-	-	-	-	-	-	16	R	22	DNQ	-	-	-	-
	BRP 2-BRM	-	-	-	-	12	7	12	R	-	-	-	-	-	-	-	-	15	6	18	R
	Lotus 24-BRM	-	-	-	-	-	-	-	-	18	R	-	-	-	-	-	-	-	-	-	-
Maurice Trintignant	BRM P57	13	R	-	-	-	-	17	11	25	DNQ	14	5	-	-	21	R	-	-	-	-

SHARED DRIVES - United States GP: Mike Spence/Jim Clark (Lotus 33-Climax) 7; Jim Clark/Mike Spence (Lotus 25-Climax) R

1964 FINAL CHAMPIONSHIP POSITIONS

	Drivers							Manufacturers	
1	John Surtees	40	15	Jo Bonnier	3		1	Ferrari	45 [49]*
2	Graham Hill	39 [41]*	16=	Chris Amon	2		2	BRM	42 [51]*
3	Jim Clark	32		Walt Hansgen	2		3	Lotus-Climax	37 [40]*
4=	Lorenzo Bandini	23		Maurice Trintignant	2		4	Brabham-Climax	30
	Richie Ginther	23	19=	Mike Hailwood	1		5	Cooper-Climax	16
6	Dan Gurney	19		Phil Hill	1		6	Brabham-BRM	7
7	Bruce McLaren	13		Pedro Rodriguez	1		7	BRP-BRM	5
8=	Peter Arundell	11		Trevor Taylor	1		8	Lotus-BRM	3
	Jack Brabham	11		*Best six results count					
10	Jo Siffert	7					*Best six results count. Points only		
11	Bob Anderson	5					awarded to first car to finish for each		
12=	Innes Ireland	4					manufacturer		
	Tony Maggs	4							
	Mike Spence	4							

After five races Clark had seemed set for a successful title defence, but his late summer was blighted by poor reliability. He led comfortably from the start at the last round in Mexico and was in a position to retain his crown when his engine failed on the very last lap. Graham Hill, leader of the championship after the penultimate round, had earlier been delayed in a collision with Bandini's Ferrari, but following Clark's retirement the Englishman was in line for the title. However, Bandini then slowed, giving his team leader Surtees second position in the race and the points he required to become World Champion.

GRAND PRIX DE MONACO

10 May 1964. Monte Carlo. 100 laps of a 1.954-mile circuit = 195.400 miles. Hot, dry and sunny. World Championship round 1

1	Graham Hill	BRM P261	100	2h41m19.5
2	Richie Ginther	BRM P261	99	
3	Peter Arundell	Lotus 25-Climax	97	
4	Jim Clark	Lotus 25-Climax	96	engine
5	Jo Bonnier	Cooper T66-Climax	96	
6	Mike Hailwood	Lotus 25-BRM	96	

Winner's average speed: 72.673 mph. Starting grid front row: Clark, 1m34.0 (pole) and Brabham, 1m34.1. Fastest lap: G Hill, 1m33.9. Leaders: Clark, laps 1-36; Gurney, 37-52; G Hill, 53-100

GROTE PRIJS VAN NEDERLAND

24 May 1964. Zandvoort. 80 laps of a 2.605-mile circuit = 208.400 miles. Hot, dry and sunny. World Championship round 2

1	Jim Clark	Lotus 25-Climax	80	2h07m35.4
2	John Surtees	Ferrari 158	80	2h08m29.0
3	Peter Arundell	Lotus 25-Climax	79	
4	Graham Hill	BRM P261	79	
5	Chris Amon	Lotus 25-BRM	79	
6	Bob Anderson	Brabham BT11-Climax	78	

Winner's average speed: 98.001 mph. Starting grid front row: Gurney, 1m31.2 (pole), Clark, 1m31.3 and G Hill, 1m31.4. Fastest lap: Clark, 1m32.8. Leaders: Clark, laps 1-80

GRAND PRIX DE BELGIQUE

14 June 1964. Spa-Francorchamps. 32 laps of an 8.761-mile circuit = 280.352 miles. Dry and overcast. World Championship round 3

1	Jim Clark	Lotus 25-Climax	32	2h06m40.5
2	Bruce McLaren	Cooper T73-Climax	32	2h06m43.9
3	Jack Brabham	Brabham BT7-Climax	32	2h07m28.6
4	Richie Ginther	BRM P261	32	2h08m39.1
5	Graham Hill	BRM P261	31	fuel pump
6	Dan Gurney	Brabham BT7-Climax	31	out of fuel

Winner's average speed: 132.790 mph. Starting grid front row: Gurney,

3m50.9 (pole), G Hill, 3m52.7 and Brabham, 3m52.8. Fastest lap: Gurney, 3m49.2. Leaders: Gurney, laps 1-2, 4-29; Surtees, 3; G Hill, 30-31; Clark, 32

GRAND PRIX DE L'AUTOMOBILE CLUB DE FRANCE

28 June 1964. Rouen-les-Essarts. 57 laps of a 4.065-mile circuit = 231.705 miles. Dry and overcast. World Championship round 4

1	Dan Gurney	Brabham BT7-Climax	57	2h07m49.1
2	Graham Hill	BRM P261	57	2h08m13.2
3	Jack Brabham	Brabham BT7-Climax	57	2h08m14.0
4	Peter Arundell	Lotus 25-Climax	57	2h08m59.7
5	Richie Ginther	BRM P261	57	2h10m01.2
6	Bruce McLaren	Cooper T73-Climax	56	

Winner's average speed: 108.766 mph. Starting grid front row: Clark, 2m09.6 (pole), Gurney, 2m10.1 and Surtees, 2m11.1. Fastest lap: Brabham, 2m11.4. Leaders: Clark, laps 1-30; Gurney, 31-57

BRITISH AND EUROPEAN GRAND PRIX

11 July 1964. Brands Hatch. 80 laps of a 2.650-mile circuit = 212.000 miles. Dry and overcast. World Championship round 5

1	Jim Clark	Lotus 25-Climax	80	2h15m07.0
2	Graham Hill	BRM P261	80	2h15m09.8
3	John Surtees	Ferrari 158	80	2h16m27.6
4	Jack Brabham	Brabham BT7-Climax	79	
5	Lorenzo Bandini	Ferrari Dino 156	78	
6	Phil Hill	Cooper T73-Climax	78	

Winner's average speed: 94.141 mph. Starting grid front row: Clark, 1m38.1 (pole), G Hill, 1m38.3 and Gurney, 1m38.4. Fastest lap: Clark, 1m38.8. Leaders: Clark, laps 1-80

GROSSER PREIS VON DEUTSCHLAND

2 August 1964. Nurburgring. 15 laps of a 14.167-mile circuit = 212.505 miles. Dry and overcast. World Championship round 6

1	John Surtees	Ferrari 158	15	2h12m04.8
2	Graham Hill	BRM P261	15	2h13m20.4
3	Lorenzo Bandini	Ferrari Dino 156	15	2h16m57.6
4	Jo Siffert	Brabham BT11-BRM	15	2h17m27.9
5	Maurice Trintignant	BRM P57	14	
6	Tony Maggs	BRM P57	14	battery

Winner's average speed: 96.535 mph. Starting grid front row: Surtees, 8m38.4 (pole), Clark, 8m38.8, Gurney, 8m39.3 and Bandini, 8m42.6. Fastest lap: Surtees, 8m39.0. Leaders: Clark, lap 1; Surtees, laps 2-3, 5-15; Gurney, 4

GROSSER PREIS VON OSTERREICH

23 August 1964. Zeltweg. 105 laps of a 1.988-mile circuit = 208.740 miles. Dry and overcast. World Championship round 7

1	Lorenzo Bandini	Ferrari Dino 156	105	2h06m18.23
2	Richie Ginther	BRM P261	105	2h06m24.41
3	Bob Anderson	Brabham BT11-Climax	102	
4	Tony Maggs	BRM P57	102	

5 Innes Ireland   BRP 2-BRM   102
6 Jo Bonnier   Brabham BT7-Climax   101

Winner's average speed: 99.161 mph. Starting grid front row: G Hill, 1m09.84 (pole), Surtees, 1m10.12, Clark, 1m10.21 and Gurney, 1m10.40. Fastest lap: Gurney, 1m10.56. Leaders: Gurney, laps 1, 8-46; Surtees, 2-7; Bandini, 47-105.

GRAN PREMIO D'ITALIA

6 September 1964. Monza. 78 laps of a 3.573-mile circuit = 278.694 miles. Dry and overcast. World Championship round 8

1	John Surtees	Ferrari 158	78	2h10m51.8
2	Bruce McLaren	Cooper T73-Climax	78	2h11m57.8
3	Lorenzo Bandini	Ferrari 158	77	
4	Richie Ginther	BRM P261	77	
5	Innes Ireland	BRP 2-BRM	77	
6	Mike Spence	Lotus 33-Climax	77	

Winner's average speed: 127.779 mph. Starting grid front row: Surtees, 1m37.4 (pole), Gurney, 1m38.2 and G Hill, 1m38.7. Fastest lap: Surtees, 1m38.8. Leaders: Gurney, laps 1, 6-7, 10, 12-14, 16, 22, 25-26, 29, 32, 37-38, 45, 47-48, 50-52, 55; Surtees, 2-5, 8-9, 11, 15, 17-21, 23-24, 27-28, 30-31, 33-36, 39-44, 46, 49, 53-54, 56-78

UNITED STATES GRAND PRIX

4 October 1964. Watkins Glen. 110 laps of a 2.350-mile circuit = 258.500 miles. Warm, dry and sunny. World Championship round 9

1	Graham Hill	BRM P261	110	2h16m38.0
2	John Surtees	Ferrari 158	110	2h17m08.5
3	Jo Siffert	Brabham BT11-BRM	109	
4	Richie Ginther	BRM P261	107	
5	Walt Hansgen	Lotus 33-Climax	107	
6	Trevor Taylor	BRP 2-BRM	106	

Winner's average speed: 113.515 mph. Starting grid front row: Clark, 1m12.65 (pole) and Surtees, 1m12.78. Fastest lap: Clark, 1m12.7. Leaders: Surtees, laps 1-12, 44; Clark, 13-43; G Hill, 45-110

GRAN PREMIO DE MEXICO

25 October 1964. Mexico City. 65 laps of a 3.107-mile circuit = 201.955 miles. Warm, dry and sunny. World Championship round 10

1	Dan Gurney	Brabham BT7-Climax	65	2h09m50.32
2	John Surtees	Ferrari 158	65	2h10m59.26
3	Lorenzo Bandini	Ferrari 1512	65	2h10m59.95
4	Mike Spence	Lotus 25-Climax	65	2h11m12.18
5	Jim Clark	Lotus 33-Climax	64	engine
6	Pedro Rodriguez	Ferrari Dino 156	64	

Winner's average speed: 93.326 mph. Starting grid front row: Clark, 1m57.24 (pole) and Gurney, 1m58.10. Fastest lap: Clark, 1m58.37. Leaders: Clark, laps 1-63; Gurney, 64-65

1965

Jim Clark, the man to beat for all but the first year of the 1.5-litre F1, fittingly became World Champion for a second time in the final year of the formula. Not only did he win six times (including both the British and Belgian races for a fourth successive year), but he also won his third attempt at the Indianapolis 500. Also, outside F1, Clark captured the French and British F2 titles for Lotus. Clark's unique season displayed a level of domination seldom seen in international motor racing, and it seemed inconceivable that this would be his last world title.

Once again British drivers dominated the series, with Graham Hill completing hat tricks of wins at both Monaco (which Clark missed to race at Indy) and Watkins Glen. The Italian Grand Prix was again the closest race of the year. The lead changed a record forty-two times between four drivers, before Hill's BRM teammate Jackie Stewart scored his maiden

1965 Bruce McLaren leads Jochen Rindt and the year's dominant driver, Jim Clark, into the Nurburgring's Karussell.

Grand Prix victory.

Reigning World Champions John Surtees and Ferrari endured a fruitless season. Richie Ginther won the closing Grand Prix in Mexico City for Honda—not only his sole win, but also a first for the marque and for Goodyear tyres.

SOUTH AFRICAN GRAND PRIX

1 January 1965. East London. 85 laps of a 2.436-mile circuit = 207.060 miles. Dry and overcast. World Championship round 1

1	Jim Clark	Lotus 33-Climax	85	2h06m46.0
2	John Surtees	Ferrari 158	85	2h07m15.0
3	Graham Hill	BRM P261	85	2h07m17.8
4	Mike Spence	Lotus 33-Climax	85	2h07m40.4
5	Bruce McLaren	Cooper T73-Climax	84	
6	Jackie Stewart	BRM P261	83	

Winner's average speed: 98.004 mph. Starting grid front row: Clark, 1m27.2 (pole), Surtees, 1m28.1 and Brabham, 1m28.3. Fastest lap: Clark, 1m27.6. Leaders: Clark, laps 1-85

GRAND PRIX DE MONACO

30 May 1965. Monte Carlo. 100 laps of a 1.954-mile circuit = 195.400 miles. Dry and overcast. World Championship round 2

1	Graham Hill	BRM P261	100	2h37m39.6
2	Lorenzo Bandini	Ferrari 1512	100	2h38m43.6
3	Jackie Stewart	BRM P261	100	2h39m21.5
4	John Surtees	Ferrari 158	99	out of fuel
5	Bruce McLaren	Cooper T77-Climax	98	
6	Jo Siffert	Brabham BT11-BRM	98	

Winner's average speed: 74.363 mph. Starting grid front row: G Hill, 1m32.5 (pole) and Brabham, 1m32.8. Fastest lap: G Hill, 1m31.7. Leaders: G Hill, laps 1-24, 65-100; Stewart, 25-29; Bandini, 30-33, 43-64; Brabham, 34-42

GRAND PRIX DE BELGIQUE ET D'EUROPE

13 June 1965. Spa-Francorchamps. 32 laps of an 8.761-mile circuit = 280.352 miles. Heavy rain. World Championship round 3

1	Jim Clark	Lotus 33-Climax	32	2h23m34.8
2	Jackie Stewart	BRM P261	32	2h24m19.6
3	Bruce McLaren	Cooper T77-Climax	31	
4	Jack Brabham	Brabham BT11-Climax	31	
5	Graham Hill	BRM P261	31	
6	Richie Ginther	Honda RA272	31	

Winner's average speed: 117.155 mph. Starting grid front row: G Hill, 3m45.4 (pole), Clark, 3m47.5 and Stewart, 3m48.8. Fastest lap: Clark, 4m12.9. Leaders: Clark, laps 1-32

GRAND PRIX DE L'AUTOMOBILE CLUB DE FRANCE

27 June 1965. Clermont-Ferrand. 40 laps of a 5.005-mile circuit = 200.200 miles. Warm, dry and sunny. World Championship round 4

1	Jim Clark	Lotus 25-Climax	40	2h14m38.4
2	Jackie Stewart	BRM P261	40	2h15m04.7
3	John Surtees	Ferrari 158	40	2h17m11.9

1965 DRIVERS' RECORDS

driver	car	ZA Q	ZA R	MC Q	MC R	B Q	B R	F Q	F R	GB Q	GB R	NL Q	NL R	D Q	D R	I Q	I R	USA Q	USA R	MEX Q	MEX R
Chris Amon	Lotus 25-BRM	-	-	-	-	-	-	8	R	-	-	-	-	16	R	-	-	-	-	-	-
	Brabham BT3-BRM	-	-	-	-	-	-	-	-	19	DNS	-	-	-	-	-	-	-	-	-	-
Bob Anderson	Brabham BT11-Climax	12	NC	9	9	19	DNS	15	9	17	R	16	R	15	DNS	-	-	-	-	-	-
Richard Attwood	Lotus 25-BRM	-	-	6	R	13	14	-	-	16	13	17	12	17	R	13	6	16	10	17	6
Giancarlo Baghetti	Brabham BT7-Climax	-	-	-	-	-	-	-	-	-	-	-	-	-	-	19	R	-	-	-	-
Lorenzo Bandini	Ferrari 1512	6	15	4	2	15	9	3	8	-	-	-	-	-	-	5	4	5	4	7	8
	Ferrari 158	-	-	-	-	-	-	-	-	9	R	12	9	7	6	-	-	-	-	-	-
Giorgio Bassi	BRM P57	-	-	-	-	-	-	-	-	-	-	-	-	-	-	22	R	-	-	-	-
Lucien Bianchi	BRM P57	-	-	-	-	17	12	-	-	-	-	-	-	-	-	-	-	-	-	-	-
Trevor Blokdyk	Cooper T59-Ford	21	DNQ	-	-	-	-	-	-	-	-	-	-	-	-	-	-	-	-	-	-
Bob Bondurant	Ferrari 158	-	-	-	-	-	-	-	-	-	-	-	-	-	-	-	-	14	9	-	-
	Lotus 33-BRM	-	-	-	-	-	-	-	-	-	-	-	-	-	-	-	-	-	-	18	R
Jo Bonnier	Brabham BT7-Climax	7	R	13	7	7	R	11	R	14	7	15	R	9	7	14	7	10	8	-	-
	Brabham BT11-Climax	-	-	-	-	-	-	-	-	-	-	-	-	-	-	-	-	-	-	12	R
Jack Brabham	Brabham BT11-Climax	3	8	2	R	10	4	-	-	8	DNS	-	-	14	5	-	-	7	3	4	R
Ronnie Bucknum	Honda RA272	-	-	15	R	11	R	16	R	-	-	-	-	-	-	6	R	12	13	9	5
Roberto Bussinello	BRM P57	-	-	-	-	-	-	-	-	-	-	-	-	21	DNQ	21	13	-	-	-	-
Dave Charlton	Lotus 20-Ford	NT	NPQ	-	-	-	-	-	-	-	-	-	-	-	-	-	-	-	-	-	-
Jim Clark	Lotus 33-Climax	1	1F	-	-	2	1F	-	-	1	1	2	1F	1	1F	1	10F	2	R	1	R
	Lotus 25-Climax	-	-	-	-	-	-	1	1F	-	-	-	-	-	-	-	-	-	-	-	-
Frank Gardner	Brabham BT11-BRM	15	12	11	R	18	R	-	-	13	8	11	11	18	R	16	R	-	-	-	-
Richie Ginther	Honda RA272	-	-	16	R	4	6	7	R	3	R	3	6	-	-	17	14	3	7	3	1
Masten Gregory	BRM P57	-	-	-	-	20	R	-	-	20	12	-	-	19	8	23	R	-	-	-	-
Brian Gubby	Lotus 24-Climax	-	-	-	-	-	-	-	-	24	DNQ	-	-	-	-	-	-	-	-	-	-
Dan Gurney	Brabham BT11-Climax	9	R	-	-	5	10	5	R	7	6	5	3	5	3	9	3	8	2	2	2F
Mike Hailwood	Lotus 25-BRM	-	-	12	R	-	-	-	-	-	-	-	-	-	-	-	-	-	-	-	-
Paul Hawkins	Brabham BT10-Ford	16	9	-	-	-	-	-	-	-	-	-	-	-	-	-	-	-	-	-	-
	Lotus 33-Climax	-	-	14	10	-	-	-	-	-	-	-	-	20	R	-	-	-	-	-	-
Graham Hill	BRM P261	5	3	1	1F	1	5	13	5	2	2F	1	4	3	2	4	2	1	1F	5	R
Denny Hulme	Brabham BT7-Climax	-	-	8	8	-	-	-	-	10	R	-	-	13	R	-	-	-	-	-	-
	Brabham BT11-Climax	-	-	-	-	-	-	6	4	-	-	7	5	-	-	12	R	-	-	-	-
Innes Ireland	Lotus 25-BRM	-	-	-	-	16	13	17	R	15	R	13	10	-	-	-	-	-	-	-	-
	Lotus 33-BRM	-	-	-	-	-	-	-	-	-	-	-	-	-	-	18	9	18	R	19	DNS
Piet de Klerk	Alfa Special	17	10	-	-	-	-	-	-	-	-	-	-	-	-	-	-	-	-	-	-
Neville Lederle	Lotus 21-Climax	22	DNQ	-	-	-	-	-	-	-	-	-	-	-	-	-	-	-	-	-	-
John Love	Cooper T55-Climax	18	R	-	-	-	-	-	-	-	-	-	-	-	-	-	-	-	-	-	-
Tony Maggs	Lotus 25-BRM	13	11	-	-	-	-	-	-	-	-	-	-	-	-	-	-	-	-	-	-
Bruce McLaren	Cooper T73-Climax	8	5	-	-	-	-	-	-	-	-	-	-	-	-	-	-	-	-	-	-
	Cooper T77-Climax	-	-	7	5	9	3	9	R	11	10	9	R	10	R	11	5	9	R	15	R
Gerhard Mitter	Lotus 25-Climax	-	-	-	-	-	-	-	-	-	-	-	-	12	R	-	-	-	-	-	-
Brausch Niemann	Lotus 22-Ford	24	DNQ	-	-	-	-	-	-	-	-	-	-	-	-	-	-	-	-	-	-
Ernest Pieterse	Lotus 21-Climax	25	DNQ	-	-	-	-	-	-	-	-	-	-	-	-	-	-	-	-	-	-
Jackie Pretorius	LDS Mk1-Alfa Romeo	NT	NPQ	-	-	-	-	-	-	-	-	-	-	-	-	-	-	-	-	-	-
David Prophet	Brabham BT10-Ford	19	14	-	-	-	-	-	-	-	-	-	-	-	-	-	-	-	-	-	-
Clive Puzey	Lotus 18/21-Climax	NT	NPQ	-	-	-	-	-	-	-	-	-	-	-	-	-	-	-	-	-	-
Ian Raby	Brabham BT3-BRM	-	-	-	-	-	-	-	-	21	11	-	-	-	-	22	DNQ	-	-	-	-
John Rhodes	Cooper T60-Climax	-	-	-	-	-	-	-	-	21	R	-	-	-	-	-	-	-	-	-	-
Jochen Rindt	Cooper T73-Climax	10	R	-	-	-	-	-	-	-	-	-	-	-	-	7	8	-	-	-	-
	Cooper T77-Climax	-	-	17	DNQ	14	11	12	R	12	14	14	R	8	4	-	-	13	6	16	R
Pedro Rodriguez	Ferrari 1512	-	-	-	-	-	-	-	-	-	-	-	-	-	-	-	-	15	5	14	7
Alan Rollinson	Cooper T71/73-Ford	-	-	-	-	-	-	-	-	23	DNQ	-	-	-	-	-	-	-	-	-	-
"Geki" Russo	Lotus 25-Climax	-	-	-	-	-	-	-	-	-	-	-	-	-	-	20	R	-	-	-	-
Ludovico Scarfiotti	Ferrari 1512	-	-	-	-	-	-	-	-	-	-	-	-	-	-	-	-	-	-	13	DNS
Doug Serrurier	LDS Mk2-Climax	23	DNQ	-	-	-	-	-	-	-	-	-	-	-	-	-	-	-	-	-	-
Jo Siffert	Brabham BT11-BRM	14	7	10	6	8	8	14	6	18	9	10	13	11	R	10	R	11	11	11	4
Moises Solana	Lotus 25-Climax	-	-	-	-	-	-	-	-	-	-	-	-	-	-	-	-	17	12	10	R
Mike Spence	Lotus 33-Climax	4	4	-	-	12	7	10	7	6	4	-	-	6	R	8	11	4	R	6	3
	Lotus 25-Climax	-	-	-	-	-	-	-	-	8	8	-	-	-	-	-	-	-	-	-	-
Jackie Stewart	BRM P261	11	6	3	3	3	2	2	2	4	5	6	2	2	R	3	1	6	R	8	R
John Surtees	Ferrari 158	2	2	5	4	6	R	4	3	-	-	-	-	-	-	-	-	-	-	-	-
	Ferrari 1512	-	-	-	-	-	-	-	-	5	3	4	7	4	R	2	R	-	-	-	-
Sam Tingle	LDS Mk1-Alfa Romeo	20	13	-	-	-	-	-	-	-	-	-	-	-	-	-	-	-	-	-	-
Nino Vaccarella	Ferrari 158	-	-	-	-	-	-	-	-	-	-	-	-	-	-	15	12	-	-	-	-

1965 FINAL CHAMPIONSHIP POSITIONS

Drivers							Manufacturers		
1	Jim Clark	54		11=	Denny Hulme	5	1	Lotus-Climax	54 (58)*
2	Graham Hill	40 (47)*			Jo Siffert	5	2	BRM	45 (61)*
3	Jackie Stewart	33 (34)*		13	Jochen Rindt	4	3	Brabham-Climax	27 (31)*
4	Dan Gurney	25		14=	Richard Attwood	2	4	Ferrari	26 (27)*
5	John Surtees	17			Ronnie Bucknum	2	5	Cooper-Climax	14
6	Lorenzo Bandini	13			Pedro Rodriguez	2	6	Honda	11
7	Richie Ginther	11			*Best six results count		7	Brabham-BRM	5
8=	Bruce McLaren	10					8	Lotus-BRM	2
	Mike Spence	10						*Best six results count. Points only	
10	Jack Brabham	9						awarded to first car to finish for each	
								manufacturer	

4	Denny Hulme	Brabham BT11-Climax	40	2h17m31.5
5	Graham Hill	BRM P261	39	
6	Jo Siffert	Brabham BT11-BRM	39	

Winner's average speed: 89.216 mph. Starting grid front row: Clark, 3m18.3 (pole), Stewart, 3m18.8 and Bandini, 3m19.1. Fastest lap: Clark, 3m18.9. Leaders: Clark, laps 1-40

BRITISH GRAND PRIX

10 July 1965. Silverstone. 80 laps of a 2.927-mile circuit = 234.160 miles. Dry and overcast. World Championship round 5

1	Jim Clark	Lotus 33-Climax	80	2h05m25.4
2	Graham Hill	BRM P261	80	2h05m28.6
3	John Surtees	Ferrari 1512	80	2h05m53.0
4	Mike Spence	Lotus 33-Climax	80	2h06m05.0
5	Jackie Stewart	BRM P261	80	2h06m40.0
6	Dan Gurney	Brabham BT11-Climax	79	

Winner's average speed: 112.017 mph. Starting grid front row: Clark, 1m30.8 (pole), G Hill, 1m31.0, Ginther, 1m31.3 and Stewart, 1m31.3. Fastest lap: G Hill, 1m32.2. Leaders: Clark, laps 1-80

GROTE PRIJS VAN NEDERLAND

18 July 1965. Zandvoort. 80 laps of a 2.605-mile circuit = 208.400 miles. Dry and overcast. World Championship round 6

1	Jim Clark	Lotus 33-Climax	80	2h03m59.1
2	Jackie Stewart	BRM P261	80	2h04m07.1
3	Dan Gurney	Brabham BT11-Climax	80	2h04m12.1
4	Graham Hill	BRM P261	80	2h04m44.2
5	Denny Hulme	Brabham BT11-Climax	79	
6	Richie Ginther	Honda RA272	79	

Winner's average speed: 100.851 mph. Starting grid front row: G Hill, 1m30.7 (pole), Clark, 1m31.0 and Ginther, 1m31.0. Fastest lap: Clark, 1m30.6. Leaders: Ginther, laps 1-2; G Hill, 3-5; Clark, 6-80

GROSSER PREIS VON DEUTSCHLAND

1 August 1965. Nurburgring. 15 laps of a 14.167-mile circuit = 212.505 miles. Dry and overcast. World Championship round 7

1	Jim Clark	Lotus 33-Climax	15	2h07m52.4
2	Graham Hill	BRM P261	15	2h08m08.3
3	Dan Gurney	Brabham BT11-Climax	15	2h08m13.8
4	Jochen Rindt	Cooper T77-Climax	15	2h11m22.0
5	Jack Brabham	Brabham BT11-Climax	15	2h12m33.6
6	Lorenzo Bandini	Ferrari 158	15	2h13m01.0

Winner's average speed: 99.710 mph. Starting grid front row: Clark, 8m22.7 (pole), Stewart, 8m26.1, G Hill, 8m26.8 and Surtees, 8m27.8. Fastest lap: Clark, 8m24.1. Leaders: Clark, laps 1-15

GRAN PREMIO D'ITALIA

12 September 1965. Monza. 76 laps of a 3.573-mile circuit = 271.548 miles. Warm, dry and sunny. World Championship round 8

1	Jackie Stewart	BRM P261	76	2h04m52.8
2	Graham Hill	BRM P261	76	2h04m56.1
3	Dan Gurney	Brabham BT11-Climax	76	2h05m09.3
4	Lorenzo Bandini	Ferrari 1512	76	2h06m08.7
5	Bruce McLaren	Cooper T77-Climax	75	

6	Richard Attwood	Lotus 25-BRM	75	

Winner's average speed: 130.468 mph. Starting grid front row: Clark, 1m35.9 (pole), Surtees, 1m36.1 and Stewart, 1m36.6. Fastest lap: Clark, 1m36.4. Leaders: Clark, 1-2, 4, 6-7, 18, 21-24, 27, 33-35, 38, 44, 46, 51, 53-54, 57; G Hill, 3, 25-26, 28, 40, 43, 45, 50, 55-56, 64, 70-71, 73-74; Stewart, 5, 8-10, 12, 14, 17, 19-20, 29-32, 36-37, 39, 41-42, 47-49, 52, 58-63, 65-69, 72, 75-76; Surtees, 11, 13, 15-16

UNITED STATES GRAND PRIX

3 October 1965. Watkins Glen. 110 laps of a 2.350-mile circuit = 258.500 miles. Windy and occasional rain. World Championship round 9

1	Graham Hill	BRM P261	110	2h20m36.1
2	Dan Gurney	Brabham BT11-Climax	110	2h20m48.6
3	Jack Brabham	Brabham BT11-Climax	110	2h21m33.6
4	Lorenzo Bandini	Ferrari 1512	109	
5	Pedro Rodriguez	Ferrari 1512	109	
6	Jochen Rindt	Cooper T77-Climax	108	

Winner's average speed: 110.312 mph. Starting grid front row: G Hill, 1m11.25 (pole) and Clark, 1m11.35. Fastest lap: G Hill, 1m11.9. Leaders: G Hill, laps 1, 5-10, 12-110; Clark, 2-4, 11

GRAN PREMIO DE MEXICO

24 October 1965. Mexico City. 65 laps of a 3.107-mile circuit = 201.955 miles. Warm, dry and sunny. World Championship round 10

1	Richie Ginther	Honda RA272	65	2h08m32.10
2	Dan Gurney	Brabham BT11-Climax	65	2h08m34.99
3	Mike Spence	Lotus 33-Climax	65	2h09m32.25
4	Jo Siffert	Brabham BT11-BRM	65	2h10m26.52
5	Ronnie Bucknum	Honda RA272	64	
6	Richard Attwood	Lotus 25-BRM	64	

Winner's average speed: 94.272 mph. Starting grid front row: Clark, 1m56.17 (pole) and Gurney, 1m56.24. Fastest lap: Gurney, 1m55.84. Leaders: Ginther, laps 1-65

1966

The new season marked the "return to power" for F1, with new rules allowing the capacity of normally aspirated engines to double to 3 litres. Although the specifications had been announced three years earlier, many teams were far from ready. Ferrari, however, was prepared for the change and so started the season as favourites once more.

Jackie Stewart's old 2-litre BRM won on the tight confines of Monte Carlo, but John Surtees confirmed Ferrari's status by dominating in Belgium. The Italians lost their impetus, however, when internal politics forced Surtees to leave and seek refuge in the Cooper team.

Jack Brabham quickly exploited this vacuum with four successive victories, enough to make him the first man to win the World Championship in a car of

1966 DRIVERS' RECORDS

driver	car	MC		B		F		GB		NL		D		I		USA		MEX	
		Q	R	Q	R	Q	R	Q	R	Q	R	Q	R	Q	R	Q	R	Q	R
Kurt Ahrens Jr	Brabham BT18-Ford	-	-	-	-	-	-	-	-	-	-	NT	F2	-	-	-	-	-	-
Chris Amon	Cooper T81-Maserati	-	-	-	-	7	8	-	-	-	-	-	-	-	-	-	-	-	-
	Brabham BT11-BRM	-	-	-	-	-	-	-	-	-	-	-	-	22	DNQ	-	-	-	-
Bob Anderson	Brabham BT11-Climax	8	R	-	-	13	7	10	NC	15	R	14	R	15	6	-	-	-	-
Peter Arundell	Lotus 43-BRM	-	-	19	DNS	17	R	-	-	-	-	-	-	-	-	-	-	-	-
	Lotus 33-BRM	-	-	-	-	-	-	20	R	16	R	16	8	13	8	-	-	18	7
	Lotus 33-Climax	-	-	-	-	-	-	-	-	-	-	-	-	-	-	NT	6	-	-
Giancarlo Baghetti	Ferrari 158/246	-	-	-	-	-	-	-	-	-	-	-	-	16	NC	-	-	-	-
Lorenzo Bandini	Ferrari 158/246	5	2F	5	3	-	-	-	-	-	-	-	-	-	-	-	-	-	-
	Ferrari 312	-	-	-	-	1	NCF	-	9	6	6	6	6	5	R	3	R	-	-
Jean-Pierre Beltoise	Matra MS5-Ford	-	-	-	-	-	-	-	-	-	-	NT	F2	-	-	-	-	-	-
Bob Bondurant	BRM P261	16	4	11	R	-	-	14	9	-	-	11	R	18	7	-	-	-	-
	Eagle AAR101-Climax	-	-	-	-	-	-	-	-	-	-	-	-	-	-	16	DSQ	-	-
	Eagle AAR102-Weslake	-	-	-	-	-	-	-	-	-	-	-	-	-	-	-	-	19	R
Jo Bonnier	Cooper T81-Maserati	14	NC	6	R	-	-	-	-	13	7	12	R	12	R	15	NC	13	6
	Brabham BT11-Climax	-	-	-	-	18	NC	-	-	-	-	-	-	-	-	-	-	-	-
	Brabham BT7-Climax	-	-	-	-	-	-	15	R	-	-	-	-	-	-	-	-	-	-
Jack Brabham	Brabham BT19-Repco	11	R	4	4	4	1	1	1F	1	1	5	1	6	R	-	-	-	-
	Brabham BT20-Repco	-	-	-	-	-	-	-	-	-	-	-	-	-	-	1	R	4	2
Ronnie Bucknum	Honda RA273	-	-	-	-	-	-	-	-	-	-	-	-	-	-	18	R	14	8
Jim Clark	Lotus 33-Climax	1	R	10	R	14	DNS	5	4	3	3	1	R	-	-	-	-	-	-
	Lotus 43-BRM	-	-	-	-	-	-	-	-	-	-	-	-	3	R	2	1	2	R
Piers Courage	Lotus 44-Ford	-	-	-	-	-	-	-	-	-	-	NT	F2	-	-	-	-	-	-
Richie Ginther	Cooper T81-Maserati	9	R	8	5	-	-	-	-	-	-	-	-	-	-	-	-	-	-
	Honda RA273	-	-	-	-	-	-	-	-	-	-	-	-	7	R	8	NC	3	4F
Dan Gurney	Eagle AAR101-Climax	-	-	15	NC	15	5	3	R	4	R	8	7	-	-	-	-	9	5
	Eagle AAR102-Weslake	-	-	-	-	-	-	-	-	-	-	-	-	19	R	14	R	-	-
Hubert Hahne	Matra MS5-BRM	-	-	-	-	-	-	-	-	-	-	NT	F2	-	-	-	-	-	-
Hans Herrmann	Brabham BT18-Ford	-	-	-	-	-	-	-	-	-	-	NT	F2	-	-	-	-	-	-
Graham Hill	BRM P261	4	3	9	R	8	R	4	3	7	2	10	4	-	-	-	-	-	-
	BRM P83	-	-	-	-	-	-	-	-	-	-	-	-	11	R	5	R	7	R
Phil Hill	Lotus 25-Climax	17	DNS*	-	-	-	-	-	-	-	-	-	-	-	-	-	-	-	-
	McLaren M3A-Ford	-	-	-	-	17	R*	-	-	-	-	-	-	-	-	-	-	-	-
	Eagle AAR101-Climax	-	-	-	-	-	-	-	-	-	-	-	-	21	DNQ	-	-	-	-
Denny Hulme	Brabham BT11-Climax	6	R	13	R	-	-	-	-	-	-	-	-	-	-	-	-	-	-
	Brabham BT20-Repco	-	-	-	-	9	3	2	2	2	2	15	RF	10	3	7	R	6	3
Jacky Ickx	Matra MS5-Ford	-	-	-	-	-	-	-	-	-	-	NT	F2	-	-	-	-	-	-
Innes Ireland	BRM P261	-	-	-	-	-	-	-	-	-	-	-	-	-	-	17	R	17	R
Chris Irwin	Brabham BT11-Climax	-	-	-	-	-	-	12	7	-	-	-	-	-	-	-	-	-	-
Chris Lawrence	Cooper T73-Ferrari	-	-	-	-	-	-	19	11	-	-	18	R	-	-	-	-	-	-
Guy Ligier	Cooper T81-Maserati	15	NC	12	NC	11	NC	17	10	17	9	NT	DNS	-	-	-	-	-	-
Bruce McLaren	McLaren M2B-Ford	10	R	-	-	-	-	-	-	-	-	-	-	-	-	11	5	15	R
	McLaren M2B-Serenissima	-	-	16	DNS	-	-	13	6	14	DNS	-	-	-	-	-	-	-	-
Gerhard Mitter	Lotus 44-Ford	-	-	-	-	-	-	-	-	-	-	NT	DNS	-	-	-	-	-	-
Silvio Moser	Brabham BT16-Ford	-	-	-	-	-	-	-	-	-	-	NT	DNS	-	-	-	-	-	-
Michael Parkes	Ferrari 312	-	-	-	-	3	2	-	-	5	R	7	R	1	2	-	-	-	-
Alan Rees	Brabham BT18-Ford	-	-	-	-	-	-	-	-	-	-	NT	F2	-	-	-	-	-	-
Jochen Rindt	Cooper T81-Maserati	7	R	2	2	5	4	7	5	6	R	9	3	8	4	9	2	5	R
Pedro Rodriguez	Lotus 33-Climax	-	-	-	-	12	R	-	-	-	-	-	-	-	-	-	-	8	R
	Lotus 44-Ford	-	-	-	-	-	-	-	-	-	-	NT	F2	-	-	-	-	-	-
	Lotus 33-BRM	-	-	-	-	-	-	-	-	-	-	-	-	-	-	10	R	-	-
"Geki" Russo	Lotus 33-Climax	-	-	-	-	-	-	-	-	-	-	-	-	20	9	-	-	-	-
Ludovico Scarfiotti	Ferrari 158/246	-	-	-	-	-	-	-	-	-	-	4	R	-	-	-	-	-	-
	Ferrari 312	-	-	-	-	-	-	-	-	-	-	-	-	2	1F	-	-	-	-
Jo Schlesser	Matra MS5-Ford	-	-	-	-	-	-	-	-	-	-	NT	F2	-	-	-	-	-	-
Jo Siffert	Brabham BT11-BRM	13	R	-	-	-	-	-	-	-	-	-	-	-	-	-	-	-	-
	Cooper T81-Maserati	-	-	14	R	6	R	11	NC	11	R	-	-	17	R	13	4	12	R
Moises Solana	Cooper T81-Maserati	-	-	-	-	-	-	-	-	-	-	-	-	-	-	-	-	16	R
Mike Spence	Lotus 33-BRM	12	R	7	R	10	R	9	R	12	5	13	R	14	5	-	-	-	-
	Lotus 25-BRM	-	-	-	-	-	-	-	-	-	-	-	-	-	-	12	R	11	DNS
Jackie Stewart	BRM P261	3	1	3	R	-	-	8	R	8	4	3	5	-	-	-	-	-	-
	BRM P83	-	-	-	-	-	-	-	-	-	-	-	-	9	R	6	R	10	R
John Surtees	Ferrari 312	2	R	1	1F	-	-	-	-	-	-	-	-	-	-	-	-	-	-
	Cooper T81-Maserati	-	-	-	-	2	R	6	R	10	R	2	2F	4	R	4	3F	1	1

driver	car	MC		B		F		GB		NL		D		I		USA		MEX	
		Q	R	Q	R	Q	R	Q	R	Q	R	Q	R	Q	R	Q	R	Q	R
John Taylor	Brabham BT11-BRM	-	-	-	-	16	6	16	8	18	8	17	R	-	-	-	-	-	-
Trevor Taylor	Shannon SH1-Climax	-	-	-	-	-	-	18	R	-	-	-	-	-	-	-	-	-	-
Vic Wilson	BRM P261	-	-	18	DNS	-	-	-	-	-	-	-	-	-	-	-	-	-	-

*Camera car for the film "Grand Prix," not competing in the Grand Prix

1966 FINAL CHAMPIONSHIP POSITIONS

Drivers

1	Jack Brabham	42 (45)*
2	John Surtees	28
3	Jochen Rindt	22 (24)*
4	Denny Hulme	18
5	Graham Hill	17
6	Jim Clark	16
7	Jackie Stewart	14
8=	Lorenzo Bandini	12
	Michael Parkes	12
10	Ludovico Scarfiotti	9
11	Richie Ginther	5
12=	Dan Gurney	4

12=	Mike Spence	4
14=	Bob Bondurant	3
	Bruce McLaren	3
	Jo Siffert	3
17=	Bob Anderson	1
	Peter Arundell	1
	Jo Bonnier	1
	John Taylor	1

*Best five results count

Manufacturers

1	Brabham-Repco	42 (49)*
2	Ferrari	31 (32)*
3	Cooper-Maserati	30 (35)*
4	BRM	22
5	Lotus-BRM	13
6	Lotus-Climax	8
7	Eagle-Climax	4
8	Honda	3
9	McLaren-Ford	2
10=	Brabham-BRM	1
	McLaren-Serenissima	1
	Brabham-Climax	1

*Best five results count. Points only awarded to first car to finish for each manufacturer

his own name. His team exclusively used the new Holden/Repco engine, which was based on an aluminium stock-block Oldsmobile. Although the Repco was not as powerful as other 3-litre units, it was reliable and proved quick enough to win.

Coventry-Climax had withdrawn from F1 at the end of 1965, leaving the British teams looking for alternative power sources. Cooper arranged to use Maserati V12 engines that had last been raced nine years previously. Their improving season was rewarded when Surtees won the last race in Mexico to finish second in the championship. Bruce McLaren's new team experimented unsuccessfully with V8s from both Ford (its Indy 500 engine) and Serenissima, while others bored out old engines to 2-litre capacity as a stopgap.

BRM eventually introduced the unreliable and complicated H16 unit, which was essentially two 1.5-litre V8s mated together. The only win for the engine was in the United States GP, where it was used in Jim Clark's Lotus 43.

GRAND PRIX DE MONACO

22 May 1966. Monte Carlo. 100 laps of a 1.954-mile circuit = 195.400 miles. Warm, dry and hazy. World Championship round 1

1	Jackie Stewart	BRM P261	100	2h33m10.6
2	Lorenzo Bandini	Ferrari 158/246	100	2h33m50.7
3	Graham Hill	BRM P261	99	
4	Bob Bondurant	BRM P261	95	

No other finishers. Winner's average speed: 76.539 mph. Starting grid front row: Clark, 1m29.9 (pole) and Surtees, 1m30.1. Fastest lap: Bandini, 1m29.8. Leaders: Surtees, laps 1-14; Stewart, 15-100

GRAND PRIX DE BELGIQUE

12 June 1966. Spa-Francorchamps. 28 laps of an 8.761-mile circuit = 245.308 miles. Wet and overcast. World Championship round 2

1	John Surtees	Ferrari 312	28	2h09m11.3
2	Jochen Rindt	Cooper T81-Maserati	28	2h09m53.4
3	Lorenzo Bandini	Ferrari 158/246	27	
4	Jack Brabham	Brabham BT19-Repco	26	
5	Richie Ginther	Cooper T81-Maserati	25	

No other finishers. Winner's average speed: 113.930 mph. Starting front

row: Surtees, 3m38.0 (pole), Rindt, 3m41.2 and Stewart, 3m41.5. Fastest lap: Surtees, 4m18.7. Leaders: Surtees, laps 1, 3, 24-28; Bandini, 2; Rindt, 4-23

GRAND PRIX DE L'AUTOMOBILE CLUB DE FRANCE ET D'EUROPE

3 July 1966. Reims. 48 laps of a 5.187-mile circuit = 248.976 miles. Very hot, dry and sunny. World Championship round 3

1	Jack Brabham	Brabham BT19-Repco	48	1h48m31.3
2	Michael Parkes	Ferrari 312	48	1h48m40.8
3	Denny Hulme	Brabham BT20-Repco	46	
4	Jochen Rindt	Cooper T81-Maserati	46	
5	Dan Gurney	Eagle AAR101-Climax	45	
6	John Taylor	Brabham BT11-BRM	45	

Winner's average speed: 137.655 mph. Starting grid front row: Bandini, 2m07.8 (pole), Surtees, 2m08.4 and Parkes, 2m09.1. Fastest lap: Bandini, 2m11.3. Leaders: Bandini, laps 1-31; Brabham, 32-48

BRITISH GRAND PRIX

16 July 1966. Brands Hatch. 80 laps of a 2.650-mile circuit = 212.000 miles. Overcast and light rain at the start, drying later. World Championship round 4

1	Jack Brabham	Brabham BT19-Repco	80	2h13m13.4
2	Denny Hulme	Brabham BT20-Repco	80	2h13m23.0
3	Graham Hill	BRM P261	79	
4	Jim Clark	Lotus 33-Climax	79	
5	Jochen Rindt	Cooper T81-Maserati	79	
6	Bruce McLaren	McLaren M2B-Serenissima	78	

Winner's average speed: 95.479 mph. Starting grid front row: Brabham, 1m34.5 (pole), Hulme, 1m34.8 and Gurney, 1m35.8. Fastest lap: Brabham, 1m37.0. Leaders: Brabham, laps 1-80

GROTE PRIJS VAN NEDERLAND

24 July 1966. Zandvoort. 90 laps of a 2.605-mile circuit = 234.450 miles. Warm, dry and sunny. World Championship round 5

1	Jack Brabham	Brabham BT19-Repco	90	2h20m32.5
2	Graham Hill	BRM P261	89	
3	Jim Clark	Lotus 33-Climax	88	
4	Jackie Stewart	BRM P261	88	
5	Mike Spence	Lotus 33-BRM	87	
6	Lorenzo Bandini	Ferrari 312	87	

Winner's average speed: 100.091 mph. Starting grid front row: Brabham, 1m28.1 (pole), Hulme, 1m28.7 and Clark, 1m28.7. Fastest lap: Hulme, 1m30.6. Leaders: Brabham, laps 1-26, 76-90; Clark, 27-75

GROSSER PREIS VON DEUTSCHLAND

7 August 1966. Nurburgring. 15 laps of a 14.167-mile circuit = 212.505 miles. Wet and overcast. World Championship round 6

1	Jack Brabham	Brabham BT19-Repco	15	2h27m03.0
2	John Surtees	Cooper T81-Maserati	15	2h27m47.4
3	Jochen Rindt	Cooper T81-Maserati	15	2h29m35.6
4	Graham Hill	BRM P261	15	2h33m44.4
5	Jackie Stewart	BRM P261	15	2h35m31.9
6	Lorenzo Bandini	Ferrari 312	15	2h37m59.4

Winner's average speed: 86.707 mph. Starting grid front row: Clark, 8m16.5 (pole), Surtees, 8m18.0, Stewart, 8m18.8 and Scarfiotti, 8m20.2. Fastest lap: Surtees, 8m49.0. Leaders: Brabham, laps 1-15

GRAN PREMIO D'ITALIA

4 September 1966. Monza. 68 laps of a 3.573-mile circuit = 242.964 miles. Warm, dry and sunny. World Championship round 7

1	Ludovico Scarfiotti	Ferrari 312	68	1h47m14.8
2	Michael Parkes	Ferrari 312	68	1h47m20.6
3	Denny Hulme	Brabham BT20-Repco	68	1h47m20.9
4	Jochen Rindt	Cooper T81-Maserati	67	
5	Mike Spence	Lotus 33-BRM	67	
6	Bob Anderson	Brabham BT11-Climax	66	

Winner's average speed: 135.928 mph. Starting grid front row: Parkes, 1m31.3 (pole), Scarfiotti, 1m31.6 and Clark, 1m31.8. Fastest lap: Scarfiotti, 1m32.4. Leaders: Bandini, lap 1; Parkes, laps 2, 8-12, 27; Surtees, 3; Brabham, 4-7; Scarfiotti, 13-26, 28-68

UNITED STATES GRAND PRIX

2 October 1966. Watkins Glen. 108 laps of a 2.350-mile circuit = 253.800 miles. Cool and dry. World Championship round 8

1	Jim Clark	Lotus 43-BRM	108	2h09m40.1
2	Jochen Rindt*	Cooper T81-Maserati	107	
3	John Surtees	Cooper T81-Maserati	107	
4	Jo Siffert	Cooper T81-Maserati	105	
5	Bruce McLaren	McLaren M2B-Ford	105	
6	Peter Arundell	Lotus 33-Climax	101	

*Rindt penalised 1 lap for completing his final lap in over twice the time of the fastest lap of the race winner, a local rule. Winner's average speed: 117.438 mph. Starting grid front row: Brabham, 1m08.42 (pole) and Clark, 1m08.53. Fastest lap: Surtees, 1m09.67. Leaders: Bandini, laps 1-9, 20-34; Brabham, 10-19, 35-55; Clark, 56-108

GRAN PREMIO DE MEXICO

23 October 1966. Mexico City. 65 laps of a 3.107-mile circuit = 201.955 miles. Warm, dry and sunny. World Championship round 9

1	John Surtees	Cooper T81-Maserati	65	2h06m35.34
2	Jack Brabham	Brabham BT20-Repco	65	2h06m43.22
3	Denny Hulme	Brabham BT20-Repco	64	
4	Richie Ginther	Honda RA273	64	
5	Dan Gurney	Eagle AAR101-Climax	64	
6	Jo Bonnier	Cooper T81-Maserati	63	

Winner's average speed: 95.722 mph. Starting grid front row: Surtees, 1m53.18 (pole) and Clark, 1m53.50. Fastest lap: Ginther, 1m53.75. Leaders: Ginther, lap 1; Brabham, laps 2-5; Surtees, 6-65

1967

Graham Hill returned to Lotus to partner with Jim Clark in one of the strongest driver line-ups yet seen. The team had an exclusive agreement to use the new Ford DFV engine that had been designed and built by Cosworth Engineering with financing from the Ford Motor Company. It would become the most successful F1 engine of all time, and continued to win races into the eighties. Clark gave the engine a stunning debut with a win at Zandvoort after Hill had retired from pole position.

The late introduction of the new engine and some initial reliability problems meant that Clark and his four wins could not prevent the Brabham team repeating their championship success. This time Denny Hulme beat his boss to the title by five points at the last race. Both drivers won twice, but the New Zealander's marginally better placings proved decisive.

The Kyalami circuit, hosting the South African GP for the first time, opened the season and almost produced a surprise win for Rhodesian privateer John Love. His old four-cylinder Cooper-Climax only lost the lead to Pedro Rodriguez's BRM when Love had to refuel six laps from the flag. Dan Gurney gave his Eagle team its only Grand Prix win at Spa when Clark and Jackie Stewart were delayed.

The Italian Grand Prix was a classic example of Jim Clark's virtuosity and another memorable slipstreaming race. In an incredible display, Clark regained a whole lap lost by an unscheduled early pit stop, and retook the lead—only to run out of fuel on the very last lap. This handed victory to John Surtees on the first appearance of the Lola-built Honda RA300.

It had been a year of tragedy for Ferrari, with Lorenzo Bandini killed in a crash at Monaco's chicane and Englishman Michael Parkes injured at Spa. This put the young New Zealander Chris Amon into the spotlight as team leader. Amon's mature performances never quite yielded a Grand Prix victory, either in 1967 or later in his career. Another youngster making a strong first impression was Jacky Ickx, who ran fourth among the F1 cars, only to retire while competing in the F2 class of the German GP.

SOUTH AFRICAN GRAND PRIX

2 January 1967. Kyalami. 80 laps of a 2.544-mile circuit = 203.520 miles. Hot, dry and sunny. World Championship round 1

1	Pedro Rodriguez	Cooper T81-Maserati	80	2h05m45.9
2	John Love	Cooper T79-Climax	80	2h06m12.3
3	John Surtees	Honda RA273	79	
4	Denny Hulme	Brabham BT20-Repco	78	
5	Bob Anderson	Brabham BT11-Climax	78	
6	Jack Brabham	Brabham BT20-Repco	76	

Winner's average speed: 97.095 mph. Starting grid front row: Brabham, 1m28.3 (pole) and Hulme, 1m28.9. Fastest lap: Hulme, 1m29.9. Leaders: Hulme, laps 1-60; Love, 61-73; Rodriguez, 74-80

GRAND PRIX DE MONACO

7 May 1967. Monte Carlo. 100 laps of a 1.954-mile circuit = 195.400 miles. Warm, dry and sunny. World Championship round 2

1	Denny Hulme	Brabham BT20-Repco	100	2h34m34.3
2	Graham Hill	Lotus 33-BRM	99	
3	Chris Amon	Ferrari 312	98	
4	Bruce McLaren	McLaren M4B-BRM	97	
5	Pedro Rodriguez	Cooper T81-Maserati	96	
6	Mike Spence	BRM P83	96	

Winner's average speed: 75.848 mph. Starting grid front row: Brabham, 1m27.6 (pole) and Bandini, 1m28.3. Fastest lap: Clark, 1m29.5. Leaders: Bandini, lap 1; Hulme, laps 2-5, 15-100; Stewart, 6-14

GROTE PRIJS VAN NEDERLAND

4 June 1967. Zandvoort. 90 laps of a 2.605-mile circuit = 234.450 miles. Dry and overcast. World Championship round 3

1	Jim Clark	Lotus 49-Ford	90	2h14m45.1
2	Jack Brabham	Brabham BT19-Repco	90	2h15m08.7
3	Denny Hulme	Brabham BT20-Repco	90	2h15m10.8
4	Chris Amon	Ferrari 312	90	2h15m12.4

Formula 1

1967 DRIVERS' RECORDS

driver	car	ZA Q	ZA R	MC Q	MC R	NL Q	NL R	B Q	B R	F Q	F R	GB Q	GB R	D Q	D R	CDN Q	CDN R	I Q	I R	USA Q	USA R	MEX Q	MEX R
Kurt Ahrens Jr	Protos-Cosworth	-	-	-	-	-	-	-	-	-	-	-	-	NT	F2	-	-	-	-	-	-	-	-
Chris Amon	Ferrari 312	-	-	14	3	9	4	5	3	7	R	6	3	8	3	4	6	4	7	4	R	2	9
Bob Anderson	Brabham BT11-Climax	10	5	17	DNQ	17	9	17	8	14	R	17	R	-	-	-	-	-	-	-	-	-	-
Richard Attwood	Cooper T81B-Maserati	-	-	-	-	-	-	-	-	-	-	-	-	-	-	14	10	-	-	-	-	-	-
Giancarlo Baghetti	Lotus 49-Ford	-	-	-	-	-	-	-	-	-	-	-	-	-	-	-	-	17	R	-	-	-	-
Lorenzo Bandini	Ferrari 312	-	-	2	R	-	-	-	-	-	-	-	-	-	-	-	-	-	-	-	-	-	-
Jean-Pierre Beltoise	Matra MS5-Ford	-	-	-	-	18	DNQ	-	-	-	-	-	-	-	-	-	-	-	-	-	-	-	-
	Matra MS7-Cosworth	-	-	-	-	-	-	-	-	-	-	-	-	-	-	-	-	-	-	18	7	14	7
Jo Bonnier	Cooper T81-Maserati	12	R	-	-	-	-	12	R	-	-	19	R	16	5	15	8	14	R	15	6	17	10
Luki Botha	Brabham BT11-Climax	17	NC	-	-	-	-	-	-	-	-	-	-	-	-	-	-	-	-	-	-	-	-
Jack Brabham	Brabham BT20-Repco	1	6	-	-	-	-	-	-	-	-	-	-	-	-	-	-	-	-	-	-	-	-
	Brabham BT19-Repco	-	-	-	-	1	R	3	2	-	-	-	-	-	-	-	-	-	-	-	-	-	-
	Brabham BT24-Repco	-	-	-	-	-	-	-	-	7	R	2	1	3	4	7	2	1	2	2	5	5	2
Dave Charlton	Brabham BT11-Climax	8	NC	-	-	-	-	-	-	-	-	-	-	-	-	-	-	-	-	-	-	-	-
Jim Clark	Lotus 43-BRM	3	R	-	-	-	-	-	-	-	-	-	-	-	-	-	-	-	-	-	-	-	-
	Lotus 33-Climax	-	-	5	RF	-	-	-	-	-	-	-	-	-	-	-	-	-	-	-	-	-	-
	Lotus 49-Ford	-	-	-	-	8	1F	1	6	4	R	1	1	1	R	1	RF	1	3F	2	1	1	1F
Piers Courage	Lotus 25-BRM	18	R	-	-	-	-	-	-	-	-	-	-	-	-	-	-	-	-	-	-	-	-
	BRM P261	-	-	13	R	-	-	-	-	-	-	16	DNS	-	-	-	-	-	-	-	-	-	-
Mike Fisher	Lotus 33-BRM	-	-	-	-	-	-	-	-	-	-	-	-	-	-	18	11	-	-	-	-	18	R
Richie Ginther	Eagle AAR102-Weslake	-	-	19	DNQ	-	-	-	-	-	-	-	-	-	-	-	-	-	-	-	-	-	-
Dan Gurney	Eagle AAR101-Climax	11	R	-	-	-	-	-	-	-	-	-	-	-	-	-	-	-	-	-	-	-	-
	Eagle AAR103-Weslake	-	-	-	-	7	R	-	-	-	-	-	-	-	-	5	3	-	-	-	-	-	-
	Eagle AAR104-Weslake	-	-	-	-	2	R	2	1F	3	R	5	R	4	RF	-	-	5	R	3	R	3	R
Hubert Hahne	Lola T100-BMW	-	-	-	-	-	-	-	-	-	-	-	-	14	R	-	-	-	-	-	-	-	-
Brian Hart	Protos-Cosworth	-	-	-	-	-	-	-	-	-	-	-	-	NT	F2	-	-	-	-	-	-	-	-
Graham Hill	Lotus 43-BRM	15	R	-	-	-	-	-	-	-	-	-	-	-	-	-	-	-	-	-	-	-	-
	Lotus 33-BRM	-	-	8	2	-	-	-	-	-	-	-	-	-	-	-	-	-	-	-	-	-	-
	Lotus 49-Ford	-	-	-	-	1	R	3	R	1	RF	2	R	13	R	2	4	8	R	1	2F	4	R
David Hobbs	BRM P261	-	-	-	-	-	-	-	-	-	-	-	-	14	8	12	9	-	-	-	-	-	-
	Lola T100-BMW	-	-	-	-	-	-	-	-	-	-	-	-	NT	F2	-	-	-	-	-	-	-	-
Denny Hulme	Brabham BT20-Repco	2	4F	4	1	7	3	-	-	-	-	-	-	-	-	-	-	-	-	-	-	-	-
	Brabham BT19-Repco	-	-	-	-	-	-	14	R	-	-	-	-	-	-	-	-	-	-	-	-	-	-
	Brabham BT24-Repco	-	-	-	-	-	-	-	-	6	2	4	2F	2	1	3	2	6	R	6	3	6	3
Jacky Ickx	Matra MS5-Cosworth	-	-	-	-	-	-	-	-	-	-	-	-	NT	F2	-	-	-	-	-	-	-	-
	Cooper T81B-Maserati	-	-	-	-	-	-	-	-	-	-	-	-	-	-	-	-	15	6	-	-	-	-
	Cooper T86-Maserati	-	-	-	-	-	-	-	-	-	-	-	-	-	-	-	-	-	-	16	R	-	-
Chris Irwin	Lotus 33-BRM	-	-	-	-	13	7	-	-	-	-	-	-	-	-	-	-	-	-	-	-	-	-
	BRM P261	-	-	-	-	-	-	-	-	15	R	-	-	13	7	-	-	-	-	-	-	-	-
	BRM P83	-	-	-	-	-	-	-	-	9	5	-	-	15	7	11	R	16	R	14	R	15	R
Tom Jones	Cooper T82-Climax	-	-	-	-	-	-	-	-	-	-	-	-	19	DNQ	-	-	-	-	-	-	-	-
Guy Ligier	Cooper T81-Maserati	-	-	-	-	-	-	18	10	15	NC	-	-	-	-	-	-	-	-	-	-	-	-
	Brabham BT20-Repco	-	-	-	-	-	-	-	-	-	-	21	10	17	6	-	-	18	R	17	R	19	11
John Love	Cooper T79-Climax	5	2	-	-	-	-	-	-	-	-	-	-	-	-	-	-	-	-	-	-	-	-
Bruce McLaren	McLaren M4B-BRM	-	-	10	4	14	R	-	-	-	-	-	-	-	-	-	-	-	-	-	-	-	-
	Eagle AAR102-Weslake	-	-	-	-	-	-	-	-	5	R	10	R	5	R	-	-	-	-	-	-	-	-
	McLaren M5A-BRM	-	-	-	-	-	-	-	-	-	-	-	-	-	-	6	7	3	R	9	R	8	13
Gerhard Mitter	Brabham BT23-Cosworth	-	-	-	-	-	-	-	-	-	-	-	-	NT	F2	-	-	-	-	-	-	-	-
Silvio Moser	Cooper T77-ATS	-	-	-	-	-	-	-	-	-	-	-	-	20	R	-	-	-	-	-	-	-	-
Jackie Oliver	Lotus 48-Cosworth	-	-	-	-	-	-	-	-	-	-	-	-	NT	F2	-	-	-	-	-	-	-	-
Michael Parkes	Ferrari 312	-	-	-	-	10	5	8	R	-	-	-	-	-	-	-	-	-	-	-	-	-	-
Al Pease	Eagle AAR101-Climax	-	-	-	-	-	-	-	-	-	-	-	-	-	-	16	NC	-	-	-	-	-	-
Brian Redman	Lola T100-Cosworth	-	-	-	-	-	-	-	-	-	-	-	-	NT	DNS	-	-	-	-	-	-	-	-
Alan Rees	Cooper T81-Maserati	-	-	-	-	-	-	-	-	-	-	15	9	-	-	-	-	-	-	-	-	-	-
	Brabham BT23-Cosworth	-	-	-	-	-	-	-	-	-	-	-	-	NT	F2	-	-	-	-	-	-	-	-
Jochen Rindt	Cooper T81-Maserati	7	R	-	-	-	-	-	-	-	-	-	-	-	-	8	R	11	4	-	-	-	-
	Cooper T81B-Maserati	-	-	15	R	4	R	4	4	8	R	-	-	-	-	-	-	-	-	8	R	-	-
	Cooper T86-Maserati	-	-	-	-	-	-	-	-	-	-	8	R	9	R	-	-	-	-	-	-	-	-
Pedro Rodriguez	Cooper T81-Maserati	4	1	16	5	5	5	13	9	13	6	9	5	10	8	-	-	-	-	-	-	-	-
	Cooper T81B-Maserati	-	-	-	-	-	-	-	-	-	-	-	-	-	-	-	-	-	-	-	-	13	6
Ludovico Scarfiotti	Ferrari 312	-	-	-	-	15	6	9	NC	-	-	-	-	-	-	-	-	-	-	-	-	-	-
	Eagle AAR103-Weslake	-	-	-	-	-	-	-	-	-	-	-	-	-	-	-	-	10	R	-	-	-	-
Jo Schlesser	Matra MS5-Cosworth	-	-	-	-	-	-	-	-	-	-	-	-	NT	F2	-	-	-	-	-	-	-	-
Johnny Servoz-Gavin	Matra MS5-Ford	-	-	11	R	-	-	-	-	-	-	-	-	-	-	-	-	-	-	-	-	-	-
Jo Siffert	Cooper T81-Maserati	16	R	9	R	16	10	16	7	11	4	18	R	12	NC	13	DNS	13	R	12	4	10	12

driver	car	ZA Q	R	MC Q	R	NL Q	R	B Q	R	F Q	R	GB Q	R	D Q	R	CDN Q	R	I Q	R	USA Q	R	MEX Q	R
Moises Solana	Lotus 49-Ford	-	-	-	-	-	-	-	-	-	-	-	-	-	-	-	-	-	-	7	R	9	R
Mike Spence	BRM P83	13	R	12	6	12	8	11	5	12	R	11	R	11	R	10	5	12	5	13	R	11	5
Jackie Stewart	BRM P83	9	R	-	-	11	R	6	2	-	-	12	R	3	R	9	R	7	R	10	R	12	R
	BRM P261	-	-	6	R	-	-	-	-	10	3	-	-	-	-	-	-	-	-	-	-	-	-
John Surtees	Honda RA273	6	3	3	R	6	R	10	R	-	-	7	6	6	4	-	-	-	-	-	-	-	-
	Honda RA300	-	-	-	-	-	-	-	-	-	-	-	-	-	-	-	-	9	1	11	R	7	4
Sam Tingle	LDS Mk3-Climax	14	R	-	-	-	-	-	-	-	-	-	-	-	-	-	-	-	-	-	-	-	-
Eppie Wietzes	Lotus 49-Ford	-	-	-	-	-	-	-	-	-	-	-	-	-	-	17	R	-	-	-	-	-	-
Jonathan Williams	Ferrari 312	-	-	-	-	-	-	-	-	-	-	-	-	-	-	-	-	-	-	-	-	16	8

1967 FINAL CHAMPIONSHIP POSITIONS

Drivers

1	Denny Hulme	51
2	Jack Brabham	46 [48]*
3	Jim Clark	41
4=	Chris Amon	20
	John Surtees	20
6=	Graham Hill	15
	Pedro Rodriguez	15
8	Dan Gurney	13
9	Jackie Stewart	10
10	Mike Spence	9
11=	John Love	6
	Jochen Rindt	6
	Jo Siffert	6
14=	Jo Bonnier	3
	Bruce McLaren	3

16=	Bob Anderson	2
	Chris Irwin	2
	Michael Parkes	2
19=	Jacky Ickx	1
	Guy Ligier	1
	Ludovico Scarfiotti	1

*Sum of best five results from the first six races and best four results from final five races

Manufacturers

1	Brabham-Repco	63 (67)*
2	Lotus-Ford	44
3	Cooper-Maserati	28
4=	Ferrari	20
	Honda	20
6	BRM	17
7	Eagle-Weslake	13
8=	Cooper-Climax	6
	Lotus-BRM	6
10	McLaren-BRM	3
11	Brabham-Climax	2

*Sum of best five results from the first six races and best four results from final five races. Points only awarded to first car to finish for each manufacturer

---

5	Michael Parkes	Ferrari 312	89	
6	Ludovico Scarfiotti	Ferrari 312	89	

Winner's average speed: 104.392 mph. Starting grid front row: Hill, 1m24.60 (pole), Gurney, 1m25.1 and Brabham, 1m25.6. Fastest lap: Clark, 1m28.08. Leaders: Hill, laps 1-10; Brabham, 11-15; Clark, 16-90

GRAND PRIX DE BELGIQUE

18 June 1967. Spa-Francorchamps. 28 laps of an 8.761-mile circuit = 245.308 miles. Warm, dry and sunny. World Championship round 4

1	Dan Gurney	Eagle AAR104-Weslake	28	1h40m49.45
2	Jackie Stewart	BRM P83	28	1h41m52.40
3	Chris Amon	Ferrari 312	28	1h42m29.40
4	Jochen Rindt	Cooper T81B-Maserati	28	1h43m03.30
5	Mike Spence	BRM P83	27	
6	Jim Clark	Lotus 49-Ford	27	

Winner's average speed: 145.982 mph. Starting grid front row: Clark, 3m28.1 (pole), Gurney, 3m31.2 and Hill, 3m32.9. Fastest lap: Gurney, 3m31.9. Leaders: Clark, laps 1-12; Stewart, 13-20; Gurney, 21-28

GRAND PRIX DE L'AUTOMOBILE CLUB DE FRANCE

2 July 1967. Le Mans-Bugatti. 80 laps of a 2.748-mile circuit = 219.840 miles. Warm, dry and sunny. World Championship round 5

1	Jack Brabham	Brabham BT24-Repco	80	2h13m21.3
2	Denny Hulme	Brabham BT24-Repco	80	2h14m10.8
3	Jackie Stewart	BRM P261	79	
4	Jo Siffert	Cooper T81-Maserati	77	
5	Chris Irwin	BRM P83	76	engine
6	Pedro Rodriguez	Cooper T81-Maserati	76	

Winner's average speed: 98.912 mph. Starting grid front row: Hill, 1m36.2 (pole), Brabham, 1m36.3 and Gurney, 1m37.0. Fastest lap: Hill, 1m36.7. Leaders: Hill, laps 1, 11-13; Brabham, 2-4, 24-80; Clark, 5-10, 14-23

BRITISH GRAND PRIX

15 July 1967. Silverstone. 80 laps of a 2.927-mile circuit = 234.160 miles. Warm, dry and sunny. World Championship round 6

1	Jim Clark	Lotus 49-Ford	80	1h59m25.6
2	Denny Hulme	Brabham BT24-Repco	80	1h59m38.4
3	Chris Amon	Ferrari 312	80	1h59m42.2
4	Jack Brabham	Brabham BT24-Repco	80	1h59m47.4
5	Pedro Rodriguez	Cooper T81-Maserati	79	
6	John Surtees	Honda RA273	78	

Winner's average speed: 117.642 mph. Starting grid front row: Clark, 1m25.3 (pole), Hill, 1m26.0, Brabham, 1m26.2 and Hulme, 1m26.3. Fastest lap: Hulme, 1m27.0. Leaders: Clark, laps 1-25, 55-80; Hill, 26-54

GROSSER PREIS VON DEUTSCHLAND

6 August 1967. Nurburgring. 15 laps of a 14.189-mile circuit = 212.835 miles. Warm, dry and sunny. World Championship round 7

1	Denny Hulme	Brabham BT24-Repco	15	2h05m55.7
2	Jack Brabham	Brabham BT24-Repco	15	2h06m34.2
3	Chris Amon	Ferrari 312	15	2h06m34.7
4	John Surtees	Honda RA273	15	2h08m21.4
5	Jo Bonnier*	Cooper T81-Maserati	15	2h14m37.8
6	Guy Ligier*	Brabham BT20-Repco	14	

*Bonnier and Ligier finished in 6th and 8th respectively behind cars in the concurrent F2 race, which were not eligible for the F1 class. Winner's average speed: 101.408 mph. Starting grid front row: Clark, 8m04.1 (pole), Hulme, 8m13.5, Stewart, 8m15.2 and Gurney, 8m16.9. Fastest lap: Gurney, 8m15.1. Leaders: Clark, laps 1-3; Gurney, 4-12; Hulme, 13-15

CANADIAN GRAND PRIX

27 August 1967. Mosport Park. 90 laps of a 2.459-mile circuit = 221.310 miles. Wet. World Championship round 8

1	Jack Brabham	Brabham BT24-Repco	90	2h40m40.0
2	Denny Hulme	Brabham BT24-Repco	90	2h41m41.9
3	Dan Gurney	Eagle AAR103-Weslake	89	
4	Graham Hill	Lotus 49-Ford	88	
5	Mike Spence	BRM P83	87	
6	Chris Amon	Ferrari 312	87	

Winner's average speed: 82.647 mph. Starting grid front row: Clark, 1m22.4 (pole), Hill, 1m22.7 and Hulme, 1m23.2. Fastest lap: Clark, 1m23.1. Leaders: Clark, laps 1-3, 58-67; Hulme, 4-57; Brabham, 68-90

GRAN PREMIO D'ITALIA E EUROPA

10 September 1967. Monza. 68 laps of a 3.573-mile circuit = 242.964 miles. Warm, dry and sunny. World Championship round 9

1	John Surtees	Honda RA300	68	1h43m45.0
2	Jack Brabham	Brabham BT24-Repco	68	1h43m45.2
3	Jim Clark	Lotus 49-Ford	68	1h44m08.1
4	Jochen Rindt	Cooper T81-Maserati	68	1h44m41.6
5	Mike Spence	BRM P83	67	
6	Jacky Ickx	Cooper T81B-Maserati	66	

Winner's average speed: 140.509 mph. Starting grid front row: Clark, 1m28.50 (pole), Brabham, 1m28.80 and McLaren, 1m29.31. Fastest lap: Clark, 1m28.5. Leaders: Gurney, laps 1-2; Clark, 3-9, 11-12, 61-67; Hulme, 10, 13-15, 17, 24-27; Brabham, 16, 59-60; Hill, 18-23, 28-58; Surtees, 68

UNITED STATES GRAND PRIX

1 October 1967. Watkins Glen. 108 laps of a 2.350-mile circuit = 253.800 miles. Warm, dry and sunny. World Championship round 10

1	Jim Clark	Lotus 49-Ford	108	2h03m13.2
2	Graham Hill	Lotus 49-Ford	108	2h03m19.5
3	Denny Hulme	Brabham BT24-Repco	107	
4	Jo Siffert	Cooper T81-Maserati	106	
5	Jack Brabham	Brabham BT24-Repco	104	
6	Jo Bonnier	Cooper T81-Maserati	101	

Winner's average speed: 123.584 mph. Starting grid front row: Hill, 1m05.48 (pole) and Clark, 1m06.07. Fastest lap: Hill, 1m06.00. Leaders: Hill, laps 1-40; Clark, 41-108

GRAN PREMIO DE MEXICO

22 October 1967. Mexico City. 65 laps of a 3.107-mile circuit = 201.955 miles. Warm, dry and sunny. World Championship round 11

1	Jim Clark	Lotus 49-Ford	65	1h59m28.70
2	Jack Brabham	Brabham BT24-Repco	65	2h00m54.06
3	Denny Hulme	Brabham BT24-Repco	64	
4	John Surtees	Honda RA300	64	
5	Mike Spence	BRM P83	63	
6	Pedro Rodriguez	Cooper T81B-Maserati	63	

Winner's average speed: 101.418 mph. Starting grid front row: Clark, 1m47.56 (pole) and Amon, 1m48.04. Fastest lap: Clark, 1m48.13. Leaders: Hill, laps 1-2; Clark, 3-65

1968 Jim Clark records his final victory at the 1968 South African Grand Prix in the unsponsored Lotus 49.

1968

On 7 April 1968, Jim Clark crashed during the Deutschland Trophae European F2 Championship race at Hockenheim. The cause is still something of a mystery, but the man who had set the pace in Formula 1 for six years was dead. Motor racing was sent into a state of shock, and then the deaths of Ludovico Scarfiotti in a hillclimb, Mike Spence during practice at Indianapolis,

and Jo Schlesser at the French GP further compounded a black year for the sport.

The responsibility for lifting the Lotus team after Hockenheim was grasped by Graham Hill, who won the next two Grands Prix and would eventually become World Champion for a second time. Lotus also gave Mario Andretti his first chance in F1 at Watkins Glen, where the young ChampCar star responded by qualifying on pole for his debut.

The Ford Cosworth DFV was now widely available, and McLaren Cars and the Ken Tyrrell-run Matra team both recorded their first wins using the engine. Bruce McLaren scored his team's first victory at Spa, while his new teammate and reigning champion Denny Hulme added two more to finish third in the Championship. Jackie Stewart was reunited with his former F3 boss Ken Tyrrell, and won three races to challenge Hill until the final event of the season. In addition, Jo Siffert, driving a Lotus 49 for Rob Walker, and Ferrari's Jacky Ickx each recorded their first Grand Prix victory.

The most visible technical development was the introduction of high aerodynamic wings, which increased cornering speeds by improving downforce.

So often the innovators, Team Lotus brought Indianapolis-style commercial sponsorship to Grand Prix racing in 1968, repainting its cars red and white in deference to Gold Leaf cigarettes. Ironically, the arrival of visible sponsorship came immediately after Jim Clark's final race and victory in the South African season-opener—truly a changing of eras.

SOUTH AFRICAN GRAND PRIX

1 January 1968. Kyalami. 80 laps of a 2.550-mile circuit = 204.000 miles. Very hot, dry and sunny. World Championship round 1

1	Jim Clark	Lotus 49-Ford	80	1h53m56.6
2	Graham Hill	Lotus 49-Ford	80	1h54m21.9
3	Jochen Rindt	Brabham BT24-Repco	80	1h54m27.0
4	Chris Amon	Ferrari 312	78	
5	Denny Hulme	McLaren M5A-BRM	78	
6	Jean-Pierre Beltoise	Matra MS7-Cosworth	77	

Winner's average speed: 107.422 mph. Starting grid front row: Clark, 1m21.6 (pole), Hill, 1m22.6 and Stewart, 1m22.7. Fastest lap: Clark, 1m23.7. Leaders: Stewart, lap 1; Clark, laps 2-80

GRAN PREMIO DE ESPANA

12 May 1968. Jarama. 90 laps of a 2.115-mile circuit = 190.386 miles. Hot, dry and sunny. World Championship round 2

1	Graham Hill	Lotus 49-Ford	90	2h15m20.1
2	Denny Hulme	McLaren M7A-Ford	90	2h15m36.0
3	Brian Redman	Cooper T86B-BRM	89	
4	Ludovico Scarfiotti	Cooper T86B-BRM	89	
5	Jean-Pierre Beltoise	Matra MS10-Ford	81	

No other finishers. Winner's average speed: 84.407 mph. Starting grid front row: Amon, 1m27.9 (pole), Rodriguez, 1m28.1 and Hulme, 1m28.3. Fastest lap: Beltoise, 1m28.3. Leaders: Rodriguez, laps 1-11; Beltoise, 12-15; Amon, 16-57; Hill, 58-90

GRAND PRIX DE MONACO

26 May 1968. Monte Carlo. 80 laps of a 1.954-mile circuit = 156.320 miles. Warm, dry and sunny. World Championship round 3

1	Graham Hill	Lotus 49B-Ford	80	2h00m32.3
2	Richard Attwood	BRM P126	80	2h00m34.5
3	Lucien Bianchi	Cooper T86B-BRM	76	
4	Ludovico Scarfiotti	Cooper T86B-BRM	76	
5	Denny Hulme	McLaren M7A-Ford	73	

No other finishers. Winner's average speed: 77.811 mph. Starting grid

1968 DRIVERS' RECORDS

Key: each race column shows Qualifying (Q) and Race result (R).

driver	car	ZA	E	MC	B	NL	F	GB	D	I	CDN	USA	MEX
		Q R	Q R	Q R	Q R	Q R	Q R	Q R	Q R	Q R	Q R	Q R	Q R
Andrea de Adamich	Ferrari 312	7 R											
Kurt Ahrens Jr	Brabham BT24-Repco								17 12				
Chris Amon	Ferrari 312	8 4	1 R		1 R	1 6	5 10	3 2	2 R	3 R	2 R	4 R	2 R
Mario Andretti	Lotus 49B-Ford									23 DNS		1 R	
Richard Attwood	BRM P126			6 2F	11 R	15 7	13 7	15 R	20 14				
Derek Bell	Ferrari 312									8 R		15 R	
Jean-Pierre Beltoise	Matra MS7-Cosworth	18 6											
	Matra MS10-Ford		5 5F										
	Matra MS11			8 R	13 8	16 2F	8 9	14 R	12 R	18 5	16 R	13 R	13 R
Lucien Bianchi	Cooper T86B-BRM			14 3	12 6	18 R			19 R		19 NC	20 R	21 R
Jo Bonnier	Cooper T81-Maserati	19 R											
	McLaren M5A-BRM			17 DNQ	16 R	19 8		20 R		19 6	18 R	18 NC	
	Honda RA301												18 5
Jack Brabham	Brabham BT24-Repco	5 R											
	Brabham BT26-Repco		14 DNS	12 R	NT R	4 R	14 R	8 R	15 5	16 R	10 R	8 R	8 10
Bill Brack	Lotus 49B-Ford										21 R		
Dave Charlton	Brabham BT11-Repco	14 R											
Jim Clark	Lotus 49-Ford	1 1F											
Piers Courage	BRM P126		11 R	11 R	7 R	14 R	15 6	16 8	8 8	17 4	15 R	14 7	19 R
Vic Elford	Cooper T86B-BRM						18 4	17 R	5 R	20 R	17 5	17 R	17 8
Frank Gardner	BRM P261								21 DNQ				
Dan Gurney	Eagle AAR104-Weslake	12 R		16 R				6 R	10 9	12 R			
	Brabham BT24-Repco						12 R						
	McLaren M7A-Ford										4 R	7 4	5 R
Hubert Hahne	Lola T100-BMW								18 10				
Graham Hill	Lotus 49-Ford	2 2	6 1										
	Lotus 49B-Ford			1 1	14 R	3 9	9 R	1 R	4 2	5 R	5 4	3 2	3 1
David Hobbs	Honda RA301								14 R				
Denny Hulme	McLaren M5A-BRM	9 5											
	McLaren M7A-Ford		3 2	10 5	5 R	7 R	4 5	11 4	11 7	7 1	6 1	5 R	4 R
Jacky Ickx	Ferrari 312	11 R	8 R		3 3	6 4	3 1	12 3	1 4	4 3	14 DNS		15 R
John Love	Brabham BT20-Repco	17 9											
Bruce McLaren	McLaren M7A-Ford		4 R	7 R	6 1	8 R	6 8	10 7	16 13	2 R	8 2	10 6	9 2
Silvio Moser	Brabham BT20-Repco			18 DNQ		17 5		19 NC	21 DNQ	22 DNQ			
Jackie Oliver	Lotus 49-Ford			13 R				2 R					
	Lotus 49B-Ford				15 5	10 NC	11 DNS		13 11	11 RF	9 R	16 DNS	14 3
Al Pease	Eagle AAR101-Climax										22 DNS		
Henri Pescarolo	Matra MS11										20 R	21 DNS	20 9
Jackie Pretorius	Brabham BT7-Climax	23 NC											
Brian Redman	Cooper T81B-Maserati	21 R											
	Cooper T86B-BRM		13 3		10 R								
Jochen Rindt	Brabham BT24-Repco	4 3	9 R	5 R									
	Brabham BT26-Repco				17 R	2 R	1 R	5 R	3 3	10 R	1 R	6 R	10 R
Pedro Rodriguez	BRM P126	10 R											
	BRM P133		2 R	9 R	8 2	11 3	10 12F	13 R	14 6		12 3	11 R	12 4
	BRM P138									15 R			
Basil van Rooyen	Cooper T75-Climax	20 R											
Ludovico Scarfiotti	Cooper T86-Maserati	15 R											
	Cooper T86B-BRM		12 4	15 4									
Jo Schlesser	Honda RA302						17 R						
Johnny Servoz-Gavin	Matra MS10-Ford			2 R						13 2	13 R		16 11
	Cooper T86B-BRM						16 R						
Jo Siffert	Cooper T81-Maserati	16 7											
	Lotus 49-Ford		10 R	3 R	9 7	13 R	12 11						
	Lotus 49B-Ford							4 1F	9 R	9 R	3 RF	12 5	1 6F
Moises Solana	Lotus 49B-Ford												11 R
Mike Spence	BRM P83	13 R											
Jackie Stewart	Matra MS9-Ford	3 R											
	Matra MS10-Ford				2 4	5 1	2 3	7 6	6 1F	6 R	11 6	2 1F	7 7
John Surtees	Honda RA300	6 8											
	Honda RA301		7 R	4 R	4 RF	9 R	7 2	9 5	7 R	1 R	7 R	9 3	6 R
Sam Tingle	LDS Mk5-Repco	22 R											
Bobby Unser	BRM P126								24 DNS				
	BRM P138											19 R	
Robin Widdows	Cooper T86B-BRM							18 R					

Formula 1

1968 FINAL CHAMPIONSHIP POSITIONS

Drivers						Manufacturers		
1	Graham Hill	48	17=	Lucien Bianchi	5	1	Lotus-Ford	62
2	Jackie Stewart	36		Vic Elford	5	2	McLaren-Ford	49
3	Denny Hulme	33	19=	Piers Courage	4	3	Matra-Ford	45
4	Jacky Ickx	27		Brian Redman	4	4	Ferrari	32
5	Bruce McLaren	22	21=	Jo Bonnier	3	5	BRM	28
6	Pedro Rodriguez	18		Dan Gurney	3	6=	Cooper-BRM	14
7=	Jo Siffert	12	23=	Jack Brabham	2		Honda	14
	John Surtees	12		Silvio Moser	2	8	Brabham-Repco	10
9	Jean-Pierre Beltoise	11				9	Matra	8
10	Chris Amon	10				10	McLaren-BRM	3
11	Jim Clark	9						
12	Jochen Rindt	8						
13=	Richard Attwood	6						
	Jackie Oliver	6						
	Ludovico Scarfiotti	6						
	Johnny Servoz-Gavin	6						

Sum of best five results from the first six races and best five results from final six races

Sum of best five results from the first six races and best five results from final six races. Points awarded only to first car to finish for each manufacturer

front row: Hill, 1m28.2 (pole) and Servoz-Gavin, 1m28.8. Fastest lap: Attwood, 1m28.1. Leaders: Servoz-Gavin, laps 1-3; Hill, 4-80

GRAND PRIX DE BELGIQUE

9 June 1968. Spa-Francorchamps. 28 laps of an 8.761-mile circuit = 245.308 miles. Dry and overcast. World Championship round 4

1	Bruce McLaren	McLaren M7A-Ford	28	1h40m02.1
2	Pedro Rodriguez	BRM P133	28	1h40m14.2
3	Jacky Ickx	Ferrari 312	28	1h40m41.7
4	Jackie Stewart*	Matra MS10-Ford	27	
5	Jackie Oliver	Lotus 49B-Ford	26	driveshaft
6	Lucien Bianchi	Cooper T86B-BRM	26	

*Stewart penalised 1 lap for completing his final lap in over twice the time of the race winner's fastest lap, a local rule. Winner's average speed: 147.133 mph. Starting grid front row: Amon, 3m28.6 (pole), Stewart, 3m32.3 and Ickx, 3m34.3. Fastest lap: Surtees, 3m30.5. Leaders: Amon, lap 1; Surtees, laps 2-10; Hulme, 11, 15; Stewart, 12-14, 16-27; McLaren, 28

GROTE PRIJS VAN NEDERLAND

23 June 1968. Zandvoort. 90 laps of a 2.605-mile circuit = 234.450 miles. Heavy showers. World Championship round 5

1	Jackie Stewart	Matra MS10-Ford	90	2h46m11.26
2	Jean-Pierre Beltoise	Matra MS11	90	2h47m45.19
3	Pedro Rodriguez	BRM P133	89	
4	Jacky Ickx	Ferrari 312	88	
5	Silvio Moser	Brabham BT20-Repco	87	
6	Chris Amon	Ferrari 312	85	

Winner's average speed: 84.645 mph. Starting grid front row: Amon, 1m23.54 (pole), Rindt, 1m23.70 and Hill, 1m23.84. Fastest lap: Beltoise, 1m45.91. Leaders: Hill, laps 1-3; Stewart, 4-90

GRAND PRIX DE FRANCE

7 July 1968. Rouen-les-Essarts. 60 laps of a 4.065-mile circuit = 243.900 miles. Wet. World Championship round 6

1	Jacky Ickx	Ferrari 312	60	2h25m40.9
2	John Surtees	Honda RA301	60	2h27m39.5
3	Jackie Stewart	Matra MS10-Ford	59	
4	Vic Elford	Cooper T86B-BRM	58	
5	Denny Hulme	McLaren M7A-Ford	58	
6	Piers Courage	BRM P126	57	

Winner's average speed: 100.452 mph. Starting grid front row: Rindt, 1m56.1 (pole), Stewart, 1m57.3 and Ickx, 1m57.7. Fastest lap: Rodriguez, 2m11.5. Leaders: Ickx, laps 1-18, 20-60; Rodriguez, 19

BRITISH GRAND PRIX

20 July 1968. Brands Hatch. 80 laps of a 2.650-mile circuit = 212.000 miles. Warm, dry and sunny. World Championship round 7

1	Jo Siffert	Lotus 49B-Ford	80	2h01m20.3
2	Chris Amon	Ferrari 312	80	2h01m24.7
3	Jacky Ickx	Ferrari 312	79	
4	Denny Hulme	McLaren M7A-Ford	79	
5	John Surtees	Honda RA301	78	
6	Jackie Stewart	Matra MS10-Ford	78	

Winner's average speed: 104.831 mph. Starting grid front row: Hill, 1m28.9 (pole), Oliver, 1m29.4 and Amon, 1m29.5. Fastest lap: Siffert, 1m29.7. Leaders: Oliver, laps 1-3, 27-43; Hill, 4-26; Siffert, 44-80

GROSSER PREIS VON DEUTSCHLAND UND EUROPA

4 August 1968. Nurburgring. 14 laps of a 14.189-mile circuit = 198.646 miles. Very wet and foggy. World Championship round 8

1	Jackie Stewart	Matra MS10-Ford	14	2h19m03.2
2	Graham Hill	Lotus 49B-Ford	14	2h23m06.4
3	Jochen Rindt	Brabham BT26-Repco	14	2h23m12.6
4	Jacky Ickx	Ferrari 312	14	2h24m58.4
5	Jack Brabham	Brabham BT26-Repco	14	2h25m24.3
6	Pedro Rodriguez	BRM P133	14	2h25m28.2

Winner's average speed: 85.714 mph. Starting grid front row: Ickx, 9m04.0 (pole), Amon, 9m14.9 and Rindt, 9m31.9. Fastest lap: Stewart, 9m36.0. Leaders: Stewart, laps 1-14

GRAN PREMIO D'ITALIA

8 September 1968. Monza. 68 laps of a 3.573-mile circuit = 242.964 miles. Hot, dry and sunny. World Championship round 9

1	Denny Hulme	McLaren M7A-Ford	68	1h40m14.8
2	Johnny Servoz-Gavin	Matra MS10-Ford	68	1h41m43.2
3	Jacky Ickx	Ferrari 312	68	1h41m43.4
4	Piers Courage	BRM P126	67	
5	Jean-Pierre Beltoise	Matra MS11	66	
6	Jo Bonnier	McLaren M5A-BRM	64	

Winner's average speed: 145.420 mph. Starting grid front row: Surtees, 1m26.07 (pole), McLaren, 1m26.11 and Amon, 1m26.21. Fastest lap: Oliver, 1m26.5. Leaders: McLaren, laps 1-6, 8-12, 14; Surtees, 7; Stewart, 13, 17-18, 27, 30, 33, 40; Siffert, 15-16; Hulme, 19-26, 28-29, 31-32, 34-39, 41-68

GRAND PRIX DU CANADA

22 September 1968. St Jovite. 90 laps of a 2.650-mile circuit = 238.500 miles. Warm, dry and sunny. World Championship round 10

1	Denny Hulme	McLaren M7A-Ford	90	2h27m11.2
2	Bruce McLaren	McLaren M7A-Ford	89	
3	Pedro Rodriguez	BRM P133	88	
4	Graham Hill	Lotus 49B-Ford	86	
5	Vic Elford	Cooper T86B-BRM	86	
6	Jackie Stewart	Matra MS10-Ford	83	

Winner's average speed: 97.223 mph. Starting grid front row: Rindt, 1m33.8 (pole), Amon, 1m33.8 and Siffert, 1m34.5. Fastest lap:

Siffert, 1m35.1. Leaders: Amon, laps 1-72; Hulme, 73-90

UNITED STATES GRAND PRIX

6 October 1968. Watkins Glen. 108 laps of a 2.350-mile circuit = 253.800 miles. Dry and overcast. World Championship round 11

1	Jackie Stewart	Matra MS10-Ford	108	1h59m20.29
2	Graham Hill	Lotus 49B-Ford	108	1h59m44.97
3	John Surtees	Honda RA301	107	
4	Dan Gurney	McLaren M7A-Ford	107	
5	Jo Siffert	Lotus 49B-Ford	105	
6	Bruce McLaren	McLaren M7A-Ford	103	

Winner's average speed: 127.604 mph. Starting grid front row: Andretti, 1m04.20 (pole) and Stewart, 1m04.27. Fastest lap: Stewart, 1m05.22. Leaders: Stewart, laps 1-108

GRAN PREMIO DE MEXICO

3 November 1968. Mexico City. 65 laps of a 3.107-mile circuit = 201.955 miles. Warm, dry and sunny. World Championship round 12

1	Graham Hill	Lotus 49B-Ford	65	1h56m43.95
2	Bruce McLaren	McLaren M7A-Ford	65	1h58m03.27
3	Jackie Oliver	Lotus 49B-Ford	65	1h58m24.60
4	Pedro Rodriguez	BRM P133	65	1h58m25.04
5	Jo Bonnier	Honda RA301	64	
6	Jo Siffert	Lotus 49B-Ford	64	

Winner's average speed: 103.804 mph. Starting grid front row: Siffert, 1m45.22 (pole) and Amon, 1m45.62. Fastest lap: Siffert, 1m44.23. Leaders: Hill, laps 1-4, 9-21, 25-65; Stewart, 5-8; Siffert, 22-24

1969

Jackie Stewart had won three Grands Prix in Ken Tyrrell's Matra-Ford in 1968, and it was no surprise when the combination dominated the new season. He won five of the first six races and went on to clinch his first title after a four-car slipstreaming battle at Monza.

The Spanish Grand Prix at Barcelona's Montjuich Park brought to a head safety concerns regarding high aerodynamic wings. Both works Lotus 49s, driven by Graham Hill and Jochen Rindt, crashed heavily after their wings collapsed from the downforce they were generating.

After an emergency meeting at Monaco, the CSI immediately banned unrestricted wings. The teams argued that this would make the cars even more dangerous, claiming that since the cars had been designed around these wings, removing them would make the cars unstable. Nevertheless, the CSI forced the changes through during the weekend of the Monaco GP.

Graham Hill won at Monaco for the fifth time, a record that would stand until Ayrton Senna's sixth victory in 1993. Emerging star Jacky Ickx won twice for Brabham to finish a distant second in the standings. The man he replaced in the team, Jochen Rindt, recorded his first GP victory at Watkins Glen for his new employer Lotus. The year ended in Mexico with Denny Hulme winning for McLaren. It would be the team's final victory before founder Bruce McLaren died while testing in June 1970.

Four-wheel-drive was seen as the next logical step in Formula 1 design, and both Matra and Lotus introduced new cars at the Dutch GP, with the McLaren version joining the grid for the British GP. Matra's system was developed by Ferguson, which had entered a four-wheel-drive car once before in 1961. This time the system proved to be an expensive distraction.

With Ferrari and BRM both uncompetitive and Matra taking a sabbatical from engine-supply, the Ford DFV engine won every round of the championship. Ferrari, which had recently sold 50% of the company to Fiat, underperformed to the extent that the marque recorded only one podium and three points finishes.

SOUTH AFRICAN GRAND PRIX

1 March 1969. Kyalami. 80 laps of a 2.550-mile circuit = 204.000 miles. Hot, dry and sunny. World Championship round 1

1	Jackie Stewart	Matra MS10-Ford	80	1h50m39.1
2	Graham Hill	Lotus 49B-Ford	80	1h50m57.9
3	Denny Hulme	McLaren M7A-Ford	80	1h51m10.9
4	Jo Siffert	Lotus 49B-Ford	80	1h51m28.3
5	Bruce McLaren	McLaren M7A-Ford	79	
6	Jean-Pierre Beltoise	Matra MS10-Ford	78	

Winner's average speed: 110.617 mph. Starting grid front row: Brabham, 1m20.0 (pole), Rindt, 1m20.2 and Hulme, 1m20.3. Fastest lap: Stewart, 1m21.6. Leaders: Stewart, laps 1-80

GRAN PREMIO DE ESPANA

4 May 1969. Montjuich Park. 90 laps of a 2.355-mile circuit = 211.950 miles. Warm, dry and sunny. World Championship round 2

1	Jackie Stewart	Matra MS80-Ford	90	2h16m53.99
2	Bruce McLaren	McLaren M7C-Ford	88	
3	Jean-Pierre Beltoise	Matra MS80-Ford	87	
4	Denny Hulme	McLaren M7A-Ford	87	
5	John Surtees	BRM P138	84	
6	Jacky Ickx	Brabham BT26-Ford	83	suspension

Winner's average speed: 92.893 mph. Starting grid front row: Rindt, 1m25.7 (pole), Amon, 1m26.2 and Hill, 1m26.6. Fastest lap: Rindt, 1m28.3. Leaders: Rindt, laps 1-19; Amon, 20-56; Stewart, 57-90

GRAND PRIX DE MONACO

18 May 1969. Monte Carlo. 80 laps of a 1.954-mile circuit = 156.320 miles. Warm, dry and overcast. World Championship round 3

1	Graham Hill	Lotus 49B-Ford	80	1h56m59.4
2	Piers Courage	Brabham BT26-Ford	80	1h57m16.7
3	Jo Siffert	Lotus 49B-Ford	80	1h57m34.0
4	Richard Attwood	Lotus 49-Ford	80	1h57m52.3
5	Bruce McLaren	McLaren M7C-Ford	79	
6	Denny Hulme	McLaren M7A-Ford	78	

Winner's average speed: 80.171 mph. Starting grid front row: Stewart, 1m24.6 (pole) and Amon, 1m25.0. Fastest lap: Stewart, 1m25.1. Leaders: Stewart, laps 1-22; Hill, 23-80

GROTE PRIJS VAN NEDERLAND

21 June 1969. Zandvoort. 90 laps of a 2.605-mile circuit = 234.450 miles. Warm, dry and sunny. World Championship round 4

1	Jackie Stewart	Matra MS80-Ford	90	2h06m42.08
2	Jo Siffert	Lotus 49B-Ford	90	2h07m06.60
3	Chris Amon	Ferrari 312	90	2h07m12.59
4	Denny Hulme	McLaren M7A-Ford	90	2h07m19.24
5	Jacky Ickx	Brabham BT26-Ford	90	2h07m19.75
6	Jack Brabham	Brabham BT26-Ford	90	2h07m52.89

Winner's average speed: 111.025 mph. Starting grid front row: Rindt, 1m20.85 (pole), Stewart, 1m21.14 and Hill, 1m22.01. Fastest lap: Stewart, 1m22.94. Leaders: Hill, laps 1-2; Rindt, 3-16; Stewart, 17-90

GRAND PRIX DE FRANCE

6 July 1969. Clermont-Ferrand. 38 laps of a 5.005-mile circuit = 190.190 miles. Warm, dry and sunny. World Championship round 5

1	Jackie Stewart	Matra MS80-Ford	38	1h56m47.4
2	Jean-Pierre Beltoise	Matra MS80-Ford	38	1h57m44.5
3	Jacky Ickx	Brabham BT26-Ford	38	1h57m44.7
4	Bruce McLaren	McLaren M7C-Ford	37	
5	Vic Elford	McLaren M7A/M7B-Ford	37	
6	Graham Hill	Lotus 49B-Ford	37	

Formula 1

1969 DRIVERS' RECORDS

driver	car	ZA		E		MC		NL		F		GB		D		I		CDN		USA		MEX	
		Q	R	Q	R	Q	R	Q	R	Q	R	Q	R	Q	R	Q	R	Q	R	Q	R	Q	R
Kurt Ahrens Jr	Brabham BT30-Cosworth	-	-	-	-	-	-	-	-	-	-	-	-	NT	F2	-	-	-	-	-	-	-	-
Chris Amon	Ferrari 312	5	R	2	R	2	R	4	3	6	10	5	R	-	-	-	-	-	-	-	-	-	-
Mario Andretti	Lotus 49B-Ford	6	R	-	-	-	-	-	-	-	-	-	-	-	-	-	-	-	-	-	-	-	-
	Lotus 63-Ford	-	-	-	-	-	-	-	-	-	-	-	-	12	R	-	-	-	-	13	R	-	-
Richard Attwood	Lotus 49-Ford	-	-	-	-	-	-	10	4	-	-	-	-	-	-	-	-	-	-	-	-	-	-
	Brabham BT30-Cosworth	-	-	-	-	-	-	-	-	-	-	-	-	NT	F2	-	-	-	-	-	-	-	-
Derek Bell	McLaren M9A-Ford	-	-	-	-	-	-	-	-	-	-	15	R	-	-	-	-	-	-	-	-	-	-
Jean-Pierre Beltoise	Matra MS10-Ford	11	6	-	-	-	-	-	-	-	-	-	-	-	-	-	-	-	-	-	-	-	-
	Matra MS80-Ford	-	-	12	3	3	R	11	8	5	2	-	-	10	6	6	3F	2	4	7	R	8	5
	Matra MS84-Ford	-	-	-	-	-	-	-	-	-	-	17	9	-	-	-	-	-	-	-	-	-	-
Jo Bonnier	Lotus 63-Ford	-	-	-	-	-	-	-	-	-	-	16	R	-	-	-	-	-	-	-	-	-	-
	Lotus 49B-Ford	-	-	-	-	-	-	-	-	-	-	-	-	14	R	-	-	-	-	-	-	-	-
Jack Brabham	Brabham BT26-Ford	1	R	5	R	8	R	8	6	-	-	-	-	-	-	7	R	6	2F	10	4	1	3
Bill Brack	BRM P138	-	-	-	-	-	-	-	-	-	-	-	-	-	-	-	-	18	NC	-	-	-	-
Tino Brambilla	Ferrari 312	-	-	-	-	-	-	-	-	-	-	-	-	-	-	15	DNS	-	-	-	-	-	-
Francois Cevert	Tecno 306-Cosworth	-	-	-	-	-	-	-	-	-	-	-	-	NT	F2	-	-	-	-	-	-	-	-
John Cordts	Brabham BT23B-Ford	-	-	-	-	-	-	-	-	-	-	-	-	-	-	-	-	19	R	-	-	-	-
Piers Courage	Brabham BT26-Ford	-	-	11	R	9	2	9	R	11	R	10	5	7	R	4	5	10	R	9	2	9	10
George Eaton	BRM P138	-	-	-	-	-	-	-	-	-	-	-	-	-	-	-	-	-	-	18	R	-	-
	BRM P139	-	-	-	-	-	-	-	-	-	-	-	-	-	-	-	-	-	-	-	-	17	R
Vic Elford	Cooper T86B-Maserati	-	-	-	-	16	7	-	-	-	-	-	-	-	-	-	-	-	-	-	-	-	-
	McLaren M7A/M7B-Ford	-	-	-	-	-	-	-	-	15	10	10	5	11	6	6	R	-	-	-	-	-	-
Hubert Hahne	BMW 269/F2	-	-	-	-	-	-	-	-	-	-	-	-	NT	DNS	-	-	-	-	-	-	-	-
Hans Herrmann	Lotus 59B-Cosworth	-	-	-	-	-	-	-	-	-	-	-	-	NT	DNS	-	-	-	-	-	-	-	-
Graham Hill	Lotus 49B-Ford	7	2	3	R	4	1	3	7	8	6	12	7	9	4	9	9	7	R	4	R	-	-
Denny Hulme	McLaren M7A-Ford	3	3	8	4	12	6	7	4	2	8	3	R	5	R	2	7	5	R	2	R	4	1
Jacky Ickx	Brabham BT26-Ford	13	R	7	6	7	R	5	5	4	3	4	2	1	1F	16	10	1	1F	8	R	2	2F
Piet de Klerk	Brabham BT20-Repco	16	R	-	-	-	-	-	-	-	-	-	-	-	-	-	-	-	-	-	-	-	-
John Love	Lotus 49-Ford	10	R	-	-	-	-	-	-	-	-	-	-	-	-	-	-	-	-	-	-	-	-
Pete Lovely	Lotus 49B-Ford	-	-	-	-	-	-	-	-	-	-	-	-	-	-	-	-	16	7	16	R	16	9
Bruce McLaren	McLaren M7A-Ford	8	5	-	-	-	-	-	-	-	-	-	-	-	-	-	-	-	-	-	-	-	-
	McLaren M7C-Ford	-	-	13	2	11	5	6	R	7	4	7	3	8	3	5	4	9	5	6	DNS	7	DNS
John Miles	Lotus 63-Ford	-	-	-	-	-	-	-	-	12	R	14	10	-	-	14	R	11	R	-	-	11	R
Gerhard Mitter	BMW 269/F2	-	-	-	-	-	-	-	-	-	-	-	-	NT	DNS	-	-	-	-	-	-	-	-
Silvio Moser	Brabham BT24-Ford	-	-	-	-	15	R	14	R	13	7	-	-	-	-	13	R	20	R	17	6	13	11
Jackie Oliver	BRM P133	14	7	10	R	13	R	13	R	-	-	13	R	-	-	-	-	-	-	-	-	-	-
	BRM P138	-	-	-	-	-	-	-	-	-	-	-	-	13	R	-	-	-	-	-	-	-	-
	BRM P139	-	-	-	-	-	-	-	-	-	-	-	-	-	-	11	R	12	R	14	R	12	6
Al Pease	Eagle AAR101-Climax	-	-	-	-	-	-	-	-	-	-	-	-	-	-	-	-	17	DSQ	-	-	-	-
Xavier Perrot	Brabham BT23C-Cosworth	-	-	-	-	-	-	-	-	-	-	-	-	NT	F2	-	-	-	-	-	-	-	-
Henri Pescarolo	Matra MS7-Cosworth	-	-	-	-	-	-	-	-	-	-	-	-	NT	F2	-	-	-	-	-	-	-	-
Dieter Quester	BMW 269/F2	-	-	-	-	-	-	-	-	-	-	-	-	NT	DNS	-	-	-	-	-	-	-	-
Jochen Rindt	Lotus 49B-Ford	2	R	1	RF	-	-	1	R	3	R	1	4	3	R	1	2	3	3	1	1F	6	R
Pedro Rodriguez	BRM P126	15	R	14	7	14	R	-	-	-	-	-	-	-	-	-	-	-	-	-	-	-	-
	Ferrari 312	-	-	-	-	-	-	-	-	-	-	8	R	-	-	12	6	13	R	12	5	15	7
Basil van Rooyen	McLaren M7A-Ford	9	R	-	-	-	-	-	-	-	-	-	-	-	-	-	-	-	-	-	-	-	-
Johnny Servoz-Gavin	Matra MS7-Cosworth	-	-	-	-	-	-	-	-	-	-	-	-	NT	F2	-	-	-	-	-	-	-	-
	Matra MS84-Ford	-	-	-	-	-	-	-	-	-	-	-	-	-	-	-	-	15	6	15	7	14	8
Jo Siffert	Lotus 49B-Ford	12	4	6	R	5	3	10	2	9	9	8	4	5	8	8	8	8	R	5	R	5	R
Jackie Stewart	Matra MS10-Ford	4	1F	-	-	-	-	-	-	-	-	-	-	-	-	-	-	-	-	-	-	-	-
	Matra MS80-Ford	-	-	4	1	1	RF	2	1F	1	1F	2	1F	2	2	3	1	4	R	3	R	3	4
Rolf Stommelen	Lotus 59B-Cosworth	-	-	-	-	-	-	-	-	-	-	-	-	NT	F2	-	-	-	-	-	-	-	-
John Surtees	BRM P138	NT	R	9	5	6	R	12	9	-	-	-	-	-	-	-	-	-	-	-	-	-	-
	BRM P139	-	-	-	-	-	-	-	-	-	-	6	R	11	DNS	10	11	14	R	11	3	10	R
Sam Tingle	Brabham BT24-Repco	17	8	-	-	-	-	-	-	-	-	-	-	-	-	-	-	-	-	-	-	-	-
Peter Westbury	Brabham BT30-Cosworth	-	-	-	-	-	-	-	-	-	-	-	-	NT	F2	-	-	-	-	-	-	-	-

1969 FINAL CHAMPIONSHIP POSITIONS

Drivers						Manufacturers		
1	Jackie Stewart	63	12	Chris Amon	4	1	Matra-Ford	66
2	Jacky Ickx	37	13=	Richard Attwood	3	2	Brabham-Ford	49 (51)*
3	Bruce McLaren	26		Vic Elford	3	3	Lotus-Ford	47
4	Jochen Rindt	22		Pedro Rodriguez	3	4	McLaren-Ford	38 (40)*
5	Jean-Pierre Beltoise	21	16=	Silvio Moser	1	5=	BRM	7
6	Denny Hulme	20		Jackie Oliver	1		Ferrari	7
7	Graham Hill	19		Johnny Servoz-Gavin	1	*Sum of best five results from the first six		
8	Piers Courage	16	Sum of best five results from the first six			races and best four results from final five		
9	Jo Siffert	15	races and best four results from final			races. Points only awarded to first car to		
10	Jack Brabham	14	five races			finish for each manufacturer		
11	John Surtees	6						

Winner's average speed: 97.709 mph. Starting grid front row: Stewart, 3m00.6 (pole) and Hulme, 3m02.4. Fastest lap: Stewart, 3m02.7. Leaders: Stewart, laps 1-38

BRITISH GRAND PRIX

19 July 1969. Silverstone. 84 laps of a 2.927-mile circuit = 245.868 miles. Dry and overcast. World Championship round 6

1	Jackie Stewart	Matra MS80-Ford	84	1h55m55.6
2	Jacky Ickx	Brabham BT26-Ford	83	
3	Bruce McLaren	McLaren M7C-Ford	83	
4	Jochen Rindt	Lotus 49B-Ford	83	
5	Piers Courage	Brabham BT26-Ford	83	
6	Vic Elford	McLaren M7A/M7B-Ford	82	

Winner's average speed: 127.254 mph. Starting grid front row: Rindt, 1m20.8 (pole), Stewart, 1m21.2 and Hulme, 1m21.5. Fastest lap: Stewart, 1m21.3. Leaders: Rindt, laps 1-5, 16-61; Stewart, 6-15, 62-84

GROSSER PREIS VON DEUTSCHLAND

3 August 1969. Nurburgring. 14 laps of a 14.189-mile circuit = 198.646 miles. Warm, dry and sunny. World Championship round 7

1	Jacky Ickx	Brabham BT26-Ford	14	1h49m55.4
2	Jackie Stewart	Matra MS80-Ford	14	1h50m53.1
3	Bruce McLaren	McLaren M7C-Ford	14	1h53m17.0
4	Graham Hill	Lotus 49B-Ford	14	1h53m54.2
5	Jo Siffert*	Lotus 49B-Ford	12	accident
6	Jean-Pierre Beltoise*	Matra MS80-Ford	12	upright

*Siffert and Beltoise were classified in 11th and 12th respectively behind cars in the concurrent F2 class, which were not eligible for the F1 class. Winner's average speed: 108.428 mph. Starting grid front row: Ickx, 7m42.1 (pole), Stewart, 7m42.4 and Rindt, 7m48.0. Fastest lap: Ickx, 7m43.8. Leaders: Stewart, laps 1-6; Ickx, 7-14

GRAN PREMIO D'ITALIA

7 September 1969. Monza. 68 laps of a 3.573-mile circuit = 242.964 miles. Warm, dry and sunny. World Championship round 8

1	Jackie Stewart	Matra MS80-Ford	68	1h39m11.26
2	Jochen Rindt	Lotus 49B-Ford	68	1h39m11.34
3	Jean-Pierre Beltoise	Matra MS80-Ford	68	1h39m11.43
4	Bruce McLaren	McLaren M7C-Ford	68	1h39m11.45
5	Piers Courage	Brabham BT26-Ford	68	1h39m44.70
6	Pedro Rodriguez	Ferrari 312	66	

Winner's average speed: 146.972 mph. Starting grid front row: Rindt, 1m25.48 (pole) and Hulme, 1m25.69. Fastest lap: Beltoise, 1m25.2. Leaders: Stewart, laps 1-6, 9-17, 19-24, 28-30, 33, 35-36, 38-68; Rindt, 7, 25-27, 31, 34, 37; Hulme, 8; Courage, 18, 32

CANADIAN GRAND PRIX

20 September 1969. Mosport Park. 90 laps of a 2.459-mile circuit = 221.310 miles. Warm, dry and sunny. World Championship round 9

1	Jacky Ickx	Brabham BT26-Ford	90	1h59m25.7
2	Jack Brabham	Brabham BT26-Ford	90	2h00m11.9
3	Jochen Rindt	Lotus 49B-Ford	90	2h00m17.7
4	Jean-Pierre Beltoise	Matra MS80-Ford	89	
5	Bruce McLaren	McLaren M7C-Ford	87	
6	Johnny Servoz-Gavin	Matra MS84-Ford	84	

Winner's average speed: 111.185 mph. Starting grid front row: Ickx, 1m17.4 (pole), Beltoise, 1m17.9 and Rindt, 1m17.9. Fastest lap: Ickx and Brabham, 1m18.1. Leaders: Rindt, laps 1-5; Stewart, 6-32; Ickx, 33-90

UNITED STATES GRAND PRIX

5 October 1969. Watkins Glen. 108 laps of a 2.350-mile circuit = 253.800 miles. Hot, dry and sunny. World Championship round 10

1	Jochen Rindt	Lotus 49B-Ford	108	1h57m56.84
2	Piers Courage	Brabham BT26-Ford	108	1h58m43.83
3	John Surtees	BRM P139	106	
4	Jack Brabham	Brabham BT26-Ford	106	
5	Pedro Rodriguez	Ferrari 312	101	
6	Silvio Moser	Brabham BT24-Ford	98	

Winner's average speed: 129.108 mph. Starting grid front row: Rindt, 1m03.62 (pole) and Hulme, 1m03.65. Fastest lap: Rindt, 1m04.34. Leaders: Rindt, laps 1-11, 21-108; Stewart, 12-20

GRAN PREMIO DE MEXICO

19 October 1969. Mexico City. 65 laps of a 3.107-mile circuit = 201.955 miles. Warm, dry and sunny. World Championship round 11

1	Denny Hulme	McLaren M7A-Ford	65	1h54m08.80
2	Jacky Ickx	Brabham BT26-Ford	65	1h54m11.36
3	Jack Brabham	Brabham BT26-Ford	65	1h54m47.28
4	Jackie Stewart	Matra MS80-Ford	65	1h54m55.84
5	Jean-Pierre Beltoise	Matra MS80-Ford	65	1h55m47.32
6	Jackie Oliver	BRM P139	63	

Winner's average speed: 106.156 mph. Starting grid front row: Brabham, 1m42.90 (pole) and Ickx, 1m43.60. Fastest lap: Ickx, 1m43.05. Leaders: Stewart, laps 1-5; Ickx, 6-9; Hulme, 10-65

1970

For the only time in its history, Formula 1 had a posthumous World Champion in 1970, when overwhelming series leader Jochen Rindt died after crashing his Lotus 72 at Parabolica during practice for the Italian Grand Prix. To complete another tragic year, Piers Courage, Rindt's great friend, died in the Dutch GP, and Bruce McLaren was killed testing a Can-Am car at Goodwood.

When Lotus perfected its new 72 model, Rindt scored four successive victories, adding to his earlier last-lap win at Monaco in a Lotus 49C. Although Rindt retired in his home race on the magnificent new Osterreichring, he was still 20 points ahead going to Monza.

Jacky Ickx scored Ferrari's first win since mid-1968 in Austria, and developed into Lotus's closest challenger as the year progressed by adding two more victories. Ferrari newcomer Clay Regazzoni won at Monza, but Rindt's points score could not be passed when his young replacement at Lotus, Emerson Fittipaldi, won the United States GP in only his fourth start.

March Engineering entered Formula 1 amid much hype and publicity. In addition to works entries, Ken Tyrrell bought a March 701 for Jackie Stewart, which he drove to victory in Spain. Meanwhile, in total secrecy, Tyrrell became a constructor in his own right. Stewart qualified the Tyrrell 001 on pole for its first Grand Prix in Canada.

Ford had been unbeaten in 1969 but faced a sterner challenge this year with Ferrari's return to form and Pedro Rodriguez's Yardley-sponsored BRM winning at Spa-Francorchamps.

Having started the season with a victory, three-time World Champion Jack Brabham ended it by retiring from the sport, with designer Ron Tauranac assuming sole ownership of the team. Dunlop tyres also withdrew from the sport at the end of the year.

1970 Jochen Rindt became the sport's only posthumous World Champion after his fatal accident at Monza.

SOUTH AFRICAN GRAND PRIX

7 March 1970. Kyalami. 80 laps of a 2.550-mile circuit = 204.000 miles. Very hot, dry and sunny. World Championship round 1

1 Jack Brabham	Brabham BT33-Ford	80	1h49m34.6
2 Denny Hulme	McLaren M14A-Ford	80	1h49m42.7
3 Jackie Stewart	March 701-Ford	80	1h49m51.7
4 Jean-Pierre Beltoise	Matra-Simca MS120	80	1h50m47.7
5 John Miles	Lotus 49C-Ford	79	
6 Graham Hill	Lotus 49C-Ford	79	

Winner's average speed: 111.703 mph. Starting grid front row: Stewart, 1m19.3 (pole), Amon, 1m19.3 and Brabham, 1m19.6. Fastest lap: Surtees and Brabham, 1m20.8. Leaders: Stewart, laps 1-19; Brabham, 20-80

GRAN PREMIO DE ESPANA

19 April 1970. Jarama. 90 laps of a 2.115-mile circuit = 190.386 miles. Very hot, dry and sunny. World Championship round 2

1 Jackie Stewart	March 701-Ford	90	2h10m58.2
2 Bruce McLaren	McLaren M14A-Ford	89	
3 Mario Andretti	March 701-Ford	89	
4 Graham Hill	Lotus 49C-Ford	89	
5 Johnny Servoz-Gavin	March 701-Ford	88	

No other finishers. Winner's average speed: 87.220 mph. Starting grid front row: Brabham, 1m23.9 (pole), Hulme, 1m24.1 and Stewart, 1m24.2. Fastest lap: Brabham, 1m24.3. Leaders: Stewart, laps 1-90

GRAND PRIX DE MONACO

10 May 1970. Monte Carlo. 80 laps of a 1.954-mile circuit = 156.320 miles. Warm, dry and sunny. World Championship round 3

1 Jochen Rindt	Lotus 49C-Ford	80	1h54m36.6

2 Jack Brabham	Brabham BT33-Ford	80	1h54m59.7
3 Henri Pescarolo	Matra-Simca MS120	80	1h55m28.0
4 Denny Hulme	McLaren M14A-Ford	80	1h56m04.9
5 Graham Hill	Lotus 49C-Ford	79	
6 Pedro Rodriguez	BRM P153	78	

Winner's average speed: 81.836 mph. Starting grid front row: Stewart, 1m24.0 (pole) and Amon, 1m24.6. Fastest lap: Rindt, 1m23.2. Leaders: Stewart, laps 1-27; Brabham, 28-79; Rindt, 80

GRAND PRIX DE BELGIQUE

7 June 1970. Spa-Francorchamps. 28 laps of an 8.761-mile circuit = 245.308 miles. Warm, dry and sunny. World Championship round 4

1 Pedro Rodriguez	BRM P153	28	1h38m09.9
2 Chris Amon	March 701-Ford	28	1h38m11.0
3 Jean-Pierre Beltoise	Matra-Simca MS120	28	1h39m53.6
4 Ignazio Giunti	Ferrari 312B	28	1h40m48.4
5 Rolf Stommelen	Brabham BT33-Ford	28	1h41m41.7
6 Henri Pescarolo	Matra-Simca MS120	27	out of fuel

Winner's average speed: 149.936 mph. Starting grid front row: Stewart, 3m28.0 (pole), Rindt, 3m30.1 and Amon, 3m30.3. Fastest lap: Amon, 3m27.4. Leaders: Amon, laps 1, 3-4; Stewart, 2; Rodriguez, 5-28

GROTE PRIJS VAN NEDERLAND

21 June 1970. Zandvoort. 80 laps of a 2.605-mile circuit = 208.400 miles. Dry and overcast. World Championship round 5

1 Jochen Rindt	Lotus 72-Ford	80	1h50m43.41
2 Jackie Stewart	March 701-Ford	80	1h51m13.41
3 Jacky Ickx	Ferrari 312B	79	
4 Clay Regazzoni	Ferrari 312B	79	
5 Jean-Pierre Beltoise	Matra-Simca MS120	79	
6 John Surtees	McLaren M7C-Ford	79	

Winner's average speed: 112.930 mph. Starting grid front row: Rindt, 1m18.50 (pole), Stewart, 1m18.73 and Ickx, 1m18.93. Fastest lap: Ickx, 1m19.23. Leaders: Ickx, laps 1-2; Rindt, 3-80

GRAND PRIX DE FRANCE

5 July 1970. Clermont-Ferrand. 38 laps of a 5.005-mile circuit = 190.190 miles. Warm, dry and sunny. World Championship round 6

1 Jochen Rindt	Lotus 72-Ford	38	1h55m57.00
2 Chris Amon	March 701-Ford	38	1h56m04.61
3 Jack Brabham	Brabham BT33-Ford	38	1h56m41.83
4 Denny Hulme	McLaren M14D-Ford	38	1h56m42.66
5 Henri Pescarolo	Matra-Simca MS120	38	1h57m16.42
6 Dan Gurney	McLaren M14A-Ford	38	1h57m16.65

Winner's average speed: 98.417 mph. Starting grid front row: Ickx, 2m58.22 (pole) and Beltoise, 2m58.70. Fastest lap: Brabham, 3m00.75. Leaders: Ickx, laps 1-14; Beltoise, 15-25; Rindt, 26-38

BRITISH GRAND PRIX

18 July 1970. Brands Hatch. 80 laps of a 2.650-mile circuit = 212.000 miles. Warm, dry and sunny. World Championship round 7

1 Jochen Rindt	Lotus 72-Ford	80	1h57m02.0
2 Jack Brabham	Brabham BT33-Ford	80	1h57m34.9
3 Denny Hulme	McLaren M14D-Ford	80	1h57m56.4
4 Clay Regazzoni	Ferrari 312B	80	1h57m56.8
5 Chris Amon	March 701-Ford	79	
6 Graham Hill	Lotus 49C-Ford	79	

Winner's average speed: 108.687 mph. Starting grid front row: Rindt, 1m24.8 (pole), Brabham, 1m24.8 and Ickx, 1m25.1. Fastest lap: Brabham, 1m25.9. Leaders: Ickx, laps 1-6; Rindt, 7-68, 80; Brabham, 69-79

GROSSER PREIS VON DEUTSCHLAND

2 August 1970. Hockenheim. 50 laps of a 4.219-mile circuit = 210.950 miles. Hot, dry and sunny. World Championship round 8

1 Jochen Rindt	Lotus 72-Ford	50	1h42m00.3
2 Jacky Ickx	Ferrari 312B	50	1h42m01.0
3 Denny Hulme	McLaren M14A-Ford	50	1h43m22.1
4 Emerson Fittipaldi	Lotus 49C-Ford	50	1h43m55.4

1970 DRIVERS' RECORDS

driver	car	ZA Q	ZA R	E Q	E R	MC Q	MC R	B Q	B R	NL Q	NL R	F Q	F R	GB Q	GB R	D Q	D R	A Q	A R	I Q	I R	CDN Q	CDN R	USA Q	USA R	MEX Q	MEX R
Andrea de Adamich	McLaren M7D-Alfa Romeo	-	-	19	DNQ	18	DNQ	-	-	-	-	15	NC	19	DNS	-	-	-	-	-	-	-	-	-	-	-	-
	McLaren M14D-Alfa Romeo	-	-	-	-	-	-	-	-	-	-	21	DNQ	-	-	-	-	23	DNQ	15	12	13	8	12	R	27	DNQ
Chris Amon	March 701-Ford	2	R	6	R	2	R	3	2F	4	R	3	2	18	5	6	R	6	8	21	7	6	3	5	5	5	4
Mario Andretti	March 701-Ford	11	R	16	3	-	-	-	-	-	-	-	-	9	R	9	R	18	R	-	-	-	-	-	-	-	-
Derek Bell	Brabham BT26-Ford	-	-	-	-	-	-	15	R	-	-	-	-	-	-	-	-	-	-	-	-	-	-	-	-	-	-
	Surtees TS7-Ford	-	-	-	-	-	-	-	-	-	-	-	-	-	-	-	-	-	-	-	-	-	-	13	6	-	-
Jean-Pierre Beltoise	Matra-Simca MS120	8	4	4	R	6	R	11	3	10	5	2	13	11	R	21	R	7	6	15	3	13	8	18	R	6	5
Jo Bonnier	McLaren M7C-Ford	-	-	-	-	-	-	-	-	-	-	-	-	-	-	-	-	24	DNQ	-	-	24	R	-	-	-	-
Jack Brabham	Brabham BT33-Ford	3	1F	1	RF	4	2	5	R	12	11	5	3F	2	2F	12	R	8	13	8	R	19	R	16	10	4	R
Francois Cevert	March 701-Ford	-	-	-	-	-	-	-	-	15	R	13	11	15	7	14	7	9	R	11	6	4	9	17	R	9	R
Dave Charlton	Lotus 49C-Ford	13	12	-	-	-	-	-	-	-	-	-	-	-	-	-	-	-	-	-	-	-	-	-	-	-	-
Piers Courage	De Tomaso 505/38-Ford	20	R	13	DNS	9	NC	12	R	9	R	-	-	-	-	-	-	-	-	-	-	-	-	-	-	-	-
George Eaton	BRM P139	23	R	-	-	-	-	-	-	-	-	-	-	-	-	-	-	-	-	-	-	-	-	-	-	-	-
	BRM P153	-	-	-	-	23	DNQ	20	DNQ	-	-	18	R	19	12	17	R	-	-	23	11	23	R	9	10	14	R
Emerson Fittipaldi	Lotus 49C-Ford	-	-	-	-	-	-	-	-	-	-	-	-	22	8	13	4	16	15	-	-	-	-	-	-	-	-
	Lotus 72-Ford	-	-	-	-	-	-	-	-	-	-	-	-	-	-	-	-	-	-	25	DNQ	-	-	3	1	18	R
Nanni Galli	McLaren M7D-Alfa Romeo	-	-	-	-	-	-	-	-	-	-	-	-	-	-	-	-	-	-	26	DNQ	-	-	-	-	-	-
Peter Gethin	McLaren M14A-Ford	-	-	-	-	-	-	-	-	-	-	11	R	-	-	17	R	21	10	17	9	11	6	21	14	10	R
Ignazio Giunti	Ferrari 312B	-	-	-	-	-	-	8	4	-	-	11	14	-	-	-	-	5	7	5	R	-	-	-	-	-	-
Dan Gurney	McLaren M14A-Ford	-	-	-	-	-	-	-	-	19	R	17	6	12	R	-	-	-	-	-	-	-	-	-	-	-	-
Hubert Hahne	March 701-Ford	-	-	-	-	-	-	-	-	-	-	-	-	-	-	25	DNQ	-	-	-	-	-	-	-	-	-	-
Graham Hill	Lotus 49C-Ford	19	6	15	4	12	5	16	R	20	NC	20	10	23	6	20	R	-	-	-	-	-	-	-	-	-	-
	Lotus 72-Ford	-	-	-	-	-	-	-	-	-	-	-	-	-	-	-	-	-	-	18	DNS	20	NC	10	R	8	R
Denny Hulme	McLaren M14A-Ford	6	2	2	R	3	4	-	-	-	-	-	-	-	-	16	3	11	R	9	4	15	R	11	7	14	3
	McLaren M14D-Ford	-	-	-	-	-	-	-	-	7	4	5	3	-	-	-	-	-	-	-	-	-	-	-	-	-	-
Gus Hutchison	Brabham BT26-Ford	-	-	-	-	-	-	-	-	-	-	-	-	-	-	-	-	-	-	-	-	-	-	22	R	-	-
Jacky Ickx	Ferrari 312B	5	R	7	R	5	R	4	8	3	3F	1	R	3	R	1	2F	3	1F	1	R	2	1	1	4F	3	1F
Piet de Klerk	Brabham BT26-Ford	21	11	-	-	-	-	-	-	-	-	-	-	-	-	-	-	-	-	-	-	-	-	-	-	-	-
John Love	Lotus 49-Ford	22	8	-	-	-	-	-	-	-	-	-	-	-	-	-	-	-	-	-	-	-	-	-	-	-	-
Pete Lovely	Lotus 49B-Ford	-	-	-	-	-	-	-	-	23	DNQ	23	DNQ	24	NC	-	-	-	-	-	-	-	-	26	DNQ	-	-
Bruce McLaren	McLaren M14A-Ford	10	R	11	2	10	R	-	-	-	-	-	-	-	-	-	-	-	-	-	-	-	-	-	-	-	-
John Miles	Lotus 49C-Ford	14	5	-	-	-	-	-	-	-	-	-	-	-	-	-	-	-	-	-	-	-	-	-	-	-	-
	Lotus 72-Ford	-	-	-	-	20	DNQ	21	DNQ	13	R	8	7	18	8	7	R	10	R	10	R	19	DNS	-	-	-	-
Silvio Moser	Bellasi F170-Ford	-	-	-	-	-	-	-	-	24	DNQ	-	-	-	-	24	DNQ	24	R	27	DNQ	-	-	-	-	-	-
Jackie Oliver	BRM P153	12	R	10	R	15	R	14	R	5	R	12	R	4	R	18	R	14	5	6	R	10	NC	7	R	13	7
Henri Pescarolo	Matra-Simca MS120	18	7	9	R	7	3	17	6	13	8	8	5	13	R	5	6	13	14	16	R	8	7	12	8	11	9
Ronnie Peterson	March 701-Ford	-	-	-	-	-	-	13	7	9	NC	16	9	9	R	14	9	19	R	-	-	14	R	16	NC	15	11
Brian Redman	Lotus 49C-Ford	NT	DNS	-	-	-	-	-	-	-	-	-	-	-	-	-	-	-	-	-	-	-	-	-	-	-	-
	De Tomaso 505/38-Ford	-	-	-	-	-	-	-	-	-	-	-	-	25	DNS	22	DNQ	-	-	-	-	-	-	-	-	-	-
Clay Regazzoni	Ferrari 312B	-	-	-	-	-	-	-	-	-	-	6	4	6	4	3	R	2	2F	3	1F	3	2F	6	13	1	2
Jochen Rindt	Lotus 49C-Ford	4	13	-	-	8	1F	2	R	-	-	-	-	-	-	-	-	-	-	-	-	-	-	-	-	-	-
	Lotus 72-Ford	-	-	8	R	-	-	-	-	1	1	1	1	6	1	1	1	1	R	12	DNS	-	-	-	-	-	-
Pedro Rodriguez	BRM P153	16	9	5	R	16	6	6	1	7	10	10	R	16	R	8	R	22	4	2	R	7	4	4	2	7	6
Tim Schenken	De Tomaso 505/38-Ford	-	-	-	-	-	-	-	-	-	-	-	-	-	-	-	-	19	R	22	R	17	NC	20	R	-	-
Johnny Servoz-Gavin	March 701-Ford	17	R	14	5	19	DNQ	-	-	-	-	-	-	-	-	-	-	-	-	-	-	-	-	-	-	-	-
Jo Siffert	March 701-Ford	9	10	21	DNQ	11	8	10	7	17	R	16	R	21	R	4	8	20	9	7	R	14	R	23	9	16	R
Alex Soler-Roig	Lotus 49C-Ford	-	-	22	DNQ	-	-	-	-	-	-	-	-	22	DNQ	-	-	-	-	-	-	-	-	-	-	-	-
	Lotus 72-Ford	-	-	-	-	-	-	-	-	18	DNQ	-	-	-	-	-	-	-	-	-	-	-	-	-	-	-	-
Jackie Stewart	March 701-Ford	1	3	3	1	1	R	1	R	2	2	4	9	8	R	7	R	4	R	4	2	-	-	-	-	-	-
	Tyrrell 001-Ford	-	-	-	-	-	-	-	-	-	-	-	-	-	-	-	-	-	-	-	-	1	R	2	R	2	R
Rolf Stommelen	Brabham BT33-Ford	15	R	17	R	17	DNQ	7	5	22	DNQ	14	7	10	DNS	11	5	17	3	20	5	18	R	19	12	17	R
John Surtees	McLaren M7C-Ford	7	RF	12	R	14	R	-	-	14	6	-	-	-	-	-	-	-	-	-	-	-	-	-	-	-	-
	Surtees TS7-Ford	-	-	-	-	-	-	-	-	-	-	-	-	20	R	15	9	12	R	10	R	5	5	8	R	15	8
Peter Westbury	BRM P153	-	-	-	-	-	-	-	-	-	-	-	-	-	-	-	-	-	-	-	-	-	-	25	DNQ	-	-
Reine Wisell	Lotus 72-Ford	-	-	-	-	-	-	-	-	-	-	-	-	-	-	-	-	-	-	-	-	-	-	9	3	12	NC

1970 FINAL CHAMPIONSHIP POSITIONS

Drivers					
1	Jochen Rindt	45	15=	Mario Andretti	4
2	Jacky Ickx	40		Reine Wisell	4
3	Clay Regazzoni	33	17=	Ignazio Giunti	3
4	Denny Hulme	27		John Surtees	3
5=	Jack Brabham	25	19=	John Miles	2
	Jackie Stewart	25		Jackie Oliver	2
7=	Chris Amon	23		Johnny Servoz-Gavin	2
	Pedro Rodriguez	23	22=	Derek Bell	1
9	Jean-Pierre Beltoise	16		Francois Cevert	1
10	Emerson Fittipaldi	12		Peter Gethin	1
11	Rolf Stommelen	10		Dan Gurney	1
12	Henri Pescarolo	8			
13	Graham Hill	7			
14	Bruce McLaren	6			

Sum of best six results from the first seven races and best five results from the final six races

Manufacturers		
1	Lotus-Ford	59
2	Ferrari	52 (55)*
3	March-Ford	48
4=	Brabham-Ford	35
	McLaren-Ford	35
6=	BRM	23
	Matra-Simca	23
8	Surtees-Ford	3

*Sum of best six results from the first seven races and best five results from the final six races. Points only awarded to first car to finish for each manufacturer

5 Rolf Stommelen Brabham BT33-Ford 49
6 Henri Pescarolo Matra-Simca MS120 49
Winner's average speed: 124.082 mph. Starting grid front row: Ickx, 1m59.5 (pole) and Rindt, 1m59.7. Fastest lap: Ickx, 2m00.5. Leaders: Ickx, laps 1-6, 10-17, 26-31, 36-43, 45-46, 48; Rindt, 7-9, 18-21, 24-25, 32-35, 44, 47, 49-50; Regazzoni, 22-23

GROSSER PREIS VON OSTERREICH

16 August 1970. Osterreichring. 60 laps of a 3.673-mile circuit = 220.380 miles. Warm, dry and sunny. World Championship round 9

1	Jacky Ickx	Ferrari 312B	60	1h42m17.32
2	Clay Regazzoni	Ferrari 312B	60	1h42m17.93
3	Rolf Stommelen	Brabham BT33-Ford	60	1h43m45.20
4	Pedro Rodriguez	BRM P153	59	
5	Jackie Oliver	BRM P153	59	
6	Jean-Pierre Beltoise	Matra-Simca MS120	59	

Winner's average speed: 129.269 mph. Starting grid front row: Rindt, 1m39.23 (pole) and Regazzoni, 1m39.70. Fastest lap: Ickx and Regazzoni, 1m40.4. Leaders: Regazzoni, lap 1; Ickx, laps 2-60

GRAN PREMIO D'ITALIA

6 September 1970. Monza. 68 laps of a 3.573-mile circuit = 242.964 miles. Hot, dry and sunny. World Championship round 10

1	Clay Regazzoni	Ferrari 312B	68	1h39m06.88
2	Jackie Stewart	March 701-Ford	68	1h39m12.61
3	Jean-Pierre Beltoise	Matra-Simca MS120	68	1h39m12.68
4	Denny Hulme	McLaren M14A-Ford	68	1h39m13.03
5	Rolf Stommelen	Brabham BT33-Ford	68	1h39m13.29
6	Francois Cevert	March 701-Ford	68	1h40m10.34

Winner's average speed: 147.081 mph. Starting grid front row: Ickx, 1m24.14 (pole) and Rodriguez, 1m24.36. Fastest lap: Regazzoni, 1m25.2. Leaders: Ickx, laps 1-3, 19-20; Rodriguez, 4, 7-8; Stewart, 5-6, 9, 11, 14-17, 26, 31, 35, 37, 42-43, 51, 53; Regazzoni, 10, 12, 32-34, 36, 38-41, 44-50, 52, 54-68; Oliver, 13, 18, 21-25, 27-28, 30; Hulme, 29

GRAND PRIX DU CANADA

20 September 1970. St Jovite. 90 laps of a 2.650-mile circuit = 238.500 miles. Warm, dry and sunny. World Championship round 11

1	Jacky Ickx	Ferrari 312B	90	2h21m18.4
2	Clay Regazzoni	Ferrari 312B	90	2h21m33.2
3	Chris Amon	March 701-Ford	90	2h22m16.3
4	Pedro Rodriguez	BRM P153	89	
5	John Surtees	Surtees TS7-Ford	89	
6	Peter Gethin	McLaren M14A-Ford	88	

Winner's average speed: 101.269 mph. Starting grid front row: Stewart, 1m31.5 (pole) and Ickx, 1m31.6. Fastest lap: Regazzoni, 1m32.2. Leaders: Stewart, laps 1-31; Ickx, 32-90

UNITED STATES GRAND PRIX

4 October 1970. Watkins Glen. 108 laps of a 2.350-mile circuit = 253.800
miles. Cool, dry and cloudy. World Championship round 12

1	Emerson Fittipaldi	Lotus 72-Ford	108	1h57m32.79
2	Pedro Rodriguez	BRM P153	108	1h58m09.18
3	Reine Wisell	Lotus 72-Ford	108	1h58m17.96
4	Jacky Ickx	Ferrari 312B	107	
5	Chris Amon	March 701-Ford	107	
6	Derek Bell	Surtees TS7-Ford	107	

Winner's average speed: 129.549 mph. Starting grid front row: Ickx, 1m03.07 (pole) and Stewart, 1m03.62. Fastest lap: Ickx, 1m02.74. Leaders: Stewart, laps 1-82; Rodriguez, 83-100; Fittipaldi, 101-108

GRAN PREMIO DE MEXICO

25 October 1970. Mexico City. 65 laps of a 3.107-mile circuit = 201.955 miles. Warm, dry and sunny. World Championship round 13

1	Jacky Ickx	Ferrari 312B	65	1h53m28.36
2	Clay Regazzoni	Ferrari 312B	65	1h54m13.82
3	Denny Hulme	McLaren M14A-Ford	65	1h54m14.33
4	Chris Amon	March 701-Ford	65	1h54m15.41
5	Jean-Pierre Beltoise	Matra-Simca MS120	65	1h54m18.47
6	Pedro Rodriguez	BRM P153	65	1h54m53.12

Winner's average speed: 106.786 mph. Starting grid front row: Regazzoni, 1m41.86 (pole) and Stewart, 1m41.88. Fastest lap: Ickx, 1m43.11. Leaders: Regazzoni, lap 1; Ickx, laps 2-65

1971

In his first full year as a constructor, Ken Tyrrell gave Jackie Stewart a car that was both quick and reliable. Stewart delivered six wins for the team—a dominating performance reminiscent of his fellow Scotsman Jim Clark. Adding to the Tyrrell success, Stewart's charismatic young teammate Francois Cevert scored his first victory at the final race of the year on the newly extended Watkins Glen circuit.

A strong challenge had been expected from Ferrari, which enjoyed a power advantage over its Ford Cosworth rivals. Race wins did materialise, at the opening Grand Prix in South Africa where Mario Andretti inherited his first victory after Denny Hulme was delayed in the closing laps, and for Jacky Ickx in Holland. But the team failed to sustain a yearlong championship challenge.

Ronnie Peterson ended his second year in the World Championship as runner-up, having joined the works March team. Although he did not win a race, he finished second on four occasions and also won the European Formula 2 Trophy for the team.

BRM scored successive victories in late summer: Jo

Siffert won in Austria despite a last lap puncture, and Peter Gethin in Italy. The latter was the closest and fastest Grand Prix victory of all time—the first five cars separated by just 0.61 seconds, at an average speed of over 150mph. But tragedy dogged the team as Siffert and Pedro Rodriguez died while competing outside the championship.

Lotus suffered its first year without a win since 1959, despite the previous success of the Lotus 72 and Emerson Fittipaldi's promise.

Major technical developments included the introduction of slick (untreaded) tyres and airboxes, which boosted power by increasing the air pressure into the engine. In addition, Lotus experimented with the Pratt & Whitney gas turbine engine. The spread of sponsorship saw the British Grand Prix supported by the Wool Marketing Board for the first time. But while slick tyres, airboxes, and race sponsorship all proved successful, gas turbines did not catch on.

SOUTH AFRICAN GRAND PRIX

6 March 1971. Kyalami. 79 laps of a 2.550-mile circuit = 201.450 miles. Hot, dry and sunny. World Championship round 1

1 Mario Andretti	Ferrari 312B	79	1h47m35.5
2 Jackie Stewart	Tyrrell 001-Ford	79	1h47m56.4
3 Clay Regazzoni	Ferrari 312B	79	1h48m06.9
4 Reine Wisell	Lotus 72C-Ford	79	1h48m44.9
5 Chris Amon	Matra-Simca MS120B	78	
6 Denny Hulme	McLaren M19A-Ford	78	

Winner's average speed: 112.341 mph. Starting grid front row: Stewart, 1m17.8 (pole), Amon, 1m18.4 and Regazzoni, 1m18.7. Fastest lap: Andretti, 1m20.3. Leaders: Regazzoni, laps 1-16; Hulme, 17-75; Andretti, 76-79

GRAN PREMIO DE ESPANA

18 April 1971. Montjuich Park. 75 laps of a 2.355-mile circuit = 176.625 miles. Hot, dry and sunny. World Championship round 2

1 Jackie Stewart	Tyrrell 003-Ford	75	1h49m03.4
2 Jacky Ickx	Ferrari 312B	75	1h49m06.8
3 Chris Amon	Matra-Simca MS120B	75	1h50m01.5
4 Pedro Rodriguez	BRM P160	75	1h50m21.3
5 Denny Hulme	McLaren M19A-Ford	75	1h50m30.4
6 Jean-Pierre Beltoise	Matra-Simca MS120B	74	

Winner's average speed: 97.174 mph. Starting grid front row: Ickx, 1m25.9 (pole), Regazzoni, 1m26.0 and Amon, 1m26.0. Fastest lap: Ickx, 1m25.1. Leaders: Ickx, laps 1-5; Stewart, 6-75

GRAND PRIX DE MONACO

23 May 1971. Monte Carlo. 80 laps of a 1.954-mile circuit = 156.320 miles. Dry and overcast. World Championship round 3

1 Jackie Stewart	Tyrrell 003-Ford	80	1h52m21.3
2 Ronnie Peterson	March 711-Ford	80	1h52m46.9
3 Jacky Ickx	Ferrari 312B	80	1h53m14.6
4 Denny Hulme	McLaren M19A-Ford	80	1h53m28.0
5 Emerson Fittipaldi	Lotus 72D-Ford	79	
6 Rolf Stommelen	Surtees TS9-Ford	79	

Winner's average speed: 83.478 mph. Starting grid front row: Stewart, 1m23.2 (pole) and Ickx, 1m24.4. Fastest lap: Stewart, 1m22.2. Leaders: Stewart, laps 1-80

GROTE PRIJS VAN NEDERLAND

20 June 1971. Zandvoort. 70 laps of a 2.605-mile circuit = 182.350 miles. Wet. World Championship round 4

1 Jacky Ickx	Ferrari 312B2	70	1h56m20.09
2 Pedro Rodriguez	BRM P160	70	1h56m28.08
3 Clay Regazzoni	Ferrari 312B2	69	
4 Ronnie Peterson	March 711-Ford	68	

5 John Surtees	Surtees TS9-Ford	68	
6 Jo Siffert	BRM P160	68	

Winner's average speed: 94.047 mph. Starting grid front row: Ickx, 1m17.42 (pole), Rodriguez, 1m17.46 and Stewart, 1m17.64. Fastest lap: Ickx, 1m34.95. Leaders: Ickx, laps 1-8, 30, 32-70; Rodriguez, 9-29, 31

GRAND PRIX DE FRANCE

4 July 1971. Paul Ricard. 55 laps of a 3.610-mile circuit = 198.550 miles. Hot, dry and sunny. World Championship round 5

1 Jackie Stewart	Tyrrell 003-Ford	55	1h46m41.68
2 Francois Cevert	Tyrrell 002-Ford	55	1h47m09.80
3 Emerson Fittipaldi	Lotus 72D-Ford	55	1h47m15.75
4 Jo Siffert	BRM P160	55	1h47m18.85
5 Chris Amon	Matra-Simca MS120B	55	1h47m22.76
6 Reine Wisell	Lotus 72D-Ford	55	1h47m57.66

Winner's average speed: 111.655 mph. Starting grid front row: Stewart, 1m50.71 (pole), Regazzoni, 1m51.53 and Ickx, 1m51.88. Fastest lap: Stewart, 1m54.09. Leaders: Stewart, laps 1-55

WOOLMARK BRITISH GRAND PRIX

17 July 1971. Silverstone. 68 laps of a 2.927-mile circuit = 199.036 miles. Warm, dry and sunny. World Championship round 6

1 Jackie Stewart	Tyrrell 003-Ford	68	1h31m31.5
2 Ronnie Peterson	March 711-Ford	68	1h32m07.6
3 Emerson Fittipaldi	Lotus 72D-Ford	68	1h32m22.0
4 Henri Pescarolo	March 711-Ford	67	
5 Rolf Stommelen	Surtees TS9-Ford	67	
6 John Surtees	Surtees TS9-Ford	67	

Winner's average speed: 130.480 mph. Starting grid front row: Regazzoni, 1m18.1 (pole), Stewart, 1m18.1 and Siffert, 1m18.2. Fastest lap: Stewart, 1m19.9. Leaders: Regazzoni, laps 1-3; Stewart, 4-68

GROSSER PREIS VON DEUTSCHLAND

1 August 1971. Nurburgring. 12 laps of a 14.189-mile circuit = 170.268 miles. Warm, dry and sunny. World Championship round 7

1 Jackie Stewart	Tyrrell 003-Ford	12	1h29m15.7
2 Francois Cevert	Tyrrell 002-Ford	12	1h29m45.8
3 Clay Regazzoni	Ferrari 312B2	12	1h29m52.8
4 Mario Andretti	Ferrari 312B2	12	1h31m20.7
5 Ronnie Peterson	March 711-Ford	12	1h31m44.8
6 Tim Schenken	Brabham BT33-Ford	12	1h32m14.3

Winner's average speed: 114.451 mph. Starting grid front row: Stewart, 7m19.0 (pole) and Ickx, 7m19.2. Fastest lap: Cevert, 7m20.1. Leaders: Stewart, laps 1-12

GROSSER PREIS VON OSTERREICH

15 August 1971. Osterreichring. 54 laps of a 3.673-mile circuit = 198.342 miles. Warm, dry and sunny. World Championship round 8

1 Jo Siffert	BRM P160	54	1h30m23.91
2 Emerson Fittipaldi	Lotus 72D-Ford	54	1h30m28.03
3 Tim Schenken	Brabham BT33-Ford	54	1h30m43.68
4 Reine Wisell	Lotus 72D-Ford	54	1h30m55.78
5 Graham Hill	Brabham BT34-Ford	54	1h31m12.34
6 Henri Pescarolo	March 711-Ford	54	1h31m48.42

Winner's average speed: 131.645 mph. Starting grid front row: Siffert, 1m37.44 (pole) and Stewart, 1m37.65. Fastest lap: Siffert, 1m38.47. Leaders: Siffert, laps 1-54

GRAN PREMIO D'ITALIA

5 September 1971. Monza. 55 laps of a 3.573-mile circuit = 196.515 miles. Hot, dry and sunny. World Championship round 9

1 Peter Gethin	BRM P160	55	1h18m12.60
2 Ronnie Peterson	March 711-Ford	55	1h18m12.61
3 Francois Cevert	Tyrrell 002-Ford	55	1h18m12.69
4 Mike Hailwood	Surtees TS9-Ford	55	1h18m12.78
5 Howden Ganley	BRM P160	55	1h18m13.21
6 Chris Amon	Matra-Simca MS120B	55	1h18m44.96

Winner's average speed: 150.759 mph. Starting grid front row: Amon, 1m22.40 (pole) and Ickx, 1m22.82. Fastest lap: Pescarolo, 1m23.80.

1971 DRIVERS' RECORDS

driver	car	ZA		E		MC		NL		F		GB		D		A		I		CDN		USA	
		Q	R	Q	R	Q	R	Q	R	Q	R	Q	R	Q	R	Q	R	Q	R	Q	R	Q	R
Andrea de Adamich	March 711-Alfa Romeo	22	13	18	R	-	-	-	-	21	R	24	NC	20	R	-	-	20	R	-	-	28	11
Chris Amon	Matra-Simca MS120B	2	5	5	3	3	4	R	5	R	9	5	9	R	16	R	-	1	6	5	10	9	12
Mario Andretti	Ferrari 312B	4	1F	8	R	20	DNQ	18	R	-	-	-	-	-	-	-	-	-	-	-	-	-	-
	Ferrari 312B2	-	-	-	-	-	-	-	-	-	-	11	4	-	-	-	-	-	-	13	13	6	DNS
Skip Barber	March 711-Ford	-	-	-	-	-	-	23	DNQ	24	NC	-	-	-	-	-	-	-	-	24	R	27	NC
Derek Bell	Surtees TS9-Ford	-	-	-	-	-	-	-	-	-	-	23	R	-	-	-	-	-	-	-	-	-	-
Jean-Pierre Beltoise	Matra-Simca MS120B	-	-	6	6	7	R	11	9	8	7	15	7	-	-	-	-	-	-	11	R	11	8
Mike Beuttler	March 711-Ford	-	-	-	-	-	-	-	-	-	-	20	R	22	DSQ	19	NC	16	R	22	NC	-	-
Jo Bonnier	McLaren M7C-Ford	23	R	-	-	-	-	-	-	-	-	23	DNQ	20	DNS	21	10	-	-	-	-	31	16
John Cannon	BRM P153	-	-	-	-	-	-	-	-	-	-	-	-	-	-	-	-	-	-	-	-	26	14
Francois Cevert	Tyrrell 002-Ford	9	R	12	7	15	R	12	R	7	2	10	10	5	2F	3	R	5	3	3	6	5	1
Dave Charlton	Brabham BT33-Ford	12	R	-	-	-	-	-	-	-	-	-	-	-	-	-	-	-	-	-	-	-	-
	Lotus 72D-Ford	-	-	-	-	-	-	NT	DNP	-	-	13	R	-	-	-	-	-	-	-	-	-	-
Chris Craft	Brabham BT33-Ford	-	-	-	-	-	-	-	-	-	-	-	-	-	-	-	-	-	-	25	DNS	30	R
Mark Donohue	McLaren M19A-Ford	-	-	-	-	-	-	-	-	-	-	-	-	-	-	-	-	-	-	8	3	19	DNS
George Eaton	BRM P160	-	-	-	-	-	-	-	-	-	-	-	-	-	-	-	-	-	-	21	15	-	-
Vic Elford	BRM P160	-	-	-	-	-	-	-	-	-	-	-	-	18	11	-	-	-	-	-	-	-	-
Emerson Fittipaldi	Lotus 72C-Ford	5	R	14	R	-	-	-	-	-	-	-	-	-	-	-	-	-	-	-	-	-	-
	Lotus 72D-Ford	-	-	-	-	17	5	-	-	17	3	4	3	8	R	5	2	-	-	4	7	2	NC
	Lotus 56B-Pratt & Whitney	-	-	-	-	-	-	-	-	-	-	-	-	-	-	-	-	18	8	-	-	-	-
Nanni Galli	March 711-Alfa Romeo	-	-	-	-	21	DNQ	20	R	-	-	-	-	21	12	15	12	-	-	-	-	-	-
	March 711-Ford	-	-	-	-	-	-	-	-	20	DNS	21	11	-	-	-	-	19	R	20	NC	25	R
Howden Ganley	BRM P153	24	R	17	10	19	DNQ	9	7	16	10	11	8	14	R	-	-	-	-	-	-	-	-
	BRM P160	-	-	-	-	-	-	-	-	-	-	-	-	-	-	14	R	4	5	9	DNS	13	4
Peter Gethin	McLaren M14A-Ford	11	R	7	8	14	R	-	-	-	-	-	-	-	-	-	-	-	-	-	-	-	-
	McLaren M19A-Ford	-	-	-	-	-	-	23	NC	19	9	14	R	19	R	-	-	-	-	-	-	-	-
	BRM P160	-	-	-	-	-	-	-	-	-	-	-	-	-	-	16	10	11	1	16	14	23	9
Mike Hailwood	Surtees TS9-Ford	-	-	-	-	-	-	-	-	-	-	-	-	-	-	-	-	17	4	-	-	15	15
Graham Hill	Brabham BT33-Ford	19	9	-	-	-	-	-	-	-	-	-	-	-	-	-	-	-	-	-	-	-	-
	Brabham BT34-Ford	-	-	15	R	9	R	16	10	4	R	16	R	13	9	8	5	14	R	15	R	20	7
David Hobbs	McLaren M19A-Ford	-	-	-	-	-	-	-	-	-	-	-	-	-	-	-	-	-	-	-	-	24	10
Denny Hulme	McLaren M19A-Ford	7	6	9	5	6	4	14	12	11	R	8	R	6	R	9	R	-	-	10	4F	3	R
Jacky Ickx	Ferrari 312B	8	8	1	2F	-	-	-	-	-	-	-	-	-	-	-	-	-	-	-	-	-	-
	Ferrari 312B2	-	-	-	-	2	3	1	1F	3	R	6	R	2	R	6	R	-	-	12	8	-	-
Jean-Pierre Jarier	March 701-Ford	-	-	-	-	-	-	-	-	-	-	-	-	-	-	-	-	-	-	24	NC	-	-
Niki Lauda	March 711-Ford	-	-	-	-	-	-	-	-	-	-	-	-	-	-	21	R	-	-	-	-	-	-
Gijs van Lennep	Surtees TS7-Ford	-	-	-	-	-	-	21	8	-	-	-	-	-	-	-	-	-	-	-	-	-	-
	Surtees TS9-Ford	-	-	-	-	-	-	-	-	-	-	-	-	-	-	-	-	-	-	-	-	29	DNS
John Love	March 701-Ford	21	R	-	-	-	-	-	-	-	-	-	-	-	-	-	-	-	-	-	-	-	-
Pete Lovely	Lotus 69-Ford	-	-	-	-	-	-	-	-	-	-	-	-	-	-	-	-	-	-	26	NC	32	NC
Helmut Marko	McLaren M7C-Ford	-	-	-	-	-	-	-	-	-	-	NT	DNQ	-	-	-	-	-	-	-	-	-	-
	BRM P153	-	-	-	-	-	-	-	-	-	-	-	-	-	-	17	11	12	R	19	12	-	-
	BRM P160	-	-	-	-	-	-	-	-	-	-	-	-	-	-	-	-	-	-	-	-	17	13
Jean Max	March 701-Ford	-	-	-	-	-	-	-	-	23	NC	-	-	-	-	-	-	-	-	-	-	-	-
Francois Mazet	March 701-Ford	-	-	-	-	-	-	-	-	24	13	-	-	-	-	-	-	-	-	-	-	-	-
Silvio Moser	Bellasi F170-Ford	-	-	-	-	-	-	-	-	-	-	-	-	-	-	-	-	22	R	-	-	-	-
Jackie Oliver	McLaren M14A-Ford	-	-	-	-	-	-	-	-	-	-	22	R	-	-	-	-	13	7	-	-	-	-
	McLaren M19A-Ford	-	-	-	-	-	-	-	-	-	-	-	-	-	-	22	9	-	-	-	-	-	-
Henri Pescarolo	March 701-Ford	18	11	-	-	-	-	-	-	-	-	-	-	-	-	-	-	-	-	-	-	-	-
	March 711-Ford	-	-	11	R	13	8	15	NC	18	R	17	4	10	R	13	6	10	RF	27	DNS	22	R
Ronnie Peterson	March 711-Ford	13	10	13	R	8	2	13	4	-	-	5	2	7	5	11	8	6	2	6	2	12	3
	March 711-Alfa Romeo	-	-	-	-	-	-	-	-	12	R	-	-	-	-	-	-	-	-	-	-	-	-
Sam Posey	Surtees TS9-Ford	-	-	-	-	-	-	-	-	-	-	-	-	-	-	-	-	-	-	-	-	18	R
Jackie Pretorius	Brabham BT26-Ford	20	R	-	-	-	-	-	-	-	-	-	-	-	-	-	-	-	-	-	-	-	-
Brian Redman	Surtees TS7-Ford	17	7	-	-	-	-	-	-	-	-	-	-	-	-	-	-	-	-	-	-	-	-
Clay Regazzoni	Ferrari 312B	3	3	2	R	-	-	-	-	-	-	-	-	-	-	-	-	-	-	-	-	-	-
	Ferrari 312B2	-	-	-	-	11	R	4	3	2	R	1	R	4	3	4	R	8	R	18	R	4	6
Peter Revson	Tyrrell 001-Ford	-	-	-	-	-	-	-	-	-	-	-	-	-	-	-	-	-	-	-	-	21	R
Pedro Rodriguez	BRM P160	10	R	5	4	5	9	2	2	5	R	-	-	-	-	-	-	-	-	-	-	-	-
Tim Schenken	Brabham BT33-Ford	-	-	21	9	18	10	19	R	14	12	7	12	9	6	7	3	9	R	17	R	16	R
Jo Siffert	BRM P153	16	R	-	-	-	-	-	-	-	-	-	-	-	-	-	-	-	-	-	-	-	-
	BRM P160	-	-	10	R	3	R	8	6	6	4	3	9	3	R	1	1F	3	9	2	9	7	2
Alex Soler-Roig	March 711-Ford	25	R	20	R	22	DNQ	17	R	22	R	-	-	-	-	-	-	-	-	-	-	-	-
Jackie Stewart	Tyrrell 001-Ford	1	2	-	-	-	-	-	-	-	-	-	-	-	-	-	-	-	-	-	-	-	-
	Tyrrell 003-Ford	-	-	4	1	1	1F	3	11	1	1F	2	1F	1	1	2	R	7	R	1	1	1	5

driver	car	ZA		E		MC		NL		F		GB		D		A		I		CDN		USA	
		Q	R	Q	R	Q	R	Q	R	Q	R	Q	R	Q	R	Q	R	Q	R	Q	R	Q	R
Rolf Stommelen	Surtees TS7-Ford	15	12	-	-	-	-	-	-	-	-	-	-	-	-	-	-	-	-	-	-	-	-
	Surtees TS9-Ford	-	-	19	R	16	6	10	DSQ	10	11	12	5	12	10	12	7	23	DNS	23	R	-	-
John Surtees	Surtees TS9-Ford	6	R	22	NC	10	7	7	5	13	8	18	6	15	7	18	R	15	R	14	11	14	17
Dave Walker	Lotus 56B-Pratt & Whitney	-	-	-	-	-	-	22	R	-	-	-	-	-	-	-	-	-	-	-	-	-	-
Reine Wisell	Lotus 72C-Ford	14	4	16	NC	12	R	-	-	-	-	-	-	-	-	-	-	-	-	-	-	-	-
	Lotus 72D-Ford	-	-	-	-	-	-	6	DSQ	15	6	-	-	17	8	10	4	-	-	7	5	10	R
	Lotus 56B-Pratt & Whitney	-	-	-	-	-	-	-	-	-	-	19	NC	-	-	-	-	-	-	-	-	-	-

1971 FINAL CHAMPIONSHIP POSITIONS

Drivers						Manufacturers		
1	Jackie Stewart	62	14=	Howden Ganley	5	1	Tyrrell-Ford	73
2	Ronnie Peterson	33		Tim Schenken	5	2	BRM	36
3	Francois Cevert	26	16=	Mark Donohue	4	3=	Ferrari	33
4=	Jacky Ickx	19		Henri Pescarolo	4		March-Ford	33 (34)*
	Jo Siffert	19	18=	Mike Hailwood	3	5	Lotus-Ford	21
6	Emerson Fittipaldi	16		Rolf Stommelen	3	6	McLaren-Ford	10
7	Clay Regazzoni	13		John Surtees	3	7	Matra-Simca	9
8	Mario Andretti	12	21	Graham Hill	2	8	Surtees-Ford	8
9=	Chris Amon	9	22	Jean-Pierre Beltoise	1	9	Brabham-Ford	5
	Peter Gethin	9	Sum of best five results from the first six			*Sum of best five results from the first six		
	Denny Hulme	9	races and best four results from the final			races and best four results from the final		
	Pedro Rodriguez	9	five races			five races. Points only awarded to first car		
	Reine Wisell	9				to finish for each manufacturer		

Leaders: Regazzoni, laps 1-3, 9; Peterson, 4-7, 10-14, 17-22, 24, 26, 33, 47-50, 54; Stewart, 8; Cevert, 15-16, 23, 31-32, 34, 36; Hailwood, 25, 27, 35, 42, 51; Siffert, 28-30; Amon, 37-41, 43-46; Gethin, 52-53, 55

CANADIAN GRAND PRIX

19 September 1971. Mosport Park. 64 laps of a 2.459-mile circuit = 157.376 miles. Race scheduled for 80 laps but stopped early due to rain. Wet. World Championship round 10

1	Jackie Stewart	Tyrrell 003-Ford	64	1h55m12.9
2	Ronnie Peterson	March 711-Ford	64	1h55m51.2
3	Mark Donohue	McLaren M19A-Ford	64	1h56m48.7
4	Denny Hulme	McLaren M19A-Ford	63	
5	Reine Wisell	Lotus 72D-Ford	63	
6	Francois Cevert	Tyrrell 002-Ford	62	

Winner's average speed: 81.956 mph. Starting grid front row: Stewart, 1m15.3 (pole), Siffert, 1m15.5 and Cevert, 1m15.7. Fastest lap: Hulme, 1m43.5. Leaders: Stewart, laps 1-17, 31-64; Peterson, 18-30

UNITED STATES GRAND PRIX

3 October 1971. Watkins Glen. 59 laps of a 3.377-mile circuit = 199.243 miles. Warm, dry and sunny. World Championship round 11

1	Francois Cevert	Tyrrell 002-Ford	59	1h43m51.991
2	Jo Siffert	BRM P160	59	1h44m32.053
3	Ronnie Peterson	March 711-Ford	59	1h44m36.061
4	Howden Ganley	BRM P160	59	1h44m48.740
5	Jackie Stewart	Tyrrell 003-Ford	59	1h44m51.994
6	Clay Regazzoni	Ferrari 312B2	59	1h45m08.417

Winner's average speed: 115.096 mph. Starting grid front row: Stewart, 1m42.642 (pole), Fittipaldi, 1m42.659 and Hulme, 1m42.925. Fastest lap: Ickx, 1m43.474. Leaders: Stewart, laps 1-13; Cevert, 14-59

1972

At age 25, Emerson Fittipaldi became the youngest World Champion to date just two years after his Grand Prix debut. The Brazilian dominated the European races and secured the title with two events to go in the three-year-old but ever more competitive Lotus 72. Lotus sponsors Players cigarettes switched marketing to their John Player Special brand, and the classic black and gold livery appeared for the first time.

Reigning champion Jackie Stewart was Fittipaldi's closest challenger, despite missing the Belgian GP with a stomach ulcer. Equipped with a new Tyrrell, Stewart soon returned to form, winning the final two Grands Prix.

Jean-Pierre Beltoise scored the only Grand Prix win of his career, dominating the Monaco Grand Prix for BRM in one of the wettest races on record. This proved to be the last victory for the once-great BRM marque. Jacky Ickx's win at the Nurburgring proved the highlight of a disappointing year for Ferrari, while Ronnie Peterson and Niki Lauda had disastrous seasons in the difficult March 721X. A more conventional car (the 721G) was introduced for the French GP, but Peterson's third in Germany was the team's only podium finish.

Bernie Ecclestone, a successful businessman who had occasionally entered ex-works Connaughts in 1958, bought the Brabham team from Ron Tauranac. On his Grand Prix debut for the team, Carlos Reutemann qualified on pole for his home Argentinian GP, and won the non-championship Brazilian race.

Denny Hulme scored McLaren's only win of the year at Kyalami, and Jody Scheckter made an impressive start in the formula for the team at the final round, running third before spinning. Chris Amon showed promise in the new V12 Matra but, as ever, he scored no victories.

Rival tyre companies Firestone and Goodyear introduced qualifying tyres in their fight for pole position. These were made of a super-soft compound of rubber, which gave improved performance, but they only lasted for a few laps and increased costs.

Formula 1

GRAN PREMIO DE LA REPUBLICA ARGENTINA

23 January 1972. Buenos Aires. 95 laps of a 2.079-mile circuit = 197.505 miles. Very hot, dry and sunny. World Championship round 1

1 Jackie Stewart	Tyrrell 003-Ford	95	1h57m58.82
2 Denny Hulme	McLaren M19A-Ford	95	1h58m24.78
3 Jacky Ickx	Ferrari 312B2	95	1h58m58.21
4 Clay Regazzoni	Ferrari 312B2	95	1h59m05.54
5 Tim Schenken	Surtees TS9B-Ford	95	1h59m07.93
6 Ronnie Peterson	March 721-Ford	94	

Winner's average speed: 100.443 mph. Starting grid front row: Reutemann, 1m12.46 (pole) and Stewart, 1m12.68. Fastest lap: Stewart, 1m13.66. Leaders: Stewart, laps 1-95

SOUTH AFRICAN GRAND PRIX

4 March 1972. Kyalami. 79 laps of a 2.550-mile circuit = 201.450 miles. Hot, dry and sunny. World Championship round 2

1 Denny Hulme	McLaren M19A-Ford	79	1h45m49.1
2 Emerson Fittipaldi	Lotus 72D-Ford	79	1h46m03.2
3 Peter Revson	McLaren M19A-Ford	79	1h46m14.9
4 Mario Andretti	Ferrari 312B2	79	1h46m27.6
5 Ronnie Peterson	March 721-Ford	79	1h46m38.1
6 Graham Hill	Brabham BT33-Ford	78	

Winner's average speed: 114.224 mph. Starting grid front row: Stewart, 1m17.0 (pole), Regazzoni, 1m17.3 and Fittipaldi, 1m17.4. Fastest lap: Hailwood, 1m18.9. Leaders: Hulme, laps 1, 57-79; Stewart, 2-44; Fittipaldi, 45-56

GRAN PREMIO DE ESPANA

1 May 1972. Jarama. 90 laps of a 2.115-mile circuit = 190.386 miles. Cold and windy with showers. World Championship round 3

1 Emerson Fittipaldi	Lotus 72D-Ford	90	2h03m41.23
2 Jacky Ickx	Ferrari 312B2	90	2h04m00.15
3 Clay Regazzoni	Ferrari 312B2	89	
4 Andrea de Adamich	Surtees TS9B-Ford	89	
5 Peter Revson	McLaren M19A-Ford	89	
6 Carlos Pace	March 711-Ford	89	

Winner's average speed: 92.355 mph. Starting grid front row: Ickx, 1m18.43 (pole), Hulme, 1m19.18 and E Fittipaldi, 1m19.26. Fastest lap: Ickx, 1m21.01. Leaders: Hulme, laps 1-4; Stewart, 5-8; Fittipaldi, 9-90

GRAND PRIX DE MONACO

14 May 1972. Monte Carlo. 80 laps of a 1.954-mile circuit = 156.320 miles. Very wet. World Championship round 4

1 Jean-Pierre Beltoise	BRM P160B	80	2h26m54.7
2 Jacky Ickx	Ferrari 312B2	80	2h27m32.9
3 Emerson Fittipaldi	Lotus 72D-Ford	79	
4 Jackie Stewart	Tyrrell 004-Ford	78	
5 Brian Redman	McLaren M19A-Ford	77	
6 Chris Amon	Matra-Simca MS120C	77	

Winner's average speed: 63.842 mph. Starting grid front row: E Fittipaldi, 1m21.4 (pole) and Ickx, 1m21.6. Fastest lap: Beltoise, 1m40.0. Leaders: Beltoise, laps 1-80

GRAND PRIX DE BELGIQUE

4 June 1972. Nivelles. 85 laps of a 2.314-mile circuit = 196.690 miles. Warm, dry and sunny. World Championship round 5

1 Emerson Fittipaldi	Lotus 72D-Ford	85	1h44m06.7
2 Francois Cevert	Tyrrell 002-Ford	85	1h44m33.3
3 Denny Hulme	McLaren M19C-Ford	85	1h45m04.8
4 Mike Hailwood	Surtees TS9B-Ford	85	1h45m18.7
5 Carlos Pace	March 711-Ford	84	
6 Chris Amon	Matra-Simca MS120C	84	

Winner's average speed: 113.353 mph. Starting grid front row: E Fittipaldi, 1m11.43 (pole), Regazzoni, 1m11.58 and Hulme, 1m11.80. Fastest lap: Amon, 1m12.12. Leaders: Regazzoni, laps 1-8; E Fittipaldi, 9-85

GRAND PRIX DE FRANCE

2 July 1972. Clermont-Ferrand. 38 laps of a 5.005-mile circuit = 190.190 miles. Warm, dry and sunny. World Championship round 6

1 Jackie Stewart	Tyrrell 003-Ford	38	1h52m21.5
2 Emerson Fittipaldi	Lotus 72D-Ford	38	1h52m49.2
3 Chris Amon	Matra-Simca MS120D	38	1h52m53.4
4 Francois Cevert	Tyrrell 002-Ford	38	1h53m10.8
5 Ronnie Peterson	March 721G-Ford	38	1h53m18.3
6 Mike Hailwood	Surtees TS9B-Ford	38	1h53m57.6

Winner's average speed: 101.563 mph. Starting grid front row: Amon, 2m53.4 (pole) and Hulme, 2m54.2. Fastest lap: Amon, 2m53.9. Leaders: Amon, laps 1-19; Stewart, 20-38

JOHN PLAYER BRITISH AND EUROPEAN GRAND PRIX

15 July 1972. Brands Hatch. 76 laps of a 2.650-mile circuit = 201.400 miles. Warm, dry and sunny. World Championship round 7

1 Emerson Fittipaldi	Lotus 72D-Ford	76	1h47m50.2
2 Jackie Stewart	Tyrrell 003-Ford	76	1h47m54.3
3 Peter Revson	McLaren M19A-Ford	76	1h49m02.7
4 Chris Amon	Matra-Simca MS120C	75	
5 Denny Hulme	McLaren M19C-Ford	75	
6 Arturo Merzario	Ferrari 312B2	75	

Winner's average speed: 112.058 mph. Starting grid front row: Ickx, 1m22.2 (pole) and E Fittipaldi, 1m22.6. Fastest lap: Stewart, 1m24.0. Leaders: Ickx, laps 1-48; E Fittipaldi, 49-76

GROSSER PREIS VON DEUTSCHLAND

30 July 1972. Nurburgring. 14 laps of a 14.189-mile circuit = 198.646 miles. Warm, dry and sunny. World Championship round 8

1 Jacky Ickx	Ferrari 312B2	14	1h42m12.3
2 Clay Regazzoni	Ferrari 312B2	14	1h43m00.6
3 Ronnie Peterson	March 721G-Ford	14	1h43m19.0
4 Howden Ganley	BRM P160C	14	1h44m32.5
5 Brian Redman	McLaren M19A-Ford	14	1h44m48.0
6 Graham Hill	Brabham BT37-Ford	14	1h45m11.9

Winner's average speed: 116.616 mph. Starting grid front row: Ickx, 7m07.0 (pole) and Stewart, 7m08.7. Fastest lap: Ickx, 7m13.6. Leaders: Ickx, laps 1-14

GROSSER PREIS VON OSTERREICH

13 August 1972. Osterreichring. 54 laps of a 3.673-mile circuit = 198.342 miles. Very hot, dry and sunny. World Championship round 9

1 Emerson Fittipaldi	Lotus 72D-Ford	54	1h29m16.66
2 Denny Hulme	McLaren M19C-Ford	54	1h29m17.84
3 Peter Revson	McLaren M19C-Ford	54	1h29m53.19
4 Mike Hailwood	Surtees TS9B-Ford	54	1h30m01.42
5 Chris Amon	Matra-Simca MS120D	54	1h30m02.30
6 Howden Ganley	BRM P160C	54	1h30m17.85

Winner's average speed: 133.298 mph. Starting grid front row: E Fittipaldi, 1m35.97 (pole) and Regazzoni, 1m36.04. Fastest lap: Hulme, 1m38.32. Leaders: Stewart, laps 1-23; E Fittipaldi, 24-54

GRAN PREMIO D'ITALIA

10 September 1972. Monza. 55 laps of a 3.588-mile circuit = 197.340 miles. Dry and overcast. World Championship round 10

1 Emerson Fittipaldi	Lotus 72D-Ford	55	1h29m58.4
2 Mike Hailwood	Surtees TS9B-Ford	55	1h30m12.9
3 Denny Hulme	McLaren M19C-Ford	55	1h30m22.2
4 Peter Revson	McLaren M19C-Ford	55	1h30m34.1
5 Graham Hill	Brabham BT37-Ford	55	1h31m04.0
6 Peter Gethin	BRM P160C	55	1h31m20.3

Winner's average speed: 131.599 mph. Starting grid front row: Ickx, 1m35.65 (pole) and Amon, 1m35.69. Fastest lap: Ickx, 1m36.3. Leaders: Ickx, laps 1-13, 17-45; Regazzoni, 14-16; E Fittipaldi, 46-55

1972 DRIVERS' RECORDS

driver	car	RA		ZA		E		MC		B		F		GB		D		A		I		CDN		USA	
		Q	R	Q	R	Q	R	Q	R	Q	R	Q	R	Q	R	Q	R	Q	R	Q	R	Q	R
Andrea de Adamich	Surtees TS9B-Ford	14	R	20	NC	13	4	18	7	10	R	13	14	20	R	20	13	13	14	21	R	15	R	19	R
Chris Amon	Matra-Simca MS120C	12	DNS	13	15	6	R	6	6	13	6F	-	-	17	4	-	-	-	-	-	-	-	-	-	-
	Matra-Simca MS120D	-	-	-	-	-	-	-	-	-	-	1	3F	-	-	8	15	6	5	2	R	10	6	7	15
Mario Andretti	Ferrari 312B2	9	R	6	4	5	R	-	-	-	-	-	-	-	-	-	-	-	-	7	7	-	-	10	6
Skip Barber	March 711-Ford	-	-	-	-	-	-	-	-	-	-	-	-	-	-	-	-	-	-	-	-	22	NC	20	16
Derek Bell	Tecno PA123	-	-	-	-	-	-	-	-	-	-	27	DNS	-	-	25	R	-	-	27	DNQ	25	DNS	30	R
Jean-Pierre Beltoise	BRM P160B	-	-	11	R	7	R	4	1F	6	R	NT	15	-	-	-	-	-	-	-	-	-	-	-	-
	BRM P160C	-	-	-	-	-	-	-	-	-	-	-	-	6	11	13	9	21	8	-	-	-	-	-	-
	BRM P180	-	-	-	-	-	-	-	-	-	-	-	-	-	-	-	-	-	-	16	8	20	R	18	R
Mike Beuttler	March 721G-Ford	-	-	-	-	26	DNQ	23	13	22	R	26	R	23	13	27	8	24	R	25	10	24	NC	21	13
Bill Brack	BRM P180	-	-	-	-	-	-	-	-	-	-	-	-	-	-	-	-	-	-	-	-	23	R	-	-
Francois Cevert	Tyrrell 002-Ford	7	R	8	9	12	R	12	NC	5	2	7	4	12	R	5	10	20	9	14	R	-	-	-	-
	Tyrrell 006-Ford	-	-	-	-	-	-	-	-	-	-	-	-	-	-	-	-	-	-	-	-	6	R	4	2
Dave Charlton	Lotus 72D-Ford	-	-	17	R	-	-	-	-	-	-	28	DNQ	24	R	26	R	-	-	-	-	-	-	-	-
Patrick Depailler	Tyrrell 004-Ford	-	-	-	-	-	-	-	-	-	-	17	NC	-	-	-	-	-	-	-	-	-	-	11	7
William Ferguson	Brabham BT33-Ford	-	-	-	-	27	DNS	-	-	-	-	-	-	-	-	-	-	-	-	-	-	-	-	-	-
Emerson Fittipaldi	Lotus 72D-Ford	5	R	3	2	3	1	1	3	1	1	8	2	2	1	3	R	1	1	6	1	4	11	9	R
Wilson Fittipaldi	Brabham BT33-Ford	-	-	-	-	14	7	21	9	-	-	-	-	-	-	-	-	-	-	-	-	-	-	-	-
	Brabham BT34-Ford	-	-	-	-	-	-	-	-	18	R	15	8	22	12	21	7	15	R	15	R	11	R	13	R
Nanni Galli	Tecno PA123	-	-	-	-	-	-	-	-	24	R	-	-	18	R	-	-	23	NC	23	R	-	-	-	-
	Ferrari 312B2	-	-	-	-	-	-	-	-	-	-	20	13	-	-	-	-	-	-	-	-	-	-	-	-
Howden Ganley	BRM P160B	13	9	16	NC	20	R	-	-	15	8	21	DNS	-	-	-	-	-	-	-	-	-	-	-	-
	BRM P180	-	-	-	-	-	-	20	R	-	-	-	-	-	-	-	-	-	-	-	-	-	-	-	-
	BRM P160C	-	-	-	-	-	-	-	-	-	-	-	-	-	-	18	4	10	6	17	11	14	10	17	R
Peter Gethin	BRM P160B	18	R	18	NC	-	-	5	R	17	R	22	DNS	16	R	-	-	-	-	-	-	-	-	-	-
	BRM P180	-	-	-	-	21	R	-	-	-	-	-	-	-	-	-	-	-	-	-	-	-	-	-	-
	BRM P160C	-	-	-	-	-	-	-	-	-	-	-	-	-	-	-	-	16	13	12	6	12	R	29	R
Mike Hailwood	Surtees TS9B-Ford	-	-	4	RF	15	R	11	R	8	4	10	6	7	R	16	R	12	4	9	2	-	-	14	17
Graham Hill	Brabham BT33-Ford	16	R	14	6	-	-	-	-	-	-	-	-	-	-	-	-	-	-	-	-	-	-	-	-
	Brabham BT37-Ford	-	-	-	-	23	10	19	12	16	R	23	10	21	R	15	6	14	R	13	5	17	8	28	11
Denny Hulme	McLaren M19A-Ford	4	2	5	1	2	R	-	-	-	-	-	-	-	-	-	-	-	-	-	-	-	-	-	-
	McLaren M19C-Ford	-	-	-	-	-	-	7	15	3	3	2	7	11	5	10	R	7	2F	5	3	2	3	3	3
Jacky Ickx	Ferrari 312B2	8	3	7	8	1	2F	2	2	4	R	4	11	1	R	1	1F	9	R	1	RF	8	12	12	5
Niki Lauda	March 721-Ford	22	11	21	7	-	-	-	-	-	-	-	-	-	-	-	-	-	-	-	-	-	-	-	-
	March 721X-Ford	-	-	-	-	25	R	22	16	25	12	-	-	-	-	-	-	-	-	-	-	-	-	-	-
	March 721G-Ford	-	-	-	-	-	-	-	-	-	-	24	R	19	9	24	R	22	10	20	13	19	DSQ	26	NC
John Love	Surtees TS9-Ford	-	-	26	16	-	-	-	-	-	-	-	-	-	-	-	-	-	-	-	-	-	-	-	-
Helmut Marko	BRM P153	19	10	23	14	-	-	-	-	-	-	-	-	-	-	-	-	-	-	-	-	-	-	-	-
	BRM P153B	-	-	-	-	-	-	17	8	23	10	-	-	-	-	-	-	-	-	-	-	-	-	-	-
	BRM P160B	-	-	-	-	-	-	-	-	-	-	6	R	-	-	-	-	-	-	-	-	-	-	-	-
Arturo Merzario	Ferrari 312B2	-	-	-	-	-	-	-	-	-	-	-	-	9	6	22	12	-	-	-	-	-	-	-	-
Francois Migault	Connew PC1-Ford	-	-	-	-	-	-	-	-	-	-	-	-	27	DNS	-	-	26	R	-	-	-	-	-	-
Jackie Oliver	BRM P160B	-	-	-	-	-	-	-	-	-	-	-	-	14	R	-	-	-	-	-	-	-	-	-	-
Carlos Pace	March 711-Ford	-	-	24	17	16	6	24	17	11	5	11	R	13	R	11	NC	18	NC	18	R	18	9	15	R
Henri Pescarolo	March 721-Ford	15	8	22	11	19	11	9	R	19	NC	12	DNS	-	-	9	R	25	DNS	26	DNQ	21	13	22	14
	Williams FX3-Ford	-	-	-	-	-	-	-	-	-	-	-	-	26	R	-	-	-	-	-	-	-	-	-	-
Ronnie Peterson	March 721-Ford	10	6	9	5	-	-	-	-	-	-	-	-	-	-	-	-	-	-	-	-	-	-	-	-
	March 721X-Ford	-	-	-	-	9	R	15	11	14	9	-	-	-	-	-	-	-	-	-	-	-	-	-	-
	March 721G-Ford	-	-	-	-	-	-	-	-	-	-	9	5	8	7	4	3	11	12	24	9	3	DSQ	27	4
Sam Posey	Surtees TS9B-Ford	-	-	-	-	-	-	-	-	-	-	-	-	-	-	-	-	-	-	-	-	-	-	23	12
Brian Redman	McLaren M19A-Ford	-	-	-	-	-	-	10	5	-	-	14	9	-	-	19	5	-	-	-	-	-	-	-	-
	BRM P180	-	-	-	-	-	-	-	-	-	-	-	-	-	-	-	-	-	-	-	-	-	-	24	R
Clay Regazzoni	Ferrari 312B2	6	4	2	12	8	3	3	R	2	R	-	-	-	-	7	2	2	R	4	R	7	5	6	8
Carlos Reutemann	Brabham BT34-Ford	1	7	15	R	-	-	-	-	-	-	-	-	-	-	-	-	-	-	-	-	-	-	-	-
	Brabham BT37-Ford	-	-	-	-	-	-	-	-	9	13	18	12	10	8	6	R	5	R	11	R	9	4	5	R
Peter Revson	McLaren M19A-Ford	3	R	12	3	11	5	-	-	7	7	-	-	3	3	-	-	-	-	-	-	-	-	-	-
	McLaren M19C-Ford	-	-	-	-	-	-	-	-	-	-	-	-	-	-	4	3	8	4	1	2	2	18	-	-
Jody Scheckter	McLaren M19A-Ford	-	-	-	-	-	-	-	-	-	-	-	-	-	-	-	-	-	-	-	-	-	-	8	9
Tim Schenken	Surtees TS9B-Ford	11	5	10	R	18	8	13	R	21	R	5	17	5	R	12	14	8	11	22	R	13	7	-	-
	Surtees TS14-Ford	-	-	-	-	-	-	-	-	-	-	-	-	-	-	-	-	-	-	-	-	-	-	32	R
Vern Schuppan	BRM P153B	-	-	-	-	-	-	-	-	-	-	26	DNS	-	-	-	-	-	-	-	-	-	-	-	-
Alex Soler-Roig	BRM P160B	21	R	-	-	22	R	-	-	-	-	-	-	-	-	-	-	-	-	-	-	-	-	-	-
Jackie Stewart	Tyrrell 003-Ford	2	1F	1	R	4	R	-	-	-	-	3	1	4	2F	2	11	-	-	-	-	-	-	-	-
	Tyrrell 004-Ford	-	-	-	-	-	-	8	4	-	-	-	-	-	-	-	-	-	-	-	-	-	-	-	-
	Tyrrell 005-Ford	-	-	-	-	-	-	-	-	-	-	-	-	-	-	-	-	3	7	3	R	5	1F	1	1F
Rolf Stommelen	Eifelland 21-Ford	-	-	25	13	17	R	25	10	20	11	16	16	25	10	14	R	17	NC	-	-	-	-	-	-

driver	car	RA Q	RA R	ZA Q	ZA R	E Q	E R	MC Q	MC R	B Q	B R	F Q	F R	GB Q	GB R	D Q	D R	A Q	A R	I Q	I R	CDN Q	CDN R	USA Q	USA R
John Surtees	Surtees TS14-Ford	-	-	-	-	-	-	-	-	-	-	-	-	-	-	-	-	-	-	19	R	-	-	25	DNS
Dave Walker	Lotus 72D-Ford	20	DSQ	19	10	24	9	14	14	12	14	25	18	15	R	23	R	19	R	-	-	-	-	31	R
Reine Wisell	BRM P153	17	R	-	-	-	-	-	-	-	-	-	-	-	-	-	-	-	-	-	-	-	-	-	-
	BRM P160B	-	-	-	-	10	R	16	R	-	-	19	R	-	-	-	-	-	-	-	-	-	-	-	-
	BRM P160C	-	-	-	-	-	-	-	-	-	-	-	-	-	-	17	R	-	-	10	12	-	-	-	-
	Lotus 72D-Ford	-	-	-	-	-	-	-	-	-	-	-	-	-	-	-	-	-	-	-	-	16	R	16	10

1972 FINAL CHAMPIONSHIP POSITIONS

Drivers

1	Emerson Fittipaldi	61
2	Jackie Stewart	45
3	Denny Hulme	39
4	Jacky Ickx	27
5	Peter Revson	23
6=	Francois Cevert	15
	Clay Regazzoni	15
8	Mike Hailwood	13
9=	Chris Amon	12
	Ronnie Peterson	12
11	Jean-Pierre Beltoise	9
12=	Mario Andretti	4
	Howden Ganley	4
	Graham Hill	4
	Brian Redman	4
16=	Andrea de Adamich	3
	Carlos Pace	3
	Carlos Reutemann	3
19	Tim Schenken	2
20=	Peter Gethin	1
	Arturo Merzario	1

Sum of best five results from the first six races and best five results from the final six races

Manufacturers

1	Lotus-Ford	61
2	Tyrrell-Ford	51
3	McLaren-Ford	47 (49)*
4	Ferrari	33
5	Surtees-Ford	18
6	March-Ford	15
7	BRM	14
8	Matra-Simca	12
9	Brabham-Ford	7

*Sum of best five results from the first six races and best five results from the final six races. Points only awarded to first car to finish for each manufacturer

CANADIAN GRAND PRIX

24 September 1972. Mosport Park. 80 laps of a 2.459-mile circuit = 196.720 miles. Dry and misty. World Championship round 11

1	Jackie Stewart	Tyrrell 005-Ford	80	1h43m16.9
2	Peter Revson	McLaren M19C-Ford	80	1h44m05.1
3	Denny Hulme	McLaren M19C-Ford	80	1h44m11.5
4	Carlos Reutemann	Brabham BT37-Ford	80	1h44m17.6
5	Clay Regazzoni	Ferrari 312B2	80	1h44m23.8
6	Chris Amon	Matra-Simca MS120D	79	

Winner's average speed: 114.282 mph. Starting grid front row: Revson, 1m13.6 (pole), Hulme, 1m13.9 and Peterson, 1m14.0. Fastest lap: Stewart, 1m15.7. Leaders: Peterson, laps 1-3; Stewart, 4-80

1973 Jackie Stewart won a third world title for Ken Tyrrell in his final year in Grand Prix racing

UNITED STATES GRAND PRIX

8 October 1972. Watkins Glen. 59 laps of a 3.377-mile circuit = 199.243 miles. Cool and dry at start, some rain later. World Championship round 12

1	Jackie Stewart	Tyrrell 005-Ford	59	1h41m45.354
2	Francois Cevert	Tyrrell 006-Ford	59	1h42m17.622
3	Denny Hulme	McLaren M19C-Ford	59	1h42m22.882
4	Ronnie Peterson	March 721G-Ford	59	1h43m07.870
5	Jacky Ickx	Ferrari 312B2	59	1h43m08.473
6	Mario Andretti	Ferrari 312B2	58	

Winner's average speed: 117.483 mph. Starting grid front row: Stewart, 1m40.481 (pole), Revson, 1m40.527 and Hulme, 1m41.084. Fastest lap: Stewart, 1m41.644. Leaders: Stewart, laps 1-59

1973

A classic contest between the Tyrrell and Lotus teams dominated 1973, with Tyrrell's Jackie Stewart crowned champion for the third time in his final year of Grand Prix racing. Despite the championship, the year ended tragically for the team when Francois Cevert, the man groomed to replace Stewart as team leader, was killed during practice for the United States GP.

Lotus retained the constructors' title with Emerson Fittipaldi and Ronnie Peterson scoring a total of seven victories for Colin Chapman's team. For Peterson, who had not won a race before, the start to his first year with Lotus proved very frustrating. The final slice of bad luck was a puncture in the closing laps of the Swedish GP, which allowed Denny Hulme's McLaren M23 to pass and denied Peterson what would have been a famous home victory.

Peterson would find that elusive first success at the next race in France. Jody Scheckter, confidently leading his third Grand Prix, was eliminated in an accident with Fittipaldi, leaving Peterson to cruise to the first of four wins. Scheckter was a true star in the making, but his inexperience showed at Silverstone, where on the second lap he spun at Woodcote in front of the field, causing a multiple-car pile-up. McLaren teammate Pete Revson won the restarted race and also triumphed in Canada.

Niki Lauda had an impressive second year in Grand Prix racing, and his performances in an increasingly uncompetitive BRM were enough to attract interest from Ferrari for the following season. The flamboyant new Hesketh team arrived with novice James Hunt and a private March 731, taking second place at Watkins Glen in a successful if unconventional first year.

Two acts of selfless heroism earned recognition from the British monarchy. In South Africa, braving flames that had engulfed the car, Mike Hailwood rescued an unconscious Clay Regazzoni from his crashed BRM. At Zandvoort, however, David Purley's similar attempt to save Roger Williamson from his overturned and burning car was sadly unsuccessful. Both Hailwood and Purley received the George Medal. Williamson was the first in a talented generation of British drivers to meet with tragic deaths over the next four years.

These accidents hastened an urgent and largely fruitful review of safety, with special emphasis placed on reducing the chance of fire after an accident. In a bid to improve safety at the start of a race, two-by-two grids became mandatory following the Dutch Grand Prix, whereas rows of up to four cars had been common in previous years.

GRAN PREMIO DE LA REPUBLICA ARGENTINA

28 January 1973. Buenos Aires. 96 laps of a 2.079-mile circuit = 199.584 miles. Hot, dry and sunny. World Championship round 1

1 Emerson Fittipaldi	Lotus 72D-Ford	96	1h56m18.22
2 Francois Cevert	Tyrrell 006-Ford	96	1h56m22.91
3 Jackie Stewart	Tyrrell 005-Ford	96	1h56m51.41
4 Jacky Ickx	Ferrari 312B2	96	1h57m00.79
5 Denny Hulme	McLaren M19C-Ford	95	
6 Wilson Fittipaldi	Brabham BT37-Ford	95	

Winner's average speed: 102.964 mph. Starting grid front row: Regazzoni, 1m10.54 (pole) and E Fittipaldi, 1m10.84. Fastest lap: E Fittipaldi, 1m11.22. Leaders: Regazzoni, laps 1-28; Cevert, 29-85; E Fittipaldi, 86-96

GRANDE PREMIO DO BRASIL

11 February 1973. Interlagos. 40 laps of a 4.946-mile circuit = 197.840 miles. Very hot, dry and sunny. World Championship round 2

1 Emerson Fittipaldi	Lotus 72D-Ford	40	1h43m55.6
2 Jackie Stewart	Tyrrell 005-Ford	40	1h44m09.1
3 Denny Hulme	McLaren M19C-Ford	40	1h45m42.0
4 Arturo Merzario	Ferrari 312B2	39	
5 Jacky Ickx	Ferrari 312B2	39	
6 Clay Regazzoni	BRM P160D	39	

Winner's average speed: 114.219 mph. Starting grid front row: Peterson, 2m30.5 (pole), E Fittipaldi, 2m30.7 and Ickx, 2m32.0. Fastest lap: E Fittipaldi and Hulme, 2m35.0. Leaders: E Fittipaldi, laps 1-40

SOUTH AFRICAN GRAND PRIX

3 March 1973. Kyalami. 79 laps of a 2.550-mile circuit = 201.450 miles. Dry and heavy cloud. World Championship round 3

1 Jackie Stewart	Tyrrell 006-Ford	79	1h43m11.07
2 Peter Revson	McLaren M19C-Ford	79	1h43m35.62
3 Emerson Fittipaldi	Lotus 72D-Ford	79	1h43m36.13
4 Arturo Merzario	Ferrari 312B2	78	
5 Denny Hulme	McLaren M23-Ford	77	
6 George Follmer	Shadow DN1A-Ford	77	

Winner's average speed: 117.140 mph. Starting grid front row: Hulme, 1m16.28 (pole), E Fittipaldi, 1m16.41 and Scheckter, 1m16.43. Fastest lap: E Fittipaldi, 1m17.10. Leaders: Hulme, laps 1-4; Scheckter, 5-6; Stewart, 7-79

GRAN PREMIO DE ESPANA

29 April 1973. Montjuich Park. 75 laps of a 2.355-mile circuit = 176.625 miles. Warm, dry and sunny. World Championship round 4

1 Emerson Fittipaldi	Lotus 72D-Ford	75	1h48m18.7
2 Francois Cevert	Tyrrell 006-Ford	75	1h49m01.4
3 George Follmer	Shadow DN1A-Ford	75	1h49m31.8
4 Peter Revson	McLaren M23-Ford	74	
5 Jean-Pierre Beltoise	BRM P160E	74	
6 Denny Hulme	McLaren M23-Ford	74	

Winner's average speed: 97.843 mph. Starting grid front row: Peterson, 1m21.8 (pole) and Hulme, 1m22.5. Fastest lap: Peterson,

1m23.8. Leaders: Peterson, laps 1-56; E Fittipaldi, 57-75

GRAND PRIX DE BELGIQUE

20 May 1973. Zolder. 70 laps of a 2.622-mile circuit = 183.540 miles. Warm, dry and sunny. World Championship round 5

1 Jackie Stewart	Tyrrell 006-Ford	70	1h42m13.43
2 Francois Cevert	Tyrrell 006-Ford	70	1h42m45.27
3 Emerson Fittipaldi	Lotus 72D-Ford	70	1h44m16.22
4 Andrea de Adamich	Brabham BT37-Ford	69	
5 Niki Lauda	BRM P160E	69	
6 Chris Amon	Tecno PA123	67	

Winner's average speed: 107.728 mph. Starting grid front row: Peterson, 1m22.46 (pole) and Hulme, 1m23.0. Fastest lap: Cevert, 1m25.42. Leaders: Peterson, lap 1; Cevert, laps 2-19; E Fittipaldi, 20-24; Stewart, 25-70

GRAND PRIX DE MONACO

3 June 1973. Monte Carlo. 78 laps of a 2.037-mile circuit = 158.886 miles. Warm, dry and sunny. World Championship round 6

1 Jackie Stewart	Tyrrell 006-Ford	78	1h57m44.3
2 Emerson Fittipaldi	Lotus 72D-Ford	78	1h57m45.6
3 Ronnie Peterson	Lotus 72D-Ford	77	
4 Francois Cevert	Tyrrell 006-Ford	77	
5 Peter Revson	McLaren M23-Ford	76	
6 Denny Hulme	McLaren M23-Ford	76	

Winner's average speed: 80.969 mph. Starting grid front row: Stewart, 1m27.5 (pole) and Peterson, 1m27.7. Fastest lap: E Fittipaldi, 1m28.1. Leaders: Cevert, lap 1; Peterson, laps 2-7; Stewart, 8-78

HITACHI SVERIGES GRAND PRIX

17 June 1973. Anderstorp. 80 laps of a 2.497-mile circuit = 199.760 miles. Warm, dry and sunny. World Championship round 7

1 Denny Hulme	McLaren M23-Ford	80	1h56m46.049
2 Ronnie Peterson	Lotus 72D-Ford	80	1h56m50.088
3 Francois Cevert	Tyrrell 006-Ford	80	1h57m00.716
4 Carlos Reutemann	Brabham BT42-Ford	80	1h57m04.117
5 Jackie Stewart	Tyrrell 006-Ford	80	1h57m12.047
6 Jacky Ickx	Ferrari 312B3	79	

Winner's average speed: 102.645 mph. Starting grid front row: Peterson, 1m23.810 (pole) and Cevert, 1m23.899. Fastest lap: Hulme, 1m26.146. Leaders: Peterson, laps 1-78; Hulme, 79-80

GRAND PRIX DE FRANCE

1 July 1973. Paul Ricard. 54 laps of a 3.610-mile circuit = 194.940 miles. Very hot, dry and sunny. World Championship round 8

1 Ronnie Peterson	Lotus 72D-Ford	54	1h41m36.52
2 Francois Cevert	Tyrrell 006-Ford	54	1h42m17.44
3 Carlos Reutemann	Brabham BT42-Ford	54	1h42m23.00
4 Jackie Stewart	Tyrrell 006-Ford	54	1h42m23.40
5 Jacky Ickx	Ferrari 312B3	54	1h42m25.42
6 James Hunt	March 731-Ford	54	1h42m59.06

Winner's average speed: 115.112 mph. Starting grid front row: Stewart, 1m48.37 (pole), Scheckter, 1m49.18 and E Fittipaldi, 1m49.36. Fastest lap: Hulme, 1m50.99. Leaders: Scheckter, laps 1-41; Peterson, 42-54

JOHN PLAYER BRITISH GRAND PRIX

14 July 1973. Silverstone. 67 laps of a 2.927-mile circuit = 196.109 miles. Race stopped after 2 laps due to accident, restarted over original distance. Dry and overcast. World Championship round 9

1 Peter Revson	McLaren M23-Ford	67	1h29m18.5
2 Ronnie Peterson	Lotus 72D-Ford	67	1h29m21.3
3 Denny Hulme	McLaren M23-Ford	67	1h29m21.5
4 James Hunt	March 731-Ford	67	1h29m21.9
5 Francois Cevert	Tyrrell 006-Ford	67	1h29m55.1
6 Carlos Reutemann	Brabham BT42-Ford	67	1h30m03.2

Winner's average speed: 131.752 mph. Starting grid front row: Peterson, 1m16.3 (pole), Hulme, 1m16.5 and Revson, 1m16.5. Fastest lap: Hunt, 1m18.6. Leaders: Peterson, laps 1-38; Revson, 39-67

Formula 1

1973 DRIVERS' RECORDS

driver	car	RA		BR		ZA		E		B		MC		S		F		GB		NL		D		A		I		CDN		USA	
		Q	R	Q	R	Q	R	Q	R	Q	R	Q	R	Q	R	Q	R	Q	R	Q	R	Q	R	Q	R	Q	R	Q	R	Q	R
Andrea de Adamich	Surtees TS9B-Ford	-	-	-	-	20	8	-	-	-	-	-	-	-	-	-	-	-	-	-	-	-	-	-	-	-	-	-	-	-	-
	Brabham BT37-Ford	-	-	-	-	-	-	17	R	18	4	26	7	-	-	13	R	-	-	-	-	-	-	-	-	-	-	-	-	-	-
	Brabham BT42-Ford	-	-	-	-	-	-	-	-	-	-	-	-	20	R	-	-	-	-	-	-	-	-	-	-	-	-	-	-	-	-
Chris Amon	Tecno PA123	-	-	-	-	-	-	-	-	15	6	12	R	-	-	29	R	19	R	-	-	-	-	23	DNS	-	-	-	-	-	-
	Tyrrell 005-Ford	-	-	-	-	-	-	-	-	-	-	-	-	-	-	-	-	-	-	-	-	-	-	-	-	-	-	11	10	13	DNS
Tom Belso	Williams IR01-Ford	-	-	-	-	-	-	-	-	-	-	-	-	22	DNS	-	-	-	-	-	-	-	-	-	-	-	-	-	-	-	-
Jean-Pierre Beltoise	BRM P160C	7	R	-	-	-	-	-	-	-	-	-	-	-	-	-	-	-	-	-	-	-	-	-	-	-	-	-	-	-	-
	BRM P160D	-	-	10	R	7	R	-	-	-	-	-	-	-	-	-	-	-	-	-	-	-	-	-	-	-	-	-	-	-	-
	BRM P160E	-	-	-	-	-	-	10	5	5	R	11	R	9	R	15	11	17	R	9	5	9	R	13	5	13	13	16	4	15	9
Mike Beuttler	March 721G-Ford	18	10	19	R	23	NC	-	-	-	-	-	-	-	-	-	-	-	-	-	-	-	-	-	-	-	-	-	-	-	-
	March 731-Ford	-	-	-	-	-	-	19	7	20	11	21	R	21	8	-	-	24	11	23	R	20	16	11	R	12	R	21	R	27	10
Luiz-Pereira Bueno	Surtees TS9B-Ford	-	-	20	12	-	-	-	-	-	-	-	-	-	-	-	-	-	-	-	-	-	-	-	-	-	-	-	-	-	-
Francois Cevert	Tyrrell 006-Ford	6	2	9	10	-	-	3	2	4	2F	4	4	2	3	4	2	7	5	3	2	3	2	10	R	11	5	6	R	5	DNS
	Tyrrell 005-Ford	-	-	-	-	NT	NC	-	-	-	-	-	-	-	-	-	-	-	-	-	-	-	-	-	-	-	-	-	-	-	-
Dave Charlton	Lotus 72D-Ford	-	-	-	-	13	R	-	-	-	-	-	-	-	-	-	-	-	-	-	-	-	-	-	-	-	-	-	-	-	-
Emerson Fittipaldi	Lotus 72D-Ford	2	1F	2	1F	2	3F	7	1	9	3	5	2F	4	12	3	R	5	R	16	R	14	6	1	R	4	2	5	2F	3	6
Wilson Fittipaldi	Brabham BT37-Ford	12	6	11	R	17	R	-	-	-	-	-	-	-	-	-	-	-	-	-	-	-	-	-	-	-	-	-	-	-	-
	Brabham BT42-Ford	-	-	-	-	-	-	12	10	19	R	9	11	13	R	19	16	13	R	13	R	13	5	16	R	16	R	10	11	26	NC
George Follmer	Shadow DN1A-Ford	-	-	-	-	21	6	14	3	11	R	20	DNS	19	14	20	R	25	R	22	10	22	R	20	R	21	10	13	17	21	14
Nanni Galli	Williams FX3B-Ford	16	R	18	9	-	-	-	-	-	-	-	-	-	-	-	-	-	-	-	-	-	-	-	-	-	-	-	-	-	-
	Williams IR01-Ford	-	-	-	-	-	-	20	11	17	R	22	R	-	-	-	-	-	-	-	-	-	-	-	-	-	-	-	-	-	-
Howden Ganley	Williams FX3B-Ford	19	NC	16	7	19	10	-	-	-	-	-	-	-	-	-	-	-	-	-	-	-	-	-	-	-	-	-	-	-	-
	Williams IR02-Ford	-	-	-	-	-	-	21	R	21	R	10	R	11	11	24	14	18	9	15	9	19	DNS	-	-	-	-	-	-	-	-
	Williams IR03-Ford	-	-	-	-	-	-	-	-	-	-	-	-	-	-	-	-	-	-	-	-	-	-	21	NC	20	R	22	6	20	12
Peter Gethin	BRM P160E	-	-	-	-	-	-	-	-	-	-	-	-	-	-	-	-	-	-	-	-	-	-	25	R	-	-	-	-	-	-
Mike Hailwood	Surtees TS14A-Ford	10	R	14	R	12	R	9	R	13	R	13	8	10	R	11	R	12	R	24	R	18	14	15	10	8	7	12	9	7	R
Graham Hill	Shadow DN1A-Ford	-	-	-	-	-	-	22	R	23	9	25	R	18	R	16	10	27	R	17	NC	21	13	22	R	22	14	17	16	19	13
Denny Hulme	McLaren M19C-Ford	8	5	5	3F	-	-	-	-	-	-	-	-	-	-	-	-	-	-	-	-	-	-	-	-	-	-	-	-	-	-
	McLaren M23-Ford	-	-	-	-	1	5	2	6	2	7	3	6	6	1F	6	8F	2	3	4	R	8	12	3	8	3	15	7	13	9	4
James Hunt	March 731-Ford	-	-	-	-	-	-	-	-	-	-	18	9	-	-	14	6	11	4F	7	3	-	-	9	R	25	DNS	15	7	4	2F
Jacky Ickx	Ferrari 312B2	3	4	3	5	11	R	-	-	-	-	-	-	-	-	-	-	-	-	-	-	-	-	-	-	-	-	-	-	-	-
	Ferrari 312B3	-	-	-	-	-	-	6	12	3	R	7	R	8	6	12	5	19	8	-	-	-	-	-	-	-	-	-	-	-	-
	McLaren M23-Ford	-	-	-	-	-	-	-	-	-	-	-	-	-	-	-	-	-	-	-	-	4	3	-	-	-	-	-	-	-	-
	Ferrari 312B3S	-	-	-	-	-	-	-	-	-	-	-	-	-	-	-	-	-	-	-	-	-	-	14	8	-	-	-	-	-	-
	Williams IR01-Ford	-	-	-	-	-	-	-	-	-	-	-	-	-	-	-	-	-	-	-	-	-	-	-	-	-	-	-	-	24	7
Jean-Pierre Jarier	March 721G-Ford	17	R	15	R	18	NC	-	-	-	-	-	-	-	-	-	-	-	-	-	-	-	-	-	-	-	-	-	-	-	-
	March 731-Ford	-	-	-	-	-	-	16	R	14	R	20	R	7	R	-	-	-	-	12	R	-	-	-	-	-	-	23	NC	18	11
Eddie Keizan	Tyrrell 004-Ford	-	-	-	-	22	NC	-	-	-	-	-	-	-	-	-	-	-	-	-	-	-	-	-	-	-	-	-	-	-	-
Niki Lauda	BRM P160C	13	R	13	8	-	-	-	-	-	-	-	-	-	-	-	-	-	-	-	-	-	-	-	-	-	-	-	-	-	-
	BRM P160D	-	-	-	-	10	R	-	-	-	-	-	-	-	-	-	-	-	-	-	-	-	-	-	-	-	-	-	-	-	-
	BRM P160E	-	-	-	-	-	-	11	R	14	5	6	R	15	13	17	9	9	12	11	R	5	R	NT	DNS	15	R	8	R	22	R
Gijs van Lennep	Williams IR01-Ford	-	-	-	-	-	-	-	-	-	-	-	-	-	-	-	-	-	-	20	6	-	-	24	9	23	R	-	-	-	-
Jochen Mass	Surtees TS14A-Ford	-	-	-	-	-	-	-	-	-	-	-	-	-	-	-	-	14	R	-	-	-	-	15	7	-	-	-	-	17	R
Graham McRae	Williams IR01-Ford	-	-	-	-	-	-	-	-	-	-	-	-	-	-	-	-	28	R	-	-	-	-	-	-	-	-	-	-	-	-
Arturo Merzario	Ferrari 312B2	14	9	17	4	15	4	-	-	-	-	-	-	-	-	-	-	-	-	-	-	-	-	-	-	-	-	-	-	-	-
	Ferrari 312B3	-	-	-	-	-	-	16	R	-	-	-	-	10	7	-	-	-	-	-	-	-	-	-	-	-	-	-	-	-	-
	Ferrari 312B3S	-	-	-	-	-	-	-	-	-	-	-	-	-	-	-	-	-	-	-	-	-	-	6	7	7	R	20	15	12	16
Jackie Oliver	Shadow DN1A-Ford	-	-	-	-	14	R	13	R	22	R	23	10	17	R	21	R	26	R	10	R	17	8	18	R	19	11	14	3	23	15
Rikky von Opel	Ensign N173-Ford	-	-	-	-	-	-	-	-	-	-	-	-	-	-	25	15	21	13	14	DNS	-	-	19	R	17	R	26	NC	28	R
Carlos Pace	Surtees TS14A-Ford	15	R	6	R	9	R	16	R	8	8	17	R	16	10	18	13	15	R	8	7	11	4F	3F	5	R	19	18	10	R	
Henri Pescarolo	March 731-Ford	-	-	-	-	18	8	-	-	-	-	-	-	-	-	-	-	-	-	-	-	-	-	-	-	-	-	-	-	-	-
	Williams IR01-Ford	-	-	-	-	-	-	23	R	-	-	12	10	-	-	-	-	-	-	-	-	-	-	-	-	-	-	-	-	-	-
Ronnie Peterson	Lotus 72D-Ford	5	R	1	R	4	11	1	RF	1	R	2	3	1	2	5	1	1	2	1	1F	2	R	2	1	1	1	1	R	1	1
Jackie Pretorius	Williams FX3B-Ford	-	-	-	-	24	R	-	-	-	-	-	-	-	-	-	-	-	-	-	-	-	-	-	-	-	-	-	-	-	-
David Purley	March 731-Ford	-	-	-	-	-	-	24	R	-	-	16	DNS	21	R	23	15	-	-	-	-	24	9	-	-	-	-	-	-	-	-
Brian Redman	Shadow DN1A-Ford	-	-	-	-	-	-	-	-	-	-	-	-	-	-	-	-	-	-	-	-	-	-	-	-	-	-	14	DSQ	-	-
Clay Regazzoni	BRM P160C	1	7	-	-	-	-	-	-	-	-	-	-	-	-	-	-	-	-	-	-	-	-	-	-	-	-	-	-	-	-
	BRM P160D	-	-	4	6	5	R	-	-	-	-	-	-	-	-	-	-	-	-	-	-	-	-	-	-	-	-	-	-	-	-
	BRM P160E	-	-	-	-	-	-	8	9	12	10	8	R	12	9	9	12	10	7	12	8	10	R	14	6	18	R	-	-	16	8
Carlos Reutemann	Brabham BT37-Ford	9	R	7	11	8	7	-	-	-	-	-	-	-	-	-	-	-	-	-	-	-	-	-	-	-	-	-	-	-	-
	Brabham BT42-Ford	-	-	-	-	-	-	15	R	7	R	19	R	5	4	8	3	8	6	5	R	6	R	5	4	10	6	4	8	2	3
Peter Revson	McLaren M19C-Ford	11	8	12	R	6	2	-	-	-	-	-	-	-	-	-	-	-	-	-	-	-	-	-	-	-	-	-	-	-	-
	McLaren M23-Ford	-	-	-	-	-	-	5	4	10	R	15	5	7	7	-	-	3	1	6	4	7	9	4	R	2	3	2	1	8	5
Jody Scheckter	McLaren M19C-Ford	-	-	-	-	3	9	-	-	-	-	-	-	-	-	-	-	-	-	-	-	-	-	-	-	-	-	-	-	-	-
	McLaren M23-Ford	-	-	-	-	-	-	-	-	-	-	-	-	-	-	2	R	6	R	-	-	-	-	-	-	-	-	3	R	11	R

driver	car	RA Q	RA R	BR Q	BR R	ZA Q	ZA R	E Q	E R	B Q	B R	MC Q	MC R	S Q	S R	F Q	F R	GB Q	GB R	NL Q	NL R	D Q	D R	A Q	A R	I Q	I R	CDN Q	CDN R	USA Q	USA R
Tim Schenken	Williams IR01-Ford	-	-	-	-	-	-	-	-	-	-	-	-	-	-	-	-	-	-	-	-	-	-	24	14	-	-	-	-	-	-
Jackie Stewart	Tyrrell 005-Ford	4	3	8	2	-	-	-	-	-	-	-	-	-	-	-	-	-	-	-	-	-	-	-	-	-	-	-	-	-	-
	Tyrrell 006-Ford	-	-	-	-	16	1	4	R	6	1	1	1	3	5	1	4	4	10	2	1	1	1	7	2	6	4F	9	5	6	DNS
Rolf Stommelen	Brabham BT42-Ford	-	-	-	-	-	-	-	-	-	-	-	-	-	-	-	-	-	-	-	-	16	11	17	R	9	12	18	12	-	-
John Watson	Brabham BT37-Ford	-	-	-	-	-	-	-	-	-	-	-	-	-	-	-	-	23	R	-	-	-	-	-	-	-	-	-	-	-	-
	Brabham BT42-Ford	-	-	-	-	-	-	-	-	-	-	-	-	-	-	-	-	-	-	-	-	-	-	-	-	-	-	-	-	25	R
Roger Williamson	March 731-Ford	-	-	-	-	-	-	-	-	-	-	-	-	-	-	-	-	22	R	18	R	-	-	-	-	-	-	-	-	-	-
Reine Wisell	March 731-Ford	-	-	-	-	-	-	-	-	-	-	-	-	14	DNS	22	R	-	-	-	-	-	-	-	-	-	-	-	-	-	-

1973 FINAL CHAMPIONSHIP POSITIONS

Drivers

	Driver	Pts			Driver	Pts			Manufacturer	Pts
1	Jackie Stewart	71		14	Jackie Oliver	4		3	McLaren-Ford	58
2	Emerson Fittipaldi	55		15=	Andrea de Adamich	3		4	Brabham-Ford	22
3	Ronnie Peterson	52			Wilson Fittipaldi	3		5	March-Ford	14
4	Francois Cevert	47		17=	Niki Lauda	2		6=	BRM	12
5	Peter Revson	38			Clay Regazzoni	2			Ferrari	12
6	Denny Hulme	26		19=	Chris Amon	1		8	Shadow-Ford	9
7	Carlos Reutemann	16			Howden Ganley	1		9	Surtees-Ford	7
8	James Hunt	14			Gijs van Lennep	1		10	Williams-Ford	2
9	Jacky Ickx	12						11	Tecno	1
10	Jean-Pierre Beltoise	9								
11	Carlos Pace	7								
12	Arturo Merzario	6								
13	George Follmer	5								

Sum of best seven results from the first eight races and best six results from the final seven races

Manufacturers

1 Lotus-Ford 92 (96)*
2 Tyrrell-Ford 82 (86)*

*Sum of best seven results from the first eight races and best six results from the final seven races. Points only awarded to first car to finish for each manufacturer

GROTE PRIJS VAN NEDERLAND

29 July 1973. Zandvoort. 72 laps of a 2.626-mile circuit = 189.072 miles. Dry and overcast. World Championship round 10

1	Jackie Stewart	Tyrrell 006-Ford	72	1h39m12.45
2	Francois Cevert	Tyrrell 006-Ford	72	1h39m28.28
3	James Hunt	March 731-Ford	72	1h40m15.46
4	Peter Revson	McLaren M23-Ford	72	1h40m21.58
5	Jean-Pierre Beltoise	BRM P160E	72	1h40m25.82
6	Gijs van Lennep	Williams IR01-Ford	70	

Winner's average speed: 114.349 mph. Starting grid front row: Peterson, 1m19.47 (pole), Stewart, 1m19.97 and Cevert, 1m20.12. Fastest lap: Peterson, 1m20.31. Leaders: Peterson, laps 1-63; Stewart, 64-72

GROSSER PREIS VON DEUTSCHLAND

5 August 1973. Nurburgring. 14 laps of a 14.189-mile circuit = 198.646 miles. Warm, dry and sunny. World Championship round 11

1	Jackie Stewart	Tyrrell 006-Ford	14	1h42m03.0
2	Francois Cevert	Tyrrell 006-Ford	14	1h42m04.6
3	Jacky Ickx	McLaren M23-Ford	14	1h42m44.2
4	Carlos Pace	Surtees TS14A-Ford	14	1h42m56.8
5	Wilson Fittipaldi	Brabham BT42-Ford	14	1h43m22.9
6	Emerson Fittipaldi	Lotus 72D-Ford	14	1h43m27.3

Winner's average speed: 116.793 mph. Starting grid front row: Stewart, 7m07.8 (pole) and Peterson, 7m08.3. Fastest lap: Pace, 7m11.4. Leaders: Stewart, laps 1-14

GROSSER PREIS VON OSTERREICH

19 August 1973. Osterreichring. 54 laps of a 3.673-mile circuit = 198.342 miles. Very hot, dry and sunny. World Championship round 12

1	Ronnie Peterson	Lotus 72D-Ford	54	1h28m48.78
2	Jackie Stewart	Tyrrell 006-Ford	54	1h28m57.79
3	Carlos Pace	Surtees TS14A-Ford	54	1h29m35.42
4	Carlos Reutemann	Brabham BT42-Ford	54	1h29m36.69
5	Jean-Pierre Beltoise	BRM P160E	54	1h30m10.38
6	Clay Regazzoni	BRM P160E	54	1h30m27.18

Winner's average speed: 133.995 mph. Starting grid front row: E Fittipaldi, 1m34.98 (pole) and Peterson, 1m35.37. Fastest lap: Pace, 1m37.29. Leaders: Peterson, laps 1-16, 49-54; E Fittipaldi, 17-48

GRAN PREMIO D'ITALIA

9 September 1973. Monza. 55 laps of a 3.588-mile circuit = 197.340 miles. Hot, dry and sunny. World Championship round 13

1	Ronnie Peterson	Lotus 72D-Ford	55	1h29m17.0
2	Emerson Fittipaldi	Lotus 72D-Ford	55	1h29m17.8
3	Peter Revson	McLaren M23-Ford	55	1h29m45.8
4	Jackie Stewart	Tyrrell 006-Ford	55	1h29m50.2
5	Francois Cevert	Tyrrell 006-Ford	55	1h30m03.2
6	Carlos Reutemann	Brabham BT42-Ford	55	1h30m16.8

Winner's average speed: 132.616 mph. Starting grid front row: Peterson, 1m34.80 (pole) and Revson, 1m35.29. Fastest lap: Stewart, 1m35.3. Leaders: Peterson, laps 1-55

CANADIAN GRAND PRIX

23 September 1973. Mosport Park. 80 laps of a 2.459-mile circuit = 196.720 miles. Wet at the start, drying later. World Championship round 14

1	Peter Revson	McLaren M23-Ford	80	1h59m04.083
2	Emerson Fittipaldi	Lotus 72D-Ford	80	1h59m36.817
3	Jackie Oliver	Shadow DN1A-Ford	80	1h59m38.588
4	Jean-Pierre Beltoise	BRM P160E	80	1h59m40.597
5	Jackie Stewart	Tyrrell 006-Ford	79	
6	Howden Ganley	Williams IR03-Ford	79	

Winner's average speed: 99.130 mph. Starting grid front row: Peterson, 1m13.697 (pole) and Revson, 1m14.737. Fastest lap: E Fittipaldi, 1m15.496. Leaders: Peterson, laps 1-2; Lauda, 3-19; E Fittipaldi, 20-32; Stewart, 33; Beltoise, 34-39; Oliver, 40-46; Revson, 47-80

UNITED STATES GRAND PRIX

7 October 1973. Watkins Glen. 59 laps of a 3.377-mile circuit = 199.243 miles. Cool and dry. World Championship round 15

1	Ronnie Peterson	Lotus 72D-Ford	59	1h41m15.779
2	James Hunt	March 731-Ford	59	1h41m16.467
3	Carlos Reutemann	Brabham BT42-Ford	59	1h41m38.729
4	Denny Hulme	McLaren M23-Ford	59	1h42m06.025
5	Peter Revson	McLaren M23-Ford	59	1h42m36.166
6	Emerson Fittipaldi	Lotus 72D-Ford	59	1h43m03.744

Winner's average speed: 118.055 mph. Starting grid front row: Peterson, 1m39.657 (pole) and Reutemann, 1m40.013. Fastest lap: Hunt, 1m41.652. Leaders: Peterson, laps 1-59

1974

Jackie Stewart's retirement from the sport heralded a major reshuffling of drivers among the teams. Tyrrell hired the relatively inexperienced partnership of Jody Scheckter and Patrick Depailler, while Emerson Fittipaldi moved to the McLaren team, which was sponsored by Marlboro for the first time. Fittipaldi's replacement at Lotus was Jacky Ickx. Meanwhile, Ferrari re-signed Clay Regazzoni and added the promising Niki Lauda from BRM.

It was a great season for the World Championship, culminating in a three-way finale in America. With two wins, Scheckter had only an outside chance of becoming champion at that final round, whereas Fittipaldi and Regazzoni entered the race equal on points. With the Ferrari delayed by faulty shock absorbers, Fittipaldi's conservative race to fourth was enough to give him a second World Championship.

Niki Lauda was the fastest driver of the year, but was forced to retire several times while leading. Although Lauda ended the season with two wins, his lack of reliability cost him a chance at the championship. Regazzoni also led a 1-2 for the Ferrari team at the Nurburgring.

Young Argentinian Carlos Reutemann won the first three Grands Prix of his career in the Gordon Murray-designed Brabham BT44. But throughout his career he failed to win his home race, despite his own best efforts and those of a partisan and patriotic crowd. In 1974, Reutemann ran out of fuel two laps from victory, handing Denny Hulme a final victory in his retirement year. Brabham's year ended with a 1-2 for the team, with Reutemann leading Carlos Pace home at Watkins Glen.

Lotus introduced the disappointing 76, but Ronnie Peterson was spectacular when the team wheeled out the aging Lotus 72, scoring three wins. Hesketh built its first Harvey Postlethwaite-designed car, and James Hunt finished on the podium on three occasions.

GRAN PREMIO DE LA REPUBLICA ARGENTINA

13 January 1974. Buenos Aires. 53 laps of a 3.709-mile circuit = 196.577 miles. Hot, dry and sunny. World Championship round 1

1	Denny Hulme	McLaren M23-Ford	53	1h41m02.01
2	Niki Lauda	Ferrari 312B3	53	1h41m11.28
3	Clay Regazzoni	Ferrari 312B3	53	1h41m22.42
4	Mike Hailwood	McLaren M23-Ford	53	1h41m33.80
5	Jean-Pierre Beltoise	BRM P160E	53	1h41m53.85
6	Patrick Depailler	Tyrrell 005-Ford	53	1h42m54.49

Winner's average speed: 116.740 mph. Starting grid front row: Peterson, 1m50.78 (pole) and Regazzoni, 1m50.96. Fastest lap: Regazzoni, 1m52.10. Leaders: Peterson, laps 1-2; Reutemann, 3-51; Hulme, 52-53

GRANDE PREMIO DO BRASIL

27 January 1974. Interlagos. 32 laps of a 4.946-mile circuit = 158.272 miles. Race scheduled for 40 laps, stopped early due to rain. Dry and cloudy at the start, rain later. World Championship round 2

1	Emerson Fittipaldi	McLaren M23-Ford	32	1h24m37.06
2	Clay Regazzoni	Ferrari 312B3	32	1h24m50.63
3	Jacky Ickx	Lotus 72D-Ford	31	
4	Carlos Pace	Surtees TS16/2-Ford	31	
5	Mike Hailwood	McLaren M23-Ford	31	
6	Ronnie Peterson	Lotus 72D-Ford	31	

Winner's average speed: 112.226 mph. Starting grid front row: Fittipaldi, 2m32.97 (pole) and Reutemann, 2m33.21. Fastest lap: Regazzoni, 2m36.05. Leaders: Reutemann, laps 1-3; Peterson, 4-15; Fittipaldi, 16-32

LUCKY STRIKE SOUTH AFRICAN GRAND PRIX

30 March 1974. Kyalami. 78 laps of a 2.550-mile circuit = 198.900 miles. Warm, dry and sunny. World Championship round 3

1	Carlos Reutemann	Brabham BT44-Ford	78	1h42m40.96
2	Jean-Pierre Beltoise	BRM P201	78	1h43m14.90
3	Mike Hailwood	McLaren M23-Ford	78	1h43m23.12
4	Patrick Depailler	Tyrrell 005-Ford	78	1h43m25.15
5	Hans-Joachim Stuck	March 741-Ford	78	1h43m27.19
6	Arturo Merzario	Williams FW02-Ford	78	1h43m37.00

Winner's average speed: 116.222 mph. Starting grid front row: Lauda, 1m16.58 (pole) and Pace, 1m16.63. Fastest lap: Reutemann, 1m18.16. Leaders: Lauda, laps 1-8; Reutemann, 9-78

GRAN PREMIO DE ESPANA

28 April 1974. Jarama. 84 laps of a 2.115-mile circuit = 177.694 miles. Race scheduled for 90 laps, stopped after two hours. Wet at the start, drying later. World Championship round 4

1	Niki Lauda	Ferrari 312B3	84	2h00m29.56
2	Clay Regazzoni	Ferrari 312B3	84	2h01m05.17
3	Emerson Fittipaldi	McLaren M23-Ford	83	
4	Hans-Joachim Stuck	March 741-Ford	82	
5	Jody Scheckter	Tyrrell 007-Ford	82	
6	Denny Hulme	McLaren M23-Ford	82	

Winner's average speed: 88.484 mph. Starting grid front row: Lauda, 1m18.44 (pole) and Peterson, 1m18.47. Fastest lap: Lauda, 1m20.83. Leaders: Peterson, laps 1-20; Lauda, 21-23, 25-84; Ickx, 24

BANG & OLUFSEN GRAND PRIX DE BELGIQUE

12 May 1974. Nivelles. 85 laps of a 2.314-mile circuit = 196.690 miles. Warm, dry and sunny. World Championship round 5

1	Emerson Fittipaldi	McLaren M23-Ford	85	1h44m20.57
2	Niki Lauda	Ferrari 312B3	85	1h44m20.92
3	Jody Scheckter	Tyrrell 007-Ford	85	1h45m06.18
4	Clay Regazzoni	Ferrari 312B3	85	1h45m12.59
5	Jean-Pierre Beltoise	BRM P201	85	1h45m28.62
6	Denny Hulme	McLaren M23-Ford	85	1h45m31.11

Winner's average speed: 113.102 mph. Starting grid front row: Regazzoni, 1m09.82 (pole) and Scheckter, 1m10.86. Fastest lap: Hulme, 1m11.31. Leaders: Regazzoni, laps 1-38; Fittipaldi, 39-85

GRAND PRIX DE MONACO

26 May 1974. Monte Carlo. 78 laps of a 2.037-mile circuit = 158.886 miles. Warm, dry and sunny. World Championship round 6

1	Ronnie Peterson	Lotus 72E-Ford	78	1h58m03.7
2	Jody Scheckter	Tyrrell 007-Ford	78	1h58m32.5
3	Jean-Pierre Jarier	Shadow DN3A-Ford	78	1h58m52.6
4	Clay Regazzoni	Ferrari 312B3	78	1h59m06.8
5	Emerson Fittipaldi	McLaren M23-Ford	77	
6	John Watson	Brabham BT42-Ford	77	

Winner's average speed: 80.747 mph. Starting grid front row: Lauda, 1m26.3 (pole) and Regazzoni, 1m26.6. Fastest lap: Peterson, 1m27.9. Leaders: Regazzoni, laps 1-20; Lauda, 21-32; Peterson, 33-78

TEXACO SVERIGES GRAND PRIX

9 June 1974. Anderstorp. 80 laps of a 2.497-mile circuit = 199.760 miles. Warm, dry and sunny. World Championship round 7

1	Jody Scheckter	Tyrrell 007-Ford	80	1h58m31.391
2	Patrick Depailler	Tyrrell 007-Ford	80	1h58m31.771
3	James Hunt	Hesketh 308-Ford	80	1h58m34.716
4	Emerson Fittipaldi	McLaren M23-Ford	80	1h59m24.898
5	Jean-Pierre Jarier	Shadow DN3A-Ford	80	1h59m47.794
6	Graham Hill	Lola T370-Ford	79	

Winner's average speed: 101.125 mph. Starting grid front row: Depailler, 1m24.758 (pole) and Scheckter, 1m25.076. Fastest lap: Depailler, 1m27.262. Leaders: Scheckter, laps 1-80

1974 DRIVERS' RECORDS

driver	car	RA Q	RA R	BR Q	BR R	ZA Q	ZA R	E Q	E R	B Q	B R	MC Q	MC R	S Q	S R	NL Q	NL R	F Q	F R	GB Q	GB R	D Q	D R	A Q	A R	I Q	I R	CDN Q	CDN R	USA Q	USA R
Chris Amon	Amon AF101-Ford							24	R			20	DNS							31	DNQ			30	DNQ						
	BRM P201																									25	NC	12	9		
Mario Andretti	Parnelli VPJ4-Ford																											16	7	3	DSQ
Ian Ashley	Token RJ02-Ford																			26	DSQ	24	NC								
	Brabham BT42-Ford																											30	DNQ	29	DNQ
Derek Bell	Surtees TS16/3-Ford																			27	DNQ	25	11	28	DNQ	28	DNQ	27	DNQ		
Tom Belso	Williams FW01-Ford					27	R																								
	Williams FW02-Ford							28	DNQ					21	8					28	DNQ										
Jean-Pierre Beltoise																															
	BRM P160E	14	5	17	10																										
	BRM P201					11	2	12	R	7	5	11	R	13	R	16	R	17	10	23	12	15	R	18	R	11	R	17	NC	NT	DNP
Vittorio Brambilla	March 741-Ford					19	10	9	DNS	31	9	15	R	17	10	15	10	16	11	18	R	23	13	20	6	13	R	29	DNQ	25	R
Dave Charlton	McLaren M23-Ford					20	19																								
Patrick Depailler	Tyrrell 005-Ford	15	6	16	8	15	4																								
	Tyrrell 006-Ford							17	8			4	9			9	8														
	Tyrrell 007-Ford									11	R			1	2F	8	6			10	R	5	R	14	R	10	11	7	5	13	6
Jose Dolhem	Surtees TS16/3-Ford																	26	DNQ							26	DNQ			26	R
Mark Donohue	Penske PC1-Ford																											24	12	14	R
Paddy Driver	Lotus 72-Ford					26	R																								
Guy Edwards	Lola T370-Ford	25	11	25	R			27	DNQ	21	12	26	8	18	7	14	R	20	15			29	DNQ								
Carlo Facetti	Brabham BT42-Ford																									27	DNQ				
Emerson Fittipaldi	McLaren M23-Ford	3	10	1	1	5	7	4	3	4	1	13	5	9	4	3	3	5	R	8	2	3	R	3	R	6	2	1	1	8	4
Howden Ganley	March 741-Ford	19	8	20	R																										
	Maki F101-Ford																			32	DNQ	NT	DNQ								
Peter Gethin	Lola T370-Ford																			21	R										
Mike Hailwood	McLaren M23-Ford	9	4	7	5	12	3	18	9	13	7	10	R	11	R	4	4	6	7	11	R	12	R								
Graham Hill	Lola T370-Ford	17	R	21	11	18	12	20	R	29	8	21	7	15	6	19	R	21	13	22	13	19	9	21	NC	21	8	20	14	24	8
David Hobbs	McLaren M23-Ford																							17	7	23	9				
Denny Hulme	McLaren M23-Ford	10	1	11	12	9	9	8	6	12	6F	12	R	12	R	9	R	11	6	19	7	7	R	10	2	19	6	14	6	17	R
James Hunt	March 731-Ford	5	R	18	9																										
	Hesketh 308-Ford					14	R	11	10	9	R	7	R	6	3	6	R	10	R	6	R	13	R	7	3	8	R	8	4	2	3
Jacky Ickx	Lotus 72D-Ford	7	R	5	3																										
	Lotus 76-Ford					10	R	5	R	16	R														22	R	16	R				
	Lotus 72E-Ford													19	R	7	R	18	11	13	5	12	3	9	5			21	13	16	R
Jean-Pierre Jabouille																															
	Williams FW01-Ford																	25	DNQ												
	Surtees TS16/3-Ford																							30	DNQ						
Jean-Pierre Jarier	Shadow DN1A-Ford	16	R	19	R																										
	Shadow DN3A-Ford							13	NC	17	13	6	3	8	5	7	R	12	12	16	R	18	8	23	8	9	R	5	R	10	10
Eddie Keizan	Tyrrell 004-Ford					24	14																								
Leo Kinnunen	Surtees TS16/1-Ford											32	DNQ			26	R			29	DNQ	34	DNQ	27	DNQ	31	DNQ				
Helmuth Koinigg	Brabham BT42-Ford																							31	DNQ						
	Surtees TS16/3-Ford																											22	10	23	R
Jacques Laffite	Williams FW02-Ford																					21	R	12	NC	17	R	18	15	11	R
Gerard Larrousse	Brabham BT42-Ford									28	R							30	DNQ												
Niki Lauda	Ferrari 312B3	8	2	3	R	1	16	1	1F	3	2	1	R	3	R	1	1	1	2	1	5F	1	R	1	R	1	R	2	RF	5	R
Gijs van Lennep	Williams FW02-Ford															30	14														
	Williams FW01-Ford																	27	DNQ												
Lella Lombardi	Brabham BT42-Ford																			29	DNQ										
Jochen Mass	Surtees TS16/2-Ford	18	R	10	17	17	R	19	R	26	R	17	DNS	22	R	20	R														
	Surtees TS16/3-Ford																	18	R	17	14	10	R								
	McLaren M23-Ford																											12	16	20	7
Arturo Merzario	Williams FW01-Ford	13	R	9	R																										
	Williams FW02-Ford					3	6	28	DNS							21	R	15	9												
	Williams FW03-Ford									7	R	6	R	14	R					15	R	16	R	9	R	15	4	19	R	15	R
Francois Migault	BRM P160E	24	R	23	16	25	15	23	R	25	16	22	R			22	14	14	NC	27	DNQ										
	BRM P201																	25	R			25	R	24	R						
John Nicholson	Lyncar 006-Ford																			31	DNQ										
Rikky von Opel	Ensign N174-Ford	26	DNS																												
	Brabham BT44-Ford					25	R	22	R	28	DNQ	20	9	23	9	28	DNQ														
Carlos Pace	Surtees TS16/2-Ford	11	R	12	4	2	11	15	13	8	R	18	R	24	R																
	Brabham BT42-Ford																	24	DNQ												
	Brabham BT44-Ford																			20	9	17	12	4	R	3	5F	9	8	4	2F
Larry Perkins	Amon AF101-Ford																							30	DNQ						

Formula 1

driver	car	RA		BR		ZA		E		B		MC		S		NL		F		GB		D		A		I		CDN		USA	
		Q	R	Q	R	Q	R	Q	R	Q	R	Q	R	Q	R	Q	R	Q	R	Q	R	Q	R	Q	R	Q	R	Q	R	Q	R
Henri Pescarolo	BRM P160E	21	9	22	14	21	18	21	12	15	R	27	R	-	-	24	R	-	-	-	-	-	-	-	-	-	-	-	-	-	-
	BRM P201	-	-	-	-	-	-	-	-	-	-	-	-	19	R	-	-	19	R	24	R	24	10	-	-	25	R	-	-	-	-
Ronnie Peterson	Lotus 72D-Ford	1	13	4	6	-	-	-	-	-	-	-	-	-	-	-	-	-	-	-	-	-	-	-	-	-	-	-	-	-	-
	Lotus 76-Ford	-	-	-	-	16	R	2	R	5	R	-	-	-	-	-	-	-	-	-	-	8	4	-	-	-	-	-	-	-	-
	Lotus 72E-Ford	-	-	-	-	-	-	-	-	3	1F	5	R	10	8F	2	1	2	10	-	-	6	R	7	1	10	3	19	R
Teddy Pilette	Brabham BT42-Ford	-	-	-	-	-	-	-	-	27	17	-	-	-	-	-	-	-	-	-	-	-	-	-	-	-	-	-	-	-	-
Tom Pryce	Token RJ02-Ford	-	-	-	-	-	-	-	-	20	R	-	-	-	-	-	-	-	-	-	-	-	-	-	-	-	-	-	-	-	-
	Shadow DN3A-Ford	-	-	-	-	-	-	-	-	-	-	-	-	-	-	11	R	3	R	5	8	11	6	16	R	22	10	13	R	18	NC
David Purley	Token RJ02-Ford	-	-	-	-	-	-	-	-	-	-	-	-	-	-	-	-	26	DNQ	-	-	-	-	-	-	-	-	-	-	-	-
Dieter Quester	Surtees TS16/3-Ford	-	-	-	-	-	-	-	-	-	-	-	-	-	-	-	-	-	-	-	-	-	-	25	9	-	-	-	-	-	-
Brian Redman	Shadow DN3A-Ford	-	-	-	-	22	7	18	18	16	R	-	-	-	-	-	-	-	-	-	-	-	-	-	-	-	-	-	-	-	-
Clay Regazzoni	Ferrari 312B3	2	3F	8	2F	6	R	3	2	1	4	2	4	4	R	2	2	4	3	7	4	2	1	8	5F	5	R	6	2	9	11
Carlos Reutemann																															
	Brabham BT44-Ford	6	7	2	7	4	1F	6	R	24	R	8	R	8	R	10	R	12	12	8	R	4	6	6	3	2	1	2	R	4	9	1	1
Peter Revson	Shadow DN3A-Ford	4	R	6	R	-	-	-	-	-	-	-	-	-	-	-	-	-	-	-	-	-	-	-	-	-	-	-	-	-	-
Richard Robarts	Brabham BT44-Ford	22	R	24	15	23	17	-	-	-	-	-	-	-	-	-	-	-	-	-	-	-	-	-	-	-	-	-	-	-	-
	Williams FW02-Ford	-	-	-	-	-	-	-	-	-	-	25	DNS	-	-	-	-	-	-	-	-	-	-	-	-	-	-	-	-	-	-
Bertil Roos	Shadow DN3A-Ford	-	-	-	-	-	-	-	-	-	-	23	R	-	-	-	-	-	-	-	-	-	-	-	-	-	-	-	-	-	-
Ian Scheckter	Lotus 72-Ford	-	-	-	-	22	13	-	-	-	-	-	-	-	-	-	-	-	-	-	-	-	-	-	-	-	-	-	-	-	-
	Hesketh 308-Ford	-	-	-	-	-	-	-	-	-	-	-	-	-	-	-	-	-	-	-	-	26	DNQ	-	-	-	-	-	-	-	-
Jody Scheckter	Tyrrell 006-Ford	12	R	14	13	8	8	-	-	-	-	-	-	-	-	-	-	-	-	-	-	-	-	-	-	-	-	-	-	-	-
	Tyrrell 007-Ford	-	-	-	-	-	-	10	5	2	3	5	2	2	1	5	5	7	4F	3	1	4	2F	5	R	12	3	3	R	6	R
Tim Schenken	Trojan T103-Ford	-	-	-	-	26	14	23	10	24	R	-	-	26	DNQ	-	-	25	R	28	DNQ	19	10	20	R	-	-	-	-
	Lotus 76-Ford	-	-	-	-	-	-	-	-	-	-	-	-	-	-	-	-	-	-	-	-	-	-	-	-	-	-	27	DSQ
Vern Schuppan	Ensign N174-Ford	-	-	-	-	-	-	14	15	25	R	-	-	17	R	23	DNQ	30	DNQ	22	R	-	-	-	-	-	-	-	-
	Ensign N173-Ford	-	-	-	-	-	-	-	-	-	-	27	DSQ	-	-	-	-	-	-	-	-	-	-	-	-	-	-	-	-
Rolf Stommelen	Lola T370-Ford	-	-	-	-	-	-	-	-	-	-	-	-	-	-	-	-	-	-	-	-	13	R	14	R	11	11	21	12
Hans-Joachim Stuck																															
	March 741-Ford	23	R	13	R	7	5	14	4	10	R	9	R	-	-	22	R	27	DNQ	9	R	20	7	15	R	18	R	23	R	28	DNQ
John Watson	Brabham BT42-Ford	20	12	15	R	13	R	16	11	19	11	23	6	14	11	13	7	14	16	13	11	-	-	-	-	-	-	-	-
	Brabham BT44-Ford	-	-	-	-	-	-	-	-	-	-	-	-	-	-	-	-	-	-	-	-	14	R	11	4	4	7	15	R	7	5
Eppie Wietzes	Brabham BT42-Ford	-	-	-	-	-	-	-	-	-	-	-	-	-	-	-	-	-	-	-	-	-	-	-	-	26	R	-	-
Mike Wilds	March 731-Ford	-	-	-	-	-	-	-	-	-	-	-	-	-	-	-	-	33	DNQ	-	-	-	-	-	-	-	-	-	-
	Ensign N174-Ford	-	-	-	-	-	-	-	-	-	-	-	-	-	-	-	-	-	-	-	-	-	-	29	DNQ	29	DNQ	28	DNQ	22	NC
Reine Wisell	March 741-Ford	-	-	-	-	-	-	-	-	-	-	16	R	-	-	-	-	-	-	-	-	-	-	-	-	-	-	-	-

1974 FINAL CHAMPIONSHIP POSITIONS

Drivers

1	Emerson Fittipaldi	55
2	Clay Regazzoni	52
3	Jody Scheckter	45
4	Niki Lauda	38
5	Ronnie Peterson	35
6	Carlos Reutemann	32
7	Denny Hulme	20
8	James Hunt	15
9	Patrick Depailler	14
10=	Mike Hailwood	12
	Jacky Ickx	12
12	Carlos Pace	11
13	Jean-Pierre Beltoise	10
14=	Jean-Pierre Jarier	6
	John Watson	6
16	Hans-Joachim Stuck	5
17	Arturo Merzario	4
18=	Vittorio Brambilla	1
	Graham Hill	1
	Tom Pryce	1

Sum of best seven results from the first eight races and best six results from the final seven races

Manufacturers

1	McLaren-Ford	73 (75)*
2	Ferrari	65
3	Tyrrell-Ford	52
4	Lotus-Ford	42
5	Brabham-Ford	35
6	Hesketh-Ford	15
7	BRM	10
8	Shadow-Ford	7
9	March-Ford	6
10	Williams-Ford	4
11	Surtees-Ford	3
12	Lola-Ford	1

*Sum of best seven results from the first eight races and best six results from the final seven races. Points only awarded to first car to finish for each manufacturer

GROTE PRIJS VAN NEDERLAND

23 June 1974. Zandvoort. 75 laps of a 2.626-mile circuit = 196.950 miles. Warm, dry and sunny. World Championship round 8

1	Niki Lauda	Ferrari 312B3	75	1h43m00.35
2	Clay Regazzoni	Ferrari 312B3	75	1h43m08.60
3	Emerson Fittipaldi	McLaren M23-Ford	75	1h43m30.62
4	Mike Hailwood	McLaren M23-Ford	75	1h43m31.64
5	Jody Scheckter	Tyrrell 007-Ford	75	1h43m34.63
6	Patrick Depailler	Tyrrell 007-Ford	75	1h43m51.86

Winner's average speed: 114.722 mph. Starting grid front row: Lauda, 1m18.31 (pole) and Regazzoni, 1m18.91. Fastest lap: Peterson, 1m21.44. Leaders: Lauda, laps 1-75

GRAND PRIX DE FRANCE

7 July 1974. Dijon-Prenois. 80 laps of a 2.044-mile circuit = 163.520 miles. Warm, dry and sunny. World Championship round 9

1	Ronnie Peterson	Lotus 72E-Ford	80	1h21m55.02
2	Niki Lauda	Ferrari 312B3	80	1h22m15.38
3	Clay Regazzoni	Ferrari 312B3	80	1h22m22.86

4	Jody Scheckter	Tyrrell 007-Ford	80	1h22m23.13
5	Jacky Ickx	Lotus 72E-Ford	80	1h22m32.56
6	Denny Hulme	McLaren M23-Ford	80	1h22m33.16

Winner's average speed: 119.770 mph. Starting grid front row: Lauda, 58.79s (pole) and Peterson, 59.08s. Fastest lap: Scheckter, 1m00.0. Leaders: Lauda, laps 1-16; Peterson, 17-80

JOHN PLAYER BRITISH GRAND PRIX

20 July 1974. Brands Hatch. 75 laps of a 2.650-mile circuit = 198.750 miles. Warm, dry and sunny. World Championship round 10

1	Jody Scheckter	Tyrrell 007-Ford	75	1h43m02.2
2	Emerson Fittipaldi	McLaren M23-Ford	75	1h43m17.5
3	Jacky Ickx	Lotus 72E-Ford	75	1h44m03.7
4	Clay Regazzoni	Ferrari 312B3	75	1h44m09.4
5*	Niki Lauda	Ferrari 312B3	74	
6	Carlos Reutemann	Brabham BT44-Ford	74	

*Lauda did not complete 74 laps due to being blocked in the pits, and he was originally classified ninth until Ferrari successfully protested the results. Winner's average speed: 115.735 mph. Starting grid front row: Lauda, 1m19.7 (pole) and Peterson, 1m19.7. Fastest lap: Lauda, 1m21.1. Leaders: Lauda, laps 1-69; Scheckter, 70-75

GROSSER PREIS VON DEUTSCHLAND UND EUROPA

4 August 1974. Nurburgring. 14 laps of a 14.189-mile circuit = 198.646 miles. Overcast with showers. World Championship round 11

1	Clay Regazzoni	Ferrari 312B3	14	1h41m35.0
2	Jody Scheckter	Tyrrell 007-Ford	14	1h42m25.7
3	Carlos Reutemann	Brabham BT44-Ford	14	1h42m58.2
4	Ronnie Peterson	Lotus 76-Ford	14	1h42m59.2
5	Jacky Ickx	Lotus 72E-Ford	14	1h43m00.0
6	Tom Pryce	Shadow DN3A-Ford	14	1h43m53.1

Winner's average speed: 117.330 mph. Starting grid front row: Lauda, 7m00.8 (pole) and Regazzoni, 7m01.1. Fastest lap: Scheckter, 7m11.1. Leaders: Regazzoni, laps 1-14

MEMPHIS GROSSER PREIS VON OSTERREICH

18 August 1974. Osterreichring. 54 laps of a 3.673-mile circuit = 198.342 miles. Very hot, dry and sunny. World Championship round 12

1	Carlos Reutemann	Brabham BT44-Ford	54	1h28m44.72
2	Denny Hulme	McLaren M23-Ford	54	1h29m27.64
3	James Hunt	Hesketh 308-Ford	54	1h29m46.26
4	John Watson	Brabham BT44-Ford	54	1h29m54.11
5	Clay Regazzoni	Ferrari 312B3	54	1h29m57.80
6	Vittorio Brambilla	March 741-Ford	54	1h29m58.54

Winner's average speed: 134.097 mph. Starting grid front row: Lauda, 1m35.40 (pole) and Reutemann, 1m35.56. Fastest lap: Regazzoni, 1m37.22. Leaders: Reutemann, laps 1-54

GRAN PREMIO D'ITALIA

8 September 1974. Monza. 52 laps of a 3.592-mile circuit = 186.784 miles. Very hot, dry and sunny. World Championship round 13

1	Ronnie Peterson	Lotus 72E-Ford	52	1h22m56.6
2	Emerson Fittipaldi	McLaren M23-Ford	52	1h22m57.4
3	Jody Scheckter	Tyrrell 007-Ford	52	1h23m21.3
4	Arturo Merzario	Williams FW03-Ford	52	1h24m24.3
5	Carlos Pace	Brabham BT44-Ford	51	
6	Denny Hulme	McLaren M23-Ford	51	

Winner's average speed: 135.117 mph. Starting grid front row: Lauda, 1m33.16 (pole) and Reutemann, 1m33.27. Fastest lap: Pace, 1m34.2. Leaders: Lauda, laps 1-29; Regazzoni, 30-40; Peterson, 41-52

LABATT'S 50 CANADIAN GRAND PRIX

22 September 1974. Mosport Park. 80 laps of a 2.459-mile circuit = 196.720 miles. Cool and dry. World Championship round 14

1	Emerson Fittipaldi	McLaren M23-Ford	80	1h40m26.136
2	Clay Regazzoni	Ferrari 312B3	80	1h40m39.170
3	Ronnie Peterson	Lotus 72E-Ford	80	1h40m40.630
4	James Hunt	Hesketh 308-Ford	80	1h40m41.805

5	Patrick Depailler	Tyrrell 007-Ford	80	1h41m21.458
6	Denny Hulme	McLaren M23-Ford	79	

Winner's average speed: 117.520 mph. Starting grid front row: Fittipaldi, 1m13.188 (pole) and Lauda, 1m13.230. Fastest lap: Lauda, 1m13.659. Leaders: Lauda, laps 1-67; Fittipaldi, 68-80

UNITED STATES GRAND PRIX

6 October 1974. Watkins Glen. 59 laps of a 3.377-mile circuit = 199.243 miles. Warm, dry and sunny. World Championship round 15

1	Carlos Reutemann	Brabham BT44-Ford	59	1h40m21.439
2	Carlos Pace	Brabham BT44-Ford	59	1h40m32.174
3	James Hunt	Hesketh 308-Ford	59	1h41m31.823
4	Emerson Fittipaldi	McLaren M23-Ford	59	1h41m39.192
5	John Watson	Brabham BT44-Ford	59	1h41m47.243
6	Patrick Depailler	Tyrrell 007-Ford	59	1h41m48.945

Winner's average speed: 119.120 mph. Starting grid front row: . Reutemann, 1m38.978 (pole) and Hunt, 1m38.995. Fastest lap: Pace, 1m40.608. Leaders: Reutemann, laps 1-59

1975 The Ferrari of new World Champion Niki Lauda leads Emerson Fittipaldi at Watkins Glen.

1975

Niki Lauda had promised to dominate Grand Prix racing in 1974, only to be thwarted by mechanical failures. In 1975 Lauda delivered, winning Ferrari its first World Championship since 1964. Designer Mauro Forghieri introduced the 312T with transverse gearbox (hence the "T" designation) to improve weight distribution. The combination of Lauda and Ferrari proved irresistible, and his five wins were backed up by Clay Regazzoni's victory at Monza.

McLaren won three times, with two of the victories coming in shortened races. The British GP was stopped when a downpour sent twelve cars sliding into the barriers. Emerson Fittipaldi took the win. Of the top six classified finishers, only two were still running at the flag!

Fittipaldi's new teammate Jochen Mass scored the only Grand Prix win of his career in the tragic Spanish GP at the end of April. Practice had been disrupted by protests from the Grand Prix Drivers' Association that the circuit, particularly its barriers, was unsafe. Their fears were realised when race leader Rolf Stommelen crashed over the barrier, killing five spectators. Lella Lombardi became the only woman in Grand Prix history to finish in the points when she took sixth in the race. It was also the first time that reduced points were awarded, since less than half of the race had been completed.

Torrential rain also shortened the Austrian GP and again forced the reduction of points. Vittorio Brambilla celebrated his only victory by crashing over the finish line! Tragedy had marred the event when a high-speed puncture caused Mark Donohue to crash in practice with fatal consequences.

James Hunt's Hesketh beat Lauda in a tremendous Dutch GP, but the financial burden of running a team without major sponsorship forced team patron Lord Hesketh to quit F1 at the end of the year. The Hesketh marque continued in Grand Prix racing, but it would never again be a force. Jody Scheckter and Tyrrell won in South Africa, but Lotus endured a fruitless year.

Brabham continued to improve, with both Carlos Reutemann and Carlos Pace winning races for the Martini-sponsored team. Pace's victory in the Brazilian GP would be the only one of his career, while Reutemann won at the Nurburgring. Jean-Pierre Jarier showed sensational early-season form for Shadow, qualifying on pole for the South American races, but was denied victory in Brazil by mechanical failure. Although Welsh teammate Tom Pryce was on pole in Britain, his promise did not translate into race wins either.

The year ended in yet another tragedy. Graham Hill had run an Embassy-sponsored team for two seasons, and in May he announced his retirement from the cockpit to concentrate on managing the concern, which had hired possibly the best young driver of the time, Tony Brise. But the new team came to an abrupt end in November, when the light plane flown by Hill crashed in fog near Elstree airfield when returning from testing at Circuit Paul Ricard. Both Hill and Brise were killed, together with designer Andy Smallman and three mechanics.

Firestone withdrew from Formula 1 early in the season, leaving Goodyear as the sole tyre supplier, and the Owen Racing Organisation ended its backing of BRM.

GRAN PREMIO DE LA REPUBLICA ARGENTINA

12 January 1975. Buenos Aires. 53 laps of a 3.709-mile circuit = 196.577 miles. Hot, dry and sunny. World Championship round 1

1	Emerson Fittipaldi	McLaren M23-Ford	53	1h39m26.29
2	James Hunt	Hesketh 308-Ford	53	1h39m32.20
3	Carlos Reutemann	Brabham BT44B-Ford	53	1h39m43.35
4	Clay Regazzoni	Ferrari 312B3	53	1h40m02.08
5	Patrick Depailler	Tyrrell 007-Ford	53	1h40m20.54
6	Niki Lauda	Ferrari 312B3	53	1h40m45.94

Winner's average speed: 118.577 mph. Starting grid front row: Pace, 1m49.21 (pole) and Pace, 1m49.64 - Jarier did not start. Fastest lap: Hunt, 1m50.91. Leaders: Reutemann, laps 1-25; Hunt, 26-34; E Fittipaldi, 35-53

GRANDE PREMIO DO BRASIL

26 January 1975. Interlagos. 40 laps of a 4.946-mile circuit = 197.840 miles. Very hot, dry and sunny. World Championship round 2

1	Carlos Pace	Brabham BT44B-Ford	40	1h44m41.17
2	Emerson Fittipaldi	McLaren M23-Ford	40	1h44m46.96
3	Jochen Mass	McLaren M23-Ford	40	1h45m17.83
4	Clay Regazzoni	Ferrari 312B3	40	1h45m24.45
5	Niki Lauda	Ferrari 312B3	40	1h45m43.05
6	James Hunt	Hesketh 308-Ford	40	1h45m46.29

Winner's average speed: 113.390 mph. Starting grid front row: Jarier, 2m29.88 (pole) and E Fittipaldi, 2m30.68. Fastest lap: Jarier, 2m34.16. Leaders: Reutemann, laps 1-4; Jarier, 5-32; Pace, 33-40

LUCKY STRIKE SOUTH AFRICAN GRAND PRIX

1 March 1975. Kyalami. 78 laps of a 2.550-mile circuit = 198.900 miles. Warm, dry and overcast. World Championship round 3

1	Jody Scheckter	Tyrrell 007-Ford	78	1h43m16.90
2	Carlos Reutemann	Brabham BT44B-Ford	78	1h43m20.64
3	Patrick Depailler	Tyrrell 007-Ford	78	1h43m33.82
4	Carlos Pace	Brabham BT44B-Ford	78	1h43m34.21
5	Niki Lauda	Ferrari 312T	78	1h43m45.54
6	Jochen Mass	McLaren M23-Ford	78	1h44m20.24

Winner's average speed: 115.548 mph. Starting grid front row: Pace, 1m16.41 (pole) and Reutemann, 1m16.48. Fastest lap: Pace, 1m17.20. Leaders: Pace, laps 1-2; J Scheckter, 3-78

GRAN PREMIO DE ESPANA

27 April 1975. Montjuich Park. 29 laps of a 2.355-mile circuit = 68.295 miles. Race scheduled for 75 laps but stopped due to serious accident, half points awarded as less than 60% of the race had been completed. Warm, dry and sunny. World Championship round 4

1	Jochen Mass	McLaren M23-Ford	29	42m53.7
2	Jacky Ickx	Lotus 72E-Ford	29	42m54.8
3	Carlos Reutemann	Brabham BT44B-Ford	28	
4	Jean-Pierre Jarier*	Shadow DN5A-Ford	28	
5	Vittorio Brambilla	March 751-Ford	28	
6	Lella Lombardi	March 751-Ford	27	

*Jarier finished, but was penalised 1 lap for passing another car while caution flags were being shown. Winner's average speed: 95.529 mph. Starting grid front row: Lauda, 1m23.4 (pole) and Regazzoni, 1m23.5. Fastest lap: Andretti, 1m25.10. Leaders: Hunt, laps 1-6; Andretti, 7-16; Stommelen, 17-21, 23-25; Pace, 22; Mass, 26-27, 29; Ickx, 28

GRAND PRIX DE MONACO

11 May 1975. Monte Carlo. 75 laps of a 2.037-mile circuit = 152.775 miles. Race scheduled for 78 laps, stopped after two hours. Rain at the start, eventually drying. World Championship round 5

1	Niki Lauda	Ferrari 312T	75	2h01m21.31
2	Emerson Fittipaldi	McLaren M23-Ford	75	2h01m24.09
3	Carlos Pace	Brabham BT44B-Ford	75	2h01m39.12
4	Ronnie Peterson	Lotus 72E-Ford	75	2h01m59.76
5	Patrick Depailler	Tyrrell 007-Ford	75	2h02m02.17
6	Jochen Mass	McLaren M23-Ford	75	2h02m03.38

Winner's average speed: 75.534 mph. Starting grid front row: Lauda, 1m26.40 (pole) and Pryce, 1m27.09. Fastest lap: Depailler, 1m28.67. Leaders: Lauda, laps 1-23, 25-75; Peterson, 24

GRAND PRIX DE BELGIQUE

25 May 1975. Zolder. 70 laps of a 2.648-mile circuit = 185.360 miles. Dry and overcast. World Championship round 6

1	Niki Lauda	Ferrari 312T	70	1h43m53.98
2	Jody Scheckter	Tyrrell 007-Ford	70	1h44m13.20
3	Carlos Reutemann	Brabham BT44B-Ford	70	1h44m35.80
4	Patrick Depailler	Tyrrell 007-Ford	70	1h44m54.06
5	Clay Regazzoni	Ferrari 312T	70	1h44m57.84
6	Tom Pryce	Shadow DN5A-Ford	70	1h45m22.43

Winner's average speed: 107.042 mph. Starting grid front row: Lauda, 1m25.43 (pole) and Pace, 1m25.47. Fastest lap: Regazzoni, 1m26.76. Leaders: Pace, laps 1-3; Brambilla, 4-5; Lauda, 6-70

POLAR SVERIGES GRAND PRIX

8 June 1975. Anderstorp. 80 laps of a 2.497-mile circuit = 199.760 miles. Warm, dry and sunny. World Championship round 7

1	Niki Lauda	Ferrari 312T	80	1h59m18.319
2	Carlos Reutemann	Brabham BT44B-Ford	80	1h59m24.607
3	Clay Regazzoni	Ferrari 312T	80	1h59m47.414
4	Mario Andretti	Parnelli VPJ4-Ford	80	2h00m02.699
5	Mark Donohue	Penske PC1-Ford	80	2h00m49.082
6	Tony Brise	Hill GH1-Ford	79	

Winner's average speed: 100.462 mph. Starting grid front row: Brambilla, 1m24.630 (pole) and Depailler, 1m25.010. Fastest lap: Lauda, 1m28.267. Leaders: Brambilla, laps 1-15; Reutemann, 16-69; Lauda, 70-80

GROTE PRIJS VAN NEDERLAND

22 June 1975. Zandvoort. 75 laps of a 2.626-mile circuit = 196.950 miles. Rain at the start, drying later. World Championship round 8

1975 DRIVERS' RECORDS

driver	car	RA	BR	ZA	E	MC	B	S	NL	F	GB	D	A	I	USA
		Q R	Q R	Q R	Q R	Q R	Q R	Q R	Q R	Q R	Q R	Q R	Q R	Q R	Q R
Chris Amon	Ensign N175-Ford	-	-	-	-	-	-	-	-	-	-	-	24 12	19 12	-
Mario Andretti	Parnelli VPJ4-Ford	10 R	18 7	6 17	4 RF	13 R	-	15 4	-	15 5	12 12	13 R	19 R	15 R	5 R
Ian Ashley	Williams FW03-Ford	-	-	-	-	-	-	-	-	-	-	20DNS	-	-	-
Vittorio Brambilla	March 741-Ford	12 9	17 R	-	-	-	-	-	-	-	-	-	-	-	-
	March 751-Ford	-	-	7 R	5 5	5 R	3 R	1 R	11 R	8 R	5 6	11 R	8 1F	9 R	6 7
Tony Brise	Williams FW03-Ford	-	-	-	-	18 7	-	-	-	-	-	-	-	-	-
	Hill GH1-Ford	-	-	-	-	-	7 R	17 6	7 7	12 7	13 15	17 R	16 15	6 R	17 R
Dave Charlton	McLaren M23-Ford	-	-	20 14	-	-	-	-	-	-	-	-	-	-	-
Jim Crawford	Lotus 72E-Ford	-	-	-	-	-	-	-	-	-	-	25 R	-	25 13	-
Patrick Depailler	Tyrrell 007-Ford	8 5	9 R	5 3	7 R	12 5F	12 4	2 12	13 9	13 6	17 9	4 9	7 11	12 7	8 R
Mark Donohue	Penske PC1-Ford	16 7	15 R	18 8	17 R	16 R	21 11	16 5	18 8	18 R	-	-	-	-	-
	March 751-Ford	-	-	-	-	-	-	-	-	-	15 5	19 R	21DNS	-	-
Harald Ertl	Hesketh 308-Ford	-	-	-	-	-	-	-	-	-	-	23 8	27 R	17 9	-
Bob Evans	Stanley BRM P201	-	-	24 15	23 R	22DNQ	20 9	23 13	20 R	25 17	-	-	25 R	20 R	-
Emerson Fittipaldi	McLaren M23-Ford	5 1	2 2	11 NC	26 DNS	2 8	7 11	8 6	R 10	4 7	1 8	R 3	9 3	3 2	2 2F
Wilson Fittipaldi	Fittipaldi FD01-Ford	23 R	-	-	-	-	-	-	-	-	-	-	-	-	-
	Fittipaldi FD02-Ford	-	-	21 13	27DNQ	21 R	26DNQ	24 12	25 17	-	-	-	-	-	-
	Fittipaldi FD03-Ford	-	-	-	-	-	-	-	-	24 11	23 R	24 R	22 R	20DNS	23 10
Hiroshi Fushida	Maki F101C-Ford	-	-	-	-	-	-	-	-	25DNS	-	28DNQ	-	-	-
Brian Henton	Lotus 72E-Ford	-	-	-	-	-	-	-	-	-	-	21 16	-	23DNS	19NC
Graham Hill	Lola T370-Ford	21 10	20 12	28DNQ	-	-	-	-	-	-	-	-	-	-	-
	Hill GH1-Ford	-	-	-	-	-	21DNQ	-	-	-	-	-	-	-	-
James Hunt	Hesketh 308-Ford	6 2F	7 6	12 R	3 R	11 R	11 R	13 R	3 1	3 2	9 4	9 R	2 2	-	-
	Hesketh 308C-Ford	-	-	-	-	-	-	-	-	-	-	-	-	8 5	15 4
Jacky Ickx	Lotus 72E-Ford	18 8	12 9	21 12	16 2	14 8	16 R	18 15	21 R	19 R	-	-	-	-	-
Jean-Pierre Jabouille	Tyrrell 007-Ford	-	-	-	-	-	-	-	-	21 12	-	-	-	-	-
Jean-Pierre Jarier	Shadow DN5A-Ford	1DNS	1 RF	13 R	10 4	3 R	10 R	3 R	10 R	4 8	11 14	12 R	-	-	-
	Shadow DN7A-Matra	-	-	-	-	-	-	-	-	-	-	-	14 R	13 R	-
Alan Jones	Hesketh 308-Ford	-	-	-	20 R	18 R	13 R	19 11	-	-	-	-	-	-	-
	Hill GH1-Ford	-	-	-	-	-	-	-	-	17 13	20 16	20 10	21 5	-	-
Eddie Keizan	Lotus 72E-Ford	-	-	22 13	-	-	-	-	-	-	-	-	-	-	-
Jacques Laffite	Williams FW02-Ford	17 R	19 11	23 NC	-	-	-	-	-	-	-	-	-	-	-
	Williams FW04-Ford	-	-	-	-	-	19DNQ	17 R	15 R	16 11	19 R	15 2	12 R	18 R	21DNS
Niki Lauda	Ferrari 312B3	4 6	4 5	-	-	-	-	-	-	-	-	-	-	-	-
	Ferrari 312T	-	-	4 5	1 R	1 1	1 1	5 1F	1 2F	1 1	3 8	1 3	1 6	1 3	1 1
Michel Leclere	Tyrrell 007-Ford	-	-	-	-	-	-	-	-	-	-	-	-	-	20 R
Gijs van Lennep	Ensign N174-Ford	-	-	-	-	-	-	22 10	-	-	-	-	-	-	-
	Ensign N175-Ford	-	-	-	-	-	-	-	-	22 15	-	24 6	-	-	-
Lella Lombardi	March 741-Ford	-	-	-	26 R	-	-	-	-	-	-	-	-	-	-
	March 751-Ford	-	-	-	-	24 6	25DNQ	23 R	24 R	23 14	26 18	22 R	25 7	22 17	24 R
	Williams FW04-Ford	-	-	-	-	-	-	-	-	-	-	-	-	-	24DNS
Brett Lunger	Hesketh 308-Ford	-	-	-	-	-	-	-	-	-	-	17 13	21 10	18 R	-
Jochen Mass	McLaren M23-Ford	13 14	10 3	16 6	11 1	15 6	15 R	14 R	8 R	7 3F	10 7	6 R	9 4	5 R	9 3
Arturo Merzario	Williams FW03-Ford	20 NC	11 R	15 R	-	-	20DNQ	19 R	-	-	-	-	-	-	-
	Williams FW04-Ford	-	-	-	25 R	-	-	-	-	-	-	-	-	-	-
	Fittipaldi FD03-Ford	-	-	-	-	-	-	-	-	-	-	-	-	26 11	-
Francois Migault	Hill GH1-Ford	-	-	-	-	22 NC	-	22 R	-	-	-	-	-	-	-
	Williams FW03-Ford	-	-	-	-	-	-	-	-	24 DNS	-	-	-	-	-
Dave Morgan	Surtees TS16/4-Ford	-	-	-	-	-	-	-	-	-	-	23 R	-	-	-
John Nicholson	Lyncar 009-Ford	-	-	-	-	-	-	-	-	-	-	26 17	-	-	-
Carlos Pace	Brabham BT44B-Ford	2 6	1 1	4F 14	R 8	3 2	8 6	R 9	5 5	R 2	2 2	R 6	R 10	R 16	R
Torsten Palm	Hesketh 308-Ford	-	-	-	-	24DNQ	-	21 10	-	-	-	-	-	-	-
Henri Pescarolo	Surtees TS16/4-Ford	-	-	-	-	NTDNP	-	-	-	-	-	-	-	-	-
Ronnie Peterson	Lotus 72E-Ford	11 R	16 15	8 10	12 R	4 4	14 R	9 9	16 15	17 10	16 R	18 R	13 5	11 R	14 5
Tom Pryce	Shadow DN3B-Ford	14 12	14 R	-	-	-	-	-	-	-	-	-	-	-	-
	Shadow DN5A-Ford	-	-	19 9	8 R	2 R	5 6	7 R	12 6	6 R	1 R	16 4	15 3	14 6	7 NC
Clay Regazzoni	Ferrari 312B3	7 4	5 4	-	-	-	-	-	-	-	-	-	-	-	-
	Ferrari 312T	-	-	9 16	2 NC	6 R	4 5F	12 3	2 3	9 R	4 13F	5 RF	5 7	2 1F	11 R
Carlos Reutemann	Brabham BT44B-Ford	3 3	8 2	2 15	3 10	9 6	3 4	2 5	4 11	14 8	R 10	1 11	14 7	4 3	R
Ian Scheckter	Tyrrell 007-Ford	-	-	17 R	-	-	-	-	-	-	-	-	-	-	-
	Williams FW04-Ford	-	-	-	-	-	-	20 R	-	-	-	-	-	-	-
	Williams FW03-Ford	-	-	-	-	-	-	-	-	19 12	-	-	-	-	-
Jody Scheckter	Tyrrell 007-Ford	9 11	8 R	3 1	13 R	7 7	9 2	8 7	4 16	2 9	6 3	3 R	10 8	4 8	10 6

driver	car	RA		BR		ZA		E		MC		B		S		NL		F		GB		D		A		I		USA	
		Q	R	Q	R	Q	R	Q	R	Q	R	Q	R	Q	R	Q	R	Q	R	Q	R	Q	R	Q	R	Q	R	Q	R
Vern Schuppan	Hill GH1-Ford	-	-	-	-	-	-	-	-	-	-	26	R	-	-	-	-	-	-	-	-	-	-	-	-	-	-	-	-
Rolf Stommelen	Lola T370-Ford	19	13	23	14	-	-	-	-	-	-	-	-	-	-	-	-	-	-	-	-	-	-	-	-	-	-	-	-
	Lola T371-Ford	-	-	-	-	14	7	-	-	-	-	-	-	-	-	-	-	-	-	-	-	-	-	-	-	-	-	-	-
	Hill GH1-Ford	-	-	-	-	-	-	9	R	-	-	-	-	-	-	-	-	-	-	-	-	-	-	26	16	23	R	-	-
Hans-Joachim Stuck	March 751-Ford	-	-	-	-	-	-	-	-	-	-	-	-	-	-	-	-	14	R	7	R	4	R	16	R	13	8	-	-
Tony Trimmer	Maki F101C-Ford	-	-	-	-	-	-	-	-	-	-	-	-	-	-	-	-	-	-	-	-	26	DNQ	30	DNQ	28	DNQ	-	-
Guy Tunmer	Lotus 72E-Ford	-	-	-	-	25	11	-	-	-	-	-	-	-	-	-	-	-	-	-	-	-	-	-	-	-	-	-	-
Joseph Vonlanthen	Williams FW03-Ford	-	-	-	-	-	-	-	-	-	-	-	-	-	-	-	-	-	-	-	-	-	-	29	R	-	-	-	-
John Watson	Surtees TS16/4-Ford	15	DSQ	13	10	10	R	6	8	17	R	18	10	10	16	14	R	14	13	18	11	-	-	18	10	-	-	-	-
	Lotus 72E-Ford	-	-	-	-	-	-	-	-	-	-	-	-	-	-	-	-	-	-	-	-	-	-	-	-	14	R	-	-
	Penske PC1-Ford	-	-	-	-	-	-	-	-	-	-	-	-	-	-	-	-	-	-	-	-	-	-	-	-	-	-	12	9
Mike Wilds	Stanley BRM P201	22	R	22	R	-	-	-	-	-	-	-	-	-	-	-	-	-	-	-	-	-	-	-	-	-	-	-	-
Roelof Wunderink	Ensign N174-Ford	-	-	-	-	-	-	19	R	23	DNQ	-	-	-	-	-	-	-	-	-	-	-	-	28	NC	27	DNQ	-	-
	Ensign N175-Ford	-	-	-	-	-	-	-	-	-	-	-	-	-	-	-	-	27	DNQ	-	-	-	-	-	-	-	-	22	R
Renzo Zorzi	Williams FW03-Ford	-	-	-	-	-	-	-	-	-	-	-	-	-	-	-	-	-	-	-	-	-	-	-	-	22	14	-	-

1975 FINAL CHAMPIONSHIP POSITIONS

Drivers

1	Niki Lauda	64.5
2	Emerson Fittipaldi	45
3	Carlos Reutemann	37
4	James Hunt	33
5	Clay Regazzoni	25
6	Carlos Pace	24
7=	Jochen Mass	20
	Jody Scheckter	20
9	Patrick Depailler	12
10	Tom Pryce	8
11	Vittorio Brambilla	6.5
12=	Jacques Laffite	6
	Ronnie Peterson	6
14	Mario Andretti	5
15	Mark Donohue	4
16	Jacky Ickx	3
17	Alan Jones	2
18	Jean-Pierre Jarier	1.5
19=	Tony Brise	1
	Gijs van Lennep	1
21	Lella Lombardi	0.5

Sum of best seven results from the first eight races and best five results from the final six races

Manufacturers

1	Ferrari	72.5
2	Brabham-Ford	54 (56)*
3	McLaren-Ford	53
4	Hesketh-Ford	33
5	Tyrrell-Ford	25
6	Shadow-Ford	9.5
7	Lotus-Ford	9
8	March-Ford	7.5
9	Williams-Ford	6
10	Parnelli-Ford	5
11	Hill-Ford	3
12	Penske-Ford	2
13	Ensign-Ford	1

*Sum of best seven results from the first eight races and best five results from the final six races. Points only awarded to first car to finish for each manufacturer

---

1	James Hunt	Hesketh 308-Ford	75	1h46m57.40
2	Niki Lauda	Ferrari 312T	75	1h46m58.46
3	Clay Regazzoni	Ferrari 312T	75	1h47m52.46
4	Carlos Reutemann	Brabham BT44B-Ford	74	
5	Carlos Pace	Brabham BT44B-Ford	74	
6	Tom Pryce	Shadow DN5A-Ford	74	

Winner's average speed: 110.484 mph. Starting grid front row: Lauda, 1m20.29 (pole) and Regazzoni, 1m20.57. Fastest lap: Lauda, 1m21.54.
Leaders: Lauda, laps 1-12; Regazzoni, 13-14; Hunt, 15-75

GRAND PRIX DE FRANCE

6 July 1975. Paul Ricard. 54 laps of a 3.610-mile circuit = 194.940 miles. Hot, dry and sunny. World Championship round 9

1	Niki Lauda	Ferrari 312T	54	1h40m18.84
2	James Hunt	Hesketh 308-Ford	54	1h40m20.43
3	Jochen Mass	McLaren M23-Ford	54	1h40m21.15
4	Emerson Fittipaldi	McLaren M23-Ford	54	1h40m58.61
5	Mario Andretti	Parnelli VPJ4-Ford	54	1h41m20.92
6	Patrick Depailler	Tyrrell 007-Ford	54	1h41m26.24

Winner's average speed: 116.598 mph. Starting grid front row: Lauda, 1m47.82 (pole) and J Scheckter, 1m48.22. Fastest lap: Mass, 1m50.60.
Leaders: Lauda, laps 1-54

JOHN PLAYER BRITISH GRAND PRIX

19 July 1975. Silverstone. 56 laps of a 2.932-mile circuit = 164.192 miles. Race scheduled for 67 laps but stopped due to numerous accidents in the heavy rain. Showers, heavy rain later. World Championship round 10

1	Emerson Fittipaldi	McLaren M23-Ford	56	1h22m05.0
2	Carlos Pace	Brabham BT44B-Ford	55	accident
3	Jody Scheckter	Tyrrell 007-Ford	55	accident
4	James Hunt	Hesketh 308-Ford	55	accident
5	Mark Donohue	March 751-Ford	55	accident
6	Vittorio Brambilla	March 751-Ford	55	

Winner's average speed: 120.019 mph. Starting grid front row: Pryce, 1m19.36 (pole) and Pace, 1m19.50. Fastest lap: Regazzoni, 1m20.9.
Leaders: Pace, laps 1-12, 22-26; Regazzoni, 13-18; Pryce, 19-20; J Scheckter, 21, 27-32; Jarier, 33-34; Hunt, 35-42; E Fittipaldi, 43-56

GROSSER PREIS VON DEUTSCHLAND

3 August 1975. Nurburgring. 14 laps of a 14.189-mile circuit = 198.646 miles. Warm, dry and sunny. World Championship round 11

1	Carlos Reutemann	Brabham BT44B-Ford	14	1h41m14.1
2	Jacques Laffite	Williams FW04-Ford	14	1h42m51.8
3	Niki Lauda	Ferrari 312T	14	1h43m37.4
4	Tom Pryce	Shadow DN5A-Ford	14	1h44m45.5
5	Alan Jones	Hill GH1-Ford	14	1h45m04.4
6	Gijs van Lennep	Ensign N175-Ford	14	1h46m19.6

Winner's average speed: 117.734 mph. Starting grid front row: Lauda, 6m58.6 (pole) and Pace, 7m00.0. Fastest lap: Regazzoni, 7m06.4. Leaders: Lauda, laps 1-9; Reutemann, 10-14

GROSSER PREIS VON OSTERREICH UND EUROPA

17 August 1975. Osterreichring. 29 laps of a 3.673-mile circuit = 106.517 miles. Race scheduled for 54 laps but stopped due to rain, half points awarded as less than 60% of the race had been completed. Very wet. World Championship round 12

1	Vittorio Brambilla	March 751-Ford	29	57m56.69
2	James Hunt	Hesketh 308-Ford	29	58m23.72
3	Tom Pryce	Shadow DN5A-Ford	29	58m31.54
4	Jochen Mass	McLaren M23-Ford	29	59m09.35

5 Ronnie Peterson	Lotus 72E-Ford	29	59m20.02
6 Niki Lauda	Ferrari 312T	29	59m26.97

Winner's average speed: 110.295 mph. Starting grid front row: Lauda, 1m34.85 (pole) and Hunt, 1m34.97. Fastest lap: Brambilla, 1m53.90. Leaders: Lauda, laps 1-14; Hunt, 15-18; Brambilla, 19-29

GRAN PREMIO D'ITALIA

7 September 1975. Monza. 52 laps of a 3.592-mile circuit = 186.784 miles. Dry and overcast. World Championship round 13

1 Clay Regazzoni	Ferrari 312T	52	1h22m42.6
2 Emerson Fittipaldi	McLaren M23-Ford	52	1h22m59.2
3 Niki Lauda	Ferrari 312T	52	1h23m05.8
4 Carlos Reutemann	Brabham BT44B-Ford	52	1h23m37.7
5 James Hunt	Hesketh 308C-Ford	52	1h23m39.7
6 Tom Pryce	Shadow DN5A-Ford	52	1h23m58.5

Winner's average speed: 135.498 mph. Starting grid front row: Lauda, 1m32.24 (pole) and Regazzoni, 1m32.75. Fastest lap: Regazzoni, 1m33.1. Leaders: Regazzoni, laps 1-52

UNITED STATES GRAND PRIX

5 October 1975. Watkins Glen. 59 laps of a 3.377-mile circuit = 199.243 miles. Cool and dry. World Championship round 14

1 Niki Lauda	Ferrari 312T	59	1h42m58.175
2 Emerson Fittipaldi	McLaren M23-Ford	59	1h43m03.118
3 Jochen Mass	McLaren M23-Ford	59	1h43m45.812
4 James Hunt	Hesketh 308C-Ford	59	1h43m47.650
5 Ronnie Peterson	Lotus 72E-Ford	59	1h43m48.161
6 Jody Scheckter	Tyrrell 007-Ford	59	1h43m48.496

Winner's average speed: 116.098 mph. Starting grid front row: Lauda, 1m42.003 (pole) and E Fittipaldi, 1m42.360. Fastest lap: E Fittipaldi, 1m43.374. Leaders: Lauda, laps 1-59

1976

Niki Lauda continued his World Championship winning form in the early races of 1976, and by mid-season a second title seemed assured. Then, on the second lap of the German Grand Prix at the Nurburgring, he crashed heavily at Bergwerk and his car burst into flames. Severely injured and badly burned, he was given the last rites in hospital. But Lauda staged a miraculous recovery, and although badly scarred, he was racing again within five weeks at the Italian GP.

It had already been an acrimonious season of disqualifications and appeals by the time of the accident, with James Hunt a constant thorn in Ferrari's side. In Spain Hunt controversially ended a run of five Ferrari victories when his McLaren was originally disqualified on a technicality but later reinstated. Then he won in Britain, before race officials ruled that he should not have participated in the restarted race after his car had been damaged in a multiple first corner accident.

Hunt had closed the gap by the time of Lauda's return, and at the last round in Japan he was just three points behind. In appallingly wet and dangerous conditions Lauda withdrew, believing his life to be more important than another championship win. Even then, Hunt appeared to have lost the title in the confusing final laps, only to learn that he had finished third—enough to become World Champion.

Though overshadowed by the championship finale, the Japanese GP also saw Mario Andretti return an improving Lotus team to the winner's circle. With Lauda sidelined, Ferrari signed Carlos Reutemann from the disappointing Brabham-Alfa Romeo team. But Reutemann made just one appearance for Ferrari

before Lauda's return. Ferrari's only other win had come early in the year when Clay Regazzoni won the first Grand Prix around the streets of Long Beach, California.

All in all it had been a remarkable season. Hunt's opportunity at McLaren had come when Emerson Fittipaldi decided to race for his family's team, a decision that prematurely halted his career as a top-line F1 driver. Fittipaldi suffered five more mediocre seasons in F1, but returned to form after coming out of retirement to race ChampCars.

Tyrrell introduced the radical six-wheel P34, which used four small front wheels to improve frontal aerodynamics. Although Jody Scheckter and Patrick Depailler finished first and second in Sweden, the car did not win again and was replaced by a conventional design after two seasons.

Ronnie Peterson quickly grew frustrated with Lotus, and after just one race returned to March, bringing that team a victory at Monza. John Watson scored Penske's only win at the Austrian GP in a victory that cost Watson his beard—the result of a bet with team owner Roger Penske!

GRANDE PREMIO DO BRASIL

25 January 1976. Interlagos. 40 laps of a 4.946-mile circuit = 197.840 miles. Very hot, dry and sunny. World Championship round 1

1 Niki Lauda	Ferrari 312T	40	1h45m16.78
2 Patrick Depailler	Tyrrell 007-Ford	40	1h45m38.25
3 Tom Pryce	Shadow DN5B-Ford	40	1h45m40.62
4 Hans-Joachim Stuck	March 761-Ford	40	1h46m44.95
5 Jody Scheckter	Tyrrell 007-Ford	40	1h47m13.24
6 Jochen Mass	McLaren M23-Ford	40	1h47m15.05

Winner's average speed: 112.751 mph. Starting grid front row: Hunt, 2m32.50 (pole) and Lauda, 2m32.52. Fastest lap: Jarier, 2m35.07. Leaders: Regazzoni, laps 1-8; Lauda, 9-40

CITIZEN GRAND PRIX OF SOUTH AFRICA

6 March 1976. Kyalami. 78 laps of a 2.550-mile circuit = 198.900 miles. Warm, dry and sunny. World Championship round 2

1 Niki Lauda	Ferrari 312T	78	1h42m18.4
2 James Hunt	McLaren M23-Ford	78	1h42m19.7
3 Jochen Mass	McLaren M23-Ford	78	1h43m04.3
4 Jody Scheckter	Tyrrell 007-Ford	78	1h43m26.8
5 John Watson	Penske PC3-Ford	77	
6 Mario Andretti	Parnelli VPJ4B-Ford	77	

Winner's average speed: 116.649 mph. Starting grid front row: Hunt, 1m16.10 (pole) and Lauda, 1m16.20. Fastest lap: Lauda, 1m17.97. Leaders: Lauda, laps 1-78

UNITED STATES GRAND PRIX WEST

28 March 1976. Long Beach. 80 laps of a 2.020-mile circuit = 161.600 miles. Warm, dry and sunny. World Championship round 3

1 Clay Regazzoni	Ferrari 312T	80	1h53m18.471
2 Niki Lauda	Ferrari 312T	80	1h54m00.885
3 Patrick Depailler	Tyrrell 007-Ford	80	1h54m08.443
4 Jacques Laffite	Ligier JS5-Matra	80	1h54m31.299
5 Jochen Mass	McLaren M23-Ford	80	1h54m40.763
6 Emerson Fittipaldi	Fittipaldi FD04-Ford	79	

Winner's average speed: 85.572 mph. Starting grid front row: Regazzoni, 1m23.099 (pole) and Depailler, 1m23.292. Fastest lap: Regazzoni, 1m23.076. Leaders: Regazzoni, laps 1-80

GRAN PREMIO DE ESPANA

2 May 1976. Jarama. 75 laps of a 2.115-mile circuit = 158.655 miles. Warm, dry and sunny. World Championship round 4

1 James Hunt*	McLaren M23-Ford	75	1h42m20.43

2	Niki Lauda	Ferrari 312T2	75	1h42m51.40
3	Gunnar Nilsson	Lotus 77-Ford	75	1h43m08.45
4	Carlos Reutemann	Brabham BT45-Alfa Romeo	74	
5	Chris Amon	Ensign N176-Ford	74	
6	Carlos Pace	Brabham BT45-Alfa Romeo	74	

*Hunt was originally disqualified because his car was found to be too wide, but was later reinstated. Winner's average speed: 93.016 mph. Starting grid front row: Hunt, 1m18.52 (pole) and Lauda, 1m18.84. Fastest lap: Mass, 1m20.93. Leaders: Lauda, laps 1-31; Hunt, 32-75.

GROTE PRIJS VAN BELGIE

16 May 1976. Zolder. 70 laps of a 2.648-mile circuit = 185.360 miles. Warm, dry and sunny. World Championship round 5

1	Niki Lauda	Ferrari 312T2	70	1h42m53.23
2	Clay Regazzoni	Ferrari 312T2	70	1h42m56.69
3	Jacques Laffite	Ligier JS5-Matra	70	1h43m28.61
4	Jody Scheckter	Tyrrell P34-Ford	70	1h44m24.31
5	Alan Jones	Surtees TS19-Ford	69	
6	Jochen Mass	McLaren M23-Ford	69	

Winner's average speed: 108.095 mph. Starting grid front row: Lauda, 1m26.55 (pole) and Regazzoni, 1m26.60. Fastest lap: Lauda, 1m25.98. Leaders: Lauda, laps 1-70

GRAND PRIX DE MONACO

30 May 1976. Monte Carlo. 78 laps of a 2.058-mile circuit = 160.524 miles. Warm, dry and mainly sunny. World Championship round 6

1	Niki Lauda	Ferrari 312T2	78	1h59m51.47
2	Jody Scheckter	Tyrrell P34-Ford	78	2h00m02.60
3	Patrick Depailler	Tyrrell P34-Ford	78	2h00m56.31
4	Hans-Joachim Stuck	March 761-Ford	77	
5	Jochen Mass	McLaren M23-Ford	77	
6	Emerson Fittipaldi	Fittipaldi FD04-Ford	77	

Winner's average speed: 80.357 mph. Starting grid front row: Lauda, 1m29.65 (pole) and Regazzoni, 1m29.91. Fastest lap: Regazzoni, 1m30.28. Leaders: Lauda, laps 1-78

GISLAVED SVERIGES GRAND PRIX

13 June 1976. Anderstorp. 72 laps of a 2.497-mile circuit = 179.784 miles. Dry and overcast. World Championship round 7

1	Jody Scheckter	Tyrrell P34-Ford	72	1h46m53.729
2	Patrick Depailler	Tyrrell P34-Ford	72	1h47m13.495
3	Niki Lauda	Ferrari 312T2	72	1h47m27.595
4	Jacques Laffite	Ligier JS5-Matra	72	1h47m49.548
5	James Hunt	McLaren M23-Ford	72	1h47m53.212
6	Clay Regazzoni	Ferrari 312T2	72	1h47m54.095

Winner's average speed: 100.912 mph. Starting grid front row: Scheckter, 1m25.659 (pole) and Andretti, 1m26.008. Fastest lap: Andretti, 1m28.002. Leaders: Andretti, laps 1-45; Scheckter, 46-72

GRAND PRIX DE FRANCE

4 July 1976. Paul Ricard. 54 laps of a 3.610-mile circuit = 194.940 miles. Hot, dry and sunny. World Championship round 8

1	James Hunt	McLaren M23-Ford	54	1h40m58.60
2	Patrick Depailler	Tyrrell P34-Ford	54	1h41m11.30
3	John Watson*	Penske PC4-Ford	54	1h41m22.15
4	Carlos Pace	Brabham BT45-Alfa Romeo	54	1h41m23.42
5	Mario Andretti	Lotus 77-Ford	54	1h41m42.52
6	Jody Scheckter	Tyrrell P34-Ford	54	1h41m53.67

*Watson was originally disqualified because of the height of his car's rear wing, but was later reinstated. Winner's average speed: 115.833 mph. Starting grid front row: Hunt, 1m47.89 (pole) and Lauda, 1m48.17. Fastest lap: Lauda, 1m51.00. Leaders: Lauda, laps 1-8; Hunt, 9-54

JOHN PLAYER BRITISH GRAND PRIX

18 July 1976. Brands Hatch. 76 laps of a 2.614-mile circuit = 198.634 miles. Race stopped after first-lap accident, restarted over original distance. Warm, dry and sunny. World Championship round 9

1	Niki Lauda	Ferrari 312T2	76	1h44m19.66
2	Jody Scheckter	Tyrrell P34-Ford	76	1h44m35.84
3	John Watson	Penske PC4-Ford	75	
4	Tom Pryce	Shadow DN5B-Ford	75	
5	Alan Jones	Surtees TS19-Ford	75	
6	Emerson Fittipaldi	Fittipaldi FD04-Ford	74	

James Hunt (McLaren M23-Ford), 1h43m27.61 finished first on the road but was disqualified for illegally taking the restart of the race. Winner's average speed: 114.236 mph. Starting grid front row: Lauda, 1m19.35 (pole) and Hunt, 1m19.41. Fastest lap: Lauda, 1m19.91 (Hunt, 1m19.82, originally set fastest lap but was subsequently disqualified). Leaders: Lauda, laps 1-76 (Hunt led laps 45-76 on the road)

GROSSER PREIS VON DEUTSCHLAND

1 August 1976. Nurburgring. 14 laps of a 14.189-mile circuit = 198.646 miles. Race stopped after Lauda's second-lap accident, restarted over original distance with the two laps of the original race disregarded. Rain at the start, drying later. World Championship round 10

1	James Hunt	McLaren M23-Ford	14	1h41m42.7
2	Jody Scheckter	Tyrrell P34-Ford	14	1h42m10.4
3	Jochen Mass	McLaren M23-Ford	14	1h42m35.1
4	Carlos Pace	Brabham BT45-Alfa Romeo	14	1h42m36.9
5	Gunnar Nilsson	Lotus 77-Ford	14	1h43m40.0
6	Rolf Stommelen	Brabham BT45-Alfa Romeo	14	1h44m13.0

Winner's average speed: 117.182 mph. Starting grid front row: Hunt, 7m06.5 (pole) and Lauda, 7m07.4. Fastest lap: Scheckter, 7m10.8. Leaders: Hunt, laps 1-14 (Peterson had led lap 1 and Mass lap 2 of the original race)

RAIFFEISEN GROSSER PREIS VON OSTERREICH

15 August 1976. Osterreichring. 54 laps of a 3.672-mile circuit = 198.288 miles. Warm, dry and mainly sunny. World Championship round 11

1	John Watson	Penske PC4-Ford	54	1h30m07.86
2	Jacques Laffite	Ligier JS5-Matra	54	1h30m18.65
3	Gunnar Nilsson	Lotus 77-Ford	54	1h30m19.84
4	James Hunt	McLaren M23-Ford	54	1h30m20.30
5	Mario Andretti	Lotus 77-Ford	54	1h30m29.35
6	Ronnie Peterson	March 761-Ford	54	1h30m42.20

Winner's average speed: 132.000 mph. Starting grid front row: Hunt, 1m35.02 (pole) and Watson, 1m35.84. Fastest lap: Hunt, 1m35.91. Leaders: Watson, laps 1-2, 12-54; Peterson, 3-9, 11; Scheckter, 10

GROTE PRIJS VAN NEDERLAND/EUROPA

29 August 1976. Zandvoort. 75 laps of a 2.626-mile circuit = 196.950 miles. Warm, dry and sunny. World Championship round 12

1	James Hunt	McLaren M23-Ford	75	1h44m52.09
2	Clay Regazzoni	Ferrari 312T2	75	1h44m53.01
3	Mario Andretti	Lotus 77-Ford	75	1h44m54.18
4	Tom Pryce	Shadow DN8A-Ford	75	1h44m59.03
5	Jody Scheckter	Tyrrell P34-Ford	75	1h45m14.55
6	Vittorio Brambilla	March 761-Ford	75	1h45m37.12

Winner's average speed: 112.684 mph. Starting grid front row: Peterson, 1m21.31 (pole) and Hunt, 1m21.39. Fastest lap: Regazzoni, 1m22.59. Leaders: Peterson, laps 1-11; Hunt, 12-75

GRAN PREMIO D'ITALIA

12 September 1976. Monza. 52 laps of a 3.604-mile circuit = 187.403 miles. Warm, dry and sunny. World Championship round 13

1	Ronnie Peterson	March 761-Ford	52	1h30m35.6
2	Clay Regazzoni	Ferrari 312T2	52	1h30m37.9
3	Jacques Laffite	Ligier JS5-Matra	52	1h30m38.6
4	Niki Lauda	Ferrari 312T2	52	1h30m55.0
5	Jody Scheckter	Tyrrell P34-Ford	52	1h30m55.1
6	Patrick Depailler	Tyrrell P34-Ford	52	1h31m11.3

Winner's average speed: 124.117 mph. Starting grid front row: Laffite, 1m41.35 (pole) and Scheckter, 1m41.38. Fastest lap: Peterson, 1m41.3. Leaders: Scheckter, laps 1-10; Peterson, 11-52

1976 DRIVERS' RECORDS

driver	car	BR		ZA		LB		E		B		MC		S		F		GB		D		A		NL		I		CDN		USA		J	
		Q	R	Q	R	Q	R	Q	R	Q	R	Q	R	Q	R	Q	R	Q	R	Q	R	Q	R	Q	R	Q	R	Q	R	Q	R	Q	R
Chris Amon	Ensign N174-Ford	-	-	18	14	17	8	-	-	-	-	-	-	-	-	-	-	-	-	-	-	-	-	-	-	-	-	-	-	-	-	-	-
	Ensign N176-Ford	-	-	-	-	-	-	10	5	8	R	12	13	3	R	-	-	6	R	17	R	-	-	-	-	-	-	-	-	-	-	-	-
	Williams FW05-Ford	-	-	-	-	-	-	-	-	-	-	-	-	-	-	-	-	-	-	-	-	-	-	-	-	-	-	26	DNS	-	-	-	-
Conny Andersson	Surtees TS19-Ford	-	-	-	-	-	-	-	-	-	-	-	-	-	-	-	-	-	-	-	-	-	-	26	R	-	-	-	-	-	-	-	-
Mario Andretti	Lotus 77-Ford	16	R	-	-	-	-	9	R	11	R	-	-	2	RF	7	5	3	R	12	12	9	5	6	3	14	R	5	3	11	R	1	1
	Parnelli VPJ4B-Ford	-	-	13	6	15	R	-	-	-	-	-	-	-	-	-	-	-	-	-	-	-	-	-	-	-	-	-	-	-	-	-	-
Ian Ashley	Stanley BRM P201B	21	R	-	-	-	-	-	-	-	-	-	-	-	-	-	-	-	-	-	-	-	-	-	-	-	-	-	-	-	-	-	-
Hans Binder	Ensign N176-Ford	-	-	-	-	-	-	-	-	-	-	-	-	-	-	-	-	-	-	-	-	19	R	-	-	-	-	-	-	-	-	-	-
	Williams FW05-Ford	-	-	-	-	-	-	-	-	-	-	-	-	-	-	-	-	-	-	-	-	-	-	-	-	-	-	-	-	-	-	25	R
Vittorio Brambilla	March 761-Ford	7	R	5	8	8	R	6	R	5	R	9	R	15	10	11	R	10	R	13	R	7	R	7	6	16	7	3	14	4	R	8	R
Warwick Brown	Williams FW05-Ford	-	-	-	-	-	-	-	-	-	-	-	-	-	-	-	-	-	-	-	-	-	-	-	-	-	-	-	-	23	14	-	-
Patrick Depailler	Tyrrell 007-Ford	9	2	6	9	2	3	-	-	-	-	-	-	-	-	-	-	-	-	-	-	-	-	-	-	-	-	-	-	-	-	-	-
	Tyrrell P34-Ford	-	-	-	-	-	-	3	R	4	R	4	3	4	2	3	2	5	R	3	R	13	R	14	7	4	6	4	2F	7	R	13	2
Guy Edwards	Hesketh 308D-Ford	-	-	-	-	-	-	-	-	29	DNQ	-	-	-	-	25	17	25	R	25	15	-	-	-	-	23	DNS	24	20	-	-	-	-
Harald Ertl	Hesketh 308D-Ford	-	-	24	15	26	DNQ	29	DNQ	24	R	24	DNQ	23	R	29	R	24	7	22	R	20	8	24	R	19	16	20	DNS	21	13	22	8
Bob Evans	Lotus 77-Ford	-	-	23	10	24	DNQ	-	-	-	-	-	-	-	-	-	-	-	-	-	-	-	-	-	-	-	-	-	-	-	-	-	-
	Brabham BT44B-Ford	-	-	-	-	-	-	-	-	-	-	-	-	-	-	-	-	-	-	22	R	-	-	-	-	-	-	-	-	-	-	-	-
Emerson Fittipaldi	Fittipaldi FD04-Ford	5	13	21	17	16	6	19	R	27	DNQ	7	6	21	R	21	R	21	6	20	13	17	R	17	R	20	15	17	R	15	9	23	R
Divina Galica	Surtees TS16/4-Ford	-	-	-	-	-	-	-	-	-	-	-	-	-	-	-	-	28	DNQ	-	-	-	-	-	-	-	-	-	-	-	-	-	-
Masahiro Hasemi	Kojima KE007-Ford	-	-	-	-	-	-	-	-	-	-	-	-	-	-	-	-	-	-	-	-	-	-	-	-	-	-	-	-	-	-	10	11F
Boy Hayje	Penske PC3-Ford	-	-	-	-	-	-	-	-	-	-	-	-	-	-	-	-	-	-	-	-	-	-	21	R	-	-	-	-	-	-	-	-
Ingo Hoffmann	Fittipaldi FD03-Ford	20	11	-	-	-	-	-	-	-	-	-	-	-	-	-	-	-	-	-	-	-	-	-	-	-	-	-	-	-	-	-	-
	Fittipaldi FD04-Ford	-	-	-	-	-	-	22	DNQ	30	DNQ	-	-	-	-	28	DNQ	-	-	-	-	-	-	-	-	-	-	-	-	-	-	-	-
Kazuyoshi Hoshino	Tyrrell 007-Ford	-	-	-	-	-	-	-	-	-	-	-	-	-	-	-	-	-	-	-	-	-	-	-	-	-	-	-	-	-	-	21	R
James Hunt	McLaren M23-Ford	1	R	1	2	3	R	1	1	3	R	14	R	8	5	1	1	2	DSQ	1	1	1	4F	2	1	27	R	1	1	1	1F	2	3
Jacky Ickx	Williams FW05-Ford	19	8	19	16	25	DNQ	21	7	28	DNQ	21	DNQ	-	-	19	10	27	DNQ	-	-	-	-	-	-	-	-	-	-	-	-	-	-
	Ensign N176-Ford	-	-	-	-	-	-	-	-	-	-	-	-	-	-	-	-	-	-	-	-	-	-	11	R	10	10	16	13	19	R	-	-
Jean-Pierre Jarier	Shadow DN5B-Ford	3	RF	15	R	7	7	15	R	14	9	10	8	14	12	15	12	23	9	23	11	18	R	20	10	17	19	18	18	16	10	15	10
Alan Jones	Surtees TS19-Ford	-	-	-	-	19	NC	20	9	16	5	19	R	18	13	18	R	19	5	14	10	15	R	16	8	18	12	21	16	18	8	20	4
Loris Kessel	Brabham BT44B-Ford	-	-	-	-	-	-	26	DNQ	23	12	-	-	26	R	30	DNQ	-	-	-	-	25	NC	-	-	-	-	-	-	-	-	-	-
	Williams FW03-Ford	-	-	-	-	-	-	-	-	-	-	-	-	-	-	-	-	-	-	-	-	-	-	-	-	NT	DNP	-	-	-	-	-	-
Masami Kuwashima	Williams FW05-Ford	-	-	-	-	-	-	-	-	-	-	-	-	-	-	-	-	-	-	-	-	-	-	-	-	-	-	-	-	-	-	26	DNS
Jacques Laffite	Ligier JS5-Matra	11	R	8	R	12	4	8	12	6	3	8	12	7	4	13	14	13	R	6	R	5	2	10	R	1	3	9	R	12	R	11	7
Niki Lauda	Ferrari 312T	2	1	2	1F	4	2	-	-	-	-	-	-	-	-	-	-	-	-	-	-	-	-	-	-	-	-	-	-	-	-	-	-
	Ferrari 312T2	-	-	-	-	-	-	2	2	1	1F	1	1	5	3	2	RF	1	1F	2	R	-	-	-	-	5	4	6	8	5	3	3	R
Michel Leclere	Williams FW05-Ford	-	-	22	13	21	DNQ	23	10	25	11	18	11	25	R	22	13	-	-	-	-	-	-	-	-	-	-	-	-	-	-	-	-
Lella Lombardi	March 761-Ford	22	14	-	-	-	-	-	-	-	-	-	-	-	-	-	-	-	-	-	-	-	-	-	-	-	-	-	-	-	-	-	-
	Brabham BT44B-Ford	-	-	-	-	-	-	-	-	-	-	-	-	-	-	-	-	30	DNQ	27	DNQ	24	12	-	-	-	-	-	-	-	-	-	-
Brett Lunger	Surtees TS19-Ford	-	-	20	11	27	DNQ	25	DNQ	26	R	-	-	24	15	23	16	18	R	24	R	16	10	-	-	24	14	23	15	24	11	-	-
Damien Magee	Brabham BT44B-Ford	-	-	-	-	-	-	-	-	-	-	-	-	-	-	27	DNQ	-	-	-	-	-	-	-	-	-	-	-	-	-	-	-	-
Jochen Mass	McLaren M23-Ford	6	6	4	3	14	5	4	RF	18	6	11	5	13	11	14	15	12	R	9	3	12	7	-	-	-	-	11	5	17	4	12	R
	McLaren M26-Ford	-	-	-	-	-	-	-	-	-	-	-	-	-	-	-	-	-	-	-	-	-	-	15	9	28	R	-	-	-	-	-	-
Arturo Merzario	March 761-Ford	-	-	-	-	23	DNQ	18	R	21	R	25	DNQ	19	14	20	9	9	R	-	-	-	-	-	-	-	-	-	-	-	-	-	-
	Williams FW05-Ford	-	-	-	-	-	-	-	-	-	-	-	-	-	-	-	-	-	-	21	R	21	R	23	R	25	DNS	25	R	25	R	19	R
Jac Nelleman	Brabham BT44B-Ford	-	-	-	-	-	-	-	-	-	-	-	-	27	DNQ	-	-	-	-	-	-	-	-	-	-	-	-	-	-	-	-	-	-
Patrick Neve	Brabham BT44B-Ford	-	-	-	-	-	-	-	-	-	-	19	R	-	-	-	-	-	-	-	-	-	-	-	-	-	-	-	-	-	-	-	-
	Ensign N176-Ford	-	-	-	-	-	-	-	-	-	-	-	-	-	-	26	18	-	-	-	-	-	-	-	-	-	-	-	-	-	-	-	-
Gunnar Nilsson	Lotus 77-Ford	-	-	25	R	20	R	7	3	22	R	16	6	6	R	12	R	14	R	16	5	4	3	13	R	12	13	15	12	20	R	16	6
Karl Oppitzhauser	March 761-Ford	-	-	-	-	-	-	-	-	-	-	-	-	-	-	-	-	-	-	NT	DNP	-	-	-	-	-	-	-	-	-	-	-	-
Carlos Pace	Brabham BT45-Alfa Romeo	10	10	14	R	13	9	11	6	9	R	13	9	10	8	5	4	16	8	7	4	8	R	9	R	3	R	10	7	10	R	6	R
Larry Perkins	Boro-Ensign N175-Ford	-	-	-	-	-	-	24	13	20	8	23	DNQ	22	R	-	-	-	-	-	-	-	-	19	R	13	R	-	-	-	-	-	-
	Brabham BT45-Alfa Romeo	-	-	-	-	-	-	-	-	-	-	-	-	-	-	-	-	-	-	-	-	-	-	-	-	-	-	19	17	13	R	17	R
Henri Pescarolo	Surtees TS19-Ford	-	-	-	-	-	-	-	-	-	-	22	DNQ	-	-	24	R	26	R	28	DNQ	22	9	22	11	22	17	22	19	26	NC	-	-
Alessandro Pesenti-Rossi	Tyrrell 007-Ford	-	-	-	-	-	-	-	-	-	-	-	-	-	-	-	-	-	-	26	14	23	11	27	DNQ	21	18	-	-	-	-	-	-
Ronnie Peterson	Lotus 77-Ford	18	R	-	-	-	-	-	-	-	-	-	-	-	-	-	-	-	-	-	-	-	-	-	-	-	-	-	-	-	-	-	-
	March 761-Ford	-	-	10	R	6	10	16	R	10	R	3	R	9	7	6	19	7	R	11	R	3	6	1	R	8	1F	2	9	3	R	9	R
Tom Pryce	Shadow DN5B-Ford	12	3	7	7	5	R	22	8	13	10	15	7	12	9	16	8	20	4	18	8	6	R	-	-	-	-	-	-	-	-	-	-
	Shadow DN8A-Ford	-	-	-	-	-	-	-	-	-	-	-	-	-	-	-	-	-	-	-	-	-	-	3	4	15	8	13	11	9	R	14	R
Clay Regazzoni	Ferrari 312T	4	7	9	R	1	1F	-	-	-	-	-	-	-	-	-	-	-	-	-	-	-	-	-	-	-	-	-	-	-	-	-	-
	Ferrari 312T2	-	-	-	-	-	-	5	11	2	2	2	14F	11	6	4	R	4	R	5	9	-	-	5	2F	9	2	12	6	14	7	7	5

driver	car	BR Q R	ZA Q R	LB Q R	E Q R	B Q R	MC Q R	S Q R	F Q R	GB Q R	D Q R	A Q R	NL Q R	I Q R	CDN Q R	USA Q R	J Q R
Carlos Reutemann	Brabham BT45-	15 12	11 R	10 R	12 4	12 R	20 R	16 R	10 11	15 R	10 R	14 R	12 R	- -	- -	- -	- -
	Alfa Romeo																
	Ferrari 312T2	- -	- -	- -	- -	- -	- -	- -	- -	- -	- -	- -	- -	7 9	- -	- -	- -
Alex Ribeiro	Hesketh 308D-Ford	- -	- -	- -	- -	- -	- -	- -	- -	- -	- -	- -	- -	- -	- -	22 12	- -
Ian Scheckter	Tyrrell 007-Ford	- -	16 R	- -	- -	- -	- -	- -	- -	- -	- -	- -	- -	- -	- -	- -	- -
Jody Scheckter	Tyrrell 007-Ford	13 5	12 4	11 R	14 R	- -	- -	- -	- -	- -	- -	- -	- -	- -	- -	- -	- -
	Tyrrell P34-Ford	- -	- -	- -	- -	7 4	5 2	1 1	9 6	8 2	8 2F	10 R	8 5	2 5	7 4	2 2	5 R
Rolf Stommelen	Brabham BT45-	- -	- -	- -	- -	- -	- -	- -	- -	- -	15 6	- -	- -	11 R	- -	- -	- -
	Alfa Romeo																
	Hesketh 308D-Ford	- -	- -	- -	- -	- -	- -	- -	- -	- -	- -	- -	- -	25 12	- -	- -	- -
Hans-Joachim Stuck																	
	March 761-Ford	14 4	17 12	18 R	17 R	15 R	6 4	20 R	17 7	17 R	4 R	11 R	18 R	6 R	8 R	6 5	18 R
Otto Stuppacher	Tyrrell 007-Ford	- -	- -	- -	- -	- -	- -	- -	- -	- -	NTDNP	- -	26 DNS	27 DNQ	27 DNQ	- -	- -
Noritake Takahara	Surtees TS19-Ford	- -	- -	- -	- -	- -	- -	- -	- -	- -	- -	- -	- -	- -	- -	24 9	
Tony Trimmer	Maki F102A-Ford	- -	- -	- -	- -	- -	- -	- -	- -	- -	- -	- -	- -	- -	- -	27 DNQ	
Emilio de Villota	Brabham BT44B-Ford	- -	- -	- -	- -	28 DNQ	- -	- -	- -	- -	- -	- -	- -	- -	- -	- -	- -
John Watson	Penske PC3-Ford	8 R	3 5	9 NC	13 R	17 7	17 10	- -	- -	- -	- -	- -	- -	- -	- -	- -	- -
	Penske PC4-Ford	- -	- -	- -	- -	- -	- -	17 R	8 3	11 3	19 7	2 1	4 R	29 11	14 10	8 6	4 R
Mike Wilds	Shadow DN3B-Ford	- -	- -	- -	- -	- -	- -	- -	- -	- -	29 DNQ	- -	- -	- -	- -	- -	- -
Emilio Zapico	Williams FW04-Ford	- -	- -	- -	- -	27 DNQ	- -	- -	- -	- -	- -	- -	- -	- -	- -	- -	- -
Renzo Zorzi	Williams FW04-Ford	17 9	- -	- -	- -	- -	- -	- -	- -	- -	- -	- -	- -	- -	- -	- -	- -

1976 FINAL CHAMPIONSHIP POSITIONS

Drivers

1	James Hunt	69
2	Niki Lauda	68
3	Jody Scheckter	49
4	Patrick Depailler	39
5	Clay Regazzoni	31
6	Mario Andretti	22
7=	Jacques Laffite	20
	John Watson	20
9	Jochen Mass	19
10	Gunnar Nilsson	11
11=	Ronnie Peterson	10
	Tom Pryce	10
13	Hans-Joachim Stuck	8
14=	Alan Jones	7
	Carlos Pace	7
16=	Emerson Fittipaldi	3
	Carlos Reutemann	3
18	Chris Amon	2
19=	Vittorio Brambilla	1
	Rolf Stommelen	1

Sum of best seven results from the first eight races and best seven results from the final eight races

Manufacturers

1	Ferrari	83
2	McLaren-Ford	74 (75)*
3	Tyrrell-Ford	71
4	Lotus-Ford	29
5=	Penske-Ford	20
	Ligier-Matra	20
7	March-Ford	19
8	Shadow-Ford	10
9	Brabham-Alfa Romeo	9
10	Surtees-Ford	7
11	Fittipaldi-Ford	3
12	Ensign-Ford	2
13	Parnelli-Ford	1

*Sum of best seven results from the first eight races and best seven results from the final eight races. Points only awarded to first car to finish for each manufacturer

LABATT'S 50 CANADIAN GRAND PRIX

3 October 1976. Mosport Park. 80 laps of a 2.459-mile circuit = 196.720 miles. Warm, dry and sunny. World Championship round 14

1	James Hunt	McLaren M23-Ford	80	1h40m09.626
2	Patrick Depailler	Tyrrell P34-Ford	80	1h40m15.957
3	Mario Andretti	Lotus 77-Ford	80	1h40m19.992
4	Jody Scheckter	Tyrrell P34-Ford	80	1h40m29.371
5	Jochen Mass	McLaren M23-Ford	80	1h40m51.437
6	Clay Regazzoni	Ferrari 312T2	80	1h40m55.882

Winner's average speed: 117.843 mph. Starting grid front row: Hunt, 1m12.389 (pole) and Peterson, 1m12.783. Fastest lap: Depailler, 1m13.817. Leaders: Peterson, laps 1-8; Hunt, 9-80

UNITED STATES GRAND PRIX

10 October 1976. Watkins Glen. 59 laps of a 3.377-mile circuit = 199.243 miles. Cool and dry. World Championship round 15

1	James Hunt	McLaren M23-Ford	59	1h42m40.741
2	Jody Scheckter	Tyrrell P34-Ford	59	1h42m48.771
3	Niki Lauda	Ferrari 312T2	59	1h43m43.065
4	Jochen Mass	McLaren M23-Ford	59	1h43m43.199
5	Hans-Joachim Stuck	March 761-Ford	59	1h43m48.719
6	John Watson	Penske PC4-Ford	59	1h43m48.931

Winner's average speed: 116.427 mph. Starting grid front row: Hunt,
1m43.622 (pole) and Scheckter, 1m43.870. Fastest lap: Hunt, 1m42.851. Leaders: Scheckter, laps 1-36, 41-45; Hunt, 37-40, 46-59

JAPANESE GRAND PRIX

24 October 1976. Fuji. 73 laps of a 2.709-mile circuit = 197.757 miles. Very wet and misty. World Championship round 16

1	Mario Andretti	Lotus 77-Ford	73	1h43m58.86
2	Patrick Depailler	Tyrrell P34-Ford	72	
3	James Hunt	McLaren M23-Ford	72	
4	Alan Jones	Surtees TS19-Ford	72	
5	Clay Regazzoni	Ferrari 312T2	72	
6	Gunnar Nilsson	Lotus 77-Ford	72	

Winner's average speed: 114.111 mph. Starting grid front row: Andretti, 1m12.77 (pole) and Hunt, 1m12.80. Fastest lap: Hasemi, 1m18.23. Leaders: Hunt, laps 1-61; Depailler, 62-63; Andretti, 64-73

1977

Mario Andretti's win at the 1976 Japanese Grand Prix had signalled the resurgence of Lotus, and for the new season team owner Colin Chapman introduced a concept that would change the sport. The new Lotus 78 "wing car" used the bodywork on either side of the cockpit to channel air under the car, generating downforce that radically boosted cornering speeds. Sliding "skirts" which extended from the bottom of the bodywork to the track surface sealed these sidepods.

"Ground effect," as it was also known, was not a new idea, but Lotus's design team, including Peter Wright and Ralph Bellamy, made it work. Mid-season engine failures robbed Andretti of vital points and the championship, but he won four times, while teammate Gunnar Nilsson scored his first victory in the wet Belgian GP.

The result of the season's first race was a surprise as Jody Scheckter gave the new Wolf marque a debut victory. Scheckter had two more wins, including the 100th victory for a Ford Cosworth DFV engine at Monaco. Jacques Laffite and Alan Jones also scored first wins for the Ligier and Shadow marques, respectively.

Two tragic events brought sadness to the sport during the spring. At the South African GP, Tom Pryce and a marshal died in a freak accident. Cresting the brow on the main straight, Pryce was unable to avoid the inexperienced marshal, who was crossing the track to a retired car. Both men were killed instantly. Just weeks later, Carlos Pace was killed in an aircraft accident in his native Brazil.

Niki Lauda, now fully recovered from the burns he suffered in 1976, produced a typically consistent season to convincingly win a second World Championship. Fittingly, his three wins included the German GP that had now moved to Hockenheim. But Lauda's relationship with the Ferrari team had grown increasingly strained, and before the Italian GP he announced that he was leaving. Before the season had finished, Lauda walked out on the team when his chief mechanic and close ally, Ermanno Cuoghi, was sacked.

Gilles Villeneuve, who had made a stunning debut at the British GP in a third McLaren, took Lauda's car for the last two races of the year. But in only his second race for Ferrari the Canadian suffered a huge accident in Japan, and after barrel-rolling wildly the car landed in a prohibited area, killing a marshal and a photographer.

Defending champion James Hunt had a disappointing start to the year. But he did win three times in the second half of the season, including a victory at the British GP after the ever-unlucky John Watson retired while leading for Brabham.

Renault returned to Grand Prix racing after an absence of almost seventy years, introducing the first turbocharged Formula 1 engine at the British GP. Although initially fragile, it started a revolution that would see a complete grid of turbocharged engines within seven years.

GRAN PREMIO DE LA REPUBLICA ARGENTINA

9 January 1977. Buenos Aires. 53 laps of a 3.709-mile circuit = 196.577 miles. Very hot, dry and sunny. World Championship round 1

1	Jody Scheckter	Wolf WR1-Ford	53	1h40m11.19
2	Carlos Pace	Brabham BT45-Alfa Romeo	53	1h40m54.43
3	Carlos Reutemann	Ferrari 312T2	53	1h40m57.21
4	Emerson Fittipaldi	Fittipaldi FD04-Ford	53	1h41m06.67
5	Mario Andretti	Lotus 78-Ford	51	wheel bearing
6	Clay Regazzoni	Ensign N177-Ford	51	

Winner's average speed: 117.727 mph. Starting grid front row: Hunt, 1m48.68 (pole) and Watson, 1m48.96. Fastest lap: Hunt, 1m51.06. Leaders: Watson, laps 1-10, 32-34; Hunt, 11-31; Pace, 35-47; J Scheckter, 48-53

GRANDE PREMIO DO BRASIL

23 January 1977. Interlagos. 40 laps of a 4.946-mile circuit = 197.840 miles. Very hot, dry and sunny. World Championship round 2

1	Carlos Reutemann	Ferrari 312T2	40	1h45m07.72
2	James Hunt	McLaren M23-Ford	40	1h45m18.43
3	Niki Lauda	Ferrari 312T2	40	1h46m55.23
4	Emerson Fittipaldi	Fittipaldi FD04-Ford	39	
5	Gunnar Nilsson	Lotus 78-Ford	39	
6	Renzo Zorzi	Shadow DN5B-Ford	39	

Winner's average speed: 112.913 mph. Starting grid front row: Hunt, 2m30.11 (pole) and Reutemann, 2m30.18. Fastest lap: Hunt, 2m34.55. Leaders: Pace, laps 1-6; Hunt, 7-22; Reutemann, 23-40

CITIZEN SOUTH AFRICAN GRAND PRIX

5 March 1977. Kyalami. 78 laps of a 2.550-mile circuit = 198.900 miles. Dry and overcast. World Championship round 3

1	Niki Lauda	Ferrari 312T2	78	1h42m21.6
2	Jody Scheckter	Wolf WR1-Ford	78	1h42m26.8
3	Patrick Depailler	Tyrrell P34-Ford	78	1h42m27.3
4	James Hunt	McLaren M23-Ford	78	1h42m31.1
5	Jochen Mass	McLaren M23-Ford	78	1h42m41.5
6	John Watson	Brabham BT45-Alfa Romeo	78	1h42m41.8

Winner's average speed: 116.589 mph. Starting grid front row: Hunt, 1m15.96 (pole) and Pace, 1m16.01. Fastest lap: Watson, 1m17.63. Leaders: Hunt, laps 1-6; Lauda, 7-78

UNITED STATES GRAND PRIX WEST

3 April 1977. Long Beach. 80 laps of a 2.020-mile circuit = 161.600 miles. Warm, dry and sunny. World Championship round 4

1	Mario Andretti	Lotus 78-Ford	80	1h51m35.470
2	Niki Lauda	Ferrari 312T2	80	1h51m36.243
3	Jody Scheckter	Wolf WR1-Ford	80	1h51m40.327
4	Patrick Depailler	Tyrrell P34-Ford	80	1h52m49.957
5	Emerson Fittipaldi	Fittipaldi FD04-Ford	80	1h52m56.378
6	Jean-Pierre Jarier	Penske PC4-Ford	79	

Winner's average speed: 86.889 mph. Starting grid front row: Lauda, 1m21.630 (pole) and Andretti, 1m21.868. Fastest lap: Lauda, 1m22.753. Leaders: J Scheckter, laps 1-76; Andretti, 77-80

GRAN PREMIO DE ESPANA

8 May 1977. Jarama. 75 laps of a 2.115-mile circuit = 158.655 miles. Warm, dry and sunny. World Championship round 5

1	Mario Andretti	Lotus 78-Ford	75	1h42m52.22
2	Carlos Reutemann	Ferrari 312T2	75	1h43m08.07
3	Jody Scheckter	Wolf WR2-Ford	75	1h43m16.73
4	Jochen Mass	McLaren M23-Ford	75	1h43m17.09
5	Gunnar Nilsson	Lotus 78-Ford	75	1h43m58.05
6	Hans-Joachim Stuck	Brabham BT45B-Alfa Romeo	74	

Winner's average speed: 92.537 mph. Starting grid front row: Andretti, 1m18.70 (pole) and Laffite, 1m19.42. Fastest lap: Laffite, 1m20.81. Leaders: Andretti, laps 1-75

GRAND PRIX DE MONACO

22 May 1977. Monte Carlo. 76 laps of a 2.058-mile circuit = 156.408 miles. Warm, dry and sunny. World Championship round 6

1	Jody Scheckter	Wolf WR1-Ford	76	1h57m52.77
2	Niki Lauda	Ferrari 312T2	76	1h57m53.66
3	Carlos Reutemann	Ferrari 312T2	76	1h58m25.57
4	Jochen Mass	McLaren M23-Ford	76	1h58m27.37
5	Mario Andretti	Lotus 78-Ford	76	1h58m28.32
6	Alan Jones	Shadow DN8A-Ford	76	1h58m29.38

Winner's average speed: 79.611 mph. Starting grid front row: Watson, 1m29.86 (pole) and J Scheckter, 1m30.27. Fastest lap: J Scheckter, 1m31.07. Leaders: J Scheckter, laps 1-76

Formula 1

driver	car	RA Q	RA R	BR Q	BR R	ZA Q	ZA R	LB Q	LB R	E Q	E R	MC Q	MC R
Conny Andersson	Stanley BRM P207	-	-	-	-	-	-	-	-	31	DNQ	-	-
Mario Andretti	Lotus 78-Ford	8	5	3	R	6	R	2	1	1	1	10	5
Ian Ashley	Hesketh 308E-Ford	-	-	-	-	-	-	-	-	-	-	-	-
Hans Binder	Surtees TS19-Ford	18	R	20	R	19	11	19	11	20	9	19	R
	Penske PC4-Ford	-	-	-	-	-	-	-	-	-	-	-	-
Michael Bleekemolen	March 761-Ford	-	-	-	-	-	-	-	-	-	-	-	-
Vittorio Brambilla	Surtees TS19-Ford	13	7	11	R	14	7	11	R	11	R	14	8
Patrick Depailler	Tyrrell P34-Ford	3	R	6	R	4	3	12	4	10	R	8	R
Bernard de Dryver	March 761-Ford	-	-	-	-	-	-	-	-	-	-	-	-
Guy Edwards	Stanley BRM P207	-	-	-	-	-	-	-	-	-	-	-	-
Harald Ertl	Hesketh 308E-Ford	-	-	-	-	-	-	-	-	18	R	23	DNQ
Emerson Fittipaldi	Fittipaldi FD04-Ford	16	4	16	4	9	10	7	5	19	14	18	R
	Fittipaldi F5-Ford	-	-	-	-	-	-	-	-	-	-	-	-
Giorgio Francia	Brabham BT45B-Alfa Romeo	-	-	-	-	-	-	-	-	-	-	-	-
Bruno Giacomelli	McLaren M23-Ford	-	-	-	-	-	-	-	-	-	-	-	-
Boy Hayje	March 761-Ford	-	-	-	21	R	-	-	28	DNQ	22	DNQ	
Brian Henton	March 761B-Ford	-	-	-	-	-	-	18	10	-	-	-	-
	March 761-Ford	-	-	-	-	-	-	-	-	29	DNQ	-	-
	Boro-Ensign N175-Ford	-	-	-	-	-	-	-	-	-	-	-	-
Hans Heyer	Penske PC4-Ford	-	-	-	-	-	-	-	-	-	-	-	-
Ingo Hoffmann	Fittipaldi FD04-Ford	19	R	19	7	-	-	-	-	-	-	-	-
Kazuyoshi Hoshino	Kojima KE009-Ford	-	-	-	-	-	-	-	-	-	-	-	-
James Hunt	McLaren M23-Ford	1	RF	1	2F	1	4	8	7	-	-	7	R
	McLaren M26-Ford	-	-	-	-	-	-	-	-	7	R	-	-
Jacky Ickx	Ensign N177-Ford	-	-	-	-	-	-	-	-	-	-	17	10
Jean-Pierre Jabouille	Renault RS01	-	-	-	-	-	-	-	-	-	-	-	-
Jean-Pierre Jarier	Penske PC4-Ford	-	-	-	-	-	-	9	6	26	DNQ	12	11
	Shadow DN8A-Ford	-	-	-	-	-	-	-	-	-	-	-	-
	Ligier JS7-Matra	-	-	-	-	-	-	-	-	-	-	-	-
Alan Jones	Shadow DN8A-Ford	-	-	-	-	-	-	14	R	14	R	11	6
Rupert Keegan	Hesketh 308E-Ford	-	-	-	-	-	-	-	-	16	R	20	12
Loris Kessel	Apollon-Williams FW03-Ford	-	-	-	-	-	-	-	-	-	-	-	-
Mikko Kozarowitsky	March 761-Ford	-	-	-	-	-	-	-	-	-	-	-	-
Jacques Laffite	Ligier JS7-Matra	15	R	14	R	12	R	5	9	2	7F	16	7
Niki Lauda	Ferrari 312T2	4	R	13	3	3	1	1	2F	3	DNS	6	2
Lamberto Leoni	Surtees TS19-Ford	-	-	-	-	-	-	-	-	-	-	-	-
Brett Lunger	March 761-Ford	-	-	-	23	14	21	R	25	10	-	-	
	McLaren M23-Ford	-	-	-	-	-	-	-	-	-	-	-	-
Jochen Mass	McLaren M23-Ford	5	R	4	R	13	5	15	R	9	4	9	4
	McLaren M26-Ford	-	-	-	-	-	-	-	-	-	-	-	-
Brian McGuire	McGuire BM1/Williams FW04-Ford	-	-	-	-	-	-	-	-	-	-	-	-
Arturo Merzario	March 761B-Ford	-	-	-	-	-	-	-	-	21	R	21	DNQ
	Shadow DN8A-Ford	-	-	-	-	-	-	-	-	-	-	-	-
Patrick Neve	March 761-Ford	-	-	-	-	-	-	-	-	22	12	-	-
Gunnar Nilsson	Lotus 78-Ford	10	DNS	10	5	10	12	16	8	12	5	13	R
Jackie Oliver	Shadow DN8A-Ford	-	-	-	-	-	-	-	-	-	-	-	-
Danny Ongais	Penske PC4-Ford	-	-	-	-	-	-	-	-	-	-	-	-
Carlos Pace	Brabham BT45-Alfa Romeo	6	2	5	R	-	-	-	-	-	-	-	-
	Brabham BT45B-Alfa Romeo	-	-	-	-	2	13	-	-	-	-	-	-
Riccardo Patrese	Shadow DN8A-Ford	-	-	-	-	-	-	-	-	-	-	15	9
Larry Perkins	Stanley BRM P207	-	-	22	R	-	-	-	-	-	-	-	-
	Stanley BRM P201B/204	-	-	-	-	22	15	-	-	-	-	-	-
	Surtees TS19-Ford	-	-	-	-	-	-	-	-	-	-	-	-
Ronnie Peterson	Tyrrell P34-Ford	14	R	8	R	7	R	10	R	15	8	4	R
Teddy Pilette	Stanley BRM P207	-	-	-	-	-	-	-	-	-	-	-	-
Tom Pryce	Shadow DN8A-Ford	9	R	12	R	15	R	-	-	-	-	-	-
David Purley	Lec CRP1-Ford	-	-	-	-	-	-	-	-	30	DNQ	-	-
Hector Rebaque	Hesketh 308E-Ford	-	-	-	-	-	-	-	-	-	-	-	-
Clay Regazzoni	Ensign N177-Ford	12	6	9	R	16	9	13	R	8	R	24	DNQ
Carlos Reutemann	Ferrari 312T2	7	3	2	1	8	8	4	R	4	2	3	3

B Q	B R	S Q	S R	F Q	F R	GB Q	GB R	D Q	D R	A Q	A R	NL Q	NL R	I Q	I R	USA Q	USA R	CDN Q	CDN R	J Q	J R
29	DNQ	30	DNQ	30	DNQ	-	-	-	-	-	-	-	-	-	-	-	-	-	-	-	-
1	R	1	6F	1	1F	6	14	7	R	3	R	1	R	4	1F	4	2	1	9F	1	R
-	-	-	-	-	-	-	-	-	-	28	DNQ	30	DNQ	30	DNQ	22	17	25	DNS	-	-
-	-	-	-	-	-	-	-	-	-	-	-	-	-	-	-	25	11	24	R	21	R
-	-	-	-	-	-	-	-	19	12	18	8	32	DNQ	-	-	-	-	-	-	-	-
-	-	-	-	-	-	-	-	-	-	-	-	-	-	34	DNQ	-	-	-	-	-	-
12	4	13	R	11	13	8	8	10	5	13	15	22	12	10	R	11	19	15	6	9	8
5	8	6	4	12	R	18	R	15	R	10	13	11	R	13	R	8	14	6	2	15	3
31	DNQ	-	-	-	-	-	-	-	-	-	-	-	-	-	-	-	-	-	-	-	-
-	-	-	-	-	-	33	NPQ	-	-	-	-	-	-	-	-	-	-	-	-	-	-
25	9	23	16	26	DNQ	-	-	-	-	-	-	-	-	-	-	-	-	-	-	-	-
-	-	18	18	-	-	-	-	-	-	-	-	-	-	-	-	-	-	-	-	-	-
16	R	-	-	22	11	22	R	28	DNQ	23	11	17	4	26	DNQ	18	13	19	R	-	-
-	-	-	-	-	-	-	-	-	-	-	-	-	-	15	R	-	-	-	-	-	-
27	15	28	DNQ	-	-	-	-	-	-	-	-	31	DNQ	-	-	-	-	-	-	-	-
-	-	-	-	-	-	29	DNQ	-	-	27	DNQ	-	-	-	-	-	-	-	-	-	-
-	-	-	-	-	-	-	-	-	-	-	-	-	-	23	DSQ	28	DNQ	-	-	-	-
-	-	-	-	-	-	-	-	27	R	-	-	-	-	-	-	-	-	-	-	-	-
-	-	-	-	-	-	-	-	-	-	-	-	-	-	-	-	-	-	-	-	11	11
9	7	3	12	2	3	1	1F	4	R	2	R	3	R	1	R	1	1	2	R	2	1
-	-	-	-	-	-	21	R	-	-	-	-	10	R	20	R	14	R	27	DNQ	-	-
26	11	17	8	19	R	20	9	12	R	18	14	21	R	18	R	-	-	-	-	-	-
-	-	-	-	-	-	-	-	-	-	-	-	-	-	-	-	16	9	-	-	-	-
-	-	-	-	-	-	-	-	-	-	-	-	-	-	-	-	-	-	-	-	17	R
17	5	11	17	10	R	12	7	17	R	14	1	13	R	16	3	13	R	7	4	12	4
19	R	24	13	14	10	13	R	23	R	20	7	26	R	23	9	20	8	26	R	-	-
-	-	-	-	-	-	-	-	-	-	-	-	-	-	33	DNQ	-	-	-	-	-	-
-	-	31	DNQ	-	-	36	NPQ	-	-	-	-	-	-	-	-	-	-	-	-	-	-
10	R	8	1	5	8	15	6	6	R	6	R	2	2	8	8	10	7	11	R	5	5
11	2	15	R	9	5	3	2	3	1F	1	2	4	1F	5	2	7	4	-	-	-	-
-	-	-	-	-	-	-	-	-	-	-	-	-	-	27	DNQ	-	-	-	-	-	-
22	DNS	22	11	25	DNQ	19	13	21	R	17	10	20	9	22	R	17	10	20	11	-	-
6	R	9	2	7	9	-	-	-	-	-	-	-	-	-	-	-	-	-	-	-	-
-	-	-	-	-	-	11	4	13	R	9	6	14	R	9	4	15	R	5	3	8	R
-	-	-	-	-	-	35	NPQ	-	-	-	-	-	-	-	-	-	-	-	-	-	-
14	14	-	-	18	R	17	R	29	DNQ	-	-	28	DNQ	NT	DNP	-	-	-	-	-	-
-	-	-	-	-	-	-	-	-	-	21	R	-	-	-	-	-	-	-	-	-	-
24	10	20	15	24	DNQ	26	10	25	DNQ	22	9	27	DNQ	24	7	24	18	21	R	-	-
3	1F	7	19	3	4	5	3	9	R	16	R	5	R	19	R	12	R	4	R	14	R
-	-	16	9	-	-	-	-	-	-	-	-	-	-	-	-	26	R	22	7	-	-
15	R	-	-	15	R	25	R	16	10	-	-	16	13	6	R	-	-	8	10	13	6
23	12	27	DNQ	27	DNQ	-	-	-	-	-	-	-	-	-	-	-	-	-	-	-	-
8	3	10	R	17	12	10	R	14	9	15	5	7	R	12	6	5	16F	3	R	18	R
-	-	-	-	-	-	-	-	30	DNQ	-	-	33	DNQ	31	DNQ	-	-	-	-	-	-
20	13	19	14	21	R	31	NPQ	-	-	-	-	-	-	-	-	-	-	-	-	-	-
32	DNQ	29	DNQ	28	DNQ	-	-	24	R	29	DNQ	32	DNQ	-	-	-	-	-	-	-	-
13	R	14	7	16	7	28	DNQ	22	R	11	R	9	R	7	5	19	5	14	R	10	R
7	R	12	3	6	6	14	15	8	4	5	4	6	6	2	R	6	6	12	R	7	2

1977 DRIVERS' RECORDS cont.

driver	car	RA Q	RA R	BR Q	BR R	ZA Q	ZA R	LB Q	LB R	E Q	E R	MC Q	MC R
Alex Ribeiro	March 761B-Ford	20	R	21	R	17	R	22	R	27	DNQ	25	DNQ
Ian Scheckter	March 761B-Ford	17	R	17	R	-	-	-	-	17	11	26	DNQ
	March 771-Ford	-	-	-	-	-	-	-	-	-	-	-	-
Jody Scheckter	Wolf WR1-Ford	11	1	15	R	5	2	3	3	-	-	2	1F
	Wolf WR2-Ford	-	-	-	-	-	-	-	-	5	3	-	-
	Wolf WR3-Ford	-	-	-	-	-	-	-	-	-	-	-	-
Vern Schuppan	Surtees TS19-Ford	-	-	-	-	-	-	-	-	-	-	-	-
Hans-Joachim Stuck	March 761B-Ford	-	-	-	-	18	R	-	-	-	-	-	-
	Brabham BT45B-Alfa Romeo	-	-	-	-	-	-	17	R	13	6	5	R
Andy Sutcliffe	March 761-Ford	-	-	-	-	-	-	-	-	-	-	-	-
Noritake Takahara	Kojima KE009-Ford	-	-	-	-	-	-	-	-	-	-	-	-
Kunimitsu Takahashi	Tyrrell 007-Ford	-	-	-	-	-	-	-	-	-	-	-	-
Patrick Tambay	Surtees TS19-Ford	-	-	-	-	-	-	-	-	-	-	-	-
	Ensign N177-Ford	-	-	-	-	-	-	-	-	-	-	-	-
Tony Trimmer	Surtees TS19-Ford	-	-	-	-	-	-	-	-	-	-	-	-
Gilles Villeneuve	McLaren M23-Ford	-	-	-	-	-	-	-	-	-	-	-	-
	Ferrari 312T2	-	-	-	-	-	-	-	-	-	-	-	-
Emilio de Villota	McLaren M23-Ford	-	-	-	-	-	-	-	-	23	13	-	-
John Watson	Brabham BT45-Alfa Romeo	2	R	7	R	11	6F	-	-	-	-	-	-
	Brabham BT45B-Alfa Romeo	-	-	-	-	-	-	6	DSQ	6	R	1	R
Renzo Zorzi	Shadow DN5B-Ford	21	R	18	6	-	-	-	-	-	-	-	-
	Shadow DN8A-Ford	-	-	-	-	20	R	20	R	24	R	-	-

1977 FINAL CHAMPIONSHIP POSITIONS

Drivers

1	Niki Lauda	72
2	Jody Scheckter	55
3	Mario Andretti	47
4	Carlos Reutemann	42
5	James Hunt	40
6	Jochen Mass	25
7	Alan Jones	22
8=	Patrick Depailler	20
	Gunnar Nilsson	20
10	Jacques Laffite	18
11	Hans-Joachim Stuck	12
12	Emerson Fittipaldi	11
13	John Watson	9
14	Ronnie Peterson	7
15=	Vittorio Brambilla	6
	Carlos Pace	6
17=	Clay Regazzoni	5
	Patrick Tambay	5
19=	Jean-Pierre Jarier	1
	Riccardo Patrese	1
	Renzo Zorzi	1

Sum of best eight results from the first nine races and best seven results from the final eight races

Manufacturers

1	Ferrari	95 (97)*
2	Lotus-Ford	62
3	McLaren-Ford	60
4	Wolf-Ford	55
5=	Brabham-Alfa Romeo	27
	Tyrrell-Ford	27
7	Shadow-Ford	23
8	Ligier-Matra	18
9	Fittipaldi-Ford	11
10	Ensign-Ford	10
11	Surtees-Ford	6
12	Penske-Ford	1

*Sum of best eight results from the first nine races and best seven results from the final eight races. Points only awarded to first car to finish for each manufacturer.

GRAND PRIX DE BELGIQUE

5 June 1977. Zolder. 70 laps of a 2.648-mile circuit = 185.360 miles. Cold and wet. World Championship round 7

1	Gunnar Nilsson	Lotus 78-Ford	70	1h55m05.71
2	Niki Lauda	Ferrari 312T2	70	1h55m19.90
3	Ronnie Peterson	Tyrrell P34-Ford	70	1h55m25.66
4	Vittorio Brambilla	Surtees TS19-Ford	70	1h55m30.69
5	Alan Jones	Shadow DN8A-Ford	70	1h56m21.18
6	Hans-Joachim Stuck	Brabham BT45B-Alfa Romeo	69	

Winner's average speed: 96.630 mph. Starting grid front row: Andretti, 1m24.64 (pole) and Watson, 1m26.18. Fastest lap: Nilsson, 1m27.54. Leaders: J Scheckter, laps 1-16; Mass, 17-18; Brambilla, 19-22; Lauda, 23-49; Nilsson, 50-70

GISLAVED SVERIGES GRAND PRIX

19 June 1977. Anderstorp. 72 laps of a 2.497-mile circuit = 179.784 miles. Warm, dry and sunny. World Championship round 8

1	Jacques Laffite	Ligier JS7-Matra	72	1h46m55.520
2	Jochen Mass	McLaren M23-Ford	72	1h47m03.969
3	Carlos Reutemann	Ferrari 312T2	72	1h47m09.889
4	Patrick Depailler	Tyrrell P34-Ford	72	1h47m11.828
5	John Watson	Brabham BT45B-Alfa Romeo	72	1h47m14.255
6	Mario Andretti	Lotus 78-Ford	72	1h47m20.797

Winner's average speed: 100.884 mph. Starting grid front row: Andretti, 1m25.404 (pole) and Watson, 1m25.545. Fastest lap: Andretti, 1m27.607. Leaders: Watson, lap 1; Andretti, laps 2-69; Laffite, 70-72

GRAND PRIX DE FRANCE

3 July 1977. Dijon-Prenois. 80 laps of a 2.361-mile circuit = 188.880 miles. Hot, dry and sunny. World Championship round 9

1	Mario Andretti	Lotus 78-Ford	80	1h39m40.13
2	John Watson	Brabham BT45B-Alfa Romeo	80	1h39m41.68
3	James Hunt	McLaren M26-Ford	80	1h40m14.00
4	Gunnar Nilsson	Lotus 78-Ford	80	1h40m51.21

	B		S		F		GB		D		A		NL		I		USA		CDN		J	
	Q	R	Q	R	Q	R	Q	R	Q	R	Q	R	Q	R	Q	R	Q	R	Q	R	Q	R
	30	DNQ	25	DNQ	23	DNQ	27	DNQ	20	8	30	DNQ	24	11	25	DNQ	23	15	23	8	23	12
	21	R	21	R	20	NC	24	R	18	R	24	R	-	-	-	-	-	-	-	-	-	-
	-	-	-	-	-	-	-	-	-	-	-	-	25	10	17	R	21	R	18	R	-	-
	-	-	4	R	-	-	4	R	-	-	-	-	-	-	3	R	-	-	9	1	-	-
	-	-	-	-	-	-	-	-	1	2	-	-	15	3	-	-	9	3	-	-	-	-
	4	R	-	-	8	R	-	-	-	-	8	R	-	-	-	-	-	-	-	-	6	10F
	-	-	-	-	-	-	23	12	19	7	25	16	29	DNQ	-	-	-	-	-	-	-	-
	18	6	5	10	13	R	7	5	5	3	4	3	19	7	11	R	2	R	13	R	4	7
	-	-	-	-	-	-	32	NPQ	-	-	-	-	-	-	-	-	-	-	-	-	-	-
	-	-	-	-	-	-	-	-	-	-	-	-	-	-	-	-	-	-	-	-	19	R
	-	-	-	-	-	-	-	-	-	-	-	-	-	-	-	-	-	-	-	-	22	9
	-	-	-	-	29	DNQ	-	-	-	-	-	-	-	-	-	-	-	-	-	-	-	-
	-	-	-	-	-	-	16	R	11	6	7	R	12	5	21	R	27	DNQ	16	5	16	R
	-	-	-	-	-	-	34	NPQ	-	-	-	-	-	-	-	-	-	-	-	-	-	-
	-	-	-	-	-	-	9	11	-	-	-	-	-	-	-	-	-	-	-	-	-	-
	-	-	-	-	-	-	-	-	-	-	-	-	-	-	-	-	-	-	17	12	20	R
	28	DNQ	26	DNQ	-	-	30	DNQ	26	DNQ	26	17	-	-	29	DNQ	-	-	-	-	-	-
	2	R	2	5	4	2	2	R	2	R	12	8F	8	R	14	R	3	12	10	R	3	R

5 Niki Lauda — Ferrari 312T2 — 80 — 1h40m54.58
6 Carlos Reutemann — Ferrari 312T2 — 79
Winner's average speed: 113.705 mph. Starting grid front row: Andretti, 1m12.21 (pole) and Hunt, 1m12.73. Fastest lap: Andretti, 1m13.75. Leaders: Hunt, laps 1-4; Watson, 5-79; Andretti, 80

JOHN PLAYER BRITISH AND EUROPEAN GRAND PRIX

16 July 1977. Silverstone. 68 laps of a 2.932-mile circuit = 199.376 miles. Warm, dry and sunny. World Championship round 10

1 James Hunt — McLaren M26-Ford — 68 — 1h31m46.06
2 Niki Lauda — Ferrari 312T2 — 68 — 1h32m04.37
3 Gunnar Nilsson — Lotus 78-Ford — 68 — 1h32m05.63
4 Jochen Mass — McLaren M26-Ford — 68 — 1h32m33.82
5 Hans-Joachim Stuck — Brabham BT45B-Alfa Romeo — 68 — 1h32m57.79
6 Jacques Laffite — Ligier JS7-Matra — 67
Winner's average speed: 130.357 mph. Starting grid front row: Hunt, 1m18.49 (pole) and Watson, 1m18.77. Fastest lap: Hunt, 1m19.60. Leaders: Watson, laps 1-49; Hunt, 50-68

GROSSER PREIS VON DEUTSCHLAND

31 July 1977. Hockenheim. 47 laps of a 4.219-mile circuit = 198.293 miles. Warm, dry and sunny. World Championship round 11

1 Niki Lauda — Ferrari 312T2 — 47 — 1h31m48.62
2 Jody Scheckter — Wolf WR2-Ford — 47 — 1h32m02.95
3 Hans-Joachim Stuck — Brabham BT45B-Alfa Romeo — 47 — 1h32m09.52
4 Carlos Reutemann — Ferrari 312T2 — 47 — 1h32m48.89
5 Vittorio Brambilla — Surtees TS19-Ford — 47 — 1h33m15.99
6 Patrick Tambay — Ensign N177-Ford — 47 — 1h33m18.43
Winner's average speed: 129.589 mph. Starting grid front row: J Scheckter, 1m53.07 (pole) and Watson, 1m53.34. Fastest lap: Lauda, 1m55.99. Leaders: J Scheckter, laps 1-12; Lauda, 13-47

GROBEL MOBEL GROSSER PREIS VON OSTERREICH

14 August 1977. Osterreichring. 54 laps of a 3.692-mile circuit = 199.368 miles. Damp at the start, drying later. World Championship round 12

1 Alan Jones — Shadow DN8A-Ford — 54 — 1h37m16.49

2 Niki Lauda — Ferrari 312T2 — 54 — 1h37m36.62
3 Hans-Joachim Stuck — Brabham BT45B-Alfa Romeo — 54 — 1h37m50.99
4 Carlos Reutemann — Ferrari 312T2 — 54 — 1h37m51.24
5 Ronnie Peterson — Tyrrell P34-Ford — 54 — 1h38m18.58
6 Jochen Mass — McLaren M26-Ford — 53
Winner's average speed: 122.972 mph. Starting grid front row: Lauda, 1m39.32 (pole) and Hunt, 1m39.45. Fastest lap: Watson, 1m40.96. Leaders: Andretti, laps 1-11; Hunt, 12-43; Jones, 44-54

GROTE PRIJS VAN NEDERLAND

28 August 1977. Zandvoort. 75 laps of a 2.626-mile circuit = 196.950 miles. Warm, dry and sunny. World Championship round 13

1 Niki Lauda — Ferrari 312T2 — 75 — 1h41m45.93
2 Jacques Laffite — Ligier JS7-Matra — 75 — 1h41m47.82
3 Jody Scheckter — Wolf WR2-Ford — 74
4 Emerson Fittipaldi — Fittipaldi F5-Ford — 74
5 Patrick Tambay — Ensign N177-Ford — 73 — out of fuel
6 Carlos Reutemann — Ferrari 312T2 — 73
Winner's average speed: 116.120 mph. Starting grid front row: Andretti, 1m18.65 (pole) and Laffite, 1m19.27. Fastest lap: Lauda, 1m19.99. Leaders: Hunt, laps 1-5; Laffite, 6-19; Lauda, 20-75

GRAN PREMIO D'ITALIA

11 September 1977. Monza. 52 laps of a 3.604-mile circuit = 187.403 miles. Warm, dry and sunny. World Championship round 14

1 Mario Andretti — Lotus 78-Ford — 52 — 1h27m50.30
2 Niki Lauda — Ferrari 312T2 — 52 — 1h28m07.26
3 Alan Jones — Shadow DN8A-Ford — 52 — 1h28m13.93
4 Jochen Mass — McLaren M26-Ford — 52 — 1h28m18.78
5 Clay Regazzoni — Ensign N177-Ford — 52 — 1h28m21.41
6 Ronnie Peterson — Tyrrell P34-Ford — 52 — 1h29m09.52
Winner's average speed: 128.010 mph. Starting grid front row: Hunt, 1m38.08 (pole) and Reutemann, 1m38.15. Fastest lap: Andretti, 1m39.10. Leaders: J Scheckter, laps 1-9; Andretti, 10-52

UNITED STATES GRAND PRIX

2 October 1977. Watkins Glen. 59 laps of a 3.377-mile circuit = 199.243 miles. Cold and wet. World Championship round 15

1	James Hunt	McLaren M26-Ford	59	1h58m23.267
2	Mario Andretti	Lotus 78-Ford	59	1h58m25.293
3	Jody Scheckter	Wolf WR2-Ford	59	1h59m42.146
4	Niki Lauda	Ferrari 312T2	59	2h00m03.882
5	Clay Regazzoni	Ensign N177-Ford	59	2h00m11.405
6	Carlos Reutemann	Ferrari 312T2	58	

Winner's average speed: 100.978 mph. Starting grid front row: Hunt, 1m40.863 (pole) and Stuck, 1m41.138. Fastest lap: Peterson, 1m51.854. Leaders: Stuck, laps 1-14; Hunt, 15-59.

LABATT'S 50 CANADIAN GRAND PRIX

9 October 1977. Mosport Park. 80 laps of a 2.459-mile circuit = 196.720 miles. Dry and overcast. World Championship round 16

1	Jody Scheckter	Wolf WR1-Ford	80	1h40m00.00
2	Patrick Depailler	Tyrrell P34-Ford	80	1h40m06.77
3	Jochen Mass	McLaren M26-Ford	80	1h40m15.76
4	Alan Jones	Shadow DN8A-Ford	80	1h40m46.69
5	Patrick Tambay	Ensign N177-Ford	80	1h41m03.26
6	Vittorio Brambilla	Surtees TS19-Ford	78	accident

Winner's average speed: 118.032 mph. Starting grid front row: Andretti, 1m11.385 (pole) and Hunt, 1m11.942. Fastest lap: Andretti, 1m13.299. Leaders: Andretti, laps 1-60, 62-78; Hunt, 61; J Scheckter, 79-80.

JAPANESE GRAND PRIX

23 October 1977. Fuji. 73 laps of a 2.709-mile circuit = 197.757 miles. Warm, dry and sunny. World Championship round 17

1	James Hunt	McLaren M26-Ford	73	1h31m51.68
2	Carlos Reutemann	Ferrari 312T2	73	1h32m54.13
3	Patrick Depailler	Tyrrell P34-Ford	73	1h32m58.07
4	Alan Jones	Shadow DN8A-Ford	73	1h32m58.29
5	Jacques Laffite	Ligier JS7-Matra	72	out of fuel
6	Riccardo Patrese	Shadow DN8A-Ford	72	

Winner's average speed: 129.167 mph. Starting grid front row: Andretti, 1m12.23 (pole) and Hunt, 1m12.39. Fastest lap: J Scheckter, 1m14.30. Leaders: Hunt, laps 1-73.

1978 The Lotus 79s of Mario Andretti and Ronnie Peterson dominated the Dutch Grand Prix and the 1978 season.

1978

Mario Andretti was finally rewarded for his patient development work at Lotus with a car in which he could dominate the World Championship. He and Ronnie Peterson scored a victory apiece in the old Lotus 78, before the 79 was introduced.

This second-generation "wing car" represented the significant advantage for which all teams strive. Andretti won another five races while Peterson added the wet Austrian GP. Peterson had been happy to re-sign with Lotus as their second driver after a disastrous year at Tyrrell. Andretti secured a deserved Championship victory, while Peterson had restored his reputation and

signed to lead the McLaren team in 1979.

However, the year of celebration for Lotus turned sour at the start of the Italian Grand Prix. Peterson's back-up Lotus 78 was involved in a multiple-car accident at the start. Although his injuries were originally not believed to be life threatening, Peterson died a day later after complications set in while doctors operated on his legs. The fastest driver of his generation, he would never be champion and paid the sport's ultimate price.

Andretti's previous teammate, Gunnar Nilsson, had left Lotus to join the new Arrows team. Sadly, his year developed into an unsuccessful fight against cancer and he never raced again. He died shortly after Peterson, in a devastating double blow for Swedish motor racing.

Arrows still made an impression, however, with Riccardo Patrese leading their second-ever race and finishing second in Sweden. But the team would only come close to victory once more before closing in 2002. The Italian was unjustly accused of causing the Monza accident and missed the US GP when other drivers refused to race with him. The London High Court also banned the original Arrows FA1 mid-season after ruling that it infringed the copyright of Shadow Cars, from whom key members of Arrows had defected.

Having switched to Michelin tyres, Ferrari was the closest challenger to Lotus. Carlos Reutemann finished third in the championship, while Villeneuve gained a popular home win in Canada when Jean-Pierre Jarier, Peterson's replacement at Lotus, retired from the lead.

Niki Lauda joined Brabham-Alfa Romeo and won two controversial races. In Sweden he drove the infamous "fan-car," which used a huge fan to generate downforce. Although the team claimed it was for cooling, the governing body believed it to be a movable aerodynamic device, and thus illegal. After Sweden the "fan-car" was banned, but the result stood. Lauda's second win came in the gloom at Monza, where he inherited victory after both Andretti and Villeneuve were penalised for jumping the start.

Tyrrell's Patrick Depailler had lost the South African GP to Peterson on the last lap, but he finally won his first Grand Prix at Monaco after John Watson retired. Emerson Fittipaldi finished second at home in Brazil, delivering the best result yet for the family team. Frank Williams and Patrick Head formed Williams Grand Prix Engineering, and Alan Jones' second at Watkins Glen showed the new team's improvement.

GRAN PREMIO DE LA REPUBLICA ARGENTINA

15 January 1978. Buenos Aires. 52 laps of a 3.709-mile circuit = 192.868 miles. Race scheduled for 53 laps but stopped early. Hot, dry and sunny. World Championship round 1

1	Mario Andretti	Lotus 78-Ford	52	1h37m04.47
2	Niki Lauda	Brabham BT45C-Alfa Romeo	52	1h37m17.68
3	Patrick Depailler	Tyrrell 008-Ford	52	1h37m18.11
4	James Hunt	McLaren M26-Ford	52	1h37m20.52
5	Ronnie Peterson	Lotus 78-Ford	52	1h38m19.32
6	Patrick Tambay	McLaren M26-Ford	52	1h38m24.37

Winner's average speed: 119.208 mph. Starting grid front row: Andretti, 1m47.75 (pole) and Reutemann,1m47.84. Fastest lap: Villeneuve, 1m49.76. Leaders: Andretti, laps 1-52.

1977-1978

GRANDE PREMIO DO BRASIL

29 January 1978. Rio de Janeiro. 63 laps of a 3.126-mile circuit = 196.938 miles. Very hot, dry and sunny. World Championship round 2

1 Carlos Reutemann	Ferrari 312T2	63	1h49m59.86
2 Emerson Fittipaldi	Fittipaldi F5A-Ford	63	1h50m48.99
3 Niki Lauda	Brabham BT45C-Alfa Romeo	63	1h50m56.88
4 Mario Andretti	Lotus 78-Ford	63	1h51m32.98
5 Clay Regazzoni	Shadow DN8A-Ford	62	
6 Didier Pironi	Tyrrell 008-Ford	62	

Winner's average speed: 107.423 mph. Starting grid front row: Peterson, 1m40.45 (pole) and Hunt, 1m40.53. Fastest lap: Reutemann, 1m43.07. Leaders: Reutemann, laps 1-63

CITIZEN SOUTH AFRICAN GRAND PRIX

4 March 1978. Kyalami. 78 laps of a 2.550-mile circuit = 198.900 miles. Hot, dry and sunny. World Championship round 3

1 Ronnie Peterson	Lotus 78-Ford	78	1h42m15.767
2 Patrick Depailler	Tyrrell 008-Ford	78	1h42m16.233
3 John Watson	Brabham BT46-Alfa Romeo	78	1h42m20.209
4 Alan Jones	Williams FW06-Ford	78	1h42m54.753
5 Jacques Laffite	Ligier JS7/9-Matra	78	1h43m24.985
6 Didier Pironi	Tyrrell 008-Ford	77	

Winner's average speed: 116.699 mph. Starting grid front row: Lauda, 1m14.65 (pole) and Andretti, 1m14.90. Fastest lap: Andretti, 1m17.09. Leaders: Andretti, laps 1-20; Scheckter, 21-26; Patrese, 27-63; Depailler, 64-77; Peterson, 78

UNITED STATES GRAND PRIX WEST

2 April 1978. Long Beach. 80.5 laps of a 2.020-mile circuit = 162.610 miles. Warm, dry and sunny. World Championship round 4

1 Carlos Reutemann	Ferrari 312T3	80	1h52m01.301
2 Mario Andretti	Lotus 78-Ford	80	1h52m12.362
3 Patrick Depailler	Tyrrell 008-Ford	80	1h52m30.252
4 Ronnie Peterson	Lotus 78-Ford	80	1h52m46.904
5 Jacques Laffite	Ligier JS7-Matra	80	1h53m24.185
6 Riccardo Patrese	Arrows FA1-Ford	79	

Winner's average speed: 87.096 mph. Starting grid front row: Reutemann, 1m20.636 (pole) and Villeneuve, 1m20.836. Fastest lap: Jones, 1m22.215. Leaders: Villeneuve, laps 1-38; Reutemann, 39-80

GRAND PRIX DE MONACO

7 May 1978. Monte Carlo. 75 laps of a 2.058-mile circuit = 154.350 miles. Warm, dry and sunny. World Championship round 5

1 Patrick Depailler	Tyrrell 008-Ford	75	1h55m14.66
2 Niki Lauda	Brabham BT46-Alfa Romeo	75	1h55m37.11
3 Jody Scheckter	Wolf WR1-Ford	75	1h55m46.95
4 John Watson	Brabham BT46-Alfa Romeo	75	1h55m48.19
5 Didier Pironi	Tyrrell 008-Ford	75	1h56m22.72
6 Riccardo Patrese	Arrows FA1-Ford	75	1h56m23.43

Winner's average speed: 80.360 mph. Starting grid front row: Reutemann, 1m28.34 (pole) and Watson, 1m28.83. Fastest lap: Lauda, 1m28.65. Leaders: Watson, laps 1-37; Depailler, 38-75

GRAND PRIX DE BELGIQUE

21 May 1978. Zolder. 70 laps of a 2.648-mile circuit = 185.360 miles. Dry and overcast. World Championship round 6

1 Mario Andretti	Lotus 79-Ford	70	1h39m52.02
2 Ronnie Peterson	Lotus 78-Ford	70	1h40m01.92
3 Carlos Reutemann	Ferrari 312T3	70	1h40m16.36
4 Gilles Villeneuve	Ferrari 312T3	70	1h40m39.06
5 Jacques Laffite	Ligier JS7/9-Matra	69	
6 Didier Pironi	Tyrrell 008-Ford	69	accident

Winner's average speed: 111.364 mph. Starting grid front row: Andretti, 1m20.90 (pole) and Reutemann, 1m21.69. Fastest lap: Peterson, 1m23.13. Leaders: Andretti, laps 1-70

GRAN PREMIO DE ESPANA

4 June 1978. Jarama. 75 laps of a 2.115-mile circuit = 158.655 miles. Warm, dry and sunny. World Championship round 7

1 Mario Andretti	Lotus 79-Ford	75	1h41m47.06
2 Ronnie Peterson	Lotus 79-Ford	75	1h42m06.62
3 Jacques Laffite	Ligier JS9-Matra	75	1h42m24.30
4 Jody Scheckter	Wolf WR5-Ford	75	1h42m47.12
5 John Watson	Brabham BT46-Alfa Romeo	75	1h42m52.98
6 James Hunt	McLaren M26-Ford	74	

Winner's average speed: 93.524 mph. Starting grid front row: Andretti, 1m16.39 (pole) and Peterson, 1m16.68. Fastest lap: Andretti, 1m20.06. Leaders: Hunt, laps 1-5; Andretti, 6-75

SVERIGES GRAND PRIX

17 June 1978. Anderstorp. 70 laps of a 2.505-mile circuit = 175.350 miles. Warm, dry and sunny. World Championship round 8

1 Niki Lauda	Brabham BT46B-Alfa Romeo	70	1h41m00.606
2 Riccardo Patrese	Arrows FA1-Ford	70	1h41m34.625
3 Ronnie Peterson	Lotus 79-Ford	70	1h41m34.711
4 Patrick Tambay	McLaren M26-Ford	69	
5 Clay Regazzoni	Shadow DN9A-Ford	69	
6 Emerson Fittipaldi	Fittipaldi F5A-Ford	69	

Winner's average speed: 104.158 mph. Starting grid front row: Andretti, 1m22.058 (pole) and Watson, 1m22.737. Fastest lap: Lauda, 1m24.836. Leaders: Andretti, laps 1-38; Lauda, 39-70

GRAND PRIX DE FRANCE

2 July 1978. Paul Ricard. 54 laps of a 3.610-mile circuit = 194.940 miles. Hot, dry and sunny. World Championship round 9

1 Mario Andretti	Lotus 79-Ford	54	1h38m51.92
2 Ronnie Peterson	Lotus 79-Ford	54	1h38m54.85
3 James Hunt	McLaren M26-Ford	54	1h39m11.72
4 John Watson	Brabham BT46-Alfa Romeo	54	1h39m28.80
5 Alan Jones	Williams FW06-Ford	54	1h39m33.73
6 Jody Scheckter	Wolf WR5-Ford	54	1h39m46.45

Winner's average speed: 118.306 mph. Starting grid front row: Watson, 1m44.41 (pole) and Andretti, 1m44.46. Fastest lap: Reutemann, 1m48.56. Leaders: Andretti, laps 1-54

JOHN PLAYER BRITISH GRAND PRIX

16 July 1978. Brands Hatch. 76 laps of a 2.614-mile circuit = 198.634 miles. Warm, dry and sunny. World Championship round 10

1 Carlos Reutemann	Ferrari 312T3	76	1h42m12.39
2 Niki Lauda	Brabham BT46-Alfa Romeo	76	1h42m13.62
3 John Watson	Brabham BT46-Alfa Romeo	76	1h42m49.64
4 Patrick Depailler	Tyrrell 008-Ford	76	1h43m25.66
5 Hans-Joachim Stuck	Shadow DN9A-Ford	75	
6 Patrick Tambay	McLaren M26-Ford	75	

Winner's average speed: 116.607 mph. Starting grid front row: Peterson, 1m16.80 (pole) and Andretti, 1m17.06. Fastest lap: Lauda, 1m18.60. Leaders: Andretti, laps 1-23; Scheckter, 24-33; Lauda, 34-59; Reutemann, 60-76

GROSSER PREIS VON DEUTSCHLAND

30 July 1978. Hockenheim. 45 laps of a 4.219-mile circuit = 189.855 miles. Very hot, dry and sunny. World Championship round 11

1 Mario Andretti	Lotus 79-Ford	45	1h28m00.90
2 Jody Scheckter	Wolf WR5-Ford	45	1h28m16.25
3 Jacques Laffite	Ligier JS9-Matra	45	1h28m28.91
4 Emerson Fittipaldi	Fittipaldi F5A-Ford	45	1h28m37.78
5 Didier Pironi	Tyrrell 008-Ford	45	1h28m58.16
6 Hector Rebaque	Lotus 78-Ford	45	1h29m38.76

Winner's average speed: 129.425 mph. Starting grid front row: Andretti, 1m51.90 (pole) and Peterson, 1m51.99. Fastest lap: Peterson, 1m55.62. Leaders: Peterson, laps 1-4; Andretti, 5-45

Formula 1

driver	car	RA Q	RA R	BR Q	BR R	ZA Q	ZA R	LB Q	LB R	MC Q	MC R	B Q	B R
Mario Andretti	Lotus 78-Ford	1	1	3	4	2	7F	4	2	4	11	-	-
	Lotus 79-Ford	-	-	-	-	-	-	-	-	-	-	1	1
Rene Arnoux	Martini MK23-Ford	-	-	-	-	27	DNQ	-	-	27	NPQ	19	9
	Surtees TS20-Ford	-	-	-	-	-	-	-	-	-	-	-	-
Hans Binder	ATS HS1-Ford	-	-	-	-	-	-	-	-	-	-	-	-
Michael Bleekemolen	ATS HS1-Ford	-	-	-	-	-	-	-	-	-	-	-	-
Vittorio Brambilla	Surtees TS19-Ford	12	18	27	DNQ	20	12	17	R	-	-	-	-
	Surtees TS20-Ford	-	-	-	-	-	-	-	-	24	DNQ	12	13
Eddie Cheever	Theodore TR1-Ford	26	DNQ	26	DNQ	-	-	-	-	-	-	-	-
	Hesketh 308E-Ford	-	-	-	-	25	R	-	-	-	-	-	-
Alberto Colombo	ATS HS1-Ford	-	-	-	-	-	-	-	-	-	-	28	DNQ
	Merzario A1-Ford	-	-	-	-	-	-	-	-	-	-	-	-
Derek Daly	Hesketh 308E-Ford	-	-	-	-	-	-	30	NPQ	26	NPQ	26	DNQ
	Ensign N177-Ford	-	-	-	-	-	-	-	-	-	-	-	-
Patrick Depailler	Tyrrell 008-Ford	10	3	11	R	12	2	12	3	5	1	13	R
Harald Ertl	Ensign N177-Ford	-	-	-	-	-	-	-	-	-	-	-	-
	ATS HS1-Ford	-	-	-	-	-	-	-	-	-	-	-	-
Emerson Fittipaldi	Fittipaldi F5A-Ford	17	9	7	2	15	R	15	8	20	9	15	R
Beppe Gabbiani	Surtees TS20-Ford	-	-	-	-	-	-	-	-	-	-	-	-
	Surtees TS19-Ford	-	-	-	-	-	-	-	-	-	-	-	-
Divina Galica	Hesketh 308E-Ford	27	DNQ	28	DNQ	-	-	-	-	-	-	-	-
Bruno Giacomelli	McLaren M26-Ford	-	-	-	-	-	-	-	-	-	-	21	8
"Gimax"	Surtees TS20-Ford	-	-	-	-	-	-	-	-	-	-	-	-
James Hunt	McLaren M26-Ford	6	4	2	R	3	R	7	R	6	R	6	R
Jacky Ickx	Ensign N177-Ford	-	-	-	-	-	-	-	-	16	R	22	12
Jean-Pierre Jabouille	Renault RS01	-	-	-	-	6	R	13	R	12	10	10	NC
Jean-Pierre Jarier	ATS HS1-Ford	11	12	16	DNS	17	8	19	11	23	DNQ	-	-
	Lotus 79-Ford	-	-	-	-	-	-	-	-	-	-	-	-
Alan Jones	Williams FW06-Ford	14	R	8	11	18	4	8	7F	10	R	11	10
Rupert Keegan	Surtees TS19-Ford	19	R	24	R	24	R	22	DNS	18	R	-	-
	Surtees TS20-Ford	-	-	-	-	-	-	-	-	-	-	25	DNQ
Jacques Laffite	Ligier JS7-Matra	8	16	14	9	-	-	14	5	-	-	-	-
	Ligier JS7/9-Matra	-	-	-	-	14	5	-	-	-	-	14	5
	Ligier JS9-Matra	-	-	-	-	-	-	-	-	15	R	-	-
Niki Lauda	Brabham BT45C-Alfa Romeo	5	2	10	3	-	-	-	-	-	-	-	-
	Brabham BT46-Alfa Romeo	-	-	-	-	1	R	3	R	3	2F	3	R
	Brabham BT46B-Alfa Romeo	-	-	-	-	-	-	-	-	-	-	-	-
Geoff Lees	Ensign N175-Ford	-	-	-	-	-	-	-	-	-	-	-	-
Lamberto Leoni	Ensign N177-Ford	22	R	17	DNS	29	DNQ	26	DNQ	-	-	-	-
Brett Lunger	McLaren M23-Ford	24	13	13	R	19	11	25	DNQ	-	-	-	-
	McLaren M26-Ford	-	-	-	-	-	-	-	-	29	NPQ	24	7
	Ensign N177-Ford	-	-	-	-	-	-	-	-	-	-	-	-
Jochen Mass	ATS HS1-Ford	13	11	20	7	16	R	16	R	21	DNQ	16	11
Arturo Merzario	Merzario A1-Ford	20	R	25	DNQ	26	R	21	R	30	NPQ	30	NPQ
Danny Ongais	Ensign N177-Ford	21	R	23	R	-	-	-	-	-	-	-	-
	Shadow DN9A-Ford	-	-	-	-	-	-	29	NPQ	-	-	-	-
Riccardo Patrese	Arrows FA1-Ford	-	-	18	10	7	R	9	6	14	6	8	R
	Arrows A1-Ford	-	-	-	-	-	-	-	-	-	-	-	-
Ronnie Peterson	Lotus 78-Ford	3	5	1	R	11	1	6	4	7	R	7	2F
	Lotus 79-Ford	-	-	-	-	-	-	-	-	-	-	-	-
Nelson Piquet	Ensign N177-Ford	-	-	-	-	-	-	-	-	-	-	-	-
	McLaren M23-Ford	-	-	-	-	-	-	-	-	-	-	-	-
	Brabham BT46-Alfa Romeo	-	-	-	-	-	-	-	-	-	-	-	-
Didier Pironi	Tyrrell 008-Ford	23	14	19	6	13	6	24	R	13	5	23	6
Bobby Rahal	Wolf WR5-Ford	-	-	-	-	-	-	-	-	-	-	-	-
	Wolf WR1-Ford	-	-	-	-	-	-	-	-	-	-	-	-
Hector Rebaque	Lotus 78-Ford	25	DNQ	22	R	22	10	28	NPQ	28	NPQ	29	NPQ
Clay Regazzoni	Shadow DN8A-Ford	16	15	15	5	28	DNQ	20	10	-	-	-	-
	Shadow DN9A-Ford	-	-	-	-	-	-	-	-	22	DNQ	18	R
Carlos Reutemann	Ferrari 312T2	2	7	4	1F	-	-	-	-	-	-	-	-
	Ferrari 312T3	-	-	-	-	9	R	1	1	1	8	2	3
Keke Rosberg	Theodore TR1-Ford	-	-	-	-	23	R	27	NPQ	25	NPQ	27	DNQ
	ATS HS1-Ford	-	-	-	-	-	-	-	-	-	-	-	-
	Wolf WR3-Ford	-	-	-	-	-	-	-	-	-	-	-	-
	Wolf WR4-Ford	-	-	-	-	-	-	-	-	-	-	-	-
	ATS D1-Ford	-	-	-	-	-	-	-	-	-	-	-	-

E		S		F		GB		D		A		NL		I		USA		CDN	
Q	R	Q	R	Q	R	Q	R	Q	R	Q	R	Q	R	Q	R	Q	R	Q	R
-	-	-	-	-	-	-	-	-	-	-	-	-	-	-	-	-	-	-	-
1	1F	1	R	2	1	2	R	1	1	2	R	1	1	1	6F	1	R	9	10
-	-	-	-	18	14	-	-	30	NPQ	26	9	23	R	-	-	21	9	16	R
-	-	-	-	-	-	-	-	-	-	30	DNQ	-	-	-	-	-	-	-	-
-	-	-	-	-	-	-	-	-	-	-	-	29	DNQ	27	DNQ	25	R	28	DNQ
16	7	18	R	19	17	25	9	20	R	21	6	22	DSQ	23	R	-	-	-	-
-	-	-	-	-	-	-	-	-	-	-	-	-	-	-	-	-	-	-	-
28	DNQ	-	-	-	-	-	-	-	-	-	-	-	-	-	-	-	-	-	-
-	-	-	-	-	-	-	-	-	-	-	-	-	-	31	NPQ	-	-	-	-
-	-	-	-	-	-	-	-	-	-	-	-	-	-	-	-	-	-	-	-
-	-	-	-	28	DNQ	15	R	-	-	19	DSQ	16	R	18	10	19	8	15	6
12	R	12	R	13	R	10	4	13	R	13	2	12	R	16	11	12	R	13	5
-	-	-	-	-	-	-	-	23	11	24	R	31	NPQ	-	-	-	-	-	-
-	-	-	-	-	-	-	-	-	-	-	-	-	-	26	DNQ	-	-	-	-
15	R	13	6	15	R	11	R	10	4	6	4	10	5	13	8	13	5	6	R
-	-	-	-	-	-	-	-	-	-	-	-	-	-	-	-	27	DNQ	-	-
-	-	-	-	-	-	-	-	-	-	-	-	-	-	-	-	-	-	24	DNQ
-	-	-	-	-	-	-	-	-	-	-	-	-	-	-	-	-	-	-	-
-	-	-	-	22	R	16	7	-	-	-	-	19	R	20	14	-	-	-	-
-	-	-	-	-	-	-	-	-	-	-	-	-	-	28	DNQ	-	-	-	-
4	6	14	8	4	3	14	R	8	DSQ	8	R	7	10	10	R	6	7	19	R
21	R	27	DNQ	-	-	-	-	-	-	-	-	-	-	-	-	-	-	-	-
11	13	10	R	11	R	12	R	9	R	3	R	9	R	3	R	9	4	22	12
-	-	-	-	-	-	-	-	26	DNQ	-	-	-	-	-	-	-	-	-	-
-	-	-	-	-	-	-	-	-	-	-	-	-	-	-	-	8	15F	1	R
18	8	9	R	14	5	6	R	6	R	15	R	11	R	6	13	3	2	5	9F
23	11	25	DNQ	23	R	29	DNQ	27	DNQ	29	DNQ	25	DNS	-	-	-	-	-	-
-	-	-	-	-	-	-	-	-	-	-	-	-	-	-	-	-	-	-	-
-	-	-	-	10	7	7	10	-	-	-	-	-	-	-	-	-	-	-	-
10	3	11	7	-	-	-	-	7	3	5	5	6	8	8	4	10	11	10	R
-	-	-	-	-	-	-	-	-	-	-	-	-	-	-	-	-	-	-	-
6	R	-	-	3	R	4	2F	3	R	12	R	3	3F	4	1	5	R	7	R
-	-	3	1F	-	-	-	-	-	-	-	-	-	-	-	-	-	-	-	-
-	-	-	-	-	-	28	DNQ	-	-	-	-	-	-	-	-	-	-	-	-
-	-	-	-	-	-	-	-	-	-	-	-	-	-	-	-	-	-	-	-
26	DNQ	26	DNQ	24	R	24	8	29	NPQ	17	8	21	R	21	R	-	-	-	-
-	-	-	-	-	-	-	-	-	-	-	-	-	-	-	-	24	13	-	-
17	9	19	13	25	13	26	NC	22	R	28	DNQ	30	DNQ	-	-	-	-	-	-
25	DNQ	22	NC	27	DNQ	23	R	28	DNQ	27	DNQ	27	R	22	R	26	R	25	DNQ
-	-	-	-	-	-	-	-	-	-	-	-	32	NPQ	-	-	-	-	-	-
8	R	5	2	12	8	5	R	14	9	-	-	-	-	-	-	-	-	-	-
-	-	-	-	-	-	-	-	-	-	16	R	13	R	12	R	-	-	12	4
2	2	4	3	5	2	1	R	2	RF	1	1F	2	2	5	R	-	-	-	-
-	-	-	-	-	-	-	-	21	R	-	-	-	-	-	-	-	-	-	-
-	-	-	-	-	-	-	-	-	-	20	R	26	R	24	9	-	-	-	-
-	-	-	-	-	-	-	-	-	-	-	-	-	-	-	-	-	-	14	11
13	12	17	R	16	10	19	R	16	5	9	R	17	R	14	R	16	10	18	7
-	-	-	-	-	-	-	-	-	-	-	-	-	-	-	-	20	12	-	-
-	-	-	-	-	-	-	-	-	-	-	-	-	-	-	-	-	-	20	R
20	R	21	12	29	DNQ	21	R	18	6	18	R	20	11	25	DNQ	23	R	26	DNQ
-	-	-	-	-	-	-	-	-	-	-	-	-	-	-	-	-	-	-	-
22	15	16	5	17	R	17	R	25	DNQ	22	NC	28	DNQ	15	NC	17	14	23	DNQ
3	R	8	10	8	18F	8	1	12	R	4	DSQ	4	7	11	3	2	1	11	3
29	NPQ	-	-	-	-	-	-	-	-	-	-	-	-	-	-	-	-	-	-
-	-	23	15	26	16	22	R	-	-	-	-	-	-	-	-	-	-	-	-
-	-	-	-	-	-	-	-	19	10	25	NC	-	-	-	-	-	-	-	-
-	-	-	-	-	-	-	-	-	-	-	-	24	R	29	NPQ	-	-	-	-
-	-	-	-	-	-	-	-	-	-	-	-	-	-	-	-	15	R	21	NC

Formula 1

1978 DRIVERS' RECORDS cont.

driver	car	RA Q	RA R	BR Q	BR R	ZA Q	ZA R	LB Q	LB R	MC Q	MC R	B Q	B R
Jody Scheckter	Wolf WR4-Ford	15	10	-	-	-	-	-	-	-	-	-	-
	Wolf WR1-Ford	-	-	12	R	5	R	-	-	9	3	-	-
	Wolf WR3-Ford	-	-	-	-	-	-	10	R	-	-	-	-
	Wolf WR5-Ford	-	-	-	-	-	-	-	-	-	-	5	R
	Wolf WR6-Ford	-	-	-	-	-	-	-	-	-	-	-	-
Rolf Stommelen	Arrows FA1-Ford	-	-	-	-	21	9	18	9	19	R	17	R
	Arrows A1-Ford	-	-	-	-	-	-	-	-	-	-	-	-
Hans-Joachim Stuck	Shadow DN8A-Ford	18	17	9	R	30	DNQ	-	-	-	-	-	-
	Shadow DN9A-Ford	-	-	-	-	-	-	23	DNS	17	R	20	R
Patrick Tambay	McLaren M26-Ford	9	6	5	R	4	R	11	12	11	7	-	-
Tony Trimmer	McLaren M23-Ford	-	-	-	-	-	-	-	-	-	-	-	-
Gilles Villeneuve	Ferrari 312T2	7	8F	6	R	-	-	-	-	-	-	-	-
	Ferrari 312T3	-	-	-	-	8	R	2	R	8	R	4	4
Emilio de Villota	McLaren M25-Ford	-	-	-	-	-	-	-	-	-	-	-	-
John Watson	Brabham BT45C-Alfa Romeo	4	R	21	8	-	-	-	-	-	-	-	-
	Brabham BT46-Alfa Romeo	-	-	-	-	10	3	5	R	2	4	9	R
	Brabham BT46B-Alfa Romeo	-	-	-	-	-	-	-	-	-	-	-	-

1978 FINAL CHAMPIONSHIP POSITIONS

Drivers

1	Mario Andretti	64
2	Ronnie Peterson	51
3	Carlos Reutemann	48
4	Niki Lauda	44
5	Patrick Depailler	34
6	John Watson	25
7	Jody Scheckter	24
8	Jacques Laffite	19
9=	Emerson Fittipaldi	17
	Gilles Villeneuve	17
11=	Alan Jones	11
	Riccardo Patrese	11
13=	James Hunt	8
	Patrick Tambay	8
15	Didier Pironi	7
16	Clay Regazzoni	4
17	Jean-Pierre Jabouille	3
18	Hans-Joachim Stuck	2
19=	Vittorio Brambilla	1
	Derek Daly	1
	Hector Rebaque	1

Sum of best seven results from the first eight races and best seven results from the final eight races

Manufacturers

1	Lotus-Ford	86
2	Ferrari	58
3	Brabham-Alfa Romeo	53
4	Tyrrell-Ford	38
5	Wolf-Ford	24
6	Ligier-Matra	19
7	Fittipaldi-Ford	17
8	McLaren-Ford	15
9=	Arrows-Ford	11
	Williams-Ford	11
11	Shadow-Ford	6
12	Renault	3
13=	Ensign-Ford	1
	Surtees-Ford	1

Sum of best seven results from the first eight races and best seven results from the final eight races. Points only awarded to first car to finish for each manufacturer

GROSSER PREIS VON OSTERREICH

13 August 1978. Osterreichring. 54 laps of a 3.692-mile circuit = 199.368 miles. Race stopped after 7 laps due to accidents in the heavy rain, restarted over remaining 47 laps. Very wet. World Championship round 12

1	Ronnie Peterson	Lotus 79-Ford	54	1h41m21.57
2	Patrick Depailler	Tyrrell 008-Ford	54	1h42m09.01
3	Gilles Villeneuve	Ferrari 312T3	54	1h43m01.33
4	Emerson Fittipaldi	Fittipaldi F5A-Ford	53	
5	Jacques Laffite	Ligier JS9-Matra	53	
6	Vittorio Brambilla	Surtees TS20-Ford	53	

Winner's average speed: 118.016 mph. Starting grid front row: Peterson, 1m37.71 (pole) and Andretti, 1m37.76. Fastest lap: Peterson, 1m43.12. Leaders: Peterson, laps 1-18, 29-54; Reutemann, 19-22; Villeneuve, 23-28

GROTE PRIJS VAN NEDERLAND

27 August 1978. Zandvoort. 75 laps of a 2.626-mile circuit = 196.950 miles. Dry but windy. World Championship round 13

1	Mario Andretti	Lotus 79-Ford	75	1h41m04.23
2	Ronnie Peterson	Lotus 79-Ford	75	1h41m04.55
3	Niki Lauda	Brabham BT46-Alfa Romeo	75	1h41m16.44
4	John Watson	Brabham BT46-Alfa Romeo	75	1h41m25.15
5	Emerson Fittipaldi	Fittipaldi F5A-Ford	75	1h41m25.73
6	Gilles Villeneuve	Ferrari 312T3	75	1h41m50.18

Winner's average speed: 116.918 mph. Starting grid front row: Andretti,

1m16.36 (pole) and Peterson, 1m16.97. Fastest lap: Lauda, 1m19.57. Leaders: Andretti, laps 1-75

GRAN PREMIO D'ITALIA

10 September 1978. Monza. 40 laps of a 3.604-mile circuit = 144.156 miles. Race scheduled for 52 laps, stopped after start-line accident and restarted over reduced distance. Warm, dry and sunny. World Championship round 14

1	Niki Lauda	Brabham BT46-Alfa Romeo	40	1h07m04.54
2	John Watson	Brabham BT46-Alfa Romeo	40	1h07m06.02
3	Carlos Reutemann	Ferrari 312T3	40	1h07m25.01
4	Jacques Laffite	Ligier JS9-Matra	40	1h07m42.07
5	Patrick Tambay	McLaren M26-Ford	40	1h07m44.93
6	Mario Andretti*	Lotus 79-Ford	40	1h07m50.87

*Andretti and Gilles Villeneuve (Ferrari 312T3), 1h07m53.02, finished first and second on the road but were penalised 1 minute for jumping the start. Winner's average speed: 128.949 mph. Starting grid front row: Andretti, 1m37.520 (pole) and Villeneuve, 1m37.866. Fastest lap: Andretti, 1m38.23. Leaders: Jabouille, laps 1-5; Lauda, 6-40 (Villeneuve led laps 1-34 and Andretti laps 35-40 on the road)

UNITED STATES GRAND PRIX

1 October 1978. Watkins Glen. 59 laps of a 3.377-mile circuit = 199.243 miles. Dry and overcast. World Championship round 15

1	Carlos Reutemann	Ferrari 312T3	59	1h40m48.800
2	Alan Jones	Williams FW06-Ford	59	1h41m08.539

E		S		F		GB		D		A		NL		I		USA		CDN	
Q	R	Q	R	Q	R	Q	R	Q	R	Q	R	Q	R	Q	R	Q	R	Q	R
-	-	-	-	-	-	-	-	-	-	-	-	-	-	-	-	-	-	-	-
-	-	-	-	-	-	-	-	-	-	-	-	-	-	-	-	-	-	-	-
9	4	6	R	7	6	3	R	4	2	7	R	-	-	-	-	-	-	-	-
-	-	-	-	-	-	-	-	-	-	-	-	15	12	9	12	11	3	2	2
19	14	24	14	21	15	27	DNQ	17	DSQ	-	-	-	-	-	-	-	-	-	-
-	-	-	-	-	-	-	-	-	-	NT	DNQ	33	NPQ	30	NPQ	22	16	27	DNQ
-	-	-	-	-	-	-	-	-	-	-	-	-	-	-	-	-	-	-	-
24	R	20	11	20	11	18	5	24	R	23	R	18	R	17	R	14	R	8	R
14	R	15	4	6	9	20	6	11	R	14	R	14	9	19	5	18	6	17	8
-	-	-	-	-	-	30	DNQ	-	-	-	-	-	-	-	-	-	-	-	-
-	-	-	-	-	-	-	-	-	-	-	-	-	-	-	-	-	-	-	-
5	10	7	9	9	12	13	R	15	8	11	3	5	6	2	7	4	R	3	1
27	DNQ	-	-	-	-	-	-	-	-	-	-	-	-	-	-	-	-	-	-
-	-	-	-	-	-	-	-	-	-	-	-	-	-	-	-	-	-	-	-
-	-	-	-	-	-	-	-	-	-	-	-	-	-	-	-	-	-	-	-
7	5	-	-	1	4	9	3	5	7	10	7	8	4	7	2	7	R	4	R
-	-	2	R	-	-	-	-	-	-	-	-	-	-	-	-	-	-	-	-

3 Jody Scheckter   Wolf WR6-Ford   59   1h41m34.501
4 Jean-Pierre Jabouille   Renault RS01   59   1h42m13.807
5 Emerson Fittipaldi   Fittipaldi F5A-Ford   59   1h42m16.889
6 Patrick Tambay   McLaren M26-Ford   59   1h42m30.010
Winner's average speed: 118.581 mph. Starting grid front row: Andretti, 1m38.114 (pole) and Reutemann, 1m39.179. Fastest lap: Jarier, 1m39.557.
Leaders: Andretti, laps 1-2; Reutemann, 3-59.

GRAND PRIX DU CANADA

8 October 1978. Montreal. 70 laps of a 2.796-mile circuit = 195.720 miles. Cool and dry. World Championship round 16

1 Gilles Villeneuve   Ferrari 312T3   70   1h57m49.196
2 Jody Scheckter   Wolf WR6-Ford   70   1h58m02.568
3 Carlos Reutemann   Ferrari 312T3   70   1h58m08.604
4 Riccardo Patrese   Arrows A1-Ford   70   1h58m13.863
5 Patrick Depailler   Tyrrell 008-Ford   70   1h58m17.754
6 Derek Daly   Ensign N177-Ford   70   1h58m43.672
Winner's average speed: 99.671 mph. Starting grid front row: Jarier, 1m38.015 (pole) and Scheckter, 1m38.026. Fastest lap: Jones, 1m38.072.
Leaders: Jarier, laps 1-49; Villeneuve, 50-70.

1979

Unsurprisingly, the pit lane at the first Grand Prix of the 1979 season was full of Lotus 79 copies. Early in the year, Ligier's JS11 was the best adaptation of ground effect principles. Jacques Laffite dominated the first two races, and Patrick Depailler, whose season was to be cruelly cut short by a hang-gliding accident, added a further victory for the team. As the season progressed, however, Ligier proved unable to sustain its challenge.

Lotus, meanwhile, found that the edge it enjoyed the previous year had vanished. Although Carlos Reutemann and Mario Andretti used the Lotus 79 to finish in the points early on, it was no longer the quickest car. Its replacement, the theoretically more advanced Lotus 80, finished third in Spain, but this proved to be false promise. The car was dropped, and the team would not win again until 1982.

Jody Scheckter moved to Ferrari after a fallow year at Wolf and formed a successful partnership with Gilles Villeneuve. The French-Canadian was quicker over a single lap, but Scheckter was more consistent. Early Villeneuve wins gave way to Scheckter victories during the year. Fittingly, Scheckter clinched the title by winning at Monza, and Villeneuve added to the Italian crowd's delirium by finishing second.

The dominant car in the second half of the season was the new Williams FW07, in which Clay Regazzoni scored the team's first victory at the British GP. Alan Jones won four more races after mid-season, but this pace was too late to mount a championship challenge.

Jean-Pierre Jabouille scored the first win for Renault and for a turbocharged engine at the French GP. But the race is best remembered for an exuberant, wheel-to-wheel battle for second position in the closing laps. Rene Arnoux and Villeneuve repeatedly passed and re-passed each other, their cars often touching and often off the road, until Villeneuve eventually won the position.

Brabham had a frustrating final year with 12-cylinder Alfa Romeo engines. At the Canadian GP the team reverted to Ford power with the new BT49. Team leader Niki Lauda controversially retired from the sport at that race (although he would return in 1982), but young Brazilian Nelson Piquet was immediately on the pace in the BT49, qualifying on the front row for the year's final race at Watkins Glen. Alfa Romeo sporadically entered a works team for the first time since 1951.

GRAN PREMIO DE LA REPUBLICA ARGENTINA

21 January 1979. Buenos Aires. 53 laps of a 3.709-mile circuit = 196.577 miles. Race stopped after first-lap accident, restarted over the original distance. Very hot, dry and sunny. World Championship round 1

1 Jacques Laffite   Ligier JS11-Ford   53   1h36m03.21
2 Carlos Reutemann   Lotus 79-Ford   53   1h36m18.15
3 John Watson   McLaren M28-Ford   53   1h37m32.02
4 Patrick Depailler   Ligier JS11-Ford   53   1h37m44.93
5 Mario Andretti   Lotus 79-Ford   52
6 Emerson Fittipaldi   Fittipaldi F5A-Ford   52
Winner's average speed: 122.792 mph. Starting grid front row: Laffite, 1m44.20 (pole) and Depailler, 1m45.24. Fastest lap: Laffite, 1m46.91.
Leaders: Depailler, laps 1-10; Laffite, 11-53.

Formula 1

1979 DRIVERS' RECORDS

driver	car	RA Q	RA R	BR Q	BR R	ZA Q	ZA R	LB Q	LB R	E Q	E R	B Q	B R	MC Q	MC R
Mario Andretti	Lotus 79-Ford	7	5	4	R	8	4	6	4	-	-	5	R	-	-
	Lotus 80-Ford	-	-	-	-	-	-	-	-	4	3	-	-	13	R
Elio de Angelis	Shadow DN9B-Ford	16	7	20	12	15	R	21	7	22	R	24	R	21	DNQ
Rene Arnoux	Renault RS01	25	R	11	R	10	R	22	DNS	11	9	18	R	-	-
	Renault RE10	-	-	-	-	-	-	-	-	-	-	-	-	19	R
Vittorio Brambilla	Alfa Romeo 177	-	-	-	-	-	-	-	-	-	-	-	-	-	-
	Alfa Romeo 179	-	-	-	-	-	-	-	-	-	-	-	-	-	-
Gianfranco Brancatelli	Kauhsen WK004-Ford	-	-	-	-	-	-	-	-	27	DNQ	-	-	-	-
	Kauhsen WK005-Ford	-	-	-	-	-	-	-	-	-	-	28	DNQ	-	-
	Merzario A2-Ford	-	-	-	-	-	-	-	-	-	-	-	-	25	NPQ
Derek Daly	Ensign N177-Ford	24	11	23	13	-	-	-	-	25	DNQ	27	DNQ	-	-
	Ensign N179-Ford	-	-	-	-	25	DNQ	26	R	-	-	-	-	24	DNQ
	Tyrrell 009-Ford	-	-	-	-	-	-	-	-	-	-	-	-	-	-
Patrick Depailler	Ligier JS11-Ford	2	4	2	2	5	R	4	5	2	1	2	R	3	5F
Emerson Fittipaldi	Fittipaldi F5A-Ford	11	6	9	11	-	-	16	R	19	11	23	9	17	R
	Fittipaldi F6-Ford	-	-	-	-	18	13	-	-	-	-	-	-	-	-
	Fittipaldi F6A-Ford	-	-	-	-	-	-	-	-	-	-	-	-	-	-
Patrick Gaillard	Ensign N179-Ford	-	-	-	-	-	-	-	-	-	-	-	-	-	-
Bruno Giacomelli	Alfa Romeo 177	-	-	-	-	-	-	-	-	-	-	14	R	-	-
	Alfa Romeo 179	-	-	-	-	-	-	-	-	-	-	-	-	-	-
James Hunt	Wolf WR7-Ford	18	R	10	R	13	8	-	-	15	R	-	-	10	R
	Wolf WR8-Ford	-	-	-	-	-	-	8	R	-	-	9	R	-	-
Jacky Ickx	Ligier JS11-Ford	-	-	-	-	-	-	-	-	-	-	-	-	-	-
Jean-Pierre Jabouille	Renault RS01	12	R	7	10	1	R	20	DNS	-	-	-	-	-	-
	Renault RE10	-	-	-	-	-	-	-	-	9	R	17	R	20	NC
Jean-Pierre Jarier	Tyrrell 009-Ford	4	R	15	DNS	9	3	7	6	12	5	11	11	6	R
Alan Jones	Williams FW06-Ford	15	9	13	R	19	R	10	3	-	-	-	-	-	-
	Williams FW07-Ford	-	-	-	-	-	-	-	-	13	R	4	R	9	R
Jacques Laffite	Ligier JS11-Ford	1	1F	1	1F	6	R	5	R	1	R	1	2	5	R
Jan Lammers	Shadow DN9B-Ford	21	R	21	14	21	R	14	R	24	12	21	10	23	DNQ
Niki Lauda	Brabham BT48-Alfa Romeo	23	R	12	R	4	6	11	R	6	R	13	R	4	R
	Brabham BT49-Ford	-	-	-	-	-	-	-	-	-	-	-	-	-	-
Geoff Lees	Tyrrell 009-Ford	-	-	-	-	-	-	-	-	-	-	-	-	-	-
Jochen Mass	Arrows A1-Ford	14	8	19	7	20	12	13	9	17	8	22	R	8	6
	Arrows A2-Ford	-	-	-	-	-	-	-	-	-	-	-	-	-	-
Arturo Merzario	Merzario A1B-Ford	22	R	26	DNQ	26	DNQ	24	R	-	-	-	-	-	-
	Merzario A2-Ford	-	-	-	-	-	-	-	-	26	DNQ	26	DNQ	-	-
Riccardo Patrese	Arrows A1-Ford	13	DNS	16	9	16	11	9	R	16	10	16	5	15	R
	Arrows A2-Ford	-	-	-	-	-	-	-	-	-	-	-	-	-	-
Nelson Piquet	Brabham BT46-Alfa Romeo	20	R	-	-	-	-	-	-	-	-	-	-	-	-
	Brabham BT48-Alfa Romeo	-	-	22	R	12	7	12	8	7	R	3	R	18	R
	Brabham BT49-Ford	-	-	-	-	-	-	-	-	-	-	-	-	-	-
Didier Pironi	Tyrrell 009-Ford	8	R	8	4	7	R	17	DSQ	10	6	12	3	7	R
Hector Rebaque	Lotus 79-Ford	19	R	25	DNQ	23	R	25	R	23	R	15	R	-	-
	Rebaque HR100-Ford	-	-	-	-	-	-	-	-	-	-	-	-	-	-
Clay Regazzoni	Williams FW06-Ford	17	10	17	15	22	9	15	R	-	-	-	-	-	-
	Williams FW07-Ford	-	-	-	-	-	-	-	-	14	R	8	R	16	2
Carlos Reutemann	Lotus 79-Ford	3	2	3	3	11	5	2	R	8	2	10	4	11	3
Alex Ribeiro	Fittipaldi F6A-Ford	-	-	-	-	-	-	-	-	-	-	-	-	-	-
Keke Rosberg	Wolf WR8-Ford	-	-	-	-	-	-	-	-	-	-	-	-	-	-
.	Wolf WR7-Ford	-	-	-	-	-	-	-	-	-	-	-	-	-	-
	Wolf WR9-Ford	-	-	-	-	-	-	-	-	-	-	-	-	-	-
	Wolf WR8/9-Ford	-	-	-	-	-	-	-	-	-	-	-	-	-	-
Jody Scheckter	Ferrari 312T3	5	R	6	6	-	-	-	-	-	-	-	-	-	-
	Ferrari 312T4	-	-	-	-	2	2	3	2	5	4	7	1	1	1
Hans-Joachim Stuck	ATS D2-Ford	26	DNQ	24	R	24	R	23	DSQ	21	14	20	8	12	R
	ATS D3-Ford	-	-	-	-	-	-	-	-	-	-	-	-	-	-
Marc Surer	Ensign N179-Ford	-	-	-	-	-	-	-	-	-	-	-	-	-	-
Patrick Tambay	McLaren M28-Ford	9	R	-	-	17	10	19	R	20	13	-	-	-	-
	McLaren M26-Ford	-	-	18	R	-	-	-	-	-	-	25	DNQ	-	-
	McLaren M28B-Ford	-	-	-	-	-	-	-	-	-	-	-	-	22	DNQ
	McLaren M28C-Ford	-	-	-	-	-	-	-	-	-	-	-	-	-	-
	McLaren M29-Ford	-	-	-	-	-	-	-	-	-	-	-	-	-	-

F		GB		D		A		NL		I		CDN		USA	
Q	R	Q	R	Q	R	Q	R	Q	R	Q	R	Q	R	Q	R
-	-	9	R	11	R	15	R	17	R	10	5	10	10	17	R
12	R	-	-	-	-	-	-	-	-	-	-	-	-	-	-
25	16	12	12	21	11	22	R	22	R	24	R	23	R	20	4
2	3F	5	2	10	R	1	6F	1	R	2	R	8	R	7	2
-	-	-	-	-	-	-	-	-	-	22	12	-	-	-	-
-	-	-	-	-	-	-	-	-	-	-	-	18	R	25	DNQ
-	-	-	-	-	-	-	-	-	-	-	-	-	-	-	-
-	-	-	-	-	-	-	-	-	-	-	-	-	-	-	-
-	-	-	-	-	-	-	-	-	-	-	-	-	-	-	-
-	-	-	-	-	-	11	8	-	-	-	-	24	R	15	R
18	R	21	R	-	-	-	-	-	-	-	-	-	-	-	-
-	-	-	-	-	-	-	-	-	-	-	-	-	-	-	-
-	-	-	-	22	R	19	R	21	R	20	8	15	8	23	7
26	DNQ	23	13	25	DNQ	24	R	25	DNQ	-	-	-	-	-	-
17	17	-	-	-	-	-	-	-	-	-	-	-	-	-	-
-	-	-	-	-	-	-	-	-	-	18	R	NT	DNP	18	R
-	-	-	-	-	-	-	-	-	-	-	-	-	-	-	-
-	-	-	-	-	-	-	-	-	-	-	-	-	-	-	-
14	R	17	6	14	R	21	R	20	5	11	R	16	R	24	R
-	-	-	-	-	-	-	-	-	-	-	-	-	-	-	-
1	1	2	R	1	R	3	R	4	R	1	14	7	R	8	R
10	5	16	3	-	-	-	-	16	R	16	6	13	R	11	R
-	-	-	-	-	-	-	-	-	-	-	-	-	-	-	-
7	4	1	R	2	1	2	1	2	1	4	9	1	1F	1	R
8	8	10	R	3	3	8	3	7	3	7	R	5	R	4	R
21	18	22	11	20	10	23	R	23	R	25	DNQ	21	9	27	DNQ
6	R	6	R	7	R	4	R	9	R	9	4	-	-	-	-
-	-	-	-	-	-	-	-	-	-	-	-	NT	DNP	-	-
-	-	-	-	16	7	-	-	-	-	-	-	-	-	-	-
-	-	-	-	-	-	-	-	-	-	-	-	-	-	-	-
22	15	20	R	18	6	20	R	18	6	21	R	25	DNQ	26	DNQ
-	-	-	-	-	-	-	-	-	-	-	-	-	-	-	-
27	DNQ	26	DNQ	26	DNQ	26	DNQ	26	DNQ	27	DNQ	29	DNQ	30	DNQ
-	-	-	-	-	-	-	-	-	-	-	-	14	R	-	-
19	14	19	R	19	R	13	R	19	R	17	13	-	-	19	R
-	-	-	-	-	-	-	-	-	-	-	-	-	-	-	-
-	-	-	-	-	-	-	-	-	-	-	-	-	-	-	-
4	R	3	R	4	12	7	R	11	4	8	R	-	-	-	-
-	-	-	-	-	-	-	-	-	-	-	-	4	R	2	RF
11	R	15	10	8	9	10	7	10	R	12	10	6	5	10	3
24	12	24	9	24	R	25	DNQ	24	7	-	-	-	-	-	-
-	-	-	-	-	-	-	-	-	-	28	DNQ	22	R	28	DNQ
-	-	-	-	-	-	-	-	-	-	-	-	-	-	-	-
9	6	4	1F	6	2	6	5	3	R	6	3F	3	3	5	R
13	13	8	8	13	R	17	R	13	R	13	7	11	R	6	R
-	-	-	-	-	-	-	-	-	-	-	-	28	DNQ	29	DNQ
16	9	-	-	17	R	-	-	-	-	23	R	-	-	-	-
-	-	14	R	-	-	-	-	-	-	-	-	-	-	-	-
-	-	-	-	-	-	12	R	8	R	-	-	27	DNQ	-	-
-	-	-	-	-	-	-	-	-	-	-	-	-	-	12	R
-	-	-	-	-	-	-	-	-	-	-	-	-	-	-	-
5	7	11	5	5	4	9	4	5	2	3	1	9	4	16	R
23	DNS	25	DNQ	23	R	-	-	-	-	-	-	-	-	-	-
-	-	-	-	-	-	18	R	15	R	15	11	12	R	14	5
-	-	-	-	-	-	-	-	-	-	26	DNQ	26	DNQ	21	R
-	-	-	-	-	-	-	-	-	-	-	-	-	-	-	-
-	-	-	-	-	-	-	-	-	-	-	-	-	-	-	-
20	10	18	7	-	-	-	-	-	-	-	-	-	-	-	-
-	-	-	-	15	R	14	10	14	R	14	R	20	R	22	R

Formula 1

1979 DRIVERS' RECORDS cont.

driver	car	RA Q	RA R	BR Q	BR R	ZA Q	ZA R	LB Q	LB R	E Q	E R	B Q	B R	MC Q	MC R
Gilles Villeneuve	Ferrari 312T3	10	R	5	5	-	-	-	-	-	-	-	-	-	-
	Ferrari 312T4	-	-	-	-	3	1F	1	1F	3	7F	6	7F	2	R
John Watson	McLaren M28-Ford	6	3	14	8	14	R	18	R	-	-	-	-	-	-
	McLaren M28B-Ford	-	-	-	-	-	-	-	-	18	R	19	6	-	-
	McLaren M28C-Ford	-	-	-	-	-	-	-	-	-	-	-	-	14	4
	McLaren M29-Ford	-	-	-	-	-	-	-	-	-	-	-	-	-	-
Ricardo Zunino	Brabham BT49-Ford	-	-	-	-	-	-	-	-	-	-	-	-	-	-

1979 FINAL CHAMPIONSHIP POSITIONS

Drivers

1	Jody Scheckter	51 (60)*
2	Gilles Villeneuve	47 (53)*
3	Alan Jones	40 (43)*
4	Jacques Laffite	36
5	Clay Regazzoni	29 (32)*
6=	Patrick Depailler	20 (22)*
	Carlos Reutemann	20 (25)*
8	Rene Arnoux	17
9	John Watson	15
10=	Mario Andretti	14
	Jean-Pierre Jarier	14
	Didier Pironi	14
13	Jean-Pierre Jabouille	9
14	Niki Lauda	4
15=	Elio de Angelis	3
	Jacky Ickx	3
	Jochen Mass	3
	Nelson Piquet	3
19=	Riccardo Patrese	2
	Hans-Joachim Stuck	2
21	Emerson Fittipaldi	1

*Sum of best four results from the first seven races and best four results from the final eight races

Manufacturers

1	Ferrari	113
2	Williams-Ford	75
3	Ligier-Ford	61
4	Lotus-Ford	39
5	Tyrrell-Ford	28
6	Renault	26
7	McLaren-Ford	15
8	Brabham-Alfa Romeo	7
9	Arrows-Ford	5
10	Shadow-Ford	3
11	ATS-Ford	2
12	Fittipaldi-Ford	1

Results for all cars entered by FOCA recognised constructors count

GRANDE PREMIO DO BRASIL

4 February 1979. Interlagos. 40 laps of a 4.946-mile circuit = 197.840 miles. Very hot, dry and sunny. World Championship round 2

1	Jacques Laffite	Ligier JS11-Ford	40	1h40m09.64
2	Patrick Depailler	Ligier JS11-Ford	40	1h40m14.92
3	Carlos Reutemann	Lotus 79-Ford	40	1h40m53.78
4	Didier Pironi	Tyrrell 009-Ford	40	1h41m35.52
5	Gilles Villeneuve	Ferrari 312T3	39	
6	Jody Scheckter	Ferrari 312T3	39	

Winner's average speed: 118.514 mph. Starting grid front row: Laffite, 2m23.07 (pole) and Depailler, 2m23.99. Fastest lap: Laffite, 2m28.76. Leaders: Laffite, laps 1-40.

SIMBA SOUTH AFRICAN GRAND PRIX

3 March 1979. Kyalami. 78 laps of a 2.550-mile circuit = 198.900 miles. Race stopped after 2 laps due to heavy rain, restarted over additional 76 laps. Occasional heavy rain. World Championship round 3

1	Gilles Villeneuve	Ferrari 312T4	78	1h41m49.96
2	Jody Scheckter	Ferrari 312T4	78	1h41m53.38
3	Jean-Pierre Jarier	Tyrrell 009-Ford	78	1h42m12.07
4	Mario Andretti	Lotus 79-Ford	78	1h42m17.84
5	Carlos Reutemann	Lotus 79-Ford	78	1h42m56.93
6	Niki Lauda	Brabham BT48-Alfa Romeo	77	

Winner's average speed: 117.192 mph. Starting grid front row: Jabouille, 1m11.80 (pole) and Scheckter, 1m12.04. Fastest lap: Villeneuve, 1m14.412. Leaders: Jabouille, lap 1; Villeneuve, laps 2-14, 53-78; Scheckter, 15-52.

LUBRI LON UNITED STATES GRAND PRIX WEST

8 April 1979. Long Beach. 80.5 laps of a 2.020-mile circuit = 162.610 miles. Warm, dry and sunny. World Championship round 4

1	Gilles Villeneuve	Ferrari 312T4	80	1h50m25.40
2	Jody Scheckter	Ferrari 312T4	80	1h50m54.78
3	Alan Jones	Williams FW06-Ford	80	1h51m25.09
4	Mario Andretti	Lotus 79-Ford	80	1h51m29.73
5	Patrick Depailler	Ligier JS11-Ford	80	1h51m48.92
6	Jean-Pierre Jarier	Tyrrell 009-Ford	79	

Winner's average speed: 88.356 mph. Starting grid front row: Villeneuve, 1m18.825 (pole) and Reutemann, 1m18.886 - Reutemann started from pit lane. Fastest lap: Villeneuve, 1m21.200. Leaders: Villeneuve, laps 1-80.

GRAN PREMIO DE ESPANA

29 April 1979. Jarama. 75 laps of a 2.115-mile circuit = 158.655 miles. Cool and dry. World Championship round 5

1	Patrick Depailler	Ligier JS11-Ford	75	1h39m11.84
2	Carlos Reutemann	Lotus 79-Ford	75	1h39m32.78
3	Mario Andretti	Lotus 80-Ford	75	1h39m39.15
4	Jody Scheckter	Ferrari 312T4	75	1h39m40.52
5	Jean-Pierre Jarier	Tyrrell 009-Ford	75	1h39m42.23
6	Didier Pironi	Tyrrell 009-Ford	75	1h40m00.27

Winner's average speed: 95.963 mph. Starting grid front row: Laffite, 1m14.50 (pole) and Depailler, 1m14.79. Fastest lap: Villeneuve, 1m16.44. Leaders: Depailler, laps 1-75.

GRAND PRIX DE BELGIQUE

13 May 1979. Zolder. 70 laps of a 2.648-mile circuit = 185.360 miles. Hot, dry and sunny. World Championship round 6

1	Jody Scheckter	Ferrari 312T4	70	1h39m59.53
2	Jacques Laffite	Ligier JS11-Ford	70	1h40m14.89
3	Didier Pironi	Tyrrell 009-Ford	70	1h40m34.70
4	Carlos Reutemann	Lotus 79-Ford	70	1h40m46.02
5	Riccardo Patrese	Arrows A1-Ford	70	1h41m03.84
6	John Watson	McLaren M28B-Ford	70	1h41m05.38

Winner's average speed: 111.225 mph. Starting grid front row: Laffite, 1m21.13 (pole) and Depailler, 1m21.20. Fastest lap: Villeneuve, 1m23.09. Leaders: Depailler, laps 1-18, 40-46; Laffite, 19-23, 47-53; Jones, 24-39; Scheckter, 54-70.

GRAND PRIX DE MONACO

27 May 1979. Monte Carlo. 76 laps of a 2.058-mile circuit = 156.408 miles. Warm, dry and sunny. World Championship round 7

F		GB		D		A		NL		I		CDN		USA	
Q	R	Q	R	Q	R	Q	R	Q	R	Q	R	Q	R	Q	R
-	-	-	-	-	-	-	-	-	-	-	-	-	-	-	-
3	2	13	14	9	8F	5	2	6	RF	5	2	2	2	3	1
-	-	-	-	-	-	-	-	-	-	-	-	-	-	-	-
-	-	-	-	-	-	-	-	-	-	-	-	-	-	-	-
15	11	-	-	-	-	-	-	-	-	-	-	-	-	-	-
-	-	7	4	12	5	16	9	12	R	19	R	17	6	13	6
-	-	-	-	-	-	-	-	-	-	-	-	19	7	9	R

1	Jody Scheckter	Ferrari 312T4	76	1h55m22.48
2	Clay Regazzoni	Williams FW07-Ford	76	1h55m22.92
3	Carlos Reutemann	Lotus 79-Ford	76	1h55m31.05
4	John Watson	McLaren M28C-Ford	76	1h56m03.79
5	Patrick Depailler	Ligier JS11-Ford	74	engine
6	Jochen Mass	Arrows A1-Ford	69	

Winner's average speed: 81.339 mph. Starting grid front row: Scheckter, 1m26.45 (pole) and Villeneuve 1m26.52. Fastest lap: Depailler, 1m28.82. Leaders: Scheckter, laps 1-76

GRAND PRIX DE FRANCE

1 July 1979. Dijon-Prenois. 80 laps of a 2.361-mile circuit = 188.880 miles. Dry and overcast. World Championship round 8

1	Jean-Pierre Jabouille	Renault RE10	80	1h35m20.42
2	Gilles Villeneuve	Ferrari 312T4	80	1h35m35.01
3	Rene Arnoux	Renault RE10	80	1h35m35.25
4	Alan Jones	Williams FW07-Ford	80	1h35m57.03
5	Jean-Pierre Jarier	Tyrrell 009-Ford	80	1h36m24.93
6	Clay Regazzoni	Williams FW07-Ford	80	1h36m25.93

Winner's average speed: 118.867 mph. Starting grid front row: Jabouille, 1m07.19 (pole) and Arnoux, 1m07.45. Fastest lap: Arnoux, 1m09.16. Leaders: Villeneuve, laps 1-46; Jabouille, 47-80

MARLBORO BRITISH GRAND PRIX

14 July 1979. Silverstone. 68 laps of a 2.932-mile circuit = 199.376 miles. Warm, dry and sunny. World Championship round 9

1	Clay Regazzoni	Williams FW07-Ford	68	1h26m11.17
2	Rene Arnoux	Renault RE10	68	1h26m35.45
3	Jean-Pierre Jarier	Tyrrell 009-Ford	67	
4	John Watson	McLaren M29-Ford	67	
5	Jody Scheckter	Ferrari 312T4	67	
6	Jacky Ickx	Ligier JS11-Ford	67	

Winner's average speed: 138.799 mph. Starting grid front row: Jones, 1m11.88 (pole) and Jabouille, 1m12.48. Fastest lap: Regazzoni, 1m14.40. Leaders: Jones, laps 1-38; Regazzoni, 39-68

GROSSER PREIS VON DEUTSCHLAND

29 July 1979. Hockenheim. 45 laps of a 4.219-mile circuit = 189.855 miles. Very hot, dry and sunny. World Championship round 10

1	Alan Jones	Williams FW07-Ford	45	1h24m48.83
2	Clay Regazzoni	Williams FW07-Ford	45	1h24m51.74
3	Jacques Laffite	Ligier JS11-Ford	45	1h25m07.22
4	Jody Scheckter	Ferrari 312T4	45	1h25m20.03
5	John Watson	McLaren M29-Ford	45	1h26m26.63
6	Jochen Mass	Arrows A2-Ford	44	

Winner's average speed: 134.309 mph. Starting grid front row: Jabouille, 1m48.48 (pole) and Jones, 1m48.75. Fastest lap: Villeneuve, 1m51.89. Leaders: Jones, laps 1-45

GROSSER PREIS VON OSTERREICH

12 August 1979. Osterreichring. 54 laps of a 3.692-mile circuit = 199.368 miles. Warm, dry and sunny. World Championship round 11

1	Alan Jones	Williams FW07-Ford	54	1h27m38.01
2	Gilles Villeneuve	Ferrari 312T4	54	1h28m14.06

3	Jacques Laffite	Ligier JS11-Ford	54	1h28m24.78
4	Jody Scheckter	Ferrari 312T4	54	1h28m25.22
5	Clay Regazzoni	Williams FW07-Ford	54	1h28m26.93
6	Rene Arnoux	Renault RE10	53	

Winner's average speed: 136.501 mph. Starting grid front row: Arnoux, 1m34.07 (pole) and Jones, 1m34.28. Fastest lap: Arnoux, 1m35.77. Leaders: Villeneuve, laps 1-3; Jones, 4-54

GROTE PRIJS VAN NEDERLAND

26 August 1979. Zandvoort. 75 laps of a 2.626-mile circuit = 196.950 miles. Dry and overcast. World Championship round 12

1	Alan Jones	Williams FW07-Ford	75	1h41m19.775
2	Jody Scheckter	Ferrari 312T4	75	1h41m41.558
3	Jacques Laffite	Ligier JS11-Ford	75	1h42m23.028
4	Nelson Piquet	Brabham BT48-Alfa Romeo	74	
5	Jacky Ickx	Ligier JS11-Ford	74	
6	Jochen Mass	Arrows A2-Ford	73	

Winner's average speed: 116.619 mph. Starting grid front row: Arnoux, 1m15.461 (pole) and Jones, 1m15.646. Fastest lap: Villeneuve, 1m19.438. Leaders: Jones, laps 1-10, 47-75; Villeneuve, 11-46

GRAN PREMIO D'ITALIA

9 September 1979. Monza. 50 laps of a 3.604-mile circuit = 180.195 miles. Warm, dry and sunny. World Championship round 13

1	Jody Scheckter	Ferrari 312T4	50	1h22m00.22
2	Gilles Villeneuve	Ferrari 312T4	50	1h22m00.68
3	Clay Regazzoni	Williams FW07-Ford	50	1h22m05.00
4	Niki Lauda	Brabham BT48-Alfa Romeo	50	1h22m54.62
5	Mario Andretti	Lotus 79-Ford	50	1h22m59.92
6	Jean-Pierre Jarier	Tyrrell 009-Ford	50	1h23m01.77

Winner's average speed: 131.844 mph. Starting grid front row: Jabouille, 1m34.580 (pole) and Arnoux, 1m34.704. Fastest lap: Regazzoni, 1m35.60. Leaders: Scheckter, laps 1, 13-50; Arnoux, 2-12

GRAND PRIX DU CANADA

30 September 1979. Montreal. 72 laps of a 2.740-mile circuit = 197.280 miles. Warm, dry and sunny. World Championship round 14

1	Alan Jones	Williams FW07-Ford	72	1h52m06.892
2	Gilles Villeneuve	Ferrari 312T4	72	1h52m07.972
3	Clay Regazzoni	Williams FW07-Ford	72	1h53m20.548
4	Jody Scheckter	Ferrari 312T4	71	
5	Didier Pironi	Tyrrell 009-Ford	71	
6	John Watson	McLaren M29-Ford	70	

Winner's average speed: 105.577 mph. Starting grid front row: Jones, 1m29.892 (pole) and Villeneuve, 1m30.554. Fastest lap: Jones, 1m31.272. Leaders: Villeneuve, laps 1-50; Jones, 51-72

TOYOTA GRAND PRIX OF THE UNITED STATES

7 October 1979. Watkins Glen. 59 laps of a 3.377-mile circuit = 199.243 miles. Cold and wet. World Championship round 15

1	Gilles Villeneuve	Ferrari 312T4	59	1h52m17.734
2	Rene Arnoux	Renault RE10	59	1h53m06.521
3	Didier Pironi	Tyrrell 009-Ford	59	1h53m10.933

4	Elio de Angelis	Shadow DN9B-Ford	59	1h53m48.246
5	Hans-Joachim Stuck	ATS D3-Ford	59	1h53m58.993
6	John Watson	McLaren M29-Ford	58	

Winner's average speed: 106.456 mph. Starting grid front row: Jones, 1m36.615 (pole) and Piquet, 1m36.914. Fastest lap: Piquet, 1m40.054. Leaders: Villeneuve, laps 1-31, 37-59; Jones, 32-36

1980

After setting the pace for the last half of the 1979 season, the Williams team updated its cars and signed Carlos Reutemann to partner Alan Jones. Once again, Jones and the FW07 proved the class of the field. The Australian withstood a strong challenge from the revitalised Brabham team to give Williams its first World Championship. Reutemann also won in Monte Carlo and consistently finished in the points.

Nelson Piquet emerged as a serious championship contender in only his second full season with Brabham. He took the series lead by winning the Italian GP, held at Imola for the only time. But engine failure ended Piquet's challenge at the season's penultimate event in Canada, where Jones won both the race and the title.

Along with Piquet, other young drivers made their mark in 1980. Didier Pironi, in his only season with Ligier, won in Belgium, crashed at Monaco while leading, and took the pole in Britain. Renault's Rene Arnoux won twice early in the year, but despite Jean-Pierre Jabouille's success in Austria, the team's turbocharged engine remained unreliable.

European F3 Champion Alain Prost signed for McLaren, and promptly outshone his more experienced team leader John Watson, scoring points finishes in his first two Grands Prix.

For Ferrari's Gilles Villeneuve it was a frustrating if spectacular season. The new Ferrari 312T5 was a step backward, and its Michelin tyres wore at an unacceptable rate. Teammate Jody Scheckter announced his retirement from the sport at the end of the year. By then the team was already looking to 1981 and were testing a new turbocharged engine.

Patrick Depailler was still recovering from his hang-gliding accident, but moved to Alfa Romeo. Sadly, just as the team appeared to be making progress under his guidance, Depailler was killed while testing at Hockenheim. His friend Jacques Laffite subsequently won an emotional victory at the German GP. Clay Regazzoni was also seriously injured when his Ensign crashed into a retired car at Long Beach.

Off the track, a war between FISA and the Formula One Constructors Association (FOCA) almost destroyed Formula 1. The Spanish GP lost its championship status when FISA-aligned teams (Alfa Romeo, Ferrari, and Renault) withdrew, while the French GP was only run after crisis talks prevented its cancellation.

GRAN PREMIO DE LA REPUBLICA ARGENTINA

13 January 1980. Buenos Aires. 53 laps of a 3.709-mile circuit = 196.577 miles. Very hot, dry and sunny. World Championship round 1

1	Alan Jones	Williams FW07-Ford	53	1h43m24.38
2	Nelson Piquet	Brabham BT49-Ford	53	1h43m48.97
3	Keke Rosberg	Fittipaldi F7-Ford	53	1h44m43.02
4	Derek Daly	Tyrrell 009-Ford	53	1h44m47.86
5	Bruno Giacomelli	Alfa Romeo 179B	52	
6	Alain Prost	McLaren M29B-Ford	52	

Winner's average speed: 114.061 mph. Starting grid front row: Jones, 1m44.17 (pole) and Laffite, 1m44.44. Fastest lap: Jones, 1m50.45. Leaders: Jones, laps 1-17, 30-53; Laffite, 18-29

GRANDE PREMIO DO BRASIL

27 January 1980. Interlagos. 40 laps of a 4.893-mile circuit = 195.720 miles. Very hot, dry and sunny. World Championship round 2

1	Rene Arnoux	Renault RE20	40	1h40m01.33
2	Elio de Angelis	Lotus 81-Ford	40	1h40m23.19
3	Alan Jones	Williams FW07B-Ford	40	1h41m07.44
4	Didier Pironi	Ligier JS11/15-Ford	40	1h41m41.46
5	Alain Prost	McLaren M29B-Ford	40	1h42m26.74
6	Riccardo Patrese	Arrows A3-Ford	39	

Winner's average speed: 117.406 mph. Starting grid front row: Jabouille, 2m21.40 (pole) and Pironi, 2m21.65. Fastest lap: Arnoux, 2m27.311. Leaders: Villeneuve, lap 1; Jabouille, laps 2-24; Arnoux, 25-40

1980 Alan Jones secured the first world title for Frank Williams in the excellent FW07.

NASHUA GRAND PRIX OF SOUTH AFRICA

1 March 1980. Kyalami. 78 laps of a 2.550-mile circuit = 198.900 miles. Warm, dry and sunny. World Championship round 3

1 Rene Arnoux	Renault RE20	78	1h36m52.54
2 Jacques Laffite	Ligier JS11/15-Ford	78	1h37m26.61
3 Didier Pironi	Ligier JS11/15-Ford	78	1h37m45.03
4 Nelson Piquet	Brabham BT49-Ford	78	1h37m53.56
5 Carlos Reutemann	Williams FW07B-Ford	77	
6 Jochen Mass	Arrows A3-Ford	77	

Winner's average speed: 123.189 mph. Starting grid front row: Jabouille, 1m10.00 (pole) and Arnoux, 1m10.21. Fastest lap: Arnoux, 1m13.15.
Leaders: Jabouille, laps 1-61; Arnoux, 62-78

TOYOTA GRAND PRIX OF LONG BEACH

30 March 1980. Long Beach. 80.5 laps of a 2.020-mile circuit = 162.610 miles. Warm, dry and sunny. World Championship round 4

1 Nelson Piquet	Brabham BT49-Ford	80	1h50m18.550
2 Riccardo Patrese	Arrows A3-Ford	80	1h51m07.762
3 Emerson Fittipaldi	Fittipaldi F7-Ford	80	1h51m37.113
4 John Watson	McLaren M29C-Ford	79	
5 Jody Scheckter	Ferrari 312T5	79	
6 Didier Pironi	Ligier JS11/15-Ford	79	

Winner's average speed: 88.448 mph. Starting grid front row: Piquet, 1m17.694 (pole) and Arnoux, 1m18.689. Fastest lap: Piquet, 1m19.830.
Leaders: Piquet, laps 1-80

GRAND PRIX DE BELGIQUE

4 May 1980. Zolder. 72 laps of a 2.648-mile circuit = 190.656 miles. Dry and windy. World Championship round 5

1 Didier Pironi	Ligier JS11/15-Ford	72	1h38m46.51
2 Alan Jones	Williams FW07B-Ford	72	1h39m33.88
3 Carlos Reutemann	Williams FW07B-Ford	72	1h40m10.63
4 Rene Arnoux	Renault RE20	71	
5 Jean-Pierre Jarier	Tyrrell 010-Ford	71	
6 Gilles Villeneuve	Ferrari 312T5	71	

Winner's average speed: 115.812 mph. Starting grid front row: Jones, 1m19.12 (pole) and Pironi, 1m19.35. Fastest lap: Laffite, 1m20.88.
Leaders: Pironi, laps 1-72

GRAND PRIX DE MONACO

18 May 1980. Monte Carlo. 76 laps of a 2.058-mile circuit = 156.408 miles. Occasional rain and overcast. World Championship round 6

1 Carlos Reutemann	Williams FW07B-Ford	76	1h55m34.365
2 Jacques Laffite	Ligier JS11/15-Ford	76	1h56m47.994
3 Nelson Piquet	Brabham BT49-Ford	76	1h56m52.091
4 Jochen Mass	Arrows A3-Ford	75	
5 Gilles Villeneuve	Ferrari 312T5	75	
6 Emerson Fittipaldi	Fittipaldi F7-Ford	74	

Winner's average speed: 81.200 mph. Starting grid front row: Pironi, 1m24.813 (pole) and Reutemann, 1m24.882. Fastest lap: Patrese, 1m26.058 (in doubt as it was raining when he set time, Reutemann, 1m27.418 set second fastest lap). Leaders: Pironi, laps 1-54; Reutemann, 55-76

GRAND PRIX DE FRANCE

29 June 1980. Paul Ricard. 54 laps of a 3.610-mile circuit = 194.940 miles. Warm, dry and windy. World Championship round 7

1 Alan Jones	Williams FW07B-Ford	54	1h32m43.42
2 Didier Pironi	Ligier JS11/15-Ford	54	1h32m47.94
3 Jacques Laffite	Ligier JS11/15-Ford	54	1h33m13.68
4 Nelson Piquet	Brabham BT49-Ford	54	1h33m58.30
5 Rene Arnoux	Renault RE20	54	1h33m59.57
6 Carlos Reutemann	Williams FW07B-Ford	54	1h34m00.16

Winner's average speed: 126.143 mph. Starting grid front row: Laffite, 1m38.88 (pole) and Arnoux, 1m39.49. Fastest lap: Jones, 1m41.45.
Leaders: Laffite, laps 1-34; Jones, 35-54

MARLBORO BRITISH GRAND PRIX

13 July 1980. Brands Hatch. 76 laps of a 2.614-mile circuit = 198.634 miles. Dry and overcast. World Championship round 8

1 Alan Jones	Williams FW07B-Ford	76	1h34m49.228
2 Nelson Piquet	Brabham BT49-Ford	76	1h35m00.235
3 Carlos Reutemann	Williams FW07B-Ford	76	1h35m02.513
4 Derek Daly	Tyrrell 010-Ford	75	
5 Jean-Pierre Jarier	Tyrrell 010-Ford	75	
6 Alain Prost	McLaren M29C-Ford	75	

Winner's average speed: 125.690 mph. Starting grid front row: Pironi, 1m11.004 (pole) and Laffite, 1m11.395. Fastest lap: Pironi, 1m12.368.
Leaders: Pironi, laps 1-18; Laffite, 19-30; Jones, 31-76

GROSSER PREIS VON DEUTSCHLAND

10 August 1980. Hockenheim. 45 laps of a 4.219-mile circuit = 189.855 miles. Dry and overcast. World Championship round 9

1 Jacques Laffite	Ligier JS11/15-Ford	45	1h22m59.73
2 Carlos Reutemann	Williams FW07B-Ford	45	1h23m02.92
3 Alan Jones	Williams FW07B-Ford	45	1h23m43.26
4 Nelson Piquet	Brabham BT49-Ford	45	1h23m44.21
5 Bruno Giacomelli	Alfa Romeo 179B	45	1h24m16.22
6 Gilles Villeneuve	Ferrari 312T5	45	1h24m28.45

Winner's average speed: 137.252 mph. Starting grid front row: Jones, 1m45.85 (pole) and Jabouille, 1m45.89. Fastest lap: Jones, 1m48.49.
Leaders: Jabouille, laps 1-26; Jones, 27-40; Laffite, 41-45

GROSSER PREIS VON OSTERREICH

17 August 1980. Osterreichring. 54 laps of a 3.692-mile circuit = 199.368 miles. Warm, dry and sunny. World Championship round 10

1 Jean-Pierre Jabouille	Renault RE20	54	1h26m15.73
2 Alan Jones	Williams FW07B-Ford	54	1h26m16.55
3 Carlos Reutemann	Williams FW07B-Ford	54	1h26m35.09
4 Jacques Laffite	Ligier JS11/15-Ford	54	1h26m57.75
5 Nelson Piquet	Brabham BT49-Ford	54	1h27m18.54
6 Elio de Angelis	Lotus 81-Ford	54	1h27m30.70

Winner's average speed: 138.671 mph. Starting grid front row: Arnoux, 1m30.27 (pole) and Jabouille, 1m31.48. Fastest lap: Arnoux, 1m32.53.
Leaders: Jones, laps 1-2; Arnoux, 3-20; Jabouille, 21-54

GROTE PRIJS VAN NEDERLAND

31 August 1980. Zandvoort. 72 laps of a 2.642-mile circuit = 190.224 miles. Warm, dry and sunny. World Championship round 11

1 Nelson Piquet	Brabham BT49-Ford	72	1h38m13.83
2 Rene Arnoux	Renault RE20	72	1h38m26.76
3 Jacques Laffite	Ligier JS11/15-Ford	72	1h38m27.26
4 Carlos Reutemann	Williams FW07B-Ford	72	1h38m29.12
5 Jean-Pierre Jarier	Tyrrell 010-Ford	72	1h39m13.85
6 Alain Prost	McLaren M30-Ford	72	1h39m36.45

Winner's average speed: 116.190 mph. Starting grid front row: Arnoux, 1m17.44 (pole) and Jabouille, 1m17.74. Fastest lap: Arnoux, 1m19.35.
Leaders: Jones, lap 1; Arnoux, lap 2; Laffite, laps 3-12; Piquet, 13-72

GRAN PREMIO D'ITALIA

14 September 1980. Imola. 60 laps of a 3.132-mile circuit = 187.920 miles. Warm, dry and sunny. World Championship round 12

1 Nelson Piquet	Brabham BT49-Ford	60	1h38m07.52
2 Alan Jones	Williams FW07B-Ford	60	1h38m36.45
3 Carlos Reutemann	Williams FW07B-Ford	60	1h39m21.19
4 Elio de Angelis	Lotus 81-Ford	59	
5 Keke Rosberg	Fittipaldi F8-Ford	59	
6 Didier Pironi	Ligier JS11/15-Ford	59	

Winner's average speed: 114.906 mph. Starting grid front row: Arnoux, 1m33.988 (pole) and Jabouille, 1m34.339. Fastest lap: Jones, 1m36.089.
Leaders: Arnoux, laps 1-2; Jabouille, 3; Piquet, 4-60

GRAND PRIX LABATT DU CANADA

28 September 1980. Montreal. 70 laps of a 2.740-mile circuit = 191.800 miles. Race stopped after first-lap accident, restarted over original dis-

Formula 1

1980 DRIVERS' RECORDS

driver	car	RA Q	RA R	BR Q	BR R	ZA Q	ZA R	LB Q	LB R	B Q	B R	MC Q	MC R	F Q	F R
Mario Andretti	Lotus 81-Ford	6	R	11	R	15	12	15	R	17	R	19	7	12	R
Elio de Angelis	Lotus 81-Ford	5	R	7	2	14	R	20	R	8	10	14	9	14	R
Rene Arnoux	Renault RE20	19	R	6	1F	2	1F	2	9	6	4	20	R	2	5
Vittorio Brambilla	Alfa Romeo 179B	-	-	-	-	-	-	-	-	-	-	-	-	-	-
Andrea de Cesaris	Alfa Romeo 179B	-	-	-	-	-	-	-	-	-	-	-	-	-	-
Eddie Cheever	Osella FA1-Ford	28	DNQ	28	DNQ	23	R	19	R	27	DNQ	22	DNQ	21	R
	Osella FA1B-Ford	-	-	-	-	-	-	-	-	-	-	-	-	-	-
Kevin Cogan	Williams FW07B-Ford	-	-	-	-	-	-	-	-	-	-	-	-	-	-
Derek Daly	Tyrrell 009-Ford	22	4	24	14	-	-	-	-	-	-	-	-	-	-
	Tyrrell 010-Ford	-	-	-	-	16	R	14	8	11	9	12	R	20	11
Patrick Depailler	Alfa Romeo 179B	23	R	21	R	7	R	3	R	10	R	7	R	10	R
Harald Ertl	ATS D4-Ford	-	-	-	-	-	-	-	-	-	-	-	-	-	-
Emerson Fittipaldi	Fittipaldi F7-Ford	24	NC	19	15	18	8	24	3	24	R	18	6	24	13
	Fittipaldi F8-Ford	-	-	-	-	-	-	-	-	-	-	-	-	-	-
Bruno Giacomelli	Alfa Romeo 179B	20	5	17	13	12	R	6	R	18	R	8	8	9	R
Jean-Pierre Jabouille	Renault RE20	9	R	1	R	1	R	11	10	5	R	16	R	6	R
Jean-Pierre Jarier	Tyrrell 009-Ford	18	R	22	12	-	-	-	-	-	-	-	-	-	-
	Tyrrell 010-Ford	-	-	-	-	13	7	12	R	9	5	9	R	16	14
Stefan Johansson	Shadow DN11A-Ford	26	DNQ	27	DNQ	-	-	-	-	-	-	-	-	-	-
Alan Jones	Williams FW07	1	1F	-	-	-	-	-	-	-	-	-	-	-	-
	Williams FW07B-Ford	-	-	10	3	8	R	5	R	1	2	3	R	4	1F
Rupert Keegan	Williams FW07-Ford	-	-	-	-	-	-	-	-	-	-	-	-	-	-
	Williams FW07B-Ford	-	-	-	-	-	-	-	-	-	-	-	-	-	-
David Kennedy	Shadow DN11A-Ford	25	DNQ	26	DNQ	27	DNQ	25	DNQ	26	DNQ	27	DNQ	-	-
	Shadow DN12A-Ford	-	-	-	-	-	-	-	-	-	-	-	-	27	DNQ
Jacques Laffite	Ligier JS11/15-Ford	2	R	5	R	4	2	13	R	3	11F	5	2	1	3
Jan Lammers	ATS D3-Ford	27	DNQ	25	DNQ	28	DNQ	-	-	-	-	-	-	-	-
	ATS D4-Ford	-	-	-	-	-	-	4	R	15	R	13	10	-	-
	Ensign N180-Ford	-	-	-	-	-	-	-	-	-	-	-	-	26	DNQ
Geoff Lees	Shadow DN11A-Ford	-	-	-	-	25	R	26	DNQ	-	-	-	-	-	-
	Shadow DN12A-Ford	-	-	-	-	-	-	-	-	25	DNQ	23	DNQ	25	DNQ
	Ensign N180-Ford	-	-	-	-	-	-	-	-	-	-	-	-	-	-
	Williams FW07B-Ford	-	-	-	-	-	-	-	-	-	-	-	-	-	-
Nigel Mansell	Lotus 81B-Ford	-	-	-	-	-	-	-	-	-	-	-	-	-	-
	Lotus 81-Ford	-	-	-	-	-	-	-	-	-	-	-	-	-	-
Jochen Mass	Arrows A3-Ford	14	R	16	10	19	6	17	7	13	R	15	4	15	10
Tiff Needell	Ensign N180-Ford	-	-	-	-	-	-	-	-	23	R	26	DNQ	-	-
Riccardo Patrese	Arrows A3-Ford	7	R	14	6	11	R	8	2	16	R	11	8F	18	9
Nelson Piquet	Brabham BT49-Ford	4	2	9	R	3	4	1	1F	7	R	4	3	8	4
Didier Pironi	Ligier JS11/15-Ford	3	R	2	4	5	3	9	6	2	1	1	R	3	2
Alain Prost	McLaren M29B-Ford	12	6	13	5	-	-	-	-	-	-	-	-	-	-
	McLaren M29C-Ford	-	-	-	-	22	DNS	-	-	19	R	10	R	7	R
	McLaren M30-Ford	-	-	-	-	-	-	-	-	-	-	-	-	-	-
Hector Rebaque	Brabham BT49-Ford	-	-	-	-	-	-	-	-	-	-	-	-	-	-
Clay Regazzoni	Ensign N180-Ford	15	NC	12	R	20	9	23	R	-	-	-	-	-	-
Carlos Reutemann	Williams FW07B-Ford	10	R	4	R	6	5	7	R	4	3	2	1	5	6
Keke Rosberg	Fittipaldi F7-Ford	13	3	15	9	24	R	22	R	21	7	24	DNQ	23	R
	Fittipaldi F8-Ford	-	-	-	-	-	-	-	-	-	-	-	-	-	-
Jody Scheckter	Ferrari 312T5	11	R	8	R	9	R	16	5	14	8	17	R	19	12
Stephen South	McLaren M29C-Ford	-	-	-	-	-	-	27	DNQ	-	-	-	-	-	-
Marc Surer	ATS D3-Ford	21	R	20	7	-	-	-	-	-	-	-	-	-	-
	ATS D4-Ford	-	-	-	-	26	DNQ	-	-	-	-	-	-	11	R
Mike Thackwell	Arrows A3-Ford	-	-	-	-	-	-	-	-	-	-	-	-	-	-
	Tyrrell 010-Ford	-	-	-	-	-	-	-	-	-	-	-	-	-	-
Gilles Villeneuve	Ferrari 312T5	8	R	3	16	10	R	10	R	12	6	6	5	17	8
John Watson	McLaren M29B-Ford	17	R	23	11	21	11	-	-	-	-	-	-	-	-
	McLaren M29C-Ford	-	-	-	-	-	-	21	4	20	NC	21	DNQ	13	7
Desire Wilson	Williams FW07-Ford	-	-	-	-	-	-	-	-	-	-	-	-	-	-
Manfred Winkelhock	Arrows A3-Ford	-	-	-	-	-	-	-	-	-	-	-	-	-	-
Ricardo Zunino	Brabham BT49-Ford	16	7	18	8	17	10	18	R	22	R	25	DNQ	22	R

GB		D		A		NL		I		CDN		USA	
Q	R	Q	R	Q	R	Q	R	Q	R	Q	R	Q	R
9	R	9	7	17	R	10	8	10	R	18	R	11	6
14	R	11	16	9	6	11	R	18	4	17	10	4	4
16	NC	3	R	1	9F	1	2F	1	10	23	R	6	7
-	-	-	-	-	-	22	R	19	R	-	-	-	-
-	-	-	-	-	-	-	-	-	-	8	R	10	R
20	R	18	R	19	R	19	R	-	-	-	-	-	-
-	-	-	-	-	-	-	-	17	12	14	R	16	R
-	-	-	-	-	-	-	-	-	-	28	DNQ	-	-
-	-	-	-	-	-	-	-	-	-	-	-	-	-
10	4	22	10	10	R	23	R	22	R	20	R	21	R
8	R	-	-	-	-	-	-	-	-	-	-	-	-
-	-	26	DNQ	-	-	-	-	-	-	-	-	-	-
-	-	-	-	-	-	-	-	-	-	-	-	-	-
22	12	12	R	23	11	21	R	15	R	16	R	19	R
6	R	19	5	8	R	8	R	4	R	4	R	1	R
13	R	2	R	2	1	2	R	2	R	13	R	-	-
-	-	-	-	-	-	-	-	-	-	-	-	-	-
11	5	23	15	13	R	17	5	12	R	15	7	22	NC
-	-	-	-	-	-	-	-	-	-	-	-	-	-
-	-	-	-	-	-	-	-	-	-	-	-	-	-
3	1	1	3F	3	2	4	11	6	2F	2	1	5	1F
18	11	-	-	-	-	-	-	-	-	-	-	-	-
-	-	25	DNQ	20	15	25	DNQ	21	11	27	DNQ	15	9
-	-	-	-	-	-	-	-	-	-	-	-	-	-
-	-	-	-	-	-	-	-	-	-	-	-	-	-
2	R	5	1	5	4	6	3	20	9	9	8	12	5
-	-	-	-	-	-	-	-	-	-	-	-	-	-
-	-	-	-	-	-	-	-	-	-	-	-	-	-
25	DNQ	24	14	25	DNQ	26	DNQ	27	DNQ	19	12	25	R
-	-	-	-	-	-	-	-	-	-	-	-	-	-
-	-	-	-	-	-	24	R	28	DNQ	-	-	-	-
-	-	-	-	-	-	-	-	-	-	-	-	27	DNQ
-	-	-	-	24	R	16	R	-	-	-	-	-	-
-	-	-	-	-	-	-	-	25	DNQ	-	-	-	-
24	13	17	8	NT	DNP	NT	DNP	-	-	21	11	24	R
-	-	-	-	-	-	-	-	-	-	-	-	-	-
21	9	10	9	18	14	14	R	7	R	11	R	20	R
5	2	6	4	7	5	5	1	5	1	1	R	2	R
1	RF	7	R	6	R	15	R	13	6	3	3F	7	3
-	-	-	-	-	-	-	-	-	-	-	-	-	-
7	6	14	11	12	7	-	-	-	-	-	-	-	-
-	-	-	-	-	-	18	6	24	7	12	R	13	DNS
17	7	15	R	14	10	13	R	9	R	10	6	8	R
-	-	-	-	-	-	-	-	-	-	-	-	-	-
4	3	4	2	4	3	3	4	3	3	5	2	3	2
26	DNQ	-	-	-	-	-	-	-	-	-	-	-	-
-	-	8	R	11	16	28	DNQ	11	5	6	9	14	10
23	10	21	13	22	13	12	9	16	8	26	DNQ	23	11
-	-	-	-	-	-	-	-	-	-	-	-	-	-
15	R	13	12	16	12	20	10	23	R	25	DNQ	17	8
-	-	-	-	-	-	27	DNQ	-	-	-	-	-	-
-	-	-	-	-	-	-	-	-	-	24	R	26	DNQ
19	R	16	6	15	8	7	7	8	R	22	5	18	R
-	-	-	-	-	-	-	-	-	-	-	-	-	-
12	8	20	R	21	R	9	R	14	R	7	4	9	NC
27	DNQ	-	-	-	-	-	-	-	-	-	-	-	-
-	-	-	-	-	-	-	-	26	DNQ	-	-	-	-
-	-	-	-	-	-	-	-	-	-	-	-	-	-

1980 FINAL CHAMPIONSHIP POSITIONS

Drivers						Manufacturers		
1	Alan Jones	67 (71)*	15=	Emerson Fittipaldi	5	1	Williams-Ford	120
2	Nelson Piquet	54		Alain Prost	5	2	Ligier-Ford	66
3	Carlos Reutemann	42 (49)*	17=	Bruno Giacomelli	4	3	Brabham-Ford	55
4	Jacques Laffite	34		Jochen Mass	4	4	Renault	38
5	Didier Pironi	32	19	Jody Scheckter	2	5	Lotus-Ford	14
6	Rene Arnoux	29	20=	Mario Andretti	1	6	Tyrrell-Ford	12
7	Elio de Angelis	13		Hector Rebaque	1	7=	Arrows-Ford	11
8	Jean-Pierre Jabouille	9	*Sum of best five results from the first				Fittipaldi-Ford	11
9	Riccardo Patrese	7	seven races and best five results from the				McLaren-Ford	11
10=	Derek Daly	6	final seven races			10	Ferrari	8
	Jean-Pierre Jarier	6				11	Alfa Romeo	4
	Keke Rosberg	6				Results for all cars entered by FOCA		
	Gilles Villeneuve	6				recognised constructors count		
	John Watson	6						

tance. Cool and dry. World Championship round 13

1	Alan Jones	Williams FW07B-Ford	70	1h46m45.53
2	Carlos Reutemann	Williams FW07B-Ford	70	1h47m01.07
3*	Didier Pironi	Ligier JS11/15-Ford	70	1h47m04.60
4	John Watson	McLaren M29C-Ford	70	1h47m16.51
5	Gilles Villeneuve	Ferrari 312T5	70	1h47m40.76
6	Hector Rebaque	Brabham BT49-Ford	69	

*Pironi penalised 1 minute for jumping the start. Winner's average speed: 107.794 mph. Starting grid front row: Piquet, 1m27.328 (pole) and Jones, 1m28.164. Fastest lap: Pironi, 1m28.769. Leaders: Jones, laps 1-2, 24-70; Piquet, 3-23 (Pironi led laps 44-70 on the road)

TOYOTA GRAND PRIX OF THE UNITED STATES

5 October 1980. Watkins Glen. 59 laps of a 3.377-mile circuit = 199.243 miles. Cool and dry. World Championship round 14

1	Alan Jones	Williams FW07B-Ford	59	1h34m36.05
2	Carlos Reutemann	Williams FW07B-Ford	59	1h34m40.26
3	Didier Pironi	Ligier JS11/15-Ford	59	1h34m48.62
4	Elio de Angelis	Lotus 81-Ford	59	1h35m05.74
5	Jacques Laffite	Ligier JS11/15-Ford	58	
6	Mario Andretti	Lotus 81-Ford	58	

Winner's average speed: 126.369 mph. Starting grid front row: Giacomelli, 1m33.291 (pole) and Piquet, 1m34.080. Fastest lap: Jones, 1m34.068. Leaders: Giacomelli, laps 1-31; Jones, 32-59.

1981

After a tortuous winter of politics, the FISA/FOCA "war" was finally resolved, and the 1981 season opened late at Long Beach. To reduce downforce and cornering speeds, sliding skirts had been banned and a minimum sidepod ground clearance of 6cm was now stipulated. Although Riccardo Patrese's Arrows qualified on pole in California, the old order appeared unchanged in the race, with Alan Jones winning for Williams.

The new ground clearance could only be measured in the pits, so systems to lower the cars and circumvent the ground clearance rule when in motion were introduced by some teams. After protests, FISA pronounced the concept legal, so everyone had to follow suit.

On the track, Brabham and Williams again disputed the championship. Carlos Reutemann defied Williams team orders to beat Jones in Brazil, and led the championship for much of the year. But the Argentinian turned in a strangely lacklustre performance at the final race in Las Vegas, allowing Nelson Piquet to snatch the title for Brabham. The outgoing champion Alan Jones, who had already announced what proved to be a tempo-

rary retirement from the sport, won the race itself for Williams. Jacques Laffite also won twice for Ligier, enough to maintain an outside chance at the title until the final race of the season.

Gilles Villeneuve made news for Ferrari, whose current car combined a powerful turbocharged engine with a truly awful chassis. After winning in Monte Carlo, Villeneuve narrowly held off four quicker cars for nearly all of the Spanish GP, scoring an incredible victory in which just 1.24 seconds separated the top five finishers!

Renault, the originators of the turbo, signed Alain Prost, who won three times. But mechanical failures again restricted the team's ability to contend for the championship.

Ron Dennis' Project 4 F2 concern merged with the ailing McLaren team to form McLaren International. The new partnership introduced the first fully carbon fibre monocoque to Grand Prix racing in the John Barnard-designed MP4/1. Backed by a patriotic home crowd, John Watson drove the car to victory in the British GP, his first win in five years. Although Lotus also used a composite chassis to delivery greater rigidity at a lower weight, the team was preoccupied with the controversial Lotus 88 concept, Colin Chapman's latest attempt to give his team a significant advantage. The car featured a conventional chassis with the bodywork suspended on a secondary chassis. But FISA ruled the second chassis was a movable aerodynamic device and thus illegal, and the car never raced.

The Belgian GP was marred by the death of Osella mechanic Giovanni Amadeo after a pit lane accident during practice. The dark mood was deepened by a start-line accident in which Arrows' chief mechanic Dave Luckett was injured. Luckett had stayed on the grid to restart Riccardo Patrese's car, and was struck by teammate Siegfried Stohr at the start.

TOYOTA GRAND PRIX OF THE UNITED STATES WEST

15 March 1981. Long Beach. 80.5 laps of a 2.020-mile circuit = 162.610 miles. Warm, dry and sunny. World Championship round 1

1	Alan Jones	Williams FW07C-Ford	80	1h50m41.33
2	Carlos Reutemann	Williams FW07C-Ford	80	1h50m50.52
3	Nelson Piquet	Brabham BT49C-Ford	80	1h51m16.25
4	Mario Andretti	Alfa Romeo 179C	80	1h51m30.64
5	Eddie Cheever	Tyrrell 010-Ford	80	1h51m48.03
6	Patrick Tambay	Theodore TY01-Ford	79	

Winner's average speed: 88.144 mph. Starting grid front row: Patrese,

1m19.39 (pole) and Jones, 1m19.40. Fastest lap: Jones, 1m20.901.
Leaders: Patrese, laps 1-24; Reutemann, 25-31; Jones, 32-80

GRANDE PREMIO DO BRASIL

29 March 1981. Rio de Janeiro. 62 laps of a 3.126-mile circuit = 193.812 miles Race scheduled for 63 laps but stopped after two hours. Wet. World Championship round 2

1 Carlos Reutemann	Williams FW07C-Ford	62	2h00m23.66
2 Alan Jones	Williams FW07C-Ford	62	2h00m28.10
3 Riccardo Patrese	Arrows A3-Ford	62	2h01m26.74
4 Marc Surer	Ensign N180B-Ford	62	2h01m40.69
5 Elio de Angelis	Lotus 81-Ford	62	2h01m50.08
6 Jacques Laffite	Ligier JS17-Matra	62	2h01m50.49

Winner's average speed: 96.589 mph. Starting grid front row: Piquet, 1m35.079 (pole) and Reutemann, 1m35.390. Fastest lap: Surer, 1m54.302. Leaders: Reutemann, laps 1-62

GRAN PREMIO DE LA REPUBLICA ARGENTINA

12 April 1981. Buenos Aires. 53 laps of a 3.709-mile circuit = 196.577 miles. Hot, dry and sunny. World Championship round 3

1 Nelson Piquet	Brabham BT49C-Ford	53	1h34m32.74
2 Carlos Reutemann	Williams FW07C-Ford	53	1h34m59.35
3 Alain Prost	Renault RE20B	53	1h35m22.72
4 Alan Jones	Williams FW07C-Ford	53	1h35m40.62
5 Rene Arnoux	Renault RE20B	53	1h36m04.59
6 Elio de Angelis	Lotus 81-Ford	52	

Winner's average speed: 124.751 mph. Starting grid front row: Piquet, 1m42.665 (pole) and Prost, 1m42.981. Fastest lap: Piquet, 1m45.287. Leaders: Piquet, laps 1-53

GRAN PREMIO DI SAN MARINO

3 May 1981. Imola. 60 laps of a 3.132-mile circuit = 187.920 miles. Cool and wet. World Championship round 4

1 Nelson Piquet	Brabham BT49C-Ford	60	1h51m23.97
2 Riccardo Patrese	Arrows A3-Ford	60	1h51m28.55
3 Carlos Reutemann	Williams FW07C-Ford	60	1h51m30.31
4 Hector Rebaque	Brabham BT49C-Ford	60	1h51m46.86
5 Didier Pironi	Ferrari 126CK	60	1h51m49.84
6 Andrea de Cesaris	McLaren M29F-Ford	60	1h52m30.58

Winner's average speed: 101.214 mph. Starting grid front row: Villeneuve, 1m34.523 (pole) and Reutemann, 1m35.229. Fastest lap: Villeneuve, 1m48.064. Leaders: Villeneuve, laps 1-14; Pironi, 15-46; Piquet, 47-60

GRAND PRIX DE BELGIQUE

17 May 1981. Zolder. 54 laps of a 2.648-mile circuit = 142.992 miles. Race scheduled for 70 laps, stopped due to accident at start. Restarted over original distance but stopped early due to rain. Warm, dry and sunny, rain later. World Championship round 5

1 Carlos Reutemann	Williams FW07C-Ford	54	1h16m31.61
2 Jacques Laffite	Ligier JS17-Matra	54	1h17m07.67
3 Nigel Mansell	Lotus 87-Ford	54	1h17m15.30
4 Gilles Villeneuve	Ferrari 126CK	54	1h17m19.25
5 Elio de Angelis	Lotus 81-Ford	54	1h17m20.81
6 Eddie Cheever	Tyrrell 010-Ford	54	1h17m24.12

Winner's average speed: 112.111 mph. Starting grid front row: Reutemann, 1m22.28 (pole) and Piquet, 1m23.13. Fastest lap: Reutemann, 1m23.30. Leaders: Pironi, laps 1-12; Jones, 13-19; Reutemann, 20-54

GRAND PRIX DE MONACO

31 May 1981. Monte Carlo. 76 laps of a 2.058-mile circuit = 156.408 miles. Warm, dry and sunny. World Championship round 6

1 Gilles Villeneuve	Ferrari 126CK	76	1h54m23.38
2 Alan Jones	Williams FW07C-Ford	76	1h55m03.29
3 Jacques Laffite	Ligier JS17-Matra	76	1h55m52.62
4 Didier Pironi	Ferrari 126CK	75	
5 Eddie Cheever	Tyrrell 010-Ford	74	
6 Marc Surer	Ensign N180B-Ford	74	

Winner's average speed: 82.040 mph. Starting grid front row: Piquet,

---

1m25.710 (pole) and Villeneuve, 1m25.788. Fastest lap: Jones, 1m27.470.
Leaders: Piquet, laps 1-53; Jones, 54-72; Villeneuve, 73-76

GRAN PREMIO DE ESPANA

21 June 1981. Jarama. 80 laps of a 2.115-mile circuit = 169.232 miles. Hot, dry and sunny. World Championship round 7

1 Gilles Villeneuve	Ferrari 126CK	80	1h46m35.01
2 Jacques Laffite	Ligier JS17-Matra	80	1h46m35.23
3 John Watson	McLaren MP4/1-Ford	80	1h46m35.59
4 Carlos Reutemann	Williams FW07C-Ford	80	1h46m36.02
5 Elio de Angelis	Lotus 87-Ford	80	1h46m36.25
6 Nigel Mansell	Lotus 87-Ford	80	1h47m03.59

Winner's average speed: 95.267 mph. Starting grid front row: Laffite, 1m13.754 (pole) and Jones, 1m14.024. Fastest lap: Jones, 1m17.818. Leaders: Jones, laps 1-13; Villeneuve, 14-80

GRAND PRIX DE FRANCE

5 July 1981. Dijon-Prenois. 80 laps of a 2.361-mile circuit = 188.880 miles. Cool and dry, rain later, drying when restarted. Race stopped after 58 laps due to rain, restarted over remaining 22 laps. World Championship round 8

1 Alain Prost	Renault RE30	80	1h35m48.13
2 John Watson	McLaren MP4/1-Ford	80	1h35m50.42
3 Nelson Piquet	Brabham BT49C-Ford	80	1h36m12.35
4 Rene Arnoux	Renault RE30	80	1h36m30.43
5 Didier Pironi	Ferrari 126CK	79	
6 Elio de Angelis	Lotus 87-Ford	79	

Winner's average speed: 118.294 mph. Starting grid front row: Arnoux, 1m05.95 (pole) and Watson, 1m06.36. Fastest lap: Prost, 1m09.14. Leaders: Piquet, laps 1-58; Prost, 59-80

MARLBORO BRITISH GRAND PRIX

18 July 1981. Silverstone. 68 laps of a 2.932-mile circuit = 199.376 miles. Warm, dry and sunny. World Championship round 9

1 John Watson	McLaren MP4/1-Ford	68	1h26m54.80
2 Carlos Reutemann	Williams FW07C-Ford	68	1h27m35.45
3 Jacques Laffite	Ligier JS17-Matra	67	
4 Eddie Cheever	Tyrrell 010-Ford	67	
5 Hector Rebaque	Brabham BT49C-Ford	67	
6 Slim Borgudd	ATS HGS1-Ford	67	

Winner's average speed: 137.638 mph. Starting grid front row: Arnoux, 1m11.000 (pole) and Prost, 1m11.046. Fastest lap: Arnoux, 1m15.067. Leaders: Prost, laps 1-16; Arnoux, 17-60; Watson, 61-68

GROSSER PREIS VON DEUTSCHLAND

2 August 1981. Hockenheim. 45 laps of a 4.219-mile circuit = 189.855 miles. Hot, dry and sunny. World Championship round 10

1 Nelson Piquet	Brabham BT49C-Ford	45	1h25m55.60
2 Alain Prost	Renault RE30	45	1h26m07.12
3 Jacques Laffite	Ligier JS17-Matra	45	1h27m00.20
4 Hector Rebaque	Brabham BT49C-Ford	45	1h27m35.29
5 Eddie Cheever	Tyrrell 011-Ford	45	1h27m46.12
6 John Watson	McLaren MP4/1-Ford	44	

Winner's average speed: 132.570 mph. Starting grid front row: Prost, 1m47.50 (pole) and Arnoux, 1m47.96. Fastest lap: Jones, 1m52.42. Leaders: Prost, laps 1-20; Jones, 21-38; Piquet, 39-45

GROSSER PREIS VON OSTERREICH

16 August 1981. Osterreichring. 53 laps of a 3.692-mile circuit = 195.676 miles. Hot, dry and sunny. World Championship round 11

1 Jacques Laffite	Ligier JS17-Matra	53	1h27m36.47
2 Rene Arnoux	Renault RE30	53	1h27m41.64
3 Nelson Piquet	Brabham BT49C-Ford	53	1h27m43.81
4 Alan Jones	Williams FW07C-Ford	53	1h27m48.51
5 Carlos Reutemann	Williams FW07C-Ford	53	1h28m08.32
6 John Watson	McLaren MP4/1-Ford	53	1h29m07.61

Winner's average speed: 134.013 mph. Starting grid front row: Arnoux, 1m32.018 (pole) and Prost, 1m32.321. Fastest lap: Laffite, 1m37.62.

1981 DRIVERS' RECORDS

driver	car	LB		BR		RA		RSM		B		MC	
		Q	R	Q	R	Q	R	Q	R	Q	R	Q	R
Michele Alboreto	Tyrrell 010-Ford	-	-	-	-	-	-	17	R	19	12	20	R
	Tyrrell 011-Ford	-	-	-	-	-	-	-	-	-	-	-	-
Mario Andretti	Alfa Romeo 179C	6	4	9	R	17	8	12	R	18	10	12	R
	Alfa Romeo 179B	-	-	-	-	-	-	-	-	-	-	-	-
Elio de Angelis	Lotus 81-Ford	13	R	10	5	10	6	-	-	14	5	-	-
	Lotus 87-Ford	-	-	-	-	-	-	-	-	-	-	6	R
Rene Arnoux	Renault RE20B	20	8	8	R	5	5	3	8	-	-	13	R
	Renault RE30	-	-	-	-	-	-	-	-	25	DNQ	-	-
Slim Borgudd	ATS D4-Ford	-	-	-	-	-	-	24	13	-	-	-	-
	ATS HGS1-Ford	-	-	-	-	-	-	-	-	27	DNQ	27	NPQ
Andrea de Cesaris	McLaren M29F-Ford	22	R	20	R	18	11	14	6	23	R	-	-
	McLaren MP4/1-Ford	-	-	-	-	-	-	-	-	-	-	11	R
Eddie Cheever	Tyrrell 010-Ford	8	5	14	NC	13	R	19	R	8	6	15	5
	Tyrrell 011-Ford	-	-	-	-	-	-	-	-	-	-	-	-
Kevin Cogan	Tyrrell 010-Ford	25	DNQ	-	-	-	-	-	-	-	-	-	-
Derek Daly	March 811-Ford	26	DNQ	NT	DNP	27	DNQ	26	DNQ	31	DNQ	28	NPQ
Giorgio Francia	Osella FA1B-Ford	-	-	-	-	-	-	-	-	-	-	-	-
Beppe Gabbiani	Osella FA1B-Ford	24	R	27	DNQ	26	DNQ	20	R	22	R	26	DNQ
Piercarlo Ghinzani	Osella FA1B-Ford	-	-	-	-	-	-	-	-	24	13	25	DNQ
Bruno Giacomelli	Alfa Romeo 179C	9	R	6	R	22	10	11	R	17	9	18	R
	Alfa Romeo 179B	-	-	-	-	-	-	-	-	-	-	-	-
Miguel Angel Guerra	Osella FA1B-Ford	27	DNQ	28	DNQ	25	DNQ	22	R	-	-	-	-
Brian Henton	Toleman TG181-Hart	-	-	-	-	-	-	30	DNQ	30	DNQ	30	NPQ
Jean-Pierre Jabouille	Ligier JS17-Matra	-	-	26	DNQ	28	DNQ	18	NC	16	R	22	DNQ
Jean-Pierre Jarier	Ligier JS17-Matra	10	R	23	7	-	-	-	-	-	-	-	-
	Osella FA1B-Ford	-	-	-	-	-	-	-	-	-	-	-	-
	Osella FA1C-Ford	-	-	-	-	-	-	-	-	-	-	-	-
Alan Jones	Williams FW07C-Ford	2	1F	3	2	3	4	8	12	6	R	7	2F
Jacques Laffite	Ligier JS17-Matra	12	R	16	6	21	R	10	R	9	2	8	3
Jan Lammers	ATS D4-Ford	21	R	25	DNQ	23	12	27	DNQ	-	-	-	-
Nigel Mansell	Lotus 81-Ford	7	R	13	11	15	R	-	-	10	3	-	-
	Lotus 87-Ford	-	-	-	-	-	-	-	-	-	-	3	R
Riccardo Patrese	Arrows A3-Ford	1	R	4	3	9	7	9	2	4	R	5	R
Nelson Piquet	Brabham BT49C-Ford	4	3	1	12	1	1F	5	1	2	R	1	R
Didier Pironi	Ferrari 126CK	11	R	17	R	12	R	6	5	3	8	17	4
Alain Prost	Renault RE20B	14	R	5	R	2	3	4	R	-	-	-	-
	Renault RE30	-	-	-	-	-	-	-	-	12	R	9	R
Hector Rebaque	Brabham BT49C-Ford	15	R	11	R	6	R	13	4	21	R	23	DNQ
Carlos Reutemann	Williams FW07C-Ford	3	2	2	1	4	2	2	3	1	1F	4	R
Keke Rosberg	Fittipaldi F8C-Ford	16	R	12	9	8	R	15	R	11	R	21	DNQ
Eliseo Salazar	March 811-Ford	29	DNQ	29	DNQ	29	DNQ	23	R	26	DNQ	29	NPQ
	Ensign N180B-Ford	-	-	-	-	-	-	-	-	-	-	-	-
Chico Serra	Fittipaldi F8C-Ford	18	7	22	R	20	R	28	DNQ	20	R	24	DNQ
Siegfried Stohr	Arrows A3-Ford	28	DNQ	21	R	19	9	25	DNQ	13	R	14	R
Marc Surer	Ensign N180B-Ford	19	R	18	4F	16	R	21	9	15	11	19	6
	Theodore TY01-Ford	-	-	-	-	-	-	-	-	-	-	-	-
Patrick Tambay	Theodore TY01-Ford	17	6	19	10	14	R	16	11	28	DNQ	16	7
	Ligier JS17-Matra	-	-	-	-	-	-	-	-	-	-	-	-
Gilles Villeneuve	Ferrari 126CK	5	R	7	R	7	R	1	7F	7	4	2	1
Jacques Villeneuve	Arrows A3-Ford	-	-	-	-	-	-	-	-	-	-	-	-
Emilio de Villota	Williams FW07-Ford	-	-	-	-	-	-	-	-	-	-	-	-
Derek Warwick	Toleman TG181-Hart	-	-	-	-	-	-	29	DNQ	29	DNQ	31	NPQ
John Watson	McLaren M29F-Ford	23	R	15	8	-	-	-	-	-	-	-	-
	McLaren MP4/1-Ford	-	-	-	-	11	R	7	10	5	7	10	R
Ricardo Zunino	Tyrrell 010-Ford	-	-	24	13	24	13	-	-	-	-	-	-

E		F		GB		D		A		NL		I		CDN		LV	
Q	R	Q	R	Q	R	Q	R	Q	R	Q	R	Q	R	Q	R	Q	R
25	DNQ	23	16	19	R	29	DNQ	22	R	-	-	-	-	-	-	-	-
-	-	-	-	-	-	-	-	-	-	25	9	22	R	22	11	17	R
8	8	-	-	11	R	12	9	13	R	7	R	13	R	16	7	10	R
-	-	10	8	-	-	-	-	-	-	-	-	-	-	-	-	-	-
10	5	8	6	22	R	14	7	9	7	9	5	11	4	7	6	15	R
17	9	1	4	1	9F	2	13	1	2	2	R	1	R	8	R	13	R
-	-	-	-	-	-	-	-	-	-	-	-	-	-	-	-	-	-
27	DNQ	27	DNQ	21	6	20	R	21	R	23	10	21	R	21	R	25	DNQ
14	R	5	11	6	R	10	R	18	8	13	DNS	16	7	13	R	14	12
20	NC	19	13	23	4	-	-	-	-	-	-	-	-	-	-	-	-
-	-	-	-	-	-	18	5	25	DNQ	22	R	17	R	14	R	19	R
22	16	20	R	17	7	21	R	19	11	19	R	19	R	20	8	27	DNQ
30	DNQ	-	-	-	-	-	-	-	-	-	-	-	-	-	-	-	-
26	DNQ	28	DNQ	30	DNQ	27	DNQ	28	DNQ	29	DNQ	26	DNQ	30	DNQ	30	DNQ
-	-	-	-	-	-	-	-	-	-	-	-	-	-	-	-	-	-
6	10	-	-	12	R	19	15	16	R	14	R	10	8	15	4	8	3
-	-	12	15	-	-	-	-	-	-	-	-	-	-	-	-	-	-
-	-	-	-	-	-	-	-	-	-	-	-	-	-	-	-	-	-
28	DNQ	26	DNQ	26	DNQ	26	DNQ	27	DNQ	26	DNQ	23	10	27	DNQ	29	DNQ
19	R	-	-	-	-	-	-	-	-	-	-	-	-	-	-	-	-
-	-	-	-	20	8	17	8	14	10	18	R	-	-	-	-	-	-
-	-	-	-	-	-	-	-	-	-	-	-	18	9	23	R	21	R
2	7F	9	17	7	R	4	11F	6	4	4	3F	5	2	3	R	2	1
1	2	6	R	14	3	7	3	4	1F	6	R	4	R	10	1	12	6
-	-	-	-	-	-	-	-	-	-	-	-	-	-	-	-	-	-
11	6	13	7	27	DNQ	15	R	11	R	17	R	12	R	5	R	9	4
12	R	18	14	10	10	13	R	10	R	10	R	20	R	18	R	11	11
9	R	4	3	3	R	6	1	7	3	3	2	6	6	1	5	4	5
13	15	14	5	4	R	5	R	8	9	12	R	8	5	12	R	18	9F
-	-	-	-	-	-	-	-	-	-	-	-	-	-	-	-	-	-
5	R	3	1F	2	R	1	2	2	R	1	1	3	1	4	R	5	2
18	R	15	9	13	5	16	4	15	R	15	4	14	R	6	R	16	R
3	4	7	10	9	2	3	R	5	5	5	R	2	3F	2	10	1	8
15	12	17	R	16	R	25	DNQ	-	-	27	DNQ	29	DNQ	25	DNQ	20	10
-	-	-	-	-	-	-	-	-	-	-	-	-	-	-	-	-	-
24	14	22	R	28	DNQ	23	NC	20	R	24	6	24	R	24	R	24	R
21	11	24	DNS	25	DNQ	30	DNQ	-	-	28	DNQ	30	DNQ	26	DNQ	26	DNQ
23	R	25	DNQ	18	R	24	12	24	R	21	7	28	DNQ	-	-	-	-
-	-	-	-	-	-	-	-	-	-	-	-	-	-	-	-	-	-
-	-	21	12	24	11	22	14	23	DNS	20	8	25	DNQ	19	9	23	R
16	13	-	-	-	-	-	-	-	-	-	-	-	-	-	-	-	-
-	-	16	R	15	R	11	R	17	R	11	R	15	R	17	R	7	R
7	1	11	R	8	R	8	10	3	R	16	R	9	R	11	3	3	R
-	-	-	-	-	-	-	-	-	-	-	-	-	-	28	DNQ	28	DNQ
NT	DNP	-	-	-	-	-	-	-	-	-	-	-	-	-	-	-	-
29	DNQ	29	DNQ	29	DNQ	28	DNQ	26	DNQ	30	DNQ	27	DNQ	29	DNQ	22	R
4	3	2	2	5	1	9	6	12	6	8	R	7	R	9	2F	6	7
-	-	-	-	-	-	-	-	-	-	-	-	-	-	-	-	-	-

1981 FINAL CHAMPIONSHIP POSITIONS

Drivers						Manufacturers		
1	Nelson Piquet	50	16	Marc Surer	4	1	Williams-Ford	95
2	Carlos Reutemann	49	17	Mario Andretti	3	2	Brabham-Ford	61
3	Alan Jones	46	18=	Slim Borgudd	1	3	Renault	54
4	Jacques Laffite	44		Andrea de Cesaris	1	4	Ligier-Matra	44
5	Alain Prost	43		Eliseo Salazar	1	5	Ferrari	34
6	John Watson	27		Patrick Tambay	1	6	McLaren-Ford	28
7	Gilles Villeneuve	25	Best 11 results count			7	Lotus-Ford	22
8	Elio de Angelis	14				8=	Alfa Romeo	10
9=	Rene Arnoux	11					Arrows-Ford	10
	Hector Rebaque	11					Tyrrell-Ford	10
11=	Eddie Cheever	10				11	Ensign-Ford	5
	Riccardo Patrese	10				12=	ATS-Ford	1
13	Didier Pironi	9					Theodore-Ford	1
14	Nigel Mansell	8						
15	Bruno Giacomelli	7						

Leaders: Villeneuve, lap 1; Prost, laps 2-26; Arnoux, 27-38; Laffite, 39-53

GROTE PRIJS VAN NEDERLAND

30 August 1981. Zandvoort. 72 laps of a 2.642-mile circuit = 190.224 miles. Warm, dry and sunny. World Championship round 12

1	Alain Prost	Renault RE30	72	1h40m22.43
2	Nelson Piquet	Brabham BT49C-Ford	72	1h40m30.67
3	Alan Jones	Williams FW07C-Ford	72	1h40m57.93
4	Hector Rebaque	Brabham BT49C-Ford	71	
5	Elio de Angelis	Lotus 87-Ford	71	
6	Eliseo Salazar	Ensign N180B-Ford	70	

Winner's average speed: 113.709 mph. Starting grid front row: Prost, 1m18.176 (pole) and Arnoux, 1m18.255. Fastest lap: Jones, 1m21.83. Leaders: Prost, laps 1-22, 24-72; Jones, 23

GRAN PREMIO D'ITALIA

13 September 1981. Monza. 52 laps of a 3.604-mile circuit = 187.403 miles. Warm, occasional rain. World Championship round 13

1	Alain Prost	Renault RE30	52	1h26m33.897
2	Alan Jones	Williams FW07C-Ford	52	1h26m56.072
3	Carlos Reutemann	Williams FW07C-Ford	52	1h27m24.484
4	Elio de Angelis	Lotus 87-Ford	52	1h28m06.799
5	Didier Pironi	Ferrari 126CK	52	1h28m08.419
6	Nelson Piquet	Brabham BT49C-Ford	51	engine

Winner's average speed: 129.893 mph. Starting grid front row: Arnoux, 1m33.467 (pole) and Reutemann, 1m34.140. Fastest lap: Reutemann, 1m37.528. Leaders: Prost, laps 1-52

GRAND PRIX LABATT DU CANADA

27 September 1981. Montreal. 63 laps of a 2.740-mile circuit = 172.620 miles. Race scheduled for 70 laps but stopped after two hours. Wet. World Championship round 14

1	Jacques Laffite	Ligier JS17-Matra	63	2h01m25.205
2	John Watson	McLaren MP4/1-Ford	63	2h01m31.438
3	Gilles Villeneuve	Ferrari 126CK	63	2h03m15.480
4	Bruno Giacomelli	Alfa Romeo 179C	62	
5	Nelson Piquet	Brabham BT49C-Ford	62	
6	Elio de Angelis	Lotus 87-Ford	62	

Winner's average speed: 85.301 mph. Starting grid front row: Piquet, 1m29.211 (pole) and Reutemann, 1m29.359. Fastest lap: Watson, 1m49.475. Leaders: Jones, laps 1-6; Prost, 7-12; Laffite, 13-63

CAESARS PALACE GRAND PRIX

17 October 1981. Caesars Palace, Las Vegas. 75 laps of a 2.268-mile circuit = 170.100 miles. Dry, hot and sunny. World Championship round 15

1	Alan Jones	Williams FW07C-Ford	75	1h44m09.077
2	Alain Prost	Renault RE30	75	1h44m29.125
3	Bruno Giacomelli	Alfa Romeo 179C	75	1h44m29.505
4	Nigel Mansell	Lotus 87-Ford	75	1h44m56.550
5	Nelson Piquet	Brabham BT49C-Ford	75	1h45m25.515
6	Jacques Laffite	Ligier JS17-Matra	75	1h45m27.252

Winner's average speed: 97.992 mph. Starting grid front row: Reutemann, 1m17.821 (pole) and Jones, 1m17.995. Fastest lap: Pironi, 1m20.156. Leaders: Jones, laps 1-75

1982 Gilles Villeneuve controversially lost to teammate Didier Pironi at Imola just two weeks before being fatally injured while qualifying in Belgium.

1982

The latest generation of Grand Prix cars continued to generate more and more downforce. To maintain the optimum attitude of the car and its aerodynamics to the track, the cars ran rock-hard springs with virtually no suspension movement. Combined with cornering forces of up to four times gravity, these cars were the most physically demanding of all time, and led to neck and back injuries for some drivers.

The season's early races were marred first by controversy and then by tragedy. As turbocharged engines became increasingly powerful, the Ford-powered teams introduced "water-cooled brakes" that allowed their cars to race under the minimum weight of 580kg. After a race, teams were allowed to replenish cooling fluids before their cars were weighed. Designers took advantage of this rule by introducing large containers, which were empty during competition but filled with water before being weighed in scrutineering. FISA ruled that the systems had nothing to do with cooling, and disqualified the first two cars from the Brazilian GP for being underweight. The ruling body finally clarified the rules in Belgium and the systems remained outlawed.

The FOCA teams (apart from Tyrrell, which had commitments to a new Italian sponsor) withdrew from the San Marino GP in protest, leaving Didier Pironi to beat Gilles Villeneuve in a controversial Ferrari 1-2. Villeneuve felt that Pironi had disobeyed team orders to steal the victory, and a feud began between the two formerly close friends.

This dispute was totally overshadowed by the accident that befell Villeneuve ten minutes from the end of final qualifying for the Belgian GP. Pushing to make the most of his last set of qualifying tyres, the Canadian clipped a slow-moving March, launching the Ferrari into a terrifying roll that left Villeneuve fatally injured. The Canadian GP was also marred by the death of rookie Ricardo Paletti in a start-line accident.

Pironi withdrew from the Belgian race, but returned to take the points lead in the championship. But a severe accident in a wet practice session at Hockenheim caused injuries that ended Pironi's career. Villeneuve's replacement, Patrick Tambay, lifted the team by winning that race.

With series leader Pironi absent, Williams driver Keke Rosberg took the World Championship, despite winning only once. McLaren's John Watson won in Belgium and from the ninth row in Detroit, but lost the title at the final round. His new teammate was none other than Niki Lauda, who won for McLaren at Long Beach and Brands Hatch. Renault continued to be fast but fragile, with both Alain Prost and Rene Arnoux winning two events.

Brabham alternated between the Ford-powered BT49 and the new BT50, which used an exclusive BMW turbo. Riccardo Patrese won a bizarre Monaco GP after spinning his BT49. Then Prost and three other drivers retired in the closing laps when placed to win. Nelson Piquet used the turbo BMW to win in Canada, and Detroit after failing to qualify in Detroit. The Brabham team also reintroduced refuelling in Grands Prix, as over a full race distance it gave a tactical advantage.

Two former World Champion teams returned to the winner's circle in 1982. Michele Alboreto won in Las Vegas for Tyrrell, while Elio de Angelis held off Rosberg in Austria by 0.05 seconds to score the last victory for Lotus before founder Colin Chapman died in December.

QUINDRINK-POINTERWARE GRAND PRIX OF SOUTH AFRICA

23 January 1982. Kyalami. 77 laps of a 2.550-mile circuit = 196.350 miles. Hot, dry and sunny. World Championship round 1

1	Alain Prost	Renault RE30B	77	1h32m08.401
2	Carlos Reutemann	Williams FW07C-Ford	77	1h32m23.347
3	Rene Arnoux	Renault RE30B	77	1h32m36.301
4	Niki Lauda	McLaren MP4/1B-Ford	77	1h32m40.514
5	Keke Rosberg	Williams FW07C-Ford	77	1h32m54.540
6	John Watson	McLaren MP4/1B-Ford	77	1h32m59.394

Winner's average speed: 127.860 mph. Starting grid front row: Arnoux, 1m06.351 (pole) and Piquet, 1m06.625. Fastest lap: Prost, 1m08.278. Leaders: Arnoux, laps 1-13, 41-67; Prost, 14-40, 68-77.

GRANDE PREMIO DO BRASIL

21 March 1982. Rio de Janeiro. 63 laps of a 3.126-mile circuit = 196.938 miles. Hot, dry and sunny. World Championship round 2

1	Alain Prost	Renault RE30B	63	1h44m33.134
2	John Watson	McLaren MP4/1B-Ford	63	1h44m36.124
3	Nigel Mansell	Lotus 91-Ford	63	1h45m09.993

4	Michele Alboreto	Tyrrell 011-Ford	63	1h45m23.895
5	Manfred Winkelhock	ATS D5-Ford	62	
6	Didier Pironi	Ferrari 126C2	62	

Nelson Piquet (Brabham BT49D-Ford), 1h43m53.760, and Keke Rosberg (Williams FW07C-Ford), 1h44m05.737, finished first and second on the road but were disqualified due to their cars being under the weight limit. Winner's average speed: 113.018 mph. Starting grid front row: Prost, 1m28.808 (pole) and Villeneuve, 1m29.173. Fastest lap: Prost, 1m37.016 (Piquet, 1m36.582 and Rosberg, 1m36.984 were disqualified). Leaders: Villeneuve, laps 1-29; Patrese, 30-32; Prost, 33-63 (Piquet led laps 30-63 with Rosberg second on the road)

TOYOTA GRAND PRIX OF LONG BEACH

4 April 1982. Long Beach. 75.5 laps of a 2.130-mile circuit = 160.815 miles. Hot, dry and sunny. World Championship round 3

1	Niki Lauda	McLaren MP4/1B-Ford	75	1h58m25.318
2	Keke Rosberg	Williams FW07C-Ford	75	1h58m39.978
3	Riccardo Patrese	Brabham BT49D-Ford	75	1h59m44.461
4	Michele Alboreto	Tyrrell 011-Ford	75	1h59m46.265
5	Elio de Angelis	Lotus 91-Ford	74	
6	John Watson	McLaren MP4/1B-Ford	74	

Gilles Villeneuve (Ferrari 126C2), 1h59m29.606, finished third on the road but was disqualified due to illegal rear wing. Winner's average speed: 81.479 mph. Starting grid front row: de Cesaris, 1m27.316 (pole) and Lauda, 1m27.436. Fastest lap: Lauda, 1m30.831. Leaders: de Cesaris, laps 1-14; Lauda, 15-75

GRAN PREMIO DI SAN MARINO

25 April 1982. Imola. 60 laps of a 3.132-mile circuit = 187.920 miles. Warm, dry and sunny. World Championship round 4

1	Didier Pironi	Ferrari 126C2	60	1h36m38.887
2	Gilles Villeneuve	Ferrari 126C2	60	1h36m39.253
3	Michele Alboreto	Tyrrell 011-Ford	60	1h37m46.571
4	Jean-Pierre Jarier	Osella FA1C-Ford	59	
5	Eliseo Salazar	ATS D5-Ford	57	

No other finishers. Manfred Winkelhock (ATS D5-Ford), 54 laps completed, finished sixth on the road but was disqualified due to his car being under the weight limit. Winner's average speed: 116.662 mph. Starting grid front row: Arnoux, 1m29.765 (pole) and Prost, 1m30.249. Fastest lap: Pironi, 1m35.036. Leaders: Arnoux, laps 1-26, 31-44; Villeneuve, 27-30, 45, 49-52, 59; Pironi, 46-48, 53-58, 60

GRAND PRIX DE BELGIQUE

9 May 1982. Zolder. 70 laps of a 2.648-mile circuit = 185.360 miles. Warm and dry. World Championship round 5

1	John Watson	McLaren MP4/1B-Ford	70	1h35m41.995
2	Keke Rosberg	Williams FW08-Ford	70	1h35m49.263
3	Eddie Cheever	Ligier JS17-Matra	69	
4	Elio de Angelis	Lotus 91-Ford	68	
5	Nelson Piquet	Brabham BT50-BMW	67	
6	Chico Serra	Fittipaldi F8D-Ford	67	

Niki Lauda (McLaren MP4/1B-Ford), 1h36m50.132, finished third on the road but disqualified due to his car being under the weight limit. Winner's average speed: 116.213 mph. Starting grid front row: Prost, 1m15.701 (pole) and Arnoux, 1m15.730. Fastest lap: Watson, 1m20.214. Leaders: Arnoux, laps 1-4; Rosberg, 5-68; Watson, 69-70

GRAND PRIX DE MONACO

23 May 1982. Monte Carlo. 76 laps of a 2.058-mile circuit = 156.408 miles. Warm and dry, rain in closing laps. World Championship round 6

1	Riccardo Patrese	Brabham BT49D-Ford	76	1h54m11.259
2	Didier Pironi	Ferrari 126C2	75	electrics
3	Andrea de Cesaris	Alfa Romeo 182	75	out of fuel
4	Nigel Mansell	Lotus 91-Ford	75	
5	Elio de Angelis	Lotus 91-Ford	75	
6	Derek Daly	Williams FW08-Ford	74	accident

Winner's average speed: 82.185 mph. Starting grid front row: Arnoux, 1m23.281 (pole) and Patrese, 1m23.791. Fastest lap: Patrese, 1m26.354. Leaders: Arnoux, laps 1-14; Prost, 15-73; Patrese, 74, 76; Pironi, 75

Formula 1

driver	car	ZA Q	R	BR Q	R	LB Q	R	RSM Q	R	B Q	R	MC Q	R	DET Q	R
Michele Alboreto	Tyrrell 011-Ford	10	7	13	4	12	4	5	3	5	R	9	10	16	R
Mario Andretti	Williams FW07C-Ford	-	-	-	-	14	R	-	-	-	-	-	-	-	-
	Ferrari 126C2	-	-	-	-	-	-	-	-	-	-	-	-	-	-
Elio de Angelis	Lotus 87B-Ford	15	8	-	-	-	-	-	-	-	-	-	-	-	-
	Lotus 91-Ford	-	-	11	R	16	5	-	-	13	4	15	5	8	R
Rene Arnoux	Renault RE30B	1	3	4	R	3	R	1	R	2	R	1	R	15	10
Mauro Baldi	Arrows A4-Ford	27	DNQ	19	10	30	DNQ	-	-	28	R	21	DNQ	24	R
	Arrows A5-Ford	-	-	-	-	-	-	-	-	-	-	-	-	-	-
Raul Boesel	March 821-Ford	21	15	17	R	23	9	-	-	26	8	29	NPQ	21	R
Slim Borgudd	Tyrrell 011-Ford	23	16	21	7	24	10	-	-	-	-	-	-	-	-
Tommy Byrne	Theodore TY02-Ford	-	-	-	-	-	-	-	-	-	-	-	-	-	-
Andrea de Cesaris	Alfa Romeo 179D	16	13	-	-	-	-	-	-	-	-	-	-	-	-
	Alfa Romeo 182	-	-	10	R	1	R	7	R	7	R	7	3	2	R
Eddie Cheever	Ligier JS17-Matra	17	R	26	R	13	R	-	-	16	3	-	-	9	2
	Ligier JS19-Matra	-	-	-	-	-	-	-	-	-	-	16	R	-	-
Derek Daly	Theodore TY01-Ford	24	14	-	-	-	-	-	-	-	-	-	-	-	-
	Theodore TY02-Ford	-	-	20	R	22	R	-	-	-	-	-	-	-	-
	Williams FW08-Ford	-	-	-	-	-	-	-	-	15	R	8	6	12	5
Teo Fabi	Toleman TG181B-Hart	NT	DNQ	27	DNQ	-	-	-	-	-	-	-	-	-	-
	Toleman TG181C-Hart	-	-	-	-	27	DNQ	10	NC	23	R	27	NPQ	-	-
Bruno Giacomelli	Alfa Romeo 179D	19	11	-	-	-	-	-	-	-	-	-	-	-	-
	Alfa Romeo 182	-	-	16	R	5	R	6	R	17	R	3	R	6	R
Roberto Guerrero	Ensign N180B-Ford	NT	DNP	-	-	-	-	-	-	-	-	-	-	-	-
	Ensign N181-Ford	-	-	28	DNQ	19	R	-	-	29	DNQ	26	DNQ	11	R
Brian Henton	Arrows A4-Ford	29	DNQ	29	DNQ	20	R	-	-	-	-	-	-	-	-
	Tyrrell 011-Ford	-	-	-	-	-	-	11	R	22	R	17	8	20	9
Jean-Pierre Jarier	Osella FA1C-Ford	26	R	23	9	10	R	9	4	18	R	25	DNQ	22	R
Rupert Keegan	March 821-Ford	-	-	-	-	-	-	-	-	-	-	-	-	-	-
Jacques Laffite	Ligier JS17-Matra	11	R	24	R	15	R	-	-	19	9	-	-	13	6
	Ligier JS19-Matra	-	-	-	-	-	-	-	-	-	-	18	R	-	-
Jan Lammers	Theodore TY02-Ford	-	-	-	-	-	-	-	-	30	DNQ	22	DNQ	NT	DNQ
Niki Lauda	McLaren MP4/1B-Ford	13	4	5	R	2	1F	-	-	4	DSQ	12	R	10	R
Geoff Lees	Theodore TY02-Ford	-	-	-	-	-	-	-	-	-	-	-	-	-	-
	Lotus 91-Ford	-	-	-	-	-	-	-	-	-	-	-	-	-	-
Nigel Mansell	Lotus 87B-Ford	18	R	-	-	-	-	-	-	-	-	-	-	-	-
	Lotus 91-Ford	-	-	14	3	17	7	-	-	9	R	11	4	7	R
Jochen Mass	March 821-Ford	22	12	22	8	21	8	-	-	27	R	23	DNQ	18	7
Roberto Moreno	Lotus 91-Ford	-	-	-	-	-	-	-	-	-	-	-	-	-	-
Ricardo Paletti	Osella FA1C-Ford	28	DNQ	31	NPQ	28	DNQ	13	R	31	NPQ	28	NPQ	23	DNS
Riccardo Patrese	Brabham BT50-BMW	4	R	-	-	-	-	-	-	11	R	-	-	-	-
	Brabham BT49D-Ford	-	-	9	R	18	3	-	-	-	-	2	1F	14	R
Nelson Piquet	Brabham BT50-BMW	2	R	-	-	-	-	-	-	10	5	13	R	28	DNQ
	Brabham BT49D-Ford	-	-	7	DSQ	6	R	-	-	-	-	-	-	-	-
Didier Pironi	Ferrari 126C2	6	18	8	6	9	R	4	1F	6	DNS	5	2	4	3
Alain Prost	Renault RE30B	5	1F	1	1F	4	R	2	R	1	R	4	7	1	NCF
Carlos Reutemann	Williams FW07C-Ford	8	2	6	R	-	-	-	-	-	-	-	-	-	-
Keke Rosberg	Williams FW07C-Ford	7	5	3	DSQ	8	2	-	-	-	-	-	-	-	-
	Williams FW08-Ford	-	-	-	-	-	-	-	-	3	2	6	R	3	4
Eliseo Salazar	ATS D5-Ford	12	9	18	R	26	R	14	5	20	R	20	R	25	R
Chico Serra	Fittipaldi F8D-Ford	25	17	25	R	29	DNQ	-	-	25	6	30	NPQ	26	11
	Fittipaldi F9-Ford	-	-	-	-	-	-	-	-	-	-	-	-	-	-
Marc Surer	Arrows A4-Ford	-	-	-	-	-	-	-	-	24	7	19	9	19	8
	Arrows A5-Ford	-	-	-	-	-	-	-	-	-	-	-	-	-	-
Patrick Tambay	Arrows A4-Ford	NT	DNP	-	-	-	-	-	-	-	-	-	-	-	-
	Ferrari 126C2	-	-	-	-	-	-	-	-	-	-	-	-	-	-
Gilles Villeneuve	Ferrari 126C2	3	R	2	R	7	DSQ	3	2	8	DNS	31	NPQ	27	DNQ
Emilio de Villota	March 821-Ford	-	-	-	-	-	-	-	-	32	NPQ	-	-	-	-
Derek Warwick	Toleman TG181B-Hart	14	R	30	DNQ	-	-	-	-	-	-	-	-	-	-
	Toleman TG181C-Hart	-	-	-	-	31	NPQ	8	DNS	21	R	24	DNQ	-	-
	Toleman TG183-Hart	-	-	-	-	-	-	-	-	-	-	-	-	-	-
John Watson	McLaren MP4/1B-Ford	9	6	12	2	11	6	-	-	12	1F	10	R	17	1
Manfred Winkelhock	ATS D5-Ford	20	10	15	5	25	R	12	DSQ	14	R	14	R	5	R

CDN		NL		GB		F		D		A		CH		I		LV	
Q	R	Q	R	Q	R	Q	R	Q	R	Q	R	Q	R	Q	R	Q	R
15	R	14	7	9	NC	15	6	7	4	8	R	12	7	11	5	3	1F
-	-	-	-	-	-	-	-	-	-	-	-	-	-	-	-	-	-
-	-	-	-	-	-	-	-	-	-	-	-	-	-	1	3	7	R
10	4	15	R	7	4	13	R	14	R	7	1	15	6	17	R	21	R
2	R	1	R	6	R	1	1	3	2	5	R	2	16	6	1F	2	R
17	8	16	6	26	9	25	R	24	R	23	6	29	DNQ	-	-	24	11
-	-	-	-	-	-	-	-	-	-	-	-	-	-	24	12	-	-
21	R	22	R	30	DNQ	30	DNQ	25	R	27	DNQ	24	R	29	DNQ	25	13
-	-	-	-	-	-	-	-	-	-	-	-	-	-	-	-	-	-
-	-	-	-	-	-	-	-	28	DNQ	26	R	28	DNQ	30	DNQ	27	R
-	-	-	-	-	-	-	-	-	-	-	-	-	-	-	-	-	-
9	6	9	R	11	R	7	R	9	R	11	R	5	10	9	10	18	9
12	10	-	-	24	R	-	-	-	-	-	-	-	-	-	-	-	-
-	-	29	DNQ	-	-	19	16	13	R	22	R	16	NC	14	6	4	3
-	-	-	-	-	-	-	-	-	-	-	-	-	-	-	-	-	-
13	7	12	5	10	5	11	7	20	R	9	R	7	9	13	R	14	6
-	-	-	-	-	-	-	-	-	-	-	-	-	-	-	-	-	-
-	-	28	DNQ	15	R	21	R	NT	DNP	17	R	23	R	22	R	28	DNQ
-	-	-	-	-	-	-	-	-	-	-	-	-	-	-	-	-	-
5	R	8	11	14	7	8	9	12	5	13	R	9	12	8	R	16	10
-	-	-	-	-	-	-	-	-	-	-	-	-	-	-	-	-	-
20	R	27	DNQ	19	R	28	DNQ	22	8	16	R	19	R	18	NC	15	DNS
-	-	-	-	-	-	-	-	-	-	-	-	-	-	-	-	-	-
26	NC	20	R	17	8F	23	10	18	7	19	R	18	11	20	R	19	8
18	R	23	14	18	R	17	R	21	R	28	DNQ	17	R	15	R	20	DNS
-	-	-	-	-	-	-	-	29	DNQ	24	R	22	R	27	DNQ	26	12
19	R	21	R	-	-	-	-	-	-	-	-	-	-	-	-	-	-
-	-	-	-	20	R	16	14	16	R	14	3	13	R	21	R	11	R
-	-	26	R	28	DNQ	27	DNQ	-	-	-	-	-	-	-	-	-	-
11	R	5	4	5	1	9	8	8	DNS	10	5	4	3	10	R	13	R
25	R	-	-	-	-	-	-	-	-	-	-	-	-	-	-	-	-
-	-	-	-	-	-	24	12	-	-	-	-	-	-	-	-	-	-
14	R	-	-	23	R	-	-	19	9	12	R	26	8	23	7	22	R
22	11	24	R	25	10	26	R	-	-	-	-	-	-	-	-	-	-
-	-	30	DNQ	-	-	-	-	-	-	-	-	-	-	-	-	-	-
23	R	-	-	-	-	-	-	-	-	-	-	-	-	-	-	-	-
-	-	10	15	2	R	4	RF	6	R	2	R	3	5	4	R	5	R
8	2	-	-	-	-	-	-	-	-	-	-	-	-	-	-	-	-
4	1	3	2	3	R	6	R	4	RF	1	RF	6	4	2	R	12	R
-	-	-	-	-	-	-	-	-	-	-	-	-	-	-	-	-	-
1	9F	4	1	4	2	3	3	1	DNS	-	-	-	-	-	-	-	-
3	R	2	R	8	6	2	2	2	R	3	8	1	2F	5	R	1	4
-	-	-	-	-	-	-	-	-	-	-	-	-	-	-	-	-	-
7	R	7	3	1	R	10	5	10	3	6	2	8	1	7	8	6	5
24	R	25	13	29	DNQ	22	R	23	R	29	DNQ	25	14	25	9	29	DNQ
29	DNQ	19	R	21	R	-	-	-	-	-	-	-	-	-	-	-	-
-	-	-	-	-	-	29	DNQ	26	11	20	7	27	DNQ	26	11	30	DNQ
16	5	17	10	22	R	20	13	27	6	21	R	-	-	19	R	-	-
-	-	-	-	-	-	-	-	-	-	-	-	14	15	-	-	17	7
-	-	6	8	13	3	5	4	5	1	4	4	10	DNS	3	2	8	DNS
28	DNQ	31	NPQ	-	-	-	-	-	-	-	-	-	-	-	-	-	-
-	-	13	RF	16	R	14	15	15	10	15	R	21	R	-	-	-	-
-	-	-	-	-	-	-	-	-	-	-	-	-	-	16	R	10	R
6	3	11	9	12	R	12	R	11	R	18	R	11	13	12	4	9	2
27	DNQ	18	12	27	DNQ	18	11	17	R	25	R	20	R	28	DNQ	23	NC

Formula 1

1982 FINAL CHAMPIONSHIP POSITIONS

Drivers						Manufacturers		
1	Keke Rosberg	44	15=	Carlos Reutemann	6	1	Ferrari	74
2=	Didier Pironi	39		Gilles Villeneuve	6	2	McLaren-Ford	69
	John Watson	39	17=	Andrea de Cesaris	5	3	Renault	62
4	Alain Prost	34		Jacques Laffite	5	4	Williams-Ford	58
5	Niki Lauda	30	19	Mario Andretti	4	5	Lotus-Ford	30
6	Rene Arnoux	28	20=	Jean-Pierre Jarier	3	6	Tyrrell-Ford	25
7=	Michele Alboreto	25		Marc Surer	3	7	Brabham-BMW	22
	Patrick Tambay	25	22=	Mauro Baldi	2	8	Ligier-Matra	20
9	Elio de Angelis	23		Bruno Giacomelli	2	9	Brabham-Ford	19
10	Riccardo Patrese	21		Eliseo Salazar	2	10	Alfa Romeo	7
11	Nelson Piquet	20		Manfred Winkelhock	2	11	Arrows-Ford	5
12	Eddie Cheever	15	26	Chico Serra	1	12	ATS-Ford	4
13	Derek Daly	8		Best 11 results count		13	Osella-Ford	3
14	Nigel Mansell	7				14	Fittipaldi-Ford	1

DETROIT GRAND PRIX

6 June 1982. Detroit. 62 laps of a 2.493-mile circuit = 154.566 miles. Race scheduled for 70 laps, stopped after 6 laps due to an accident, restarted over remaining 64 laps but stopped after two hours. Warm, dry and sunny. World Championship round 7

1	John Watson	McLaren MP4/1B-Ford	62	1h58m41.043
2	Eddie Cheever	Ligier JS17-Matra	62	1h58m56.769
3	Didier Pironi	Ferrari 126C2	62	1h59m09.120
4	Keke Rosberg	Williams FW08-Ford	62	1h59m53.019
5	Derek Daly	Williams FW08-Ford	62	2h00m04.800
6	Jacques Laffite	Ligier JS17-Matra	61	

Winner's average speed: 78.140 mph. Starting grid front row: Prost, 1m48.537 (pole) and de Cesaris, 1m48.872. Fastest lap: Prost, 1m50.438. Leaders: Prost, laps 1-22; Rosberg, 23-36; Watson, 37-62

GRAND PRIX LABATT DU CANADA

13 June 1982. Montreal. 70 laps of a 2.740-mile circuit = 191.800 miles. Race stopped after start-line accident, restarted over original distance. Cold but dry. World Championship round 8

1	Nelson Piquet	Brabham BT50-BMW	70	1h46m39.577
2	Riccardo Patrese	Brabham BT49D-Ford	70	1h46m53.376
3	John Watson	McLaren MP4/1B-Ford	70	1h47m41.413
4	Elio de Angelis	Lotus 91-Ford	69	
5	Marc Surer	Arrows A4-Ford	69	
6	Andrea de Cesaris	Alfa Romeo 182	68	out of fuel

Winner's average speed: 107.895 mph. Starting grid front row: Pironi, 1m27.509 (pole) and Arnoux, 1m27.895. Fastest lap: Pironi, 1m28.323. Leaders: Pironi, lap 1; Arnoux, laps 2-8; Piquet, 9-70

GROTE PRIJS VAN NEDERLAND

3 July 1982. Zandvoort. 72 laps of a 2.642-mile circuit = 190.224 miles. Warm, dry and sunny. World Championship round 9

1	Didier Pironi	Ferrari 126C2	72	1h38m03.254
2	Nelson Piquet	Brabham BT50-BMW	72	1h38m24.903
3	Keke Rosberg	Williams FW08-Ford	72	1h38m25.619
4	Niki Lauda	McLaren MP4/1B-Ford	72	1h39m26.974
5	Derek Daly	Williams FW08-Ford	71	
6	Mauro Baldi	Arrows A4-Ford	71	

Winner's average speed: 116.399 mph. Starting grid front row: Arnoux, 1m14.233 (pole) and Prost, 1m14.660. Fastest lap: Warwick, 1m19.780. Leaders: Prost, laps 1-4; Pironi, 5-72

MARLBORO BRITISH GRAND PRIX

18 July 1982. Brands Hatch. 76 laps of a 2.614-mile circuit = 198.634 miles. Hot, dry and sunny. World Championship round 10

1	Niki Lauda	McLaren MP4/1B-Ford	76	1h35m33.812
2	Didier Pironi	Ferrari 126C2	76	1h35m59.538
3	Patrick Tambay	Ferrari 126C2	76	1h36m12.248
4	Elio de Angelis	Lotus 91-Ford	76	1h36m15.054
5	Derek Daly	Williams FW08-Ford	76	1h36m15.242
6	Alain Prost	Renault RE30B	76	1h36m15.448

Winner's average speed: 124.713 mph. Starting grid front row: Rosberg, 1m09.540 (pole) and Patrese, 1m09.627 - Rosberg started from the back of the grid. Fastest lap: Henton, 1m13.028. Leaders: Piquet, laps 1-9; Lauda, 10-76

GRAND PRIX DE FRANCE

25 July 1982. Paul Ricard. 54 laps of a 3.610-mile circuit = 194.940 miles. Hot, dry and sunny. World Championship round 11

1	Rene Arnoux	Renault RE30B	54	1h33m33.217
2	Alain Prost	Renault RE30B	54	1h33m50.525
3	Didier Pironi	Ferrari 126C2	54	1h34m15.345
4	Patrick Tambay	Ferrari 126C2	54	1h34m49.458
5	Keke Rosberg	Williams FW08-Ford	54	1h35m04.211
6	Michele Alboreto	Tyrrell 011-Ford	54	1h35m05.556

Winner's average speed: 125.023 mph. Starting grid front row: Arnoux, 1m34.406 (pole) and Prost, 1m34.688. Fastest lap: Patrese, 1m40.075. Leaders: Arnoux, laps 1-2, 24-54; Patrese, 3-7; Piquet, 8-23

GROSSER PREIS VON DEUTSCHLAND

8 August 1982. Hockenheim. 45 laps of a 4.224-mile circuit = 190.062 miles. Hot, dry and sunny. World Championship round 12

1	Patrick Tambay	Ferrari 126C2	45	1h27m25.178
2	Rene Arnoux	Renault RE30B	45	1h27m41.557
3	Keke Rosberg	Williams FW08-Ford	44	
4	Michele Alboreto	Tyrrell 011-Ford	44	
5	Bruno Giacomelli	Alfa Romeo 182	44	
6	Marc Surer	Arrows A4-Ford	44	

Winner's average speed: 130.448 mph. Starting grid front row: Pironi, 1m47.947 (pole) and Prost, 1m48.890 - Pironi did not start. Fastest lap: Piquet, 1m54.035. Leaders: Arnoux, lap 1; Piquet, laps 2-18; Tambay, 19-45

GROSSER PREIS VON OSTERREICH

15 August 1982. Osterreichring. 53 laps of a 3.692-mile circuit = 195.676 miles. Hot, dry and sunny. World Championship round 13

1	Elio de Angelis	Lotus 91-Ford	53	1h25m02.212
2	Keke Rosberg	Williams FW08-Ford	53	1h25m02.262
3	Jacques Laffite	Ligier JS19-Matra	52	
4	Patrick Tambay	Ferrari 126C2	52	
5	Niki Lauda	McLaren MP4/1B-Ford	52	
6	Mauro Baldi	Arrows A4-Ford	52	

Winner's average speed: 138.064 mph. Starting grid front row: Piquet, 1m27.612 (pole) and Patrese, 1m27.971. Fastest lap: Piquet, 1m33.699. Leaders: Piquet, lap 1; Patrese, laps 2-27; Prost, 28-48; de Angelis, 49-53

GRAND PRIX DE SUISSE

29 August 1982. Dijon-Prenois, France. 80 laps of a 2.361-mile circuit =
188.880 miles. Hot, dry and sunny. World Championship round 14

1	Keke Rosberg	Williams FW08-Ford	80	1h32m41.087
2	Alain Prost	Renault RE30B	80	1h32m45.529
3	Niki Lauda	McLaren MP4/1B-Ford	80	1h33m41.430
4	Nelson Piquet	Brabham BT50-BMW	79	
5	Riccardo Patrese	Brabham BT50-BMW	79	
6	Elio de Angelis	Lotus 91-Ford	79	

Winner's average speed: 122.272 mph. Starting grid front row: Prost,
1m01.380 (pole) and Arnoux, 1m01.740. Fastest lap: Prost, 1m07.477.
Leaders: Arnoux, lap 1; Prost, laps 2-78; Rosberg, 79-80

GRAN PREMIO D'ITALIA

12 September 1982. Monza. 52 laps of a 3.604-mile circuit = 187.403
miles. Hot, dry and sunny. World Championship round 15

1	Rene Arnoux	Renault RE30B	52	1h22m25.734
2	Patrick Tambay	Ferrari 126C2	52	1h22m39.798
3	Mario Andretti	Ferrari 126C2	52	1h23m14.186
4	John Watson	McLaren MP4/1B-Ford	52	1h23m53.579
5	Michele Alboreto	Tyrrell 011-Ford	51	
6	Eddie Cheever	Ligier JS19-Matra	51	

Winner's average speed: 136.411 mph. Starting grid front row: Andretti,
1m28.473 (pole) and Piquet, 1m28.508. Fastest lap: Arnoux, 1m33.619.
Leaders: Arnoux, laps 1-52

CAESARS PALACE GRAND PRIX

25 September 1982. Caesars Palace, Las Vegas. 75 laps of a 2.268-mile
circuit = 170.100 miles. Hot, dry and sunny. World Championship
round 16

1	Michele Alboreto	Tyrrell 011-Ford	75	1h41m56.888
2	John Watson	McLaren MP4/1B-Ford	75	1h42m24.180
3	Eddie Cheever	Ligier JS19-Matra	75	1h42m53.338
4	Alain Prost	Renault RE30B	75	1h43m05.536
5	Keke Rosberg	Williams FW08-Ford	75	1h43m08.263
6	Derek Daly	Williams FW08-Ford	74	

Winner's average speed: 100.110 mph. Starting grid front row: Prost,
1m16.356 (pole) and Arnoux, 1m16.786. Fastest lap: Alboreto, 1m19.639.
Leaders: Prost, laps 1, 15-51; Arnoux, 2-14; Alboreto, 52-75

1983

In 1983 Grand Prix racing enjoyed a season free from
the controversy and tragedy that had marred the previous season. It was a year of change: new rules stipulated that the underside of the car between the two axles
had to be flat, rendering the "wing car" dead. Teams
partially compensated for the reduction in downforce by
using larger wings, and the cars were now less painful
to drive.

A turbocharged engine won the World Championship
for the first time, but the victors were not turbo pioneers
Renault. Alain Prost led the series for most of the season, but lost out to Nelson Piquet's Brabham-BMW at
the final race. At one stage the Renault team leader had
held an apparently secure 14-point lead, but a run of
late-season successes gave Brabham the title.

The turbo revolution continued, with new engines
built by Alfa Romeo, Porsche (financed by Techniques
d'Avant Garde for McLaren), and Honda (for newcomers
Spirit and then Williams). In addition, both BMW and
Renault supplied second teams. The venerable, normally aspirated Ford Cosworth engine recorded its last
three victories, all on temporary street circuits. At Long
Beach, John Watson came from twenty-second position
on the grid to win—a championship record. Keke
Rosberg was masterful during the damp opening laps

at Monte Carlo, and Michele Alboreto scored the last
victory for the engine and for team owner Ken Tyrrell
in Detroit.

The Belgian Grand Prix returned to a superbly
modified Spa-Francorchamps circuit for the first time
since 1970. Andrea de Cesaris dominated the race
before his Alfa Romeo engine failed, leaving Prost to
take the victory.

Rene Arnoux joined Patrick Tambay at Ferrari, and
after a slow start to the year, won in Canada and
Germany to join the championship race. When Piquet
and Prost collided while battling for the lead in
Holland, Arnoux inherited the win and appeared
poised to overtake Prost's points lead. But Arnoux's
chances evaporated in the penultimate round at
Brands Hatch when he was delayed by a spin. Tambay
won at Imola in the number 27 Ferrari made famous
by the late Gilles Villeneuve.

Mid-race pit stops for fuel, reintroduced by
Brabham in 1982, proved an advantage and were
adopted by the rest of the field. Bizarrely, second position was not awarded for the Brazilian GP after
Rosberg was disqualified for a push start in the pits—
uniquely the cars behind him were not elevated in the
official results.

GRANDE PREMIO DO BRASIL

13 March 1983. Rio de Janeiro. 63 laps of a 3.126-mile circuit = 196.938
miles. Hot, dry and sunny. World Championship round 1

1	Nelson Piquet	Brabham BT52-BMW	63	1h48m27.731
2	*not awarded			
3	Niki Lauda	McLaren MP4/1C-Ford	63	1h49m19.614
4	Jacques Laffite	Williams FW08C-Ford	63	1h49m41.682
5	Patrick Tambay	Ferrari 126C2B	63	1h49m45.848
6	Marc Surer	Arrows A6-Ford	63	1h49m45.938

*Keke Rosberg (Williams FW08C-Ford), 1h48m48.362, finished second but
was disqualified for a push start during a pit stop, other competitors not
elevated. Winner's average speed: 108.944 mph. Starting grid front row:
Rosberg, 1m34.526 (pole) and Prost, 1m34.672. Fastest lap: Piquet,
1m39.829. Leaders: Rosberg, laps 1-6; Piquet, 7-63

TOYOTA GRAND PRIX OF LONG BEACH

27 March 1983. Long Beach. 75 laps of a 2.035-mile circuit = 152.625
miles. Hot, dry and sunny. World Championship round 2

1	John Watson	McLaren MP4/1C-Ford	75	1h53m34.889
2	Niki Lauda	McLaren MP4/1C-Ford	75	1h54m02.882
3	Rene Arnoux	Ferrari 126C2B	75	1h54m48.527
4	Jacques Laffite	Williams FW08C-Ford	74	
5	Marc Surer	Arrows A6-Ford	74	
6	Johnny Cecotto	Theodore N183-Ford	74	

Winner's average speed: 80.625 mph. Starting grid front row: Tambay,
1m26.117 (pole) and Arnoux, 1m26.935. Fastest lap: Lauda, 1m28.330.
Leaders: Tambay, laps 1-25; Laffite, 26-44; Watson, 45-75

GRAND PRIX DE FRANCE

17 April 1983. Paul Ricard. 54 laps of a 3.610-mile circuit = 194.940
miles. Cool and dry. World Championship round 3

1	Alain Prost	Renault RE40	54	1h34m13.913
2	Nelson Piquet	Brabham BT52-BMW	54	1h34m43.633
3	Eddie Cheever	Renault RE40	54	1h34m54.145
4	Patrick Tambay	Ferrari 126C2B	54	1h35m20.793
5	Keke Rosberg	Williams FW08C-Ford	53	
6	Jacques Laffite	Williams FW08C-Ford	53	

Winner's average speed: 124.124 mph. Starting grid front row: Prost,
1m36.672 (pole) and Cheever, 1m38.980. Fastest lap: Prost, 1m42.695.
Leaders: Prost, laps 1-29, 33-54; Piquet, 30-32

1983 DRIVERS' RECORDS

driver	car	BR Q	BR R	LB Q	LB R	F Q	F R	RSM Q	RSM R	MC Q	MC R	B Q	B R
Kenneth Acheson	RAM-March 01-Ford	-	-	-	-	-	-	-	-	-	-	-	-
Michele Alboreto	Tyrrell 011-Ford	11	R	7	9	15	8	13	R	11	R	17	14
	Tyrrell 012-Ford	-	-	-	-	-	-	-	-	-	-	-	-
Elio de Angelis	Lotus 92-Ford	13	DSQ	-	-	-	-	-	-	-	-	-	-
	Lotus 93T-Renault	-	-	5	R	5	R	9	R	19	R	13	9
	Lotus 94T-Renault	-	-	-	-	-	-	-	-	-	-	-	-
Rene Arnoux	Ferrari 126C2B	6	10	2	3	4	7	1	3	2	R	5	R
	Ferrari 126C3	-	-	-	-	-	-	-	-	-	-	-	-
Mauro Baldi	Alfa Romeo 183T	10	R	21	R	8	R	10	10	13	6	12	R
Raul Boesel	Ligier JS21-Ford	17	R	26	7	25	R	25	9	18	R	26	13
Thierry Boutsen	Arrows A6-Ford	-	-	-	-	-	-	-	-	-	-	18	R
Johnny Cecotto	Theodore N183-Ford	19	14	17	6	17	11	23	R	27	NPQ	25	10
Andrea de Cesaris	Alfa Romeo 183T	28	DNQ	19	R	7	12	8	R	7	R	3	RF
Eddie Cheever	Renault RE30C	8	R	15	R	-	-	-	-	-	-	-	-
	Renault RE40	-	-	-	-	2	3	6	R	3	R	8	3
Corrado Fabi	Osella FA1D-Ford	24	R	27	DNQ	23	R	26	R	24	DNQ	24	R
	Osella FA1E-Alfa Romeo	-	-	-	-	-	-	-	-	-	-	-	-
Piercarlo Ghinzani	Osella FA1D-Ford	27	DNQ	28	DNQ	28	DNQ	-	-	-	-	-	-
	Osella FA1E-Alfa Romeo	-	-	-	-	-	-	28	DNQ	26	DNQ	27	DNQ
Bruno Giacomelli	Toleman TG183B-Hart	15	R	14	R	13	13	17	R	21	DNQ	16	8
Roberto Guerrero	Theodore N183-Ford	14	NC	18	R	22	R	21	R	28	NPQ	14	R
Jean-Pierre Jarier	Ligier JS21-Ford	12	R	10	R	20	9	19	R	9	R	21	R
Stefan Johansson	Spirit 201-Honda	-	-	-	-	-	-	-	-	-	-	-	-
Alan Jones	Arrows A6-Ford	-	-	12	R	-	-	-	-	-	-	-	-
Jacques Laffite	Williams FW08C-Ford	18	4	4	4	19	6	16	7	8	R	11	6
	Williams FW09-Honda	-	-	-	-	-	-	-	-	-	-	-	-
Niki Lauda	McLaren MP4/1C-Ford	9	3	23	2F	12	R	18	R	22	DNQ	15	R
	McLaren MP4/1E-TAG Porsche	-	-	-	-	-	-	-	-	-	-	-	-
Nigel Mansell	Lotus 92-Ford	22	12	13	12	18	R	15	12	14	R	19	R
	Lotus 94T-Renault	-	-	-	-	-	-	-	-	-	-	-	-
	Lotus 93T-Renault	-	-	-	-	-	-	-	-	-	-	-	-
Jonathan Palmer	Williams FW08C-Ford	-	-	-	-	-	-	-	-	-	-	-	-
Riccardo Patrese	Brabham BT52-BMW	7	R	11	10	3	R	5	RF	17	R	6	R
	Brabham BT52B-BMW	-	-	-	-	-	-	-	-	-	-	-	-
Nelson Piquet	Brabham BT52-BMW	4	1F	20	R	6	2	2	R	6	2F	4	4
	Brabham BT52B-BMW	-	-	-	-	-	-	-	-	-	-	-	-
Alain Prost	Renault RE30C	2	7	-	-	-	-	-	-	-	-	-	-
	Renault RE40	-	-	8	11	1	1F	4	2	1	3	1	1
Keke Rosberg	Williams FW08C-Ford	1	DSQ	3	R	16	5	11	4	5	1	9	5
	Williams FW09-Honda	-	-	-	-	-	-	-	-	-	-	-	-
Eliseo Salazar	RAM-March 01-Ford	26	15	25	R	27	DNQ	27	DNQ	25	DNQ	28	DNQ
Jean-Louis Schlesser	RAM-March 01-Ford	-	-	-	-	29	DNQ	-	-	-	-	-	-
Chico Serra	Arrows A6-Ford	23	9	-	-	26	R	20	8	15	7	-	-
Danny Sullivan	Tyrrell 011-Ford	21	11	9	8	24	R	22	R	20	5	23	12
	Tyrrell 012-Ford	-	-	-	-	-	-	-	-	-	-	-	-
Marc Surer	Arrows A6-Ford	20	6	16	5	21	10	12	6	12	R	10	11
Patrick Tambay	Ferrari 126C2B	3	5	1	R	11	4	3	1	4	4	2	2
	Ferrari 126C3	-	-	-	-	-	-	-	-	-	-	-	-
Jacques Villeneuve	RAM-March 01-Ford	-	-	-	-	-	-	-	-	-	-	-	-
Derek Warwick	Toleman TG183B-Hart	5	8	6	R	9	R	14	R	10	R	22	7
John Watson	McLaren MP4/1C-Ford	16	R	22	1	14	R	24	5	23	DNQ	20	R
	McLaren MP4/1E-TAG Porsche	-	-	-	-	-	-	-	-	-	-	-	-
Manfred Winkelhock	ATS D6-BMW	25	16	24	R	10	R	7	11	16	R	7	R

1983

DET Q	DET R	CDN Q	CDN R	GB Q	GB R	D Q	D R	A Q	A R	NL Q	NL R	I Q	I R	EU Q	EU R	ZA Q	ZA R
-	-	-	-	29	DNQ	27	DNQ	29	DNQ	29	DNQ	29	DNQ	27	DNQ	24	12
6	1	17	8	16	13	16	R	18	R	-	-	-	-	-	-	-	-
-	-	-	-	-	-	-	-	-	-	18	6	24	R	26	R	18	R
-	-	-	-	-	-	-	-	-	-	-	-	-	-	-	-	-	-
4	R	11	R	-	-	-	-	-	-	-	-	-	-	-	-	-	-
-	-	-	-	4	R	11	R	12	R	3	R	8	5	1	R	11	R
1	R	1	1	-	-	-	-	-	-	-	-	-	-	-	-	-	-
-	-	-	-	1	5	2	1F	2	2	10	1F	3	2	5	9	4	R
25	12	26	10	11	7	7	R	9	R	12	5	10	R	15	R	17	R
23	10	24	R	22	R	25	R	27	DNQ	24	10	27	DNQ	23	15	23	NC
10	7	15	7	17	15	14	9	19	13	21	14	18	R	18	11	20	9
26	R	23	R	27	DNQ	22	11	28	DNQ	28	DNQ	26	12	-	-	-	-
8	R	8	R	9	8	3	2	11	R	8	R	6	R	14	4	9	2
-	-	-	-	-	-	-	-	-	-	-	-	-	-	-	-	-	-
7	R	6	2	7	R	6	R	8	4	11	R	7	3	7	10	14	6
27	DNQ	25	R	-	-	-	-	-	-	-	-	-	-	-	-	-	-
-	-	-	-	28	DNQ	28	DNQ	26	10	25	11	25	R	28	DNQ	25	R
-	-	-	-	-	-	-	-	-	-	-	-	-	-	-	-	-	-
24	R	28	DNQ	26	R	26	R	25	11	27	DNQ	23	R	24	R	26	R
17	9	10	R	12	R	10	R	7	R	13	13	14	7	12	6	16	R
11	NC	21	R	21	16	24	R	21	R	20	12	21	13	21	12	-	-
19	R	16	R	25	10	19	8	20	7	22	R	19	9	22	DNS	21	10
-	-	-	-	14	R	13	R	16	12	16	7	17	R	19	14	-	-
-	-	-	-	-	-	-	-	-	-	-	-	-	-	-	-	-	-
20	5	13	R	20	12	15	6	24	R	17	R	28	DNQ	29	DNQ	-	-
-	-	-	-	-	-	-	-	-	-	-	-	-	-	-	-	10	R
18	R	19	R	15	6	18	DSQ	14	6	-	-	-	-	-	-	-	-
-	-	-	-	-	-	-	-	-	-	19	R	13	R	13	R	12	11
14	6	18	R	-	-	-	-	-	-	-	-	-	-	-	-	-	-
-	-	-	-	18	4	-	-	3	5	5	R	11	8	3	3F	7	NC
-	-	-	-	-	-	17	R	-	-	-	-	-	-	-	-	-	-
-	-	-	-	-	-	-	-	-	-	-	-	-	-	25	13	-	-
15	R	5	R	-	-	-	-	-	-	-	-	-	-	-	-	-	-
-	-	-	-	5	R	8	3	6	R	6	9	1	R	2	7	3	1
2	4	3	R	-	-	-	-	-	-	-	-	-	-	-	-	-	-
-	-	-	-	6	2	4	13	4	3	1	R	4	1F	4	1	2	3F
-	-	-	-	-	-	-	-	-	-	-	-	-	-	-	-	-	-
13	8	2	5	3	1F	5	4	5	1F	4	R	5	R	8	2	5	R
12	2	9	4	13	11	12	10	15	8	23	R	16	11	16	R	-	-
-	-	-	-	-	-	-	-	-	-	-	-	-	-	-	-	6	5
-	-	-	-	-	-	-	-	-	-	-	-	-	-	-	-	-	-
-	-	-	-	-	-	-	-	-	-	-	-	-	-	-	-	-	-
16	R	22	DSQ	23	14	21	12	23	R	26	R	22	R	-	-	-	-
-	-	-	-	-	-	-	-	-	-	-	-	-	-	20	R	19	7
5	11	14	R	19	17	20	7	22	R	14	8	20	10	17	R	22	8
3	R	4	3F	-	-	-	-	-	-	-	-	-	-	-	-	-	-
-	-	-	-	2	3	1	R	1	R	2	2	2	4	6	R	1	R
-	-	27	DNQ	-	-	-	-	-	-	-	-	-	-	-	-	-	-
9	R	12	R	10	R	9	R	10	R	7	4	12	6	11	5	13	4
21	3F	20	6	24	9	23	5	17	9	15	3	-	-	-	-	-	-
-	-	-	-	-	-	-	-	-	-	-	-	15	R	10	R	15	DSQ
22	R	7	9	8	R	NT	DNQ	13	R	9	DSQ	9	R	9	8	8	R

Formula 1

1983 FINAL CHAMPIONSHIP POSITIONS

Drivers							Manufacturers		
1	Nelson Piquet	59		14	Derek Warwick	9	1	Ferrari	89
2	Alain Prost	57		15	Marc Surer	4	2	Renault	79
3	Rene Arnoux	49		16	Mauro Baldi	3	3	Brabham-BMW	72
4	Patrick Tambay	40		17=	Elio de Angelis	2	4	Williams-Ford	36
5	Keke Rosberg	27			Danny Sullivan	2	5	McLaren-Ford	34
6=	Eddie Cheever	22		19=	Johnny Cecotto	1	6	Alfa Romeo	18
	John Watson	22			Bruno Giacomelli	1	7	Tyrrell-Ford	12
8	Andrea de Cesaris	15		Best 11 results count			8	Lotus-Renault	11
9	Riccardo Patrese	13					9	Toleman-Hart	10
10	Niki Lauda	12					10	Arrows-Ford	4
11	Jacques Laffite	11					11	Williams-Honda	2
12=	Michele Alboreto	10					12=	Lotus-Ford	1
	Nigel Mansell	10						Theodore-Ford	1

GRAN PREMIO DI SAN MARINO

1 May 1983. Imola. 60 laps of a 3.132-mile circuit = 187.920 miles. Warm, dry and sunny. World Championship round 4

1	Patrick Tambay	Ferrari 126C2B	60	1h37m52.460
2	Alain Prost	Renault RE40	60	1h38m41.241
3	Rene Arnoux	Ferrari 126C2B	59	
4	Keke Rosberg	Williams FW08C-Ford	59	
5	John Watson	McLaren MP4/1C-Ford	59	
6	Marc Surer	Arrows A6-Ford	59	

Winner's average speed: 115.201 mph. Starting grid front row: Arnoux, 1m31.238 (pole) and Piquet, 1m31.964. Fastest lap: Patrese, 1m34.437. Leaders: Arnoux, laps 1-5; Patrese, 6-34; Tambay, 35-60

GRAND PRIX DE MONACO

15 May 1983. Monte Carlo. 76 laps of a 2.058-mile circuit = 156.408 miles. Warm and damp at the start, drying later. World Championship round 5

1	Keke Rosberg	Williams FW08C-Ford	76	1h56m38.121
2	Nelson Piquet	Brabham BT52-BMW	76	1h56m56.596
3	Alain Prost	Renault RE40	76	1h57m09.487
4	Patrick Tambay	Ferrari 126C2B	76	1h57m42.418
5	Danny Sullivan	Tyrrell 011-Ford	74	
6	Mauro Baldi	Alfa Romeo 183T	74	

Winner's average speed: 80.460 mph. Starting grid front row: Prost, 1m24.840 (pole) and Arnoux, 1m25.182. Fastest lap: Piquet, 1m27.283. Leaders: Prost, lap 1; Rosberg, laps 2-76

GRAND PRIX DE BELGIQUE

22 May 1983. Spa-Francorchamps. 40 laps plus 0.407 miles (start and finish at different places on circuit) of a 4.312-mile circuit = 172.891 miles. Warm, dry and sunny. World Championship round 6

1	Alain Prost	Renault RE40	40	1h27m11.502
2	Patrick Tambay	Ferrari 126C2B	40	1h27m34.684
3	Eddie Cheever	Renault RE40	40	1h27m51.371
4	Nelson Piquet	Brabham BT52-BMW	40	1h27m53.797
5	Keke Rosberg	Williams FW08C-Ford	40	1h28m01.982
6	Jacques Laffite	Williams FW08C-Ford	40	1h28m44.609

Winner's average speed: 119.136 mph. Starting grid front row: Prost, 2m04.615 (pole) and Tambay, 2m04.626. Fastest lap: de Cesaris, 2m07.493. Leaders: de Cesaris, laps 1-18; Prost, 19-22, 24-40; Piquet, 23

DETROIT GRAND PRIX

5 June 1983. Detroit. 60 laps of a 2.500-mile circuit = 150.000 miles. Warm, dry and sunny. World Championship round 7

1	Michele Alboreto	Tyrrell 011-Ford	60	1h50m53.669
2	Keke Rosberg	Williams FW08C-Ford	60	1h51m01.371
3	John Watson	McLaren MP4/1C-Ford	60	1h51m02.952
4	Nelson Piquet	Brabham BT52-BMW	60	1h52m05.854
5	Jacques Laffite	Williams FW08C-Ford	60	1h52m26.272
6	Nigel Mansell	Lotus 92-Ford	59	

Winner's average speed: 81.158 mph. Starting grid front row: Arnoux, 1m44.734 (pole) and Piquet, 1m44.933. Fastest lap: Watson, 1m47.668. Leaders: Piquet, laps 1-9, 32-50; Arnoux, 10-31; Alboreto, 51-60

GRAND PRIX LABATT DU CANADA

12 June 1983. Montreal. 70 laps of a 2.740-mile circuit = 191.800 miles. Hot, dry and sunny. World Championship round 8

1	Rene Arnoux	Ferrari 126C2B	70	1h48m31.838
2	Eddie Cheever	Renault RE40	70	1h49m13.867
3	Patrick Tambay	Ferrari 126C2B	70	1h49m24.448
4	Keke Rosberg	Williams FW08C-Ford	70	1h49m48.886
5	Alain Prost	Renault RE40	69	
6	John Watson	McLaren MP4/1C-Ford	69	

Winner's average speed: 106.035 mph. Starting grid front row: Arnoux, 1m28.729 (pole) and Prost, 1m28.830. Fastest lap: Tambay, 1m30.851. Leaders: Arnoux, laps 1-35, 39-70; Patrese, 36-38

MARLBORO BRITISH GRAND PRIX

16 July 1983. Silverstone. 67 laps of a 2.932-mile circuit = 196.444 miles. Hot, dry and sunny. World Championship round 9

1	Alain Prost	Renault RE40	67	1h24m39.780
2	Nelson Piquet	Brabham BT52B-BMW	67	1h24m58.941
3	Patrick Tambay	Ferrari 126C3	67	1h25m06.026
4	Nigel Mansell	Lotus 94T-Renault	67	1h25m18.732
5	Rene Arnoux	Ferrari 126C3	67	1h25m38.654
6	Niki Lauda	McLaren MP4/1C-Ford	66	

Winner's average speed: 139.218 mph. Starting grid front row: Arnoux, 1m09.462 (pole) and Tambay, 1m10.104. Fastest lap: Prost, 1m14.212. Leaders: Tambay, laps 1-19; Prost, 20-36, 42-67; Piquet, 37-41

GROSSER PREIS VON DEUTSCHLAND

7 August 1983. Hockenheim. 45 laps of a 4.224-mile circuit = 190.062 miles. Warm, dry and sunny. World Championship round 10

1	Rene Arnoux	Ferrari 126C3	45	1h27m10.319
2	Andrea de Cesaris	Alfa Romeo 183T	45	1h28m20.971
3	Riccardo Patrese	Brabham BT52B-BMW	45	1h28m54.412
4	Alain Prost	Renault RE40	45	1h29m11.069
5	John Watson	McLaren MP4/1C-Ford	44	
6	Jacques Laffite	Williams FW08C-Ford	44	

Niki Lauda (McLaren MP4/1C-Ford), 44 laps completed, finished fifth on the road but disqualified due to reversing in the pits. Winner's average speed: 130.819 mph. Starting grid front row: Tambay, 1m49.328 (pole) and Arnoux, 1m49.435. Fastest lap: Arnoux, 1m53.938. Leaders: Tambay, lap 1; Arnoux, laps 2-23, 31-45; Piquet, 24-30

GROSSER PREIS VON OSTERREICH

14 August 1983. Osterreichring. 53 laps of a 3.692-mile circuit = 195.676 miles. Hot, dry and sunny. World Championship round 11

1	Alain Prost	Renault RE40	53	1h24m32.745
2	Rene Arnoux	Ferrari 126C3	53	1h24m39.580

3	Nelson Piquet	Brabham BT52B-BMW	53	1h25m00.404
4	Eddie Cheever	Renault RE40	53	1h25m01.140
5	Nigel Mansell	Lotus 94T-Renault	52	
6	Niki Lauda	McLaren MP4/1C-Ford	51	

Winner's average speed: 138.866 mph. Starting grid front row: Tambay, 1m29.871 (pole) and Arnoux, 1m29.935. Fastest lap: Prost, 1m33.961. Leaders: Tambay, laps 1-21; Arnoux, 22-27, 38-47; Piquet, 28-37; Prost, 48-53

GROTE PRIJS VAN NEDERLAND

28 August 1983. Zandvoort. 72 laps of a 2.642-mile circuit = 190.224 miles. Cool and dry. World Championship round 12

1	Rene Arnoux	Ferrari 126C3	72	1h38m41.950
2	Patrick Tambay	Ferrari 126C3	72	1h39m02.789
3	John Watson	McLaren MP4/1C-Ford	72	1h39m25.691
4	Derek Warwick	Toleman TG183B-Hart	72	1h39m58.789
5	Mauro Baldi	Alfa Romeo 183T	72	1h40m06.242
6	Michele Alboreto	Tyrrell 012-Ford	71	

Winner's average speed: 115.639 mph. Starting grid front row: Piquet, 1m15.630 (pole) and Tambay, 1m16.370. Fastest lap: Arnoux, 1m19.863. Leaders: Piquet, laps 1-41; Arnoux, 42-72

GRAN PREMIO D'ITALIA

11 September 1983. Monza. 52 laps of a 3.604-mile circuit = 187.403 miles. Warm, dry and sunny. World Championship round 13

1	Nelson Piquet	Brabham BT52B-BMW	52	1h23m10.880
2	Rene Arnoux	Ferrari 126C3	52	1h23m21.092
3	Eddie Cheever	Renault RE40	52	1h23m29.492
4	Patrick Tambay	Ferrari 126C3	52	1h23m39.903
5	Elio de Angelis	Lotus 94T-Renault	52	1h24m04.560
6	Derek Warwick	Toleman TG183B-Hart	52	1h24m24.228

Winner's average speed: 135.177 mph. Starting grid front row: Patrese, 1m29.122 (pole) and Tambay, 1m29.650. Fastest lap: Piquet, 1m34.431. Leaders: Patrese, laps 1-3; Piquet, 4-52

JOHN PLAYER GRAND PRIX OF EUROPE

25 September 1983. Brands Hatch. 76 laps of a 2.614-mile circuit = 198.634 miles. Hot, dry and sunny. World Championship round 14

1	Nelson Piquet	Brabham BT52B-BMW	76	1h36m45.865
2	Alain Prost	Renault RE40	76	1h36m52.436
3	Nigel Mansell	Lotus 94T-Renault	76	1h37m16.180
4	Andrea de Cesaris	Alfa Romeo 183T	76	1h37m20.261
5	Derek Warwick	Toleman TG183B-Hart	76	1h37m30.780
6	Bruno Giacomelli	Toleman TG183B-Hart	76	1h37m38.055

Winner's average speed: 123.165 mph. Starting grid front row: de Angelis, 1m12.092 (pole) and Patrese, 1m12.458. Fastest lap: Mansell, 1m14.342. Leaders: Patrese, laps 1-10; Piquet, 11-76

SOUTHERN SUN HOTELS GRAND PRIX OF SOUTH AFRICA

15 October 1983. Kyalami. 77 laps of a 2.550-mile circuit = 196.350 miles. Hot, dry and sunny. World Championship round 15

1	Riccardo Patrese	Brabham BT52B-BMW	77	1h33m25.708
2	Andrea de Cesaris	Alfa Romeo 183T	77	1h33m35.027
3	Nelson Piquet	Brabham BT52B-BMW	77	1h33m47.677
4	Derek Warwick	Toleman TG183B-Hart	76	
5	Keke Rosberg	Williams FW09-Honda	76	
6	Eddie Cheever	Renault RE40	76	

Winner's average speed: 126.096 mph. Starting grid front row: Tambay, 1m06.554 (pole) and Piquet, 1m06.792. Fastest lap: Piquet, 1m09.948. Leaders: Piquet, laps 1-59; Patrese, 60-77

1984

After running a close second for Renault in the 1983 season, Alain Prost surprisingly left the team and joined Niki Lauda in the new John Barnard-designed McLaren MP4/2-TAG Porsche. Prost won seven times in 1984, but it still wasn't enough to make him France's first World

Champion. Lauda won only five events, but clinched a third world title by just half a point at the final Grand Prix in Portugal.

Nelson Piquet's Brabham-BMW was often as quick as the McLarens, but poor reliability limited him to just two wins, both in North America, and McLaren remained unbeaten once the series had returned to Europe.

Derek Warwick almost won his first race for Renault in Brazil, and teammate Patrick Tambay led in France, but ultimately neither was successful. Ferrari hired Michele Alboreto, the first Italian to drive for the marque since 1973, and he scored their only win, defeating Warwick in Belgium.

The Toleman-Hart team replaced the departing Warwick with the reigning British F3 Champion, Ayrton Senna. At Imola a dispute between the team and its tyre supplier resulted in his failure to qualify, but the Brazilian's performance for the remainder of the year marked him as a future World Champion.

Senna almost recorded his first Grand Prix win in torrential rain at Monaco. The race was stopped early (half-points being awarded) as the Brazilian closed in on race leader Prost. Nigel Mansell, in his fourth season at Lotus, was also denied victory at Monte Carlo when he crashed while leading. It was Mansell's Lotus teammate Elio de Angelis who provided the most consistent challenge to the McLarens, leading in Germany and finishing in the points eleven times to finish third in the Championship.

Controversy enveloped Tyrrell, the only team still using a normally aspirated engine. After Stefan Bellof and Martin Brundle impressed by achieving podium finishes in Monaco and Detroit, respectively, FISA took fuel samples from the team at the latter race and found them to be illegal. The team was excluded from the championship and all of its 1984 results disqualified.

Fuel stops were outlawed on safety grounds, and fuel capacity was reduced. This often led to cars grinding to an embarrassing halt in the closing laps of a race after using the last of their precious 220 litres of fuel.

GRANDE PREMIO DO BRASIL

25 March 1984. Rio de Janeiro. 61 laps of a 3.126-mile circuit = 190.686 miles. Hot, dry and sunny. World Championship round 1

1	Alain Prost	McLaren MP4/2-TAG Porsche	61	1h42m34.492
2	Keke Rosberg	Williams FW09-Honda	61	1h43m15.006
3	Elio de Angelis	Lotus 95T-Renault	61	1h43m33.620
4	Eddie Cheever	Alfa Romeo 184T	60	
5	Patrick Tambay	Renault RE50	59	out of fuel
6	Thierry Boutsen	Arrows A6-Ford	59	

Martin Brundle (Tyrrell 012-Ford), 60 laps completed, finished fifth on the road but was disqualified due to illegal fuel found at Detroit GP. Winner's average speed: 111.540 mph. Starting grid front row: de Angelis, 1m28.392 (pole) and Alboreto, 1m28.898. Fastest lap: Prost, 1m36.499. Leaders: Alboreto, laps 1-11; Lauda, 12-37; Prost, 38, 51-61; Warwick, 39-50

NATIONAL PANASONIC GRAND PRIX OF SOUTH AFRICA

7 April 1984. Kyalami. 75 laps of a 2.550-mile circuit = 191.250 miles. Hot, dry and sunny. World Championship round 2

1	Niki Lauda	McLaren MP4/2-TAG Porsche	75	1h29m23.43
2	Alain Prost	McLaren MP4/2-TAG Porsche	75	1h30m29.38

Formula 1

1984 DRIVERS' RECORDS

driver	car	BR Q	BR R	ZA Q	ZA R	B Q	B R	RSM Q	RSM R	F Q	F R	MC Q	MC R
Michele Alboreto	Ferrari 126C4	2	R	10	11	1	1	13	R	10	R	4	6
Philippe Alliot	RAM 02-Hart	25	R	23	R	27	DNQ	23	R	23	R	27	DNQ
Elio de Angelis	Lotus 95T-Renault	1	3	7	7	5	5	11	3	2	5	11	5
Rene Arnoux	Ferrari 126C4	10	R	15	R	2	3F	6	2	11	4	3	3
Mauro Baldi	Spirit 101B-Hart	23	R	21	8	25	R	24	8	25	R	26	DNQ
Stefan Bellof	Tyrrell 012-Ford	22	R	25	R	21	DSQ	21	DSQ	21	R	20	DSQ
Gerhard Berger	ATS D7-BMW	-	-	-	-	-	-	-	-	-	-	-	-
Thierry Boutsen	Arrows A6-Ford	20	6	27	12	-	-	20	5	-	-	-	-
	Arrows A7-BMW	-	-	-	-	17	R	-	-	15	11	24	DNQ
Martin Brundle	Tyrrell 012-Ford	18	DSQ	26	DSQ	22	R	22	DSQ	24	DSQ	22	DNQ
Johnny Cecotto	Toleman TG183B-Hart	17	R	19	R	16	R	19	NC	-	-	-	-
	Toleman TG184-Hart	-	-	-	-	-	-	-	-	19	R	18	R
Andrea de Cesaris	Ligier JS23-Renault	14	R	14	5	13	R	12	6	27	10	7	R
	Ligier JS23B-Renault	-	-	-	-	-	-	-	-	-	-	-	-
Eddie Cheever	Alfa Romeo 184T	12	4	16	R	11	R	8	7	17	R	23	DNQ
Corrado Fabi	Brabham BT53-BMW	-	-	-	-	-	-	-	-	-	-	15	R
Teo Fabi	Brabham BT53-BMW	15	R	6	R	18	R	9	R	18	9	-	-
Jo Gartner	Osella FA1E-Alfa Romeo	-	-	-	-	-	-	26	R	-	-	-	-
	Osella FA1F-Alfa Romeo	-	-	-	-	-	-	-	-	-	-	-	-
Piercarlo Ghinzani	Osella FA1F-Alfa Romeo	21	R	20	DNS	20	R	27	DNQ	26	12	19	7
Francois Hesnault	Ligier JS23-Renault	19	R	17	10	23	R	17	R	14	DNS	17	R
Stefan Johansson	Tyrrell 012-Ford	-	-	-	-	-	-	-	-	-	-	-	-
	Toleman TG184-Hart	-	-	-	-	-	-	-	-	-	-	-	-
Jacques Laffite	Williams FW09-Honda	13	R	11	R	15	R	15	R	12	8	16	8
	Williams FW09B-Honda	-	-	-	-	-	-	-	-	-	-	-	-
Niki Lauda	McLaren MP4/2-TAG Porsche	6	R	8	1	14	R	5	R	9	1	8	R
Nigel Mansell	Lotus 95T-Renault	5	R	3	R	10	R	18	R	6	3	2	R
Pierluigi Martini	Toleman TG183B-Hart	-	-	-	-	-	-	-	-	-	-	-	-
Jonathan Palmer	RAM 01-Hart	26	8	22	R	-	-	-	-	-	-	-	-
	RAM 02-Hart	-	-	-	-	26	10	25	9	22	13	25	DNQ
Riccardo Patrese	Alfa Romeo 184T	11	R	18	4	7	R	10	R	16	R	14	R
Nelson Piquet	Brabham BT53-BMW	7	R	1	R	9	9	1	RF	3	R	9	R
Alain Prost	McLaren MP4/2-TAG Porsche	4	1F	5	2	8	R	2	1	5	7F	1	1
Keke Rosberg	Williams FW09-Honda	9	2	2	R	3	4	3	R	4	6	10	4
	Williams FW09B-Honda	-	-	-	-	-	-	-	-	-	-	-	-
Huub Rothengatter	Spirit 101B-Hart	-	-	-	-	-	-	-	-	-	-	-	-
	Spirit 101C-Ford	-	-	-	-	-	-	-	-	-	-	-	-
Ayrton Senna	Toleman TG183B-Hart	16	R	13	6	19	6	28	DNQ	-	-	-	-
	Toleman TG184-Hart	-	-	-	-	-	-	-	-	13	R	13	2F
Philippe Streiff	Renault RE50	-	-	-	-	-	-	-	-	-	-	-	-
Marc Surer	Arrows A6-Ford	24	7	24	9	24	8	-	-	20	R	21	DNQ
	Arrows A7-BMW	-	-	-	-	-	-	16	R	-	-	-	-
Patrick Tambay	Renault RE50	8	5	4	RF	12	7	14	R	1	2	6	R
Mike Thackwell	RAM 02-Hart	-	-	-	-	-	-	-	-	-	-	-	-
	Tyrrell 012-Ford	-	-	-	-	-	-	-	-	-	-	-	-
Derek Warwick	Renault RE50	3	R	9	3	4	2	4	4	7	R	5	R
Manfred Winkelhock	ATS D7-BMW	27	DNQ	12	R	6	R	7	R	8	R	12	R
	Brabham BT53-BMW	-	-	-	-	-	-	-	-	-	-	-	-

3 Derek Warwick — Renault RE50 — 74
4 Riccardo Patrese — Alfa Romeo 184T — 73
5 Andrea de Cesaris — Ligier JS23-Renault — 73
6 Ayrton Senna — Toleman TG183B-Hart — 72
Winner's average speed: 128.369 mph. Starting grid front row: Piquet, 1m04.871 (pole) and Rosberg, 1m05.058. Fastest lap: Tambay, 1m08.877. Leaders: Rosberg, lap 1; Piquet, laps 2-20; Lauda, 21-75

5 Elio de Angelis — Lotus 95T-Renault — 69
6 Ayrton Senna — Toleman TG183B-Hart — 68
Stefan Bellof (Tyrrell 012-Ford), 69 laps completed, finished sixth on the road but was disqualified due to illegal fuel found at Detroit GP. Winner's average speed: 115.209 mph. Starting grid front row: Alboreto, 1m14.846 (pole) and Arnoux, 1m15.398. Fastest lap: Arnoux, 1m19.294. Leaders: Alboreto, laps 1-70

GRAND PRIX DE BELGIQUE

29 April 1984. Zolder. 70 laps of a 2.648-mile circuit = 185.360 miles. Warm, dry and sunny. World Championship round 3

1 Michele Alboreto — Ferrari 126C4 — 70 — 1h36m32.048
2 Derek Warwick — Renault RE50 — 70 — 1h37m14.434
3 Rene Arnoux — Ferrari 126C4 — 70 — 1h37m41.851
4 Keke Rosberg — Williams FW09-Honda — 69 — out of fuel

GRAN PREMIO DI SAN MARINO

6 May 1984. Imola. 60 laps of a 3.132-mile circuit = 187.920 miles. Warm, dry and sunny. World Championship round 4

1 Alain Prost — McLaren MP4/2-TAG Porsche — 60 — 1h36m53.679
2 Rene Arnoux — Ferrari 126C4 — 60 — 1h37m07.095
3 Elio de Angelis — Lotus 95T-Renault — 59 — out of fuel

CDN		DET		DAL		GB		D		A		NL		I		EU		P	
Q	R	Q	R	Q	R	Q	R	Q	R	Q	R	Q	R	Q	R	Q	R	Q	R
6	R	4	R	9	R	9	5	6	R	12	3	9	R	11	2	5	2F	8	4
26	10	20	R	24	DNS	24	R	22	R	25	11	26	10	23	R	25	R	27	R
3	4	5	2	2	3	4	4	2	R	3	R	3	4	3	R	23	R	5	5
5	5	15	R	4	2	13	6	10	6	15	7	15	11F	14	R	6	5	17	9
-	-	-	-	-	-	-	-	-	-	-	-	-	-	-	-	24	8	25	15
22	R	16	R	17	R	26	DSQ	-	-	28	DNQ	24	DSQ	-	-	-	-	-	-
-	-	-	-	-	-	-	-	20	12	-	-	20	6	18	R	-	-	23	13
-	-	-	-	-	-	-	-	-	-	-	-	-	-	-	-	-	-	-	-
18	R	13	R	20	R	12	R	15	R	17	5	11	R	19	10	11	9	18	R
21	DSQ	11	DSQ	27	DNQ	-	-	-	-	-	-	-	-	-	-	-	-	-	-
-	-	-	-	-	-	-	-	-	-	-	-	-	-	-	-	-	-	-	-
20	9	17	R	15	R	NT	DNP	-	-	-	-	-	-	-	-	-	-	-	-
10	R	12	R	16	R	19	10	11	7	18	R	14	R	16	R	-	-	-	-
-	-	-	-	-	-	-	-	-	-	-	-	-	-	-	-	17	7	20	12
11	11	8	R	14	R	18	R	18	R	16	R	17	13	10	9	13	R	14	17
16	R	-	-	11	7	-	-	-	-	-	-	-	-	-	-	-	-	-	-
-	-	23	3	-	-	14	R	8	R	7	4	10	5	5	R	10	R	-	-
-	-	-	-	-	-	-	-	-	-	-	-	-	-	-	-	-	-	-	-
-	-	-	-	-	-	27	R	23	R	22	R	23	12	24	5	22	R	24	16
19	R	26	R	18	5	21	9	21	R	23	R	21	R	22	7	20	R	22	R
13	R	18	R	19	R	20	R	17	R	21	8	20	7	18	R	19	10	21	R
-	-	-	-	-	-	25	R	26	DSQ	27	DNQ	25	DSQ	-	-	-	-	-	-
-	-	-	-	-	-	-	-	-	-	-	-	-	-	17	4	26	R	10	11
17	R	19	5	25	4	-	-	-	-	-	-	-	-	-	-	-	-	-	-
-	-	-	-	-	-	16	R	12	R	11	R	8	R	13	R	14	R	15	14
8	2	10	R	5	RF	3	1F	7	2	4	1F	6	2	4	1F	5	4	11	2F
7	6	3	R	1	6	8	R	16	4	8	R	12	3	7	R	8	R	6	R
-	-	-	-	-	-	-	-	-	-	-	-	-	-	27	DNQ	-	-	-	-
-	-	-	-	-	-	-	-	-	-	-	-	-	-	-	-	-	-	-	-
-	-	24	R	26	R	23	R	25	R	24	9	22	9	26	R	21	R	26	R
14	R	25	R	21	R	17	12	20	R	13	10	18	R	9	3	9	6	12	8
1	1F	1	1	12	R	1	7	5	R	1	2	2	R	1	R	1	3F	1	6
2	3	2	4	7	R	2	R	1	1F	2	R	1	1	2	R	2	1	2	1
15	R	21	R	8	1	-	-	-	-	-	-	-	-	-	-	-	-	-	-
-	-	-	-	-	-	5	R	19	R	9	R	7	8	6	R	4	R	4	R
24	NC	-	-	23	R	22	NC	24	9	26	NC	27	R	25	8	-	-	-	-
-	-	27	DNQ	-	-	-	-	-	-	-	-	-	-	-	-	-	-	-	-
-	-	-	-	-	-	-	-	-	-	-	-	-	-	-	-	-	-	-	-
9	7	7	R	6	R	7	3	9	R	10	R	13	R	-	-	-	-	3	3
-	-	-	-	-	-	-	-	-	-	-	-	-	-	-	-	-	-	13	R
23	R	22	R	-	-	-	-	-	-	-	-	-	-	-	-	-	-	-	-
-	-	-	-	22	R	15	11	14	R	19	6	19	R	15	R	16	R	16	R
NT	DNP	9	R	10	R	10	8	4	5	5	R	5	6	8	R	3	R	7	7
25	R	-	-	-	-	-	-	-	-	-	-	-	-	-	-	-	-	-	-
-	-	-	-	-	-	-	-	27	DNQ	-	-	-	-	-	-	-	-	-	-
4	R	6	RF	3	R	6	2	3	3	6	R	4	R	12	R	7	R	9	R
12	8	14	R	13	8	11	R	13	R	14	DNS	16	R	21	DNS	-	-	-	-
-	-	-	-	-	-	-	-	-	-	-	-	-	-	-	-	-	-	19	10

1984 FINAL CHAMPIONSHIP POSITIONS

Drivers

1	Niki Lauda	72
2	Alain Prost	71.5
3	Elio de Angelis	34
4	Michele Alboreto	30.5
5	Nelson Piquet	29
6	Rene Arnoux	27
7	Derek Warwick	23
8	Keke Rosberg	20.5
9=	Nigel Mansell	13
	Ayrton Senna	13
11	Patrick Tambay	11
12	Teo Fabi	9
13	Riccardo Patrese	8
14=	Thierry Boutsen	5
	Jacques Laffite	5
16=	Andrea de Cesaris	3
	Eddie Cheever	3
	Stefan Johansson	3
19	Piercarlo Ghinzani	2
20	Marc Surer	1

Best 11 results count

Manufacturers

1	McLaren-TAG Porsche	143.5
2	Ferrari	57.5
3	Lotus-Renault	47
4	Brabham-BMW	38
5	Renault	34
6	Williams-Honda	25.5
7	Toleman-Hart	16
8	Alfa Romeo	11
9=	Arrows-BMW	3
	Arrows-Ford	3
	Ligier-Renault	3
12	Osella-Alfa Romeo	2

4	Derek Warwick	Renault RE50	59	
5	Thierry Boutsen	Arrows A6-Ford	59	
6	Andrea de Cesaris	Ligier JS23-Renault	58	out of fuel

Stefan Bellof (Tyrrell 012-Ford), 59 laps completed, finished fifth on the road but was disqualified due to illegal fuel found at Detroit GP. Winner's average speed: 116.366 mph. Starting grid front row: Piquet, 1m28.517 (pole) and Prost, 1m28.628. Fastest lap: Piquet, 1m33.275. Leaders: Prost, laps 1-60

GRAND PRIX DE FRANCE

20 May 1984. Dijon-Prenois. 79 laps of a 2.361-mile circuit = 186.519 miles. Warm, dry and sunny. World Championship round 5

1	Niki Lauda	McLaren MP4/2-		
		TAG Porsche	79	1h31m11.951
2	Patrick Tambay	Renault RE50	79	1h31m19.105
3	Nigel Mansell	Lotus 95T-Renault	79	1h31m35.920
4	Rene Arnoux	Ferrari 126C4	79	1h31m55.657
5	Elio de Angelis	Lotus 95T-Renault	79	1h32m18.076
6	Keke Rosberg	Williams FW09-Honda	78	

Winner's average speed: 122.711 mph. Starting grid front row: Tambay, 1m02.200 (pole) and de Angelis, 1m02.336. Fastest lap: Prost, 1m05.257. Leaders: Tambay, laps 1-40, 55-61; Lauda, 41-54, 62-79

GRAND PRIX DE MONACO

3 June 1984. Monte Carlo. 31 laps of a 2.058-mile circuit = 63.798 miles. Race scheduled for 78 laps but stopped due to heavy rain, half points awarded as less than 60% of race distance was completed. Cool and very wet. World Championship round 6

1	Alain Prost	McLaren MP4/2-		
		TAG Porsche	31	1h01m07.740
2	Ayrton Senna	Toleman TG184-Hart	31	1h01m15.186
3	Rene Arnoux	Ferrari 126C4	31	1h01m36.817
4	Keke Rosberg	Williams FW09-Honda	31	1h01m42.986
5	Elio de Angelis	Lotus 95T-Renault	31	1h01m52.179
6	Michele Alboreto	Ferrari 126C4	30	

Stefan Bellof (Tyrrell 012-Ford), 1h01m28.881, finished third on the road but was disqualified due to illegal fuel found at Detroit GP. Winner's average speed: 62.620 mph. Starting grid front row: Prost, 1m22.661 (pole) and Mansell, 1m22.752. Fastest lap: Senna, 1m54 334. Leaders: Prost, laps 1-10, 16-31; Mansell, 11-15

GRAND PRIX LABATT DU CANADA

17 June 1984. Montreal. 70 laps of a 2.740-mile circuit = 191.800 miles. Hot, dry and sunny. World Championship round 7

1	Nelson Piquet	Brabham BT53-BMW	70	1h46m23.748
2	Niki Lauda	McLaren MP4/2-		
		TAG Porsche	70	1h46m26.360
3	Alain Prost	McLaren MP4/2-		
		TAG Porsche	70	1h47m51.780
4	Elio de Angelis	Lotus 95T-Renault	69	
5	Rene Arnoux	Ferrari 126C4	68	
6	Nigel Mansell	Lotus 95T-Renault	68	

Winner's average speed: 108.162 mph. Starting grid front row: Piquet, 1m25.442 (pole) and Prost, 1m26.198. Fastest lap: Piquet, 1m28.763. Leaders: Piquet, laps 1-70

DETROIT GRAND PRIX

24 June 1984. Detroit. 63 laps of a 2.500-mile circuit = 157.500 miles. Race stopped by a first-lap accident, restarted over original distance. Hot, dry and sunny. World Championship round 8

1	Nelson Piquet	Brabham BT53-BMW	63	1h55m41.842
2	Elio de Angelis	Lotus 95T-Renault	63	1h56m14.480
3	Teo Fabi	Brabham BT53-BMW	63	1h57m08.370
4	Alain Prost	McLaren MP4/2-		
		TAG Porsche	63	1h57m37.100
5	Jacques Laffite	Williams FW09-Honda	62	

No other finishers. Martin Brundle (Tyrrell 012-Ford), 1h55m42.679, finished second on the road but was disqualified due to illegal fuel. Winner's average speed: 81.679 mph. Starting grid front row: Piquet, 1m40.980 (pole) and Prost, 1m41.640. Fastest lap: Warwick,

1m46.221. Leaders: Piquet, laps 1-63

DALLAS GRAND PRIX

8 July 1984. Fair Park. 67 laps of a 2.424-mile circuit = 162.408 miles. Race scheduled for 78 laps, stopped after two hours. Very hot, dry and sunny. World Championship round 9

1	Keke Rosberg	Williams FW09-Honda	67	2h01m22.617
2	Rene Arnoux	Ferrari 126C4	67	2h01m45.081
3	Elio de Angelis	Lotus 95T-Renault	66	
4	Jacques Laffite	Williams FW09-Honda	65	
5	Piercarlo Ghinzani	Osella FA1F-Alfa Romeo	65	
6	Nigel Mansell	Lotus 95T-Renault	64	gearbox

Winner's average speed: 80.283 mph. Starting grid front row: Mansell, 1m37.041 (pole) and de Angelis, 1m37.635. Fastest lap: Lauda, 1m45.353. Leaders: Mansell, laps 1-35; Rosberg, 36-48, 57-67; Prost, 49-56

JOHN PLAYER SPECIAL BRITISH GRAND PRIX

22 July 1984. Brands Hatch. 71 laps of a 2.614-mile circuit = 185.566 miles. Race scheduled for 75 laps, stopped after 11 laps due to an accident, restarted over an additional 60 laps. Hot, dry and sunny. World Championship round 10

1	Niki Lauda	McLaren MP4/2-		
		TAG Porsche	71	1h29m28.532
2	Derek Warwick	Renault RE50	71	1h30m10.655
3	Ayrton Senna	Toleman TG184-Hart	71	1h30m31.860
4	Elio de Angelis	Lotus 95T-Renault	70	
5	Michele Alboreto	Ferrari 126C4	70	
6	Rene Arnoux	Ferrari 126C4	70	

Winner's average speed: 124.436 mph. Starting grid front row: Piquet, 1m10.869 (pole) and Prost, 1m11.076. Fastest lap: Lauda, 1m13.191. Leaders: Piquet, laps 1-11; Prost, 12-37; Lauda, 38-71

GROSSER PREIS VON DEUTSCHLAND

5 August 1984. Hockenheim. 44 laps of a 4.224-mile circuit = 185.838 miles. Warm, dry and sunny. World Championship round 11

1	Alain Prost	McLaren MP4/2-		
		TAG Porsche	44	1h24m43.210
2	Niki Lauda	McLaren MP4/2-		
		TAG Porsche	44	1h24m46.359
3	Derek Warwick	Renault RE50	44	1h25m19.633
4	Nigel Mansell	Lotus 95T-Renault	44	1h25m34.873
5	Patrick Tambay	Renault RE50	44	1h25m55.159
6	Rene Arnoux	Ferrari 126C4	43	

Winner's average speed: 131.613 mph. Starting grid front row: Prost, 1m47.012 (pole) and de Angelis, 1m47.065. Fastest lap: Prost, 1m53.538. Leaders: de Angelis, laps 1-7; Piquet, 8-21; Prost, 22-44

GROSSER PREIS VON OSTERREICH

19 August 1984. Osterreichring. 51 laps of a 3.692-mile circuit = 188.292 miles. Race stopped on first lap due to false start, restarted over original distance. Warm, dry and sunny. World Championship round 12

1	Niki Lauda	McLaren MP4/2-		
		TAG Porsche	51	1h21m12.851
2	Nelson Piquet	Brabham BT53-BMW	51	1h21m36.376
3	Michele Alboreto	Ferrari 126C4	51	1h22m01.849
4	Teo Fabi	Brabham BT53-BMW	51	1h22m09.163
5	Thierry Boutsen	Arrows A7-BMW	50	
6	Marc Surer	Arrows A7-BMW	50	

Winner's average speed: 139.108 mph. Starting grid front row: Piquet, 1m26.173 (pole) and Prost, 1m26.203. Fastest lap: Lauda, 1m32.882. Leaders: Piquet, laps 1-39; Lauda, 40-51

GROTE PRIJS VAN NEDERLAND

26 August 1984. Zandvoort. 71 laps of a 2.642-mile circuit = 187.582 miles. Warm, dry and sunny. World Championship round 13

| 1 | Alain Prost | McLaren MP4/2- | | |
| | | TAG Porsche | 71 | 1h37m21.468 |

2	Niki Lauda	McLaren MP4/2-		
		TAG Porsche	71	1h37m31.751
3	Nigel Mansell	Lotus 95T-Renault	71	1h38m41.012
4	Elio de Angelis	Lotus 95T-Renault	70	
5	Teo Fabi	Brabham BT53-BMW	70	
6	Patrick Tambay	Renault RE50	70	

Winner's average speed: 115.604 mph. Starting grid front row: Prost, 1m13.567 (pole) and Piquet, 1m13.872. Fastest lap: Arnoux, 1m19.465. Leaders: Piquet, laps 1-10; Prost, 11-71

GRAN PREMIO D'ITALIA

9 September 1984. Monza. 51 laps of a 3.604-mile circuit = 183.799 miles. Hot, dry and sunny. World Championship round 14

1	Niki Lauda	McLaren MP4/2-		
		TAG Porsche	51	1h20m29.065
2	Michele Alboreto	Ferrari 126C4	51	1h20m53.314
3	Riccardo Patrese	Alfa Romeo 184T	50	
4	Stefan Johansson	Toleman TG184-Hart	49	
5*	Jo Gartner	Osella FA1F-Alfa Romeo	49	
6*	Gerhard Berger	ATS D7-BMW	49	

*Not entered in the World Championship, no points awarded. Winner's average speed: 137.019 mph. Starting grid front row: Piquet, 1m26.584 (pole) and Prost, 1m26.671. Fastest lap: Lauda, 1m31.912. Leaders: Piquet, laps 1-15; Tambay, 16-42; Lauda, 43-51

GROSSER PREIS VON EUROPA

7 October 1984. Nurburgring. 67 laps of a 2.822-mile circuit = 189.074 miles. Cold and dry. World Championship round 15

1	Alain Prost	McLaren MP4/2-		
		TAG Porsche	67	1h35m13.284
2	Michele Alboreto	Ferrari 126C4	67	1h35m37.195
3	Nelson Piquet	Brabham BT53-BMW	67	1h35m38.206
4	Niki Lauda	McLaren MP4/2-		
		TAG Porsche	67	1h35m56.370
5	Rene Arnoux	Ferrari 126C4	67	1h36m14.714
6	Riccardo Patrese	Alfa Romeo 184T	66	

Winner's average speed: 119.138 mph. Starting grid front row: Piquet, 1m18.871 (pole) and Prost, 1m19.175. Fastest lap: Piquet and Alboreto, 1m23.146. Leaders: Prost, laps 1-67

GRANDE PREMIO DE PORTUGAL

21 October 1984. Estoril. 70 laps of a 2.703-mile circuit = 189.210 miles. Hot, dry and sunny. World Championship round 16

1	Alain Prost	McLaren MP4/2-		
		TAG Porsche	70	1h41m11.753
2	Niki Lauda	McLaren MP4/2-		
		TAG Porsche	70	1h41m25.178
3	Ayrton Senna	Toleman TG184-Hart	70	1h41m31.795
4	Michele Alboreto	Ferrari 126C4	70	1h41m32.070
5	Elio de Angelis	Lotus 95T-Renault	70	1h42m43.922
6	Nelson Piquet	Brabham BT53-BMW	69	

Winner's average speed: 112.184 mph. Starting grid front row: Piquet, 1m21.703 (pole) and Prost, 1m21.774. Fastest lap: Lauda, 1m22.996. Leaders: Rosberg, laps 1-8; Prost, 9-70

1985

After coming so close in the two previous seasons, Alain Prost finally became the first Frenchman to win the World Championship. He clinched the title with six wins and with two races to spare. At Zandvoort, teammate Niki Lauda won by under three-tenths from Prost in his final year as a Grand Prix driver.

Prost's closest challenger was Ferrari's Michele Alboreto, who led the series after a win in Canada in June. But Prost re-established his supremacy on the quick circuits that followed, beating Alboreto by more

1985 Alain Prost continued McLaren's success by becoming France's first World Champion in 1985

than a lap at Silverstone. A series of three retirements finally ended Alboreto's hopes. Ferrari replaced Rene Arnoux with the highly rated but underused Stefan Johansson after just one race. The Swede led at Imola, but his race performances were often hampered by poor grid positions.

Ayrton Senna moved to Lotus and proved to be the quickest driver in Formula 1. But although he scored a tremendous first victory in the wet Portuguese GP, for most of the season he was unlucky and had to wait until September for a second win at Spa. The meeting had actually started in June, but was postponed after first qualifying when the newly laid track surface broke up, rendering the course's fast corners highly dangerous.

Senna's Lotus teammate Elio de Angelis managed one win (at San Marino, after Prost's McLaren had been disqualified) and a pole, but after six years with the team he signed for Brabham at the end of the season. In their continuing search for Grand Prix success, Pirelli supplied their tyres to Brabham. Nelson Piquet won in France, but otherwise did not figure strongly in his final year with the team.

Williams-Honda was the quickest combination by the end of the season, with three successive victories. Nigel Mansell finally won his first Grand Prix at Brands Hatch after more than seventy unsuccessful attempts. He followed it up with victory in the South African GP, a race which some teams boycotted for political reasons. Keke Rosberg, who had previously won in Detroit, completed the Williams hat trick at the final round, held for the first time in Australia.

After nine seasons the Renault team withdrew from racing at the end of the season. They would continue to supply Lotus, Ligier, and Tyrrell with their turbocharged engines. Toleman had a troubled season that was delayed by problems securing a tyre contract. The team was eventually bought by its sponsor, Benetton, and the cars would be known as Benettons for 1986.

JOHN PLAYER SPECIAL GRANDE PREMIO DO BRASIL

7 April 1985. Rio de Janeiro. 61 laps of a 3.126-mile circuit = 190.686 miles. Hot, dry and sunny. World Championship round 1

1	Alain Prost	McLaren MP4/2B-		
		TAG Porsche	61	1h41m26.115
2	Michele Alboreto	Ferrari 156/85	61	1h41m29.374
3	Elio de Angelis	Lotus 97T-Renault	60	
4	Rene Arnoux	Ferrari 156/85	59	

Formula 1

1985 DRIVERS' RECORDS

driver	car	BR Q	BR R	P Q	P R	RSM Q	RSM R	MC Q	MC R	CDN Q	CDN R	DET Q	DET R
Kenneth Acheson	RAM 03-Hart	-	-	-	-	-	-	-	-	-	-	-	-
Michele Alboreto	Ferrari 156/85	1	2	5	2	4	RF	3	2F	3	1	3	3
Philippe Alliot	RAM 03-Hart	20	9	20	R	21	R	23	DNQ	21	R	23	R
Elio de Angelis	Lotus 97T-Renault	3	3	4	4	3	1	9	3	1	5	8	5
Rene Arnoux	Ferrari 156/85	7	4	-	-	-	-	-	-	-	-	-	-
Mauro Baldi	Spirit 101D-Hart	24	R	24	R	26	R	-	-	-	-	-	-
Stefan Bellof	Tyrrell 012-Ford	-	-	21	6	24	R	22	DNQ	23	11	19	4
	Tyrrell 014-Renault	-	-	-	-	-	-	-	-	-	-	-	-
Gerhard Berger	Arrows A8-BMW	19	R	17	R	10	R	11	R	12	13	24	11
Thierry Boutsen	Arrows A8-BMW	12	11	16	R	5	2	6	9	7	9	21	7
Martin Brundle	Tyrrell 012-Ford	21	8	22	R	25	9	18	10	24	12	18	R
	Tyrrell 014-Renault	-	-	-	-	-	-	-	-	-	-	-	-
Ivan Capelli	Tyrrell 014-Renault	-	-	-	-	-	-	-	-	-	-	-	-
Andrea de Cesaris	Ligier JS25-Renault	13	R	8	R	13	R	8	4	15	14	17	10
Eddie Cheever	Alfa Romeo 185T	18	R	14	R	12	R	4	R	11	17	7	9
	Alfa Romeo 184TB	-	-	-	-	-	-	-	-	-	-	-	-
Christian Danner	Zakspeed 841	-	-	-	-	-	-	-	-	-	-	-	-
Teo Fabi	Toleman TG185-Hart	-	-	-	-	-	-	20	R	18	R	13	R
Piercarlo Ghinzani	Osella FA1G-Alfa Romeo	22	12	-	-	22	NC	21	DNQ	22	R	22	R
	Osella FA1F-Alfa Romeo	-	-	26	9	-	-	-	-	-	-	-	-
	Toleman TG185-Hart	-	-	-	-	-	-	-	-	-	-	-	-
Francois Hesnault	Brabham BT54-BMW	17	R	19	R	20	R	25	DNQ	-	-	-	-
	Renault RE60	-	-	-	-	-	-	-	-	-	-	-	-
Stefan Johansson	Tyrrell 012-Ford	23	7	-	-	-	-	-	-	-	-	-	-
	Ferrari 156/85	-	-	11	8	15	6	15	R	4	2	9	2
Alan Jones	Lola THL1-Hart	-	-	-	-	-	-	-	-	-	-	-	-
Jacques Laffite	Ligier JS25-Renault	15	6	18	R	16	R	16	6	19	8	16	12
Niki Lauda	McLaren MP4/2B-TAG Porsche	9	R	7	R	8	4	14	R	17	R	12	R
Nigel Mansell	Williams FW10-Honda	5	R	9	5	7	5	2	7	16	6	2	R
Pierluigi Martini	Minardi M185-Ford	25	R	25	R	-	-	-	-	-	-	-	-
	Minardi M185-Motori Moderni	-	-	-	-	19	R	26	DNQ	25	R	25	R
Jonathan Palmer	Zakspeed 841	-	-	23	R	17	DNS	19	11	-	-	-	-
Riccardo Patrese	Alfa Romeo 185T	14	R	13	R	18	R	12	R	13	10	14	R
	Alfa Romeo 184TB	-	-	-	-	-	-	-	-	-	-	-	-
Nelson Piquet	Brabham BT54-BMW	8	R	10	R	9	8	13	R	9	R	10	6
Alain Prost	McLaren MP4/2B-TAG Porsche	6	1F	2	R	6	DSQ	5	1	5	3	4	R
Keke Rosberg	Williams FW10-Honda	2	R	3	R	2	R	7	8	8	4	5	1
Huub Rothengatter	Osella FA1G-Alfa Romeo	-	-	-	-	-	-	-	-	-	-	-	-
Ayrton Senna	Lotus 97T-Renault	4	R	1	1F	1	7	1	R	2	16F	1	RF
Philippe Streiff	Ligier JS25-Renault	-	-	-	-	-	-	-	-	-	-	-	-
	Tyrrell 014-Renault	-	-	-	-	-	-	-	-	-	-	-	-
Marc Surer	Brabham BT54-BMW	-	-	-	-	-	-	-	-	20	15	11	8
Patrick Tambay	Renault RE60	11	5	12	3	11	3	17	R	10	7	15	R
	Renault RE60B	-	-	-	-	-	-	-	-	-	-	-	-
Derek Warwick	Renault RE60	10	10	6	7	14	10	10	5	6	R	6	R
	Renault RE60B	-	-	-	-	-	-	-	-	-	-	-	-
John Watson	McLaren MP4/2B-TAG Porsche	-	-	-	-	-	-	-	-	-	-	-	-
Manfred Winkelhock	RAM 03-Hart	16	13	15	NC	23	R	24	DNQ	14	R	20	R

5 Patrick Tambay   Renault RE60   59
6 Jacques Laffite   Ligier JS25-Renault   59
Winner's average speed: 112.793 mph. Starting grid front row: Alboreto, 1m27.768 (pole) and Rosberg, 1m27.864. Fastest lap: Prost, 1m36.702. Leaders: Rosberg, laps 1-9; Alboreto, 10-18; Prost, 19-61

GRANDE PREMIO DE PORTUGAL

21 April 1985. Estoril. 67 laps of a 2.703-mile circuit = 181.101 miles. Race scheduled for 69 laps, stopped after two hours. Cold and very wet. World Championship round 2

1 Ayrton Senna   Lotus 97T-Renault   67   2h00m28.006
2 Michele Alboreto   Ferrari 156/85   67   2h01m30.984
3 Patrick Tambay   Renault RE60   66
4 Elio de Angelis   Lotus 97T-Renault   66
5 Nigel Mansell   Williams FW10-Honda   65

6 Stefan Bellof   Tyrrell 012-Ford   65
Winner's average speed: 90.200 mph. Starting grid front row: Senna, 1m21.007 (pole) and Prost, 1m21.420. Fastest lap: Senna, 1m44.121. Leaders: Senna, laps 1-67

GRAN PREMIO DI SAN MARINO

5 May 1985. Imola. 60 laps of a 3.132-mile circuit = 187.920 miles. Warm, dry and sunny. World Championship round 3

1 Elio de Angelis   Lotus 97T-Renault   60   1h34m35.955
2 Thierry Boutsen   Arrows A8-BMW   59
3 Patrick Tambay   Renault RE60   59
4 Niki Lauda   McLaren MP4/2B-TAG Porsche   59
5 Nigel Mansell   Williams FW10-Honda   58
6 Stefan Johansson   Ferrari 156/85   57   out of fuel

F Q	F R	GB Q	GB R	D Q	D R	A Q	A R	NL Q	NL R	I Q	I R	B Q	B R	EU Q	EU R	ZA Q	ZA R	AUS Q	AUS R
-	-	-	-	-	-	23	R	27	DNQ	24	R	-	-	-	-	-	-	-	-
3	R	6	2	8	1	9	3	16	4	7	13	4	R	15	R	15	R	5	R
23	R	21	R	21	R	21	R	25	R	26	R	20	R	23	R	-	-	-	-
7	5	8	NC	7	R	7	5	11	5	6	6	9	R	9	5	6	R	10	DSQ
-	-	-	-	-	-	-	-	-	-	-	-	-	-	-	-	-	-	-	-
26	13	26	11	-	-	-	-	-	-	-	-	-	-	-	-	-	-	-	-
-	-	-	-	19	8	22	7	22	R	-	-	-	-	-	-	-	-	-	-
9	R	17	8	17	7	17	R	14	9	11	R	8	7	19	10	11	5	7	6
12	9	19	R	15	4	16	8	8	R	14	9	6	10	12	6	10	6	11	R
-	-	-	-	26	10	27	DNQ	-	-	-	-	-	-	-	-	-	-	-	-
21	R	20	7	-	-	-	-	21	7	18	8	21	13	16	R	17	7	17	NC
-	-	-	-	-	-	-	-	-	-	-	-	-	-	24	R	-	-	22	4
13	R	7	R	14	R	18	R	18	R	-	-	-	-	-	-	-	-	-	-
18	10	-	-	-	-	-	-	-	-	-	-	-	-	-	-	-	-	-	-
-	-	22	R	18	R	20	R	20	R	17	R	19	R	18	11	14	R	13	R
-	-	-	-	-	-	-	-	-	-	-	-	22	R	25	R	-	-	-	-
19	14	9	R	1	R	6	R	5	R	15	12	11	R	20	R	7	R	24	R
24	15	25	R	-	-	-	-	-	-	-	-	-	-	-	-	-	-	-	-
-	-	-	-	-	-	-	-	-	-	-	-	-	-	-	-	-	-	-	-
-	-	-	-	-	-	19	R	15	R	21	R	16	R	14	R	13	R	21	R
-	-	-	-	-	-	-	-	-	-	-	-	-	-	-	-	-	-	-	-
-	-	-	-	23	R	-	-	-	-	-	-	-	-	-	-	-	-	-	-
-	-	-	-	-	-	-	-	-	-	-	-	-	-	-	-	-	-	-	-
16	4	11	R	2	9	12	4	17	R	10	5	5	R	13	R	16	4	15	5
-	-	-	-	-	-	-	-	-	-	25	R	-	-	22	R	18	DNS	19	R
15	R	16	3	13	3	15	R	13	R	20	R	17	11	10	RF	-	-	20	2
6	R	10	R	12	5F	3	R	10	1	16	R	NT	DNP	-	-	8	R	16	R
8	DNS	5	R	10	6	2	R	7	6	3	11F	7	2	3	1	1	1	2	R
-	-	-	-	-	-	-	-	-	-	-	-	-	-	-	-	-	-	-	-
25	R	23	R	27	11	26	R	24	R	23	R	24	12	26	R	20	R	23	8
22	R	24	R	24	R	25	R	23	R	-	-	-	-	-	-	-	-	-	-
17	11	14	9	-	-	-	-	-	-	-	-	-	-	-	-	-	-	-	-
-	-	-	-	9	R	10	R	19	R	13	R	15	R	11	9	12	R	14	R
5	1	2	4	6	R	5	R	1	4	2	3	5	2	2	R	2	9	9	R
4	3	3	1F	3	2	1	1F	3	2F	5	1	1	3F	6	4	9	3	4	R
1	2F	1	R	4	12	4	R	2	R	2	R	10	4	4	3	3	2F	3	1F
-	-	-	-	25	R	24	9	26	NC	22	R	23	NC	27	DNQ	21	R	25	7
2	R	4	10	5	R	14	2	4	3	1	3	2	1	1	2	4	R	1	R
-	-	-	-	-	-	-	-	-	-	19	10	18	9	5	8	-	-	18	3
-	-	-	-	-	-	-	-	-	-	-	-	-	-	-	-	19	R	-	-
14	8	15	6	11	R	11	6	9	10	9	4	12	8	7	R	5	R	6	R
-	-	-	-	-	-	-	-	-	-	-	-	-	-	-	-	-	-	-	-
10	6	13	R	16	R	8	10	6	R	8	7	13	R	17	12	-	-	8	R
11	7	-	-	-	-	-	-	-	-	-	-	-	-	-	-	-	-	-	-
-	-	12	5	20	R	13	R	12	R	12	R	14	6	8	R	-	-	12	R
-	-	-	-	-	-	-	-	-	-	-	-	-	-	-	-	21	7	-	-
20	12	18	R	22	R	-	-	-	-	-	-	-	-	-	-	-	-	-	-

1985 FINAL CHAMPIONSHIP POSITIONS

Drivers

1	Alain Prost	73 (76)*
2	Michele Alboreto	53
3	Keke Rosberg	40
4	Ayrton Senna	38
5	Elio de Angelis	33
6	Nigel Mansell	31
7	Stefan Johansson	26
8	Nelson Piquet	21
9	Jacques Laffite	16
10	Niki Lauda	14
11=	Thierry Boutsen	11
	Patrick Tambay	11
13=	Marc Surer	5
	Derek Warwick	5
15=	Stefan Bellof	4
	Philippe Streiff	4
17=	Rene Arnoux	3
	Gerhard Berger	3
	Ivan Capelli	3
	Andrea de Cesaris	3

*Best 11 results count

Manufacturers

1	McLaren-TAG Porsche	90
2	Ferrari	82
3=	Lotus-Renault	71
	Williams-Honda	71
5	Brabham-BMW	26
6	Ligier-Renault	23
7	Renault	16
8	Arrows-BMW	14
9	Tyrrell-Ford	4
10	Tyrrell-Renault	3

Formula 1

Alain Prost (McLaren MP4/2B-TAG Porsche), 1h33m57.118, finished first on the road but was disqualified due to his car being under weight limit. Winner's average speed: 119.189 mph. Starting grid front row: Senna, 1m27.327 (pole) and Rosberg, 1m27.354. Fastest lap: Alboreto, 1m30.961. Leaders: Senna, laps 1-56; Johansson, 57; de Angelis, 58-60 (Prost led laps 58-60 on the road)

GRAND PRIX DE MONACO

19 May 1985. Monte Carlo. 78 laps of a 2.058-mile circuit = 160.524 miles. Cool and dry, light rain later. World Championship round 4

1	Alain Prost	McLaren MP4/2B-TAG Porsche	78	1h51m58.034
2	Michele Alboreto	Ferrari 156/85	78	1h52m05.575
3	Elio de Angelis	Lotus 97T-Renault	78	1h53m25.205
4	Andrea de Cesaris	Ligier JS25-Renault	77	
5	Derek Warwick	Renault RE60	77	
6	Jacques Laffite	Ligier JS25-Renault	77	

Winner's average speed: 86.020 mph. Starting grid front row: Senna, 1m20.450 (pole) and Mansell, 1m20.536. Fastest lap: Alboreto, 1m22.637. Leaders: Senna, laps 1-13; Alboreto, 14-17, 24-31; Prost, 18-23, 32-78

GRAND PRIX DE BELGIQUE

2 June 1985. Race postponed until 15 September due to unsafe track conditions. Spa-Francorchamps

RACE POSTPONED

Starting grid front row (after one qualifying session): Alboreto, 1m56.046 (pole) and de Angelis, 1m56.277

GRAND PRIX LABATT DU CANADA

16 June 1985. Montreal. 70 laps of a 2.740-mile circuit = 191.800 miles. Cool and dry. World Championship round 5

1	Michele Alboreto	Ferrari 156/85	70	1h46m01.813
2	Stefan Johansson	Ferrari 156/85	70	1h46m03.770
3	Alain Prost	McLaren MP4/2B-TAG Porsche	70	1h46m06.154
4	Keke Rosberg	Williams FW10-Honda	70	1h46m29.634
5	Elio de Angelis	Lotus 97T-Renault	70	1h46m45.162
6	Nigel Mansell	Williams FW10-Honda	70	1h47m19.691

Winner's average speed: 108.535 mph. Starting grid front row: de Angelis, 1m24.567 (pole) and Senna, 1m24.816. Fastest lap: Senna, 1m27.445. Leaders: de Angelis, laps 1-15; Alboreto, 16-70

DETROIT GRAND PRIX

23 June 1985. Detroit. 63 laps of a 2.500-mile circuit = 157.500 miles. Hot, dry and sunny. World Championship round 6

1	Keke Rosberg	Williams FW10-Honda	63	1h55m39.851
2	Stefan Johansson	Ferrari 156/85	63	1h56m37.400
3	Michele Alboreto	Ferrari 156/85	63	1h56m43.021
4	Stefan Bellof	Tyrrell 012-Ford	63	1h56m46.076
5	Elio de Angelis	Lotus 97T-Renault	63	1h57m06.817
6	Nelson Piquet	Brabham BT54-BMW	62	

Winner's average speed: 81.702 mph. Starting grid front row: Senna, 1m42.051 (pole) and Mansell, 1m43.249. Fastest lap: Senna, 1m45.612. Leaders: Senna, laps 1-7; Rosberg, 8-63

GRAND PRIX DE FRANCE

7 July 1985. Paul Ricard. 53 laps of a 3.610-mile circuit = 191.330 miles. Hot, dry and sunny. World Championship round 7

1	Nelson Piquet	Brabham BT54-BMW	53	1h31m46.266
2	Keke Rosberg	Williams FW10-Honda	53	1h31m52.926
3	Alain Prost	McLaren MP4/2B-TAG Porsche	53	1h31m55.551
4	Stefan Johansson	Ferrari 156/85	53	1h32m39.757
5	Elio de Angelis	Lotus 97T-Renault	53	1h32m39.956
6	Patrick Tambay	Renault RE60B	53	1h33m01.433

Winner's average speed: 125.092 mph. Starting grid front row: Rosberg, 1m32.462 (pole) and Senna, 1m32.835. Fastest lap: Rosberg, 1m39.914. Leaders: Rosberg, laps 1-10; Piquet, 11-53

MARLBORO BRITISH GRAND PRIX

21 July 1985. Silverstone. 65 laps of a 2.932-mile circuit = 190.580 miles. Race scheduled for 66 laps, stopped early in error. Warm, dry and sunny. World Championship round 8

1	Alain Prost	McLaren MP4/2B-TAG Porsche	65	1h18m10.436
2	Michele Alboreto	Ferrari 156/85	64	
3	Jacques Laffite	Ligier JS25-Renault	64	
4	Nelson Piquet	Brabham BT54-BMW	64	
5	Derek Warwick	Renault RE60B	64	
6	Marc Surer	Brabham BT54-BMW	63	

Winner's average speed: 146.274 mph. Starting grid front row: Rosberg, 1m05.591 (pole) and Piquet, 1m06.249. Fastest lap: Prost, 1m09.886. Leaders: Senna, laps 1-57, 59; Prost, 58, 60-65

GROSSER PREIS VON DEUTSCHLAND

4 August 1985. Nurburgring. 67 laps of a 2.822-mile circuit = 189.074 miles. Cool and dry. World Championship round 9

1	Michele Alboreto	Ferrari 156/85	67	1h35m31.337
2	Alain Prost	McLaren MP4/2B-TAG Porsche	67	1h35m42.998
3	Jacques Laffite	Ligier JS25-Renault	67	1h36m22.491
4	Thierry Boutsen	Arrows A8-BMW	67	1h36m26.616
5	Niki Lauda	McLaren MP4/2B-TAG Porsche	67	1h36m45.309
6	Nigel Mansell	Williams FW10-Honda	67	1h36m48.157

Winner's average speed: 118.762 mph. Starting grid front row: Fabi, 1m17.429 (pole) and Johansson, 1m18.616. Fastest lap: Lauda, 1m22.806. Leaders: Rosberg, laps 1-15, 27-44; Senna, 16-26; Alboreto, 45-67

GROSSER PREIS VON OSTERREICH

18 August 1985. Osterreichring. 52 laps of a 3.692-mile circuit = 191.984 miles. Race stopped after first-lap accident, restarted over original distance. Warm, dry and sunny. World Championship round 10

1	Alain Prost	McLaren MP4/2B-TAG Porsche	52	1h20m12.583
2	Ayrton Senna	Lotus 97T-Renault	52	1h20m42.585
3	Michele Alboreto	Ferrari 156/85	52	1h20m46.939
4	Stefan Johansson	Ferrari 156/85	52	1h20m51.656
5	Elio de Angelis	Lotus 97T-Renault	52	1h21m34.675
6	Marc Surer	Brabham BT54-BMW	51	

Winner's average speed: 143.612 mph. Starting grid front row: Prost, 1m25.490 (pole) and Mansell, 1m26.052. Fastest lap: Prost, 1m29.241. Leaders: Prost, laps 1-26, 40-52; Lauda, 27-39

GROTE PRIJS VAN NEDERLAND

25 August 1985. Zandvoort. 70 laps of a 2.642-mile circuit = 184.940 miles. Cool and dry. World Championship round 11

1	Niki Lauda	McLaren MP4/2B-TAG Porsche	70	1h32m29.263
2	Alain Prost	McLaren MP4/2B-TAG Porsche	70	1h32m29.495
3	Ayrton Senna	Lotus 97T-Renault	70	1h33m17.754
4	Michele Alboreto	Ferrari 156/85	70	1h33m18.100
5	Elio de Angelis	Lotus 97T-Renault	69	
6	Nigel Mansell	Williams FW10-Honda	69	

Winner's average speed: 119.977 mph. Starting grid front row: Piquet, 1m11.074 (pole) and Rosberg, 1m11.647. Fastest lap: Prost, 1m16.538. Leaders: Rosberg, laps 1-19; Prost, 20-33; Lauda, 34-70

GRAN PREMIO D'ITALIA

8 September 1985. Monza. 51 laps of a 3.604-mile circuit = 183.799 miles. Hot, dry and sunny. World Championship round 12

1	Alain Prost	McLaren MP4/2B-TAG Porsche	51	1h17m59.451
2	Nelson Piquet	Brabham BT54-BMW	51	1h18m51.086
3	Ayrton Senna	Lotus 97T-Renault	51	1h18m59.841

4	Marc Surer	Brabham BT54-BMW	51	1h19m00.060
5	Stefan Johansson	Ferrari 156/85	50	out of fuel
6	Elio de Angelis	Lotus 97T-Renault	50	

Winner's average speed: 141.400 mph. Starting grid front row: Senna, 1m25.084 (pole) and Rosberg, 1m25.230. Fastest lap: Mansell, 1m28.283. Leaders: Rosberg, laps 1-27, 40-44; Prost, 28-39, 45-51.

GRAND PRIX DE BELGIQUE

15 September 1985. Race originally scheduled for 2 June but meeting abandoned due to unsafe track conditions, only cars entered for that race allowed to compete. Spa-Francorchamps. 43 laps of a 4.318-mile circuit = 185.670 miles. Cool and wet, drying later. World Championship round 13

1	Ayrton Senna	Lotus 97T-Renault	43	1h34m19.893
2	Nigel Mansell	Williams FW10-Honda	43	1h34m48.315
3	Alain Prost	McLaren MP4/2B-TAG Porsche	43	1h35m15.002
4	Keke Rosberg	Williams FW10-Honda	43	1h35m35.183
5	Nelson Piquet	Brabham BT54-BMW	42	
6	Derek Warwick	Renault RE60B	42	

Winner's average speed: 118.096 mph. Starting grid front row: Prost, 1m55.306 (pole) and Senna, 1m55.403. Fastest lap: Prost, 2m01.730. Leaders: Senna, laps 1-8, 10-43; de Angelis, 9

SHELL OILS GRAND PRIX OF EUROPE

6 October 1985. Brands Hatch. 75 laps of a 2.614-mile circuit = 196.020 miles. Warm, dry and sunny. World Championship round 14

1	Nigel Mansell	Williams FW10-Honda	75	1h32m58.109
2	Ayrton Senna	Lotus 97T-Renault	75	1h33m19.505
3	Keke Rosberg	Williams FW10-Honda	75	1h33m56.642
4	Alain Prost	McLaren MP4/2B-TAG Porsche	75	1h34m04.230
5	Elio de Angelis	Lotus 97T-Renault	74	
6	Thierry Boutsen	Arrows A8-BMW	73	

Winner's average speed: 126.507 mph. Starting grid front row: Senna, 1m07.169 (pole) and Piquet, 1m07.482. Fastest lap: Laffite, 1m11.526. Leaders: Senna, laps 1-8; Mansell, 9-75

SOUTHERN HOTELS GRAND PRIX OF SOUTH AFRICA

19 October 1985. Kyalami. 75 laps of a 2.550-mile circuit = 191.250 miles. Hot, dry and sunny. World Championship round 15

1	Nigel Mansell	Williams FW10-Honda	75	1h28m22.866
2	Keke Rosberg	Williams FW10-Honda	75	1h28m30.438
3	Alain Prost	McLaren MP4/2B-TAG Porsche	75	1h30m14.660
4	Stefan Johansson	Ferrari 156/85	74	
5	Gerhard Berger	Arrows A8-BMW	74	
6	Thierry Boutsen	Arrows A8-BMW	74	

Winner's average speed: 129.835 mph. Starting grid front row: Mansell, 1m02.366 (pole) and Piquet, 1m02.490. Fastest lap: Rosberg, 1m08.149. Leaders: Mansell, laps 1-75

MITSUBISHI AUSTRALIAN GRAND PRIX

3 November 1985. Adelaide. 82 laps of a 2.347-mile circuit = 192.454 miles. Hot, dry and sunny. World Championship round 16

1	Keke Rosberg	Williams FW10-Honda	82	2h00m40.473
2	Jacques Laffite	Ligier JS25-Renault	82	2h01m26.603
3	Philippe Streiff	Ligier JS25-Renault	82	2h02m09.009
4	Ivan Capelli	Tyrrell 014-Renault	81	
5	Stefan Johansson	Ferrari 156/85	81	
6	Gerhard Berger	Arrows A8-BMW	81	

Winner's average speed: 95.689 mph. Starting grid front row: Senna, 1m19.843 (pole) and Mansell, 1m20.537. Fastest lap: Rosberg, 1m23.758. Leaders: Rosberg, laps 1-42, 45-53, 62-82; Senna, 43-44, 54-55, 58-61; Lauda, 56-57

1986

Alain Prost became the first driver to successfully defend his World Championship since Jack Brabham in 1960, in a season that climaxed in a classic three-way title fight at the final round in Adelaide. Prost appeared to have little chance against the powerful Williams-Hondas of Nigel Mansell and the pre-season favourite Nelson Piquet. But with just eighteen laps remaining and the title in his grasp, Mansell suffered a spectacular 180 mph puncture that ended his hopes. Piquet was then forced to change tyres as a precaution, handing the race and championship to a surprised but ecstatic Prost.

Williams' year had begun badly when team founder Frank Williams was paralysed in a road accident. But once the season started, Mansell was a revelation, driving with newly found maturity and speed, winning four times and overshadowing his more illustrious new teammate.

However, as the Williams teammates fought a tense battle for supremacy, Prost also won four races and finished in the points on all but three occasions. Although his McLaren was at times no match for the Williams (he was a lapped third at Brands Hatch), Prost's consistency won out over the full season.

Ayrton Senna was the fourth major title protagonist. He beat Mansell by half a car-length in a dash to the finish line at Spain's new venue in Jerez. Another victory in Detroit kept him in the championship until the end of the European season. Senna was on pole and led at half of the season's events, but ultimately his Lotus-Renault could not match his pace.

Gerhard Berger scored a first victory in Mexico after several impressive performances in the powerful Benetton-BMW. While the Goodyear-equipped cars all made tyre stops, Berger ran without pitting to give Pirelli a rare success. Teo Fabi qualified on pole twice for Benetton, but never led a lap.

This was also the year of the low-line Brabham BT55. In order to reduce frontal area and lower the centre of gravity, the car's BMW engine lay almost flat in the chassis and was mated to a new compact, seven-speed Weismann gearbox. However, the car suffered gearbox and overheating problems and failed to impress. Tragedy also touched the team when Elio de Angelis was killed in May while testing a BT55 at Circuit Paul Ricard.

Jacques Laffite also suffered career-ending injuries at the start of the British GP—the very race in which he equalled Graham Hill's long-standing record for Grand Prix starts. Keke Rosberg also retired from Formula 1 after a disappointing year at McLaren.

Finally, F1 held a race in communist Europe for the first time at the new Hungaroring outside Budapest, where a huge crowd witnessed a great race between Senna and Piquet.

GRANDE PREMIO DO BRASIL

23 March 1986. Rio de Janeiro. 61 laps of a 3.126-mile circuit = 190.686 miles. Hot, dry and sunny. World Championship round 1

1	Nelson Piquet	Williams FW11-Honda	61	1h39m32.583
2	Ayrton Senna	Lotus 98T-Renault	61	1h40m07.410
3	Jacques Laffite	Ligier JS27-Renault	61	1h40m32.342

Formula 1

1986 DRIVERS' RECORDS

driver	car	BR Q	BR R	E Q	E R	RSM Q	RSM R	MC Q	MC R	B Q	B R	CDN Q	CDN R
Michele Alboreto	Ferrari F186	6	R	13	R	5	10	4	R	9	4	11	8
Philippe Alliot	Ligier JS27-Renault	-	-	-	-	-	-	-	-	-	-	-	-
Elio de Angelis	Brabham BT55-BMW	14	8	15	R	19	R	20	R	-	-	-	-
Rene Arnoux	Ligier JS27-Renault	4	4	6	R	8	R	12	5	7	R	5	6
Allen Berg	Osella FA1F-Alfa Romeo	-	-	-	-	-	-	-	-	-	-	-	-
	Osella FA1G-Alfa Romeo	-	-	-	-	-	-	-	-	-	-	-	-
	Osella FA1H-Alfa Romeo	-	-	-	-	-	-	-	-	-	-	-	-
Gerhard Berger	Benetton B186-BMW	16	6	7	6	9	3	5	R	2	10	7	R
Thierry Boutsen	Arrows A8-BMW	15	R	19	7	12	7	14	8	14	R	12	R
	Arrows A9-BMW	-	-	-	-	-	-	-	-	-	-	-	-
Martin Brundle	Tyrrell 014-Renault	17	5	12	R	13	8	-	-	-	-	-	-
	Tyrrell 015-Renault	-	-	-	-	-	-	10	R	12	R	19	9
Alex Caffi	Osella FA1F-Alfa Romeo	-	-	-	-	-	-	-	-	-	-	-	-
Ivan Capelli	AGS JH21C-Motori Moderni	-	-	-	-	-	-	-	-	-	-	-	-
Andrea de Cesaris	Minardi M185B-Motori Moderni	22	R	24	R	23	R	25	DNQ	19	R	21	R
	Minardi M186-Motori Moderni	-	-	-	-	-	-	-	-	-	-	-	-
Eddie Cheever	Lola THL2-Ford	-	-	-	-	-	-	-	-	-	-	-	-
Christian Danner	Osella FA1F-Alfa Romeo	24	R	23	R	25	R	24	DNQ	25	R	25	R
	Arrows A8-BMW	-	-	-	-	-	-	-	-	-	-	-	-
	Arrows A9-BMW	-	-	-	-	-	-	-	-	-	-	-	-
Johnny Dumfries	Lotus 98T-Renault	11	9	10	R	17	R	22	DNQ	13	R	16	R
Teo Fabi	Benetton B186-BMW	12	10	9	5	10	R	16	R	6	7	15	R
Piercarlo Ghinzani	Osella FA1G-Alfa Romeo	23	R	21	R	26	R	21	DNQ	24	R	23	R
	Osella FA1H-Alfa Romeo	-	-	-	-	-	-	-	-	-	-	-	-
Stefan Johansson	Ferrari F186	8	R	11	R	7	4	15	10	11	3	18	R
Alan Jones	Lola THL1-Hart	19	R	17	R	-	-	-	-	-	-	-	-
	Lola THL2-Ford	-	-	-	-	21	R	18	R	16	11	13	10
Jacques Laffite	Ligier JS27-Renault	5	3	8	R	14	R	7	6	17	5	8	7
Nigel Mansell	Williams FW11-Honda	3	R	3	2F	3	R	2	4	5	1	1	1
Alessandro Nannini	Minardi M185B-Motori Moderni	25	R	25	DNS	18	R	26	DNQ	22	R	20	R
	Minardi M186-Motori Moderni	-	-	-	-	-	-	-	-	-	-	-	-
Jonathan Palmer	Zakspeed 861	21	R	16	R	20	R	19	12	20	13	22	R
Riccardo Patrese	Brabham BT55-BMW	10	R	14	R	16	6	6	R	15	8	9	R
	Brabham BT54-BMW	-	-	-	-	-	-	-	-	-	-	-	-
Nelson Piquet	Williams FW11-Honda	2	1F	2	R	2	2F	11	7	1	R	3	3F
Alain Prost	McLaren MP4/2C-TAG Porsche	9	R	4	3	4	1	1	1F	3	6F	4	2
Keke Rosberg	McLaren MP4/2C-TAG Porsche	7	R	5	4	6	5	9	2	8	6	6	4
Huub Rothengatter	Zakspeed 861	-	-	-	-	24	R	23	DNQ	23	R	24	12
Ayrton Senna	Lotus 98T-Renault	1	2	1	1	1	R	3	3	4	2	2	5
Philippe Streiff	Tyrrell 014-Renault	18	7	20	R	22	R	-	-	-	-	17	11
	Tyrrell 015-Renault	-	-	-	-	-	-	13	11	18	12	-	-
Marc Surer	Arrows A8-BMW	20	R	22	R	15	9	17	9	21	9	-	-
Patrick Tambay	Lola THL1-Hart	13	R	18	8	11	R	-	-	-	-	-	-
	Lola THL2-Ford	-	-	-	-	-	-	8	R	10	R	14	DNS
Derek Warwick	Brabham BT55-BMW	-	-	-	-	-	-	-	-	-	-	10	R

4 Rene Arnoux   Ligier JS27-Renault   61   1h41m01.012
5 Martin Brundle   Tyrrell 014-Renault   60
6 Gerhard Berger   Benetton B186-BMW   59

Winner's average speed: 114.937 mph. Starting grid front row: Senna, 1m25.501 (pole) and Piquet, 1m26.266. Fastest lap: Piquet, 1m33.546. Leaders: Senna, laps 1-2, 19, 41; Piquet, 3-18, 27-40, 42-61; Prost, 20-26

GRAN PREMIO TIO PEPE DE ESPANA

13 April 1986. Jerez. 72 laps of a 2.621-mile circuit = 188.705 miles. Warm, dry and sunny. World Championship round 2

1 Ayrton Senna   Lotus 98T-Renault   72   1h48m47.735
2 Nigel Mansell   Williams FW11-Honda   72   1h48m47.749
3 Alain Prost   McLaren MP4/2C-TAG Porsche   72   1h49m09.287
4 Keke Rosberg   McLaren MP4/2C-TAG Porsche   71
5 Teo Fabi   Benetton B186-BMW   71
6 Gerhard Berger   Benetton B186-BMW   71

Winner's average speed: 104.069 mph. Starting grid front row: Senna, 1m21.605 (pole) and Piquet, 1m22.431. Fastest lap: Mansell, 1m27.176. Leaders: Senna, laps 1-39, 63-72; Mansell, 40-62

GRAN PREMIO DI SAN MARINO

27 April 1986. Imola. 60 laps of a 3.132-mile circuit = 187.920 miles. Warm, dry and sunny. World Championship round 3

1 Alain Prost   McLaren MP4/2C-TAG Porsche   60   1h32m28.408
2 Nelson Piquet   Williams FW11-Honda   60   1h32m36.053
3 Gerhard Berger   Benetton B186-BMW   59
4 Stefan Johansson Ferrari F186   59
5 Keke Rosberg   McLaren MP4/2C-TAG Porsche   58   out of fuel
6 Riccardo Patrese Brabham BT55-BMW   58   out of fuel

Winner's average speed: 121.929 mph. Starting grid front row: Senna, 1m25.050 (pole) and Piquet, 1m25.569. Fastest lap: Piquet, 1m28.667. Leaders: Piquet, laps 1-28; Rosberg, 29-33; Prost, 34-60

GRAND PRIX DE MONACO

11 May 1986. Monte Carlo. 78 laps of a 2.068-mile circuit = 161.304

DET		F		GB		D		H		A		I		P		MEX		AUS	
Q	R	Q	R	Q	R	Q	R	Q	R	Q	R	Q	R	Q	R	Q	R	Q	R
11	4	6	8	12	R	10	R	15	R	9	2	9	R	13	5	12	R	9	R
-	-	-	-	-	-	14	R	12	9	11	R	14	R	11	R	10	6	8	8
4	R	4	5	8	4	8	4	9	R	12	10	11	R	10	7	13	15	5	7
25	R	-	-	-	-	26	12	26	R	26	R	-	-	27	13	26	16	26	NC
-	-	26	R	-	-	-	-	-	-	-	-	-	-	-	-	-	-	-	-
12	R	8	R	4	R	4	10F	11	R	2	7F	4	5	4	R	4	1	6	R
13	R	21	NC	13	NC	-	-	22	R	-	-	13	7	21	10	21	7	22	R
-	-	-	-	-	-	21	R	-	-	18	R	-	-	-	-	-	-	-	-
16	R	15	10	11	5	15	R	16	6	17	R	20	10	19	R	16	11	16	4
-	-	-	-	-	-	-	-	-	-	-	-	27	NC	-	-	-	-	-	-
-	-	-	-	-	-	-	-	-	-	-	-	25	R	25	R	-	-	-	-
23	R	23	R	21	R	23	R	-	-	23	R	-	-	-	-	-	-	-	-
-	-	-	-	-	-	-	-	20	R	-	-	21	R	16	R	22	8	11	R
10	R	-	-	-	-	-	-	-	-	-	-	-	-	-	-	-	-	-	-
19	R	18	11	23	R	17	R	-	-	22	6	16	8	22	11	20	9	24	R
-	-	-	-	-	-	-	-	21	R	-	-	-	-	-	-	-	-	-	-
14	7	12	R	10	7	12	R	8	5	15	R	17	R	15	9	17	R	14	6
17	R	9	R	7	R	9	R	13	R	1	R	1	RF	5	8	9	R	13	10
22	R	-	-	24	R	25	R	23	R	25	11	26	R	24	R	25	R	25	R
-	-	25	R	-	-	-	-	-	-	-	-	-	-	-	-	-	-	-	-
5	R	10	R	18	R	11	11	7	4	14	3	12	3	8	6	14	12	12	3
21	R	20	R	14	R	19	9	10	R	16	4	18	6	17	R	15	R	15	R
6	2	11	6	19	R	-	-	-	-	-	-	-	-	-	-	-	-	-	-
2	5	2	1F	2	1F	6	3	4	3	6	R	3	2	2	1F	3	5	1	R
24	R	19	R	20	R	22	R	17	R	-	-	19	R	18	R	24	14	18	R
-	-	-	-	-	-	-	-	19	R	-	-	-	-	-	-	-	-	-	-
20	8	22	R	22	9	16	R	24	10	21	R	22	R	20	12	18	10	21	9
8	6	16	7	-	-	7	R	14	R	4	R	10	R	9	R	5	13	19	R
-	-	-	-	-	-	15	R	-	-	-	-	-	-	-	-	-	-	-	-
3	RF	3	3	1	2	5	1	2	1F	7	R	6	1	6	3	2	4F	2	2F
7	3	5	2	6	3	2	6	3	R	5	1	2	R	3	2	6	2	4	1
9	R	7	4	5	R	1	5	5	R	3	9	8	4	7	R	11	R	7	R
26	DNS	24	R	25	R	24	R	25	R	24	8	24	R	26	R	23	DNS	23	R
1	1	1	R	3	R	3	2	1	2	8	R	5	R	1	4	1	3	3	R
18	9	17	R	16	6	18	R	18	8	20	R	23	9	23	R	19	R	10	5
-	-	13	R	17	R	13	8	6	7	13	5	15	R	14	NC	8	R	17	NC
15	10	14	9	9	8	20	7	19	R	10	DNS	7	R	12	R	7	R	20	R

1986 FINAL CHAMPIONSHIP POSITIONS

Drivers

1	Alain Prost	72 (74)*
2	Nigel Mansell	70 (72)*
3	Nelson Piquet	69
4	Ayrton Senna	55
5	Stefan Johansson	23
6	Keke Rosberg	22
7	Gerhard Berger	17
8=	Michele Alboreto	14
	Rene Arnoux	14
	Jacques Laffite	14
11	Martin Brundle	8
12	Alan Jones	4
13=	Johnny Dumfries	3
	Philippe Streiff	3
15=	Teo Fabi	2
	Riccardo Patrese	2
	Patrick Tambay	2
18=	Philippe Alliot	1
	Christian Danner	1

*Best 11 results count

Manufacturers

1	Williams-Honda	141
2	McLaren-TAG Porsche	96
3	Lotus-Renault	58
4	Ferrari	37
5	Ligier-Renault	29
6	Benetton-BMW	19
7	Tyrrell-Renault	11
8	Lola-Ford	6
9	Brabham-BMW	2
10	Arrows-BMW	1

miles. Warm, dry and sunny. World Championship round 4

1	Alain Prost	McLaren MP4/2C-		
		TAG Porsche	78	1h55m41.060
2	Keke Rosberg	McLaren MP4/2C-		
		TAG Porsche	78	1h56m06.082
3	Ayrton Senna	Lotus 98T-Renault	78	1h56m34.706
4	Nigel Mansell	Williams FW11-Honda	78	1h56m52.462
5	Rene Arnoux	Ligier JS27-Renault	77	
6	Jacques Laffite	Ligier JS27-Renault	77	

Winner's average speed: 83.661 mph. Starting grid front row: Prost, 1m22.627 (pole) and Mansell, 1m23.047. Fastest lap: Prost, 1m26.607. Leaders: Prost, laps 1-34, 42-78; Senna, 35-41

GRAND PRIX DE BELGIQUE

25 May 1986. Spa-Francorchamps. 43 laps of a 4.312-mile circuit = 185.416 miles. Hot, dry and sunny. World Championship round 5

1	Nigel Mansell	Williams FW11-Honda	43	1h27m57.925
2	Ayrton Senna	Lotus 98T-Renault	43	1h28m17.752
3	Stefan Johansson	Ferrari F186	43	1h28m24.517
4	Michele Alboreto	Ferrari F186	43	1h28m27.559
5	Jacques Laffite	Ligier JS27-Renault	43	1h29m08.615
6	Alain Prost	McLaren MP4/2C-		
		TAG Porsche	43	1h30m15.697

Winner's average speed: 126.470 mph. Starting grid front row: Piquet, 1m54.331 (pole) and Berger, 1m54.468. Fastest lap: Prost, 1m59.282. Leaders: Piquet, laps 1-16; Senna, 17-21; Johansson, 22-23; Mansell, 24-43

GRAND PRIX LABATT DU CANADA

15 June 1986. Montreal. 69 laps of a 2.740-mile circuit = 189.060 miles. Hot and dry. World Championship round 6

1	Nigel Mansell	Williams FW11-Honda	69	1h42m26.415
2	Alain Prost	McLaren MP4/2C-		
		TAG Porsche	69	1h42m47.074
3	Nelson Piquet	Williams FW11-Honda	69	1h43m02.677
4	Keke Rosberg	McLaren MP4/2C-		
		TAG Porsche	69	1h44m02.088
5	Ayrton Senna	Lotus 98T-Renault	68	
6	Rene Arnoux	Ligier JS27-Renault	68	

Winner's average speed: 110.734 mph. Starting grid front row: Mansell, 1m24.118 (pole) and Senna, 1m24.188. Fastest lap: Piquet, 1m25.443. Leaders: Mansell, laps 1-16, 22-30, 32-69; Rosberg, 17-21; Prost, 31

DETROIT GRAND PRIX

22 June 1986. Detroit. 63 laps of a 2.500-mile circuit = 157.500 miles. Hot, dry and windy. World Championship round 7

1	Ayrton Senna	Lotus 98T-Renault	63	1h51m12.847
2	Jacques Laffite	Ligier JS27-Renault	63	1h51m43.864
3	Alain Prost	McLaren MP4/2C-		
		TAG Porsche	63	1h51m44.671
4	Michele Alboreto	Ferrari F186	63	1h52m43.783
5	Nigel Mansell	Williams FW11-Honda	62	
6	Riccardo Patrese	Brabham BT55-BMW	62	

Winner's average speed: 84.971 mph. Starting grid front row: Senna, 1m38.301 (pole) and Mansell, 1m38.839. Fastest lap: Piquet, 1m41.233. Leaders: Senna, laps 1-2, 8-14, 40-63; Mansell, 3-7; Arnoux, 15-17; Laffite, 18-30; Piquet, 31-39

GRAND PRIX DE FRANCE

6 July 1986. Paul Ricard. 80 laps of a 2.369-mile circuit = 189.520 miles. Warm, dry and sunny. World Championship round 8

1	Nigel Mansell	Williams FW11-Honda	80	1h37m19.272
2	Alain Prost	McLaren MP4/2C-		
		TAG Porsche	80	1h37m36.400
3	Nelson Piquet	Williams FW11-Honda	80	1h37m56.817
4	Keke Rosberg	McLaren MP4/2C-		
		TAG Porsche	80	1h38m07.975
5	Rene Arnoux	Ligier JS27-Renault	79	
6	Jacques Laffite	Ligier JS27-Renault	79	

Winner's average speed: 116.842 mph. Starting grid front row: Senna, 1m06.526 (pole) and Mansell, 1m06.755. Fastest lap: Mansell, 1m09.993. Leaders: Mansell, laps 1-25, 37-53, 59-80; Prost, 26-36, 54-58

SHELL OILS BRITISH GRAND PRIX

13 July 1986. Brands Hatch. 75 laps of a 2.614-mile circuit = 196.020 miles. Race stopped after first-lap accident, restarted over original distance. Warm, dry and sunny. World Championship round 9

1	Nigel Mansell	Williams FW11-Honda	75	1h30m38.471
2	Nelson Piquet	Williams FW11-Honda	75	1h30m44.045
3	Alain Prost	McLaren MP4/2C-		
		TAG Porsche	74	
4	Rene Arnoux	Ligier JS27-Renault	73	
5	Martin Brundle	Tyrrell 015-Renault	72	
6	Philippe Streiff	Tyrrell 015-Renault	72	

Winner's average speed: 129.756 mph. Starting grid front row: Piquet, 1m06.961 (pole) and Mansell, 1m07.399. Fastest lap: Mansell, 1m09.593. Leaders: Piquet, laps 1-22; Mansell, 23-75

GROSSER PREIS VON DEUTSCHLAND

27 July 1986. Hockenheim. 44 laps of a 4.224-mile circuit = 185.838 miles. Hot, dry and sunny. World Championship round 10

1	Nelson Piquet	Williams FW11-Honda	44	1h22m08.263
2	Ayrton Senna	Lotus 98T-Renault	44	1h22m23.700
3	Nigel Mansell	Williams FW11-Honda	44	1h22m52.843
4	Rene Arnoux	Ligier JS27-Renault	44	1h23m23.439
5	Keke Rosberg	McLaren MP4/2C-		
		TAG Porsche	43	out of fuel
6	Alain Prost	McLaren MP4/2C-		
		TAG Porsche	43	out of fuel

Winner's average speed: 135.751 mph. Starting grid front row: Rosberg, 1m42.013 (pole) and Prost, 1m42.166. Fastest lap: Berger, 1m46.604. Leaders: Senna, lap 1; Rosberg, laps 2-5, 15-19, 28-38; Piquet, 6-14, 21-27, 39-44; Prost, 20

MAGYAR NAGYDIJ (HUNGARIAN GRAND PRIX)

10 August 1986. Hungaroring. 76 laps of a 2.494-mile circuit = 189.544 miles. Race scheduled for 77 laps, stopped after two hours. Hot, dry and sunny. World Championship round 11

1	Nelson Piquet	Williams FW11-Honda	76	2h00m34.508
2	Ayrton Senna	Lotus 98T-Renault	76	2h00m52.181
3	Nigel Mansell	Williams FW11-Honda	75	
4	Stefan Johansson	Ferrari F186	75	
5	Johnny Dumfries	Lotus 98T-Renault	74	
6	Martin Brundle	Tyrrell 015-Renault	74	

Winner's average speed: 94.320 mph. Starting grid front row: Senna, 1m29.450 (pole) and Piquet, 1m29.785. Fastest lap: Piquet, 1m31.001. Leaders: Senna, laps 1-11, 36-56; Piquet, 12-35, 57-76

GROSSER PREIS VON OSTERREICH

17 August 1986. Osterreichring. 52 laps of a 3.692-mile circuit = 191.984 miles. Hot, dry and sunny. World Championship round 12

1	Alain Prost	McLaren MP4/2C-		
		TAG Porsche	52	1h21m22.531
2	Michele Alboreto	Ferrari F186	51	
3	Stefan Johansson	Ferrari F186	50	
4	Alan Jones	Lola THL2-Ford	50	
5	Patrick Tambay	Lola THL2-Ford	50	
6	Christian Danner	Arrows A8-BMW	49	

Winner's average speed: 141.554 mph. Starting grid front row: Fabi, 1m23.549 (pole) and Berger, 1m23.743. Fastest lap: Berger, 1m29.444. Leaders: Berger, laps 1-25; Mansell, 26-28; Prost, 29-52

GRAN PREMIO D'ITALIA

7 September 1986. Monza. 51 laps of a 3.604-mile circuit = 183.799 miles. Hot, dry and sunny. World Championship round 13

| 1 | Nelson Piquet | Williams FW11-Honda | 51 | 1h17m42.889 |
| 2 | Nigel Mansell | Williams FW11-Honda | 51 | 1h17m52.717 |

3	Stefan Johansson	Ferrari F186	51	1h18m05.804
4	Keke Rosberg	McLaren MP4/2C- TAG Porsche	51	1h18m36.698
5	Gerhard Berger	Benetton B186-BMW	50	
6	Alan Jones	Lola THL2-Ford	49	

Winner's average speed: 141.903 mph. Starting grid front row: Fabi, 1m24.078 (pole) and Prost, 1m24.514 - Fabi started from the back of the grid, Prost from the pit lane. Fastest lap: Fabi, 1m28.099. Leaders: Berger, laps 1-6, 25-26; Mansell, 7-24, 27-37; Piquet, 38-51

GRANDE PREMIO DE PORTUGAL

21 September 1986. Estoril. 70 laps of a 2.703-mile circuit = 189.210 miles. Hot, dry and sunny. World Championship round 14

1	Nigel Mansell	Williams FW11-Honda	70	1h37m21.900
2	Alain Prost	McLaren MP4/2C- TAG Porsche	70	1h37m40.672
3	Nelson Piquet	Williams FW11-Honda	70	1h38m11.174
4	Ayrton Senna	Lotus 98T-Renault	69	out of fuel
5	Michele Alboreto	Ferrari F186	69	
6	Stefan Johansson	Ferrari F186	69	

Winner's average speed: 116.598 mph. Starting grid front row: Senna, 1m16.673 (pole) and Mansell, 1m17.489. Fastest lap: Mansell, 1m20.943. Leaders: Mansell, laps 1-70

GRAN PREMIO DE MEXICO

12 October 1986. Mexico City. 68 laps of a 2.747-mile circuit = 186.796 miles. Hot, dry and humid. World Championship round 15

1	Gerhard Berger	Benetton B186-BMW	68	1h33m18.700
2	Alain Prost	McLaren MP4/2C- TAG Porsche	68	1h33m44.138
3	Ayrton Senna	Lotus 98T-Renault	68	1h34m11.213
4	Nelson Piquet	Williams FW11-Honda	67	
5	Nigel Mansell	Williams FW11-Honda	67	
6	Philippe Alliot	Ligier JS27-Renault	67	

Winner's average speed: 120.111 mph. Starting grid front row: Senna, 1m16.990 (pole) and Piquet, 1m17.279. Fastest lap: Piquet, 1m19.360. Leaders: Piquet, laps 1-31; Senna, 32-35; Berger, 36-68

FOSTER'S AUSTRALIAN GRAND PRIX

26 October 1986. Adelaide. 82 laps of a 2.347-mile circuit = 192.454 miles. Warm, dry and sunny. World Championship round 16

1	Alain Prost	McLaren MP4/2C- TAG Porsche	82	1h54m20.388
2	Nelson Piquet	Williams FW11-Honda	82	1h54m24.593
3	Stefan Johansson	Ferrari F186	81	
4	Martin Brundle	Tyrrell 015-Renault	81	
5	Philippe Streiff	Tyrrell 015-Renault	80	out of fuel
6	Johnny Dumfries	Lotus 98T-Renault	80	

Winner's average speed: 100.991 mph. Starting grid front row: Mansell, 1m18.403 (pole) and Piquet, 1m18.714. Fastest lap: Piquet, 1m20.787. Leaders: Piquet, laps 1-6, 63-64; Rosberg, 7-62; Prost, 65-82

1987

For the second year in a row, Nigel Mansell failed to win the World Championship in dramatic fashion. Mansell's speed was never in question: he recorded more wins (six) and more pole positions (eight) than any of his rivals. But his Williams teammate Nelson Piquet finished in the points more often, so when Mansell was injured in a spectacular practice accident in Japan, the Brazilian's third World Championship was confirmed.

The year began badly for Piquet when a huge practice accident at Tamburello prevented him from starting at Imola. But a combination of podium finishes, lucky wins in Germany and Hungary, and a more convincing display at Monza ultimately gave him an unassailable lead. The high point for Mansell came at Silverstone,

1987 Nelson Piquet clinched a third world title in 1987 despite losing to Williams teammate Nigel Mansell in an epic race at Silverstone.

where he came from twenty-eight seconds behind Piquet to snatch victory from his teammate with a breath-taking passing manoeuvre.

McLaren used the TAG Porsche engine for a final season, but suffered as development of the unit slowed. Alain Prost was still able to win three times, including a brilliant victory in Portugal, which established a new record of 28 victories in his Grand Prix career.

Ferrari's Gerhard Berger almost won at Estoril before spinning out of the lead just three laps from the finish under pressure from Prost. Berger raised hopes of a championship challenge in 1988 by winning the final two Grands Prix of the year.

Ayrton Senna scored the first victories for the Lotus's "active" (computer controlled) suspension system in Monaco and Detroit. Despite this technical advance and a switch to Honda engines, the team was unable to give him consistently competitive machinery. Senna announced he would be moving to McLaren at the end of the year, and Lotus never won a race again.

The Austrian GP was held on the spectacular Osterreichring circuit for the last time in a race that was stopped twice by start-line accidents. Problems with the circuit's narrow starting straight meant it would not be used again for F1 until it was reopened as the much-modified A1 Ring.

1987 was a transitional season with turbocharged engines being gradually replaced by a new normally aspirated formula. Jonathan Palmer won the Jim Clark Cup for entries complying with the new regulations.

GRANDE PREMIO DO BRASIL

12 April 1987. Rio de Janeiro. 61 laps of a 3.126-mile circuit = 190.686 miles. Hot and dry. World Championship round 1

1	Alain Prost	McLaren MP4/3- TAG Porsche	61	1h39m45.141
2	Nelson Piquet	Williams FW11B-Honda	61	1h40m25.688
3	Stefan Johansson	McLaren MP4/3- TAG Porsche	61	1h40m41.899
4	Gerhard Berger	Ferrari F187	61	1h41m24.376
5	Thierry Boutsen	Benetton B187-Ford	60	
6	Nigel Mansell	Williams FW11B-Honda	60	

Winner's average speed: 114.696 mph. Starting grid front row: Mansell, 1m26.128 (pole) and Piquet, 1m26.567. Fastest lap: Piquet, 1m33.861. Leaders: Piquet, laps 1-7, 17-20; Senna, 8-12; Prost, 13-16, 21-61

1987 DRIVERS' RECORDS

driver	car	BR		RSM		B		MC		DET		F		GB	
		Q	R	Q	R	Q	R	Q	R	Q	R	Q	R	Q	R
Michele Alboreto	Ferrari F187	9	8	7	3	5	R	5	3	7	R	8	R	7	R
Philippe Alliot	Lola LC87-Ford	-	-	23	10	22	8	18	R	20	R	23	R	21	R
Rene Arnoux	Ligier JS29B-Megatron BMW	-	-	14	DNS	16	6	22	11	21	10	-	-	-	-
	Ligier JS29C-Megatron BMW	-	-	-	-	-	-	-	-	-	-	13	R	16	R
Gerhard Berger	Ferrari F187	7	4	6	R	4	R	8	4	12	4	6	R	8	R
Thierry Boutsen	Benetton B187-Ford	6	5	12	R	7	R	9	R	4	R	5	R	5	7
Martin Brundle	Zakspeed 861	19	R	-	-	-	-	-	-	15	R	-	-	-	-
	Zakspeed 871	-	-	16	5	18	R	14	7	-	-	18	R	17	NC
Alex Caffi	Osella FA1I-Alfa Romeo	21	R	21	12	26	R	16	R	19	R	20	R	20	R
Adrian Campos	Minardi M187-Motori Moderni	16	DSQ	18	R	19	R	24	DNS	25	R	21	R	19	R
Ivan Capelli	March 87P-Ford	23	DNS	-	-	-	-	-	-	-	-	-	-	-	-
	March 871-Ford	-	-	24	R	21	R	19	6	22	R	22	R	24	R
Andrea de Cesaris	Brabham BT56-BMW	13	R	15	R	13	3	21	R	17	R	11	R	9	R
Eddie Cheever	Arrows A10-Megatron BMW	14	R	10	R	11	4	6	R	6	6	14	R	14	R
Yannick Dalmas	Lola LC87-Ford	-	-	-	-	-	-	-	-	-	-	-	-	-	-
Christian Danner	Zakspeed 861	17	9	19	7	-	-	-	-	-	-	-	-	-	-
	Zakspeed 871	-	-	-	-	20	R	NT	DNQ	16	8	19	R	18	R
Teo Fabi	Benetton B187-Ford	4	R	5	RF	9	R	12	8	8	R	7	5	6	6
Pascal Fabre	AGS JH22-Ford	22	12	26	13	25	10	25	13	26	12	26	9	25	9
Franco Forini	Osella FA1I-Alfa Romeo	-	-	-	-	-	-	-	-	-	-	-	-	-	-
Piercarlo Ghinzani	Ligier JS29B-Megatron BMW	-	-	20	R	17	7	20	12	23	NC	-	-	-	-
	Ligier JS29C-Megatron BMW	-	-	-	-	-	-	-	-	-	-	17	R	NT	DNC
Stefan Johansson	McLaren MP4/3-TAG Porsche	10	3	9	4	10	2	7	R	11	7	9	8	10	R
Nicola Larini	Coloni FC187-Ford	-	-	-	-	-	-	-	-	-	-	-	-	-	-
Nigel Mansell	Williams FW11B-Honda	1	6	2	1	1	R	1	R	1	5	1	1	2	1F
Stefano Modena	Brabham BT56-BMW	-	-	-	-	-	-	-	-	-	-	-	-	-	-
Roberto Moreno	AGS JH22-Ford	-	-	-	-	-	-	-	-	-	-	-	-	-	-
Satoru Nakajima	Lotus 99T-Honda	12	7	13	6	15	5	17	10	24	R	16	NC	12	4
Alessandro Nannini	Minardi M187-Motori Moderni	15	R	17	R	14	R	13	R	18	R	15	R	15	R
Jonathan Palmer	Tyrrell 016-Ford	18	10	25	R	24	R	15	5	13	11	24	7	23	8
Riccardo Patrese	Brabham BT56-BMW	11	R	8	9	8	R	10	R	9	9	12	R	11	R
	Williams FW11B-Honda	-	-	-	-	-	-	-	-	-	-	-	-	-	-
Nelson Piquet	Williams FW11B-Honda	2	2F	3	DNS	2	R	3	2	3	2	4	2F	1	2
Alain Prost	McLaren MP4/3-TAG Porsche	5	1	4	R	6	1F	4	9	5	3	2	3	4	R
Ayrton Senna	Lotus 99T-Honda	3	R	1	2	3	R	2	1F	2	1F	3	4	3	3
Philippe Streiff	Tyrrell 016-Ford	20	11	22	8	23	9	23	R	14	R	25	6	22	R
Gabriele Tarquini	Osella FA1H-Alfa Romeo	-	-	27	R	-	-	-	-	-	-	-	-	-	-
Derek Warwick	Arrows A10-Megatron BMW	8	R	11	11	12	R	11	R	10	R	10	R	13	5

1987 Ayrton Senna scores the last victory for Lotus at the Detroit Grand Prix.

GRAN PREMIO DI SAN MARINO

3 May 1987. Imola. 59 laps of a 3.132-mile circuit = 184.788 miles. Warm and dry. World Championship round 2

1 Nigel Mansell — Williams FW11B-Honda — 59 — 1h31m24.076
2 Ayrton Senna — Lotus 99T-Honda — 59 — 1h31m51.621
3 Michele Alboreto — Ferrari F187 — 59 — 1h32m03.220
4 Stefan Johansson — McLaren MP4/3-TAG Porsche — 59 — 1h32m24.664
5 Martin Brundle — Zakspeed 871 — 57
6 Satoru Nakajima — Lotus 99T-Honda — 57

Winner's average speed: 121.303 mph. Starting grid front row: Senna, 1m25.826 (pole) and Mansell, 1m25.946. Fastest lap: Fabi, 1m29.246.
Leaders: Senna, laps 1, 25-26; Mansell, 2-21, 27-59; Alboreto, 22-24

GRAND PRIX DE BELGIQUE

17 May 1987. Spa-Francorchamps. 43 laps of a 4.312-mile circuit = 185.416 miles. Race stopped after one lap due to an accident, restarted over the original distance. Cool, dry and cloudy. World Championship round 3

1 Alain Prost — McLaren MP4/3-TAG Porsche — 43 — 1h27m03.217
2 Stefan Johansson — McLaren MP4/3-TAG Porsche — 43 — 1h27m27.981
3 Andrea de Cesaris — Brabham BT56-BMW — 42 — out of fuel
4 Eddie Cheever — Arrows A10-Megatron BMW — 42
5 Satoru Nakajima — Lotus 99T-Honda — 42
6 Rene Arnoux — Ligier JS29B-Megatron BMW — 41

Winner's average speed: 127.794 mph. Starting grid front row: Mansell, 1m52.026 (pole) and Piquet, 1m53.416. Fastest lap: Prost, 1m57.153.
Leaders: Piquet, laps 1-9; Prost, 10-43

D		H		A		I		P		E		MEX		J		AUS	
Q	R	Q	R	Q	R	Q	R	Q	R	Q	R	Q	R	Q	R	Q	R
5	R	5	R	6	R	8	R	6	R	4	15	9	R	4	4	6	2
21	6	15	R	22	12	23	R	19	R	17	6	24	6	19	R	17	R
-	-	-	-	-	-	-	-	-	-	-	-	-	-	-	-	-	-
12	R	19	R	16	10	15	10	18	R	14	R	18	R	18	R	20	R
10	R	2	R	3	R	3	4	1	2F	3	RF	2	R	1	1	1	1F
6	R	7	4	4	4	6	5	9	14	8	16	4	R	3	5	5	3
-	-	-	-	-	-	-	-	-	-	-	-	-	-	-	-	-	-
19	NC	22	R	17	DSQ	17	R	17	R	20	11	13	R	16	R	16	R
26	R	21	R	21	R	21	R	25	R	27	DNQ	26	R	24	R	27	DNQ
18	R	24	R	19	R	20	R	20	R	24	14	19	R	22	R	26	R
-	-	-	-	-	-	-	-	-	-	-	-	-	-	-	-	-	-
24	R	18	10	23	11	25	13	22	9	19	12	20	R	21	R	23	R
7	R	13	R	10	R	10	R	13	R	10	R	10	R	11	R	10	8
15	R	11	8	12	R	13	R	11	6	13	8	12	4	13	9	11	R
-	-	-	-	-	-	-	-	-	-	-	-	23	9	23	14	21	5
-	-	-	-	-	-	-	-	-	-	-	-	-	-	-	-	-	-
20	R	23	R	20	9	16	9	16	R	22	R	17	R	17	R	24	7
9	R	12	R	5	3	7	7	10	4	6	6	6	5	6	R	9	R
25	R	26	13	26	NC	28	DNQ	27	DNQ	25	R	27	DNQ	-	-	-	-
-	-	-	-	-	-	26	R	26	R	28	DNQ	-	-	-	-	-	-
-	-	-	-	-	-	-	-	-	-	-	-	-	-	-	-	-	-
17	R	25	12	18	8	19	8	23	R	23	R	21	R	25	13	22	R
8	2	8	R	14	7	11	6	8	5	11	3	15	R	10	3	8	R
-	-	-	-	-	-	27	DNQ	-	-	26	R	-	-	-	-	-	-
1	RF	1	14	2	1F	2	3	2	R	2	1	1	1	7	DNS	-	-
-	-	-	-	-	-	-	-	-	-	-	-	-	-	-	-	15	R
-	-	-	-	-	-	-	-	-	-	-	-	-	-	27	R	25	6
14	R	17	R	13	13	14	11	15	8	18	9	16	R	12	6	14	R
16	R	20	11	15	R	18	16	14	11	21	R	14	R	15	R	13	R
23	5	16	7	24	14	22	14	24	10	16	R	22	7	20	8	19	4
11	R	10	5	8	R	9	R	7	R	9	13	8	3	9	11	-	-
-	-	-	-	-	-	-	-	-	-	-	-	-	-	-	-	7	9
4	1	3	1F	1	2	1	1	4	3	1	4	3	2F	5	15	3	R
3	7	4	3	9	6	5	15	3	1	7	2	5	R	2	7F	2	R
2	3	6	2	7	5	4	2F	5	7	5	5	7	R	8	2	4	DSQ
22	4	14	9	25	R	24	12	21	12	15	7	25	8	26	12	18	R
-	-	-	-	-	-	-	-	-	-	-	-	-	-	-	-	-	-
13	R	9	6	11	R	12	R	12	13	12	10	11	R	14	10	12	R

1987 FINAL CHAMPIONSHIP POSITIONS

Drivers

1	Nelson Piquet	73 (76)*
2	Nigel Mansell	61
3	Ayrton Senna	57
4	Alain Prost	46
5	Gerhard Berger	36
6	Stefan Johansson	30
7	Michele Alboreto	17
8	Thierry Boutsen	16
9	Teo Fabi	12
10	Eddie Cheever	8
11=	Satoru Nakajima	7
	Jonathan Palmer	7
13	Riccardo Patrese	6
14=	Andrea de Cesaris	4
	Philippe Streiff	4
16=	Philippe Alliot	3
	Derek Warwick	3
18	Martin Brundle	2
19=	Rene Arnoux	1
	Ivan Capelli	1
	Roberto Moreno	1

*Best 11 results count

Manufacturers

1	Williams-Honda	137
2	McLaren-TAG Porsche	76
3	Lotus-Honda	64
4	Ferrari	53
5	Benetton-Ford	28
6=	Arrows-Megatron BMW	11
	Tyrrell-Ford	11
8	Brabham-BMW	10
9	Lola-Ford	3
10	Zakspeed	2
11=	Ligier-Megatron BMW	1
	March-Ford	1
	AGS-Ford	1

Formula 1

GRAND PRIX DE MONACO

31 May 1987. Monte Carlo. 78 laps of a 2.068-mile circuit = 161.304 miles. Warm, dry and sunny. World Championship round 4

1 Ayrton Senna	Lotus 99T-Honda	78	1h57m54.085
2 Nelson Piquet	Williams FW11B-Honda	78	1h58m27.297
3 Michele Alboreto	Ferrari F187	78	1h59m06.924
4 Gerhard Berger	Ferrari F187	77	
5 Jonathan Palmer	Tyrrell 016-Ford	76	
6 Ivan Capelli	March 871-Ford	76	

Winner's average speed: 82.088 mph. Starting grid front row: Mansell, 1m23.039 (pole) and Senna, 1m23.711. Fastest lap: Senna, 1m27.685. Leaders: Mansell, laps 1-29; Senna, 30-78

DETROIT GRAND PRIX

21 June 1987. Detroit. 63 laps of a 2.500-mile circuit = 157.500 miles. Warm, dry and humid. World Championship round 5

1 Ayrton Senna	Lotus 99T-Honda	63	1h50m16.358
2 Nelson Piquet	Williams FW11B-Honda	63	1h50m50.177
3 Alain Prost	McLaren MP4/3-TAG Porsche	63	1h51m01.685
4 Gerhard Berger	Ferrari F187	63	1h51m18.959
5 Nigel Mansell	Williams FW11B-Honda	62	
6 Eddie Cheever	Arrows A10-Megatron BMW	60	out of fuel

Winner's average speed: 85.697 mph. Starting grid front row: Mansell, 1m39.264 (pole) and Senna, 1m40.607. Fastest lap: Senna, 1m40.464. Leaders: Mansell, laps 1-33; Senna, 34-63

GRAND PRIX DE FRANCE

5 July 1987. Paul Ricard. 80 laps of a 2.369-mile circuit = 189.520 miles. Hot, dry and sunny. World Championship round 6

1 Nigel Mansell	Williams FW11B-Honda	80	1h37m03.839
2 Nelson Piquet	Williams FW11B-Honda	80	1h37m11.550
3 Alain Prost	McLaren MP4/3-TAG Porsche	80	1h37m59.094
4 Ayrton Senna	Lotus 99T-Honda	79	
5 Teo Fabi	Benetton B187-Ford	77	
6 Philippe Streiff	Tyrrell 016-Ford	76	driveshaft

Winner's average speed: 117.152 mph. Starting grid front row: Mansell, 1m06.454 (pole) and Prost, 1m06.877. Fastest lap: Piquet, 1m09.548. Leaders: Mansell, laps 1-35, 46-80; Piquet, 36-45

SHELL OILS BRITISH GRAND PRIX

12 July 1987. Silverstone. 65 laps of a 2.969-mile circuit = 192.985 miles. Warm, dry and sunny. World Championship round 7

1 Nigel Mansell	Williams FW11B-Honda	65	1h19m11.780
2 Nelson Piquet	Williams FW11B-Honda	65	1h19m13.698
3 Ayrton Senna	Lotus 99T-Honda	64	
4 Satoru Nakajima	Lotus 99T-Honda	63	
5 Derek Warwick	Arrows A10-Megatron BMW	63	
6 Teo Fabi	Benetton B187-Ford	63	

Winner's average speed: 146.208 mph. Starting grid front row: Piquet, 1m07.110 (pole) and Mansell, 1m07.180. Fastest lap: Mansell, 1m09.832. Leaders: Piquet, laps 1-62; Mansell, 63-65

GROSSER PREIS VON DEUTSCHLAND

26 July 1987. Hockenheim. 44 laps of a 4.224-mile circuit = 185.838 miles. Warm, dry and sunny. World Championship round 8

1 Nelson Piquet	Williams FW11B-Honda	44	1h21m25.091
2 Stefan Johansson	McLaren MP4/3-TAG Porsche	44	1h23m04.682
3 Ayrton Senna	Lotus 99T-Honda	43	
4 Philippe Streiff	Tyrrell 016-Ford	43	
5 Jonathan Palmer	Tyrrell 016-Ford	43	
6 Philippe Alliot	Lola LC87-Ford	42	

Winner's average speed: 136.951 mph. Starting grid front row: Mansell, 1m42.616 (pole) and Senna, 1m42.873. Fastest lap: Mansell, 1m45.716.

Leaders: Senna, lap 1; Mansell, laps 2-7, 19-22; Prost, 8-18, 23-39; Piquet, 40-44

MAGYAR NAGYDIJ (HUNGARIAN GRAND PRIX)

9 August 1987. Hungaroring. 76 laps of a 2.494-mile circuit = 189.544 miles. Hot, dry and sunny. World Championship round 9

1 Nelson Piquet	Williams FW11B-Honda	76	1h59m26.793
2 Ayrton Senna	Lotus 99T-Honda	76	2h00m04.520
3 Alain Prost	McLaren MP4/3-TAG Porsche	76	2h00m54.249
4 Thierry Boutsen	Benetton B187-Ford	75	
5 Riccardo Patrese	Brabham BT56-BMW	75	
6 Derek Warwick	Arrows A10-Megatron BMW	74	

Winner's average speed: 95.211 mph. Starting grid front row: Mansell, 1m28.047 (pole) and Berger, 1m28.549. Fastest lap: Piquet, 1m30.149. Leaders: Mansell, laps 1-70; Piquet, 71-76

GROSSER PREIS VON OSTERREICH

16 August 1987. Osterreichring. 52 laps of a 3.692-mile circuit = 191.984 miles. Race stopped twice by firstlap accidents, restarted over original distance on both occasions. Hot and dry. World Championship round 10

1 Nigel Mansell	Williams FW11B-Honda	52	1h18m44.898
2 Nelson Piquet	Williams FW11B-Honda	52	1h19m40.602
3 Teo Fabi	Benetton B187-Ford	51	
4 Thierry Boutsen	Benetton B187-Ford	51	
5 Ayrton Senna	Lotus 99T-Honda	50	
6 Alain Prost	McLaren MP4/3-TAG Porsche	50	

Winner's average speed: 146.277 mph. Starting grid front row: Piquet, 1m23.357 (pole) and Mansell, 1m23.459. Fastest lap: Mansell, 1m28.318. Leaders: Piquet, laps 1-20; Mansell, 21-52

GRAN PREMIO D'ITALIA

6 September 1987. Monza. 50 laps of a 3.604-mile circuit = 180.195 miles. Hot, dry and sunny. World Championship round 11

1 Nelson Piquet	Williams FW11B-Honda	50	1h14m47.707
2 Ayrton Senna	Lotus 99T-Honda	50	1h14m49.513
3 Nigel Mansell	Williams FW11B-Honda	50	1h15m36.743
4 Gerhard Berger	Ferrari F187	50	1h15m45.686
5 Thierry Boutsen	Benetton B187-Ford	50	1h16m09.226
6 Stefan Johansson	McLaren MP4/3-TAG Porsche	50	1h16m16.494

Winner's average speed: 144.551 mph. Starting grid front row: Piquet, 1m23.460 (pole) and Mansell, 1m23.559. Fastest lap: Senna, 1m26.796. Leaders: Piquet, laps 1-23, 43-50; Senna, 24-42

GRANDE PREMIO DE PORTUGAL

20 September 1987. Estoril. 70 laps of a 2.703-mile circuit = 189.210 miles. Race stopped after one lap due to an accident, restarted over original distance. Hot, dry and sunny. World Championship round 12

1 Alain Prost	McLaren MP4/3-TAG Porsche	70	1h37m03.906
2 Gerhard Berger	Ferrari F187	70	1h37m24.399
3 Nelson Piquet	Williams FW11B-Honda	70	1h38m07.210
4 Teo Fabi	Benetton B187-Ford	69	out of fuel
5 Stefan Johansson	McLaren MP4/3-TAG Porsche	69	
6 Eddie Cheever	Arrows A10-Megatron BMW	68	

Winner's average speed: 116.959 mph. Starting grid front row: Berger, 1m17.620 (pole) and Mansell, 1m17.951. Fastest lap: Berger, 1m19.282. Leaders: Mansell, lap 1; Berger, laps 2-33, 36-67; Alboreto, 34-35; Prost, 68-70

GRAN PREMIO TIO PEPE DE ESPANA

27 September 1987. Jerez. 72 laps of a 2.621-mile circuit = 188.705 miles. Hot, dry and sunny. World Championship round 13

1 Nigel Mansell	Williams FW11B-Honda	72	1h49m12.692
2 Alain Prost	McLaren MP4/3-TAG Porsche	72	1h49m34.917

3	Stefan Johansson	McLaren MP4/3- TAG Porsche	72	1h49m43.510
4	Nelson Piquet	Williams FW11B-Honda	72	1h49m44.142
5	Ayrton Senna	Lotus 99T-Honda	72	1h50m26.199
6	Philippe Alliot	Lola LC87-Ford	71	

Winner's average speed: 103.673 mph. Starting grid front row: Piquet, 1m22.461 (pole) and Mansell, 1m23.081. Fastest lap: Berger, 1m26.986. Leaders: Mansell, laps 1-72.

GRAN PREMIO DE MEXICO

18 October 1987. Mexico City. 63 laps of a 2.747-mile circuit = 173.061 miles. Race scheduled for 68 laps, stopped after 30 laps due to an accident, restarted over an additional 33 laps. Hot, dry and sunny. World Championship round 14

1	Nigel Mansell	Williams FW11B-Honda	63	1h26m24.207
2	Nelson Piquet	Williams FW11B-Honda	63	1h26m50.383
3	Riccardo Patrese	Brabham BT56-BMW	63	1h27m51.086
4	Eddie Cheever	Arrows A10- Megatron BMW	63	1h28m05.559
5	Teo Fabi	Benetton B187-Ford	61	
6	Philippe Alliot	Lola LC87-Ford	60	

Winner's average speed: 120.176 mph. Starting grid front row: Mansell, 1m18.383 (pole) and Berger, 1m18.426. Fastest lap: Piquet, 1m19.132. Leaders: Berger, laps 1, 15-20; Boutsen, 2-14; Mansell, 21-63.

FUJI TELEVISION JAPANESE GRAND PRIX

1 November 1987. Suzuka. 51 laps of a 3.641-mile circuit = 185.691 miles. Cool, dry and cloudy. World Championship round 15

1	Gerhard Berger	Ferrari F187	51	1h32m58.072
2	Ayrton Senna	Lotus 99T-Honda	51	1h33m15.456
3	Stefan Johansson	McLaren MP4/3- TAG Porsche	51	1h33m15.766
4	Michele Alboreto	Ferrari F187	51	1h34m18.513
5	Thierry Boutsen	Benetton B187-Ford	51	1h34m23.648
6	Satoru Nakajima	Lotus 99T-Honda	51	1h34m34.551

Winner's average speed: 119.842 mph. Starting grid front row: Berger, 1m40.042 (pole) and Prost, 1m40.652. Fastest lap: Prost, 1m43.844. Leaders: Berger, laps 1-24, 26-51; Senna, 25.

FOSTER'S AUSTRALIAN GRAND PRIX

15 November 1987. Adelaide. 82 laps of a 2.347-mile circuit = 192.454 miles. Hot, dry and sunny. World Championship round 16

1	Gerhard Berger	Ferrari F187	82	1h52m56.144
2	Michele Alboreto	Ferrari F187	82	1h54m04.028
3	Thierry Boutsen	Benetton B187-Ford	81	
4	Jonathan Palmer	Tyrrell 016-Ford	80	
5*	Yannick Dalmas	Lola LC87-Ford	79	
6	Roberto Moreno	AGS JH22-Ford	79	

*Not entered in the World Championship, no points awarded. Ayrton Senna (Lotus 99T-Honda), 1h53m30.989, finished second on the road but was disqualified due to his car having oversized brake ducts. Winner's average speed: 102.246 mph. Starting grid front row: Berger, 1m17.267 (pole) and Prost, 1m17.967. Fastest lap: Berger, 1m20.416. Leaders: Berger, laps 1-82.

1988

McLaren dominated Grand Prix racing in 1988 on a scale that had not been seen since Alberto Ascari's days with Ferrari. The team now included Ayrton Senna and Alain Prost, two of the greatest drivers ever, and they were free to race, unfettered by team orders. They were soon embroiled in an epic battle for the World Championship that would not be decided until October in Japan. At this final race, Senna came back to score a brilliant victory after stalling at the start to clinch the title.

Together its drivers won all but one Grand Prix,

and McLaren only lost at Monza after Senna crashed with Williams's Jean-Louis Schlesser while lapping him two laps from victory. The Brazilian's misfortune handed victory to the turbocharged Ferraris of Gerhard Berger and Michele Alboreto in the first Italian Grand Prix since the death of Enzo Ferrari in August. But it was small consolation for the pre-season favourites who had been so comprehensively beaten by McLaren during the season.

1988 was the final year for turbochargers in F1, with the total reintroduction of normally aspirated engines scheduled for the following season. While other manufacturers concentrated on developing power for the future, Honda continued to improve their current unit, and the low-line McLaren MP4/4-Honda proved to be all-conquering.

Elsewhere, Nelson Piquet moved to Lotus-Honda with disappointing results, never finishing higher than third. Honda's decision to supply McLaren and Lotus's acceptance of Satoru Nakajima as Piquet's teammate resulted in Williams losing its engine supply. Instead the team used normally aspirated Judd engines while looking for a new long-term technical partner. Nigel Mansell's impressive displays at a wet Silverstone and at Jerez resulted in second place finishes, but the British driver decided to move to Ferrari for 1989, in search of an elusive world title.

Apart from Mansell, there were a number of other teams and drivers making their mark in the normally aspirated ranks. Alessandro Nannini joined Thierry Boutsen at Benetton, and both drivers were consistent points scorers, with five podium finishes giving Boutsen fourth place in the championship. Ivan Capelli also impressed in the nimble Leyton House March, finishing second in Portugal and briefly leading in Japan.

GRANDE PREMIO DO BRASIL

3 April 1988. Rio de Janeiro. 60 laps of a 3.126-mile circuit = 187.560 miles. Race scheduled for 61 laps, but reduced due to an unscheduled second parade lap. Hot, dry and cloudy. World Championship round 1

1	Alain Prost	McLaren MP4/4-Honda	60	1h36m06.857
2	Gerhard Berger	Ferrari F187/88C	60	1h36m16.730
3	Nelson Piquet	Lotus 100T-Honda	60	1h37m15.438
4	Derek Warwick	Arrows A10B- Megatron BMW	60	1h37m20.205
5	Michele Alboreto	Ferrari F187/88C	60	1h37m21.413
6	Satoru Nakajima	Lotus 100T-Honda	59	

Winner's average speed: 117.086 mph. Starting grid front row: Senna, 1m28.096 (pole) and Mansell, 1m28.632 - Senna started from the pit lane. Fastest lap: Berger, 1m32.943. Leaders: Prost, laps 1-60.

GRAN PREMIO DI SAN MARINO

1 May 1988. Imola. 60 laps of a 3.132-mile circuit = 187.920 miles. Warm, dry and cloudy. World Championship round 2

1	Ayrton Senna	McLaren MP4/4-Honda	60	1h32m41.264
2	Alain Prost	McLaren MP4/4-Honda	60	1h32m43.598
3	Nelson Piquet	Lotus 100T-Honda	59	
4	Thierry Boutsen	Benetton B188-Ford	59	
5	Gerhard Berger	Ferrari F187/88C	59	
6	Alessandro Nannini	Benetton B188-Ford	59	

Winner's average speed: 121.647 mph. Starting grid front row: Senna, 1m27.148 (pole) and Prost, 1m27.919. Fastest lap: Prost, 1m29.685. Leaders: Senna, laps 1-60.

Formula 1

driver	car	BR		RSM		MC		MEX		CDN		DET	
		Q	R	Q	R	Q	R	Q	R	Q	R	Q	R
Michele Alboreto	Ferrari F187/88C	6	5	10	18	4	3	5	4	4	R	3	R
Philippe Alliot	Lola LC88-Ford	16	R	15	17	13	R	13	R	17	10	14	R
Rene Arnoux	Ligier JS31-Judd	18	R	29	DNQ	20	R	20	R	20	R	20	R
Julian Bailey	Tyrrell 017-Ford	27	DNQ	21	R	30	DNQ	29	DNQ	23	R	23	9
Gerhard Berger	Ferrari F187/88C	4	2F	5	5	3	2	3	3	3	R	2	R
Thierry Boutsen	Benetton B188-Ford	7	7	8	4	16	8	11	8	7	3	5	3
Martin Brundle	Williams FW12-Judd	-	-	-	-	-	-	-	-	-	-	-	-
Alex Caffi	Dallara 3087-Ford	31	NPQ	-	-	-	-	-	-	-	-	-	-
	Dallara F188-Ford	-	-	24	R	17	R	23	R	31	NPQ	22	8
Adrian Campos	Minardi M188-Ford	23	R	22	16	29	DNQ	30	DNQ	27	DNQ	-	-
Ivan Capelli	March 881-Judd	9	R	9	R	22	10	10	16	14	5	21	DNS
Andrea de Cesaris	Rial ARC1-Ford	14	R	16	R	19	R	12	R	12	9	12	4
Eddie Cheever	Arrows A10B-Megatron BMW	15	8	7	7	9	R	7	6	8	R	15	R
Yannick Dalmas	Lola LC88-Ford	17	R	19	12	21	7	22	9	29	DNQ	25	7
Piercarlo Ghinzani	Zakspeed 881	28	DNQ	25	R	23	R	18	15	22	14	30	DNQ
Mauricio Gugelmin	March 881-Judd	13	R	20	15	14	R	16	R	18	R	13	R
Stefan Johansson	Ligier JS31-Judd	21	9	28	DNQ	26	R	24	10	25	R	18	R
Nicola Larini	Osella FA1I-Alfa Romeo	29	DNQ	-	-	-	-	-	-	-	-	-	-
	Osella FA1L-Alfa Romeo	-	-	NT	DNP	25	9	28	DNQ	28	DNQ	27	R
Oscar Larrauri	EuroBrun ER188-Ford	26	DNS	27	DNQ	18	R	26	13	24	R	24	R
Nigel Mansell	Williams FW12-Judd	2	R	11	R	5	R	14	R	9	R	6	R
Pierluigi Martini	Minardi M188-Ford	-	-	-	-	-	-	-	-	-	-	16	6
Stefano Modena	EuroBrun ER188-Ford	24	R	26	NC	NT	DNP	NT	DNP	15	12	19	R
Satoru Nakajima	Lotus 100T-Honda	10	6	12	8	27	DNQ	6	R	13	11	28	DNQ
Alessandro Nannini	Benetton B188-Ford	12	R	4	6	6	R	8	7	5	R	7	R
Jonathan Palmer	Tyrrell 017-Ford	22	R	23	14	10	5	27	DNQ	19	6	17	5
Riccardo Patrese	Williams FW12-Judd	8	R	6	13	8	6	17	R	11	R	10	R
Nelson Piquet	Lotus 100T-Honda	5	3	3	3	11	R	4	R	6	4	8	R
Alain Prost	McLaren MP4/4-Honda	3	1	2	2F	2	1	2	1F	2	2	4	2F
Pierre-Henri Raphanel	Lola LC88-Ford	-	-	-	-	-	-	-	-	-	-	-	-
Luis Perez Sala	Minardi M188-Ford	20	R	18	11	15	R	25	11	21	13	26	R
Jean-Louis Schlesser	Williams FW12-Judd	-	-	-	-	-	-	-	-	-	-	-	-
Bernd Schneider	Zakspeed 881	30	DNQ	30	DNQ	28	DNQ	15	R	30	DNQ	29	DNQ
Ayrton Senna	McLaren MP4/4-Honda	1	DSQ	1	1	1	RF	1	2	1	1F	1	1
Philippe Streiff	AGS JH23-Ford	19	R	13	10	12	DNS	19	12	10	R	11	R
Aguri Suzuki	Lola LC88-Ford	-	-	-	-	-	-	-	-	-	-	-	-
Gabriele Tarquini	Coloni FC188-Ford	25	R	17	R	24	R	21	14	26	8	31	NPQ
	Coloni FC188B-Ford	-	-	-	-	-	-	-	-	-	-	-	-
Derek Warwick	Arrows A10B-Megatron BMW	11	4	14	9	7	4	9	5	16	R	9	R

GRAND PRIX DE MONACO

15 May 1988. Monte Carlo. 78 laps of a 2.068-mile circuit = 161.304 miles. Warm, dry and cloudy. World Championship round 3

1 Alain Prost   McLaren MP4/4-Honda   78   1h57m17.077
2 Gerhard Berger   Ferrari F187/88C   78   1h57m37.530
3 Michele Alboreto   Ferrari F187/88C   78   1h57m58.306
4 Derek Warwick   Arrows A10B-Megatron BMW   77
5 Jonathan Palmer   Tyrrell 017-Ford   77
6 Riccardo Patrese   Williams FW12-Judd   77

Winner's average speed: 82.519 mph. Starting grid front row: Senna, 1m23.998 (pole) and Prost, 1m25.425. Fastest lap: Senna, 1m26.321. Leaders: Senna, laps 1-66; Prost, 67-78.

GRAN PREMIO DE MEXICO

29 May 1988. Mexico City. 67 laps of a 2.747-mile circuit = 184.049 miles. Hot, dry and sunny. World Championship round 4

1 Alain Prost   McLaren MP4/4-Honda   67   1h30m15.737
2 Ayrton Senna   McLaren MP4/4-Honda   67   1h30m22.841
3 Gerhard Berger   Ferrari F187/88C   67   1h31m13.051
4 Michele Alboreto   Ferrari F187/88C   66
5 Derek Warwick   Arrows A10B-Megatron BMW   66
6 Eddie Cheever   Arrows A10B-Megatron BMW   66

Winner's average speed: 122.343 mph. Starting grid front row: Senna, 1m17.468 (pole) and Prost, 1m18.097. Fastest lap: Prost, 1m18.608. Leaders: Prost, laps 1-67.

GRAND PRIX DU CANADA

12 June 1988. Montreal. 69 laps of a 2.728-mile circuit = 188.232 miles. Hot, dry and sunny. World Championship round 5

1 Ayrton Senna   McLaren MP4/4-Honda   69   1h39m46.618
2 Alain Prost   McLaren MP4/4-Honda   69   1h39m52.552
3 Thierry Boutsen   Benetton B188-Ford   69   1h40m38.027
4 Nelson Piquet   Lotus 100T-Honda   68
5 Ivan Capelli   March 881-Judd   68
6 Jonathan Palmer   Tyrrell 017-Ford   67

Winner's average speed: 113.192 mph. Starting grid front row: Senna, 1m21.681 (pole) and Prost, 1m21.863. Fastest lap: Senna, 1m24.973. Leaders: Prost, laps 1-18; Senna, 19-69.

DETROIT GRAND PRIX

19 June 1988. Detroit. 63 laps of a 2.500-mile circuit = 157.500 miles. Hot, dry and sunny. World Championship round 6

1 Ayrton Senna   McLaren MP4/4-Honda   63   1h54m56.035
2 Alain Prost   McLaren MP4/4-Honda   63   1h55m34.748
3 Thierry Boutsen   Benetton B188-Ford   62

F Q	F R	GB Q	GB R	D Q	D R	H Q	H R	B Q	B R	I Q	I R	P Q	P R	E Q	E R	J Q	J R	AUS Q	AUS R
4	3	2	17	4	4	15	R	4	R	4	2F	7	5	10	R	9	11	12	R
18	R	22	14	20	R	20	12	16	R	9	20	R	20	R	12	14	19	9	24	10
27	DNQ	25	18	17	17	25	R	17	R	24	13	23	10	19	R	23	17	23	R
28	DNQ	24	16	29	DNQ	29	DNQ	30	DNQ	26	12	27	DNQ	29	DNQ	26	14	28	DNQ
3	4	1	9	3	3	9	4	3	RF	3	1	4	RF	8	6	3	4	4	R
5	R	12	R	9	6	3	3	6	DSQ	8	6	13	3	4	9	10	3	10	5
-	-	-	-	-	-	-	-	12	7	-	-	-	-	-	-	-	-	-	-
14	12	21	11	19	15	10	R	15	8	21	R	17	7	18	10	21	R	11	R
-	-	-	-	-	-	-	-	-	-	-	-	-	-	-	-	-	-	-	-
10	9	6	R	7	5	4	R	14	3	11	5	3	2	6	R	4	R	9	6
12	10	14	R	14	13	18	R	19	R	18	R	12	R	23	R	14	R	15	8
13	11	13	7	15	10	14	R	11	6	5	3	18	R	25	R	15	R	18	R
19	13	23	13	21	R	17	9	23	R	25	R	15	R	16	11	-	-	-	-
NT	DNQ	28	DNQ	23	14	30	DNQ	24	R	16	R	28	DNQ	30	DNQ	29	DNQ	26	R
16	8	5	4	10	8	8	5	13	R	13	8	5	R	11	7	13	10	19	R
29	DNQ	29	DNQ	28	DNQ	24	R	20	11	28	DNQ	24	R	21	R	27	DNQ	22	9
-	-	-	-	-	-	-	-	-	-	-	-	-	-	-	-	-	-	-	-
24	R	26	19	18	R	31	NPQ	26	R	17	R	25	12	14	R	24	R	31	NPQ
26	R	27	DNQ	26	16	27	DNQ	31	NPQ	31	NPQ	31	NPQ	28	DNQ	28	DNQ	25	R
9	R	11	2F	11	R	2	R	-	-	-	-	6	R	3	2	8	R	3	R
22	15	19	15	30	DNQ	16	R	28	DNQ	14	R	14	R	20	R	17	13	14	7
20	14	20	12	25	R	26	11	29	DNQ	30	DNQ	29	DNQ	26	13	30	DNQ	20	R
8	7	10	10	8	9	19	7	8	R	12	R	16	R	15	R	6	7	13	R
6	6	8	3	6	18F	5	R	7	DSQ	9	9	9	R	5	3	12	5	8	R
23	R	17	R	24	11	21	R	21	12	27	DNQ	22	R	22	R	16	12	17	R
15	R	15	8	13	R	6	6	5	R	10	7	11	R	7	5	11	6	6	4
7	5	7	5	5	R	13	8	9	4	7	R	8	R	9	8	5	R	5	3
1	1F	4	R	2	2	7	2F	2	2	2	R	1	1	2	1F	2	2	2	1F
-	-	-	-	-	-	-	-	-	-	-	-	-	-	-	-	-	-	29	DNQ
25	NC	18	R	27	DNQ	11	10	27	DNQ	19	R	19	8	24	12	22	15	21	R
-	-	-	-	-	-	-	-	-	-	22	11	-	-	-	-	-	-	-	-
21	R	30	DNQ	22	12	28	DNQ	25	R	15	R	30	DNQ	27	DNQ	25	R	30	DNQ
2	2	3	1	1	1	1	1	1	1	1	1	10	2	6	1	4	1	1F	1	2
17	R	16	R	16	R	23	R	18	10	23	R	21	9	13	R	18	8	16	R
-	-	-	-	-	-	-	-	-	-	-	-	-	-	-	-	-	-	20	16
31	NPQ	31	NPQ	31	NPQ	22	13	22	NC	-	-	-	-	-	-	-	-	-	-
-	-	-	-	-	-	-	-	-	-	-	29	DNQ	26	11	31	NPQ	31	NPQ	27	DNQ
11	R	9	6	12	7	12	R	10	5	6	4	10	4	17	R	7	R	7	R

1988 FINAL CHAMPIONSHIP POSITIONS

Drivers

1	Ayrton Senna	90 (94)*
2	Alain Prost	87 (105)*
3	Gerhard Berger	41
4	Thierry Boutsen	27
5	Michele Alboreto	24
6	Nelson Piquet	22
7=	Ivan Capelli	17
	Derek Warwick	17
9=	Nigel Mansell	12
	Alessandro Nannini	12
11	Riccardo Patrese	8
12	Eddie Cheever	6
13=	Mauricio Gugelmin	5
	Jonathan Palmer	5
15	Andrea de Cesaris	3
16=	Pierluigi Martini	1
	Satoru Nakajima	1

*Best 11 results count

Manufacturers

1	McLaren-Honda	199
2	Ferrari	65
3	Benetton-Ford	39
4=	Arrows-Megatron BMW	23
	Lotus-Honda	23
6	March-Judd	22
7	Williams-Judd	20
8	Tyrrell-Ford	5
9	Rial-Ford	3
10	Minardi-Ford	1

4 Andrea de Cesaris   Rial ARC1-Ford   62
5 Jonathan Palmer   Tyrrell 017-Ford   62
6 Pierluigi Martini   Minardi M188-Ford   62

Winner's average speed: 82.221 mph. Starting grid front row: Senna, 1m40.606 (pole) and Berger, 1m41.464. Fastest lap: Prost, 1m44.836. Leaders: Senna, laps 1-63

GRAND PRIX DE FRANCE

3 July 1988. Paul Ricard. 80 laps of a 2.369-mile circuit = 189.520 miles. Hot, dry and sunny. World Championship round 7

1 Alain Prost   McLaren MP4/4-Honda 80   1h37m37.328
2 Ayrton Senna   McLaren MP4/4-Honda 80   1h38m09.080
3 Michele Alboreto   Ferrari F187/88C   80   1h38m43.833
4 Gerhard Berger   Ferrari F187/88C   79
5 Nelson Piquet   Lotus 100T-Honda   79
6 Alessandro Nannini   Benetton B188-Ford   79

Winner's average speed: 116.482 mph. Starting grid front row: Prost, 1m07.589 (pole) and Senna, 1m08.067. Fastest lap: Prost, 1m11.737. Leaders: Prost, laps 1-36, 61-80; Senna, 37-60

BRITISH GRAND PRIX

10 July 1988. Silverstone. 65 laps of a 2.969-mile circuit = 192.985 miles. Cool and wet. World Championship round 8

1 Ayrton Senna   McLaren MP4/4-Honda 65   1h33m16.367
2 Nigel Mansell   Williams FW12-Judd   65   1h33m39.711
3 Alessandro Nannini   Benetton B188-Ford   65   1h34m07.581
4 Mauricio Gugelmin   March 881-Judd   65   1h34m27.745
5 Nelson Piquet   Lotus 100T-Honda   65   1h34m37.202
6 Derek Warwick   Arrows A10B-
                        Megatron BMW   64

Winner's average speed: 124.142 mph. Starting grid front row: Berger, 1m10.133 (pole) and Alboreto, 1m10.332. Fastest lap: Mansell, 1m23.308. Leaders: Berger, laps 1-13; Senna, 14-65

GROSSER PREIS VON DEUTSCHLAND

24 July 1988. Hockenheim. 44 laps of a 4.224-mile circuit = 185.838 miles. Cool and wet. World Championship round 9

1 Ayrton Senna   McLaren MP4/4-Honda 44   1h32m54.188
2 Alain Prost   McLaren MP4/4-Honda 44   1h33m07.797
3 Gerhard Berger   Ferrari F187/88C   44   1h33m46.283
4 Michele Alboreto   Ferrari F187/88C   44   1h34m35.100
5 Ivan Capelli   March 881-Judd   44   1h34m43.794
6 Thierry Boutsen   Benetton B188-Ford   43

Winner's average speed: 120.021 mph. Starting grid front row: Senna, 1m44.596 (pole) and Prost, 1m44.873. Fastest lap: Nannini, 2m03.032. Leaders: Senna, laps 1-44

MAGYAR NAGYDIJ (HUNGARIAN GRAND PRIX)

7 August 1988. Hungaroring. 76 laps of a 2.494-mile circuit = 189.544 miles. Hot, dry and sunny. World Championship round 10

1 Ayrton Senna   McLaren MP4/4-Honda 76   1h57m47.081
2 Alain Prost   McLaren MP4/4-Honda 76   1h57m47.610
3 Thierry Boutsen   Benetton B188-Ford   76   1h58m18.491
4 Gerhard Berger   Ferrari F187/88C   76   1h59m15.751
5 Mauricio Gugelmin   March 881-Judd   75
6 Riccardo Patrese   Williams FW12-Judd   75

Winner's average speed: 96.554 mph. Starting grid front row: Senna, 1m27.635 (pole) and Mansell, 1m27.743. Fastest lap: Prost, 1m30.639. Leaders: Senna, laps 1-76

GRAND PRIX DE BELGIQUE

28 August 1988. Spa-Francorchamps. 43 laps of a 4.312-mile circuit = 185.416 miles. Warm, dry and cloudy. World Championship round 11

1 Ayrton Senna   McLaren MP4/4-Honda 43   1h28m00.549
2 Alain Prost   McLaren MP4/4-Honda 43   1h28m31.019
3 Ivan Capelli   March 881-Judd   43   1h29m16.317
4 Nelson Piquet   Lotus 100T-Honda   43   1h29m24.177
5 Derek Warwick   Arrows A10B-
                        Megatron BMW   43   1h29m25.904

6 Eddie Cheever   Arrows A10B-
                        Megatron BMW   42

Thierry Boutsen, 1h29m00.230, and Alessandro Nannini (both Benetton B188-Ford), 1h29m09.143, finished third and fourth on the road but were disqualified due to illegal fuel. Winner's average speed: 126.407 mph. Starting grid front row: Senna, 1m53.718 (pole) and Prost, 1m54.128. Fastest lap: Berger, 2m00.772. Leaders: Senna, laps 1-43

GRAN PREMIO D'ITALIA

11 September 1988. Monza. 51 laps of a 3.604-mile circuit = 183.799 miles. Hot, dry and sunny. World Championship round 12

1 Gerhard Berger   Ferrari F187/88C   51   1h17m39.744
2 Michele Alboreto   Ferrari F187/88C   51   1h17m40.246
3 Eddie Cheever   Arrows A10B-
                        Megatron BMW   51   1h18m15.276
4 Derek Warwick   Arrows A10B-
                        Megatron BMW   51   1h18m15.858
5 Ivan Capelli   March 881-Judd   51   1h18m32.266
6 Thierry Boutsen   Benetton B188-Ford   51   1h18m39.622

Winner's average speed: 141.998 mph. Starting grid front row: Senna, 1m25.974 (pole) and Prost, 1m26.277. Fastest lap: Alboreto, 1m29.070. Leaders: Senna, laps 1-49; Berger, 50-51

GRANDE PREMIO DE PORTUGAL

25 September 1988. Estoril. 70 laps of a 2.703-mile circuit = 189.210 miles. Hot, dry and sunny. World Championship round 13

1 Alain Prost   McLaren MP4/4-Honda 70   1h37m40.958
2 Ivan Capelli   March 881-Judd   70   1h37m50.511
3 Thierry Boutsen   Benetton B188-Ford   70   1h38m25.577
4 Derek Warwick   Arrows A10B-
                        Megatron BMW   70   1h38m48.377
5 Michele Alboreto   Ferrari F187/88C   70   1h38m52.842
6 Ayrton Senna   McLaren MP4/4-Honda 70   1h38m59.227

Winner's average speed: 116.219 mph. Starting grid front row: Prost, 1m17.411 (pole) and Senna, 1m17.869. Fastest lap: Berger, 1m21.961. Leaders: Senna, lap 1; Prost, laps 2-70

GRAN PREMIO DE ESPANA

2 October 1988. Jerez. 72 laps of a 2.621-mile circuit = 188.705 miles. Hot, dry and sunny. World Championship round 14

1 Alain Prost   McLaren MP4/4-Honda 72   1h48m43.851
2 Nigel Mansell   Williams FW12-Judd   72   1h49m10.083
3 Alessandro Nannini   Benetton B188-Ford   72   1h49m19.297
4 Ayrton Senna   McLaren MP4/4-Honda 72   1h49m30.561
5 Riccardo Patrese   Williams FW12-Judd   72   1h49m31.281
6 Gerhard Berger   Ferrari F187/88C   72   1h49m35.664

Winner's average speed: 104.131 mph. Starting grid front row: Senna, 1m24.067 (pole) and Prost, 1m24.134. Fastest lap: Prost, 1m27.845. Leaders: Prost, laps 1-72

FUJI TELEVISION JAPANESE GRAND PRIX

30 October 1988. Suzuka. 51 laps of a 3.641-mile circuit = 185.691 miles. Cool and mainly dry, some drizzle. World Championship round 15

1 Ayrton Senna   McLaren MP4/4-Honda 51   1h33m26.173
2 Alain Prost   McLaren MP4/4-Honda 51   1h33m39.536
3 Thierry Boutsen   Benetton B188-Ford   51   1h34m02.282
4 Gerhard Berger   Ferrari F187/88C   51   1h34m52.887
5 Alessandro Nannini   Benetton B188-Ford   51   1h34m56.776
6 Riccardo Patrese   Williams FW12-Judd   51   1h35m03.788

Winner's average speed: 119.241 mph. Starting grid front row: Senna, 1m41.853 (pole) and Prost, 1m42.177. Fastest lap: Senna, 1m46.326. Leaders: Prost, laps 1-15, 17-27; Capelli, 16; Senna, 28-51

AUSTRALIAN GRAND PRIX

13 November 1988. Adelaide. 82 laps of a 2.347-mile circuit = 192.454 miles. Hot, dry and cloudy. World Championship round 16

1 Alain Prost   McLaren MP4/4-Honda 82   1h53m14.676
2 Ayrton Senna   McLaren MP4/4-Honda 82   1h53m51.463
3 Nelson Piquet   Lotus 100T-Honda   82   1h54m02.222

4	Riccardo Patrese	Williams FW12-Judd	82	1h54m34.764
5	Thierry Boutsen	Benetton B188-Ford	81	
6	Ivan Capelli	March 881-Judd	81	

Winner's average speed: 101.967 mph. Starting grid front row: Senna, 1m17.748 (pole) and Prost, 1m17.880. Fastest lap: Prost, 1m21.216. Leaders: Prost, laps 1-13, 26-82; Berger, 14-25

1989

A new 3.5-litre normally aspirated engine formula was introduced in 1989, ending the turbocharger era in Formula 1. McLaren-Honda remained the team to beat, with Ayrton Senna and Alain Prost continuing their stormy but successful partnership. Senna won more often (six wins to four) but Prost consistently finished in the points as his rival retired, giving the Frenchman the championship lead.

A bitter season reached its climax in a controversial Japanese GP. Senna needed to win to retain hopes of keeping his World Championship crown. But Suzuka was one of the few races in which Prost was able to outpace his normally quicker teammate, leading narrowly for the majority of the race.

On the forty-seventh lap, Senna made an ambitious passing manoeuvre into the chicane, Prost turned into the corner early to block Senna's advance and the cars collided. Prost stepped from his car but Senna returned to the track, pitted, retook the lead and won. However, he was subsequently disqualified for not rejoining the circuit at the point at which he had left it, and Prost was declared World Champion!

Nigel Mansell and the first John Barnard-designed Ferrari made a winning debut at the Brazilian GP. But the car's revolutionary semi-automatic gearbox suffered reliability problems that prevented an effective challenge for the title. Mansell also won brilliantly from twelfth on the grid in Hungary, on a circuit where passing is nearly impossible. He was suspended from the Spanish GP after ignoring black flags incurred for reversing in the pit-lane during the previous week's Portuguese GP.

Ferrari teammate Gerhard Berger recovered from a fiery accident at Imola's Tamburello corner to win in Portugal. No victory could have been more popular. The race was also notable for Minardi's most competitive day: Pierluigi Martini qualified and finished fifth, and even led briefly.

Renault made a winning return to Grand Prix racing with Williams, whose new driver Thierry Boutsen was successful in the wet Canadian and Australian GPs. Riccardo Patrese added six podium finishes to give Williams-Renault second place in the Constructors' Championship.

Johnny Herbert, still in pain from injuries sustained during the 1988 Brands Hatch F3000 race, made a stunning debut in Brazil for Benetton, finishing fourth ahead of teammate Alessandro Nannini. But Herbert's unhealed injuries increasingly restricted his performances as the season wore on, and he was eventually replaced by Emanuele Pirro before mid-season. Nannini benefited from Senna's Japanese disqualification to record the only Grand Prix victory of his career.

Jean Alesi was the most promising newcomer, running second and finishing fourth in his first race

for Tyrrell at the French GP. Further points-scoring performances at Monza and Jerez marked him as a star of the future. In contrast, triple World Champion Nelson Piquet had a lacklustre season for Lotus, even failing to qualify at Spa.

1989 A bitter championship season was decided when the McLarens of Alain Prost and Ayrton Senna clashed at Suzuka's chicane.

GRANDE PREMIO DO BRASIL

26 March 1989. Rio de Janeiro. 61 laps of a 3.126-mile circuit = 190.686 miles. Very hot, dry and sunny. World Championship round 1

1	Nigel Mansell	Ferrari 640	61	1h38m58.744
2	Alain Prost	McLaren MP4/5-Honda	61	1h39m06.553
3	Mauricio Gugelmin	March 881-Judd	61	1h39m08.114
4	Johnny Herbert	Benetton B188-Ford	61	1h39m09.237
5	Derek Warwick	Arrows A11-Ford	61	1h39m16.610
6	Alessandro Nannini	Benetton B188-Ford	61	1h39m16.985

Winner's average speed: 115.592 mph. Starting grid front row: Senna, 1m25.302 (pole) and Patrese, 1m26.172. Fastest lap: Patrese, 1m32.507. Leaders: Patrese, laps 1-15, 21-22; Mansell, 16-20, 28-44, 47-61; Prost, 23-27, 45-46

GRAN PREMIO KRONENBOURG DI SAN MARINO

23 April 1989. Imola. 58 laps of a 3.132-mile circuit = 181.656 miles. Race scheduled for 61 laps, stopped after three laps due to an accident, restarted over an additional 55 laps. Warm, dry and sunny. World Championship round 2

1	Ayrton Senna	McLaren MP4/5-Honda	58	1h26m51.245
2	Alain Prost	McLaren MP4/5-Honda	58	1h27m31.517
3	Alessandro Nannini	Benetton B188-Ford	57	
4	Thierry Boutsen	Williams FW12C-Renault	57	
5	Derek Warwick	Arrows A11-Ford	57	
6	Jonathan Palmer	Tyrrell 018-Ford	57	

Winner's average speed: 125.490 mph. Starting grid front row: Senna, 1m26.010 (pole) and Prost, 1m26.235. Fastest lap: Prost, 1m26.795. Leaders: Senna, laps 1-58

GRAND PRIX DE MONACO

7 May 1989. Monte Carlo. 77 laps of a 2.068-mile circuit = 159.236 miles. Warm, dry and sunny. World Championship round 3

1	Ayrton Senna	McLaren MP4/5-Honda	77	1h53m33.251
2	Alain Prost	McLaren MP4/5-Honda	77	1h54m25.780
3	Stefano Modena	Brabham BT58-Judd	76	
4	Alex Caffi	Dallara F189-Ford	75	
5	Michele Alboreto	Tyrrell 018-Ford	75	
6	Martin Brundle	Brabham BT58-Judd	75	

Winner's average speed: 84.137 mph. Starting grid front row: Senna, 1m22.308 (pole) and Prost, 1m23.456. Fastest lap: Prost, 1m25.501. Leaders: Senna, laps 1-77

Formula 1

1989 DRIVERS' RECORDS

driver	car	BR		RSM		MC		MEX		USA		CDN	
		Q	R	Q	R	Q	R	Q	R	Q	R	Q	R
Michele Alboreto	Tyrrell 017B-Ford	20	10	-	-	-	-	-	-	-	-	-	-
	Tyrrell 018-Ford	-	-	27	DNQ	12	5	7	3	9	R	20	R
	Lola LC89-Lamborghini	-	-	-	-	-	-	-	-	-	-	-	-
Jean Alesi	Tyrrell 018-Ford	-	-	-	-	-	-	-	-	-	-	-	-
Philippe Alliot	Lola LC88C-Lamborghini	26	12	-	-	-	-	-	-	-	-	-	-
	Lola LC89-Lamborghini	-	-	20	R	17	R	16	NC	12	R	10	R
Rene Arnoux	Ligier JS33-Ford	28	DNQ	28	DNQ	21	12	25	14	29	DNQ	22	5
Paolo Barilla	Minardi M189-Ford	-	-	-	-	-	-	-	-	-	-	-	-
Gerhard Berger	Ferrari 640	3	R	5	R	-	-	6	R	8	R	4	R
Eric Bernard	Lola LC89-Lamborghini	-	-	-	-	-	-	-	-	-	-	-	-
Enrico Bertaggia	Coloni C3-Ford	-	-	-	-	-	-	-	-	-	-	-	-
Thierry Boutsen	Williams FW12C-Renault	4	R	6	4	3	10	8	R	16	6	6	1
	Williams FW13-Renault	-	-	-	-	-	-	-	-	-	-	-	-
Martin Brundle	Brabham BT58-Judd	13	R	22	R	4	6	20	9	5	R	31	NPQ
Alex Caffi	Dallara F189-Ford	31	NPQ	9	7	9	4	19	13	6	R	8	6
Ivan Capelli	March 881-Judd	7	R	13	R	-	-	-	-	-	-	-	-
	March CG891-Judd	-	-	-	-	22	11	4	R	11	R	21	R
Andrea de Cesaris	Dallara F189-Ford	15	13	16	10	10	13	12	R	13	8	9	3
Eddie Cheever	Arrows A11-Ford	24	R	21	9	20	7	24	7	17	3	16	R
Yannick Dalmas	Lola LC88C-Lamborghini	27	DNQ	-	-	-	-	-	-	-	-	-	-
	Lola LC89-Lamborghini	-	-	26	DNS	28	DNQ	29	DNQ	30	DNQ	28	DNQ
	AGS JH23B-Ford	-	-	-	-	-	-	-	-	-	-	-	-
	AGS JH24-Ford	-	-	-	-	-	-	-	-	-	-	-	-
Christian Danner	Rial ARC2-Ford	17	14	29	DNQ	27	DNQ	23	12	26	4	23	8
Martin Donnelly	Arrows A11-Ford	-	-	-	-	-	-	-	-	-	-	-	-
Gregor Foitek	EuroBrun ER188B-Judd	29	DNQ	32	NPQ	35	NPQ	32	NPQ	33	NPQ	33	NPQ
	EuroBrun ER189-Judd	-	-	-	-	-	-	-	-	-	-	-	-
	Rial ARC2-Ford	-	-	-	-	-	-	-	-	-	-	-	-
Bertrand Gachot	Onyx ORE1-Ford	38	NPQ	31	NPQ	34	NPQ	31	NPQ	39	NPQ	32	NPQ
	Rial ARC2-Ford	-	-	-	-	-	-	-	-	-	-	-	-
Piercarlo Ghinzani	Osella FA1M-Ford	32	NPQ	33	NPQ	30	NPQ	NT	NPQ	31	NPQ	34	NPQ
Olivier Grouillard	Ligier JS33-Ford	22	9	10	DSQ	16	R	11	8	27	DNQ	30	DNQ
Mauricio Gugelmin	March 881-Judd	12	3	19	R	-	-	-	-	-	-	-	-
	March CG891-Judd	-	-	-	-	14	R	28	DNQ	18	DSQ	17	R
Johnny Herbert	Benetton B188-Ford	10	4	23	11	24	14	18	15	25	5	29	DNQ
	Tyrrell 018-Ford	-	-	-	-	-	-	-	-	-	-	-	-
Stefan Johansson	Onyx ORE1-Ford	37	NPQ	34	NPQ	31	NPQ	21	R	19	R	18	DSQ
Nicola Larini	Osella FA1M-Ford	19	DSQ	14	12	32	NPQ	33	NPQ	34	NPQ	15	R
Oscar Larrauri	EuroBrun ER189-Judd	-	-	-	-	-	-	-	-	-	-	-	-
JJ Lehto	Onyx ORE1-Ford	-	-	-	-	-	-	-	-	-	-	-	-
Nigel Mansell	Ferrari 640	6	1	3	R	5	R	3	RF	4	R	5	DSQ
Pierluigi Martini	Minardi M188B-Ford	16	R	11	R	11	R	-	-	-	-	-	-
	Minardi M189-Ford	-	-	-	-	-	-	22	R	15	R	11	R
Stefano Modena	Brabham BT58-Judd	14	R	17	R	8	3	9	R	10	7	7	R
Roberto Moreno	Coloni FC188C-Ford	30	DNQ	30	DNQ	25	R	30	DNQ	28	DNQ	-	-
	Coloni C3-Ford	-	-	-	-	-	-	-	-	-	-	26	R
Satoru Nakajima	Lotus 101-Judd	21	8	24	NC	29	DNQ	15	R	23	R	27	DNQ
Alessandro Nannini	Benetton B188-Ford	11	6	7	3	15	8	13	4	3	R	13	DSQ
	Benetton B189-Ford	-	-	-	-	-	-	-	-	-	-	-	-
Jonathan Palmer	Tyrrell 017B-Ford	18	7	-	-	-	-	-	-	-	-	-	-
	Tyrrell 018-Ford	-	-	25	6	23	9	14	R	21	9	14	RF
Riccardo Patrese	Williams FW12C-Renault	2	RF	4	R	7	15	5	2	14	2	3	2
	Williams FW13-Renault	-	-	-	-	-	-	-	-	-	-	-	-
Nelson Piquet	Lotus 101-Judd	9	R	8	R	19	R	26	11	22	R	19	4
Emanuele Pirro	Benetton B188-Ford	-	-	-	-	-	-	-	-	-	-	-	-
	Benetton B189-Ford	-	-	-	-	-	-	-	-	-	-	-	-
Alain Prost	McLaren MP4/5-Honda	5	2	2	2F	2	2F	2	5	2	1	1	R
Pierre-Henri Raphanel	Coloni FC188C-Ford	34	NPQ	36	NPQ	18	R	38	NPQ	32	NPQ	-	-
	Coloni C3-Ford	-	-	-	-	-	-	-	-	-	-	39	NPQ
	Rial ARC2-Ford	-	-	-	-	-	-	-	-	-	-	-	-
Luis Perez Sala	Minardi M188B-Ford	23	R	15	R	26	R	-	-	-	-	-	-
	Minardi M189-Ford	-	-	-	-	-	-	27	DNQ	20	R	24	R
Bernd Schneider	Zakspeed 891-Yamaha	25	R	38	NPQ	33	NPQ	35	NPQ	37	NPQ	35	NPQ
Ayrton Senna	McLaren MP4/5-Honda	1	11	1	1	1	1	1	1	1	RF	2	7
Aguri Suzuki	Zakspeed 891-Yamaha	36	NPQ	37	NPQ	37	NPQ	36	NPQ	38	NPQ	38	NPQ

F Q	F R	GB Q	GB R	D Q	D R	H Q	H R	B Q	B R	I Q	I R	P Q	P R	E Q	E R	J Q	J R	AUS Q	AUS R
-	-	-	-	-	-	-	-	-	-	-	-	-	-	-	-	-	-	-	-
-	-	-	-	-	-	-	-	-	-	-	-	-	-	-	-	-	-	-	-
-	-	-	-	26	R	26	R	22	R	13	R	21	11	33	NPQ	28	DNQ	32	NPQ
16	4	22	R	10	10	11	9	-	-	10	5	-	-	9	4	18	R	15	R
-	-	-	-	-	-	-	-	-	-	-	-	-	-	-	-	-	-	-	-
7	R	12	R	15	R	32	NPQ	11	16	7	R	17	9	5	6	8	R	19	R
18	R	27	DNQ	23	11	27	DNQ	17	R	23	9	23	13	27	DNQ	27	DNQ	26	R
-	-	-	-	-	-	-	-	-	-	-	-	-	-	-	-	19	R	-	-
6	R	4	R	4	R	6	R	3	R	2	2	2	1F	2	2	3	R	14	R
15	11	13	R	-	-	-	-	-	-	-	-	-	-	-	-	-	-	-	-
-	-	-	-	-	-	-	-	39	NPQ	39	NPQ	37	NPQ	38	NPQ	NT	NPQ	39	NPQ
5	R	7	10	6	R	4	3	4	4	6	3	-	-	-	-	-	-	-	-
-	-	-	-	-	-	-	-	-	-	-	-	8	R	21	R	7	3	5	1
32	NPQ	20	R	12	8	15	12	20	R	12	6	10	8	8	R	13	5	12	R
26	R	32	NPQ	20	R	3	7	12	R	20	11	7	R	23	R	15	9	10	R
-	-	-	-	-	-	-	-	-	-	-	-	-	-	-	-	-	-	-	-
12	R	8	R	22	R	14	R	19	12	18	R	24	R	19	R	17	R	16	R
27	DNQ	25	R	21	7	18	R	18	11	17	R	19	R	15	7	16	10	9	-
25	7	28	DNQ	25	12	16	5	24	R	27	DNQ	26	R	22	R	24	8	22	R
-	-	-	-	-	-	-	-	-	-	-	-	-	-	-	-	-	-	-	-
-	-	35	NPQ	31	NPQ	33	NPQ	-	-	-	-	-	-	-	-	-	-	-	-
-	-	-	-	-	-	-	-	37	NPQ	38	NPQ	38	NPQ	35	NPQ	38	NPQ	37	NPQ
29	DNQ	30	DNQ	29	DNQ	29	DNQ	29	DNQ	28	DNQ	30	DNQ	-	-	-	-	-	-
14	12	-	-	-	-	-	-	-	-	-	-	-	-	-	-	-	-	-	-
38	NPQ	33	NPQ	-	-	-	-	38	NPQ	-	-	-	-	-	-	-	-	-	-
-	-	-	-	37	NPQ	37	NPQ	-	-	-	-	-	-	-	-	-	-	-	-
-	-	-	-	-	-	-	-	-	-	-	-	-	-	29	DNQ	-	-	-	-
11	13	21	12	28	DNQ	21	R	23	R	22	R	-	-	-	-	-	-	-	-
-	-	-	-	-	-	-	-	-	-	-	-	-	-	-	-	30	DNQ	29	DNQ
35	NPQ	34	NPQ	34	NPQ	22	R	32	NPQ	34	NPQ	32	NPQ	25	R	31	NPQ	21	R
17	6	24	7	11	R	28	DNQ	26	13	21	R	28	DNQ	24	R	23	R	24	R
-	-	-	-	-	-	-	-	-	-	-	-	-	-	-	-	-	-	-	-
10	NCF	6	R	14	R	13	R	9	7	25	R	14	10	26	R	20	7	25	7
-	-	-	-	-	-	-	-	-	-	-	-	-	-	-	-	-	-	-	-
-	-	-	-	-	-	-	-	16	R	-	-	27	DNQ	-	-	-	-	-	-
13	5	31	NPQ	24	R	24	R	15	8	31	NPQ	12	3	31	NPQ	33	NPQ	31	NPQ
31	NPQ	17	R	32	NPQ	31	NPQ	31	NPQ	24	R	39	NPQ	11	R	10	R	11	R
-	-	-	-	-	-	-	-	-	-	37	NPQ	33	NPQ	37	NPQ	35	NPQ	35	NPQ
-	-	-	-	-	-	-	-	-	-	-	-	31	NPQ	17	R	36	NPQ	17	R
3	2	3	2F	3	3	12	1F	6	3	3	R	3	R	-	-	4	R	7	R
-	-	-	-	-	-	-	-	-	-	-	-	-	-	-	-	-	-	-	-
23	R	11	5	13	9	10	R	14	9	15	7	5	5	4	R	-	-	3	6
22	R	14	R	16	R	8	11	8	R	30	DNQ	11	14	12	R	9	R	8	8
30	DNQ	23	R	35	NPQ	36	NPQ	33	NPQ	33	NPQ	15	R	32	NPQ	32	NPQ	34	NPQ
19	R	16	8	18	R	20	R	27	DNQ	19	10	25	7	18	R	12	R	23	4F
-	-	-	-	-	-	-	-	-	-	-	-	-	-	-	-	-	-	-	-
4	R	9	3	7	R	7	R	7	5	8	R	13	4	14	R	6	1	4	2
-	-	-	-	-	-	-	-	-	-	-	-	-	-	-	-	-	-	-	-
9	10	18	R	19	R	19	13	21	14	14	R	18	6	13	10	26	R	27	DNQ
8	3	5	R	5	4	1	R	5	R	5	4	-	-	6	5	-	-	-	-
-	-	-	-	-	-	-	-	-	-	-	-	6	R	-	-	5	2	6	3
20	8	10	4	8	5	17	6	28	DNQ	11	R	20	R	7	8	11	4	18	R
24	9	26	11	-	-	-	-	-	-	-	-	-	-	-	-	-	-	-	-
-	-	-	-	9	R	25	8	13	10	9	R	16	R	10	R	22	R	13	5
1	1	2	1	2	2	5	4	2	2F	4	1F	4	2	3	3	2	RF	2	R
-	-	-	-	-	-	-	-	-	-	-	-	-	-	-	-	-	-	-	-
36	NPQ	37	NPQ	36	NPQ	39	NPQ	-	-	-	-	-	-	-	-	-	-	-	-
-	-	-	-	-	-	-	-	30	DNQ	29	DNQ	29	DNQ	28	DNQ	29	DNQ	30	DNQ
-	-	-	-	-	-	-	-	-	-	-	-	-	-	-	-	-	-	-	-
28	DNQ	15	6	27	DNQ	23	R	25	15	26	8	9	12	20	R	14	R	28	DNQ
34	NPQ	36	NPQ	39	NPQ	34	NPQ	35	NPQ	35	NPQ	36	NPQ	34	NPQ	21	R	33	NPQ
2	R	1	R	1	1F	2	2	1	1	1	R	1	R	1	1F	1	DSQ	1	R
37	NPQ	38	NPQ	38	NPQ	38	NPQ	36	NPQ	36	NPQ	35	NPQ	36	NPQ	34	NPQ	36	NPQ

Formula 1

1989 DRIVERS' RECORDS (cont.)

driver	car	BR		RSM		MC		MEX		USA		CDN	
		Q	R	Q	R	Q	R	Q	R	Q	R	Q	R
Gabriele Tarquini	AGS JH23B-Ford	-	-	18	8	13	R	17	6	24	7	25	R
	AGS JH24-Ford	-	-	-	-	-	-	-	-	-	-	-	-
Derek Warwick	Arrows A11-Ford	8	5	12	5	6	R	10	R	10	R	12	R
Volker Weidler	Rial ARC2-Ford	33	NPQ	39	NPQ	36	NPQ	34	NPQ	36	NPQ	37	NPQ
Joachim Winkelhock	AGS JH23B-Ford	35	NPQ	35	NPQ	38	NPQ	37	NPQ	35	NPQ	36	NPQ

1989 FINAL CHAMPIONSHIP POSITIONS

Drivers

1	Alain Prost	76 (81)*
2	Ayrton Senna	60
3	Riccardo Patrese	40
4	Nigel Mansell	38
5	Thierry Boutsen	37
6	Alessandro Nannini	32
7	Gerhard Berger	21
8	Nelson Piquet	12
9	Jean Alesi	8
10	Derek Warwick	7
11=	Michele Alboreto	6
	Eddie Cheever	6
	Stefan Johansson	6
14=	Johnny Herbert	5
	Pierluigi Martini	5
16=	Martin Brundle	4
	Alex Caffi	4
	Andrea de Cesaris	4
	Mauricio Gugelmin	4
	Stefano Modena	4

21=	Christian Danner	3
	Satoru Nakajima	3
23=	Rene Arnoux	2
	Jonathan Palmer	2
	Emanuele Pirro	2
26=	Philippe Alliot	1
	Olivier Grouillard	1
	Luis Perez Sala	1
	Gabriele Tarquini	1
*Best 11 results count		

Manufacturers

1	McLaren-Honda	141
2	Williams-Renault	77
3	Ferrari	59
4	Benetton-Ford	39
5	Tyrrell-Ford	16
6	Lotus-Judd	15
7	Arrows-Ford	13
8=	Dallara-Ford	8
	Brabham-Judd	8
10=	Onyx-Ford	6
	Minardi-Ford	6
12	March-Judd	4
13=	Rial-Ford	3
	Ligier-Ford	3
15=	AGS-Ford	1
	Lola-Lamborghini	1

GRAN PREMIO DE MEXICO

28 May 1989. Mexico City. 69 laps of a 2.747-mile circuit = 189.543 miles. Race stopped after two laps due to an accident, restarted over original distance. Hot, dry and sunny. World Championship round 4

1	Ayrton Senna	McLaren MP4/5-Honda 69		1h35m21.431
2	Riccardo Patrese	Williams FW12-Renault	69	1h35m36.991
3	Michele Alboreto	Tyrrell 018-Ford	69	1h35m52.685
4	Alessandro Nannini	Benetton B188-Ford	69	1h36m06.926
5	Alain Prost	McLaren MP4/5-Honda 69		1h36m17.544
6	Gabriele Tarquini	AGS JH23B-Ford	68	

Winner's average speed: 119.263 mph. Starting grid front row: Senna, 1m17.876 (pole) and Prost, 1m18.773. Fastest lap: Mansell, 1m20.420. Leaders: Senna, laps 1-69

ICEBERG UNITED STATES GRAND PRIX

4 June 1989. Phoenix. 75 laps of a 2.360-mile circuit = 177.000 miles. Race scheduled for 81 laps, stopped after two hours. Hot, dry and sunny. World Championship round 5

1	Alain Prost	McLaren MP4/5-Honda 75		2h01m33.133
2	Riccardo Patrese	Williams FW12-Renault	75	2h02m12.829
3	Eddie Cheever	Arrows A11-Ford	75	2h02m16.343
4	Christian Danner	Rial ARC2-Ford	74	
5	Johnny Herbert	Benetton B188-Ford	74	
6	Thierry Boutsen	Williams FW12-Renault	74	

Winner's average speed: 87.370 mph. Starting grid front row: Senna, 1m30.108 (pole) and Prost, 1m31.517. Fastest lap: Senna, 1m33.969. Leaders: Senna, laps 1-33; Prost, 34-75

GRAND PRIX MOLSON DU CANADA

18 June 1989. Montreal. 69 laps of a 2.728-mile circuit = 188.232 miles. Cool and wet. World Championship round 6

1	Thierry Boutsen	Williams FW12C-Renault	69	2h01m24.073
2	Riccardo Patrese	Williams FW12C-Renault	69	2h01m54.080
3	Andrea de Cesaris	Dallara F189-Ford	69	2h03m00.722
4	Nelson Piquet	Lotus 101-Judd	69	2h03m05.557
5	Rene Arnoux	Ligier JS33-Ford	68	
6	Alex Caffi	Dallara F189-Ford	67	

Winner's average speed: 93.030 mph. Starting grid front row: Prost, 1m20.973 (pole) and Senna, 1m21.049. Fastest lap: Palmer, 1m31.925. Leaders: Prost, lap 1; Senna, laps 2-3, 39-66; Patrese, 4-34; Warwick, 35-38; Boutsen, 67-69

RHONE-POULENC GRAND PRIX DE FRANCE

9 July 1989. Paul Ricard. 80 laps of a 2.369-mile circuit = 189.520 miles. Race stopped after first-lap accident, restarted over original distance. Hot, dry and sunny. World Championship round 7

1	Alain Prost	McLaren MP4/5-Honda	80	1h38m29.411
2	Nigel Mansell	Ferrari 640	80	1h39m13.428
3	Riccardo Patrese	Williams FW12C-Renault	80	1h39m36.332
4	Jean Alesi	Tyrrell 018-Ford	80	1h39m42.643
5	Stefan Johansson	Onyx ORE1-Ford	79	
6	Olivier Grouillard	Ligier JS33-Ford	79	

Winner's average speed: 115.455 mph. Starting grid front row: Prost, 1m07.203 (pole) and Senna, 1m07.228. Fastest lap: Gugelmin, 1m12.090. Leaders: Prost, laps 1-80

F		GB		D		H		B		I		P		E		J		AUS	
Q	R	Q	R	Q	R	Q	R	Q	R	Q	R	Q	R	Q	R	Q	R	Q	R
21	R	-	-	33	NPQ	-	-	-	-	-	-	-	-	-	-	-	-	-	-
-	-	29	DNQ	-	-	35	NPQ	34	NPQ	32	NPQ	34	NPQ	30	NPQ	37	NPQ	38	NPQ
-	-	19	9	17	6	9	10	10	6	16	R	22	R	16	9	25	6	20	R
33	NPQ	39	NPQ	30	DNQ	30	DNQ	-	-	-	-	-	-	-	-	-	-	-	-
39	NPQ	-	-	-	-	-	-	-	-	-	-	-	-	-	-	-	-	-	-

SHELL BRITISH GRAND PRIX

16 July 1989. Silverstone. 64 laps of a 2.969-mile circuit = 190.016 miles. Warm, dry and sunny. World Championship round 8

1	Alain Prost	McLaren MP4/5-Honda	64	1h19m22.131
2	Nigel Mansell	Ferrari 640	64	1h19m41.500
3	Alessandro Nannini	Benetton B189-Ford	64	1h20m10.150
4	Nelson Piquet	Lotus 101-Judd	64	1h20m28.866
5	Pierluigi Martini	Minardi M189-Ford	63	
6	Luis Perez Sala	Minardi M189-Ford	63	

Winner's average speed: 143.645 mph. Starting grid front row: Senna, 1m09.099 (pole) and Prost, 1m09.266. Fastest lap: Mansell, 1m12.017.
Leaders: Senna, laps 1-10; Prost, 11-64.

GROSSER MOBIL 1 PREIS VON DEUTSCHLAND

30 July 1989. Hockenheim. 45 laps of a 4.224-mile circuit = 190.062 miles. Warm and cloudy. World Championship round 9

1	Ayrton Senna	McLaren MP4/5-Honda	45	1h21m43.302
2	Alain Prost	McLaren MP4/5-Honda	45	1h22m01.453
3	Nigel Mansell	Ferrari 640	45	1h23m06.556
4	Riccardo Patrese	Williams FW12C-Renault	44	
5	Nelson Piquet	Lotus 101-Judd	44	
6	Derek Warwick	Arrows A11-Ford	44	

Winner's average speed: 139.543 mph. Starting grid front row: Senna, 1m42.300 (pole) and Prost, 1m43.295. Fastest lap: Senna, 1m45.884.
Leaders: Senna, laps 1-19, 43-45; Prost, 20-42.

POP 84 MAGYAR NAGYDIJ (HUNGARIAN GRAND PRIX)

13 August 1989. Hungaroring. 77 laps of a 2.466-mile circuit = 189.882 miles. Hot, dry and sunny. World Championship round 10

1	Nigel Mansell	Ferrari 640	77	1h49m38.650
2	Ayrton Senna	McLaren MP4/5-Honda	77	1h50m04.617
3	Thierry Boutsen	Williams FW12C-Renault	77	1h50m17.004
4	Alain Prost	McLaren MP4/5-Honda	77	1h50m22.827
5	Eddie Cheever	Arrows A11-Ford	77	1h50m23.756
6	Nelson Piquet	Lotus 101-Judd	77	1h50m50.689

Winner's average speed: 103.908 mph. Starting grid front row: Patrese, 1m19.726 (pole) and Senna, 1m20.039. Fastest lap: Mansell, 1m22.637.
Leaders: Patrese, laps 1-52; Senna, 53-57; Mansell, 58-77

CHAMPION GRAND PRIX DE BELGIQUE

27 August 1989. Spa-Francorchamps. 44 laps of a 4.312-mile circuit = 189.728 miles. Cool and wet. World Championship round 11

1	Ayrton Senna	McLaren MP4/5-Honda	44	1h40m54.196
2	Alain Prost	McLaren MP4/5-Honda	44	1h40m55.500
3	Nigel Mansell	Ferrari 640	44	1h40m56.020
4	Thierry Boutsen	Williams FW12C-Renault	44	1h41m48.614
5	Alessandro Nannini	Benetton B189-Ford	44	1h42m03.001
6	Derek Warwick	Arrows A11-Ford	44	1h42m12.512

Winner's average speed: 112.818 mph. Starting grid front row: Senna, 1m50.867 (pole) and Prost, 1m51.463. Fastest lap: Prost, 2m11.571.
Leaders: Senna, laps 1-44

COCA COLA GRAN PREMIO D'ITALIA

10 September 1989. Monza. 53 laps of a 3.604-mile circuit = 191.007 miles. Hot, dry and sunny. World Championship round 12

1	Alain Prost	McLaren MP4/5-Honda	53	1h19m27.550
2	Gerhard Berger	Ferrari 640	53	1h19m34.876
3	Thierry Boutsen	Williams FW12C-Renault	53	1h19m42.525
4	Riccardo Patrese	Williams FW12C-Renault	53	1h20m06.272
5	Jean Alesi	Tyrrell 018-Ford	52	
6	Martin Brundle	Brabham BT58-Judd	52	

Winner's average speed: 144.230 mph. Starting grid front row: Senna, 1m23.720 (pole) and Berger, 1m24.734. Fastest lap: Prost, 1m28.107.
Leaders: Senna, laps 1-44; Prost, 45-53

GRANDE PREMIO DE PORTUGAL

24 September 1989. Estoril. 71 laps of a 2.703-mile circuit = 191.913 miles. Hot, dry and sunny. World Championship round 13

1	Gerhard Berger	Ferrari 640	71	1h36m48.546
2	Alain Prost	McLaren MP4/5-Honda	71	1h37m21.183
3	Stefan Johansson	Onyx ORE1-Ford	71	1h37m43.871
4	Alessandro Nannini	Benetton B189-Ford	71	1h38m10.915
5	Pierluigi Martini	Minardi M189-Ford	70	
6	Jonathan Palmer	Tyrrell 018-Ford	70	

Winner's average speed: 118.943 mph. Starting grid front row: Senna, 1m15.468 (pole) and Berger, 1m16.059. Fastest lap: Berger, 1m18.986.
Leaders: Berger, laps 1-23, 41-71; Mansell, 24-39; Martini, 40

GRAN PREMIO TIO PEPE DE ESPANA

1 October 1989. Jerez. 73 laps of a 2.621-mile circuit = 191.326 miles. Hot, dry and sunny. World Championship round 14

1	Ayrton Senna	McLaren MP4/5-Honda	73	1h47m48.264
2	Gerhard Berger	Ferrari 640	73	1h48m15.315
3	Alain Prost	McLaren MP4/5-Honda	73	1h48m42.052
4	Jean Alesi	Tyrrell 018-Ford	72	
5	Riccardo Patrese	Williams FW12C-Renault	72	
6	Philippe Alliot	Lola LC89-Lamborghini	72	

Winner's average speed: 106.485 mph. Starting grid front row: Senna, 1m20.291 (pole) and Berger, 1m20.565. Fastest lap: Senna, 1m25.779.
Leaders: Senna, laps 1-73

FUJI TELEVISION JAPANESE GRAND PRIX

22 October 1989. Suzuka. 53 laps of a 3.641-mile circuit = 192.973 miles. Warm, dry and sunny. World Championship round 15

1	Alessandro Nannini	Benetton B189-Ford	53	1h35m06.277
2	Riccardo Patrese	Williams FW13-Renault	53	1h35m18.181
3	Thierry Boutsen	Williams FW13-Renault	53	1h35m19.723
4	Nelson Piquet	Lotus 101-Judd	53	1h36m50.502
5	Martin Brundle	Brabham BT58-Judd	52	
6	Derek Warwick	Arrows A11-Ford	52	

Ayrton Senna (McLaren MP4/5-Honda), 1h35m03.980, finished first on the road but was disqualified for rejoining the circuit at the wrong place after his accident with Prost. Winner's average speed: 121.744 mph. Starting grid front row: Senna, 1m38.041 (pole) and Prost, 1m39.771. Fastest lap: Prost, 1m43.506. Leaders: Prost, laps 1-20, 24-46; Senna, 21-23; Nannini,

47-53 (Senna led laps 47-48 and 51-53 on the road but was disqualified for infringement on lap 46)

5 November 1989. Adelaide. 70 laps of a 2.347-mile circuit = 164.290 miles. Race scheduled for 81 laps, stopped on first lap due to rain, restarted over original distance but stopped after two hours. Cool and wet. World Championship round 16

1 Thierry Boutsen	Williams FW13-Renault	70	2h00m17.421
2 Alessandro Nannini	Benetton B189-Ford	70	2h00m46.079
3 Riccardo Patrese	Williams FW13-Renault	70	2h00m55.104
4 Satoru Nakajima	Lotus 101-Judd	70	2h00m59.752
5 Emanuele Pirro	Benetton B189-Ford	68	
6 Pierluigi Martini	Minardi M189-Ford	67	

Winner's average speed: 81.947 mph. Starting grid front row: Senna, 1m16.665 (pole) and Prost, 1m17.403. Fastest lap: Nakajima, 1m38.480. Leaders: Senna, laps 1-13; Boutsen, 14-70

1990 Ayrton Senna leads Gerhard Berger and Nigel Mansell at the start of the Australian Grand Prix.

1990

Alain Prost moved to Ferrari to escape the bitterness of his McLaren partnership with Ayrton Senna. But the penultimate race in the 1990 championship would be a case of déjà vu. At the Japanese GP, the roles of the previous year's event were reversed. Prost, who needed to score points to remain in the championship, made the better start. But in a clear act of retribution, Senna drove his former teammate off the road. The championship was Senna's, but the circumstances would taint the victory.

Tyrrell's Jean Alesi continued his impressive graduation to Grand Prix racing, nearly defeating Senna in the opening GP in Phoenix, and securing another second place finish at Monaco. Alesi was such a hot property that at one point during the season, three teams (Tyrrell, Williams, and Ferrari) all believed that they had signed him for 1991. His eventual choice of Ferrari would prove fateful: had he moved to Williams instead, Alesi might have retired from F1 with a World Championship rather than a solitary race win.

Senna and Prost overshadowed their respective teammates, Gerhard Berger and Nigel Mansell, throughout the year. Berger should have won in Japan but spun out of the lead while passing the aftermath of the Senna/Prost contretemps. After failing to finish the British GP, an emotional Mansell announced he was quitting the sport. But when Williams failed to sign Alesi, the team tempted Mansell out of retirement before he had even stopped racing! In Portugal, after nearly crashing into his teammate at the start, Mansell scored the sole victory of a disappointing year.

After struggling in the early season, Leyton House (formerly March) surprised the Grand Prix circus at Paul Ricard by nearly finishing first and second. Unfortunately for the team, Mauricio Gugelmin retired and Prost just caught Ivan Capelli to score Ferrari's one-hundredth Grand Prix victory.

Riccardo Patrese and Thierry Boutsen both won a race for Williams-Renault as Renault developed its V10 engine. Boutsen won in Hungary by holding off a train of quicker cars for the whole race. Meanwhile, Nelson Piquet resurrected his career at Benetton, winning the final two races to finish third in the championship. Teammate Alessandro Nannini suffered a helicopter accident in which his right arm was severed. Despite successful surgery, his Grand Prix career was over.

Lotus, now using Lamborghini engines, suffered another frustrating year. The season nearly ended in tragedy for the team's promising newcomer, Martin Donnelly, who was critically injured during practice at Jerez. Initial fears for his life proved ill founded, but he too would not race at this level again. Sponsor Camel announced they would withdraw their support of Lotus at the end of the year, forcing the team to the brink of extinction.

11 March 1990. Phoenix. 72 laps of a 2.360-mile circuit = 169.920 miles. Cool, dry and cloudy. World Championship round 1

1 Ayrton Senna	McLaren MP4/5B-Honda	72	1h52m32.829
2 Jean Alesi	Tyrrell 018-Ford	72	1h52m41.514
3 Thierry Boutsen	Williams FW13B-Renault	72	1h53m26.909
4 Nelson Piquet	Benetton B189B-Ford	72	1h53m41.187
5 Stefano Modena	Brabham BT58-Judd	72	1h53m42.332
6 Satoru Nakajima	Tyrrell 018-Ford	71	

Winner's average speed: 90.586 mph. Starting grid front row: Berger, 1m28.664 (pole) and Martini, 1m28.731. Fastest lap: Berger, 1m31.050. Leaders: Alesi, laps 1-34; Senna, 35-72

25 March 1990. Interlagos. 71 laps of a 2.687-mile circuit = 190.777 miles. Hot, dry and sunny. World Championship round 2

1 Alain Prost	Ferrari 641	71	1h37m21.258
2 Gerhard Berger	McLaren MP4/5B-Honda	71	1h37m34.822
3 Ayrton Senna	McLaren MP4/5B-Honda	71	1h37m58.980
4 Nigel Mansell	Ferrari 641	71	1h38m08.524
5 Thierry Boutsen	Williams FW13B-Renault	70	
6 Nelson Piquet	Benetton B189B-Ford	70	

Winner's average speed: 117.577 mph. Starting grid front row: Senna, 1m17.277 (pole) and Berger, 1m17.888. Fastest lap: Berger, 1m19.899. Leaders: Senna, laps 1-32, 35-40; Berger, 33-34; Prost, 41-71

13 May 1990. Imola. 61 laps of a 3.132-mile circuit = 191.052 miles. Warm, dry and sunny. World Championship round 3

1 Riccardo Patrese	Williams FW13B-Renault	61	1h30m55.478
2 Gerhard Berger	McLaren MP4/5B-Honda	61	1h31m00.595
3 Alessandro Nannini	Benetton B190-Ford	61	1h31m01.718
4 Alain Prost	Ferrari 641/2	61	1h31m02.321
5 Nelson Piquet	Benetton B190-Ford	61	1h31m48.590
6 Jean Alesi	Tyrrell 019-Ford	60	

Winner's average speed: 126.073 mph. Starting grid front row: Senna,

1m23.220 (pole) and Berger, 1m23.781. Fastest lap: Nannini, 1m27.156.
Leaders: Senna, laps 1-3; Boutsen, 4-17; Berger, 18-50; Patrese, 51-61

GRAND PRIX DE MONACO

27 May 1990. Monte Carlo. 78 laps of a 2.068-mile circuit = 161.304 miles. Race stopped after first-lap accident, restarted over original distance. Warm, dry and sunny. World Championship round 4

1	Ayrton Senna	McLaren MP4/5B-Honda	78	1h52m46.982
2	Jean Alesi	Tyrrell 019-Ford	78	1h52m48.069
3	Gerhard Berger	McLaren MP4/5B-Honda	78	1h52m49.055
4	Thierry Boutsen	Williams FW13B-Renault	77	
5	Alex Caffi	Arrows A11B-Ford	76	
6	Eric Bernard	Lola 90-Lamborghini	76	

Winner's average speed: 85.813 mph. Starting grid front row: Senna, 1m21.314 (pole) and Prost, 1m21.776. Fastest lap: Senna, 1m24.468. Leaders: Senna, laps 1-78

GRAND PRIX MOLSON DU CANADA

10 June 1990. Montreal. 70 laps of a 2.728-mile circuit = 190.960 miles. Warm and cloudy, damp track, drying. World Championship round 5

1	Ayrton Senna	McLaren MP4/5B-Honda	70	1h42m56.400
2	Nelson Piquet	Benetton B190-Ford	70	1h43m06.897
3	Nigel Mansell	Ferrari 641/2	70	1h43m09.785
4	Gerhard Berger*	McLaren MP4/5B-Honda	70	1h43m11.254
5	Alain Prost	Ferrari 641/2	70	1h43m12.220
6	Derek Warwick	Lotus 102-Lamborghini	68	

*Berger penalised 1 minute for jumping the start. Winner's average speed: 111.304 mph. Starting grid front row: Senna, 1m20.399 (pole) and Berger, 1m20.465. Fastest lap: Berger, 1m22.077. Leaders: Senna, laps 1-11, 15-70; Nannini, 12-14 (Berger led laps 15-70 on the road)

GRAN PREMIO DE MEXICO

24 June 1990. Mexico City. 69 laps of a 2.747-mile circuit = 189.543 miles. Warm, dry and cloudy. World Championship round 6

1	Alain Prost	Ferrari 641/2	69	1h32m35.783
2	Nigel Mansell	Ferrari 641/2	69	1h33m01.134
3	Gerhard Berger	McLaren MP4/5B-Honda	69	1h33m01.313
4	Alessandro Nannini	Benetton B190-Ford	69	1h33m16.882
5	Thierry Boutsen	Williams FW13B-Renault	69	1h33m22.452
6	Nelson Piquet	Benetton B190-Ford	69	1h33m22.726

Winner's average speed: 122.819 mph. Starting grid front row: Berger, 1m17.227 (pole) and Patrese, 1m17.498. Fastest lap: Prost, 1m17.958. Leaders: Senna, laps 1-60; Prost, 61-69

RHONE-POULENC GRAND PRIX DE FRANCE

8 July 1990. Paul Ricard. 80 laps of a 2.369-mile circuit = 189.520 miles. Hot, dry and sunny. World Championship round 7

1	Alain Prost	Ferrari 641/2	80	1h33m29.606
2	Ivan Capelli	Leyton House CG901-Judd	80	1h33m38.232
3	Ayrton Senna	McLaren MP4/5B-Honda	80	1h33m41.212
4	Nelson Piquet	Benetton B190-Ford	80	1h34m10.813
5	Gerhard Berger	McLaren MP4/5B-Honda	80	1h34m11.825
6	Riccardo Patrese	Williams FW13B-Renault	80	1h34m38.957

Winner's average speed: 121.626 mph. Starting grid front row: Mansell, 1m04.402 (pole) and Berger, 1m04.512. Fastest lap: Mansell, 1m08.012. Leaders: Berger, laps 1-27; Senna, 28-29; Mansell, 30-31; Patrese, 32; Capelli, 33-77; Prost, 78-80

FOSTER'S BRITISH GRAND PRIX

15 July 1990. Silverstone. 64 laps of a 2.969-mile circuit = 190.016 miles. Hot, dry and sunny. World Championship round 8

1	Alain Prost	Ferrari 641/2	64	1h18m30.999
2	Thierry Boutsen	Williams FW13B-Renault	64	1h19m10.091
3	Ayrton Senna	McLaren MP4/5B-Honda	64	1h19m14.087
4	Eric Bernard	Lola 90-Lamborghini	64	1h19m46.301
5	Nelson Piquet	Benetton B190-Ford	64	1h19m55.002
6	Aguri Suzuki	Lola 90-Lamborghini	63	

Winner's average speed: 145.204 mph. Starting grid front row: Mansell, 1m07.428 (pole) and Senna, 1m08.071. Fastest lap: Mansell, 1m11.291. Leaders: Senna, laps 1-11; Mansell, 12-21, 28-42; Berger, 22-27; Prost, 43-64

GROSSER MOBIL 1 PREIS VON DEUTSCHLAND

29 July 1990. Hockenheim. 45 laps of a 4.227-mile circuit = 190.211 miles. Hot, dry and sunny. World Championship round 9

1	Ayrton Senna	McLaren MP4/5B-Honda	45	1h20m47.164
2	Alessandro Nannini	Benetton B190-Ford	45	1h20m53.684
3	Gerhard Berger	McLaren MP4/5B-Honda	45	1h20m55.717
4	Alain Prost	Ferrari 641/2	45	1h21m32.424
5	Riccardo Patrese	Williams FW13B-Renault	45	1h21m35.192
6	Thierry Boutsen	Williams FW13B-Renault	45	1h22m08.655

Winner's average speed: 141.270 mph. Starting grid front row: Senna, 1m40.198 (pole) and Berger, 1m40.434. Fastest lap: Boutsen, 1m45.602. Leaders: Senna, laps 1-17, 34-45; Nannini, 18-33

MAGYAR NAGYDIJ (HUNGARIAN GRAND PRIX)

12 August 1990. Hungaroring. 77 laps of a 2.466-mile circuit = 189.882 miles. Hot, dry and sunny. World Championship round 10

1	Thierry Boutsen	Williams FW13B-Renault	77	1h49m30.597
2	Ayrton Senna	McLaren MP4/5B-Honda	77	1h49m30.885
3	Nelson Piquet	Benetton B190-Ford	77	1h49m58.490
4	Riccardo Patrese	Williams FW13B-Renault	77	1h50m02.430
5	Derek Warwick	Lotus 102-Lamborghini	77	1h50m44.841
6	Eric Bernard	Lola 90-Lamborghini	77	1h50m54.905

Winner's average speed: 104.035 mph. Starting grid front row: Boutsen, 1m17.919 (pole) and Patrese, 1m17.955. Fastest lap: Patrese, 1m22.058. Leaders: Boutsen, laps 1-77

GRAND PRIX DE BELGIQUE

26 August 1990. Spa-Francorchamps. 44 laps of a 4.312-mile circuit = 189.728 miles. Race stopped twice by first-lap accidents, restarted over original distance on both occasions. Warm, dry and cloudy. World Championship round 11

1	Ayrton Senna	McLaren MP4/5B-Honda	44	1h26m31.997
2	Alain Prost	Ferrari 641/2	44	1h26m35.547
3	Gerhard Berger	McLaren MP4/5B-Honda	44	1h27m00.459
4	Alessandro Nannini	Benetton B190-Ford	44	1h27m21.334
5	Nelson Piquet	Benetton B190-Ford	44	1h28m01.647
6	Mauricio Gugelmin	Leyton House CG901-Judd	44	1h28m20.848

Winner's average speed: 131.553 mph. Starting grid front row: Senna, 1m50.365 (pole) and Berger, 1m50.948. Fastest lap: Prost, 1m55.087. Leaders: Senna, laps 1-44

COCA COLA GRAN PREMIO D'ITALIA

9 September 1990. Monza. 53 laps of a 3.604-mile circuit = 191.007 miles. Race stopped after first-lap accident, restarted over original distance. Hot, dry and sunny. World Championship round 12

1	Ayrton Senna	McLaren MP4/5B-Honda	53	1h17m57.878
2	Alain Prost	Ferrari 641/2	53	1h18m03.932
3	Gerhard Berger	McLaren MP4/5B-Honda	53	1h18m05.282
4	Nigel Mansell	Ferrari 641/2	53	1h18m54.097
5	Riccardo Patrese	Williams FW13B-Renault	53	1h19m23.152
6	Satoru Nakajima	Tyrrell 019-Ford	52	

Winner's average speed: 146.995 mph. Starting grid front row: Senna, 1m22.533 (pole) and Prost, 1m22.935. Fastest lap: Senna, 1m26.254. Leaders: Senna, laps 1-53

GRANDE PREMIO DE PORTUGAL

23 September 1990. Estoril. 61 laps of a 2.703-mile circuit = 164.883 miles. Race scheduled for 71 laps, stopped due to an accident. Hot, dry and sunny. World Championship round 13

1	Nigel Mansell	Ferrari 641/2	61	1h22m11.014
2	Ayrton Senna	McLaren MP4/5B-Honda	61	1h22m13.822
3	Alain Prost	Ferrari 641/2	61	1h22m15.203
4	Gerhard Berger	McLaren MP4/5B-Honda	61	1h22m16.910

Formula 1

driver	car	USA Q	USA R	BR Q	BR R	RSM Q	RSM R	MC Q	MC R	CDN Q	CDN R	MEX Q	MEX R
Michele Alboreto	Arrows A11B-Ford	21	10	23	R	29	DNQ	27	DNQ	14	R	17	17
Jean Alesi	Tyrrell 018-Ford	4	2	7	7	-	-	-	-	-	-	-	-
	Tyrrell 019-Ford	-	-	-	-	7	6	3	2	8	R	6	7
Philippe Alliot	Ligier JS33B-Ford	NT	DNQ	10	12	17	9	18	R	17	R	22	18
Paolo Barilla	Minardi M189-Ford	14	R	17	R	-	-	-	-	-	-	-	-
	Minardi M190-Ford	-	-	-	-	27	11	19	R	29	DNQ	16	14
Gerhard Berger	McLaren MP4/5B-Honda	1	RF	2	2F	2	2	5	3	2	4F	1	3
Eric Bernard	Lola LC89-Lamborghini	15	8	11	R	-	-	-	-	-	-	-	-
	Lola 90-Lamborghini	-	-	-	-	14	13	24	6	23	9	25	R
Thierry Boutsen	Williams FW13B-Renault	9	3	3	5	4	R	6	4	6	R	5	5
David Brabham	Brabham BT59-Judd	-	-	-	-	30	DNQ	25	R	30	DNQ	21	R
Gary Brabham	Life F190	34	NPQ	NT	NPQ	-	-	-	-	-	-	-	-
Alex Caffi	Arrows A11B-Ford	-	-	25	R	28	DNQ	22	5	26	8	29	DNQ
Ivan Capelli	Leyton House CG901-Judd	26	R	29	DNQ	19	R	23	R	24	10	27	DNQ
Andrea de Cesaris	Dallara F190-Ford	3	R	9	R	18	R	12	R	25	R	15	13
Yannick Dalmas	AGS JH24-Ford	32	NPQ	26	R	-	-	-	-	-	-	-	-
	AGS JH25-Ford	-	-	-	-	NT	DNP	32	NPQ	32	NPQ	31	NPQ
Martin Donnelly	Lotus 102-Lamborghini	19	DNS	14	R	12	8	11	R	12	R	12	8
Gregor Foitek	Brabham BT58-Judd	23	R	22	R	-	-	-	-	-	-	-	-
	Onyx ORE2-Ford	-	-	-	-	24	R	20	7	21	R	23	15
	Monteverdi ORE2-Ford	-	-	-	-	-	-	-	-	-	-	-	-
Bertrand Gachot	Coloni C3B-Subaru	35	NPQ	33	NPQ	31	NPQ	34	NPQ	33	NPQ	33	NPQ
	Coloni C3B-Ford	-	-	-	-	-	-	-	-	-	-	-	-
Bruno Giacomelli	Life F190	-	-	-	-	33	NPQ	35	NPQ	35	NPQ	35	NPQ
	Life F190-Judd	-	-	-	-	-	-	-	-	-	-	-	-
Olivier Grouillard	Osella FA1M-Ford	8	R	21	R	-	-	-	-	-	-	-	-
	Osella FA1Me-Ford	-	-	-	-	23	R	28	DNQ	15	13	20	19
Mauricio Gugelmin	Leyton House CG901-Judd	25	14	30	DNQ	13	R	29	DNQ	28	DNQ	28	DNQ
Johnny Herbert	Lotus 102-Lamborghini	-	-	-	-	-	-	-	-	-	-	-	-
Stefan Johansson	Onyx ORE1-Ford	27	DNQ	27	DNQ	-	-	-	-	-	-	-	-
Claudio Langes	EuroBrun ER189-Judd	33	NPQ	34	NPQ	-	-	-	-	-	-	-	-
	EuroBrun ER189B-Judd	-	-	-	-	32	NPQ	33	NPQ	34	NPQ	34	NPQ
Nicola Larini	Ligier JS33B-Ford	13	R	20	11	21	10	17	R	20	R	24	16
JJ Lehto	Onyx ORE1-Ford	NT	DNQ	28	DNQ	-	-	-	-	-	-	-	-
	Onyx ORE2-Ford	-	-	-	-	26	12	26	R	22	R	26	R
	Monteverdi ORE2-Ford	-	-	-	-	-	-	-	-	-	-	-	-
Nigel Mansell	Ferrari 641	17	R	5	4	-	-	-	-	-	-	-	-
	Ferrari 641/2	-	-	-	-	5	R	7	R	7	3	4	2
Pierluigi Martini	Minardi M189-Ford	2	7	8	9	-	-	-	-	-	-	-	-
	Minardi M190-Ford	-	-	-	-	10	DNS	8	R	16	R	7	12
Stefano Modena	Brabham BT58-Judd	10	5	12	R	-	-	-	-	-	-	-	-
	Brabham BT59-Judd	-	-	-	-	15	R	14	R	10	7	10	11
Gianni Morbidelli	Dallara F190-Ford	28	DNQ	16	14	-	-	-	-	-	-	-	-
	Minardi M190-Ford	-	-	-	-	-	-	-	-	-	-	-	-
Roberto Moreno	EuroBrun ER189-Judd	16	13	32	NPQ	-	-	-	-	-	-	-	-
	EuroBrun ER189B-Judd	-	-	-	-	25	R	30	DNQ	27	DNQ	30	DNQ
	Benetton B190-Ford	-	-	-	-	-	-	-	-	-	-	-	-
Satoru Nakajima	Tyrrell 018-Ford	11	6	19	8	-	-	-	-	-	-	-	-
	Tyrrell 019-Ford	-	-	-	-	20	R	21	R	13	11	9	R
Alessandro Nannini	Benetton B189B-Ford	22	11	15	10	-	-	-	-	-	-	-	-
	Benetton B190-Ford	-	-	-	-	9	3F	16	R	4	R	14	4
Riccardo Patrese	Williams FW13B-Renault	12	9	4	13	3	1	4	R	9	R	2	9
Nelson Piquet	Benetton B189B-Ford	6	4	13	6	-	-	-	-	-	-	-	-
	Benetton B190-Ford	-	-	-	-	8	5	10	DSQ	5	2	8	6
Emanuele Pirro	Dallara F190-Ford	-	-	-	-	22	R	9	R	19	R	18	R
Alain Prost	Ferrari 641	7	R	6	1	-	-	-	-	-	-	-	-
	Ferrari 641/2	-	-	-	-	6	4	2	R	3	5	13	1F
Bernd Schneider	Arrows A11-Ford	20	12	-	-	-	-	-	-	-	-	-	-
	Arrows A11B-Ford	-	-	-	-	-	-	-	-	-	-	-	-
Ayrton Senna	McLaren MP4/5B-Honda	5	1	1	3	1	R	1	1F	1	1	3	20
Aguri Suzuki	Lola LC89-Lamborghini	18	R	18	R	-	-	-	-	-	-	-	-
	Lola 90-Lamborghini	-	-	-	-	16	R	15	R	18	12	19	R
Gabriele Tarquini	AGS JH24-Ford	31	NPQ	31	NPQ	-	-	-	-	-	-	-	-
	AGS JH25-Ford	-	-	-	-	NT	NPQ	31	NPQ	31	NPQ	32	NPQ
Derek Warwick	Lotus 102-Lamborghini	24	R	24	R	11	7	13	R	11	6	11	10

F		GB		D		H		B		I		P		E		J		AUS	
Q	R	Q	R	Q	R	Q	R	Q	R	Q	R	Q	R	Q	R	Q	R	Q	R
18	10	25	R	19	R	22	12	26	13	22	12	19	9	26	10	25	R	27	DNQ
-	-	-	-	-	-	-	-	-	-	-	-	-	-	-	-	-	-	-	-
13	R	6	8	8	11	6	R	9	8	5	R	8	8	4	R	7	DNS	5	8
12	9	22	13	24	DSQ	21	14	27	DNQ	20	13	21	R	13	R	21	10	19	11
-	-	-	-	-	-	-	-	-	-	-	-	-	-	-	-	-	-	-	-
27	DNQ	24	12	28	DNQ	23	15	25	R	28	DNQ	28	DNQ	28	DNQ	-	-	-	-
2	5	3	14	2	3	3	16	2	3	3	3	4	4	5	R	4	R	2	4
-	-	-	-	-	-	-	-	-	-	-	-	-	-	-	-	-	-	-	-
11	8	8	4	12	R	12	6	15	9	13	R	10	R	18	R	17	R	23	R
8	R	4	2	6	6F	1	1	4	R	6	R	7	R	7	4	5	5	9	5
25	15	28	DNQ	21	R	28	DNQ	24	R	29	DNQ	26	R	27	DNQ	23	R	25	R
-	-	-	-	-	-	-	-	-	-	-	-	-	-	-	-	-	-	-	-
22	R	17	7	18	9	26	9	19	10	21	9	17	13	-	-	24	9	29	DNQ
7	2	10	R	10	7	16	R	12	7	16	R	12	R	19	R	13	R	14	R
21	DSQ	23	R	30	DNQ	10	R	20	R	25	10	18	R	17	R	26	R	15	R
-	-	-	-	-	-	-	-	-	-	-	-	-	-	-	-	-	-	-	-
26	17	32	NPQ	29	DNQ	27	DNQ	29	DNQ	24	NC	25	R	24	9	29	DNQ	28	DNQ
17	12	14	R	20	R	18	7	22	12	11	R	15	R	23	DNS	-	-	-	-
-	-	-	-	-	-	-	-	-	-	-	-	-	-	-	-	-	-	-	-
29	DNQ	30	DNQ	-	-	-	-	-	-	-	-	-	-	-	-	-	-	-	-
-	-	-	-	26	R	30	DNQ	-	-	-	-	-	-	-	-	-	-	-	-
34	NPQ	34	NPQ	-	-	-	-	-	-	-	-	-	-	-	-	-	-	-	-
-	-	-	-	33	NPQ	32	NPQ	30	DNQ	30	DNQ	30	DNQ	30	DNQ	30	DNQ	30	DNQ
NT	NPQ	35	NPQ	35	NPQ	35	NPQ	33	NPQ	33	NPQ	-	-	-	-	-	-	-	-
-	-	-	-	-	-	-	-	-	-	-	-	NT	NPQ	33	NPQ	-	-	-	-
-	-	-	-	-	-	-	-	-	-	-	-	-	-	-	-	-	-	-	-
31	NPQ	27	DNQ	27	DNQ	31	NPQ	23	16	23	R	27	DNQ	21	R	27	DNQ	22	13
10	R	15	DNS	14	R	17	8	14	6	10	R	14	12	12	8	16	R	16	R
-	-	-	-	-	-	-	-	-	-	-	-	-	-	-	-	15	R	18	R
-	-	-	-	-	-	-	-	-	-	-	-	-	-	-	-	-	-	-	-
33	NPQ	33	NPQ	34	NPQ	34	NPQ	32	NPQ	32	NPQ	32	NPQ	32	NPQ	-	-	-	-
19	14	21	10	22	10	25	11	21	14	26	11	23	10	20	7	18	7	12	10
30	DNQ	29	DNQ	-	-	-	-	-	-	-	-	-	-	-	-	-	-	-	-
-	-	-	-	25	NC	29	DNQ	-	-	-	-	-	-	-	-	-	-	-	-
1	18F	1	RF	4	R	5	17	5	R	4	4	1	1	3	2	3	R	3	2F
-	-	-	-	-	-	-	-	-	-	-	-	-	-	-	-	-	-	-	-
23	R	18	R	15	R	14	R	16	15	15	R	16	11	11	R	11	8	10	9
-	-	-	-	-	-	-	-	-	-	-	-	-	-	-	-	-	-	-	-
20	13	20	9	17	R	20	R	13	17	17	R	24	R	25	R	22	R	17	12
-	-	-	-	-	-	-	-	-	-	-	-	-	-	-	-	20	R	20	R
32	NPQ	31	NPQ	32	NPQ	33	NPQ	31	NPQ	31	NPQ	31	NPQ	31	NPQ	-	-	-	-
-	-	-	-	-	-	-	-	-	-	-	-	-	-	-	-	9	2	8	7
15	R	12	R	13	R	15	R	10	R	14	6	20	DNS	14	R	14	6	13	R
-	-	-	-	-	-	-	-	-	-	-	-	-	-	-	-	-	-	-	-
5	16	13	R	9	2	7	R	6	4	8	8	9	6	9	3	-	-	-	-
6	6	7	R	5	5	2	4F	7	R	7	5	5	7F	6	5F	8	4F	6	6
-	-	-	-	-	-	-	-	-	-	-	-	-	-	-	-	-	-	-	-
9	4	11	5	7	R	9	3	8	5	9	7	6	5	8	R	6	1	7	1
24	R	19	11	23	R	13	10	17	R	19	R	13	15	16	R	19	R	21	R
-	-	-	-	-	-	-	-	-	-	-	-	-	-	-	-	-	-	-	-
4	1	5	1	3	4	8	R	3	2F	2	2	2	3	2	1	2	R	4	3
-	-	-	-	-	-	-	-	-	-	-	-	-	-	29	DNQ	-	-	-	-
3	3	2	3	1	1	4	2	1	1	1	1F	3	2	1	R	1	R	1	R
14	7	9	6	11	R	19	R	11	R	18	R	11	14	15	6	10	3	24	R
-	-	-	-	-	-	-	-	-	-	-	-	-	-	-	-	-	-	-	-
28	DNQ	26	R	31	NPQ	24	13	28	DNQ	27	DNQ	29	DNQ	22	R	28	DNQ	26	R
16	11	16	R	16	8	11	5	18	11	12	R	22	R	10	R	12	R	11	R

1990 FINAL CHAMPIONSHIP POSITIONS

Drivers						Manufacturers	
1	Ayrton Senna	78	14=	Satoru Nakajima	3	1 McLaren-Honda	121
2	Alain Prost	71 (73)*		Derek Warwick	3	2 Ferrari	110
3=	Gerhard Berger	43	16=	Alex Caffi	2	3 Benetton-Ford	71
	Nelson Piquet	43 (44)*		Stefano Modena	2	4 Williams-Renault	57
5	Nigel Mansell	37	18	Mauricio Gugelmin	1	5 Tyrrell-Ford	16
6	Thierry Boutsen	34	*Best 11 results count			6 Leyton House-Judd	7
7	Riccardo Patrese	23				7 Lotus-Lamborghini	3
8	Alessandro Nannini	21				8= Arrows-Ford	2
9	Jean Alesi	13				Brabham-Judd	2
10=	Ivan Capelli	6				Lola Lamborghini, 11 points,	
	Roberto Moreno	6				excluded from the championship	
	Aguri Suzuki	6				due to incorrect entry	
13	Eric Bernard	5					

5 Nelson Piquet   Benetton B190-Ford   61   1h23m08.432
6 Alessandro Nannini   Benetton B190-Ford   61   1h23m09.263
Winner's average speed: 120.377 mph. Starting grid front row: Mansell,
1m13.557 (pole) and Prost, 1m13.595. Fastest lap: Patrese, 1m18.306.
Leaders: Senna, laps 1-28, 32-49; Berger, 29-31; Mansell, 50-61

GRAN PREMIO TIO PEPE DE ESPANA

30 September 1990. Jerez. 73 laps of a 2.621-mile circuit = 191.326
miles. Hot, dry and sunny. World Championship round 14

1 Alain Prost   Ferrari 641/2   73   1h48m01.461
2 Nigel Mansell   Ferrari 641/2   73   1h48m23.525
3 Alessandro Nannini   Benetton B190-Ford   73   1h48m36.335
4 Thierry Boutsen   Williams FW13B-
                        Renault   73   1h48m44.757
5 Riccardo Patrese   Williams FW13B-
                        Renault   73   1h48m58.991
6 Aguri Suzuki   Lola 90-Lamborghini 73   1h49m05.189
Winner's average speed: 106.268 mph. Starting grid front row: Senna,
1m18.387 (pole) and Prost, 1m18.824. Fastest lap: Patrese, 1m24.513.
Leaders: Senna, laps 1-26; Piquet, 27-28; Prost, 29-73

FUJI TELEVISION JAPANESE GRAND PRIX

21 October 1990. Suzuka. 53 laps of a 3.641-mile circuit = 192.973 miles.
Hot, dry and sunny. World Championship round 15

1 Nelson Piquet   Benetton B190-Ford   53   1h34m36.824
2 Roberto Moreno   Benetton B190-Ford   53   1h34m44.047
3 Aguri Suzuki   Lola 90-Lamborghini 53   1h34m59.293
4 Riccardo Patrese   Williams FW13B-
                        Renault   53   1h35m13.082
5 Thierry Boutsen   Williams FW13B-
                        Renault   53   1h35m23.708
6 Satoru Nakajima   Tyrrell 019-Ford   53   1h35m49.174
Winner's average speed: 122.375 mph. Starting grid front row: Senna,
1m36.996 (pole) and Prost, 1m37.228. Fastest lap: Patrese, 1m44.233.
Leaders: Berger, lap 1; Mansell, laps 2-26; Piquet, 27-53

FOSTER'S AUSTRALIAN GRAND PRIX

4 November 1990. Adelaide. 81 laps of a 2.347-mile circuit = 190.107
miles. Hot, dry and sunny. World Championship round 16

1 Nelson Piquet   Benetton B190-Ford   81   1h49m44.570
2 Nigel Mansell   Ferrari 641/2   81   1h49m47.690
3 Alain Prost   Ferrari 641/2   81   1h50m21.829
4 Gerhard Berger   McLaren MP4/5B-
                        Honda   81   1h50m31.432
5 Thierry Boutsen   Williams FW13B-
                        Renault   81   1h51m35.730
6 Riccardo Patrese   Williams FW13B-
                        Renault   80
Winner's average speed: 103.938 mph. Starting grid front row: Senna,
1m15.671 (pole) and Berger, 1m16.244. Fastest lap: Mansell, 1m18.203.
Leaders: Senna, laps 1-61; Piquet, 62-81

1991

Ayrton Senna effectively clinched his third World Championship by winning the first four races of the year, while Nigel Mansell and Riccardo Patrese struggled to sort out their state-of-the-art, but still unreliable, Williams-Renaults. The Brazilian sealed the series with three more victories, including the wet and shortened Australian GP. With the championship settled, Senna pulled over at the last corner of the Japanese GP to let Gerhard Berger win his first race for McLaren.

Mansell came tantalisingly close to winning in Canada, only to retire on the last corner, handing victory to Nelson Piquet's Benetton. The Williams-Renaults finally held together in Mexico, but it was Patrese who took the victory. Although Mansell eventually scored the first of five wins in France, he was unable to close the gap on Senna in the championship.

Ferrari had a poor year, and team leader Alain Prost was dropped for the final race after publicly criticising the organization. It was the first year since his debut season in 1980 that Prost had failed to win a Grand Prix. Jean Alesi came closest to giving Ferrari victory, but retired while leading in Belgium.

Tyrrell replaced Alesi with Stefano Modena and switched to Honda V10 power. Modena's second place in Montreal was the highlight in an otherwise disappointing season.

The 7Up-sponsored Jordan team made a major impact in its first season in Grand Prix racing. Andrea de Cesaris might have won at Spa but for engine failure in the closing laps. Bertrand Gachot also showed promise, but was jailed prior to his home Belgian GP for spraying CS gas into the face of a London taxi driver. Eddie Jordan replaced Gachot with the young Mercedes-Benz sports car driver Michael Schumacher, and the German proved so sensational in practice that Benetton stole him prior to the next race.

Lotus fought back from the brink of liquidation, with Julian Bailey and the promising F3 graduate Mika Hakkinen scoring points at Imola.

A new scoring system awarding 10 points for a win was introduced for the first time.

ICEBERG UNITED STATES GRAND PRIX

10 March 1991. Phoenix. 81 laps of a 2.312-mile circuit = 187.272 miles.
Race scheduled for 82 laps, stopped after two hours. Warm, dry and
overcast. World Championship round 1

1 Ayrton Senna	McLaren MP4/6-Honda	81	2h00m47.828
2 Alain Prost	Ferrari 642	81	2h01m04.150
3 Nelson Piquet	Benetton B190B-Ford	81	2h01m05.204
4 Stefano Modena	Tyrrell 020-Honda	81	2h01m13.237
5 Satoru Nakajima	Tyrrell 020-Honda	80	
6 Aguri Suzuki	Lola L91-Ford	79	

Winner's average speed: 93.018 mph. Starting grid front row: Senna, 1m21.434 (pole) and Prost, 1m22.555. Fastest lap: Alesi, 1m26.758.
Leaders: Senna, laps 1-81.

GRANDE PREMIO DO BRASIL

24 March 1991. Interlagos. 71 laps of a 2.687-mile circuit = 190.777 miles. Warm and overcast, wet in closing laps. World Championship round 2

1 Ayrton Senna	McLaren MP4/6-Honda	71	1h38m28.128
2 Riccardo Patrese	Williams FW14-Renault	71	1h38m31.119
3 Gerhard Berger	McLaren MP4/6-Honda	71	1h38m33.544
4 Alain Prost	Ferrari 642	71	1h38m47.497
5 Nelson Piquet	Benetton B190B-Ford	71	1h38m50.088
6 Jean Alesi	Ferrari 642	71	1h38m51.769

Winner's average speed: 116.246 mph. Starting grid front row: Senna, 1m16.392 (pole) and Patrese, 1m16.775. Fastest lap: Mansell, 1m20.436.
Leaders: Senna, laps 1-71.

GRAN PREMIO DI SAN MARINO

28 April 1991. Imola. 61 laps of a 3.132-mile circuit = 191.052 miles. Warm and sunny, wet track, drying. World Championship round 3

1 Ayrton Senna	McLaren MP4/6-Honda	61	1h35m14.750
2 Gerhard Berger	McLaren MP4/6-Honda	61	1h35m16.425
3 JJ Lehto	Dallara F191-Judd	60	
4 Pierluigi Martini	Minardi M191-Ferrari	59	
5 Mika Hakkinen	Lotus 102B-Judd	58	
6 Julian Bailey	Lotus 102B-Judd	58	

Winner's average speed: 120.353 mph. Starting grid front row: Senna, 1m21.877 (pole) and Patrese, 1m21.957. Fastest lap: Berger, 1m26.531.
Leaders: Patrese, laps 1-9; Senna, 10-61.

GRAND PRIX DE MONACO

12 May 1991. Monte Carlo. 78 laps of a 2.068-mile circuit = 161.304 miles. Warm, dry and sunny. World Championship round 4

1 Ayrton Senna	McLaren MP4/6-Honda	78	1h53m02.334
2 Nigel Mansell	Williams FW14-Renault	78	1h53m20.682
3 Jean Alesi	Ferrari 642	78	1h53m49.789
4 Roberto Moreno	Benetton B191-Ford	77	
5 Alain Prost	Ferrari 642	77	
6 Emanuele Pirro	Dallara F191-Judd	77	

Winner's average speed: 85.619 mph. Starting grid front row: Senna, 1m20.344 (pole) and Modena, 1m20.809. Fastest lap: Prost, 1m24.368.
Leaders: Senna, laps 1-78.

GRAND PRIX MOLSON DU CANADA

2 June 1991. Montreal. 69 laps of a 2.753-mile circuit = 189.957 miles. Hot, dry and sunny. World Championship round 5

1 Nelson Piquet	Benetton B191-Ford	69	1h38m51.490
2 Stefano Modena	Tyrrell 020-Honda	69	1h39m23.322
3 Riccardo Patrese	Williams FW14-Renault	69	1h39m33.707
4 Andrea de Cesaris	Jordan 191-Ford	69	1h40m11.700
5 Bertrand Gachot	Jordan 191-Ford	69	1h40m13.841
6 Nigel Mansell	Williams FW14-Renault	68	ignition

Winner's average speed: 115.291 mph. Starting grid front row: Patrese, 1m19.837 (pole) and Mansell, 1m20.225. Fastest lap: Mansell, 1m22.385.
Leaders: Mansell, laps 1-68; Piquet, 69.

GRAN PREMIO DE MEXICO

16 June 1991. Mexico City. 67 laps of a 2.747-mile circuit = 184.049 miles. Race scheduled for 69 laps, but reduced after two false starts. Warm, dry and sunny. World Championship round 6

1 Riccardo Patrese	Williams FW14-Renault	67	1h29m52.205

2 Nigel Mansell	Williams FW14-Renault	67	1h29m53.541
3 Ayrton Senna	McLaren MP4/6-Honda	67	1h30m49.561
4 Andrea de Cesaris	Jordan 191-Ford	66	
5 Roberto Moreno	Benetton B191-Ford	66	throttle
6 Eric Bernard	Lola L91-Ford	66	

Winner's average speed: 122.877 mph. Starting grid front row: Patrese, 1m16.696 (pole) and Mansell, 1m16.978. Fastest lap: Mansell, 1m16.788.
Leaders: Mansell, laps 1-14; Patrese, 15-67.

RHONE-POULENC GRAND PRIX DE FRANCE

7 July 1991. Magny-Cours. 72 laps of a 2.654-mile circuit = 191.088 miles. Warm, dry and overcast. World Championship round 7

1 Nigel Mansell	Williams FW14-Renault	72	1h38m00.056
2 Alain Prost	Ferrari 643	72	1h38m05.059
3 Ayrton Senna	McLaren MP4/6-Honda	72	1h38m34.990
4 Jean Alesi	Ferrari 643	72	1h38m35.976
5 Riccardo Patrese	Williams FW14-Renault	71	
6 Andrea de Cesaris	Jordan 191-Ford	71	

Winner's average speed: 116.992 mph. Starting grid front row: Patrese, 1m14.559 (pole) and Prost, 1m14.789. Fastest lap: Mansell, 1m19.168.
Leaders: Prost, laps 1-21, 32-54; Mansell, 22-31, 55-72.

BRITISH GRAND PRIX

14 July 1991. Silverstone. 59 laps of a 3.247-mile circuit = 191.573 miles. Hot, dry and sunny. World Championship round 8

1 Nigel Mansell	Williams FW14-Renault	59	1h27m35.479
2 Gerhard Berger	McLaren MP4/6-Honda	59	1h28m17.772
3 Alain Prost	Ferrari 643	59	1h28m35.629
4 Ayrton Senna	McLaren MP4/6-Honda	58	out of fuel
5 Nelson Piquet	Benetton B191-Ford	58	
6 Bertrand Gachot	Jordan 191-Ford	58	

Winner's average speed: 131.227 mph. Starting grid front row: Mansell, 1m20.939 (pole) and Senna, 1m21.618. Fastest lap: Mansell, 1m26.379.
Leaders: Mansell, laps 1-59.

GROSSER MOBIL 1 PREIS VON DEUTSCHLAND

28 July 1991. Hockenheim. 45 laps of a 4.227-mile circuit = 190.211 miles. Hot, dry and sunny. World Championship round 9

1 Nigel Mansell	Williams FW14-Renault	45	1h19m29.661
2 Riccardo Patrese	Williams FW14-Renault	45	1h19m43.440
3 Jean Alesi	Ferrari 643	45	1h19m47.279
4 Gerhard Berger	McLaren MP4/6-Honda	45	1h20m02.312
5 Andrea de Cesaris	Jordan 191-Ford	45	1h20m47.198
6 Bertrand Gachot	Jordan 191-Ford	45	1h21m10.226

Winner's average speed: 143.565 mph. Starting grid front row: Mansell, 1m37.087 (pole) and Senna, 1m37.274. Fastest lap: Patrese, 1m43.569.
Leaders: Mansell, laps 1-18, 21-45; Alesi, 19-20.

MAGYAR NAGYDIJ (HUNGARIAN GRAND PRIX)

11 August 1991. Hungaroring. 77 laps of a 2.466-mile circuit = 189.882 miles. Hot, dry and sunny. World Championship round 10

1 Ayrton Senna	McLaren MP4/6-Honda	77	1h49m12.796
2 Nigel Mansell	Williams FW14-Renault	77	1h49m17.395
3 Riccardo Patrese	Williams FW14-Renault	77	1h49m28.390
4 Gerhard Berger	McLaren MP4/6-Honda	77	1h49m34.652
5 Jean Alesi	Ferrari 643	77	1h49m44.185
6 Ivan Capelli	Leyton House CG911-Ilmor	76	

Winner's average speed: 104.318 mph. Starting grid front row: Senna, 1m16.147 (pole) and Patrese, 1m17.379. Fastest lap: Gachot, 1m21.547.
Leaders: Senna, laps 1-77.

GRAND PRIX DE BELGIQUE

25 August 1991. Spa-Francorchamps. 44 laps of a 4.312-mile circuit = 189.728 miles. Hot, dry and sunny. World Championship round 11

1 Ayrton Senna	McLaren MP4/6-Honda	44	1h27m17.669
2 Gerhard Berger	McLaren MP4/6-Honda	44	1h27m19.570

1991 DRIVERS' RECORDS

driver	car	USA Q	USA R	BR Q	BR R	RSM Q	RSM R	MC Q	MC R	CDN Q	CDN R	MEX Q	MEX R
Michele Alboreto	Footwork A11C-Porsche	25	R	29	DNQ	30	DNQ	-	-	-	-	-	-
	Footwork FA12-Porsche	-	-	-	-	-	-	25	R	21	R	26	R
	Footwork FA12-Ford	-	-	-	-	-	-	-	-	-	-	-	-
Jean Alesi	Ferrari 642	6	12F	5	6	7	R	9	3	7	R	4	R
	Ferrari 643	-	-	-	-	-	-	-	-	-	-	-	-
Julian Bailey	Lotus 102B-Judd	30	DNQ	30	DNQ	26	6	27	DNQ	-	-	-	-
Fabrizio Barbazza	AGS JH25-Ford	-	-	-	-	28	DNQ	28	DNQ	27	DNQ	30	DNQ
	AGS JH25B-Ford	-	-	-	-	-	-	-	-	-	-	-	-
	AGS JH27-Ford	-	-	-	-	-	-	-	-	-	-	-	-
Michael Bartels	Lotus 102B-Judd	-	-	-	-	-	-	-	-	-	-	-	-
Gerhard Berger	McLaren MP4/6-Honda	7	R	4	3	5	2F	6	R	6	R	5	R
Eric Bernard	Lola L91-Ford	19	R	11	R	17	R	21	9	19	R	18	6
Mark Blundell	Brabham BT59Y-Yamaha	24	R	25	R	-	-	-	-	-	-	-	-
	Brabham BT60Y-Yamaha	-	-	-	-	23	8	22	R	29	DNQ	12	R
Thierry Boutsen	Ligier JS35-Lamborghini	20	R	18	10	24	7	16	7	16	R	14	8
	Ligier JS35B-Lamborghini	-	-	-	-	-	-	-	-	-	-	-	-
Martin Brundle	Brabham BT59Y-Yamaha	12	11	26	12	-	-	-	-	-	-	-	-
	Brabham BT60Y-Yamaha	-	-	-	-	18	11	NT	DNQ	20	R	17	R
Alex Caffi	Footwork A11C-Porsche	28	DNQ	27	DNQ	-	-	-	-	-	-	-	-
	Footwork FA12-Porsche	-	-	-	-	29	DNQ	NT	DNQ	-	-	-	-
	Footwork FA12-Ford	-	-	-	-	-	-	-	-	-	-	-	-
Ivan Capelli	Leyton House CG911-Ilmor	18	R	15	R	22	R	18	R	13	R	22	R
Andrea de Cesaris	Jordan 191-Ford	31	NPQ	13	R	11	R	10	R	11	4	11	4
Pedro Chaves	Coloni C4-Ford	32	NPQ	33	NPQ	34	NPQ	33	NPQ	34	NPQ	32	NPQ
Erik Comas	Ligier JS35-Lamborghini	27	DNQ	23	R	19	10	23	10	26	8	27	DNQ
	Ligier JS35B-Lamborghini	-	-	-	-	-	-	-	-	-	-	-	-
Bertrand Gachot	Jordan 191-Ford	14	10	10	R	12	R	24	8	14	5	20	R
	Lola L91-Ford	-	-	-	-	-	-	-	-	-	-	-	-
Olivier Grouillard	Fomet FA1Me-Ford	33	NPQ	34	NPQ	-	-	-	-	-	-	-	-
	Fomet F1-Ford	-	-	-	-	32	NPQ	34	NPQ	31	NPQ	10	R
	AGS JH27-Ford	-	-	-	-	-	-	-	-	-	-	-	-
Mauricio Gugelmin	Leyton House CG911-Ilmor	23	R	8	R	15	12	15	R	23	R	21	R
Mika Hakkinen	Lotus 102B-Judd	13	R	22	9	25	5	26	9	24	R	24	9
Naoki Hattori	Coloni C4-Ford	-	-	-	-	-	-	-	-	-	-	-	-
Johnny Herbert	Lotus 102B-Judd	-	-	-	-	-	-	-	-	30	DNQ	25	10
Stefan Johansson	AGS JH25-Ford	29	DNQ	28	DNQ	-	-	-	-	-	-	-	-
	Footwork FA12-Porsche	-	-	-	-	-	-	-	-	25	R	29	DNQ
	Footwork FA12-Ford	-	-	-	-	-	-	-	-	-	-	-	-
Nicola Larini	Lamborghini 291	17	7	32	NPQ	33	NPQ	31	NPQ	32	NPQ	NT	NPQ
JJ Lehto	Dallara F191-Judd	10	R	19	R	16	3	13	11	17	R	16	R
Nigel Mansell	Williams FW14-Renault	4	R	3	RF	4	R	5	2	2	6F	2	2F
Pierluigi Martini	Minardi M191-Ferrari	15	9	20	R	9	4	14	12	18	7	15	R
Stefano Modena	Tyrrell 020-Honda	11	4	9	R	6	R	2	R	9	2	8	11
Gianni Morbidelli	Minardi M191-Ferrari	26	R	21	8	8	R	17	R	15	R	23	7
	Ferrari 643	-	-	-	-	-	-	-	-	-	-	-	-
Roberto Moreno	Benetton B190B-Ford	8	R	14	7	-	-	-	-	-	-	-	-
	Benetton B191-Ford	-	-	-	-	13	R	8	4	5	R	9	5
	Jordan 191-Ford	-	-	-	-	-	-	-	-	-	-	-	-
	Minardi M191-Ferrari	-	-	-	-	-	-	-	-	-	-	-	-
Satoru Nakajima	Tyrrell 020-Honda	16	5	16	R	10	R	11	R	12	10	13	12
Riccardo Patrese	Williams FW14-Renault	3	R	2	2	2	R	3	R	1	3	1	1
Nelson Piquet	Benetton B190B-Ford	5	3	7	5	-	-	-	-	-	-	-	-
	Benetton B191-Ford	-	-	-	-	14	R	4	4	8	1	6	R
Emanuele Pirro	Dallara F191-Judd	9	R	12	11	31	NPQ	12	6	10	9	33	NPQ
Eric van de Poele	Lamborghini 291	34	NPQ	31	NPQ	21	9	32	NPQ	33	NPQ	31	NPQ
Alain Prost	Ferrari 642	2	2	6	4	3	DNS	7	5F	4	R	7	R
	Ferrari 643	-	-	-	-	-	-	-	-	-	-	-	-
Michael Schumacher	Jordan 191-Ford	-	-	-	-	-	-	-	-	-	-	-	-
	Benetton B191-Ford	-	-	-	-	-	-	-	-	-	-	-	-
Ayrton Senna	McLaren MP4/6-Honda	1	1	1	1	1	1	1	1	3	R	3	3
Aguri Suzuki	Lola L91-Ford	21	6	17	DNS	20	R	19	R	22	R	19	R
Gabriele Tarquini	AGS JH25-Ford	22	8	24	R	27	DNQ	20	R	28	DNQ	28	DNQ
	AGS JH25B-Ford	-	-	-	-	-	-	-	-	-	-	-	-
	AGS JH27-Ford	-	-	-	-	-	-	-	-	-	-	-	-
	Fomet F1-Ford	-	-	-	-	-	-	-	-	-	-	-	-
Karl Wendlinger	Leyton House CG911-Ilmor	-	-	-	-	-	-	-	-	-	-	-	-
Alessandro Zanardi	Jordan 191-Ford	-	-	-	-	-	-	-	-	-	-	-	-

F		GB		D		H		B		I		P		E		J		AUS	
Q	R	Q	R	Q	R	Q	R	Q	R	Q	R	Q	R	Q	R	Q	R	Q	R
-	-	-	-	-	-	-	-	-	-	-	-	-	-	-	-	-	-	-	-
25	R	26	R	27	DNQ	28	DNQ	31	NPQ	27	DNQ	24	15	24	R	27	DNQ	15	13
-	-	-	-	-	-	-	-	-	-	-	-	-	-	-	-	-	-	-	-
6	4	6	R	6	3	6	5	5	R	6	R	6	3	7	4	6	R	7	R
-	-	-	-	-	-	-	-	-	-	-	-	-	-	-	-	-	-	-	-
28	DNQ	29	DNQ	33	NPQ	33	NPQ	34	NPQ	31	NPQ	-	-	-	-	-	-	-	-
-	-	-	-	-	-	-	-	-	-	-	-	31	NPQ	32	NPQ	-	-	-	-
-	-	-	-	28	DNQ	30	DNQ	-	-	28	DNQ	-	-	29	DNQ	-	-	-	-
5	R	4	2	3	4	5	4	4	2	3	4	2	R	1	R	1	1	2	3F
23	R	21	R	25	R	21	R	20	R	24	R	27	DNQ	23	R	NT	DNP	-	-
17	R	12	R	21	12	20	R	13	6	11	12	15	R	12	R	30	NPQ	17	17
-	-	-	-	-	-	-	-	-	-	-	-	-	-	-	-	-	-	-	-
16	12	19	R	17	9	19	17	18	11	21	R	20	16	26	R	17	9	20	R
-	-	-	-	-	-	-	-	-	-	-	-	-	-	-	-	-	-	-	-
24	R	14	R	15	11	10	R	16	9	19	13	19	12	11	10	19	5	28	DNQ
-	-	-	-	-	-	-	-	-	-	-	-	-	-	-	-	-	-	-	-
-	-	-	-	32	NPQ	32	NPQ	29	DNQ	33	NPQ	33	NPQ	31	NPQ	26	10	23	15
15	R	16	R	12	R	9	6	12	R	12	8	9	17	8	R	-	-	-	-
13	6	13	R	7	5	17	7	11	13	14	7	14	8	17	R	11	R	12	8
34	NPQ	34	NPQ	34	NPQ	34	NPQ	33	NPQ	NT	NPQ	34	NPQ	NT	DNP	-	-	-	-
14	11	27	DNQ	26	R	25	10	26	R	22	11	23	11	25	R	20	R	22	18
19	R	17	6	11	6	16	9F	-	-	-	-	-	-	-	-	-	-	-	-
-	-	-	-	-	-	-	-	-	-	-	-	-	-	-	-	-	-	30	DNQ
21	R	31	NPQ	31	NPQ	27	DNQ	23	10	26	R	32	NPQ	-	-	-	-	-	-
-	-	-	-	-	-	-	-	-	-	-	-	-	-	33	NPQ	-	-	-	-
9	7	9	R	16	R	13	11	15	R	18	15	7	7	13	7	18	8	14	14
27	DNQ	25	12	23	R	26	14	24	R	25	14	26	14	21	R	21	R	25	19
-	-	-	-	-	-	-	-	-	-	-	-	-	-	-	-	31	NPQ	32	NPQ
20	10	24	14	-	-	-	-	21	7	-	-	22	R	-	-	23	R	21	11
-	-	-	-	-	-	-	-	-	-	-	-	-	-	-	-	-	-	-	-
30	DNQ	28	DNQ	-	-	-	-	-	-	-	-	-	-	-	-	-	-	-	-
32	NPQ	32	NPQ	24	R	24	16	28	DNQ	23	16	29	DNQ	28	DNQ	28	DNQ	19	R
26	R	11	13	20	R	12	R	14	R	20	R	18	R	15	8	12	R	11	12
4	1F	1	1F	1	1	3	2	3	R	2	1	4	DSQ	2	1	3	R	3	2
12	9	23	9	10	R	18	R	9	12	10	R	8	4	19	13	7	R	10	R
11	R	10	7	14	13	8	12	10	R	13	R	12	R	14	16	14	6	9	10
10	R	20	11	19	R	23	13	19	R	17	9	13	9	16	14	8	R	-	-
-	-	-	-	-	-	-	-	-	-	-	-	-	-	-	-	-	-	8	6
-	-	-	-	-	-	-	-	-	-	-	-	-	-	-	-	-	-	-	-
8	R	7	R	9	8	15	8	8	4F	-	-	-	-	-	-	-	-	-	-
-	-	-	-	-	-	-	-	-	-	9	R	16	10	-	-	-	-	-	-
18	R	15	8	13	R	14	15	22	R	15	R	21	13	18	17	15	R	24	R
1	5	3	R	4	2F	2	3	17	5	4	R	1	1F	4	3F	5	3	4	5
-	-	-	-	-	-	-	-	-	-	-	-	-	-	-	-	-	-	-	-
7	8	8	5	8	8	11	R	6	3	8	6	11	5	10	11	10	7	5	4
31	NPQ	18	10	18	10	7	R	25	8	16	10	17	R	9	15	16	R	13	7
33	NPQ	33	NPQ	30	DNQ	29	DNQ	30	DNQ	29	DNQ	30	DNQ	30	DNQ	29	DNQ	29	DNQ
-	-	-	-	-	-	-	-	-	-	-	-	-	-	-	-	-	-	-	-
2	2	5	3	5	R	4	R	2	R	5	3	5	R	6	2	4	4	-	-
-	-	-	-	-	-	-	-	7	R	-	-	-	-	-	-	-	-	-	-
-	-	-	-	-	-	-	-	-	-	7	5	10	6	5	6	9	R	6	R
3	3	2	4	2	7	1	1	1	1	1	2F	3	2	3	5	2	2F	1	1
22	R	22	R	22	R	22	R	27	DNQ	30	DNQ	25	R	27	DNQ	25	R	27	DNQ
-	-	-	-	-	-	-	-	-	-	-	-	-	-	-	-	-	-	-	-
29	DNQ	30	DNQ	29	DNQ	31	NPQ	32	NPQ	-	-	-	-	-	-	-	-	-	-
-	-	-	-	-	-	-	-	-	-	32	NPQ	28	DNQ	-	-	-	-	-	-
-	-	-	-	-	-	-	-	-	-	-	-	-	-	22	12	24	11	31	NPQ
-	-	-	-	-	-	-	-	-	-	-	-	-	-	-	-	22	R	26	20
-	-	-	-	-	-	-	-	-	-	-	-	-	-	20	9	13	R	16	9

1991 FINAL CHAMPIONSHIP POSITIONS

Drivers							Manufacturers		
1	Ayrton Senna	96		JJ Lehto	4		1	McLaren-Honda	139
2	Nigel Mansell	72		Michael Schumacher	4		2	Williams-Renault	125
3	Riccardo Patrese	53	15=	Martin Brundle	2		3	Ferrari	55.5
4	Gerhard Berger	43		Mika Hakkinen	2		4	Benetton-Ford	38.5
5	Alain Prost	34		Satoru Nakajima	2		5	Jordan-Ford	13
6	Nelson Piquet	26.5	18=	Julian Bailey	1		6	Tyrrell-Honda	12
7	Jean Alesi	21		Eric Bernard	1		7	Minardi-Ferrari	6
8	Stefano Modena	10		Mark Blundell	1		8	Dallara-Judd	5
9	Andrea de Cesaris	9		Ivan Capelli	1		9=	Lotus-Judd	3
10	Roberto Moreno	8		Emanuele Pirro	1			Brabham-Yamaha	3
11	Pierluigi Martini	6		Aguri Suzuki	1		11	Lola-Ford	2
12=	Bertrand Gachot	4	24	Gianni Morbidelli	0.5		12	Leyton House-Ilmor	1

3	Nelson Piquet	Benetton B191-Ford	44	1h27m49.845
4	Roberto Moreno	Benetton B191-Ford	44	1h27m54.979
5	Riccardo Patrese	Williams FW14-Renault	44	1h28m14.856
6	Mark Blundell	Brabham BT60Y-Yamaha	44	1h28m57.704

Winner's average speed: 130.405 mph. Starting grid front row: Senna, 1m47.811 (pole) and Prost, 1m48.821. Fastest lap: Moreno, 1m55.161. Leaders: Senna, laps 1-14, 31-44; Mansell, 15-16, 18-21; Piquet, 17; Alesi, 22-30

COCA COLA GRAN PREMIO D'ITALIA

8 September 1991. Monza. 53 laps of a 3.604-mile circuit = 191.007 miles. Warm, dry and hazy. World Championship round 12

1	Nigel Mansell	Williams FW14-Renault	53	1h17m54.319
2	Ayrton Senna	McLaren MP4/6-Honda	53	1h18m10.581
3	Alain Prost	Ferrari 643	53	1h18m11.148
4	Gerhard Berger	McLaren MP4/6-Honda	53	1h18m22.038
5	Michael Schumacher	Benetton B191-Ford	53	1h18m28.782
6	Nelson Piquet	Benetton B191-Ford	53	1h18m39.919

Winner's average speed: 147.107 mph. Starting grid front row: Senna, 1m21.114 (pole) and Mansell, 1m21.247. Fastest lap: Senna, 1m26.061. Leaders: Senna, laps 1-25, 27-33; Patrese, 26; Mansell, 34-53

GRANDE PREMIO DE PORTUGAL

22 September 1991. Estoril. 71 laps of a 2.703-mile circuit = 191.913 miles. Warm, dry and sunny. World Championship round 13

1	Riccardo Patrese	Williams FW14-Renault	71	1h35m42.304
2	Ayrton Senna	McLaren MP4/6-Honda	71	1h36m03.245
3	Jean Alesi	Ferrari 643	71	1h36m35.858
4	Pierluigi Martini	Minardi M191-Ferrari	71	1h36m45.802
5	Nelson Piquet	Benetton B191-Ford	71	1h36m52.337
6	Michael Schumacher	Benetton B191-Ford	71	1h36m58.886

Winner's average speed: 120.315 mph. Starting grid front row: Patrese, 1m13.001 (pole) and Berger, 1m13.221. Fastest lap: Patrese, 1m18.350 (Mansell set a fastest lap of 1m18.179 after he had been disqualified). Leaders: Patrese, laps 1-17, 30-71; Mansell, 18-29

GRAN PREMIO TIO PEPE DE ESPANA

29 September 1991. Catalunya. 65 laps of a 2.950-mile circuit = 191.731 miles. Warm and overcast, damp track, drying. World Championship round 14

1	Nigel Mansell	Williams FW14-Renault	65	1h38m41.541
2	Alain Prost	Ferrari 643	65	1h38m52.872
3	Riccardo Patrese	Williams FW14-Renault	65	1h38m57.450
4	Jean Alesi	Ferrari 643	65	1h39m04.313
5	Ayrton Senna	McLaren MP4/6-Honda	65	1h39m43.943
6	Michael Schumacher	Benetton B191-Ford	65	1h40m01.009

Winner's average speed: 116.563 mph. Starting grid front row: Berger, 1m18.751 (pole) and Mansell, 1m18.970. Fastest lap: Patrese, 1m22.837. Leaders: Berger, laps 1-8, 12-20; Mansell, 9, 21-65; Patrese, 10, Senna, 11

FUJI TELEVISION JAPANESE GRAND PRIX

20 October 1991. Suzuka. 53 laps of a 3.641-mile circuit = 192.973 miles. Warm, dry and sunny. World Championship round 15

1	Gerhard Berger	McLaren MP4/6-Honda	53	1h32m10.695
2	Ayrton Senna	McLaren MP4/6-Honda	53	1h32m11.039
3	Riccardo Patrese	Williams FW14-Renault	53	1h33m07.426
4	Alain Prost	Ferrari 643	53	1h33m31.456
5	Martin Brundle	Brabham BT60Y-Yamaha	52	
6	Stefano Modena	Tyrrell 020-Honda	52	

Winner's average speed: 125.609 mph. Starting grid front row: Berger, 1m34.700 (pole) and Senna, 1m34.898. Fastest lap: Senna, 1m41.532. Leaders: Berger, laps 1-17, 53; Senna, 18-21, 24-52; Patrese, 22-23

FOSTER'S AUSTRALIAN GRAND PRIX

3 November 1991. Adelaide. 14 laps of a 2.347-mile circuit = 32.858 miles. Race scheduled for 81 laps, stopped due to heavy rain, half points awarded as less than 60% of the race had been completed. Very wet. World Championship round 16

1	Ayrton Senna	McLaren MP4/6-Honda	14	24m34.899
2	Nigel Mansell	Williams FW14-Renault	14	24m36.158
3	Gerhard Berger	McLaren MP4/6-Honda	14	24m40.019
4	Nelson Piquet	Benetton B191-Ford	14	25m05.002
5	Riccardo Patrese	Williams FW14-Renault	14	25m25.436
6	Gianni Morbidelli	Ferrari 643	14	25m25.968

Winner's average speed: 80.201 mph. Starting grid front row: Senna, 1m14.041 (pole) and Berger, 1m14.385. Fastest lap: Berger, 1m41.141. Leaders: Senna, laps 1-14

1992

The 1992 season was finally Nigel Mansell's year. With the Williams FW14B-Renault now sorted and reliable, there was never any doubt who would be World Champion. Williams was so dominant in the early part of the season that its drivers led every mile until lap 71 of the sixth round. Mansell made an exceptional start to the season with five successive Grand Prix victories, and added four more to clinch the title. His win at Silverstone in July sparked a patriotic crowd invasion while other cars were still running at speed.

But this overwhelming success would soon create turmoil for the team. Despite finishing second in the championship, Mansell's teammate Riccardo Patrese would not be retained at Williams for 1993. Both Ayrton Senna and Alain Prost (who was taking the year off) vied to join Mansell in what was clearly the best drive available. The Brazilian even offered to drive for free, but it was Prost who was eventually signed. Mansell, unhappy with his treatment by the team during negotiations

1992 Nigel Mansell's Williams FW14B dominated the 1992 World Championship to finally secure the title.

with Prost, decided to move to ChampCars in 1993 rather than defend his World Championship.

Despite being at the height of his powers, Ayrton Senna had to be content with just three wins for McLaren. When Mansell was delayed in the Monaco GP in the pits, Senna held off the returning Williams to equal Graham Hill's record of five victories in the principality. Gerhard Berger lived in Senna's shadow, but scored a couple of victories after his teammate and the Williams duo had retired.

Michael Schumacher continued his outstanding introduction to Formula 1 with Benetton. His victory in Belgium a year after his debut, and another ten top-six finishes gave the German third in the championship. Teammate Martin Brundle could not match Schumacher in practice, but often raced well. He nearly won in Canada, held off Senna in Britain, and finished second at Monza.

Ferrari's fortunes sunk yet further in 1992: Jean Alesi finished no higher than third, while former Leyton House star Ivan Capelli was sacked before the end of a disastrous season.

Mika Hakkinen and Johnny Herbert enjoyed an increasingly competitive season with Lotus, giving the team fifth in the Constructors' Championship. Although Hakkinen gained the results, Herbert was usually quicker, but was forced to retire from all but four races.

Giovanna Amati attempted to become the first female Grand Prix driver since Lella Lombardi raced in the 1976 Austrian GP, but Damon Hill replaced her when she failed to qualify the uncompetitive Brabham for the first three races.

Max Mosley was elected President of FISA, succeeding Jean-Marie Balestre.

YELLOW PAGES SOUTH AFRICAN GRAND PRIX

1 March 1992. Kyalami. 72 laps of a 2.648-mile circuit = 190.656 miles. Warm, dry and overcast. World Championship round 1

1	Nigel Mansell	Williams FW14B-Renault	72	1h36m45.320
2	Riccardo Patrese	Williams FW14B-Renault	72	1h37m09.680
3	Ayrton Senna	McLaren MP4/6B-Honda	72	1h37m19.995
4	Michael Schumacher	Benetton B191B-Ford	72	1h37m33.183
5	Gerhard Berger	McLaren MP4/6B-Honda	72	1h37m58.954
6	Johnny Herbert	Lotus 102D-Ford	71	

Winner's average speed: 118.230 mph. Starting grid front row: Mansell, 1m15.486 (pole) and Senna, 1m16.227. Fastest lap: Mansell, 1m17.578. Leaders: Mansell, laps 1-72

GRAN PREMIO DE MEXICO

22 March 1992. Mexico City. 69 laps of a 2.747-mile circuit = 189.543 miles. Hot, dry and sunny. World Championship round 2

1	Nigel Mansell	Williams FW14B-Renault	69	1h31m53.587
2	Riccardo Patrese	Williams FW14B-Renault	69	1h32m06.558
3	Michael Schumacher	Benetton B191B-Ford	69	1h32m15.016
4	Gerhard Berger	McLaren MP4/6B-Honda	69	1h32m26.934
5	Andrea de Cesaris	Tyrrell 020B-Ilmor	68	
6	Mika Hakkinen	Lotus 102D-Ford	68	

Winner's average speed: 123.759 mph. Starting grid front row: Mansell, 1m16.346 (pole) and Patrese, 1m16.362. Fastest lap: Berger, 1m17.711. Leaders: Mansell, laps 1-69

GRANDE PREMIO DO BRASIL

5 April 1992. Interlagos. 71 laps of a 2.687-mile circuit = 190.777 miles. Hot, dry and sunny. World Championship round 3

1	Nigel Mansell	Williams FW14B-Renault	71	1h36m51.856
2	Riccardo Patrese	Williams FW14B-Renault	71	1h37m21.186
3	Michael Schumacher	Benetton B191B-Ford	70	
4	Jean Alesi	Ferrari F92A	70	
5	Ivan Capelli	Ferrari F92A	70	
6	Michele Alboreto	Footwork FA13-Mugen	70	

Winner's average speed: 118.172 mph. Starting grid front row: Mansell, 1m15.703 (pole) and Patrese, 1m16.894. Fastest lap: Patrese, 1m19.490. Leaders: Patrese, laps 1-31; Mansell, 32-71

GRAN PREMIO TIO PEPE DE ESPANA

3 May 1992. Catalunya. 65 laps of a 2.950-mile circuit = 191.731 miles. Cool and wet. World Championship round 4

1	Nigel Mansell	Williams FW14B-Renault	65	1h56m10.674
2	Michael Schumacher	Benetton B192-Ford	65	1h56m34.588
3	Jean Alesi	Ferrari F92A	65	1h56m37.136
4	Gerhard Berger	McLaren MP4/7A-Honda	65	1h57m31.321
5	Michele Alboreto	Footwork FA13-Mugen	64	
6	Pierluigi Martini	Dallara F192-Ferrari	63	

Winner's average speed: 99.019 mph. Starting grid front row: Mansell, 1m20.190 (pole) and Schumacher, 1m21.195. Fastest lap: Mansell, 1m42.503. Leaders: Mansell, laps 1-65

GRAN PREMIO ICEBERG DI SAN MARINO

17 May 1992. Imola. 60 laps of a 3.132-mile circuit = 187.920 miles. Hot, dry and sunny. World Championship round 5

1	Nigel Mansell	Williams FW14B-Renault	60	1h28m40.927
2	Riccardo Patrese	Williams FW14B-Renault	60	1h28m50.378
3	Ayrton Senna	McLaren MP4/7A-Honda	60	1h29m29.911
4	Martin Brundle	Benetton B192-Ford	60	1h29m33.934
5	Michele Alboreto	Footwork FA13-Mugen	59	
6	Pierluigi Martini	Dallara F192-Ferrari	59	

Winner's average speed: 127.142 mph. Starting grid front row: Mansell, 1m21.842 (pole) and Patrese, 1m22.895. Fastest lap: Patrese, 1m26.100. Leaders: Mansell, laps 1-60

GRAND PRIX DE MONACO

31 May 1992. Monte Carlo. 78 laps of a 2.068-mile circuit = 161.304 miles. Warm, dry and sunny. World Championship round 6

1	Ayrton Senna	McLaren MP4/7A-Honda	78	1h50m59.372
2	Nigel Mansell	Williams FW14B-Renault	78	1h50m59.587
3	Riccardo Patrese	Williams FW14B-Renault	78	1h51m31.215
4	Michael Schumacher	Benetton B192-Ford	78	1h51m38.666
5	Martin Brundle	Benetton B192-Ford	78	1h52m20.719
6	Bertrand Gachot	Larrousse LC92-Lamborghini	77	

Winner's average speed: 87.200 mph. Starting grid front row: Mansell, 1m19.495 (pole) and Patrese, 1m20.368. Fastest lap: Mansell, 1m21.598. Leaders: Mansell, laps 1-70; Senna, 71-78

1992 DRIVERS' RECORDS

driver	car	ZA Q	R	MEX Q	R	BR Q	R	E Q	R	RSM Q	R	MC Q	R
Michele Alboreto	Footwork FA13-Mugen	17	10	25	13	14	6	16	5	9	5	11	7
Jean Alesi	Ferrari F92A	5	R	10	R	6	4	8	3	7	R	4	R
	Ferrari F92AT	-	-	-	-	-	-	-	-	-	-	-	-
Giovanna Amati	Brabham BT60B-Judd	30	DNQ	30	DNQ	30	DNQ	-	-	-	-	-	-
Paul Belmondo	March CG911-Ilmor	27	DNQ	28	DNQ	28	DNQ	23	12	24	13	30	DNQ
Gerhard Berger	McLaren MP4/6B-Honda	3	5	5	4F	-	-	-	-	-	-	-	-
	McLaren MP4/7A-Honda	-	-	-	-	4	R	7	4	4	R	5	R
Enrico Bertaggia	Coloni C4B-Judd	NT	DNP	-	-	-	-	-	-	-	-	-	-
	Andrea Moda S192-Judd	-	-	NT	DNP	-	-	-	-	-	-	-	-
Thierry Boutsen	Ligier JS37-Renault	14	R	22	10	10	R	14	R	10	R	22	12
Martin Brundle	Benetton B191B-Ford	8	R	4	R	7	R	-	-	-	-	-	-
	Benetton B192-Ford	-	-	-	-	-	-	6	R	6	4	7	5
Alex Caffi	Coloni C4B-Judd	NT	DNP	-	-	-	-	-	-	-	-	-	-
	Andrea Moda S192-Judd	-	-	NT	DNP	-	-	-	-	-	-	-	-
Ivan Capelli	Ferrari F92A	9	R	20	R	11	5	5	10	8	R	8	R
	Ferrari F92AT	-	-	-	-	-	-	-	-	-	-	-	-
Andrea de Cesaris	Tyrrell 020B-Ilmor	10	R	11	5	13	R	11	R	14	14	10	R
Andrea Chiesa	Fondmetal GR01-Ford	28	DNQ	23	R	27	DNQ	20	R	28	DNQ	29	DNQ
	Fondmetal GR02-Ford	-	-	-	-	-	-	-	-	-	-	-	-
Erik Comas	Ligier JS37-Renault	13	7	26	9	15	R	10	R	13	9	23	10
Christian Fittipaldi	Minardi M191B-Lamborghini	20	R	17	R	20	R	22	11	-	-	-	-
	Minardi M192-Lamborghini	-	-	-	-	-	-	-	-	25	R	17	8
Bertrand Gachot	Larrousse LC92-Lamborghini	22	R	13	11	18	R	24	R	19	R	15	6
Olivier Grouillard	Tyrrell 020B-Ilmor	12	R	16	R	17	R	15	R	20	8	24	R
Mauricio Gugelmin	Jordan 192-Yamaha	23	11	8	R	21	R	17	R	18	7	13	R
Mika Hakkinen	Lotus 102D-Ford	21	9	18	6	24	10	21	R	27	DNQ	-	-
	Lotus 107-Ford	-	-	-	-	-	-	-	-	-	-	14	R
Johnny Herbert	Lotus 102D-Ford	11	6	12	7	26	R	26	R	-	-	-	-
	Lotus 107-Ford	-	-	-	-	-	-	-	-	26	R	9	R
Damon Hill	Brabham BT60B-Judd	-	-	-	-	-	-	30	DNQ	29	DNQ	28	DNQ
Ukyo Katayama	Larrousse LC92-Lamborghini	18	12	24	12	25	9	27	DNQ	17	R	31	NPQ
Jan Lammers	March CG911-Ilmor	-	-	-	-	-	-	-	-	-	-	-	-
Nicola Larini	Ferrari F92A	-	-	-	-	-	-	-	-	-	-	-	-
JJ Lehto	Dallara F192-Ferrari	24	R	7	8	16	8	12	R	16	11	20	9
Nigel Mansell	Williams FW14B-Renault	1	1F	1	1	1	1	1	1F	1	1	1	2F
Pierluigi Martini	Dallara F192-Ferrari	25	R	9	R	8	R	13	6	15	6	18	R
Perry McCarthy	Andrea Moda S192-Judd	-	-	-	-	NT	NPQ	NT	NPQ	32	NPQ	NT	NPQ
Stefano Modena	Jordan 192-Yamaha	29	DNQ	15	R	12	R	29	DNQ	23	R	21	R
Gianni Morbidelli	Minardi M191B-Lamborghini	19	R	21	R	23	7	25	R	-	-	-	-
	Minardi M192-Lamborghini	-	-	-	-	-	-	-	-	21	R	12	R
Roberto Moreno	Andrea Moda S192-Judd	-	-	-	-	31	NPQ	31	NPQ	31	NPQ	26	R
Emanuele Naspetti	March CG911-Ilmor	-	-	-	-	-	-	-	-	-	-	-	-
Riccardo Patrese	Williams FW14B-Renault	4	2	2	2	2	2F	4	R	2	2F	2	3
Eric van de Poele	Brabham BT60B-Judd	26	13	29	DNQ	29	DNQ	28	DNQ	30	DNQ	27	DNQ
	Fondmetal GR02-Ford	-	-	-	-	-	-	-	-	-	-	-	-
Michael Schumacher	Benetton B191B-Ford	6	4	3	3	5	3	-	-	-	-	-	-
	Benetton B192-Ford	-	-	-	-	-	-	2	2	5	R	6	4
Ayrton Senna	McLaren MP4/6B-Honda	2	3	6	R	-	-	-	-	-	-	-	-
	McLaren MP4/7A-Honda	-	-	-	-	3	R	3	9	3	3	3	1
Aguri Suzuki	Footwork FA13-Mugen	16	8	27	DNQ	22	R	19	7	11	10	19	11
Gabriele Tarquini	Fondmetal GR01-Ford	15	R	14	R	19	R	18	R	22	R	25	R
	Fondmetal GR02-Ford	-	-	-	-	-	-	-	-	-	-	-	-
Karl Wendlinger	March CG911-Ilmor	7	R	19	R	9	R	9	8	12	12	16	R
Alessandro Zanardi	Minardi M192-Lamborghini	-	-	-	-	-	-	-	-	-	-	-	-

	CDN		F		GB		D		H		B		I		P		J		AUS
Q	R	Q	R	Q	R	Q	R	Q	R	Q	R	Q	R	Q	R	Q	R	Q	R
16	7	14	7	12	7	17	9	7	7	14	R	16	7	8	6	24	15	11	R
8	3	6	R	8	R	5	5	9	R	-	-	-	-	-	-	-	-	-	-
-	-	-	-	-	-	-	-	-	-	5	R	3	R	10	R	15	5	6	4
-	-	-	-	-	-	-	-	-	-	-	-	-	-	-	-	-	-	-	-
20	14	27	DNQ	28	DNQ	22	13	17	9	-	-	-	-	-	-	-	-	-	-
-	-	-	-	-	-	-	-	-	-	-	-	-	-	-	-	-	-	-	-
4	1F	4	R	5	5	4	R	5	3	6	R	5	4	4	2	4	2	4	1
-	-	-	-	-	-	-	-	-	-	-	-	-	-	-	-	-	-	-	-
21	10	9	R	13	10	8	7	8	R	7	R	8	R	11	8	10	R	22	5
-	-	-	-	-	-	-	-	-	-	-	-	-	-	-	-	-	-	-	-
7	R	7	3	6	3	9	4	6	5	9	4	9	2	6	4	13	3	8	3
-	-	-	-	-	-	-	-	-	-	-	-	-	-	-	-	-	-	-	-
9	R	8	R	14	9	12	R	10	6	12	R	-	-	-	-	-	-	-	-
-	-	-	-	-	-	-	-	-	-	-	-	7	R	16	R	-	-	-	-
14	5	19	R	18	R	20	R	19	8	13	8	21	6	12	9	9	4	7	R
29	DNQ	-	-	29	DNQ	29	DNQ	-	-	-	-	-	-	-	-	-	-	-	-
-	-	26	R	-	-	-	-	-	-	-	-	-	-	-	-	-	-	-	-
22	6	10	5	10	8	7	6	11	R	NT	DNP	15	R	14	R	8	R	9	R
-	-	-	-	-	-	-	-	-	-	-	-	-	-	-	-	-	-	-	-
25	13	28	DNQ	-	-	-	-	-	-	27	DNQ	27	DNQ	26	12	12	6	17	9
19	DSQ	13	R	11	R	25	14	15	R	20	18	10	R	13	R	18	R	21	R
26	12	22	11	20	11	14	R	22	R	22	R	18	R	15	R	21	R	13	R
24	R	24	R	24	R	23	15	21	10	24	14	26	R	20	R	25	R	20	R
-	-	-	-	-	-	-	-	-	-	-	-	-	-	-	-	-	-	-	-
10	R	11	4	9	6	13	R	16	4	8	6	11	R	7	5	7	R	10	7
-	-	-	-	-	-	-	-	-	-	-	-	-	-	-	-	-	-	-	-
6	R	12	6	7	R	11	R	13	R	10	13	13	R	9	R	6	R	12	13
30	DNQ	30	DNQ	26	16	30	DNQ	25	11	-	-	-	-	-	-	-	-	-	-
11	R	18	R	16	R	16	R	20	R	26	17	23	9	25	R	20	11	26	R
-	-	-	-	-	-	-	-	-	-	-	-	-	-	-	-	23	R	25	12
-	-	-	-	-	-	-	-	-	-	-	-	-	-	-	-	11	12	19	11
23	9	17	9	19	13	21	10	28	DNQ	16	7	14	11	19	R	22	9	24	R
3	R	1	1F	1	1F	1	1	2	2F	1	2	1	RF	1	1	1	RF	1	R
15	8	25	10	22	15	18	11	26	R	19	R	22	8	21	R	19	10	14	R
NT	NPQ	NT	DNP	32	NPQ	NT	NPQ	NT	NPQ	29	DNQ	-	-	-	-	-	-	-	-
17	R	20	R	23	R	27	DNQ	24	R	17	15	28	DNQ	24	13	17	7	15	6
-	-	-	-	-	-	-	-	-	-	-	-	-	-	-	-	-	-	-	-
13	11	16	8	25	R	26	12	27	DNQ	23	16	12	R	18	14	14	14	16	10
31	NPQ	NT	DNP	31	NPQ	31	NPQ	30	DNQ	28	DNQ	-	-	-	-	-	-	-	-
-	-	-	-	-	-	-	-	-	-	21	12	24	R	23	11	26	13	23	R
2	R	2	2	2	2	2	8F	1	R	4	3	4	5	2	R	2	1	3	R
28	DNQ	29	DNQ	30	DNQ	28	DNQ	-	-	-	-	-	-	-	-	-	-	-	-
-	-	-	-	-	-	-	-	18	R	15	10	25	R	-	-	-	-	-	-
5	2	5	R	4	4	6	3	4	R	3	1F	6	3	5	7	5	R	5	2F
-	-	-	-	-	-	-	-	-	-	-	-	-	-	-	-	-	-	-	-
1	R	3	R	3	R	3	2	3	1	2	5	2	1	3	3F	3	R	2	R
27	DNQ	15	R	17	12	15	R	14	R	25	9	19	R	17	10	16	8	18	8
-	-	-	-	-	-	-	-	-	-	-	-	-	-	-	-	-	-	-	-
18	R	23	R	15	14	19	R	12	R	11	R	20	R	-	-	-	-	-	-
12	4	21	R	21	R	21	R	10	16	23	R	18	11	17	10	22	R	-	-
-	-	-	-	27	DNQ	24	R	29	DNQ	-	-	-	-	-	-	-	-	-	-

1992 FINAL CHAMPIONSHIP POSITIONS

Drivers						Manufacturers		
1	Nigel Mansell	108	14=	Thierry Boutsen	2	1	Williams-Renault	164
2	Riccardo Patrese	56		Johnny Herbert	2	2	McLaren-Honda	99
3	Michael Schumacher	53		Pierluigi Martini	2	3	Benetton-Ford	91
4	Ayrton Senna	50	17=	Christian Fittipaldi	1	4	Ferrari	21
5	Gerhard Berger	49		Bertrand Gachot	1	5	Lotus-Ford	13
6	Martin Brundle	38		Stefano Modena	1	6	Tyrrell-Ilmor	8
7	Jean Alesi	18				7=	Footwork-Mugen	6
8	Mika Hakkinen	11					Ligier-Renault	6
9	Andrea de Cesaris	8				9	March-Ilmor	3
10	Michele Alboreto	6				10	Dallara-Ferrari	2
11	Erik Comas	4				11=	Larrousse-Lamborghini	1
12=	Ivan Capelli	3					Minardi-Lamborghini	1
	Karl Wendlinger	3					Jordan-Yamaha	1

GRAND PRIX MOLSON DU CANADA

14 June 1992. Montreal. 69 laps of a 2.753-mile circuit = 189.957 miles. Hot, dry and sunny. World Championship round 7

1	Gerhard Berger	McLaren MP4/7A-Honda	69	1h37m08.299
2	Michael Schumacher	Benetton B192-Ford	69	1h37m20.700
3	Jean Alesi	Ferrari F92A	69	1h38m15.626
4	Karl Wendlinger	March CG911-Ilmor	68	
5	Andrea de Cesaris	Tyrrell 020B-Ilmor	68	
6	Erik Comas	Ligier JS37-Renault	68	

Winner's average speed: 117.332 mph. Starting grid front row: Senna, 1m19.775 (pole) and Patrese, 1m19.872. Fastest lap: Berger, 1m22.325. Leaders: Senna, laps 1-37; Berger, 38-69

RHONE-POULENC GRAND PRIX DE FRANCE

5 July 1992. Magny-Cours. 69 laps of a 2.641-mile circuit = 182.229 miles. Race scheduled for 72 laps, stopped after 18 laps due to rain, restarted over an additional 51 laps. Warm, dry and overcast, turning wet. World Championship round 8

1	Nigel Mansell	Williams FW14B-Renault	69	1h38m08.459
2	Riccardo Patrese	Williams FW14B-Renault	69	1h38m54.906
3	Martin Brundle	Benetton B192-Ford	69	1h39m21.038
4	Mika Hakkinen	Lotus 107-Ford	68	
5	Erik Comas	Ligier JS37-Renault	68	
6	Johnny Herbert	Lotus 107-Ford	68	

Winner's average speed: 111.409 mph. Starting grid front row: Mansell, 1m13.864 (pole) and Patrese, 1m14.332. Fastest lap: Mansell, 1m17.070. Leaders: Patrese, laps 1-20; Mansell, 21-69

BRITISH GRAND PRIX

12 July 1992. Silverstone. 59 laps of a 3.247-mile circuit = 191.573 miles. Hot, dry and sunny. World Championship round 9

1	Nigel Mansell	Williams FW14B-Renault	59	1h25m42.991
2	Riccardo Patrese	Williams FW14B-Renault	59	1h26m22.085
3	Martin Brundle	Benetton B192-Ford	59	1h26m31.386
4	Michael Schumacher	Benetton B192-Ford	59	1h26m36.258
5	Gerhard Berger	McLaren MP4/7A-Honda	59	1h26m38.786
6	Mika Hakkinen	Lotus 107-Ford	59	1h27m03.129

Winner's average speed: 134.098 mph. Starting grid front row: Mansell, 1m18.965 (pole) and Patrese, 1m20.884. Fastest lap: Mansell, 1m22.539. Leaders: Mansell, laps 1-59

GROSSER MOBIL 1 PREIS VON DEUTSCHLAND

26 July 1992. Hockenheim. 45 laps of a 4.235-mile circuit = 190.575 miles. Hot, dry and sunny. World Championship round 10

1	Nigel Mansell	Williams FW14B-Renault	45	1h18m22.032
2	Ayrton Senna	McLaren MP4/7A-Honda	45	1h18m26.532
3	Michael Schumacher	Benetton B192-Ford	45	1h18m56.494
4	Martin Brundle	Benetton B192-Ford	45	1h18m58.991
5	Jean Alesi	Ferrari F92A	45	1h19m34.639
6	Erik Comas	Ligier JS37-Renault	45	1h19m58.530

Winner's average speed: 145.909 mph. Starting grid front row: Mansell, 1m37.960 (pole) and Patrese, 1m38.310. Fastest lap: Patrese, 1m41.591. Leaders: Mansell, laps 1-14, 20-45; Patrese, 15-19

MARLBORO MAGYAR NAGYDIJ (HUNGARIAN GRAND PRIX)

16 August 1992. Hungaroring. 77 laps of a 2.466-mile circuit = 189.882 miles. Hot, dry and sunny. World Championship round 11

1	Ayrton Senna	McLaren MP4/7A-Honda	77	1h46m19.216
2	Nigel Mansell	Williams FW14B-Renault	77	1h46m59.355
3	Gerhard Berger	McLaren MP4/7A-Honda	77	1h47m09.998
4	Mika Hakkinen	Lotus 107-Ford	77	1h47m13.529
5	Martin Brundle	Benetton B192-Ford	77	1h47m16.714
6	Ivan Capelli	Ferrari F92A	76	

Winner's average speed: 107.157 mph. Starting grid front row: Patrese, 1m15.476 (pole) and Mansell, 1m15.643. Fastest lap: Mansell, 1m18.308. Leaders: Patrese, laps 1-38; Senna, 39-77

GRAND PRIX DE BELGIQUE

30 August 1992. Spa-Francorchamps. 44 laps of a 4.312-mile circuit = 189.728 miles. Warm, dry and overcast at the start, rain later before drying again. World Championship round 12

1	Michael Schumacher	Benetton B192-Ford	44	1h36m10.721
2	Nigel Mansell	Williams FW14B-Renault	44	1h36m47.316
3	Riccardo Patrese	Williams FW14B-Renault	44	1h36m54.618
4	Martin Brundle	Benetton B192-Ford	44	1h36m56.780
5	Ayrton Senna	McLaren MP4/7A-Honda	44	1h37m19.090
6	Mika Hakkinen	Lotus 107-Ford	44	1h37m20.751

Winner's average speed: 118.360 mph. Starting grid front row: Mansell, 1m50.545 (pole) and Senna, 1m52.743. Fastest lap: Schumacher, 1m53.791. Leaders: Senna, laps 1, 7-10; Mansell, 2-3, 11-33; Patrese, 4-6; Schumacher, 34-44

PIONEER GRAN PREMIO D'ITALIA

13 September 1992. Monza. 53 laps of a 3.604-mile circuit = 191.007 miles. Hot, dry and sunny. World Championship round 13

1	Ayrton Senna	McLaren MP4/7A-Honda	53	1h18m15.349
2	Martin Brundle	Benetton B192-Ford	53	1h18m32.399
3	Michael Schumacher	Benetton B192-Ford	53	1h18m39.722
4	Gerhard Berger	McLaren MP4/7A-Honda	53	1h19m40.839
5	Riccardo Patrese	Williams FW14B-Renault	53	1h19m48.507
6	Andrea de Cesaris	Tyrrell 020B-Ilmor	52	

Winner's average speed: 146.448 mph. Starting grid front row: Mansell, 1m22.221 (pole) and Senna, 1m22.822. Fastest lap: Mansell, 1m26.119. Leaders: Mansell, laps 1-19; Patrese, 20-47; Senna, 48-53

SG GIGANTE GRANDE PREMIO DE PORTUGAL

27 September 1992. Estoril. 71 laps of a 2.703-mile circuit = 191.913 miles. Warm, dry and sunny. World Championship round 14

1	Nigel Mansell	Williams FW14B-Renault	71	1h34m46.659
2	Gerhard Berger	McLaren MP4/7A-Honda	71	1h35m24.192
3	Ayrton Senna	McLaren MP4/7A-Honda	70	

4 Martin Brundle	Benetton B192-Ford	70
5 Mika Hakkinen	Lotus 107-Ford	70
6 Michele Alboreto	Footwork FA13-Mugen	70

Winner's average speed: 121.493 mph. Starting grid front row: Mansell, 1m13.041 (pole) and Patrese, 1m13.672. Fastest lap: Senna, 1m16.272. Leaders: Mansell, laps 1-71.

FUJI TELEVISION JAPANESE GRAND PRIX

25 October 1992. Suzuka. 53 laps of a 3.641-mile circuit = 192.973 miles. Warm, dry and cloudy. World Championship round 15

1 Riccardo Patrese	Williams FW14B-Renault	53	1h33m09.553
2 Gerhard Berger	McLaren MP4/7A-Honda	53	1h33m23.282
3 Martin Brundle	Benetton B192-Ford	53	1h34m25.056
4 Andrea de Cesaris	Tyrrell 020B-Ilmor	52	
5 Jean Alesi	Ferrari F92A	52	
6 Christian Fittipaldi	Minardi M192-Lamborghini	52	

Winner's average speed: 124.286 mph. Starting grid front row: Mansell, 1m37.360 (pole) and Patrese, 1m38.219. Fastest lap: Mansell, 1m40.646. Leaders: Mansell, laps 1-35; Patrese, 36-53.

FOSTER'S AUSTRALIAN GRAND PRIX

8 November 1992. Adelaide. 81 laps of a 2.347-mile circuit = 190.107 miles. Warm, dry and overcast. World Championship round 16

1 Gerhard Berger	McLaren MP4/7A-Honda	81	1h46m54.786
2 Michael Schumacher	Benetton B192-Ford	81	1h46m55.527
3 Martin Brundle	Benetton B192-Ford	81	1h47m48.942
4 Jean Alesi	Ferrari F92AT	80	
5 Thierry Boutsen	Ligier JS37-Renault	80	
6 Stefano Modena	Jordan 192-Yamaha	80	

Winner's average speed: 106.689 mph. Starting grid front row: Mansell, 1m13.732 (pole) and Senna, 1m14.202. Fastest lap: Schumacher, 1m16.078. Leaders: Mansell, laps 1-18; Patrese, 19-50; Berger, 51-81.

1993

In 1993 Alain Prost returned from a year off to replace Nigel Mansell in the all-conquering Williams team. Although he would once again win the World Championship, Prost received little credit from the press. Every time he added to his record number of GP victories it was attributed to the Williams car; but when he lost the blame fell squarely on the Frenchman's shoulders. Nevertheless, by the end of the season Prost had won seven races, always qualified on the front row, and collected his fourth title by a 26-point margin.

Highly regarded by the team and by Renault, Prost still felt pressure from the F1 governing body and the media. When it became obvious in Portugal that Ayrton Senna would be joining Williams for 1994, he announced his retirement, just a day before clinching his fourth title.

At McLaren, Senna started the year without the Honda engines he had used for the last six years, and with the seemingly impossible task of wresting the championship away from Williams. A combination of Senna's brilliance, the heavy rain in which he thrived, and a nimble McLaren-Ford gave the Brazilian victories in Brazil and at Donington, as well as the championship lead after six rounds.

Senna gave the performance of his career at Donington Park, passing four cars on the opening lap and out-thinking his rivals in the treacherous conditions. But after this, Prost gathered momentum and victories, and despite Senna driving as forcefully as he could, the title slipped away from him.

Both Williams and McLaren turned to two relatively inexperienced drivers to back up their stars. After near

misses at Silverstone and Hockenheim, Damon Hill captured the first of three successive wins for Williams in Hungary. But McLaren's choice, American ChampCar Champion Michael Andretti, struggled in F1 and eventually relinquished his ride immediately after a year-best third at Monza. Andretti's disappointing performance was highlighted by his replacement, Mika Hakkinen, who immediately out-qualified Senna and would end the year by taking third place for McLaren in Japan.

Benetton's Michael Schumacher only won once in Portugal, but further enhanced his credentials by finishing on the podium eight other times in 1993. Riccardo Patrese replaced Brundle as the German's teammate, but failed to match Schumacher's pace in a disappointing final season in Grand Prix racing. Patrese retired from the formula after a record 256 races.

Jean Alesi continued to be spectacular, especially in practice. But although he led in Portugal and was normally quicker than teammate Gerhard Berger, it was another season without a win for Ferrari. The team hired former rally co-driver Jean Todt to bring organisation to its racing programme. Although Ferrari would not regain the championship for another seven years, Todt's recruitment was a vital step in returning the team to full competitiveness.

Mercedes-Benz re-entered Formula 1 with Swiss sports car team Sauber, but after a points finish at the first round, the alliance's potential went unfulfilled. Jordan's fortunes improved after replacing Yamaha's disappointing engine with a Hart unit at the start of the year. Rubens Barrichello made a strong showing at Donington, while Eddie Irvine's debut for the team at Suzuka was even more dramatic: he finished sixth and had a widely reported post-race physical altercation with Senna, after the Jordan repassed and blocked the McLaren while being lapped.

PANASONIC SOUTH AFRICAN GRAND PRIX

14 March 1993. Kyalami. 72 laps of a 2.648-mile circuit = 190.656 miles. Hot, dry and cloudy, rain in the closing laps. World Championship round 1

1 Alain Prost	Williams FW15C-Renault	72	1h38m45.082
2 Ayrton Senna	McLaren MP4/8-Ford	72	1h40m04.906
3 Mark Blundell	Ligier JS39-Renault	71	
4 Christian Fittipaldi	Minardi M193-Ford	71	
5 JJ Lehto	Sauber C12-Ilmor	70	
6 Gerhard Berger	Ferrari F93A	69	engine

Winner's average speed: 115.840 mph. Starting grid front row: Prost, 1m15.696 (pole) and Senna, 1m15.784. Fastest lap: Prost, 1m19.492. Leaders: Senna, laps 1-23; Prost, 24-72.

GRANDE PREMIO DO BRASIL

28 March 1993. Interlagos. 71 laps of a 2.687-mile circuit = 190.777 miles. Dry and overcast, wet in mid-race laps. World Championship round 2

1 Ayrton Senna	McLaren MP4/8-Ford	71	1h51m15.485
2 Damon Hill	Williams FW15C-Renault	71	1h51m32.110
3 Michael Schumacher	Benetton B193-Ford	71	1h52m00.921
4 Johnny Herbert	Lotus 107B-Ford	71	1h52m02.042
5 Mark Blundell	Ligier JS39-Renault	71	1h52m07.612
6 Alessandro Zanardi	Lotus 107B-Ford	70	

Winner's average speed: 102.883 mph. Starting grid front row: Prost, 1m15.866 (pole) and Hill, 1m16.859. Fastest lap: Schumacher, 1m20.024. Leaders: Prost, laps 1-29; Hill, 30-41; Senna, 42-71.

Formula 1

driver	car	ZA Q	R	BR Q	R	EU Q	R	RSM Q	R	E Q	R	MC Q	R
Michele Alboreto	Lola T93/30-Ferrari	25	R	25	11	24	11	26	DNQ	26	DNQ	24	R
Jean Alesi	Ferrari F93A	5	R	9	8	9	R	9	R	8	R	5	3
Philippe Alliot	Larrousse LH93-Lamborghini	11	R	11	7	15	R	14	5	13	R	15	12
Michael Andretti	McLaren MP4/8-Ford	9	R	5	R	6	R	6	R	7	R	9	8
Marco Apicella	Jordan 193-Hart	-	-	-	-	-	-	-	-	-	-	-	-
Luca Badoer	Lola T93/30-Ferrari	26	R	21	12	26	DNQ	24	7	22	R	26	DNQ
Fabrizio Barbazza	Minardi M193-Ford	24	R	24	R	20	6	25	6	25	R	25	11
Rubens Barrichello	Jordan 193-Hart	14	R	14	R	12	10	13	R	17	12	16	9
Gerhard Berger	Ferrari F93A	15	6	13	R	8	R	8	R	11	6	7	14
Mark Blundell	Ligier JS39-Renault	8	3	10	5	21	R	7	R	12	7	21	R
Thierry Boutsen	Jordan 193-Hart	-	-	-	-	19	R	19	R	21	11	23	R
Martin Brundle	Ligier JS39-Renault	12	R	16	R	22	R	10	3	18	R	13	6
Ivan Capelli	Jordan 193-Hart	18	R	26	DNQ	-	-	-	-	-	-	-	-
Andrea de Cesaris	Tyrrell 020C-Yamaha	23	R	23	R	25	R	18	R	24	DSQ	19	10
	Tyrrell 021-Yamaha	-	-	-	-	-	-	-	-	-	-	-	-
Erik Comas	Larrousse LH93-Lamborghini	19	R	17	10	17	9	17	R	14	9	10	R
Christian Fittipaldi	Minardi M193-Ford	13	4	20	R	16	7	23	R	20	8	17	5
Jean-Marc Gounon	Minardi M193-Ford	-	-	-	-	-	-	-	-	-	-	-	-
Mika Hakkinen	McLaren MP4/8-Ford	-	-	-	-	-	-	-	-	-	-	-	-
Johnny Herbert	Lotus 107B-Ford	17	R	12	4	11	4	12	8	10	R	14	R
Damon Hill	Williams FW15C-Renault	4	R	2	2	2	2	2	R	2	R	4	2
Eddie Irvine	Jordan 193-Hart	-	-	-	-	-	-	-	-	-	-	-	-
Ukyo Katayama	Tyrrell 020C-Yamaha	21	R	22	R	18	R	22	R	23	R	22	R
	Tyrrell 021-Yamaha	-	-	-	-	-	-	-	-	-	-	-	-
Pedro Lamy	Lotus 107B-Ford	-	-	-	-	-	-	-	-	-	-	-	-
JJ Lehto	Sauber C12-Ilmor	6	5	7	R	7	R	16	4	9	R	11	R
	Sauber C12	-	-	-	-	-	-	-	-	-	-	-	-
Pierluigi Martini	Minardi M193-Ford	-	-	-	-	-	-	-	-	-	-	-	-
Emanuele Naspetti	Jordan 193-Hart	-	-	-	-	-	-	-	-	-	-	-	-
Riccardo Patrese	Benetton B193-Ford	7	R	6	R	-	-	-	-	-	-	-	-
	Benetton B193B-Ford	-	-	-	-	10	5	11	R	5	4	6	R
Alain Prost	Williams FW15C-Renault	1	1F	1	R	1	3	1	1F	1	1	1	4F
Michael Schumacher	Benetton B193-Ford	3	R	4	3F	-	-	-	-	-	-	-	-
	Benetton B193B-Ford	-	-	-	-	3	R	3	2	4	3F	2	R
Ayrton Senna	McLaren MP4/8-Ford	2	2	3	1	4	1F	4	R	2	3	3	1
Aguri Suzuki	Footwork FA13B-Mugen	20	R	19	R	-	-	-	-	-	-	-	-
	Footwork FA14-Mugen	-	-	-	-	23	R	21	9	19	10	18	R
Toshio Suzuki	Larrousse LH93-Lamborghini	-	-	-	-	-	-	-	-	-	-	-	-
Derek Warwick	Footwork FA13B-Mugen	22	7	18	9	-	-	-	-	-	-	-	-
	Footwork FA14-Mugen	-	-	-	-	14	R	15	R	16	13	12	R
Karl Wendlinger	Sauber C12-Ilmor	10	R	8	R	5	R	5	R	6	R	8	13
	Sauber C12	-	-	-	-	-	-	-	-	-	-	-	-
Alessandro Zanardi	Lotus 107B-Ford	16	R	15	6	13	8	20	R	15	R	20	7

SEGA EUROPEAN GRAND PRIX

11 April 1993. Donington Park. 76 laps of a 2.500-mile circuit = 190.000 miles. Cool and very wet. World Championship round 3

1	Ayrton Senna	McLaren MP4/8-Ford	76	1h50m46.570
2	Damon Hill	Williams FW15C-Renault	76	1h52m09.769
3	Alain Prost	Williams FW15C-Renault	75	
4	Johnny Herbert	Lotus 107B-Ford	75	
5	Riccardo Patrese	Benetton B193B-Ford	74	
6	Fabrizio Barbazza	Minardi M193-Ford	74	

Winner's average speed: 102.910 mph. Starting grid front row: Prost, 1m10.458 (pole) and Hill, 1m10.762. Fastest lap: Senna, 1m18.029 (time set on a lap through the pit-lane). Leaders: Senna, laps 1-18, 20-34, 39-76; Prost, 19, 35-38

GRAN PREMIO DI SAN MARINO

25 April 1993. Imola. 61 laps of a 3.132-mile circuit = 191.052 miles. Cool, damp and overcast, drying later. World Championship round 4

1	Alain Prost	Williams FW15C-Renault	61	1h33m20.413
2	Michael Schumacher	Benetton B193B-Ford	61	1h33m52.823
3	Martin Brundle	Ligier JS39-Renault	60	
4	JJ Lehto	Sauber C12-Ilmor	59	engine
5	Philippe Alliot	Larrousse LH93-Lamborghini	59	
6	Fabrizio Barbazza	Minardi M193-Ford	59	

Winner's average speed: 122.810 mph. Starting grid front row: Prost, 1m22.070 (pole) and Hill, 1m22.168. Fastest lap: Prost, 1m26.128. Leaders: Hill, laps 1-11; Prost, 12-61

GRAN PREMIO DE ESPANA

9 May 1993. Catalunya. 65 laps of a 2.950-mile circuit = 191.731 miles. Hot, dry and sunny. World Championship round 5

1	Alain Prost	Williams FW15C-Renault	65	1h32m27.685
2	Ayrton Senna	McLaren MP4/8-Ford	65	1h32m44.558
3	Michael Schumacher	Benetton B193B-Ford	65	1h32m54.810
4	Riccardo Patrese	Benetton B193B-Ford	64	
5	Michael Andretti	McLaren MP4/8-Ford	64	
6	Gerhard Berger	Ferrari F93A	63	

Winner's average speed: 124.418 mph. Starting grid front row: Prost, 1m17.809 (pole) and Hill, 1m18.346. Fastest lap: Schumacher, 1m20.989. Leaders: Hill, laps 1-10; Prost, 11-65

CDN		F		GB		D		H		B		I		P		J		AUS	
Q	R	Q	R	Q	R	Q	R	Q	R	Q	R	Q	R	Q	R	Q	R	Q	R
26	DNQ	26	DNQ	26	DNQ	26	16	25	R	25	14	21	R	25	R	-	-	-	-
6	R	6	R	12	9	10	7	8	R	4	R	3	2	5	4	14	R	7	4
15	R	10	9	24	11	23	12	19	8	18	12	16	9	20	10	-	-	-	-
12	14	16	6	11	R	12	R	11	R	14	8	9	3	-	-	-	-	-	-
-	-	-	-	-	-	-	-	-	-	-	-	23	R	-	-	-	-	-	-
25	15	22	R	25	R	25	R	26	R	24	13	25	10	26	14	-	-	-	-
23	R	24	R	-	-	-	-	-	-	-	-	-	-	-	-	-	-	-	-
14	R	8	7	15	10	17	R	16	R	13	R	19	R	15	13	12	5	13	11
5	4	14	14	13	R	9	6	6	3	16	10	6	R	8	R	5	R	6	5
10	R	4	R	9	7	5	3	12	7	15	11	14	R	10	R	17	7	14	9
24	12	20	11	23	R	24	13	24	9	20	R	-	-	-	-	-	-	-	-
7	5	3	5	6	14	6	8	13	5	11	7	12	R	11	6	15	9	8	6
-	-	-	-	-	-	-	-	-	-	-	-	-	-	-	-	-	-	-	-
19	R	25	15	-	-	-	-	-	-	-	-	-	-	-	-	-	-	-	-
-	-	-	-	21	NC	19	R	22	11	17	R	18	13	17	12	18	R	15	13
13	8	9	16	17	R	16	R	18	R	19	R	20	6	22	11	21	R	21	12
17	9	23	8	19	12	20	11	14	R	22	R	24	8	24	9	-	-	-	-
-	-	-	-	-	-	-	-	-	-	-	-	-	-	3	R	24	R	22	R
-	-	-	-	-	-	-	-	-	-	-	-	-	-	3	R	3	3	5	R
20	10	19	R	7	4	13	10	20	R	10	5	7	R	14	R	19	11	20	R
2	3	1	2	2	RF	2	15	2	1	2	1	2	1F	1	3F	6	4	3	3F
-	-	-	-	-	-	-	-	-	-	-	-	-	-	-	-	8	6	19	R
22	17	21	R	22	13	-	-	-	-	-	-	-	-	-	-	-	-	-	-
-	-	-	-	-	-	21	R	23	10	23	15	17	14	21	R	13	R	18	R
-	-	-	-	-	-	-	-	-	-	-	-	26	11	18	R	20	13	23	R
11	7	18	R	16	8	18	R	15	R	9	9	-	-	-	-	-	-	-	-
-	-	-	-	-	-	-	-	-	-	-	-	13	R	12	7	11	8	12	R
-	-	-	-	20	R	22	14	7	R	21	R	22	7	19	8	22	10	16	R
-	-	-	-	-	-	-	-	-	-	-	-	-	-	23	R	-	-	-	-
-	-	-	-	-	-	-	-	-	-	-	-	-	-	-	-	-	-	-	-
4	R	12	10	5	3	7	5	5	2	8	6	10	5	7	R	10	R	9	8
1	1	2	1	1	1	1	1	1	12F	1	3F	1	12	2	2	1	2F	2	2
-	-	-	-	-	-	-	-	-	-	-	-	-	-	-	-	-	-	-	-
3	2F	7	3F	3	2	3	2F	3	R	3	2	5	R	6	1	4	R	4	R
8	R	5	4	4	5	4	4	4	R	5	4	4	R	4	R	2	1	1	1
-	-	-	-	-	-	-	-	-	-	-	-	-	-	-	-	-	-	-	-
16	13	13	12	10	R	8	R	10	R	6	R	8	R	16	R	9	R	10	7
-	-	-	-	-	-	-	-	-	-	-	-	-	-	-	-	23	12	24	14
-	-	-	-	-	-	-	-	-	-	-	-	-	-	-	-	-	-	-	-
18	16	15	13	8	6	11	17	9	4	7	R	11	R	9	R	7	14	17	10
9	6	11	R	18	R	14	9	17	6	12	R	-	-	-	-	-	-	-	-
-	-	-	-	-	-	-	-	-	-	-	-	15	4	13	5	16	R	11	15
21	11	17	R	14	R	15	R	21	R	NT	DNP	-	-	-	-	-	-	-	-

1993 FINAL CHAMPIONSHIP POSITIONS

Drivers

1	Alain Prost	99
2	Ayrton Senna	73
3	Damon Hill	69
4	Michael Schumacher	52
5	Riccardo Patrese	20
6	Jean Alesi	16
7	Martin Brundle	13
8	Gerhard Berger	12
9	Johnny Herbert	11
10	Mark Blundell	10
11=	Michael Andretti	7
	Karl Wendlinger	7
13=	Christian Fittipaldi	5
	JJ Lehto	5
15=	Mika Hakkinen	4
	Derek Warwick	4
17=	Philippe Alliot	2
	Fabrizio Barbazza	2
	Rubens Barrichello	2
20=	Erik Comas	1
	Eddie Irvine	1
	Alessandro Zanardi	1

Manufacturers

1	Williams-Renault	168
2	McLaren-Ford	84
3	Benetton-Ford	72
4	Ferrari	28
5	Ligier-Renault	23
6=	Lotus-Ford	12
	Sauber-Ilmor	12
8	Minardi-Ford	7
9	Footwork-Mugen	4
10=	Jordan-Hart	3
	Larrousse-Lamborghini	3

GRAND PRIX DE MONACO

23 May 1993. Monte Carlo. 78 laps of a 2.068-mile circuit = 161.304 miles. Warm, dry and cloudy. World Championship round 6

1	Ayrton Senna	McLaren MP4/8-Ford	78	1h52m10.947
2	Damon Hill	Williams FW15C-Renault	78	1h53m03.065
3	Jean Alesi	Ferrari F93A	78	1h53m14.309
4	Alain Prost	Williams FW15C-Renault	77	
5	Christian Fittipaldi	Minardi M193-Ford	76	
6	Martin Brundle	Ligier JS39-Renault	76	

Winner's average speed: 86.272 mph. Starting grid front row: Prost, 1m20.557 (pole) and Schumacher, 1m21.190. Fastest lap: Prost, 1m23.604. Leaders: Prost, laps 1-11; Schumacher, 12-32; Senna, 33-78

MOLSON GRAND PRIX DU CANADA

13 June 1993. Montreal. 69 laps of a 2.753-mile circuit = 189.957 miles. Hot, dry and sunny. World Championship round 7

1	Alain Prost	Williams FW15C-Renault	69	1h36m41.822
2	Michael Schumacher	Benetton B193B-Ford	69	1h36m56.349
3	Damon Hill	Williams FW15C-Renault	69	1h37m34.507
4	Gerhard Berger	Ferrari F93A	68	
5	Martin Brundle	Ligier JS39-Renault	68	
6	Karl Wendlinger	Sauber C12-Ilmor	68	

Winner's average speed: 117.867 mph. Starting grid front row: Prost, 1m18.987 (pole) and Hill, 1m19.491. Fastest lap: Schumacher, 1m21.500. Leaders: Hill, laps 1-5; Prost, 6-69

RHONE-POULENC GRAND PRIX DE FRANCE

4 July 1993. Magny-Cours. 72 laps of a 2.641-mile circuit = 190.152 miles. Warm, dry and cloudy. World Championship round 8

1	Alain Prost	Williams FW15C-Renault	72	1h38m35.241
2	Damon Hill	Williams FW15C-Renault	72	1h38m35.583
3	Michael Schumacher	Benetton B193B-Ford	72	1h38m56.450
4	Ayrton Senna	McLaren MP4/8-Ford	72	1h39m07.646
5	Martin Brundle	Ligier JS39-Renault	72	1h39m09.036
6	Michael Andretti	McLaren MP4/8-Ford	71	

Winner's average speed: 115.726 mph. Starting grid front row: Hill, 1m14.382 (pole) and Prost, 1m14.524. Fastest lap: Schumacher, 1m19.256. Leaders: Hill, laps 1-26; Prost, 27-72

BRITISH GRAND PRIX

11 July 1993. Silverstone. 59 laps of a 3.247-mile circuit = 191.573 miles. Cool, dry and cloudy. World Championship round 9

1	Alain Prost	Williams FW15C-Renault	59	1h25m38.189
2	Michael Schumacher	Benetton B193B-Ford	59	1h25m45.849
3	Riccardo Patrese	Benetton B193B-Ford	59	1h26m55.671
4	Johnny Herbert	Lotus 107B-Ford	59	1h26m56.596
5	Ayrton Senna	McLaren MP4/8-Ford	58	out of fuel
6	Derek Warwick	Footwork FA14-Mugen	58	

Winner's average speed: 134.223 mph. Starting grid front row: Prost, 1m19.006 (pole) and Hill, 1m19.134. Fastest lap: Hill, 1m22.515. Leaders: Hill, laps 1-41; Prost, 42-59

GROSSER MOBIL 1 PREIS VON DEUTSCHLAND

25 July 1993. Hockenheim. 45 laps of a 4.235-mile circuit = 190.575 miles. Warm, dry and sunny. World Championship round 10

1	Alain Prost	Williams FW15C-Renault	45	1h18m40.885
2	Michael Schumacher	Benetton B193B-Ford	45	1h18m57.549
3	Mark Blundell	Ligier JS39-Renault	45	1h19m40.234
4	Ayrton Senna	McLaren MP4/8-Ford	45	1h19m49.114
5	Riccardo Patrese	Benetton B193B-Ford	45	1h20m12.401
6	Gerhard Berger	Ferrari F93A	45	1h20m15.639

Winner's average speed: 145.327 mph. Starting grid front row: Prost, 1m38.748 (pole) and Hill, 1m38.905. Fastest lap: Schumacher, 1m41.859. Leaders: Hill, laps 1-7, 10-43; Prost, 8-9, 44-45

MARLBORO MAGYAR NAGYDIJ (HUNGARIAN GRAND PRIX)

15 August 1993. Hungaroring. 77 laps of a 2.466-mile circuit = 189.882

miles. Hot, dry and sunny. World Championship round 11

1	Damon Hill	Williams FW15C-Renault	77	1h47m39.098
2	Riccardo Patrese	Benetton B193B-Ford	77	1h48m51.013
3	Gerhard Berger	Ferrari F93A	77	1h48m57.140
4	Derek Warwick	Footwork FA14-Mugen	76	
5	Martin Brundle	Ligier JS39-Renault	76	
6	Karl Wendlinger	Sauber C12-Ilmor	76	

Winner's average speed: 105.831 mph. Starting grid front row: Prost, 1m14.631 (pole) and Hill, 1m14.835 - Prost started from the back of the grid. Fastest lap: Prost, 1m19.633. Leaders: Hill, laps 1-77

GRAND PRIX DE BELGIQUE

29 August 1993. Spa-Francorchamps. 44 laps of a 4.312-mile circuit = 189.728 miles. Hot, dry and sunny. World Championship round 12

1	Damon Hill	Williams FW15C-Renault	44	1h24m32.124
2	Michael Schumacher	Benetton B193B-Ford	44	1h24m35.792
3	Alain Prost	Williams FW15C-Renault	44	1h24m47.112
4	Ayrton Senna	McLaren MP4/8-Ford	44	1h26m11.887
5	Johnny Herbert	Lotus 107B-Ford	43	
6	Riccardo Patrese	Benetton B193B-Ford	43	

Winner's average speed: 134.662 mph. Starting grid front row: Prost, 1m47.571 (pole) and Hill, 1m48.466. Fastest lap: Prost, 1m51.095. Leaders: Prost, laps 1-30; Hill, 31-44

PIONEER GRAN PREMIO D'ITALIA

12 September 1993. Monza. 53 laps of a 3.604-mile circuit = 191.007 miles. Hot, dry and sunny. World Championship round 13

1	Damon Hill	Williams FW15C-Renault	53	1h17m07.509
2	Jean Alesi	Ferrari F93A	53	1h17m47.521
3	Michael Andretti	McLaren MP4/8-Ford	52	
4	Karl Wendlinger	Sauber C12	52	
5	Riccardo Patrese	Benetton B193B-Ford	52	
6	Erik Comas	Larrousse LH93-Lamborghini	51	

Winner's average speed: 148.595 mph. Starting grid front row: Prost, 1m21.179 (pole) and Hill, 1m21.491. Fastest lap: Hill, 1m23.575. Leaders: Prost, laps 1-48; Hill, 49-53

GRANDE PREMIO DE PORTUGAL

26 September 1993. Estoril. 71 laps of a 2.703-mile circuit = 191.913 miles. Warm, dry and sunny. World Championship round 14

1	Michael Schumacher	Benetton B193B-Ford	71	1h32m46.309
2	Alain Prost	Williams FW15C-Renault	71	1h32m47.291
3	Damon Hill	Williams FW15C-Renault	71	1h32m54.515
4	Jean Alesi	Ferrari F93A	71	1h33m53.914
5	Karl Wendlinger	Sauber C12	70	
6	Martin Brundle	Ligier JS39-Renault	70	

Winner's average speed: 124.119 mph. Starting grid front row: Hill, 1m11.494 (pole) and Prost, 1m11.683 - Hill started from the back of the grid. Fastest lap: Hill, 1m14.859. Leaders: Alesi, laps 1-19; Prost, 20-29; Schumacher, 30-71

FUJI TELEVISION JAPANESE GRAND PRIX

24 October 1993. Suzuka. 53 laps of a 3.641-mile circuit = 192.973 miles. Dry and clear, then cool and wet. World Championship round 15

1	Ayrton Senna	McLaren MP4/8-Ford	53	1h40m27.912
2	Alain Prost	Williams FW15C-Renault	53	1h40m39.347
3	Mika Hakkinen	McLaren MP4/8-Ford	53	1h40m54.054
4	Damon Hill	Williams FW15C-Renault	53	1h41m51.450
5	Rubens Barrichello	Jordan 193-Hart	53	1h42m03.013
6	Eddie Irvine	Jordan 193-Hart	53	1h42m14.333

Winner's average speed: 115.248 mph. Starting grid front row: Prost, 1m37.154 (pole) and Senna, 1m37.284. Fastest lap: Prost, 1m41.176. Leaders: Senna, laps 1-13, 21-53; Prost, 14-20

FOSTER'S AUSTRALIAN GRAND PRIX

7 November 1993. Adelaide. 79 laps of a 2.347-mile circuit = 185.413 miles. Warm, dry and sunny. World Championship round 16

1	Ayrton Senna	McLaren MP4/8-Ford	79	1h43m27.476
2	Alain Prost	Williams FW15C-Renault	79	1h43m36.735
3	Damon Hill	Williams FW15C-Renault	79	1h44m01.378
4	Jean Alesi	Ferrari F93A	78	
5	Gerhard Berger	Ferrari F93A	78	
6	Martin Brundle	Ligier JS39-Renault	78	

Winner's average speed: 107.530 mph. Starting grid front row: Senna, 1m13.371 (pole) and Prost, 1m13.807. Fastest lap: Hill, 1m15.381.
Leaders: Senna, laps 1-23, 29-79; Prost, 24-28

1994

Certain years in the history of motor racing are over-shadowed by a single terrible weekend. The year 1955 is forever remembered for the Le Mans tragedy, and 1968 for the death of Jim Clark. The death of Ayrton Senna at Imola on 1 May 1994 seemed inconceivable, and coming just twenty-four hours after rookie Roland Ratzenberger had died in practice, it shook the sport to its core. Seemingly indestructible and arguably the most talented driver of all time, the Brazilian was killed at Imola's dauntingly fast Tamburello corner while leading the San Marino Grand Prix. His death robbed Formula 1 of its greatest star, just as Michael Schumacher's challenge had started to gather momentum.

These tragedies were compounded by a series of other accidents in which drivers were injured: Karl Wendlinger, Pedro Lamy, Jean Alesi, JJ Lehto and Andrea Montermini were all sidelined in one of the sport's blackest summers.

Widely acknowledged as the fastest driver of his generation, Senna was driving a Williams-Renault, then the best car in F1. A fourth world title seemed all but assured. His death refocused attention on the dangers of the sport: circuits were changed and controversial new safety measures (including revised wings, airboxes, and a 10cm wooden step on the underside of the cars) were gradually introduced to reduce speeds.

In 1968 Graham Hill had lifted the spirits of Lotus after Clark's death; and now it fell to his son to lead the Williams team. Damon Hill was thirty-seven points behind a dominant Michael Schumacher by the British Grand Prix in July, but that race proved the turning point. Hill won his home race (a feat never achieved by his father) and Schumacher was excluded from the results and banned for two further races for ignoring a black flag issued after he overtook Hill on the parade lap.

But worse things were still to come for Benetton. Jos Verstappen in the second car was temporarily engulfed in a frightening fireball during a German GP fuel stop, and Schumacher was disqualified in Belgium for an infringement of the new stepped flat-bottom rules.

Hill won both races from which Schumacher had been banned, and a dramatic victory in Japan brought the Williams driver to within a point of the German before the final race in Australia. The championship would be decided in suitably controversial circumstances: while fighting for the lead in Adelaide, Schumacher and Hill collided. With both drivers out of the race, Michael Schumacher became Germany's first World Champion.

In the wake of Senna's death, Williams elevated their test driver David Coulthard to the race team. His performance improved as the season progressed, but a returning Nigel Mansell replaced him for France and

1994 Ayrton Senna leads on his debut for Williams but his death at Imola robbed the sport of its greatest star.

the final three races. The former World Champion qualified on pole in Australia and inherited victory when Hill and Schumacher crashed.

Gerhard Berger scored Ferrari's first victory since 1990 at Hockenheim, a race in which opening-lap accidents forced ten cars to retire. Teammate Jean Alesi had a frustrating season and was often outpaced by Berger. The Frenchman qualified on pole at Monza only for gearbox problems to rob him of a first victory.

McLaren used Peugeot engines in 1994, but they proved both underpowered and unreliable. Despite this, Mika Hakkinen finished on the podium six times to clinch fourth in the World Championship. Jordan continued its progress in Formula 1, and 22-year-old Rubens Barrichello benefited from changeable weather conditions in Belgium to become the youngest driver ever to qualify on pole.

After a ten-year ban, refuelling stops were reintroduced, placing greater emphasis on race strategy and less on overtaking skills.

GRANDE PREMIO DO BRASIL

27 March 1994. Interlagos. 71 laps of a 2.667-mile circuit = 189.357 miles. Warm, dry and overcast. World Championship round 1

1	Michael Schumacher	Benetton B194-Ford	71	1h35m38.759
2	Damon Hill	Williams FW16-Renault	70	
3	Jean Alesi	Ferrari 412T1	70	
4	Rubens Barrichello	Jordan 194-Hart	70	
5	Ukyo Katayama	Tyrrell 022-Yamaha	69	
6	Karl Wendlinger	Sauber C13-Mercedes-Benz	69	

Winner's average speed: 118.786 mph. Starting grid front row: Senna, 1m15.962 (pole) and Schumacher, 1m16.290. Fastest lap: Schumacher, 1m18.455. Leaders: Senna, laps 1-21; Schumacher, 22-71

PACIFIC GRAND PRIX

17 April 1994. TI Circuit, Aida. 83 laps of a 2.314-mile circuit = 192.062 miles. Warm, dry and sunny. World Championship round 2

1	Michael Schumacher	Benetton B194-Ford	83	1h46m01.693
2	Gerhard Berger	Ferrari 412T1	83	1h47m16.993
3	Rubens Barrichello	Jordan 194-Hart	82	
4	Christian Fittipaldi	Footwork FA15-Ford	82	
5	Heinz-Harald Frentzen	Sauber C13-Mercedes-Benz	82	
6	Erik Comas	Larrousse LH94-Ford	80	

Winner's average speed: 108.685 mph. Starting grid front row: Senna, 1m10.218 (pole) and Schumacher, 1m10.440. Fastest lap: Schumacher, 1m14.023. Leaders: Schumacher, laps 1-83

Formula 1

driver	car	BR Q	BR R	PAC Q	PAC R	RSM Q	RSM R	MC Q	MC R	E Q	E R	CDN Q	CDN R
Philippe Adams	Lotus 109-Mugen	-	-	-	-	-	-	-	-	-	-	-	-
Michele Alboreto	Minardi M193B-Ford	22	R	15	R	15	R	12	6	14	R	18	11
Jean Alesi	Ferrari 412T1	3	3	-	-	-	-	5	5	6	4	2	3
	Ferrari 412T1B	-	-	-	-	-	-	-	-	-	-	-	-
Philippe Alliot	McLaren MP4/9-Peugeot	-	-	-	-	-	-	-	-	-	-	-	-
	Larrousse LH94-Ford	-	-	-	-	-	-	-	-	-	-	-	-
Rubens Barrichello	Jordan 194-Hart	14	4	8	3	NT	DNP	15	R	5	R	6	7
Paul Belmondo	Pacific PR01-Ilmor	NT	DNQ	28	DNQ	27	DNQ	24	R	26	R	27	DNQ
Olivier Beretta	Larrousse LH94-Ford	23	R	21	R	22	R	18	8	17	DNS	22	R
Gerhard Berger	Ferrari 412T1	17	R	5	2	3	R	3	3	7	R	3	4
	Ferrari 412T1B	-	-	-	-	-	-	-	-	-	-	-	-
Eric Bernard	Ligier JS39B-Renault	20	R	18	10	17	12	21	R	20	8	24	13
	Lotus 109-Mugen	-	-	-	-	-	-	-	-	-	-	-	-
Mark Blundell	Tyrrell 022-Yamaha	12	R	12	R	12	9	10	R	11	3	13	10
David Brabham	Simtek S941-Ford	26	12	25	R	24	R	22	R	24	10	25	14
Martin Brundle	McLaren MP4/9-Peugeot	18	R	6	R	13	8	8	2	8	R	12	R
Andrea de Cesaris	Jordan 194-Hart	-	-	-	-	20	R	14	4	-	-	-	-
	Sauber C13-Mercedes-Benz	-	-	-	-	-	-	-	-	-	-	14	R
Erik Comas	Larrousse LH94-Ford	13	9	16	6	18	R	13	10	16	R	21	R
David Coulthard	Williams FW16-Renault	-	-	-	-	-	-	-	-	9	R	5	5
	Williams FW16B-Renault	-	-	-	-	-	-	-	-	-	-	-	-
Yannick Dalmas	Larrousse LH94-Ford	-	-	-	-	-	-	-	-	-	-	-	-
Jean-Denis Deletraz	Larrousse LH94-Ford	-	-	-	-	-	-	-	-	-	-	-	-
Christian Fittipaldi	Footwork FA15-Ford	11	R	9	4	16	R	6	R	21	R	16	DSQ
Heinz-Harald Frentzen	Sauber C13-Mercedes-Benz	5	R	11	5	7	7	NT	DNP	12	R	10	R
Bertrand Gachot	Pacific PR01-Ilmor	25	R	27	DNQ	25	R	23	R	25	R	26	R
Jean-Marc Gounon	Simtek S941-Ford	-	-	-	-	-	-	-	-	-	-	-	-
Mika Hakkinen	McLaren MP4/9-Peugeot	8	R	4	R	8	3	2	R	3	R	8	R
Johnny Herbert	Lotus 107C-Mugen	21	7	23	7	19	10	16	R	-	-	-	-
	Lotus 109-Mugen	-	-	-	-	-	-	-	-	22	R	17	8
	Ligier JS39B-Renault	-	-	-	-	-	-	-	-	-	-	-	-
	Benetton B194-Ford	-	-	-	-	-	-	-	-	-	-	-	-
Damon Hill	Williams FW16-Renault	4	2	3	R	4	6F	4	R	2	1	4	2
	Williams FW16B-Renault	-	-	-	-	-	-	-	-	-	-	-	-
Taki Inoue	Simtek S941-Ford	-	-	-	-	-	-	-	-	-	-	-	-
Eddie Irvine	Jordan 194-Hart	16	R	-	-	-	-	-	-	13	6	7	R
Ukyo Katayama	Tyrrell 022-Yamaha	10	5	14	R	9	5	11	R	10	R	9	R
Franck Lagorce	Ligier JS39B-Renault	-	-	-	-	-	-	-	-	-	-	-	-
Pedro Lamy	Lotus 107C-Mugen	24	10	24	8	21	R	19	11	-	-	-	-
Nicola Larini	Ferrari 412T1	-	-	7	R	6	2	-	-	-	-	-	-
JJ Lehto	Benetton B194-Ford	-	-	-	-	5	R	17	7	4	R	20	6
	Sauber C13-Mercedes-Benz	-	-	-	-	-	-	-	-	-	-	-	-
Nigel Mansell	Williams FW16-Renault	-	-	-	-	-	-	-	-	-	-	-	-
	Williams FW16B-Renault	-	-	-	-	-	-	-	-	-	-	-	-
Pierluigi Martini	Minardi M193B-Ford	15	8	17	R	14	R	9	R	-	-	15	9
	Minardi M194-Ford	-	-	-	-	-	-	-	-	18	5	-	-
Andrea Montermini	Simtek S941-Ford	-	-	-	-	-	-	-	-	27	DNQ	-	-
Gianni Morbidelli	Footwork FA15-Ford	6	R	13	R	11	R	7	R	15	R	11	R
Hideki Noda	Larrousse LH94-Ford	-	-	-	-	-	-	-	-	-	-	-	-
Olivier Panis	Ligier JS39B-Renault	19	11	22	9	23	11	20	9	19	7	19	12
Roland Ratzenberger	Simtek S941-Ford	27	DNQ	26	11	26	DNS	-	-	-	-	-	-
Mika Salo	Lotus 109-Mugen	-	-	-	-	-	-	-	-	-	-	-	-
Domenico Schiattarella	Simtek S941-Ford	-	-	-	-	-	-	-	-	-	-	-	-
Michael Schumacher	Benetton B194-Ford	2	1F	2	1F	2	1	1	1F	1	2F	1	1F
Ayrton Senna	Williams FW16-Renault	1	R	1	R	1	R	-	-	-	-	-	-
Aguri Suzuki	Jordan 194-Hart	-	-	20	R	-	-	-	-	-	-	-	-
Jos Verstappen	Benetton B194-Ford	9	R	10	R	-	-	-	-	-	-	-	-
Karl Wendlinger	Sauber C13-Mercedes-Benz	7	6	19	R	10	4	NT	DNP	-	-	-	-
Alessandro Zanardi	Lotus 107C-Mugen	-	-	-	-	-	-	-	-	23	9	23	R
	Lotus 109-Mugen	-	-	-	-	-	-	-	-	-	-	-	-

F		GB		D		H		B		I		P		EU		J		AUS	
Q	R	Q	R	Q	R	Q	R	Q	R	Q	R	Q	R	Q	R	Q	R	Q	R
-	-	-	-	-	-	-	-	26	R	-	-	25	16	-	-	-	-	-	-
21	R	16	R	23	R	20	7	18	9	22	R	19	13	20	14	21	R	16	R
4	R	4	2	2	R	13	R	5	R	1	R	5	R	16	10	7	3	8	6
-	-	-	-	-	-	14	R	-	-	-	-	-	-	-	-	-	-	-	-
-	-	-	-	-	-	-	-	19	R	-	-	-	-	-	-	-	-	-	-
7	R	6	4	10	R	10	R	1	R	16	4	8	4	5	12	10	R	5	4
28	DNQ	28	DNQ	27	DNQ	28	DNQ	28	DNQ	28	DNQ	28	DNQ	28	DNQ	28	DNQ	27	DNQ
25	R	24	14	24	7	25	9	-	-	-	-	-	-	-	-	-	-	-	-
-	-	-	-	-	-	-	-	-	-	-	-	-	-	-	-	-	-	-	-
5	3	3	R	1	1	4	12	11	R	2	2	1	R	6	5	11	R	11	2
15	R	23	13	14	3	18	10	16	10	12	7	21	10	-	-	-	-	-	-
-	-	-	-	-	-	-	-	-	-	-	-	-	-	22	18	-	-	-	-
17	10	11	R	7	R	11	5	12	5	21	R	12	R	14	13	13	R	13	R
24	R	25	15	25	R	23	11	21	R	26	R	24	R	23	R	24	12	24	R
12	R	9	R	13	R	6	4	13	R	15	5	7	6	15	R	9	R	9	3
-	-	-	-	-	-	-	-	-	-	-	-	-	-	-	-	-	-	-	-
11	6	17	R	18	R	17	R	15	R	8	R	17	R	18	R	-	-	-	-
20	R	22	R	22	6	21	8	22	R	24	8	22	R	24	R	22	9	-	-
-	-	7	5	6	RF	-	-	-	-	-	-	-	-	-	-	-	-	-	-
-	-	-	-	-	-	3	R	7	4	5	6	3	2F	-	-	-	-	-	-
-	-	-	-	-	-	-	-	-	-	23	R	23	14	-	-	-	-	-	-
-	-	-	-	-	-	-	-	-	-	-	-	-	-	-	-	-	-	25	R
18	8	19	9	17	4	16	14	24	R	19	R	11	8	19	17	18	8	19	8
10	4	20	7	9	R	8	R	9	R	11	R	9	R	4	6	3	6	10	7
27	DNQ	27	DNQ	28	DNQ	27	DNQ	27	DNQ	27	DNQ	27	DNQ	27	DNQ	27	DNQ	28	DNQ
26	9	26	16	26	R	26	R	25	11	25	R	26	15	-	-	-	-	-	-
9	R	5	3	8	R	-	-	8	2	7	3	4	3	9	3	8	7	4	12
-	-	-	-	-	-	-	-	-	-	-	-	-	-	-	-	-	-	-	-
19	7	21	11	15	R	24	R	20	12	4	R	20	11	-	-	-	-	-	-
-	-	-	-	-	-	-	-	-	-	-	-	-	-	7	8	-	-	-	-
-	-	-	-	-	-	-	-	-	-	-	-	-	-	-	-	5	R	7	R
1	2F	1	1F	3	8	-	-	-	-	-	-	-	-	-	-	-	-	-	-
-	-	-	-	-	-	2	2	3	1F	3	1F	2	1	2	2	2	1F	3	R
-	-	-	-	-	-	-	-	-	-	-	-	-	-	-	-	26	R	-	-
6	R	12	DNS	11	R	7	R	4	R	9	R	13	7	10	4	6	5	6	R
14	R	8	6	5	R	5	R	23	R	14	R	6	R	13	7	14	R	15	R
-	-	-	-	-	-	-	-	-	-	-	-	-	-	-	-	20	R	20	11
-	-	-	-	-	-	-	-	-	-	-	-	-	-	-	-	-	-	-	-
-	-	-	-	-	-	-	-	-	-	-	-	-	-	-	-	-	-	-	-
-	-	-	-	-	-	-	-	20	9	14	R	-	-	-	-	-	-	-	-
-	-	-	-	-	-	-	-	-	-	-	-	-	-	-	-	15	R	17	10
2	R	-	-	-	-	-	-	-	-	-	-	-	-	-	-	-	-	-	-
-	-	-	-	-	-	-	-	-	-	-	-	-	-	3	R	4	4	1	1
16	5	13	10	20	R	15	R	10	8	18	R	18	12	17	15	16	R	18	9
-	-	-	-	-	-	-	-	-	-	-	-	-	-	-	-	-	-	-	-
22	R	15	R	16	5	19	R	14	6	17	R	16	9	8	11	12	R	21	R
-	-	-	-	-	-	-	-	-	-	-	-	-	-	25	R	23	R	23	R
13	R	14	12	12	2	9	6	17	7	6	10	15	DSQ	11	9	19	11	12	5
-	-	-	-	-	-	-	-	-	-	-	-	-	-	-	-	25	10	22	R
-	-	-	-	-	-	-	-	-	-	-	-	-	-	26	19	-	-	26	R
3	1	2	DSQ	4	R	1	1F	2	DSQ	-	-	-	-	1	1F	1	2	2	RF
-	-	-	-	-	-	-	-	-	-	-	-	-	-	-	-	-	-	-	-
8	R	10	8	19	R	12	3	6	3	10	R	10	5	12	R	-	-	-	-
-	-	-	-	-	-	-	-	-	-	-	-	-	-	-	-	-	-	-	-
23	R	18	R	21	R	22	13	-	-	13	R	-	-	21	16	17	13	14	R

Formula 1

1994 FINAL CHAMPIONSHIP POSITIONS

Drivers							Manufacturers		
1	Michael Schumacher	92		14=	Christian Fittipaldi	6	1	Williams-Renault	118
2	Damon Hill	91			Eddie Irvine	6	2	Benetton-Ford	103
3	Gerhard Berger	41			Nicola Larini	6	3	Ferrari	71
4	Mika Hakkinen	26		17	Ukyo Katayama	5	4	McLaren-Peugeot	42
5	Jean Alesi	24		18=	Eric Bernard	4	5	Jordan-Hart	28
6	Rubens Barrichello	19			Andrea de Cesaris	4	6=	Ligier-Renault	13
7	Martin Brundle	16			Pierluigi Martini	4		Tyrrell-Yamaha	13
8	David Coulthard	14			Karl Wendlinger	4	8	Sauber-Mercedes-Benz	12
9	Nigel Mansell	13		22	Gianni Morbidelli	3	9	Footwork-Ford	9
10	Jos Verstappen	10		23	Erik Comas	2	10	Minardi-Ford	5
11	Olivier Panis	9		24=	Michele Alboreto	1	11	Larrousse-Ford	2
12	Mark Blundell	8			JJ Lehto	1			
13	Heinz-Harald Frentzen	7							

GRAN PREMIO DI SAN MARINO

1 May 1994. Imola. 58 laps of a 3.132-mile circuit = 181.656 miles. Race scheduled for 61 laps, stopped after 5 laps due to Senna's accident, restarted over an additional 53 laps. Hot, dry and sunny. World Championship round 3

1	Michael Schumacher	Benetton B194-Ford	58	1h28m28.642
2	Nicola Larini	Ferrari 412T1	58	1h29m23.584
3	Mika Hakkinen	McLaren MP4/9-Peugeot	58	1h29m39.321
4	Karl Wendlinger	Sauber C13-Mercedes-Benz	58	1h29m42.300
5	Ukyo Katayama	Tyrrell 022-Yamaha	57	
6	Damon Hill	Williams FW16-Renault	57	

Winner's average speed: 123.188 mph. Starting grid front row: Senna, 1m21.548 (pole) and Schumacher, 1m21.885. Fastest lap: Hill, 1m24.335. Leaders: Senna, laps 1-5; Schumacher, 6-13, 15-58; Berger, 14 (Berger led laps 6-14, Hakkinen, 15-18 and Larini, 19-23 on the road)

GRAND PRIX DE MONACO

15 May 1994. Monte Carlo. 78 laps of a 2.068-mile circuit = 161.304 miles. Hot, dry and sunny. World Championship round 4

1	Michael Schumacher	Benetton B194-Ford	78	1h49m55.372
2	Martin Brundle	McLaren MP4/9-Peugeot	78	1h50m32.650
3	Gerhard Berger	Ferrari 412T1	78	1h51m12.196
4	Andrea de Cesaris	Jordan 194-Hart	77	
5	Jean Alesi	Ferrari 412T1	77	
6	Michele Alboreto	Minardi M193B-Ford	77	

Winner's average speed: 88.046 mph. Starting grid front row: Schumacher, 1m18.560 (pole) and Hakkinen, 1m19.488. Fastest lap: Schumacher, 1m21.076. Leaders: Schumacher, laps 1-78

GRAN PREMIO MARLBORO DE ESPANA

29 May 1994. Catalunya. 65 laps of a 2.950-mile circuit = 191.731 miles. Hot, dry and sunny. World Championship round 5

1	Damon Hill	Williams FW16-Renault	65	1h36m14.374
2	Michael Schumacher	Benetton B194-Ford	65	1h36m38.540
3	Mark Blundell	Tyrrell 022-Yamaha	65	1h37m41.343
4	Jean Alesi	Ferrari 412T1	64	
5	Pierluigi Martini	Minardi M194-Ford	64	
6	Eddie Irvine	Jordan 194-Hart	64	

Winner's average speed: 119.533 mph. Starting grid front row: Schumacher, 1m21.908 (pole) and Hill, 1m22.559. Fastest lap: Schumacher, 1m25.155. Leaders: Schumacher, laps 1-22, 41-45; Hakkinen, 23-30; Hill, 31-40, 46-65

GRAND PRIX MOLSON DU CANADA

12 June 1994. Montreal. 69 laps of a 2.765-mile circuit = 190.785 miles. Hot, dry and cloudy. World Championship round 6

1	Michael Schumacher	Benetton B194-Ford	69	1h44m31.887
2	Damon Hill	Williams FW16-Renault	69	1h45m11.547
3	Jean Alesi	Ferrari 412T1	69	1h45m45.275

4	Gerhard Berger	Ferrari 412T1	69	1h45m47.496
5	David Coulthard	Williams FW16-Renault	68	
6	JJ Lehto	Benetton B194-Ford	68	

Christian Fittipaldi (Footwork FA12-Ford), 68 laps completed, finished sixth on the road but disqualified due to his car being under the weight limit. Winner's average speed: 109.509 mph. Starting grid front row: Schumacher, 1m26.178 (pole) and Alesi, 1m26.319. Fastest lap: Schumacher, 1m28.927. Leaders: Schumacher, laps 1-69

GRAND PRIX DE FRANCE

3 July 1994. Magny-Cours. 72 laps of a 2.641-mile circuit = 190.152 miles. Hot, dry and sunny. World Championship round 7

1	Michael Schumacher	Benetton B194-Ford	72	1h38m35.704
2	Damon Hill	Williams FW16-Renault	72	1h38m48.346
3	Gerhard Berger	Ferrari 412T1B	72	1h39m28.469
4	Heinz-Harald Frentzen	Sauber C13-Mercedes-Benz	71	
5	Pierluigi Martini	Minardi M193B-Ford	70	
6	Andrea de Cesaris	Sauber C13-Mercedes-Benz	70	

Winner's average speed: 115.717 mph. Starting grid front row: Hill, 1m16.282 (pole) and Mansell, 1m16.359. Fastest lap: Hill, 1m19.678. Leaders: Schumacher, laps 1-37, 45-72; Hill, 38-44

BRITISH GRAND PRIX

10 July 1994. Silverstone. 60 laps of a 3.210-mile circuit = 192.600 miles. Hot, dry and sunny. World Championship round 8

1	Damon Hill	Williams FW16-Renault	60	1h30m03.640
2	Jean Alesi	Ferrari 412T1B	60	1h31m11.768
3	Mika Hakkinen	McLaren MP4/9-Peugeot	60	1h31m44.299
4	Rubens Barrichello	Jordan 194-Hart	60	1h31m45.391
5	David Coulthard	Williams FW16-Renault	59	
6	Ukyo Katayama	Tyrrell 022-Yamaha	59	

Michael Schumacher (Benetton B194-Ford), 1h30m22.418, finished second on the road but disqualified for ignoring the black flag. Winner's average speed: 128.314 mph. Starting grid front row: Hill, 1m24.960 (pole) and Schumacher, 1m24.963. Fastest lap: Hill, 1m27.100. Leaders: Hill, laps 1-15, 22-60; Berger, 16-21 (Schumacher led laps 15-17 and 22-26 on the road but was disqualified)

GROSSER MOBIL 1 PREIS VON DEUTSCHLAND

31 July 1994. Hockenheim. 45 laps of a 4.239-mile circuit = 190.755 miles. Hot, dry and sunny. World Championship round 9

1	Gerhard Berger	Ferrari 412T1B	45	1h22m37.272
2	Olivier Panis	Ligier JS39B-Renault	45	1h23m32.051
3	Eric Bernard	Ligier JS39B-Renault	45	1h23m42.314
4	Christian Fittipaldi	Footwork FA15-Ford	45	1h23m58.881
5	Gianni Morbidelli	Footwork FA15-Ford	45	1h24m07.816
6	Erik Comas	Larrousse LH94-Ford	45	1h24m22.717

Winner's average speed: 138.527 mph. Starting grid front row: Berger,

1m43.582 (pole) and Alesi, 1m44.012. Fastest lap: Coulthard, 1m46.211.
Leaders: Berger, laps 1-45

MARLBORO MAGYAR NAGYDIJ (HUNGARIAN GRAND PRIX)

14 August 1994. Hungaroring. 77 laps of a 2.465-mile circuit = 189.805 miles. Hot, dry and sunny. World Championship round 10

1 Michael Schumacher	Benetton B194-Ford	77	1h48m00.185
2 Damon Hill	Williams FW16B-Renault	77	1h48m21.012
3 Jos Verstappen	Benetton B194-Ford	77	1h49m10.514
4 Martin Brundle	McLaren MP4/9-Peugeot	76	electrics
5 Mark Blundell	Tyrrell 022-Yamaha	76	
6 Olivier Panis	Ligier JS39B-Renault	76	

Winner's average speed: 105.444 mph. Starting grid front row:
Schumacher, 1m18.258 (pole) and Hill, 1m18.824. Fastest lap:
Schumacher, 1m20.881. Leaders: Schumacher, laps 1-16, 26-77; Hill,
17-25

GRAND PRIX DE BELGIQUE

28 August 1994. Spa-Francorchamps. 44 laps of a 4.350-mile circuit = 191.400 miles. Warm, dry and sunny. World Championship round 11

1 Damon Hill	Williams FW16B-Renault	44	1h28m47.170
2 Mika Hakkinen	McLaren MP4/9-Peugeot	44	1h29m38.551
3 Jos Verstappen	Benetton B194-Ford	44	1h29m57.623
4 David Coulthard	Williams FW16B-Renault	44	1h30m32.957
5 Mark Blundell	Tyrrell 022-Yamaha	43	
6 Gianni Morbidelli	Footwork FA15-Ford	43	

Michael Schumacher (Benetton B194-Ford), 1h28m33.508, finished first
on the road but disqualified due to stepped flat-bottom infringement.
Winner's average speed: 129.344 mph. Starting grid front row: Barrichello,
2m21.163 (pole) and Schumacher, 2m21.494. Fastest lap: Hill, 1m57.117.
Leaders: Alesi, laps 1-2; Hill, 3-11, 37-44; Coulthard, 12-13, 18-36;
Barrichello, 14-17 (Schumacher led laps 1-28 and 30-44 on the road but
was disqualified, Coulthard led lap 29 on the road)

GRAN PREMIO D'ITALIA

11 September 1994. Monza. 53 laps of a 3.604-mile circuit = 191.007 miles. Race stopped after first-lap accident, restarted over original distance. Hot, dry and sunny. World Championship round 12

1 Damon Hill	Williams FW16B-Renault	53	1h18m02.754
2 Gerhard Berger	Ferrari 412T1B	53	1h18m07.684
3 Mika Hakkinen	McLaren MP4/9-Peugeot	53	1h18m28.394
4 Rubens Barrichello	Jordan 194-Hart	53	1h18m53.388
5 Martin Brundle	McLaren MP4/9-Peugeot	53	1h19m28.329
6 David Coulthard	Williams FW16B-Renault	52	out of fuel

Winner's average speed: 146.842 mph. Starting grid front row: Alesi,
1m23.844 (pole) and Berger, 1m23.978. Fastest lap: Hill, 1m25.930.
Leaders: Alesi, laps 1-14; Berger, 15-23; Hill, 24, 29-53; Coulthard, 25, 27-
28; Hakkinen, 26

GRANDE PREMIO DE PORTUGAL

25 September 1994. Estoril. 71 laps of a 2.709-mile circuit = 192.339 miles. Warm, dry and sunny. World Championship round 13

1 Damon Hill	Williams FW16B-Renault	71	1h41m10.165
2 David Coulthard	Williams FW16B-Renault	71	1h41m10.768
3 Mika Hakkinen	McLaren MP4/9-Peugeot	71	1h41m30.358
4 Rubens Barrichello	Jordan 194-Hart	71	1h41m38.168
5 Jos Verstappen	Benetton B194-Ford	71	1h41m39.550
6 Martin Brundle	McLaren MP4/9-Peugeot	71	1h42m02.867

Winner's average speed: 114.069 mph. Starting grid front row: Berger,
1m20.608 (pole) and Hill, 1m20.766. Fastest lap: Coulthard, 1m22.446.
Leaders: Berger, laps 1-7; Coulthard, 8-17, 26-27; Hill, 18, 28-71; Alesi,
19-22; Barrichello, 23-25

GRAN PREMIO DE EUROPA

16 October 1994. Jerez. 69 laps of a 2.751-mile circuit = 189.819 miles. Hot, dry and sunny. World Championship round 14

1 Michael Schumacher	Benetton B194-Ford	69	1h40m26.689
2 Damon Hill	Williams FW16B-Renault	69	1h40m51.378

3 Mika Hakkinen	McLaren MP4/9-Peugeot	69	1h41m36.337
4 Eddie Irvine	Jordan 194-Hart	69	1h41m45.135
5 Gerhard Berger	Ferrari 412T1B	68	
6 Heinz-Harald Frentzen	Sauber C13-Mercedes-Benz	68	

Winner's average speed: 113.387 mph. Starting grid front row:
Schumacher, 1m22.762 (pole) and Hill, 1m22.892. Fastest lap:
Schumacher, 1m25.040. Leaders: Hill, laps 1-17, 33-34; Schumacher, 18-
32, 35-69

FUJI TELEVISION JAPANESE GRAND PRIX

6 November 1994. Suzuka. 50 laps of a 3.641-mile circuit = 182.050 miles. Race scheduled for 53 laps, stopped after 13 laps due to an accident and heavy rain, restarted over an additional 37 laps. Very wet. World Championship round 15

1 Damon Hill	Williams FW16B-Renault	50	1h55m53.532
2 Michael Schumacher	Benetton B194-Ford	50	1h55m56.897
3 Jean Alesi	Ferrari 412T1B	50	1h56m45.577
4 Nigel Mansell	Williams FW16B-Renault	50	1h56m49.606
5 Eddie Irvine	Jordan 194-Hart	50	1h57m35.639
6 Heinz-Harald Frentzen	Sauber C13-Mercedes-Benz	50	1h57m53.395

Winner's average speed: 94.251 mph. Starting grid front row:
Schumacher, 1m37.209 (pole) and Hill, 1m37.696. Fastest lap: Hill,
1m56.597. Leaders: Schumacher, laps 1-18, 36-40; Hill, 19-35, 41-50

AUSTRALIAN GRAND PRIX

13 November 1994. Adelaide. 81 laps of a 2.347 mile-circuit = 190.107 miles. Warm, dry and overcast. World Championship round 16

1 Nigel Mansell	Williams FW16B-Renault	81	1h47m51.480
2 Gerhard Berger	Ferrari 412T1B	81	1h47m53.991
3 Martin Brundle	McLaren MP4/9-Peugeot	81	1h48m43.967
4 Rubens Barrichello	Jordan 194-Hart	81	1h49m02.010
5 Olivier Panis	Ligier JS39B-Renault	80	
6 Jean Alesi	Ferrari 412T1B	80	

Winner's average speed: 105.754 mph. Starting grid front row: Mansell,
1m16.179 (pole) and Schumacher, 1m16.197. Fastest lap: Schumacher,
1m17.140. Leaders: Schumacher, laps 1-35; Mansell, 36-53, 64-81;
Berger, 54-63

1995

With Formula 1 still recovering from the tragedies of the previous spring, Michael Schumacher firmly established himself as the best driver in the world. Schumacher displayed all the attributes of a Grand Prix driver who would dominate his generation—he was tactically aware, ruthless and, above all, quick. Benetton joined Williams in adopting Renault engines for the new season, and these two teams would once again fight it out for the World Championship.

Conventional wisdom was that the Williams FW17 was the better car, but Benetton had the best driver, and generally out-manoeuvred Williams with superior race strategy. The result was nine Grand Prix victories for Schumacher, who took his second world title by a 33-point margin.

The contest between Schumacher and Williams's Damon Hill was a sometimes bitter one, with the German accusing his rival of "brake testing" him while running in traffic in France. The animosity grew two weeks later at the British GP when they crashed together as Hill attempted to take the lead. The two cars again made contact during the races at Spa and Monza, earning a rebuke from F1 ringmaster Bernie Ecclestone.

Having joined Benetton for the final two races of 1994, Johnny Herbert continued as Schumacher's

Formula 1

1995 Michael Schumacher successfully defended the world title in 1995 and confirmed himself as the leading driver of his generation.

teammate. He benefited from the collision between Schumacher and Hill at Silverstone to score a popular home victory, and followed up with another win at Monza.

Williams passed up an opportunity to sign Nigel Mansell, preferring to invest in the youth of David Coulthard. Though unquestionably fast, Coulthard's season was marred by mistakes. Even so, he defeated both Schumacher and Hill in a straight fight in Portugal and took third position in the championship.

Gerhard Berger and Jean Alesi remained at Ferrari for another season of frustration. But Alesi scored his first win in Canada when Schumacher experienced gearbox trouble—Ferrari's sole triumph of the year.

Schumacher's Canadian misfortunes also benefited the Jordan team, with drivers Rubens Barrichello and Eddie Irvine finishing on the podium. This was the team's first year with a works Peugeot engine, and the combination proved fast but unreliable. Irvine also suffered a frightening fire during refuelling at the Belgian GP.

McLaren, now using engines from Mercedes-Benz, signed Nigel Mansell in his return to full-time F1 racing. But the combination quickly turned into a disaster, and Mansell only raced twice before finally leaving the sport. In contrast, his teammate Mika Hakkinen confirmed his talent by finishing second in Italy and Japan. However, the Finn was seriously injured practicing for the Australian Grand Prix, but he made a full recovery.

Heinz-Harald Frentzen showed maturity in the Sauber, now powered by the works Ford engine that had won the championship 12 months previously. Several fine performances, including a podium at Monza, suggested that he could challenge Schumacher if armed with a competitive car.

GRANDE PREMIO DO BRASIL

26 March 1995. Interlagos. 71 laps of a 2.667-mile circuit = 189.357 miles. Warm, dry and overcast. World Championship round 1

1*	Michael Schumacher	Benetton B195-Renault	71	1h38m34.154
2*	David Coulthard	Williams FW17-Renault	71	1h38m42.214
3	Gerhard Berger	Ferrari 412T2	70	
4	Mika Hakkinen	McLaren MP4/10-Mercedes-Benz	70	
5	Jean Alesi	Ferrari 412T2	70	
6	Mark Blundell	McLaren MP4/10-Mercedes-Benz	70	

*No manufacturers' points awarded due to fuel irregularities. Winner's

average speed: 115.263 mph. Starting grid front row: Hill, 1m20.081 (pole) and Schumacher, 1m20.382. Fastest lap: Schumacher, 1m20.921. Leaders: Schumacher, laps 1-17, 31-35, 47-71; Hill, 18-21, 23-30; Coulthard, 22, 36-46

MARLBORO GRAN PREMIO DE LA REPUBLICA ARGENTINA

9 April 1995. Buenos Aires. 72 laps of a 2.645-mile circuit = 190.440 miles. Race stopped after first-lap accidents, restarted over original distance. Warm, dry and overcast. World Championship round 2

1	Damon Hill	Williams FW17-Renault	72	1h53m14.532
2	Jean Alesi	Ferrari 412T2	72	1h53m20.939
3	Michael Schumacher	Benetton B195-Renault	72	1h53m47.908
4	Johnny Herbert	Benetton B195-Renault	71	
5	Heinz-Harald Frentzen	Sauber C14-Ford	70	
6	Gerhard Berger	Ferrari 412T2	70	

Winner's average speed: 100.902 mph. Starting grid front row: Coulthard, 1m53.241 (pole) and Hill, 1m54.057. Fastest lap: Schumacher, 1m30.522. Leaders: Coulthard, laps 1-5; Schumacher, 6-10, 17; Hill, 11-16, 26-72; Alesi, 18-25

GRAN PREMIO DI SAN MARINO

30 April 1995. Imola. 63 laps of a 3.064-mile circuit = 193.032 miles. Cool, dry and cloudy. World Championship round 3

1	Damon Hill	Williams FW17-Renault	63	1h41m42.552
2	Jean Alesi	Ferrari 412T2	63	1h42m01.062
3	Gerhard Berger	Ferrari 412T2	63	1h42m25.668
4	David Coulthard	Williams FW17-Renault	63	1h42m34.442
5	Mika Hakkinen	McLaren MP4/10-Mercedes-Benz	62	
6	Heinz-Harald Frentzen	Sauber C14-Ford	62	

Winner's average speed: 113.873 mph. Starting grid front row: Schumacher, 1m27.274 (pole) and Berger, 1m27.282. Fastest lap: Berger, 1m29.568. Leaders: Schumacher, laps 1-9; Coulthard, 10; Berger, 11-21; Hill, 22-63

GRAN PREMIO MARLBORO DE ESPANA

14 May 1995. Catalunya. 65 laps of a 2.937-mile circuit = 190.905 miles. Warm, dry and sunny. World Championship round 4

1	Michael Schumacher	Benetton B195-Renault	65	1h34m20.507
2	Johnny Herbert	Benetton B195-Renault	65	1h35m12.495
3	Gerhard Berger	Ferrari 412T2	65	1h35m25.744
4	Damon Hill	Williams FW17-Renault	65	1h36m22.256
5	Eddie Irvine	Jordan 195-Peugeot	64	
6	Olivier Panis	Ligier JS41-Mugen	64	

Winner's average speed: 121.413 mph. Starting grid front row: Schumacher, 1m21.452 (pole) and Alesi, 1m22.052. Fastest lap: Hill, 1m24.531. Leaders: Schumacher, laps 1-65

GRAND PRIX DE MONACO

28 May 1995. Monte Carlo. 78 laps of a 2.068-mile circuit = 161.304 miles. Race stopped after first-lap accident, restarted over original distance. Warm, dry and sunny. World Championship round 5

1	Michael Schumacher	Benetton B195-Renault	78	1h53m11.258
2	Damon Hill	Williams FW17-Renault	78	1h53m46.075
3	Gerhard Berger	Ferrari 412T2	78	1h54m22.705
4	Johnny Herbert	Benetton B195-Renault	77	
5	Mark Blundell	McLaren MP4/10-Mercedes-Benz	77	
6	Heinz-Harald Frentzen	Sauber C14-Ford	76	

Winner's average speed: 85.506 mph. Starting grid front row: Hill, 1m21.952 (pole) and Schumacher, 1m22.742. Fastest lap: Alesi, 1m24.621. Leaders: Hill, laps 1-23; Schumacher, 24-35, 37-78; Alesi, 36

GRAND PRIX MOLSON DU CANADA

11 June 1995. Montreal. 69 laps of a 2.765-mile circuit = 190.785 miles. Organisers declared positions after 68 laps due to track invasion. Warm, dry and cloudy. World Championship round 6

1	Jean Alesi	Ferrari 412T2	69	1h46m31.131
2	Rubens Barrichello	Jordan 195-Peugeot	69	1h47m03.020

3	Eddie Irvine	Jordan 195-Peugeot	69	1h47m04.603
4	Olivier Panis	Ligier JS41-Mugen	69	1h47m07.839
5	Michael Schumacher	Benetton B195-Renault	69	1h47m08.393
6	Gianni Morbidelli	Footwork FA16-Hart	68	

Winner's average speed: 107.465 mph. Starting grid front row: Schumacher, 1m27.661 (pole) and Hill, 1m28.039. Fastest lap: Schumacher, 1m29.174. Leaders: Schumacher, laps 1-57; Alesi, 58-69.

GRAND PRIX DE FRANCE

2 July 1995. Magny-Cours. 72 laps of a 2.641-mile circuit = 190.152 miles. Warm, dry and hazy. World Championship round 7

1	Michael Schumacher	Benetton B195-Renault	72	1h38m28.429
2	Damon Hill	Williams FW17-Renault	72	1h38m59.738
3	David Coulthard	Williams FW17-Renault	72	1h39m31.255
4	Martin Brundle	Ligier JS41-Mugen	72	1h39m31.722
5	Jean Alesi	Ferrari 412T2	72	1h39m46.298
6	Rubens Barrichello	Jordan 195-Peugeot	71	

Winner's average speed: 115.859 mph. Starting grid front row: Hill, 1m17.225 (pole) and Schumacher, 1m17.512. Fastest lap: Schumacher, 1m20.218. Leaders: Hill, laps 1-21; Schumacher, 22-72.

BRITISH GRAND PRIX

16 July 1995. Silverstone. 61 laps of a 3.210-mile circuit = 195.810 miles. Warm, cloudy and windy. World Championship round 8

1	Johnny Herbert	Benetton B195-Renault	61	1h34m35.093
2	Jean Alesi	Ferrari 412T2	61	1h34m51.572
3	David Coulthard	Williams FW17-Renault	61	1h34m58.981
4	Olivier Panis	Ligier JS41-Mugen	61	1h36m08.261
5	Mark Blundell	McLaren MP4/10-Mercedes-Benz	61	1h36m23.265
6	Heinz-Harald Frentzen	Sauber C14-Ford	60	

Winner's average speed: 124.212 mph. Starting grid front row: Hill, 1m28.124 (pole) and Schumacher, 1m28.397. Fastest lap: Hill, 1m29.752. Leaders: Hill, laps 1-22, 32-41; Schumacher, 23-31, 42-45; Herbert, 46-48, 51-61; Coulthard, 49-50

GROSSER MOBIL 1 PREIS VON DEUTSCHLAND

30 July 1995. Hockenheim. 45 laps of a 4.239-mile circuit = 190.755 miles. Hot, dry and sunny. World Championship round 9

1	Michael Schumacher	Benetton B195-Renault	45	1h22m56.043
2	David Coulthard	Williams FW17-Renault	45	1h23m02.031
3	Gerhard Berger	Ferrari 412T2	45	1h24m04.140
4	Johnny Herbert	Benetton B195-Renault	45	1h24m19.479
5	Jules Boullion	Sauber C14-Ford	44	
6	Aguri Suzuki	Ligier JS41-Mugen	44	

Winner's average speed: 138.005 mph. Starting grid front row: Hill, 1m44.385 (pole) and Schumacher, 1m44.465. Fastest lap: Schumacher, 1m48.824. Leaders: Hill, lap 1; Schumacher, laps 2-19, 24-45; Coulthard, 20-23

MAGYAR NAGYDIJ (HUNGARIAN GRAND PRIX)

13 August 1995. Hungaroring. 77 laps of a 2.465-mile circuit = 189.805 miles. Hot, dry and sunny. World Championship round 10

1	Damon Hill	Williams FW17-Renault	77	1h46m25.271
2	David Coulthard	Williams FW17-Renault	77	1h46m59.119
3	Gerhard Berger	Ferrari 412T2	76	
4	Johnny Herbert	Benetton B195-Renault	76	
5	Heinz-Harald Frentzen	Sauber C14-Ford	76	
6	Olivier Panis	Ligier JS41-Mugen	76	

Winner's average speed: 107.012 mph. Starting grid front row: Hill, 1m16.982 (pole) and Coulthard, 1m17.366. Fastest lap: Hill, 1m20.247. Leaders: Hill, laps 1-77

GRAND PRIX DE BELGIQUE

27 August 1995. Spa-Francorchamps. 44 laps of a 4.329-mile circuit = 190.476 miles. Dry at the start, rain showers later. World Championship round 11

1	Michael Schumacher	Benetton B195-Renault	44	1h36m47.875
2	Damon Hill	Williams FW17-Renault	44	1h37m07.368

3	Martin Brundle	Ligier JS41-Mugen	44	1h37m12.873
4	Heinz-Harald Frentzen	Sauber C14-Ford	44	1h37m14.847
5	Mark Blundell	McLaren MP4/10B-Mercedes-Benz	44	1h37m21.647
6	Rubens Barrichello	Jordan 195-Peugeot	44	1h37m27.549

Winner's average speed: 118.066 mph. Starting grid front row: Berger, 1m54.392 (pole) and Alesi, 1m54.631. Fastest lap: Coulthard, 1m53.412. Leaders: Herbert, laps 1, 4-5; Alesi, 2-3; Coulthard, 6-13; Hill, 14-15, 19-21, 24; Schumacher, 16-18, 22-23, 25-44

PIONEER GRAN PREMIO D'ITALIA

10 September 1995. Monza. 53 laps of a 3.604-mile circuit = 191.007 miles. Race stopped after first-lap accident, restarted over original distance. Warm, dry and sunny. World Championship round 12

1	Johnny Herbert	Benetton B195-Renault	53	1h18m27.916
2	Mika Hakkinen	McLaren MP4/10B-Mercedes-Benz	53	1h18m45.695
3	Heinz-Harald Frentzen	Sauber C14-Ford	53	1h18m52.237
4	Mark Blundell	McLaren MP4/10B-Mercedes-Benz	53	1h18m56.139
5	Mika Salo	Tyrrell 023-Yamaha	52	
6	Jules Boullion	Sauber C14-Ford	52	

Winner's average speed: 146.057 mph. Starting grid front row: Coulthard, 1m24.462 (pole) and Schumacher, 1m25.026. Fastest lap: Berger, 1m26.419. Leaders: Coulthard, laps 1-13; Berger, 14-24; Alesi, 25, 30-45; Barrichello, 26; Hakkinen, 27; Herbert, 28-29, 46-53

GRANDE PREMIO DE PORTUGAL

24 September 1995. Estoril. 71 laps of a 2.709-mile circuit = 192.339 miles. Race stopped after first-lap accident, restarted over original distance. Warm, dry and sunny. World Championship round 13

1	David Coulthard	Williams FW17-Renault	71	1h41m52.145
2	Michael Schumacher	Benetton B195-Renault	71	1h41m59.393
3	Damon Hill	Williams FW17-Renault	71	1h42m14.266
4	Gerhard Berger	Ferrari 412T2	71	1h43m17.024
5	Jean Alesi	Ferrari 412T2	71	1h43m17.574
6	Heinz-Harald Frentzen	Sauber C14-Ford	70	

Winner's average speed: 113.286 mph. Starting grid front row: Coulthard, 1m20.537 (pole) and Hill, 1m20.905. Fastest lap: Coulthard, 1m23.220. Leaders: Coulthard, laps 1-38, 44-71; Hill, 39-43

GROSSER PREIS VON EUROPA

1 October 1995. Nurburgring. 67 laps of a 2.831-mile circuit = 189.677 miles. Race scheduled for 68 laps, reduced due to extra parade lap. Damp and overcast. World Championship round 14

1	Michael Schumacher	Benetton B195-Renault	67	1h39m59.044
2	Jean Alesi	Ferrari 412T2	67	1h40m01.728
3	David Coulthard	Williams FW17B-Renault	67	1h40m34.426
4	Rubens Barrichello	Jordan 195-Peugeot	66	
5	Johnny Herbert	Benetton B195-Renault	66	
6	Eddie Irvine	Jordan 195-Peugeot	66	

Winner's average speed: 113.824 mph. Starting grid front row: Coulthard, 1m18.738 (pole) and Hill, 1m18.972. Fastest lap: Schumacher, 1m21.180. Leaders: Coulthard, laps 1-12; Alesi, 13-64; Schumacher, 65-67

PACIFIC GRAND PRIX

22 October 1995. TI Circuit, Aida. 83 laps of a 2.314-mile circuit = 192.062 miles. Warm, dry and sunny. World Championship round 15

1	Michael Schumacher	Benetton B195-Renault	83	1h48m49.972
2	David Coulthard	Williams FW17B-Renault	83	1h49m04.892
3	Damon Hill	Williams FW17B-Renault	83	1h49m38.305
4	Gerhard Berger	Ferrari 412T2	82	
5	Jean Alesi	Ferrari 412T2	82	
6	Johnny Herbert	Benetton B195-Renault	82	

Winner's average speed: 105.885 mph. Starting grid front row: Coulthard, 1m14.013 (pole) and Hill, 1m14.213. Fastest lap: Schumacher, 1m16.374. Leaders: Coulthard, laps 1-48; Schumacher, 49-83

Formula 1

1995 DRIVERS' RECORDS

driver	car	BR Q	BR R	RA Q	RA R	RSM Q	RSM R	E Q	E R	MC Q	MC R	CDN Q	CDN R
Jean Alesi	Ferrari 412T2	6	5	6	2	5	2	2	R	5	RF	5	1
Luca Badoer	Minardi M195-Ford	18	R	13	R	20	14	21	R	16	R	19	8
Rubens Barrichello	Jordan 195-Peugeot	16	R	10	R	10	R	8	7	11	R	9	2
Gerhard Berger	Ferrari 412T2	5	3	8	6	2	3F	3	3	4	3	4	R
Mark Blundell	McLaren MP4/10-Mercedes-Benz	9	6	17	R	-	-	-	-	10	5	10	R
	McLaren MP4/10B-Mercedes-Benz	-	-	-	-	-	-	-	-	-	-	-	-
	McLaren MP4/10C-Mercedes-Benz	-	-	-	-	-	-	-	-	-	-	-	-
"Jules" Boullion	Sauber C14-Ford	-	-	-	-	-	-	-	-	19	8	18	R
Martin Brundle	Ligier JS41-Mugen	-	-	-	-	-	-	11	9	8	R	14	R
David Coulthard	Williams FW17-Renault	3	2	1	R	3	4	4	R	3	R	3	R
	Williams FW17B-Renault	-	-	-	-	-	-	-	-	-	-	-	-
Jean-Denis Deletraz	Pacific PR02-Ford	-	-	-	-	-	-	-	-	-	-	-	-
Pedro Diniz	Forti FG01-Ford	25	10	25	NC	26	NC	26	R	22	10	24	R
Heinz-Harald Frentzen	Sauber C14-Ford	14	R	9	5	14	6	12	8	14	6	12	R
Bertrand Gachot	Pacific PR02-Ford	20	R	23	R	22	R	24	R	21	R	20	R
Mika Hakkinen	McLaren MP4/10-Mercedes-Benz	7	4	5	R	6	5	9	R	6	R	7	R
	McLaren MP4/10B-Mercedes-Benz	-	-	-	-	-	-	-	-	-	-	-	-
	McLaren MP4/10C-Mercedes-Benz	-	-	-	-	-	-	-	-	-	-	-	-
Johnny Herbert	Benetton B195-Renault	4	R	11	4	8	7	7	2	7	4	6	R
Damon Hill	Williams FW17-Renault	1	R	2	1	4	1	5	4F	1	2	2	R
	Williams FW17B-Renault	-	-	-	-	-	-	-	-	-	-	-	-
Taki Inoue	Footwork FA16-Hart	21	R	26	R	19	R	18	R	26	R	22	9
Eddie Irvine	Jordan 195-Peugeot	8	R	4	R	7	8	6	5	9	R	8	3
Ukyo Katayama	Tyrrell 023-Yamaha	11	R	15	8	15	R	17	R	15	R	16	R
Pedro Lamy	Minardi M195-Ford	-	-	-	-	-	-	-	-	-	-	-	-
Giovanni Lavaggi	Pacific PR02-Ford	-	-	-	-	-	-	-	-	-	-	-	-
Jan Magnussen	McLaren MP4/10B-Mercedes-Benz	-	-	-	-	-	-	-	-	-	-	-	-
Nigel Mansell	McLaren MP4/10B-Mercedes-Benz	-	-	-	-	9	10	10	R	-	-	-	-
Pierluigi Martini	Minardi M195-Ford	17	DNS	16	R	18	12	19	14	18	7	17	R
Andrea Montermini	Pacific PR02-Ford	22	9	22	R	24	R	23	DNS	25	DSQ	21	R
Gianni Morbidelli	Footwork FA16-Hart	13	R	12	R	11	13	14	11	13	9	13	6
Roberto Moreno	Forti FG01-Ford	23	R	24	NC	25	NC	25	R	24	R	23	R
Olivier Panis	Ligier JS41-Mugen	10	R	18	7	12	9	15	6	12	R	11	4
Massimiliano Papis	Footwork FA16-Hart	-	-	-	-	-	-	-	-	-	-	-	-
Mika Salo	Tyrrell 023-Yamaha	12	7	7	R	13	R	13	10	17	R	15	7
Domenico Schiattarella	Simtek S951-Ford	26	R	20	9	23	R	22	15	20	R	-	-
Michael Schumacher	Benetton B195-Renault	2	1F	3	3F	1	R	1	1	2	1	1	5F
Aguri Suzuki	Ligier JS41-Mugen	15	8	19	R	16	11	-	-	-	-	-	-
Gabriele Tarquini	Tyrrell 023-Yamaha	-	-	-	-	-	-	-	-	-	-	-	-
Jos Verstappen	Simtek S951-Ford	24	R	14	R	17	R	16	12	23	R	-	-
Karl Wendlinger	Sauber C14-Ford	19	R	21	R	21	R	20	13	-	-	-	-

1995 FINAL CHAMPIONSHIP POSITIONS

Drivers

1	Michael Schumacher	102
2	Damon Hill	69
3	David Coulthard	49
4	Johnny Herbert	45
5	Jean Alesi	42
6	Gerhard Berger	31
7	Mika Hakkinen	17
8	Olivier Panis	16
9	Heinz-Harald Frentzen	15
10	Mark Blundell	13
11	Rubens Barrichello	11
12	Eddie Irvine	10
13	Martin Brundle	7
14=	Gianni Morbidelli	5
	Mika Salo	5
16	"Jules" Boullion	3
17=	Pedro Lamy	1
	Aguri Suzuki	1

Manufacturers

1	Benetton-Renault*	137
2	Williams-Renault*	112
3	Ferrari	73
4	McLaren-Mercedes-Benz	30
5	Ligier-Mugen	24
6	Jordan-Peugeot	21
7	Sauber-Ford	18
8=	Footwork-Hart	5
	Tyrrell-Yamaha	5
9	Minardi-Ford	1

*Williams and Benetton lost their manu-
facturers points from the Brazilian Grand
Prix for fuel irregularities

F		GB		D		H		B		I		P		EU		PAC		J		AUS	
Q	R	Q	R	Q	R	Q	R	Q	R	Q	R	Q	R	Q	R	Q	R	Q	R	Q	R
4	5	6	2	10	R	6	R	2	R	5	R	7	5	6	2	4	5	2	R	5	R
17	13	18	10	16	R	12	8	19	R	18	R	18	14	18	11	16	15	18	9	15	DNS
5	6	9	11	5	R	14	7	12	6	6	R	8	11	11	4	11	R	10	7	7	R
7	12	4	R	4	3	4	3	1	R	3	RF	4	4	4	R	5	4	5	R	4	R
13	11	10	5	–	–	–	–	–	–	–	–	–	–	–	–	–	–	–	–	–	–
–	–	–	–	8	R	13	R	6	5	9	4	12	9	–	–	10	9	24	7	10	4
–	–	–	–	–	–	–	–	–	–	–	–	–	–	10	R	–	–	–	–	–	–
15	R	16	9	14	5	19	10	14	11	14	6	14	12	13	R	15	R	–	–	–	–
9	4	11	R	–	–	8	R	13	3	11	R	9	8	12	7	–	–	–	–	11	R
3	3	3	3	3	2	2	2	5	RF	1	R	1	1F	1	3	1	2	6	R	2	R
–	–	–	–	–	–	–	–	–	–	–	–	24	R	24	15	–	–	–	–	–	–
23	R	20	R	21	R	23	R	24	13	23	9	22	16	22	13	21	17	21	R	21	7
12	10	12	6	11	R	11	5	10	4	10	3	5	6	8	R	8	7	8	6	8	6
22	R	21	12	–	–	–	–	–	–	–	–	–	–	–	–	24	R	23	R	23	8
8	7	8	R	–	–	–	–	–	–	–	–	–	–	–	–	–	–	–	–	–	–
–	–	–	–	7	R	5	R	3	R	7	2	13	R	–	–	–	–	3	2	24	DNS
–	–	–	–	–	–	–	–	–	–	–	–	9	8	–	–	–	–	–	–	–	–
10	R	5	1	9	4	9	4	4	7	8	1	6	7	7	5	7	6	9	3	8	R
1	2	1	RF	1	R	1	1F	8	2	4	R	2	3	–	–	–	–	–	–	–	–
–	–	–	–	–	–	–	–	–	–	–	–	–	–	2	R	2	3	4	R	1	1F
18	R	19	R	19	R	18	R	18	12	20	8	19	15	21	R	20	R	19	12	19	R
11	9	7	R	6	9	7	13	7	12	–	R	10	10	5	6	6	11	7	4	9	R
19	R	14	R	17	7	17	R	15	R	17	10	16	R	–	–	17	14	14	R	16	R
–	–	–	–	15	9	17	10	19	R	17	R	16	9	14	13	17	11	17	6	–	–
–	–	–	–	24	R	24	R	23	R	24	R	–	–	–	–	–	–	–	–	–	–
–	–	–	–	–	–	–	–	–	–	–	–	–	–	–	–	12	10	–	–	–	–
20	R	15	7	20	R	–	–	–	–	–	–	–	–	–	–	–	–	–	–	–	–
21	NC	24	R	23	8	22	12	21	R	21	R	21	R	20	R	23	R	20	R	22	R
16	14	–	–	–	–	–	–	–	–	–	–	–	–	–	–	19	R	15	R	13	3
24	16	22	R	22	R	21	R	22	14	22	R	23	17	23	R	22	16	22	R	20	R
6	8	13	4	12	R	10	6	9	9	13	R	11	R	14	R	9	8	11	5	12	2
–	–	–	–	17	R	15	R	20	R	20	R	15	7	20	R	17	12	–	–	–	–
14	15	23	8	13	R	16	R	11	8	16	5	15	13	15	10	18	12	12	6	14	5
–	–	–	–	–	–	–	–	–	–	–	–	–	–	–	–	–	–	–	–	–	–
2	1F	2	R	2	1F	3	11	16	1	2	R	3	2	3	1F	3	1F	1	1F	3	R
–	–	18	6	–	–	–	–	–	–	–	–	–	–	–	–	–	–	–	–	–	–
–	–	–	–	–	–	–	–	–	–	–	–	19	14	–	–	–	–	–	–	–	–
–	–	–	–	–	–	–	–	–	–	–	–	–	–	–	–	–	–	16	10	18	R

FUJI TELEVISION JAPAN GRAND PRIX

29 October 1995. Suzuka. 53 laps of a 3.641-mile circuit = 192.973 miles. Wet and overcast at the start, drying. World Championship round 16

1	Michael Schumacher	Benetton B195-Renault	53	1h36m52.930
2	Mika Hakkinen	McLaren MP4/10B-Mercedes-Benz	53	1h37m12.267
3	Johnny Herbert	Benetton B195-Renault	53	1h38m16.734
4	Eddie Irvine	Jordan 195-Peugeot	53	1h38m35.066
5	Olivier Panis	Ligier JS41-Mugen	52	
6	Mika Salo	Tyrrell 023-Yamaha	52	

Winner's average speed: 119.510 mph. Starting grid front row: Schumacher, 1m38.023 (pole) and Alesi, 1m38.888. Fastest lap: Schumacher, 1m42.976. Leaders: Schumacher, laps 1-10, 12-31, 36-53; Hakkinen, 11; Hill, 32-35.

AUSTRALIAN GRAND PRIX

12 November 1995. Adelaide. 81 laps of a 2.347-mile circuit = 190.107 miles. Warm, dry and sunny. World Championship round 17

1	Damon Hill	Williams FW17B-Renault	81	1h49m15.946
2	Olivier Panis	Ligier JS41-Mugen	79	
3	Gianni Morbidelli	Footwork FA16-Hart	79	
4	Mark Blundell	McLaren MP4/10B-Mercedes-Benz	79	
5	Mika Salo	Tyrrell 023-Yamaha	78	
6	Pedro Lamy	Minardi M195-Ford	78	

Winner's average speed: 104.392 mph. Starting grid front row: Hill, 1m15.505 (pole) and Coulthard, 1m15.628. Fastest lap: Hill, 1m17.943. Leaders: Coulthard, laps 1-19; Schumacher, 20-21; Hill, 22-81.

1996

With Michael Schumacher seduced by the prospect of returning Ferrari to World Championship success (and a reputed $25m annual salary), Williams started 1996 as overwhelming F1 favourites. Damon Hill emerged from two years in the German's shadow with six wins and the title 28 years after his father Graham's second championship win. Even so, Hill would be dropped from the 1997 Williams line-up.

For this season Hill was joined at Williams by another son with a famous racing name. Jacques Villeneuve, the son of Gilles, arrived as reigning ChampCar champion and Indianapolis 500 winner, and immediately qualified on pole for his debut in Australia, and would have won but for falling oil pressure. He later withstood pressure from Schumacher at the Nurburgring to win on only his fourth start, and scored another three wins to challenge Hill until the very last race.

Schumacher finished third in the championship in his first season at Ferrari. He scored three wins, starting in Spain with a wet-weather performance to rank among the greatest ever. He also scored victories at Monza and Belgium, but poor reliability and an uncharacteristic mistake at Monaco prevented a sustained challenge.

Benetton not only suffered from the loss of Schumacher, but also the reliability that had helped secure the title a year earlier. Jean Alesi and Gerhard Berger arrived from Ferrari: Alesi would have won in Monaco but for suspension failure, and a blown engine within three laps of the finish at Hockenheim denied Berger a certain win.

Although McLaren would also endure a year without victory, the team was boosted by the remarkable return of Mika Hakkinen after his life-threatening injuries at the final race of 1995. His drive to third at Monza after being delayed by a broken front wing was the highlight of a promising season. David Coulthard led at Imola after a demon start and finished second at Monaco when he could have won. Here Olivier Panis profited from the misfortunes of others, and with some opportune passing, scored Ligier's first victory in 15 years.

The most memorable moments in a poor season for Jordan were Martin Brundle's huge accident in the opening laps in Melbourne and Rubens Barrichello qualifying on the front row for his home race three weeks later. Heinz-Harald Frentzen was in the spotlight after he was named Hill's replacement at Williams, but his final year with Sauber had been a disappointment.

Entry into Formula 1 was now restricted to twelve team franchises, although all twelve have yet to be filled.

TRANSURBAN AUSTRALIAN GRAND PRIX

10 March 1996. Albert Park. 58 laps of a 3.295-mile circuit = 191.110 miles. Race stopped after first-lap accident, restarted over original distance. Warm, dry and sunny. World Championship round 1

1	Damon Hill	Williams FW18-Renault	58	1h32m50.491
2	Jacques Villeneuve	Williams FW18-Renault	58	1h33m28.511
3	Eddie Irvine	Ferrari F310	58	1h33m53.062
4	Gerhard Berger	Benetton B196-Renault	58	1h34m07.528
5	Mika Hakkinen	McLaren MP4/11-Mercedes-Benz	58	1h34m25.562
6	Mika Salo	Tyrrell 024-Yamaha	57	

Winner's average speed: 123.507 mph. Starting grid front row: Villeneuve, 1m32.371 (pole) and Hill, 1m32.509. Fastest lap: Villeneuve, 1m33.421. Leaders: Villeneuve, laps 1-29, 33-53; Hill, 30-32, 54-58

GRANDE PREMIO DO BRASIL

31 March 1996. Interlagos. 71 laps of a 2.667-mile circuit = 189.357 miles. Heavy rain at the start, drying later. World Championship round 2

1	Damon Hill	Williams FW18-Renault	71	1h49m52.976
2	Jean Alesi	Benetton B196-Renault	71	1h50m10.958
3	Michael Schumacher	Ferrari F310	70	
4	Mika Hakkinen	McLaren MP4/11-Mercedes-Benz	70	
5	Mika Salo	Tyrrell 024-Yamaha	70	
6	Olivier Panis	Ligier JS43-Mugen	70	

Winner's average speed: 103.396 mph. Starting grid front row: Hill, 1m18.111 (pole) and Barrichello, 1m19.092. Fastest lap: Hill, 1m21.547. Leaders: Hill, laps 1-39, 43-71; Alesi, 40-42

GRAN PREMIO MARLBORO DE ARGENTINA

7 April 1996. Buenos Aires. 72 laps of a 2.645-mile circuit = 190.440 miles. Warm, dry and sunny. World Championship round 3

1	Damon Hill	Williams FW18-Renault	72	1h54m55.322
2	Jacques Villeneuve	Williams FW18-Renault	72	1h55m07.489
3	Jean Alesi	Benetton B196-Renault	72	1h55m10.076
4	Rubens Barrichello	Jordan 196-Peugeot	72	1h55m50.453
5	Eddie Irvine	Ferrari F310	72	1h56m00.313
6	Jos Verstappen	Footwork FA17-Hart	72	1h56m04.235

Winner's average speed: 99.427 mph. Starting grid front row: Hill, 1m30.346 (pole) and Schumacher, 1m30.598. Fastest lap: Alesi, 1m29.413. Leaders: Hill, laps 1-72

GROSSER PREIS VON EUROPA

28 April 1996. Nurburgring. 67 laps of a 2.831-mile circuit = 189.677 miles. Warm, dry and cloudy. World Championship round 4

1	Jacques Villeneuve	Williams FW18-Renault	67	1h33m26.473
2	Michael Schumacher	Ferrari F310	67	1h33m27.235
3	David Coulthard	McLaren MP4/11-Mercedes-Benz	67	1h33m59.307
4	Damon Hill	Williams FW18-Renault	67	1h33m59.984
5	Rubens Barrichello	Jordan 196-Peugeot	67	1h34m00.186
6	Martin Brundle	Jordan 196-Peugeot	67	1h34m22.040

Winner's average speed: 121.794 mph. Starting grid front row: Hill, 1m18.941 (pole) and Villeneuve, 1m19.721. Fastest lap: Hill, 1m21.363. Leaders: Villeneuve, laps 1-67

GRAN PREMIO DI SAN MARINO

5 May 1996. Imola. 63 laps of a 3.064-mile circuit = 193.032 miles. Warm, dry and sunny. World Championship round 5

1	Damon Hill	Williams FW18-Renault	63	1h35m26.156
2	Michael Schumacher	Ferrari F310	63	1h35m42.616
3	Gerhard Berger	Benetton B196-Renault	63	1h36m13.047
4	Eddie Irvine	Ferrari F310	63	1h36m27.739
5	Rubens Barrichello	Jordan 196-Peugeot	63	1h36m44.646
6	Jean Alesi	Benetton B196-Renault	62	

Winner's average speed: 121.358 mph. Starting grid front row: Schumacher, 1m26.890 (pole) and Hill, 1m27.105. Fastest lap: Hill, 1m28.931. Leaders: Coulthard, laps 1-19; Schumacher, 20; Hill, 21-63

GRAND PRIX DE MONACO

19 May 1996. Monte Carlo. 75 laps of a 2.068-mile circuit = 155.100 miles. Race scheduled for 78 laps, stopped after two hours. Rain at the start, drying later. World Championship round 6

1	Olivier Panis	Ligier JS43-Mugen	75	2h00m45.629
2	David Coulthard	McLaren MP4/11-Mercedes-Benz	75	2h00m50.457
3	Johnny Herbert	Sauber C15-Ford	75	2h01m23.132
4	Heinz-Harald Frentzen	Sauber C15-Ford	74	
5	Mika Salo	Tyrrell 024-Yamaha	70	accident
6	Mika Hakkinen	McLaren MP4/11-Mercedes-Benz	70	accident

Winner's average speed: 77.062 mph. Starting grid front row:
Schumacher, 1m20.356 (pole) and Hill, 1m20.866. Fastest lap: Alesi,
1m25.205. Leaders: Hill, laps 1-27, 30-40; Alesi, 28-29, 41-59; Panis,
60-75

GRAN PREMIO MARLBORO DE ESPANA

2 June 1996. Catalunya. 65 laps of a 2.937-mile circuit = 190.905 miles.
Heavy rain. World Championship round 7

1	Michael Schumacher	Ferrari F310	65	1h59m49.307
2	Jean Alesi	Benetton B196-Renault	65	2h00m34.609
3	Jacques Villeneuve	Williams FW18-Renault	65	2h00m37.695
4	Heinz-Harald Frentzen	Sauber C15-Ford	64	
5	Mika Hakkinen	McLaren MP4/11-Mercedes-Benz	64	
6	Pedro Diniz	Ligier JS43-Mugen	63	

Winner's average speed: 95.594 mph. Starting grid front row: Hill,
1m20.650 (pole) and Villeneuve, 1m21.084. Fastest lap: Schumacher,
1m45.517. Leaders: Villeneuve, laps 1-11; Schumacher, 12-65

GRAND PRIX MOLSON DU CANADA

16 June 1996. Montreal. 69 laps of a 2.747-mile circuit = 189.543 miles.
Warm, dry and sunny. World Championship round 8

1	Damon Hill	Williams FW18-Renault	69	1h36m03.465
2	Jacques Villeneuve	Williams FW18-Renault	69	1h36m07.648
3	Jean Alesi	Benetton B196-Renault	69	1h36m58.121
4	David Coulthard	McLaren MP4/11-Mercedes-Benz	69	1h37m07.138
5	Mika Hakkinen	McLaren MP4/11-Mercedes-Benz	68	
6	Martin Brundle	Jordan 196-Peugeot	68	

Winner's average speed: 118.393 mph. Starting grid front row: Hill,
1m21.059 (pole) and Villeneuve, 1m21.079. Fastest lap: Villeneuve,
1m21.916. Leaders: Hill, laps 1-27, 36-69; Villeneuve, 28-35

GRAND PRIX DE FRANCE

30 June 1996. Magny-Cours. 72 laps of a 2.641-mile circuit = 190.152
miles. Warm, dry and sunny. World Championship round 9

1	Damon Hill	Williams FW18-Renault	72	1h36m28.795
2	Jacques Villeneuve	Williams FW18-Renault	72	1h36m36.922
3	Jean Alesi	Benetton B196-Renault	72	1h37m15.237
4	Gerhard Berger	Benetton B196-Renault	72	1h37m15.654
5	Mika Hakkinen	McLaren MP4/11-Mercedes-Benz	72	1h37m31.569
6	David Coulthard	McLaren MP4/11-Mercedes-Benz	71	

Winner's average speed: 118.254 mph. Starting grid front row:
Schumacher, 1m15.989 (pole) and Hill, 1m16.058. Fastest lap: Villeneuve,
1m18.610. Leaders: Hill, laps 1-27, 31-72; Villeneuve, 28-30

BRITISH GRAND PRIX

14 July 1996. Silverstone. 61 laps of a 3.152-mile circuit = 192.272 miles.
Hot, dry and sunny. World Championship round 10

1	Jacques Villeneuve	Williams FW18-Renault	61	1h33m00.874
2	Gerhard Berger	Benetton B196-Renault	61	1h33m19.900
3	Mika Hakkinen	McLaren MP4/11-Mercedes-Benz	61	1h33m51.704
4	Rubens Barrichello	Jordan 196-Peugeot	61	1h34m07.590
5	David Coulthard	McLaren MP4/11-Mercedes-Benz	61	1h34m23.381
6	Martin Brundle	Jordan 196-Peugeot	60	

Winner's average speed: 124.027 mph. Starting grid front row: Hill,
1m26.875 (pole) and Villeneuve, 1m27.070. Fastest lap: Villeneuve,
1m29.288. Leaders: Villeneuve, laps 1-23, 31-61; Alesi, 24-30

GROSSER MOBIL 1 PREIS VON DEUTSCHLAND

28 July 1996. Hockenheim. 45 laps of a 4.239-mile circuit = 190.755
miles. Warm, dry and sunny. World Championship round 11

1	Damon Hill	Williams FW18-Renault	45	1h21m43.417

2	Jean Alesi	Benetton B196-Renault	45	1h21m54.869
3	Jacques Villeneuve	Williams FW18-Renault	45	1h22m17.343
4	Michael Schumacher	Ferrari F310	45	1h22m24.934
5	David Coulthard	McLaren MP4/11-Mercedes-Benz	45	1h22m25.613
6	Rubens Barrichello	Jordan 196-Peugeot	45	1h23m25.516

Winner's average speed: 140.049 mph. Starting grid front row: Hill,
1m43.912 (pole) and Berger, 1m44.299. Fastest lap: Hill, 1m46.504.
Leaders: Berger, laps 1-23, 35-42; Hill, 24-34, 43-45

MARLBORO MAGYAR NAGYDIJ (HUNGARIAN GRAND PRIX)

11 August 1996. Hungaroring. 77 laps of a 2.465-mile circuit = 189.805
miles. Warm, dry and sunny. World Championship round 12

1	Jacques Villeneuve	Williams FW18-Renault	77	1h46m21.134
2	Damon Hill	Williams FW18-Renault	77	1h46m21.905
3	Jean Alesi	Benetton B196-Renault	77	1h47m45.346
4	Mika Hakkinen	McLaren MP4/11-Mercedes-Benz	76	
5	Olivier Panis	Ligier JS43-Mugen	76	
6	Rubens Barrichello	Jordan 196-Peugeot	75	

Winner's average speed: 107.081 mph. Starting grid front row:
Schumacher, 1m17.129 (pole) and Hill, 1m17.182. Fastest lap: Hill,
1m20.093. Leaders: Schumacher, laps 1-18; Villeneuve, 19-21, 25-58,
64-77; Hill, 22-24, 59-63

GRAND PRIX DE BELGIQUE

25 August 1996. Spa-Francorchamps. 44 laps of a 4.329-mile circuit =
190.476 miles. Warm, dry and sunny. World Championship round 13

1	Michael Schumacher	Ferrari F310	44	1h28m15.125
2	Jacques Villeneuve	Williams FW18-Renault	44	1h28m20.727
3	Mika Hakkinen	McLaren MP4/11-Mercedes-Benz	44	1h28m30.835
4	Jean Alesi	Benetton B196-Renault	44	1h28m34.250
5	Damon Hill	Williams FW18-Renault	44	1h28m44.304
6	Gerhard Berger	Benetton B196-Renault	44	1h28m45.021

Winner's average speed: 129.499 mph. Starting grid front row: Villeneuve,
1m50.574 (pole) and Hill, 1m50.980. Fastest lap: Berger, 1m53.067.
Leaders: Villeneuve, laps 1-14, 30-32; Coulthard, 15-21; Hakkinen, 22-23;
Schumacher, 24-29, 33-44

PIONEER GRAN PREMIO D'ITALIA

8 September 1996. Monza. 53 laps of a 3.585-mile circuit = 190.005
miles. Hot, dry and sunny. World Championship round 14

1	Michael Schumacher	Ferrari F310	53	1h17m43.632
2	Jean Alesi	Benetton B196-Renault	53	1h18m01.897
3	Mika Hakkinen	McLaren MP4/11-Mercedes-Benz	53	1h18m50.267
4	Martin Brundle	Jordan 196-Peugeot	53	1h19m08.849
5	Rubens Barrichello	Jordan 196-Peugeot	53	1h19m09.107
6	Pedro Diniz	Ligier JS43-Mugen	52	

Winner's average speed: 146.671 mph. Starting grid front row: Hill,
1m24.204 (pole) and Villeneuve, 1m24.521. Fastest lap: Schumacher,
1m26.110. Leaders: Hill, laps 1-5; Alesi, 6-30; Schumacher, 31-53

GRANDE PREMIO DE PORTUGAL

22 September 1996. Estoril. 70 laps of a 2.709-mile circuit = 189.630
miles. Warm, dry and sunny. World Championship round 15

1	Jacques Villeneuve	Williams FW18-Renault	70	1h40m22.915
2	Damon Hill	Williams FW18-Renault	70	1h40m42.881
3	Michael Schumacher	Ferrari F310	70	1h41m16.680
4	Jean Alesi	Benetton B196-Renault	70	1h41m18.024
5	Eddie Irvine	Ferrari F310	70	1h41m50.304
6	Gerhard Berger	Benetton B196-Renault	70	1h41m56.056

Winner's average speed: 113.345 mph. Starting grid front row: Hill,
1m20.330 (pole) and Villeneuve, 1m20.339. Fastest lap: Villeneuve,
1m22.873. Leaders: Hill, laps 1-17, 22-33, 36-48; Alesi, 18-21; Villeneuve,
34-35, 49-70

1996 DRIVERS' RECORDS

driver	car	AUS Q	R	BR Q	R	RA Q	R	EU Q	R	RSM Q	R	MC Q	R
Jean Alesi	Benetton B196-Renault	6	R	5	2	4	3F	4	R	5	6	3	RF
Luca Badoer	Forti FG01B-Ford	21	DNQ	19	11	21	R	22	DNQ	-	-	21	R
	Forti FG03-Ford	-	-	-	-	-	-	-	-	21	10	-	-
Rubens Barrichello	Jordan 196-Peugeot	8	R	2	R	6	4	5	5	9	5	6	R
Gerhard Berger	Benetton B196-Renault	7	4	8	R	5	R	8	9	7	3	4	R
Martin Brundle	Jordan 196-Peugeot	19	R	6	12	15	R	11	6	12	R	16	R
David Coulthard	McLaren MP4/11-Mercedes-Benz	13	R	14	R	9	7	6	3	4	R	5	2
Pedro Diniz	Ligier JS43-Mugen	20	10	22	8	18	R	17	10	17	7	17	R
Giancarlo Fisichella	Minardi M195B-Ford	16	R	-	-	-	-	18	13	19	R	18	R
Heinz-Harald Frentzen	Sauber C15-Ford	9	8	9	R	11	R	10	R	10	R	9	4
Mika Hakkinen	McLaren MP4/11-Mercedes-Benz	5	5	7	4	8	R	9	8	11	8	8	6
Johnny Herbert	Sauber C15-Ford	14	R	12	R	17	9	12	7	15	R	13	3
Damon Hill	Williams FW18-Renault	2	1	1	1F	1	1	1	4F	2	1F	2	R
Eddie Irvine	Ferrari F310	3	3	10	7	10	5	7	R	6	4	7	7
Ukyo Katayama	Tyrrell 024-Yamaha	15	11	16	9	13	R	16	DSQ	16	R	15	R
Pedro Lamy	Minardi M195B-Ford	17	R	18	10	19	R	19	12	18	9	19	R
Giovanni Lavaggi	Minardi M195B-Ford	-	-	-	-	-	-	-	-	-	-	-	-
Tarso Marques	Minardi M195B-Ford	-	-	21	R	14	R	-	-	-	-	-	-
Andrea Montermini	Forti FG01B-Ford	22	DNQ	20	R	22	10	21	DNQ	-	-	-	-
	Forti FG03-Ford	-	-	-	-	-	-	-	-	22	DNQ	22	DNS
Olivier Panis	Ligier JS43-Mugen	11	7	15	6	12	8	15	R	13	R	14	1
Ricardo Rosset	Footwork FA17-Hart	18	9	17	R	20	R	20	11	20	R	20	R
Mika Salo	Tyrrell 024-Yamaha	10	6	11	5	16	R	14	DSQ	8	R	11	5
Michael Schumacher	Ferrari F310	4	R	4	3	2	R	3	2	1	2	1	R
Jos Verstappen	Footwork FA17-Hart	12	R	13	R	7	6	13	R	14	R	12	R
Jacques Villeneuve	Williams FW18-Renault	1	2F	3	R	3	2	2	1	3	11	10	R

1996 FINAL CHAMPIONSHIP POSITIONS

Drivers						Manufacturers	
1	Damon Hill	97	10	Eddie Irvine	11	1 Williams-Renault	175
2	Jacques Villeneuve	78	11	Martin Brundle	8	2 Ferrari	70
3	Michael Schumacher	59	12	Heinz-Harald Frentzen	7	3 Benetton-Renault	68
4	Jean Alesi	47	13	Mika Salo	5	4 McLaren-Mercedes-Benz	49
5	Mika Hakkinen	31	14	Johnny Herbert	4	5 Jordan-Peugeot	22
6	Gerhard Berger	21	15	Pedro Diniz	2	6 Ligier-Mugen	15
7	David Coulthard	18	16	Jos Verstappen	1	7 Sauber-Ford	11
8	Rubens Barrichello	14				8 Tyrrell-Yamaha	5
9	Olivier Panis	13				9 Footwork-Hart	1

FUJI TELEVISION JAPANESE GRAND PRIX

13 October 1996. Suzuka. 52 laps of a 3.641-mile circuit = 189.332 miles.
Warm, dry and sunny. World Championship round 16

1	Damon Hill	Williams FW18-Renault	52	1h32m33.791
2	Michael Schumacher	Ferrari F310	52	1h32m35.674
3	Mika Hakkinen	McLaren MP4/11-Mercedes-Benz	52	1h32m37.003
4	Gerhard Berger	Benetton B196-Renault	52	1h33m00.317
5	Martin Brundle	Jordan 196-Peugeot	52	1h33m40.911
6	Heinz-Harald Frentzen	Sauber C15-Ford	52	1h33m54.977

Winner's average speed: 122.726 mph. Starting grid front row: Villeneuve, 1m38.909 (pole) and Hill, 1m39.370. Fastest lap: Villeneuve, 1m44.043. Leaders: Hill, laps 1-52

1997

Jacques Villeneuve has been happy to cultivate an image as F1's anti-hero. Always cocky, quick, and unconventional, in 1997 he fulfilled the promise of his first season with seven wins, and entered the final race at Jerez just one point behind Michael Schumacher's increasingly competitive Ferrari.

Schumacher may be the leading driver of his generation, but his actions at Jerez drew condemnation from all corners of the sport. On lap 48 of the title-deciding race, Villeneuve passed him for the lead. An FIA hearing later ruled that Schumacher responded by deliberately driving into Villeneuve in an attempt to eliminate his rival and protect his points lead. He was stripped of all of his season's points and second position in the championship for driving outside the rules. Meanwhile, Villeneuve finished third in the race to clinch the title.

Villeneuve outperformed his Williams teammate Heinz-Harald Frentzen, who despite a victory at Imola and podium finishes in six other races, experienced a season hampered by mistakes and incorrect strategies.

E		CDN		F		GB		D		H		B		I		P		J	
Q	R	Q	R	Q	R	Q	R	Q	R	Q	R	Q	R	Q	R	Q	R	Q	R
4	2	4	3	3	3	5	R	5	2	5	3	7	4	6	2	3	4	9	R
-	-	-	-	-	-	-	-	-	-	-	-	-	-	-	-	-	-	-	-
21	DNQ	20	R	20	R	22	DNQ	-	-	-	-	-	-	-	-	-	-	-	-
7	R	8	R	10	9	6	4	9	6	13	6	10	R	10	5	9	R	11	9
5	R	7	R	4	4	7	2	2	13	6	R	5	6F	8	R	5	6	4	4
15	R	9	6	8	8	6	10	10	10	12	R	8	R	9	4	10	9	10	5
14	R	10	4	7	6	9	5	7	5	9	R	4	R	5	R	8	13	8	8
17	6	18	R	11	R	17	R	11	R	15	R	15	R	14	6	18	R	16	R
19	R	16	8	17	R	18	11	-	-	-	-	-	-	-	-	-	-	-	-
11	4	12	R	12	R	11	8	13	8	10	R	11	R	13	R	11	7	7	6
10	5	6	5	5	5	4	3	4	R	7	4	6	3	4	3	7	R	5	3
9	R	15	7	16	DSQ	13	9	14	R	8	R	12	R	12	9	12	8	13	10
1	R	1	1	2	1	1	R	1	1F	2	2F	2	5	1	R	1	2	2	1
6	R	5	R	22	R	10	R	8	R	4	R	9	R	7	R	6	5	6	R
16	R	17	R	14	R	12	R	16	R	14	7	17	8	16	10	14	12	14	R
18	R	19	R	18	12	19	R	18	12	19	R	19	10	18	R	19	16	18	12
-	-	-	-	-	-	-	-	20	DNQ	20	10	20	DNQ	20	R	20	15	20	DNQ
22	DNQ	22	R	21	R	21	DNQ	-	-	-	-	-	-	-	-	-	-	-	-
8	R	11	R	9	7	16	R	12	7	11	5	14	R	11	R	15	10	12	7
20	R	21	R	19	11	20	R	19	11	18	8	18	9	19	R	17	14	19	13
12	DSQ	14	R	13	10	14	7	15	9	16	R	13	7	17	R	13	11	15	R
3	1F	3	R	1	DNS	3	R	3	4	1	9	3	1	3	1F	4	3	3	2
13	R	13	R	15	R	15	10	17	R	17	R	16	R	15	8	16	R	17	11
2	3	2	2F	6	2F	2	1F	6	3	3	1	1	2	2	7	2	1F	1	RF

1997 Jacques Villeneuve and Michael Schumacher clash at the Jerez championship showdown, handing the title to Villeneuve.

Defending champion Damon Hill moved to Arrows, but the combination struggled until Hungary, where he led convincingly until mechanical failure on the last lap robbed him of Arrows's first victory.

McLaren returned to the winners' circle after 49 races when David Coulthard won in Australia, the first race for new sponsor West. He logged another victory at Monza, while teammate Mika Hakkinen won for the first time at Jerez when both Villeneuve and Coulthard (who was obeying team orders) let him through in the closing laps.

At Jordan, youth took precedence over experience in 1997. The team hired Giancarlo Fisichella and Ralf Schumacher, two drivers with a total of eight previous races between them. They collided at the Argentinian GP, but Ralf recovered to become the youngest podium finisher ever at the age of 21.

Technical gurus Ross Brawn and Rory Byrne left Benetton to join Ferrari, but Gerhard Berger did score the marque's final GP victory in Germany.

Olivier Panis impressed in the Bridgestone-shod Prost (formerly Ligier), but his season was cut short by injuries sustained in Montreal. Replacement Jarno Trulli confirmed the car's potential by finishing fourth in Germany and leading a week later in Austria. Rubens Barrichello finished second in Monte Carlo for Jackie Stewart's new Ford-backed team, but despite good qualifying performances, the team was hampered by poor reliability.

QANTAS AUSTRALIAN GRAND PRIX

9 March 1997. Albert Park. 58 laps of a 3.295-mile circuit = 191.110 miles. Warm, dry and sunny. World Championship round 1

1 David Coulthard	McLaren MP4/12-Mercedes-Benz	58	1h30m28.718
2 Michael Schumacher	Ferrari F310B	58	1h30m48.764
3 Mika Hakkinen	McLaren MP4/12-Mercedes-Benz	58	1h30m50.895
4 Gerhard Berger	Benetton B197-Renault	58	1h30m51.559
5 Olivier Panis	Prost JS45-Mugen	58	1h31m29.026
6 Nicola Larini	Sauber C16-Petronas Ferrari	58	1h32m04.758

Winner's average speed: 126.733 mph. Starting grid front row: Villeneuve, 1m29.369 (pole) and Frentzen, 1m31.123. Fastest lap: Frentzen, 1m30.585. Leaders: Frentzen, laps 1-17, 33-39; Coulthard, 18-32, 40-58

GRANDE PREMIO DO BRASIL

30 March 1997. Interlagos. 72 laps of a 2.667-mile circuit = 192.024 miles. Race stopped on first lap as a stranded car could not be moved from the grid, restarted over original distance. Humid and overcast. World Championship round 2

1 Jacques Villeneuve Williams FW19-Renault 72 1h36m06.990

Formula 1

1997 DRIVERS' RECORDS

driver	car	AUS Q	AUS R	BR Q	BR R	RA Q	RA R	RSM Q	RSM R	MC Q	MC R	E Q	E R
Jean Alesi	Benetton B197-Renault	8	R	6	6	11	7	14	5	9	R	4	3
Rubens Barrichello	Stewart SF1-Ford	11	R	11	R	5	R	13	R	10	2	17	R
Gerhard Berger	Benetton B197-Renault	10	4	3	2	12	6F	11	R	17	9	6	10
David Coulthard	McLaren MP4/12-Mercedes-Benz	4	1	12	10	10	R	10	R	5	R	3	6
Pedro Diniz	Arrows A18-Yamaha	22	10	16	R	22	R	17	R	16	R	21	R
Giancarlo Fisichella	Jordan 197-Peugeot	14	R	7	8	9	R	6	4	4	4	8	9F
Norberto Fontana	Sauber C16-Petronas Ferrari	-	-	-	-	-	-	-	-	-	-	-	-
Heinz-Harald Frentzen	Williams FW19-Renault	2	8F	8	9	2	R	2	1F	1	R	2	8
Mika Hakkinen	McLaren MP4/12-Mercedes-Benz	6	3	4	4	17	5	8	6	8	R	5	7
Johnny Herbert	Sauber C16-Petronas Ferrari	7	R	13	7	8	4	7	R	7	R	10	5
Damon Hill	Arrows A18-Yamaha	20	DNS	9	17	13	R	15	R	13	R	15	R
Eddie Irvine	Ferrari F310B	5	R	14	16	7	2	9	3	15	3	11	12
Ukyo Katayama	Minardi M197-Hart	15	R	18	18	21	R	22	11	20	10	20	R
Nicola Larini	Sauber C16-Petronas Ferrari	13	6	19	11	14	R	12	7	11	R	-	-
Jan Magnussen	Stewart SF1-Ford	19	R	20	R	15	10	16	R	19	7	22	13
Tarso Marques	Minardi M197-Hart	-	-	-	-	-	-	-	-	-	-	-	-
Gianni Morbidelli	Sauber C16-Petronas Ferrari	-	-	-	-	-	-	-	-	-	-	13	14
Shinji Nakano	Prost JS45-Mugen	16	7	15	14	20	R	18	R	21	R	16	R
Olivier Panis	Prost JS45-Mugen	9	5	5	3	3	R	4	8	12	4	12	2
Ricardo Rosset	Lola T97/30-Ford	24	DNQ	NT	DNP	-	-	-	-	-	-	-	-
Mika Salo	Tyrrell 025-Ford	18	R	22	13	19	8	19	9	14	5	14	R
Michael Schumacher	Ferrari F310B	3	2	2	5	4	R	3	2	2	1F	7	4
Ralf Schumacher	Jordan 197-Peugeot	12	R	10	R	6	3	5	R	6	R	9	R
Vincenzo Sospiri	Lola T97/30-Ford	23	DNQ	NT	DNP	-	-	-	-	-	-	-	-
Jarno Trulli	Minardi M197-Hart	17	9	17	12	18	9	20	DNS	18	R	18	15
	Prost JS45-Mugen	-	-	-	-	-	-	-	-	-	-	-	-
Jos Verstappen	Tyrrell 025-Ford	21	R	21	15	16	R	21	10	22	8	19	11
Jacques Villeneuve	Williams FW19-Renault	1	R	1	1F	1	1	1	R	3	R	1	1
Alexander Wurz	Benetton B197-Renault	-	-	-	-	-	-	-	-	-	-	-	-

1997 FINAL CHAMPIONSHIP POSITIONS

Drivers

1	Jacques Villeneuve	81
2	Heinz-Harald Frentzen	42
3=	Jean Alesi	36
	David Coulthard	36
5=	Gerhard Berger	27
	Mika Hakkinen	27
7	Eddie Irvine	24
8	Giancarlo Fisichella	20
9	Olivier Panis	16
10	Johnny Herbert	15
11	Ralf Schumacher	13
12	Damon Hill	7
13	Rubens Barrichello	6

14	Alexander Wurz	4
15	Jarno Trulli	3
16=	Pedro Diniz	2
	Shinji Nakano	2
	Mika Salo	2
19	Nicola Larini	1

Michael Schumacher scored 78 points but was excluded from the championship for trying to drive into Jacques Villeneuve at the final race of the season. His drivers' points were taken away; the manufacturers' points and his race results remained unaffected.

Manufacturers

1	Williams-Renault	123
2	Ferrari	102
3	Benetton-Renault	67
4	McLaren-Mercedes-Benz	63
5	Jordan-Peugeot	33
6	Prost-Mugen	21
7	Sauber-Petronas Ferrari	16
8	Arrows-Yamaha	9
9	Stewart-Ford	6
10	Tyrrell-Ford	2

2 Gerhard Berger Benetton B197-Renault 72 1h36m11.180
3 Olivier Panis Prost JS45-Mugen 72 1h36m22.860
4 Mika Hakkinen McLaren MP4/12-Mercedes-Benz 72 1h36m40.023
5 Michael Schumacher Ferrari F310B 72 1h36m40.721
6 Jean Alesi Benetton B197-Renault 72 1h36m41.010
Winner's average speed: 119.870 mph. Starting grid front row: Villeneuve, 1m16.004 (pole) and M Schumacher, 1m16.594. Fastest lap: Villeneuve, 1m18.397. Leaders: Villeneuve, laps 1-45, 49-72; Berger, 46-48

GRAN PREMIO MARLBORO DE ARGENTINA

13 April 1997. Buenos Aires. 72 laps of a 2.645-mile circuit = 190.440 miles. Hot, dry and sunny. World Championship round 3

1 Jacques Villeneuve Williams FW19-Renault 72 1h52m01.715
2 Eddie Irvine Ferrari F310B 72 1h52m02.694
3 Ralf Schumacher Jordan 197-Peugeot 72 1h52m13.804
4 Johnny Herbert Sauber C16-Petronas Ferrari 72 1h52m31.634
5 Mika Hakkinen McLaren MP4/12-Mercedes-Benz 72 1h52m32.066
6 Gerhard Berger Benetton B197-Renault 72 1h52m33.108
Winner's average speed: 101.995 mph. Starting grid front row: Villeneuve, 1m24.473 (pole) and Frentzen, 1m25.271. Fastest lap: Berger, 1m27.981. Leaders: Villeneuve, laps 1-38, 45-72; Irvine, 39-44

GRAN PREMIO DI SAN MARINO

27 April 1997. Imola. 62 laps of a 3.064-mile circuit = 189.968 miles. Warm, dry and sunny. World Championship round 4

1 Heinz-Harald Frentzen Williams FW19-Renault 62 1h31m00.673
2 Michael Schumacher Ferrari F310B 62 1h31m01.910
3 Eddie Irvine Ferrari F310B 62 1h32m19.016
4 Giancarlo Fisichella Jordan 197-Peugeot 62 1h32m24.061
5 Jean Alesi Benetton B197-Renault 61
6 Mika Hakkinen McLaren MP4/12-Mercedes-Benz 61

CDN		F		GB		D		H		B		I		A		LUX		J		EU	
Q	R	Q	R	Q	R	Q	R	Q	R	Q	R	Q	R	Q	R	Q	R	Q	R	Q	R
8	2	8	5	11	2	6	6	9	11	2	8	1	2	15	R	10	2	7	5	10	13
3	R	13	R	21	R	12	R	11	R	12	R	11	13	5	14	9	R	12	R	12	R
-	-	-	-	-	-	1	1F	7	8	15	6	7	7	18	10	7	4	5	8	8	4
5	7F	9	7	6	4	8	R	8	R	10	R	6	1	10	2	6	R	11	10	6	2
16	8	16	R	16	R	16	R	19	R	8	7	17	R	17	13	15	5	16	12	13	R
6	3	11	9	10	7	2	11	13	R	4	2	3	4	14	4	4	R	9	7	17	11
-	-	20	R	22	9	18	9	-	-	-	-	-	-	-	-	-	-	-	-	18	14
4	4	2	2	2	R	5	R	6	RF	7	3	2	3	4	3	3	3F	6	2F	3	6F
9	R	10	R	3	R	3	4	R	5	DSQ	5	9F	2	R	1	R	4	4	5	5	1
13	5	14	8	9	R	14	R	10	3	11	4	12	R	12	8	16	7	8	6	14	8
15	9	17	12	12	6	13	8	3	2	9	13	14	R	7	7	13	8	17	11	4	R
12	R	5	3	7	R	10	R	5	9	17	10	10	8	8	R	14	R	3	3	7	5
22	R	21	11	18	R	22	R	20	10	20	14	21	R	19	11	22	R	19	R	19	17
-	-	-	-	-	-	-	-	-	-	-	-	-	-	-	-	-	-	-	-	-	-
21	R	15	R	15	R	15	R	17	R	18	12	13	R	6	R	12	R	14	R	11	9
-	-	22	R	20	10	21	R	22	12	22	R	22	14	NT	DNQ	18	R	20	R	20	15
18	10	-	-	-	-	-	-	15	R	13	9	18	12	13	9	19	9	18	DNS	-	-
19	6	12	R	14	11	17	7	16	6	R	R	15	11	16	R	17	R	15	R	15	10
10	11	-	-	-	-	-	-	-	-	-	-	-	-	-	-	11	6	10	R	9	7
-	-	-	-	-	-	-	-	-	-	-	-	-	-	-	-	-	-	-	-	-	-
17	R	19	R	17	R	19	R	21	13	19	11	19	R	21	R	20	10	22	R	21	12
1	1	1	1F	4	RF	4	2	1	4	3	1	9	6	9	6	5	R	2	1	2	R
7	R	3	6	5	5	7	5	14	5	6	R	8	R	11	5	8	R	13	9	16	R
-	-	-	-	-	-	-	-	-	-	-	-	-	-	-	-	-	-	-	-	-	-
20	R	-	-	-	-	-	-	-	-	-	-	-	-	-	-	-	-	-	-	-	-
-	-	6	10	13	8	11	4	12	7	14	15	16	10	3	R	-	-	-	-	-	-
14	R	18	R	19	R	20	10	18	R	21	R	20	R	20	12	21	R	21	13	22	16
2	R	4	4	1	1	9	R	2	1	1	5F	4	5	1	1F	2	1	1	DSQ	1	3
11	R	7	R	8	3	-	-	-	-	-	-	-	-	-	-	-	-	-	-	-	-

Winner's average speed: 125.238 mph. Starting grid front row: Villeneuve, 1m23.303 (pole) and Frentzen, 1m23.646. Fastest lap: Frentzen, 1m25.531. Leaders: Villeneuve, laps 1-25; Frentzen, 26-43, 45-62; M Schumacher, 44

GRAND PRIX DE MONACO

11 May 1997. Monte Carlo. 62 laps of a 2.092-mile circuit = 129.704 miles. Race scheduled for 78 laps, stopped after two hours. Wet and cloudy. World Championship round 5

1	Michael Schumacher	Ferrari F310B	62	2h00m05.654
2	Rubens Barrichello	Stewart SF1-Ford	62	2h00m58.960
3	Eddie Irvine	Ferrari F310B	62	2h01m27.762
4	Olivier Panis	Prost JS45-Mugen	62	2h01m50.056
5	Mika Salo	Tyrrell 025-Ford	61	
6	Giancarlo Fisichella	Jordan 197-Peugeot	61	

Winner's average speed: 64.801 mph. Starting grid front row: Frentzen, 1m18.216 (pole) and M Schumacher, 1m18.235. Fastest lap: M Schumacher, 1m53.315. Leaders: M Schumacher, laps 1-62

GRAN PREMIO MARLBORO DE ESPANA

25 May 1997. Catalunya. 64 laps of a 2.937-mile circuit = 187.968 miles. Warm, dry and sunny. World Championship round 6

1	Jacques Villeneuve	Williams FW19-Renault	64	1h30m35.896
2	Olivier Panis	Prost JS45-Mugen	64	1h30m41.700
3	Jean Alesi	Benetton B197-Renault	64	1h30m48.430
4	Michael Schumacher	Ferrari F310B	64	1h30m53.875
5	Johnny Herbert	Sauber C16-Petronas Ferrari	64	1h31m03.882
6	David Coulthard	McLaren MP4/12-Mercedes-Benz	64	1h31m05.640

Winner's average speed: 124.485 mph. Starting grid front row: Villeneuve, 1m16.525 (pole) and Frentzen, 1m16.791. Fastest lap: Fisichella, 1m22.242. Leaders: Villeneuve, laps 1-20, 22-45, 47-64; Alesi, 21; M Schumacher, 46

GRAND PRIX PLAYER'S DU CANADA

15 June 1997. Montreal. 54 laps of a 2.747-mile circuit = 148.338 miles. Race scheduled for 69 laps, stopped after an accident. Hot, dry and sunny. World Championship round 7

1	Michael Schumacher	Ferrari F310B	54	1h17m40.646
2	Jean Alesi	Benetton B197-Renault	54	1h17m43.211
3	Giancarlo Fisichella	Jordan 197-Peugeot	54	1h17m43.865
4	Heinz-Harald Frentzen	Williams FW19-Renault	54	1h17m44.414
5	Johnny Herbert	Sauber C16-Petronas Ferrari	54	1h17m45.362
6	Shinji Nakano	Prost JS45-Mugen	54	1h18m17.347

Winner's average speed: 114.580 mph. Starting grid front row: M Schumacher, 1m18.095 (pole) and Villeneuve, 1m18.108. Fastest lap: Coulthard, 1m19.635. Leaders: M Schumacher, laps 1-27, 40-43, 52-54; Coulthard, 28-39, 44-51

GRAND PRIX DE FRANCE

29 June 1997. Magny-Cours. 72 laps of a 2.641-mile circuit = 190.152 miles. Warm and overcast at the start, rain later. World Championship round 8

1	Michael Schumacher	Ferrari F310B	72	1h38m50.492
2	Heinz-Harald Frentzen	Williams FW19-Renault	72	1h39m14.029
3	Eddie Irvine	Ferrari F310B	72	1h40m05.293
4	Jacques Villeneuve	Williams FW19-Renault	72	1h40m12.276
5	Jean Alesi	Benetton B197-Renault	72	1h40m13.227
6	Ralf Schumacher	Jordan 197-Peugeot	72	1h40m20.363

Winner's average speed: 115.428 mph. Starting grid front row: M Schumacher, 1m14.548 (pole) and Frentzen, 1m14.749. Fastest lap: M Schumacher, 1m17.910. Leaders: M Schumacher, laps 1-22, 24-46, 48-72; Frentzen, 23, 47

RAC BRITISH GRAND PRIX

13 July 1997. Silverstone. 59 laps of a 3.194-mile circuit = 188.446 miles. Hot, dry and sunny. World Championship round 9

1	Jacques Villeneuve	Williams FW19-Renault	59	1h28m01.665
2	Jean Alesi	Benetton B197-Renault	59	1h28m11.870
3	Alexander Wurz	Benetton B197-Renault	59	1h28m12.961
4	David Coulthard	McLaren MP4/12-Mercedes-Benz	59	1h28m32.894
5	Ralf Schumacher	Jordan 197-Peugeot	59	1h28m33.545
6	Damon Hill	Arrows A18-Yamaha	59	1h29m15.217

Winner's average speed: 128.445 mph. Starting grid front row: Villeneuve, 1m21.598 (pole) and Frentzen, 1m21.732. Fastest lap: M Schumacher, 1m24.475. Leaders: Villeneuve, laps 1-22, 38-44, 53-59; M Schumacher, 23-37; Hakkinen, 45-52

GROSSER MOBIL 1 PREIS VON DEUTSCHLAND

27 July 1997. Hockenheim. 45 laps of a 4.239-mile circuit = 190.755 miles. Hot, dry and sunny. World Championship round 10

1	Gerhard Berger	Benetton B197-Renault	45	1h20m59.046
2	Michael Schumacher	Ferrari F310B	45	1h21m16.573
3	Mika Hakkinen	McLaren MP4/12-Mercedes-Benz	45	1h21m23.816
4	Jarno Trulli	Prost JS45-Mugen	45	1h21m26.211
5	Ralf Schumacher	Jordan 197-Peugeot	45	1h21m29.041
6	Jean Alesi	Benetton B197-Renault	45	1h21m33.763

Winner's average speed: 141.328 mph. Starting grid front row: Berger, 1m41.873 (pole) and Fisichella, 1m41.896. Fastest lap: Berger, 1m45.747. Leaders: Berger, laps 1-17, 25-45; Fisichella, 18-24

MARLBORO MAGYAR NAGYDIJ (HUNGARIAN GRAND PRIX)

10 August 1997. Hungaroring. 77 laps of a 2.465-mile circuit = 189.805 miles. Hot, dry and sunny. World Championship round 11

1	Jacques Villeneuve	Williams FW19-Renault	77	1h45m47.149
2	Damon Hill	Arrows A18-Yamaha	77	1h45m56.228
3	Johnny Herbert	Sauber C16-Petronas Ferrari	77	1h46m07.594
4	Michael Schumacher	Ferrari F310B	77	1h46m17.650
5	Ralf Schumacher	Jordan 197-Peugeot	77	1h46m17.864
6	Shinji Nakano	Prost JS45-Mugen	77	1h46m28.661

Winner's average speed: 107.654 mph. Starting grid front row: M Schumacher, 1m14.672 (pole) and Villeneuve, 1m14.859. Fastest lap: Frentzen, 1m18.372. Leaders: M Schumacher, laps 1-10; Hill, 11-25, 30-76; Frentzen, 26-29; Villeneuve, 77

GRAND PRIX DE BELGIQUE

24 August 1997. Spa-Francorchamps. 44 laps of a 4.329-mile circuit = 190.476 miles. Wet at the start, drying later. World Championship round 12

1	Michael Schumacher	Ferrari F310B	44	1h33m46.717
2	Giancarlo Fisichella	Jordan 197-Peugeot	44	1h34m13.470
3	Heinz-Harald Frentzen	Williams FW19-Renault	44	1h34m18.189
4	Johnny Herbert	Sauber C16-Petronas Ferrari	44	1h34m25.742
5	Jacques Villeneuve	Williams FW19-Renault	44	1h34m28.820
6	Gerhard Berger	Benetton B197-Renault	44	1h34m50.458

Mika Hakkinen (McLaren MP4/12-Mercedes-Benz), 1h34m17.573, finished third on the road but was disqualified due to irregular fuel in practice. Winner's average speed: 121.867 mph. Starting grid front row: Villeneuve, 1m49.450 (pole) and Alesi, 1m49.759. Fastest lap: Villeneuve, 1m52.692. Leaders: Villeneuve, laps 1-4; M Schumacher, 5-44

GRAN PREMIO CAMPARI D'ITALIA

7 September 1997. Monza. 53 laps of a 3.585-mile circuit = 190.005 miles. Hot, dry and sunny. World Championship round 13

1	David Coulthard	McLaren MP4/12-Mercedes-Benz	53	1h17m04.609
2	Jean Alesi	Benetton B197-Renault	53	1h17m06.546
3	Heinz-Harald Frentzen	Williams FW19-Renault	53	1h17m08.952
4	Giancarlo Fisichella	Jordan 197-Peugeot	53	1h17m10.480
5	Jacques Villeneuve	Williams FW19-Renault	53	1h17m11.025
6	Michael Schumacher	Ferrari F310B	53	1h17m16.090

Winner's average speed: 147.908 mph. Starting grid front row: Alesi, 1m22.990 (pole) and Frentzen, 1m23.042. Fastest lap: Hakkinen, 1m24.808. Leaders: Alesi, laps 1-31; Hakkinen, 32-33; M Schumacher, 34; Coulthard, 35-53

GROSSER PREIS VON OSTERREICH

21 September 1997. A1 Ring. 71 laps of a 2.684-mile circuit = 190.564 miles. Hot, dry and sunny. World Championship round 14

1	Jacques Villeneuve	Williams FW19-Renault	71	1h27m35.999
2	David Coulthard	McLaren MP4/12-Mercedes-Benz	71	1h27m38.908
3	Heinz-Harald Frentzen	Williams FW19-Renault	71	1h27m39.961
4	Giancarlo Fisichella	Jordan 197-Peugeot	71	1h27m48.126
5	Ralf Schumacher	Jordan 197-Peugeot	71	1h28m07.858
6	Michael Schumacher	Ferrari F310B	71	1h28m09.409

Winner's average speed: 130.523 mph. Starting grid front row: Villeneuve, 1m10.304 (pole) and Hakkinen, 1m10.398. Fastest lap: Villeneuve, 1m11.814. Leaders: Trulli, laps 1-37; Villeneuve, 38-40, 44-71; M Schumacher, 41-42; Coulthard, 43

GROSSER PREIS VON LUXEMBURG

28 September 1997. Nurburgring. 67 laps of a 2.831-mile circuit = 189.677 miles. Warm, dry and sunny. World Championship round 15

1	Jacques Villeneuve	Williams FW19-Renault	67	1h31m27.843
2	Jean Alesi	Benetton B197-Renault	67	1h31m39.613
3	Heinz-Harald Frentzen	Williams FW19-Renault	67	1h31m41.323
4	Gerhard Berger	Benetton B197-Renault	67	1h31m44.259
5	Pedro Diniz	Arrows A18-Yamaha	67	1h32m10.990
6	Olivier Panis	Prost JS45-Mugen	67	1h32m11.593

Winner's average speed: 124.427 mph. Starting grid front row: Hakkinen, 1m16.602 (pole) and Villeneuve, 1m16.691. Fastest lap: Frentzen, 1m18.805. Leaders: Hakkinen, laps 1-28, 32-43; Coulthard, 29-31; Villeneuve, 44-67

FUJI TELEVISION JAPANESE GRAND PRIX

12 October 1997. Suzuka. 53 laps of a 3.641-mile circuit = 192.973 miles. Hot, dry and sunny. World Championship round 16

1	Michael Schumacher	Ferrari F310B	53	1h29m48.446
2	Heinz-Harald Frentzen	Williams FW19-Renault	53	1h29m49.824
3	Eddie Irvine	Ferrari F310B	53	1h30m14.830
4	Mika Hakkinen	McLaren MP4/12-Mercedes-Benz	53	1h30m15.575
5	Jean Alesi	Benetton B197-Renault	53	1h30m28.849
6	Johnny Herbert	Sauber C16-Petronas Ferrari	53	1h30m30.076

Jacques Villeneuve (Williams FW19-Renault), 1h30m28.222, finished fifth on the road but was disqualified for not slowing for yellow flags during practice. Winner's average speed: 128.925 mph. Starting grid front row: Villeneuve, 1m36.071 (pole) and M Schumacher, 1m36.133. Fastest lap: Frentzen, 1m38.942. Leaders: M Schumacher, laps 1, 17-18, 25-33, 38-53; Irvine, 2-16, 22-24; Frentzen, 19-21, 34-37 (Villeneuve led laps 1-2 and 17-20 on the road but had been disqualified for a practice rule infringement)

GRAND PRIX OF EUROPE

26 October 1997. Jerez. 69 laps of a 2.752-mile circuit = 189.888 miles. Warm, dry and sunny. World Championship round 17

1	Mika Hakkinen	McLaren MP4/12-Mercedes-Benz	69	1h38m57.771
2	David Coulthard	McLaren MP4/12-Mercedes-Benz	69	1h38m59.425
3	Jacques Villeneuve	Williams FW19-Renault	69	1h38m59.574
4	Gerhard Berger	Benetton B197-Renault	69	1h38m59.690
5	Eddie Irvine	Ferrari F310B	69	1h39m01.560
6	Heinz-Harald Frentzen	Williams FW19-Renault	69	1h39m02.308

Winner's average speed: 115.127 mph. Starting grid front row: Villeneuve, 1m21.072 (pole) and M Schumacher, 1m21.072 - Villeneuve on pole as he set time first. Fastest lap: Frentzen, 1m23.135. Leaders: M Schumacher, laps 1-21, 28-42, 45-47; Villeneuve, 22, 43-44, 48-68; Frentzen, 23-27; Hakkinen, 69

1998 Mika Hakkinen returned McLaren to World Championship glory with victory in Japan.

1998

The promise shown by McLaren in 1997 was confirmed by victory in 1998, when the team won its first World Championship in seven years. Ron Dennis hired Williams designer Adrian Newey, and the resulting Bridgestone-shod MP4/13-Mercedes was the class of the field. Drivers Mika Hakkinen and David Coulthard lapped the field in Melbourne's opening race, with the only problem occurring when Hakkinen mistakenly attempted a pit stop only to be waved through, but his teammate observed a pre-race agreement and let the Finn through to win.

It was in 1998 that Hakkinen emerged as a true star, eclipsing Coulthard on all but three circuits. His victory over Michael Schumacher at the Nurburgring proved decisive in his championship campaign, and it showed he could compete as an equal with F1's most established star. Coulthard won at Imola, but ultimately was unable to match the Finn's pace now that the world title was at stake.

Michael Schumacher again had a chance of scoring a first title for Ferrari at the last race, thanks to a record that included six wins. When his Ferrari stalled on the Japanese GP grid, he sliced through the field, climbing from twenty-first to third before a puncture ended his race and confirmed Hakkinen's championship.

Erstwhile champions Williams endured a season without victory for the first time in a decade. Deprived of works Renault engines, Jacques Villeneuve and Heinz-Harald Frentzen could only finish on the podium on three occasions.

Giancarlo Fisichella moved to Benetton and finished second in Monte Carlo and Montreal. He also qualified alongside Jean Alesi's Sauber on the front row for the Austrian GP, but the two collided during the race.

The season began poorly for Jordan, but at the wet Belgian race Damon Hill and Ralf Schumacher took advantage of a car that suited the conditions. And when Michael Schumacher crashed into the McLaren of Coulthard when obscured by spray, the Jordan drivers

scored a 1-2 finish that would be Hill's final victory. The race had started with 13 cars being involved in the biggest first-lap accident in 25 years, though thankfully there were no injuries.

The Tyrrell team was sold to British American Tobacco and entered the championship for the last time before becoming British American Racing in 1999. Teams introduced ugly "x-wings" in the search for increased downforce, but these were banned on aesthetic grounds.

QANTAS AUSTRALIAN GRAND PRIX

8 March 1998. Albert Park. 58 laps of a 3.295-mile circuit = 191.110 miles. Warm, dry and sunny. World Championship round 1

1	Mika Hakkinen	McLaren MP4/13-Mercedes-Benz	58	1h31m45.996
2	David Coulthard	McLaren MP4/13-Mercedes-Benz	58	1h31m46.698
3	Heinz-Harald Frentzen	Williams FW20-Mecachrome	57	
4	Eddie Irvine	Ferrari F300	57	
5	Jacques Villeneuve	Williams FW20-Mecachrome	57	
6	Johnny Herbert	Sauber C17-Petronas Ferrari	57	

Winner's average speed: 124.954 mph. Starting grid front row: Hakkinen, 1m30.010 (pole) and Coulthard, 1m30.053. Fastest lap: Hakkinen, 1m31.649. Leaders: Hakkinen, laps 1-23, 25-35, 56-58; Coulthard, 24, 36-55

GRANDE PREMIO DO BRASIL

29 March 1998. Interlagos. 72 laps of a 2.667-mile circuit = 192.024 miles. Humid and overcast. World Championship round 2

1	Mika Hakkinen	McLaren MP4/13-Mercedes-Benz	72	1h37m11.747
2	David Coulthard	McLaren MP4/13-Mercedes-Benz	72	1h37m12.849
3	Michael Schumacher	Ferrari F300	72	1h38m12.297
4	Alexander Wurz	Benetton B198-Playlife	72	1h38m19.200
5	Heinz-Harald Frentzen	Williams FW20-Mecachrome	71	
6	Giancarlo Fisichella	Benetton B198-Playlife	71	

Winner's average speed: 118.538 mph. Starting grid front row: Hakkinen, 1m17.092 (pole) and Coulthard, 1m17.757. Fastest lap: Hakkinen, 1m19.337. Leaders: Hakkinen, laps 1-72

GRAN PREMIO MARLBORO DE ARGENTINA

12 April 1998. Buenos Aires. 72 laps of a 2.645-mile circuit = 190.440 miles. Cool and overcast. World Championship round 3

1	Michael Schumacher	Ferrari F300	72	1h48m36.175
2	Mika Hakkinen	McLaren MP4/13-Mercedes-Benz	72	1h48m59.073
3	Eddie Irvine	Ferrari F300	72	1h49m33.920
4	Alexander Wurz	Benetton B198-Playlife	72	1h49m44.309
5	Jean Alesi	Sauber C17-Petronas Ferrari	72	1h49m54.461
6	David Coulthard	McLaren MP4/13-Mercedes-Benz	72	1h49m55.926

Winner's average speed: 105.213 mph. Starting grid front row: Coulthard, 1m25.852 (pole) and M Schumacher, 1m26.251. Fastest lap: Wurz, 1m28.179. Leaders: Coulthard, laps 1-4; M Schumacher, 5-28, 43-72; Hakkinen, 29-42

GRAN PREMIO DI SAN MARINO

26 April 1998. Imola. 62 laps of a 3.064-mile circuit = 189.968 miles. Warm, dry and sunny. World Championship round 4

1	David Coulthard	McLaren MP4/13-Mercedes-Benz	62	1h34m24.593
2	Michael Schumacher	Ferrari F300	62	1h34m29.147

1998 DRIVERS' RECORDS

driver	car	AUS		BR		RA		RSM		E		MC	
		Q	R	Q	R	Q	R	Q	R	Q	R	Q	R
Jean Alesi	Sauber C17-Petronas Ferrari	12	R	15	9	11	5	12	6	14	10	11	12
Rubens Barrichello	Stewart SF2-Ford	14	R	13	R	14	10	17	R	9	5	14	R
David Coulthard	McLaren MP4/13-Mercedes-Benz	2	2	2	2	1	6	1	1	2	2	2	R
Pedro Diniz	Arrows A19	20	R	22	R	18	R	18	R	15	R	12	6
Giancarlo Fisichella	Benetton B198-Playlife	7	R	7	6	10	7	10	R	4	R	3	2
Heinz-Harald Frentzen	Williams FW20-Mecachrome	6	3	3	5	6	9	8	5	13	8	5	R
Mika Hakkinen	McLaren MP4/13-Mercedes-Benz	1	1F	1	1F	3	2	2	R	1	1F	1	1F
Johnny Herbert	Sauber C17-Petronas Ferrari	5	6	14	11	12	R	11	R	7	7	9	7
Damon Hill	Jordan 198-Mugen	10	8	11	DSQ	9	8	7	10	8	R	15	8
Eddie Irvine	Ferrari F300	8	4	6	8	4	3	4	3	6	R	7	3
Jan Magnussen	Stewart SF2-Ford	18	R	16	10	22	R	20	R	18	12	17	R
Shinji Nakano	Minardi M198-Ford	22	R	18	R	19	13	21	R	20	14	19	9
Olivier Panis	Prost AP01-Peugeot	21	9	9	R	15	15	13	11	12	16	18	R
Ricardo Rosset	Tyrrell 026-Ford	19	R	21	R	21	14	22	R	22	DNQ	22	DNQ
Mika Salo	Arrows A19	16	R	20	R	17	R	14	9	17	R	8	4
Michael Schumacher	Ferrari F300	3	R	4	3	2	1	3	2F	3	3	4	10
Ralf Schumacher	Jordan 198-Mugen	9	R	8	R	5	R	9	7	11	11	16	R
Toranosuke Takagi	Tyrrell 026-Ford	13	R	17	R	13	12	15	R	21	13	20	11
Jarno Trulli	Prost AP01-Peugeot	15	R	12	R	16	11	16	R	16	9	10	R
Esteban Tuero	Minardi M198-Ford	17	R	19	R	20	R	19	8	19	15	21	R
Jos Verstappen	Stewart SF2-Ford	-	-	-	-	-	-	-	-	-	-	-	-
Jacques Villeneuve	Williams FW20-Mecachrome	4	5	10	7	7	R	6	4	10	6	13	5
Alexander Wurz	Benetton B198-Playlife	11	7	5	4	8	4F	5	R	5	4	4	R

1998 FINAL CHAMPIONSHIP POSITIONS

Drivers

1	Mika Hakkinen	100
2	Michael Schumacher	86
3	David Coulthard	56
4	Eddie Irvine	47
5	Jacques Villeneuve	21
6	Damon Hill	20
7=	Heinz-Harald Frentzen	17
	Alexander Wurz	17
9	Giancarlo Fisichella	16
10	Ralf Schumacher	14
11	Jean Alesi	9
12	Rubens Barrichello	4
13=	Pedro Diniz	3
	Mika Salo	3
15=	Johnny Herbert	1
	Jan Magnussen	1
	Jarno Trulli	1

Manufacturers

1	McLaren-Mercedes-Benz	156
2	Ferrari	133
3	Williams-Mecachrome	38
4	Jordan-Mugen	34
5	Benetton-Playlife	33
6	Sauber-Petronas Ferrari	10
7	Arrows	6
8	Stewart-Ford	5
9	Prost-Peugeot	1

3	Eddie Irvine	Ferrari F300	62	1h35m16.368
4	Jacques Villeneuve	Williams FW20-Mecachrome	62	1h35m19.183
5	Heinz-Harald Frentzen	Williams FW20-Mecachrome	62	1h35m42.069
6	Jean Alesi	Sauber C17-Petronas Ferrari	61	

Winner's average speed: 120.730 mph. Starting grid front row: Coulthard, 1m25.973 (pole) and Hakkinen, 1m26.075. Fastest lap: M Schumacher, 1m29.345. Leaders: Coulthard, laps 1-62

GRAN PREMIO MARLBORO DE ESPANA

10 May 1998. Catalunya. 65 laps of a 2.937-mile circuit = 190.905 miles. Hot, dry and sunny. World Championship round 5

1	Mika Hakkinen	McLaren MP4/13-Mercedes-Benz	65	1h33m37.621
2	David Coulthard	McLaren MP4/13-Mercedes-Benz	65	1h33m47.060
3	Michael Schumacher	Ferrari F300	65	1h34m24.716
4	Alexander Wurz	Benetton B198-Playlife	65	1h34m40.159
5	Rubens Barrichello	Stewart SF2-Ford	64	
6	Jacques Villeneuve	Williams FW20-Mecachrome	64	

Winner's average speed: 122.340 mph. Starting grid front row: Hakkinen, 1m20.262 (pole) and Coulthard, 1m20.996. Fastest lap: Hakkinen, 1m24.275. Leaders: Hakkinen, laps 1-26, 28-45, 47-65; Coulthard, 27, 46

GRAND PRIX DE MONACO

24 May 1998. Monte Carlo. 78 laps of a 2.092-mile circuit = 163.176 miles. Hot, dry and sunny. World Championship round 6

1	Mika Hakkinen	McLaren MP4/13-Mercedes-Benz	78	1h51m23.595
2	Giancarlo Fisichella	Benetton B198-Playlife	78	1h51m35.070
3	Eddie Irvine	Ferrari F300	78	1h52m04.973
4	Mika Salo	Arrows A19	78	1h52m23.958
5	Jacques Villeneuve	Williams FW20-Mecachrome	77	
6	Pedro Diniz	Arrows A19	77	

Winner's average speed: 87.892 mph. Starting grid front row: Hakkinen, 1m19.798 (pole) and Coulthard, 1m20.137. Fastest lap: Hakkinen, 1m22.948. Leaders: Hakkinen, laps 1-78

GRAND PRIX PLAYER'S DU CANADA

7 June 1998. Montreal. 69 laps of a 2.747-mile circuit = 189.543 miles. Race stopped due to first-lap accident, restarted over original distance. Cool and overcast. World Championship round 7

1	Michael Schumacher	Ferrari F300	69	1h40m57.355
2	Giancarlo Fisichella	Benetton B198-Playlife	69	1h41m14.017
3	Eddie Irvine	Ferrari F300	69	1h41m57.414

CDN		F		GB		A		D		H		B		I		LUX		J	
Q	R	Q	R	Q	R	Q	R	Q	R	Q	R	Q	R	Q	R	Q	R	Q	R
9	R	11	7	8	R	2	R	11	10	11	7	10	3	8	5	11	10	12	7
13	5	14	10	18	R	5	R	13	R	14	R	14	R	13	10	12	11	16	R
1	R	3	6F	4	R	14	2F	2	2F	2	2	2	7	4	R	5	3	3	3
19	9	17	14	13	R	13	R	18	R	12	11	16	5	20	R	17	R	18	R
4	2	9	9	11	5	1	R	8	7	8	7	8	R	11	8	4	6	10	8
7	R	8	15	6	R	7	R	10	9	7	5	9	4	12	7	7	5	5	5
2	R	1	3	1	2	3	1	1	1	1	1	6	1	3	4F	3	1F	2	1
12	R	13	8	9	R	18	8	12	R	15	10	12	R	15	R	13	R	11	10
10	R	7	R	7	R	15	7	5	4	4	4	3	1	14	6	10	9	8	4
8	3	4	2	5	3	8	4	6	8	5	R	5	R	5	2	2	4	4	2
20	6	-	-	-	-	-	-	-	-	-	-	-	-	-	-	-	-	-	-
18	7	21	17	21	8	21	11	20	R	19	15	21	8	21	R	20	15	20	R
15	R	16	11	16	R	10	R	16	15	20	12	15	R	9	R	15	12	13	11
22	8	18	R	22	R	22	12	22	DNP	22	DNQ	22	R	18	12	22	R	22	DNQ
17	R	19	13	14	R	6	R	17	14	13	R	18	R	16	R	16	14	15	R
3	1F	2	1	2	1F	4	3	9	5	3	1F	4	RF	1	1	1	2	1	RF
5	R	6	16	10	6	9	5	4	6	10	9	8	2	6	3	6	R	7	R
16	R	20	R	19	9	20	R	15	13	18	14	19	R	19	9	19	16	17	R
14	R	12	R	15	R	16	10	14	12	16	R	13	6	10	13	14	R	14	12
21	R	22	R	20	R	19	R	21	16	21	R	22	R	22	11	21	NC	21	R
-	-	15	12	17	R	12	R	19	R	17	13	17	R	17	R	18	13	19	R
6	10	5	4	3	7	11	6	3	3	6	3	6	R	2	R	9	8	6	6
11	4	10	5	12	4	17	9	7	11	9	R	11	R	7	R	8	7	9	9

4 Alexander Wurz   Benetton B198-Playlife 69   1h42m00.587
5 Rubens Barrichello   Stewart SF2-Ford   69   1h42m18.868
6 Jan Magnussen   Stewart SF2-Ford   68
Winner's average speed: 112.649 mph. Starting grid front row: Coulthard, 1m18.213 (pole) and Hakkinen, 1m18.282. Fastest lap: M Schumacher, 1m19.379. Leaders: Coulthard, laps 1-18; M Schumacher, 19, 44-69; Fisichella, 20-43

GRAND PRIX MOBIL 1 DE FRANCE

28 June 1998. Magny-Cours. 71 laps of a 2.641-mile circuit = 187.511 miles. Hot, dry and sunny. World Championship round 8

1	Michael Schumacher	Ferrari F300	71	1h34m45.026
2	Eddie Irvine	Ferrari F300	71	1h35m04.601
3	Mika Hakkinen	McLaren MP4/13-Mercedes-Benz	71	1h35m04.773
4	Jacques Villeneuve	Williams FW20-Mecachrome	71	1h35m51.991
5	Alexander Wurz	Benetton B198-Playlife	70	
6	David Coulthard	McLaren MP4/13-Mercedes-Benz	70	

Winner's average speed: 118.740 mph. Starting grid front row: Hakkinen, 1m14.929 (pole) and M Schumacher, 1m15.159. Fastest lap: Coulthard, 1m17.523. Leaders: M Schumacher, laps 1-22, 24-71; Irvine, 23

RAC BRITISH GRAND PRIX

12 July 1998. Silverstone. 60 laps of a 3.194-mile circuit = 191.640 miles. Dry and windy at the start, heavy rain later. World Championship round 9

1	Michael Schumacher	Ferrari F300	60	1h47m02.450
2	Mika Hakkinen	McLaren MP4/13-Mercedes-Benz	60	1h47m24.915
3	Eddie Irvine	Ferrari F300	60	1h47m31.649
4	Alexander Wurz	Benetton B198-Playlife	59	
5	Giancarlo Fisichella	Benetton B198-Playlife	59	
6	Ralf Schumacher	Jordan 198-Mugen	59	

Winner's average speed: 107.421 mph. Starting grid front row: Hakkinen, 1m23.271 (pole) and M Schumacher, 1m23.720. Fastest lap: M Schumacher, 1m35.704. Leaders: Hakkinen, laps 1-50; M Schumacher, 51-60

GROSSER PREIS VON OSTERREICH

26 July 1998. A1 Ring. 71 laps of a 2.684-mile circuit = 190.564 miles. Hot, dry and sunny. World Championship round 10

1	Mika Hakkinen	McLaren MP4/13-Mercedes-Benz	71	1h30m44.086
2	David Coulthard	McLaren MP4/13-Mercedes-Benz	71	1h30m49.375
3	Michael Schumacher	Ferrari F300	71	1h31m23.178
4	Eddie Irvine	Ferrari F300	71	1h31m28.062
5	Ralf Schumacher	Jordan 198-Mugen	71	1h31m34.740
6	Jacques Villeneuve	Williams FW20-Mecachrome	71	1h31m37.288

Winner's average speed: 126.014 mph. Starting grid front row: Fisichella, 1m29.598 (pole) and Alesi, 1m30.317. Fastest lap: Coulthard, 1m12.878. Leaders: Hakkinen, laps 1-34, 37-71; Coulthard, 35-36

GROSSER MOBIL 1 PREIS VON DEUTSCHLAND

2 August 1998. Hockenheim. 45 laps of a 4.239-mile circuit = 190.755 miles. Hot, dry and sunny. World Championship round 11

1	Mika Hakkinen	McLaren MP4/13-Mercedes-Benz	45	1h20m47.984
2	David Coulthard	McLaren MP4/13-Mercedes-Benz	45	1h20m48.410
3	Jacques Villeneuve	Williams FW20-Mecachrome	45	1h20m50.561
4	Damon Hill	Jordan 198-Mugen	45	1h20m55.169
5	Michael Schumacher	Ferrari F300	45	1h21m00.597
6	Ralf Schumacher	Jordan 198-Mugen	45	1h21m17.722

Winner's average speed: 141.650 mph. Starting grid front row: Hakkinen, 1m41.838 (pole) and Coulthard, 1m42.347. Fastest lap: Coulthard, 1m46.116. Leaders: Hakkinen, laps 1-25, 28-45; Coulthard, 26-27

MARLBORO MAGYAR NAGYDIJ (HUNGARIAN GRAND PRIX)

16 August 1998. Hungaroring. 77 laps of a 2.465-mile circuit = 189.805 miles. Hot, dry and sunny. World Championship round 12

1	Michael Schumacher	Ferrari F300	77	1h45m25.550
2	David Coulthard	McLaren MP4/13-Mercedes-Benz	77	1h45m34.983

3 Jacques Villeneuve   Williams FW20-
      Mecachrome   77   1h46m09.994
4 Damon Hill   Jordan 198-Mugen   77   1h46m20.626
5 Heinz-Harald Frentzen   Williams FW20-
      Mecachrome   77   1h46m22.060
6 Mika Hakkinen   McLaren MP4/13-
      Mercedes-Benz   76

Winner's average speed: 108.022 mph. Starting grid front row: Hakkinen, 1m16.973 (pole) and Coulthard, 1m17.131. Fastest lap: M Schumacher, 1m19.286. Leaders: Hakkinen, laps 1-46; M Schumacher, 47-77

30 August 1998. Spa-Francorchamps. 44 laps of a 4.329-mile circuit = 190.476 miles. Race stopped after a first-lap accident, restarted over original distance. Cool and heavy rain. World Championship round 13

1 Damon Hill   Jordan 198-Mugen   44   1h43m47.407
2 Ralf Schumacher   Jordan 198-Mugen   44   1h43m48.339
3 Jean Alesi   Sauber C17-
      Petronas Ferrari   44   1h43m54.647
4 Heinz-Harald Frentzen   Williams FW20-
      Mecachrome   44   1h44m19.650
5 Pedro Diniz   Arrows A19   44   1h44m39.089
6 Jarno Trulli   Prost AP01-Peugeot   42

Winner's average speed: 110.112 mph. Starting grid front row: Hakkinen, 1m48.682 (pole) and Coulthard, 1m48.845. Fastest lap: M Schumacher, 2m03.766. Leaders: Hill, laps 1-7, 26-44; M Schumacher, 8-25

13 September 1998. Monza. 53 laps of a 3.585-mile circuit = 190.005 miles. Warm, dry and sunny. World Championship round 14

1 Michael Schumacher   Ferrari F300   53   1h17m09.672
2 Eddie Irvine   Ferrari F300   53   1h17m47.649
3 Ralf Schumacher   Jordan 198-Mugen   53   1h17m50.824
4 Mika Hakkinen   McLaren MP4/13-
      Mercedes-Benz   53   1h18m05.343
5 Jean Alesi   Sauber C17-
      Petronas Ferrari   53   1h18m11.544
6 Damon Hill   Jordan 198-Mugen   53   1h18m16.360

Winner's average speed: 147.747 mph. Starting grid front row: M Schumacher, 1m25.289 (pole) and Villeneuve, 1m25.561. Fastest lap: Hakkinen, 1m25.139. Leaders: Hakkinen, laps 1-7, 32-34; Coulthard, 8-16; M Schumacher, 17-31, 35-53

27 September 1998. Nurburgring. 67 laps of a 2.831-mile circuit = 189.677 miles. Cool and overcast. World Championship round 15

1 Mika Hakkinen   McLaren MP4/13-
      Mercedes-Benz   67   1h32m14.789
2 Michael Schumacher   Ferrari F300   67   1h32m17.000
3 David Coulthard   McLaren MP4/13-
      Mercedes-Benz   67   1h32m48.952
4 Eddie Irvine   Ferrari F300   67   1h33m12.971
5 Heinz-Harald Frentzen   Williams FW20-
      Mecachrome   67   1h33m15.036
6 Giancarlo Fisichella   Benetton B198-Playlife   67   1h33m16.148

Winner's average speed: 123.372 mph. Starting grid front row: M Schumacher, 1m18.561 (pole) and Irvine, 1m18.907. Fastest lap: Hakkinen, 1m20.450. Leaders: M Schumacher, laps 1-24; Hakkinen, 25-67

1 November 1998. Suzuka. 51 laps of a 3.641-mile circuit = 185.691 miles. Race scheduled for 53 laps, start aborted twice by stalled cars on the grid, restarted over reduced distance. Warm, dry and sunny. World Championship round 16

1 Mika Hakkinen   McLaren MP4/13-
      Mercedes-Benz   51   1h27m22.535
2 Eddie Irvine   Ferrari F300   51   1h27m29.026
3 David Coulthard   McLaren MP4/13-
      Mercedes-Benz   51   1h27m50.197

4 Damon Hill   Jordan 198-Mugen   51   1h28m36.026
5 Heinz-Harald Frentzen   Williams FW20-
      Mecachrome   51   1h28m36.392
6 Jacques Villeneuve   Williams FW20-
      Mecachrome   51   1h28m38.402

Winner's average speed: 127.512 mph. Starting grid front row: M Schumacher, 1m36.293 (pole) and Hakkinen, 1m36.471 - Schumacher started from the back of the grid. Fastest lap: M Schumacher, 1m40.190. Leaders: Hakkinen, laps 1-51

1999

Nobody seemed to want to win the 1999 World Championship. One by one, would-be champions came to the fore, only to be robbed or throw their title chances away. As the field entered the first lap of the British GP, the year looked like another straightforward battle between Michael Schumacher and Mika Hakkinen. But Schumacher crashed heavily attempting to pass teammate Eddie Irvine, breaking his leg and ruling himself out for three months.

Irvine took up the challenge of trying to score Ferrari's first driver's title in two decades. He won four races and scored points in 10 others, giving him the lead for the championship going into the season's last race in Japan.

Mika Hakkinen should have claimed a second successive world title long before the finale at Suzuka. His eleven pole positions were proof of his speed, and with Schumacher sidelined he appeared to have a clear run at the title. But after first-half victories in Brazil, Spain, and Canada, Hakkinen's progress was halted by a string of setbacks. First a wheel fell off at Silverstone; a week later in Austria he was spun out the lead by teammate David Coulthard. The bad luck continued at Hockenheim, where a puncture-induced crash at 190-mph suddenly left him trailing Irvine in the points. But Hakkinen rallied to win in Hungary, and despite a costly spin at Monza, came all the way back to dominate in Japan and capture the championship.

David Coulthard endured another year in Hakkinen's shadow. Technical failures denied him deserved victories in France and Malaysia (where he forcefully passed Schumacher), but the Finn generally outperformed him again. Coulthard won twice (luckily at Silverstone and from the front at Spa) and was heading for a victory at the Nurburgring, which would have taken him to within three points of the series lead. But his shot at the championship came to a sudden end when he spun off the damp track.

Jordan's Heinz-Harald Frentzen had briefly emerged as a challenger with wins at Magny-Cours and Monza. But an electrical failure while leading at the Nurburgring and an uncompetitive run in Malaysia ended his hopes. Still, third place in both the drivers' and constructors' championships represented a significant step forward for the team and re-established Frentzen as a leading contender.

Ralf Schumacher, who outperformed new Williams teammate and reigning ChampCar Champion Alessandro Zanardi all year, would have won at the Nurburgring but for a puncture. This left Johnny Herbert to score the only win for the Stewart-Ford team.

That was much more than Jacques Villeneuve and British American Racing achieved. The team arrived amid unprecedented hype but never finished in the points. However, they ended the year on a positive note by announcing a works Honda engine supply for 2000.

QANTAS AUSTRALIAN GRAND PRIX

7 March 1999. Albert Park. 57 laps of a 3.295-mile circuit = 187.815 miles. Warm, dry and sunny. World Championship round 1

1 Eddie Irvine	Ferrari F399	57	1h35m01.659
2 Heinz-Harald Frentzen	Jordan 199-Mugen	57	1h35m02.686
3 Ralf Schumacher	Williams FW21-Supertec	57	1h35m08.671
4 Giancarlo Fisichella	Benetton B199-Playlife	57	1h35m35.077
5 Rubens Barrichello	Stewart SF3-Ford	57	1h35m56.357
6 Pedro de la Rosa	Arrows A20	57	1h36m25.976

Winner's average speed: 118.585 mph. Starting grid front row: Hakkinen, 1m30.462 (pole) and Coulthard, 1m30.946. Fastest lap: M Schumacher, 1m32.112. Leaders: Hakkinen, laps 1-17; Irvine, 18-57

GRANDE PREMIO MARLBORO DO BRASIL

11 April 1999. Interlagos. 72 laps of a 2.667-mile circuit = 192.024 miles. Hot, dry and sunny. World Championship round 2

1 Mika Hakkinen	McLaren MP4/14-Mercedes-Benz	72	1h38m03.765
2 Michael Schumacher	Ferrari F399	72	1h38m08.710
3 Heinz-Harald Frentzen	Jordan 199-Mugen	71	fuel pressure
4 Ralf Schumacher	Williams FW21-Supertec	71	
5 Eddie Irvine	Ferrari F399	71	
6 Olivier Panis	Prost AP02-Peugeot	71	

Winner's average speed: 117.490 mph. Starting grid front row: Hakkinen, 1m16.568 (pole) and Coulthard, 1m16.715. Fastest lap: Hakkinen, 1m18.448. Leaders: Hakkinen, laps 1-3, 38-72; Barrichello, 4-26; M Schumacher, 27-37

GRAN PREMIO WARSTEINER DI SAN MARINO

2 May 1999. Imola. 62 laps of a 3.064-mile circuit = 189.968 miles. Hot, dry and sunny. World Championship round 3

1 Michael Schumacher	Ferrari F399	62	1h33m44.792
2 David Coulthard	McLaren MP4/14-Mercedes-Benz	62	1h33m49.057
3 Rubens Barrichello	Stewart SF3-Ford	61	
4 Damon Hill	Jordan 199-Mugen	61	
5 Giancarlo Fisichella	Benetton B199-Playlife	61	
6 Jean Alesi	Sauber C18-Petronas Ferrari	61	

Winner's average speed: 121.584 mph. Starting grid front row: Hakkinen, 1m26.362 (pole) and Coulthard, 1m26.384. Fastest lap: M Schumacher, 1m28.547. Leaders: Hakkinen, laps 1-17; Coulthard, 18-35; M Schumacher, 36-62

GRAND PRIX DE MONACO

16 May 1999. Monte Carlo. 78 laps of a 2.092-mile circuit = 163.176 miles. Hot, dry and sunny. World Championship round 4

1 Michael Schumacher	Ferrari F399	78	1h49m31.812
2 Eddie Irvine	Ferrari F399	78	1h50m02.288
3 Mika Hakkinen	McLaren MP4/14-Mercedes-Benz	78	1h50m09.295
4 Heinz-Harald Frentzen	Jordan 199-Mugen	78	1h50m25.821
5 Giancarlo Fisichella	Benetton B199-Playlife	77	
6 Alexander Wurz	Benetton B199-Playlife	77	

Winner's average speed: 89.387 mph. Starting grid front row: Hakkinen, 1m20.547 (pole) and M Schumacher, 1m20.611. Fastest lap: Hakkinen, 1m22.259. Leaders: M Schumacher, laps 1-78

GRAN PREMIO MARLBORO DE ESPANA

30 May 1999. Catalunya. 65 laps of a 2.937-mile circuit = 190.905 miles. Hot, dry and sunny. World Championship round 5

1 Mika Hakkinen	McLaren MP4/14-Mercedes-Benz	65	1h34m13.665
2 David Coulthard	McLaren MP4/14-Mercedes-Benz	65	1h34m19.903
3 Michael Schumacher	Ferrari F399	65	1h34m24.510
4 Eddie Irvine	Ferrari F399	65	1h34m43.847
5 Ralf Schumacher	Williams FW21-Supertec	65	1h35m40.873
6 Jarno Trulli	Prost AP02-Peugeot	64	

Winner's average speed: 121.560 mph. Starting grid front row: Hakkinen, 1m22.088 (pole) and Irvine, 1m22.219. Fastest lap: M Schumacher, 1m24.982. Leaders: Hakkinen, laps 1-23, 27-44, 46-65; Coulthard, 24-26, 45

AIR CANADA GRAND PRIX DU CANADA

13 June 1999. Montreal. 69 laps of a 2.747-mile circuit = 189.543 miles. Very hot, dry and sunny. World Championship round 6

1 Mika Hakkinen	McLaren MP4/14-Mercedes-Benz	69	1h41m35.727
2 Giancarlo Fisichella	Benetton B199-Playlife	69	1h41m36.509
3 Eddie Irvine	Ferrari F399	69	1h41m37.524
4 Ralf Schumacher	Williams FW21-Supertec	69	1h41m38.119
5 Johnny Herbert	Stewart SF3-Ford	69	1h41m38.532
6 Pedro Diniz	Sauber C18-Petronas Ferrari	69	1h41m39.438

Winner's average speed: 111.940 mph. Starting grid front row: M Schumacher, 1m19.298 (pole) and Hakkinen, 1m19.327. Fastest lap: Irvine, 1m20.382. Leaders: M Schumacher, laps 1-29; Hakkinen, 30-69

GRAND PRIX MOBIL 1 DE FRANCE

27 June 1999. Magny-Cours. 72 laps of a 2.641-mile circuit = 190.152 miles. Dry and overcast at the start, heavy rain later. World Championship round 7

1 Heinz-Harald Frentzen	Jordan 199-Mugen	72	1h58m24.343
2 Mika Hakkinen	McLaren MP4/14-Mercedes-Benz	72	1h58m35.435
3 Rubens Barrichello	Stewart SF3-Ford	72	1h59m07.775
4 Ralf Schumacher	Williams FW21-Supertec	72	1h59m09.818
5 Michael Schumacher	Ferrari F399	72	1h59m12.224
6 Eddie Irvine	Ferrari F399	72	1h59m13.244

Winner's average speed: 96.356 mph. Starting grid front row: Barrichello, 1m38.441 (pole) and Alesi, 1m38.881. Fastest lap: Coulthard, 1m19.227. Leaders: Barrichello, laps 1-5, 10-43, 55-59; Coulthard, 6-9; M Schumacher, 44-54; Hakkinen, 60-65; Frentzen, 66-72

RAC BRITISH GRAND PRIX

11 July 1999. Silverstone. 60 laps of a 3.194-mile circuit = 191.640 miles. Race stopped on first lap by cars stalled on the grid, restarted over original distance. Hot, dry and sunny. World Championship round 8

1 David Coulthard	McLaren MP4/14-Mercedes-Benz	60	1h32m30.144
2 Eddie Irvine	Ferrari F399	60	1h32m31.973
3 Ralf Schumacher	Williams FW21-Supertec	60	1h32m57.555
4 Heinz-Harald Frentzen	Jordan 199-Mugen	60	1h32m57.933
5 Damon Hill	Jordan 199-Mugen	60	1h33m08.750
6 Pedro Diniz	Sauber C18-Petronas Ferrari	60	1h33m23.787

Winner's average speed: 124.304 mph. Starting grid front row: Hakkinen, 1m24.804 (pole) and M Schumacher, 1m25.223. Fastest lap: Hakkinen, 1m28.309. Leaders: Hakkinen, laps 1-24; Irvine, 25-26; Coulthard, 27-42, 46-60; Frentzen, 43-44; Hill, 45

GROSSER PREIS VON OSTERREICH

25 July 1999. A1 Ring. 71 laps of a 2.684-mile circuit = 190.564 miles. Warm and overcast. World Championship round 9

1 Eddie Irvine	Ferrari F399	71	1h28m12.438
2 David Coulthard	McLaren MP4/14-Mercedes-Benz	71	1h28m12.751
3 Mika Hakkinen	McLaren MP4/14-Mercedes-Benz	71	1h28m34.720
4 Heinz-Harald Frentzen	Jordan 199-Mugen	71	1h29m05.241
5 Alexander Wurz	Benetton B199-Playlife	71	1h29m18.796
6 Pedro Diniz	Sauber C18-Petronas Ferrari	71	1h29m23.371

Formula 1

1999 DRIVERS' RECORDS

driver	car	AUS Q	AUS R	BR Q	BR R	RSM Q	RSM R	MC Q	MC R	E Q	E R	CDN Q	CDN R
Jean Alesi	Sauber C18-Petronas Ferrari	16	R	14	R	13	6	14	R	5	R	8	R
Luca Badoer	Minardi M01-Ford	21	R	-	-	22	8	20	R	22	R	21	10
Rubens Barrichello	Stewart SF3-Ford	4	5	3	R	6	3	5	9	7	DSQ	5	R
David Coulthard	McLaren MP4/14-Mercedes-Benz	2	R	2	R	2	2	3	R	3	2	4	7
Pedro Diniz	Sauber C18-Petronas Ferrari	14	R	15	R	15	R	15	R	12	R	18	6
Giancarlo Fisichella	Benetton B199-Playlife	7	4	5	R	16	5	9	5	13	9	7	2
Heinz-Harald Frentzen	Jordan 199-Mugen	5	2	8	3	7	R	6	4	8	R	6	11
Marc Gene	Minardi M01-Ford	22	R	20	9	21	9	22	R	21	R	22	8
Mika Hakkinen	McLaren MP4/14-Mercedes-Benz	1	R	1	1F	1	R	1	3F	1	1	2	1
Johnny Herbert	Stewart SF3-Ford	13	R	10	R	12	10	13	R	14	R	10	5
Damon Hill	Jordan 199-Mugen	9	R	7	R	8	4	17	R	11	7	14	R
Eddie Irvine	Ferrari F399	6	1	6	5	4	R	4	2	2	4	3	3F
Olivier Panis	Prost AP02-Peugeot	20	R	12	6	11	R	18	R	15	R	15	9
Pedro de la Rosa	Arrows A20	18	6	17	R	18	R	21	R	19	11	20	R
Mika Salo	BAR 01-Supertec	-	-	-	-	19	7	12	R	16	8	-	-
	Ferrari F399	-	-	-	-	-	-	-	-	-	-	-	-
Stephane Sarrazin	Minardi M01-Ford	-	-	18	R	-	-	-	-	-	-	-	-
Michael Schumacher	Ferrari F399	3	8F	4	2	3	1F	2	1	4	3F	1	R
Ralf Schumacher	Williams FW21-Supertec	8	3	11	4	9	R	16	R	10	5	13	4
Toranosuke Takagi	Arrows A20	17	7	19	8	20	R	19	R	20	12	19	R
Jarno Trulli	Prost AP02-Peugeot	12	R	13	R	14	R	7	7	9	6	9	R
Jacques Villeneuve	BAR 01-Supertec	11	R	21	R	5	R	8	R	6	R	16	R
Alexander Wurz	Benetton B199-Playlife	10	R	9	7	17	R	10	6	18	10	11	R
Alessandro Zanardi	Williams FW21-Supertec	15	R	16	R	10	11	11	8	17	R	12	R
Ricardo Zonta	BAR 01-Supertec	19	R	NT	DNP	-	-	-	-	-	-	17	R

Winner's average speed: 129.625 mph. Starting grid front row: Hakkinen, 1m10.954 (pole) and Coulthard, 1m11.153. Fastest lap: Hakkinen, 1m12.107. Leaders: Coulthard, laps 1-39; Irvine, 40-71

GROSSER MOBIL 1 PREIS VON DEUTSCHLAND

1 August 1999. Hockenheim. 45 laps of a 4.239-mile circuit = 190.755 miles. Hot, dry and sunny. World Championship round 10

1	Eddie Irvine	Ferrari F399	45	1h21m58.594
2	Mika Salo	Ferrari F399	45	1h21m59.601
3	Heinz-Harald Frentzen	Jordan 199-Mugen	45	1h22m03.789
4	Ralf Schumacher	Williams FW21-Supertec	45	1h22m11.403
5	David Coulthard	McLaren MP4/14-Mercedes-Benz	45	1h22m15.417
6	Olivier Panis	Prost AP02-Peugeot	45	1h22m28.473

Winner's average speed: 139.617 mph. Starting grid front row: Hakkinen, 1m42.950 (pole) and Frentzen, 1m43.000. Fastest lap: Coulthard, 1m45.270. Leaders: Hakkinen, laps 1-24; Salo, 25; Irvine, 26-45

MARLBORO MAGYAR NAGYDIJ (HUNGARIAN GRAND PRIX)

15 August 1999. Hungaroring. 77 laps of a 2.465-mile circuit = 189.805 miles. Hot, dry and sunny. World Championship round 11

1	Mika Hakkinen	McLaren MP4/14-Mercedes-Benz	77	1h46m23.536
2	David Coulthard	McLaren MP4/14-Mercedes-Benz	77	1h46m33.242
3	Eddie Irvine	Ferrari F399	77	1h46m50.764
4	Heinz-Harald Frentzen	Jordan 199-Mugen	77	1h46m55.351
5	Rubens Barrichello	Stewart SF3-Ford	77	1h47m07.344
6	Damon Hill	Jordan 199-Mugen	77	1h47m19.262

Winner's average speed: 107.041 mph. Starting grid front row: Hakkinen, 1m18.156 (pole) and Irvine, 1m18.263. Fastest lap: Coulthard, 1m20.699. Leaders: Hakkinen, laps 1-77

GRAND PRIX FOSTER'S DE BELGIQUE

29 August 1999. Spa-Francorchamps. 44 laps of a 4.329-mile circuit = 190.476 miles. Hot, dry and sunny. World Championship round 12

1	David Coulthard	McLaren MP4/14-Mercedes-Benz	44	1h25m43.057
2	Mika Hakkinen	McLaren MP4/14-Mercedes-Benz	44	1h25m53.526
3	Heinz-Harald Frentzen	Jordan 199-Mugen	44	1h26m16.490
4	Eddie Irvine	Ferrari F399	44	1h26m28.005
5	Ralf Schumacher	Williams FW21-Supertec	44	1h26m31.124
6	Damon Hill	Jordan 199-Mugen	44	1h26m37.973

Winner's average speed: 133.328 mph. Starting grid front row: Hakkinen, 1m50.329 (pole) and Coulthard, 1m50.484. Fastest lap: Hakkinen, 1m53.955. Leaders: Coulthard, laps 1-44

GRAN PREMIO CAMPARI D'ITALIA

12 September 1999. Monza. 53 laps of a 3.585-mile circuit = 190.005 miles. Hot, dry and sunny. World Championship round 13

1	Heinz-Harald Frentzen	Jordan 199-Mugen	53	1h17m02.923
2	Ralf Schumacher	Williams FW21-Supertec	53	1h17m06.195
3	Mika Salo	Ferrari F399	53	1h17m14.855
4	Rubens Barrichello	Stewart SF3-Ford	53	1h17m20.553
5	David Coulthard	McLaren MP4/14-Mercedes-Benz	53	1h17m21.065
6	Eddie Irvine	Ferrari F399	53	1h17m30.325

Winner's average speed: 147.962 mph. Starting grid front row: Hakkinen, 1m22.432 (pole) and Frentzen, 1m22.926. Fastest lap: R Schumacher, 1m25.579. Leaders: Hakkinen, laps 1-29; Frentzen, 30-35, 37-53; Salo, 36

GROSSER PREIS WARSTEINER VON EUROPA

26 September 1999. Nurburgring. 66 laps of a 2.831-mile circuit = 186.846 miles. Dry at the start, rain later. World Championship round 14

1	Johnny Herbert	Stewart SF3-Ford	66	1h41m54.314
2	Jarno Trulli	Prost AP02-Peugeot	66	1h42m16.953

F		GB		A		D		H		B		I		EU		MAL		J	
Q	R	Q	R	Q	R	Q	R	Q	R	Q	R	Q	R	Q	R	Q	R	Q	R
2	R	10	14	17	R	21	8	11	16	16	9	13	9	16	R	15	7	10	6
20	10	21	R	19	13	19	10	19	14	20	R	19	R	19	R	21	R	22	R
1	3	7	8	5	R	6	R	8	5	7	10	7	4	15	3	6	5	13	8
4	RF	3	1	2	2	3	5F	3	2F	2	1	3	5	2	R	3	R	3	R
11	R	12	6	16	6	16	R	12	R	18	R	16	R	13	R	17	R	17	11
7	R	17	7	12	12	10	R	4	R	13	11	17	R	6	R	11	11	14	14
5	1	5	4	4	4	2	3	5	4	3	3	2	1	1	R	14	6	4	4
19	R	22	15	22	11	15	9	22	17	21	16	20	R	20	6	19	9	20	R
14	2	1	RF	1	3F	1	R	1	1	1	2F	1	R	3	5F	4	3	2	1
9	R	11	12	6	14	17	11	10	11	10	R	15	R	14	1	5	4	8	7
18	R	6	5	11	8	8	8	6	6	4	6	9	10	7	R	9	R	12	R
17	6	4	2	3	1	5	1	2	3	6	4	8	6	9	7	2	1	5	3
3	8	15	13	18	10	7	6	14	10	17	13	10	11	5	9	12	R	6	R
21	12	20	R	21	R	20	R	20	15	22	R	21	R	22	R	20	R	21	13
-	-	-	-	-	-	-	-	-	-	-	-	-	-	-	-	-	-	-	-
-	-	-	-	7	9	4	2	18	12	9	7	6	3	12	R	-	-	-	-
-	-	-	-	-	-	-	-	-	-	-	-	-	-	-	-	-	-	-	-
6	5	2	R	-	-	-	-	-	-	-	-	-	-	-	-	1	2F	1	2F
16	4	8	3	8	R	11	4	16	9	5	5	5	2F	4	4	8	R	9	5
22	11	19	16	20	R	22	R	21	R	19	R	22	R	21	R	22	R	19	R
8	7	14	9	13	7	9	R	13	8	12	12	12	R	10	2	18	DNS	7	R
12	R	9	R	9	R	12	R	9	R	11	15	11	8	8	10	10	R	11	9
13	R	18	10	10	5	13	7	7	7	15	14	14	R	11	R	7	8	15	10
15	R	13	11	14	R	14	R	15	R	8	4	7	R	18	R	16	10	16	R
10	9	16	R	15	15	18	R	17	13	14	R	18	R	17	8	13	R	18	12

1999 FINAL CHAMPIONSHIP POSITIONS

Drivers

1	Mika Hakkinen	76
2	Eddie Irvine	74
3	Heinz-Harald Frentzen	54
4	David Coulthard	48
5	Michael Schumacher	44
6	Ralf Schumacher	35
7	Rubens Barrichello	21
8	Johnny Herbert	15
9	Giancarlo Fisichella	13
10	Mika Salo	10
11=	Damon Hill	7
	Jarno Trulli	7
13=	Pedro Diniz	3
	Alexander Wurz	3
15=	Jean Alesi	2
	Olivier Panis	2
17=	Marc Gene	1
	Pedro de la Rosa	1

Manufacturers

1	Ferrari	128
2	McLaren-Mercedes-Benz	124
3	Jordan-Mugen	61
4	Stewart-Ford	36
5	Williams-Mecachrome	35
6	Benetton-Playlife	16
7	Prost-Peugeot	9
8	Sauber-Petronas Ferrari	5
9=	Arrows	1
	Minardi-Ford	1

3 Rubens Barrichello — Stewart SF3-Ford — 66 — 1h42m17.180
4 Ralf Schumacher — Williams FW 21-Supertec — 66 — 1h42m33.822
5 Mika Hakkinen — McLaren MP4/14-Mercedes-Benz — 66 — 1h42m57.264
6 Marc Gene — Minardi M01-Ford — 66 — 1h42m59.468
Winner's average speed: 110.012 mph. Starting grid front row: Frentzen, 1m19.910 (pole) and Coulthard, 1m20.176. Fastest lap: Hakkinen, 1m21.282. Leaders: Frentzen, laps 1-32; Coulthard, 33-37; R Schumacher, 38-44, 49; Fisichella, 45-48; Herbert, 50-66.

PETRONAS MALAYSIAN GRAND PRIX

17 October 1999. Sepang. 56 laps of a 3.444-mile circuit = 192.864 miles. Hot, humid and sunny. World Championship round 15

1 Eddie Irvine — Ferrari F399 — 56 — 1h36m38.494
2 Michael Schumacher — Ferrari F399 — 56 — 1h36m39.534
3 Mika Hakkinen — McLaren MP4/14-Mercedes-Benz — 56 — 1h36m48.237
4 Johnny Herbert — Stewart SF3-Ford — 56 — 1h36m56.032
5 Rubens Barrichello — Stewart SF3-Ford — 56 — 1h37m10.790
6 Heinz-Harald Frentzen — Jordan 199-Mugen — 56 — 1h37m13.378
Winner's average speed: 119.739 mph. Starting grid front row: M Schumacher, 1m39.688 (pole) and Irvine, 1m40.635. Fastest lap: M Schumacher, 1m40.267. Leaders: M Schumacher, laps 1-3, 26-28, 42-52; Irvine, 4-25, 29-41, 53-56

FUJI TELEVISION JAPANESE GRAND PRIX

31 October 1999. Suzuka. 53 laps of a 3.641-mile circuit = 192.973 miles. Warm, dry and sunny. World Championship round 16

1 Mika Hakkinen — McLaren MP4/14-Mercedes-Benz — 53 — 1h31m18.785
2 Michael Schumacher — Ferrari F399 — 53 — 1h31m23.800
3 Eddie Irvine — Ferrari F399 — 53 — 1h32m54.473
4 Heinz-Harald Frentzen — Jordan 199-Mugen — 53 — 1h32m57.420
5 Ralf Schumacher — Williams FW21-Supertec — 53 — 1h32m58.279
6 Jean Alesi — Sauber C18-Petronas Ferrari — 52
Winner's average speed: 126.799 mph. Starting grid front row: M Schumacher, 1m37.470 (pole) and Hakkinen, 1m37.820. Fastest lap: M Schumacher, 1m41.319. Leaders: Hakkinen, laps 1-19, 23-53; M Schumacher, 20-22.

2000

Michael Schumacher finally gave Ferrari its first drivers' World Championship since 1979 in another yearlong battle with Mika Hakkinen's McLaren. Schumacher won the season's first two races after Hakkinen had retired from the lead, and then narrowly beat the Finn at Imola.

Schumacher's prospects for a third title appeared more doubtful after first-lap accidents at the A1 Ring and Hockenheim, and resounding defeats to Hakkinen in Hungary and Belgium. But he returned to form by beating Hakkinen at Monza and capitalizing on McLaren's misfortunes at the US GP, now run on an excellent road course at the Indianapolis Motor Speedway. A seventh victory at the season's penultimate event in Japan was enough to clinch the title for Schumacher, and he won again at the final race in Malaysia. Schumacher's new Ferrari partner, Rubens Barrichello, scored an emotional first win from eighteenth on the grid in the Hockenheim rain.

David Coulthard scored prestigious wins in Britain, Monte Carlo, and France to close in on Schumacher's lead, but his challenge ultimately faded. Just five days before the Spanish GP, Coulthard survived a plane crash in which both pilots were killed. His second-place finish was a testament to the Scot's courage and resolve.

2000 was the first year since 1988 in which only two teams had won races. Even so, Williams had an increasingly promising first year using BMW power. A 19-year-old Jenson Button was especially impressive, out-qualifying teammate Ralf Schumacher on seven occasions and taking third on the grid at Spa.

The Mugen Honda-powered Jordan team was fast enough to finish third in the championship for a second successive year. Jordan was the only team other than Ferrari and McLaren to qualify on the front row, but poor reliability blighted its challenge. British American Racing took a great step forward in their first year with works Honda engines, showing improved reliability and helping Jacques Villeneuve to a series of points finishes.

Stewart Grand Prix had been sold to Ford in 1999, was renamed Jaguar and repainted in British Racing Green. Eddie Irvine signed from Ferrari but it was a bad year, its car hampered by engine problems and poor aerodynamics. Prost also struggled, and ended Peugeot's last year in the sport without a point—officially F1's worst team.

QANTAS AUSTRALIAN GRAND PRIX

12 March 2000. Albert Park. 58 laps of a 3.295-mile circuit = 191.110 miles. Hot, dry and sunny. World Championship round 1

1 Michael Schumacher	Ferrari F1-2000	58	1h34m01.967
2 Rubens Barrichello	Ferrari F1-2000	58	1h34m13.402
3 Ralf Schumacher	Williams FW22-BMW	58	1h34m21.996
4 Jacques Villeneuve	BAR 02-Honda	58	1h34m46.434
5 Giancarlo Fisichella	Benetton B200-Playlife	58	1h34m47.152
6 Ricardo Zonta	BAR 02-Honda	58	1h34m48.455

Mika Salo (Sauber C19-Petronas Ferrari), 1h34m47.611, finished sixth on the road but was disqualified due to an illegal front wing. Winner's average speed: 121.943 mph. Starting grid front row: Hakkinen, 1m30.556 (pole) and Coulthard, 1m30.910. Fastest lap: Barrichello, 1m31.481. Leaders: Hakkinen, laps 1-18; M Schumacher, 19-29, 36-44, 46-58; Frentzen, 30-35; Barrichello, 45

GRANDE PREMIO MARLBORO DO BRASIL

26 March 2000. Interlagos. 71 laps of a 2.667-mile circuit = 189.357 miles. Hot, dry and overcast. World Championship round 2

1 Michael Schumacher	Ferrari F1-2000	71	1h31m35.271
2 Giancarlo Fisichella	Benetton B200-Playlife	71	1h32m15.169
3 Heinz-Harald Frentzen	Jordan EJ10-Mugen	71	1h32m17.539
4 Jarno Trulli	Jordan EJ10-Mugen	71	1h32m48.051
5 Ralf Schumacher	Williams FW22-BMW	70	
6 Jenson Button	Williams FW22-BMW	70	

David Coulthard (McLaren MP4/15-Mercedes-Benz) finished second on the road but was disqualified due to illegal front wing. Winner's average speed: 124.049 mph. Starting grid front row: Hakkinen, 1m14.111 (pole) and Coulthard, 1m14.285. Fastest lap: M Schumacher, 1m14.755. Leaders: Hakkinen, laps 1, 23-29; M Schumacher, 2-20, 30-71; Barrichello, 21-22

GRAN PREMIO WARSTEINER DI SAN MARINO

9 April 2000. Imola. 62 laps of a 3.064-mile circuit = 189.968 miles. Warm, dry and overcast. World Championship round 3

1 Michael Schumacher	Ferrari F1-2000	62	1h31m39.776
2 Mika Hakkinen	McLaren MP4/15-Mercedes-Benz	62	1h31m40.944
3 David Coulthard	McLaren MP4/15-Mercedes-Benz	62	1h32m30.784
4 Rubens Barrichello	Ferrari F1-2000	62	1h33m09.052
5 Jacques Villeneuve	BAR 02-Honda	61	
6 Mika Salo	Sauber C19-Petronas Ferrari	61	

Winner's average speed: 124.348 mph. Starting grid front row: Hakkinen, 1m24.714 (pole) and M Schumacher, 1m24.805. Fastest lap: Hakkinen, 1m26.523. Leaders: Hakkinen, laps 1-44; M Schumacher, 45-62

FOSTER'S BRITISH GRAND PRIX

23 April 2000. Silverstone. 60 laps of a 3.194-mile circuit = 191.640 miles. Warm, dry and sunny. World Championship round 4

1 David Coulthard	McLaren MP4/15-Mercedes-Benz	60	1h28m50.108
2 Mika Hakkinen	McLaren MP4/15-Mercedes-Benz	60	1h28m51.585
3 Michael Schumacher	Ferrari F1-2000	60	1h29m10.025
4 Ralf Schumacher	Williams FW22-BMW	60	1h29m31.420
5 Jenson Button	Williams FW22-BMW	60	1h29m47.867
6 Jarno Trulli	Jordan EJ10-Mugen	60	1h30m09.381

Winner's average speed: 129.435 mph. Starting grid front row: Barrichello, 1m25.703 (pole) and Frentzen, 1m25.706. Fastest lap: Hakkinen, 1m26.217. Leaders: Barrichello, laps 1-30, 33-35; Coulthard, 31-32, 42-60; M Schumacher, 36-38; Frentzen, 39-41

GRAN PREMIO MARLBORO DE ESPANA

7 May 2000. Catalunya. 65 laps of a 2.937-mile circuit = 190.905 miles. Warm, dry and sunny. World Championship round 5

1 Mika Hakkinen	McLaren MP4/15-Mercedes-Benz	65	1h33m55.390
2 David Coulthard	McLaren MP4/15-Mercedes-Benz	65	1h34m11.456
3 Rubens Barrichello	Ferrari F1-2000	65	1h34m24.502
4 Ralf Schumacher	Williams FW22-BMW	65	1h34m32.701
5 Michael Schumacher	Ferrari F1-2000	65	1h34m43.373
6 Heinz-Harald Frentzen	Jordan EJ10-Mugen	65	1h35m17.315

Winner's average speed: 121.954 mph. Starting grid front row: M Schumacher, 1m20.974 (pole) and Hakkinen, 1m21.052. Fastest lap: Hakkinen, 1m24.470. Leaders: M Schumacher, laps 1-23, 27-41; Hakkinen, 24-26, 42-65

GROSSER WARSTEINER PREIS VON EUROPA

21 May 2000. Nurburgring. 67 laps of a 2.831-mile circuit = 189.677 miles. Dry and cloudy at the start, heavy rain later. World Championship round 6

1 Michael Schumacher	Ferrari F1-2000	67	1h42m00.307
2 Mika Hakkinen	McLaren MP4/15-Mercedes-Benz	67	1h42m14.129
3 David Coulthard	McLaren MP4/15-Mercedes-Benz	66	
4 Rubens Barrichello	Ferrari F1-2000	66	
5 Giancarlo Fisichella	Benetton B200-Playlife	66	
6 Pedro de la Rosa	Arrows A21-Supertec	66	

Winner's average speed: 111.569 mph. Starting grid front row: Coulthard, 1m17.529 (pole) and M Schumacher, 1m17.667. Fastest lap: M Schumacher, 1m22.269. Leaders: Hakkinen, laps 1-10, 36-45; M Schumacher, 11-15, 17-35, 46-67; Barrichello, 16

GRAND PRIX DE MONACO

4 June 2000. Monte Carlo. 78 laps of a 2.092-mile circuit = 163.176 miles. Start aborted by an engine failure on the grid, restart aborted due to failure in starting light procedure and a separate first-lap accident, restarted over original distance. Hot, dry and sunny. World Championship round 7

1 David Coulthard	McLaren MP4/15-Mercedes-Benz	78	1h49m28.213
2 Rubens Barrichello	Ferrari F1-2000	78	1h49m44.102
3 Giancarlo Fisichella	Benetton B200-Playlife	78	1h49m46.735
4 Eddie Irvine	Jaguar R1-Cosworth	78	1h50m34.137
5 Mika Salo	Sauber C19-Petronas Ferrari	78	1h50m48.988
6 Mika Hakkinen	McLaren MP4/15-Mercedes-Benz	77	

Winner's average speed: 89.436 mph. Starting grid front row: M Schumacher, 1m19.475 (pole) and Trulli, 1m19.746. Fastest lap: Hakkinen, 1m21.571. Leaders: M Schumacher, laps 1-55; Coulthard, 56-78

GRAND PRIX AIR CANADA

18 June 2000. Montreal. 69 laps of a 2.747-mile circuit = 189.543 miles. Dry and cloudy at the start, heavy rain later. World Championship round 8

1 Michael Schumacher	Ferrari F1-2000	69	1h41m12.313
2 Rubens Barrichello	Ferrari F1-2000	69	1h41m12.487
3 Giancarlo Fisichella	Benetton B200-Playlife	69	1h41m27.678
4 Mika Hakkinen	McLaren MP4/15-Mercedes-Benz	69	1h41m30.874
5 Jos Verstappen	Arrows A21-Supertec	69	1h42m04.521
6 Jarno Trulli	Jordan EJ10-Mugen	69	1h42m14.000

Winner's average speed: 112.371 mph. Starting grid front row: M Schumacher, 1m18.439 (pole) and Coulthard, 1m18.537. Fastest lap: Hakkinen, 1m19.049. Leaders: M Schumacher, laps 1-34, 43-69; Barrichello, 35-42

MOBIL 1 GRAND PRIX DE FRANCE

2 July 2000. Magny-Cours. 72 laps of a 2.641-mile circuit = 190.152 miles. Hot, dry and sunny. World Championship round 9

1 David Coulthard	McLaren MP4/15-Mercedes-Benz	72	1h38m05.538
2 Mika Hakkinen	McLaren MP4/15-Mercedes-Benz	72	1h38m20.286
3 Rubens Barrichello	Ferrari F1-2000	72	1h38m37.947
4 Jacques Villeneuve	BAR 02-Honda	72	1h39m06.860
5 Ralf Schumacher	Williams FW22-BMW	72	1h39m09.519
6 Jarno Trulli	Jordan EJ10-Mugen	72	1h39m21.143

Winner's average speed: 116.310 mph. Starting grid front row: M Schumacher, 1m15.632 (pole) and Coulthard, 1m15.734. Fastest lap: Coulthard, 1m19.479. Leaders: M Schumacher, laps 1-24, 26-39; Coulthard, 25, 40-72

GROSSER A1 PREIS VON OSTERREICH

16 July 2000. A1 Ring. 71 laps of a 2.684-mile circuit = 190.564 miles. Hot, dry and sunny. World Championship round 10

1 Mika Hakkinen	McLaren MP4/15-Mercedes-Benz	71	1h28m15.818
2 David Coulthard	McLaren MP4/15-Mercedes-Benz	71	1h28m28.353

3 Rubens Barrichello	Ferrari F1-2000	71	1h28m46.613
4 Jacques Villeneuve	BAR 02-Honda	70	
5 Jenson Button	Williams FW22-BMW	70	
6 Mika Salo	Sauber C19-Petronas Ferrari	70	

Winner's average speed: 129.542 mph. Starting grid front row: Hakkinen, 1m10.410 (pole) and Coulthard, 1m10.795. Fastest lap: Coulthard, 1m11.783. Leaders: Hakkinen, laps 1-38, 43-71; Coulthard, 39-42

GROSSER MOBIL 1 PREIS VON DEUTSCHLAND

30 July 2000. Hockenheim. 45 laps of a 4.239-mile circuit = 190.755 miles. Dry and cloudy at the start, heavy rain later. World Championship round 11

1 Rubens Barrichello	Ferrari F1-2000	45	1h25m34.418
2 Mika Hakkinen	McLaren MP4/15-Mercedes-Benz	45	1h25m41.870
3 David Coulthard	McLaren MP4/15-Mercedes-Benz	45	1h25m55.586
4 Jenson Button	Williams FW22-BMW	45	1h25m57.103
5 Mika Salo	Sauber C19-Petronas Ferrari	45	1h26m01.530
6 Pedro de la Rosa	Arrows A21-Supertec	45	1h26m03.498

Winner's average speed: 133.748 mph. Starting grid front row: Coulthard, 1m45.697 (pole) and M Schumacher, 1m47.063. Fastest lap: Barrichello, 1m44.300. Leaders: Hakkinen, laps 1-25, 28-35; Coulthard, 26-27; Barrichello, 36-45

MARLBORO MAGYAR NAGYDIJ (HUNGARIAN GRAND PRIX)

13 August 2000. Hungaroring. 77 laps of a 2.465-mile circuit = 189.805 miles. Hot, dry and sunny. World Championship round 12

1 Mika Hakkinen	McLaren MP4/15-Mercedes-Benz	77	1h45m33.869
2 Michael Schumacher	Ferrari F1-2000	77	1h45m41.786
3 David Coulthard	McLaren MP4/15-Mercedes-Benz	77	1h45m42.324
4 Rubens Barrichello	Ferrari F1-2000	77	1h46m18.026
5 Ralf Schumacher	Williams FW22-BMW	77	1h46m24.306
6 Heinz-Harald Frentzen	Jordan EJ10-Mugen	77	1h46m41.968

Winner's average speed: 107.880 mph. Starting grid front row: M Schumacher, 1m17.514 (pole) and Coulthard, 1m17.886. Fastest lap: Hakkinen, 1m20.028. Leaders: Hakkinen, laps 1-31, 33-77; Coulthard, 32

FOSTER'S GRAND PRIX DE BELGIQUE

27 August 2000. Spa-Francorchamps. 44 laps of a 4.329-mile circuit = 190.476 miles. Wet at the start, drying later. World Championship round 13

1 Mika Hakkinen	McLaren MP4/15-Mercedes-Benz	44	1h28m14.494
2 Michael Schumacher	Ferrari F1-2000	44	1h28m15.598
3 Ralf Schumacher	Williams FW22-BMW	44	1h28m52.590
4 David Coulthard	McLaren MP4/15-Mercedes-Benz	44	1h28m57.775
5 Jenson Button	Williams FW22-BMW	44	1h29m04.408
6 Heinz-Harald Frentzen	Jordan EJ10-Mugen	44	1h29m10.478

Winner's average speed: 129.514 mph. Starting grid front row: Hakkinen, 1m50.646 (pole) and Trulli, 1m51.419 (started behind the safety car). Fastest lap: Barrichello, 1m53.803. Leaders: Hakkinen, laps 1-12, 23-27, 41-44; M Schumacher, 13-22, 28-40

GRAN PREMIO CAMPARI D'ITALIA

10 September 2000. Monza. 53 laps of a 3.599-mile circuit = 190.747 miles. Hot, dry and sunny. World Championship round 14

1 Michael Schumacher	Ferrari F1-2000	53	1h27m31.638
2 Mika Hakkinen	McLaren MP4/15-Mercedes-Benz	53	1h27m35.448
3 Ralf Schumacher	Williams FW22-BMW	53	1h28m24.070
4 Jos Verstappen	Arrows A21-Supertec	53	1h28m31.576
5 Alexander Wurz	Benetton B200-Playlife	53	1h28m39.064
6 Ricardo Zonta	BAR 02-Honda	53	1h28m40.931

Winner's average speed: 130.757 mph. Starting grid front row: M Schumacher, 1m23.770 (pole) and Barrichello, 1m23.797. Fastest lap:

2000 DRIVERS' RECORDS

driver	car	AUS Q	AUS R	BR Q	BR R	RSM Q	RSM R	GB Q	GB R	E Q	E R	EU Q	EU R
Jean Alesi	Prost AP03-Peugeot	17	R	15	R	15	R	15	10	17	R	17	9
Rubens Barrichello	Ferrari F1-2000	4	2F	4	R	4	4	1	R	3	3	4	4
Luciano Burti	Jaguar R1-Cosworth	-		-		-		-		-		-	
Jenson Button	Williams FW22-BMW	21	R	9	6	18	R	6	5	10	17	11	10
David Coulthard	McLaren MP4/15-Mercedes-Benz	2	R	2	DSQ	3	3	4	1	4	2	1	3
Pedro Diniz	Sauber C19-Petronas Ferrari	19	R	20	DNS	10	8	13	11	15	R	15	7
Giancarlo Fisichella	Benetton B200-Playlife	9	5	5	2	19	11	12	7	13	9	7	5
Heinz-Harald Frentzen	Jordan EJ10-Mugen	5	R	7	3	6	R	2	17	8	6	10	R
Marc Gene	Minardi M02-Fondmetal Ford	18	8	18	R	21	R	21	14	20	14	20	R
Mika Hakkinen	McLaren MP4/15-Mercedes-Benz	1	R	1	R	1	2F	3	2F	2	1F	3	2
Nick Heidfeld	Prost AP03-Peugeot	15	9	19	R	22	R	17	R	19	16	22	DNQ
Johnny Herbert	Jaguar R1-Cosworth	20	R	17	R	17	10	14	12	14	13	16	11
Eddie Irvine	Jaguar R1-Cosworth	7	R	6	R	7	7	9	13	9	11	8	R
Gaston Mazzacane	Minardi M02-Fondmetal Ford	22	R	21	10	20	13	22	15	21	15	21	8
Pedro de la Rosa	Arrows A21-Supertec	12	R	16	8	13	R	19	R	22	R	12	6
Mika Salo	Sauber C19-Petronas Ferrari	10	DSQ	22	DNS	12	6	18	8	12	7	19	R
Michael Schumacher	Ferrari F1-2000	3	1	3	1F	2	1	5	3	1	5	2	1F
Ralf Schumacher	Williams FW22-BMW	11	3	11	5	5	R	7	4	5	4	5	R
Jarno Trulli	Jordan EJ10-Mugen	6	R	12	4	8	15	11	6	7	12	6	R
Jos Verstappen	Arrows A21-Supertec	13	R	14	7	16	14	8	R	11	R	13	R
Jacques Villeneuve	BAR 02-Honda	8	4	10	R	9	5	10	16	6	R	9	R
Alexander Wurz	Benetton B200-Playlife	14	7	13	R	11	9	20	9	18	10	14	12
Ricardo Zonta	BAR 02-Honda	16	6	8	9	14	12	16	R	16	8	18	R

2000 FINAL CHAMPIONSHIP POSITIONS

Drivers

1	Michael Schumacher	108
2	Mika Hakkinen	89
3	David Coulthard	73
4	Rubens Barrichello	62
5	Ralf Schumacher	24
6	Giancarlo Fisichella	18
7	Jacques Villeneuve	17
8	Jenson Button	12
9	Heinz-Harald Frentzen	11
10=	Mika Salo	6
	Jarno Trulli	6
12	Jos Verstappen	5
13	Eddie Irvine	4
14	Ricardo Zonta	3
15=	Pedro de la Rosa	2
	Alexander Wurz	2

Manufacturers

1	Ferrari	170
2	McLaren-Mercedes-Benz*	152
3	Williams-BMW	36
4=	Benetton-Playlife	20
	BAR-Honda	20
6	Jordan-Mugen	17
7	Arrows-Supertec	7
8	Sauber-Petronas Ferrari	6
9	Jaguar-Cosworth	4

*McLaren were deducted Mika Hakkinen's manufacturer's points from the Austrian Grand Prix for a technical infringement

Hakkinen, 1m25.595. Leaders: M Schumacher, laps 1-39, 43-53; Hakkinen, 40-42

SAP UNITED STATES GRAND PRIX

24 September 2000. Indianapolis. 73 laps of a 2.607-mile circuit = 190.311 miles. Cool, damp and overcast at the start, drying. World Championship round 15

1	Michael Schumacher	Ferrari F1-2000	73	1h36m30.883
2	Rubens Barrichello	Ferrari F1-2000	73	1h36m43.001
3	Heinz-Harald Frentzen	Jordan EJ10-Mugen	73	1h36m48.251
4	Jacques Villeneuve	BAR 02-Honda	73	1h36m48.819
5	David Coulthard	McLaren MP4/15-Mercedes-Benz	73	1h36m59.696
6	Ricardo Zonta	BAR 02-Honda	73	1h37m22.577

Winner's average speed: 118.310 mph. Starting grid front row: M Schumacher, 1m14.266 (pole) and Coulthard, 1m14.392. Fastest lap: Coulthard, 1m14.711. Leaders: Coulthard, laps 1-6; M Schumacher, 7-73

FUJI TELEVISION JAPANESE GRAND PRIX

8 October 2000. Suzuka. 53 laps of a 3.641-mile circuit = 192.973 miles. Cool and overcast at the start, light rain later. World Championship round 16

1	Michael Schumacher	Ferrari F1-2000	53	1h29m53.435
2	Mika Hakkinen	McLaren MP4/15-Mercedes-Benz	53	1h29m55.272
3	David Coulthard	McLaren MP4/15-Mercedes-Benz	53	1h31m03.349
4	Rubens Barrichello	Ferrari F1-2000	53	1h31m12.626
5	Jenson Button	Williams FW22-BMW	53	1h31m19.129
6	Jacques Villeneuve	BAR 02-Honda		

Winner's average speed: 128.805 mph. Starting grid front row: M Schumacher, 1m35.825 (pole) and Hakkinen, 1m35.834. Fastest lap: Hakkinen, 1m39.189. Leaders: Hakkinen, laps 1-21, 25-36; M Schumacher, 22-23, 37-53; Coulthard, 24

PETRONAS MALAYSIAN GRAND PRIX

22 October 2000. Sepang. 56 laps of a 3.444-mile circuit = 192.864 miles. Hot, humid and sunny. World Championship round 17

1	Michael Schumacher	Ferrari F1-2000	56	1h35m54.235
2	David Coulthard	McLaren MP4/15-Mercedes-Benz	56	1h35m54.967
3	Rubens Barrichello	Ferrari F1-2000	56	1h36m12.679
4	Mika Hakkinen	McLaren MP4/15-Mercedes-Benz	56	1h36m29.504

MC		CDN		F		A		D		H		B		I		USA		J		MAL	
Q	R	Q	R	Q	R	Q	R	Q	R	Q	R	Q	R	Q	R	Q	R	Q	R	Q	R
7	R	17	R	18	14	17	R	20	R	14	R	17	R	19	12	20	R	17	R	18	11
6	2	3	2	3	3	3	3	18	1F	5	4	10	RF	2	R	4	2	4	4	4	3
-	-	-	-	-	-	21	11	-	-	-	-	-	-	-	-	-	-	-	-	-	-
14	R	18	11	10	8	18	5	16	4	8	9	3	5	12	R	6	R	5	5	16	R
3	1	2	7	2	1F	2	2F	1	3	2	3	5	4	5	R	2	5F	3	3	3	2
19	R	19	10	15	11	11	9	19	R	13	R	15	11	16	8	9	8	20	11	20	R
8	3	10	3	14	9	8	R	3	R	7	R	11	R	9	11	15	R	12	14	13	9
4	10	5	R	8	7	15	R	17	R	6	6	8	6	8	R	7	3	8	R	10	R
21	R	20	16	21	15	20	8	22	R	21	15	21	14	21	9	22	12	21	R	21	R
5	6F	4	4F	4	2	1	1	4	2	3	1F	1	1	3	2F	3	R	2	2F	2	4F
18	8	21	R	16	12	13	R	13	12	19	R	14	R	20	R	16	9	16	R	19	R
11	9	11	R	11	R	16	7	8	R	17	R	9	8	18	R	19	11	10	7	12	R
10	4	16	13	6	13	NT	DNP	10	10	10	8	12	10	14	R	17	7	7	8	7	6
22	R	22	12	22	R	22	12	21	11	22	R	22	17	22	10	21	R	22	15	22	13
16	R	9	R	13	R	12	R	5	6	15	16	16	16	10	R	18	R	13	12	14	R
13	5	15	R	12	10	9	6	15	5	9	10	18	9	15	7	14	R	19	10	17	8
1	R	1	1	1	R	4	R	2	R	1	2	4	2	1	1	1	1	1	1	1	1
9	R	12	14	5	5	19	R	14	7	4	5	6	3	7	3	10	R	6	R	8	R
2	R	7	6	9	6	5	R	6	9	12	7	2	R	6	R	5	R	15	13	9	12
15	R	13	5	20	R	10	R	11	R	20	13	20	15	11	4	13	R	14	R	15	10
17	7	6	15	7	4	7	4	9	8	16	12	7	7	4	R	8	4	9	6	6	5
12	R	14	9	17	R	14	10	7	R	11	11	19	13	13	5	11	10	11	R	5	7
20	R	8	8	19	R	6	R	12	R	18	14	13	12	17	6	12	6	18	9	11	R

2001 Despite racing wheel-to-wheel with Michael Schumacher, and victory at Monza in his first year, Juan Pablo Montoya was unable to halt Ferrari in 2001.

5 Jacques Villeneuve   BAR 02-Honda   56   1h37m04.927
6 Eddie Irvine   Jaguar R1-Cosworth   56   1h37m06.803
Winner's average speed: 120.661 mph. Starting grid front row: M Schumacher, 1m37.397 (pole) and Hakkinen, 1m37.860. Fastest lap: Hakkinen, 1m38.543. Leaders: Hakkinen, laps 1-2; Coulthard, 3-17; M Schumacher, 18-24, 26-39, 42-56; Barrichello, 25, 40-41

2001

For the first time since joining Ferrari, Michael Schumacher was armed with the best car in the field. The result was a year in which he broke Alain Prost's long-standing record for grand prix wins and clinched a fourth World Championship in August. He also broke records for grand prix points scored during a season and over a career. Only Ayrton Senna's 65 pole positions and Juan Manuel Fangio's five world titles now prevented Schumacher from holding every F1 record.

David Coulthard led McLaren-Mercedes' effort by winning in Brazil and Austria, but the combination was increasingly unable to match Ferrari as the year progressed. Mika Hakkinen also won twice later in the season, but seemed strangely off the pace and announced

2001 DRIVERS' RECORDS

driver	car	AUS Q	AUS R	MAL Q	MAL R	BR Q	BR R	RSM Q	RSM R	E Q	E R	A Q	A R
Jean Alesi	Prost AP04-Acer Ferrari	14	9	13	9	15	8	14	9	15	10	20	10
	Jordan EJ11-Honda	-	-	-	-	-	-	-	-	-	-	-	-
Fernando Alonso	Minardi PS01-European Ford	19	12	21	13	19	R	18	R	18	13	18	R
Rubens Barrichello	Ferrari F2001	2	3	2	2	6	R	6	3	4	R	4	3
Enrique Bernoldi	Arrows A22-Asiatech	18	R	22	R	16	R	16	10	16	R	15	R
Luciano Burti	Jaguar R2-Cosworth	21	8	15	10	14	R	15	11	-	-	-	-
	Prost AP04-Acer Ferrari	-	-	-	-	-	-	-	-	14	11	17	11
Jensen Button	Benetton B201-Renault	16	14	17	11	20	10	21	12	21	15	21	R
David Coulthard	McLaren MP4/16-Mercedes-Benz	6	2	8	3	5	1	1	2	3	5	7	1F
Tomas Enge	Prost AP04-Acer Ferrari	-	-	-	-	-	-	-	-	-	-	-	-
Giancarlo Fisichella	Benetton B201-Renault	17	13	16	R	18	6	19	R	19	14	19	R
Heinz-Harald Frentzen	Jordan EJ11-Honda	4	5	9	4	8	11	9	6	8	R	11	R
	Prost AP04-Acer Ferrari	-	-	-	-	-	-	-	-	-	-	-	-
Mika Hakkinen	McLaren MP4/16-Mercedes-Benz	3	R	4	6F	3	R	2	4	2	9	8	R
Nick Heidfeld	Sauber C20-Petronas Ferrari	10	4	11	R	9	3	12	7	10	6	6	9
Eddie Irvine	Jaguar R2-Cosworth	12	11	12	R	13	R	13	R	13	R	13	7
Tarso Marques	Minardi PS01-European Ford	22	R	20	14	22	9	22	R	22	16	22	R
Gaston Mazzacane	Prost AP04-Acer Ferrari	20	R	19	12	21	R	20	R	-	-	-	-
Juan Pablo Montoya	Williams FW23-BMW	11	R	6	R	4	R	7	R	12	2	2	R
Olivier Panis	BAR 03-Honda	9	7	10	R	11	4	8	8	11	7	10	5
Kimi Raikkonen	Sauber C20-Petronas Ferrari	13	6	14	R	10	R	10	R	9	8	9	4
Pedro de la Rosa	Jaguar R2-Cosworth	-	-	-	-	-	-	-	-	20	R	14	R
Michael Schumacher	Ferrari F2001	1	1F	1	1	1	2	4	R	1	1F	1	2
Ralf Schumacher	Williams FW23-BMW	5	R	3	5	2	RF	3	1F	5	R	3	R
Jarno Trulli	Jordan EJ11-Honda	7	R	5	8	7	5	5	5	6	4	5	DSQ
Jos Verstappen	Arrows A22-Asiatech	15	R	18	7	17	R	17	R	17	12	16	6
Jacques Villeneuve	BAR 03-Honda	8	R	7	R	12	7	11	R	7	3	12	8
Alex Yoong	Minardi PS01-European Ford	-	-	-	-	-	-	-	-	-	-	-	-
Ricardo Zonta	Jordan EJ11-Honda	-	-	-	-	-	-	-	-	-	-	-	-

2001 FINAL CHAMPIONSHIP POSITIONS

Drivers						Manufacturers		
1	Michael Schumacher	123	12=	Heinz-Harald Frentzen	6	1	Ferrari	179
2	David Coulthard	65		Eddie Irvine	6	2	McLaren-Mercedes-Benz	102
3	Rubens Barrichello	56	14=	Jean Alesi	5	3	Williams-BMW	80
4	Ralf Schumacher	49		Olivier Panis	5	4	Sauber-Petronas Ferrari	21
5	Mika Hakkinen	37	16	Pedro de la Rosa	3	5	Jordan-Honda	19
6	Juan Pablo Montoya	31	17	Jenson Button	2	6	BAR-Honda	17
7=	Nick Heidfeld	12	18	Jos Verstappen	1	7	Benetton-Renault	10
	Jarno Trulli	12				8	Jaguar-Cosworth	9
	Jacques Villeneuve	12				9	Prost-Acer Ferrari	4
10	Kimi Raikkonen	9				10	Arrows-Asiatech	1
11	Giancarlo Fisichella	8						

he would take a year off in 2002.

A second challenge to Ferrari came from the increasingly competitive Williams-BMW. Ralf Schumacher scored the first of three victories for the team at Imola, their first win since 1997. New teammate Juan Pablo Montoya announced his arrival by passing Michael Schumacher in Brazil. Although he took time to adapt to F1, as the year ended Montoya was increasingly the team's quicker driver, having demonstrated his championship potential by winning at Monza.

To make way for the highly rated Montoya, Williams loaned Jenson Button to Benetton. But the change proved disastrous for the young Englishman. The team struggled while developing a revolutionary new Renault engine, and while Giancarlo Fisichella got the most out of the car, Button generally could not match his teammate's pace. This was Benetton's final season in F1,

with new owners Renault set to take over in 2002.

It was a good year for newcomers to F1: not only did Montoya win in his first season, but Minardi's Fernando Alonso and Sauber's Kimi Raikkonen both showed great promise. Raikkonen and Nick Heidfeld gave Sauber their best year in the category, and the young Finn signed to replace Hakkinen at McLaren for 2002.

Honda supplied both BAR and Jordan with works engines, prompting a battle for supremacy between the teams. Jordan emerged the winner two weeks after the season ended when Jarno Trulli, who had been disqualified for a technical infringement, was confirmed as finishing fourth in Indianapolis. Jordan had replaced a disappointing Heinz-Harald Frentzen with Jean Alesi midseason, but the Frenchman announced his retirement from F1 after he failed to earn an extension to his contract for 2002.

MC		CDN		EU		F		GB		D		H		B		I		USA		J	
Q	R	Q	R	Q	R	Q	R	Q	R	Q	R	Q	R	Q	R	Q	R	Q	R	Q	R
11	6	16	5	14	15	19	12	14	11	14	6	-	-	-	-	-	-	-	-	-	-
-	-	-	-	-	-	-	-	-	-	-	-	12	10	13	6	16	8	9	7	11	R
18	R	21	R	21	14	21	17	21	16	21	10	18	R	20	R	21	13	17	R	18	11
4	2	5	R	4	5	8	3	6	3	6	2	3	2	5	5	2	2	5	15	4	5
20	9	17	R	18	R	20	R	20	14	19	8	20	R	21	12	18	R	19	13	20	14
-	-	-	-	-	-	-	-	-	-	-	-	-	-	-	-	-	-	-	-	-	-
21	R	19	8	17	12	15	10	16	R	16	R	19	R	18	R	-	-	-	-	-	-
17	7	20	R	20	13	17	16	18	15	18	5	17	R	15	R	11	R	10	9	9	7
1	5F	3	R	5	3	3	4F	3	R	5	R	2	3	9	2	6	R	7	3	7	3
-	-	-	-	-	-	-	-	-	-	-	-	-	-	-	-	20	12	21	14	19	R
10	R	18	R	15	11	16	11	19	13	17	4	15	R	8	3	14	10	12	8	6	17
13	R	-	-	8	R	7	8	5	7	-	-	-	-	-	-	-	-	-	-	-	-
-	-	-	-	-	-	-	-	-	-	-	-	16	R	4	9	12	R	15	10	15	12
3	R	8	3	6	6	4	DNS	2	1F	3	R	6	5F	7	4	7	R	4	1	5	4
12	R	6	R	13	R	11	9	11	R	13	7	11	R	11	11	17	9	13	11	17	13
15	10	7	4	9	10	13	7	7	5	8	R	9	7	12	R	9	7	11	R	12	R
14	R	14	6	16	8	14	14	13	12	9	R	13	11	10	R	10	5	16	12	16	R
2	1	1	2	1	2	1	1	2	4	R	1	1	3	1F	3	4	1	2	1	1	1
5	R	2	1F	2	4	1	2	10	R	2	1	4	2	7	4	3F	2	R	3	3	6F
8	R	4	11	7	R	5	5	4	R	10	R	5	R	16	R	5	R	8	4	8	8
19	8	13	10	19	R	18	13	17	10	20	R	21	12	19	10	19	R	20	R	21	15
9	4	9	R	11	9	10	R	12	8	12	3	10	9	6	8	15	6	18	R	14	10
-	-	-	-	-	-	-	-	-	-	-	-	-	-	-	-	22	R	22	R	22	16
-	-	12	7	-	-	-	-	-	-	15	R	-	-	-	-	-	-	-	-	-	-

The dangers of the sport were brought sharply into focus by three accidents. Australian GP marshal Graham Beveridge was killed by debris from Villeneuve's car in an accident with Ralf Schumacher, and Prost's Luciano Burti was fortunate to survive frightening crashes at both Hockenheim and Spa.

QANTAS AUSTRALIAN GRAND PRIX

4 March 2001. Albert Park. 58 laps of a 3.295-mile circuit = 191.110 miles. Hot, dry and sunny. World Championship round 1

1	Michael Schumacher	Ferrari F2001	58	1h38m26.533
2	David Coulthard	McLaren MP4/16-Mercedes-Benz	58	1h38m28.251
3	Rubens Barrichello	Ferrari F2001	58	1h39m00.024
4	Nick Heidfeld	Sauber C20-Petronas Ferrari	58	1h39m38.012
5	Heinz-Harald Frentzen	Jordan EJ11-Honda	58	1h39m39.340
6	Kimi Raikkonen	Sauber C20-Petronas Ferrari	58	1h39m50.676

Winner's average speed: 116.481 mph. Starting grid front row: M Schumacher, 1m26.892 (pole) and Barrichello, 1m27.263. Fastest lap: M Schumacher, 1m28.214. Leaders: M Schumacher, laps 1-36, 41-58; Coulthard, 37-40.

PETRONAS MALAYSIAN GRAND PRIX

18 March 2001. Sepang. 55 laps of a 3.444-mile circuit = 189.420 miles. Hot, dry and sunny at the start, heavy rain later before drying. World Championship round 2

1	Michael Schumacher	Ferrari F2001	55	1h47m34.801
2	Rubens Barrichello	Ferrari F2001	55	1h47m58.461
3	David Coulthard	McLaren MP4/16-Mercedes-Benz	55	1h48m03.356
4	Heinz-Harald Frentzen	Jordan EJ11-Honda	55	1h48m21.344
5	Ralf Schumacher	Williams FW23-BMW	55	1h48m23.034
6	Mika Hakkinen	McLaren MP4/16-Mercedes-Benz	55	1h48m23.407

Winner's average speed: 105.644 mph. Starting grid front row: M Schumacher, 1m35.220 (pole) and Barrichello, 1m35.319. Fastest lap: Hakkinen, 1m40.962. Leaders: M Schumacher, laps 1-2, 16-55; Trulli, 3; Coulthard, 4-15.

GRANDE PREMIO MARLBORO DO BRASIL

1 April 2001. Interlagos. 71 laps of a 2.667-mile circuit = 189.357 miles. Hot, dry and sunny at the start, rain later. World Championship round 3

1	David Coulthard	McLaren MP4/16-Mercedes-Benz	71	1h39m00.834
2	Michael Schumacher	Ferrari F2001	71	1h39m16.998
3	Nick Heidfeld	Sauber C20-Petronas Ferrari	70	
4	Olivier Panis	BAR 03-Honda	70	
5	Jarno Trulli	Jordan EJ11-Honda	70	
6	Giancarlo Fisichella	Benetton B201-Renault	70	

Winner's average speed: 114.746 mph. Starting grid front row: M Schumacher, 1m13.780 (pole) and R Schumacher, 1m14.090. Fastest lap: R Schumacher, 1m15.693. Leaders: M Schumacher, laps 1-2, 48-49; Montoya, 3-38; Coulthard, 39-47, 50-71.

GRAN PREMIO WARSTEINER DI SAN MARINO

15 April 2001. Imola. 62 laps of a 3.064-mile circuit = 189.968 miles. Warm, dry and sunny. World Championship round 4

1	Ralf Schumacher	Williams FW23-BMW	62	1h30m44.817
2	David Coulthard	McLaren MP4/16-Mercedes-Benz	62	1h30m49.169
3	Rubens Barrichello	Ferrari F2001	62	1h31m19.583
4	Mika Hakkinen	McLaren MP4/16-Mercedes-Benz	62	1h31m21.132
5	Jarno Trulli	Jordan EJ11-Honda	62	1h32m10.375

6 Heinz-Harald Frentzen Jordan EJ11-Honda   61
Winner's average speed: 125.603 mph. Starting grid front row: Coulthard, 1m23.054 (pole) and Hakkinen, 1m23.282. Fastest lap: R Schumacher, 1m25.524. Leaders: R Schumacher, laps 1-62

GRAN PREMIO MARLBORO DE ESPANA

29 April 2001. Catalunya. 65 laps of a 2.937-mile circuit = 190.905 miles. Dry, windy and sunny. World Championship round 5

1 Michael Schumacher	Ferrari F2001	65	1h31m03.305
2 Juan Pablo Montoya	Williams FW23-BMW	65	1h31m44.042
3 Jacques Villeneuve	BAR 03-Honda	65	1h31m52.930
4 Jarno Trulli	Jordan EJ11-Honda	65	1h31m54.557
5 David Coulthard	McLaren MP4/16-Mercedes-Benz	65	1h31m54.920
6 Nick Heidfeld	Sauber C20-Petronas Ferrari	65	1h32m05.197

Winner's average speed: 125.795 mph. Starting grid front row: M Schumacher, 1m18.201 (pole) and Hakkinen, 1m18.286. Fastest lap: M Schumacher, 1m21.151. Leaders: M Schumacher, laps 1-22, 28-43, 65; Hakkinen, 23-27, 44-64

GROSSER A1 PREIS VON OSTERREICH

13 May 2001. A1 Ring. 71 laps of a 2.684-mile circuit = 190.564 miles. Warm, dry and sunny. World Championship round 6

1 David Coulthard	McLaren MP4/16-Mercedes-Benz	71	1h27m45.927
2 Michael Schumacher	Ferrari F2001	71	1h27m48.117
3 Rubens Barrichello	Ferrari F2001	71	1h27m48.454
4 Kimi Raikkonen	Sauber C20-Petronas Ferrari	71	1h28m27.520
5 Olivier Panis	BAR 03-Honda	71	1h28m39.702
6 Jos Verstappen	Arrows A22-Asiatech	70	

Winner's average speed: 130.277 mph. Starting grid front row: M Schumacher, 1m09.562 (pole) and Montoya, 1m09.686. Fastest lap: Coulthard, 1m10.843. Leaders: Montoya, laps 1-15; Barrichello, 16-46; Coulthard, 47-71

GRAND PRIX DE MONACO

27 May 2001. Monte Carlo. 78 laps of a 2.092-mile circuit = 163.176 miles. Hot, dry and sunny. World Championship round 7

1 Michael Schumacher	Ferrari F2001	78	1h47m22.561
2 Rubens Barrichello	Ferrari F2001	78	1h47m22.992
3 Eddie Irvine	Jaguar R2-Cosworth	78	1h47m53.259
4 Jacques Villeneuve	BAR 03-Honda	78	1h47m55.015
5 David Coulthard	McLaren MP4/16-Mercedes-Benz	77	
6 Jean Alesi	Prost AP04-Acer Ferrari	77	

Winner's average speed: 91.180 mph. Starting grid front row: Coulthard, 1m17.430 (pole) and M Schumacher, 1m17.631 - Coulthard started from the back of the grid. Fastest lap: Coulthard, 1m19.424. Leaders: M Schumacher, laps 1-54, 60-78; Barrichello, 55-59

GRAND PRIX AIR CANADA

10 June 2001. Montreal. 69 laps of a 2.747-mile circuit = 189.543 miles. Hot, dry and sunny. World Championship round 8

1 Ralf Schumacher	Williams FW23-BMW	69	1h34m31.522
2 Michael Schumacher	Ferrari F2001	69	1h34m51.757
3 Mika Hakkinen	McLaren MP4/16-Mercedes-Benz	69	1h35m12.194
4 Kimi Raikkonen	Sauber C20-Petronas Ferrari	69	1h35m39.638
5 Jean Alesi	Prost AP04-Acer Ferrari	69	1h35m41.957
6 Pedro de la Rosa	Jaguar R2-Cosworth	68	

Winner's average speed: 120.312 mph. Starting grid front row: M Schumacher, 1m15.782 (pole) and R Schumacher, 1m16.297. Fastest lap: R Schumacher, 1m17.205. Leaders: M Schumacher, laps 1-44; R Schumacher, 45-69

GROSSER WARSTEINER PREIS VON EUROPA

24 June 2001. Nurburgring. 67 laps of a 2.831-mile circuit = 189.677 miles. Hot, dry and sunny. World Championship round 9

1 Michael Schumacher	Ferrari F2001	67	1h29m42.724
2 Juan Pablo Montoya	Williams FW23-BMW	67	1h29m46.941
3 David Coulthard	McLaren MP4/16-Mercedes-Benz	67	1h30m07.717
4 Ralf Schumacher	Williams FW23-BMW	67	1h30m16.069
5 Rubens Barrichello	Ferrari F2001	67	1h30m28.219
6 Mika Hakkinen	McLaren MP4/16-Mercedes-Benz	67	1h30m47.592

Winner's average speed: 126.857 mph. Starting grid front row: M Schumacher, 1m14.960 (pole) and R Schumacher, 1m15.226. Fastest lap: Montoya, 1m18.354. Leaders: M Schumacher, laps 1-28, 30-67; Montoya, 29

GRAND PRIX MOBIL 1 DE FRANCE

1 July 2001. Magny-Cours. 72 laps of a 2.641-mile circuit = 190.152 miles. Hot, dry and sunny. World Championship round 10

1 Michael Schumacher	Ferrari F2001	72	1h33m35.636
2 Ralf Schumacher	Williams FW23-BMW	72	1h33m46.035
3 Rubens Barrichello	Ferrari F2001	72	1h33m52.017
4 David Coulthard	McLaren MP4/16-Mercedes-Benz	72	1h33m52.742
5 Jarno Trulli	Jordan EJ11-Honda	72	1h34m43.921
6 Nick Heidfeld	Sauber C20-Petronas Ferrari	71	

Winner's average speed: 121.900 mph. Starting grid front row: R Schumacher, 1m12.989 (pole) and M Schumacher, 1m12.999. Fastest lap: Coulthard, 1m16.088. Leaders: R Schumacher, laps 1-23; Coulthard, 26; Montoya, 27-30, 46-50; M Schumacher, 24-25, 31-45, 51-72

FOSTER'S BRITISH GRAND PRIX

15 July 2001. Silverstone. 60 laps of a 3.194-mile circuit = 191.640 miles. Warm, dry and cloudy. World Championship round 11

1 Mika Hakkinen	McLaren MP4/16-Mercedes-Benz	60	1h25m33.770
2 Michael Schumacher	Ferrari F2001	60	1h26m07.416
3 Rubens Barrichello	Ferrari F2001	60	1h26m33.051
4 Juan Pablo Montoya	Williams FW23-BMW	60	1h26m42.542
5 Kimi Raikkonen	Sauber C20-Petronas Ferrari	59	
6 Nick Heidfeld	Sauber C20-Petronas Ferrari	59	

Winner's average speed: 134.385 mph. Starting grid front row: M Schumacher, 1m20.447 (pole) and Hakkinen, 1m20.529. Fastest lap: Hakkinen, 1m23.405. Leaders: M Schumacher, laps 1-4; Hakkinen, 5-21, 25-60; Montoya, 22-24

GROSSER MOBIL 1 PREIS VON DEUTSCHLAND

29 July 2001. Hockenheim. 45 laps of a 4.239-mile circuit = 190.755 miles. Race stopped due to first-lap accident, restarted over original distance. Very hot, dry and sunny. World Championship round 12

1 Ralf Schumacher	Williams FW23-BMW	45	1h18m17.873
2 Rubens Barrichello	Ferrari F2001	45	1h19m03.990
3 Jacques Villeneuve	BAR 03-Honda	45	1h19m20.679
4 Giancarlo Fisichella	Benetton B201-Renault	45	1h19m21.350
5 Jenson Button	Benetton B201-Renault	45	1h19m23.327
6 Jean Alesi	Prost AP04-Acer Ferrari	45	1h19m23.823

Winner's average speed: 146.176 mph. Starting grid front row: Montoya, 1m38.117 (pole) and R Schumacher, 1m38.136. Fastest lap: Montoya, 1m41.808. Leaders: Montoya, laps 1-22; R Schumacher, 23-45

MARLBORO MAGYAR NAGYDIJ (HUNGARIAN GRAND PRIX)

19 August 2001. Hungaroring. 77 laps of a 2.465-mile circuit = 189.805 miles. Very hot, dry and sunny. World Championship round 13

1 Michael Schumacher	Ferrari F2001	77	1h41m49.675

2	Rubens Barrichello	Ferrari F2001	77	1h41m53.038
3	David Coulthard	McLaren MP4/16-		
		Mercedes-Benz	77	1h41m53.615
4	Ralf Schumacher	Williams FW23-BMW	77	1h42m39.362
5	Mika Hakkinen	McLaren MP4/16-		
		Mercedes-Benz	77	1h42m59.968
6	Nick Heidfeld	Sauber C20-		
		Petronas Ferrari	76	

Winner's average speed: 111.839 mph. Starting grid front row: M
Schumacher, 1m14.059 (pole) and Coulthard, 1m14.860. Fastest lap:
Hakkinen, 1m16.723. Leaders: M Schumacher, laps 1-28, 33-52, 55-77;
Barrichello, 29-30; Coulthard, 31-32, 53-54

FOSTER'S GRAND PRIX DE BELGIQUE

2 September 2001. Spa-Francorchamps. 36 laps of a 4.329-mile circuit =
155.844 miles. Race scheduled for 44 laps, start aborted twice due to
cars stalling on the grid, restarted race stopped due to accident after 4
laps and restarted as new race over 36 laps. Warm, dry and cloudy.
World Championship round 14

1	Michael Schumacher	Ferrari F2001	36	1h08m05.002
2	David Coulthard	McLaren MP4/16-		
		Mercedes-Benz	36	1h08m15.100
3	Giancarlo Fisichella	Benetton B201-Renault	36	1h08m32.744
4	Mika Hakkinen	McLaren MP4/16-		
		Mercedes-Benz	36	1h08m41.089
5	Rubens Barrichello	Ferrari F2001	36	1h08m59.523
6	Jean Alesi	Jordan EJ11-Honda	36	1h09m04.686

Winner's average speed: 137.341 mph. Starting grid front row: Montoya,
1m52.072 (pole) and R Schumacher, 1m52.959 - Montoya started from the
back of the grid. Fastest lap: M Schumacher, 1m49.758. Leaders: M
Schumacher, laps 1-36

GRAN PREMIO CAMPARI D'ITALIA

16 September 2001. Monza. 53 laps of a 3.599-mile circuit = 190.747
miles. Warm, dry and sunny. World Championship round 15

1	Juan Pablo Montoya	Williams FW23-BMW	53	1h16m58.493
2	Rubens Barrichello	Ferrari F2001	53	1h17m03.668
3	Ralf Schumacher	Williams FW23-BMW	53	1h17m15.828
4	Michael Schumacher	Ferrari F2001	53	1h17m23.484
5	Pedro de la Rosa	Jaguar R2-Cosworth	53	1h18m13.477
6	Jacques Villeneuve	BAR 03-Honda	53	1h18m20.962

Winner's average speed: 148.683 mph. Starting grid front row: Montoya,
1m22.216 (pole) and Barrichello, 1m22.528. Fastest lap: R Schumacher,
1m25.073. Leaders: Montoya, laps 1-8, 20-28, 42-53; Barrichello, 9-19, 36-
41; R Schumacher, 29-35

SAP UNITED STATES GRAND PRIX

30 September 2001. Indianapolis. 73 laps of a 2.607-mile circuit =
190.311 miles. Warm, dry and sunny. World Championship round 16

1	Mika Hakkinen	McLaren MP4/16-		
		Mercedes-Benz	73	1h32m42.840
2	Michael Schumacher	Ferrari F2001	73	1h32m53.886
3	David Coulthard	McLaren MP4/16-		
		Mercedes-Benz	73	1h32m54.883
4	Jarno Trulli	Jordan EJ11-Honda	73	1h33m40.263
5	Eddie Irvine	Jaguar R2-Cosworth	73	1h33m55.274
6	Nick Heidfeld	Sauber C20-		
		Petronas Ferrari	73	1h33m55.836

Winner's average speed: 123.160 mph. Starting grid front row: M
Schumacher, 1m11.708 (pole) and R Schumacher, 1m11.986 (Hakkinen,
1m11.945, originally qualified second but his fastest time was disqualified
due to a pit lane violation). Fastest lap: Montoya, 1m14.448. Leaders: M
Schumacher, laps 1-4, 27-33, 36-38; Barrichello, 5-26, 46-49; Montoya,
34-35; Hakkinen, 39-45, 50-73

FUJI TELEVISION JAPANESE GRAND PRIX

14 October 2001. Suzuka. 53 laps of a 3.641-mile circuit = 192.973 miles.
Warm, dry and sunny. World Championship round 17

1	Michael Schumacher	Ferrari F2001	53	1h27m33.298

2	Juan Pablo Montoya	Williams FW23-BMW	53	1h27m36.452
3	David Coulthard	McLaren MP4/16-		
		Mercedes-Benz	53	1h27m56.560
4	Mika Hakkinen	McLaren MP4/16-		
		Mercedes-Benz	53	1h28m08.837
5	Rubens Barrichello	Ferrari F2001	53	1h28m09.842
6	Ralf Schumacher	Williams FW23-BMW	53	1h28m10.420

Winner's average speed: 132.241 mph. Starting grid front row: M
Schumacher, 1m32.484 (pole) and Montoya, 1m33.184. Fastest lap: R
Schumacher, 1m36.944. Leaders: M Schumacher, laps 1-18, 24-36, 39-
53; Montoya, 19-21, 37-38; R Schumacher, 22-23

2002

Ferrari's stranglehold on Formula 1 tightened in a
season of increasing domination and yet more
records. Michael Schumacher equalled Juan Manuel
Fangio's long-standing record of five World
Championship victories, and by a wide margin. He finished every lap of the season, every race on the podium, and won eleven times—each a feat that establish-
es a new benchmark. Ferrari scored as many points
as the rest of the field combined.

Although the team started the year with the 2001 car,
it still dominated the Australian Grand Prix. Ferrari
introduced the F2002 after Schumacher could only finish third in Malaysia, his worst result of the year. The car
proved so dominant that Schumacher and teammate
Rubens Barrichello would only lose once more. But
Ferrari angered F1 fans and the establishment by
imposing team orders as early as the Austrian GP, when
it demanded that Barrichello relinquish the lead. This
race had been Barrichello's finest in F1: he outpaced
Schumacher in qualifying and again in the race before
pulling over after the last corner. Barrichello did win
four races later in the season, but the suspicion always
lingered that his teammate was paying him back for
Austria.

Following the promise of 2001, Williams-BMW
proved a major disappointment. Ralf Schumacher did
lead a one-two for the team in Malaysia but it was their
only win. Juan Pablo Montoya qualified on pole for seven
races. His last pole of the year at Monza set a new
record for a single Grand Prix qualifying lap, 161.423
mph, eclipsing the previous best set by Keke Rosberg at
Silverstone in 1985. But despite having the most powerful engine in Formula 1, the combination of the Williams
chassis and Michelin tyres did not have the pace over a
race distance to challenge Ferrari. Ferrari enjoyed being
the only leading team supplied tyres by Bridgestone,
while Williams shared Michelin with McLaren-
Mercedes.

David Coulthard held off Michael Schumacher at
Monaco to give McLaren their only win of the year, but
he could only finish fifth in the championship. Kimi
Raikkonen replaced countryman Mika Hakkinen, who
was on sabbatical, as Coulthard's teammate and
emerged as a true star of the future. He would have won
at Magny-Cours had he not run wide in a corner after
slipping on oil late in the race. That allowed
Schumacher by, and Raikonnen had to settle for second
place. Spectacular wheel-to-wheel dices with Montoya
at Hockenheim and Hungaroring further demonstrated
that Raikkonen has championship potential. Meanwhile,
at mid-season Hakkinen confirmed his expected retire-

ment from the sport.

Apart from these three teams only Eddie Irvine's improving Jaguar recorded a podium finish, a third at Monza. Jenson Button re-established himself with a series of points finishes and with Jarno Trulli earned Renault fourth place in the championship. In the first and last races of the season local drivers earned their place in the media spotlight. Minardi's Mark Webber and Jordan's Takuma Sato were ecstatic to finish fifth in Australia and Japan respectively.

Toyota made their long-awaited debut in the formula, and competition with the Honda-powered BAR and Jordan teams to be the top Japanese manufacturer became one of the year's sub-plots. Mika Salo finished sixth in two early races for Toyota, but both BAR and Jordan passed their rivals as the year progressed.

The effects of an uncertain world economy were felt in F1 with several teams struggling to find sufficient sponsorship. Prost went out of business before the season began and Arrows, financially hobbled, sat out the last five races.

QANTAS AUSTRALIAN GRAND PRIX

3 March 2002. Albert Park. 58 laps of a 3.295-mile circuit = 191.110 miles. Warm, dry and overcast. World Championship round 1

1	Michael Schumacher	Ferrari F2001	58	1h35m36.792
2	Juan Pablo Montoya	Williams FW24-BMW	58	1h35m55.419
3	Kimi Raikkonen	McLaren MP4/17-		
		Mercedes-Benz	58	1h36m01.858
4	Eddie Irvine	Jaguar R3-Cosworth	57	
5	Mark Webber	Minardi PS02-Asiatech	56	
6	Mika Salo	Toyota TF102	56	

Winner's average speed: 119.927 mph. Starting grid front row: Barrichello, 1m25.843 (pole) and M Schumacher, 1m25.848. Fastest lap: Raikkonen, 1m28.541. Leaders: Coulthard, laps 1-10; M Schumacher, 11, 17-58; Montoya, 12-16

PETRONAS MALAYSIAN GRAND PRIX

17 March 2002. Sepang. 56 laps of a 3.444-mile circuit = 192.864 miles. Very hot, dry and cloudy. World Championship round 2

1	Ralf Schumacher	Williams FW24-BMW	56	1h34m12.912
2	Juan Pablo Montoya	Williams FW24-BMW	56	1h34m52.611
3	Michael Schumacher	Ferrari F2001	56	1h35m14.706
4	Jenson Button	Renault R202	56	1h35m22.678
5	Nick Heidfeld	Sauber C21-		
		Petronas Ferrari	55	
6	Felipe Massa	Sauber C21-		
		Petronas Ferrari	55	

Winner's average speed: 122.823 mph. Starting grid front row: M Schumacher, 1m35.266 (pole) and Montoya, 1m35.497. Fastest lap: Montoya, 1m38.049. Leaders: Barrichello, laps 1-21, 32-35; R Schumacher, 22-31, 36-56

GRANDE PREMIO DO BRASIL

31 March 2002. Interlagos. 71 laps of a 2.667-mile circuit = 189.357 miles. Very hot, dry and sunny. World Championship round 3

1	Michael Schumacher	Ferrari F2002	71	1h31m43.663
2	Ralf Schumacher	Williams FW24-BMW	71	1h31m44.251
3	David Coulthard	McLaren MP4/17-		
		Mercedes-Benz	71	1h32m42.773
4	Jenson Button	Renault R202	71	1h32m50.546
5	Juan Pablo Montoya	Williams FW24-BMW	71	1h32m51.226
6	Mika Salo	Toyota TF102	70	

Winner's average speed: 123.860 mph. Starting grid front row: Montoya, 1m13.114 (pole) and M Schumacher, 1m13.241. Fastest lap: Montoya, 1m16.079. Leaders: M Schumacher, laps 1-13, 17-39, 45-71; Barrichello, 14-16; R Schumacher, 40-44

GRAN PREMIO DI SAN MARINO

14 April 2002. Imola. 62 laps of a 3.064-mile circuit = 189.968 miles. Warm, dry and cloudy. World Championship round 4

1	Michael Schumacher	Ferrari F2002	62	1h29m10.789
2	Rubens Barrichello	Ferrari F2002	62	1h29m28.696
3	Ralf Schumacher	Williams FW24-BMW	62	1h29m30.544
4	Juan Pablo Montoya	Williams FW24-BMW	62	1h29m55.514
5	Jenson Button	Renault R202	62	1h30m34.184
6	David Coulthard	McLaren MP4/17-		
		Mercedes-Benz	61	

Winner's average speed: 127.810 mph. Starting grid front row: M Schumacher, 1m21.091 (pole) and Barrichello, 1m21.155. Fastest lap: Barrichello, 1m24.170. Leaders: M Schumacher, laps 1-31, 33-46, 48-62; Barrichello, 32, 47

GRAN PREMIO MARLBORO DE ESPANA

28 April 2002. Catalunya. 65 laps of a 2.937-mile circuit = 190.905 miles. Warm, dry and cloudy. World Championship round 5

1	Michael Schumacher	Ferrari F2002	65	1h30m29.981
2	Juan Pablo Montoya	Williams FW24-BMW	65	1h31m05.610
3	David Coulthard	McLaren MP4/17-		
		Mercedes-Benz	65	1h31m12.604
4	Nick Heidfeld	Sauber C21-		
		Petronas Ferrari	65	1h31m36.677
5	Felipe Massa	Sauber C21-		
		Petronas Ferrari	65	1h31m48.954
6	Heinz-Harald Frentzen	Arrows A23-Cosworth	65	1h31m50.410

Winner's average speed: 126.567 mph. Starting grid front row: M Schumacher, 1m16.364 (pole) and Barrichello, 1m16.690 - Barrichello did not start. Fastest lap: M Schumacher, 1m20.355. Leaders: M Schumacher, laps 1-65

GROSSER A1 PREIS VON OSTERREICH

12 May 2002. A1 Ring. 71 laps of a 2.684-mile circuit = 190.564 miles. Warm, dry and overcast. World Championship round 6

1	Michael Schumacher	Ferrari F2002	71	1h33m51.562
2	Rubens Barrichello	Ferrari F2002	71	1h33m51.744
3	Juan Pablo Montoya	Williams FW24-BMW	71	1h34m09.292
4	Ralf Schumacher	Williams FW24-BMW	71	1h34m10.010
5	Giancarlo Fisichella	Jordan EJ12-Honda	71	1h34m41.527
6	David Coulthard	McLaren MP4/17-		
		Mercedes-Benz	71	1h34m42.234

Winner's average speed: 121.819 mph. Starting grid front row: Barrichello, 1m08.082 (pole) and R Schumacher, 1m08.364. Fastest lap: M Schumacher, 1m09.298. Leaders: Barrichello, laps 1-61, 63-70; M Schumacher, 62, 71

GRAND PRIX DE MONACO

26 May 2002. Monte Carlo. 78 laps of a 2.092-mile circuit = 163.176 miles. Warm, dry and sunny. World Championship round 7

1	David Coulthard	McLaren MP4/17-		
		Mercedes-Benz	78	1h45m39.055
2	Michael Schumacher	Ferrari F2002	78	1h45m40.104
3	Ralf Schumacher	Williams FW24-BMW	78	1h46m56.504
4	Jarno Trulli	Renault R202	77	
5	Giancarlo Fisichella	Jordan EJ12-Honda	77	
6	Heinz-Harald Frentzen	Arrows A23-Cosworth	77	

Winner's average speed: 92.669 mph. Starting grid front row: Montoya, 1m16.676 (pole) and Coulthard, 1m17.068. Fastest lap: Barrichello, 1m18.023. Leaders: Coulthard, laps 1-78

GRAND PRIX AIR CANADA

9 June 2002. Montreal. 70 laps of a 2.703-mile circuit = 189.210 miles. Hot, dry and overcast. World Championship round 8

1	Michael Schumacher	Ferrari F2002	70	1h33m36.111
2	David Coulthard	McLaren MP4/17-		
		Mercedes-Benz	70	1h33m37.243

3 Rubens Barrichello	Ferrari F2002	70	1h33m43.193
4 Kimi Raikkonen	McLaren MP4/17-		
	Mercedes-Benz	70	1h34m13.674
5 Giancarlo Fisichella	Jordan EJ12-Honda	70	1h34m18.923
6 Jarno Trulli	Renault R202	70	1h34m25.059

Winner's average speed: 121.286 mph. Starting grid front row: Montoya, 1m12.836 (pole) and M Schumacher, 1m13.018. Fastest lap: Montoya, 1m15.960. Leaders: Barrichello, laps 1-25; M Schumacher, 26-37, 51-70; Montoya, 38-50

GROSSER ALLIANZ PREIS VON EUROPA

23 June 2002. Nurburgring. 60 laps of a 3.196-mile circuit = 191.760 miles. Warm, dry and overcast. World Championship round 9

1 Rubens Barrichello	Ferrari F2002	60	1h35m07.426
2 Michael Schumacher	Ferrari F2002	60	1h35m07.720
3 Kimi Raikkonen	McLaren MP4/17-		
	Mercedes-Benz	60	1h35m53.861
4 Ralf Schumacher	Williams FW24-BMW	60	1h36m14.389
5 Jenson Button	Renault R202	60	1h36m24.370
6 Felipe Massa	Sauber C21-		
	Petronas Ferrari	59	

Winner's average speed: 120.954 mph. Starting grid front row: Montoya, 1m29.906 (pole) and R Schumacher, 1m29.915. Fastest lap: M Schumacher, 1m32.226. Leaders: Barrichello, laps 1-60

FOSTER'S BRITISH GRAND PRIX

7 July 2002. Silverstone. 60 laps of a 3.194-mile circuit = 191.640 miles. Warm, dry and overcast at the start, rain later before drying again. World Championship round 10

1 Michael Schumacher	Ferrari F2002	60	1h31m45.015
2 Rubens Barrichello	Ferrari F2002	60	1h31m59.593
3 Juan Pablo Montoya	Williams FW24-BMW	60	1h32m16.676
4 Jacques Villeneuve	BAR 04-Honda	59	
5 Olivier Panis	BAR 04-Honda	59	
6 Nick Heidfeld	Sauber C21-		
	Petronas Ferrari	59	

Winner's average speed: 125.323 mph. Starting grid front row: Montoya, 1m18.998 (pole) and Barrichello, 1m19.032. Fastest lap: Barrichello, 1m23.083. Leaders: Montoya, laps 1-15; M Schumacher, 16-60

MOBIL 1 GRAND PRIX DE FRANCE

21 July 2002. Magny-Cours. 72 laps of a 2.641-mile circuit = 190.152 miles. Hot, dry and cloudy. World Championship round 11

1 Michael Schumacher	Ferrari F2002	72	1h32m09.837
2 Kimi Raikkonen	McLaren MP4/17-		
	Mercedes-Benz	72	1h32m10.941
3 David Coulthard	McLaren MP4/17-		
	Mercedes-Benz	72	1h32m41.812
4 Juan Pablo Montoya	Williams FW24-BMW	72	1h32m50.512
5 Ralf Schumacher	Williams FW24-BMW	72	1h32m51.609
6 Jenson Button	Renault R202	71	

Winner's average speed: 123.792 mph. Starting grid front row: Montoya, 1m11.985 (pole) and M Schumacher, 1m12.008. Fastest lap: Coulthard, 1m15.045. Leaders: Montoya, laps 1-23, 36-42; M Schumacher, 24-25, 29-35, 68-72; Raikkonen, 26, 43-49, 55-67; Coulthard, 27-28, 50-54

GROSSER MOBIL 1 PREIS VON DEUTSCHLAND

28 July 2002. Hockenheim. 67 laps of a 2.842-mile circuit = 190.414 miles. Hot, dry and sunny. World Championship round 12

1 Michael Schumacher	Ferrari F2002	67	1h27m52.078
2 Juan Pablo Montoya	Williams FW24-BMW	67	1h28m02.581
3 Ralf Schumacher	Williams FW24-BMW	67	1h28m06.544
4 Rubens Barrichello	Ferrari F2002	67	1h28m15.273
5 David Coulthard	McLaren MP4/17-		
	Mercedes-Benz	66	
6 Nick Heidfeld	Sauber C21-		
	Petronas Ferrari	66	

Winner's average speed: 130.023 mph. Starting grid front row: M Schumacher, 1m14.389 (pole) and R Schumacher, 1m14.570. Fastest lap:

M Schumacher, 1m16.462. Leaders: M Schumacher, laps 1-26, 31-47, 49-67; R Schumacher, 27-29, 48; Montoya, 30

MARLBORO MAGYAR NAGYDIJ (HUNGARIAN GRAND PRIX)

18 August 2002. Hungaroring. 77 laps of a 2.465-mile circuit = 189.805 miles. Very hot, dry and sunny. World Championship round 13

1 Rubens Barrichello	Ferrari F2002	77	1h41m49.001
2 Michael Schumacher	Ferrari F2002	77	1h41m49.435
3 Ralf Schumacher	Williams FW24-BMW	77	1h42m02.357
4 Kimi Raikkonen	McLaren MP4/17-		
	Mercedes-Benz	77	1h42m18.480
5 David Coulthard	McLaren MP4/17-		
	Mercedes-Benz	77	1h42m26.801
6 Giancarlo Fisichella	Jordan EJ12-Honda	77	1h42m57.805

Winner's average speed: 111.851 mph. Starting grid front row: Barrichello, 1m13.333 (pole) and M Schumacher, 1m13.392. Fastest lap: M Schumacher, 1m16.207. Leaders: Barrichello, laps 1-32, 34-77; R Schumacher, 33

FOSTER'S GRAND PRIX DE BELGIQUE

1 September 2002. Spa-Francorchamps. 44 laps of a 4.316-mile circuit = 189.904 miles. Cool, dry and sunny. World Championship round 14

1 Michael Schumacher	Ferrari F2002	44	1h21m20.634
2 Rubens Barrichello	Ferrari F2002	44	1h21m22.611
3 Juan Pablo Montoya	Williams FW24-BMW	44	1h21m39.079
4 David Coulthard	McLaren MP4/17-		
	Mercedes-Benz	44	1h21m39.992
5 Ralf Schumacher	Williams FW24-BMW	44	1h22m17.074
6 Eddie Irvine	Jaguar R3B-Cosworth	44	1h22m38.004

Winner's average speed: 140.075 mph. Starting grid front row: M Schumacher, 1m43.726 (pole) and Raikkonen, 1m44.150. Fastest lap: M Schumacher, 1m47.176. Leaders: M Schumacher, laps 1-16, 18-44; Barrichello, 17

GRAN PREMIO VODAFONE D'ITALIA

15 September 2002. Monza. 53 laps of a 3.599-mile circuit = 190.747 miles. Hot, dry and sunny. World Championship round 15

1 Rubens Barrichello	Ferrari F2002	53	1h16m19.982
2 Michael Schumacher	Ferrari F2002	53	1h16m20.237
3 Eddie Irvine	Jaguar R3B-Cosworth	53	1h17m12.561
4 Jarno Trulli	Renault R202	53	1h17m18.201
5 Jenson Button	Renault R202	53	1h17m27.752
6 Olivier Panis	BAR 04-Honda	53	1h17m28.473

Winner's average speed: 149.933 mph. Starting grid front row: Montoya, 1m20.264 (pole) and M Schumacher, 1m20.521. Fastest lap: Barrichello, 1m23.657. Leaders: R Schumacher, laps 1-3; Montoya, 4; Barrichello, 5-19, 29-53; M Schumacher, 20-28

2002 Michael Schumacher and Rubens Barrichello enjoyed a record-breaking season, and first and second in the championship.

Formula 1

2002 DRIVERS' RECORDS

driver	car	AUS Q	AUS R	MAL Q	MAL R	BR Q	BR R	RSM Q	RSM R	E Q	E R	A Q	A R	MC Q	MC R
Rubens Barrichello	Ferrari F2001	1	R	3	R	8	R	-	-	-	-	-	-	-	-
	Ferrari F2002	-	-	-	-	-	-	2	2F	2	DNS	1	2	5	7F
Enrique Bernoldi	Arrows A23-Cosworth	17	DSQ	16	R	21	R	20	R	14	R	12	R	15	12
Jenson Button	Renault R202	11	R	8	4	7	4	9	5	6	12	13	7	8	R
David Coulthard	McLaren MP4/17-Mercedes-Benz	4	R	6	R	4	3	6	6	7	3	8	6	2	1
Anthony Davidson	Minardi PS02-Asiatech	-	-	-	-	-	-	-	-	-	-	-	-	-	-
Giancarlo Fisichella	Jordan EJ12-Honda	8	R	9	13	14	R	15	R	12	R	15	5	11	5
Heinz-Harald Frentzen	Arrows A23-Cosworth	15	DSQ	11	11	18	R	13	R	10	6	11	11	12	6
	Sauber C21-Petronas Ferrari	-	-	-	-	-	-	-	-	-	-	-	-	-	-
Nick Heidfeld	Sauber C21-Petronas Ferrari	10	R	7	5	9	R	7	10	8	4	5	R	17	8
Eddie Irvine	Jaguar R3-Cosworth	19	4	20	R	13	7	18	R	22	R	20	R	21	9
	Jaguar R3B-Cosworth	-	-	-	-	-	-	-	-	-	-	-	-	-	-
Felipe Massa	Sauber C21-Petronas Ferrari	9	R	14	6	12	R	11	8	11	5	7	R	13	R
Allan McNish	Toyota TF102	16	R	19	7	16	R	17	R	19	8	14	9	10	R
Juan Pablo Montoya	Williams FW24-BMW	6	2	2	2F	1	5F	4	4	4	2	4	3	1	R
Olivier Panis	BAR 04-Honda	12	R	18	R	17	R	12	R	13	R	9	R	18	R
Kimi Raikkonen	McLaren MP4/17-Mercedes-Benz	5	3F	5	R	5	12	5	R	5	R	6	R	6	R
Pedro de la Rosa	Jaguar R3-Cosworth	20	8	17	10	11	8	21	R	16	R	19	R	20	10
	Jaguar R3B-Cosworth	-	-	-	-	-	-	-	-	-	-	-	-	-	-
Mika Salo	Toyota TF102	14	6	10	12	10	6	16	R	17	9	10	8	9	R
Takuma Sato	Jordan EJ12-Honda	22	R	15	9	19	9	14	R	18	R	18	R	16	R
Michael Schumacher	Ferrari F2001	2	1	1	3	-	-	-	-	-	-	-	-	-	-
	Ferrari F2002	-	-	-	-	2	1	1	1	1	1F	3	1F	3	2
Ralf Schumacher	Williams FW24-BMW	3	R	4	1	3	2	3	3	3	11	2	4	4	3
Jarno Trulli	Renault R202	7	R	12	R	6	R	8	9	9	10	16	R	7	4
Jacques Villeneuve	BAR 04-Honda	13	R	13	8	15	10	10	7	15	7	17	10	14	R
Mark Webber	Minardi PS02-Asiatech	18	5	21	R	20	11	19	11	20	DNS	21	12	19	11
Alex Yoong	Minardi PS02-Asiatech	21	7	22	R	22	13	22	DNQ	21	DNS	22	R	22	R

2002 FINAL CHAMPIONSHIP POSITIONS

Drivers

	Driver	Points
1	Michael Schumacher	144
2	Rubens Barrichello	77
3	Juan Pablo Montoya	50
4	Ralf Schumacher	42
5	David Coulthard	41
6	Kimi Raikkonen	24
7	Jenson Button	14
8	Jarno Trulli	9
9	Eddie Irvine	8
10=	Giancarlo Fisichella	7
	Nick Heidfeld	7
12=	Felipe Massa	4
	Jacques Villeneuve	4
14	Olivier Panis	3
15=	Heinz-Harald Frentzen	2
	Mika Salo	2
	Takuma Sato	2
	Mark Webber	2

Manufacturers

	Manufacturer	Points
1	Ferrari	221
2	Williams-BMW	92
3	McLaren-Mercedes-Benz	65
4	Renault	23
5	Sauber-Petronas Ferrari	11
6	Jordan-Honda	9
7	Jaguar-Cosworth	8
8	BAR-Honda	7
9=	Arrows-Cosworth	2
	Minardi-Asiatech	2
	Toyota	2

SAP UNITED STATES GRAND PRIX

29 September 2002. Indianapolis. 73 laps of a 2.607-mile circuit = 190.311 miles. Warm, dry and sunny. World Championship round 16

1	Rubens Barrichello	Ferrari F2002	73	1h31m07.934
2	Michael Schumacher	Ferrari F2002	73	1h31m07.945
3	David Coulthard	McLaren MP4/17-Mercedes-Benz	73	1h31m15.733
4	Juan Pablo Montoya	Williams FW24-BMW	73	1h31m17.845
5	Jarno Trulli	Renault R202	73	1h32m04.781
6	Jacques Villeneuve	BAR 04-Honda	73	1h32m06.146

Winner's average speed: 125.298 mph. Starting grid front row: M Schumacher, 1m10.790 (pole) and Barrichello, 1m11.058. Fastest lap: Barrichello, 1m12.738. Leaders: M Schumacher, laps 1-26, 29-48, 51-72; Barrichello, 27-28, 49-50, 73

FUJI TELEVISION JAPANESE GRAND PRIX

13 October 2002. Suzuka. 53 laps of a 3.617-mile circuit = 191.701 miles. Hot, dry and sunny. World Championship round 17

1	Michael Schumacher	Ferrari F2002	53	1h26m59.698
2	Rubens Barrichello	Ferrari F2002	53	1h27m00.205
3	Kimi Raikkonen	McLaren MP4/17-Mercedes-Benz	53	1h27m22.990
4	Juan Pablo Montoya	Williams FW24-BMW	53	1h27m35.973
5	Takuma Sato	Jordan EJ12-Honda	53	1h28m22.392
6	Jenson Button	Renault R202	52	

Winner's average speed: 132.215 mph. Starting grid front row: M Schumacher, 1m31.317 (pole) and Barrichello, 1m31.749. Fastest lap: M Schumacher, 1m36.125. Leaders: M Schumacher, laps 1-20, 22-53; Barrichello, 21

CDN		EU		GB		F		D		H		B		I		USA		J	
Q	R	Q	R	Q	R	Q	R	Q	R	Q	R	Q	R	Q	R	Q	R	Q	R
-	-	-	-	-	-	-	-	-	-	-	-	-	-	-	-	-	-	-	-
3	3	4	1	2	2F	3	DNS	3	4	1	1	3	2	4	1F	2	1F	2	2
17	R	21	10	18	R	21	DNQ	18	R	-	-	NT	DNP	-	-	-	-	-	-
13	15	8	5	12	12	7	6	13	R	9	R	10	R	17	5	14	8	10	6
8	2	5	R	6	10	6	3F	9	5	10	5	6	4	7	7	3	3	3	R
-	-	-	-	-	-	-	-	-	-	20	R	20	R	-	-	-	-	-	-
6	5	18	R	17	7	NT	DNP	6	R	5	6	14	R	12	8	9	7	8	R
19	13	15	13	16	R	20	DNQ	15	R	-	-	NT	DNP	-	-	-	-	-	-
-	-	-	-	-	-	-	-	-	-	-	-	-	-	-	-	11	13	-	-
7	12	9	7	10	6	10	7	10	6	8	9	18	10	15	10	10	9	12	7
14	R	17	R	-	-	-	-	-	-	-	-	-	-	-	-	-	-	-	-
-	-	-	-	19	R	9	R	16	R	16	R	8	6	5	3	13	10	14	9
12	9	11	6	11	9	12	R	14	7	7	7	17	R	14	R	-	-	15	R
20	R	13	14	15	R	17	11	17	R	18	14	13	9	13	R	16	15	18	DNS
1	RF	1	R	1	3	1	4	4	2	4	11	5	3	1	R	4	4	6	4
11	8	12	9	13	5	11	R	7	R	12	12	15	12	16	6	12	12	16	R
5	4	6	3	5	R	4	2	5	R	11	4	2	R	6	R	6	R	4	3
16	R	16	11	-	-	-	-	-	-	-	-	-	-	-	-	-	-	-	-
-	-	-	-	21	11	15	9	20	R	15	13	11	R	8	R	17	R	17	R
18	R	10	R	8	R	16	R	19	9	17	15	9	7	10	11	19	14	13	8
15	10	14	16	14	R	14	R	12	8	14	10	16	11	18	12	15	11	7	5
-	-	-	-	-	-	-	-	-	-	-	-	-	-	-	-	-	-	-	-
2	1	3	2F	3	1	2	1	1	1F	2	2F	1	1F	2	2	1	2	1	1F
4	7	2	4	4	8	5	5	2	3	3	3	4	5	3	R	5	16	5	11
10	6	7	8	7	R	8	R	8	R	6	8	7	R	11	4	8	5	11	R
9	R	19	12	9	4	13	R	11	R	13	R	12	8	9	9	7	6	9	R
21	11	20	15	20	R	18	8	21	R	19	16	19	R	19	R	18	R	19	10
22	14	22	R	22	DNQ	19	10	22	DNQ	-	-	-	-	20	13	20	R	20	R

2002 Rubens Barrichello pips World Champion Michael Schumacher to the line in a staged finish to the United States GP.

MANUFACTURERS A-Z

Note: On a number of occasions a constructor has changed its name in deference to a major sponsor. In this section they can be found listed under their original names unless the team was sold AND there was a major change of personnel. For example, when its sponsor Benetton bought Toleman, owner Ted Toleman left the organisation just as the Stewart family moved aside when the team developed into Jaguar. In these cases separate entries have been included for Toleman and Benetton, Stewart and Jaguar. Conversely Arrows/Footwork and March/Leyton House are found under Arrows and March respectively as they reverted to their original names when the commercial arrangement had finished.

Note: the drivers listed in this section are ranked by the number of wins achieved for that constructor, followed by points and then starts if equal.

AFM

Alex von Falkenhausen Motorenbau

Grand Prix Debut:	1952 Swiss GP	Stuck (retired)
Last Grand Prix:	1953 Italian GP	Stuck (14th)
Principal:	Alex von Falkenhausen	
Base:	Munich	

WORLD CHAMPIONSHIP RECORD

Starts:	4	
Best result:	14th	1953 Italian GP (Stuck)
Best qualifying:	14th	1952 Swiss GP (Stuck)

AFM GRAND PRIX DRIVERS

Driver	Nat	Start (DNS/DNQ)	1st	2nd	3rd	4th	5th	6th	PP	FL	Points
Hans Stuck	D	3	-	-	-	-	-	-	-	-	-
Gunther Bechem	D	1	-	-	-	-	-	-	-	-	-
Theo Fitzau	D	1	-	-	-	-	-	-	-	-	-
Willi Heeks	D	1	-	-	-	-	-	-	-	-	-
Helmut Niedermayr	D	1	-	-	-	-	-	-	-	-	-
Ludwig Fischer	D	- (1)	-	-	-	-	-	-	-	-	-
Willi Krakau	D	- (1)	-	-	-	-	-	-	-	-	-

AFM GRAND PRIX CARS

Type	Year	Engine	Designer
1	1952	BMW 328 S6	Alex von Falkenhausen
2	1953	BMW 328 S6	Alex von Falkenhausen
4	1952	Kuchen V8	Alex von Falkenhausen
6	1952	BMW 328 S6	Alex von Falkenhausen
7	1952	BMW 328 S6	Alex von Falkenhausen
8	1952	BMW 328 S6	Alex von Falkenhausen

AGS

Automobiles Gonfaronaise Sportive

Grand Prix Debut:	1986 Italian GP	Capelli (retired)
Last Grand Prix:	1991 Monaco GP	Tarquini (retired)
Principal:	Henri Julien, 1970-89; Cyril de Rouvre, 1989-91 when AGS applied for receivership; Gabriele Rafanelli and Patrizio Cantu, bought assets in 1991	
Base:	Gonfaron, 1970-89; Le Luc-en-Provence, 1990-91	

WORLD CHAMPIONSHIP RECORD

Starts:	47	
Points:	2	
Best result:	6th	1987 Australian GP (Moreno), 1989 Mexican GP (Tarquini)
Best qualifying:	10th	1988 Canadian GP (Streiff)

Best World Championship position:		
Drivers:	19th in 1987 (Moreno)	
Constructors:	11th in 1987	

MAJOR SPONSORS

1986-87	El Charro
1988	Bouygues
1989	Faure
1990	Ted Lapidus

AGS GRAND PRIX DRIVERS

Driver	Nat	Start (DNS/DNQ)	1st	2nd	3rd	4th	5th	6th	PP	FL	Points
Gabriele Tarquini	I	13 (31)	-	-	-	-	-	1	-	-	1
Roberto Moreno	BR	2	-	-	-	-	-	1	-	-	1
Philippe Streiff	F	15 (1)	-	-	-	-	-	-	-	-	-
Pascal Fabre	F	11 (3)	-	-	-	-	-	-	-	-	-
Yannick Dalmas	F	5 (20)	-	-	-	-	-	-	-	-	-
Ivan Capelli	I	2	-	-	-	-	-	-	-	-	-
Fabrizio Barbazza	I	- (12)	-	-	-	-	-	-	-	-	-
Joachim Winkelhock	D	- (7)	-	-	-	-	-	-	-	-	-
Stefan Johansson	S	- (2)	-	-	-	-	-	-	-	-	-
Olivier Grouillard	F	- (1)	-	-	-	-	-	-	-	-	-

AGS GRAND PRIX CARS

Type	Year	Engine	Designer
JH21C	1986	Motori Moderni V6 tc	Christian Vanderpleyn
JH22	1987	Ford DFZ V8	Christian Vanderpleyn
JH23	1988	Ford DFZ V8	Christian Vanderpleyn
JH23B	1989	Ford DFR V8	Christian Vanderpleyn
JH24	1989	Ford DFR V8	Claude Galopin
JH25	1990	Ford DFR V8	Michel Costa
JH25B	1991	Ford DFR V8	Michel Costa/ Christian Vanderpleyn
JH26	1991	Ford DFR V8	Michel Costa
Never built due to lack of finance			
JH27	1991	Ford DFR V8	Mario Tollentino

Alfa Romeo

Grand Prix Debut:	1950 British GP	Farina (1st), Fagioli (2nd), Parnell (3rd), Fangio (retired)
Last Grand Prix:	1985 Australian GP	Patrese (retired), Cheever (retired)
Base:	Portello, near Milan	
Works teams:	Alfa Corse prior to 1963; Autodelta, 1963-82; Euroracing, 1983-85 (Autodelta continued to manufacturer chassis, engines and gearboxes)	
Team Principal:	Autodelta: Carlo Chiti, 1979-84; Giovanni Tonti, 1984-85 Euroracing: Paolo Pavenello	

WORLD CHAMPIONSHIP RECORD

Starts:	112	
Points:	214	
Wins:	10	1950 British GP (Farina), Monaco GP (Fangio), Swiss GP (Farina), Belgian GP (Fangio), French GP (Fangio), Italian GP (Farina), 1951 Swiss GP (Fangio), Belgian GP

Pole positions:	12	(Farina), French GP (Fagioli/Fangio) and Spanish GP (Fangio) 1950 British GP (Farina), Monaco GP (Fangio), Swiss GP (Fangio), Belgian GP (Farina), French GP (Fangio), Italian GP (Fangio), 1951 Swiss GP (Fangio), Belgian GP (Fangio), French GP (Fangio), Italian GP (Fangio), 1980 United States GP (Giacomelli), 1982 Long Beach GP (de Cesaris)
Fastest laps:	14	1950 British GP (Farina), Monaco GP (Fangio), Swiss GP (Farina), Belgian GP (Farina), French GP (Fangio), Italian GP (Fangio), 1951 Swiss GP (Fangio), Belgian GP (Fangio), French GP (Fangio), British GP (Farina), German GP (Fangio), Italian GP (Farina), Spanish GP (Fangio), 1983 Belgian GP (de Cesaris)
Laps/miles in the lead:		701.6 laps/2978 miles
World Champions:		
Drivers:		Twice - 1950 (Farina) and 1951 (Fangio)

Best World Championship position:
Constructors: 6th in 1983

ALFA ROMEO GRAND PRIX DRIVERS

Driver	Nat	Start (DNS/DNQ)	1st	2nd	3rd	4th	5th	6th	PP	FL	Points
Juan Manuel Fangio	RA	13	6	2	-	-	-	-	8	8	64
Giuseppe Farina	I	13	4	-	3	1	1	-	2	5	52
Luigi Fagioli	I	7	1	4	1	-	-	-	-	-	32
Andrea de Cesaris	I	32 (1)	-	2	1	1	-	1	1	1	20
Bruno Giacomelli	I	49 (1)	-	-	1	1	3	-	1	-	13
Riccardo Patrese	I	32	-	-	1	1	-	1	-	-	8
Felice Bonetto	I	4	-	-	1	1	1	-	-	-	7
Reg Parnell	GB	1	-	-	1	-	-	-	-	-	4
Eddie Cheever	USA	31 (1)	-	-	-	1	-	-	-	-	3
Mario Andretti	USA	15	-	-	-	1	-	-	-	-	3
Mauro Baldi	I	15	-	-	-	1	1	-	-	-	3
Consalvo Sanesi	I	5	-	-	-	1	-	1	-	-	3
Emanuel de Graffenried	CH	3	-	-	-	-	1	1	-	-	2
Patrick Depailler	F	8	-	-	-	-	-	-	-	-	-
Vittorio Brambilla	I	4 (1)	-	-	-	-	-	-	-	-	-
Piet de Klerk	ZA	2	-	-	-	-	-	-	-	-	-
Paul Pietsch	D	1	-	-	-	-	-	-	-	-	-
Piero Taruffi	I	1	-	-	-	-	-	-	-	-	-

ALFA ROMEO GRAND PRIX CARS

Type	Year	Engine	Designer
158	1950*	Alfa Romeo S8 sc	Gioacchino Colombo
159	1950	Alfa Romeo S8 sc	Gioacchino Colombo
Alfa Special	1963	Alfa Romeo Giulietta S4	Piet de Klerk
A private "special" built by de Klerk for South African racing			
177	1979	Alfa Romeo 115-12 F12	Carlo Chiti
179	1979	Alfa Romeo 1260 V12	Carlo Chiti/ Robert Choulet
179B	1980	Alfa Romeo 1260 V12	Carlo Chiti/ Robert Choulet
179C	1981	Alfa Romeo 1260 V12	Carlo Chiti/ Robert Choulet
179D	1982	Alfa Romeo 1260 V12	Carlo Chiti/ Robert Choulet
182	1982	Alfa Romeo 1260 V12	Gerard Ducarouge
183T	1983	Alfa Romeo 890T V8 tc	Gerard Ducarouge
184T	1984	Alfa Romeo 890T V8 tc	Luigi Marmiroli/ Mario Tollentino/ Bruno Zava
184TB	1985	Alfa Romeo 890T V8 tc	Luigi Marmiroli/ Mario Tollentino/ Bruno Zava
185T	1985	Alfa Romeo 890T V8 tc	John Gentry

*Championship debut, the 158 first raced in 1938

Alta

Grand Prix Debut:	1950 British GP	Kelly (not classified), Crossley (retired)
Last Grand Prix:	1952 British GP	G Whitehead (12th)
Principal:	Geoffrey Taylor	
Base:	Tolworth, near Kingston-upon-Thames	

WORLD CHAMPIONSHIP RECORD

Starts:	5	
Best result:	9th	1950 Belgian GP (Crossley)
Best qualifying:	12th	1950 Belgian GP (Crossley), 1952 British GP (G Whitehead)

ALTA GRAND PRIX DRIVERS

Driver	Nat	Start (DNS/DNQ)	1st	2nd	3rd	4th	5th	6th	PP	FL	Points
Geoffrey Crossley	GB	2	-	-	-	-	-	-	-	-	-
Joe Kelly	IRL	2	-	-	-	-	-	-	-	-	-
Graham Whitehead	GB	1	-	-	-	-	-	-	-	-	-
Peter Whitehead	GB	1	-	-	-	-	-	-	-	-	-

ALTA GRAND PRIX CARS

Type	Year	Engine	Designer
GP	1950*	Alta GP S4 sc	Geoffrey Taylor
F2	1952	Alta F2 S4	Geoffrey Taylor

*Championship debut, the GP first raced in 1948

Amon

Only Grand Prix:	1974 Spanish GP	Amon (retired)
Principals:	Chris Amon and John Dalton	
Base:	Reading	

WORLD CHAMPIONSHIP RECORD

Starts:	1	
Best result:	No finishes	
Best qualifying:	20th	1974 Monaco GP (Amon) - did not start

AMON GRAND PRIX DRIVERS

Driver	Nat	Start (DNS/DNQ)	1st	2nd	3rd	4th	5th	6th	PP	FL	Points
Chris Amon	NZ	1 (3)	-	-	-	-	-	-	-	-	-
Larry Perkins	AUS	- (1)	-	-	-	-	-	-	-	-	-

AMON GRAND PRIX CARS

Type	Year	Engine	Designer
AF101	1974	Ford DFV V8	Gordon Fowell

Andrea Moda

Bought Coloni in 1991 and ran Coloni C4Bs until the Simtek-built Andrea Moda S192 was ready; also see Coloni and Simtek

Only Grand Prix:	1992 Monaco GP	Moreno (retired)
Principal:	Andrea Sassetti	
Base:	Constructor: Banbury (GB); Team: Perugia (I)	

WORLD CHAMPIONSHIP RECORD

Starts:	1	
Best result:	No finishes	
Best qualifying:	26th	1992 Monaco GP (Moreno)

ANDREA MODA GRAND PRIX DRIVERS

Driver	Nat	Start (DNS/DNQ)	1st	2nd	3rd	4th	5th	6th	PP	FL	Points
Roberto Moreno	BR	1 (9)	-	-	-	-	-	-	-	-	-
Perry McCarthy	GB	- (10)	-	-	-	-	-	-	-	-	-
Enrico Bertaggia	I	- (1)	-	-	-	-	-	-	-	-	-
Alex Caffi	I	- (1)	-	-	-	-	-	-	-	-	-

ANDREA MODA GRAND PRIX CARS

Type	Year	Engine	Designer
S192	1992	Judd GV V10	Nick Wirth

Arrows

Cars were officially named after major sponsor/shareholder Footwork from 1991-96

Grand Prix Debut:	1978 Brazilian GP	Patrese (10th)
Last Grand Prix:	2002 German GP	Bernoldi (retired), Frentzen (retired)
Principals:	Jackie Oliver, 1978-90; Watara Ohasi/Footwork and Jackie Oliver, 1991-96; Tom Walkinshaw, 1996-2002. Arrows founded by Franco Ambrosio, Alan Rees, Oliver, Dave Wass and Tony Southgate	
Base:	Milton Keynes, 1978-96; Leafield, 1996-2002	

WORLD CHAMPIONSHIP RECORD

Starts:	382	
Points:	167	
Best result:	2nd	1978 Swedish GP (Patrese), 1980 Long Beach GP (Patrese), 1981 San Marino GP (Patrese), 1985 San Marino GP (Boutsen), 1997 Hungarian GP (Hill)
Pole positions:	1	1981 Long Beach GP (Patrese)
Fastest laps:	1	1980 Monaco GP (Patrese)
Laps/miles in the lead:	127.5 laps/308 miles	

Best World Championship position:

Drivers:	7th in 1988 (Warwick)
Constructors:	4th in 1988

MAJOR SPONSORS

1978	Varig, Warsteiner
1979-80	Warsteiner
1981	Ragno, Beta
1982	Ragno
1984-85	Barclay
1986	Barclay, USF&G
1987-89	USF&G
1990-93	Footwork
1994	Uliveto, Tecnotest
1995	Unimat, Hype
1996	Power Horse, Philips, Hype
1997-98	Danka, Parmalat
1999	Repsol, T-minus, Baan
2000	Orange, Repsol YPF, Eurobet, Chello
2001	Orange, Eurobet, Chello, Red Bull
2002	Orange, Red Bull

ARROWS GRAND PRIX DRIVERS

Driver	Nat	Start (DNS/DNQ)	1st	2nd	3rd	4th	5th	6th	PP	FL	Points
Derek Warwick	GB	63	-	-	-	5	5	6	-	-	31
Riccardo Patrese	I	57 (1)	-	3	1	1	1	3	1	1	30
Eddie Cheever	USA	46 (2)	-	-	2	2	1	4	-	-	20
Thierry Boutsen	B	57 (1)	-	1	-	1	2	3	-	-	16
Marc Surer	CH	47 (1)	-	-	-	-	2	4	-	-	8

Driver	Nat	Start	1st	2nd	3rd	4th	5th	6th	PP	FL	Points
Gianni Morbidelli	I	26	-	-	1	-	1	2	-	-	8
Jos Verstappen	NL	50	-	-	-	1	1	2	-	-	7
Jochen Mass	D	24 (4)	-	-	-	1	-	4	-	-	7
Damon Hill	GB	16 (1)	-	1	-	-	-	1	-	-	7
Michele Alboreto	I	38 (9)	-	-	-	2	2	-	-	-	6
Christian Fittipaldi	BR	16	-	-	-	2	-	-	-	-	6
Pedro Diniz	BR	33	-	-	-	-	2	1	-	-	5
Pedro de la Rosa	E	33	-	-	-	-	-	3	-	-	3
Gerhard Berger	A	16	-	-	-	1	1	-	-	-	3
Mika Salo	SF	16	-	-	-	1	-	-	-	-	3
Alex Caffi	I	13 (8)	-	-	-	1	-	-	-	-	2
Mauro Baldi	I	11 (4)	-	-	-	-	2	-	-	-	2
Heinz-Harald Frentzen	D	11 (2)	-	-	-	-	2	-	-	-	2
Christian Danner	D	10	-	-	-	-	-	1	-	-	1
Aguri Suzuki	J	30 (2)	-	-	-	-	-	-	-	-	-
Enrique Bernoldi	BR	28 (2)	-	-	-	-	-	-	-	-	-
Taki Inoue	J	17	-	-	-	-	-	-	-	-	-
Ricardo Rosset	BR	16	-	-	-	-	-	-	-	-	-
Toranosuke Takagi	J	16	-	-	-	-	-	-	-	-	-
Siegfried Stohr	I	9 (4)	-	-	-	-	-	-	-	-	-
Rolf Stommelen	D	9 (3)	-	-	-	-	-	-	-	-	-
Massimiliano Papis	I	7	-	-	-	-	-	-	-	-	-
Chico Serra	BR	4	-	-	-	-	-	-	-	-	-
Stefan Johansson	S	1 (3)	-	-	-	-	-	-	-	-	-
Brian Henton	GB	1 (2)	-	-	-	-	-	-	-	-	-
Bernd Schneider	D	1 (1)	-	-	-	-	-	-	-	-	-
Alan Jones	AUS	1	-	-	-	-	-	-	-	-	-
Martin Donnelly	GB	1	-	-	-	-	-	-	-	-	-
Jacques Villeneuve sr	CDN	- (2)	-	-	-	-	-	-	-	-	-
Manfred Winkelhock	D	- (1)	-	-	-	-	-	-	-	-	-
Mike Thackwell	NZ	- (1)	-	-	-	-	-	-	-	-	-
Patrick Tambay	F	- (1)	-	-	-	-	-	-	-	-	-

ARROWS GRAND PRIX CARS

Type	Year	Engine	Designer
FA1	1978	Ford DFV V8	Tony Southgate/Dave Wass
London High Court ruled that the FA1 was an illegal copy of the Shadow DN9			
A1	1978	Ford DFV V8	Tony Southgate/Dave Wass
A2	1979	Ford DFV V8	Tony Southgate/Dave Wass
A3	1980	Ford DFV V8	Tony Southgate/Dave Wass
A4	1982	Ford DFV V8	Dave Wass
A5	1982	Ford DFV V8	Dave Wass
A6	1983	Ford DFV V8	Dave Wass
A7	1984	BMW M12/13 S4 tc	Dave Wass
A8	1985	BMW M12/13 S4 tc	Dave Wass
A9	1986	BMW M12/13 S4 tc	Dave Wass
A10	1987	Megatron BMW M12/13 S4 tc	Ross Brawn
A10B	1988	Megatron BMW M12/13 S4 tc	Ross Brawn
A11	1989	Ford DFR V8	Ross Brawn/James Robinson
A11B	1990	Ford DFR V8	Alan Jenkins/James Robinson/Ross Brawn
A11C*	1991	Porsche V12	Alan Jenkins
FA12*	1991	Porsche V12, Ford DFR V8	Alan Jenkins
FA13*	1992	Mugen MF-351H V10	Alan Jenkins
FA13B*	1993	Mugen MF-351H V10	Alan Jenkins
FA14*	1993	Mugen MF-351HB V10	Alan Jenkins
FA15*	1994	Ford HB V8	Alan Jenkins
FA16*	1995	Hart 830 V8	Alan Jenkins
FA17*	1996	Hart 830 V8	Alan Jenkins
A18	1997	Yamaha OX11A V10	Frank Dernie

Type	Year	Engine	Designer
A19	1998	Arrows V10	John Barnard
A20	1999	Arrows V10	Mike Coughlan
A21	2000	Mecachrome FB02 V10	Mike Coughlan/Eghbal Hamidy
A22	2001	Asiatech 001 V10	Mike Coughlan
A23	2002	Cosworth CR3 V10	Mike Coughlan

*Footwork

Aston-Butterworth

Grand Prix Debut:	1952 Belgian GP Montgomerie-Charrington (retired)
Last Grand Prix:	1952 German GP Aston (retired)
Principal:	Bill Aston
Base:	Frimley, Surrey

WORLD CHAMPIONSHIP RECORD

Starts:	2	
Best result:	No finishes	
Best qualifying:	15th	1952 Belgian GP (Montgomerie-Charrington)

ASTON-BUTTERWORTH GRAND PRIX DRIVERS

Driver	Nat	Start (DNS/DNQ)	1st	2nd	3rd	4th	5th	6th	PP	FL	Points
Bill Aston	GB	1 (2)	-	-	-	-	-	-	-	-	-
Robin Montgomerie-Charrington	USA	1	-	-	-	-	-	-	-	-	-

ASTON-BUTTERWORTH GRAND PRIX CARS

Type	Year	Engine	Designer
NB41	1952	Butterworth F4	Bill Aston

Aston Martin

Grand Prix Debut:	1959 Dutch GP	Shelby (retired), Salvadori (retired)
Last Grand Prix:	1960 British GP	Trintignant (11th), Salvadori (retired)
Principal:	David Brown	
Base:	Feltham	

WORLD CHAMPIONSHIP RECORD

Starts:	5	
Best result:	6th	1959 British GP (Salvadori), Portuguese GP (Salvadori)
Best qualifying:	2th	1959 British GP (Salvadori)

ASTON MARTIN GRAND PRIX DRIVERS

Driver	Nat	Start (DNS/DNQ)	1st	2nd	3rd	4th	5th	6th	PP	FL	Points
Roy Salvadori	GB	5 (1)	-	-	-	-	-	2	-	-	-
Carroll Shelby	USA	4	-	-	-	-	-	-	-	-	-
Maurice Trintignant	F	1	-	-	-	-	-	-	-	-	-

ASTON MARTIN GRAND PRIX CARS

Type	Year	Engine	Designer
DBR4/250	1959	Aston Martin DBR4 S6	Ted Cutting
DBR5/250	1960	Aston Martin DBR4 S6	Ted Cutting

ATS

ATS Wheels

Grand Prix Debut:	1978 Argentinian GP Mass (11th), Jarier (12th)
Last Grand Prix:	1984 Portuguese GP Berger (13th)
Principal:	Hans-Gunther Schmidt

Base:	Bicester (GB)

WORLD CHAMPIONSHIP RECORD

Starts:	89	
Points:	7	
Best result:	5th	1979 United States GP (Stuck), 1982 Brazilian GP (Winkelhock), San Marino GP (Salazar)
Best qualifying:	4th	1980 Long Beach GP (Lammers)

Best World Championship position:

Drivers:	18th in 1981 (Borgudd)
Constructors:	11th in 1979

ATS WHEELS GRAND PRIX DRIVERS

Driver	Nat	Start (DNS/DNQ)	1st	2nd	3rd	4th	5th	6th	PP	FL	Points
Manfred Winkelhock	D	38 (7)	-	-	-	-	1	-	-	-	2
Eliseo Salazar	RCH	13 (3)	-	-	-	-	1	-	-	-	2
Hans-Joachim Stuck	D	12 (3)	-	-	-	-	1	-	-	-	2
Slim Borgudd	S	7 (5)	-	-	-	-	-	1	-	1	1
Jochen Mass	D	10 (3)	-	-	-	-	-	-	-	-	-
Marc Surer	CH	9 (2)	-	-	-	-	-	-	-	-	-
Jan Lammers	NL	5 (5)	-	-	-	-	-	-	-	-	-
Keke Rosberg	SF	5	-	-	-	-	-	-	-	-	-
Gerhard Berger	A	4	-	-	-	-	-	-	1*	-	-
Jean-Pierre Jarier	F	3 (3)	-	-	-	-	-	-	-	-	-
Michael Bleekemolen	NL	1 (3)	-	-	-	-	-	-	-	-	-
Alberto Colombo	I	- (2)	-	-	-	-	-	-	-	-	-
Harald Ertl	A	- (2)	-	-	-	-	-	-	-	-	-
Hans Binder	A	- (1)	-	-	-	-	-	-	-	-	-

*not entered in World Championship so ineligible for points

ATS WHEELS GRAND PRIX CARS

Type	Year	Engine	Designer
HS1	1978	Ford DFV V8	Geoff Ferris/Robin Herd/John Gentry

Based on the Ferris-designed Penske PC4, modified by Herd and Gentry

Type	Year	Engine	Designer
D1	1978	Ford DFV V8	John Gentry
D2	1979	Ford DFV V8	John Gentry/Giacomo Caliri
D3	1979	Ford DFV V8	Nigel Stroud
D4	1980	Ford DFV V8	Gustav Brunner/Tim Wardrop
HGS1	1981	Ford DFV V8	Herve Guilpin/Tim Wardrop
D5	1982	Ford DFV V8	Herve Guilpin/Don Halliday
Modified HGS1			
D6	1983	BMW M12/13 S4 tc	Gustav Brunner
D7	1984	BMW M12/13 S4 tc	Gustav Brunner

ATS

Automobili Turismo e Sport

Grand Prix Debut:	1963 Belgian GP	P Hill (retired), Baghetti (retired)
Last Grand Prix:	1964 Italian GP	Cabral (retired)
Principals:	Carlo Chiti and Romolo Tavoni	
Base:	Bologna	

WORLD CHAMPIONSHIP RECORD

Starts:	6	
Best result:	11th	1963 Italian GP (P Hill)
Best qualifying:	13th	1963 Dutch GP (P Hill)

AUTOMOBILI TURISMO E SPORT GRAND PRIX DRIVERS

Driver	Nat	Start (DNS/DNQ)	1st	2nd	3rd	4th	5th	6th	PP	FL	Points
Giancarlo Baghetti	I	5	-	-	-	-	-	-			
Phil Hill	USA	5	-	-	-	-	-	-			
Mario Araujo de Cabral	P	1	-	-	-	-	-	-			

AUTOMOBILI TURISMO E SPORT GRAND PRIX CARS

Type	Year	Engine	Designer
100	1963	ATS V8	Carlo Chiti

BAR
British American Racing

Grand Prix Debut: 1999 Australian GP   Villeneuve (retired), Zonta (retired)
Latest Grand Prix: 2002 Japanese GP   Panis (retired), Villeneuve (retired)
Principal: Craig Pollock, 1999-2001; David Richards, 2002 to date
Base: Brackley, Northamptonshire

WORLD CHAMPIONSHIP RECORD

Starts: 67
Points: 44
Best result: 3rd   2001 Spanish GP (Villeneuve), German GP (Villeneuve)
Best qualifying: 4th   2000 Italian GP (Villeneuve)

Best World Championship position:
Drivers: 7th in 2000 (Villeneuve)
Constructors: 4th in 2000

MAJOR SPONSORS

1999	Lucky Strike, 555
2000 to date	Lucky Strike

BAR GRAND PRIX DRIVERS

Driver	Nat	Starts (DNS/DNQ)	1st	2nd	3rd	4th	5th	6th	PP	FL	Points
Jacques Villeneuve	CDN	67	-	-	2	6	2	3	-	-	33
Olivier Panis	F	34	-	-	-	1	2	1	-	-	8
Ricardo Zonta	BR	29 (1)	-	-	-	-	-	3	-	-	3
Mika Salo	SF	3	-	-	-	-	-	-	-	-	-

BAR GRAND PRIX CARS

Type	Year	Engine	Designer
01	1999	Supertec FB01 V10	Malcolm Oastler
02	2000	Honda RA001E V10	Malcolm Oastler
03	2001	Honda RA001E V10	Malcolm Oastler
04	2002	Honda RA002E V10	Malcolm Oastler

Bellasi

Grand Prix Debut: 1970 Austrian GP   Moser (retired)
Last Grand Prix: 1971 Italian GP   Moser (retired)
Principal: Vittorio Bellasi

WORLD CHAMPIONSHIP RECORD

Starts: 2
Best result: No finishes
Best qualifying: 21st   1970 French GP (Moser) - did not qualify. 1971 Italian GP Moser qualified 22nd but started

BELLASI GRAND PRIX DRIVERS

Driver	Nat	Starts (DNS/DNQ)	1st	2nd	3rd	4th	5th	6th	PP	FL	Points
Silvio Moser	CH	2 (4)	-	-	-	-	-	-	-	-	-

BELLASI GRAND PRIX CARS

Type	Year	Engine	Designer
F170	1970	Ford DFV V8	Vittorio Bellasi

Benetton
Bought Toleman in 1986, bought by Renault in 2000, renamed Renault for 2002 season; also see Toleman and Renault

Grand Prix Debut: 1986 Brazilian GP   Berger (6th), Fabi (10th)
Last Grand Prix: 2001 Japanese GP   Button (7th), Fisichella (retired)
Principal: Peter Collins, 1986-89; Flavio Briatore, 1990-97; David Richards, 1997-98; Rocco Benetton, 1999-2000; Briatore 2000-2001
Base: Witney, 1986-92; Enstone 1992-2001

WORLD CHAMPIONSHIP RECORD

Starts: 260
Points: 861.5
Wins: 27   1986 Mexican GP (Berger), 1989 Japanese GP (Nannini),.1990 Japanese GP (Piquet), Australian GP (Piquet), 1991 Canadian GP (Piquet), 1992 Belgian GP (Schumacher), 1993 Portuguese GP (Schumacher), 1994 Brazilian GP (Schumacher), Pacific GP (Schumacher), San Marino GP (Schumacher), Monaco GP (Schumacher), Canadian GP (Schumacher), French GP (Schumacher), Hungarian GP (Schumacher), European GP (Schumacher), 1995 Brazilian GP (Schumacher), Spanish GP (Schumacher), Monaco GP (Schumacher), French GP (Schumacher), British GP (Herbert), German GP (Schumacher), Belgian GP (Schumacher), Italian GP (Herbert), European GP (Schumacher), Pacific GP (Schumacher), Japanese GP (Schumacher), 1997 German GP (Berger)

Pole positions: 15   1986 Austrian GP (Fabi), Italian GP (Fabi), 1994 Monaco GP (Schumacher), Spanish GP (Schumacher), Canadian GP (Schumacher), Hungarian GP (Schumacher), European GP (Schumacher), Japanese GP (Schumacher), 1995 San Marino GP (Schumacher), Spanish GP (Schumacher), Canadian GP (Schumacher), Japanese GP (Schumacher), 1997 German GP (Berger), Italian GP (Alesi), 1998 Austrian GP (Fisichella)

Fastest laps: 36   1986 German GP (Berger), Austrian GP (Berger), Italian GP (Fabi), 1987 San Marino GP (Fabi), 1988 German GP (Nannini), 1990 San Marino GP (Nannini), 1991 Belgian GP (Moreno), 1992 Belgian GP (Schumacher), Australian GP (Schumacher), 1993 Brazilian GP (Schumacher), Spanish GP (Schumacher), Canadian GP (Schumacher), French GP (Schumacher), German GP (Schumacher), 1994 Brazilian GP (Schumacher), Pacific GP (Schumacher), Monaco GP (Schumacher), Spanish GP (Schumacher), Canadian GP (Schumacher), Hungarian GP (Schumacher), European GP (Schumacher), Australian GP (Schumacher), 1995 Brazilian GP (Schumacher), Argentinian GP (Schumacher), Canadian GP (Schumacher), French GP (Schumacher), German GP (Schumacher), European GP (Schumacher), Pacific GP (Schumacher), Japanese GP (Schumacher), 1996 Argentinian GP (Alesi), Monaco GP (Alesi), Belgian

GP (Berger), 1997 Argentinian GP (Berger), German GP (Berger), 1998 Argentinian GP (Wurz)

Laps/miles in the lead: 1504 laps/4385 miles

World Champions

Drivers: Twice - 1994 (Schumacher) and 1995 (Schumacher)
Constructors: Once - 1995

MAJOR SPONSORS

1986-90	Benetton
1991-93	Camel, Benetton
1994	Mild Seven, Benetton
1995	Mild Seven, Bitburger, Benetton
1996	Mild Seven, Hype, Kingfisher, Benetton
1997-98	Mild Seven, Korean Air, FedEx, Benetton
1999	Mild Seven, Korean Air, Benetton
2000	Mild Seven, Korean Air, Marconi, Benetton
2001	Mild Seven, Marconi, Elf, D2

BENETTON GRAND PRIX DRIVERS

Driver	Nat	Starts	1st	2nd	3rd	4th	5th	6th	PP	FL	Points
		(DNS/DNQ)									
Michael Schumacher	D	68	19	11	8	3	2	2	10	23	303
Nelson Piquet	BR	32	3	1	3	3	7	3	-	-	70.5
Gerhard Berger	A	46	2	2	2	6	1	6	1	5	65
Johnny Herbert	GB	24 (1)	2	1	1	5	2	1	-	-	50
Alessandro Nannini	I	46	1	2	6	4	2	4	-	2	65
Jean Alesi	F	33	-	8	5	2	3	3	1	2	83
Giancarlo Fisichella	I	66	-	4	3	2	5	3	1	-	55
Thierry Boutsen	B	32	-	-	6	3	4	2	-	-	43
Martin Brundle	GB	16	-	1	4	4	2	-	-	-	38
Alexander Wurz	A	52	-	-	1	5	3	1	-	1	26
Riccardo Patrese	I	16	-	1	1	1	3	1	-	-	20
Teo Fabi	I	32	-	-	1	1	3	1	2	2	14
Roberto Moreno	BR	13	-	1	-	2	1	-	-	1	14
Jos Verstappen	NL	10	-	-	2	-	1	-	-	-	10
Jenson Button	GB	17	-	-	-	-	1	-	-	-	2
Emanuele Pirro	I	10	-	-	-	-	1	-	-	-	2
JJ Lehto	SF	6	-	-	-	-	-	1	-	-	1

BENETTON GRAND PRIX CARS

Type	Year	Engine	Designer
B186	1986	BMW M12/13 S4 tc	Rory Byrne
B187	1987	Ford TEC V6 tc	Rory Byrne
B188	1988	Ford DFR V8	Rory Byrne
B189	1989	Ford HB V8	Rory Byrne
B189B	1990	Ford HB V8	Rory Byrne
B190	1990	Ford HB V8	Rory Byrne/John Barnard
B190B	1991	Ford HB V8	Rory Byrne/John Barnard
B191	1991	Ford HB V8	John Barnard/Gordon Kimball/Ross Brawn/Rory Byrne
B191B	1992	Ford HB V8	John Barnard/Gordon Kimball/Ross Brawn/Rory Byrne
B192	1992	Ford HB V8	Ross Brawn
B193	1993	Ford HB V8	Ross Brawn
B193B	1993	Ford HB V8	Ross Brawn
B194	1994	Ford Zetec-R V8	Ross Brawn
B195	1995	Renault RS7 V10	Ross Brawn
B196	1996	Renault RS8 V10	Ross Brawn
B197	1997	Renault RS9 V10	Pat Symonds/Nick Wirth
B198	1998	Playlife GC37/01 V10*	Pat Symonds/Nick Wirth
B199	1999	Playlife FB01 V10*	Pat Symonds/Nick Wirth
B200	2000	Playlife FB02 V10*	Pat Symonds/Tim Densham
B201	2001	Renault RS21 V10	Mike Gascoyne/Pat Symonds/Tim Densham

*manufactured by Mecachrome

BMW

Bayerische Motoren Werke

Grand Prix Debut:	1952 German GP	Balsa (retired), Bechem (retired)	
Last Grand Prix:	1953 German GP	Krause (14th)	
Base:	Munich		

WORLD CHAMPIONSHIP RECORD

Starts: 2
Best result: 14th 1953 German GP (Krause)
Best qualifying: 26th 1953 German GP (Krause)

BMW GRAND PRIX DRIVERS

Driver	Nat	Starts	1st	2nd	3rd	4th	5th	6th	PP	FL	Points
		(DNS/DNQ)									
Marcel Balsa	F	1	-	-	-	-	-	-	-	-	-
Gunther Bechem	D	1	-	-	-	-	-	-	-	-	-
Rudolf Krause	DDR	1	-	-	-	-	-	-	-	-	-
Hubert Hahne	D	- (1)	-	-	-	-	-	-	-	-	-
Harry Merkel	D	- (1)	-	-	-	-	-	-	-	-	-
Gerhard Mitter	D	- (1)	-	-	-	-	-	-	-	-	-
Dieter Quester	A	- (1)	-	-	-	-	-	-	-	-	-

BMW GRAND PRIX CARS

Type	Year	Engine	Designer
"Eigenbau"	1952	BMW 328 S6	Various, "Eigenbau" meaning special in German
269/F2 F2 car	1969	BMW M20 S4	Len Terry

Brabham

Grand Prix Debut:	1962 German GP	J Brabham (retired)
Last Grand Prix:	1992 Hungarian GP	D Hill (11th)
Principals:	Jack Brabham and Ron Tauranac, 1962-70; Ron Tauranac, 1971; Bernie Ecclestone, 1972-87; no team in 1988; Joachim Luhti, 1989; Dennis Nursey/Middlebridge Group, 1990-92	
Base:	Chessington, 1962-89; Milton Keynes, 1990-92	

WORLD CHAMPIONSHIP RECORD

Starts:	394	
Points:	983	
Wins:	35	1964 French GP (Gurney), Mexican GP (Gurney), 1966 French GP (Brabham), British GP (Brabham), Dutch GP (Brabham), German GP (Brabham), 1967 Monaco GP (Hulme), French GP (Brabham), German GP (Hulme), Canadian GP (Brabham), 1969 German GP (Ickx), Canadian GP (Ickx), 1970 South African GP (Brabham), 1974 South African GP (Reutemann), Austrian GP (Reutemann), United States GP (Reutemann), 1975 Brazilian GP (Pace), German GP (Reutemann), 1978 Swedish GP (Lauda), Italian GP (Lauda), 1980 Long Beach GP (Piquet), Dutch GP (Piquet), Italian GP (Piquet), 1981 Argentinian GP (Piquet), San Marino GP (Piquet), German GP (Piquet), 1982 Monaco GP (Patrese), Canadian GP (Piquet), 1983 Brazilian GP (Piquet), Italian GP (Piquet), European GP (Piquet), South African GP (Patrese), 1984 Canadian GP (Nelson Piquet), Detroit GP (Piquet), 1985 French GP (Piquet)
Pole positions:	39	1964 Dutch GP (Gurney), Belgian GP (Gurney), 1966 British GP (Brabham), Dutch GP (Brabham), United States GP (Brabham), 1967 South African GP (Brabham), Monaco GP (Brabham), 1968 French GP (Rindt), Canadian GP (Rindt), 1969 South African GP (Brabham), German GP (Ickx), Canadian GP (Ickx), Mexican GP (Brabham), 1970 Spanish GP

(Brabham), 1972 Argentinian GP (Reutemann), 1974 United States GP (Reutemann), 1975 South African GP (Pace), 1977 Monaco GP (Watson), 1978 South African GP (Lauda), French GP (Watson), 1980 Long Beach GP (Piquet), Canadian GP (Piquet), 1981 Brazilian GP (Piquet), Argentinian GP (Piquet), Monaco GP (Piquet), Canadian GP (Piquet), 1982 Austrian GP (Piquet), 1983 Dutch GP (Piquet), Italian GP (Patrese), 1984 South African GP (Piquet), San Marino GP (Piquet), Canadian GP (Piquet), Detroit GP (Piquet), British GP (Piquet), Austrian GP (Piquet), Italian GP (Piquet), European GP (Piquet), Portuguese GP (Piquet), 1985 Dutch GP (Piquet)

Fastest laps: 41 1963 South African GP (Gurney), 1964 Belgian GP (Gurney), French GP (J Brabham), Austrian GP (Gurney), 1965 Mexican GP (Gurney), 1966 British GP (J Brabham), Dutch GP (Hulme), 1967 South African GP (Hulme), British GP (Hulme), 1969 German GP (Ickx), Canadian GP (Ickx), and (J Brabham), Mexican GP (Ickx), 1970 South African GP (J Brabham), Spanish GP (J Brabham), French GP (J Brabham), British GP (J Brabham), 1974 South African GP (Reutemann), Italian GP (Pace), United States GP (Pace), 1975 South African GP (Pace), 1977 South African GP (Watson), Austrian GP (Watson), 1978 Monaco GP (Lauda), Swedish GP (Lauda), British GP (Lauda), Dutch GP (Lauda), 1979 United States GP (Piquet), 1980 Long Beach GP (Piquet), 1981 Argentinian GP (Piquet), 1982 Monaco GP (Patrese), French GP (Patrese), German GP (Piquet), Austrian GP (Piquet), 1983 Brazilian GP (Piquet), San Marino GP (Patrese), Monaco GP (Piquet), Italian GP (Piquet), South African GP (Piquet), 1984 San Marino GP (Piquet), Canadian GP (Piquet), European GP (Piquet)

Laps/miles in the lead: 2723.5 laps/8252 miles

World Champions:

Drivers: Four times - 1966 (Brabham), 1967 (Hulme), 1981 (Piquet) and 1983 (Piquet)

Constructors: Twice - 1966 and 1967

MAJOR SPONSORS

1968	Caltex
1970	Auto Motor und Sport
1972	Bardahl, Esso, YPF
1973	Bardahl, Ceramica Pagnossin, Hexagon, YPF
1974	Hitachi
1975-77	Martini
1978-84	Parmalat
1985-86	Olivetti
1989	Bioptron
1992	Yamazen

BRABHAM GRAND PRIX DRIVERS

Driver	Nat	Starts (DNS/DNQ)	1st	2nd	3rd	4th	5th	6th	PP	FL	Points
Nelson Piquet	BR	106 (1)	13	9	7	8	5	3	18	12	236
Jack Brabham	AUS	80 (2)	7	9	5	9	4	2	8	7	174
Carlos Reutemann	RA	66	4	2	6	6	-	3	2	1	91
Denny Hulme	NZ	26	2	4	6	2	1	-	-	3	74
Dan Gurney	USA	30	2	4	4	-	1	3	2	4	63
Niki Lauda	A	29 (1)	2	3	2	1	-	1	1	4	48
Riccardo Patrese	I	61	2	1	3	-	2	2	1	3	42
Jacky Ickx	B	11	2	2	1	-	1	1	2	3	37
Carlos Pace	BR	39 (1)	1	3	1	3	2	1	1	3	45
John Watson	GB	50	-	2	2	4	3	2	2	2	40
Piers Courage	GB	10	-	2	-	-	2	-	-	-	16
Hector Rebaque	MEX	21 (1)	-	-	-	3	1	1	-	-	12
Jo Siffert	CH	20	-	-	1	2	-	2	-	-	12

Driver	Nat	Start	1st	2nd	3rd	4th	5th	6th	PP	FL	Points
Hans-Joachim Stuck	D	14	-	-	2	-	1	2	-	-	12
Rolf Stommelen	D	16 (3)	-	-	1	-	3	1	-	-	11
Teo Fabi	I	12	-	-	1	1	1	-	-	-	9
Bob Anderson	RSR	23 (4)	-	-	1	-	1	2	-	-	8
Jochen Rindt	A	13	-	-	2	-	-	-	2	-	8
Stefano Modena	I	32 (1)	-	-	1	1	-	-	-	-	6
Martin Brundle	GB	28 (4)	-	-	-	-	2	2	-	-	6
Graham Hill	GB	23	-	-	-	-	2	2	-	-	6
Marc Surer	CH	12	-	-	-	1	-	2	-	-	5
Tim Schenken	AUS	10	-	-	1	-	-	1	-	-	5
Andrea de Cesaris	I	16	-	-	1	-	-	-	-	-	4
Wilson Fittipaldi	BR	25	-	-	-	-	1	1	-	-	3
Silvio Moser	CH	9 (4)	-	-	-	-	1	1	-	-	3
Andrea de Adamich	I	5	-	-	-	1	-	-	-	-	3
Jo Bonnier	S	20	-	-	-	-	-	1	-	-	1
Mark Blundell	GB	14 (2)	-	-	-	-	-	1	-	-	1
Guy Ligier	F	5	-	-	-	-	-	1	-	-	1
John Taylor	GB	4	-	-	-	-	1	-	-	-	1
Derek Warwick	GB	10 (1)	-	-	-	-	-	-	-	-	-
David Brabham	AUS	8 (6)	-	-	-	-	-	-	-	-	-
Ricardo Zunino	RA	8 (1)	-	-	-	-	-	-	-	-	-
Frank Gardner	AUS	8	-	-	-	-	-	-	-	-	-
Rikky von Opel	FL	4 (2)	-	-	-	-	-	-	-	-	-
Elio de Angelis	I	4	-	-	-	-	-	-	-	-	-
Loris Kessel	CH	3 (2)	-	-	-	-	-	-	-	-	-
Francois Hesnault	F	3 (1)	-	-	-	-	-	-	-	-	-
Kurt Ahrens jr	D	3	-	-	-	-	-	-	-	-	-
Dave Charlton	ZA	3	-	-	-	-	-	-	-	-	-
Corrado Fabi	I	3	-	-	-	-	-	-	-	-	-
Larry Perkins	AUS	3	-	-	-	-	-	-	-	-	-
Richard Robarts	GB	3	-	-	-	-	-	-	-	-	-
Damon Hill	GB	2 (6)	-	-	-	-	-	-	-	-	-
Ian Raby	GB	2 (2)	-	-	-	-	-	-	-	-	-
Gregor Foitek	CH	2	-	-	-	-	-	-	-	-	-
Piet de Klerk	ZA	2	-	-	-	-	-	-	-	-	-
Jackie Pretorius	ZA	2	-	-	-	-	-	-	-	-	-
David Prophet	GB	2	-	-	-	-	-	-	-	-	-
Hap Sharp	USA	2	-	-	-	-	-	-	-	-	-
Eric van de Poele	B	1 (9)	-	-	-	-	-	-	-	-	-
Lella Lombardi	I	1 (3)	-	-	-	-	-	-	-	-	-
Chris Craft	GB	1 (1)	-	-	-	-	-	-	-	-	-
Gerard Larrousse	F	1 (1)	-	-	-	-	-	-	-	-	-
Richard Attwood	GB	1	-	-	-	-	-	-	-	-	-
Giancarlo Baghetti	I	1	-	-	-	-	-	-	-	-	-
Derek Bell	GB	1	-	-	-	-	-	-	-	-	-
Luki Botha	ZA	1	-	-	-	-	-	-	-	-	-
John Cordts	CDN	1	-	-	-	-	-	-	-	-	-
Bob Evans	GB	1	-	-	-	-	-	-	-	-	-
Paul Hawkins	AUS	1	-	-	-	-	-	-	-	-	-
Hans Herrmann	D	1	-	-	-	-	-	-	-	-	-
Gus Hutchison	USA	1	-	-	-	-	-	-	-	-	-
Chris Irwin	GB	1	-	-	-	-	-	-	-	-	-
John Love	RSR	1	-	-	-	-	-	-	-	-	-
Patrick Neve	B	1	-	-	-	-	-	-	-	-	-
Xavier Perrot	CH	1	-	-	-	-	-	-	-	-	-
Teddy Pilette	B	1	-	-	-	-	-	-	-	-	-
Alan Rees	GB	1	-	-	-	-	-	-	-	-	-
Sam Tingle	RSR	1	-	-	-	-	-	-	-	-	-
Peter Westbury	GB	1	-	-	-	-	-	-	-	-	-
Eppie Wietzes	CDN	1	-	-	-	-	-	-	-	-	-
Manfred Winkelhock	D	1	-	-	-	-	-	-	-	-	-
Giovanna Amati	I	- (3)	-	-	-	-	-	-	-	-	-
Chris Amon	NZ	- (2)	-	-	-	-	-	-	-	-	-
Ian Ashley	GB	- (2)	-	-	-	-	-	-	-	-	-
Carlo Facetti	I	- (1)	-	-	-	-	-	-	-	-	-
William Ferguson	ZA	- (1)	-	-	-	-	-	-	-	-	-
Giorgio Francia	I	- (1)	-	-	-	-	-	-	-	-	-
Helmuth Koinigg	A	- (1)	-	-	-	-	-	-	-	-	-
Damien Magee	GB	- (1)	-	-	-	-	-	-	-	-	-
Jac Nelleman	DK	- (1)	-	-	-	-	-	-	-	-	-
"Geki" Russo	I	- (1)	-	-	-	-	-	-	-	-	-

Driver	Nat	Start	1st	2nd	3rd	4th	5th	6th	PP	FL	Points
Emilio de Villota	E	- (1)	-	-	-	-	-	-	-	-	-

BRABHAM GRAND PRIX CARS

Type	Year	Engine	Designer
BT3	1962	Climax V8, BRM V8	Ron Tauranac
BT6	1963	Ford S4	Ron Tauranac
BT7	1963	Climax V8	Ron Tauranac
BT10	1964	Ford SCA S4	Ron Tauranac
BT11	1964	Climax V8, BRM V8, Repco V8	Ron Tauranac
BT16	1966	Ford SCA S4	Ron Tauranac
BT18	1966	Ford SCA S4	Ron Tauranac
BT19	1966	Repco 620 V8	Ron Tauranac
BT20	1966	Repco 620 V8	Ron Tauranac
BT23B	1969	Ford S4	Ron Tauranac
BT23C	1969	Ford S4	Ron Tauranac
BT24	1967	Repco V8, Ford DFV V8	Ron Tauranac
BT26	1968	Repco 860 V8, Ford DFV V8	Ron Tauranac
BT30	1969	Ford S4	Ron Tauranac
BT33	1970	Ford DFV V8	Ron Tauranac
BT34	1971	Ford DFV V8	Ron Tauranac

Lobster-claw Brabham with twin-radiators mounted as part of front wing

Type	Year	Engine	Designer
BT37	1972	Ford DFV V8	Ralph Bellamy
BT39	1972	Weslake V12	Ralph Bellamy

Prototype Weslake-powered car, never raced

Type	Year	Engine	Designer
BT42	1973	Ford DFV V8	Gordon Murray
BT44	1974	Ford DFV V8	Gordon Murray
BT44B	1975	Ford DFV V8	Gordon Murray
BT45	1976	Alfa Romeo 115-12 F12	Gordon Murray
BT45B	1977	Alfa Romeo 115-12 F12	Gordon Murray
BT45C	1978	Alfa Romeo 115-12 F12	Gordon Murray
BT46	1978	Alfa Romeo 115-12 F12	Gordon Murray
BT46B	1978	Alfa Romeo 115-12 F12	Gordon Murray

"Fan-car", raced once (winning) but subsequently banned

Type	Year	Engine	Designer
BT48	1979	Alfa Romeo 1260 V12	Gordon Murray/ David North
BT49	1979	Ford DFV V8	Gordon Murray/ David North
BT49B	1980	Ford DFV V8	Gordon Murray/ David North

Used Weismann gearbox, soon abandoned

Type	Year	Engine	Designer
BT49C	1981	Ford DFV V8	Gordon Murray/ David North
BT49D	1982	Ford DFV V8	Gordon Murray/ David North
BT50	1982	BMW M12/13 S4 tc	Gordon Murray/ David North
BT51	1981	BMW M12/13 S4 tc	Gordon Murray/ David North

Ground-effect car, never raced as new rules banned sliding skirts and rendered it obsolete

Type	Year	Engine	Designer
BT52	1983	BMW M12/13 S4 tc	Gordon Murray/ David North
BT52B	1983	BMW M12/13 S4 tc	Gordon Murray/ David North
BT53	1984	BMW M12/13 S4 tc	Gordon Murray/ David North
BT54	1985	BMW M12/13 S4 tc	Gordon Murray/ David North
BT55	1986	BMW M12/13 S4 tc	Gordon Murray/ David North

Lowline car featuring Weismann gearbox

Type	Year	Engine	Designer
BT56	1987	BMW M12/13 S4 tc	John Baldwin/ Sergio Rinland/ David North
BT58	1989	Judd CV V8	Sergio Rinland/ John Baldwin
BT59	1990	Judd EV V8	Sergio Rinland
BT59Y	1991	Yamaha OX99 V12	Sergio Rinland
BT60Y	1991	Yamaha OX99 V12	Sergio Rinland
BT60B	1992	Judd GV V10	Sergio Rinland/ Tim Densham

British American Racing

see BAR

BRM

British Racing Motors

Grand Prix Debut: 1951 British GP   Parnell (5th), Walker (7th)
Last Grand Prix: 1977 South African GP Perkins (15th)
Principals: Raymond Mays, 1950-51; Sir Alfred Owen, 1952-74; Jean Owen and Louis Stanley, 1974-79 (entered as Stanley-BRM from 1975); John Jordan, 1980-82 (entered as Jordan-BRM in British F1); John Mangoletsi (entered in World Sports Cars), 1992
Base: Bourne, Lincolnshire

WORLD CHAMPIONSHIP RECORD

Grand Prix Started: 197
Points: 537.5
Wins: 17 — 1959 Dutch GP (Bonnier), 1962 Dutch GP (Hill), German GP (Hill), Italian GP (Hill), South African GP (Hill), 1963 Monaco GP (Hill), United States GP (Hill), 1964 Monaco GP (Hill), United States GP (Hill), 1965 Monaco GP (Hill), Italian GP (Stewart), United States GP (Hill), 1966 Monaco GP (Stewart), 1970 Belgian GP (Rodriguez), 1971 Austrian GP (Siffert), Italian GP (Gethin), 1972 Monaco GP (Beltoise)
Pole positions: 11 — 1959 Dutch GP (Bonnier), 1962 Belgian GP (Hill), 1963 Belgian GP (Hill), United States GP (Hill), 1964 Austrian GP (Hill), 1965 Monaco GP (Hill), Belgian GP (Hill), Dutch GP (Hill), United States GP (Hill), 1971 Austrian GP (Siffert), 1973 Argentinian GP (Regazzoni)
Fastest laps: 15 — 1959 French GP (Moss), British GP (Moss), 1960 British GP (Hill), 1961 British GP (Brooks), 1962 French GP (Hill), German GP (Hill), Italian GP (Hill), 1964 Monaco GP (Hill), 1965 Monaco GP (Hill), British GP (Hill), United States GP (Hill), 1968 Monaco GP (Attwood), French GP (Rodriguez), 1971 Austrian GP (Siffert), 1972 Monaco GP (Beltoise)
Laps/miles in the lead: 1342 laps/3786 miles
World Champions:
Drivers: Once - 1962 (G Hill)
Constructors: Once - 1962

BRM GRAND PRIX DRIVERS

Driver	Nat	Starts (DNS/DNQ)	1st	2nd	3rd	4th	5th	6th	PP	FL	Points
Graham Hill	GB	64	10	9	7	5	4	2	8	8	193
Jackie Stewart	GB	29	2	4	2	1	2	1	-	-	58
Pedro Rodriguez	MEX	33	1	3	2	4	-	3	-	1	50
Jean-Pierre Beltoise	F	40 (1)	1	1	-	1	5	-	-	1	28
Jo Siffert	CH	11	1	1	-	1	-	1	1	1	19
Jo Bonnier	S	17	1	-	1	3	-	1	-	1	17
Peter Gethin	GB	15 (1)	1	-	-	-	-	1	-	-	10
Richie Ginther	USA	29	-	6	3	5	2	-	-	-	67
Harry Schell	USA	16	-	1	-	1	5	1	-	-	19
Howden Ganley	NZ	19 (3)	-	-	-	2	1	1	-	-	9
Mike Spence	GB	12	-	-	-	-	4	1	-	-	9
Stirling Moss	GB	2	-	1	-	-	-	-	-	2	7.5
Jean Behra	F	9	-	-	1	1	-	-	-	-	7
Tony Brooks	GB	9 (1)	-	-	1	-	1	-	-	1	6
John Surtees	GB	9 (1)	-	-	1	-	1	-	-	-	6
Richard Attwood	GB	6 (1)	-	1	-	-	-	-	-	1	6
Piers Courage	GB	12 (1)	-	-	1	-	1	-	-	-	4
Tony Maggs	ZA	3 (2)	-	-	1	-	1	-	-	-	4

Formula 1

Driver	Nat	Start	1st	2nd	3rd	4th	5th	6th	PP	FL	Points
Jackie Oliver	GB	24	-	-	-	-	1	1	-	-	3
Bob Bondurant	USA	5	-	-	-	1	-	-	-	-	3
Niki Lauda	A	14 (1)	-	-	-	1	-	-	-	-	2
Clay Regazzoni	CH	14	-	-	-	-	2	1	-	-	2
Chris Irwin	GB	8	-	-	-	1	-	-	-	-	2
Maurice Trintignant	F	6 (1)	-	-	-	1	-	-	-	-	2
Lorenzo Bandini	I	3	-	-	-	1	-	-	-	-	2
Reg Parnell	GB	1 (1)	-	-	-	1	-	-	-	-	2
Henri Pescarolo	F	12	-	-	-	-	-	-	-	-	-
George Eaton	CDN	11 (2)	-	-	-	-	-	-	-	-	-
Francois Migault	F	10 (1)	-	-	-	-	-	-	-	-	-
Ron Flockhart	GB	9 (1)	-	-	-	-	1	-	-	-	-
Helmut Marko	A	9	-	-	-	-	-	-	-	-	-
Bob Evans	GB	8 (1)	-	-	-	-	-	-	-	-	-
Dan Gurney	USA	7	-	-	-	-	-	-	-	-	-
Giancarlo Baghetti	I	6	-	-	-	-	-	-	-	-	-
Reine Wisell	S	6	-	-	-	-	-	-	-	-	-
Masten Gregory	USA	4	-	-	-	-	-	-	-	-	-
Chris Amon	NZ	2	-	-	-	-	-	-	-	-	-
Bill Brack	CDN	2	-	-	-	-	-	-	-	-	-
David Hobbs	GB	2	-	-	-	-	-	-	-	-	-
Innes Ireland	GB	2	-	-	-	-	-	-	-	-	-
Larry Perkins	AUS	2	-	-	-	-	-	-	-	-	-
Alex Soler-Roig	E	2	-	-	-	-	-	-	-	-	-
Mike Wilds	GB	2	-	-	-	-	-	-	-	-	-
Roberto Bussinello	I	1 (1)	-	-	-	-	-	-	-	-	-
Mike Hawthorn	GB	1 (1)	-	-	-	-	-	-	-	-	-
Bobby Unser	USA	1 (1)	-	-	-	-	-	-	-	-	-
Ian Ashley	GB	1	-	-	-	-	-	-	-	-	-
Giorgio Bassi	I	1	-	-	-	-	-	-	-	-	-
Lucien Bianchi	B	1	-	-	-	-	-	-	-	-	-
John Cannon	CDN	1	-	-	-	-	-	-	-	-	-
Vic Elford	GB	1	-	-	-	-	-	-	-	-	-
Jack Fairman	GB	1	-	-	-	-	-	-	-	-	-
Hans Herrmann	D	1	-	-	-	-	-	-	-	-	-
Bruce Johnstone	ZA	1	-	-	-	-	-	-	-	-	-
Les Leston	GB	1	-	-	-	-	-	-	-	-	-
Herbert MacKay-Fraser	USA	1	-	-	-	-	-	-	-	-	-
Brian Redman	GB	1	-	-	-	-	-	-	-	-	-
Moises Solana	MEX	1	-	-	-	-	-	-	-	-	-
Peter Walker	GB	1	-	-	-	-	-	-	-	-	-
Conny Andersson	S	- (4)	-	-	-	-	-	-	-	-	-
Teddy Pilette	B	- (3)	-	-	-	-	-	-	-	-	-
Guy Edwards	GB	- (1)	-	-	-	-	-	-	-	-	-
Frank Gardner	AUS	- (1)	-	-	-	-	-	-	-	-	-
Jackie Lewis	GB	- (1)	-	-	-	-	-	-	-	-	-
Ken Richardson	GB	- (1)	-	-	-	-	-	-	-	-	-
Roy Salvadori	GB	- (1)	-	-	-	-	-	-	-	-	-
Vern Schuppan	AUS	- (1)	-	-	-	-	-	-	-	-	-
Peter Westbury	GB	- (1)	-	-	-	-	-	-	-	-	-
Vic Wilson	GB	- (1)	-	-	-	-	-	-	-	-	-

BRM GRAND PRIX CARS

Type	Year	Engine	Designer
P15	1951	BRM 15 V16 sc	Peter Berthon
P25	1956	BRM 256 S4	Peter Berthon/Stuart Tresilian
P25 (58)	1958	BRM 258 S4	Peter Berthon/Stuart Tresilian
P25 (59)	1959	BRM 259 S4	Peter Berthon/Stuart Tresilian/Tony Rudd
P48	1960	BRM 259 S4	Tony Rudd
P48/57	1961	Climax FPF S4	Tony Rudd
P48/57 (62)	1962	BRM 56 V8	Tony Rudd
P57	1962	BRM 56 V8	Tony Rudd
P61	1963	BRM 56 V8	Tony Rudd
P261	1964	BRM 56 V8	Tony Rudd
P67 4-wheel-drive	1964	BRM 56 V8	Tony Rudd
P83	1966	BRM 75 H16	Tony Rudd
P126	1968	BRM 101 V12	Len Terry
P133	1968	BRM 101 V12	Len Terry
P138	1968	BRM P142 V12	Len Terry
P139	1969	BRM P142 V12	Len Terry
P153	1970	BRM P142 V12	Tony Southgate
P160	1971	BRM P142 V12	Tony Southgate
P153B	1972	BRM P142 V12	Tony Southgate
P160B	1972	BRM P142 V12	Tony Southgate
P160C	1972	BRM P142 V12	Tony Southgate
P180	1972	BRM P142 V12	Tony Southgate
P160D	1973	BRM P142 V12	Tony Southgate
P160E	1973	BRM P142 V12	Tony Southgate/Mike Pilbeam
P201	1974	BRM P142 V12	Mike Pilbeam
P201*	1975	BRM P200 V12	Mike Pilbeam
P201B*	1976	BRM P200 V12	Mike Pilbeam
P207*	1977	BRM P202 V12	Len Terry
P201B/204*	1977	BRM P200 V12	Mike Pilbeam

*Stanley-BRM

BRP

British Racing Partnership

Grand Prix Debut:	1963 Belgian GP Ireland (retired)
Last Grand Prix:	1964 Mexican GP Ireland (12th), Taylor (retired)
Principals:	Alfred Moss and Ken Gregory
Base:	Highgate, North London

WORLD CHAMPIONSHIP RECORD

Starts:	13	
Points:	11	
Best result:	4th	1963 Dutch GP (Ireland), Italian GP (Ireland)
Best qualifying:	7th	1963 Belgian GP (Ireland), Dutch GP (Ireland)

Best World Championship position:

Drivers:	9th in 1963 (Ireland)
Constructors:	6th in 1963

BRP GRAND PRIX DRIVERS

Driver	Nat	Starts (DNS/DNQ)	1st	2nd	3rd	4th	5th	6th	PP	FL	Points
Innes Ireland	GB	12	-	-	-	2	2	-	-	-	10
Trevor Taylor	GB	6 (1)	-	-	-	-	-	1	-	-	1

BRP GRAND PRIX CARS

Type	Year	Engine	Designer
1	1963	BRM V8	Tony Robinson
2	1964	BRM V8	Tony Robinson

Bugatti

Only World Championship

Grand Prix:	1956 French GP Trintignant (retired)
Principal:	Genevieve Bugatti (founder Ettore Bugatti had died in 1947)
Base:	Molsheim

WORLD CHAMPIONSHIP RECORD

Starts:	1	
Best result:	No finishes	
Best qualifying:	18th	1956 French GP (Trintignant)

BUGATTI GRAND PRIX DRIVERS

Driver	Nat	Starts (DNS/DNQ)	1st	2nd	3rd	4th	5th	6th	PP	FL	Points
Maurice Trintignant	F	1	-	-	-	-	-	-	-	-	-

BUGATTI GRAND PRIX CARS

Type	Year	Engine	Designer
T251	1956	Bugatti 251 S8	Gioacchino Colombo

Cisitalia

Principals: Piero Dusio and Piero Taruffi
Base: Turin

WORLD CHAMPIONSHIP RECORD

Starts: None

CISITALIA GRAND PRIX DRIVERS

Driver	Nat	Starts (DNS/DNQ)	1st	2nd	3rd	4th	5th	6th	PP	FL	Points
Piero Dusio	I	- (1)	-	-	-	-	-	-	-	-	-

CISITALIA GRAND PRIX CARS

Type	Year	Engine	Designer
D46	1952	BPM	Dante Giacosa

Coloni

Also see Andrea Moda

Grand Prix Debut: 1987 Spanish GP   Larini (retired)
Last Grand Prix: 1989 Portuguese GP Moreno (retired)
Principal: Enzo Coloni, 1987-91; Andrea Sassetti, 1991-92
(Sassetti changed name to Andrea Moda for 1992)
Base: Perugia

WORLD CHAMPIONSHIP RECORD

Starts: 13
Best result: 8th   1988 Canadian GP (Tarquini)
Best qualifying: 15th   1989 Portuguese GP (Moreno)

MAJOR SPONSORS

1989	Himont

COLONI GRAND PRIX DRIVERS

Driver	Nat	Starts (DNS/DNQ)	1st	2nd	3rd	4th	5th	6th	PP	FL	Points
Gabriele Tarquini	I	8 (8)	-	-	-	-	-	-	-	-	-
Roberto Moreno	BR	4 (12)	-	-	-	-	-	-	-	-	-
Pierre-Henri Raphanel	F	1 (9)	-	-	-	-	-	-	-	-	-
Nicola Larini	I	1 (1)	-	-	-	-	-	-	-	-	-
Bertrand Gachot	B	- (16)	-	-	-	-	-	-	-	-	-
Pedro Chaves	P	- (14)	-	-	-	-	-	-	-	-	-
Enrico Bertaggia	I	- (7)	-	-	-	-	-	-	-	-	-
Alex Caffi	I	- (1)	-	-	-	-	-	-	-	-	-
Naoki Hattori	J	- (2)	-	-	-	-	-	-	-	-	-

COLONI GRAND PRIX CARS

Type	Year	Engine	Designer
FC187	1987	Ford DFZ V8	Roberto Ori
FC188	1988	Ford DFZ V8	Roberto Ori
FC188B	1988	Ford DFZ V8	Roberto Ori
FC188C	1989	Ford DFR V8	Roberto Ori
C3	1989	Ford DFR V8	Christian Vanderpleyn/ Michel Costa
C3B	1990	Subaru F12, Ford DFR V8	Christian Vanderpleyn/ Paul Burgess

Type	Year	Engine	Designer
C4	1991	Ford DFR V8	Coloni Technical Department/ Perugia University
C4B	1992	Judd GV V10	Coloni Technical Department/ Perugia University

Connaught

Grand Prix Debut: 1952 British GP   Poore (4th), Thompson (5th), Downing (9th), McAlpine (16th)
Last Grand Prix: 1959 United States GP   Said (retired)
Principals: Rodney Clarke, Mike Oliver and Kenneth McAlpine
Base: Send, Surrey

WORLD CHAMPIONSHIP RECORD

Starts: 17
Points: 17
Best result: 3rd   1956 Italian GP (Flockhart)
Best qualifying: 5th   1952 British GP (Downing)

Best World Championship position:
Drivers: 10th in 1956 (Fairman)
Constructors: -

CONNAUGHT GRAND PRIX DRIVERS

Driver	Nat	Starts (DNS/DNQ)	1st	2nd	3rd	4th	5th	6th	PP	FL	Points
Jack Fairman	GB	4 (1)	-	-	-	1	1	-	-	-	5
Ron Flockhart	GB	1	-	-	1	-	-	-	-	-	4
Dennis Poore	GB	2	-	-	-	1	-	-	-	-	3
Stuart Lewis-Evans	GB	1	-	-	-	1	-	-	-	-	3
Eric Thompson	GB	1	-	-	-	-	1	-	-	-	2
Kenneth McAlpine	GB	7	-	-	-	-	-	-	-	-	-
Roy Salvadori	GB	5	-	-	-	-	-	-	-	-	-
Johnny Claes	B	4	-	-	-	-	-	-	-	-	-
"B Bira"	SM	3	-	-	-	-	-	-	-	-	-
Ivor Bueb	GB	2	-	-	-	-	-	-	-	-	-
Ken Downing	GB	2	-	-	-	-	-	-	-	-	-
Leslie Marr	GB	2	-	-	-	-	-	-	-	-	-
Stirling Moss	GB	2	-	-	-	-	-	-	-	-	-
Tony Rolt	GB	2	-	-	-	-	-	-	-	-	-
Don Beauman	GB	1	-	-	-	-	-	-	-	-	-
Les Leston	GB	1	-	-	-	-	-	-	-	-	-
Andre Pilette	B	1	-	-	-	-	-	-	-	-	-
John Riseley-Prichard	GB	1	-	-	-	-	-	-	-	-	-
Bob Said	USA	1	-	-	-	-	-	-	-	-	-
Archie Scott-Brown	GB	1	-	-	-	-	-	-	-	-	-
Piero Scotti	I	1	-	-	-	-	-	-	-	-	-
Ian Stewart	GB	1	-	-	-	-	-	-	-	-	-
Leslie Thorne	GB	1	-	-	-	-	-	-	-	-	-
Desmond Titterington	GB	1	-	-	-	-	-	-	-	-	-
Peter Walker	GB	1	-	-	-	-	-	-	-	-	-
Bill Whitehouse	GB	1	-	-	-	-	-	-	-	-	-
Bernie Ecclestone	GB	- (1)	-	-	-	-	-	-	-	-	-
Paul Emery	GB	- (1)	-	-	-	-	-	-	-	-	-
Bruce Kessler	USA	- (1)	-	-	-	-	-	-	-	-	-

CONNAUGHT GRAND PRIX CARS

Type	Year	Engine	Designer
A	1952	Lea-Francis S4	Rodney Clarke
B	1955	Alta GP S4	Rodney Clarke
C	1959	Alta GP S4	Rodney Clarke

Connew

Only Grand Prix: 1972 Austrian GP   Migault (retired)
Principal: Peter Connew
Base: Romford, Essex

WORLD CHAMPIONSHIP RECORD

Starts:	1
Best result:	No finishes
Best qualifying:	26th 1972 Austrian GP (Migault)

MAJOR SPONSORS

1972	Darnval

CONNEW GRAND PRIX DRIVERS

Driver	Nat	Starts	1st	2nd	3rd	4th	5th	6th	PP	FL	Points
		(DNS/DNQ)									
Francois Migault	F	1 (1)	-	-	-	-	-	-	-	-	-

CONNEW GRAND PRIX CARS

Type	Year	Engine	Designer
PC1	1972	Ford DFV V8	Peter Connew

Cooper

Grand Prix Debut:	1950 Monaco GP	Schell (retired)
Last Grand Prix:	1969 Monaco GP	Elford (7th)
Principals:	Charles and John Cooper, 1950 until Charles' death in 1964; John Cooper, 1965; Chipstead Motor Group (Jonathan Sieff and Roy Salvadori), 1965-69	
Base:	Surbiton, Surrey, 1950-65; Byfleet, 1966-69	

WORLD CHAMPIONSHIP RECORD

Starts:	129
Points:	494.5
Wins:	16 1958 Argentinian GP (Moss), Monaco GP (Trintignant), 1959 Monaco GP (Brabham), British GP (Brabham), Portuguese GP (Moss), Italian GP (Moss), United States GP (McLaren), 1960 Argentinian GP (McLaren), Dutch GP (Brabham), Belgian GP (Brabham), French GP (Brabham), British GP (Brabham), Portuguese GP (Brabham), 1962 Monaco GP (McLaren), 1966 Mexican GP (Surtees), 1967 South African GP (Rodriguez)
Pole positions:	11 1959 Monaco GP (Moss), British GP (Brabham), Portuguese GP (Moss), Italian GP (Moss), United States GP (Moss), 1960 Argentinian GP (Moss), Belgian GP (Brabham), French GP (Brabham), British GP (Brabham), 1961 United States GP (Brabham), 1966 Mexican GP (Surtees)
Fastest laps:	14 1959 Monaco GP (Brabham), Dutch GP (Moss), British GP (McLaren), Portuguese GP (Moss), United States GP (Trintignant), 1960 Argentinian GP (Moss), Monaco GP (McLaren), Belgian GP (Brabham), French GP (Brabham), United States GP (Brabham), 1961 United States GP (Brabham), 1962 Dutch GP (McLaren), 1966 German GP (Surtees), United States GP (Surtees)

Laps/miles in the lead: 829 laps/2822 miles

World Champions:
Drivers:	Twice - 1959 (J Brabham) and 1960 (J Brabham)
Constructors:	Twice - 1959 and 1960

COOPER GRAND PRIX DRIVERS

Driver	Nat	Starts	1st	2nd	3rd	4th	5th	6th	PP	FL	Points
		(DNS/DNQ)									
Jack Brabham	AUS	39	7	1	2	4	-	4	5	5	84
Bruce McLaren	NZ	64	3	7	10	4	7	3	-	3	136.5
Stirling Moss	GB	11	3	-	1	-	-	1	5	3	26
Maurice Trintignant	F	25	1	1	3	2	1	-	-	1	31
John Surtees	GB	15	1	1	1	-	2	-	1	2	23
Pedro Rodriguez	MEX	8	1	-	-	-	2	2	-	-	15

Driver	Nat	Start	1st	2nd	3rd	4th	5th	6th	PP	FL	Points
Jochen Rindt	A	28 (1)	-	2	1	5	1	1	-	-	34
Tony Maggs	ZA	19	-	2	1	-	2	2	-	-	22
Roy Salvadori	GB	22	-	1	1	1	2	3	-	-	19
Jo Bonnier	S	27	-	-	-	-	4	4	-	-	12
Masten Gregory	USA	12 (4)	-	1	1	-	-	-	-	-	10
Olivier Gendebien	B	5	-	1	1	-	-	-	-	-	10
Mike Hawthorn	GB	5	-	-	1	2	-	-	-	-	10
Jo Siffert	CH	18 (1)	-	-	-	3	-	-	-	-	9
Tony Brooks	GB	6	-	-	-	1	2	-	-	-	7
Lucien Bianchi	B	10 (1)	-	-	1	-	-	2	-	-	6
John Love	RSR	4 (1)	-	1	-	-	-	-	-	-	6
Ludovico Scarfiotti	I	3	-	-	-	2	-	-	-	-	6
Vic Elford	GB	8	-	-	-	1	1	-	-	-	5
Brian Redman	GB	3	-	-	1	-	-	-	-	-	4
Jackie Lewis	GB	9	-	-	-	1	-	-	-	-	3
Henry Taylor	GB	5 (1)	-	-	-	1	-	-	-	-	3
Giulio Cabianca	I	1	-	-	1	-	-	-	-	-	3
Carlos Menditeguy	RA	1	-	-	1	-	-	-	-	-	3
Phil Hill	USA	10	-	-	-	-	-	2	-	-	2
Alan Brown	GB	8 (1)	-	-	-	1	1	-	-	-	2
Richie Ginther	USA	2	-	-	-	1	-	-	-	-	2
Jacky Ickx	B	2	-	-	-	-	1	-	-	-	1
Ian Burgess	GB	12 (2)	-	-	-	-	1	-	-	-	-
Guy Ligier	F	7 (1)	-	-	-	-	-	-	-	-	-
Ken Wharton	GB	6	-	-	-	-	-	-	-	-	-
Eric Brandon	GB	5	-	-	-	-	-	-	-	-	-
Jack Fairman	GB	5	-	-	-	-	-	-	-	-	-
Bob Gerard	GB	5	-	-	-	-	1	-	-	-	-
Lorenzo Bandini	I	4	-	-	-	-	-	-	-	-	-
Chris Bristow	GB	4	-	-	-	-	-	-	-	-	-
Mario Araujo de Cabral	P	3 (1)	-	-	-	-	-	-	-	-	-
Bernard Collomb	F	3	-	-	-	-	-	-	-	-	-
Gino Munaron	I	3	-	-	-	-	-	-	-	-	-
Harry Schell	USA	3	-	-	-	-	-	-	-	-	-
Giorgio Scarlatti	I	2 (1)	-	-	-	-	-	-	-	-	-
Colin Davis	GB	2	-	-	-	-	-	-	-	-	-
Dick Gibson	GB	2	-	-	-	-	-	-	-	-	-
Chris Lawrence	GB	2	-	-	-	-	-	-	-	-	-
Tony Marsh	GB	2	-	-	-	-	-	-	-	-	-
Brian Naylor	GB	2	-	-	-	-	-	-	-	-	-
Wolfgang Seidel	D	2	-	-	-	-	-	-	-	-	-
Hap Sharp	USA	2	-	-	-	-	-	-	-	-	-
Peter Whitehead	GB	2	-	-	-	-	-	-	-	-	-
Trevor Blokdyk	ZA	1 (1)	-	-	-	-	-	-	-	-	-
Ivor Bueb	GB	1 (1)	-	-	-	-	-	-	-	-	-
Ron Flockhart	GB	1 (1)	-	-	-	-	-	-	-	-	-
Keith Greene	GB	1 (1)	-	-	-	-	-	-	-	-	-
Bruce Halford	GB	1 (1)	-	-	-	-	-	-	-	-	-
Chris Amon	NZ	1	-	-	-	-	-	-	-	-	-
Peter Ashdown	GB	1	-	-	-	-	-	-	-	-	-
Richard Attwood	GB	1	-	-	-	-	-	-	-	-	-
John Barber	GB	1	-	-	-	-	-	-	-	-	-
Edgar Barth	DDR	1	-	-	-	-	-	-	-	-	-
Carel Godin de Beaufort	NL	1	-	-	-	-	-	-	-	-	-
Roberto Bonomi	RA	1	-	-	-	-	-	-	-	-	-
Tommy Bridger	GB	1	-	-	-	-	-	-	-	-	-
Robert la Caze	MA	1	-	-	-	-	-	-	-	-	-
George Constantine	USA	1	-	-	-	-	-	-	-	-	-
Tony Crook	GB	1	-	-	-	-	-	-	-	-	-
Chuck Daigh	USA	1	-	-	-	-	-	-	-	-	-
Piero Drogo	YV	1	-	-	-	-	-	-	-	-	-
Paul England	AUS	1	-	-	-	-	-	-	-	-	-
Christian Goethals	B	1	-	-	-	-	-	-	-	-	-
Horace Gould	GB	1	-	-	-	-	-	-	-	-	-
Andre Guelfi	F	1	-	-	-	-	-	-	-	-	-
Walt Hansgen	USA	1	-	-	-	-	-	-	-	-	-
Mike Harris	RSR	1	-	-	-	-	-	-	-	-	-
Hans Herrmann	D	1	-	-	-	-	-	-	-	-	-

Driver	Nat	Start	1st	2nd	3rd	4th	5th	6th	PP	FL	Points
Pete Lovely	USA	1	-	-	-	-	-	-	-	-	-
Timmy Mayer	USA	1	-	-	-	-	-	-	-	-	-
Mike McDowell	GB	1	-	-	-	-	-	-	-	-	-
Silvio Moser	CH	1	-	-	-	-	-	-	-	-	-
David Murray	GB	1	-	-	-	-	-	-	-	-	-
Massimo Natili	I	1	-	-	-	-	-	-	-	-	-
Rodney Nuckey	GB	1	-	-	-	-	-	-	-	-	-
Arthur Owen	GB	1	-	-	-	-	-	-	-	-	-
Reg Parnell	GB	1	-	-	-	-	-	-	-	-	-
Roger Penske	USA	1	-	-	-	-	-	-	-	-	-
Francois Picard	F	1	-	-	-	-	-	-	-	-	-
Renato Pirocchi	I	1	-	-	-	-	-	-	-	-	-
Alan Rees	GB	1	-	-	-	-	-	-	-	-	-
John Rhodes	GB	1	-	-	-	-	-	-	-	-	-
Basil van Rooyen	ZA	1	-	-	-	-	-	-	-	-	-
Adolfo Schwelm Cruz	RA	1	-	-	-	-	-	-	-	-	-
Johnny Servoz-Gavin	F	1	-	-	-	-	-	-	-	-	-
Moises Solana	MEX	1	-	-	-	-	-	-	-	-	-
Jimmy Stewart	GB	1	-	-	-	-	-	-	-	-	-
John Taylor	GB	1	-	-	-	-	-	-	-	-	-
Mike Taylor	GB	1	-	-	-	-	-	-	-	-	-
Alfonso Thiele	USA	1	-	-	-	-	-	-	-	-	-
Alessandro de Tomaso	RA	1	-	-	-	-	-	-	-	-	-
Wolfgang von Trips	D	1	-	-	-	-	-	-	-	-	-
Robin Widdows	GB	1	-	-	-	-	-	-	-	-	-
Vic Wilson	GB	1	-	-	-	-	-	-	-	-	-
Tino Brambilla	I	-	(1)	-	-	-	-	-	-	-	-
Alain de Chagny	B	-	(1)	-	-	-	-	-	-	-	-
Frank Dochnal	USA	-	(1)	-	-	-	-	-	-	-	-
Helmut Glockler	D	-	(1)	-	-	-	-	-	-	-	-
Tom Jones	USA	-	(1)	-	-	-	-	-	-	-	-
Les Leston	GB	-	(1)	-	-	-	-	-	-	-	-
Jean Lucienbonnet	F	-	(1)	-	-	-	-	-	-	-	-
Bill Moss	GB	-	(1)	-	-	-	-	-	-	-	-
Tim Parnell	GB	-	(1)	-	-	-	-	-	-	-	-
Lance Reventlow	USA	-	(1)	-	-	-	-	-	-	-	-
Alan Rollinson	GB	-	(1)	-	-	-	-	-	-	-	-
Jean-Claude Rudaz	CH	-	(1)	-	-	-	-	-	-	-	-
Trevor Taylor	GB	-	(1)	-	-	-	-	-	-	-	-

COOPER GRAND PRIX CARS

Type	Year	Engine	Designer
T12 F3 car	1950	JAP twin	Owen Maddock
T20	1952	Bristol BS S6	Owen Maddock
T23	1953	Bristol BS S6, Bristol 401 S6 (1954)	Owen Maddock
T24	1953	Alta F2 S4, Alta GP S4 (1954)	Owen Maddock
T40	1955	Bristol 401 S6	Jack Brabham
T41	1957	Climax FWB S4	Owen Maddock
T43	1957	Climax FPF S4, Bristol 401 S6, OSCA	Owen Maddock
T45	1958	Climax FPF S4, Maserati 250S S4	Owen Maddock
T51	1959	Climax FPF S4, Maserati 250S S4, Borgward 30, Ferrari 555/F1, * Ferrari 625LM S4*	Owen Maddock

*Ferrari-engined cars known as the Cooper-Castellotti

Type	Year	Engine	Designer
T53	1960	Climax FPF S4, Maserati 250S S4, Alfa Romeo S4	Owen Maddock
T55	1961	Climax FPF S4	Owen Maddock
T58	1961	Climax FWMV V8	Owen Maddock

Type	Year	Engine	Designer
T59	1962	Climax FPF S4, Ford S4	Owen Maddock
T60	1962	Climax FMWV V8	Owen Maddock
T66	1963	Climax FMWV V8	Owen Maddock
T71/73	1964	Ford S4	Owen Maddock
T73	1964	Climax FMWV V8, Ferrari 250GT V12	Eddie Strait
T75	1968	Climax S4	Eddie Strait
T77	1965	Climax FMWV V8, ATS V8	Eddie Strait
T79	1967	Climax FPF S4	Eddie Strait
Ex-Tasman Cup car used by John Love			
T81	1966	Maserati 9/F1 V12	Derrick White
T81B	1967	Maserati 9/F1 V12	Derrick White
T86	1967	Maserati 10/F1 V12	Derrick White
T86B	1968	BRM V12, Maserati 10/F1 V12	Derrick White/Tony Robinson
T86C	1968	Alfa Romeo T33 V8	Derrick White/Tony Robinson
Test vehicle for Alfa Romeo, did not race			

Dallara

Grand Prix Debut:	1988 San Marino GP Caffi (retired)
Last Grand Prix:	1992 Australian GP Lehto (retired), Martini (retired)
Principal:	Gianpaolo Dallara
Base:	Parma
Works team:	Scuderia Italia
Principal:	Beppe Lucchini
Base:	Brescia

WORLD CHAMPIONSHIP RECORD

Starts:	78
Points:	15
Best result:	3rd 1989 Canadian GP (de Cesaris), 1991 San Marino GP (Lehto)
Best qualifying:	3rd 1989 Hungarian GP (Caffi), 1990 United States GP (de Cesaris)
Best World Championship position:	
Drivers:	12th in 1991 (Lehto)
Constructors:	8th in 1989 and 1991

DALLARA GRAND PRIX DRIVERS

Driver	Nat	Starts (DNS/DNQ)	1st	2nd	3rd	4th	5th	6th	PP	FL	Points
JJ Lehto	SF	31 (1)	-	-	1	-	-	-	-	-	4
Andrea de Cesaris	I	30 (2)	-	-	1	-	-	-	-	-	4
Alex Caffi	I	28 (4)	-	-	-	1	-	-	-	-	4
Pierluigi Martini	I	16	-	-	-	-	2	-	-	-	2
Emanuele Pirro	I	27 (3)	-	-	-	-	-	1	-	-	1
Gianni Morbidelli	I	1 (1)	-	-	-	-	-	-	-	-	-

DALLARA GRAND PRIX CARS

Type	Year	Engine	Designer
3087 F3000 car	1988	Ford DFV V8	Gianpaolo Dallara
F188	1988	Ford DFZ V8	Sergio Rinland
F189	1989	Ford DFR V8	Gianpaolo Dallara/ Mario Tolentino
F190	1990	Ford DFR V8	Gianpaolo Dallara/ Christian Vanderpleyn
F191	1991	Judd GV V10	Gianpaolo Dallara/ Nigel Couperthwaite
F192	1992	Ferrari Tipo 036 V12	Gianpaolo Dallara

De Tomaso
see Tomaso

Eagle

Grand Prix Debut:	1966 Belgian GP	Gurney (not classified)
Last Grand Prix:	1969 Canadian GP	Pease (disqualified)
Principal:	Dan Gurney	
Base:	Rye, Sussex and Santa Ana, California	

WORLD CHAMPIONSHIP RECORD

Starts:	25	
Points:	17	
Wins:	1	1967 Belgian GP (Gurney)
Best qualifying:	2nd	1967 Dutch GP (Gurney), Belgian GP (Gurney)
Fastest laps:	2	1967 Belgian GP (Gurney), German GP (Gurney)
Laps/miles in the lead:	19 laps/205 miles	

Best World Championship position:

Drivers:	8th in 1967 (Gurney)	
Constructors:	7th in 1966 and 1967	

EAGLE GRAND PRIX DRIVERS

Driver	Nat	Starts (DNS/DNQ)	1st	2nd	3rd	4th	5th	6th	PP	FL	Points
Dan Gurney	USA	24	1	-	1	-	2	-	-	2	17
Bruce McLaren	NZ	3	-	-	-	-	-	-	-	-	-
Bob Bondurant	USA	2	-	-	-	-	-	-	-	-	-
Al Pease	CDN	2 (1)	-	-	-	-	-	-	-	-	-
Ludovico Scarfiotti	I	1	-	-	-	-	-	-	-	-	-
Richie Ginther	USA	- (1)	-	-	-	-	-	-	-	-	-
Phil Hill	USA	- (1)	-	-	-	-	-	-	-	-	-

EAGLE GRAND PRIX CARS

Type	Year	Engine	Designer
AAR101	1966	Climax FPF S4	Len Terry
AAR102	1966	Weslake 58 V12	Len Terry
AAR103	1967	Weslake 58 V12	Len Terry
AAR104	1967	Weslake 58 V12	Len Terry

Eifelland

Grand Prix Debut:	1972 South African GP	Stommelen (13th)
Last Grand Prix:	1972 Austrian GP	Stommelen (not classified)
Principal:	Gunther Henerici of Eifelland Caravans	

WORLD CHAMPIONSHIP RECORD

Starts:	8	
Best result:	10th	1972 Monaco GP (Stommelen), British GP (Stommelen)
Best qualifying:	14th	1972 German GP (Stommelen)

MAJOR SPONSORS

1972	Eifelland Caravans

EIFELLAND GRAND PRIX DRIVERS

Driver	Nat	Starts (DNS/DNQ)	1st	2nd	3rd	4th	5th	6th	PP	FL	Points
Rolf Stommelen	D	8	-	-	-	-	-	-	-	-	-

EIFELLAND GRAND PRIX CARS

Type	Year	Engine	Designer
21	1972	Ford DFV V8	Luigi Colani

A March 721 with radical but unsuccessful new bodywork designed by Colani.

Emeryson

Grand Prix Debut:	1956 British GP	Emery (retired)
Last Grand Prix:	1962 Italian GP	Settember (retired)
Principal:	Paul Emery	
Base:	London, 1956-60; Send, Surrey (ex-Connaught factory), 1960-62	

WORLD CHAMPIONSHIP RECORD

Starts:	4	
Best result:	10th	1962 Dutch GP (Seidel)
Best qualifying:	19th	1962 British GP (Settember)

EMERYSON GRAND PRIX DRIVERS

Driver	Nat	Starts (DNS/DNQ)	1st	2nd	3rd	4th	5th	6th	PP	FL	Points
Tony Settember	USA	2	-	-	-	-	-	-	-	-	-
Paul Emery	GB	1	-	-	-	-	-	-	-	-	-
Wolfgang Seidel	D	1	-	-	-	-	-	-	-	-	-
Lucien Bianchi	B	- (1)	-	-	-	-	-	-	-	-	-
Olivier Gendebien	B	- (1)	-	-	-	-	-	-	-	-	-
Andre Pilette	B	- (1)	-	-	-	-	-	-	-	-	-

EMERYSON GRAND PRIX CARS

Type	Year	Engine	Designer
Mk1	1956	Alta GP S4	Paul Emery
Mk2	1961	Maserati 150S S4, Climax FPF S4	Paul Emery

EMW
Eisenacher Motoren Werke

Only Grand Prix:	1953 German GP	Barth (retired)
Base:	Eisenach	

WORLD CHAMPIONSHIP RECORD

Starts:	1	
Best result:	No finishes	
Best qualifying:	24th	1953 German GP (Barth)

EMW GRAND PRIX DRIVERS

Driver	Nat	Starts (DNS/DNQ)	1st	2nd	3rd	4th	5th	6th	PP	FL	Points
Edgar Barth	DDR	1	-	-	-	-	-	-	-	-	-

EMW GRAND PRIX CARS

Type	Year	Engine	Designer
EMW	1953	BMW 328 S6	-

ENB
Ecurie Nationale Belge

Only Grand Prix:	1962 German GP	Bianchi (16th)
Principal:	Jacques Swaters	
Base:	Brussels	

WORLD CHAMPIONSHIP RECORD

Starts:	1	
Best result:	16th	1962 German GP (Bianchi)
Best qualifying:	25th	1962 German GP (Bianchi)

ENB GRAND PRIX DRIVERS

Driver	Nat	Starts (DNS/DNQ)	1st	2nd	3rd	4th	5th	6th	PP	FL	Points
Lucien Bianchi	B	1	-	-	-	-	-	-	-	-	-

ENB GRAND PRIX CARS

Type	Year	Engine	Designer
1962	1962	Maserati 150S S4	Paul Emery

Ensign

Including Boro. Bought by Theodore in 1983;
also see Theodore

Grand Prix Debut:	1973 French GP	von Opel (15th)
Last Grand Prix:	1982 Italian GP	Guerrero (not classified)
Principal:	Mo Nunn	
Base:	Walsall, 1973-80; Chasetown, Staffordshire, 1981-82	

WORLD CHAMPIONSHIP RECORD

Starts:	99	
Points:	19	
Best result:	4th	1981 Brazilian GP (Surer)
Best qualifying:	3rd	1976 Swedish GP (Amon)
Fastest laps:	1	1981 Brazilian GP (Surer)

Best World Championship position:

Drivers:	16th in 1981 (Surer)
Constructors:	10th in 1977

MAJOR SPONSORS

1974	Dempster, Theodore Racing
1975	HB Alarms
1976	F&S Properties, First National City, John Day Models, Norris Industries, Raiffeisenkasse, Tissot
1977	Tissot, Castrol
1978	Tissot, Interscope, Mopar
1979	Rainbow Jeans
1980	Unipart
1982	Caribu

ENSIGN GRAND PRIX DRIVERS

Driver	Nat	Starts (DNS/DNQ)	1st	2nd	3rd	4th	5th	6th	PP	FL	Points
Clay Regazzoni	CH	19 (2)	-	-	-	-	2	1	-	-	5
Patrick Tambay	F	7 (1)	-	-	-	-	2	1	-	-	5
Marc Surer	CH	7 (2)	-	-	-	1	-	1	-	1	4
Chris Amon	NZ	10	-	-	-	-	1	-	-	-	2
Derek Daly	IRL	9 (5)	-	-	-	-	-	1	-	-	1
Eliseo Salazar	RCH	8 (1)	-	-	-	-	-	1	-	-	1
Gijs van Lennep	NL	3	-	-	-	-	-	1	-	-	1
Roberto Guerrero	USA	8 (7)	-	-	-	-	-	-	-	-	-
Jacky Ickx	B	8 (1)	-	-	-	-	-	-	-	-	-
Rikky von Opel	FL	6 (2)	-	-	-	-	-	-	-	-	-
Larry Perkins	AUS	5 (1)	-	-	-	-	-	-	-	-	-
Vern Schuppan	AUS	5 (2)	-	-	-	-	-	-	-	-	-
Jan Lammers	NL	3 (5)	-	-	-	-	-	-	-	-	-
Roelof Wunderink	NL	3 (3)	-	-	-	-	-	-	-	-	-
Harald Ertl	A	2 (1)	-	-	-	-	-	-	-	-	-
Patrick Gaillard	F	2 (3)	-	-	-	-	-	-	-	-	-
Danny Ongais	USA	2	-	-	-	-	-	-	-	-	-
Hans Binder	A	1	-	-	-	-	-	-	-	-	-
Brian Henton	GB	1 (1)	-	-	-	-	-	-	-	-	-
Geoff Lees	GB	1 (2)	-	-	-	-	-	-	-	-	-
Lamberto Leoni	I	1 (3)	-	-	-	-	-	-	-	-	-
Brett Lunger	USA	1	-	-	-	-	-	-	-	-	-
Tiff Needell	GB	1 (1)	-	-	-	-	-	-	-	-	-
Patrick Neve	B	1	-	-	-	-	-	-	-	-	-
Nelson Piquet	BR	1	-	-	-	-	-	-	-	-	-
Mike Wilds	GB	1 (3)	-	-	-	-	-	-	-	-	-

ENSIGN GRAND PRIX CARS

Type	Year	Engine	Designer
N173	1973	Ford DFV V8	Mo Nunn
N174	1974	Ford DFV V8	Mo Nunn
N175	1975	Ford DFV V8	Dave Baldwin/Mo Nunn
Run by 1974-sponsors HB as a Boro-Ensign in 1976			
N176	1976	Ford DFV V8	Dave Baldwin/Mo Nunn
N177	1977	Ford DFV V8	Dave Baldwin/Mo Nunn
N179	1979	Ford DFV V8	Dave Baldwin/Mo Nunn/ Shahab Ahmed
N180	1980	Ford DFV V8	Ralph Bellamy/Nigel Bennett
N180B	1981	Ford DFV V8	Ralph Bellamy/Nigel Bennett
N181	1982	Ford DFV V8	Nigel Bennett

ERA

English Racing Automobiles

Grand Prix Debut:	1950 British GP	Gerard (6th), Harrison (7th), Walker/Rolt (retired), Johnson (retired)
Last Grand Prix:	1952 Dutch GP	Moss (retired)
Principals:	Raymond Mays, Humphrey Cook and Peter Berthon (Founders). Leslie Johnson, 1947-52	
Base:	Bourne, Lincolnshire, 1933-39; Dunstable, 1947-52	

WORLD CHAMPIONSHIP RECORD

Starts:	7	
Best result:	6th	1950 British GP (Gerard), Monaco GP (Gerard)
Best qualifying:	10th	1950 British GP (Walker), 1951 British GP (Gerard), 1952 Belgian GP (Moss)

ERA GRAND PRIX DRIVERS

Driver	Nat	Starts (DNS/DNQ)	1st	2nd	3rd	4th	5th	6th	PP	FL	Points
Bob Gerard	GB	3	-	-	-	-	-	2	-	-	-
Cuth Harrison	GB	3	-	-	-	-	-	-	-	-	-
Stirling Moss	GB	3	-	-	-	-	-	-	-	-	-
Leslie Johnson	GB	1	-	-	-	-	-	-	-	-	-
Tony Rolt	GB	1	-	-	-	-	-	-	-	-	-
Brian Shawe-Taylor	GB	1	-	-	-	-	-	-	-	-	-
Peter Walker	GB	1	-	-	-	-	-	-	-	-	-

ERA GRAND PRIX CARS

Type	Year	Engine	Designer
A-type	1950*	ERA S6 sc	Reid Railton/Peter Berthon
B-type	1950*	ERA S6 sc	Reid Railton/Peter Berthon
C-type	1950*	ERA S6 sc	Reid Railton/Peter Berthon
E-type	1950*	ERA S6 sc	Reid Railton/Peter Berthon
G-type	1952	Bristol BS S6	David Hodkin

*Championship debut, the A-type first raced in 1934, B-type in 1935, C-type in 1936 and E-type in 1939

EuroBrun

Grand Prix Debut:	1988 Brazilian GP	Modena (retired)
Last Grand Prix:	1990 San Marino GP	Moreno (retired)
Principals:	Paolo Pavanello and Walter Brun	
Base:	Senago, near Milan (I)	

WORLD CHAMPIONSHIP RECORD

Starts:	14	
Best result:	11th	1988 Hungarian GP (Modena)
Best qualifying:	15th	1988 Canadian GP (Modena)

EUROBRUN GRAND PRIX DRIVERS

Driver	Nat	Starts	1st	2nd	3rd	4th	5th	6th	PP	FL	Points
		(DNS/DNQ)									
Stefano Modena	I	10 (6)	-	-	-	-	-	-	-	-	-
Oscar Larrauri	RA	7 (14)	-	-	-	-	-	-	-	-	-
Roberto Moreno	BR	2 (12)	-	-	-	-	-	-	-	-	-
Gregor Foitek	CH	- (11)	-	-	-	-	-	-	-	-	-
Claudio Langes	I	- (14)	-	-	-	-	-	-	-	-	-

EUROBRUN GRAND PRIX CARS

Type	Year	Engine	Designer
ER188	1988	Ford DFZ V8	Mario Tolentino/Bruno Zava
ER188B	1989	Judd CV V8	Mario Tolentino/Bruno Zava/ George Ryton
ER189	1989	Judd CV V8	George Ryton/Roberto Ori
ER189B	1990	Judd CV V8	George Ryton/Roberto Ori

Ferguson

Only Grand Prix: 1961 British GP   Fairman/Moss (disqualified)
Principal: Harry Ferguson
Base: Coventry

WORLD CHAMPIONSHIP RECORD

Starts: 1
Best result: No finishes
Best qualifying: 20th   1961 British GP (Fairman)

FERGUSON GRAND PRIX DRIVERS

Driver	Nat	Starts	1st	2nd	3rd	4th	5th	6th	PP	FL	Points
		(DNS/DNQ)									
Jack Fairman	GB	1	-	-	-	-	-	-	-	-	-
Stirling Moss	GB	1	-	-	-	-	-	-	-	-	-

FERGUSON GRAND PRIX CARS

Type	Year	Engine	Designer
P99 4-wheel-drive	1961	Climax FPF S4	Claude Hill

Ferrari

Grand Prix Debut: 1950 Monaco GP   Ascari (2nd), Sommer (4th), Villoresi (retired)
Latest Grand Prix: 2002 Japanese GP   Schumacher (1st), Barrichello (2nd)
Principal: Enzo Ferrari, 1929 until his death in August 1988; Cesare Fiorio, 1989-June 1991; Piero Ferrari, June 1991-92; Luca di Montezemolo, 1992 to date
Base: Modena, 1929-40; Maranello, 1945 to date

WORLD CHAMPIONSHIP RECORD

Starts: 669
Points: 3830.27
Wins: 159 1951 British GP (Gonzalez), German GP (Ascari), Italian GP (Ascari), 1952 Swiss GP (Taruffi), Belgian GP (Ascari), French GP (Ascari), British GP (Ascari), German GP (Ascari), Dutch GP (Ascari), Italian GP (Ascari), 1953 Argentinian GP (Ascari), Dutch GP (Ascari), Belgian GP (Ascari), French GP (Hawthorn), British GP (Ascari), German GP (Farina), Swiss GP (Ascari), 1954 British GP (Gonzalez), Spanish GP (Hawthorn), 1955 Monaco GP (Trintignant), 1956 Argentinian GP (Musso/Fangio), Belgian GP (Collins), French GP (Collins), British GP (Fangio), German GP (Fangio), 1958 French GP (Hawthorn), British GP

(Collins), 1959 French GP (Brooks), German GP (Brooks), 1960 Italian GP (Hill), 1961 Dutch GP (von Trips), Belgian GP (Hill), French GP (Baghetti), British GP (von Trips), Italian GP (Hill), 1963 German GP (Surtees), 1964 German GP (Surtees), Austrian GP (Bandini), Italian GP (Surtees), 1966 Belgian GP (Surtees), Italian GP (Scarfiotti), 1968 French GP (Ickx), 1970 Austrian GP (Ickx), Italian GP (Regazzoni), Canadian GP (Ickx), Mexican GP (Ickx), 1971 South African GP (Andretti), Dutch GP (Ickx), 1972 German GP (Ickx), 1974 Spanish GP (Lauda), Dutch GP (Lauda), German GP (Regazzoni), 1975 Monaco GP (Lauda), Belgian GP (Lauda), Swedish GP (Lauda), French GP (Lauda), Italian GP (Regazzoni), United States GP (Lauda), 1976 Brazilian GP (Lauda), South African GP (Lauda), Long Beach GP (Regazzoni), Belgian GP (Lauda), Monaco GP (Lauda), British GP (Lauda), 1977 Brazilian GP (Reutemann), South African GP (Lauda), German GP (Lauda), Dutch GP (Lauda), 1978 Brazilian GP (Reutemann), Long Beach GP (Reutemann), British GP (Reutemann), United States GP (Reutemann), Canadian GP (Villeneuve), 1979 South African GP (Villeneuve), Long Beach GP (Villeneuve), Belgian GP (Scheckter), Monaco GP (Scheckter), Italian GP (Scheckter), United States GP (Villeneuve), 1981 Monaco GP (Villeneuve), Spanish GP (Villeneuve), 1982 San Marino GP (Pironi), Dutch GP (Pironi), German GP (Tambay), 1983 San Marino GP (Tambay), Canadian GP (Arnoux), German GP (Arnoux), Dutch GP (Arnoux), 1984 Belgian GP (Alboreto), 1985 Canadian GP (Alboreto), German GP (Alboreto), 1987 Japanese GP (Berger), Australian GP (Berger), 1988 Italian GP (Berger), 1989 Brazilian GP (Mansell), Hungarian GP (Mansell), Portuguese GP (Berger), 1990 Brazilian GP (Prost), Mexican GP (Prost), French GP (Prost), British GP (Prost), Portuguese GP (Mansell), Spanish GP (Prost), 1994 German GP (Berger), 1995 Canadian GP (Alesi), 1996 Spanish GP (Schumacher), Belgian GP (Schumacher), Italian GP (Schumacher), 1997 Monaco GP (Schumacher), Canadian GP (Schumacher), French GP (Schumacher), Belgian GP (Schumacher), Japanese GP (Schumacher), 1998 Argentinian GP (Schumacher), Canadian GP (Schumacher), French GP (Schumacher), British GP (Schumacher), Hungarian GP (Schumacher), Italian GP (Schumacher), 1999 Australian GP (Irvine), San Marino GP (Schumacher), Monaco GP (Schumacher), Austrian GP (Irvine), German GP (Irvine), Malaysian GP (Irvine), 2000 Australian GP (Schumacher), Brazilian GP (Schumacher), San Marino GP (Schumacher), European GP (Schumacher), Canadian GP (Schumacher), German GP (Barrichello), Italian GP (Schumacher), United States GP (Schumacher), Japanese GP (Schumacher), Malaysian GP (Schumacher), 2001 Australian GP (Schumacher), Malaysian GP (Schumacher), Spanish GP (Schumacher), Monaco GP (Schumacher), European GP (Schumacher), French GP (Schumacher), Hungarian GP (Schumacher), Belgian GP (Schumacher), Japanese GP (Schumacher), 2002 Australian GP (Schumacher), Brazilian GP (Schumacher), San Marino GP (Schumacher), Spanish GP (Schumacher), Austrian GP (Schumacher), Canadian GP (Schumacher), European GP (Barrichello), British GP (Schumacher), French GP (Schumacher), German GP (Schumacher), Hungarian GP (Barrichello), Belgian GP (Schumacher), Italian GP (Barrichello), United States GP (Barrichello),

Manufacturers 'E-F'

Japanese GP (Schumacher)

Pole positions: 158 1951 British GP (Gonzalez), German GP (Ascari), Spanish GP (Ascari), 1952 Swiss GP (Farina), Belgian GP (Ascari), French GP (Ascari), British GP (Farina), German GP (Ascari), Dutch GP (Ascari), Italian GP (Ascari), 1953 Argentinian GP (Ascari), Dutch GP (Ascari), French GP (Ascari), British GP (Ascari), German GP (Ascari), Italian GP (Ascari), 1954 Argentinian GP (Farina), Swiss GP (Gonzalez), 1955 Argentinian GP (Gonzalez), 1956 Argentinian GP (Fangio), Monaco GP (Fangio), Belgian GP (Fangio), French GP (Fangio), German GP (Fangio), Italian GP (Fangio), 1958 Belgian GP (Hawthorn), French GP (Hawthorn), German GP (Hawthorn), Moroccan GP (Hawthorn), 1959 French GP (Brooks), German GP (Brooks), 1960 Italian GP (Hill), 1961 Dutch GP (Hill), Belgian GP (Hill), French GP (Hill), British GP (Hill), German GP (Hill), Italian GP (von Trips), 1963 Italian GP (Surtees), 1964 German GP (Surtees), Italian GP (Surtees), 1966 Belgian GP (Surtees), French GP (Bandini), Italian GP (Parkes), 1968 Spanish GP (Amon), Belgian GP (Amon), Dutch GP (Amon), German GP (Ickx), 1970 French GP (Ickx), German GP (Ickx), Italian GP (Ickx), United States GP (Ickx), Mexican GP (Regazzoni), 1971 Spanish GP (Ickx), Dutch GP (Ickx), British GP (Regazzoni), 1972 Spanish GP (Ickx), British GP (Ickx), German GP (Ickx), Italian GP (Ickx), 1974 South African GP (Lauda), Spanish GP (Lauda), Belgian GP (Regazzoni), Monaco GP (Lauda), Dutch GP (Lauda), French GP (Lauda), British GP (Lauda), German GP (Lauda), Austrian GP (Lauda), Italian GP (Lauda), 1975 Spanish GP (Lauda), Monaco GP (Lauda), Belgian GP (Lauda), Dutch GP (Lauda), French GP (Lauda), German GP (Lauda), Austrian GP (Lauda), Italian GP (Lauda), United States GP (Lauda), 1976 Long Beach GP (Regazzoni), Belgian GP (Lauda), Monaco GP (Lauda), British GP (Lauda), 1977 Long Beach GP (Lauda), Austrian GP (Lauda), 1978 Long Beach GP (Reutemann), Monaco GP (Reutemann), 1979 Long Beach GP (Villeneuve), Monaco GP (Scheckter), 1981 San Marino GP (Villeneuve), 1982 Canadian GP (Pironi), German GP (Pironi), Italian GP (Andretti), 1983 Long Beach GP (Tambay), San Marino GP (Arnoux), Detroit GP (Arnoux), Canadian GP (Arnoux), British GP (Arnoux), German GP (Tambay), Austrian GP (Tambay), South African GP (Tambay), 1984 Belgian GP (Alboreto), 1985 Brazilian GP (Alboreto), 1987 Portuguese GP (Berger), Japanese GP (Berger), Australian GP (Berger), 1988 British GP (Berger), 1990 French GP (Mansell), British GP (Mansell), Portuguese GP (Mansell), 1994 German GP (Berger), Italian GP (Alesi), Portuguese GP (Berger), 1995 Belgian GP (Berger), 1996 San Marino GP (Schumacher), Monaco GP (Schumacher), French GP (Schumacher), Hungarian GP (Schumacher), 1997 Canadian GP (Schumacher), French GP (Schumacher), Hungarian GP (Schumacher), 1998 Italian GP (Schumacher), Luxembourg GP (Schumacher), Japanese GP (Schumacher), 1999 Canadian GP (Schumacher), Malaysian GP (Schumacher), Japanese GP (Schumacher), 2000 British GP (Barrichello), Spanish GP (Schumacher), Monaco GP (Schumacher), Canadian GP (Schumacher), French GP (Schumacher), Hungarian GP (Schumacher), Italian GP (Schumacher), United States GP (Schumacher), Japanese GP (Schumacher), Malaysian GP (Schumacher), 2001 Australian GP (Schumacher), Malaysian GP (Schumacher), Brazilian GP (Schumacher), Spanish GP (Schumacher), Austrian GP (Schumacher), Canadian GP (Schumacher), European GP (Schumacher), British GP (Schumacher), Hungarian GP (Schumacher), United States GP (Schumacher), Japanese GP (Schumacher), 2002 Australian GP (Barrichello), Malaysian GP (Schumacher), San Marino GP (Schumacher), Spanish GP (Schumacher), Austrian GP (Barrichello), German GP (Schumacher), Hungarian GP (Barrichello), Belgian GP (Schumacher), United States GP (Schumacher), Japanese GP (Schumacher)

Fastest laps: 160 1952 Swiss GP (Taruffi), Belgian GP (Ascari), French GP (Ascari), British GP (Ascari), German GP (Ascari), Dutch GP (Ascari), Italian GP (Ascari), 1953 Argentinian GP (Ascari), Dutch GP (Villoresi), French GP (Ascari), British GP (Ascari), German GP (Ascari), Swiss GP (Ascari), 1954 Argentinian GP (Gonzalez), British GP (Gonzalez), and (Hawthorn), Italian GP (Gonzalez), 1956 Argentinian GP (Fangio), Monaco GP (Fangio), French GP (Fangio), German GP (Fangio), 1957 French GP (Musso), 1958 Monaco GP (Hawthorn), Belgian GP (Hawthorn), French GP (Hawthorn), British GP (Hawthorn), Portuguese GP (Hawthorn), Italian GP (Hill), 1959 German GP (Brooks), Italian GP (Hill), 1960 Belgian GP (Hill), Italian GP (Hill), 1961 Monaco GP (Ginther), Belgian GP (Ginther), French GP (Hill), German GP (Hill), Italian GP (Baghetti), 1963 Monaco GP (Surtees), British GP (Surtees), German GP (Surtees), 1964 German GP (Surtees), Italian GP (Surtees), 1966 Monaco GP (Bandini), Belgian GP (Surtees), French GP (Bandini), Italian GP (Scarfiotti), 1970 Dutch GP (Ickx), German GP (Ickx), Austrian GP (Ickx), and (Regazzoni), Italian GP (Regazzoni), Canadian GP (Regazzoni), United States GP (Ickx), Mexican GP (Ickx), 1971 South African GP (Andretti), Spanish GP (Ickx), Dutch GP (Ickx), United States GP (Ickx), 1972 Spanish GP (Ickx), German GP (Ickx), Italian GP (Ickx), 1974 Argentinian GP (Regazzoni), Brazilian GP (Regazzoni), Spanish GP (Lauda), British GP (Lauda), Austrian GP (Regazzoni), Canadian GP (Lauda), 1975 Belgian GP (Regazzoni), Swedish GP (Lauda), Dutch GP (Lauda), British GP (Regazzoni), German GP (Regazzoni), Italian GP (Regazzoni), 1976 South African GP (Lauda), Long Beach GP (Regazzoni), Belgian GP (Lauda), Monaco GP (Regazzoni), French GP (Lauda), British GP (Lauda), Dutch GP (Regazzoni), 1977 Long Beach GP (Lauda), German GP (Lauda), Dutch GP (Lauda), 1978 Argentinian GP (Villeneuve), Brazilian GP (Reutemann), French GP (Reutemann), 1979 South African GP (Villeneuve), Long Beach GP (Villeneuve), Spanish GP (Villeneuve), Belgian GP (Villeneuve), German GP (Villeneuve), Dutch GP (Villeneuve), 1981 San Marino GP (Villeneuve), Las Vegas GP (Pironi), 1982 San Marino GP (Pironi), Canadian GP (Pironi), 1983 Canadian GP (Tambay), German GP (Arnoux), Dutch GP (Arnoux), 1984 Belgian GP (Arnoux), Dutch GP (Arnoux), European GP (Alboreto), 1985 San Marino GP (Alboreto), Monaco GP (Alboreto), 1987 Portuguese GP (Berger), Spanish GP (Berger), Australian GP (Berger), 1988 Brazilian GP (Berger), Belgian GP (Berger), Italian GP (Alboreto), Portuguese GP (Berger), 1989 Mexican GP (Mansell), British GP (Mansell), Hungarian GP (Mansell), Portuguese GP (Berger), 1990 Mexican GP (Prost), French GP (Mansell), British GP (Mansell), Belgian GP (Prost), Australian GP (Mansell), 1991 United States GP (Alesi), Monaco GP (Prost), 1995 San Marino GP (Berger), Monaco GP (Alesi), Italian GP (Berger), 1996 Spanish GP (Schumacher), Italian GP (Schumacher), 1997 Monaco GP (Schumacher), French GP (Schumacher), British GP (Schumacher),

1998 San Marino GP (Schumacher), Canadian GP (Schumacher), British GP (Schumacher), Hungarian GP (Schumacher), Belgian GP (Schumacher), Japanese GP (Schumacher), 1999 Australian GP (Schumacher), San Marino GP (Schumacher), Spanish GP (Schumacher), Canadian GP (Irvine), Malaysian GP (Schumacher), Japanese GP (Schumacher), 2000 Australian GP (Barrichello), Brazilian GP (Schumacher), European GP (Schumacher), German GP (Barrichello), Belgian GP (Barrichello), 2001 Australian GP (Schumacher), Spanish GP (Schumacher), Belgian GP (Schumacher), 2002 San Marino GP (Barrichello), Spanish GP (Schumacher), Austrian GP (Schumacher), Monaco GP (Barrichello), European GP (Schumacher), British GP (Barrichello), German GP (Schumacher), Hungarian GP (Schumacher), Belgian GP (Schumacher), Italian GP (Barrichello), United States GP (Barrichello), Japanese GP (Schumacher)

Laps/miles in the lead: 10182 laps/33421 miles

World Champions:

Drivers: Twelve times - 1952 (Ascari), 1953 (Ascari), 1956 (Fangio), 1958 (Hawthorn), 1961 (P Hill), 1964 (Surtees), 1975 (Lauda), 1977 (Lauda), 1979 (Scheckter), 2000 (Schumacher), 2001 (Schumacher) and 2002 (Schumacher)

Constructors: Twelve times - 1961, 1964, 1975, 1976, 1977, 1979, 1982, 1983, 1999, 2000, 2001 and 2002

MAJOR SPONSORS

1997-99	Marlboro (as major sponsor)
2000-2001	Marlboro, Shell
2002 to date	Marlboro, Vodafone, Shell

FERRARI GRAND PRIX DRIVERS

Driver	Nat	Starts (DNS/DNQ)	1st	2nd	3rd	4th	5th	6th	PP	FL	Points
Michael Schumacher	D	109 (1)	45	23	8	4	4	2	40	28	642
Niki Lauda	A	57 (1)	15	12	5	2	4	2	23	12	242.5
Alberto Ascari	I	26 (1)	13	4	-	2	1	1	13	11	139.5
Jacky Ickx	B	55 (1)	6	4	6	4	3	1	11	11	121
Gilles Villeneuve	CDN	66 (1)	6	5	2	2	3	3	2	8	107
Rubens Barrichello	BR	49 (2)	5	14	10	5	3	-	4	8	195
Gerhard Berger	A	96	5	8	11	11	3	5	7	9	182
Alain Prost	F	30 (1)	5	5	4	4	2	-	-	3	107
Carlos Reutemann	RA	34	5	2	6	2	-	3	2	2	90
Clay Regazzoni	CH	73	4	11	8	8	4	3	4	13	169
Eddie Irvine	GB	65	4	6	13	6	4	2	-	1	156
John Surtees	GB	30	4	5	4	2	-	-	4	6	88
Michele Alboreto	I	80	3	9	7	7	4	1	2	4	138.5
Mike Hawthorn	GB	35	3	9	4	5	2	3	4	6	113.64
Phil Hill	USA	31	3	5	8	2	-	1	6	6	96
Rene Arnoux	F	32	3	4	4	2	3	2	4	4	79
Nigel Mansell	GB	31	3	5	3	2	-	-	3	6	75
Jody Scheckter	ZA	28 (1)	3	3	-	4	2	1	1	-	62
Peter Collins	GB	20	3	3	3	1	1	1	-	-	47
Juan Manuel Fangio	RA	7	3	2	-	2	-	-	6	4	34.5
Patrick Tambay	F	21 (2)	2	3	3	5	1	-	4	1	65
Jose Froilan Gonzalez	RA	15	2	6	3	1	1	-	3	3	56.64
Wolfgang von Trips	D	25 (1)	2	2	2	3	4	3	1	-	56
Didier Pironi	F	25 (2)	2	2	2	1	3	1	2	3	48
Tony Brooks	GB	7	2	1	1	-	-	-	2	1	27
Jean Alesi	F	79	1	6	9	7	8	2	1	2	121
Giuseppe Farina	I	20 (1)	1	9	3	2	1	1	3	-	75.33

Driver	Nat	Start	1st	2nd	3rd	4th	5th	6th	PP	FL	Points
Lorenzo Bandini	I	35	1	2	5	2	3	3	1	2	56
Maurice Trintignant	F	17 (1)	1	2	2	2	3	1	-	-	33.33
Luigi Musso	I	15	1	4	-	1	-	-	-	1	32
Piero Taruffi	I	13	1	2	1	1	2	1	-	1	32
Mario Andretti	USA	12 (2)	1	-	1	2	-	1	1	1	20
Giancarlo Baghetti	I	8	1	-	-	1	1	-	-	1	14
Ludovico Scarfiotti	I	6 (2)	1	-	-	-	-	2	-	1	11
Stefan Johansson	S	31	-	2	4	5	2	2	-	-	49
Luigi Villoresi	I	20 (2)	-	2	6	2	-	3	-	1	43
Chris Amon	NZ	27	-	1	5	2	-	2	3	-	34
Richie Ginther	USA	10	-	2	2	-	1	2	-	2	24
Michael Parkes	GB	6	-	2	-	-	1	-	1	-	14
Eugenio Castellotti	I	11	-	1	1	1	1	1	-	-	13.5
Dan Gurney	USA	4	-	1	1	1	-	-	-	1	13
Rudolf Fischer	CH	7 (1)	-	1	-	1	-	-	-	-	10
Mika Salo	SF	6	-	1	1	-	-	-	-	-	10
Paul Frere	B	3	-	1	-	1	-	-	-	-	9
Olivier Gendebien	B	8	-	-	-	2	1	2	-	-	8
Cliff Allison	GB	6 (1)	-	1	-	-	1	-	-	-	8
Arturo Merzario	I	11	-	-	-	2	-	1	-	-	7
Willy Mairesse	B	10	-	1	1	1	-	-	-	-	7
Pedro Rodriguez	MEX	8	-	-	-	2	2	-	-	-	6
Nicola Larini	I	4	-	1	-	-	-	-	-	-	6
Peter Whitehead	GB	7 (2)	-	-	1	-	-	-	-	-	4
Ricardo Rodriguez	MEX	5 (1)	-	-	1	-	1	-	-	-	4
Robert Manzon	F	5 (1)	-	-	1	-	-	-	-	-	4
Alfonso de Portago	E	5	-	1	-	1	-	-	-	-	4
Umberto Maglioli	I	6	-	2	-	-	1	-	-	-	3.33
Ivan Capelli	I	14	-	-	-	1	1	1	-	-	3
Ignazio Giunti	I	4	-	-	1	-	-	-	-	-	3
Raymond Sommer	F	2	-	-	1	-	-	-	-	-	3
Reg Parnell	GB	2	-	-	1	-	-	-	-	-	3
Dorino Serafini	I	1	-	1	-	-	-	-	-	-	3
Jean Behra	F	3	-	-	-	1	-	-	-	-	2
Gianni Morbidelli	I	1	-	-	-	-	1	-	-	-	0.5
Louis Rosier	F	15	-	-	-	-	-	-	-	-	-
Jacques Swaters	B	5 (1)	-	-	-	-	-	-	-	-	-
Peter Hirt	CH	4	-	-	-	-	-	-	-	-	-
Piero Carini	I	3	-	-	-	-	-	-	-	-	-
Charles de Tornaco	B	2 (2)	-	-	-	-	-	-	-	-	-
Andre Simon	F	2	-	-	-	-	1	-	-	-	-
Derek Bell	GB	2	-	-	-	-	-	-	-	-	-
Giorgio Scarlatti	I	1 (1)	-	-	-	-	-	-	-	-	-
Alejandro de Tomaso	RA	1	-	-	-	-	-	-	-	-	-
Andre Pilette	B	1	-	-	-	1	-	-	-	-	-
Andrea de Adamich	I	1	-	-	-	-	-	-	-	-	-
Bob Bondurant	USA	1	-	-	-	-	-	-	-	-	-
Cesare Perdisa	I	1	-	-	-	-	-	-	-	-	-
Chico Landi	BR	1	-	-	-	-	-	-	-	-	-
Clemente Biondetti	I	1	-	-	-	-	-	-	-	-	-
Gianfranco Comotti	I	1	-	-	-	-	-	-	-	-	-
Harry Schell	USA	1	-	-	-	-	-	-	-	-	-
Johnny Claes	B	1	-	-	-	-	-	-	-	-	-
Jonathan Williams	GB	1	-	-	-	-	-	-	-	-	-
Kurt Adolff	D	1	-	-	-	-	-	-	-	-	-
Max de Terra	CH	1	-	-	-	-	-	-	-	-	-
Nanni Galli	I	1	-	-	-	-	-	-	-	-	-
Nino Vaccarella	I	1	-	-	-	-	-	-	-	-	-
Roger Laurent	B	1	-	-	-	1	-	-	-	-	-
Roy Salvadori	GB	1	-	-	-	-	-	-	-	-	-
Rudolf Schoeller	CH	1	-	-	-	-	-	-	-	-	-
Hans Stuck	D	- (1)	-	-	-	-	-	-	-	-	-
Tino Brambilla	I	- (1)	-	-	-	-	-	-	-	-	-

FERRARI GRAND PRIX CARS

Type	Year	Engine	Designer
125	1950#	Ferrari 125/F1 V12 sc	Gioacchino Colombo
166I	1950	Jaguar XK120 S6	Aurelio Lampredi; modified by Clemente Biondetti
275	1950	Ferrari 275/F1 V12	Aurelio Lampredi

Type	Year	Engine	Designer
375	1950	Ferrari 375/F1 V12	Aurelio Lampredi
212	1951	Ferrari 212 S4	Giocchino Colombo
500	1952	Ferrari 500/F2 S4	Aurelio Lampredi
166/F2	1952	Ferrari 166/F2 V12	Aurelio Lampredi
212 (52)	1952	Ferrari 166/F2 V12	Aurelio Lampredi
125/F2	1952	Ferrari 166/F2 V12	Aurelio Lampredi
166C	1953	Ferrari 166/F2 V12	Aurelio Lampredi
553	1953	Ferrari 553/F2 S4	Aurelio Lampredi
625	1954	Ferrari 625/F1 S4	Aurelio Lampredi
553 Squalo	1954	Ferrari 555/F1 S4	Aurelio Lampredi
625 (555)	1954	Ferrari 625/555 S4	Aurelio Lampredi
625 (735/555)	1954	Ferrari 735/555 S4	Aurelio Lampredi
555 Super-squalo	1955	Ferrari 555/F1 S4	Aurelio Lampredi
D50*	1955	Lancia DS50 V8	Vittorio Jano

The Lancia-Ferrari D50 was also known as Ferrari 801 in 1956

Type	Year	Engine	Designer
Dino 246	1958	Ferrari 246/F1 V6	Vittorio Jano/Carlo Chiti
Dino 156	1958	Ferrari 156/F1 V6	Vittorio Jano/Carlo Chiti
Dino 246P	1960	Ferrari 246/F1 V6	Carlo Chiti
Dino 156P	1960	Ferrari 156/F1 V6	Carlo Chiti
Dino 156	1963	Ferrari 156/F1 V6	Mauro Forghieri
158	1964	Ferrari 158/F1 V8	Mauro Forghieri
1512	1964	Ferrari 1512/F1 F12	Mauro Forghieri
158/246	1966	Ferrari 246/F1 V6	Mauro Forghieri
312	1966	Ferrari 312 V12	Mauro Forghieri
312B	1970	Ferrari 312B Boxer F12	Mauro Forghieri
312B2	1971	Ferrari 312B Boxer F12	Mauro Forghieri
312B3	1973	Ferrari 312B Boxer F12	Mauro Forghieri/Franco Rocchi
312B3S	1973	Ferrari 312B Boxer F12	Mauro Forghieri/Franco Rocchi
312T	1975	Ferrari 312B Boxer F12	Mauro Forghieri/Franco Rocchi
312T2	1976	Ferrari 312B Boxer F12	Mauro Forghieri/Franco Rocchi
312T3	1978	Ferrari 312B Boxer F12	Mauro Forghieri
312T4	1979	Ferrari 312B Boxer F12	Mauro Forghieri
312T5	1980	Ferrari 312B Boxer F12	Mauro Forghieri
126CK	1981	Ferrari 126C V6 tc	Mauro Forghieri/Antonio Tomaini
126C2	1982	Ferrari 126C V6 tc	Harvey Postlethwaite
126C2B	1983	Ferrari 126C V6 tc	Harvey Postlethwaite
126C3	1983	Ferrari 126C V6 tc	Harvey Postlethwaite
126C4	1984	Ferrari 126C V6 tc	Harvey Postlethwaite/Mauro Forghieri
156/85	1985	Ferrari 126C V6 tc	Harvey Postlethwaite/Antonio Tomaini/Ildo Renzetti
F186	1986	Ferrari F186 V6 tc	Harvey Postlethwaite
F187	1987	Ferrari Tipo 033 V6 tc	Gustav Brunner
F187/88C	1988	Ferrari Tipo 033B V6 tc	Gustav Brunner
640	1989	Ferrari Tipo 034 V12	John Barnard
641	1990	Ferrari Tipo 036 V12	John Barnard
641/2	1990	Ferrari Tipo 036 V12	John Barnard
642	1991	Ferrari Tipo 036 V12	Steve Nichols
643	1991	Ferrari Tipo 036 V12	Steve Nichols
F92A	1992	Ferrari Tipo 036 V12	Steve Nichols
F92AT	1992	Ferrari Tipo 036 V12	Steve Nichols
F93A	1993	Ferrari Tipo 036 V12	George Ryton/John Barnard
412T1	1994	Ferrari Tipo 043 V12	John Barnard
412T1B	1994	Ferrari Tipo 043 V12	John Barnard
412T2	1995	Ferrari Tipo 044 V12	John Barnard
F310	1996	Ferrari Tipo 046 V10	John Barnard
F310B	1997	Ferrari Tipo 046 V10	John Barnard
F300	1998	Ferrari Tipo 047 V10	Ross Brawn
F399	1999	Ferrari Tipo 048 V10	Ross Brawn
F1-2000	2000	Ferrari Tipo 049 V10	Ross Brawn
F2001	2001	Ferrari Tipo 050 V10	Ross Brawn
F2002	2002	Ferrari Tipo 051 V10	Ross Brawn

*Lancia-Ferrari. #Championship debut, the 125 first raced in 1948

Fittipaldi

Bought Walter Wolf Racing in 1980

Grand Prix Debut: 1975 Argentinian GP W Fittipaldi (retired)
Last Grand Prix: 1982 Italian GP Serra (11th)
Principals: Wilson Fittipaldi, 1975; Wilson and Emerson Fittipaldi, 1976-82
Base: Sao Paulo and Reading, Berkshire

WORLD CHAMPIONSHIP RECORD

Starts: 103
Points: 44
Best result: 2nd 1978 Brazilian GP (E Fittipaldi)
Best qualifying: 5th 1976 Brazilian GP (E Fittipaldi)

Best World Championship position:
Drivers: 9th in 1978 (E Fittipaldi)
Constructors: 7th in 1978

MAJOR SPONSORS

1975-79	Copersucar
1980	Skol Brasil

FITTIPALDI GRAND PRIX DRIVERS

Driver	Nat	Starts	1st	2nd	3rd	4th	5th	6th	PP	FL	Points
		(DNS/DNQ)									
Emerson Fittipaldi	BR	74 (3)	-	1	1	5	3	6	-	-	37
Keke Rosberg	SF	20 (8)	-	-	1	-	1	-	-	-	6
Chico Serra	BR	14 (15)	-	-	-	-	-	1	-	-	1
Wilson Fittipaldi	BR	10 (3)	-	-	-	-	-	-	-	-	-
Ingo Hoffmann	BR	3 (3)	-	-	-	-	-	-	-	-	-
Arturo Merzario	I	1	-	-	-	-	-	-	-	-	-
Alex Ribeiro	BR	- (2)	-	-	-	-	-	-	-	-	-

FITTIPALDI GRAND PRIX CARS

Type	Year	Engine	Designer
FD01	1975	Ford DFV V8	Richard Divila
FD02	1975	Ford DFV V8	Richard Divila
FD03	1975	Ford DFV V8	Richard Divila
FD04	1976	Ford DFV V8	Richard Divila
F5	1977	Ford DFV V8	David Baldwin
F5A	1978	Ford DFV V8	David Baldwin/Giacomo Caliri
F6	1979	Ford DFV V8	Ralph Bellamy
F6A	1979	Ford DFV V8	Ralph Bellamy
F7	1980	Ford DFV V8	Harvey Postlethwaite

Formerly Wolf WR7, WR8 and WR9 chassis, renamed when Fittipaldi bought Wolf

Type	Year	Engine	Designer
F8	1980	Ford DFV V8	Harvey Postlethwaite
F8C	1981	Ford DFV V8	Harvey Postlethwaite/Gary Thomas
F8D	1982	Ford DFV V8	Harvey Postlethwaite/Gary Thomas/Tim Wright
F9	1982	Ford DFV V8	Richard Divila/Tim Wright

Fondmetal

Bought Osella in 1991; also see Osella

Grand Prix Debut: 1991 Mexican GP Grouillard (retired)
Last Grand Prix: 1992 Italian GP Tarquini (retired), van de Poele (retired)
Principal: Gabriele Rumi
Base: Constructor: Bicester (GB); Team: Palosco, near Bergamo (I)

WORLD CHAMPIONSHIP RECORD

Starts:	19	
Best result:	10th	1991 Belgian GP (Grouillard), 1992 Belgian GP (van de Poele)
Best qualifying:	10th	1991 Mexican GP (Grouillard)

MAJOR SPONSORS

1991-92	Fondmetal Wheels

FONDMETAL GRAND PRIX DRIVERS

Driver	Nat	Starts (DNS/DNQ)	1st	2nd	3rd	4th	5th	6th	PP	FL	Points
Gabriele Tarquini	I	15 (1)	-	-	-	-	-	-	-	-	-
Olivier Grouillard	F	4 (9)	-	-	-	-	-	-	-	-	-
Andrea Chiesa	CH	3 (7)	-	-	-	-	-	-	-	-	-
Eric van de Poele	B	3	-	-	-	-	-	-	-	-	-

FONDMETAL GRAND PRIX CARS

Type	Year	Engine	Designer
FA1Me*	1991	Ford DFR V8	Antonio Tomaini
Formerly Osella FA1Me, renamed Fomet when Fondmetal bought Osella			
F1*	1991	Ford DFR V8	Tino Belli/Riccardo Rosa/ Tim Holloway
GR01	1992	Ford HB V8	Tino Belli/Riccardo Rosa/ Tim Holloway
GR02	1992	Ford HB V8	Sergio Rinland
*Fomet			

Footwork

See Arrows

Forti

Grand Prix Debut:	1995 Brazilian GP	Diniz (10th), Moreno (retired)
Last Grand Prix:	1996 French GP	Montermini (retired), Badoer (retired)
Principal:	Guido Forti	
Base:	Alessandria	

WORLD CHAMPIONSHIP RECORD

Starts:	23	
Best result:	7th	1995 Australian GP (Diniz)
Best qualifying:	19th	1996 Brazilian GP (Badoer)

MAJOR SPONSORS

1995	Parmalat
1996	Hudson, Finfirst, TAT, Shannon

FORTI GRAND PRIX DRIVERS

Driver	Nat	Starts (DNS/DNQ)	1st	2nd	3rd	4th	5th	6th	PP	FL	Points
Pedro Diniz	BR	17	-	-	-	-	-	-	-	-	-
Roberto Moreno	BR	17	-	-	-	-	-	-	-	-	-
Luca Badoer	I	6 (4)	-	-	-	-	-	-	-	-	-
Andrea Montermini	I	4 (6)	-	-	-	-	-	-	-	-	-

FORTI GRAND PRIX CARS

Type	Year	Engine	Designer
FG01	1995	Ford ED V8	Giorgio Stirano
FG01B	1996	Ford Zetec-R V8	Giorgio Stirano
FG03	1996	Ford Zetec-R V8	George Ryton

Frazer-Nash

Grand Prix Debut:	1952 Swiss GP	Wharton (4th)
Last Grand Prix:	1952 Dutch GP	Wharton (retired)
Base:	Isleworth	

WORLD CHAMPIONSHIP RECORD

Starts:	4	
Points:	3	
Best result:	4th	1952 Swiss GP (Wharton)
Best qualifying:	7th	1952 Belgian GP (Wharton), Dutch GP (Wharton)
Best World Championship position:		
Drivers:	13th in 1952 (Wharton)	
Constructors:	-	

FRAZER-NASH GRAND PRIX DRIVERS

Driver	Nat	Starts (DNS/DNQ)	1st	2nd	3rd	4th	5th	6th	PP	FL	Points
Ken Wharton	GB	3	-	-	-	1	-	-	-	-	3
Tony Crook	GB	1	-	-	-	-	-	-	-	-	-

FRAZER-NASH GRAND PRIX CARS

Type	Year	Engine	Designer
FN48	1952	Bristol BS S6	HJ Aldington
421	1952	BMW 328 S6, Bristol BS S6	HJ Aldington

Fry

Principal:	David Fry

WORLD CHAMPIONSHIP RECORD

Starts:	None

FRY GRAND PRIX DRIVERS

Driver	Nat	Starts (DNS/DNQ)	1st	2nd	3rd	4th	5th	6th	PP	FL	Points
Michael Parkes	GB	- (1)	-	-	-	-	-	-	-	-	-

FRY GRAND PRIX CARS

Type	Year	Engine	Designer
Fry	1959	Climax FPF S4	David Fry

Gilby

Grand Prix Debut:	1961 British GP	Greene (15th)
Last Grand Prix:	1963 British GP	Raby (retired)
Principal:	Sid Greene	
Base:	Ongar	

WORLD CHAMPIONSHIP RECORD

Starts:	3	
Best result:	15th	1961 British GP (Greene)
Best qualifying:	19th	1962 German GP (Greene), 1963 British GP (Raby)

GILBY GRAND PRIX DRIVERS

Driver	Nat	Starts (DNS/DNQ)	1st	2nd	3rd	4th	5th	6th	PP	FL	Points
Keith Greene	GB	2 (1)	-	-	-	-	-	-	-	-	-
Ian Raby	GB	1 (2)	-	-	-	-	-	-	-	-	-

GILBY GRAND PRIX CARS

Type	Year	Engine	Designer
Gilby	1961	Climax FPF S4, BRM 56 V8	Len Terry

Gordini

Grand Prix Debut:	1950 Monaco GP	Manzon (retired), Trintignant (retired)
Last Grand Prix:	1956 Italian GP	Simon (9th), Manzon (retired), da Silva Ramos (retired)
Principal:	Amedee Gordini	
Base:	Paris	

WORLD CHAMPIONSHIP RECORD

Starts:	40	
Points:	30.14	
Best result:	3rd	1952 Swiss GP (Behra), Belgian GP (Manzon)
Best qualifying:	3rd	1952 Swiss GP (Manzon), German GP (Trintignant)
Fastest laps:	1	1954 British GP (Behra)
Laps/miles in the lead:	1 lap/9 miles	

Best World Championship position:

Drivers:	6th in 1952 (Manzon)
Constructors:	-

GORDINI GRAND PRIX DRIVERS

Driver	Nat	Starts (DNS/DNQ)	1st	2nd	3rd	4th	5th	6th	PP	FL	Points
Robert Manzon	F	23	-	-	1	2	1	-	-	-	12
Jean Behra	F	20	-	-	1	-	1	2	-	1	6.14
Maurice Trintignant	F	19	-	-	-	3	2	-	-	-	6
Hermanos da Silva Ramos	F/BR	7	-	-	-	-	1	-	-	-	2
Andre Pilette	B	5 (1)	-	-	-	-	1	1	-	-	2
Elie Bayol	F	4	-	-	-	-	1	1	-	-	2
Harry Schell	USA	7	-	-	-	-	-	-	-	-	-
Jacques Pollet	F	5	-	-	-	-	-	-	-	-	-
Andre Simon	F	5	-	-	-	-	-	1	-	-	-
"B Bira"	SM	4	-	-	-	-	-	-	-	-	-
Clemar Bucci	RA	4	-	-	-	-	-	-	-	-	-
Paul Frere	B	4	-	-	-	-	-	-	-	-	-
Johnny Claes	B	3 (1)	-	-	-	-	-	-	-	-	-
Roberto Mieres	RA	3	-	-	-	-	-	1	-	-	-
Fred Wacker	USA	3 (2)	-	-	-	-	-	1	-	-	-
Georges Berger	B	2	-	-	-	-	-	-	-	-	-
Pablo Birger	RA	2	-	-	-	-	-	-	-	-	-
Aldo Gordini	F	1	-	-	-	-	-	-	-	-	-
Jesus Iglesias	RA	1	-	-	-	-	-	-	-	-	-
Roger Loyer	F	1	-	-	-	-	-	-	-	-	-
Jean Lucas	F	1	-	-	-	-	-	-	-	-	-
Carlos Menditeguy	RA	1	-	-	-	-	-	-	-	-	-
Andre Milhoux	B	1	-	-	-	-	-	-	-	-	-
Robert O'Brien	USA	1	-	-	-	-	-	-	-	-	-
Mike Sparken	USA	1	-	-	-	-	-	-	-	-	-
Max de Terra	CH	1	-	-	-	-	-	-	-	-	-

GORDINI GRAND PRIX CARS

Type	Year	Engine	Designer
11*	1951#	Simca 15C S4	Amedee Gordini
11 (52)*	1952	Simca 508S S4	Amedee Gordini
15*	1950#	Simca 15C S4 sc	Amedee Gordini
15 (52)*	1952	Gordini 18 S4	Amedee Gordini
16S*	1952	Gordini 20 S6	Amedee Gordini
16	1952	Gordini 20 S6	Amedee Gordini
16 (53)	1953	Gordini 16 S6	Amedee Gordini
16 (54)	1954	Gordini 23 S6	Amedee Gordini

Type	Year	Engine	Designer
32	1955	Gordini 25 S8	Amedee Gordini

*Simca-Gordini. #Championship debut, the 11 first raced in 1946 and the 15 in 1947

Greifzu

Only Grand Prix:	1952 German GP	Krause (retired)
Principal:	Paul Greifzu	

WORLD CHAMPIONSHIP RECORD

Starts:	1	
Best result:	No finishes	
Best qualifying:	No time set	

GREIFZU GRAND PRIX DRIVERS

Driver	Nat	Starts (DNS/DNQ)	1st	2nd	3rd	4th	5th	6th	PP	FL	Points
Rudolf Krause	DDR	1	-	-	-	-	-	-	-	-	-

GREIFZU GRAND PRIX CARS

Type	Year	Engine	Designer
Greifzu	1952	BMW 328 S6	Paul Greifzu

Heck

Also known as Klodwig

Grand Prix Debut:	1952 German GP	Klodwig (retired)
Last Grand Prix:	1953 German GP	Klodwig (15th)
Principal:	Ernst Klodwig	
Base:	East Berlin	

WORLD CHAMPIONSHIP RECORD

Starts:	2	
Best result:	15th	1953 German GP (Klodwig)
Best qualifying:	32nd	1953 German GP (Klodwig)

HECK GRAND PRIX DRIVERS

Driver	Nat	Starts (DNS/DNQ)	1st	2nd	3rd	4th	5th	6th	PP	FL	Points
Ernst Klodwig	DDR	2	-	-	-	-	-	-	-	-	-

HECK GRAND PRIX CARS

Type	Year	Engine	Designer
Heck Rear-engined	1952	BMW 328 S6	Ernst Klodwig

Hesketh

Grand Prix Debut:	1974 South African GP	Hunt (retired)
Last Grand Prix:	1978 South African GP	Cheever (retired)
Principal:	Lord Alexander Fermor-Hesketh, 1974-75 (sold equipment to Wolf-Williams Racing); Anthony "Bubbles" Horsley, 1976-78	
Base:	Towcester	

WORLD CHAMPIONSHIP RECORD

Starts:	52	
Points:	48	
Wins:	1	1975 Dutch GP (Hunt)
Best qualifying:	2nd	1974 United States GP (Hunt), 1975 Austrian GP (Hunt)
Fastest laps:	1	1975 Argentinian GP (Hunt)
Laps/miles in the lead:	88 laps/246 miles	

Best World Championship position:
Drivers: 4th in 1975 (Hunt)
Constructors: 4th in 1975

MAJOR SPONSORS

1974-75	none
1976	Penthouse, Rizla
1977	British Air Ferries, Penthouse, Rizla, Heyco, Marlboro, Obex Oil
1978	Olympus Cameras

HESKETH GRAND PRIX DRIVERS

Driver	Nat	Starts (DNS/DNQ)	1st	2nd	3rd	4th	5th	6th	PP	FL	Points
James Hunt	GB	27	1	3	3	3	1	1	-	1	48
Harald Ertl	A	17 (6)	-	-	-	-	-	-	-	-	-
Rupert Keegan	GB	12	-	-	-	-	-	-	-	-	-
Guy Edwards	GB	4 (2)	-	-	-	-	-	-	-	-	-
Alan Jones	AUS	4	-	-	-	-	-	-	-	-	-
Brett Lunger	USA	3	-	-	-	-	-	-	-	-	-
Hector Rebaque	MEX	1 (5)	-	-	-	-	-	-	-	-	-
Ian Ashley	GB	1 (4)	-	-	-	-	-	-	-	-	-
Torsten Palm	S	1 (1)	-	-	-	-	-	-	-	-	-
Eddie Cheever	USA	1	-	-	-	-	-	-	-	-	-
Alex Ribeiro	BR	1	-	-	-	-	-	-	-	-	-
Rolf Stommelen	D	1	-	-	-	-	-	-	-	-	-
Derek Daly	IRL	- (3)	-	-	-	-	-	-	-	-	-
Divina Galica	GB	- (2)	-	-	-	-	-	-	-	-	-
Ian Scheckter	ZA	- (1)	-	-	-	-	-	-	-	-	-

HESKETH GRAND PRIX CARS

Type	Year	Engine	Designer
308	1974	Ford DFV V8	Harvey Postlethwaite
308B	1975	Ford DFV V8	Harvey Postlethwaite
308C	1975	Ford DFV V8	Harvey Postlethwaite
Renamed Williams FW05 when sold to Wolf-Williams Racing			
308D	1976	Ford DFV V8	Harvey Postlethwaite
308E	1977	Ford DFV V8	Frank Dernie/Nigel Stroud

Hill

Grand Prix Debut: 1975 Spanish GP — Stommelen (retired), Migault (not classified)
Last Grand Prix: 1975 United States GP — Brise (retired)
Principal: Graham Hill
Base: West London

WORLD CHAMPIONSHIP RECORD

Starts:	10	
Points:	3	
Best result:	5th	1975 German GP (Jones)
Best qualifying:	6th	1975 Italian GP (Brise)
Laps/miles in the lead:	8 laps/19 miles	

Best World Championship position:
Drivers: 17th in 1975 (Jones)
Constructors: 11th in 1975

MAJOR SPONSORS

1975	Embassy

HILL GRAND PRIX DRIVERS

Driver	Nat	Starts (DNS/DNQ)	1st	2nd	3rd	4th	5th	6th	PP	FL	Points
Alan Jones	AUS	4	-	-	-	-	1	-	-	-	2
Tony Brise	GB	9	-	-	-	-	-	1	-	-	1
Rolf Stommelen	D	3	-	-	-	-	-	-	-	-	-
Francois Migault	F	2	-	-	-	-	-	-	-	-	-

Driver	Nat	Start	1st	2nd	3rd	4th	5th	6th	PP	FL	Points
Vern Schuppan	AUS	1	-	-	-	-	-	-	-	-	-
Graham Hill	GB	- (1)	-	-	-	-	-	-	-	-	-

HILL GRAND PRIX CARS

Type	Year	Engine	Designer
GH1	1975	Ford DFV V8	Andy Smallman
Originally Lola T371, renamed Hill GH1			
GH2	1975	Ford DFV V8	Andy Smallman
Never raced due to closure of team in 1975			

Honda

Grand Prix Debut: 1964 German GP — Bucknum (13th)
Last Grand Prix: 1968 Mexican GP — Bonnier (5th), Surtees (retired)
Principal: Soichiro Honda
Base: Tokyo, 1964; Amsterdam, 1965-66; Slough, 1967-68

WORLD CHAMPIONSHIP RECORD

Starts:	35	
Points:	50	
Wins:	2	1965 Mexican GP (Ginther), 1967 Italian GP (Surtees)
Pole positions:	1	1968 Italian GP (Surtees)
Fastest laps:	2	1966 Mexican GP (Ginther), 1968 Belgian GP (Surtees)
Laps/miles in the lead:	79 laps/296 miles	

Best World Championship position:
Drivers: 4th in 1967 (Surtees)
Constructors: 4th in 1967

HONDA GRAND PRIX DRIVERS

Driver	Nat	Starts (DNS/DNQ)	1st	2nd	3rd	4th	5th	6th	PP	FL	Points
John Surtees	GB	21	1	1	2	2	1	1	1	1	32
Richie Ginther	USA	11	1	-	-	1	-	2	-	1	14
Ronnie Bucknum	USA	11	-	-	-	-	1	-	-	-	2
Jo Bonnier	S	1	-	-	-	-	1	-	-	-	2
David Hobbs	GB	1	-	-	-	-	-	-	-	-	-
Jo Schlesser	F	1	-	-	-	-	-	-	-	-	-

HONDA GRAND PRIX CARS

Type	Year	Engine	Designer
RA270	1963	Honda RA271 V12	Yoshio Nakamura
Test chassis, never raced			
RA271	1964	Honda RA271 V12	Yoshio Nakamura
RA272	1965	Honda RA271 V12	Yoshio Nakamura
RA273	1966	Honda RA273 V12	Yoshio Nakamura
RA300	1967	Honda RA273 V12	Eric Bradley/John Surtees
Based on Lola T190 Champcar monocoque			
RA301	1968	Honda RA273 V12	Eric Bradley/John Surtees/ Nakamura/Derrick White. Further modified by Len Terry
RA302	1968	Honda RA302 V8	Yoshio Nakamura
Air-cooled			

HWM
Hersham and Walton Motors

Grand Prix Debut: 1951 Swiss GP — Moss (8th), Abecassis (retired)
Last Grand Prix: 1954 French GP — Macklin (retired)
Principals: John Heath and George Abecassis
Base: Walton-on-Thames

WORLD CHAMPIONSHIP RECORD

Starts:	14	
Points:	2	
Best result:	5th	1952 Belgian GP (Frere)
Best qualifying:	6th	1952 Swiss GP (Collins)

Best World Championship position:

Drivers:	16th in 1952 (Frere)
Constructors:	-

HWM GRAND PRIX DRIVERS

Driver	Nat	Starts (DNS/DNQ)	1st	2nd	3rd	4th	5th	6th	PP	FL	Points
Paul Frere	B	4	-	-	-	1	-	-	-	-	2
Lance Macklin	GB	12 (1)	-	-	-	-	-	-	-	-	-
Peter Collins	GB	8 (2)	-	-	-	-	1	-	-	-	-
Tony Gaze	AUS	3 (1)	-	-	-	-	-	-	-	-	-
Yves Giraud-Cabantous	F	3	-	-	-	-	-	-	-	-	-
Duncan Hamilton	GB	3	-	-	-	-	-	-	-	-	-
George Abecassis	GB	2	-	-	-	-	-	-	-	-	-
Stirling Moss	GB	2	-	-	-	-	-	-	-	-	-
Johnny Claes	B	1	-	-	-	-	-	-	-	-	-
Jack Fairman	GB	1	-	-	-	-	-	-	-	-	-
John Fitch	USA	1	-	-	-	-	-	-	-	-	-
Roger Laurent	B	1	-	-	-	-	-	-	-	-	-
Dries van der Lof	NL	1	-	-	-	-	-	-	-	-	-
Albert Scherrer	CH	1	-	-	-	-	-	-	-	-	-
Ted Whiteaway	GB	- (1)	-	-	-	-	-	-	-	-	-

HWM GRAND PRIX CARS

Type	Year	Engine	Designer
51	1951	Alta F2 S4	John Heath
51/52	1952	Alta F2 S4	John Heath
52	1952	Alta F2 S4	John Heath
53	1953	Alta F2 S4	John Heath
52/53	1953	Alta F2 S4	John Heath
54	1954	Alta GP S4	John Heath

Jaguar

Bought Stewart in 1999; also see Stewart

Grand Prix Debut:	2000 Australian GP Irvine (retired), Herbert (retired)
Latest Grand Prix:	2002 Japanese GP Irvine (9th), de la Rosa (retired)
Principal:	Neil Ressler, 2000; Bobby Rahal, December 2000-August 2001; Niki Lauda, August 2001-November 2002; Tony Purnell, November 2002 to date
Base:	Milton Keynes

WORLD CHAMPIONSHIP RECORD

Starts:	51	
Points:	21	
Best result:	3rd	2001 Monaco GP (Irvine), 2002 Italian GP (Irvine)
Best qualifying:	5th	2002 Italian GP (Irvine)

Best World Championship position:

Drivers:	9th in 2002 (Irvine)
Constructors:	7th in 2002

MAJOR SPONSORS

2000	HSBC, Beck's, Lear, DHL
2001 to date	HSBC, Beck's, Lear, AT&T Business

JAGUAR GRAND PRIX DRIVERS

Driver	Nat	Starts (DNS/DNQ)	1st	2nd	3rd	4th	5th	6th	PP	FL	Points
Eddie Irvine	GB	50 (1)	-	-	2	2	1	2	-	-	18
Pedro de la Rosa	E	30	-	-	-	-	1	1	-	-	3
Johnny Herbert	GB	17	-	-	-	-	-	-	-	-	-
Luciano Burti	BR	5	-	-	-	-	-	-	-	-	-

JAGUAR GRAND PRIX CARS

Type	Year	Engine	Designer
R1	2000	Cosworth CR2 V10	Gary Anderson
R2	2001	Cosworth CR3 V10	Gary Anderson
R3	2002	Cosworth CR3 V10	Steve Nichols/John Russell
R3B	2002	Cosworth CR3 V10	Steve Nichols/Mark Hanford/Ben Agathangelou

JBW

Grand Prix Debut:	1959 British GP	Naylor (retired)
Last Grand Prix:	1961 Italian GP	Naylor (retired)
Principal:	Brian Naylor	
Base:	Stockport, Cheshire	

WORLD CHAMPIONSHIP RECORD

Starts:	5	
Best result:	13th	1960 British GP (Naylor)
Best qualifying:	7th	1960 Italian GP (Naylor)

JBW GRAND PRIX DRIVERS

Driver	Nat	Starts (DNS/DNQ)	1st	2nd	3rd	4th	5th	6th	PP	FL	Points
Brian Naylor	GB	5 (1)	-	-	-	-	-	-	-	-	-

JBW GRAND PRIX CARS

Type	Year	Engine	Designer
1959	1959	Maserati 250S S4	Fred Wilkinson
1960	1961	Climax FPF S4, Maserati 150S S4	Fred Wilkinson

Jordan

Grand Prix Debut:	1991 United States GP	Gachot (10th)
Latest Grand Prix:	2002 Japanese GP	Sato (5th), Fisichella (retired)
Principal:	Eddie Jordan	
Base:	Silverstone	

WORLD CHAMPIONSHIP RECORD

Starts:	197	
Points:	261	
Wins:	3	1998 Belgian GP (Hill), 1999 French GP (Frentzen), Italian GP (Frentzen)
Pole positions:	2	1994 Belgian GP (Barrichello), 1999 European GP (Frentzen)
Fastest laps:	2	1991 Hungarian GP (Gachot), 1997 Spanish GP (Fisichella)
Laps/miles in the lead:	116 laps/405 miles	

Best World Championship position:

Drivers:	3rd in 1999 (Frentzen)
Constructors:	3rd in 1999

MAJOR SPONSORS

1991	7Up/Fuji
1992-94	Sasol
1995	Total

1996-2001	Benson & Hedges
2002	DHL/Deutsch Post/Benson & Hedges

JORDAN GRAND PRIX DRIVERS

Driver	Nat	Starts (DNS/DNQ)	1st	2nd	3rd	4th	5th	6th	PP	FL	Points
Heinz-Harald Frentzen	D	43 (1)	2	1	5	6	1	5	1	-	71
Damon Hill	GB	32	1	-	-	4	1	3	-	-	27
Rubens Barrichello	BR	64 (1)	-	1	1	8	4	4	1	-	46
Giancarlo Fisichella	I	33 (1)	-	1	1	3	3	2	-	1	27
Ralf Schumacher	D	33	-	1	2	-	5	3	-	-	27
Jarno Trulli	I	34	-	-	-	3	3	3	-	-	18
Eddie Irvine	GB	31 (1)	-	-	1	2	2	3	-	-	17
Andrea de Cesaris	I	17	-	-	-	3	1	1	-	-	12
Martin Brundle	GB	16	-	-	-	1	1	3	-	-	8
Bertrand Gachot	B	10	-	-	-	-	1	2	-	1	4
Takuma Sato	J	17	-	-	-	-	1	-	-	-	2
Stefano Modena	I	12 (4)	-	-	-	-	-	1	-	-	1
Jean Alesi	F	5	-	-	-	-	-	1	-	-	1
Mauricio Gugelmin	BR	16	-	-	-	-	-	-	-	-	-
Thierry Boutsen	B	10	-	-	-	-	-	-	-	-	-
Alessandro Zanardi	I	3	-	-	-	-	-	-	-	-	-
Ricardo Zonta	BR	2	-	-	-	-	-	-	-	-	-
Roberto Moreno	BR	2	-	-	-	-	-	-	-	-	-
Ivan Capelli	I	1 (1)	-	-	-	-	-	-	-	-	-
Aguri Suzuki	J	1	-	-	-	-	-	-	-	-	-
Emanuele Naspetti	I	1	-	-	-	-	-	-	-	-	-
Marco Apicella	I	1	-	-	-	-	-	-	-	-	-
Michael Schumacher	D	1	-	-	-	-	-	-	-	-	-

JORDAN GRAND PRIX CARS

Type	Year	Engine	Designer
191	1991	Ford HB V8	Gary Anderson
192	1992	Yamaha OX99 V12	Gary Anderson
193	1993	Hart 1035 V10	Gary Anderson
194	1994	Hart 1035 V10	Gary Anderson/ Steve Nichols
195	1995	Peugeot A10 V10	Gary Anderson
196	1996	Peugeot A12 V10	Gary Anderson
197	1997	Peugeot A14 V10	Gary Anderson
198	1998	Mugen MF310C V10	Gary Anderson
199	1999	Mugen MF301HD V10	Mike Gascoyne
EJ10	2000	Mugen MF301HE V10	Mike Gascoyne
EJ11	2001	Honda RA001E V10	Tim Holloway
EJ12	2002	Honda RA002E V10	Eghbal Hamidy

Kauhsen

Principal: Willi Kauhsen

WORLD CHAMPIONSHIP RECORD

Starts: None
Best qualifying: 27th 1979 Spanish GP (Brancatelli)

KAUHSEN GRAND PRIX DRIVERS

Driver	Nat	Starts (DNS/DNQ)	1st	2nd	3rd	4th	5th	6th	PP	FL	Points
Gianfranco Brancatelli	I	- (2)	-	-	-	-	-	-	-	-	-

KAUHSEN GRAND PRIX CARS

Type	Year	Engine	Designer
WK004	1979	Ford DFV V8	Klaus Kapitza
WK005	1979	Ford DFV V8	Klaus Kapitza

Klenk

Only Grand Prix:	1954 German GP Helfrich (retired)
Principal:	Hans Klenk
Base:	Stuttgart

WORLD CHAMPIONSHIP RECORD

Starts: 1
Best result: No finishes
Best qualifying: 21st 1954 German GP (Helfrich)

KLENK GRAND PRIX DRIVERS

Driver	Nat	Starts (DNS/DNQ)	1st	2nd	3rd	4th	5th	6th	PP	FL	Points
Theo Helfrich	D	1	-	-	-	-	-	-	-	-	-

KLENK GRAND PRIX CARS

Type	Year	Engine	Designer
Meteor	1954	BMW 328 S6	Hans Klenk

Kojima

Grand Prix Debut:	1976 Japanese GP	Hasemi (11th)
Last Grand Prix:	1977 Japanese GP	Hoshino (11th), Takahara (retired)
Principal:	Matsuhisa Kojima	
Base:	Kyoto	

WORLD CHAMPIONSHIP RECORD

Starts:	2	
Best result:	11th	1976 Japanese GP (Hasemi), 1977 Japanese GP (Hoshino)
Best qualifying:	10th	1976 Japanese GP (Hasemi)
Fastest laps:	1	1976 Japanese GP (Hasemi)

KOJIMA GRAND PRIX DRIVERS

Driver	Nat	Starts (DNS/DNQ)	1st	2nd	3rd	4th	5th	6th	PP	FL	Points
Masahiro Hasemi	J	1	-	-	-	-	-	-	-	1	-
Kazuyoshi Hoshino	J	1	-	-	-	-	-	-	-	-	-
Noritake Takahara	J	1	-	-	-	-	-	-	-	-	-

KOJIMA GRAND PRIX CARS

Type	Year	Engine	Designer
KE007	1976	Ford DFV V8	Masao Ono
KE009	1977	Ford DFV V8	Masao Ono

Kurtis

Only Grand Prix:	1959 United States GP Ward (retired)
Principal:	Frank Kurtis
Base:	Glendale, California

WORLD CHAMPIONSHIP RECORD

Starts: 1
Best result: No finishes
Best qualifying: 19th 1959 United States GP (Ward)

KURTIS GRAND PRIX DRIVERS

Driver	Nat	Starts (DNS/DNQ)	1st	2nd	3rd	4th	5th	6th	PP	FL	Points
Rodger Ward	USA	1	-	-	-	-	-	-	-	-	-

KURTIS GRAND PRIX CARS

Type	Year	Engine	Designer
Roadster	1959	Offenhauser S4	Frank Kurtis

Lamborghini

Grand Prix Debut:	1991 United States GP	Larini (7th)
Last Grand Prix:	1991 Australian GP	Larini (retired)
Principal:	Mauro Forghieri	
Base:	Modena	

WORLD CHAMPIONSHIP RECORD

Starts:	6	
Best result:	7th	1991 United States GP (Larini)
Best qualifying:	17th	1991 United States GP (Larini)

LAMBORGHINI GRAND PRIX DRIVERS

Driver	Nat	Starts 1st (DNS/DNQ)	2nd	3rd	4th	5th	6th	PP	FL	Points
Nicola Larini	I	5 (11)	-	-	-	-	-	-	-	-
Eric van de Poele	B	1 (15)	-	-	-	-	-	-	-	-

LAMBORGHINI GRAND PRIX CARS

Type	Year	Engine	Designer
291	1991	Lamborghini 3512 V12	Mauro Forghieri/ Mario Tollentino/ Peter Wyss

Lago-Talbot

Grand Prix Debut:	1950 British GP	Giraud-Cabantous (4th), Rosier (5th), Etancelin (8th), Claes (11th), Martin (retired)
Last Grand Prix:	1951 Spanish GP	Rosier (7th), Etancelin (8th), Claes (retired), Grignard (retired), Giraud-Cabantous (retired), Chiron (retired)
Principal:	Antonio Lago	
Base:	Suresnes	

WORLD CHAMPIONSHIP RECORD

Starts:	13	
Points:	25	
Best result:	3rd	1950 Swiss GP (Rosier), Belgian GP (Rosier)
Best qualifying:	4th	1950 Monaco GP (Etancelin), French GP (Etancelin)
Laps/miles in the lead:	5 laps/44 miles	

Best World Championship position:

Drivers:	4th in 1950 (Rosier)
Constructors:	-

LAGO-TALBOT GRAND PRIX DRIVERS

Driver	Nat	Starts 1st (DNS/DNQ)	2nd	3rd	4th	5th	6th	PP	FL	Points
Louis Rosier	F	13	-	-	2	2	1	1	-	-	16
Yves Giraud-Cabantous	F	10	-	-	-	1	1	-	-	-	5
Philippe Etancelin	F	11	-	-	-	-	2	-	-	-	3
Eugene Chaboud	F	3	-	-	-	-	1	-	-	-	1
Johnny Claes	B	13	-	-	-	-	-	-	-	-	-
Louis Chiron	MC	6	-	-	-	-	1	-	-	-	-
"Pierre Levegh"	F	6	-	-	-	-	-	-	-	-	-
Guy Mairesse	F	3	-	-	-	-	-	-	-	-	-
Raymond Sommer	F	3	-	-	-	-	-	-	-	-	-
Duncan Hamilton	GB	2	-	-	-	-	-	-	-	-	-
Henri Louveau	F	2	-	-	-	-	-	-	-	-	-

Driver	Nat	Start	1st	2nd	3rd	4th	5th	6th	PP	FL	Points
Eugene Martin	F	2	-	-	-	-	-	-	-	-	-
Jacques Swaters	B	2	-	-	-	-	-	-	-	-	-
Jose Froilan Gonzalez	RA	1	-	-	-	-	-	-	-	-	-
Georges Grignard	F	1	-	-	-	-	-	-	-	-	-
Andre Pilette	B	1	-	-	-	-	1	-	-	-	-
Charles Pozzi	F	1	-	-	-	-	1	-	-	-	-
Harry Schell	USA	1	-	-	-	-	-	-	-	-	-

LAGO-TALBOT GRAND PRIX CARS

Type	Year	Engine	Designer
T26C	1950*	Talbot 23CV S6	Antonio Lago/Carlo Marchetti
T26C-GS	1950*	Talbot 23CV S6	Antonio Lago/Carlo Marchetti
T26C-DA	1950	Talbot 23CV S6	Antonio Lago/Carlo Marchetti

*Championship debut, the T26C first raced in 1948 and the T26C-GS in 1939

Lancia

Cars sold to Ferrari in 1955 and renamed Lancia-Ferrari; also see Ferrari

Grand Prix Debut:	1954 Spanish GP	Ascari (retired), Villoresi (retired)
Last Grand Prix:	1955 Belgian GP	Castellotti (retired)
Principal:	Vincenzo Lancia and Claudio Fogolin (founders in 1906). Gianni Lancia	
Base:	Turin	

WORLD CHAMPIONSHIP RECORD

Starts:	4	
Points:	9	
Best result:	2nd	1955 Monaco GP (Castellotti)
Pole positions:	2	1954 Spanish GP (Ascari), 1955 Belgian GP (Castellotti)
Fastest laps:	1	1954 Spanish GP (Ascari)
Laps/miles in the lead:	21 laps/62 miles	

Best World Championship positions:

Drivers:	3rd in 1955 (Castellotti - his 12 points included 6 for Ferrari)
Constructors:	-

LANCIA GRAND PRIX DRIVERS

Driver	Nat	Starts 1st (DNS/DNQ)	2nd	3rd	4th	5th	6th	PP	FL	Points
Eugenio Castellotti	I	3	-	1	-	-	-	-	1	-	6
Luigi Villoresi	I	3	-	-	-	-	1	-	-	-	2
Alberto Ascari	I	3	-	-	-	-	-	-	1	1	1
Louis Chiron	MC	1	-	-	-	-	1	-	-	-	-

LANCIA GRAND PRIX CARS

Type	Year	Engine	Designer
D50	1954	Lancia DS50 V8	Vittorio Jano

Larrousse

Grand Prix Debut:	1992 South African GP	Katayama (12th), Gachot (retired)
Last Grand Prix:	1994 Australian GP	Noda (retired), Deletraz (retired)
Principal:	Gerard Larrousse	
Base:	Constructor: Bicester (GB); Team: Signes, near Circuit Paul Ricard (F)	

WORLD CHAMPIONSHIP RECORD

Starts:	48
Points:	6

Best result: 5th   1993 San Marino GP (Alliot)
Best qualifying: 9th   1993 French GP (Comas)

Best World Championship position:
Drivers: 17th in 1992 (Gachot), and 1993 (Alliot)
Constructors: 10th in 1993

MAJOR SPONSORS

1992	Venturi, Central Park
1993	Central Park
1994	Tourtel, Kronenbourg

LARROUSSE GRAND PRIX DRIVERS

Driver	Nat	Starts (DNS/DNQ)	1st	2nd	3rd	4th	5th	6th	PP	FL	Points
Erik Comas	F	31	-	-	-	-	-	3	-	-	3
Philippe Alliot	F	15	-	-	-	-	1	-	-	-	2
Bertrand Gachot	B	16	-	-	-	-	-	1	-	-	1
Ukyo Katayama	J	14 (2)	-	-	-	-	-	-	-	-	-
Olivier Beretta	MC	9 (1)	-	-	-	-	-	-	-	-	-
Hideki Noda	J	3	-	-	-	-	-	-	-	-	-
Yannick Dalmas	F	2	-	-	-	-	-	-	-	-	-
Toshio Suzuki	J	2	-	-	-	-	-	-	-	-	-
Jean-Denis Deletraz	CH	1	-	-	-	-	-	-	-	-	-

Note: Results and records do not include those achieved in Equipe Larrousse Lolas

LARROUSSE GRAND PRIX CARS

Type	Year	Engine	Designer
LC92	1992	Lamborghini 3512 V12	Tino Belli/ Tim Holloway/ Robin Herd
LH93	1993	Lamborghini 3512 V12	Tino Belli/ Tim Holloway/ Robin Herd
LH94	1994	Ford HB V8	Tino Belli/ Tim Holloway/ Robin Herd

LDS
LD Serrurier

Grand Prix Debut: 1962 South African GP   Serrurier (retired)
Last Grand Prix: 1968 South African GP   Tingle (retired)
Principal: Doug Serrurier
Base: Alberton, Transvaal

WORLD CHAMPIONSHIP RECORD

Starts: 5
Best result: 11th   1963 South African GP (Serrurier)
Best qualifying: 14th   1962 South African GP (Serrurier), 1967 South African GP (Tingle)

LDS GRAND PRIX DRIVERS

Driver	Nat	Starts (DNS/DNQ)	1st	2nd	3rd	4th	5th	6th	PP	FL	Points
Sam Tingle	RSR	4	-	-	-	-	-	-	-	-	-
Doug Serrurier	ZA	2 (1)	-	-	-	-	-	-	-	-	-
Jackie Pretorius	ZA	- (1)	-	-	-	-	-	-	-	-	-

LDS GRAND PRIX CARS

Type	Year	Engine	Designer
Mk1	1962	Alfa Romeo	Doug Serrurier
Mk2	1965	Climax FPF S4	Doug Serrurier
Mk3	1967	Climax FPF S4	Doug Serrurier
Mk5	1968	Repco V8	Doug Serrurier

Lec

Grand Prix Debut: 1977 Belgian GP   Purley (13th)
Last Grand Prix: 1977 French GP   Purley (retired)
Principal: David Purley
Base: Bognor Regis, Sussex

WORLD CHAMPIONSHIP RECORD

Starts: 3
Best result: 13th   1977 Belgian GP (Purley)
Best qualifying: 19th   1977 Swedish GP (Purley)

MAJOR SPONSORS

1977	Lec Refrigeration, Mopar

LEC GRAND PRIX DRIVERS

Driver	Nat	Starts (DNS/DNQ)	1st	2nd	3rd	4th	5th	6th	PP	FL	Points
David Purley	GB	3 (2)	-	-	-	-	-	-	-	-	-

LEC GRAND PRIX CARS

Type	Year	Engine	Designer
CRP1	1977	Ford DFV V8	Mike Pilbeam

Leyton House
See March

Life

Principal: Ernesto Vita

WORLD CHAMPIONSHIP RECORD

Starts: None
Best qualifying: 33rd   1990 San Marino GP (Giacomelli), Belgian GP (Giacomelli), Italian GP (Giacomelli), Spanish GP (Giacomelli)

LIFE GRAND PRIX DRIVERS

Driver	Nat	Starts (DNS/DNQ)	1st	2nd	3rd	4th	5th	6th	PP	FL	Points
Bruno Giacomelli	I	- (12)	-	-	-	-	-	-	-	-	-
Gary Brabham	AUS	- (2)	-	-	-	-	-	-	-	-	-

LIFE GRAND PRIX CARS

Type	Year	Engine	Designer
F190	1990	Life W12, Judd CV V8	Richard Divila/ Gianni Marelli

Designed and built by First Racing

Ligier
Team sold to Alain Prost in 1997; also see Prost

Grand Prix Debut: 1976 Brazilian GP   Laffite (retired)
Last Grand Prix: 1996 Japanese GP   Panis (7th), Diniz (retired)
Principal: Guy Ligier, 1976-92; Cyril de Rouvre, 1993-94; Flavio Briatore/Benetton Formula, 1994-96
Base: Vichy, 1976-88; Magny Cours, 1989-96

WORLD CHAMPIONSHIP RECORD

Starts: 326
Points: 388
Wins: 9   1977 Swedish GP (Laffite), 1979 Argentinian

	GP (Laffite), Brazilian GP (Laffite), Spanish GP (Depailler), 1980 Belgian GP (Pironi), German GP (Laffite), 1981 Austrian GP (Laffite), Canadian GP (Laffite), 1996 Monaco GP (Panis)	
Pole positions:	9 1976 Italian GP (Laffite), 1979 Argentinian GP (Laffite), Brazilian GP (Laffite), Spanish GP (Laffite), Belgian GP (Laffite), 1980 Monaco GP (Pironi), French GP (Laffite), British GP (Pironi), 1981 Spanish GP (Laffite)	
Fastest laps:	9 1977 Spanish GP (Laffite), 1979 Argentinian GP (Laffite), Brazilian GP (Laffite), Monaco GP (Depailler), 1980 Belgian GP (Laffite), British GP (Pironi), Canadian GP (Pironi), 1981 Austrian GP (Laffite), 1985 European GP (Laffite)	
Laps/miles in the lead:	537 laps/1558 miles	

Best World Championship position:

Drivers:	4th in 1979, 1980 and 1981 (all Laffite)
Constructors:	2nd in 1980

MAJOR SPONSORS

1976-80	Gitanes
1981-82	Talbot, Gitanes
1983	Gitanes
1984	LOTO, Gitanes
1985	Gitanes, Candy
1986-91	LOTO, Gitanes
1992	Gitanes Blondes, LOTO
1993-95	Gitanes Blondes
1996	Gauloises, Parmalat

LIGIER GRAND PRIX DRIVERS

Driver	Nat	Starts (DNS/DNQ)	1st	2nd	3rd	4th	5th	6th	PP	FL	Points
Jacques Laffite	F	132	6	9	16	4	7	8	7	6	206
Olivier Panis	F	49	1	2	-	2	3	4	-	-	38
Didier Pironi	F	14	1	1	3	1	-	2	2	2	32
Patrick Depailler	F	7	1	1	-	1	2	-	-	1	22
Martin Brundle	GB	27	-	-	2	1	3	3	-	-	20
Rene Arnoux	F	53 (10)	-	-	3	3	2	-	-	-	17
Eddie Cheever	USA	14 (1)	-	1	2	-	-	1	-	-	15
Mark Blundell	GB	16	-	-	2	-	1	-	-	-	10
Andrea de Cesaris	I	27	-	-	-	1	1	1	-	-	6
Erik Comas	F	28 (4)	-	-	-	-	1	2	-	-	4
Eric Bernard	F	13	-	-	1	-	-	-	-	-	4
Philippe Streiff	F	4	-	-	1	-	-	-	-	-	4
Jacky Ickx	B	8	-	-	-	-	1	1	-	-	3
Thierry Boutsen	B	32	-	-	-	-	1	-	-	-	2
Pedro Diniz	BR	16	-	-	-	-	2	-	-	-	2
Philippe Alliot	F	21 (2)	-	-	-	-	-	1	-	-	1
Olivier Grouillard	F	12 (4)	-	-	-	-	-	1	-	-	1
Aguri Suzuki	J	5 (1)	-	-	-	-	-	1	-	-	1
Jean-Pierre Jarier	F	17 (1)	-	-	-	-	-	-	-	-	-
Nicola Larini	I	16	-	-	-	-	-	-	-	-	-
Francois Hesnault	F	15 (1)	-	-	-	-	-	-	-	-	-
Piercarlo Ghinzani	I	14 (1)	-	-	-	-	-	-	-	-	-
Raul Boesel	BR	13 (2)	-	-	-	-	-	-	-	-	-
Stefan Johansson	S	10 (6)	-	-	-	-	-	-	-	-	-
Patrick Tambay	F	8	-	-	-	-	-	-	-	-	-
Jean-Pierre Jabouille	F	3 (3)	-	-	-	-	-	-	-	-	-
Franck Lagorce	F	2	-	-	-	-	-	-	-	-	-
Johnny Herbert	GB	1	-	-	-	-	-	-	-	-	-

LIGIER GRAND PRIX CARS

Type	Year	Engine	Designer
JS5	1976	Matra MS73 V12	Gerard Ducarouge/ Michel Beaujon/Paul Carillo
JS7	1977	Matra MS76 V12	Gerard Ducarouge/ Michel Beaujon/Paul Carillo
JS7/9	1978	Matra MS76 V12	Gerard Ducarouge/ Michel Beaujon/Paul Carillo
JS9	1978	Matra MS78 V12	Gerard Ducarouge/ Michel Beaujon/Paul Carillo
JS11	1979	Ford DFV V8	Gerard Ducarouge/ Michel Beaujon/Paul Carillo
JS11/15	1980	Ford DFV V8	Gerard Ducarouge/ Michel Beaujon
JS17*	1981	Matra MS81 V12	Gerard Ducarouge/ Michel Beaujon
JS19*	1982	Matra MS81 V12	Michel Beaujon/ Jean-Pierre Jabouille
JS21	1983	Ford DFV V8	Michel Beaujon/ Claude Galopin
JS23	1984	Renault EF4 V6 tc	Michel Beaujon/ Claude Galopin
JS23B	1984	Renault EF4 V6 tc	Michel Beaujon/ Claude Galopin
JS25	1985	Renault EF4B V6 tc	Michel Tetu/Michel Beaujon
JS27	1986	Renault EF4B/ EF15 V6 tc	Michel Tetu
JS29	1987	Alfa Romeo 415T S4 tc	Michel Tetu
JS29B	1987	Megatron BMW M12/13 S4 tc	Michel Tetu
JS29C	1987	Megatron BMW M12/13 S4 tc	Michel Tetu
JS31	1988	Judd CV V8	Michel Tetu
JS33	1989	Ford DFR V8	Michel Beaujon/ Richard Divila/Ken Anderson
JS33B	1990	Ford DFR V8	Michel Beaujon/ Richard Divila/Ken Anderson
JS35	1991	Lamborghini 3512 V12	Michel Beaujon/ Claude Galopin/Richard Divila
JS35B	1991	Lamborghini 3512 V12	Michel Beaujon/Frank Dernie
JS37	1992	Renault RS3 V10	Frank Dernie
JS39	1993	Renault RS5 V10	Gerard Ducarouge/John Davis
JS39B	1994	Renault RS5 V10	Gerard Ducarouge/John Davis
JS41	1995	Mugen MF301 V10	Frank Dernie
JS43	1996	Mugen MF301HA V10	Frank Dernie

Never raced due to Alfa Romeo withdrawing after Ligier's Rene Arnoux publicly criticised the poor performance of their new engine

*officially Talbot-Ligier. Note: "JS" designation refers to Jo Schlesser

Lola

Grand Prix Debut:	1962 Dutch GP	Salvadori (retired), Surtees (retired)
Last Grand Prix:	1993 Portuguese GP	Badoer (14th), Alboreto (retired)
Principal:	Eric Broadley	
Base:	Bromley, 1956-65; Slough, 1965-70; Huntingdon, 1970-97	

WORLD CHAMPIONSHIP RECORD

Starts:	149	
Points:	43	
Best result:	2nd	1962 British GP (Surtees), German GP (Surtees)
Pole positions:	1	1962 Dutch GP (Surtees)

Best World Championship position:

Drivers:	4th in 1962 (Surtees)
Constructors:	4th in 1962

MAJOR SPONSORS

1997	MasterCard, Pennzoil

LOLA GRAND PRIX DRIVERS

Driver	Nat	Starts 1st (DNS/DNQ)	2nd	3rd	4th	5th	6th	PP	FL	Points
John Surtees	GB	9	-	2	-	1	2	-	1	-	19
Aguri Suzuki	J	28 (5)	-	-	1	-	-	3	-	-	7
Eric Bernard	F	31 (2)	-	-	-	1	-	3	-	-	6
Philippe Alliot	F	46	-	-	-	-	-	4	-	-	4
Alan Jones	AUS	19 (1)	-	-	-	1	-	1	-	-	4
Patrick Tambay	F	14 (1)	-	-	-	-	1	-	-	-	2
Graham Hill	GB	17 (1)	-	-	-	-	-	1	-	-	1
Yannick Dalmas	F	16 (7)	-	-	-	-	1*	-	-	-	-
Michele Alboreto	I	14 (6)	-	-	-	-	-	-	-	-	-
Luca Badoer	I	12 (2)	-	-	-	-	-	-	-	-	-
Guy Edwards	GB	7 (2)	-	-	-	-	-	-	-	-	-
Roy Salvadori	GB	7 (1)	-	-	-	-	-	-	-	-	-
Rolf Stommelen	D	7	-	-	-	-	-	-	-	-	-
Chris Amon	NZ	5 (2)	-	-	-	-	-	-	-	-	-
Bob Anderson	RSR	2	-	-	-	-	-	-	-	-	-
Hubert Hahne	D	2	-	-	-	-	-	-	-	-	-
Masten Gregory	USA	2	-	-	-	-	-	-	-	-	-
David Hobbs	GB	1	-	-	-	-	-	-	-	-	-
Eddie Cheever	USA	1	-	-	-	-	-	-	-	-	-
John Campbell-Jones	GB	1	-	-	-	-	-	-	-	-	-
Lucien Bianchi	B	1	-	-	-	-	-	-	-	-	-
Maurice Trintignant	F	1	-	-	-	-	-	-	-	-	-
Mike Hailwood	GB	1	-	-	-	-	-	-	-	-	-
Peter Gethin	GB	1	-	-	-	-	-	-	-	-	-
Ricardo Rosset	BR	- (2)	-	-	-	-	-	-	-	-	-
Vincenzo Sospiri	I	- (2)	-	-	-	-	-	-	-	-	-
Bertrand Gachot	B	- (1)	-	-	-	-	-	-	-	-	-
Brian Redman	GB	- (1)	-	-	-	-	-	-	-	-	-
Pierre-Henri Raphanel	F	- (1)	-	-	-	-	-	-	-	-	-

*Not entered in World Championship so ineligible for points.

LOLA GRAND PRIX CARS

Type	Year	Engine	Designer
Mk4	1962	Climax FMWV V8	Eric Broadley
Mk4A	1962	Climax FMWV V8	Eric Broadley
T100	1967	BMW S4	Eric Broadley
F2 car			
T370	1974	Ford DFV V8	Andy Smallman
T371	1975	Ford DFV V8	Andy Smallman
Renamed Hill GH1			
THL1*	1985	Hart 415T S4 tc	Neil Oatley/ Ross Brawn/ John Baldwin
THL2*	1986	Ford TEC V6 tc	Neil Oatley/ Ross Brawn/ John Baldwin
LC87	1987	Ford DFZ V8	Eric Broadley/ Ralph Bellamy
LC88	1988	Ford DFZ V8	Eric Broadley/ Chris Murphy
LC88C	1989	Lamborghini 3512 V12	Eric Broadley/ Chris Murphy
LC89	1989	Lamborghini 3512 V12	Eric Broadley/ Chris Murphy/ Gerard Ducarouge
90	1990	Lamborghini 3512 V12	Eric Broadley/ Chris Murphy/ Gerard Ducarouge
L91	1991	Ford DFR V8	Eric Broadley/ Mark Williams/ Bruce Ashmore
T93/30	1993	Ferrari V12	Eric Broadley

Type	Year	Engine	Designer
T97/30	1997	Ford Zetec-R V8	Eric Broadley

*Designed and built for Carl Haas by FORCE in Colnbrook. As Lola's North American importer, Haas named them Lolas

Lotus

Grand Prix Debut: 1958 Monaco GP — Allison (6th), G Hill (retired)
Last Grand Prix: 1994 Australian GP — Zanardi (retired), Salo (retired)
Principal: Colin Chapman, 1952-82; Peter Warr, 1982-90; Tony Rudd, 1990; Peter Collins and Peter Wright, 1991-94
Base: Hornsey, North London, 1952-59; Cheshunt, Hertfordshire, 1959-67; Wymondham, Norfolk, 1967-94

WORLD CHAMPIONSHIP RECORD

Starts: 491
Points: 1514
Wins: 79 — 1960 Monaco GP (Moss), United States GP (Moss), 1961 Monaco GP (Moss), German GP (Moss), United States GP (Ireland), 1962 Belgian GP (Clark), British GP (Clark), United States GP (Clark), 1963 Belgian GP (Clark), Dutch GP (Clark), French GP (Clark), British GP (Clark), Italian GP (Clark), Mexican GP (Clark), South African GP (Clark), 1964 Dutch GP (Clark), Belgian GP (Clark), British GP (Clark), 1965 South African GP (Clark), Belgian GP (Clark), French GP (Clark), British GP (Clark), Dutch GP (Clark), German GP (Clark), 1966 United States GP (Clark), 1967 Dutch GP (Clark), British GP (Clark), United States GP (Clark), Mexican GP (Clark), 1968 South African GP (Clark), Spanish GP (Hill), Monaco GP (Hill), British GP (Siffert), Mexican GP (Hill), 1969 Monaco GP (Hill), United States GP (Rindt), 1970 Monaco GP (Rindt), Dutch GP (Rindt), French GP (Rindt), British GP (Rindt), German GP (Rindt), United States GP (Fittipaldi), 1972 Spanish GP (Fittipaldi), Belgian GP (Fittipaldi), British GP (Fittipaldi), Austrian GP (Fittipaldi), Italian GP (Fittipaldi), 1973 Argentinian GP (Fittipaldi), Brazilian GP (Fittipaldi), Spanish GP (Fittipaldi), French GP (Peterson), Austrian GP (Peterson), Italian GP (Peterson), United States GP (Peterson), 1974 Monaco GP (Peterson), French GP (Peterson), Italian GP (Peterson), 1976 Japanese GP (Andretti), 1977 Long Beach GP (Andretti), Spanish GP (Andretti), Belgian GP (Nilsson), French GP (Andretti), Italian GP (Andretti), 1978 Argentinian GP (Andretti), South African GP (Peterson), Belgian GP (Andretti), Spanish GP (Andretti), French GP (Andretti), German GP (Andretti), Austrian GP (Peterson), Dutch GP (Andretti), 1982 Austrian GP (de Angelis), 1985 Portuguese GP (Senna), San Marino GP (de Angelis), Belgian GP (Senna), 1986 Spanish GP (Senna), Detroit GP (Senna), 1987 Monaco GP (Senna), Detroit GP (Senna)

Pole positions: 107 — 1960 Monaco GP (Moss), Dutch GP (Moss), Portuguese GP (Surtees), United States GP (Moss), 1961 Monaco GP (Moss), 1962 Monaco GP (Clark), French GP (Clark), British GP (Clark), Italian GP (Clark), United States GP (Clark), South African GP (Clark), 1963 Monaco GP (Clark), Dutch GP (Clark), French GP (Clark), British GP (Clark),

German GP (Clark), Mexican GP (Clark), South African GP (Clark), 1964 Monaco GP (Clark), French GP (Clark), British GP (Clark), United States GP (Clark), Mexican GP (Clark), 1965 South African GP (Clark), French GP (Clark), British GP (Clark), German GP (Clark), Italian GP (Clark), Mexican GP (Clark), 1966 Monaco GP (Clark), German GP (Clark), 1967 Dutch GP (Hill), Belgian GP (Clark), French GP (Hill), British GP (Clark), German GP (Clark), Canadian GP (Clark), Italian GP (Clark), United States GP (Hill), Mexican GP (Clark), 1968 South African GP (Clark), Monaco GP (Hill), British GP (Hill), United States GP (Andretti), Mexican GP (Siffert), 1969 Spanish GP (Rindt), Dutch GP (Rindt), British GP (Rindt), Italian GP (Rindt), United States GP (Rindt), 1970 Dutch GP (Rindt), British GP (Rindt), Austrian GP (Rindt), 1972 Monaco GP (Fittipaldi), Belgian GP (Fittipaldi), Austrian GP (Fittipaldi), 1973 Brazilian GP (Peterson), Spanish GP (Peterson), Belgian GP (Peterson), Swedish GP (Peterson), British GP (Peterson), Dutch GP (Peterson), Austrian GP (Fittipaldi), Italian GP (Peterson), Canadian GP (Peterson), United States GP (Peterson), 1974 Argentinian GP (Peterson), 1976 Japanese GP (Andretti), 1977 Spanish GP (Andretti), Belgian GP (Andretti), Swedish GP (Andretti), French GP (Andretti), Dutch GP (Andretti), Canadian GP (Andretti), Japanese GP (Andretti), 1978 Argentinian GP (Andretti), Brazilian GP (Peterson), Belgian GP (Andretti), Spanish GP (Andretti), Swedish GP (Andretti), British GP (Peterson), German GP (Andretti), Austrian GP (Peterson), Dutch GP (Andretti), Italian GP (Andretti), United States GP (Andretti), Canadian GP (Jarier), 1983 European GP (de Angelis), 1984 Brazilian GP (de Angelis), Dallas GP (Mansell), 1985 Portuguese GP (Senna), San Marino GP (Senna), Monaco GP (Senna), Canadian GP (de Angelis), Detroit GP (Senna), Italian GP (Senna), European GP (Senna), Australian GP (Senna), 1986 Brazilian GP (Senna), Spanish GP (Senna), San Marino GP (Senna), Detroit GP (Senna), French GP (Senna), Hungarian GP (Senna), Portuguese GP (Senna), Mexican GP (Senna), 1987 San Marino GP (Senna)

Fastest laps: 71

1960 Dutch GP (Moss), Belgian GP (Ireland), Portuguese GP (Surtees), 1961 Monaco GP (Moss), Dutch GP (Clark), 1962 Monaco GP (Clark), Belgian GP (Clark), British GP (Clark), United States GP (Clark), South African GP (Clark), 1963 Belgian GP (Clark), Dutch GP (Clark), French GP (Clark), Italian GP (Clark), United States GP (Clark), Mexican GP (Clark), 1964 Dutch GP (Clark), British GP (Clark), United States GP (Clark), Mexican GP (Clark), 1965 South African GP (Clark), Belgian GP (Clark), French GP (Clark), Dutch GP (Clark), German GP (Clark), Italian GP (Clark), 1967 Monaco GP (Clark), Dutch GP (Clark), French GP (G Hill), Canadian GP (Clark), Italian GP (Clark), United States GP (G Hill), Mexican GP (Clark), 1968 South African GP (Clark), British GP (Siffert), Italian GP (Oliver), Canadian GP (Siffert), Mexican GP (Siffert), 1969 Spanish GP (Rindt), United States GP (Rindt), 1970 Monaco GP (Rindt), 1973 Argentinian GP (Fittipaldi), Brazilian GP

(Fittipaldi), South African GP (Fittipaldi), Spanish GP (Peterson), Monaco GP (Fittipaldi), Dutch GP (Peterson), Canadian GP (Fittipaldi), 1974 Monaco GP (Peterson), Dutch GP (Peterson), 1976 Swedish GP (Andretti), 1977 Belgian GP (Nilsson), Swedish GP (Andretti), French GP (Andretti), Italian GP (Andretti), Canadian GP (Andretti), 1978 South African GP (Andretti), Belgian GP (Peterson), Spanish GP (Andretti), German GP (Peterson), Austrian GP (Peterson), Italian GP (Andretti), United States GP (Jarier), 1983 European GP (Mansell), 1985 Portuguese GP (Senna), Canadian GP (Senna), Detroit GP (Senna), 1987 Monaco GP (Senna), Detroit GP (Senna), Italian GP (Senna), 1989 Australian GP (Nakajima)

Laps/miles in the lead: 5498 laps/16285 miles

World Champions:

Drivers: Six times - 1963 (Clark), 1965 (Clark), 1968 (G Hill), 1970 (Rindt), 1972 (Fittipaldi) and 1978 (Andretti)

Constructors: Seven times - 1963, 1965, 1968, 1970, 1972, 1973 and 1978

MAJOR SPONSORS

1968-71	Gold Leaf
1972-77	John Player Special
1978	John Player Special, Olympus
1979	Martini
1980-81	Essex, John Player Special, Courage (British GP only)
1982-84	John Player Special
1985	John Player Special, Olympus
1986	John Player Special, deLonghi
1987	Camel, deLonghi
1988	Camel, Epson
1989	Camel, Epson, PIAA
1990	Camel
1992-93	Castrol, Hitachi
1994	Hitachi, Loctite, Miller Genuine Draft

LOTUS GRAND PRIX DRIVERS

Driver	Nat	Starts (DNS/DNQ)	1st	2nd	3rd	4th	5th	6th	PP	FL	Points
Jim Clark	GB	72 (1)	25	1	6	4	3	1	33	28	274
Mario Andretti	USA	79 (1)	11	2	3	3	6	3	17	8	147
Ronnie Peterson	S	59	9	6	3	3	3	1	13	7	144
Emerson Fittipaldi	BR	42 (1)	9	6	5	1	1	2	4	5	144
Ayrton Senna	BR	48	6	10	6	2	3	-	16	6	150
Jochen Rindt	A	19 (1)	6	1	1	1	-	-	8	3	67
Graham Hill	GB	60 (1)	4	6	-	4	1	4	5	2	89
Stirling Moss	GB	12 (1)	4	-	-	2	-	-	4	2	40
Elio de Angelis	I	90	2	2	5	10	17	6	3	-	119
Innes Ireland	GB	36 (3)	2	1	2	1	2	2	-	1	37
Gunnar Nilsson	S	31 (1)	1	-	3	1	3	1	-	1	31
Jo Siffert	CH	35 (2)	1	1	1	1	2	2	1	3	28
Nigel Mansell	GB	59 (2)	-	-	5	4	1	4	1	1	38
Nelson Piquet	BR	31 (1)	-	-	3	5	3	1	-	-	34
Carlos Reutemann	RA	15	-	2	2	1	1	-	-	-	25
Mike Spence	GB	24 (1)	-	1	3	2	1	-	-	-	18
Jacky Ickx	B	24	-	1	2	-	2	-	-	-	15
Johnny Herbert	GB	54 (1)	-	-	-	3	1	2	-	-	13
Mika Hakkinen	SF	30 (2)	-	-	2	2	3	-	-	-	13
Reine Wisell	S	14	-	1	2	1	1	-	-	-	13
Peter Arundell	GB	11 (2)	-	2	1	-	1	-	-	-	12
Satoru Nakajima	J	43 (5)	-	-	2	1	3	-	1	-	11
Trevor Taylor	GB	20	-	1	-	-	1	-	-	-	7
Jackie Oliver	GB	8 (2)	-	1	-	1	-	-	1	6
John Surtees	GB	4	-	1	-	-	-	1	1	6

Formula 1

Driver	Nat	Start	1st	2nd	3rd	4th	5th	6th	PP	FL	Points
Richard Attwood	GB	9	-	-	-	1	-	2	-	-	5
Derek Warwick	GB	16	-	-	-	-	1	1	-	-	3
Johnny Dumfries	GB	15 (1)	-	-	-	-	1	1	-	-	3
Jim Hall	USA	11 (1)	-	-	-	-	1	1	-	-	3
Cliff Allison	GB	9 (1)	-	-	-	1	1	2	-	-	3
Jack Brabham	AUS	6	-	-	-	-	1	1	-	-	3
John Miles	GB	12 (3)	-	-	-	-	1	-	-	-	2
Chris Amon	NZ	11 (1)	-	-	-	-	1	-	-	-	2
Walt Hansgen	USA	1	-	-	-	-	1	-	-	-	2
Alessandro Zanardi	I	21 (1)	-	-	-	-	-	1	-	-	1
Hector Rebaque	MEX	18 (9)	-	-	-	-	-	1	-	-	1
Masten Gregory	USA	11 (1)	-	-	-	-	-	1	-	-	1
Mike Hailwood	GB	11	-	-	-	-	-	1	-	-	1
Julian Bailey	GB	1 (3)	-	-	-	-	-	1	-	-	1
Neville Lederle	ZA	1 (1)	-	-	-	-	-	1	-	-	1
Ron Flockhart	GB	1	-	-	-	-	-	1	-	-	1
Martin Donnelly	GB	12 (2)	-	-	-	-	-	-	-	-	-
Dave Walker	AUS	11	-	-	-	-	-	-	-	-	-
Pedro Lamy	P	8	-	-	-	-	-	-	-	-	-
Alan Stacey	GB	7	-	-	-	-	-	-	-	-	-
Maurice Trintignant	F	7	-	-	-	-	-	-	-	-	-
Pete Lovely	USA	6 (4)	-	-	-	-	-	-	-	-	-
Dave Charlton	ZA	6 (3)	-	-	-	-	-	-	-	-	-
Pedro Rodriguez	MEX	6	-	-	-	-	-	-	-	-	-
Moises Solana	MEX	6	-	-	-	-	-	-	-	-	-
Peter Revson	USA	4 (2)	-	-	-	-	-	-	-	-	-
Wolfgang Seidel	D	4 (2)	-	-	-	-	-	-	-	-	-
Lucien Bianchi	B	4	-	-	-	-	-	-	-	-	-
Gerry Ashmore	GB	3 (1)	-	-	-	-	-	-	-	-	-
Henry Taylor	GB	3 (1)	-	-	-	-	-	-	-	-	-
Tony Maggs	ZA	3	-	-	-	-	-	-	-	-	-
Ian Burgess	GB	2 (2)	-	-	-	-	-	-	-	-	-
Brian Henton	GB	2 (1)	-	-	-	-	-	-	-	-	-
Tony Marsh	GB	2 (1)	-	-	-	-	-	-	-	-	-
Michel May	CH	2 (1)	-	-	-	-	-	-	-	-	-
Gerhard Mitter	D	2 (1)	-	-	-	-	-	-	-	-	-
Tim Parnell	GB	2 (1)	-	-	-	-	-	-	-	-	-
Ernest Pieterse	ZA	2 (1)	-	-	-	-	-	-	-	-	-
David Piper	GB	2 (1)	-	-	-	-	-	-	-	-	-
Philippe Adams	B	2	-	-	-	-	-	-	-	-	-
Jo Bonnier	S	2	-	-	-	-	-	-	-	-	-
Piers Courage	GB	2	-	-	-	-	-	-	-	-	-
Jim Crawford	GB	2	-	-	-	-	-	-	-	-	-
Mike Fisher	USA	2	-	-	-	-	-	-	-	-	-
Paul Hawkins	AUS	2	-	-	-	-	-	-	-	-	-
Jean-Pierre Jarier	F	2	-	-	-	-	-	-	1	1	-
John Love	RSR	2	-	-	-	-	-	-	-	-	-
Willy Mairesse	B	2	-	-	-	-	-	-	-	-	-
"Geki" Russo	I	2	-	-	-	-	-	-	-	-	-
Mika Salo	SF	2	-	-	-	-	-	-	-	-	-
Hap Sharp	USA	2	-	-	-	-	-	-	-	-	-
Jay Chamberlain	USA	1 (2)	-	-	-	-	-	-	-	-	-
Bernard Collomb	F	1 (2)	-	-	-	-	-	-	-	-	-
Tony Shelly	NZ	1 (2)	-	-	-	-	-	-	-	-	-
Paddy Driver	ZA	1 (1)	-	-	-	-	-	-	-	-	-
Bob Evans	GB	1 (1)	-	-	-	-	-	-	-	-	-
Phil Hill	USA	1 (1)	-	-	-	-	-	-	-	-	-
Brausch Niemann	ZA	1 (1)	-	-	-	-	-	-	-	-	-
Nino Vaccarella	I	1 (1)	-	-	-	-	-	-	-	-	-
Giancarlo Baghetti	I	1	-	-	-	-	-	-	-	-	-
Eric Bernard	F	1	-	-	-	-	-	-	-	-	-
Bob Bondurant	USA	1	-	-	-	-	-	-	-	-	-
Bill Brack	CDN	1	-	-	-	-	-	-	-	-	-
Ivor Bueb	GB	1	-	-	-	-	-	-	-	-	-
John Campbell-Jones	GB	1	-	-	-	-	-	-	-	-	-
Olivier Gendebien	B	1	-	-	-	-	-	-	-	-	-
Bruce Halford	GB	1	-	-	-	-	-	-	-	-	-
Chris Irwin	GB	1	-	-	-	-	-	-	-	-	-
Eddie Keizan	ZA	1	-	-	-	-	-	-	-	-	-
Geoff Lees	GB	1	-	-	-	-	-	-	-	-	-
Roger Penske	USA	1	-	-	-	-	-	-	-	-	-
Alberto Rodriguez Larreta	RA	1	-	-	-	-	-	-	-	-	-
Lloyd Ruby	USA	1	-	-	-	-	-	-	-	-	-
Peter Ryan	CDN	1	-	-	-	-	-	-	-	-	-
Ian Scheckter	ZA	1	-	-	-	-	-	-	-	-	-
Tim Schenken	AUS	1	-	-	-	-	-	-	-	-	-
Heinz Schiller	CH	1	-	-	-	-	-	-	-	-	-
Rob Schroeder	USA	1	-	-	-	-	-	-	-	-	-
Gaetano Starrabba	I	1	-	-	-	-	-	-	-	-	-
Rolf Stommelen	D	1	-	-	-	-	-	-	-	-	-
Guy Tunmer	ZA	1	-	-	-	-	-	-	-	-	-
Rodger Ward	USA	1	-	-	-	-	-	-	-	-	-
John Watson	GB	1	-	-	-	-	-	-	-	-	-
Eppie Wietzes	CDN	1	-	-	-	-	-	-	-	-	-
Michael Bartels	D	- (4)	-	-	-	-	-	-	-	-	-
Alex Soler-Roig	E	- (3)	-	-	-	-	-	-	-	-	-
Andre Pilette	B	- (2)	-	-	-	-	-	-	-	-	-
Brian Gubby	GB	- (1)	-	-	-	-	-	-	-	-	-
Dan Gurney	USA	- (1)	-	-	-	-	-	-	-	-	-
Hans Herrmann	D	- (1)	-	-	-	-	-	-	-	-	-
Kurt Kuhnke	D	- (1)	-	-	-	-	-	-	-	-	-
Roberto Moreno	BR	- (1)	-	-	-	-	-	-	-	-	-
Ernesto Prinoth	I	- (1)	-	-	-	-	-	-	-	-	-
Clive Puzey	ZA	- (1)	-	-	-	-	-	-	-	-	-
Brian Redman	GB	- (1)	-	-	-	-	-	-	-	-	-
Gunther Seifert	D	- (1)	-	-	-	-	-	-	-	-	-
Mike Taylor	GB	- (1)	-	-	-	-	-	-	-	-	-

LOTUS GRAND PRIX CARS

Type	Year	Engine	Designer
12	1958	Climax FPF S4	Colin Chapman
16	1958	Climax FPF S4	Colin Chapman
18	1960	Climax FPF S4, Maserati 250S S4, Borgward S4	Colin Chapman
18/21	1961	Climax FPF S4	Colin Chapman
20	1965	Ford 109E S4	Colin Chapman
Formula Junior car			
21	1961	Climax FPF S4	Colin Chapman
22	1963	Ford 109E S4	Colin Chapman
Formula Junior car			
24	1962	Climax FMWV V8, BRM 56 V8	Colin Chapman
25	1962	Climax FMWV V8, BRM 56 V8	Colin Chapman
First monocoque Lotus			
33	1964	Climax FMWV V8, BRM 56 V8	Len Terry/Colin Chapman
43	1966	BRM 75 H16	Colin Chapman
44	1966	Ford SCA S4	Colin Chapman
F2 car			
48	1967	Ford FVA S4	Colin Chapman
F2 car			
49	1967	Ford DFV V8	Colin Chapman/Maurice Philippe
49B	1968	Ford DFV V8	Colin Chapman/Maurice Philippe
49C	1970	Ford DFV V8	Colin Chapman/Maurice Philippe
59B	1969	Cosworth, Pratt & Whitney turbine	Colin Chapman/Maurice Philippe
F2 car fitted with gas turbine engine raced in 1971			
63	1969	Ford DFV V8	Maurice Philippe
4-wheel-drive			
69	1971	Ford FVA S4	Dave Baldwin
F2 car			
72	1970	Ford DFV V8	Colin Chapman/Maurice Philippe

Type	Year	Engine	Designer
72C	1971	Ford DFV V8	Colin Chapman/ Maurice Philippe
72D	1971	Ford DFV V8	Colin Chapman/ Maurice Philippe
72E	1974	Ford DFV V8	Colin Chapman/ Maurice Philippe
76	1974	Ford DFV V8	Colin Chapman/ Ralph Bellamy
77	1976	Ford DFV V8	Geoff Aldridge/ Martin Ogilvie
78	1977	Ford DFV V8	Ralph Bellamy/ Martin Ogilvie/Peter Wright
79	1978	Ford DFV V8	Martin Ogilvie/Geoff Aldridge
80	1979	Ford DFV V8	Martin Ogilvie/ Geoff Aldridge/Peter Wright
81	1980	Ford DFV V8	Martin Ogilvie/Peter Wright
81B	1980	Ford DFV V8	Martin Ogilvie/Peter Wright
87	1981	Ford DFV V8	Colin Chapman/ Martin Ogilvie/Peter Wright
87B	1982	Ford DFV V8	Colin Chapman/ Martin Ogilvie/Peter Wright
91	1982	Ford DFV V8	Colin Chapman/Martin Ogilvie
92	1983	Ford DFV V8	Colin Chapman/Martin Ogilvie
93T	1983	Renault EF1/EF4B V6 tc	Colin Chapman/Martin Ogilvie
94T	1983	Renault EF1/EF4B V6 tc	Gerard Ducarouge/ Martin Ogilvie
95T	1984	Renault EF4B V6 tc	Gerard Ducarouge/ Martin Ogilvie
97T	1985	Renault EF4B/EF15 V6 tc	Gerard Ducarouge/ Martin Ogilvie
98T	1986	Renault EF15B V6 tc	Gerard Ducarouge/ Martin Ogilvie
99T	1987	Honda RA166E V6 tc	Gerard Ducarouge/ Martin Ogilvie
100T	1988	Honda RA168E V6 tc	Gerard Ducarouge/ Martin Ogilvie
101	1989	Judd CV V8	Frank Dernie/Mike Coghlan
102	1990	Lamborghini 3512 V12	Frank Dernie
102B	1991	Judd EV V8	Frank Coppuck
102C	1991	Isuzu V12	Frank Coppuck
Test chassis for new Isuzu engine, never raced			
102D	1992	Ford HB V8	Frank Coppuck
107	1992	Ford HB V8	Chris Murphy
107B	1993	Ford HB V8	Chris Murphy
107C	1994	Mugen MF-351HB V10	Chris Murphy
109	1994	Mugen MF-351HB V10	Chris Murphy

Lyncar

Only Grand Prix: 1975 British GP   Nicholson (17th)
Principal: Martin Slater
Base: Slough, Berkshire

WORLD CHAMPIONSHIP RECORD

Starts: 1
Best result: 17th   1975 British GP (Nicholson)
Best qualifying: 26th   1975 British GP (Nicholson)

MAJOR SPONSORS

1974-75   Pinch

LYNCAR GRAND PRIX DRIVERS

Driver	Nat	Starts (DNS/DNQ)	1st	2nd	3rd	4th	5th	6th	PP	FL	Points
John Nicholson	NZ	1 (1)	-	-	-	-	-	-	-	-	-

LYNCAR GRAND PRIX CARS

Type	Year	Engine	Designer
006	1974	Ford DFV V8	Martin Slater
009	1975	Ford DFV V8	Martin Slater

Maki

Principal: Kenji Mimura

WORLD CHAMPIONSHIP RECORD

Starts: None
Best qualifying: 25th   1975 Dutch GP (Fushida)

MAJOR SPONSORS

1975   Citizen
1976   Hotstuff

MAKI GRAND PRIX DRIVERS

Driver	Nat	Starts (DNS/DNQ)	1st	2nd	3rd	4th	5th	6th	PP	FL	Points
Tony Trimmer	GB	- (4)	-	-	-	-	-	-	-	-	-
Hiroshi Fushida	J	- (2)	-	-	-	-	-	-	-	-	-
Howden Ganley	NZ	- (2)	-	-	-	-	-	-	-	-	-

MAKI GRAND PRIX CARS

Type	Year	Engine	Designer
F101	1974	Ford DFV V8	Kenji Mimura/Masao Ono
F101C	1975	Ford DFV V8	Kenji Mimura/Masao Ono
F102A	1976	Ford DFV V8	Kenji Mimura/Masao Ono

March

During 1990-91 cars were officially named after major sponsor/shareholder Leyton House, renamed March again in 1992. For RAM-March see RAM

Grand Prix Debut: 1970 South African GP   Stewart (3rd), Siffert (10th), Amon (retired), Andretti (retired), Servoz-Gavin (retired)
Last Grand Prix: 1992 Australian GP   Lammers (12th), Naspetti (retired)
Principals: Robin Herd, 1969-89; Akira Akagi/Leyton House, 1990-91; Ken Marrable, 1992; March was founded by Max Mosley, Alan Rees, Graham Croaker and Robin Herd in 1969
Base: Bicester

WORLD CHAMPIONSHIP RECORD

Starts: 227
Points: 193
Wins: 3   1970 Spanish GP (Stewart), 1975 Austrian GP (Brambilla), 1976 Italian GP (Peterson)
Pole positions: 5   1970 South African GP (Stewart), Monaco GP (Stewart), Belgian GP (Stewart), 1975 Swedish GP (Brambilla), 1976 Dutch GP (Peterson)
Fastest laps: 7   1970 Belgian GP (Amon), 1971 Italian GP (Pescarolo), 1973 British GP (Hunt), United States GP (Hunt), 1975 Austrian GP

Laps/miles in the lead: (Brambilla), 1976 Italian GP (Peterson), 1989 French GP (Gugelmin)
338 laps/927 miles

Best World Championship position:
Drivers: 2nd in 1971 (Peterson)
Constructors: 3rd in 1970 and 1971

1970-72	STP
1973	STP, Wheatcroft Racing
1974	Beta, Jagermeister
1975	Beta, Elf, Lavazza
1976	Beta, Duckhams, First National City, Jagermeister, John Day Models, Lavazza, Monaco Fine Arts, Ovoro, Theodore Racing
1977	Hollywood, Lexington, Rothmans, Sportsman Lager
1981	Guinness, Rizla
1982	Rizla, Rothmans
1987-91	Leyton House
1992	Uliveto

Driver	Nat	Starts (DNS/DNQ)	1st	2nd	3rd	4th	5th	6th	PP	FL	Points
Ronnie Peterson	S	47	1	4	2	2	3	2	1	1	55
Jackie Stewart	GB	10	1	2	1	-	-	-	3	-	25
Vittorio Brambilla	I	41 (2)	1	-	-	1	3	1	1	8.5
Ivan Capelli	I	74 (4)	-	2	1	-	3	3	-	-	25
Chris Amon	NZ	13	-	2	1	1	2	-	-	1	23
James Hunt	GB	9 (1)	-	1	1	1	-	1	-	2	14
Hans-Joachim Stuck	D	34 (2)	-	-	3	2	-	-	-	-	13
Mauricio Gugelmin	BR	58 (6)	-	1	1	1	1	-	1	10
Henri Pescarolo	F	19 (4)	-	-	1	-	1	-	1	4
Mario Andretti	USA	5	-	1	-	-	-	-	-	4
Karl Wendlinger	A	16	-	-	-	1	-	-	-	-	3
Carlos Pace	BR	11	-	-	-	1	1	-	-	3
Mark Donohue	USA	2 (1)	-	-	-	1	-	-	-	2
Johnny Servoz-Gavin	F	2 (1)	-	-	-	1	-	-	-	2
Francois Cevert	F	9	-	-	-	-	1	-	1
Lella Lombardi	I	11 (1)	-	-	-	-	1	-	0.5
Mike Beuttler	GB	28 (1)	-	-	-	-	-	-	-
Ian Scheckter	ZA	13 (1)	-	-	-	-	-	-	-
Niki Lauda	A	13	-	-	-	-	-	-	-
Jo Siffert	CH	12 (1)	-	-	-	-	-	-	-
Jean-Pierre Jarier	F	11	-	-	-	-	-	-	-
Raul Boesel	BR	10 (5)	-	-	-	-	-	-	-
Alex Ribeiro	BR	9 (8)	-	-	-	-	-	-	-
Arturo Merzario	I	9 (6)	-	-	-	-	-	-	-
Jochen Mass	D	9 (1)	-	-	-	-	-	-	-
Derek Daly	IRL	8 (7)	-	-	-	-	-	-	-
Patrick Neve	B	8 (3)	-	-	-	-	-	-	-
Nanni Galli	I	7 (2)	-	-	-	-	-	-	-
Andrea de Adamich	I	7	-	-	-	-	-	-	-
Paul Belmondo	F	5 (6)	-	-	-	-	-	-	-
Skip Barber	USA	5 (1)	-	-	-	-	-	-	-
Emanuele Naspetti	I	5	-	-	-	-	-	-	-
David Purley	GB	4 (1)	-	-	-	-	-	-	-
Alex Soler-Roig	E	4 (1)	-	-	-	-	-	-	-
Rupert Keegan	GB	3 (2)	-	-	-	-	-	-	-
Brett Lunger	USA	3	-	-	-	-	-	-	-
Boy Hayje	NL	2 (4)	-	-	-	-	-	-	-
Reine Wisell	S	2 (1)	-	-	-	-	-	-	-
Howden Ganley	NZ	2	-	-	-	-	-	-	-
Jan Lammers	NL	2	-	-	-	-	-	-	-
Roger Williamson	GB	2	-	-	-	-	-	-	-
Eliseo Salazar	RCH	1 (5)	-	-	-	-	-	-	-
Brian Henton	GB	1 (3)	-	-	-	-	-	-	-
John Love	RSR	1	-	-	-	-	-	-	-
Jean Max	F	1	-	-	-	-	-	-	-
Francois Mazet	F	1	-	-	-	-	-	-	-

Driver	Nat	Start (DNS/DNQ)	1st	2nd	3rd	4th	5th	6th	PP	FL	Points
Emilio de Villota	E	- (5)	-	-	-	-	-	-	-	-	-
Mikko Kozarowitsky	SF	- (2)	-	-	-	-	-	-	-	-	-
Michael Bleekemolen	NL	- (1)	-	-	-	-	-	-	-	-	-
Bernard de Dryver	B	- (1)	-	-	-	-	-	-	-	-	-
Hubert Hahne	D	- (1)	-	-	-	-	-	-	-	-	-
Karl Oppitzhauser	A	- (1)	-	-	-	-	-	-	-	-	-
Andy Sutcliffe	GB	- (1)	-	-	-	-	-	-	-	-	-
Mike Wilds	GB	- (1)	-	-	-	-	-	-	-	-	-

Type	Year	Engine	Designer
701	1970	Ford DFV V8	Robin Herd/Peter Wright
711	1971	Ford DFV V8, Alfa Romeo T33 V8	Robin Herd/Geoff Ferris/ Frank Costin
721	1972	Ford DFV V8	Robin Herd
721G	1972	Ford DFV V8	Robin Herd
721X	1972	Ford DFV V8	Robin Herd
731	1973	Ford DFV V8	Robin Herd
741	1974	Ford DFV V8	Robin Herd
751	1975	Ford DFV V8	Robin Herd
761	1976	Ford DFV V8	Robin Herd
761B	1977	Ford DFV V8	Robin Herd/Martin Walters
771	1977	Ford DFV V8	Robin Herd/Martin Walters
811	1981	Ford DFV V8	Robin Herd/Adrian Reynard/ Alan Mertens
821	1982	Ford DFV V8	Adrian Reynard
87P	1987	Ford DFZ V8	Gordon Coppuck/Tim Holloway/Andy Brown
871	1987	Ford DFZ V8	Gordon Coppuck/ Tim Holloway/Andy Brown
881	1988	Judd CV V8	Adrian Newey
CG891	1989	Judd EV V8	Adrian Newey
CG901*	1990	Judd EV V8	Adrian Newey/Gustav Brunner
CG911*	1991	Ilmor 2175A V10	Chris Murphy/Gustav Brunner

*Leyton House (CG911 renamed March in 1992). Note: CG designation refers to Cesare Garibaldi of Genoa Racing

Martini

Grand Prix Debut: 1978 Belgian GP   Arnoux (9th)
Last Grand Prix: 1978 Dutch GP   Arnoux (retired)
Principal: Tico Martini
Base: Magny-Cours

Starts: 4
Best result: 9th   1978 Belgian GP (Arnoux), Austrian GP (Arnoux)
Best qualifying: 18th   1978 French GP (Arnoux)

1978	Silver Match, RMO, Elf

Driver	Nat	Starts (DNS/DNQ)	1st	2nd	3rd	4th	5th	6th	PP	FL	Points
Rene Arnoux	F	4 (3)	-	-	-	-	-	-	-	-	-

Type	Year	Engine	Designer
MK23	1978	Ford DFV V8	Tico Martini

Note: The MK designation stands for Martini-Knight in reference to the Knight family, who operate the racing school at Magny-Cours

Maserati

Grand Prix Debut: 1950 British GP   Hampshire (9th), Fry/
Shaw-Taylor (10th),"Bira"
(retired), Murray (retired),
de Graffenried (retired),
Chiron (retired)

Last Grand Prix: 1960 United States GP   Drake (13th)

Principals: Alfieri Maserati 1926-32; Ernesto Maserati, 1932-37;
Adolfo Orsi, 1938-60; founded by brothers Alfieri,
Bindo, Carlo, Ettore, Ernesto and Mario Maserati

Base: Bologna, 1926-37; Modena, 1937 to date

WORLD CHAMPIONSHIP RECORD

Starts: 68

Points: 312.92

Wins: 9 1953 Italian GP (Fangio), 1954 Argentinian GP
(Fangio), Belgian GP (Fangio), 1956 Monaco GP
(Moss), Italian GP (Moss), 1957 Argentinian GP
(Fangio), Monaco GP (Fangio), French GP (Fangio),
German GP (Fangio)

Pole positions: 10 1953 Belgian GP (Fangio), Swiss GP (Fangio), 1954
Belgian GP (Fangio), 1956 British GP (Moss), 1957
Argentinian GP (Moss), Monaco GP (Fangio), French
GP (Fangio), German GP (Fangio), Pescara GP
(Fangio), 1958 Argentinian GP (Fangio)

Fastest laps: 15 1952 Italian GP (Gonzalez), 1953 Belgian GP
(Gonzalez), French GP (Fangio), British GP
(Gonzalez), Italian GP (Fangio), 1954 Belgian GP
(Fangio), British GP (Marimon), (Moss), and (Ascari),
1955 Dutch GP (Mieres), 1956 Belgian GP (Moss),
British GP (Moss), Italian GP (Moss), 1957
Argentinian GP (Moss), Monaco GP (Fangio),
German GP (Fangio), 1958 Argentinian GP (Fangio)

Laps/miles in the lead: 832 laps/2948 miles

World Champions:

Drivers: Twice - 1954 (Fangio - including 40.14 of his 57.14
points for Mercedes-Benz) and 1957 (Fangio)

Best World Championship position:

Constructors: 5th in 1958

MASERATI GRAND PRIX DRIVERS

Driver	Nat	Starts (DNS/DNQ)	1st	2nd	3rd	4th	5th	6th	PP	FL	Points
Juan Manuel Fangio	RA	19	7	5	-	3	-	-	8	6	99
Stirling Moss	GB	14	2	1	2	-	1	-	2	5	33.14
Jean Behra	F	20	-	2	5	1	2	4	-	-	36
Jose Froilan Gonzalez	RA	9	-	1	3	1	-	-	-	3	21
Roberto Mieres	RA	14	-	-	-	3	2	1	-	1	13
Luigi Musso	I	9 (1)	-	1	1	-	1	-	-	-	12
Felice Bonetto	I	11 (2)	-	-	1	2	2	1	-	-	10.5
Harry Schell	USA	21	-	-	1	1	2	3	-	-	10
Masten Gregory	USA	8	-	-	1	3	-	1	-	-	10
Onofre Marimon	RA	11 (1)	-	-	2	-	-	-	-	1	8.14
"B Bira"	SM	12	-	-	-	2	1	1	-	-	8
Emanuel de Graffenried	CH	19 (1)	-	-	-	1	2	3	-	-	7
Chico Godia-Sales	E	13 (1)	-	-	-	2	-	1	-	-	6
Carlos Menditeguy	RA	8 (1)	-	-	1	-	1	-	-	-	6
Cesare Perdisa	I	6 (1)	-	-	2	-	1	-	-	-	5
Luigi Villoresi	I	8 (1)	-	-	-	-	2	1	-	-	4
Sergio Mantovani	I.	7 (1)	-	-	-	-	2	-	-	-	4
Louis Chiron	MC	6 (1)	-	-	1	-	-	-	-	-	4
Mike Hawthorn	GB	1 (1)	-	-	1	-	-	-	-	-	4
Horace Gould	GB	13 (3)	-	-	-	-	1	-	-	-	2
Louis Rosier	F	10	-	-	-	-	1	1	-	-	2
Oscar Galvez	RA	1	-	-	-	-	1	-	-	-	2

Driver	Nat	Start	1st	2nd	3rd	4th	5th	6th	PP	FL	Points
Hermann Lang	D	1	-	-	-	-	1	-	-	-	2
Gerino Gerini	I	6 (1)	-	-	-	1	-	-	-	-	1.5
Chico Landi	BR	5	-	-	-	1	-	-	-	-	1.5
Giorgio Scarlatti	I	8 (1)	-	-	-	-	1	1	-	-	1
Alberto Ascari	I	2	-	-	-	-	-	-	-	1	0.14
Jo Bonnier	S	12	-	-	-	-	-	-	-	-	-
Luigi Piotti	I	6 (2)	-	-	-	-	1	-	-	-	-
Bruce Halford	GB	6	-	-	-	-	-	-	-	-	-
Roy Salvadori	GB	6	-	-	-	-	-	-	-	-	-
Hans Herrmann	D	4 (1)	-	-	-	-	-	-	-	-	-
Ken Wharton	GB	4 (1)	-	-	-	-	1	-	-	-	-
Gino Bianco	BR	4	-	-	-	-	-	-	-	-	-
Franco Rol	I	4	-	-	-	-	-	-	-	-	-
Carroll Shelby	USA	4	-	-	1	-	-	-	-	-	-
Maria Teresa de Filippis	I	3 (1)	-	-	-	-	-	-	-	-	-
David Murray	GB	3 (1)	-	-	-	-	-	-	-	-	-
Andre Simon	F	3 (1)	-	-	-	-	-	-	-	-	-
Antonio Branca	CH	3	-	-	-	-	-	-	-	-	-
Heitel Cantoni	U	3	-	-	-	-	-	-	-	-	-
Umberto Maglioli	I	3	-	-	-	-	-	-	-	-	-
Ottorino Volonterio	CH	3	-	-	-	-	-	-	-	-	-
Giulio Cabianca	I	2	-	-	-	-	-	-	-	-	-
Peter Collins	GB	2	-	-	-	-	-	-	-	-	-
Jorge Daponte	RA	2	-	-	-	-	-	-	-	-	-
David Hampshire	GB	2	-	-	-	-	-	-	-	-	-
Fritz d'Orey	BR	2	-	-	-	-	-	-	-	-	-
Wolfgang Seidel	D	2	-	-	-	-	-	-	-	-	-
Alberto Uria	U	2	-	-	-	-	-	1	-	-	-
Johnny Claes	B	1 (1)	-	-	-	-	-	-	-	-	-
Lance Macklin	GB	1 (1)	-	-	-	-	-	-	-	-	-
Troy Ruttman	USA	1 (1)	-	-	-	-	-	-	-	-	-
Cliff Allison	GB	1	-	-	-	-	-	-	-	-	-
Carel Godin de Beaufort	NL	1	-	-	-	-	-	-	-	-	-
Jack Brabham	AUS	1	-	-	-	-	-	-	-	-	-
Clemar Bucci	RA	1	-	-	-	-	-	-	-	-	-
Ivor Bueb	GB	1	-	-	-	-	-	-	-	-	-
Ettore Chimeri	YV	1	-	-	-	-	-	-	-	-	-
Gianfranco Comotti	I	1	-	-	-	-	-	-	-	-	-
Antonio Creus	E	1	-	-	-	-	-	-	-	-	-
Bob Drake	USA	1	-	-	-	-	-	-	-	-	-
Nasif Estefano	RA	1	-	-	-	-	-	-	-	-	-
Philippe Etancelin	F	1	-	-	-	-	-	-	-	-	-
John Fitch	USA	1	-	-	-	-	-	-	-	-	-
Jan Flinterman	NL	1	-	-	-	-	-	-	-	-	-
Ron Flockhart	GB	1	-	-	-	-	-	-	-	-	-
Philip Fotheringham-Parker	GB	1	-	-	-	-	-	-	-	-	-
Joe Fry	GB	1	-	-	-	-	-	-	-	-	-
Oscar Gonzalez	U	1	-	-	-	-	-	1	-	-	-
Phil Hill	USA	1	-	-	-	-	-	-	-	-	-
John James	GB	1	-	-	-	-	-	-	-	-	-
Gino Munaron	I	1	-	-	-	-	-	-	-	-	-
Nello Pagani	I	1	-	-	-	-	-	-	-	-	-
Reg Parnell	GB	1	-	-	-	-	-	-	-	-	-
Paul Pietsch	D	1	-	-	-	-	-	-	-	-	-
Brian Shawe-Taylor	GB	1	-	-	-	-	-	-	-	-	-
Piero Taruffi	I	1	-	-	-	-	-	-	-	-	-
Maurice Trintignant	F	1	-	-	-	-	-	-	-	-	-
Peter Walker	GB	1	-	-	-	-	-	-	-	-	-
Ken Kavanagh	AUS	- (2)	-	-	-	-	-	-	-	-	-
Andre Testut	MC	- (2)	-	-	-	-	-	-	-	-	-
Astrubel Bayardo	ROU	- (1)	-	-	-	-	-	-	-	-	-
Phil Cade	USA	- (1)	-	-	-	-	-	-	-	-	-
Alberto Crespo	RA	- (1)	-	-	-	-	-	-	-	-	-
Juan Jover	E	- (1)	-	-	-	-	-	-	-	-	-
Alfredo Pian	RA	- (1)	-	-	-	-	-	-	-	-	-
Giovanni de Riu	I	- (1)	-	-	-	-	-	-	-	-	-

MASERATI GRAND PRIX CARS

Type	Year	Engine	Designer
4CL	1950	Maserati 4CL S4	Ernesto Maserati
4CLT/48	1950	Maserati 4CL S4, OSCA V12	Alberto Massimino
Also known as the "San Remo" Maserati			
4CLT/48- Anzani	1955	Anzani S4	Amedeo Ruggeri
4CLT/48- Plate	1952	Maserati 4CL/ Plate S4	Engine modified by Enrico Plate
4CLT/50- Milano	1950	Speluzzi S4	Engine modified by Mario Speluzzi
A6GCM	1952	Maserati A6GC S6	Alberto Massimino
A6SSG	1953	Maserati A6GC S6	Alberto Massimino/ Gioacchino Colombo
250F	1954	Maserati 250/F1 S6	Gioacchino Colombo/ Vittorio Bellentani
250F (V12)	1957	Maserati 250-T2 V12	Gioacchino Colombo/ Vittorio Bellentani

Matra
Mecanique-Aviation-Traction

Grand Prix Debut: 1966 German GP Beltoise, Hahne, Schlesser, Ickx (all raced in F2 class)
Last Grand Prix: 1972 United States GP Amon (15th)
Principal: Michel Chassagny
Works teams: Matra Sports and Matra International
Team Principal: Matra Sports: Jean-Luc Lagardere and Claude de Guezec
Matra International: Ken Tyrrell
Base: Velizy

WORLD CHAMPIONSHIP RECORD

Starts: 62
Points: 184
Wins: 9 1968 Dutch GP (Stewart), German GP (Stewart), United States GP (Stewart), 1969 South African GP (Stewart), Spanish GP (Stewart), Dutch GP (Stewart), French GP (Stewart), British GP (Stewart), Italian GP (Stewart)
Pole positions: 4 1969 Monaco GP (Stewart), French GP (Stewart), 1971 Italian GP (Amon), 1972 French GP (Amon)
Fastest laps: 12 1968 Spanish GP (Beltoise), Dutch GP (Beltoise), German GP (Stewart), United States GP (Stewart), 1969 South African GP (Stewart), Monaco GP (Stewart), Dutch GP (Stewart), French GP (Stewart), British GP (Stewart), Italian GP (Beltoise), 1972 Belgian GP (Amon), French GP (Amon)

Laps/miles in the lead: 668 laps/2249 miles

World Champions:
Drivers: Once - 1969 (Stewart)
Constructors: Once - 1969

MAJOR SPONSORS

1966-72 Elf

MATRA GRAND PRIX DRIVERS

Driver	Nat	Starts (DNS/DNQ)	1st	2nd	3rd	4th	5th	6th	PP	FL	Points
Jackie Stewart	GB	21	9	1	1	2	-	2	2	7	99
Jean-Pierre Beltoise	F	46 (1)	-	2	4	2	5	5	-	3	49
Chris Amon	NZ	21 (1)	-	-	2	1	3	4	2	2	21
Henri Pescarolo	F	16 (1)	-	-	1	-	1	2	-	-	8
Johnny Servoz-Gavin	F	9	-	1	-	-	-	1	-	-	7
Jacky Ickx	B	2	-	-	-	-	-	-	-	-	-

Driver	Nat	Start	1st	2nd	3rd	4th	5th	6th	PP	FL	Points
Jo Schlesser	F	2	-	-	-	-	-	-	-	-	-
Hubert Hahne	D	1	-	-	-	-	-	-	-	-	-

MATRA GRAND PRIX CARS

Type	Year	Engine	Designer
MS5	1966	BRM 71, Ford SCA S4	Bernard Boyer
MS7	1967	Ford FVA S4	Bernard Boyer
MS9	1968	Ford DFV V8	Bernard Boyer
MS10	1968	Ford DFV V8	Bernard Boyer
MS11	1968	Matra V12	Bernard Boyer
MS80	1969	Ford DFV V8	Bernard Boyer
MS84	1969	Ford DFV V8	Bernard Boyer/ Derek Gardner
4-wheel-drive			
MS120*	1970	Matra MS12 V12	Bernard Boyer
MS120B*	1971	Matra MS12 V12	Bernard Boyer
MS120C*	1972	Matra MS71 V12	Bernard Boyer
MS120D*	1972	Matra MS71 V12	Bernard Boyer
*Matra-Simca			

McLaren

Grand Prix Debut: 1966 Monaco GP McLaren (retired)
Latest Grand Prix: 2002 Japanese GP Raikkonen (3rd), Coulthard (retired)
Principal: Bruce McLaren, 1966 until his death in June 1970; Teddy Mayer, 1970-80; Ron Dennis and Mayer, September 1980-82; Dennis, 1982 to date
Base: Feltham, 1963-64; Colnbrook, 1965-81; Woking, 1981 to date

WORLD CHAMPIONSHIP RECORD

Starts: 543
Points: 2756.5
Wins: 135 1968 Belgian GP (McLaren), Italian GP (Hulme), Canadian GP (Hulme), 1969 Mexican GP (Hulme), 1972 South African GP (Hulme), 1973 Swedish GP (Hulme), British GP (Revson), Canadian GP (Revson), 1974 Argentinian GP (Hulme), Brazilian GP (Fittipaldi), Belgian GP (Fittipaldi), Canadian GP (Fittipaldi), 1975 Argentinian GP (Fittipaldi), Spanish GP (Mass), British GP (Fittipaldi), 1976 Spanish GP (Hunt), French GP (Hunt), German GP (Hunt), Dutch GP (Hunt), Canadian GP (Hunt), United States GP (Hunt), 1977 British GP (Hunt), United States GP (Hunt), Japanese GP (Hunt), 1981 British GP (Watson), 1982 Long Beach GP (Lauda), Belgian GP (Watson), Detroit GP (Watson), British GP (Lauda), 1983 Long Beach GP (Watson), 1984 Brazilian GP (Prost), South African GP (Lauda), San Marino GP (Lauda), French GP (Lauda), Monaco GP (Prost), British GP (Lauda), German GP (Prost), Austrian GP (Lauda), Dutch GP (Prost), Italian GP (Lauda), European GP (Prost), Portuguese GP (Prost), 1985 Brazilian GP (Prost), Monaco GP (Prost), British GP (Prost), Austrian GP (Prost), Dutch GP (Lauda), Italian GP (Prost), 1986 San Marino GP (Prost), Monaco GP (Prost), Austrian GP (Prost), Australian GP (Prost), 1987 Brazilian GP (Prost), Belgian GP (Prost), Portuguese GP (Prost), 1988 Brazilian GP (Prost), San Marino GP (Senna), Monaco GP (Prost), Mexican GP (Prost), Canadian GP (Senna), Detroit GP (Senna), French GP (Prost), British GP (Senna), German GP (Senna), Hungarian GP (Senna), Belgian GP (Senna), Portuguese GP (Prost), Spanish GP (Prost), Japanese GP (Senna), Australian GP (Prost), 1989 San Marino GP (Senna), Monaco GP (Senna), Mexican GP (Senna), United States GP (Prost),

French GP (Prost), British GP (Prost), German GP (Senna), Belgian GP (Senna), Italian GP (Prost), Spanish GP (Senna), 1990 United States GP (Senna), Monaco GP (Senna), Canadian GP (Senna), German GP (Senna), Belgian GP (Senna), Italian GP (Senna), 1991 United States GP (Senna), Brazilian GP (Senna), San Marino GP (Senna), Monaco GP (Senna), Hungarian GP (Senna), Belgian GP (Senna), Japanese GP (Berger), Australian GP (Senna), 1992 Monaco GP (Senna), Canadian GP (Berger), Hungarian GP (Senna), Italian GP (Senna), Australian GP (Berger), 1993 Brazilian GP (Senna), European GP (Senna), Monaco GP (Senna), Japanese GP (Senna), Australian GP (Senna), 1997 Australian GP (Coulthard), Italian GP (Coulthard), European GP (Hakkinen), 1998 Australian GP (Hakkinen), Brazilian GP (Hakkinen), San Marino GP (Coulthard), Spanish GP (Hakkinen), Monaco GP (Hakkinen), Austrian GP (Hakkinen), German GP (Hakkinen), Luxembourg GP (Hakkinen), Japanese GP (Hakkinen), 1999 Brazilian GP (Hakkinen), Spanish GP (Hakkinen), Canadian GP (Hakkinen), British GP (Coulthard), Hungarian GP (Hakkinen), Belgian GP (Coulthard), Japanese GP (Hakkinen), 2000 British GP (Coulthard), Spanish GP (Hakkinen), Monaco GP (Coulthard), French GP (Coulthard), Austrian GP (Hakkinen), Hungarian GP (Hakkinen), Belgian GP (Hakkinen), 2001 Brazilian GP (Coulthard), Austrian GP (Coulthard), British GP (Hakkinen), United States GP (Hakkinen), 2002 Monaco GP (Coulthard)

Pole positions: 112 1972 Canadian GP (Revson), 1973 South African GP (Hulme), 1974 Brazilian GP (Fittipaldi), Canadian GP (Fittipaldi), 1976 Brazilian GP (Hunt), South African GP (Hunt), Spanish GP (Hunt), French GP (Hunt), German GP (Hunt), Austrian GP (Hunt), Canadian GP (Hunt), United States GP (Hunt), 1977 Argentinian GP (Hunt), Brazilian GP (Hunt), South African GP (Hunt), British GP (Hunt), Italian GP (Hunt), United States GP (Hunt), 1984 Monaco GP (Prost), German GP (Prost), Dutch GP (Prost), 1985 Austrian GP (Prost), Belgian GP (Prost), 1986 Monaco GP (Prost), German GP (Rosberg), 1988 Brazilian GP (Senna), San Marino GP (Senna), Monaco GP (Senna), Mexican GP (Senna), Canadian GP (Senna), Detroit GP (Senna), French GP (Prost), German GP (Senna), Hungarian GP (Senna), Belgian GP (Senna), Italian GP (Senna), Portuguese GP (Prost), Spanish GP (Senna), Japanese GP (Senna), Australian GP (Senna), 1989 Brazilian GP (Senna), San Marino GP (Senna), Monaco GP (Senna), Mexican GP (Senna), United States GP (Senna), Canadian GP (Prost), French GP (Prost), British GP (Senna), German GP (Senna), Belgian GP (Senna), Italian GP (Senna), Portuguese GP (Senna), Spanish GP (Senna), Japanese GP (Senna), Australian GP (Senna), 1990 United States GP (Berger), Brazilian GP (Senna), San Marino GP (Senna), Monaco GP (Senna), Canadian GP (Senna), Mexican GP (Berger), German GP (Senna), Belgian GP (Senna), Italian GP (Senna), Spanish GP (Senna), Japanese GP (Senna), Australian GP (Senna), 1991 United States GP (Senna), Brazilian GP (Senna), San Marino GP (Senna), Monaco GP (Senna), Hungarian GP (Senna), Belgian GP (Senna), Italian GP (Senna), Spanish GP (Berger), Japanese GP (Berger), Australian GP (Senna), 1992 Canadian GP (Senna), 1993 Australian GP (Senna), 1997 Luxembourg GP (Hakkinen), 1998 Australian GP (Hakkinen), Brazilian GP (Hakkinen), Argentinian GP (Coulthard), San Marino GP (Coulthard), Spanish GP (Hakkinen), Monaco GP (Hakkinen), Canadian GP (Coulthard), French GP (Hakkinen), British GP (Hakkinen), German GP (Hakkinen), Hungarian GP (Hakkinen), Belgian GP (Hakkinen), 1999 Australian GP (Hakkinen), Brazilian GP (Hakkinen), San Marino GP (Hakkinen), 1999 Monaco GP (Hakkinen), Spanish GP (Hakkinen), British GP (Hakkinen), Austrian GP (Hakkinen), German GP (Hakkinen), Hungarian GP (Hakkinen), Belgian GP (Hakkinen), Italian GP (Hakkinen), 2000 Australian GP (Hakkinen), Brazilian GP (Hakkinen), San Marino GP (Hakkinen), European GP (Coulthard), Austrian GP (Hakkinen), German GP (Coulthard), Belgian GP (Hakkinen), 2001 San Marino GP (Coulthard), Monaco GP (Coulthard)

Fastest laps: 109 1970 South African GP (Surtees), 1971 Canadian GP (Hulme), 1972 Austrian GP (Hulme), 1973 Brazilian GP (Hulme), Swedish GP (Hulme), French GP (Hulme), 1974 Belgian GP (Hulme), 1975 French GP (Mass), United States GP (Fittipaldi), 1976 Spanish GP (Mass), Austrian GP (Hunt), United States GP (Hunt), 1977 Argentinian GP (Hunt), Brazilian GP (Hunt), British GP (Hunt), 1981 Canadian GP (Watson), 1982 Long Beach GP (Lauda), Belgian GP (Watson), 1983 Long Beach GP (Lauda), Detroit GP (Watson), 1984 Brazilian GP (Prost), French GP (Prost), Dallas GP (Lauda), British GP (Lauda), German GP (Prost), Austrian GP (Lauda), Italian GP (Lauda), Portuguese GP (Lauda), 1985 Brazilian GP (Prost), British GP (Prost), German GP (Lauda), Austrian GP (Prost), Dutch GP (Prost), Belgian GP (Prost), 1986 Monaco GP (Prost), Belgian GP (Prost), 1987 Belgian GP (Prost), Japanese GP (Prost), 1988 San Marino GP (Prost), Monaco GP (Senna), Mexican GP (Prost), Canadian GP (Senna), Detroit GP (Prost), French GP (Prost), Hungarian GP (Prost), Spanish GP (Prost), Japanese GP (Senna), Australian GP (Prost), 1989 San Marino GP (Prost), Monaco GP (Prost), United States GP (Senna), German GP (Senna), Belgian GP (Prost), Italian GP (Prost), Spanish GP (Senna), Japanese GP (Prost), 1990 United States GP (Berger), Brazilian GP (Berger), Monaco GP (Senna), Canadian GP (Berger), Italian GP (Senna), 1991 San Marino GP (Berger), Italian GP (Senna), Japanese GP (Senna), Australian GP (Berger), 1992 Mexican GP (Berger), Canadian GP (Berger), Portuguese GP (Senna), 1993 European GP (Senna), 1997 Canadian GP (Coulthard), Italian GP (Hakkinen), 1998 Australian GP (Hakkinen), Brazilian GP (Hakkinen), Spanish GP (Hakkinen), Monaco GP (Hakkinen), French GP (Coulthard), Austrian GP (Coulthard), German GP (Coulthard), Italian GP (Hakkinen), Luxembourg GP (Hakkinen), 1999 Brazilian GP (Hakkinen), Monaco GP (Hakkinen), French GP (Coulthard), British GP (Hakkinen), Austrian GP (Hakkinen), German GP (Coulthard), Hungarian GP (Coulthard), Belgian GP (Hakkinen), European GP (Hakkinen), 2000 San Marino GP (Hakkinen), British GP (Hakkinen), Spanish GP (Hakkinen), Monaco GP (Hakkinen), Canadian GP (Hakkinen), French GP (Coulthard), Austrian GP (Coulthard), Hungarian GP (Hakkinen), Italian GP (Hakkinen), United States GP (Coulthard), Japanese GP (Hakkinen), Malaysian GP (Hakkinen), 2001 Malaysian GP (Hakkinen), Austrian GP (Coulthard), Monaco GP (Coulthard), French GP (Coulthard), British GP (Hakkinen), Hungarian GP (Hakkinen), 2002 Australian GP (Raikkonen), French GP (Coulthard)

Laps/miles in the lead: 7768 laps/22619 miles

World Champions:
Drivers: Eleven times - 1974 (Fittipaldi), 1976 (Hunt), 1984 (Lauda), 1985 (Prost), 1986 (Prost), 1988 (Senna),

Formula 1

1989 (Prost), 1990 (Senna), 1991 (Senna), 1998 (Hakkinen) and 1999 (Hakkinen)

Constructors: Eight times - 1974, 1984, 1985, 1988, 1989, 1990, 1991 and 1998

MAJOR SPONSORS

1972-73	Yardley
1974	Texaco, Marlboro, Yardley
1975	Marlboro, Texaco
1976-77	Marlboro
1978-79	Marlboro, Lowenbrau (North American races only)
1979-96	Marlboro
1997 to date	West

McLAREN GRAND PRIX DRIVERS

Driver	Nat	Starts (DNS/DNQ)	1st	2nd	3rd	4th	5th	6th	PP	FL	Points
Ayrton Senna	BR	96	35	12	8	5	3	1	46	12	451
Alain Prost	F	107 (2)	30	21	12	3	2	6	10	24	458.5
Mika Hakkinen	SF	131 (2)	20	14	17	11	8	6	26	25	407
David Coulthard	GB	116	11	20	17	5	9	6	7	14	337
James Hunt	GB	49	9	2	3	3	1	1	14	5	117
Niki Lauda	A	58 (3)	8	5	2	4	2	2	-	8	128
Denny Hulme	NZ	86	6	5	10	9	7	9	1	6	174
Emerson Fittipaldi	BR	28 (1)	5	6	2	3	1	-	2	1	100
John Watson	GB	73 (2)	4	4	5	5	3	8	-	3	109
Gerhard Berger	A	48	3	7	8	9	3	-	4	7	135
Peter Revson	USA	23	2	2	4	3	3	-	1	-	61
Jochen Mass	D	49	1	1	6	6	4	5	-	2	64
Bruce McLaren	NZ	33 (4)	1	4	2	3	4	2	-	-	60
Stefan Johansson	S	16	-	2	3	1	1	1	-	-	30
Kimi Raikkonen	SF	17	-	1	3	2	-	-	-	1	24
Keke Rosberg	SF	16	-	1	-	4	2	-	1	-	22
Martin Brundle	GB	16	-	1	1	1	1	1	-	-	16
Mark Blundell	GB	15	-	-	-	2	3	1	-	-	13
Mike Hailwood	GB	11	-	-	1	2	1	-	-	-	12
Patrick Tambay	F	28 (2)	-	-	-	1	1	3	-	-	8
Michael Andretti	USA	13	-	-	1	-	1	1	-	-	7
Dan Gurney	USA	6	-	-	-	1	-	1	-	-	4
Brian Redman	GB	3	-	-	-	-	2	-	-	-	4
Mark Donohue	USA	1 (1)	-	-	1	-	-	-	-	-	4
Jacky Ickx	B	1	-	-	1	-	-	-	-	-	4
Vic Elford	GB	4	-	-	-	-	1	1	-	-	3
Andrea de Cesaris	I	14 (1)	-	-	-	-	1	-	-	-	1
Peter Gethin	GB	14	-	-	-	-	1	-	-	-	1
Jo Bonnier	S	10 (4)	-	-	-	-	1	-	-	-	1
John Surtees	GB	4	-	-	-	-	1	1	-	1	1
Brett Lunger	GB	17 (5)	-	-	-	-	-	-	-	-	-
Bruno Giacomelli	I	6	-	-	-	-	-	-	-	-	-
Jody Scheckter	ZA	6	-	-	-	-	-	-	-	-	-
Andrea de Adamich	I	4 (6)	-	-	-	-	-	-	-	-	-
David Hobbs	GB	3	-	-	-	-	-	-	-	-	-
Jackie Oliver	GB	3	-	-	-	-	-	-	-	-	-
Nelson Piquet	BR	3	-	-	-	-	-	-	-	-	-
Emilio de Villota	E	2 (6)	-	-	-	-	-	-	-	-	-
Dave Charlton	ZA	2	-	-	-	-	-	-	-	-	-
Nigel Mansell	GB	2	-	-	-	-	-	-	-	-	-
Basil van Rooyen	ZA	1	-	-	-	-	-	-	-	-	-
Derek Bell	GB	1	-	-	-	-	-	-	-	-	-
Gilles Villeneuve	CDN	1	-	-	-	-	-	-	-	-	-
Jan Magnussen	DK	1	-	-	-	-	-	-	-	-	-
Philippe Alliot	F	1	-	-	-	-	-	-	-	-	-
Helmut Marko	A	- (1)	-	-	-	-	-	-	-	-	-
Nanni Galli	I	- (1)	-	-	-	-	-	-	-	-	-
Stephen South	GB	- (1)	-	-	-	-	-	-	-	-	-
Tony Trimmer	GB	- (1)	-	-	-	-	-	-	-	-	-

McLAREN GRAND PRIX CARS

Type	Year	Engine	Designer
M2B	1966	Ford 406 V8, Serenissima V8	Robin Herd
M3A	1966	Ford 406 V8	Robin Herd
M4B	1967	BRM V8	Robin Herd
M5A	1967	BRM V12	Robin Herd
M7A	1968	Ford DFV V8	Robin Herd/Gordon Coppuck
M7A/M7B	1969	Ford DFV V8	Robin Herd/Gordon Coppuck
M7C	1969	Ford DFV V8	Robin Herd/Gordon Coppuck
M7D	1970	Alfa Romeo T33 V8	Robin Herd/Gordon Coppuck
M9A	1969	Ford DFV V8	Jo Marquart
M14A	1970	Ford DFV V8	Jo Marquart
M14D	1970	Ford DFV V8, Alfa Romeo T33 V8	Jo Marquart
M19A	1971	Ford DFV V8	Ralph Bellamy
M19C	1972	Ford DFV V8	Ralph Bellamy
M23	1973	Ford DFV V8	Gordon Coppuck
M25	1978	Ford DFV V8	Gordon Coppuck
M26	1976	Ford DFV V8	Gordon Coppuck
M28	1979	Ford DFV V8	Gordon Coppuck
M28B	1979	Ford DFV V8	Gordon Coppuck
M28C	1979	Ford DFV V8	Gordon Coppuck
M29	1979	Ford DFV V8	Gordon Coppuck
M29B	1980	Ford DFV V8	Gordon Coppuck
M29C	1980	Ford DFV V8	Gordon Coppuck
M29F	1981	Ford DFV V8	Gordon Coppuck/John Baldwin
M30	1980	Ford DFV V8	Gordon Coppuck
MP4/1	1981	Ford DFV V8	John Barnard
MP4/1B	1982	Ford DFV V8	John Barnard
MP4/1C	1983	Ford DFV V8	John Barnard
MP4/1E	1983	TAG Porsche P01 V6 tc	John Barnard
MP4/2	1984	TAG Porsche P01 V6 tc	John Barnard
MP4/2B	1985	TAG Porsche P01 V6 tc	John Barnard
MP4/2C	1986	TAG Porsche P01 V6 tc	John Barnard
MP4/3	1987	TAG Porsche P01 V6 tc	Steve Nichols
MP4/4	1988	Honda RA168E V6 tc	Steve Nichols/Gordon Murray
MP4/5	1989	Honda RA101E V10	Neil Oatley
MP4/5B	1990	Honda RA101E V10	Neil Oatley
MP4/6	1991	Honda RA121E V12	Neil Oatley
MP4/6B	1992	Honda RA121E V12	Neil Oatley
MP4/7A	1992	Honda RA122E V12	Neil Oatley
MP4/8	1993	Ford HB V8	Neil Oatley
MP4/9	1994	Peugeot A4/A6 V10	Neil Oatley
MP4/10	1995	Mercedes-Benz FO110 V10	Neil Oatley
MP4/10B	1995	Mercedes-Benz FO110 V10	Neil Oatley
MP4/10C	1995	Mercedes-Benz FO110 V10	Neil Oatley
MP4/11	1996	Mercedes-Benz FO110 V10	Neil Oatley
MP4/12	1997	Mercedes-Benz FO110E/F V10	Neil Oatley
MP4/13	1998	Mercedes-Benz FO110G V10	Adrian Newey
MP4/14	1999	Mercedes-Benz FO110H V10	Adrian Newey
MP4/15	2000	Mercedes-Benz FO110J V10	Adrian Newey
MP4/16	2001	Mercedes-Benz FO110K V10	Adrian Newey
MP4/17	2002	Mercedes-Benz FO110M V10	Adrian Newey

Mercedes-Benz

Grand Prix Debut:	1954 French GP
Last Grand Prix:	1955 Italian GP
Principal:	Alfred Neubauer
Base:	Unterturkheim, Stuttgart

Fangio (1st), Kling (2nd), Herrmann (retired)

Fangio (1st), Taruffi (2nd), Kling (retired), Moss (retired)

WORLD CHAMPIONSHIP RECORD

Starts:	12	
Points:	139.14	
Wins:	9	1954 French GP (Fangio), German GP (Fangio), Swiss GP (Fangio), Italian GP (Fangio), 1955 Argentinian GP (Fangio), Belgian GP (Fangio), Dutch GP (Fangio), British GP (Moss), Italian GP (Fangio)
Pole positions:	8	1954 French GP (Fangio), British GP (Fangio), German GP (Fangio), Italian GP (Fangio), 1955 Monaco GP (Fangio), Dutch GP (Fangio), British GP (Moss), Italian GP (Fangio)
Fastest laps:	9	1954 French GP (Herrmann), British GP (Fangio), German GP (Kling), Swiss GP (Fangio), 1955 Argentinian GP (Fangio), Monaco GP (Fangio), Belgian GP (Fangio), British GP (Moss), Italian GP (Moss)
Laps/miles in the lead:	589 laps/2472 miles	
World Champions:	Twice - 1954 (Fangio - 17 points of his 57.14 were scored for Maserati) and 1955 (Fangio)	

MERCEDES-BENZ GRAND PRIX DRIVERS

Driver	Nat	Starts (DNS/DNQ)	1st	2nd	3rd	4th	5th	6th	PP	FL	Points
Juan Manuel Fangio	RA	12	8	1	1	1	-	-	7	5	81.14
Stirling Moss	GB	6	1	2	-	1	-	-	1	2	23
Karl Kling	D	11	-	1	1	2	1	-	-	1	17
Hans Herrmann	D	6	-	-	1	2	-	-	-	1	9
Piero Taruffi	I	2	-	1	-	1	-	-	-	-	9
Hermann Lang	D	1	-	-	-	-	-	-	-	-	-
Andre Simon	F	1	-	-	-	-	-	-	-	-	-

MERCEDES-BENZ GRAND PRIX CARS

Type	Year	Engine	Designer
W196	1954	Mercedes-Benz M196 S8	Hans Scherenberg/ Ludwig Kraus/ Hans Gassmann

Merzario

Grand Prix Debut:	1978 Argentinian GP
Last Grand Prix:	1979 Long Beach GP
Principal:	Arturo Merzario
Base:	Como

Merzario (retired)

Merzario (retired)

WORLD CHAMPIONSHIP RECORD

Starts:	10	
Best result:	No finishes	
Best qualifying:	20th	1978 Argentinian GP (Merzario)

MAJOR SPONSORS

1978–79	Flor Bath

MERZARIO GRAND PRIX DRIVERS

Driver	Nat	Starts (DNS/DNQ)	1st	2nd	3rd	4th	5th	6th	PP	FL	Points
Arturo Merzario	I	10 (20)	-	-	-	-	-	-	-	-	-
Gianfranco Brancatelli	I	- (1)	-	-	-	-	-	-	-	-	-
Alberto Colombo	I	- (1)	-	-	-	-	-	-	-	-	-

MERZARIO GRAND PRIX CARS

Type	Year	Engine	Designer
A1	1978	Ford DFV V8	Arturo Merzario/ Gianfranco Palazzoli
A1B	1979	Ford DFV V8	Arturo Merzario
A2	1979	Ford DFV V8	Arturo Merzario/ Simon Hadfield
A4	1979	Ford DFV V8	Arturo Merzario/ Simon Hadfield/ Gianpaolo Dallara

Minardi

Grand Prix Debut:	1985 Brazilian GP
Latest Grand Prix:	2002 Japanese GP
Principals:	Giancarlo Minardi, 1985-93; Minardi and Beppe Lucchini (of Scuderia Italia), 1994-96; Minardi, 1997-2000; Paul Stoddart, 2001 to date
Base:	Faenza

Martini (retired)

Webber (10th), Yoong (retired)

WORLD CHAMPIONSHIP RECORD

Starts:	287	
Points:	30	
Best result:	4th	1991 San Marino GP (Martini), Portuguese GP (Martini), 1993 South African GP (Fittipaldi)
Best qualifying:	2nd	1990 United States GP (Martini)
Laps/miles in the lead:	1 lap/3 miles	

Best World Championship position:

Drivers:	11th in 1991 (Martini)
Constructors:	7th in 1991

MAJOR SPONSORS

1985-86	Simod
1987	Simod, Lois, Reporter
1988	Lois, Cimarron
1989	SCM, Lois
1990-92	SCM
1993	Beta
1994	Lucchini, Beta
1995-96	Doimo, Valleverde, Mercatone Uno
1997	Mild Seven, Fondmetal, Doimo, Roces
1998	Fondmetal, Doimo, Roces
1999	Fondmetal, Telefonica
2000	Telefonica
2001	European Aviation, Magnum
2002 to date	GoKL, Magnum, European Aviation

MINARDI GRAND PRIX DRIVERS

Driver	Nat	Starts (DNS/DNQ)	1st	2nd	3rd	4th	5th	6th	PP	FL	Points
Pierluigi Martini	I	102 (5)	-	-	2	4	2	-	-	16	
Christian Fittipaldi	BR	24 (3)	-	-	1	1	1	-	-	6	
Mark Webber	AUS	16 (1)	-	-	-	-	1	-	-	2	
Fabrizio Barbazza	I	8	-	-	-	-	2	-	-	2	
Marc Gene	E	33	-	-	-	-	1	-	-	1	
Luis Perez Sala	E	26 (6)	-	-	-	-	1	-	-	1	
Pedro Lamy	P	24	-	-	-	-	1	-	-	1	
Michele Alboreto	I	16	-	-	-	-	1	-	-	1	
Gianni Morbidelli	I	32 (1)	-	-	-	-	-	-	-	-	
Luca Badoer	I	31 (1)	-	-	-	-	-	-	-	-	
Alessandro Nannini	I	30 (2)	-	-	-	-	-	-	-	-	
Tarso Marques	BR	24 (2)	-	-	-	-	-	-	-	-	
Adrian Campos	E	17 (4)	-	-	-	-	-	-	-	-	
Fernando Alonso	E	17	-	-	-	-	-	-	-	-	
Gaston Mazzacane	RA	17	-	-	-	-	-	-	-	-	
Ukyo Katayama	J	17	-	-	-	-	-	-	-	-	
Esteban Tuero	RA	16	-	-	-	-	-	-	-	-	

Driver	Nat	Start	1st	2nd	3rd	4th	5th	6th	PP	FL	Points
Shinji Nakano	J	16	-	-	-	-	-	-	-	-	-
Andrea de Cesaris	I	15 (1)	-	-	-	-	-	-	-	-	-
Alex Yoong	MAL	14 (4)	-	-	-	-	-	-	-	-	-
Paolo Barilla	I	9 (6)	-	-	-	-	-	-	-	-	-
Giancarlo Fisichella	I	8	-	-	-	-	-	-	-	-	-
Jarno Trulli	I	6 (1)	-	-	-	-	-	-	-	-	-
Giovanni Lavaggi	I	3 (3)	-	-	-	-	-	-	-	-	-
Anthony Davidson	GB	2	-	-	-	-	-	-	-	-	-
Jean-Marc Gounon	F	2	-	-	-	-	-	-	-	-	-
Alessandro Zanardi	I	1 (2)	-	-	-	-	-	-	-	-	-
Roberto Moreno	BR	1	-	-	-	-	-	-	-	-	-
Stephane Sarrazin	F	1	-	-	-	-	-	-	-	-	-

MINARDI GRAND PRIX CARS

Type	Year	Engine	Designer
M185	1985	Ford DFV V8,	
		Motori Moderni V6 tc	Giacomo Caliri
M185B	1986	Motori Moderni V6 tc	Giacomo Caliri
M186	1986	Motori Moderni V6 tc	Giacomo Caliri
M187	1987	Motori Moderni V6 tc	Giacomo Caliri
M188	1988	Ford DFZ V8	Giacomo Caliri/Aldo Costa
M188B	1989	Ford DFR V8	Giacomo Caliri/Aldo Costa
M189	1989	Ford DFR V8	Aldo Costa/
			Nigel Couperthwaite
M190	1990	Ford DFR V8	Aldo Costa/Vincenzo Emiliani
M191	1991	Ferrari Tipo 036 V12	Aldo Costa
M191B	1992	Lamborghini 3512 V12	Aldo Costa
M192	1992	Lamborghini 3512 V12	Aldo Costa
M193	1993	Ford HB V8	Aldo Costa/Gustav Brunner
M193B	1994	Ford HB V8	Aldo Costa/Gustav Brunner
M195	1995	Ford ED V8	Aldo Costa
M195B	1996	Ford ED V8	Aldo Costa/Gabriele Tredozi
M197	1997	Hart 830 V8	Gabriele Tredozi
M198	1998	Ford Zetec-R V10	Gustav Brunner
M01	1999	Ford Zetec-R V10	Gustav Brunner
M02	2000	Ford Zetec-R V10	Gustav Brunner
PS01	2001	Ford Zetec-R V10	Gustav Brunner
PS02	2002	Asiatech AT02 V10	Gustav Brunner

Monteverdi

see Onyx

Onyx

Includes Monteverdi

Grand Prix Debut:	1989 Mexican GP	Johansson (retired)
Last Grand Prix:	1990 German GP	Lehto (not classified), Foitek (retired). Cars were officially renamed Monteverdi for this final race
Principals:	Mike Earle and Joe Chamberlain, 1989; Jean-Pierre van Rossem/Moneytron, 1989-90; Peter Monteverdi, 1990	
Base:	Littlehampton	

WORLD CHAMPIONSHIP RECORD

Starts:	17	
Points:	6	
Best result:	3rd	1989 Portuguese GP (Johansson)
Best qualifying:	11th	1989 French GP (Gachot)

Best World Championship position:

Drivers:	11th in 1989 (Johansson)
Constructors:	10th in 1989

MAJOR SPONSORS

1989	Moneytron
1990	Moneytron, Monteverdi

ONYX GRAND PRIX DRIVERS

Driver	Nat	Starts (DNS/DNQ)	1st	2nd	3rd	4th	5th	6th	PP	FL	Points
Stefan Johansson	S	8 (10)	-	-	1	-	1	-	-	-	6
JJ Lehto	SF	7 (7)	-	-	-	-	-	-	-	-	-
Bertrand Gachot	B	5 (7)	-	-	-	-	-	-	-	-	-
Gregor Foitek	CH	5 (3)	-	-	-	-	-	-	-	-	-

ONYX GRAND PRIX CARS

Type	Year	Engine	Designer
ORE1	1989	Ford DFR V8	Alan Jenkins/Bernie Marcus
ORE2	1990	Ford DFR V8	Alan Jenkins/Bernie Marcus

Officially renamed Monteverdi ORE2 for its final Grand Prix

OSCA

Officine Specializate Costruzione Automobili (Fratelli Maserati)

Grand Prix Debut:	1951 Italian GP	Rol (9th)
Last Grand Prix:	1953 Italian GP	Chiron (10th), Bayol (retired)
Principal:	Ernesto Maserati	
Base:	San Lazzaro di Savena, near Bologna	

WORLD CHAMPIONSHIP RECORD

Starts:	4	
Best result:	9th	1951 Italian GP (Rol)
Best qualifying:	10th	1952 Italian GP (Bayol)

OSCA GRAND PRIX DRIVERS

Driver	Nat	Starts (DNS/DNQ)	1st	2nd	3rd	4th	5th	6th	PP	FL	Points
Elie Bayol	F	3 (1)	-	-	-	-	-	-	-	-	-
Louis Chiron	MC	2 (2)	-	-	-	-	-	-	-	-	-
Franco Rol	I	1	-	-	-	-	-	-	-	-	-
Giulio Cabianca	I	- (1)	-	-	-	-	-	-	-	-	-
Luigi Piotti	I	- (1)	-	-	-	-	-	-	-	-	-

OSCA GRAND PRIX CARS

Type	Year	Engine	Designer
4500G	1951	OSCA V12	Ernesto Maserati/Bindo Maserati/ Ettore Maserati
20	1952	OSCA S6	Ernesto Maserati/Bindo Maserati/ Ettore Maserati

Osella

Team sold to Fondmetal in 1991; also see Fondmetal

Grand Prix Debut:	1980 South African GP	Cheever (retired)
Last Grand Prix:	1990 Australian GP	Grouillard (13th)
Principal:	Enzo Osella	
Base:	Volpiano, near Turin	

WORLD CHAMPIONSHIP RECORD

Starts:	132	
Points:	5	
Best result:	4th	1982 San Marino GP (Jarier)
Best qualifying:	8th	1990 United States GP (Grouillard)

Best World Championship position:

Drivers:	19th in 1984 (Ghinzani)
Constructors:	12th in 1984

MAJOR SPONSORS

1980-81	Denim
1982	Denim, Saima
1983-85	Kelemata
1986	Landis & Gyr
1987	Landis & Gyr, Stievani
1988	Stievani
1989-90	Fondmetal

OSELLA GRAND PRIX DRIVERS

Driver	Nat	Starts	1st	2nd	3rd	4th	5th	6th	PP	FL	Points
		(DNS/DNQ)									
Jean-Pierre Jarier	F	20 (3)	-	-	-	1	-	-	-	-	3
Piercarlo Ghinzani	I	47 (26)	-	-	-	-	1	-	-	-	2
Nicola Larini	I	18 (14)	-	-	-	-	-	-	-	-	-
Alex Caffi	I	15 (2)	-	-	-	-	-	-	-	-	-
Eddie Cheever	USA	10 (4)	-	-	-	-	-	-	-	-	-
Olivier Grouillard	F	9 (7)	-	-	-	-	-	-	-	-	-
Corrado Fabi	I	9 (6)	-	-	-	-	-	-	-	-	-
Allen Berg	CDN	9	-	-	-	-	-	-	-	-	-
Jo Gartner	A	8	-	-	-	-	1*	-	-	-	-
Huub Rothengatter	NL	7 (1)	-	-	-	-	-	-	-	-	-
Christian Danner	D	5 (1)	-	-	-	-	-	-	-	-	-
Beppe Gabbiani	I	3 (12)	-	-	-	-	-	-	-	-	-
Ricardo Paletti	I	2 (6)	-	-	-	-	-	-	-	-	-
Franco Forini	CH	2 (1)	-	-	-	-	-	-	-	-	-
Miguel Angel Guerra	RA	1 (3)	-	-	-	-	-	-	-	-	-
Gabriele Tarquini	I	1	-	-	-	-	-	-	-	-	-
Giorgio Francia	I	- (1)	-	-	-	-	-	-	-	-	-

*not entered in World Championship so ineligible for points

OSELLA GRAND PRIX CARS

Type	Year	Engine	Designer
FA1	1980	Ford DFV V8	Enzo Osella/Giorgio Stirano
FA1B	1980	Ford DFV V8	Enzo Osella/Giorgio Stirano/ Giorgio Valentini
FA1C	1981	Ford DFV V8	Enzo Osella/Giorgio Valentini/ Herve Guilpin
FA1D	1983	Ford DFV V8	Enzo Osella/ Giuseppe Petrotta/ Herve Guilpin
FA1E	1983	Alfa Romeo 1260 V12	Tony Southgate
FA1F	1984	Alfa Romeo 890T V8 tc	Giuseppe Petrotta
FA1G	1985	Alfa Romeo 890T V8 tc	Giuseppe Petrotta
FA1H	1986	Alfa Romeo 890T V8 tc	Giuseppe Petrotta
FA1I	1987	Alfa Romeo 890T V8 tc	Giuseppe Petrotta
FA1L	1988	Alfa Romeo 890T V8 tc*	Antonio Tomaini
FA1M	1989	Ford DFR V8	Antonio Tomaini
FA1Me	1990	Ford DFR V8	Antonio Tomaini

Renamed Fomet FA1Me when company sold to Fondmetal
*engine officially renamed Osella

Pacific

Grand Prix Debut:	1994 Brazilian GP	Gachot (retired)
Last Grand Prix:	1995 Australian GP	Gachot (8th), Montermini (retired)
Principal:	Keith Wiggins	
Base:	Thetford, Norfolk	

WORLD CHAMPIONSHIP RECORD

Starts:	22	
Best result:	8th 1995 German GP	(Montermini), Australian GP (Gachot)
Best qualifying:	20th 1995 Brazilian GP	(Gachot), Canadian GP (Gachot), European GP (Montermini), Japanese GP (Montermini)

MAJOR SPONSORS

1994-95	Ursus

PACIFIC GRAND PRIX DRIVERS

Driver	Nat	Starts	1st	2nd	3rd	4th	5th	6th	PP	FL	Points
		(DNS/DNQ)									
Bertrand Gachot	B	16 (11)	-	-	-	-	-	-	-	-	-
Andrea Montermini	I	16 (1)	-	-	-	-	-	-	-	-	-
Giovanni Lavaggi	I	4	-	-	-	-	-	-	-	-	-
Paul Belmondo	F	2 (14)	-	-	-	-	-	-	-	-	-
Jean-Denis Deletraz	CH	2	-	-	-	-	-	-	-	-	-

PACIFIC GRAND PRIX CARS

Type	Year	Engine	Designer
PR01	1994	Ilmor 2175A V10	Rory Byrne/Paul Brown
Originally designed and built by Reynard Racing Cars			
PR02	1995	Ford ED V8	Frank Coppuck

Parnelli

Grand Prix Debut:	1974 Canadian GP	Andretti (7th)
Last Grand Prix:	1976 Long Beach GP Andretti (retired)	
Principals:	Velco Miletich and Rufus Parnelli Jones	
Base:	Torrance, California	

WORLD CHAMPIONSHIP RECORD

Starts:	16	
Points:	6	
Best result:	4th	1975 Swedish GP (Andretti)
Best qualifying:	3rd	1974 United States GP (Andretti)
Fastest laps:	1	1975 Spanish GP (Andretti)
Laps/miles in the lead:	10 laps/24 miles	

Best World Championship position:

Drivers:	14th in 1975 (Andretti). Andretti finished 6th in 1976 scoring 1 point for Parnelli and 21 for Lotus
Constructors:	10th in 1975

MAJOR SPONSORS

1974	Viceroy
1976	American Wheels

PARNELLI GRAND PRIX DRIVERS

Driver	Nat	Starts	1st	2nd	3rd	4th	5th	6th	PP	FL	Points
		(DNS/DNQ)									
Mario Andretti	USA	16	-	-	-	1	1	1	-	1	6

PARNELLI GRAND PRIX CARS

Type	Year	Engine	Designer
VPJ4	1974	Ford DFV V8	Maurice Philippe
VPJ4B	1976	Ford DFV V8	Maurice Philippe

Penske

Grand Prix Debut:	1974 Canadian GP	Donohue (12th)
Last Grand Prix:	1977 Canadian GP	Ongais (7th)

Principal: Roger Penske
Base: Reading, Pennsylvania (USA) and Poole (GB)

WORLD CHAMPIONSHIP RECORD

Starts: 40
Points: 23
Wins: 1 1976 Austrian GP (Watson)
Best qualifying: 2nd 1976 Austrian GP (Watson)
Laps/miles in the lead: 45 laps/165 miles

Best World Championship position:
Drivers: 7th in 1976 (Watson)
Constructors: 5th in 1976

MAJOR SPONSORS

1974-76 First National City

PENSKE GRAND PRIX DRIVERS

Driver	Nat	Starts (DNS/DNQ)	1st	2nd	3rd	4th	5th	6th	PP	FL	Points
John Watson	GB	17	1	-	2	-	1	1	-	-	20
Mark Donohue	USA	11	-	-	-	1	-	-	-	-	2
Jean-Pierre Jarier	F	10 (1)	-	-	-	-	1	-	-	1
Hans Binder	A	2 (1)	-	-	-	-	-	-	-	-	-
Danny Ongais	USA	2	-	-	-	-	-	-	-	-	-
Boy Hayje	NL	1	-	-	-	-	-	-	-	-	-
Hans Heyer	D	1	-	-	-	-	-	-	-	-	-

PENSKE GRAND PRIX CARS

Type	Year	Engine	Designer
PC1	1974	Ford DFV V8	Geoff Ferris
PC3	1976	Ford DFV V8	Geoff Ferris
PC4	1976	Ford DFV V8	Geoff Ferris

Porsche

Grand Prix Debut: 1957 German GP Barth, de Beaufort and Maglioli (all raced in F2 class)
Last Grand Prix: 1964 Dutch GP de Beaufort (retired)
Principal: Ferry Porsche
Base: Zuffenhausen, Stuttgart

WORLD CHAMPIONSHIP RECORD

Starts: 33
Points: 50
Wins: 1 1962 French GP (Gurney)
Pole positions: 1 1962 German GP (Gurney)
Laps/miles in the lead: 20 laps/107 miles

Best World Championship position:
Drivers: 3rd in 1961 (Gurney)
Constructors: 3rd in 1961

PORSCHE GRAND PRIX DRIVERS

Driver	Nat	Starts (DNS/DNQ)	1st	2nd	3rd	4th	5th	6th	PP	FL	Points
Dan Gurney	USA	15	1	3	1	-	2	1	1	-	36
Jo Bonnier	S	15	-	-	-	-	2	2	-	-	6
Carel Godin de Beaufort	NL	26 (3)	-	-	-	-	4	-	-	-	4
Gerhard Mitter	D	2	-	-	-	1	-	-	-	-	3
Hans Herrmann	D	4	-	-	-	-	-	1	-	-	1
Edgar Barth	DDR	3	-	-	-	-	-	-	-	-	-
Wolfgang von Trips	D	1 (1)	-	-	-	-	-	-	-	-	-
Harry Blanchard	USA	1	-	-	-	-	-	-	-	-	-
Fred Gamble	USA	1	-	-	-	-	-	-	-	-	-
Masten Gregory	USA	1	-	-	-	-	-	-	-	-	-

Driver	Nat	Start	1st	2nd	3rd	4th	5th	6th	PP	FL	Points
Umberto Maglioli	I	1	-	-	-	-	-	-	-	-	-
Ben Pon	NL	1	-	-	-	-	-	-	-	-	-
Nino Vaccarella	I	1	-	-	-	-	-	-	-	-	-
Heini Walter	CH	1	-	-	-	-	-	-	-	-	-
Jean Behra	F	- (1)	-	-	-	-	-	-	-	-	-
Maria Teresa de Filippis	I	- (1)	-	-	-	-	-	-	-	-	-

PORSCHE GRAND PRIX CARS

Type	Year	Engine	Designer
550RS	1957	Porsche 547 F4	Wilhelm Hild
718 RSK	1958	Porsche 547 F4	Wilhelm Hild
Behra-Porsche	1959	Porsche RSK F4	Valerio Colotti
718	1959	Porsche RSK F4	Wilhelm Hild/Hans Mezger/ Helmuth Bott
787	1961	Porsche RSK F4	Wilhelm Hild
804	1962	Porsche 753 F8	Hans Honich/Hans Mezger
Air cooled			

Prost

Bought Ligier in 1997; also see Ligier

Grand Prix Debut: 1997 Australian GP Panis (5th), Nakano (7th)
Last Grand Prix: 2001 Japanese GP Frentzen (12th), Enge (retired)
Principals: Alain Prost, 1997-2000; Alain Prost and Pedro Diniz, 2001
Base: Magny-Cours, 1996; Guyancourt, Paris, 1997-2001

WORLD CHAMPIONSHIP RECORD

Starts: 83
Points: 35
Best result: 2nd 1997 Spanish GP (Panis), 1999 European GP (Trulli)
Best qualifying: 3rd 1997 Argentinian GP (Panis), Austrian GP (Trulli), 1999 French GP (Panis)
Laps/miles in the lead: 37 laps/99 miles

Best World Championship position:
Drivers: 9th in 1997 (Panis)
Constructors: 6th in 1997

MAJOR SPONSORS

1997- 99 Gauloises
2000 Gauloises, Yahoo
2001 PSN, Acer, Adecco, Parmalat

PROST GRAND PRIX DRIVERS

Driver	Nat	Starts (DNS/DNQ)	1st	2nd	3rd	4th	5th	6th	PP	FL	Points
Olivier Panis	F	42	-	1	1	1	3	-	-	18
Jarno Trulli	I	38 (1)	-	1	-	1	-	2	-	-	11
Jean Alesi	F	29	-	-	-	-	1	2	-	-	4
Shinji Nakano	J	17	-	-	-	-	-	2	-	-	2
Nick Heidfeld	D	16 (1)	-	-	-	-	-	-	-	-	-
Luciano Burti	BR	10	-	-	-	-	-	-	-	-	-
Heinz-Harald Frentzen	D	5	-	-	-	-	-	-	-	-	-
Gaston Mazzacane	RA	4	-	-	-	-	-	-	-	-	-
Tomas Enge	CS	3	-	-	-	-	-	-	-	-	-

PROST GRAND PRIX CARS

Type	Year	Engine	Designer
JS45	1997	Mugen MF301HA/ V10	Loic Bigois
AP01	1998	Peugeot A16 V10	Loic Bigois
AP02	1999	Peugeot A18 V10	Loic Bigois/John Barnard

Type	Year	Engine	Designer
AP03	2000	Peugeot A20 V10	Alan Jenkins/Loic Bigois/John Barnard
AP04	2001	Ferrari Tipo 049 V10*	Henri Durand/John Barnard
*badged Acer			

Protos

Only Grand Prix: 1967 German GP Hart and Ahrens (both raced in F2 class)

Principal: Ron Harris

WORLD CHAMPIONSHIP RECORD

Starts: 1
Best result: No finishes
Best qualifying: No time set

PROTOS GRAND PRIX DRIVERS

Driver	Nat	Starts (DNS/DNQ)	1st	2nd	3rd	4th	5th	6th	PP	FL	Points
Kurt Ahrens jr	D	1	-	-	-	-	-	-	-	-	-
Brian Hart	GB	1	-	-	-	-	-	-	-	-	-

PROTOS GRAND PRIX CARS

Type	Year	Engine	Designer
Protos	1967	Ford FVA S4	Frank Costin/Brian Hart
F2 car, wooden chassis			

RAM

Grand Prix Debut: 1983 Brazilian GP Salazar (15th)
Last Grand Prix: 1985 European GP Alliot (retired)
Principals: John MacDonald and Mick Ralph
Base: Bicester

WORLD CHAMPIONSHIP RECORD

Starts: 31
Best result: 8th 1984 Brazilian GP (Palmer)
Best qualifying: 14th 1985 Canadian GP (Winkelhock)

MAJOR SPONSORS

1984-85 Skoal Bandit

RAM GRAND PRIX DRIVERS

Driver	Nat	Starts (DNS/DNQ)	1st	2nd	3rd	4th	5th	6th	PP	FL	Points
Philippe Alliot	F	26 (4)	-	-	-	-	-	-	-	-	-
Jonathan Palmer	GB	14 (1)	-	-	-	-	-	-	-	-	-
Manfred Winkelhock	D	8 (1)	-	-	-	-	-	-	-	-	-
Kenneth Acheson	GB	3 (7)	-	-	-	-	-	-	-	-	-
Eliseo Salazar	RCH	2 (4)	-	-	-	-	-	-	-	-	-
Mike Thackwell	NZ	1	-	-	-	-	-	-	-	-	-
Jean-Louis Schlesser	F	- (1)	-	-	-	-	-	-	-	-	-
Jacques Villeneuve	CDN	- (1)	-	-	-	-	-	-	-	-	-

RAM GRAND PRIX CARS

Type	Year	Engine	Designer
01*	1983	Ford DFV V8	Dave Kelly
01	1984	Hart 415T S4 tc	Dave Kelly
02	1984	Hart 415T S4 tc	Dave Kelly
03	1985	Hart 415T S4 tc	Gustav Brunner/Sergio Rinland/Tim Feast

*RAM-March

Rebaque

Only Grand Prix: 1979 Canadian GP Rebaque (retired)
Principal: Hector Rebaque
Base: Constructor: Poole. Team: Leamington-Spa

WORLD CHAMPIONSHIP RECORD

Starts: 1
Best result: No finishes
Best qualifying: 22nd 1979 Canadian GP (Rebaque)

REBAQUE GRAND PRIX DRIVERS

Driver	Nat	Starts (DNS/DNQ)	1st	2nd	3rd	4th	5th	6th	PP	FL	Points
Hector Rebaque	MEX	1 (2)	-	-	-	-	-	-	-	-	-

REBAQUE GRAND PRIX CARS

Type	Year	Engine	Designer
HR100	1979	Ford DFV V8	Geoff Ferris
Designed and built by Penske Cars			

Renault

Bought Benetton in 2000; also see Benetton

Grand Prix Debut: 1977 British GP Jabouille (retired)
Latest Grand Prix: 2002 Japanese GP Button (6th), Trulli (retired)
Principals: Francois Castaing and Bernard Dudot, 1977-85; Flavio Briatore, 2002 to date
Base: Viry-Chatillon, 1977-85; Enstone (GB), 2002 to date

WORLD CHAMPIONSHIP RECORD

Starts: 140
Points: 335
Wins: 15 1979 French GP (Jabouille), 1980 Brazilian GP (Arnoux), South African GP (Arnoux), Austrian GP (Jabouille), 1981 French GP (Prost), Dutch GP (Prost), Italian GP (Prost), 1982 South African GP (Prost), Brazilian GP (Prost), French GP (Arnoux), Italian GP (Arnoux), 1983 French GP (Prost), Belgian GP (Prost), British GP (Prost), Austrian GP (Prost)
Pole positions: 31 1979 South African GP (Jabouille), French GP (Jabouille), German GP (Jabouille), Austrian GP (Arnoux), Dutch GP (Arnoux), Italian GP (Jabouille), 1980 Brazilian GP (Jabouille), South African GP (Jabouille), Austrian GP (Arnoux), Dutch GP (Arnoux), Italian GP (Arnoux), 1981 French GP (Arnoux), British GP (Arnoux), German GP (Prost), Austrian GP (Arnoux), Dutch GP (Prost), Italian GP (Arnoux), 1982 South African GP (Arnoux), Brazilian GP (Prost), San Marino GP (Arnoux), Belgian GP (Prost), Monaco GP (Arnoux), Detroit GP (Prost), Dutch GP (Arnoux), French GP (Arnoux), Swiss GP (Prost), Las Vegas GP (Prost), 1983 French GP (Prost), Monaco GP (Prost), Belgian GP (Prost), 1984 French GP (Tambay)
Fastest laps: 18 1979 French GP (Arnoux), Austrian GP (Arnoux), 1980 Brazilian GP (Arnoux), South African GP (Arnoux), Austrian GP (Arnoux), Dutch GP (Arnoux), 1981 French GP (Prost), British GP (Arnoux), 1982 South African GP (Prost), Brazilian GP (Prost), Detroit GP (Prost), Swiss GP (Prost), Italian GP (Arnoux), 1983 French GP (Prost), British GP (Prost), Austrian GP (Prost), 1984 South African GP (Tambay), Detroit GP (Warwick)
Laps/miles in the lead: 1220 laps/3707 miles

Best World Championship position:
Drivers: 2nd in 1983 (Prost)
Constructors: 2nd in 1983

RENAULT GRAND PRIX DRIVERS

Driver	Nat	Starts (DNS/DNQ)	1st	2nd	3rd	4th	5th	6th	PP	FL	Points
Alain Prost	F	46	9	6	2	2	1	1	10	8	134
Rene Arnoux	F	58 (2)	4	5	2	2	2	1	14	8	85
Jean-Pierre Jabouille	F	45 (2)	2	-	-	1	-	-	6	-	21
Derek Warwick	GB	31	-	2	2	1	2	1	-	1	28
Patrick Tambay	F	30 (1)	-	1	2	-	3	2	1	1	22
Eddie Cheever	USA	15	-	1	3	1	-	1	-	-	22
Jenson Button	GB	17	-	-	-	2	3	2	-	-	14
Jarno Trulli	I	17	-	-	-	2	1	1	-	-	9
Francois Hesnault	F	1	-	-	-	-	-	-	-	-	-
Philippe Streiff	F	1	-	-	-	-	-	-	-	-	-

RENAULT GRAND PRIX CARS

Type	Year	Engine	Designer
RS01	1977	Renault EF1 V6 tc	Andre de Cortanze/ Marcel Hubert
RE10	1979	Renault EF1 V6 tc	Michel Tetu
RE20	1980	Renault EF1 V6 tc	Michel Tetu
RE20B	1981	Renault EF1 V6 tc	Michel Tetu
RE30	1981	Renault EF1 V6 tc	Michel Tetu
RE30B	1982	Renault EF1 V6 tc	Michel Tetu
RE30C	1983	Renault EF1 V6 tc	Michel Tetu
RE40	1983	Renault EF1 V6 tc	Michel Tetu
RE50	1984	Renault EF4 V6 tc	Michel Tetu
RE60	1985	Renault EF4B V6 tc	Michel Tetu/ Jean-Marc d'Adda/ Bernard Touret
RE60B	1985	Renault EF15 V6 tc	Jean-Marc d'Adda/ Bernard Touret
R202	2002	Renault RS22	Mike Gascoyne/Tim Densham

Rial

Grand Prix Debut:	1988 Brazilian GP	de Cesaris (retired)
Last Grand Prix:	1989 Canadian GP	Danner (8th)
Principal:	Hans-Gunther Schmidt	
Base:	Ludwigshafen	

WORLD CHAMPIONSHIP RECORD

Starts:	20	
Points:	6	
Best result:	4th	1988 Detroit GP (de Cesaris), 1989 United States GP (Danner)
Best qualifying:	12th	1988 Mexican GP (de Cesaris), Canadian GP (de Cesaris), Detroit GP (de Cesaris), French GP (de Cesaris), Portuguese GP (de Cesaris)

Best World Championship position:

Drivers:	15th in 1988 (de Cesaris)
Constructors:	9th in 1988

RIAL GRAND PRIX DRIVERS

Driver	Nat	Starts (DNS/DNQ)	1st	2nd	3rd	4th	5th	6th	PP	FL	Points
Andrea de Cesaris	I	16	-	-	-	1	-	-	-	-	3
Christian Danner	D	4 (9)	-	-	-	1	-	-	-	-	3
Volker Weidler	D	- (10)	-	-	-	-	-	-	-	-	-
Pierre-Henri Raphanel	F	- (6)	-	-	-	-	-	-	-	-	-
Bertrand Gachot	B	- (2)	-	-	-	-	-	-	-	-	-
Gregor Foitek	CH	- (1)	-	-	-	-	-	-	-	-	-

RIAL GRAND PRIX CARS

Type	Year	Engine	Designer
ARC1	1988	Ford DFZ V8	Gustav Brunner
ARC2	1989	Ford DFR V8	Gustav Brunner/ Stefan Fober/Bob Bell

Sauber

Grand Prix Debut:	1993 South African GP	Lehto (5th), Wendlinger (retired)
Latest Grand Prix:	2002 Japanese GP	Heidfeld (7th), Massa (retired)
Principal:	Peter Sauber	
Base:	Hinwil	

WORLD CHAMPIONSHIP RECORD

Starts:	163	
Points:	122	
Best result:	3rd	1995 Italian GP (Frentzen), 1996 Monaco GP (Herbert), 1997 Hungarian GP (Herbert), 1998 Belgian GP (Alesi), 2001 Brazilian GP (Heidfeld)
Best qualifying:	2nd	1998 Austrian GP (Alesi), 1999 French GP (Alesi)

Best World Championship position:

Drivers:	7th in 2001 (Heidfeld)
Constructors:	4th in 2001

SAUBER GRAND PRIX DRIVERS

Driver	Nat	Starts (DNS/DNQ)	1st	2nd	3rd	4th	5th	6th	PP	FL	Points
Heinz-Harald Frentzen	D	49 (1)	-	-	1	4	3	7	-	-	29
Johnny Herbert	GB	49	-	-	2	2	2	2	-	-	20
Nick Heidfeld	D	34	-	-	1	2	1	7	-	-	19
Jean Alesi	F	32	-	-	1	-	2	3	-	-	11
Karl Wendlinger	A	25 (1)	-	-	-	2	1	3	-	-	11
Kimi Raikkonen	SF	17	-	-	-	2	1	1	-	-	9
Mika Salo	SF	16 (1)	-	-	-	-	2	2	-	-	6
JJ Lehto	SF	18	-	-	-	1	1	-	-	-	5
Felipe Massa	BR	16	-	-	-	-	1	2	-	-	4
Pedro Diniz	BR	32 (1)	-	-	-	-	-	3	-	-	3
"Jules" Boullion	F	11	-	-	-	-	1	1	-	-	3
Andrea de Cesaris	I	9	-	-	-	-	-	1	-	-	1
Nicola Larini	I	5	-	-	-	-	1	-	-	-	1
Gianni Morbidelli	I	7 (1)	-	-	-	-	-	-	-	-	-
Norberto Fontana	RA	4	-	-	-	-	-	-	-	-	-

SAUBER GRAND PRIX CARS

Type	Year	Engine	Designer
C12	1993	Ilmor 2175A V10, Sauber V10	Leo Ress
C13	1994	Mercedes-Benz 2175A V10	Leo Ress

Type	Year	Engine	Designer
C14	1995	Ford Zetec-R V10	Leo Ress
C15	1996	Ford Zetec-R V10	Leo Ress
C16	1997	Ferrari Tipo 046 V10*	Leo Ress
C17	1998	Ferrari Tipo 046 V10*	Leo Ress
C18	1999	Ferrari Tipo 047 V10*	Leo Ress
C19	2000	Ferrari Tipo 048 V10*	Leo Ress/ Sergio Rinland
C20	2001	Ferrari Tipo 049 V10*	Sergio Rinland/Heinz Haller/Willy Rampf
C21	2002	Ferrari Tipo 051 V10*	Willy Rampf

*badged Petronas

Scarab

Grand Prix Debut: 1960 Belgian GP   Daigh (retired), Reventlow (retired)
Last Grand Prix: 1960 United States GP Daigh (10th)
Principal: Lance Reventlow
Base: Culver City

WORLD CHAMPIONSHIP RECORD

Starts: 2
Best result: 10th   1960 United States GP (Daigh)
Best qualifying: 16th   1960 Dutch GP (Daigh) - did not start, Belgian GP (Reventlow)

SCARAB GRAND PRIX DRIVERS

Driver	Nat	Starts (DNS/DNQ)	1st	2nd	3rd	4th	5th	6th	PP	FL	Points
Chuck Daigh	USA	2 (3)	-	-	-	-	-	-	-	-	-
Lance Reventlow	USA	1 (2)	-	-	-	-	-	-	-	-	-
Richie Ginther	USA	- (1)	-	-	-	-	-	-	-	-	-

SCARAB GRAND PRIX CARS

Type	Year	Engine	Designer
Scarab	1960	Scarab S4	Dick Troutmann/Tom Barnes

Scirocco

Grand Prix Debut: 1963 Belgian GP   Settember (8th)
Last Grand Prix: 1964 Belgian GP   Pilette (retired)
Principal: Hugh Powell
Base: West London

WORLD CHAMPIONSHIP RECORD

Starts: 5
Best result: 8th   1963 Belgian GP (Settember)
Best qualifying: 18th   1963 British GP (Settember)

SCIROCCO GRAND PRIX DRIVERS

Driver	Nat	Starts (DNS/DNQ)	1st	2nd	3rd	4th	5th	6th	PP	FL	Points
Tony Settember	USA	4 (1)	-	-	-	-	-	-	-	-	-
Ian Burgess	GB	2	-	-	-	-	-	-	-	-	-
Andre Pilette	B	1 (1)	-	-	-	-	-	-	-	-	-

SCIROCCO GRAND PRIX CARS

Type	Year	Engine	Designer
01	1963	BRM 56 V8	Hugh Aiden-Jones/ Paul Emery
02	1963	BRM 56 V8, Climax FMWV V8	Hugh Aiden-Jones/ Paul Emery

Shadow

Grand Prix Debut: 1973 South African GP Follmer (6th), Oliver (retired)
Last Grand Prix: 1980 South African GP Lees (retired)
Principal: Don Nichols
Base: Northampton

WORLD CHAMPIONSHIP RECORD

Starts: 104
Points: 68.5
Wins: 1   1977 Austrian GP (Jones)
Pole positions: 3   1975 Argentinian GP (Jarier), Brazilian GP (Jarier), British GP (Pryce)
Fastest laps: 2   1975 Brazilian GP (Jarier), 1976 Brazilian GP (Jarier)
Laps/miles in the lead: 50 laps/208 miles
Best World Championship position:
Drivers: 7th in 1977 (Jones)
Constructors: 6th in 1975

MAJOR SPONSORS

1973-75	UOP (Universal Oil Products)
1976	Benihana, Bic, Lucky Strike, Tabatip
1977	Ambrosio, Tabatip
1978	Villiger
1979	Interscope, Samson
1980	Theodore, Interlekt

SHADOW GRAND PRIX DRIVERS

Driver	Nat	Starts (DNS/DNQ)	1st	2nd	3rd	4th	5th	6th	PP	FL	Points
Alan Jones	AUS	14	1	-	1	2	1	1	-	-	22
Tom Pryce	GB	41	-	-	2	3	-	4	1	-	19
Jean-Pierre Jarier	F	44 (1)	-	-	1	1	1	-	2	2	7.5
George Follmer	USA	12 (1)	-	-	1	-	-	1	-	-	5
Jackie Oliver	GB	14	-	-	1	-	-	-	-	-	4
Clay Regazzoni	CH	11 (5)	-	-	-	-	2	-	-	-	4
Elio de Angelis	I	14 (1)	-	-	-	1	-	-	-	-	3
Hans-Joachim Stuck	D	14 (2)	-	-	-	-	1	-	-	-	2
Riccardo Patrese	I	9	-	-	-	-	-	1	-	-	1
Renzo Zorzi	I	5	-	-	-	-	-	1	-	-	1
Jan Lammers	NL	12 (3)	-	-	-	-	-	-	-	-	-
Graham Hill	GB	12	-	-	-	-	-	-	-	-	-
Brian Redman	GB	4	-	-	-	-	-	-	-	-	-
Peter Revson	USA	2	-	-	-	-	-	-	-	-	-
Geoff Lees	GB	1 (4)	-	-	-	-	-	-	-	-	-
Arturo Merzario	I	1	-	-	-	-	-	-	-	-	-
Bertil Roos	S	1	-	-	-	-	-	-	-	-	-
David Kennedy	IRL	- (7)	-	-	-	-	-	-	-	-	-
Stefan Johansson	S	- (2)	-	-	-	-	-	-	-	-	-
Danny Ongais	USA	- (2)	-	-	-	-	-	-	-	-	-
Mike Wilds	GB	- (1)	-	-	-	-	-	-	-	-	-

SHADOW GRAND PRIX CARS

Type	Year	Engine	Designer
DN1A	1973	Ford DFV V8	Tony Southgate
DN3A	1974	Ford DFV V8	Tony Southgate
DN3B	1975	Ford DFV V8	Tony Southgate
DN5A	1975	Ford DFV V8	Tony Southgate
DN5B	1976	Ford DFV V8	Tony Southgate
DN7A	1975	Matra MS73 V12	Tony Southgate
DN8A	1976	Ford DFV V8	Tony Southgate/Dave Wass
DN9A	1978	Ford DFV V8	Tony Southgate/John Baldwin
DN9B	1979	Ford DFV V8	Richard Owen/John Gentry
DN11A	1980	Ford DFV V8	John Gentry/Richard Owen/ Vic Morris
DN12A	1980	Ford DFV V8	Vic Morris/Chuck Greameger

Shannon

Only Grand Prix: 1966 British GP   Taylor (retired)
Principals: Hugh Aiden-Jones and Paul Emery

WORLD CHAMPIONSHIP RECORD

Starts: 1
Best result: No finishes
Best qualifying: 18th   1966 British GP (Taylor)

SHANNON GRAND PRIX DRIVERS

Driver	Nat	Starts (DNS/DNQ)	1st	2nd	3rd	4th	5th	6th	PP	FL	Points
Trevor Taylor	GB	1	-	-	-	-	-	-	-	-	-

SHANNON GRAND PRIX CARS

Type	Year	Engine	Designer
SH1	1966	Climax FPE V8	Hugh Aiden-Jones/ Paul Emery

Simtek

Grand Prix Debut: 1994 Brazilian GP   Brabham (12th)
Last Grand Prix: 1995 Monaco GP   Schiattarella (retired), Verstappen (retired)
Principal: Nick Wirth
Base: Banbury

WORLD CHAMPIONSHIP RECORD

Starts: 21
Best result: 9th   1994 French GP (Gounon), 1995 Argentinian GP (Schiattarella)
Best qualifying: 14th   1995 Argentinian GP (Verstappen)

MAJOR SPONSORS

1994-95   MTV

SIMTEK GRAND PRIX DRIVERS

Driver	Nat	Starts (DNS/DNQ)	1st	2nd	3rd	4th	5th	6th	PP	FL	Points
David Brabham	AUS	16	-	-	-	-	-	-	-	-	-
Domenico Schiattarella	I	7	-	-	-	-	-	-	-	-	-
Jean-Marc Gounon	F	7	-	-	-	-	-	-	-	-	-
Jos Verstappen	NL	5	-	-	-	-	-	-	-	-	-
Roland Ratzenberger	A	1 (2)	-	-	-	-	-	-	-	-	-
Taki Inoue	J	1	-	-	-	-	-	-	-	-	-
Andrea Montermini	I	- (1)	-	-	-	-	-	-	-	-	-

SIMTEK GRAND PRIX CARS

Type	Year	Engine	Designer
S941	1994	Ford HB V8	Nick Wirth
S951	1995	Ford ED V8	Nick Wirth

Spirit

Grand Prix Debut: 1983 British GP   Johansson (retired)
Last Grand Prix: 1985 San Marino GP   Baldi (retired)
Principals: John Wickham and Gordon Coppuck
Base: Bicester

WORLD CHAMPIONSHIP RECORD

Starts: 23

Best result: 7th   1983 Dutch GP (Johansson)
Best qualifying: 13th   1983 German GP (Johansson)

SPIRIT GRAND PRIX DRIVERS

Driver	Nat	Starts (DNS/DNQ)	1st	2nd	3rd	4th	5th	6th	PP	FL	Points
Mauro Baldi	I	10 (1)	-	-	-	-	-	-	-	-	-
Huub Rothengatter	NL	7 (1)	-	-	-	-	-	-	-	-	-
Stefan Johansson	S	6	-	-	-	-	-	-	-	-	-

SPIRIT GRAND PRIX CARS

Type	Year	Engine	Designer
201	1983	Honda RA163E V6 tc	Gordon Coppuck/ John Baldwin
Converted F2 car			
101B	1984	Hart 415T S4 tc	Gordon Coppuck
101C	1984	Ford DFV V8	Gordon Coppuck
101D	1985	Hart 415T S4 tc	Gordon Coppuck

Stebro

Only Grand Prix: 1963 United States GP   Broeker (7th)

WORLD CHAMPIONSHIP RECORD

Starts: 1
Best result: 7th   1963 United States GP (Broeker)
Best qualifying: 21st   1963 United States GP (Broeker)

STEBRO GRAND PRIX DRIVERS

Driver	Nat	Starts (DNS/DNQ)	1st	2nd	3rd	4th	5th	6th	PP	FL	Points
Peter Broeker	CDN	1	-	-	-	-	-	-	-	-	-

STEBRO GRAND PRIX CARS

Type	Year	Engine	Designer
4	1963	Ford 105E S4	-

Stewart

Sold to Jaguar in 1999; also see Jaguar

Grand Prix Debut: 1997 Australian GP   Barrichello (retired), Magnussen (retired)
Last Grand Prix: 1999 Japanese GP   Herbert (7th), Barrichello (8th)
Principals: Jackie and Paul Stewart
Base: Milton Keynes

WORLD CHAMPIONSHIP RECORD

Starts: 49
Points: 47
Wins: 1   1999 European GP (Herbert)
Pole positions: 1   1999 French GP (Barrichello)
Laps/miles in the lead: 84 laps/226 miles

Best World Championship position:
Drivers: 7th in 1999 (Barrichello)
Constructors: 4th in 1999

MAJOR SPONSORS

1997	HSBC, Visit Malaysia, Texaco
1998	HSBC, Texaco, MCI
1999	HSBC, MCI, Texaco, Lear

STEWART GRAND PRIX DRIVERS

Driver	Nat	Starts	1st	2nd	3rd	4th	5th	6th	PP	FL	Points
		(DNS/DNQ)									
Johnny Herbert	GB	16	1	-	-	1	1	-	-	-	15
Rubens Barrichello	BR	49	-	1	3	1	5	-	1	-	31
Jan Magnussen	DK	24	-	-	-	-	1	-	-	-	1
Jos Verstappen	NL	9	-	-	-	-	-	-	-	-	-

STEWART GRAND PRIX CARS

Type	Year	Engine	Designer
SF1	1997	Ford Zetec-R V10	Alan Jenkins
SF2	1998	Ford Zetec-R V10	Alan Jenkins
SF3	1999	Ford CR-1 V10	Gary Anderson

Surtees

Grand Prix Debut:	1970 British GP	Surtees (retired)
Last Grand Prix:	1978 Canadian GP	Arnoux (retired)
Principal:	John Surtees
Base:	Edenbridge, Kent

WORLD CHAMPIONSHIP RECORD

Starts:	118	
Points:	54	
Best result:	2nd	1972 Italian GP (Hailwood)
Best qualifying:	2nd	1974 South African GP (Pace)
Fastest laps:	3	1972 South African GP (Hailwood), 1973 German GP (Pace), Austrian GP (Pace)
Laps/miles in the lead:	9 laps/28 miles	

Best World Championship position:

Drivers:	8th in 1972 (Hailwood)
Constructors:	5th in 1972

MAJOR SPONSORS

1971	Brooke Bond Oxo, Rob Walker, AMS, Eifelland
1972	Brooke Bond Oxo, Rob Walker, Ceramica Pagnossin, Flame Out
1973	Brooke Bond Oxo, Rob Walker, Ceramica Pagnossin, Fina
1974	Bang & Olufsen, Fina, Memphis
1975	Matchbox, National
1976	Campari, Chesterfield, Durex, Theodore
1977	Beta, Durex
1978	Beta, Durex, British Air Ferries

SURTEES GRAND PRIX DRIVERS

Driver	Nat	Starts	1st	2nd	3rd	4th	5th	6th	PP	FL	Points
		(DNS/DNQ)									
Mike Hailwood	GB	27	-	1	-	3	-	1	-	1	16
Carlos Pace	BR	22	-	-	1	2	-	-	-	2	10
Vittorio Brambilla	I	29 (2)	-	-	-	1	1	2	-	-	7
Alan Jones	AUS	14	-	-	-	1	2	-	-	-	7
John Surtees	GB	19 (1)	-	-	-	-	2	1	-	-	5
Andrea de Adamich	I	13	-	-	-	1	-	-	-	-	3
Rolf Stommelen	D	9 (1)	-	-	-	1	1	-	-	-	3
Tim Schenken	AUS	12	-	-	-	-	1	-	-	-	2
Derek Bell	GB	3 (4)	-	-	-	-	-	1	-	-	1
Jochen Mass	D	13 (1)	-	-	-	-	-	-	-	-	-
John Watson	GB	11	-	-	-	-	-	-	-	-	-
Brett Lunger	USA	10 (2)	-	-	-	-	-	-	-	-	-
Hans Binder	A	9	-	-	-	-	-	-	-	-	-
Henri Pescarolo	F	7 (3)	-	-	-	-	-	-	-	-	-
Rupert Keegan	GB	6 (7)	-	-	-	-	-	-	-	-	-
Vern Schuppan	AUS	3 (1)	-	-	-	-	-	-	-	-	-
Rene Arnoux	F	2	-	-	-	-	-	-	-	-	-
Helmuth Koinigg	A	2	-	-	-	-	-	-	-	-	-
Sam Posey	USA	2	-	-	-	-	-	-	-	-	-
Leo Kinnunen	SF	1 (5)	-	-	-	-	-	-	-	-	-
Larry Perkins	AUS	1 (2)	-	-	-	-	-	-	-	-	-
Jose Dolhem	F	1 (2)	-	-	-	-	-	-	-	-	-
Gijs van Lennep	NL	1 (1)	-	-	-	-	-	-	-	-	-
Conny Andersson	S	1	-	-	-	-	-	-	-	-	-
Luis-Pereira Bueno	BR	1	-	-	-	-	-	-	-	-	-
John Love	RSR	1	-	-	-	-	-	-	-	-	-
Dave Morgan	GB	1	-	-	-	-	-	-	-	-	-
Dieter Quester	A	1	-	-	-	-	-	-	-	-	-
Brian Redman	GB	1	-	-	-	-	-	-	-	-	-
Noritake Takahara	J	1	-	-	-	-	-	-	-	-	-
Beppe Gabbiani	I	- (2)	-	-	-	-	-	-	-	-	-
Divina Galica	GB	- (1)	-	-	-	-	-	-	-	-	-
"Gimax"	I	- (1)	-	-	-	-	-	-	-	-	-
Jean-Pierre Jabouille	F	- (1)	-	-	-	-	-	-	-	-	-
Lamberto Leoni	I	- (1)	-	-	-	-	-	-	-	-	-
Patrick Tambay	F	- (1)	-	-	-	-	-	-	-	-	-
Tony Trimmer	GB	- (1)	-	-	-	-	-	-	-	-	-

SURTEES GRAND PRIX CARS

Type	Year	Engine	Designer
TS7	1970	Ford DFV V8	John Surtees/Peter Connew/ Shahab Ahmed
TS9	1971	Ford DFV V8	John Surtees/Peter Connew/ Shahab Ahmed
TS9B	1972	Ford DFV V8	John Surtees/Peter Connew/ Shahab Ahmed
TS14	1972	Ford DFV V8	John Surtees
TS14A	1973	Ford DFV V8	John Surtees
TS16/1	1974	Ford DFV V8	John Surtees
TS16/2	1974	Ford DFV V8	John Surtees
TS16/3	1974	Ford DFV V8	John Surtees
TS16/4	1975	Ford DFV V8	John Surtees
TS19	1976	Ford DFV V8	John Surtees/Ken Sears
TS20	1978	Ford DFV V8	John Surtees/Ken Sears

Talbot

see Lago-Talbot

Tec-Mec

Studio Technica-Meccanica

Only Grand Prix:	1959 United States GP d'Orey (retired)
Principal:	Valerio Colotti
Base:	Modena

WORLD CHAMPIONSHIP RECORD

Starts:	1	
Best result:	No finishes	
Best qualifying:	17th	1959 United States GP (d'Orey)

TEC-MEC GRAND PRIX DRIVERS

Driver	Nat	Starts	1st	2nd	3rd	4th	5th	6th	PP	FL	Points
		(DNS/DNQ)									
Fritz d'Orey	BR	1	-	-	-	-	-	-	-	-	-

TEC-MEC GRAND PRIX CARS

Type	Year	Engine	Designer
F415	1959	Maserati 250F S6	Valerio Colotti

Tecno

Grand Prix Debut: 1969 German GP   Cevert (F2 class)
Last Grand Prix: 1973 Dutch GP   Amon (retired)
Principals: Luciano and Gianfranco Pederzani
Base: Bologna

WORLD CHAMPIONSHIP RECORD

Starts: 11
Points: 1
Best result: 6th   1973 Belgian GP (Amon)
Best qualifying: 12th   1973 Monaco GP (Amon)
Best World Championship position:
Drivers: 19th in 1973 (Amon)
Constructors: 11th in 1973

MAJOR SPONSORS

1972-73	Martini

TECNO GRAND PRIX DRIVERS

Driver	Nat	Starts (DNS/DNQ)	1st	2nd	3rd	4th	5th	6th	PP	FL	Points
Chris Amon	NZ	4 (1)	-	-	-	-	-	1	-	-	1
Nanni Galli	I	4	-	-	-	-	-	-	-	-	-
Derek Bell	GB	2 (3)	-	-	-	-	-	-	-	-	-
Francois Cevert	F	1	-	-	-	-	-	-	-	-	-

TECNO GRAND PRIX CARS

Type	Year	Engine	Designer
306	1969	Cosworth	Gianfranco Pederzani/ Luciano Pederzani
PA123	1972	Tecno Series P F12	Gianfranco Pederzani/ Luciano Pederzani
PA123 (73)	1973	Tecno Series P F12	Alan McCall

Theodore

Took over Ensign in 1983; also see Ensign

Grand Prix Debut: 1978 South African GP Rosberg (retired)
Last Grand Prix: 1983 European GP   Guerrero (12th)
Principal: Teddy Yip
Base: Woking, 1978; Northampton, 1981-82; Chasetown, Staffordshire, 1983

WORLD CHAMPIONSHIP RECORD

Starts: 33
Points: 2
Best result: 6th   1981 Long Beach GP (Tambay), 1983 Long Beach GP (Cecotto)
Best qualifying: 11th   1983 Detroit GP (Guerrero)

Best World Championship position:
Drivers: 18th in 1981 (Tambay)
Constructors: 12th in 1981 and 1983

MAJOR SPONSORS

1981-82	Theodore
1983	Cafe do Colombia

THEODORE GRAND PRIX DRIVERS

Driver	Nat	Starts (DNS/DNQ)	1st	2nd	3rd	4th	5th	6th	PP	FL	Points
Johnny Cecotto	YV	9 (4)	-	-	-	-	-	1	-	-	1
Patrick Tambay	F	6 (1)	-	-	-	-	-	1	-	-	1
Roberto Guerrero	USA	13 (1)	-	-	-	-	-	-	-	-	-
Marc Surer	CH	6 (2)	-	-	-	-	-	-	-	-	-
Derek Daly	IRL	3	-	-	-	-	-	-	-	-	-

Driver	Nat	Start	1st	2nd	3rd	4th	5th	6th	PP	FL	Points
Tommy Byrne	IRL	2 (3)	-	-	-	-	-	-	-	-	-
Jan Lammers	NL	1 (5)	-	-	-	-	-	-	-	-	-
Keke Rosberg	SF	1 (4)	-	-	-	-	-	-	-	-	-
Geoff Lees	GB	1	-	-	-	-	-	-	-	-	-
Eddie Cheever	USA	- (2)	-	-	-	-	-	-	-	-	-

THEODORE GRAND PRIX CARS

Type	Year	Engine	Designer
TR1	1978	Ford DFV V8	Ron Tauranac/Len Bailey
TR2	1981	Ford DFV V8	Vic Morris/Chuck Greameger
Formerly Shadow DN12A, renamed Theodore TR2. Only raced in the non-championship South African GP			
TY01	1981	Ford DFV V8	Tony Southgate
TY02	1982	Ford DFV V8	Tony Southgate
N183	1983	Ford DFV V8	Nigel Bennett

Token

Grand Prix Debut: 1974 Belgian GP   Pryce (retired)
Last Grand Prix: 1974 Austrian GP   Ashley (not classified)
Principals: Tony Vlassopoulo and Ken Grob
Base: Woking, Surrey

WORLD CHAMPIONSHIP RECORD

Starts: 3
Best result: No finishes
Best qualifying: 20th   1974 Belgian GP (Pryce)

MAJOR SPONSORS

1974	Harper, ShellSport

TOKEN GRAND PRIX DRIVERS

Driver	Nat	Starts (DNS/DNQ)	1st	2nd	3rd	4th	5th	6th	PP	FL	Points
Ian Ashley	GB	2	-	-	-	-	-	-	-	-	-
Tom Pryce	GB	1	-	-	-	-	-	-	-	-	-
David Purley	GB	- (1)	-	-	-	-	-	-	-	-	-

TOKEN GRAND PRIX CARS

Type	Year	Engine	Designer
RJ02	1974	Ford DFV V8	Ray Jessop

Commissioned and built by Rondel Racing (owned by Ron Dennis and Neil Trundle). Project sold to Token when money ran out. Renamed Safir after new owners in 1975 but only used in non-championship races

Toleman

Team sold to Benetton in 1985; also see Benetton

Grand Prix Debut: 1981 Italian GP   Henton (10th)
Last Grand Prix: 1985 Australian GP   Fabi (retired), Ghinzani (retired)
Principal: Ted Toleman
Base: Witney, Oxfordshire

WORLD CHAMPIONSHIP RECORD

Starts: 57
Points: 26
Best result: 2nd   1984 Monaco GP (Senna)
Pole positions: 1   1985 German GP (Fabi)
Fastest laps: 2   1982 Dutch GP (Warwick), 1984 Monaco GP (Senna)

Best World Championship position:
Drivers: 9th in 1984 (Senna)
Constructors: 7th in 1984

MAJOR SPONSORS

1981-83	Candy
1984	Segafredo
1985	Benetton

TOLEMAN GRAND PRIX DRIVERS

Driver	Nat	Starts (DNS/DNQ)	1st	2nd	3rd	4th	5th	6th	PP	FL	Points
Ayrton Senna	BR	14 (1)	-	1	2	-	-	2	-	1	13
Derek Warwick	GB	26 (15)	-	-	-	2	1	1	-	1	9
Stefan Johansson	S	3	-	-	-	1	-	-	-	-	3
Bruno Giacomelli	I	14 (1)	-	-	-	-	-	1	-	-	1
Teo Fabi	I	20 (7)	-	-	-	-	-	-	1	-	-
Johnny Cecotto	YV	9 (1)	-	-	-	-	-	-	-	-	-
Piercarlo Ghinzani	I	7									
Brian Henton	GB	1 (11)	-	-	-	-	-	-	-	-	-
Pierluigi Martini	I	- (1)	-	-	-	-	-	-	-	-	-

TOLEMAN GRAND PRIX CARS

Type	Year	Engine	Designer
TG181	1981	Hart 415T S4 tc	Rory Byrne/John Gentry
TG181B	1982	Hart 415T S4 tc	Rory Byrne/John Gentry
TG181C	1982	Hart 415T S4 tc	Rory Byrne/John Gentry
TG183	1982	Hart 415T S4 tc	Rory Byrne/John Gentry
TG183B	1983	Hart 415T S4 tc	Rory Byrne/John Gentry
TG184	1984	Hart 415T S4 tc	Rory Byrne/John Gentry
TG185	1985	Hart 415T S4 tc	Rory Byrne

de Tomaso

Grand Prix Debut:	1961 French GP	Scarlatti (retired)
Last Grand Prix:	1970 United States GP	Schenken (retired)
Principal:	Alejandro de Tomaso	
Base:	Modena	

WORLD CHAMPIONSHIP RECORD

Starts:	10	
Best result:	No finishes	
Best qualifying:	9th	1970 Monaco GP (Courage), Dutch GP (Courage)

DE TOMASO GRAND PRIX DRIVERS

Driver	Nat	Starts (DNS/DNQ)	1st	2nd	3rd	4th	5th	6th	PP	FL	Points
Piers Courage	GB	4 (1)	-	-	-	-	-	-	-	-	-
Tim Schenken	AUS	4	-	-	-	-	-	-	-	-	-
Roberto Lippi	I	1 (2)	-	-	-	-	-	-	-	-	-
Roberto Bussinello	I	1	-	-	-	-	-	-	-	-	-
Giorgio Scarlatti	I	1	-	-	-	-	-	-	-	-	-
Nino Vaccarella	I	1	-	-	-	-	-	-	-	-	-
Nasif Estefano	RA	- (2)	-	-	-	-	-	-	-	-	-
Brian Redman	GB	- (2)	-	-	-	-	-	-	-	-	-

DE TOMASO GRAND PRIX CARS

Type	Year	Engine	Designer
F1/001	1961	OSCA S4	Alejandro de Tomaso
F1/002	1961	OSCA S4, Ferrari V6	Alejandro de Tomaso
F1/003	1961	Alfa Romeo Giulietta S4	Alejandro de Tomaso
F1/004	1961	Alfa Romeo Giulietta S4	Alejandro de Tomaso
F1/801	1962	de Tomaso F8	Alberto Massimino
505/38	1970	Ford DFV V8	Gianpaolo Dallara

Toyota

Grand Prix Debut:	2002 Australian GP	Salo (6th), McNish (retired)
Latest Grand Prix:	2002 Japanese GP	Salo (8th)

Principle:	Ove Andersson
Base:	Cologne

WORLD CHAMPIONSHIP RECORD

Starts:	17	
Points:	2	
Best result:	6th	2002 Australian GP (Salo), 2002 Brazilian GP (Salo)
Best qualifying:	8th	2002 British GP (Salo)

Best World Championship position:

Drivers:	15th in 2002 (Salo)
Constructors:	9th in 2002

MAJOR SPONSORS

2002 to date	Panasonic

TOYOTA GRAND PRIX DRIVERS

Driver	Nat	Starts	1st	2nd	3rd	4th	5th	6th	PP	FL	Points
Mika Salo	SF	17	-	-	-	-	-	2	-	-	2
Allan McNish	GB	16 (1)	-	-	-	-	-	-	-	-	-

TOYOTA GRAND PRIX CARS

Type	Year	Engine	Designer
TF102	2002	Toyota RVX02	Gustav Brunner

Trojan

Grand Prix Debut:	1974 Spanish GP	Schenken (14th)
Last Grand Prix:	1974 Italian GP	Schenken (retired)
Principal:	Peter Agg	
Base:	Croydon, Surrey	

WORLD CHAMPIONSHIP RECORD

Starts:	6	
Best result:	10th	1974 Belgian GP (Schenken), Austrian GP (Schenken)
Best qualifying:	19th	1974 Austrian GP (Schenken)

MAJOR SPONSORS

1974	Suzuki, Homelite

TROJAN GRAND PRIX DRIVERS

Driver	Nat	Starts (DNS/DNQ)	1st	2nd	3rd	4th	5th	6th	PP	FL	Points
Tim Schenken	AUS	6 (2)	-	-	-	-	-	-	-	-	-

TROJAN GRAND PRIX CARS

Type	Year	Engine	Designer
T103	1974	Ford DFV V8	Ron Tauranac

Tyrrell

Sold to British American Racing (BAR) in 1998; also see BAR

Grand Prix Debut:	1970 Canadian GP	Stewart (retired)
Last Grand Prix:	1998 Japanese GP	Takagi (retired)
Principal:	Ken Tyrrell, 1970-97; Craig Pollock/British American Tobacco, 1998	
Base:	Ockham, Surrey	

WORLD CHAMPIONSHIP RECORD

Starts:	430
Points:	711

Formula 1

MAJOR SPONSORS

1970-76	Elf
1977-78	Elf, Citibank
1979-80	Candy
1981	Ceramica Imola, Michelob
1982	Candy, Denim
1983	Benetton
1986-87	Data General
1989	Camel
1990	Epson, PIAA
1991	Braun, Epson, PIAA
1992	Calbee, Club Angle
1993	Cabin, Calbee
1994	Mild Seven, Calbee, Club Angle, Fondmetal Wheels
1995	Nokia, Mild Seven
1996	Mild Seven, Korean Air
1997-98	PIAA

TYRRELL GRAND PRIX DRIVERS

Driver	Nat	Starts (DNS/DNQ)	1st	2nd	3rd	4th	5th	6th	PP	FL	Points
Jackie Stewart	GB	39 (1)	15	4	1	3	3	-	12	8	178
Jody Scheckter	ZA	45	4	7	3	4	5	2	1	3	114
Michele Alboreto	I	46 (3)	2	-	2	3	2	2	-	1	41
Patrick Depailler	F	80	1	9	7	5	4	5	1	3	119
Francois Cevert	F	37 (1)	1	10	2	2	2	1	-	2	88
Didier Pironi	F	31	-	-	2	1	3	4	-	-	21
Jean Alesi	F	23 (1)	-	2	-	2	1	1	-	-	21
Jean-Pierre Jarier	F	26 (1)	-	-	2	-	5	2	-	-	20
Jonathan Palmer	GB	45 (3)	-	-	1	4	3	-	1	14
Mika Salo	SF	50	-	-	-	-	5	2	-	-	12
Stefano Modena	I	16	-	1	-	1	-	1	-	-	10

Driver	Nat	Start	1st	2nd	3rd	4th	5th	6th	PP	FL	Points
Eddie Cheever	USA	14 (1)	-	-	1	3	1	-	-	10
Martin Brundle	GB	38 (3)	-	-	-	1	2	1	-	-	8
Andrea de Cesaris	I	32	-	-	-	1	2	1	-	-	8
Mark Blundell	GB	16	-	-	1	-	2	-	-	-	8
Philippe Streiff	F	33	-	-	-	1	1	2	-	-	7
Ronnie Peterson	S	17	-	-	1	-	1	1	-	1	7
Derek Daly	IRL	17	-	-	-	2	-	-	-	-	6
Ukyo Katayama	J	64	-	-	-	-	2	1	-	-	5
Satoru Nakajima	J	31 (1)	-	-	-	-	1	3	-	-	5
Stefan Bellof	D	20 (2)	-	-	-	1	-	1	-	-	4
Ivan Capelli	I	2	-	-	-	1	-	-	-	-	3
Danny Sullivan	USA	15	-	-	-	-	1	-	-	-	2
Jos Verstappen	NL	17	-	-	-	-	-	-	-	-	-
Olivier Grouillard	F	16	-	-	-	-	-	-	-	-	-
Toranosuke Takagi	J	16	-	-	-	-	-	-	-	-	-
Brian Henton	GB	13	-	-	-	-	-	-	-	1	-
Ricardo Rosset	BR	11 (5)	-	-	-	-	-	-	-	-	-
Julian Bailey	GB	6 (10)	-	-	-	-	-	-	-	-	-
Stefan Johansson	S	4 (1)	-	-	-	-	-	-	-	-	-
Alessandro Pesenti-Rossi	I	3 (1)	-	-	-	-	-	-	-	-	-
Slim Borgudd	S	3	-	-	-	-	-	-	-	-	-
Eddie Keizan	ZA	2	-	-	-	-	-	-	-	-	-
Ian Scheckter	ZA	2	-	-	-	-	-	-	-	-	-
Ricardo Zunino	RA	2	-	-	-	-	-	-	-	-	-
Mike Thackwell	NZ	1 (2)	-	-	-	-	-	-	-	-	-
Chris Amon	NZ	1 (1)	-	-	-	-	-	-	-	-	-
Johnny Herbert	GB	1 (1)	-	-	-	-	-	-	-	-	-
Gabriele Tarquini	I	1	-	-	-	-	-	-	-	-	-
Geoff Lees	GB	1	-	-	-	-	-	-	-	-	-
Jean-Pierre Jabouille	F	1	-	-	-	-	-	-	-	-	-
Kazuyoshi Hoshino	J	1	-	-	-	-	-	-	-	-	-
Kunimitsu Takahashi	J	1	-	-	-	-	-	-	-	-	-
Michel Leclere	F	1	-	-	-	-	-	-	-	-	-
Peter Revson	USA	1	-	-	-	-	-	-	-	-	-
Otto Stuppacher	A	- (4)	-	-	-	-	-	-	-	-	-
Kevin Cogan	USA	- (1)	-	-	-	-	-	-	-	-	-

TYRRELL GRAND PRIX CARS

Type	Year	Engine	Designer
001	1970	Ford DFV V8	Derek Gardner
002	1971	Ford DFV V8	Derek Gardner
003	1971	Ford DFV V8	Derek Gardner
004	1972	Ford DFV V8	Derek Gardner
005	1972	Ford DFV V8	Derek Gardner
006	1972	Ford DFV V8	Derek Gardner
007	1974	Ford DFV V8	Derek Gardner
P34	1976	Ford DFV V8	Derek Gardner
Six-wheel car			
008	1978	Ford DFV V8	Maurice Philippe
009	1979	Ford DFV V8	Maurice Philippe
010	1980	Ford DFV V8	Maurice Philippe
011	1981	Ford DFV V8	Maurice Philippe/Brian Lisles
012	1983	Ford DFY V8	Maurice Philippe/Brian Lisles
014	1985	Renault EF4B/EF15 V6 tc	Maurice Philippe/Brian Lisles
015	1986	Renault EF4B/EF15 V6 tc	Maurice Philippe/Brian Lisles
016	1987	Ford DFZ V8	Brian Lisles/Maurice Philippe
017	1988	Ford DFZ V8	Brian Lisles/Maurice Philippe/Graham Heard
017B	1989	Ford DFR V8	Brian Lisles/Graham Heard
018	1989	Ford DFR V8	Harvey Postlethwaite/Jean-Claude Migeot
019	1990	Ford DFR V8	Harvey Postlethwaite/Jean-Claude Migeot
020	1991	Honda RA101E V10	George Ryton

Type	Year	Engine	Designer
020B	1992	Ilmor 2175A V10	Harvey Postlethwaite/ George Ryton
020C	1993	Yamaha OX10A V10	Harvey Postlethwaite/ George Ryton
021	1993	Yamaha OX10A V10	Mike Coughlan
022	1994	Yamaha OX10A V10	Harvey Postlethwaite/ Jean-Claude Migeot
023	1995	Yamaha OX10C V10	Harvey Postlethwaite
024	1996	Yamaha OX11A V10	Harvey Postlethwaite
025	1997	Ford ED4 V8	Harvey Postlethwaite
026	1998	Ford Zetec-R V10	Harvey Postlethwaite

Vanwall

Grand Prix Debut:	1954 British GP	Collins (retired)
Last Grand Prix:	1960 French GP	Brooks (retired)
Principal:	Tony Vandervell
Base:	Acton, West London

WORLD CHAMPIONSHIP RECORD

Starts:	28
Points:	108
Wins:	9 1957 British GP (Brooks/Moss), Pescara GP (Moss), Italian GP (Moss), 1958 Dutch GP (Moss), Belgian GP (Brooks), German GP (Brooks), Portuguese GP (Moss), Italian GP (Brooks), Moroccan GP (Moss)
Pole positions:	7 1957 British GP (Moss), Italian GP (Lewis-Evans), 1958 Monaco GP (Brooks), Dutch GP (Lewis-Evans), British GP (Moss), Portuguese GP (Moss), Italian GP (Moss)
Fastest laps:	6 1957 British GP (Moss), Pescara GP (Moss), Italian GP (Brooks), 1958 Dutch GP (Moss), German GP (Moss), Moroccan GP (Moss)
Laps/miles in the lead:	371 laps/1732 miles

World Champions:
Constructors: Once - 1958

Best World Championship position:
Drivers: 2nd in 1957 (Moss) and 1958 (Moss - including 8 points of his 41 in a Cooper-Climax)

VANWALL GRAND PRIX DRIVERS

Driver	Nat	Starts (DNS/DNQ)	1st	2nd	3rd	4th	5th	6th	PP	FL	Points
Stirling Moss	GB	14	6	1	-	-	1	-	4	5	57
Tony Brooks	GB	16	4	1	-	-	-	-	1	1	35
Stuart Lewis-Evans	GB	13	-	-	2	1	1	-	2	-	13
Harry Schell	USA	7	-	-	-	1	-	-	-	-	3
Maurice Trintignant	F	4	-	-	-	-	-	-	-	-	-
Mike Hawthorn	GB	3	-	-	-	-	-	-	-	-	-
Peter Collins	GB	2 (1)	-	-	-	-	-	-	-	-	-
Ken Wharton	GB	2	-	-	-	-	-	-	-	-	-
Jose Froilan Gonzalez	RA	1	-	-	-	-	-	-	-	-	-
Roy Salvadori	GB	1	-	-	-	-	-	-	-	-	-
Piero Taruffi	I	1	-	-	-	-	-	-	-	-	-
Colin Chapman	GB	- (1)	-	-	-	-	-	-	-	-	-

VANWALL GRAND PRIX CARS

Type	Year	Engine	Designer
Special	1954	Vanwall S4	Owen Maddock
VW1-4	1955	Vanwall S4	Frank Costin/Colin Chapman
VW5-7	1957	Vanwall S4	Frank Costin/Colin Chapman
VW9-10	1958	Vanwall S4	Frank Costin/Colin Chapman
VW11	1960	Vanwall S4	Frank Costin/Valerio Colotti

Veritas

Grand Prix Debut:	1951 Swiss GP	Hirt (retired)
Last Grand Prix:	1953 German GP	Herrmann (9th), Helfrich (12th), Seidel (16th), Karch (retired), Heeks (retired), Bauer (retired), Loof (retired)
Principal:	Ernst Loof	
Base:	Messkirch, 1948-49; Nurburgring, 1950-56	

WORLD CHAMPIONSHIP RECORD

Starts:	6	
Best result:	7th	1952 German GP (Riess)
Best qualifying:	7th	1952 German GP (Pietsch)

VERITAS GRAND PRIX DRIVERS

Driver	Nat	Starts (DNS/DNQ)	1st	2nd	3rd	4th	5th	6th	PP	FL	Points
Theo Helfrich	D	2	-	-	-	-	-	-	-	-	-
Arthur Legat	B	2	-	-	-	-	-	-	-	-	-
Toni Ulmen	D	2	-	-	-	-	-	-	-	-	-
Erwin Bauer	D	1	-	-	-	-	-	-	-	-	-
Adolf Brudes	D	1	-	-	-	-	-	-	-	-	-
Willi Heeks	D	1	-	-	-	-	-	-	-	-	-
Hans Herrmann	D	1	-	-	-	-	-	-	-	-	-
Peter Hirt	CH	1	-	-	-	-	-	-	-	-	-
Oswald Karch	D	1	-	-	-	-	-	-	-	-	-
Hans Klenk	D	1	-	-	-	-	-	-	-	-	-
Ernst Loof	D	1	-	-	-	-	-	-	-	-	-
Josef Peters	D	1	-	-	-	-	-	-	-	-	-
Paul Pietsch	D	1	-	-	-	-	-	-	-	-	-
Fritz Riess	D	1	-	-	-	-	-	-	-	-	-
Wolfgang Seidel	D	1	-	-	-	-	-	-	-	-	-

VERITAS GRAND PRIX CARS

Type	Year	Engine	Designer
Meteor	1951	Veritas S6, BMW 328 S6	Ernst Loof
RS	1952	Veritas S6, BMW 328 S6	Ernst Loof

Williams

Grand Prix Debut:	1972 British GP	Pescarolo (retired)
Latest Grand Prix:	2002 Japanese GP	Montoya (4th), Schumacher (11th)
Principals:	Frank Williams Racing Cars: Frank Williams, 1969-1974; Walter Wolf and Williams, 1975 until September 1976 when Williams left the company Williams Grand Prix Engineering: Williams and Patrick Head, 1977 to date	
Base:	Frank Williams Racing Cars: Reading, 1969-76 (became Walter Wolf Racing) Williams Grand Prix Engineering: Didcot, 1977-95; Grove, 1995 to date	

WORLD CHAMPIONSHIP RECORD

Starts:	455
Points:	2209.5
Wins:	108 1979 British GP (Regazzoni), German GP (Jones), Austrian GP (Jones), Dutch GP (Jones), Canadian GP (Jones), 1980 Argentinian GP (Jones), Monaco GP (Reutemann), French GP (Jones), British GP (Jones), Canadian GP (Jones), United States GP (Jones), 1981 Long Beach GP (Jones), Brazilian GP (Reutemann), Belgian GP (Reutemann), Las Vegas GP (Jones), 1982 Swiss GP (Rosberg), 1983 Monaco GP (Rosberg), 1984 Dallas GP (Rosberg), 1985 Detroit GP (Rosberg), European GP (Mansell), South African

Formula 1

GP (Mansell), Australian GP (Rosberg), 1986
Brazilian GP (Piquet), Belgian GP (Mansell),
Canadian GP (Mansell), French GP (Mansell), British
GP (Mansell), German GP (Piquet), Hungarian GP
(Piquet), Italian GP (Piquet), Portuguese GP
(Mansell), 1987 San Marino GP (Mansell), French GP
(Mansell), British GP (Mansell), German GP (Piquet),
Hungarian GP (Piquet), Austrian GP (Mansell),
Italian GP (Piquet), Spanish GP (Mansell), Mexican
GP (Mansell), 1989 Canadian GP (Boutsen),
Australian GP (Boutsen), 1990 San Marino GP
(Patrese), Hungarian GP (Boutsen), 1991 Mexican
GP (Patrese), French GP (Mansell), British GP
(Mansell), German GP (Mansell), Italian GP
(Mansell), Portuguese GP (Patrese), Spanish GP
(Mansell), 1992 South African GP (Mansell), Mexican
GP (Mansell), Brazilian GP (Mansell), Spanish GP
(Mansell), San Marino GP (Mansell), French GP
(Mansell), British GP (Mansell), German GP
(Mansell), Portuguese GP (Mansell), Japanese GP
(Riccardo Patrese), 1993 South African GP (Prost),
San Marino GP (Prost), Spanish GP (Prost),
Canadian GP (Prost), French GP (Prost), British GP
(Prost), German GP (Prost), Hungarian GP (Hill),
Belgian GP (Hill), Italian GP (Hill), 1994 Spanish GP
(Hill), British GP (Hill), Belgian GP (Hill), Italian GP
(Hill), Portuguese GP (Hill), Japanese GP (Hill),
Australian GP (Mansell), 1995 Argentinian GP (Hill),
San Marino GP (Hill), Hungarian GP (Hill),
Portuguese GP (Coulthard), Australian GP (Hill),
1996 Australian GP (Hill), Brazilian GP (Hill),
Argentinian GP (Hill), European GP (Villeneuve), San
Marino GP (Hill), Canadian GP (Hill), French GP
(Hill), British GP (Villeneuve), German GP (Hill),
Hungarian GP (Villeneuve), Portuguese GP
(Villeneuve), Japanese GP (Hill), 1997 Brazilian GP
(Villeneuve), Argentinian GP (Villeneuve), San Marino
GP (Frentzen), Spanish GP (Villeneuve), British GP
(Villeneuve), Hungarian GP (Villeneuve), Austrian GP
(Villeneuve), Luxembourg GP (Villeneuve), 2001 San
Marino GP (Schumacher), Canadian GP
(Schumacher), German GP (Schumacher), Italian GP
(Montoya), 2002 Malaysian GP (Schumacher)

Pole positions: 119 1979 British GP (Jones), Canadian GP (Jones),
United States GP (Jones), 1980 Argentinian GP
(Jones), Belgian GP (Jones), German GP (Jones),
1981 Belgian GP (Reutemann), Las Vegas GP
(Reutemann), 1982 British GP (Rosberg), 1983
Brazilian GP (Rosberg), 1985 French GP (Rosberg),
British GP (Rosberg), South African GP (Mansell),
1986 Belgian GP (Piquet), Canadian GP (Mansell),
British GP (Piquet), Australian GP (Mansell), 1987
Brazilian GP (Mansell), Belgian GP (Mansell),
Monaco GP (Mansell), Detroit GP (Mansell), French
GP (Mansell), British GP (Piquet), German GP
(Mansell), Hungarian GP (Mansell), Austrian GP
(Piquet), Italian GP (Piquet), Spanish GP (Piquet),
Mexican GP (Mansell), 1989 Hungarian GP (Patrese),
1990 Hungarian GP (Boutsen), 1991 Canadian GP
(Patrese), Mexican GP (Patrese), French GP
(Patrese), British GP (Mansell), German GP
(Mansell), Portuguese GP (Patrese), 1992 South
African GP (Mansell), Mexican GP (Mansell),
Brazilian GP (Mansell), Spanish GP (Mansell), San
Marino GP (Mansell), Monaco GP (Mansell), French
GP (Mansell), British GP (Mansell), German GP
(Mansell), Hungarian GP (Patrese), Belgian GP
(Mansell), Italian GP (Mansell), Portuguese GP
(Mansell), Japanese GP (Mansell), Australian GP
(Mansell), 1993 South African GP (Prost), Brazilian
GP (Prost), European GP (Prost), San Marino GP
(Prost), Spanish GP (Prost), Monaco GP (Prost),

Canadian GP (Prost), French GP (Hill), British GP
(Prost), German GP (Prost), Hungarian GP (Prost),
Belgian GP (Prost), Italian GP (Prost), Portuguese
GP (Hill), Japanese GP (Prost), 1994 Brazilian GP
(Senna), Pacific GP (Senna), San Marino GP (Senna),
French GP (Hill), British GP (Hill), Australian GP
(Mansell), 1995 Brazilian GP (Hill), Argentinian GP
(Coulthard), Monaco GP (Hill), French GP (Hill),
British GP (Hill), German GP (Hill), Hungarian GP
(Hill), Italian GP (Coulthard), Portuguese GP
(Coulthard), European GP (Coulthard), Pacific GP
(Coulthard), Australian GP (Hill), 1996 Australian GP
(Villeneuve), Brazilian GP (Hill), Argentinian GP (Hill),
European GP (Hill), Spanish GP (Hill), Canadian GP
(Hill), British GP (Hill), German GP (Hill), Belgian GP
(Villeneuve), Italian GP (Hill), Portuguese GP (Hill),
Japanese GP (Villeneuve), 1997 Australian GP
(Villeneuve), Brazilian GP (Villeneuve), Argentinian
GP (Villeneuve), San Marino GP (Villeneuve), Monaco
GP (Frentzen), Spanish GP (Villeneuve), British GP
(Villeneuve), Belgian GP (Villeneuve), Austrian GP
(Villeneuve), Japanese GP (Villeneuve), European GP
(Villeneuve), 2001 French GP (Schumacher), German
GP (Montoya), Belgian GP (Montoya), Italian GP
(Montoya), 2002 Brazilian GP (Montoya), Monaco GP
(Montoya), Canadian GP (Montoya), European GP
(Montoya), British GP (Montoya), French GP
(Montoya), Italian GP (Montoya)

Fastest laps: 121 1978 Long Beach GP (Jones), Canadian GP (Jones),
1979 British GP (Regazzoni), Italian GP (Regazzoni),
Canadian GP (Jones), 1980 Argentinian GP (Jones),
French GP (Jones), German GP (Jones), Italian GP
(Jones), United States GP (Jones), 1981 Long Beach
GP (Jones), Belgian GP (Reutemann), Monaco GP
(Jones), Spanish GP (Jones), German GP (Jones),
Dutch GP (Jones), Italian GP (Reutemann), 1985
French GP (Rosberg), Italian GP (Mansell), South
African GP (Rosberg), Australian GP (Rosberg), 1986
Brazilian GP (Piquet), Spanish GP (Mansell), San
Marino GP (Piquet), Canadian GP (Piquet), Detroit
GP (Piquet), French GP (Mansell), British GP
(Mansell), Hungarian GP (Piquet), Portuguese GP
(Mansell), Mexican GP (Piquet), Australian GP
(Piquet), 1987 Brazilian GP (Piquet), French GP
(Piquet), British GP (Mansell), German GP (Mansell),
Hungarian GP (Piquet), Austrian GP (Mansell),
Mexican GP (Piquet), 1988 British GP (Mansell), 1989
Brazilian GP (Patrese), 1990 German GP (Boutsen),
Hungarian GP (Patrese), Portuguese GP (Patrese),
Spanish GP (Patrese), Japanese GP (Patrese), 1991
Brazilian GP (Mansell), Canadian GP (Mansell),
Mexican GP (Mansell), French GP (Mansell), British
GP (Mansell), German GP (Patrese), Portuguese GP
(Patrese), Spanish GP (Patrese), 1992 South African
GP (Mansell), Brazilian GP (Patrese), Spanish GP
(Mansell), San Marino GP (Patrese), Monaco GP
(Mansell), French GP (Mansell), British GP (Mansell),
German GP (Patrese), Hungarian GP (Mansell),
Italian GP (Mansell), Japanese GP (Mansell), 1993
South African GP (Prost), San Marino GP (Prost),
Monaco GP (Prost), British GP (Hill), Hungarian GP
(Prost), Belgian GP (Prost), Italian GP (Hill),
Portuguese GP (Coulthard), Japanese GP (Prost),
Australian GP (Hill), 1994 San Marino GP (Hill),
French GP (Hill), British GP (Hill), German GP
(Coulthard), Belgian GP (Hill), Italian GP (Hill),
Portuguese GP (Coulthard), Japanese GP (Hill), 1995
Spanish GP (Hill), British GP (Hill), Hungarian GP
(Hill), Belgian GP (Coulthard), Portuguese GP
(Coulthard), Australian GP (Hill), 1996 Australian GP
(Villeneuve), Brazilian GP (Hill), European GP (Hill),
San Marino GP (Hill), Canadian GP (Villeneuve),

French GP (Villeneuve), British GP (Villeneuve), German GP (Hill), Hungarian GP (Hill), Portuguese GP (Villeneuve), Japanese GP (Villeneuve), 1997 Australian GP (Frentzen), Brazilian GP (Villeneuve), San Marino GP (Frentzen), Hungarian GP (Frentzen), Belgian GP (Villeneuve), Austrian GP (Villeneuve), Luxembourg GP (Frentzen), Japanese GP (Frentzen), European GP (Frentzen), 1999 Italian GP (Schumacher), 2001 Brazilian GP (Schumacher), San Marino GP (Schumacher), Canadian GP (Schumacher), European GP (Juan Montoya), German GP (Juan Montoya), Italian GP (Schumacher), United States GP (Montoya), Japanese GP (Schumacher), 2002 Malaysian GP (Montoya), Brazilian GP (Montoya), Canadian GP (Montoya)

Laps/miles in the lead: 7138 laps/20672 miles
World Champions:
Drivers: Seven times - 1980 (Jones), 1982 (Rosberg), 1987 (Piquet), 1992 (Mansell), 1993 (Prost), 1996 (Hill) 1997 (Villeneuve)
Constructors: Nine times - 1980, 1981, 1986, 1987, 1992, 1993, 1994, 1996 and 1997

MAJOR SPONSORS

1972	Politoys, Motul
1973-74	Iso, Marlboro
1975	Ambrozium H7, Lavazza
1976	Walter Wolf, Mapfre
1978	Saudia Airlines
1979	Saudia Airlines, Albilad, TAG
1980-81	Saudia Airlines, Leyland, TAG
1982-83	Saudia Airlines, TAG
1984	Saudia Airlines, Denim, Mobil
1985-87	Canon, ICI, Denim
1988-90	Canon, ICI, Barclay
1991-92	Canon, Labatt's, Camel
1993	Canon, Sega, Camel
1994-97	Rothmans
1998-99	Winfield
2000-July 2002	Compaq, Castrol, Allianz
July 2002 to date	Hewlett Packard, Castrol, Allianz

WILLIAMS GRAND PRIX DRIVERS

Driver	Nat	Starts (DNS/DNQ)	1st	2nd	3rd	4th	5th	6th	PP	FL	Points
Nigel Mansell	GB	95 (2)	28	12	3	2	5	5	28	22	369
Damon Hill	GB	65	21	14	5	3	1	1	20	19	326
Jacques Villeneuve	CDN	49	11	5	5	3	4	3	13	9	180
Alan Jones	AUS	60	11	7	4	4	1	-	6	13	171
Nelson Piquet	BR	31 (1)	7	10	4	2	-	6	11	145
Alain Prost	F	16	7	3	2	1	-	-	13	6	99
Keke Rosberg	SF	62	5	7	3	7	6	1	4	3	131.5
Riccardo Patrese	I	81	4	12	8	5	9	5	6	11	180
Ralf Schumacher	D	67	4	3	10	11	9	1	1	6	150
Carlos Reutemann	RA	31	3	7	6	2	2	1	2	2	104
Thierry Boutsen	B	32	3	1	4	4	4	2	1	1	71
Juan Pablo Montoya	CO	34	1	7	3	5	1	-	10	6	81
David Coulthard	GB	25	1	5	3	2	2	1	5	4	63
Heinz-Harald Frentzen	D	33	1	2	5	2	5	1	1	6	59
Clay Regazzoni	CH	15	1	2	2	-	1	1	-	2	32
Jacques Laffite	F	44 (4)	-	1	-	3	2	3	-	-	22
Jenson Button	GB	17	-	-	-	1	4	1	-	-	12
Derek Daly	IRL	12	-	-	-	-	3	2	-	-	8
Arturo Merzario	I	25 (3)	-	-	-	1	-	1	-	-	4
Howden Ganley	NZ	14 (1)	-	-	-	-	-	1	-	-	1
Gijs van Lennep	NL	4 (1)	-	-	-	-	-	1	-	-	1
Alessandro Zanardi	I	16	-	-	-	-	-	-	-	-	-
Michel Leclere	F	6 (1)	-	-	-	-	-	-	-	-	-
Jacky Ickx	B	5 (4)	-	-	-	-	-	-	-	-	-

Driver	Nat	Start	1st	2nd	3rd	4th	5th	6th	PP	FL	Points
Nanni Galli	I	5	-	-	-	-	-	-	-	-	-
Rupert Keegan	GB	4 (3)	-	-	-	-	-	-	-	-	-
Ayrton Senna	BR	3	-	-	-	-	-	3	-	-	-
Henri Pescarolo	F	3	-	-	-	-	-	-	-	-	-
Tom Belso	DK	2 (3)	-	-	-	-	-	-	-	-	-
Ian Scheckter	ZA	2	-	-	-	-	-	-	-	-	-
Renzo Zorzi	I	2	-	-	-	-	-	-	-	-	-
Damien Magee	GB	1	-	-	-	-	-	-	-	-	-
Graham McRae	NZ	1	-	-	-	-	-	-	-	-	-
Hans Binder	A	1	-	-	-	-	-	-	-	-	-
Jackie Pretorius	ZA	1	-	-	-	-	-	-	-	-	-
Jean-Louis Schlesser	F	1	-	-	-	-	-	-	-	-	-
Jonathan Palmer	GB	1	-	-	-	-	-	-	-	-	-
Joseph Vonlanthen	CH	1	-	-	-	-	-	-	-	-	-
Mario Andretti	USA	1	-	-	-	-	-	-	-	-	-
Martin Brundle	GB	1	-	-	-	-	-	-	-	-	-
Tim Schenken	AUS	1	-	-	-	-	-	-	-	-	-
Tony Brise	GB	1	-	-	-	-	-	-	-	-	-
Warwick Brown	AUS	1	-	-	-	-	-	-	-	-	-
Loris Kessel	CH	- (2)	-	-	-	-	-	-	-	-	-
Chris Amon	NZ	- (1)	-	-	-	-	-	-	-	-	-
Desire Wilson	ZA	- (1)	-	-	-	-	-	-	-	-	-
Emilio Zapico	E	- (1)	-	-	-	-	-	-	-	-	-
Emilio de Villota	E	- (1)	-	-	-	-	-	-	-	-	-
Francois Migault	F	- (1)	-	-	-	-	-	-	-	-	-
Geoff Lees	GB	- (1)	-	-	-	-	-	-	-	-	-
Ian Ashley	GB	- (1)	-	-	-	-	-	-	-	-	-
Jean-Pierre Jabouille	F	- (1)	-	-	-	-	-	-	-	-	-
Kevin Cogan	USA	- (1)	-	-	-	-	-	-	-	-	-
Lella Lombardi	I	- (1)	-	-	-	-	-	-	-	-	-
Masami Kuwashima	J	- (1)	-	-	-	-	-	-	-	-	-
Richard Robarts	GB	- (1)	-	-	-	-	-	-	-	-	-

WILLIAMS GRAND PRIX CARS

Type	Year	Engine	Designer
FX3*	1972	Ford DFV V8	Len Bailey
FX3B*	1973	Ford DFV V8	Len Bailey
IR01**	1973	Ford DFV V8	John Clarke
Renamed FW01			
IR02**	1973	Ford DFV V8	John Clarke
Renamed FW02			
IR03**	1973	Ford DFV V8	John Clarke
Renamed FW03			
FW01	1974	Ford DFV V8	John Clarke
FW02	1974	Ford DFV V8	John Clarke
FW03	1974	Ford DFV V8	John Clarke
Sold and renamed Apollon-Ford in 1977			
FW04	1975	Ford DFV V8	Ray Stokoe
Sold and renamed McGuire BM1-Ford in 1977			
FW05	1976	Ford DFV V8	Harvey Postlethwaite
Formerly Hesketh 308C			
FW06	1978	Ford DFV V8	Patrick Head
FW07	1979	Ford DFV V8	Patrick Head
FW07B	1980	Ford DFV V8	Patrick Head
FW07C	1981	Ford DFV V8	Patrick Head/Frank Dernie
FW08	1982	Ford DFV V8	Patrick Head/Frank Dernie
FW08C	1983	Ford DFV V8	Patrick Head/Frank Dernie
FW09	1983	Honda RA163E V6 tc	Patrick Head/Frank Dernie
FW09B	1984	Honda RA163E V6 tc	Patrick Head/Frank Dernie
FW10	1985	Honda RA163E V6 tc	Patrick Head/Frank Dernie
FW11	1986	Honda RA166E V6 tc	Patrick Head/Frank Dernie
FW11B	1987	Honda RA167E V6 tc	Patrick Head/Frank Dernie
FW12	1988	Judd CV V8	Patrick Head/Frank Dernie
FW12C	1989	Renault RS01 V10	Patrick Head/ Enrique Scalabroni
FW13	1989	Renault RS01 V10	Patrick Head/ Enrique Scalabroni
FW13B	1990	Renault RS02 V10	Patrick Head/ Enrique Scalabroni

Type	Year	Engine	Designer
FW14	1991	Renault RS03 V10	Patrick Head/Adrian Newey
FW14B	1992	Renault RS03 V10	Patrick Head/Adrian Newey
FW15C	1993	Renault RS05 V10	Patrick Head/Adrian Newey
FW16	1994	Renault RS06 V10	Patrick Head/Adrian Newey
FW16B	1994	Renault RS06 V10	Patrick Head/Adrian Newey
FW17	1995	Renault RS07 V10	Patrick Head/Adrian Newey
FW17B	1995	Renault RS07 V10	Patrick Head/Adrian Newey
FW18	1996	Renault RS08 V10	Patrick Head/Adrian Newey
FW19	1997	Renault RS09 V10	Patrick Head
FW20	1998	Mecachrome GC37/01 V10	Patrick Head
FW21	1999	Mecachrome FB01 V10	Patrick Head
FW22	2000	BMW E41 V10	Patrick Head
FW23	2001	BMW E41 V10	Patrick Head
FW24	2002	BMW P82 V10	Patrick Head/Gavin Fisher/ Geoff Willis

*officially known as Politoys. **officially known as Iso-Marlboro

Wolf

Team sold to Fittipaldi in 1980; also see Fittipaldi

Grand Prix Debut: 1977 Argentinian GP   Scheckter (1st)
Last Grand Prix: 1979 United States GP   Rosberg (retired)
Principal: Walter Wolf
Base: Reading

WORLD CHAMPIONSHIP RECORD

Starts:	47	
Points:	79	
Wins:	3	1977 Argentinian GP (Scheckter), Monaco GP (Scheckter), Canadian GP (Scheckter)
Pole positions:	1	1977 German GP (Scheckter)
Fastest laps:	2	1977 Monaco GP (Scheckter), Japanese GP (Scheckter)
Laps/miles in the lead:	213 laps/504 miles	

Best World Championship position:
Drivers: 2nd in 1977 (Scheckter)
Constructors: 4th in 1977

MAJOR SPONSORS

1977-78	Castrol
1979	Olympus

WOLF GRAND PRIX DRIVERS

Driver	Nat	Starts (DNS/DNQ)	1st	2nd	3rd	4th	5th	6th	PP	FL	Points
Jody Scheckter	ZA	33	3	4	6	1	-	1	1	2	79
Keke Rosberg	SF	10 (2)	-	-	-	-	-	-	-	-	-
James Hunt	GB	7	-	-	-	-	-	-	-	-	-
Bobby Rahal	USA	2	-	-	-	-	-	-	-	-	-

1950 Giuseppe Farina is congratulated after winning the very first World Championship Grand Prix.

WOLF GRAND PRIX CARS

Type	Year	Engine	Designer
WR1-WR4	1977	Ford DFV V8	Harvey Postlethwaite
WR5, WR6	1978	Ford DFV V8	Harvey Postlethwaite
WR7-WR9	1979	Ford DFV V8	Harvey Postlethwaite
Renamed Fittipaldi F7 when team was sold			

Zakspeed

Grand Prix Debut:	1985 Portuguese GP	Palmer (retired)
Last Grand Prix:	1989 Japanese GP	Schneider (retired)
Principal:	Erich Zakowski	
Base:	Niederzissen	

WORLD CHAMPIONSHIP RECORD

Starts:	53	
Points:	2	
Best result:	5th	1987 San Marino GP (Brundle)
Best qualifying:	13th	1987 Mexican GP (Brundle)

Best World Championship position:

Drivers:	18th in 1987 (Brundle)
Constructors:	10th in 1987

MAJOR SPONSORS

1985-89	West

ZAKSPEED GRAND PRIX DRIVERS

Driver	Nat	Starts (DNS/DNQ)	1st	2nd	3rd	4th	5th	6th	PP	FL	Points
Martin Brundle	GB	16	-	-	-	-	1	-	-	-	2
Jonathan Palmer	GB	23 (1)	-	-	-	-	-	-	-	-	-
Christian Danner	D	17 (1)	-	-	-	-	-	-	-	-	-
Huub Rothengatter	NL	11 (3)	-	-	-	-	-	-	-	-	-
Bernd Schneider	D	8 (24)	-	-	-	-	-	-	-	-	-
Piercarlo Ghinzani	I	8 (8)	-	-	-	-	-	-	-	-	-
Aguri Suzuki	J	- (16)	-	-	-	-	-	-	-	-	-

ZAKSPEED GRAND PRIX CARS

Type	Year	Engine	Designer
841	1985	Zakspeed S4 tc	Paul Brown
861	1986	Zakspeed S4 tc	Paul Brown
871	1987	Zakspeed S4 tc	Chris Murphy/Heinz Zollinir
881	1988	Zakspeed S4 tc	Chris Murphy/Heinz Zollinir
891	1989	Yamaha OX88 V8	Gustav Brunner/Nino Frisson/ Peter Wyss

2002 Michael Schumacher celebrates victory in the latest race covered in this edition.

Records

AVERAGE AGE OF GRAND PRIX FIELD

1950	40 years 256 days	1968	31 years 141 days	1986	31 years 148 days
1951	39 years 350 days	1969	31 years 160 days	1987	30 years 209 days
1952	36 years 312 days	1970	30 years 338 days	1988	30 years 256 days
1953	36 years 167 days	1971	31 years 128 days	1989	30 years 341 days
1954	34 years 297 days	1972	31 years 1 day	1990	30 years 277 days
1955	35 years 22 days	1973	31 years 170 days	1991	30 years 178 days
1956	34 years 233 days	1974	30 years 346 days	1992	30 years 59 days
1957	32 years 323 days	1975	30 years 168 days	1993	30 years 290 days
1958	32 years 11 days	1976	30 years 287 days	1994	29 years 149 days
1959	31 years 217 days	1977	31 years 24 days	1995	29 years 207 days
1960	31 years 159 days	1978	31 years 131 days	1996	29 years 81 days
1961	30 years 243 days	1979	31 years 37 days	1997	28 years 197 days
1962	30 years 199 days	1980	30 years 351 days	1998	28 years 145 days
1963	30 years 216 days	1981	30 years 97 days	1999	29 years 178 days
1964	31 years 92 days	1982	30 years 2 days	2000	28 years 296 days
1965	30 years 349 days	1983	30 years 78 days	2001	28 years 99 days
1966	32 years 79 days	1984	30 years 76 days	2002	28 years 344 days
1967	31 years 225 days	1985	30 years 215 days		

GRAND PRIX STARTS

Riccardo Patrese	256	Ronnie Peterson	123	Maurice Trintignant	82
Gerhard Berger	210	Pierluigi Martini	118	Marc Surer	81
Andrea de Cesaris	208	Jacky Ickx	116	Stefan Johansson	79
Nelson Piquet	204	Alan Jones	116	Piercarlo Ghinzani	76
Jean Alesi	201	Jacques Villeneuve	116	Alessandro Nannini	76
Alain Prost	199	Damon Hill	115	Vittorio Brambilla	74
Michele Alboreto	194	Keke Rosberg	114	Mauricio Gugelmin	74
Nigel Mansell	187	Patrick Tambay	114	Satoru Nakajima	74
Michael Schumacher	178	Denny Hulme	112	Hans-Joachim Stuck	74
Graham Hill	176	Jody Scheckter	112	Jim Clark	72
Jacques Laffite	176	John Surtees	111	Carlos Pace	72
Niki Lauda	171	Mika Salo	110	Stefano Modena	70
Thierry Boutsen	163	Philippe Alliot	109	Didier Pironi	70
Rubens Barrichello	162	Elio de Angelis	108	Bruno Giacomelli	69
Johnny Herbert	162	Giancarlo Fisichella	107	Gianni Morbidelli	67
Mika Hakkinen	161	Jochen Mass	105	Gilles Villeneuve	67
Ayrton Senna	161	Jo Bonnier	104	Stirling Moss	66
Martin Brundle	158	Bruce McLaren	100	Teo Fabi	64
John Watson	152	Ralf Schumacher	100	Aguri Suzuki	64
Rene Arnoux	149	Jackie Stewart	99	Pedro de la Rosa	63
Eddie Irvine	146	Pedro Diniz	98	JJ Lehto	62
Carlos Reutemann	146	Chris Amon	96	Mark Blundell	61
Derek Warwick	146	Jo Siffert	96	Jochen Rindt	60
Emerson Fittipaldi	144	Patrick Depailler	95	Erik Comas	59
David Coulthard	141	Ukyo Katayama	95	Arturo Merzario	57
Heinz-Harald Frentzen	141	Jarno Trulli	95	Henri Pescarolo	57
Jean-Pierre Jarier	133	Ivan Capelli	93	Alex Caffi	56
Eddie Cheever	132	James Hunt	92	Harry Schell	56
Clay Regazzoni	132	Jos Verstappen	91	Pedro Rodriguez	55
Mario Andretti	128	Jean-Pierre Beltoise	86	Rolf Stommelen	54
Jack Brabham	126	Dan Gurney	86	Philippe Streiff	53
Olivier Panis	125	Jonathan Palmer	83	Jean Behra	52

Records

GRAND PRIX STARTS (cont.)

Richie Ginther	52	Huub Rothengatter	25	Silvio Moser	12
Alexander Wurz	52	David Brabham	24	Brian Redman	12
Jenson Button	51	Tarso Marques	24	Giorgio Scarlatti	12
Juan Manuel Fangio	51	Luigi Musso	24	Johnny Servoz-Gavin	12
Mike Hailwood	50	Eliseo Salazar	24	Peter Arundell	11
Nick Heidfeld	50	Raul Boesel	23	"Jules" Boullion	11
Innes Ireland	50	Johnny Claes	23	Ronnie Bucknum	11
Jackie Oliver	50	Yannick Dalmas	23	Dave Charlton	11
Luca Badoer	49	Jan Lammers	23	George Eaton	11
Derek Daly	49	Emanuel de Graffenried	22	Guy Edwards	11
Jean-Pierre Jabouille	49	Reine Wisell	22	Pascal Fabre	11
Nicola Larini	49	Giancarlo Baghetti	21	Paul Frere	11
Phil Hill	48	Roberto Guerrero	21	Jim Hall	11
Francois Cevert	47	Gaston Mazzacane	21	Karl Kling	11
Bertrand Gachot	47	Stefan Bellof	20	Onofre Marimon	11
Roy Salvadori	47	Andrea Montermini	20	Larry Perkins	11
Manfred Winkelhock	47	"B Bira"	19	Andre Simon	11
Eric Bernard	45	Harald Ertl	19	Dave Walker	11
Mike Hawthorn	45	Brian Henton	19	Slim Borgudd	10
Lorenzo Bandini	42	Francois Hesnault	19	Tony Brise	10
Roberto Moreno	42	Johnny Cecotto	18	Bob Evans	10
Tom Pryce	42	Hans Herrmann	18	Chris Irwin	10
Olivier Grouillard	41	Taki Inoue	18	Umberto Maglioli	10
Hector Rebaque	41	Ian Scheckter	18	Carlos Menditeguy	10
Karl Wendlinger	41	Chico Serra	18	Patrick Neve	10
Alessandro Zanardi	41	Piero Taruffi	18	Rikky von Opel	10
Christian Fittipaldi	40	Fernando Alonso	17	Alex Ribeiro	10
Tony Brooks	38	Richard Attwood	17	Ludovico Scarfiotti	10
Masten Gregory	38	Lucien Bianchi	17	Wolfgang Seidel	10
Louis Rosier	38	Adrian Campos	17	Peter Whitehead	10
Gabriele Tarquini	38	Nanni Galli	17	Ricardo Zunino	10
Emanuele Pirro	37	Roberto Mieres	17	Paolo Barilla	9
Mauro Baldi	36	Takuma Sato	17	Derek Bell	9
Christian Danner	36	Cliff Allison	16	Olivier Beretta	9
Mike Spence	36	Ian Burgess	16	Allen Berg	9
Wilson Fittipaldi	35	Felipe Massa	16	Bob Bondurant	9
Howden Ganley	35	Allan McNish	16	Jean-Marc Gounon	9
Brett Lunger	34	Esteban Tuero	16	Jackie Lewis	9
Juan Pablo Montoya	34	Mark Webber	16	John Love	9
Kimi Raikkonen	34	Felice Bonetto	15	Helmut Marko	9
Tim Schenken	34	Luciano Burti	15	Andre Pilette	9
Giuseppe Farina	33	Louis Chiron	15	Bernd Schneider	9
Marc Gene	33	Johnny Dumfries	15	Vern Schuppan	9
Shinji Nakano	33	Danny Sullivan	15	Siegfried Stohr	9
Peter Collins	32	Ken Wharton	15	Fabrizio Barbazza	8
Pedro Lamy	32	Eugenio Castellotti	14	Alan Brown	8
Toranosuke Takagi	32	Mark Donohue	14	Frank Gardner	8
Alberto Ascari	31	Olivier Gendebien	14	Jo Gartner	8
Gunnar Nilsson	31	Horace Gould	14	Bob Gerard	8
Luigi Villoresi	31	Stuart Lewis-Evans	14	Bruce Halford	8
Ricardo Zonta	31	Alex Yoong	14	Gijs van Lennep	8
Andrea de Adamich	30	Michael Andretti	13	Carroll Shelby	8
Peter Gethin	30	Hans Binder	13	Moises Solana	8
Peter Revson	30	Martin Donnelly	13	Henry Taylor	8
Carel Godin de Beaufort	28	Vic Elford	13	Julian Bailey	7
Enrique Bernoldi	28	Ron Flockhart	13	Elie Bayol	7
Mike Beuttler	28	Yves Giraud-Cabantous	13	Paul Belmondo	7
Piers Courage	28	Chico Godia-Sales	13	Luigi Fagioli	7
Robert Manzon	28	Lance Macklin	13	Rudolf Fischer	7
Ricardo Rosset	27	Francois Migault	13	Gregor Foitek	7
Trevor Taylor	27	Philippe Etancelin	12	David Hobbs	7
Wolfgang von Trips	27	Corrado Fabi	12	Oscar Larrauri	7
Jose Froilan Gonzalez	26	Jack Fairman	12	Giovanni Lavaggi	7
Luis Perez Sala	26	George Follmer	12	Michel Leclere	7
Bob Anderson	25	Guy Ligier	12	Pete Lovely	7
Rupert Keegan	25	Lella Lombardi	12	Sergio Mantovani	7
Tony Maggs	25	Willy Mairesse	12	Kenneth McAlpine	7
Jan Magnussen	25	John Miles	12	Brian Naylor	7

Formula 1

GRAND PRIX STARTS (cont.)

Miguel Angel Guerra	1	Dave Morgan	1	Heinz Schiller	1
Mike Harris	1	Massimo Natili	1	Jean-Louis Schlesser	1
Brian Hart	1	Tiff Needell	1	Rudolf Schoeller	1
Masahiro Hasemi	1	John Nicholson	1	Rob Schroeder	1
Hans Heyer	1	Helmut Niedermayr	1	Adolfo Schwelm Cruz	1
Gus Hutchison	1	Brausch Niemann	1	Archie Scott-Brown	1
Jesus Iglesias	1	Rodney Nuckey	1	Piero Scotti	1
John James	1	Robert O'Brien	1	Dorino Serafini	1
Leslie Johnson	1	Arthur Owen	1	Tony Shelly	1
Bruce Johnstone	1	Nello Pagani	1	Mike Sparken	1
Oswald Karch	1	Torsten Palm	1	Gaetano Starrabba	1
Leo Kinnunen	1	Xavier Perrot	1	Ian Stewart	1
Hans Klenk	1	Josef Peters	1	Jimmy Stewart	1
Alberto Rodriguez Larreta	1	Francois Picard	1	Kunimitsu Takahashi	1
Gerard Larrousse	1	Teddy Pilette	1	Mike Taylor	1
Neville Lederle	1	Renato Pirocchi	1	Alfonso Thiele	1
Lamberto Leoni	1	Ben Pon	1	Eric Thompson	1
Roberto Lippi	1	Charles Pozzi	1	Leslie Thorne	1
Dries van der Lof	1	Dieter Quester	1	Desmond Titterington	1
Ernst Loof	1	Pierre-Henri Raphanel	1	Guy Tunmer	1
Roger Loyer	1	Roland Ratzenberger	1	Bobby Unser	1
Jean Lucas	1	Lance Reventlow	1	Joseph Vonlanthen	1
Mike MacDowel	1	John Rhodes	1	Heini Walter	1
Herbert MacKay-Fraser	1	Fritz Riess	1	Peter Westbury	1
Damien Magee	1	John Riseley-Prichard	1	Graham Whitehead	1
Jean Max	1	Bertil Roos	1	Bill Whitehouse	1
Timmy Mayer	1	Lloyd Ruby	1	Robin Widdows	1
Francois Mazet	1	Troy Ruttman	1	Jonathan Williams	1
Graham McRae	1	Peter Ryan	1	Vic Wilson	1
Andre Milhoux	1	Bob Said	1		
Robin Montgomerie-Charrington	1	Stephane Sarrazin	1		
		Albert Scherrer	1		

YOUNGEST DRIVERS TO START A GRAND PRIX

19 years 182 days	Mike Thackwell	Retired	1980 Canadian GP	20 years 52 days	Jenson Button	Retired	2000 Australian GP
19 years 208 days	Ricardo Rodriguez	Retired	1961 Italian GP	20 years 52 days	Eddie Cheever	Retired	1978 South African GP
19 years 217 days	Fernando Alonso	12th	2001 Australian GP	20 years 72 days	Tarso Marques	Retired	1996 Brazilian GP
19 years 320 days	Esteban Tuero	Retired	1998 Australian GP	20 years 194 days	Peter Collins	Retired	1952 Swiss GP
19 years 324 days	Chris Amon	Retired	1963 Belgian GP	20 years 295 days	Rubens Barrichello	Retired	1993 South African GP

OLDEST DRIVERS TO START A GRAND PRIX

55 years 337 days	Heitel Cantoni	11th	1952 Italian GP	52 years 292 days	Adolf Brudes	Retired	1952 German GP
55 years 292 days	Louis Chiron	6th	1955 Monaco GP	52 years 260 days	Hans Stuck	14th	1953 Italian GP
55 years 190 days	Philippe Etancelin	8th	1952 French GP	52 years 127 days	Bill Aston	Retired	1952 German GP
54 years 232 days	Arthur Legat	Retired	1953 Belgian GP	52 years 15 days	Clemente Biondetti	Retired	1950 Italian GP
53 years 21 days	Luigi Fagioli	1st	1951 French GP	50 years 273 days	Louis Rosier	5th	1956 German GP

Formula 1

DID NOT START

Drivers with the greatest number of occasions on which they appeared during a F1 weekend but did not start the Grand Prix, whether it is because they failed to qualify, suffered a mechanical failure or another reason.

Gabriele Tarquini	40	Andrea Chiesa	7	Rubens Barrichello	3
Bertrand Gachot	37	Teo Fabi	7	Carel Godin de Beaufort	3
Piercarlo Ghinzani	35	Damon Hill	7	Tom Belso	3
Roberto Moreno	34	Jean-Pierre Jabouille	7	Gianfranco Brancatelli	3
Arturo Merzario	29	David Kennedy	7	Tommy Byrne	3
Yannick Dalmas	27	Geoff Lees	7	Dave Charlton	3
Nicola Larini	26	Clay Regazzoni	7	Louis Chiron	3
Bernd Schneider	25	Ricardo Rosset	7	Peter Collins	3
Stefan Johansson	24	Hans-Joachim Stuck	7	Alberto Colombo	3
Eric van de Poele	24	Marc Surer	7	Chuck Daigh	3
Aguri Suzuki	24	Joachim Winkelhock	7	Pascal Fabre	3
Michele Alboreto	21	Andrea de Adamich	6	Christian Fittipaldi	3
Alex Caffi	21	Paolo Barilla	6	Wilson Fittipaldi	3
Olivier Grouillard	21	David Brabham	6	Patrick Gaillard	3
Paul Belmondo	20	Andrea de Cesaris	6	Divina Galica	3
Brian Henton	18	Corrado Fabi	6	Nanni Galli	3
Jan Lammers	18	Howden Ganley	6	Horace Gould	3
Hector Rebaque	17	Mauricio Gugelmin	6	Miguel Angel Guerra	3
Pierre-Henri Raphanel	16	Jacky Ickx	6	Johnny Herbert	3
Derek Warwick	16	Niki Lauda	6	Graham Hill	3
Rene Arnoux	15	Pierluigi Martini	6	Ingo Hoffmann	3
Derek Daly	15	Satoru Nakajima	6	Innes Ireland	3
Gregor Foitek	15	Ricardo Paletti	6	Giovanni Lavaggi	3
Chico Serra	15	Luis Perez Sala	6	Francois Migault	3
Pedro Chaves	14	Tony Trimmer	6	John Miles	3
Beppe Gabbiani	14	Mauro Baldi	5	Gianni Morbidelli	3
Bruno Giacomelli	14	Slim Borgudd	5	Patrick Neve	3
Claudio Langes	14	Vittorio Brambilla	5	Teddy Pilette	3
Oscar Larrauri	14	Ivan Capelli	5	Luigi Piotti	3
Keke Rosberg	14	Johnny Cecotto	5	Nelson Piquet	3
Julian Bailey	13	Guy Edwards	5	Emanuele Pirro	3
Eliseo Salazar	13	Emerson Fittipaldi	5	Alain Prost	3
Emilio de Villota	13	Masten Gregory	5	Lance Reventlow	3
Chris Amon	12	Leo Kinnunen	5	Roy Salvadori	3
Fabrizio Barbazza	12	Lella Lombardi	5	Giorgio Scarlatti	3
Rupert Keegan	12	Jonathan Palmer	5	Mike Thackwell	3
Eddie Cheever	11	Andre Pilette	5	Jacques Villeneuve sr	3
Christian Danner	11	Huub Rothengatter	5	Luigi Villoresi	3
Stefano Modena	11	Mike Wilds	5	Roelof Wunderink	3
Jean-Pierre Jarier	10	Bob Anderson	4	Alessandro Zanardi	3
Perry McCarthy	10	Conny Andersson	4	Cliff Allison	2
Alex Ribeiro	10	Michael Bartels	4	Peter Arundell	2
Patrick Tambay	10	Michael Bleekemolen	4	Bill Aston	2
Volker Weidler	10	Jo Bonnier	4	Stefan Bellof	2
Harald Ertl	9	Ian Burgess	4	Jean-Pierre Beltoise	2
Brett Lunger	9	Adrian Campos	4	Eric Bernard	2
Jochen Mass	9	Erik Comas	4	Enrique Bernoldi	2
Andrea Montermini	9	Heinz-Harald Frentzen	4	Lucien Bianchi	2
Rolf Stommelen	9	Mika Hakkinen	4	Hans Binder	2
Manfred Winkelhock	9	Boy Hayje	4	Mark Blundell	2
Luca Badoer	8	Loris Kessel	4	Felice Bonetto	2
Enrico Bertaggia	8	Jacques Laffite	4	Gary Brabham	2
Roberto Guerrero	8	Lamberto Leoni	4	Jack Brabham	2
JJ Lehto	8	Pete Lovely	4	Tino Brambilla	2
Silvio Moser	8	Nigel Mansell	4	Jay Chamberlain	2
Henri Pescarolo	8	Bruce McLaren	4	Johnny Claes	2
Kenneth Acheson	7	Rikky von Opel	4	Kevin Cogan	2
Philippe Alliot	7	Larry Perkins	4	Bernard Collomb	2
Ian Ashley	7	David Purley	4	Piers Courage	2
Derek Bell	7	Ian Raby	4	Jose Dolhem	2
Raul Boesel	7	Brian Redman	4	Martin Donnelly	2
Martin Brundle	7	Vern Schuppan	4	Mark Donohue	2
		Jo Siffert	4	George Eaton	2
		Alex Soler-Roig	4	Nasif Estefano	2
		Siegfried Stohr	4	Bob Evans	2
		Otto Stuppacher	4	Maria Teresa de Filippis	2
		Alex Yoong	4	Giorgio Francia	2
		Giovanna Amati	3	Hiroshi Fushida	2
		Mario Andretti	3	Richie Ginther	2

DID NOT START (cont.)

Keith Greene	2	Pedro Diniz	1	Gunnar Nilsson	1
Hubert Hahne	2	Frank Dochnal	1	Karl Oppitzhauser	1
Naoki Hattori	2	Paddy Driver	1	Carlos Pace	1
Mike Hawthorn	2	Bernard de Dryver	1	Torsten Palm	1
Hans Herrmann	2	Johnny Dumfries	1	Michael Parkes	1
Francois Hesnault	2	Piero Dusio	1	Reg Parnell	1
Phil Hill	2	Bernie Ecclestone	1	Riccardo Patrese	1
Eddie Irvine	2	Paul Emery	1	Al Pease	1
Ukyo Katayama	2	Carlo Facetti	1	Cesare Perdisa	1
Ken Kavanagh	2	Jack Fairman	1	Alessandro Pesenti-Rossi	1
Mikko Kozarowitsky	2	Giuseppe Farina	1	Alfredo Pian	1
Gijs van Lennep	2	William Ferguson	1	Ernest Pieterse	1
Roberto Lippi	2	Ludwig Fischer	1	David Piper	1
Lance Macklin	2	Rudolf Fischer	1	Jackie Pretorius	1
Tony Maggs	2	Giancarlo Fisichella	1	Ernesto Prinoth	1
Tarso Marques	2	Ron Flockhart	1	Clive Puzey	1
Gerhard Mitter	2	George Follmer	1	Dieter Quester	1
Alessandro Nannini	2	Franco Forini	1	Ken Richardson	1
Jackie Oliver	2	Frank Gardner	1	Giovanni de Riu	1
Danny Ongais	2	Tony Gaze	1	Richard Robarts	1
Tim Parnell	2	Olivier Gendebien	1	Ricardo Rodriguez	1
Didier Pironi	2	Gerino Gerini	1	Alan Rollinson	1
Roland Ratzenberger	2	Peter Gethin	1	Jean-Claude Rudaz	1
Peter Revson	2	"Gimax"	1	"Geki" Russo	1
Jochen Rindt	2	Helmut Glockler	1	Troy Ruttman	1
Ludovico Scarfiotti	2	Chico Godia-Sales	1	Mika Salo	1
Ian Scheckter	2	Emanuel de Graffenried	1	Jody Scheckter	1
Tim Schenken	2	Brian Gubby	1	Jean-Louis Schlesser	1
Wolfgang Seidel	2	Dan Gurney	1	Michael Schumacher	1
Tony Shelly	2	Bruce Halford	1	Gunther Seiffert	1
Vincenzo Sospiri	2	Jim Hall	1	Ayrton Senna	1
John Surtees	2	Nick Heidfeld	1	Doug Serrurier	1
Henry Taylor	2	James Hunt	1	Johnny Servoz-Gavin	1
Trevor Taylor	2	Alan Jones	1	Tony Settember	1
Andre Testut	2	Tom Jones	1	Andre Simon	1
Charles de Tornaco	2	Juan Jover	1	Stephen South	1
Maurice Trintignant	2	Bruce Kessler	1	Mike Spence	1
Wolfgang von Trips	2	Helmuth Koinigg	1	Jackie Stewart	1
Jarno Trulli	2	Willi Krakau	1	Philippe Streiff	1
Fred Wacker	2	Kurt Kuhnke	1	Hans Stuck	1
John Watson	2	Masami Kuwashima	1	Andy Sutcliffe	1
Peter Whitehead	2	Gerard Larrousse	1	Jacques Swaters	1
Jean Alesi	1	Michel Leclere	1	Mike Taylor	1
Elio de Angelis	1	Neville Lederle	1	Bobby Unser	1
Alberto Ascari	1	Les Leston	1	Nino Vaccarella	1
Gerry Ashmore	1	Jackie Lewis	1	Gilles Villeneuve	1
Richard Attwood	1	Guy Ligier	1	Mark Webber	1
Skip Barber	1	John Love	1	Karl Wendlinger	1
Astrubel Bayardo	1	"Jean Lucienbonnet"	1	Peter Westbury	1
Elie Bayol	1	Damien Magee	1	Ken Wharton	1
Jean Behra	1	Sergio Mantovani	1	Ted Whiteaway	1
Olivier Beretta	1	Robert Manzon	1	Desire Wilson	1
Mike Beuttler	1	Onofre Marimon	1	Vic Wilson	1
Trevor Blokdyk	1	Helmut Marko	1	Reine Wisell	1
Thierry Boutsen	1	Tony Marsh	1	Emilio Zapico	1
Tony Brooks	1	Michel May	1	Ricardo Zonta	1
Alan Brown	1	Brian McGuire	1	Ricardo Zunino	1
Ivor Bueb	1	Allan McNish	1		
Roberto Bussinello	1	Carlos Menditeguy	1		
Giulio Cabianca	1	Harry Merkel	1		
Mario Araujo de Cabral	1	Bill Moss	1		
Phil Cade	1	Stirling Moss	1		
Francois Cevert	1	David Murray	1		
Eugene Chaboud	1	Luigi Musso	1		
Alain de Chagny	1	Brian Naylor	1		
Colin Chapman	1	Tiff Needell	1		
Jim Clark	1	Jac Nelleman	1		
Chris Craft	1	John Nicholson	1		
Alberto Crespo	1	Brausch Niemann	1		

Formula 1

WINS

Michael Schumacher	64	Rene Arnoux	7	Jean-Pierre Jabouille	2
Alain Prost	51	Tony Brooks	6	Peter Revson	2
Ayrton Senna	41	Jacques Laffite	6	Pedro Rodriguez	2
Nigel Mansell	31	Riccardo Patrese	6	Jo Siffert	2
Jackie Stewart	27	Jochen Rindt	6	Patrick Tambay	2
Jim Clark	25	John Surtees	6	Maurice Trintignant	2
Niki Lauda	25	Gilles Villeneuve	6	Wolfgang von Trips	2
Juan Manuel Fangio	24	Michele Alboreto	5	Jean Alesi	1
Nelson Piquet	23	Rubens Barrichello	5	Giancarlo Baghetti	1
Damon Hill	22	Giuseppe Farina	5	Lorenzo Bandini	1
Mika Hakkinen	20	Clay Regazzoni	5	Jean-Pierre Beltoise	1
Stirling Moss	16	Keke Rosberg	5	Jo Bonnier	1
Jack Brabham	14	John Watson	5	Vittorio Brambilla	1
Emerson Fittipaldi	14	Dan Gurney	4	Francois Cevert	1
Graham Hill	14	Eddie Irvine	4	Luigi Fagioli	1
Alberto Ascari	13	Bruce McLaren	4	Peter Gethin	1
Mario Andretti	12	Ralf Schumacher	4	Richie Ginther	1
David Coulthard	12	Thierry Boutsen	3	Innes Ireland	1
Alan Jones	12	Peter Collins	3	Jochen Mass	1
Carlos Reutemann	12	Heinz-Harald Frentzen	3	Juan Pablo Montoya	1
Jacques Villeneuve	11	Mike Hawthorn	3	Luigi Musso	1
Gerhard Berger	10	Johnny Herbert	3	Alessandro Nannini	1
James Hunt	10	Phil Hill	3	Gunnar Nilsson	1
Ronnie Peterson	10	Didier Pironi	3	Carlos Pace	1
Jody Scheckter	10	Elio de Angelis	2	Olivier Panis	1
Denny Hulme	8	Patrick Depailler	2	Ludovico Scarfiotti	1
Jacky Ickx	8	Jose Froilan Gonzalez	2	Piero Taruffi	1

YOUNGEST DRIVERS TO WIN A GRAND PRIX

22 years 103 days	Bruce McLaren	1959 United States GP	24 years 130 days	Jody Scheckter	1974 Swedish GP
23 years 187 days	Jacky Ickx	1968 French GP	24 years 142 days	Elio de Angelis	1982 Austrian GP
23 years 239 days	Michael Schumacher	1992 Belgian GP	24 years 181 days	David Coulthard	1995 Portuguese GP
23 years 296 days	Emerson Fittipaldi	1970 United States GP	24 years 210 days	Peter Collins	1956 Belgian GP
24 years 86 days	Mike Hawthorn	1953 French GP	25 years 20 days	Jacques Villeneuve	1996 European GP

OLDEST DRIVERS TO WIN A GRAND PRIX

53 years 21 days	Luigi Fagioli	1951 French GP	41 years 96 days	Nigel Mansell	1994 Australian GP
46 years 277 days	Giuseppe Farina	1953 German GP	40 years 199 days	Maurice Trintignant	1958 Monaco GP
46 years 42 days	Juan Manuel Fangio	1957 German GP	40 years 92 days	Graham Hill	1969 Monaco GP
45 years 219 days	Piero Taruffi	1952 Swiss GP	39 years 312 days	Clay Regazzoni	1979 British GP
43 years 339 days	Jack Brabham	1970 South African GP	39 years 36 days	Carlos Reutemann	1981 Belgian GP

MOST POINTS SCORED

Michael Schumacher	945	Jim Clark	274	Jacky Ickx	181
Alain Prost	798.5	Rubens Barrichello	272	Mario Andretti	180
Ayrton Senna	614	Jack Brabham	261	John Surtees	180
Nelson Piquet	485.5	Jody Scheckter	255	James Hunt	179
Nigel Mansell	482	Denny Hulme	248	Ralf Schumacher	177
Niki Lauda	420.5	Jean Alesi	241	John Watson	169
Mika Hakkinen	420	Jacques Laffite	228	Heinz-Harald Frentzen	161
David Coulthard	400	Jacques Villeneuve	213	Keke Rosberg	159.5
Gerhard Berger	385	Clay Regazzoni	212	Patrick Depailler	141
Damon Hill	360	Alan Jones	206	Alberto Ascari	140.64
Jackie Stewart	360	Ronnie Peterson	206	Dan Gurney	133
Carlos Reutemann	310	Bruce McLaren	196.5	Thierry Boutsen	132
Graham Hill	289	Eddie Irvine	191	Mike Hawthorn	127.64
Emerson Fittipaldi	281	Stirling Moss	186.64	Giuseppe Farina	127.33
Riccardo Patrese	281	Michele Alboreto	186.5	Elio de Angelis	122
Juan Manuel Fangio	278.64	Rene Arnoux	181	Jochen Rindt	109

Records

MOST POINTS SCORED (cont.)

Richie Ginther	107	Robert Manzon	16	Sergio Mantovani	4
Gilles Villeneuve	107	Satoru Nakajima	16	Felipe Massa	4
Patrick Tambay	103	Vittorio Brambilla	15.5	Alfonso de Portago	4
Didier Pironi	101	Derek Daly	15	Ricardo Rodriguez	4
Martin Brundle	98	Roberto Moreno	15	Peter Whitehead	4
Johnny Herbert	98	Giancarlo Baghetti	14	Umberto Maglioli	3.33
Phil Hill	98	Bruno Giacomelli	14	Bob Bondurant	3
Francois Cevert	89	Jonathan Palmer	14	"Jules" Boullion	3
Stefan Johansson	88	Michael Parkes	14	Giulio Cabianca	3
Chris Amon	83	Rolf Stommelen	14	Johnny Dumfries	3
Giancarlo Fisichella	82	Karl Wendlinger	14	Philippe Etancelin	3
Juan Pablo Montoya	81	Roberto Mieres	13	Wilson Fittipaldi	3
Jose Froilan Gonzalez	77.64	Jackie Oliver	13	Ignazio Giunti	3
Jean-Pierre Beltoise	77	Hector Rebaque	13	Jim Hall	3
Tony Brooks	75	Reine Wisell	13	Jackie Lewis	3
Maurice Trintignant	72.33	Peter Arundell	12	Gerhard Mitter	3
Jochen Mass	71	Christian Fittipaldi	12	Silvio Moser	3
Pedro Rodriguez	71	Henri Pescarolo	12	Emanuele Pirro	3
Derek Warwick	71	Cliff Allison	11	Dennis Poore	3
Eddie Cheever	70	Richard Attwood	11	Eliseo Salazar	3
Jo Siffert	68	Paul Frere	11	Consalvo Sanesi	3
Alessandro Nannini	65	Peter Gethin	11	Dorino Serafini	3
Olivier Panis	64	Arturo Merzario	11	Raymond Sommer	3
Peter Revson	61	Philippe Streiff	11	Henry Taylor	3
Andrea de Cesaris	59	Eric Bernard	10	Ken Wharton	3
Lorenzo Bandini	58	Pedro Diniz	10	Ricardo Zonta	3
Carlos Pace	58	Rudolf Fischer	10	Fabrizio Barbazza	2
Wolfgang von Trips	56	Howden Ganley	10	Elie Bayol	2
Jean Behra	51.14	Mauricio Gugelmin	10	Alan Brown	2
Luigi Villoresi	49	Hans Herrmann	10	Ronnie Bucknum	2
Peter Collins	47	JJ Lehto	10	Oscar Galvez	2
Innes Ireland	47	Emanuel de Graffenried	9	Piercarlo Ghinzani	2
Luigi Musso	44	Carlos Menditeguy	9	Horace Gould	2
Piero Taruffi	41	Reg Parnell	9	Walt Hansgen	2
Jo Bonnier	39	Johnny Servoz-Gavin	9	Chris Irwin	2
Jarno Trulli	38	Gianni Morbidelli	8.5	Hermann Lang	2
Kimi Raikkonen	33	Onofre Marimon	8.14	Gijs van Lennep	2
Mika Salo	33	Bob Anderson	8	John Miles	2
Mark Blundell	32	"B Bira"	8	Shinji Nakano	2
Luigi Fagioli	32	Mark Donohue	8	Andre Pilette	2
Harry Schell	32	Vic Elford	8	Takuma Sato	2
Jean-Pierre Jarier	31.5	Brian Redman	8	Hermano da Silva Ramos	2
Ivan Capelli	31	Aguri Suzuki	8	Danny Sullivan	2
Gunnar Nilsson	31	Trevor Taylor	8	Eric Thompson	2
Mike Hailwood	29	Philippe Alliot	7	Mark Webber	2
Hans-Joachim Stuck	29	Michael Andretti	7	Manfred Winkelhock	2
Jenson Button	28	Erik Comas	7	Gerino Gerini	1.5
Mike Spence	27	Nicola Larini	7	Chico Landi	1.5
Tony Maggs	26	Willy Mairesse	7	Julian Bailey	1
Alexander Wurz	26	Tim Schenken	7	Derek Bell	1
Teo Fabi	23	Andrea de Adamich	6	Slim Borgudd	1
Masten Gregory	21	Lucien Bianchi	6	Tony Brise	1
Jean-Pierre Jabouille	21	Alex Caffi	6	Johnny Cecotto	1
Piers Courage	20	Chico Godia-Sales	6	Eugene Chaboud	1
Eugenio Castellotti	19.5	John Love	6	Marc Gene	1
Nick Heidfeld	19	Pedro de la Rosa	6	Olivier Grouillard	1
Tom Pryce	19	Mauro Baldi	5	Pedro Lamy	1
Roy Salvadori	19	Jack Fairman	5	Neville Lederle	1
Olivier Gendebien	18	Ron Flockhart	5	Guy Ligier	1
Pierluigi Martini	18	George Follmer	5	Jan Magnussen	1
Louis Rosier	18	Bertrand Gachot	5	Luis Perez Sala	1
Felice Bonetto	17.5	Yves Giraud-Cabantous	5	Giorgio Scarlatti	1
Karl Kling	17	Ukyo Katayama	5	Chico Serra	1
Stefano Modena	17	Cesare Perdisa	5	Gabriele Tarquini	1
Ludovico Scarfiotti	17	Carel Godin de Beaufort	4	John Taylor	1
Marc Surer	17	Stefan Bellof	4	Alessandro Zanardi	1
Jos Verstappen	17	Louis Chiron	4	Renzo Zorzi	1
Stuart Lewis-Evans	16	Christian Danner	4	Lella Lombardi	0.5

Formula 1

YOUNGEST DRIVERS TO SCORE POINTS

20 years 66 days	Jenson Button	6th	2000 Brazilian GP
20 years 122 days	Ricardo Rodriguez	4th	1962 Belgian GP
20 years 309 days	Chris Amon	5th	1964 Dutch GP
20 years 325 days	Felipe Massa	6th	2002 Malaysian GP
21 years 138 days	Kimi Raikkonen	6th	2001 Australian GP

OLDEST DRIVERS TO SCORE POINTS

53 years 247 days	Philippe Etancelin	5th	1950 Italian GP
53 years 21 days	Luigi Fagioli	1st	1951 French GP
50 years 289 days	Louis Chiron	3rd	1950 Monaco GP
50 years 273 days	Louis Rosier	5th	1956 German GP
50 years 76 days	Felice Bonetto	4th	1953 Swiss GP

HIGHEST POINTS PER START

Juan Manuel Fangio	5.464	Mario Andretti	1.406	Reine Wisell	0.591
Michael Schumacher	5.309	Keke Rosberg	1.399	Willy Mairesse	0.583
Luigi Fagioli	4.571	Eugenio Castellotti	1.393	Mike Hailwood	0.580
Alberto Ascari	4.537	Lorenzo Bandini	1.381	Mark Donohue	0.571
Alain Prost	4.013	Eddie Irvine	1.308	Sergio Mantovani	0.571
Giuseppe Farina	3.858	Jacques Laffite	1.295	Robert Manzon	0.571
Ayrton Senna	3.814	Pedro Rodriguez	1.291	Harry Schell	0.571
Jim Clark	3.806	Olivier Gendebien	1.286	Hans Herrmann	0.556
Jackie Stewart	3.636	Rene Arnoux	1.215	Masten Gregory	0.553
Damon Hill	3.130	Jean Alesi	1.199	Jenson Button	0.549
Dorino Serafini	3.000	Felice Bonetto	1.167	Michael Andretti	0.538
Jose Froilan Gonzalez	2.986	Stuart Lewis-Evans	1.143	Eddie Cheever	0.530
David Coulthard	2.837	Heinz-Harald Frentzen	1.142	Mark Blundell	0.525
Mike Hawthorn	2.836	Elio de Angelis	1.130	Olivier Panis	0.512
Stirling Moss	2.828	Stefan Johansson	1.114	Alexander Wurz	0.500
Mika Hakkinen	2.609	John Watson	1.112	Derek Warwick	0.486
Nigel Mansell	2.578	Riccardo Patrese	1.098	Louis Rosier	0.474
Niki Lauda	2.459	Peter Arundell	1.091	Chico Godia-Sales	0.462
Juan Pablo Montoya	2.382	Tony Maggs	1.040	Tom Pryce	0.452
Nelson Piquet	2.380	Giulio Cabianca	1.000	Jean-Pierre Jabouille	0.429
Michael Parkes	2.333	Paul Frere	1.000	"B Bira"	0.421
Piero Taruffi	2.278	Walt Hansgen	1.000	Jack Fairman	0.417
Jody Scheckter	2.277	Hermann Lang	1.000	George Follmer	0.417
Denny Hulme	2.214	Neville Lederle	1.000	Emanuel de Graffenried	0.409
Carlos Reutemann	2.123	Gunnar Nilsson	1.000	Roy Salvadori	0.404
Wolfgang von Trips	2.074	Jean Behra	0.983	Jarno Trulli	0.400
Jack Brabham	2.071	Kimi Raikkonen	0.971	Peter Whitehead	0.400
Richie Ginther	2.058	Michele Alboreto	0.961	Hans-Joachim Stuck	0.392
Phil Hill	2.042	Innes Ireland	0.940	Ron Flockhart	0.385
Peter Revson	2.033	Patrick Tambay	0.904	Yves Giraud-Cabantous	0.385
Oscar Galvez	2.000	Carlos Menditeguy	0.900	Nick Heidfeld	0.380
Eric Thompson	2.000	Jean-Pierre Beltoise	0.895	Jo Bonnier	0.375
Tony Brooks	1.974	Maurice Trintignant	0.882	Henry Taylor	0.375
Bruce McLaren	1.965	Chris Amon	0.865	Peter Gethin	0.367
Emerson Fittipaldi	1.951	Alessandro Nannini	0.855	Teo Fabi	0.359
James Hunt	1.946	Thierry Boutsen	0.810	Roberto Moreno	0.357
Francois Cevert	1.894	Carlos Pace	0.806	Lucien Bianchi	0.353
Jacques Villeneuve	1.836	Alfonso de Portago	0.800	Karl Wendlinger	0.341
Gerhard Berger	1.833	Ricardo Rodriguez	0.800	Bob Bondurant	0.333
Luigi Musso	1.833	Giancarlo Fisichella	0.766	Ivan Capelli	0.333
Jochen Rindt	1.817	Roberto Mieres	0.765	Eugene Chaboud	0.333
Alan Jones	1.776	Ignazio Giunti	0.750	Jackie Lewis	0.333
Ralf Schumacher	1.770	Johnny Servoz-Gavin	0.750	Umberto Maglioli	0.333
Ludovico Scarfiotti	1.700	Mike Spence	0.750	Bob Anderson	0.320
Rubens Barrichello	1.679	Onofre Marimon	0.740	Hector Rebaque	0.317
Ronnie Peterson	1.675	Piers Courage	0.714	Derek Daly	0.306
Graham Hill	1.642	Cesare Perdisa	0.714	Christian Fittipaldi	0.300
John Surtees	1.622	Jo Siffert	0.708	Mika Salo	0.300
Clay Regazzoni	1.606	Cliff Allison	0.688	Trevor Taylor	0.296
Gilles Villeneuve	1.597	Jochen Mass	0.676	Elie Bayol	0.286
Luigi Villoresi	1.581	Giancarlo Baghetti	0.667	Howden Ganley	0.286
Jacky Ickx	1.560	John Love	0.667	Hermano da Silva Ramos	0.286
Dan Gurney	1.547	Brian Redman	0.667	Andrea de Cesaris	0.284
Karl Kling	1.545	Richard Attwood	0.647	"Jules" Boullion	0.273
Reg Parnell	1.500	Martin Brundle	0.620	Jim Hall	0.273
Dennis Poore	1.500	Vic Elford	0.615	Louis Chiron	0.267
Patrick Depailler	1.484	Johnny Herbert	0.605	Jackie Oliver	0.260
Peter Collins	1.469	Gerhard Mitter	0.600	Rolf Stommelen	0.259
Didier Pironi	1.443	Consalvo Sanesi	0.600	Fabrizio Barbazza	0.250
Rudolf Fischer	1.429	Raymond Sommer	0.600	Alan Brown	0.250

HIGHEST POINTS PER START (cont.)

Driver	Pts	Driver	Pts	Driver	Pts
Philippe Etancelin	0.250	Jos Verstappen	0.187	Pedro Diniz	0.102
Gerino Gerini	0.250	Ronnie Bucknum	0.182	Slim Borgudd	0.100
Chico Landi	0.250	Jonathan Palmer	0.169	Tony Brise	0.100
Gijs van Lennep	0.250	John Miles	0.167	Ricardo Zonta	0.097
Felipe Massa	0.250	JJ Lehto	0.161	Pedro de la Rosa	0.095
Silvio Moser	0.250	Pierluigi Martini	0.153	Wilson Fittipaldi	0.086
Stefano Modena	0.243	Julian Bailey	0.143	Guy Ligier	0.083
Jean-Pierre Jarier	0.237	Carel Godin de Beaufort	0.143	Giorgio Scarlatti	0.083
Eric Bernard	0.222	Horace Gould	0.143	Emanuele Pirro	0.081
Andre Pilette	0.222	Nicola Larini	0.143	Philippe Alliot	0.064
Satoru Nakajima	0.216	Renzo Zorzi	0.143	Shinji Nakano	0.061
Henri Pescarolo	0.211	Mauro Baldi	0.139	Johnny Cecotto	0.056
Marc Surer	0.210	Mauricio Gugelmin	0.135	Chico Serra	0.056
Vittorio Brambilla	0.209	Danny Sullivan	0.133	Ukyo Katayama	0.053
Philippe Streiff	0.208	Gianni Morbidelli	0.127	Manfred Winkelhock	0.043
Tim Schenken	0.206	Eliseo Salazar	0.125	Lella Lombardi	0.042
Bruno Giacomelli	0.203	Aguri Suzuki	0.125	Jan Magnussen	0.040
Andrea de Adamich	0.200	Mark Webber	0.125	Luis Perez Sala	0.038
Stefan Bellof	0.200	Erik Comas	0.119	Pedro Lamy	0.031
Johnny Dumfries	0.200	Takuma Sato	0.118	Marc Gene	0.030
Chris Irwin	0.200	Derek Bell	0.111	Piercarlo Ghinzani	0.026
John Taylor	0.200	Christian Danner	0.111	Gabriele Tarquini	0.026
Ken Wharton	0.200	Alex Caffi	0.107	Olivier Grouillard	0.024
Arturo Merzario	0.193	Bertrand Gachot	0.106	Alessandro Zanardi	0.024

POLE POSITIONS

Driver	No	Driver	No	Driver	No
Ayrton Senna	65	Jochen Rindt	10	Michele Alboreto	2
Michael Schumacher	50	Riccardo Patrese	8	Jean Alesi	2
Jim Clark	33	John Surtees	8	Heinz-Harald Frentzen	2
Alain Prost	33	Jacques Laffite	7	Stuart Lewis-Evans	2
Nigel Mansell	32	Rubens Barrichello	6	Jo Siffert	2
Juan Manuel Fangio	29	Emerson Fittipaldi	6	Gilles Villeneuve	2
Mika Hakkinen	26	Phil Hill	6	John Watson	2
Niki Lauda	24	Jean-Pierre Jabouille	6	Lorenzo Bandini	1
Nelson Piquet	24	Alan Jones	6	Jo Bonnier	1
Damon Hill	20	Carlos Reutemann	6	Thierry Boutsen	1
Mario Andretti	18	Chris Amon	5	Vittorio Brambilla	1
Rene Arnoux	18	Giuseppe Farina	5	Eugenio Castellotti	1
Jackie Stewart	17	Clay Regazzoni	5	Andrea de Cesaris	1
Stirling Moss	16	Keke Rosberg	5	Patrick Depailler	1
Alberto Ascari	14	Patrick Tambay	5	Giancarlo Fisichella	1
James Hunt	14	Mike Hawthorn	4	Bruno Giacomelli	1
Ronnie Peterson	14	Didier Pironi	4	Denny Hulme	1
Jack Brabham	13	Elio de Angelis	3	Carlos Pace	1
Graham Hill	13	Tony Brooks	3	Michael Parkes	1
Jacky Ickx	13	Teo Fabi	3	Tom Pryce	1
Jacques Villeneuve	13	Jose Froilan Gonzalez	3	Peter Revson	1
Gerhard Berger	12	Dan Gurney	3	Ralf Schumacher	1
David Coulthard	12	Jean-Pierre Jarier	3	Wolfgang von Trips	1
Juan Pablo Montoya	10	Jody Scheckter	3		

YOUNGEST DRIVERS TO QUALIFY ON POLE

Age	Driver	Result	Race
22 years 96 days	Rubens Barrichello	Retired	1994 Belgian GP
22 years 308 days	Andrea de Cesaris	Retired	1982 Long Beach GP
23 years 215 days	Jacky Ickx	4th	1968 German GP
24 years 13 days	David Coulthard	Retired	1995 Argentinian GP
24 years 250 days	Eugenio Castellotti	Retired	1955 Belgian GP
24 years 297 days	Chris Amon	Retired	1968 Spanish GP
24 years 336 days	Jacques Villeneuve	2nd	1996 Australian GP
25 years 31 days	Ayrton Senna	1st	1985 Portuguese GP
25 years 35 days	Niki Lauda	16th	1974 South African GP
25 years 131 days	Michael Schumacher	1st	1994 Monaco GP

Formula 1

OLDEST DRIVERS TO QUALIFY ON POLE

47 years 80 days	Giuseppe Farina	2nd	1954 Argentinian GP
46 years 209 days	Juan Manuel Fangio	4th	1958 Argentinian GP
44 years 17 days	Jack Brabham	Retired	1970 Spanish GP
42 years 196 days	Mario Andretti	3rd	1982 Italian GP
41 years 96 days	Nigel Mansell	1st	1994 Australian GP
39 years 189 days	Carlos Reutemann	8th	1981 Las Vegas GP
39 years 155 days	Graham Hill	Retired	1968 British GP
38 years 243 days	Alain Prost	2nd	1993 Japanese GP
38 years 122 days	Riccardo Patrese	Retired	1992 Hungarian GP
37 years 335 days	Gerhard Berger	1st	1997 German GP

FRONT ROW QUALIFICATIONS

Ayrton Senna	87	Juan Pablo Montoya	13	Teo Fabi	3
Alain Prost	86	Jody Scheckter	13	Innes Ireland	3
Michael Schumacher	85	Heinz-Harald Frentzen	12	Jean-Pierre Jarier	3
Nigel Mansell	56	Jose Froilan Gonzalez	12	Karl Kling	3
Jim Clark	48	Tony Brooks	11	Robert Manzon	3
Juan Manuel Fangio	48	Jean-Pierre Jabouille	11	Pedro Rodriguez	3
Damon Hill	47	Jacques Laffite	11	Jean-Pierre Beltoise	2
Nelson Piquet	44	John Watson	11	Andrea de Cesaris	2
Graham Hill	42	Jean Alesi	10	Francois Cevert	2
Jackie Stewart	42	Jean Behra	10	Giancarlo Fisichella	2
Mika Hakkinen	39	Keke Rosberg	10	Willy Mairesse	2
Jack Brabham	38	Ralf Schumacher	10	Michael Parkes	2
Stirling Moss	37	Phil Hill	9	Tom Pryce	2
David Coulthard	36	Patrick Tambay	9	Roy Salvadori	2
Rene Arnoux	34	Peter Collins	8	Ludovico Scarfiotti	2
Gerhard Berger	32	Richie Ginther	8	Maurice Trintignant	2
Niki Lauda	31	Gilles Villeneuve	8	Jarno Trulli	2
Riccardo Patrese	28	Eugenio Castellotti	7	Felice Bonetto	1
Giuseppe Farina	27	Patrick Depailler	7	Thierry Boutsen	1
Alberto Ascari	25	Bruce McLaren	7	Vittorio Brambilla	1
Jacky Ickx	25	Carlos Pace	7	Eddie Cheever	1
Ronnie Peterson	25	Elio de Angelis	6	Olivier Gendebien	1
Mario Andretti	24	Luigi Musso	6	Bruno Giacomelli	1
James Hunt	24	Didier Pironi	6	Masten Gregory	1
Denny Hulme	23	Lorenzo Bandini	5	Stefan Johansson	1
Jacques Villeneuve	23	Jo Bonnier	5	Pierluigi Martini	1
Carlos Reutemann	22	Stuart Lewis-Evans	5	Stefano Modena	1
Dan Gurney	21	Peter Revson	5	Jackie Oliver	1
Clay Regazzoni	21	Harry Schell	5	Reg Parnell	1
John Surtees	21	Jo Siffert	5	Kimi Raikkonen	1
Chris Amon	19	Luigi Villoresi	5	Ricardo Rodriguez	1
Jochen Rindt	18	Michele Alboreto	4	Consalvo Sanesi	1
Mike Hawthorn	17	Luigi Fagioli	4	Johnny Servoz-Gavin	1
Rubens Barrichello	16	Eddie Irvine	4	Hans-Joachim Stuck	1
Emerson Fittipaldi	16	Piero Taruffi	4	Trevor Taylor	1
Alan Jones	13	Wolfgang von Trips	4		

FASTEST LAPS

Michael Schumacher	51	Jacky Ickx	14	Jose Froilan Gonzalez	6
Alain Prost	41	Alberto Ascari	13	Dan Gurney	6
Nigel Mansell	29	Alan Jones	13	Mike Hawthorn	6
Jim Clark	28	Rene Arnoux	12	Phil Hill	6
Mika Hakkinen	25	Jack Brabham	12	Jacques Laffite	6
Niki Lauda	24	John Surtees	11	Juan Pablo Montoya	6
Juan Manuel Fangio	23	Mario Andretti	10	Ralf Schumacher	6
Nelson Piquet	23	Graham Hill	10	Michele Alboreto	5
Gerhard Berger	21	Denny Hulme	9	Giuseppe Farina	5
Damon Hill	19	Ronnie Peterson	9	Carlos Pace	5
Stirling Moss	19	Jacques Villeneuve	9	Didier Pironi	5
Ayrton Senna	19	Rubens Barrichello	8	Carlos Reutemann	5
David Coulthard	18	James Hunt	8	Jody Scheckter	5
Riccardo Patrese	15	Gilles Villeneuve	8	John Watson	5
Clay Regazzoni	15	Emerson Fittipaldi	6	Jean Alesi	4
Jackie Stewart	15	Heinz-Harald Frentzen	6	Jean-Pierre Beltoise	4

FASTEST LAPS (cont.)

Patrick Depailler	4		Giancarlo Baghetti	1		Roberto Moreno	1
Jo Siffert	4		Jean Behra	1		Luigi Musso	1
Chris Amon	3		Thierry Boutsen	1		Satoru Nakajima	1
Tony Brooks	3		Vittorio Brambilla	1		Gunnar Nilsson	1
Richie Ginther	3		Andrea de Cesaris	1		Jackie Oliver	1
Jean-Pierre Jarier	3		Giancarlo Fisichella	1		Jonathan Palmer	1
Bruce McLaren	3		Bertrand Gachot	1		Henri Pescarolo	1
Jochen Rindt	3		Mauricio Gugelmin	1		Kimi Raikkonen	1
Keke Rosberg	3		Mike Hailwood	1		Pedro Rodriguez	1
Lorenzo Bandini	2		Masahiro Hasemi	1		Ludovico Scarfiotti	1
Francois Cevert	2		Brian Henton	1		Marc Surer	1
Teo Fabi	2		Hans Herrmann	1		Piero Taruffi	1
Jochen Mass	2		Innes Ireland	1		Maurice Trintignant	1
Alessandro Nannini	2		Eddie Irvine	1		Luigi Villoresi	1
Patrick Tambay	2		Karl Kling	1		Alexander Wurz	1
Derek Warwick	2		Onofre Marimon	1			
Richard Attwood	1		Roberto Mieres	1			

YOUNGEST DRIVERS TO RECORD THE FASTEST RACE LAP

21 years 321 days	Bruce McLaren	3rd	1959 British GP
22 years 137 days	Kimi Raikkonen	3rd	2002 Australian GP
23 years 126 days	David Coulthard	Retired	1994 German GP
23 years 239 days	Michael Schumacher	1st	1992 Belgian GP
23 years 356 days	Andrea de Cesaris	Retired	1983 Belgian GP

OLDEST DRIVERS TO RECORD THE FASTEST RACE LAP

46 years 210 days	Juan Manuel Fangio	4th	1958 Argentinian GP
45 years 219 days	Piero Taruffi	1st	1952 Swiss GP
44 years 321 days	Giuseppe Farina	3rd	1951 Italian GP
44 years 107 days	Jack Brabham	2nd	1970 British GP
44 years 22 days	Luigi Villoresi	Retired	1953 Dutch GP

LAPS IN THE LEAD

Michael Schumacher	3629	Didier Pironi	268	Giancarlo Fisichella	35
Ayrton Senna	2981	Jose Froilan Gonzalez	266	Andrea de Cesaris	32.6
Alain Prost	2712	Mike Hawthorn	225	Vittorio Brambilla	32
Nigel Mansell	2089	Michele Alboreto	219	Elio de Angelis	31
Jim Clark	1945	Dan Gurney	200	Bruno Giacomelli	31
Jackie Stewart	1913	Ralf Schumacher	193	Alessandro Nannini	26
Niki Lauda	1657	Patrick Tambay	193	Eugenio Castellotti	21
Nelson Piquet	1567.5	Juan Pablo Montoya	187	Gunnar Nilsson	21
Mika Hakkinen	1485	Jean-Pierre Jabouille	185	Kimi Raikkonen	21
Damon Hill	1381	Chris Amon	183	Karl Kling	18
Juan Manuel Fangio	1353	Phil Hill	165	Harry Schell	17
Stirling Moss	1181	Thierry Boutsen	164	Olivier Panis	16
Graham Hill	1103	Patrick Depailler	164	Derek Warwick	16
Alberto Ascari	930	Eddie Irvine	158	Hans-Joachim Stuck	14
David Coulthard	872	Wolfgang von Trips	156	Masten Gregory	13
Jack Brabham	825	Heinz-Harald Frentzen	151	John Love	13
Mario Andretti	793	Lorenzo Bandini	143	Luigi Fagioli	8
Ronnie Peterson	707	Tony Brooks	140	Rolf Stommelen	8
Gerhard Berger	692	Jo Bonnier	139	Giancarlo Baghetti	7
Jody Scheckter	674	Francois Cevert	129	Michael Parkes	7
Carlos Reutemann	650	Peter Collins	127	Luigi Musso	6
James Hunt	634	Richie Ginther	116	Mike Hailwood	5
Jacques Villeneuve	627	Jean Behra	107	Stuart Lewis-Evans	5
Alan Jones	616	Jean-Pierre Beltoise	101	Jochen Mass	5
Riccardo Patrese	572.5	Jo Siffert	99	Raymond Sommer	5
Jacky Ickx	529	Pedro Rodriguez	86	Trevor Taylor	4
Rubens Barrichello	521	Jean-Pierre Jarier	79	Olivier Gendebien	3
Keke Rosberg	511	Maurice Trintignant	78	Peter Gethin	3
Rene Arnoux	507	Peter Revson	63	Stefan Johansson	3
Gilles Villeneuve	500	Ludovico Scarfiotti	55	Willy Mairesse	3
Emerson Fittipaldi	478	Carlos Pace	50	Johnny Servoz-Gavin	3
Denny Hulme	435	Ivan Capelli	46	Piers Courage	2
Jochen Rindt	387	Piero Taruffi	46	Roberto Mieres	2
Clay Regazzoni	360	Johnny Herbert	44	Tom Pryce	2
Giuseppe Farina	334	Innes Ireland	43	Mika Salo	2
John Surtees	311	Bruce McLaren	41	Luigi Villoresi	2
John Watson	287	Carlos Menditeguy	39	Felice Bonetto	1
Jacques Laffite	283	Jarno Trulli	38	Pierluigi Martini	1
Jean Alesi	268	Jackie Oliver	37		

Formula 1

MILES IN THE LEAD

Michael Schumacher	10481	Jose Froilan Gonzalez	933	Bruno Giacomelli	105
Ayrton Senna	8473	Phil Hill	917	Elio de Angelis	103
Alain Prost	7838	Tony Brooks	826	Jarno Trulli	103
Jim Clark	6312	Jean Alesi	810	Alessandro Nannini	101
Nigel Mansell	5988	John Watson	769	Innes Ireland	101
Juan Manuel Fangio	5805	Didier Pironi	697	Eugenio Castellotti	96
Jackie Stewart	5692	Ralf Schumacher	614	Carlos Menditeguy	95
Nelson Piquet	4628	Jean-Pierre Jabouille	607	Vittorio Brambilla	94
Niki Lauda	4593	Patrick Tambay	592	Harry Schell	60
Mika Hakkinen	4457	Peter Collins	588	Gunnar Nilsson	56
Damon Hill	4018	Michele Alboreto	582	Kimi Raikkonen	55
Stirling Moss	3961	Juan Pablo Montoya	579	Derek Warwick	48
Alberto Ascari	3675	Chris Amon	529	Hans-Joachim Stuck	47
Graham Hill	2968	Eddie Irvine	527	Raymond Sommer	44
Jack Brabham	2826	Wolfgang von Trips	490	Masten Gregory	42
David Coulthard	2574	Heinz-Harald Frentzen	471	Luigi Musso	41
Mario Andretti	2201	Richie Ginther	458	Giancarlo Baghetti	36
Gerhard Berger	2139	Thierry Boutsen	411	Trevor Taylor	35
Carlos Reutemann	2059	Lorenzo Bandini	400	Olivier Panis	33
Ronnie Peterson	2059	Patrick Depailler	381	John Love	33
James Hunt	2006	Pedro Rodriguez	366	Luigi Fagioli	31
Jacky Ickx	1940	Francois Cevert	348	Olivier Gendebien	26
Alan Jones	1844	Jo Bonnier	340	Willy Mairesse	26
Jacques Villeneuve	1820	Jo Siffert	324	Michael Parkes	25
Jody Scheckter	1772	Jean-Pierre Jarier	281	Rolf Stommelen	19
Giuseppe Farina	1642	Jean Behra	273	Mike Hailwood	18
Riccardo Patrese	1608	Jean-Pierre Beltoise	235	Stuart Lewis-Evans	18
Rene Arnoux	1598	Piero Taruffi	208	Luigi Villoresi	18
Rubens Barrichello	1523	Ludovico Scarfiotti	197	Jochen Mass	12
Emerson Fittipaldi	1389	Carlos Pace	183	Stefan Johansson	12
Keke Rosberg	1342	Peter Revson	168	Peter Gethin	11
John Surtees	1334	Maurice Trintignant	162	Mika Salo	8
Gilles Villeneuve	1279	Johnny Herbert	142	Piers Courage	7
Denny Hulme	1189	Bruce McLaren	116	Tom Pryce	6
Jochen Rindt	1185	Ivan Capelli	110	Johnny Servoz-Gavin	6
Clay Regazzoni	1150	Andrea de Cesaris	109	Roberto Mieres	5
Mike Hawthorn	1018	Karl Kling	108	Felice Bonetto	3
Dan Gurney	988	Giancarlo Fisichella	107	Pierluigi Martini	3
Jacques Laffite	946	Jackie Oliver	106		

YOUNGEST DRIVERS TO FINISH IN A PODIUM POSITION

21 years 288 days	Ralf Schumacher	3rd	1997 Argentinian GP
21 years 307 days	Elio de Angelis	2nd	1980 Brazilian GP
21 years 321 days	Bruce McLaren	3rd	1959 British GP
21 years 328 days	Rubens Barrichello	3rd	1994 Pacific GP
22 years 137 days	Kimi Raikkonen	3rd	2002 Australian GP

OLDEST DRIVERS TO FINISH IN A PODIUM POSITION

53 years 21 days	Luigi Fagioli	1st	1951 French GP
50 years 289 days	Louis Chiron	3rd	1950 Monaco GP
50 years 363 days	Felice Bonetto	3rd	1953 Dutch GP
48 years 335 days	Piero Taruffi	2nd	1955 Italian GP
48 years 218 days	Giuseppe Farina	3rd	1955 Belgian GP

YOUNGEST DRIVERS TO FINISH A GRAND PRIX

19 years 217 days	Fernando Alonso	12th	2001 Australian GP
19 years 345 days	Chris Amon	7th	1963 French GP
20 years 4 days	Esteban Tuero	8th	1998 San Marino GP
20 years 66 days	Jenson Button	6th	2000 Brazilian GP
20 years 122 days	Ricardo Rodriguez	4th	1962 Belgian GP

OLDEST DRIVERS TO FINISH A GRAND PRIX

55 years 337 days	Heitel Cantoni	11th	1952 Italian GP
55 years 292 days	Louis Chiron	6th	1955 Monaco GP
55 years 190 days	Philippe Etancelin	8th	1952 French GP
53 years 233 days	Arthur Legat	13th	1952 Belgian GP
53 years 21 days	Luigi Fagioli	1st	1951 French GP

CLOSEST FINISHES

0.01 seconds	Peter Gethin	1971 Italian GP		0.1	Juan Manuel Fangio	1954 French GP
0.011	Rubens Barrichello	2002 United States GP		0.1	Giancarlo Baghetti	1961 French GP
0.014	Ayrton Senna	1986 Spanish GP		0.174	Michael Schumacher	2000 Canadian GP
0.050	Elio de Angelis	1982 Austrian GP		0.182	Michael Schumacher	2002 Austrian GP
0.08	Jackie Stewart	1969 Italian GP		0.2	Stirling Moss	1955 British GP

Other Records

Most world championships:
Five, Juan Manuel Fangio and Michael Schumacher

Race with the youngest average age:
27 years 156 days, 1997 French GP

Race with the oldest average age: 42 years 285 days, 1951 Belgian GP

Fewest starters in a race: Ten, 1958 Argentinian GP

Most starters in a race: 34, 1953 German GP

Widest championship-winning margin:
67 points, Michael Schumacher, 2002

Narrowest championship-winning margin:
0.5 points, Niki Lauda, 1984

Most wins in a season: Eleven, Michael Schumacher, 2002

Most successive wins at the start of a season:
Five, Nigel Mansell, 1992

Most successive wins: Nine, Alberto Ascari, 1952-53

Most points in a season: 144, Michael Schumacher, 2002

Most pole positions in a season: 14, Nigel Mansell, 1992

Most fastest laps in a season: Nine, Mika Hakkinen, 2000

Most laps/miles in the lead in a season:
692 laps/2039 miles, Nigel Mansell, 1992

Fastest race: 150.759 mph, 1971 Italian GP

Slowest race: 61.331 mph, 1950 Monaco GP

Longest circuit used: 16.032 miles, Pescara, 1957

Shortest circuit used: 1.954 miles, Monte Carlo, 1955-72

Most lead changes during a single race: 43, 1965 Italian GP

Most races without a win: 208, Andrea de Cesaris

Most races without scoring a point: 49, Luca Badoer

Manufacturers' Records

MOST STARTS

Ferrari*	669	Wolf	47	Aston Martin	5
McLaren	543	Gordini	40	JBW	5
Lotus	491	Penske	40	LDS	5
Williams	455	Honda	35	Scirocco	5
Tyrrell	430	Porsche	33	AFM	4
Brabham	394	Theodore	33	Emeryson	4
Arrows	382	RAM	31	Frazer-Nash	4
Ligier	326	Vanwall	28	Lancia	4
Minardi	287	Eagle	25	Martini	4
Benetton	260	Forti	23	OSCA	4
March	227	Spirit	23	Gilby	3
BRM	197	Pacific	22	Lec	3
Jordan	197	Simtek	21	Token	3
Sauber	163	Rial	20	Aston	2
Lola	149	Fondmetal	19	BMW	2
Renault	140	Connaught	17	Bellasi	2
Osella	132	Onyx	17	Heck	2
Cooper	129	Toyota	17	Kojima	2
Surtees	118	Parnelli	16	Scarab	2
Alfa Romeo	112	EuroBrun	14	Amon	1
Shadow	104	HWM	14	Andrea Moda	1
Fittipaldi	103	BRP	13	Bugatti	1
Ensign	99	Coloni	13	Connew	1
ATS Wheels	89	Talbot	13	EMW	1
Prost	83	Mercedes-Benz	12	ENB	1
Dallara	78	Tecno	11	Ferguson	1
Maserati	68	De Tomaso	10	Greifzu	1
BAR	67	Hill	10	Klenk	1
Matra	62	Merzario	10	Kurtis	1
Toleman	57	Eifelland	8	Lyncar	1
Zakspeed	53	ERA	7	Protos	1
Hesketh	52	ATS (Automobili Turismo e Sport)	6	Rebaque	1
Jaguar	51	Lamborghini	6	Shannon	1
Stewart	49	Trojan	6	Stebro	1
Larrousse	48	Veritas	6	Tec-Mec	1
AGS	47	Alta	5	*also raced in 1952 Indianapolis 500	

Formula 1

MOST WINS

Ferrari	159	Renault	15	Wolf	3
McLaren	135	Alfa Romeo	10	Honda	2
Williams	108	Ligier	9	Eagle	1
Lotus	79	Maserati	9	Hesketh	1
Brabham	35	Matra	9	Penske	1
Benetton	27	Mercedes-Benz	9	Porsche	1
Tyrrell	23	Vanwall	9	Shadow	1
BRM	17	Jordan	3	Stewart	1
Cooper	16	March	3		

MOST POINTS

Ferrari	3830.27	Wolf	79	Dallara	15
McLaren	2756.5	Shadow	68.5	BRP	11
Williams	2209.5	Surtees	54	Lancia	9
Lotus	1514	Honda	50	ATS Wheels	7
Brabham	983	Porsche	50	Larrousse	6
Benetton	861.5	Hesketh	48	Onyx	6
Tyrrell	711	Stewart	47	Parnelli	6
BRM	537.5	BAR	44	Rial	6
Cooper	494.5	Fittipaldi	44	Osella	5
Ligier	388	Lola	43	Frazer-Nash	3
Renault	335	Prost	35	Hill	3
Maserati	312.92	Gordini	30.14	AGS	2
Jordan	261	Minardi	30	HWM	2
Alfa Romeo	214	Toleman	26	Theodore	2
March	193	Talbot	25	Toyota	2
Matra	184	Penske	23	Zakspeed	2
Arrows	167	Jaguar	21	Tecno	1
Mercedes-Benz	139.14	Ensign	19		
Sauber	122	Connaught	17		
Vanwall	108	Eagle	17		

HIGHEST POINTS PER START

Mercedes-Benz	11.595	Honda	1.429	Prost	0.422
Ferrari	5.725	Jordan	1.325	Jaguar	0.412
McLaren	5.076	Ligier	1.190	Parnelli	0.375
Williams	4.856	Connaught	1.000	Onyx	0.353
Maserati	4.602	Stewart	0.959	Hill	0.300
Vanwall	3.857	Hesketh	0.923	Rial	0.300
Cooper	3.833	March	0.850	Lola	0.289
Benetton	3.313	BRP	0.846	Dallara	0.192
Lotus	3.084	Gordini	0.754	Ensign	0.192
Matra	2.968	Frazer-Nash	0.750	HWM	0.143
BRM	2.728	Sauber	0.748	Larrousse	0.125
Brabham	2.495	Eagle	0.680	Toyota	0.118
Renault	2.393	Shadow	0.659	Minardi	0.105
Lancia	2.250	BAR	0.657	Tecno	0.091
Talbot	1.923	Penske	0.575	ATS Wheels	0.079
Alfa Romeo	1.911	Surtees	0.458	Theodore	0.061
Wolf	1.681	Toleman	0.456	AGS	0.043
Tyrrell	1.653	Arrows	0.437	Osella	0.038
Porsche	1.515	Fittipaldi	0.427	Zakspeed	0.038

POLE POSITIONS

Ferrari	158	Cooper	11	Arrows	1
Williams	119	Maserati	10	Honda	1
McLaren	112	Ligier	9	Lola	1
Lotus	107	Mercedes-Benz	8	Porsche	1
Brabham	39	Vanwall	7	Stewart	1
Renault	31	March	5	Toleman	1
Benetton	15	Matra	4	Wolf	1
Tyrrell	14	Shadow	3		
Alfa Romeo	12	Jordan	2		
BRM	11	Lancia	2		

FASTEST LAPS

Ferrari	160	Cooper	14	Toleman	2
Williams	121	Matra	12	Wolf	2
McLaren	109	Ligier	9	Arrows	1
Lotus	71	Mercedes-Benz	9	Ensign	1
Brabham	41	March	7	Gordini	1
Benetton	36	Vanwall	6	Hesketh	1
Tyrrell	20	Surtees	3	Kojima	1
Renault	18	Eagle	2	Lancia	1
Maserati	15	Honda	2	Parnelli	1
BRM	15	Jordan	2		
Alfa Romeo	14	Shadow	2		

MOST LAPS IN THE LEAD

Ferrari	10182	Matra	668	Penske	45
McLaren	7768	Mercedes-Benz	589	Prost	37
Williams	7138	Ligier	537	Lancia	21
Lotus	5498	Vanwall	371	Porsche	20
Brabham	2723.5	March	338	Eagle	19
Benetton	1504	Wolf	213	Parnelli	10
Tyrrell	1493	Arrows	127.5	Surtees	9
BRM	1342	Jordan	116	Hill	8
Renault	1220	Hesketh	88	Talbot	5
Maserati	832	Stewart	84	Gordini	1
Cooper	829	Honda	79	Minardi	1
Alfa Romeo	701.6	Shadow	50		

MOST MILES IN THE LEAD

Ferrari	33421	Mercedes-Benz	2472	Eagle	205
McLaren	22619	Matra	2249	Penske	165
Williams	20672	Vanwall	1732	Porsche	107
Lotus	16285	Ligier	1558	Prost	99
Brabham	8252	March	927	Lancia	62
Benetton	4385	Wolf	504	Talbot	44
Tyrrell	4191	Jordan	405	Surtees	28
BRM	3786	Arrows	308	Parnelli	24
Renault	3707	Honda	296	Hill	19
Alfa Romeo	2978	Hesketh	246	Gordini	9
Maserati	2948	Stewart	226	Minardi	3
Cooper	2822	Shadow	208		

Engine Records

MOST STARTS

Ferrari (inc. Petronas and Acer)	671	Zakspeed	51	ATS	7
Ford	524	Ilmor	49	Veritas	6
Renault	320	Mecachrome (inc. Playlife		Aston Martin	5
Honda	237	and Supertec)	49	ERA	4
Alfa Romeo	225	Motori Moderni	44	Lancia	4
BRM	189	Asiatech	33	Sauber	4
BMW (inc. Megatron)	164	Gordini	33	Speluzzi	4
Mercedes-Benz	160	Repco	33	Kuchen	3
Mugen	147	Arrows	32	Pratt & Whitney	3
Hart	145	Vanwall	28	Butterworth	2
Matra	125	Alta	26	Scarab	2
Yamaha	116	Weslake	18	Borgward	1
Peugeot	115	Bristol	17	Bugatti	1
Maserati	108	Toyota	17	JAP	1
Porsche (inc. TAG)	105	Talbot	13	Jaguar	1
Climax	97	Simca	11	Offenhauser	1
Lamborghini	80	Lea-Francis	10	Serenissima	1
Judd	68	Tecno	10		
Cosworth	56	OSCA	8		

MOST WINS

Ford	175	Porsche (inc. TAG)	26	Repco	8
Ferrari	159	BRM	18	Mugen	4
Renault	95	BMW	14	Matra	3
Honda	71	Alfa Romeo	12	Weslake	1
Climax	40	Maserati	11		
Mercedes-Benz	40	Vanwall	9		

MOST POINTS

Ford	4615	Repco	175	Alta	14
Ferrari (inc. Petronas and Acer)	3914.27	Mecachrome (inc. Playlife and Supertec)	149	Weslake	13
				Lancia	9
Renault	2050	Peugeot	128	Arrows	7
Honda	1296.5	Vanwall	108	Lea-Francis	5
Mercedes-Benz	902.14	Judd	86	Sauber	5
Climax	866.5	Hart	63	Simca	5
BRM	607.5	Yamaha	36	Asiatech	3
Porsche (inc. TAG)	455.5	Gordini	25.14	Speluzzi	2
BMW (inc. Megatron)	450	Talbot	25	Toyota	2
Maserati	393.92	Cosworth	24	Zakspeed	2
Alfa Romeo	330	Lamborghini	20	Serenissima	1
Mugen	182	Ilmor	19	Tecno	1
Matra	175	Bristol	15		

POLE POSITIONS

Ferrari	158	Alfa Romeo	15	Hart	2
Ford	139	BRM	11	Lancia	2
Renault	135	Maserati	11	Mecachrome (inc. Playlife and Supertec)	1
Honda	74	Porsche (inc. TAG)	8		
Climax	44	Repco	7	Mugen	1
Mercedes-Benz	41	Vanwall	7		
BMW	26	Matra	4		

Tyre Records

MOST STARTS

Goodyear	492	Michelin	145	Engelbert	61
Pirelli	200	Firestone	110	Avon	27
Dunlop	176	Bridgestone	102	Continental	13

MOST WINS

Goodyear	368	Michelin	65	Continental	10
Dunlop	83	Pirelli	44	Engelbert	8
Bridgestone	70	Firestone	38		

MOST POINTS

Goodyear	9474.5	Michelin	1433.5	Engelbert	313.13
Dunlop	1989	Pirelli	1162.2	Continental	147.14
Bridgestone	1684	Firestone	969	Avon	8

POLE POSITIONS

Goodyear	358	Michelin	68	Engelbert	12
Dunlop	76	Firestone	49	Continental	8
Bridgestone	69	Pirelli	46		

NON-CHAMPIONSHIP F1 RACES

1950

10.04.50	Grand Prix de Pau (Pau)	Juan Manuel Fangio	RA	Maserati 4CLT/48	58.245
10.04.50	Richmond Trophy (Goodwood)	Reg Parnell	GB	Maserati 4CLT/48	77.609
16.04.50	Gran Premio di San Remo (San Remo)	Juan Manuel Fangio	RA	Alfa Romeo 158	58.873
30.04.50	Grand Prix de Paris (Montlhery)	Georges Grignard	F	Lago-Talbot T26C	93.118
15.06.50	British Empire Trophy (Douglas)	Bob Gerard	GB	ERA B-type	70.246
09.07.50	Gran Premio di Bari (Bari)	Giuseppe Farina	I	Alfa Romeo 158	80.182
13.07.50	JCC Jersey Road Race (St Helier)	Peter Whitehead	GB	Ferrari 125	91.000
16.07.50	Grand Prix d'Albi (Albi)	Louis Rosier	F	Lago-Talbot T26C	99.725
23.07.50	Grote Prijs van Nederland (Zandvoort)	Louis Rosier	F	Lago-Talbot T26C-DA	76.616
30.07.50	Grand Prix des Nations (Geneva)	Juan Manuel Fangio	RA	Alfa Romeo 158	79.293
07.08.50	Nottingham Trophy (Gamston)	David Hampshire	GB	Maserati 4CLT/48	91.100
12.08.50	Ulster Trophy (Dundrod)	Peter Whitehead	GB	Ferrari 125	84.326
15.08.50	Gran Premio di Pescara (Pescara)	Juan Manuel Fangio	RA	Alfa Romeo 158	84.168
26.08.50	International Trophy (Silverstone)	Giuseppe Farina	I	Alfa Romeo 158	90.157
30.09.50	Goodwood Trophy (Goodwood)	Reg Parnell	GB	BRM P15	81.704
29.10.50	Gran Premio do Penya Rhin (Montjuich Park)	Alberto Ascari	I	Ferrari 375	56.409

1951

11.03.51	Gran Premio di Siracusa (Syracuse, Sicily)	Luigi Villoresi	I	Ferrari 375	90.713
26.03.51	Grand Prix de Pau (Pau)	Luigi Villoresi	I	Ferrari 375	57.264
26.03.51	Richmond Trophy (Goodwood)	"B Bira"	SM	Maserati 4CLT/48	86.838
22.04.51	Gran Premio di San Remo (San Remo)	Alberto Ascari	I	Ferrari 375	63.195
29.04.51	Grand Prix de Bordeaux (Bordeaux)	Louis Rosier	F	Lago-Talbot T26C-DA	60.203
05.05.51	International Trophy (Silverstone)	Reg Parnell	GB	Ferrari 375	61.899
20.05.51	Grand Prix de Paris (Bois de Bologne)	Giuseppe Farina	I	Maserati 4CLT/48	67.332
02.06.51	Ulster Trophy (Dundrod)	Giuseppe Farina	I	Alfa Romeo 159	91.456
21.07.51	Scottish Grand Prix (Winfield)	Philip Fotheringham-Parker	GB	Maserati 4CLT/48	75.519
22.07.51	Grote Prijs van Nederland (Zandvoort)	Louis Rosier	F	Lago-Talbot T26C-DA	78.445
05.08.51	Grand Prix d'Albi (Albi)	Maurice Trintignant	F	Simca-Gordini 15	101.299
15.08.51	Gran Premio di Pescara (Pescara)	Jose Froilan Gonzalez	RA	Ferrari 375	85.506
02.09.51	Gran Premio di Bari (Bari)	Juan Manuel Fangio	RA	Alfa Romeo 159	83.889
29.09.51	Goodwood Trophy (Goodwood)	Giuseppe Farina	I	Alfa Romeo 159	95.115

1952

06.04.52	Gran Premio del Valentino (Valentino Park)	Luigi Villoresi	I	Ferrari 375	74.294
14.04.52	Richmond Trophy (Goodwood)	Jose Froilan Gonzalez	RA	Ferrari 375	88.238
11.05.52	Elaintarha Ajot (Helsinki)	Roger Laurent	B	Lago-Talbot T26C	61.484
01.06.52	Grand Prix d'Albi (Albi)	Louis Rosier	F	Ferrari 375	101.972
07.06.52	Ulster Trophy (Dundrod)	Piero Taruffi	I	Ferrari 375	81.432
02.08.52	Daily Mail Trophy (Boreham)	Luigi Villoresi	I	Ferrari 375	82.830
14.09.52	Skarpnacksloppet (Skarpnack)	Gunnar Carlsson	S	Mercury Special-Ford	59.053

1953

10.05.53	Elaintarha Ajot (Helsinki)	Rodney Nuckey	GB	Cooper T23-Bristol	64.471
31.05.53	Grand Prix d'Albi (Albi)	Louis Rosier	F	Ferrari 375	105.514
28.06.53	Grand Prix de Rouen (Rouen-les-Essarts)	Giuseppe Farina	I	Ferrari 500	84.446
13.09.53	Skarpnacksloppet (Skarpnack)	Erik Lundgren	S	Ford Special	60.541

1954

11.04.54	Gran Premio di Siracusa (Syracuse, Sicily)	Giuseppe Farina	I	Ferrari 625	97.087
19.04.54	Grand Prix de Pau (Pau)	Jean Behra	F	Gordini 16 (54)	62.299
19.04.54	Lavant Cup (Goodwood)	Reg Parnell	GB	Ferrari 625	88.758
09.05.54	Grand Prix de Bordeaux (Bordeaux)	Jose Froilan Gonzalez	RA	Ferrari 625	60.614
15.05.54	International Trophy (Silverstone)	Jose Froilan Gonzalez	RA	Ferrari 553 Squalo	92.780

22.05.54	Gran Premio di Bari (Bari)	Jose Froilan Gonzalez	RA	Ferrari 625	152.669
05.06.54	Curtis Trophy (Snetterton)	Roy Salvadori	GB	Maserati 250F	88.178
06.06.54	Gran Premio di Roma (Castel Fusano)	Onofre Marimon	RA	Maserati 250F	106.177
06.06.54	Grand Prix des Frontieres (Chimay)	"B Bira"	SM	Maserati 250F	98.539
07.06.54	BARC Formula 1 Race (Goodwood)	Reg Parnell	GB	Ferrari 625	87.591
07.06.54	Cornwall MRC Formula 1 Race (Davidstow)	John Riseley-Prichard	GB	Connaught A-Lea-Francis	74.210
19.06.54	Crystal Palace Trophy (Crystal Palace)	Reg Parnell	GB	Ferrari 625	72.881
11.07.54	Grand Prix de Rouen (Rouen-les-Essarts)	Maurice Trintignant	F	Ferrari 625	81.892
25.07.54	Grand Prix de Caen (Caen)	Maurice Trintignant	F	Ferrari 625	88.445
02.08.54	August Trophy (Crystal Palace)	Reg Parnell	GB	Ferrari 625	74.597
02.08.54	Cornwall MRC Formula 1 Race (Davidstow)	John Coombs	GB	Lotus 8-Lea-Francis	76.649
07.08.54	International Gold Cup (Oulton Park)	Stirling Moss	GB	Maserati 250F	83.468
14.08.54	Redex Trophy (Snetterton)	Reg Parnell	GB	Ferrari 625	88.755
15.08.54	Gran Premio di Pescara (Pescara)	Luigi Musso	I	Maserati 250F	87.493
28.08.54	Joe Fry Memorial Trophy (Castle Combe)	Horace Gould	GB	Cooper T23-Bristol (GP)	83.566
12.09.54	Circuit de Cadours (Cadours)	Jean Behra	F	Gordini 16 (54)	75.971
19.09.54	Grosser Preis von Berlin (Avus)	Karl Kling	D	Mercedes-Benz W196	132.612
25.09.54	Goodwood Trophy (Goodwood)	Stirling Moss	GB	Maserati 250F	91.489
02.10.54	Daily Telegraph Trophy (Aintree)	Stirling Moss	GB	Maserati 250F	85.435

1955

27.03.55	Gran Premio del Valentino (Valentino Park)	Alberto Ascari	I	Lancia D50	87.860
11.04.55	Grand Prix de Pau (Pau)	Jean Behra	F	Maserati 250F	62.138
11.04.55	Glover Trophy (Goodwood)	Roy Salvadori	GB	Maserati 250F	89.247
24.04.55	Grand Prix de Bordeaux (Bordeaux)	Jean Behra	F	Maserati 250F	64.688
07.05.55	International Trophy (Silverstone)	Peter Collins	GB	Maserati 250F	95.938
08.05.55	Gran Premio di Napoli (Posillipo)	Alberto Ascari	I	Lancia D50	68.721
29.05.55	Grand Prix d'Albi (Albi)	Andre Simon	F	Maserati 250F	81.690
29.05.55	Curtis Trophy (Snetterton)	Roy Salvadori	GB	Maserati 250F	89.357
30.05.55	Cornwall MRC Formula 1 Race (Davidstow)	Leslie Marr	GB	Connaught B-Alta	85.538
30.07.55	London Trophy (Crystal Palace)	Mike Hawthorn	GB	Maserati 250F	77.381
06.08.55	Daily Record Trophy (Charterhall)	Bob Gerard	GB	Maserati 250F	83.285
13.08.55	Redex Trophy (Snetterton)	Harry Schell	USA	Vanwall VW2	81.100
03.09.55	Daily Telegraph Trophy (Aintree)	Roy Salvadori	GB	Maserati 250F	83.721
24.09.55	International Gold Cup (Oulton Park)	Stirling Moss	GB	Maserati 250F	85.941
01.10.55	Avon Trophy (Castle Combe)	Harry Schell	USA	Vanwall VW2	86.071
23.10.55	Gran Premio di Siracusa (Syracuse, Sicily)	Tony Brooks	GB	Connaught B-Alta	100.792

1956

05.02.56	Gran Premio de la Ciudad de Buenos Aires (Mendoza)	Juan Manuel Fangio	RA	Lancia-Ferrari D50	83.090
02.04.56	Glover Trophy (Goodwood)	Stirling Moss	GB	Maserati 250F	94.349
15.04.56	Gran Premio di Siracusa (Syracuse, Sicily)	Juan Manuel Fangio	RA	Lancia-Ferrari D50	98.784
21.04.56	BARC 200 (Aintree)	Stirling Moss	GB	Maserati 250F	84.273
05.05.56	International Trophy (Silverstone)	Stirling Moss	GB	Vanwall VW2	100.466
06.05.56	Gran Premio di Napoli (Posillipo)	Robert Manzon	F	Gordini 16 (54)	64.975
24.06.56	Aintree 100 (Aintree)	Horace Gould	GB	Maserati 250F	83.081
22.07.56	Vanwall Trophy (Snetterton)	Roy Salvadori	GB	Maserati 250F	92.340
26.08.56	Grand Prix de Caen (Caen)	Harry Schell	USA	Maserati 250F	80.346
14.10.56	BRSCC Formula 1 Race (Brands Hatch)	Archie Scott-Brown	GB	Connaught B-Alta	73.777

1957

27.01.57	Gran Premio de la Ciudad de Buenos Aires (Buenos Aires)	Juan Manuel Fangio	RA	Maserati 250F	71.669
07.04.57	Gran Premio di Siracusa (Syracuse, Sicily)	Peter Collins	GB	Lancia-Ferrari D50	104.211
22.04.57	Grand Prix de Pau (Pau)	Jean Behra	F	Maserati 250F	62.804
22.04.57	Glover Trophy (Goodwood)	Stuart Lewis-Evans	GB	Connaught B-Alta	90.655
28.04.57	Gran Premio di Napoli (Posillipo)	Peter Collins	GB	Lancia-Ferrari D50	70.058
14.07.57	Grand Prix de Reims (Reims)	Luigi Musso	I	Lancia-Ferrari D50	124.046
28.07.57	Grand Prix de Caen (Caen)	Jean Behra	F	BRM P25	91.486
14.09.57	International Trophy (Silverstone)	Jean Behra	F	BRM P25	99.946
22.09.57	Gran Premio di Modena (Modena)	Jean Behra	F	Maserati 250F	83.209
27.10.57	Grand Prix du Maroc (Ain Diab)	Jean Behra	F	Maserati 250F	112.652

1958

07.04.58	Glover Trophy (Goodwood)	Mike Hawthorn	GB	Ferrari Dino 246	94.885
13.04.58	Gran Premio di Siracusa (Syracuse, Sicily)	Luigi Musso	I	Ferrari Dino 246	102.009
19.04.58	BARC 200 (Aintree)	Stirling Moss	GB	Cooper T45-Climax	85.664
03.05.58	International Trophy (Silverstone)	Peter Collins	GB	Ferrari Dino 246	101.817
20.07.58	Grand Prix de Caen (Caen)	Stirling Moss	GB	Cooper T45-Climax	93.914

1959

30.03.59	Glover Trophy (Goodwood)	Stirling Moss	GB	Cooper T51-Climax	90.314
18.04.59	BARC 200 (Aintree)	Jean Behra	F	Ferrari Dino 246	88.763
02.05.59	International Trophy (Silverstone)	Jack Brabham	AUS	Cooper T51-Climax	102.730
26.09.59	International Gold Cup (Oulton Park)	Stirling Moss	GB	Cooper T51-Climax	96.294
10.10.59	Silver City Trophy (Snetterton)	Ron Flockhart	GB	BRM P25	101.710

1960

18.04.60	Glover Trophy (Goodwood)	Innes Ireland	GB	Lotus 18-Climax	100.387
14.05.60	International Trophy (Silverstone)	Innes Ireland	GB	Lotus 18-Climax	108.831
01.08.60	Silver City Trophy (Brands Hatch)	Jack Brabham	AUS	Cooper T53-Climax	92.863
17.09.60	Lombank Trophy (Snetterton)	Innes Ireland	GB	Lotus 18-Climax	102.730
24.09.60	International Gold Cup (Oulton Park)	Stirling Moss	GB	Lotus 18-Climax	93.858

1961

26.03.61	Lombank Trophy (Snetterton)	Jack Brabham	AUS	Cooper T53-Climax	101.067
03.04.61	Glover Trophy (Goodwood)	John Surtees	GB	Cooper T53-Climax	95.747
03.04.61	Grand Prix de Pau (Pau)	Jim Clark	GB	Lotus 18-Climax	63.517
09.04.61	Grand Prix de Bruxelles (Heysel)	Jack Brabham	AUS	Cooper T53-Climax	80.357
16.04.61	Grosser Preis von Wien (Aspern)	Stirling Moss	GB	Lotus 18-Climax	85.673
22.04.61	BARC 200 (Aintree)	Jack Brabham	AUS	Cooper T55-Climax	78.066
25.04.61	Gran Premio di Siracusa (Syracuse, Sicily)	Giancarlo Baghetti	I	Ferrari Dino 156	106.105
14.05.61	Gran Premio di Napoli (Posillipo)	Giancarlo Baghetti	I	Ferrari Dino 156	67.281
22.05.61	London Trophy (Crystal Palace)	Roy Salvadori	GB	Cooper T53-Climax	82.552
03.06.61	Silver City Trophy (Brands Hatch)	Stirling Moss	GB	Lotus 18/21-Climax	91.770
23.07.61	Grosser Preis der Solitude (Solitude)	Innes Ireland	GB	Lotus 21-Climax	105.202
20.08.61	Kannonloppet (Karlskoga)	Stirling Moss	GB	Lotus 18/21-Climax	72.498
26.08.61	Grand Prix Danmark (Roskildering)	Stirling Moss	GB	Lotus 18/21-Climax	59.723
03.09.61	Gran Premio di Modena (Modena)	Stirling Moss	GB	Lotus 18/21-Climax	88.081
17.09.61	Flugplatzrennen (Zeltweg)	Innes Ireland	GB	Lotus 21-Climax	91.429
23.09.61	International Gold Cup (Oulton Park)	Stirling Moss	GB	Ferguson P99-Climax	88.828
01.10.61	Lewis-Evans Trophy (Brands Hatch)	Tony Marsh	GB	BRM P48-Climax	91.152
10.10.61	Coppa Italia (Vallelunga)	Giancarlo Baghetti	I	Porsche 718	65.145
09.12.61	Rand Grand Prix (Kyalami)	Jim Clark	GB	Lotus 21-Climax	90.543
17.12.61	Natal Grand Prix (Westmead)	Jim Clark	GB	Lotus 21-Climax	90.479
26.12.61	South African Grand Prix (East London)	Jim Clark	GB	Lotus 21-Climax	92.200

1962

02.01.62	Cape Grand Prix (Killarney)	Trevor Taylor	GB	Lotus 21-Climax	81.505
01.04.62	Grand Prix de Bruxelles (Heysel)	Willy Mairesse	B	Ferrari Dino 156	80.789
14.04.62	Lombank Trophy (Snetterton)	Jim Clark	GB	Lotus 24-Climax	101.086
23.04.62	Lavant Cup (Goodwood)	Bruce McLaren	NZ	Cooper T55-Climax	99.050
23.04.62	Glover Trophy (Goodwood)	Graham Hill	GB	BRM P57	102.648
23.04.62	Grand Prix de Pau (Pau)	Maurice Trintignant	F	Lotus 18/21-Climax	64.477
28.04.62	BARC 200 (Aintree)	Jim Clark	GB	Lotus 24-Climax	92.653
12.05.62	International Trophy (Silverstone)	Graham Hill	GB	BRM P57	99.730
20.05.62	Gran Premio di Napoli (Posillipo)	Willy Mairesse	B	Ferrari Dino 156	69.963
11.06.62	International 2000 Guineas (Mallory Park)	John Surtees	GB	Lola Mk4-Climax	93.375
11.06.62	Crystal Palace Trophy (Crystal Palace)	Innes Ireland	GB	Lotus 24-BRM	86.342
01.07.62	Grand Prix de Reims (Reims)	Bruce McLaren	NZ	Cooper T60-Climax	127.025
15.07.62	Grosser Preis der Solitude (Solitude)	Dan Gurney	USA	Porsche 804	100.677
12.08.62	Kannonloppet (Karlskoga)	Masten Gregory	USA	Lotus 24-BRM	78.292

19.08.62	Gran Premio del Mediterraneo (Enna)	Lorenzo Bandini	I	Ferrari Dino 156	128.892
25.08.62	Grand Prix Danmark (Roskildering)	Jack Brabham	AUS	Lotus 24-Climax	59.965
01.09.62	International Gold Cup (Oulton Park)	Jim Clark	GB	Lotus 25-Climax	97.702
04.11.62	Gran Premio de Mexico (Mexico City)	Jim Clark/Trevor Taylor	GB	Lotus 25-Climax	90.314
15.12.62	Rand Grand Prix (Kyalami)	Jim Clark	GB	Lotus 25-Climax	94.467
22.12.62	Natal Grand Prix (Westmead)	Trevor Taylor	GB	Lotus 25-Climax	93.356

1963

30.03.63	Lombank Trophy (Snetterton)	Graham Hill	GB	BRM P57	95.467
15.04.63	Glover Trophy (Goodwood)	Innes Ireland	GB	Lotus 24-BRM	102.439
15.04.63	Grand Prix de Pau (Pau)	Jim Clark	GB	Lotus 25-Climax	61.619
21.04.63	Gran Premio d'Imola (Imola)	Jim Clark	GB	Lotus 25-Climax	99.380
25.04.63	Gran Premio di Siracusa (Syracuse, Sicily)	Jo Siffert	CH	Lotus 24-BRM	92.436
27.04.63	BARC 200 (Aintree)	Graham Hill	GB	BRM P57	94.392
11.05.63	International Trophy (Silverstone)	Jim Clark	GB	Lotus 25-Climax	108.125
19.05.63	Gran Premio di Roma (Vallelunga)	Bob Anderson	RSR	Lola Mk4-Climax	77.874
28.07.63	Grosser Preis der Solitude (Solitude)	Jack Brabham	AUS	Brabham BT3-Climax	106.213
11.08.63	Kannonloppet (Karlskoga)	Jim Clark	GB	Lotus 25-Climax	69.417
18.08.63	Gran Premio del Mediterraneo (Enna)	John Surtees	GB	Ferrari Dino 156	137.653
01.09.63	Grosser Preis von Osterreich (Zeltweg)	Jack Brabham	AUS	Brabham BT3-Climax	96.286
21.09.63	International Gold Cup (Oulton Park)	Jim Clark	GB	Lotus 25-Climax	98.337
14.12.63	Rand Grand Prix (Kyalami)	John Surtees	GB	Ferrari Dino 156	95.182

1964

14.03.64	Daily Mirror Trophy (Snetterton)	Innes Ireland	GB	BRP 1-BRM	78.077
30.03.64	News of the World Trophy (Goodwood)	Jim Clark	GB	Lotus 25-Climax	104.909
12.04.64	Gran Premio di Siracusa (Syracuse, Sicily)	John Surtees	GB	Ferrari 158	104.519
18.04.64	BARC 200 (Aintree)	Jack Brabham	AUS	Brabham BT7-Climax	93.457
02.05.64	International Trophy (Silverstone)	Jack Brabham	AUS	Brabham BT7-Climax	110.355
19.07.64	Grosser Preis der Solitude (Solitude)	Jim Clark	GB	Lotus 33-Climax	91.435
16.08.64	Gran Premio del Mediterraneo (Enna)	Jo Siffert	CH	Brabham BT11-BRM	137.698
12.12.64	Rand Grand Prix (Kyalami)	Graham Hill	GB	Brabham BT11-BRM	92.161

1965

13.03.65	Daily Mail Race of Champions (Brands Hatch)	Mike Spence	GB	Lotus 33-Climax	96.583
04.04.65	Gran Premio di Siracusa (Syracuse, Sicily)	Jim Clark	GB	Lotus 33-Climax	112.601
19.04.65	Sunday Mirror Trophy (Goodwood)	Jim Clark	GB	Lotus 25-Climax	105.067
15.05.65	International Trophy (Silverstone)	Jackie Stewart	GB	BRM P261	111.664
15.08.65	Gran Premio del Mediterraneo (Enna-Pergusa)	Jo Siffert	CH	Brabham BT11-BRM	139.308
04.12.65	Rand Grand Prix (Kyalami)	Jack Brabham	AUS	Brabham BT11-Climax	97.613

1966

01.01.66	South African Grand Prix (Kyalami)	Mike Spence	GB	Lotus 33-Climax (2.0)	102.150
01.05.66	Gran Premio di Siracusa (Syracuse, Sicily)	John Surtees	GB	Ferrari 312	117.001
14.05.66	International Trophy (Silverstone)	Jack Brabham	AUS	Brabham BT19-Repco	116.063
17.09.66	International Gold Cup (Oulton Park)	Jack Brabham	AUS	Brabham BT19-Repco	100.041

1967

12.03.67	Race of Champions (Brands Hatch)	Dan Gurney	USA	Eagle T1G-Weslake	98.589
15.04.67	Spring Trophy (Oulton Park)	Jack Brabham	AUS	Brabham BT20-Repco	104.944
29.04.67	International Trophy (Silverstone)	Michael Parkes	GB	Ferrari 312	114.650
21.05.67	Syracuse Grand Prix (Syracuse, Sicily)	Ludovico Scarfiotti*	I	Ferrari 312	116.034
		Michael Parkes*	GB	Ferrari 312	
16.09.67	International Gold Cup (Oulton Park)	Jack Brabham	AUS	Brabham BT24-Repco	106.319
12.11.67	Gran Premio de Espana (Jarama)	Jim Clark	GB	Lotus 49-Ford	125.291

*dead heat

1968

17.03.68	Race of Champions (Brands Hatch)	Bruce McLaren	NZ	McLaren M7A-Ford	100.773
25.04.68	International Trophy (Silverstone)	Denny Hulme	NZ	McLaren M7A-Ford	122.176
17.08.68	International Gold Cup (Oulton Park)	Jackie Stewart	GB	Matra MS10-Ford	109.256

1969

16.03.69	Race of Champions (Brands Hatch)	Jackie Stewart	GB	Matra MS80-Ford	108.646
30.03.69	International Trophy (Silverstone)	Jack Brabham	AUS	Brabham BT26A-Ford	107.002
13.04.69	Gran Premio de Madrid (Jarama)	Keith Holland	GB	Lola T142-Chevrolet	79.956
16.08.69	International Gold Cup (Oulton Park)	Jacky Ickx	B	Brabham BT26A-Ford	109.570

1970

22.03.70	Race of Champions (Brands Hatch)	Jackie Stewart	GB	March 701-Ford	109.108
26.04.70	International Trophy (Silverstone)	Chris Amon	NZ	March 701-Ford	124.186
22.08.70	International Gold Cup (Oulton Park)	John Surtees	GB	Surtees TS7-Ford	110.803

1971

24.01.71	Gran Premio de la Republica Argentina (Buenos Aires)	Chris Amon	NZ	Matra-Simca MS120	97.209
21.03.71	Daily Mail Race of Champions (Brands Hatch)	Clay Regazzoni	CH	Ferrari 312B2	108.041
28.03.71	Questor Grand Prix (Ontario)	Mario Andretti	USA	Ferrari 312B	109.692
09.04.71	Rothmans International Trophy (Oulton Park)	Pedro Rodriguez	MEX	BRM P160	115.128
08.05.71	GKN/Daily Express International Trophy (Silverstone)	Graham Hill	GB	Brabham BT34-Ford	128.527
13.06.71	Jochen Rindt Memorial Trophy (Hockenheim)	Jacky Ickx	B	Ferrari 312B	126.218
21.08.71	Rothmans Gold Cup (Oulton Park)	John Surtees	GB	Surtees TS9-Ford	114.955
24.10.71	Rothmans World Championship Victory Race (Brands Hatch)	Peter Gethin	GB	BRM P160	111.822

1972

19.03.72	STP/Daily Mail Race of Champions (Brands Hatch)	Emerson Fittipaldi	BR	Lotus 72D-Ford	112.215
30.03.72	Grande Premio do Brasil (Interlagos)	Carlos Reutemann	RA	Brabham BT34-Ford	112.882
23.04.72	GKN/Daily Express Trophy (Silverstone)	Emerson Fittipaldi	BR	Lotus 72D-Ford	131.806
29.05.72	Rothmans Gold Cup (Oulton Park)	Denny Hulme	NZ	McLaren M19A-Ford	115.725
18.06.72	Grand Premio della Republica Italia (Vallelunga)	Emerson Fittipaldi	BR	Lotus 72D-Ford	97.839
28.08.72	Rothmans £50,000 (Brands Hatch)	Emerson Fittipaldi	BR	Lotus 72D-Ford	109.836
22.10.72	John Player Challenge Trophy (Brands Hatch)	Jean-Pierre Beltoise	F	BRM P180	106.360

1973

18.03.73	Daily Mail Race of Champions (Brands Hatch)	Peter Gethin	GB	Chevron B24-Chevrolet*	110.837
08.04.73	GKN/Daily Express International Trophy (Silverstone)	Jackie Stewart	GB	Tyrrell 006-Ford	132.827

*F5000 car

1974

03.02.74	Grande Premio Presidenta Medici (Brasilia)	Emerson Fittipaldi	BR	McLaren M23-Ford	108.348
17.03.74	Simoniz/Daily Mail Race of Champions (Brands Hatch)	Jacky Ickx	B	Lotus 72D-Ford	99.958

| 7.04.74 | Daily Express International Trophy (Silverstone) | James Hunt | GB | Hesketh 308-Ford | 133.577 |

1975

16.03.75	British Airways/Daily Mail Race of Champions (Brands Hatch)	Tom Pryce	GB	Shadow DN5A-Ford	113.792
13.04.75	Daily Express International Trophy (Silverstone)	Niki Lauda	A	Ferrari 312T	134.335
24.08.75	Grand Prix de Suisse (Dijon-Prenois)	Clay Regazzoni	CH	Ferrari 312T	79.867

1976

| 14.03.76 | Daily Mail Race of Champions (Brands Hatch) | James Hunt | GB | McLaren M23-Ford | 108.111 |
| 11.04.76 | Graham Hill International Trophy (Silverstone) | James Hunt | GB | McLaren M23-Ford | 132.579 |

1977

| 20.03.77 | Marlboro/Daily Mail Race of Champions (Brands Hatch) | James Hunt | GB | McLaren M23-Ford | 116.363 |

1978

| 19.03.78 | Daily Express International Trophy (Silverstone) | Keke Rosberg | SF | Theodore TR1-Ford | 96.637 |

1979

| 15.04.79 | Marlboro/Daily Mail Race of Champions (Brands Hatch) | Gilles Villeneuve | CDN | Ferrari 312T3 | 117.718 |
| 16.09.79 | Gran Premio di Dino Ferrari (Imola) | Niki Lauda | A | Brabham BT48-Alfa Romeo | 118.026 |

1980

| 01.06.80 | Gran Premio de Espana (Jarama) | Alan Jones | AUS | Williams FW07B-Ford | 98.358 |

1981

| 07.02.81 | Nashua Grand Prix of South Africa (Kyalami) | Carlos Reutemann | RA | Williams FW07B-Ford | 112.306 |

1983

| 10.04.83 | Marlboro Race of Champions (Brands Hatch) | Keke Rosberg | SF | Williams FW08C-Ford | 117.787 |

Early Grand Prix Racing

1933 Achille Varzi and Baconin Borzacchini lead at the start of the 1933 Monaco Grand Prix.

City to City Races 1894-1903

Although there had been an unsuccessful attempt to organise a motoring competition near Paris as early as 1887, motor racing was officially born on 22 July 1894 when twenty-one cars left the Porte Maillot in Paris for the eighty-mile trip to Rouen. The *Petit Journal*-sponsored event was a reliability trial, with first prize of 5000 francs awarded to the driver of the first car that completed the course safely and at low running cost. Another stipulation was that each car should have both a driver and a mechanic, and when the first driver to finish, Count de Dion, did not have a mechanic he forfeited the spoils of victory.

Within twelve months a newly formed committee (which would become the Automobile Club de France in 1896) organised the first true race from Paris to Bordeaux and back. This set the format for the inter-city races that would dominate racing for eight years.

Each year the ACF chose a new destination for their Paris races, and in 1903 this was Madrid. Cars had to weigh under 1000kg, so to have the largest possible engines, designers built light (and fragile) chassis. On the first day's run to Bordeaux, an estimated three million spectators lined the roads to watch these huge cars, some of which were capable of over 80 mph in a straight line. Unfortunately, their brakes were not as effective, and after a series of fearful accidents left five competitors and numerous spectators dead, the event was abandoned.

The searing heat, blinding dust, and poor crowd control had turned the Paris-Madrid race into a disaster, and the ACF turned to closed circuit racing for the future, albeit on courses of over 50 miles in length.

1894

PARIS-ROUEN

22 June 1894. 78.75 miles

1	Jules de Dion*	de Dion	6h48m00
2	Georges Lemaitre	Peugeot	6h51m30
3	Doriot	Peugeot	7h04m30
4	Paul Panhard	Panhard	7h21m30
5	Emile Levassor	Panhard	7h43m30
6	Kraeutler	Peugeot	7h46m30

*Ineligible for first prize as not accompanied by a mechanic. Winner's average speed: 11.58 mph

1895

PARIS-BORDEAUX-PARIS

11-13 June 1895. 732 miles

1	Emile Levassor*	Panhard	48h48m00
2	Rigoulot*	Peugeot	54h35m00
3	A Koechlin	Peugeot	59h48m00
4	Doriot	Peugeot	59h49m00
5	driver unknown	Roger	64h30m00
6	Emile Mayade	Panhard	72h14m00

*Ineligible for first prize as a their cars were two-seaters and only four-seaters were eligible. Winner's average speed: 15.00 mph

1896

PARIS-MARSEILLE-PARIS

24 September-3 October 1896. 1062.5 miles

1	Emile Mayade	Panhard	67h42m58
2	Merkel	Panhard	68h11m05
3	Viet	de Dion tricycle	71h01m05
4	d'Hostingue	Panhard	71h23m22
5	Collomb	de Dion tricycle	73h30m12
6	Berlet	Peugeot	75h29m24

Winner's average speed: 15.69 mph

1897

PARIS-DIEPPE

24 July 1897. 106.2 miles

1	Paul Jamin	Bollee	4h13m33
2	Jules de Dion	de Dion	4h19m34
3	Gilles Hourgieres	Panhard	4h36m00
4	Fernand Charron	Panhard	4h38m31
5	Pellier	Bollee	4h43m55
6	Bertrand	de Dion	4h45m15

Winner's average speed: 25.13 mph

1898

PARIS-AMSTERDAM-PARIS

7-13 July 1898. 889.25 miles

1	Fernand Charron	Panhard	33h04m34
2	Leonce Girardot	Panhard	33h25m18
3	Etienne Giraud	Bollee	34h08m58
4	Rene de Knyff	Panhard	34h58m50
5	M Loysel	Bollee	35h19m09
6	Adam	Panhard	35h45m57

Winner's average speed: 26.88 mph

1899

PARIS-BORDEAUX

24 May 1899. 351 miles

1	Fernand Charron	Panhard	11h43m20
2	Rene de Knyff	Panhard	11h51m26
3	Leonce Girardot	Panhard	12h32m35
4	Archambault	Panhard	12h37m45
5	Gilles Hourgieres	Panhard	13h03m44
6	Antony	Mors	13h17m43

Winner's average speed: 29.94 mph

TOUR DE FRANCE AUTOMOBILE

16-24 July 1899. 1350 miles

1	Rene de Knyff	Panhard	44h43m39.2
2	Leonce Girardot	Panhard	49h37m39.4
3	Gaston de Chasseloup-Laubat	Panhard	49h44m18.0
4	Pinson	Panhard	52h34m17.8
5	Castelnau	Bollee	53h29m07.0
6	George Heath	Panhard	58h47m26.0

Winner's average speed: 30.18 mph

1900

PARIS-TOULOUSE-PARIS

25-28 July 1900. 837.1 miles

1 Alfred Levegh	Mors	20h50m09
2 Pinson	Panhard	22h11m01
3 Carl Voight	Panhard	22h11m51
4 Etienne Giraud	Panhard	22h55m32
5 Georges Teste	de Dion	23h54m01
6 Antony	Mors	26h46m27

Winner's average speed: 40.18 mph

1901

PARIS-BORDEAUX

29 May 1901. 327.6 miles

1 Henri Fournier	Mors	6h10m44
2 Maurice Farman	Panhard	6h41m15
3 Carl Voight	Panhard	7h15m11
4 Pinson	Panhard	7h45m51
5 Axt	Panhard	7h46m17
6 Etienne Giraud	Panhard	8h08m48

Winner's average speed: 53.02 mph

PARIS-BERLIN

27-29 June 1901. 687 miles

1 Henri Fournier	Mors	15h33m06
2 Leonce Girardot	Panhard	16h38m38
3 Rene de Knyff	Panhard	16h40m02
4 Brasier	Mors	17h14m35
5 Henri Farman	Panhard	17h46m06
6 Fernand Charron	Panhard	18h20m57

Winner's average speed: 44.18 mph

1902

PARIS-VIENNA

26-29 June 1902. 615.4 miles

1 Marcel Renault	Renault	15h47m43.8
2 Henri Farman	Panhard	16h00m30.2
3 J Edmond	Darracq	16h10m16.2
4 Louis Zborowski	Mercedes	16h13m29.6
5 Maurice Farman	Panhard	16h19m29.4
6 Paul Baras	Darracq	17h04m52.0

Winner's average speed: 38.96 mph

1903

PARIS-MADRID

24 May 1903. 342 miles (stopped at Bordeaux due to fatal accidents)

1 Fernand Gabriel	Mors	5h14m31.2
2 Louis Renault	Renault	5h29m39.2
3 Jacques Salleron	Mors	5h47m01.8
4 Charles Jarrott	de Dietrich	5h52m55.0
5 Pierre de Crawhez	Panhard	5h54m11.4
6 John Warden	Mercedes	5h55m30.8

Winner's average speed: 65.24 mph

Gordon Bennett Cup

The promotional value of motor racing was recognised early in its history. In 1899 James Gordon Bennett of the *New York Herald's* European edition announced the first Coupe Internationale, now better known as the Gordon Bennett Trophy.

National teams of up to three competitors could enter, provided drivers and riding mechanics were members of the national motoring organisation and all of the car's components were made in that country. These requirements led Mercedes to build cars both in Germany and Austria in 1904-05 to gain more entries. The winning country won the right to hold the following year's race.

Although not well supported at first, by 1904 six nations competed, and the Automobile Club de France were forced to organise an elimination race to decide their entries from a field of twenty-nine. This pressure for French entries finally forced the Trophy to be abandoned after the 1905 race. The ACF decided to replace it with a new event in which all manufacturers, irrespective of nationality, could enter up to three cars—the birth of Grand Prix racing.

1900

14 June 1900. Paris-Lyon. 353.35 miles

1 Fernand Charron	Panhard 40		9h09m00
2 Leonce Girardot	Panhard 40		10h36m23

No other finishers. Winner's average speed: 38.617 mph

1901

29 May 1901. Paris-Bordeaux. 327.60 miles

1 Leonce Girardot	Panhard 40		8h50m59

No other finishers. Winner's average speed: 37.018 mph

1902

26-28 June 1902. Paris-Innsbruck (part of the Paris-Vienna race). 351.46 miles

1 Selwyn Edge	Napier 50		11h02m52.6

No other finishers. Winner's average speed: 31.812 mph

1903

2 July 1903. Athy, Ireland. 3 laps of the 40-mile circuit A and 4 laps of the 51.88-mile circuit B = 327.52 miles

1 Camille Jenatzy	Mercedes 90hp	7	6h39m00
2 Rene de Knyff	Panhard 70	7	6h50m40
3 Henri Farman	Panhard 70	7	6h51m44
4 Fernand Gabriel	Mors Z	7	7h11m33

No other finishers. Winner's average speed: 49.245 mph. Fastest lap: Circuit A: Foxhall Keene (Mercedes 90hp), 46m03; Circuit B: Gabriel, 1h00m19

1904

17 June 1904. Homburg, Germany. 4 laps of a 79.465 mile-circuit = 317.860 miles

1 Leon Thery	Richard-Brasier	4	5h50m01.4
2 Camille Jenatzy	Mercedes 60	4	6h01m29.4
3 Henri Rougier	Turcat-Mery	4	6h47m09.8
4 Pierre de Caters	Mercedes 60	4	6h47m30.0

1904 Leon Thery's victorious Richard-Brasier about to start the Gordon Bennett Trophy.

5	Edgar Braun	Mercedes 60	4	6h59m47.8
6	Lucien Hautvast	Pipe	4	7h02m35.0

Winner's average speed: 54.487 mph. Fastest lap: Thery, 1h26m22.2

1905

5 July 1905. Auvergne, France. 4 laps of a 85.350 mile-circuit = 341.400 miles

1	Leon Thery	Richard-Brasier	4	7h02m42.6
2	Felice Nazzaro	Fiat	4	7h10m09.2
3	Alessandro Cagno	Fiat	4	7h21m22.6
4	Gustave Caillois	Richard-Brasier	4	7h27m06.4
5	Christian Werner	Mercedes	4	8h03m30.0
6	Arthur Duray	de Dietrich 24/28	4	8h05m00.0

Winner's average speed: 48.459 mph. Fastest lap: Vincenzo Lancia (Fiat), 1h34m57

Grand Prix Racing 1906-49

The first Grand Prix was held over two days in June on the roads near Le Mans. The event had the desired effect of allowing French motor manufacturers more entries, and the Hungarian Ferenc Szisz gave Renault the honour of winning the first-ever Grand Prix, despite a strong challenge from Felice Nazzaro's Fiat.

Although an American event was organised in 1908, it was not until after World War I that other European nations followed suit. The format became established during the twenties as circuits in Italy, Belgium, Spain, Britain, and Germany (albeit for sports cars) all staged Grands Prix.

The Depression saw fields dwindle and works teams withdraw, but new rules introduced in 1934 heralded an era dominated by the state-backed German teams, whose government hoped to reap political capital from success in the sport. These years did, however, provide some of the best racing ever seen between legendary drivers such as Rudolf Caracciola, Bernd Rosemeyer, and Tazio Nuvolari. A European Championship was also inaugurated in 1935 as a forerunner to today's World Championship.

Rather than face inevitable defeat in Grand Prix racing, Alfa Romeo turned its attention to Voiturette racing, the equivalent of the later F2 or F3000 categories. In 1938 the company's supercharged 158 "Alfetta" began to win in the second formula, and after peace was restored to Europe, it was eligible for the new category, now named Formula 1 for the first time.

WORLD CHAMPIONSHIP

The first World Championship of Grand Prix racing was held in 1925 as a manufacturers title, with the Indianapolis 500 joining national Grands Prix as qualifying rounds.

year	constructor	qualifying races
1925	Alfa Romeo	Indianapolis 500, Belgian GP, French GP, and Italian GP
1926	Bugatti	Indianapolis 500, French GP, European GP, Spanish GP, English GP, and Italian GP
1927	Delage	Indianapolis 500, French GP, Spanish GP, Italian GP, and English GP

EUROPEAN CHAMPIONSHIP

In 1935 the German national authority suggested that for the first time an official champion driver should be chosen for Grand Prix racing. Points were awarded as follows:

1 to 1st	5 to those who have completed 50% of race
2 to 2nd	6 to those who have completed 25% of race
3 to 3rd	7 to those who have completed less than 25% of race
4 to 4th and all those to have completed over 75% of race	8 to those who did not start

with the champion having scored the fewest points.

However, when applied to the 1939 season, this system makes Hermann Muller European Champion rather than Hermann Lang, as was declared at the time.

year	driver	nat	car	qualifying rounds
1935	Rudolf Caracciola	D	Mercedes-Benz W25B	Belgian GP, German GP, Swiss GP, Italian GP, and Spanish GP
1936	Bernd Rosemeyer	D	Auto Union C	Monaco GP, German GP, Swiss GP, and Italian GP
1937	Rudolf Caracciola	D	Mercedes-Benz W125	Belgian GP, German GP, Monaco GP, Swiss GP, and Italian GP
1938	Rudolf Caracciola	D	Mercedes-Benz W154	French GP, German GP, Swiss GP, and Italian GP
1939*	Hermann Lang	D	Mercedes-Benz W163	Belgian GP, French GP, German GP, and Swiss GP
or	Hermann Muller	D	Auto Union D	

*champion in doubt due to scoring inconsistency

Rules

1906	1000kg maximum weight
1907	9.4mpg fuel consumption limit
1908	1100kg minimum weight. Cylinder bore limited to 155mm for 4 cylinder engines and 127mm for 6 cylinders
1909-11	**NO GRAND PRIX RACING**
1912	1750mm minimum width
1913	800kg minimum weight, 1100kg maximum weight. 14mpg fuel consumption limit
1914	4500cc maximum engine capacity. 1100kg maximum weight
1915-20	**NO GRAND PRIX RACING**
1921	3000cc maximum engine capacity. 800kg minimum weight
1922-24	2000cc maximum engine capacity. 650kg minimum weight
1925	Engine capacity and minimum weight unchanged. Riding mechanics banned but cars still required to have two seats
1926	1500cc maximum engine capacity. 600kg minimum weight
1927	Engine capacity unchanged. 700kg minimum weight. Two seats no longer required
1928	550kg minimum weight, 750kg maximum
1929	900kg minimum weight, commercial fuel stipulated
1930	1100cc minimum engine capacity. 900kg minimum weight. 30% benzole fuel allowed
1931	Minimum race duration of 10 hours. No engine or weight restrictions
1932	Race duration between 5 and 10 hours. No engine or weight restrictions
1933	500 km maximum. No engine or weight restrictions
1934-37	750kg minimum weight
1938-39	4500cc for normally aspirated and 3000cc supercharged maximum engine capacity. 400-850kg minimum weight depending on engine size
1945-46	No standardised rules
1947-53	Formula 1. 4500cc normally aspirated and 1500cc supercharged maximum engine capacity

1906 Ferenc Szisz's Renault wins the very first Grand Prix in the countryside around Le Mans.

1906

GRAND PRIX DE L'AUTOMOBILE CLUB DE FRANCE

26-27 June 1906. Le Mans. 12 laps of a 64.120 mile-circuit = 769.440 miles

1	Ferenc Szisz	Renault AK	12	12h14m07.0
2	Felice Nazzaro	Fiat 130hp	12	12h46m26.4
3	Albert Clement	Clement-Bayard 100hp	12	12h49m46.2
4	Jules Barillier	Brasier 105hp	12	13h53m00.0
5	Vincenzo Lancia	Fiat 130hp	12	14h22m11.0
6	George Heath	Panhard 130	12	14h47m45.4

Winner's average speed: 62.887 mph. Fastest lap: Paul Baras (Brasier 105hp), 52m25.4

1907

GRAND PRIX DE L'AUTOMOBILE CLUB DE FRANCE

2 July 1907. Dieppe. 10 laps of a 47.840 mile-circuit = 478.400 miles

1	Felice Nazzaro	Fiat	10	6h46m33.0
2	Ferenc Szisz	Renault AK	10	6h53m10.6
3	Paul Baras	Brasier	10	7h05m05.6
4	Fernand Gabriel	Lorraine-Dietrich	10	7h11m39.0
5	Victor Rigal	Darracq	10	7h12m36.4
6	Gustave Caillois	Darracq	10	7h15m58.6

Winner's average speed: 70.604 mph. Fastest lap: Arthur Duray (Lorraine-Dietrich), 37m59.8

1908

GRAND PRIX DE L'AUTOMOBILE CLUB DE FRANCE

7 July 1908. Dieppe. 10 laps of a 47.840 mile-circuit = 478.400 miles

1	Christian Lautenschlager	Mercedes	10	6h55m43.8
2	Victor Hemery	Benz	10	7h04m24.0
3	Rene Hanriot	Benz	10	7h05m13.0
4	Victor Rigal	Clement-Bayard	10	7h30m36.6
5	Willy Poge	Mercedes	10	7h32m31.0
6	Carl Jorns	Opel	10	7h39m40.0

Winner's average speed: 69.045 mph. Fastest lap: Otto Salzer (Mercedes), 36m31.0

AMERICAN GRAND PRIZE

26 November 1908. Savannah. 16 laps of a 25.130 mile-circuit = 402.080 miles

1	Louis Wagner	Fiat	16	6h10m31.0
2	Victor Hemery	Benz 150hp	16	6h11m27.0
3	Felice Nazzaro	Fiat	16	6h18m47.0
4	Rene Hanriot	Benz 150hp	16	6h26m12.0
5	Lucien Hautvast	Clement-Bayard	16	6h34m06.0
6	Louis Strang	Renault	16	6h43m37.0

Winner's average speed: 65.111 mph. Fastest lap: Ralph de Palma (Fiat), 21m36.0

1910

AMERICAN GRAND PRIZE

12 November 1910. Savannah. 24 laps of a 17.300 mile-circuit = 415.200 miles

1	David Bruce-Brown	Benz	24	5h53m05.4
2	Victor Hemery	Benz	24	5h53m06.8
3	Bob Burman	Marquette-Buick	24	6h11m23.5
4	Ralph Mulford	Lozier	24	6h26m12.7
5	Joe Horan	Lozier 6	24	6h30m02.7
6	Ray Harroun/ Joe Dawson	Marmon	24	6h30m22.2

Winner's average speed: 70.554 mph. Fastest lap: Felice Nazzaro (Fiat), 13m42.0

1912 Georges Boillot and the Peugeot L76 were the class of the 1912 Grand Prix de l'Automobile Club de France.

1911

AMERICAN GRAND PRIZE

30 November 1911. Savannah. 24 laps of a 17.140 mile-circuit = 411.360 miles

1 David Bruce-Brown	Fiat S74	24	5h31m29.1
2 Eddie Hearne	Benz	24	5h33m33.1
3 Ralph de Palma	Mercedes	24	5h34m40.8
4 Caleb Bragg	Fiat S74	24	5h51m55.3
5 Lou Disbrow	Pope-Hartford	24	6h26m44.0
6 Bill Mitchell	Abbott Detroit-Continental	24	

Winner's average speed: 74.458 mph. Fastest lap: Victor Hemery (Benz), 12m36.0

1912

GRAND PRIX DE L'AUTOMOBILE CLUB DE FRANCE

25-26 June 1912. Dieppe. 20 laps of a 47.840 mile-circuit = 956.800 miles

1 Georges Boillot	Peugeot L76	20	13h58m02.6
2 Louis Wagner	Fiat S74	20	14h11m08.4
3 Victor Rigal	Sunbeam	20	14h38m36.0
4 Dario Resta	Sunbeam	20	14h39m51.8
5 Emil Medinger	Sunbeam	20	15h59m41.4
6 Joseph Christiaens	Excelsior	20	16h23m38.8

Winner's average speed: 68.502 mph. Fastest lap: David Bruce-Brown (Fiat S74), 36m32.0

AMERICAN GRAND PRIZE

5 October 1912. Milwaukee. 52 laps of a 7.880 mile-circuit = 409.760 miles

1 Caleb Bragg	Fiat S74	52	5h59m27.4
2 Erwin Bergdoll	Benz	52	6h14m58.4
3 Gil Anderson	Stutz	52	6h15m22.5
4 Barney Oldfield	Fiat S74	52	6h19m54.7
5 Ralph de Palma	Mercedes	51	accident
6 George Clark	Mercedes	51	

Winner's average speed: 68.396 mph. Fastest lap: Teddy Tetzlaff (Fiat S74), 6m07.0

1913

GRAND PRIX DE L'AUTOMOBILE CLUB DE FRANCE

12 July 1913. Amiens. 29 laps of a 19.650 mile-circuit = 569.850 miles

1 Georges Boillot	Peugeot EX3	29	7h53m56.8

2 Jules Goux	Peugeot EX3	29	7h56m22.4
3 Jean Chassagne	Sunbeam	29	8h06m20.2
4 Paul Bablot	Delage Y	29	8h16m13.6
5 Albert Guyot	Delage Y	29	8h17m58.8
6 Dario Resta	Sunbeam	29	8h21m38.4

Winner's average speed: 72.141 mph. Fastest lap: Bablot, 15m22

1914

AMERICAN GRAND PRIZE

28 February 1914. Santa Monica. 48 laps of a 8.417 mile-circuit = 404.016 miles

1 Eddie Pullen	Mercer	48	5h13m30.0
2 Guy Ball	Marmon	48	5h53m23.0
3 William Taylor	Alco	48	6h08m29.0
4 Ralph de Palma	Mercedes	48	6h09m08.0
5 Gil Anderson	Stutz	45	piston
6 Huntley Gordon	Mercer	41	

Winner's average speed: 77.324 mph. Fastest lap: Teddy Tetzlaff (Fiat S74), 5m49.0

GRAND PRIX DE L'AUTOMOBILE CLUB DE FRANCE

4 July 1914. Lyon. 20 laps of a 23.380 mile-circuit = 467.600 miles

1 Christian Lautenschlager	Mercedes GP	20	7h08m18.4
2 Louis Wagner	Mercedes GP	20	7h09m54.2
3 Otto Salzer	Mercedes GP	20	7h13m15.8
4 Jules Goux	Peugeot EX5	20	7h17m47.2
5 Dario Resta	Sunbeam	20	7h28m17.4
6 Dragutin Esser	Nagant	20	7h40m28.2

Winner's average speed: 65.504 mph. Fastest lap: Max Sailer (Mercedes GP), 20m06.0

1915

AMERICAN GRAND PRIZE

27 February 1915. San Francisco. 104 laps of a 3.840 mile-circuit = 399.360 miles

1 Dario Resta	Peugeot EX3	104	7h07m53.0
2 Howdy Wilcox	Stutz	104	7h14m36.0
3 Hughie Hughes	Ono	104	7h21m46.0
4 Gil Anderson	Stutz	104	7h30m21.0
5 Lou Disbrow	Simplex ZIP 90hp	104	7h31m38.0

No other finishers. Winner's average speed: 56.000 mph. Fastest lap: not published

1916

AMERICAN GRAND PRIZE

18 November 1916. Santa Monica. 48 laps of a 8.417 mile-circuit = 404.016 miles

1 Howdy Wilcox/			
Johnny Aitken	Peugeot EX5	48	4h42m47.0
2 Earl Cooper	Stutz	48	4h48m59.0
3 AH Patterson	Hudson 6	48	5h09m39.0
4 Clyde Roades	Hudson 6	48	5h54m05.0
5 William Weightman/			
Eddie Rickenbacher	Duesenberg	45	

No other finishers. Winner's average speed: 85.723 mph. Fastest lap: Ed Ruckstell (Mercer), no time published

1921

GRAND PRIX DE L'AUTOMOBILE CLUB DE FRANCE

26 July 1921. Le Mans. 30 laps of a 10.726 mile-circuit = 321.780 miles

1 Jimmy Murphy	Duesenberg	30	4h07m11.4
2 Ralph de Palma	Ballot 3L	30	4h22m10.6
3 Jules Goux	Ballot 2LS	30	4h28m38.2
4 Andre Dubonnet	Duesenberg	30	4h30m19.2
5 Andre Boillot	Sunbeam	30	4h35m17.4
6 Albert Guyot	Duesenberg	30	4h38m13.0

Winner's average speed: 78.105 mph. Starting grid front row: de Palma and Emile Mathis (Mathis) - positions drawn. Fastest lap: Murphy, 7m43.0

GRAN PREMIO D'ITALIA

4 September 1921. Brescia. 30 laps of a 10.750 mile-circuit = 322.500 miles

1 Jules Goux	Ballot 3L	30	3h35m09.0
2 Jean Chassagne	Ballot 3L	30	3h40m52.0
3 Louis Wagner	Fiat 802	30	3h45m33.0

No other finishers. Winner's average speed: 89.937 mph. Starting grid front row: Started in numerical order every 60 seconds, numbers drawn. Fastest lap: Pietro Bordino (Fiat 802), 6m54.2

1921 Jimmy Murphy (Duesenberg) scored a significant American win at the French Grand Prix at Le Mans.

1922

GRAND PRIX DE L'AUTOMOBILE CLUB DE FRANCE

16 July 1922. Strasbourg. 60 laps of a 8.300 mile-circuit = 498.000 miles

1 Felice Nazzaro	Fiat 804	60	6h17m17.0
2 Pierre de Vizcaya	Bugatti T30	60	7h15m09.8
3 Piero Marco	Bugatti T30	60	7h48m04.2
4 Pietro Bordino	Fiat 804	58	accident
5 Jacques Mones-Maury	Bugatti T30	57	

No other finishers. Winner's average speed: 79.198 mph. Starting grid front row: F Nazzaro - positions drawn. Fastest lap: Bordino, 5m43

GRAN PREMIO D'ITALIA

3 September 1922. Monza. 80 laps of a 6.214 mile-circuit = 497.120 miles

1 Pietro Bordino	Fiat 804	80	5h43m13.0
2 Felice Nazzaro	Fiat 804	80	5h51m35.0
3 Pierre de Vizcaya	Bugatti T30	76	

No other finishers. Winner's average speed: 86.905 mph. Starting grid front row: Franz Heim (Heim) and Nazzaro - positions drawn. Fastest lap: Bordino, 4m05.0

1923

GRAND PRIX DE L'AUTOMOBILE CLUB DE FRANCE

2 June 1923. Tours. 35 laps of a 14.180 mile-circuit = 496.300 miles

1 Henry Segrave	Sunbeam	35	6h35m19.6
2 Albert Divo	Sunbeam	35	6h54m25.8
3 Ernst Friedrich	Bugatti T30	35	7h00m22.4
4 Kenelm Lee Guinness	Sunbeam	35	7h02m03.0
5 Andre Lefebvre	Voisin Laboratoire	35	7h50m29.2

No other finishers. Winner's average speed: 75.325 mph. Starting grid front row: Rene Thomas (Delage 2LCV) and Lee Guinness - positions drawn. Fastest lap: Pietro Bordino (Fiat 805), 9m36

GRAN PREMIO D'ITALIA E EUROPA

9 September 1923. Monza. 80 laps of a 6.214 mile-circuit = 497.120 miles

1 Carlo Salamano	Fiat 805	80	5h27m38.4
2 Felice Nazzaro	Fiat 805	80	5h28m02.0
3 Jimmy Murphy	Miller 122	80	5h32m51.0
4 Ferdinando Minoia	Benz RH	76	
5 Franz Horner	Benz RH	71	
6 Martin de Alsaga	Miller 122	70	

Winner's average speed: 91.037 mph. Starting grid front row: Minoia, Pietro Bordino (Fiat 805) and Eugenio Silvani (Voisin Laboratoire) - positions drawn, rolling start. Fastest lap: Bordino, 3m44

GRAN PREMIO DE ESPANA

28 October 1923. Sitges. 200 laps of a 1.243 mile-circuit = 248.600 miles. Race scheduled for 300 laps but reduced after rain delayed start

1 Albert Divo	Sunbeam	200	2h33m50.0
2 Louis Zborowski	Miller 122	200	2h34m46.0
3 Alfonso Carreras	Elizalde 511	200	3h26m35.0
4 Jose dos Santos-Mora	Diatto 20S	200	
5 Jose Feliu	Elizalde 511	200	

No other finishers. Winner's average speed: 96.962 mph. Starting grid front row: n/a. Fastest lap: Zborowski, 45.8s

1924

GRAND PRIX DE L'AUTOMOBILE CLUB DE FRANCE ET EUROPE

3 August 1924. Lyon. 35 laps of a 14.380 mile-circuit = 503.300 miles

1 Giuseppe Campari	Alfa Romeo P2	35	7h05m34.8
2 Albert Divo	Delage 2LCV	35	7h06m40.2
3 Robert Benoist	Delage 2LCV	35	7h17m00.8
4 Louis Wagner	Alfa Romeo P2	35	7h25m10.8
5 Henry Segrave	Sunbeam	35	7h28m56.0
6 Rene Thomas	Delage 2LCV	35	7h37m27.4

Winner's average speed: 70.957 mph. Starting grid front row: Segrave and Divo - positions drawn. Fastest lap: Segrave, 11m19.0

GRAN PREMIO DE SAN SEBASTIAN

25 September 1924. Lasarte. 35 laps of a 11.029 mile-circuit = 386.015 miles

1 Henry Segrave	Sunbeam	35	6h01m19.0

2	Meo Costantini	Bugatti T35	35	6h02m44.0
3	Andre Morel	Delage 2LCV	35	6h03m47.0
4	Albert Divo	Delage 2LCV	35	6h11m11.0
5	Pierre de Vizcaya	Bugatti T35	35	6h29m09.0
6	Jean Chassagne	Bugatti T35	35	6h46m30.0

Winner's average speed: 64.101 mph. Starting grid front row: n/a. Fastest lap: Costantini, 9m13.8

GRAN PREMIO D'ITALIA

19 October 1924. Monza. 80 laps of a 6.214 mile-circuit = 497.120 miles

1	Antonio Ascari	Alfa Romeo P2	80	5h02m05.0
2	Louis Wagner	Alfa Romeo P2	80	5h18m05.0
3	Giuseppe Campari/			
	Cesare Pastore	Alfa Romeo P2	80	5h21m59.0
4	Ferdinando Minoia	Alfa Romeo P2	80	5h22m43.4
5	Jules Goux	Rolland Pilain-Schmid	80	6h10m22.0
6	Giulio Foresti	Rolland Pilain-Schmid	80	6h32m03.0

Winner's average speed: 98.738 mph. Starting grid front row: Ascari, Christian Werner (Mercedes M72/94) and Goux - positions drawn. Fastest lap: Ascari, 3m43.6

1925

GRAND PRIX DE BELGIQUE ET EUROPE

28 June 1925. Spa-Francorchamps. 54 laps of a 9.310 mile-circuit = 502.740 miles

1	Antonio Ascari	Alfa Romeo P2	54	6h42m57.0
2	Giuseppe Campari	Alfa Romeo P2	54	7h04m55.0

No other finishers. Winner's average speed: 74.859 mph. Starting grid front row: Rene Thomas (Delage 2LCV), Ascari and Robert Benoist (Delage 2LCV) - positions drawn. Fastest lap: Ascari, 6m51.2

GRAND PRIX DE L'AUTOMOBILE CLUB DE FRANCE

26 July 1925. Montlhery. 80 laps of a 7.767 mile-circuit = 621.360 miles

1	Robert Benoist/			
	Albert Divo	Delage 2LCV	80	8h54m41.2
2	Louis Wagner/			
	Paul Torchy	Delage 2LCV	80	9h02m27.4
3	Giulio Masetti	Sunbeam	80	9h06m15.2
4	Meo Costantini	Bugatti T35	80	9h07m38.4
5	Jules Goux	Bugatti T35	80	9h15m11.2
6	Ferdinand de Vizcaya	Bugatti T35	80	9h20m48.4

Winner's average speed: 69.726 mph. Starting grid front row: Pierre de Vizcaya (Bugatti T35), Giuseppe Campari (Alfa Romeo P2) and Henry Segrave (Sunbeam) - positions drawn, rolling start. Fastest lap: Divo, 5m48.0

GRAN PREMIO D'ITALIA

6 September 1925. Monza. 80 laps of a 6.214 mile-circuit = 497.120 miles

1	Gastone Brilli-Peri	Alfa Romeo P2	80	5h14m33.3
2	Giuseppe Campari/			
	Giovanni Minozzi	Alfa Romeo P2	80	5h33m30.2
3	Meo Costantini	Bugatti T39	80	5h44m40.9
4	Tommy Milton	Duesenberg 122	80	5h46m40.5
5	Peter de Paolo	Alfa Romeo P2	80	5h48m10.3
6	Ferdinand de Vizcaya	Bugatti T37	80	5h50m49.4

Winner's average speed: 94.823 mph. Starting grid front row: Emilio Materassi (Diatto GP), Albert Guyot (Rolland Pilain-McCollum), Campari and Alfieri Maserati (Diatto 20S) - positions drawn. Fastest lap: Peter Kreis (Duesenberg), 3m36.7

GRAN PREMIO DE SAN SEBASTIAN

19 September 1925. Lasarte. 40 laps of a 11.029 mile-circuit = 441.160 miles

1	Albert Divo/			
	Andre Morel	Delage 2LCV	40	5h45m01.0

2	Robert Benoist	Delage 2LCV	40	5h55m43.0
3	Rene Thomas	Delage 2LCV	40	5h56m26.0
4	Pierre de Vizcaya	Bugatti T35	40	6h01m40.0
5	Ferdinand de Vizcaya	Bugatti T35	40	6h11m33.0

No other finishers. Winner's average speed: 76.720 mph. Starting grid front row: n/a. Fastest lap: Meo Costantini (Bugatti T35), 8m00.0

1926

GRAND PRIX DE L'AUTOMOBILE CLUB DE FRANCE

27 June 1926. Miramas. 100 laps of a 3.107 mile-circuit = 310.700 miles

1	Jules Goux	Bugatti T39A	100	4h38m43.8

No other finishers, only three cars started. Winner's average speed: 66.882 mph. Starting grid front row: Pierre de Vizcaya, Meo Costantini, and Goux (all Bugatti T37A) - positions drawn. Fastest lap: Goux, 2m24

GROSSER PREIS VON DEUTSCHLAND

11 July 1926. Avus. Sports car race. 20 laps of a 12.160-mile circuit = 243.200 miles

1	Rudolf Caracciola	Mercedes M72/94	20	2h54m17.8
2	Christian Riecken	NAG	20	2h57m33.2
3	Willy Cleer	Alfa Romeo RL6	20	3h00m16.8
4	Pierre Clause	Bignan	20	3h02m07.4
5	Georg Kloble	NSU	20	3h07m27.0
6	Max zu Schaumburg-			
	Lippe	OM Superba	20	3h10m57.4

Winner's average speed: 83.719 mph. Starting grid front row: n/a. Fastest lap: Ferdinando Minoia (OM 856), time not published

GRAN PREMIO DE EUROPA

18 July 1926. Lasarte. 45 laps of a 11.029 mile-circuit = 496.305 miles

1	Jules Goux	Bugatti T39A	45	6h51m52.0
2	Edmond Bourlier/			
	Robert Senechal	Delage 15S8	45	6h59m42.0
3	Meo Costantini	Bugatti T39A	45	7h28m18.0
4	Andre Morel/Edmond Bourlier/			
	Louis Wagner	Delage 15S8	40	
5	Ferdinando Minoia	Bugatti T39A	40	

No other finishers. Winner's average speed: 72.301 mph. Starting grid front row: Robert Benoist (Delage 15S8) and Goux - positions drawn. Fastest lap: Wagner, 8m53.5

GRAN PREMIO DE ESPANA

25 July 1926. Lasarte. 40 laps of a 11.029 mile-circuit = 441.160 miles

1	Meo Costantini	Bugatti T35	40	5h35m47.0
2	Jules Goux	Bugatti T35	40	5h52m15.0
3	Louis Wagner/			
	Robert Benoist	Delage 2LCV	40	5h56m57.0
4	Ferdinando Minoia	Bugatti T35	40	5h57m27.0

| 5 Ferry | Bugatti T35 | 33 | |

No other finishers. Winner's average speed: 78.829 mph. Starting grid front row: n/a. Fastest lap: Costantini, no time published

ENGLISH GRAND PRIX

7 August 1926. Brooklands. 110 laps of a 2.616 mile-circuit = 287.760 miles

1 Robert Senechal/			
Louis Wagner	Delage 15S8	110	4h00m56.0
2 Malcolm Campbell	Bugatti T39A	110	4h10m44.0
3 Robert Benoist/			
Andre Dubonnet	Delage 15S8	110	4h18m08.0

No other finishers. Winner's average speed: 71.661 mph. Starting grid front row: in line across track. Fastest lap: Henry Segrave (Talbot T700), 1m49.5

GRAN PREMIO D'ITALIA

5 September 1926. Monza. 60 laps of a 6.214 mile-circuit = 372.840 miles

| 1 "Sabipa" | Bugatti T39A | 60 | 4h20m29.0 |
| 2 Meo Costantini | Bugatti T39A | 60 | 4h27m01.4 |

No other finishers. Winner's average speed: 85.880 mph. Starting grid front row: Emilio Materassi (Maserati 26), Roberto Serboli (Chiribiri 12/16), and Jules Goux (Bugatti T39A) - positions drawn. Fastest lap: Costantini, 3m47.0

1927

GRAND PRIX DE L'AUTOMOBILE CLUB DE FRANCE

3 July 1927. Montlhery. 48 laps of a 7.767 mile-circuit = 372.816 miles

1 Robert Benoist	Delage 15S8	48	4h45m41.2
2 Edmond Bourlier	Delage 15S8	48	4h53m55.6
3 Andre Morel	Delage 15S8	48	5h11m31.4
4 "W Williams"/			
Jules Moriceau	Talbot T700	48	5h24m30.0

No other finishers. Winner's average speed: 78.299 mph. Starting grid front row: George Eyston (Halford), Albert Divo (Talbot T700) and Benoist - positions drawn. Fastest lap: Benoist, 5m41.0

GROSSER PREIS VON DEUTSCHLAND

17 July 1927. Nurburgring. Sports car race. 18 laps of a 17.563 mile-circuit = 316.134 miles

1 Otto Merz	Mercedes-Benz S	18	4h59m35.6
2 Christian Werner	Mercedes-Benz S	18	5h02m54.6
3 Willy Walb	Mercedes-Benz S	18	5h10m49.0
4 Elizabeth Junek	Bugatti	18	5h40m07.6
5 Hugo Urban-Emmerich	Talbot	18	6h00m32.0
6 Willy Cleer	Bugatti	18	6h07m11.0

Winner's average speed: 63.313 mph. Starting grid front row: n/a. Fastest lap: Werner, 15m51.6

GRAN PREMIO DE ESPANA

31 July 1927. Lasarte. 40 laps of a 11.029 mile-circuit = 441.160 miles

1 Robert Benoist	Delage 15S8	40	5h20m45.0
2 Caberto Conelli	Bugatti T39A	40	5h23m02.0
3 Edmond Bourlier	Delage 15S8	40	5h28m12.0

No other finishers. Winner's average speed: 82.524 mph. Starting grid front row: n/a. Fastest lap: Benoist, 7m33.0

GRAN PREMIO D'ITALIA E EUROPA

4 September 1927. Monza. 60 laps of a 6.214 mile-circuit = 372.840 miles

1 Robert Benoist	Delage 15S8	60	3h26m59.7
2 Giuseppe Morandi	OM 865	60	3h49m32.5
3 Earl Cooper/			
Peter Kreis	Miller 91	60	4h02m05.7
4 Ferdinando Minoia	OM 865	60	4h02m28.5

No other finishers. Winner's average speed: 108.072 mph. Starting grid

front row: Minoia, Benoist and Kreis - positions drawn. Fastest lap: Benoist, 3m57.24

ENGLISH GRAND PRIX

1 October 1927. Brooklands. 125 laps of a 2.616 mile-circuit = 327.000 miles

1 Robert Benoist	Delage 15S8	125	3h49m14.6
2 Edmond Bourlier	Delage 15S8	125	3h49m21.6
3 Albert Divo	Delage 15S8	125	3h52m20.0
4 Louis Chiron	Bugatti T39A	125	4h17m50.0
5 Emilio Materassi	Bugatti T39A	118	

No other finishers. Winner's average speed: 85.586 mph. Starting grid front row: in line across track. Fastest lap: not published

1928

GRAND PRIX DE L'AUTOMOBILE CLUB DE FRANCE

1 July 1928. St Gaudens. Sports car handicap race. 10 laps of a 16.156 mile-circuit = 161.560 miles

1 "W Williams"	Bugatti T35C	10	2h27m40.8
2 Andre Rousseau	Salmson	10	2h30m04.6
3 Edouard Brisson	Stutz	10	2h31m13.4
4 Lucien Desvaux	Lombard	10	2h31m28.4
5 Georges Casse	Salmson	10	2h38m36.0
6 Henri Stoffel	Chrysler	10	2h40m14.0

Note: time shown includes the handicap. Winner's average speed: 65.639 mph. Starting grid front row: n/a. Fastest lap: "Williams", 10m48

GROSSER PREIS VON DEUTSCHLAND

15 July 1928. Nurburgring. Sports car race. 18 laps of a 17.563 mile-circuit = 316.134 miles

1 Rudolf Caracciola/			
Christian Werner	Mercedes-Benz SS	18	4h54m24.0
2 Otto Merz	Mercedes-Benz SS	18	4h56m02.0
3 Christian Werner/			
Willy Walb	Mercedes-Benz SS	18	5h04m23.0
4 Gastone Brilli-Peri	Bugatti	18	5h05m16.0
5 Georg Kimpel/			
Adolff Rosenberger	Mercedes-Benz SS	18	5h06m29.0
6 Louis Chiron	Bugatti	18	5h17m26.0

Winner's average speed: 64.429 mph. Starting grid front row: n/a. Fastest lap: Caracciola, 15m13.2

GRAN PREMIO DE SAN SEBASTIAN

25 July 1928. Lasarte. 40 laps of a 11.029 mile-circuit = 441.160 miles

1 Louis Chiron	Bugatti T35C	40	5h20m30.0
2 Robert Benoist	Bugatti T35B	40	5h22m56.5
3 Marcel Lehoux	Bugatti T35C	40	5h32m35.0
4 Goffredo Zehender	Bugatti T37A	40	5h42m23.7
5 Manuel Blancas	Bugatti T35B	40	6h04m46.8
6 Torres	Bugatti T37A	29	

Winner's average speed: 82.588 mph. Starting grid front row: n/a. Fastest lap: Chiron, 6m50.6

GRAN PREMIO DE ESPANA

29 July 1928. Lasarte. Handicap race. 15 laps of a 11.029 mile-circuit = 165.435 miles

1 Louis Chiron	Bugatti T35C	15	2h25m00.0
2 Georges Bouriano	Bugatti T35	15	2h30m14.0
3 Delemer	EHP	15	2h30m37.0
4 Christian	Lombard	15	2h35m43.0
5 Robert Laly	Aries	15	2h35m51.0
6 Cyril de Vere	Chrysler	15	2h36m24.0

Note: time shown includes the handicap. Winner's average speed: 68.456 mph. Starting grid front row: n/a. Fastest lap: Bouriano, no time available

GRAN PREMIO D'ITALIA E EUROPA

9 September 1928. Monza. 60 laps of a 6.214 mile-circuit = 372.840 miles

1	Louis Chiron	Bugatti T35C	60	3h45m08.6
2	Achille Varzi/			
	Giuseppe Campari	Alfa Romeo P2	60	3h47m29.0
3	Tazio Nuvolari	Bugatti T35C	60	3h59m27.6
4	Guy Drouet	Bugatti T35B	60	3h59m37.8
5	Aymo Maggi	Maserati 26R	60	4h10m29.0
6	Ernesto Maserati	Maserati 26R	55	

Winner's average speed: 99.361 mph. Starting grid front row: Baconin Borzacchini (Maserati 26B), Giuliio Foresti (Bugatti T35C), Emilio Materassi (Talbot T700), "W Williams" (Bugatti T35B), and Gastone Brilli-Peri (Talbot T700). Fastest lap: Luigi Arcangeli (Talbot T700), 3m37.4

1929

GRAND PRIX DE MONACO

14 April 1929. Monte Carlo. 100 laps of a 1.976 mile-circuit = 197.600 miles

1	"W Williams"	Bugatti T35B	100	3h56m11.0
2	Georges Bouriano	Bugatti T35C	100	3h57m28.8
3	Rudolf Caracciola	Mercedes-Benz SSK	100	3h58m33.6
4	"Georges Philippe"	Bugatti T35C	99	
5	Rene Dreyfus	Bugatti T37A	97	
6	Philippe Etancelin	Bugatti T35C	96	

Winner's average speed: 50.198 mph. Starting grid front row: Etancelin, Christian Dauvergne (Bugatti T35C) and Marcel Lehoux (Bugatti T35B) - positions drawn. Fastest lap: "Williams", 2m15.0

GRAND PRIX DE L'AUTOMOBILE CLUB DE FRANCE

30 June 1929. Le Mans. 37 laps of a 10.153 mile-circuit = 375.661 miles

1	"W Williams"	Bugatti T35B	37	4h33m01.2
2	Andre Boillot	Peugeot 174S	37	4h34m20.0
3	Caberto Conelli	Bugatti T35C	37	4h34m28.0
4	Albert Divo	Bugatti T35B	37	4h41m27.4
5	Robert Senechal	Bugatti T35B	37	4h58m27.8
6	Robert Gauthier	Bugatti T35C	37	5h18m38.4

Winner's average speed: 82.557 mph. Starting grid front row: Raoul de Rovin (Bugatti T35B) and Jean Chassagne (Ballot RH2) - positions drawn. Fastest lap: "Williams," 7m01.0

GROSSER PREIS VON DEUTSCHLAND

14 July 1929. Nurburgring. Sports car race. 18 laps of a 17.563 mile-circuit = 316.134 miles

1	Louis Chiron	Bugatti T35C	18	4h46m06.4
2	"Georges Philippe"	Bugatti T35C	18	4h57m52.2
3	August Momberger/			
	Max Arco-Zinneberg	Mercedes-Benz SSK	18	5h00m37.8
4	Guy Bouriat	Bugatti T35C	18	5h03m28.4
5	Mario Lepori	Bugatti	18	
6	W Rosenstein/			
	Adolff Rosenberger	Mercedes-Benz SSK	18	

Winner's average speed: 66.297 mph. Starting grid front row: n/a. Fastest lap: Chiron, 15m06.0

GRAN PREMIO DE ESPANA

25 July 1929. Lasarte. 40 laps of a 11.029 mile-circuit = 441.160 miles

1	Louis Chiron	Bugatti T35B	40	5h57m06.0
2	"Georges Philippe"/			
	Guy Bouriat	Bugatti T35C	40	6h02m59.0
3	Marcel Lehoux	Bugatti T35C	40	6h04m18.0
4	Rene Dreyfus	Bugatti T35C	40	6h09m51.0
5	Edmond Bourlier	Bugatti T35B	40	6h19m05.0
6	Jean de Maleplane	Bugatti T35C	40	6h32m05.0

Winner's average speed: 74.124 mph. Starting grid front row: n/a. Fastest lap: Chiron, 7m26.0

GRAN PREMIO DI MONZA

15 September 1929. Monza. Final: 22 laps of a 2.796 mile-circuit = 61.512 miles

1	Achille Varzi	Alfa Romeo P2	22	31m38.4
2	Tazio Nuvolari	Talbot T700	22	33m15.0
3	August Momberger	Mercedes-Benz SS	22	34m17.2
4	Gastone Brilli-Peri	Alfa Romeo P2	22	34m18.3
5	Federico Caflisch	Mercedes-Benz SS	22	34m20.0
6	Alfieri Maserati	Maserati V4	22	34m48.2

Winner's average speed: 116.647 mph. Starting grid front row: A Maserati, Momberger, Caflisch, Luigi Arcangeli (Talbot T700) and Nuvolari - positions drawn. Fastest lap: A Maserati, 1m21.0

1930

GRAND PRIX DE MONACO

6 April 1930. Monte Carlo. 100 laps of a 1.976 mile-circuit = 197.600 miles

1	Rene Dreyfus	Bugatti T35B	100	3h41m02.6
2	Louis Chiron	Bugatti T35C	100	3h41m24.4
3	Guy Bouriat	Bugatti T35C	100	3h49m20.4
4	Goffredo Zehender	Bugatti T35B	100	3h54m39.6
5	Michel Dore	Bugatti T37A	100	4h12m06.6
6	Hans Stuber	Bugatti T35C	94	

Winner's average speed: 53.637 mph. Starting grid front row: Baconin Borzacchini (Maserati 26B), Bobby Bowes (Frazer Nash-Anzani) and "W Williams" (Bugatti T35C)-positions drawn-Bowes did not start. Fastest lap: Dreyfus, 2m07.0

GRAND PRIX DE BELGIQUE ET D'EUROPE

20 July 1930. Spa-Francorchamps. 40 laps of a 9.236 mile-circuit = 369.440 miles

1	Louis Chiron	Bugatti T35C	40	5h08m34.6
2	Guy Bouriat	Bugatti T35C	40	5h09m34.0
3	Albert Divo	Bugatti T35C	40	5h13m54.0
4	Arthur Duray	Aries	40	5h22m26.0
5	Goffredo Zehender	Imperia	40	5h25m19.0
6	Charles Montier	Montier Speciale-Ford	40	5h30m30.0

Winner's average speed: 71.834 mph. Starting grid front row: n/a. Fastest lap: Bouriat, 7m05.0

GRAN PREMIO DI MONZA

7 September 1930. Monza. Final: 35 laps of a 4.263 mile-circuit = 149.205 miles

1	Achille Varzi	Maserati 26M	35	1h35m46.2
2	Luigi Arcangeli	Maserati 26M	35	1h35m46.4
3	Ernesto Maserati	Maserati V4	35	1h36m10.4
4	Giovanni Minozzi	Bugatti T35C	35	1h39m23.2
5	Luigi Fagioli	Maserati 26M	35	1h39m23.6
6	Philippe Etancelin	Bugatti T35C	35	1h39m49.8

Winner's average speed: 93.477 mph. Starting grid front row: Arcangeli, Baconin Borzacchini (Alfa Romeo P2) and Fagioli - positions decided by heat results. Fastest lap: Varzi, 2m32.6

GRAND PRIX DE L'AUTOMOBILE CLUB DE FRANCE

21 September 1930. Pau. 25 laps of a 9.860 mile-circuit = 246.500 miles

1	Philippe Etancelin	Bugatti T35C	25	2h43m18.4
2	Tim Birkin	Bentley 4.5	25	2h46m44.6
3	Juan Zanelli	Bugatti T35B	25	2h46m58.8
4	Stanislav Czaykowski	Bugatti T35C	25	2h51m27.0
5	Jean de l'Espee	Bugatti T35C	25	2h54m28.8
6	Robert Senechal	Delage 15S8	25	2h56m28.6

Winner's average speed: 90.566 mph. Starting grid front row: Marcel Lehoux (Bugatti T35B), Czaykowski and Louis Casali (La Perle) - positions drawn. Fastest lap: "W Williams" (Bugatti T35C), 6m10.0

MASARYKUV OKRUH (CZECH GRAND PRIX)

21 September 1930. Brno. 17 laps of a 18.109 mile-circuit = 307.853 miles

1	Hermann zu Leiningen/Heinrich-Joachim von Morgen	Bugatti T35B	17	4h54m13.0
2	Ernst-Gunther Burgaller	Bugatti T35B	17	4h57m08.9
3	Tazio Nuvolari/Baconin Borzacchini	Alfa Romeo P2	17	5h26m13.9
4	Jan Kubicek	Bugatti T35	17	5h33m31.9
5	Milos Bondy	Bugatti T35	17	5h38m57.3

No other finishers. Winner's average speed: 62.781 mph. Starting front row: n/a. Fastest lap: Rudolf Caracciola (Mercedes-Benz SSK), 15m27.2

GRAN PREMIO DE ESPANA

5 October 1930. Lasarte. 30 laps of a 11.029 mile-circuit = 330.870 miles

1	Achille Varzi	Maserati 26M	30	3h43m05.0
2	Aymo Maggi	Maserati 26M	30	4h05m03.0
3	Henri Stoffel	Peugeot 174S	30	4h08m48.0
4	Rene Ferrand	Peugeot 174S	30	4h10m10.0
5	Max Fourny	Bugatti T35C	30	4h13m58.0
6	Jean de Maleplane	Bugatti T35C	30	4h14m48.0

Winner's average speed: 88.990 mph. Starting grid front row: n/a. Fastest lap: Varzi, 7m05.6

1931

GRAND PRIX DE MONACO

19 April 1931. Monte Carlo. 100 laps of a 1.976 mile-circuit = 197.600 miles

1	Louis Chiron	Bugatti T51	100	3h39m09.2
2	Luigi Fagioli	Maserati 26M	100	3h43m04.6
3	Achille Varzi	Bugatti T51	100	3h43m13.2
4	Guy Bouriat	Bugatti T51	98	
5	Goffredo Zehender	Alfa Romeo 6C-1750	97	
6	Andre Boillot	Peugeot 174S	96	

Winner's average speed: 54.099 mph. Starting grid front row: Rene Dreyfus (Maserati 26M), Hans Stuber (Bugatti T35C) and Bernd Ackerl (Bugatti T37A) - positions drawn. Fastest lap: Chiron and Fagioli, 2m07

GRAN PREMIO D'ITALIA

24 May 1931. Monza. Race scheduled for 10 hours. 155 laps of a 6.214 mile-circuit = 963.170 miles

1	Giuseppe Campari/Tazio Nuvolari	Alfa Romeo 8C "Monza"	155	10 hours
2	Ferdinando Minoia/Baconin Borzacchini	Alfa Romeo 8C "Monza"	153	
3	Albert Divo/Guy Bouriat	Bugatti T51	152	
4	Jean-Pierre Wimille/Jean Gaupillat	Bugatti T51	138	
5	Boris Ivanowski/Henri Stoffel	Mercedes-Benz SSKL	134	
6	Francesco Pirola/Johnny Lurani	Alfa Romeo 6C-1500	129	

Winner's average speed: 96.317 mph. Starting grid front row: Campari, Wimille and Robert Senechal (Delage 15S8) - positions drawn. Fastest lap: Campari, 3m32.8

GRAND PRIX DE L'AUTOMOBILE CLUB DE FRANCE

21 June 1931. Montlhery. Race scheduled for 10 hours. 101 laps of a 7.767 mile-circuit = 784.467 miles

1	Achille Varzi/Louis Chiron	Bugatti T51	101	10 hours
2	Giuseppe Campari/Baconin Borzacchini	Alfa Romeo 8C "Monza"	97	

3	Clemente Biondetti/Luigi Parenti	Maserati 26M	94	
4	Tim Birkin/George Eyston	Maserati 26M	94	
5	Robert Senechal	Delage 15S8	91	
6	Ferdinando Minoia/Goffredo Zehender	Alfa Romeo 8C "Monza"	91	

Winner's average speed: 78.447 mph. Starting grid front row: n/a. Fastest lap: Luigi Fagioli (Maserati 26M), 5m29.0

GRAND PRIX DE BELGIQUE

12 July 1931. Spa-Francorchamps. Race scheduled for 10 hours. 88 laps of a 9.236 mile-circuit = 812.768 miles

1	"W Williams"/Caberto Conelli	Bugatti T51	88	10 hours
2	Tazio Nuvolari/Baconin Borzacchini	Alfa Romeo 8C "Monza"	88	
3	Ferdinando Minoia/Giovanni Minozzi	Alfa Romeo 6C-1750	85	
4	Tim Birkin/Brian Lewis	Alfa Romeo 8C "Monza" LM	83	
5	Henri Stoffel/Boris Ivanowski	Mercedes-Benz SSK	81	
6	Jean Pesato/Pierre Felix	Alfa Romeo 6C-1750	73	

Winner's average speed: 81.277 mph. Starting grid front row: Minoia, "Williams" and Albert Divo (Bugatti T51) - positions drawn. Fastest lap: Louis Chiron (Bugatti T51), 6m18.6

GROSSER PREIS VON DEUTSCHLAND

19 July 1931. Nurburgring. Formula Libre. 22 laps of a 14.167 mile-circuit = 311.674 miles

1	Rudolf Caracciola	Mercedes-Benz SSKL	22	4h38m10.0
2	Louis Chiron	Bugatti T51	22	4h39m28.0
3	Achille Varzi	Bugatti T51	22	4h42m10.0
4	Tazio Nuvolari	Alfa Romeo 8C "Monza"	22	4h43m54.0
5	Otto Merz	Mercedes-Benz SSKL	22	4h43m54.0
6	Hans Stuck	Mercedes-Benz SSKL	22	4h47m34.0

Winner's average speed: 67.227 mph. Starting grid front row: Manfred von Brauchitsch (Mercedes-Benz SSKL), Ernst-Gunther Burgaller (Bugatti T35B), and Heinrich-Joachim von Morgen (Bugatti T35B) - positions drawn. Fastest lap: Varzi, 11m48.0

MASARYKUV OKRUH (CZECH GRAND PRIX)

27 September 1931. Brno. 17 laps of a 18.109 mile-circuit = 307.853 miles

1	Louis Chiron	Bugatti T51	17	4h12m07.5
2	Hans Stuck	Mercedes-Benz SSKL	17	4h26m10.4
3	Heinrich-Joachim von Morgen	Bugatti T35B	17	4h30m01.0
4	Georg-Kristian Lobkowicz	Bugatti T51	17	4h33m50.5
5	Hermann zu Leiningen	Bugatti T35C	17	5h00m06.7
6	Tivador Zichy	Bugatti T35C	17	5h05m43.6

Winner's average speed: 73.262 mph. Starting grid front row: Luigi Fagioli (Maserati 26M), 15m14.4 (pole), Baconin Borzacchini (Alfa Romeo 8C "Monza"), 15m17.3, and Achille Varzi (Bugatti T51), 15m24.2. Fastest lap: Chiron, 14m24.8

1932

GRAND PRIX DE MONACO

17 April 1932. Monte Carlo. 100 laps of a 1.976 mile-circuit = 197.600 miles

1	Tazio Nuvolari	Alfa Romeo 8C "Monza"	100	3h32m25.3
2	Rudolf Caracciola	Alfa Romeo 8C "Monza"	100	3h32m28.0
3	Luigi Fagioli	Maserati 26M	100	3h34m43.0
4	Earl Howe	Bugatti T51	98	

5 Goffredo Zehender   Alfa Romeo 8C "Monza"   96
6 Marcel Lehoux   Bugatti T51   95
Winner's average speed: 55.814 mph. Starting grid front row: "W Williams" (Bugatti T51), Philippe Etancelin (Alfa Romeo 8C "Monza"), and Amedeo Ruggeri (Maserati 26M) - positions drawn. Fastest lap: Achille Varzi (Bugatti T51), 2m02.0

GRAN PREMIO D'ITALIA

5 June 1932. Monza. Race scheduled for 5 hours. 83 laps of a 6.214 mile-circuit = 515.762 miles

1 Tazio Nuvolari	Alfa Romeo Tipo-B "P3"	83	5 hours
2 Luigi Fagioli	Maserati V5	82	
3 Baconin Borzacchini/Attilio Marinoni/			
Rudolf Caracciola	Alfa Romeo 8C "Monza"	82	
4 Giuseppe Campari	Alfa Romeo Tipo-B "P3"	82	
5 Rene Dreyfus	Bugatti T51	82	
6 Albert Divo/Guy Bouriat	Bugatti T51	81	

Winner's average speed: 103.152 mph. Starting grid front row: Luigi Castelbarco (Maserati 26M), Marcel Lehoux (Bugatti T51), and Borzacchini - positions drawn. Fastest lap: Nuvolari, 3m22.6

GRAND PRIX DE L'AUTOMOBILE CLUB DE FRANCE

3 July 1932. Reims. Race scheduled for 5 hours. 92 laps of a 4.865 mile-circuit = 447.580 miles

1 Tazio Nuvolari	Alfa Romeo Tipo-B "P3"	92	5 hours
2 Baconin Borzacchini	Alfa Romeo Tipo-B "P3"	92	
3 Rudolf Caracciola	Alfa Romeo Tipo-B "P3"	92	
4 Louis Chiron	Bugatti T51	91	
5 Rene Dreyfus	Bugatti T51	90	
6 "W Williams"	Bugatti T51	90	

Winner's average speed: 89.516 mph. Starting grid front row: Max Fourny (Bugatti T35C), Philippe Etancelin (Alfa Romeo 8C "Monza"), and Jean Gaupillat (Bugatti T51) - positions drawn. Fastest lap: Nuvolari, 3m00.0

GROSSER PREIS VON DEUTSCHLAND

17 July 1932. Nurburgring. 25 laps of a 14.167 mile-circuit = 354.175 miles

1 Rudolf Caracciola	Alfa Romeo Tipo-B "P3"	25	4h47m22.8
2 Tazio Nuvolari	Alfa Romeo Tipo-B "P3"	25	4h47m53.0
3 Baconin Borzacchini	Alfa Romeo Tipo-B "P3"	25	4h54m33.0
4 Rene Dreyfus	Bugatti T51	25	5h01m05.4

No other finishers. Winner's average speed: 73.946 mph. Starting grid front row: n/a. Fastest lap: Nuvolari, 10m49.4

MASARYKUV OKRUH (CZECH GRAND PRIX)

4 September 1932. Brno. 17 laps of a 18.109 mile-circuit = 307.853 miles

1 Louis Chiron	Bugatti T51	17	4h37m29.7
2 Luigi Fagioli	Maserati 8C-3000	17	4h42m30.5
3 Tazio Nuvolari	Alfa Romeo 8C "Monza"	17	5h06m20.1
4 Antonio Brivio	Alfa Romeo 8C "Monza"	17	5h08m03.0
5 V Stasny	Bugatti T35B	17	5h31m01.0

No other finishers. Winner's average speed: 66.564 mph. Starting grid front row: n/a. Fastest lap: Chiron, 14m44.9

1933

GRAND PRIX DE MONACO

23 April 1933. Monte Carlo. 100 laps of a 1.976 mile-circuit = 197.600 miles

1 Achille Varzi	Bugatti T51	100	3h27m49.4
2 Baconin Borzacchini	Alfa Romeo 8C "Monza"	100	3h29m49.4
3 Rene Dreyfus	Bugatti T51	99	
4 Louis Chiron	Alfa Romeo 8C "Monza"	97	
5 Carlo Felice Trossi	Alfa Romeo 8C "Monza"	97	
6 Goffredo Zehender	Maserati 8CM	94	

Winner's average speed: 57.048 mph. Starting grid front row: Varzi, 2m02.0 (pole), Chiron, 2m03.0, and Borzacchini, 2m03.0. Fastest lap: Varzi, 1m59.0

GRAND PRIX DE L'AUTOMOBILE CLUB DE FRANCE

11 June 1933. Montlhery. 40 laps of a 7.767 mile-circuit = 310.680 miles

1 Giuseppe Campari	Maserati 8C-3000	40	3h48m45.4
2 Philippe Etancelin	Alfa Romeo 8C "Monza"	40	3h49m37.4
3 George Eyston	Alfa Romeo 8C "Monza"	39	
4 Raymond Sommer	Alfa Romeo 8C "Monza"	39	
5 Guy Moll	Alfa Romeo 8C "Monza"	38	
6 Julio Villars	Alfa Romeo 8C "Monza"	34	

Winner's average speed: 81.487 mph. Starting grid front row: Juan Zanelli (Alfa Romeo 8C "Monza"), Pierre Felix (Alfa Romeo 8C "Monza"), and Earl Howe (Bugatti T51) - positions drawn. Fastest lap: Campari, 5m23.0

GRAND PRIX DE BELGIQUE

9 July 1933. Spa-Francorchamps. 40 laps of a 9.236 mile-circuit = 369.440 miles

1 Tazio Nuvolari	Maserati 8CM	40	4h09m11.0
2 Achille Varzi	Bugatti T51	40	4h12m26.0
3 Rene Dreyfus	Bugatti T51	40	4h12m59.0
4 Marcel Lehoux	Bugatti T51	40	4h13m28.0
5 Eugenio Siena	Alfa Romeo 8C "Monza"	40	4h17m10.0
6 "W Williams"	Bugatti T51	39	

Winner's average speed: 88.956 mph. Starting grid front row: Louis Chiron (Alfa Romeo 8C "Monza"), Lehoux, and Guy Moll (Alfa Romeo 8C "Monza") - positions drawn. Fastest lap: Nuvolari, 6m00.0

GRAN PREMIO D'ITALIA

10 September 1933. Monza. 50 laps of a 6.214 mile-circuit = 310.700 miles

1 Luigi Fagioli	Alfa Romeo Tipo-B "P3"	50	2h51m41.0
2 Tazio Nuvolari	Maserati 8CM	50	2h52m21.2
3 Goffredo Zehender	Maserati 8CM	48	
4 Marcel Lehoux	Alfa Romeo 8C "Monza"	47	
5 Eugenio Siena/			
Antonio Brivio	Alfa Romeo 8C "Monza"	47	
6 Luigi Castelbarco	Alfa Romeo 8C "Monza"	47	

Winner's average speed: 108.584 mph. Starting grid front row: Robert Brunet (Bugatti T51), Jean Gaupillat (Bugatti T51), Luigi Premoli (PBM-Maserati), and Siena - positions drawn. Fastest lap: Fagioli, 3m13.2

MASARYKUV OKRUH (CZECH GRAND PRIX)

17 September 1933. Brno. 17 laps of a 18.109 mile-circuit = 307.853 miles

1 Louis Chiron	Alfa Romeo Tipo-B "P3"	17	4h50m22.6
2 Luigi Fagioli	Alfa Romeo Tipo-B "P3"	17	4h54m02.0
3 Jean-Pierre Wimille	Alfa Romeo 8C "Monza"	17	5h00m04.0
4 Rene Dreyfus	Bugatti T51	17	5h02m12.0
5 Zdenek Pohl	Bugatti T35B	16	
6 Laszlo Hartmann	Bugatti T51	16	

Winner's average speed: 63.611 mph. Starting grid front row: n/a. Fastest lap: Fagioli, 15m21.0

GRAN PREMIO DE ESPANA

24 September 1933. Lasarte. 30 laps of a 11.029 mile-circuit = 330.870 miles

1 Louis Chiron	Alfa Romeo Tipo-B "P3"	30	3h50m57.8
2 Luigi Fagioli	Alfa Romeo Tipo-B "P3"	30	3h55m22.0
3 Marcel Lehoux	Bugatti T51	30	4h12m50.0
4 Achille Varzi	Bugatti T59	30	4h14m14.0
5 Jean-Pierre Wimille	Alfa Romeo 8C "Monza"	30	4h15m57.0
6 Rene Dreyfus	Bugatti T59	29	

Winner's average speed: 85.954 mph. Starting grid front row: n/a. Fastest lap: Tazio Nuvolari (Maserati 8CM), 6m41.2

1934

GRAND PRIX DE MONACO

2 April 1934. Monte Carlo. 100 laps of a 1.976 mile-circuit = 197.600 miles

1934 Louis Chiron's Alfa Romeo takes the lead of the French Grand Prix against the new and fancied German teams.

1	Guy Moll	Alfa Romeo Tipo-B "P3"	100	3h31m31.4
2	Louis Chiron	Alfa Romeo Tipo-B "P3"	100	3h32m33.4
3	Rene Dreyfus	Bugatti T59	99	
4	Marcel Lehoux	Alfa Romeo Tipo-B "P3"	99	
5	Tazio Nuvolari	Bugatti T59	98	
6	Achille Varzi	Alfa Romeo Tipo-B "P3"	98	

Winner's average speed: 56.051 mph. Starting grid front row: Carlo Felice Trossi (Alfa Romeo Tipo-B "P3"), 1m58.0 (pole), Philippe Etancelin (Maserati 8CM), 1m59.0, and Dreyfus - 1m59.0. Fastest lap: Trossi, 2m02.0.

GRAND PRIX DE L'AUTOMOBILE CLUB DE FRANCE

1 July 1934. Montlhery. 40 laps of a 7.767 mile-circuit = 310.680 miles

1	Louis Chiron	Alfa Romeo Tipo-B "P3"	40	3h39m14.6
2	Achille Varzi	Alfa Romeo Tipo-B "P3"	40	3h42m31.9
3	Carlo Felice Trossi/			
	Guy Moll	Alfa Romeo Tipo-B "P3"	40	3h43m23.8
4	Robert Benoist	Bugatti T59	36	

No other finishers. Winner's average speed: 85.023 mph. Starting grid front row: Hermann zu Leiningen (Auto Union A), Hans Stuck (Auto Union A), and Varzi - positions drawn, Leiningen did not start. Fastest lap: Chiron, 5m06.0.

GROSSER PREIS VON DEUTSCHLAND

15 July 1934. Nurburgring. 25 laps of a 14.167 mile-circuit = 354.175 miles

1	Hans Stuck	Auto Union A	25	4h38m19.2
2	Luigi Fagioli	Mercedes-Benz W25A	25	4h40m26.2
3	Louis Chiron	Alfa Romeo Tipo-B "P3"	25	4h46m32.8
4	Tazio Nuvolari	Maserati 8CM	25	4h55m10.2
5	Hanns Geier	Mercedes-Benz W25A	25	4h59m05.4
6	Goffredo Zehender	Maserati 8CM	25	5h14m46.8

Winner's average speed: 76.353 mph. Starting grid front row: Renato Balestrero (Alfa Romeo 8C "Monza"), Hugh Hamilton (Maserati 8CM), and Giovanni Minozzi (Alfa Romeo 8C "Monza") - positions drawn. Fastest lap: Stuck, 10m43.8

GRAND PRIX DE BELGIQUE

29 July 1934. Spa-Francorchamps. 40 laps of a 9.290 mile-circuit = 371.600 miles

1	Rene Dreyfus	Bugatti T59	40	4h15m03.8
2	Antonio Brivio	Bugatti T59	40	4h16m54.8

3	Raymond Sommer	Maserati 8CM	39	
4	Robert Benoist	Bugatti T59	37	
5	Charles Montier	Montier Speciale-Ford	30	

No other finishers. Winner's average speed: 87.414 mph. Starting grid front row: Brivio, Louis Chiron (Alfa Romeo Tipo-B "P3"), and Dreyfus - positions drawn. Fastest lap: Brivio, 5m45.0

GRAND PRIX DE SUISSE

26 August 1934. Bremgarten. 70 laps of a 4.524 mile-circuit = 316.680 miles

1	Hans Stuck	Auto Union A	70	3h37m57.6
2	August Momberger	Auto Union A	69	
3	Rene Dreyfus	Bugatti T59	69	
4	Achille Varzi/			
	Carlo Felice Trossi	Alfa Romeo Tipo-B "P3"	69	
5	Louis Chiron	Alfa Romeo Tipo-B "P3"	69	
6	Luigi Fagioli	Mercedes-Benz W25A	68	

Winner's average speed: 87.176 mph. Starting grid front row: Goffredo Zehender (Maserati 4CM), Varzi, and Stuck - positions drawn, Zehender did not start. Fastest lap: Stuck, 3m00.0

GRAN PREMIO D'ITALIA

9 September 1934. Monza. 116 laps of a 2.690 mile-circuit = 312.040 miles

1	Rudolf Caracciola/			
	Luigi Fagioli	Mercedes-Benz W25A	116	4h45m47.0
2	Hans Stuck/			
	Hermann zu Leiningen	Auto Union A	115	
3	Carlo Felice Trossi/			
	Gianfranco Comotti	Alfa Romeo Tipo-B "P3"	114	
4	Louis Chiron	Alfa Romeo Tipo-B "P3"	113	
5	Tazio Nuvolari	Maserati 6C-34	113	
6	Gianfranco Comotti/			
	Attilio Marinoni	Alfa Romeo Tipo-B "P3"	113	

Winner's average speed: 65.513 mph. Starting grid front row: Caracciola, Achille Varzi (Alfa Romeo Tipo-B "P3"), and Antonio Brivio (Bugatti T59) - positions drawn, Brivio did not start. Fastest lap: Stuck, 2m13.6

GRAN PREMIO DE ESPANA

23 September 1934. Lasarte. 30 laps of a 11.029 mile-circuit = 330.870 miles

1	Luigi Fagioli	Mercedes-Benz W25A	30	3h19m41.6
2	Rudolf Caracciola	Mercedes-Benz W25A	30	3h20m24.4
3	Tazio Nuvolari	Bugatti T59	30	3h20m48.0
4	Hermann zu Leiningen/			
	Hans Stuck	Auto Union A	30	3h21m03.0
5	Achille Varzi/			
	Louis Chiron	Alfa Romeo Tipo-B "P3"	30	3h21m49.0
6	Jean-Pierre Wimille	Bugatti T59	30	3h26m21.8

Winner's average speed: 99.413 mph. Starting grid front row: Stuck, Wimille, and Caracciola - positions drawn. Fastest lap: Stuck, 6m20.0

MASARYKUV OKRUH (CZECH GRAND PRIX)

30 September 1934. Brno. 17 laps of a 18.109 mile-circuit = 307.853 miles

1	Hans Stuck	Auto Union A	17	3h53m27.9
2	Luigi Fagioli	Mercedes-Benz W25A	17	3h56m24.5
3	Tazio Nuvolari	Maserati 6C-34	17	3h57m14.1
4	Hermann zu Leiningen	Auto Union A	17	4h02m05.2
5	Achille Varzi	Alfa Romeo Tipo-B "P3"	17	4h04m08.9
6	Ernst Henne/			
	Hanns Geier	Mercedes-Benz W25A	17	4h12m12.6

Winner's average speed: 79.118 mph. Starting grid front row: Louis Chiron (Alfa Romeo Tipo-B "P3"), Varzi, and Laszlo Hartmann (Bugatti T51) - positions drawn. Fastest lap: Fagioli, 13m16.2

1935

GRAND PRIX DE MONACO

22 April 1935. Monte Carlo. 100 laps of a 1.976 mile-circuit = 197.600 miles

1	Luigi Fagioli	Mercedes-Benz W25B	100	3h23m49.8
2	Rene Dreyfus	Alfa Romeo Tipo-B "P3"	100	3h24m21.3
3	Antonio Brivio	Alfa Romeo Tipo-B "P3"	100	3h24m56.2
4	Philippe Etancelin	Maserati 6C-34	99	
5	Louis Chiron	Alfa Romeo Tipo-B "P3"	97	
6	Raymond Sommer	Alfa Romeo Tipo-B "P3"	94	

Winner's average speed: 58.166 mph. Starting grid front row: Rudolf Caracciola (Mercedes-Benz W25B), 1m56.6 (pole), Manfred von Brauchitsch (Mercedes-Benz W25B), 1m57.0 and Fagioli, 1m57.3. Fastest lap: Fagioli, 1m58.4

GRAND PRIX DE L'AUTOMOBILE CLUB DE FRANCE

23 June 1935. Montlhery. 40 laps of a 7.767 mile-circuit = 310.680 miles

1	Rudolf Caracciola	Mercedes-Benz W25B	40	4h00m54.6
2	Manfred von			
	Brauchitsch	Mercedes-Benz W25B	40	4h00m55.1
3	Goffredo Zehender	Maserati 6C-34	38	
4	Luigi Fagioli	Mercedes-Benz W25B	37	
5	Achille Varzi/			
	Bernd Rosemeyer	Auto Union B	35	
6	Raymond Sommer	Maserati 8CM	35	

Winner's average speed: 77.377 mph. Starting grid front row: Varzi, 5m20.1 (pole), Tazio Nuvolari (Alfa Romeo Tipo-B "P3"), 5m23.6, and Hans Stuck (Auto Union B), 5m28.8. Fastest lap: Nuvolari, 5m29.1

GRAND PRIX DE BELGIQUE

14 July 1935. Spa-Francorchamps. 34 laps of a 9.290 mile-circuit = 315.860 miles. European Championship round 1

1	Rudolf Caracciola	Mercedes-Benz W25B	34	3h12m31.0
2	Luigi Fagioli/Manfred von			
	Brauchitsch	Mercedes-Benz W25B	34	3h14m08.0
3	Louis Chiron	Alfa Romeo Tipo-B "P3"	34	3h14m47.0
4	Rene Dreyfus/			
	Attilio Marinoni	Alfa Romeo Tipo-B "P3"	34	3h17m54.0
5	Robert Benoist	Bugatti T59	31	
6	Piero Taruffi	Bugatti T59	31	

Winner's average speed: 98.441 mph. Starting grid front row: Marcel Lehoux (Maserati 8CM) and Dreyfus - positions drawn. Fastest lap:

von Brauchitsch, 5m23

GROSSER PREIS VON DEUTSCHLAND

28 July 1935. Nurburgring. 22 laps of a 14.167 mile-circuit = 311.674 miles. European Championship round 2

1	Tazio Nuvolari	Alfa Romeo Tipo-B "P3"	22	4h08m04.1
2	Hans Stuck	Auto Union B	22	4h10m18.4
3	Rudolf Caracciola	Mercedes-Benz W25B	22	4h11m13.1
4	Bernd Rosemeyer	Auto Union B	22	4h12m51.0
5	Manfred von			
	Brauchitsch	Mercedes-Benz W25B	22	4h14m17.4
6	Luigi Fagioli	Mercedes-Benz W25B	22	4h15m58.3

Winner's average speed: 75.384 mph. Starting grid front row: Renato Balestrero (Alfa Romeo 8C "Monza"), Nuvolari, and Stuck - positions drawn. Fastest lap: von Brauchitsch, 10m32.0

GRAND PRIX DE SUISSE

25 August 1935. Bremgarten. 70 laps of a 4.524 mile-circuit = 316.680 miles. European Championship round 3

1	Rudolf Caracciola	Mercedes-Benz W25B	70	3h31m12.2
2	Luigi Fagioli	Mercedes-Benz W25B	70	3h31m48.1
3	Bernd Rosemeyer	Auto Union B	70	3h32m20.0
4	Achille Varzi	Auto Union B	69	
5	Tazio Nuvolari	Alfa Romeo Tipo-B "P3"	68	
6	Hermann Lang	Mercedes-Benz W25B	67	

Winner's average speed: 89.964 mph. Starting grid front row: Varzi, 2m41.8 (pole), Caracciola, 2m42.8 and Hans Stuck (Auto Union B), 2m43.6. Fastest lap: Caracciola, 2m44.4

GRAN PREMIO D'ITALIA

8 September 1935. Monza. 73 laps of a 4.320 mile-circuit = 315.360 miles. European Championship round 4

1	Hans Stuck	Auto Union B	73	3h40m09.0
2	Rene Dreyfus/			
	Tazio Nuvolari	Alfa Romeo Tipo-C "8C-35"	73	3h41m50.0
3	Paul Pietsch/			
	Bernd Rosemeyer	Auto Union B	70	
4	Attilio Marinoni	Alfa Romeo Tipo-B "P3"	68	
5	Piero Taruffi	Bugatti T59	49	

No other finishers. Winner's average speed: 85.949 mph. Starting grid front row: Rudolf Caracciola (Mercedes-Benz W25B), Taruffi and Giuseppe Farina (Maserati V8RI)—positions drawn, Farina did not start. Fastest lap: Nuvolari, 2m49.8

GRAN PREMIO DE ESPANA

22 September 1935. Lasarte. 30 laps of a 11.029 mile-circuit = 330.870 miles. European Championship round 5

1	Rudolf Caracciola	Mercedes-Benz W25B	30	3h09m59.4
2	Luigi Fagioli	Mercedes-Benz W25B	30	3h10m42.4
3	Manfred von			
	Brauchitsch	Mercedes-Benz W25B	30	3h12m14.2
4	Jean-Pierre Wimille	Bugatti T59	30	3h12m54.8
5	Bernd Rosemeyer	Auto Union B	30	3h15m51.0
6	Robert Benoist	Bugatti T59	29	

Winner's average speed: 104.491 mph. Starting grid front row: Wimille, Rosemeyer and Achille Varzi (Auto Union B) - positions drawn. Fastest lap: Varzi, 5m58.0

MASARYKUV OKRUH (CZECH GRAND PRIX)

29 September 1935. Brno. 17 laps of a 18.109 mile-circuit = 307.853 miles

1	Bernd Rosemeyer	Auto Union B	17	3h44m10.6
2	Tazio Nuvolari	Alfa Romeo Tipo-C "8C-35"	17	3h50m48.4
3	Louis Chiron	Alfa Romeo Tipo-B "P3"	17	3h50m52.2
4	Antonio Brivio	Alfa Romeo Tipo-B "P3"	17	3h52m12.0
5	Laszlo Hartmann	Maserati 8CM	15	

No other finishers. Winner's average speed: 82.396 mph. Starting grid front row: n/a. Fastest lap: Achille Varzi (Auto Union B), 12m49.0

DONINGTON GRAND PRIX

5 October 1935. Donington Park. 120 laps of a 2.550 mile-circuit = 306.000 miles

1	Richard Shuttleworth	Alfa Romeo Tipo-B "P3"	120	4h47m12.0
2	Earl Howe	Bugatti T59	120	4h47m57.8
3	Charlie Martin	Bugatti T59	120	4h49m47.4
4	Bill Everitt/Gino Rovere	Maserati 6C-34	120	4h53m59.0
5	"B Bira"	ERA B-type	120	4h58m16.0
6	Roy Eccles/Pat Fairfield	Bugatti T59	120	4h59m33.0

Winner's average speed: 63.928 mph. Starting grid front row: Raymond Sommer (Alfa Romeo Tip-B "P3"), 2m04.0 (pole), Giuseppe Farina (Maserati V8RI), 2m08.4, and Percy Maclure (Riley 2000/6), 2m14.0. Fastest lap: Farina, 2m08.4

1936

GRAND PRIX DE MONACO

13 April 1936. Monte Carlo. 100 laps of a 1.976 mile-circuit = 197.600 miles. European Championship round 1

1	Rudolf Caracciola	Mercedes-Benz W25C	100	3h49m20.4
2	Achille Varzi	Auto Union C	100	3h51m09.5
3	Hans Stuck	Auto Union C	99	
4	Tazio Nuvolari	Alfa Romeo Tipo-C "8C-35"	99	
5	Antonio Brivio/ Giuseppe Farina	Alfa Romeo Tipo-C "8C-35"	97	
6	Jean-Pierre Wimille	Bugatti T59	97	

Winner's average speed: 51.696 mph. Starting grid front row: Louis Chiron (Mercedes-Benz W25C), 1m53.2 (pole), Nuvolari, 1m53.7 and Caracciola, 1m54.0. Fastest lap: Stuck, 2m07.4

MAGYAR NAGYDIJ (HUNGARIAN GRAND PRIX)

21 June 1936. Budapest. 50 laps of a 3.100 mile-circuit = 155.000 miles

1	Tazio Nuvolari	Alfa Romeo Tipo-C "8C-35"	50	2h14m03.46
2	Bernd Rosemeyer	Auto Union C	50	2h14m17.69
3	Achille Varzi	Auto Union C	49	
4	Mario Tadini	Alfa Romeo Tipo-C "8C-35"	47	
5	Hans Stuck/ Ernst von Delius	Auto Union C	46	
6	Austin Dobson	Alfa Romeo Tipo-B "P3"	45	

Winner's average speed: 69.373 mph. Starting grid front row: Rosemeyer and Stuck-positions drawn. Fastest lap: Nuvolari, 2m35.68

GRAND PRIX DE L'AUTOMOBILE CLUB DE FRANCE

28 June 1936. Montlhery. Sports cars. 80 laps of a 7.767 mile-circuit = 621.360 miles

1	Jean-Pierre Wimille/ Raymond Sommer	Bugatti T57G	80	7h58m53.7
2	"Michel Paris"/ Marcel Mongin	Delahaye 135	80	7h59m44.3
3	Robert Brunet/ Goffredo Zehender	Delahaye 135	80	8h00m25.6
4	Laury Schell/ Rene Carriere	Delahaye 135	79	
5	Albert Perrot/Dhome	Delahaye 135	78	
6	Pierre Veyron/ "W Williams"	Bugatti T57G	78	

Winner's average speed: 77.849 mph. Starting grid front row: n/a. Fastest lap: Rene Dreyfus (Talbot), 5m36.0

GROSSER PREIS VON DEUTSCHLAND

26 July 1936. Nurburgring. 22 laps of a 14.167 mile-circuit = 311.674 miles. European Championship round 2

1	Bernd Rosemeyer	Auto Union C	22	3h48m39.6
2	Hans Stuck	Auto Union C	22	3h52m36.4
3	Antonio Brivio	Alfa Romeo Tipo-C "8C-35"	22	3h57m05.0
4	Rudolf Hasse	Auto Union C	22	3h59m13.2

5	Luigi Fagioli/ Rudolf Caracciola	Mercedes-Benz W25C	21	
6	Ernst von Delius	Auto Union C	21	

Winner's average speed: 81.783 mph. Starting grid front row: Tazio Nuvolari (Alfa Romeo Tipo-C "8C-35"), Stuck, and Jean-Pierre Wimille (Bugatti T59) - positions drawn. Fastest lap: Rosemeyer, 9m56.6

GRAND PRIX DE SUISSE

23 August 1936. Bremgarten. 70 laps of a 4.524 mile-circuit = 316.680 miles. European Championship round 3

1	Bernd Rosemeyer	Auto Union C	70	3h09m01.6
2	Achille Varzi	Auto Union C	70	3h09m54.2
3	Hans Stuck	Auto Union C	69	
4	Hermann Lang/ Luigi Fagioli	Mercedes-Benz W25C	69	
5	Rudolf Hasse	Auto Union C	67	

No other finishers. Winner's average speed: 100.519 mph. Starting grid front row: Rudolf Caracciola (Mercedes-Benz W25C), 2m37.9 (pole), Rosemeyer, 2m39.3, and Varzi, 2m39.5. Fastest lap: Rosemeyer, 2m34.5

GRAN PREMIO D'ITALIA

13 September 1936. Monza. 72 laps of a 4.320 mile-circuit = 311.040 miles. European Championship round 4

1	Bernd Rosemeyer	Auto Union C	72	3h43m25.0
2	Tazio Nuvolari	Alfa Romeo Tipo-C "8C-35"	72	3h45m30.3
3	Ernst von Delius	Auto Union C	70	
4	Rene Dreyfus	Alfa Romeo Tipo-C "8C-35"	70	
5	Carlo Maria Pintacuda	Alfa Romeo Tipo-C "8C-35"	68	
6	Piero Dusio	Maserati 6C-34	59	

Winner's average speed: 83.532 mph. Starting grid front row: Rosemeyer, 2m56.4 (pole), Hans Stuck (Auto Union C), 2m58.8, and Nuvolari, 3m00.6. Fastest lap: Rosemeyer, 2m59.6

DONINGTON GRAND PRIX

3 October 1936. Donington Park. 120 laps of a 2.550 mile-circuit = 306.000 miles

1	Hans Ruesch/ Dick Seaman	Alfa Romeo Tipo-C "8C-35"	120	4h25m22.0
2	Charlie Martin	Alfa Romeo Tipo-B "P3"	120	4h28m25.0
3	Peter Whitehead/ Peter Walker	ERA B-type	120	4h31m35.0
4	Reggie Tongue	ERA B-type	120	4h32m29.0
5	"B Bira"	Maserati 8CM	120	4h33m19.0
6	Austin Dobson	Alfa Romeo Tipo-B "P3"	120	4h35m00.0

Winner's average speed: 69.187 mph. Starting grid front row: George Cholmondley-Tapper (Maserati 8CM), Tommy Clarke (Delahaye 135), Percy Maclure (Riley 2000/6), and Reg Parnell (MG K3 Magnette) - positions drawn. Fastest lap: not published

1937

GRAND PRIX DE L'AUTOMOBILE CLUB DE FRANCE

4 July 1937. Montlhery. Sports cars. 40 laps of a 7.767 mile-circuit = 310.680 miles

1	Louis Chiron	Talbot T150C	40	3h46m06.1
2	Gianfranco Comotti	Talbot T150C	40	3h48m12.5
3	Albert Divo	Talbot T150C	40	3h49m48.9
4	Rene Carriere	Delahaye 135	39	
5	Raymond Sommer	Talbot T150C	38	
6	Eugene Chaboud/ Jean Tremoulet	Delahaye 135	33	

Winner's average speed: 82.444 mph. Starting grid front row: n/a. Fastest lap: Chiron, 5m29.7

GRAND PRIX DE BELGIQUE

11 July 1937. Spa-Francorchamps. 34 laps of a 9.290 mile-circuit = 315.860 miles. European Championship round 1

1937 Manfred von Brauchitsch's Mercedes-Benz W125 airborne during the Donington Grand Prix.

1 Rudolf Hasse	Auto Union C	34	3h01m29.0
2 Hans Stuck	Auto Union C	34	3h02m24.0
3 Hermann Lang	Mercedes-Benz W125	34	3h04m07.0
4 Manfred von Brauchitsch	Mercedes-Benz W125	34	3h04m25.0
5 Raymond Sommer	Alfa Romeo 12C-36	34	3h05m54.0

No other finishers. Winner's average speed: 104.426 mph. Starting grid front row: von Brauchitsch , Lang, and Stuck - positions drawn. Fastest lap: Lang, 5m05.6

GROSSER PREIS VON DEUTSCHLAND

25 July 1937. Nurburgring. 22 laps of a 14.167 mile-circuit = 311.674 miles. European Championship round 2

1 Rudolf Caracciola	Mercedes-Benz W125	22	3h46m00.1
2 Manfred von Brauchitsch	Mercedes-Benz W125	22	3h46m46.3
3 Bernd Rosemeyer	Auto Union C	22	3h47m01.4
4 Tazio Nuvolari	Alfa Romeo 12C-36	22	3h50m04.0
5 Rudolf Hasse	Auto Union C	22	3h51m25.1
6 Christian Kautz	Mercedes-Benz W125	22	3h52m10.3

Winner's average speed: 82.745 mph. Starting grid front row: Rosemeyer, 9m46.2 (pole), Hermann Lang (Mercedes-Benz W125), 9m52.2, and von Brauchitsch, 9m55.1. Fastest lap: Rosemeyer, 9m53.4

GRAND PRIX DE MONACO

8 August 1937. Monte Carlo. 100 laps of a 1.976 mile-circuit = 197.600 miles. European Championship round 3

1 Manfred von Brauchitsch	Mercedes-Benz W125	100	3h07m23.9
2 Rudolf Caracciola	Mercedes-Benz W125	100	3h08m48.2
3 Christian Kautz	Mercedes-Benz W125	98	
4 Hans Stuck/ Bernd Rosemeyer	Auto Union C	97	
5 Goffredo Zehender	Mercedes-Benz W125	97	
6 Giuseppe Farina	Alfa Romeo 12C-36	97	

Winner's average speed: 63.266 mph. Starting grid front row: Caracciola, 1m47.5 (pole), von Brauchitsch, 1m48.4, and Rosemeyer, 1m49.0. Fastest lap: Caracciola, 1m46.5

GRAND PRIX DE SUISSE

22 August 1937. Bremgarten. 50 laps of a 4.524 mile-circuit = 226.200 miles. European Championship round 4

1 Rudolf Caracciola	Mercedes-Benz W125	50	2h17m39.3
2 Hermann Lang	Mercedes-Benz W125	50	2h18m28.7
3 Manfred von Brauchitsch	Mercedes-Benz W125	50	2h18m45.7
4 Hans Stuck	Auto Union C	50	2h18m50.8
5 Tazio Nuvolari/ Bernd Rosemeyer	Auto Union C	50	2h19m00.5
6 Christian Kautz	Mercedes-Benz W125	49	

Winner's average speed: 98.594 mph. Starting grid front row: Caracciola, 2m32.0 (pole), Rosemeyer, 2m32.5, and Stuck, 2m34.3. Fastest lap: Rosemeyer, 2m36.1

GRAN PREMIO D'ITALIA

12 September 1937. Livorno. 50 laps of a 4.340 mile-circuit = 217.000 miles. European Championship round 5

1 Rudolf Caracciola	Mercedes-Benz W125	50	2h44m54.4
2 Hermann Lang	Mercedes-Benz W125	50	2h44m54.8
3 Bernd Rosemeyer	Auto Union C	50	2h46m19.8
4 Dick Seaman	Mercedes-Benz W125	49	
5 Hermann Muller	Auto Union C	49	
6 Achille Varzi	Auto Union C	49	

Winner's average speed: 78.954 mph. Starting grid front row: Caracciola, 3m11.0 (pole), Varzi, 3m13.6, and Rosemeyer, 3m14.2. Fastest lap: Lang and Caracciola, 3m11.2

MASARYKUV OKRUK (CZECH GRAND PRIX)

26 September 1937. Brno. 15 laps of a 18.109 mile-circuit = 271.635 miles

1 Rudolf Caracciola	Mercedes-Benz W125	15	3h09m25.3
2 Manfred von Brauchitsch	Mercedes-Benz W125	15	3h10m01.7
3 Hermann Muller/ Bernd Rosemeyer	Auto Union C	15	3h10m07.1
4 Dick Seaman	Mercedes-Benz W125	15	3h10m43.8
5 Tazio Nuvolari	Alfa Romeo 12C-36	14	
6 Antonio Brivio	Alfa Romeo 12C-36	14	

Winner's average speed: 86.041 mph. Starting grid front row: Nuvolari and Hermann Lang (Mercedes-Benz W125) - positions drawn. Fastest lap: Caracciola, 11m59.3

DONINGTON GRAND PRIX

2 October 1937. Donington Park. 80 laps of a 3.125 mile-circuit = 250.000 miles

1 Bernd Rosemeyer	Auto Union C	80	3h01m02.2
2 Manfred von Brauchitsch	Mercedes-Benz W125	80	3h01m40.0
3 Rudolf Caracciola	Mercedes-Benz W125	80	3h02m18.8
4 Hermann Muller	Auto Union C	80	3h04m50.0
5 Rudolf Hasse	Auto Union C	80	3h09m50.0
6 "B Bira"	Maserati 8CM	78	

Winner's average speed: 82.856 mph. Starting grid front row: von Brauchitsch, 2m10.4 (pole), Rosemeyer, 2m11.4, Hermann Lang (Mercedes-Benz W125), 2m14.3, and Dick Seaman (Mercedes-Benz W125), 2m15.4. Fastest lap: Rosemeyer and von Brauchitsch, 2m11.4

1938

GRAND PRIX DE L'AUTOMOBILE CLUB DE FRANCE

3 July 1938. Reims. 64 laps of a 4.865 mile-circuit = 311.360 miles. European Championship round 1

1 Manfred von Brauchitsch	Mercedes-Benz W154	64	3h04m38.5
2 Rudolf Caracciola	Mercedes-Benz W154	64	3h06m19.6
3 Hermann Lang	Mercedes-Benz W154	63	
4 Rene Carriere	Talbot T26SS	54	

No other finishers. Winner's average speed: 101.178 mph. Starting front row: Lang, 2m39.2 (pole), and von Brauchitsch, 2m40.7. Fastest lap: Lang, 2m45.1

GROSSER PREIS VON DEUTSCHLAND

24 July 1938. Nurburgring. 22 laps of a 14.167 mile-circuit = 311.674 miles. European Championship round 2

1 Dick Seaman	Mercedes-Benz W154	22	3h51m46.2
2 Rudolf Caracciola/ Hermann Lang	Mercedes-Benz W154	22	3h55m06.1
3 Hans Stuck	Auto Union D	22	4h00m42.3
4 Hermann Muller/ Tazio Nuvolari	Auto Union D	22	4h01m19.1
5 Rene Dreyfus	Delahaye 145	21	
6 Paul Pietsch	Maserati 4CM	20	

Winner's average speed: 80.685 mph. Starting grid front row: Manfred von Brauchitsch (Mercedes-Benz W154), 9m48.4 (pole), Lang, 9m54.1, and Seaman, 10m01.2. Fastest lap: Seaman, 10m09.1

GRAND PRIX DE SUISSE

21 August 1938. Bremgarten. 50 laps of a 4.524 mile-circuit = 226.200 miles. European Championship round 3

1 Rudolf Caracciola	Mercedes-Benz W154	50	2h32m07.8
2 Dick Seaman	Mercedes-Benz W154	50	2h32m33.8
3 Manfred von Brauchitsch	Mercedes-Benz W154	50	2h33m11.6
4 Hans Stuck	Auto Union D	48	
5 Giuseppe Farina	Alfa Romeo 312	48	
6 Piero Taruffi	Alfa Romeo 308	47	

Winner's average speed: 89.213 mph. Starting grid front row: Seaman, 2m38.8 (pole), Hermann Lang (Mercedes-Benz W154), 2m42.0, and Caracciola, 2m42.2. Fastest lap: Seaman, 2m50.8

GRAN PREMIO D'ITALIA

11 September 1938. Monza. 60 laps of a 4.350 mile-circuit = 261.000 miles. European Championship round 4

1 Tazio Nuvolari	Auto Union D	60	2h41m39.6
2 Giuseppe Farina	Alfa Romeo 316	58	
3 Rudolf Caracciola/Manfred von Brauchitsch	Mercedes-Benz W154	57	
4 Clemente Biondetti	Alfa Romeo 316	56	
5 Pietro Ghersi	Alfa Romeo 308	47	

Carlo Felice Trossi (Maserati 8 CTF), 56 laps completed, finished 5th but was disqualified. No other finishers. Winner's average speed: 96.870 mph. Starting grid front row: Hermann Lang (Mercedes-Benz W154), 2m32.4 (pole), von Brauchitsch, 2m33.1, Caracciola, 2m33.3, and Hermann Muller (Auto Union D), 2m34.4. Fastest lap: Lang, 2m34.2

DONINGTON GRAND PRIX

22 October 1938. Donington Park. 80 laps of a 3.125 mile-circuit = 250.000 miles

1 Tazio Nuvolari	Auto Union D	80	3h06m22.0
2 Hermann Lang	Mercedes-Benz W154	80	3h08m00.0
3 Dick Seaman	Mercedes-Benz W154	79	
4 Hermann Muller	Auto Union D	79	
5 Manfred von Brauchitsch	Mercedes-Benz W154	79	
6 Arthur Dobson	ERA B-type	74	

Winner's average speed: 80.486 mph. Starting grid front row: Lang, 2m11.0 (pole), Nuvolari, 2m11.2, von Brauchitsch, 2m11.4, and Seaman, 2m12.2. Fastest lap: Nuvolari, 2m14.4

1939

GRAND PRIX DE BELGIQUE

26 June 1939. Spa-Francorchamps. 34 laps of a 9.060 mile-circuit = 308.040 miles. European Championship round 1

1 Hermann Lang	Mercedes-Benz W163	34	3h20m21.1
2 Rudolf Hasse	Auto Union D	34	3h20m37.9
3 Manfred von Brauchitsch	Mercedes-Benz W163	34	3h22m14.0
4 Raymond Sommer	Alfa Romeo 312	32	
5 Robert Mazaud	Delahaye 135	30	
6 Louis Gerard	Delahaye 135	29	

Winner's average speed: 92.250 mph. Starting grid front row: Giuseppe Farina (Alfa Romeo 316), Lang, and Hermann Muller (Auto Union D) - positions drawn. Fastest lap: Lang, 5m19.9

GRAND PRIX DE L'AUTOMOBILE CLUB DE FRANCE

9 July 1939. Reims. 51 laps of a 4.865 mile-circuit = 248.115 miles. European Championship round 2

1 Hermann Muller	Auto Union D	51	2h21m11.8
2 Georg Meier	Auto Union D	50	
3 Rene le Begue	Talbot T26C	48	
4 Philippe Etancelin	Talbot T26C	48	
5 Raymond Sommer	Alfa Romeo 308	47	
6 Hans Stuck	Auto Union D	47	

Winner's average speed: 105.434 mph. Starting grid front row: Hermann Lang (Mercedes-Benz W163), 2m27.7 (pole), Rudolf Caracciola (Mercedes-Benz W163), 2m29.6, and Tazio Nuvolari (Auto Union D), 2m29.9. Fastest lap: Lang, 2m32.2

GROSSER PREIS VON DEUTSCHLAND

23 July 1939. Nurburgring. 22 laps of a 14.167 mile-circuit = 311.674 miles. European Championship round 3

1 Rudolf Caracciola	Mercedes-Benz W163	22	4h08m41.8
2 Hermann Muller	Auto Union D	22	4h09m39.6
3 Paul Pietsch	Maserati 8CTF	21	
4 Rene Dreyfus	Delahaye 145	20	
5 "Georges Raph"	Delahaye 145	19	
6 Robert Mazaud	Delahaye 135	19	

Winner's average speed: 75.194 mph. Starting grid front row: Hermann Lang (Mercedes-Benz W163), 9m43.1 (pole), Manfred von Brauchitsch (Mercedes-Benz W163), 9m51.0, and Caracciola, 9m56.0. Fastest lap: Caracciola, 10m24.2

GRAND PRIX DE SUISSE

20 August 1939. Bremgarten. Final: 30 laps of a 4.524 mile-circuit = 135.720 miles. European Championship round 4

Top: 1948 Maserati teammates Luigi Villoresi and Alberto Ascari celebrate victory at Silverstone's first British Grand Prix. **Middle: 1921** Left-to-right: Henry Segrave, eventual winner Jimmy Murphy and Andre Dubonnet in the pits. **Bottom: 1929** "W Williams" won the first Monaco Grand Prix for Bugatti.

1	Hermann Lang	Mercedes-Benz W163	30	1h24m47.6
2	Rudolf Caracciola	Mercedes-Benz W163	30	1h24m50.7
3	Manfred von Brauchitsch	Mercedes-Benz W163	30	1h25m57.5
4	Hermann Muller	Auto Union D	30	1h27m01.3
5	Tazio Nuvolari	Auto Union D	30	1h27m08.6
6	Giuseppe Farina	Alfa Romeo 158	29	

Winner's average speed: 96.036 mph. Starting grid front row: Lang (pole), Caracciola and von Brauchitsch - positions based on heat results. Fastest lap: Lang, 2m38.4 (Caracciola, 2m36 in the second qualifying heat)

YUGOSLAVIAN GRAND PRIX

3 September 1939. Kalemagdan Park, Belgrade. 50 laps of a 1.734 mile-circuit = 86.700 miles

1	Tazio Nuvolari	Auto Union D	50	1h04m03.8
2	Manfred von Brauchitsch	Mercedes-Benz W163	50	1h04m11.4
3	Hermann Muller	Auto Union D	50	1h04m34.4

No other finishers. Winner's average speed: 81.201 mph. Starting grid front row: von Brauchitsch, 1m14.2 (pole) and Hermann Lang (Mercedes-Benz W163), 1m15.0. Fastest lap: Muller, 1m14.0

1947

GRAND PRIX DE SUISSE

8 June 1947. Bremgarten. Final: 30 laps of a 4.524 mile-circuit = 135.720 miles

1	Jean-Pierre Wimille	Alfa Romeo 158	30	1h25m09.1
2	Achille Varzi	Alfa Romeo 158	30	1h25m53.8
3	Carlo Felice Trossi	Alfa Romeo 158	30	1h26m26.5
4	Raymond Sommer	Maserati 4CL	29	
5	Consalvo Sanesi	Alfa Romeo 158	29	
6	Luigi Villoresi	Maserati 4CL	29	

Winner's average speed: 95.632 mph. Starting grid front row: Wimille (pole), Varzi, and Sanesi - positions based on heat results. Fastest lap: Wimille, 2m47.0

GRAND PRIX DE BELGIQUE ET D'EUROPE

29 June 1947. Spa-Francorchamps. 35 laps of a 9.060 mile-circuit = 317.100 miles

1	Jean-Pierre Wimille	Alfa Romeo 158	35	3h18m28.64
2	Achille Varzi	Alfa Romeo 158	34	
3	Carlo Felice Trossi/Giovanni-Battista Guidotti	Alfa Romeo 158	33	
4	Bob Gerard/Cuth Harrison	ERA B	32	
5	Maurice Trintignant	Delage 3L	31	
6	Louis Rosier	Lago-Talbot T150SS	30	

Winner's average speed: 95.860 mph. Starting grid front row: Wimille, 5m12.5 (pole), Varzi, and Louis Chiron (Lago-Talbot T26C). Fastest lap: Wimille, 5m18.0

GRAN PREMIO D'ITALIA

7 September 1947. Milan. 100 laps of a 2.144 mile-circuit = 214.400 miles

1	Carlo Felice Trossi	Alfa Romeo 158	100	3h02m52.0
2	Achille Varzi	Alfa Romeo 158	100	3h02m52.1
3	Consalvo Sanesi	Alfa Romeo 158	99	
4	Alessandro Gaboardi	Alfa Romeo 158	95	
5	Alberto Ascari	Maserati 4CLT	94	
6	Henri Louveau	Delage 3L	91	

Winner's average speed: 70.346 mph. Starting grid front row: Sanesi, 1m44.0 (pole), Trossi, 1m44.8, and Luigi Villoresi (Maserati 4CLT), 1m45.4. Fastest lap: Trossi, 1m44.0

GRAND PRIX DE L'AUTOMOBILE CLUB DE FRANCE

21 September 1947. Lyon. 70 laps of a 4.490 mile-circuit = 314.300 miles

1	Louis Chiron	Lago-Talbot T26C	70	4h03m40.7
2	Henri Louveau	Maserati 4CLT	70	4h05m18.6
3	Eugene Chaboud	Talbot T150C	69	
4	Louis Rosier	Talbot T150C	69	
5	Charles Pozzi	Delahaye 135S	67	
6	Gianfranco Comotti	Talbot T150C	62	

Winner's average speed: 77.389 mph. Starting grid front row: Louveau, 3m17.9 (pole), Chiron, 3m18.3, and Chaboud, 3m23.1. Fastest lap: Alberto Ascari (Maserati 4CLT), Luigi Villoresi (Maserati 4CLT) and "Georges Raph" (Maserati 4CL), 3m17.5

1948

GRAND PRIX DE MONACO

16 May 1948. Monte Carlo. 100 laps of a 1.976 mile-circuit = 197.600 miles

1	Giuseppe Farina	Maserati 4CLT	100	3h18m26.9
2	Louis Chiron	Lago-Talbot T26C	100	3h19m02.1
3	Emanuel de Graffenried	Maserati 4CL	98	
4	Maurice Trintignant	Simca-Gordini 15	98	
5	Alberto Ascari/Luigi Villoresi	Maserati 4CLT	97	
6	Yves Giraud-Cabantous	Talbot T150C	95	

Winner's average speed: 59.744 mph. Starting grid front row: Farina, 1m53.8 (pole), Jean-Pierre Wimille (Simca-Gordini 11), 1m54.2, and Villoresi, 1m54.3. Fastest lap: Farina, 1m53.9

GRAND PRIX DE SUISSE ET D'EUROPE

4 July 1948. Bremgarten. 40 laps of a 4.524 mile-circuit = 180.960 miles

1	Carlo Felice Trossi	Alfa Romeo 158	40	1h59m17.3
2	Jean-Pierre Wimille	Alfa Romeo 158	40	1h59m17.5
3	Luigi Villoresi	Maserati 4CLT/48	40	2h01m54.6
4	Consalvo Sanesi	Alfa Romeo 158	39	
5	Alberto Ascari	Maserati 4CLT/48	39	
6	Louis Chiron	Lago-Talbot T26C	38	

Winner's average speed: 91.020 mph. Starting grid front row: Wimille, 2m54.2 (pole), Giuseppe Farina (Maserati 4CLT), 2m54.3, and Villoresi, 2m56.7. Fastest lap: Wimille, 2m51.0

GRAND PRIX DE L'AUTOMOBILE CLUB DE FRANCE

18 July 1948. Reims. 64 laps of a 4.856 mile-circuit = 310.784 miles

1	Jean-Pierre Wimille	Alfa Romeo 158	64	3h01m07.5
2	Consalvo Sanesi	Alfa Romeo 158	64	3h01m32.0
3	Alberto Ascari	Alfa Romeo 158	64	3h01m32.5
4	Gianfranco Comotti	Lago-Talbot T26C	62	
5	"Georges Raph"	Lago-Talbot T26C	62	
6	Louis Rosier	Lago-Talbot T26C	60	

Winner's average speed: 102.951 mph. Starting grid front row: Wimille, 2m35.2 (pole), Ascari, 2m44.7, and Sanesi, 2m51.2. Fastest lap: Wimille, 2m41.2

GRAN PREMIO D'ITALIA

5 September 1948. Turin. 75 laps of a 2.980 mile-circuit = 223.500 miles

1	Jean-Pierre Wimille	Alfa Romeo 158	75	3h10m42.4
2	Luigi Villoresi	Maserati 4CLT/48	74	
3	Raymond Sommer	Ferrari 125	73	
4	Alberto Ascari	Maserati 4CLT/48	72	
5	Reg Parnell	Maserati 4CLT	72	
6	Louis Rosier	Lago-Talbot T26C	70	

Winner's average speed: 70.317 mph. Starting grid front row: Wimille, 2m16.6 (pole), Carlo Felice Trossi (Alfa Romeo 158), 2m18.4, Villoresi, 2m20.0, and Sommer, 2m20.4. Fastest lap: Wimille, 2m22.4

BRITISH GRAND PRIX

2 October 1948. Silverstone. 65 laps of a 3.670 mile-circuit = 238.550 miles

1	Luigi Villoresi	Maserati 4CLT/48	65	3h18m03.0
2	Alberto Ascari	Maserati 4CLT/48	65	3h18m17.0
3	Bob Gerard	ERA B type	65	3h20m06.0
4	Louis Rosier	Lago-Talbot T26C	65	3h22m38.6
5	"B Bira"	Maserati 4CLT/48	64	
6	John Bolster/ Peter Bell	ERA B type	63	

Winner's average speed: 72.270 mph. Starting grid front row: Louis Chiron (Lago-Talbot T26C), 2m56.0 (pole), Emanuel de Graffenried (Maserati 4CL), 2m57.0, Philippe Etancelin (Lago-Talbot T26C), 2m58.0, Gerard, 2m58.2, and Leslie Johnson (ERA E), 2m58.6. Fastest lap: Villoresi, 2m52.0

1949

BRITISH GRAND PRIX

14 May 1949. Silverstone. 100 laps of a 3.000 mile-circuit = 300.000 miles

1	Emanuel de Graffenried	Maserati 4CLT/48	100	3h52m50.2
2	Bob Gerard	ERA B type	100	3h53m55.4
3	Louis Rosier	Lago-Talbot T26C	99	
4	David Hampshire/ Billy Cotton	ERA B type	99	
5	Philippe Etancelin	Lago-Talbot T26C	97	
6	Fred Ashmore	Maserati 4CLT/48	97	

Winner's average speed: 77.307 mph. Starting grid front row: Luigi Villoresi (Maserati 4CLT/48), 2m09.8 (pole), "B Bira" (Maserati 4CLT/48), 2m10.2, Peter Walker (ERA B type), 2m13.2, de Graffenried, 2m13.6 and Gerard, 2m14.4. Fastest lap: "Bira", 2m10.4

GRAND PRIX DE BELGIQUE

19 June 1949. Spa-Francorchamps. 35 laps of a 9.060 mile-circuit = 317.100 miles

1	Louis Rosier	Lago-Talbot T26C	35	3h15m17.7
2	Luigi Villoresi	Ferrari 125	35	3h16m06.8
3	Alberto Ascari	Ferrari 125	35	3h19m28.4
4	Peter Whitehead	Ferrari 125	35	3h20m35.6
5	Johnny Claes	Lago-Talbot T26C	34	
6	Fred Ashmore	Maserati 4CLT/48	33	

Winner's average speed: 97.422 mph. Starting grid front row: Villoresi, Juan Manuel Fangio (Maserati 4CLT/48), and Philippe Etancelin (Lago-Talbot T26C) - positions drawn. Fastest lap: Giuseppe Farina (Maserati 4CLT/48), 5m19.0

GRAND PRIX DE SUISSE

3 July 1949. Bremgarten. 40 laps of a 4.524 mile-circuit = 180.960 miles

1	Alberto Ascari	Ferrari 125	40	1h59m24.6
2	Luigi Villoresi	Ferrari 125	40	2h00m21.2
3	Raymond Sommer	Lago-Talbot T26C	40	2h00m41.3
4	Philippe Etancelin	Lago-Talbot T26C	40	2h01m07.9
5	"B Bira"	Maserati 4CLT/48	40	2h01m31.3
6	Louis Rosier	Lago-Talbot T26C	40	2h01m52.9

Winner's average speed: 90.927 mph. Starting grid front row: Giuseppe Farina (Maserati 4CLT/48), 2m50.4 (pole), "Bira," 2m53.2, and Ascari, 2m54.7. Fastest lap: Farina, 2m52.2

GRAND PRIX DE FRANCE

17 July 1949. Reims. 64 laps of a 4.856 mile-circuit = 310.784 miles

1	Louis Chiron	Lago-Talbot T26C	64	3h06m33.7
2	"B Bira"	Maserati 4CLT/48	64	3h06m51.3
3	Peter Whitehead	Ferrari 125	64	3h07m22.2
4	Louis Rosier	Lago-Talbot T26C	64	3h07m30.4
5	Raymond Sommer	Lago-Talbot T26C	61	
6	Eugene Chaboud	Delahaye 135	58	

Winner's average speed: 99.951 mph. Starting grid front row: Luigi Villoresi (Ferrari 125), 2m42 (pole), Juan Manuel Fangio (Maserati 4CLT/48), and Rosier. Fastest lap: Whitehead, 2m46.2

GRAND PRIX DE L'AUTOMOBILE CLUB DE FRANCE

7 August 1949. St Gaudens. Sports cars. 46 laps of a 6.835 mile-circuit = 314.410 miles

1	Charles Pozzi	Delahaye 135S	46	3h34m02.2
2	John Heath	Alta	45	
3	Jose Scaron	Simca-Gordini T8	44	
4	Louis Chiron/Paul Vallee	Lago-Talbot Monoplace Decallee	44	
5	Henri Louveau	Delage D6S	44	
6	Auguste Veuillet	Delage D6S	43	

Winner's average speed: 88.137 mph. Starting grid front row: Raymond Sommer (Lago-Talbot T26GS), 4m00. Fastest lap: Sommer, 4m18.4

GRAN PREMIO D'ITALIA E EUROPA

11 September 1949. Monza. 80 laps of a 3.915 mile-circuit = 313.200 miles

1	Alberto Ascari	Ferrari 125	80	2h58m53.6
2	Philippe Etancelin	Lago-Talbot T26C	79	
3	"B Bira"	Maserati 4CLT/48	77	
4	Emanuel de Graffenried	Maserati 4CLT/48	76	
5	Raymond Sommer	Ferrari 125	75	
6	Cuth Harrison	ERA B type	75	

Winner's average speed: 105.046 mph. Starting grid front row: Ascari, 2m05.0 (pole), Luigi Villoresi (Ferrari 125), 2m05.4, Giuseppe Farina (Maserati 4CLT/48), 2m07.8, and Sommer, 2m09.8. Fastest lap: Ascari, 2m06.8

CZECH GRAND PRIX

25 September 1949. Brno. 20 laps of a 11.060 mile-circuit = 221.200 miles

1	Peter Whitehead	Ferrari 125	20	2h48m41.0
2	Philippe Etancelin	Lago-Talbot T26C	20	2h49m16.6
3	Franco Cortese	Ferrari 125	20	2h53m30.4
4	"Pierre Levegh"	Lago-Talbot T26C	19	
5	Henri Louveau	Maserati 4CLT	19	
6	Johnny Claes	Lago-Talbot T26C	19	

Winner's average speed: 78.680 mph. Starting grid front row: "B Bira" (Maserati 4CLT/48) and Giuseppe Farina (Maserati 4CLT/48) - positions drawn. Fastest lap: "Bira" and Emanuel de Graffenried (Maserati 4CLT/48), 8m03.0

European Formula 2 Championship

1967 Jochen Rindt on the way to victory for Roy Winkelmann Racing at Silverstone.

European Formula 2 Championship

Since the very earliest days of motor racing there had been a small car class, whether it was termed "light car class" or later "voiturette". Formula 2 was created as a less-powerful supporting category to Formula 1 in 1948. The World Championship was held for Formula 2 in 1952 and 1953 (see page 15) when there were not enough F1 constructors, but it was not until new 1600cc engines were introduced in 1967 that a European Championship was organised for the category.

Although Grand Prix drivers often used to compete in F2, it was decided at this time that the new European Champion should be a younger driver on his way up to Formula 1, and experienced drivers were ineligible to score Championship points (see Graded Drivers below). But the series gave newcomers the opportunity to compare their skills with the likes of Jim Clark, Jackie Stewart, and the formula's acknowledged master, Jochen Rindt.

The maximum engine capacity was increased to 2000cc in 1972, and the Championship was held until the dwindling number of competitors led to its replacement after the 1984 season by the newly announced Formula 3000 category. Critics claimed that F2 had failed to foster enough new Grand Prix stars (no F2 champion went on to win the world title) and that the best prospects such as Alain Prost, Ayrton Senna, and Nelson Piquet bypassed the formula by moving straight from F3 to Grand Prix racing.

Graded Drivers

A driver was A-graded by the FIA when he had finished in the top six in at least two Grands Prix, or in the top three in two or more World Sports Car events, or a combination of these during the previous two seasons. In addition, the European F2 Champion was graded for one season, and World Champions for five years. (A) indicates A-graded drivers in the results

below; points were awarded to the top six non-graded drivers to finish, all of which are listed.

Rules

1948-53	2000cc normally aspirated or 500cc super charged engine capacity
1957-60	1500cc normally aspirated engine capacity
1964-66	1000cc normally aspirated engine capacity, maximum of 4 cylinders
1967-71	1300-1600cc normally aspirated engine capacity, maximum of 6 cylinders, engine block from a type of car of which at least 500 had been built in the last year
1972-75	2000cc normally aspirated engine capacity, engine block and cylinder head from a type of car of which at least 1000 had been built
1976-84	2000cc normally aspirated engine capacity, pure racing engines allowed, maximum 6 cylinders

Points

9-6-4-3-2-1 awarded to the top six eligible finishers

1981 European Formula 2 Championship contenders Geoff Lees (left) and Thierry Boutsen.

FIA EUROPEAN FORMULA 2 CHAMPIONS

year	driver	nat	team	car
1967	Jacky Ickx	B	Tyrrell Racing Organisation	Matra MS5-Ford/Matra MS7-Ford
1968	Jean-Pierre Beltoise	F	Matra Sports	Matra MS7-Ford
1969	Johnny Servoz-Gavin	F	Tyrrell Racing Organisation	Matra MS7-Ford
1970	Clay Regazzoni	CH	Tecno Racing Team	Tecno 68-Ford/Tecno 70-Ford
1971	Ronnie Peterson	S	March Engineering	March 712M-Ford
1972	Mike Hailwood	GB	Team Surtees	Surtees TS10-Ford
1973	Jean-Pierre Jarier	F	March Engineering	March 732-BMW
1974	Patrick Depailler	F	March Engineering	March 742-BMW
1975	Jacques Laffite	F	Automobiles Martini	Martini MK16-BMW
1976	Jean-Pierre Jabouille	F	Equipe Elf	Elf 2J-Renault
1977	Rene Arnoux	F	Automobiles Martini	Martini MK22-Renault
1978	Bruno Giacomelli	I	March Engineering	March 782-BMW
1979	Marc Surer	CH	March Engineering	March 792-BMW
1980	Brian Henton	GB	Toleman Group Motorsport	Toleman TG280-Hart/Toleman TG280B-Hart
1981	Geoff Lees	GB	Ralt Racing	Ralt RH6/81-Honda
1982	Corrado Fabi	I	March Engineering	March 822-BMW
1983	Jonathan Palmer	GB	Ralt Racing	Ralt RH6/83-Honda
1984	Mike Thackwell	NZ	Ralt Racing	Ralt RH6/84-Honda

1967

GUARDS 100

24 March 1967. Snetterton. Two 10-lap qualifying heats. Final: 40 laps of a 2.710-mile circuit = 108.400 miles. European F2 Trophy round 1

1	Jochen Rindt (A)	Brabham BT23-Ford	40	59m40.6
2	Graham Hill (A)	Lotus 48-Ford	40	59m40.6
3	Alan Rees	Brabham BT23-Ford	40	1h00m23.0
4	Denny Hulme (A)	Brabham BT23-Ford	40	1h00m35.8
5	Bruce McLaren (A)	McLaren M4A-Ford	40	1h00m49.0
6	Jack Brabham (A)	Brabham BT23-Ford	40	1h01m04.0
7	Piers Courage	McLaren M4A-Ford	39	
8	Ian Raby	Brabham BT14-Lotus	32	

Winner's average speed: 108.987 mph. Pole position: Rindt, based on heat results. Fastest lap: Rindt and Hill, 1m28.2

WILLS TROPHY/BARC 200

27 March 1967. Silverstone. Aggregate of two 20-lap heats. 40 laps of a 2.927-mile circuit = 117.080 miles. European F2 Trophy round 2

1	Jochen Rindt (A)	Brabham BT23-Ford	40	1h00m13.0
2	Alan Rees	Brabham BT23-Ford	40	1h00m29.0
3	John Surtees (A)	Lola T100-Ford	40	1h00m37.0
4	Bruce McLaren (A)	McLaren M4A-Ford	40	1h00m48.2
5	Jackie Stewart (A)	Matra MS5-Ford	40	1h00m53.2
6	Frank Gardner	Brabham BT23-Ford	40	1h01m21.2
7	Jacky Ickx	Matra MS5-Ford	40	1h01m39.2
8	Robin Widdows	Brabham BT23-Ford	40	1h02m01.6
9	Mike Spence (A)	Lotus 33-Ford	40	1h02m03.8
10	Jack Brabham (A)	Brabham BT23-Ford	39	
11	Philip Robinson	Alexis 8-Lotus	36	
12	Graham Hill (A)	Lotus 48-Ford	34	
13	Ian Raby	Brabham BT14-Lotus	34	

Winner's average speed: 116.659 mph. Pole position: Rindt, 1m29.2. Fastest lap: Rindt and Hill, 1m29.2

EIFELRENNEN

23 April 1967. Nurburgring. 30 laps of a 4.814-mile circuit = 144.420 miles. European F2 Trophy round 3

1	Jochen Rindt (A)	Brabham BT23-Ford	30	1h35m46.4
2	John Surtees (A)	Lola T100-BMW	30	1h36m03.3
3	Jacky Ickx	Matra MS5-Ford	30	1h36m03.8
4	Hubert Hahne	Lola T100-BMW	30	1h37m27.8
5	Piers Courage	McLaren M4A-Ford	30	1h37m28.2
6	Bruce McLaren (A)	McLaren M4A-Ford	29	
7	Chris Irwin	Lola T100-Ford	29	
8	Gerhard Mitter	Brabham BT23-Ford	28	
9	Alan Rees	Brabham BT23-Ford	28	

Winner's average speed: 90.476 mph. Pole position: Jim Clark (Lotus 48-Ford), 2m49.6. Fastest lap: Rindt, 3m07.8

DEUTSCHLAND TROPHAE

9 July 1967. Hockenheim. Aggregate of a 15-lap and 30-lap heat. 45 laps of a 4.206-mile circuit = 189.270 miles. European F2 Trophy round 4

1	Frank Gardner	Brabham BT23-Ford	45	1h32m48.3
2	Brian Hart	Protos 16-Ford	45	1h33m28.1
3	Piers Courage	McLaren M4A-Ford	45	1h33m50.8
4	Robin Widdows	Brabham BT23-Ford	43	
5	Ian Raby	Brabham BT14-Lotus	42	
6	Alan Rollinson	Cooper T82-Ford	42	

Winner's average speed: 122.366 mph. Pole position: Chris Irwin (Lola T100-Ford), 2m01.5. Fastest lap: Hart, 2m00.0

FLUGPLATZRENNEN TULLN-LANGENLEBARN

16 July 1967. Tulln-Langenlebarn. 50 laps of a 1.780-mile circuit = 89.000 miles. European F2 Trophy round 5

1	Jochen Rindt (A)	Brabham BT23-Ford	50	54m44.40
2	Jack Brabham (A)	Brabham BT23-Ford	50	54m45.80
3	Jean-Pierre Beltoise	Matra MS5-Ford	50	55m07.54
4	Frank Gardner	Brabham BT23-Ford	50	55m21.79
5	Jacky Ickx	Matra MS7-Ford	50	55m23.61
6	Graham Hill (A)	Lotus 48-Ford	50	55m30.65
7	Chris Irwin	Lola T100-Ford	50	55m36.86
8	Johnny Servoz-Gavin	Matra MS5-Ford	49	
9	Piers Courage	McLaren M4A-Ford	49	

Winner's average speed: 97.552 mph. Pole position: Beltoise, 1m05.3. Fastest lap: Jim Clark (Lotus 48-Ford), 1m04.24

GRAN PREMIO DE MADRID

23 July 1967. Jarama. 55 laps of a 2.115-mile circuit = 116.347 miles. European F2 Trophy round 6

1	Jim Clark (A)	Lotus 48-Ford	55	1h25m29.1
2	Jackie Stewart (A)	Matra MS7-Ford	55	1h25m37.0
3	Chris Irwin	Lola T100-Ford	55	1h26m43.2
4	Jack Brabham (A)	Brabham BT23-Ford	55	1h26m53.7
5	Johnny Servoz-Gavin	Matra MS5-Ford	54	
6	Brian Redman	Lola T100-Ford	54	
7	Pedro Rodriguez (A)	Protos 16-Ford	54	
8	Piers Courage	McLaren M4A-Ford	54	
9	Robin Widdows	Brabham BT23-Ford	52	
10	Frank Gardner	Brabham BT23-Ford	51	fire extinguisher

Winner's average speed: 81.661 mph. Pole position: Graham Hill (Lotus 48-Ford), 1m31.3. Fastest lap: Clark, 1m30.7

GROTE PRIJS VAN ZANDVOORT

30 July 1967. Zandvoort. 15-lap qualifying heat. Final: 30 laps of a 2.605-mile circuit = 78.150 miles. European F2 Trophy round 7

1	Jacky Ickx	Matra MS5-Ford	30	44m43.2
2	Piers Courage	McLaren M4A-Ford	30	44m58.1
3	Frank Gardner	Brabham BT23-Ford	30	45m16.1
4	Jean-Pierre Beltoise	Matra MS7-Ford	30	45m44.1
5	Alan Rees	Brabham BT23-Ford	30	45m59.7
6	Brian Hart	Protos 16-Ford	30	46m02.0

Winner's average speed: 104.852 mph. Pole position: Ickx, based on heat results. Fastest lap: Ickx, 1m27.8

GRAN PREMIO DEL MEDITERRANEO

20 August 1967. Enna-Pergusa. Aggregate of two 40-lap heats. 80 laps of a 2.983-mile circuit = 238.640 miles. European F2 Trophy round 8

1	Jackie Stewart (A)	Matra MS7-Ford	80	1h40m19.2
2	Jean-Pierre Beltoise	Matra MS5-Ford	80	1h40m19.9
3	Jacky Ickx	Matra MS5-Ford	80	1h40m20.2
4	Jo Schlesser	Matra MS5-Ford	80	1h41m08.6
5	Johnny Servoz-Gavin	Matra MS5-Ford	80	1h41m13.9
6	Alan Rees	Brabham BT23-Ford	79	
7	Graham Hill (A)	Lotus 48-Ford	78	
8	Brian Hart	Protos 16-Ford	77	

Winner's average speed: 142.727 mph. Pole position: Stewart, 1m13.5. Fastest lap: Ickx, 1m13.3

GUARDS INTERNATIONAL TROPHY

28 August 1967. Brands Hatch. Two 10-lap qualifying heats. Final: 40 laps of a 2.650-mile circuit = 106.000 miles. European F2 Trophy round 9

1	Jochen Rindt (A)	Brabham BT23-Ford	40	1h02m44.2
2	Jackie Stewart (A)	Matra MS7-Ford	40	1h03m03.6
3	Jo Schlesser	Matra MS5-Ford	40	1h03m15.4
4	Frank Gardner	Brabham BT23-Ford	40	1h03m30.8
5	Jacky Ickx	Matra MS5-Ford	40	1h03m49.8
6*	Jackie Oliver	Lotus 48-Ford	40	1h04m15.0
7	Graham Hill (A)	Lotus 48-Ford	40	1h04m15.4
8	Brian Redman	Lola T100-Ford	39	
9	Hubert Hahne	Lola T100-BMW	39	

*including 1m penalty for jumping the start. Winner's average speed: 101.376 mph. Pole position: Rindt, based on heat results. Fastest lap: Rindt, 1m33.0

GRAN PREMIO DI ROMA

8 October 1967. Vallelunga. Aggregate of two 30-lap heats. 60 laps of a 1.988-mile circuit = 119.280 miles. European F2 Trophy round 10

1	Jacky Ickx	Matra MS7-Ford	60	1h20m27.8
2	Jean-Pierre Beltoise	Matra MS5-Ford	60	1h20m52.0
3	Johnny Servoz-Gavin	Matra MS7-Ford	60	1h21m25.1
4	Frank Gardner	Brabham BT23C-Ford	60	1h21m55.0
5	Brian Redman	Lola T100-Ford	60	1h21m59.6
6	Jean-Pierre Jaussaud	Matra MS5-Ford	60	1h22m24.1

Winner's average speed: 88.945 mph. Pole position: Ickx, 1m18.4. Fastest lap: Ickx, 1m18.7

1967 FINAL CHAMPIONSHIP POSITIONS

1	Jacky Ickx	41 (45)*	12=	Hubert Hahne	7
2	Frank Gardner	34 (35)*		Ian Raby	7
3	Jean-Pierre Beltoise	27	14	Jackie Oliver	3
4	Piers Courage	24	15=	Gerhard Mitter	2
5	Alan Rees	23		Philip Robinson	2
6=	Chris Irwin	15	17=	Jean-Pierre Jaussaud	1
	Johnny Servoz-Gavin	15		Alan Rollinson	1
8	Jo Schlesser	13	(A) Graded driver ineligible for		
9=	Brian Hart	8	points. *Best six results count		
	Brian Redman	8			
	Robin Widdows	8			

1968 Tino Brambilla leads Andrea de Adamich, Peter Gethin and Clay Regazzoni at Vallelunga.

1968

DEUTSCHLAND TROPHAE

7 April 1968. Hockenheim. Aggregate of two 20-lap heats. 40 laps of a 4.206-mile circuit = 168.240 miles. European F2 Trophy round 1

1	Jean-Pierre Beltoise	Matra MS7-Ford	40	1h25m49.7
2	Henri Pescarolo	Matra MS7-Ford	40	1h25m51.8
3	Piers Courage	Brabham BT23C-Ford	40	1h26m51.9
4	Chris Lambert	Brabham BT23C-Ford	40	1h27m13.0
5	Chris Amon (A)	Ferrari 166	40	1h28m30.3
6	Jo Schlesser	McLaren M4A-Ford	40	1h28m30.6
7	Robin Widdows	McLaren M4A-Ford	39	

Winner's average speed: 117.612 mph. Pole position: Beltoise, 1m59.3. Fastest lap: Pescarolo, 2m00.1

BARC THRUXTON TROPHY

15 April 1968. Thruxton. Two 15-lap qualifying heats. Final: 54 laps of a 2.356-mile circuit = 127.224 miles. European F2 Trophy round 2

1	Jochen Rindt (A)	Brabham BT23C-Ford	54	1h09m45.6
2	Jean-Pierre Beltoise	Matra MS7-Ford	54	1h09m53.0
3	Derek Bell	Brabham BT23C-Ford	54	1h10m18.8

4	Jackie Oliver	Lotus 48-Ford	53	
5	Kurt Ahrens Jr	Brabham BT23C-Ford	53	
6	Chris Williams	Lola T100-Ford	52	
7	Alan Rees	Brabham BT23C-Ford	52	

Winner's average speed: 109.424 mph. Pole position: Rindt, based on heat times. Fastest lap: Rindt, 1m16.0

GRAN PREMIO DE MADRID

28 April 1968. Jarama. 60 laps of a 2.115-mile circuit = 126.924 miles. European F2 Trophy round 3

1	Jean-Pierre Beltoise	Matra MS7-Ford	60	1h30m09.7
2	Jochen Rindt (A)	Brabham BT23C-Ford	60	1h30m28.4
3	Kurt Ahrens Jr	Brabham BT23C-Ford	60	1h31m12.4
4	Henri Pescarolo	Matra MS7-Ford	60	1h31m14.0
5	Clay Regazzoni	Tecno TF68-Ford	59	
6	Jorge de Bagration	Lola T100-Ford	57	
7	Brian Hart	Merlyn 12-Ford	57	

Winner's average speed: 84.464 mph. Pole position: Beltoise, 1m28.7. Fastest lap: Beltoise, 1m28.2

HOLTS LONDON TROPHY

3 June 1968. Crystal Palace. Two 22-lap qualifying heats. Final: 90 laps of a 1.390-mile circuit = 125.100 miles. European F2 Trophy round 4

1	Jochen Rindt (A)	Brabham BT23C-Ford	90	1h20m06.8
2	Brian Redman	Lola T100-Ford	90	1h20m37.0
3	Clay Regazzoni	Tecno TF68-Ford	89	
4	Jackie Oliver	Lotus 48-Ford	89	
5	Jo Schlesser	McLaren M4A-Ford	88	accident
6	Jean-Pierre Jaussaud	Tecno TF68-Ford	85	

No other finishers. Winner's aversage speed: 93.692 mph. Pole position: Rindt, based on heat results. Fastest lap: Rindt 52.0s

FLUGPLATZRENNEN TULLN-LANGENLEBARN

14 July 1968. Tulln-Langenlebarn. Aggregate of two 35-lap heats. 70 laps of a 1.780-mile circuit = 124.600 miles. European F2 Trophy round 5

1	Jochen Rindt (A)	Brabham BT23C-Ford	70	1h15m24.63
2	Jean-Pierre Beltoise	Matra MS7-Ford	70	1h15m57.15
3	Henri Pescarolo	Matra MS7-Ford	70	1h16m18.01
4	Kurt Ahrens Jr	Brabham BT23C-Ford	70	1h16m31.38
5	Jackie Oliver	Lotus 48-Ford	70	1h17m03.22
6	Tino Brambilla	Brabham BT23-Ford	70	1h17m22.10
7	Derek Bell	Ferrari 166	69	

Winner's average speed: 99.137 mph. Pole position: Rindt, 1m03.27. Fastest lap: Rindt, 1m03.2

GROTE PRIJS VAN ZANDVOORT

28 July 1968. Zandvoort. Two 20-lap qualifying heats. Final: 50 laps of a 2.605-mile circuit = 130.250 miles. European F2 Trophy round 6

1	Jean-Pierre Beltoise	Matra MS7-Ford	50	1h13m52.18
2	Henri Pescarolo	Matra MS7-Ford	50	1h13m52.24
3	Richard Attwood	Tecno TF68-Ford	50	1h13m52.32
4	Silvio Moser	Tecno TF68-Ford	49	
5	Eric Offenstadt	Tecno TF68-Ford	49	
6	Robin Widdows	McLaren M4A-Ford	49	

Winner's average speed: 105.794 mph. Pole position: Derek Bell (Ferrari 166), based on heat times. Fastest lap: Attwood, 1m26.84

GRAN PREMIO DEL MEDITERRANEO

25 August 1968. Enna-Pergusa. 50 laps of a 2.983-mile circuit = 149.150 miles. European F2 Trophy round 7

1	Jochen Rindt (A)	Brabham BT23C-Ford	50	1h02m40.6
2	Piers Courage	Brabham BT23C-Ford	50	1h02m40.6
3	Tino Brambilla	Ferrari 166	50	1h02m40.6
4	Clay Regazzoni	Tecno TF68-Ford	50	1h02m40.6
5	Derek Bell	Ferrari 166	50	1h02m41.5
6	Jacky Ickx (A)	Ferrari 166	50	1h02m43.8
7	Brian Hart	Brabham BT23C-Ford	50	1h02m44.0
8	Henri Pescarolo	Matra MS7-Ford	50	1h02m52.4

Winner's average speed: 142.780 mph. Pole position: Pescarolo, 1m13.7. Fastest lap: Rindt, 1m12.8

PREIS VON HESSEN UND WURTTEMBERG

13 October 1968. Hockenheim. 35 laps of a 4.206-mile circuit = 147.210 miles. European F2 Trophy round 8

1	Tino Brambilla	Ferrari 166	35	1h11m40.2
2	Henri Pescarolo	Matra MS7-Ford	35	1h11m40.4
3	Derek Bell	Ferrari 166	35	1h11m40.6
4	Jackie Oliver	Lotus 48-Ford	35	1h11m41.3
5	David Hobbs	Lola T100-Ford	35	1h11m42.4
6	Brian Hart	Brabham BT23C-Ford	35	1h11m42.6

Winner's average speed: 123.240 mph. Pole position: Jochen Rindt (Brabham BT23C-Ford), 1m58.7. Fastest lap: Brambilla, 1m59.0

GRAN PREMIO DI ROMA

27 October 1968. Vallelunga. Aggregate of two 40-lap heats. 80 laps of a 1.988-mile circuit = 159.040 miles. European F2 Trophy round 9

1	Tino Brambilla	Ferrari 166	80	1h43m02.7
2	Andrea de Adamich	Ferrari 166	80	1h43m08.1
3	Peter Gethin	Brabham BT23C-Ford	80	1h43m10.4
4	Jean-Pierre Beltoise	Matra MS7-Ford	80	1h43m51.6
5	Henri Pescarolo	Matra MS7-Ford	80	1h44m05.0
6	Derek Bell	Ferrari 166	80	1h44m08.0

Winner's average speed: 92.604 mph. Pole position: Brambilla, 1m16.3, based on average of three quickest laps. Fastest lap: Brambilla, 1m16.2

1968 FINAL CHAMPIONSHIP POSITIONS

1	Jean-Pierre Beltoise	48	15=	Chris Lambert	3
2	Henri Pescarolo	30 (31)*		Silvio Moser	3
3	Tino Brambilla	26	17=	Jorge de Bagration	2
4	Derek Bell	15		David Hobbs	2
5	Jackie Oliver	14		Jean-Pierre Jaussaud	2
6=	Kurt Ahrens Jr	13		Eric Offenstadt	2
	Piers Courage	13		Robin Widdows	2
	Clay Regazzoni	13		Chris Williams	2
9	Brian Redman	9	23	Alan Rees	1
10	Andrea de Adamich	6		(A) Graded driver ineligible for
11	Jo Schlesser	5		points. *Best six results count
12=	Richard Attwood	4		
	Peter Gethin	4		
	Brian Hart	4		

1969

WILLS TROPHY/BARC 200

7 April 1969. Thruxton. Two 15-lap qualifying heats. Final: 50 laps of a 2.356-mile circuit = 117.800 miles. European F2 Trophy round 1

1	Jochen Rindt (A)	Lotus 59-Ford	50	1h02m44.6
2	Jackie Stewart (A)	Matra MS7-Ford	50	1h03m14.8
3	Jean-Pierre Beltoise (A)	Matra MS7-Ford	50	1h03m57.4
4	Henri Pescarolo	Matra MS7-Ford	49	
5	Johnny Servoz-Gavin	Matra MS7-Ford	49	
6	Tino Brambilla	Ferrari 166	48	
7	Piers Courage (A)	Brabham BT23C-Ford	48	
8	Francois Cevert	Tecno TF68-Ford	48	
9	Enzo Corti	Brabham BT23-Ford	48	
10	Clay Regazzoni	Ferrari 166	47	

Winner's average speed: 112.649 mph. Pole position: Stewart, based on heat times. Fastest lap: Rindt, 1m14.0

JIM CLARK-RENNEN/DEUTSCHLAND TROPHAE

13 April 1969. Hockenheim. Aggregate of two 20-lap heats. 40 laps of a 4.206-mile circuit = 168.240 miles. European F2 Trophy round 2

1	Jean-Pierre Beltoise (A)	Matra MS7-Ford	40	1h21m39.6
2	Hubert Hahne	Lola T102-BMW	40	1h21m40.2
3	Piers Courage (A)	Brabham BT23C-Ford	40	1h21m43.8

4	Kurt Ahrens Jr	Brabham BT30-Ford	40	1h22m01.1
5*	Henri Pescarolo	Matra MS7-Ford	40	1h22m20.3
6*	Johnny Servoz-Gavin	Matra MS7-Ford	40	1h22m01.4
7*	Alan Rollinson	Lotus 59-Ford	40	1h22m03.0
8	Nanni Galli	Tecno TF68-Ford	40	1h22m23.6

*Positions decided by points awarded for heats. Winner's average speed: 123.615 mph. Pole position: Pescarolo, 2m08.9. Fastest lap: Beltoise, 1m59.1

EIFELRENNEN

27 April 1969. Nurburgring. 10 laps of a 14.189-mile circuit = 141.890 miles. European F2 Trophy round 3

1	Jackie Stewart (A)	Matra MS7-Ford	10	1h21m40.4
2	Jo Siffert (A)	Lola T102-BMW	10	1h22m56.4
3	Jean-Pierre Beltoise (A)	Matra MS7-Ford	10	1h23m11.7
4	Hubert Hahne	Lola T102-BMW	10	1h23m52.4
5	Derek Bell	Ferrari 166	10	1h23m55.7
6	Johnny Servoz-Gavin	Matra MS7-Ford	10	1h24m05.3
7	Francois Cevert	Tecno TF68-Ford	10	1h24m49.9
8	Malcolm Guthrie	Brabham BT23C-Ford	10	1h28m18.5
9	Werner Lindermann	Brabham BT23-Ford	9	

Winner's average speed: 104.237 mph. Pole position: Siffert, 9m03.8. Fastest lap: Stewart, 8m05.3

GRAN PREMIO DE MADRID

11 May 1969. Jarama. 60 laps of a 2.115-mile circuit = 126.924 miles. European F2 Trophy round 4

1	Jackie Stewart (A)	Matra MS7-Ford	60	1h29m36.7
2	Jean-Pierre Beltoise (A)	Matra MS7-Ford	60	1h29m37.2
3	Piers Courage (A)	Brabham BT23C-Ford	60	1h29m57.2
4	Johnny Servoz-Gavin	Matra MS7-Ford	59	
5	Hubert Hahne	Lola T102-BMW	59	
6	Tino Brambilla	Ferrari 166	59	
7	Peter Westbury	Brabham BT30-Ford	59	
8	Derek Bell	Ferrari 166	58	
9	Nanni Galli	Tecno TF68-Ford	58	

Winner's average speed: 84.983 mph. Pole position: Beltoise, 1m28.6. Fastest lap: Stewart and Beltoise, 1m28.4

FLUGPLATZRENNEN TULLN-LANGENLEBARN

13 July 1969. Tulln-Langenlebarn. Aggregate of two 35-lap heats. 70 laps of a 1.780-mile circuit = 124.600 miles. European F2 Trophy round 5

1	Jochen Rindt (A)	Lotus 59-Ford	70	1h13m22.02
2	Jackie Stewart (A)	Matra MS7-Ford	70	1h13m24.64
3	Graham Hill (A)	Lotus 59-Ford	70	1h13m42.12
4	Jean-Pierre Beltoise (A)	Matra MS7-Ford	70	1h13m59.74
5	Francois Cevert	Tecno TF68-Ford	70	1h14m33.40
6	Nanni Galli	Tecno TF68-Ford	70	1h14m45.39
7	Hubert Hahne	BMW 269/F2	69	
8	Xavier Perrot	Brabham BT23C-Ford	69	
9	Peter Westbury	Brabham BT30-Ford	64	engine
10	Werner Lindermann	Brabham BT23-Ford	63	

Winner's average speed: 101.899 mph. Pole position: Rindt, 1m02.1. Fastest lap: Rindt, 1m01.7

GRAN PREMIO DEL MEDITERRANEO

24 August 1969. Enna-Pergusa. Aggregate of two 31-lap heats. 62 laps of a 2.983-mile circuit = 184.946 miles. European F2 Trophy round 6

1	Piers Courage (A)	Brabham BT30-Ford	62	1h17m58.0
2	Johnny Servoz-Gavin	Matra MS7-Ford	62	1h17m58.7
3	Francois Cevert	Tecno TF68-Ford	62	1h17m59.3
4	Clay Regazzoni	Tecno TF69-Ford	62	1h18m00.3
4	Robin Widdows	Brabham BT23C-Ford	62	1h18m28.5
6	Graham Hill (A)	Lotus 59-Ford	62	1h18m57.1
7	Alan Rollinson	Brabham BT30-Ford	62	1h18m58.6
8	Patrick Dal Bo	Pygmee MDB12-Ford	62	1h19m25.8

Winner's average speed: 142.327 mph. Pole position: Regazzoni, 1m13.5. Fastest lap: Hill, 1m12.9

GRAN PREMIO DI ROMA

12 October 1969. Vallelunga. Aggregate of two 40-lap heats. 80 laps of a 1.988-mile circuit = 159.040 miles. European F2 Trophy round 7

1	Johnny Servoz-Gavin	Matra MS7-Ford	80	1h42m43.4
2	Peter Westbury	Brabham BT30-Ford	79	
3	John Miles	Lotus 59-Ford	79	
4	Derek Bell	Brabham BT30-Ford	78	
5	Franco Bernabei	Brabham BT23C-Ford	77	
6	John Pollock	Lotus 48-Ford	76	

Winner's average speed: 92.894 mph. Pole position: Servoz-Gavin, 1m15.49. Fastest lap: Servoz-Gavin, 1m15.7

1969 European Formula 2 Champion Johnny Servoz-Gavin.

1969 FINAL CHAMPIONSHIP POSITIONS

1	Johnny Servoz-Gavin	37 (40)*	13=	Xavier Perrot	3
				Robin Widdows	3
2	Hubert Hahne	28	15=	Franco Bernabei	2
3	Francois Cevert	21		Enzo Corti	2
4	Henri Pescarolo	13		Malcolm Guthrie	2
5=	Derek Bell	11		Werner Lindermann	2
	Peter Westbury	11	19=	Patrick Dal Bo	1
7=	Tino Brambilla	8		John Pollock	1
	Nanni Galli	8		(A) Graded driver ineligible for	
9	Kurt Ahrens Jr	6		points. *Best five results count	
10	Clay Regazzoni	5			
11=	John Miles	4			
	Alan Rollinson	4			

1970

WILLS TROPHY/BARC 200

30 March 1970. Thruxton. Two 20-lap qualifying heats. Final: 46 laps of a 2.356-mile circuit = 108.376 miles. European F2 Trophy round 1

1	Jochen Rindt (A)	Lotus 69-Ford	46	57m41.0
2	Jackie Stewart (A)	Brabham BT30-Ford	46	57m53.4
3	Derek Bell	Brabham BT30-Ford	45	
4	Robin Widdows	Brabham BT30-Ford	45	
5	Alistair Walker	Brabham BT23C-Ford	45	
6	Jacky Ickx (A)	BMW 270/F2	44	
7	Dieter Quester	BMW 269/F2	44	
8	Clay Regazzoni	Tecno TF69-Ford	44	
9	Tommy Reid	Brabham BT30-Ford	44	

Winner's average speed: 112.729 mph. Pole position: Rindt, based on heat times. Fastest lap: Rindt, 1m14.0

JIM CLARK-RENNEN/DEUTSCHLAND TROPHAE

12 April 1970. Hockenheim. Points awarded for two 20-lap heats. 40 laps of a 4.206-mile circuit = 168.240 miles. European F2 Trophy round 2

1	Clay Regazzoni	Tecno TF69-Ford	40	1h22m01.3
2	Tetsu Ikuzawa	Lotus 69-Ford	40	1h22m01.6
3	Derek Bell	Brabham BT30-Ford	40	1h22m03.1
4	Hubert Hahne	BMW 269/F2	40	1h22m16.2
5*	Emerson Fittipaldi	Lotus 69-Ford	40	1h22m17.4
6*	Rolf Stommelen (A)	March 702-Ford	40	1h22m16.9
7	Peter Gaydon	Brabham BT30-Ford	40	1h22m43.0

*positions decided by points awarded for heats. Winner's average speed: 123.070 mph. Pole position: Jochen Rindt (Lotus 69-Ford), 1m58.5. Fastest lap: Dieter Quester (BMW 269/F2), 1m58.7

GRAN PREMIO DE BARCELONA

26 April 1970. Montjuich Park. 45 laps of a 2.355-mile circuit = 105.975 miles. European F2 Trophy round 3

1	Derek Bell	Brabham BT30-Ford	45	1h08m07.6
2	Henri Pescarolo	Brabham BT30-Ford	45	1h08m29.9
3	Emerson Fittipaldi	Lotus 69-Ford	44	
4	Robin Widdows	Brabham BT30-Ford	44	
5	Dieter Quester	BMW 269/F2	44	
6	Carlos Reutemann	Brabham BT30-Ford	44	

Winner's average speed: 93.333 mph. Pole position: Pescarolo, 1m29.7. Fastest lap: Bell, 1m29.5

GRAND PRIX DE ROUEN-LES-ESSARTS

28 June 1970. Rouen-les-Essarts. Two 15-lap qualifying heats. Final: 25 laps of a 4.065-mile circuit = 101.625 miles. European F2 Trophy round 4

1	Jo Siffert (A)	BMW 270/F2	25	51m24.3
2	Clay Regazzoni	Tecno TF69-Ford	25	51m24.4
3	Emerson Fittipaldi	Lotus 69-Ford	25	51m24.5
4	Jacky Ickx (A)	BMW 270/F2	25	51m25.0
5	Tim Schenken	Brabham BT30-Ford	25	51m25.3
6	Ronnie Peterson	March 702-Ford	25	51m25.7
7	Derek Bell	Brabham BT30-Ford	25	51m26.2
8	Jack Brabham (A)	Brabham BT30-Ford	25	51m26.7
9	Jochen Rindt (A)	Lotus 69-Ford	25	51m35.6
10	Peter Westbury	Brabham BT30-Ford	25	51m35.8

Winner's average speed: 118.617 mph. Pole position: Regazzoni, based on heat results. Fastest lap: Schenken, 2m00.8

GRAN PREMIO DEL MEDITERRANEO

23 August 1970. Enna-Pergusa. Aggregate of two 31-lap heats. 62 laps of a 3.010-mile circuit = 186.620 miles. European F2 Trophy round 5

1	Clay Regazzoni	Tecno TF70-Ford	62	1h28m03.5
2	Jo Siffert (A)	BMW 270/F2	62	1h28m03.8
3	Jacky Ickx (A)	BMW 270/F2	62	1h28m04.1
4	Peter Westbury	Brabham BT30-Ford	62	1h28m10.0
5	Emerson Fittipaldi	Lotus 69-Ford	62	1h29m18.6
6	Rolf Stommelen (A)	Brabham BT30-Ford	62	1h29m28.0
7	Derek Bell	Brabham BT30-Ford	60	
8	Jean-Pierre Jabouille	Pygmee MDB15-Ford	59	

No other finishers. Winner's average speed: 127.157 mph. Pole position: Ickx, 1m22.8. Fastest lap: Regazzoni, 1m23.5

FLUGPLATZRENNEN TULLN-LANGENLEBARN

13 September 1970. Tulln-Langenlebarn. Aggregate of two 35-lap heats. 70 laps of a 1.780-mile circuit = 124.600 miles. European F2 Trophy round 6

1	Jacky Ickx (A)	BMW 270/F2	70	1h13m45.82
2	Jack Brabham (A)	Brabham BT30-Ford	70	1h13m49.68
3	Francois Cevert	Tecno TF70-Ford	70	1h14m17.33
4	Derek Bell	Brabham BT30-Ford	70	1h14m39.12
5	Ronnie Peterson	March 702-Ford	70	1h15m05.94
6	Vittorio Brambilla	Brabham BT23-Ford	69	
7	Tetsu Ikuzawa	Lotus 69-Ford	69	

8 Alistair Walker　　　　Brabham BT30-Ford　　68

Winner's average speed: 101.351 mph. Pole position: Clay Regazzoni (Tecno TF70-Ford), 1m01.5. Fastest lap: Cevert, 1m01.6

GRAN PREMIO CITTI DI IMOLA

27 September 1970. Imola Aggregate of two 28-lap heats. 56 laps of a 3.118-mile circuit = 174.608 miles. European F2 Trophy round 7

1	Clay Regazzoni	Tecno TF70-Ford	56	1h30m50.3
2	Emerson Fittipaldi	Lotus 69-Ford	56	1h30m58.2
3	Derek Bell	Brabham BT30-Ford	56	1h31m12.3
4	Ronnie Peterson	March 702-Ford	56	1h31m12.8
5	Rolf Stommelen (A)	Brabham BT30-Ford	56	1h31m21.8
6	Mike Goth	Brabham BT30-Ford	56	1h32m50.4
7	Tetsu Ikuzawa	Lotus 69-Ford	56	1h33m01.4

Winner's average speed: 115.331 mph. Pole position: Regazzoni, 1m36.34. Fastest lap: Jacky Ickx (BMW 270/F2), 1m35.5

PREIS VON HESSEN UND WURTTEMBERG

11 October 1970. Hockenheim. 35 laps of a 4.206-mile circuit = 147.210 miles. European F2 Trophy round 8

1	Dieter Quester	BMW 270/F2	35	1h16m34.4
2	Clay Regazzoni	Tecno TF70-Ford	35	1h16m36.1
3	Ronnie Peterson	March 702-Ford	35	1h17m03.3
4	Emerson Fittipaldi	Lotus 69-Ford	35	1h17m03.6
5	Carlos Reutemann	Brabham BT30-Ford	35	1h17m42.9
6	Derek Bell	Brabham BT30-Ford	35	1h17m46.9

Winner's average speed: 115.348 mph. Pole position: Peterson, 2m09.0. Fastest lap: Quester, 2m08.7

1970 FINAL CHAMPIONSHIP POSITIONS

1	Clay Regazzoni	44	12	Tim Schenken	4
2	Derek Bell	35 (38)*	13=	Vittorio Brambilla	3
3	Emerson Fittipaldi	25		Hubert Hahne	3
4=	Ronnie Peterson	14		Carlos Reutemann	3
	Dieter Quester	14	16=	Mike Goth	2
6=	Francois Cevert	9		Jean-Pierre Jabouille	2
	Tetsu Ikuzawa	9	18=	Peter Gaydon	1
	Robin Widdows	9		Tommy Reid	1
9	Peter Westbury	7	(A) Graded driver ineligible for		
10	Henri Pescarolo	6	points. *Best six results count		
11	Alistair Walker	5			

1971

JIM CLARK-RENNEN

4 April 1971. Hockenheim. Aggregate of two 20-lap heats. 40 laps of a 4.219-mile circuit = 168.760 miles. European F2 Trophy round 1

1	Francois Cevert	Tecno TF71-Ford	40	1h27m09.8
2	Graham Hill (A)	Brabham BT36-Ford	40	1h27m14.7
3	Carlos Reutemann	Brabham BT30-Ford	40	1h27m21.5
4	Wilson Fittipaldi	Lotus 69-Ford	40	1h27m31.7
5	Tim Schenken	Brabham BT36-Ford	40	1h27m34.8
6	Gerry Birrell	Lotus 69-Ford	40	1h28m36.1
7	Brian Hart	Brabham BT30-Ford	40	1h28m38.5

Winner's average speed: 116.168 mph. Pole position: Ronnie Peterson (March 712M-Ford), 2m08.0. Fastest lap: Peterson, 2m04.4

YELLOW PAGES JOCHEN RINDT TROPHY

12 April 1971. Thruxton. Two 28-lap qualifying heats. Final: 50 laps of a 2.356-mile circuit = 117.800 miles. European F2 Trophy round 2

1	Graham Hill (A)	Brabham BT36-Ford	50	1h02m36.2
2	Ronnie Peterson	March 712M-Ford	50	1h02m36.8
3	Derek Bell	March 712M-Ford	50	1h02m56.0
4	Francois Cevert	Tecno TF71-Ford	50	1h03m15.6
5	Tim Schenken	Brabham BT36-Ford	50	1h03m16.0

6 Wilson Fittipaldi　　　Lotus 69-Ford　　50　　1h03m37.6
7 Alistair Walker　　　　Brabham BT30-Ford　49

Winner's average speed: 112.901 mph. Pole position: Henri Pescarolo (March 712M-Ford), based on heat results. Fastest lap: Peterson, 1m13.4

EIFELRENNEN

2 May 1971. Nurburgring. 10 laps of a 14.189-mile circuit = 141.890 miles. European F2 Trophy round 3

1	Francois Cevert	Tecno TF71-Ford	10	1h20m19.2
2	Emerson Fittipaldi (A)	Lotus 69-Ford	10	1h20m37.0
3	Carlos Reutemann	Brabham BT30-Ford	10	1h20m42.1
4	Peter Westbury	Brabham BT36-Ford	10	1h20m48.2
5	Graham Hill (A)	Brabham BT36-Ford	10	1h20m48.4
6	Niki Lauda	March 712M-Ford	10	1h21m08.8
7	Wilson Fittipaldi	Lotus 69-Ford	10	1h21m43.7
8	Helmut Marko	Lola T240-Ford	10	1h21m54.7

Winner's average speed: 105.994 mph. Pole position: Derek Bell (March 712M-Ford), 7m59.7. Fastest lap: Ronnie Peterson (March 712M-Ford), 7m57.1

GRAN PREMIO DE MADRID

16 May 1971. Jarama. 60 laps of a 2.115-mile circuit = 126.924 miles. European F2 Trophy round 4

1	Emerson Fittipaldi (A)	Lotus 69-Ford	60	1h29m42.9
2	Dieter Quester	March 712M-BMW	60	1h29m57.7
3	Carlos Reutemann	Brabham BT30-Ford	60	1h30m12.3
4	John Cannon	March 712M-Ford	60	1h30m17.0
5	Jean-Pierre Jaussaud	March 712M-Ford	60	1h30m37.4
6	Wilson Fittipaldi	Lotus 69-Ford	60	1h30m42.9
7	Niki Lauda	March 712M-Ford	60	1h30m46.4

Winner's average speed: 84.885 mph. Pole position: Ronnie Peterson (March 712M-Ford), 1m28.0. Fastest lap: Tim Schenken (Brabham BT36-Ford), 1m28.2

HILTON TRANSPORT LONDON TROPHY

31 May 1971. Crystal Palace. Two 45-lap qualifying heats. Final: 50 laps of a 1.390-mile circuit = 69.500 miles. European F2 Trophy round 5

1	Emerson Fittipaldi (A)	Lotus 69-Ford	50	42m03.0
2	Tim Schenken	Brabham BT36-Ford	50	42m07.4
3	Ronnie Peterson	March 712M-Ford	50	42m08.2
4	Jean-Pierre Jaussaud	March 712M-Ford	50	42m08.8
5	Carlos Reutemann	Brabham BT30-Ford	49	
6	Gerry Birrell	Lotus 69-Ford	49	
7	Silvio Moser	Brabham BT30-Ford	49	

Winner's average speed: 99.168 mph. Pole position: E Fittipaldi, based on heat times. Fastest lap: Schenken, Peterson, Jaussaud and E Fittipaldi, 49.6s

GRAND PRIX DE ROUEN-LES-ESSARTS

27 June 1971. Rouen-les-Essarts. Two 16-lap qualifying heats. Final: 25 laps of a 4.065-mile circuit = 101.625 miles. European F2 Trophy round 6

1	Ronnie Peterson	March 712M-Ford	25	55m36.3
2	Dieter Quester	March 712M-BMW	25	55m42.8
3	Graham Hill (A)	Brabham BT36-Ford	25	55m43.6
4	Niki Lauda	March 712M-Ford	25	56m01.1
5	Francois Migault	Lotus 69-Ford	25	56m41.8
6	Tim Schenken	Brabham BT36-Ford	22	engine
7	Carlos Pace	March 712M-Ford	22	fuel starvation

Carlos Reutemann (Brabham BT30-Ford), 57m46.8, and Francois Mazet (Chevron B18-Ford), 23 laps completed, finished sixth and seventh respectively but were disqualified. Winner's average speed: 109.657 mph. Pole position: Francois Cevert (Tecno TF71-Ford), based on heat results. Fastest lap: Cevert, 2m11.0

MANTORP PARK FORMELA 2 TROFEN

8 August 1971. Mantorp Park. Aggregate of two 36-lap heats. 72 laps of a 2.543-mile circuit = 183.096 miles. European F2 Trophy round 7

1	Ronnie Peterson	March 712M-Ford	72	1h46m08.2

2	Tim Schenken	Brabham BT36-Ford	72	1h46m43.7
3	Carlos Reutemann	Brabham BT36-Ford	72	1h46m50.1
4	Wilson Fittipaldi	March 712M-Ford	72	1h47m25.2
5	John Watson	Brabham BT30-Ford	72	1h47m50.6
6	Gerry Birrell	Lotus 69-Ford	72	1h47m57.7

Winner's average speed: 103.506 mph. Pole position: Peterson, 1m38.0. Fastest lap: Peterson, 1m27.1

FLUGPLATZRENNEN TULLN-LANGENLEBARN

12 September 1971. Tulln-Langenlebarn. Aggregate of two 35-lap heats. 70 laps of a 1.780-mile circuit = 124.600 miles. European F2 Trophy round 8

1	Ronnie Peterson	March 712M-Ford	70	1h24m32.26
2	Tim Schenken	Brabham BT36-Ford	70	1h24m59.91
3	Dieter Quester	March 712M-BMW	70	1h25m12.94
4	Wilson Fittipaldi	March 712M-Ford	70	1h25m44.29
5	John Watson	Brabham BT30-Ford	69	
6	Bob Wollek	Brabham BT36-Ford	69	

Winner's average speed: 88.434 mph. Pole position: Peterson, 1m00.48. Fastest lap: Schenken, 1m10.79

GRAND PRIX D'ALBI

26 September 1971. Albi. 63 laps of a 2.090-mile circuit = 131.670 miles. European F2 Trophy round 9

1	Emerson Fittipaldi (A)	Lotus 69-Ford	63	1h16m49.1
2	Carlos Reutemann	Brabham BT36-Ford	63	1h17m49.6
3	Jean-Pierre Jarier	March 712M-Ford	63	1h17m59.5
4	Francois Migault	March 712M-Ford	62	
5	Graham Hill (A)	Brabham BT36-Ford	61	
6	Ronnie Peterson	March 712M-Ford	61	
7	Jean-Pierre Jaussaud	March 712M-Ford	58	
8	Peter Westbury	Brabham BT36-Ford	57	

Winner's average speed: 102.843 mph. Pole position: Reutemann, 1m11.0. Fastest lap: Reutemann, 1m11.7

GRAN PREMIO DI ROMA

10 October 1971. Vallelunga. Aggregate of two 35-lap heats. 70 laps of a 1.988-mile circuit = 139.160 miles. European F2 Trophy round 10

1	Ronnie Peterson	March 712M-Ford	70	1h25m57.2
2	Dieter Quester	March 712M-BMW	70	1h26m07.0
3	Carlos Reutemann	Brabham BT36-Ford	70	1h26m38.9
4	Mike Beuttler	March 712M-Ford	70	1h26m51.2
5	Gerry Birrell	Lotus 69-Ford	70	1h27m07.7
6	John Watson	Brabham BT30-Ford	70	1h27m10.0

Winner's average speed: 97.141 mph. Pole position: Emerson Fittipaldi (Lotus 69-Ford), 1m11.75. Fastest lap: E Fittipaldi, 1m12.8

GRAN PREMIO DI MADUNINA

17 October 1971. Vallelunga. 65 laps of a 1.988-mile circuit = 129.220 miles. European F2 Trophy round 11

1	Mike Beuttler	March 712M-Ford	65	1h19m49.1
2	Dieter Quester	March 712M-BMW	65	1h20m00.1
3	Jean-Pierre Jarier	March 712M-Ford	65	1h20m45.4
4	Carlos Ruesch	Brabham BT36-Ford	65	1h20m59.6
5	Vittorio Brambilla	March 712M-Ford	65	1h21m01.0
6	Silvio Moser	Brabham BT36-Ford	64	

Winner's average speed: 97.136 mph. Pole position: Emerson Fittipaldi (Lotus 69-Ford), 1m11.98. Fastest lap: Beuttler and Quester, 1m12.5

1971 FINAL CHAMPIONSHIP POSITIONS

Drivers			18=	Vittorio Brambilla	2
1	Ronnie Peterson	54		Silvio Moser	2
2	Carlos Reutemann	38	19=	Brian Hart	1
3	Dieter Quester	31		Helmut Marko	1
4	Tim Schenken	29		Carlos Pace	1
5	Francois Cevert	22		Alistair Walker	1
6	Wilson Fittipaldi	16		Bob Wollek	1
7	Mike Beuttler	12		(A) Graded driver ineligible for	
8	Jean-Pierre Jarier	10		points. Best ten results count	
9	Jean-Pierre Jaussaud	9			
10	Niki Lauda	8			
11=	Gerry Birrell	7			
	Francois Migault	7			
13	Derek Bell	6			
14=	John Watson	5			
	Peter Westbury	5			
16	John Cannon	4			
17	Carlos Ruesch	3			

1972

JOHN PLAYER FORMULA 2 CHAMPIONSHIP RACE

12 March 1972. Mallory Park. Aggregate of two 50-lap heats. 100 laps of a 1.350-mile circuit = 135.000 miles. European F2 Trophy round 1

1	Dave Morgan	Brabham BT35-Ford	100	1h14m32.8
2	Niki Lauda	March 722-Ford	100	1h14m36.0
3	Carlos Reutemann	Brabham BT38-Ford	100	1h14m42.0
4	Jody Scheckter	McLaren M21-Ford	100	1h15m15.0
5	Mike Hailwood	Surtees TS10-Ford	99	
6	Xavier Perrot	March 722-Ford	99	

Winner's average speed: 108.657 mph. Pole position: Ronnie Peterson (March 722-Ford), 43.4s. Fastest lap: Peterson, 43.0s

ESSO UNIFLO JOCHEN RINDT TROPHY

3 April 1972. Thruxton. Two 28-lap qualifying heats. Final: 50 laps of a 2.356-mile circuit = 117.800 miles. European F2 Trophy round 2

1	Ronnie Peterson (A)	March 722-Ford	50	1h00m19.4
2	Francois Cevert (A)	March 722-Ford	50	1h00m44.0
3	Niki Lauda	March 722-Ford	49	
4	Patrick Dal Bo	Pygmee MDB17-Ford	48	
5	Claudio Francisci	Brabham BT38-Ford	47	

No other finishers. Winner's average speed: 117.169 mph. Pole position: Peterson, based on heat times. Fastest lap: Peterson, 1m11.6

JIM CLARK-RENNEN

16 April 1972. Hockenheim. Aggregate of two 20-lap heats. 40 laps of a 4.219-mile circuit = 168.760 miles. European F2 Trophy round 3

1	Jean-Pierre Jaussaud	Brabham BT38-Ford	40	1h25m24.2
2	Mike Beuttler	March 722-Ford	40	1h25m37.5
3	Bob Wollek	Brabham BT38-Ford	40	1h25m43.8
4	Xavier Perrot	March 722-Ford	40	1h28m05.3
5	Tom Belso	Brabham BT38-Ford	40	1h29m31.0
6	John Wingfield	Brabham BT36-Ford	39	

Winner's average speed: 118.562 mph. Pole position: Niki Lauda (March 722-Ford), 2m08.0. Fastest lap: Patrick Depailler (Alpine A367-Ford), 2m06.0

GRAND PRIX DE PAU

7 May 1972. Pau. Two 37-lap qualifying heats. Final: 70 laps of a 1.715-mile circuit = 120.050 miles. European F2 Trophy round 4

1	Peter Gethin	Chevron B20-Ford	70	1h33m40.8
2	Patrick Depailler	March 722-Ford	70	1h33m41.7
3	David Purley	March 722-Ford	68	
4	Jean-Pierre Jaussaud	Brabham BT38-Ford	66	

5	Mike Hailwood	Surtees TS10-Ford	66
6	Reine Wisell (A)	GRD 272-Ford	65
7	Bob Wollek	Brabham BT38-Ford	64

Winner's average speed: 76.889 mph. Pole position: Gethin, based on heat results. Fastest lap: Gethin, 1m16.1

GREATER LONDON TROPHY

29 May 1972. Crystal Palace. Two 45-lap qualifying heats. Final: 50 laps of a 1.390-mile circuit = 69.500 miles. European F2 Trophy round 5

1	Jody Scheckter	McLaren M21-Ford	50	41m32.4
2	Mike Hailwood	Surtees TS10-Ford	50	41m34.6
3	Carlos Reutemann	Brabham BT38-Ford	50	41m35.8
4	Vic Elford	Chevron B20-Ford	50	41m37.0
5	Francois Cevert (A)	March 722-Ford	50	41m44.2
6	Jean-Pierre Beltoise (A)	Brabham BT38-Ford	50	42m14.0
7	Patrick Depailler	March 722-Ford	50	42m15.8
8	Jochen Mass	March 722-Ford	50	42m16.2

Winner's average speed: 100.385 mph. Pole position: Hailwood, based on heat times. Fastest lap: Cevert and Scheckter, 48.6s

JOCHEN RINDT-RENNEN

11 June 1972. Hockenheim. Points awarded for two 15-lap heats. 30 laps of a 4.219-mile circuit = 126.570 miles. European F2 Trophy round 6

1	Emerson Fittipaldi (A)	Lotus 69-Ford	30	1h13m39.2
2	Jean-Pierre Jaussaud	Brabham BT38-Ford	30	1h15m05.6
3	Ronnie Peterson (A)	March 722-Ford	30	1h15m28.6
4*	Mike Beuttler	March 722-Ford	30	1h15m59.1
5*	Xavier Perrot	March 722-Ford	30	1h15m57.8
6*	Tim Schenken (A)	Brabham BT38-Ford	30	1h15m58.9
7*	Carlos Reutemann	Brabham BT38-Ford	30	1h16m33.2
8*	Dave Morgan	Brabham BT38-Ford	28	
9*	Carlos Ruesch	Surtees TS10-Ford	30	1h16m43.8

*positions decided by points awarded for heats. Winner's average speed: 103.107 mph. Pole position: Niki Lauda (March 722-Ford), 2m02.9. Fastest lap: E Fittipaldi, 2m22.7

GRAND PRIX DE ROUEN-LES-ESSARTS

25 June 1972. Rouen-les-Essarts. Two 20-lap qualifying heats. Final: 30 laps of a 3.444-mile circuit = 103.320 miles. European F2 Trophy round 7

1	Emerson Fittipaldi (A)	Lotus 69-Ford	30	54m20.0
2	Mike Hailwood	Surtees TS10-Ford	30	54m28.0
3	Carlos Reutemann	Brabham BT38-Ford	30	54m47.4
4	Dave Morgan	Brabham BT38-Ford	30	54m58.6
5	John Watson	Tui BH2-Ford	30	55m01.6
6	Francois Cevert (A)	March 722-Ford	30	55m02.7
7	Graham Hill (A)	Brabham BT38-Ford	30	55m37.3
8	Jose Dolhem	March 722-Ford	29	
9	Bob Wollek	Brabham BT38-Ford	27	

Winner's average speed: 114.096 mph. Pole position: E Fittipaldi, based heats results. Fastest lap: Hailwood, 1m46.8

JOCHEN RINDT-RENNEN

9 July 1972. Osterreichring. 34 laps of a 3.673-mile circuit = 124.882 miles. European F2 Trophy round 8

1	Emerson Fittipaldi (A)	Lotus 69-Ford	34	59m23.51
2	Mike Hailwood	Surtees TS10-Ford	34	59m39.52
3	Carlos Reutemann	Brabham BT38-Ford	34	1h00m10.03
4	Dave Morgan	Brabham BT38-Ford	34	1h00m10.59
5	Patrick Depailler	March 722-Ford	34	1h00m11.37
6	Bob Wollek	Brabham BT38-Ford	34	1h00m29.57
7	Carlos Ruesch	Surtees TS10-Ford	34	1h00m39.40

Winner's average speed: 126.161 mph. Pole position: E Fittipaldi, 1m42.57. Fastest lap: E Fittipaldi, 1m43.48

GRAN PREMIO SHELL DI IMOLA

23 July 1972. Imola. Aggregate of two 28-lap heats. 56 laps of a 3.118-mile circuit = 174.608 miles. European F2 Trophy round 9

1	John Surtees (A)	Surtees TS10-Ford	56	1h28m08.2
2	Bob Wollek	Brabham BT38-Ford	56	1h28m16.7
3	Niki Lauda	March 722-Ford	56	1h28m32.2
4	Andrea de Adamich	Surtees TS10-Ford	56	1h28m38.6
5	Graham Hill (A)	Brabham BT38-Ford	56	1h29m26.0
6	Jody Scheckter	McLaren M21-Ford	56	1h29m48.7
7	Jean-Pierre Jaussaud	Brabham BT38-Ford	53	
8	John Watson	Tui BH2-Ford	52	

Winner's average speed: 118.866 mph. Pole position: Jaussaud, 1m32.05. Fastest lap: Peter Gethin (Chevron B20-Ford), 1m31.9

HITACHI MANTORP GRAND PRIX

6 August 1972. Mantorp Park. Aggregate of two 36-lap heats. 72 laps of a 2.543-mile circuit = 183.096 miles. European F2 Trophy round 10

1	Mike Hailwood	Surtees TS10-Ford	72	1h45m51.1
2	Jean-Pierre Jabouille	March 722-Ford	72	1h45m57.3
3	Jean-Pierre Jaussaud	Brabham BT38-Ford	72	1h46m41.4
4	Brett Lunger	March 722-Ford	72	1h47m33.4
5	Carlos Ruesch	Surtees TS10-Ford	71	
6	Carlos Reutemann	Brabham BT38-Ford	71	

Winner's average speed: 103.784 mph. Pole position: Peter Gethin (Chevron B20-Ford), 1m25.6. Fastest lap: Gethin, 1m25.9

GRAN PREMIO DEL MEDITERRANEO

20 August 1972. Enna-Pergusa. Aggregate of two 32-lap heats. 64 laps of a 3.011-mile circuit = 192.704 miles. European F2 Trophy round 11

1	Henri Pescarolo (A)	Brabham BT38-Ford	64	1h33m22.8
2	Patrick Depailler	March 722-Ford	64	1h33m46.2
3	Carlos Ruesch	Surtees TS10-Ford	64	1h34m10.6
4	Wilson Fittipaldi	Brabham BT38-Ford	62	
5	Hiroshi Kazato	March 722-Ford	62	
6	Carlos Reutemann	Brabham BT38-Ford	61	
7	Jean-Pierre Jaussaud	Brabham BT38-Ford	61	

Winner's average speed: 123.819 mph. Pole position: Mike Hailwood (Surtees TS10-Ford), 1m25.7. Fastest lap: Carlos Pace (Surtees TS10-Ford), 1m25.1

SALZBURGER FESTSPIELPREIS

3 September 1972. Salzburgring. Aggregate of two 30-lap heats. 60 laps of a 2.633-mile circuit = 157.980 miles. European F2 Trophy round 12

1	Mike Hailwood	Surtees TS10-Ford	60	1h13m31.76
2	Carlos Pace	Surtees TS10-Ford	60	1h13m32.94
3	Dave Morgan	Brabham BT38-Ford	60	1h13m42.78
4	Graham Hill (A)	Brabham BT38-Ford	60	1h13m46.89
5	Peter Gethin	Chevron B20-Ford	60	1h14m39.38
6	Niki Lauda	March 722-Ford	60	1h14m47.21
7	Patrick Depailler	March 722-Ford	60	1h15m09.56

Winner's average speed: 128.912 mph. Pole position: Pace, 1m12.15. Fastest lap: Hailwood, 1m11.89

GRAND PRIX D'ALBI

24 September 1972. Albi. Two 28-lap qualifying heats. Final: 32 laps of a 2.090-mile circuit = 66.880 miles. European F2 Trophy round 13

1	Jean-Pierre Jaussaud	Brabham BT38-Ford	32	37m53.5
2	Patrick Depailler	March 722-Ford	32	37m53.7
3	Bob Wollek	Brabham BT38-Ford	32	38m11.4
4	Tom Belso	Brabham BT38-Ford	32	38m15.2
5	James Hunt	March 712M-Ford	32	38m18.6
6	Carlos Ruesch	Surtees TS10-Ford	32	38m30.4

Winner's average speed: 105.902 mph. Pole position: Depailler, based on heat results. Fastest lap: Depailler, 1m10.1

PREIS VON HESSEN UND WURTTEMBERG

1 October 1972. Hockenheim. 32 laps of a 4.219-mile circuit = 135.008 miles. European F2 Trophy round 14

| 1 | Tim Schenken (A) | Brabham BT38-Ford | 32 | 1h07m22.7 |
| 2 | Mike Hailwood | Surtees TS10-Ford | 32 | 1h07m40.6 |

3	Ronnie Peterson (A)	March 722-Ford	32	1h07m42.8
4	Wilson Fittipaldi	Brabham BT38-Ford	32	1h07m43.1
5	Graham Hill (A)	Brabham BT38-Ford	32	1h07m56.5
6	Tino Brambilla	March 712M-Ford	32	1h07m59.7
7	Henri Pescarolo (A)	Brabham BT38-Ford	32	1h08m13.8
8	James Hunt	March 712M-Ford	32	1h08m18.1
9	Niki Lauda	March 722-Ford	32	1h08m30.3
10	Jean-Pierre Jabouille	Alpine A367-Ford	32	1h08m49.0

Winner's average speed: 120.224 mph. Pole position: Emerson Fittipaldi (Lotus 69-Ford), 2m03.4. Fastest lap: E Fittipaldi, 2m05.0

1972 FINAL CHAMPIONSHIP POSITIONS

1	Mike Hailwood	55	17=	Tom Belso	5
2	Jean-Pierre Jaussaud	37		James Hunt	5
3	Patrick Depailler	27	19=	Andrea de Adamich	4
4	Carlos Reutemann	26		Tino Brambilla	4
5	Niki Lauda	25		Claudio Francisci	4
6	Dave Morgan	23		David Purley	4
7	Bob Wollek	21		John Watson	4
8	Jody Scheckter	15	24=	Vic Elford	3
9=	Mike Beuttler	12		Hiroshi Kazato	3
	Peter Gethin	12		Brett Lunger	3
11	Carlos Ruesch	11	27	Jose Dolhem	2
12	Wilson Fittipaldi	10	28=	Jochen Mass	1
13	Xavier Perrot	8		John Wingfield	1
14	Jean-Pierre Jabouille	7	(A) Graded driver ineligible for		
15=	Patrick Dal Bo	6	points. Best ten results count		
	Carlos Pace	6			

1973

RADIO LUXEMBOURG TROPHY

11 March 1973. Mallory Park. Aggregate of two 50-lap heats. 100 laps of a 1.350-mile circuit = 135.000 miles. European F2 Championship round 1 ("B" race)

1	Jean-Pierre Jarier	March 732-BMW	100	1h12m09.8
2	Mike Hailwood (A)	Surtees TS15-Ford	100	1h13m05.4
3	Dave McConnell	Surtees TS15-Ford	97	
4	Dave Morgan	Chevron B25-Ford	95	
5	John Lepp	Chevron B25-Ford	94	
6	Vittorio Brambilla	March 712M-BMW	94	
7	Bob Salisbury	Surtees TS15-Ford	92	

Winner's average speed: 112.245 mph. Pole position: Jean-Pierre Beltoise (March 732-BMW), 42.5s. Fastest lap: Jarier, 41.8s

JIM CLARK-RENNEN

8 April 1973. Hockenheim. Aggregate of two 20-lap heats. 40 laps of a 4.219-mile circuit = 168.760 miles. European F2 Championship round 2 ("A" race)

1	Jean-Pierre Jarier	March 732-BMW	40	1h22m27.0
2	Patrick Depailler	Alpine A367-Ford	40	1h22m46.9
3	Derek Bell	Surtees TS15-Ford	40	1h23m59.4
4	Henri Pescarolo (A)	Motul M1-Ford	40	1h24m55.5
5	Wilson Fittipaldi	Brabham BT40-Ford	40	1h25m20.8
6	Colin Vandervell	March 732-BMW	40	1h25m53.4
7	Jacques Coulon	March 732-BMW	39	

Winner's average speed: 122.809 mph. Pole position: Jean-Pierre Beltoise (March 732-BMW), 2m02.8. Fastest lap: Jarier, 2m02.4

ESSO UNIFLO JOCHEN RINDT TROPHY

23 April 1973. Thruxton. Two 28-lap qualifying heats. Final: 50 laps of a 2.356-mile circuit = 117.800 miles. European F2 Championship round 3 ("A" race)

1	Henri Pescarolo (A)	Motul M1-Ford	50	1h01m45.4
2	Bob Wollek	Motul M1-Ford	50	1h02m00.2
3	Mike Beuttler	March 732-BMW	50	1h02m01.8

4	Gerry Birrell	Chevron B25-Ford	50	1h02m21.0
5	Dave Morgan	Chevron B25-Ford	50	1h02m33.0
6	Jean-Pierre Jaussaud	Motul M1-Ford	50	1h03m21.8
7	Vittorio Brambilla	March 732-BMW	49	

Winner's average speed: 114.449 mph. Pole position: Patrick Depailler (Alpine A367-Ford), based on heat times. Fastest lap: Jacques Coulon (March 732-BMW), 1m11.2

EIFELRENNEN

29 April 1973. Nurburgring. 10 laps of a 14.189-mile circuit = 141.890 miles. European F2 Championship round 4 ("A" race)

1	Reine Wisell (A)	GRD 273-Ford	10	1h31m22.9
2	Tim Schenken (A)	Motul M1-Ford	10	1h31m25.1
3	Patrick Depailler	Alpine A367-Ford	10	1h31m40.5
4	Derek Bell	Surtees TS15-Ford	10	1h32m09.0
5	Vittorio Brambilla	March 732-BMW	10	1h32m11.7
6	Bob Wollek	Motul M1-Ford	10	1h32m46.5
7	Richard Scott	Scott 1-Ford	10	1h33m48.5
8	Silvio Moser	Surtees TS10-Ford	10	1h35m49.2

Winner's average speed: 93.163 mph. Pole position: Hans-Joachim Stuck (March 732-BMW), 7m30.5. Fastest lap: Bell, 8m36.7

GRAND PRIX DE PAU

6 May 1973. Pau. Two 20-lap qualifying heats. Final: 70 laps of a 1.715-mile circuit = 120.050 miles. European F2 Championship round 5 ("B" race)

1	Francois Cevert (A)	Alpine A367-Ford	70	1h30m49.77
2	Jean-Pierre Jarier	March 732-BMW	70	1h31m14.44
3	Tim Schenken (A)	Motul M1-Ford	70	1h31m25.70
4	Mike Beuttler	March 732-BMW	69	
5	Bob Wollek	Motul M1-Ford	69	
6	Jean-Pierre Jaussaud	Motul M1-Ford	69	
7	Roger Williamson	GRD 273-Ford	68	
8	Sten Gunnarsson	GRD 273-Ford	68	

Winner's average speed: 79.302 mph. Pole position: Patrick Depailler (Alpine A367-Ford), based on heat results. Fastest lap: Jean-Pierre Beltoise (March 732-BMW), 1m15.0

SWEDISH GOLD CUP

20 May 1973. Kinnekulle. Aggregate of two 48-lap heats. 96 laps of a 1.286-mile circuit = 123.456 miles. European F2 Championship round 6 ("B" race)

1	Jochen Mass	Surtees TS15-Ford	96	1h20m49.3
2	Patrick Depailler	Alpine A367-Ford	96	1h21m20.4
3	Tim Schenken (A)	Motul M1-Ford	96	1h21m48.8
4	Sten Gunnarsson	GRD 273-Ford	94	
5	Hakan Dahlqvist	GRD 273-Ford	93	

No other finishers. Winner's average speed: 91.651 mph. Pole position: Mass, 48.6s. Fastest lap: Mass, 49.5s

GRAND PRIX DE GB

10 June 1973. Nivelles. Aggregate of two 28-lap heats. 56 laps of a 2.314-mile circuit = 129.584 miles. European F2 Championship round 7 ("A" race)

1	Jean-Pierre Jarier	March 732-BMW	56	1h10m33.35
2	Jochen Mass	Surtees TS15-Ford	56	1h10m57.23
3	Vittorio Brambilla	March 732-BMW	56	1h11m07.65
4	Mike Beuttler	March 732-BMW	56	1h11m36.97
5	Colin Vandervell	March 732-BMW	56	1h11m37.42
6	Dave Morgan	Chevron B25-Ford	56	1h12m03.73

Winner's average speed: 110.197 mph. Pole position: Jarier, 1m14.32. Fastest lap: Mass, 1m14.17

JOCHEN RINDT-RENNEN

17 June 1973. Hockenheim. Aggregate of two 20-lap heats. 40 laps of a 4.219-mile circuit = 168.760 miles. European F2 Championship round 8 ("B" race)

1	Jochen Mass	Surtees TS15-Ford	40	1h22m20.7
2	Colin Vandervell	March 732-BMW	40	1h22m31.4

3	Jacques Coulon	March 732-BMW	40	1h23m04.7
4	Vittorio Brambilla	March 732-BMW	40	1h23m54.4
5	Henri Pescarolo (A)	Motul M1-Ford	40	1h24m48.4
6	Hiroshi Kazato	GRD 273-Ford	40	1h25m58.2
7	Silvio Moser	Surtees TS10-Ford	40	1h26m23.5

Winner's average speed: 122.966 mph. Pole position: Mass, 2m01.6.
Fastest lap: Mass, 2m02.7

GRAND PRIX DE ROUEN-LES-ESSARTS

24 June 1973. Rouen-les-Essarts. Two 20-lap qualifying heats. Final: 30 laps of a 3.444-mile circuit = 103.320 miles. European F2 Championship round 9 ("A" race)

1	Jean-Pierre Jarier	March 732-BMW	30	56m20.7
2	Jochen Mass	Surtees TS15-Ford	30	56m40.0
3	Tim Schenken (A)	Motul M1-Ford	30	56m41.4
4	Jacques Coulon	March 732-BMW	30	57m03.6
5	Wilson Fittipaldi	Brabham BT40-BMW	30	57m10.6
6	Patrick Depailler	Alpine A367-Ford	30	57m40.9
7	Brett Lunger	Chevron B25-Ford	29	

Winner's average speed: 110.022 mph. Pole position: Jarier, based on heat results. Fastest lap: Jarier, 1m49.3

GRAN PREMIO DELLA LOTTERIA DI MONZA

29 June 1973. Monza. Aggregate of two 20-lap heats. 40 laps of a 3.573-mile circuit = 142.920 miles. European F2 Championship round 10 ("B" race)

1	Roger Williamson	March 732-BMW	40	1h09m05.6
2	Patrick Depailler	Alpine A367-Ford	40	1h09m22.0
3	Jacques Coulon	March 732-BMW	40	1h10m25.6
4	Derek Bell	Surtees TS15-Ford	39	
5	Hiroshi Kazato	GRD 273-Ford	37	

No other finishers. Winner's average speed: 124.110 mph. Pole position: Williamson, 1m42.2. Fastest lap: Williamson, 1m41.0

MANTORP PARK F2 TROFEN

29 July 1973. Mantorp Park. Aggregate of two 36-lap heats. 72 laps of a 2.543-mile circuit = 183.096 miles. European F2 Championship round 11 ("A" race)

1	Jean-Pierre Jarier	March 732-BMW	72	1h42m05.0
2	Jochen Mass	Surtees TS15-Ford	72	1h42m25.7
3	John Watson	Chevron B25-Ford	72	1h42m30.6
4	Patrick Depailler	Alpine A367-Ford	72	1h42m50.6
5	Tom Pryce	Motul M1-Ford	72	1h43m17.6
6	Jean-Pierre Jaussaud	Motul M1-Ford	72	1h43m43.1

Winner's average speed: 107.616 mph. Pole position: Depailler, 1m22.8.
Fastest lap: Depailler, 1m24.0

KANNONLOPPET

12 August 1973. Karlskoga. Two 36-lap qualifying heats. Final: 48 laps of a 1.864-mile circuit = 89.472 miles. European F2 Championship round 12 ("B" race)

1	Jean-Pierre Jarier	March 732-BMW	48	59m14.4
2	Peter Gethin	Chevron B25-Ford	48	59m14.6
3	Torsten Palm	Surtees TS15-Ford	48	59m16.9
4	Tim Schenken (A)	Motul M1-Ford	48	1h00m01.4
5	Ronnie Peterson (A)	Lotus 74-Ford	48	1h00m10.8
6	Jacques Coulon	March 732-BMW	48	1h00m20.0
7	Colin Vandervell	March 732-BMW	47	engine
8	Bill Gubelmann	March 732-BMW	47	

Winner's average speed: 90.620 mph. Pole position: Gethin, based on heat results. Fastest lap: Palm, 1m12.8

GRAN PREMIO DEL MEDITERRANEO

26 August 1973. Enna-Pergusa. Aggregate of two 30-lap heats. 60 laps of a 3.011-mile circuit = 180.660 miles. European F2 Championship round 13 ("A" race)

1	Jean-Pierre Jarier	March 732-BMW	60	1h23m53.6
2	Vittorio Brambilla	March 732-BMW	60	1h24m22.8
3	Jochen Mass	Surtees TS15-Ford	60	1h25m07.3

4	Tim Schenken (A)	Motul M1-Ford	60	1h25m47.0
5	Bob Wollek	Motul M1-Ford	60	1h25m49.2
6	Bill Gubelmann	March 732-BMW	59	
7	Ronnie Peterson (A)	Lotus 74-Ford	58	
8	Gabriele Serblin	Brabham BT40-Ford	55	

Winner's average speed: 129.207 mph. Pole position: Jarier, 1m22.73.
Fastest lap: Patrick Depailler (Alpine A367-Ford), 1m22.4

SALZBURGER FESTSPIELPREIS

2 September 1973. Salzburgring. 50 laps of a 2.633-mile circuit = 131.650 miles. European F2 Championship round 14 ("B" race)

1	Vittorio Brambilla	March 732-BMW	50	59m47.28
2	Patrick Depailler	Alpine A367-Ford	50	59m49.13
3	Jacques Coulon	March 732-BMW	50	1h00m23.69
4	Carlos Pace (A)	Surtees TS15-Ford	50	1h00m43.40
5	Bill Gubelmann	March 732-BMW	49	
6	Roland Binder	March 732-BMW	49	
7	Kurt Rieder	March 732-BMW	49	

Winner's average speed: 132.117 mph. Pole position: Depailler, 1m10.67.
Fastest lap: Depailler, 1m10.84

NORISRING-RENNEN

9 September 1973. Norisring. Aggregate of two 60-lap heats. 120 laps of a 1.429-mile circuit = 171.480 miles. European F2 Championship round 15 ("B" race)

1	Tim Schenken (A)	Motul M1-Ford	120	1h46m40.9
2	Tom Pryce	Motul M1-Ford	120	1h47m59.1
3	Henri Pescarolo (A)	Motul M1-BMW	116	
4	Gunnar Nilsson	GRD 273-Ford	112	
5	Bob Wollek	Motul M1-Ford	112	

No other finishers. Winner's average speed: 96.444 mph. Pole position: Jean-Pierre Jarier (March 732-BMW), 51.2s. Fastest lap: Jarier, 51.9s

GRAND PRIX D'ALBI

16 September 1973. Albi. 56 laps of a 2.090-mile circuit = 117.040 miles. European F2 Championship round 16 ("A" race)

1	Vittorio Brambilla	March 732-BMW	56	1h04m59.2
2	Jean-Pierre Jarier	March 732-BMW	56	1h05m02.6
3	Jean-Pierre Beltoise (A)	March 732-BMW	56	1h05m03.6
4	Jacques Coulon	March 732-BMW	56	1h05m29.6
5	Jean-Pierre Jabouille	Alpine A367-Ford	56	1h05m48.6
6	Jochen Mass	Surtees TS15-Ford	56	1h05m49.8
7	Tim Schenken (A)	Motul M1-Ford	56	1h05m56.6
8	Bertil Roos	GRD 273-Ford	55	

Winner's average speed: 108.059 mph. Pole position: V Brambilla, 1m08.3.
Fastest lap: Beltoise, 1m08.9

GRAN PREMIO DI ROMA

14 October 1973. Vallelunga. Aggregate of two 35-lap heats. 70 laps of a 1.988-mile circuit = 139.160 miles. European F2 Championship round 17 ("A" race)

1	Jacques Coulon	March 732-BMW	70	1h24m40.0
2	Vittorio Brambilla	March 732-BMW	70	1h25m10.6
3	Joseph Vonlanthen	GRD 273-Ford	67	
4	Roland Binder	March 732-BMW	63	

No other finishers. Winner's average speed: 98.617 mph. Pole position: V Brambilla, 1m11.35. Fastest lap: V Brambilla, 1m10.7

1973 FINAL CHAMPIONSHIP POSITIONS

1	Jean-Pierre Jarier	78	10=	Tom Pryce	11
2	Jochen Mass	42		Roger Williamson	11
3	Patrick Depailler	38	12	Dave Morgan	8
4	Vittorio Brambilla	35 (44)*	13=	Wilson Fittipaldi	6
5	Jacques Coulon	33		Peter Gethin	6
6	Bob Wollek	23		Bill Gubelmann	6
7	Mike Beuttler	15		Jean-Pierre Jaussaud	6
8	Derek Bell	13		Dave McConnell	6
9	Colin Vandervell	12		Gunnar Nilsson	6

1973 FINAL CHAMPIONSHIP POSITIONS (cont.)

19=	Roland Binder	5	31=	Brett Lunger	1
	Sten Gunnarsson	5		Kurt Rieder	1
21=	Gerry Birrell	4		Bertil Roos	1
	Hiroshi Kazato	4		Bob Salisbury	1
	Torsten Palm	4		Gabriele Serblin	1
	Joseph Vonlanthen	4		(A) Graded driver ineligible for	
	John Watson	4		points. *Best nine "A" and four	
26=	Hakan Dahlqvist	3		"B" results count, Brambilla	
	Jean-Pierre Jabouille	3		won at the Salzburgring, but as	
	John Lepp	3		it was his fifth "B" race he could	
29=	Silvio Moser	2		not count the points	
	Richard Scott	2			

1974

GRAN PREMIO DE BARCELONA

24 March 1974. Montjuich Park. 54 laps of a 2.355-mile circuit = 127.170 miles. European F2 Championship round 1

1	Hans-Joachim Stuck	March 742-BMW	54	1h18m47.68
2	Patrick Depailler	March 742-BMW	54	1h18m51.50
3	Jean-Pierre Jabouille	Alpine A367-BMW	54	1h19m45.65
4	Gabriele Serblin	March 742-BMW	54	1h20m02.75
5	Andy Sutcliffe	March 732-BMW	53	
6	Michel Leclere	Alpine A367-BMW	53	

Winner's average speed: 96.837 mph. Pole position: Stuck, 1m25.8. Fastest lap: Stuck, 1m25.58

JIM CLARK-RENNEN

7 April 1974. Hockenheim. Aggregate of two 20-lap heats. 40 laps of a 4.219-mile circuit = 168.760 miles. European F2 Championship round 2

1	Hans-Joachim Stuck	March 742-BMW	40	1h21m37.1
2	John Watson	Surtees TS15-Ford	40	1h22m38.2
3	Michel Leclere	Alpine A367-BMW	40	1h22m39.2
4	Patrick Depailler	March 742-BMW	40	1h22m41.2
5	Patrick Tambay	Alpine A367-BMW	40	1h22m56.2
6	Bertil Roos	Chevron B27-Ford	40	1h23m00.1

Winner's average speed: 124.060 mph. Pole position: Stuck, 2m00.2. Fastest lap: Stuck, 2m00.9

GRAND PRIX DE PAU

5 May 1974. Pau. 75 laps of a 1.715-mile circuit = 128.625 miles. European F2 Championship round 3

1	Patrick Depailler	March 742-BMW	75	1h54m33.57
2	Jacques Laffite	March 742-BMW	74	
3	Andy Sutcliffe	March 732-BMW	74	
4	Jean-Pierre Jabouille	Alpine A367-BMW	74	
5	Michel Leclere	Alpine A367-BMW	74	
6	Tim Schenken (A)	Surtees TS15A-BMW	73	
7	David Purley	March 742-BMW	72	

Winner's average speed: 67.367 mph. Pole position: Depailler, 1m16.1. Fastest lap: Laffite, 1m28.6

SALZBURGER FESTSPIELPREIS

2 June 1974. Salzburgring. 50 laps of a 2.633-mile circuit = 131.650 miles. European F2 Championship round 4

1	Jacques Laffite	March 742-BMW	50	1h00m33.00
2	David Purley	Chevron B27-Ford	50	1h00m37.98
3	Jose Dolhem	Surtees TS15-Ford	50	1h00m38.58
4	Patrick Tambay	Alpine A367-BMW	50	1h01m32.00
5	Maurizio Flammini	March 742-BMW	49	
6	Torsten Palm	GRD 274-BMW	49	

Winner's average speed: 130.454 mph. Pole position: Tom Pryce (Chevron B27-Ford), 1m11.68. Fastest lap: Dolhem, 1m11.47

RHEIN POKAL/JOCHEN RINDT-TROPHAE

9 June 1974. Hockenheim. Aggregate of two 20-lap heats, second heat stopped after 15 laps due to heavy rain. 35 laps of a 4.219-mile circuit = 147.665 miles. European F2 Championship round 5

1	Jean-Pierre Jabouille	Alpine A367-BMW	35	1h11m43.9
2	Jacques Laffite	March 742-BMW	35	1h11m56.0
3	Hans-Joachim Stuck	March 742-BMW	35	1h12m01.3
4	Tom Pryce	Chevron B27-BMW	35	1h12m22.9
5	Michel Leclere	March 742-BMW	35	1h13m21.6
6	Andy Sutcliffe	March 732-BMW	35	1h13m30.7

Winner's average speed: 123.514 mph. Pole position: Stuck, 2m00.1. Fastest lap: Jabouille, 2m01.2

GRAN PREMIO DI MUGELLO

14 July 1974. Mugello. Aggregate of two 25-lap heats. 50 laps of a 3.259-mile circuit = 162.950 miles. European F2 Championship round 6

1	Patrick Depailler	March 742-BMW	50	1h32m46.4
2	Jean-Pierre Paoli	March 742-BMW	50	1h33m04.2
3	Tom Pryce	Chevron B27-BMW	50	1h33m50.9
4	Jacques Coulon	March 742-BMW	50	1h34m13.2
5	Giancarlo Martini	March 742-BMW	50	1h35m41.4
6	Brian Henton	March 742-BMW	49	

Winner's average speed: 105.386 mph. Pole position: Jacques Laffite (March 742-BMW), 1m46.5. Fastest lap: Jean-Pierre Jabouille (Alpine A367-BMW), 1m49.8

KANNONLOPPET

11 August 1974. Karlskoga. 68 laps of a 1.864-mile circuit = 126.752 miles. European F2 Championship round 7

1	Ronnie Peterson (A)	March 742-BMW	68	1h23m00.4
2	Patrick Depailler	March 742-BMW	68	1h23m00.7
3	Jacques Laffite	March 742-BMW	68	1h23m19.7
4	Masami Kuwashima	March 742-BMW	68	1h23m20.0
5	Gabriele Serblin	March 742-BMW	67	
6	Alain Cudini	Alpine A367-BMW	67	
7	Torsten Palm	GRD 273-BMW	67	

Winner's average speed: 91.621 mph. Pole position: Depailler, 1m11.2. Fastest lap: Depailler, 1m12.1

GRAN PREMIO DEL MEDITERRANEO

25 August 1974. Enna-Pergusa. Aggregate of two 30-lap heats. 60 laps of a 3.011-mile circuit = 180.660 miles. European F2 Championship round 8

1	Hans-Joachim Stuck	March 742-BMW	60	1h24m31.9
2	David Purley	Chevron B27-BMW	60	1h25m34.6
3	Gabriele Serblin	March 742-BMW	60	1h25m55.2
4	Michel Leclere	Alpine A367-BMW	59	accident
5	Duilio Truffo	March 742-BMW	58	
6	Cosimo Turizio	March 742-BMW	58	

Winner's average speed: 128.231 mph. Pole position: Stuck, 1m22.4. Fastest lap: Stuck, 1m22.6

PREIS VON HESSEN UND WURTTEMBERG

29 September 1974. Hockenheim. Aggregate of two 20-lap heats. 40 laps of a 4.219-mile circuit = 168.760 miles. European F2 Championship round 9

1	Patrick Depailler	March 742-BMW	40	1h23m26.4
2	Hans-Joachim Stuck	March 742-BMW	40	1h23m34.7
3	Jean-Pierre Jabouille	Alpine A367-BMW	40	1h23m52.5
4	Patrick Tambay	Alpine A367-BMW	40	1h24m38.5
5	Jacques Coulon	March 742-BMW	40	1h24m55.7
6	Alessandro Pesenti-Rossi	March 732-BMW	40	1h27m28.2

Winner's average speed: 121.352 mph. Pole position: Jabouille, 2m00.7. Fastest lap: Jabouille, 2m01.2

GRAN PREMIO DI ROMA

13 October 1974. Vallelunga. Aggregate of two 35-lap heats. 70 laps of a 1.988-mile circuit = 139.160 miles. European F2 Championship round 10

1	Patrick Depailler	March 742-BMW	70	1h22m48.59
2	Hans-Joachim Stuck	March 742-BMW	70	1h23m35.72
3	Jacques Laffite	March 742-BMW	70	1h23m37.30
4	Patrick Tambay	Alpine A367-BMW	70	1h24m35.83
5	Tom Pryce	Chevron B27-BMW	70	1h24m43.38
6	Tim Schenken (A)	Surtees TS15A-BMW	69	
7	Alessandro Pesenti-Rossi	March 732-BMW	68	

Winner's average speed: 100.829 mph. Pole position: Depailler, 1m09.94. Fastest lap: Depailler, 1m09.79

1974 FINAL CHAMPIONSHIP POSITIONS

1	Patrick Depailler	54	14=	Jose Dolhem	4
2	Hans-Joachim Stuck	43		Masami Kuwashima	4
3	Jacques Laffite	31	16=	Alain Cudini	2
4	Jean-Pierre Jabouille	20		Maurizio Flammini	2
5	David Purley	13		Giancarlo Martini	2
6	Michel Leclere	12		Torsten Palm	2
7	Patrick Tambay	11		Alessandro Pesenti-Rossi	2
8	Gabriele Serblin	10		Duilio Truffo	2
9	Tom Pryce	9	22=	Brian Henton	1
10	Andy Sutcliffe	7		Bertil Roos	1
11=	Jean-Pierre Paoli	6		Cosimo Turizio	1
	John Watson	6	(A) Graded driver ineligible for		
13	Jacques Coulon	5	points		

1975

GRANDE PREMIO DO ESTORIL

9 March 1975. Estoril. 50 laps of a 2.703-mile circuit = 135.150 miles. European F2 Championship round 1

1	Jacques Laffite	Martini MK16-BMW	50	1h35m05.83
2	Joseph Vonlanthen	March 742-BMW	50	1h35m36.02
3	Lamberto Leoni	March 752-BMW	50	1h35m36.40
4	Giorgio Francia	Osella FA2-BMW	49	
5	Duilio Truffo	March 742-BMW	49	
6	Giancarlo Martini	March 752-BMW	48	

Winner's average speed: 85.271 mph. Pole position: Michel Leclere (March 752-BMW), 1m34.61. Fastest lap: Francia, 1m44.06

WELLA EUROPEAN TROPHY/JOCHEN RINDT TROPHY

31 March 1975. Thruxton. Aggregate of two 30-lap heats. 60 laps of a 2.356-mile circuit = 141.360 miles. European F2 Championship round 2

1	Jacques Laffite	Martini MK16-BMW	60	1h13m07.8
2	Patrick Tambay	March 752-BMW	60	1h13m51.4
3	Giancarlo Martini	March 752-BMW	59	
4	Hector Rebaque	Chevron B29-Ford	59	
5	Jean-Pierre Jabouille	Elf 2J-BMW	59	
6	Duilio Truffo	Osella FA2-BMW	59	

Winner's average speed: 115.980 mph. Pole position: Laffite, 1m10.1. Fastest lap: Brian Henton (March 752-Ford) and Laffite, 1m11.0

JIM CLARK-RENNEN

13 April 1975. Hockenheim. Aggregate of two 20-lap heats. 40 laps of a 4.219-mile circuit = 168.760 miles. European F2 Championship round 3

1	Gerard Larrousse	Alpine A367-BMW	40	1h22m57.9
2	Hans-Joachim Stuck (A)	March 752-BMW	40	1h23m22.2
3	Brian Henton	March 752-Ford	40	1h24m01.4
4	Loris Kessel	March 742-BMW	40	1h24m38.8
5	Giorgio Francia	Osella FA2-BMW	40	1h24m51.2

6	Claude Bourgoignie	March 752-BMW	40	1h25m07.9
7	Alessandro Pesenti-Rossi	March 742-BMW	40	1h25m29.1

Winner's average speed: 122.047 mph. Pole position: Patrick Tambay (March 752-BMW), 2m12.3. Fastest lap: Jacques Laffite (Martini MK16-BMW), 2m01.7

EIFELRENNEN/PREIS VON RADIO TELE-LUXEMBOURG

26 April 1975. Nurburgring. Aggregate of two 7-lap heats. 14 laps of a 14.189-mile circuit = 198.646 miles. European F2 Championship round 4

1	Jacques Laffite	Martini MK16-BMW	14	1h46m24.2
2	Patrick Tambay	March 752-BMW	14	1h47m39.0
3	Harald Ertl	Chevron B27-BMW	14	1h47m54.0
4	Jean-Pierre Jabouille	Elf 2J-BMW	14	1h51m06.2
5	Sandro Cinotti	March 752-BMW	14	1h51m07.6
6	Giorgio Francia	Osella FA2-BMW	14	1h51m09.0

Winner's average speed: 112.015 mph. Pole position: Laffite, 7m21.7. Fastest lap: Hans-Joachim Stuck (March 752-BMW), 7m24.5

GRAND PRIX DE PAU

19 May 1975. Pau. 73 laps of a 1.715-mile circuit = 125.195 miles. European F2 Championship round 5

1	Jacques Laffite	Martini MK16-BMW	73	1h32m10.7
2	Jean-Pierre Jabouille	Elf 2J-BMW	73	1h32m27.2
3	Patrick Depailler (A)	March 752-BMW	73	1h33m07.1
4	Gerard Larrousse	Alpine A367-BMW	72	
5	Michel Leclere	March 752-BMW	72	
6	Duilio Truffo	Osella FA2-BMW	72	
7	Claude Bourgoignie	March 752-BMW	72	

Winner's average speed: 81.491 mph. Pole position: Laffite, 1m13.61. Fastest lap: Laffite, 1m14.68

RHEIN POKAL/JOCHEN RINDT TROPHAE

8 June 1975. Hockenheim. Aggregate of two 20-lap heats. 40 laps of a 4.219-mile circuit = 168.760 miles. European F2 Championship round 6

1	Jacques Laffite	Martini MK16-BMW	40	1h22m51.2
2	Claude Bourgoignie	March 752-BMW	40	1h23m42.0
3	Maurizio Flammini	March 742-BMW	40	1h24m01.2
4	Loris Kessel	March 742-BMW	40	1h24m25.7
5	Giorgio Francia	Osella FA2-BMW	40	1h24m38.5
6	Duilio Truffo	Osella FA2-BMW	40	1h25m05.5

Winner's average speed: 122.211 mph. Pole position: Laffite, 2m01.1. Fastest lap: Michel Leclere (March 752-BMW), 2m01.6

SALZBURGER FESTSPIELPREIS

15 June 1975. Salzburgring. 55 laps of a 2.633-mile circuit = 144.815 miles. European F2 Championship round 7

1	Jean-Pierre Jabouille	Elf 2J-BMW	55	1h06m23.48
2	Hans Binder	March 752-BMW	55	1h06m28.24
3	Gabriele Serblin	March 752-BMW	55	1h06m45.93
4	Claude Bourgoignie	March 752-BMW	55	1h07m01.46
5	Giorgio Francia	Osella FA2-BMW	55	1h07m29.87
6	Maurizio Flammini	March 742-BMW	55	1h07m29.87

Winner's average speed: 130.874 mph. Pole position: Michel Leclere (March 752-BMW), 1m10.54. Fastest lap: Jabouille, 1m10.97

GRAND PRIX DE ROUEN-LES-ESSARTS

29 June 1975. Rouen-les-Essarts. 40 laps of a 3.444-mile circuit = 137.760 miles. European F2 Championship round 8

1	Michel Leclere	March 752-BMW	40	1h13m30.48
2	Patrick Tambay	March 752-BMW	40	1h13m37.13
3	Claude Bourgoignie	March 752-BMW	40	1h14m44.42
4	Jean-Pierre Jaussaud	March 752-Ford	40	1h14m46.25
5	Bernard de Dryver	March 752-BMW	39	

No other finishers. Winner's average speed: 112.445 mph. Pole position: Jean-Pierre Jabouille (Elf 2J-BMW), 1m47.28. Fastest lap: Jaussaud, 1m48.74

TROFEO ETIENNE AIGNER/GRAN PREMIO DI MUGELLO

13 July 1975. Mugello. Aggregate of two 25-lap heats. 50 laps of a 3.259-mile circuit = 162.950 miles. European F2 Championship round 9

1	Maurizio Flammini	March 742-BMW	50	1h34m26.2
2	Alessandro Pesenti-Rossi	March 742-BMW	50	1h34m37.1
3	"Gianfranco"	March 742-BMW	50	1h36m49.3
4	Carlo Giorgio	March 742-Ford	50	1h37m30.4
5	Duilio Truffo	Osella FA2-BMW	49	
6	Bernard de Dryver	March 752-BMW	49	

Winner's average speed: 103.530 mph. Pole position: Truffo, 1m48.31. Fastest lap: Truffo, 1m50.5

GRAN PREMIO DEL MEDITERRANEO

27 July 1975. Enna-Pergusa. Aggregate of two 30-lap heats. 60 laps of a 3.076-mile circuit = 184.560 miles. European F2 Championship round 10

1	Jacques Laffite	Martini MK16-BMW	60	1h39m58.3
2	Gerard Larrousse	Alpine A367-BMW	60	1h40m03.3
3	Gabriele Serblin	March 752-BMW	60	1h41m20.3
4	Giorgio Francia	Osella FA2-BMW	60	1h41m44.7
5	Duilio Truffo	Osella FA2-BMW	60	1h41m56.3
6	Alessandro Pesenti-Rossi	March 742-BMW	60	1h42m32.1

Winner's average speed: 110.767 mph. Pole position: Patrick Tambay (March 752-BMW), 1m35.66. Fastest lap: Michel Leclere (March 752-BMW), 1m36.4

BRDC EUROPEAN TROPHY

31 August 1975. Silverstone. 50 laps of a 2.932-mile circuit = 146.600 miles. European F2 Championship round 11

1	Michel Leclere	March 752-BMW	50	1h11m05.56
2	Gerard Larrousse	Elf 2J-BMW	50	1h11m12.46
3	Brian Henton	Pilbeam R18-Ford	50	1h11m15.31
4	Patrick Tambay	March 752-BMW	50	1h12m04.12
5	Gabriele Serblin	March 752-BMW	50	1h12m13.66
6	Giancarlo Martini	March 752-BMW	50	1h12m14.77

Winner's average speed: 123.726 mph. Pole position: Leclere, 1m23.24. Fastest lap: Jean-Pierre Jabouille (Elf 2J-BMW), 1m24.15

ELF GROTE PRIJS VAN LIMBORG

14 September 1975. Zolder. Aggregate of two 24-lap heats. 48 laps of a 2.648-mile circuit = 127.104 miles. European F2 Championship round 12

1	Michel Leclere	March 752-BMW	48	1h12m46.82
2	Patrick Tambay	March 752-BMW	48	1h13m14.40
3	Maurizio Flammini	March 742-BMW	48	1h13m39.89
4	Hans Binder	Chevron B29-BMW	48	1h14m22.85
5	Giorgio Francia	Osella FA2-BMW	48	1h14m34.76
6	Ray Mallock	March 742-Ford	48	1h15m20.22

Winner's average speed: 104.784 mph. Pole position: Jacques Laffite (Martini MK16-BMW), 1m28.75. Fastest lap: Gerard Larrousse (Elf 2J-BMW), 1m28.69

GRAND PRIX DE NOGARO

28 September 1975. Nogaro. 65 laps of a 1.939-mile circuit = 126.035 miles. European F2 Championship round 13

1	Patrick Tambay	March 752-BMW	65	1h20m44.08
2	Michel Leclere	March 752-BMW	65	1h20m52.60
3	Jean-Pierre Jabouille	Elf 2J-BMW	65	1h21m29.78
4	Jean-Pierre Jaussaud	March 752-BMW	64	
5	Alessandro Pesenti-Rossi	March 742-BMW	64	
6	Alberto Colombo	March 752-BMW	64	

Winner's average speed: 93.666 mph. Pole position: Tambay, 1m12.62. Fastest lap: Jabouille, 1m13.21

GRAN PREMIO DI ROMA

12 October 1975. Vallelunga. Aggregate of two 35-lap heats. 70 laps of a 1.988-mile circuit = 139.160 miles. European F2 Championship round 14

1	Vittorio Brambilla	March 752-BMW	70	1h26m08.7
2	Jacques Laffite	Martini MK16-BMW	70	1h26m48.0
3	Maurizio Flammini	March 752-BMW	70	1h26m49.0
4	Alessandro Pesenti-Rossi	March 742-BMW	70	1h27m21.3
5	Giancarlo Martini	March 752-BMW	70	1h27m55.6
6	Gerard Larrousse	Elf 2J-BMW	69	

Winner's average speed: 96.925 mph. Pole position: Michel Leclere (March 752-BMW), 1m10.23. Fastest lap: Laffite, 1m10.81

1975 FINAL CHAMPIONSHIP POSITIONS

1	Jacques Laffite	60	15	Giancarlo Martini	8
2=	Michel Leclere	36	16	Loris Kessel	7
	Patrick Tambay	36	17=	Jean-Pierre Jaussaud	6
4	Gerard Larrousse	26		Joseph Vonlanthen	6
5	Jean-Pierre Jabouille	24	19=	Harald Ertl	4
6	Maurizio Flammini	22		"Gianfranco"	4
7=	Claude Bourgoignie	16		Lamberto Leoni	4
	Giorgio Francia	16	22=	Bernard de Dryver	3
9	Alessandro Pesenti-Rossi	13		Carlo Giorgio	3
				Hector Rebaque	3
10=	Brian Henton	10	25	Sandro Cinotti	2
	Gabriele Serblin	10	26=	Alberto Colombo	1
	Duilio Truffo	10		Ray Mallock	1
13=	Hans Binder	9	(A) Graded driver ineligible for		
	Vittorio Brambilla	9	points		

1976

JIM CLARK-RENNEN

11 April 1976. Hockenheim. Aggregate of two 20-lap heats. 40 laps of a 4.219-mile circuit = 168.760 miles. European F2 Championship round 1

1	Hans-Joachim Stuck (A)	March 762-BMW	40	1h21m45.6
2	Rene Arnoux	Martini MK16-Renault	40	1h23m03.0
3	Patrick Tambay	Martini MK19-Renault	40	1h23m15.4
4	Willi Deutsch	March 762-BMW	40	1h23m20.2
5	Roberto Marazzi	Chevron B35-BMW	40	1h23m56.7
6	Harald Ertl	March 752-BMW	40	1h24m42.9
7	Hans Heyer	Toj F201-BMW	40	1h25m12.3

Winner's average speed: 123.845 mph. Pole position: Stuck, 1m58.9 (pole). Fastest lap: Stuck, 1m59.8

JOCHEN RINDT TROPHY

19 April 1976. Thruxton. 55 laps of a 2.356-mile circuit = 129.580 miles. European F2 Championship round 2

1	Maurizio Flammini	March 762-BMW	55	1h06m51.54
2	Alex Ribeiro	March 762-BMW	55	1h07m18.35
3	Patrick Tambay	Martini MK19-Renault	55	1h07m19.72
4	Eddie Cheever	March 752-Hart	55	1h07m29.10
5	Ingo Hoffmann	March 762-Hart	54	
6	Francois Migault	Osella FA2-BMW	54	

Winner's average speed: 116.287 mph. Pole position: Flammini, 1m10.22. Fastest lap: Jean-Pierre Jabouille (Elf 2J-Renault), 1m10.88

GRAN PREMIO DI ROMA

9 May 1976. Vallelunga. 65 laps of a 1.988-mile circuit = 129.220 miles. European F2 Championship round 3

1	Jean-Pierre Jabouille	Elf 2J-Renault	65	1h18m03.1
2	Patrick Tambay	Martini MK19-Renault	65	1h18m12.2
3	Alex Ribeiro	March 762-BMW	65	1h18m20.1
4	Michel Leclere	Elf 2J-Renault	65	1h18m27.0

5 Alessandro
  Pesenti-Rossi   March 762-BMW   65   1h18m41.2
6 Jean-Pierre Jaussaud Chevron B35-Chrysler 65   1h18m58.9
Winner's average speed: 99.334 mph. Pole position: Jabouille, 1m09.40.
Fastest lap: Rene Arnoux (Martini MK19-Renault), 1m10.7

SALZBURGER FESTSPIELPREIS

23 May 1976. Salzburgring. 50 laps of a 2.635-mile circuit = 131.750 miles. European F2 Championship round 4

1 Michel Leclere	Elf 2J-Renault	50	1h04m28.82
2 Maurizio Flammini	March 762-BMW	50	1h04m34.43
3 Patrick Tambay	Martini MK19-Renault	50	1h04m36.42
4 Rene Arnoux	Martini MK19-Renault	50	1h04m40.63
5 Alex Ribeiro	March 762-BMW	50	1h04m45.78
6 Jean-Pierre Jabouille	Elf 2J-Renault	50	1h05m27.56

Winner's average speed: 122.596 mph. Pole position: Flammini, 1m24.05.
Fastest lap: Arnoux, 1m14.95

GRAND PRIX DE PAU

7 June 1976. Pau. 73 laps of a 1.715-mile circuit = 125.195 miles. European F2 Championship round 5

1 Rene Arnoux	Martini MK19-Renault	73	1h32m11.58
2 Jacques Laffite (A)	Chevron B35-BMW	73	1h32m54.49
3 Jean-Pierre Jabouille	Elf 2J-Renault	72	
4 Jean-Pierre Jarier (A)	Chevron B35-Hart	72	
5 Giancarlo Martini	March 762-BMW	72	
6 Alex Ribeiro	March 762-BMW	71	
7 Klaus Ludwig	March 762-Hart	70	
8 Freddy Kottulinsky	Ralt RT1-BMW	69	

Winner's average speed: 81.478 mph. Pole position: Patrick Tambay (Martini MK19-Renault), 1m13.77. Fastest lap: Laffite, 1m14.37

DMV RHEIN POKAL

20 June 1976. Hockenheim. Aggregate of two 20-lap heats. 40 laps of a 4.219-mile circuit = 168.760 miles. European F2 Championship round 6

1 Hans-Joachim Stuck (A)	March 762-BMW	40	1h21m27.6
2 Michel Leclere	Elf 2J-Renault	40	1h21m34.3
3 Patrick Tambay	Martini MK19-Renault	40	1h21m40.8
4 Jean-Pierre Jabouille	Elf 2J-Renault	40	1h21m43.1
5 Rene Arnoux	Martini MK19-Renault	40	1h21m58.9
6 Giancarlo Martini	March 762-BMW	40	1h23m05.0
7 Maurizio Flammini	March 762-BMW	40	1h23m15.4

Winner's average speed: 124.301 mph. Pole position: Stuck, 1m59.9.
Fastest lap: Leclere, 2m00.7

GRAND PRIX DE ROUEN-LES-ESSARTS

27 June 1976. Rouen-les-Essarts. 38 laps of a 3.444-mile circuit = 130.872 miles. European F2 Championship round 7

1 Maurizio Flammini	March 762-BMW	38	1h09m59.27
2 Jean-Pierre Jabouille	Elf 2J-Renault	38	1h10m12.81
3 Giancarlo Martini	March 762-BMW	38	1h10m29.18
4 Keke Rosberg	Toj F201-BMW	38	1h10m41.75
5 Roberto Marazzi	Chevron B35-BMW	38	1h10m54.42
6 Ingo Hoffmann	March 762-Hart	38	1h11m07.80

Winner's average speed: 112.196 mph. Pole position: Alex Ribeiro (March 762-BMW), 1m47.19. Fastest lap: Rene Arnoux (Martini MK19-Renault), 1m47.55

GRAN PREMIO ETIENNE AIGNER DI MUGELLO

11 July 1976. Mugello. 43 laps of a 3.259-mile circuit = 140.137 miles. European F2 Championship round 8

1 Jean-Pierre Jabouille	Elf 2J-Renault	43	1h19m28.8
2 Rene Arnoux	Martini MK19-Renault	43	1h19m31.4
3 Patrick Tambay	Martini MK19-Renault	43	1h19m52.7
4 Alex Ribeiro	March 762-BMW	43	1h20m01.8
5 Giancarlo Martini	March 762-BMW	43	1h20m20.5
6 Maurizio Flammini	March 762-BMW	43	1h20m30.9

Winner's average speed: 105.790 mph. Pole position: Jabouille, 1m48.20.
Fastest lap: Arnoux, 1m49.8

GRAN PREMIO DEL MEDITERRANEO

25 July 1976. Enna-Pergusa. Aggregate of two 30-lap heats. 60 laps of a 3.076-mile circuit = 184.560 miles. European F2 Championship round 9

1 Rene Arnoux	Martini MK19-Renault	60	1h36m12.9
2 Alex Ribeiro	March 762-BMW	60	1h36m17.4
3 Eddie Cheever	March 762-Hart	60	1h37m37.1
4 Jean-Pierre Jabouille	Elf 2J-Renault	60	1h38m04.7
5 Hans Binder	Chevron B35-BMW	60	1h38m06.0
6 Markus Hotz	March 762-BMW	59	

Winner's average speed: 115.092 mph. Pole position: Patrick Tambay (Martini MK19-Renault), 1m33.16. Fastest lap: Ribeiro, 1m34.2

GRANDE PREMIO DO ESTORIL

8 August 1976. Estoril. 50 laps of a 2.703-mile circuit = 135.150 miles. European F2 Championship round 10

1 Rene Arnoux	Martini MK19-Renault	50	1h20m19.77
2 Jean-Pierre Jabouille	Elf 2J-Renault	50	1h20m42.22
3 Alex Ribeiro	March 762-BMW	50	1h20m46.53
4 Hans Binder	Chevron B35-BMW	50	1h20m47.65
5 Eddie Cheever	March 752-Hart	50	1h21m17.19
6 Alberto Colombo	March 762-BMW	50	1h21m32.32

Winner's average speed: 100.947 mph. Pole position: Arnoux, 1m34.01.
Fastest lap: Arnoux, 1m34.55

GRAND PRIX DE NOGARO

19 September 1976. Nogaro. 65 laps of a 1.939-mile circuit = 126.035 miles. European F2 Championship round 11

1 Patrick Tambay	Martini MK19-Renault	65	1h20m12.91
2 Jacques Laffite (A)	Chevron B35-Hart	65	1h20m29.24
3 Michel Leclere	Elf 2J-Renault	65	1h20m37.15
4 Hans Binder	Chevron B35-BMW	65	1h20m40.61
5 Alex Ribeiro	March 762-BMW	65	1h21m24.41
6 Klaus Ludwig	March 762-Hart	65	1h21m24.83
7 Rolf Stommelen (A)	March 762-BMW	65	1h21m25.18
8 Eddie Cheever	Ralt RT1-Hart	65	1h21m31.63

Winner's average speed: 94.273 mph. Pole position: Jean-Pierre Jabouille (Elf 2J-Renault), 1m11.84. Fastest lap: Tambay, 1m12.92

TEXACO GOLD POKAL

26 September 1976. Hockenheim. Aggregate of two 20-lap heats. 40 laps of a 4.219-mile circuit = 168.760 miles. European F2 Championship round 12

1 Jean-Pierre Jabouille	Elf 2J-Renault	40	1h22m32.9
2 Michel Leclere	Elf 2J-Renault	40	1h22m36.5
3 Rene Arnoux	Martini MK19-Renault	40	1h22m38.0
4 Hans Binder	Chevron B35-BMW	40	1h23m15.6
5 Keke Rosberg	Toj F201-BMW	40	1h23m48.2
6 Jochen Mass (A)	Chevron B35-BMW	40	1h23m51.8
7 Giorgio Francia	Chevron B35-BMW	40	1h24m03.9

Winner's average speed: 122.663 mph. Pole position: Jabouille, 1m58.6.
Fastest lap: Arnoux, 2m00.8

1976 FINAL CHAMPIONSHIP POSITIONS

1	Jean-Pierre Jabouille	53	14	Ingo Hoffmann	3
2	Rene Arnoux	52	15=	Harald Ertl	3
3	Patrick Tambay	39		Alessandro Pesenti-Rossi	2
4	Michel Leclere	33	17=	Alberto Colombo	1
5	Alex Ribeiro	31		Giorgio Francia	1
6	Maurizio Flammini	26		Hans Heyer	1
7=	Hans Binder	12		Markus Hotz	1
	Giancarlo Martini	12		Jean-Pierre Jaussaud	1
9	Eddie Cheever	10		Freddy Kottulinsky	1
10=	Roberto Marazzi	5		Francois Migault	1
	Keke Rosberg	5		(A) Graded driver ineligible for
12=	Willi Deutsch	4		points
	Klaus Ludwig	4			

1977

DAILY EXPRESS INTERNATIONAL TROPHY

6 March 1977. Silverstone. 47 laps of a 2.932-mile circuit = 137.804 miles. European F2 Championship round 1

1 Rene Arnoux	Martini MK22-Renault	47	1h05m45.52
2 Ray Mallock	Chevron B40-Hart	47	1h06m00.23
3 Patrick Neve	March 772P-BMW	47	1h06m03.61
4 Ingo Hoffmann	Ralt RT1-BMW	47	1h06m21.43
5 Alberto Colombo	March 772-BMW	47	1h06m23.37
6 Riccardo Patrese	Chevron B35-BMW	47	1h06m25.27

Eddie Cheever (Ralt RT1-BMW), 1h06m06.47, finished fourth on the road but was penalised 1 minute for jumping the start. Winner's average speed: 125.736 mph. Pole position: Michel Leclere (Elf 2J-Renault), 1m21.85. Fastest lap: Neve, 1m21.85

PHILIPS CAR RADIO JOCHEN RINDT TROPHY

11 April 1977. Thruxton. 55 laps of a 2.356-mile circuit = 129.580 miles. European F2 Championship round 2

1 Brian Henton	Boxer PR276-Hart	55	1h05m59.43
2 Eddie Cheever	Ralt RT1-BMW	55	1h06m03.27
3 Alex Ribeiro	March 772P-BMW	55	1h06m40.08
4 Alberto Colombo	March 772-BMW	55	1h06m40.20
5 Riccardo Patrese	Chevron B35-BMW	55	1h06m54.44
6 Hans Royer	Chevron B35-Hart	54	

Winner's average speed: 117.817 mph. Pole position: Ribeiro, 1m08.87. Fastest lap: Henton, 1m10.67

JIM CLARK-RENNEN/MARTINI GOLD CUP

17 April 1977. Hockenheim. Aggregate of two 20-lap heats. 40 laps of a 4.219-mile circuit = 168.760 miles. European F2 Championship round 3

1 Jochen Mass (A)	March 772P-BMW	40	1h21m20.4
2 Rene Arnoux	Martini MK22-Renault	40	1h21m30.4
3 Riccardo Patrese	Chevron B35-BMW	40	1h21m33.1
4 Alessandro Pesenti-Rossi	March 772-Hart	40	1h22m32.8
5 Brian Henton	Boxer PR276-Hart	40	1h22m38.7
6 Alberto Colombo	March 772-Hart	40	1h22m44.8
7 Jacques Laffite (A)	Chevron B40-Hart	40	1h22m51.9
8 Keke Rosberg	Chevron B40-Hart	40	1h23m06.6

Winner's average speed: 124.485 mph. Pole position: Mass, 1m59.6. Fastest lap: Eddie Cheever (Ralt RT1-BMW), 2m00.4

EIFELRENNEN/VALVOLINE CUP

1 May 1977. Nurburgring. 9 laps of a 14.189-mile circuit = 127.701 miles. European F2 Championship round 4

1 Jochen Mass (A)	March 772P-BMW	9	1h06m41.1
2 Eddie Cheever	Ralt RT1-BMW	9	1h06m54.3
3 Keke Rosberg	Chevron B40-Hart	9	1h07m00.5

1977 Rene Arnoux leads at the start at Nogaro.

4 Didier Pironi	Martini MK22-Renault	9	1h07m02.6
5 Rene Arnoux	Martini MK22-Renault	9	1h07m05.3
6 Bruno Giacomelli	March 772-Hart	9	1h07m19.8
7 Ingo Hoffmann	Ralt RT1-BMW	9	1h07m42.6

Winner's average speed: 114.899 mph. Pole position: Riccardo Patrese (Chevron B35-BMW), 7m15.3. Fastest lap: Mass, 7m20.3

GRAN PREMIO DI ROMA

15 May 1977. Vallelunga. 65 laps of a 1.988-mile circuit = 129.220 miles. European F2 Championship round 5

1 Bruno Giacomelli	March 772P-BMW	65	1h16m57.36
2 Didier Colombo	Martini MK22-Renault	65	1h17m41.88
3 Eddie Cheever	Ralt RT1-BMW	65	1h17m51.61
4 Alessandro Pesenti-Rossi	March 772-Hart	65	1h17m53.73
5 Alberto Colombo	March 772-Hart	65	1h18m04.57
6 Luciano Pavesi	Ralt RT1-Hart	64	

Winner's average speed: 100.748 mph. Pole position: Giacomelli, 1m09.02. Fastest lap: Giacomelli, 1m10.38

GRAND PRIX DE PAU

30 May 1977. Pau. 59 laps of a 1.715-mile circuit = 101.185 miles. Race scheduled for 73 laps but stopped due to numerous accidents in the heavy rain. European F2 Championship round 6

1 Rene Arnoux	Martini MK22-Renault	59	1h14m52.52
2* Didier Pironi	Martini MK22-Renault	59	1h14m52.94
3* Riccardo Patrese	Chevron B40-BMW	59	1h15m11.06
4 Alberto Colombo	March 772-BMW	58	accident
5 Gaudenzio Mantova	March 762-BMW	58	
6 Ricardo Zunino	March 772-Hart	57	accident

*crashed on next lap. Winner's average speed: 81.083 mph. Pole position: Patrick Tambay (Chevron B40-Hart), 1m13.38. Fastest lap: Pironi, 1m14.57

GRAN PREMIO ETIENNE AIGNER DI MUGELLO

19 June 1977. Mugello. 42 laps of a 3.259-mile circuit = 136.878 miles. European F2 Championship round 7

1 Bruno Giacomelli	March 772P-BMW	42	1h16m36.5
2 Riccardo Patrese	Chevron B40-BMW	42	1h16m55.9
3 Alberto Colombo	March 772-BMW	42	1h17m06.5
4 Alessandro Pesenti-Rossi	March 772-BMW	42	1h17m17.6
5 Marc Surer	March 762-BMW	42	1h17m44.7
6 Bernard de Dryver	March 778-BMW	42	1h17m46.2

Winner's average speed: 107.203 mph. Pole position: Patrese, 1m47.20. Fastest lap: Pesenti-Rossi, 1m48.4

GRAND PRIX DE ROUEN-LES-ESSARTS

26 June 1977. Rouen-les-Essarts. 38 laps of a 3.444-mile circuit = 130.872 miles. European F2 Championship round 8

1 Eddie Cheever	Ralt RT1-BMW	38	1h08m36.19
2 Riccardo Patrese	Chevron B40-BMW	38	1h08m43.79
3 Didier Pironi	Martini MK22-Renault	38	1h08m45.74
4 Gianfranco Brancatelli	Ralt RT1-Ferrari	38	1h09m32.54
5 Ingo Hoffmann	Ralt RT1-BMW	38	1h09m42.96
6 Alberto Colombo	March 772-BMW	38	1h09m59.42

Winner's average speed: 114.460 mph. Pole position: Cheever, 1m45.7. Fastest lap: Hoffmann, 1m47.05

GRAND PRIX DE NOGARO

10 July 1977. Nogaro. 65 laps of a 1.939-mile circuit = 126.035 miles. European F2 Championship round 9

1 Rene Arnoux	Martini MK22-Renault	65	1h20m42.60
2 Riccardo Patrese	Chevron B40-BMW	65	1h21m10.29
3 Ingo Hoffmann	Ralt RT1-BMW	65	1h21m22.13
4 Bruno Giacomelli	March 772P-BMW	65	1h21m46.37
5 Eddie Cheever	Ralt RT1-BMW	65	1h21m53.54
6 Alberto Colombo	March 772-BMW	65	1h21m58.51

Winner's average speed: 93.695 mph. Pole position: Arnoux, 1m12.27. Fastest lap: Patrese, 1m13.79

GRAN PREMIO DEL MEDITERRANEO

24 July 1977. Enna-Pergusa. Aggregate of two 30-lap heats. 60 laps of a 3.076-mile circuit = 184.560 miles. European F2 Championship round 10

1	Keke Rosberg	Chevron B40-Hart	60	1h36m18.0
2	Rene Arnoux	Martini MK22-Renault	60	1h37m07.8
3	Ingo Hoffmann	Ralt RT1-BMW	60	1h37m15.8
4	Didier Pironi	Martini MK22-Renault	60	1h37m52.2
5	Gaudenzio Mantova	March 762-BMW	60	1h37m59.3
6	"Gianfranco"	March 762-BMW	60	1h38m39.1

Winner's average speed: 114.991 mph. Pole position: Rosberg, 1m33.08. Fastest lap: Riccardo Patrese (Chevron B40-BMW), 1m33.9

GRAN PREMIO DEL ADRIATICO

7 August 1977. Misano. Aggregate of two 30-lap heats. 60 laps of a 2.167-mile circuit = 130.020 miles. European F2 Championship round 11

1	Lamberto Leoni	Chevron B40-Ferrari	60	1h13m44.8
2	Eddie Cheever	Ralt RT1-BMW	60	1h13m47.5
3	Ingo Hoffmann	Ralt RT1-BMW	60	1h14m07.4
4	Alessandro Pesenti-Rossi	March 772-BMW	60	1h14m21.1
5	Didier Pironi	Martini MK22-Renault	60	1h14m30.7
6	Clay Regazzoni (A)	Chevron B40-Hart	60	1h14m47.6
7	Patrick Bardinon	March 772-BMW	60	1h15m02.6

Winner's average speed: 105.784 mph. Pole position: Bruno Giacomelli (March 772P-BMW), 1m11.5. Fastest lap: Giacomelli, 1m12.3

GRANDE PREMIO DO ESTORIL

2 October 1977. Estoril. 50 laps of a 2.703-mile circuit = 135.150 miles. European F2 Championship round 12

1	Didier Pironi	Martini MK22-Renault	50	1h19m29.30
2	Rene Arnoux	Martini MK22-Renault	50	1h19m46.65
3	Eddie Cheever	Ralt RT1-BMW	50	1h19m47.22
4	Keke Rosberg	Chevron B40-Hart	50	1h19m47.52
5	Derek Daly	Chevron B40-Hart	50	1h19m55.49
6	Riccardo Patrese	Chevron B40-BMW	50	1h19m56.18

Winner's average speed: 102.015 mph. Pole position: Pironi, 1m33.05. Fastest lap: Daly, 1m34.16

BRSCC FORMULA 2 TROPHY

30 October 1977. Donington Park. 65 laps of a 1.957-mile circuit = 127.225 miles. European F2 Championship round 13

1	Bruno Giacomelli	March 782/772P-BMW	65	1h12m40.35
2	Keke Rosberg	Chevron B40-Hart	65	1h13m08.04
3	Didier Pironi	Martini MK22-Renault	65	1h13m25.36
4	Marc Surer	March 772P-BMW	65	1h13m28.88
5	Danny Sullivan	Boxer PR276-Hart	65	1h13m35.35
6	Rene Arnoux	Martini MK22-Renault	65	1h14m04.05

Winner's average speed: 105.039 mph. Pole position: Giacomelli, 1m05.00. Fastest lap: Giacomelli, 1m06.19

1977 FINAL CHAMPIONSHIP POSITIONS

1	Rene Arnoux	52	14=	Gaudenzio Mantova	4
2	Eddie Cheever	40		Patrick Neve	4
3	Didier Pironi	38		Alex Ribeiro	4
4=	Bruno Giacomelli	32	17	Gianfranco Brancatelli	3
	Riccardo Patrese	32	18=	Derek Daly	2
6	Keke Rosberg	25		Danny Sullivan	2
7=	Alberto Colombo	18	20=	Patrick Bardinon	1
	Ingo Hoffmann	18		Bernard de Dryver	1
9	Alessandro Pesenti-Rossi	13		"Gianfranco"	1
				Luciano Pavesi	1
10	Brian Henton	12		Hans Royer	1
11	Lamberto Leoni	9		Ricardo Zunino	1
12	Ray Mallock	6	(A) Graded driver ineligible for		
13	Marc Surer	5	points		

1978

PHILIPS CAR STEREO JOCHEN RINDT TROPHY

27 March 1978. Thruxton. 55 laps of a 2.356-mile circuit = 129.580 miles. European F2 Championship round 1

1	Bruno Giacomelli	March 782-BMW	55	1h06m13.77
2	Marc Surer	March 782-BMW	55	1h06m17.12
3	Rad Dougall	March 782-BMW	55	1h06m24.66
4	Eddie Cheever	March 782-BMW	55	1h06m25.37
5	Manfred Winkelhock	March 782-BMW	55	1h06m30.70
6	Derek Daly	Chevron B42-Hart	55	1h06m57.57

Winner's average speed: 117.392 mph. Pole position: Giacomelli, 1m09.13. Fastest lap: Giacomelli, 1m10.86

JIM CLARK-RENNEN

9 April 1978. Hockenheim. Aggregate of two 20-lap heats. 40 laps of a 4.219-mile circuit = 168.760 miles. European F2 Championship round 2

1	Bruno Giacomelli	March 782-BMW	40	1h20m22.0
2	Marc Surer	March 782-BMW	40	1h20m31.9
3	Jean-Pierre Jarier (A)	March 782-BMW	40	1h20m46.6
4	Ingo Hoffmann	March 782-BMW	40	1h20m52.2
5	Alberto Colombo	March 782-BMW	40	1h21m02.2
6	Alex Ribeiro	March 782-Hart	40	1h21m23.5
7	Jochen Mass (A)	Chevron B42-Hart	40	1h21m56.2
8	Keke Rosberg	Chevron B42-Hart	40	1h22m00.0

Winner's average speed: 125.993 mph. Pole position: Giacomelli, 1m59.0. Fastest lap: Giacomelli and Surer, 1m59.4

EIFELRENNEN

30 April 1978. Nurburgring. 9 laps of a 14.189-mile circuit = 127.701 miles. European F2 Championship round 3

1	Alex Ribeiro	March 782-Hart	9	1h06m34.2
2	Keke Rosberg	Chevron B42-Hart	9	1h06m34.3
3	Eddie Cheever	March 782-BMW	9	1h06m34.8
4	Marc Surer	March 782-BMW	9	1h06m42.2
5	Brian Henton	March 782-Hart	9	1h06m45.2
6	Ingo Hoffmann	March 782-BMW	9	1h06m45.8

Winner's average speed: 115.098 mph. Pole position: Bruno Giacomelli (March 782-BMW), 7m11.5. Fastest lap: Rosberg, 7m17.3

GRAND PRIX DE PAU

15 May 1978. Pau. 73 laps of a 1.715-mile circuit = 125.195 miles. European F2 Championship round 4

1	Bruno Giacomelli	March 782-BMW	73	1h33m11.73
2	Eje Elgh	Chevron B42-Hart	73	1h33m33.47
3	Marc Surer	March 782-BMW	73	1h33m45.98
4	Piero Necchi	March 782-BMW	73	1h34m04.56
5	Eddie Cheever	March 782-BMW	73	1h34m25.16
6	Patrick Tambay (A)	Chevron B42-Hart	72	engine
7	Roberto Marazzi	March 782-BMW	70	

Winner's average speed: 80.602 mph. Pole position: Brian Henton (March 782-Hart), 1m13.64. Fastest lap: Giacomelli, 1m14.45

GRAN PREMIO ETIENNE AIGNER DI MUGELLO

28 May 1978. Mugello. 42 laps of a 3.259-mile circuit = 136.878 miles. European F2 Championship round 5

1	Derek Daly	Chevron B42-Hart	42	1h15m39.7
2	Marc Surer	March 782-BMW	42	1h15m40.1
3	Bruno Giacomelli	March 782-BMW	42	1h15m41.2
4	Ingo Hoffmann	March 782-BMW	42	1h16m39.1
5	Alberto Colombo	March 782-BMW	42	1h16m45.3
6	Arturo Merzario (A)	Chevron B42-Hart	42	1h16m48.8
7	Eddie Cheever	March 782-BMW	42	1h16m50.2

Winner's average speed: 108.545 mph. Pole position: Giacomelli, 1m45.54. Fastest lap: Cheever, 1m46.70

GRAN PREMIO DI ROMA

4 June 1978. Vallelunga. 65 laps of a 1.988-mile circuit = 129.220 miles.
European F2 Championship round 6

1 Derek Daly	Chevron B42-Hart	65	1h17m12.2
2 Bruno Giacomelli	March 782-BMW	65	1h17m13.2
3 Piero Necchi	March 782-BMW	65	1h17m15.0
4 Manfred Winkelhock	March 782-BMW	65	1h17m47.4
5 Beppe Gabbiani	Chevron B42-Ferrari	65	1h17m47.7
6 Ricardo Zunino	March 782-BMW	65	1h17m48.5

Winner's average speed: 100.426 mph. Pole position: Giacomelli, 1m08.48.
Fastest lap: Giacomelli, 1m10.0

GRAND PRIX DE ROUEN-LES-ESSARTS

18 June 1978. Rouen-les-Essarts. 38 laps of a 3.444-mile circuit =
130.872 miles. European F2 Championship round 7

1 Bruno Giacomelli	March 782-BMW	38	1h08m43.2
2 Eddie Cheever	March 782-BMW	38	1h08m55.1
3 Marc Surer	March 782-BMW	38	1h09m27.7
4 Alberto Colombo	March 782-BMW	38	1h09m42.6
5 Ricardo Zunino	March 782-BMW	38	1h09m45.9
6 Eje Elgh	Chevron B42-Hart	38	1h09m47.4

Winner's average speed: 114.265 mph. Pole position: Giacomelli, 1m58.79.
Fastest lap: Ingo Hoffmann (March 782-BMW), 1m46.31

£50,000 EUROPEAN CHAMPIONSHIP TROPHY

25 June 1978. Donington Park. Aggregate of two 40-lap heats. 80 laps of
a 1.957-mile circuit = 156.584 miles. European F2 Championship round 8

1 Keke Rosberg	Chevron B42-Hart	80	1h29m51.43
2 Piero Necchi	March 782-BMW	80	1h29m56.61
3 Marc Surer	March 782-BMW	80	1h30m08.88
4 Ingo Hoffmann	March 782-BMW	80	1h30m15.23
5 Manfred Winkelhock	March 782-BMW	80	1h30m48.60
6 Rad Dougall	March 782-BMW	80	1h31m09.65

Winner's average speed: 104.555 mph. Pole position: Bruno Giacomelli
(March 782-BMW), 1m04.68. Fastest lap: Brian Henton (March 782-Hart),
1m04.91

GRAND PRIX DE NOGARO

9 July 1978. Nogaro. 65 laps of a 1.939-mile circuit = 126.035 miles.
European F2 Championship round 9

1 Bruno Giacomelli	March 782-BMW	65	1h19m12.23
2 Marc Surer	March 782-BMW	65	1h19m28.43
3 Derek Daly	Chevron B42-Hart	65	1h19m41.43
4 Alberto Colombo	March 782-BMW	65	1h19m42.64
5 Ingo Hoffmann	March 782-BMW	65	1h19m56.67
6 Geoff Lees	Chevron B42-Hart	65	1h20m05.32

Winner's average speed: 95.476 mph. Pole position: Giacomelli, 1m10.59.
Fastest lap: Giacomelli, 1m12.39

GRAN PREMIO DEL MEDITERRANEO

23 July 1978. Enna-Pergusa. 41 laps of a 3.076-mile circuit = 126.116
miles. European F2 Championship round 10

1 Bruno Giacomelli	March 782-BMW	41	1h04m05.6
2 Eddie Cheever	March 782-BMW	41	1h04m13.3
3 Derek Daly	Chevron B42-Hart	41	1h04m19.9
4 Piercarlo Ghinzani	March 782-BMW	41	1h04m33.4
5 Ricardo Zunino	March 782-BMW	41	1h04m47.9
6 Brian Henton	March 782-Hart	41	1h05m00.4

Winner's average speed: 118.062 mph. Pole position: Daly, 1m31.34.
Fastest lap: Daly, 1m31.5

GRAN PREMIO DEL ADRIATICO

6 August 1978. Misano. 60 laps of a 2.167-mile circuit = 130.020 miles.
European F2 Championship round 11

1 Bruno Giacomelli	March 782-BMW	60	1h13m45.09
2 Marc Surer	March 782-BMW	60	1h13m53.49
3 Elio de Angelis	Chevron B42-Hart	60	1h14m16.08
4 Geoff Lees	Chevron B42-Hart	60	1h14m27.58
5 Arturo Merzario (A)	Chevron B42-Hart	60	1h14m32.57
6 Eddie Cheever	March 782-BMW	60	1h14m43.18
7 Ricardo Zunino	March 782-BMW	60	1h14m50.73

Winner's average speed: 105.777 mph. Pole position: Brian Henton (March
782-Hart), 1m11.67. Fastest lap: Giacomelli, 1m12.7

PREIS VON HESSEN UND WURTTEMBERG

24 September 1978. Hockenheim. Aggregate of two 20-lap heats. 40 laps
of a 4.219-mile circuit = 168.760 miles. European F2 Championship
round 12

1 Bruno Giacomelli	March 782-BMW	40	1h20m29.02
2 Marc Surer	March 782-BMW	40	1h20m35.39
3 Manfred Winkelhock	March 782-BMW	40	1h21m15.64
4 Stephen South	March 782-Hart	40	1h21m19.09
5 Ricardo Zunino	March 782-BMW	40	1h21m23.42
6 Eje Elgh	Chevron B42-Hart	40	1h21m24.06

Winner's average speed: 125.809 mph. Pole position: Surer, 1m 58.68.
Fastest lap: Derek Daly (Chevron B42-Hart), 1m59.17

1978 FINAL CHAMPIONSHIP POSITIONS

1	Bruno Giacomelli	78 (82)*	13	Rad Dougall	5
2	Marc Surer	48 (51)*	14=	Elio de Angelis	4
3	Derek Daly	27		Geoff Lees	4
4	Eddie Cheever	24	16=	Piercarlo Ghinzani	3
5	Keke Rosberg	16		Brian Henton	3
6=	Ingo Hoffmann	13		Stephen South	3
	Piero Necchi	13	19	Beppe Gabbiani	2
8=	Alberto Colombo	11	20	Roberto Marazzi	1
	Alex Ribeiro	11		(A) Graded driver ineligible for	
	Manfred Winkelhock	11		points. *Best nine results count	
11=	Eje Elgh	8			
	Ricardo Zunino	8			

1979

MARLBORO/DAILY EXPRESS INTERNATIONAL TROPHY

25 March 1979. Silverstone. 40 laps of a 2.932-mile circuit = 117.280
miles. Race scheduled for 47 laps, stopped after two laps due to an accident, restarted as a new race over reduced distance. European F2
Championship round 1

1 Eddie Cheever	Osella FA2/79-BMW	40	1h01m42.52
2 Derek Daly	March 792-BMW	40	1h01m42.85
3 Brian Henton	Ralt RT2-Hart	40	1h02m16.61
4 Bobby Rahal	Chevron B48-Hart	40	1h02m39.45
5 Stephen South	March 792-BMW	40	1h03m07.98
6 Alberto Colombo	March 782-BMW	39	

Winner's average speed: 114.033 mph. Pole position: Cheever, 1m19.81.
Fastest lap: Daly, 1m30.01

JIM CLARK-RENNEN/MARTINI GOLD CUP

8 April 1979. Hockenheim. Aggregate of two 20-lap heats. 40 laps of a
4.219-mile circuit = 168.760 miles. European F2 Championship round 2

1 Keke Rosberg	March 792-BMW	40	1h20m27.1
2 Rad Dougall	March 782-Hart	40	1h20m54.3
3 Miguel Angel Guerra	March 792-BMW	40	1h21m07.1
4 Brian Henton	Ralt RT2-Hart	40	1h21m12.4
5 Eddie Cheever	Osella FA2/79-BMW	40	1h21m28.0
6 Teo Fabi	March 792-BMW	40	1h21m28.4

Winner's average speed: 125.859 mph. Pole position: Marc Surer (March
792-BMW), 1m56.9. Fastest lap: Stephen South (March 792-BMW),
1m59.0

PHILIPS CAR RADIO JOCHEN RINDT TROPHY

16 April 1979. Thruxton. 55 laps of a 2.356-mile circuit = 129.580 miles. European F2 Championship round 3

1	Rad Dougall	March 782-Hart	55	1h04m10.31
2	Derek Daly	March 792-BMW	55	1h04m53.27
3	Alberto Colombo	March 782-BMW	55	1h05m02.32
4	Miguel Angel Guerra	March 792-BMW	55	1h05m07.39
5	Bobby Rahal	Chevron B48-Hart	55	1h05m19.68
6	Huub Rothengatter	Chevron B48-Hart	54	

Winner's average speed: 121.156 mph. Pole position: Dougall, 1m07.97. Fastest lap: Marc Surer (March 792-BMW), 1m09.11

EIFELRENNEN/GROSSER PREIS VON RTL

29 April 1979. Nurburgring. 9 laps of a 14.189-mile circuit = 127.701 miles. European F2 Championship round 4

1	Marc Surer	March 792-BMW	9	1h12m46.7
2	Brian Henton	March 782-Hart	9	1h13m31.0
3	Manfred Winkelhock	Ralt RT1-BMW	9	1h13m47.3
4	Siegfried Stohr	Chevron B48-BMW	9	1h13m53.7
5	Huub Rothengatter	Chevron B48-Hart	9	1h13m53.9
6	Rad Dougall	March 782-Hart	9	1h14m14.1

Winner's average speed: 105.279 mph. Pole position: Keke Rosberg (March 792-BMW), 7m06.9. Fastest lap: Winkelhock, 7m29.1

GRAN PREMIO DI ROMA

13 May 1979. Vallelunga. 65 laps of a 1.988-mile circuit = 129.220 miles. European F2 Championship round 5

1	Marc Surer	March 792-BMW	65	1h16m34.9
2	Siegfried Stohr	Chevron B48-BMW	65	1h17m09.4
3	Maurizio Flammini	March 792-BMW	65	1h17m17.5
4	Bobby Rahal	Chevron B48-Hart	65	1h17m21.5
5	Rad Dougall	March 782-Hart	65	1h17m32.8
6	Andrea de Cesaris	March 792-BMW	64	

Winner's average speed: 101.241 mph. Pole position: Stephen South (March 792-BMW), 1m08.04. Fastest lap: Brian Henton (March 782-Hart), 1m09.5

GRAN PREMIO VANUCCI DI MUGELLO

20 May 1979. Mugello. 42 laps of a 3.259-mile circuit = 136.878 miles. European F2 Championship round 6

1	Brian Henton	Ralt RT2-Hart	42	1h15m46.8
2	Beppe Gabbiani	March 792-BMW	42	1h15m59.8
3	Eje Elgh	March 792-BMW	42	1h16m05.0
4	Teo Fabi	March 792-BMW	42	1h16m11.7
5	Derek Warwick	March 792-Hart	42	1h16m18.5
6	Bobby Rahal	Chevron B48-Hart	42	1h16m20.6

Winner's average speed: 108.375 mph. Pole position: Henton, 1m44.74. Fastest lap: Gabbiani, 1m47.0

GRAND PRIX DE PAU

4 June 1979. Pau. 73 laps of a 1.715-mile circuit = 125.195 miles. European F2 Championship round 7

1	Eddie Cheever	Osella FA2/79-BMW	73	1h54m30.32
2	Siegfried Stohr	Chevron B48-BMW	73	1h54m58.40
3	Marc Surer	March 792-BMW	72	
4	Beppe Gabbiani	March 792-BMW	72	
5	Patrick Gaillard	Chevron B48-Hart	72	
6	Miguel Angel Guerra	March 792-BMW	71	

Winner's average speed: 65.601 mph. Pole position: Surer, 1m13.25. Fastest lap: Cheever, 1m31.52

PREIS VON HESSEN UND WURTTEMBERG

10 June 1979. Hockenheim. Aggregate of two 20-lap heats. 40 laps of a 4.219-mile circuit = 168.760 miles. European F2 Championship round 8

1	Stephen South	March 792-BMW	40	1h20m56.57
2	Derek Daly	March 792-BMW	40	1h21m09.49
3	Beppe Gabbiani	March 792-BMW	40	1h21m34.21
4	Patrick Gaillard	Chevron B48-Hart	40	1h21m58.17
5	Marc Surer	March 792-BMW	40	1h22m13.40
6	Bobby Rahal	Chevron B48-Hart	40	1h22m26.08

Winner's average speed: 125.096 mph. Pole position: South, 1m58.36. Fastest lap: Alberto Colombo (March 782-BMW), 1m59.98

GROTE PRIJS VAN ZANDVOORT

15 July 1979. Zandvoort. 50 laps of a 2.626-mile circuit = 131.300 miles. European F2 Championship round 9

1	Eddie Cheever	Osella FA2/79-BMW	50	1h09m37.86
2	Teo Fabi	March 792-BMW	50	1h09m39.16
3	Marc Surer	March 792-BMW	50	1h09m39.87
4	Alberto Colombo	March 782-BMW	50	1h09m50.11
5	Brian Henton	Ralt RT2-Hart	50	1h09m56.07
6	Eje Elgh	March 792-BMW	50	1h10m01.90

Winner's average speed: 113.139 mph. Pole position: Henton, 1m20.21. Fastest lap: Cheever, 1m21.70

GRAN PREMIO DEL MEDITERRANEO

29 July 1979. Enna-Pergusa. 45 laps of a 3.076-mile circuit = 138.420 miles. European F2 Championship round 10

1	Eje Elgh	March 792-BMW	45	1h11m02.9
2	Derek Daly	March 792-BMW	45	1h11m18.8
3	Stephen South	March 792-BMW	45	1h11m23.2
4	Teo Fabi	March 792-BMW	45	1h11m38.6
5	Eddie Cheever	Osella FA2/79-BMW	45	1h11m56.2
6	Rad Dougall	Ralt RT2-Hart	45	1h12m04.7

Brian Henton (Ralt RT2-Hart), 1h10m59.2, finished first on the road but was disqualified for missing the chicane at the start. Winner's average speed: 116.895 mph. Pole position: Henton, 1m31.45. Fastest lap: South, 1m33.20

GRAN PREMIO DEL ADRIATICO

5 August 1979. Misano. 60 laps of a 2.167-mile circuit = 130.020 miles. European F2 Championship round 11

1	Brian Henton	Ralt RT2-Hart	60	1h14m29.0
2	Beppe Gabbiani	March 792-BMW	60	1h15m25.3
3	Marc Surer	March 792-BMW	60	1h15m31.4
4	Juan Traverso	March 792-Hart	59	
5	Siegfried Stohr	March 792-BMW	58	
6	Eddie Cheever	Osella FA2/79-BMW	58	

Winner's average speed: 104.738 mph. Pole position: Henton, 1m11.63. Fastest lap: Henton, 1m13.2

£50,000 EUROPEAN CHAMPIONSHIP TROPHY

19 August 1979. Donington Park. 65 laps of a 1.957-mile circuit = 127.225 miles. European F2 Championship round 12

1	Derek Daly	March 792-BMW	65	1h11m53.20
2	Marc Surer	March 792-BMW	65	1h11m56.10
3	Stephen South	March 792-BMW	65	1h12m28.37
4	Brian Henton	Ralt RT2-Hart	65	1h12m36.01
5	Eje Elgh	March 792-BMW	65	1h12m44.57
6	Oscar Pedersoli	March 782-BMW	65	1h12m56.29

Winner's average speed: 106.188 mph. Pole position: Daly, 1m04.05. Fastest lap: Daly, 1m05.34

1979 FINAL CHAMPIONSHIP POSITIONS

1	Marc Surer	38	Miguel Angel Guerra	8
2	Brian Henton	36	15	Patrick Gaillard	5
3	Derek Daly	33	16=	Maurizio Flammini	4
4	Eddie Cheever	32		Manfred Winkelhock	4
5=	Rad Dougall	19	18=	Huub Rothengatter	3
	Beppe Gabbiani	19		Juan Traverso	3
	Stephen South	19	20	Derek Warwick	2
8	Siegfried Stohr	17	21=	Andrea de Cesaris	1
9	Eje Elgh	16		Oscar Pedersoli	1
10	Teo Fabi	13	Best nine results count	
11	Bobby Rahal	10		
12	Keke Rosberg	9		
13=	Alberto Colombo	8		

1980

P&O FERRIES JOCHEN RINDT TROPHY

7 April 1980. Thruxton. 55 laps of a 2.356-mile circuit = 129.580 miles.
European F2 Championship round 1

1	Brian Henton	Toleman TG280-Hart	55	1h04m10.56
2	Derek Warwick	Toleman TG280-Hart	55	1h04m14.25
3	Andrea de Cesaris	March 802-BMW	55	1h04m57.29
4	Chico Serra	March 802-BMW	55	1h05m20.68
5	Oscar Pedersoli	March 782-BMW	54	
6	Huub Rothengatter	Toleman TG280-Hart	54	

Winner's average speed: 121.148 mph. Pole position: Warwick, 1m07.60.
Fastest lap: Henton, 1m09.04.

JIM CLARK-RENNEN

13 April 1980. Hockenheim. 27 laps of a 4.219-mile circuit = 113.913
miles. Race scheduled for 30 laps, stopped due to Markus Hottinger's
fatal accident. European F2 Championship round 2

1	Teo Fabi	March 802-BMW	27	54m28.99
2	Brian Henton	Toleman TG280-Hart	27	54m37.88
3	Alberto Colombo	March 782-BMW	27	54m43.74
4	Chico Serra	March 802-BMW	26	
5	Huub Rothengatter	Toleman TG280-Hart	26	
6	Oscar Pedersoli	March 782-BMW	26	

Winner's average speed: 125.448 mph. Pole position: Andrea de Cesaris
(March 802-BMW), 1m56.73. Fastest lap: Mike Thackwell (March 802-
BMW), 1m59.23

EIFELRENNEN

27 April 1980. Nurburgring. 9 laps of a 14.189-mile circuit = 127.701
miles. European F2 Championship round 3

1	Teo Fabi	March 802-BMW	9	1h08m08.51
2	Brian Henton	Toleman TG280-Hart	9	1h08m42.19
3	Derek Warwick	Toleman TG280-Hart	9	1h08m45.16
4	Siegfried Stohr	Toleman TG280-Hart	9	1h09m15.33
5	Jochen Dauer	Chevron B48-BMW	9	1h09m46.38
6	Huub Rothengatter	Toleman TG280-Hart	9	1h09m53.65

Winner's average speed: 112.443 mph. Pole position: Richard Dallest (AGS
JH17-BMW), 8m56.56. Fastest lap: Mike Thackwell (March 802-BMW),
7m23.65

GRAN PREMIO DI ROMA

12 May 1980. Vallelunga. 65 laps of a 1.988-mile circuit = 129.220 miles.
European F2 Championship round 4

1	Brian Henton	Toleman TG280-Hart	65	1h15m56.1
2	Andrea de Cesaris	March 802-BMW	65	1h16m00.5
3	Derek Warwick	Toleman TG280-Hart	65	1h16m02.3
4	Mike Thackwell	March 802-BMW	65	1h16m25.9
5	Siegfried Stohr	Toleman TG280-Hart	65	1h16m45.5

6	Alberto Colombo	March 782-BMW	65	1h16m51.6

Winner's average speed: 102.103 mph. Pole position: Warwick, 1m07.69.
Fastest lap: Henton, 1m09.2

GRAND PRIX DE PAU

26 May 1980. Pau. 73 laps of a 1.715-mile circuit = 125.195 miles.
European F2 Championship round 5

1	Richard Dallest	AGS JH17-BMW	73	1h34m03.57
2	Siegfried Stohr	Toleman TG280-Hart	73	1h34m05.08
3	Brian Henton	Toleman TG280-Hart	73	1h34m38.49
4	Mike Thackwell	March 802-BMW	73	1h34m53.64
5	Miguel Angel Guerra	Minardi GM75-BMW	72	
6	Alberto Colombo	March 782-BMW	71	

Winner's average speed: 79.861 mph. Pole position: Derek Warwick
(Toleman TG280-Hart), 1m12.09. Fastest lap: Henton, 1m14.59

MARLBORO FORMULA 2 TROPHY

8 June 1980. Silverstone. 47 laps of a 2.932-mile circuit = 137.804 miles.
European F2 Championship round 6

1	Derek Warwick	Toleman TG280-Hart	47	1h03m18.66
2	Andrea de Cesaris	March 802-BMW	47	1h03m34.33
3	Mike Thackwell	March 802-BMW	47	1h03m45.49
4	Teo Fabi	March 802-BMW	47	1h04m07.89
5	Huub Rothengatter	Toleman TG280-Hart	47	1h04m11.41
6	Miguel Angel Guerra	Minardi GM75-BMW	47	1h04m29.02

Winner's average speed: 130.597 mph. Pole position: Brian Henton
(Toleman TG280B-Hart), 1m18.50. Fastest lap: Henton, 1m19.11

GRAND PRIX DE BELGIQUE FORMULE 2

22 June 1980. Zolder. 50 laps of a 2.648-mile circuit = 132.400 miles.
European F2 Championship round 7

1	Huub Rothengatter	Toleman TG280-Hart	50	1h13m44.61
2	Brian Henton	Toleman TG280B-Hart	50	1h14m03.63
3	Siegfried Stohr	Toleman TG280-Hart	50	1h14m04.73
4	Derek Warwick	Toleman TG280-Hart	50	1h14m35.04
5	Miguel Angel Guerra	Minardi GM75-BMW	50	1h14m36.90
6	Mike Thackwell	March 802-BMW	50	1h15m00.87

Winner's average speed: 107.725 mph. Pole position: Teo Fabi (March 802-
BMW), 1m26.12. Fastest lap: Henton, 1m26.97

GRAN PREMIO MARLBORO DI MUGELLO

6 July 1980. Mugello. 42 laps of a 3.259-mile circuit = 136.878 miles.
European F2 Championship round 8

1	Brian Henton	Toleman TG280B-Hart	42	1h15m22.6
2	Derek Warwick	Toleman TG280B-Hart	42	1h15m22.7
3	Teo Fabi	March 802-BMW	42	1h16m07.6
4	Miguel Angel Guerra	Minardi GM75-BMW	42	1h16m09.1
5	Andrea de Cesaris	March 802-BMW	42	1h16m17.2
6	Siegfried Stohr	Toleman TG280-Hart	42	1h16m44.3

Winner's average speed: 108.955 mph. Pole position: Warwick, 1m42.46.
Fastest lap: Warwick, 1m46.5

1980 The new Toleman team of Brian Henton (#7) and Derek Warwick
dominate the 1980 European F2 Championship.

GROTE PRIJS VAN ZANDVOORT

20 July 1980. Zandvoort. 45 laps of a 2.642-mile circuit = 118.890 miles.
European F2 Championship round 9

1	Richard Dallest	AGS JH17-BMW	45	1h15m53.593
2	Derek Warwick	Toleman TG280B-Hart	45	1h15m57.238
3	Teo Fabi	March 802-BMW	45	1h16m16.347
4	Chico Serra	March 802-BMW	45	1h16m29.465
5	Nigel Mansell	Ralt RH6/80-Honda	45	1h16m48.814
6	Beppe Gabbiani	Maurer MM80-BMW	45	1h17m14.801

Winner's average speed: 93.993 mph. Pole position: Dallest, 1m37.249.
Fastest lap: Brian Henton (Toleman TG280B-Hart), 1m35.631

GRAN PREMIO DEL MEDITERRANEO

2 August 1980. Enna-Pergusa. 45 laps of a 3.076-mile circuit = 138.420
miles. European F2 Championship round 10

1	Siegfried Stohr	Toleman TG280-Hart	45	1h10m39.79
2	Brian Henton	Toleman TG280B-Hart	45	1h10m49.46
3	Manfred Winkelhock	March 802-BMW	45	1h11m10.26
4	Huub Rothengatter	Toleman TG280-Hart	45	1h11m15.73
5	Richard Dallest	AGS JH15-BMW	45	1h11m16.23
6	Andrea de Cesaris	March 802-BMW	45	1h11m30.87

Winner's average speed: 117.532 mph. Pole position: Stohr, 1m31.40.
Fastest lap: Teo Fabi (March 802-BMW), 1m31.26

GRAN PREMIO DEL ADRIATICO

10 August 1980. Misano. 60 laps of a 2.167-mile circuit = 130.020 miles.
European F2 Championship round 11

1	Andrea de Cesaris	March 802-BMW	60	1h12m39.38
2	Brian Henton	Toleman TG280B-Hart	60	1h12m40.55
3	Derek Warwick	Toleman TG280B-Hart	60	1h13m01.36
4	Huub Rothengatter	Toleman TG280-Hart	60	1h13m25.93
5	Miguel Angel Guerra	Minardi GM75-BMW	60	1h13m31.00
6	Alberto Colombo	Toleman TG280-Hart	60	1h13m48.76

Winner's average speed: 107.371 mph.
Fastest lap: Henton, 1m11.22

PREIS VON HESSEN UND WURTTEMBERG

28 September 1980. Hockenheim. 30 laps of a 4.219-mile circuit =
126.570 miles. European F2 Championship round 12

1	Teo Fabi	March 802-BMW	30	59m41.06
2	Nigel Mansell	Ralt RH6/80-Honda	30	1h00m01.38
3	Siegfried Stohr	Toleman TG280-Hart	30	1h00m26.26
4	Richard Dallest	AGS JH17-BMW	30	1h00m28.71
5	Alberto Colombo	Toleman TG280-Hart	30	1h01m25.77
6	Fredy Schnarwiler	March 802-BMW	30	1h01m46.91

Winner's average speed: 127.239 mph. Pole position: Fabi, 1m56.10.
Fastest lap: Fabi, 1m57.09

1980 FINAL CHAMPIONSHIP POSITIONS

1	Brian Henton	61	10=	Alberto Colombo	9
2	Derek Warwick	42		Chico Serra	9
3	Teo Fabi	38	12	Nigel Mansell	8
4	Siegfried Stohr	29	13	Manfred Winkelhock	4
5	Andrea de Cesaris	28	14	Oscar Pedersoli	3
6	Richard Dallest	23	15	Jochen Dauer	2
7	Huub Rothengatter	21	16=	Beppe Gabbiani	1
8	Mike Thackwell	11		Fredy Schnarwiler	1
9	Miguel Angel Guerra	10		Best nine results count	

1981

MARLBORO/DAILY EXPRESS INTERNATIONAL TROPHY

29 March 1981. Silverstone. 47 laps of a 2.932-mile circuit = 137.804

miles. European F2 Championship round 1

1	Mike Thackwell	Ralt RH6/81-Honda	47	1h11m44.67
2	Ricardo Paletti	March 812-BMW	47	1h12m20.86
3	Corrado Fabi	March 812-BMW	46	
4	Jim Crawford	Toleman TG280-Hart	46	
5	Carlo Rossi	Toleman TG280-Hart	46	
6	Brian Robinson	Chevron B42-Hart	46	

Winner's average speed: 115.246 mph. Pole position: Thackwell, 1m18.59.
Fastest lap: Geoff Lees (Ralt RH6/81-Honda), 1m23.82

JIM CLARK-RENNEN

5 April 1981. Hockenheim. 30 laps of a 4.219-mile circuit = 126.570
miles. European F2 Championship round 2

1	Stefan Johansson	Toleman T850-Hart	30	1h00m28.05
2	Manfred Winkelhock	Ralt RT2-BMW	30	1h00m29.19
3	Mike Thackwell	Ralt RH6/81-Honda	30	1h00m42.62
4	Eje Elgh	Maurer MM81-BMW	30	1h00m44.87
5	Geoff Lees	Ralt RH6/81-Honda	30	1h00m45.79
6	Carlo Rossi	Toleman TG280-Hart	30	1h00m56.00

Winner's average speed: 125.591 mph. Pole position: Lees, 1m57.14.
Fastest lap: Ricardo Paletti (March 812-BMW), 1m59.26

P&O FERRIES JOCHEN RINDT TROPHY

20 April 1981. Thruxton. 55 laps of a 2.356-mile circuit = 129.580 miles.
European F2 Championship round 3

1	Roberto Guerrero	Maurer MM81-BMW	55	1h04m02.40
2	Eje Elgh	Maurer MM81-BMW	55	1h04m11.69
3	Ricardo Paletti	March 812-BMW	55	1h04m43.60
4	Johnny Cecotto	Minardi FLY281-BMW	55	1h04m59.61
5	Christian Danner	March 812-BMW	55	1h06m01.69
6*	Piero Necchi	March 812-BMW	54	

*including 1m penalty. Winner's average speed: 121.405 mph. Pole position: Thierry Boutsen (March 812-BMW), 1m06.38. Fastest lap: Marc Surer (March 812-BMW), 1m08.00

EIFELRENNEN

26 April 1981. Nurburgring. 9 laps of a 14.189-mile circuit = 127.701
miles. European F2 Championship round 4

1	Thierry Boutsen	March 812-BMW	9	1h05m04.63
2	Eje Elgh	Maurer MM81-BMW	9	1h06m06.56
3	Corrado Fabi	March 812-BMW	9	1h06m06.81
4	Stefan Johansson	Toleman T850-Hart	9	1h06m10.26
5	Geoff Lees	Ralt RH6/81-Honda	9	1h06m37.78
6	Kenneth Acheson	Toleman T850-Hart	9	1h07m05.24

Winner's average speed: 117.738 mph. Pole position: Fabi, 7m10.25.
Fastest lap: Boutsen, 7m10.33

GRAN PREMIO DI ROMA

10 May 1981. Vallelunga. 65 laps of a 1.988-mile circuit = 129.220 miles.
European F2 Championship round 5

1	Eje Elgh	Maurer MM81-BMW	65	1h16m01.14
2	Stefan Johansson	Toleman T850-Hart	65	1h16m04.42
3	Thierry Boutsen	March 812-BMW	65	1h16m07.74
4	Corrado Fabi	March 812-BMW	65	1h16m13.19
5	Geoff Lees	Ralt RH6/81-Honda	65	1h16m24.13
6	Ricardo Paletti	March 812-BMW	65	1h16m53.09

Winner's average speed: 101.990 mph. Pole position: Elgh, 1m07.79.
Fastest lap: Fabi, 1m09.06

GRAND PREMIO DI MUGELLO

24 May 1981. Mugello. 42 laps of a 3.259-mile circuit = 136.878 miles.
European F2 Championship round 6

1	Corrado Fabi	March 812-BMW	42	1h15m20.99
2	Geoff Lees	Ralt RH6/81-Honda	42	1h15m22.40
3	Piero Necchi	March 812-BMW	42	1h15m31.82
4	Eje Elgh	Maurer MM81-BMW	42	1h15m32.95

| 5 Mike Thackwell | Ralt RH6/81-Honda | 42 | 1h15m57.14 |
| 6 Roberto Guerrero | Maurer MM81-BMW | 42 | 1h16m08.59 |

Winner's average speed: 108.994 mph. Pole position: Thierry Boutsen (March 812-BMW), 1m42.82. Fastest lap: Necchi, 1m46.27

GRAND PRIX DE PAU

8 June 1981. Pau. 73 laps of a 1.715-mile circuit = 125.195 miles. European F2 Championship round 7

1 Geoff Lees	Ralt RH6/81-Honda	73	1h33m13.91
2 Thierry Boutsen	March 812-BMW	73	1h33m14.43
3 Piero Necchi	March 812-BMW	73	1h34m11.87
4 Carlo Rossi	Toleman TG280-Hart	72	
5 Eje Elgh	Maurer MM81-BMW	72	
6 Mike Thackwell	Ralt RH6/81-Honda	72	

Winner's average speed: 80.570 mph. Pole position: Michele Alboreto (Minardi FLY281-BMW), 1m13.07. Fastest lap: Lees, 1m15.00

GRAN PREMIO DEL MEDITERRANEO

26 July 1981. Enna-Pergusa. 45 laps of a 3.076-mile circuit = 138.420 miles. Race stopped after first-lap accident, restarted over original distance. European F2 Championship round 8

1 Thierry Boutsen	March 812-BMW	45	1h10m09.82
2 Huub Rothengatter	March 812-BMW	45	1h10m13.12
3 Michele Alboreto	Minardi FLY281-BMW	45	1h10m24.58
4 Roberto Guerrero	Maurer MM81-BMW	45	1h10m28.63
5 Eje Elgh	Maurer MM81-BMW	45	1h10m37.44
6 Jo Gartner	Toleman TG280-BMW	45	1h11m18.66

Winner's average speed: 118.369 mph. Pole position: Boutsen, 1m30.92. Fastest lap: Boutsen, 1m32.05

GRAND PRIX DE BELGIQUE FORMULE 2

9 August 1981. Spa-Francorchamps. 30 laps of a 4.312-mile circuit = 129.360 miles. European F2 Championship round 9

1 Geoff Lees	Ralt RH6/81-Honda	30	1h10m02.68
2 Thierry Boutsen	March 812-BMW	30	1h10m11.65
3 Eje Elgh	Maurer MM81-BMW	30	1h10m47.18
4 Corrado Fabi	March 812-BMW	30	1h10m48.95
5 Manfred Winkelhock	Maurer MM81-BMW	30	1h10m57.46
6 Jim Crawford	Toleman TG280-Hart	30	1h11m19.35

Winner's average speed: 110.809 mph. Pole position: Boutsen, 2m15.39. Fastest lap: Lees, 2m16.81

JOHN HOWITT TROPHY

16 August 1981. Donington Park. 70 laps of a 1.957-mile circuit = 137.011 miles. European F2 Championship round 10

1 Geoff Lees	Ralt RH6/81-Honda	70	1h16m49.82
2 Corrado Fabi	March 812-BMW	70	1h17m00.58
3 Manfred Winkelhock	Maurer MM81-BMW	70	1h17m18.58
4 Stefan Johansson	Toleman TG280B-Hart	70	1h17m41.10
5 Mike Thackwell	Ralt RH6/81-Honda	70	1h17m45.49
6 Johnny Cecotto	March 812-BMW	70	1h17m54.78

Winner's average speed: 106.998 mph. Pole position: Winkelhock, 1m02.74. Fastest lap: Lees and Fabi, 1m05.10

GRAN PREMIO DEL ADRATICO

6 September 1981. Misano. 60 laps of a 2.167-mile circuit = 130.020 miles. European F2 Championship round 11

1 Michele Alboreto	Minardi FLY281-BMW	60	1h12m03.74
2 Geoff Lees	Ralt RH6/81-Honda	60	1h12m12.98
3 Mike Thackwell	Ralt RH6/81-Honda	60	1h12m54.50
4 Roberto Guerrero	Maurer MM81-BMW	60	1h12m55.01
5 Richard Dallest	AGS JH18-BMW	60	1h12m55.32
6 Johnny Cecotto	March 812-BMW	60	1h13m15.33

Winner's average speed: 108.256 mph. Pole position: Thierry Boutsen (March 812-BMW), 1m10.49. Fastest lap: Alboreto and Lees, 1m11.01

MANTORP PARK F2 TROFEN

20 September 1981. Mantorp Park. 65 laps of a 1.942-mile circuit =

126.230 miles. European F2 Championship round 12

1 Stefan Johansson	Toleman TG280B-Hart	65	1h20m08.8
2 Geoff Lees	Ralt RH6/81-Honda	65	1h20m15.3
3 Kenneth Acheson	Toleman T850-Hart	65	1h20m44.5
4 Thierry Boutsen	March 812-BMW	65	1h20m45.8
5 Richard Dallest	AGS JH18-BMW	65	1h21m05.3
6 Johnny Cecotto	March 812-BMW	65	1h21m20.5

Winner's average speed: 94.499 mph. Pole position: Corrado Fabi (March 812-BMW), 1m10.09. Fastest lap: Cecotto, 1m11.69

1981 FINAL CHAMPIONSHIP POSITIONS

1	Geoff Lees	51	12=	Johnny Cecotto	6
2	Thierry Boutsen	37		Carlo Rossi	6
3	Eje Elgh	35		Huub Rothengatter	6
4	Stefan Johansson	30	15	Kenneth Acheson	5
5	Corrado Fabi	29	16=	Jim Crawford	4
6	Mike Thackwell	22		Richard Dallest	4
7	Roberto Guerrero	16	18	Christian Danner	2
8	Michele Alboreto	13	19=	Jo Gartner	1
9	Manfred Winkelhock	12		Brian Robinson	1
10	Ricardo Paletti	11		Best nine results count	
11	Piero Necchi	9			

1982

MARLBORO/DAILY EXPRESS INTERNATIONAL TROPHY

21 March 1982. Silverstone. 47 laps of a 2.932-mile circuit = 137.804 miles. European F2 Championship round 1

1 Stefan Bellof	Maurer MM82-BMW	47	1h11m51.38
2 Satoru Nakajima	March 812-Honda	47	1h12m12.64
3 Beppe Gabbiani	Maurer MM82-BMW	47	1h12m12.76
4 Roberto del Castello	Toleman TG280-BMW	47	1h12m19.06
5 Alessandro Nannini	Minardi FLY281B-BMW	47	1h12m22.86
6 Jo Gartner	March 822-BMW	47	1h12m58.08

Winner's average speed: 115.066 mph. Pole position: Stefan Johansson (Spirit 201-Honda), 1m20.91. Fastest lap: Christian Danner (March 822-BMW), 1m29.35

JIM CLARK-RENNEN

4 April 1982. Hockenheim. 30 laps of a 4.227-mile circuit = 126.810 miles. European F2 Championship round 2

1 Stefan Bellof	Maurer MM82-BMW	30	1h03m03.44
2 Thierry Boutsen	Spirit 201-Honda	30	1h03m08.23
3 Corrado Fabi	March 822-BMW	30	1h03m16.34
4 Johnny Cecotto	March 822-BMW	30	1h03m16.60
5 Beppe Gabbiani	Maurer MM82-BMW	30	1h03m28.13
6 Thierry Tassin	Toleman DS1-Hart	30	1h03m35.79

Winner's average speed: 120.662 mph. Pole position: Bellof, 2m02.05. Fastest lap: Bellof, 2m04.21

P&O FERRIES JOCHEN RINDT TROPHY

12 April 1982. Thruxton. 55 laps of a 2.356-mile circuit = 129.580 miles. European F2 Championship round 3

1 Johnny Cecotto	March 822-BMW	55	1h03m49.22
2 Kenneth Acheson	Ralt RH6/82-Honda	55	1h04m01.00
3 Thierry Boutsen	Spirit 201-Honda	55	1h04m05.09
4 Beppe Gabbiani	Maurer MM82-BMW	55	1h04m17.21
5 Philippe Streiff	AGS JH19-BMW	55	1h04m20.26
6 Richard Dallest	March 822-BMW	55	1h04m28.37

Winner's average speed: 121.823 mph. Pole position: Stefan Johansson (Spirit 201-Honda), 1m05.33. Fastest lap: Cecotto, 1m07.37

EIFELRENNEN

25 April 1982. Nurburgring. 9 laps of a 14.189-mile circuit = 127.701

miles. European F2 Championship round 4

1	Thierry Boutsen	Spirit 201-Honda	9	1h05m01.37
2	Corrado Fabi	March 822-BMW	9	1h05m01.54
3	Johnny Cecotto	March 822-BMW	9	1h05m59.35
4	Kenneth Acheson	Ralt RH6/82-Honda	9	1h06m02.15
5	Stefan Bellof	Maurer MM82-BMW	9	1h06m10.75
6	Stefan Johansson	Spirit 201-Honda	9	1h06m13.77

Winner's average speed: 117.836 mph. Pole position: Thierry Tassin (Toleman DS1-Hart), 8m21.02. Fastest lap: Bellof, 9m06.51

GRAN PREMIO DI MUGELLO

9 May 1982. Mugello. 42 laps of a 3.259-mile circuit = 136.878 miles. European F2 Championship round 5

1	Corrado Fabi	March 822-BMW	42	1h14m32.79
2	Johnny Cecotto	March 822-BMW	42	1h14m36.92
3	Stefan Johansson	Spirit 201-Honda	42	1h14m42.87
4	Thierry Boutsen	Spirit 201-Honda	42	1h14m44.05
5	Jonathan Palmer	Ralt RH6/82-Honda	42	1h14m56.67
6	Kenneth Acheson	Ralt RH6/82-Honda	42	1h15m30.82

Winner's average speed: 110.169 mph. Pole position: Johansson, 1m57.87. Fastest lap: Fabi, 1m44.21

GRAN PREMIO DI ROMA

16 May 1982. Vallelunga. 65 laps of a 1.988-mile circuit = 129.220 miles. European F2 Championship round 6

1	Corrado Fabi	March 822-BMW	65	1h15m45.40
2	Philippe Streiff	AGS JH19-BMW	65	1h15m56.23
3	Pascal Fabre	AGS JH19-BMW	65	1h16m36.31
4	Stefan Johansson	Spirit 201-Honda	64	
5	Jonathan Palmer	Ralt RH6/82-Honda	64	
6	Thierry Boutsen	Spirit 201-Honda	64	

Winner's average speed: 102.343 mph. Pole position: Johansson, 1m07.10. Fastest lap: Stefan Bellof (Maurer MM82-BMW), 1m08.63

GRAND PRIX DE PAU

31 May 1982. Pau. 73 laps of a 1.715-mile circuit = 125.195 miles. European F2 Championship round 7

1	Johnny Cecotto	March 822-BMW	73	1h31m00.03
2	Thierry Boutsen	Spirit 201-Honda	73	1h31m15.93
3	Mike Thackwell	March 822-BMW	73	1h32m17.02
4	Frank Jelinski	Maurer MM82-BMW	72	
5	Kenneth Acheson	Ralt RH6/82-Honda	72	
6	Jonathan Palmer	Ralt RH6/82-Honda	72	

Winner's average speed: 82.546 mph. Pole position: Boutsen, 1m11.23. Fastest lap: Acheson, 1m12.37

GRAND PRIX DE BELGIQUE FORMULE 2

13 June 1982. Spa-Francorchamps. 23 laps of a 4.312-mile circuit = 99.176 miles. Race scheduled for 30 laps, stopped due to heavy rain. European F2 Championship round 8

1	Thierry Boutsen	Spirit 201-Honda	23	58m17.47
2	Johnny Cecotto	March 822-BMW	23	58m40.06
3	Mike Thackwell	March 822-BMW	23	59m05.44
4	Philippe Streiff	AGS JH19-BMW	23	59m11.00
5	Corrado Fabi	March 822-BMW	23	59m14.17
6	Jonathan Palmer	Ralt RH6/82-Honda	23	1h00m07.55

Winner's average speed: 102.083 mph. Pole position: Stefan Johansson (Spirit 201-Honda), 2m13.10. Fastest lap: Thackwell, 2m29.48

RHEIN POKAL-RENNEN

20 June 1982. Hockenheim. 30 laps of a 4.227-mile circuit = 126.810 miles. European F2 Championship round 9

1	Corrado Fabi	March 822-BMW	30	1h03m04.32
2	Beppe Gabbiani	Maurer MM82-BMW	30	1h03m06.92
3	Stefan Bellof	Maurer MM82-BMW	30	1h03m08.52
4	Stefan Johansson	Spirit 201-Honda	30	1h03m46.63
5	Frank Jelinski	Maurer MM82-BMW	30	1h03m49.83
6	Johnny Cecotto	March 822-BMW	30	1h03m51.26

Winner's average speed: 120.634 mph. Pole position: Thierry Boutsen (Spirit 201-Honda), 2m02.00. Fastest lap: Fabi, 2m04.28

JOHN HOWITT TROPHY

4 July 1982. Donington Park. 70 laps of a 1.957-mile circuit = 137.011 miles. European F2 Championship round 10

1	Corrado Fabi	March 822-BMW	70	1h15m42.11
2	Johnny Cecotto	March 822-BMW	70	1h15m42.70
3	Jonathan Palmer	Ralt RH6/82-Honda	70	1h15m57.70
4	Beppe Gabbiani	Maurer MM82-BMW	70	1h16m08.49
5	Philippe Streiff	AGS JH19-BMW	70	1h16m12.60
6	Stefan Bellof	Maurer MM82-BMW	70	1h16m15.95

Winner's average speed: 108.593 mph. Pole position: Palmer, 1m02.21. Fastest lap: Fabi, 1m03.82

MANTORP PARK F2 TROFEN

18 July 1982. Mantorp Park. 65 laps of a 1.942-mile circuit = 126.230 miles. European F2 Championship round 11

1	Johnny Cecotto	March 822-BMW	65	1h18m28.40
2	Philippe Streiff	AGS JH19-BMW	65	1h18m53.80
3	Beppe Gabbiani	Maurer MM82-BMW	65	1h18m58.10
4	Thierry Boutsen	Spirit 201-Honda	65	1h19m29.11
5	Christian Danner	March 822-BMW	65	1h19m31.80
6	Pascal Fabre	AGS JH19-BMW	64	

Winner's average speed: 96.514 mph. Pole position: Corrado Fabi (March 822-BMW), 1m09.40. Fastest lap: not published

GRAN PREMIO DEL MEDITERRANEO

1 August 1982. Enna-Pergusa. 45 laps of a 3.076-mile circuit = 138.420 miles. European F2 Championship round 12

1	Thierry Boutsen	Spirit 201-Honda	45	1h09m22.15
2	Stefan Bellof	Maurer MM82-BMW	45	1h09m26.42
3	Johnny Cecotto	March 822-BMW	45	1h10m32.23
4	Philippe Streiff	AGS JH19-BMW	45	1h10m43.61
5	Frank Jelinski	Maurer MM82-BMW	45	1h10m45.07
6	Christian Danner	March 822-BMW	44	

Winner's average speed: 119.725 mph. Pole position: Boutsen, 1m30.44. Fastest lap: Bellof, 1m30.75

GRAN PREMIO DEL ADRIATICO

7 August 1982. Misano. 60 laps of a 2.167-mile circuit = 130.020 miles. European F2 Championship round 13

1	Corrado Fabi	March 822-BMW	60	1h18m25.19
2	Alessandro Nannini	Minardi FLY281B-BMW	60	1h18m35.58
3	Beppe Gabbiani	Maurer MM82-BMW	60	1h18m40.28
4	Christian Danner	March 822-BMW	60	1h18m55.21
5	Stefan Bellof	Maurer MM82-BMW	60	1h18m56.33
6	Thierry Boutsen	Spirit 201-Honda	60	1h19m10.60

Winner's average speed: 99.480 mph. Pole position: Fabi, 1m08.68. Fastest lap: Bellof, 1m10.89

1982 FINAL CHAMPIONSHIP POSITIONS

1	Corrado Fabi	57	12	Frank Jelinski	7
2	Johnny Cecotto	56 (57)*	13=	Christian Danner	6
3	Thierry Boutsen	50 (51)*		Satoru Nakajima	6
4	Stefan Bellof	33	15	Pascal Fabre	5
5	Beppe Gabbiani	26	16	Roberto del Castello	3
6	Philippe Streiff	22	17=	Richard Dallest	1
7	Kenneth Acheson	12		Jo Gartner	1
8	Stefan Johansson	11		Thierry Tassin	1
9	Jonathan Palmer	10		*Best nine results count	
10=	Alessandro Nannini	8			
	Mike Thackwell	8			

1983

MARLBORO/DAILY EXPRESS INTERNATIONAL TROPHY

20 March 1983. Silverstone. 47 laps of a 2.932-mile circuit = 137.804 miles. European F2 Championship round 1

1	Beppe Gabbiani	March 832-BMW	47	1h08m30.71
2	Mike Thackwell	Ralt RH6/83-Honda	47	1h08m57.31
3	Christian Danner	March 832-BMW	47	1h09m40.25
4	Stefan Bellof	Maurer MM83-BMW	46	throttle cable
5	Philippe Streiff	AGS JH19B-BMW	46	
6	Lamberto Leoni	March 832-BMW	46	

Winner's average speed: 120.683 mph. Pole position: Dave Scott (March 832-BMW), 1m16.95. Fastest lap: Bellof, 1m19.93

P&O FERRIES JOCHEN RINDT TROPHY

4 April 1983. Thruxton. 55 laps of a 2.356-mile circuit = 129.580 miles. European F2 Championship round 2

1	Beppe Gabbiani	March 832-BMW	55	1h03m54.06
2	Mike Thackwell	Ralt RH6/83-Honda	55	1h04m01.91
3	Jonathan Palmer	Ralt RH6/83-Honda	55	1h04m08.57
4	Thierry Tassin	March 832-BMW	55	1h04m24.64
5	Philippe Alliot	Martini 001-BMW	55	1h04m42.34
6	Frank Jelinski	Maurer MM82-BMW	54	

Winner's average speed: 121.669 mph. Pole position: Thackwell, 1m05.78. Fastest lap: Thackwell, 1m07.70

JIM CLARK-RENNEN

10 April 1983. Hockenheim. 30 laps of a 4.227-mile circuit = 126.810 miles. European F2 Championship round 3

1	Jonathan Palmer	Ralt RH6/83-Honda	30	1h02m25.22
2	Christian Danner	March 832-BMW	30	1h02m47.52
3	Mike Thackwell	Ralt RH6/83-Honda	30	1h03m15.02
4	Jo Gartner	Spirit 201-BMW	30	1h03m20.50
5	Alessandro Nannini	Minardi M283-BMW	30	1h03m53.14
6	Thierry Tassin	March 832-BMW	30	1h03m56.36

Winner's average speed: 121.893 mph. Pole position: Lamberto Leoni (March 832-BMW), 2m14.43. Fastest lap: Palmer, 2m03.76

EIFELRENNEN

24 April 1983. Nurburgring. 9 laps of a 12.944-mile circuit = 116.496 miles. European F2 Championship round 4

1	Beppe Gabbiani	March 832-BMW	9	58m46.44
2	Alessandro Nannini	Minardi FLY281B-BMW	9	58m53.41
3	Christian Danner	March 832-BMW	9	58m58.26
4	Jonathan Palmer	Ralt RH6/83-Honda	9	59m34.28
5	Alain Ferte	Maurer MM83-BMW	9	59m39.53
6	Thierry Tassin	March 832-BMW	9	59m40.64

Winner's average speed: 118.926 mph. Pole position: Danner, 6m26.19. Fastest lap: Danner, 6m28.03

GRAN PREMIO DI ROMA

8 May 1983. Vallelunga. 65 laps of a 1.988-mile circuit = 129.220 miles. European F2 Championship round 5

1	Beppe Gabbiani	March 832-BMW	65	1h14m59.60
2	Jonathan Palmer	Ralt RH6/83-Honda	65	1h15m09.85
3	Mike Thackwell	Ralt RH6/83-Honda	65	1h15m28.87
4	Thierry Tassin	March 832-BMW	65	1h15m29.34
5	Philippe Streiff	AGS JH19B-BMW	65	1h15m43.82
6	Guido Dacco	Toleman T850-BMW	64	

Winner's average speed: 103.385 mph. Pole position: Gabbiani, 1m06.16. Fastest lap: Gabbiani, 1m08.14

GRAND PRIX DE PAU

23 May 1983. Pau. 73 laps of a 1.715-mile circuit = 125.195 miles. European F2 Championship round 6

1	Jo Gartner	Spirit 201-BMW	73	1h45m18.65
2	Kenneth Acheson	Maurer MM83-BMW	73	1h45m44.56
3	Jonathan Palmer	Ralt RH6/83-Honda	73	1h46m12.61
4	Thierry Tassin	March 832-BMW	73	1h46m24.58
5	Christian Danner	March 832-BMW	73	1h46m24.89
6	Rolf Biland	March 832-BMW	69	

Alain Ferte (Maurer MM83-BMW), 1h45m08.06, and Stefan Bellof (Maurer MM83-BMW), 1h45m30.81, finished first and third on the road but were disqualified due to their cars being under the weight limit. Winner's average speed: 71.329 mph. Pole position: Bellof, 1m11.87. Fastest lap: not available (Bellof, 1m13.12 was subsequently disqualified)

GRAN PREMIO DE MADRID

12 June 1983. Jarama. 65 laps of a 2.115-mile circuit = 137.501 miles. European F2 Championship round 7

1	Mike Thackwell	Ralt RH6/83-Honda	65	1h28m50.80
2	Stefan Bellof	Maurer MM83-BMW	65	1h28m53.16
3	Jonathan Palmer	Ralt RH6/83-Honda	65	1h29m06.29
4	Philippe Streiff	AGS JH19B-BMW	65	1h29m25.62
5	Alain Ferte	Maurer MM83-BMW	65	1h29m29.99
6	Enrique Mansilla	March 832-BMW	65	1h29m43.15

Winner's average speed: 92.857 mph. Pole position: Palmer, 1m16.79. Fastest lap: Thackwell, 1m20.02

DONINGTON PARK EUROPEAN F2 TROPHY

25 June 1983. Donington Park. 70 laps of a 1.957-mile circuit = 137.011 miles. European F2 Championship round 8

1	Jonathan Palmer	Ralt RH6/83-Honda	70	1h16m39.02
2	Mike Thackwell	Ralt RH6/83-Honda	70	1h16m57.39
3	Philippe Streiff	AGS JH19B-BMW	70	1h17m18.12
4	Kazuyoshi Hoshino	March 832-BMW	70	1h17m23.96
5	Christian Danner	March 832-BMW	70	1h17m35.50
6	Dave Scott	March 832-BMW	69	

Winner's average speed: 107.249 mph. Pole position: Palmer, 1m00.93. Fastest lap: Thackwell, 1m04.69

TROFEO RICARDO PALETTI

24 July 1983. Misano. 58 laps of a 2.167-mile circuit = 125.686 miles. European F2 Championship round 9

1	Jonathan Palmer	Ralt RH6/83-Honda	58	1h09m37.74
2	Pierluigi Martini	Minardi M283-BMW	58	1h10m41.61
3	Roberto del Castello	March 832-BMW	58	1h10m50.60
4	Guido Dacco	March 832-BMW	57	
5	Fulvio Ballabio	AGS JH19B-BMW	57	
6	Fredy Lienhard	March 832-BMW	55	

Winner's average speed: 108.305 mph. Pole position: Philippe Alliot (Martini 001-BMW), 1m09.21. Fastest lap: Alliot, 1m10.95

GRAN PREMIO DEL MEDITERRANEO

31 July 1983. Enna-Pergusa. 45 laps of a 3.076-mile circuit = 138.420 miles. European F2 Championship round 10

1	Jonathan Palmer	Ralt RH6/83-Honda	45	1h10m11.30
2	Philippe Streiff	AGS JH19B-BMW	45	1h10m18.07
3	Mike Thackwell	Ralt RH6/83-Honda	45	1h10m24.63
4	Beppe Gabbiani	March 832-BMW	45	1h10m45.71
5	Jo Gartner	Spirit 201-BMW	45	1h10m58.19
6	Michel Ferte	Martini 001-BMW	45	1h10m59.94

Winner's average speed: 118.327 mph. Pole position: Thackwell, 1m30.82. Fastest lap: Alessandro Nannini (Minardi M283-BMW), 1m31.37

GRAND PRIX DE BELGIQUE FORMULE 2

21 August 1983. Zolder. 46 laps of a 2.648-mile circuit = 121.808 miles. Race scheduled for 48 laps, stopped after first-lap accident, restarted over reduced distance. European F2 Championship round 11

1	Jonathan Palmer	Ralt RH6/83-Honda	46	1h06m12.03
2	Mike Thackwell	Ralt RH6/83-Honda	46	1h06m22.86
3	Philippe Streiff	AGS JH19B-BMW	46	1h06m55.98
4	Christian Danner	March 832-BMW	46	1h06m57.41
5	Philippe Alliot	Martini 001-BMW	46	1h07m06.03
6	Enrique Mansilla	March 832-BMW	46	1h07m26.92

Winner's average speed: 110.399 mph. Pole position: Palmer, 1m24.09.
Fastest lap: Palmer, 1m25.09

GRAN PREMIO DI MUGELLO

4 September 1983. Mugello. 42 laps of a 3.259-mile circuit = 136.878 miles. European F2 Championship round 12

1	Jonathan Palmer	Ralt RH6/83-Honda	42	1h14m58.38
2	Mike Thackwell	Ralt RH6/83-Honda	42	1h14m58.70
3	Philippe Streiff	AGS JH19B-BMW	42	1h16m06.00
4	Alessandro Nannini	Minardi M283-BMW	42	1h16m27.42
5	Dave Scott	March 832-BMW	42	1h16m32.69
6	Fulvio Ballabio	AGS JH19-BMW	41	

Winner's average speed: 109.542 mph. Pole position: Palmer, 1m40.73.
Fastest lap: Palmer, 1m45.69

1983 FINAL CHAMPIONSHIP POSITIONS

1	Jonathan Palmer	68 (75)*	16=	Fulvio Ballabio	3
2	Mike Thackwell	51		Kazuyoshi Hoshino	3
3	Beppe Gabbiani	39		Dave Scott	3
4	Philippe Streiff	25	19	Enrique Mansilla	2
5	Christian Danner	21	20=	Rolf Biland	1
6	Jo Gartner	14		Michel Ferte	1
7=	Alessandro Nannini	11		Frank Jelinski	1
	Thierry Tassin	11		Lamberto Leoni	1
9	Stefan Bellof	9		Fredy Lienhard	1
10=	Kenneth Acheson	6		*Best nine results count	
	Pierluigi Martini	6			
12=	Philippe Alliot	4			
	Roberto del Castello	4			
	Guido Dacco	4			
	Alain Ferte	4			

1984

MARLBORO/DAILY EXPRESS INTERNATIONAL TROPHY

1 April 1984. Silverstone. 47 laps of a 2.932-mile circuit = 137.804 miles. European F2 Championship round 1

1	Mike Thackwell	Ralt RH6/84-Honda	47	1h01m04.11
2	Roberto Moreno	Ralt RH6/84-Honda	47	1h01m38.25
3	Michel Ferte	Martini 002-BMW	46	
4	Thierry Tassin	March 842-BMW	46	
5	Pascal Fabre	March 842-BMW	46	
6	Emanuele Pirro	March 842-BMW	46	

Winner's average speed: 135.393 mph. Pole position: Moreno, 1m14.82.
Fastest lap: Thackwell, 1m16.00

JIM CLARK-RENNEN

8 April 1984. Hockenheim. 30 laps of a 4.227-mile circuit = 126.810 miles. European F2 Championship round 2

1	Roberto Moreno	Ralt RH6/84-Honda	30	1h01m43.63
2	Mike Thackwell	Ralt RH6/84-Honda	30	1h01m44.16
3	Michel Ferte	Martini 002-BMW	30	1h02m16.49
4	Emanuele Pirro	March 842-BMW	30	1h02m23.55
5	Philippe Streiff	AGS JH19C-BMW	30	1h02m26.35
6	Christian Danner	March 842-BMW	30	1h02m28.37

Winner's average speed: 123.262 mph. Pole position: Ferte, 2m00.19.
Fastest lap: Thackwell, 2m01.21

P&O FERRIES JOCHEN RINDT TROPHY

23 April 1984. Thruxton. 55 laps of a 2.356-mile circuit = 129.580 miles. European F2 Championship round 3

1	Mike Thackwell	Ralt RH6/84-Honda	55	1h03m11.78
2	Christian Danner	March 842-BMW	55	1h03m33.05
3	Philippe Streiff	AGS JH19C-BMW	55	1h04m22.51
4	Emanuele Pirro	March 842-BMW	54	

5	Thierry Tassin	March 842-BMW	54
6	Didier Theys	Martini 002-BMW	54

Winner's average speed: 123.026 mph. Pole position: Thackwell, 1m05.68.
Fastest lap: Thackwell, 1m07.38

GRAN PREMIO DI ROMA

13 May 1984. Vallelunga. 65 laps of a 1.988-mile circuit = 129.220 miles. European F2 Championship round 4

1	Mike Thackwell	Ralt RH6/84-Honda	65	1h15m59.41
2	Roberto Moreno	Ralt RH6/84-Honda	65	1h16m17.87
3	Christian Danner	March 842-BMW	65	1h16m37.94
4	Michel Ferte	Martini 002-BMW	64	
5	Pascal Fabre	March 842-BMW	64	
6	Didier Theys	Martini 002-BMW	64	

Winner's average speed: 102.029 mph. Pole position: Thackwell, 1m05.69.
Fastest lap: Thackwell, 1m07.38

TROFEO BANCA TOSCANA/GRAN PREMIO DI MUGELLO

19 May 1984. Mugello. 42 laps of a 3.259-mile circuit = 136.878 miles. European F2 Championship round 5

1	Mike Thackwell	Ralt RH6/84-Honda	42	1h13m38.89
2	Michel Ferte	Martini 002-BMW	42	1h14m58.89
3	Christian Danner	March 842-BMW	42	1h15m00.93
4	Emanuele Pirro	March 842-BMW	42	1h15m15.35
5	Thierry Tassin	March 842-BMW	41	
6	Didier Theys	Martini 002-BMW	41	

Winner's average speed: 111.512 mph. Pole position: Danner, 1m39.45.
Fastest lap: Thackwell, 1m43.92

GRAND PRIX DE PAU

11 June 1984. Pau. 73 laps of a 1.715-mile circuit = 125.195 miles. European F2 Championship round 6

1	Mike Thackwell	Ralt RH6/84-Honda	73	1h29m39.73
2	Philippe Streiff	AGS JH19C-BMW	73	1h30m20.59
3	Roberto Moreno	Ralt RH6/84-Honda	73	1h30m23.45
4	Christian Danner	March 842-BMW	73	1h30m41.70
5	Alain Ferte	Martini 002-BMW	73	1h30m48.82
6	Pierre Petit	March 842-BMW	72	

Winner's average speed: 83.778 mph. Pole position: Thackwell, 1m10.51.
Fastest lap: Thackwell, 1m12.65

RHEIN POKAL-RENNEN

24 June 1984. Hockenheim. 30 laps of a 4.227-mile circuit = 126.810 miles. European F2 Championship round 7

1	Pascal Fabre	March 842-BMW	30	1h02m20.22
2	Thierry Tassin	March 842-BMW	30	1h02m27.14
3	Michel Ferte	Martini 002-BMW	30	1h02m28.63
4	Alessandro Nannini	Minardi M283-BMW	30	1h02m29.28
5	Pierre Petit	March 842-BMW	30	1h03m10.93
6	Roberto del Castello	Minardi M283-BMW	30	1h03m11.49

Winner's average speed: 122.056 mph. Pole position: Mike Thackwell (Ralt RH6/84-Honda), 2m00.33. Fastest lap: Thackwell, 2m01.73

GRAN PREMIO DEL ADRIATICO

22 July 1984. Misano. 58 laps of a 2.167-mile circuit = 125.686 miles. European F2 Championship round 8

1	Mike Thackwell	Ralt RH6/84-Honda	58	1h08m15.71
2	Philippe Streiff	AGS JH19C-BMW	57	
3	Pierre Petit	March 842-BMW	57	
4	Thierry Tassin	March 842-BMW	57	
5	Guido Dacco	March 832-BMW	57	
6	Christian Danner	March 842-BMW	57	

Winner's average speed: 110.474 mph. Pole position: Roberto Moreno (Ralt RH6/84-Honda), 1m08.72. Fastest lap: Moreno, 1m08.5

GRAN PREMIO DEL MEDITERRANEO

29 July 1984. Enna-Pergusa. 45 laps of a 3.076-mile circuit = 138.420 miles. European F2 Championship round 9

1	Mike Thackwell	Ralt RH6/84-Honda	45	1h08m55.21
2	Roberto Moreno	Ralt RH6/84-Honda	45	1h08m57.71
3	Alessandro Nannini	Minardi M283-BMW	45	1h09m27.21
4	Pierre Petit	March 842-BMW	45	1h09m27.23
5	Michel Ferte	Martini 002-BMW	45	1h10m11.07
6	Emanuele Pirro	March 842-BMW	45	1h10m21.32

Winner's average speed: 120.505 mph. Pole position: Thackwell, 1m29.48.
Fastest lap: Thackwell, 1m30.09

DERBY EVENING TELEGRAPH TROPHY

27 August 1984. Donington Park. 70 laps of a 1.957-mile circuit = 137.011 miles. European F2 Championship round 10

1	Roberto Moreno	Ralt RH6/84-Honda	70	1h16m32.37
2	Emanuele Pirro	March 842-BMW	70	1h16m46.50
3	Christian Danner	March 842-BMW	70	1h16m47.76
4	Mike Thackwell	Ralt RH6/84-Honda	70	1h16m51.35
5	Thierry Tassin	March 842-BMW	70	1h16m59.21
6	"Pierre Chauvet"	March 842-BMW	69	

Winner's average speed: 107.404 mph. Pole position: Thackwell, 1m01.06.
Fastest lap: Thackwell, 1m04.37

DAILY MAIL TROPHY

23 September 1984. Brands Hatch. 47 laps of a 2.614-mile circuit = 122.839 miles. Race scheduled for 50 laps, stopped after 31 laps due to rain, restarted over an additional 16 laps. European F2 Championship round 11

1	Philippe Streiff	AGS JH19C-BMW	47	1h09m11.39
2	Michel Ferte	Martini 002-BMW	47	1h10m21.48
3	Roberto Moreno	Ralt RH6/84-Honda	47	1h10m32.38
4	Tomas Kaiser	March 842-BMW	47	1h10m34.84
5	Alessandro Nannini	Minardi M283-BMW	47	1h10m51.63
6	Emanuele Pirro	March 842-BMW	46	

Winner's average speed: 106.524 mph. Pole position: Moreno, 1m16.63.
Fastest lap: Moreno, 1m18.57

1984 FINAL CHAMPIONSHIP POSITIONS

1	Mike Thackwell	72	10	Alessandro Nannini	9
2	Roberto Moreno	44	11=	Tomas Kaiser	3
3	Michel Ferte	29		Didier Theys	3
4	Philippe Streiff	27	13=	Guido Dacco	2
5	Christian Danner	23		Alain Ferte	2
6=	Emanuele Pirro	18	15=	Roberto del Castello	1
	Thierry Tassin	18		"Pierre Chauvet"	1
8	Pascal Fabre	13		Best nine results count	
9	Pierre Petit	10			

1984 Mike Thackwell, the final European Formula 2 champion, and the Ralt RH6/84-Honda at Donington Park.

Records

STARTS

Alberto Colombo	74	Tetsu Ikuzawa	24	Didier Pironi	13	Andy Sutcliffe	7
Mike Thackwell	52	Jochen Mass	24	Johnny Servoz-Gavin	13	Adrian Wilkins	7
Beppe Gabbiani	50	Hans Binder	23	Cosimo Turizio	13	Wink Bancroft	6
Brian Henton	49	Derek Daly	23	Kurt Ahrens Jr	12	Mike Beckwith	6
Jean-Pierre Jabouille	49	Willi Deutsch	23	Andrea de Cesaris	12	Tom Belso	6
Guido Dacco	48	Jonathan Palmer	23	Nanni Galli	12	Max Bonnin	6
Christian Danner	47	Siegfried Stohr	23	Roberto Guerrero	12	Warren Booth	6
Eddie Cheever	46	John Watson	23	Masami Kuwashima	12	Helmut Bross	6
Michel Leclere	43	Jacques Coulon	22	Wolfgang Locher	12	John Cannon	6
Jean-Pierre Jaussaud	42	Bill Gubelmann	22	Alan Rees	12	Christian Ethuin	6
Giancarlo Martini	41	Fredy Schnarwiler	22	Chico Serra	12	Divina Galica	6
Eje Elgh	40	Derek Warwick	22	Rolf Stommelen	12	Markus Hotz	6
Patrick Tambay	39	Stefan Bellof	21	Andrea de Adamich	11	James Hunt	6
Patrick Depailler	37	Roland Binder	21	Fulvio Ballabio	11	Franz Konrad	6
Jean-Pierre Beltoise	36	Piers Courage	21	Harald Brutschin	11	Kim Mather	6
Maurizio Flammini	36	Giorgio Francia	21	Claudio Francisci	11	Hans Meier	6
Jo Gartner	36	Peter Gethin	21	Frank Gardner	11	Jean-Pierre Paoli	6
Tim Schenken	36	Tomas Kaiser	21	Robs Lamplough	11	Luciano Pavesi	6
Philippe Streiff	36	Hiroshi Kazato	21	Roberto Moreno	11	Bruno Pescia	6
Richard Dallest	35	Freddy Kottulinsky	21	Jackie Oliver	11	Alain Serpaggi	6
Alessandro Nannini	35	Pierre Petit	21	Guido Pardini	11	Alfred Amweg	5
Roberto del Castello	33	Carlo Rossi	21	Emanuele Pirro	11	Johnny Blades	5
Marc Surer	33	Niki Lauda	20	Bobby Rahal	11	Hans-Georg Burger	5
Derek Bell	32	Xavier Perrot	20	Juan Traverso	11	John Cardwell	5
Vittorio Brambilla	32	Alessandro Pesenti-Rossi	20	Alistair Walker	11	Jim Clark	5
Ingo Hoffmann	32	Robin Widdows	20	Michele Alboreto	10	Alain Couderc	5
Jacques Laffite	32	Reine Wisell	20	Philippe Alliot	10	Jochen Dauer	5
Piero Necchi	31	Claude Bourgoignie	19	Alain Ferte	10	Bernard Devaney	5
Tino Brambilla	30	Pascal Fabre	19	Sten Gunnarsson	10	Giancarlo Gagliardi	5
"Pierre Chauvet"	30	Emerson Fittipaldi	19	Chris Irwin	10	Walter Habegger	5
Miguel Angel Guerra	30	Jochen Rindt	19	Gerard Larrousse	10	Beat Jans	5
Henri Pescarolo	30	Mike Beuttler	18	Gaudenzio Mantova	10	Max Mosley	5
Ronnie Peterson	30	Dave Morgan	18	Francois Migault	10	Satoru Nakajima	5
Manfred Winkelhock	30	David Purley	18	Alan Rollinson	10	Guillermo Ortega	5
Kenneth Acheson	29	Sandro Cinotti	17	Jody Scheckter	10	Hector Rebaque	5
Graham Hill	29	Frank Jelinski	17	Dave Scott	10	Brian Redman	5
Bernard de Dryver	28	Geoff Lees	17	Jackie Stewart	10	Pedro Rodriguez	5
Lamberto Leoni	28	Ray Mallock	17	Aldo Bertuzzi	9	Bertil Roos	5
Silvio Moser	28	Arturo Merzario	17	Norman Dickson	9	Giovanni Salvati	5
Carlos Reutemann	28	Ricardo Paletti	17	Sewi Hopfer	9	Peter Scharmann	5
Alex Ribeiro	28	Carlos Ruesch	17	Chris Lambert	9	Danny Sullivan	5
Keke Rosberg	28	Duilio Truffo	17	Jurg Lienhard	9	John Surtees	5
Huub Rothengatter	28	Gerry Birrell	16	Brett Lunger	9	Hannelore Werner	5
Johnny Cecotto	27	Mike Hailwood	16	Enrique Mansilla	9	Giacomo Agostini	4
Francois Cevert	27	Brian Hart	16	Paul Smith	9	Dieter Braun	4
"Gianfranco"	27	Jacky Ickx	16	Bernd Terbeck	9	Brian Cullen	4
Peter Westbury	27	Roberto Marazzi	16	Colin Vandervell	9	Andrew Fletcher	4
Rene Arnoux	26	Paolo Barilla	15	Roger Williamson	9	Gunther Gebhardt	4
Jose Dolhem	26	Loris Kessel	15	Paolo Bozzetto	8	Ian Grob	4
Wilson Fittipaldi	26	Richard Scott	15	Jack Brabham	8	Mikko Kozarowitsky	4
Jean-Pierre Jarier	26	Jo Siffert	15	Enzo Corti	8	Cocho Lopez	4
Stefan Johansson	26	Gianfranco Brancatelli	14	Bruno Frey	8	Corrado Manfredini	4
Joseph Vonlanthen	26	Jim Crawford	14	Patrick Gaillard	8	Nigel Mansell	4
Ricardo Zunino	26	Michel Ferte	14	Boy Hayje	8	Helmut Marko	4
Thierry Boutsen	25	Carlo Giorgio	14	Helmut Henzler	8	Roland Minder	4
Corrado Fabi	25	Klaus Ludwig	14	Patrick Neve	8	Tiff Needell	4
Bruno Giacomelli	25	Riccardo Patrese	14	Jean-Louis Schlesser	8	Lorenzo Niccolini	4
Oscar Pedersoli	25	Tom Pryce	14	Jorg Siegrist	8	Eric Offenstadt	4
Dieter Quester	25	Stephen South	14	Didier Theys	8	Adam Potocki	4
Clay Regazzoni	25	John Wingfield	14	Rolf Biland	7	Walter Raus	4
Gabriele Serblin	25	Elio de Angelis	13	Don Briedenbach	7	Jeremy Richardson	4
Hans-Joachim Stuck	25	Ariel Bakst	13	J David Briggs	7	Philip Robinson	4
Thierry Tassin	25	Patrick Dal Bo	13	Malcolm Guthrie	7	Roland Salamon	4
Bob Wollek	25	Piercarlo Ghinzani	13	Cliff Hansen	7	Bob Salisbury	4
Rad Dougall	24	Hubert Hahne	13	Markus Hottinger	7	Manfred Schurti	4
Harald Ertl	24	Xavier Lapeyre	13	Werner Lindermann	7	Chris Amon	3
Teo Fabi	24	Carlos Pace	13	Stefano Livio	7	Mika Arpiainen	3
				Francois Mazet	7	Eddy Bianchi	3
				Brendan McInerney	7	Paul Blum	3
				Torsten Palm	7	Bernard Chevanne	3
				Ian Raby	7	Juan Cochesa	3
				Jo Schlesser	7	Bruno Corradi	3

Formula 2

STARTS (cont.)

Alain Cudini	3	Hans-Peter Pandur	2
Lian Duarte	3	John Pollock	2
Peter Gaydon	3	Antonio Prado	2
Kazuyoshi Hoshino	3	Brian Robinson	2
Oscar Larrauri	3	Marco Rocca	2
Fredy Lienhard	3	Vern Schuppan	2
Guy Ligier	3	"Shangry La"	2
Freddy Link	3	Willy Siller	2
Ricardo Londono-Bridge	3	Harry Stiller	2
Willi Lovato	3	Peter Stuertz	2
Dave McConnell	3	Trevor Taylor	2
Bruce McLaren	3	Hermann Unold	2
Chris Meek	3	Emilio de Villota	2
Gerhard Mitter	3	Dave Walker	2
Bob Muir	3	Mike Walker	2
Herbert Muller	3	Tom Walkinshaw	2
Gunnar Nilsson	3	Chris Williams	2
Anders Olofsson	3	Gregg Young	2
Axel Plankenhorn	3	John l'Amie	1
Ferrante Ponti	3	"M Arriva"	1
Alain Prost	3	Jorge de Bagration	1
Tommy Reid	3	Ken Bailey	1
Richard Robarts	3	Roy Baker	1
Hans Royer	3	Pasquale Barberio	1
Adrian Russell	3	Dick Barker	1
Peter Schindler	3	Eugenio Baturone	1
Alex Soler-Roig	3	Franco Bernabei	1
Marc Sourd	3	Jean Blanc	1
Eugen Strahl	3	Maxime Bochet	1
Patrick Studer	3	Gino Bollinger	1
Ted Wentz	3	Jo Bonnier	1
Jonathan Williams	3	Willy Braillard	1
Richard Attwood	2	Marco Brand	1
Walter Baltisser	2	Max Busslinger	1
Patrick Bardinon	2	Benedicto Caldarella	1
Dieter Basche	2	Romeo Camathias	1
Gerd Biechteler	2	Roberto Campominosi	1
Graham Birrell	2	Mario Casoni	1
Michael Bleekemolen	2	Andre Chevalley	1
Bernd Brutschin	2	David Cole	1
Francesco Cerulli Irelli	2	Derek Cook	1
Enzo Coloni	2	Mike Costin	1
Stanley Dickens	2	Chris Craft	1
Spartico Dini	2	Paul Craven	1
Jorg Dubler	2	Hakan Dahlqvist	1
Bruno Eichmann	2	Allan Deacon	1
Bob Evans	2	Pierre Dieudonne	1
Carlo Facetti	2	Rudolf Dotsch	1
Jean-Claude Favre	2	Guy Edwards	1
Roby Filannino	2	Vic Elford	1
Helmut Gall	2	Robert Ellice	1
"Gimax"	2	Roberto Farnetti	1
Tom Gloy	2	Laurent Ferrier	1
Mike Goth	2	Julian Gerard	1
David Hobbs	2	Harald Grohs	1
Gunther Huber	2	Ami Guichard	1
Denny Hulme	2	Henning Hagenbauer	1
Bill Ivy	2	Armin Hahne	1
Carlos Jarque	2	Bert Hawthorne	1
Helmut Kalenborn	2	Hans Heyer	1
Rupert Keegan	2	Howdy Holmes	1
Peter Korda	2	Francy Jerancic	1
Michael Korten	2	Reinhold Joest	1
Motoharu Kurosawa	2	Alan Jones	1
Graeme Lawrence	2	Eddie Jordan	1
Bob Marsland	2	Paul Keller	1
Jean Max	2	James King	1
Graham McRae	2	Wolfgang Klein	1
Sergio Mignotti	2	Helmuth Koinigg	1
John Miles	2	Gernot Lamby	1
Lionel Noghes	2	Jan Lammers	1

Gijs van Lennep	1	Ettore Ricci	1
John Lepp	1	Kurt Rieder	1
Arie Luyendyk	1	Tony Rouff	1
Arthur Mallock	1	Georges Schafer	1
Pierluigi Martini	1	Rob Slotemaker	1
Bo Martinsson	1	Moises Solana	1
Keiji Matsumoto	1	Mike Spence	1
Iain McLaren	1	Bartl Stadler	1
Jimmy Mieusset	1	Wyatt Stanley	1
Fausto Morello	1	Hubert Striebig	1
Valentino Musetti	1	Marcel Tarres	1
Piero Nappi	1	Danilo Tesini	1
Brian Nelson	1	Jimmy Veitch	1
John Nicholson	1	Gilles Villeneuve	1
John Nielsen	1	Francesco Vinto	1
Gunnar Nordstrom	1	Udo Wagenhauser	1
Gunnar Palm	1	Peter Wardle	1
Walter Pedrazzi	1	Cyd Williams	1
Alain Peltier	1	Peter Williams	1
Larry Perkins	1	Bernhard Wissler	1
Gianluigi Picchi	1	Severo Zampatti	1
Roy Pike	1		
Herve Regout	1		

WINS

Jochen Rindt	12	Stefan Johansson	2
Bruno Giacomelli	11	Roberto Moreno	2
Mike Thackwell	9	Henri Pescarolo	2
Jean-Pierre Jarier	7	Tim Schenken	2
Jacques Laffite	7	Marc Surer	2
Rene Arnoux	6	Patrick Tambay	2
Corrado Fabi	6	Michele Alboreto	1
Emerson Fittipaldi	6	Derek Bell	1
Brian Henton	6	Mike Beuttler	1
Jonathan Palmer	6	Andrea de Cesaris	1
Ronnie Peterson	6	Jim Clark	1
Thierry Boutsen	5	Jacques Coulon	1
Jean-Pierre Jabouille	5	Piers Courage	1
Hans-Joachim Stuck	5	Rad Dougall	1
Jean-Pierre Beltoise	4	Pascal Fabre	1
Eddie Cheever	4	Frank Gardner	1
Patrick Depailler	4	Jo Gartner	1
Beppe Gabbiani	4	Peter Gethin	1
Michel Leclere	4	Roberto Guerrero	1
Jochen Mass	4	Graham Hill	1
Vittorio Brambilla	3	Gerard Larrousse	1
Johnny Cecotto	3	Lamberto Leoni	1
Francois Cevert	3	Dave Morgan	1
Derek Daly	3	Didier Pironi	1
Teo Fabi	3	Dieter Quester	1
Maurizio Flammini	3	Alex Ribeiro	1
Jacky Ickx	3	Huub Rothengatter	1
Geoff Lees	3	Jody Scheckter	1
Clay Regazzoni	3	Johnny Servoz-Gavin	1
Keke Rosberg	3	Jo Siffert	1
Jackie Stewart	3	Stephen South	1
Stefan Bellof	2	Siegfried Stohr	1
Tino Brambilla	2	Philippe Streiff	1
Richard Dallest	2	John Surtees	1
Eje Elgh	2	Derek Warwick	1
Mike Hailwood	2	Roger Williamson	1
Jean-Pierre Jaussaud	2	Reine Wisell	1

YOUNGEST DRIVERS TO WIN

19 years 168 days	Eddie Cheever	1977 Rouen
19 years 364 days	Mike Thackwell	1981 Silverstone
20 years 42 days	Corrado Fabi	1981 Mugello
21 years 72 days	Andrea de Cesaris	1980 Misano

Records

OLDEST DRIVERS TO WIN

42 years 56 days	Graham Hill	1971 Thruxton
38 years 163 days	John Surtees	1972 Imola
37 years 335 days	Vittorio Brambilla	1975 Vallelunga
35 years 281 days	Frank Gardner	1967 Hockenheim

MOST POINTS SCORED

Name	Pts	Name	Pts	Name	Pts	Name	Pts
Mike Thackwell	164	Michel Ferte	30	Silvio Moser	7	Kazuyoshi Hoshino	3
Brian Henton	123	Alessandro Pesenti-Rossi	30	Carlos Pace	7	Tomas Kaiser	3
Patrick Depailler	119	Huub Rothengatter	30	Ian Raby	7	Chris Lambert	3
Bruno Giacomelli	114	Thierry Tassin	30	Andy Sutcliffe	7	John Lepp	3
Jean-Pierre Jabouille	109	Andrea de Cesaris	29	Guido Dacco	6	Hector Rebaque	3
Eddie Cheever	106	Richard Dallest	28	Jose Dolhem	6	Dave Scott	3
Rene Arnoux	104	Alessandro Nannini	28	Harald Ertl	6	Didier Theys	3
Marc Surer	94	Gerard Larrousse	26	Alain Ferte	6	Juan Traverso	3
Jacques Laffite	91	Emerson Fittipaldi	25	Bill Gubelmann	6	Jorge de Bagration	2
Thierry Boutsen	88	Rad Dougall	24	Roberto Marazzi	6	Franco Bernabei	2
Jean-Pierre Jarier	88	Alan Rees	24	Pierluigi Martini	6	Sandro Cinotti	2
Beppe Gabbiani	87	Kenneth Acheson	23	Dave McConnell	6	Enzo Corti	2
Corrado Fabi	86	Peter Westbury	23	Satoru Nakajima	6	Alain Cudini	2
Patrick Tambay	86	Peter Gethin	22	Gunnar Nilsson	6	Jochen Dauer	2
Jonathan Palmer	85	Giancarlo Martini	22	Torsten Palm	6	Mike Goth	2
Derek Bell	83	Piero Necchi	22	Jean-Pierre Paoli	6	Malcolm Guthrie	2
Michel Leclere	81	Stephen South	22	Carlo Rossi	6	David Hobbs	2
Jean-Pierre Beltoise	75	Robin Widdows	22	Alistair Walker	6	Werner Lindermann	2
Philippe Streiff	74	Hans Binder	21	Tom Belso	5	Enrique Mansilla	2
Ronnie Peterson	68	Gabriele Serblin	21	Roland Binder	5	Gerhard Mitter	2
Carlos Reutemann	67	Tom Pryce	20	Patrick Gaillard	5	Eric Offenstadt	2
Johnny Cecotto	63	Kurt Ahrens Jr	19	"Gianfranco"	5	Philip Robinson	2
Derek Daly	62	John Watson	19	Sten Gunnarsson	5	Bertil Roos	2
Jean-Pierre Jaussaud	62	Pascal Fabre	18	James Hunt	5	Richard Scott	2
Clay Regazzoni	62	Miguel Angel Guerra	18	Alan Rollinson	5	Danny Sullivan	2
Eje Elgh	59	Emanuele Pirro	18	Philippe Alliot	4	Chris Williams	2
Vittorio Brambilla	58	Jo Schlesser	18	Elio de Angelis	4	Patrick Bardinon	1
Mike Hailwood	55	Giorgio Francia	17	Richard Attwood	4	Rolf Biland	1
Geoff Lees	55	Jackie Oliver	17	John Cannon	4	"Pierre Chauvet"	1
Keke Rosberg	55	David Purley	17	Jim Crawford	4	Peter Gaydon	1
Johnny Servoz-Gavin	55	Brian Redman	17	Willi Deutsch	4	Hans Heyer	1
Maurizio Flammini	54	Claude Bourgoignie	16	Bernard de Dryver	4	Markus Hotz	1
Francois Cevert	52	Jo Gartner	16	Claudio Francisci	4	Freddy Kottulinsky	1
Christian Danner	52	Roberto Guerrero	16	Masami Kuwashima	4	Fredy Lienhard	1
Teo Fabi	51	Chris Irwin	15	Klaus Ludwig	4	Helmut Marko	1
Henri Pescarolo	50	Jody Scheckter	15	Brett Lunger	4	Luciano Pavesi	1
Alberto Colombo	48	Lamberto Leoni	14	Gaudenzio Mantova	4	John Pollock	1
Alex Ribeiro	46	Carlos Ruesch	14	John Miles	4	Tommy Reid	1
Siegfried Stohr	46	Michele Alboreto	13	Patrick Neve	4	Kurt Rieder	1
Jacky Ickx	45	Brian Hart	13	Oscar Pedersoli	4	Brian Robinson	1
Dieter Quester	45	Duilio Truffo	12	Fulvio Ballabio	3	Hans Royer	1
Bob Wollek	45	Colin Vandervell	12	Gianfranco Brancatelli	3	Bob Salisbury	1
Roberto Moreno	44	Gerry Birrell	11	Hakan Dahlqvist	3	Fredy Schnarwiler	1
Derek Warwick	44	Ricardo Paletti	11	Vic Elford	3	Cosimo Turizio	1
Jochen Mass	43	Xavier Perrot	11	Piercarlo Ghinzani	3	John Wingfield	1
Hans-Joachim Stuck	43	Roger Williamson	11	Carlo Giorgio	3		
Stefan Bellof	42	Andrea de Adamich	10				
Stefan Johansson	41	Pierre Petit	10				
Mike Beuttler	39	Bobby Rahal	10				
Tino Brambilla	38	Joseph Vonlanthen	10				
Jacques Coulon	38	Tetsu Ikuzawa	9				
Hubert Hahne	38	Chico Serra	9				
Didier Pironi	38	Ricardo Zunino	9				
Piers Courage	37	Roberto del Castello	8				
Frank Gardner	35	Nanni Galli	8				
Ingo Hoffmann	34	Frank Jelinski	8				
Niki Lauda	33	Nigel Mansell	8				
Tim Schenken	33	Francois Migault	8				
Wilson Fittipaldi	32	Patrick Dal Bo	7				
Riccardo Patrese	32	Hiroshi Kazato	7				
Dave Morgan	31	Loris Kessel	7				
Manfred Winkelhock	31	Ray Mallock	7				

HIGHEST POINTS PER START

Pierluigi Martini	6.000	Derek Daly	2.696
Bruno Giacomelli	4.560	Gerard Larrousse	2.600
Johnny Servoz-Gavin	4.231	Derek Bell	2.594
Rene Arnoux	4.000	Jo Schlesser	2.571
Roberto Moreno	4.000	Brian Henton	2.510
Jonathan Palmer	3.696	Clay Regazzoni	2.480
Thierry Boutsen	3.520	Andrea de Cesaris	2.417
Corrado Fabi	3.440	Carlos Reutemann	2.393
Mike Hailwood	3.438	Johnny Cecotto	2.333
Brian Redman	3.400	Eddie Cheever	2.304
Jean-Pierre Jarier	3.385	Riccardo Patrese	2.286
Geoff Lees	3.235	Ronnie Peterson	2.267
Patrick Depailler	3.216	Jean-Pierre Jabouille	2.224
Frank Gardner	3.182	Patrick Tambay	2.205
Mike Thackwell	3.154	Mike Beuttler	2.167
Hakan Dahlqvist	3.000	Michel Ferte	2.143
Vic Elford	3.000	Teo Fabi	2.125
John Lepp	3.000	Jean-Pierre Beltoise	2.083
Hubert Hahne	2.923	Philippe Streiff	2.056
Didier Pironi	2.923	Richard Attwood	2.000
Marc Surer	2.848	Jorge de Bagration	2.000
Jacques Laffite	2.844	Stefan Bellof	2.000
Jacky Ickx	2.813	Franco Bernabei	2.000

HIGHEST POINTS PER START (cont.)

Nigel Mansell	2.000	John Watson	0.826
Dave McConnell	2.000	Carlos Ruesch	0.824
John Miles	2.000	Brian Hart	0.813
Gunnar Nilsson	2.000	Giorgio Francia	0.810
Alan Rees	2.000	Richard Dallest	0.800
Siegfried Stohr	2.000	Francois Migault	0.800
Derek Warwick	2.000	Alessandro Nannini	0.800
Keke Rosberg	1.964	Kenneth Acheson	0.793
Francois Cevert	1.926	Chico Serra	0.750
Michel Leclere	1.884	Piero Necchi	0.742
Vittorio Brambilla	1.813	Duilio Truffo	0.706
Dieter Quester	1.800	Gerry Birrell	0.688
Bob Wollek	1.800	John Cannon	0.667
Jochen Mass	1.792	Alain Cudini	0.667
Piers Courage	1.762	Nanni Galli	0.667
Beppe Gabbiani	1.740	Gerhard Mitter	0.667
Jacques Coulon	1.727	Alberto Colombo	0.649
Dave Morgan	1.722	Ricardo Paletti	0.647
Hans-Joachim Stuck	1.720	Patrick Gaillard	0.625
Henri Pescarolo	1.667	Alain Ferte	0.600
Niki Lauda	1.650	Miguel Angel Guerra	0.600
Alex Ribeiro	1.643	Hector Rebaque	0.600
Emanuele Pirro	1.636	Xavier Perrot	0.550
Kurt Ahrens Jr	1.583	Alistair Walker	0.545
Stefan Johansson	1.577	Patrick Dal Bo	0.538
Stephen South	1.571	Carlos Pace	0.538
Jackie Oliver	1.545	Giancarlo Martini	0.537
Maurizio Flammini	1.500	Patrick Bardinon	0.500
Chris Irwin	1.500	Sten Gunnarsson	0.500
Alessandro Pesenti-Rossi	1.500	Lamberto Leoni	0.500
Jody Scheckter	1.500	Patrick Neve	0.500
Jean-Pierre Jaussaud	1.476	Eric Offenstadt	0.500
Eje Elgh	1.475	John Pollock	0.500
Tom Pryce	1.429	Brian Robinson	0.500
Roberto Guerrero	1.333	Philip Robinson	0.500
Colin Vandervell	1.333	Alan Rollinson	0.500
Emerson Fittipaldi	1.316	Pierre Petit	0.476
Michele Alboreto	1.300	Frank Jelinski	0.471
Tino Brambilla	1.267	Loris Kessel	0.467
Wilson Fittipaldi	1.231	Jo Gartner	0.444
Roger Williamson	1.222	Brett Lunger	0.444
Satoru Nakajima	1.200	Ray Mallock	0.412
Thierry Tassin	1.200	Philippe Alliot	0.400
Christian Danner	1.106	Jochen Dauer	0.400
Robin Widdows	1.100	Gaudenzio Mantova	0.400
Huub Rothengatter	1.071	Bertil Roos	0.400
Ingo Hoffmann	1.063	Danny Sullivan	0.400
Peter Gethin	1.048	Joseph Vonlanthen	0.385
Manfred Winkelhock	1.033	Tetsu Ikuzawa	0.375
Rad Dougall	1.000	Roberto Marazzi	0.375
Mike Goth	1.000	Didier Theys	0.375
Hans Heyer	1.000	Claudio Francisci	0.364
David Hobbs	1.000	Ricardo Zunino	0.346
Kazuyoshi Hoshino	1.000	Peter Gaydon	0.333
Jean-Pierre Paoli	1.000	Hiroshi Kazato	0.333
Ian Raby	1.000	Masami Kuwashima	0.333
Kurt Rieder	1.000	Chris Lambert	0.333
Andy Sutcliffe	1.000	Fredy Lienhard	0.333
Chris Williams	1.000	Tommy Reid	0.333
Pascal Fabre	0.947	Hans Royer	0.333
David Purley	0.944	Elio de Angelis	0.308
Tim Schenken	0.917	Dave Scott	0.300
Hans Binder	0.913	Jim Crawford	0.286
Andrea de Adamich	0.909	Malcolm Guthrie	0.286
Bobby Rahal	0.909	Werner Lindermann	0.286
Torsten Palm	0.857	Klaus Ludwig	0.286
Peter Westbury	0.852	Carlo Rossi	0.286
Claude Bourgoignie	0.842	Fulvio Ballabio	0.273
Gabriele Serblin	0.840	Bill Gubelmann	0.273
Tom Belso	0.833	Juan Traverso	0.273
James Hunt	0.833	Enzo Corti	0.250

Harald Ertl	0.250	Luciano Pavesi	0.167
Helmut Marko	0.250	Oscar Pedersoli	0.160
Silvio Moser	0.250	Rolf Biland	0.143
Bob Salisbury	0.250	Bernard de Dryver	0.143
Roberto del Castello	0.242	Tomas Kaiser	0.143
Roland Binder	0.238	Richard Scott	0.133
Jose Dolhem	0.231	Guido Dacco	0.125
Piercarlo Ghinzani	0.231	Sandro Cinotti	0.118
Enrique Mansilla	0.222	Cosimo Turizio	0.077
Gianfranco Brancatelli	0.214	John Wingfield	0.071
Carlo Giorgio	0.214	Freddy Kottulinsky	0.048
"Gianfranco"	0.185	Fredy Schnarwiler	0.045
Willi Deutsch	0.174	"Pierre Chauvet"	0.033
Markus Hotz	0.167		

POLE POSITIONS

Bruno Giacomelli	11	Maurizio Flammini	2
Jochen Rindt	10	Mike Hailwood	2
Mike Thackwell	9	Niki Lauda	2
Thierry Boutsen	8	Riccardo Patrese	2
Patrick Depailler	8	Alex Ribeiro	2
Brian Henton	8	Keke Rosberg	2
Ronnie Peterson	7	Stephen South	2
Hans-Joachim Stuck	7	Jackie Stewart	2
Jean-Pierre Beltoise	6	Michele Alboreto	1
Emerson Fittipaldi	6	Philippe Alliot	1
Jean-Pierre Jabouille	6	Tino Brambilla	1
Jacques Laffite	6	Andrea de Cesaris	1
Patrick Tambay	6	Francois Cevert	1
Stefan Johansson	5	Jim Clark	1
Michel Leclere	5	Rad Dougall	1
Jonathan Palmer	5	Eje Elgh	1
Corrado Fabi	4	Michel Ferte	1
Jean-Pierre Jarier	4	Beppe Gabbiani	1
Henri Pescarolo	4	Graham Hill	1
Clay Regazzoni	4	Chris Irwin	1
Derek Warwick	4	Jean-Pierre Jaussaud	1
Peter Gethin	3	Geoff Lees	1
Jacky Ickx	3	Lamberto Leoni	1
Jochen Mass	3	Carlos Pace	1
Roberto Moreno	3	Didier Pironi	1
Marc Surer	3	Tom Pryce	1
Rene Arnoux	2	Carlos Reutemann	1
Derek Bell	2	Dave Scott	1
Stefan Bellof	2	Johnny Servoz-Gavin	1
Vittorio Brambilla	2	Jo Siffert	1
Eddie Cheever	2	Siegfried Stohr	1
Richard Dallest	2	Thierry Tassin	1
Derek Daly	2	Duilio Truffo	1
Christian Danner	2	Roger Williamson	1
Teo Fabi	2	Manfred Winkelhock	1

FASTEST LAPS

Mike Thackwell	15	Hans-Joachim Stuck	5
Brian Henton	12	Eddie Cheever	4
Jochen Rindt	11	Jacky Ickx	4
Bruno Giacomelli	9	Jean-Pierre Jarier	4
Patrick Depailler	7	Jochen Mass	4
Jean-Pierre Jabouille	7	Tim Schenken	4
Ronnie Peterson	7	Francois Cevert	3
Rene Arnoux	6	Peter Gethin	3
Stefan Bellof	6	Graham Hill	3
Jacques Laffite	6	Michel Leclere	3
Jean-Pierre Beltoise	5	Jonathan Palmer	3
Derek Daly	5	Dieter Quester	3
Corrado Fabi	5	Marc Surer	3
Emerson Fittipaldi	5	Derek Bell	2
Geoff Lees	5	Thierry Boutsen	2

FASTEST LAPS (cont.)

Tino Brambilla	2	Giorgio Francia	1
Johnny Cecotto	2	Brian Hart	1
Jim Clark	2	Gerard Larrousse	1
Christian Danner	2	Alessandro Nannini	1
Teo Fabi	2	Piero Necchi	1
Beppe Gabbiani	2	Patrick Neve	1
Mike Hailwood	2	Carlos Pace	1
Ingo Hoffmann	2	Ricardo Paletti	1
Jean-Pierre Jaussaud	2	Torsten Palm	1
Roberto Moreno	2	Henri Pescarolo	1
Riccardo Patrese	2	Alessandro Pesenti-Rossi	1
Stephen South	2	Didier Pironi	1
Jackie Stewart	2	Clay Regazzoni	1
Kenneth Acheson	1	Carlos Reutemann	1
Michele Alboreto	1	Keke Rosberg	1
Philippe Alliot	1	Jody Scheckter	1
Richard Attwood	1	Johnny Servoz-Gavin	1
Mike Beuttler	1	Patrick Tambay	1
Vittorio Brambilla	1	Duilio Truffo	1
Alberto Colombo	1	Derek Warwick	1
Jacques Coulon	1	Roger Williamson	1
Jose Dolhem	1	Manfred Winkelhock	1

CLOSEST FINISHES

0 seconds*	Jochen Rindt	1967 Snetterton
0**	Jochen Rindt	1968 Enna-Pergusa
0.06	Jean-Pierre Beltoise	1968 Zandvoort
0.1	Jo Siffert	1970 Rouen
0.1	Alex Ribeiro	1978 Nurburgring
0.1	Brian Henton	1980 Mugello
0.17	Thierry Boutsen	1982 Nurburgring
0.2	Tino Brambilla	1968 Hockenheim
0.2	Jean-Pierre Jaussaud	1972 Albi
0.2	Jean-Pierre Jarier	1973 Karlskoga

*First two cars (Rindt and Graham Hill) both credited with the same time; **First four cars (Rindt, Piers Courage, Tino Brambilla, and Clay Regazzoni) all credited with the same time

Other Records

Fewest starters in a race: Nine, 1973 Kinnekulle
Most starters in a race: 37, 1971 Nurburgring
Widest championship-winning margin: 36 points, Jean-Pierre Jarier, 1973
Narrowest championship-winning margin: 1 point, Jean-Pierre Jabouille, 1976 and Corrado Fabi, 1982
Most wins in a season: Eight, Bruno Giacomelli, 1978
Most successive wins: Five, Jonathan Palmer, 1983
Most points in a season: 82, Bruno Giacomelli, 1978
Fastest race: 142.780 mph, 1968 Enna-Pergusa
Slowest race: 65.601 mph, 1979 Pau

Manufacturers' Records

WINS

March	77	Spirit	4
Ralt	23	AGS	3
Brabham	18	Alpine	3
Martini	14	BMW	3
Lotus	10	Osella	3
Matra	10	Ferrari	2
Toleman	8	Motul	2
Chevron	6	Boxer	1
Elf	5	GRD	1
Surtees	5	McLaren	1
Tecno	5	Minardi	1
Maurer	4		

POINTS

March	1966	Osella	57
Brabham	454	Ferrari	56
Ralt	450	McLaren	46
Martini	280	Motul	40
Chevron	264	GRD	27
Matra	233	BMW	21
Toleman	207	Boxer	14
Surtees	154	Pygmee	9
Maurer	144	Protos	8
Tecno	132	Toj	6
Elf	117	Pilbeam	4
AGS	109	Tui	4
Alpine	104	Alexis	2
Lotus	78	Scott	2
Spirit	76	Cooper	1
Lola	70	Merlyn	1
Minardi	61		

Engine Records

WINS

BMW	94	Hart	17
Ford	60	Renault	12
Honda	23	Ferrari	3

POINTS

BMW	2444	Renault	267
Ford	1556	Ferrari	70
Hart	437	Lotus	9
Honda	413	Chrysler	1

Team Records

WINS

March Engineering	57	ASCA	2
Ralt Racing	20	Brian Lewis (inc. Boxer)	2
Automobiles Martini	15	Fred Opert Racing	2
Roy Winkelmann Racing	11	Scuderia Ferrari	2
Elf Switzerland	7	Trivellato Racing	2
Toleman Group Motorsport	7	Team Beta/Brambilla	2
Tyrrell Racing Organisation	6	Wheatcroft Racing	2
Project 4 Racing	5	Alex Ribeiro	1
Rondel Racing	5	Bob Sparshott Automotive	1
Team Surtees	5	Clarke-Mordaunt-Guthrie	1
Tecno Racing Team	5	Edward Reeves	1
Docking/Spitzley	4	John Coombs Racing	1
Team Lotus	4	Emco Sports/Jo Gartner	1
Matra Sports	4	Jochen Rindt	1
Maurer	4	Motor Racing Developments	1
Onyx Race Engineering	4	Bruce McLaren	1
AGS	3	Motor Racing	1
BMW	3	Minardi Team	1
Team Bardahl	3	Pierre Robert	1
Chevron Cars	3	Project 3 Racing	1
Osella Squadra Corse	3	Team Tiga	1
Spirit Racing	3	Frank Williams Racing Cars	1

International Formula 3000 Championship

2001 Tomas Enge leads Bas Leinders and eventual champion Justin Wilson at the start of the Barcelona race.

International Formula 3000 Championship

Formula 3000 had first been proposed in 1983 as a competing category to F2, but it was not until 1985 that the first series was organised. It retained F2 chassis regulations, but instead employed 3000cc engines—hence the Formula 3000 designation.

Most competitors opted for power from the Ford Cosworth DFV that had been the mainstay of British Grand Prix teams since the late sixties. Although the championship suffered from a lack of competitors in its first year (with only eleven cars starting at Pau), it was soon well supported, enjoying full grids from its second season on.

Even so, teams have always complained that the series is poorly promoted, and with costs spiralling major changes were introduced for the 1996 season to help reduce budgets. New Lola chassis powered by detuned 3-litre Zytek (née Judd) engines became mandatory. The championship now supports Formula 1 races exclusively, robbing the calendar of classic second-division events at Pau, Enna, and others.

No Formula 3000 champion has gone on to win the Formula 1 title, a failing shared with the preceding Formula 2 series. This is a trend that Juan Pablo Montoya and Nick Heidfeld will be looking to redress in the years to come.

Rules

1985	Single seater cars using 3000cc normally aspirated engine capacity
1986-95	Technical rules unchanged, Avon tyres mandatory
1996 to date	Lola chassis and 3000cc Zytek normally aspirated engines mandatory

Points

| 1985-96 | 9-6-4-3-2-1 awarded to the top six finishers |
| 1997-2002 | 10-6-4-3-2-1 awarded to the top six finishers |

1985

MARLBORO/DAILY EXPRESS INTERNATIONAL TROPHY

24 March 1985. Silverstone. 44 laps of a 2.932 mile-circuit = 129.008 miles. FIA F3000 Championship round 1

1	Mike Thackwell	Ralt RB20-Cosworth	44	1h07m41.01
2	John Nielsen	Ralt RB20-Cosworth	44	1h08m13.35
3	Michel Ferte	March 85B-Cosworth	44	1h09m09.77
4	Christian Danner	March 85B-Cosworth	43	
5	Gabriele Tarquini	March 85B-Cosworth	42	
6	Roberto Moreno	Tyrrell 012-Cosworth	42	

Winner's average speed: 114.363 mph. Pole position: M Ferte, 1m17.92. Fastest lap: Nielsen, 1m27.64

TOWNSEND THORESEN JOCHEN RINDT TROPHY

8 April 1985. Thruxton. 54 laps of a 2.356 mile-circuit = 127.224 miles. FIA F3000 Championship round 2

1	Emanuele Pirro	March 85B-Cosworth	54	1h05m00.83
2	Mike Thackwell	Ralt RB20-Cosworth	54	1h05m03.31
3	Michel Ferte	March 85B-Cosworth	54	1h05m14.44
4	Tomas Kaiser	March 85B-Cosworth	54	1h06m09.18
5	Gabriele Tarquini	March 85B-Cosworth	53	
6	Christian Danner	March 85B-Cosworth	53	

Winner's average speed: 117.413 mph. Pole position: Thackwell, 1m06.33. Fastest lap: Danner, 1m09.40

ESTORIL F3000

20 April 1985. Estoril. 47 laps of a 2.703 mile-circuit = 127.041 miles. FIA F3000 Championship round 3

1	John Nielsen	Ralt RB20-Cosworth	47	1h12m44.424
2	Michel Ferte	March 85B-Cosworth	47	1h12m57.792
3	Gabriele Tarquini	March 85B-Cosworth	47	1h13m36.616
4	Emanuele Pirro	March 85B-Cosworth	47	1h14m14.674
5	Roberto Moreno	Tyrrell 012-Cosworth	46	
6	Olivier Grouillard	March 85B-Cosworth	46	

Winner's average speed: 104.790 mph. Pole position: Mike Thackwell (Ralt RB20-Cosworth), 1m30.180. Fastest lap: Thackwell, 1m30.306

EIFELRENNEN

28 April 1985. Nurburgring. Cancelled due to snow on race day

NO RACE

Pole position: Mike Thackwell (Ralt RB20-Cosworth), 1m28.47

GRAN PREMIO DI ROMA

12 May 1985. Vallelunga. 65 laps of a 1.988 mile-circuit = 129.220 miles.

FIA INTERNATIONAL FORMULA 3000 CHAMPIONS

Year	Driver	Nat	Team	Car
1985	Christian Danner	D	Bob Sparshott Automotive	March 85B-Cosworth
1986	Ivan Capelli	I	Genoa Racing	March 86B-Cosworth
1987	Stefano Modena	I	Onyx Race Engineering	March 87B-Cosworth
1988	Roberto Moreno	BR	Bromley Motorsport	Reynard 88D-Cosworth
1989	Jean Alesi	F	Eddie Jordan Racing	Reynard 89D-Mugen
1990	Erik Comas	F	DAMS	Lola T90/50-Mugen
1991	Christian Fittipaldi	BR	Pacific Racing	Reynard 91D-Mugen
1992	Luca Badoer	I	Team Crypton	Reynard 92D-Cosworth
1993	Olivier Panis	F	DAMS	Reynard 93D-Cosworth
1994	Jules Boullion	F	DAMS	Reynard 94D-Cosworth
1995	Vincenzo Sospiri	I	Super Nova Racing	Reynard 95D-Cosworth
1996	Jorg Muller	D	RSM Marko	Lola T96/50-Zytek
1997	Ricardo Zonta	BR	Super Nova Racing	Lola T96/50-Zytek
1998	Juan Pablo Montoya	CO	Super Nova Racing	Lola T96/50-Zytek
1999	Nick Heidfeld	D	West Competition (McLaren)	Lola B99/50-Zytek
2000	Bruno Junqueiro	BR	Petrobras Junior Team	Lola B99/50-Zytek
2001	Justin Wilson	GB	Coca-Cola Nordic Racing	Lola B99/50-Zytek
2002	Sebastien Bourdais	F	Super Nova Racing	Lola B2/50-Zytek

FIA F3000 Championship round 4

1	Emanuele Pirro	March 85B-Cosworth	65	1h15m14.83
2	John Nielsen	Ralt RB20-Cosworth	65	1h15m36.66
3	Christian Danner	March 85B-Cosworth	65	1h15m37.12
4	Olivier Grouillard	March 85B-Cosworth	65	1h15m37.74
5	Philippe Streiff	AGS JH20-Cosworth	65	1h16m03.81
6	Johnny Dumfries	March 85B-Cosworth	65	1h16m15.34

Winner's average speed: 103.036 mph. Pole position: Mike Thackwell (Ralt RB20-Cosworth), 1m05.88. Fastest lap: Pirro, 1m08.36

GRAND PRIX DE PAU

27 May 1985. Pau. 72 laps of a 1.715 mile-circuit = 123.480 miles. FIA F3000 Championship round 5

1	Christian Danner	March 85B-Cosworth	72	1h30m28.63
2	Emanuele Pirro	March 85B-Cosworth	72	1h31m10.38
3	Lamberto Leoni	Williams FW08C-Cosworth	72	1h31m28.25
4	Olivier Grouillard	March 85B-Cosworth	72	1h32m32.13
5	Philippe Streiff	AGS JH20-Cosworth	71	

No other finishers. Winner's average speed: 81.886 mph. Pole position: Pirro, 1m12.65. Fastest lap: Danner, 1m13.26

GRAND PRIX DE BELGIQUE FORMULE 3000

2 June 1985. Spa-Francorchamps. 29 laps of a 4.318 mile-circuit = 125.219 miles. FIA F3000 Championship round 6

1	Mike Thackwell	Ralt RB20-Cosworth	29	1h11m56.510
2	Alain Ferte	March 85B-Cosworth	29	1h12m46.546
3	Christian Danner	March 85B-Cosworth	29	1h12m55.153
4	Gabriele Tarquini	March 85B-Cosworth	29	1h12m57.814
5	Guido Dacco	March 85B-Cosworth	29	1h13m37.044
6	Juan Manuel Fangio II	Lola T950-Cosworth	29	1h13m52.332

Winner's average speed: 104.434 mph. Pole position: Michel Ferte (March 85B-Cosworth), 2m11.195. Fastest lap: Thackwell, 2m26.769

DIJON-PRENOIS F3000

30 June 1985. Dijon-Prenois. 55 laps of a 2.361 mile-circuit = 129.855 miles. FIA F3000 Championship round 7

1	Christian Danner	March 85B-Cosworth	55	1h08m54.10
2	Mike Thackwell	Ralt RB20-Cosworth	55	1h09m16.96
3	John Nielsen	Ralt RB20-Cosworth	55	1h10m04.59
4	Alain Ferte	March 85B-Cosworth	55	1h10m05.05
5	Guido Dacco	March 85B-Cosworth	54	
6	Philippe Alliot	March 85B-Cosworth	54	

Winner's average speed: 113.079 mph. Pole position: Nielsen, 1m10.21. Fastest lap: Thierry Tassin (March 85B-Cosworth), 1m13.80

GRAN PREMIO DEL MEDITERRANEO

28 July 1985. Enna-Pergusa. 40 laps of a 3.076 mile-circuit = 123.040 miles. FIA F3000 Championship round 8

1	Mike Thackwell	Ralt RB20-Cosworth	40	1h01m58.99
2	Emanuele Pirro	March 85B-Cosworth	40	1h01m59.62
3	Christian Danner	March 85B-Cosworth	40	1h02m20.10
4	Gabriele Tarquini	March 85B-Cosworth	40	1h02m51.85
5	Mario Hytten	March 85B-Cosworth	40	1h02m52.61
6	Guido Dacco	March 85B-Cosworth	40	1h02m53.32

Winner's average speed: 119.103 mph. Pole position: Thackwell, 1m29.52. Fastest lap: Danner, 1m31.29

OSTERREICHRING F3000

17 August 1985. Osterreichring. 31 laps of a 3.692 mile-circuit = 114.452 miles. FIA F3000 Championship round 9

1	Ivan Capelli	March 85B-Cosworth	31	53m56.114
2	John Nielsen	Ralt RB20-Cosworth	31	53m56.698
3	Lamberto Leoni	March 85B-Cosworth	31	54m12.296
4	Emanuele Pirro	March 85B-Cosworth	31	54m19.762
5	Philippe Streiff	AGS JH20-Cosworth	31	54m22.483
6	Thierry Tassin	March 85B-Cosworth	31	54m25.584

Winner's average speed: 127.322 mph. Pole position: Christian Danner (March 85B-Cosworth), 1m39.780. Fastest lap: Mike Thackwell (Ralt RB20-Cosworth), 1m42.244

ZANDVOORT F3000

24 August 1985. Zandvoort. 48 laps of a 2.642 mile-circuit = 126.816 miles. FIA F3000 Championship round 10

1	Christian Danner	March 85B-Cosworth	48	1h15m19.023
2	Mike Thackwell	Ralt RB20-Cosworth	48	1h15m23.404
3	Philippe Streiff	AGS JH20-Cosworth	48	1h15m51.264
4	John Nielsen	Ralt RB20-Cosworth	48	1h16m14.199
5	Emanuele Pirro	March 85B-Cosworth	47	
6	Guido Dacco	March 85B-Cosworth	47	

Winner's average speed: 101.026 mph. Pole position: Danner, 1m21.450. Fastest lap: Danner, 1m23.645

DONINGTON PARK F3000

22 September 1985. Donington Park. 40 laps of a 2.500 mile-circuit = 100.000 miles. FIA F3000 Championship round 11

1	Christian Danner	March 85B-Cosworth	40	59m17.83
2	Mario Hytten	March 85B-Cosworth	40	59m27.96
3	Ivan Capelli	March 85B-Cosworth	40	59m28.47
4	Michel Ferte	March 85B-Cosworth	40	59m35.67
5	Philippe Streiff	AGS JH20-Cosworth	40	59m41.23
6	Alain Ferte	March 85B-Cosworth	40	59m41.52

Winner's average speed: 101.185 mph. Pole position: Mike Thackwell (Ralt RB20-Cosworth), 1m23.59. Fastest lap: Capelli, 1m27.60

1985 Christian Danner's championship winning BS Automotive March at the formula's opening race at Silverstone.

1985 FINAL CHAMPIONSHIP POSITIONS

1	Christian Danner	51 (52)*	12	Olivier Grouillard	7
2	Mike Thackwell	45	13	Guido Dacco	6
3	Emanuele Pirro	38	14=	Tomas Kaiser	3
4	John Nielsen	34		Roberto Moreno	3
5	Michel Ferte	17	16=	Philippe Alliot	1
6	Gabriele Tarquini	14		Johnny Dumfries	1
7	Ivan Capelli	13		Juan Manuel Fangio II	1
8	Philippe Streiff	12		Thierry Tassin	1
9	Alain Ferte	10		*Best eight results count	
10=	Mario Hytten	8			
	Lamberto Leoni	8			

1986

DAILY EXPRESS INTERNATIONAL TROPHY

13 April 1986. Silverstone. 24 laps of a 2.932 mile-circuit = 70.368 miles. Race scheduled for 44 laps, stopped after 2 laps due to an accident, restarted over an additional 39 laps, stopped after another serious accident after 22 laps of second heat, results declared with half points awarded. FIA F3000 Championship round 1

1	Pascal Fabre	Lola T86/50-Cosworth	24	35m33.97
2	Emanuele Pirro	March 86B-Cosworth	24	35m35.19
3	John Nielsen	Ralt RT20-Honda	24	35m50.26

4	Mike Thackwell	Lola T86/50-Cosworth	24	35m51.50
5	Tomas Kaiser	Lola T86/50-Cosworth	24	36m01.06
6	Alessandro Santin	Lola T86/50-Cosworth	24	36m01.32

Winner's average speed: 118.711 mph. Pole position: Fabre, 1m19.83. Fastest lap: Fabre, 1m26.65.

GRAN PREMIO DI ROMA

4 May 1986. Vallelunga. 64 laps of a 1.988 mile-circuit = 127.232 miles. FIA F3000 Championship round 2

1	Ivan Capelli	March 86B-Cosworth	64	1h14m24.22
2	Pascal Fabre	Lola T86/50-Cosworth	64	1h14m42.88
3	Emanuele Pirro	March 86B-Cosworth	64	1h14m43.23
4	Mauricio Gugelmin	March 86B-Cosworth	64	1h14m45.77
5	Satoru Nakajima	Ralt RT20-Honda	64	1h14m46.02
6	Alessandro Santin	Lola T86/50-Cosworth	64	1h15m16.90

Winner's average speed: 102.601 mph. Pole position: Capelli, 1m07.13. Fastest lap: Capelli, 1m08.27

GRAND PRIX DE PAU

19 May 1986. Pau. 73 laps of a 1.715 mile-circuit = 125.195 miles. FIA F3000 Championship round 3

1	Mike Thackwell	Ralt RT20-Honda	73	1h31m17.92
2	Emanuele Pirro	March 86B-Cosworth	73	1h32m11.07
3	Michel Ferte	March 86B-Cosworth	73	1h32m31.14
4	Richard Dallest	AGS JH20B-Cosworth	72	
5	Luis Perez Sala	Ralt RT20-Cosworth	72	
6	John Jones	March 86B-Cosworth	71	

Winner's average speed: 82.276 mph. Pole position: Pirro, 1m11.83. Fastest lap: Pirro, 1m13.70

GRAND PRIX DE BELGIQUE FORMULE 3000

24 May 1986. Spa-Francorchamps. 28 laps of a 4.318 mile-circuit = 120.901 miles. FIA F3000 Championship round 4

1	Philippe Alliot	March 86B-Cosworth	28	1h02m03.562
2	John Nielsen	Ralt RT20-Honda	28	1h02m06.078
3	Ivan Capelli	March 86B-Cosworth	28	1h02m12.390
4	Luis Perez Sala	Ralt RT20-Cosworth	28	1h02m26.430
5	Michel Ferte	March 86B-Cosworth	28	1h02m43.260
6	Pierre-Henri Raphanel	March 86B-Cosworth	28	1h02m49.760

Winner's average speed: 116.889 mph. Pole position: Alliot, 2m09.87. Fastest lap: Nielsen, 2m11.139

TROFEO ELIO DE ANGELIS

8 June 1986. Imola. 39 laps of a 3.132 mile-circuit = 122.148 miles. FIA F3000 Championship round 5

1	Pierluigi Martini	Ralt RT20-Cosworth	39	1h05m48.56
2	Ivan Capelli	March 86B-Cosworth	39	1h05m49.37
3	Alain Ferte	March 86B-Cosworth	39	1h06m14.84
4	Gabriele Tarquini	March 85B-Cosworth	39	1h06m26.00
5	Luis Perez Sala	Ralt RT20-Cosworth	39	1h06m26.55
6	Franco Forini	March 86B-Cosworth	39	1h06m54.62

Winner's average speed: 111.365 mph. Pole position: Capelli, 1m39.25. Fastest lap: Michel Ferte (March 86B-Cosworth), 1m39.60

EURO MUGELLO

29 June 1986. Mugello. 38 laps of a 3.259 mile-circuit = 123.842 miles. FIA F3000 Championship round 6

1	Pierluigi Martini	Ralt RT20-Cosworth	38	1h10m48.43
2	Michel Ferte	March 86B-Cosworth	38	1h10m48.85
3	Ivan Capelli	March 86B-Cosworth	38	1h10m54.34
4	Olivier Grouillard	Lola T86/50-Cosworth	38	1h10m59.80
5	Satoru Nakajima	Ralt RT20-Honda	38	1h11m12.92
6	Emanuele Pirro	March 86B-Cosworth	38	1h11m33.71

Winner's average speed: 104.940 mph. Pole position: Martini, 1m44.73. Fastest lap: Martini, 1m49.35

GRAN PREMIO DEL MEDITERRANEO

20 July 1986. Enna-Pergusa. 40 laps of a 3.076 mile-circuit = 123.040 miles. FIA F3000 Championship round 7

1	Luis Perez Sala	Ralt RT20-Cosworth	40	1h01m42.72
2	Pierluigi Martini	Ralt RT20-Cosworth	40	1h01m49.52
3	Pascal Fabre	Lola T86/50-Cosworth	40	1h01m50.63
4	Tomas Kaiser	Lola T86/50-Cosworth	40	1h01m55.66
5	Claudio Langes	Lola T86/50-Cosworth	40	1h01m57.17
6	John Nielsen	Ralt RT20-Honda	40	1h02m04.46

Winner's average speed: 119.627 mph. Pole position: Ivan Capelli (March 86B-Cosworth), 1m29.75. Fastest lap: Mike Thackwell (Lola T86/50-Cosworth), 1m30.92

OSTERREICHRING F3000

16 August 1986. Osterreichring. 34 laps of a 3.692 mile-circuit = 125.528 miles. FIA F3000 Championship round 8

1	Ivan Capelli	March 86B-Cosworth	34	58m47.530
2	John Nielsen	Ralt RT20-Honda	34	58m49.688
3	Gabriele Tarquini	March 85B-Cosworth	34	59m22.944
4	Satoru Nakajima	Ralt RT20-Honda	34	59m23.120
5	Luis Perez Sala	Ralt RT20-Cosworth	34	59m27.301
6	Olivier Grouillard	Lola T86/50-Cosworth	34	59m31.762

Winner's average speed: 128.107 mph. Pole position: Nielsen, 1m40.527. Fastest lap: Nielsen, 1m42.704

HALFORDS BIRMINGHAM SUPERPRIX

25 August 1986. Birmingham. 24 laps of a 2.470 mile-circuit = 59.280 miles. Race scheduled for 52 laps, stopped due to accidents in the heavy rain, half points awarded. FIA F3000 Championship round 9

1	Luis Perez Sala	Ralt RT20-Cosworth	24	42m24.40
2	Pierluigi Martini	Ralt RT20-Cosworth	24	42m27.72
3	Michel Ferte	March 86B-Cosworth	24	42m29.70
4	Eliseo Salazar	Lola T86/50-Cosworth	24	42m37.63
5	Pascal Fabre	Lola T86/50-Cosworth	24	43m07.83
6	Russell Spence	March 86B-Cosworth	24	43m20.19

Winner's average speed: 83.870 mph. Pole position: Martini, 1m22.16. Fastest lap: Salazar, 1m42.62

LE MANS F3000

28 September 1986. Le Mans-Bugatti. 47 laps of a 2.635 mile-circuit = 123.845 miles. FIA F3000 Championship round 10

1	Emanuele Pirro	March 86B-Cosworth	47	1h10m36.43
2	Michel Ferte	March 86B-Cosworth	47	1h10m42.95
3	Pierre-Henri Raphanel	March 86B-Cosworth	47	1h10m48.83
4	Ivan Capelli	March 86B-Cosworth	47	1h10m56.28
5	Luis Perez Sala	Ralt RT20-Cosworth	47	1h11m49.00
6	Claudio Langes	Lola T86/50-Cosworth	47	1h12m04.01

Winner's average speed: 105.240 mph. Pole position: Pirro, 1m27.31. Fastest lap: Pirro, 1m29.20

JARAMA F3000

5 October 1986. Jarama. 58 laps of a 2.115 mile-circuit = 122.693 miles. Race scheduled for 62 laps, stopped after 43 laps due to rain, restarted over and additional 15 laps. FIA F3000 Championship round 11

1*	Pierluigi Martini	Ralt RT20-Cosworth	58	1h18m03.50
2	Emanuele Pirro	March 86B-Cosworth	58	1h18m05.49
3	Michel Ferte	March 86B-Cosworth	58	1h18m15.92
4	Ivan Capelli	March 86B-Cosworth	58	1h18m36.42
5	John Nielsen	Ralt RT20-Honda	58	1h18m44.42
6	Mauricio Gugelmin	March 86B-Cosworth	58	1h18m48.07

*Originally disqualified because the team worked on the car between heats, later reinstated but time estimated, as it was not published. Winner's average speed: 94.268 mph. Pole position: Pirro, 1m18.17. Fastest lap: M Ferte, 1m19.51

1986 FINAL CHAMPIONSHIP POSITIONS

1	Ivan Capelli	38		13= Alain Ferte	4
2	Pierluigi Martini	36		Olivier Grouillard	4
3	Emanuele Pirro	29		Mauricio Gugelmin	4
4	Luis Perez Sala	24.5		Tomas Kaiser	4
5	Michel Ferte	24		17= Richard Dallest	3
6	John Nielsen	17		Claudio Langes	3
7	Pascal Fabre	15.5		19= Eliseo Salazar	1.5
8	Mike Thackwell	10.5		Alessandro Santin	1.5
9	Philippe Alliot	9		21= Franco Forini	1
10=	Satoru Nakajima	7		John Jones	1
	Gabriele Tarquini	7		23 Russell Spence	0.5
12	Pierre-Henri Raphanel	5			

1987

MARLBORO INTERNATIONAL TROPHY

12 April 1987. Silverstone. 42 laps of a 2.969 mile-circuit = 124.698 miles. FIA F3000 Championship round 1

1	Mauricio Gugelmin	Ralt RT21-Honda	42	57m07.10
2	Michel Trolle	Lola T87/50-Cosworth	42	57m20.73
3	Roberto Moreno	Ralt RT21-Honda	42	57m21.81
4	Stefano Modena	March 87B-Cosworth	42	57m22.83
5	Pierluigi Martini	Ralt RT21-Cosworth	42	57m51.33
6	Alfonso Garcia de Vinuesa	Lola T87/50-Cosworth	42	57m55.32

Winner's average speed: 130.989 mph. Pole position: Moreno, 1m19.08. Fastest lap: Moreno, 1m20.66

GRAN PREMIO DI ROMA

10 May 1987. Vallelunga. 61 laps of a 1.988 mile-circuit = 121.268 miles. Race scheduled for 64 laps, stopped due to an accident after 19 laps, restarted over an additional 42 laps. FIA F3000 Championship round 2

1	Stefano Modena	March 87B-Cosworth	61	1h10m06.20
2	Luis Perez Sala	Lola T87/50-Cosworth	61	1h10m18.53
3	Mauricio Gugelmin	Ralt RT21-Honda	61	1h10m40.72
4	Pierre-Henri Raphanel	March 87B-Cosworth	61	1h10m43.25
5	John Jones	Lola T87/50-Cosworth	61	1h11m08.83
6	Mark Blundell	Lola T86/50-Cosworth	61	1h11m12.10

Olivier Grouillard (March 87B-Cosworth), 1h10m44.000, finished fifth on the road but was disqualified for car being underweight. Winner's average speed: 103.791 mph. Pole position: Yannick Dalmas (March 87B-Cosworth), 1m06.30. Fastest lap: Modena, 1m08.05

SPA-FRANCORCHAMPS F3000

16 May 1987. Spa-Francorchamps. 16 laps of a 4.318 mile-circuit = 69.086 miles. Race scheduled for 29 laps but stopped due to accident, half points awarded. FIA F3000 Championship round 3

1	Michel Trolle	Lola T87/50-Cosworth	16	38m57.67
2	Mark Blundell	Lola T86/50-Cosworth	16	39m00.72
3	Roberto Moreno	Ralt RT21-Honda	16	39m07.52
4	Andy Wallace	March 87B-Cosworth	16	39m10.31
5	Marco Apicella	Dallara 3087-Cosworth	16	39m25.46
6	Gary Evans	Ralt RT21-Cosworth	16	39m51.52

Winner's average speed: 106.393 mph. Pole position: Moreno, 2m23.77. Fastest lap: Luis Perez Sala (Lola T87/50-Cosworth), 2m15.99

GRAND PRIX DE PAU

8 June 1987. Pau. 72 laps of a 1.715 mile-circuit = 123.480 miles. FIA F3000 Championship round 4

1	Yannick Dalmas	March 87B-Cosworth	72	1h30m14.55
2	John Jones	Lola T87/50-Cosworth	72	1h30m24.47
3	Michel Ferte	Lola T87/50-Cosworth	72	1h30m24.80
4	Olivier Grouillard	March 87B-Cosworth	72	1h30m41.11
5	Paul Belmondo	Lola T87/50-Cosworth	72	1h30m50.10
6	Lamberto Leoni	March 87B-Cosworth	72	1h30m52.40

Winner's average speed: 82.099 mph. Pole position: Pierre-Henri Raphanel (March 87B-Cosworth), 1m11.88. Fastest lap: Roberto Moreno (Ralt RT21-Honda), 1m13.64

DONINGTON PARK F3000

28 June 1987. Donington Park. 50 laps of a 2.500 mile-circuit = 125.000 miles. FIA F3000 Championship round 5

1	Luis Perez Sala	Lola T87/50-Cosworth	50	1h12m16.41
2	Stefano Modena	March 87B-Cosworth	50	1h12m23.08
3	Pierre-Henri Raphanel	March 87B-Cosworth	50	1h12m40.12
4	Roberto Moreno	Ralt RT21-Honda	50	1h12m45.03
5	Michel Trolle	Lola T87/50-Cosworth	50	1h13m05.07
6	Michel Ferte	Lola T87/50-Cosworth	50	1h13m07.06

Winner's average speed: 103.772 mph. Pole position: Sala, 1m23.84. Fastest lap: Yannick Dalmas (March 87B-Cosworth), 1m25.60

GRAN PREMIO DEL MEDITERRANEO

19 July 1987. Enna-Pergusa. 41 laps of a 3.076 mile-circuit = 126.116 miles. FIA F3000 Championship round 6

1	Roberto Moreno	Ralt RT21-Honda	41	1h03m09.90
2	Pierluigi Martini	Ralt RT20-Cosworth	41	1h03m12.15
3	Gabriele Tarquini	March 87B-Cosworth	41	1h03m12.53
4	Julian Bailey	Lola T87/50-Cosworth	41	1h03m12.93
5	Lamberto Leoni	March 87B-Cosworth	41	1h03m13.80
6	Stefano Modena	March 87B-Cosworth	41	1h03m26.16

Winner's average speed: 119.797 mph. Pole position: Mauricio Gugelmin (Ralt RT21-Honda), 1m29.46. Fastest lap: Leoni, 1m30.93

BRANDS HATCH F3000

23 August 1987. Brands Hatch. 45 laps of a 2.614 mile-circuit = 117.612 miles. Race scheduled for 48 laps, stopped due to accident. FIA F3000 Championship round 7

1	Julian Bailey	Lola T87/50-Cosworth	45	59m09.96
2	Mauricio Gugelmin	Ralt RT21-Honda	45	59m12.09
3	Roberto Moreno	Ralt RT21-Honda	45	59m21.91
4	Stefano Modena	March 87B-Cosworth	45	59m24.23
5	Yannick Dalmas	March 87B-Cosworth	45	59m24.66
6	Mark Blundell	Lola T86/50-Cosworth	45	59m29.22

Winner's average speed: 119.270 mph. Pole position: Moreno, 1m16.46. Fastest lap: Dalmas, 1m17.33

HALFORDS BIRMINGHAM SUPERPRIX

31 August 1987. Birmingham. 51 laps of a 2.470 mile-circuit = 125.970 miles. FIA F3000 Championship round 8

1	Stefano Modena	March 87B-Cosworth	51	1h11m44.52
2	Roberto Moreno	Ralt RT21-Honda	51	1h11m55.94
3	Mauricio Gugelmin	Ralt RT21-Honda	51	1h11m57.82
4	Luis Perez Sala	Lola T87/50-Cosworth	51	1h12m00.64
5	Andy Wallace	Lola T87/50-Cosworth	51	1h12m17.29
6	Olivier Grouillard	March 87B-Cosworth	51	1h12m17.55

Winner's average speed: 105.353 mph. Pole position: Gugelmin, 1m21.77. Fastest lap: Moreno, 1m22.91

IMOLA F3000

13 September 1987. Imola. 40 laps of a 3.132 mile-circuit = 125.280 miles. FIA F3000 Championship round 9

1	Stefano Modena	March 87B-Cosworth	40	1h06m13.38
2	Gabriele Tarquini	March 87B-Cosworth	40	1h06m31.96
3	Luis Perez Sala	Lola T87/50-Cosworth	40	1h06m34.07
4	Lamberto Leoni	March 87B-Judd	40	1h06m36.99
5	Roberto Moreno	Ralt RT21-Honda	40	1h06m44.46
6	Andy Wallace	Lola T87/50-Cosworth	40	1h06m48.60

Winner's average speed: 113.507 mph. Pole position: Moreno, 1m36.59. Fastest lap: Tarquini, 1m38.29

LE MANS F3000

27 September 1987. Le Mans-Bugatti. 47 laps of a 2.635 mile-circuit = 123.845 miles. FIA F3000 Championship round 10

1	Luis Perez Sala	Lola T87/50-Cosworth	47	1h12m49.12
2	Russell Spence	March 87B-Cosworth	47	1h13m07.21
3	Michel Trolle	Lola T87/50-Cosworth	47	1h13m11.48
4	Lamberto Leoni	March 87B-Judd	47	1h13m17.92
5	Gabriele Tarquini	March 87B-Cosworth	47	1h13m26.69
6	Julian Bailey	Lola T87/50-Cosworth	47	1h13m32.71

Winner's average speed: 102.044 mph. Pole position: Sala, 1m30.35. Fastest lap: Sala, time not published.

JARAMA F3000

11 October 1987. Jarama. 61 laps of a 2.115 mile-circuit = 129.039 miles. FIA F3000 Championship round 11

1	Yannick Dalmas	March 87B-Cosworth	61	1h23m21.289
2	Mauricio Gugelmin	Ralt RT21-Honda	61	1h23m35.931
3	Russell Spence	March 87B-Cosworth	61	1h23m45.770
4	Lamberto Leoni	March 87B-Judd	61	1h23m46.670
5	Luis Perez Sala	Lola T87/50-Cosworth	61	1h23m47.930
6	Stefano Modena	March 87B-Cosworth	61	1h24m13.010

Winner's average speed: 92.884 mph. Pole position: John Jones (Lola T87/50-Cosworth), 1m28.188. Fastest lap: Dalmas, 1m20.092

1987 FINAL CHAMPIONSHIP POSITIONS

1	Stefano Modena	40(41)*	14=	Mark Blundell	5
2	Luis Perez Sala	33		Michel Ferte	5
3	Roberto Moreno	30	16	Andy Wallace	4.5
4	Mauricio Gugelmin	29	17	Olivier Grouillard	4
5	Yannick Dalmas	20	18	Paul Belmondo	2
6	Michel Trolle	16.5	19=	Marco Apicella	1
7	Julian Bailey	13		Alfonso Garcia	
8=	Lamberto Leoni	12		de Vinuesa	1
	Gabriele Tarquini	12	21	Gary Evans	0.5
10	Russell Spence	10		*Best seven results count	
11=	John Jones	8			
	Pierluigi Martini	8			
13	Pierre-Henri				
	Raphanel	7			

1988 Roberto Moreno wins the 1988 Formula 3000 Championship for Bromley Motorsport and Reynard.

1988

JEREZ F3000

17 April 1988. Jerez. 47 laps of a 2.621 mile-circuit = 123.182 miles. FIA F3000 Championship round 1

1	Johnny Herbert	Reynard 88D-Cosworth	47	1h17m20.02
2	Mark Blundell	Lola T88/50-Cosworth	47	1h17m29.33
3	Michel Trolle	Lola T88/50-Cosworth	47	1h17m52.04
4	Fabien Giroix	Lola T88/50-Cosworth	47	1h18m28.83
5	Olivier Grouillard	Lola T88/50-Cosworth	47	1h18m30.93
6	Eric Bernard	Ralt RT22-Judd	47	1h18m37.89

Winner's average speed: 95.572 mph. Pole position: Herbert, 1m32.85. Fastest lap: Trolle, 1m37.09

GRAN PREMIO DI ROMA

8 May 1988. Vallelunga. 63 laps of a 1.988 mile-circuit = 125.244 miles. FIA F3000 Championship round 2

1	Gregor Foitek	Lola T88/50-Cosworth	63	1h13m49.83
2	Bertrand Gachot	Reynard 88D-Cosworth	63	1h13m56.02
3	Olivier Grouillard	Lola T88/50-Cosworth	63	1h13m58.41
4	Roberto Moreno	Reynard 88D-Cosworth	63	1h13m58.61
5	Mark Blundell	Lola T88/50-Cosworth	63	1h13m59.04
6	Michel Trolle	Lola T88/50-Cosworth	63	1h14m26.60

Winner's average speed: 101.782 mph. Pole position: Foitek, 1m06.52. Fastest lap: Trolle, 1m08.26

GRAND PRIX DE PAU

23 May 1988. Pau. 72 laps of a 1.715 mile-circuit = 123.480 miles. FIA F3000 Championship round 3

1	Roberto Moreno	Reynard 88D-Cosworth	72	1h29m01.76
2	Jean Alesi	Reynard 88D-Cosworth	72	1h29m23.79
3	Pierluigi Martini	March 88B-Judd	72	1h29m24.71
4	Eric Bernard	Ralt RT22-Judd	72	1h29m25.22
5	Marco Apicella	March 88B-Judd	72	1h29m26.30
6	Pierre-Henri Raphanel	Reynard 88D-Cosworth	72	1h29m54.24

Winner's average speed: 83.218 mph. Pole position: Moreno, 1m10.86. Fastest lap: Apicella, 1m12.72

INTERNATIONAL TROPHY

5 June 1988. Silverstone. 42 laps of a 2.969 mile-circuit = 124.698 miles. FIA F3000 Championship round 4

1	Roberto Moreno	Reynard 88D-Cosworth	42	56m33.83
2	Bertrand Gachot	Reynard 88D-Cosworth	42	56m55.62
3	Pierre-Henri Raphanel	Reynard 88D-Cosworth	42	57m04.42
4	Gregor Foitek	Lola T88/50-Cosworth	42	57m13.53
5	Jean Alesi	Reynard 88D-Cosworth	42	57m16.59
6	Marco Apicella	March 88B-Judd	42	57m16.85

Winner's average speed: 132.273 mph. Pole position: Gachot, 1m19.61. Fastest lap: Moreno, 1m19.70

MONZA F3000

26 June 1988. Monza. 31 laps of a 3.604 mile-circuit = 111.721 miles. Race scheduled for 34 laps, stopped after 13 laps due to an accident, restarted over an additional 18 laps. FIA F3000 Championship round 5

1	Roberto Moreno	Reynard 88D-Cosworth	31	51m40.552
2	Marco Apicella	March 88B-Judd	31	51m58.147
3	Johnny Herbert	Reynard 88D-Cosworth	31	52m14.330
4	Gregor Foitek	Lola T88/50-Cosworth	31	52m32.430
5	Claudio Langes	Lola T88/50-Cosworth	31	52m41.410
6	Andrea Chiesa	Lola T87/50-Cosworth	31	52m46.530

Winner's average speed: 129.717 mph. Pole position: Moreno, 1m37.22. Fastest lap: Herbert, 1m38.120

GRAN PREMIO DE MEDITERRANEO

17 July 1988. Enna-Pergusa. 37 laps of a 3.076 mile-circuit = 113.812 miles. Race scheduled for 41 laps, stopped after 3 laps due to an accident, restarted over an additional 34 laps. FIA F3000 Championship round 6

1	Pierluigi Martini	March 88B-Judd	37	56m20.62
2	Olivier Grouillard	Lola T88/50-Cosworth	37	56m24.67
3	Michel Trolle	Lola T88/50-Cosworth	37	56m32.45
4	Claudio Langes	Lola T88/50-Cosworth	37	56m35.82
5	Pierre-Henri Raphanel	Reynard 88D-Cosworth	37	56m41.33
6	Jean Alesi	Reynard 88D-Cosworth	37	56m45.11

Winner's average speed: 121.198 mph. Pole position: Grouillard, 1m29.07. Fastest lap: Martini, 1m30.14

BRANDS HATCH F3000

21 August 1988. Brands Hatch. 42 laps of a 2.600 mile-circuit = 109.208 miles. Race scheduled for 48 laps, stopped after 22 laps due to an accident, restarted over an additional 20 laps. FIA F3000 Championship round 7

1	Martin Donnelly	Reynard 88D-Cosworth	42	54m14.20
2	Pierluigi Martini	March 88B-Judd	42	54m42.97
3	Mark Blundell	Lola T88/50-Cosworth	42	54m45.26
4	Paolo Barilla	Reynard 88D-Cosworth	42	54m56.15
5	Cor Euser	Reynard 88D-Cosworth	42	55m09.47
6*	Volker Weidler	March 88B-Cosworth	42	55m42.35

Eric Bernard (Reynard 88D-Cosworth), 55m17.47, finished sixth but was disqualified due to an illegal rear wing. *Includes 1 minute penalty. Winner's average speed: 120.813 mph. Pole position: Johnny Herbert (Reynard 88D-Cosworth), 1m14.77. Fastest lap: Donnelly, 1m15.88

HALFORDS BIRMINGHAM SUPERPRIX

29 August 1988. Birmingham. 43 laps of a 2.470 mile-circuit = 106.210 miles. Race stopped twice due to first-lap accidents, restarted on both occasions over original distance. FIA F3000 Championship round 8

1	Roberto Moreno	Reynard 88D-Cosworth	43	1h00m19.78
2	Martin Donnelly	Reynard 88D-Cosworth	43	1h00m27.48
3	Pierluigi Martini	March 88B-Judd	43	1h00m41.48
4	Volker Weidler	March 88B-Cosworth	43	1h00m57.48
5	Bertrand Gachot	Reynard 88D-Cosworth	43	1h00m58.16
6	Michel Ferte	Lola T88/50-Cosworth	43	1h01m31.24

Eric Bernard (Reynard 88D-Cosworth), 1h01m08.3, finished sixth but was disqualified due to his car being under the weight limit. Winner's average speed: 105.630 mph. Pole position: Olivier Grouillard (Lola T88/50-Cosworth), 1m21.81 - did not start. Fastest lap: Donnelly, 1m23.33

LE MANS F3000

25 September 1988. Le Mans-Bugatti. 47 laps of a 2.635 mile-circuit = 123.845 miles. FIA F3000 Championship round 9

1	Olivier Grouillard	Lola T88/50-Cosworth	47	1h12m15.23
2	Martin Donnelly	Reynard 88D-Cosworth	47	1h12m22.55
3	Jean-Denis Deletraz	Lola T88/50-Cosworth	47	1h12m53.22
4	Bertrand Gachot	Reynard 88D-Cosworth	47	1h12m54.02
5	Roberto Moreno	Reynard 88D-Cosworth	47	1h13m03.69
6	Pierre-Henri Raphanel	Reynard 88D-Cosworth	47	1h13m24.65

Winner's average speed: 102.842 mph. Pole position: Grouillard, 1m28.86. Fastest lap: Grouillard, 1m31.14

ZOLDER F3000

16 October 1988. Zolder. 49 laps of a 2.606 mile-circuit = 127.694 miles. FIA F3000 Championship round 10

1	Olivier Grouillard	Lola T88/50-Cosworth	49	1h13m30.27
2	Mark Blundell	Lola T88/50-Cosworth	49	1h13m30.49
3	Jean-Denis Deletraz	Lola T88/50-Cosworth	49	1h14m00.16
4	Eric Bernard	Reynard 88D-Cosworth	49	1h14m00.62
5	Roberto Moreno	Reynard 88D-Cosworth	49	1h14m01.56
6	Bertrand Gachot	Reynard 88D-Cosworth	49	1h14m56.28

Winner's average speed: 104.234 mph. Pole position: Martin Donnelly (Reynard 88D-Cosworth), 1m27.75. Fastest lap: Grouillard, 1m28.27

DIJON-PRENOIS F3000

23 October 1988. Dijon-Prenois. 54 laps of a 2.361 mile-circuit = 127.494 miles. FIA F3000 Championship round 11

1	Martin Donnelly	Reynard 88D-Cosworth	54	1h04m57.03
2	Eric Bernard	Reynard 88D-Cosworth	54	1h04m58.65
3	Olivier Grouillard	Lola T88/50-Cosworth	54	1h05m05.67
4	Bertrand Gachot	Reynard 88D-Cosworth	54	1h05m07.58
5	Jean Alesi	Reynard 88D-Cosworth	54	1h05m18.89
6	Volker Weidler	March 88B-Cosworth	54	1h05m18.96

Winner's average speed: 117.776 mph. Pole position: Roberto Moreno

(Reynard 88D-Cosworth), 1m07.61. Fastest lap: Mark Blundell (Lola T88/50-Cosworth), 1m10.74

1988 FINAL CHAMPIONSHIP POSITIONS

1	Roberto Moreno	43	13=	Jean-Denis Deletraz	8
2	Olivier Grouillard	34		Pierre-Henri Raphanel	8
3	Martin Donnelly	30	15=	Claudio Langes	5
4	Pierluigi Martini	23		Volker Weidler	5
5	Bertrand Gachot	21	17=	Paolo Barilla	3
6	Mark Blundell	18		Fabien Giroix	3
7	Gregor Foitek	15	19	Cor Euser	2
8=	Eric Bernard	13	20=	Andrea Chiesa	1
	Johnny Herbert	13		Michel Ferte	1
10	Jean Alesi	11			
11=	Marco Apicella	9			
	Michel Trolle	9			

1989

MOTORING NEWS INTERNATIONAL TROPHY

9 April 1989. Silverstone. 41 laps of a 2.969 mile-circuit = 121.729 miles. FIA F3000 Championship round 1

1	Thomas Danielsson	Reynard 89D-Cosworth	41	55m31.92
2	Philippe Favre	Lola T89/50-Cosworth	41	55m32.50
3	Mark Blundell	Reynard 89D-Cosworth	41	55m55.89
4	Jean Alesi	Reynard 89D-Mugen	41	55m56.57
5	Erik Comas	Lola T89/50-Mugen	41	56m03.10
6	Eric van de Poele	Lola T89/50-Cosworth	41	56m07.36

JJ Lehto (Reynard 89D-Mugen), 55m38.84, finished third but was disqualified due to an illegal rev limiter. Winner's average speed: 131.523 mph. Pole position: Favre, 1m17.41. Fastest lap: Favre, 1m20.19 (Lehto, 1m20.01, set fastest lap but was disqualified)

GRAN PREMIO DI ROMA

30 April 1989. Vallelunga. 64 laps of a 1.988 mile-circuit = 127.232 miles. FIA F3000 Championship round 2

1	Fabrizio Giovanardi	Leyton March 89B-Judd	64	1h13m08.797
2	Andrea Chiesa	Reynard 89D-Cosworth	64	1h13m13.706
3	Eric van de Poele	Lola T89/50-Cosworth	64	1h13m24.010
4	Erik Comas	Lola T89/50-Mugen	64	1h13m28.040
5	Emanuele Naspetti	Reynard 89D-Cosworth	64	1h13m36.510
6	Alain Ferte	Reynard 89D-Cosworth	64	1h13m45.780

Martin Donnelly (Reynard 89D-Mugen), 1h13m01.404, finished first but was disqualified as nosecone had not passed crash test. Winner's average speed: 104.890 mph. Pole position: Donnelly, 1m04.97. Fastest lap: Marco Apicella (Reynard 89D-Judd), 1m06.772

GRAND PRIX DE PAU

15 May 1989. Pau. 72 laps of a 1.715 mile-circuit = 123.480 miles. Race stopped twice due to first-lap accidents, restarted on both occasions over original distance. FIA F3000 Championship round 3

1	Jean Alesi	Reynard 89D-Mugen	72	1h28m51.90
2	Marco Apicella	Reynard 89D-Judd	72	1h29m00.99
3	Thomas Danielsson	Reynard 89D-Mugen	72	1h29m26.63
4	JJ Lehto	Reynard 89D-Mugen	72	1h29m26.67
5	Alain Ferte	Reynard 89D-Cosworth	71	
6	Mark Blundell	Reynard 89D-Cosworth	70	

Winner's average speed: 83.371 mph. Pole position: Apicella, 1m10.65. Fastest lap: Apicella and Eric Bernard (Lola T89/50-Mugen), 1m11.93

JEREZ F3000

4 June 1989. Jerez. 48 laps of a 2.621 mile-circuit = 125.803 miles. FIA F3000 Championship round 4

1	Eric Bernard	Lola T89/50-Mugen	48	1h18m28.48
2	Erik Comas	Lola T89/50-Mugen	48	1h18m48.52
3	Marco Apicella	Reynard 89D-Judd	48	1h18m50.93
4	Eric van de Poele	Lola T89/50-Cosworth	48	1h19m10.77

5	Jean Alesi	Reynard 89D-Mugen	48	1h19m13.31
6	JJ Lehto	Reynard 89D-Mugen	48	1h19m20.00

Winner's average speed: 96.186 mph. Pole position: Bernard, 1m31.84.
Fastest lap: Bernard, 1m34.79

GRAN PREMIO DEL MEDITERRANEO

23 July 1989. Enna-Pergusa. 39 laps of a 3.076 mile-circuit = 119.964 miles. FIA F3000 Championship round 5

1	Andrea Chiesa	Reynard 89D-Cosworth	39	58m54.516
2	Claudio Langes	Lola T89/50-Cosworth	39	58m55.128
3	Eddie Irvine	Reynard 89D-Mugen	39	58m55.690
4	Marco Apicella	Reynard 89D-Judd	39	59m36.650
5	Gary Evans	Reynard 89D-Cosworth	39	59m57.930

No other finishers. Winner's average speed: 122.187 mph. Pole position: Jean Alesi (Reynard 89D-Mugen), 1m26.55. Fastest lap: Martin Donnelly (Reynard 89D-Mugen), 1m28.860

BRANDS HATCH F3000

20 August 1989. Brands Hatch. 48 laps of a 2.600 mile-circuit = 124.810 miles. FIA F3000 Championship round 6

1	Martin Donnelly	Reynard 89D-Mugen	48	1h02m03.76
2	Jean Alesi	Reynard 89D-Mugen	48	1h02m17.06
3	Erik Comas	Lola T89/50-Mugen	48	1h02m20.46
4	Eric Bernard	Lola T89/50-Mugen	48	1h02m53.63
5	Gary Brabham	Leyton March 89B-Judd	48	1h03m02.56
6	Claudio Langes	Reynard 89D-Cosworth	48	1h03m04.22

Winner's average speed: 120.662 mph. Pole position: Comas, 1m14.33.
Fastest lap: Bernard, 1m15.51

HALFORDS BIRMINGHAM SUPERPRIX

28 August 1989. Birmingham. 51 laps of a 2.470 mile-circuit = 125.970 miles. FIA F3000 Championship round 7

1	Jean Alesi	Reynard 89D-Mugen	51	1h11m48.98
2	Marco Apicella	Reynard 89D-Judd	51	1h11m49.42
3	Martin Donnelly	Reynard 89D-Mugen	51	1h12m26.68
4	Eric Bernard	Lola T89/50-Mugen	51	1h12m44.32
5	Mark Blundell	Reynard 89D-Cosworth	51	1h13m04.64
6	Eddie Irvine	Reynard 89D-Mugen	51	1h13m10.66

Winner's average speed: 105.243 mph. Pole position: Alesi, 1m20.66.
Fastest lap: Alesi, 1m23.03

SPA-FRANCORCHAMPS F3000

16 September 1989. Spa-Francorchamps. 28 laps of a 4.312 mile-circuit = 120.736 miles. FIA F3000 Championship round 8

1	Jean Alesi	Reynard 89D-Mugen	28	1h02m40.93
2	Erik Comas	Lola T89/50-Mugen	28	1h02m57.02
3	Marco Apicella	Reynard 89D-Judd	28	1h03m17.46
4	Eric van de Poele	Lola T89/50-Cosworth	28	1h03m17.65
5	JJ Lehto	Reynard 89D-Mugen	28	1h03m17.81
6	Thomas Danielsson	Reynard 89D-Cosworth	28	1h04m07.15

Winner's average speed: 115.570 mph. Pole position: Comas, 2m22.35.
Fastest lap: Comas, 2m11.45

LE MANS F3000

24 September 1989. Le Mans-Bugatti. 45 laps of a 2.750 mile-circuit = 123.750 miles. FIA F3000 Championship round 9

1	Erik Comas	Lola T89/50-Mugen	45	1h10m54.30
2	Eric van de Poele	Lola T89/50-Cosworth	45	1h11m05.68
3	Eric Bernard	Lola T89/50-Mugen	45	1h11m06.35
4	Eddie Irvine	Reynard 89D-Mugen	45	1h11m12.38
5	Stephane Proulx	Lola T89/50-Cosworth	45	1h11m13.74
6	Jean Alesi	Reynard 89D-Mugen	45	1h11m14.46

Winner's average speed: 104.718 mph. Pole position: Bernard, 1m30.47.
Fastest lap: Comas, 1m33.42

DIJON-PRENOIS F3000

22 October 1989. Dijon-Prenois. 54 laps of a 2.361 mile-circuit = 127.494 miles. FIA F3000 Championship round 10

1	Erik Comas	Lola T89/50-Mugen	54	1h05m07.20
2	Eric Bernard	Lola T89/50-Mugen	54	1h05m15.42
3	Andrew Gilbert-Scott	Lola T89/50-Cosworth	54	1h05m33.24
4	Eddie Irvine	Reynard 89D-Mugen	54	1h06m03.42
5	Eric van de Poele	Lola T89/50-Cosworth	54	1h06m11.32
6	Mark Blundell	Reynard 89D-Cosworth	54	1h06m15.00

Winner's average speed: 117.470 mph. Pole position: Bernard, 1m08.96.
Fastest lap: Comas, 1m10.43

1989 FINAL CHAMPIONSHIP POSITIONS

1	Jean Alesi	39*	13=	Philippe Favre	6
2	Erik Comas	39		JJ Lehto	6
3	Eric Bernard	25	15	Andrew Gilbert-Scott	4
4	Marco Apicella	23	16	Alain Ferte	3
5	Eric van de Poele	19	17=	Gary Brabham	2
6	Andrea Chiesa	15		Gary Evans	2
7	Thomas Danielsson	14		Emanuele Naspetti	2
8	Martin Donnelly	13		Stephane Proulx	2
9	Eddie Irvine	11		*Alesi was champion due to	
10	Fabrizio Giovanardi	9		winning more races	
11	Mark Blundell	8			
12	Claudio Langes	7			

1990

DONINGTON 200 GOLD CUP

22 April 1990. Donington Park. 50 laps of a 2.500 mile-circuit = 125.000 miles. FIA F3000 Championship round 1

1	Erik Comas	Lola T90/50-Mugen	50	1h12m15.34
2	Andrea Chiesa	Lola T90/50-Mugen	50	1h12m41.20
3	John Jones	Lola T90/50-Mugen	50	1h12m42.17
4	Antonio Tamburini	Reynard 90D-Cosworth	50	1h12m42.74
5	Richard Dean	Reynard 90D-Mugen	50	1h12m54.30
6	Eric van de Poele	Reynard 90D-Cosworth	50	1h13m19.01

Winner's average speed: 103.798 mph. Pole position: Andrea Montermini (Reynard 90D-Mugen), 1m20.18. Fastest lap: Stephane Proulx (Lola T90/50-Mugen), 1m22.29

INTERNATIONAL TROPHY

19 May 1990. Silverstone. 41 laps of a 2.969 mile-circuit = 121.729 miles. FIA F3000 Championship round 2

1	Allan McNish	Lola T90/50-Mugen	41	54m23.21
2	Erik Comas	Lola T90/50-Mugen	41	54m25.22
3	Marco Apicella	Reynard 90D-Mugen	41	54m34.06
4	Andrea Montermini	Reynard 90D-Mugen	41	54m51.52
5	Eric van de Poele	Reynard 90D-Cosworth	41	54m52.51
6	Eddie Irvine	Reynard 90D-Mugen	41	54m53.05

Winner's average speed: 134.293 mph. Pole position: McNish, 1m16.53.
Fastest lap: McNish, 1m18.31

GRAND PRIX DE PAU

4 June 1990. Pau. 69 laps of a 1.715 mile-circuit = 118.335 miles. Race stopped after a first-lap accident, restarted over original distance, stopped after 10 laps due to an accident, restarted over an additional 59 laps. FIA F3000 Championship round 3

1	Eric van de Poele	Reynard 90D-Cosworth	69	1h24m18.72
2	Fabrizio Giovanardi	Reynard 90D-Mugen	69	1h24m39.02
3	Gianni Morbidelli	Lola T90/50-Cosworth	69	1h24m55.50
4	John Jones	Lola T90/50-Mugen	69	1h25m22.14
5	Franck Freon	Lola T89/50-Cosworth	65	accident
6	Allan McNish	Lola T90/50-Mugen	65	accident

Winner's average speed: 84.212 mph. Pole position: Erik Comas (Lola T90/50-Mugen), 1m10.55. Fastest lap: Marco Apicella (Reynard 90D-Mugen), 1m11.71

JEREZ F3000

17 June 1990. Jerez. 48 laps of a 2.621 mile-circuit = 125.803 miles. FIA F3000 Championship round 4

1	Erik Comas	Lola T90/50-Mugen	48	1h18m07.02
2	Marco Apicella	Reynard 90D-Mugen	48	1h18m08.29
3	Andrea Montermini	Reynard 90D-Mugen	48	1h18m38.13
4	Fabrizio Barbazza	Leyton March 90B-Cosworth	48	1h19m01.81
5	Andrea Chiesa	Lola T90/50-Mugen	48	1h19m07.40
6	Fabrizio Giovanardi	Reynard 90D-Mugen	48	1h19m09.19

Winner's average speed: 96.627 mph. Pole position: Comas, 1m30.44. Fastest lap: Apicella, 1m35.22

MONZA F3000

24 June 1990. Monza. 34 laps of a 3.604 mile-circuit = 122.533 miles. FIA F3000 Championship round 5

1	Erik Comas	Lola T90/50-Mugen	34	55m19.12
2	Eddie Irvine	Reynard 90D-Mugen	34	55m20.82
3	Gary Brabham	Lola T90/50-Cosworth	34	55m22.64
4	Gianni Morbidelli	Lola T90/50-Cosworth	34	55m23.77
5	Marco Apicella	Reynard 90D-Mugen	34	55m26.52
6	Allan McNish	Lola T90/50-Mugen	34	55m28.33

Winner's average speed: 132.902 mph. Pole position: Damon Hill (Lola T90/50-Cosworth), 1m34.53. Fastest lap: Hill, 1m35.66

GRAN PREMIO DEL MEDITERRANEO

22 July 1990. Enna-Pergusa. 36 laps of a 3.076 mile-circuit = 110.736 miles. FIA F3000 Championship round 6

1	Gianni Morbidelli	Lola T90/50-Cosworth	36	55m27.219
2	Allan McNish	Lola T90/50-Mugen	36	56m14.083
3	Gary Brabham	Lola T90/50-Cosworth	36	56m40.320
4	Eddie Irvine	Reynard 90D-Mugen	36	56m41.140
5	Heinz-Harald Frentzen	Reynard 90D-Mugen	36	56m44.740
6	Fabrizio Giovanardi	Reynard 90D-Mugen	36	57m13.850

Winner's average speed: 119.815 mph. Pole position: Damon Hill (Lola T90/50-Cosworth), 1m25.62. Fastest lap: Hill, 1m29.423

HOCKENHEIM F3000

28 July 1990. Hockenheim. 29 laps of a 4.227 mile-circuit = 122.580 miles. FIA F3000 Championship round 7

1	Eddie Irvine	Reynard 90D-Mugen	29	58m14.604
2	Marco Apicella	Reynard 90D-Mugen	29	58m19.442
3	Jean-Marc Gounon	Reynard 90D-Mugen	29	58m47.400
4	Erik Comas	Lola T90/50-Mugen	29	58m54.160
5	Karl Wendlinger	Lola T90/50-Cosworth	29	59m08.180
6	Heinz-Harald Frentzen	Reynard 90D-Mugen	29	59m09.410

Winner's average speed: 126.277 mph. Pole position: Damon Hill (Lola T90/50-Cosworth), 1m56.146. Fastest lap: Apicella, 1m59.397

BRANDS HATCH F3000

19 August 1990. Brands Hatch. 48 laps of a 2.600 mile-circuit = 124.810 miles. FIA F3000 Championship round 8

1	Allan McNish	Lola T90/50-Mugen	48	1h09m09.68
2	Damon Hill	Lola T90/50-Cosworth	48	1h09m19.75
3	Eddie Irvine	Reynard 90D-Mugen	48	1h09m32.17
4	Pedro Chaves	Reynard 90D-Cosworth	48	1h09m45.96
5	Andrea Chiesa	Lola T90/50-Mugen	48	1h09m52.50
6	Jean-Marc Gounon	Reynard 90D-Mugen	48	1h10m03.21

Marco Apicella (Reynard 90D-Mugen) finished third but was disqualified due to illegal fuel. Winner's average speed: 108.277 mph. Pole position: Irvine, 1m12.70. Fastest lap: Michael Bartels (Reynard 90D-Mugen), 1m15.56

HALFORDS BIRMINGHAM SUPERPRIX

27 August 1990. Birmingham. 51 laps of a 2.470 mile-circuit = 125.970 miles. FIA F3000 Championship round 9

1	Eric van de Poele	Reynard 90D-Cosworth	51	1h11m47.02

2	Andrea Chiesa	Lola T90/50-Mugen	51	1h12m05.96
3	Didier Artzet	Reynard 90D-Cosworth	51	1h12m06.68
4	Jean-Marc Gounon	Reynard 90D-Mugen	51	1h12m07.51
5	Fabrizio Giovanardi	Reynard 90D-Mugen	51	1h12m20.81
6	Emanuele Naspetti	Reynard 90D-Mugen	51	1h12m30.47

Winner's average speed: 105.291 mph. Pole position: Marco Apicella (Reynard 90D-Mugen), 1m20.95. Fastest lap: Apicella, 1m22.93

LE MANS F3000

23 September 1990. Le Mans-Bugatti. 45 laps of a 2.750 mile-circuit = 123.750 miles. FIA F3000 Championship round 10

1	Erik Comas	Lola T90/50-Mugen	45	1h11m41.65
2	Andrea Montermini	Reynard 90D-Mugen	45	1h11m52.77
3	Eddie Irvine	Reynard 90D-Mugen	45	1h11m58.58
4	Jean-Marc Gounon	Reynard 90D-Mugen	45	1h11m58.79
5	Andrea Chiesa	Lola T90/50-Mugen	45	1h11m59.97
6	Paul Belmondo	Reynard 90D-Mugen	45	1h12m00.47

Winner's average speed: 103.565 mph. Pole position: Comas, 1m30.60. Fastest lap: Philippe Gache (Lola T89/50-Cosworth), 1m33.21

GRAND PRIX DE NOGARO

7 October 1990. Nogaro. 55 laps of a 2.259 mile-circuit = 124.245 miles. FIA F3000 Championship round 11

1	Eric van de Poele	Reynard 90D-Cosworth	55	1h20m27.81
2	Erik Comas	Lola T90/50-Mugen	55	1h20m38.84
3	Gianni Morbidelli	Lola T90/50-Cosworth	55	1h20m54.16
4	Antonio Tamburini	Reynard 90D-Cosworth	55	1h21m13.87
5	Marco Apicella	Reynard 90D-Mugen	55	1h21m14.28
6	Michael Bartels	Reynard 90D-Mugen	55	1h21m16.10

Winner's average speed: 92.647 mph. Pole position: Morbidelli, 1m18.61. Fastest lap: Comas, 1m20.30

1990 FINAL CHAMPIONSHIP POSITIONS

1	Erik Comas	51	13=	Damon Hill	6
2	Eric van de Poele	30		Antonio Tamburini	6
3	Eddie Irvine	27	15	Didier Artzet	4
4	Allan McNish	26	16=	Fabrizio Barbazza	3
5=	Marco Apicella	20		Pedro Chaves	3
	Gianni Morbidelli	20		Heinz-Harald Frentzen	3
7	Andrea Chiesa	18	19=	Richard Dean	2
8	Andrea Montermini	13		Franck Freon	2
9	Jean-Marc Gounon	11		Karl Wendlinger	2
10	Fabrizio Giovanardi	10	22=	Michael Bartels	1
11	Gary Brabham	8		Paul Belmondo	1
12	John Jones	7		Emanuele Naspetti	1

1991

GRAN PREMIO DI ROMA

14 April 1991. Vallelunga. 60 laps of a 1.988 mile-circuit = 119.280 miles. Race stopped after 37 laps due to an accident, restarted over an additional 23 laps. FIA F3000 Championship round 1

1	Alessandro Zanardi	Reynard 91D-Mugen	60	1h06m05.152
2	Christian Fittipaldi	Reynard 91D-Mugen	60	1h06m16.800
3	Antonio Tamburini	Reynard 91D-Mugen	60	1h06m20.876
4	Damon Hill	Lola T91/50-Cosworth	60	1h06m22.937
5	Giuseppe Bugatti	Reynard 91D-Mugen	60	1h06m37.009
6	Alain Menu	Reynard 91D-Cosworth	60	1h06m41.183

Winner's average speed: 108.295 mph. Pole position: Fittipaldi, 1m03.236. Fastest lap: Zanardi, 1m04.939

GRAND PRIX DE PAU

20 May 1991. Pau. 72 laps of a 1.715 mile-circuit = 123.480 miles. FIA F3000 Championship round 2

1	Jean-Marc Gounon	Ralt RT23-Cosworth	72	1h26m31.24

2	Christian Fittipaldi	Reynard 91D-Mugen	72	1h26m43.39
3	Eric Helary	Reynard 91D-Cosworth	72	1h26m48.49
4	Marco Apicella	Lola T91/50-Mugen	72	1h26m54.65
5	Fabrizio Giovanardi	Lola T91/50-Cosworth	72	1h26m55.89
6	Alain Menu	Reynard 91D-Cosworth	72	1h26m56.10

Winner's average speed: 85.630 mph. Pole position: Alessandro Zanardi (Reynard 91D-Mugen), 1m09.48. Fastest lap: Andrea Montermini (Ralt RT23-Cosworth), 1m10.47

JEREZ F3000

9 June 1991. Jerez. 48 laps of a 2.621 mile-circuit = 125.803 miles. FIA F3000 Championship round 3

1	Christian Fittipaldi	Reynard 91D-Mugen	48	1h18m15.69
2	Alessandro Zanardi	Reynard 91D-Mugen	48	1h18m23.44
3	Andrea Montermini	Ralt RT23-Cosworth	48	1h18m24.06
4	Antonio Tamburini	Reynard 91D-Mugen	48	1h18m24.62
5	Karl Wendlinger	Reynard 91D-Cosworth	48	1h18m29.58
6	Jean-Marc Gounon	Ralt RT23-Cosworth	48	1h18m58.02

Winner's average speed: 96.448 mph. Pole position: Fittipaldi, 1m30.38. Fastest lap: Fittipaldi, 1m35.19

EURO MUGELLO

23 June 1991. Mugello. 38 laps of a 3.259 mile-circuit = 123.842 miles. FIA F3000 Championship round 4

1	Alessandro Zanardi	Reynard 91D-Mugen	38	1h03m08.380
2	Marco Apicella	Lola T91/50-Mugen	38	1h03m14.825
3	Christian Fittipaldi	Reynard 91D-Mugen	38	1h03m29.075
4	Vincenzo Sospiri	Lola T91/50-Cosworth	38	1h03m32.985
5	Allan McNish	Lola T91/50-Mugen	38	1h03m39.145
6	Heinz-Harald Frentzen	Lola T91/50-Mugen	38	1h03m40.940

Winner's average speed: 117.684 mph. Pole position: Zanardi, 1m35.096. Fastest lap: Zanardi, 1m38.367

GRAN PREMIO DEL MEDITERRANEO

7 July 1991. Enna-Pergusa. 40 laps of a 3.076 mile-circuit = 123.040 miles. FIA F3000 Championship round 5

1	Emanuele Naspetti	Reynard 91D-Cosworth	40	59m34.254
2	Marco Apicella	Lola T91/50-Mugen	40	59m41.389
3	Giuseppe Bugatti	Reynard 91D-Mugen	40	59m51.130
4	Antonio Tamburini	Reynard 91D-Mugen	40	59m53.402
5	Heinz-Harald Frentzen	Lola T91/50-Mugen	40	59m54.265
6	Jean-Marc Gounon	Ralt RT23-Cosworth	40	1h00m20.320*

*Includes 1 minute penalty for jumping the start. Winner's average speed: 123.926 mph. Pole position: Naspetti, 1m26.086. Fastest lap: Gounon, 1m27.786

HOCKENHEIM F3000

27 July 1991. Hockenheim. 29 laps of a 4.227 mile-circuit = 122.580 miles. FIA F3000 Championship round 6

1	Emanuele Naspetti	Reynard 91D-Cosworth	29	57m19.217
2	Vincenzo Sospiri	Lola T91/50-Cosworth	29	57m22.174
3	Karl Wendlinger	Reynard 91D-Cosworth	29	57m35.040
4	Christian Fittipaldi	Reynard 91D-Mugen	29	57m43.329
5	Jean-Marc Gounon	Ralt RT23-Cosworth	29	57m47.817
6	Antonio Tamburini	Reynard 91D-Mugen	29	57m49.544

Winner's average speed: 128.311 mph. Pole position: Andrea Montermini (Ralt RT23-Cosworth), 1m54.327. Fastest lap: Montermini, 1m56.969

BRANDS HATCH FORMULA 3000 TROPHY

18 August 1991. Brands Hatch. 48 laps of a 2.600 mile-circuit = 124.810 miles. FIA F3000 Championship round 7

1	Emanuele Naspetti	Reynard 91D-Cosworth	48	1h00m26.28
2	Alessandro Zanardi	Reynard 91D-Mugen	48	1h00m27.96
3	Christian Fittipaldi	Reynard 91D-Mugen	48	1h00m56.89
4	Marco Apicella	Lola T91/50-Mugen	48	1h01m04.04
5	Antonio Tamburini	Reynard 91D-Mugen	48	1h01m05.15
6	Damon Hill	Lola T91/50-Cosworth	48	1h01m08.52

Winner's average speed: 123.905 mph. Pole position: Zanardi, 1m12.44. Fastest lap: Naspetti, 1m13.86

SPA-FRANCORCHAMPS F3000

24 August 1991. Spa-Francorchamps. 29 laps of a 4.312 mile-circuit = 125.048 miles. FIA F3000 Championship round 8

1	Emanuele Naspetti	Reynard 91D-Cosworth	29	1h03m09.82
2	Alessandro Zanardi	Reynard 91D-Mugen	29	1h03m10.99
3	Laurent Aiello	Lola T91/50-Mugen	29	1h03m30.07
4	Eric Helary	Reynard 91D-Cosworth	29	1h03m31.14
5	Heinz-Harald Frentzen	Lola T91/50-Mugen	29	1h03m31.95
6	Fabrizio Giovanardi	Reynard 91D-Cosworth	29	1h03m38.95

Winner's average speed: 118.785 mph. Pole position: Aiello, 2m05.74. Fastest lap: Naspetti, 2m09.21

LE MANS F3000

22 September 1991. Le Mans-Bugatti. 45 laps of a 2.753 mile-circuit = 123.885 miles. FIA F3000 Championship round 9

1	Antonio Tamburini	Reynard 91D-Mugen	45	1h24m09.87
2	Christian Fittipaldi	Reynard 91D-Mugen	45	1h25m05.56
3	Andrea Montermini	Ralt RT23-Cosworth	45	1h25m15.30
4	Damon Hill	Lola T91/50-Cosworth	45	1h25m48.26
5	Philippe Gache	Lola T89/50-Cosworth	44	
6	Gabriel Furlan	Reynard 91D-Judd	44	

Winner's average speed: 88.316 mph. Pole position: Fittipaldi, 1m30.65. Fastest lap: Tamburini, 1m49.60

GRAND PRIX DE NOGARO

6 October 1991. Nogaro. 55 laps of a 2.259 mile-circuit = 124.245 miles. FIA F3000 Championship round 10

1	Christian Fittipaldi	Reynard 91D-Mugen	55	1h14m26.15
2	Alessandro Zanardi	Reynard 91D-Mugen	55	1h14m30.37
3	Damon Hill	Reynard 91D-Cosworth	55	1h15m00.66
4	Fabrizio Giovanardi	Reynard 91D-Cosworth	55	1h15m15.49
5	Eric Helary	Reynard 91D-Cosworth	55	1h15m20.13
6	Emanuele Naspetti	Reynard 91D-Cosworth	55	1h15m32.71

Winner's average speed: 100.149 mph. Pole position: Fittipaldi, 1m17.76. Fastest lap: Zanardi, 1m20.16

1991 FINAL CHAMPIONSHIP POSITIONS

1	Christian Fittipaldi	47	11=	Giuseppe Bugatti	6
2	Alessandro Zanardi	42		Fabrizio Giovanardi	6
3	Emanuele Naspetti	37		Karl Wendlinger	6
4	Antonio Tamburini	22	14	Heinz-Harald Frentzen	5
5	Marco Apicella	18	15	Laurent Aiello	4
6	Jean-Marc Gounon	13	16=	Philippe Gache	2
7	Damon Hill	11		Allan McNish	2
8=	Eric Helary	9		Alain Menu	2
	Vincenzo Sospiri	9	19	Gabriel Furlan	1
10	Andrea Montermini	8			

1992

BRDC INTERNATIONAL TROPHY

10 May 1992. Silverstone. 37 laps of a 3.247 mile-circuit = 120.139 miles. FIA F3000 Championship round 1

1	Jordi Gene	Reynard 92D-Mugen	37	59m21.470
2	Rubens Barrichello	Reynard 92D-Judd	37	59m39.169
3	Olivier Panis	Lola T92/50-Cosworth	37	59m55.192
4	Jean-Marc Gounon	Lola T92/50-Cosworth	37	1h00m01.193
5	Luca Badoer	Reynard 92D-Cosworth	37	1h00m02.677
6	Emanuele Naspetti	Reynard 92D-Cosworth	37	1h00m22.346

Winner's average speed: 121.439 mph. Pole position: Gene, 1m54.518. Fastest lap: Barrichello, 1m34.904

GRAND PRIX DE PAU

8 June 1992. Pau. 72 laps of a 1.715 mile-circuit = 123.480 miles. FIA F3000 Championship round 2

1	Emanuele Naspetti	Reynard 92D-Cosworth	72	1h25m38.91
2	Michael Bartels	Reynard 92D-Cosworth	72	1h25m47.76
3	Rubens Barrichello	Reynard 92D-Judd	72	1h25m57.02
4	Vittorio Zoboli	Reynard 92D-Cosworth	72	1h26m02.10
5	Giuseppe Bugatti	Reynard 92D-Mugen	71	
6	Luca Badoer	Reynard 92D-Cosworth	71	

Winner's average speed: 86.502 mph. Pole position: Andrea Montermini (Reynard 92D-Judd), 1m08.60. Fastest lap: Naspetti, 1m09.82

BARCELONA F3000

21 June 1992. Catalunya. 43 laps of a 2.950 mile-circuit = 126.837 miles. FIA F3000 Championship round 3

1	Andrea Montermini	Reynard 92D-Judd	43	1h06m51.154
2	Rubens Barrichello	Reynard 92D-Judd	43	1h07m04.061
3	Jordi Gene	Reynard 92D-Mugen	43	1h07m12.181
4	Emmanuel Collard	Lola T92/50-Cosworth	43	1h07m15.825
5	Allan McNish	Reynard 92D-Mugen	43	1h07m16.316
6	Luca Badoer	Reynard 92D-Cosworth	43	1h07m16.572

Winner's average speed: 113.836 mph. Pole position: Montermini, 1m29.565. Fastest lap: Emanuele Naspetti (Reynard 92D-Cosworth), 1m30.536

GRAN PREMIO DEL MEDITERRANEO

12 July 1992. Enna-Pergusa. 40 laps of a 3.076 mile-circuit = 123.040 miles. FIA F3000 Championship round 4

1	Luca Badoer	Reynard 92D-Cosworth	40	58m20.958
2	Emanuele Naspetti	Reynard 92D-Cosworth	40	58m42.445
3	Andrea Montermini	Reynard 92D-Judd	40	58m44.749
4	Michael Bartels	Reynard 92D-Cosworth	40	58m54.717
5	Alessandro Zampedri	Reynard 92D-Cosworth	40	59m01.754
6	Jerome Policand	Lola T92/50-Cosworth	40	59m15.437

Winner's average speed: 126.521 mph. Pole position: Badoer, 1m24.708. Fastest lap: Badoer, 1m26.242

HOCKENHEIM F3000

25 July 1992. Hockenheim. 29 laps of a 4.235 mile-circuit = 122.815 miles. FIA F3000 Championship round 5

1	Luca Badoer	Reynard 92D-Cosworth	29	56m24.640
2	Michael Bartels	Reynard 92D-Cosworth	29	56m32.508
3	Allan McNish	Reynard 92D-Mugen	29	56m35.068
4	Emanuele Naspetti	Reynard 92D-Cosworth	29	56m46.874
5	Jordi Gene	Reynard 92D-Mugen	29	56m49.284
6	Rubens Barrichello	Reynard 92D-Judd	29	56m50.742

Winner's average speed: 130.630 mph. Pole position: Badoer, 1m53.483. Fastest lap: Badoer, 1m55.381

NURBURGRING F3000

23 August 1992. Nurburgring. 45 laps of a 2.822 mile-circuit = 126.990 miles. FIA F3000 Championship round 6

1	Luca Badoer	Reynard 92D-Cosworth	45	1h06m10.45
2	Michael Bartels	Reynard 92D-Cosworth	45	1h06m23.66
3	Rubens Barrichello	Reynard 92D-Cosworth	45	1h06m24.52
4	Emmanuel Collard	Lola T92/50-Cosworth	45	1h06m35.14
5	Laurent Aiello	Reynard 92D-Mugen	45	1h06m36.23
6	Jean-Marc Gounon	Lola T92/50-Cosworth	45	1h06m48.87

Winner's average speed: 115.142 mph. Pole position: Emanuele Naspetti (Reynard 92D-Cosworth), 1m25.72. Fastest lap: Barrichello, 1m26.98

SPA-FRANCORCHAMPS F3000

29 August 1992. Spa-Francorchamps. 25 laps of a 4.312 mile-circuit = 107.800 miles. Race stopped after 3 laps due to an accident, restarted over an additional 22 laps. FIA F3000 Championship round 7

1	Andrea Montermini	Reynard 92D-Cosworth	25	53m48.61
2	Jordi Gene	Reynard 92D-Mugen	25	54m06.21
3	Michael Bartels	Reynard 92D-Cosworth	25	54m18.66
4	David Coulthard	Reynard 92D-Judd	25	54m29.35
5	Rubens Barrichello	Reynard 92D-Cosworth	25	54m29.75
6	Laurent Aiello	Reynard 92D-Mugen	25	54m30.26

Winner's average speed: 120.200 mph. Pole position: Montermini, 2m06.78. Fastest lap: Montermini, 2m07.29

ALBACETE F3000

13 September 1992. Albacete. 57 laps of a 2.236 mile-circuit = 127.452 miles. FIA F3000 Championship round 8

1	Andrea Montermini	Reynard 92D-Cosworth	57	1h20m36.22
2	Luca Badoer	Reynard 92D-Cosworth	57	1h20m41.61
3	Emmanuel Collard	Lola T92/50-Cosworth	57	1h20m47.96
4	Paul Stewart	Reynard 92D-Judd	57	1h21m33.87
5	Allan McNish	Reynard 92D-Mugen	57	1h21m51.54
6	Rubens Barrichello	Reynard 92D-Cosworth	57	1h21m52.63

Winner's average speed: 94.873 mph. Pole position: Badoer, 1m18.54. Fastest lap: Montermini, 1m21.94

GRAND PRIX DE NOGARO

11 October 1992. Nogaro. 55 laps of a 2.259 mile-circuit = 124.245 miles. FIA F3000 Championship round 9

1	Luca Badoer	Reynard 92D-Cosworth	55	1h14m39.94
2	Jean-Marc Gounon	Lola T92/50-Cosworth	55	1h14m51.37
3	David Coulthard	Reynard 92D-Judd	55	1h14m52.35
4	Andrea Montermini	Reynard 92D-Cosworth	55	1h14m54.09
5	Alessandro Zampedri	Reynard 92D-Cosworth	55	1h15m12.67
6	Rubens Barrichello	Reynard 92D-Cosworth	55	1h15m20.67

Winner's average speed: 99.841 mph. Pole position: Badoer, 1m17.69. Fastest lap: Badoer, 1m20.58

MAGNY-COURS F3000

18 October 1992. Magny-Cours. 47 laps of a 2.641 mile-circuit = 124.127 miles. FIA F3000 Championship round 10

1	Jean-Marc Gounon	Lola T92/50-Cosworth	47	1h08m13.148
2	Olivier Panis	Lola T92/50-Cosworth	47	1h08m13.522
3	David Coulthard	Reynard 92D-Judd	47	1h08m14.452
4	Emmanuel Collard	Lola T92/50-Cosworth	47	1h08m20.324
5	Rubens Barrichello	Reynard 92D-Cosworth	47	1h08m21.212
6	Giampiero Simoni	Reynard 92D-Judd	47	1h08m41.368

Winner's average speed: 109.172 mph. Pole position: Luca Badoer (Reynard 92D-Cosworth), 1m24.270. Fastest lap: Coulthard, 1m25.759

1992 FINAL CHAMPIONSHIP POSITIONS

1	Luca Badoer	46		11	Allan McNish	8
2	Andrea Montermini	34		12	Alessandro Zampedri	4
3	Rubens Barrichello	27		13=	Laurent Aiello	3
4	Michael Bartels	25			Paul Stewart	3
5	Jordi Gene	21			Vittorio Zoboli	3
6=	Jean-Marc Gounon	19		16	Giuseppe Bugatti	2
	Emanuele Naspetti	19		17=	Jerome Policand	1
8	Emmanuel Collard	13			Giampiero Simoni	1
9	David Coulthard	11				
10	Olivier Panis	10				

1993

TOM WHEATCROFT CUP

3 May 1993. Donington Park. 46 laps of a 2.500 mile-circuit = 115.000 miles. Race stopped after 2 laps, restarted over an additional 44 laps. FIA F3000 Championship round 1

1	Olivier Beretta	Reynard 93D-Cosworth	46	1h03m01.35
2	Pedro Lamy	Reynard 93D-Cosworth	46	1h03m07.41
3	Olivier Panis	Reynard 93D-Cosworth	46	1h03m08.84
4	Massimiliano Papis	Reynard 93D-Cosworth	46	1h03m28.15
5	Paul Stewart	Reynard 93D-Cosworth	46	1h03m42.23
6	Giampiero Simoni	Reynard 93D-Judd	46	1h03m47.64

Winner's average speed: 109.485 mph. Pole position: Beretta, 1m19.55. Fastest lap: Gil de Ferran (Reynard 93D-Cosworth), 1m20.97

BRDC INTERNATIONAL TROPHY

9 May 1993. Silverstone. 37 laps of a 3.247 mile-circuit = 120.139 miles. FIA F3000 Championship round 2

1	Gil de Ferran	Reynard 93D-Cosworth	37	1h00m20.32
2	David Coulthard	Reynard 93D-Cosworth	37	1h00m29.86
3	Michael Bartels	Reynard 93D-Cosworth	37	1h00m37.81
4	Franck Lagorce	Reynard 93D-Cosworth	37	1h00m38.68
5	Paul Stewart	Reynard 93D-Cosworth	37	1h00m45.20
6	Olivier Panis	Reynard 93D-Cosworth	37	1h00m47.01

Alessandro Zampedri (Reynard 93D-Cosworth), 1h00m45.45, finished sixth but was disqualified as his car was under the weight limit. Winner's average speed: 119.465 mph. Pole position: de Ferran, 1m33.20. Fastest lap: Coulthard, 1m35.78

GRAND PRIX DE PAU

31 May 1993. Pau. 72 laps of a 1.715 mile-circuit = 123.480 miles. Race stopped after a first-lap accident, restarted over original distance. FIA F3000 Championship round 3

1	Pedro Lamy	Reynard 92D-Cosworth	72	1h25m55.83
2	David Coulthard	Reynard 93D-Cosworth	72	1h26m31.37
3	Paul Stewart	Reynard 93D-Cosworth	72	1h26m33.66
4	Olivier Beretta	Reynard 93D-Cosworth	72	1h26m35.38
5	Massimiliano Papis	Reynard 93D-Cosworth	72	1h26m53.85
6	Vincenzo Sospiri	Reynard 93D-Judd	72	1h27m04.06

Winner's average speed: 86.219 mph. Pole position: Lamy, 1m09.28. Fastest lap: Olivier Panis (Reynard 93D-Cosworth), 1m10.07

GRAN PREMIO DEL MEDITERRANEO

18 July 1993. Enna-Pergusa. 37 laps of a 3.076 mile-circuit = 113.812 miles. Race stopped after 10 laps, restarted over an additional 27 laps. FIA F3000 Championship round 4

1	David Coulthard	Reynard 93D-Cosworth	37	53m47.53
2	Vincenzo Sospiri	Reynard 93D-Judd	37	54m16.34
3	Jerome Policand	Reynard 92D-Judd	37	54m48.05
4	Jan Lammers	Reynard 93D-Cosworth	37	54m58.08
5	Enrico Bertaggia	Reynard 92D-Cosworth	37	55m53.42
6	Andrea Gilardi	Reynard 92D-Cosworth	37	56m02.56

Winner's average speed: 126.946 mph. Pole position: Michael Bartels (Reynard 93D-Cosworth), 1m24.34. Fastest lap: Coulthard, 1m26.59

HOCKENHEIM F3000

24 July 1993. Hockenheim. 26 laps of a 4.235 mile-circuit = 110.110 miles. Race stopped after 2 laps due to an accident, restarted over an additional 24 laps. FIA F3000 Championship round 5

1	Olivier Panis	Reynard 93D-Cosworth	26	51m01.607
2	Pedro Lamy	Reynard 92D-Cosworth	26	51m07.422
3	Vincenzo Sospiri	Reynard 93D-Judd	26	51m27.440
4	Olivier Beretta	Reynard 93D-Cosworth	26	51m28.410
5	Paolo delle Piane	Reynard 93D-Cosworth	26	51m41.264
6	Andrea Gilardi	Reynard 92D-Cosworth	26	52m12.670

Winner's average speed: 129.473 mph. Pole position: Lamy, 1m52.922. Fastest lap: Panis, 1m55.950

NURBURGRING F3000

22 August 1993. Nurburgring. 45 laps of a 2.822 mile-circuit = 126.990 miles. FIA F3000 Championship round 6

1	Olivier Panis	Reynard 93D-Cosworth	45	1h06m52.13
2	Gil de Ferran	Reynard 93D-Cosworth	45	1h07m02.50
3	Alessandro Zampedri	Reynard 93D-Cosworth	45	1h07m08.81
4	Pedro Lamy	Reynard 92D-Cosworth	45	1h07m10.11
5	Olivier Beretta	Reynard 93D-Cosworth	45	1h07m14.98
6	Vincenzo Sospiri	Reynard 93D-Judd	45	1h07m17.78

Winner's average speed: 113.945 mph. Pole position: Panis, 1m24.03. Fastest lap: Lamy, 1m27.63

SPA-FRANCORCHAMPS F3000

28 August 1993. Spa-Francorchamps. 29 laps of a 4.312 mile-circuit = 125.048 miles. FIA F3000 Championship round 7

1	Olivier Panis	Reynard 93D-Cosworth	29	1h01m57.34
2	Gil de Ferran	Reynard 93D-Cosworth	29	1h01m58.39
3	David Coulthard	Reynard 93D-Cosworth	29	1h02m01.15
4	Pedro Lamy	Reynard 92D-Cosworth	29	1h02m10.53
5	Vincenzo Sospiri	Reynard 93D-Judd	29	1h02m18.93
6	Paul Stewart	Reynard 93D-Cosworth	29	1h02m19.91

Winner's average speed: 121.101 mph. Pole position: Panis, 2m04.026. Fastest lap: Lamy, 2m06.94

MAGNY-COURS F3000

3 October 1993. Magny-Cours. 47 laps of a 2.641 mile-circuit = 124.127 miles. FIA F3000 Championship round 8

1	Franck Lagorce	Reynard 93D-Cosworth	47	1h17m20.577
2	Jules Boullion	Reynard 93D-Cosworth	47	1h18m26.430
3	Pedro Lamy	Reynard 92D-Cosworth	47	1h18m38.326
4	Nicolas Leboissetier	Reynard 92D-Cosworth	47	1h18m46.381
5	Vincenzo Sospiri	Reynard 93D-Judd	47	1h18m49.419
6	Paul Stewart	Reynard 93D-Cosworth	47	1h18m57.416

Winner's average speed: 96.293 mph. Pole position: Emmanuel Collard (Reynard 93D-Cosworth), 1m24.44. Fastest lap: Lagorce, 1m27.577

GRAND PRIX DE NOGARO

10 October 1993. Nogaro. 55 laps of a 2.259 mile-circuit = 124.245 miles. FIA F3000 Championship round 9

1	Franck Lagorce	Reynard 93D-Cosworth	55	1h14m44.597
2	Jules Boullion	Reynard 93D-Cosworth	55	1h14m45.044
3	Emmanuel Collard	Reynard 93D-Cosworth	55	1h14m45.705
4	Olivier Beretta	Reynard 93D-Cosworth	55	1h15m33.083
5	Yvan Muller	Reynard 92D-Judd	55	1h16m01.082
6	Massimiliano Papis	Reynard 93D-Cosworth	55	1h16m05.677

Winner's average speed: 99.737 mph. Pole position: Lagorce, 1m17.342. Fastest lap: Boullion, 1m20.250

1993 FINAL CHAMPIONSHIP POSITIONS

1	Olivier Panis	32	11=	Michael Bartels	4
2	Pedro Lamy	31		Emmanuel Collard	4
3	David Coulthard	25		Jerome Policand	4
4=	Gil de Ferran	21		Alessandro Zampedri	4
	Franck Lagorce	21	15=	Jan Lammers	3
6	Olivier Beretta	20		Nicolas Leboissetier	3
7	Vincenzo Sospiri	16	17=	Enrico Bertaggia	2
8	Jules Boullion	12		Andrea Gilardi	2
9	Paul Stewart	10		Yvan Muller	2
10	Massimiliano Papis	6		Paolo delle Piane	2
			21	Giampiero Simoni	1

1994

AUTOSPORT INTERNATIONAL TROPHY

2 May 1994. Silverstone. 38 laps of a 3.247 mile-circuit = 123.386 miles. FIA F3000 Championship round 1

1	Franck Lagorce	Reynard 94D-Cosworth	38	1h01m56.79
2	David Coulthard	Reynard 94D-Cosworth	38	1h02m00.89
3	Gil de Ferran	Reynard 94D-Judd	38	1h02m04.31
4	Vincenzo Sospiri	Reynard 94D-Cosworth	38	1h02m37.98
5	Hideki Noda	Reynard 94D-Cosworth	38	1h02m39.61
6	Didier Cottaz	Reynard 94D-Judd	38	1h02m40.65

Winner's average speed: 119.509 mph. Pole position: Lagorce, 1m33.83. Fastest lap: Lagorce, 1m37.67

GRAND PRIX DE PAU

23 May 1994. Pau. 71 laps of a 1.715 mile-circuit = 121.765 miles. FIA F3000 Championship round 2

1	Gil de Ferran	Reynard 94D-Judd	71	1h25m39.27
2	Vincenzo Sospiri	Reynard 94D-Cosworth	71	1h25m44.74

3 Didier Cottaz   Reynard 94D-Judd   71   1h25m51.12
4 Jules Boullion   Reynard 94D-Cosworth 71   1h25m52.83
5 Franck Lagorce   Reynard 94D-Cosworth 71   1h26m23.34
6 Guillaume Gomez   Reynard 94D-Cosworth 70

Winner's average speed: 85.295 mph. Pole position: de Ferran, 1m09.63.
Fastest lap: Sospiri, 1m11.39

BARCELONA F3000

28 May 1994. Catalunya. 41 laps of a 2.950 mile-circuit = 120.938 miles. FIA F3000 Championship round 3

1 Massimiliano Papis   Reynard 94D-Judd   41   1h05m41.393
2 Fabrizio de Simone   Reynard 94D-Judd   41   1h06m04.825
3 Vincenzo Sospiri   Reynard 94D-Cosworth   41   1h06m05.302
4 Jordi Gene   Lola T94/50-Cosworth   41   1h06m13.991
5 Franck Lagorce   Reynard 94D-Cosworth   41   1h06m15.529
6 Marc Goossens   Lola T94/50-Cosworth   41   1h06m27.295

Winner's average speed: 110.462 mph. Pole position: Papis, 1m30.889.
Fastest lap: Jules Boullion (Reynard 94D-Cosworth), 1m34.639

GRAN PREMIO DEL MEDITERRANEO

17 July 1994. Enna-Pergusa. 41 laps of a 3.076 mile-circuit = 126.116 miles. FIA F3000 Championship round 4

1 Gil de Ferran   Reynard 94D-Judd   41   57m41.731
2 Franck Lagorce   Reynard 94D-Cosworth   41   57m52.357
3 Hideki Noda   Reynard 94D-Cosworth   41   57m55.845
4 Massimiliano Papis   Reynard 94D-Judd   41   58m13.860
5 Jerome Policand   Reynard 94D-Cosworth   41   58m19.358
6 Christian Pescatori Reynard 93D-Cosworth   41   58m24.122

Winner's average speed: 131.153 mph. Pole position: Lagorce, 1m24.159.
Fastest lap: Pescatori, 1m25.157

HOCKENHEIM F3000

30 July 1994. Hockenheim. 29 laps of a 4.235 mile-circuit = 122.815 miles. FIA F3000 Championship round 5

1 Franck Lagorce   Reynard 94D-Cosworth   29   58m07.686
2 Jules Boullion   Reynard 94D-Cosworth   29   58m15.484
3 Gil de Ferran   Reynard 94D-Judd   29   58m28.089
4 Vincenzo Sospiri   Reynard 94D-Cosworth   29   58m38.724
5 Marc Goossens   Lola T94/50-Cosworth   29   58m46.652
6 Wim Eyckmans   Reynard 94D-Cosworth   29   58m55.587

Winner's average speed: 126.770 mph. Pole position: Guillaume Gomez (Reynard 94D-Cosworth), 1m55.880. Fastest lap: Lagorce, 1m59.278

SPA-FRANCORCHAMPS F3000

27 August 1994. Spa-Francorchamps. 27 laps of a 4.350 mile-circuit = 117.450 miles. FIA F3000 Championship round 6

1 Jules Boullion   Reynard 94D-Cosworth   27   1h11m34.525
2 Didier Cottaz   Reynard 94D-Judd   27   1h11m51.464
3 Kenny Brack   Reynard 94D-Judd   27   1h12m12.698
4 Guillaume Gomez   Reynard 94D-Cosworth   27   1h12m22.004
5 Gil de Ferran   Reynard 94D-Judd   27   1h12m26.967
6 Fabrizio de Simone   Reynard 94D-Cosworth   27   1h12m38.048

Winner's average speed: 98.456 mph. Pole position: Franck Lagorce (Reynard 94D-Cosworth), 2m07.685. Fastest lap: Tarso Marques (Reynard 94D-Cosworth), 2m32.38

ESTORIL F3000

24 September 1994. Estoril. 44 laps of a 2.709 mile-circuit = 119.196 miles. FIA F3000 Championship round 7

1 Jules Boullion   Reynard 94D-Cosworth   44   1h08m11.419
2 Vincenzo Sospiri   Reynard 94D-Cosworth   44   1h08m32.879
3 Guillaume Gomez   Reynard 94D-Cosworth   44   1h08m35.054
4 Pedro Diniz   Reynard 94D-Cosworth   44   1h08m37.572
5 Didier Cottaz   Reynard 94D-Judd   44   1h08m38.358
6 Kenny Brack   Reynard 94D-Judd   44   1h08m40.463

Winner's average speed: 104.879 mph. Pole position: Emmanuel Clerico (Reynard 94D-Cosworth), 1m28.852. Fastest lap: Clerico, 1m31.193

MAGNY-COURS F3000

2 October 1994. Magny-Cours. 48 laps of a 2.641 mile-circuit = 126.768 miles. FIA F3000 Championship round 8

1 Jules Boullion   Reynard 94D-Cosworth   48   1h10m41.298
2 Franck Lagorce   Reynard 94D-Cosworth   48   1h10m45.661
3 Guillaume Gomez   Reynard 94D-Cosworth   48   1h10m53.138
4 Tarso Marques   Reynard 94D-Cosworth   48   1h11m51.018
5 Vincenzo Sospiri   Reynard 94D-Cosworth   48   1h11m56.800
6 Massimiliano Papis   Reynard 94D-Judd   48   1h12m03.743

Winner's average speed: 107.600 mph. Pole position: Lagorce, 1m37.332.
Fastest lap: Lagorce, 1m27.211

1994 FINAL CHAMPIONSHIP POSITIONS

1	Jules Boullion	36		11	Kenny Brack	5
2	Franck Lagorce	34		12=	Pedro Diniz	3
3	Gil de Ferran	28			Jordi Gene	3
4	Vincenzo Sospiri	24			Marc Goossens	3
5=	Didier Cottaz	13			Tarso Marques	3
	Massimiliano Papis	13		16	Jerome Policand	2
7	Guillaume Gomez	12		17=	Wim Eyckmans	1
8	Fabrizio de Simone	7			Christian Pescatori	1
9=	David Coulthard	6				
	Hideki Noda	6				

1995

AUTOSPORT INTERNATIONAL TROPHY

7 May 1995. Silverstone. 40 laps of a 3.210-mile circuit = 128.400 miles. FIA F3000 Championship round 1

1 Ricardo Rosset   Reynard 95D-Cosworth   40   1h08m13.35
2 Vincenzo Sospiri   Reynard 95D-Cosworth   40   1h08m21.12
3 Allan McNish   Reynard 95D-Cosworth   40   1h08m21.71
4 Marc Goossens   Lola T95/50-Cosworth   40   1h08m24.48
5 Kenny Brack   Reynard 95D-Judd   40   1h08m41.07
6 Christian Pescatori Reynard 95D-Cosworth   40   1h09m03.90

Winner's average speed: 112.925 mph. Pole position: Rosset, 1m38.023.
Fastest lap: Tarso Marques (Reynard 95D-Cosworth), 1m40.95

BARCELONA F3000

13 May 1995. Catalunya. 43 laps of a 2.937-mile circuit = 126.291 miles. FIA F3000 Championship round 2

1 Vincenzo Sospiri   Reynard 95D-Cosworth   43   1h06m56.018
2 Ricardo Rosset   Reynard 95D-Cosworth   43   1h06m58.248
3 Tarso Marques   Reynard 95D-Cosworth   43   1h07m00.215
4 Emmanuel Clerico   Reynard 95D-Cosworth   43   1h07m03.397
5 Marc Goossens   Lola T95/50-Cosworth   43   1h07m21.676
6 Christophe Tinseau   Reynard 95D-Judd   43   1h07m26.992

Winner's average speed: 113.209 mph. Pole position: Allan McNish (Reynard 95D-Cosworth), 1m29.922. Fastest lap: Clerico, 1m31.597

GRAND PRIX DE PAU

5 June 1995. Pau. 72 laps of a 1.715-mile circuit = 123.480 miles. FIA F3000 Championship round 3

1 Vincenzo Sospiri   Reynard 95D-Cosworth   72   1h26m47.823
2 Allan McNish   Reynard 95D-Cosworth   72   1h26m50.614
3 Marc Goossens   Lola T95/50-Cosworth   72   1h26m51.453
4 Kenny Brack   Reynard 95D-Judd   72   1h26m59.347
5 Jean-Philippe Belloc   Reynard 95D-Cosworth   72   1h27m14.707
6 Didier Cottaz   Reynard 95D-Cosworth   72   1h27m15.767

Winner's average speed: 85.358 mph. Pole position: Tarso Marques (Reynard 95D-Cosworth), 1m09.171. Fastest lap: Emmanuel Clerico (Reynard 95D-Cosworth), 1m10.801

1995 Vincenzo Sospiri celebrates victory in Barcelona.

GRAN PREMIO DEL MEDITERRANEO

23 July 1995. Enna-Pergusa. 40 laps of a 3.076-mile circuit = 123.040 miles. FIA F3000 Championship round 4

1 Ricardo Rosset	Reynard 95D-Cosworth	40	1h02m15.387
2 Vincenzo Sospiri	Reynard 95D-Cosworth	40	1h02m27.601
3 Christian Pescatori	Reynard 95D-Cosworth	40	1h02m33.290
4 Marco Campos	Lola T95/50-Cosworth	40	1h02m46.200
5 Fabrizio de Simone	Reynard 95D-Judd	40	1h02m50.253
6 Jerome Policand	Lola T95/50-Cosworth	40	1h03m03.222

Winner's average speed: 118.580 mph. Pole position: Kenny Brack (Reynard 95D-Judd), 1m29.853. Fastest lap: Rosset, 1m31.149

HOCKENHEIM F3000

29 July 1995. Hockenheim. 29 laps of a 4.239-mile circuit = 122.931 miles. FIA F3000 Championship round 5

1 Marc Goossens	Lola T95/50-Cosworth	29	58m04.329
2 Kenny Brack	Reynard 95D-Judd	29	58m08.063
3 Guillaume Gomez	Reynard 95D-Cosworth	29	58m16.513
4 Emmanuel Clerico	Reynard 95D-Cosworth	29	58m17.928
5 Marcos Gueiros	Reynard 95D-Judd	29	58m28.362
6 Allan McNish	Reynard 95D-Cosworth	29	58m33.598

Winner's average speed: 127.012 mph. Pole position: Gomez, 1m55.843. Fastest lap: Ricardo Rosset (Reynard 95D-Cosworth), 1m58.633

SPA-FRANCORCHAMPS F3000

27 August 1995. Spa-Francorchamps. 28 laps of a 4.329-mile circuit = 121.212 miles. FIA F3000 Championship round 6

1 Vincenzo Sospiri	Reynard 95D-Cosworth	28	59m03.485
2 Christophe Bouchut	Lola T95/50-Cosworth	28	59m06.830
3 Guillaume Gomez	Reynard 95D-Cosworth	28	59m07.324
4 Ricardo Rosset	Reynard 95D-Cosworth	28	59m29.433
5 Tarso Marques	Reynard 95D-Cosworth	28	59m34.082
6 Emmanuel Clerico	Reynard 95D-Cosworth	28	59m41.850

Winner's average speed: 123.145 mph. Pole position: Allan McNish (Reynard 95D-Cosworth), 2m03.989. Fastest lap: Gomez, 2m04.022

ESTORIL F3000

23 September 1995. Estoril. 46 laps of a 2.709-mile circuit = 124.614 miles. FIA F3000 Championship round 7

1 Tarso Marques	Reynard 95D-Cosworth	46	1h11m49.521
2 Emmanuel Clerico	Reynard 95D-Cosworth	46	1h11m56.200
3 Kenny Brack	Reynard 95D-Judd	46	1h12m05.565
4 Jerome Policand	Lola T95/50-Cosworth	46	1h12m17.750
5 Ricardo Rosset	Reynard 95D-Cosworth	46	1h12m18.845
6 Christian Pescatori	Reynard 95D-Cosworth	46	1h12m42.809

Winner's average speed: 104.098 mph. Pole position: Marques, 1m28.938. Fastest lap: Guillaume Gomez (Reynard 95D-Cosworth), 1m32.421

MAGNY-COURS F3000

15 October 1995. Magny-Cours. 47 laps of a 2.641-mile circuit = 124.127 miles. FIA F3000 Championship round 8

1 Kenny Brack	Reynard 95D-Judd	47	1h08m59.65
2 Marc Goossens	Lola T95/50-Cosworth	47	1h09m08.15
3 Jean-Philippe Belloc	Reynard 95D-Cosworth	47	1h09m14.64
4 Vincenzo Sospiri	Reynard 95D-Cosworth	47	1h09m14.82
5 Emmanuel Clerico	Reynard 95D-Cosworth	47	1h09m15.54
6 Christian Pescatori	Reynard 95D-Cosworth	47	1h09m30.02

Winner's average speed: 107.946 mph. Pole position: Brack, 1m25.10. Fastest lap: Tarso Marques (Reynard 95D-Cosworth), 1m26.88

1995 FINAL CHAMPIONSHIP POSITIONS

1	Vincenzo Sospiri	42	10=	Jean-Philippe Belloc	6
2	Ricardo Rosset	29		Christophe Bouchut	6
3=	Kenny Brack	24	12	Jerome Policand	4
	Marc Goossens	24	13	Marco Campos	3
5=	Emmanuel Clerico	15	14=	Marcos Gueiros	2
	Tarso Marques	15		Fabrizio de Simone	2
7	Allan McNish	11	16=	Didier Cottaz	1
8	Guillaume Gomez	8		Christophe Tinseau	1
9	Christian Pescatori	7			

1996

NURBURGRING F3000

11 May 1996. Nurburgring. 43 laps of a 2.831-mile circuit = 121.733 miles. FIA F3000 Championship round 1

1 Kenny Brack	Lola T96/50-Zytek	43	1h07m04.880
2 Jorg Muller	Lola T96/50-Zytek	43	1h07m06.810
3 Marcos Gueiros	Lola T96/50-Zytek	43	1h07m22.260
4 Tom Kristensen	Lola T96/50-Zytek	43	1h07m22.600
5 Pedro Couceiro	Lola T96/50-Zytek	43	1h07m57.120
6 Laurent Redon	Lola T96/50-Zytek	43	1h08m01.520

Winner's average speed: 108.882 mph. Pole position: Brack, 1m30.57. Fastest lap: Brack and Muller, 1m32.62

GRAND PRIX DE PAU

27 May 1996. Pau. 72 laps of a 1.715-mile circuit = 123.480 miles. FIA F3000 Championship round 2

1 Jorg Muller	Lola T96/50-Zytek	72	1h28m55.055
2 Kenny Brack	Lola T96/50-Zytek	72	1h29m00.329
3 Ricardo Zonta	Lola T96/50-Zytek	71	
4 Cristiano da Matta	Lola T96/50-Zytek	71	
5 Patrick Lemarie	Lola T96/50-Zytek	71	
6 Luca Rangoni	Lola T96/50-Zytek	71	

Winner's average speed: 83.322 mph. Pole position: Tom Kristensen (Lola T96/50-Zytek), 1m11.734. Fastest lap: Kristensen, 1m13.012

GRAN PREMIO DEL MEDITERRANEO

21 July 1996. Enna-Pergusa. 40 laps of a 3.076-mile circuit = 123.040 miles. FIA F3000 Championship round 3

1 Marc Goossens	Lola T96/50-Zytek	40	1h03m33.989
2 Jorg Muller	Lola T96/50-Zytek	40	1h03m51.050
3 Christophe Tinseau	Lola T96/50-Zytek	40	1h03m56.070
4 Marcos Gueiros	Lola T96/50-Zytek	40	1h03m57.330
5 Cristiano da Matta	Lola T96/50-Zytek	40	1h03m59.780
6 Oliver Tichy	Lola T96/50-Zytek	40	1h04m13.080

Winner's average speed: 116.137 mph. Pole position: Goossens, 1m33.232. Fastest lap: Muller, 1m33.253

HOCKENHEIM F3000

27 July 1996. Hockenheim. 29 laps of a 4.239-mile circuit = 122.931 miles. FIA F3000 Championship round 4

1 Kenny Brack	Lola T96/50-Zytek	29	59m58.82
2 Jorg Muller	Lola T96/50-Zytek	29	1h00m03.77
3 Marcos Gueiros	Lola T96/50-Zytek	29	1h00m17.16
4 Christophe Tinseau	Lola T96/50-Zytek	29	1h00m21.91
5 Tom Kristensen	Lola T96/50-Zytek	29	1h00m32.46

6 Ricardo Zonta   Lola T96/50-Zytek   29   1h00m33.35
Winner's average speed: 122.971 mph. Pole position: Brack, 2m01.08.
Fastest lap: Brack, 2m03.41

AUTOSPORT INTERNATIONAL TROPHY

17 August 1996. Silverstone. 40 laps of a 3.152-mile circuit = 126.080 miles. FIA F3000 Championship round 5

1 Kenny Brack   Lola T96/50-Zytek   40   1h09m17.948
2 Tom Kristensen   Lola T96/50-Zytek   40   1h09m18.929
3 Ricardo Zonta   Lola T96/50-Zytek   40   1h09m27.183
4 Marcos Gueiros   Lola T96/50-Zytek   40   1h09m37.814
5 Christian Pescatori Lola T96/50-Zytek   40   1h09m41.162
6 Christophe Tinseau   Lola T96/50-Zytek   40   1h09m47.189
Winner's average speed: 109.162 mph. Pole position: Brack, 1m40.485.
Fastest lap: Kristensen, 1m43.180

SPA-FRANCORCHAMPS F3000

24 August 1996. Spa-Francorchamps. 22 laps of a 4.329-mile circuit = 95.238 miles. FIA F3000 Championship round 6

1 Jorg Muller   Lola T96/50-Zytek   22   48m24.693
2 Marc Goossens   Lola T96/50-Zytek   22   48m33.300
3 Tom Kristensen   Lola T96/50-Zytek   22   48m33.988
4 Christian Pescatori Lola T96/50-Zytek   22   48m37.219
5 Kenny Brack   Lola T96/50-Zytek   22   48m40.649
6 Christophe Tinseau   Lola T96/50-Zytek   22   48m45.148
Winner's average speed: 118.035 mph. Pole position: Tom Kristensen (Lola T96/50-Zytek), 2m10.580. Fastest lap: Muller, 2m10.731

MAGNY-COURS F3000

14 September 1996. Magny-Cours. 47 laps of a 2.641-mile circuit = 124.127 miles. FIA F3000 Championship round 7

1 Marc Goossens   Lola T96/50-Zytek   47   1h10m45.670
2 Kenny Brack   Lola T96/50-Zytek   47   1h11m02.844
3 Jorg Muller   Lola T96/50-Zytek   47   1h11m13.119
4 Laurent Redon   Lola T96/50-Zytek   47   1h11m21.973
5 Cristiano da Matta   Lola T96/50-Zytek   47   1h11m31.639
6 Thomas Biagi   Lola T96/50-Zytek   47   1h11m35.312
Winner's average speed: 105.250 mph. Pole position: Goossens, 1m27.681.
Fastest lap: Brack, 1m29.078

ESTORIL F3000

21 September 1996. Estoril. 46 laps of a 2.709-mile circuit = 124.614 miles. FIA F3000 Championship round 8

1 Ricardo Zonta   Lola T96/50-Zytek   46   1h14m55.143
2 Jorg Muller   Lola T96/50-Zytek   46   1h14m57.688
3 Kenny Brack   Lola T96/50-Zytek   46   1h15m03.663
4 Marc Goossens   Lola T96/50-Zytek   46   1h15m27.094
5 Fabrizio Gollin   Lola T96/50-Zytek   46   1h15m27.946
6 Thomas Biagi   Lola T96/50-Zytek   46   1h15m44.877
Winner's average speed: 99.799 mph. Pole position: Muller, 1m33.545.
Fastest lap: Zonta, 1m35.623

MUGELLO F3000

28 September 1996. Mugello. 38 laps of a 3.259-mile circuit = 123.842 miles. FIA F3000 Championship round 9

1 Ricardo Zonta   Lola T96/50-Zytek   38   1h05m44.337
2 Jorg Muller   Lola T96/50-Zytek   38   1h05m44.581
3 Kenny Brack   Lola T96/50-Zytek   38   1h05m58.383
4 Tom Kristensen   Lola T96/50-Zytek   38   1h05m58.886
5 Thomas Biagi   Lola T96/50-Zytek   38   1h06m23.580
6 Marc Goossens   Lola T96/50-Zytek   38   1h06m32.933
Winner's average speed: 113.031 mph. Pole position: Zonta, 1m40.036.
Fastest lap: Zonta, 1m42.478

HOCKENHEIM F3000

12 October 1996. Hockenheim. 29 laps of a 4.239-mile circuit = 122.931 miles. FIA F3000 Championship round 10

1 Christophe Tinseau   Lola T96/50-Zytek   29   59m24.317

2 Marcos Gueiros   Lola T96/50-Zytek   29   59m34.041
3 Oliver Tichy   Lola T96/50-Zytek   29   59m40.581
4 Laurent Redon   Lola T96/50-Zytek   29   59m44.724
5 Elton Julian   Lola T96/50-Zytek   29   59m51.563
6 Cyrille Sauvage   Lola T96/50-Zytek   29   59m53.765
Kenny Brack (Lola T96/50-Zytek) finished first on the road but was disqualified for ignoring black flag. Winner's average speed: 124.162 mph. Pole position: Jorg Muller (Lola T96/50-Zytek), 1m59.402. Fastest lap: Muller, 2m00.413

1996 FINAL CHAMPIONSHIP POSITIONS

1	Jorg Muller	52	10=	Christian Pescatori	5
2	Kenny Brack	49		Oliver Tichy	5
3	Marc Goossens	28	12	Thomas Biagi	4
4	Ricardo Zonta	27	13=	Pedro Couceiro	2
5	Marcos Gueiros	20		Fabrizio Gollin	2
6=	Tom Kristensen	18		Elton Julian	2
	Christophe Tinseau	18		Patrick Lemarie	2
8=	Cristiano da Matta	7	17=	Luca Rangoni	1
	Laurent Redon	7		Cyrille Sauvage	1

1997

AUTOSPORT INTERNATIONAL TROPHY

11 May 1997. Silverstone. 40 laps of a 3.194-mile circuit = 127.760 miles. FIA F3000 Championship round 1

1 Tom Kristensen   Lola T96/50-Zytek   40   1h21m22.689
2 Pedro Couceiro   Lola T96/50-Zytek   40   1h21m27.037
3 Jamie Davies   Lola T96/50-Zytek   40   1h21m27.289
4 Jason Watt   Lola T96/50-Zytek   40   1h21m30.381
5 Dino Morelli   Lola T96/50-Zytek   40   1h21m31.896
6 Patrick Lemarie   Lola T96/50-Zytek   40   1h21m32.730
Ricardo Zonta (Lola T96/50-Zytek), 1h21m15.501, finished first on the road but was disqualified for illegal gearbox. Winner's average speed: 94.197 mph. Pole position: Zonta, 1m40.463. Fastest lap: Marc Gene (Lola T96/50-Zytek), 1m53.745

GRAND PRIX DE PAU

19 May 1997. Pau. 75 laps of a 1.715-mile circuit = 128.625 miles. FIA F3000 Championship round 2

1 Juan Pablo Montoya   Lola T96/50-Zytek   75   1h32m44.230
2 Tom Kristensen   Lola T96/50-Zytek   75   1h33m19.303
3 Jamie Davies   Lola T96/50-Zytek   75   1h33m21.430
4 Laurent Redon   Lola T96/50-Zytek   75   1h33m32.085
5 Cyrille Sauvage   Lola T96/50-Zytek   75   1h33m32.792
6 Soheil Ayari   Lola T96/50-Zytek   75   1h33m53.950
Winner's average speed: 83.219 mph. Pole position: Montoya, 1m12.607.
Fastest lap: Montoya, 1m12.697

HELSINKI F3000

25 May 1997. Helsinki. 65 laps of a 1.976-mile circuit = 128.440 miles. FIA F3000 Championship round 3

1 Soheil Ayari   Lola T96/50-Zytek   65   1h38m32.881
2 Oliver Tichy   Lola T96/50-Zytek   65   1h38m52.205
3 Dino Morelli   Lola T96/50-Zytek   65   1h38m57.056
4 Patrick Lemarie   Lola T96/50-Zytek   65   1h38m59.256
5 Rui Aguas   Lola T96/50-Zytek   65   1h39m40.160
6 Stephen Watson   Lola T96/50-Zytek   65   1h39m56.579
Winner's average speed: 78.199 mph. Pole position: Juan Pablo Montoya (Lola T96/50-Zytek), 1m23.968. Fastest lap: Montoya, 1m25.466

NURBURGRING F3000

29 June 1997. Nurburgring. 4 laps of a 2.831-mile circuit = 11.324 miles. Race stopped due to an accident in the heavy rain, half points awarded. FIA F3000 Championship round 4

1	Ricardo Zonta	Lola T96/50-Zytek	4	7m57.334
2	Jason Watt	Lola T96/50-Zytek	4	7m59.522
3	Tom Kristensen	Lola T96/50-Zytek	4	8m02.206
4	Juan Pablo Montoya	Lola T96/50-Zytek	4	8m15.156
5	Max Wilson	Lola T96/50-Zytek	4	8m16.667
6	Gonzalo Rodriguez	Lola T96/50-Zytek	4	8m18.057

Winner's average speed: 85.404 mph. Pole position: Zonta, 1m31.294. Fastest lap: Zonta, 1m56.523

GRAN PREMIO DEL MEDITERRANEO

20 July 1997. Enna-Pergusa. 41 laps of a 3.076-mile circuit = 126.116 miles. FIA F3000 Championship round 5

1	Jamie Davies	Lola T96/50-Zytek	41	1h04m48.310
2	Ricardo Zonta	Lola T96/50-Zytek	41	1h05m12.572
3	Max Wilson	Lola T96/50-Zytek	41	1h05m20.311
4	Craig Lowndes	Lola T96/50-Zytek	41	1h05m21.297
5	Kurt Mollekens	Lola T96/50-Zytek	41	1h05m30.141
6	Laurent Redon	Lola T96/50-Zytek	41	1h05m36.323

Winner's average speed: 116.765 mph. Pole position: Davies, 1m32.846. Fastest lap: Davies, 1m33.500

HOCKENHEIM F3000

26 July 1997. Hockenheim. 31 laps of a 4.239-mile circuit = 131.409 miles. FIA F3000 Championship round 6

1	Ricardo Zonta	Lola T96/50-Zytek	31	1h04m33.262
2	Max Wilson	Lola T96/50-Zytek	31	1h04m36.688
3	Jamie Davies	Lola T96/50-Zytek	31	1h04m38.694
4	Jason Watt	Lola T96/50-Zytek	31	1h04m46.683
5	Juan Pablo Montoya	Lola T96/50-Zytek	31	1h04m52.926
6	Kurt Mollekens	Lola T96/50-Zytek	31	1h05m21.671

Winner's average speed: 122.138 mph. Pole position: Tom Kristensen (Lola T96/50-Zytek), 2m01.579. Fastest lap: Montoya, 2m03.508

A1 RING F3000

3 August 1997. A1 Ring. 48 laps of a 2.684-mile circuit = 128.832 miles. FIA F3000 Championship round 7

1	Juan Pablo Montoya	Lola T96/50-Zytek	48	1h12m39.794
2	Ricardo Zonta	Lola T96/50-Zytek	48	1h12m40.263
3	Laurent Redon	Lola T96/50-Zytek	48	1h13m17.414
4	Rui Aguas	Lola T96/50-Zytek	48	1h13m21.284
5	Oliver Tichy	Lola T96/50-Zytek	48	1h13m22.944
6	Tom Kristensen	Lola T96/50-Zytek	48	1h13m40.253

Winner's average speed: 106.380 mph. Pole position: Montoya, 1m24.225. Fastest lap: Zonta, 1m24.161

SPA-FRANCORCHAMPS F3000

23 August 1997. Spa-Francorchamps. 29 laps of a 4.329-mile circuit = 125.541 miles. FIA F3000 Championship round 8

1	Jason Watt	Lola T96/50-Zytek	29	1h05m19.036
2	Max Wilson	Lola T96/50-Zytek	29	1h05m19.322
3	Boris Derichebourg	Lola T96/50-Zytek	29	1h05m39.915
4	Cyrille Sauvage	Lola T96/50-Zytek	29	1h05m40.995
5	Ricardo Zonta	Lola T96/50-Zytek	29	1h05m49.462
6	Stephen Watson	Lola T96/50-Zytek	29	1h05m51.693

Winner's average speed: 115.321 mph. Pole position: Tom Kristensen (Lola T96/50-Zytek), 2m29.405. Fastest lap: Rui Aguas (Lola T96/50-Zytek), 2m13.517

GRAN PREMIO DI MUGELLO

28 September 1997. Mugello. 40 laps of a 3.259-mile circuit = 130.360 miles. FIA F3000 Championship round 9

1	Ricardo Zonta	Lola T96/50-Zytek	40	1h09m03.576
2	Jason Watt	Lola T96/50-Zytek	40	1h09m19.080
3	Juan Pablo Montoya	Lola T96/50-Zytek	40	1h09m20.956
4	Max Wilson	Lola T96/50-Zytek	40	1h09m34.793
5	Laurent Redon	Lola T96/50-Zytek	40	1h09m34.919
6	Soheil Ayari	Lola T96/50-Zytek	40	1h09m39.608

Winner's average speed: 113.259 mph. Pole position: Zonta, 1m40.372. Fastest lap: Zonta, 1m42.448

JEREZ F3000

25 October 1997. Jerez. 44 laps of a 2.752-mile circuit = 121.088 miles. FIA F3000 Championship round 10

1	Juan Pablo Montoya	Lola T96/50-Zytek	44	1h13m47.224
2	Oliver Tichy	Lola T96/50-Zytek	44	1h14m13.144
3	Gareth Rees	Lola T96/50-Zytek	44	1h14m18.272
4	Werner Lupberger	Lola T96/50-Zytek	44	1h14m30.585
5	Rui Aguas	Lola T96/50-Zytek	44	1h14m36.630
6	Christian Horner	Lola T96/50-Zytek	44	1h14m45.683

Cyrille Sauvage (Lola T96/50-Zytek), 1h13m52.493, finished second on the road but was disqualified due to parc ferme irregularity. Winner's average speed: 98.463 mph. Pole position: Ricardo Zonta (Lola T96/50-Zytek), 1m36.473. Fastest lap: Zonta, 1m39.010

1997 FINAL CHAMPIONSHIP POSITIONS

1	Ricardo Zonta	39	13	Cyrille Sauvage	5
2	Juan Pablo Montoya	37.5	14=	Boris Derichebourg	4
3	Jason Watt	25		Patrick Lemarie	4
4	Jamie Davies	22		Gareth Rees	4
5	Max Wilson	20	17=	Craig Lowndes	3
6	Tom Kristensen	19		Werner Lupberger	3
7	Oliver Tichy	14		Kurt Mollekens	3
8	Soheil Ayari	12	20	Stephen Watson	2
9	Laurent Redon	10	21	Christian Horner	1
10	Rui Aguas	7	22	Gonzalo Rodriguez	0.5
11=	Pedro Couceiro	6			
	Dino Morelli	6			

1998

OSCHERSLEBEN F3000

11 April 1998. Oschersleben. 56 laps of a 2.279-mile circuit = 127.624 miles. FIA F3000 Championship round 1

1	Stephane Sarrazin	Lola T96/50-Zytek	56	1h24m52.384
2	Nick Heidfeld	Lola T96/50-Zytek	56	1h25m03.667
3	Jamie Davies	Lola T96/50-Zytek	56	1h25m28.870
4	Thomas Biagi	Lola T96/50-Zytek	56	1h25m32.885
5	Cyrille Sauvage	Lola T96/50-Zytek	56	1h25m42.857
6	Gaston Mazzacane	Lola T96/50-Zytek	56	1h25m45.684

Paolo Ruberti (Lola T96/50-Zytek), 1h25m25.602, finished third on the road but was disqualified due to a bodywork infringement. Winner's average speed: 90.222 mph. Pole position: Juan Pablo Montoya (Lola T96/50-Zytek), 1m18.475. Fastest lap: Montoya, 1m20.387

IMOLA F3000

26 April 1998. Imola. 42 laps of a 3.064-mile circuit = 128.688 miles. FIA F3000 Championship round 2

1	Jason Watt	Lola T96/50-Zytek	42	1h16m38.513
2	Kurt Mollekens	Lola T96/50-Zytek	42	1h16m39.081
3	Gonzalo Rodriguez	Lola T96/50-Zytek	42	1h16m39.517
4	Nick Heidfeld	Lola T96/50-Zytek	42	1h16m41.324
5	Andre Couto	Lola T96/50-Zytek	42	1h16m47.626
6	Boris Derichebourg	Lola T96/50-Zytek	42	1h16m48.900

Winner's average speed: 100.745 mph. Pole position: Juan Pablo Montoya (Lola T96/50-Zytek), 1m40.695. Fastest lap: Rodriguez, 1m41.814

BARCELONA F3000

9 May 1998. Catalunya. 44 laps of a 2.937-mile circuit = 129.228 miles. FIA F3000 Championship round 3

1	Juan Pablo Montoya	Lola T96/50-Zytek	44	1h12m50.057
2	Kurt Mollekens	Lola T96/50-Zytek	44	1h12m57.817
3	Boris Derichebourg	Lola T96/50-Zytek	44	1h12m59.450
4	Dominik Schwager	Lola T96/50-Zytek	44	1h13m00.281
5	Soheil Ayari	Lola T96/50-Zytek	44	1h13m00.814
6	Max Wilson	Lola T96/50-Zytek	44	1h13m19.340

Winner's average speed: 106.456 mph. Pole position: Montoya, 1m35.289. Fastest lap: Nick Heidfeld (Lola T96/50-Zytek), 1m37.267

AUTOSPORT INTERNATIONAL TROPHY

16 May 1998. Silverstone. 40 laps of a 3.194-mile circuit = 127.760 miles. FIA F3000 Championship round 4

1	Juan Pablo Montoya	Lola T96/50-Zytek	40	1h10m08.886
2	Nick Heidfeld	Lola T96/50-Zytek	40	1h10m21.792
3	Jason Watt	Lola T96/50-Zytek	40	1h10m34.186
4	Gareth Rees	Lola T96/50-Zytek	40	1h10m35.162
5	Max Wilson	Lola T96/50-Zytek	40	1h10m35.499
6	Gaston Mazzacane	Lola T96/50-Zytek	40	1h10m39.644

Winner's average speed: 109.277 mph. Pole position: Montoya, 1m38.602. Fastest lap: Montoya, 1m41.366

GRAND PRIX DE MONACO F3000

23 May 1998. Monte Carlo. 50 laps of a 2.092-mile circuit = 104.600 miles. FIA F3000 Championship round 5

1	Nick Heidfeld	Lola T96/50-Zytek	50	1h18m04.955
2	Gonzalo Rodriguez	Lola T96/50-Zytek	50	1h18m08.817
3	Jamie Davies	Lola T96/50-Zytek	50	1h18m24.466
4	Stephane Sarrazin	Lola T96/50-Zytek	50	1h18m31.562
5	Kurt Mollekens	Lola T96/50-Zytek	50	1h18m53.173
6	Juan Pablo Montoya	Lola T96/50-Zytek	50	1h19m16.516

Winner's average speed: 80.376 mph. Pole position: Jason Watt (Lola T96/50-Zytek), 1m30.925. Fastest lap: Montoya, 1m31.602

GRAND PRIX DE PAU

1 June 1998. Pau. 75 laps of a 1.715-mile circuit = 128.625 miles. FIA F3000 Championship round 6

1	Juan Pablo Montoya	Lola T96/50-Zytek	75	1h33m10.179
2	Max Wilson	Lola T96/50-Zytek	74	
3	Nick Heidfeld	Lola T96/50-Zytek	74	
4	Gareth Rees	Lola T96/50-Zytek	74	
5	Kurt Mollekens	Lola T96/50-Zytek	74	
6	Andre Couto	Lola T96/50-Zytek	74	

Winner's average speed: 82.833 mph. Pole position: Montoya, 1m12.086. Fastest lap: Montoya, 1m12.953

A1 RING F3000

25 July 1998. A1 Ring. 48 laps of a 2.684-mile circuit = 128.832 miles. FIA F3000 Championship round 7

1	Soheil Ayari	Lola T96/50-Zytek	48	1h11m04.222
2	Juan Pablo Montoya	Lola T96/50-Zytek	48	1h11m25.272
3	Jason Watt	Lola T96/50-Zytek	48	1h11m31.823
4	Gonzalo Rodriguez	Lola T96/50-Zytek	48	1h11m32.593
5	Nicolas Minassian	Lola T96/50-Zytek	48	1h11m35.195
6	Bruno Junqueira	Lola T96/50-Zytek	48	1h11m37.352

Winner's average speed: 108.764 mph. Pole position: Ayari, 1m23.948. Fastest lap: Ayari, 1m24.139

HOCKENHEIM F3000

1 August 1998. Hockenheim. 31 laps of a 4.239-mile circuit = 131.409 miles. Race stopped after first-lap accident, restarted over original distance. FIA F3000 Championship round 8

1	Nick Heidfeld	Lola T96/50-Zytek	31	1h12m57.599
2	Jason Watt	Lola T96/50-Zytek	31	1h13m27.801
3	Juan Pablo Montoya	Lola T96/50-Zytek	31	1h13m43.345
4	Kevin McGarrity	Lola T96/50-Zytek	31	1h14m04.219
5	Bruno Junqueira	Lola T96/50-Zytek	31	1h14m16.979
6	Gareth Rees	Lola T96/50-Zytek	31	1h14m18.696

Winner's average speed: 108.067 mph. Pole position: Heidfeld, 1m59.620. Fastest lap: Heidfeld, 2m01.464

HUNGARORING F3000

15 August 1998. Hungaroring. 52 laps of a 2.465-mile circuit = 128.180 miles. FIA F3000 Championship round 9

1	Nick Heidfeld	Lola T96/50-Zytek	52	1h20m14.689
2	Stephane Sarrazin	Lola T96/50-Zytek	52	1h20m17.407
3	Juan Pablo Montoya	Lola T96/50-Zytek	52	1h20m43.145
4	Nicolas Minassian	Lola T96/50-Zytek	52	1h20m52.686
5	Andre Couto	Lola T96/50-Zytek	52	1h20m58.174
6	Oliver Martini	Lola T96/50-Zytek	52	1h21m01.147

Winner's average speed: 95.842 mph. Pole position: Sarrazin, 1m29.471. Fastest lap: Heidfeld, 1m31.174

SPA-FRANCORCHAMPS F3000

29 August 1998. Spa-Francorchamps. 29 laps of a 4.329-mile circuit = 125.541 miles. FIA F3000 Championship round 10

1	Gonzalo Rodriguez	Lola T96/50-Zytek	29	1h03m10.530
2	Juan Pablo Montoya	Lola T96/50-Zytek	29	1h03m10.565
3	Soheil Ayari	Lola T96/50-Zytek	29	1h03m14.885
4	Nick Heidfeld	Lola T96/50-Zytek	29	1h03m24.026
5	Alex Muller	Lola T96/50-Zytek	29	1h03m31.761
6	Marcelo Battistuzzi	Lola T96/50-Zytek	29	1h03m46.427

Winner's average speed: 119.231 mph. Pole position: Montoya, 2m07.690. Fastest lap: Ayari, 2m09.792

GRAN PREMIO DEL MEDITERRANEO

6 September 1998. Enna-Pergusa. 41 laps of a 3.076-mile circuit = 126.116 miles. FIA F3000 Championship round 11

1	Juan Pablo Montoya	Lola T96/50-Zytek	41	1h04m29.540
2	Nick Heidfeld	Lola T96/50-Zytek	41	1h04m34.990
3	Soheil Ayari	Lola T96/50-Zytek	41	1h04m39.897
4	Gareth Rees	Lola T96/50-Zytek	41	1h04m41.186
5	Oliver Martini	Lola T96/50-Zytek	41	1h04m41.726
6	Werner Lupberger	Lola T96/50-Zytek	41	1h04m52.169

Winner's average speed: 117.331 mph. Pole position: Heidfeld, 1m32.127. Fastest lap: Montoya, 1m33.212

NURBURGRING F3000

26 September 1998. Nurburgring. 45 laps of a 2.831-mile circuit = 127.395 miles. FIA F3000 Championship round 12

1	Gonzalo Rodriguez	Lola T96/50-Zytek	45	1h12m37.085
2	Jason Watt	Lola T96/50-Zytek	45	1h13m02.665
3	Juan Pablo Montoya	Lola T96/50-Zytek	45	1h13m03.378
4	Kurt Mollekens	Lola T96/50-Zytek	45	1h13m15.870
5	Andre Couto	Lola T96/50-Zytek	45	1h13m16.797
6	Tomas Enge	Lola T96/50-Zytek	45	1h13m19.408

Winner's average speed: 105.259 mph. Pole position: Montoya, 1m31.973. Fastest lap: Rodriguez, 1m32.857

1998 FINAL CHAMPIONSHIP POSITIONS

1	Juan Pablo Montoya	65	14=	Thomas Biagi	3
2	Nick Heidfeld	58		Bruno Junqueira	3
3	Gonzalo Rodriguez	33		Oliver Martini	3
4	Jason Watt	30		Kevin McGarrity	3
5	Soheil Ayari	20		Dominik Schwager	3
6=	Kurt Mollekens	19	21=	Gaston Mazzacane	2
	Stephane Sarrazin	19		Alex Muller	2
8	Gareth Rees	10		Cyrille Sauvage	2
9	Max Wilson	9	24=	Marcelo Battistuzzi	1
10	Jamie Davies	8		Tomas Enge	1
11	Andre Couto	7		Werner Lupberger	1
12=	Boris Derichebourg	5			
	Nicolas Minassian	5			

1999

IMOLA F3000

1 May 1999. Imola. 42 laps of a 3.064-mile circuit = 128.688 miles. FIA F3000 Championship round 1

1	Nick Heidfeld	Lola B99/50-Zytek	42	1h11m29.942
2	Kevin McGarrity	Lola B99/50-Zytek	42	1h11m51.922
3	Fabrice Walfrisch	Lola B99/50-Zytek	42	1h11m53.346
4	Stephane Sarrazin	Lola B99/50-Zytek	42	1h12m04.542
5	Gonzalo Rodriguez	Lola B99/50-Zytek	42	1h12m13.382
6	Justin Wilson	Lola B99/50-Zytek	42	1h12m20.596

Winner's average speed: 107.992 mph. Pole position: Max Wilson (Lola B99/50-Zytek), 1m39.092. Fastest lap: Heidfeld, 1m40.199

GRAND PRIX DE MONACO F3000

15 May 1999. Monte Carlo. 50 laps of a 2.092-mile circuit = 104.600 miles. FIA F3000 Championship round 2

1	Gonzalo Rodriguez	Lola B99/50-Zytek	50	1h18m22.018
2	Jason Watt	Lola B99/50-Zytek	50	1h19m02.112
3	Max Wilson	Lola B99/50-Zytek	50	1h19m05.281
4	Oliver Gavin	Lola B99/50-Zytek	50	1h19m10.529
5	Norberto Fontana	Lola B99/50-Zytek	50	1h19m16.191
6	Bruno Junqueira	Lola B99/50-Zytek	50	1h19m17.433

Winner's average speed: 80.085 mph. Pole position: Nick Heidfeld (Lola B99/50-Zytek), 1m30.087. Fastest lap: Stephane Sarrazin (Lola B99/50-Zytek), 1m30.640

BARCELONA F3000

29 May 1999. Catalunya. 44 laps of a 2.937-mile circuit = 129.228 miles. FIA F3000 Championship round 3

1	Nick Heidfeld	Lola B99/50-Zytek	44	1h13m16.982
2	Gonzalo Rodriguez	Lola B99/50-Zytek	44	1h13m19.984
3	Andre Couto	Lola B99/50-Zytek	44	1h14m12.504
4	Bruno Junqueira	Lola B99/50-Zytek	44	1h14m13.742
5	Stephane Sarrazin	Lola B99/50-Zytek	44	1h14m15.965
6	Justin Wilson	Lola B99/50-Zytek	44	1h14m21.452

Winner's average speed: 105.805 mph. Pole position: Heidfeld, 1m32.491. Fastest lap: Heidfeld, 1m35.731

MAGNY-COURS F3000

26 June 1999. Magny-Cours. 49 laps of a 2.641-mile circuit = 129.409 miles. FIA F3000 Championship round 4

1	Nick Heidfeld	Lola B99/50-Zytek	49	1h25m56.738
2	Tomas Enge	Lola B99/50-Zytek	49	1h26m09.261
3	David Saelens	Lola B99/50-Zytek	49	1h26m45.335
4	Jeffrey van Hooydonk	Lola B99/50-Zytek	49	1h26m45.894
5	Stephane Sarrazin	Lola B99/50-Zytek	49	1h26m54.486
6	Bas Leinders	Lola B99/50-Zytek	49	1h26m55.077

Winner's average speed: 90.342 mph. Pole position: Bruno Junqueira (Lola B99/50-Zytek), 1m27.112. Fastest lap: Soheil Ayari (Lola B99/50-Zytek), 1m29.555

SILVERSTONE INTERNATIONAL TROPHY

10 July 1999. Silverstone. 40 laps of a 3.194-mile circuit = 127.760 miles. FIA F3000 Championship round 5

1	Nicolas Minassian	Lola B99/50-Zytek	40	1h07m48.722
2	Bruno Junqueira	Lola B99/50-Zytek	40	1h07m51.437
3	Nick Heidfeld	Lola B99/50-Zytek	40	1h07m52.998
4	Soheil Ayari	Lola B99/50-Zytek	40	1h08m06.193
5	Norberto Fontana	Lola B99/50-Zytek	40	1h08m07.455
6	Franck Montagny	Lola B99/50-Zytek	40	1h08m17.085

Winner's average speed: 113.042 mph. Pole position: Minassian, 1m37.711. Fastest lap: Heidfeld, 1m40.929

A1 RING F3000

24 July 1999. A1 Ring. 48 laps of a 2.684-mile circuit = 128.832 miles. FIA F3000 Championship round 6

1	Nick Heidfeld	Lola B99/50-Zytek	48	1h07m50.994
2	Soheil Ayari	Lola B99/50-Zytek	48	1h07m59.051
3	Nicolas Minassian	Lola B99/50-Zytek	48	1h08m08.199
4	Jason Watt	Lola B99/50-Zytek	48	1h08m30.758
5	Andrea Piccini	Lola B99/50-Zytek	48	1h08m32.011
6	Stephane Sarrazin	Lola B99/50-Zytek	48	1h08m32.475

Winner's average speed: 113.927 mph. Pole position: Heidfeld, 1m23.206. Fastest lap: Heidfeld, 1m23.243

HOCKENHEIM F3000

31 July 1999. Hockenheim. 31 laps of a 4.239-mile circuit = 131.409 miles. FIA F3000 Championship round 7

1	Bruno Junqueira	Lola B99/50-Zytek	31	1h01m17.627
2	Max Wilson	Lola B99/50-Zytek	31	1h01m18.631
3	Stephane Sarrazin	Lola B99/50-Zytek	31	1h01m22.063
4	Gonzalo Rodriguez	Lola B99/50-Zytek	31	1h01m25.536
5	Enrique Bernoldi	Lola B99/50-Zytek	31	1h01m42.449
6	Franck Montagny	Lola B99/50-Zytek	31	1h01m52.361

Winner's average speed: 128.635 mph. Pole position: Wilson, 1m59.828. Fastest lap: Rodriguez, 2m01.472

HUNGARORING F3000

14 August 1999. Hungaroring. 52 laps of a 2.465-mile circuit = 128.180 miles. FIA F3000 Championship round 8

1	Stephane Sarrazin	Lola B99/50-Zytek	52	1h19m43.676
2	Nick Heidfeld	Lola B99/50-Zytek	52	1h19m44.468
3	Franck Montagny	Lola B99/50-Zytek	52	1h19m56.489
4	Soheil Ayari	Lola B99/50-Zytek	52	1h19m57.994
5	Nicolas Minassian	Lola B99/50-Zytek	52	1h19m59.342
6	Jason Watt	Lola B99/50-Zytek	52	1h20m01.049

Marc Goosens (Lola B99/50-Zytek), 1h19m56.123, finished third on the road but was disqualified due to an illegal damper. Winner's average speed: 96.463 mph. Pole position: Fabrice Walfrisch (Lola B99/50-Zytek), 1m29.261. Fastest lap: Heidfeld, 1m30.801

SPA-FRANCORCHAMPS F3000

28 August 1999. Spa-Francorchamps. 30 laps of a 4.329-mile circuit = 129.870 miles. FIA F3000 Championship round 9

1	Jason Watt	Lola B99/50-Zytek	30	1h13m57.599
2	Gonzalo Rodriguez	Lola B99/50-Zytek	30	1h14m00.462
3	Nicolas Minassian	Lola B99/50-Zytek	30	1h14m01.237
4	Nick Heidfeld	Lola B99/50-Zytek	30	1h14m04.095
5	David Saelens	Lola B99/50-Zytek	30	1h14m10.020
6	Ricardo Mauricio	Lola B99/50-Zytek	30	1h14m14.468

Winner's average speed: 105.357 mph. Pole position: Watt, 2m08.829. Fastest lap: Rodriguez, 2m08.993

NURBURGRING F3000

25 September 1999. Nurburgring. 45 laps of a 2.831-mile circuit = 127.395 miles. FIA F3000 Championship round 10

1	Jason Watt	Lola B99/50-Zytek	45	1h09m35.500
2	Nick Heidfeld	Lola B99/50-Zytek	45	1h09m36.002
3	Max Wilson	Lola B99/50-Zytek	45	1h09m49.464
4	Soheil Ayari	Lola B99/50-Zytek	45	1h09m51.679
5	David Saelens	Lola B99/50-Zytek	45	1h10m23.870
6	Jamie Davies	Lola B99/50-Zytek	45	1h10m25.108

Winner's average speed: 109.836 mph. Pole position: Watt, 1m31.098. Fastest lap: Heidfeld, 1m31.876

1999 FINAL CHAMPIONSHIP POSITIONS

1	Nick Heidfeld	59	13=	Andre Couto	4
2	Jason Watt	30		Norberto Fontana	4
3	Gonzalo Rodriguez	27		Fabrice Walfrisch	4
4	Stephane Sarrazin	22	16=	Oliver Gavin	3
5=	Bruno Junqueira	20		Jeffrey van Hooydonk	3
	Nicolas Minassian	20	18=	Enrique Bernoldi	2
7	Soheil Ayari	15		Andrea Piccini	2
8	Max Wilson	14		Justin Wilson	2
9	David Saelens	8	21=	Jamie Davies	1
10=	Tomas Enge	6		Bas Leinders	1
	Kevin McGarrity	6		Ricardo Mauricio	1
	Franck Montagny	6			

2000

IMOLA F3000

8 April 2000. Imola. 42 laps of a 3.064-mile circuit = 128.688 miles. FIA F3000 Championship round 1

1	Nicolas Minassian	Lola B99/50-Zytek	42	1h11m06.106
2	Bruno Junqueira	Lola B99/50-Zytek	42	1h11m08.404
3	Mark Webber	Lola B99/50-Zytek	42	1h11m08.838
4	Jaime Melo Jr	Lola B99/50-Zytek	42	1h11m11.038
5	Tomas Enge	Lola B99/50-Zytek	42	1h11m12.004
6	Fabrizio Gollin	Lola B99/50-Zytek	42	1h11m22.271

Winner's average speed: 108.595 mph. Pole position: Junqueira, 1m38.038. Fastest lap: Stephane Sarrazin (Lola B99/50-Zytek), 1m40.429

SILVERSTONE INTERNATIONAL TROPHY

22 April 2000. Silverstone. 40 laps of a 3.194-mile circuit = 127.760 miles. FIA F3000 Championship round 2

1	Mark Webber	Lola B99/50-Zytek	40	1h22m24.239
2	Darren Manning	Lola B99/50-Zytek	40	1h22m25.187
3	Justin Wilson	Lola B99/50-Zytek	40	1h22m29.219
4	Enrique Bernoldi	Lola B99/50-Zytek	40	1h22m36.090
5	Bruno Junqueira	Lola B99/50-Zytek	40	1h22m40.736
6	Soheil Ayari	Lola B99/50-Zytek	40	1h22m54.966

Winner's average speed: 93.025 mph. Pole position: Manning, 1m56.776. Fastest lap: Stephane Sarrazin (Lola B99/50-Zytek), 1m54.304

BARCELONA F3000

6 May 2000. Catalunya. 44 laps of a 2.937-mile circuit = 129.228 miles. FIA F3000 Championship round 3

1	Bruno Junqueira	Lola B99/50-Zytek	44	1h11m52.069
2	Nicolas Minassian	Lola B99/50-Zytek	44	1h11m55.632
3	David Saelens	Lola B99/50-Zytek	44	1h12m02.847
4	Jeffrey van Hooydonk	Lola B99/50-Zytek	44	1h12m04.400
5	Justin Wilson	Lola B99/50-Zytek	44	1h12m05.920
6	Franck Montagny	Lola B99/50-Zytek	44	1h12m07.756

Winner's average speed: 107.888 mph. Pole position: Enrique Bernoldi (Lola B99/50-Zytek), 1m33.280. Fastest lap: Mark Webber (Lola B99/50-Zytek), 1m36.740

NURBURGRING F3000

20 May 2000. Nurburgring. 45 laps of a 2.831-mile circuit = 127.395 miles. FIA F3000 Championship round 4

1	Bruno Junqueira	Lola B99/50-Zytek	45	1h24m07.832
2	Fabrizio Gollin	Lola B99/50-Zytek	45	1h24m18.714
3	Andre Couto	Lola B99/50-Zytek	45	1h25m06.370
4	Sebastien Bourdais	Lola B99/50-Zytek	45	1h25m06.952
5	Stephane Sarrazin	Lola B99/50-Zytek	45	1h25m36.257
6	Jaime Melo Jr	Lola B99/50-Zytek	44	

Andreas Scheld (Lola B99/50-Zytek), 1h24m12.629, finished second on the road but was disqualified due to illegal front wing. Winner's average speed: 90.855 mph. Pole position: David Saelens (Lola B99/50-Zytek), 1m30.043. Fastest lap: Junqueira, 1m32.151

GRAND PRIX DE MONTE CARLO F3000

3 June 2000. Monte Carlo. 50 laps of a 2.092-mile circuit = 104.600 miles. FIA F3000 Championship round 5

1	Bruno Junqueira	Lola B99/50-Zytek	50	1h19m08.755
2	Jamie Davies	Lola B99/50-Zytek	50	1h19m10.359
3	David Saelens	Lola B99/50-Zytek	50	1h19m16.480
4	Kevin McGarrity	Lola B99/50-Zytek	50	1h19m17.010
5	Nicolas Minassian	Lola B99/50-Zytek	50	1h19m19.910
6	Franck Montagny	Lola B99/50-Zytek	50	1h19m20.514

Winner's average speed: 79.297 mph. Pole position: Saelens, 1m29.178. Fastest lap: Fernando Alonso (Lola B99/50-Zytek), 1m30.539

MAGNY-COURS F3000

1 July 2000. Magny-Cours. 49 laps of a 2.641-mile circuit = 129.409 miles. FIA F3000 Championship round 6

1	Nicolas Minassian	Lola B99/50-Zytek	49	1h15m44.627
2	Sebastien Bourdais	Lola B99/50-Zytek	49	1h15m48.186
3	David Saelens	Lola B99/50-Zytek	49	1h15m52.563
4	Franck Montagny	Lola B99/50-Zytek	49	1h15m59.057
5	Tomas Enge	Lola B99/50-Zytek	49	1h16m00.360
6	Stephane Sarrazin	Lola B99/50-Zytek	49	1h16m07.858

Winner's average speed: 102.511 mph. Pole position: Bourdais, 1m27.071. Fastest lap: Mark Webber (Lola B99/50-Zytek), 1m30.105

A1 RING F3000

15 July 2000. A1 Ring. 48 laps of a 2.684-mile circuit = 128.832 miles. FIA F3000 Championship round 7

1	Nicolas Minassian	Lola B99/50-Zytek	48	1h10m42.354
2	Justin Wilson	Lola B99/50-Zytek	48	1h10m43.768
3	Darren Manning	Lola B99/50-Zytek	48	1h10m48.263
4	Mark Webber	Lola B99/50-Zytek	48	1h10m48.490
5	Jaime Melo Jr	Lola B99/50-Zytek	48	1h10m49.304
6	Fernando Alonso	Lola B99/50-Zytek	48	1h10m49.575

Winner's average speed: 109.325 mph. Pole position: Jeffrey van Hooydonk (Lola B99/50-Zytek), 1m33.336. Fastest lap: Tomas Enge (Lola B99/50-Zytek), 1m23.461

HOCKENHEIM F3000

29 July 2000. Hockenheim. 31 laps of a 4.239-mile circuit = 131.409 miles. FIA F3000 Championship round 8

1	Tomas Enge	Lola B99/50-Zytek	31	1h14m50.567
2	Tomas Scheckter	Lola B99/50-Zytek	31	1h14m56.883
3	Mark Webber	Lola B99/50-Zytek	31	1h15m06.890
4	Andrea Piccini	Lola B99/50-Zytek	31	1h15m08.811
5	Kristian Kolby	Lola B99/50-Zytek	31	1h15m10.896
6	Enrique Bernoldi	Lola B99/50-Zytek	31	1h15m20.002

Winner's average speed: 105.348 mph. Pole position: Enge, 2m11.990. Fastest lap: Darren Manning (Lola B99/50-Zytek), 2m04.173

HUNGARORING F3000

12 August 2000. Hungaroring. 52 laps of a 2.465-mile circuit = 128.180 miles. FIA F3000 Championship round 9

1	Bruno Junqueira	Lola B99/50-Zytek	52	1h21m30.052
2	Fernando Alonso	Lola B99/50-Zytek	52	1h21m30.647
3	Ricardo Mauricio	Lola B99/50-Zytek	52	1h21m35.865
4	Nicolas Minassian	Lola B99/50-Zytek	52	1h21m41.193
5	Justin Wilson	Lola B99/50-Zytek	52	1h21m42.557
6	Enrique Bernoldi	Lola B99/50-Zytek	52	1h21m48.154

Winner's average speed: 94.365 mph. Pole position: Junqueira, 1m27.531. Fastest lap: Marc Goossens (Lola B99/50-Zytek), 1m30.320

SPA-FRANCORCHAMPS F3000

26 August 2000. Spa-Francorchamps. 30 laps of a 4.329-mile circuit = 129.870 miles. FIA F3000 Championship round 10

1	Fernando Alonso	Lola B99/50-Zytek	30	1h08m04.964
2	Marc Goossens	Lola B99/50-Zytek	30	1h08m19.565
3	Nicolas Minassian	Lola B99/50-Zytek	30	1h08m20.300
4	David Saelens	Lola B99/50-Zytek	30	1h08m27.136
5	Justin Wilson	Lola B99/50-Zytek	30	1h08m32.933

6 Tomas Enge   Lola B99/50-Zytek   30   1h08m43.419
Winner's average speed: 114.452 mph. Pole position: Alonso, 2m07.184.
Fastest lap: Alonso, 2m10.096

2000 FINAL CHAMPIONSHIP POSITIONS

1	Bruno Junqueira	48		Jaime Melo Jr	6
2	Nicolas Minassian	45		Tomas Scheckter	6
3	Mark Webber	21	15=	Enrique Bernoldi	5
4	Fernando Alonso	17		Franck Montagny	5
5	Justin Wilson	16	17=	Andre Couto	4
6=	Tomas Enge	15		Ricardo Mauricio	4
	David Saelens	15	19=	Jeffrey van Hooydonk	3
8	Darren Manning	10		Kevin McGarrity	3
9	Sebastien Bourdais	9		Andrea Piccini	3
10	Fabrizio Gollin	7		Stephane Sarrazin	3
11=	Jamie Davies	6	23	Kristian Kolby	2
	Marc Goossens	6	24	Soheil Ayari	1

2001

INTERLAGOS F3000

31 March 2001. Interlagos. 35 laps of a 2.667-mile circuit = 93.345 miles.
FIA F3000 Championship round 1

1	Justin Wilson	Lola B99/50-Zytek	35	53m48.503
2	Jaime Melo Jr	Lola B99/50-Zytek	35	53m56.152
3	Sebastien Bourdais	Lola B99/50-Zytek	35	54m05.962
4	David Saelens	Lola B99/50-Zytek	35	54m10.418
5	Joel Camathias	Lola B99/50-Zytek	35	54m15.601
6	Fabrizio Gollin	Lola B99/50-Zytek	35	54m17.070

Winner's average speed: 104.086 mph. Pole position: Melo, 1m26.732.
Fastest lap: Antonio Pizzonia (Lola B99/50-Zytek), 1m27.755

IMOLA F3000

14 April 2001. Imola. 31 laps of a 3.064-mile circuit = 94.984 miles. FIA
F3000 Championship round 2

1	Mark Webber	Lola B99/50-Zytek	31	56m45.779
2	Darren Manning	Lola B99/50-Zytek	31	56m49.082
3	Tomas Enge	Lola B99/50-Zytek	31	56m49.869
4	Antonio Pizzonia	Lola B99/50-Zytek	31	56m55.537
5	Patrick Friesacher	Lola B99/50-Zytek	31	56m55.950
6	Justin Wilson	Lola B99/50-Zytek	31	56m56.712

Winner's average speed: 100.401 mph. Pole position: Webber, 1m38.518.
Fastest lap: Webber, 1m40.232

BARCELONA F3000

28 April 2001. Catalunya. 32 laps of a 2.937-mile circuit = 93.984 miles.
FIA F3000 Championship round 3

1	Tomas Enge	Lola B99/50-Zytek	32	52m00.457
2	Bas Leinders	Lola B99/50-Zytek	32	52m02.668
3	Justin Wilson	Lola B99/50-Zytek	32	52m03.663
4	Mario Haberfeld	Lola B99/50-Zytek	32	52m09.721
5	David Saelens	Lola B99/50-Zytek	32	52m20.588
6	Antonio Pizzonia	Lola B99/50-Zytek	32	52m21.291

Winner's average speed: 108.427 mph. Pole position: Wilson, 1m33.931.
Fastest lap: Wilson, 1m36.230

A1 RING F3000

12 May 2001. A1 Ring. 35 laps of a 2.684-mile circuit = 93.940 miles. FIA
F3000 Campionship round 4

1	Justin Wilson	Lola B99/50-Zytek	35	51m57.144
2	Bas Leinders	Lola B99/50-Zytek	35	51m57.599
3	Tomas Enge	Lola B99/50-Zytek	35	51m58.093
4	Antonio Pizzonia	Lola B99/50-Zytek	35	51m59.211
5	Jaime Melo Jr	Lola B99/50-Zytek	35	52m08.893
6	Andrea Piccini	Lola B99/50-Zytek	35	52m11.559

Winner's average speed: 108.492 mph. Pole position: Sebastien
Bourdais (Lola B99/50-Zytek), 1m23.240. Fastest lap: Giorgio Pantano
(Lola B99/50-Zytek), 1m24.003

GRAND PRIX DE MONTE CARLO F3000

26 May 2001. Monte Carlo. 45 laps of a 2.092-mile circuit = 94.140 miles.
FIA F3000 Championship round 5

1	Mark Webber	Lola B99/50-Zytek	45	1h13m21.073
2	Justin Wilson	Lola B99/50-Zytek	45	1h13m21.966
3	Stephane Sarrazin	Lola B99/50-Zytek	45	1h13m28.320
4	Sebastien Bourdais	Lola B99/50-Zytek	45	1h13m29.810
5	Ricardo Sperafico	Lola B99/50-Zytek	45	1h13m38.171
6	Ricardo Mauricio	Lola B99/50-Zytek	45	1h13m45.110

Winner's average speed: 77.005 mph. Pole position: Webber, 1m29.643.
Fastest lap: Webber, 1m30.462

NURBURGRING F3000

23 June 2001. Nurburgring. 33 laps of a 2.831-mile circuit = 93.423
miles. FIA F3000 Championship round 6

1	Tomas Enge	Lola B99/50-Zytek	33	50m50.598
2	Mark Webber	Lola B99/50-Zytek	33	50m56.224
3	Ricardo Sperafico	Lola B99/50-Zytek	33	50m59.261
4	David Saelens	Lola B99/50-Zytek	33	51m09.285
5	Ricardo Mauricio	Lola B99/50-Zytek	33	51m11.431
6	Antonio Pizzonia	Lola B99/50-Zytek	33	51m12.354

Winner's average speed: 110.248 mph. Pole position: Enge, 1m30.433.
Fastest lap: Giorgio Pantano (Lola B99/50-Zytek), 1m31.669

MAGNY-COURS F3000

30 June 2001. Magny-Cours. 36 laps of a 2.641-mile circuit = 95.076
miles. FIA F3000 Championship round 7

1	Mark Webber	Lola B99/50-Zytek	36	54m39.769
2	Justin Wilson	Lola B99/50-Zytek	36	54m47.223
3	Tomas Enge	Lola B99/50-Zytek	36	54m49.562
4	Patrick Friesacher	Lola B99/50-Zytek	36	55m00.824
5	Darren Manning	Lola B99/50-Zytek	36	55m03.118
6	Sebastien Bourdais	Lola B99/50-Zytek	36	55m03.905

Winner's average speed: 104.359 mph. Pole position: Enge, 1m27.436.
Fastest lap: Webber, 1m29.826

SILVERSTONE F3000

14 July 2001. Silverstone. 30 laps of a 3.194-mile circuit = 95.820 miles.
FIA F3000 Championship round 8

1	Sebastien Bourdais	Lola B99/50-Zytek	30	50m56.439
2	Justin Wilson	Lola B99/50-Zytek	30	50m57.365
3	Antonio Pizzonia	Lola B99/50-Zytek	30	51m00.781
4	Mark Webber	Lola B99/50-Zytek	30	51m03.982
5	Tomas Enge	Lola B99/50-Zytek	30	51m04.732
6	Darren Manning	Lola B99/50-Zytek	30	51m07.310

Winner's average speed: 112.861 mph. Pole position: Enge, 1m38.312.
Fastest lap: Bourdais, 1m40.456

HOCKENHEIM F3000

28 July 2001. Hockenheim. 22 laps of a 4.239-mile circuit = 93.258 miles.
FIA F3000 Championship round 9

1	Antonio Pizzonia	Lola B99/50-Zytek	22	44m47.547
2	Justin Wilson	Lola B99/50-Zytek	22	44m52.535
3	Ricardo Sperafico	Lola B99/50-Zytek	22	44m56.343
4	Sebastien Bourdais	Lola B99/50-Zytek	22	45m01.751
5	Tomas Enge	Lola B99/50-Zytek	22	45m05.363
6	Bas Leinders	Lola B99/50-Zytek	22	45m06.328

Winner's average speed: 124.920 mph. Pole position: Ricardo Sperafico,
1m59.526. Fastest lap: Enge, 2m00.795

HUNGARORING F3000

18 August 2001. Hungaroring. 38 laps of a 2.465-mile circuit = 93.670
miles. FIA F3000 Championship round 10

1	Justin Wilson	Lola B99/50-Zytek	38	58m00.190
2	Ricardo Mauricio	Lola B99/50-Zytek	38	58m05.784
3	Sebastien Bourdais	Lola B99/50-Zytek	38	58m08.683
4	Patrick Friesacher	Lola B99/50-Zytek	38	58m14.718
5	Giorgio Pantano	Lola B99/50-Zytek	38	58m16.941
6	Bas Leinders	Lola B99/50-Zytek	38	58m21.117

Winner's average speed: 96.895 mph. Pole position: Wilson, 1m27.695.
Fastest lap: Pantano, 1m30.196

SPA-FRANCORCHAMPS F3000

1 September 2001. Spa-Francorchamps. 22 laps of a 4.329-mile circuit = 95.238 miles. FIA F3000 Championship round 11

1	Ricardo Sperafico	Lola B99/50-Zytek	22	51m48.919
2	Justin Wilson	Lola B99/50-Zytek	22	52m00.504
3	Ricardo Mauricio	Lola B99/50-Zytek	22	52m05.901
4	Tomas Enge	Lola B99/50-Zytek	22	52m07.171
5	Marc Goossens	Lola B99/50-Zytek	22	52m20.784
6	Sebastien Bourdais	Lola B99/50-Zytek	22	52m21.701

Winner's average speed: 110.282 mph. Pole position: Ricardo Sperafico, 2m13.129. Fastest lap: Mario Haberfeld (Lola B99/50-Zytek), 2m08.781

MONZA F3000

15 September 2001. Monza. 24 laps of a 3.599-mile circuit = 86.376 miles. FIA F3000 Championship round 12

1	Giorgio Pantano	Lola B99/50-Zytek	24	43m58.618
2	Justin Wilson	Lola B99/50-Zytek	24	43m59.553
3	Ricardo Sperafico	Lola B99/50-Zytek	24	44m00.205
4	Bas Leinders	Lola B99/50-Zytek	24	44m03.033
5	David Saelens	Lola B99/50-Zytek	24	44m08.787
6	Ricardo Mauricio	Lola B99/50-Zytek	24	44m12.150

Mario Haberfeld (Lola 99/50-Zytek), 44m04.181, finished fifth on the road but was penalised 25 seconds for cutting a corner. Winner's average speed: 117.847 mph. Pole position: Antonio Pizzonia (Lola B99/50-Zytek), 1m40.033. Fastest lap: Pizzonia, 1m40.885

2001 FINAL CHAMPIONSHIP POSITIONS

1	Justin Wilson	71	11	Darren Manning	9
2=	Tomas Enge	39	12=	Patrick Friesacher	8
	Mark Webber	39		Jaime Melo Jr	8
4	Sebastien Bourdais	26	14	Stephane Sarrazin	4
5	Ricardo Sperafico	24	15	Mario Haberfeld	3
6	Antonio Pizzonia	22	16=	Joel Carnathias	2
7	Bas Leinders	17		Marc Goossens	2
8	Ricardo Mauricio	14	18=	Fabrizio Gollin	1
9	Giorgio Pantano	12		Andrea Piccini	1
10	David Saelens	10			

2002

INTERLAGOS F3000

30 March 2002. Interlagos. 35 laps of a 2.667-mile circuit = 93.345 miles. FIA F3000 Championship round 1

1	Rodrigo Sperafico	Lola B2/50-Zytek	35	53m24.481
2	Mario Haberfeld	Lola B2/50-Zytek	35	53m25.219
3	Ricardo Mauricio	Lola B2/50-Zytek	35	53m28.381
4	Antonio Pizzonia	Lola B2/50-Zytek	35	53m29.700
5	Bjorn Wirdheim	Lola B2/50-Zytek	35	53m29.911
6	Enrico Toccacelo	Lola B2/50-Zytek	35	53m31.025

Winner's average speed: 104.866 mph. Pole position: Sebastien Bourdais (Lola B2/50-Zytek), 1m26.056. Fastest lap: Bourdais, 1m27.323

IMOLA F3000

13 April 2002. Imola. 31 laps of a 3.064-mile circuit = 94.984 miles. FIA F3000 Championship round 2

1	Sebastien Bourdais	Lola B2/50-Zytek	31	51m39.076
2	Rodrigo Sperafico	Lola B2/50-Zytek	31	51m40.161
3	Giorgio Pantano	Lola B2/50-Zytek	31	51m51.717
4	Antonio Pizzonia	Lola B2/50-Zytek	31	51m56.283
5	Patrick Friesacher	Lola B2/50-Zytek	31	51m57.014
6	Tomas Enge	Lola B2/50-Zytek	31	52m03.188

Winner's average speed: 110.337 mph. Pole position: Bourdais, 1m53.951. Fastest lap: Pantano, 1m38.936

BARCELONA F3000

27 April 2002. Catalunya. 32 laps of a 2.937-mile circuit = 93.984 miles. FIA F3000 Championship round 3

1	Giorgio Pantano	Lola B2/50-Zytek	32	51m44.572
2	Tomas Enge	Lola B2/50-Zytek	32	51m45.560
3	Sebastien Bourdais	Lola B2/50-Zytek	32	51m52.731
4	Ricardo Mauricio	Lola B2/50-Zytek	32	51m56.532
5	Mario Haberfeld	Lola B2/50-Zytek	32	52m04.256
6	Enrico Toccacelo	Lola B2/50-Zytek	32	52m04.956

Winner's average speed: 108.982 mph. Pole position: Bourdais, 1m32.779. Fastest lap: Bourdais, 1m35.307

A1 RING F3000

11 May 2002. A1 Ring. 35 laps of a 2.684-mile circuit = 93.940 miles. FIA F3000 Championship round 4

1	Tomas Enge	Lola B2/50-Zytek	35	48m53.862
2	Bjorn Wirdheim	Lola B2/50-Zytek	35	48m57.579
3	Mario Haberfeld	Lola B2/50-Zytek	35	48m58.729
4	Giorgio Pantano	Lola B2/50-Zytek	35	48m59.459
5	Patrick Friesacher	Lola B2/50-Zytek	35	49m03.825
6	Enrico Toccacelo	Lola B2/50-Zytek	35	49m04.535

Winner's average speed: 115.269 mph. Pole position: Enge, 1m22.190. Fastest lap: Enge, 1m22.794

GRAND PRIX DE MONTE CARLO F3000

25 May 2002. Monte Carlo. 45 laps of a 2.092-mile circuit = 94.140 miles. FIA F3000 Championship round 5

1	Sebastien Bourdais	Lola B2/50-Zytek	45	1h07m40.545
2	Patrick Friesacher	Lola B2/50-Zytek	45	1h07m58.971
3	Tomas Enge	Lola B2/50-Zytek	45	1h08m08.174
4	Antonio Pizzonia	Lola B2/50-Zytek	45	1h08m08.985
5	Ricardo Sperafico	Lola B2/50-Zytek	45	1h08m15.345
6	Mario Haberfeld	Lola B2/50-Zytek	45	1h09m09.245

Alex Muller (Lola B2/50-Zytek), 1h09m00.900, finished sixth on the road but was disqualified for car being under weight. Winner's average speed: 83.463 mph. Pole position: Bourdais, 1m28.258. Fastest lap: Enge, 1m28.964

NURBURGRING F3000

22 June 2002. Nurburgring. 30 laps of a 3.196-mile circuit = 95.880 miles. FIA F3000 Championship round 6

1	Sebastien Bourdais	Lola B2/50-Zytek	30	54m55.289
2	Ricardo Sperafico	Lola B2/50-Zytek	30	54m59.057
3	Antonio Pizzonia	Lola B2/50-Zytek	30	55m26.051
4	Patrick Friesacher	Lola B2/50-Zytek	30	55m33.794
5	Rob Nguyen	Lola B2/50-Zytek	30	55m37.605
6	Bjorn Wirdheim	Lola B2/50-Zytek	30	55m39.133

Winner's average speed: 108.089 mph. Pole position: Bourdais, 1m46.323. Fastest lap: Tomas Enge (Lola B2/50-Zytek), 1m48.597

INTERNATIONAL TROPHY

6 July 2002. Silverstone. 30 laps of a 3.194-mile circuit = 95.820 miles. FIA F3000 Championship round 7

1	Tomas Enge	Lola B2/50-Zytek	30	49m45.388
2	Sebastien Bourdais	Lola B2/50-Zytek	30	49m58.304
3	Ricardo Sperafico	Lola B2/50-Zytek	30	50m02.988
4	Giorgio Pantano	Lola B2/50-Zytek	30	50m04.330
5	Antonio Pizzonia	Lola B2/50-Zytek	30	50m10.609
6	Bjorn Wirdheim	Lola B2/50-Zytek	30	50m20.610

Winner's average speed: 115.547 mph. Pole position: Enge, 1m36.529. Fastest lap: Enge, 1m38.416

MAGNY-COURS F3000

20 July 2002. Magny-Cours. 35 laps of a 2.641-mile circuit = 92.435 miles. FIA F3000 Championship round 8

1	Tomas Enge	Lola B2/50-Zytek	35	54m58.076
2	Sebastien Bourdais	Lola B2/50-Zytek	35	54m59.213
3	Giorgio Pantano	Lola B2/50-Zytek	35	55m00.034
4	Antonio Pizzonia	Lola B2/50-Zytek	35	55m02.668

5	Mario Haberfeld	Lola B2/50-Zytek	35	55m02.924
6	Enrico Toccacelo	Lola B2/50-Zytek	35	55m11.591

Winner's average speed: 100.897 mph. Pole position: Enge, 1m25.394.
Fastest lap: Enge, 1m27.802

HOCKENHEIM F3000

27 July 2002. Hockenheim. 33 laps of a 2.842-mile circuit = 93.786 miles. FIA F3000 Championship round 9

1	Giorgio Pantano	Lola B2/50-Zytek	33	50m00.768
2	Bjorn Wirdheim	Lola B2/50-Zytek	33	50m09.545
3	Rodrigo Sperafico	Lola B2/50-Zytek	33	50m24.251
4	Mario Haberfeld	Lola B2/50-Zytek	33	50m26.984
5	Tiago Monteiro	Lola B2/50-Zytek	33	50m28.108
6	Ricardo Sperafico	Lola B2/50-Zytek	33	50m34.577

Winner's average speed: 112.514 mph. Pole position: Pantano, 1m27.789.
Fastest lap: Ricardo Sperafico, 1m29.654

HUNGARORING F3000

17 August 2002. Hungaroring. 38 laps of a 2.465-mile circuit = 93.670 miles. FIA F3000 Championship round 10

1	Enrico Toccacelo	Lola B2/50-Zytek	38	59m25.829
2	Giorgio Pantano	Lola B2/50-Zytek	38	59m27.352
3	Sebastien Bourdais	Lola B2/50-Zytek	38	59m27.747
4	Bjorn Wirdheim	Lola B2/50-Zytek	38	59m29.850
5	Ricardo Sperafico	Lola B2/50-Zytek	38	59m30.441
6	Patrick Friesacher	Lola B2/50-Zytek	38	59m35.594

Tomas Enge (Lola B2/50-Zytek), 59m24.642, finished first on the road but was disqualified after failing a drugs test. Winner's average speed: 94.568 mph. Pole position: Enge, 1m28.120. Fastest lap: Ricardo Sperafico, 1m29.846

SPA FRANCORCHAMPS F3000

31 August 2002. Spa-Francorchamps. 22 laps of a 4.316-mile circuit = 94.952 miles. FIA F3000 Championship round 11

1	Giorgio Pantano	Lola B2/50-Zytek	22	47m06.609
2	Sebastien Bourdais	Lola B2/50-Zytek	22	47m07.035
3	Ricardo Sperafico	Lola B2/50-Zytek	22	47m07.680
4	Tomas Enge	Lola B2/50-Zytek	22	47m21.494
5	Ricardo Mauricio	Lola B2/50-Zytek	22	47m23.368
6	Nicolas Kiesa	Lola B2/50-Zytek	22	47m26.152

Winner's average speed: 120.932 mph. Pole position: Bourdais, 2m04.626.
Fastest lap: Bourdais, 2m07.133

MONZA F3000

14 September 2002. Monza. 26 laps of a 3.599-mile circuit = 93.574 miles. FIA F3000 Championship round 12

1	Bjorn Wirdheim	Lola B2/50-Zytek	26	44m57.538
2	Tomas Enge	Lola B2/50-Zytek	26	44m59.846
3	Giorgio Pantano	Lola B2/50-Zytek	26	44m59.879
4	Ricardo Sperafico	Lola B2/50-Zytek	26	45m00.851
5	Nicolas Kiesa	Lola B2/50-Zytek	26	45m01.653
6	Zsolt Baumgartner	Lola B2/50-Zytek	26	45m02.393

Antonio Pizzonia (Lola B2/50-Zytek), 44m59.118, finished second on the road but was disqualified due to illegal wing. Winner's average speed: 124.879 mph. Pole position: Wirdheim, 1m37.857. Fastest lap: Pantano, 1m39.287

2002 FINAL CHAMPIONSHIP POSITIONS

1	Sebastien Bourdais	56		11	Ricardo Mauricio	9
2	Giorgio Pantano	54		12	Nicolas Kiesa	3
3	Tomas Enge	50		13=	TiagoMonteiro	2
4	Bjorn Wirdheim	29			Rob Nguyen	2
5	Ricardo Sperafico	22		15	Zsolt Baumgartner	1
6	Rodrigo Sperafico	20				
7=	Mario Haberfeld	18				
	Antonio Pizzonia	18				
9=	Patrick Friesacher	14				
	Enrico Toccacelo	14				

1989 Jean Alesi leads Marco Apicella during their dice for the lead of the 1989 Birmingham Super Prix.

1998 Juan Pablo Montoya included the Formula 3000 Championship title en route to Grand Prix racing.

Drivers' Records

STARTS

Marco Apicella	52	Lamberto Leoni	27	Jean-Denis Deletraz	20
Fabrizio Gollin	48	Roberto Moreno	27	Andrew Gilbert-Scott	20
Paul Belmondo	45	Andrea Piccini	27	Mauricio Gugelmin	20
Tomas Enge	45	Gonzalo Rodriguez	27	Werner Lupberger	20
Soheil Ayari	40	Stephen Watson	27	Franck Montagny	20
Marc Goossens	39	Christian Pescatori	26	Stephane Proulx	20
Ricardo Mauricio	37	Russell Spence	26	Laurent Redon	20
Andrea Chiesa	36	Paul Stewart	26	Alessandro Santin	20
Mario Haberfeld	36	Kenny Brack	25	Ricardo Zonta	20
Allan McNish	36	Alain Ferte	25	Laurent Aiello	19
Paolo delle Piane	36	Fabrizio Giovanardi	25	Zsolt Baumgartner	19
Michel Ferte	35	Gareth Rees	25	Olivier Beretta	19
Vincenzo Sospiri	35	Fabrice Walfrisch	25	Eric Bernard	19
Jerome Policand	34	Patrick Friesacher	24	Heinz-Harald Frentzen	19
Sebastien Bourdais	33	Philippe Gache	24	Jordi Gene	19
Claudio Langes	33	Hideki Noda	24	Derek Hill	19
Cyrille Sauvage	33	Giorgio Pantano	24	Eddie Irvine	19
Jamie Davies	32	Antonio Pizzonia	24	Paolo Barilla	18
Olivier Grouillard	32	Ricardo Sperafico	24	Enrique Bernoldi	18
Pierre-Henri Raphanel	32	Oliver Tichy	24	Pedro Chaves	18
Justin Wilson	32	Giuseppe Bugatti	23	Pedro Couceiro	18
Michael Bartels	31	Boris Derichebourg	23	Gregor Foitek	18
Bruno Junqueira	31	Antonio Tamburini	23	Marcos Gueiros	18
Pierluigi Martini	31	Jean-Philippe Belloc	22	Kurt Mollekens	18
Nicolas Minassian	31	Guillaume Gomez	22	Olivier Panis	18
Andrea Montermini	31	Nick Heidfeld	22	Christophe Tinseau	18
Emanuele Naspetti	31	Darren Manning	22	Andy Wallace	18
Gabriele Tarquini	31	Kevin McGarrity	22	Alessandro Zampedri	18
Jason Watt	31	Juan Pablo Montoya	22	"Jules" Boullion	17
Andre Couto	30	John Nielsen	22	Ivan Capelli	17
Gary Evans	30	Emanuele Pirro	22	Emmanuel Clerico	17
David Saelens	30	Mark Webber	22	Cor Euser	17
Max Wilson	30	Thomas Biagi	21	Gil de Ferran	17
Phil Andrews	29	Mario Hytten	21	Jeffrey van Hooydonk	17
Jean-Marc Gounon	29	Alex Muller	21	Viktor Maslov	17
Gaston Mazzacane	29	Eric van de Poele	21	Jaime Melo jr	17
Stephane Sarrazin	29	Luis Perez Sala	21	Dino Morelli	17
Mark Blundell	28	Rodrigo Sperafico	21	Massimiliano Papis	17
John Jones	28	Jean Alesi	20	Michel Trolle	17
Bas Leinders	28	Emmanuel Collard	20	Vittorio Zoboli	17
Damon Hill	27	Erik Comas	20	Rui Aguas	16
Tomas Kaiser	27	David Coulthard	20	Giovanni Bonanno	16

Records

STARTS (cont.)

Name	Starts	Name	Starts	Name	Starts
Didier Cottaz	16	Gabriel Furlan	9	Domenico Gitto	4
Pedro Diniz	16	Oliver Gavin	9	Marco Greco	4
Tom Kristensen	16	Eric Helary	9	Jonny Kane	4
Franck Lagorce	16	Guido Knycz	9	Jeff MacPherson	4
Patrick Lemarie	16	Kristian Kolby	9	Cathy Muller	4
Fabrizio de Simone	16	Nicolas Leboissetier	9	Andrej Pavicevic	4
Mike Thackwell	16	JJ Lehto	9	Tomas Scheckter	4
Enrico Toccacelo	16	Yvan Muller	9	Fermin Velez	4
Gary Brabham	15	Carl Rosenblad	9	James Weaver	4
Martin Donnelly	15	Marco Campos	8	Giovanni Aloi	3
Gregoire de Galzain	15	Roberto Colciago	8	Slim Borgudd	3
Tarso Marques	15	David Cook	8	Roberto del Castello	3
James Taylor	15	Johnny Dumfries	8	Richard Dallest	3
Giovanna Amati	14	Garry Formato	8	Franck Freon	3
Fabrizio Barbazza	14	Taki Inoue	8	Markus Friesacher	3
Marcelo Battistuzzi	14	Pedro Lamy	8	Claude-Yves Gosselin	3
Thomas Danielsson	14	Massimo Monti	8	Wolf Henzler	3
Norberto Fontana	14	Ricardo Rosset	8	Ross Hockenhull	3
Mikke van Hool	14	Brian Smith	8	Ken Johnson	3
Christian Horner	14	Alexandre Sperafico	8	Mauro Martini	3
Oliver Martini	14	Philippe Alliot	7	Hidetoshi Mitsusada	3
Paolo Ruberti	14	Julian Bailey	7	Polo Villamil	3
Eliseo Salazar	14	Anthony Beltoise	7	Paul Warwick	3
Giampiero Simoni	14	Christophe Bouchut	7	Aldo Bertuzzi	2
Volker Weidler	14	Ryan Briscoe	7	Max Busslinger	2
Severino Nardozi	13	Giambattista Busi	7	Dominic Chappell	2
Jari Nurminen	13	"Constantino jr"	7	Patrick Crinelli	2
Joel Camathias	12	Juan Manuel Fangio II	7	Thierry Delubac	2
"Pierre Chauvet"	12	Antonio Garcia	7	David Dussau	2
Guido Dacco	12	Frederic Gosparini	7	Alain Filhol	2
Elton Julian	12	Altfrid Heger	7	Franco Forini	2
Nicolas Kiesa	12	Satoru Nakajima	7	Beppe Gabbiani	2
Gabriele Lancieri	12	Steve Robertson	7	Stephane de Groodt	2
Giovanni Montanari	12	Franco Scapini	7	Naoki Hattori	2
Tiago Monteiro	12	Giorgio Vinella	7	Marc Hynes	2
Rob Nguyen	12	Richard Dean	6	Ukyo Katayama	2
Tony Schmidt	12	Johnny Herbert	6	Eric Lang	2
Bjorn Wirdheim	12	David Hunt	6	Giovanni Lavaggi	2
Didier Artzet	11	Alain Menu	6	Sergio Paese	2
Yannick Dalmas	11	Yves Olivier	6	Mark Skaife	2
Christian Danner	11	Peter Olsson	6	Aguri Suzuki	2
Bertrand Gachot	11	Marc Rostan	6	Gianfranco Tacchino	2
Stefano Modena	11	Emiliano Spataro	6	David Velay	2
Gianni Morbidelli	11	David Terrien	6	Alex Yoong	2
Dominik Schwager	11	Esteban Tuero	6	Peter Zakowski	2
Philippe Streiff	11	Fabiano Vandone	6	Kenneth Acheson	1
Karl Wendlinger	11	Adrian Campos	5	Mark Albon	1
Alessandro Zanardi	11	Eric Cheli	5	Alexandre de Andrade	1
Luca Badoer	10	Dominique Delestre	5	Massimiliano Angelelli	1
Rubens Barrichello	10	Fabien Giroix	5	Claudio Antonioli	1
Enrico Bertaggia	10	Jacques Goudchaux	5	Steve Arnold	1
Wim Eyckmans	10	Justin Keen	5	Fulvio Ballabio	1
Pascal Fabre	10	Nicola Larini	5	Andrea Boldrini	1
Philippe Favre	10	Perry McCarthy	5	Cary Bren	1
Christian Fittipaldi	10	Andreas Scheld	5	Tommy Byrne	1
Bertrand Godin	10	Thomas Schie	5	Gianluca Calcagni	1
Akira Iida	10	Norman Simon	5	Paulo Carcasci	1
Jan Lammers	10	Felice Tedeschi	5	Dave Coyne	1
Craig Lowndes	10	Gabriele Varano	5	Tim Davies	1
Cristiano da Matta	10	Alfonso de Vinuesa	5	Corrado Fabi	1
Ananda Mikola	10	Eric Angelvy	4	Hans Fertl	1
Jorg Muller	10	Thed Bjork	4	Yann Goudy	1
Mark Shaw	10	David Brabham	4	Jean-Philippe Grand	1
Thierry Tassin	10	Jonathan Cochet	4	Jaroslav Janis	1
Christijan Albers	9	Nicolas Filiberti	4	Steve Kempton	1
Fernando Alonso	9	Marc Gene	4	Peter Kox	1
Steven Andskar	9	Andrea Gilardi	4	Gilles Lempereur	1

Formula 3000

YOUNGEST DRIVERS TO START

18 years 74 days	Jaroslav Janis	2001 Monza
18 years 103 days	Tarso Marques	1994 Silverstone
18 years 118 days	Esteban Tuero	1996 Silverstone
18 years 172 days	Polo Villamil	1998 Barcelona
18 years 253 days	Fernando Alonso	2000 Imola

OLDEST DRIVERS TO START

45 years 95 days	"Pierre Chauvet"	1988 Dijon-Prenois
44 years 312 days	Guido Dacco	1987 Enna-Pergusa
42 years 343 days	James Taylor	1998 Nurburgring
42 years 265 days	Valentino Musetti	1985 Donington Park
39 years 3 days	Jan Lammers	1995 Pau

WINS

Nick Heidfeld	7	Stefano Modena	3	Jamie Davies	1
Juan Pablo Montoya	7	Andrea Montermini	3	Pascal Fabre	1
Erik Comas	6	Olivier Panis	3	Gregor Foitek	1
Tomas Enge	6	Emanuele Pirro	3	Jordi Gene	1
Bruno Junqueira	5	Eric van de Poele	3	Fabrizio Giovanardi	1
Roberto Moreno	5	Gonzalo Rodriguez	3	Mauricio Gugelmin	1
Emanuele Naspetti	5	Vincenzo Sospiri	3	Johnny Herbert	1
Ricardo Zonta	5	Justin Wilson	3	Eddie Irvine	1
Luca Badoer	4	Soheil Ayari	2	Tom Kristensen	1
Sebastien Bourdais	4	Yannick Dalmas	2	Pedro Lamy	1
Kenny Brack	4	Christian Fittipaldi	2	Tarso Marques	1
Christian Danner	4	Jean-Marc Gounon	2	Gianni Morbidelli	1
Franck Lagorce	4	Olivier Grouillard	2	John Nielsen	1
Pierluigi Martini	4	Allan McNish	2	Massimiliano Papis	1
Nicolas Minassian	4	Jorg Muller	2	Antonio Pizzonia	1
Giorgio Pantano	4	Ricardo Rosset	2	Ricardo Sperafico	1
Luis Perez Sala	4	Stephane Sarrazin	2	Rodrigo Sperafico	1
Mike Thackwell	4	Alessandro Zanardi	2	Antonio Tamburini	1
Jason Watt	4	Philippe Alliot	1	Christophe Tinseau	1
Mark Webber	4	Fernando Alonso	1	Enrico Toccacelo	1
Jean Alesi	3	Julian Bailey	1	Michel Trolle	1
"Jules" Boullion	3	Olivier Beretta	1	Bjorn Wirdheim	1
Ivan Capelli	3	Eric Bernard	1		
Martin Donnelly	3	Andrea Chiesa	1		
Gil de Ferran	3	David Coulthard	1		
Marc Goossens	3	Thomas Danielsson	1		

YOUNGEST DRIVERS TO WIN

19 years 27 days	Fernando Alonso	2000 Spa-Francorchamps
19 years 247 days	Tarso Marques	1995 Estoril
20 years 140 days	Allan McNish	1990 Silverstone
20 years 141 days	Christian Fittipaldi	1991 Jerez
20 years 181 days	Ricardo Zonta	1996 Estoril

OLDEST DRIVERS TO WIN

31 years 300 days	Philippe Alliot	1986 Spa-Francorchamps
30 years 150 days	Kenny Brack	1996 Silverstone
30 years 45 days	Olivier Grouillard	1988 Zolder
29 years 309 days	Tom Kristensen	1997 Silverstone
29 years 291 days	Jean-Marc Gounon	1992 Magny-Cours

Records

MOST POINTS SCORED

Name	Points	Name	Points	Name	Points
Nick Heidfeld	117	Marcos Gueiros	22	Patrick Lemarie	6
Tomas Enge	111	Kurt Mollekens	22	Dino Morelli	6
Juan Pablo Montoya	102.5	Bertrand Gachot	21	Hideki Noda	6
Sebastien Bourdais	91	Mario Haberfeld	21	Andrea Piccini	6
Vincenzo Sospiri	91	Olivier Beretta	20	Tomas Scheckter	6
Erik Comas	90	Yannick Dalmas	20	Volker Weidler	5
Justin Wilson	89	Guillaume Gomez	20	Andy Wallace	4.5
Jason Watt	85	Lamberto Leoni	20	Didier Artzet	4
Kenny Brack	78	Gianni Morbidelli	20	Norberto Fontana	4
Roberto Moreno	76	Pierre-Henri Raphael	20	Andrew Gilbert-Scott	4
Marco Apicella	71	Rodrigo Sperafico	20	Werner Lupberger	4
Bruno Junqueira	71	Darren Manning	19	Fabrice Walfrisch	4
Nicolas Minassian	70	Massimiliano Papis	19	Fabrizio Barbazza	3
Pierluigi Martini	67	Oliver Tichy	19	Paolo Barilla	3
Emanuele Pirro	67	Christophe Tinseau	19	Paul Belmondo	3
Giorgio Pantano	66	Bas Leinders	18	Marco Campos	3
Ricardo Zonta	66	Tarso Marques	18	Pedro Chaves	3
Marc Goossens	63	Fernando Alonso	17	Richard Dallest	3
Gonzalo Rodriguez	60.5	Emmanuel Collard	17	Pedro Diniz	3
Mark Webber	60	Alain Ferte	17	Oliver Gavin	3
Emanuele Naspetti	59	Damon Hill	17	Fabien Giroix	3
Luis Perez Sala	57.5	Laurent Redon	17	Nicolas Kiesa	3
Mike Thackwell	55.5	John Jones	16	Jan Lammers	3
Franck Lagorce	55	Pascal Fabre	15.5	Nicolas Leboissetier	3
Andrea Montermini	55	Emmanuel Clerico	15	Craig Lowndes	3
Christian Danner	52	Andre Couto	15	Oliver Martini	3
Jorg Muller	52	Gregor Foitek	15	Dominik Schwager	3
Ivan Capelli	51	Claudio Langes	15	Vittorio Zoboli	3
John Nielsen	51	Didier Cottaz	14	Gary Evans	2.5
Jean Alesi	50	Thomas Danielsson	14	Enrico Bertaggia	2
Gil de Ferran	49	Jaime Melo Jr	14	Joel Camathias	2
Olivier Grouillard	49	Gareth Rees	14	Richard Dean	2
Eric van de Poele	49	Enrico Toccacelo	14	Cor Euser	2
Soheil Ayari	48	Julian Bailey	13	Franck Freon	2
"Jules" Boullion	48	Johnny Herbert	13	Philippe Gache	2
Stephane Sarrazin	48	Christian Pescatori	13	Andrea Gilardi	2
Michel Ferte	47	Paul Stewart	13	Elton Julian	2
Christian Fittipaldi	47	Kevin McGarrity	12	Kristian Kolby	2
Allan McNish	47	Philippe Streiff	12	Gaston Mazzacane	2
Luca Badoer	46	Franck Montagny	11	Alain Menu	2
Ricardo Sperafico	46	Jerome Policand	11	Tiago Monteiro	2
Martin Donnelly	43	Russell Spence	10.5	Alex Muller	2
Jean-Marc Gounon	43	Philippe Alliot	10	Yvan Muller	2
Max Wilson	43	Gary Brabham	10	Rob Nguyen	2
David Coulthard	42	Fabrizio Gollin	10	Paolo delle Piane	2
Olivier Panis	42	Boris Derichebourg	9	Stephane Proulx	2
Alessandro Zanardi	42	Eric Helary	9	Giampiero Simoni	2
Stefano Modena	41	Fabrizio de Simone	9	Stephen Watson	2
Antonio Pizzonia	40	Giuseppe Bugatti	8	Eliseo Salazar	1.5
Eric Bernard	38	Pedro Couceiro	8	Alessandro Santin	1.5
Eddie Irvine	38	Jean-Denis Deletraz	8	Marcelo Battistuzzi	1
Jamie Davies	37	Heinz-Harald Frentzen	8	Zsolt Baumgartner	1
Tom Kristensen	37	Mario Hytten	8	Johnny Dumfries	1
Andrea Chiesa	34	Cyrille Sauvage	8	Wim Eyckmans	1
Mauricio Gugelmin	33	Karl Wendlinger	8	Juan Manuel Fangio II	1
David Saelens	33	Alessandro Zampedri	8	Franco Forini	1
Gabriele Tarquini	33	Rui Aguas	7	Gabriel Furlan	1
Mark Blundell	31	Laurent Aiello	7	Christian Horner	1
Pedro Lamy	31	Enrique Bernoldi	7	Luca Rangoni	1
Michael Bartels	30	Thomas Biagi	7	Thierry Tassin	1
Ricardo Rosset	29	Tomas Kaiser	7	Alfonso de Vinuesa	1
Bjorn Wirdheim	29	Cristiano da Matta	7		
Ricardo Mauricio	28	Satoru Nakajima	7		
Antonio Tamburini	28	Jean-Philippe Belloc	6		
Rubens Barrichello	27	Christophe Bouchut	6		
Michel Trolle	25.5	Guido Dacco	6		
Fabrizio Giovanardi	25	Philippe Favre	6		
Jordi Gene	24	Jeffrey van Hooydonk	6		
Patrick Friesacher	22	JJ Lehto	6		

Formula 3000

HIGHEST POINTS PER START

Name	Points	Name	Points	Name	Points
Nick Heidfeld	5.318	Kurt Mollekens	1.222	Marco Campos	0.375
Jorg Muller	5.200	Antonio Tamburini	1.217	Patrick Lemarie	0.375
Christian Danner	4.727	Soheil Ayari	1.200	Laurent Aiello	0.368
Christian Fittipaldi	4.700	Tarso Marques	1.200	Didier Artzet	0.364
Juan Pablo Montoya	4.659	Jamie Davies	1.156	Volker Weidler	0.357
Luca Badoer	4.600	Massimiliano Papis	1.118	Jeffrey van Hooydonk	0.353
Erik Comas	4.500	Mark Blundell	1.107	Dino Morelli	0.353
Pedro Lamy	3.875	David Saelens	1.100	Giuseppe Bugatti	0.348
Alessandro Zanardi	3.818	Philippe Streiff	1.091	Thomas Biagi	0.333
Stefano Modena	3.727	Gabriele Tarquini	1.065	Richard Dean	0.333
Ricardo Rosset	3.625	Christophe Tinseau	1.056	Oliver Gavin	0.333
Mike Thackwell	3.469	Olivier Beretta	1.053	Nicolas Leboissetier	0.333
Franck Lagorce	3.438	Richard Dallest	1.000	Alain Menu	0.333
Ricardo Zonta	3.300	Thomas Danielsson	1.000	Jerome Policand	0.324
Kenny Brack	3.120	Fabrizio Giovanardi	1.000	Jan Lammers	0.300
Emanuele Pirro	3.045	Eric Helary	1.000	Craig Lowndes	0.300
Ivan Capelli	3.000	Satoru Nakajima	1.000	Norberto Fontana	0.286
Gil de Ferran	2.882	Luca Rangoni	1.000	Jean-Philippe Belloc	0.273
Martin Donnelly	2.867	Michael Bartels	0.968	Dominik Schwager	0.273
"Jules" Boullion	2.824	Rodrigo Sperafico	0.952	Tomas Kaiser	0.259
Roberto Moreno	2.815	Andrea Chiesa	0.944	Nicolas Kiesa	0.250
Justin Wilson	2.781	Patrick Friesacher	0.917	Hideki Noda	0.250
Sebastien Bourdais	2.758	Guillaume Gomez	0.909	Andy Wallace	0.250
Giorgio Pantano	2.750	Emmanuel Clerico	0.882	Cyrille Sauvage	0.242
Jason Watt	2.742	Didier Cottaz	0.875	Kristian Kolby	0.222
Luis Perez Sala	2.738	Enrico Toccacelo	0.875	Yvan Muller	0.222
Mark Webber	2.727	Darren Manning	0.864	Andrea Piccini	0.222
Rubens Barrichello	2.700	Christophe Bouchut	0.857	Fabrizio Barbazza	0.214
Vincenzo Sospiri	2.600	Emmanuel Collard	0.850	Oliver Martini	0.214
Jean Alesi	2.500	Laurent Redon	0.850	Fabrizio Gollin	0.208
Tomas Enge	2.467	Gregor Foitek	0.833	Enrico Bertaggia	0.200
Bjorn Wirdheim	2.417	Jaime Melo jr	0.824	Andrew Gilbert-Scott	0.200
Olivier Panis	2.333	Oliver Tichy	0.792	Werner Lupberger	0.200
Eric van de Poele	2.333	Ricardo Mauricio	0.757	Alfonso de Vinuesa	0.200
John Nielsen	2.318	Lamberto Leoni	0.741	Pedro Diniz	0.188
Tom Kristensen	2.313	Karl Wendlinger	0.727	Vittorio Zoboli	0.176
Bruno Junqueira	2.290	Cristiano da Matta	0.700	Paolo Barilla	0.167
Nicolas Minassian	2.258	Alain Ferte	0.680	Joel Camathias	0.167
Gonzalo Rodriguez	2.241	Gary Brabham	0.667	Pedro Chaves	0.167
Johnny Herbert	2.167	Franck Freon	0.667	Elton Julian	0.167
Pierluigi Martini	2.161	JJ Lehto	0.667	Tiago Monteiro	0.167
David Coulthard	2.100	Bas Leinders	0.643	Rob Nguyen	0.167
Eric Bernard	2.000	Damon Hill	0.630	Fabrice Walfrisch	0.160
Eddie Irvine	2.000	Pierre-Henri Raphanel	0.625	Juan Manuel Fangio II	0.143
Ricardo Sperafico	1.917	Philippe Favre	0.600	Giampiero Simoni	0.143
Bertrand Gachot	1.909	Fabien Giroix	0.600	Johnny Dumfries	0.125
Emanuele Naspetti	1.903	Mario Haberfeld	0.583	Cor Euser	0.118
Fernando Alonso	1.889	John Jones	0.571	Gabriel Furlan	0.111
Julian Bailey	1.857	Fabrizio de Simone	0.563	Eliseo Salazar	0.107
Yannick Dalmas	1.818	Gareth Rees	0.560	Wim Eyckmans	0.100
Gianni Morbidelli	1.818	Franck Montagny	0.550	Stephane Proulx	0.100
Andrea Montermini	1.774	Kevin McGarrity	0.545	Thierry Tassin	0.100
Antonio Pizzonia	1.667	Andre Couto	0.500	Alex Muller	0.095
Stephane Sarrazin	1.655	Guido Dacco	0.500	Gary Evans	0.083
Mauricio Gugelmin	1.650	Franco Forini	0.500	Philippe Gache	0.083
Marc Goossens	1.615	Andrea Gilardi	0.500	Alessandro Santin	0.075
Pascal Fabre	1.550	Christian Pescatori	0.500	Stephen Watson	0.074
Olivier Grouillard	1.531	Paul Stewart	0.500	Marcelo Battistuzzi	0.071
Tomas Scheckter	1.500	Claudio Langes	0.455	Christian Horner	0.071
Michel Trolle	1.500	Pedro Couceiro	0.444	Gaston Mazzacane	0.069
Jean-Marc Gounon	1.483	Alessandro Zampedri	0.444	Paul Belmondo	0.067
Max Wilson	1.433	Rui Aguas	0.438	Paolo delle Piane	0.056
Philippe Alliot	1.429	Heinz-Harald Frentzen	0.421	Zsolt Baumgartner	0.053
Marco Apicella	1.365	Russell Spence	0.404		
Michel Ferte	1.343	Jean-Denis Deletraz	0.400		
Allan McNish	1.306	Boris Derichebourg	0.391		
Jordi Gene	1.263	Enrique Bernoldi	0.389		
Marcos Gueiros	1.222	Mario Hytten	0.381		

Records

POLE POSITIONS

Juan Pablo Montoya	10	Martin Donnelly	2	Enrique Bernoldi	1
Sebastien Bourdais	8	Gil de Ferran	2	Emmanuel Clerico	1
Tomas Enge	8	Michel Ferte	2	Emmanuel Collard	1
Roberto Moreno	7	Guillaume Gomez	2	Yannick Dalmas	1
Luca Badoer	5	Marc Goossens	2	Jamie Davies	1
Kenny Brack	5	Mauricio Gugelmin	2	Pascal Fabre	1
Erik Comas	5	Johnny Herbert	2	Philippe Favre	1
Nick Heidfeld	5	Pedro Lamy	2	Gregor Foitek	1
Franck Lagorce	5	Tarso Marques	2	Bertrand Gachot	1
Andrea Montermini	5	Pierluigi Martini	2	Jordi Gene	1
Mike Thackwell	5	Jorg Muller	2	Jeffrey van Hooydonk	1
Ricardo Zonta	5	Emanuele Naspetti	2	Eddie Irvine	1
Christian Fittipaldi	4	John Nielsen	2	John Jones	1
Tom Kristensen	4	Olivier Panis	2	Darren Manning	1
Emanuele Pirro	4	David Saelens	2	Jaime Melo Jr	1
Eric Bernard	3	Luis Perez Sala	2	Nicolas Minassian	1
Ivan Capelli	3	Ricardo Sperafico	2	Gianni Morbidelli	1
Olivier Grouillard	3	Mark Webber	2	Giorgio Pantano	1
Damon Hill	3	Justin Wilson	2	Massimiliano Papis	1
Bruno Junqueira	3	Max Wilson	2	Antonio Pizzonia	1
Allan McNish	3	Laurent Aiello	1	Pierre-Henri Raphanel	1
Jason Watt	3	Philippe Alliot	1	Ricardo Rosset	1
Alessandro Zanardi	3	Fernando Alonso	1	Stephane Sarrazin	1
Jean Alesi	2	Soheil Ayari	1	Fabrice Walfrisch	1
Marco Apicella	2	Michael Bartels	1	Bjorn Wirdheim	1
Christian Danner	2	Olivier Beretta	1		

FASTEST LAPS

Nick Heidfeld	9	Rubens Barrichello	2	Bruno Junqueira	1
Juan Pablo Montoya	8	"Jules" Boullion	2	Lamberto Leoni	1
Tomas Enge	7	Ivan Capelli	2	Darren Manning	1
Marco Apicella	6	Michel Ferte	2	Allan McNish	1
Ricardo Zonta	6	Guillaume Gomez	2	Stefano Modena	1
Giorgio Pantano	5	Olivier Grouillard	2	Christian Pescatori	1
Mark Webber	5	Damon Hill	2	Stephane Proulx	1
Sebastien Bourdais	4	Tom Kristensen	2	Eliseo Salazar	1
Erik Comas	4	Pedro Lamy	2	Vincenzo Sospiri	1
Christian Danner	4	Pierluigi Martini	2	Antonio Tamburini	1
Franck Lagorce	4	Olivier Panis	2	Gabriele Tarquini	1
Andrea Montermini	4	Antonio Pizzonia	2	Thierry Tassin	1
Roberto Moreno	4	Ricardo Rosset	2	Justin Wilson	1
Jorg Muller	4	Luis Perez Sala	2		
Emanuele Naspetti	4	Ricardo Sperafico	2		
Gonzalo Rodriguez	4	Michel Trolle	2		
Mike Thackwell	4	Rui Aguas	1		
Soheil Ayari	3	Jean Alesi	1		
Luca Badoer	3	Michael Bartels	1		
Eric Bernard	3	Mark Blundell	1		
Kenny Brack	3	Jamie Davies	1		
Emmanuel Clerico	3	Pascal Fabre	1		
David Coulthard	3	Philippe Favre	1		
Yannick Dalmas	3	Gil de Ferran	1		
Martin Donnelly	3	Christian Fittipaldi	1		
Tarso Marques	3	Philippe Gache	1		
John Nielsen	3	Marc Gene	1		
Emanuele Pirro	3	Marc Goossens	1		
Stephane Sarrazin	3	Jean-Marc Gounon	1		
Alessandro Zanardi	3	Mario Haberfeld	1		
Fernando Alonso	2	Johnny Herbert	1		

CLOSEST FINISHES

0.035 seconds	Gonzalo Rodriguez	1998 Spa-Francorchamps	0.426	Giorgio Pantano	2002 Spa-Francorchamps
0.22	Olivier Grouillard	1988 Zolder	0.44	Jean Alesi	1989 Birmingham
0.244	Ricardo Zonta	1996 Mugello	0.447	Franck Lagorce	1993 Nogaro
0.286	Jason Watt	1997 Spa-Francorchamps	0.455	Justin Wilson	2001 A1-Ring
0.374	Jean-Marc Gounon	1992 Magny-Cours			
0.42	Pierluigi Martini	1986 Mugello			

Other Records

Fewest starters in a race: 11, 1985 Pau
Most starters in a race: 35, 1998 Barcelona and 1998 Silverstone
Widest championship-winning margin: 32 points, Justin Wilson, 2001
Narrowest championship-winning margin: 0 points, Jean Alesi, 1989.
Alesi won the title as he had won more races than rival Erik Comas

Most wins in a season: Four, Christian Danner, 1985; Roberto Moreno, 1988; Erik Comas, 1990; Emanuele Naspetti, 1991; Luca Badoer, 1992; Juan Pablo Montoya, 1998; Nick Heidfeld, 1999; Bruno Junqueira, 2000
Most successive wins: Four, Emanuele Naspetti, 1991
Most points in a season: 71, Justin Wilson, 2001
Fastest race: 152.946 mph, 1993 Enna-Pergusa
Slowest race: 77.005 mph, 2001 Monte Carlo

Manufacturers' Records

WINS

Lola	96*
Reynard	59
March	18
Ralt	13

*including 76 wins scored since F3000 became a one-make category

POINTS

Lola	2230.5*	Tyrrell	3
Reynard	1377	Dallara	1
March	456	*including 1641 points scored	
Ralt	265	since F3000 became a one-make	
AGS	15	category	
Williams	4		

Engine Records

WINS

Cosworth	80
Zytek	64*
Mugen	20
Judd	7
Honda	3

*all scored since F3000 became a one-make category

POINTS

Cosworth	1871.5
Zytek	1641*
Mugen	504
Judd	243
Honda	92

*including 1641 points scored since F3000 became a one-make category

Teams' Records

WINS

Super Nova Racing*	35	Pacific Racing	5	Durango Corse	2
DAMS	21	RSM Marko	5	First Racing	2
Forti Corse	9	Arden International	4	Madgwick International	2
Team Astromega	8	BS Automotive	4	3001 International	1
Eddie Jordan Racing	8	Bromley Motorsport	4	Auto Sport Racing	1
McLaren International	8	Coloni Motorsport	4	European Aviation	1
Ralt Racing	7	Il Barone Rampante	3	Kid Jensen Racing	1
Nordic Racing	6	GDBA Motorsport	3	Mythos Racing	1
Onyx Race Engineering	6	Genoa Racing	3	Roni Motorsport	1
Apomatox 3000	5	Lola Motorsport	3	*including Petrobras Junior and	
Team Crypton	5	ORECA	3	Den Bla Avis	
GA Motorsport	5	Paul Stewart Racing	3		
Luciano Pavesi Racing	5	Draco Engineering	2		

European Formula 3 Championship

1984 European Champion Ivan Capelli leads the field at the Silverstone.

European Formula 3 Championship

Formula 3 has always been an important stepping-stone to the top echelons of the sport. The new category was introduced in Britain after World War II, using low-cost 500cc motorcycle engines mounted in small, nimble chassis. Although national championships were organised throughout Europe from the fifties, it was not until 1975 that a European championship was introduced by the FIA. By that time the category stipulated 2000cc normally aspirated engines based on road car units.

A decade later the European championship was replaced by a one-off, end-of-season race between the top national championship contenders. However, this too has disappeared from the calendar. But the championships in Britain, France, and Germany still provide a fertile breeding ground for future Formula 1 stars. While F2 and F3000 have yet to produce a World Champion, Ayrton Senna, Alain Prost (despite three earlier F2 starts), and Nelson Piquet, among others, all graduated directly to Formula 1 after championship success in F3.

1979 Slim Borgudd leads Alain Prost and Michael Bleekemolen at Zandvoort.

Rules

1975-84   2000cc maximum engine capacity. Normally aspirated stock-block engines. Maximum 4 cylinders

Points

1975-84   9-6-4-3-2-1 points awarded to the top six finishers

FIA EUROPEAN FORMULA 3 CHAMPIONS

year	driver	nat	team	car
1975	Larry Perkins	AUS	Team Cowangie	Ralt RT1-Ford
1976	Riccardo Patrese	I	Trivellato Racing	Chevron B34-Toyota
1977	Piercarlo Ghinzani	I	AFMP Euroracing	March 773-Toyota
1978	Jan Lammers	NL	Roger Heavens Racing	Ralt RT1-Toyota
1979	Alain Prost	F	Automobiles Martini	Martini MK27-Renault
1980	Michele Alboreto	I	Euroracing	March 803-Alfa Romeo/March 803B-Alfa Romeo
1981	Mauro Baldi	I	Euroracing	March 813-Alfa Romeo
1982	Oscar Larrauri	RA	Euroracing	Euroracing 101-Alfa Romeo
1983	Pierluigi Martini	I	Luciano Pavesi	Ralt RT3-Alfa Romeo
1984	Ivan Capelli	I	Enzo Coloni Racing	Martini MK42-Alfa Romeo

FIA FORMULA 3 EUROPEAN CUP

When the European F3 Championship was cancelled, FISA replaced it with a one-off race to decide the European Champion. The top six from each national series were invited. Run at Paul Ricard (1985), Imola (1986), Silverstone (1987), Nurburgring (1988), Misano (1989), and Le Mans (1990); it was due to be held at Donington Park for 1991 but the event was cancelled.

1985	Alex Caffi	I	Enzo Coloni Racing	Dallara 385-Alfa Romeo
1986	Stefano Modena	I	Seresina/Ferdinando Ravarotto	Reynard 863-Alfa Romeo
1987	Steve Kempton	GB	Reynard Research & Development	Reynard 873-Alfa Romeo
1988	Joachim Winkelhock	D	WTS Racing	Reynard 883-Volkswagen
1989	Gianni Morbidelli	I	Forti Corse	Dallara 389-Alfa Romeo
1990	Alessandro Zanardi	I	RC Motorsport	Dallara 390-Alfa Romeo
1991	RACE CANCELLED			

EFDA EUROPEAN FORMULA 3 EUROSERIES

The new F3 Euroseries was an attempt by Dan Partel of the European Formula Drivers Association to reintroduce a European Championship for the category. However, it was cancelled by FISA after just one season.

1987	Dave Coyne	GB	Bross Druck Chemie	Reynard 873-Volkswagen

Race Winnners

1975

date	race	driver	nat	car	mph
10.05.75	Monte Carlo	Renzo Zorzi	I	GRD 374-Lancia	75.515
01.06.75	Nurburgring	Freddy Kottulinsky	S	Modus M1-BMW	104.260
08.06.75	Anderstorp	Conny Andersson	S	March 753-Toyota	92.390
29.06.75	Monza	Larry Perkins	AUS	Ralt RT1-Ford	116.799
02.08.75	Djurslandring	Terry Perkins	AUS	Ralt RT1-Ford	n/a

1976

date	race	driver	nat	car	mph
04.04.76	Nurburgring	Conny Andersson	S	March 753-Toyota	101.282
19.04.76	Zandvoort	Riccardo Patrese	I	Chevron B34-Toyota	102.642
09.05.76	Mantorp Park	Gianfranco Brancatelli	I	March 763-Toyota	101.219
23.05.76	Avus	Conny Andersson	S	March 763-Toyota	n/a*
13.06.76	Enna-Pergusa	Riccardo Patrese	I	Chevron B34-Toyota	101.092
27.06.76	Monza	Riccardo Patrese	I	Chevron B34-Toyota	112.524
25.07.76	Croix-en-Ternois	Conny Andersson	S	March 763-Toyota	76.756
22.08.76	Kassel-Calden	Riccardo Patrese	I	Chevron B34-Toyota	n/a*
04.09.76	Knutstorp	Conny Andersson	S	March 763-Toyota	78.517
03.10.76	Vallelunga	Gianfranco Brancatelli	I	March 763-Toyota	93.691

*Race decided by points awarded for results in the two heats

1977

date	race	driver	nat	car	mph
20.03.77	Paul Ricard	Beppe Gabbiani	I	Chevron B38-Toyota	91.573
27.03.77	Nurburgring	Piercarlo Ghinzani	I	March 773-Toyota	88.897
11.04.77	Zandvoort	Anders Olofsson	S	Ralt RT1-Toyota	103.263
24.04.77	Zolder	Piercarlo Ghinzani	I	March 773-Toyota	93.748
08.05.77	Osterreichring	Anders Olofsson	S	Ralt RT1-Toyota	106.234
29.05.77	Imola	Piercarlo Ghinzani	I	March 773-Toyota	101.789
12.06.77	Enna-Pergusa	Oscar Pedersoli	I	Ralt RT1-Toyota	107.930
26.06.77	Monza	Elio de Angelis	I	Ralt RT1-Toyota	113.476
24.07.77	Croix-en-Ternois	Derek Daly	IRL	Chevron B38-Toyota	77.363
07.08.77	Knutstorp	Anders Olofsson	S	Ralt RT1-Toyota	79.956
21.08.77	Kassel-Calden	Nelson Piquet	BR	Ralt RT1-Toyota	101.603
27.08.77	Donington Park	Brett Riley	NZ	March 773-Toyota	98.142
18.09.77	Jarama	Nelson Piquet	BR	Ralt RT1-Toyota	85.291
09.10.77	Vallelunga	Oscar Pedersoli	I	Ralt RT1-Toyota	94.230

1978

date	race	driver	nat	car	mph
27.03.78	Zandvoort	Jan Lammers	NL	Ralt RT1-Toyota	104.335
02.04.78	Nurburgring	Anders Olofsson	S	Ralt RT1-Toyota	106.484
16.04.78	Osterreichring	Anders Olofsson	S	Ralt RT1-Toyota	113.861
23.04.78	Zolder	Teo Fabi	I	March 783-Toyota	78.357
14.05.78	Imola	Patrick Gaillard	F	Chevron B43-Toyota	103.190
27.05.78	Nurburgring	Patrick Gaillard	F	Chevron B43-Toyota	107.655
04.06.78	Dijon-Prenois	Teo Fabi	I	March 783-Toyota	103.986
25.06.78	Monza	Jan Lammers	NL	Ralt RT1-Toyota	94.510
02.07.78	Enna-Pergusa	Michael Bleekemolen	NL	Chevron B43-Toyota	109.640
16.07.78	Magny-Cours	Jan Lammers	NL	Ralt RT1-Toyota	98.401
06.08.78	Knutstorp	Anders Olofsson	S	Ralt RT1-Toyota	79.498
13.08.78	Karlskoga	Jan Lammers	NL	Ralt RT1-Toyota	86.959
26.08.78	Donington Park	Derek Warwick	GB	Ralt RT1-Toyota	99.330
03.09.78	Kassel-Calden	Anders Olofsson	S	Ralt RT1-Toyota	102.505
17.09.78	Jarama	Alain Prost	F	Martini MK21B-Renault	86.456
08.10.78	Vallelunga	Teo Fabi	I	March 783-Toyota	95.659

1979

date	race	driver	nat	car	mph
18.03.79	Vallelunga	Piercarlo Ghinzani	I	March 793-Alfa Romeo	95.095
15.04.79	Osterreichring	Alain Prost	F	Martini MK27-Renault	116.432
22.04.79	Zolder	Alain Prost	F	Martini MK27-Renault	98.906
01.05.79	Magny-Cours	Alain Prost	F	Martini MK27-Renault	98.542
20.05.79	Donington Park	Brett Riley	NZ	March 783/793-Triumph	80.856
04.06.79	Zandvoort	Alain Prost	F	Martini MK27-Renault	104.428

European Formula 3

date	race	driver	nat	car	mph
17.06.79	Enna-Pergusa	Piercarlo Ghinzani	I	March 793-Alfa Romeo	105.790
24.06.79	Monza	Mike Thackwell	NZ	March 793-Toyota	114.082
05.08.79	Knutstorp	Alain Prost	F	Martini MK27-Renault	80.125
12.08.79	Kinnekulle	Richard Dallest	F	Martini MK27-Toyota	88.822
09.09.79	Jarama	Alain Prost	F	Martini MK27-Renault	86.280
07.10.79	Kassel-Calden	Michael Korten	D	March 793-Toyota	101.264

1980

date	race	driver	nat	car	mph
30.03.80	Nurburgring	Thierry Boutsen	B	Martini MK31-Toyota	105.972
06.04.80	Osterreichring	Michele Alboreto	I	March 803-Alfa Romeo	116.658
20.04.80	Zolder	Thierry Boutsen	B	Martini MK31-Toyota	95.201
27.04.80	Magny-Cours	Thierry Boutsen	B	Martini MK31-Toyota	98.781
26.05.80	Zandvoort	Mauro Baldi	I	Martini MK31-Toyota	100.396
01.06.80	La Chatre	Michele Alboreto	I	March 803-Alfa Romeo	79.525
15.06.80	Mugello	Corrado Fabi	I	March 803-Alfa Romeo	101.170
29.06.80	Monza	Michele Alboreto	I	March 803-Alfa Romeo	113.443
27.07.80	Misano	Mauro Baldi	I	Martini MK31-Toyota	100.742
10.08.80	Knutstorp	Corrado Fabi	I	March 803-Alfa Romeo	77.576
07.09.80	Silverstone	Mike White	ZA	March 803B-Toyota	119.763
21.09.80	Jarama	Mauro Baldi	I	Martini MK31-Toyota	88.399
05.10.80	Kassel-Calden	Michele Alboreto	I	March 803B-Alfa Romeo	104.960
12.10.80	Zolder	Philippe Streiff	F	Martini MK31-Toyota	100.839

1981

date	race	driver	nat	car	mph
15.03.81	Vallelunga	Mauro Baldi	I	March 813-Alfa Romeo	96.240
29.03.81	Nurburgring	Oscar Larrauri	RA	March 813-Toyota	94.370
05.04.81	Donington Park	Mike White	ZA	March 813-Alfa Romeo	100.797
19.04.81	Osterreichring	Mauro Baldi	I	March 813-Alfa Romeo	119.129
26.04.81	Zolder	Mauro Baldi	I	March 813-Alfa Romeo	102.901
03.05.81	Magny-Cours	Philippe Alliot	F	Martini MK34-Alfa Romeo	101.259
24.05.81	La Chatre	Philippe Alliot	F	Martini MK34-Alfa Romeo	80.550
08.06.81	Zandvoort	Mauro Baldi	I	March 813-Alfa Romeo	102.672
21.06.81	Silverstone	Roberto Moreno	BR	Ralt RT3/81-Toyota	122.634
28.06.81	Croix-en-Ternois	Mauro Baldi	I	March 813-Alfa Romeo	77.980
19.07.81	Misano	Mauro Baldi	I	March 813-Alfa Romeo	87.162
09.08.81	Knutstorp	Mauro Baldi	I	March 813-Alfa Romeo	80.037
06.09.81	Jarama	Alain Ferte	F	Martini MK34-Alfa Romeo	89.297
20.09.81	Imola	Mauro Baldi	I	March 813-Alfa Romeo	101.749
04.10.81	Mugello	Emanuele Pirro	I	Martini MK34-Toyota	102.792

1982

date	race	driver	nat	car	mph
14.03.82	Mugello	Oscar Larrauri	RA	Euroracing 101-Alfa Romeo	102.980
28.03.82	Nurburgring	Oscar Larrauri	RA	Euroracing 101-Alfa Romeo	98.467
04.04.82	Donington Park	James Weaver	GB	Ralt RT3/81-Toyota	100.903
18.04.82	Zolder	Oscar Larrauri	RA	Euroracing 101-Alfa Romeo	101.655
02.05.82	Magny-Cours	Alain Ferte	F	Martini MK37-Alfa Romeo	101.525
16.05.82	Osterreichring	Emanuele Pirro	I	Euroracing 101-Alfa Romeo	118.335
31.05.82	Zandvoort	Oscar Larrauri	RA	Euroracing 101-Alfa Romeo	102.130
13.06.82	Silverstone	Emanuele Pirro	I	Euroracing 101-Alfa Romeo	121.741
27.06.82	Monza	Oscar Larrauri	RA	Euroracing 101-Alfa Romeo	115.625
04.07.82	Enna-Pergusa	Oscar Larrauri	RA	Euroracing 101-Alfa Romeo	111.011
18.07.82	La Chatre	Philippe Alliot	F	Martini MK37-Alfa Romeo	81.150
08.08.82	Knutstorp	Oscar Larrauri	RA	Euroracing 101-Alfa Romeo	80.131
05.09.82	Nogaro	James Weaver	GB	Ralt RT3/82-Toyota	91.950
12.09.82	Jarama	James Weaver	GB	Ralt RT3/82-Toyota	89.057
03.10.82	Kassel-Calden	Emanuele Pirro	I	Euroracing 101-Alfa Romeo	87.381

1983

date	race	driver	nat	car	mph
13.03.83	Vallelunga	Emanuele Pirro	I	Ralt RT3/83-Alfa Romeo	96.920
17.04.83	Zolder	Emanuele Pirro	I	Ralt RT3/83-Alfa Romeo	102.348
01.05.83	Magny-Cours	John Nielsen	DK	Ralt RT3/83-Volkswagen	97.829
22.05.83	Osterreichring	Tommy Byrne	IRL	Ralt RT3/83-Toyota	119.329
05.06.83	La Chatre	Roberto Ravaglia	I	Ralt RT3/83-Toyota	80.154
12.06.83	Silverstone	Martin Brundle	GB	Ralt RT3/83-Toyota	122.400
26.06.83	Monza	John Nielsen	DK	Ralt RT3/83-Volkswagen	116.290

date	race	driver	nat	car	mph
10.07.83	Misano	Tommy Byrne	IRL	Ralt RT3/83-Toyota	101.984
31.07.83	Zandvoort	John Nielsen	DK	Ralt RT3/83-Volkswagen	101.668
07.08.83	Knutstorp	John Nielsen	DK	Ralt RT3/83-Volkswagen	80.671
04.09.83	Nogaro	Pierluigi Martini	I	Ralt RT3/83-Alfa Romeo	91.849
11.09.83	Jarama	Pierluigi Martini	I	Ralt RT3/83-Alfa Romeo	89.404
25.09.83	Imola	Pierluigi Martini	I	Ralt RT3/83-Alfa Romeo	103.857
09.10.83	Donington Park	Martin Brundle	GB	Ralt RT3/83-Toyota	93.242
23.10.83	Croix-en-Ternois	Pierluigi Martini	I	Ralt RT3/83-Alfa Romeo	79.694

1984

date	race	driver	nat	car	mph
25.03.84	Donington Park	Johnny Dumfries	GB	Ralt RT3/83-Volkswagen	85.842
15.04.84	Zolder	John Nielsen	DK	Ralt RT3/84-Volkswagen	102.885
01.05.84	Magny-Cours	Ivan Capelli	I	Martini MK42-Alfa Romeo	102.472
13.05.84	La Chatre	Ivan Capelli	I	Martini MK42-Alfa Romeo	81.067
27.05.84	Osterreichring	Gerhard Berger	A	Ralt RT3/84-Alfa Romeo	120.560
10.06.84	Silverstone	Johnny Dumfries	GB	Ralt RT3/83-Volkswagen	124.430
17.06.84	Nurburgring	Johnny Dumfries	GB	Ralt RT3/83-Volkswagen	103.697
24.06.84	Monza	Gerhard Berger	A	Ralt RT3/84-Alfa Romeo	115.723
08.07.84	Enna-Pergusa	Ivan Capelli	I	Martini MK42-Alfa Romeo	112.675
15.07.84	Mugello	Ivan Capelli	I	Martini MK42-Alfa Romeo	104.569
19.08.84	Knutstorp	Claudio Langes	I	Ralt RT3/84-Toyota	80.082
16.09.84	Nogaro	John Nielsen	DK	Ralt RT3/84-Volkswagen	94.408
21.10.84	Jarama	Johnny Dumfries	GB	Ralt RT3/83-Volkswagen	90.527

1981 Left to right: Enzo Coloni, Michele Alboreto, Corrado Fabi, and Philippe Alliot head a packed field at Mugello.

Le Mans 24 Hours

1976 Jacky Ickx, the most successful driver in Le Mans history, shares the front row with Renault's Jean-Pierre Jabouille.

Le Mans 24 Hours

Rules

The Le Mans 24 Hours has been the leading sports car race of the year since it was first held in 1923. It normally adopted current World Championship rules until the series was abandoned in 1992. A mixture of racing sports cars, GTS (silhouette), and road-based GT cars has competed since then. The organisers have attempted to equalise the power-to-weight ratio of the different classes with their fuel capacity and minimum weight restrictions.

The race currently has two pure Prototype classes. LMP900 is for Le Mans prototypes with a minimum weight of 900 kg and maximum engine capacity of 6000cc normally aspirated or 4000cc turbocharged. LMP675 has a minimum weight limit of 675 kg and maximum engine capacity of 3400cc normally aspirated or 2000cc turbocharged. GTP is as LMP900, but enclosed cockpits and narrower tyres are stipulated. GTS is for silhouette GT cars, and less tuned pure GT entries complete the classes.

1923

26-27 May 1923. 128 laps of a 10.726 mile-circuit = 1372.928 miles

1	Andre Lagache/ Rene Leonard	Chenard & Walcker "Sport"	128
2	Raoul Bachmann/		
	Christian Dauvergne	Chenard & Walcker "Sport"	124
3	Raymond de Tornaco/Paul Gros	Bignan 11HP "Desmo"	120
4=	John Duff/Frank Clement	Bentley "Sport"	112
4=	Philippe de Marne/Jean Martin	Bignan 11HP "Commercial"	112
4=	Andre Dils/Nicolas Caerels	Excelsior "Albert 1er"	112

Winner's average speed: 57.205 mph. Class winners: 5001-8000cc: Dils/Caerels; 3001-5000cc: Gerard de Courcelles/Andre Rossignol (Lorraine Dietrich B3-6); 2001-3000cc: Lagache/Leonard; 1501-2000cc: de Tornaco/Gros; 1101-1500cc: Max de Pourtales/Sosthene de la Rochefoucauld (Bugatti T16S); 751-1100cc: Georges Casse/Lucien Desvaux (Salmson AL). Fastest lap: Clement, 9m39

1924

14-15 June 1924. 120 laps of a 10.726 mile-circuit = 1287.120 miles

1	John Duff/Frank Clement	Bentley "Sport"	120
2	Henri Stoffel/Edouard Brisson	Lorraine-Dietrich B3-6	119
3	Gerard de Courcelles/		
	Andre Rossignol	Lorraine-Dietrich B3-6	119
4	Andre Pisard/"Chavee"	Chenard & Walcker 2-litre	111
5	Christian Dauvergne/		
	Manso de Zuniga	Chenard & Walcker 2-litre	108
6	Gaston Delalande/		
	Georges Guignard	Rolland Pilain C23	106

Winner's average speed: 53.630 mph. Class winners: 3001-5000cc: Stoffel/Brisson; 2001-3000cc: Duff/Clement; 1501-2000cc: Pisard/"Chavee"; 1101-1500cc: no finishers; 751-1100cc: Fernand Gabriel/Henri Lapierre (Aries 8-10CV). Fastest lap: Andre Lagache (Chenard & Walcker), 9m19

1925

20-21 June 1925. 129 laps of a 10.726 mile-circuit = 1383.654 miles

1	Gerard de Courcelles/		
	Andre Rossignol	Lorraine-Dietrich B3-6	129

2	Jean Chassagne/		
	Sammy Davis	Sunbeam "Sport" DA8206	125
3	Stalter/Edouard Brisson	Lorraine-Dietrich B3-6	124
4=	Tino Danieli/Mario Danieli	OM 665S "Superba"	120
4=	Giulio Foresti/Aime Vassiaux	OM 665S "Superba"	120
6	Louis Wagner/Charles Flohot	Aries 3-litre	119

Winner's average speed: 57.652 mph. Class winners: 3001-5000cc: de Courcelles/Rossignol; 2001-3000cc: Chassagne/Davis; 1501-2000cc: Danieli/Danieli and Foresti/Vassiaux; 1101-1500cc: Louis Balart/Robert Doutrebente (Corre la Licorne W15); 751-1101cc: Raymond Glazmann/Manso de Zuniga (Chenard & Walcker). Fastest lap: Andre Lagache (Chenard & Walcker), 9m10

1926

12-13 June 1926. 147 laps of a 10.726 mile-circuit = 1576.722 miles

1	Robert Bloch/Andre Rossignol	Lorraine-Dietrich B3-6	147
2	Gerard de Courcelles/		
	Marcel Mongin	Lorraine-Dietrich B3-6	146
3	Stalter/Edouard Brisson	Lorraine-Dietrich B3-6	139
4	Ferdinando Minoia/Giulio Foresti	OM 665SS "Superba"	134
5	Tino Danieli/Mario Danieli	OM 665SS "Superba"	131
6	Pierre Tabourin/Auguste Lefranc	Theo Schneider 25SP	118

Winner's average speed: 65.697 mph. Class winners: 3001-5000cc: Bloch/Rossignol; 2001-3000cc: no finishers; 1501-2000cc: Minoia/Foresti; 1101-1500cc: Henri de Costier/Pierre Bussienne (EHP DS); 751-1100cc: Georges Casse/Andre Rousseau (Salmson GS). Fastest lap: de Courcelles, 9m03

1927

18-19 June 1927. 137 laps of a 10.726 mile-circuit = 1469.462 miles

1	Sammy Davis/JD Benjafield	Bentley "Sport"	137
2	Andre de Victor/J Hasley	Salmson GS	117
3	Georges Casse/Andre Rousseau	Salmson GS	115
4	Lucien Desvaux/Fernand Vallon	SCAP 1.5-litre	110
5	Guy Bouriat/Pierre Bussienne	EHP DS-Cime	108
6	Andre Marandet/		
	Gonzague Lecureul	SARA BDE	106

Winner's average speed: 61.228 mph. Class winners: 3001-5000cc: no finishers; 2001-3000cc: Davis/Benjafield; 1501-2000cc: no finishers; 1101-1500cc: Desvaux/Vallon; 751-1100cc: de Victor/Hasley. Fastest lap: Frank Clement (Bentley "Super Sport"), 8m46

1928

16-17 June 1928. 154 laps of a 10.726 mile-circuit = 1651.804 miles

1	Woolf Barnato/Bernard Rubin	Bentley 4.4	154
2	Edouard Brisson/Robert Bloch	Stutz DV "Black Hawk"	153
3	Henri Stoffel/Andre Rossignol	Chrysler 72	144
4	Jean Ghica Cantacuzino/		
	G Ghica Cantacuzino	Chrysler 72	139
5	Tim Birkin/Jean Chassagne	Bentley 4.4	135
6	Maurice Harvey/Harold Purdy	Alvis TA	132

Winner's average speed: 68.825 mph. Class winners: 3001-5000cc: Barnato/Rubin; 2001-3000cc no finishers; 1501-2000cc: Robert Benoist/Christian Dauvergne (Itala 65S); 1101-1500cc: Harvey/Purdy; 751-1100cc: Michel Dore/Jean Treunet (BNC). Fastest lap: Birkin, 8m07

1929

15-16 June 1929. 173 laps of a 10.153 mile-circuit = 1756.469 miles

1	Woolf Barnato/Tim Birkin	Bentley "Speed Six"	173
2	Jack Dunfee/Glen Kidston	Bentley 4.4	166
3	JD Benjafield/Andre d'Erlanger	Bentley 4.4	158
4	Frank Clement/Jean Chassagne	Bentley 4.4	156
5	Guy Bouriat/"Georges Philippe"	Stutz DV sc	152
6	Henri Stoffel/Robert Benoist	Chrysler 75	151

Winner's average speed: 73.186 mph. Class winners: 5001-8000cc:
Barnato/Birkin; 3001-5000cc: Dunfee/Kidston; 1501-2000cc: no finishers;
1101-1500cc: Kenneth Peacock/Sammy Newsome (Lea-Francis "Hyper
Sport"); 751-1100cc: Louis Balart/Louis Debeugny (Tracta). Fastest lap:
Birkin, 7m21

1930

21-22 June 1930. 178 laps of a 10.153 mile-circuit = 1807.234 miles

1	Woolf Barnato/Glen Kidston	Bentley "Speed Six"	178
2	Frank Clement/Richard Watney	Bentley "Speed Six"	172
3	Brian Lewis/Hugh Eaton	Talbot GB-90	161
4	John Hindmarsh/ Tim Rose-Richards	Talbot GB-90	159
5	Earl Howe/Leslie Callingham	Alfa Romeo 6C Sport	158
6	Kenneth Peacock/ Sammy Newsome	Lea-Francis S	139

Winner's average speed: 75.301 mph. Class winners: 5001-8000cc:
Barnato/Kidston; 3001-5000cc: no finishers; 2001-3000cc: Lewis/Eaton;
1501-2000cc: Peacock/Newsome; 751-1100cc: Jean-Albert
Gregoire/Fernand Vallon (Tracta A29). Fastest lap: Tim Birkin (Bentley 4.4),
6m48

1931

13-14 June 1931. 183 laps of a 10.153 mile-circuit = 1857.999 miles

1	Earl Howe/Tim Birkin	Alfa Romeo 8C	183
2	Boris Ivanowski/Henri Stoffel	Mercedes-Benz SSK	176
3	Tim Rose-Richards/ AC Saunders Davies	Talbot T105	172
4	Robert Trebor/Louis Balart	Lorraine-Dietrich B3-6	149
5	Augustus Bertelli/ Maurice Harvey	Aston Martin LM5	139
6	Just-Emile Vernet/ Fernand Vallon	Caban Speciale-Ruby	127

Winner's average speed: 77.417 mph. Class winners: 5001-8000cc:
Ivanowski/Stoffel; 3001-5000cc: Trebor/Balart. 2001-3000cc: Howe/Birkin;
1101-1500cc: Bertelli/Harvey; 751-1100cc: Vernet/Vallon. Fastest lap:
Ivanowski, 7m02

1932

18-19 June 1932. 218 laps of an 8.378 mile-circuit = 1826.404 miles

1	Raymond Sommer/ Luigi Chinetti	Alfa Romeo 8C	218
2	Franco Cortese/ Giovanni-Battista Guidotti	Alfa Romeo 8C	216
3	Brian Lewis/Tim Rose-Richards	Talbot T105	180
4	Odette Siko/"Sabipa"	Alfa Romeo 6C	179
5	Sammy Newsome/ Henken Widengren	Aston Martin 1.5-litre	174
6	Jean Sebilleau/ Georges Delaroche	Bugatti T40	172

Winner's average speed: 76.100 mph. Class winners: 5001-8000cc and
3001-5000cc: no finishers; 2001-3000cc: Sommer/Chinetti; 1501-2000cc:
Siko/"Sabipa"; 1101-1500cc: Newsome/Widengren; 751-1100cc: Charles
Martin/Auguste Bodoignet (Amilcar CO). Fastest lap: Ferdinando Minoia
(Alfa Romeo 8C), 5m41

1933

17-18 June 1933. 233 laps of an 8.378 mile-circuit = 1952.074 miles

1	Raymond Sommer/ Tazio Nuvolari	Alfa Romeo 8C	233
2	Luigi Chinetti/Philippe Varent	Alfa Romeo 8C	232
3	Brian Lewis/Tim Rose-Richards	Alfa Romeo 8C	225
4	Bill van der Becke/ Kenneth Peacock	Riley 9 "Brooklands"	191

5	Pat Driscoll/ Clifton Penn-Hughes	Aston Martin Ulster	188
6	Ludovic Ford/Maurice Baumer	MG Midget C	176

Winner's average speed: 81.336 mph. Class winners: 5001-8000cc and
3001-5000cc: no finishers; 2001-3000cc: Sommer/Nuvolari; 1501-2000cc:
Andre Rousseau/Francois Paco (Alfa Romeo 6C); 1101-1500cc:
Driscoll/Penn-Hughes; 751-1100cc: van der Becke/Peacock; up to 750cc:
Ford/Baumer. Fastest lap: Sommer, 5m31.4

1934

16-17 June 1934. 213 laps of an 8.378 mile-circuit = 1784.514 miles

1	Philippe Etancelin/ Luigi Chinetti	Alfa Romeo 8C	213
2	Jean Sebilleau/ Georges Delaroche	Riley 9 MPH Racing	200
3	Fred Dixon/Cyril Paul	Riley 9 MPH Racing	199
4	Roy Eccles/Charlie Martin	MG Magnette K3	197
5	Bill van der Becke/ Kenneth Peacock	Riley 9 "Brooklands"	195
6	Sammy Newsome/ Percy Maclure	Riley Ulster Imp	195

Winner's average speed: 74.355 mph. Class winners: 3001-5000cc: no finishers; 2001-3000cc: Etancelin/Chinetti; 1501-2000cc: no finishers; 1101-
1500cc: Sebilleau/Delaroche; 751-1100cc: Eccles/Martin; up to 750cc: no
finishers. Fastest lap: Etancelin, 5m41.0

1935

15-16 June 1935. 222 laps of an 8.378 mile-circuit = 1859.916 miles

1	John Hindmarsh/Luis Fontes	Lagonda Rapide	222
2	"Helde"/Henri Stoffel	Alfa Romeo 8C	222
3	Charlie Martin/ Charles Brackenbury	Aston Martin Ulster	215
4	Bill van der Becke/ Cliff Richardson	Riley 9 MPH	208
5	"Michel Paris"/Marcel Mongin	Delahaye 135	207
6	Guy Don/Jean Desvignes	Alfa Romeo 6C	204

Winner's average speed: 77.497 mph. Class winners: over 4000cc:
Hindmarsh/Fontes; 3001-4000cc: 1501-2000cc: Philippe Maillard-
Brune/Charles Druck (MG Magnette K3); "Helde"/Stoffel; 1001-1500cc:
Martin/Brackenbury; up to 1000cc: Stanley Barnes/Archie Langley (Singer
LM Replica). Fastest lap: Earl Howe (Alfa Romeo 8C), 5m47.9

1937 The Bugattis lead in the rain.

1937

19-20 June 1937. 244 laps of an 8.378 mile-circuit = 2044.232 miles

1	Jean-Pierre Wimille/ Robert Benoist	Bugatti T57G	244
2	Joseph Paul/Marcel Mongin	Delahaye 135S	236
3	Rene Dreyfus/Henri Stoffel	Delahaye 135S	232

4 Louis Gerard/
   Jacques de Valence   Delage D6   215
5 JM Skeffington/
   RC Murton-Neale   Aston Martin Ulster   205
6 Peter Orsich/Rudolf Sauerwein Adler Trumpf   205

Winner's average speed: 85.176 mph. Class winners: 3001-5000cc: Wimille/Benoist; 2001-3000cc: Gerard/de Valence; 1501-2000cc: no finishers; 1101-1500cc: Skeffington/Murton-Neale; 751-1100cc: Just-Emile Vernet/Suzanne Largeot (Simca); up to 750cc: Jean Viale/Albert Alin (Simca 5). Fastest lap: Wimille, 5m13.0

1938

18-19 June 1938. 235 laps of an 8.378 mile-circuit = 1968.830 miles

1 Eugene Chaboud/
   Jean Tremoulet   Delahaye 135S   235
2 Gaston Serraud/
   Yves Giraud-Cabantous   Delahaye 135S   233
3 Jean Prenant/Andre Morel   Lago-Talbot SS   219
4 Louis Villeneuve/Rene Biolay Delahaye 135S   218
5 Charles de Cortanze/
   Marcel Contet   Peugeot 402DS   214
6 Peter Orsich/Rudolf Sauerwein Adler Super Trumpf 211

Winner's average speed: 82.035 mph. Class winners: 3001-5000cc: Chaboud/Tremoulet; 2001-3000cc: no finishers; 1501-2000cc: de Cortanze/Contet; 1101-1500cc: Hans-Otto Lhoer/Paul von Guillaume (Adler Trumpf); 751-1101cc: Jacques Savoye/Pierre Savoye (Singer Speciale); up to 750cc: Maurice Aime/Charles Plantivaux (Simca 5). Fastest lap: Raymond Sommer (Alfa Romeo 8C-2900B), 5m13.8

1939

17-18 June 1939. 248 laps of an 8.378 mile-circuit = 2077.744 miles

1 Jean-Pierre Wimille/Pierre Veyron Bugatti T57C   248
2 Louis Gerard/Georges Monneret Delage 3L   245
3 Arthur Dobson/Charles Brackenbury Lagonda V12   239
4 Lord Selsdon/Lord Waleran Lagonda V12   238
5 Paul von Schaumburg-Lippe/
   Fritz Wencher   BMW 328 "Touring"   236
6 Louis Villeneuve/Rene Biolay Delahaye 135S   235

Winner's average speed: 86.573 mph. Class winners: 3001-5000cc: Wimille/Veyron; 2001-3000cc: Gerard/Monneret; 1501-2000cc: von Schaumburg-Lippe/Wencher; 1101-1500cc: Peter Clark/Marcus Chambers (HRG-Singer); 751-1100cc: Amedee Gordini/Roger Scaron (Simca 8). Fastest lap: Robert Mazaud (Delahaye 135S), 5m12.1

1949

25-26 June 1949. 235 laps of an 8.378 mile-circuit = 1968.830 miles

1 Luigi Chinetti/Lord Selsdon Ferrari 166MM   235
2 Henri Louveau/Juan Jover   Delage D6S   234
3 Norbert Culpan/HJ Aldington Frazer-Nash RLM-Bristol 224
4 Louis Gerard/Chico Godia-Sales Delage D6S   212
5 Georges Grignard/Robert Brunet Delahaye 135S   210
6 "Soltan" Hay/Tommy Wisdom   Bentley Corniche   210

Winner's average speed: 82.035 mph. Class winners: 3001-5000cc: Grignard/Brunet; 2001-3000cc: Louveau/Jover; 1501-2000cc: Chinetti/Selsdon; 1101-1500cc: Erik Thompson/Jack Fairman (HRG Lightweight LM); 751-1100cc: Jean de Montremy/Eugene Dussous (Monopole Sport-Simca); 501-750cc: Otto Krattner/Frank Sutner (Aero Minor). Fastest lap: Andre Simon (Delahaye 175S), 5m12.5

1950

24-25 June 1950. 256 laps of an 8.378 mile-circuit = 2144.768 miles

1 Louis Rosier/Jean-Louis Rosier Lago-Talbot T26C-GS 256
2 Pierre Meyrat/Guy Mairesse Lago-Talbot monoplace 254
3 Sydney Allard/Tom Cole   Allard J2-Cadillac   251

4 Tony Rolt/Duncan Hamilton   Healey-Nash   250
5 George Abecassis/
   Lance Macklin   Aston Martin DB2   249
6 Charles Brackenbury/
   Reg Parnell   Aston Martin DB2   244

Winner's average speed: 89.365 mph. Class winners: 5001-8000cc: Allard/Cole; 3001-5000cc: Rosier/Rosier; 2001-3000cc: Abecassis/Macklin; 1501-2000cc: TASO Mathieson/Dick Stoop (Frazer-Nash MM-Bristol); 1101-1500cc: Tommy Wisdom/Tom Wise (Jowett Jupiter Javelin); 751-1100cc Jean Sandt/Herve Coatalen (Renault 4CV); 501-750cc: Maurice Gastonides/Henk Hoogeven (Aero Minor). Fastest lap: L Rosier, 4m53.5

1951

23-24 June 1951. 267 laps of an 8.378 mile-circuit = 2236.926 miles

1 Peter Walker/Peter Whitehead Jaguar XK120C   267
2 Pierre Meyrat/Guy Mairesse Lago-Talbot T26C-GS   258
3 Lance Macklin/Eric Thompson Aston Martin DB2   257
4 "Pierre Levegh"/Rene Marchand Lago-Talbot monoplace 256
5 George Abecassis/
   Brian Shawe-Taylor   Aston Martin DB2   255
6 Tony Rolt/Duncan Hamilton   Healey Sport Coupe-Nash 255

Winner's average speed: 93.205 mph. Class winners: 5001-8000cc: John Fitch/Phil Walters (Cunningham C2R-Chrysler); 3001-5000cc: Walker/Whitehead; 2001-3000cc: Macklin/Thompson; 1501-2000cc: Johnny Lurani/Giovanni Bracco (Lancia Aurelia B20); 1101-1500cc: Marcel Becquart/Gordon Wilkins (Jowett Jupiter); 751-1100cc: Auguste Veuillet/Edmond Mouche (Porsche 356); 501-750cc: Francois Landon/Andre Briat (Renault 4CV). Fastest lap: Stirling Moss (Jaguar XK120C), 4m46.8

1952

14-15 June 1952. 276 laps of an 8.378 mile-circuit = 2312.328 miles

1 Hermann Lang/Fritz Riess   Mercedes-Benz 300SL   276
2 Theo Helfrich/
   Helmut Niedermayr   Mercedes-Benz 300SL   275
3 Leslie Johnson/Tommy Wisdom Healey-Nash 4-litre   261
4 Briggs Cunningham/Bill Spear Cunningham C4R-Chrysler 251
5 Andre Simon/Lucien Vincent Ferrari 340 America   249
6 Luigi Valenzano/"Ippocampo" Lancia Aurelia B20   247

Winner's average speed: 96.347 mph. Class winners: 5001-8000cc: Cunningham/Spear; 3001-5000cc: Johnson/Wisdom; 2001-3000cc: Lang/Riess; 1501-2000cc: no finishers; 1101-1500cc: Marcel Becquart/Gordon Wilkins (Jowett R1 Jupiter); 751-1100cc: Auguste Veuillet/Edmond Mouche (Porsche 356); 501-750cc: Jean Hemard/Eugene Dussous (Monopole X84). Fastest lap: Alberto Ascari (Ferrari 250S), 4m40.5

1953

13-14 June 1953. 302 laps of an 8.378 mile-circuit = 2530.156 miles

1 Tony Rolt/Duncan Hamilton   Jaguar XK120C   302
2 Peter Walker/Stirling Moss Jaguar XK120C   299
3 Phil Walters/John Fitch   Cunningham C5R-Chrysler 297
4 Peter Whitehead/Ian Stewart Jaguar XK120C   296
5 Paolo Marzotto/Giannino Marzotto Ferrari 340MM   293
6 Maurice Trintignant/Harry Schell Gordini T24S   292

Winner's average speed: 105.423 mph. Class winners: 5001-8000cc: Walters/Fitch; 3001-5000cc: Rolt/Hamilton; 2001-3000cc: Trintignant/Schell; 1501-2000cc: Ken Wharton/Laurence Mitchell (Frazer-Nash LMR); 1101-1500cc: Richard von Frankenburg/Paul Frere (Porsche 550); 751-1100cc: Mario Damonte/"Helde" (OSCA MT4); 501-750cc: Rene Bonnet/Andre Moynet (DB HBR-Panhard). Fastest lap: Alberto Ascari (Ferrari 375MM), 4m27.4

1954

12-13 June 1954. 300 laps of an 8.378 mile-circuit = 2513.400 miles

1	Maurice Trintignant/		
	Jose Froilan Gonzalez	Ferrari 375 Plus	300
2	Tony Rolt/Duncan Hamilton	Jaguar D-type	300
3	Bill Spear/Sherwood Johnston	Cunningham C4R-Chrysler	282
4	Roger Laurent/Jacques Swaters	Jaguar XK120C	276
5	Briggs Cunningham/		
	John Benett	Cunningham C4R-Chrysler	272
6	Andre Guelfi/Jacques Pollet	Gordini T30S	262

Winner's average speed: 104.725 mph. Class winners: 5001-8000cc: Spear/Johnston; 3001-5000cc: Trintignant/Gonzalez; 2001-3000cc: Guelfi/Pollet; 1501-2000cc: Peter Wilson/Jim Mayers (Bristol 450); 1101-1500cc: Johnny Claes/Pierre Stasse (Porsche 550 Spyder); 751-1100cc: Zora Arkus Duntov/Gustave Olivier (Porsche 550 Spyder); 501-750cc: Rene Bonnet/Elie Bayol (DB HBR-Panhard). Fastest lap: Gonzalez, 4m16.8

1955

11-12 June 1955. 306 laps of an 8.378 mile-circuit = 2563.668 miles

1	Mike Hawthorn/Ivor Bueb	Jaguar D-type	306
2	Peter Collins/Paul Frere	Aston Martin DB3S	301
3	Johnny Claes/Jacques Swaters	Jaguar D-type	295
4	Helmuth Polensky/		
	Richard von Frankenberg	Porsche 550	283
5	Wolfgang Seidel/		
	Olivier Gendebien	Porsche 550	275
6	Helmut Glockler/Jaroslav Juhan	Porsche 550	272

Winner's average speed: 106.820 mph. Class winners: 3001-5000cc: Hawthorn/Bueb; 2001-3000cc: Collins/Frere; 1501-2000cc: Peter Wilson/Jim Mayers (Bristol 450C); 1101-1500cc: Polensky/von Frankenberg; 751-1100cc: Zora Arkus Duntov/Auguste Veuillet (Porsche 550 Spyder); 501-750cc: Louis Cornet/Robert Mougin (DB HBR-Panhard). Pole position: Eugenio Castellotti (Ferrari 121LM), 4m41.1. Fastest lap: Hawthorn, 4m06.6

1956

28-29 July 1956. 299 laps of an 8.365 mile-circuit = 2501.135 miles

1	Ninian Sanderson/		
	Ron Flockhart	Jaguar D-type	299
2	Stirling Moss/Peter Collins	Aston Martin DB3S	298
3	Maurice Trintignant/		
	Olivier Gendebien	Ferrari 625LM	292
4	Jacques Swaters/		
	Freddy Rousselle	Jaguar D-type	283
5	Wolfgang von Trips/		
	Richard von Frankenberg	Porsche RS550A	281
6	Mike Hawthorn/Ivor Bueb	Jaguar D-type	279

Winner's average speed: 104.214 mph. Class winners: 3001-5000cc: Sanderson/Flockhart; 2001-3000cc: Moss/Collins; 1501-2000cc: no finishers; 1101-1500cc: von Trips/von Frankenberg; 751-1100cc: Reg Bicknell/Peter Jopp (Lotus XI); 501-750cc: Gerard Laureau/Paul Armagnac (DB HBR5-Panhard). Fastest lap: Hawthorn, 4m20.0

1957

22-23 June 1957. 326 laps of an 8.365 mile-circuit = 2726.990 miles

1	Ivor Bueb/Ron Flockhart	Jaguar D-type	326
2	Ninian Sanderson/		
	John Lawrence	Jaguar D-type	318
3	Jean Lucas/"Mary"	Jaguar D-type	316
4	Paul Frere/Freddy Rousselle	Jaguar D-type	309
5	Stuart Lewis-Evans/		
	Martino Severi	Ferrari 315S	299
6	Duncan Hamilton/		
	Masten Gregory	Jaguar D-type	298

Winner's average speed: 113.625 mph. Class winners: 3001-5000cc: Bueb/Flockhart; 2001-3000cc: Jean-Paul Colas/Jean Kerguen (Aston Martin DB3S); 1501-2000cc: Lucien Bianchi/Georges Harris (Ferrari 550TR); 1101-1500cc: Ed Hugus/Carel Godin de Beaufort (Porsche 550RS); 751-1100cc: Herbert MacKay-Fraser/Jay Chamberlain (Lotus XI); 501-750cc: Cliff Allison/Keith Hall (Lotus XI). Fastest lap: Mike Hawthorn (Ferrari 335MM), 3m58.7

1958

21-22 June 1958. 304 laps of an 8.365 mile-circuit = 2542.960 miles

1	Olivier Gendebien/Phil Hill	Ferrari 250TR	304
2	Peter Whitehead/		
	Graham Whitehead	Aston Martin DB3S	292
3	Jean Behra/Hans Herrmann	Porsche 718 RSK	290
4	Edgar Barth/Paul Frere	Porsche 718 RSK	289
5	Carel Godin de Beaufort/		
	Herbert Linge	Porsche 550 RS	287
6	"Beurlys"/Alain de Chagny	Ferrari 250TR	278

Winner's average speed: 105.957 mph. Class winners: 2001-3000cc: Gendebien/Hill; 1501-2000cc: Behra/Herrmann; 1101-1500cc: Barth/Frere; 751-1100cc: no finishers; 501-750cc: Alejandro de Tomaso/Colin Davis (OSCA S750TN). Fastest lap: Mike Hawthorn (Ferrari 250TR), 4m08.0

1959

20-21 June 1959. 322 laps of an 8.365 mile-circuit = 2693.530 miles

1	Roy Salvadori/Carroll Shelby	Aston Martin DBR1	322
2	Maurice Trintignant/Paul Frere	Aston Martin DBR1	322
3	"Beurlys"/"Elde"	Ferrari 250GT	297
4	Andre Pilette/Georges Arents	Ferrari 250GT	296
5	Bob Grossman/Fernand Tavano	Ferrari 250GT California	294
6	Lino Fayen/Gino Munaron	Ferrari 250GT	293

Winner's average speed: 112.230 mph. Class winners: 2001-3000cc: Salvadori/Shelby; 1501-2000cc: Ted Whiteaway/John Turner (AC Ace-Bristol); 1101-1500cc: Peter Lumsden/Peter Riley (Lotus Elite); 751-1100cc: no finishers; 501-750cc: Louis Cornet/Rene Cotton (DB HBR4-Panhard); GT: "Beurlys"/"Elde". Fastest lap: Jean Behra (Ferrari 250GT), 4m00.9

1960

25-26 June 1960. 313 laps of an 8.365 mile-circuit = 2618.245 miles

1	Olivier Gendebien/Paul Frere	Ferrari 250TR	313
2	Ricardo Rodriguez/Andre Pilette	Ferrari 250TR	309
3	Roy Salvadori/Jim Clark	Aston Martin DBR1	305
4	Fernand Tavano/"Loustel"	Ferrari 250GT	301
5	Georges Arents/Alan Connell	Ferrari 250GT	299
6	"Elde"/Pierre Noblet	Ferrari 250GT	299

Winner's average speed: 109.094 mph. Class winners: 4001-5000cc: John Fitch/Bob Grossman (Chevrolet Corvette); 2001-3000cc: Gendebien/Frere; 1601-2000cc: Ted Lund/Colin Escott (MGA); 1301-1600cc: Herbert Linge/Heini Walter (Porsche 356B Carrera GTL); 1001-1300cc: Roger Masson/Claude Laurent (Lotus Elite); 851-1000cc: Jack Dalton/John Colgate (Austin Healey Sprite); 701-850cc: Gerard Laureau/Paul Armagnac (DB HBR4-Panhard); GT: Tavano/"Loustel". Fastest lap: Masten Gregory (Maserati T61), 4m04.0

1961

10-11 June 1961. 332 laps of an 8.365 mile-circuit = 2777.180 miles

1	Olivier Gendebien/Phil Hill	Ferrari 250TR	332
2	Willy Mairesse/Michael Parkes	Ferrari 250TR	329
3	Pierre Noblet/Jean Guichet	Ferrari 250GT	316
4	Augie Pabst/Richard Thompson	Maserati T63	310
5	Masten Gregory/Bob Holbert	Porsche RS61	308
6	Bob Grossman/Andre Pilette	Ferrari 250GT	308

Winner's average speed: 115.716 mph. Class winners: 2001-3000cc: Gendebien/Hill; 1601-2000cc: Gregory/Holbert; 1301-1600cc: Herbert Linge/Ben Pon (Porsche 356B Carrera GTL); 851-1300cc: Bill Allen/Trevor Taylor (Lotus Elite); 701-850cc: Denny Hulme/Angus Hyslop (Fiat-Abarth 850S); GT: Noblet/Guichet. Fastest lap: Ricardo Rodriguez (Ferrari 250TR), 3m59.09

1962

23-24 June 1962. 330 laps of an 8.365 mile-circuit = 2760.450 miles

1	Olivier Gendebien/Phil Hill	Ferrari 330LM	330
2	Jean Guichet/Pierre Noblet	Ferrari 250GTO	325
3	"Elde"/"Beurlys"	Ferrari 250GTO	312
4	Briggs Cunningham/ Roy Salvadori	Jaguar E-type	309
5	Peter Lumsden/Peter Sargent	Jaguar E-type	309
6	Bob Grossman/ "Fireball" Roberts	Ferrari 250TR "Experimantal"	296

Winner's average speed: 115.019 mph. Class winners: 3001-4000cc: Gendebien/Hill; 2001-3000cc: Guichet/Noblet; 1601-2000cc: Chris Lawrence/Richard Shepherd-Barron (Morgan Plus 4); 1301-1600cc: Edgar Barth/Hans Herrmann (Porsche 356B Carrera GTL); 1001-1300cc: David Hobbs/Frank Gardner (Lotus Elite); 851-1000cc: Bernard Consten/Jose Rosinski (Rene Bonnet Djet); 701-850cc: Andre Guillaudin/Alain Bertaut (CD Dyna-Panhard); GT: Guichet/Noblet. Pole position: P Hill, 3m55.1. Fastest lap: P Hill, 3m57.3

1963

15-16 June 1963. 338 laps of an 8.365 mile-circuit = 2827.370 miles

1	Ludovico Scarfiotti/ Lorenzo Bandini	Ferrari 250P	338
2	"Beurlys"/ Gerald Langlois van Ophem	Ferrari 250GTO	322
3	Michael Parkes/ Umberto Maglioli	Ferrari 250P	322
4	"Elde"/Pierre Dumay	Ferrari 250GTO	321
5	Jack Sears/Mike Salmon	Ferrari 330LMB	313

6	Masten Gregory/David Piper	Ferrari 250GTO	311

Winner's average speed: 117.807 mph. Class winners: 4001-5000cc: Peter Bolton/Ninian Sanderson (AC Cobra); 3001-4000cc: Sears/Salmon; 2001-3000cc: Scarfiotti/Bandini; 1601-2000cc: Edgar Barth/Herbert Linge (Porsche 718); 1301-1600cc: no finishers; 1001-1300cc: John Wagstaff/Patrick Ferguson (Lotus Elite); GT: "Beurlys"/van Ophem. Pole position: Pedro Rodriguez (Ferrari 330TR), 3m50.9. Fastest lap: John Surtees (Ferrari 250P), 3m53.3

1964

20-21 June 1964. 348 laps of an 8.365 mile-circuit = 2911.020 miles

1	Jean Guichet/Nino Vaccarella	Ferrari 275P	348
2	Jo Bonnier/Graham Hill	Ferrari 330P	343
3	John Surtees/Lorenzo Bandini	Ferrari 330P	323
4	Dan Gurney/Bob Bondurant	AC Cobra Daytona-Ford	333
5	Lucien Bianchi/"Beurlys"	Ferrari 250GTO	332
6	Innes Ireland/Tony Maggs	Ferrari 250GTO	327

Winner's average speed: 121.293 mph. Class winners: over 5000cc: Edgar Berney/Pierre Noblet (Iso Rivolta); 4001-5000cc: Gurney/Bondurant; 3001-4000cc: Guichet/Vaccarella; 2001-3000cc: Bianchi/"Beurlys"; 1601-2000cc: Robert Buchet/Guy Ligier (Porsche 904GTS); 1301-1600cc: Roberto Bussinello/Bruno Deserti (Alfa Romeo Giulia TZ); 1151-1300cc: Clive Hunt/John Wagstaff (Lotus Elite); 1001-1150cc: Henry Morrogh/Roger de Lageneste (Alpine M64-Renault); GT: Gurney/Bondurant. Pole position: Surtees, 3m42.0. Fastest lap: Phil Hill (Ford GT40), 3m49.2

1965

19-20 June 1965. 347 laps of an 8.365 mile-circuit = 2902.655 miles

1	Masten Gregory/Jochen Rindt	Ferrari 275LM	347
2	Pierre Dumay/Gustave Gosselin	Ferrari 275LM	341
3	Willy Mairesse/"Beurlys"	Ferrari 250GTB	338
4	Herbert Linge/Peter Nocker	Porsche 904/6	334
5	Gerhard Koch/Anton Fischaber	Porsche 904GTS	324
6	Dieter Spoerry/Peter Boller	Ferrari 275LM	323

Winner's average speed: 120.944 mph. Class winners: over 5000cc: Regis Fraissinet/Jean de Mortimart (Iso Grifo A3C); 4001-5000cc: Pedro

1967 Dan Gurney (left) and Jo Siffert spray champagne at the end of the race.

Rodriguez/Nino Vaccarella (Ferrari 365P2); 3001-4000cc: Gregory/Rindt; 1601-2000cc: Linge/Nocker; 1301-1600cc: no finishers; 1151-1300cc: Paul Hawkins/John Rhodes (Austin Healey Sebring Sprite); 1001-1150cc: Jean-Jacques Thuner/Simo Lampinen (Triumph Spitfire); GT: Mairesse/"Beurlys". Pole position: Phil Hill (Ford GT40), 3m33.0. Fastest lap: P Hill, 3m37.5

1966

17-18 June 1966. 359 laps of an 8.365 mile-circuit = 3003.035 miles

1	Bruce McLaren/Chris Amon	Ford GT40 Mk2	359
2	Ken Miles/Denny Hulme	Ford GT40 Mk2	359
3	Ronnie Bucknum/		
	Dick Hutcherson	Ford GT40 Mk2	347
4	Jo Siffert/Colin Davis	Porsche 906 Carrera 6LH	338
5	Hans Herrmann/Herbert Linge	Porsche 906 Carrera 6LH	337
6	Udo Schutz/Piet de Klerk	Porsche 906 Carrera 6LH	336

Winner's average speed. 125.126 mph. Class winners. over 5000cc: McLaren/Amon; 3001-5000cc: Piers Courage/Roy Pike (Ferrari 275GTB/C); 1601-2000cc: Siffert/Davis; 1151-1300cc: Henry Grandsire/Leo Cella (Alpine A210-Renault); 1001-1150cc: no finishers; Sports: Gunther Klass/Rolf Stommelen (Porsche 906/6); GT: Courage/Pike. Pole position: Dan Gurney (Ford GT40 Mk2), 3m30.6. Fastest lap: Gurney, 3m30.6

1967

10-11 June 1967. 388 laps of an 8.365 mile-circuit = 3245.620 miles

1	Dan Gurney/AJ Foyt Jr	Ford GT40 Mk4	388
2	Ludovico Scarfiotti/		
	Michael Parkes	Ferrari 330P4	384
3	Willy Mairesse/"Beurlys"	Ferrari 330P4	377
4	Bruce McLaren/Mark Donohue	Ford GT40 Mk4	359
5	Jo Siffert/Hans Herrmann	Porsche 907/6	358
6	Rolf Stommelen/		
	Jochen Neerpasch	Porsche 910/6	351

Winner's average speed: 135.234 mph. Class winners: over 5000cc: Gurney/Foyt; 3001-5000cc: Scarfiotti/Parkes; 1601-2000cc: Siffert/Herrmann; 1301-1600cc: Jean Vinatier/Mauro Bianchi (Alpine A210-Renault); 1151-1300cc: Henry Grandsire/Jose Rosinski (Alpine A210-Renault); 1001-1150cc: no finishers; Sports: Vic Elford/Ben Pon (Porsche 906/6); GT: Rico Steinemann/Dieter Spoerry (Ferrari 275GTB). Pole position: McLaren, 3m24.4. Fastest lap: Denny Hulme (Ford GT40 Mk4) and Mario Andretti (Ford GT40 Mk4), 3m23.6

1968

28-29 September 1968. 330 laps of an 8.369 mile-circuit = 2761.770 miles

1	Pedro Rodriguez/Lucien Bianchi	Ford GT40	330
2	Dieter Spoerry/		
	Rico Steinemann	Porsche 907/8	325
3	Rolf Stommelen/		
	Jochen Neerpasch	Porsche 908LH	324
4	Ignazio Giunti/Nanni Galli	Alfa Romeo T33/2	321
5	Carlo Facetti/Spartico Dini	Alfa Romeo T33/2	314
6	Mario Casoni/Giampiero Biscaldi	Alfa Romeo T33/2	304

Winner's average speed: 115.074 mph. Class winners: 3001-5000cc: Rodriguez/Bianchi; 2501-3000cc: Stommelen/Neerpasch; 2001-2500cc: Spoerry/Steinemann; 1601-2000cc: Giunti/Galli; 1151-1600cc: Herve le Guellec/Alain Serpaggi (Alpine A210-Renault); 1001-1150cc: Jean-Claude Andruet/Jean-Pierre Nicolas (Alpine A210-Renault); Sports: Rodriguez/Bianchi; Sports-Prototype: Spoerry/Steinemann; GT: Jean-Pierre Gaban/Roger Vanderschrick (Porsche 911T). Pole position: Jo Siffert (Porsche 908LH), 3m35.4. Fastest lap: Stommelen, 3m38.1

1969

14-15 June 1969. 371 laps of an 8.369 mile-circuit = 3104.899 miles

1	Jacky Ickx/Jackie Oliver	Ford GT40	371
2	Hans Herrmann/		
	Gerard Larrousse	Porsche 908LH	371
3	David Hobbs/Mike Hailwood	Ford GT40	367
4	Jean-Pierre Beltoise/		
	Piers Courage	Matra-Simca MS650	367
5	Jean Guichet/Nino Vaccarella	Matra-Simca MS630	358
6	Helmut Kelleners/		
	Reinhold Joest	Ford GT40	340

Winner's average speed: 129.371 mph. Class winners: 3001-5000cc: Ickx/Oliver; 2501-3000cc: Herrmann/Larrousse; 1601-2000cc: Christian Poirot/Pierre Maublanc (Porsche 910); 1151-1600cc: no finishers; 1001-1150cc: Alain Serpaggi/Christian Ethuin (Alpine A210-Renault); Sports: Ickx/Oliver; Sports-Prototype: Herrmann/Larrousse; GT: Jean-Pierre Gaban/Yves Deprez (Porsche 911S). Pole position: Rolf Stommelen (Porsche 917LH), 3m22.9. Fastest lap: Vic Elford (Porsche 917LH), 3m27.2

1970

13-14 June 1970. 342 laps of an 8.369 mile-circuit = 2862.198 miles

1	Hans Herrmann/		
	Richard Attwood	Porsche 917K	342
2	Gerard Larrousse/Willi Kauhsen	Porsche 917LH	337
3	Rudi Lins/Helmut Marko	Porsche 908/2LH	334
4	Sam Posey/Ronnie Bucknum	Ferrari 512S	312
5	Hughes de Fierlandt/		
	Alistair Walker	Ferrari 512S	304
6	Guy Chasseuil/		
	Claude Ballot-Lena	Porsche 914/6	284

Winner's average speed: 119.258 mph. Class winners: over 5000cc: Henri Greder/Jean-Paul Rouget (Chevrolet Corvette); 3001-5000cc: Herrmann/Attwood; 2501-3000cc: Lins/Marko; 2001-2500cc: Nicolas Koob/Erwin Kremer (Porsche 911S); 1601-2000cc: Chasseuil/Ballot-Lena; Sports: Herrmann/Attwood; Sports-Prototype: Lins/Marko; GT: Greder/Rouget. Pole position: Vic Elford (Porsche 917LH), 3m19.8. Fastest lap: Elford, 3m21.0

1971

12-13 June 1971. 396 laps of an 8.369 mile-circuit = 3314.124 miles

1	Helmut Marko/Gijs van Lennep	Porsche 917K	396
2	Herbert Muller/Richard Attwood	Porsche 917K	394
3	Sam Posey/Tony Adamowicz	Ferrari 512M	365
4	Chris Craft/David Weir	Ferrari 512M	354
5	Bob Grossman/Luigi Chinetti Jr	Ferrari 365 GTB4	313
6	Raymond Touroul/		
	"Andre Anselme"	Porsche 911S	305

Note: first rolling start. Winner's average speed: 138.089 mph. Class winners: 3001-5000cc: Marko/van Lennep; 2501-3000cc: no finishers; 2001-2500cc: Touroul/"Anselme"; 1601-2000cc: Walter Brun/Peter Mattli (Porsche 907); Sports: Marko/van Lennep; Prototype: Brun/Mattli; GT: Touroul/"Anselme". Pole position: Pedro Rodriguez (Porsche 917LH), 3m13.9. Fastest lap: Jackie Oliver (Porsche 917LH), 3m18.4

1972

10-11 June 1972. 343 laps of an 8.476 mile-circuit = 2907.268 miles

1	Henri Pescarolo/Graham Hill	Matra-Simca MS670	343
2	Francois Cevert/Howden Ganley	Matra-Simca MS670	333
3	Reinhold Joest/		
	Michel Weber/Mario Casoni	Porsche 908LH	324
4	Andrea de Adamich/		
	Nino Vaccarella	Alfa Romeo T33TT/3	306
5	Jean-Claude Andruet/		
	Claude Ballot-Lena	Ferrari 365 GTB4 Daytona	305
6	Sam Posey/Tony Adamowicz	Ferrari 365 GTB4 Daytona	303

Winner's average speed: 121.136 mph. Class winners: Sports 2001-3000cc: Pescarolo/Hill; Sports up to 2000cc: Rene Lignonet/Barrie Smith (Lola T290-Ford); GT: Andruet/Ballot-Lena; Special Touring: Gerry

Birrell/Claude Bourgoignie (Ford Capri RS2600). Pole position: Cevert, 3m42.2. Fastest lap: Gijs van Lennep (Lola T280-Ford), 3m46.9

1973

9-10 June 1973. 355 laps of an 8.476 mile-circuit = 3008.980 miles

1	Henri Pescarolo/		
	Gerard Larrousse	Matra-Simca MS670B	355
2	Arturo Merzario/Carlos Pace	Ferrari 312P	349
3	Jean-Pierre Jabouille/		
	Jean-Pierre Jaussaud	Matra-Simca MS670B	331
4	Gijs van Lennep/Herbert Muller	Porsche Carrera RSR	328
5	Juan Fernandez/Bernard Cheneviere/		
	Paco Torredemer	Porsche 908/3	319
6	Vic Elford/Claude Ballot-Lena	Ferrari 365 GTB4 Daytona	316

Winner's average speed: 125.374 mph. Class winners: Sports 2501-3000cc: Pescarolo/Larrousse; Sports 2001-2500cc: no finishers; Sports up to 2000cc: no finishers; GT over 5000cc: Henri Greder/"Marie-Claude Beaumont" (Chevrolet Corvette); GT 3001-5000cc: Elford/Ballot-Lena; GT up to 3000cc: Erwin Kremer/Clemens Schickentanz/Paul Keller (Porsche 911 Carrera RSR); Special Touring: Dieter Quester/Toine Hezemans (BMW 3.0 CSL). Pole position: Merzario, 3m37.5. Fastest lap: Francois Cevert (Matra-Simca MS670B), 3m39.6

1974

15-16 June 1974. 337 laps of an 8.476 mile-circuit = 2856.412 miles

1	Henri Pescarolo/		
	Gerard Larrousse	Matra-Simca MS670B	337
2	Gijs van Lennep/Herbert Muller	Porsche Carrera RSR turbo	331
3	Jean-Pierre Jabouille/		
	Francois Migault	Matra-Simca MS670B	324
4	Mike Hailwood/Derek Bell	Mirage GR7-Ford	317
5	Cyrille Grandet/		
	Dominique Bardini	Ferrari 365 GTB4 Daytona	313
6	David Heinz/Alain Cudini	Ferrari 365 GTB4 Daytona	312

Winner's average speed: 119.017 mph. Class winners: Sports 2001-3000cc: Pescarolo/Larrousse; Sports up to 2000cc: "Christine"/Marie Laurent/Yvette Fontaine (Chevron B23-Ford); GT over 5000cc: Henri Greder/"Marie-Claude Beaumont" (Chevrolet Corvette); GT up to 5000cc: Grandet/Bardini; Special Touring: Jean-Claude Aubriet/"Depnic" (BMW 3.0 CSL). Pole position: Pescarolo, 3m35.8. Fastest lap: Jean-Pierre Jarier (Matra-Simca MS680), 3m42.7

1975

14-15 June 1975. 336 laps of an 8.476 mile-circuit = 2847.936 miles

1	Jacky Ickx/Derek Bell	Mirage GR8-Ford	336
2	Guy Chasseuil/		
	Jean-Louis Lafosse	Ligier JS2-Ford	335
3	Vern Schuppan/		
	Jean-Pierre Jaussaud	Mirage GR8-Ford	330
4	Reinhold Joest/		
	Mario Casoni/Jurgen Barth	Porsche 908/3LH	325
5	John Fitzpatrick/Gijs van Lennep/Manfred Schurti/		
	Toine Hezemans	Porsche Carrera RSR	315
6	Nick Faure/		
	John Cooper/"Beurlys"	Porsche Carrera RSR	311

Winner's average speed: 118.664 mph. Class winners: Sports 2001-3000cc: Ickx/Bell; Sports up to 2000cc: Michele Mouton/Marianne Hopfner/Christine Dacremont (Moynet LM75-Chrysler/Simca); GT: Fitzpatrick/van Lennep/Schurti/Hezemans; GTS: Gerhard Maurer/Christian Beez/Eugen Stahl (Porsche 911 Carrera RS); GTX: Bernard Beguin/Peter Zbinden/Claude Haldi (Porsche 911 turbo); Special Touring: Daniel Brillat/Giancarlo Gagliardi/Michel Degoumois (BMW 2002). Pole position: Ickx, 3m49.4. Fastest lap: Chris Craft (Lola T380-Ford), 3m53.8

1976

12-13 June 1976. 349 laps of an 8.476 mile-circuit = 2958.124 miles

1	Jacky Ickx/Gijs van Lennep	Porsche 936	349
2	Jean-Louis Lafosse/		
	Francois Migault	Mirage GR8-Ford	338
3	Chris Craft/Alain de Cadenet	Lola T380LM-Ford	337
4	Rolf Stommelen/		
	Manfred Schurti	Porsche 935	331
5	Derek Bell/Vern Schuppan	Mirage GR8-Ford	326
6	Alain Cudini/		
	Raymond Touroul/Rene Boubet	Porsche Carrera RSR	314

Winner's average speed: 123.255 mph. Class winners: Group 6/Sports 2001-3000cc: Ickx/van Lennep; Group 6/Sports up to 2000cc: Francois Trisconi/Georges Morand/Andre Chevalley (Lola T292-Ford); Group 5: Stommelen/Schurti; Group 4/GT: "Segolen"/Marcel Ouviere/"Ladagi" (Porsche 911 Carrera RS); Group 2/Special Touring: no finishers; GTP: Henri Pescarolo/Jean-Pierre Beltoise (Inaltera GT-Ford); GTX: no finishers; IMSA GT: Jean-Pierre Laffeach/John Rulon-Miller/Tom Waugh (Porsche 911 Carrera RSR); NASCAR: no finishers. Pole position: Jean-Pierre Jabouille (Alpine A442-Renault), 3m33.1. Fastest lap: Jabouille, 3m43.0

1977

11-12 June 1977. 342 laps of an 8.476 mile-circuit = 2898.792 miles

1	Jacky Ickx/Jurgen Barth/		
	Hurley Haywood	Porsche 936	342
2	Vern Schuppan/		
	Jean-Pierre Jarier	Mirage GR8-Renault	331
3	Claude Ballot-Lena/Peter Gregg	Porsche 935	315
4	Jean Ragnotti/Jean Rondeau	Inaltera GTP-Ford	315
5	Alain de Cadenet/Chris Craft	Lola T380LM-Ford	315
6	Michel Pignard/Alfred Dufrenne/		
	Jacques Henry	Chevron B36-Chrysler	303

Winner's average speed: 120.783 mph. Class winners: Group 6/Sports 2001-3000cc: Ickx/Barth/Haywood; Group 6/Sports up to 2000cc: Pignard/Dufrenne/Henry; Group 5: Ballot-Lena/Gregg; Group 4/GT: Bob Wollek/Philippe Gurdjian/JP Wielemans (Porsche 934); GTP: Ragnotti/Rondeau; GTX: no finishers; IMSA GT: Jean Xhenceval/Pierre Dieudonne/Spartaco Dini (BMW 3.0 CSL). Pole position: Jean-Pierre Jabouille (Alpine A442-Renault), 3m31.7. Fastest lap: Ickx, 3m36.5

1978

10-11 June 1978. 369 laps of an 8.476 mile-circuit = 3127.644 miles

1	Didier Pironi/		
	Jean-Pierre Jaussaud	Alpine A442B-Renault	369
2	Bob Wollek/Jurgen Barth/		
	Jacky Ickx	Porsche 936	364
3	Hurley Haywood/		
	Peter Gregg/Reinhold Joest	Porsche 935	362
4	Guy Frequelin/Jean Ragnotti/Jose Dolhem/		
	Jean-Pierre Jabouille	Alpine A442B-Renault	358
5	Brian Redman/		
	Dick Barbour/John Paul	Porsche 935	337
6	Jim Busby/Chris Cord/		
	Rick Knoop	Porsche 935	336

Winner's average speed: 130.319 mph. Class winners: Group 6/Sports 2001-3000cc: Pironi/Jaussaud; Group 6/Sports up to 2000cc: Michel Pignard/Laurent Ferrier/Lucien Rossiaud (Chevron B36-Chrysler); Group 5: Busby/Cord/Knoop; Group 4/GT: Anny-Charlotte Verney/Xavier Lapeyre/Francois Servanin/Hubert Striebig (Porsche 911 Carrera RSR); GTP: Jean Rondeau/Jacky Haran/Bernard Darniche (Rondeau M378-Ford); IMSA GTX: Redman/Barbour/Paul. Pole position: Ickx, 3m27.6. Fastest lap: Jabouille, 3m34.2

1979

9-10 June 1979. 306 laps of an 8.467 mile-circuit = 2590.902 miles

1	Klaus Ludwig/Bill Whittington/		
	Don Whittington	Porsche 935-K3	306
2	Rolf Stommelen/		
	Dick Barbour/Paul Newman	Porsche 935	299
3	Laurent Ferrier/Francois Servanin/		
	Francois Trisconi	Porsche 935	292
4	Angelo Pallavicini/		
	Herbert Muller/Marco Vanoli	Porsche 934	291
5	Bernard Darniche/		
	Jean Ragnotti	Rondeau M379-Ford	287
6	Herve Poulain/Marcel Mignot/		
	Manfred Winkelhock	BMW M1 Coupe	284

Winner's average speed: 107.954 mph. Class winners: Group 6/Sports 2001-3000cc: Darniche/Ragnotti; Group 6/Sports up to 2000cc: Tony Charnell/Richard Jones/Robin Smith (Chevron B36-Ford); Group 5: Ludwig/Whittington/Whittington; Group 4/GT: Pallavicini/Muller/Vanoli; GTP: Max Mamers/Jean-Daniel Raulet (WM P79-Peugeot); IMSA GTX: Stommelen/Barbour/Newman. Pole position: Bob Wollek (Porsche 936), 3m30.07. Fastest lap: Jacky Ickx (Porsche 936), 3m36.01

1980

14-15 June 1980. 338 laps of an 8.467 mile-circuit = 2861.846 miles

1	Jean-Pierre Jaussaud/		
	Jean Rondeau	Rondeau M379B-Ford	338
2	Jacky Ickx/Reinhold Joest	Porsche 936/80	336
3	Jean-Michel Martin/		
	Philippe Martin/Gordon Spice	Rondeau M379B-Ford	329
4	Guy Frequelin/Roger Dorchy	WM P79/80-Peugeot	318
5	John Fitzpatrick/		
	Brian Redman/Dick Barbour	Porsche 935-K3	317
6	Jurgen Barth/Manfred Schurti	Porsche 924 Carrera	316

Winner's average speed: 119.244 mph. Class winners: Group 6/Sports 2001-3000cc: Jaussaud/Rondeau; Group 6/Sports up to 2000cc: Bruno Sotty/Philippe Hesnault/Daniel Laurent (Chevron B36-Chrysler); Group 5: Dieter Schornstein/Harald Grohs/Gotz von Tschirnhaus (Porsche 935); Group 4/GT: Thierry Perrier/Roger Carmillet (Porsche 911SC); GTP over 3000cc: Frequelin/Dorchy; GTP up to 3000cc: Martin/Martin/Spice; IMSA GTX: Fitzpatrick/Redman/Barbour. Pole position: Henri Pescarolo/Jean Ragnotti (Rondeau M379B-Ford), 3m47.9-based on average of both drivers. Fastest lap: Ickx, 3m40.6

1981

13-14 June 1981. 354 laps of an 8.467 mile-circuit = 2997.318 miles

1	Jacky Ickx/Derek Bell	Porsche 936/81	354
2	Jacky Haran/Jean-Louis		
	Schlesser/Philippe Streiff	Rondeau M379C-Ford	340
3	Gordon Spice/Francois Migault	Rondeau M379C-Ford	335
4	John Cooper/Dudley Wood/		
	Claude Bourgoignie	Porsche 935-K3	330
5	Claude Ballot-Lena/		
	Jean-Claude Andruet	Ferrari 512BB	328
6	Anny-Charlotte Verney/Ralph Kent-Cooke/		
	Bob Garretson	Porsche 935-K3	327

Winner's average speed: 124.888 mph. Class winners: Group 6/Sports over 2000cc: Ickx/Bell; Group 6/Sports up to 2000cc: Jean-Philippe Grand/Yves Courage (Lola T298-BMW); Group 5 over 2000cc: Cooper/Wood/Bourgoignie; Group 5 up to 2000cc: Eddie Cheever/Michele Alboreto/Carlo Facetti (Lancia Beta Monte Carlo); Group 4/GT: Thierry Perrier/Valentin Bertapalle/Bernard Salam (Porsche 934); GTP over 3000cc: Jurgen Barth/Walter Rohrl (Porsche 944LM); GTP up to 3000cc: Haran/Schlesser/Streiff; IMSA GTX: Ballot-Lena/Andruet; IMSA GTO: Manfred Schurti/Andy Rouse (Porsche 924 Carrera GTR). Pole position: Ickx, 3m29.44. Fastest lap: Hurley Haywood (Porsche 936/81), 3m34.0

1982

19-20 June 1982. 359 laps of an 8.467 mile-circuit = 3039.653 miles

1	Jacky Ickx/Derek Bell	Porsche 956	359
2	Jochen Mass/Vern Schuppan	Porsche 956	356
3	Hurley Haywood/		
	Al Holbert/Jurgen Barth	Porsche 956	340
4	John Fitzpatrick/David Hobbs	Porsche 935-K4	329
5	Dany Snobeck/		
	Francois Servanin/Rene Metge	Porsche 935-K3	325
6	Pierre Dieudonne/Carson Baird/		
	Jean-Paul Libert	Ferrari 512BB	322

Winner's average speed: 126.652 mph. Class winners: Group C: Ickx/Bell; Group 5: John Cooper/Paul Smith/Claude Bourgoignie (Porsche 935-K3); Group 4/GT: Richard Cleare/Tony Dron/Richard Jones (Porsche 934); IMSA GTX: Fitzpatrick/Hobbs; IMSA GT: Jim Busby/Doc Bundy (Porsche 924 Carrera GTR). Pole position: Ickx, 3m28.40. Fastest lap: Jean Ragnotti (Rondeau M382C-Ford), 3m36.9

1983

18-19 June 1983. 370 laps of an 8.467 mile-circuit = 3132.790 miles

1	Vern Schuppan/Hurley Haywood/		
	Al Holbert	Porsche 956	370
2	Jacky Ickx/Derek Bell	Porsche 956	370
3	Mario Andretti/Michael Andretti/		
	Philippe Alliot	Porsche 956	364
4	Volkert Merl/Clemens Schickentanz/		
	Maurizio de Narvaez	Porsche 956	361
5	John Fitzpatrick/Guy Edwards/		
	Rupert Keegan	Porsche 956	358
6	Klaus Ludwig/		
	Stefan Johansson/Bob Wollek	Porsche 956	354

Winner's average speed: 130.533 mph. Class winners: Group C: Schuppan/Haywood/Holbert; Group C Junior: Yoshimi Katayama/Yojiro Terada/Takashi Yorino (Mazda 717C); Group B: John Cooper/Paul Smith/David Ovey (Porsche 930). Pole position: Ickx, 3m16.36. Fastest lap: Ickx, 3m29.7

1984

16-17 June 1984. 359 laps of an 8.467 mile-circuit = 3039.653 miles

1	Klaus Ludwig/Henri Pescarolo	Porsche 956	359
2	Jean Rondeau/John Paul Jr/		
	Preston Henn	Porsche 956	357
3	David Hobbs/Philippe Streiff/		
	Sarel van der Merwe	Porsche 956	350
4	Walter Brun/Bob Akin/		
	Leopold von Bayern	Porsche 956	339
5	Volkert Merl/Dieter Schornstein/		
	"John Winter"	Porsche 956	339
6	Vern Schuppan/Alan Jones/		
	Jean-Pierre Jarier	Porsche 956	336

Winner's average speed: 126.652 mph. Class winners: Group C: Ludwig/Pescarolo; Group C Junior: Yoshimi Katayama/John Morton/John O'Steen (Lola T616-Mazda); Group B: Pierre de Thoisy/Jean-Francois Yvon/Philippe Dagoreau (BMW M1); IMSA GTP: no finishers; IMSA GTX: no finishers; IMSA GTO: Thierry Perrier/Valentin Bertapelle/Raymond Touroul (Porsche 911SC). Pole position: Bob Wollek (Lancia LC2), 3m17.11. Fastest lap: Alessandro Nannini (Lancia LC2), 3m28.9

1985

15-16 June 1985. 373 laps of an 8.467 mile-circuit = 3158.191 miles

1	Klaus Ludwig/Paolo Barilla/		
	"John Winter"	Porsche 956	373
2	Jonathan Palmer/		
	James Weaver/Richard Lloyd	Porsche 956GTI	370

3 Derek Bell/Hans-Joachim Stuck   Porsche 962C   366
4 David Hobbs/Jo Gartner/
   Guy Edwards   Porsche 956   365
5 Sarel van der Merwe/
   George Fouche/Mario Hytten   Porsche 956   360
6 Bob Wollek/Alessandro Nannini/
   Lucio Cesario   Lancia LC2   359

Winner's average speed: 131.591 mph. Class winners: Group C1: Ludwig/Barilla/"Winter"; Group C2: Gordon Spice/Ray Bellm/Mark Galvin (Tiga GC85-Ford); Group B: Edgar Doren/Martin Birrane/Jean-Paul Libert (BMW M1); IMSA GTP: Bob Tullius/Chip Robinson/Claude Ballot-Lena (Jaguar XJR-5). Pole position: Stuck, 3m14.80. Fastest lap: Jochen Mass (Porsche 962C), 3m25.1

1986

31 May-1 June 1986. 367 laps of an 8.406 mile-circuit = 3085.002 miles

1 Hans-Joachim Stuck/
   Derek Bell/Al Holbert   Porsche 962C   367
2 Oscar Larrauri/Joel Gouhier/
   Jesus Pareja   Porsche 962C   359
3 George Follmer/John Morton/
   Kemper Miller   Porsche 956   354
4 Emilio de Villota/George Fouche/
   Fermin Velez   Porsche 956   348
5 Jurgen Laessig/Fulvio Ballabio/
   Dudley Wood   Porsche 956   344
6 Siegfried Brunn/Ernst Schuster/
   Rudi Seher   Porsche 936CJ   343

Winner's average speed: 128.542 mph. Class winners: Group C1: Stuck/Bell/Holbert; Group C2: Ian Harrower/Evan Clements/Tom Dodd-Noble (Gebhardt JC843-Ford); Group B: no finishers; IMSA GTP: Lionel Robert/Jack Newsum/Richard Cleare (March 85G-Nissan); IMSA GTX: Rene Metge/Claude Ballot-Lena (Porsche 961). Pole position: Jochen Mass (Porsche 962C), 3m15.99. Fastest lap: Klaus Ludwig (Porsche 956), 3m23.3

1987

13-14 June 1987. 354 laps of an 8.410 mile-circuit = 2977.140 miles

1 Derek Bell/Hans-Joachim Stuck/
   Al Holbert   Porsche 962C   354
2 Jurgen Laessig/Pierre Yver/
   Bernard de Dryver   Porsche 962C   334
3 Pierre-Henri Raphanel/
   Herve Regout/Yves Courage   Cougar C20-Porsche 331
4 George Fouche/Franz Konrad/
   Wayne Taylor   Porsche 962C   326
5 Eddie Cheever/Raul Boesel/
   Jan Lammers   Jaguar XJR-8LM 324
6 Gordon Spice/Fermin Velez/
   Philippe de Henning   Spice SE87C-Ford 320

Winner's average speed: 124.048 mph. Class winners: Group C1: Bell/Stuck/Holbert; Group C2: Spice/Velez/de Henning; IMSA GTP: David Kennedy/Pierre Dieudonne/Mark Galvin (Mazda 757); IMSA GTX: no finishers. Pole position: Bob Wollek (Porsche 962C), 3m21.09. Fastest lap: Johnny Dumfries (Sauber C9-Mercedes-Benz), 3m25.04

1988

11-12 June 1988. 394 laps of an 8.410 mile-circuit = 3313.540 miles

1 Johnny Dumfries/Andy Wallace/
   Jan Lammers   Jaguar XJR-9LM 394
2 Hans-Joachim Stuck/
   Klaus Ludwig/Derek Bell   Porsche 962C   394
3 Stanley Dickens/Frank Jelinski/
   "John Winter"   Porsche 962C   385
4 Derek Daly/Larry Perkins/
   Kevin Cogan   Jaguar XJR-9LM 383

5 David Hobbs/Didier Theys/
   Franz Konrad   Porsche 962C   380
6 Mario Andretti/Michael Andretti/
   John Andretti   Porsche 962C   375

Winner's average speed: 137.732 mph. Class winners: Group C1: Dumfries/Wallace/Lammers; Group C2: Gordon Spice/Ray Bellm/Pierre de Thoisy (Spice SE88C-Ford); IMSA GTP: Yojiro Terada/David Kennedy/Pierre Dieudonne (Mazda 757). Pole position: Stuck, 3m15.64. Fastest lap: Stuck, 3m22.50

1989

10-11 June 1989. 389 laps of an 8.410 mile-circuit = 3271.490 miles

1 Jochen Mass/Manuel Reuter/
   Stanley Dickens   Sauber C9/88-Mercedes-Benz 389
2 Mauro Baldi/Kenneth Acheson/
   Gianfranco Brancatelli   Sauber C9/88-Mercedes-Benz 384
3 Bob Wollek/
   Hans-Joachim Stuck   Porsche 962C   382
4 Jan Lammers/Patrick Tambay/
   Andrew Gilbert-Scott   Jaguar XJR-9LM   380
5 Jean-Louis Schlesser/Jean-Pierre Jabouille/
   Alain Cudini   Sauber C9/88-Mercedes-Benz 378
6 Henri Pescarolo/Jean-Louis Ricci/
   Claude Ballot-Lena   Porsche 962C   371

Winner's average speed: 136.312 mph. Class winners: Group C1: Mass/Reuter/Dickens; Group C2: Jean-Claude Andruet/Philippe Farjon/Shunji Kasuya (Cougar C20LM-Porsche); IMSA GTP: David Kennedy/Pierre Dieudonne/Chris Hodgetts (Mazda 767B). Pole position: Schlesser, 3m15.04. Fastest lap: Alain Ferte (Jaguar XJR-9LM), 3m21.27

1990

16-17 June 1990. 359 laps of an 8.450 mile-circuit = 3033.550 miles

1 Martin Brundle/John Nielsen/
   Price Cobb   Jaguar XJR-12   359
2 Jan Lammers/Andy Wallace/
   Franz Konrad   Jaguar XJR-12   355
3 Tiff Needell/David Sears/
   Anthony Reid   Porsche 962C   352
4 Frank Jelinski/Derek Bell/
   Hans-Joachim Stuck   Porsche 962C   350
5 Masahiro Hasemi/Kazuyoshi Hoshino/
   Toshio Suzuki   Nissan R89C   348
6 Geoff Lees/Hitoshi Ogawa/
   Masanori Sekiya   Toyota 90CV   347

Winner's average speed: 126.398 mph. Class winners: Group C1: Brundle/Nielsen/Cobb; Group C2: Richard Piper/Olindo Iacobelli/Mike Youles (Spice SE89C-Ford); IMSA GTP: Yoshimi Katayama/Takashi Yorino/Yojiro Terada (Mazda 767B). Pole position: Mark Blundell (Nissan R90CK), 3m27.02. Fastest lap: Steve Millen (Nissan R90CK), 3m40.03

1991 Weidler/Herbert/Gachot's rotary-engine Mazda 787B scores the first Japanese win at Le Mans.

1991

22-23 June 1991. 362 laps of an 8.451 mile-circuit = 3059.262 miles

1	Volker Weidler/Johnny Herbert/		
	Bertrand Gachot	Mazda 787B	362
2	Raul Boesel/Michel Ferte/		
	Davy Jones	Jaguar XJR-12	360
3	Teo Fabi/Bob Wollek/		
	Kenneth Acheson	Jaguar XJR-12	358
4	Derek Warwick/John Nielsen/		
	Andy Wallace	Jaguar XJR-12	356
5	Karl Wendlinger/Michael Schumacher/		
	Fritz Kreutzpointner	Mercedes-Benz C11	355
6	David Kennedy/Stefan Johansson/		
	Maurizio Sandro Sala	Mazda 787B	355

Winner's average speed: 127.593 mph. Class winners: Group C1 category 1: Naoki Nagasaka/Hisashi Yokoshima/Kiyoshi Misaki (Spice SE90C-Ford); Group C1 category 2: Weidler/Herbert/Gachot. Pole position: Jean-Louis Schlesser, 3m31.250 (Mercedes-Benz C11). Fastest lap: Schumacher, 3m35.564

1992

20-21 June 1992. 352 laps of an 8.451 mile-circuit = 2974.752 miles

1	Derek Warwick/		
	Yannick Dalmas/Mark Blundell	Peugeot 905B	352
2	Masanori Sekiya/Pierre-Henri Raphanel/		
	Kenneth Acheson	Toyota TS010	346
3	Mauro Baldi/Philippe Alliot/		
	Jean-Pierre Jabouille	Peugeot 905B	345
4	Johnny Herbert/Volker Weidler/Bertrand Gachot/		
	Maurizio Sandro Sala	Mazda MXR01	336
5	George Fouche/Steven Andskar/		
	Stefan Johansson	Toyota 92CV	336
6	Bob Wollek/Henri Pescarolo/		
	Jean-Louis Ricci	Cougar C28S-Porsche	335

Winner's average speed: 123.869 mph. Class winners: Group C1 category 1: Warwick/Dalmas/Blundell; Group C1 category 2: Fouche/Andskar/Johansson; Group C1 category 3: Wollek/Pescarolo/Ricci; National sports-prototype: no finishers. Pole position: Alliot, 3m21.209. Fastest lap: Jan Lammers (Toyota TS010), 3m32.295

1993

19-20 June 1993. 375 laps of an 8.451 mile-circuit = 3169.125 miles

1	Eric Helary/Christophe Bouchut/		
	Geoff Brabham	Peugeot 905B	375
2	Thierry Boutsen/		
	Yannick Dalmas/Teo Fabi	Peugeot 905B	374
3	Philippe Alliot/Mauro Baldi/		
	Jean-Pierre Jabouille	Peugeot 905B	367
4	Eddie Irvine/Toshio Suzuki/		
	Masanori Sekiya	Toyota TS010	364
5	Roland Ratzenberger/		
	Mauro Martini/Naoki Nagasaka	Toyota 92CV	363
6	George Fouche/Eje Elgh/		
	Steven Andskar	Toyota 92CV	358

Winner's average speed: 132.580 mph. Class winners: Group C1 category 1: Helary/Bouchut/Brabham; Group C1 category 2: Ratzenberger/Martini/Nagasaka; GT: Joel Gouhier/Dominique Dupuy/Jurgen Barth (Porsche 911 Carrera RSR); Le Mans prototype: Patrick Gonin/Bernard Santal/Alain Lamouille (WR LM93-Peugeot). Pole position: Alliot, 3m24.94. Fastest lap: Sekiya, 3m27.47

1994

18-19 June 1994. 344 laps of an 8.451 mile-circuit = 2907.144 miles

1	Yannick Dalmas/Hurley Haywood/		
	Mauro Baldi	Dauer 962LM-Porsche	344
2	Eddie Irvine/Mauro Martini/		
	Jeff Krosnoff	Toyota 94CV	343
3	Hans-Joachim Stuck/		
	Danny Sullivan/Thierry Boutsen	Dauer 962LM-Porsche	343
4	Steven Andskar/		
	George Fouche/Bob Wollek	Toyota 94CV	328
5	Steve Millen/Johnny O'Connell/		
	John Morton	Nissan 300ZX	317
6	Derek Bell/Robin Donovan/		
	Jurgen Laessig	Kremer K8-Porsche	316

Winner's average speed: 121.131 mph. Class winners: Group C1 category 2: Irvine/Martini/Krosnoff; Le Mans prototype: no finishers; GT1: Dalmas/Haywood/Baldi; GT2: Jesus Pareja/Dominique Dupuy/Carlos Palau (Porsche 911 Carrera RSR); IMSA GTS: Millen/O'Connell/Morton. Pole position: Alain Ferte (Cougar C32LM-Porsche), 3m51.05. Fastest lap: Boutsen, 3m52.54

1995

17-18 June 1995. 298 laps of an 8.453-mile circuit = 2518.994 miles

1	Yannick Dalmas/JJ Lehto/		
	Masanori Sekiya	McLaren F1 GTR-BMW	298
2	Mario Andretti/Eric Helary/		
	Bob Wollek	Courage C34-Porsche	298
3	Derek Bell/Justin Bell/		
	Andy Wallace	McLaren F1 GTR-BMW	296
4	Ray Bellm/Mark Blundell/		
	Maurizio Sandro Sala	McLaren F1 GTR-BMW	291
5	Jean-Denis Deletraz/Fabien		
	Giroix/Olivier Grouillard	McLaren F1 GTR-BMW	290
6	Christophe Bouchut/Thierry Boutsen/		
	Hans-Joachim Stuck	Kremer K8-Porsche	289

Winner's average speed: 104.958 mph. Class winners: WSC prototype: Andretti/Helary/Wollek; Le Mans prototype (LMP): Patrice Roussel/Edouard Sezionale/Bernard Santal (Debora LMP295-Ford); GT1: Dalmas/Lehto/Sekiya; GT2: Keiichi Tsuchiya/Akira Iida/Kunimitsu Takahashi (Honda NSX). Pole position: William David (WR LM94-Peugeot), 3m46.05. Fastest lap: David, 3m51.41

1996

15-16 June 1996. 354 laps of an 8.453-mile circuit = 2992.362 miles

1	Davy Jones/Manuel Reuter/		
	Alexander Wurz	Porsche WSC95	354
2	Thierry Boutsen/Hans-Joachim		
	Stuck/Bob Wollek	Porsche 911 GT1	353
3	Yannick Dalmas/Scott Goodyear/		
	Karl Wendlinger	Porsche 911 GT1	341
4	Thomas Bscher/		
	Peter Kox/John Nielsen	McLaren F1 GTR-BMW	338
5	David Brabham/Lindsay Owen-		
	Jones/Pierre-Henri Raphanel	McLaren F1 GTR-BMW	335
6	Derek Bell/Olivier Grouillard/		
	Andy Wallace	McLaren F1 GTR-BMW	328

Winner's average speed: 124.653 mph. Class winners: LMP1: Jones/Reuter/Wurz; LMP2: Franck Freon/Yojiro Terada/Jim Downing (Kudzu DLM-Mazda); IMSA WSC: no finishers; GT1: Boutsen/Stuck/Wollek; GT2: Ralf Kelleners/Bruno Eichmann/Guy Martinolle (Porsche 911 GT2). Pole position: Pierluigi Martini (Porsche WSC95), 3m46.682. Fastest lap: Eric van de Poele (Ferrari 333SP), 3m47.495

1997

14-15 June 1997. 361 laps of an 8.453-mile circuit = 3051.533 miles

1	Michele Alboreto/Stefan Johansson/Tom Kristensen	Porsche WSC95	361
2	Jean-Marc Gounon/Anders Olofsson/ Pierre-Henri Raphanel	McLaren F1 GTR-BMW	360
3	Eric Helary/Peter Kox/ Roberto Ravaglia	McLaren F1 GTR-BMW	358
4	Didier Cottaz/Marc Goossens/ Jerome Policand	Courage C41-Porsche	336
5	Patrice Gouselard/Armin Hahne/Pedro Lamy	Porsche 911 GT1	331
6	Gianpiero Moretti/ Massimiliano Papis/Didier Theys	Ferrari 333SP	321

Winner's average speed: 126.911 mph. Class winners: LMP: Alboreto/Johansson/Kristensen; GT1: Gounon/Olofsson/Raphanel; GT2: Michel Neugarten/Guy Martinolle/Jean-Claude Lagniez (Porsche 911 GT2). Pole position: Alboreto, 3m41.581. Fastest lap: Kristensen, 3m45.068

1998

6-7 June 1998. 351 laps of an 8.453-mile circuit = 2967.003 miles

1	Laurent Aiello/Allan McNish/ Stephane Ortelli	Porsche 911 GT1-98	351
2	Uwe Alzen/Jorg Muller/ Bob Wollek	Porsche 911 GT1-98	350
3	Kazuyoshi Hoshino/Masahiko Kageyama/Aguri Suzuki	Nissan R390 GT1	347
4	Bill Auberlen/ Steve O'Rourke/Tim Sugden	McLaren F1 GTR-BMW	347
5	Michael Krumm/ Franck Lagorce/John Nielsen	Nissan R390 GT1	342
6	Erik Comas/Jan Lammers/ Andrea Montermini	Nissan R390 GT1	342

Winner's average speed: 123.625 mph. LMP1: Wayne Taylor/Eric van de Poele/Fermin Velez (Ferrari 333SP); LMP2: no finishers; GT1: Aiello/McNish/Ortelli; GT2: Justin Bell/Luca Drudi/David Donohue (Chrysler Viper GTS-R). Pole position: Bernd Schneider (Mercedes-Benz CLK-LM), 3m35.544. Fastest lap: Martin Brundle (Toyota GT One), 3m41.809

1999

12-13 June 1999. 365 laps of an 8.453-mile circuit = 3085.345 miles

1	Yannick Dalmas/Pierluigi Martini/Joachim Winkelhock	BMW V12 LMR	365
2	Ukyo Katayama/Toshio Suzuki/ Keiichi Tsuchiya	Toyota GT-One	364
3	Frank Biela/Emanuele Pirro/ Didier Theys	Audi R8R	360
4	Laurent Aiello/Michele Alboreto/Rinaldo Capello	Audi R8R	346
5	Bill Auberlen/Thomas Bscher/ Steve Soper	BMW V12 LM98	345
6	Alex Caffi/Andrea Montermini/ Domenico Schiattarella	Courage C52-Nissan	342

Winner's average speed: 128.556 mph. LMP1: Dalmas/Martini/Winkelhock; LMP2: no finishers. GTP: Katayama/Suzuki/Tsuchiya; GTS: Olivier Beretta/Karl Wendlinger/Dominique Dupuy (Chrysler Viper GTS-R); GT: Uwe Alzen/Patrick Huisman/Luca Riccitelli (Porsche 996 GT3-R). Pole position: Martin Brundle (Toyota GT-One), 3m29.930. Fastest lap: Katayama, 3m35.032

2000

17-18 June 2000. 368 laps of an 8.453-mile circuit = 3110.704 miles

1	Frank Biela/Tom Kristensen/ Emanuele Pirro	Audi R8	368
2	Laurent Aiello/Allan McNish/ Stephane Ortelli	Audi R8	367
3	Christian Abt/Michele Alboreto/ Rinaldo Capello	Audi R8	365
4	Sebastien Bourdais/Emmanuel Clerico/ Olivier Grouillard	Courage C52-Peugeot	344
5	Hiroki Katoh/Johnny O'Connell/ Pierre-Henri Raphanel	Panoz LMP Roadster S	342
6	Masahiko Kageyama/Masemi Kageyama/ Toshio Suzuki	Panoz LMP Roadster S	340

Winner's average speed: 129.613 mph. LMP900 (LMP1): Biela/Kristensen/Pirro; LMP675 (LMP2): Scott Maxwell/John Graham/Greg Wilkins (Lola B2K/40-Nissan); GTS: Olivier Beretta/Karl Wendlinger/Dominique Dupuy (Chrysler Viper GTS-R); GT: Hideo Fukuyama/Atsushi Yogo/Bruno Lambert (Porsche 911 GT3-R). Pole position: McNish, 3m36.124. Fastest lap: McNish, 3m37.359

2001

16-17 June 2001. 321 laps of an 8.453-mile circuit = 2713.413 miles

1	Frank Biela/Tom Kristensen/ Emanuele Pirro	Audi R8	321
2	Laurent Aiello/Rinaldo Capello/ Christian Pescatori	Audi R8	320
3	Butch Leitzinger/ Eric van de Poele/Andy Wallace	Bentley EXP "Speed Eight"	306
4	Olivier Beretta/Pedro Lamy/ Karl Wendlinger	Chrysler-Mopar LMP	298
5	Jean-Denis Deletraz/ Pascal Fabre/Jordi Gene	Reynard 2KQ-Volkswagen	284
6	Fabio Babini/Luca Drudi/ Gabrio Rosa	Porsche 911 GT3-RS	283

Winner's average speed: 112.427 mph. LMP900 (LMP1): Biela/Kristensen/Pirro; LMP675 (LMP2): Deletraz/Fabre/Gene; LM-GTP: Leitzinger/van de Poele/Wallace; GTS: Ron Fellows/Johnny O'Connell/Scott Pruett (Chevrolet Corvette C5-R); GT: Babini/Drudi/Rosa. Pole position: Capello, 3m32.429. Fastest lap: Aiello, 3m39.046

2002

15 June 2002. Le Mans. 375 laps of an 8.451-mile circuit = 3169.125 miles

1	Frank Biela/Tom Kristensen/ Emanuele Pirro	Audi R8	375
2	Rinaldo Capello/Johnny Herbert/ Christian Pescatori	Audi R8	374
3	Michael Krumm/Philipp Peter/ Marco Werner	Audi R8	372
4	Butch Leitzinger/ Eric van de Poele/Andy Wallace	Bentley EXP "Speed Eight"	362
5	Olivier Beretta/Erik Comas/ Pedro Lamy	Dallara LMP-Judd	359
6	Nicolas Minassian/Franck Montagny/Stephane Sarrazin	Dallara LMP-Judd	359

Winner's average speed: 132.047 mph. LMP900 (LMP1): Biela/Kristensen/Pirro; LMP675 (LMP2): Jean-Denis Deletraz/Walter Lechner jr/Christophe Pillon (Reynard 2KQ-Volkswagen). LM-GTP: Leitzinger/van de Poele/Wallace; GTS: Ron Fellows/Oliver Gavin/Johnny O'Connell (Chevrolet Corvette C5-R); GT: Timo Bernhard/Kevin Buchler/Lucas Luhr (Porsche 911 GT3-RS). Pole position: Capello, 3m29.905. Fastest lap: Kristensen, 3m33.483

Drivers' Records

WINS					
Jacky Ickx	6	Christophe Bouchut	1	Pierluigi Martini	1
Derek Bell	5	Geoff Brabham	1	Jochen Mass	1
Yannick Dalmas	4	Martin Brundle	1	Bruce McLaren	1
Olivier Gendebien	4	Eugene Chaboud	1	Allan McNish	1
Tom Kristensen	4	Frank Clement	1	John Nielsen	1
Henri Pescarolo	4	Price Cobb	1	Tazio Nuvolari	1
Woolf Barnato	3	Gerard de Courcelles	1	Jackie Oliver	1
Frank Biela	3	Sammy Davis	1	Stephane Ortelli	1
Luigi Chinetti	3	Stanley Dickens	1	Didier Pironi	1
Hurley Haywood	3	John Duff	1	Fritz Riess	1
Phil Hill	3	Johnny Dumfries	1	Jochen Rindt	1
Al Holbert	3	Philippe Etancelin	1	Pedro Rodriguez	1
Klaus Ludwig	3	Luis Fontes	1	Tony Rolt	1
Emanuele Pirro	3	AJ Foyt Jr	1	Jean Rondeau	1
Tim Birkin	2	Paul Frere	1	Jean-Louis Rosier	1
Ivor Bueb	2	Bertrand Gachot	1	Louis Rosier	1
Ron Flockhart	2	Jose Froilan Gonzalez	1	Bernard Rubin	1
Jean-Pierre Jaussaud	2	Masten Gregory	1	Roy Salvadori	1
Gerard Larrousse	2	Jean Guichet	1	Ninian Sanderson	1
Gijs van Lennep	2	Dan Gurney	1	Ludovico Scarfiotti	1
Manuel Reuter	2	Duncan Hamilton	1	Vern Schuppan	1
Andre Rossignol	2	Mike Hawthorn	1	Masanori Sekiya	1
Raymond Sommer	2	Eric Helary	1	Peter Selsdon	1
Hans-Joachim Stuck	2	Johnny Herbert	1	Carroll Shelby	1
Jean-Pierre Wimille	2	Hans Herrmann	1	Jean Tremoulet	1
Laurent Aiello	1	Graham Hill	1	Maurice Trintignant	1
Michele Alboreto	1	John Hindmarsh	1	Nino Vaccarella	1
Chris Amon	1	Earl Howe	1	Pierre Veyron	1
Richard Attwood	1	Ed Hugus	1	Peter Walker	1
Mauro Baldi	1	Stefan Johansson	1	Andy Wallace	1
Lorenzo Bandini	1	Davy Jones	1	Derek Warwick	1
Paolo Barilla	1	Glen Kidston	1	Volker Weidler	1
Jurgen Barth	1	Andre Lagache	1	Peter Whitehead	1
JD Benjafield	1	Jan Lammers	1	Bill Whittington	1
Robert Benoist	1	Hermann Lang	1	Don Whittington	1
Lucien Bianchi	1	JJ Lehto	1	Joachim Winkelhock	1
Robert Bloch	1	Rene Leonard	1	"John Winter"	1
Mark Blundell	1	Helmut Marko	1	Alexander Wurz	1

Manufacturers' Records

WINS					
Porsche (inc. Dauer-Porsche)	16	Lorraine-Dietrich	2	McLaren	1
Ferrari	9	Peugeot	2	Mercedes-Benz	1
Jaguar	7	Alpine	1	Mirage	1
Bentley	5	Aston Martin	1	Rondeau	1
Alfa Romeo	4	BMW	1	Sauber	1
Ford	4	Chenard & Walcker	1	Talbot	1
Audi	3	Delahaye	1		
Matra	3	Lagonda	1		
Bugatti	2	Mazda	1		

Other Records

Most starts: 33, Henri Pescarolo
Most pole positions: Five, Jacky Ickx
Closest finish: 120 metres, 1969, Jacky Ickx (excludes "staged" finishes)
Widest winning margin: 217 miles in 1927
Most starters: 60, 1950 and 1951
Fewest starters: 17, 1930

Most finishers: 30, 1923 (out of 33 starters) and 1951
Fewest finishers: six, 1931
Furthest distance covered by winning car: 3314.124 miles, 1971
Shortest distance covered by winning car: 1287.120 miles, 1924
100% record: Woolf Barnato raced at Le Mans on three occasions, winning each time

World Sports Car Championship

1971 Nino Vaccarella/Toine Hezemans (Alfa Romeo T33/3) head for victory in the Targa Florio.

World Sports Car Championship

More than any other major series, World Championship Sports Car racing has had a history of success and failure, boom and decline. The original series was organised by the FIA for manufacturers in 1953 and featured the classic long-distance races of the time.

During the fifties the championship attracted competition from Ferrari, Jaguar, Aston Martin, Mercedes-Benz, Cunningham, Lancia, Alfa Romeo, Maserati and others. But by 1961 all serious challenges to Ferrari (who had been champions for all but two seasons to date) had dwindled and the series was cancelled.

With the FIA's attention turning to Grand Touring cars, the organisers of the Sebring 12 Hours, Targa Florio, Nurburgring 1000 kms and Le Mans 24 Hours joined forces to promote the Speed World Challenge for Sports Cars. It proved a success and was adopted by the FIA in 1963 and developed into a full World Championship for Makes.

Ferrari continued to dominate until Ford perfected the spectacular GT40 into a race-winning force in 1965. World Championship victories for Ford followed in 1966 and under new regulations in 1968.

Porsche, destined to become the most successful Sports Car manufacturer, introduced the 917 in 1969. The car withstood a renewed challenge from Ferrari to win three successive championships from 1969-71, prompting another new formula for 1972. Although this change brought Ferrari back to the fore, the company withdrew from Sports Car racing at the end of 1973 to concentrate on Formula 1.

Matra, Alfa Romeo and Renault all made brief and successful forays into Sports Car racing during the seventies, but Porsche remained the mainstay of the category. In 1976 and 1977 separate series were organised for Group 5 and Group 6 cars, but Sports Car racing had entered a period of decline due to the confusion between the championships and a lack of interest from sponsors, spectators and most manufacturers alike.

A drivers championship was introduced in 1981, and new Group C rules were adopted a year later. Although Porsche continued to extend its unrivalled record with the 956 and 962 Group C cars, the company faced renewed challenges in the late eighties, first from Jaguar and then from Mercedes-Benz.

To reflect the number of privateers running Porsches, a Teams Championship replaced the manufacturers title in 1985. After Brun Motorsport won the 1986 series for Porsche, Jaguar and Sauber-Mercedes dominated the series.

But the introduction of new 3.5-litre engines during a transitional period starting in 1989 alienated the privateer teams that had been the backbone of the Group C years. The championship was abandoned after a final under-supported year in 1992.

1953 Peter Collins and Pat Griffith win the 1953 Tourist Trophy for Aston Martin.

Rules

World Sports Car Championship (1953-61)

1953-55	Prototypes, racing Sports Cars and production cars. No engine limit. Minimum homologation for production cars of 100
1956-57	Prototypes only. 2500cc maximum engine capacity
1958-61	Prototypes only. 3000cc maximum engine capacity

Speed World Challenge (1962-63)

1962	Prototypes and Grand Touring Cars. 4000cc maximum engine capacity for prototypes
1963	GT Prototypes and Grand Touring Cars. No engine limit

International Championship for Makes (1964-71)

1964-65	Prototypes and Grand Touring Cars. No engine limit
1966-67	Group 6 (Sports-prototypes), (Group 5) Special Touring Cars and Group 4 (Sports Cars). Minimum homologation for Group 4 of 50. No engine limit. Two divisions: above 2000cc and up to 2000cc
1968-69	Groups 6 (Sports-prototypes), 4 (Sports Cars) and 3 (Special GT). Stockblock engines only in Group 4. 3000cc maximum engine capacity for Group 6, 5000cc for Group 4, no engine limit for Group 3
1970-71	Groups 6 (Sports-prototypes), 5 (Sports Cars) and 4 (Special GT). Minimum homologation for Group 5 of 25. 3000cc maximum engine capacity for Group 6, 5000cc for Group 5, no engine limit for Group 4

World Championship for Makes (1972-81)

1972-75	Groups 5 (Sports Cars) and 4 (Special GT). 3000cc maximum engine capacity for Group 5, no engine limit for Group 4
1976-77	Group 5 (Special Production cars) in three divisions: up to 6000cc, 3000cc and 2000cc
1978-80	Group 5 (Special Production cars) in two divisions: over and up to 2000cc
1981	Group 5 (Special Production cars) in three divisions: over and up to 2000cc, and IMSA GTX

World Sports Car Championship (1976-77)

1976-77	Groups 6 (Sports-prototypes) and 5 (Sports Cars). 5000cc maximum engine capacity for stockblocks, 3000cc for normally aspirated racing engines or 2140cc for turbocharged racing engines in Group 6, 3000cc for Group 5

World Endurance Championship (1982-85)

| 1982-84 | Group C (Sports-prototypes). No engine limit. Maximum fuel consumption of 60 litres per 100 kms |
| 1985 | Group C (Sports-prototypes). No engine limit. Maximum fuel consumption of 51 litres per 100 kms |

World Sports-Prototype Championship (1986-90)

| 1986-88 | 1985 rules: Group C (Sports-prototypes). No engine limit. Maximum fuel consumption of 51 litres per 100 kms |
| 1989-90 | Categories 1 (3.5-litre sports-prototypes) and 2 (old Group C). Category 1: 3500cc maximum engine capacity. Normally aspirated engines. Maximum 12 cylinders. No fuel restriction |

World Sports Car Championship (1991-92)

| 1991-92 | Categories 1 (3.5-litre sports-prototypes) and 2 (old Group C). Category 1: 3500cc maximum engine capacity. Normally aspirated engines. Maximum 12 cylinders. No fuel restriction |

Points

World Sports Car Championship (1953-61)

1953-57	8-6-4-3-2-1 points awarded to the top six finishers. Best result per marque at each race counted
1958	8-6-4-3-2-1 points awarded to the top six finishers except for the shorter, four-hour Tourist Trophy, where 4-3-2-1 points awarded to top four finishers. Best result per marque at each race counted
1959-60	8-6-4-3-2-1 points awarded to the top six finishers. Best result per marque at each race counted
1961	8-6-4-3-2-1 points awarded to the top six finishers except at races of under 1000 kms or 6 hours where half points were awarded. Best result per marque at each race counted

Speed World Challenge (1962-63)

| 1962-63 | 10-9-8-6-5-4-3-2 points awarded to the top eight finishers plus 1 point to all other finishers. Best result per marque at each race counted. Each marque had to compete in every round to qualify for points |

International Championship for Makes (1964-71)

1964-67	9-6-4-3-2-1 points awarded to the top six finishers. Best result per marque at each race counted
1968	8-6-4-3-2-1 points awarded to the top six finishers except at Zeltweg where half points were awarded. Best result per marque at each race counted
1969-71	8-6-4-3-2-1 points awarded to the top six finishers. Best result per marque at each race counted

World Championship for Makes (1972-81)

| 1972-80 | 20-15-12-10-8-6-4-3-2-1 points awarded to the top ten finishers. Best result per marque at each race counted |
| 1981 | Manufacturers title: 20-15-12-10-8-6-4-3-2-1 points awarded to the top ten finishers in both over 2000cc and under 2000cc classes. Best result per marque at each race in each class counted. Drivers title: 20-19-18-17-16-15-14-13-12-11-10-9-8-7-6-5-4-3-2-1 points awarded to the top twenty finishers plus bonus points awarded as follows: no bonus to category 1 (Group 6 over 2000cc) 1 bonus point to category 2 (Group 5 over 2000cc, IMSA GTP over 2000cc, Group C over 2000cc, IMSA GTX over 2000cc, IMSA AAGT) |

2 bonus points to category 3 (Group 6 under 2000cc, Group 5 under 2000cc, Group 4 over 2000cc, IMSA GTO, IMSA GTX under 2000cc)
3 bonus points to category 4 (IMSA GTP under 2000cc, Group 2 over 2000cc, IMSA GTU, Group C under 2000cc)
4 bonus points to category 5 (Group 4 under 2000cc, Group 1 over 2000cc)
5 bonus points to category 6 (Group 2 under 2000cc, Group 1 under 2000cc, IMSA RS)

World Endurance Championship (1982-85)

1982-85	20-15-12-10-8-6-4-3-2-1 points awarded to the top ten finishers. Best result per marque at each race counted. Bonus points awarded in drivers championship as follows: no bonus to category 1 (Group C, Group 6 over 2000cc, Group 5 over 2000cc, IMSA GTX over 2000cc) 1 bonus point to category 2 (Group B over 2000cc, Group 6 under 2000cc, Group 5 under 2000cc, Group 4 over 2000cc, IMSA GTO) 2 bonus points to category 3 (IMSA GTU, Group 2 over 2000cc, Group 3 over 2000cc) 3 bonus points to category 4 (Group B under 2000cc, Group 4 under 2000cc, Group 2 under 2000cc, Group 3 under 2000cc)
1983-84	Both manufacturers and drivers titles: 20-15-12-10-8-6-4-3-2-1 points awarded to the top ten finishers. Best result per marque at each race counted
1985	Both teams and drivers titles: 20-15-12-10-8-6-4-3-2-1 points awarded to the top ten finishers. Best result per team at each race counted

World Sports-Prototype Championship (1986-90)

1986	20-15-12-10-8-6-4-3-2-1 points awarded to the top ten finishers. Best result per marque at each race counted
1987	20-15-12-10-8-6-4-3-2-1 points awarded to the top ten finishers. Group C2 drivers scored 2 bonus points for finishing in the top ten. Best result per marque at each race counted
1988	60-45-36-30-24-18-12-9-6-3 points awarded to the top ten finishers at 24-hour races (Le Mans); 40-30-24-20-16-12-8-6-4-2 points awarded to the top ten finishers at 800-1000 kms races (Jerez, Monza, Silverstone, Brands Hatch, Nurburgring, Spa and Fuji); 20-15-12-10-8-6-4-3-2-1 points awarded to the top ten finishers at sprint races (Jarama, Brno and Sandown Park). Drivers had to complete at least 30% of their car's total race distance to qualify for points and could only drive in one car. C2 drivers awarded bonus points for finishing in the top ten overall as follows: 6 points at 24-hour races; 4 at 800-1000 kms races; and 2 at sprint races
1989	20-15-12-10-8-6-4-3-2-1 points awarded to the top ten finishers. Drivers had to complete at least 30% of their car's total race distance to qualify for points and could only drive in one car
1990	9-6-4-3-2-1 points awarded to the top six finishers. Drivers had to complete at least 30% of their car's total race distance to qualify for points and could only drive in one car

World Sports Car Championship (1991-92)

| 1991-92 | 20-15-12-10-8-6-4-3-2-1 points awarded to the top ten finishers. Drivers had to complete at least 30% of their car's total race distance to qualify for points and could only drive in one car. Car had to be entered in championship to qualify in points |

WORLD SPORTS CAR CHAMPIONS

Drivers

year	champion	nat	team	car
1981	Bob Garretson	USA	Cooke-Woods Racing/	
			Garretson Racing/Varde Racing	Porsche 935/Porsche 935-K3/Mazda RX7
1982	Jacky Ickx	B	Rothmans Porsche	Porsche 956
1983	Jacky Ickx	B	Rothmans Porsche	Porsche 956
1984	Stefan Bellof	D	Rothmans Porsche	Porsche 956
1985	Derek Bell/Hans-Joachim Stuck	GB/D	Rothmans Porsche	Porsche 962C
1986	Derek Bell	GB	Rothmans Porsche	Porsche 962C
1987	Raul Boesel	BR	Silk Cut Jaguar (TWR)	Jaguar XJR-8
1988	Martin Brundle	GB	Silk Cut Jaguar (TWR)	Jaguar XJR-9
1989	Jean-Louis Schlesser	F	Team Sauber Mercedes	Sauber C9/88-Mercedes-Benz
1990	Mauro Baldi/Jean-Louis Schlesser	I/F	Team Sauber Mercedes	Sauber C9/88-Mercedes-Benz/Mercedes-Benz C11
1991	Teo Fabi	I	Silk Cut Jaguar (TWR)	Jaguar XJR-14/Jaguar XJR-12
1992	Yannick Dalmas/Derek Warwick	F/GB	Peugeot Talbot Sport	Peugeot 905B

Manufacturers

year	championship	manufacturer/team	year	championship	manufacturer/team
1953	World Sports Car Championship	Ferrari	1978	World Championship for Makes	Porsche
1954	World Sports Car Championship	Ferrari	1979	World Championship for Makes	Porsche
1955	World Sports Car Championship	Mercedes-Benz	1980	World Championship for Makes	Porsche
1956	World Sports Car Championship	Ferrari	1981	World Championship for Makes	Lancia
1957	World Sports Car Championship	Ferrari	1982	World Endurance Championship	Porsche
1958	World Sports Car Championship	Ferrari	1983	World Endurance Championship	Porsche
1959	World Sports Car Championship	Aston Martin	1984	World Endurance Championship	Porsche
1960	World Sports Car Championship	Ferrari	1985	World Endurance	
1961	World Sports Car Championship	Ferrari		Championship for Teams	Rothmans Porsche
1962	Speed World Challenge	Ferrari	1986	World Sports-Prototype	
1963	Speed and Endurance World Challenge	Ferrari		Championship for Teams	Brun Motorsport
1964	International Championship for Makes	Ferrari	1987	World Sports-Prototype	
1965	International Championship for Makes	Ferrari		Championship for Teams	Silk Cut Jaguar (TWR)
1966	International Championship for Makes	Ford	1988	World Sports-Prototype	
1967	International Championship for Makes	Ferrari		Championship for Teams	Silk Cut Jaguar (TWR)
1968	International Championship for Makes	Ford	1989	World Sports-Prototype	
1969	International Championship for Makes	Porsche		Championship for Teams	Team Sauber Mercedes
1970	International Championship for Makes	Porsche	1990	World Sports-Prototype	
1971	International Championship for Makes	Porsche		Championship for Teams	Team Sauber Mercedes
1972	World Championship for Makes	Ferrari	1991	World Sports Car	
1973	World Championship for Makes	Matra-Simca		Championship for Teams	Silk Cut Jaguar (TWR)
1974	World Championship for Makes	Matra-Simca	1992	World Sports Car	
1975	World Championship for Makes	Alfa Romeo		Championship for Teams	Peugeot Talbot Sport
1976	World Championship for Makes	Porsche			
	World Championship for Sports Cars	Porsche			
1977	World Championship for Makes	Porsche			
	World Championship for Sports Cars	Alfa Romeo			

Group C2 Drivers

year	champion	nat	car
1985	Gordon Spice	GB	Tiga GC85-Ford
1986	Gordon Spice/Ray Bellm	GB	Spice SE86C-Ford
1987	Gordon Spice/Fermin Velez	GB/E	Spice SE86C-Ford
1988	Gordon Spice/Ray Bellm	GB	Spice SE88C-Ford
1989	Nick Adams/Fermin Velez	GB/E	Spice SE89C-Ford

Group C2 Manufacturers/Teams

year	manufacturer/team
1983	Alba-Giannini
1984	Alba-Giannini
1985	Spice Engineering
1986	Ecurie Ecosse
1987	Spice Engineering
1988	Spice Engineering
1989	Chamberlain Engineering

1953

World Sports Car Championship

12 HOURS OF SEBRING

8 March 1953. Sebring. 173 laps of a 5.200-mile circuit = 899.600 miles.
World Sports Car Championship round 1

1	John Fitch/Phil Walters	Cunningham C4R-Chrysler	173	12h00m03
2	George Abecassis/Reg Parnell	Aston Martin DB3	172	
3	Sherwood Johnston/Bob Wilder	Jaguar XK120C	162	
4	Bob Gegan/Harry Gray	Jaguar XK120C	155	
5	Briggs Cunningham/Bill Lloyd	OSCA MT4	153	
6	Charles Hassan/Ed Lunken	Ferrari 166MM	153	

Winner's average speed: 74.961 mph

MILLE MIGLIA

26 April 1953. Brescia-Rome-Brescia. 939.515 miles. World Sports Car
Championship round 2

1	Giannino Marzotto/ Marco Crosara	Ferrari 340MM	10h37m19
2	Juan Manuel Fangio/ Giulio Sala	Alfa Romeo 6C-3000 CM	10h49m03
3	Felice Bonetto/U Peruzzi	Lancia D20	11h07m40
4	Tom Cole/Mario Vandelli	Ferrari 340MM	11h20m39
5	Reg Parnell/ Louis Klementaski	Aston Martin DB3	11h32m43
6	Guerino Bertocchi/ Emilio Giletti	Maserati A6GCS	11h38m42

Winner's average speed: 88.450 mph

24 HEURES DU MANS

13-14 June 1953. Le Mans. 302 laps of an 8.378-mile circuit = 2530.156
miles. World Sports Car Championship round 3

1	Duncan Hamilton/Tony Rolt	Jaguar XK120C	302	24 hours
2	Stirling Moss/Peter Walker	Jaguar XK120C	299	
3	John Fitch/Phil Walters	Cunningham C5R-Chrysler	297	
4	Ian Stewart/Peter Whitehead	Jaguar XK120C	296	
5	Giannino Marzotto/Paolo Marzotto	Ferrari 340MM	293	
6	Harry Schell/Maurice Trintignant	Gordini T24S	292	

Winner's average speed: 105.423 mph. Pole position: Alberto Ascari
(Ferrrari 375MM), 4m31.0 (Le Mans start). Fastest lap: Ascari, 4m27.4

24 HEURES DE SPA-FRANCORCHAMPS

25-26 July 1953. Spa-Francorchamps. 260 laps of an 8.774-mile circuit =
2281.240 miles. World Sports Car Championship round 4

1	Giuseppe Farina/ Mike Hawthorn	Ferrari 340MM	260	24h02m07.085
2	Guy Gale/ James Scott-Douglas	Jaguar XK120C	242	
3	Hermann Roosdorp/ Toni Ulmen	Jaguar XK120C	231	
4	Marc Gignoux/ Claude Storez	DB HBR-Panhard	211	
5	Wladimir Narichkine/ Viegas Vallagao	Mercedes-Benz 220	192	
6	Averseng/Marcel Lauga	Simca Aronde	191	

Winner's average speed: 94.912 mph. Pole position: Hawthorn, 4m39.0.
Fastest lap: Farina, 4m44.0

NURBURGRING 1000 KM-RENNEN

30 August 1953. Nurburgring. 44 laps of a 14.167-mile circuit = 623.348
miles. World Sports Car Championship round 5

1	Alberto Ascari/Giuseppe Farina	Ferrari 375MM	44	8h20m44
2	Roy Salvadori/Ian Stewart	Jaguar XK120C	44	8h35m44
3	Franz-Eugen Hammernick/ Adolf Brudes	Borgward Hansa 1500RS	44	8h40m03

4	Walter Schlutter/Richard Trenkel	Porsche 550	43	
5	Josef Peters/Wolfgang Seidel	Veritas Comet RS	44	
6	John Lawrence/Jimmy Stewart	Jaguar XK120C	41	

Winner's average speed: 74.692 mph. Pole position: Jean Manuel Fangio
(Lancia D24), 10m12.8 (Le Mans start). Fastest lap: Robert Manzon
(Lancia D24), 10m23.0

TOURIST TROPHY

5 September 1953. Dundrod. 111 laps of a 7.416-mile circuit = 823.176
miles. World Sports Car Championship round 6

1	Peter Collins/Pat Griffith	Aston Martin DB3S	106	9h37m12
2	Reg Parnell/Eric Thompson	Aston Martin DB3S	106	9h40m35
3	Stirling Moss/Peter Walker	Jaguar XK120C	103	
4	Graham Whitehead/ Tony Gaze	Aston Martin DB3	102	
5	Robert Dickson/ Desmond Titterington	Aston Martin DB3	101	
6	Ken Wharton/Ernie Robb	Frazer-Nash MkII	101	

Handicap race, overall result counted towards the World Championship.
Overall winner's average speed: 85.569 mph. Pole position: Moss, 5m02.0.
Fastest lap: Walker, 5m01.0. Handicap race result (which decided the
Tourist Trophy): 1 Collins/Griffith; 2 Parnell/Thompson; 3 Wharton/Robb; 4
Moss/Walker; 5 Whitehead/Gaze; 6 Dickson/Titterington

CARRERA PANAMERICANA

19-23 November 1953. Tuxla Gutierrez-Ciudad Juarez, Mexico. 1911.962
miles. World Sports Car Championship round 7

1	Juan Manuel Fangio/ Gino Bronzoni	Lancia D24	18h11m00
2	Piero Taruffi/Luigi Maggio	Lancia D24	18h18m51
3	Eugenio Castellotti/ Carlo Luoni	Lancia D23	18h24m52
4	Guido Mancini/ Fabrizio Serena	Ferrari 375MM	19h40m29
5	Louis Rosier	Lago-Talbot T26C-GS	20h11m22
6	Umberto Maglioli/ Mario Ricci/Forese Salviati	Ferrari 375MM	20h16m28

Winner's average speed: 105.149 mph

1953 FINAL CHAMPIONSHIP POSITIONS

Manufacturers				
			9 Porsche	3
1	Ferrari	27 (30)*	10= Lago-Talbot	2
2	Jaguar	24 (28)*	OSCA	2
3	Aston Martin	16	Veritas	2
4=	Cunningham-Chrysler	12	13= Frazer Nash	1
	Lancia	12	Gordini	1
6	Alfa Romeo	6	Maserati	1
7=	Borgward	4	*Best four results count	
	Panhard-DB	4		

1954

World Sports Car Championship

1000 KM DE LA CIUDAD DE BUENOS AIRES

24 January 1954. Buenos Aires. 106 laps of a 5.888-mile circuit = 624.128
miles. World Sports Car Championship round 1

1	Giuseppe Farina/ Umberto Maglioli	Ferrari 375MM	106	6h41m50.8
2	Harry Schell/ Alfonso de Portago	Ferrari 250MM Vignale	103	
3	Peter Collins/Pat Griffith	Aston Martin DB3S	102	
4	James Scott-Douglas/ Ninian Sanderson	Jaguar XK120C	100	
5	Luis Milan/Elpidio Tortone	Ferrari 625TF	99	

6 Emilio Giletti/Luigi Musso   Maserati A6GCS   97
Winner's average speed: 93.189 mph. Fastest lap: Farina, 3m34.6

12 HOURS OF SEBRING

7 March 1954. Sebring. 168 laps of a 5.200-mile circuit = 873.600 miles. World Sports Car Championship round 2

1 Stirling Moss/Bill Lloyd	OSCA MT4	167	12h04m16.7
2 Porfirio Rubirosa/			
Gino Valenzano	Lancia D24	163	
3 Lance Macklin/			
George Huntoon	Austin Healey 100S	163	
4 James Simpson/			
George Colby	OSCA MT4	163	
5 Otto Linton/Harry Beck	OSCA MT4	161	
6 WK Carpenter/John van Driel	Kieft Sport-Bristol	158	

Piero Taruffi/Robert Manzon (Lancia D24), 161 laps, finished sixth on the road but disqualified for outside assistance. Winner's average speed: 72.370 mph. Pole position: Phil Walters (Ferrari 375MM), 3m32.02 (Le Mans start). Fastest lap: Alberto Ascari (Lancia D24), 3m32.0

MILLE MIGLIA

1-2 May 1954. Brescia-Rome-Brescia. 992.332 miles. World Sports Car Championship round 3

1 Alberto Ascari	Lancia D24	11h26m10
2 Vittorio Marzotto	Ferrari 500 Mondial	12h00m01
3 Luigi Musso/Augusto Zocco	Maserati A6GCS	12h00m10
4 Clemente Biondetti	Ferrari 250MM	
	Pinin Farina	12h15m36
5 Bruno Venezian/M Orlandi	Maserati A6GCS	12h27m43
6 Hans Herrmann/		
Herbert Linge	Porsche 550 Spyder	12h35m44

Winner's average speed: 86.772 mph

24 HEURES DU MANS

12-13 June 1954. Le Mans. 300 laps of an 8.378-mile circuit = 2513.400 miles. World Sports Car Championship round 4

1 Maurice Trintignant/			
Jose Froilan Gonzalez	Ferrari 375 Plus	300	24 hours
2 Tony Rolt/Duncan Hamilton	Jaguar D-type	299	
3 Bill Spear/	Cunningham		
Sherwood Johnston	C4R-Chrysler	282	
4 Roger Laurent/			
Jacques Swaters	Jaguar XK120C	276	
5 Briggs Cunningham/	Cunningham		
John Bennett	C4R-Chrysler	272	
6 Andre Guelfi/Jacques Pollet	Gordini T30S	262	

Winner's average speed: 104.725 mph. Fastest lap: Gonzalez, 4m16.8

TOURIST TROPHY

11 September 1954. Dundrod. 94 laps of a 7.416-mile circuit = 697.104 miles. World Sports Car Championship round 5

1 Mike Hawthorn/			
Maurice Trintignant	Ferrari 750S Monza	94	7h14m13
2 Juan Manuel Fangio/			
Piero Taruffi	Lancia D24	84	
3 Robert Manzon/			
Eugenio Castellotti	Lancia D24	82	
4 George Abecassis/			
James Mayers	HWM-Jaguar	79	
5 Luigi Musso/			
Sergio Mantovani	Maserati A6GCS	79	
6 Peter Whitehead/			
Ken Wharton	Jaguar D-type	79	

Handicap race, overall result counted towards the World Championship. Overall winner's average speed: 96.326 mph. Pole position: Alberto Ascari (Lancia D24), 4m54.0 (Le Mans start). Fastest lap: Hawthorn, 4m49.0. Handicap race result (which decided the Tourist Trophy): 1 Gerard Laureau/Paul Armagnac (DB HBR-Panhard); 2 Hawthorn/Trintignant; 3 Musso/Mantovani; 4 Fangio/Taruffi; 5

Whitehead/Wharton; 6 Manzon/Castellotti

CARRERA PANAMERICANA

19-23 November 1954. Tuxla Gutierrez-Ciudad Juarez, Mexico. 1907.490 miles. World Sports Car Championship round 6

1 Umberto Maglioli	Ferrari 375 Plus		17h40m26
2 Phil Hill/Richie Ginther	Ferrari 375MM		18h04m54
3 Hans Herrmann	Porsche 550 Spyder		
4 Jaroslav Juhan	Porsche 550 Spyder		
5 Franco Cornacchia/			
Enrico Peruchini	Ferrari 250 Monza		
6 Luigi Chinetti/			
John Shakespeare	Ferrari 375MM		

Winner's average speed: 107.927 mph

1954 FINAL CHAMPIONSHIP POSITIONS

Manufacturers			7	Porsche	5
1	Ferrari	32 (38)*	8=	Aston Martin	4
2	Lancia	20		Austin Healey	4
3	Jaguar	11		Cunningham-Chrysler	4
4=	Maserati	8	11	Kieft-Bristol	1
	OSCA	8	*Best four results count		
6	Gordini	6			

1955
World Sports Car Championship

1000 KM DE LA CIUDAD DE BUENOS AIRES

23 January 1955. Buenos Aires. 58 laps of a 10.648-mile circuit = 617.584 miles. World Sports Car Championship round 1

1 Enrique Saenz Valiente/			
Jose Maria Ibanez	Ferrari 375 Plus	58	6h35m15.4
2 Carlos Najurieta/			
Oscar Rivero	Ferrari 375MM	58	6h41m12.1
3 Ricardo Grandio/			
Jose M Faraoni	Maserati A6GCS	56	
4 Jaroslav Juhan/			
Jorge Salas Chaves	Porsche 550 Spyder	56	
5 Elie Bayol/Harry Schell	Gordini T24S	54	
6 Jorge Camano/			
Oscar Camano	Ferrari 212	54	

Winner's average speed: 93.749 mph. Pole position: Saenz Valiente, 6m06.3. Fastest lap: Jose Froilan Gonzalez (Ferrari 118LM), 6m06.1

12 HOURS OF SEBRING

13 March 1955. Sebring. 182 laps of a 5.200-mile circuit = 946.400 miles. World Sports Car Championship round 2

1 Mike Hawthorn/Phil Walters	Jaguar D-type	182	12h00m03.7
2 Phil Hill/Carroll Shelby	Ferrari 750S Monza	182	12h00m29.1
3 Bill Spear/			
Sherwood Johnston	Maserati 300S	180	
4 Gino Valenzano/			
Cesare Perdisa	Maserati 300S	178	
5 Piero Taruffi/Harry Schell	Ferrari 750S Monza	177	
6 Stirling Moss/Lance Macklin	Austin Healey 100S	176	

Winner's average speed: 78.860 mph. Pole position: Hawthorn, 3m38.0 (Le Mans start). Fastest lap: Johnston, 3m38.8

MILLE MIGLIA

30 April-1 May 1955. Brescia-Rome-Brescia. 992.332 miles. World Sports Car Championship round 3

1 Stirling Moss/		
Denis Jenkinson	Mercedes-Benz 300SLR	10h07m48
2 Juan Manuel Fangio	Mercedes-Benz 300SLR	10h39m33

3	Umberto Maglioli/			
	Luciano Monteferrario	Ferrari 118LM		10h52m47
4	Francesco Giardini	Maserati A6GCS		11h15m32
5	John Fitch/Kurt Gesell	Mercedes-Benz 300SL		11h29m21
6	Sergio Sighinolfi	Ferrari 750S Monza		11h33m27

Winner's average speed: 97.960 mph

24 HEURES DU MANS

11-12 June 1955. Le Mans. 306 laps of an 8.378-mile circuit = 2563.668 miles. World Sports Car Championship round 4

1	Mike Hawthorn/Ivor Bueb	Jaguar D-type	306	24 hours
2	Peter Collins/Paul Frere	Aston Martin DB3S	301	
3	Johnny Claes/			
	Jacques Swaters	Jaguar D-type	295	
4	Helmut Polensky/			
	Richard von Frankenberg	Porsche 550 Spyder	283	
5	Wolfgang Seidel/			
	Olivier Gendebien	Porsche 550 Spyder	275	
6	Helmut Glockler/			
	Jaroslav Juhan	Porsche 550 Spyder	272	

Winner's average speed: 106.820 mph. Pole position: Eugenio Castellotti (Ferrari 121LM), 4m14.1 (Le Mans start). Fastest lap: Hawthorn, 4m06.6

1955 Karl Kling finishes second for the dominant Mercedes team at the Tourist Trophy.

TOURIST TROPHY

17 September 1955. Dundrod. 84 laps of a 7.416-mile circuit = 622.944 miles. World Sports Car Championship round 5

1	Stirling Moss/John Fitch	Mercedes-Benz 300SLR	84	7h03m11
2	Juan Manuel Fangio/			
	Karl Kling	Mercedes-Benz 300SLR	83	
3	Wolfgang von Trips/			
	Andre Simon /Karl Kling	Mercedes-Benz 300SLR	82	
4	Peter Walker/			
	Dennis Poore	Aston Martin DB3S	81	
5	Luigi Musso/			
	Franco Bordoni	Maserati 300S	79	
6	Eugenio Castellotti/			
	Piero Taruffi	Ferrari 750S Monza	79	

Winner's average speed: 88.323 mph. Pole position: Moss, 4m48.0 (Le Mans start). Fastest lap: Mike Hawthorn (Jaguar D-type), 4m42.0

TARGA FLORIO

16 October 1955. Madonie (Piccolo). 13 laps of a 44.739-mile circuit = 581.607 miles. World Sports Car Championship round 6

1	Stirling Moss/Peter Collins	Mercedes-Benz 300SLR	13	9h43m14.0
2	Juan Manuel Fangio/			
	Karl Kling	Mercedes-Benz 300SLR	13	9h47m55.4
3	Eugenio Castellotti/			
	Robert Manzon	Ferrari 860 Monza	13	9h53m20.8

4	Desmond Titterington/			
	John Fitch	Mercedes-Benz 300SLR	13	9h54m53.4
5	Carlo Manzini/			
	Francesco Giardini	Maserati A6GCS	13	10h41m15.0
6	Giuseppe Musso/			
	Giuseppe Rossi	Maserati A6GCS	13	10h48m53.2

Winner's average speed: 59.833 mph. Fastest lap: Moss, 43m07.4

1955 FINAL CHAMPIONSHIP POSITIONS

Manufacturers				
			6 Porsche	6
1 Mercedes-Benz	24		7 Gordini	2
2 Ferrari	22 [23]*		8 Austin Healey	1
3 Jaguar	16		*Best four results count	
4 Maserati	13 [15]*			
5 Aston Martin	9			

1956
World Sports Car Championship

1000 KM DE LA CIUDAD DE BUENOS AIRES

29 January 1956. Buenos Aires. 106 laps of a 5.888-mile circuit = 624.128 miles. World Sports Car Championship round 1

1	Stirling Moss/			
	Carlos Menditeguy	Maserati 300S	106	6h29m37.9
2	Olivier Gendebien/Phil Hill	Ferrari 860 Monza	104	
3	Jean Behra/			
	Jose Froilan Gonzalez	Maserati 300S	101	
4	Alejandro de Tomaso/			
	Carlo Tomasi	Maserati 150S	94	
5	Enrique Muro/Julio Pola	Ferrari 500 Mondial	93	
6	Eduardo Kovacs/Raul Jaras	Mercedes-Benz 300SL	90	

Winner's average speed: 96.110 mph. Pole position: Juan Manuel Fangio (Ferrari 410 Plus), 3m29.4. Fastest lap: Peter Collins (Ferrari 410 Plus), 3m26.4

12 HOURS OF SEBRING

24 March 1956. Sebring. 194 laps of a 5.200-mile circuit = 1008.800 miles. World Sports Car Championship round 2

1	Juan Manuel Fangio/			
	Eugenio Castellotti	Ferrari 860 Monza	194	12h00m31.198
2	Luigi Musso/Harry Schell	Ferrari 860 Monza	192	
3	Bob Sweikert/Jack Ensley	Jaguar D-type	188	
4	Roy Salvadori/			
	Carroll Shelby	Aston Martin DB3S	186	
5	Jean Behra/Piero Taruffi /			
	Cesare Perdisa	Maserati 300S	186	
6	Hans Herrmann/			
	Wolfgang von Trips	Porsche 550	182	

Winner's average speed: 84.006 mph. Pole position: Fangio, 3m27.2 (Le Mans start). Fastest lap: Mike Hawthorn (Jaguar D-type), 3m29.7

MILLE MIGLIA

28-29 April 1956. Brescia-Rome-Brescia. 992.332 miles. World Sports Car Championship round 3

1	Eugenio Castellotti	Ferrari 290MM		11h37m10
2	Peter Collins/			
	Louis Klementaski	Ferrari 860 Monza		11h48m28
3	Luigi Musso	Ferrari 860 Monza		12h11m49
4	Juan Manuel Fangio	Ferrari 290MM		12h26m50
5	Olivier Gendebien/			
	Jacques Washer	Ferrari 250GT		12h29m58
6	Paul Metternich/			
	Wittigo Einseidel	Mercedes-Benz 300SL		12h36m38

Winner's average speed: 85.403 mph

NURBURGRING 1000 KM-RENNEN

27 May 1956. Nurburgring. 44 laps of a 14.167-mile circuit = 623.348 miles. World Sports Car Championship round 4

1	Stirling Moss/Jean Behra/			
	Harry Schell/Piero Taruffi	Maserati 300S	44	7h43m54.5
2	Juan Manuel Fangio/			
	Eugenio Castellotti	Ferrari 860 Monza	44	7h44m20.7
3	Phil Hill/Olivier Gendebien/			
	Alfonso de Portago	Ferrari 290MM	44	7h53m55.9
4	Wolfgang von Trips/			
	Umberto Maglioli	Porsche 550RS	44	8h01m45.9
5	Peter Collins/Tony Brooks	Aston Martin DB3S	43	
6	Hans Herrmann/			
	Richard von Frankenberg	Porsche 550RS	44*	8h06m10.2

*Each class leader completed the full 44-lap distance. Winner's average speed: 80.621 mph. Pole position: Fangio, 10m03.6 (Le Mans start). Fastest lap: Fangio, 10m05.3

SVERIGES GRAND PRIX

12 August 1956. Kristianstad. 153 laps of a 4.062-mile circuit = 621.486 miles. World Sports Car Championship round 5

1	Maurice Trintignant/			
	Phil Hill	Ferrari 290MM	153	6h33m47.7
2	Peter Collins/			
	Wolfgang von Trips	Ferrari 290MM	153	6h34m27.6
3	Alfonso de Portago/Mike Hawthorn/Duncan Hamilton/			
	Peter Collins	Ferrari 860 Monza	152	
4*	John Kvarnstrom/			
	Erik Lundgren	Ferrari 750S Monza	148	
5*	Allan Borgefors/Carl-Gunnar			
	Hammarlund	Ferrari 375MM	147	
6	Peter Whitehead/			
	Graham Whitehead	Jaguar D-type	145	

*GT cars ineligible for points, sixth-placed Jaguar awarded points for fourth. Winner's average speed: 94.692 mph. Pole position: Stirling Moss (Maserati 300S), 2m23.3 (Le Mans start). Fastest lap: Collins, 2m26.2

1956 FINAL CHAMPIONSHIP POSITIONS

Manufacturers		6 Mercedes-Benz	2
1 Ferrari	24 [36]*	*Best three results count	
2 Maserati	18		
3 Jaguar	7		
4 Aston Martin	5		
5 Porsche	4		

1957
World Sports Car Championship

1000 KM DE LA CIUDAD DE BUENOS AIRES

20 January 1957. Buenos Aires. 98 laps of a 6.350-mile circuit = 622.300 miles. World Sports Car Championship round 1

1	Masten Gregory/Eugenio Castellotti/			
	Luigi Musso	Ferrari 290MM	98	6h10m29.9
2	Jean Behra/Carlos Menditeguy/			
	Stirling Moss	Maserati 300S	98	6h11m53.4
3	Alfonso de Portago/Peter Collins/Eugenio Castellotti/			
	Wolfgang von Trips	Ferrari 290MM	98	6h12m59.6
4	Ninian Sanderson/			
	Roberto Mieres	Jaguar D-type	95	
5	Luigi Piotti/			
	Roberto Bonomi	Maserati 300S	91	
6	Alejandro de Tomaso/			
	Isabel Haskell	OSCA MT4	88	

Winner's average speed: 100.778 mph. Pole position: Juan Manuel Fangio (Maserati 450S), 3m36.1. Fastest lap: Moss, 3m36.0

12 HOURS OF SEBRING

23 March 1957. Sebring. 197 laps of a 5.200-mile circuit = 1024.400 miles. World Sports Car Championship round 2

1	Juan Manuel Fangio/			
	Jean Behra	Maserati 450S	197	12h00m3.374
2	Stirling Moss/			
	Harry Schell	Maserati 300S	195	
3	Mike Hawthorn/Ivor Bueb	Jaguar D-type	193	
4	Masten Gregory/			
	Lou Brero	Ferrari 290S	193	
5	Walt Hansgen/Russ Boss	Jaguar D-type	188	
6	Peter Collins/			
	Maurice Trintignant	Ferrari 315S	187	

Winner's average speed: 85.360 mph. Pole position: Fangio, 3m25.8 (Le Mans start). Fastest lap: Behra, 3m24.5

MILLE MIGLIA

11-12 May 1957. Brescia-Rome-Brescia. 992.332 miles. World Sports Car Championship round 3

1	Piero Taruffi	Ferrari 315S	10h27m47
2	Wolfgang von Trips	Ferrari 315S	10h30m48
3	Olivier Gendebien/		
	Jacques Washer	Ferrari 250GT	10h35m53
4	Giorgio Scarlatti	Maserati 300S	11h00m58
5	Umberto Maglioli	Porsche 550RS	11h14m07
6	Camillo Luglio/		
	Umberto Carli	Ferrari 250GT	11h26m58

Winner's average speed: 94.842 mph

ADAC 1000 KM-RENNEN

26 May 1957. Nurburgring. 44 laps of a 14.167-mile circuit = 623.348 miles. World Sports Car Championship round 4

1	Tony Brooks/			
	Noel Cunningham-Reid	Aston Martin DBR1	44	7h33m38.2
2	Peter Collins/			
	Olivier Gendebien	Ferrari 335S	44	7h37m51.9
3	Mike Hawthorn/			
	Maurice Trintignant	Ferrari 315S	44	7h39m27.2
4	Umberto Maglioli/			
	Edgar Barth	Porsche 550RS	44	7h47m17.2
5	Juan Manuel Fangio/Stirling Moss/Chico Godia-Sales/			
	Horace Gould	Maserati 300S	43	
6	Roy Salvadori/			
	Les Leston	Aston Martin DBR1	43	

Winner's average speed: 82.447 mph. Pole position: Fangio, 9m43.5 (Le Mans start). Fastest lap: Moss, 9m49.9

24 HEURES DU MANS

22-23 June 1957. Le Mans. 326 laps of an 8.365-mile circuit = 2726.990 miles. World Sports Car Championship round 5

1	Ivor Bueb/Ron Flockhart	Jaguar D-type	326	24 hours
2	Ninian Sanderson/			
	John Lawrence	Jaguar D-type	318	
3	Jean Lucas/"Mary"	Jaguar D-type	316	
4	Paul Frere/			
	Freddy Rousselle	Jaguar D-type	309	
5	Stuart Lewis-Evans/			
	Martino Severi	Ferrari 315S	299	
6	Duncan Hamilton/			
	Masten Gregory	Jaguar D-type	298	

Winner's average speed: 113.625 mph. Pole position: Juan Manuel Fangio (Maserati 450S), 3m58.1 (Le Mans start). Fastest lap: Mike Hawthorn (Ferrari 335S), 3m58.7

SVERIGES GRAND PRIX

11 August 1957. Kristianstad. 145 laps of a 4.062-mile circuit = 588.990 miles. World Sports Car Championship round 6

1 Jean Behra/Stirling Moss	Maserati 450S	145	6h01m01.1
2 Phil Hill/Peter Collins	Ferrari 335S	144	
3 Jo Bonnier/Giorgio Scarlatti/Harry Schell/			
Stirling Moss	Maserati 300S	138	
4 Mike Hawthorn/			
Luigi Musso	Ferrari 335S	134	
5 Alain de Chagny/			
Claude Dubois	Jaguar D-type	132	
6 Carl-Otto Bremer/			
Esko Keinanen	Ferrari 750S Monza	132	

Winner's average speed: 97.888 mph. Pole position: Behra, 2m22.5. Fastest lap: Behra, 2m20.9

GRAN PREMIO DE VENEZUELA

3 November 1957. Caracas. 101 laps of a 6.170-mile circuit = 623.170 miles. World Sports Car Championship round 7

1 Peter Collins/Phil Hill	Ferrari 335S	101	6h31m55.8
2 Luigi Musso/Mike Hawthorn	Ferrari 335S	100	
3 Wolfgang von Trips/			
Wolfgang Seidel	Ferrari 250TR	99	
4 Maurice Trintignant/			
Olivier Gendebien	Ferrari 250TR	97	
5 Fritz Huschke			
von Hanstein/Edgar Barth	Porsche 718 RSK	91	
6 Mauricio Marcotulli/			
Ettore Chimeri	Maserati 300S	91	

Winner's average speed: 95.400 mph. Pole position: Stirling Moss (Maserati 450S), 3m41.1. Fastest lap: Moss, 3m38.4

1957 FINAL CHAMPIONSHIP POSITIONS

Manufacturers		6 OSCA	1
1 Ferrari	30 (41)*	*Best four results count	
2 Maserati	25 (28)*		
3 Jaguar	17		
4 Aston Martin	8		
5 Porsche	7		

1958
World Sports Car Championship

1000 KM DE LA CIUDAD DE BUENOS AIRES

26 January 1958. Buenos Aires. 106 laps of a 5.888-mile circuit = 624.128 miles. World Sports Car Championship round 1

1 Peter Collins/Phil Hill	Ferrari 250TR	106	6h19m55.4
2 Wolfgang von Trips/Olivier			
Gendebien/Luigi Musso	Ferrari 250TR	106	6h23m08.0
3 Stirling Moss/Jean Behra	Porsche 718 RSK	106	6h23m17.8
4 Piero Drogo/			
Sergio Gonzalez	Ferrari 250TR	102	
5 Roberto Mieres/Edgar			
Barth/Antonio von Dory	Porsche 550RS	99	
6 Luciano Mantovani/			
Gino Munaron	Ferrari 500TR	98	

Winner's average speed: 98.566 mph. Pole position: P Hill, 3m27.5. Fastest lap: Collins, 3m25.9

12 HOURS OF SEBRING

22 March 1958. Sebring. 200 laps of a 5.200-mile circuit = 1040.000 miles. World Sports Car Championship round 2

1 Peter Collins/Phil Hill	Ferrari 250TR	200	12h01m22.6
2 Luigi Musso/			
Olivier Gendebien	Ferrari 250TR	199	
3 Harry Schell/			
Wolfgang Seidel	Porsche 718 RSK	193	

4 Sam Weiss/			
Dave Tallakson	Lotus 11-Climax	179	
5 Bruce Kessler/Paul O'Shea/			
David Cunningham	Ferrari 250GT	179	
6 Colin Chapman/			
Cliff Allison	Lotus 11-Climax	179	

Winner's average speed: 86.501 mph. Pole position: Mike Hawthorn (Ferrari 250TR), 3m21.0 (Le Mans start). Fastest lap: Stirling Moss (Aston Martin DBR1), 3m20.3

TARGA FLORIO

11 May 1958. Madonie (Piccolo). 14 laps of a 44.739-mile circuit = 626.346 miles. World Sports Car Championship round 3

1 Luigi Musso/			
Olivier Gendebien	Ferrari 250TR	14	10h37m58.1
2 Jean Behra/			
Giorgio Scarlatti	Porsche 718 RSK	14	10h43m37.9
3 Mike Hawthorn/			
Wolfgang von Trips	Ferrari 250TR	14	10h44m29.3
4 Peter Collins/Phil Hill	Ferrari 250TR	14	11h10m01.4
5 Giulio Cabianca/			
Franco Bordoni	OSCA MT4	14	11h25m35.7
6 Fritz Huschke von			
Hanstein/Antonio Pucci	Porsche 356A Carrera	14	11h34m04.6

Winner's average speed: 58.907 mph. Fastest lap: Stirling Moss (Aston Martin DBR1), 42m17.5

ADAC 1000 KM-RENNEN

1 June 1958. Nurburgring. 44 laps of a 14.167-mile circuit = 623.348 miles. World Sports Car Championship round 4

1 Stirling Moss/			
Jack Brabham	Aston Martin DBR1	44	7h23m33
2 Mike Hawthorn/			
Peter Collins	Ferrari 250TR	44	7h27m17
3 Wolfgang von Trips/			
Olivier Gendebien	Ferrari 250TR	44	7h33m15
4 Luigi Musso/Phil Hill	Ferrari 250TR	43	
5 Wolfgang Seidel/Gino			
Munaron/Luigi Musso	Ferrari 250TR	42	
6 Richard von Frankenberg/			
Carel Godin de Beaufort/			
Edgar Barth	Porsche 550RS	44*	

*Each class leader completed the full 44-lap distance. Winner's average speed: 84.322 mph. Pole position: Hawthorn, 9m43.1. Fastest lap: Moss, 9m43.0

24 HEURES DU MANS

21-22 June 1958. Le Mans. 304 laps of an 8.365-mile circuit = 2542.960 miles. World Sports Car Championship round 5

1 Olivier Gendebien/			
Phil Hill	Ferrari 250TR	304	24 hours
2 Peter Whitehead/			
Graham Whitehead	Aston Martin DB3S	292	
3 Jean Behra/			
Hans Herrmann	Porsche 718 RSK	290	
4 Edgar Barth/Paul Frere	Porsche 718 RSK	289	
5 Carel Godin de Beaufort/			
Herbert Linge	Porsche 550RS	287	
6 "Beurlys"/			
Alain de Chagny	Ferrari 250TR	278	

Winner's average speed: 105.957 mph. Pole position: Stirling Moss (Aston Martin DBR1), 4m07.3 (Le Mans start). Fastest lap: Mike Hawthorn (Ferrari 250TR), 4m08.0

RAC TOURIST TROPHY

13 September 1958. Goodwood. 148 laps of a 2.400-mile circuit = 355.200 miles. Half points awarded due to short race distance. World Sports Car Championship round 6

1 Stirling Moss/Tony Brooks	Aston Martin DBR1	148	4h01m17.0
2 Roy Salvadori/ Jack Brabham	Aston Martin DBR1	148	4h01m17.4
3 Carroll Shelby/ Stuart Lewis-Evans	Aston Martin DBR1	148	4h01m17.8
4 Jean Behra/Edgar Barth	Porsche 718 RSK	144	
5 Masten Gregory/ Innes Ireland	Jaguar D-type	143	
6 Peter Blond/ Duncan Hamilton	Jaguar D-type	142	

Winner's average speed: 88.328 mph. Pole position: Moss, 1m32.0. Fastest lap: Moss, 1m32.6

1958 FINAL CHAMPIONSHIP POSITIONS

Manufacturers				
1 Ferrari	32 (38)*	4 Lotus-Climax	3
2= Aston Martin	18	5 OSCA	2
Porsche	18 (19)*	*Best four results count	

1959
World Sports Car Championship

12 HOURS OF SEBRING

21 March 1959. Sebring. 188 laps of a 5.200-mile circuit = 977.600 miles. World Sports Car Championship round 1

1 Dan Gurney/Chuck Daigh/Phil Hill/ Olivier Gendebien	Ferrari 250TR	188	12h02m31.8
2 Jean Behra/Cliff Allison	Ferrari 250TR	187	
3 Jo Bonnier/ Wolfgang von Trips	Porsche 718 RSK	184	
4 Bob Holbert/Don Sesslar	Porsche 718 RSK	182	
5 John Fitch/Edgar Barth	Porsche 718 RSK	181	
6 Ed Martin/ Lance Reventlow	Ferrari 250TR	174	

Winner's average speed: 81.181 mph. Pole position: Behra, 3m24.0 (Le Mans start). Fastest lap: Behra, 3m21.6

TARGA FLORIO

24 May 1959. Madonie (Piccolo). 14 laps of a 44.739-mile circuit = 626.346 miles. World Sports Car Championship round 2

1 Edgar Barth/ Wolfgang Seidel	Porsche 718 RSK	14	11h02m21.8
2 Herbert Linge/Eberhard Mahle/ Paul-Ernst Strahle	Porsche 550RS	14	11h24m20.2
3 Antonio Pucci/Fritz Huschke von Hanstein	Porsche 356A Carrera	14	11h31m44.0
4 Paul-Ernst Strahle/Herbert Linge/ Eberhard Mahle	Porsche 356A Carrera	14	11h36m00.0
5 Mennato Boffa/ Piero Drogo	Maserati A6G	14	11h41m20.0
6 Colin Davis/Mario Sannino/ Dario Sepe	Alfa Romeo Giulietta SV	14	12h04m09.0

Winner's average speed: 56.737 mph. Pole position: Umberto Maglioli (Porsche 718 RSK), 45m51.0. Fastest lap: Jo Bonnier (Porsche 718 RSK), 43m11.6

ADAC 1000 KM-RENNEN

7 June 1959. Nurburgring. 44 laps of a 14.167-mile circuit = 623.348 miles. World Sports Car Championship round 3

1 Stirling Moss/ Jack Fairman	Aston Martin DBR1	44	7h33m18
2 Olivier Gendebien/ Phil Hill	Ferrari 250TR	44	7h33m59
3 Tony Brooks/Jean Behra	Ferrari 250TR	44	7h36m45
4 Umberto Maglioli/ Hans Herrmann	Porsche 718 RSK	44	7h40m57
5 Dan Gurney/Cliff Allison	Ferrari 250TR	43	
6 Heini Walter/ Arthur Heuberger	Porsche 718 RSK	42	

Winner's average speed: 82.508 mph. Pole position: Behra, 9m37.4. Fastest lap: Moss, 9m32.0

24 HEURES DU MANS

20-21 June 1959. Le Mans. 322 laps of an 8.365-mile circuit = 2693.530 miles. World Sports Car Championship round 4

1 Roy Salvadori/ Carroll Shelby	Aston Martin DBR1	322	24 hours
2 Maurice Trintignant/ Paul Frere	Aston Martin DBR1	322	
3 "Beurlys"/"Elde"	Ferrari 250GT	297	
4 Andre Pilette/ Georges Arents	Ferrari 250GT	296	
5 Bob Grossman/ Fernand Tavano	Ferrari 250GT California	294	
6 Lino Fayen/ Gino Munaron	Ferrari 250GT	293	

Winner's average speed: 112.230 mph. Pole position: Dan Gurney (Ferrari 250TR), 4m03.3 (Le Mans start). Fastest lap: Jean Behra (Ferrari 250TR), 4m00.9

RAC TOURIST TROPHY

5 September 1959. Goodwood. 224 laps of a 2.400-mile circuit = 537.600 miles. World Sports Car Championship round 5

1 Carroll Shelby/Jack Fairman/ Stirling Moss	Aston Martin DBR1	224	6h00m46.8
2 Jo Bonnier/ Wolfgang von Trips	Porsche 718 RSK	223	
3 Tony Brooks/Phil Hill/Cliff Allison/ Olivier Gendebien	Ferrari 250TR	223	
4 Maurice Trintignant/ Paul Frere	Aston Martin DBR1	221	
5 Dan Gurney/Tony Brooks	Ferrari 250TR	220	
6 Peter Ashdown/ Alan Ross	Lola Mk1-Climax	210	

Winner's average speed: 89.406 mph. Pole position: Moss, 1m31.2. Fastest lap: Brooks, 1m31.8

1959 FINAL CHAMPIONSHIP POSITIONS

Manufacturers				
1 Aston Martin	24	4 Maserati	2
2= Ferrari	18 (22)*	5= Alfa Romeo	1
Porsche	18 (21)*	Lola-Climax	1
		*Best three results count	

1960
World Sports Car Championship

1000 KM DE LA CIUDAD DE BUENOS AIRES

31 January 1960. Buenos Aires. 106 laps of a 5.888-mile circuit = 624.128 miles. World Sports Car Championship round 1

1 Phil Hill/Cliff Allison	Ferrari 250TR	106	6h17m12.1
2 Wolfgang von Trips/ Richie Ginther	Ferrari 250TR	105	
3 Jo Bonnier/Graham Hill	Porsche 718 RSK	101	
4 Celso Lara-Barberis/ Christian Bino Heins	Maserati 300S	101	
5 Pedro von Dory/Antonio von Dory/ Juan Manuel Bordeu	Porsche 718 RSK	100	

6 Christian Goethals/
Kurt Delfosse   Porsche 718 RSK   100
Winner's average speed: 99.278 mph. Pole position: P Hill, 3m23.1.
Fastest lap: Dan Gurney (Maserati Tipo 61), 3m22.4

12 HOURS OF SEBRING

26 March 1960. Sebring. 196 laps of a 5.200-mile circuit = 1019.200 miles. World Sports Car Championship round 2

1 Olivier Gendebien/			
Hans Herrmann	Porsche 718 RS60	196	12h00m03.03
2 Bob Holbert/			
Roy Scheckter	Porsche 718 RS60	187	
3 Jack Nethercutt/			
Pete Lovely	Ferrari 250TR	186	
4 Ed Hugus/Augie Pabst	Ferrari 250TR	185	
5 George Reed/			
Alan Connell jr	Ferrari 250GT California	185	
6 William Sturgis/			
Fritz d'Orey	Ferrari 250GT	183	

Winner's average speed: 84.927 mph. Pole position: Masten Gregory (Maserati Tipo 61), 3m19.0 (Le Mans start). Fastest lap: Chuck Daigh (Ferrari 250TR), 3m18.14

TARGA FLORIO

8 May 1960. Madonie (Piccolo). 10 laps of a 44.739-mile circuit = 447.390 miles. World Sports Car Championship round 3

1 Jo Bonnier/			
Hans Herrmann	Porsche 718 RS60	10	7h33m08.2
2 Wolfgang von Trips/			
Phil Hill	Ferrari Dino 246S	10	7h39m11.0
3 Olivier Gendebien/			
Hans Herrmann	Porsche 718 RS60	10	7h41m46.0
4 Willy Mairesse/Ludovico Scarfiotti/			
Giulio Cabianca	Ferrari Dino 246S	10	7h44m49.0
5 Edgar Barth/Graham Hill	Porsche 718 RS60	10	7h59m11.6
6 Herbert Linge/Paul-Ernst Strahle/			
Dieter Lissmann	Porsche 356B Carrera GTL	10	8h10m06.2

Winner's average speed: 59.239 mph. Pole position: Bonnier, 42m26.0.
Fastest lap: Bonnier, 42m46.0

ADAC 1000 KM-RENNEN

22 May 1960. Nurburgring. 44 laps of a 14.167-mile circuit = 623.348 miles. World Sports Car Championship round 4

1 Stirling Moss/Dan Gurney	Maserati Tipo 61	44	7h31m40.5
2 Jo Bonnier/			
Olivier Gendebien	Porsche 718 RS60	44	7h34m32.9
3 Cliff Allison/Willy Mairesse/			
Phil Hill	Ferrari 250TR	44	7h35m44.1
4 Hans Herrmann/			
Maurice Trintignant	Porsche 718 RS60	44	7h37m57.7
5 Gino Munaron/			
Masten Gregory	Maserati Tipo 61	43	
6 Heini Walter/			
Thomas Losinger	Porsche 718 RSK	42	

Winner's average speed: 82.805 mph. Pole position: Bonnier, 9m43.6.
Fastest lap: Moss, 9m37.0

24 HEURES DU MANS

25-26 June 1960. Le Mans. 313 laps of an 8.365-mile circuit = 2618.245 miles. World Sports Car Championship round 5

1 Olivier Gendebien/			
Paul Frere	Ferrari 250TR	313	24 hours
2 Ricardo Rodriguez/			
Andre Pilette	Ferrari 250TR	309	
3 Roy Salvadori/Jim Clark	Aston Martin DBR1	305	
4 Fernand Tavano/			
Pierre Dumay	Ferrari 250GT	301	

5 Georges Arents/
Alan Connell jr   Ferrari 250GT   299
6 "Elde"/Pierre Noblet   Ferrari 250GT   299
Winner's average speed: 109.094 mph. Pole position: Dan Gurney (Jaguar E2A), 4m04.5 (Le Mans start). Fastest lap: Masten Gregory (Maserati Tipo 61), 4m04.0

1960 FINAL CHAMPIONSHIP POSITIONS

Manufacturers		4 Aston Martin	4
1 Ferrari	22 (30)*	*Best three results count. Ferrari	
2 Porsche	22 (26)*	won championship due to their	
3 Maserati	11	greater number of total points	

1961

World Sports Car Championship

12 HOURS OF SEBRING

25 March 1961. Sebring. 208 laps of a 5.200-mile circuit = 1081.600 miles. World Sports Car Championship round 1

1 Phil Hill/			
Olivier Gendebien	Ferrari 250TR	208	12h02m11
2 Willy Mairesse/Giancarlo Baghetti/Richie Ginther/			
Wolfgang von Trips	Ferrari 250TR	208	
3 Pedro Rodriguez/			
Ricardo Rodriguez	Ferrari 250TR	207	
4 Hap Sharp/Ronnie Hissom	Ferrari 250TR	203	
5 Bob Holbert/Roger Penske	Porsche 718 RS61	199	
6 Jim Hall/			
George Constantine	Ferrari Dino 246S	199	

Winner's average speed: 89.861 mph. Pole position: von Trips (Ferrari Dino 246SP), 3m15.7 (Le Mans start). Fastest lap: Stirling Moss (Maserati Tipo 61), 3m13.2

TARGA FLORIO

30 April 1961. Madonie (Piccolo). 10 laps of a 44.739-mile circuit = 447.390 miles. World Sports Car Championship round 2

1 Wolfgang von Trips/			
Olivier Gendebien	Ferrari Dino 246SP	10	6h57m39.2
2 Jo Bonnier/Dan Gurney	Porsche 718 RS61	10	7h02m03.5
3 Hans Herrmann/			
Edgar Barth	Porsche 718 RS61	10	7h14m14.0
4 Nino Vaccarella/			
Maurice Trintignant	Maserati Tipo 63	10	7h28m49.6
5 Umberto Maglioli/			
Giorgio Scarlatti	Maserati Tipo 63	10	7h40m04.2
6 Antonio Pucci/			
Paul-Ernst Strahle	Porsche 356B Carrera GTL	10	7h48m25.8

Winner's average speed: 64.272 mph. Pole position: Bonnier, 42m40.0.
Fastest lap: von Trips, 40m03.2

ADAC 1000 KM-RENNEN

28 May 1961. Nurburgring. 44 laps of a 14.167-mile circuit = 623.348 miles. World Sports Car Championship round 3

1 Masten Gregory/			
Lucky Casner	Maserati Tipo 61	44	7h51m39.2
2 Pedro Rodriguez/			
Ricardo Rodriguez	Ferrari 250TR	43	
3 Wolfgang von Trips/Olivier Gendebien/			
Richie Ginther	Ferrari Dino 246SP	43	
4 Carlo Abate/Colin Davis	Ferrari 250GT	43	
5 Willy Mairesse/			
Giancarlo Baghetti	Ferrari 250GT	43	
6 Fritz Hahnl/Helmut Zick	Porsche 356B Carrera GTL	43	

Winner's average speed: 79.297 mph. Pole position: von Trips, 9m33.7.
Fastest lap: Phil Hill (Ferrari Dino 246SP), 9m15.8

24 HEURES DU MANS

10-11 June 1961. Le Mans. 332 laps of an 8.365-mile circuit = 2777.180 miles. World Sports Car Championship round 4

1 Olivier Gendebien/			
Phil Hill	Ferrari 250TR	332	24 hours
2 Willy Mairesse/			
Michael Parkes	Ferrari 250TR	329	
3 Pierre Noblet/			
Jean Guichet	Ferrari 250GT	316	
4 Augie Pabst/			
Richard Thompson	Maserati Tipo 63	310	
5 Masten Gregory/			
Bob Holbert	Porsche 718 RS61	308	
6 Bob Grossman/			
Andre Pilette	Ferrari 250GT	308	

Winner's average speed: 115.716 mph. Pole position: Richie Ginther (Ferrari Dino 246SP), 4m02.8 (Le Mans start). Fastest lap: Ricardo Rodriguez (Ferrari 250TR), 3m59.9

4 ORE DI PESCARA

15 August 1961. Pescara. 22 laps of a 16.032-mile circuit = 352.704 miles. Half points awarded due to short race distance. World Sports Car Championship round 5

1 Lorenzo Bandini/			
Giorgio Scarlatti	Ferrari 250TR	22	4 hours
2 Edgar Barth/			
Karl Orthuber	Porsche 718 RS61	21	
3 Mennato Boffa	Maserati Tipo 60	21	
4 Georges Arents/			
George Hamill	Ferrari 250TR	21	
5 Colin Davis	OSCA 1.6S	21	
6 Sergio Bettoja/"Kim"	Ferrari 250GT	21	

Winner's average speed: 88.176 mph. Pole position: Giancarlo Baghetti (Ferrari Dino 246SP), 9m49.4 (but cars were started in number order). Fastest lap: Richie Ginther (Ferrari Dino 246SP), 9m55.5

1961 FINAL CHAMPIONSHIP POSITIONS

Manufacturers		3 Porsche	11 (14)*
1 Ferrari	24 (34)*	4 OSCA	1
2 Maserati	14 (16)*	*Best three results count	

1962
Speed World Challenge

12 HOURS OF SEBRING

24 March 1962. Sebring. 206 laps of a 5.200-mile circuit = 1071.200 miles. Speed World Challenge round 1

1 Jo Bonnier/			
Lucien Bianchi	Ferrari 250TR	206	12h01m59.4
2 Phil Hill/			
Olivier Gendebien	Ferrari 250GTO	196	
3 Bruce Jennings/Frank Rand/			
Bill Wuesthoff	Porsche 718 RS60	195	
4 George Hamill/			
Fabrizio Serena	Ferrari 250GT	190	
5 Bruce McLaren/			
Roger Penske	Cooper T61-Maserati	190	
6 Hap Sharp/			
Ronnie Hissom/Jim Hall	Chaparral 1-Chevrolet	189	

Winner's average speed: 89.021 mph. Pole position: n/a, Le Mans start. Fastest lap: Pedro Rodriguez (Ferrari Dino 246SP), 3m12.4

TARGA FLORIO

6 May 1962. Madonie (Piccolo). 10 laps of a 44.739-mile circuit = 447.390 miles. Speed World Challenge round 2

1 Willy Mairesse/Ricardo Rodriguez/			
Olivier Gendebien	Ferrari Dino 246SP	10	7h02m56.6
2 Giancarlo Baghetti/			
Lorenzo Bandini	Ferrari Dino 196SP	10	7h14m24.0
3 Jo Bonnier/			
Nino Vaccarella	Porsche 718 GTR	10	7h17m20.0
4 Giorgio Scarlatti/			
Pietro Ferraro	Ferrari 250GTO	10	7h22m08.1
5 Roger Delageneste/			
Jean Rolland	Ferrari 250GTO	10	7h44m33.0
6 Hans Herrmann/			
Herbert Linge	Porsche 356B Carrera GTL	10	7h45m26.0

Winner's average speed: 63.468 mph. Pole position: Bonnier (Porsche 718 WRS), 42m06.2. Fastest lap: Mairesse, 40m00.3

ADAC 1000 KM-RENNEN

27 May 1962. Nurburgring. 44 laps of a 14.167-mile circuit = 623.348 miles. Speed World Challenge round 3

1 Olivier Gendebien/			
Phil Hill	Ferrari Dino 246SP	44	7h33m27.7
2 Willy Mairesse/			
Michael Parkes	Ferrari 250GTO	44	7h35m49.2
3 Graham Hill/			
Hans Herrmann	Porsche 718 WRS	44	7h42m24.6
4 Bruce McLaren/			
Tony Maggs	Aston Martin DBR1	42	
5 Peter Nocker/			
Wolfgang Seidel	Ferrari 250GT	41	
6 Edgar Barth/			
Herbert Linge	Porsche 356B Carrera GTL	41	

Winner's average speed: 82.479 mph. Pole position: P Hill, 9m25.5. Fastest lap: P Hill, 9m31.9

24 HEURES DU MANS

23-24 June 1962. Le Mans. 330 laps of an 8.365-mile circuit = 2760.450 miles. Speed World Challenge round 4

1 Olivier Gendebien/			
Phil Hill	Ferrari 330LM	330	24 hours
2 Jean Guichet/			
Pierre Noblet	Ferrari 250GTO	325	
3 "Elde"/"Beurlys"	Ferrari 250GTO	312	
4 Briggs Cunningham/			
Roy Salvadori	Jaguar E-type	309	
5 Peter Lumsden/			
Peter Sargent	Jaguar E-type	309	
6 Bob Grossman/			
"Fireball" Roberts	Ferrari 250GTO	296	

Winner's average speed: 115.019 mph. Pole position: P Hill, 3m55.1 (Le Mans start). Fastest lap: P Hill, 3m57.3

1962 FINAL CHAMPIONSHIP POSITIONS

Manufacturers		(Only manufacturers who
1 Ferrari	39	competed in every round were
2 Porsche	35	eligible)
3 Alfa Romeo	25	

1963
Speed and Endurance World Challenge

12 HOURS OF SEBRING

23 March 1963. Sebring. 209 laps of a 5.200-mile circuit = 1086.800 miles. Speed and Endurance World Challenge round 1

1 John Surtees/			
Ludovico Scarfiotti	Ferrari 250P	209	12h01m15.6
2 Willy Mairesse/Nino Vaccarella/			
Lorenzo Bandini	Ferrari 250P	208	
3 Pedro Rodriguez/			
Graham Hill	Ferrari 330LM	207	
4 Roger Penske/			
Augie Pabst	Ferrari 250GTO	203	
5 Carlo Abate/			
Juan Manuel Bordeu	Ferrari 250GTO	197	
6 Innes Ireland/			
Richie Ginther	Ferrari 250GTO	196	

Winner's average speed: 90.408 mph. Pole position: none, Le Mans start.
Fastest lap: Surtees, 3m11.4

TARGA FLORIO

5 May 1963. Madonie (Piccolo). 10 laps of a 44.739-mile circuit = 447.390 miles. Speed and Endurance World Challenge round 2

1 Jo Bonnier/Carlo Abate	Porsche 718 GTR	10	6h55m45.2
2 Willy Mairesse/Ludovico Scarfiotti/			
Lorenzo Bandini	Ferrari Dino 196SP	10	6h55m57.0
3 Edgar Barth/			
Herbert Linge	Porsche 356B GT/2	10	7h25m19.4
4 Maurizio Grana/			
Gianni Bulgari	Ferrari 250GTO	10	7h26m31.4
5 Antonio Pucci/			
Paul-Ernst Strahle	Porsche 356B Carrera 2	10	7h33m37.2
6 Juan Manuel Bordeu/			
Giorgio Scarlatti	Ferrari 250GTO	10	7h40m16.2

Winner's average speed: 64.566 mph. Pole position: Umberto Maglioli (Porsche 718 WRS), 42m48.0. Fastest lap: Michael Parkes (Ferrari 250P), 40m04.1

ADAC 1000 KM-RENNEN

19 May 1963. Nurburgring. 44 laps of a 14.167-mile circuit = 623.348 miles. Speed and Endurance World Challenge round 3

1 John Surtees/			
Willy Mairesse	Ferrari 250P	44	7h32m18.4
2 Jean Guichet/			
Pierre Noblet	Ferrari 250GTO	44	7h40m03.0
3 Carlo Abate/			
Umberto Maglioli	Ferrari 250TR	43	
4 Edgar Barth/Herbert Linge/Ben Pon/			
Hans-Joachim Walter	Porsche 356B GT/2	43	
5 "Elde"/Gerald Langlois			
van Ophem	Ferrari 250GT	41	
6 David Piper/Ed Cantrell	Ferrari 250GTO	41	

Winner's average speed: 82.689 mph. Pole position: Surtees, 9m13.1.
Fastest lap: Surtees, 9m16.0

24 HEURES DU MANS

15-16 June 1963. Le Mans. 338 laps of an 8.365-mile circuit = 2827.370 miles. Speed and Endurance World Challenge round 4

1 Ludovico Scarfiotti/			
Lorenzo Bandini	Ferrari 250P	338	24 hours
2 "Beurlys"/Gerald Langlois			
van Ophem	Ferrari 250GTO	322	
3 Michael Parkes/			
Umberto Maglioli	Ferrari 250P	322	
4 "Elde"/Pierre Dumay	Ferrari 250GTO	321	
5 Jack Sears/Mike Salmon	Ferrari 330LMB	313	
6 Masten Gregory/			
David Piper	Ferrari 250GTO	311	

Winner's average speed: 117.807 mph. Pole position: P Rodriguez, 3m50.9 (Le Mans start). Fastest lap: Surtees (Ferrari 250P), 3m53.3

1963 FINAL CHAMPIONSHIP POSITIONS

Manufacturers		4 Alfa Romeo	10
1 Ferrari	39	(Only manufacturers who	
2 Porsche	35	competed in every round were	
3 Jaguar	22	eligible)	

1964

International Championship of Makes

DAYTONA CONTINENTAL

16 February 1964. Daytona. 327 laps of a 3.810-mile circuit = 1245.870 miles. International Championship of Makes round 1

1 Phil Hill/Pedro Rodriguez	Ferrari 250GTO	327	12h40m25.8
2 David Piper/			
Lucien Bianchi	Ferrari 250GTO	323	
3 Bob Grossman/			
Walt Hansgen	Ferrari 250GTO	319	
4 Dan Gurney/Bob Johnson	AC Cobra-Ford	311	
5 Ulf Norinder/			
John Cannon	Ferrari 250GTO	311	
6 Edgar Barth/Herbert Linge/			
Jo Bonnier	Porsche 356 Carrera 2	311	

Winner's average speed: 98.303 mph. Pole position: Bob Holbert/Dave MacDonald (AC Cobra Daytona-Ford), 2m08.8. Fastest lap: MacDonald, 2m08.2

12 HOURS OF SEBRING

21 March 1964. Sebring. 214 laps of a 5.200-mile circuit = 1112.800 miles. International Championship of Makes round 2

1 Michael Parkes/			
Umberto Maglioli	Ferrari 275P	214	12h00m04.8
2 Ludovico Scarfiotti/			
Nino Vaccarella	Ferrari 275P	213	
3 John Surtees/			
Lorenzo Bandini	Ferrari 330P	212	
4 Bob Holbert/			
Dave MacDonald	AC Cobra Daytona-Ford	209	
5 Lew Spencer/			
Bob Bondurant	AC Cobra-Ford	205	
6 Jo Schlesser/Phil Hill	AC Cobra-Ford	203	

Winner's average speed: 92.723 mph. Pole position: Surtees, 3m04.2.
Fastest lap: Surtees, 3m06.2

TARGA FLORIO

26 April 1964. Madonie (Piccolo). 10 laps of a 44.739-mile circuit = 447.390 miles. International Championship of Makes round 3

1 Antonio Pucci/Colin Davis	Porsche 904GTS	10	7h10m53.6
2 Gianni Balzarini/			
Herbert Linge	Porsche 904GTS	10	7h23m15.3
3 Roberto Bussinello/			
Nino Todaro	Alfa Romeo Giulia TZ	10	7h27m07.0
4 "Kim"/Alfonso Thiele	Alfa Romeo Giulia TZ	10	7h27m38.2
5 Claudio Ferlaino/			
Luigi Taramazzo	Ferrari 250GTO	10	7h28m38.2
6 Edgar Barth/			
Umberto Maglioli	Porsche 904/8	10	7h29m16.4

Winner's average speed: 62.297 mph. Pole position: Jo Bonnier (Porsche 718 RS Spyder), 41m14.0. Fastest lap: Davis, 41m10.8

GRAND PRIX DE SPA-FRANCORCHAMPS

17 May 1964. Spa-Francorchamps. 36 laps of an 8.761-mile circuit = 315.396 miles. International Championship of Makes round 4

1 Michael Parkes	Ferrari 250GTO	36	2h32m05.2
2 Jean Guichet	Ferrari 250GTO	36	
3 Lorenzo Bandini	Ferrari 250GTO	36	

4 David Piper	Ferrari 250GTO	36	
5 Edgar Barth	Porsche 904GTS	35	
6 Gerald Langlois			
van Ophem	Ferrari 250GTO	35	

Winner's average speed: 124.427 mph. Pole position: Parkes, 4m09.0.
Fastest lap: Phil Hill (AC Cobra Daytona-Ford), 4m04.5

ADAC 1000 KM-RENNEN

31 May 1964. Nurburgring. 44 laps of a 14.167-mile circuit = 623.348
miles. International Championship of Makes round 5

1 Ludovico Scarfiotti/			
Nino Vaccarella	Ferrari 275P	44	7h08m27
2 Michael Parkes/			
Jean Guichet	Ferrari 250GTO	43	
3 Ben Pon/Gerhard Koch	Porsche 904GTS	43	
4 Lucien Bianchi/Gerald Langlois			
van Ophem	Ferrari 250GTO	43	
5 Jo Bonnier/			
Richie Ginther	Porsche 904/8	42	
6 Herbert Muller/			
Andre Knorr	Porsche 904GTS	42	

Winner's average speed: 87.293 mph. Pole position: John Surtees (Ferrari
275P), 8m57.9. Fastest lap: Surtees, 9m09.0

24 HEURES DU MANS

21-22 June 1964. Le Mans. 348 laps of an 8.365-mile circuit = 2911.020
miles. International Championship of Makes round 6

1 Jean Guichet/			
Nino Vaccarella	Ferrari 275P	348	24 hours
2 Jo Bonnier/Graham Hill	Ferrari 330P	343	
3 John Surtees/			
Lorenzo Bandini	Ferrari 330P	323	
4 Dan Gurney/	AC Cobra		
Bob Bondurant	Daytona-Ford	333	
5 Lucien Bianchi/"Beurlys"	Ferrari 250GTO	332	
6 Innes Ireland/			
Tony Maggs	Ferrari 250GTO	327	

Winner's average speed: 121.293 mph. Pole position: Surtees, 3m42.0 (Le
Mans start). Fastest lap: Phil Hill (Ford GT40), 3m49.2

12 HEURES DE REIMS

5 July 1964. Reims. 293 laps of a 5.187-mile circuit = 1519.791 miles.
International Championship of Makes round 7

1 Graham Hill/Jo Bonnier	Ferrari 250LM	293	12 hours
2 John Surtees/			
Lorenzo Bandini	Ferrari 250LM	277	
3 Michael Parkes/			
Ludovico Scarfiotti	Ferrari 250GTO	253	
4 David Piper/Tony Maggs	Ferrari 250GTO	243	
5 Nasif Estefano/			
Andrea Vianini	Porsche 904GTS	242	
6 Gerhard Koch/			
Gerhard Mitter	Porsche 904GTS	240	

Winner's average speed: 126.649 mph. Pole position: Surtees, 2m19.2.
Fastest lap: G Hill, 2m19.2

TOURIST TROPHY

29 August 1964. Goodwood. 130 laps of a 2.400-mile circuit = 312.000
miles. International Championship of Makes round 8

1 Graham Hill	Ferrari 330P	130	3h12m43.6
2 David Piper	Ferrari 250LM	129	
3 Dan Gurney	AC Cobra		
	Daytona-Ford	129	
4 Jack Sears	AC Cobra-Ford	127	
5 Bob Olthoff	AC Cobra-Ford	126	
6 Innes Ireland	Ferrari 250GTO	125	

Winner's average speed: 97.132 mph. Pole position: Bruce McLaren
(Cooper T61-Oldsmobile), 1m23.2. Fastest lap: McLaren, 1m23.8

1000 KM DE PARIS

11 October 1964. Montlhery. 129 laps of a 4.837-mile circuit = 623.973
miles. International Championship of Makes round 9

1 Graham Hill/Jo Bonnier	Ferrari 330P	129	6h32m53.1
2 Pedro Rodriguez/			
Jo Schlesser	Ferrari 250GTO	127	
3 Edgar Barth/Colin Davis	Porsche 904/8	126	
4 Tony Maggs/David Piper	Ferrari 250GTO	126	
5 Lucien Bianchi/Gerald Langlois			
van Ophem	Ferrari 250GTO	125	
6 Rob Slotemaker/			
David van Lennep	Porsche 904GTS	124	

Winner's average speed: 95.291 mph. Pole position: G Hill, 2m43.6.
Fastest lap: Jackie Stewart (Ferrari 250GTO), 2m45.1

1964 FINAL CHAMPIONSHIP POSITIONS

Manufacturers		4 Alfa Romeo	4
1 Ferrari	54 (74)*	*Best six results count	
2 Porsche	22		
3 AC Cobra-Ford	13		

1965

International Championship of Makes

DAYTONA CONTINENTAL

28 February 1965. Daytona. 327 laps of a 3.810-mile circuit = 1245.870
miles. International Championship of Makes round 1

1 Ken Miles/Lloyd Ruby	Ford GT40	327	12h27m09.0
2 Jo Schlesser/Bob Johnson/			
Harold Keck	AC Cobra Daytona-Ford	322	
3 Richie Ginther/			
Bob Bondurant	Ford GT40	319	
4 Rick Muther/			
John Timanus	AC Cobra Daytona-Ford	318	
5 Charles Kolb/			
Roger Heftler	Porsche 904GTS	313	
6 Ed Leslie/Allen Grant	AC Cobra Daytona-Ford	312	

Winner's average speed: 100.050 mph. Pole position: John Surtees
(Ferrari 330P2), 2m00.6. Fastest lap: Walt Hansgen (Ferrari 330P), 2m01.8

12 HOURS OF SEBRING

27 March 1965. Sebring. 196 laps of a 5.200-mile circuit = 1019.200
miles. International Championship of Makes round 2

1 Jim Hall/Hap Sharp	Chaparral 2A-Chevrolet*	196	12h01m47.0
2 Bruce McLaren/			
Ken Miles	Ford GT40	192	
3 David Piper/Tony Maggs	Ferrari 250LM	190	
4 Jo Schlesser/			
Bob Bondurant	AC Cobra Daytona-Ford	187	
5 Lake Underwood/			
Gunther Klass	Porsche 904GTS	185	
6 Ben Pon/Joe Buzzetta	Porsche 904GTS	185	

*Sports-racing car, ineligible for points. Winner's average speed: 84.723
mph. Pole position: Hall, 2m57.6. Fastest lap: Hall, 2m59.3

1000 KM DI MONZA/TROFEO FILIPPO CARACCIOLO

25 April 1965. Monza. 100 laps of a 6.214-mile circuit = 621.370 miles.
International Championship of Makes round 3

1 Michael Parkes/			
Jean Guichet	Ferrari 275P2	100	4h56m08.0
2 John Surtees/			
Ludovico Scarfiotti	Ferrari 330P2	100	4h57m59.9
3 Bruce McLaren/			
Ken Miles	Ford GT40	96	
4 Ben Pon/Rob Slotemaker	Porsche 904GTS	92	

5 Pierre Noblet/
Mario Casoni ... Iso Grifo A3C-Chevrolet ... 92
6 Innes Ireland/
Mike Salmon ... Ferrari 250LM ... 91

Winner's average speed: 125.897 mph. Pole position: Parkes, 2m46.9. Fastest lap: Surtees, 2m47.2

TOURIST TROPHY

1 May 1965. Oulton Park. 138 laps of a 2.761-mile circuit = 381.018 miles. Aggregate of two 2-hour heats. International Championship of Makes round 4

1 Denny Hulme	Brabham BT8-Climax*	138	4h03m01.400
2 David Hobbs	Lola T70-Ford*	137	
3 David Piper	Ferrari 250LM*	133	
4 John Whitmore	AC Cobra-Ford	130	
5 Peter Sutcliffe	Ferrari 250LM	130	
6 Allen Grant	AC Cobra-Ford	128	

*Sports-Racing class, ineligible for points. Winner's average speed: 94.069 mph. Pole position: John Surtees (Lola T70-Chevrolet), 1m36.6. Fastest lap: Bruce McLaren (McLaren/Elva M1A-Oldsmobile), 1m39.0

TARGA FLORIO

9 May 1965. Madonie (Piccolo). 10 laps of a 44.739-mile circuit = 447.390 miles. International Championship of Makes round 5

1 Nino Vaccarella/			
Lorenzo Bandini	Ferrari 275P2	10	7h01m12.4
2 Colin Davis/			
Gerhard Mitter	Porsche 904/8	10	7h05m34.0
3 Umberto Maglioli/			
Herbert Linge	Porsche 904/6	10	7h06m58.0
4 Jo Bonnier/Graham Hill	Porsche 904/8	10	7h10m08.0
5 Antonio Pucci/			
Gunther Klass	Porsche 904GTS	10	7h11m07.0
6 Hans Herrmann/			
Leo Cella	Fiat Abarth 1600 OT	10	7h17m23.0

Winner's average speed: 63.730 mph. Pole position: Vaccarella, 39m30.0. Fastest lap: Vaccarella, 39m21.0

GRAND PRIX DE SPA-FRANCORCHAMPS

16 May 1965. Spa-Francorchamps. 36 laps of an 8.761-mile circuit = 315.396 miles. International Championship of Makes round 6

1 Willy Mairesse	Ferrari 250LM	36	2h29m45.7
2 David Piper	Ferrari 250LM	36	2h31m43.5
3 Ben Pon	Porsche 904GTS	36	2h32m37.4
4 Peter Sutcliffe	Ferrari 250GTO	36	2h32m43.8
5 Bob Bondurant	AC Cobra Daytona-Ford	36	2h32m49.8
6 Mike Salmon	Ferrari 250GTO	35	

Winner's average speed: 126.359 mph. Pole position: Michael Parkes (Ferrari 330P), 3m59.7. Fastest lap: Parkes, 4m01.3

ADAC 1000 KM-RENNEN

23 May 1965. Nurburgring. 44 laps of a 14.167-mile circuit = 623.348 miles. International Championship of Makes round 7

1 John Surtees/			
Ludovico Scarfiotti	Ferrari 330P2	44	6h53m05.4
2 Michael Parkes/			
Jean Guichet	Ferrari 275P2	44	6h53m50.2
3 Jo Bonnier/Jochen Rindt	Porsche 904/8	44	7h00m59.6
4 Lorenzo Bandini/			
Nino Vaccarella	Ferrari Dino 166P	43	
5 Umberto Maglioli/			
Herbert Linge	Porsche 904/6	43	
6 Peter Nocker/			
Gunther Klass	Porsche 904/6	43	

Winner's average speed: 90.539 mph. Pole position: Surtees, 8m53.1. Fastest lap: Surtees, 8m50.5

24 HEURES DU MANS

19-20 June 1965. Le Mans. 347 laps of an 8.365-mile circuit = 2902.655

miles. International Championship of Makes round 8

1 Masten Gregory/Jochen Rindt/			
Ed Hugus	Ferrari 250LM	347	24 hours
2 Pierre Dumay/			
Gustave Gosselin	Ferrari 250LM	342	
3 Willy Mairesse/"Beurlys"	Ferrari 275GTB	338	
4 Herbert Linge/			
Peter Nocker	Porsche 904/6	334	
5 Gerhard Koch/			
Anton Fischhaber	Porsche 904GTS	324	
6 Dieter Spoerry/			
Armand Boller	Ferrari 250LM	323	

Winner's average speed: 120.944 mph. Pole position: Phil Hill (Ford GT40 Mk2), 3m33.0 (Le Mans start). Fastest lap: P Hill, 3m37.5

12 HEURES DE REIMS

3-4 July 1965. Reims. 284 laps of a 5.187-mile circuit = 1473.108 miles. International Championship of Makes round 9

1 Pedro Rodriguez/			
Jean Guichet	Ferrari 365P2	284	12 hours
2 John Surtees/			
Michael Parkes	Ferrari 365P2	282	
3 Willy Mairesse/"Beurlys"	Ferrari 250LM	279	
4 David Piper/			
Richard Attwood	Ferrari 250LM	273	
5 Bob Bondurant/			
Jo Schlesser	AC Cobra Daytona-Ford	270	
6 Mike de'Udy/Paul Hawkins	Porsche 904GTS	261	

Winner's average speed: 122.759 mph. Pole position: Rodriguez, 2m18.5. Fastest lap: Surtees, 2m17.9

1965 FINAL CHAMPIONSHIP POSITIONS

Manufacturers		4 Ford	22
1 Ferrari	54 (66)*	8 Iso Grifo	2
2= AC Cobra-Ford	23	9 Fiat-Abarth	1
Porsche	23 (26)*	*Best six results count	

1966

International Championship of Makes

DAYTONA 24 HOURS

5-6 February 1966. Daytona. 678 laps of a 3.810-mile circuit = 2583.180 miles. International Championship of Makes round 1

1 Ken Miles/Lloyd Ruby	Ford GT40 Mk2	678	24h00m07.6
2 Dan Gurney/Jerry Grant	Ford GT40 Mk2	670	
3 Walt Hansgen/			
Mark Donohue	Ford GT40 Mk2	669	
4 Pedro Rodriguez/			
Mario Andretti	Ferrari 365P2/3	664	
5 Bruce McLaren/			
Chris Amon	Ford GT40 Mk2	652	
6 Hans Herrmann/			
Herbert Linge	Porsche 906	623	

Winner's average speed: 107.623 mph. Pole position: Miles, 1m57.8. Fastest lap: Gurney, 1m57.7

12 HOURS OF SEBRING

26 March 1966. Sebring. 228 laps of a 5.200-mile circuit = 1185.600 miles. International Championship of Makes round 2

1 Lloyd Ruby/Ken Miles	Ford GT40 Roadster	228	12h01m16.1
2 Walt Hansgen/			
Mark Donohue	Ford GT40 Mk2	216	
3 Peter Revson/			
Skip Scott	Ford GT40	213	

4 Hans Herrmann/Joe Buzzetta/
   Gerhard Mitter   Porsche 906   209
5 Lorenzo Bandini/
   Ludovico Scarfiotti   Ferrari Dino 206P   206
6 Jo Siffert/Charles Vogele Porsche 906   205

Dan Gurney/Jerry Grant (Ford GT40 Mk2), 227 laps, finished second on the road but was disqualified for outside assistance. Winner's average speed: 98.626 mph. Pole position: Gurney, 2m45.6. Fastest lap: Gurney, 2m54.8

1966 John Surtees/Mike Parkes (Ferrari 330P3) were victorious at Monza in 1966.

1000 KM DI MONZA/TROFEO FILIPPO CARACCIOLO

25 April 1966. Monza. 100 laps of a 6.214-mile circuit = 621.370 miles. International Championship of Makes round 3

1 John Surtees/
   Michael Parkes   Ferrari 330P3   100   6h05m11.6
2 John Whitmore/
   Masten Gregory   Ford GT40   99
3 Herbert Muller/
   Willy Mairesse   Ford GT40   98
4 Gerhard Mitter/
   Hans Herrmann   Porsche 906   98
5 Jo Siffert/Charles Vogele Porsche 906   96
6 Guy Ligier/Henri Greder Ford GT40   95

Winner's average speed: 102.089 mph. Pole position: Parkes, 2m58.1. Fastest lap: Surtees, 3m26.7

TARGA FLORIO

8 May 1966. Madonie (Piccolo). 10 laps of a 44.739-mile circuit = 447.390 miles. International Championship of Makes round 4

1 Willy Mairesse/
   Herbert Muller   Porsche 906   10   7h16m32.3
2 Jean Guichet/
   Giancarlo Baghetti   Ferrari Dino 206S 10   7h25m02.2
3 Antonio Pucci/
   Vincenzo Arena   Porsche 906   10   7h34m08.0
4 Enrico Pinto/
   Nino Todaro   Alfa Romeo Giulia TZ 10 7h45m24.2
5 Claude Bourillot/
   Umberto Maglioli   Porsche 906   10   7h51m55.0
6 Roger Delageneste/
   Jose Rosinski   Alpine A110-Renault 10 7h52m33.8

Winner's average speed: 61.492 mph. Pole position: Gunther Klass (Porsche 906), 39m05.7. Fastest lap: Gerhard Mitter (Porsche 906), 40m19.0

1000 KM DE SPA-FRANCORCHAMPS

22 May 1966. Spa-Francorchamps. 71 laps of an 8.761-mile circuit = 622.031 miles. International Championship of Makes round 5

1 Michael Parkes/
   Ludovico Scarfiotti   Ferrari 330P3   71   4h43m24.0
2 John Whitmore/
   Frank Gardner   Ford GT40 Mk2 70

3 Skip Scott/Peter Revson Ford GT40   69
4 Peter Sutcliffe/
   Brian Redman   Ford GT40   68
5 Innes Ireland/
   Chris Amon   Ford GT40   67
6 Richard Attwood/
   Jean Guichet   Ferrari Dino 206S 67

Winner's average speed: 131.693 mph. Pole position: Parkes, 3m47.4. Fastest lap: Parkes, 3m46.4

ADAC 1000 KM-RENNEN

5 June 1966. Nurburgring. 44 laps of a 14.167-mile circuit = 623.348 miles. International Championship of Makes round 6

1 Phil Hill/Jo Bonnier   Chaparral 2D-Chevrolet 44 6h58m47.6
2 Ludovico Scarfiotti/
   Lorenzo Bandini   Ferrari Dino 206S 44 6h59m29.2
3 Pedro Rodriguez/
   Richie Ginther   Ferrari Dino 206S 44 7h00m02.4
4 Bob Bondurant/
   Paul Hawkins   Porsche 906   44 7h06m52.8
5 Guy Ligier/Jo Schlesser Ford GT40   43
6 Peter Sutcliffe/
   John Taylor   Ford GT40   43

Winner's average speed: 89.306 mph. Pole position: John Surtees (Ferrari 330P3), 8m31.9. Fastest lap: Surtees, 8m37.0

24 HEURES DU MANS

17-18 June 1966. Le Mans. 359 laps of an 8.365-mile circuit = 3003.035 miles. International Championship of Makes round 7

1 Bruce McLaren/
   Chris Amon   Ford GT40 Mk2 359 24 hours
2 Ken Miles/Denny Hulme Ford GT40 Mk2 359 24 hours
3 Ronnie Bucknum/
   Dick Hutcherson   Ford GT40 Mk2 347
4 Jo Siffert/Colin Davis Porsche 906/6LH 338
5 Hans Herrmann/
   Herbert Linge   Porsche 906/6LH 337
6 Udo Schutz/Piet de Klerk Porsche 906/6LH 336

Winner's average speed: 125.126 mph. Pole position: Dan Gurney (Ford GT40 Mk2), 3m30.6 (Le Mans start). Fastest lap: Gurney, 3m30.6

1966 FINAL CHAMPIONSHIP POSITIONS

Manufacturers

1 Ford	39 (41)*	4 Chaparral-Chevrolet 9
2 Ferrari	33 (35)*	5 Alfa Romeo 3
3 Porsche	21 (22)*	6 Alpine-Renault 1
		*Best five results count

1967

International Championship of Makes

DAYTONA 24 HOURS

4-5 February 1967. Daytona. 666 laps of a 3.810-mile circuit = 2537.460 miles. International Championship of Makes round 1

1 Lorenzo Bandini/
   Chris Amon   Ferrari 330P4 666 24h00m32.0
2 Michael Parkes/
   Ludovico Scarfiotti   Ferrari 330P4 663
3 Pedro Rodriguez/
   Jean Guichet   Ferrari 412P 637
4 Hans Herrmann/
   Jo Siffert   Porsche 910 618
5 Dieter Spoerry/
   Rico Steinemann   Porsche 906/6LH 608
6 Jacky Ickx/
   Richard Thompson   Ford GT40 601

1967 Bruce McLaren and Mario Andretti's Ford GT40 wins the Sebring 12 Hours.

Winner's average speed: 105.688 mph. Pole position: Dan Gurney (Ford GT40 Mk2), 1m55.10. Fastest lap: Phil Hill (Chaparral 2F-Chevrolet), 1m55.69.

12 HOURS OF SEBRING

1 April 1967. Sebring. 238 laps of a 5.200-mile circuit = 1237.600 miles. International Championship of Makes round 2

1	Mario Andretti/			
	Bruce McLaren	Ford GT40 Mk4	238	12h01m28.2
2	AJ Foyt jr/Lloyd Ruby	Ford GT40 Mk2	226	engine
3	Gerhard Mitter/			
	Scooter Patrick	Porsche 910	226	
4	Hans Herrmann/			
	Jo Siffert	Porsche 910	223	
5	Umberto Maglioli/			
	Nino Vaccarella	Ford GT40	223	
6	Dieter Spoerry/			
	Rico Steinemann	Porsche 906/6LH	218	

Winner's average speed: 102.923 mph. Pole position: Andretti, 2m48.0. Fastest lap: Mike Spence (Chaparral 2F-Chevrolet), 2m48.6

1000 KM DI MONZA/TROFEO FILIPPO CARACCIOLO

25 April 1967. Monza. 100 laps of a 6.214-mile circuit = 621.370 miles. International Championship of Makes round 3

1	Chris Amon/			
	Lorenzo Bandini	Ferrari 330P4	100	5h07m43.0
2	Ludovico Scarfiotti/			
	Michael Parkes	Ferrari 330P4	100	5h10m59.2
3	Gerhard Mitter/			
	Jochen Rindt	Porsche 910	96	
4	Herbert Muller/			
	Nino Vaccarella	Ferrari 412P	95	
5	Hans Herrmann/			
	Jo Siffert	Porsche 910	95	
6	Jo Schlesser/Guy Ligier	Ford GT40	95	

Winner's average speed: 121.158 mph. Pole position: Mike Spence (Chaparral 2F-Chevrolet), 2m53.8. Fastest lap: Bandini, 2m55.8

1000 KM DE SPA-FRANCORCHAMPS

1 May 1967. Spa-Francorchamps. 71 laps of an 8.761-mile circuit = 622.031 miles. International Championship of Makes round 4

1	Jacky Ickx/			
	Richard Thompson	Mirage Mk1-Ford	71	5h09m46.5
2	Jo Siffert/			
	Hans Herrmann	Porsche 910	70	
3	Richard Attwood/			
	Lucien Bianchi	Ferrari 412P	70	
4	Paul Hawkins/			
	Jackie Epstein	Lola T70 Mk3-Chevrolet	69	
5	Michael Parkes/			
	Ludovico Scarfiotti	Ferrari 330P4	69	
6	Peter Sutcliffe/			
	Brian Redman	Ford GT40	68	

Winner's average speed: 120.481 mph. Pole position: Phil Hill (Chaparral 2F-Chevrolet), 3m35.6. Fastest lap: Mike Spence (Chaparral 2F-Chevrolet), 4m03.5

TARGA FLORIO

14 May 1967. Madonie (Piccolo). 10 laps of a 44.739-mile circuit = 447.390 miles. International Championship of Makes round 5

1	Paul Hawkins/			
	Rolf Stommelen	Porsche 910	10	6h37m01.0
2	Leo Cella/			
	Giampiero Biscaldi	Porsche 910	10	6h37m48.2
3	Jochen Neerpasch/			
	Vic Elford	Porsche 910	10	6h41m03.8
4	Vittorio Venturi/			
	Jonathan Williams	Ferrari Dino 206P	10	6h52m10.2
5	Henri Greder/			
	Jean-Michel Giorgi	Ford GT40	10	7h20m36.6
6	Hans Herrmann/			
	Jo Siffert	Porsche 910	9	

Winner's average speed: 67.613 mph. Pole position: Nino Vaccarella (Ferrari 330P4), 37m12.2. Fastest lap: Herbert Muller (Ferrari 412P), 37m09.0

ADAC 1000 KM-RENNEN

28 May 1967. Nurburgring. 44 laps of a 14.189-mile circuit = 624.316 miles. International Championship of Makes round 6

1	Udo Schutz/Joe Buzzetta	Porsche 910	44	6h54m12.9
2	Paul Hawkins/			
	Gerhard Koch	Porsche 910	44	6h54m13.1
3	Jochen Neerpasch/			
	Vic Elford	Porsche 910	44	6h58m32.6
4	Gerhard Mitter/			
	Lucien Bianchi	Porsche 910	43	electrics
5	Andrea de Adamich/Nanni Galli/Roberto Bussinello/			
	Teodoro Zeccoli	Alfa Romeo T33	43	
6	Hans-Dieter Dechent/			
	Robert Huhn	Porsche 906	42	

Winner's average speed: 90.434 mph. Pole position: Phil Hill (Chaparral 2F-Chevrolet), 8m31.9. Fastest lap: P Hill, 8m42.1

24 HEURES DU MANS

10-11 June 1967. Le Mans. 387 laps of an 8.365-mile circuit = 3237.255 miles. International Championship of Makes round 7

1	Dan Gurney/AJ Foyt Jr	Ford GT40 Mk4	387	24 hours
2	Ludovico Scarfiotti/			
	Michael Parkes	Ferrari 330P4	384	
3	Willy Mairesse/"Beurlys"	Ferrari 330P4	377	
4	Bruce McLaren/			
	Mark Donohue	Ford GT40 Mk4	359	
5	Jo Siffert/			
	Hans Herrmann	Porsche 907	358	
6	Rolf Stommelen/			
	Jochen Neerpasch	Porsche 910	351	

Winner's average speed: 134.886 mph. Pole position: McLaren, 3m24.4 (Le Mans start). Fastest lap: Denny Hulme and Mario Andretti (both Ford GT40 Mk4), 3m23.6

BOAC 6 HOURS

30 July 1967. Brands Hatch. 211 laps of a 2.650-mile circuit = 559.150 miles. International Championship of Makes round 8

1	Mike Spence/Phil Hill	Chaparral 2F-Chevrolet	211	6h00m26.0
2	Jackie Stewart/			
	Chris Amon	Ferrari 330P4	211	6h01m24.6
3	Jo Siffert/			
	Bruce McLaren	Porsche 910	209	

4 Hans Herrmann/			
Jochen Neerpasch	Porsche 907	206	
5 Ludovico Scarfiotti/			
Peter Sutcliffe	Ferrari 330P4	206	
6 Paul Hawkins/			
Jonathan Williams	Ferrari 330P4	204	

Winner's average speed: 93.080 mph. Pole position: Denny Hulme (Lola T70 Mk3-Chevrolet), 1m36.6. Fastest lap: Hulme, 1m37.2

1967 FINAL CHAMPIONSHIP POSITIONS

Manufacturers		6 Lola-Chevrolet	3
1 Ferrari	34 (37)*	7 Alfa Romeo	2
2 Porsche	32 (41)*	*Best five results count	
3 Ford	22 (23)*		
4= Chaparral-Chevrolet	9		
Mirage-Ford	9		

1968
International Championship of Makes

DAYTONA 24 HOURS

3-4 February 1968. Daytona. 673 laps of a 3.810-mile circuit = 2564.130 miles. International Championship of Makes round 1

1 Vic Elford/Jochen Neerpasch/Rolf Stommelen/Jo Siffert/			
Hans Herrmann	Porsche 907	673	24h01m54.700
2 Jo Siffert/			
Hans Herrmann	Porsche 907	668	
3 Joe Buzzetta/			
Jo Schlesser	Porsche 907	659	
4 Jerry Titus/			
Ronnie Bucknum	Ford Mustang	629	
5 Udo Schutz/			
Nino Vaccarella	Alfa Romeo T33/2	617	
6 Mario Andretti/			
Lucien Bianchi	Alfa Romeo T33/2	609	

Winner's average speed: 106.697 mph. Pole position: Jacky Ickx (Ford GT40), 1m54.91. Fastest lap: Ickx, 1m56.86

12 HOURS OF SEBRING

23 March 1968. Sebring. 237 laps of a 5.200-mile circuit = 1232.400 miles. International Championship of Makes round 2

1 Hans Herrmann/			
Jo Siffert	Porsche 907	237	12h01m19.225
2 Vic Elford/			
Jochen Neerpasch	Porsche 907	227	
3 Mark Donohue/			
Craig Fisher	Chevrolet Camaro	221	
4 Joseph Welch/Bob Johnson/			
Craig Fisher	Chevrolet Camaro	217	
5 Jerry Titus/			
Ronnie Bucknum	Ford Mustang	217	
6 David Morgan/			
Hap Sharp	Chevrolet Corvette Stingray	208	

Winner's average speed: 102.512 mph. Pole position: Herrmann, 2m49.4. Fastest lap: Scooter Patrick (Lola T70 Mk3B-Chevrolet), 2m49.0

BOAC 6 HOURS

7 April 1968. Brands Hatch. 218 laps of a 2.650-mile circuit = 577.700 miles. International Championship of Makes round 3

1 Jacky Ickx/			
Brian Redman	Ford GT40	218	6h01m13.0
2 Ludovico Scarfiotti/			
Gerhard Mitter	Porsche 907	218	6h01m35.0
3 Vic Elford/			
Jochen Neerpasch	Porsche 907	216	

4 Paul Hawkins/			
David Hobbs	Ford GT40	210	
5 Pedro Rodriguez/			
Roy Pierpoint	Ferrari 250LM	209	
6 Jo Bonnier/			
Sten Axelsson	Lola T70 Mk3-Chevrolet	207	

Winner's average speed: 95.959 mph. Pole position: Jo Siffert (Porsche 907), 1m34.6. Fastest lap: Bruce McLaren (Ford 3L), time n/a

1000 KM DI MONZA/TROFEO FILIPPO CARACCIOLO

25 April 1968. Monza. 100 laps of a 6.214-mile circuit = 621.370 miles. International Championship of Makes round 4

1 Paul Hawkins/			
David Hobbs	Ford GT40	100	5h18m23.4
2 Rolf Stommelen/			
Jochen Neerpasch	Porsche 907L	100	5h20m15.8
3 Patrick Depailler/			
Andre de Cortanze	Alpine A211-Renault	97	
4 Gerhard Koch/Rudi Lins	Porsche 910	95	
5 Antonio Nicodemi/			
Carlo Facetti	Porsche 910	94	
6 Andre Wicky/			
Jean-Pierre Hanrioud	Porsche 910	92	

Winner's average speed: 117.096 mph. Pole position: Jacky Ickx (Ford GT40), 2m57.0. Fastest lap: Ickx, 2m56.5

TARGA FLORIO

5 May 1968. Madonie (Piccolo). 10 laps of a 44.739-mile circuit = 447.390 miles. International Championship of Makes round 5

1 Vic Elford/			
Umberto Maglioli	Porsche 907	10	6h28m47.9
2 Nanni Galli/			
Ignazio Giunti	Alfa Romeo T33/2	10	6h31m30.7
3 Mario Casoni/			
Lucien Bianchi	Alfa Romeo T33/2	10	6h37m55.1
4 Hans Herrmann/			
Jochen Neerpasch	Porsche 907	10	6h38m48.7
5 Teddy Pilette/			
Rob Slotemaker	Alfa Romeo T33/2	10	6h55m28.8
6 Giancarlo Baghetti/			
Giampiero Biscaldi	Alfa Romeo T33/2	10	7h00m08.5

Winner's average speed: 69.042 mph. Pole position: Elford, 36m47.7. Fastest lap: Elford, 36m02.3

ADAC 1000 KM-RENNEN

19 May 1968. Nurburgring. 44 laps of a 14.189-mile circuit = 624.316 miles. International Championship of Makes round 6

1 Jo Siffert/Vic Elford	Porsche 908	44	6h34m06.3
2 Hans Herrmann/			
Rolf Stommelen	Porsche 907	44	6h37m07.8
3 Jacky Ickx/Paul Hawkins	Ford GT40	44	6h37m57.5
4 Jochen Neerpasch/			
Joe Buzzetta	Porsche 907	44	6h42m22.9
5 Nanni Galli/			
Ignazio Giunti	Alfa Romeo T33/2	43	
6 David Hobbs/			
Brian Redman	Ford GT40	43	

Winner's average speed: 95.048 mph. Pole position: Siffert, 8m32.8. Fastest lap: Siffert, 8m33.0

1000 KM DE SPA-FRANCORCHAMPS

26 May 1968. Spa-Francorchamps. 71 laps of an 8.761-mile circuit = 622.031 miles. International Championship of Makes round 7

1 Jacky Ickx/			
Brian Redman	Ford GT40	71	5h05m19.3
2 Gerhard Mitter/			
Jo Schlesser	Porsche 907	70	
3 Hans Herrmann/			
Rolf Stommelen	Porsche 908	69	

4	Paul Hawkins/			
	David Hobbs	Ford GT40	67	
5	Gerhard Koch/Rudi Lins	Porsche 910	67	
6	Dieter Spoerry/			
	Rico Steinemann	Porsche 910	66	

Winner's average speed: 122.238 mph. Pole position: Frank Gardner (Ford 3L), 3m36.3. Fastest lap: Schlesser, 4m00.3.

WATKINS GLEN 6 HOURS

14 July 1968. Watkins Glen. 286 laps of a 2.350-mile circuit = 672.100 miles. International Championship of Makes round 8

1	Jacky Ickx/			
	Lucien Bianchi	Ford GT40	286	6h00m26.08
2	David Hobbs/			
	Paul Hawkins	Ford GT40	267	
3	Richard Thompson/			
	Ray Heppenstall	Howmet TX turbine	267	
4	Werner Frank/			
	Ralph Tritchmann	Porsche 906/6LH	257	
5	Jim Locke/Bob Bailey	Porsche 906/6LH	257	
6	Hans Herrmann/Tetsu Ikuzawa/			
	Jo Siffert	Porsche 908	257	

Winner's average speed: 111.882 mph. Pole position: Siffert, 1m10.2. Fastest lap: Ickx, 1m11.1

GROSSER PREIS VON ÖSTERREICH

25 August 1968. Zeltweg. 157 laps of a 1.988-mile circuit = 312.116 miles. Half points awarded. International Championship of Makes round 9

1	Jo Siffert	Porsche 908	157	2h55m17.79
2	Hans Herrmann/			
	Kurt Ahrens jr	Porsche 908	157	2h55m30.23
3	Paul Hawkins	Ford GT40	152	
4	Teddy Pilette	Alfa Romeo T33/2	152	
5	Willi Kauhsen/			
	Karl von Wendt	Porsche 910	147	
6	Rico Steinemann/			
	Dieter Spoerry	Porsche 910	147	

Winner's average speed: 106.830 mph. Pole position: Siffert, 1m04.86. Fastest lap: Siffert, 1m04.82

24 HEURES DU MANS

28-29 September 1968. Le Mans. 330 laps of an 8.369-mile circuit = 2761.770 miles. International Championship of Makes round 10

1	Pedro Rodriguez/			
	Lucien Bianchi	Ford GT40	330	24 hours
2	Dieter Spoerry/			
	Rico Steinemann	Porsche 907	325	
3	Rolf Stommelen/			
	Jochen Neerpasch	Porsche 908	324	
4	Ignazio Giunti/Nanni Galli	Alfa Romeo T33/2	321	
5	Carlo Facetti/			
	Spartico Dini	Alfa Romeo T33/2	314	
6	Mario Casoni/			
	Giampiero Biscaldi	Alfa Romeo T33/2	304	

Winner's average speed: 115.074 mph. Pole position: Jo Siffert (Porsche 908), 3m35.4 (Le Mans start). Fastest lap: Stommelen, 3m38.1

1967 FINAL CHAMPIONSHIP POSITIONS

Manufacturers			7	Ferrari	2
1	Ford	45 (56)*	8	Lola-Chevrolet	1
2	Porsche	42 (67.5)*	*Best five results count		
3	Alfa Romeo	14.5			
4=	Alpine-Renault	4			
	Chevrolet	4			
	Howmet	4			

1969

International Championship of Makes

DAYTONA 24 HOURS

1-2 February 1969. Daytona. 626 laps of a 3.810-mile circuit = 2385.060 miles. International Championship of Makes round 1

1	Mark Donohue/			
	Chuck Parsons	Lola T70 Mk3B-Chevrolet	626	24h01m35.303
2	Lothar Motschenbacher/			
	Ed Leslie	Lola T70 Mk3-Chevrolet	596	
3	Jon Ward/Jerry Titus	Pontiac Firebird	591	
4	Bruce Jennings/Herb Wetanson/			
	Tony Adamowicz	Porsche 911T	583	
5	Bert Everett/Alan Johnson/			
	Linley Coleman	Porsche 911	581	
6	John Gunn/Bob Beatty/			
	Hubert Kleinpeter	Chevron B8-BMW	579	

Winner's average speed: 99.268 mph. Pole position: Vic Elford (Porsche 908L), 1m52.2. Fastest lap: Elford, time n/a

12 HOURS OF SEBRING

22 March 1969. Sebring. 239 laps of a 5.200-mile circuit = 1242.800 miles. International Championship of Makes round 2

1	Jacky Ickx/Jackie Oliver	Ford GT40	239	12h01m25.121
2	Chris Amon/			
	Mario Andretti	Ferrari 312P	238	
3	Rolf Stommelen/Joe Buzzetta/			
	Kurt Ahrens Jr	Porsche 908/2	235	
4	Alex Soler-Roig/Rudi Lins	Porsche 907	233	
5	Gerhard Mitter/			
	Udo Schutz	Porsche 908/2	232	
6	Ed Leslie/			
	Lothar Motschenbacher	Lola T70 Mk3-Chevrolet	229	

Winner's average speed: 103.363 mph. Pole position: Andretti, 2m40.14. Fastest lap: Amon, 2m41.88

BOAC 6 HOURS

13 April 1969. Brands Hatch. 227 laps of a 2.650-mile circuit = 601.550 miles. International Championship of Makes round 3

1	Jo Siffert/Brian Redman	Porsche 908/2	227	6h00m08.4
2	Vic Elford/			
	Richard Attwood	Porsche 908/2	225	
3	Gerhard Mitter/			
	Udo Schutz	Porsche 908/2	223	
4	Chris Amon/			
	Pedro Rodriguez	Ferrari 312P	223	
5	David Hobbs/			
	Mike Hailwood	Ford GT40	207	
6	Hans Herrmann/			
	Rolf Stommelen	Porsche 908/2	205	

Winner's average speed: 100.219 mph. Pole position: Siffert, 1m28.8. Fastest lap: Siffert, time n/a

1000 KM DI MONZA/TROFEO FILIPPO CARACCIOLO

25 April 1969. Monza. 100 laps of a 6.214-mile circuit = 621.370 miles. International Championship of Makes round 4

1	Jo Siffert/Brian Redman	Porsche 908L	100	4h53m41.2
2	Hans Herrmann/			
	Kurt Ahrens jr	Porsche 908L	99	
3	Gerhard Koch/			
	Hans-Dieter Dechent	Porsche 907	92	
4	Helmut Kelleners/			
	Reinhold Joest	Ford GT40	92	
5	Andrea de Adamich/	Lola T70 Mk3B-		
	Frank Gardner	Chevrolet	92	
6	Patrick Depailler/			
	Jean-Pierre Jabouille	Alpine A220-Renault	91	accident

Winner's average speed: 126.945 mph. Pole position: Chris Amon (Ferrari

312P), 2m48.2. Fastest lap: Pedro Rodriguez (Ferrari 312P), 2m48.1

(Porsche 917LH), 3m27.2

TARGA FLORIO

4 May 1969. Madonie (Piccolo). 10 laps of a 44.739-mile circuit = 447.390 miles. International Championship of Makes round 5

1 Gerhard Mitter/			
Udo Schutz	Porsche 908/2	10	6h07m45.7
2 Vic Elford/			
Umberto Maglioli	Porsche 908/2	10	6h10m34.0
3 Hans Herrmann/			
Rolf Stommelen	Porsche 908/2	10	6h21m26.7
4 Karl von Wendt/			
Willi Kauhsen	Porsche 908/2	10	6h35m33.5
5 Enrico Pinto/			
Giovanni Alberti	Alfa Romeo T33/2	10	6h46m35.3
6 Gerhard Koch/			
Hans-Dieter Dechent	Porsche 907	9	

Winner's average speed: 72.991 mph. Pole position: Elford, 35m54.7. Fastest lap: Elford, 35m08.2

1000 KM DE SPA-FRANCORCHAMPS

11 May 1969. Spa-Francorchamps. 71 laps of an 8.761-mile circuit = 622.031 miles. International Championship of Makes round 6

1 Jo Siffert/Brian Redman	Porsche 908L	71	4h24m19.6
2 Pedro Rodriguez/			
David Piper	Ferrari 312P	71	4h27m52.1
3 Vic Elford/Kurt Ahrens Jr	Porsche 908L	70	
4 Rolf Stommelen/			
Hans Herrmann	Porsche 908L	67	
5 Jo Bonnier/			
Herbert Muller	Lola T70 Mk3B-Chevrolet	67	
6 Teddy Pilette/			
Rob Slotemaker	Alfa Romeo T33/2	65	

Winner's average speed: 141.196 mph. Pole position: Paul Hawkins (Lola T70 Mk3B-Chevrolet), 3m42.5 - Siffert (Porsche 917) set 3m41.9 but the car was withdrawn. Fastest lap: Redman, 3m37.1

ADAC 1000 KM-RENNEN

1 June 1969. Nurburgring. 44 laps of a 14.189-mile circuit = 624.316 miles. International Championship of Makes round 7

1 Jo Siffert/Brian Redman	Porsche 908/2	44	6h11m02.3
2 Rolf Stommelen/			
Hans Herrmann	Porsche 908/2	44	6h15m04.2
3 Vic Elford/Kurt Ahrens Jr	Porsche 908/2	44	6h16m09.8
4 Richard Attwood/			
Rudi Lins	Porsche 908/2	43	
5 Willi Kauhsen/			
Karl von Wendt	Porsche 908/2	42	
6 Helmut Kelleners/			
Reinhold Joest	Ford GT40	41	

Winner's average speed: 100.957 mph. Pole position: Siffert, 8m00.2. Fastest lap: Chris Amon (Ferrari 312P), 8m03.3

24 HEURES DU MANS

14-15 June 1969. Le Mans. 371 laps of an 8.369-mile circuit = 3104.899 miles. International Championship of Makes round 8

1 Jacky Ickx/Jackie Oliver	Ford GT40	371	24 hours
2 Hans Herrmann/			
Gerard Larrousse	Porsche 908L	371	
3 David Hobbs/			
Mike Hailwood	Ford GT40	367	
4 Jean-Pierre Beltoise/			
Piers Courage	Matra-Simca MS650	367	
5 Jean Guichet/			
Nino Vaccarella	Matra-Simca MS630	358	
6 Reinhold Joest/			
Helmut Kelleners	Ford GT40	340	

Winner's average speed: 129.371 mph. Pole position: Rolf Stommelen (Porsche 917LH), 3m22.9 (Le Mans start). Fastest lap: Vic Elford

WATKINS GLEN 6 HOURS

12 July 1969. Watkins Glen. 291 laps of a 2.350-mile circuit = 683.850 miles. International Championship of Makes round 9

1 Jo Siffert/Brian Redman	Porsche 908/2	291	6h01m10.1
2 Vic Elford/			
Richard Attwood	Porsche 908/2	291	6h02m45.2
3 Rudi Lins/Joe Buzzetta	Porsche 908/2	282	
4 Johnny Servoz-Gavin/			
Pedro Rodriguez	Matra-Simca MS650	267	
5 Helmut Kelleners/			
Reinhold Joest	Ford GT40	265	
6 Dick Smothers/Fred Baker/			
Lou Sell	Porsche 906/6LH	257	

Winner's average speed: 113.606 mph. Pole position: Siffert, 1m08.47. Fastest lap: Elford, 1m09.13

GROSSER PREIS VON OSTERREICH

10 August 1969. Osterreichring. 170 laps of a 3.673-mile circuit = 624.410 miles. International Championship of Makes round 10

1 Jo Siffert/Kurt Ahrens Jr	Porsche 917	170	5h23m36.6
2 Jo Bonnier/			
Herbert Muller	Lola T70 Mk3B-Chevrolet	170	5h24m44.13
3 Richard Attwood/			
Brian Redman	Porsche 917K	169	
4 Masten Gregory/			
Richard Brostrom	Porsche 908/2	168	
5 Rudi Lins/			
Gerard Larrousse	Porsche 908/2	168	
6 Karl von Wendt/			
Willi Kauhsen	Porsche 908/2	166	

Winner's average speed: 115.769 mph. Pole position: Jacky Ickx (Mirage M3-Ford), 1m47.6. Fastest lap: Ickx, 1m46.6

1969 FINAL CHAMPIONSHIP POSITIONS

Manufacturers			
		6 Pontiac	4
1 Porsche	45 (76)*	7 Alfa Romeo	3
2 Ford	25 (26)*	8= Alpine-Renault	1
3 Lola-Chevrolet	20	Chevron-BMW	1
4 Ferrari	15	*Best five results count	
5 Matra-Simca	6		

1970

International Championship of Makes

DAYTONA 24 HOURS

31 January-1 February 1970. Daytona. 724 laps of a 3.810-mile circuit = 2758.440 miles. International Championship of Makes round 1

1 Pedro Rodriguez/Leo Kinnunen/			
Brian Redman	Porsche 917K	724	24h00m52.1
2 Jo Siffert/Brian Redman	Porsche 917K	679	
3 Mario Andretti/Jacky Ickx/			
Arturo Merzario	Ferrari 512S	676	
4 Michael Parkes/			
Sam Posey	Ferrari 312P	647	
5 David Piper/			
Tony Adamowicz	Ferrari 312P	632	
6 Jerry Thompson/			
John Mahler	Chevrolet Corvette	608	

Winner's average speed: 114.866 mph. Pole position: Andretti, 1m51.6. Fastest lap: Siffert, 1m48.7

12 HOURS OF SEBRING

21 March 1970. Sebring. 248 laps of a 5.200-mile circuit = 1289.600 miles. International Championship of Makes round 2

1 Ignazio Giunti/Nino Vaccarella/			
Mario Andretti	Ferrari 512S	248	12h01m11.2
2 Steve McQueen/			
Peter Revson	Porsche 908/2	248	12h01m32.3
3 Masten Gregory/			
Toine Hezemans	Alfa Romeo T33/3	247	
4 Pedro Rodriguez/Leo Kinnunen/			
Jo Siffert	Porsche 917K	244	
5 Henri Pescarolo/			
Johnny Servoz-Gavin	Matra-Simca MS650	242	
6 Michael Parkes/			
Chuck Parsons	Ferrari 312P	240	

Winner's average speed: 107.290 mph. Pole position: Andretti, 2m33.50. Fastest lap: Kinnunen, 2m32.77

BOAC 1000 KMS

12 April 1970. Brands Hatch. 235 laps of a 2.650-mile circuit = 622.750 miles. International Championship of Makes round 3

1 Pedro Rodriguez/			
Leo Kinnunen	Porsche 917K	235	6h45m29.6
2 Vic Elford/Denny Hulme	Porsche 917K	230	
3 Richard Attwood/			
Hans Herrmann	Porsche 917K	227	
4 Gijs van Lennep/			
Hans Laine	Porsche 908/2	227	
5 Chris Amon/			
Arturo Merzario	Ferrari 512S	225	
6 Gerard Larrousse/			
Gerhard Koch	Porsche 908/2	217	

Winner's average speed: 92.147 mph. Pole position: Amon, 1m28.6. Fastest lap: Jo Siffert (Porsche 917K), time n/a

1000 KM DI MONZA

25 April 1970. Monza. 174 laps of a 3.573-mile circuit = 621.702 miles. International Championship of Makes round 4

1 Pedro Rodriguez/			
Leo Kinnunen	Porsche 917K	174	4h18m01.7
2 Ignazio Giunti/Nino Vaccarella/			
Chris Amon	Ferrari 512S	174	4h19m27.6
3 John Surtees/			
Peter Schetty	Ferrari 512S	171	
4 Chris Amon/			
Arturo Merzario	Ferrari 512S	171	
5 Jean-Pierre Beltoise/			
Jack Brabham	Matra-Simca MS650	169	
6 Henri Pescarolo/			
Johnny Servoz-Gavin	Matra-Simca MS650	169	

Winner's average speed: 144.566 mph. Pole position: Jo Siffert (Porsche 917K), 1m25.21. Fastest lap: Vic Elford (Porsche 917K), 1m24.80

TARGA FLORIO

3 May 1970. Madonie (Piccolo). 11 laps of a 44.739-mile circuit = 492.129 miles. International Championship of Makes round 5

1 Jo Siffert/Brian Redman	Porsche 908/3	11	6h35m30.0
2 Pedro Rodriguez/			
Leo Kinnunen	Porsche 908/3	11	6h37m12.5
3 Nino Vaccarella/			
Ignazio Giunti	Ferrari 512S	11	6h39m05.2
4 Gijs van Lennep/			
Hans Laine	Porsche 908/2	11	6h44m51.7
5 Richard Attwood/			
Bjorn Waldegaard	Porsche 908/3	11	6h45m01.6
6 Herbert Muller/			
Michael Parkes	Ferrari 512S	10	

Winner's average speed: 74.659 mph. Pole position: Siffert, 34m10.0. Fastest lap: Kinnunen, 33m36.0

1000 KM DE SPA-FRANCORCHAMPS

17 May 1970. Spa-Francorchamps. 71 laps of an 8.761-mile circuit = 622.031 miles. International Championship of Makes round 6

1 Jo Siffert/Brian Redman	Porsche 917K	71	4h09m47.8
2 Jacky Ickx/John Surtees	Ferrari 512S	71	4h12m23.3
3 Vic Elford/Kurt Ahrens jr	Porsche 917K	70	
4 Ignazio Giunti/			
Nino Vaccarella	Ferrari 512S	68	
5 Gijs van Lennep/			
Hans Laine	Porsche 917K	68	
6 Richard Attwood/			
Hans Herrmann	Porsche 917K	68	

Winner's average speed: 149.409 mph. Pole position: Pedro Rodriguez (Porsche 917K), 3m19.8. Fastest lap: Rodriguez, 3m16.5

ADAC 1000 KM-RENNEN

31 May 1970. Nurburgring. 44 laps of a 14.189-mile circuit = 624.316 miles. International Championship of Makes round 7

1 Vic Elford/Kurt Ahrens jr	Porsche 908/3	44	6h05m21.2
2 Hans Herrmann/			
Richard Attwood	Porsche 908/3	44	6h10m34.8
3 John Surtees/			
Nino Vaccarella	Ferrari 512S	43	
4 Herbert Muller/			
Michael Parkes	Ferrari 512S	42	
5 Gerard Larrousse/			
Helmut Marko	Porsche 908/2	42	
6 Rudi Lins/Willi Kauhsen	Porsche 908/2	42	

Winner's average speed: 102.528 mph. Pole position: Jo Siffert (Porsche 908/3), 7m43.3. Fastest lap: Pedro Rodriguez (Porsche 908/3), 7m50.4

24 HEURES DU MANS

13-14 June 1970. Le Mans. 342 laps of an 8.369-mile circuit = 2862.198 miles. International Championship of Makes round 8

1 Hans Herrmann/			
Richard Attwood	Porsche 917K	342	24 hours
2 Gerard Larrousse/			
Willi Kauhsen	Porsche 917LH	337	
3 Rudi Lins/Helmut Marko	Porsche 908/2	334	
4 Sam Posey/			
Ronnie Bucknum	Ferrari 512S	312	
5 Hugues de Fierlandt/			
Alistair Walker	Ferrari 512S	304	
6 Guy Chasseuil/			
Claude Ballot-Lena	Porsche 914/6GT	284	

Winner's average speed: 119.258 mph. Pole position: Kurt Ahrens jr (Porsche 917LH), 3m19.8 (Le Mans start). Fastest lap: Vic Elford (Porsche 917LH), 3m21.05

WATKINS GLEN 6 HOURS

11 July 1970. Watkins Glen. 308 laps of a 2.350-mile circuit = 723.800 miles. International Championship of Makes round 9

1 Pedro Rodriguez/			
Leo Kinnunen	Porsche 917K	308	6h00m47.7
2 Jo Siffert/Brian Redman	Porsche 917K	308	6h01m31.9
3 Mario Andretti/			
Ignazio Giunti	Ferrari 512S	305	
4 Vic Elford/Denny Hulme	Porsche 917K	302	
5 Jacky Ickx/Peter Schetty	Ferrari 512S	299	
6 Richard Attwood/			
Kurt Ahrens jr	Porsche 917K	295	

Winner's average speed: 120.368 mph. Pole position: Siffert, 1m06.3. Fastest lap: Rodriguez, 1m04.9

OSTERREICHRING 1000 KM-RENNEN

11 October 1970. Osterreichring. 170 laps of a 3.673-mile circuit = 624.410 miles. International Championship of Makes round 10

1 Jo Siffert/Brian Redman	Porsche 917K	170	5h08m04.67

2	Andrea de Adamich/			
	Henri Pescarolo	Alfa Romeo T33/3	168	engine
3	Gerard Larrousse/			
	Rudi Lins	Porsche 908/2	167	
4	Vic Elford/			
	Richard Attwood	Porsche 917K	162	
5	Reinhold Joest/			
	Gerold Pankl	Porsche 908/2	162	
6	Niki Lauda/Peter Peter	Porsche 908/2	161	

Winner's average speed: 121.608 mph. Pole position: Pedro Rodriguez
(Porsche 917K), 1m40.48. Fastest lap: Jacky Ickx (Ferrari 512S), 1m40.0

1970 FINAL CHAMPIONSHIP POSITIONS

Manufacturers

1	Porsche	63 (87)*	4	Matra-Simca	4
2	Ferrari	37 (42)*	5	Chevrolet	1
3	Alfa Romeo	10		*Best seven results count	

1971
International Championship of Makes

1000 KM DE LA CIUDAD DE BUENOS AIRES

10 January 1971. Buenos Aires. 165 laps of a 3.709-mile circuit = 611.985
miles. International Championship of Makes round 1

1	Jo Siffert/Derek Bell	Porsche 917K	165	5h25m25.94
2	Pedro Rodriguez/			
	Jackie Oliver	Porsche 917K	164	
3	Nanni Galli/			
	Rolf Stommelen	Alfa Romeo T33/3	163	
4	Andrea de Adamich/			
	Henri Pescarolo	Alfa Romeo T33/3	161	
5	Jose Juncadella/			
	Carlos Pairetti	Ferrari 512S	155	
6	Gustave Gosselin/			
	Hugues de Fierlandt	Ferrari 512S	153	

Winner's average speed: 112.832 mph. Pole position: Rodriguez, 1m52.70.
Fastest lap: Siffert, 1m51.53

1971 The winning Porsche 917K of Pedro Rodriguez and Jackie Oliver
leads on Daytona's banking.

DAYTONA 24 HOURS

30-31 January 1971. Daytona. 688 laps of a 3.810-mile circuit = 2621.280
miles. International Championship of Makes round 2

1	Pedro Rodriguez/Jackie Oliver	Porsche 917K	688	24h00m58.0
2	Ronnie Bucknum/Tony Adamowicz	Ferrari 512S	687	
3	Mark Donohue/David Hobbs	Ferrari 512M	674	
4	Tony de Lorenzo/Don Yenko/			
	John Mahler	Chevrolet Corvette	613	
5	Luigi Chinetti jr/Nestor Veiga/			
	Alain de Cadenet	Ferrari 312P	584	
6	David Heinz/Or Costanzo	Chevrolet Corvette	581	

Winner's average speed: 109.147 mph. Pole position: Donohue, 1m42.42.
Fastest lap: Donohue, 1m41.25

12 HOURS OF SEBRING

20 March 1971. Sebring. 260 laps of a 5.200-mile circuit = 1352.000
miles. International Championship of Makes round 3

1	Vic Elford/			
	Gerard Larrousse	Porsche 917K	260	12h01m03.77
2	Nanni Galli/			
	Rolf Stommelen	Alfa Romeo T33/3	257	
3	Andrea de Adamich/Henri Pescarolo/			
	Nino Vaccarella	Alfa Romeo T33/3	248	
4	Pedro Rodriguez/			
	Jackie Oliver	Porsche 917K	248	
5	Jo Siffert/Derek Bell*	Porsche 917K	244	
6	Mark Donohue/			
	David Hobbs	Ferrari 512M	243	

*Includes 4-lap penalty for outside assistance. Winner's average speed:
112.501 mph. Pole position: Donohue, 2m31.65. Fastest lap: Siffert,
2m30.46

BOAC 1000 KMS

4 April 1971. Brands Hatch. 235 laps of a 2.650-mile circuit = 622.750
miles. International Championship of Makes round 4

1	Andrea de Adamich/			
	Henri Pescarolo	Alfa Romeo T33/3	235	6h24m32.2
2	Jacky Ickx/			
	Clay Regazzoni	Ferrari 312PB	232	
3	Jo Siffert/Derek Bell	Porsche 917K	229	
4	Herbert Muller/			
	Rene Herzog	Ferrari 512M	228	
5	Jose Juncadella/			
	David Hobbs	Ferrari 512M	227	
6	Reinhold Joest/			
	Willi Kauhsen	Porsche 917K	221	

Winner's average speed: 97.169 mph. Pole position: Regazzoni, 1m27.4.
Fastest lap: Regazzoni, time n/a

1000 KM DI MONZA

25 April 1971. Monza. 174 laps of a 3.573-mile circuit = 621.702 miles.
International Championship of Makes round 5

1	Pedro Rodriguez/			
	Jackie Oliver	Porsche 917K	174	4h14m32.6
2	Jo Siffert/Derek Bell	Porsche 917K	172	
3	Andrea de Adamich/			
	Henri Pescarolo	Alfa Romeo T33/3	169	
4	Rolf Stommelen/			
	Toine Hezemans	Alfa Romeo T33/3	168	
5	Nino Vaccarella/Toine Hezemans/			
	Rolf Stommelen	Alfa Romeo T33/3	167	
6	Herbert Muller/			
	Rene Herzog	Ferrari 512M	165	

Winner's average speed: 146.545 mph. Pole position: Vic Elford (Porsche
917K), 1m32.93. Fastest lap: Rodriguez, 1m24.0

1000 KM DE SPA-FRANCORCHAMPS

9 May 1971. Spa-Francorchamps. 71 laps of an 8.761-mile circuit =
622.031 miles. International Championship of Makes round 6

1	Pedro Rodriguez/			
	Jackie Oliver	Porsche 917K	71	4h01m09.7
2	Jo Siffert/Derek Bell	Porsche 917K	71	4h01m10.1
3	Andrea de Adamich/			
	Henri Pescarolo	Alfa Romeo T33/3	67	
4	Reinhold Joest/			
	Willi Kauhsen	Porsche 917K	66	
5	Claude Ballot-Lena/			
	Guy Chasseuil	Porsche 908/2	60	
6	Teddy Pilette/		Lola T70 Mk3B-		
	Gustave Gosselin	Chevrolet	58	

Winner's average speed: 154.759 mph. Pole position: Bell, 3m16.0. Fastest lap: Siffert, 3m14.6

TARGA FLORIO

16 May 1971. Madonie (Piccolo). 11 laps of a 44.739-mile circuit = 492.129 miles. International Championship of Makes round 7

1	Nino Vaccarella/			
	Toine Hezemans	Alfa Romeo T33/3	11	6h35m46.2
2	Andrea de Adamich/			
	Gijs van Lennep	Alfa Romeo T33/3	11	6h36m57.9
3	Jo Bonnier/			
	Richard Attwood	Lola T212-Ford	11	7h00m05.2
4	Bernard Cheneviere/			
	Paul Keller	Porsche 911S	10	
5	Michael Parkes/			
	Peter Westbury	Lola T212-Ford	10	
6	Giulio Pucci/Dieter Schmid	Porsche 911S	10	

Winner's average speed: 74.608 mph. Pole position: Vaccarella, 34m14.2. Fastest lap: Vic Elford (Porsche 908/3), 33m45.6

ADAC 1000 KM-RENNEN

30 May 1971. Nurburgring. 44 laps of a 14.189-mile circuit = 624.316 miles. International Championship of Makes round 8

1	Vic Elford/Gerard Larrousse	Porsche 908/3	44	5h51m49.3
2	Pedro Rodriguez/Jo Siffert	Porsche 908/3	44	5h53m33.4
3	Helmut Marko/			
	Gijs van Lennep	Porsche 908/3	44	5h53m33.5
4	Andrea de Adamich/			
	Henri Pescarolo	Alfa Romeo T33/3	44	5h56m20.0
5	Toine Hezemans/			
	Nino Vaccarella	Alfa Romeo T33/3	42	
6	Reinhold Joest/Willi Kauhsen	Porsche 917K	40	

Winner's average speed: 106.471 mph. Pole position: Jacky Ickx (Ferrari 312PB), 7m36.1. Fastest lap: Ickx, 7m40.8

24 HEURES DU MANS

12-13 June 1971. Le Mans. 396 laps of an 8.369-mile circuit = 3314.124 miles. International Championship of Makes round 9

1	Helmut Marko/			
	Gijs van Lennep	Porsche 917K	396	24 hours
2	Herbert Muller/			
	Richard Attwood	Porsche 917K	394	
3	Sam Posey/			
	Tony Adamowicz	Ferrari 512M	365	
4	Chris Craft/David Weir	Ferrari 512M	354	
5	Bob Grossman/			
	Luigi Chinetti Jr	Ferrari 365 GTB4 Daytona	313	
6	Raymond Touroul/			
	"Andre Anselme"	Porsche 911S	305	

Winner's average speed: 138.089 mph. Pole position: Pedro Rodriguez (Porsche 917LH), 3m13.9 - rolling start used for the first time. Fastest lap: Jackie Oliver (Porsche 917LH), 3m18.4

OSTERREICHRING 1000 KM-RENNEN

27 June 1971. Osterreichring. 170 laps of a 3.673-mile circuit = 624.410 miles. International Championship of Makes round 10

1	Pedro Rodriguez/			
	Richard Attwood	Porsche 917K	170	5h04m26.01
2	Toine Hezemans/			
	Nino Vaccarella	Alfa Romeo T33/3	168	
3	Rolf Stommelen/			
	Nanni Galli	Alfa Romeo T33/3	168	
4	"Pam"/Mario Casoni	Ferrari 512M	159	
5	"Pooky"/Ennio Bonomelli	Porsche 910	140	
6	Clemens Schickentanz/			
	Peter Kersten	Porsche 911S	139	

Winner's average speed: 123.063 mph. Pole position: Rodriguez, 1m39.49. Fastest lap: Rodriguez, 1m39.35

WATKINS GLEN 6 HOURS

24 July 1971. Watkins Glen. 279 laps of a 2.430-mile circuit = 677.970 miles. International Championship of Makes round 11

1	Andrea de Adamich/			
	Ronnie Peterson	Alfa Romeo T33/3	279	6h00m25.063
2	Jo Siffert/			
	Gijs van Lennep	Porsche 917K	277	
3	Derek Bell/			
	Richard Attwood	Porsche 917K	259	
4	Vic Elford/Nanni Galli	Alfa Romeo T33/3	258	accident
5	Alain de Cadenet/			
	Lothar Motschenbacher	Ferrari 512M	253	
6	John Greenwood/			
	Bob Johnson	Chevrolet Corvette	229	

Winner's average speed: 112.864 mph. Pole position: Mark Donohue (Ferrari 512M), 1m07.740. Fastest lap: Bell, 1m08.297

1971 FINAL CHAMPIONSHIP POSITIONS

Manufacturers		4=	Chevrolet	4
1 Porsche	63 (85)*		Lola-Ford	4
2 Alfa Romeo	47 (54)*	6	Lola-Chevrolet	1
3 Ferrari	24 (25)*		*Best even results count	

1972

World Championship of Makes

1000 KM DE LA CIUDAD DE BUENOS AIRES

9 January 1972. Buenos Aires. 168 laps of a 3.709-mile circuit = 623.112 miles. World Championship of Makes round 1

1	Ronnie Peterson/			
	Tim Schenken	Ferrari 312PB	168	5h45m58.22
2	Clay Regazzoni/			
	Brian Redman	Ferrari 312PB	168	5h48m02.97
3	Giovanni Alberti/Carlo Facetti/			
	Andrea de Adamich	Alfa Romeo T33/3	162	
4	Vic Elford/Helmut Marko	Alfa Romeo T33TT/3	160	
5	Jose Juncadella/			
	John Hine	Chevron B19-Ford	158	
6	Juan Fernandez/			
	Jorge de Bagration	Porsche 908/3	157	

Winner's average speed: 108.063 mph. Pole position: Peterson, 1m58.59. Fastest lap: Reine Wisell (Lola T280-Ford), 1m58.39

6 HOURS OF DAYTONA

6 February 1972. Daytona. 194 laps of a 3.810-mile circuit = 739.140 miles. World Championship of Makes round 2

1	Jacky Ickx/Mario Andretti	Ferrari 312PB	194	6h01m40.4
2	Ronnie Peterson/			
	Tim Schenken	Ferrari 312PB	192	
3	Vic Elford/Helmut Marko	Alfa Romeo T33TT/3	190	
4	Clay Regazzoni/			
	Brian Redman	Ferrari 312PB	179	
5	Andrea de Adamich/			
	Nanni Galli	Alfa Romeo T33/3	175	
6	Hubert Kleinpeter/			
	Tom Waugh	Lola T212-Ford	166	

Winner's average speed: 122.620 mph. Pole position: Andretti, 1m44.22. Fastest lap: Redman, time n/a

12 HOURS OF SEBRING

25 March 1972. Sebring. 259 laps of a 5.200-mile circuit = 1346.800 miles. World Championship of Makes round 3

1	Jacky Ickx/Mario Andretti	Ferrari 312PB	259	12h04m41.006
2	Ronnie Peterson/			
	Tim Schenken	Ferrari 312PB	257	

3 Toine Hezemans/			
Nino Vaccarella	Alfa Romeo T33TT/3	233	
4 David Heinz/Bob Johnson	Chevrolet Corvette	221	
5 Peter Gregg/			
Hurley Haywood	Porsche 911S	215	
6 Jo Bonnier/Reine Wisell/			
Gerard Larrousse	Lola T212-Ford	213	

Winner's average speed: 111.508 mph. Pole position: Andretti, 2m31.44. Fastest lap: Schenken, 2m33.80

BOAC 1000 KMS

16 April 1972. Brands Hatch. 235 laps of a 2.650-mile circuit = 622.750 miles. World Championship of Makes round 4

1 Jacky Ickx/Mario Andretti	Ferrari 312PB	235	5h55m27.5
2 Ronnie Peterson/			
Tim Schenken	Ferrari 312PB	234	
3 Rolf Stommelen/			
Peter Revson	Alfa Romeo T33TT/3	233	
4 Vic Elford/			
Andrea de Adamich	Alfa Romeo T33TT/3	231	
5 Clay Regazzoni/			
Brian Redman	Ferrari 312PB	220	
6 Helmut Marko/			
Nanni Galli	Alfa Romeo T33TT/3	220	

Francois Migault/Brian Robinson (Chevron B21-Ford), 220 laps, finished fifth on the road but disqualified as car was underweight. Winner's average speed: 105.118 mph. Pole position: Regazzoni, 1m26.6. Fastest lap: Ickx, Peterson and Regazzoni, 1m27.4

1000 KM DI MONZA/TROFEO FILIPPO CARACCIOLO

25 April 1972. Monza. 174 laps of a 3.573-mile circuit = 621.702 miles. World Championship of Makes round 5

1 Jacky Ickx/			
Clay Regazzoni	Ferrari 312PB	174	5h52m05.6
2 Reinhold Joest/			
Gerhard Schuler	Porsche 908/3	170	
3 Ronnie Peterson/			
Tim Schenken	Ferrari 312PB	165	
4 Peter Mattli/Herve Bayard	Porsche 907	153	
5 Ugo Locatelli/"Pal Joe"	De Tomaso Pantera-Ford	147	
6 Eris Tondelli/			
Mauro Formento	Chevron B19-Ford	129	

Winner's average speed: 105.944 mph. Pole position: Peterson, 1m24.75. Fastest lap: Peterson, 1m46.1

1000 KM DE SPA-FRANCORCHAMPS

7 May 1972. Spa-Francorchamps. 71 laps of an 8.761-mile circuit = 622.031 miles. World Championship of Makes round 6

1 Brian Redman/			
Arturo Merzario	Ferrari 312PB	71	4h17m19.1
2 Jacky Ickx/Clay Regazzoni	Ferrari 312PB	70	
3 John Hine/John Bridges	Chevron B19/21-Ford	66	
4 Derek Bell/			
Gijs van Lennep	Mirage M6-Ford	64	
5 Gerard Larrousse/			
Hugues de Fierlandt	Lola T280-Ford	64	
6 Peter Humble/Nick May	Chevron B19/21-Ford	60	

Winner's average speed: 145.042 mph. Pole position: Ickx, 3m20.4. Fastest lap: Ickx, 3m20.7

TARGA FLORIO

21 May 1972. Madonie (Piccolo). 11 laps of a 44.739-mile circuit = 492.129 miles. World Championship of Makes round 7

1 Arturo Merzario/			
Sandro Munari	Ferrari 312PB	11	6h27m48.0
2 Helmut Marko/			
Nanni Galli	Alfa Romeo T33TT/3	11	6h28m04.9

3 Andrea de Adamich/			
Toine Hezemans	Alfa Romeo T33TT/3	11	6h46m12.2
4 Antonio Zadra/			
Enrico Pasolini	Lola T290-Ford	10	
5 Pino Pica/Gabriele Gottifredi	Porsche 911S	10	
6 Gunther Steckkonig/			
Giulio Pucci	Porsche 911S	9	accident

Winner's average speed: 76.142 mph. Pole position: Merzario, 33m59.7. Fastest lap: Marko, 33m41.0

ADAC 1000 KM-RENNEN

28 May 1972. Nurburgring. 44 laps of a 14.189-mile circuit = 624.316 miles. World Championship of Makes round 8

1 Ronnie Peterson/			
Tim Schenken	Ferrari 312PB	44	6h01m40.2
2 Brian Redman/Arturo Merzario	Ferrari 312PB	44	6h06m09.9
3 Andrea de Adamich/			
Helmut Marko	Alfa Romeo T33TT/3	43	
4 Derek Bell/Gijs van Lennep	Mirage M6-Ford	42	
5 John Hine/John Bridges	Chevron B21-Ford	41	
6 Gerard Larrousse/Jo Bonnier	Lola T290-Ford	39	

Winner's average speed: 103.572 mph. Pole position: Peterson, 7m56.1. Fastest lap: Rolf Stommelen (Alfa Romeo T33TT/3), 7m42.2

24 HEURES DU MANS

10-11 June 1972. Le Mans. 343 laps of an 8.476-mile circuit = 2907.268 miles. World Championship of Makes round 9

1 Henri Pescarolo/			
Graham Hill	Matra-Simca MS670	343	24 hours
2 Francois Cevert/			
Howden Ganley	Matra-Simca MS670	333	
3 Reinhold Joest/Michael Weber/			
Mario Casoni	Porsche 908L	324	
4 Andrea de Adamich/			
Nino Vaccarella	Alfa Romeo T33TT/3	306	
5 Jean-Claude Andruet/			
Claude Ballot-Lena	Ferrari 365 GTB4 Daytona	305	
6 Sam Posey/			
Tony Adamowicz	Ferrari 365 GTB4 Daytona	303	

Winner's average speed: 121.136 mph. Pole position: Cevert, 3m42.2. Fastest lap: Gijs van Lennep (Lola T280-Ford), 3m46.9

OSTERREICHRING 1000 KM-RENNEN

25 June 1972. Osterreichring. 170 laps of a 3.673-mile circuit = 624.410 miles. World Championship of Makes round 10

1 Jacky Ickx/Brian Redman	Ferrari 312PB	170	4h58m46.28
2 Helmut Marko/			
Carlos Pace	Ferrari 312PB	169	
3 Ronnie Peterson/			
Tim Schenken	Ferrari 312PB	166	
4 Arturo Merzario/			
Sandro Munari	Ferrari 312PB	164	
5 Rolf Stommelen/			
Toine Hezemans	Chevron B21-BMW	164	
6 Jose Juncadella/			
John Bridges	Chevron B21-Ford	158	

Winner's average speed: 125.396 mph. Pole position: Derek Bell (Mirage M6-Ford), 1m40.60. Fastest lap: Ickx, 1m41.88

WATKINS GLEN 6 HOURS

22 July 1972. Watkins Glen. 195 laps of a 3.377-mile circuit = 658.515 miles. World Championship of Makes round 11

1 Jacky Ickx/Mario Andretti	Ferrari 312PB	195	6h01m11.276
2 Ronnie Peterson/			
Tim Schenken	Ferrari 312PB	195	6h01m25.300
3 Derek Bell/Carlos Pace	Mirage M6-Ford	181	
4 Tony Dean/Bob Brown	Porsche 908/2	171	

5 Reinhold Joest/
  Mario Casoni   Porsche 908/3   166
6 Jean-Pierre Jarier/   Ferrari 365 GTB4
  Gregg Young   Daytona   156
Winner's average speed: 109.392 mph. Pole position: Schenken, 1m47.387. Fastest lap: Ickx, 1m47.204

1972 FINAL CHAMPIONSHIP POSITIONS

Manufacturers			
1 Ferrari	160 (208)*	8 Chevrolet	14
2 Alfa Romeo	85	9 de Tomaso-Ford	12
3 Porsche	66 (71)*	10 Chevron-BMW	8
4 Lola-Ford	48	11 Ford	5
5 Chevron-Ford	45	12 Osella-Abarth	4
6 Mirage-Ford	32	13 Lola-Alfa Romeo	3
7 Matra-Simca	20	*Best eight results count	

1973
World Championship of Makes

DAYTONA 24 HOURS

3-4 February 1973. Daytona. 670 laps of a 3.810-mile circuit = 2552.700 miles. World Championship of Makes round 1

1 Peter Gregg/
  Hurley Haywood   Porsche 911 Carrera RSR 670   24h01m11.9
2 Milt Minter/
  Francois Migault   Ferrari 365 GTB4 Daytona 648
3 David Heinz/Bob McClure/
  Dana English   Chevrolet Corvette   642
4 George Stone/Bruce Jennings/
  Mike Downs   Porsche 911S   638
5 Luigi Chinetti jr/Bob Grossman/
  Wilbur Shaw jr   Ferrari 365 GTB4 Daytona 632
6 John Fitzpatrick/Erwin Kremer/
  Paul Keller   Porsche 911S   630
Winner's average speed: 106.274 mph. Pole position: Derek Bell (Mirage M6-Ford), 1m45.512. Fastest lap: Mike Hailwood (Mirage M6-Ford), 1m49.604

6 ORE DI VALLELUNGA

25 March 1973. Vallelunga. 290 laps of a 1.988-mile circuit = 576.520 miles. World Championship of Makes round 2

1 Henri Pescarolo/Gerard Larrousse/
  Francois Cevert   Matra-Simca MS670 290   6 hours
2 Tim Schenken/
  Carlos Reutemann   Ferrari 312PB   289
3 Jacky Ickx/Brian Redman Ferrari 312PB   289
4 Carlos Pace/
  Arturo Merzario   Ferrari 312PB   288
5 Reinhold Joest/
  Mario Casoni   Porsche 908/3   272
6 Reine Wisell/
  Jean-Louis Lafosse   Lola T282-Ford   268
Winner's average speed: 96.087 mph. Pole position: Cevert, 1m08.55. Fastest lap: Schenken, 1m09.7

1000 KM DE DIJON

15 April 1973. Dijon-Prenois. 312 laps of a 2.044-mile circuit = 637.728 miles. World Championship of Makes round 3

1 Henri Pescarolo/
  Gerard Larrousse   Matra-Simca MS670 312   5h34m37.1
2 Jacky Ickx/Brian Redman Ferrari 312PB   311
3 Jean-Pierre Beltoise/
  Francois Cevert   Matra-Simca MS670 308

4 Carlos Pace/
  Arturo Merzario   Ferrari 312PB   308
5 Mike Hailwood/
  Vern Schuppan   Mirage M6-Ford   303
6 Reine Wisell/
  Jean-Louis Lafosse   Lola T282-Ford   290
Winner's average speed: 114.350 mph. Pole position: Cevert, 59.4s. Fastest lap: Cevert, 1m00.6

1000 KM DI MONZA/TROFEO FILIPPO CARACCIOLO

25 April 1973. Monza. 174 laps of a 3.573-mile circuit = 621.702 miles. World Championship of Makes round 4

1 Jacky Ickx/Brian Redman Ferrari 312PB   174   4h07m34.4
2 Tim Schenken/
  Carlos Reutemann   Ferrari 312PB   171
3 Henri Pescarolo/
  Gerard Larrousse   Matra-Simca MS670 164
4 Giancarlo Gagliardi/
  "Pooky"   Lola T290-Ford   150
5 Carlo Facetti/"Pam"   Alfa Romeo T33TT/3 149
6 Giorgio Schon/"Pal Joe" Lola T290-Abarth   145
Winner's average speed: 150.671 mph. Pole position: Francois Cevert (Matra-Simca MS670), 1m21.13. Fastest lap: Cevert, 1m21.9

1000 KM DE SPA-FRANCORCHAMPS

6 May 1973. Spa-Francorchamps. 71 laps of an 8.761-mile circuit = 622.031 miles. World Championship of Makes round 5

1 Derek Bell/Mike Hailwood Mirage M6-Ford   71   4h05m43.5
2 Mike Hailwood/Vern Schuppan/
  Howden Ganley   Mirage M6-Ford   69
3 Henri Pescarolo/Gerard Larrousse/
  Chris Amon   Matra-Simca MS670 68
4 Arturo Merzario/
  Carlos Pace   Ferrari 312PB   67
5 Gijs van Lennep/
  Herbert Muller   Porsche 911 Carrera RSR 63
6 Carlos Santos/
  Carlos Mendoza   Lola T292-Ford   62
Winner's average speed: 151.885 mph. Pole position: Jacky Ickx (Ferrari 312PB), 3m12.7. Fastest lap: Pescarolo, 3m13.4

TARGA FLORIO

13 May 1973. Madonie (Piccolo). 11 laps of a 44.739-mile circuit = 492.129 miles. World Championship of Makes round 6

1 Gijs van Lennep/
  Herbert Muller   Porsche 911 Carrera RSR 11   6h54m19.9
2 Sandro Munari/
  Jean-Claude Andruet   Lancia Stratos   11   7h00m30.5
3 Leo Kinnunen/
  Claude Haldi   Porsche 911 Carrera RSR 11   7h12m42.5
4 Luigi Moreschi/
  "Frank McBoden"   Chevron B21-Ford   11   7h17m34.4
5 Silvio Moser/
  Antonio Nicodemi   Lola T290-Ford   11   7h25m35.5
6 Gunther Steckkonig/
  Giulio Pucci   Porsche 911 Carrera RSR 11   7h27m29.9
Winner's average speed: 71.266 mph. Pole position: Arturo Merzario (Ferrari 312PB), 33m38.5. Fastest lap: Rolf Stommelen (Alfa Romeo T33TT/12), 34m13.1

ADAC 1000 KM-RENNEN

27 May 1973. Nurburgring. 44 laps of a 14.189-mile circuit = 624.316 miles. World Championship of Makes round 7

1 Jacky Ickx/Brian Redman Ferrari 312PB   44   5h36m53.4
2 Arturo Merzario/
  Carlos Pace   Ferrari 312PB   44   5h36m53.5
3 John Burton/
  John Bridges   Chevron B23-Ford   40

4 Claude Haldi/
  Bernard Cheneviere   Porsche 908/3   40
5 Gijs van Lennep/
  Herbert Muller   Porsche 911 Carrera RSR 40
6 John Fitzpatrick/
  Gerry Birrell   Ford Capri RS2600   39
Winner's average speed: 111.190 mph. Pole position: Francois Cevert
(Matra-Simca MS670), 7m12.8. Fastest lap: Cevert, 7m20.3

24 HEURES DU MANS

9-10 June 1973. Le Mans. 355 laps of an 8.476-mile circuit = 3008.980
miles. World Championship of Makes round 8

1 Henri Pescarolo/
  Gerard Larrousse   Matra-Simca MS670B   355   24 hours
2 Arturo Merzario/
  Carlos Pace   Ferrari 312PB   349
3 Jean-Pierre Jabouille/
  Jean-Pierre Jaussaud Matra-Simca MS670B   331
4 Gijs van Lennep/
  Herbert Muller   Porsche 911 Carrera RSR 328
5 Juan Fernandez/Bernard Cheneviere/
  Paco Torredemer   Porsche 908/3   319
6 Vic Elford/
  Claude Ballot-Lena   Ferrari 365 GTB4 Daytona 316
Winner's average speed: 125.374 mph. Pole position: Merzario, 3m37.5.
Fastest lap: Francois Cevert (Matra-Simca MS670B), 3m39.6

OSTERREICHRING 1000 KM-RENNEN

24 June 1973. Osterreichring. 170 laps of a 3.673-mile circuit = 624.410
miles. World Championship of Makes round 9

1 Henri Pescarolo/
  Gerard Larrousse   Matra-Simca MS670 170 4h48m57.80
2 Jean-Pierre Beltoise/
  Francois Cevert   Matra-Simca MS670 170 4h49m44.43
3 Jacky Ickx/Brian Redman Ferrari 312PB   169
4 Mike Hailwood/John Watson Mirage M6-Ford   167
5 Derek Bell/Howden Ganley Mirage M6-Ford   166
6 Arturo Merzario/Carlos Pace Ferrari 312PB   164
Winner's average speed: 129.652 mph. Pole position: Cevert, 1m37.64.
Fastest lap: Cevert, 1m38.30

WATKINS GLEN 6 HOURS

21 July 1973. Watkins Glen. 199 laps of a 3.377-mile circuit = 672.023
miles. World Championship of Makes round 10

1 Henri Pescarolo/
  Gerard Larrousse   Matra-Simca MS670 199 6h00m20.938
2 Jacky Ickx/
  Brian Redman   Ferrari 312PB   197
3 Arturo Merzario/
  Carlos Pace   Ferrari 312PB   196
4 Derek Bell/
  Howden Ganley   Mirage M6-Ford   180
5 Mike Hailwood/
  John Watson   Mirage M6-Ford   179
6 Mark Donohue/
  George Follmer   Porsche 911 Carrera RSR 178
Winner's average speed: 111.895 mph. Pole position: Francois Cevert
(Matra-Simca MS670B), 1m42.273. Fastest lap: Cevert, 1m43.847

1973 FINAL CHAMPIONSHIP POSITIONS

Manufacturers			
1 Matra-Simca	124	7 Lancia	15
2 Ferrari	115 (137)*	8 Chevrolet	14
3 Porsche	82 (91)*	9 Alfa Romeo	13
4 Mirage-Ford	48	10= BMW	6
5 Lola-Ford/Abarth	36	Ford	6
6 Chevron-Ford	30	*Best seven results count	

1974
World Championship of Makes

1000 KM DI MONZA/TROFEO FILIPPO CARACCIOLO

25 April 1974. Monza. 174 laps of a 3.588-mile circuit = 624.312 miles.
World Championship of Makes round 1

1 Arturo Merzario/
  Mario Andretti   Alfa Romeo T33TT/12 174 4h45m57.4
2 Rolf Stommelen/
  Jacky Ickx   Alfa Romeo T33TT/12 170
3 Carlo Facetti/
  Andrea de Adamich Alfa Romeo T33TT/12 166
4 Mike Hailwood/
  Derek Bell   Mirage GR7-Ford   166
5 Gijs van Lennep/
  Herbert Muller   Porsche 911 Carrera RSR 165
6 Pino Pica/
  Giorgio Pianta   Lola T282-Ford   161
Winner's average speed: 130.994 mph. Pole position: Merzario, 1m28.26.
Fastest lap: Bell, 1m31.3

1000 KM DE SPA-FRANCORCHAMPS

5 May 1974. Spa-Francorchamps. 71 laps of an 8.761-mile circuit =
622.031 miles. World Championship of Makes round 2

1 Jacky Ickx/
  Jean-Pierre Jarier Matra-Simca MS670C 71 4h12m15.6
2 Mike Hailwood/
  Derek Bell   Mirage GR7-Ford   71 4h15m10.6
3 Gijs van Lennep/
  Herbert Muller   Porsche 911 Carrera RSR 66
4 John Fitzpatrick/
  Jurgen Barth   Porsche 911 Carrera RSR 62
5 Clemens Schickentanz/
  Willi Kauhsen   Porsche 911 Carrera RSR 62
6 Paul Keller/Hans Heyer Porsche 911 Carrera RSR 62
Winner's average speed: 147.950 mph. Pole position: Bell, 3m23.9. Fastest
lap: Ickx, 3m19.7

ADAC 1000 KM-RENNEN

19 May 1974. Nurburgring. 33 laps of a 14.189-mile circuit = 468.237
miles. Race distance reduced due to oil crisis. World Championship of
Makes round 3

1 Jean-Pierre Beltoise/
  Jean-Pierre Jarier Matra-Simca MS670C 33 4h07m24.1
2 Rolf Stommelen/
  Carlos Reutemann Alfa Romeo T33TT/12 32
3 Carlo Facetti/
  Andrea de Adamich Alfa Romeo T33TT/12 32
4 James Hunt/Vern Schuppan/
  Derek Bell   Mirage GR7-Ford   32
5 Henri Pescarolo/
  Gerard Larrousse Matra-Simca MS670C 31
6 Gijs van Lennep/
  Herbert Muller   Porsche 911 Carrera RSR 30
Winner's average speed: 113.557 mph. Pole position: Pescarolo, 7m10.8.
Fastest lap: Jarier, 7m15.9

1000 KM DI IMOLA

2 June 1974. Imola. 198 laps of a 3.144-mile circuit = 622.512 miles.
World Championship of Makes round 4

1 Henri Pescarolo/
  Gerard Larrousse Matra-Simca MS670C 198 6h13m36.0
2 Rolf Stommelen/
  Carlos Reutemann Alfa Romeo T33TT/12 196
3 Carlo Facetti/
  Andrea de Adamich Alfa Romeo T33TT/12 189
4 Jean-Pierre Beltoise/
  Jean-Pierre Jarier Matra-Simca MS670C 184 engine

5 Paul Keller/Hans Heyer   Porsche 911 Carrera RSR   177
6 Giovanni Borri/
   Giorgio Schon   Porsche 911 Carrera RSR   173
Winner's average speed: 99.975 mph. Pole position: Beltoise, 1m40.17.
Fastest lap: Larrousse, 1m40.8

24 HEURES DU MANS

15-16 June 1974. Le Mans. 337 laps of an 8.476-mile circuit = 2856.412 miles. World Championship of Makes round 5

1 Henri Pescarolo/
   Gerard Larrousse   Matra-Simca MS670B   337   24 hours
2 Gijs van Lennep/
   Herbert Muller   Porsche 911 Carrera RSR   331
3 Jean-Pierre Jabouille/
   Francois Migault   Matra-Simca MS670B   324
4 Mike Hailwood/
   Derek Bell   Mirage GR7-Ford   317
5 Cyrille Grandet/
   "Dominique Bardini"   Ferrari 365 GTB4 Daytona   313
6 David Heinz/
   Alain Cudini   Ferrari 365 GTB4 Daytona   312
Winner's average speed: 119.017 mph. Pole position: Larrousse, 3m35.8.
Fastest lap: Jean-Pierre Jarier (Matra-Simca MS680), 3m42.7

OSTERREICHRING 1000 KM-RENNEN

30 June 1974. Osterreichring. 170 laps of a 3.673-mile circuit = 624.410 miles. World Championship of Makes round 6

1 Henri Pescarolo/
   Gerard Larrousse   Matra-Simca MS670C   170   4h51m20.27
2 Carlo Facetti/
   Andrea de Adamich   Alfa Romeo T33TT/12   167
3 Jean-Pierre Beltoise/
   Jean-Pierre Jarier   Matra-Simca MS670C   166
4 Mike Hailwood/
   Derek Bell   Mirage GR7-Ford   166
5 Jacky Ickx/Arturo Merzario/
   Vittorio Brambilla   Alfa Romeo T33TT/12   152   engine
6 Gijs van Lennep/
   Herbert Muller   Porsche 911 Carrera RSR 151
Winner's average speed: 128.595 mph. Pole position: Larrousse, 1m35.97.
Fastest lap: Ickx, 1m35.81

WATKINS GLEN 6 HOURS

13 July 1974. Watkins Glen. 193 laps of a 3.377-mile circuit = 651.761 miles. World Championship of Makes round 7

1 Jean-Pierre Beltoise/
   Jean-Pierre Jarier   Matra-Simca MS670C   193   6h01m33.800
2 Gijs van Lennep/
   Herbert Muller   Porsche 911 Carrera RSR   184
3 Peter Gregg/
   Hurley Haywood   Porsche 911 Carrera RSR   176
4 Ludwig Heimrath/
   Jim Cook   Porsche 911 Carrera RSR   172
5 Maurice Carter/
   Tony de Lorenzo   Chevrolet Camaro   168
6 Jacques Bienvenue/
   Marc Dancose   Porsche 911 Carrera RSR   164
Mario Andretti/Arturo Merzario (Alfa Romeo T33TT/12), 171 laps, finished
fifth on the road but disqualified for outside assistance. Winner's average
speed: 108.157 mph. Pole position: Gerard Larrousse (Matra-Simca
MS670C), 1m43.698. Fastest lap: Beltoise, 1m44.005

1000 KM DU CASTELLET

15 August 1974. Paul Ricard. 130 laps of a 3.610-mile circuit = 469.300 miles. Race distance reduced due to oil crisis. World Championship of Makes round 8

1 Jean-Pierre Beltoise/
   Jean-Pierre Jarier   Matra-Simca MS670C   130   4h10m57.7
2 Henri Pescarolo/
   Gerard Larrousse   Matra-Simca MS670C   127
3 Jacky Ickx/Derek Bell   Mirage GR7-Ford   125
4 Reinhold Joest/
   Mario Casoni   Porsche 908/3   119
5 Paul Blancpain/
   Knut-Holger Lehmann   Porsche 908/3   114
6 Guy Chasseuil/
   Francois Migault   Ligier JS2-Maserati   114
Winner's average speed: 112.200 mph. Pole position: Jarier, 1m49.1.
Fastest lap: Beltoise, 1m50.6

BRITISH AIRWAYS 1000 KMS

29 September 1974. Brands Hatch. 235 laps of a 2.650-mile circuit = 622.750 miles. World Championship of Makes round 9

1 Jean-Pierre Beltoise/
   Jean-Pierre Jarier   Matra-Simca MS670C   235   5h47m33.01
2 Henri Pescarolo/
   Gerard Larrousse   Matra-Simca MS670C   235   5h47m35.80
3 Derek Bell/
   David Hobbs   Mirage GR7-Ford   224
4 Peter Gethin/
   Brian Redman   Chevron B26-Hart   224
5 Herbert Muller/   Porsche 911
   Gijs van Lennep   Carrera RSR   219
6 Jurgen Barth/Claude Haldi Porsche 908/3   213
Winner's average speed: 107.510 mph. Pole position: Beltoise, 1m23.3.
Fastest lap: Jarier, 1m22.5

KYALAMI 9 HOURS

9 November 1974. Kyalami. 235 laps of a 2.550-mile circuit = 599.250 miles. Race distance reduced to 6 hours due to oil crisis. World Championship of Makes round 10

1 Henri Pescarolo/
   Gerard Larrousse   Matra-Simca MS670C   235   6 hours
2 Jean-Pierre Beltoise/
   Jean-Pierre Jarier   Matra-Simca MS670C   235
3 Derek Bell/David Hobbs   Mirage GR7-Ford   229
4 John Lepp/Guy Tunmer   Chevron B26-Ford   217
5 Jochen Mass/
   Toine Hezemans   Ford Capri RS3100   215
6 Rolf Stommelen/John Fitzpatrick/
   Tim Schenken   Porsche 911 Carrera RSR   214
Winner's average speed: 99.875 mph. Pole position: Beltoise, 1m18.03.
Fastest lap: Larrousse, 1m19.3

1974 FINAL CHAMPIONSHIP POSITIONS

Manufacturers		11= BMW	3
1 Matra-Simca	140 (180)*	March-Ford	3
2 Mirage-Ford	81 (91)*	13 Mazda	2
3 Porsche	76 (94)*	14= Alpine-Renault	1
4 Alfa Romeo	65	AMS-Ford	1
5 Chevron-Ford/Hart	30	Ecosse-Ford	1
6 Ligier-Maserati	12	*Best seven results count	
7 Lola-Ford	10		
8= Chevrolet	8		
Ferrari	8		
Ford	8		

1975
World Championship of Makes

DAYTONA 24 HOURS

1-2 February 1975. Daytona. 684 laps of a 3.870-mile circuit = 2647.080 miles. World Championship of Makes round 1

1	Peter Gregg/ Hurley Haywood	Porsche 911 Carrera RSR	684	24h00m43.0
2	Michael Keyser/Bill Sprowls/ Andreas Contreras	Porsche 911 Carrera RSR	669	
3	Charlie Kemp/ Carson Baird	Porsche 911 Carrera RSR	668	
4	George Dyer/ Jacques Bienvenue	Porsche 911 Carrera RSR	665	
5	Bill Webbe/George Dickinson/ Harry Theodoracopulos	Porsche 911 Carrera RSR	623	
6	John Graves/John O'Steen/ Dave Helmick	Porsche 911 Carrera RSR	619	

Winner's average speed: 110.240 mph. Pole position: John Greenwood (Chevrolet Corvette), 1m55.223. Fastest lap: Greenwood, 1m57.300

1000 KM DI MUGELLO

23 March 1975. Mugello. 150 laps of a 3.259-mile circuit = 488.850 miles. Race distance reduced due to oil crisis. World Championship of Makes round 2

1	Gerard Larrousse/ Jean-Pierre Jabouille	Alpine A442-Renault	150	4h47m34.7
2	Arturo Merzario/ Jacky Ickx	Alfa Romeo T33TT/12	149	
3	Gijs van Lennep/ Herbert Muller	Porsche 908/3	149	
4	Henri Pescarolo/ Derek Bell	Alfa Romeo T33TT/12	148	
5	John Hine/Ian Grob	Chevron B31-Hart	144	
6	Lella Lombardi/ "Marie-Claude Beaumont"	Alpine A441-Renault	144	

Winner's average speed: 101.993 mph. Pole position: Merzario, 1m48.83. Fastest lap: Jabouille, 1m49.8

1000 KM DE DIJON

6 April 1975. Dijon-Prenois. 245 laps of a 2.044-mile circuit = 500.780 miles. Race distance reduced due to oil crisis. World Championship of Makes round 3

1	Arturo Merzario/ Jacques Laffite	Alfa Romeo T33TT/12	245	4h27m28.8
2	Reinhold Joest/ Mario Casoni	Porsche 908/3	238	
3	John Hine/Ian Grob	Chevron B31-Hart	234	
4	Henri Pescarolo/ Derek Bell	Alfa Romeo T33TT/12	225	
5	Toine Hezemans/ John Fitzpatrick	Porsche 911 Carrera RSR	220	
6	Francois Migault/ Jean-Pierre Jarier	Ligier JS2-Ford	219	

Winner's average speed: 112.333 mph. Pole position: Gerard Larrousse (Alpine A442-Renault), 1m00.9. Fastest lap: Merzario, 1m01.5

1000 KM DI MONZA/TROFEO FILIPPO CARACCIOLO

20 April 1975. Monza. 174 laps of a 3.592-mile circuit = 625.008 miles. World Championship of Makes round 4

1	Arturo Merzario/ Jacques Laffite	Alfa Romeo T33TT/12	174	4h43m21.8
2	Reinhold Joest/ Mario Casoni	Porsche 908/3	171	
3	Gerard Larrousse/ Jean-Pierre Jabouille	Alpine A442-Renault	170	
4	Lella Lombardi/ "Marie-Claude Beaumont"	Alpine A441-Renault	166	

5	Jurgen Barth/Ernst Kraus	Porsche 908/3	162	
6	Toine Hezemans/Manfred Schurti/ John Fitzpatrick	Porsche 911 Carrera RSR	159	

Winner's average speed: 132.341 mph. Pole position: Jochen Mass (Mirage GR7-Ford), 1m28.97. Fastest lap: Larrousse, 1m30.2

1000 KM DE SPA-FRANCORCHAMPS

4 May 1975. Spa-Francorchamps. 54 laps of an 8.761-mile circuit = 473.094 miles. Race distance reduced due to oil crisis. World Championship of Makes round 5

1	Henri Pescarolo/ Derek Bell	Alfa Romeo T33TT/12	54	3h32m54.4
2	Jacky Ickx/ Arturo Merzario	Alfa Romeo T33TT/12	53	
3	Alain Peltier/Sigi Muller	BMW 3.0 CSL	49	
4	Claude Haldi/ Bernard Beguin	Porsche 911 Carrera RSR	48	
5	Claude Ballot-Lena/ Jean-Claude Andruet	Porsche 911 Carrera RSR	48	
6	Clemens Schickentanz/Hartwig Bertrams/ Reine Wisell	Porsche 911 Carrera RSR	48	

Winner's average speed: 133.324 mph. Pole position: Bell, 3m20.4. Fastest lap: Ickx, 3m25.5

COPPA FLORIO

18 May 1975. Enna-Pergusa. 207 laps of a 3.011-mile circuit = 623.277 miles. World Championship of Makes round 6

1	Arturo Merzario/ Jochen Mass	Alfa Romeo T33TT/12	207	5h05m25.7
2	Henri Pescarolo/ Derek Bell	Alfa Romeo T33TT/12	206	
3	Reinhold Joest/ Mario Casoni	Porsche 908/3	184	
4	Hartwig Bertrams/Reine Wisell/ Clemens Schickentanz	Porsche 911 Carrera RSR	182	
5	Clemens Schickentanz/Hartwig Bertrams/ Reine Wisell	Porsche 911 Carrera RSR	182	
6	Giancarlo Gagliardi/ "Bramen"	Chevron B31-Ford	175	

Winner's average speed: 122.440 mph. Pole position: Merzario, 1m21.76. Fastest lap: Merzario, 1m24.1

ADAC 1000 KM-RENNEN

1 June 1975. Nurburgring. 44 laps of a 14.189-mile circuit = 624.316 miles. World Championship of Makes round 7

1	Arturo Merzario/ Jacques Laffite	Alfa Romeo T33TT/12	44	5h41m14.1
2	Tim Schenken/ Howden Ganley	Mirage GR7-Ford	44	5h41m54.0
3	Herbert Muller/ Leo Kinnunen	Porsche 908/3	43	
4	Gerard Larrousse/ Jean-Pierre Jabouille	Alpine A442-Renault	43	
5	Jurgen Barth/ Ernst Kraus	Porsche 908/3	42	
6	Jochen Mass/ Jody Scheckter	Alfa Romeo T33TT/12	42	

Winner's average speed: 109.775 mph. Pole position: Jabouille, 7m12.1. Fastest lap: Larrousse, 7m20.8

OSTERREICHRING 1000 KM-RENNEN

29 June 1975. Osterreichring. 103 laps of a 3.673-mile circuit = 378.319 miles. Race stopped due to rain. World Championship of Makes round 8

1	Henri Pescarolo/ Derek Bell	Alfa Romeo T33TT/12	103	3h34m50.88
2	Arturo Merzario/ Vittorio Brambilla	Alfa Romeo T33TT/12	103	3h36m13.28
3	Reinhold Joest/ Mario Casoni	Porsche 908/3	102	

4 Jurgen Barth/Ernst Kraus   Porsche 908/3   92
5 Dave Morgan/John Lepp   March 75S-Hart   90
6 Manfred Mohr/
   Martino Finotto   Lola T294-Ferrari   87
Winner's average speed: 105.652 mph. Pole position: Gerard Larrousse
(Alpine A442-Renault), 1m36.35. Fastest lap: Jody Scheckter (Alpine A442-
Renault), 1m41.21

WATKINS GLEN 6 HOURS

12 July 1975. Watkins Glen. 152 laps of a 3.377-mile circuit = 513.304 miles. World Championship of Makes round 9

1 Henri Pescarolo/
   Derek Bell   Alfa Romeo T33TT/12   152 6h01m23.900
2 Mario Andretti/
   Arturo Merzario   Alfa Romeo T33TT/12   152 6h02m43.932
3 Gerard Larrousse/
   Jean-Pierre Jarier   Alpine A442-Renault   149
4 Reinhold Joest/
   Mario Casoni   Porsche 908/3   149
5 Robert Hagestad/
   Hurley Haywood   Porsche 911 Carrera RSR 143
6 Brian Redman/Sam Posey   BMW 3.0 CSL   142
Winner's average speed: 85.220 mph. Pole position: Jody Scheckter
(Alpine A442-Renault), 1m42.890. Fastest lap: Larrousse, 1m45.956

1975 FINAL CHAMPIONSHIP POSITIONS

Manufacturers					
1	Alfa Romeo	140 (155)*	7	March-Hart	12
2	Porsche	98 (118)*	8=	Ligier-Ford	10
3	Alpine-Renault	54		Lola-Ford/Ferrari	10
4	Chevron-Ford/Hart	35	10	Ferrari	4
5	BMW	18	11	Chevrolet	2
6	Mirage-Ford	15		*Best seven results count	

1976
World Championship of Makes

6 ORE ETIENNE AIGNER

21 March 1976. Mugello. 174 laps of a 3.259-mile circuit = 567.066 miles. World Championship of Makes round 1

1 Jacky Ickx/Jochen Mass   Porsche 935   174 6h00m53.3
2 Bob Wollek/Hans Heyer   Porsche 935   168
3 Leo Kinnunen/
   Egon Evertz   Porsche 934   162
4 Reinhold Joest/Jurgen Barth/
   Willi Bartels   Porsche 911 Carrera RSR 161
5 Kenneth Leim/
   Kurt Simonsen   Porsche 911 Carrera RSR 157
6 Rolf Stommelen/
   Tim Schenken   Porsche 934   155
Winner's average speed: 94.278 mph. Pole position: Ickx, 1m55.28. Fastest
lap: Ickx, 1m58.07

6 ORE DI VALLELUNGA/TROFEO IGNAZIO GIUNTI

4 April 1976. Vallelunga. 269 laps of a 1.988 mile-circuit = 534.772 miles. World Championship of Makes round 2

1 Jacky Ickx/Jochen Mass   Porsche 935   269 6 hours
2 Harald Grohs/Sam Posey/
   Hugues de Fierlandt   BMW 3.5 CSL   253
3 Kenneth Leim/
   Kurt Simonsen   Porsche 911 Carrera RSR 244
4 John Fitzpatrick/
   Tom Walkinshaw   BMW 3.5 CSL   242

5 Giorgio Schon/Luigi Tommasi/
   Giuseppe Bianco   Porsche 934   242
6 Michele di Gioia/
   Vittorio Bernasconi   Porsche 911 Carrera RSR 241
Winner's average speed: 89.129 mph. Pole position: Mass, 1m14.7.
Fastest lap: Ickx, 1m16.9

SILVERSTONE 6 HOURS

9 May 1976. Silverstone. 217 laps of a 2.932-mile circuit = 636.244 miles. World Championship of Makes round 3

1 John Fitzpatrick/
   Tom Walkinshaw   BMW 3.5 CSL   217 6 hours
2 Bob Wollek/Hans Heyer   Porsche 935   217
3 Leo Kinnunen/
   Egon Evertz   Porsche 934/5   215
4 Harald Grohs/
   Hugues de Fierlandt   BMW 3.5 CSL   213
5 Lella Lombardi/
   Heinz Martin   Porsche 934   205
6 Umberto Grano/
   Martino Finotto   Ford Escort RS   199
Winner's average speed: 106.041 mph. Pole position: Jochen Mass
(Porsche 935), 1m26.85. Fastest lap: Jacky Ickx (Porsche 935), 1m28.19

ADAC 1000 KM-RENNEN

30 May 1976. Nurburgring. 47 laps of a 14.189-mile circuit = 666.883 miles. World Championship of Makes round 4

1 Dieter Quester/
   Albrecht Krebs   BMW 3.5 CSL   47   6h38m20.6
2 Toine Hezemans/
   Tim Schenken   Porsche 934/5   47   6h42m14.2
3 Derek Bell/Reinhard Stenzel/
   Helmut Kelleners   Porsche 934   46
4 Claude Haldi/
   Markus Hotz   Porsche 934/5   46
5 Gijs van Lennep/
   Hartwig Bertrams   Porsche 934/5   45
6 Helmut Bross/
   Eberhard Sindel   Porsche 934   44
Winner's average speed: 100.448 mph. Pole position: Manfred Schurti
(Porsche 935), 7m37.7. Fastest lap: Rolf Stommelen (Porsche 935),
8m02.7

MARTHA 1000

27 June 1976. Osterreichring. 187 laps of a 3.673 mile-circuit = 686.851 miles. World Championship of Makes 5

1 Dieter Quester/
   Gunnar Nilsson   BMW 3.5 CSL   187 6h00m16.43
2 John Fitzpatrick/
   Tom Walkinshaw   BMW 3.5 CSL   186
3 Claude Haldi/
   Peter Zbinden   Porsche 934/5   182
4 Derek Bell/
   Vern Schuppan   Porsche 935   175
5 Girolama Capra/
   Gabriele Gottifredi   Porsche 934   169
6 Norbert Neumann/
   Kalli Hufstadt   BMW 2002 Ti   166
Winner's average speed: 114.388 mph. Pole position: Jacky Ickx (Porsche
935), 1m43.96. Fastest lap: Bell, 1m49.80

WATKINS GLEN 6 HOURS

10 July 1976. Watkins Glen. 174 laps of a 3.377-mile circuit = 587.598 miles. World Championship of Makes round 6

1 Rolf Stommelen/
   Manfred Schurti   Porsche 935   174 6h00m28.60
2 Leo Kinnunen/Egon Evertz/
   Toine Hezemans   Porsche 934/5   173
3 Jacky Ickx/Jochen Mass   Porsche 935   173

4 Peter Gregg/
Hurley Haywood BMW 3.5 CSL 170
5 Dieter Quester/
Ronnie Peterson BMW 3.5 CSL 166
6 John O'Steen/Dave Helmick/
John Graves Porsche 911 Carrera RSR 164
Winner's average speed: 97.804 mph. Pole position: Mass, 1m55.249.
Fastest lap: Stommelen, 1m55.53

6 HEURES DE L'AUTOMOBILE CLUB DE FRANCE

4 September 1976. Dijon-Prenois. 310 laps of a 2.044-mile circuit =
633.640 miles. World Championship of Makes round 7

1 Jacky Ickx/Jochen Mass Porsche 935 310 6 hours
2 Bob Wollek/Hans Heyer Porsche 935 309
3 Rolf Stommelen/
Manfred Schurti Porsche 935 303
4 Leo Kinnunen/
Egon Evertz Porsche 934/5 300
5 Claude Haldi/
Herbert Muller Porsche 934/5 297
6 Dieter Quester/Ronnie Peterson/
Albrecht Krebs BMW 3.5 CSL 296
Winner's average speed: 105.607 mph. Pole position: Peterson, 1m05.23.
Fastest lap: Ickx, 1m06.84

1976 FINAL CHAMPIONSHIP POSITIONS

Manufacturers		5= Lancia	3
1 Porsche	95 (122)*	MG	3
2 BMW	85 (92)*	*Best five results count	
3 Ford	8		
4 de Tomaso-Ford	5		

1976

World Championship for Sports Cars

ADAC GOODYEAR 300 KM-RENNEN

4 April 1976. Nurburgring. 11 laps of a 14.189-mile circuit = 156.079
miles. World Championship for Sports Cars round 1

1 Reinhold Joest Porsche 908/3 11 1h44m15.8
2* Toine Hezemans Porsche 934 11 1h47m24.9
3 Helmut Bross Lola T294-BMW 11 1h47m25.3
4* Helmut Kelleners Porsche 934 11 1h47m44.0
5 Rolf Stommelen Porsche 936 11 1h48m06.2
6 Stanislav Sterzel March 75S-BMW 11 1h49m13.1
*Not entered in the championship and ineligible for points. Winner's aver-
age speed: 89.129 mph. Pole position: Patrick Depailler (Alpine A442-
Renault), 7m16.09. Fastest lap: Stommelen, 9m11.6

4 ORE DI MONZA/TROFEO FILIPPO CARRACCIOLO

25 April 1976. Monza. 153 laps of a 3.592-mile circuit = 549.576 miles.
World Championship for Sports Cars round 2

1 Jacky Ickx/
Jochen Mass Porsche 936 153 4h00m54.4
2 Henri Pescarolo/
Jean-Pierre Jarier Alpine A442-Renault 152
3 Jurgen Barth/Horst Godel/
Reinhold Joest Porsche 908/3 132
4 "Amphicar"/
Armando Floridia Osella PA4-BMW 132
5 Danilo Tesini/"Mici" Osella PA4-BMW 130
6 Ermanno Pettiti/
Roby Filannino Osella PA4-BMW 129
Winner's average speed: 136.877 mph. Pole position: Mass, 1m32.23.
Fastest lap: Jarier, 1m29.6

500 KM DI IMOLA/TROFEO IGNAZIO GIUNTI

23 May 1976. Imola. 100 laps of a 3.144-mile circuit = 314.400 miles.
World Championship for Sports Cars round 3

1 Jacky Ickx/Jochen Mass Porsche 936 100 2h59m57.90
2 Arturo Merzario/
Vittorio Brambilla Alfa Romeo T33SC/12 96
3 Jurgen Barth/Horst Godel/
Reinhold Joest Porsche 908/3 94
4 Ermanno Pettiti/
Roby Filannino Osella PA4-BMW 93
5 "Amphicar"/
Armando Floridia Osella PA4-BMW 92
6 Ian Bracey/
Tony Birchenough Lola T294-Ford 91
Winner's average speed: 104.820 mph. Pole position: Jean-Pierre Jarier
(Alpine A442-Renault), 1m40.23. Fastest lap: Jarier, 1m42.30

COPPA FLORIO

27 June 1976. Enna-Pergusa. 102 laps of a 3.076-mile circuit = 313.752
miles. World Championship for Sports Cars round 4

1 Jochen Mass/
Rolf Stommelen Porsche 936 102 2h57m48.90
2 Ermanno Pettiti/
Roby Filannino Osella PA4-BMW 92
3 Stanislav Sterzel/"Gimax" March 75S-BMW 92
4 Pasquale Barberio/
Carlo Bilotti Osella PA4-BMW 90
5 Jurgen Barth/Horst Godel Porsche 908/3 90
6 "Amphicar"/
Armando Floridia Osella PA4-BMW 89
Winner's average speed: 105.869 mph. Pole position: Jacques Laffite
(Alpine A442-Renault), 1m35.56. Fastest lap: Jean-Pierre Jarier (Alpine
A442-Renault), 1m36.00

PLAYER'S 200

22 August 1976. Mosport Park. 80 laps of a 2.459-mile circuit = 196.720
miles. World Championship for Sports Cars round 5

1* Jackie Oliver Shadow DN4A-Chevrolet 80 1h45m57.592
2* George Follmer McLaren M20-Chevrolet 80 1h46m05.450
3 Jacky Ickx Porsche 936 80 1h46m43.767
4 Patrick Depailler Alpine A442-Renault 79
5 Vern Schuppan Mirage GR8-Ford 77
6 Tony Cicale Chevron B26-Ford 75
*Not entered in the championship and ineligible for points. Winner's aver-
age speed: 111.393 mph. Pole position: Oliver, 1m15.520 (pole, car ineligible for championship points). Fastest lap: Oliver, 1m16.240

500 KM DE L'AUTOMOBILE CLUB DE FRANCE

5 September 1976. Dijon-Prenois. 152 laps of a 2.044-mile circuit =
310.688 miles. World Championship for Sports Cars round 6

1 Jacky Ickx/Jochen Mass Porsche 936 152 2h41m23.89
2 Patrick Depailler/
Jacques Laffite Alpine A442-Renault 152 2h41m49.98
3 Jean-Pierre Jabouille/
Jean-Pierre Jarier Alpine A442-Renault 148
4 Reinhold Joest/
Jurgen Barth Porsche 908/3 144
5 Xavier Lapeyre/
Alain Cudini Lola T286-Ford 144
6 Bob Wollek/Horst Godel Porsche 908/3 140
Winner's average speed: 115.499 mph. Pole position: Depailler, 1m00.09.
Fastest lap: Mass, 1m01.18

SALZBURGRING ELAN TROPHAE

19 September 1976. Salzburgring. 70 laps of a 2.635-mile circuit =
184.450 miles. World Championship for Sports Cars round 7

1 Jochen Mass Porsche 936 70 1h28m25.24

2 Reinhold Joest	Porsche 908/3	68	
3 Dieter Quester	Osella PA4-BMW	65	
4 Jurgen Barth	Porsche 908/3	65	
5 Eugen Strahl	Sauber C5-BMW	65	
6 Giorgio Pianta	Osella Abarth SE027-BMW	63	

Winner's average speed: 125.163 mph. Pole position: Vittorio Brambilla (Alfa Romeo T33SC/12), 1m22.89. Fastest lap: Brambilla, 1m13.23

1976 FINAL CHAMPIONSHIP POSITIONS

Manufacturers			8 Mirage-Ford	12
1 Porsche	100 (140)*		9= KMW-Porsche	8
2= Alpine-Renault	47		McLaren-Chevrolet	8
Osella-BMW	47		Sauber-BMW	8
4 Lola-BMW/Ford	40		12 Rex-Ford	6
5 March-BMW	28		13 Cheetah-BMW	2
6 Chevron-Chrysler/Ford	23		*Best five results count	
7 Alfa Romeo	15			

1977
World Championship of Makes

DAYTONA 24 HOURS

5-6 February 1977. Daytona. 681 laps of a 3.870-mile circuit = 2635.470 miles. World Championship of Makes round 1

1 John Graves/Hurley Haywood/				
Dave Helmick	Porsche 911 Carrera RSR	681	24h02m06.174	
2 Martino Finotto/Carlo Facetti/				
Romeo Camathias	Porsche 935	679		
3 Reinhold Joest/Bob Wollek/				
Albrecht Krebs	Porsche 935	670		
4 George Dyer/				
Brad Frisselle	Porsche 911 Carrera RSR	663		
5 Paul Newman/Elliott Forbes-Robinson/				
Milt Minter	Ferrari 365 GTB4 Daytona	631		
6 John Carusso/Luis Sereix/				
Emory Donaldson	Chevrolet Corvette	628		

Winner's average speed: 109.651 mph. Pole position: Jochen Mass (Porsche 935), 1m48.289. Fastest lap: Jacky Ickx (Porsche 935), 1m52.004

6 ORE DI MUGELLO

20 March 1977. Mugello. 161 laps of a 3.259-mile circuit = 524.699 miles. World Championship of Makes round 2

1 Rolf Stommelen/				
Manfred Schurti	Porsche 935	161	6h00m12.56	
2 Martino Finotto/Carlo Facetti/				
Romeo Camathias	Porsche 935	155		
3 Vittorio Coggiola/				
Piero Monticone	Porsche 935	154		
4 Arturo Merzario/				
Giuseppe Bianco	Porsche 934	149		
5 "Amphicar"/				
Luigi Moreschi	Porsche 911 Carrera RSR	147		
6 Klaus Utz/Rolf Biland	Porsche 911 Carrera RSR	145		

Winner's average speed: 87.399 mph. Pole position: Jochen Mass (Porsche 935), 2m11.2. Fastest lap: Mass, 1m57.2

KOSSET 6 HOURS

15 May 1977. Silverstone. 230 laps of a 2.932-mile circuit = 674.360 miles. World Championship of Makes round 3

1 Jacky Ickx/Jochen Mass	Porsche 935	230	6 hours	
2 Bob Wollek/				
John Fitzpatrick	Porsche 935	228		
3 Rolf Stommelen/				
Toine Hezemans	Porsche 935	222		

4 Ronnie Peterson/				
Helmut Kelleners	BMW 320i	215		
5 Franz Konrad/				
Peter Hahnlein	Porsche 935	214		
6 Martino Finotto/				
Carlo Facetti	Porsche 935	211		

Winner's average speed: 112.393 mph. Pole position: Mass, 1m25.91. Fastest lap: Mass, 1m27.28

ADAC 1000 KM-RENNEN

29 May 1977. Nurburgring. 44 laps of a 14.189 mile-circuit = 624.316 miles. World Championship of Makes round 4

1 Toine Hezemans/Tim Schenken/				
Rolf Stommelen	Porsche 935	44	5h58m30.5	
2 Bob Wollek/				
John Fitzpatrick	Porsche 935	43		
3 Marc Surer/				
Manfred Winkelhock	BMW 320i	43		
4 Franz Konrad/Paul Keller	Porsche 935	42		
5 Dieter Schornstein/				
Gotz von Tschirnhaus	Porsche 934/5	41		
6 Manfred Schurti/				
Helmut Kelleners	Porsche 935	41		

Winner's average speed: 104.486 mph. Pole position: Jacky Ickx (Porsche 935), 7m31.9. Fastest lap: Stommelen, 7m40.1

WATKINS GLEN 6 HOURS

9 July 1977. Watkins Glen. 173 laps of a 3.377-mile circuit = 584.221 miles. World Championship of Makes round 5

1 Jacky Ickx/Jochen Mass	Porsche 935	173	6h01m56.685	
2 George Follmer/				
Brett Lunger	Porsche 935	170		
3 Hurley Haywood/				
Robert Hagestad	Porsche 934	169		
4 Dick Barbour/				
Johnny Rutherford	Porsche 934	166		
5 Ted Field/Danny Ongais	Porsche 934	165		
6 Peter Gregg/Claude Ballot-Lena/				
John Gunn	Porsche 934	163		

Winner's average speed: 96.847 mph. Pole position: Mass, 1m52.518. Fastest lap: Mass, 1m53.277

MOLSON DIAMOND 6 HOURS

20 August 1977. Mosport Park. 240 laps of a 2.459-mile circuit = 590.160 miles. World Championship of Makes round 6

1 Ludwig Heimrath/				
Paul Miller	Porsche 934	240	5h59m58.827	
2 Gilles Villeneuve/				
Eddie Cheever	BMW 320i	234		
3 Bob Tullius/				
Brian Fuerstenau	Jaguar XJS	229		
4 John Bauer/Tom Spalding/				
Elliott Forbes-Robinson	Porsche 911	227		
5 Harry Bytzek/Klaus Bytzek/				
Rudi Bartling	Porsche 911 Carrera RSR	224		
6 Howard Meister/				
Hal Shaw	Porsche 911 Carrera RSR	224		

Peter Gregg/Bob Wollek (Porsche 934), 243 laps, 5h59m51.288, finished first on the road but was disqualified for illegal suspension. Winner's average speed: 98.365 mph. Pole position: Jacky Ickx (Porsche 935), 1m20.123. Fastest lap: Ickx, 1m21.948

BRANDS HATCH 6 HOURS

25 September 1977. Brands Hatch. 103 laps of a 2.614-mile circuit = 269.201 miles. Race scheduled for 6 hours but reduced due to heavy rain, half points awarded. World Championship of Makes round 7

1 Jacky Ickx/				
Jochen Mass	Porsche 935	103	2h44m30.80	

2 Manfred Schurti/
  Edgar Doren   Porsche 935   101
3 Franz Konrad/Bob Wollek/
  Reinhold Joest   Porsche 935   97
4 Bob Wollek/Nick Faure   Porsche 935   95
5 Eberhard Sindel/
  Gunther Steckkonig   Porsche 935   94
6 Claude Haldi/
  Angelo Pallavicini   Porsche 934   82

Winner's average speed: 98.181 mph. Pole position: Ickx, 1m26.25. Fastest lap: n/a

PREIS VON HESSEN UND WURTTEMBURG

8 October 1977. Hockenheim. 165 laps of a 4.219-mile circuit = 696.135 miles. Aggregate of two 3-hour heats. World Championship of Makes round 8

1 Bob Wollek/John Fitzpatrick Porsche 935-K2   165   6h04m07.1
2 Claude Ballot-Lena/
  Jean-Louis Lafosse   Porsche 935   157
3 Marc Surer/Eddie Cheever BMW 320i   156
4 Claude Haldi/Werner Christmann/
  Bob Wollek   Porsche 935   155
5 Volkert Merl/Peter Hahnlein/
  Franz Konrad   Porsche 935   151
6 Eberhard Sindel/
  Gunther Steckkonig   Porsche 934/5   150

Winner's average speed: 114.710 mph. Pole position: Wollek, 2m02.0. Fastest lap: Jacky Ickx (Porsche 935), 2m03.2

6 ORE DI VALLELUNGA

23 October 1977. Vallelunga. 249 laps of a 1.988-mile circuit = 495.012 miles. World Championship of Makes round 9

1 Luigi Moreschi/"Dino"   Porsche 935   249   6h00m07.1
2 Vittorio Coggiola/
  Piero Monticone   Porsche 935   248
3 Maurizio Micangeli/
  Carlo Pietromarchi   De Tomaso Pantera-Ford 241
4 Kenneth Leim/
  Lella Lombardi   Porsche 911 Carrera RSR 240
5 Michele di Gioia/
  Guido Agazzotti Cavazza Porsche 911 Carrera RSR 238
6 Franco Bernabei/Gianluigi Picchi/
  Bruno del Fante   Porsche 911 Carrera RSR 227

Winner's average speed: 82.475 mph. Pole position: Carlo Facetti (Porsche 935), 1m16.23. Fastest lap: Facetti, 1m17.2

1977 FINAL CHAMPIONSHIP POSITIONS

Manufacturers		6	Chevrolet	7
1 Porsche	140 (180)*	7=	Fiat	3
2 BMW	49		Lancia	3
3 de Tomaso-Ford	12	9	Ford	2
4 Jaguar	10		*Best seven results count	
5 Ferrari	8			

1977

World Championship for Sports Cars

500 KM DE L'AUTOMOBILE CLUB DE FRANCE

17 April 1977. Dijon-Prenois. 132 laps of a 2.361-mile circuit = 311.652 miles. World Championship for Sports Cars round 1

1 Arturo Merzario/
  Jean-Pierre Jarier   Alfa Romeo T33SC/12 132 3h02m18.4
2 "Amphicar"/
  Giuseppe Virgilio   Osella PA5-BMW   125
3 Alain de Cadenet/
  Ernst Berg   Lola T294-Ford   123

4 Giovanni Bormida/
  Ermanno Pettiti   Osella PA5-BMW   122
5 Michel Pignard/Jean-Louis Bos/
  Fred Stadler   Chevron B36-Chrysler 119   accident
6 Sandro Plastina/Mario Luini/
  Jean-Pierre Pochon   Cheetah G601-BMW 116

Winner's average speed: 102.570 mph. Pole position: Vittorio Brambilla (Alfa Romeo T33SC/12), 1m16.21. Fastest lap: Merzario, 1m17.4

500 KM DI MONZA/TROFEO FILIPPO CARACCIOLO

25 April 1977. Monza. 85 laps of a 3.604-mile circuit = 306.332 miles. World Championship for Sports Cars round 2

1 Vittorio Brambilla   Alfa Romeo T33SC/12 85 2h40m06.0
2 Giorgio Francia/
  Silvio Artina   Osella PA5-BMW   84
3 Danilo Tesini/
  "Gianfranco"   Osella PA5-BMW   81
4 Peter Hoffmann   McLaren M8F-Chevrolet 81
5 Luigi Colzani/
  Gabriele Ciuti   Osella PA4-BMW   80
6 Giorgio Schon/"Pal Joe" Osella PA5-BMW   79

Winner's average speed: 114.803 mph. Pole position: Brambilla, 1m42.53. Fastest lap: Arturo Merzario (Alfa Romeo T33SC/12), 1m45.8

TROFEO IGNAZIO GIUNTI/400 KM DI VALLELUNGA

29 May 1977. Vallelunga. 125 laps of a 1.988-mile circuit = 248.500 miles. World Championship for Sports Cars round 3

1 Vittorio Brambilla   Alfa Romeo T33SC/12 125 2h36m17.2
2 Arturo Merzario   Alfa Romeo T33SC/12 124
3 Giorgio Francia   Osella PA5-BMW   123
4 Claudio Francisci   Chevron B31-Ford 120
5 "Amphicar"/
  Luigi Moreschi   Osella PA5-BMW   119
6 Danilo Tesini/
  "Gianfranco"   Osella PA5-BMW   118

Winner's average speed: 95.402 mph. Pole position: Brambilla, 1m10.8. Fastest lap: Brambilla, 1m12.2

COPPA FLORIO

19 June 1977. Enna-Pergusa. 100 laps of a 3.076-mile circuit = 307.600 miles. World Championship for Sports Cars round 4

1 Arturo Merzario   Alfa Romeo T33SC/12 100 2h57m40.2
2 Eugen Strahl/
  Peter Bernhard   Sauber C5-BMW   97
3 Giampaolo Ceraolo/
  Pasquale Anastasio Osella PA5-Ford   94
4 Fabio Siliprandi/
  Antonio de Castro   Chevron B36-Ford 89
5 Corrado Manfredini/
  Mario Casoni   Lola T294-Ford   88
6 Adelino Zenone/
  Marco de Bartoli   Osella PA4-BMW   88

Winner's average speed: 103.878 mph. Pole position: Merzario, 1m35.7. Fastest lap: Merzario, 1m39.1

GRANDE PREMIO COSTA DEL SOL

10 July 1977. Estoril. 89 laps of a 2.703-mile circuit = 240.567 miles. World Championship for Sports Cars round 5

1 Arturo Merzario   Alfa Romeo T33SC/12 89 2h30m56.68
2 Vittorio Brambilla   Alfa Romeo T33SC/12 89 2h30m56.79
3 Spartico Dini/
  Giorgio Francia   Alfa Romeo T33SC/12 86
4 Chris Craft   Lola T296-Ford   84
5 Eugen Strahl/
  Peter Bernhard   Sauber C5-BMW   82
6 Ian Bracey/
  Tony Birchenough   Lola T294-Ford   73

Winner's average speed: 95.625 mph. Pole position: Merzario, 1m38.43. Fastest lap: Brambilla, 1m37.73

500 KM DU CASTELLET

24 July 1977. Paul Ricard. 150 laps of a 2.028-mile circuit = 304.200 miles. World Championship for Sports Cars round 6

1 Arturo Merzario/			
Jean-Pierre Jarier	Alfa Romeo T33SC/12	150	3h23m14.9
2 Jorg Obermoser/			
Pierre-Francois Rousselot	Toj SC302-Ford	148	
3 Jean-Pierre Jaussaud/			
Jacques Henry	Chevron B31-Chysler	145	
4 Tony Charnell/Robin Smith	Chevron B31-Ford	144	
5 Eugen Strahl/			
Peter Bernhard	Sauber C5-BMW	142	
6 Georges Morand/Frederic Alliot/			
Christian Blanc	Lola T296-Ford	141	

Winner's average speed: 89.801 mph. Pole position: Vittorio Brambilla (Alfa Romeo T33SC/12), 1m15.5. Fastest lap: Brambilla, 1m17.3

250 KM DI IMOLA

4 September 1977. Imola. 50 laps of a 3.144-mile circuit = 157.200 miles. World Championship for Sports Cars round 7

1 Vittorio Brambilla	Alfa Romeo T33SC/12	50	1h29m43.5
2 Giorgio Francia	Osella PA5-BMW	49	
3 Lella Lombardi/			
Giovanni Anzeloni	Osella PA5-BMW	47	
4 Francesco Cerulli Irelli	AMS 277-Ford	47	
5 Renzo Zorzi/			
Giuseppe Piazzi	Chevron B36-BMW	47	
6 Duilio Ghislotti/			
Romeo Camathias	Lola T296-BMW	46	

Winner's average speed: 105.121 mph. Pole position: Brambilla, 1m41.73. Fastest lap: Arturo Merzario (Alfa Romeo T33SC/12), 1m43.4

SALZBURGER FESTSPIELPREIS

18 September 1977. Salzburgring. 70 laps of a 2.635-mile circuit = 184.450 miles. World Championship for Sports Cars round 8

1 Vittorio Brambilla	Alfa Romeo T33SC/12	70	1h27m26.79
2 Arturo Merzario	Alfa Romeo T33SC/12	69	
3 Spartico Dini/			
Giorgio Francia	Alfa Romeo T33SC/12	68	
4 Guy Edwards/			
Ray Mallock	Lola T296-Ford	65	
5 Herbert Muller	March 76S-BMW	64	
6 Duilio Ghislotti/			
Romeo Camathias	Lola T296-BMW	62	

Winner's average speed: 126.557 mph. Pole position: Brambilla, 1m12.65. Fastest lap: Brambilla, 1m12.45

1977 FINAL CHAMPIONSHIP POSITIONS

Manufacturers			7	AMS-Ford	15
1	Alfa Romeo	120 (160)*	8	McLaren-Chevrolet	13
2	Osella-BMW/Ford	73	9	March-BMW	8
3=	Lola-Ford/BMW	43	10=	Cheetah-BMW	6
	Chevron-Chrysler/Ford	43		Porsche	6
5	Sauber-BMW	31	*Best six results count		
6	Toj-Ford	17			

1978

World Championship for Makes

DAYTONA 24 HOURS

3-4 February 1978. Daytona. 680 laps of a 3.870-mile circuit = 2631.600 miles. World Championship for Makes round 1

1 Rolf Stommelen/Toine Hezemans/			
Peter Gregg	Porsche 935	680	24h00m45.4

2 Dick Barbour/Johnny Rutherford/			
Manfred Schurti	Porsche 935	650	
3 Diego Febles/Alec Poole	Porsche 911 Carrera RSR	645	
4 Bonky Fernandez/John Paul/			
Phil Currin	Porsche 911 Carrera RSR	637	
5 "John Winter"/Dieter Schornstein/			
Josef Brambring	Porsche 935	635	
6 Steve Earle/Bob Akin/			
Rick Knoop	Porsche 911 Carrera RSR	632	

Winner's average speed: 109.592 mph. Pole position: Danny Ongais (Porsche 935), 2m01.152. Fastest lap: Stommelen, 1m51.845

6 ORE DI MUGELLO

19 March 1978. Mugello. 176 laps of a 3.259-mile circuit = 573.584 miles. World Championship for Makes round 2

1 Toine Hezemans/John Fitzpatrick/			
Hans Heyer	Porsche 935	176	6h01m49.4
2 Franz Konrad/Reinhold Joest/			
Volkert Merl	Porsche 935	175	
3 Dieter Quester/Derek Bell	BMW 320i	174	
4 Claude Haldi/			
Herbert Muller	Porsche 935	174	
5 Martino Finotto/			
Carlo Facetti	Porsche 935	174	
6 Bo Emanuelsson/			
Anders Olofsson	BMW 320i	174	

Winner's average speed: 95.116 mph. Pole position: Fitzpatrick, 1m55.42. Fastest lap: Hezemans, 1m56.90

4 HEURES DE DIJON

16 April 1978. Dijon-Prenois. 169 laps of a 2.361-mile circuit = 399.009 miles. World Championship for Makes round 3

1 Bob Wollek/			
Henri Pescarolo	Porsche 935	169	4h00m55.85
2 John Fitzpatrick/Hans Heyer/			
Toine Hezemans	Porsche 935	166	
3 Giorgio Francia/			
Eddie Cheever	BMW 320i	165	
4 Bo Emanuelsson/			
Ingvar Carlsson	BMW 320i	165	
5 Jean-Louis Lafosse/			
Claude Ballot-Lena	Porsche 935	162	
6 Dieter Schornstein/			
"John Winter"	Porsche 935	157	

Winner's average speed: 99.367 mph. Pole position: Hezemans, 1m20.44. Fastest lap: Hezemans, 1m21.70

SILVERSTONE 6 HOURS

14 May 1978. Silverstone. 235 laps of a 2.932-mile circuit = 689.020 miles. World Championship for Makes round 4

1 Jacky Ickx/Jochen Mass	Porsche 935	235	6 hours
2 Bob Wollek/			
Henri Pescarolo	Porsche 935	228	
3 Harald Grohs/			
Eddy Joosen	BMW 320i	219	
4 Freddy Kottulinsky/			
Markus Hotz	BMW 320i	219	
5 Dieter Schornstein/			
"John Winter"/Bob Wollek	Porsche 935	218	
6 Franz Konrad/			
Volkert Merl	Porsche 935	202	

Winner's average speed: 114.837 mph. Pole position: Ickx, 1m22.38. Fastest lap: Mass, 1m23.88

ADAC 1000 KM-RENNEN

28 May 1978. Nurburgring. 44 laps of a 14.189-mile circuit = 624.316 miles. Aggregate of two 22-lap heats. World Championship for Makes round 5

1 Klaus Ludwig/Hans Heyer/
  Toine Hezemans   Porsche 935   44   5h55m46.6
2 Jacky Ickx/
  Manfred Schurti   Porsche 935   44   5h56m45.2
3 Bob Wollek/
  Henri Pescarolo   Porsche 935   44   6h01m03.2
4 Franz Konrad/Volkert Merl/
  Ralf-Dieter Schreiber Porsche 935 44   6h05m09.3
5 Reinhold Joest/
  Jurgen Barth   Porsche 935   44   6h06m24.4
6 Hans-Joachim Stuck/
  Markus Hottinger   BMW 320i   44   6h07m53.2

Winner's average speed: 105.288 mph. Pole position: Hezemans, 7m36.2.
Fastest lap: Wollek, 7m45.0

6 ORE DI MISANO

25 June 1978. Misano. 261 laps of a 2.167-mile circuit = 565.587 miles.
World Championship for Makes round 6

1 Bob Wollek/
  Henri Pescarolo   Porsche 935   261   6h00m56.6
2 Vittorio Coggiola/
  Piero Monticone   Porsche 935   255
3 Franz Konrad/
  Volkert Merl   Porsche 935   255
4 Harald Grohs/
  Patrick Neve   BMW 320i   255
5 Dieter Quester/
  Wolfgang Wolf   BMW 320i   246
6 Freddy Kottulinsky/
  Markus Hotz   BMW 320i   240

Winner's average speed: 94.018 mph. Pole position: Wollek, 1m16.64.
Fastest lap: John Fitzpatrick (Porsche 935), 1m18.3

WATKINS GLEN 6 HOURS

8 July 1978. Watkins Glen. 146 laps of a 3.377-mile circuit = 493.042
miles. Race interupted due to rain storm. World Championship for
Makes round 7

1 Toine Hezemans/John Fitzpatrick/
  Peter Gregg   Porsche 935   146   6h01m54.999
2 Dick Barbour/Manfred Schurti/
  Rolf Stommelen   Porsche 935   146   6h02m25.132
3 Hans-Joachim Stuck/
  Dieter Quester   BMW 320i   138
4 Hal Shaw/Monte Shelton Porsche 935 136
5 Chris Cord/Jim Adams Chevrolet Monza 132
6 Otis Chandler/
  John Thomas jr   Porsche 935   132

Winner's average speed: 81.738 mph. Pole position: Stommelen,
1m53.611. Fastest lap: Fitzpatrick, 1m54.700

6 ORE DI VALLELUNGA

3 September 1978. Vallelunga. 267 laps of a 1.988-mile circuit = 530.796
miles. World Championship for Makes round 8

1 Bob Wollek/
  Henri Pescarolo   Porsche 935   267   6h01m00.4
2 Toine Hezemans/Hans Heyer/
  John Fitzpatrick   Porsche 935   267   6h02m21.6
3 Klaus Ludwig/John Fitzpatrick/
  Toine Hezemans   Porsche 935   266
4 Marc Surer/
  Freddy Kottulinsky BMW 320i   261
5 Carlo Facetti/Piercarlo Ghinzani/
  Luigi Moreschi   Porsche 935   254
6 Dieter Schornstein/
  "John Winter"   Porsche 935   247

Winner's average speed: 88.219 mph. Pole position: Jacky Ickx (Porsche
935), 1m12.8. Fastest lap: Ickx, 1m15.4

1978 FINAL CHAMPIONSHIP POSITIONS

Manufacturers		5	Chevrolet	2
1 Porsche	120 (160)*	6	Fiat	1
2 BMW	68 (74)*	*Best six result count		
3= Ferrari	3			
de Tomaso-Ford	3			

1979
World Championship for Makes

PEPSI-COLA DAYTONA 24 HOURS

3-4 February 1979. Daytona. 684 laps of a 3.870-mile circuit = 2647.080
miles. World Championship for Makes round 1

1 Danny Ongais/Hurley Haywood/
  Ted Field   Porsche 935   684   24h00m24.87
2 John Morton/
  Tony Adamowicz   Ferrari 365 GTB4 Daytona 635
3 Rick Mears/Bruce Canepa/
  Monte Shelton   Porsche 935   627
4 Don Whittington/Jurgen Barth/
  Bill Whittington   Porsche 935   622
5 Yoshimi Katayama/Yojiro Terada/
  Takashi Yorino   Mazda RX-7   617
6 Walt Bohren/Jim Downing/
  Roger Mandeville   Mazda RX-7   615

Winner's average speed: 110.263 mph. Pole position: Carlo Facetti
(Porsche 935), 1m46.113. Fastest lap: Peter Gregg (Porsche 935),
1m49.477

6 ORE DI MUGELLO

18 March 1979. Mugello. 138 laps of a 3.259-mile circuit = 449.742 miles.
World Championship for Makes round 2

1 John Fitzpatrick/Manfred Schurti/
  Bob Wollek   Porsche 935   138   5h15m47.5
2 Bob Wollek/Jacky Ickx/
  Manfred Schurti   Porsche 935   136
3 Carlo Facetti/
  Martino Finotto   Porsche 935   136
4 Giorgio Francia/
  Lella Lombardi   Osella PA6-BMW   133
5 Angelo Pallavicini/
  Marco Vanoli   Porsche 911 Carrera RSR 122
6 Enzo Calderari/
  Willi Spavetti   Porsche 911 Carrera RSR 120

Winner's average speed: 85.450 mph. Pole position: Francia, 1m52.97.
Fastest lap: Facetti, 1m57.90

6 HEURES DE DIJON

22 April 1979. Dijon-Prenois. 255 laps of a 2.361-mile circuit = 602.055
miles. World Championship for Makes round 3

1 Reinhold Joest/Volkert Merl/
  Mario Ketterer   Porsche 908/4   255   6h00m03.4
2 Jacky Ickx/Bob Wollek/
  Manfred Schurti   Porsche 935   251
3 Dieter Schornstein/
  Edgar Doren   Porsche 935   239
4 Claude Haldi/
  Herbert Lowe   Porsche 935   235
5 Peter Hahnlein/Franz Gschwender/
  Klaus Boehm   Porsche 935   232
6 Mario Luini/Philippe Roux/
  Philippe Jeanneret Cheetah G501-Ford   232

Winner's average speed: 100.327 mph. Pole position: Joest, 1m17.77.
Fastest lap: Joest, 1m18.6

RIVET SUPPLY 6 HOURS

6 May 1979. Silverstone. 228 laps of a 2.932-mile circuit = 668.496 miles. World Championship for Makes round 4

1 John Fitzpatrick/Bob Wollek/
  Hans Heyer — Porsche 935 — 228 — 6 hours
2 Alain de Cadenet/
  Francois Migault — De Cadenet LM-Ford — 221
3 Dieter Schornstein/
  Edgar Doren — Porsche 935 — 216
4 Jean-Pierre Delauney/
  Cyrille Grandet — Porsche 911 Carrera RSR — 209
5 Manfred Schurti/John Fitzpatrick/
  Bob Wollek — Porsche 935 — 209
6 Peter Zbinden/Eddi Kofel — Porsche 934 — 209

Winner's average speed: 111.416 mph. Pole position: Jochen Mass (Porsche 936), 1m20.13. Fastest lap: Mass, 1m23.25

ADAC 1000-KM RENNEN

3 June 1979. Nurburgring. 44 laps of a 14.189-mile circuit = 624.316 miles. World Championship for Makes round 5

1 Manfred Schurti/John Fitzpatrick/
  Bob Wollek — Porsche 935 — 44 — 5h57m35.1
2 Klaus Ludwig/
  Axel Plankenhorn — Porsche 935 — 44 — 5h57m46.8
3 Henri Pescarolo/
  Brian Redman — Porsche 935 — 43
4 Dieter Schornstein/Edgar Doren/
  Gotz von Tschirnhaus — Porsche 935 — 43
5 Volkert Merl/Derek Bell/
  Rolf Stommelen — Porsche 935 — 41 — spun
6 Eckhart Schimpf/
  Hans-Georg Burger — BMW 320i — 41

Winner's average speed: 104.755 mph. Pole position: Stommelen, 7m32.2. Fastest lap: Stommelen, 7m41.9

24 HEURES DU MANS

9-10 June 1979. Le Mans. 306 laps of an 8.467-mile circuit = 2590.902 miles. World Championship for Makes round 6

1 Klaus Ludwig/Bill Whittington/
  Don Whittington — Porsche 935-K3 — 306 — 24 hours
2 Rolf Stommelen/Dick Barbour/
  Paul Newman — Porsche 935 — 299
3 Laurent Ferrier/Francois Servanin/
  Francois Trisconi — Porsche 935 — 292
4 Angelo Pallavicini/Herbert Muller/
  Marco Vanoli — Porsche 934 — 291
5 Bernard Darniche/
  Jean Ragnotti — Rondeau M379-Ford — 287
6 Herve Poulain/Marcel Mignot/
  Manfred Winkelhock — BMW M1 — 284

Winner's average speed: 107.954 mph. Pole position: Bob Wollek (Porsche 936), 3m30.07. Fastest lap: Jacky Ickx (Porsche 936), 3m36.01

COPPA FLORIO

24 June 1979. Enna-Pergusa. 180 laps of a 3.076-mile circuit = 553.680 miles. World Championship for Makes round 7

1 Lella Lombardi/
  Enrico Grimaldi — Osella PA7-BMW — 148 — 6h01m35.6
2 Riccardo Patrese/
  Carlo Facetti — Lancia Beta Monte Carlo — 179
3 Angelo Pallavicini/
  Marco Vanoli — Porsche 911 Carrera RSR — 177
4 Daniel Brillat/
  Jean-Pierre Aeschlimann — Cheetah G601-BMW — 176
5 Felice Besenzoni/
  Luciano del Ben — Ferrari 308GTB — 173
6 Jacono Veninata/
  Giovanni Cascone — Osella PA6-Ford — 170

Winner's average speed: 91.873 mph. Pole position: Patrese, 1m39.32. Fastest lap: Lombardi, 1m42.5

WATKINS GLEN 6 HOURS

7 July 1979. Watkins Glen. 175 laps of a 3.377-mile circuit = 590.975 miles. World Championship for Makes round 8

1 Don Whittington/Klaus Ludwig/
  Bill Whittington — Porsche 935-K3 — 175 — 6h00m09.97
2 Rolf Stommelen/Dick Barbour/
  Paul Newman — Porsche 935 — 171
3 Rob McFarlin/Bob Akin/
  Roy Woods — Porsche 935 — 170
4 Elliott Forbes-Robinson/Randy Townsend/
  Brett Lunger — Porsche 935 — 169
5 John Paul/Al Holbert — Porsche 935 — 167
6 Bob Tullius/
  Brian Fuerstenau — Triumph TR8 — 162

Winner's average speed: 98.450 mph. Pole position: Stommelen, 1m50.354. Fastest lap: Stommelen, 1m54.763

RIVET SUPPLY 6 HOURS

5 August 1979. Brands Hatch. 231 laps of a 2.614-mile circuit = 603.742 miles. World Championship for Makes round 9

1 Reinhold Joest/
  Volkert Merl — Porsche 908/4 — 231 — 6h00m04.9
2 Klaus Ludwig/
  Axel Plankenhorn — Porsche 935-K3 — 229
3 Tony Charnell/
  Martin Raymond — Chevron B36-Ford — 220
4 Dieter Schornstein/
  Edgar Doren — Porsche 935 — 218
5 Riccardo Patrese/
  Walter Rohrl — Lancia Beta Monte Carlo — 214
6 Alain de Cadenet/
  Francois Migault — De Cadenet LM-Ford — 212

Winner's average speed: 100.601 mph. Pole position: Joest, 1m26.67. Fastest lap: n/a

TROFEO IGNAZIO GIUNTI/6 ORE DI VALLELUNGA

16 September 1979. Vallelunga. 265 laps of a 1.988-mile circuit = 526.820 miles. World Championship for Makes round 10

1 Lella Lombardi/
  Giorgio Francia — Osella PA7-BMW — 265 — 6h00m19.3
2 Enzo Coloni/Pasquale Barberio/
  Geraldo Vatielli — Osella PA6-BMW — 261
3 "Gero"/"Robin Hood" — Osella PA3-Ford — 250
4 Bernard Verdier/
  Bruno Sotty — Chevron B36-Chrysler — 248
5 "Tore"/Marco Rocca — Osella PA7-BMW — 245
6 Luigi Moreschi/
  "Amphicar" — Osella PA7-BMW — 245

Winner's average speed: 87.725 mph. Pole position: Coloni, 1m12.65. Fastest lap: Maurizio Flammini (Chevron B36-BMW), 1m13.08

1979 FINAL CHAMPIONSHIP POSITIONS

Manufacturers - over 2000cc		Manufacturers - 2000cc	
1 Porsche	140 (180)*	1 Lancia	50
2 Ferrari	30	2 BMW	32
3 de Tomaso-Ford	6	3= Ford	30
4 Triumph	4	Porsche	30
5 BMW	1	5 Fiat	20
*Best seven results count		6 Volkswagen	6
		7 Audi	2
		Manufacturers - overall	
		1 Porsche	

1980
World Championship for Makes

DAYTONA 24 HOURS

3-4 February 1980. Daytona. 715 laps of a 3.870-mile circuit = 2767.050 miles. World Championship for Makes round 1

1	Rolf Stommelen/Reinhold Joest/			
	Volkert Merl	Porsche 935	715	24h01m13.33
2	John Paul/Al Holbert	Porsche 935-K3	682	
3	Ted Field/Danny Ongais/			
	Milt Minter	Porsche 935-K3	664	
4	Maurice Carter/Craig Carter/			
	Murray Edwards	Chevrolet Camaro	636	
5	William Koll/Jim Cook/			
	Greg Lacava	Porsche 914/6	632	
6	Tony Garcia/Alberto Vadia Jr/			
	Terry Herman	Porsche 911 Carrera RSR	630	

Winner's average speed: 115.196 mph. Pole position: Don Whittington (Porsche 935-K3), 1m44.110. Fastest lap: Bill Whittington (Porsche 935-K3], 1m47.964

DAILY MAIL BRANDS HATCH 6 HOURS

16 March 1980. Brands Hatch. 147 laps of a 2.614-mile circuit = 384.199 miles. Race scheduled for 6 hours but stopped after 111 laps due to Martin Raymond's fatal accident, restarted for an additional 1 hour. World Championship for Makes round 2

1	Riccardo Patrese/			
	Walter Rohrl	Lancia Beta Monte Carlo	147	3h51m57.00
2	Eddie Cheever/			
	Michele Alboreto	Lancia Beta Monte Carlo	146	
3	Alain de Cadenet/			
	Desire Wilson	De Cadenet LM-Ford	145	
4	Martino Finotto/			
	Carlo Facetti	Lancia Beta Monte Carlo	143	
5	Dudley Wood/John Cooper/			
	Peter Lovett	Porsche 935-K3	139	
6	Adrian Yates-Smith/			
	Barrie Williams	Porsche 911SC	135	

Winner's average speed: 99.383 mph. Pole position: Joest, 1m25.42. Fastest lap: n/a

6 ORE DI MUGELLO

13 April 1980. Mugello. 177 laps of a 3.259-mile circuit = 576.843 miles. World Championship for Makes round 3

1	Riccardo Patrese/			
	Eddie Cheever	Lancia Beta Monte Carlo	177	6h01m07.7
2	Michele Alboreto/			
	Walter Rohrl	Lancia Beta Monte Carlo	176	
3	Marcelo Gallo/"Gimax"	Osella PA8-BMW	173	
4	Martino Finotto/			
	Carlo Facetti	Lancia Beta Monte Carlo	171	
5	Geraldo Vatielli/			
	Paolo Giangrossi	Osella PA7-Ford	170	
6	Didier Pironi/			
	Dieter Quester	BMW M1	167	

Winner's average speed: 95.840 mph. Pole position: Vittorio Brambilla (Osella PA8-BMW), 1m51.77. Fastest lap: Brambilla, 1m53.8

6 ORE DI MONZA/TROFEO FILIPPO CARACCIOLO

27 April 1980. Monza. 183 laps of a 3.604-mile circuit = 659.514 miles. World Championship for Makes round 4

1	Alain de Cadenet/			
	Desire Wilson	De Cadenet LM-Ford	183	6h01m08.8
2	Henri Pescarolo/			
	Jurgen Barth	Porsche 935-K3	183	6h01m18.7
3	Riccardo Patrese/			
	Walter Rohrl	Lancia Beta Monte Carlo	182	

4	Dieter Schornstein/			
	Harald Grohs	Porsche 935	180	
5	Eddie Cheever/			
	Piercarlo Ghinzani	Lancia Beta Monte Carlo	176	
6	Ruggero Parpinelli/			
	Silvano Frisori	Osella PA6-Ford	170	

Winner's average speed: 109.570 mph. Pole position: Renzo Zorzi (Capoferri M1-Ford), 1m45.95. Fastest lap: Zorzi, 1m48.60

SILVERSTONE 6 HOURS

11 May 1980. Silverstone. 235 laps of a 2.932-mile circuit = 689.020 miles. World Championship for Makes round 5

1	Alain de Cadenet/			
	Desire Wilson	De Cadenet LM-Ford	235*	6 hours
2	Jurgen Barth/			
	Siegfried Brunn	Porsche 908/3	235	6 hours
3	John Paul/Brian Redman/			
	John Paul jr	Porsche 935	234	
4	Michele Alboreto/			
	Walter Rohrl	Lancia Beta Monte Carlo	232	
5	Dieter Schornstein/			
	Harald Grohs	Porsche 935	229	
6	Edgar Doren/Jurgen Laessig/			
	Gerhard Holup	Porsche 935-K3	225	

*Includes 1-lap penalty for missing the Woodcote chicane. Winner's average speed: 114.837 mph. Pole position: John Fitzpatrick (Porsche 935-K3), 1m22.09. Fastest lap: Fitzpatrick, 1m25.53

ADAC 1000 KM-RENNEN

25 May 1980. Nurburgring. 44 laps of a 14.189-mile circuit = 624.316 miles. World Championship for Makes round 6

1	Rolf Stommelen/			
	Jurgen Barth	Porsche 908/4	44	5h52m15.1
2	John Fitzpatrick/Axel Plankenhorn/			
	Dick Barbour	Porsche 935-K3	44	5h52m56.0
3	Hans-Joachim Stuck/			
	Nelson Piquet	BMW M1	44	5h53m10.2
4	Riccardo Patrese/			
	Hans Heyer	Lancia Beta Monte Carlo	44	5h55m48.0
5	Bob Wollek/			
	Manfred Schurti	Porsche 935	44	5h56m24.9
6	Eddie Cheever/			
	Piercarlo Ghinzani	Lancia Beta Monte Carlo	43	

Winner's average speed: 106.341 mph. Pole position: Stommelen, 7m26.0. Fastest lap: Fitzpatrick, 7m34.3

24 HEURES DU MANS

14-15 June 1980. Le Mans. 338 laps of an 8.467-mile circuit = 2861.846 miles. World Championship for Makes round 7

1	Jean-Pierre Jaussaud/			
	Jean Rondeau	Rondeau M379B-Ford	338	24 hours
2	Jacky Ickx/Reinhold Joest	Porsche 936/80	336	
3	Jean-Michel Martin/Philippe Martin/			
	Gordon Spice	Rondeau M379B-Ford	329	
4	Guy Frequelin/			
	Roger Dorchy	WM P79/80-Peugeot	318	
5	John Fitzpatrick/Brian Redman/			
	Dick Barbour	Porsche 935-K3	317	
6	Jurgen Barth/			
	Manfred Schurti	Porsche 924 Carrera	316	

Winner's average speed: 119.244 mph. Pole position: Henri Pescarolo/Jean Ragnotti, 3m47.9 (Rondeau M379B-Ford) - position based on average time of both drivers best lap. Fastest lap: Ickx, 3m40.6

WATKINS GLEN 6 HOURS

5 July 1980. Watkins Glen. 139 laps of a 3.377-mile circuit = 469.403 miles. World Championship for Makes round 8

1	Riccardo Patrese/			
	Hans Heyer	Lancia Beta Monte Carlo	139	6h02m15.393

2	Eddie Cheever/			
	Michele Alboreto	Lancia Beta Monte Carlo	138	
3	John Fitzpatrick/			
	Brian Redman	Porsche 935-K3	134	
4	Ted Field/Danny Ongais	Porsche 935-K3	133	
5	Jurgen Barth/Volkert Merl	Porsche 935	133	
6	Martino Finotto/			
	Piercarlo Ghinzani	Lancia Beta Monte Carlo	133	

Winner's average speed: 77.747 mph. Pole position: Bobby Rahal (Porsche 935-K3), 1m51.638. Fastest lap: Ongais, 1m53.471

MOLSON CANADIAN 1000

17 August 1980. Mosport Park. 245 laps of a 2.459-mile circuit = 602.455 miles. World Championship for Makes round 9

1	John Fitzpatrick/			
	Brian Redman	Porsche 935-K3	245	6h00m11.807
2	John Paul/John Paul jr	Porsche 935	245	6h01m31.000
3	Ted Field/Danny Ongais	Porsche 935	244	
4	Hans Heyer/Walter Rohrl	Lancia Beta Monte Carlo	241	
5	Rick Mears/			
	Skeeter McKitterick	Porsche 935-K3	237	
6	Bob Akin/Paul Miller/			
	Kees Nierop	Porsche 935-K3	234	

Winner's average speed: 100.354 mph. Pole position: Fitzpatrick, 1m20.015. Fastest lap: Ongais, 1m19.96

6 ORE DI VALLELUNGA

7 September 1980. Vallelunga. 271 laps of a 1.988-mile circuit = 538.748 miles. World Championship for Makes round 10

1	Giorgio Francia/			
	Roberto Marazzi	Osella PA8-BMW	271	6h01m13.5
2	Siegfried Brunn/Derek Bell	Porsche 908/3	267	
3	Riccardo Patrese/			
	Eddie Cheever	Lancia Beta Monte Carlo	266	
4	Edgar Doren/			
	Jurgen Laessig	Porsche 935-K3	263	
5	Silvano Frisori/			
	Ruggero Parpinelli	Osella PA6-Ford	262	
6	Claudio Francisci/"Gimax"	Osella PA8-BMW	262	

Winner's average speed: 89.487 mph. Pole position: Francia, 1m12.06. Fastest lap: Vittorio Brambilla (Osella PA8-BMW), 1m15.1

1000 KM DE DIJON

28 September 1980. Dijon-Prenois. 180 laps of a 2.361-mile circuit = 424.980 miles. Race scheduled for 264 laps but reduced when fog delayed start. World Championship for Makes round 11

1	Henri Pescarolo/			
	Jurgen Barth	Porsche 935-K3	180	4h25m35.23
2	Claude Haldi/			
	Bernard Beguin	Porsche 935	178	
3	Christian Justice/			
	Victor Cheli	Chevron B36-Chrysler	177	
4	John Cooper/Dudley Wood	Porsche 935-K3	173	
5	Noel del Bello/Rene Boccard	Lola T298-Chrysler	172	
6	Francois Servanin/			
	Laurent Ferrier	BMW M1	172	

Winner's average speed: 96.009 mph. Pole position: Vittorio Brambilla (Osella PA8-BMW), 1m18.62. Fastest lap: Edgar Doren (Porsche 935-K3), 1m21.16

1980 FINAL CHAMPIONSHIP POSITIONS

Manufacturers - over 2000cc			2	BMW	59
1	Porsche	160 (210)*	3	Porsche	15
2	Lancia	40	4	Ford	4
3	Opel	3	*Best seven results count		
*Best seven results count			**Manufacturers - overall**		
Manufacturers - 2000cc			1	Porsche	
1	Lancia	160 (200)*			

1981
World Endurance Championship

PEPSI-COLA DAYTONA 24 HOURS

31 January-1 February 1981. Daytona. 708 laps of a 3.870-mile circuit = 2739.960 miles. World Endurance Championship round 1

1	Bob Garretson/Bobby Rahal/			
	Brian Redman	Porsche 935-K3	708	24h01m36.871
2	Bob Akin/Derek Bell/			
	Craig Siebert	Porsche 935	695	
3	William Koll/Jeff Kline/			
	Rob McFarlin	Porsche 911SC	644	
4	Frank Carney/Dick Davenport/			
	Rameau Johnson	Datsun ZX	626	
5	Carlo Facetti/Martino Finotto/			
	Emanuele Pirro	Lancia Beta Monte Carlo	609	
6	Hans-Joachim Stuck/Alf Gebhardt/			
	Walter Brun	BMW M1	608	

Winner's average speed: 114.037 mph. Pole position: Rolf Stommelen (Porsche 935), 1m43.104. Fastest lap: Facetti, 1m48.14

COCA-COLA 12 HOURS OF SEBRING

21 March 1981. Sebring. 245 laps of a 5.200-mile circuit = 1274.000 miles. World Endurance Championship round 2

1	Bruce Leven/Hurley Haywood/			
	Al Holbert	Porsche 935	245	12h00m49.855
2	Roy Woods/Ralph Kent-Cooke/			
	Skeeter McKitterick	Porsche 935-K3	242	
3	Marty Hinze/Milt Minter/			
	Bill Whittington	Porsche 935	240	
4	Howard Meister/Rolf Stommelen/			
	Harald Grohs	Porsche 935	233	
5	Chuck Kendall/Pete Smith/			
	Dennis Aase	Porsche 911 Carrera RSR	218	
6	Gianpiero Moretti/Charles Mendez/			
	Maurizio de Narvaez	Porsche 935	213	

Winner's average speed: 106.044 mph. Pole position: John Fitzpatrick (Porsche 935), 2m28.675. Fastest lap: John Paul jr (Porsche 935), 2m28.65

6 ORE DI MUGELLO

12 April 1981. Mugello. 177 laps of a 3.259-mile circuit = 576.843 miles. World Endurance Championship round 3

1	Lella Lombardi/			
	Giorgio Francia	Osella PA9-BMW	177	6h00m24.74
2	John Cooper/Dudley Wood	Porsche 935-K3	168	
3	Anton Fischhaber/			
	Mario Ketterer	BMW 320i	160	
4	Christian Bussi/			
	Jacques Guerin	Porsche 935	160	
5	Francois Servanin/Laurent Ferrier/Pierre-			
	Francois Rousselot	BMW M1	160	
6	Mario Benusiglio/			
	Luigi de Angelis	Osella PA8-Ford	160	

Michele Alboreto/Piercarlo Ghinzani (Lancia Beta Monte Carlo), 168 laps, finished third on the road but disqualified as gearbox casing was changed during race. Winner's average speed: 96.031 mph. Pole position: Francia, 1m52.57. Fastest lap: Alboreto, 1m56.79

1000 KM DI MONZA/TROFEO FILIPPO CARACCIOLO

26 April 1981. Monza. 173 laps of a 3.604-mile circuit = 623.475 miles. World Endurance Championship round 4

1	Edgar Doren/			
	Jurgen Laessig	Porsche 935-K3	173	6h33m48.8
2	Lella Lombardi/			
	Giorgio Francia	Osella PA9-BMW	172	
3	"Gimax"/Luigi Moreschi	Osella PA9-BMW	171	
4	Teo Fabi/Dieter Quester	BMW M1	170	
5	Siegfried Brunn/Eddie Jordan	Porsche 908/4	170	

6 Francois Servanin/Laurent Ferrier/Pierre-
Francois Rousselot   BMW M1   167
Winner's average speed: 94.989 mph. Pole position: Carlo Facetti (Ferrari 308GTB), 1m46.69. Fastest lap: Harald Grohs (Porsche 935), 2m01.8

LOS ANGELES TIMES/TOYOTA 6 HOUR GRAND PRIX OF ENDURANCE

26 April 1981. Riverside. 199 laps of a 3.250 mile-circuit = 646.750 miles. World Endurance Championship round 5

1	John Fitzpatrick/ Jim Busby	Porsche 935-K3	199	6h00m46.114
2	John Paul/John Paul jr	Porsche 935	199	6h01m19.098
3	Bobby Rahal/ Brian Redman	Porsche 935-K3	197	
4	Bob Garretson/Roy Woods/ Ralph Kent-Cooke	Porsche 935-K3	190	
5	Hurley Haywood/ Bruce Leven	Porsche 935	189	
6	David Hobbs/Marc Surer/ John Morton	BMW M1C	188	

Winner's average speed: 107.562 mph. Pole position: Paul jr, 1m38.090. Fastest lap: Paul jr, 1m40.710

SILVERSTONE 6 HOURS

10 May 1981. Silverstone. 205 laps of a 2.932-mile circuit = 601.060 miles. World Endurance Championship round 6

1	Dieter Schornstein/Harald Grohs/ Walter Rohrl	Porsche 935	205	6 hours
2	Derek Bell/Steve O'Rourke/ David Hobbs	BMW M1	203	
3	Siegfried Brunn/ Eddie Jordan	Porsche 908/4	203	
4	Lella Lombardi/ Giorgio Francia	Osella PA9-BMW	200	
5	Edgar Doren/ Jurgen Laessig	Porsche 935-K3	199	
6	Bob Akin/Bobby Rahal/ Peter Lovett	Porsche 935-K3	198	

Winner's average speed: 100.177 mph. Pole position: Jochen Mass (Porsche 908/80), 1m21.32. Fastest lap: Jordan, 1m26.02

ADAC 1000 KM-RENNEN

24 May 1981. Nurburgring. 17 laps of a 14.189-mile circuit = 241.213 miles. Race scheduled for 44 laps but stopped early due to Herbert Muller's fatal accident, half points awarded. World Endurance Championship round 7

1	Hans-Joachim Stuck/ Nelson Piquet	BMW M1	17	2h16m50.86
2	Reinhold Joest/ Jochen Mass	Porsche 908/80	17	2h17m10.85
3	Bob Wollek/Preston Henn*/ Adrian Yates-Smith*	Porsche 935-K3	17	2h18m15.59
4	Hans Heyer/ Piercarlo Ghinzani	Lancia Beta Monte Carlo	17	2h18m18.70
5	Edgar Doren/ Jurgen Laessig	Porsche 935	17	2h21m05.72
6	Volkert Merl/Jurgen Barth	Porsche 908/4	16	

*Only Wollek had driven when the race was stopped. Winner's average speed: 105.758 mph. Pole position: Manfred Winkelhock (Ford Capri), 7m18.49. Fastest lap: Mass, 7m33.53

24 HEURES DU MANS

13-14 June 1981. Le Mans. 354 laps of an 8.467-mile circuit = 2997.318 miles. World Endurance Championship round 8

1	Jacky Ickx/Derek Bell	Porsche 936/81	354	24 hours
2	Jacky Haran/Jean-Louis Schlesser/ Philippe Streiff	Rondeau M379C-Ford	340	
3	Gordon Spice/ Francois Migault	Rondeau M379C-Ford	335	
4	John Cooper/Dudley Wood/ Claude Bourgoignie	Porsche 935-K3	330	

5	Claude Ballot-Lena/ Jean-Claude Andruet	Ferrari 512BB	328
6	Anny-Charlotte Verney/Ralph Kent-Cooke/ Bob Garretson	Porsche 935-K3	327

Winner's average speed: 124.888 mph. Pole position: Ickx, 3m29.44. Fastest lap: Hurley Haywood (Porsche 936/81), 3m34.0

COPPA FLORIO/6 ORE ENNA-PERGUSA

28 June 1981. Enna-Pergusa. 202 laps of a 3.076-mile circuit = 621.352 miles. World Endurance Championship round 9

1	Guy Edwards/ Emilio de Villota	Lola T600-Ford	202	6h00m49.39
2	Giorgio Francia/ Lella Lombardi	Osella PA9-BMW	200	
3	"Gimax"/Luigi Moreschi	Osella PA9-BMW	194	
4	Edgar Doren/ Angelo Pallavicini	Porsche 934	178	
5	Duilio Truffo/ Fabrizio Violati	Ferrari 512BB	173	
6	Enrico Uncini/ Gabriele Ciuti	Osella PA7-BMW	169	

Winner's average speed: 103.322 mph. Pole position: Martino Finotto (Ferrari 308GTB), 1m36.08. Fastest lap: de Villota, 1m38.45

DAYTONA 6 HOURS/CHAMPION SPARK PLUG CHALLENGE

5 July 1981. Daytona. 152 laps of a 3.870-mile circuit = 588.240 miles. World Endurance Championship round 10

1	Roger Mandeville/ Amos Johnson	Mazda RX-3	152	6h00m29.73
2	Jim Downing/Tom Waugh	Mazda RX-3	152	6h00m45.55
3	Jack Dunham/ Hurley Haywood	Mazda RX-3	147	
4	Fred Stiff/VJ Elmore	Mazda RX-3	145	
5	Chuck Ulinski/ML Speer/ Ray Ratcliff	Mazda RX-3	145	
6	Jim Nealon/Bill Jobe	Mazda RX-3	145	

Winner's average speed: 97.905 mph. Pole position: Irv Hoerr (American Motors Spirit), 2m14.272. Fastest lap: Downing, 2m16.620

WATKINS GLEN 6 HOURS

12 July 1981. Watkins Glen. 173 laps of a 3.377-mile circuit = 584.221 miles. World Endurance Championship round 11

1	Riccardo Patrese/ Michele Alboreto	Lancia Beta Monte Carlo	173	6h00m28.053
2	Andrea de Cesaris/ Henri Pescarolo	Lancia Beta Monte Carlo	171	
3	Rick Mears/Johnny Rutherford/ Bob Garretson	Porsche 935-K3	168	
4	John Fitzpatrick/ Jim Busby	Porsche 935-K3	160	
5	Preston Henn/Marty Hinze/ Dale Whittington	Porsche 935-K3	157	
6	Gianpiero Moretti/ Bobby Rahal	Porsche 935	157	

Winner's average speed: 97.244 mph. Pole position: Bill Whittington (Porsche 935-K3), 1m48.583. Fastest lap: John Paul jr (Porsche 935), 1m52.831

24 HEURES DE SPA-FRANCORCHAMPS

25-26 July 1981. Spa-Francorchamps. 456 laps of a 4.312-mile circuit = 1966.272 miles. World Endurance Championship round 12

1	Pierre Dieudonne/ Tom Walkinshaw	Mazda RX-7	456	24 hours
2	Eddy Joosen/Dirk Vermeersch/ Jean-Claude Andruet	BMW 530i	454	
3	Vince Woodman/Jonathan Buncombe/ Peter Clark	Ford Capri	453	
4	Jean Xhenceval/Daniel Herregods/ Umberto Grano	BMW 530i	451	

5 Marc Duez/Jeff Allam/Chuck Nicholson/
Win Percy   Mazda RX-7   445
6 Les Blackburn/Bob Akin/
John Morrison   Ford Capri   435
Winner's average speed: 81.928 mph. Pole position: Claude Bourgoignie
(Chevrolet Camaro), 2m51.25. Fastest lap: Bourgoignie, 2m54.4

MOLSON 1000

16 August 1981. Mosport Park. 229 laps of a 2.459-mile circuit = 563.111
miles. World Endurance Championship round 13

1 Rolf Stommelen/
Harald Grohs   Porsche 935   229   6h00m43.972
2 Brian Redman/
Eppie Wietzes   Lola T600-Chevrolet   229   6h01m06.708
3 Ted Field/Bill Whittington   Porsche 935-K3   222
4 Preston Henn/Edgar Doren   Porsche 935-K3   219
5 David Cowart/
Kemper Miller   BMW M1   218
6 John Fitzpatrick/
Jim Busby   Porsche 935-K3   218
Winner's average speed: 93.661 mph. Pole position: Stommelen,
1m18.956. Fastest lap: B Whittington, 1m20.657

PABST 500 MILES

23 August 1981. Elkhart Lake. 125 laps of a 4.048-mile circuit = 506.000
miles. World Endurance Championship round 14

1 Rolf Stommelen/
Harald Grohs   Porsche 935   125   4h44m35.38
2 Brian Redman/Sam Posey   Lola T600-Chevrolet   125   4h45m26.00
3 Chris Cord/Jim Adams   Lola T600-Chevrolet   121
4 Bob Garretson/Tom Gloy   Porsche 935-K3   119
5 Gianpiero Moretti/
Bobby Rahal   Porsche 935   118
6 John Fitzpatrick/
Jim Busby   Porsche 935-K3   118
Winner's average speed: 106.680 mph. Pole position: Stommelen,
2m08.359. Fastest lap: John Paul jr (Porsche 935), 2m10.25

FLYING TIGERS 1000

27 September 1981. Brands Hatch. 238 laps of a 2.614-mile circuit =
622.037 miles. World Endurance Championship round 15

1 Guy Edwards/
Emilio de Villota   Lola T600-Ford   238   6h13m30.7
2 Bob Garretson/
Bobby Rahal   Porsche 935-K3   230
3 Derek Bell/Chris Craft   BMW M1   227
4 John Cooper/Dudley Wood   Porsche 935-K3   226
5 Lella Lombardi/
Giorgio Francia   Osella PA9-BMW   226
6 Dieter Schornstein/
Harald Grohs   Porsche 935   221
Winner's average speed: 99.922 mph. Pole position: Manfred Winkelhock
(Ford C100), 1m25.5. Fastest lap: n/a

1981 FINAL CHAMPIONSHIP POSITIONS

Drivers				
1	Bob Garretson	132	11= John Cooper	72.5
2	Harald Grohs	116.5	Dudley Wood	72.5
3	Derek Bell	113	13 Fred Stiff	71.5
4=	Giorgio Francia	101	14 Lee Mueller	63
	Lella Lombardi	101	15 Rolf Stommelen	60
6	Bobby Rahal	98	16= Amos Johnson	59
7	Edgar Doren	97.5	Roger Mandeville	59
8	Bob Akin	89	Bill Whittington	59
9	Brian Redman	85	19= Michele Alboreto	58
10	Hurley Haywood	75	David Hobbs	58

1981 FINAL CHAMPIONSHIP POSITIONS (cont.)

Manufacturers - over 2000cc			2	BMW	22.5
1	Porsche	100 (107.5)*	3	Opel	6
2	BMW	52	4	Ford	4
3	Ferrari	18	5	Toyota	3
4	Lancia	6	6	Porsche	2
5	Morgan	2	7	Audi	1.5

*Best five results count   *Best five results count

Manufacturers - 2000cc			Manufacturers - overall	
1	Lancia	100 (110)*	1	Lancia

1982

World Endurance Championship

1000 KM DI MONZA/TROFEO FILIPPO CARACCIOLO

18 April 1982. Monza. 173 laps of a 3.604-mile circuit = 623.475 miles.
World Endurance Championship round 1

1 Henri Pescarolo/Giorgio Francia/
Jean Rondeau   Rondeau M382C-Ford   173   5h33m56.2
2 Rolf Stommelen/
Ted Field   Porsche 935-K3   172
3 Gabriele Ciuti/Mario Benusiglio/
Giuseppe Piazzi   Osella PA7-BMW   167
4 Volkert Merl/
Dieter Schornstein   Porsche 935   167
5 Mario Casoni/Joe Castellano/
Mark Thatcher   Lancia Beta Monte Carlo   163
6 Guy Frequelin/Roger Dorchy/
Jean-Daniel Raulet   WM P82-Peugeot   162
Winner's average speed: 112.023 mph. Pole position: Riccardo Patrese
(Lancia LC1), 1m39.91. Fastest lap: Patrese, 1m44.3

PACE PETROLEUM 6 HOURS

16 May 1982. Silverstone. 240 laps of a 2.932-mile circuit = 703.680
miles. World Endurance Championship round 2

1 Riccardo Patrese/
Michele Alboreto   Lancia LC1   240   6h00m15.42
2 Jacky Ickx/Derek Bell   Porsche 956   237
3 Jean-Michel Martin/Philippe Martin/
Bob Wollek   Porsche 936C   231
4 Giorgio Francia/
Duilio Truffo   Osella PA9-BMW   228
5 Henri Pescarolo/
Gordon Spice   Rondeau M382C-Ford   227
6 Ray Mallock/Mike Salmon   Nimrod NRA/C2-
Aston Martin   227
Winner's average speed: 117.196 mph. Pole position: Ickx, 1m16.91.
Fastest lap: Patrese, 1m21.18

ADAC 1000 KM-RENNEN

30 May 1982. Nurburgring. 44 laps of a 14.189-mile circuit = 624.316
miles. World Endurance Championship round 3

1 Riccardo Patrese/Michele Alboreto/
Teo Fabi   Lancia LC1   44   5h54m10.83
2 Henri Pescarolo/
Rolf Stommelen   Rondeau M382C-Ford   43
3 Helmut Kelleners/Enzo Calderari/
Umberto Grano   BMW M1   41
4 Mario Ketterer/Anton Fischhaber/
Eckhart Schimpf   BMW 320i   39
5 Richard Lloyd/Tony Dron/
Hans Volker   Porsche 924 Carrera GTR   39
6 Armin Hahne/
Heinz Becker   Mazda RX-7   39

World Sports Car Championship

Winner's average speed: 105.762 mph. Pole position: Klaus Ludwig (Ford C100), 7m16.57. Fastest lap: Manfred Winkelhock (Ford C100), 7m23.97

24 HEURES DU MANS

19-20 June 1982. Le Mans. 359 laps of an 8.467-mile circuit = 3039.653 miles. World Endurance Championship round 4

1	Jacky Ickx/Derek Bell	Porsche 956	359	24 hours
2	Jochen Mass/ Vern Schuppan	Porsche 956	356	
3	Hurley Haywood/Al Holbert/ Jurgen Barth	Porsche 956	340	
4	John Fitzpatrick/ David Hobbs	Porsche 935-K4	329	
5	Dany Snobeck/Francois Servanin/ Rene Metge	Porsche 935-K3	325	
6	Pierre Dieudonne/Carson Baird/ Jean-Paul Libert	Ferrari 512BB	322	

Winner's average speed: 126.652 mph. Pole position: Ickx, 3m28.40. Fastest lap: Jean Ragnotti (Rondeau M382C-Ford), 3m36.9

TROPHEE DINERS CLUB/1000 KM DE SPA-FRANCORCHAMPS

5 September 1982. Spa-Francorchamps. 144 laps of a 4.312-mile circuit = 620.928 miles. World Endurance Championship round 5

1	Jacky Ickx/Jochen Mass	Porsche 956	144	6h06m04.14
2	Derek Bell/ Vern Schuppan	Porsche 956	141	
3	Riccardo Patrese/ Teo Fabi	Lancia LC1	140	
4	Jean-Michel Martin/ Philippe Martin	Porsche 936C	134	
5	Francois Migault/ Gordon Spice	Rondeau M382C-Ford	133	
6	Giorgio Francia/ Luigi Moreschi	Osella PA9-BMW	132	

Winner's average speed: 101.772 mph. Pole position: Ickx, 2m15.12. Fastest lap: Michele Alboreto (Lancia LC1), 2m21.18

TROFEO BANCA TOSCANA

19 September 1982. Mugello. 191 laps of a 3.259-mile circuit = 622.469 miles. World Endurance Championship round 6

1	Michele Alboreto/ Piercarlo Ghinzani	Lancia LC1	191	6h18m40.05
2	Corrado Fabi/ Alessandro Nannini	Lancia LC1	191	6h20m12.21
3	Bob Wollek/Hans Heyer/ Henri Pescarolo	Porsche 936C	184	
4	Giorgio Francia/ Luigi Moreschi	Osella PA9-BMW	175	
5	Walter Brun/ Sigi Muller Jr	Sauber C6-Ford	175	
6	Dieter Schornstein/Volkert Merl/ Bob Wollek	Porsche 935	175	

Winner's average speed: 98.630 mph. Pole position: Riccardo Patrese (Lancia LC1), 1m45.29. Fastest lap: Teo Fabi and Ghinzani (both Lancia LC1), 1m47.88

FUJI 6 HOURS

3 October 1982. Fuji. 260 laps of a 2.709-mile circuit = 704.340 miles. World Endurance Championship round 7

1	Jacky Ickx/Jochen Mass	Porsche 956	260	6h00m41.05
2	Riccardo Patrese/ Teo Fabi	Lancia LC1	258	
3	Masakazu Nakamura/ Kiyoshi Misaki	March 75SC-Toyota	243	
4	Naoki Nagasaka/ Fumiyasu Sato	BMW M1	238	
5	Kaoru Hoshino/Nobuhide Tachi/ Aguri Suzuki	Toyota Celica C	234	

1982 Jacky Ickx secured his first World Sports Car Championship by beating Riccardo Patrese at Brands Hatch.

6	Tom Walkinshaw/Takashi Yorino/ Masanori Sekiya	Mazda RX-7 254i	228

Winner's average speed: 117.167 mph. Pole position: Michele Alboreto (Lancia LC1), 1m12.39. Fastest lap: n/a

SHELL OILS 1000 KMS

17 October 1982. Brands Hatch. 211 laps of a 2.614-mile circuit = 551.470 miles. Race stopped after 9 laps due to heavy rain, restarted over an additional 202 laps, aggregate result. World Endurance Championship round 8

1	Jacky Ickx/Derek Bell	Porsche 956	211	5h35m01.6
2	Riccardo Patrese/ Teo Fabi	Lancia LC1	211	5h35m06.3
3	David Hobbs/John Fitzpatrick/ Bob Wollek	Porsche 935-K4	202	
4	Jonathan Palmer/ Desire Wilson	Ford C100	201	
5	Marc Surer/Klaus Ludwig/ Manfred Winkelhock	Ford C100	200	
6	John Paul Jr/ Frank Jelinski	Kremer CK5-Porsche	198	

Winner's average speed: 98.763 mph. Pole position: Surer, 1m27.50. Fastest lap: Ickx, 1m21.00

1982 FINAL CHAMPIONSHIP POSITIONS

Drivers					
1	Jacky Ickx	95	18	Hans Heyer	17
2	Riccardo Patrese	87	19=	Corrado Fabi	16
3	Derek Bell	70		Volkert Merl	16
4	Teo Fabi	66		Alessandro Nannini	16
5	Michele Alboreto	63		Dieter Schornstein	16
6	Henri Pescarolo	61		Gordon Spice	16
7	Jochen Mass	55		Drivers who change cars during	
8	Giorgio Francia	49		a race ineligible for points	
9=	Vern Schuppan	30			
	Rolf Stommelen	30		**Manufacturers**	
11	Bob Wollek	24	1	Porsche	75
12=	John Fitzpatrick	22	2	Rondeau-Ford	62
	David Hobbs	22	3	Nimrod-Aston Martin	24
	Jean-Michel Martin	22	4	WM-Peugeot	21
	Philippe Martin	22	5=	Ford	10
16	Piercarlo Ghinzani	21		Sauber-Ford	10
17	Luigi Moreschi	18	7	Lola-Ford	3

1983

World Endurance Championship

1000 KM DI MONZA/TROFEO FILIPPO CARACCIOLO

10 April 1983. Monza. 173 laps of a 3.604-mile circuit = 623.475 miles.
World Endurance Championship round 1

1	Bob Wollek/			
	Thierry Boutsen	Porsche 956	173	5h12m06.09
2	Jacky Ickx/Jochen Mass	Porsche 956	173	5h13m19.80
3	Rolf Stommelen/Hans Heyer/			
	Clemens Schickentanz	Porsche 956	170	
4	Axel Plankenhorn/Jurgen Barth/			
	Jurgen Laessig	Porsche 956	163	
5	John Fitzpatrick/			
	David Hobbs	Porsche 956	161	
6	Jan Lammers/Tiff Needell/			
	Richard Lloyd	Porsche 956	161	

Winner's average speed: 119.860 mph. Pole position: Piercarlo Ghinzani
(Lancia LC2), 1m35.86. Fastest lap: Fitzpatrick, 1m40.40

GRAND PRIX INTERNATIONAL 1000 KMS

8 May 1983. Silverstone. 212 laps of a 2.932-mile circuit = 621.584 miles.
World Endurance Championship round 2

1	Derek Bell/Stefan Bellof	Porsche 956	212	5h02m42.93
2	Bob Wollek/			
	Stefan Johansson	Porsche 956	212	5h03m36.14
3	Jan Lammers/			
	Thierry Boutsen	Porsche 956	205	
4	Jurgen Laessig/Axel Plankenhorn/			
	Harald Grohs	Porsche 956	201	
5	Alan Jones/			
	Vern Schuppan	Porsche 956	201	
6	Tony Dron/Richard Cleare Kremer CK5-Porsche 197			

Winner's average speed: 123.202 mph. Pole position: Bellof, 1m13.15.
Fastest lap: Riccardo Patrese (Lancia LC2), 1m18.39

ADAC BITBURGER 1000 KM-RENNEN

29 May 1983. Nurburgring. 44 laps of a 12.944-mile circuit = 569.536
miles. Race stopped after 26 laps due to an accident, restarted over an
additional 18 laps, aggregate result. World Endurance Championship
round 2

1	Jochen Mass/Jacky Ickx	Porsche 956	44	5h26m34.63
2	Bob Wollek/			
	Stefan Johansson	Porsche 956	44	5h30m34.99
3	Keke Rosberg/Jan Lammers/			
	Jonathan Palmer	Porsche 956	43	
4	Hans Heyer/Axel Plankenhorn/			
	Jurgen Laessig	Porsche 956	42	
5	Oscar Larrauri/			
	Massimo Sigala	Lancia LC1	40	
6	John Fitzpatrick/			
	David Hobbs	Porsche 956	39	

Winner's average speed: 104.637 mph. Pole position: Stefan Bellof
(Porsche 956), 6m11.13. Fastest lap: Bellof, 6m25.91

24 HEURES DU MANS

18-19 June 1983. Le Mans. 370 laps of an 8.467-mile circuit = 3132.790
miles. World Endurance Championship round 4

1	Vern Schuppan/Hurley Haywood/			
	Al Holbert	Porsche 956	370	24 hours
2	Jacky Ickx/Derek Bell	Porsche 956	370	
3	Mario Andretti/Michael Andretti/			
	Philippe Alliot	Porsche 956	364	
4	Volkert Merl/Clemens Schickentanz/			
	Maurizio de Narvaez	Porsche 956	361	
5	John Fitzpatrick/Guy Edwards/			
	Rupert Keegan	Porsche 956	358	

6	Klaus Ludwig/Stefan Johansson/			
	Bob Wollek	Porsche 956	354	

Winner's average speed: 130.533 mph. Pole position: Ickx, 3m16.56.
Fastest lap: Ickx, 3m29.70

TROPHEE DINERS CLUB/1000 KM DE SPA-FRANCORCHAMPS

4 September 1983. Spa-Francorchamps. 144 laps of a 4.312-mile circuit
= 620.928 miles. World Endurance Championship round 5

1	Jacky Ickx/Jochen Mass	Porsche 956	144	5h44m33.52
2	Derek Bell/Stefan Bellof	Porsche 956	144	5h45m36.54
3	John Fitzpatrick/			
	David Hobbs	Porsche 956	139	
4	Hans-Joachim Stuck/Harald Grohs/			
	Walter Brun	Porsche 956	138	
5	Jurgen Laessig/Axel Plankenhorn/			
	Herve Regout	Porsche 956	136	
6	Giorgio Francia/			
	Paolo Barilla	Lancia LC2	134	

Winner's average speed: 108.126 mph. Pole position: Ickx, 2m09.38.
Fastest lap: Bellof, 2m14.11

FUJI 1000 KMS

2 October 1983. Fuji. 225 laps of a 2.709-mile circuit = 609.525 miles.
Race scheduled for 230 laps, stopped due to accident. World Endurance
Championship round 6

1	Derek Bell/Stefan Bellof	Porsche 956	225	4h57m06.36
2	Jacky Ickx/Jochen Mass	Porsche 956	225	4h57m56.29
3	Vern Schuppan/			
	Naohiro Fujita	Porsche 956	219	
4	Henri Pescarolo/			
	Thierry Boutsen	Porsche 956	218	
5	Bob Wollek/Hans Heyer	Porsche 956	209	
6	Kenji Takahashi/			
	Clemens Schickentanz	Porsche 956	203	

Winner's average speed: 123.092 mph. Pole position: Bellof, 1m10.02.
Fastest lap: Bellof, 1m19.228

CASTROL 1000 KMS

10 December 1983. Kyalami. 244 laps of a 2.550-mile circuit = 622.200
miles. World Endurance Championship round 7

1	Derek Bell/Stefan Bellof	Porsche 956	244	5h44m06.33
2	Riccardo Patrese/			
	Alessandro Nannini	Lancia LC2	240	
3	Jacky Ickx/Jochen Mass	Porsche 956	236	
4	Dieter Schornstein/"John Winter"/			
	Bob Wollek	Porsche 956	228	
5	Jonathan Palmer/			
	Jan Lammers	Porsche 956	225	
6	Sarel van der Merwe/Tony Martin/			
	Graham Duxbury	Porsche 956	224	

Winner's average speed: 108.490 mph. Pole position: Bellof, 1m10.88.
Fastest lap: Bellof, 1m15.59

1983 Wollek/Johansson (Joest Porsche) edges ahead of the works
Porsche and Lancia teams at the start at Silverstone

1983 FINAL CHAMPIONSHIP POSITIONS

Drivers			Manufacturers		
1	Jacky Ickx	97	1	Porsche	100 (140)*
2	Derek Bell	94	2	Lancia	32
3	Jochen Mass	82	3=	March-Nissan	4
4	Stefan Bellof	75		Nimrod-Aston Martin	4
5	Bob Wollek	64	5	Sauber-BMW	3
6	Thierry Boutsen	44	6	Dome-Toyota	2
7	Jan Lammers	43	7	URD-BMW	1
8=	Jurgen Laessig	42	*Best five results count		
	Axel Plankenhorn	42			
10	Vern Schuppan	40	**Manufacturers –**		
11	Stefan Johansson	36	**Group C Junior**		
12	Hans Heyer	30	1	Alba-Giannini	75
13=	John Fitzpatrick	29			
	David Hobbs	29	**Manufacturers – Group B**		
15	Clemens Schickentanz	28	1	Porsche	82 (94)*
16	Al Holbert	24	*Best five results count		
17	Jonathan Palmer	23			
18	Riccardo Patrese	21			
19=	Harald Grohs	20			
	Hurley Haywood	20			

1984 Stefan Bellof leads at the Nurburgring.

1984
World Endurance Championship

1000 KM DI MONZA/TROFEO FILIPPO CARACCIOLO

23 April 1984. Monza. 173 laps of a 3.604-mile circuit = 623.475 miles. World Endurance Championship round 1

1	Derek Bell/Stefan Bellof	Porsche 956	173	5h06m15.60
2	Jacky Ickx/Jochen Mass	Porsche 956	173	5h06m39.56
3	Mauro Baldi/Paolo Barilla	Lancia LC2	168	
4	Hans-Joachim Stuck/Harald Grohs/			
	Walter Brun	Porsche 956	167	
5	Jonathan Palmer/			
	Jan Lammers	Porsche 956	159	
6	Dieter Schornstein/			
	Volkert Merl	Porsche 956	155	

Winner's average speed: 122.146 mph. Pole position: Bellof, 1m35.85. Fastest lap: Riccardo Patrese (Lancia LC2), 1m38.00

GRAND PRIX INTERNATIONAL 1000 KMS

13 May 1984. Silverstone. 212 laps of a 2.932-mile circuit = 621.584 miles. World Endurance Championship round 2

1	Jacky Ickx/Jochen Mass	Porsche 956	212	5h05m21.20
2	Klaus Ludwig/			
	Henri Pescarolo	Porsche 956	210	

3	Rupert Keegan/		
	Guy Edwards	Porsche 956	207
4	Paolo Barilla/Mauro Baldi	Lancia LC2	206
5	Jonathan Palmer/		
	Jan Lammers	Porsche 956	203
6	Franz Konrad/		
	David Sutherland	Porsche 956	202

Winner's average speed: 122.137 mph. Pole position: Riccardo Patrese (Lancia LC2), 1m13.84. Fastest lap: Mass, 1m16.76

24 HEURES DU MANS

16-17 June 1984. Le Mans. 359 laps of an 8.467-mile circuit = 3039.653 miles. World Endurance Championship round 3

1	Klaus Ludwig/			
	Henri Pescarolo	Porsche 956B	359	24 hours
2	Jean Rondeau/John Paul Jr/			
	Preston Henn	Porsche 956	357	
3	David Hobbs/Philippe Streiff/			
	Sarel van der Merwe	Porsche 956	350	
4	Walter Brun/Bob Akin/			
	Leopold von Bayern	Porsche 956B	339	
5	Volkert Merl/Dieter Schornstein/			
	"John Winter"	Porsche 956	339	
6	Vern Schuppan/Alan Jones/			
	Jean-Pierre Jarier	Porsche 956B	336	

Winner's average speed: 126.652 mph. Pole position: Bob Wollek (Lancia LC2), 3m17.11. Fastest lap: Alessandro Nannini (Lancia LC2), 3m28.90

ADAC 1000 KM-RENNEN

15-Jul-1984. Nurburgring. 207 laps of a 2.822-mile circuit = 584.154 miles. Race scheduled for 220 laps but stopped after 6 hours. World Endurance Championship round 4

1	Stefan Bellof/Derek Bell	Porsche 956	207	6h00m43.59
2	Thierry Boutsen/			
	David Hobbs	Porsche 956	207	6h00m59.27
3	Alessandro Nannini/			
	Paolo Barilla	Lancia LC2	206	
4	Jonathan Palmer/Jan Lammers/			
	Christian Danner	Porsche 956	205	
5	Marc Surer/			
	Manfred Winkelhock	Porsche 956	204	
6	Oscar Larrauri/			
	Massimo Sigala	Porsche 956	203	

Winner's average speed: 97.163 mph. Pole position: Bellof, 1m28.68. Fastest lap: Palmer, 1m32.75

BRITISH AEROSPACE 1000 KMS

29 July 1984. Brands Hatch. 238 laps of a 2.614-mile circuit = 622.037 miles. World Endurance Championship round 5

1	Jonathan Palmer/			
	Jan Lammers	Porsche 956	238	5h41m46.33
2	Jochen Mass/			
	Henri Pescarolo	Porsche 956B	236	
3	Thierry Boutsen/Rupert Keegan/			
	Guy Edwards	Porsche 962C	234	
4	David Sutherland/Desire Wilson/			
	George Fouche	Porsche 956	229	
5	Stefan Bellof/			
	Harald Grohs	Porsche 956	224	
6	David Hobbs/Guy Edwards/			
	Thierry Boutsen	Porsche 956	222	

Winner's average speed: 109.202 mph. Pole position: Palmer, 1m17.32. Fastest lap: Palmer and Bob Wollek (Lancia LC2), 1m21.03

BUDWEISER GT 1000 KMS

5 August 1984. Mosport Park. 253 laps of a 2.459-mile circuit = 622.127 miles. World Endurance Championship round 6

1	Jacky Ickx/Jochen Mass	Porsche 956	253	6h00m41.411
2	David Hobbs/Rupert Keegan/			
	Franz Konrad	Porsche 956B	245	

3 Almo Coppelli/
  Guido Dacco   Alba AR2-Giannini 229
4 Stefan Bellof/Derek Bell Porsche 956 221
5 Pasquale Barberio/Maurizio Gellini/
  Geraldo Vatielli   Alba AR3-Ford 217
6 Martino Finotto/Carlo Facetti/
  Alfredo Sebastiani   Alba AR2-Giannini 204

Winner's average speed: 103.489 mph. Pole position: Bellof, 1m12.107.
Fastest lap: Bellof, 1m13.874

1000 KM DE SPA-FRANCORCHAMPS ROTHMANS

2 September 1984. Spa-Francorchamps. 144 laps of a 4.312-mile circuit = 620.928 miles. World Endurance Championship round 7

1 Stefan Bellof/Derek Bell Porsche 956 144 5h53m17.19
2 Jochen Mass/Jacky Ickx Porsche 956 144 5h54m14.90
3 Hans-Joachim Stuck/Harald Grohs/
  Walter Brun   Porsche 956B 142
4 Massimo Sigala/
  Oscar Larrauri   Porsche 956 141
5 Jurgen Laessig/Herve Regout/
  Philippe Martin   Porsche 956 141
6 Vern Schuppan/
  John Watson   Porsche 956 139

Winner's average speed: 105.455 mph. Pole position: Thierry Boutsen (Porsche 956B), 2m09.63. Fastest lap: Bellof, 2m15.57

1000 KM DI IMOLA

16 September 1984. Imola. 199 laps of a 3.132-mile circuit = 623.268 miles. World Endurance Championship round 8

1 Stefan Bellof/
  Hans-Joachim Stuck Porsche 956B 199 5h54m56.32
2 Jonathan Palmer/
  Jan Lammers   Porsche 956GTi 199 5h55m30.53
3 Jochen Mass/Henri Pescarolo/
  Hans Heyer   Porsche 956B 197
4 Walter Brun/George Fouche/
  Leopold von Bayern Porsche 956B 195
5 Oscar Larrauri/
  Massimo Sigala   Porsche 956 193
6 Harald Grohs/Herve Regout/
  Jurgen Laessig   Porsche 956 191

Winner's average speed: 105.359 mph. Pole position: Riccardo Patrese (Lancia LC2), 1m37.82. Fastest lap: Pierluigi Martini (Lancia LC2), 1m37.84

FUJI 1000 KMS

30 September 1984. Fuji. 226 laps of a 2.709-mile circuit = 612.234 miles. World Endurance Championship round 9

1 Stefan Bellof/
  John Watson   Porsche 956 226 5h30m00.37
2 Jochen Mass/Jacky Ickx Porsche 956 226 5h30m32.67
3 Hans-Joachim Stuck/
  Vern Schuppan   Porsche 956 224
4 Stefan Johansson/
  Henri Pescarolo   Porsche 956 222
5 Manfred Winkelhock/
  Mike Thackwell   Porsche 956 216
6 Naoki Nagasaka/
  Keiichi Suzuki   Lotec M1C-BMW 209

Winner's average speed: 111.313 mph. Pole position: Bellof, 1m17.49.
Fastest lap: n/a

KYALAMI 1000 KMS

3 November 1984. Kyalami. 244 laps of a 2.550-mile circuit = 622.200 miles. World Endurance Championship round 10

1 Riccardo Patrese/
  Alessandro Nannini Lancia LC2 244 5h38m13.92
2 Bob Wollek/Paolo Barilla Lancia LC2 242

3 George Santana/Hanni van der Linde/
  Errol Shearsby   Nissan Skyline 202
4 Ben Morganrood/Johann Coetzee/
  Willie Hapburn   Mazda RX-7 201
5 Nicola Bianco/
  Arnold Chatz   Alfa Romeo GTV6 200
6 Paul Moni/Mick Formato Alfa Romeo GTV6 193

Winner's average speed: 110.374 mph. Pole position: Wollek, 1m12.96.
Fastest lap: Patrese/Nannini, 1m16.18 - organisers did not publish which driver set time

SANDOWN PARK 1000 KMS

2 December 1984. Sandown Park. 206 laps of a 2.425-mile circuit = 499.550 miles. Race scheduled for 257 laps, stopped after 6 hours. World Endurance Championship round 11

1 Stefan Bellof/Derek Bell Porsche 956 206 6h01m30.3
2 Jochen Mass/Jacky Ickx Porsche 956 203
3 Jonathan Palmer/
  Jan Lammers   Porsche 956GTi 202
4 Sarel van der Merwe/
  George Fouche   Porsche 956 200
5 Manfred Winkelhock/
  Rusty French   Porsche 956B 200
6 Colin Bond/
  Andrew Miedecke   Porsche 962C 198

Winner's average speed: 82.912 mph. Pole position: Bellof, 1m31.6.
Fastest lap: Bellof, 1m34.4

1984 FINAL CHAMPIONSHIP POSITIONS

	Drivers			Manufacturers	
1	Stefan Bellof	138 (139)*	1	Porsche	120 (152)*
2	Jochen Mass	127 (131)*	2	Lancia	57
3	Jacky Ickx	104	3	Alba-Giannini	12
4=	Derek Bell	91	4	Alba-Ford	8
	Henri Pescarolo	91	5=	Lotec-BMW	6
6=	Jan Lammers	75		Tiga-Ford	6
	Jonathan Palmer	75	7	Rondeau-Ford	5
8=	David Hobbs	54	8=	Dome-Toyota	4
	Hans-Joachim Stuck	54		Lola-Mazda	4
10	Paolo Barilla	49	10	March-Mazda	3
11	Walter Brun	47	11	BMW	2
12	Rupert Keegan	44	12=	Ecosse-Ford	1
13	Klaus Ludwig	39		Lola-Chevrolet	1
14	Dieter Schornstein	38	*Best six results count		
15	Harald Grohs	36			
16	Alessandro Nannini	35	**Manufacturers - Group C2**		
17	George Fouche	34	1	Alba-Giannini	82 (90)*
18	"John Winter"	32	*Best six results count		
19=	Mauro Baldi	28			
	Oscar Larrauri	28	**Manufacturers - Group B**		
	Massimo Sigala	28	1	BMW	100
*Best eight results count					

1985

World Endurance Championship

6 ORE DI MUGELLO

14 April 1985. Mugello. 190 laps of a 3.259-mile circuit = 619.210 miles. World Endurance Championship round 1

1 Jacky Ickx/Jochen Mass Porsche 962C 190 5h59m52.21
2 Marc Surer/
  Manfred Winkelhock Porsche 962C 190 6h00m22.05
3 Stefan Bellof/
  Thierry Boutsen   Porsche 962C 189
4 Mauro Baldi/Bob Wollek Lancia LC2 186
5 Klaus Ludwig/George Fouche/
  Gianni Mussato   Porsche 956B 184

6 Mike Thackwell/Herve Regout/
   Jurgen Laessig   Porsche 956   179
Derek Bell/Hans-Joachim Stuck (Porsche 962C), 186 laps, finished fourth on the road but disqualified as last lap too slow. Winner's average speed: 103.239 mph. Pole position: Riccardo Patrese (Lancia LC2), 1m39.07. Fastest lap: Patrese, 1m45.79

1000 KM DI MONZA/TROFEO FILIPPO CARACCIOLO

28 April 1985. Monza. 138 laps of a 3.604-mile circuit = 497.338 miles. Race scheduled for 173 laps but stopped when a tree fell across the track. World Endurance Championship round 2

1 Manfred Winkelhock/
   Marc Surer   Porsche 962C   138   4h04m41.43
2 Hans-Joachim Stuck/
   Derek Bell   Porsche 956   138   4h05m13.07
3 Riccardo Patrese/
   Alessandro Nannini   Lancia LC2   138
4 Jochen Mass/Jacky Ickx   Porsche 962C   138
5 Jonathan Palmer/
   Jan Lammers   Porsche 956GTi   134
6 Oscar Larrauri/Massimo Sigala/
   Renzo Zorzi   Porsche 956   129
Stefan Bellof/Thierry Boutsen (Porsche 962C), 138 laps, finished fifth on the road but disqualified due to illegal refuelling system. Winner's average speed: 121.951 mph. Pole position: Patrese, 1m31.00. Fastest lap: Boutsen/Bellof, 1m39.35 - the organisers did not publish which driver set time

SILVERSTONE 1000 KMS

12 May 1985. Silverstone. 212 laps of a 2.932-mile circuit = 621.584 miles. World Endurance Championship round 3

1 Jochen Mass/Jacky Ickx   Porsche 962C   212   4h54m03.22
2 Derek Bell/
   Hans-Joachim Stuck   Porsche 956   211
3 Riccardo Patrese/
   Alessandro Nannini   Lancia LC2   210
4 Manfred Winkelhock/
   Marc Surer   Porsche 962C   210
5 Jonathan Palmer/
   Jan Lammers   Porsche 956GTi   207
6 Klaus Ludwig/Paolo Barilla/
   Paul Belmondo   Porsche 956   206
Winner's average speed: 126.831 mph. Pole position: Patrese, 1m10.84. Fastest lap: Palmer, 1m15.96

24 HEURES DU MANS

15-16 June 1985. Le Mans. 373 laps of an 8.467-mile circuit = 3158.191 miles. World Endurance Championship round 4

1 Klaus Ludwig/Paolo Barilla/
   "John Winter"   Porsche 956B   373   24 hours
2 Jonathan Palmer/James Weaver/
   Richard Lloyd   Porsche 956GTi   370
3 Derek Bell/
   Hans-Joachim Stuck   Porsche 962C   366
4 David Hobbs/Jo Gartner/
   Guy Edwards   Porsche 956B   365
5 Sarel van der Merwe/George Fouche/
   Mario Hytten   Porsche 956B   360
6 Bob Wollek/Alessandro Nannini/
   Lucio Cesario   Lancia LC2   359
Winner's average speed: 131.591 mph. Pole position: Stuck, 3m14.80. Fastest lap: Jochen Mass (Porsche 962C), 3m25.10

DUSCHFRISCH 1000 KM-RENNEN

14 July 1985. Hockenheim. 147 laps of a 4.227-mile circuit = 621.369 miles. World Endurance Championship round 5

1 Derek Bell/
   Hans-Joachim Stuck   Porsche 962C   147   5h23m00.68
2 Oscar Larrauri/
   Massimo Sigala   Porsche 956   147   5h23m40.59

3 Klaus Ludwig/
   Paolo Barilla   Porsche 956B   145
4 Bob Wollek/Mauro Baldi   Lancia LC2   145
5 Jonathan Palmer/
   David Hobbs   Porsche 956GTi   143
6 Gerhard Berger/
   Walter Brun   Porsche 956   142
Winner's average speed: 115.421 mph. Pole position: Jochen Mass (Porsche 962C), 1m55.18. Fastest lap: Stefan Bellof (Porsche 956B), 2m00.66

BUDWEISER GT 1000 KMS

11 August 1985. Mosport Park. 253 laps of a 2.459-mile circuit = 622.127 miles. World Endurance Championship round 6

1 Derek Bell/
   Hans-Joachim Stuck   Porsche 962C   253   5h55m41.988
2 Jochen Mass/Jacky Ickx   Porsche 962C   253   5h57m06.848
3 Martin Brundle/Mike Thackwell/
   Jean-Louis Schlesser   Jaguar XJR-6   234
4 Ludwig Heimrath/Ludwig Heimrath Jr/
   Kees Kroesemeijer   Porsche 956   234
5 Gordon Spice/Ray Bellm   Tiga GC85-Ford   231
6 Frank Jelinski/
   John Graham   Gebhardt 853-Ford   225
Winner's average speed: 104.941 mph. Pole position: Stuck, 1m09.775. Fastest lap: Stuck, 1m12.915

1000 KM DE SPA-FRANCORCHAMPS

1 September 1985. Spa-Francorchamps. 122 laps of a 4.312-mile circuit = 526.064 miles. Race scheduled for 145 laps but stopped after Stefan Bellof's fatal accident. World Endurance Championship round 7

1 Bob Wollek/Mauro Baldi/
   Riccardo Patrese   Lancia LC2   122   5h00m23.420
2 Hans-Joachim Stuck/
   Derek Bell   Porsche 962C   122   5h02m37.860
3 Klaus Ludwig/
   Paolo Barilla   Porsche 956B   121
4 Alessandro Nannini/Riccardo Patrese/
   Mauro Baldi   Lancia LC2   121
5 Martin Brundle/
   Mike Thackwell   Jaguar XJR-6   120
6 Marc Duez/"John Winter"/
   Volker Weidler   Porsche 956   120
Winner's average speed: 105.076 mph. Pole position: Patrese, 2m05.91. Fastest lap: Jochen Mass (Porsche 962C), 2m10.73

SHELL GEMINI 1000 KMS

22 September 1985. Brands Hatch. 238 laps of a 2.614-mile circuit = 622.037 miles. World Endurance Championship round 8

1 Derek Bell/
   Hans-Joachim Stuck   Porsche 962C   238   5h34m26.02
2 Jochen Mass/Jacky Ickx   Porsche 962C   238   5h34m38.01
3 Bob Wollek/Andrea de Cesaris/
   Mauro Baldi   Lancia LC2   237
4 Riccardo Patrese/
   Alessandro Nannini   Lancia LC2   233
5 Vern Schuppan/
   Al Holbert   Porsche 956   224
6 Ray Mallock/Mike Wilds/
   David Leslie   Ecosse C285-Ford   219
Winner's average speed: 111.598 mph. Pole position: Patrese, 1m14.66. Fastest lap: de Cesaris, 1m19.11

FUJI 1000 KMS

6 October 1985. Fuji. 62 laps of a 2.709-mile circuit = 167.958 miles. Race scheduled for 226 laps, stopped after 2 hours due to heavy rain, half points awarded. World Endurance Championship round 9

1 Kazuyoshi Hoshino/Keiji Matsumoto*/
   Akira Hagiwara*   March 85G-Nissan   62   2h01m10.79

2 Osamu Nakako/Emanuele Pirro*/
Akio Morimoto*   Le Mans 05C-Nissan 61
3 Satoru Nakajima/
Masanori Sekiya   Dome 85C-Toyota 61
4 Naoki Nagasaka/
Taku Akaike*   Dome 85C-Toyota 61
5 Masahiro Hasemi/
Takao Wada*   March 85G-Nissan 60
6 Vern Schuppan/George Fouche*/
Keiichi Suzuki*   Porsche 956 60

*Had not driven when race was stopped. Winner's average speed: 83.161 mph. Pole position: Hans-Joachim Stuck (Porsche 962C), 1m15.92. Fastest lap: n/a

SELANGOR 800 KMS

1 December 1985. Shah Alam. 217 laps of a 2.295-mile circuit = 498.015 miles. World Endurance Championship round 10

1 Jochen Mass/Jacky Ickx Porsche 962C   217   5h32m03.34
2 Mike Thackwell/John Nielsen/
Jan Lammers   Jaguar XJR-6   217   5h33m25.73
3 Vern Schuppan/
James Weaver   Porsche 956   208
4 Franz Konrad/
Andrew Miedecke   Porsche 956   205
5 Oscar Larrauri/Massimo Sigala/
Frank Jelinski   Porsche 956   195
6 Richard Piper/Ian Harrower/
Evan Clements   Gebhardt 843-Ford 191

Winner's average speed: 89.988 mph. Pole position: Mass, 1m21.33. Fastest lap: Mass, 1m24.52

1985 FINAL CHAMPIONSHIP POSITIONS

Drivers		Teams		
1= Derek Bell	117	1 Rothmans Porsche	107	
Hans-Joachim Stuck	117	2 Martini Lancia	58	
3= Jacky Ickx	101	3 Joest Racing	50	
Jochen Mass	101	4 Porsche Kremer Racing	43	
5= Klaus Ludwig	58	5 Richard Lloyd Racing	31	
Bob Wollek	58	6 Brun Motorsport	28	
7 Paolo Barilla	52	7= Jaguar (TWR)	20	
8 Alessandro Nannini	50	Obermaier Racing	20	
9= Marc Surer	45	9 Spice Engineering	16	
Manfred Winkelhock	45	10= Fitzpatrick		
11 Mike Thackwell	43	Porsche Team	10	
12 Jonathan Palmer	39	Hoshino Racing	10	
13 Mauro Baldi	36			
14 Riccardo Patrese	34	Drivers - C2		
15 Jan Lammers	31	1= Ray Bellm	130	
16=Ray Bellm	30	Gordon Spice	130	
Gordon Spice	30			
18 Oscar Larrauri	29	Teams - C2		
19 James Weaver	27	1 Spice Engineering	110	
20=Vern Schuppan	23			
Massimo Sigala	23			

1986
World Sports-Prototype Championship

KOUROS CUP/TROFEO FILIPPO CARACCIOLO

20 April 1986. Monza. 63 laps of a 3.604-mile circuit = 227.046 miles. World Sports-Prototype Championship round 1

1 Hans-Joachim Stuck/
Derek Bell   Porsche 962C   63   1h48m40.29
2 Andrea de Cesaris/
Alessandro Nannini   Lancia LC2   63   1h49m29.39
3 Massimo Sigala/
Walter Brun   Porsche 956   61

4 Oscar Larrauri/
Jesus Pareja   Porsche 962C   61
5 Drake Olson/
Thierry Boutsen   Porsche 962C   61
6 Jochen Mass/Bob Wollek Porsche 962C   61

Winner's average speed: 125.357 mph. Pole position: de Cesaris, 1m32.32. Fastest lap: Nannini, 1m36.96

KOUROS 1000 KMS

5 May 1986. Silverstone. 212 laps of a 2.932-mile circuit = 621.584 miles. World Sports-Prototype Championship round 2

1 Derek Warwick/
Eddie Cheever   Jaguar XJR-6   212   4h48m55.37
2 Derek Bell/
Hans-Joachim Stuck   Porsche 962C   210
3 Jo Gartner/Tiff Needell Porsche 962C   207
4 James Weaver/
Klaus Niedzwiedz   Porsche 956GTi 206
5 Emilio de Villota/
Fermin Velez   Porsche 956B   206
6 George Follmer/John Morton/
Paolo Barilla   Porsche 956   205

Winner's average speed: 129.083 mph. Pole position: Andrea de Cesaris (Lancia LC2), 1m10.81. Fastest lap: de Cesaris, 1m13.95

24 HEURES DU MANS

31 May-1 June 1986. Le Mans. 367 laps of an 8.406-mile circuit = 3085.002 miles. World Sports-Prototype Championship round 3

1 Hans-Joachim Stuck/Derek Bell/
Al Holbert   Porsche 962C   367   24 hours
2 Oscar Larrauri/Joel Gouhier/
Jesus Pareja   Porsche 962C   359
3 George Follmer/John Morton/
Kemper Miller   Porsche 956   354
4 Emilio de Villota/George Fouche/
Fermin Velez   Porsche 956   348
5 Jurgen Laessig/Fulvio Ballabio/
Dudley Wood   Porsche 956   344
6 Siegfried Brunn/Ernst Schuster/
Rudi Seher   Porsche 936CJ 343

Winner's average speed: 128.542 mph. Pole position: Jochen Mass (Porsche 962C), 3m15.99. Fastest lap: Klaus Ludwig (Porsche 956B), 3m23.3

200 MEILEN VON NURNBERG

29 June 1986. Norisring. 79 laps of a 1.429-mile circuit = 112.891 miles. World Sports-Prototype Championship round 4

1 Klaus Ludwig   Porsche 956B   79   1h07m00.36
2 Eddie Cheever   Jaguar XJR-6   79   1h07m08.03
3 Derek Warwick   Jaguar XJR-6   79
4 Frank Jelinski   Porsche 962C   78
5 James Weaver   Porsche 962C   78
6 Walter Brun   Porsche 962C   78

Winner's average speed: 101.087 mph. Pole position: Hans-Joachim Stuck (Porsche 962C), 46.54s. Fastest lap: Stuck, 48.28s

SHELL GEMINI 1000 KMS

20 July 1986. Brands Hatch. 236 laps of a 2.614-mile circuit = 616.810 miles. Race scheduled for 238 laps but stopped early due to additional parade laps. World Sports-Prototype Championship round 5

1 Bob Wollek/Mauro Baldi Porsche 956GTi 236   5h53m44.43
2 Hans-Joachim Stuck/Derek Bell/
Klaus Ludwig   Porsche 956B   232
3 Thierry Boutsen/
Frank Jelinski   Porsche 956   231
4 Derek Warwick/
Jean-Louis Schlesser Jaguar XJR-6   231
5 Paolo Barilla/"John Winter"/
Klaus Ludwig   Porsche 956   230

6 Eddie Cheever/
Gianfranco Brancatelli   Jaguar XJR-6   230
Winner's average speed: 104.621 mph. Pole position: Stuck, 1m16.27.
Fastest lap: Wollek, 1m18.68

TROFEO SILK CUT

3 August 1986. Jerez. 86 laps of a 2.621-mile circuit = 225.397 miles.
World Sports-Prototype Championship round 6

1 Oscar Larrauri/
Jesus Pareja   Porsche 962C   86   2h27m47.34
2 Walter Brun/Frank Jelinski Porsche 956 86 2h28m23.24
3 Derek Warwick/
Jan Lammers   Jaguar XJR-6   84
4 Fulvio Ballabio/Dudley Wood/
Jurgen Laessig   Porsche 956   82
5 Gordon Spice/Ray Bellm   Spice SE86C-Ford 79
6 Evan Clements/
Ian Harrower   Gebhardt 843-Ford   78
Winner's average speed: 91.508 mph. Pole position: Jelinski, 1m33.48.
Fastest lap: Larrauri, 1m38.09

ADAC KOUROS 1000 KM-RENNEN

24 August 1986. Nurburgring. 121 laps of a 2.822-mile circuit = 341.462
miles. Race scheduled for 221 laps, stopped after 22 laps due to heavy
rain, restarted over 3 hours, aggregate result. World Sports-Prototype
Championship round 7

1 Mike Thackwell/
Henri Pescarolo   Sauber C8-Mercedes-Benz 121 3h42m30.02
2 Mauro Baldi/
Klaus Niedzwiedz Porsche 956GTi 119
3 Emilio de Villota/
Fermin Velez   Porsche 956   119
4 Jurgen Laessig/Fulvio Ballabio/
Harald Grohs   Porsche 956   115
5 Ray Mallock/
Marc Duez   Ecosse C286-Rover   115
6 Walter Lechner/Ernst Franzmeier/
Max Payne   Gebhardt 853-Ford   112
Winner's average speed: 92.080 mph. Pole position: Thierry Boutsen
(Porsche 962C), 1m27.27. Fastest lap: Niedzwiedz, 1m34.82

1000 KM DE SPA-FRANCORCHAMPS KOUROS

15 September 1986. Spa-Francorchamps. 145 laps of a 4.312-mile circuit
= 625.240 miles. World Sports-Prototype Championship round 8

1 Thierry Boutsen/
Frank Jelinski   Porsche 962C   145   5h35m54.54
2 Derek Warwick/
Jan Lammers   Jaguar XJR-6   145   5h35m55.34
3 Derek Bell/
Hans-Joachim Stuck Porsche 962C 145
4 Paolo Barilla/
Klaus Ludwig   Porsche 956B   144
5 Eddie Cheever/
Jean-Louis Schlesser Jaguar XJR-6 143
6 Mike Thackwell/
Henri Pescarolo   Sauber C8-
Mercedes-Benz   140
Winner's average speed: 111.680 mph. Pole position: Boutsen, 2m06.87.
Fastest lap: Cheever, 2m09.38

FUJI 1000 KMS

6 October 1986. Fuji. 226 laps of a 2.759-mile circuit = 623.534 miles.
World Sports-Prototype Championship round 9

1 Paolo Barilla/
Piercarlo Ghinzani Porsche 956B 226 5h29m25.332
2 Frank Jelinski/
Stanley Dickens   Porsche 956   225
3 Eddie Cheever/
Derek Warwick   Jaguar XJR-6   225
4 Bruno Giacomelli/
Volker Weidler   Porsche 962C   224
5 Kris Nissen/Harald Grohs/
"John Winter"   Porsche 956   223
6 Vern Schuppan/George Fouche/
Keiichi Suzuki   Porsche 956   223
Winner's average speed: 113.569 mph. Pole position: Oscar Larrauri
(Porsche 962C), 1m16.519. Fastest lap: n/a

1986 FINAL CHAMPIONSHIP POSITIONS

Drivers		
1	Derek Bell	82*
2	Hans-Joachim Stuck	82
3	Derek Warwick	81
4	Frank Jelinski	74
5	Eddie Cheever	61
6=	Oscar Larrauri	50
	Jesus Pareja	50
8	Paolo Barilla	44
9	Thierry Boutsen	41
10	Mauro Baldi	38
11	Walter Brun	37
12=	Fulvio Ballabio	35
	Jurgen Laessig	35
14=	Fermin Velez	34
	Emilio de Villota	34
16	Henri Pescarolo	31
17	Klaus Ludwig	30
18=	Mike Thackwell	29
	Bob Wollek	29
20	Klaus Niedzwiedz	28

not compete together. Bell
finished 11th, Stuck 15th.

Teams		
1	Brun Motorsport	57
2	Joest Racing	48
3=	Rothmans Porsche	47
	Silk Cut Jaguar (TWR)	47
5	Fitzpatrick Porsche Team	30
6	Kouros Sauber	29
7	Richard Lloyd Racing	28
8=	Porsche Kremer Racing	18
	Obermaier Racing	18
10	Ecurie Ecosse	8

Drivers - C2		
1=	Ray Bellm	105
	Gordon Spice	105

Teams - C2		
1	Ecurie Ecosse	70

*Bell was declared champion
due to finishing higher than
Stuck at the Norisring. It was
the only event at which they did

1987
World Sports-Prototype Championship

GRAN PREMIO FORTUNA

22 March 1987. Jarama. 109 laps of a 2.115-mile circuit = 230.579 miles.
World Sports-Prototype Championship round 1

1 Jan Lammers/
John Watson   Jaguar XJR-8   109   2h29m56.303
2 Hans-Joachim Stuck/
Derek Bell   Porsche 962C   109   2h29m57.935
3 Eddie Cheever/
Raul Boesel   Jaguar XJR-8   109
4 Volker Weidler/
Kris Nissen   Porsche 962C   106
5 Oscar Larrauri/
Jesus Pareja   Porsche 962C   106
6 Massimo Sigala/
Gianfranco Brancatelli Porsche 962C 105
Winner's average speed: 92.269 mph. Pole position: Cheever, 1m14.541.
Fastest lap: Stuck, 1m17.871

JEREZ 1000 KMS

29 March 1987. Jerez. 211 laps of a 2.621-mile circuit = 553.010 miles. Race scheduled for 237 laps, stopped after 6 hours. World Sports-Prototype Championship round 2

1	Eddie Cheever/ Raul Boesel	Jaguar XJR-8	211	6h01m15.46
2	Kris Nissen/ Volker Weidler	Porsche 962C	208	
3	Hans-Joachim Stuck/ Derek Bell	Porsche 962C	205	
4	Fermin Velez/ Gordon Spice	Spice SE86C-Ford	199	
5	Ray Mallock/David Leslie	Ecosse C286-Ford	199	
6	Gianfranco Brancatelli/ Massimo Sigala	Porsche 962C	188	

Winner's average speed: 91.847 mph. Pole position: Stuck, 1m29.19. Fastest lap: n/a

1000 KM DI MONZA/TROFEO FILIPPO CARACCIOLO

12 April 1987. Monza. 173 laps of a 3.604-mile circuit = 623.475 miles. World Sports-Prototype Championship round 3

1	Jan Lammers/ John Watson	Jaguar XJR-8	173	5h03m55.37
2	Hans-Joachim Stuck/ Derek Bell	Porsche 962C	171	
3	Frank Jelinski/Jesus Pareja/ Oscar Larrauri*	Porsche 962C	168	
4	"John Winter"/Stanley Dickens*/ Klaus Ludwig	Porsche 962C	167	
5	Gianfranco Brancatelli/ Massimo Sigala	Porsche 962C	165	
6	Bob Wollek/Jochen Mass	Porsche 962C	159	

*Larrauri and Dickens drove less than 30% of the race, ineligible for points. Winner's average speed: 123.085 mph. Pole position: Stuck, 1m32.17. Fastest lap: Lammers, 1m37.16

AUTOGLASS 1000 KMS

10 May 1987. Silverstone. 210 laps of a 2.969-mile circuit = 623.490 miles. World Sports-Prototype Championship round 4

1	Eddie Cheever/ Raul Boesel	Jaguar XJR-8	210	5h03m06.22
2	Jan Lammers/ John Watson	Jaguar XJR-8	210	5h03m12.36
3	Hans-Joachim Stuck/ Derek Bell	Porsche 962C	209	
4	Jochen Mass/ Bob Wollek	Porsche 962C	202	
5	Walter Brun/Uwe Schafer	Porsche 962C	200	
6	Ray Mallock/David Leslie	Ecosse C286-Ford	191	

Winner's average speed: 123.421 mph. Pole position: Stuck, 1m15.11. Fastest lap: Cheever, 1m18.12

24 HEURES DU MANS

13-14 June 1987. Le Mans. 355 laps of an 8.410-mile circuit = 2985.550 miles. World Sports-Prototype Championship round 5

1	Derek Bell/Hans-Joachim Stuck/ Al Holbert	Porsche 962C	355	24 hours
2	Jurgen Laessig/Pierre Yver/ Bernard de Dryver	Porsche 962C	335	
3	Pierre-Henri Raphanel/Herve Regout/ Yves Courage	Cougar C20-Porsche	332	
4	George Fouche/Franz Konrad/ Wayne Taylor	Porsche 962C	327	
5	Eddie Cheever/Raul Boesel/ Jan Lammers	Jaguar XJR-8LM	325	
6	Gordon Spice/Fermin Velez/ Philippe de Henning	Spice SE87C-Ford	321	

Winner's average speed: 124.398 mph. Pole position: Bob Wollek (Porsche 962C), 3m21.09. Fastest lap: Johnny Dumfries (Sauber C9-Mercedes-Benz), 3m25.04

200 MEILEN VON NURNBERG

28 June 1987. Norisring. 154 laps of a 1.429-mile circuit = 220.066 miles. Aggregate of two 77-lap heats. World Sports-Prototype Championship round 6

1	Mauro Baldi/ Jonathan Palmer	Porsche 962GTi	154	2h09m39.95
2	Oscar Larrauri/ Jochen Mass*	Porsche 962C	151	
3	"John Winter"/ Stanley Dickens	Porsche 962C	150	
4	Eddie Cheever/ Raul Boesel	Jaguar XJR-8	147	
5	Jurgen Laessig/Pierre Yver	Porsche 962C	146	
6	Fermin Velez/ Gordon Spice	Spice SE86C-Ford	143	

*Mass drove less than 30% of the race, ineligible for points. Frank Jelinski/Klaus Ludwig (Porsche 962C), 153 laps, finished second on the road but disqualified due to illegal fuel tank. Winner's average speed: 101.831 mph. Pole position: Hans-Joachim Stuck (Porsche 962C), 47.07s. Fastest lap: Ludwig, 49.03s

SHELL GEMINI 1000 KMS

26 July 1987. Brands Hatch. 238 laps of a 2.614-mile circuit = 622.037 miles. World Sports-Prototype Championship round 7

1	Raul Boesel/John Nielsen	Jaguar XJR-8	238	5h33m48.51
2	Mauro Baldi/ Johnny Dumfries	Porsche 962GTi	238	5h35m01.51
3	Jan Lammers/ John Watson	Jaguar XJR-8	229	
4	Hans-Joachim Stuck/ Derek Bell	Porsche 962C	228	
5	Jochen Mass/ Oscar Larrauri	Porsche 962C	228	
6	Kris Nissen/ Volker Weidler	Porsche 962C	225	

Winner's average speed: 111.807 mph. Pole position: Lammers, 1m14.44. Fastest lap: Lammers, 1m16.44

ADAC 1000 KM-RENNEN

30 August 1987. Nurburgring. 221 laps of a 2.822-mile circuit = 623.662 miles. World Sports-Prototype Championship round 8

1	Eddie Cheever/ Raul Boesel	Jaguar XJR-8	221	5h55m53.12**
2	Derek Bell/ Hans-Joachim Stuck	Porsche 962C	218	
3	Jochen Mass/Oscar Larrauri	Porsche 962C	216	
4	Frank Jelinski/"John Winter"*/ Stanley Dickens	Porsche 962C	212	
5	Mauro Baldi/Jonathan Palmer	Porsche 962GTi	211	
6	Hans-Peter Kaufmann/Franz Hunkeler/ Jesus Pareja*	Porsche 962C	208	

*"Winter" and Pareja drove less than 30% of the race, ineligible for points. ** Including 1 minute penalty for jumping the start. Winner's average speed: 105.145 mph. Pole position: Baldi, 1m25.43. Fastest lap: Klaus Ludwig (Porsche 962C), 1m29.51

1000 KM DE SPA-FRANCORCHAMPS KOUROS

13 September 1987. Spa-Francorchamps. 142 laps of a 4.312-mile circuit = 612.304 miles. Race stopped after 6 hours. World Sports-Prototype Championship round 9

1	Martin Brundle/Johnny Dumfries/ Raul Boesel	Jaguar XJR-8	142	6h00m16.18
2	Jan Lammers/ John Watson	Jaguar XJR-8	141	

3 Jochen Mass/
  Oscar Larrauri   Porsche 962C   140
4 Eddie Cheever/
  John Nielsen   Jaguar XJR-8   140
5 Hans-Joachim Stuck/Derek Bell/
  Bob Wollek   Porsche 962C   139
6 Frank Jelinski/"John Winter"*/
  Stanley Dickens*   Porsche 962C   138

*"Winter" and Dickens drove less than 30% of the race, ineligible for points. Winner's average speed: 101.974 mph. Pole position: Mike Thackwell (Sauber C9-Mercedes-Benz), 2m04.04. Fastest lap: Thackwell, 2m09.30

FUJI 1000 KMS

27 September 1987. Fuji. 224 laps of a 2.759-mile circuit = 618.016 miles. World Sports-Prototype Championship round 10

1 Jan Lammers/
  John Watson   Jaguar XJR-8   224   5h40m55.634
2 Raul Boesel/
  Johnny Dumfries   Jaguar XJR-8   224   5h41m52.124
3 Mauro Baldi/
  Mike Thackwell   Porsche 962GTi   221
4 Jochen Mass/
  Oscar Larrauri   Porsche 962C   218
5 Frank Jelinski/Stanley Dickens/Bob Wollek /
  "John Winter"*   Porsche 962C   218
6 Derek Bell/
  Geoff Brabham   Porsche 962C   218

*"Winter" drove less than 30% of the race, ineligible for points. Winner's average speed: 108.765 mph. Pole position: Takao Wada (Nissan R86V), 1m19.021. Fastest lap: Geoff Lees (Toyota 87C), 1m23.096

1987 FINAL CHAMPIONSHIP POSITIONS

Drivers

1	Raul Boesel	127 (145)*	6	Porsche Kremer Racing	41
2=	Jan Lammers	102	7	Spice Engineering	39
	John Watson	102	8	Primagaz Racing (Courage	
4	Eddie Cheever	100		and Obermaier)	31
5=	Derek Bell	99 (113)*	9	Ecurie Ecosse	28
	Hans-Joachim Stuck	99 (107)*	10	Mazdaspeed	8
7	Oscar Larrauri	69	11	Rothmans Porsche Japan	6
8=	Mauro Baldi	58	12=	Cosmik/GP Motorsport	4
	Jochen Mass	58		Kelmar Racing	4
10=	Gordon Spice	50		Kouros Sauber	4
	Fermin Velez	50	15	Dauer Racing	3
12=	Frank Jelinski	40	16=	From A Racing	2
	David Leslie	40		Richard Cleare Racing	2
	Ray Mallock	40	18=	Tiga Team Dana Ford	1
15	Jesus Pareja	38		Trust Engineering	1
16	Johnny Dumfries	35		URD Junior Team	1
17	John Nielsen	32			
18=	Kris Nissen	31	**Drivers - C2**		
	Jonathan Palmer	31	1=	Gordon Spice	140 (170)*
	Volker Weidler	31		Fermin Velez	140 (170)*

*Best seven results count

*Best seven results count

Teams - C2

1	Spice Engineering	170

Teams

1	Silk Cut Jaguar (TWR)	178
2	Brun Motorsport	91
3	Rothmans Porsche	74
4	Joest Racing	63
5	Brittain Lloyd Racing	58

1988
World Sports-Prototype Championship

JEREZ 800 KMS

6 March 1988. Jerez. 190 laps of a 2.621-mile circuit = 497.971 miles. World Sports-Prototype Championship round 1

1 Jean-Louis Schlesser/   Sauber C9/88-
  Mauro Baldi/Jochen Mass Mercedes-Benz   190   5h18m03.15
2 John Nielsen/Andy Wallace/
  John Watson   Jaguar XJR-9   190   5h18m27.68
3 Bob Wollek/Klaus Ludwig   Porsche 962C   188
4 James Weaver/Derek Bell   Porsche 962GTi   184
5 Frank Jelinski/
  "John Winter"   Porsche 962C   183
6 Manuel Reuter/
  Uwe Schafer   Porsche 962BM   183

Winner's average speed: 93.941 mph. Pole position: Schlesser, 1m28.67. Fastest lap: n/a

JARAMA 360 KMS

13 March 1988. Jarama. 109 laps of a 2.115-mile circuit = 230.579 miles. World Sports-Prototype Championship round 2

1 Eddie Cheever/
  Martin Brundle   Jaguar XJR-9   109   2h30m04.979
2 Jean-Louis Schlesser/
  Mauro Baldi   Sauber C9/88-Mercedes-Benz 109 2h30m24.252
3 John Nielsen/
  John Watson   Jaguar XJR-9   107
4 Uwe Schafer/
  Manuel Reuter   Porsche 962BM   107
5 Kris Nissen/
  Volker Weidler   Porsche 962C   106
6 Oscar Larrauri/
  Jesus Pareja   Porsche 962C   106

Winner's average speed: 92.180 mph. Pole position: Schlesser, 1m14.350. Fastest lap: Schlesser, 1m18.464

1000 KM DI MONZA/TROFEO FILIPPO CARACCIOLO

10 April 1988. Monza. 173 laps of a 3.604-mile circuit = 623.475 miles. World Sports-Prototype Championship round 3

1 Martin Brundle/
  Eddie Cheever   Jaguar XJR-9   173   4h52m13.52
2 Jean-Louis Schlesser/Mauro Baldi/
  Jochen Mass   Sauber C9/88-Mercedes-Benz 172
3 Oscar Larrauri/
  Massimo Sigala   Porsche 962C   171
4 Frank Jelinski/
  "John Winter"   Porsche 962C   168
5 Klaus Ludwig/
  Bob Wollek   Porsche 962C   164
6 Volker Weidler/
  Bruno Giacomelli   Porsche 962C   164

Winner's average speed: 128.012 mph. Pole position: Schlesser, 1m31.69. Fastest lap: Schlesser, 1m35.75

AUTOSPORT 1000 KMS

8 May 1988. Silverstone. 210 laps of a 2.969-mile circuit = 623.490 miles. World Sports-Prototype Championship round 4

1 Eddie Cheever/
  Martin Brundle   Jaguar XJR-9   210   4h50m48.59
2 Jean-Louis Schlesser/
  Jochen Mass   Sauber C9/88-Mercedes-Benz 210 4h51m24.20
3 Mauro Baldi/
  James Weaver   Sauber C9/88-Mercedes-Benz 208
4 Bob Wollek/Philippe Streiff/
  David Hobbs   Porsche 962C   201
5 Frank Jelinski/Stanley Dickens/
  "John Winter"   Porsche 962C   198
6 Thorkyld Thyrring/
  Almo Coppelli   Spice SE88C-Ford 191

Derek Bell/Tiff Needell (Porsche 962GTi), 205 laps, finished fourth on the road but disqualified due to illegal fuel tank. Winner's average speed: 128.639 mph. Pole position: Schlesser, 1m15.02. Fastest lap: Baldi, 1m18.24

24 HEURES DU MANS

11-12 June 1988. Le Mans. 394 laps of an 8.410-mile circuit = 3313.540 miles. World Sports-Prototype Championship round 5

1	Johnny Dumfries/Andy Wallace/			
	Jan Lammers	Jaguar XJR-9LM	394	24h03m28.26
2	Hans-Joachim Stuck/Klaus Ludwig/			
	Derek Bell	Porsche 962C	394	24h06m05.11
3	Stanley Dickens/Frank Jelinski/			
	"John Winter"	Porsche 962C	385	
4	Derek Daly/Larry Perkins/			
	Kevin Cogan	Jaguar XJR-9LM	383	
5	David Hobbs/Didier Theys/			
	Franz Konrad	Porsche 962C	380	
6	Mario Andretti/Michael Andretti/			
	John Andretti	Porsche 962C	375	

Winner's average speed: 137.732 mph. Pole position: Stuck, 3m15.64. Fastest lap: Stuck, 3m22.50

GRAND PRIX CSSR

10 July 1988. Brno. 67 laps of a 3.357-mile circuit = 224.919 miles. World Sports-Prototype Championship round 6

1	Jean-Louis Schlesser/	Sauber C9/88-		
	Jochen Mass	Mercedes-Benz	67	2h06m40.62
2	Martin Brundle/			
	John Nielsen	Jaguar XJR-9	67	2h07m00.67
3	Jan Lammers/			
	Johnny Dumfries	Jaguar XJR-9	67	2h07m48.89
4	Mauro Baldi/	Sauber C9/88-		
	James Weaver	Mercedes-Benz	67	2h08m17.73
5	Bob Wollek/			
	"John Winter"	Porsche 962C	66	
6	Franz Konrad/			
	Jurgen Barth	Porsche 962C	65	

Winner's average speed: 106.532 mph. Pole position: Schlesser, 1m46.44. Fastest lap: Baldi, 1m49.77

BRANDS HATCH 1000 KMS

24 July 1988. Brands Hatch. 240 laps of a 2.600-mile circuit = 624.048 miles. World Sports-Prototype Championship round 7

1	John Nielsen/Martin Brundle/			
	Andy Wallace	Jaguar XJR-9	240	5h33m23.08
2	Klaus Ludwig/			
	Bob Wollek	Porsche 962C	239	
3	Mauro Baldi/	Sauber C9/88-		
	Jean-Louis Schlesser	Mercedes-Benz	235	
4	Gordon Spice/			
	Ray Bellm	Spice SE88C-Ford	224	
5	Almo Coppelli/			
	Thorkyld Thyring	Spice SE88C-Ford	224	
6	Costas Los/			
	Wayne Taylor	Spice SE87C-Ford	219	

Winner's average speed: 112.311 mph. Pole position: Baldi, 1m14.17. Fastest lap: Schlesser, 1m15.82

ADAC 1000 KM-RENNEN

3 September 1988. Nurburgring. 2 heats of 91 laps and 109 laps respectively = 200 laps of a 2.822-mile circuit = 564.400 miles. World Sports-Prototype Championship round 8

1	Jean-Louis Schlesser/	Sauber C9/88-		
	Jochen Mass	Mercedes-Benz	200	5h53m00.60
2	Eddie Cheever/			
	Martin Brundle	Jaguar XJR-9	199	
3	Bob Wollek/Paolo Barilla	Porsche 962C	196	
4	Frank Jelinski/			
	"John Winter"	Porsche 962C	194	

5	Manuel Reuter/		
	Jesus Pareja	Porsche 962C	193
6	Walter Brun/		
	Harald Huysman	Porsche 962C	192

Winner's average speed: 95.929 mph. Pole position: Mauro Baldi (Sauber C9/88-Mercedes-Benz), 1m24.92. Fastest lap: Schlesser, 1m28.55

1000 KM DE SPA-FRANCORCHAMPS

18 September 1988. Spa-Francorchamps. 142 laps of a 4.312-mile circuit = 612.304 miles. Race scheduled for 145 laps, stopped after 6 hours. World Sports-Prototype Championship round 9

1	Mauro Baldi/	Sauber C9/88-		
	Stefan Johansson	Mercedes-Benz	142	6h01m34.23
2	Jan Lammers/			
	Martin Brundle	Jaguar XJR-9	142	6h01m58.79
3	Jochen Mass/	Sauber C9/88-		
	Jean-Louis Schlesser	Mercedes-Benz	139	
4	Oscar Larrauri/			
	Manuel Reuter	Porsche 962C	138	
5	Thorkyld Thyring/			
	Almo Coppelli	Spice SE88C-Ford	134	
6	Gordon Spice/Ray Bellm	Spice SE88C-Ford	132	

Winner's average speed: 101.607 mph. Pole position: Baldi, 2m02.25. Fastest lap: Lammers, 2m22.12

FUJI 1000 KMS

9 October 1988. Fuji. 224 laps of a 2.759-mile circuit = 618.016 miles. World Sports-Prototype Championship round 10

1	Martin Brundle/			
	Eddie Cheever	Jaguar XJR-9	224	5h28m05.941
2	Klaus Ludwig/Price Cobb	Porsche 962C	223	
3	Frank Jelinski/			
	"John Winter"	Porsche 962C	221	
4	Stanley Dickens/			
	Hideki Okada	Porsche 962C	221	
5	Jochen Mass/Kenneth Acheson/			
	Jean-Louis Schlesser	Sauber C9/88-		
		Mercedes-Benz	220	
6	Kunimitsu Takahashi/			
	Kazuo Mogi	Porsche 962C	217	

Winner's average speed: 113.018 mph. Pole position: Okada, 1m18.210. Fastest lap: Ludwig, 1m21.795

LUCAS SUPERSPRINT 360

20 November 1988. Sandown Park. 93 laps of a 2.425-mile circuit = 225.525 miles. World Sports-Prototype Championship round 11

1	Jean-Louis Schlesser/	Sauber C9/88-		
	Jochen Mass	Mercedes-Benz	93	2h30m51.35
2	Mauro Baldi/	Sauber C9/88-		
	Stefan Johansson	Mercedes-Benz	93	2h30m56.00
3	Eddie Cheever/			
	Martin Brundle	Jaguar XJR-9	93	2h32m28.51
4	Jan Lammers/			
	Johnny Dumfries	Jaguar XJR-9	92	
5	Gordon Spice/Ray Bellm	Spice SE88C-Ford	88	
6	Neil Crang/			
	Tim Lee-Davey	Porsche 962C	88	

Winner's average speed: 89.698 mph. Pole position: Schlesser, 1m28.62. Fastest lap: Schlesser, 1m33.58

1988 FINAL CHAMPIONSHIP POSITIONS

Drivers

1	Martin Brundle	240 (267)*
2	Jean-Louis Schlesser	208 (259)*
3	Mauro Baldi	188 (198)*
4	Eddie Cheever	182
5	Jochen Mass	180
6	Klaus Ludwig	145
7	"John Winter"	140 (143)*
8	Frank Jelinski	135
9	Bob Wollek	122
10	Jan Lammers	118
11	John Nielsen	97
12=	Ray Bellm	88 (94)*
	Gordon Spice	88 (94)*
14	Johnny Dumfries	88
15	Stanley Dickens	72
16=	Almo Coppelli	67
	Thorkild Thyrring	67
18	Manuel Reuter	58
19	Stefan Johansson	55
20	James Weaver	54

*Best seven results count

Teams

1	Silk Cut Jaguar (TWR)	357
2	AEG Sauber Mercedes	278
3	Joest Racing	189
4	Brun Motorsport	94
5	Spice Engineering	78

6	Porsche System Engineering	75
7	Swiss Team Salamin	38
8	Porsche Kremer Racing	37
9	Richard Lloyd Racing	28
10	From A Racing	20
11	GP Motorsport	18
12	Chamberlain Engineering	16
13=	Alpha/Nova Engineering	12
	Team Davey	12
15	Kelmar Racing	9
16=	Obermaier Racing	8
	Rothmans Team Schuppan	8
18=	ADA Engineering	4
	Lucky Strike Schanche	4
	Mazdaspeed	4
	Nissan Motorsport	4
22	Takefuji Team Schuppan	3
23	Trust Engineering	2
24	Maurer Design	1

Drivers - C2

1=	Ray Bellm	260 (300)*
	Gordon Spice	260 (300)*

*Best seven results count

Teams - C2

1	Spice Engineering	390

1989

World Sports-Prototype Championship

SUZUKA 480 KMS

9 April 1989. Suzuka. 82 laps of a 3.641-mile circuit = 298.562 miles. World Sports-Prototype Championship round 1

1	Jean-Louis Schlesser/ Mauro Baldi	Sauber C9/88-Mercedes-Benz	82	2h48m58.453
2	Kenneth Acheson	Sauber C9/88-Mercedes-Benz	82	2h49m04.634
3	Bob Wollek/Frank Jelinski	Porsche 962C	82	
4	Toshio Suzuki/ Kazuyoshi Hoshino	Nissan R88C	81	
5	John Nielsen/ Andy Wallace	Jaguar XJR-9	81	
6	Paolo Barilla/ Hitoshi Ogawa	Toyota 89CV	81	

Winner's average speed: 106.015 mph. Pole position: Geoff Lees (Toyota 89CV), 1m50.635. Fastest lap: Jan Lammers (Jaguar XJR-9), 1m57.549

COUPE DE DIJON

21 May 1989. Dijon-Prenois. 127 laps of a 2.361-mile circuit = 299.847 miles. World Sports-Prototype Championship round 2

1	Bob Wollek/Frank Jelinski	Porsche 962C	127	2h42m21.903
2	Jean-Louis Schlesser/ Jochen Mass	Sauber C9/88-Mercedes-Benz	127	2h43m00.298
3	Mauro Baldi/ Kenneth Acheson	Sauber C9/88-Mercedes-Benz	127	
4	Johnny Dumfries/ Geoff Lees	Toyota 88C	126	
5	Derek Bell/ Tiff Needell	Porsche 962GTi	124	
6	Pascal Fabre/ Jean-Louis Bousquet	Cougar C22S-Porsche	123	

Winner's average speed: 110.805 mph. Pole position: Schlesser, 1m07.275. Fastest lap: Baldi, 1m11.739

TROFEO REPSOL

25 June 1989. Jarama. 145 laps of a 2.115-mile circuit = 306.733 miles. World Sports-Prototype Championship round 3

1	Jochen Mass/ Jean-Louis Schlesser	Sauber C9/88-Mercedes-Benz	145	3h26m13.882
2	Jan Lammers/ Patrick Tambay	Jaguar XJR-9	144	
3	Oscar Larrauri/ Jesus Pareja*	Porsche 962C	143	
4	Thorkyld Thyrring/ Wayne Taylor	Spice SE89C-Ford	143	
5	Mauro Baldi/ Kenneth Acheson	Sauber C9/88-Mercedes-Benz	143	
6	John Nielsen/ Andy Wallace	Jaguar XJR-9	142	

*Pareja drove less than 30% of the race, ineligible for points. Winner's average speed: 89.239 mph. Pole position: Baldi, 1m15.580. Fastest lap: Baldi, 1m20.970

BRANDS HATCH TROPHY

23 July 1989. Brands Hatch. 115 laps of a 2.600-mile circuit = 299.023 miles. World Sports-Prototype Championship round 4

1	Mauro Baldi/ Kenneth Acheson	Sauber C9/88-Mercedes-Benz	115	2h41m37.754
2	Bob Wollek/ Frank Jelinski	Porsche 962C	115	2h42m54.796
3	Jean-Louis Schlesser/ Jochen Mass	Sauber C9/88-Mercedes-Benz	114	
4	David Leslie/ Brian Redman	Aston Martin AMR1	112	
5	Jan Lammers/ Patrick Tambay	Jaguar XJR-11	111	
6	Walter Brun/ Jesus Pareja	Porsche 962C	111	

Winner's average speed: 111.003 mph. Pole position: Lammers, 1m12.927. Fastest lap: Baldi, 1m16.111

ADAC TROPHAE

20 August 1989. Nurburgring. 106 laps of a 2.822-mile circuit = 299.132 miles. World Sports-Prototype Championship round 5

1	Jean-Louis Schlesser/ Jochen Mass	Sauber C9/88-Mercedes-Benz	106	2h47m14.599
2	Mauro Baldi/ Kenneth Acheson	Sauber C9/88-Mercedes-Benz	106	2h47m16.677
3	George Fouche/ Giovanni Lavaggi	Porsche 962-CK6	104	
4	Walter Brun/ Jesus Pareja	Porsche 962C	104	
5	John Nielsen/ Andy Wallace	Jaguar XJR-11	104	
6	Oscar Larrauri/ Franz Konrad	Porsche 962C	104	

Winner's average speed: 107.316 mph. Pole position: Baldi, 1m23.125. Fastest lap: Schlesser, 1m29.281

WHEATCROFT GOLD CUP

3 September 1989. Donington Park. 120 laps of a 2.500-mile circuit = 300.000 miles. World Sports-Prototype Championship round 6

1	Jochen Mass/ Jean-Louis Schlesser	Sauber C9/88-Mercedes-Benz	120	2h57m50.883
2	Kenneth Acheson/ Mauro Baldi	Sauber C9/88-Mercedes-Benz	120	2h58m42.777
3	Julian Bailey/ Mark Blundell	Nissan R89C	120	
4	Bob Wollek/ Frank Jelinski	Porsche 962C	119	

5 Oscar Larrauri/
  Harald Huysman   Porsche 962C   119
6 David Leslie/Michael Roe Aston Martin AMR1 118
Winner's average speed: 101.210 mph. Pole position: Baldi, 1m19.123.
Fastest lap: Bailey, 1m24.500

COUPE DE SPA

17 September 1989. Spa-Francorchamps. 70 laps of a 4.312-mile circuit
= 301.840 miles. World Sports-Prototype Championship round 7

1 Mauro Baldi/
  Kenneth Acheson   Mercedes-Benz   70   2h39m16.453
2 Bob Wollek/
  Frank Jelinski   Porsche 962C   70   2h41m32.434
3 Julian Bailey/
  Mark Blundell   Nissan R89C   69
4 Oscar Larrauri/
  Roland Ratzenberger Porsche 962C   68
5 Wayne Taylor/
  Thorkyld Thyrring   Spice SE89C-Ford   68
6 Henri Pescarolo/
  Jean-Louis Ricci   Porsche 962C   68
Winner's average speed: 113.706 mph. Pole position: Baldi, 2m05.900.
Fastest lap: Baldi, 2m07.863

TROFEO HERMANOS RODRIGUEZ

29 October 1989. Mexico City. 109 laps of a 2.747-mile circuit = 299.423
miles. World Sports-Prototype Championship round 8

1 Jean-Louis Schlesser/
  Jochen Mass   Mercedes-Benz   109   2h51m17.986
2 Oscar Larrauri/
  Harald Huysman   Porsche 962C   109   2h51m54.429
3 Henri Pescarolo/
  Frank Jelinski   Porsche 962C   109
4 Derek Bell/
  Tiff Needell   Porsche 962GTi   108
5 Andy Wallace/
  Alain Ferte   Jaguar XJR-9   108
6 Patrick Tambay/
  Jan Lammers   Jaguar XJR-9   108
Winner's average speed: 104.877 mph. Pole position: Mauro Baldi (Sauber
C9/88-Mercedes-Benz), 1m22.571. Fastest lap: Schlesser, 1m25.120

1989 FINAL CHAMPIONSHIP POSITIONS

Drivers			Teams		
1	Jean-Louis		1	Team Sauber Mercedes	155
	Schlesser	115 (127)*	2	Joest Racing	84
2	Jochen Mass	107	3	Brun Motorsport	66
3	Mauro Baldi	102 (110)*	4	Silk Cut Jaguar (TWR)	57
4	Kenneth Acheson	97 (105)*	5	Nissan Motorsport	37
5	Frank Jelinski	84	6	Aston Martin	26
6	Bob Wollek	72	7	Toyota Team TOM's	25
7	Oscar Larrauri	54	8	Porsche Kremer Racing	21
8=	Jan Lammers	30	9	Spice Engineering	19
	Patrick Tambay	30	10	Richard Lloyd Racing	18
	Andy Wallace	30	11	Courage Competition	16
11	Julian Bailey	27	12	Porsche Almeras	5
	Mark Blundell	27	13=	Chamberlain	
13	Harald Huysman	25		Engineering	3
14=	Henri Pescarolo	24		France Promoteam	3
	Brian Redman	24		Mazdaspeed	3
16=	David Leslie	22	16	Obermaier Racing	1
	John Nielsen	22			
18=	Walter Brun	20	**Drivers - C2**		
	Jesus Pareja	20	1=	Nick Adams	107
20=	Johnny Dumfries	19		Fermin Velez	107
	Thorkild Thyrring	19			
*Best six results count			**Teams - C2**		
			1	Chamberlain	
				Engineering	120

1990
World Sports-Prototype Championship

FUJI FILM CUP

8 April 1990. Suzuka. 82 laps of a 3.641-mile circuit = 298.562 miles.
World Sports-Prototype Championship round 1

1 Jean-Louis Schlesser/   Sauber C9/88-
  Mauro Baldi   Mercedes-Benz 82   2h43m45.429
2 Jochen Mass/   Sauber C9/88-
  Karl Wendlinger   Mercedes-Benz 82   2h44m27.762
3 Masahiro Hasemi/
  Anders Olofsson   Nissan R89C   81
4 Geoff Lees/Hitoshi Ogawa Toyota 90CV   81
5 Kunimitsu Takahashi/
  Kazuo Mogi   Porsche 962C   80
6 Oscar Larrauri/
  Harald Huysman   Porsche 962C   80
Winner's average speed: 109.392 mph. Pole position: Lees, 1m48.716.
Fastest lap: Martin Brundle (Jaguar XJR-11), 1m53.732

TROFEO FILIPPO CARACCIOLO

29 April 1990. Monza. 83 laps of a 3.604-mile circuit = 299.124 miles.
World Sports-Prototype Championship round 2

1 Mauro Baldi/
  Jean-Louis Schlesser   Mercedes-Benz C11 83   2h17m11.736
2 Jochen Mass/
  Karl Wendlinger   Mercedes-Benz C11 83   2h17m29.348
3 Martin Brundle/
  Alain Ferte   Jaguar XJR-11 83
4 Jan Lammers/
  Andy Wallace   Jaguar XJR-11 82
5 Bob Wollek/
  Frank Jelinski   Porsche 962C   82
6 Wayne Taylor/
  Eric van de Poele   Spice SE90C-Ford 81
Winner's average speed: 130.816 mph. Pole position: Baldi, 1m29.165.
Fastest lap: Mass, 1m33.426

BRITISH EMPIRE TROPHY

20 May 1990. Silverstone. 101 laps of a 2.969-mile circuit = 299.869
miles. World Sports-Prototype Championship round 3

1 Martin Brundle/
  Alain Ferte   Jaguar XJR-11 101 2h19m39.467
2 Jan Lammers/
  Andy Wallace   Jaguar XJR-11 100
3 Bruno Giacomelli/
  Fermin Velez   Spice SE90C-Ford 100
4 Bob Wollek/
  Frank Jelinski   Porsche 962C   99
5 Bernd Schneider/
  Steven Andskar   Porsche 962-CK6 98
6 Oscar Larrauri/
  Harald Huysman   Porsche 962BM 97
Winner's average speed: 128.830 mph. Pole position: Jean-Louis
Schlesser (Mercedes-Benz C11), 1m12.073. Fastest lap: Schlesser,
1m16.649

COUPE DE SPA

3 June 1990. Spa-Francorchamps. 70 laps of a 4.312-mile circuit =
301.840 miles. World Sports-Prototype Championship round 4

1 Jochen Mass/
  Karl Wendlinger   Mercedes-Benz C11 70   2h42m54.880
2 Jan Lammers/
  Andy Wallace   Jaguar XJR-11 70   2h44m25.656
3 Julian Bailey/
  Kenneth Acheson   Nissan R90C   70
4 Tim Harvey/Fermin Velez Spice SE90C-Ford 69
5 Oscar Larrauri/
  Harald Huysman   Porsche 962BM 69

6 Steven Andskar/
  Manuel Reuter   Porsche 962GTi   69
Winner's average speed: 111.165 mph. Pole position: Mauro Baldi
(Mercedes-Benz C11), 1m59.350. Fastest lap: Baldi, 2m06.211

COUPE DE DIJON

22 July 1990. Dijon-Prenois. 127 laps of a 2.361-mile circuit = 299.847
miles. Race stopped after first lap accident, restarted over full distance.
World Sports-Prototype Championship round 5

1 Jean-Louis Schlesser/
  Mauro Baldi   Mercedes-Benz C11 127   2h39m03.603
2 Jochen Mass/
  Michael Schumacher   Mercedes-Benz C11 127   2h39m07.448
3 Julian Bailey/
  Mark Blundell   Nissan R90C   126
4 Jan Lammers/
  Andy Wallace   Jaguar XJR-11   125
5 Martin Brundle/
  Alain Ferte   Jaguar XJR-11   125
6 Wayne Taylor/
  Eliseo Salazar   Spice SE90C-Ford   124
Winner's average speed: 113.107 mph. Pole position: Schlesser,
1m05.527. Fastest lap: Schlesser, 1m08.973

ADAC SPORTSWAGEN TROPHAE

19 August 1990. Nurburgring. 106 laps of a 2.822-mile circuit = 299.132
miles. World Sports-Prototype Championship round 6

1 Mauro Baldi/
  Jean-Louis Schlesser   Mercedes-Benz C11 106   2h39m15.913
2 Jochen Mass/
  Michael Schumacher   Mercedes-Benz C11 106   2h39m38.475
3 Martin Brundle/
  Alain Ferte   Jaguar XJR-11   105
4 Jan Lammers/
  Andy Wallace   Jaguar XJR-11   105
5 Mark Blundell   Nissan R90C   103
6 Bob Wollek/
  Frank Jelinski   Porsche 962C   103
Winner's average speed: 112.692 mph. Pole position: Schlesser,
1m20.344. Fastest lap: Schlesser, 1m26.092

SHELL DONINGTON TROPHY

2 September 1990. Donington Park. 120 laps of a 2.500-mile circuit =
300.000 miles. World Sports-Prototype Championship round 7

1 Jean-Louis Schlesser/
  Mauro Baldi   Mercedes-Benz C11 120   2h53m40.919
2 Jochen Mass/
  Heinz-Harald Frentzen Mercedes-Benz C11 120   2h55m03.134
3 Tim Harvey/Cor Euser   Spice SE90C-Ford   118
4 Kenneth Acheson/
  Gianfranco Brancatelli Nissan R90C   117
5 Eric van de Poele/
  Bruno Giacomelli   Spice SE90C-Ford   117
6 Julian Bailey/
  Mark Blundell   Nissan R90C   117
Martin Brundle (Jaguar XJR-11), 119 laps, finished third on the road but
disqualified for illegal refuelling. Winner's average speed: 103.638 mph.
Pole position: Baldi, 1m16.952. Fastest lap: Baldi, 1m23.597

MONDIAL PLAYERS LTEE

23 September 1990. Montreal. 61 laps of a 2.728-mile circuit = 166.408
miles. Race scheduled for 110 laps but stopped due to accident, half
points awarded. World Sports-Prototype Championship round 8

1 Mauro Baldi/
  Jean-Louis Schlesser   Mercedes-Benz C11 61   1h44m42.012
2 Mark Blundell/
  Julian Bailey   Nissan R90C   61   1h44m48.460
3 Manuel Reuter/
  Steven Andskar*   Porsche 962GTi   61   1h46m05.576

4 Bernd Schneider/
  Jurgen Barth*   Porsche 962-CK6   61   1h46m06.153
5 Kenneth Acheson/
  Gianfranco Brancatelli* Nissan R90C   61   1h46m33.317
6 Bob Wollek/
  Frank Jelinski   Porsche 962C   61   1h46m34.385
*Had not driven when race was stopped. Winner's average speed: 95.363
mph. Pole position: Schlesser, 1m25.407. Fastest lap: Baldi, 1m28.725

TROFEO HERMANOS RODRIGUEZ

7 October 1990. Mexico City. 109 laps of a 2.747-mile circuit = 299.423
miles. World Sports-Prototype Championship round 9

1 Jochen Mass/
  Michael Schumacher   Mercedes-Benz C11 109   2h47m54.970
2 Julian Bailey/
  Mark Blundell   Nissan R90C   107
3 Andy Wallace/Davy Jones Jaguar XJR-11   107
4 Gianfranco Brancatelli/
  Kenneth Acheson   Nissan R90C   106
5 Hans-Joachim Stuck/
  Jonathan Palmer   Porsche 962C   106
6 Bob Wollek/
  Frank Jelinski   Porsche 962C   105
Mauro Baldi/Jean-Louis Schlesser (Mercedes-Benz 11), 2h47m33.785,
finished first on the road but disqualified due to illegal refuelling. Winner's
average speed: 106.990 mph. Pole position: Martin Brundle (Jaguar XJR-
11), 1m20.626. Fastest lap: Schumacher, 1m23.250

1990 FINAL CHAMPIONSHIP POSITIONS

Drivers				
1=	Mauro Baldi	49.5	Heinz-Harald Frentzen	6
	Jean-Louis Schlesser	49.5	Bruno Giacomelli	6
3	Jochen Mass	48	20= Cor Euser	4
4	Andy Wallace	25	Masahiro Hasemi	4
5=	Jan Lammers	21	Davy Jones	4
	Michael Schumacher	21	Oscar Larrauri	4
	Karl Wendlinger	21	Anders Olofsson	4
8	Martin Brundle	19	**Teams**	
9	Julian Bailey	18	1 Team Sauber Mercedes	67.5
10	Mark Blundell	16	2 Silk Cut Jaguar (TWR)	30
11	Kenneth Acheson	11	3 Nissan Motorsport	26
12	Alain Ferte	10	4 Spice Engineering	13
13=	Frank Jelinski	7.5	5 Joest Racing	8.5
	Bob Wollek	7.5	6 Porsche Kremer Racing	5.5
15=	Tim Harvey	7	7 Brun Motorsport	4
	Fermin Velez	7	8= Richard Lloyd Racing	3
17=	Gianfranco Brancatelli	6	Toyota Team TOM's	3

1991

World Sports Car Championship

FUJI FILM CUP

14 April 1991. Suzuka. 74 laps of a 3.641-mile circuit = 269.434 miles.
World Sports Car Championship round 1

1 Mauro Baldi/
  Philippe Alliot   Peugeot 905   74   2h25m01.688
2 Jean-Louis Schlesser/
  Jochen Mass   Mercedes-Benz C11 73
3 Manuel Reuter/
  Harri Toivonen   Porsche 962-CK6   72
4 Charles Zwolsman/
  Cor Euser   Spice SE90C-Ford   72
5 George Fouche/
  Steven Andskar   Porsche 962C   71
6 David Kennedy/
  Maurizio Sandro Sala   Mazda 787B   71
Oscar Larrauri/Bernard Santal (Porsche 962C), 71 laps, finished fifth on
the road but disqualified due to illegal refuelling. Winner's average speed:

111.468 mph. Pole position: Derek Warwick (Jaguar XJR-14), 1m48.084. Fastest lap: Warwick, 1m49.148

TROFEO FILIPPO CARACCIOLO

5 May 1991. Monza. 75 laps of a 3.604-mile circuit = 270.293 miles. World Sports Car Championship round 2

1 Martin Brundle/			
Derek Warwick	Jaguar XJR-14	75	2h05m42.844
2 Teo Fabi/Martin Brundle	Jaguar XJR-14	74	
3 Jean-Louis Schlesser/			
Jochen Mass	Mercedes-Benz C11	73	
4 Cor Euser/			
Charles Zwolsman	Spice SE90C-Ford	71	
5 Manuel Reuter/			
Harri Toivonen	Porsche 962-CK6	71	
6 Oscar Larrauri/			
Massimo Sigala	Porsche 962C	69	

Winner's average speed: 129.003 mph. Pole position: Fabi, 1m33.672. Fastest lap: Brundle, 1m29.182

CASTROL BRDC EMPIRE TROPHY

19 May 1991. Silverstone. 83 laps of a 3.247-mile circuit = 269.501 miles. World Sports Car Championship round 3

1 Derek Warwick*/Teo Fabi	Jaguar XJR-14	83	2h12m30.045
2 Karl Wendlinger/			
Michael Schumacher	Mercedes-Benz C291	82	
3 Martin Brundle	Jaguar XJR-14	79	
4 Jean-Louis Schlesser/			
Jochen Mass	Mercedes-Benz C11	79	
5 Cor Euser/Richard Piper	Spice SE90C-Ford	78	
6 Philippe Alliot/			
Mauro Baldi	Peugeot 905	78	

*Warwick not entered in car, ineligible for points. Winner's average speed: 122.037 mph. Pole position: Fabi, 1m27.478. Fastest lap: Brundle, 1m29.372

24 HEURES DU MANS

22-23 June 1991. Le Mans. 362 laps of an 8.453-mile circuit = 3059.986 miles. World Sports Car Championship round 4

1 Volker Weidler/Johnny Herbert/			
Bertrand Gachot*	Mazda 787B	362	23h58m35.912
2 Raul Boesel/Michel Ferte*/			
Davy Jones	Jaguar XJR-12	360	
3 Teo Fabi/Kenneth Acheson/			
Bob Wollek	Jaguar XJR-12	358	
4 Derek Warwick/John Nielsen/			
Andy Wallace	Jaguar XJR-12	356	
5 Karl Wendlinger/Michael Schumacher/			
Fritz Kreutzpointner	Mercedes-Benz C11	355	
6 David Kennedy/Stefan Johansson/			
Maurizio Sandro Sala	Mazda 787B	355	

*Gachot and Ferte drove insufficient distance to be eligible for points. Winner's average speed: 127.624 mph. Pole position: Philippe Alliot (Peugeot 905), 3m35.058 due to championship regulations, fastest qualifier: Jean-Louis Schlesser (Mercedes-Benz C11), 3m31.270. Fastest lap: Schumacher, 3m35.564

ADAC SPORTSWAGON TROPHAE

18 August 1991. Nurburgring. 95 laps of a 2.822-mile circuit = 268.090 miles. World Sports Car Championship round 5

1 David Brabham/			
Derek Warwick	Jaguar XJR-14	95	2h23m41.028
2 Teo Fabi/David Brabham	Jaguar XJR-14	95	2h23m45.937
3 Manuel Reuter/			
Harri Toivonen	Porsche 962-CK6	89	
4 Jurgen Oppermann/			
Otto Altenbach	Porsche 962C	89	
5 Maurizio Sandro Sala/			
David Kennedy	Mazda 787B	89	

6 Lionel Robert/			
Francois Migault*	Cougar C26S-Porsche	89	

*Includes 1 minute penalty for overtaking another car while yellow flags were being shown. Winner's average speed: 111.950 mph. Pole position: Fabi, 1m19.519. Fastest lap: Fabi, 1m21.533

SWC MAGNY-COURS

15 September 1991. Magny-Cours. 101 laps of a 2.654-mile circuit = 268.054 miles. World Sports Car Championship round 6

1 Yannick Dalmas/			
Keke Rosberg	Peugeot 905B	101	2h31m38.258
2 Philippe Alliot/			
Mauro Baldi	Peugeot 905B	101	2h32m21.078
3 Teo Fabi/David Brabham	Jaguar XJR-14	99	
4 Cor Euser/			
Charles Zwolsman	Spice SE90C-Ford	95	
5 David Brabham/			
Derek Warwick	Jaguar XJR-14	94	
6 Manuel Reuter/			
Harri Toivonen	Porsche 962-CK6	93	

Winner's average speed: 106.064 mph. Pole position: Dalmas, 1m21.821. Fastest lap: Alliot, 1m25.823

TROFEO HERMANOS RODRIGUEZ

6 October 1991. Mexico City. 98 laps of a 2.747-mile circuit = 269.206 miles. World Sports Car Championship round 7

1 Keke Rosberg/			
Yannick Dalmas	Peugeot 905B	98	2h29m25.811
2 Philippe Alliot/			
Mauro Baldi	Peugeot 905B	97	
3 Bernd Schneider/			
"John Winter"	Porsche 962C	94	
4 Cor Euser/			
Charles Zwolsman	Spice SE90C-Ford	93	
5 Derek Bell/			
Gianpiero Moretti	Porsche 962C	92	
6 David Brabham/			
Derek Warwick	Jaguar XJR-14	92	

Winner's average speed: 108.093 mph. Pole position: Alliot, 1m19.229. Fastest lap: Michael Schumacher (Mercedes-Benz C291), 1m21.611

WSC AUTOPOLIS

27 October 1991. Autopolis. 93 laps of a 2.904-mile circuit = 270.072 miles. World Sports Car Championship round 8

1 Michael Schumacher/			
Karl Wendlinger	Mercedes-Benz C291	93	2h26m36.699
2 Derek Warwick	Jaguar XJR-14	93	2h27m07.187
3 Teo Fabi/David Brabham	Jaguar XJR-14	93	2h28m15.860
4 Mauro Baldi/			
Philippe Alliot	Peugeot 905B	92	
5 Jean-Louis Schlesser/			
Jochen Mass	Mercedes-Benz C291	92	
6 Geoff Lees/			
Andy Wallace*	Toyota TS010	90	

*Toyota not entered in the championship, ineligible for points. Winner's average speed: 110.525 mph. Pole position: Fabi, 1m27.188. Fastest lap: Yannick Dalmas (Peugeot 905B), 1m30.615

1991 FINAL CHAMPIONSHIP POSITIONS

Drivers

				Michael Schumacher	43
1	Teo Fabi	86		Karl Wendlinger	43
2	Derek Warwick	79	12	Harri Toivonen	41
3=	Philippe Alliot	69	13=	Yannick Dalmas	40
	Mauro Baldi	69		Keke Rosberg	40
5	Cor Euser	54	15	Maurizio Sandro Sala	31
6	Charles Zwolsman	46	16=	Johnny Herbert	20
7=	Jochen Mass	45		Volker Weidler	20
	Jean-Louis Schlesser	45	18=	David Brabham	18
9=	Manuel Reuter	43	19=	David Kennedy	16

1991 FINAL CHAMPIONSHIP POSITIONS (cont.)

Jesus Pareja	16	5	Mazdaspeed	47
		6	Porsche Kremer Racing	43
Teams		7	Courage Competition	28
1 Silk Cut Jaguar (TWR)	108	8	Swiss Team Salamin	26
2 Peugeot Talbot Sport	79	9	Brun Motorsport	22
3 Team Sauber Mercedes	70	10	Konrad Motorsport	6
4 Euro Racing	54			

1992
World Sports Car Championship

TROFEO FILIPPO CARACCIOLO

26 April 1992. Monza. 87 laps of a 3.604-mile circuit = 313.539 miles. World Sports Car Championship round 1

1 Geoff Lees/Hitoshi Ogawa	Toyota TS010	87	2h16m42.659	
2 Derek Warwick/				
Yannick Dalmas	Peugeot 905B	85		accident
3 Bernard Thuner/				
Ferdinand de Lesseps	Spice SE89C-Ford	76		
4 Almo Coppelli/				
Frank Kramer	Gebhardt C91-Ford	75		
5 Luigi Taverna/				
Alessandro Gini	Spice SE90C-Ford	60		clutch
6 Raineri Randaccio/				
"Stingbrace"	Spice SE90C-Ford	46		

Winner's average speed: 137.607 mph. Pole position: Dalmas, 1m26.019. Fastest lap: Mauro Baldi (Peugeot 905B), 1m29.386.

CASTROL BRDC EMPIRE TROPHY

10 May 1992. Silverstone. 96 laps of a 3.247-mile circuit = 311.712 miles. World Sports Car Championship round 2

1 Derek Warwick/				
Yannick Dalmas	Peugeot 905B	96	2h32m29.226	
2 Maurizio Sandro Sala/				
Johnny Herbert	Mazda MXR01	94		
3 Will Hoy/				
Ferdinand de Lesseps	Spice SE89C-Ford	85		
4 Raineri Randaccio/				
"Stingbrace"	Spice SE90C-Ford	76		
5 Geoff Lees/Hitoshi Ogawa	Toyota TS010	55		electrics
6 Cor Euser/				
Charles Zwolsman	Lola T92/10-Judd	29		gearbox

Stefan Johansson/Jesus Pareja (Lola T92/10-Judd), 90 laps, finished third on the road but disqualified illegal fuel. Winner's average speed: 122.651 mph. Pole position: Warwick, 1m24.421. Fastest lap: Dalmas, 1m29.043

24 HEURES DU MANS

21-22 June 1992. Le Mans. 352 laps of an 8.453-mile circuit = 2975.456 miles. World Sports Car Championship round 3

1 Derek Warwick/Yannick Dalmas/				
Mark Blundell	Peugeot 905B	352	24h00m54.765	
2 Masanori Sekiya/Pierre-Henri Raphanel/				
Kenneth Acheson	Toyota TS010	346		
3 Mauro Baldi/Philippe Alliot/				
Jean-Pierre Jabouille	Peugeot 905B	345		
4 Johnny Herbert/Volker Weidler/				
Bertrand Gachot/Maurizio Sandro Sala				
	Mazda MXR01	336		
5 George Fouche/Steven Andskar/				
Stefan Johansson	Toyota 92CV	336		
6 Bob Wollek/Henri Pescarolo/				
Jean-Louis Ricci	Cougar C28LM-Porsche	335		

Winner's average speed: 123.899 mph. Pole position: Alliot, 3m21.209. Fastest lap: Jan Lammers (Toyota TS010), 3m32.295

TRITON SHOWERS TROPHY

19 July 1992. Donington Park. 125 laps of a 2.500-mile circuit = 312.500 miles. World Sports Car Championship round 4

1 Mauro Baldi/Philippe Alliot	Peugeot 905B	125	2h54m03.868
2 Derek Warwick/			
Yannick Dalmas	Peugeot 905B	125	2h54m04.444
3 Geoff Lees/David Brabham	Toyota TS010	125	2h54m32.016
4 Phil Andrews/			
Heinz-Harald Frentzen	Lola T92/10-Judd	119	
5 Maurizio Sandro Sala/			
Alex Caffi	Mazda MXR01	112	
6 Ferdinand de Lesseps/			
Will Hoy	Spice SE89C-Ford	111	

Winner's average speed: 107.719 mph. Pole position: Warwick, 1m15.285. Fastest lap: Warwick, 1m19.380

FUJI FILM CUP

30 August 1992. Suzuka. 171 laps of a 3.641-mile circuit = 622.611 miles. World Sports Car Championship round 5

1 Derek Warwick/			
Yannick Dalmas	Peugeot 905B	171	5h30m09.627
2 Geoff Lees/Jan Lammers/			
David Brabham	Toyota TS010	170	
3 Mauro Baldi/Philippe Alliot	Peugeot 905B	163	
4 Mauro Martini/Katsutomo Kaneishi/			
Jeff Krosnoff	Nissan R91CK	163	
5 Jesus Pareja/			
Hideshi Matsuda	Lola T92/10-Judd	160	
6 Ferdinand de Lesseps/Nick Adams/			
Masahiro Kimoto	Spice SE89C-Ford	144	

Winner's average speed: 113.147 mph. Pole position: Alliot, 1m43.957. Fastest lap: Alliot, 1m50.660

SWC MAGNY-COURS

18 October 1992. Magny-Cours. 118 laps of a 2.641-mile circuit = 311.638 miles. Race rescheduled for 199 laps but stopped early. World Sports Car Championship round 6

1 Philippe Alliot/Mauro Baldi	Peugeot 905B	118	2h44m19.617
2 Christophe Bouchut/			
Eric Helary	Peugeot 905B	116	
3 Geoff Lees/Jan Lammers	Toyota TS010	114	
4 Andy Wallace/			
David Brabham	Toyota TS010	113	
5 Derek Warwick/			
Yannick Dalmas	Peugeot 905B	113	
6 Alex Caffi/			
Maurizio Sandro Sala	Mazda MXR01	107	

Winner's average speed: 113.787 mph. Pole position: Alliot, 1m16.415. Fastest lap: Alliot, 1m20.34

1992 FINAL CHAMPIONSHIP POSITIONS

Drivers				
1= Yannick Dalmas	98	16= Kenneth Acheson	15
Derek Warwick	98	Christophe Bouchut	15
3= Philippe Alliot	64	Eric Helary	15
Mauro Baldi	64	Pierre-Henri Raphanel	15
5 Geoff Lees	59	20 Alex Caffi	14
6 Jan Lammers	35		
7 Ferdinand de Lesseps	34	**Teams**	
8 Maurizio Sandro Sala	29	1 Peugeot Talbot Sport	115
9 Johnny Herbert	25	2 Toyota Team TOM's	74
10 David Brabham	22	3 Mazdaspeed	39
11 Hitoshi Ogawa	20	4 Chamberlain	
12= Will Hoy	18	Engineering	34
Andy Wallace	18	5 Euro Racing	26
14 Raineri Randaccio	17	6 Team SCI	17
15 Heinz-Harald Frentzen	16		

1992 The Peugeot team dominated the final year of the World Sports Car Championship.

Drivers' Records

WINS

Jacky Ickx	37	Hans Herrmann	5	Ken Miles	3
Jochen Mass	32	Jan Lammers	5	Ronnie Peterson	3
Derek Bell	21	Michael Parkes	5	Lloyd Ruby	3
Henri Pescarolo	21	Ludovico Scarfiotti	5	Tim Schenken	3
Mauro Baldi	17	Nino Vaccarella	5	Maurice Trintignant	3
Brian Redman	17	Michele Alboreto	4	Kenneth Acheson	2
Jean-Louis Schlesser	15	Jean-Pierre Beltoise	4	Andrea de Adamich	2
Phil Hill	14	Vittorio Brambilla	4	Kurt Ahrens jr	2
Jo Siffert	14	Giorgio Francia	4	Alberto Ascari	2
Gerard Larrousse	12	Peter Gregg	4	Richard Attwood	2
Stirling Moss	12	Mike Hawthorn	4	Paolo Barilla	2
Olivier Gendebien	11	Hans Heyer	4	Jurgen Barth	2
Arturo Merzario	11	Graham Hill	4	Thierry Boutsen	2
Pedro Rodriguez	11	Al Holbert	4	Tony Brooks	2
Rolf Stommelen	11	Reinhold Joest	4	Ivor Bueb	2
Bob Wollek	11	Leo Kinnunen	4	Alain de Cadenet	2
Stefan Bellof	9	Umberto Maglioli	4	Johnny Dumfries	2
Eddie Cheever	9	Willy Mairesse	4	Guy Edwards	2
John Fitzpatrick	9	Manfred Schurti	4	Teo Fabi	2
Martin Brundle	8	John Surtees	4	Jack Fairman	2
Riccardo Patrese	8	John Watson	4	John Fitch	2
Hans-Joachim Stuck	8	Philippe Alliot	3	Piercarlo Ghinzani	2
Mario Andretti	7	Chris Amon	3	Paul Hawkins	2
Jean-Pierre Jarier	7	Jean Behra	3	Frank Jelinski	2
Derek Warwick	7	Lucien Bianchi	3	Gijs van Lennep	2
Jo Bonnier	6	Eugenio Castellotti	3	Bruce McLaren	2
Vic Elford	6	Juan Manuel Fangio	3	Herbert Muller	2
Hurley Haywood	6	Giuseppe Farina	3	Luigi Musso	2
Toine Hezemans	6	Masten Gregory	3	John Nielsen	2
Klaus Ludwig	6	Harald Grohs	3	Jonathan Palmer	2
Jackie Oliver	6	Jean Guichet	3	Dieter Quester	2
Lorenzo Bandini	5	Dan Gurney	3	Walter Rohrl	2
Raul Boesel	5	Jacques Laffite	3	Jean Rondeau	2
Peter Collins	5	Lella Lombardi	3	Keke Rosberg	2
Yannick Dalmas	5	Volkert Merl	3	Michael Schumacher	2

World Sports Car Championship

WINS (cont.)

Udo Schutz	2	Jose Froilan Gonzalez	1	Alessandro Nannini	1
Carroll Shelby	2	John Graves	1	Jochen Neerpasch	1
Piero Taruffi	2	Pat Griffith	1	Gunnar Nilsson	1
Emilio de Villota	2	Enrico Grimaldi	1	Hitoshi Ogawa	1
Tom Walkinshaw	2	Akira Hagiwara	1	Danny Ongais	1
Andy Wallace	2	Mike Hailwood	1	Jesus Pareja	1
Phil Walters	2	Jim Hall	1	Chuck Parsons	1
Karl Wendlinger	2	Duncan Hamilton	1	Nelson Piquet	1
Bill Whittington	2	Ludwig Heimrath	1	Antonio Pucci	1
Don Whittington	2	Dave Helmick	1	Bobby Rahal	1
Desire Wilson	2	Johnny Herbert	1	Clay Regazzoni	1
Carlo Abate	1	David Hobbs	1	Jochen Rindt	1
Cliff Allison	1	Kazuyoshi Hoshino	1	Ricardo Rodriguez	1
Edgar Barth	1	Ed Hugus	1	Tony Rolt	1
Mark Blundell	1	Denny Hulme	1	Enrique Saenz Valiente	1
David Brabham	1	Jose Maria Ibanez	1	Roy Salvadori	1
Jack Brabham	1	Jean-Pierre Jabouille	1	Giorgio Scarlatti	1
Gino Bronzoni	1	Jean-Pierre Jaussaud	1	Harry Schell	1
Jim Busby	1	Denis Jenkinson	1	Dieter Schornstein	1
Joe Buzzetta	1	Stefan Johansson	1	Vern Schuppan	1
Lucky Casner	1	Amos Johnson	1	Wolfgang Seidel	1
Francois Cevert	1	Mario Ketterer	1	Hap Sharp	1
Marco Crosara	1	Albrecht Krebs	1	Mike Spence	1
Noel Cunningham-Reid	1	Jurgen Laessig	1	Marc Surer	1
Chuck Daigh	1	Oscar Larrauri	1	Mike Thackwell	1
Colin Davis	1	Geoff Lees	1	Richard Thompson	1
Pierre Dieudonne	1	Bruce Leven	1	Wolfgang von Trips	1
"Dino"	1	Bill Lloyd	1	Volker Weidler	1
Mark Donohue	1	Roger Mandeville	1	Manfred Winkelhock	1
Edgar Doren	1	Roberto Marazzi	1	"John Winter"	1
Alain Ferte	1	Helmut Marko	1		
Ted Field	1	Giannino Marzotto	1		
Ron Flockhart	1	Keiji Matsumoto	1		
AJ Foyt jr	1	Carlos Menditeguy	1		
Paul Frere	1	Paul Miller	1		
Bertrand Gachot	1	Gerhard Mitter	1		
Bob Garretson	1	Luigi Moreschi	1		
Ignazio Giunti	1	Sandro Munari	1		

POLE POSITIONS

Jacky Ickx	19	John Fitzpatrick	4	Kurt Ahrens jr	1
Jochen Mass	14	Mike Hawthorn	4	Michele Alboreto	1
Jo Siffert	13	Ronnie Peterson	4	Giancarlo Baghetti	1
Mauro Baldi	12	Jean Behra	3	Claude Bourgoignie	1
Jean-Louis Schlesser	11	Jean-Pierre Beltoise	3	Martin Brundle	1
Riccardo Patrese	10	Thierry Boutsen	3	Eugenio Castellotti	1
Hans-Joachim Stuck	10	Mark Donohue	3	Eddie Cheever	1
Stefan Bellof	9	Carlo Facetti	3	Enzo Coloni	1
Vittorio Brambilla	9	Giorgio Francia	3	Martino Finotto	1
John Surtees	9	Reinhold Joest	3	Frank Gardner	1
Juan Manuel Fangio	8	Nino Vaccarella	3	Piercarlo Ghinzani	1
Arturo Merzario	8	Derek Warwick	3	Richie Ginther	1
Rolf Stommelen	8	Chris Amon	2	John Greenwood	1
Francois Cevert	7	Alberto Ascari	2	Masten Gregory	1
Phil Hill	7	Andrea de Cesaris	2	Jim Hall	1
Stirling Moss	7	Yannick Dalmas	2	Paul Hawkins	1
Pedro Rodriguez	7	Patrick Depailler	2	Hans Herrmann	1
Mario Andretti	6	Toine Hezemans	2	Graham Hill	1
Bob Wollek	6	Jean-Pierre Jarier	2	Irv Hoerr	1
Philippe Alliot	5	Jan Lammers	2	Bob Holbert	1
Derek Bell	5	Geoff Lees	2	Denny Hulme	1
Jo Bonnier	5	Umberto Maglioli	2	Jean-Pierre Jabouille	1
Dan Gurney	5	Bruce McLaren	2	Frank Jelinski	1
Gerard Larrousse	5	Henri Pescarolo	2	Gunther Klass	1
Michael Parkes	5	Clay Regazzoni	2	Jacques Laffite	1
Vic Elford	4	Wolfgang von Trips	2	Oscar Larrauri	1
Teo Fabi	4	Manfred Winkelhock	2	Klaus Ludwig	1

POLE POSITIONS (cont.)

Dave MacDonald	1	Jean Ragnotti	1	Marc Surer	1
Ken Miles	1	Bobby Rahal	1	Mike Thackwell	1
Hideki Okada	1	Enrique Saenz Valiente	1	Takao Wada	1
Jackie Oliver	1	Jody Scheckter	1	Phil Walters	1
Danny Ongais	1	Tim Schenken	1	Bill Whittington	1
Jonathan Palmer	1	Manfred Schurti	1	Don Whittington	1
John Paul jr	1	Mike Spence	1	Renzo Zorzi	1

FASTEST LAPS

Jacky Ickx	25	Alberto Ascari	2	Masten Gregory	1
Jochen Mass	12	Jean-Pierre Beltoise	2	Harald Grohs	1
Stirling Moss	11	Jo Bonnier	2	Mike Hailwood	1
Mauro Baldi	10	Andrea de Cesaris	2	Jim Hall	1
Jean-Louis Schlesser	10	Eddie Cheever	2	Walt Hansgen	1
Rolf Stommelen	10	Yannick Dalmas	2	Hurley Haywood	1
John Surtees	10	Teo Fabi	2	Graham Hill	1
Stefan Bellof	9	Giuseppe Farina	2	Jean-Pierre Jabouille	1
Vic Elford	8	Jose Froilan Gonzalez	2	Reinhold Joest	1
Phil Hill	8	Toine Hezemans	2	Sherwood Johnston	1
Jo Siffert	8	Denny Hulme	2	Eddie Jordan	1
Vittorio Brambilla	7	Leo Kinnunen	2	Oscar Larrauri	1
Pedro Rodriguez	7	Jackie Oliver	2	Geoff Lees	1
Francois Cevert	6	Danny Ongais	2	Gijs van Lennep	1
Mike Hawthorn	6	Ronnie Peterson	2	Lella Lombardi	1
Jean-Pierre Jarier	6	Brian Redman	2	Dave MacDonald	1
Arturo Merzario	6	Clay Regazzoni	2	Willy Mairesse	1
Riccardo Patrese	6	Tim Schenken	2	Robert Manzon	1
John Fitzpatrick	5	Mike Spence	2	Helmut Marko	1
Jan Lammers	5	Derek Warwick	2	Pierluigi Martini	1
Gerard Larrousse	5	Bill Whittington	2	Gerhard Mitter	1
Jean Behra	4	Mario Andretti	1	Herbert Muller	1
Dan Gurney	4	Julian Bailey	1	Klaus Niedzwiedz	1
Klaus Ludwig	4	Lorenzo Bandini	1	Scooter Patrick	1
John Paul jr	4	Claude Bourgoignie	1	Henri Pescarolo	1
Hans-Joachim Stuck	4	Thierry Boutsen	1	Jean Ragnotti	1
Philippe Alliot	3	Tony Brooks	1	Ricardo Rodriguez	1
Derek Bell	3	Chuck Daigh	1	Jody Scheckter	1
Martin Brundle	3	Colin Davis	1	Jo Schlesser	1
Peter Collins	3	Mark Donohue	1	Jackie Stewart	1
Carlo Facetti	3	Edgar Doren	1	Mike Thackwell	1
Bruce McLaren	3	Jim Downing	1	Wolfgang von Trips	1
Alessandro Nannini	3	Johnny Dumfries	1	Nino Vaccarella	1
Jonathan Palmer	3	Juan Manuel Fangio	1	Emilio de Villota	1
Michael Parkes	3	Maurizio Flammini	1	Peter Walker	1
Michael Schumacher	3	Piercarlo Ghinzani	1	Manfred Winkelhock	1
Bob Wollek	3	Richie Ginther	1	Reine Wisell	1
Michele Alboreto	2	John Greenwood	1	Renzo Zorzi	1
Chris Amon	2	Peter Gregg	1		

Manufacturers' Records

WINS

Porsche	126	Aston Martin	7	Alpine	1
Ferrari	63	Maserati	6	Brabham	1
Mercedes-Benz		BMW	4	Cunningham	1
(including Sauber-Mercedes)	25	Osella	4	March	1
Jaguar	23	Chaparral	3	OSCA	1
Alfa Romeo	19	Lola	3	Shadow	1
Matra	15	Mazda	3	Toyota	1
Ford	13	De Cadenet	2		
Lancia	11	Mirage	2		
Peugeot	8	Rondeau	2		

World Sports Car Championship

1968 The start of the Le Mans 24 hours at which Ford clinched the World Sports Car Championship.

FIA GT Championship

2002 The Ferrari 360 Modena of Christian Pescatori and Andrea Bertolini in action at Estoril.

FIA GT Championship

The BPR Organisation launched a new GT series in 1994 in an attempt to fill the gap left after the demise of the World Sports Car Championship two years earlier. It was originally a non-championship series of events attracting an assortment of private Porsches, Venturis, Lotuses and Ferraris, but for 1995 the series was awarded full championship status.

The BMW-powered McLaren F1 dominated the early championships but the introduction of the Porsche 911 GT1 towards the end of 1997 took the category to a new, more professional level. The AMG Mercedes-Benz team dominated the final two GT1 years (winning every race in 1998) before organisers switched to the GT2 class for 1999.

Lister Storm won the 2000 championship and the Prodrive team have developed the Ferrari 550 Marenello into a race winner but the private Chrysler Viper GTS-Rs have proved the mainstay of the series.

FIA GT CHAMPIONS

GT1/Overall Drivers Champions

year	driver	nat	team	car
1995	John Nielsen/Thomas Bscher	DK/D	West Competition (Dave Price)	McLaren F1 GTR-BMW
1996	Ray Bellm/James Weaver	GB	GTC Motorsport	McLaren F1 GTR-BMW
1997	Bernd Schneider	D	AMG Motorenbau	Mercedes-Benz CLK-GTR
1998	Klaus Ludwig/Ricardo Zonta	D/BR	AMG Motorenbau	Mercedes-Benz CLK-GTR / Mercedes-Benz CLK-LM
1999	Karl Wendlinger/Olivier Beretta	A/MC	Viper Team ORECA	Chrysler Viper GTS-R
2000	Julian Bailey/Jamie Campbell-Walter	GB	Lister Storm Racing	Lister Storm GT
2001	Christophe Bouchut/Jean-Philippe Belloc	F	Larbre Competition	Chrysler Viper GTS-R
2002	Christophe Bouchut	F	Larbre Competition	Chrysler Viper GTS-R

GT2 Champions

year	driver	nat	team	car
1995	Lilian Bryner/Enzo Calderari	CH	Stadler	Porsche 911 GT2
1996	Bruno Eichmann/Gerd Ruch	CH/D	Roock Racing	Porsche 911 GT2
1997	Justin Bell	GB	Viper Team ORECA	Chrysler Viper GTS-R
1998	Olivier Beretta/Pedro Lamy	MC/P	Viper Team ORECA	Chrysler Viper GTS-R

N-GT Champions

year	driver	nat	team	car
2000	Christophe Bouchut/Patrice Goueslard	F	Larbre Competition	Porsche 911 GT3-R
2001	David Terrien/Christian Pescatori	F/I	JMB Competition	Ferrari 360 Modena
2002	Stephane Ortelli	F	Freisinger Motorsport	Porsche 911 GT3-RS

European GT Champions

year	driver	nat	team	car
1995	John Nielsen/Thomas Bscher	DK/D	West Competition (Dave Price)	McLaren F1 GTR-BMW
1996	Ray Bellm/James Weaver	GB	GTC Motorsport	McLaren F1 GTR-BMW
1997	NO SERIES			
1998	Thomas Bscher/Geoff Lees	D/GB	GTC Motorsport	McLaren F1 GTR-BMW

BPR ran a European Championship in 1995-96. Patrick Peter broke away from the main GT championship to run his own one-off 1998 GTR Euroseries, which was abandoned due to lack of entries after 5 rounds

Race Winners

1994

Non-championship

date	race	drivers	nat	car	mph
06.03.94	Paul Ricard	Jean-Pierre Jarier/Jesus Pareja/Bob Wollek	F/E/F	Porsche 911 turbo SLM	102.224
09.04.94	Jarama	Dominique Dupuy/Jean-Pierre Jarier/Jesus Pareja	F/F/E	Porsche 911 turbo SLM	83.178
01.05.94	Dijon-Prenois	Michel Ferte/Michel Neugarten	F/B	Venturi 600LM	96.157
29.05.94	Montlhery	Jean-Claude Basso/Henri Pescarolo	F	Venturi 600LM	81.710
10.07.94	Vallelunga	Luciano della Noce/Anders Olofsson	I/S	Ferrari F40	88.050
23.07.94	Spa-Francorchamps	Michel Ferte/Michel Neugarten	F/B	Venturi 600LM	94.454
28.08.94	Suzuka	Jean-Pierre Jarier/Jesus Pareja/Bob Wollek	F/E/F	Porsche 911 turbo SLM	91.886
13.11.94	Zhuhai	Jean-Pierre Jarier/Jacques Laffite/Bob Wollek	F	Porsche 911 turbo SLM	80.219

1995

date	race	drivers	nat	car	mph
26.02.95	Jerez	Ray Bellm/Maurizio Sandro Sala	GB/BR	McLaren F1 GTR-BMW	84.537
12.03.95	Paul Ricard	Ray Bellm/Maurizio Sandro Sala	GB/BR	McLaren F1 GTR-BMW	101.560
26.03.95	Monza	Thomas Bscher/John Nielsen	D/DK	McLaren F1 GTR-BMW	111.925
09.04.95	Jarama	Ray Bellm/Maurizio Sandro Sala	GB/BR	McLaren F1 GTR-BMW	85.212

date	race	drivers	nat	car	mph
23.04.95	Nurburgring	Ray Bellm/Maurizio Sandro Sala	GB/BR	McLaren F1 GTR-BMW	93.959
08.05.95	Donington Park	Thomas Bscher/John Nielsen	D/DK	McLaren F1 GTR-BMW	90.816
14.05.95	Montlhery	Detlef Hubner/Stefan Oberndorfer	D	Porsche 911 GT2	83.799
02.07.95	Anderstorp	Michel Ferte/Olivier Thevenin	F	Ferrari F40	91.656
27.08.95	Suzuka	Ray Bellm/Maurizio Sandro Sala/Masanori Sekiya	GB/BR/J	McLaren F1 GTR-BMW	93.777
17.09.95	Silverstone	Olivier Grouillard/Andy Wallace	F/GB	McLaren F1 GTR-BMW	79.967
08.10.95	Nogaro	Olivier Grouillard/Andy Wallace	F/GB	McLaren F1 GTR-BMW	84.526
05.11.95	Zhuhai	Olivier Grouillard/Andy Wallace	F/GB	McLaren F1 GTR-BMW	82.870

1996

date	race	drivers	nat	car	mph
03.03.96	Paul Ricard	Ray Bellm/James Weaver	GB	McLaren F1 GTR-BMW	108.349
24.03.96	Monza	Thomas Bscher/John Nielsen	D/DK	McLaren F1 GTR-BMW	113.705
14.04.96	Jarama	Ray Bellm/James Weaver	GB	McLaren F1 GTR-BMW	87.410
12.05.96	Silverstone	Olivier Grouillard/Andy Wallace	GB	McLaren F1 GTR-BMW	98.270
30.06.96	Nurburgring	Thomas Bscher/Peter Kox	D/NL	McLaren F1 GTR-BMW	97.507
14.07.96	Anderstorp	Luciano della Noce/Anders Olofsson	I/S	Ferrari F40 GT-E	94.382
25.08.96	Suzuka	Ray Bellm/JJ Lehto/James Weaver	GB/SF/GB	McLaren F1 GTR-BMW	98.616
08.09.96	Brands Hatch	Thierry Boutsen/Hans-Joachim Stuck	B/D	Porsche 911 GT1	107.593
22.09.96	Spa-Francorchamps	Thierry Boutsen/Hans-Joachim Stuck	B/D	Porsche 911 GT1	107.336
06.10.96	Nogaro	Ray Bellm/James Weaver	GB	McLaren F1 GTR-BMW	86.772
03.11.96	Zhuhai	Emmanuel Collard/Ralf Kelleners	D	Porsche 911 GT1	99.541

1997

date	race	drivers	nat	car	mph
13.04.97	Hockenheim	JJ Lehto/Steve Soper	SF/GB	McLaren F1 GTR-BMW	119.135
11.05.97	Silverstone	Peter Kox/Roberto Ravaglia	NL/I	McLaren F1 GTR-BMW	83.176
25.05.97	Helsinki	JJ Lehto/Steve Soper	SF/GB	McLaren F1 GTR-BMW	74.211
29.06.97	Nurburgring	Klaus Ludwig/Bernd Schneider	D	Mercedes-Benz CLK-GTR	103.956
20.07.97	Spa-Francorchamps	JJ Lehto/Steve Soper	SF/GB	McLaren F1 GTR-BMW	108.443
03.08.97	A1 Ring	Klaus Ludwig/Bernd Maylander/Bernd Schneider	D	Mercedes-Benz CLK-GTR	107.614
24.08.97	Suzuka	Alessandro Nannini/Bernd Schneider/Marcel Tiemann	I/D/D	Mercedes-Benz CLK-GTR	103.908
14.09.97	Donington Park	Bernd Schneider/Alexander Wurz	D/A	Mercedes-Benz CLK-GTR	99.363
28.09.97	Mugello	JJ Lehto/Steve Soper	SF/GB	McLaren F1 GTR-BMW	106.570
19.10.97	Sebring	Klaus Ludwig/Bernd Schneider	D	Mercedes-Benz CLK-GTR	83.851
26.10.97	Laguna Seca	Klaus Ludwig/Bernd Schneider	D	Mercedes-Benz CLK-GTR	96.560

1998

date	race	drivers	nat	car	mph
12.04.98	Oschersleben	Klaus Ludwig/Ricardo Zonta	D/BR	Mercedes-Benz CLK-GTR	96.388
17.05.98	Silverstone	Bernd Schneider/Mark Webber	D/AUS	Mercedes-Benz CLK-GTR	107.647
28.06.98	Hockenheim	Bernd Schneider/Mark Webber	D/AUS	Mercedes-Benz CLK-LM	122.852
12.07.98	Dijon-Prenois	Klaus Ludwig/Ricardo Zonta	D/BR	Mercedes-Benz CLK-LM	112.451
19.07.98	Hungaroring	Bernd Schneider/Mark Webber	D/AUS	Mercedes-Benz CLK-LM	92.600
23.08.98	Suzuka	Bernd Schneider/Mark Webber	D/AUS	Mercedes-Benz CLK-LM	107.664
06.09.98	Donington Park	Bernd Schneider/Mark Webber	D/AUS	Mercedes-Benz CLK-LM	101.345
20.09.98	A1 Ring	Klaus Ludwig/Ricardo Zonta	D/BR	Mercedes-Benz CLK-LM	111.471
18.10.98	Homestead	Klaus Ludwig/Ricardo Zonta	D/BR	Mercedes-Benz CLK-LM	94.022
25.10.98	Laguna Seca	Klaus Ludwig/Ricardo Zonta	D/BR	Mercedes-Benz CLK-LM	98.683

1999

date	race	drivers	nat	car	mph
11.04.99	Monza	Olivier Beretta/Karl Wendlinger	MC/A	Chrysler Viper GTS-R	115.377
09.05.99	Silverstone	Olivier Beretta/Karl Wendlinger	MC/A	Chrysler Viper GTS-R	96.306
27.06.99	Hockenheim	Jean-Philippe Belloc/Dominique Dupuy	F	Chrysler Viper GTS-R	87.709
04.07.99	Hungaroring	Jean-Philippe Belloc/Dominique Dupuy	F	Chrysler Viper GTS-R	84.623
18.07.99	Zolder	Olivier Beretta/Karl Wendlinger	MC/A	Chrysler Viper GTS-R	91.932
08.08.99	Oschersleben	Olivier Beretta/Karl Wendlinger	MC/A	Chrysler Viper GTS-R	88.818
05.09.99	Donington Park	Olivier Beretta/Karl Wendlinger	MC/A	Chrysler Viper GTS-R	91.969
26.09.99	Homestead	Paul Belmondo/Emmanuel Clerico	F	Chrysler Viper GTS-R	89.121
03.10.99	Watkins Glen	Jean-Philippe Belloc/David Donohue	F/USA	Chrysler Viper GTS-R	107.714
28.11.99	Zhuhai	Olivier Beretta/Karl Wendlinger	MC/A	Chrysler Viper GTS-R	93.344

2000 The championship winning Lister Storm of Julian Bailey leads the wet Estoril FIA GT race.

2000

date	race	drivers	nat	car	mph
26.03.00	Valencia	Julian Bailey/Jamie Campbell-Walter	GB	Lister Storm	90.336
02.04.00	Estoril	Julian Bailey/Jamie Campbell-Walter	GB	Lister Storm	65.876
16.04.00	Monza	David Hart/Mike Hezemans	NL	Chrysler Viper GTS-R	114.499
14.05.00	Silverstone	Julian Bailey/Jamie Campbell-Walter	GB	Lister Storm	99.282
02.07.00	Hungaroring	Boris Derichebourg/Vincent Vosse	F/B	Chrysler Viper GTS-R	84.615
23.07.00	Zolder	Julian Bailey/Jamie Campbell-Walter	GB	Lister Storm	93.131
06.08.00	A1 Ring	Tom Coronel/Mike Hezemans	NL	Chrysler Viper GTS-R	101.233
02.09.00	Lausitzring	Hubert Haupt/Wolfgang Kaufmann	D	Porsche 911 GT2	73.149
17.09.00	Brno	David Hart/Mike Hezemans	NL	Chrysler Viper GTS-R	82.785
22.10.00	Magny-Cours	Julian Bailey/Jamie Campbell-Walter	GB	Lister Storm	93.106

2001

01.04.01	Monza	Jamie Campbell-Walter/Tom Coronel	GB/NL	Lister Storm	114.625
16.04.01	Brno	Jean-Philippe Belloc/Christophe Bouchut	F	Chrysler Viper GTS-R	86.018
01.05.01	Magny-Cours	Jamie Campbell-Walter/Tom Coronel	GB/NL	Lister Storm	94.064
13.05.01	Silverstone	Jean-Philippe Belloc/Christophe Bouchut	F	Chrysler Viper GTS-R	98.669
20.05.01	Zolder	Jean-Philippe Belloc/Christophe Bouchut	F	Chrysler Viper GTS-R	82.246
01.07.01	Hungaroring	Jeroen Bleekemolen/Mike Hezemans	NL	Chrysler Viper GTS-R	83.207
28.07.01	Spa 24 hrs	Jean-Philippe Belloc/Christophe Bouchut/Marc Duez	F/F/B	Chrysler Viper GTS-R	95.054
26.08.01	A1 Ring	Peter Kox/Rickard Rydell	NL/S	Ferrari 550M	102.792
09.09.01	Nurburgring	Jamie Campbell-Walter/Mike Jordan	GB	Lister Storm	91.368
30.09.01	Jarama	Alain Menu/Rickard Rydell	CH/S	Ferrari 550M	87.979
21.10.01	Estoril	Jeroen Bleekemolen/Mike Hezemans	NL	Chrysler Viper GTS-R	77.471

2002

21.04.02	Magny-Cours	Jamie Campbell-Walter/Nicolaus Springer	GB/D	Lister Storm GT	95.067
05.05.02	Silverstone	Fabio Babini/Marc Duez	I/B	Chrysler Viper GTS-R	100.997
19.05.02	Brno	Jamie Campbell-Walter/Nicolaus Springer	GB/D	Lister Storm GT	94.315
02.06.02	Jarama	Jean-Denis Deletraz/Andrea Piccini	CH/I	Ferrari 550M	88.895
30.06.02	Anderstorp	Jean-Denis Deletraz/Andrea Piccini	CH/I	Ferrari 550M	69.645
14.07.02	Oschersleben	Jean-Denis Deletraz/Andrea Piccini	CH/I	Ferrari 550M	91.028
04.08.02	Spa 24 hrs	Christophe Bouchut/Sebastien Bourdais/David Terrien/Vincent Vosse	F/F/F/B	Chrysler Viper GTS-R	94.446
22.09.02	Enna-Pergusa	Jamie Campbell-Walter/Nicolaus Springer	GB/D	Lister Storm GT	103.422
06.10.02	Donington Park	Mike Hezemans/Anthony Kumpen	NL/B	Chrysler Viper GTS-R	93.975
20.10.02	Estoril	Jean-Denis Deletraz/Andrea Piccini	CH/I	Ferrari 550M	86.312

Sports Racing World Cup

2002 The 2002 Sports-Racing Champion Jan Lammers leads at Dijon for Racing for Holland.

Sports-Racing World Cup

Sports Car entrepreneur John Mangoletsi launched the new International Sports Racing Series in the summer of 1997, and the championship won full FIA recognition in October 2000. Renamed the FIA World Sports Car Championship (the reuse of the once-defunct title illustrates the organisers' ambitions) the series is for open top sports-racing cars, with a focus on cost control, and weight handicaps aimed at keeping the racing close.

Nevertheless, since the championship's first full year in 1998 the Ferrari 333SP was the class of the field, winning 60% of the races. In 2001, however, the first new sports car in two decades from the Japanese Dome concern ended the year in a winning streak and in 2002 became the first concern other than Ferrari to be crowned champions.

FIA SPORTS CAR CHAMPIONS

Overall Drivers Champions

year	driver	nat	team	car
1998	Emmanuel Collard/Vincenzo Sospiri	F/I	JMB Competition	Ferrari 333SP
1999	Emmanuel Collard/Vincenzo Sospiri	F/I	JMB Competition	Ferrari 333SP
2000	Christian Pescatori/David Terrien	I/F	JMB Competition	Ferrari 333SP
2001	Marco Zadra	I	BMS Scuderia Italia	Ferrari 333SP
2002	Jan Lammers/Val Hillebrand	NL/B	Racing Team Holland	Dome S101-Judd

Known as International Sports Racing Series 1998, Sports Racing World Cup 1999-2000, FIA Sports Car World Championship 2001

SRL class (formerly SR2)

year	driver	nat	team	car
1998	Jean-Claude de Castelli	F	Waterair Bonnet Sport	Debora LMP296-BMW
1999	Angelo Lancellotti	I	Tampolli Engineering	Tampolli RS2/RTA99-Alfa Romeo
2000	Peter Owen/Mark Smithson	GB	Redman Bright Engineering	Pilbeam MP84-Nissan
2001	Thed Bjork/Larry Oberto	S/USA	SRTS	Lola B2K-Nissan
2002	Piergiuseppe Peroni/Mirko Savoldi	I	Lucchini Engineering	Lucchini 2001-Alfa Romeo

Race Winners

1997

Non-championship

date	race	drivers	nat	car	mph
06.07.97	Donington Park	Stefan Johansson/Pierluigi Martini	S/I	Porsche WSC95	99.066
01.08.97	Zolder	Fredy Lienhard/Didier Theys	CH/B	Ferrari 333SP	96.757
09.11.97	Jarama	Didier Cottaz/Jerome Policand	F/CH	Courage C41-Porsche	91.452

1998

International Sports Racing Series

13.04.98	Paul Ricard	Fredy Lienhard/Didier Theys	CH/B	Ferrari 333SP	100.480
17.05.98	Brno	Emmanuel Collard/Vincenzo Sospiri	F/I	Ferrari 333SP	97.262
05.07.98	Misano	Emmanuel Collard/Vincenzo Sospiri	F/I	Ferrari 333SP	99.404
19.07.98	Donington Park	Emmanuel Collard/Vincenzo Sospiri	F/I	Ferrari 333SP	97.768
16.08.98	Anderstorp	Emmanuel Collard/Vincenzo Sospiri	F/I	Ferrari 333SP	95.943
06.09.98	Nurburgring	Emmanuel Collard/Vincenzo Sospiri	F/I	Ferrari 333SP	99.830
20.09.98	Le Mans-Bugatti	Emmanuel Collard/Vincenzo Sospiri	F/I	Ferrari 333SP	96.025
06.12.98	Kyalami	Garry Formato/Jerome Policand	ZA/CH	Riley & Scott MkIII-Ford	95.259

1999

Sports Racing World Cup

28.03.99	Catalunya	Emmanuel Collard/Vincenzo Sospiri	F/I	Ferrari 333SP	99.672
11.04.99	Monza	Emmanuel Collard/Vincenzo Sospiri	F/I	Ferrari 333SP	123.710
16.05.99	Spa-Francorchamps	Mauro Baldi/Laurent Redon	I/F	Ferrari 333SP	112.250
27.06.99	Enna-Pergusa	Emanuele Moncini/Christian Pescatori	I	Ferrari 333SP	113.388
18.07.99	Donington Park	Eric Bernard/Jean-Marc Gounon	F	Lola B98/10-Judd	98.947
01.08.99	Brno	Jean-Marc Gounon/Christophe Tinseau	F	Lola B98/10-Judd	102.463
05.09.99	Nurburgring	Eric Bernard/Jean-Marc Gounon	F	Lola B98/10-Judd	106.371
19.09.99	Magny-Cours	Giovanni Lavaggi/Gaston Mazzacane	I/RA	Ferrari 333SP	79.230
28.11.99	Kyalami	Eric Bernard/Jean-Marc Gounon	F	Lola B98/10-Judd	80.262

2000

Sports Racing World Cup

date	race	drivers	nat	car	mph
26.03.00	Catalunya	Christian Pescatori/David Terrien	I/F	Ferrari 333SP	104.913
16.04.00	Monza	Mauro Baldi/Garry Formato	I/ZA	Riley & Scott MkIII-Judd	115.590
21.05.00	Spa-Francorchamps	Filippo Francioni/Salvatore Ronca	I	Lucchini SP99-Alfa Romeo	87.559
30.06.00	Daytona	Andy Wallace/James Weaver	GB	Riley & Scott MkIII-Ford	103.825
09.07.00	Elkhart Lake	Mauro Baldi/Fredy Lienhard/Didier Theys	I/CH/B	Ferrari 333SP-Judd	112.561
06.08.00	Brno	Christian Pescatori/David Terrien	I/F	Ferrari 333SP	99.476
27.08.00	Donington Park	Christian Pescatori/David Terrien	I/F	Ferrari 333SP	94.881
17.09.00	Nurburgring	Christian Pescatori/David Terrien	I/F	Ferrari 333SP	90.642
01.10.00	Magny-Cours	Christian Pescatori/David Terrien	I/F	Ferrari 333SP	99.346
26.11.00	Kyalami	Garry Formato/Ralf Kelleners	ZA/D	Lola B98/K2000-Ford	92.635

2001 The Scuderia Italia Ferrari 333SP of Christian Pescatori and Marco Zadra wins at Barcelona.

2001

Sports Car World Championship

08.04.01	Catalunya	Christian Pescatori/Marco Zadra	I	Ferrari 333SP	102.619
22.04.01	Monza	Giovanni Lavaggi/Christian Vann	I/GB	Ferrari 333SP	117.793
13.05.01	Spa-Francorchamps	Jean-Marc Gounon/Marco Zadra	F/I	Ferrari 333SP	109.751
01.07.01	Brno	Hiroki Katoh/John Nielsen	J/DK	Dome S101-Judd	98.116
29.07.01	Magny-Cours	Jules Boullion/Laurent Redon	F	Courage C60-Peugeot	99.265
26.08.01	Donington Park	Ben Collins/Werner Lupberger	GB/ZA	Ascari A410-Judd	98.085
01.09.01	Mondello Park	Hiroki Katoh/John Nielsen	J/DK	Dome S101-Judd	80.962
16.09.01	Nurburgring	Val Hillebrand/Jan Lammers	B/NL	Dome S101-Judd	100.771

2002

Sports Car World Championship

07.04.02	Catalunya	Jules Boullion/Sebastien Bourdais	F	Courage C60-Peugeot	95.100
14.04.02	Estoril	Olivier Beretta/Nicolas Minassian	MC/F	Dallara LMP-Judd	98.132
18.05.02	Brno	Val Hillebrand/Jan Lammers	B/NL	Dome S101-Judd	103.003
30.06.02	Magny-Cours	Val Hillebrand/Jan Lammers	B/NL	Dome S101-Judd	100.356
18.08.02	Dijon-Prenois	Val Hillebrand/Jan Lammers	B/NL	Dome S101-Judd	111.360
22.09.02	Spa-Francorchamps	Jules Boullion/Sebastien Bourdais	F	Courage C60-Peugeot	113.442

Indianapolis 500

1988 Danny Sullivan's Penske-Chevrolet leads into Turn 1 at the start of the 1988 Indianapolis 500.

Indianapolis 500

Rules

1911-12	9800cc maximum engine capacity
1913-14	7400cc maximum engine capacity
1915-19	4900cc maximum engine capacity
1920-22	3000cc maximum engine capacity
1923-25	2000cc maximum engine capacity
1926-29	1500cc maximum engine capacity
1930-33	6000cc supercharged production engines
1934	6000cc supercharged production engines. 45-gallon maximum fuel limit
1935	6000cc supercharged production engines. 42.5-gallon maximum fuel limit
1936	No maximum engine capacity. 37.5-gallon maximum fuel limit
1937	As 1936, commercial pump fuel compulsory
1938-56	4500cc normally aspirated and 3000cc supercharged maximum engine capacity
1957-68	4200cc normally aspirated and 2800cc supercharged maximum engine capacity
1969-70	4200cc normally aspirated, 2650cc turbocharged and 5000cc stockblock rocker arm normally aspirated maximum engine capacity
1971	4200cc normally aspirated, 2650cc turbocharged and 5878cc stockblock normally aspirated maximum engine capacity
1972-78	4500cc normally aspirated, 2650cc turbocharged and 5878cc stockblock normally aspirated maximum engine capacity
1979-84	4500cc normally aspirated, 2650cc turbocharged, 5878cc stockblock normally aspirated and 3430cc stockblock supercharged maximum engine capacity
1985-96	2650cc turbocharged and 3430cc stockblock supercharged maximum engine capacity. Normally aspirated engines fazed out
1997 to date	Production-based 3500cc normally aspirated maximum engine capacity

NOTE: From 1979 until the implementation of full Indy Racing League rules in 1997 the maximum manifold intake pressure restrictions differed between the Indianapolis 500 and the other championship races favouring stockblock engines.

1911

30 May 1911. 200 laps of a 2.500 mile-circuit = 500.000 miles

1	Ray Harroun/Cyrus Patschke	Marmon Wasp	200	6h42m08
2	Ralph Mulford	Lozier	200	6h43m51
3	David Bruce-Brown	Fiat	200	6h52m29
4	Spencer Wishart/Dave Murphy	Mercedes	200	6h52m57
5	Joe Dawson/Cyrus Patschke	Marmon	200	6h54m34
6	Ralph de Palma	Simplex	200	7h02m02

Winner's average speed: 74.602 mph. Starting grid front row: Strang (pole), de Palma, H Endicott and Aitken - positions decided by date of entry

1912

30 May 1912. 200 laps of a 2.500 mile-circuit = 500.000 miles

1	Joe Dawson/Don Herr	National	200	6h21m06.0
2	Teddy Tetzlaff/Caleb Bragg	Fiat	200	6h31m29.0
3	Hughie Hughes	Mercer	200	6h33m09.0
4	Charles Merz/William Knipper	Stutz-Wisconsin	200	6h34m40.0
5	Bill Endicott/Harry Endicott	Schacht-Wisconsin	200	6h46m28.2
6	Len Zengel/William Knipper	Schacht-Wisconsin	200	6h50m28.4

Winner's average speed: 78.719 mph. Starting grid front row: Anderson,

80.93 mph (pole), Zengel, 78.85 mph, Tetzlaff, 84.24 mph and de Palma, 86.02 mph - positions decided by date of entry. Fastest qualifier: Bruce-Brown, 88.45 mph

1913

30 May 1913. 200 laps of a 2.500 mile-circuit = 500.000 miles

1	Jules Goux	Peugeot L76	200	6h35m05.00
2	Spencer Wishart/Ralph de Palma	Mercer	200	6h48m13.40
3	Charles Merz/Earl Cooper	Stutz-Wisconsin	200	6h48m49.25
4	Albert Guyot	Sunbeam	200	7h02m58.95
5	Theodore Pilette	Mercedes-Knight	200	7h20m13.00
6	Howdy Wilcox/Frank Fox	Pope-Hartford	200	7h23m26.55

Winner's average speed: 75.933 mph. Starting grid front row: Bragg, 87.34 mph (pole), Guyot, 80.75 mph, Liesaw, 78.02 mph and B Evans, 82.01 mph - positions drawn. Fastest qualifier: Tower, 88.23 mph

1914

30 May 1914. 200 laps of a 2.500 mile-circuit = 500.000 miles

1	Rene Thomas	Delage	200	6h03m45
2	Arthur Duray	Peugeot	200	6h10m24
3	Albert Guyot	Delage	200	6h14m01
4	Jules Goux	Peugeot	200	6h17m24
5	Barney Oldfield/Gil Anderson	Stutz	200	6h23m51
6	Joseph Christiaens	Excelsior	200	6h27m24

Winner's average speed: 82.474 mph. Starting grid front row: Chassagne, 88.31 mph (pole), Tetzlaff, 96.36 mph, Wilcox, 90.76 mph and Chandler, 87.54 mph - positions drawn. Fastest qualifier: Boillot, 99.86 mph

1915

31 May 1915. 200 laps of a 2.500 mile-circuit = 500.000 miles

1	Ralph de Palma	Mercedes	200	5h33m55.51
2	Dario Resta	Peugeot	200	5h37m24.94
3	Gil Anderson/Johnny Aitken	Stutz	200	5h42m27.58
4	Earl Cooper/Johnny Aitken	Stutz	200	5h46m19.36
5	Eddie O'Donnell	Duesenberg	200	6h08m13.27
6	Bob Burman	Peugeot	200	6h13m19.61

Winner's average speed: 89.840 mph. Starting grid front row: Wilcox, 98.90 mph (pole), R de Palma, 98.58 mph, Resta, 98.47 mph and E Cooper, 96.77 mph

1916

30 May 1916. 120 laps of a 2.500 mile-circuit = 300.000 miles. Race distance reduced due to World War 1

1	Dario Resta	Peugeot	120	3h34m17
2	Wilbur d'Alene	Duesenberg	120	3h36m15
3	Ralph Mulford	Peugeot	120	3h37m56
4	Joseph Christiaens	Sunbeam	120	3h46m36
5	Barney Oldfield	Delage	120	3h47m19
6	Pete Henderson/Eddie Rickenbacher	Maxwell	120	3h49m56

Winner's average speed: 84.001 mph. Starting grid front row: Aitken, 96.69 mph (pole), Rickenbacher, 96.44 mph, Anderson, 95.94 mph and Resta, 94.40 mph

1919

30 May 1919. 200 laps of a 2.500 mile-circuit = 500.000 miles

1	Howdy Wilcox	Peugeot	200	5h40m42.87
2	Eddie Hearne	Stutz	200	5h44m29.04
3	Jules Goux	Peugeot-Premier	200	5h49m06.18
4	Albert Guyot	Ballot	200	5h55m16.27
5	Tom Alley	Bender	200	6h05m03.92

6 Ralph de Palma   Packard   200   6h10m10.92
Winner's average speed: 88.050 mph. Starting grid front row: Thomas,
104.70 mph (pole), Wilcox, 100.01 mph, Guyot, 98.30 mph and R de Palma,
98.20 mph

1920

30 May 1920. 200 laps of a 2.500 mile-circuit = 500.000 miles

1 Gaston Chevrolet   Frontenac   200   5h40m16.14
2 Rene Thomas   Ballot   200   5h43m02.29
3 Tommy Milton   Duesenberg   200   5h46m43.38
4 Jimmy Murphy   Duesenberg   200   5h52m31.37
5 Ralph de Palma   Ballot   200   6h05m19.15
6 Eddie Hearne   Duesenberg   200   6h14m19.16
Winner's average speed: 88.166 mph. Starting grid front row: R de Palma,
99.15 mph (pole), Boyer, 96.90 mph, L Chevrolet, 96.30 mph and
Chassagne, 95.45 mph

1921

30 May 1921. 200 laps of a 2.500 mile-circuit = 500.000 miles

1 Tommy Milton   Frontenac   200   5h34m44.65
2 Roscoe Sarles   Duesenberg   200   5h38m34.03
3 Percy Ford/Jules Ellingboe Frontenac   200   5h52m50.30
4 Eddie Miller/Jimmy Murphy   Duesenberg   200   5h54m24.98
5 Ora Haibe   Sunbeam   200   5h55m58.20
6 Albert Guyot/Joe Boyer/
   Eddie Miller   Duesenberg   200   6h01m17.70
Winner's average speed: 89.621 mph. Starting grid front row: R de Palma,
100.75 mph (pole), Sarles, 98.35 mph, Boyer, 96.65 mph and Hearne, 96.18
mph

1922

30 May 1922. 200 laps of a 2.500 mile-circuit = 500.000 miles

1 Jimmy Murphy   Duesenberg-Miller 200   5h17m30.79
2 Harry Hartz   Duesenberg   200   5h20m44.39
3 Eddie Hearne   Ballot   200   5h22m26.06
4 Ralph de Palma   Duesenberg   200   5h31m04.65
5 Ora Haibe/Jules Ellingboe   Duesenberg   200   5h31m13.45
6 Jerry Wonderlich/
   Jules Ellingboe   Duesenberg   200   5h37m52.84
Winner's average speed: 94.484 mph. Starting grid front row: Murphy,
100.50 mph (pole), Hartz, 99.97 mph and de Palma, 99.55 mph

1923

30 May 1923. 200 laps of a 2.500 mile-circuit = 500.000 miles

1 Tommy Milton/Howdy Wilcox Miller   200   5h29m50.17
2 Harry Hartz   Miller   200   5h33m05.09
3 Jimmy Murphy   Miller   200   5h40m36.64
4 Eddie Hearne/Earl Cooper   Miller   200   5h46m14.23
5 Lora Corum   Ford T-Fronty Ford 200   6h03m16.81
6 Frank Elliott/Dave Lewis   Miller   200   6h04m52.87
Winner's average speed: 90.954 mph. Starting grid front row: Milton,
108.17 mph (pole), Hartz, 103.70 mph and Resta, 98.02 mph

1924

30 May 1924. 200 laps of a 2.500 mile-circuit = 500.000 miles

1 Lora Corum/Joe Boyer   Duesenberg   200   5h05m23.51
2 Earl Cooper   Miller   200   5h06m47.18
3 Jimmy Murphy   Miller   200   5h08m25.39
4 Harry Hartz   Miller   200   5h10m44.39
5 Bennett Hill   Miller   200   5h11m00.07
6 Peter de Paolo   Duesenberg   200   5h18m08.55
Winner's average speed: 98.234 mph. Starting grid front row: Murphy,

108.037 mph (pole), Hartz, 107.130 mph and Milton, 105.200 mph

1925

30 May 1925. 200 laps of a 2.500 mile-circuit = 500.000 miles

1 Peter de Paolo/Norman Batten Duesenberg 200   4h56m39.47
2 Dave Lewis/Bennett Hill   Miller   200   4h57m33.15
3 "Red" Shafer/Wade Morton Duesenberg   200   4h59m26.79
4 Harry Hartz   Miller   200   5h03m21.59
5 Tommy Milton   Miller   200   5h08m25.72
6 "Leon Duray"/Fred Comer   Miller   200   5h09m34.01
Winner's average speed: 101.127 mph. Starting grid front row: "Duray",
113.196 mph (pole), de Paolo, 113.083 mph and Hartz, 112.433 mph

1926

31 May 1926. 160 laps of a 2.500 mile-circuit = 400.000 miles. Race
stopped due to rain

1 Frank Lockhart   Miller   160   4h10m14.95
2 Harry Hartz   Miller   158
3 Cliff Woodbury   Miller   158
4 Fred Comer/Wade Morton   Miller   155
5 Peter de Paolo   Duesenberg   153
6 Frank Elliott/"Leon Duray" Miller   152
Winner's average speed: 95.904 mph. Starting grid front row: Cooper,
111.735 mph (pole), Hartz, 109.542 mph and "Duray", 109.186 mph

1927

30 May 1927. 200 laps of a 2.500 mile-circuit = 500.000 miles

1 George Souders   Duesenberg   200   5h07m33.08
2 Earl de Vore/Zeke Meyer   Miller   200   5h19m35.95
3 Tony Gulotta/Peter de Paolo Miller   200   5h22m05.88
4 Wilbur Shaw/Louis Meyer   Miller   200   5h22m12.05
5 Dave Evans/Steve Nemish   Duesenberg   200   5h30m27.71
6 Robert McDonough/
   Peter de Paolo   Cooper-Miller   200   5h31m49.34
Winner's average speed: 97.545 mph. Starting grid front row: Lockhart,
120.100 mph (pole), de Paolo, 119.510 mph and "Duray", 118.788 mph

1928

30 May 1928. 200 laps of a 2.500 mile-circuit = 500.000 miles

1 Louis Meyer   Miller   200   5h01m33.75
2 Lou Moore/Louis Schneider Miller   200   5h02m17.64
3 George Souders   Miller   200   5h06m01.04
4 Ray Keech/Wilbur Shaw   Miller   200   5h21m28.45
5 Norman Batten/Zeke Meyer Fengler-Miller 200   5h21m47.51
6 Babe Stapp/Ralph Hepburn Miller   200   5h23m50.41
Winner's average speed: 99.482 mph. Starting grid front row: "Duray",
122.391 mph (pole), Woodbury, 120.418 mph and Bergere, 119.956 mph

1929

30 May 1929. 200 laps of a 2.500 mile-circuit = 500.000 miles

1 Ray Keech   Miller   200   5h07m25.42
2 Louis Meyer   Miller   200   5h13m49.21
3 Jimmy Gleason/Thane Houser/
   Ernest Triplett   Duesenberg   200   5h20m10.46
4 Carl Marchese   Miller   200   5h20m42.95
5 Fred Winnai/Lora Corum/
   Roscoe Ford   Duesenberg   200   5h37m52.05
6 "Speed" Gardner/
   Chet Gardner   Miller   200   5h39m24.27
Winner's average speed: 97.585 mph. Starting grid front row: Woodbury,
120.599 mph (pole), "Duray", 119.087 mph and Hepburn, 116.543 mph

1930

30 May 1930. 200 laps of a 2.500 mile-circuit = 500.000 miles

1	Billy Arnold	Summers-Miller	200	4h58m39.72
2	"Shorty" Cantlon/			
	Herman Schurch	Stevens-Miller	200	5h05m57.18
3	Louis Schneider	Stevens-Miller	200	5h10m04.21
4	Louis Meyer	Stevens-Miller	200	5h14m57.07
5	Bill Cummings/Fred Winnai	Stevens-		
		Duesenberg	200	5h20m35.11
6	Dave Evans	Stevens-Miller	200	5h24m04.50

Winner's average speed: 100.448 mph. Starting grid front row: Arnold, 113.268 mph (pole), Meyer, 111.290 mph and Cantlon, 109.810 mph

1931

30 May 1931. 200 laps of a 2.500 mile-circuit = 500.000 miles

1	Louis Schneider	Stevens-Miller	200	5h10m27.93
2	Fred Frame	Duesenberg	200	5h11m11.12
3	Ralph Hepburn/Peter Kreis	Miller	200	5h18m23.35
4	Myron Stevens/Zeke Meyer	Stevens-Miller	200	5h18m40.09
5	Russell Snowberger	Snowberger-		
		Studebaker	200	5h18m50.70
6	Jimmy Gleason/Wilbur Shaw	Duesenberg	200	5h20m29.76

Winner's average speed: 96.629 mph. Starting grid front row: Snowberger, 112.796 mph (pole), Cummings, 112.563 mph and Bost, 112.125 mph. Fastest qualifier: Arnold, 116.080 mph

1932

30 May 1932. 200 laps of a 2.500 mile-circuit = 500.000 miles

1	Fred Frame	Wetteroth-Miller	200	4h48m03.79
2	Howdy Wilcox II	Stevens-Miller	200	4h48m47.45
3	Cliff Bergere	Rigling-		
		Studebaker	200	4h52m13.24
4	Bob Carey	Stevens-Miller	200	4h55m57.90
5	Russell Snowberger	Snowberger-		
		Hupmobile	200	4h57m38.72
6	Zeke Meyer	Rigling-		
		Studebaker	200	5h04m38.52

Winner's average speed: 104.144 mph. Starting grid front row: Moore, 117.363 mph (pole), Arnold, 116.290 mph and Saulpaugh, 114.369 mph

1933

30 May 1933. 200 laps of a 2.500 mile-circuit = 500.000 miles

1	Louis Meyer	Miller	200	4h48m00.75
2	Wilbur Shaw	Stevens-Miller	200	4h54m42.64
3	Lou Moore	Duesenberg-Miller	200	4h55m16.79
4	Chet Gardner	Stevens-Miller	200	4h56m29.71
5	"Stubby" Stubblefield	Rigling-Buick	200	4h57m43.82
6	Dave Evans	Rigling-		
		Studebaker	200	4h58m43.82

Winner's average speed: 104.162 mph. Starting grid front row: Cummings, 118.521 mph (pole), Brisko, 118.388 mph and Frame, 117.864 mph

1934

30 May 1934. 200 laps of a 2.500 mile-circuit = 500.000 miles

1	Bill Cummings	Miller	200	4h46m05.20
2	Mauri Rose	Stevens-Miller	200	4h46m32.43
3	Lou Moore/Wilbur Shaw	Miller	200	4h52m19.63
4	"Deacon" Litz/Babe Stapp	Miller	200	4h57m46.27
5	Joe Russo	Duesenberg	200	5h00m19.21
6	Al Miller/Zeke Meyer	Rigling-Buick	200	5h05m18.08

Winner's average speed: 104.863 mph. Starting grid front row: Petillo, 119.329 mph (pole), Shaw, 117.647 mph and Brisko, 116.894 mph

1935

30 May 1935. 200 laps of a 2.500 mile-circuit = 500.000 miles

1	Kelly Petillo	Wetteroth-		
		Offenhauser	200	4h42m22.71
2	Wilbur Shaw	Shaw-Offenhauser	200	4h43m02.73
3	Bill Cummings	Miller	200	4h46m22.48
4	Floyd Roberts	Miller	200	4h50m37.05
5	Ralph Hepburn/Gene Haustein	Miller	200	4h50m45.73
6	"Shorty" Cantlon/Bill Winn	Stevens-Miller	200	4h56m37.07

Winner's average speed: 106.240 mph. Starting grid front row: Mays, 120.736 mph (pole), Gordon, 119.481 mph and Roberts, 118.671 mph

1936

30 May 1936. 200 laps of a 2.500 mile-circuit = 500.000 miles

1	Louis Meyer	Stevens-Miller	200	4h35m03.39
2	Ted Horn	Wetteroth-Miller	200	4h37m20.54
3	"Doc" MacKenzie/Kelly Petillo	Wetteroth-		
		Offenhauser	200	4h39m10.36
4	Mauri Rose	Miller	200	4h39m39.85
5	Chet Miller	Summers-Miller	200	4h40m35.17
6	Ray Pixley	Miller	200	4h45m01.58

Winner's average speed: 109.069 mph. Starting grid front row: Mays, 119.644 mph (pole), Stapp, 118.945 mph and Miller, 117.675 mph

1937

30 May 1937. 200 laps of a 2.500 mile-circuit = 500.000 miles

1	Wilbur Shaw	Shaw-Offenhauser	200	4h24m07.80
2	Ralph Hepburn/	Stevens-		
	Bob Swanson	Offenhauser	200	4h24m09.96
3	Ted Horn	Wetteroth-Miller	200	4h24m28.87
4	Louis Meyer	Miller	200	4h30m55.70
5	Cliff Bergere/George Barringer	Stevens-		
		Offenhauser	200	4h35m23.60
6	Bill Cummings/Chet Miller	Miller-Offenhauser	200	4h40m03.03

Winner's average speed: 113.580 mph. Starting grid front row: Cummings, 123.455 mph (pole), Shaw, 122.791 mph and Ardinger, 121.983 mph. Fastest qualifier: Snyder, 125.287 mph

1938

30 May 1938. 200 laps of a 2.500 mile-circuit = 500.000 miles

1	Floyd Roberts	Wetteroth-Miller	200	4h15m58.40
2	Wilbur Shaw	Shaw-		
		Offenhauser	200	4h19m33.67
3	Chet Miller	Summers-		
		Offenhauser	200	4h20m59.51
4	Ted Horn	Wetteroth-Miller	200	4h27m22.39
5	Chet Gardner	Rigling-		
		Offenhauser	200	4h31m57.48
6	Herb Ardinger/Russell Snowberger/			
	Cliff Bergere	Miller Ford-		
		Offenhauser	199	

Winner's average speed: 117.200 mph. Starting grid front row: Roberts, 125.681 mph (pole), Snowberger, 124.027 mph and Mays, 122.845 mph. Fastest qualifier: Householder, 125.769 mph

1939

30 May 1939. 200 laps of a 2.500 mile-circuit = 500.000 miles

1	Wilbur Shaw	Maserati 8CTF	200	4h20m47.39
2	Jimmy Snyder	Adams-Sparks	200	4h22m35.61
3	Cliff Bergere	Miller Ford-Offenhauser	200	4h23m51.40
4	Ted Horn	Miller	200	4h28m08.82

1939 Wilbur Shaw poses with the winning Boyle Special Maserati.

5 Babe Stapp	Alfa Romeo Tipo-C "8C-35"	200	4h29m42.68
6 George Barringer	Weil-Offenhauser	200	4h30m12.60

Winner's average speed: 115.035 mph. Starting grid front row: Snyder, 130.138 mph (pole), Meyer, 130.067 mph and Shaw, 128.977 mph

1940

30 May 1940. 200 laps of a 2.500 mile-circuit = 500.000 miles

1 Wilbur Shaw	Maserati 8CTF	200	4h22m31.17
2 Rex Mays	Stevens-Winfield	200	4h23m45.31
3 Mauri Rose	Wetteroth-Offenhauser	200	4h24m08.96
4 Ted Horn	Miller	199	
5 Joel Thorne	Adams-Sparks	197	
6 Bob Swanson	Stevens-Sampson	196	

Winner's average speed: 114.277 mph. Starting grid front row: Mays, 127.850 mph (pole), Shaw, 127.065 mph and Rose, 125.624 mph

1941

30 May 1941. 200 laps of a 2.500 mile-circuit = 500.000 miles

1 Floyd Davis/ Mauri Rose	Wetteroth-Offenhauser	200	4h20m36.24
2 Rex Mays	Stevens-Winfield	200	4h22m06.19
3 Ted Horn	Adams-Sparks	200	4h23m28.39
4 Ralph Hepburn	Miller Ford-Novi	200	4h24m00.79
5 Cliff Bergere	Wetteroth-Offenhauser	200	4h24m15.10
6 Chet Miller	Miller	200	4h28m02.75

Winner's average speed: 115.117 mph. Starting grid front row: Rose, 128.691 mph (pole), Mays, 128.301 mph and Shaw, 127.836 mph

1946

30 May 1946. 200 laps of a 2.500 mile-circuit = 500.000 miles

1 George Robson	Adams-Sparks	200	4h21m26.70
2 Jimmy Jackson	Miller-Offenhauser	200	4h22m00.74
3 Ted Horn	Maserati 8CTF	200	4h33m19.60
4 Emil Andres	Maserati	200	4h35m28.65
5 Joie Chitwood/Sam Hanks	Wetteroth-Offenhauser	200	4h36m45.30
6 Louis Durant	Alfa Romeo	200	4h45m30.88

Winner's average speed: 114.747 mph. Starting grid front row: Bergere, 126.471 mph (pole), Russo, 126.183 mph and Hanks, 124.762 mph. Fastest qualifier: Hepburn, 133.944 mph

1947

30 May 1947. 200 laps of a 2.500 mile-circuit = 500.000 miles

1 Mauri Rose	Deidt-Offenhauser	200	4h17m52.17

2 Bill Holland	Deidt-Offenhauser	200	4h18m24.29
3 Ted Horn	Maserati	200	4h20m52.55
4 Herb Ardinger/Cliff Bergere	Kurtis-Novi	200	4h24m32.52
5 Jimmy Jackson	Miller-Offenhauser	200	4h25m52.65
6 Rex Mays	Kurtis-Winfield	200	4h30m08.05

Winner's average speed: 116.338 mph. Starting grid front row: Horn, 126.564 mph (pole), Bergere, 124.957 mph and Rose, 124.040 mph. Fastest qualifier: Holland, 128.755 mph

1948

30 May 1948. 200 laps of a 2.500 mile-circuit = 500.000 miles

1 Mauri Rose	Deidt-Offenhauser	200	4h10m23.33
2 Bill Holland	Deidt-Offenhauser	200	4h11m47.40
3 Duke Nalon	Kurtis-Novi	200	4h14m09.78
4 Ted Horn	Maserati	200	4h14m34.47
5 Mack Hellings	Kurtis KK2000-Offenhauser	200	4h24m38.52
6 Hal Cole	Kurtis KK2000-Offenhauser	200	4h28m50.86

Winner's average speed: 119.814 mph. Starting grid front row: Mays, 130.577 mph (pole), Holland, 129.515 mph and Rose, 129.129 mph. Fastest qualifier: Nalon, 131.603 mph

1949

30 May 1949. 200 laps of a 2.500 mile-circuit = 500.000 miles

1 Bill Holland	Deidt-Offenhauser	200	4h07m15.97
2 Johnnie Parsons	Kurtis-Offenhauser	200	4h10m26.97
3 George Connor	Lesovsky-Offenhauser	200	4h10m50.78
4 Myron Fohr	Marchese-Offenhauser	200	4h12m32.65
5 Joie Chitwood	Kurtis KK2000-Offenhauser	200	4h12m36.97
6 Jimmy Jackson	Deidt-Offenhauser	200	4h14m31.00

Winner's average speed: 121.327 mph. Starting grid front row: Nalon, 132.939 mph (pole), Mays, 129.552 mph and McGrath, 128.884 mph

1950

30 May 1950. 138 laps of a 2.500 mile-circuit = 345.000 miles. Race stopped due to rain

1 Johnnie Parsons	Kurtis-Offenhauser	138	2h46m55.97
2 Bill Holland	Deidt-Offenhauser	137	
3 Mauri Rose	Deidt-Offenhauser	137	
4 Cecil Green	Kurtis KK3000-Offenhauser	137	
5 Joie Chitwood/ Tony Bettenhausen	Kurtis KK2000-Offenhauser	136	
6 Lee Wallard	Moore-Offenhauser	136	

Winner's average speed: 124.002 mph. Starting grid front row: Faulkner, 134.343 mph (pole), Agabashian, 132.792 mph and Rose, 132.319 mph

1951

30 May 1951. 200 laps of a 2.500 mile-circuit = 500.000 miles

1 Lee Wallard	Kurtis-Offenhauser	200	3h57m38.05
2 Mike Nazaruk	Kurtis-Offenhauser	200	3h59m25.31
3 Manuel Ayulo/ Jack McGrath	Kurtis KK3000-Offenhauser	200	4h00m29.42
4 Andy Linden	Sherman-Offenhauser	200	4h02m18.06
5 Bobby Ball	Schroeder-Offenhauser	200	4h02m30.27
6 Henry Banks	Moore-Offenhauser	200	4h03m18.02

Winner's average speed: 126.244 mph. Starting grid front row: Nalon, 136.498 mph (pole), Wallard, 135.039 mph and McGrath, 134.303 mph. Fastest qualifier: Faulkner, 136.872 mph

1952

30 May 1952. 200 laps of a 2.500 mile-circuit = 500.000 miles

1 Troy Ruttman	Kuzma-Offenhauser	200	3h52m41.88
2 Jim Rathmann	Kurtis KK3000- Offenhauser	200	3h56m44.24
3 Sam Hanks	Kurtis KK3000- Offenhauser	200	3h58m53.48
4 Duane Carter	Lesovsky-Offenhauser	200	3h59m30.21
5 Art Cross	Kurtis KK4000- Offenhauser	200	4h01m22.08
6 Jimmy Bryan	Kurtis KK3000- Offenhauser	200	4h02m06.23

Winner's average speed: 128.922 mph. Starting grid front row:
Agabashian, 138.010 mph (pole), Linden, 137.002 mph and McGrath,
136.664 mph. Fastest qualifier: Miller, 139.034 mph

1953

30 May 1953. 200 laps of a 2.500 mile-circuit = 500.000 miles

1 Bill Vukovich	Kurtis KK500A- Offenhauser	200	3h53m01.69
2 Art Cross	Kurtis KK4000- Offenhauser	200	3h56m32.56
3 Sam Hanks/ Duane Carter	Kurtis KK4000- Offenhauser	200	3h57m13.24
4 Fred Agabashian/ Paul Russo	Kurtis KK500B- Offenhauser	200	3h57m40.91
5 Jack McGrath	Kurtis KK4000- Offenhauser	200	4h00m51.33
6 Jimmy Daywalt	Kurtis KK3000- Offenhauser	200	4h01m11.88

Winner's average speed: 128.740 mph. Starting grid front row: Vukovich,
138.392 mph (pole), Agabashian, 137.546 mph and McGrath, 136.602 mph

1954

31 May 1954. 200 laps of a 2.500 mile-circuit = 500.000 miles

1 Bill Vukovich	Kurtis KK500A-Offenhauser	200	3h49m17.27
2 Jimmy Bryan	Kuzma-Offenhauser	200	3h50m27.26
3 Jack McGrath	Kurtis KK500C-Offenhauser	200	3h50m36.97
4 Troy Ruttman/ Duane Carter	Kurtis KK500A-Offenhauser	200	3h52m09.90
5 Mike Nazaruk	Kurtis KK500C-Offenhauser	200	3h52m41.85
6 Fred Agabashian	Kurtis KK500C-Offenhauser	200	3h53m04.83

Winner's average speed: 130.840 mph. Starting grid front row: McGrath,
141.033 mph (pole), Daywalt, 139.789 mph and Bryan, 139.665 mph

1955

30 May 1955. 200 laps of a 2.500 mile-circuit = 500.000 miles

1 Bob Sweikert	Kurtis KK500D-Offenhauser	200	3h53m59.53
2 Tony Bettenhausen/ Paul Russo	Kurtis KK500C-Offenhauser	200	3h56m43.11
3 Jimmy Davies	Kurtis KK500B-Offenhauser	200	3h57m31.89
4 Johnny Thomson	Kuzma-Offenhauser	200	3h57m38.44
5 Walt Faulkner/ Bill Homeier	Kurtis KK500C-Offenhauser	200	3h59m16.66
6 Andy Linden	Kurtis KK4000-Offenhauser	200	3h59m57.47

Winner's average speed: 128.209 mph. Starting grid front row: Hoyt,
140.045 mph (pole), Bettenhausen, 139.985 mph and McGrath, 142.580
mph. Fastest qualifier: McGrath

1956

30 May 1956. 200 laps of a 2.500 mile-circuit = 500.000 miles

1 Pat Flaherty	Watson-Offenhauser	200	3h53m28.84
2 Sam Hanks	Kurtis KK500C-Offenhauser	200	3h53m49.30
3 Don Freeland	Phillips-Offenhauser	200	3h54m59.07
4 Johnnie Parsons	Kuzma-Offenhauser	200	3h56m54.48
5 Dick Rathmann	Kurtis KK500C-Offenhauser	200	3h57m50.65
6 Bob Sweikert	Kuzma-Offenhauser	200	3h59m03.84

Winner's average speed: 128.490 mph. Starting grid front row: Flaherty,
145.596 mph (pole), J Rathmann, 145.120 mph and O'Connor, 144.980 mph

1957

30 May 1957. 200 laps of a 2.500 mile-circuit = 500.000 miles

1 Sam Hanks	Epperly-Offenhauser	200	3h41m14.25
2 Jim Rathmann	Epperly-Offenhauser	200	3h41m35.75
3 Jimmy Bryan	Kuzma-Offenhauser	200	3h43m28.25
4 Paul Russo	Kurtis 500F-Novi	200	3h44m11.10
5 Andy Linden	Kurtis KK500G-Offenhauser	200	3h44m28.55
6 Johnny Boyd	Kurtis KK500G-Offenhauser	200	3h45m49.55

Winner's average speed: 135.601 mph. Starting grid front row: O'Connor,
143.948 mph (pole), Sachs, 143.822 mph and Ruttman, 142.772 mph.
Fastest qualifier: Russo, 144.817 mph

1958

30 May 1958. 200 laps of a 2.500 mile-circuit = 500.000 miles

1 Jimmy Bryan	Epperly-Offenhauser	200	3h44m13.80
2 George Amick	Epperly-Offenhauser	200	3h44m41.45
3 Johnny Boyd	Kurtis KK500G-Offenhauser	200	3h45m23.75
4 Tony Bettenhausen	Epperly-Offenhauser	200	3h45m45.60
5 Jim Rathmann	Epperly-Offenhauser	200	3h45m49.45
6 Jimmy Reece	Watson-Offenhauser	200	3h46m30.75

Winner's average speed: 133.791 mph. Starting grid front row: D
Rathmann, 145.974 mph (pole), Elisian, 145.926 mph and Reece, 145.513
mph

1959

30 May 1959. 200 laps of a 2.500 mile-circuit = 500.000 miles

1 Rodger Ward	Watson-Offenhauser	200	3h40m49.20
2 Jim Rathmann	Watson-Offenhauser	200	3h41m12.47
3 Johnny Thomson	Lesovsky-Offenhauser	200	3h41m39.85
4 Tony Bettenhausen	Epperly-Offenhauser	200	3h42m36.25
5 Paul Goldsmith	Epperly-Offenhauser	200	3h42m55.60
6 Johnny Boyd	Kurtis KK500G-Offenhauser	200	3h44m06.23

Winner's average speed: 135.857 mph. Starting grid front row: Thomson,
145.908 mph (pole), Sachs, 145.425 mph and J Rathmann, 144.433 mph

1960

30 May 1960. 200 laps of a 2.500 mile-circuit = 500.000 miles

1 Jim Rathmann	Watson-Offenhauser	200	3h36m11.36
2 Rodger Ward	Watson-Offenhauser	200	3h36m24.03
3 Paul Goldsmith	Epperly-Offenhauser	200	3h39m18.58
4 Don Branson	Phillips-Offenhauser	200	3h39m19.28
5 Johnny Thomson	Lesovsky-Offenhauser	200	3h39m22.65
6 Eddie Johnson	Trevis-Offenhauser	200	3h40m21.88

Winner's average speed: 138.767 mph. Starting grid front row: Sachs,
146.592 mph (pole), J Rathmann, 146.371 mph and Ward, 145.560 mph.
Fastest qualifier: Hurtubise, 149.056 mph

1961

30 May 1961. 200 laps of a 2.500 mile-circuit = 500.000 miles

1	AJ Foyt Jr	Watson-Offenhauser	200	3h35m37.49
2	Eddie Sachs	Ewing-Offenhauser	200	3h35m45.77
3	Rodger Ward	Watson-Offenhauser	200	3h36m32.68
4	Shorty Templeman	Watson-Offenhauser	200	3h39m10.84
5	Al Keller	Phillips-Offenhauser	200	3h40m31.94
6	Chuck Stevenson	Epperly-Offenhauser	200	3h41m00.45

Winner's average speed: 139.131 mph. Starting grid front row: Sachs, 147.481 mph (pole), Branson, 146.843 mph and Hurtubise, 146.306 mph

1962

30 May 1962. 200 laps of a 2.500 mile-circuit = 500.000 miles

1	Rodger Ward	Watson-Offenhauser	200	3h33m50.33
2	Len Sutton	Watson-Offenhauser	200	3h34m01.85
3	Eddie Sachs	Ewing-Offenhauser	200	3h34m10.26
4	Don Davis	Lesovsky-Offenhauser	200	3h34m38.46
5	Bobby Marshman	Epperly-Offenhauser	200	3h36m09.27
6	Jim McElreath	Kurtis-Offenhauser	200	3h36m22.02

Winner's average speed: 140.293 mph. Starting grid front row: Jones, 150.370 mph (pole), Ward, 149.371 mph and Marshman, 149.347 mph

1963

30 May 1963. 200 laps of a 2.500 mile-circuit = 500.000 miles

1	Parnelli Jones	Watson-Offenhauser	200	3h29m35.40
2	Jim Clark	Lotus 29-Ford	200	3h30m09.24
3	AJ Foyt Jr	Trevis-Offenhauser	200	3h30m57.34
4	Rodger Ward	Watson-Offenhauser	200	3h32m37.80
5	Don Branson	Watson-Offenhauser	200	3h32m58.11
6	Jim McElreath	Watson-Offenhauser	200	3h32m58.43

Winner's average speed: 143.137 mph. Starting grid front row: Jones, 151.153 mph (pole), Hurtubise, 150.257 mph and Branson, 150.188 mph

1964

30 May 1964. 200 laps of a 2.500 mile-circuit = 500.000 miles

1	AJ Foyt Jr	Watson-Offenhauser	200	3h23m35.83
2	Rodger Ward	Watson-Offenhauser	200	3h25m00.18
3	Lloyd Ruby	Watson-Offenhauser	200	3h27m52.31
4	Johnny White	Watson-Offenhauser	200	3h29m29.30
5	Johnny Boyd	Kuzma-Offenhauser	200	3h30m45.31
6	Bud Tingelstad	Trevis-Offenhauser	198	

Winner's average speed: 147.350 mph. Starting grid front row: Clark, 158.828 mph (pole), Marshman, 157.857 mph and Ward, 156.406 mph

1963 Jim Clark and the Lotus-Ford team went close to victory in 1963 before winning two years later.

1965

31 May 1965. 200 laps of a 2.500 mile-circuit = 500.000 miles

1	Jim Clark	Lotus 38-Ford	200	3h19m05.34
2	Parnelli Jones	Kuzma/Lotus 34-Ford	200	3h21m04.32
3	Mario Andretti	Brawner/Brabham-Ford	200	3h21m10.70
4	Al Miller	Lotus 29-Ford	200	3h24m39.89
5	Gordon Johncock	Watson-Offenhauser	200	3h24m53.62
6	Mick Rupp	Gerhardt-Offenhauser	198	

Winner's average speed: 150.686 mph. Starting grid front row: Foyt, 161.233 mph (pole), Clark, 160.729 mph and Gurney, 158.898 mph

1966 Graham Hill took a late victory In the 1966 Indy 500.

1966

30 May 1966. 200 laps of a 2.500 mile-circuit = 500.000 miles

1	Graham Hill	Lola T90-Ford	200	3h27m52.53
2	Jim Clark	Lotus 38-Ford	200	3h28m33.66
3	Jim McElreath	Brabham-Ford	200	3h28m42.42
4	Gordon Johncock	Gerhardt-Ford	200	3h29m40.00
5	Mel Kenyon	Gerhardt-Offenhauser	198	
6	Jackie Stewart	Lola T90-Ford	190	oil pressure

Winner's average speed: 144.317 mph. Starting grid front row: Andretti, 165.899 mph (pole), Clark, 164.114 mph and Snider, 162.521 mph

1967

30 May 1967. 200 laps of a 2.500 mile-circuit = 500.000 miles

1	AJ Foyt jr	Coyote/Lotus 34-Ford	200	3h18m24.22
2	Al Unser	Lola T90-Ford	198	
3	Joe Leonard	Coyote/Lotus 34-Ford	197	
4	Denny Hulme	Eagle 67-Ford	197	
5	Jim McElreath	Moore-Ford	197	
6	Parnelli Jones	Granatelli turbine	196	

Winner's average speed: 151.207 mph. Starting grid front row: Andretti, 168.982 mph (pole), Gurney, 167.224 mph and Johncock, 166.559 mph

1968

30 May 1968. 200 laps of a 2.500 mile-circuit = 500.000 miles

1	Bobby Unser	Eagle 68-Drake/ Offenhauser	200	3h16m13.76
2	Dan Gurney	Eagle 68-Ford/Weslake	200	3h17m07.57
3	Mel Kenyon	Gerhardt-Drake/ Offenhauser	200	3h21m02.43
4	Denny Hulme	Eagle 68-Ford	200	3h21m08.71
5	Lloyd Ruby	Mongoose-Drake/ Offenhauser	200	3h21m58.83
6	Ronnie Duman	Brabham-Drake/ Offenhauser	199	

Winner's average speed: 152.882 mph. Starting grid front row: Leonard, 171.559 mph (pole), Hill, 171.208 mph and B Unser, 169.507 mph

1969

30 May 1969. 200 laps of a 2.500 mile-circuit = 500.000 miles

1 Mario Andretti	Brawner/Hawk III-Ford	200	3h11m14.71
2 Dan Gurney	Eagle 69-Ford/Weslake	200	3h13m07.74
3 Bobby Unser	Lola T152-Offenhauser	200	3h14m41.45
4 Mel Kenyon	Gerhardt-Offenhauser	200	3h17m08.32
5 Peter Revson	Brabham BT25-Repco	197	
6 Joe Leonard	Eagle 69-Ford	193	

Winner's average speed: 156.867 mph. Starting grid front row: Foyt, 170.568 mph (pole), Andretti, 169.851 mph and B Unser, 169.683 mph

1970

30 May 1970. 200 laps of a 2.500 mile-circuit = 500.000 miles

1 Al Unser	Colt 70-Ford	200	3h12m37.04
2 Mark Donohue	Lola T153-Ford	200	3h13m09.23
3 Dan Gurney	Eagle 70-Offenhauser	200	3h15m49.25
4 Donnie Allison	Eagle 70-Ford	200	3h16m21.86
5 Jim McElreath	Coyote-Ford	200	3h17m07.95
6 Mario Andretti	McNamara T500-Ford	199	

Winner's average speed: 155.749 mph. Starting grid front row: A Unser, 170.221 mph (pole), Rutherford, 170.213 mph and Foyt, 170.004 mph

1971

29 May 1971. 200 laps of a 2.500 mile-circuit = 500.000 miles

1 Al Unser	Colt 71-Ford	200	3h10m11.56
2 Peter Revson	McLaren M16-Offenhauser	200	3h10m34.44
3 AJ Foyt Jr	Coyote-Ford	200	3h12m13.37
4 Jim Malloy	Eagle 70-Offenhauser	200	3h14m04.65
5 Bill Vukovich Jr	Brabham BT32-Offenhauser	200	3h14m05.77
6 Donnie Allison	Coyote-Ford	199	

Winner's average speed: 157.735 mph. Starting grid front row: Revson, 178.696 mph (pole), Donohue, 177.087 mph and B Unser, 175.816 mph

1972

27 May 1972. 200 laps of a 2.500 mile-circuit = 500.000 miles

1 Mark Donohue	McLaren M16B-Offenhauser	200	3h04m05.54
2 Al Unser	Parnelli-Offenhauser	200	3h07m16.49
3 Joe Leonard	Parnelli-Offenhauser	200	3h08m17.51
4 Sam Sessions	Lola-Ford	200	3h09m22.88
5 Sam Posey	Eagle 72-Offenhauser	198	
6 Lloyd Ruby	Atlanta-Foyt/Ford	196	

Winner's average speed: 162.962 mph. Starting grid front row: B Unser, 195.940 mph (pole), Revson, 192.885 mph and Donohue, 191.408 mph

1973

28 May 1973. 133 laps of a 2.500 mile-circuit = 332.500 miles. Race stopped due to rain

1 Gordon Johncock	Eagle 73-Offenhauser	133	2h05m26.59
2 Bill Vukovich Jr	Eagle 73-Offenhauser	133	2h06m51.50
3 Roger McCluskey	McLaren M16B-Offenhauser	131	
4 Mel Kenyon	Eagle 73-Foyt/Ford	131	
5 Gary Bettenhausen	McLaren M16C-Offenhauser	130	
6 Steve Krisiloff	Kingfish-Offenhauser	129	

Winner's average speed: 159.036 mph. Starting grid front row: Rutherford, 198.413 mph (pole), B Unser, 198.183 mph and Donohue, 197.412 mph

1974

26 May 1974. 200 laps of a 2.500 mile-circuit = 500.000 miles

1 Johnny Rutherford	McLaren M16C/D-Offenhauser	200	3h09m10.06
2 Bobby Unser	Eagle 74-Offenhauser	200	3h09m32.38
3 Bill Vukovich Jr	Eagle 74-Offenhauser	199	
4 Gordon Johncock	Eagle 74-Offenhauser	198	
5 David Hobbs	McLaren M16C/D-Offenhauser	196	
6 Jim McElreath	Eagle 74-Offenhauser	194	

Winner's average speed: 158.589 mph. Starting grid front row: Foyt, 191.632 mph (pole), Dallenbach, 189.683 mph and Hiss, 187.490 mph

1975

25 May 1975. 174 laps of a 2.500 mile-circuit = 435.000 miles. Race stopped due to rain

1 Bobby Unser	Eagle 75-Offenhauser	174	2h54m55.08
2 Johnny Rutherford	McLaren M16E-Offenhauser	174	2h55m59.08
3 AJ Foyt Jr	Coyote-Foyt/Ford	174	2h56m43.70
4 Pancho Carter	Eagle 75-Offenhauser	169	
5 Roger McCluskey	Riley-Offenhauser	167	
6 Bill Vukovich Jr	Eagle 75-Offenhauser	166	

Winner's average speed: 149.213 mph. Starting grid front row: Foyt, 193.976 mph (pole), Johncock, 191.652 mph and B Unser, 191.073 mph

1976

30 May 1976. 102 laps of a 2.500 mile-circuit = 255.000 miles. Race stopped due to rain

1 Johnny Rutherford	McLaren M16E-Offenhauser	102	1h42m52.48
2 AJ Foyt Jr	Coyote-Foyt/Ford	102	1h43m07.84
3 Gordon Johncock	Wildcat-DGS/Offenhauser	102	1h44m37.43
4 Wally Dallenbach	Wildcat-DGS/Offenhauser	101	
5 Pancho Carter	Eagle 76-Offenhauser	101	
6 Tom Sneva	McLaren M16C/D-Offenhauser	101	

Winner's average speed: 148.725 mph. Starting grid front row: Rutherford, 188.957 mph (pole), Johncock, 188.531 mph and Sneva, 186.355 mph. Fastest qualifier: Andretti, 189.404 mph

1977

29 May 1977. 200 laps of a 2.500 mile-circuit = 500.000 miles

1 AJ Foyt jr	Coyote-Foyt/Ford	200	3h05m57.16
2 Tom Sneva	McLaren M24-Cosworth	200	3h06m25.79
3 Al Unser	Parnelli VPJ6B-Cosworth	199	
4 Wally Dallenbach	Wildcat-DGS/Offenhauser	199	
5 Johnny Parsons Jr	Wildcat-DGS/Offenhauser	193	
6 Tom Bigelow	Watson-Offenhauser	192	

Winner's average speed: 161.331 mph. Starting grid front row: Sneva, 198.884 mph (pole), B Unser, 197.618 mph and A Unser, 195.950 mph

1978

28 May 1978. 200 laps of a 2.500 mile-circuit = 500.000 miles

1 Al Unser	Lola T500-Cosworth	200	3h05m54.99
2 Tom Sneva	Penske PC6-Cosworth	200	
3 Gordon Johncock	Wildcat-DGS/Offenhauser	199	
4 Steve Krisiloff	Wildcat-DGS/Offenhauser	198	
5 Wally Dallenbach	McLaren M24-Cosworth	196	out of fuel
6 Bobby Unser	Eagle 78-Cosworth	195	

Winner's average speed: 161.363 mph. Starting grid front row: Sneva, 202.156 mph (pole), Ongais, 200.122 mph and Mears, 200.078 mph

1978 Al Unser took one of four wins in 1978, a record he shares with AJ Foyt and Rick Mears.

1979

27 May 1979. 200 laps of a 2.500 mile-circuit = 500.000 miles

1 Rick Mears	Penske PC6-Cosworth	200	3h08m47.97
2 AJ Foyt Jr	Parnelli VPJ6C-Cosworth	200	3h09m33.66
3 Mike Mosley	Eagle 79-Cosworth	200	3h09m36.00
4 Danny Ongais	Parnelli VPJ6B-Cosworth	199	
5 Bobby Unser	Penske PC7-Cosworth	199	
6 Gordon Johncock	Penske PC6-Cosworth	197	

Winner's average speed: 158.899 mph. Starting grid front row: Mears, 193.736 mph (pole), Sneva, 192.998 mph and A Unser, 192.503 mph

1980

25 May 1980. 200 laps of a 2.500 mile-circuit = 500.000 miles

1 Johnny Rutherford	Chaparral 2K-Cosworth	200	3h29m59.55
2 Tom Sneva	McLaren M24-Cosworth	200	3h30m29.49
3 Gary Bettenhausen	Wildcat Mk2-DGS/Offenhauser	200	3h30m32.90
4 Gordon Johncock	Penske PC6-Cosworth	200	3h30m33.17
5 Rick Mears	Penske PC9-Cosworth	199	
6 Pancho Carter	Penske PC7-Cosworth	199	

Winner's average speed: 142.862 mph. Starting grid front row: Rutherford, 192.256 mph (pole), Andretti, 191.012 mph and B Unser, 189.994 mph

1981

24 May 1981. 200 laps of a 2.500 mile-circuit = 500.000 miles

1 Bobby Unser	Penske PC9B-Cosworth	200	3h35m41.78
2 Mario Andretti	Wildcat Mk8-Cosworth	200	3h35m46.96
3 Vern Schuppan	McLaren M24B-Cosworth	199	
4 Kevin Cogan	Phoenix-Cosworth	197	
5 Geoff Brabham	Penske PC9-Cosworth	197	
6 Sheldon Kinser	Longhorn LR01-Cosworth	195	

Winner's average speed: 139.084 mph. Starting grid front row: B Unser, 200.546 mph (pole), Mosley, 197.141 mph and Foyt, 196.078 mph. Fastest qualifier: Sneva, 200.691 mph

1982

30 May 1982. 200 laps of a 2.500 mile-circuit = 500.000 miles

1 Gordon Johncock	Wildcat Mk8B-Cosworth	200	3h05m09.14	
2 Rick Mears	Penske PC10-Cosworth	200	3h05m09.30	
3 Pancho Carter	March 82C-Cosworth	199		
4 Tom Sneva	March 82C-Cosworth	197		engine
5 Al Unser	Longhorn LR03-Cosworth	197		
6 Don Whittington	March 81C-Cosworth	196		

Winner's average speed: 162.029 mph. Starting grid front row: Mears, 207.004 mph (pole), Cogan, 204.082 mph and Foyt, 203.332 mph

1983

29 May 1983. 200 laps of a 2.500 mile-circuit = 500.000 miles

1 Tom Sneva	March 83C-Cosworth	200	3h05m03.066
2 Al Unser*	Penske PC11-Cosworth	200	3h05m14.240
3 Rick Mears	Penske PC11-Cosworth	200	3h05m24.928
4 Geoff Brabham	Penske PC10-Cosworth	199	
5 Kevin Cogan	March 83C-Cosworth	198	
6 Howdy Holmes	March 83C-Cosworth	198	

*Including 2-lap penalty for passing under yellow flag. Winner's average speed: 162.117 mph. Starting grid front row: Fabi, 207.395 mph (pole), Mosley, 205.372 mph and Mears, 204.301 mph

1984

27 May 1984. 200 laps of a 2.500 mile-circuit = 500.000 miles

1 Rick Mears	March 84C-Cosworth	200	3h03m21.660
2 Roberto Guerrero	March 84C-Cosworth	198	
3 Al Unser	March 84C-Cosworth	198	
4 Al Holbert	March 84C-Cosworth	198	
5 Michael Andretti	March 84C-Cosworth	198	
6 AJ Foyt Jr	March 84C-Cosworth	198	

Winner's average speed: 163.612 mph. Starting grid front row: Sneva, 210.029 mph (pole), Holmes, 207.977 mph and Mears, 207.847 mph

1985

26 May 1985. 200 laps of a 2.500 mile-circuit = 500.000 miles

1 Danny Sullivan	March 85C-Cosworth	200	3h16m06.069
2 Mario Andretti	Lola T900-Cosworth	200	3h16m08.546
3 Roberto Guerrero	March 85C-Cosworth	200	
4 Al Unser	March 85C-Cosworth	199	
5 Johnny Parsons Jr	March 85C-Cosworth	198	
6 Johnny Rutherford	March 85C-Cosworth	198	

Winner's average speed: 152.982 mph. Starting grid front row: Carter, 212.583 mph (pole), Brayton, 212.354 mph and Rahal, 211.818 mph

1986

31 May 1986. 200 laps of a 2.500 mile-circuit = 500.000 miles

1 Bobby Rahal	March 86C-Cosworth	200	2h55m43.480
2 Kevin Cogan	March 86C-Cosworth	200	2h55m44.921
3 Rick Mears	March 86C-Cosworth	200	
4 Roberto Guerrero	March 86C-Cosworth	200	
5 Al Unser Jr	Lola T86/00-Cosworth	199	
6 Michael Andretti	March 86C-Cosworth	199	

Winner's average speed: 170.722 mph. Starting grid front row: Mears, 216.828 mph (pole), Sullivan, 215.382 mph and Michael Andretti, 214.522 mph

1987

24 May 1987. 200 laps of a 2.500 mile-circuit = 500.000 miles

1 Al Unser	March 86C-Cosworth	200	3h04m59.147
2 Roberto Guerrero	March 87C-Cosworth	200	3h05m03.634
3 Fabrizio Barbazza	March 87C-Cosworth	198	
4 Al Unser Jr	March 87C-Cosworth	196	
5 Gary Bettenhausen	March 86C-Cosworth	195	
6 Dick Simon	Lola T87/00-Cosworth	193	

Winner's average speed: 162.175 mph. Starting grid front row: Mario Andretti, 215.390 mph (pole), Rahal, 213.316 mph and Mears, 211.467 mph

1988

29 May 1988. 200 laps of a 2.500 mile-circuit = 500.000 miles

1 Rick Mears	Penske PC17-Chevrolet	200	3h27m10.204

2 Emerson Fittipaldi	March 88C-Chevrolet	200	3h27m17.280
3 Al Unser	Penske PC17-Chevrolet	199	
4 Michael Andretti	March 88C-Cosworth	199	
5 Bobby Rahal	Lola T88/00-Judd	199	
6 Jim Crawford	Lola T87/00-Buick	198	

Winner's average speed: 144.809 mph. Starting grid front row: Mears, 219.198 mph (pole), Sullivan, 216.214 mph and A Unser sr, 215.270 mph

1989

28 May 1989. 200 laps of a 2.500 mile-circuit = 500.000 miles

1 Emerson Fittipaldi	Penske PC18-Chevrolet	200	2h59m01.040
2 Al Unser Jr	Lola T89/00-Chevrolet	198	accident
3 Raul Boesel	Lola T89/00-Judd	194	
4 Mario Andretti	Lola T89/00-Chevrolet	193	
5 AJ Foyt Jr	Lola T89/00-Cosworth	193	
6 Scott Brayton	Lola T89/00-Buick	193	

Winner's average speed: 167.582 mph. Starting grid front row: Mears, 223.885 mph (pole), Unser sr, 223.471 mph and Fittipaldi, 222.329 mph

1990

27 May 1990. 200 laps of a 2.500 mile-circuit = 500.000 miles

1 Arie Luyendyk	Lola T90/00-Chevrolet	200	2h41m18.248
2 Bobby Rahal	Lola T90/00-Chevrolet	200	2h41m29.282
3 Emerson Fittipaldi	Penske PC19-Chevrolet	200	
4 Al Unser Jr	Lola T90/00-Chevrolet	199	
5 Rick Mears	Penske PC19-Chevrolet	198	
6 AJ Foyt Jr	Lola T90/00-Chevrolet	194	

Winner's average speed: 185.984 mph. Starting grid front row: Fittipaldi, 225.301 mph (pole), Mears, 224.215 mph and Luyendyk, 223.304 mph

1991

26 May 1991. 200 laps of a 2.500 mile-circuit = 500.000 miles

1 Rick Mears	Penske PC20-Chevrolet	200	2h50m00.791
2 Michael Andretti	Lola T91/00-Chevrolet	200	2h50m03.940
3 Arie Luyendyk	Lola T91/00-Chevrolet	199	
4 Al Unser Jr	Lola T91/00-Chevrolet	198	
5 John Andretti	Lola T91/00-Chevrolet	197	
6 Gordon Johncock	Lola T90/00-Cosworth	188	

Winner's average speed: 176.457 mph. Starting grid front row: Mears, 224.113 mph (pole), Foyt, 222.443 mph and Mario Andretti, 221.818 mph. Fastest qualifier: G Bettenhausen, 224.468 mph

1992

24 May 1992. 200 laps of a 2.500 mile-circuit = 500.000 miles

1 Al Unser Jr	Galmer G92-Chevrolet	200	3h43m04.991
2 Scott Goodyear	Lola T92/00-Chevrolet	200	3h43m05.034
3 Al Unser	Lola T92/00-Buick	200	3h43m15.226
4 Eddie Cheever	Lola T92/00-Ford	200	3h43m15.271
5 Danny Sullivan	Galmer G92-Chevrolet	199	
6 Bobby Rahal	Lola T92/00-Chevrolet	199	

Winner's average speed: 134.479 mph. Starting grid front row: Guerrero, 232.482 mph (pole), Cheever, 229.639 mph and Mario Andretti, 229.503 mph - Guerrero did not take the green flag having spun during the parade laps

1993

30 May 1993. 200 laps of a 2.500 mile-circuit = 500.000 miles

1 Emerson Fittipaldi	Penske PC22-Chevrolet	200	3h10m49.860
2 Arie Luyendyk	Lola T93/00-Ford	200	3h10m52.722
3 Nigel Mansell	Lola T93/00-Ford	200	3h10m54.608
4 Raul Boesel	Lola T93/00-Ford	200	3h10m54.977
5 Mario Andretti	Lola T93/00-Ford	200	3h10m55.264

6 Scott Brayton	Lola T93/00-Ford	200	3h10m57.743

Winner's average speed: 157.207 mph. Starting grid front row: Luyendyk, 223.967 mph (pole), Mario Andretti, 223.414 mph and Boesel, 222.379 mph

1994

29 May 1994. 200 laps of a 2.500 mile-circuit = 500.000 miles

1 Al Unser Jr	Penske PC23-Mercedes-Benz	200	3h06m29.006
2 Jacques Villeneuve	Reynard 94I-Ford	200	3h06m37.610
3 Bobby Rahal	Penske PC22-Ilmor	199	
4 Jimmy Vasser	Reynard 94I-Ford	199	
5 Robby Gordon	Lola T94/00-Ford	199	
6 Michael Andretti	Reynard 94I-Ford	198	

Winner's average speed: 160.872 mph. Starting grid front row: Unser Jr, 228.011 mph (pole), Boesel, 227.618 mph and Fittipaldi, 227.303 mph

1995

28 May 1995. 200 laps of a 2.500-mile circuit = 500.000 miles

1 Jacques Villeneuve*	Reynard 95I-Ford	200	3h15m17.561
2 Christian Fittipaldi	Reynard 95I-Ford	200	3h15m20.042
3 Bobby Rahal	Lola T95/00-Mercedes-Benz	200	3h15m20.527
4 Eliseo Salazar	Lola T95/00-Ford	200	3h15m22.329
5 Robby Gordon	Reynard 95I-Ford	200	3h15m32.466
6 Mauricio Gugelmin	Reynard 95I-Ford	200	3h15m34.638

*Includes 2-lap penalty for passing under yellow flag. Winner's average speed: 153.616 mph. Starting grid front row: Brayton, 231.604 mph (pole), Luyendyk, 231.031 mph and Goodyear, 230.759 mph

1996

26 May 1996. 200 laps of a 2.500-mile circuit = 500.000 miles

1 Buddy Lazier	Reynard 95I-Ford	200	3h22m45.753
2 Davy Jones	Lola T95/00-Mercedes-Benz	200	3h22m46.448
3 Richie Hearn	Reynard 95I-Ford	200	
4 Alessandro Zampedri	Reynard 95I-Ford	200	
5 Roberto Guerrero	Reynard 95I-Ford	198	accident
6 Eliseo Salazar	Lola T95/00-Ford	197	accident

Winner's average speed: 147.956 mph. Starting grid front row: Stewart, 233.100 mph (pole), Jones, 232.882 mph and Salazar, 232.684 mph - Brayton had qualified on pole at 233.718 mph but subsequently suffered a fatal accident

1997

26-27 May 1997. 200 laps of a 2.500-mile circuit = 500.000 miles. Race stopped after 15 laps due to rain. Restarted over remaining 185 laps

1 Arie Luyendyk	G-Force GF01-Aurora	200	3h25m43.388
2 Scott Goodyear	G-Force GF01-Aurora	200	3h25m43.958
3 Jeff Ward	G-Force GF01-Aurora	200	
4 Buddy Lazier	Dallara IR7-Aurora	200	
5 Tony Stewart	G-Force GF01-Aurora	200	
6 Davey Hamilton	G-Force GF01-Aurora	199	

Winner's average speed: 145.827 mph. Starting grid front row: Luyendyk, 218.263 mph (pole), Stewart, 218.020 mph and Sospiri, 216.820 mph

1998

24 May 1998. 200 laps of a 2.500-mile circuit = 500.000 miles

1 Eddie Cheever	Dallara IR7-Aurora	200	3h26m40.524
2 Buddy Lazier	Dallara IR7-Aurora	200	3h26m43.715
3 Steve Knapp	G-Force GF01-Aurora	200	
4 Davey Hamilton	G-Force GF01-Aurora	199	
5 Robby Unser	Dallara IR7-Aurora	198	

2000 Juan Pablo Montoya celebrates victory with the traditional milk.

6 Kenny Brack   Dallara IR7-Aurora   198
Winner's average speed: 145.155 mph. Starting grid front row: Boat, 223.503 mph (pole), Ray, 221.120 mph and Brack, 220.980 mph

1999

30 May 1999. 200 laps of a 2.500-mile circuit = 500.000 miles

1	Juan Pablo Montoya			
1	Kenny Brack	Dallara IR7-Aurora	200	3h15m51.182
2	Jeff Ward	Dallara IR7-Aurora	200	3h15m57.744
3	Billy Boat	Dallara IR7-Aurora	200	
4	Robby Gordon	Dallara IR7-Aurora	200	
5	Robby McGehee	Dallara IR7-Aurora	199	
6	Robbie Buhl	Dallara IR7-Aurora	199	

Winner's average speed: 153.176 mph. Starting grid front row: Luyendyk, 225.179mph (pole), Ray, 225.073 mph and Boat, 223.469 mph

2000

28 May 2000. 200 laps of a 2.500-mile circuit = 500.000 miles

1	Juan Pablo Montoya	G-Force GF05-Aurora	200	2h58m59.431
2	Buddy Lazier	Dallara IR0-Aurora	200	2h59m06.615
3	Eliseo Salazar	G-Force GF05-Aurora	200	2h59m15.133
4	Jeff Ward	G-Force GF05-Aurora	200	2h59m17.844
5	Eddie Cheever	Dallara IR0-Infiniti	200	2h59m18.157
6	Robby Gordon	Dallara IR0-Aurora	200	2h59m18.505

Winner's average speed: 167.607 mph. Starting grid front row: Ray, 223.471 mph (pole), Montoya, 223.372 mph and Salazar, 223.231 mph

2001

27 May 2001. 200 laps of a 2.500-mile circuit = 500.000 miles

1	Helio Castro-Neves	Dallara IR0-Aurora	200	3h31m54.180
2	Gil de Ferran	Dallara IR0-Aurora	200	3h31m55.917

3	Michael Andretti	Dallara IR0-Aurora	200	3h31m59.916
4	Jimmy Vasser	G-Force GF05-Aurora	200	3h32m08.165
5	Bruno Junqueira	G-Force GF05-Aurora	200	3h32m21.436
6	Tony Stewart	G-Force GF05-Aurora	200	3h32m31.741

Winner's average speed: 141.574 mph. Starting grid front row: Sharp, 226.037 mph (pole), Ray, 225.194 mph and Gordon, 224.994 mph

2002

26 May 2002. 200 laps of a 2.500-mile circuit = 500.000 miles

1	Helio Castro-Neves	Dallara IR0-Chevrolet	200	3h00m10.871
2	Paul Tracy	Dallara IR0-Chevrolet	200	3h00m10.909
3	Felipe Giaffone	G-Force GF05-Chevrolet	200	3h00m11.000
4	Alex Barron	Dallara IR0-Chevrolet	200	3h00m12.275
5	Eddie Cheever	Dallara IR0-Infiniti	200	3h00m13.326
6	Richie Hearn	Dallara IR0-Chevrolet	200	3h00m14.074

Winner's average speed: 166.499 mph. Starting grid front row: Junqueira, 231.342 mph (pole), Buhl, 231.033 mph and Boesel, 230.613 mph

2002 Helio Castro-Neves took a close second successive victory in 2002.

Clockwise from top left: 2002 The Borg Warner Trophy is among the most sought after in motor racing. **2002** Polewinner Bruno Junqueira leads the field away from the grid for America's greatest race. **1969** Mario Andretti enjoyed his only Indianapolis win.

STARTS

Name	Starts	Name	Starts	Name	Starts
AJ Foyt jr	35	Jim Hurtubise	10	Lyn St James	7
Mario Andretti	29	Buddy Lazier	10	Len Sutton	7
Al Unser	27	Harry McQuinn	10	Ira Vail	7
Gordon Johncock	24	Ralph Mulford	10	Jimmy Vasser	7
Johnny Rutherford	24	Duke Nalon	10	Salt Walther	7
George Snider	22	Ralph de Palma	10	Frank Wearne	7
Gary Bettenhausen	21	Johnnie Parsons	10	Gil Anderson	6
Bobby Unser	19	Kelly Petillo	10	Herb Ardinger	6
Roger McCluskey	18	"Red" Shafer	10	Manuel Ayulo	6
Lloyd Ruby	18	Bud Tingelstad	10	Billy Boat	6
Pancho Carter	17	Louis Tomei	10	Buzz Calkins	6
Arie Luyendyk	17	Henry Banks	9	Wesley Crawford	6
Dick Simon	17	Tom Bigelow	9	Derek Daly	6
Tom Sneva	17	Jimmy Bryan	9	Cliff Durant	6
Cliff Bergere	16	Bill Cummings	9	Jules Ellingboe	6
Chet Miller	16	Fred Frame	9	Pat Flaherty	6
Ralph Hepburn	15	Bobby Grim	9	Paul Goldsmith	6
Eddie Johnson	15	Dan Gurney	9	Stephan Gregoire	6
Jim McElreath	15	Joe Leonard	9	Davey Hamilton	6
Rick Mears	15	Zeke Meyer	9	Bob Harkey	6
Mike Mosley	15	Lou Moore	9	Harry Hartz	6
Mauri Rose	15	Dick Rathmann	9	Howdy Holmes	6
Paul Russo	15	Chuck Stevenson	9	Jimmy Jackson	6
Russell Snowberger	15	Don Branson	8	Jerry Karl	6
Al Unser Jr	15	Bob Christie	8	Al Keller	6
Rodger Ward	15	Earl Cooper	8	Sheldon Kinser	6
Tony Bettenhausen	14	Jim Crawford	8	Dave Lewis	6
Scott Brayton	14	Jimmy Daywalt	8	Al Putnam	6
George Connor	14	Larry Dickson	8	Greg Ray	6
Roberto Guerrero	14	"Leon Duray"	8	Jimmy Reece	6
Tony Gulotta	14	Teo Fabi	8	Eliseo Salazar	6
Jim Rathmann	14	Stan Fox	8	Louis Schneider	6
Wilbur Shaw	14	Don Freeland	8	Jack Turner	6
Michael Andretti	13	Chet Gardner	8	Jeff Ward	6
Raul Boesel	13	Robby Gordon	8	Spider Webb	6
Eddie Cheever	13	Bennett Hill	8	Carl Williams	6
Wally Dallenbach	13	Mel Kenyon	8	Jerry Wonderlich	6
Louis Meyer	13	Jack McGrath	8	Billy Arnold	5
Bobby Rahal	13	Tommy Milton	8	George Bailey	5
Babe Stapp	13	Eddie Sachs	8	Paul Bost	5
Johnny Boyd	12	Scott Sharp	8	Joe Boyer	5
Frank Brisko	12	Johnny Thomson	8	Bob Burman	5
"Shorty" Cantlon	12	Billy de Vore	8	Jim Clark	5
Kevin Cogan	12	Billy Winn	8	Jimmy Davies	5
Sam Hanks	12	Fred Winnai	8	Mark Donohue	5
"Deacon" Litz	12	Tom Alley	7	Ronnie Duman	5
Rex Mays	12	John Andretti	7	Ed Elisian	5
Johnny Parsons Jr	12	George Barringer	7	Walt Faulkner	5
Troy Ruttman	12	Robbie Buhl	7	Dennis Firestone	5
Danny Sullivan	12	Bill Cheesbourg	7	Chip Ganassi	5
Bill Vukovich Jr	12	Joie Chitwood	7	Spike Gehlhausen	5
Fred Agabashian	11	Duke Dinsmore	7	Jimmy Gleason	5
Tony Bettenhausen Jr	11	Mark Dismore	7	Jules Goux	5
Duane Carter	11	Dominic Dobson	7	Michael Groff	5
Emerson Fittipaldi	11	Frank Elliott	7	Albert Guyot	5
Scott Goodyear	11	Dave Evans	7	Ira Hall	5
Eddie Hearne	11	Josele Garza	7	Al Herman	5
Steve Krisiloff	11	Ora Haibe	7	Bill Holland	5
Al Miller	11	Mel Hansen	7	Davy Jones	5
Danny Ongais	11	Parnelli Jones	7	Art Klein	5
Bob Veith	11	Peter Kreis	7	Arnie Knepper	5
Howdy Wilcox	11	Andy Linden	7	Randy Lewis	5
Emil Andres	10	Robert McDonough	7	"Doc" MacKenzie	5
Geoff Brabham	10	Wade Morton	7	John Martin	5
Lora Corum	10	Peter de Paolo	7	Jimmy Murphy	5
Jerry Grant	10	John Paul Jr	7	Pat O'Connor	5
Gene Hartley	10	Sam Sessions	7	Art Pollard	5
Ted Horn	10	Johnny Seymour	7	Peter Revson	5

Records

Eddie Rickenbacher	5	Dempsey Wilson	4	Johnny Sawyer	3
Floyd Roberts	5	Spencer Wishart	4	Bill Schindler	3
Jerry Sneva	5	Cliff Woodbury	4	Sam Schmidt	3
Jimmy Snyder	5	Cale Yarborough	4	Jeret Schroeder	3
Tony Stewart	5	Charles van Acker	3	Vern Schuppan	3
"Stubby" Stubblefield	5	Johnny Aitken	3	Herman Schurch	3
Bob Sweikert	5	Wilbur d'Alene	3	Bob Scott	3
Shorty Templeman	5	Jeff Andretti	3	Bill Sheffler	3
Paul Tracy	5	Tom Bagley	3	Bob Swanson	3
Ernest Triplett	5	Andre Boillot	3	Marshall Teague	3
Johnny Unser	5	Ronnie Bucknum	3	Didier Theys	3
Rich Vogler	5	Bill Cantrell	3	Joe Thomas	3
Bill Vukovich	5	Michael Chandler	3	Johnny Tolan	3
Bill Whittington	5	William Chandler	3	Earl de Vore	3
Don Whittington	5	Steve Chassey	3	Bill Vukovich III	3
Tony Willman	5	Hal Cole	3	Stan Wattles	3
Norman Batten	4	Ray Crawford	3	Lee Roy Yarbrough	3
Donnie Beechler	4	Airton Dare	3	Alessandro Zampedri	3
Jack Brabham	4	Joe Dawson	3	Bobby Allison	2
Kenny Brack	4	Louis Durant	3	Donnie Allison	2
Caleb Bragg	4	Bill Endicott	3	Red Amick	2
Walt Brown	4	Harry Endicott	3	Les Anderson	2
Larry Cannon	4	Frank Farmer	3	Keith Andrews	2
Jimmy Caruthers	4	Gil de Ferran	3	Ernie Ansterberg	2
Jean Chassagne	4	Sarah Fisher	3	Al Aspen	2
Louis Chevrolet	4	George Follmer	3	Eric Bachelart	2
Fred Comer	4	George Fonder	3	Bobby Ball	2
Art Cross	4	Kenneth Fowler	3	Charles Bauman	2
Floyd Davis	4	"Speed" Gardner	3	Pat Bedard	2
Rick Decker	4	Allan Gordon	3	John Boling	2
Lou Disbrow	4	Janet Guthrie	3	David Bruce-Brown	2
Harry Grant	4	Jim Guthrie	3	Harry Butcher	2
Marco Greco	4	Richie Hearn	3	Jack le Cain	2
Cliff Griffith	4	Ludwig Heimrath Jr	3	Ray Campbell	2
Willie Haupt	4	Graham Hill	3	Tyce Carlson	2
Gene Haustein	4	Tommy Hinnershitz	3	Willie Carlson	2
Mack Hellings	4	Jackie Holmes	3	Helio Castro-Neves	2
Mike Hiss	4	Bill Homeier	3	Arthur Chevrolet	2
David Hobbs	4	Sam Hornish Jr	3	Gaston Chevrolet	2
Thane Houser	4	Cliff Hucul	3	Joseph Christiaens	2
Jerry Hoyt	4	Joe Huff	3	Allen Crowe	2
Hughie Hughes	4	John Jenkins	3	Don Davis	2
Denny Hulme	4	Stefan Johansson	3	Bill Denver	2
Chuck Hulse	4	Luther Johnson	3	Paul Durant	2
William Knipper	4	Jimmy Kite	3	Bob Evans	2
Lee Kunzman	4	Steve Knapp	3	"Dusty" Fahrnow	2
John Mahler	4	Fred Lecklider	3	Adrian Fernandez	2
Jim Malloy	4	Mike Magill	3	Chet Fillip	2
Bobby Marshman	4	Johnny Mantz	3	Myron Fohr	2
Hideshi Matsuda	4	Cy Marshall	3	Gene Force	2
Hiro Matsushita	4	Robby McGehee	3	Billy Foster	2
Johnny McDowell	4	Dr Jack Miller	3	Frank Fox	2
Charles Merz	4	Rocky Moran	3	Malcolm Fox	2
Al Miller	4	Rick Muther	3	Lee Frayer	2
Tero Palmroth	4	Mike Nazaruk	3	Roland Free	2
Scott Pruett	4	Cal Niday	3	Billy Garrett	2
George Robson	4	Eddie O'Donnell	3	Juan Gaudino	2
Joe Russo	4	Ed Pimm	3	Elmer George	2
Roscoe Sarles	4	Bill Puterbaugh	3	Felipe Giaffone	2
William Shattuc	4	Cornelius van Ranst	3	Cecil Green	2
Teddy Tetzlaff	4	Eldon Rasmussen	3	Mauricio Gugelmin	2
Rene Thomas	4	Dario Resta	3	Norman Hall	2
Joel Thorne	4	Raoul Riganti	3	Pete Halsmer	2
Lee Wallard	4	Hal Robson	3	Walt Hansgen	2
Chuck Weyant	4	"Ebb" Rose	3	Fred Harder	2
Doc Williams	4	Eddie Russo	3	Douglas Hawkes	2

Indianapolis 500

STARTS (cont.)

Pete Henderson	2	Dennis Vitolo	2	Jack Curtner	1
Don Herr	2	Bruce Walkup	2	Bertrand de Cystria	1
Bryan Herta	2	Bentley Warren	2	Dany Day	1
Ronnie Householder	2	Wayne Weiler	2	Ernest Delaney	1
Ray Howard	2	Lou Wilson	2	Bert Dingley	1
George Howie	2	Len Zengel	2	Rene Dreyfus	1
Joe James	2	Denny Zimmerman	2	John Duff	1
Bobby Johns	2	George Abell	1	Len Duncan	1
Herm Johnson	2	Bert Adams	1	Arthur Duray	1
Bernard Jourdain	2	Walt Ader	1	Don Edmunds	1
Bruno Junqueira	2	George Ainslee	1	Ernest Eldridge	1
Ray Keech	2	Bill Albertson	1	Fred Ellis	1
Danny Kladis	2	Michele Alboreto	1	Billy Engelhart	1
Chris Kneifel	2	Leslie Allen	1	Wim Eyckmans	1
Harry Knight	2	Martin de Alsaga	1	Milt Fankhouse	1
Henry Kohlert	2	Bill Alsup	1	WH Farr	1
Johnny Kreiger	2	George Amick	1	Harlan Fengler	1
Phil Krueger	2	Frank Armi	1	Dick Ferguson	1
Jud Larson	2	Charles Arnold	1	George Fernic	1
Jaques Lazier	2	Chuck Arnold	1	Ira Fetterman	1
Bayliss Levrett	2	Alberto Ascari	1	Christian Fittipaldi	1
Billy Liesaw	2	Sonny Ates	1	Louis Fontaine	1
Frank Lockhart	2	George C Babcock	1	Carl Forberg	1
Al Loquasto	2	Paul Bablot	1	Percy Ford	1
Art Malone	2	"Cannonball" Baker	1	Roscoe Ford	1
Nigel Mansell	2	Salvatore Barbarino	1	Aldo Franchi	1
Mel Marquette	2	Fabrizio Barbazza	1	Dario Franchitti	1
"Ernie McCoy"	2	Alex Barron	1	Howard Frey	1
Larry McCoy Jr	2	Charles Basle	1	Ernest Friderich	1
Jim McWithey	2	Ralph Beardsley	1	Philippe Gache	1
Roger Mears	2	Rene le Begue	1	Racin Gardner	1
Roberto Moreno	2	Fred Belcher	1	Affonso Giaffone	1
Alfred Moss	2	CW Belt	1	Ray Gilhooley	1
Antoine Mourre	2	Charles Bigelow	1	Tom Gloy	1
Steve Nemish	2	Mark Billman	1	Harry Goetz	1
Barney Oldfield	2	Art Bisch	1	Frank Goode	1
Lee Oldfield	2	Georges Boillot	1	Joe Gosek	1
Jan Opperman	2	Joseph Bonedeo	1	Masten Gregory	1
Jimmy Patterson	2	Brian Bonner	1	Arthur Greiner	1
Jack Petticord	2	Pietro Bordino	1	Robbie Groff	1
Jean Porporato	2	Baconin Borzacchini	1	Carlos Guerrero	1
Eddie Pullen	2	Claude Bourbonnais	1	Dean Hall	1
Bill Rader	2	Riley Brett	1	Howard Hall	1
Willy T Ribbs	2	SF Brock	1	Scott Harrington	1
Larry Rice	2	WW Brown	1	Ray Harroun	1
Tim Richmond	2	Eddie Burbach	1	Shigeaki Hattori	1
Jochen Rindt	2	Claude Burton	1	Hurley Haywood	1
Red Roberts	2	Jack Buxton	1	Jon Herb	1
"Chuck Rodee"	2	Joe Caccia	1	Jack Hewitt	1
Billy Roe	2	Bob Carey	1	Denny Hickey	1
Sam Ross	2	Ray Cariens	1	Jim Hickman	1
Jimmy Rossi	2	Ted Chamberlain	1	George Hill	1
Joe Saldana	2	Louis Chiron	1	Jim Hill	1
Bryan Saulpaugh	2	George Clark	1	Andy Hillenburg	1
Swede Savage	2	Fred Clemons	1	Kurt Hitke	1
Carl Scarborough	2	Harry Cobe	1	Sam Hoffman	1
Benny Shoaff	2	Louis le Cocq	1	Al Holbert	1
Gordon Smiley	2	Jim Coffey	1	John Hollansworth Jr	1
George Souders	2	Gary Congdon	1	Ralph Holmes	1
William Spence	2	Joe Cooper	1	Joe Horan	1
Jackie Stewart	2	Al Cotey	1	Norm Houser	1
Phil Threshie	2	GC Cox	1	Glenn Howard	1
Jack Tower	2	Charles Crawford	1	Bill Hunt	1
Robby Unser	2	Larry Crockett	1	Harris Insinger	1
Fermin Velez	2	Letterio Cucinotta	1	Joe Jagersberger	1
Jacques Villeneuve	2	Terry Curley	1	Rupert Jeffkins	1

Records

Art Johnson	1	Don Orstrander	1	Louis Wagner	1
Ben Jones	1	John de Palma	1	Clay Weatherly	1
Bubby Jones	1	Sam Palmer	1	Louie Webb	1
Herbert Jones	1	Massimiliano Papis	1	Greg Weld	1
John Jones	1	Phil Pardee	1	Bob Wente	1
MC Jones	1	Edward Parker	1	Christian Werner	1
Walter Jones	1	Cyrus Patschke	1	Neil Whalen	1
Will Jones	1	"Bunny" Phillips	1	Johnny White	1
Michel Jourdain Jr	1	Theodore Pilette	1	Dale Whittington	1
Tony Kanaan	1	Nelson Piquet	1	Jimmy Wilburn	1
Bert Karnatz	1	Ray Pixley	1	Howdy Wilcox II	1
Charles Keene	1	Sam Posey	1	George Wingerter	1
Mel Keneally	1	Ted Prappas	1	Cory Witherill	1
IJ Kilpatrick	1	Willard Prentiss	1	JJ Yeley	1
Steve Kinser	1	Francis Quinn	1	Louis Zborowski	1
Charles Kirkpatrick	1	"Noel van Raalte"	1	Paolo Zuccarelli	1
Tom Klausler	1	Roger Rager	1		
Barney Kloepfer	1	E Rawlings	1		
Dave Koetzla	1	Elmer Ray	1		
Randy Lanier	1	Hector Rebaque	1		
Christian Lautenschlager	1	Laurent Redon	1		
Bob Lazier	1	Clay Regazzoni	1		
Greg Leffler	1	Andre Ribeiro	1		
Jason Leffler	1	Jim Rigsby	1		
Bill Lindau	1	CL Rogers	1		
George Lynch	1	Pete Romsevich	1		
Herb Lytle	1	Tom Rooney	1		
Dave MacDonald	1	Mick Rupp	1		
"Bon" MacDougall	1	Karl Sailer	1		
Jeff MacPherson	1	Max Sailer	1		
George Mack	1	"Mike Salay"	1		
"Bill Mackey"	1	Bob Sall	1		
Ed Madden	1	Everett Saylor	1		
John Mais	1	Tomas Scheckter	1		
Carl Marchese	1	Gus Schrader	1		
George Mason	1	Glenn Schultz	1		
Bob Mathouser	1	Louis Schwitzer	1		
Joe Matson	1	Bill Scott	1		
Johnny Mauro	1	Johnny Shackelford	1		
Jack McCarver	1	Elmer Shannon	1		
JJ McCoy	1	Harold Shaw	1		
JC McDonald	1	AJ Shepherd	1		
Frank McGurk	1	EH Sherwood	1		
Herschell McKee	1	Bill Simpson	1		
Graham McRae	1	Ted Simpson	1		
Al Melcher	1	Vincenzo Sospiri	1		
Ned Meyers	1	Lester Spangler	1		
Andy Michner	1	Myron Stevens	1		
Eddie Miller	1	Louis Strang	1		
Nicolas Minassian	1	Harry Thicksten	1		
Juan Pablo Montoya	1	Arthur Thurman	1		
Charles Moran	1	Brian Till	1		
Jules Moriceau	1	Omar Toft	1		
Brad Murphey	1	Rick Treadway	1		
Dave Murphy	1	Marion Trexler	1		
Harry Nichols	1	Vincenzo Trucco	1		
Joe Nikrent	1	Jack Turner	1		
Johnny O'Connell	1	Jerry Unser	1		
Bobby Olivero	1	Jules de Vigne	1		
Homer Ormsby	1	Jacques Villeneuve	1		
Len Ormsby	1	Luigi Villoresi	1		
Tom Orr	1	Pierre de Vizcaya	1		

WINS

AJ Foyt Jr	4	Jimmy Bryan	1	Jimmy Murphy	1
Rick Mears	4	Eddie Cheever	1	Ralph de Palma	1
Al Unser	4	Gaston Chevrolet	1	Peter de Paolo	1
Louis Meyer	3	Jim Clark	1	Johnnie Parsons	1
Mauri Rose	3	Lora Corum	1	Cyrus Patschke	1
Johnny Rutherford	3	Bill Cummings	1	Kelly Petillo	1
Wilbur Shaw	3	Floyd Davis	1	Bobby Rahal	1
Bobby Unser	3	Joe Dawson	1	Jim Rathmann	1
Helio Castro-Neves	2	Mark Donohue	1	Dario Resta	1
Emerson Fittipaldi	2	Pat Flaherty	1	Floyd Roberts	1
Gordon Johncock	2	Fred Frame	1	George Robson	1
Arie Luyendyk	2	Jules Goux	1	Troy Ruttman	1
Tommy Milton	2	Sam Hanks	1	Louis Schneider	1
Al Unser Jr	2	Ray Harroun	1	Tom Sneva	1
Bill Vukovich	2	Don Herr	1	George Souders	1
Rodger Ward	2	Graham Hill	1	Danny Sullivan	1
Howdy Wilcox	2	Bill Holland	1	Bob Sweikert	1
Mario Andretti	1	Parnelli Jones	1	Rene Thomas	1
Billy Arnold	1	Ray Keech	1	Jacques Villeneuve	1
Norman Batten	1	Buddy Lazier	1	Lee Wallard	1
Joe Boyer	1	Frank Lockhart	1		
Kenny Brack	1	Juan Pablo Montoya	1		

POLE POSITIONS

Rick Mears	6	Cliff Bergere	1	Pat O'Connor	1
AJ Foyt Jr	4	Billy Boat	1	Kelly Petillo	1
Rex Mays	4	Caleb Bragg	1	Dick Rathmann	1
Mario Andretti	3	Pancho Carter	1	Greg Ray	1
Arie Luyendyk	3	Jean Chassagne	1	Peter Revson	1
Johnny Rutherford	3	Jim Clark	1	Floyd Roberts	1
Tom Sneva	3	Earl Cooper	1	Mauri Rose	1
Scott Brayton	2	Teo Fabi	1	Scott Sharp	1
Bill Cummings	2	Walt Faulkner	1	Russell Snowberger	1
"Leon Duray"	2	Emerson Fittipaldi	1	Jimmy Snyder	1
Parnelli Jones	2	Pat Flaherty	1	Louis Strang	1
Jimmy Murphy	2	Roberto Guerrero	1	Rene Thomas	1
Duke Nalon	2	Ted Horn	1	Johnny Thomson	1
Ralph de Palma	2	Jerry Hoyt	1	Al Unser	1
Eddie Sachs	2	Bruno Junqueira	1	Al Unser Jr	1
Bobby Unser	2	Joe Leonard	1	Bill Vukovich	1
Fred Agabashian	1	Frank Lockhart	1	Howdy Wilcox	1
Johnny Aitken	1	Jack McGrath	1	Cliff Woodbury	1
Gil Anderson	1	Tommy Milton	1		
Billy Arnold	1	Lou Moore	1		

OTHER RECORDS

Youngest winner: 22 years 81 days, Troy Ruttman, 1952
Oldest winner: 47 years 360 days, Al Unser Sr, 1987
Most laps led in a race: 198 laps, Billy Arnold, 1930
Least laps led by the winning driver: 2 laps, Joe Dawson, 1912
Most laps in the lead in total: 644 laps, Al Unser Sr
Most lead changes in a race: 29, 1960
Consecutive wins: 2, Wilbur Shaw, 1939-40; Mauri Rose, 1947-48; Bill Vukovich, 1953-54; Al Unser, 1970-71, Helio Castro-Neves, 2001-02
Narrowest race-winner margin: 0.038s, Helio Castro-Neves, 2002
Widest race-winning margin: 13m08.0, Jules Goux, 1913
Fastest race: 185.981 mph, Arie Luyendyk, 1990
Slowest race: 74.602 mph, Ray Harroun/Cyrus Patschke, 1911

Rookies to have won the race: Ray Harroun, 1911; Cyrus Patschke (relief), 1911; Don Herr (relief), 1912; Jules Goux, 1913; Rene Thomas, 1914; Norman Batten (relief), 1925; Frank Lockhart, 1926; George Souders, 1927; Graham Hill, 1966; Juan Pablo Montoya, 2000 and Helio Castro-Neves, 2001
Wins from pole position: Jimmy Murphy, 1922; Tommy Milton, 1923; Billy Arnold, 1930; Floyd Roberts, 1938; Bill Vukovich, 1953; Pat Flaherty, 1956; Parnelli Jones, 1963; Al Unser, 1970; Johnny Rutherford, 1976; Rick Mears, 1979; Johnny Rutherford, 1980; Bobby Unser, 1981; Rick Mears, 1988; Rick Mears, 1991; Al Unser Jr, 1994; Arie Luyendyk, 1997

North American Indycar Championships

1990 Al Unser jr leads Michael Andretti, Bobby Rahal, Emerson Fittipaldi and Teo Fabi at Laguna Seca.

North American Indycar and Champcar Championships

The Indycar Championship was the first international racing series in the world, and for most of the century it was North America's leading competition. However, the 1996 split between championship organisers CART (Championship Auto Racing Teams) and its traditional centrepiece race the Indianapolis 500 has ended the millennium with two championships and open-wheel racing in North America weakened. Legal disputes also forced the CART series to be known as Champcars as its rival denied any reference to Indy.

The American Automobile Association (AAA) inaugurated a championship in 1916 and a series has been contested every year since except when suspended due to world wars. Italian Dario Resta was crowned inaugural champion, the only non-American to win the series before CART became the sanctioning body in 1979.

The Indianapolis 500 has always taken centre stage during the month of May with qualification, practice and race taking the whole month. During the fifties and sixties the championships also encompassed a hillclimb (Pikes Peak), road courses and short ovals (both paved and on dirt) making it the most versatile of competitions.

The United States Auto Club (USAC) replaced the AAA as the governing body in 1956, a period in which front-engined Offenhauser roadsters dominated. However, a British invasion of new cars with engines behind the driver began in the early-sixties and culminated Indianapolis 500 victories for Jim Clark's Lotus and Graham Hill's Lola in 1965 and '66 respectively.

The European influence continued into the seventies as McLaren joined Lola in the series. However, in 1979 the teams, disenchanted with USAC's organisation, formed their own series under the CART banner. USAC tried to run a series also that year, but it was an uncompetitive affair and from 1980 CART ran the undisputed championship.

USAC, who still organised the Indy 500, shattered an uneasy peace in the mid-nineties when they announced a breakaway oval-only series, the Indy Racing League. Although generally less competitive than CART in its first five years, the IRL has gradually gained in strength with the Indianapolis month of May still a highlight of American motorsport. As the top echelons of North American open wheel racing remain at war NASCAR continues to grow at their expense.

Rules

1911-12	9800cc maximum engine capacity
1913-14	7400cc maximum engine capacity
1915-19	4900cc maximum engine capacity
1920-22	3000cc maximum engine capacity
1923-25	2000cc maximum engine capacity
1926-29	1500cc maximum engine capacity

1965 The Lotus-Ford of seven-time USAC Champion AJ Foyt Jr at Indianapolis. He has also won a record 67 Indycar races.

1930-33	6000cc supercharged production engines
1934	6000cc supercharged production engines. 45-gallon maximum fuel limit
1935	6000cc supercharged production engines. 42.5-gallon maximum fuel limit
1936	No maximum engine capacity. 37.5-gallon maximum fuel limit
1937	As 1936, commercial pump fuel compulsory
1938-56	4500cc normally aspirated and 3000cc supercharged maximum engine capacity
1957-68	4200cc normally aspirated and 2800cc supercharged maximum engine capacity
1969-70	4200cc normally aspirated, 2650cc turbocharged and 5000cc stockblock rocker arm normally aspirated maximum engine capacity
1971	4200cc normally aspirated, 2650cc turbocharged and 5878cc stockblock normally aspirated maximum engine capacity
1972-79 (USAC)	4500cc normally aspirated, 2650cc turbocharged and 5878cc stockblock normally aspirated maximum engine capacity

CART

1979 to date	2650cc turbocharged, 3430cc stockblock supercharged maximum engine capacity. Stockblock engines phased out

IRL

1995-96	2650cc turbocharged maximum engine capacity
1997 to date	Production-based 3500cc normally aspirated maximum engine capacity

NOTE: From 1979 until the implementation of full Indy Racing League rules in 1997 the maximum manifold intake pressure restrictions differed between the Indianapolis 500 and the other championship races favouring stockblock engines at Indy.

ALL TIME "INDYCAR" WINS (Including Indianapolis 500, CART, IRL and all Indycar championship races)

	overall	Indy 500	AAA/USAC	CART	IRL
AJ Foyt jr	67	4	67*	-	-
Mario Andretti	52	1	33	19	-
Michael Andretti	42	-	-	42	-
Al Unser	39	4	35	4	-
Bobby Unser	35	3	25*	10	-
Al Unser Jr	33	2	-	31	2
Rick Mears	29	4	3	26	-
Johnny Rutherford	27	3	17	10	-
Rodger Ward	26	2	26	-	-
Gordon Johncock	25	2	20*	5	-
Ralph de Palma	24	1	24	-	-
Bobby Rahal	24	1	-	24	-
Tommy Milton	23	2	23	-	-
Tony Bettenhausen	22	-	22	-	-
Emerson Fittipaldi	22	2	-	22	-
Earl Cooper	21	-	21	-	-
Jimmy Bryan	19	1	19	-	-
Jimmy Murphy	19	1	19	-	-
Paul Tracy	19	-	-	19	-
Ralph Mulford	17	-	17	-	-
Danny Sullivan	17	1	-	17	-
Alessandro Zanardi	15	-	-	15	-
Tom Sneva	13	1	3	10	-
Eddie Hearne	11	-	11	-	-
Cristiano da Matta	11	-	-	11	-
Juan Pablo Montoya	11	1	-	10	1
Johnnie Parsons	11	1	11	-	-
Louis Chevrolet	10	-	10	-	-
Dario Franchitti	10	-	-	10	-
Frank Lockhart	10	1	10	-	-
Peter de Paolo	10	1	10	-	-
Dario Resta	10	1	10	-	-
Jimmy Vasser	10	-	-	10	-
Kenny Brack	9	1	-	5	4
Helio Castro-Neves	9	2	-	6	3
Gil de Ferran	9	-	-	7	2
Sam Hornish Jr	8	-	-	-	8
Buddy Lazier	8	1	-	-	8
Rex Mays	8	-	8	-	-
Louis Meyer	8	3	8	-	-
Eddie Sachs	8	-	8	-	-
Wilbur Shaw	8	3	8	-	-
Johnny Aitken	7	-	7	-	-
Adrian Fernandez	7	-	-	7	-
Dan Gurney	7	-	7	-	-
Harry Hartz	7	-	7	-	-
Arie Luyendyk	7	2	-	3	4
Eddie Rickenbacher	7	-	7	-	-
Lloyd Ruby	7	-	7	-	-
Scott Sharp	7	-	-	-	7
Johnny Thomson	7	-	7	-	-
Don Branson	6	-	6	-	-
Bob Burman	6	-	6	-	-
Bill Cummings	6	1	6	-	-
Bennett Hill	6	-	6	-	-
Parnelli Jones	6	1	6	-	-
Joe Leonard	6	-	6	-	-
Danny Ongais	6	-	6	-	-
Mauri Rose	6	3	6	-	-
Roscoe Sarles	6	-	6	-	-
Eddie Cheever	5	1	-	-	5
Wally Dallenbach	5	-	5	-	-
Frank Elliott	5	-	5	-	-
Teo Fabi	5	-	-	5	-
Scott Goodyear	5	-	-	2	3
Ted Horn	5	-	5	-	-
Jud Larson	5	-	5	-	-

	overall	Indy 500	AAA/USAC	CART	IRL
Dave Lewis	5	-	5	-	-
Nigel Mansell	5	-	-	5	-
Roger McCluskey	5	-	5	-	-
Jim McElreath	5	-	5	-	-
Greg Moore	5	-	-	5	-
Mike Mosley	5	-	4	1	-
Eddie Pullen	5	-	5	-	-
Greg Ray	5	-	-	-	5
Jacques Villeneuve Jr	5	1	-	5	-
Gary Bettenhausen	4	-	4	-	-
"Shorty" Cantlon	4	-	4	-	-
Gaston Chevrolet	4	1	4	-	-
Lou Disbrow	4	-	4	-	-
"Leon Duray"	4	-	4	-	-
Myron Fohr	4	-	4	-	-
Sam Hanks	4	1	4	-	-
Ray Harroun	4	1	4	-	-
Hughie Hughes	4	-	4	-	-
Jim Hurtubise	4	-	4	-	-
Ray Keech	4	1	4	-	-
Jack McGrath	4	-	4	-	-
Kelly Petillo	4	1	4	-	-
Al Rogers	4	-	4	-	-
Chuck Stevenson	4	-	4	-	-
Bob Sweikert	4	1	4	-	-
Bill Vukovich	4	2	4	-	-
Howdy Wilcox	4	2	4	-	-
Bill Winn	4	-	4	-	-
George Amick	3	-	3	-	-
Gil Anderson	3	-	3	-	-
Billy Arnold	3	1	3	-	-
Mark Blundell	3	-	-	3	-
Joe Boyer	3	1	3	-	-
Patrick Carpentier	3	-	-	3	-
Jimmy Davies	3	-	3	-	-
Bert Dingley	3	-	3	-	-
Mark Donohue	3	1	3	-	-
Cliff Durant	3	-	3	-	-
Bill Endicott	3	-	3	-	-
Walt Faulkner	3	-	3	-	-
Pat Flaherty	3	1	3	-	-
Bill Holland	3	1	3	-	-
Bruno Junqueira	3	-	-	3	-
Charles Merz	3	-	3	-	-
Eddie O'Donnell	3	-	3	-	-
Massimiliano Papis	3	-	-	3	-
Jim Rathmann	3	1	3	-	-
Andre Ribeiro	3	-	-	3	-
Tony Stewart	3	-	-	-	3
Len Sutton	3	-	3	-	-
Teddy Tetzlaff	3	-	3	-	-
Tom Alley	2	-	2	-	-
Manuel Ayulo	2	-	2	-	-
Norman Batten	2	1	2	-	-
Pietro Bordino	2	-	2	-	-
Robbie Buhl	2	-	-	-	2
Bob Carey	2	-	2	-	-
Jim Clark	2	1	2	-	-
Joe Dawson	2	1	2	-	-
Harlan Fengler	2	-	2	-	-
Ira Fetterman	2	-	2	-	-

*including 1981 Indianapolis and Pocono 500 and the 1982 Indianapolis 500 which were organised by USAC and did not count towards the championship

North American Indycar Championships

	overall	Indy 500	AAA/USAC	CART	IRL
Christian Fittipaldi	2	-	-	2	-
Robby Gordon	2	-	-	2	-
Harry Grant	2	-	2	-	-
Roberto Guerrero	2	-	-	2	-
Mel Hansen	2	-	2	-	-
Don Herr	2	1	2	-	-
Harvey Herrick	2	-	2	-	-
Bryan Herta	2	-	-	2	-
Tom Kincaid	2	-	2	-	-
Robert McDonough	2	-	2	-	-
Lou Moore	2	-	2	-	-
Roberto Moreno	2	-	-	2	-
Pat O'Connor	2	-	2	-	-
Barney Oldfield	2	-	2	-	-
John Paul Jr	2	-	-	1	1
Art Pollard	2	-	2	-	-
Scott Pruett	2	-	-	2	-
George Robertson	2	-	2	-	-
Paul Russo	2	-	2	-	-
Troy Ruttman	2	1	2	-	-
Babe Stapp	2	-	2	-	-
Joe Thomas	2	-	2	-	-
Louis Unser	2	-	2	-	-
Lee Wallard	2	1	2	-	-
Cliff Woodbury	2	-	2	-	-
Charles van Acker	1	-	1	-	-
Walt Ader	1	-	1	-	-
Fred Agabashian	1	-	1	-	-
Emil Andres	1	-	1	-	-
John Andretti	1	-	-	1	-
Keith Andrews	1	-	1	-	-
Charles Arnold	1	-	1	-	-
Dick Atkins	1	-	1	-	-
Bobby Ball	1	-	1	-	-
Henry Banks	1	-	1	-	-
Alex Barron	1	-	-	-	1
Erwin Bergdoll	1	-	1	-	-
Charles Bigelow	1	-	1	-	-
Art Bisch	1	-	1	-	-
Billy Boat	1	-	-	-	1
Walt Brown	1	-	1	-	-
David Bruce-Brown	1	-	1	-	-
Ronnie Bucknum	1	-	1	-	-
Dave Buick	1	-	1	-	-
Buzz Calkins	1	-	-	-	1
Willie Carlson	1	-	1	-	-
Pancho Carter	1	-	-	1	-
Kevin Cogan	1	-	-	1	-
Fred Comer	1	-	1	-	-
George Connor	1	-	1	-	-
Lora Corum	1	1	1	-	-
Howard Covey	1	-	1	-	-
Airton Dare	1	-	-	-	1
Floyd Davis	1	1	1	-	-
Duke Dinsmore	1	-	1	-	-
Mark Dismore	1	-	-	-	1
Scott Dixon	1	-	-	1	-
Mario Dominguez	1	-	-	1	-
WE Ferguson	1	-	1	-	-
Bob Finney	1	-	1	-	-
Jack Fleming	1	-	1	-	-
George Follmer	1	-	1	-	-
Fred Frame	1	1	1	-	-
Frank Gelnaw	1	-	1	-	-
Elmer George	1	-	1	-	-
Felipe Giaffone	1	-	-	-	1
Jimmy Gleason	1	-	1	-	-
Jules Goux	1	1	1	-	-
Bobby Grim	1	-	1	-	-
Mauricio Gugelmin	1	-	-	1	-
Jim Guthrie	1	-	-	-	1
George Hammond	1	-	1	-	-
Harris Hanshue	1	-	1	-	-
Richie Hearn	1	-	-	-	1
Pete Henderson	1	-	1	-	-
George Hill	1	-	1	-	-
Graham Hill	1	1	1	-	-
John Jenkins	1	-	1	-	-
George Joermann	1	-	1	-	-
Van Johnson	1	-	1	-	-
Tony Kanaan	1	-	-	1	-
Bruce Keene	1	-	1	-	-
Art Klein	1	-	1	-	-
William Knipper	1	-	1	-	-
Jaques Lazier	1	-	-	-	1
Frank Lescault	1	-	1	-	-
Al Livingstone	1	-	1	-	-
Leigh Lynch	1	-	1	-	-
Herb Lytle	1	-	1	-	-
Johnny Mantz	1	-	1	-	-
Bobby Marshman	1	-	1	-	-
Joe Matson	1	-	1	-	-
Eaton McMillian	1	-	1	-	-
Mike Nazaruk	1	-	1	-	-
Joe Nikrent	1	-	1	-	-
Louis Nikrent	1	-	1	-	-
Tazio Nuvolari	1	-	1	-	-
Jim Packard	1	-	1	-	-
Cyrus Patschke	1	1	1	-	-
Hector Rebaque	1	-	-	1	-
Peter Revson	1	-	1	-	-
Floyd Roberts	1	1	1	-	-
Mortimer Roberts	1	-	1	-	-
George Robson	1	1	1	-	-
Bernd Rosemeyer	1	-	1	-	-
Grover Ruckstell	1	-	1	-	-
Eliseo Salazar	1	-	-	-	1
Swede Savage	1	-	1	-	-
Tomas Scheckter	1	-	-	-	1
Bill Schindler	1	-	1	-	-
Sam Schmidt	1	-	-	-	1
Louis Schneider	1	1	1	-	-
Arthur See	1	-	1	-	-
"Red" Shafer	1	-	1	-	-
William Sharp	1	-	1	-	-
Jimmy Snyder	1	-	1	-	-
George Souders	1	1	1	-	-
Louis Strang	1	-	1	-	-
"Stubby" Stubblefield	1	-	1	-	-
William Taylor	1	-	1	-	-
Rene Thomas	1	1	1	-	-
Bud Tingelstad	1	-	1	-	-
Ira Vail	1	-	1	-	-
Wes Vandervoort	1	-	1	-	-
Jacques Villeneuve sr	1	-	-	1	-
Earl de Vore	1	-	1	-	-
Bill Vukovich Jr	1	-	1	-	-
Jeff Ward	1	-	-	-	1
Spencer Wishart	1	-	1	-	-
Len Zengel	1	-	1	-	-

INDYCAR CHAMPIONS

AAA National Champions

year	driver	nat	car
1916	Dario Resta	I	Peugeot
1920	Gaston Chevrolet	USA	Frontenac
1921	Tommy Milton	USA	Durant-Duesenberg/Frontenac/Durant-Miller
1922	Jimmy Murphy	USA	Duesenberg-Miller
1923	Eddie Hearne	USA	Miller
1924	Jimmy Murphy	USA	Miller
1925	Peter de Paolo	USA	Duesenberg
1926	Harry Hartz	USA	Miller
1927	Peter de Paolo	USA	Miller
1928	Louis Meyer	USA	Miller
1929	Louis Meyer	USA	Miller
1930	Billy Arnold	USA	Summers-Miller
1931	Louis Schneider	USA	Stevens-Miller
1932	Bob Carey	USA	Stevens-Miller
1933	Louis Meyer	USA	Miller
1934	Bill Cummings	USA	Miller
1935	Kelly Petillo	USA	Wetteroth-Offenhauser
1936	Mauri Rose	USA	Miller-Offenhauser
1937	Wilbur Shaw	USA	Shaw/Stevens-Offenhauser
1938	Floyd Roberts	USA	Wetteroth-Offenhauser
1939	Wilbur Shaw	USA	Maserati
1940	Rex Mays	USA	Stevens-Winfield
1941	Rex Mays	USA	Stevens-Winfield
1946	Ted Horn	USA	Horn-Offenhauser/Maserati
1947	Ted Horn	USA	Horn-Offenhauser/Maserati
1948	Ted Horn	USA	Horn-Offenhauser/Maserati
1949	Johnnie Parsons	USA	Kurtis-Offenhauser
1950	Henry Banks	USA	Maserati-Offenhauser/Moore-Offenhauser
1951	Tony Bettenhausen	USA	Deidt-Offenhauser/Kurtis-Offenhauser
1952	Chuck Stevenson	USA	Kurtis KK4000-Offenhauser
1953	Sam Hanks	USA	Kurtis KK4000-Offenhauser
1954	Jimmy Bryan	USA	Kuzma-Offenhauser
1955	Bob Sweikert	USA	Kurtis KK500D-Offenhauser/Watson-Offenhauser

USAC National Championship

year	driver	nat	team	car
1956	Jimmy Bryan	USA	Dean Van Lines	Kuzma-Offenhauser
1957	Jimmy Bryan	USA	Dean Van Lines	Kuzma-Offenhauser
1958	Tony Bettenhausen	USA	John Zink jr*	Epperly-Offenhauser/Kurtis KK4000-Offenhauser/Watson-Offenhauser
1959	Rodger Ward	USA	Leader Cards	Watson-Offenhauser
1960	AJ Foyt Jr	USA	Bowes Seal Fast	Meskowski-Offenhauser
1961	AJ Foyt Jr	USA	Bowes Seal Fast	Watson/Trevis-Offenhauser/Meskowski-Offenhauser
1962	Rodger Ward	USA	Leader Cards	Watson-Offenhauser
1963	AJ Foyt Jr	USA	Sheraton-Thompson	Meskowski-Offenhauser/Watson/Trevis-Offenhauser
1964	AJ Foyt Jr	USA	Sheraton-Thompson	Watson-Offenhauser/Meskowski-Offenhauser
1965	Mario Andretti	USA	Dean Racing Enterprises	Hawk-Ford/Kuzma-Offenhauser
1966	Mario Andretti	USA	Dean Racing Enterprises	Hawk-Ford/Kuzma-Offenhauser
1967	AJ Foyt Jr	USA	Sheraton-Thompson	Coyote-Ford/Meskowski-Offenhauser
1968	Bobby Unser	USA	Leader Cards	Eagle 68-Ford/Eagle 68-Offenhauser/Unser-Chevrolet
1969	Mario Andretti	USA	STP Granatelli	Hawk-Ford/Kuzma-Offenhauser
1970	Al Unser	USA	Vel's Parnelli Jones	Colt/Lola 70-Ford/King-Ford
1971	Joe Leonard	USA	Vel's Parnelli Jones	Colt 71-Ford
1972	Joe Leonard	USA	Vel's Parnelli Jones	Parnelli-Offenhauser
1973	Roger McCluskey	USA	Lindsey Hopkins	McLaren M16B-Offenhauser
1974	Bobby Unser	USA	All-American Racers	Eagle 74-Offenhauser
1975	AJ Foyt Jr	USA	Gilmore-Foyt Racing	Coyote-Ford
1976	Gordon Johncock	USA	Patrick Racing	Wildcat-Offenhauser
1977	Tom Sneva	USA	Penske Racing	McLaren M24-Cosworth
1978	Tom Sneva	USA	Penske Racing	Penske PC6-Cosworth
1979	AJ Foyt Jr	USA	Gilmore-Foyt Racing	Parnelli VPJ6C-Cosworth/Coyote-Ford

*also drown for Jones & Maley and Hardwood Special

INDYCAR CHAMPIONS (cont.)

NOTE: In 1926-27 the Secretary of the AAA Contest Board Val Haresnape retrospectively announced champions for 1909-15 and 1917-19 based on all AAA races, whether they be a 5-mile dash, class result or city-to-city marathon. The confusion was compounded in 1951 when historian Russ Catlin further revised the official AAA records. He published new champions for 1902-08, amended the 1909 Haresnape champion from Bert Dingley to George Robertson and gave the 1920 series to Tommy Milton rather than to true winner Gaston Chevrolet. His calculations were again based on all AAA races and not just championship events.

A championship awarded forty-nine years late cannot be considered genuine. However, I have included the Haresnape and Catlin revisions below, as well as all relevant race results since 1909 to complete this section, and to explain some championship listings published elsewhere.

HARESNAPE-CREATED CHAMPIONS

year	driver	nat	car
1909	Bert Dingley	USA	Chalmers Detroit
1910	Ray Harroun	USA	Marmon
1911	Ralph Mulford	USA	Lozier
1912	Ralph de Palma	USA	Mercedes
1913	Earl Cooper	USA	Stutz
1914	Ralph de Palma	USA	Mercedes
1915	Earl Cooper	USA	Stutz
1917	Earl Cooper	USA	Stutz
1918	Ralph Mulford	USA	Frontenac
1919	Howard Wilcox	USA	Peugeot
1920	Tommy Milton	USA	Duesenberg/Frontenac

CATLIN-ADDED CHAMPIONS (plus revision for 1909)

year	driver	nat
1902	Harry Harkness	USA
1903	Barney Oldfield	USA
1904	George Heath	USA
1905	Victor Hemery	F
1906	Joe Tracy	USA
1907	Eddie Bald	USA
1908	Louis Strang	USA
1909	George Robertson	USA

Race Winners

AAA NATIONAL CHAMPIONSHIP

NOTE: 1909-16 and 1917-19 are races included in the AAA revisions of 1926-27 and 1951

1909

date	race	driver	nat	car	mph
12.06.09	Portland	Howard Covey	USA	Cadillac	55.757
12.06.09	Portland	Charles Arnold	USA	Pope-Hartford	57.276
12.06.09	Portland	Bert Dingley	USA	Chalmers-Detroit	58.600
18.06.09	Crown Point	Joe Matson	USA	Chalmers-Detroit	51.463
19.06.09	Crown Point	Louis Chevrolet	USA	Buick	49.288
05.07.09	Denver	Eaton McMillian	USA	Colburn	38.978
10.07.09	Santa Monica	Harris Hanshue	USA	Apperson	64.453
10.07.09	Santa Monica	Bert Dingley	USA	Chalmers-Detroit	55.429
19.08.09	Indianapolis	Bob Burman	USA	Buick	53.772
20.08.09	Indianapolis	Louis Strang	USA	Buick	64.739
21.08.09	Indianapolis	Leigh Lynch	USA	Jackson	57.983
06.09.09	Lowell	Bob Burman	USA	Buick	55.514
07.09.09	Lowell	William Knipper	USA	Chalmers-Detroit	51.500
07.09.09	Lowell	Louis Chevrolet	USA	Buick	54.200
08.09.09	Lowell	George Robertson	USA	Simplex	54.201
29.09.09	Riverhead	Ralph de Palma	USA	Fiat	62.430
29.09.09	Riverhead	Frank Lescault	USA	Palmer Singer	62.000
29.09.09	Riverhead	William Sharp	USA	Sharp Arrow	63.400
29.09.09	Riverhead	Louis Chevrolet	USA	Buick	70.300
29.09.09	Riverhead	Arthur See	USA	Maxwell	60.000
09.10.09	Philadelphia	George Robertson	USA	Simplex	55.485
24.10.09	San Leandro	Jack Fleming	USA	Pope-Hartford	76.516
30.10.09	Vanderbilt Cup (Long Island)	Harry Grant	USA	Alco	62.796
06.11.09	Los Angeles-Phoenix	Joe Nikrent	USA	Buick	24.967

1910

date	race	driver	nat	car	mph
05.05.10	Atlanta	Ray Harroun	USA	Marmon	65.746
06.05.10	Atlanta	Bill Endicott	USA	Cole	59.500
06.05.10	Atlanta	Herb Lytle	USA	American	74.380
07.05.10	Atlanta	Tom Kincaid/Johnny Aitken	USA	National	65.788
27.05.10	Indianapolis	Tom Kincaid	USA	National	71.669

date	race	driver	nat	car	mph
28.05.10	Indianapolis	Ray Harroun	USA	Marmon	72.058
30.05.10	Indianapolis	Ray Harroun	USA	Marmon	70.551
02.07.10	Indianapolis	Bob Burman	USA	Marquette-Buick	74.447
04.07.10	Indianapolis	Joe Dawson	USA	Marmon	73.468
26.08.10	Elgin	Dave Buick	USA	Marmon	55.206
26.08.10	Elgin	Al Livingstone	USA	National	60.852
27.08.10	Elgin	Ralph Mulford	USA	Lozier	62.770
03.09.10	Indianapolis	Eddie Hearne	USA	Benz	75.030
03.09.10	Indianapolis	Howdy Wilcox	USA	National	72.238
05.09.10	Indianapolis	Eddie Hearne	USA	Benz	78.851
05.09.10	Indianapolis	Johnny Aitken	USA	National	71.466
01.10.10	Long Island	Bill Endicott	USA	Cole	54.930
01.10.10	Long Island	Frank Gelnaw	USA	Falcar	58.443
01.10.10	Vanderbilt Cup (Long Island)	Harry Grant	USA	Alco	65.181

1911

date	race	driver	nat	car	mph
22.02.11	Oakland	Charles Bigelow	USA	Mercer	57.143
22.02.11	Oakland	Charles Merz	USA	National	66.801
22.02.11	Oakland	Bert Dingley	USA	Pope-Hartford	65.755
28.03.11	Jacksonville	Lou Disbrow	USA	Pope-Hartford	79.558
30.05.11	Indianapolis 500	Ray Harroun/Cyrus Patschke	USA	Marmon Wasp	74.602
04.07.11	Bakersfield	Harvey Herrick	USA	National	48.596
25.08.11	Elgin	Hughie Hughes	USA	Mercer	64.824
25.08.11	Elgin	Don Herr	USA	National	65.836
26.08.11	Elgin	Len Zengel	USA	National	66.606
09.09.11	Cincinnati	John Jenkins	USA	Cole	54.096
09.09.11	Cincinnati	Eddie Hearne	USA	Fiat	56.684
09.10.11	Philadelphia	Erwin Bergdoll	USA	Benz	61.151
09.10.11	Philadelphia	Ralph Mulford	USA	Lozier	60.184
09.10.11	Philadelphia	Lou Disbrow	USA	National	58.311
09.10.11	Philadelphia	Hughie Hughes	USA	Mercer	57.925
14.10.11	Santa Monica	Bruce Keene	USA	Marmon	68.780
14.10.11	Santa Monica	Charles Merz	USA	National	74.425
14.10.11	Santa Monica	Louis Nikrent	USA	Buick	59.211
14.10.11	Santa Monica	Harvey Herrick	USA	National	74.629
27.11.11	Vanderbilt Cup (Savannah)	Ralph Mulford	USA	Lozier	74.076
30.11.11	American GP (Savannah)	David Bruce-Brown	USA	Fiat S74	74.548

1912

date	race	driver	nat	car	mph
04.05.12	Santa Monica	George Joermann	USA	Maxwell	61.871
04.05.12	Santa Monica	Ralph de Palma	USA	Mercer	69.542
04.05.12	Santa Monica	Teddy Tetzlaff	USA	Fiat	78.721
30.05.12	Indianapolis 500	Joe Dawson/Don Herr	USA	National	78.719
05.07.12	Tacoma	Eddie Pullen	USA	Mercer	62.183
05.07.12	Tacoma	Earl Cooper	USA	Stutz	66.889
05.07.12	Tacoma	Teddy Tetzlaff	USA	Fiat	69.380
06.07.12	Tacoma	Teddy Tetzlaff	USA	Fiat	65.681
25.08.12	Columbus	Spencer Wishart	USA	Mercer	57.672
30.08.12	Elgin	Hughie Hughes	USA	Mercer	65.261
30.08.12	Elgin	Charles Merz	USA	Stutz	66.328
31.08.12	Elgin	Ralph de Palma	USA	Mercedes	68.579
31.08.12	Elgin	Ralph de Palma	USA	Mercedes	69.125
02.10.12	Vanderbilt Cup (Milwaukee)	Ralph de Palma	USA	Mercedes	68.980
03.10.12	Milwaukee	Bill Endicott	USA	Mason	55.699
03.10.12	Milwaukee	Mortimer Roberts	USA	Mason	58.799
05.11.12	Brighton Beach	Ralph Mulford	USA	Mason	58.718

1913

date	race	driver	nat	car	mph
01.01.13	San Diego	George Hill	USA	Fiat	46.196
02.03.13	San Diego	Willie Carlson	USA	Benz	59.247
30.05.13	Indianapolis 500	Jules Goux	F	Peugeot L76	75.933
04.07.13	Columbus	Ralph Mulford	USA	Mason	59.465
05.07.13	Tacoma	Earl Cooper	USA	Stutz	70.571

date	race	driver	nat	car	mph
07.07.13	Tacoma	Earl Cooper	USA	Stutz	71.275
28.07.13	Galveston	Lou Disbrow	USA	Simplex	71.443
29.07.13	Galveston	WE Ferguson	USA	Peugeot	71.443
30.07.13	Galveston	Lou Disbrow	USA	Simplex	69.098
09.08.13	Santa Monica	Earl Cooper	USA	Stutz	73.967
29.08.13	Elgin	Ralph de Palma	USA	Mercer	67.513
30.08.13	Elgin	Gil Anderson	USA	Stutz	72.383
09.09.13	Corona	Earl Cooper	USA	Stutz	75.031
09.09.13	Corona	Earl Cooper	USA	Stutz	74.177

1914

date	race	driver	nat	car	mph
26.02.14	Vanderbilt Cup (Santa Monica)	Ralph de Palma	USA	Mercedes	75.000
28.02.14	American GP (Santa Monica)	Eddie Pullen	USA	Mercer	77.324
30.05.14	Indianapolis 500	Rene Thomas	F	Delage	82.474
03.07.14	Tacoma	Hughie Hughes	USA	Maxwell	74.285
04.07.14	Tacoma	Earl Cooper	USA	Stutz	73.321
04.07.14	Sioux City	Eddie Rickenbacher	USA	Duesenberg	78.591
30.07.14	Galveston	Ralph Mulford	USA	Peugeot	88.253
01.08.14	Galveston	Ralph Mulford	USA	Peugeot	59.900
03.08.14	Galveston	Ralph Mulford	USA	Peugeot	63.091
21.08.14	Elgin	Ralph de Palma	USA	Mercedes	74.934
22.08.14	Elgin	Ralph de Palma	USA	Mercedes	74.543
26.09.14	Kalamazoo	Bob Burman	USA	Peugeot	63.499
22.10.14	Galesburg	Ralph Mulford	USA	Duesenberg	64.580
24.10.14	Minneapolis	Tom Alley	USA	Duesenberg	65.574
26.11.14	Corona	Eddie Pullen	USA	Mercer	87.927

1915

date	race	driver	nat	car	mph
09.01.15	San Diego	Earl Cooper	USA	Stutz	65.335
03.02.15	Glendale	Eddie O'Donnell	USA	Duesenberg	47.531
07.02.15	Ascot Park	Eddie O'Donnell	USA	Duesenberg	59.104
27.02.15	American GP (San Francisco)	Dario Resta	I	Peugeot EX3	56.130
06.03.15	Vanderbilt Cup (San Francisco)	Dario Resta	I	Peugeot EX3	66.400
17.03.15	Venice	Barney Oldfield	USA	Maxwell	67.143
20.03.15	Tucson	Barney Oldfield	USA	Maxwell	67.121
29.04.15	Oklahoma City	Bob Burman	USA	Peugeot	68.007
31.05.15	Indianapolis 500	Ralph de Palma	USA	Mercedes	89.840
09.06.15	Galesburg	Eddie O'Donnell	USA	Duesenberg	62.500
26.06.15	Maywood Speedway, Chicago	Dario Resta	I	Peugeot EX3	97.582
03.07.15	Sioux City	Eddie Rickenbacher	USA	Maxwell	74.705
04.07.15	Tacoma	Grover Ruckstell	USA	Mercer	84.722
05.07.15	Tacoma	Eddie Pullen	USA	Mercer	84.966
05.07.15	Omaha Speedway	Eddie Rickenbacher	USA	Maxwell	91.122
09.07.15	Burlington	Bob Burman	USA	Peugeot	47.061
07.08.15	Des Moines	Ralph Mulford	USA	Duesenberg	86.919
07.08.15	Maywood Speedway, Chicago	Dario Resta	I	Peugeot EX3	101.862
20.08.15	Elgin	Earl Cooper	USA	Stutz	74.941
21.08.15	Elgin	Gil Anderson	USA	Stutz	77.212
28.08.15	Kalamazoo	Ralph de Palma	USA	Stutz	64.155
04.09.15	Twin City	Earl Cooper	USA	Stutz	86.334
18.09.15	Narragansett Park, Providence	Eddie Rickenbacher	USA	Maxwell	67.105
09.10.15	Sheepshead Bay	Gil Anderson	USA	Stutz	102.589
02.11.15	Sheepshead Bay	Dario Resta	I	Peugeot EX3	105.395
20.11.15	Phoenix	Earl Cooper	USA	Stutz	64.390
25.11.15	San Francisco	Earl Cooper	USA	Stutz	57.417

1916

date	race	driver	nat	car	mph
13.05.16	Sheepshead Bay	Eddie Rickenbacher	USA	Maxwell	96.240
30.05.16	Indianapolis 500	Dario Resta	I	Peugeot	84.001
10.06.16	Maywood Speedway, Chicago	Dario Resta	I	Peugeot	98.615
24.06.16	Des Moines	Ralph de Palma	USA	Mercedes	93.162
04.07.16	Twin City	Ralph de Palma	USA	Mercedes	91.075
15.07.16	Omaha Speedway	Dario Resta	I	Peugeot	99.194
05.08.16	Tacoma	Eddie Rickenbacher	USA	Maxwell	89.255

date	race	driver	nat	car	mph
04.09.16	Cincinnati	Johnny Aitken	USA	Peugeot EX3	97.059
09.09.16	Indianapolis	Johnny Aitken	USA	Peugeot EX3	89.440
30.09.16	Sheepshead Bay	Johnny Aitken	USA	Peugeot EX3	104.846
14.10.16	Maywood Speedway, Chicago	Dario Resta	I	Peugeot	103.966
28.10.16	Sheepshead Bay	Johnny Aitken	USA	Peugeot EX3	105.956
16.11.16	Vanderbilt Cup (Santa Monica)	Dario Resta	I	Peugeot	87.155
18.11.16	American GP (Santa Monica)	Howdy Wilcox/Johnny Aitken	USA	Peugeot EX5	85.723
30.11.16	Ascot Park	Eddie Rickenbacher	USA	Duesenberg	67.538

1917

date	race	driver	nat	car	mph
04.03.17	Ascot Park	Earl Cooper	USA	Stutz	68.363
10.05.17	Uniontown	William Taylor	USA	Newman-Stutz	89.246
30.05.17	Cincinnati	Louis Chevrolet	USA	Frontenac	102.181
16.06.17	Maywood Speedway, Chicago	Earl Cooper	USA	Stutz	103.107
04.07.17	Omaha Speedway	Ralph Mulford	USA	Hudson	101.256
14.07.17	Twin City	Earl Cooper	USA	Stutz	97.297
14.07.17	Twin City	Ira Vail	USA	Hudson	96.264
03.09.17	Tacoma	Earl Cooper	USA	Stutz	87.146
03.09.17	Maywood Speedway, Chicago	Ralph de Palma	USA	Packard 299	106.572
03.09.17	Maywood Speedway, Chicago	Louis Chevrolet	USA	Frontenac	106.210
08.09.17	Uniontown	Frank Elliott	USA	Delage-Miller	90.685
15.09.17	Narragansett Park, Providence	Ralph Mulford	USA	Frontenac	75.630
15.09.17	Narragansett Park, Providence	Tommy Milton	USA	Duesenberg	75.885
15.09.17	Narragansett Park, Providence	Tommy Milton	USA	Duesenberg	70.835
22.09.17	Sheepshead Bay	Louis Chevrolet	USA	Frontenac	110.396
13.10.17	Maywood Speedway, Chicago	Tom Alley	USA	Alley-Miller	105.556
13.10.17	Maywood Speedway, Chicago	Ralph Mulford	USA	Frontenac	105.960
13.10.17	Maywood Speedway, Chicago	Pete Henderson	USA	Roamer	109.608
29.10.17	Uniontown	Eddie Hearne	USA	Duesenberg	92.855
29.11.17	Ascot Park	Louis Chevrolet	USA	Frontenac	76.433
29.11.17	Ascot Park	Eddie Hearne	USA	Duesenberg	71.576

1918

date	race	driver	nat	car	mph
16.05.18	Uniontown	Tommy Milton	USA	Duesenberg	101.301
16.05.18	Uniontown	Ralph Mulford	USA	Frontenac	97.484
16.05.18	Uniontown	Eddie Hearne	USA	Frontenac	96.272
16.05.18	Uniontown	Louis Chevrolet	USA	Frontenac	94.952
16.05.18	Uniontown	Ralph Mulford	USA	Frontenac	96.927
04.07.18	Tacoma	Cliff Durant	USA	Stutz	98.966
04.07.18	Tacoma	Cliff Durant	USA	Stutz	97.954
04.07.18	Tacoma	Eddie Hearne	USA	Duesenberg	94.290
18.07.18	Uniontown	Louis Chevrolet	USA	Frontenac	94.572
28.07.18	Maywood Speedway, Chicago	Ralph de Palma	USA	Packard 299	110.735
28.07.18	Maywood Speedway, Chicago	Ralph de Palma	USA	Packard 299	106.425
17.08.18	Sheepshead Bay	Ralph de Palma	USA	Packard 299	111.180
17.08.18	Sheepshead Bay	Ralph de Palma	USA	Packard 299	108.959
17.08.18	Sheepshead Bay	Ralph de Palma	USA	Packard 299	109.144
02.09.18	Uniontown	Ralph Mulford	USA	Frontenac	96.173

1919

date	race	driver	nat	car	mph
15.03.19	Santa Monica	Cliff Durant	USA	Chevrolet	82.006
23.03.19	Ascot Park	Roscoe Sarles	USA	Duesenberg	70.848
19.05.19	Uniontown	Tommy Milton	USA	Duesenberg	96.215
30.05.19	Indianapolis 500	Howdy Wilcox	USA	Peugeot	88.050
14.06.19	Sheepshead Bay	Tommy Milton	USA	Duesenberg	112.430
14.06.19	Sheepshead Bay	Ralph Mulford	USA	Frontenac	110.137
14.06.19	Sheepshead Bay	Ralph de Palma	USA	Packard 299	113.679
04.07.19	Tacoma	Louis Chevrolet	USA	Frontenac	97.317
04.07.19	Sheepshead Bay	Gaston Chevrolet	USA	Frontenac	110.527
19.07.19	Uniontown	Tommy Milton	USA	Duesenberg	100.891
19.07.19	Uniontown	Dave Lewis	USA	Duesenberg	98.301
19.07.19	Uniontown	Ira Fetterman	USA	Peerless	99.877
19.07.19	Uniontown	Roscoe Sarles	USA	Miller	93.968
19.07.19	Uniontown	Tommy Milton	USA	Duesenberg	101.250

North American Indycar Championships

date	race	driver	nat	car	mph
23.08.19	Elgin	Tommy Milton	USA	Duesenberg	73.745
01.09.19	Uniontown	Gaston Chevrolet/Joe Boyer	USA	Frontenac	93.537
20.09.19	Sheepshead Bay	Gaston Chevrolet	USA	Frontenac	108.998
12.10.19	Cincinnati	Joe Boyer	USA	Frontenac	101.818

1920

date	race	driver	nat	car	mph
28.02.20	Beverly Hills	Jimmy Murphy	USA	Duesenberg	103.243
10.04.20	Beverly Hills*	Art Klein	USA	Peugeot	110.837
10.04.20	Beverly Hills*	Jimmy Murphy	USA	Duesenberg	110.294
10.04.20	Beverly Hills*	Tommy Milton	USA	Duesenberg	111.801
30.05.20	Indianapolis 500	Gaston Chevrolet	USA	Frontenac	88.166
19.06.20	Uniontown*	Tommy Milton	USA	Duesenberg	94.578
05.07.20	Tacoma	Tommy Milton	USA	Duesenberg	94.099
28.08.20	Elgin	Ralph de Palma	USA	Ballot	78.673
06.09.20	Uniontown*	Tommy Milton	USA	Duesenberg	96.601
02.10.20	Fresno*	Jimmy Murphy	USA	Duesenberg	96.360
25.11.20	Beverly Hills	Roscoe Sarles	USA	Duesenberg	103.199

*non-championship race but included in AAA revisions

1921

date	race	driver	nat	car	mph
27.02.21	Beverly Hills	Ralph de Palma	USA	Ballot	106.509
27.02.21	Beverly Hills	Roscoe Sarles	USA	Duesenberg	107.271
27.02.21	Beverly Hills	Jimmy Murphy	USA	Duesenberg	103.806
27.02.21	Beverly Hills	Tommy Milton	USA	Durant-Duesenberg	104.287
27.02.21	Beverly Hills	Ralph de Palma	USA	Ballot	107.399
10.04.21	Beverly Hills	Ralph de Palma	USA	Ballot	106.383
10.04.21	Beverly Hills	Eddie Pullen	USA	Duesenberg	107.914
10.04.21	Beverly Hills	Joe Thomas	USA	Duesenberg	105.882
10.04.21	Beverly Hills	Jimmy Murphy	USA	Duesenberg	107.399
10.04.21	Beverly Hills	Jimmy Murphy	USA	Duesenberg	109.290
30.04.21	Fresno	Joe Thomas	USA	Duesenberg	100.409
30.05.21	Indianapolis 500	Tommy Milton	USA	Frontenac	89.621
18.06.21	Uniontown	Roscoe Sarles	USA	Duesenberg	97.755
04.07.21	Tacoma	Tommy Milton	USA	Durant-Miller	97.403
14.08.21	Santa Rosa	Eddie Hearne	USA	Duesenberg	110.674
05.09.21	Uniontown	Ira Fetterman	USA	Duesenberg	99.803
01.10.21	Fresno	Earl Cooper	USA	Duesenberg	100.784
23.10.21	Santa Rosa	Roscoe Sarles	USA	Duesenberg	110.339
24.11.21	Beverly Hills	Eddie Hearne	USA	Duesenberg	110.362
11.12.21	San Carlos	Jimmy Murphy	USA	Duesenberg	110.958

1922

date	race	driver	nat	car	mph
05.03.22	Beverly Hills	Tommy Milton	USA	Durant-Miller	110.837
02.04.22	Beverly Hills	Pietro Bordino	I	Fiat 802	114.943
02.04.22	Beverly Hills	Tommy Milton	USA	Durant-Miller	115.237
02.04.22	Beverly Hills	Jimmy Murphy	USA	Duesenberg	114.213
02.04.22	Beverly Hills	Frank Elliott	USA	Miller	114.504
02.04.22	Beverly Hills	Tommy Milton	USA	Durant-Miller	115.311
16.04.22	San Carlos	Harry Hartz	USA	Duesenberg	111.616
27.04.22	Fresno	Jimmy Murphy	USA	Duesenberg	102.857
07.05.22	Santa Rosa	Pietro Bordino	I	Fiat 802	114.405
07.05.22	Santa Rosa	Jimmy Murphy	USA	Duesenberg-Miller	115.339
30.05.22	Indianapolis 500	Jimmy Murphy	USA	Duesenberg-Miller	94.484
17.06.22	Uniontown	Jimmy Murphy	USA	Duesenberg-Miller	102.258
04.07.22	Tacoma	Jimmy Murphy	USA	Duesenberg-Miller	97.603
06.08.22	Santa Rosa	Frank Elliott	USA	Miller	116.152
06.08.22	Santa Rosa	Frank Elliott	USA	Miller	113.208
17.09.22	Kansas City	Tommy Milton	USA	Miller	107.218
30.09.22	Fresno	Bennett Hill	USA	Miller	102.541
03.12.22	Beverly Hills	Jimmy Murphy	USA	Miller	114.606

1923

date	race	driver	nat	car	mph
25.02.23	Beverly Hills	Jimmy Murphy	USA	Miller	115.628
26.04.23	Fresno	Jimmy Murphy	USA	Miller	103.567
30.05.23	Indianapolis 500	Tommy Milton/Howdy Wilcox	USA	Miller	90.954
04.07.23	Kansas City	Eddie Hearne	USA	Miller	106.118
04.09.23	Altoona	Eddie Hearne	USA	Miller	111.501
29.09.23	Fresno	Harry Hartz	USA	Miller	103.647
21.10.23	Kansas City	Harlan Fengler	USA	Miller	112.847
29.11.23	Beverly Hills	Bennett Hill	USA	Miller	112.430

1924

date	race	driver	nat	car	mph
24.02.24	Beverly Hills	Harlan Fengler	USA	Miller	116.060
30.05.24	Indianapolis 500	LL Corum/Joe Boyer	USA	Duesenberg	98.234
14.06.24	Altoona	Jimmy Murphy	USA	Miller	114.548
04.07.24	Kansas City	Jimmy Murphy	USA	Miller	114.421
01.09.24	Altoona	Jimmy Murphy	USA	Miller	114.382
15.09.24	Syracuse	"Red" Shafer	USA	Duesenberg	78.658
02.10.24	Fresno	Earl Cooper	USA	Miller	105.613
25.10.24	Charlotte	Tommy Milton	USA	Miller	118.171
14.12.24	Culver City	Bennett Hill	USA	Miller	126.786

1925

date	race	driver	nat	car	mph
01.03.25	Culver City	Tommy Milton	USA	Miller	126.886
30.04.25	Fresno	Peter de Paolo	USA	Duesenberg	104.875
11.05.25	Charlotte	Earl Cooper	USA	Miller	122.034
30.05.25	Indianapolis 500	Peter de Paolo/Norman Batten	USA	Duesenberg	101.127
13.06.25	Altoona	Peter de Paolo	USA	Duesenberg	115.605
11.07.25	Laurel	Peter de Paolo	USA	Duesenberg	123.300
07.09.25	Altoona	Robert McDonough	USA	Miller	118.196
26.10.25	Laurel	Robert McDonough	USA	Miller	126.003
31.10.25	Salem	Peter de Paolo	USA	Duesenberg	126.006
11.11.25	Charlotte	Tommy Milton	USA	Duesenberg	124.971
29.11.25	Culver City	Frank Elliott	USA	Miller	127.874

1926

date	race	driver	nat	car	mph
22.02.26	Miami	Peter de Paolo	USA	Duesenberg	129.296
21.03.26	Culver City	Bennett Hill	USA	Miller	131.295
01.05.26	Atlantic City	Harry Hartz	USA	Miller	134.092
10.05.26	Charlotte	Earl de Vore	USA	Miller	120.088
31.05.26	Indianapolis 500	Frank Lockhart	USA	Miller	95.904
12.06.26	Altoona	Dave Lewis	USA	Miller	112.435
05.07.26	Salem	Peter de Paolo	USA	Duesenberg	128.249
05.07.26	Salem	Earl Cooper	USA	Miller	116.562
17.07.26	Atlantic City	Harry Hartz	USA	Miller	128.659
17.07.26	Atlantic City	Norman Batten	USA	Miller	120.755
17.07.26	Atlantic City	Fred Comer	USA	Miller	124.742
17.07.26	Atlantic City	Harry Hartz	USA	Miller	123.411
23.08.26	Charlotte	Earl Cooper	USA	Miller	128.848
23.08.26	Charlotte	Dave Lewis	USA	Miller	125.320
23.08.26	Charlotte	Frank Lockhart	USA	Miller	122.549
23.08.26	Charlotte	Frank Lockhart	USA	Miller	120.878
18.09.26	Altoona	Frank Lockhart	USA	Miller	116.379
02.10.26	Fresno	Bennett Hill	USA	Miller	106.257
02.10.26	Fresno	Frank Lockhart	USA	Miller	100.739
12.10.26	Salem	Bennett Hill	USA	Miller	129.977
12.10.26	Salem	"Leon Duray"	USA	Miller	130.393
12.10.26	Salem	Harry Hartz	USA	Miller	123.261
11.11.26	Charlotte	Frank Lockhart	USA	Miller	132.548
11.11.26	Charlotte	Dave Lewis	USA	Miller	127.119
11.11.26	Charlotte	Harry Hartz	USA	Miller	129.403
11.11.26	Charlotte	"Leon Duray"	USA	Miller	122.045

1927

date	race	driver	nat	car	mph
06.03.27	Culver City	"Leon Duray"	USA	Miller	124.712
07.05.27	Atlantic City	Dave Lewis	USA	Miller	130.059
30.05.27	Indianapolis 500	George Souders	USA	Duesenberg	97.545
11.06.27	Altoona	Peter de Paolo	USA	Miller	116.565
04.07.27	Salem	Peter de Paolo	USA	Miller	124.348
05.09.27	Altoona	Frank Lockhart	USA	Miller	116.705
19.09.27	Charlotte	Frank Lockhart	USA	Miller	127.540
19.09.27	Charlotte	Peter de Paolo	USA	Miller	126.050
19.09.27	Charlotte	Babe Stapp	USA	Miller	119.915
12.10.27	Salem	Frank Lockhart	USA	Miller	125.739
12.10.27	Salem	Frank Lockhart	USA	Miller	126.701

1928

date	race	driver	nat	car	mph
30.05.28	Indianapolis 500	Louis Meyer	USA	Miller	99.482
10.06.28	Detroit	Ray Keech	USA	Miller	77.664
04.07.28	Salem	"Leon Duray"	USA	Miller	130.751
04.07.28	Salem	Ray Keech	USA	Miller	122.742
19.08.28	Altoona	Louis Meyer	USA	Miller	116.637
01.09.28	Syracuse	Ray Keech	USA	Miller	75.314
12.10.28	Salem	Cliff Woodbury	USA	Miller	117.005

1929

date	race	driver	nat	car	mph
30.05.29	Indianapolis 500	Ray Keech	USA	Miller	97.585
09.06.29	Detroit	Cliff Woodbury	USA	Miller	76.224
15.06.29	Altoona	Louis Meyer	USA	Miller	119.000
31.08.29	Syracuse	Wilbur Shaw	USA	Miller	81.066
02.09.29	Altoona	Louis Meyer	USA	Miller	109.476

1930

date	race	driver	nat	car	mph
03.05.30	Langhorne	Bill Cummings	USA	Miller	77.320
30.05.30	Indianapolis 500	Billy Arnold	USA	Summers-Miller	100.448
09.06.30	Detroit	Wilbur Shaw	USA	Smith-Miller	68.256
14.06.30	Altoona	Billy Arnold	USA	Summers-Miller	111.173
22.06.30	Akron	"Shorty" Cantlon	USA	Stevens-Miller	67.771
04.07.30	Bridgeville	Wilbur Shaw	USA	Smith-Miller	66.790
01.09.30	Altoona	Billy Arnold	USA	Summers-Miller	113.261
06.09.30	Syracuse	Bill Cummings	USA	Duesenberg	83.484

1931

date	race	driver	nat	car	mph
30.05.31	Indianapolis 500	Louis Schneider	USA	Stevens-Miller	96.629
14.06.31	Detroit	Louis Meyer	USA	Stevens-Miller	75.472
04.07.31	Altoona	Lou Moore	USA	Miller	112.853
07.09.31	Altoona	Jimmy Gleason	USA	Duesenberg	117.801
07.09.31	Altoona	"Shorty" Cantlon	USA	Stevens-Miller	114.068
07.09.31	Altoona	"Shorty" Cantlon	USA	Stevens-Miller	109.656
12.09.31	Syracuse	Lou Moore	USA	Miller	74.077

1932

date	race	driver	nat	car	mph
30.05.32	Indianapolis 500	Fred Frame	USA	Wetteroth-Miller	104.144
05.06.32	Detroit	Bob Carey	USA	Stevens-Miller	71.625
19.06.32	Roby	"Stubby" Stubblefield	USA	Adams-Miller	76.271
02.07.32	Syracuse	Bob Carey	USA	Stevens-Miller	81.158
10.09.32	Detroit	Mauri Rose	USA	Stevens-Miller	74.457
13.11.32	Oakland	Bill Cummings	USA	Miller	90.452

1933

date	race	driver	nat	car	mph
30.05.33	Indianapolis 500	Louis Meyer	USA	Miller	104.162
11.06.33	Detroit	Bill Cummings	USA	Miller	73.907
09.09.33	Syracuse	Bill Cummings	USA	Miller	81.874

1934

30.05.34	Indianapolis 500	Bill Cummings	USA	Miller	104.863
25.08.34	Springfield	Bill Winn	USA	Miller	77.771
09.09.34	Syracuse	"Shorty" Cantlon	USA	Weil-Miller	79.893
23.12.34	Mines Field	Kelly Petillo	USA	Stevens/Summers-Sparks	81.494

1935

30.05.35	Indianapolis 500	Kelly Petillo	USA	Wetteroth-Offenhauser	106.240
04.07.35	St Paul	Kelly Petillo	USA	Wetteroth-Offenhauser	77.270
24.08.35	Springfield	Bill Winn	USA	Duesenberg-Miller	80.393
02.09.35	Syracuse	Bill Winn	USA	Duesenberg-Miller	83.546
07.09.35	Altoona	Louis Meyer	USA	Stevens-Miller	86.559
13.10.35	Langhorne	Kelly Petillo	USA	Wetteroth-Offenhauser	91.900

1936

30.05.36	Indianapolis 500	Louis Meyer	USA	Stevens-Miller	109.069
20.06.36	Goshen	Rex Mays	USA	Stevens/Summers-Sparks	76.410
15.09.36	Syracuse	Mauri Rose	USA	Miller-Offenhauser	82.378
12.10.36	Vanderbilt Cup (Roosevelt Raceway)	Tazio Nuvolari	I	Alfa Romeo 12C-36	65.503

1937

30.05.37	Indianapolis 500	Wilbur Shaw	USA	Shaw-Offenhauser	113.580
05.07.37	Vanderbilt Cup (Roosevelt Raceway)	Bernd Rosemeyer	D	Auto Union C	82.234
12.09.37	Syracuse	Bill Winn	USA	Weil-Miller	87.491

1938

30.05.38	Indianapolis 500	Floyd Roberts	USA	Wetteroth-Miller	117.200
10.09.38	Syracuse	Jimmy Snyder	USA	Lencki-Offenhauser	84.211

1939

30.05.39	Indianapolis 500	Wilbur Shaw	USA	Maserati 8CTF	115.035
27.08.39	Milwaukee	Babe Stapp	USA	Stevens-Miller	83.663
02.09.39	Syracuse	Mauri Rose	USA	Wetteroth-Offenhauser	74.906

1940

30.05.40	Indianapolis 500	Wilbur Shaw	USA	Maserati 8CTF	114.277
24.08.40	Springfield	Rex Mays	USA	Stevens-Winfield	87.464
02.09.40	Syracuse	Rex Mays	USA	Stevens-Winfield	85.268

1941

30.05.41	Indianapolis 500	Floyd Davis/Mauri Rose	USA	Wetteroth-Offenhauser	115.117
24.08.41	Milwaukee	Rex Mays	USA	Stevens-Winfield	82.248
01.09.41	Syracuse	Rex Mays	USA	Stevens-Winfield	84.567

North American Indycar Championships

1946

date	race	driver	nat	car	mph
30.05.46	Indianapolis 500	George Robson	USA	Adams-Sparks	114.747
30.06.46	Langhorne	Rex Mays	USA	Stevens-Winfield	85.144
02.09.46	Lakewood Park, Atlanta	George Connor	USA	Kurtis-Offenhauser	not published
15.09.46	Indiana State Fair	Rex Mays	USA	Stevens-Winfield	78.888
22.09.46	Milwaukee	Rex Mays	USA	Stevens-Winfield	84.814
06.10.46	Goshen	Tony Bettenhausen	USA	Wetteroth-Offenhauser	77.644

1947

date	race	driver	nat	car	mph
30.05.47	Indianapolis 500	Mauri Rose	USA	Deidt-Offenhauser	116.338
08.06.47	Milwaukee	Bill Holland	USA	Wetteroth-Offenhauser	87.280
22.06.47	Langhorne	Bill Holland	USA	Wetteroth-Offenhauser	87.728
04.07.47	Lakewood Park, Atlanta	Walt Ader	USA	Adams-Offenhauser	75.224
13.07.47	Bainbridge	Ted Horn	USA	Horn-Offenhauser	85.378
27.07.47	Milwaukee	Charles van Acker	USA	Stevens-Offenhauser	85.960
17.08.47	Goshen	Tony Bettenhausen	USA	Stevens-Offenhauser	80.062
24.08.47	Milwaukee	Ted Horn	USA	Horn-Offenhauser	84.336
01.09.47	Pikes Peak	Louis Unser	USA	Maserati	45.598
28.09.47	Springfield	Tony Bettenhausen	USA	Stevens-Offenhauser	92.519
02.10.47	Arlington Downs, Dallas	Ted Horn	USA	Horn-Offenhauser	85.097

1948

date	race	driver	nat	car	mph
25.04.48	Arlington Downs, Dallas	Ted Horn	USA	Horn-Offenhauser	78.539
30.05.48	Indianapolis 500	Mauri Rose	USA	Deidt-Offenhauser	119.814
06.06.48	Milwaukee	Emil Andres	USA	Kurtis-Offenhauser	85.320
20.06.48	Langhorne	Walt Brown	USA	Kurtis-Offenhauser	89.649
15.08.48	Milwaukee	Johnny Mantz	USA	Kurtis-Offenhauser	85.327
21.08.48	Springfield	Ted Horn	USA	Horn-Offenhauser	90.520
29.08.48	Milwaukee	Tony Bettenhausen/Myron Fohr	USA	Marchese-Offenhauser	86.734
04.09.48	Du Quoin	Lee Wallard	USA	Meyer-Offenhauser	88.387
06.09.48	Lakewood Park, Atlanta	Mel Hansen	USA	Wetteroth-Offenhauser	79.278
06.09.48	Pikes Peak	Al Rogers	USA	Offenhauser	47.065
19.09.48	Springfield	Myron Fohr	USA	Marchese-Offenhauser	88.692
10.10.48	Du Quoin	Johnnie Parsons	USA	Kurtis-Offenhauser	83.571

1949

date	race	driver	nat	car	mph
24.04.49	Arlington Downs, Dallas	Johnnie Parsons	USA	Kurtis-Offenhauser	not published
30.05.49	Indianapolis 500	Bill Holland	USA	Deidt-Offenhauser	121.327
05.06.49	Milwaukee	Myron Fohr	USA	Marchese-Offenhauser	83.615
19.06.49	Trenton	Myron Fohr	USA	Marchese-Offenhauser	75.765
20.08.49	Springfield	Mel Hansen	USA	Lesovsky-Offenhauser	87.912
28.08.49	Milwaukee	Johnnie Parsons	USA	Kurtis-Offenhauser	85.817
03.09.49	Du Quoin	Tony Bettenhausen	USA	Kurtis-Offenhauser	90.068
05.09.49	Pikes Peak	Al Rogers	USA	Offenhauser	46.868
10.09.49	Syracuse	Johnnie Parsons	USA	Kurtis-Offenhauser	86.196
11.09.49	Detroit	Tony Bettenhausen	USA	Kurtis-Offenhauser	81.264
25.09.49	Springfield	Johnnie Parsons	USA	Kurtis-Offenhauser	91.720
16.10.49	Langhorne	Johnnie Parsons	USA	Kurtis-Offenhauser	93.623
30.10.49	Sacramento	Fred Agabashian	USA	Kurtis-Offenhauser	84.486
06.11.49	Del Mar	Jimmy Davies	USA	Ewing-Offenhauser	85.359

1950

date	race	driver	nat	car	mph
30.05.50	Indianapolis 500	Johnnie Parsons	USA	Kurtis-Offenhauser	124.002
11.06.50	Milwaukee	Tony Bettenhausen	USA	Wetteroth-Offenhauser	85.027
25.06.50	Langhorne	Jack McGrath	USA	Kurtis KK3000-Offenhauser	88.517
19.08.50	Springfield	Paul Russo	USA	Nichels-Offenhauser	91.278
27.08.50	Milwaukee	Walt Faulkner	USA	Kurtis KK2000-Offenhauser	87.315
04.09.50	Pikes Peak	Al Rogers	USA	Coniff-Offenhauser	47.617
09.09.50	Syracuse	Jack McGrath	USA	Kurtis KK3000-Offenhauser	87.350
10.09.50	Detroit	Henry Banks	USA	Moore-Offenhauser	82.853

date	race	driver	nat	car	mph
01.10.50	Springfield	Tony Bettenhausen	USA	Kurtis-Offenhauser	87.637
15.10.50	Sacramento	Duke Dinsmore	USA	Kurtis KK2000-Offenhauser	82.474
12.11.50	Phoenix	Jimmy Davies	USA	Ewing-Offenhauser	78.020
26.11.50	Bay Meadows	Tony Bettenhausen	USA	Kurtis-Offenhauser	86.163
10.12.50	Darlington	Johnnie Parsons	USA	Nichels-Offenhauser	104.541

1951

date	race	driver	nat	car	mph
30.05.51	Indianapolis 500	Lee Wallard	USA	Kurtis-Offenhauser	126.244
10.06.51	Milwaukee	Tony Bettenhausen	USA	Kurtis-Offenhauser	90.041
24.06.51	Langhorne	Tony Bettenhausen	USA	Kurtis-Offenhauser	92.374
04.07.51	Darlington	Walt Faulkner	USA	Kuzma-Offenhauser	104.719
18.08.51	Springfield	Tony Bettenhausen	USA	Kurtis-Offenhauser	90.054
26.08.51	Milwaukee	Walt Faulkner	USA	Kuzma-Offenhauser	91.342
01.09.51	Du Quoin	Tony Bettenhausen	USA	Kurtis-Offenhauser	88.311
03.09.51	Du Quoin	Tony Bettenhausen	USA	Kurtis-Offenhauser	87.425
03.09.51	Pikes Peak	Al Rogers	USA	Offenhauser	47.597
08.09.51	Syracuse	Tony Bettenhausen	USA	Kurtis-Offenhauser	not published
09.09.51	Detroit	Paul Russo	USA	Nichels-Offenhauser	83.639
23.09.51	Centennial Park, Denver	Tony Bettenhausen	USA	Kurtis-Offenhauser	86.643
21.10.51	San Jose	Tony Bettenhausen	USA	Kurtis-Offenhauser	80.645
04.11.51	Phoenix	Johnnie Parsons	USA	Kurtis KK4000-Offenhauser	84.626
11.11.51	Bay Meadows	Johnnie Parsons	USA	Kurtis KK4000-Offenhauser	87.708

1952

date	race	driver	nat	car	mph
30.05.52	Indianapolis 500	Troy Ruttman	USA	Kuzma-Offenhauser	128.922
08.06.52	Milwaukee	Mike Nazaruk	USA	Kurtis-Offenhauser	92.255
04.07.52	Raleigh	Troy Ruttman	USA	Kuzma-Offenhauser	89.109
16.08.52	Springfield	Bill Schindler	USA	Nichels-Offenhauser	94.336
24.08.52	Milwaukee	Chuck Stevenson	USA	Kurtis KK4000-Offenhauser	81.392
30.08.52	Detroit	Bill Vukovich	USA	Kuzma-Offenhauser	81.559
01.09.52	Pikes Peak	George Hammond	USA	Kurtis-Offenhauser	47.897
01.09.52	Du Quoin	Chuck Stevenson	USA	Kurtis KK4000-Offenhauser	88.409
06.09.52	Syracuse	Jack McGrath	USA	Kurtis KK4000-Offenhauser	89.073
28.09.52	Centennial Park, Denver	Bill Vukovich	USA	Kuzma-Offenhauser	87.357
02.11.52	San Jose	Bobby Ball	USA	Kurtis KK4000-Offenhauser	not published
11.11.52	Phoenix	Johnnie Parsons	USA	Kurtis KK4000-Offenhauser	85.878

1953

date	race	driver	nat	car	mph
30.05.53	Indianapolis 500	Bill Vukovich	USA	Kurtis KK500A-Offenhauser	128.740
07.06.53	Milwaukee	Jack McGrath	USA	Kurtis KK4000-Offenhauser	93.634
21.06.53	Springfield	Rodger Ward	USA	Kurtis-Offenhauser	89.483
04.07.53	Detroit	Rodger Ward	USA	Kurtis-Offenhauser	82.257
22.08.53	Springfield	Sam Hanks	USA	Kurtis KK4000-Offenhauser	91.162
30.08.53	Milwaukee	Chuck Stevenson	USA	Kuzma-Offenhauser	89.580
07.09.53	Du Quoin	Sam Hanks	USA	Kurtis KK4000-Offenhauser	89.984
07.09.53	Pikes Peak	Louis Unser	USA	Kurtis-Offenhauser	48.840
12.09.53	Syracuse	Tony Bettenhausen	USA	Kurtis-Offenhauser	74.089
26.09.53	Indiana State Fairgrounds	Bob Sweikert	USA	Kuzma-Offenhauser	87.192
25.10.53	Sacramento	Jimmy Bryan	USA	Kurtis KK4000-Offenhauser	79.786
11.11.53	Phoenix	Tony Bettenhausen	USA	Kurtis-Offenhauser	83.916

1954

date	race	driver	nat	car	mph
31.05.54	Indianapolis 500	Bill Vukovich	USA	Kurtis KK500A-Offenhauser	130.840
06.06.54	Milwaukee	Chuck Stevenson	USA	Kuzma-Offenhauser	97.527
20.06.54	Langhorne	Jimmy Bryan	USA	Kuzma-Offenhauser	97.545
05.07.54	Darlington	Manuel Ayulo	USA	Kuzma-Offenhauser	122.665
21.08.54	Springfield	Jimmy Davies	USA	Ewing-Offenhauser	92.546
29.08.54	Milwaukee	Manuel Ayulo	USA	Kuzma-Offenhauser	96.261
06.09.54	Du Quoin	Sam Hanks	USA	Kurtis-Offenhauser	88.029
06.09.54	Pikes Peak	Keith Andrews	USA	Offenhauser	50.843
11.09.54	Syracuse	Bob Sweikert	USA	Kurtis KK4000-Offenhauser	90.339

date	race	driver	nat	car	mph
18.09.54	Indiana State Fairgrounds	Jimmy Bryan	USA	Kuzma-Offenhauser	85.395
17.10.54	Sacramento	Jimmy Bryan	USA	Kuzma-Offenhauser	86.940
07.11.54	Phoenix	Jimmy Bryan	USA	Kuzma-Offenhauser	84.524
14.11.54	Las Vegas	Jimmy Bryan	USA	Kuzma-Offenhauser	84.818

1955

date	race	driver	nat	car	mph
30.05.55	Indianapolis 500	Bob Sweikert	USA	Kurtis KK500D-Offenhauser	128.209
05.06.55	Milwaukee	Johnny Thomson	USA	Kuzma-Offenhauser	98.844
19.06.55	Langhorne	Jimmy Bryan	USA	Kuzma-Offenhauser	95.727
20.08.55	Springfield	Jimmy Bryan	USA	Kuzma-Offenhauser	90.524
28.08.55	Milwaukee	Pat Flaherty	USA	Kurtis KK500B-Offenhauser	95.033
05.09.55	Du Quoin	Jimmy Bryan	USA	Kuzma-Offenhauser	93.530
05.09.55	Pikes Peak	Bob Finney	USA	Lincoln	51.607
10.09.55	Syracuse	Bob Sweikert	USA	Watson-Offenhauser	89.928
17.09.55	Indiana State Fairgrounds	Jimmy Bryan	USA	Kuzma-Offenhauser	83.978
16.10.55	Sacramento	Jimmy Bryan	USA	Kuzma-Offenhauser	86.207
06.11.55	Phoenix	Jimmy Bryan	USA	Kuzma-Offenhauser	83.862

USAC NATIONAL CHAMPIONSHIP

1956

date	race	driver	nat	car	mph
30.05.56	Indianapolis 500	Pat Flaherty	USA	Watson-Offenhauser	128.490
10.06.56	Milwaukee	Pat Flaherty	USA	Watson-Offenhauser	98.847
24.06.56	Langhorne	George Amick	USA	Kuzma-Offenhauser	95.201
04.07.56	Darlington	Pat O'Connor	USA	Templeton-Offenhauser	124.066
14.07.56	Lakewood Park, Atlanta	Eddie Sachs	USA	Hillegass-Offenhauser	not published
19.08.56	Springfield	Jimmy Bryan	USA	Kuzma-Offenhauser	88.471
26.08.56	Milwaukee	Jimmy Bryan	USA	Kuzma-Offenhauser	92.733
03.09.56	Du Quoin	Jimmy Bryan	USA	Kuzma-Offenhauser	91.706
08.09.56	Syracuse	Tony Bettenhausen	USA	Kuzma-Offenhauser	90.804
15.09.56	Indiana State Fairgrounds	Jimmy Bryan	USA	Kuzma-Offenhauser	80.727
21.10.56	Sacramento	Jud Larson	USA	Watson-Offenhauser	86.797
12.11.56	Phoenix	George Amick	USA	Lesovsky-Offenhauser	91.826

1957

date	race	driver	nat	car	mph
30.05.57	Indianapolis 500	Sam Hanks	USA	Epperly-Offenhauser	135.601
02.06.57	Langhorne	Johnny Thomson	USA	Kuzma-Offenhauser	100.174
09.06.57	Milwaukee	Rodger Ward	USA	Lesovsky-Offenhauser	97.789
23.06.57	Detroit	Jimmy Bryan	USA	Kuzma-Offenhauser	80.232
04.07.57	Lakewood Park, Atlanta	George Amick	USA	Lesovsky-Offenhauser	89.995
17.08.57	Springfield	Rodger Ward	USA	Lesovsky-Offenhauser	96.015
25.08.57	Milwaukee	Jim Rathmann	USA	Epperly-Offenhauser	98.134
02.09.57	Du Quoin	Jud Larson	USA	Watson-Offenhauser	90.948
07.09.57	Syracuse	Elmer George	USA	Watson-Offenhauser	94.295
14.09.57	Indiana State Fairgrounds	Jud Larson	USA	Watson-Offenhauser	91.751
29.09.57	Trenton	Pat O'Connor	USA	Kuzma-Offenhauser	100.279
20.10.57	Sacramento	Rodger Ward	USA	Lesovsky-Offenhauser	90.965
11.11.57	Phoenix	Jimmy Bryan	USA	Kuzma-Offenhauser	86.001

1958

date	race	driver	nat	car	mph
30.03.58	Trenton	Len Sutton	USA	Kuzma-Offenhauser	95.527
30.05.58	Indianapolis 500	Jimmy Bryan	USA	Epperly-Offenhauser	133.791
08.06.58	Milwaukee	Art Bisch	USA	Kuzma-Offenhauser	94.013
15.06.58	Langhorne	Eddie Sachs	USA	Kuzma-Offenhauser	91.976
04.07.58	Lakewood Park, Atlanta	Jud Larson	USA	Watson-Offenhauser	87.146
16.08.58	Springfield	Johnny Thomson	USA	Kuzma-Offenhauser	98.137
24.08.58	Milwaukee	Rodger Ward	USA	Lesovsky-Offenhauser	97.809
01.09.58	Du Quoin	Johnny Thomson	USA	Kuzma-Offenhauser	94.753
06.09.58	Syracuse	Johnny Thomson	USA	Kuzma-Offenhauser	94.953
13.09.58	Indiana State Fairgrounds	Eddie Sachs	USA	Kuzma-Offenhauser	92.142

date	race	driver	nat	car	mph
28.09.58	Trenton	Rodger Ward	USA	Lesovsky-Offenhauser	99.368
26.10.58	Sacramento	Johnny Thomson	USA	Kuzma-Offenhauser	89.175
11.11.58	Phoenix	Jud Larson	USA	Lesovsky-Offenhauser	92.738

1959

date	race	driver	nat	car	mph
04.04.59	Daytona	Jim Rathmann	USA	Watson-Offenhauser	170.261
19.04.59	Trenton	Tony Bettenhausen	USA	Kuzma-Offenhauser	91.161
30.05.59	Indianapolis 500	Rodger Ward	USA	Watson-Offenhauser	135.857
07.06.59	Milwaukee	Johnny Thomson	USA	Lesovsky-Offenhauser	98.609
14.06.59	Langhorne	Van Johnson	USA	Kurtis KK4000-Offenhauser	99.553
22.08.59	Springfield	Len Sutton	USA	Kuzma-Offenhauser	95.186
30.08.59	Milwaukee	Rodger Ward	USA	Watson-Offenhauser	96.317
07.09.59	Du Quoin	Rodger Ward	USA	Watson-Offenhauser	93.268
12.09.59	Syracuse	Eddie Sachs	USA	Meskowski-Offenhauser	94.121
19.09.59	Indiana State Fairgrounds	Rodger Ward	USA	Watson-Offenhauser	91.033
27.09.59	Trenton	Eddie Sachs	USA	Meskowski-Offenhauser	97.398
18.10.59	Phoenix	Tony Bettenhausen	USA	Kuzma-Offenhauser	88.458
25.10.59	Sacramento	Jim Hurtubise	USA	Kuzma-Offenhauser	86.464

1960

date	race	driver	nat	car	mph
10.04.60	Trenton	Rodger Ward	USA	Watson-Offenhauser	95.486
30.05.60	Indianapolis 500	Jim Rathmann	USA	Watson-Offenhauser	138.767
05.06.60	Milwaukee	Rodger Ward	USA	Watson-Offenhauser	99.465
19.06.60	Langhorne	Jim Hurtubise	USA	Kuzma-Offenhauser	100.786
20.08.60	Springfield	Jim Packard	USA	Lesovsky-Offenhauser	90.909
28.08.60	Milwaukee	Len Sutton	USA	Watson-Offenhauser	100.131
05.09.60	Du Quoin	AJ Foyt jr	USA	Meskowski-Offenhauser	93.351
10.09.60	Syracuse	Bobby Grim	USA	Meskowski-Offenhauser	93.258
17.09.60	Indiana State Fairgrounds	AJ Foyt Jr	USA	Meskowski-Offenhauser	89.286
25.09.60	Trenton	Eddie Sachs	USA	Kuzma-Offenhauser	99.223
30.10.60	Sacramento	AJ Foyt Jr	USA	Meskowski-Offenhauser	84.796
20.11.60	Phoenix	AJ Foyt Jr	USA	Meskowski-Offenhauser	89.078

1961

date	race	driver	nat	car	mph
09.04.61	Trenton	Eddie Sachs	USA	Kuzma-Offenhauser	98.680
30.05.61	Indianapolis 500	AJ Foyt Jr	USA	Watson-Offenhauser	139.131
04.06.61	Milwaukee	Rodger Ward	USA	Watson-Offenhauser	103.860
18.06.61	Langhorne	AJ Foyt Jr	USA	Meskowski-Offenhauser	99.601
20.08.61	Milwaukee	Lloyd Ruby	USA	Watson-Offenhauser	101.638
21.08.61	Springfield	Jim Hurtubise	USA	Kuzma-Offenhauser	97.459
04.09.61	Du Quoin	AJ Foyt Jr	USA	Meskowski-Offenhauser	92.755
09.09.61	Syracuse	Rodger Ward	USA	Watson-Offenhauser	95.090
16.09.61	Indiana State Fairgrounds	AJ Foyt Jr	USA	Meskowski-Offenhauser	92.370
24.09.61	Trenton	Eddie Sachs	USA	Kuzma-Offenhauser	101.013
29.10.61	Sacramento	Rodger Ward	USA	Watson-Offenhauser	88.779
19.11.61	Phoenix	Parnelli Jones	USA	Kuzma-Offenhauser	not published

1962

date	race	driver	nat	car	mph
08.04.62	Trenton	AJ Foyt Jr	USA	Meskowski-Offenhauser	101.102
30.05.62	Indianapolis 500	Rodger Ward	USA	Watson-Offenhauser	140.293
10.06.62	Milwaukee	AJ Foyt Jr	USA	Watson/Trevis-Offenhauser	100.860
01.07.62	Langhorne	AJ Foyt Jr	USA	Meskowski-Offenhauser	93.187
22.07.62	Trenton	Rodger Ward	USA	Watson-Offenhauser	100.977
19.08.62	Springfield	Jim Hurtubise	USA	Kuzma-Offenhauser	92.625
19.08.62	Milwaukee	Rodger Ward	USA	Watson-Offenhauser	100.015
26.08.62	Langhorne	Don Branson	USA	Watson-Offenhauser	104.800
08.09.62	Syracuse	Rodger Ward	USA	Watson-Offenhauser	95.572
15.09.62	Indiana State Fairgrounds	Parnelli Jones	USA	Kuzma-Offenhauser	90.612
23.09.62	Trenton	Don Branson	USA	Watson-Offenhauser	102.529
28.10.62	Sacramento	AJ Foyt Jr	USA	Meskowski-Offenhauser	95.260
18.11.62	Phoenix	Bobby Marshman	USA	Meskowski-Offenhauser	92.122

1963

date	race	driver	nat	car	mph
21.04.63	Trenton	AJ Foyt Jr	USA	Meskowski-Offenhauser	102.492
30.05.63	Indianapolis 500	Parnelli Jones	USA	Watson-Offenhauser	143.137
09.06.63	Milwaukee	Rodger Ward	USA	Watson-Offenhauser	100.585
23.06.63	Langhorne	AJ Foyt Jr	USA	Meskowski-Offenhauser	104.135
28.07.63	Trenton	AJ Foyt Jr	USA	Watson/Trevis-Offenhauser	100.403
17.08.63	Springfield	Rodger Ward	USA	Watson-Offenhauser	95.557
18.08.63	Milwaukee	Jim Clark	GB	Lotus 29-Ford	104.452
02.09.63	Du Quoin	AJ Foyt Jr	USA	Meskowski-Offenhauser	95.234
14.09.63	Indiana State Fairgrounds	Rodger Ward	USA	Watson-Offenhauser	93.545
22.09.63	Trenton	AJ Foyt Jr	USA	Watson/Trevis-Offenhauser	101.358
27.10.63	Sacramento	Rodger Ward	USA	Watson-Offenhauser	92.174
17.11.63	Phoenix	Rodger Ward	USA	Watson-Offenhauser	85.026

1964

date	race	driver	nat	car	mph
22.03.64	Phoenix	AJ Foyt Jr	USA	Watson-Offenhauser	107.536
19.04.64	Trenton	AJ Foyt Jr	USA	Watson-Offenhauser	104.530
30.05.64	Indianapolis 500	AJ Foyt Jr	USA	Watson-Offenhauser	147.350
07.06.64	Milwaukee	AJ Foyt Jr	USA	Watson-Offenhauser	100.346
21.06.64	Langhorne	AJ Foyt Jr	USA	Meskowski-Offenhauser	102.552
19.07.64	Trenton	AJ Foyt Jr	USA	Watson-Offenhauser	105.590
22.08.64	Springfield	AJ Foyt Jr	USA	Meskowski-Offenhauser	95.238
23.08.64	Milwaukee	Parnelli Jones	USA	Lotus 34-Ford	104.751
07.09.64	Du Quoin	AJ Foyt Jr	USA	Meskowski-Offenhauser	97.800
26.09.64	Indiana State Fairgrounds	AJ Foyt Jr	USA	Meskowski-Offenhauser	89.056
27.09.64	Trenton	Parnelli Jones	USA	Lotus 34-Ford	96.415
25.10.64	Sacramento	AJ Foyt Jr	USA	Meskowski-Offenhauser	91.451
22.11.64	Phoenix	Lloyd Ruby	USA	Halibrand-Offenhauser	107.736

1965

date	race	driver	nat	car	mph
28.03.65	Phoenix	Don Branson	USA	Watson-Offenhauser	106.456
25.04.65	Trenton	Jim McElreath	USA	Brabham-Offenhauser	97.186
31.05.65	Indianapolis 500	Jim Clark	GB.	Lotus 38-Ford	150.686
06.06.65	Milwaukee	Parnelli Jones	USA	Kuzma/Lotus 34-Ford	101.747
20.06.65	Langhorne	Jim McElreath	USA	Brabham-Offenhauser	89.109
04.07.65	Pikes Peak	Al Unser	USA	Eisert/Lotus 34-Ford	57.652
18.07.65	Trenton	AJ Foyt Jr	USA	Bignotti/Lotus 34-Ford	98.361
25.07.65	Indianapolis Raceway Park	Mario Andretti	USA	Hawk-Ford	101.657
01.08.65	Atlanta	Johnny Rutherford	USA	Watson-Ford	143.807
08.08.65	Langhorne	Jim McElreath	USA	Brabham-Offenhauser	104.858
14.08.65	Milwaukee	Joe Leonard	USA	Hallibrand-Ford	97.277
21.08.65	Springfield	AJ Foyt Jr	USA	Meskowski-Offenhauser	96.174
22.08.65	Milwaukee	Gordon Johncock	USA	Gerhardt-Offenhauser	100.453
06.09.65	Du Quoin	Don Branson	USA	Watson-Offenhauser	88.792
18.09.65	Indiana State Fairgrounds	AJ Foyt Jr	USA	Meskowski-Offenhauser	84.849
26.09.65	Trenton	AJ Foyt Jr	USA	Bignotti/Lotus 34-Ford	99.953
24.10.65	Sacramento	Don Branson	USA	Watson-Offenhauser	86.320
21.11.65	Phoenix	AJ Foyt Jr	USA	Bignotti/Lotus 34-Ford	99.986

1966

date	race	driver	nat	car	mph
20.03.66	Phoenix	Jim McElreath	USA	Brabham-Ford	98.819
24.04.66	Trenton	Rodger Ward	USA	Lola T90-Drake/Offenhauser	99.905
30.05.66	Indianapolis 500	Graham Hill	GB	Lola T90-Ford	144.317
05.06.66	Milwaukee	Mario Andretti	USA	Brawner/Brabham-Ford	95.655
12.06.66	Langhorne	Mario Andretti	USA	Brawner/Brabham-Ford	98.690
26.06.66	Atlanta	Mario Andretti	USA	Brawner/Brabham-Ford	141.362
04.07.66	Pikes Peak	Bobby Unser	USA	Unser-Chevrolet	60.081
24.07.66	Indianapolis Raceway Park	Mario Andretti	USA	Brawner/Brabham-Ford	95.373
07.08.66	Langhorne	Roger McCluskey	USA	Eagle 66-Ford	108.494
20.08.66	Springfield	Don Branson	USA	Watson-Offenhauser	95.243
27.08.66	Milwaukee	Mario Andretti	USA	Brawner/Brabham-Ford	104.060
05.09.66	Du Quoin	Bud Tingelstad	USA	Meskowski-Offenhauser	95.102
10.09.66	Indiana State Fairgrounds	Mario Andretti	USA	Kuzma-Offenhauser	96.582

date	race	driver	nat	car	mph
25.09.66	Trenton	Mario Andretti	USA	Brawner/Brabham-Ford	105.127
23.10.66	Sacramento	Dick Atkins	USA	Watson-Offenhauser	88.568
20.11.66	Phoenix	Mario Andretti	USA	Brawner/Brabham-Ford	104.686

1967

09.04.67	Phoenix	Lloyd Ruby	USA	Mongoose-Drake/Offenhauser	86.295
23.04.67	Trenton	Mario Andretti	USA	Brawner/Hawk-Ford	109.838
30.05.67	Indianapolis 500	AJ Foyt Jr	USA	Coyote/Lotus 34-Ford	151.207
04.06.67	Milwaukee	Gordon Johncock	USA	Gerhardt-Ford	98.643
18.06.67	Langhorne	Lloyd Ruby	USA	Lotus 38-Ford	113.380
25.06.67	Pikes Peak	Wes Vandervoort	USA	Chevrolet	58.254
01.07.67	Mosport Park	Bobby Unser	USA	Eagle 67-Ford	99.609
01.07.67	Mosport Park	Bobby Unser	USA	Eagle 67-Ford	not published
23.07.67	Indianapolis Raceway Park	Mario Andretti	USA	Brawner/Hawk-Ford	113.611
30.07.67	Langhorne	Mario Andretti	USA	Brawner/Hawk-Ford	113.184
06.08.67	St Jovite	Mario Andretti	USA	Brawner/Hawk-Ford	87.151
06.08.67	St Jovite	Mario Andretti	USA	Brawner/Hawk-Ford	92.401
19.08.67	Springfield	AJ Foyt Jr	USA	Meskowski-Offenhauser	86.326
20.08.67	Milwaukee	Mario Andretti	USA	Brawner/Hawk-Ford	105.386
04.09.67	Du Quoin	AJ Foyt Jr	USA	Meskowski-Offenhauser	93.578
09.09.67	Indiana State Fairgrounds	Mario Andretti	USA	Kuzma-Offenhauser	95.546
24.09.67	Trenton	AJ Foyt Jr	USA	Coyote-Ford	92.223
01.10.67	Sacramento	AJ Foyt Jr	USA	Meskowski-Offenhauser	87.712
22.10.67	Hanford	Gordon Johncock	USA	Gerhardt-Ford	127.523
19.11.67	Phoenix	Mario Andretti	USA	Brawner/Hawk-Ford	109.872
26.11.67	Riverside	Dan Gurney	USA	Eagle 67-Ford/Weslake	107.995

1968

17.03.68	Hanford	Gordon Johncock	USA	Gerhardt-Drake/Offenhauser	121.511
31.03.68	Stardust, Las Vegas	Bobby Unser	USA	Eagle 68-Ford	113.269
07.04.68	Phoenix	Bobby Unser	USA	Eagle 68-Drake/Offenhauser	100.938
21.04.68	Trenton	Bobby Unser	USA	Eagle 68-Drake/Offenhauser	103.397
30.05.68	Indianapolis 500	Bobby Unser	USA	Eagle 68-Drake/Offenhauser	152.882
09.06.68	Milwaukee	Lloyd Ruby	USA	Mongoose-Drake/Offenhauser	100.739
15.06.68	Mosport Park	Dan Gurney	USA	Eagle 68-Ford/Weslake	103.993
15.06.68	Mosport Park	Dan Gurney	USA	Eagle 68-Ford/Weslake	106.784
23.06.68	Langhorne	Gordon Johncock	USA	Gerhardt-Drake/Offenhauser	103.464
30.06.68	Pikes Peak	Bobby Unser	USA	Unser-Chevrolet	62.609
07.07.68	Castle Rock	AJ Foyt Jr	USA	Coyote-Ford	83.168
13.07.68	Nazareth	Al Unser	USA	Ward-Offenhauser	99.558
21.07.68	Indianapolis Raceway Park	Al Unser	USA	Lola T150-Ford	96.795
21.07.68	Indianapolis Raceway Park	Al Unser	USA	Lola T150-Ford	86.768
28.07.68	Langhorne	Al Unser	USA	Lola T150-Ford	107.651
28.07.68	Langhorne	Al Unser	USA	Lola T150-Ford	124.875
04.08.68	St Jovite	Mario Andretti	USA	Brawner/Hawk-Ford	96.492
04.08.68	St Jovite	Mario Andretti	USA	Brawner/Hawk-Ford	90.022
17.08.68	Springfield	Roger McCluskey	USA	Meskowski-Offenhauser	90.046
18.08.68	Milwaukee	Lloyd Ruby	USA	Mongoose-Drake/Offenhauser	108.735
02.09.68	Du Quoin	Mario Andretti	USA	Kuzma-Offenhauser	91.518
07.09.68	Indiana State Fairgrounds	AJ Foyt Jr	USA	Meskowski-Offenhauser	93.294
22.09.68	Trenton	Mario Andretti	USA	Brawner-Drake/Offenhauser	104.543
29.09.68	Sacramento	AJ Foyt Jr	USA	Meskowski-Offenhauser	87.118
13.10.68	Michigan	Ronnie Bucknum	USA	Eagle 68-Drake/Offenhauser	161.812
03.11.68	Hanford	AJ Foyt Jr	USA	Coyote-Ford	134.416
17.11.68	Phoenix	Gary Bettenhausen	USA	Gerhardt-Drake/Offenhauser	104.972
01.12.68	Riverside	Dan Gurney	USA	Eagle 68-Ford/Weslake	112.548

1969

30.03.69	Phoenix	George Follmer	USA	Gilbert-Chevrolet	109.866
13.04.69	Hanford	Mario Andretti	USA	Brawner/Hawk III-Ford	not published
30.05.69	Indianapolis 500	Mario Andretti	USA	Brawner/Hawk III-Ford	156.867
08.06.69	Milwaukee	Art Pollard	USA	Gerhardt-Drake/Offenhauser	112.156
15.06.69	Langhorne	Bobby Unser	USA	Eagle 69-Drake/Offenhauser	112.425

North American Indycar Championships

date	race	driver	nat	car	mph
29.06.69	Pikes Peak	Mario Andretti	USA	King-Chevrolet	58.424
06.07.69	Castle Rock	Gordon Johncock	USA	Eagle 69-Ford	84.337
12.07.69	Nazareth	Mario Andretti	USA	Kuzma-Offenhauser	105.851
19.07.69	Trenton	Mario Andretti	USA	Brawner/Hawk III-Ford	139.591
27.07.69	Indianapolis Raceway Park	Dan Gurney	USA	Eagle 69-Ford	92.275
27.07.69	Indianapolis Raceway Park	Peter Revson	USA	Brabham-Repco	94.967
17.08.69	Milwaukee	Al Unser	USA	Lola T152-Ford	106.758
18.08.69	Springfield	Mario Andretti	USA	Kuzma-Offenhauser	96.642
24.08.69	Dover Downs	Art Pollard	USA	Gerhardt-Plymouth	124.978
01.09.69	Du Quoin	Al Unser	USA	King-Ford	94.724
06.09.69	Indiana State Fairgrounds	AJ Foyt Jr	USA	Meskowski-Ford	93.609
14.09.69	Brainerd	Gordon Johncock	USA	Eagle 69-Ford	110.436
14.09.69	Brainerd	Dan Gurney	USA	Eagle 69-Ford	114.894
21.09.69	Trenton	Mario Andretti	USA	Brawner/Hawk III-Ford	134.382
28.09.69	Sacramento	Al Unser	USA	King-Ford	93.526
19.10.69	Seattle	Mario Andretti	USA	Brawner/Hawk III-Ford	85.164
19.10.69	Seattle	Al Unser	USA	Lola T152-Ford	83.486
15.11.69	Phoenix	Al Unser	USA	Lola T152-Ford	110.109
07.12.69	Riverside	Mario Andretti	USA	Brawner/Hawk III-Ford	107.786

1970

date	race	driver	nat	car	mph
28.03.70	Phoenix	Al Unser	USA	Colt 70-Ford	not published
04.04.70	Sears Point	Dan Gurney	USA	Eagle 70-Ford	86.972
26.04.70	Trenton	Lloyd Ruby	USA	Mongoose-Drake/Offenhauser	135.967
30.05.70	Indianapolis 500	Al Unser	USA	Colt 70-Ford	155.749
07.06.70	Milwaukee	Joe Leonard	USA	Colt 70-Ford	108.299
16.06.70	Langhorne	Bobby Unser	USA	Eagle 70-Drake/Offenhauser	106.302
28.06.70	Castle Rock	Mario Andretti	USA	McNamara T500-Ford	84.013
04.07.70	Michigan	Gary Bettenhausen	USA	Gerhardt-Drake/Offenhauser	140.625
26.07.70	Indianapolis Raceway Park	Al Unser	USA	Colt 70-Ford	92.799
22.08.70	Springfield	Al Unser	USA	King-Ford	62.301
23.08.70	Milwaukee	Al Unser	USA	Colt 70-Ford	114.304
06.09.70	Ontario	Jim McElreath	USA	Coyote-Ford	160.106
07.09.70	Du Quoin	Al Unser	USA	King-Ford	98.155
12.09.70	Indiana State Fairgrounds	Al Unser	USA	King-Ford	97.994
19.09.70	Sedalia	Al Unser	USA	King-Ford	98.039
03.10.70	Trenton	Al Unser	USA	Colt 70-Ford	137.639
04.10.70	Sacramento	Al Unser	USA	King-Ford	93.376
21.11.70	Phoenix	Swede Savage	USA	Eagle 70-Ford	116.807

1971

date	race	driver	nat	car	mph
28.02.71	Rafaela (RA)	Al Unser	USA	Colt 71-Ford	166.851
28.02.71	Rafaela (RA)	Al Unser	USA	Colt 71-Ford	148.764
27.03.71	Phoenix	Al Unser	USA	Colt 71-Ford	111.565
25.04.71	Trenton	Mike Mosley	USA	Eagle 71-Ford	132.562
29.05.71	Indianapolis 500	Al Unser	USA	Colt 71-Ford	157.735
06.06.71	Milwaukee	Al Unser	USA	Colt 71-Ford	114.912
03.07.71	Pocono	Mark Donohue	USA	McLaren M16A-Drake/Offenhauser	138.650
18.07.71	Michigan	Mark Donohue	USA	McLaren M16A-Drake/Offenhauser	146.074
15.08.71	Milwaukee	Bobby Unser	USA	Eagle 71-Drake/Offenhauser	109.384
05.09.71	Ontario	Joe Leonard	USA	Colt 71-Ford	152.355
03.10.71	Trenton	Bobby Unser	USA	Eagle 71-Drake/Offenhauser	140.778
23.10.71	Phoenix	AJ Foyt Jr	USA	Coyote-Ford	110.701

1972

date	race	driver	nat	car	mph
18.03.72	Phoenix	Bobby Unser	USA	Eagle 72-Offenhauser	102.825
23.04.72	Trenton	Gary Bettenhausen	USA	McLaren M16B-Offenhauser	145.642
27.05.72	Indianapolis 500	Mark Donohue	USA	McLaren M16B-Offenhauser	162.962
04.06.72	Milwaukee	Bobby Unser	USA	Eagle 72-Offenhauser	109.131
16.07.72	Michigan	Joe Leonard	USA	Parnelli-Offenhauser	139.316
29.07.72	Pocono	Joe Leonard	USA	Parnelli-Offenhauser	154.781
13.08.72	Milwaukee	Joe Leonard	USA	Parnelli-Offenhauser	111.652

date	race	driver	nat	car	mph
03.09.72	Ontario	Roger McCluskey	USA	McLaren M16B-Offenhauser	148.995
24.09.72	Trenton	Bobby Unser	USA	Eagle 72-Offenhauser	143.880
04.11.72	Phoenix	Bobby Unser	USA	Eagle 72-Offenhauser	127.618

1973

date	race	driver	nat	car	mph
07.04.73	Texas World Speedway	Al Unser	USA	Parnelli-Offenhauser	153.224
15.04.73	Trenton	AJ Foyt Jr	USA	Coyote-Foyt/Ford	138.359
15.04.73	Trenton	Mario Andretti	USA	Parnelli-Offenhauser	149.626
28.05.73	Indianapolis 500	Gordon Johncock	USA	Eagle 73-Offenhauser	159.036
10.06.73	Milwaukee	Bobby Unser	USA	Eagle 73-Offenhauser	113.957
01.07.73	Pocono	AJ Foyt Jr	USA	Coyote-Foyt/Ford	144.948
15.07.73	Michigan	Roger McCluskey	USA	McLaren M16B-Offenhauser	161.146
12.08.73	Milwaukee	Wally Dallenbach	USA	Eagle 73-Offenhauser	108.320
26.08.73	Ontario	Wally Dallenbach	USA	Eagle 73-Offenhauser	179.919
26.08.73	Ontario	Johnny Rutherford	USA	McLaren M16C-Offenhauser	164.162
02.09.73	Ontario	Wally Dallenbach	USA	Eagle 73-Offenhauser	157.660
16.09.73	Michigan	Bill Vukovich Jr	USA	Eagle 73-Offenhauser	134.026
16.09.73	Michigan	Johnny Rutherford	USA	McLaren M16C-Offenhauser	157.243
23.09.73	Trenton	Gordon Johncock	USA	Eagle 73-Offenhauser	135.025
06.10.73	Texas World Speedway	Gary Bettenhausen	USA	McLaren M16C-Offenhauser	181.910
03.11.73	Phoenix	Gordon Johncock	USA	Eagle 73-Offenhauser	115.015

1974

date	race	driver	nat	car	mph
03.03.74	Ontario	AJ Foyt Jr	USA	Coyote-Foyt/Ford	176.873
03.03.74	Ontario	Johnny Rutherford	USA	McLaren M16C/D-Offenhauser	172.673
10.03.74	Ontario	Bobby Unser	USA	Eagle 74-Offenhauser	157.017
17.03.74	Phoenix	Mike Mosley	USA	Eagle 74-Offenhauser	116.681
07.04.74	Trenton	Bobby Unser	USA	Eagle 74-Offenhauser	128.708
26.05.74	Indianapolis 500	Johnny Rutherford	USA	McLaren M16C/D-Offenhauser	158.589
09.06.74	Milwaukee	Johnny Rutherford	USA	McLaren M16C/D-Offenhauser	110.226
30.06.74	Pocono	Johnny Rutherford	USA	McLaren M16C/D-Offenhauser	156.701
21.07.74	Michigan	Bobby Unser	USA	Eagle 74-Offenhauser	141.717
11.08.74	Milwaukee	Gordon Johncock	USA	Eagle 74-Offenhauser	118.752
15.09.74	Michigan	Al Unser	USA	Eagle 74-Offenhauser	142.141
22.09.74	Trenton	AJ Foyt Jr	USA	Coyote-Foyt/Ford	135.372
22.09.74	Trenton	Bobby Unser	USA	Eagle 74-Offenhauser	156.069
02.11.74	Phoenix	Gordon Johncock	USA	Eagle 74-Offenhauser	124.202

1975

date	race	driver	nat	car	mph
02.03.75	Ontario	AJ Foyt Jr	USA	Coyote-Foyt/Ford	177.085
02.03.75	Ontario	Wally Dallenbach	USA	Eagle 75-Offenhauser	150.305
09.03.75	Ontario	AJ Foyt Jr	USA	Coyote-Foyt/Ford	154.344
16.03.75	Phoenix	Johnny Rutherford	USA	McLaren M16D-Offenhauser	110.971
06.04.75	Trenton	AJ Foyt Jr	USA	Coyote-Foyt/Ford	154.646
25.05.75	Indianapolis 500	Bobby Unser	USA	Eagle 75-Offenhauser	149.213
08.06.75	Milwaukee	AJ Foyt Jr	USA	Coyote-Foyt/Ford	114.042
29.06.75	Pocono	AJ Foyt Jr	USA	Coyote-Foyt/Ford	140.712
20.07.75	Michigan	AJ Foyt Jr	USA	Coyote-Foyt/Ford	158.907
17.08.75	Milwaukee	Mike Mosley	USA	Eagle 75-Offenhauser	114.393
13.09.75	Michigan	Tom Sneva	USA	McLaren M16C-Offenhauser	176.160
21.09.75	Trenton	Gordon Johncock	USA	Wildcat-Offenhauser	123.511
09.11.75	Phoenix	AJ Foyt Jr	USA	Coyote-Foyt/Ford	111.055

1976

date	race	driver	nat	car	mph
14.03.76	Phoenix	Bobby Unser	USA	Eagle 76-Offenhauser	107.918
02.05.76	Trenton	Johnny Rutherford	USA	McLaren M16E-Offenhauser	147.499
30.05.76	Indianapolis 500	Johnny Rutherford	USA	McLaren M16E-Offenhauser	148.725
13.06.76	Milwaukee	Mike Mosley	USA	Eagle 76-Offenhauser	121.557
27.06.76	Pocono	Al Unser	USA	Parnelli VPJ6B-Cosworth	143.622
18.07.76	Michigan	Gordon Johncock	USA	Wildcat-DGS/Offenhauser	165.033
01.08.76	Texas World Speedway	AJ Foyt Jr	USA	Coyote-Foyt/Ford	172.885

North American Indycar Championships

date	race	driver	nat	car	mph
15.08.76	Trenton	Gordon Johncock	USA	Wildcat-DGS/Offenhauser	135.929
22.08.76	Milwaukee	Al Unser	USA	Parnelli VPJ6B-Cosworth	121.907
05.09.76	Ontario	Bobby Unser	USA	Eagle 76-Offenhauser	143.246
18.09.76	Michigan	AJ Foyt Jr	USA	Coyote-Foyt/Ford	164.068
31.10.76	Texas World Speedway	Johnny Rutherford	USA	McLaren M16E-Offenhauser	150.313
07.11.76	Phoenix	Al Unser	USA	Parnelli VPJ6B-Cosworth	107.695

1977

date	race	driver	nat	car	mph
06.03.77	Ontario	AJ Foyt Jr	USA	Coyote-Foyt/Ford	154.073
27.03.77	Phoenix	Johnny Rutherford	USA	McLaren M24-Cosworth	111.395
02.04.77	Texas World Speedway	Tom Sneva	USA	McLaren M24-Cosworth	157.711
30.04.77	Trenton	Wally Dallenbach	USA	Wildcat-DGS/Offenhauser	151.288
29.05.77	Indianapolis 500	AJ Foyt Jr	USA	Coyote-Foyt/Ford	161.331
12.06.77	Milwaukee	Johnny Rutherford	USA	McLaren M24-Cosworth	92.962
26.06.77	Pocono	Tom Sneva	USA	McLaren M24-Cosworth	152.131
03.07.77	Mosport Park	AJ Foyt Jr	USA	Coyote-Foyt/Ford	90.723
17.07.77	Michigan	Danny Ongais	USA	Parnelli VPJ6B-Cosworth	149.152
31.07.77	Texas World Speedway	Johnny Rutherford	USA	McLaren M24-Cosworth	164.191
21.08.77	Milwaukee	Johnny Rutherford	USA	McLaren M24-Cosworth	103.798
04.09.77	Ontario	Al Unser	USA	Parnelli VPJ6B-Cosworth	152.074
17.09.77	Michigan	Gordon Johncock	USA	Wildcat-DGS/Offenhauser	175.250
29.10.77	Phoenix	Gordon Johncock	USA	Wildcat-DGS/Offenhauser	108.596

1978

date	race	driver	nat	car	mph
18.03.78	Phoenix	Gordon Johncock	USA	Wildcat Mk2-DGS/Offenhauser	116.757
26.03.78	Ontario	Danny Ongais	USA	Parnelli VPJ6B-Cosworth	162.810
15.04.78	Texas World Speedway	Danny Ongais	USA	Parnelli VPJ6B-Cosworth	173.594
23.04.78	Trenton	Gordon Johncock	USA	Wildcat Mk2-DGS/Offenhauser	130.988
28.05.78	Indianapolis 500	Al Unser	USA	Lola T500-Cosworth	161.363
11.06.78	Mosport Park	Danny Ongais	USA	Parnelli VPJ6B-Cosworth	87.164
18.06.78	Milwaukee	Rick Mears	USA	Penske PC6-Cosworth	120.677
25.06.78	Pocono	Al Unser	USA	Lola T500-Cosworth	142.261
16.07.78	Michigan	Johnny Rutherford	USA	McLaren M24B-Cosworth	159.941
23.07.78	Atlanta	Rick Mears	USA	Penske PC6-Cosworth	143.286
06.08.78	Texas World Speedway	AJ Foyt Jr	USA	Coyote-Foyt/Ford	159.060
20.08.78	Milwaukee	Danny Ongais	USA	Parnelli VPJ6B-Cosworth	108.385
03.09.78	Ontario	Al Unser	USA	Lola T500-Cosworth	145.158
16.09.78	Michigan	Danny Ongais	USA	Parnelli VPJ6B-Cosworth	146.246
23.09.78	Trenton	Mario Andretti	USA	Penske PC6-Cosworth	120.080
01.10.78	Silverstone (GB)	AJ Foyt Jr	USA	Coyote-Foyt/Ford	104.361
07.10.78	Brands Hatch (GB)	Rick Mears	USA	Penske PC6-Cosworth	95.789
28.10.78	Phoenix	Johnny Rutherford	USA	McLaren M24B-Cosworth	120.974

1979

date	race	driver	nat	car	mph
25.03.79	Ontario	AJ Foyt Jr	USA	Parnelli VPJ6C-Cosworth	154.279
08.04.79	Texas World Speedway	AJ Foyt Jr	USA	Coyote-Foyt/Ford	129.575
27.05.79	Indianapolis 500	Rick Mears	USA	Penske PC6-Cosworth	158.899
10.06.79	Milwaukee	AJ Foyt Jr	USA	Parnelli VPJ6C-Cosworth	108.955
24.06.79	Pocono	AJ Foyt Jr	USA	Parnelli VPJ6C-Cosworth	134.995
29.07.79	Texas World Speedway	AJ Foyt Jr	USA	Parnelli VPJ6C-Cosworth	162.934
12.08.79	Milwaukee	Roger McCluskey	USA	Lola T500B-Cosworth	117.135

CART Championship

2002 Jimmy Vasser leads Cristiano da Matta and Michael Andretti in the 197 mph Fontana CART race - the fastest race in history.

CART CHAMPCAR WORLD SERIES

year	driver	nat	team	car
1979	Rick Mears	USA	Penske Racing	Penske PC7-Cosworth/Penske PC6-Cosworth
1980	Johnny Rutherford	USA	Chaparral Racing	Chaparral 2K-Cosworth
1981	Rick Mears	USA	Penske Racing	Penske PC9B-Cosworth
1982	Rick Mears	USA	Penske Racing	Penske PC10-Cosworth
1983	Al Unser	USA	Penske Racing	Penske PC11-Cosworth/Penske PC10B-Cosworth
1984	Mario Andretti	USA	Newman-Haas Racing	Lola T800-Cosworth
1985	Al Unser	USA	Penske Racing	March 85C-Cosworth
1986	Bobby Rahal	USA	Truesports	March 86C-Cosworth
1987	Bobby Rahal	USA	Truesports	Lola T87/00-Cosworth
1988	Danny Sullivan	USA	Penske Racing	Penske PC17-Cosworth
1989	Emerson Fittipaldi	BR	Patrick Racing	Penske PC17-Chevrolet/Penske PC18-Chevrolet
1990	Al Unser Jr	USA	Galles-Kraco Racing	Lola T90/00-Chevrolet
1991	Michael Andretti	USA	Newman-Haas Racing	Lola T91/00-Chevrolet
1992	Bobby Rahal	USA	Rahal-Hogan Racing	Lola T92/00-Chevrolet
1993	Nigel Mansell	GB	Newman-Haas Racing	Lola T93/00-Ford
1994	Al Unser Jr	USA	Penske Racing	Penske PC23-Ilmor/Penske PC23-Mercedes-Benz
1995	Jacques Villeneuve	CDN	Forsythe-Green Racing	Reynard 95I-Ford
1996	Jimmy Vasser	USA	Chip Ganassi Racing	Reynard 96I-Honda
1997	Alessandro Zanardi	I	Chip Ganassi Racing	Reynard 97I-Honda
1998	Alessandro Zanardi	I	Chip Ganassi Racing	Reynard 98I-Honda
1999	Juan Pablo Montoya	CO	Chip Ganassi Racing	Reynard 99I-Honda
2000	Gil de Ferran	BR	Penske Racing	Reynard 2KI-Honda
2001	Gil de Ferran	BR	Penske Racing	Reynard 01I-Honda
2002	Cristiano da Matta	BR	Newman-Haas Racing	Lola B2/00-Toyota

1979

JIMMY BRYAN 150

11 March 1979. Phoenix. 150 laps of a 1.000-mile circuit = 150.000 miles. SCCA/CART Indycar Championship round 1

1	Gordon Johncock	Penske PC6-Cosworth	150	1h15m23.016
2	Rick Mears	Penske PC7-Cosworth	150	1h15m24.000
3	Johnny Rutherford	McLaren M24B-Cosworth	150	
4	Al Unser	Lola T500-Cosworth	150	
5	Bobby Unser	Penske PC7-Cosworth	149	
6	Mike Mosley	Eagle 79-Cosworth	148	

Winner's average speed: 119.389 mph. Pole position: B Unser, 145.666 mph

GOULD TWIN DIXIE 250 FIRST RACE

22 April 1979. Atlanta. 82 laps of a 1.522-mile circuit = 124.804 miles. SCCA/CART Indycar Championship round 2

1	Johnny Rutherford	McLaren M24B-Cosworth	82	47m28
2	Lee Kunzman	Parnelli VPJ6C-Cosworth	82	
3	Tom Sneva	McLaren M24-Cosworth	82	
4	Gordon Johncock	Penske PC6-Cosworth	82	
5	Rick Mears	Penske PC6-Cosworth	82	
6	Al Unser	Lola T500-Cosworth	82	

Winner's average speed: 157.758 mph. Pole position: Rutherford, 201.693 mph

GOULD TWIN DIXIE 250 SECOND RACE

22 April 1979. Atlanta. 82 laps of a 1.522-mile circuit = 124.804 miles. SCCA/CART Indycar Championship round 3

1	Johnny Rutherford	McLaren M24B-Cosworth	82	45m40
2	Rick Mears	Penske PC6-Cosworth	82	
3	Al Unser	Lola T500-Cosworth	82	
4	Bobby Unser	Penske PC6-Cosworth	82	
5	Tom Sneva	McLaren M24-Cosworth	81	
6	Danny Ongais	Parnelli VPJ6B-Cosworth	81	

Winner's average speed: 163.976 mph. Pole position: Rutherford (positions based on result of first race)

INDIANAPOLIS 500

27 May 1979. Indianapolis. 200 laps of a 2.500-mile circuit = 500.000 miles. SCCA/CART Indycar Championship round 4

1	Rick Mears	Penske PC6-Cosworth	200	3h08m47.970
2	AJ Foyt Jr	Parnelli VPJ6C-Cosworth	200	3h09m33.660
3	Mike Mosley	Eagle 79-Cosworth	200	3h09m36.000
4	Danny Ongais	Parnelli VPJ6B-Cosworth	199	
5	Bobby Unser	Penske PC7-Cosworth	199	
6	Gordon Johncock	Penske PC6-Cosworth	197	

Winner's average speed: 158.899 mph. Pole position: Mears, 193.736 mph. Fastest lap: Mosley, 193.216 mph

TRENTON TWIN INDY FIRST RACE

10 June 1979. Trenton. 67 laps of a 1.500-mile circuit = 100.500 miles. SCCA/CART Indycar Championship round 5

1	Bobby Unser	Penske PC7-Cosworth	67	49m50.0
2	Al Unser	Chaparral 2K-Cosworth	67	49m51.5
3	Gordon Johncock	Penske PC6-Cosworth	67	
4	Wally Dallenbach	Penske PC6-Cosworth	66	
5	Rick Mears	Penske PC6-Cosworth	66	
6	Tom Sneva	McLaren M24-Cosworth	66	

Winner's average speed: 121.003 mph. Pole position: Johncock, 172.298 mph

TRENTON TWIN INDY SECOND RACE

10 June 1979. Trenton. 67 laps of a 1.500-mile circuit = 100.500 miles. SCCA/CART Indycar Championship round 6

1	Bobby Unser	Penske PC7-Cosworth	67	40m46
2	Wally Dallenbach	Penske PC6-Cosworth	67	40m52
3	Johnny Rutherford	McLaren M24B-Cosworth	67	
4	Tom Bagley	Penske PC6-Cosworth	67	
5	Gordon Johncock	Penske PC6-Cosworth	66	
6	Danny Ongais	Parnelli VPJ6B-Cosworth	66	

Winner's average speed: 147.915 mph. Pole position: B Unser (positions based on results of first race)

NORTON 250 FIRST RACE

15 July 1979. Michigan. 63 laps of a 2.000-mile circuit = 126.000 miles.
SCCA/CART Indycar Championship round 7

1 Gordon Johncock	Penske PC6-Cosworth	63	44m13
2 Mike Mosley	Eagle 79-Cosworth	63	
3 Johnny Rutherford	McLaren M24B-Cosworth	63	
4 Rick Mears	Penske PC7-Cosworth	63	
5 Wally Dallenbach	Penske PC6-Cosworth	63	
6 Tom Bagley	Penske PC6-Cosworth	62	

Winner's average speed: 170.976 mph. Pole position: Bobby Unser
(Penske PC7-Cosworth), 203.879 mph

NORTON 250 SECOND RACE

15 July 1979. Michigan. 63 laps of a 2.000-mile circuit = 126.000 miles.
SCCA/CART Indycar Championship round 8

1 Bobby Unser	Penske PC7-Cosworth	63	48m40
2 Tom Sneva	McLaren M24-Cosworth	63	
3 Al Unser	Chaparral 2K-Cosworth	63	
4 Gordon Johncock	Penske PC6-Cosworth	63	
5 Rick Mears	Penske PC7-Cosworth	62	
6 Tom Bagley	Penske PC6-Cosworth	62	

Winner's average speed: 155.342 mph. Pole position: Johncock (positions
based on results of first race)

KENT OIL 150

5 August 1979. Watkins Glen. 62 laps of a 2.430-mile circuit = 150.660
miles. SCCA/CART Indycar Championship round 9

1 Bobby Unser	Penske PC7-Cosworth	62	1h14m42.000
2 Rick Mears	Penske PC7-Cosworth	62	1h15m01.171
3 Gordon Johncock	Penske PC6-Cosworth	62	
4 Danny Ongais	Parnelli VPJ6B-Cosworth	62	
5 Al Unser	Chaparral 2K-Cosworth	62	
6 Tom Bagley	Penske PC6-Cosworth	60	

Winner's average speed: 121.012 mph. Pole position: A Unser, 135.657
mph

DITZLER 150

19 August 1979. Trenton. 100 laps of a 1.500-mile circuit = 150.000 miles.
SCCA/CART Indycar Championship round 10

1 Rick Mears	Penske PC7-Cosworth	100	1h09m20
2 Bobby Unser	Penske PC7-Cosworth	100	
3 Tom Sneva	McLaren M24-Cosworth	100	
4 Wally Dallenbach	Penske PC6-Cosworth	100	
5 Johnny Rutherford	McLaren M24B-Cosworth	99	
6 Al Unser	Lola T500-Cosworth	99	

Winner's average speed: 129.808 mph. Pole position: B Unser, 171.277
mph

CALIFORNIA 500

2 September 1979. Ontario. 200 laps of a 2.500-mile circuit = 500.000
miles. SCCA/CART Indycar Championship round 11

1 Bobby Unser	Penske PC7-Cosworth	200	3h24m22
2 Rick Mears	Penske PC7-Cosworth	200	
3 Mario Andretti	Penske PC6-Cosworth	200	
4 Johnny Rutherford	McLaren M24B-Cosworth	199	
5 Al Unser	Chaparral 2K-Cosworth	197	
6 Danny Ongais	Parnelli VPJ6B-Cosworth	196	

Winner's average speed: 146.795 mph. Pole position: Mears, 203.046 mph

GOULD GRAND PRIX

15 September 1979. Michigan. 75 laps of a 2.000-mile circuit = 150.000
miles. SCCA/CART Indycar Championship round 12

1 Bobby Unser	Penske PC7-Cosworth	75	51m22.0
2 Tom Sneva	McLaren M24-Cosworth	75	51m32.6
3 Rick Mears	Penske PC7-Cosworth	74	out of fuel
4 Johnny Rutherford	McLaren M24B-Cosworth	74	
5 Tom Bagley	Penske PC6-Cosworth	74	
6 Wally Dallenbach	Penske PC6-Cosworth	73	engine

Winner's average speed: 175.211 mph. Pole position: B Unser, 35.294s

RICH'S INDY ATLANTA CLASSIC

30 September 1979. Atlanta. 100 laps of a 1.522-mile circuit = 152.200
miles. SCCA/CART Indycar Championship round 13

1 Rick Mears	Penske PC7-Cosworth	100	50m09
2 Gordon Johncock	Penske PC6-Cosworth	99	out of fuel
3 Bobby Unser	Penske PC7-Cosworth	99	
4 Wally Dallenbach	Penske PC6-Cosworth	99	
5 Al Unser	Chaparral 2K-Cosworth	97	
6 Joe Saldana	Eagle 79-Offenhauser	90	

Winner's average speed: 182.094 mph. Pole position: B Unser, 26.975s

1979 Al and Bobby Unser lead at the start at Phoenix in 1979, the first
year of the CART series.

MILLER HIGH LIFE 150

20 October 1979. Phoenix. 150 laps of a 1.000-mile circuit = 150.000
miles. SCCA/CART Indycar Championship round 14

1 Al Unser	Chaparral 2K-Cosworth	150	1h13m03.00
2 Bobby Unser	Penske PC7-Cosworth	150	1h13m08.76
3 Rick Mears	Penske PC7-Cosworth	148	
4 Gordon Johncock	Penske PC6-Cosworth	148	
5 Tom Sneva	McLaren M24-Cosworth	147	
6 Johnny Rutherford	McLaren M24B-Cosworth	146	

Winner's average speed: 123.203 mph. Pole position: B Unser, 24.33s

1979 FINAL CHAMPIONSHIP POSITIONS

1	Rick Mears	4060	7	Tom Sneva	1360
2	Bobby Unser	3780	8	Tom Bagley	1208
3	Gordon Johncock	2211	9	Wally Dallenbach	1149
4	Johnny Rutherford	2163	10	Mike Mosley	1121
5	Al Unser	2085			
6	Danny Ongais	1443			

1980

DATSUN 200

13 April 1980. Ontario. 80 laps of a 2.500-mile circuit = 200.000 miles.
CART/PPG Indycar World Series round 1

1 Johnny Rutherford	Chaparral 2K-Cosworth	80	1h14m04
2 Tom Sneva	McLaren M24-Cosworth	79	
3 Gordon Johncock	Wildcat Mk4-Cosworth	79	
4 Spike Gehlhausen	Penske PC7-Cosworth	78	
5 Tom Bagley	Penske PC6-Cosworth	77	
6 Gordon Smiley	Penske PC6-Cosworth	77	

Winner's average speed: 162.016 mph. Pole position: Rutherford, 45.73s

INDIANAPOLIS 500

26 May 1980. Indianapolis. 200 laps of a 2.500-mile circuit = 500.000 miles. CART/PPG Indycar World Series round 2

1	Johnny Rutherford	Chaparral 2K-Cosworth	200	3h29m59.56
2	Tom Sneva	McLaren M24-Cosworth	200	3h30m29.48
3	Gary Bettenhausen	Wildcat Mk2-Offenhauser	200	3h30m32.90
4	Gordon Johncock	Penske PC6-Cosworth	200	3h30m33.17
5	Rick Mears	Penske PC9-Cosworth	199	
6*	Pancho Carter	Penske PC7-Cosworth	199	

*Carter penalised 1 lap. Winner's average speed: 142.862 mph. Pole position: Rutherford, 192.256 mph. Fastest lap: Rutherford, 190.074 mph

GOULD REX MAYS 150

8 June 1980. Milwaukee. 150 laps of a 1.032-mile circuit = 154.800 miles. CART/PPG Indycar World Series round 3

1	Bobby Unser	Penske PC9-Cosworth	150	1h19m48.36
2	Johnny Rutherford	Chaparral 2K-Cosworth	150	1h19m54.87
3	Gordon Johncock	Phoenix 80-Cosworth	150	
4	Pancho Carter	Penske PC7-Cosworth	147	
5	Rick Mears	Penske PC9-Cosworth	147	
6	Tom Sneva	McLaren M24-Cosworth	146	

Winner's average speed: 116.382 mph. Pole position: Johncock, 27.377s

TRUE-VALUE HARDWARE 500

22 June 1980. Pocono. 200 laps of a 2.500-mile circuit = 500.000 miles. CART/PPG Indycar World Series round 4

1	Bobby Unser	Penske PC9-Cosworth	200	3h18m04.81
2	Johnny Rutherford	Chaparral 2K-Cosworth	200	3h18m25.84
3	Tom Sneva	McLaren M24-Cosworth	198	
4	Bill Alsup	Penske PC7-Cosworth	194	
5	Vern Schuppan	Wildcat Mk2-Offenhauser	193	
6	Pancho Carter	Lightning-Cosworth	193	

Winner's average speed: 151.454 mph. Pole position: B Unser, 185.491 mph

RED ROOF INNS 150

13 July 1980. Mid-Ohio. 65 laps of a 2.400-mile circuit = 156.000 miles. CART/PPG Indycar World Series round 5

1	Johnny Rutherford	Chaparral 2K-Cosworth	65	1h48m04.93
2	Gordon Johncock	Phoenix 80-Cosworth	65	1h48m27.98
3	Bill Alsup	Penske PC7-Cosworth	64	
4	Roger Mears	King-Chevrolet	63	
5	Vern Schuppan	Wildcat Mk2-Offenhauser	61	
6	Tom Gloy	Penske PC6-Cosworth	60	

Winner's average speed: 86.601 mph. Pole position: Al Unser (Longhorn LR01-Cosworth), 1m24.87

NORTON 200

20 July 1980. Michigan. 100 laps of a 2.000-mile circuit = 200.000 miles. CART/PPG Indycar World Series round 6

1	Johnny Rutherford	Chaparral 2K-Cosworth	100	1h20m48.00
2	Bobby Unser	Penske PC9-Cosworth	100	1h21m01.25
3	Pancho Carter	Penske PC7-Cosworth	100	1h21m06.20
4	Rick Mears	Penske PC9-Cosworth	100	1h21m17.00
5	Gordon Johncock	Wildcat Mk4-Cosworth	99	
6	Tom Sneva	McLaren M24-Cosworth	99	

Winner's average speed: 148.515 mph. Pole position: B Unser, 37.405s

KENT OIL 150

3 August 1980. Watkins Glen. 62 laps of a 2.430-mile circuit = 150.660 miles. CART/PPG Indycar World Series round 7

1	Bobby Unser	Penske PC9-Cosworth	62	1h30m51.00
2	Rick Mears	Penske PC9-Cosworth	62	1h30m51.45
3	Danny Ongais	Parnelli VPJ6B-Cosworth	62	1h30m56.00
4	Tom Sneva	McLaren M24-Cosworth	62	
5	Johnny Rutherford	Chaparral 2K-Cosworth	62	
6	Tom Bagley	Phoenix 80-Cosworth	62	

Winner's average speed: 99.500 mph. Pole position: Al Unser (Longhorn LR01-Cosworth), 1m06.085

TONY BETTENHAUSEN 200

10 August 1980. Milwaukee. 200 laps of a 1.032-mile circuit = 206.400 miles. CART/PPG Indycar World Series round 8

1	Johnny Rutherford	Chaparral 2K-Cosworth	200	1h54m13
2*	Rick Mears	Penske PC9-Cosworth	199	
3*	Bobby Unser	Penske PC9-Cosworth	197	
4	Tom Bagley	Phoenix 80-Cosworth	197	
5	Spike Gehlhausen	Penske PC7-Cosworth	194	
6	Bill Tempero	Eagle-Chevrolet	192	

*Mears and Unser penalised 1 lap. Winner's average speed: 108.426 mph. Pole position: Rutherford, 26.128s

CALIFORNIA 500

31 August 1980. Ontario. 200 laps of a 2.500-mile circuit = 500.000 miles. CART/PPG Indycar World Series round 9

1	Bobby Unser	Penske PC9-Cosworth	200	3h11m51.00
2	Johnny Rutherford	Chaparral 2K-Cosworth	200	3h11m59.53
3	Rick Mears	Penske PC9-Cosworth	199	
4	Al Unser	Longhorn LR01-Cosworth	193	
5	Tom Gloy	Penske PC6-Cosworth	190	
6	Dennis Firestone	Penske PC6-Cosworth	190	

Winner's average speed: 156.372 mph. Pole position: B Unser, 195.200 mph

GOULD GRAND PRIX

20 September 1980. Michigan. 75 laps of a 2.000-mile circuit = 150.000 miles. CART/PPG Indycar World Series round 10

1	Mario Andretti	Penske PC9-Cosworth	75	53m44.0
2	Bobby Unser	Penske PC9-Cosworth	75	53m44.8
3	Rick Mears	Penske PC9-Cosworth	75	53m51.0
4	Johnny Rutherford	Chaparral 2K-Cosworth	75	53m55.0
5	Al Unser	Longhorn LR01-Cosworth	73	
6	Tom Sneva	Phoenix 80-Cosworth	73	

Winner's average speed: 167.494 mph. Pole position: Andretti, 36.769s

COPA MEXICO 150

26 October 1980. Mexico City. 60 laps of a 2.479-mile circuit = 148.740 miles. CART/PPG Indycar World Series round 11

1	Rick Mears	Penske PC9-Cosworth	60	1h16m43
2	Bobby Unser	Penske PC9-Cosworth	60	1h16m50
3	Al Unser	Longhorn LR01-Cosworth	60	1h17m34
4	Tom Sneva	McLaren M24-Cosworth	59	
5	Dennis Firestone	Penske PC6-Cosworth	57	
6	Jim McElreath	Eagle-Offenhauser	55	

Winner's average speed: 116.329 mph. Pole position: B Unser, 1m11.839

MILLER HIGH LIFE 150

8 November 1980. Phoenix. 150 laps of a 1.000-mile circuit = 150.000 miles. CART/PPG Indycar World Series round 12

1	Tom Sneva	Phoenix 80-Cosworth	150	1h30m04.0
2	Mario Andretti	Penske PC9-Cosworth	150	1h30m13.1
3	Gary Bettenhausen	Orbitor Mk1-Cosworth	146	
4	Sheldon Kinser	Watson-Cosworth	146	
5	Dennis Firestone	Penske PC6-Cosworth	145	
6	Pete Halsmer	McLaren M24-Cosworth	145	

Winner's average speed: 99.926 mph. Pole position: Andretti, 25.194s

1980 FINAL CHAMPIONSHIP POSITIONS

1	Johnny Rutherford	4723	7	Bill Alsup	1214
2	Bobby Unser	3714	8	Al Unser	1153
3	Tom Sneva	2930	9	Gary Bettenhausen	1057
4	Rick Mears	2866	10	Vern Schuppan	806
5	Pancho Carter	1855			
6	Gordon Johncock	1572			

1981

KRACO CAR STEREO 150

22 March 1981. Phoenix. 150 laps of a 1.000-mile circuit = 150.000 miles. CART/PPG Indycar World Series round 1

1 Johnny Rutherford	Chaparral 2K-Cosworth	150	1h17m08
2 Bobby Unser	Penske PC9B-Cosworth	150	1h17m30
3 Tom Sneva	Phoenix 00-Cosworth	149	
4 Rick Mears	Penske PC9B-Cosworth	147	
5 Bill Alsup	Penske PC7-Cosworth	145	
6 Gordon Johncock	Wildcat Mk8-Cosworth	144	fuel pump

Winner's average speed: 116.681 mph. Pole position: B Unser, 25.165s

GOULD REX MAYS 150

7 June 1981. Milwaukee. 150 laps of a 1.032-mile circuit = 154.800 miles. CART/PPG Indycar World Series round 2

1 Mike Mosley	Eagle 81-Chevrolet	150	1h19m03.55
2 Kevin Cogan	Phoenix 80-Cosworth	150	
3 Mario Andretti	Wildcat Mk8-Cosworth	148	
4 Tom Sneva	Phoenix 80-Cosworth	147	
5 Al Unser	Longhorn LR02-Cosworth	146	
6 Johnny Rutherford	Chaparral 2K-Cosworth	146	

Winner's average speed: 117.482 mph. Pole position: Gordon Johncock (Wildcat Mk8-Cosworth), 26.726s

KRACO TWIN 125 FIRST RACE

28 June 1981. Atlanta. 83 laps of a 1.522-mile circuit = 126.326 miles. CART/PPG Indycar World Series round 3

1 Rick Mears	Penske PC9B-Cosworth	83	51m29
2 Johnny Rutherford	Chaparral 2K-Cosworth	83	51m32
3 Mario Andretti	Wildcat Mk8-Cosworth	83	
4 Gordon Johncock	Wildcat Mk8-Cosworth	83	
5 Pancho Carter	Penske PC7-Cosworth	83	
6 Al Unser	Longhorn LR02-Cosworth	83	

Winner's average speed: 147.224 mph. Pole position: Rutherford, 27.326s

KRACO TWIN 125 SECOND RACE

28 June 1981. Atlanta. 83 laps of a 1.522-mile circuit = 126.326 miles. CART/PPG Indycar World Series round 4

1 Rick Mears	Penske PC9B-Cosworth	83	45m20.0
2 Mario Andretti	Wildcat Mk8-Cosworth	83	45m21.7
3 Johnny Rutherford	Chaparral 2K-Cosworth	83	
4 Gordon Johncock	Wildcat Mk8-Cosworth	83	
5 Pancho Carter	Penske PC7-Cosworth	83	
6 Bobby Unser	Penske PC9B-Cosworth	83	

Winner's average speed: 167.196 mph. Pole position: Mears (positions based on results of first race)

NORTON MICHIGAN 500

25 July 1981. Michigan. 250 laps of a 2.000-mile circuit = 500.000 miles. CART/PPG Indycar World Series round 5

1 Pancho Carter	Penske PC7-Cosworth	250	3h45m45
2 Tony Bettenhausen Jr	McLaren M24B-Cosworth	250	3h45m47
3 Rick Mears	Penske PC9B-Cosworth	248	
4 Bill Alsup	Penske PC9B-Cosworth	247	
5 Tom Bigelow	Penske PC7-Chevrolet	247	
6 Gary Bettenhausen	Wildcat Mk8-Cosworth	247	

Winner's average speed: 132.890 mph. Pole position: Tom Sneva (March 81C-Cosworth), 35.757s

LOS ANGELES TIMES CALIFORNIA 500 KMS

30 August 1981. Riverside. 95 laps of a 3.250-mile circuit = 308.750 miles. CART/PPG Indycar World Series round 6

1 Rick Mears	Penske PC9B-Cosworth	95	2h43m40.98
2 Gordon Johncock	Wildcat Mk8-Cosworth	95	2h43m42.37
3 Bill Alsup	Penske PC9B-Cosworth	94	
4 Michael Chandler	Penske PC7-Cosworth	94	

5 Bob Lazier	Penske PC7-Cosworth	92	
6 Dick Simon	Watson-Cosworth	90	

Winner's average speed: 113.176 mph. Pole position: Geoff Brabham (Eagle 81-Chevrolet), 1m31.695

AB DICK TONY BETTENHAUSEN 200

5 September 1981. Milwaukee. 200 laps of a 1.032-mile circuit = 206.400 miles. CART/PPG Indycar World Series round 7

1 Tom Sneva	March 81C-Cosworth	200	1h41m41
2 Rick Mears	Penske PC9B-Cosworth	200	1h41m45
3 Bobby Unser	Penske PC9B-Cosworth	199	
4 Johnny Rutherford	Chaparral 2K-Cosworth	198	
5 Al Unser	Longhorn LR02-Cosworth	197	
6 Gordon Johncock	Wildcat Mk8-Cosworth	197	

Winner's average speed: 121.790 mph. Pole position: Rutherford, 26.492s

DETROIT NEWS GRAND PRIX

20 September 1981. Michigan. 74 laps of a 2.000-mile circuit = 148,000 miles. CART/PPG Indycar World Series round 8

1 Rick Mears	Penske PC9B-Cosworth	74	1h10m30
2 Mario Andretti	Wildcat Mk8-Cosworth	74	
3 Al Unser	Eagle 81-Cosworth	74	
4 Bill Alsup	Penske PC9B-Cosworth	74	
5 Gordon Johncock	Wildcat Mk8-Cosworth	74	
6 Dick Ferguson	Penske PC7-Cosworth	74	

Winner's average speed: 125.957 mph. Pole position: Mears, 35.980s

WATKINS GLEN 200

4 October 1981. Watkins Glen. 60 laps of a 3.377-mile circuit = 202.620 miles. CART/PPG Indycar World Series round 9

1 Rick Mears	Penske PC9B-Cosworth	60	1h52m17
2 Johnny Rutherford	Chaparral 2K-Cosworth	59	
3 Bill Alsup	Penske PC7-Cosworth	59	
4 Bob Lazier	Penske PC7-Cosworth	58	
5 Steve Chassey	Eagle-Chevrolet	56	
6 Rocky Moran	Eagle 81-Chevrolet	55	out of fuel

Winner's average speed: 108.273 mph. Pole position: Mario Andretti (Wildcat Mk8-Cosworth), 1m56.167

COPA MEXICO 150

18 October 1981. Mexico City. 59 laps of a 2.479-mile circuit = 146.261 miles. CART/PPG Indycar World Series round 10

1 Rick Mears	Penske PC9B-Cosworth	59	1h24m48
2 Al Unser	Longhorn LR02-Cosworth	59	1h24m53
3 Gordon Johncock	Wildcat Mk8-Cosworth	59	
4 Bob Lazier	March 81C-Cosworth	59	
5 Bill Alsup	Penske PC9B-Cosworth	58	
6 Pancho Carter	Penske PC7-Cosworth	58	

Winner's average speed: 103.487 mph. Pole position: Bobby Unser (Penske PC9B-Cosworth), 1m11.538

MILLER HIGH LIFE 150

31 October 1981. Phoenix. 150 laps of a 1.000-mile circuit = 150.000 miles. CART/PPG Indycar World Series round 11

1 Tom Sneva	March 81C-Cosworth	150	1h20m10
2 Bobby Unser	Penske PC9B-Cosworth	150	1h20m11
3 Gordon Johncock	Wildcat Mk8-Cosworth	150	
4 Mario Andretti	Wildcat Mk8-Cosworth	150	
5 Pancho Carter	Penske PC7-Cosworth	148	
6 Josele Garza	Penske PC9-Cosworth	148	

Winner's average speed: 112.266 mph. Pole position: B Unser, 24.211s

1981 FINAL CHAMPIONSHIP POSITIONS

1	Rick Mears	304	7	Bobby Unser	99
2	Bill Alsup	177	8	Tom Sneva	96
3	Pancho Carter	168	9	Bob Lazier	92
4	Gordon Johncock	142	10	Al Unser	90
5	Johnny Rutherford	120			
6	Tony Bettenhausen Jr	107			

1982

KRACO CAR STEREO 150

28 March 1982. Phoenix. 150 laps of a 1.000-mile circuit = 150.000 miles. CART/PPG Indycar World Series round 1

1	Rick Mears	Penske PC10-Cosworth	150	1h15m48.231
2	Mario Andretti	Wildcat Mk8B-Cosworth	150	1h15m52.431
3	Kevin Cogan	Penske PC10-Cosworth	149	
4	Johnny Rutherford	Chaparral 2K-Cosworth	149	
5	Gordon Johncock	Wildcat Mk8B-Cosworth	147	
6	Pancho Carter	March 82C-Cosworth	147	

Winner's average speed: 118.727 mph. Pole position: Mears, 23.977s

STROH'S 200

1 May 1982. Atlanta. 132 laps of a 1.522-mile circuit = 200.904 miles. CART/PPG Indycar World Series round 2

1	Rick Mears	Penske PC10-Cosworth	132	1h13m10.00
2	Gordon Johncock	Wildcat Mk8B-Cosworth	132	1h13m17.69
3	Danny Sullivan	March 82C-Cosworth	125	
4	Roger Mears	Penske PC7-Cosworth	125	
5	Bill Alsup	Penske PC9C-Cosworth	121	
6	Herm Johnson	Eagle 81-Chevrolet	115	

Winner's average speed: 164.750 mph. Pole position: Mears, 26.798s

GOULD REX MAYS 150

13 June 1982. Milwaukee. 150 laps of a 1.032-mile circuit = 154.800 miles. CART/PPG Indycar World Series round 3

1	Gordon Johncock	Wildcat Mk8B-Cosworth	150	1h10m52.69
2	AJ Foyt Jr	March 82C-Cosworth	150	1h11m04.49
3	Rick Mears	Penske PC10-Cosworth	149	
4	Tom Sneva	March 82C-Cosworth	149	
5	Kevin Cogan	Penske PC10-Cosworth	146	
6	Johnny Parsons Jr	March 82C-Cosworth	146	

Winner's average speed: 131.042 mph. Pole position: Johncock, 25.266s

BUDWEISER CLEVELAND 500

4 July 1982. Cleveland. 125 laps of a 2.485-mile circuit = 310.625 miles. CART/PPG Indycar World Series round 4

1	Bobby Rahal	March 82C-Cosworth	125	3h03m44
2	Mario Andretti	Wildcat Mk8B-Cosworth	125	3h04m05
3	Al Unser	Longhorn LR03-Cosworth	125	
4	Rick Mears	Penske PC10-Cosworth	124	
5	Gordon Johncock	Wildcat Mk8B-Cosworth	124	
6	Geoff Brabham	March 82C-Cosworth	123	

Winner's average speed: 101.438 mph. Pole position: Kevin Cogan (Penske PC10-Cosworth), 1m12.20

NORTON MICHIGAN 500

18 July 1982. Michigan. 250 laps of a 2.000-mile circuit = 500.000 miles. CART/PPG Indycar World Series round 5

1	Gordon Johncock	Wildcat Mk8B-Cosworth	250	3h14m54.00
2	Mario Andretti	Wildcat Mk8B-Cosworth	250	3h15m18.72
3	Bobby Rahal	March 82C-Cosworth	245	
4	Al Unser	Longhorn LR03-Cosworth	245	
5	Tom Bigelow	Eagle 81-Chevrolet	241	
6	Gary Bettenhausen	Penske PC7-Chevrolet	241	

Winner's average speed: 153.925 mph. Pole position: Rick Mears

PROVIMI VEAL TONY BETTENHAUSEN 200

1 August 1982. Milwaukee. 200 laps of a 1.032-mile circuit = 206.400 miles. CART/PPG Indycar World Series round 6

1	Tom Sneva	March 82C-Cosworth	200	1h49m57.545
2	Bobby Rahal	March 82C-Cosworth	199	
3	Mario Andretti	Wildcat Mk8B-Cosworth	199	
4	Howdy Holmes	March 82C-Cosworth	197	
5	Kevin Cogan	Penske PC10-Cosworth	197	
6	Pancho Carter	March 82C-Cosworth	196	

Winner's average speed: 112.624 mph. Pole position: Rick Mears (Penske PC10-Cosworth), 25.028s

DOMINO'S PIZZA POCONO 500

15 August 1982. Pocono. 200 laps of a 2.500-mile circuit = 500.000 miles. CART/PPG Indycar World Series round 7

1	Rick Mears	Penske PC10-Cosworth	200	3h25m39
2	Kevin Cogan	Penske PC10-Cosworth	200	3h25m41
3	Bobby Rahal	March 82C-Cosworth	197	
4	Geoff Brabham	March 82C-Cosworth	197	
5	Tony Bettenhausen Jr	March 82C-Cosworth	195	
6	Gordon Johncock	Wildcat Mk8B-Cosworth	193	gearbox

Winner's average speed: 145.879 mph. Pole position: Mears, 44.780s

AIRCAL 500 KMS

29 August 1982. Riverside. 95 laps of a 3.250-mile circuit = 308.750 miles. CART/PPG Indycar World Series round 8

1	Rick Mears	Penske PC10-Cosworth	95	2h42m14
2	Tom Sneva	March 82C-Cosworth	95	2h43m20
3	Johnny Rutherford	March 82C-Cosworth	93	
4	Roger Mears	Penske PC7-Cosworth	90	
5	Al Unser Jr	March 82C-Cosworth	86	fuel feed
6	Greg Leffler	Eagle 81-Chevrolet	78	valve

Winner's average speed: 114.187 mph. Pole position: Kevin Cogan (Penske PC10-Cosworth), 1m30.365

ROAD AMERICA 200

19 September 1982. Elkhart Lake. 50 laps of a 4.048-mile circuit = 202.400 miles. CART/PPG Indycar World Series round 9

1	Hector Rebaque	March 82C-Cosworth	50	1h49m56.09
2	Al Unser	Longhorn LR03B-Cosworth	49	out of fuel
3	Bobby Rahal	March 82C-Cosworth	49	
4	Josele Garza	Penske PC9-Cosworth	49	
5	Rick Mears	Penske PC10-Cosworth	48	
6	Phil Krueger	King-Chevrolet	45	

Winner's average speed: 110.465 mph. Pole position: Mears, 1m57.710

DETROIT NEWS GRAND PRIX

26 September 1982. Michigan. 75 laps of a 2.000-mile circuit = 150.000 miles. CART/PPG Indycar World Series round 10

1	Bobby Rahal	March 82C-Cosworth	75	1h04m03
2	Mario Andretti	Wildcat Mk8B-Cosworth	75	1h04m16
3	Geoff Brabham	March 82C-Cosworth	74	
4	Tony Bettenhausen Jr	March 82C-Cosworth	74	
5	Howdy Holmes	March 82C-Cosworth	74	
6	Bill Alsup	Penske PC9C-Cosworth	74	

Winner's average speed: 140.515 mph. Pole position: Rick Mears (Penske PC10-Cosworth), 34.881s

MILLER HIGH LIFE 150

6 November 1982. Phoenix. 150 laps of a 1.000-mile circuit = 150.000 miles. CART/PPG Indycar World Series round 11

1	Tom Sneva	March 82C-Cosworth	150	1h21m05
2	Rick Mears	Penske PC10-Cosworth	150	1h21m11
3	Mario Andretti	Wildcat Mk8B-Cosworth	150	
4	Kevin Cogan	Penske PC10-Cosworth	148	
5	Bobby Rahal	March 82C-Cosworth	148	

6 Tony Bettenhausen Jr March 82C-Cosworth 147
Winner's average speed: 110.997 mph. Pole position: Mears, 23.881s

1982 FINAL CHAMPIONSHIP POSITIONS

1	Rick Mears	294	7	Al Unser	125
2	Bobby Rahal	242	8	Geoff Brabham	110
3	Mario Andretti	188	9	Roger Mears	103
4	Gordon Johncock	186	10	Tony Bettenhausen Jr	80
5	Tom Sneva	144			
6	Kevin Cogan	136			

1983

KRACO DIXIE 200

17 April 1983. Atlanta. 132 laps of a 1.522-mile circuit = 200.904 miles. CART/PPG Indycar World Series round 1

1	Gordon Johncock	Wildcat Mk9-Cosworth	132	1h22m29.295
2	Al Unser	Penske PC11-Cosworth	132	1h22m53.000
3	John Paul Jr	Penske PC10-Cosworth	131	
4	Pete Halsmer	Penske PC10-Cosworth	130	
5	Mario Andretti	Lola T700-Cosworth	128	
6	Al Unser Jr	Eagle 83-Cosworth	127	

Winner's average speed: 146.133 mph. Pole position: Rick Mears (Penske PC11-Cosworth), 26.730s

INDIANAPOLIS 500

29 May 1983. Indianapolis. 200 laps of a 2.500-mile circuit = 500.000 miles. CART/PPG Indycar World Series round 2

1	Tom Sneva	March 83C-Cosworth	200	3h05m03.066
2*	Al Unser	Penske PC11-Cosworth	200	3h05m14.240
3	Rick Mears	Penske PC11-Cosworth	200	3h05m24.928
4	Geoff Brabham	Penske PC10-Cosworth	199	
5	Kevin Cogan	March 83C-Cosworth	198	
6	Howdy Holmes	March 83C-Cosworth	198	

*penalised 2 laps. Winner's average speed: 162.117 mph. Pole position: Teo Fabi (March 83C-Cosworth), 207.395 mph. Fastest lap: Fabi, 45.568s

DANA REX MAYS 150

12 June 1983. Milwaukee. 150 laps of a 1.032-mile circuit = 154.800 miles. CART/PPG Indycar World Series round 3

1	Tom Sneva	March 83C-Cosworth	150	1h17m31
2	Al Unser	Penske PC11-Cosworth	150	1h17m32
3	Rick Mears	Penske PC11-Cosworth	150	
4	Teo Fabi	March 83C-Cosworth	149	
5	Mike Mosley	March 83C-Cosworth	148	
6*	Bobby Rahal	March 83C-Cosworth	147	

*Rahal penalised 1 lap. Winner's average speed: 119.819 mph. Pole position: Fabi, 26.259s

BUDWEISER CLEVELAND 500

3 July 1983. Cleveland. 125 laps of a 2.485-mile circuit = 310.625 miles. CART/PPG Indycar World Series round 4

1	Al Unser	Penske PC11-Cosworth	125	2h51m54
2	Pete Halsmer	Penske PC10-Cosworth	125	2h52m25
3	Teo Fabi	March 83C-Cosworth	124	
4	Mike Mosley	March 83C-Cosworth	124	
5	Tom Sneva	March 83C-Cosworth	123	
6	Roger Mears	Penske PC10-Cosworth	121	

Winner's average speed: 108.421 mph. Pole position: Mario Andretti (Lola T700-Cosworth), 1m13.516

NORTON MICHIGAN 500

17 July 1983. Michigan. 250 laps of a 2.000-mile circuit = 500.000 miles. CART/PPG Indycar World Series round 5

1	John Paul Jr	Penske PC10-Cosworth	250	3h42m27
2	Al Unser	Penske PC11-Cosworth	250	3h42m42
3	Mario Andretti	Lola T700-Cosworth	250	
4	Rick Mears	Penske PC11-Cosworth	249	accident
5	Bobby Rahal	March 82C-Cosworth	249	
6	Pancho Carter	March 82C-Cosworth	248	

Winner's average speed: 134.862 mph. Pole position: Teo Fabi (March 83C-Cosworth), 35.621s

PROVIMI VEAL 200

31 July 1983. Elkhart Lake. 50 laps of a 4.048-mile circuit = 202.400 miles. CART/PPG Indycar World Series round 6

1	Mario Andretti	Lola T700-Cosworth	50	2h00m42.75
2	Al Unser Jr	Eagle 83-Cosworth	50	2h00m58.73
3	Al Unser	Penske PC11-Cosworth	50	
4	Tom Sneva	Theodore T83-Cosworth	49	
5	John Paul Jr	Penske PC10-Cosworth	49	
6	Steve Chassey	Eagle 82-Chevrolet	49	

Winner's average speed: 100.603 mph. Pole position: Andretti, 1m58.898

DOMINO'S PIZZA 500

14 August 1983. Pocono. 200 laps of a 2.500-mile circuit = 500.000 miles. CART/PPG Indycar World Series round 7

1	Teo Fabi	March 83C-Cosworth	200	3h42m28
2	Al Unser Jr	March 83C-Cosworth	200	3h42m32
3	Rick Mears	Penske PC10B-Cosworth	200	
4	Mike Mosley	March 83C-Cosworth	199	
5	Bobby Rahal	March 83C-Cosworth	199	
6	Pancho Carter	March 82C-Cosworth	198	

Winner's average speed: 134.852 mph. Pole position: Tom Sneva (March 83C-Cosworth), 46.912s

LOS ANGELES TIMES/BUDWEISER 500

28 August 1983. Riverside. 95 laps of a 3.250-mile circuit = 308.750 miles. CART/PPG Indycar World Series round 8

1	Bobby Rahal	March 83C-Cosworth	95	2h45m28
2	Teo Fabi	March 83C-Cosworth	95	2h45m56
3	John Paul Jr	Penske PC10-Cosworth	95	
4	Al Unser Jr	Eagle 83-Cosworth	94	
5	Tom Sneva	March 83C-Cosworth	93	
6	Tom Klausler	Schkee DB6-Chevrolet	90	

Winner's average speed: 111.956 mph. Pole position: Fabi, 1m30.887

ESCORT RADAR WARNING 200

11 September 1983. Mid-Ohio. 84 laps of a 2.400-mile circuit = 201.600 miles. CART/PPG Indycar World Series round 9

1	Teo Fabi	March 83C-Cosworth	84	2h01m49
2	Mario Andretti	Lola T700-Cosworth	84	2h02m15
3	Bobby Rahal	March 83C-Chevrolet	84	
4	Al Unser	Penske PC10B-Cosworth	83	
5	Danny Ongais	March 83C-Cosworth	83	
6	Kevin Cogan	Theodore T83-Cosworth	83	

Winner's average speed: 99.297 mph. Pole position: Rahal, 1m21.364

DETROIT NEWS GRAND PRIX 200

18 September 1983. Michigan. 100 laps of a 2.000-mile circuit = 200.000 miles. CART/PPG Indycar World Series round 10

1	Rick Mears	Penske PC10B-Cosworth	100	1h05m49
2	Bobby Rahal	March 83C-Cosworth	100	1h05m57
3	Teo Fabi	March 83C-Cosworth	99	
4	Mario Andretti	Lola T700-Cosworth	99	
5	Al Unser	Penske PC10B-Cosworth	98	
6	Chip Ganassi	Wildcat Mk9B-Cosworth	98	

Winner's average speed: 182.325 mph. Pole position: Rahal, 35.075s

CAESARS PALACE GRAND PRIX

9 October 1983. Caesars Palace. 178 laps of a 1.125-mile circuit = 200.250 miles. CART/PPG Indycar World Series round 11

1	Mario Andretti	Lola T700-Cosworth	178	2h17m48
2	John Paul Jr	Penske PC10-Cosworth	178	2h17m50
3	Chip Ganassi	Wildcat Mk9B-Cosworth	177	
4	Al Unser	Penske PC10B-Cosworth	177	
5	Pete Halsmer	Penske PC10-Cosworth	177	
6	Pancho Carter	March 82C-Cosworth	176	

Winner's average speed: 87.192 mph. Pole position: Paul Jr, 34.888s

CRIBARI WINES 300 KMS

23 October 1983. Laguna Seca. 98 laps of a 1.900-mile circuit = 186.200 miles. CART/PPG Indycar World Series round 12

1	Teo Fabi	March 83C-Cosworth	98	1h44m28
2	Mario Andretti	Lola T700-Cosworth	98	1h44m50
3	Chip Ganassi	Wildcat Mk9B-Cosworth	98	1h44m54
4	Al Unser Jr	Eagle 83-Cosworth	98	1h45m21
5	Howdy Holmes	March 83C-Cosworth	96	
6	Roger Mears	Penske PC10-Cosworth	94	

Winner's average speed: 106.943 mph. Pole position: Fabi, 56.920s

MILLER HIGH LIFE 150

29 October 1983. Phoenix. 150 laps of a 1.000-mile circuit = 150.000 miles. CART/PPG Indycar World Series round 13

1	Teo Fabi	March 83C-Cosworth	150	1h11m03
2	Mario Andretti	Lola T700-Cosworth	150	1h11m12
3	Tom Sneva	March 83C-Cosworth	149	
4	Al Unser	Penske PC10B-Cosworth	148	
5	Chip Ganassi	Wildcat Mk9B-Cosworth	148	
6	Kevin Cogan	March 83C-Cosworth	148	

Winner's average speed: 126.671 mph. Pole position: Fabi, 24.947s

1983 FINAL CHAMPIONSHIP POSITIONS

1	Al Unser	151	7	Al Unser jr	89
2	Teo Fabi	146	8	John Paul jr	84
3	Mario Andretti	133	9	Chip Ganassi	56
4	Tom Sneva	96	10	Pancho Carter	53
5	Bobby Rahal	94			
6	Rick Mears	92			

1984

TOYOTA GRAND PRIX OF LONG BEACH

1 April 1984. Long Beach. 112 laps of a 1.670-mile circuit = 187.040 miles. CART/PPG Indycar World Series round 1

1	Mario Andretti	Lola T800-Cosworth	112	2h15m23.0
2	Geoff Brabham	March 84C-Cosworth	112	2h16m26.2
3	Tom Sneva	March 84C-Cosworth	111	
4	Jim Crawford	Theodore RK83-Cosworth	111	
5	Emerson Fittipaldi	March 83C-Cosworth	110	
6	Jacques Villeneuve	March 83C-Cosworth	110	

Winner's average speed: 82.894 mph. Pole position: Andretti, 1m06.263

DANA JIMMY BRYAN 150

15 April 1984. Phoenix. 150 laps of a 1.000-mile circuit = 150.000 miles. CART/PPG Indycar World Series round 2

1	Tom Sneva	March 84C-Cosworth	150	1h14m39.42
2	Howdy Holmes	March 84C-Cosworth	150	1h15m04.20
3	Michael Andretti	March 84C-Cosworth	149	
4	Dick Simon	March 84C-Cosworth	148	
5	Danny Ongais	March 84C-Cosworth	148	
6	Danny Sullivan	Shierson DSR1-Cosworth	146	

Winner's average speed: 120.551 mph. Pole position: Sneva, 24.070s

INDIANAPOLIS 500

27 May 1984. Indianapolis. 200 laps of a 2.500-mile circuit = 500.000 miles. CART/PPG Indycar World Series round 3

1	Rick Mears	March 84C-Cosworth	200	3h03m21.66
2	Roberto Guerrero	March 84C-Cosworth	198	
3	Al Unser	March 84C-Cosworth	198	
4	Al Holbert	March 84C-Cosworth	198	
5	Michael Andretti	March 84C-Cosworth	198	
6	AJ Foyt Jr	March 84C-Cosworth	197	

Winner's average speed: 163.612 mph. Pole position: Tom Sneva (March 84C-Cosworth), 210.029 mph. Fastest lap: Gordon Johncock (March 84C-Cosworth), 204.815 mph

DANA REX MAYS CLASSIC 200

3 June 1984. Milwaukee. 200 laps of a 1.032-mile circuit = 206.400 miles. CART/PPG Indycar World Series round 4

1	Tom Sneva	March 84C-Cosworth	200	1h41m40.128
2	Rick Mears	March 84C-Cosworth	200	1h41m44.000
3	Al Unser Jr	March 84C-Cosworth	200	
4	Michael Andretti	March 84C-Cosworth	199	
5	Al Unser	March 84C-Cosworth	199	
6	Gordon Johncock	March 84C-Cosworth	197	

Winner's average speed: 121.807 mph. Pole position: Mears, 25.173s

STROH'S GI JOE'S 200

17 June 1984. Portland. 104 laps of a 1.915-mile circuit = 199.160 miles. CART/PPG Indycar World Series round 5

1	Al Unser Jr	March 84C-Cosworth	104	1h53m17.39
2	Geoff Brabham	March 84C-Cosworth	104	1h53m57.00
3	Teo Fabi	March 84C-Cosworth	104	
4	Derek Daly	March 84C-Cosworth	103	
5	Tom Sneva	March 84C-Cosworth	102	
6	Jacques Villeneuve	March 83C-Cosworth	100	

Winner's average speed: 105.478 mph. Pole position: Mario Andretti (Lola T800-Cosworth), 59.437s

MEADOWLANDS GRAND PRIX

1 July 1984. Meadowlands. 100 laps of a 1.682-mile circuit = 168.200 miles. CART/PPG Indycar World Series round 6

1	Mario Andretti	Lola T800-Cosworth	100	2h04m59.4
2	Danny Sullivan	Lola T800-Cosworth	100	2h06m11.1
3	Geoff Brabham	March 84C-Cosworth	99	
4	Al Unser Jr	March 84C-Cosworth	99	
5	Al Holbert	March 84C-Cosworth	98	
6	Tom Sneva	March 84C-Cosworth	98	

Winner's average speed: 80.742 mph. Pole position: Andretti, 1m03.067

BUDWEISER CLEVELAND GRAND PRIX

8 July 1984. Cleveland. 88 laps of a 2.485-mile circuit = 218.680 miles. CART/PPG Indycar World Series round 7

1	Danny Sullivan	Lola T800-Cosworth	88	1h50m17
2	Chip Ganassi	March 84C-Cosworth	86	
3	Michael Andretti	March 84C-Cosworth	86	
4	Rick Mears	March 84C-Cosworth	86	
5	Roberto Guerrero	March 84C-Cosworth	86	
6	Derek Daly	March 84C-Cosworth	85	

Winner's average speed: 118.974 mph. Pole position: Mario Andretti (Lola T800-Cosworth), 1m10.637

NORTON MICHIGAN 500

22 July 1984. Michigan. 250 laps of a 2.000-mile circuit = 500.000 miles. CART/PPG Indycar World Series round 8

1	Mario Andretti	Lola T800-Cosworth	250	3h44m45.00
2	Tom Sneva	March 84C-Cosworth	250	3h44m45.14
3	Rick Mears	March 84C-Cosworth	250	
4	Gordon Johncock	March 84C-Cosworth	250	
5	Roberto Guerrero	March 84C-Cosworth	250	

6 Pancho Carter	March 84C-Cosworth	249	accident

Winner's average speed: 133.482 mph. Pole position: Andretti, 34.109s

PROVIMI VEAL 200

5 August 1984. Elkhart Lake. 50 laps of a 4.048-mile circuit = 202.400 miles. CART/PPG Indycar World Series round 9

1 Mario Andretti	Lola T800-Cosworth	50	1h43m08.409
2 Bobby Rahal	March 84C-Cosworth	50	1h44m13.249
3 Al Unser	March 84C-Cosworth	50	
4 Rick Mears	March 84C-Cosworth	49	
5 Geoff Brabham	March 84C-Cosworth	49	
6 John Paul Jr	March 84C-Cosworth	49	

Winner's average speed: 117.743 mph. Pole position: Andretti, 1m55.187

DOMINO'S PIZZA POCONO 500

19 August 1984. Pocono. 200 laps of a 2.500-mile circuit = 500.000 miles. CART/PPG Indycar World Series round 10

1 Danny Sullivan	Lola T800-Cosworth	200	3h38m29.69
2 Rick Mears	March 84C-Cosworth	200	3h38m29.96
3 Bobby Rahal	March 84C-Cosworth	200	
4 Tom Sneva	March 84C-Cosworth	200	
5 Danny Ongais	March 84C-Cosworth	199	
6 Scott Brayton	March 84C-Cosworth	199	

Winner's average speed: 137.303 mph. Pole position: Mears, 44.363s

ESCORT RADAR WARNING 200

2 September 1984. Mid-Ohio. 84 laps of a 2.400-mile circuit = 201.600 miles. CART/PPG Indycar World Series round 11

1 Mario Andretti	Lola T800-Cosworth	84	1h59m50.11
2 Bobby Rahal	March 84C-Cosworth	84	2h00m28.01
3 Danny Sullivan	Lola T800-Cosworth	83	
4 Emerson Fittipaldi	March 84C-Cosworth	82	
5 Rick Mears	March 84C-Cosworth	82	
6 Howdy Holmes	March 84C-Cosworth	82	

Winner's average speed: 100.939 mph. Pole position: Andretti, 1m22.215

MOLSON BREWERIES 200

9 September 1984. Sanair. 225 laps of a 0.826-mile circuit = 185.850 miles. CART/PPG Indycar World Series round 12

1 Danny Sullivan	Lola T800-Cosworth	225	1h39m49.43
2 Bobby Rahal	March 84C-Cosworth	225	1h39m59.77
3 Michael Andretti	March 84C-Cosworth	225	
4 Josele Garza	March 84C-Cosworth	224	
5 Johnny Rutherford	March 84C-Cosworth	224	
6 Al Unser Jr	March 84C-Cosworth	224	

Winner's average speed: 111.707 mph. Pole position: Rahal, 20.718s

DETROIT NEWS GRAND PRIX 200

23-24 September 1984. Michigan. 100 laps of a 2.000-mile circuit = 200.000 miles. Race stopped after 33 laps due to rain, restarted over an additional 67 laps. CART/PPG Indycar World Series round 13

1 Mario Andretti	Lola T800-Cosworth	100	1h11m12.42
2 Tom Sneva	March 84C-Cosworth	100	1h11m13.82
3 Danny Ongais	March 84C-Cosworth	100	
4 Al Unser	March 84C-Cosworth	100	
5 Bobby Rahal	March 84C-Cosworth	100	
6 Al Unser Jr	March 84C-Cosworth	100	

Winner's average speed: 168.523 mph. Pole position: Johnny Rutherford (March 84C-Cosworth), 33.459s

STROH'S BOBBY BALL 150

14 October 1984. Phoenix. 150 laps of a 1.000-mile circuit = 150.000 miles. CART/PPG Indycar World Series round 14

1 Bobby Rahal	March 84C-Cosworth	150	1h31m47.49
2 Al Unser Jr	March 84C-Cosworth	150	1h31m48.30
3 Michael Andretti	March 84C-Cosworth	150	
4 Tom Sneva	March 84C-Cosworth	150	
5 Danny Ongais	March 84C-Cosworth	150	

6 Corrado Fabi	Lola T800-Cosworth	149	

Winner's average speed: 98.048 mph. Pole position: Jacques Villeneuve (March 84C-Cosworth), 23.155s

QUINN'S COOLER 300 KMS

21 October 1984. Laguna Seca. 98 laps of a 1.900-mile circuit = 186.200 miles. CART/PPG Indycar World Series round 15

1 Bobby Rahal	March 84C-Cosworth	98	1h33m47.97
2 Mario Andretti	Lola T800-Cosworth	98	1h34m01.14
3 Michael Andretti	March 84C-Cosworth	98	
4 Al Unser Jr	March 84C-Cosworth	98	
5 Geoff Brabham	March 84C-Cosworth	97	
6 Al Unser	March 84C-Cosworth	97	

Winner's average speed: 119.105 mph. Pole position: Mario Andretti, 54.030s

CAESARS PALACE GRAND PRIX

11 November 1984. Caesars Palace. 178 laps of a 1.125-mile circuit = 200.250 miles. CART/PPG Indycar World Series round 16

1 Tom Sneva	March 84C-Cosworth	178	2h08m13.55
2 Mario Andretti	Lola T800-Cosworth	178	2h08m20.02
3 John Paul Jr	March 84C-Cosworth	178	
4 Al Unser Jr	March 84C-Cosworth	177	
5 Geoff Brabham	March 84C-Cosworth	177	
6 Roberto Guerrero	March 84C-Cosworth	176	

Winner's average speed: 93.702 mph. Pole position: Danny Sullivan (Lola T800-Cosworth), 32.952s

1984 FINAL CHAMPIONSHIP POSITIONS

1	Mario Andretti	176	8	Geoff Brabham	87
2	Tom Sneva	163	9	Al Unser	76
3	Bobby Rahal	137	10	Danny Ongais	53
4=	Rick Mears	110			
	Danny Sullivan	110			
6	Al Unser jr	103			
7	Michael Andretti	102			

1985

TOYOTA GRAND PRIX OF LONG BEACH

14 April 1985. Long Beach. 90 laps of a 1.670-mile circuit = 150.300 miles. CART/PPG Indycar World Series round 1

1 Mario Andretti	Lola T900-Cosworth	90	1h42m50.07
2 Emerson Fittipaldi	March 85C-Cosworth	90	1h43m50.30
3 Danny Sullivan	March 85C-Cosworth	89	out of fuel
4 Jim Crawford	Lola T900-Cosworth	89	
5 Al Unser	March 85C-Cosworth	89	
6 Geoff Brabham	March 85C-Cosworth	88	

Winner's average speed: 87.694 mph. Pole position: Andretti, 1m05.213

INDIANAPOLIS 500

26 May 1985. Indianapolis. 200 laps of a 2.500-mile circuit = 500.000 miles. CART/PPG Indycar World Series round 2

1 Danny Sullivan	March 85C-Cosworth	200	3h16m06.069
2 Mario Andretti	Lola T900-Cosworth	200	3h16m08.546
3 Roberto Guerrero	March 85C-Cosworth	200	
4*Al Unser	March 85C-Cosworth	199	
5 Johnny Parsons Jr	March 85C-Cosworth	198	
6*Johnny Rutherford	March 85C-Cosworth	198	

*Unser and Rutherford penalised 1 lap. Winner's average speed: 152.982 mph. Pole position: Pancho Carter (March 85C-Buick), 212.583 mph

MILLER AMERICAN REX MAYS 200

2 June 1985. Milwaukee. 200 laps of a 1.032-mile circuit = 206.400 miles. CART/PPG Indycar World Series round 3

1	Mario Andretti	Lola T900-Cosworth	200	1h36m38.89
2	Tom Sneva	Eagle 85-Cosworth	200	1h36m51.61
3	Rick Mears	March 85C-Cosworth	200	
4	Danny Sullivan	March 85C-Cosworth	199	
5	Pancho Carter	March 85C-Cosworth	196	
6	Roberto Guerrero	March 85C-Cosworth	196	

Winner's average speed: 128.135 mph. Pole position: Andretti, 24.389s

STROH'S GI JOE'S 200

16 June 1985. Portland. 104 laps of a 1.915-mile circuit = 199.160 miles. CART/PPG Indycar World Series round 4

1	Mario Andretti	Lola T900-Cosworth	104	1h51m35.524
2	Al Unser Jr	Lola T900-Cosworth	104	1h52m13.024
3	Emerson Fittipaldi	March 85C-Cosworth	104	
4	Al Unser	March 85C-Cosworth	103	
5	Kevin Cogan	March 85C-Cosworth	102	
6	Scott Brayton	March 85C-Cosworth	102	

Winner's average speed: 107.083 mph. Pole position: Danny Sullivan (March 85C-Cosworth), 59.932s

UNITED STATES GRAND PRIX AT THE MEADOWLANDS

30 June 1985. Meadowlands. 100 laps of a 1.682-mile circuit = 168.200 miles. CART/PPG Indycar World Series round 5

1	Al Unser Jr	Lola T900-Cosworth	100	1h51m55.51
2	Emerson Fittipaldi	March 85C-Cosworth	100	1h52m32.09
3	Al Unser	March 85C-Cosworth	100	
4	Michael Andretti	March 85C-Cosworth	100	
5	Bruno Giacomelli	March 85C-Cosworth	99	
6	Tom Sneva	Eagle 85-Cosworth	99	

Winner's average speed: 90.167 mph. Pole position: Mario Andretti (Lola T900-Cosworth), 1m01.504

BUDWEISER CLEVELAND GRAND PRIX

7 July 1985. Cleveland. 88 laps of a 2.485-mile circuit = 218.680 miles. CART/PPG Indycar World Series round 6

1	Al Unser Jr	Lola T900-Cosworth	88	1h45m31.850
2	Geoff Brabham	March 85C-Cosworth	88	1h45m45.997
3	Al Unser	March 85C-Cosworth	88	
4	Jacques Villeneuve	March 85C-Cosworth	88	
5	Arie Luyendyk	Lola T900-Cosworth	88	
6	Josele Garza	March 85C-Cosworth	88	

Winner's average speed: 124.331 mph. Pole position: Bobby Rahal (March 85C-Cosworth), 1m07.793

MICHIGAN 500

28 July 1985. Michigan. 250 laps of a 2.000-mile circuit = 500.000 miles. CART/PPG Indycar World Series round 7

1	Emerson Fittipaldi	March 85C-Cosworth	250	3h53m58.33
2	Al Unser	March 85C-Cosworth	250	3h53m58.73
3	Tom Sneva	Eagle 85-Cosworth	249	
4	Johnny Rutherford	March 85C-Cosworth	248	
5	Ed Pimm	Eagle 85-Cosworth	248	
6	Bobby Rahal	March 85C-Cosworth	247	

Winner's average speed: 128.220 mph. Pole position: Rick Mears (March 85C-Cosworth), 33.689s

PROVIMI VEAL 200

4 August 1985. Elkhart Lake. 50 laps of a 4.048-mile circuit = 202.400 miles. CART/PPG Indycar World Series round 8

1	Jacques Villeneuve	March 85C-Cosworth	50	1h45m12.15
2	Michael Andretti	March 85C-Cosworth	50	1h45m22.17
3	Alan Jones	Lola T900-Cosworth	50	
4	Bobby Rahal	March 85C-Cosworth	50	
5	Emerson Fittipaldi	March 85C-Cosworth	50	
6	Arie Luyendyk	Lola T900-Cosworth	50	

Winner's average speed: 115.435 mph. Pole position: Danny Sullivan (March 85C-Cosworth), 1m52.029

DOMINO'S PIZZA 500

18 August 1985. Pocono. 200 laps of a 2.500-mile circuit = 500.000 miles. CART/PPG Indycar World Series round 9

1	Rick Mears	March 85C-Cosworth	200	3h17m47.44
2	Al Unser Jr	Lola T900-Cosworth	200	3h17m49.62
3	Al Unser	March 85C-Cosworth	200	
4	Bobby Rahal	March 85C-Cosworth	200	
5	Danny Sullivan	March 85C-Cosworth	199	
6	Emerson Fittipaldi	March 85C-Cosworth	197	

Winner's average speed: 151.676 mph. Pole position: Mears, 44.219s

ESCORT RADAR WARNING 200

1 September 1985. Mid-Ohio. 84 laps of a 2.400-mile circuit = 201.600 miles. CART/PPG Indycar World Series round 10

1	Bobby Rahal	March 85C-Cosworth	84	1h52m23.20
2	Danny Sullivan	March 85C-Cosworth	84	1h53m19.33
3	Jacques Villeneuve	March 85C-Cosworth	84	
4	Al Unser Jr	Lola T900-Cosworth	83	
5	Bill Whittington	March 85C-Cosworth	83	
6	Bruno Giacomelli	March 85C-Cosworth	83	

Winner's average speed: 107.628 mph. Pole position: Rahal, 1m15.267

GRAND PRIX MOLSON INDY

8 September 1985. Sanair. 225 laps of a 0.826-mile circuit = 185.850 miles. CART/PPG Indycar World Series round 11

1	Johnny Rutherford	March 85C-Cosworth	225	2h03m54.37
2	Pancho Carter	March 85C-Cosworth	225	2h03m54.47
3	Al Unser Jr	Lola T900-Cosworth	225	
4	Geoff Brabham	March 85C-Cosworth	225	
5	Danny Sullivan	March 85C-Cosworth	224	
6	Josele Garza	March 85C-Cosworth	223	

Winner's average speed: 89.996 mph. Pole position: Bobby Rahal (March 85C-Cosworth), 20.252s

DETROIT NEWS GRAND PRIX 200

22 September 1985. Michigan. 100 laps of a 2.000-mile circuit = 200.000 miles. CART/PPG Indycar World Series round 12

1	Bobby Rahal	March 85C-Cosworth	100	1h13m19.45
2	Rick Mears	March 85C-Cosworth	100	1h13m20.16
3	Ed Pimm	Eagle 85-Cosworth	100	
4	Kevin Cogan	March 85C-Cosworth	99	
5	Tom Sneva	Eagle 85-Cosworth	99	
6	Josele Garza	March 85C-Cosworth	99	

Winner's average speed: 163.657 mph. Pole position: Rahal, 33.605s

STROH'S 300 KMS

6 October 1985. Laguna Seca. 98 laps of a 1.900-mile circuit = 186.200 miles. CART/PPG Indycar World Series round 13

1	Bobby Rahal	March 85C-Cosworth	98	1h38m56.09
2	Al Unser	March 85C-Cosworth	98	1h39m08.81
3	Al Unser Jr	Lola T900-Cosworth	98	1h39m11.88
4	Roberto Guerrero	March 85C-Cosworth	98	1h39m17.55
5	Jan Lammers	Lola T800-Cosworth	97	
6	Bruno Giacomelli	March 85C-Cosworth	97	

Winner's average speed: 112.923 mph. Pole position: Rahal, 54.164s

DANA JIMMY BRYAN 150

13 October 1985. Phoenix. 150 laps of a 1.000-mile circuit = 150.000 miles. CART/PPG Indycar World Series round 14

1	Al Unser	March 85C-Cosworth	150	1h14m35.99
2	Al Unser Jr	Lola T900-Cosworth	149	
3	Mario Andretti	Lola T900-Cosworth	149	
4	Danny Sullivan	March 85C-Cosworth	149	
5	Michael Andretti	March 85C-Cosworth	149	
6	Bobby Rahal	March 85C-Cosworth	149	

Winner's average speed: 120.644 mph. Pole position: A Unser, 22.238s

BEATRICE INDY CHALLENGE

9 November 1985. Tamiami Park. 112 laps of a 1.784-mile circuit = 199.808 miles. CART/PPG Indycar World Series round 15

1	Danny Sullivan	March 85C-Cosworth	112	2h04m59.41
2	Bobby Rahal	March 85C-Cosworth	112	2h05m16.21
3	Al Unser Jr	Lola T900-Cosworth	112	
4	Al Unser	March 85C-Cosworth	112	
5	Roberto Moreno	March 85C-Cosworth	112	
6	Danny Ongais	March 85C-Cosworth	110	

Winner's average speed: 95.915 mph. Pole position: Rahal, 56.408s

1985 FINAL CHAMPIONSHIP POSITIONS

1	Al Unser	151	8	Jacques Villeneuve	54
2	Al Unser Jr	150	9	Michael Andretti	53
3	Bobby Rahal	134	10=	Rick Mears	51
4	Danny Sullivan	126		Johnny Rutherford	51
5	Mario Andretti	114			
6	Emerson Fittipaldi	104			
7	Tom Sneva	66			

1986 Bobby Rahal and the TrueSports team won the first of back-to-back Championships in 1986.

1986

DANA 200

6 April 1986. Phoenix. 200 laps of a 1.000-mile circuit = 200.000 miles. CART/PPG Indycar World Series round 1

1	Kevin Cogan	March 86C-Cosworth	200	1h39m42.76
2	Tom Sneva	March 86C-Cosworth	199	
3	Emerson Fittipaldi	March 86C-Cosworth	199	
4	Danny Sullivan	March 86C-Cosworth	198	
5	Johnny Rutherford	March 86C-Cosworth	198	
6	Arie Luyendyk	Lola T86/00-Cosworth	196	

Winner's average speed: 120.346 mph. Pole position: Mario Andretti (Lola T86/00-Cosworth), 21.716s

TOYOTA GRAND PRIX OF LONG BEACH

13 April 1986. Long Beach. 95 laps of a 1.670-mile circuit = 158.650 miles. CART/PPG Indycar World Series round 2

1	Michael Andretti	March 86C-Cosworth	95	1h57m34.18	
2	Al Unser Jr	Lola T86/00-Cosworth	95	1h57m34.56	
3	Geoff Brabham	Lola T86/00-Cosworth	95		
4	Tom Sneva	March 86C-Cosworth	94		
5	Mario Andretti	Lola T86/00-Cosworth	94		
6	Roberto Moreno	Lola T86/00-Cosworth	93		engine

Winner's average speed: 80.965 mph. Pole position: Danny Sullivan (March 86C-Cosworth), 1m06.565

INDIANAPOLIS 500

31 May 1986. Indianapolis. 200 laps of a 2.500-mile circuit = 500.000 miles. CART/PPG Indycar World Series round 3

1	Bobby Rahal	March 86C-Cosworth	200	2h55m43.480
2	Kevin Cogan	March 86C-Cosworth	200	2h55m44.921
3	Rick Mears	March 86C-Cosworth	200	2h55m45.361
4	Roberto Guerrero	March 86C-Cosworth	200	2h55m54.025
5	Al Unser Jr	Lola T86/00-Cosworth	199	
6	Michael Andretti	March 86C-Cosworth	199	

Winner's average speed: 170.722 mph. Pole position: Mears, 216.828 mph. Fastest lap: Rahal, 43.031s

MILLER AMERICAN 200

8 June 1986. Milwaukee. 200 laps of a 1.032-mile circuit = 206.400 miles. CART/PPG Indycar World Series round 4

1	Michael Andretti	March 86C-Cosworth	200	1h42m45
2	Tom Sneva	March 86C-Cosworth	199	out of fuel
3	Rick Mears	March 86C-Cosworth	199	
4	Johnny Rutherford	March 86C-Cosworth	199	
5	Mario Andretti	Lola T86/00-Cosworth	198	
6	Bobby Rahal	March 86C-Cosworth	198	

Winner's average speed: 120.526 mph. Pole position: Michael Andretti, 23.544s

BUDWEISER GI JOE'S 200

15 June 1986. Portland. 104 laps of a 1.915-mile circuit = 199.160 miles. CART/PPG Indycar World Series round 5

1	Mario Andretti	Lola T86/00-Cosworth	104	1h50m53.48
2	Michael Andretti	March 86C-Cosworth	104	1h50m53.55
3	Al Unser Jr	Lola T86/00-Cosworth	104	
4	Tom Sneva	March 86C-Cosworth	102	accident
5	Jacques Villeneuve	March 86C-Cosworth	102	accident
6	Ed Pimm	March 86C-Cosworth	101	

Winner's average speed: 107.760 mph. Pole position: Emerson Fittipaldi (March 86C-Cosworth), 1m13.275

CHASE GRAND PRIX AT THE MEADOWLANDS

29 June 1986. Meadowlands. 100 laps of a 1.682-mile circuit = 168.200 miles. CART/PPG Indycar World Series round 6

1	Danny Sullivan	March 86C-Cosworth	100	1h49m17.54
2	Emerson Fittipaldi	March 86C-Cosworth	100	1h49m28.43
3	Bobby Rahal	March 86C-Cosworth	100	1h49m49.55
4	Roberto Guerrero	March 86C-Cosworth	100	1h50m06.22
5	Jacques Villeneuve	March 86C-Cosworth	99	
6	Randy Lanier	March 86C-Cosworth	95	

Winner's average speed: 92.340 mph. Pole position: Michael Andretti (March 86C-Cosworth), 1m00.535

BUDWEISER CLEVELAND GRAND PRIX

6 July 1986. Cleveland. 88 laps of a 2.485-mile circuit = 218.680 miles. CART/PPG Indycar World Series round 7

1	Danny Sullivan	March 86C-Cosworth	88	1h43m01.17
2	Michael Andretti	March 86C-Cosworth	88	1h43m45.42
3	Mario Andretti	Lola T86/00-Cosworth	88	
4	Rick Mears	March 86C-Cosworth	88	
5	Tom Sneva	March 86C-Cosworth	88	
6	Raul Boesel	Lola T86/00-Cosworth	85	

Winner's average speed: 127.362 mph. Pole position: Sullivan, 1m06.063

MOLSON INDY TORONTO

20 July 1986. Toronto. 103 laps of a 1.784-mile circuit = 183.752 miles. CART/PPG Indycar World Series round 8

1	Bobby Rahal	March 86C-Cosworth	103	2h05m50.51
2	Danny Sullivan	March 86C-Cosworth	103	2h05m52.76
3	Mario Andretti	Lola T86/00-Cosworth	103	2h06m18.03
4	Al Unser Jr	Lola T86/00-Cosworth	103	2h06m25.96
5	Kevin Cogan	March 86C-Cosworth	103	2h06m55.98
6	Arie Luyendyk	March 86C-Cosworth	102	

Winner's average speed: 87.611 mph. Pole position: Emerson Fittipaldi (March 86C-Cosworth), 1m00.312

MICHIGAN 500

2 August 1986. Michigan. 250 laps of a 2.000-mile circuit = 500.000 miles. CART/PPG Indycar World Series round 9

1	Johnny Rutherford	March 86C-Cosworth	250	3h38m45.32
2	Josele Garza	March 86C-Cosworth	250	3h38m47.14
3	Pancho Carter	Lola T86/00-Cosworth	248	
4	Geoff Brabham	Lola T86/00-Honda	239	accident
5	Raul Boesel	Lola T86/00-Cosworth	239	
6	Roberto Moreno	Lola T86/00-Cosworth	238	

Winner's average speed: 137.140 mph. Pole position: Rick Mears (March 86C-Cosworth), 32.229s

DOMINO'S PIZZA 500

17 August 1986. Pocono. 200 laps of a 2.500-mile circuit = 500.000 miles. CART/PPG Indycar World Series round 10

1	Mario Andretti	Lola T86/00-Cosworth	200	3h17m13.8
2	Kevin Cogan	March 86C-Cosworth	199	
3	Pancho Carter	Lola T86/00-Cosworth	198	
4	AJ Foyt Jr	March 86C-Cosworth	197	
5	Raul Boesel	March 86C-Cosworth	197	
6	Al Unser Jr	Lola T86/00-Cosworth	195	

Winner's average speed: 152.107 mph. Pole position: Michael Andretti (March 86C-Cosworth), 43.748s

ESCORT RADAR WARNING 200

31 August 1986. Mid-Ohio. 84 laps of a 2.400-mile circuit = 201.600 miles. CART/PPG Indycar World Series round 11

1	Bobby Rahal	March 86C-Cosworth	84	1h56m18.62
2	Roberto Guerrero	March 86C-Cosworth	84	1h56m19.44
3	Danny Sullivan	March 86C-Cosworth	84	
4	Kevin Cogan	March 86C-Cosworth	84	
5	Al Unser Jr	Lola T86/00-Cosworth	83	
6	Derek Daly	March 86C-Cosworth	82	

Winner's average speed: 103.998 mph. Pole position: Mario Andretti (Lola T86/00-Cosworth), 1m16.237

MOLSON INDY MONTREAL

7 September 1986. Sanair. 225 laps of a 0.826-mile circuit = 185.850 miles. CART/PPG Indycar World Series round 12

1	Bobby Rahal	March 86C-Cosworth	225	1h48m05.83
2	Al Unser Jr	Lola T86/00-Cosworth	225	1h48m19.57
3	Emerson Fittipaldi	March 86C-Cosworth	223	
4	Kevin Cogan	March 86C-Cosworth	223	
5	Danny Sullivan	March 86C-Cosworth	221	
6	Michael Andretti	March 86C-Cosworth	219	

Winner's average speed: 103.157 mph. Pole position: Rick Mears (Penske PC15-Chevrolet), 20.074s

PEPSI COLA 250

28 September 1986. Michigan. 125 laps of a 2.000-mile circuit = 250 miles. CART/PPG Indycar World Series round 13

1	Bobby Rahal	March 86C-Cosworth	125	1h22m33.20
2	Michael Andretti	March 86C-Cosworth	125	1h22m36.45
3	Emerson Fittipaldi	March 86C-Cosworth	125	1h22m38.27
4	Kevin Cogan	March 86C-Cosworth	125	1h22m38.38
5	Tom Sneva	March 86C-Cosworth	125	1h22m41.82
6	Roberto Moreno	Lola T86/00-Cosworth	124	

Winner's average speed: 181.701 mph. Pole position: Rick Mears (March 86C-Chevrolet), 32.810s

RACE FOR LIFE 200

21 September, 4 October 1986. Elkhart Lake. 50 laps of a 4.048-mile circuit = 202.400 miles. Race scheduled for 21 September, cancelled due to rain, restarted on 4 October. CART/PPG Indycar World Series round 14

1	Emerson Fittipaldi	March 86C-Cosworth	50	2h26m38.4
2	Michael Andretti	March 86C-Cosworth	50	2h26m38.7
3	Rick Mears	March 86C-Chevrolet	50	
4	Roberto Guerrero	March 86C-Cosworth	50	
5	Bobby Rahal	March 86C-Cosworth	50	
6	Danny Sullivan	March 86C-Cosworth	50	

Winner's average speed: 82.815 mph. Pole position: Rahal, 1m55.829

CHAMPION SPARK PLUG 300 KMS

12 October 1986. Laguna Seca. 98 laps of a 1.900-mile circuit = 186.200 miles. CART/PPG Indycar World Series round 15

1	Bobby Rahal	March 86C-Cosworth	98	1h33m20.34
2	Danny Sullivan	March 86C-Cosworth	98	1h33m21.75
3	Michael Andretti	March 86C-Cosworth	98	1h33m40.85
4	Mario Andretti	Lola T86/00-Cosworth	98	1h33m47.03
5	Roberto Guerrero	March 86C-Cosworth	98	1h34m10.41
6	Geoff Brabham	Lola T86/00-Cosworth	98	1h34m13.23

Winner's average speed: 119.693 mph. Pole position: Mario Andretti, 53.036s

CIRCLE K FIESTA BOWL 200

19 October 1986. Phoenix. 200 laps of a 1.000-mile circuit = 200.000 miles. CART/PPG Indycar World Series round 16

1	Michael Andretti	March 86C-Cosworth	200	1h29m06.16
2	Danny Sullivan	March 86C-Cosworth	200	1h29m26.38
3	Bobby Rahal	March 86C-Cosworth	199	
4	Mario Andretti	Lola T86/00-Cosworth	199	
5	Emerson Fittipaldi	March 86C-Cosworth	198	
6	Al Unser Jr	Lola T86/00-Cosworth	193	

Winner's average speed: 134.676 mph. Pole position: Rahal, 22.097s

NISSAN INDY CHALLENGE

9 November 1986. Tamiami Park. 112 laps of a 1.784-mile circuit = 199.808 miles. CART/PPG Indycar World Series round 17

1	Al Unser Jr	Lola T86/00-Cosworth	112	1h52m45.38
2	Roberto Guerrero	March 86C-Cosworth	112	1h53m20.74
3	Rick Mears	Penske PC15-Chevrolet	110	
4	Kevin Cogan	March 86C-Cosworth	110	
5	Geoff Brabham	Lola T86/00-Cosworth	109	out of fuel
6	Jacques Villeneuve	March 86C-Cosworth	109	

Winner's average speed: 106.322 mph. Pole position: Guerrero, 56.814s

1986 FINAL CHAMPIONSHIP POSITIONS

1	Bobby Rahal	179	7	Emerson Fittipaldi	103
2	Michael Andretti	171	8	Rick Mears	89
3	Danny Sullivan	147	9	Roberto Guerrero	87
4	Al Unser jr	137	10	Tom Sneva	82
5	Mario Andretti	136			
6	Kevin Cogan	115			

1987

TOYOTA GRAND PRIX OF LONG BEACH

5 April 1987. Long Beach. 95 laps of a 1.670-mile circuit = 158.650 miles. CART/PPG Indycar World Series round 1

1	Mario Andretti	Lola T87/00-Chevrolet	95	1h51m33.036
2	Al Unser Jr	March 87C-Cosworth	94	
3	Tom Sneva	March 87C-Cosworth	94	
4	Michael Andretti	March 87C-Cosworth	93	
5	Josele Garza	March 87C-Cosworth	93	
6	Chip Robinson	March 86C-Cosworth	92	

Winner's average speed: 85.333 mph. Pole position: Mario Andretti, 1m05.886

CHECKER 200

12 April 1987. Phoenix. 200 laps of a 1.000-mile circuit = 200.000 miles. CART/PPG Indycar World Series round 2

1	Roberto Guerrero	March 87C-Cosworth	200	1h26m56.62
2	Bobby Rahal	Lola T87/00-Cosworth	200	1h27m05.24
3	Arie Luyendyk	March 87C-Cosworth	199	
4	Michael Andretti	March 87C-Cosworth	199	
5	Mario Andretti	Lola T87/00-Chevrolet	198	
6	Josele Garza	March 87C-Cosworth	196	

Winner's average speed: 138.020 mph. Pole position: Mario Andretti, 21.832s

INDIANAPOLIS 500

24 May 1987. Indianapolis. 200 laps of a 2.500-mile circuit = 500.000 miles. CART/PPG Indycar World Series round 3

1	Al Unser	March 86C-Cosworth	200	3h04m59.147
2	Roberto Guerrero	March 87C-Cosworth	200	3h05m03.634
3	Fabrizio Barbazza	March 87C-Cosworth	198	
4	Al Unser Jr	March 87C-Cosworth	196	
5	Gary Bettenhausen	March 86C-Cosworth	195	
6	Dick Simon	Lola T87/00-Cosworth	193	

Winner's average speed: 162.175 mph. Pole position: Mario Andretti (Lola T87/00-Chevrolet), 215.390 mph. Fastest lap: Guerrero, 205.011 mph

MILLER AMERICAN 200

31 May 1987. Milwaukee. 200 laps of a 1.032-mile circuit = 206.400 miles. CART/PPG Indycar World Series round 4

1	Michael Andretti	March 87C-Cosworth	200	1h47m17.0
2	Bobby Rahal	Lola T87/00-Cosworth	200	1h47m23.3
3	Derek Daly	Lola T87/00-Cosworth	198	
4	Arie Luyendyk	March 87C-Cosworth	198	
5	Al Unser Jr	March 87C-Cosworth	197	
6	AJ Foyt Jr	Lola T87/00-Cosworth	196	

Winner's average speed: 115.433 mph. Pole position: Roberto Guerrero (March 87C-Cosworth), 23.544s

BUDWEISER GI JOE'S 200

14 June 1987. Portland. 104 laps of a 1.915-mile circuit = 199.160 miles. CART/PPG Indycar World Series round 5

1	Bobby Rahal	Lola T87/00-Cosworth	104	1h50m02.53
2	Michael Andretti	March 87C-Cosworth	104	1h50m08.92
3	Rick Mears	Penske PC16-Chevrolet	102	
4	Fabrizio Barbazza	March 87C-Cosworth	102	
5	Scott Brayton	March 87C-Cosworth	102	
6	Josele Garza	March 87C-Cosworth	102	

Winner's average speed: 108.591 mph. Pole position: Roberto Guerrero (March 87C-Cosworth), 59.207s

CHASE GRAND PRIX AT THE MEADOWLANDS

28 June 1987. Meadowlands. 100 laps of a 1.682-mile circuit = 168.200 miles. CART/PPG Indycar World Series round 6

1	Bobby Rahal	Lola T87/00-Cosworth	100	1h57m18.316
2	Mario Andretti	Lola T87/00-Chevrolet	100	1h57m22.110
3	Emerson Fittipaldi	March 87C-Chevrolet	100	
4	Geoff Brabham	March 87C-Honda	100	
5	Michael Andretti	March 87C-Cosworth	99	
6	Arie Luyendyk	March 87C-Cosworth	99	

Winner's average speed: 86.032 mph. Pole position: Mario Andretti, 1m01.097

BUDWEISER CLEVELAND GRAND PRIX

5 July 1987. Cleveland. 80 laps of a 2.485-mile circuit = 198.800 miles. CART/PPG Indycar World Series round 7

1	Emerson Fittipaldi	March 87C-Chevrolet	80	1h32m40.695
2	Bobby Rahal	Lola T87/00-Cosworth	80	1h32m51.314
3	Al Unser Jr	March 87C-Cosworth	80	1h33m03.814
4	Danny Sullivan	March 86C-Chevrolet	80	1h33m08.753
5	Roberto Guerrero	March 87C-Cosworth	80	1h33m11.467
6	Michael Andretti	March 87C-Cosworth	80	1h33m37.865

Winner's average speed: 128.703 mph. Pole position: Guerrero, 1m05.509

MOLSON INDY TORONTO

19 July 1987. Toronto. 103 laps of a 1.784-mile circuit = 183.752 miles. CART/PPG Indycar World Series round 8

1	Emerson Fittipaldi	March 87C-Chevrolet	103	1h54m35.918
2	Danny Sullivan	March 86C-Chevrolet	103	1h54m44.270
3	Bobby Rahal	Lola T87/00-Cosworth	103	1h55m10.233
4	Roberto Guerrero	March 87C-Cosworth	101	
5	Michael Andretti	March 87C-Cosworth	100	
6	Tom Sneva	March 87C-Cosworth	99	spun

Winner's average speed: 96.206 mph. Pole position: Rahal, 1m00.930

MARLBORO 500

2 August 1987. Michigan. 250 laps of a 2.000-mile circuit = 500.000 miles. CART/PPG Indycar World Series round 9

1	Michael Andretti	March 87C-Cosworth	250	2h54m56.071
2	Al Unser	March 86C-Cosworth	250	2h55m05.181
3	Bobby Rahal	Lola T87/00-Cosworth	250	
4	Danny Sullivan	March 86C-Chevrolet	248	
5	Arie Luyendyk	March 87C-Cosworth	247	
6	Fabrizio Barbazza	March 87C-Cosworth	246	

Winner's average speed: 171.493 mph. Pole position: Michael Andretti, 33.406s

QUAKER STATE 500

16 August 1987. Pocono. 200 laps of a 2.500-mile circuit = 500.000 miles. CART/PPG Indycar World Series round 10

1	Rick Mears	March 86C-Chevrolet	200	3h11m50.92
2	Geoff Brabham	March 87C-Honda	200	3h12m08.24
3	Roberto Guerrero	March 87C-Cosworth	200	3h12m14.76
4	Arie Luyendyk	March 87C-Cosworth	198	
5	Bobby Rahal	Lola T87/00-Cosworth	198	
6	Pancho Carter	March 87C-Cosworth	197	

Winner's average speed: 156.373 mph. Pole position: Mario Andretti (Lola T87/00-Chevrolet), 44.795s

LIVING WELL/PROVIMI VEAL 200

30 August 1987. Elkhart Lake. 50 laps of a 4.048-mile circuit = 202.400 miles. CART/PPG Indycar World Series round 11

1	Mario Andretti	Lola T87/00-Chevrolet	50	1h39m52.26
2	Geoff Brabham	March 87C-Honda	50	1h40m33.34
3	Al Unser Jr	March 87C-Cosworth	50	1h41m21.13
4	Arie Luyendyk	March 87C-Cosworth	50	1h41m49.93
5	Danny Sullivan	March 86C-Chevrolet	49	
6	John Andretti	March 87C-Cosworth	49	

Winner's average speed: 121.597 mph. Pole position: Mario Andretti, 1m52.687

ESCORT RADAR WARNING 200

6 September 1987. Mid-Ohio. 84 laps of a 2.400-mile circuit = 201.600 miles. CART/PPG Indycar World Series round 12

1	Roberto Guerrero	March 87C-Cosworth	84	1h51m58.7
2	Bobby Rahal	Lola T87/00-Cosworth	84	1h52m24.6
3	Danny Sullivan	March 86C-Chevrolet	84	
4	Rick Mears	March 86C-Chevrolet	84	
5	Kevin Cogan	March 87C-Chevrolet	84	
6	Emerson Fittipaldi	March 87C-Chevrolet	84	

Winner's average speed: 108.021 mph. Pole position: Guerrero, 1m15.585

BOSCH SPARK PLUG GRAND PRIX

20 September 1987. Nazareth. 200 laps of a 0.946-mile circuit = 189.200 miles. CART/PPG Indycar World Series round 13

1	Michael Andretti	March 87C-Cosworth	200	1h33m02.65
2	Bobby Rahal	Lola T87/00-Cosworth	199	
3	Rick Mears	March 86C-Chevrolet	198	
4	Arie Luyendyk	March 87C-Cosworth	198	
5	Kevin Cogan	March 87C-Chevrolet	198	
6	Al Unser Jr	March 87C-Cosworth	197	

Winner's average speed: 122.007 mph. Pole position: Michael Andretti, 21.926s

CART

CHAMPION SPARK PLUG 300 KMS

11 October 1987. Laguna Seca. 98 laps of a 1.900-mile circuit = 186.200 miles. CART/PPG Indycar World Series round 14

1	Bobby Rahal	Lola T87/00-Cosworth	98	1h33m58.682
2	Danny Sullivan	March 86C-Chevrolet	98	1h34m22.299
3	Rick Mears	March 86C-Chevrolet	97	
4	Al Unser Jr	March 87C-Cosworth	97	
5	Geoff Brabham	March 87C-Honda	96	
6	Arie Luyendyk	March 87C-Cosworth	96	

Winner's average speed: 118.879 mph. Pole position: Mario Andretti (Lola T87/00-Chevrolet), 52.926s

NISSAN INDY CHALLENGE

1 November 1987. Tamiami Park. 103 laps of a 1.784-mile circuit = 183.752 miles. CART/PPG Indycar World Series round 15

1	Michael Andretti	March 87C-Cosworth	103	1h56m12.55
2	Al Unser Jr	March 87C-Cosworth	103	1h57m08.86
3	Geoff Brabham	March 87C-Honda	103	1h57m47.16
4	Mario Andretti	Lola T87/00-Chevrolet	102	
5	Rick Mears	March 86C-Chevrolet	102	
6	Raul Boesel	March 87C-Cosworth	101	

Winner's average speed: 94.873 mph. Pole position: Mario Andretti, 56.027s

1987 FINAL CHAMPIONSHIP POSITIONS

1	Bobby Rahal	188	7	Arie Luyendyk	98
2	Michael Andretti	158	8	Geoff Brabham	90
3	Al Unser jr	107	9	Danny Sullivan	87
4	Roberto Guerrero	106	10	Emerson Fittipaldi	78
5	Rick Mears	102			
6	Mario Andretti	100			

1988

CHECKER 200

10 April 1988. Phoenix. 200 laps of a 1.000-mile circuit = 200.000 miles. CART/PPG Indycar World Series round 1

1	Mario Andretti	Lola T88/00-Chevrolet	200	1h38m22.000
2	Roberto Guerrero	Lola T88/00-Cosworth	200	1h38m36.026
3	Michael Andretti	March 88C-Cosworth	200	
4	AJ Foyt Jr	Lola T88/00-Cosworth	198	
5	Raul Boesel	March 88C-Cosworth	198	
6	Tony Bettenhausen Jr	Lola T87/00-Cosworth	195	

Winner's average speed: 121.993 mph. Pole position: Rick Mears (Penske PC17-Chevrolet), 21.723s

TOYOTA GRAND PRIX OF LONG BEACH

17 April 1988. Long Beach. 95 laps of a 1.670-mile circuit = 158.650 miles. CART/PPG Indycar World Series round 2

1	Al Unser Jr	March 88C-Chevrolet	95	1h53m47.34
2	Bobby Rahal	Lola T88/00-Judd	94	
3	Kevin Cogan	March 87C-Cosworth	94	
4	Raul Boesel	March 88C-Cosworth	93	
5	Derek Daly	Lola T88/00-Cosworth	93	
6	Rocky Moran	March 87C-Cosworth	93	

Winner's average speed: 83.655 mph. Pole position: Danny Sullivan (Penske PC17-Chevrolet), 1m06.607

INDIANAPOLIS 500

29 May 1988. Indianapolis. 200 laps of a 2.500-mile circuit = 500.000 miles. CART/PPG Indycar World Series round 3

1	Rick Mears	Penske PC17-Chevrolet	200	3h27m10.204
2	Emerson Fittipaldi	March 88C-Chevrolet	200	3h27m17.276
3	Al Unser	Penske PC17-Chevrolet	199	

4	Michael Andretti	March 88C-Cosworth	199	
5	Bobby Rahal	Lola T88/00-Judd	199	
6	Jim Crawford	Lola T87/00-Buick	198	

Winner's average speed: 144.809 mph. Pole position: Mears, 219.198 mph. Fastest lap: Mears, 42.956s

MILLER HIGH LIFE 200

5 June 1988. Milwaukee. 200 laps of a 1.032-mile circuit = 206.400 miles. CART/PPG Indycar World Series round 4

1	Rick Mears	Penske PC17-Chevrolet	200	1h37m42.28
2	Danny Sullivan	Penske PC17-Chevrolet	200	1h37m48.07
3	Emerson Fittipaldi	March 88C-Chevrolet	199	
4	Raul Boesel	March 88C-Cosworth	198	
5	AJ Foyt Jr	Lola T88/00-Cosworth	198	
6	Bobby Rahal	Lola T88/00-Judd	197	

Winner's average speed: 126.749 mph. Pole position: Michael Andretti (March 88C-Cosworth), 23.016s

BUDWEISER GI JOE'S 200

19 June 1988. Portland. 104 laps of a 1.915-mile circuit = 199.160 miles. CART/PPG Indycar World Series round 5

1	Danny Sullivan	Penske PC17-Chevrolet	104	1h57m17.42
2	Arie Luyendyk	Lola T88/00-Cosworth	104	1h57m34.60
3	Emerson Fittipaldi	March 88C-Chevrolet	104	
4	Al Unser Jr	March 88C-Chevrolet	104	
5	Mario Andretti	Lola T88/00-Chevrolet	103	
6	Rick Mears	Penske PC17-Chevrolet	103	

Winner's average speed: 101.881 mph. Pole position: Sullivan, 58.298s

BUDWEISER CLEVELAND GRAND PRIX

3 July 1988. Cleveland. 80 laps of a 2.485-mile circuit = 198.800 miles. CART/PPG Indycar World Series round 6

1	Mario Andretti	Lola T88/00-Chevrolet	80	1h35m46.316
2	Bobby Rahal	Lola T88/00-Judd	80	1h35m47.226
3	Danny Sullivan	Penske PC17-Chevrolet	80	
4	Al Unser Jr	March 88C-Chevrolet	80	
5	Raul Boesel	Lola T88/00-Cosworth	79	
6	Derek Daly	Lola T88/00-Cosworth	79	

Winner's average speed: 124.546 mph. Pole position: Sullivan, 1m04.664

MOLSON INDY TORONTO

17 July 1988. Toronto. 103 laps of a 1.784-mile circuit = 183.752 miles. CART/PPG Indycar World Series round 7

1	Al Unser Jr	March 88C-Chevrolet	103	1h59m34.620
2	Danny Sullivan	Penske PC17-Chevrolet	103	1h59m46.797
3	Michael Andretti	March 88C-Cosworth	103	
4	Emerson Fittipaldi	Lola T88/00-Chevrolet	103	
5	Bobby Rahal	Lola T88/00-Judd	102	
6	Rick Mears	Penske PC17-Chevrolet	102	

Winner's average speed: 92.201 mph. Pole position: Sullivan, 1m00.274

MARLBORO GRAND PRIX AT THE MEADOWLANDS

24 July 1988. Meadowlands. 150 laps of a 1.217-mile circuit = 182.550 miles. CART/PPG Indycar World Series round 8

1	Al Unser Jr	March 88C-Chevrolet	150	1h50m14.68
2	Mario Andretti	Lola T88/00-Chevrolet	149	gearbox
3	Rick Mears	Penske PC17-Chevrolet	149	
4	Danny Sullivan	Penske PC17-Chevrolet	148	
5	Bobby Rahal	Lola T88/00-Judd	146	
6	Michael Andretti	March 88C-Chevrolet	145	

Winner's average speed: 99.352 mph. Pole position: Emerson Fittipaldi (Lola T87/00-Chevrolet), 38.556s

MARLBORO 500

7 August 1988. Michigan. 250 laps of a 2.000-mile circuit = 500.000 miles. CART/PPG Indycar World Series round 9

1	Danny Sullivan	Penske PC17-Chevrolet	250	2h46m03.82
2	Bobby Rahal	Lola T88/00-Judd	249	

3 Michael Andretti	Lola T88/00-Cosworth	247
4 Tony Bettenhausen Jr	Lola T87/00-Cosworth	240
5 Phil Krueger	March 86C-Cosworth	239
6 Gordon Johncock	Lola T88/00-Cosworth	237

Winner's average speed: 180.654 mph. Pole position: Rick Mears (Penske PC17-Chevrolet), 32.963s

QUAKER STATE 500

21 August 1988. Pocono. 200 laps of a 2.500-mile circuit = 500.000 miles. CART/PPG Indycar World Series round 10

1 Bobby Rahal	Lola T88/00-Judd	200	3h44m21.673
2 Al Unser Jr	March 88C-Chevrolet	200	3h44m38.720
3 Roberto Guerrero	Lola T88/00-Cosworth	199	
4 Derek Daly	Lola T88/00-Cosworth	199	
5 Raul Boesel	Lola T88/00-Cosworth	197	
6 Gordon Johncock	Lola T88/00-Cosworth	195	

Winner's average speed: 133.713 mph. Pole position: Rick Mears (Penske PC17-Chevrolet), 43.996s

ESCORT RADAR WARNING 200

4 September 1988. Mid-Ohio. 84 laps of a 2.400-mile circuit = 201.600 miles. CART/PPG Indycar World Series round 11

1 Emerson Fittipaldi	Lola T87/00-Chevrolet	84	2h14m18.486
2 Mario Andretti	Lola T88/00-Chevrolet	84	2h14m26.190
3 Rick Mears	Penske PC17-Chevrolet	84	
4 Al Unser Jr	March 88C-Chevrolet	83	
5 Danny Sullivan	Penske PC17-Chevrolet	83	
6 Raul Boesel	Lola T88/00-Cosworth	83	

Winner's average speed: 90.062 mph. Pole position: Sullivan, 1m16.619

BRIGGS & STRATTON 200

11 September 1988. Elkhart Lake. 50 laps of a 4.048-mile circuit = 202.400 miles. CART/PPG Indycar World Series round 12

1 Emerson Fittipaldi	Lola T87/00-Chevrolet	50	1h38m11.24
2 Bobby Rahal	Lola T88/00-Judd	50	1h38m12.31
3 Mario Andretti	Lola T88/00-Chevrolet	50	
4 Danny Sullivan	Penske PC17-Chevrolet	50	
5 Michael Andretti	Lola T88/00-Cosworth	50	
6 Derek Daly	Lola T88/00-Cosworth	49	

Winner's average speed: 123.682 mph. Pole position: Sullivan, 1m51.567

BOSCH SPARK PLUG GRAND PRIX

25 September 1988. Nazareth. 200 laps of a 0.946-mile circuit = 189.200 miles. CART/PPG Indycar World Series round 13

1 Danny Sullivan	Penske PC17-Chevrolet	200	1h20m47.630
2 Michael Andretti	Lola T88/00-Cosworth	200	1h20m59.836
3 Mario Andretti	Lola T88/00-Chevrolet	199	
4 Teo Fabi	March 88C-Porsche	198	
5 Raul Boesel	Lola T88/00-Cosworth	198	
6 Roberto Guerrero	March 87C-Cosworth	197	

Winner's average speed: 140.506 mph. Pole position: Sullivan, 20.911s

CHAMPION SPARK PLUG 300 KMS

16 October 1988. Laguna Seca. 84 laps of a 2.214-mile circuit = 185.976 miles. CART/PPG Indycar World Series round 14

1 Danny Sullivan	Penske PC17-Chevrolet	84	1h58m35.660
2 Michael Andretti	Lola T88/00-Cosworth	84	1h58m38.444
3 Mario Andretti	Lola T88/00-Chevrolet	84	
4 Bobby Rahal	Lola T88/00-Judd	84	
5 Rick Mears	Penske PC17-Chevrolet	84	
6 Al Unser Jr	March 88C-Chevrolet	84	

Winner's average speed: 94.090 mph. Pole position: Sullivan, 1m14.293

NISSAN INDY CHALLENGE

6 November 1988. Tamiami Park. 112 laps of a 1.784-mile circuit = 199.808 miles. CART/PPG Indycar World Series round 15

| 1 Al Unser Jr | March 88C-Chevrolet | 112 | 1h58m08.832 |
| 2 Rick Mears | Penske PC17-Chevrolet | 112 | 1h59m01.878 |

3 Didier Theys	Lola T88/00-Cosworth	111
4 Kevin Cogan	March 88C-Cosworth	110
5 Danny Sullivan	Penske PC17-Chevrolet	108
6 Bernard Jourdain	March 86C-Cosworth	108

Winner's average speed: 101.471 mph. Pole position: Sullivan, 55.062s

1988 FINAL CHAMPIONSHIP POSITIONS

1	Danny Sullivan	182		8	Raul Boesel	89
2	Al Unser Jr	149		9	Derek Daly	53
3	Bobby Rahal	136		10=	Teo Fabi	44
4	Rick Mears	129			John Jones	44
5	Mario Andretti	126				
6	Michael Andretti	119				
7	Emerson Fittipaldi	105				

1989

AUTOWORKS 200

9 April 1989. Phoenix. 200 laps of a 1.000-mile circuit = 200.000 miles. CART/PPG Indycar World Series round 1

1 Rick Mears	Penske PC18-Chevrolet	200	1h35m09.205
2 Al Unser Jr	Lola T89/00-Chevrolet	199	
3 Danny Sullivan	Penske PC18-Chevrolet	199	
4 Michael Andretti	Lola T89/00-Chevrolet	199	
5 Emerson Fittipaldi	Penske PC17-Chevrolet	199	
6 Teo Fabi	March 89P-Porsche	198	

Winner's average speed: 126.112 mph. Pole position: Mears, 21.617s

TOYOTA GRAND PRIX OF LONG BEACH

16 April 1989. Long Beach. 95 laps of a 1.670-mile circuit = 158.650 miles. CART/PPG Indycar World Series round 2

1 Al Unser Jr	Lola T89/00-Chevrolet	95	1h51m19.786
2 Michael Andretti	Lola T89/00-Chevrolet	95	1h51m32.163
3 Emerson Fittipaldi	Penske PC17-Chevrolet	95	
4 Bobby Rahal	Lola T89/00-Cosworth	94	
5 Rick Mears	Penske PC18-Chevrolet	94	
6 Raul Boesel	Lola T89/00-Judd	93	

Winner's average speed: 85.503 mph. Pole position: Unser Jr, 1m06.255

INDIANAPOLIS 500

28 May 1989. Indianapolis. 200 laps of a 2.500-mile circuit = 500.000 miles. CART/PPG Indycar World Series round 3

1 Emerson Fittipaldi	Penske PC18-Chevrolet	200	2h59m01.04
2 Al Unser Jr	Lola T89/00-Chevrolet	198	accident
3 Raul Boesel	Lola T89/00-Judd	194	
4 Mario Andretti	Lola T89/00-Chevrolet	193	
5 AJ Foyt Jr	Lola T89/00-Cosworth	193	
6 Scott Brayton	Lola T89/00-Buick	193	

Winner's average speed: 167.582 mph. Pole position: Rick Mears (Penske PC18-Chevrolet), 223.885 mph. Fastest lap: Fittipaldi, 40.455s

MILLER HIGH LIFE 200

4 June 1989. Milwaukee. 200 laps of a 1.032-mile circuit = 206.400 miles. CART/PPG Indycar World Series round 4

1 Rick Mears	Penske PC18-Chevrolet	200	1h32m11.666
2 Michael Andretti	Lola T89/00-Chevrolet	200	1h32m22.502
3 Teo Fabi	March 89P-Porsche	198	
4 Raul Boesel	Lola T89/00-Judd	198	
5 Scott Pruett	Lola T89/00-Judd	197	
6 Arie Luyendyk	Lola T89/00-Cosworth	195	

Winner's average speed: 134.325 mph. Pole position: Mears, 22.385s

VALVOLINE DETROIT GRAND PRIX

18 June 1989. Detroit. 62 laps of a 2.500-mile circuit = 155 miles.
CART/PPG Indycar World Series round 5

1 Emerson Fittipaldi	Penske PC18-Chevrolet	62	2h02m11.349
2 Scott Pruett	Lola T89/00-Judd	62	2h02m40.893
3 Mario Andretti	Lola T89/00-Chevrolet	62	
4 Teo Fabi	March 89P-Porsche	62	
5 Rick Mears	Penske PC18-Chevrolet	61	
6 Arie Luyendyk	Lola T89/00-Cosworth	61	

Winner's average speed: 76.112 mph. Pole position: Michael Andretti (Lola T89/00-Chevrolet), 1m41.681

BUDWEISER GI JOE'S 200

25 June 1989. Portland. 104 laps of a 1.915-mile circuit = 199.160 miles.
CART/PPG Indycar World Series round 6

1 Emerson Fittipaldi	Penske PC18-Chevrolet	104	1h55m20.286
2 Bobby Rahal	Lola T89/00-Cosworth	104	1h55m40.647
3 Arie Luyendyk	Lola T89/00-Cosworth	104	
4 Teo Fabi	March 89P-Porsche	103	
5 Scott Pruett	Lola T89/00-Judd	103	
6 Michael Andretti	Lola T89/00-Chevrolet	102	

Winner's average speed: 103.605 mph. Pole position: Fabi, 57.634s

BUDWEISER CLEVELAND GRAND PRIX

2 July 1989. Cleveland. 80 laps of a 2.485-mile circuit = 198.800 miles.
CART/PPG Indycar World Series round 7

1 Emerson Fittipaldi	Penske PC18-Chevrolet	80	1h32m56.878
2 Mario Andretti	Lola T89/00-Chevrolet	80	1h33m13.828
3 Bobby Rahal	Lola T89/00-Cosworth	80	
4 Teo Fabi	March 89P-Porsche	80	
5 Rick Mears	Penske PC18-Chevrolet	80	
6 Scott Pruett	Lola T89/00-Judd	79	

Winner's average speed: 128.330 mph. Pole position: Michael Andretti (Lola T89/00-Chevrolet), 1m04.636

MARLBORO GRAND PRIX AT THE MEADOWLANDS

16 July 1989. Meadowlands. 145 laps of a 1.217-mile circuit = 176.465 miles. CART/PPG Indycar World Series round 8

1 Bobby Rahal	Lola T89/00-Cosworth	145	2h09m20.21
2 Emerson Fittipaldi	Penske PC18-Chevrolet	145	2h09m26.39
3 Scott Pruett	Lola T89/00-Judd	143	
4 Rick Mears	Penske PC18-Chevrolet	143	
5 Al Unser Jr	Lola T89/00-Chevrolet	142	
6 Raul Boesel	Lola T89/00-Judd	141	

Winner's average speed: 81.863 mph. Pole position: Fittipaldi, 37.219s

MOLSON INDY TORONTO

23 July 1989. Toronto. 103 laps of a 1.784-mile circuit = 183.752 miles.
CART/PPG Indycar World Series round 9

1 Michael Andretti	Lola T89/00-Chevrolet	103	2h01m00.94
2 Emerson Fittipaldi	Penske PC18-Chevrolet	103	2h01m13.02
3 Danny Sullivan	Penske PC18-Chevrolet	102	
4 Teo Fabi	March 89P-Porsche	101	
5 Rick Mears	Penske PC18-Chevrolet	101	
6 Scott Pruett	Lola T89/00-Judd	101	

Winner's average speed: 91.105 mph. Pole position: Fittipaldi, 59.499s

MARLBORO 500

6 August 1989. Michigan. 250 laps of a 2.000-mile circuit = 500.000 miles.
CART/PPG Indycar World Series round 10

1 Michael Andretti	Lola T89/00-Chevrolet	250	3h07m15.239
2 Teo Fabi	March 89P-Porsche	249	
3 Mario Andretti	Lola T89/00-Chevrolet	249	
4 Al Unser Jr	Lola T89/00-Chevrolet	249	
5 Derek Daly	Lola T89/00-Judd	247	
6 Arie Luyendyk	Lola T89/00-Cosworth	246	

Winner's average speed: 160.210 mph. Pole position: Emerson Fittipaldi (Penske PC18-Chevrolet), 32.753s

QUAKER STATE 500

20 August 1989. Pocono. 200 laps of a 2.500-mile circuit = 500.000 miles.
CART/PPG Indycar World Series round 11

1 Danny Sullivan	Penske PC18-Chevrolet	200	2h55m43.550
2 Rick Mears	Penske PC18-Chevrolet	200	2h55m47.776
3 Michael Andretti	Lola T89/00-Chevrolet	200	
4 Teo Fabi	March 89P-Porsche	200	
5 Mario Andretti	Lola T89/00-Chevrolet	199	
6 Arie Luyendyk	Lola T89/00-Cosworth	198	

Winner's average speed: 170.720 mph. Pole position: Emerson Fittipaldi (Penske PC18-Chevrolet), 42.510s

RED ROOF INNS 200

3 September 1989. Mid-Ohio. 84 laps of a 2.400-mile circuit = 201.600 miles. CART/PPG Indycar World Series round 12

1 Teo Fabi	March 89P-Porsche	84	1h54m46.081
2 Al Unser Jr	Lola T89/00-Chevrolet	84	1h54m54.058
3 Michael Andretti	Lola T89/00-Chevrolet	84	
4 Emerson Fittipaldi	Penske PC18-Chevrolet	84	
5 Danny Sullivan	Penske PC18-Chevrolet	84	
6 Rick Mears	Penske PC18-Chevrolet	83	

Winner's average speed: 105.395 mph. Pole position: Fabi, 1m15.678

BRIGGS & STRATTON 200

10 September 1989. Elkhart Lake. 50 laps of a 4.048-mile circuit = 202.400 miles. CART/PPG Indycar World Series round 13

1 Danny Sullivan	Penske PC18-Chevrolet	50	1h37m43.06
2 Teo Fabi	March 89P-Porsche	50	1h38m24.97
3 Rick Mears	Penske PC18-Chevrolet	50	
4 Arie Luyendyk	Lola T89/00-Cosworth	50	
5 Emerson Fittipaldi	Penske PC18-Chevrolet	50	
6 Michael Andretti	Lola T89/00-Chevrolet	49	out of fuel

Winner's average speed: 124.276 mph. Pole position: Sullivan, 1m50.367

BOSCH SPARK PLUG GRAND PRIX

24 September 1989. Nazareth. 200 laps of a 0.946-mile circuit = 189.200 miles. CART/PPG Indycar World Series round 14

1 Emerson Fittipaldi	Penske PC18-Chevrolet	200	1h29m02.852
2 Rick Mears	Penske PC18-Chevrolet	200	1h29m07.348
3 Danny Sullivan	Penske PC18-Chevrolet	200	
4 Al Unser Jr	Lola T89/00-Chevrolet	199	
5 Michael Andretti	Lola T89/00-Chevrolet	196	
6 Scott Pruett	Lola T89/00-Judd	195	

Winner's average speed: 127.482 mph. Pole position: Mears, 20.610s

CHAMPION SPARK PLUG 300 KMS

15 October 1989. Laguna Seca. 84 laps of a 2.214-mile circuit = 185.976 miles. CART/PPG Indycar World Series round 15

1 Rick Mears	Penske PC18-Chevrolet	84	1h58m29.341
2 Mario Andretti	Lola T89/00-Chevrolet	84	1h58m31.187
3 Al Unser Jr	Lola T89/00-Chevrolet	84	
4 Scott Pruett	Lola T89/00-Judd	84	
5 Emerson Fittipaldi	Penske PC18-Chevrolet	84	
6 Bobby Rahal	Lola T89/00-Cosworth	84	

Winner's average speed: 94.174 mph. Pole position: Mears, 1m12.348

1989 FINAL CHAMPIONSHIP POSITIONS

1	Emerson Fittipaldi	196	7	Danny Sullivan	107
2	Rick Mears	186	8	Scott Pruett	101
3	Michael Andretti	150	9	Bobby Rahal	88
4	Teo Fabi	141	10	Arie Luyendyk	75
5	Al Unser Jr	136			
6	Mario Andretti	110			

1990

AUTOWORKS 200

8 April 1990. Phoenix. 200 laps of a 1.000-mile circuit = 200.000 miles. CART/PPG Indycar World Series round 1

1 Rick Mears	Penske PC19-Chevrolet	200	1h35m01.112
2 Bobby Rahal	Lola T90/00-Chevrolet	200	1h35m08.368
3 Al Unser Jr	Lola T90/00-Chevrolet	200	
4 Mario Andretti	Lola T90/00-Chevrolet	199	
5 Emerson Fittipaldi	Penske PC19-Chevrolet	199	
6 Danny Sullivan	Penske PC19-Chevrolet	199	

Winner's average speed: 126.291 mph. Pole position: Mears, 21.407s

TOYOTA GRAND PRIX OF LONG BEACH

22 April 1990. Long Beach. 95 laps of a 1.670-mile circuit = 158.650 miles. CART/PPG Indycar World Series round 2

1 Al Unser Jr	Lola T90/00-Chevrolet	95	1h53m00.937
2 Emerson Fittipaldi	Penske PC19-Chevrolet	95	1h53m02.661
3 Danny Sullivan	Penske PC19-Chevrolet	95	
4 Michael Andretti	Lola T90/00-Chevrolet	95	
5 Mario Andretti	Lola T90/00-Chevrolet	95	
6 Rick Mears	Penske PC19-Chevrolet	94	

Winner's average speed: 84.227 mph. Pole position: Unser Jr, 1m06.798

INDIANAPOLIS 500

27 May 1990. Indianapolis. 200 laps of a 2.500-mile circuit = 500.000 miles. CART/PPG Indycar World Series round 3

1 Arie Luyendyk	Lola T90/00-Chevrolet	200	2h41m18.404
2 Bobby Rahal	Lola T90/00-Chevrolet	200	2h41m29.282
3 Emerson Fittipaldi	Penske PC19-Chevrolet	200	2h42m00.123
4 Al Unser Jr	Lola T90/00-Chevrolet	199	
5 Rick Mears	Penske PC19-Chevrolet	198	
6 AJ Foyt Jr	Lola T90/00-Chevrolet	194	

Winner's average speed: 185.981 mph. Pole position: Fittipaldi, 225.301 mph. Fastest lap: Fittipaldi and Luyendyk, 40.436s

MILLER GENUINE DRAFT 200

3 June 1990. Milwaukee. 200 laps of a 1.032-mile circuit = 206.400 miles. CART/PPG Indycar World Series round 4

1 Al Unser Jr	Lola T90/00-Chevrolet	200	1h29m46.393
2 Rick Mears	Penske PC19-Chevrolet	200	1h29m47.122
3 Emerson Fittipaldi	Penske PC19-Chevrolet	200	
4 Bobby Rahal	Lola T90/00-Chevrolet	200	
5 Michael Andretti	Lola T90/00-Chevrolet	200	
6 Raul Boesel	Lola T89/00-Judd	196	

Winner's average speed: 137.948 mph. Pole position: Mears, 22.865s

VALVOLINE DETROIT GRAND PRIX

17 June 1990. Detroit. 62 laps of a 2.500-mile circuit = 155 miles. CART/PPG Indycar World Series round 5

1 Michael Andretti	Lola T90/00-Chevrolet	62	1h49m32.249
2 Bobby Rahal	Lola T90/00-Chevrolet	62	1h51m20.775
3 Eddie Cheever	Penske PC18-Chevrolet	61	
4 Rick Mears	Penske PC19-Chevrolet	61	
5 Arie Luyendyk	Lola T90/00-Chevrolet	61	
6 Raul Boesel	Lola T89/00-Judd	60	

Winner's average speed: 84.902 mph. Pole position: Michael Andretti, 1m42.154

BUDWEISER GI JOE'S 200

24 June 1990. Portland. 104 laps of a 1.915-mile circuit = 199.160 miles. CART/PPG Indycar World Series round 6

1 Michael Andretti	Lola T90/00-Chevrolet	104	1h48m22.036
2 Mario Andretti	Lola T90/00-Chevrolet	104	1h48m25.956
3 Al Unser Jr	Lola T90/00-Chevrolet	104	
4 Danny Sullivan	Penske PC19-Chevrolet	104	
5 Rick Mears	Penske PC19-Chevrolet	104	
6 Arie Luyendyk	Lola T90/00-Chevrolet	103	

Winner's average speed: 110.269 mph. Pole position: Sullivan, 56.655s

BUDWEISER CLEVELAND GRAND PRIX

8 July 1990. Cleveland. 85 laps of a 2.106-mile circuit = 179.010 miles. CART/PPG Indycar World Series round 7

1 Danny Sullivan	Penske PC19-Chevrolet	85	1h47m24.658
2 Bobby Rahal	Lola T90/00-Chevrolet	85	1h47m29.878
3 Emerson Fittipaldi	Penske PC19-Chevrolet	85	
4 Mario Andretti	Lola T90/00-Chevrolet	85	
5 John Andretti	March 90P-Porsche	85	
6 Arie Luyendyk	Lola T90/00-Chevrolet	84	

Winner's average speed: 99.995 mph. Pole position: Rick Mears (Penske PC19-Chevrolet), 1m01.215

MARLBORO GRAND PRIX AT THE MEADOWLANDS

15 July 1990. Meadowlands. 150 laps of a 1.217-mile circuit = 182.550 miles. CART/PPG Indycar World Series round 8

1 Michael Andretti	Lola T90/00-Chevrolet	150	1h52m34.777
2 Rick Mears	Penske PC19-Chevrolet	150	1h53m13.088
3 Teo Fabi	March 90P-Porsche	149	
4 Arie Luyendyk	Lola T90/00-Chevrolet	146	
5 AJ Foyt Jr	Lola T90/00-Chevrolet	145	
6 Emerson Fittipaldi	Penske PC19-Chevrolet	143	

Winner's average speed: 97.291 mph. Pole position: Michael Andretti, 38.213s

MOLSON INDY TORONTO

22 July 1990. Toronto. 94 laps of a 1.784-mile circuit = 167.696 miles. Race scheduled for 103 laps, stopped due to rain. CART/PPG Indycar World Series round 9

1 Al Unser Jr	Lola T90/00-Chevrolet	94	2h15m26.000
2 Michael Andretti	Lola T90/00-Chevrolet	94	2h16m04.100
3 Eddie Cheever	Lola T90/00-Chevrolet	93	
4 Danny Sullivan	Penske PC19-Chevrolet	93	
5 Arie Luyendyk	Lola T90/00-Chevrolet	93	
6 Mario Andretti	Lola T90/00-Chevrolet	93	

Winner's average speed: 74.293 mph. Pole position: Sullivan, 59.883s

MARLBORO 500

5 August 1990. Michigan. 250 laps of a 2.000-mile circuit = 500.000 miles. CART/PPG Indycar World Series round 10

1 Al Unser Jr	Lola T90/00-Chevrolet	250	2h38m07.291
2 Bobby Rahal	Lola T90/00-Chevrolet	250	2h38m32.750
3 Mario Andretti	Lola T90/00-Chevrolet	249	
4 Eddie Cheever	Penske PC18-Chevrolet	242	
5 Roberto Guerrero	Lola T90/00-Alfa Romeo	240	
6 AJ Foyt Jr	Lola T90/00-Chevrolet	240	

Winner's average speed: 189.727 mph. Pole position: Emerson Fittipaldi (Penske PC19-Chevrolet), 32.316s

TEXACO/HAVOLINE GRAND PRIX OF DENVER

26 August 1990. Denver. 80 laps of a 1.900-mile circuit = 152 miles. CART/PPG Indycar World Series round 11

1 Al Unser Jr	Lola T90/00-Chevrolet	80	2h08m00.753
2 Danny Sullivan	Penske PC19-Chevrolet	80	2h08m28.749
3 Bobby Rahal	Lola T90/00-Chevrolet	80	
4 Mario Andretti	Lola T90/00-Chevrolet	80	
5 Michael Andretti	Lola T90/00-Chevrolet	79	
6 John Andretti	March 90P-Porsche	79	

Winner's average speed: 71.243 mph. Pole position: Teo Fabi (March 90P-Porsche), 1m26.622

MOLSON INDY VANCOUVER

2 September 1990. Vancouver. 97 laps of a 1.704-mile circuit = 165.288 miles. CART/PPG Indycar World Series round 12

1 Al Unser Jr	Lola T90/00-Chevrolet	97	2h08m13.233
2 Danny Sullivan	Penske PC19-Chevrolet	97	2h08m23.234

3 Mario Andretti   Lola T90/00-Chevrolet   97
4 Rick Mears   Penske PC19-Chevrolet   97
5 John Andretti   March 90P-Porsche   97
6 Emerson Fittipaldi   Penske PC19-Chevrolet   96

Winner's average speed: 77.345 mph. Pole position: Michael Andretti (Lola T90/00-Chevrolet), 1m02.253

RED ROOF INNS 200

16 September 1990. Mid-Ohio. 89 laps of a 2.258-mile circuit = 200.962 miles. CART/PPG Indycar World Series round 13

1 Michael Andretti   Lola T90/00-Chevrolet   89   2h19m27.000
2 Mario Andretti   Lola T90/00-Chevrolet   89   2h19m34.631
3 Al Unser Jr   Lola T90/00-Chevrolet   89
4 Eddie Cheever   Lola T90/00-Chevrolet   89
5 Danny Sullivan   Penske PC19-Chevrolet   89
6 Bobby Rahal   Lola T90/00-Chevrolet   88

Winner's average speed: 86.466 mph. Pole position: Michael Andretti, 1m10.038

TEXACO/HAVOLINE 200

23 September 1990. Elkhart Lake. 50 laps of a 4.048-mile circuit = 202.400 miles. CART/PPG Indycar World Series round 14

1 Michael Andretti   Lola T90/00-Chevrolet   50   1h53m00.148
2 Emerson Fittipaldi   Penske PC19-Chevrolet   50   1h53m02.497
3 Rick Mears   Penske PC19-Chevrolet   50   1h53m07.270
4 Al Unser Jr   Lola T90/00-Chevrolet   50   1h53m08.230
5 Mario Andretti   Lola T90/00-Chevrolet   50   1h53m23.110
6 Arie Luyendyk   Lola T90/00-Chevrolet   50   1h53m40.960

Winner's average speed: 107.467 mph. Pole position: Danny Sullivan (Penske PC19-Chevrolet), 1m49.682

BOSCH SPARK PLUG GRAND PRIX

7 October 1990. Nazareth. 200 laps of a 0.946-mile circuit = 189.200 miles. CART/PPG Indycar World Series round 15

1 Emerson Fittipaldi   Penske PC19-Chevrolet   200   1h46m28.636
2 Rick Mears   Penske PC19-Chevrolet   200   1h46m29.003
3 Bobby Rahal   Lola T90/00-Chevrolet   199
4 Mario Andretti   Lola T90/00-Chevrolet   198
5 Michael Andretti   Lola T90/00-Chevrolet   198
6 Eddie Cheever   Lola T90/00-Chevrolet   196

Winner's average speed: 106.614 mph. Pole position: Rahal, 20.462s

CHAMPION SPARK PLUG 300 KMS

21 October 1990. Laguna Seca. 84 laps of a 2.214-mile circuit = 185.976 miles. CART/PPG Indycar World Series round 16

1 Danny Sullivan   Penske PC19-Chevrolet   84   1h47m45.206
2 Al Unser Jr   Lola T90/00-Chevrolet   84   1h48m14.794
3 Michael Andretti   Lola T90/00-Chevrolet   84   1h48m34.040
4 Rick Mears   Penske PC19-Chevrolet   84   1h48m34.620
5 Bobby Rahal   Lola T90/00-Chevrolet   84   1h48m52.090
6 Emerson Fittipaldi   Penske PC19-Chevrolet   84   1h48m53.050

Winner's average speed: 103.556 mph. Pole position: Sullivan, 1m12.384

1990 FINAL CHAMPIONSHIP POSITIONS

1	Al Unser Jr	210	7	Mario Andretti	136
2	Michael Andretti	181	8	Arie Luyendyk	90
3	Rick Mears	168	9	Eddie Cheever	80
4	Bobby Rahal	153	10	John Andretti	51
5	Emerson Fittipaldi	144			
6	Danny Sullivan	139			

1991

GOLD COAST INDY CAR GRAND PRIX

17 March 1991. Surfers Paradise. 65 laps of a 2.794-mile circuit = 181.610 miles. CART/PPG Indycar World Series round 1

1 John Andretti   Lola T91/00-Chevrolet   65   2h12m54.820
2 Bobby Rahal   Lola T91/00-Chevrolet   65   2h13m07.524
3 Rick Mears   Penske PC20-Chevrolet   65
4 Danny Sullivan   Lola T91/00-Alfa Romeo   65
5 Scott Pruett   Truesports 91C-Judd   65
6 Scott Brayton   Lola T91/00-Chevrolet   65

Winner's average speed: 81.983 mph. Pole position: Michael Andretti (Lola T91/00-Chevrolet), 1m40.047

TOYOTA GRAND PRIX OF LONG BEACH

14 April 1991. Long Beach. 95 laps of a 1.670-mile circuit = 158.650 miles. CART/PPG Indycar World Series round 2

1 Al Unser Jr   Lola T91/00-Chevrolet   95   1h57m14.162
2 Bobby Rahal   Lola T91/00-Chevrolet   95   1h57m18.054
3 Eddie Cheever   Lola T91/00-Chevrolet   94
4 Rick Mears   Penske PC20-Chevrolet   94
5 Arie Luyendyk   Lola T91/00-Chevrolet   93
6 Ted Prappas   Lola T89/00-Judd   93

Winner's average speed: 81.195 mph. Pole position: Michael Andretti (Lola T91/00-Chevrolet), 1m06.306

VALVOLINE 200

21 April 1991. Phoenix. 200 laps of a 1.000-mile circuit = 200.000 miles. CART/PPG Indycar World Series round 3

1 Arie Luyendyk   Lola T91/00-Chevrolet   200   1h32m18.994
2 Bobby Rahal   Lola T91/00-Chevrolet   200   1h32m21.604
3 Emerson Fittipaldi   Penske PC20-Chevrolet   200
4 Michael Andretti   Lola T91/00-Chevrolet   200
5 Rick Mears   Penske PC20-Chevrolet   199
6 Al Unser Jr   Lola T91/00-Chevrolet   199

Winner's average speed: 129.988 mph. Pole position: Mears, 21.386s

INDIANAPOLIS 500

26 May 1991. Indianapolis. 200 laps of a 2.500-mile circuit = 500.000 miles. CART/PPG Indycar World Series round 4

1 Rick Mears   Penske PC20-Chevrolet   200   2h50m00.791
2 Michael Andretti   Lola T91/00-Chevrolet   200   2h50m03.940
3 Arie Luyendyk   Lola T91/00-Chevrolet   199
4 Al Unser Jr   Lola T91/00-Chevrolet   198
5 John Andretti   Lola T91/00-Chevrolet   197
6 Gordon Johncock   Lola T90/00-Cosworth   188

Winner's average speed: 176.457 mph. Pole position: Mears, 224.113 mph. Fastest qualifier: Gary Bettenhausen (Lola T91/00-Buick), 224.468 mph. Fastest lap: Luyendyk, 40.508s

MILLER GENUINE DRAFT 200

2 June 1991. Milwaukee. 200 laps of a 1.032-mile circuit = 206.400 miles. CART/PPG Indycar World Series round 5

1 Michael Andretti   Lola T91/00-Chevrolet   200   1h29m10.902
2 John Andretti   Lola T91/00-Chevrolet   200   1h29m33.383
3 Mario Andretti   Lola T91/00-Chevrolet   199
4 Bobby Rahal   Lola T91/00-Chevrolet   198
5 Danny Sullivan   Lola T91/00-Alfa Romeo   197
6 Scott Brayton   Lola T91/00-Chevrolet   196

Winner's average speed: 138.863 mph. Pole position: Rick Mears (Penske PC20-Chevrolet), 22.186s. Fastest lap: Scott Pruett (Truesports 91C-Judd), 24.251s

VALVOLINE DETROIT GRAND PRIX

16 June 1991. Detroit. 62 laps of a 2.500-mile circuit = 155 miles. CART/PPG Indycar World Series round 6

1	Emerson Fittipaldi	Penske PC20-Chevrolet	62	1h57m59.050
2	Bobby Rahal	Lola T91/00-Chevrolet	62	1h57m59.337
3	Arie Luyendyk	Lola T91/00-Chevrolet	62	1h58m03.396
4	Al Unser Jr	Lola T91/00-Chevrolet	62	1h58m15.586
5	Rick Mears	Penske PC20-Chevrolet	62	1h58m23.047
6	John Andretti	Lola T91/00-Chevrolet	62	1h58m39.390

Winner's average speed: 78.824 mph. Pole position: Michael Andretti (Lola T91/00-Chevrolet), 1m41.442

BUDWEISER GI JOE'S 200

23 June 1991. Portland. 104 laps of a 1.922-mile circuit = 199.888 miles. CART/PPG Indycar World Series round 7

1	Michael Andretti	Lola T91/00-Chevrolet	104	1h44m06.044
2	Emerson Fittipaldi	Penske PC20-Chevrolet	104	1h44m10.569
3	Bobby Rahal	Lola T91/00-Chevrolet	104	1h44m42.932
4	Al Unser Jr	Lola T91/00-Chevrolet	104	1h44m51.117
5	Mario Andretti	Lola T91/00-Chevrolet	104	1h45m04.234
6	Rick Mears	Penske PC20-Chevrolet	103	out of fuel

Winner's average speed: 115.208 mph. Pole position: Fittipaldi, 56.497s

BUDWEISER CLEVELAND GRAND PRIX

7 July 1991. Cleveland. 85 laps of a 2.106-mile circuit = 179.010 miles. CART/PPG Indycar World Series round 8

1	Michael Andretti	Lola T91/00-Chevrolet	85	1h42m47.919
2	Emerson Fittipaldi	Penske PC20-Chevrolet	85	1h42m50.169
3	Bobby Rahal	Lola T91/00-Chevrolet	85	
4	Al Unser Jr	Lola T91/00-Chevrolet	85	
5	Arie Luyendyk	Lola T91/00-Chevrolet	85	
6	Mario Andretti	Lola T91/00-Chevrolet	85	

Winner's average speed: 104.482 mph. Pole position: Fittipaldi, 1m00.553

MARLBORO GRAND PRIX AT THE MEADOWLANDS

14 July 1991. Meadowlands. 150 laps of a 1.217-mile circuit = 182.550 miles. CART/PPG Indycar World Series round 9

1	Bobby Rahal	Lola T91/00-Chevrolet	150	1h54m37.807
2	Al Unser Jr	Lola T91/00-Chevrolet	150	1h54m44.761
3	Rick Mears	Penske PC20-Chevrolet	150	1h55m10.483
4	John Andretti	Lola T91/00-Chevrolet	150	1h55m18.704
5	Eddie Cheever	Lola T91/00-Chevrolet	148	
6	Danny Sullivan	Lola T91/00-Alfa Romeo	147	

Winner's average speed: 95.551 mph. Pole position: Mears, 37.772s

MOLSON INDY TORONTO

21 July 1991. Toronto. 103 laps of a 1.784-mile circuit = 183.752 miles. CART/PPG Indycar World Series round 10

1	Michael Andretti	Lola T91/00-Chevrolet	103	1h50m57.274
2	Mario Andretti	Lola T91/00-Chevrolet	103	1h51m13.024
3	Bobby Rahal	Lola T91/00-Chevrolet	103	1h51m42.793
4	Scott Pruett	Truesports 91C-Judd	102	
5	John Andretti	Lola T91/00-Chevrolet	101	
6	Scott Brayton	Lola T91/00-Chevrolet	101	

Winner's average speed: 99.366 mph. Pole position: Michael Andretti, 59.077s

MARLBORO 500

4 August 1991. Michigan. 250 laps of a 2.000-mile circuit = 500.000 miles. CART/PPG Indycar World Series round 11

1	Rick Mears	Penske PC20-Chevrolet	250	2h59m23.650
2	Arie Luyendyk	Lola T91/00-Chevrolet	250	2h59m26.793
3	Al Unser Jr	Lola T91/00-Chevrolet	246	
4	Mario Andretti	Lola T91/00-Chevrolet	245	engine
5	Tony Bettenhausen Jr	Penske PC19-Chevrolet	245	
6	John Andretti	Lola T91/00-Chevrolet	241	

Winner's average speed: 167.230 mph. Pole position: Mears, 31.976s

TEXACO/HAVOLINE GRAND PRIX OF DENVER

25 August 1991. Denver. 70 laps of a 1.900-mile circuit = 133 miles. CART/PPG Indycar World Series round 12

1	Al Unser Jr	Lola T91/00-Chevrolet	70	1h57m06.583
2	Emerson Fittipaldi	Penske PC20-Chevrolet	70	1h58m16.159
3	Michael Andretti	Lola T91/00-Chevrolet	70	
4	Eddie Cheever	Lola T91/00-Chevrolet	70	
5	Scott Pruett	Truesports 91C-Judd	69	
6	Willy T Ribbs	Lola T90/00-Cosworth	69	

Winner's average speed: 68.141 mph. Pole position: Michael Andretti, 1m25.896

MOLSON INDY VANCOUVER

1 September 1991. Vancouver. 100 laps of a 1.677-mile circuit = 167.700 miles. CART/PPG Indycar World Series round 13

1	Michael Andretti	Lola T91/00-Chevrolet	100	1h47m10.182
2	Bobby Rahal	Lola T91/00-Chevrolet	100	1h47m21.740
3	Al Unser Jr	Lola T91/00-Chevrolet	100	1h47m34.270
4	Mario Andretti	Lola T91/00-Chevrolet	99	
5	Scott Pruett	Truesports 91C-Judd	99	
6	Rick Mears	Penske PC20-Chevrolet	98	

Winner's average speed: 93.888 mph. Pole position: Michael Andretti, 57.385s

PIONEER ELECTRONICS 200

15 September 1991. Mid-Ohio. 89 laps of a 2.258-mile circuit = 200.962 miles. CART/PPG Indycar World Series round 14

1	Michael Andretti	Lola T91/00-Chevrolet	89	1h59m49.943
2	Emerson Fittipaldi	Penske PC20-Chevrolet	89	1h59m53.467
3	Bobby Rahal	Lola T91/00-Chevrolet	89	1h59m58.086
4	Scott Pruett	Truesports 91C-Judd	89	2h00m00.614
5	Al Unser Jr	Lola T91/00-Chevrolet	89	2h00m01.771
6	Rick Mears	Penske PC20-Chevrolet	89	2h00m02.132

Winner's average speed: 100.622 mph. Pole position: Michael Andretti, 1m09.475

TEXACO/HAVOLINE 200

22 September 1991. Elkhart Lake. 50 laps of a 4.048-mile circuit = 202.400 miles. CART/PPG Indycar World Series round 15

1	Michael Andretti	Lola T91/00-Chevrolet	50	1h35m05.010
2	Al Unser Jr	Lola T91/00-Chevrolet	50	1h35m10.767
3	Mario Andretti	Lola T91/00-Chevrolet	50	1h35m39.659
4	Bobby Rahal	Lola T91/00-Chevrolet	50	1h35m43.917
5	Arie Luyendyk	Lola T91/00-Chevrolet	50	1h36m36.121
6	Emerson Fittipaldi	Penske PC20-Chevrolet	49	

Winner's average speed: 127.719 mph. Pole position: Rahal, 1m47.090. Fastest lap: Michael Andretti, 1m50.454

BOSCH SPARK PLUG GRAND PRIX

6 October 1991. Nazareth. 200 laps of a 0.946-mile circuit = 189.200 miles. CART/PPG Indycar World Series round 16

1	Arie Luyendyk	Lola T91/00-Chevrolet	200	1h31m23.223
2	Bobby Rahal	Lola T91/00-Chevrolet	200	1h31m23.920
3	Michael Andretti	Lola T91/00-Chevrolet	200	1h31m36.270
4	Al Unser Jr	Lola T91/00-Chevrolet	200	1h31m37.060
5	Mario Andretti	Lola T91/00-Chevrolet	200	1h31m44.380
6	Eddie Cheever	Lola T91/00-Chevrolet	198	

Winner's average speed: 124.219 mph. Pole position: Rick Mears (Penske PC20-Chevrolet), 20.141s

CHAMPION SPARK PLUG 300 KMS

20 October 1991. Laguna Seca. 84 laps of a 2.214-mile circuit = 185.976 miles. CART/PPG Indycar World Series round 17

1	Michael Andretti	Lola T91/00-Chevrolet	84	1h47m42.217
2	Al Unser Jr	Lola T91/00-Chevrolet	84	1h47m51.450
3	Mario Andretti	Lola T91/00-Chevrolet	84	1h47m57.400
4	Emerson Fittipaldi	Penske PC20-Chevrolet	84	1h47m59.220
5	Rick Mears	Penske PC20-Chevrolet	84	1h48m06.880
6	Eddie Cheever	Lola T91/00-Chevrolet	84	1h48m51.490

Winner's average speed: 103.604 mph. Pole position: Michael Andretti, 1m12.095

1991 FINAL CHAMPIONSHIP POSITIONS

1	Michael Andretti	234	7	Mario Andretti	132
2	Bobby Rahal	200	8	John Andretti	105
3	Al Unser Jr	197	9	Eddie Cheever	91
4	Rick Mears	144	10	Scott Pruett	67
5	Emerson Fittipaldi	140			
6	Arie Luyendyk	134			

1992

DAIKYO INDYCAR GRAND PRIX

22 March 1992. Surfers Paradise. 65 laps of a 2.794-mile circuit = 181.610 miles. PPG Indycar World Series round 1

1	Emerson Fittipaldi	Penske PC21-Chevrolet	65	2h20m32.477
2	Rick Mears	Penske PC21-Chevrolet	65	2h20m35.810
3	Bobby Rahal	Lola T92/00-Chevrolet	65	
4	Al Unser Jr	Galmer G92-Chevrolet	65	
5	Danny Sullivan	Galmer G92-Chevrolet	65	
6	John Andretti	Lola T92/00-Chevrolet	65	

Winner's average speed: 77.533 mph. Pole position: Unser Jr, 1m38.744

VALVOLINE 200

5 April 1992. Phoenix. 200 laps of a 1.000-mile circuit = 200.000 miles. PPG Indycar World Series round 2

1	Bobby Rahal	Lola T92/00-Chevrolet	200	1h31m56.123
2	Eddie Cheever	Lola T92/00-Ford	200	1h32m18.473
3	Emerson Fittipaldi	Penske PC21-Chevrolet	199	
4	Paul Tracy	Penske PC20-Chevrolet	198	
5	Al Unser Jr	Galmer G92-Chevrolet	197	
6	John Andretti	Lola T92/00-Chevrolet	197	

Winner's average speed: 130.526 mph. Pole position: Michael Andretti (Lola T91/00-Ford), 20.952s. Fastest lap: Rick Mears (Penske PC21-Chevrolet), 21.915s

TOYOTA GRAND PRIX OF LONG BEACH

12 April 1992. Long Beach. 105 laps of a 1.586-mile circuit = 166.530 miles. PPG Indycar World Series round 3

1	Danny Sullivan	Galmer G92-Chevrolet	105	1h48m56.715
2	Bobby Rahal	Lola T92/00-Chevrolet	105	1h48m57.311
3	Emerson Fittipaldi	Penske PC21-Chevrolet	105	1h48m58.440
4	Al Unser Jr	Galmer G92-Chevrolet	105	1h49m20.490
5	Scott Goodyear	Lola T92/00-Chevrolet	104	
6	Rick Mears	Penske PC21-Chevrolet	103	

Winner's average speed: 91.714 mph. Pole position: Michael Andretti (Lola T92/00-Ford), 53.872s

INDIANAPOLIS 500

24 May 1992. Indianapolis. 200 laps of a 2.500-mile circuit = 500.000 miles. PPG Indycar World Series round 4

1	Al Unser Jr	Galmer G92-Chevrolet	200	3h43m04.991
2	Scott Goodyear	Lola T92/00-Chevrolet	200	3h43m05.034
3	Al Unser	Lola T92/00-Buick	200	3h43m15.226
4	Eddie Cheever	Lola T92/00-Ford	200	3h43m15.271
5	Danny Sullivan	Galmer G92-Chevrolet	199	
6	Bobby Rahal	Lola T92/00-Chevrolet	199	

Winner's average speed: 134.479 mph. Pole position: Roberto Guerrero (Lola T92/00-Buick), 232.482 mph, spun on the parade lap and did not take the green flag. Fastest lap: Michael Andretti (Lola T92/00-Ford), 39.281s

ITT AUTOMOTIVE DETROIT GRAND PRIX

7 June 1992. Belle Isle. 77 laps of a 2.100-mile circuit = 161.700 miles. PPG Indycar World Series round 5

1	Bobby Rahal	Lola T92/00-Chevrolet	77	1h58m20.020
2	Raul Boesel	Lola T92/00-Chevrolet	77	1h58m28.557

3	Stefan Johansson	Penske PC20-Chevrolet	77	1h58m31.160
4	Michael Andretti	Lola T92/00-Ford	77	
5	Danny Sullivan	Galmer G92-Chevrolet	76	
6	Teo Fabi	Lola T92/00-Ford	76	

Winner's average speed: 81.989 mph. Pole position: Michael Andretti, 1m14.340

BUDWEISER GI JOE'S 200

21 June 1992. Portland. 102 laps of a 1.967-mile circuit = 200.634 miles. PPG Indycar World Series round 6

1	Michael Andretti	Lola T92/00-Ford	102	1h53m25.246
2	Emerson Fittipaldi	Penske PC21-Chevrolet	102	1h53m33.653
3	Al Unser Jr	Galmer G92-Chevrolet	102	1h56m05.899
4	Eddie Cheever	Lola T92/00-Ford	101	
5	John Andretti	Lola T92/00-Chevrolet	101	
6	Mario Andretti	Lola T92/00-Ford	101	

Winner's average speed: 106.136 mph. Pole position: Fittipaldi, 1m00.658

MILLER GENUINE DRAFT 200

28 June 1992. Milwaukee. 200 laps of a 1.032-mile circuit = 206.400 miles. PPG Indycar World Series round 7

1	Michael Andretti	Lola T92/00-Ford	200	1h26m56.201
2	Bobby Rahal	Lola T92/00-Chevrolet	200	1h27m21.099
3	Scott Brayton	Lola T92/00-Chevrolet	198	
4	Emerson Fittipaldi	Penske PC21-Chevrolet	197	
5	Eddie Cheever	Lola T92/00-Ford	197	
6	Mario Andretti	Lola T92/00-Ford	197	

Winner's average speed: 142.448 mph. Pole position: Rahal, 22.096s

NEW ENGLAND 200

5 July 1992. New Hampshire. 200 laps of a 1.058-mile circuit = 211.600 miles. PPG Indycar World Series round 8

1	Bobby Rahal	Lola T92/00-Chevrolet	200	1h35m00.885
2	Michael Andretti	Lola T92/00-Ford	199	
3	Scott Goodyear	Lola T92/00-Chevrolet	199	
4	Rick Mears	Penske PC21-Chevrolet	199	
5	John Andretti	Lola T92/00-Chevrolet	197	
6	Scott Pruett	Truesports 92C-Chevrolet	196	

Winner's average speed: 133.621 mph. Pole position: Rahal, 22.279s. Fastest lap: Michael Andretti, 162.614 mph

MOLSON INDY TORONTO

19 July 1992. Toronto. 103 laps of a 1.784-mile circuit = 183.752 miles. PPG Indycar World Series round 9

1	Michael Andretti	Lola T92/00-Ford	103	1h52m21.974
2	Bobby Rahal	Lola T92/00-Chevrolet	103	1h52m42.807
3	Danny Sullivan	Galmer G92-Chevrolet	102	
4	Mario Andretti	Lola T92/00-Ford	102	
5	John Andretti	Lola T92/00-Chevrolet	102	
6	Scott Goodyear	Lola T92/00-Chevrolet	101	

Winner's average speed: 98.118 mph. Pole position: Rahal, 59.057s

MARLBORO 500

2 August 1992. Michigan. 250 laps of a 2.000-mile circuit = 500.000 miles. PPG Indycar World Series round 10

1	Scott Goodyear	Lola T92/00-Ford	250	2h48m53.699
2	Paul Tracy	Penske PC21-Chevrolet	250	2h48m59.631
3	Raul Boesel	Lola T92/00-Chevrolet	249	
4	Al Unser Jr	Galmer G92-Chevrolet	249	
5	Scott Pruett	Truesports 92C-Chevrolet	249	
6	John Andretti	Lola T92/00-Chevrolet	249	

Winner's average speed: 177.625 mph. Pole position: Mario Andretti (Lola T92/00-Ford), 31.284s

BUDWEISER CLEVELAND GRAND PRIX

9 August 1992. Cleveland. 85 laps of a 2.106-mile circuit = 179.010 miles. PPG Indycar World Series round 11

1	Emerson Fittipaldi	Penske PC21-Chevrolet	85	1h30m38.527

2	Michael Andretti	Lola T92/00-Ford	85	1h30m54.557
3	Al Unser Jr	Galmer G92-Chevrolet	85	
4	Bobby Rahal	Lola T92/00-Chevrolet	85	
5	Mario Andretti	Lola T92/00-Ford	84	
6	Raul Boesel	Lola T92/00-Chevrolet	84	

Winner's average speed: 118.495 mph. Pole position: Fittipaldi, 59.732s

TEXACO/HAVOLINE 200

23 August 1992. Elkhart Lake. 50 laps of a 4.048-mile circuit = 202.400 miles. PPG Indycar World Series round 12

1	Emerson Fittipaldi	Penske PC21-Chevrolet	50	1h48m26.677
2	Al Unser Jr	Galmer G92-Chevrolet	50	1h48m27.452
3	Bobby Rahal	Lola T92/00-Chevrolet	50	1h48m27.770
4	Michael Andretti	Lola T92/00-Ford	50	1h48m30.830
5	Mario Andretti	Lola T92/00-Ford	50	1h48m34.540
6	John Andretti	Lola T92/00-Ford	50	1h48m38.370

Winner's average speed: 111.983 mph. Pole position: Paul Tracy (Penske PC21-Chevrolet), 1m48.211. Fastest lap: Fittipaldi, 1m49.690

MOLSON INDY VANCOUVER

30 August 1992. Vancouver. 100 laps of a 1.677-mile circuit = 167.700 miles. PPG Indycar World Series round 13

1	Michael Andretti	Lola T92/00-Ford	100	1h41m50.788
2	Al Unser Jr	Galmer G92-Chevrolet	100	1h42m45.346
3	Stefan Johansson	Penske PC20-Chevrolet	99	
4	Scott Pruett	Truesports 92C-Chevrolet	99	
5	Scott Goodyear	Lola T92/00-Ford	97	
6	Mario Andretti	Lola T92/00-Ford	97	

Winner's average speed: 98.796 mph. Pole position: Michael Andretti, 54.514s. Fastest lap: Emerson Fittipaldi (Penske PC21-Chevrolet), 56.696s

PIONEER ELECTRONICS 200

13 September 1992. Mid-Ohio. 89 laps of a 2.258-mile circuit = 200.962 miles. PPG Indycar World Series round 14

1	Emerson Fittipaldi	Penske PC21-Chevrolet	89	1h51m23.444
2	Paul Tracy	Penske PC21-Chevrolet	89	1h51m33.443
3	Al Unser Jr	Galmer G92-Chevrolet	89	1h52m15.306
4	John Andretti	Lola T92/00-Ford	89	1h52m52.766
5	Mario Andretti	Lola T92/00-Ford	88	
6	Stefan Johansson	Penske PC20-Chevrolet	88	

Winner's average speed: 108.247 mph. Pole position: Michael Andretti (Lola T92/00-Ford), 1m08.766

BOSCH SPARK PLUG GRAND PRIX

4 October 1992. Nazareth. 200 laps of a 0.946-mile circuit = 189.200 miles. PPG Indycar World Series round 15

1	Bobby Rahal	Lola T92/00-Chevrolet	200	1h33m07.969
2	Michael Andretti	Lola T92/00-Ford	200	1h33m08.757
3	Paul Tracy	Penske PC21-Chevrolet	200	1h33m18.150
4	Scott Goodyear	Lola T92/00-Chevrolet	200	1h33m22.940
5	Mario Andretti	Lola T92/00-Ford	199	
6	Raul Boesel	Lola T92/00-Chevrolet	197	

Winner's average speed: 121.890 mph. Pole position: Michael Andretti, 19.842s. Fastest lap: Rahal, 20.380s

TOYOTA MONTEREY GRAND PRIX/KODALUX PROCESSING 300

18 October 1992. Laguna Seca. 84 laps of a 2.214-mile circuit = 185.976 miles. PPG Indycar World Series round 16

1	Michael Andretti	Lola T92/00-Ford	84	1h51m35.423
2	Mario Andretti	Lola T92/00-Ford	84	1h51m40.138
3	Bobby Rahal	Lola T92/00-Chevrolet	84	1h51m44.660
4	Eddie Cheever	Lola T92/00-Ford	84	1h51m58.850
5	John Andretti	Lola T92/00-Chevrolet	84	1h52m13.720
6	Raul Boesel	Lola T92/00-Chevrolet	84	1h52m16.090

Winner's average speed: 99.996 mph. Pole position: Michael Andretti, 1m11.185

1992 FINAL CHAMPIONSHIP POSITIONS

1	Bobby Rahal	196	7	Danny Sullivan	99
2	Michael Andretti	192	8	John Andretti	94
3	Al Unser Jr	169	9=	Raul Boesel	80
4	Emerson Fittipaldi	151		Eddie Cheever	80
5	Scott Goodyear	108			
6	Mario Andretti	105			

1993

AUSTRALIAN FAI INDYCAR GRAND PRIX

21 March 1993. Surfers Paradise. 65 laps of a 2.794-mile circuit = 181.610 miles. PPG Indycar World Series round 1

1	Nigel Mansell	Lola T93/00-Ford	65	1h52m02.886
2	Emerson Fittipaldi	Penske PC22-Chevrolet	65	1h52m07.999
3	Robby Gordon	Lola T92/00-Ford	65	1h52m08.476
4	Mario Andretti	Lola T93/00-Ford	65	1h52m17.533
5	Arie Luyendyk	Lola T93/00-Ford	65	1h52m50.106
6	Bobby Rahal	Rahal-Hogan RH001-Chevrolet	64	

Winner's average speed: 97.249 mph. Pole position: Mansell, 1m38.555. Fastest lap: Mansell, time n/a

VALVOLINE 200

4 April 1993. Phoenix. 200 laps of a 1.000-mile circuit = 200.000 miles. PPG Indycar World Series round 2

1	Mario Andretti	Lola T93/00-Ford	200	1h36m53.630
2	Raul Boesel	Lola T93/00-Ford	199	
3	Jimmy Vasser	Lola T92/00-Chevrolet	197	
4	Al Unser Jr	Lola T93/00-Chevrolet	197	
5	Teo Fabi	Lola T93/00-Chevrolet	196	
6	Arie Luyendyk	Lola T93/00-Ford	195	

Winner's average speed: 123.847 mph. Pole position: Scott Goodyear (Lola T93/00-Ford), 20.833s

TOYOTA GRAND PRIX OF LONG BEACH

18 April 1993. Long Beach. 105 laps of a 1.586-mile circuit = 166.530 miles. PPG Indycar World Series round 3

1	Paul Tracy	Penske PC22-Chevrolet	105	1h47m36.418
2	Bobby Rahal	Rahal-Hogan RH001-Chevrolet	105	1h47m49.076
3	Nigel Mansell	Lola T93/00-Ford	105	1h47m55.883
4	Teo Fabi	Lola T93/00-Chevrolet	105	1h48m29.331
5	Roberto Guerrero	Lola T93/00-Chevrolet	104	
6	Robbie Buhl	Lola T92/00-Chevrolet	104	

Winner's average speed: 92.855 mph. Pole position: Mansell, 52.903s. Fastest lap: Tracy, time n/a

INDIANAPOLIS 500

30 May 1993. Indianapolis. 200 laps of a 2.500-mile circuit = 500.000 miles. PPG Indycar World Series round 4

1	Emerson Fittipaldi	Penske PC22-Chevrolet	200	3h10m49.860
2	Arie Luyendyk	Lola T93/00-Ford	200	3h10m52.722
3	Nigel Mansell	Lola T93/00-Ford	200	3h10m54.608
4	Raul Boesel	Lola T93/00-Ford	200	3h10m54.977
5	Mario Andretti	Lola T93/00-Ford	200	3h10m55.264
6	Scott Brayton	Lola T93/00-Ford	200	3h10m57.743

Winner's average speed: 157.207 mph. Pole position: Luyendyk, 223.967 mph. Fastest lap: Fittipaldi, 41.90s

MILLER GENUINE DRAFT 200

6 June 1993. Milwaukee. 200 laps of a 1.032-mile circuit = 206.400 miles. PPG Indycar World Series round 5

1	Nigel Mansell	Lola T93/00-Ford	200	1h48m08.245
2	Raul Boesel	Lola T93/00-Ford	200	1h48m08.759
3	Emerson Fittipaldi	Penske PC22-Chevrolet	200	1h48m12.696

4	Bobby Rahal	Lola T93/00-Chevrolet	200	1h48m21.541
5	Al Unser Jr	Lola T93/00-Chevrolet	198	
6	Scott Brayton	Lola T93/00-Ford	198	

Winner's average speed: 114.521 mph. Pole position: Boesel, 21.719s.
Fastest lap: Boesel, 23.478s

ITT AUTOMOTIVE DETROIT GRAND PRIX

13 June 1993. Belle Isle. 77 laps of a 2.100-mile circuit = 161.700 miles.
PPG Indycar World Series round 6

1	Danny Sullivan	Lola T93/00-Chevrolet	77	1h56m43.678
2	Raul Boesel	Lola T93/00-Ford	77	1h56m55.884
3	Mario Andretti	Lola T93/00-Ford	77	1h56m59.249
4	Andrea Montermini	Lola T92/00-Chevrolet	77	1h57m01.031
5	Bobby Rahal	Lola T93/00-Chevrolet	77	1h57m01.311
6	Al Unser Jr	Lola T93/00-Chevrolet	77	1h57m07.709

Winner's average speed: 83.116 mph. Pole position: Nigel Mansell (Lola
T93/00-Ford), 1m10.902

BUDWEISER GI JOE'S 200

27 June 1993. Portland. 102 laps of a 1.967-mile circuit = 200.634 miles.
PPG Indycar World Series round 7

1	Emerson Fittipaldi	Penske PC22-Chevrolet	102	2h03m54.620
2	Nigel Mansell	Lola T93/00-Ford	102	2h03m58.979
3	Paul Tracy	Penske PC22-Chevrolet	102	2h04m04.889
4	Bobby Rahal	Lola T93/00-Chevrolet	101	
5	Al Unser Jr	Lola T93/00-Chevrolet	101	
6	Mario Andretti	Lola T93/00-Ford	101	

Winner's average speed: 97.151 mph. Pole position: Mansell, 1m00.902

BUDWEISER CLEVELAND GRAND PRIX

11 July 1993. Cleveland. 85 laps of a 2.106-mile circuit = 179.010 miles.
PPG Indycar World Series round 8

1	Paul Tracy	Penske PC22-Chevrolet	85	1h34m27.254
2	Emerson Fittipaldi	Penske PC22-Chevrolet	85	1h34m45.344
3	Nigel Mansell	Lola T93/00-Ford	85	1h34m49.271
4	Stefan Johansson	Penske PC22-Chevrolet	84	
5	Mario Andretti	Lola T93/00-Ford	84	
6	Robby Gordon	Lola T93/00-Ford	84	

Winner's average speed: 113.712 mph. Pole position: Tracy, 59.168s

MOLSON INDY TORONTO

18 July 1993. Toronto. 103 laps of a 1.784-mile circuit = 183.752 miles.
PPG Indycar World Series round 9

1	Paul Tracy	Penske PC22-Chevrolet	103	1h53m58.951
2	Emerson Fittipaldi	Penske PC22-Chevrolet	103	1h54m11.975
3	Danny Sullivan	Lola T93/00-Chevrolet	103	1h54m13.151
4	Bobby Rahal	Lola T93/00-Chevrolet	103	1h54m13.744
5	Al Unser Jr	Lola T93/00-Chevrolet	103	1h54m14.225
6	Robby Gordon	Lola T93/00-Ford	103	1h54m45.750

Winner's average speed: 96.726 mph. Pole position: Fittipaldi, 58.256s

MARLBORO 500

1 August 1993. Michigan. 250 laps of a 2.000-mile circuit = 500.000 miles.
PPG Indycar World Series round 10

1	Nigel Mansell	Lola T93/00-Ford	250	2h39m24.131
2	Mario Andretti	Lola T93/00-Ford	250	2h39m33.565
3	Arie Luyendyk	Lola T93/00-Ford	249	
4	Raul Boesel	Lola T93/00-Ford	248	
5	Scott Goodyear	Lola T93/00-Ford	247	
6	Teo Fabi	Lola T93/00-Chevrolet	246	

Winner's average speed: 188.203 mph. Pole position: Mario Andretti,
30.733s

NEW ENGLAND 200

8 August 1993. New Hampshire. 200 laps of a 1.058-mile circuit =
211.600 miles. PPG Indycar World Series round 11

1	Nigel Mansell	Lola T93/00-Ford	200	1h37m33.033
2	Paul Tracy	Penske PC22-Chevrolet	200	1h37m33.487

3	Emerson Fittipaldi	Penske PC22-Chevrolet	200	1h37m41.830
4	Roberto Guerrero	Lola T93/00-Chevrolet	199	
5	Robby Gordon	Lola T93/00-Ford	199	
6	Scott Brayton	Lola T93/00-Ford	198	

Winner's average speed: 130.148 mph. Pole position: Mansell, 22.504s

TEXACO/HAVOLINE 200

22 August 1993. Elkhart Lake. 50 laps of a 4.048-mile circuit = 202.400
miles. PPG Indycar World Series round 12

1	Paul Tracy	Penske PC22-Chevrolet	50	1h41m20.689
2	Nigel Mansell	Lola T93/00-Ford	50	1h41m48.148
3	Bobby Rahal	Lola T93/00-Chevrolet	50	1h42m00.207
4	Raul Boesel	Lola T93/00-Ford	50	1h42m12.446
5	Emerson Fittipaldi	Penske PC22-Chevrolet	50	1h42m20.845
6	Eddie Cheever	Lola T93/00-Ford	50	1h43m12.493

Winner's average speed: 119.829 mph. Pole position: Tracy, 1m47.405

MOLSON INDY VANCOUVER

29 August 1993. Vancouver. 102 laps of a 1.648-mile circuit = 168.096
miles. PPG Indycar World Series round 13

1	Al Unser Jr	Lola T93/00-Chevrolet	102	1h49m52.452
2	Bobby Rahal	Lola T93/00-Chevrolet	102	1h50m03.651
3	Stefan Johansson	Penske PC22-Chevrolet	102	1h50m26.789
4	Scott Goodyear	Lola T93/00-Ford	102	1h50m35.008
5	Mario Andretti	Lola T93/00-Ford	102	1h50m39.545
6	Nigel Mansell	Lola T93/00-Ford	101	

Winner's average speed: 91.794 mph. Pole position: Goodyear, 53.791s

PIONEER ELECTONICS 200

12 September 1993. Mid-Ohio. 89 laps of a 2.258-mile circuit = 200.962
miles. PPG Indycar World Series round 14

1	Emerson Fittipaldi	Penske PC22-Chevrolet	89	1h56m59.188
2	Robby Gordon	Lola T93/00-Ford	89	1h57m15.857
3	Scott Goodyear	Lola T93/00-Ford	89	1h57m19.745
4	Raul Boesel	Lola T93/00-Ford	89	1h57m20.278
5	Arie Luyendyk	Lola T93/00-Ford	89	1h57m21.155
6	Bobby Rahal	Lola T93/00-Chevrolet	89	1h57m34.896

Winner's average speed: 103.069 mph. Pole position: Nigel Mansell (Lola
T93/00-Ford), 1m08.428

BOSCH SPARK PLUG GRAND PRIX

19 September 1993. Nazareth. 200 laps of a 0.946-mile circuit = 189.200
miles. PPG Indycar World Series round 15

1	Nigel Mansell	Lola T93/00-Ford	200	1h15m37.273
2	Scott Goodyear	Lola T93/00-Ford	200	1h15m56.539
3	Paul Tracy	Penske PC22-Chevrolet	198	
4	Robby Gordon	Lola T93/00-Ford	198	
5	Emerson Fittipaldi	Penske PC22-Chevrolet	198	
6	Bobby Rahal	Lola T93/00-Chevrolet	196	

Winner's average speed: 150.117 mph. Pole position: Mansell-qualifying
cancelled due to rain, started in championship order

1993 Nigel Mansell gave up the opportunity to defend his F1 crown to win
the CART title in 1993 for Newman-Haas Racing.

TOYOTA MONTEREY GRAND PRIX

3 October 1993. Laguna Seca. 84 laps of a 2.214-mile circuit = 185.976 miles. PPG Indycar World Series round 16

1 Paul Tracy	Penske PC22-Chevrolet	84	1h44m58.169
2 Emerson Fittipaldi	Penske PC22-Chevrolet	84	1h45m25.660
3 Arie Luyendyk	Lola T93/00-Ford	84	1h45m44.338
4 Scott Goodyear	Lola T93/00-Ford	84	1h46m00.729
5 Al Unser Jr	Lola T93/00-Chevrolet	84	1h46m09.991
6 Stefan Johansson	Penske PC22-Chevrolet	83	

Winner's average speed: 106.303 mph. Pole position: Fittipaldi, 1m10.976

1993 FINAL CHAMPIONSHIP POSITIONS

1	Nigel Mansell	191	7	Al Unser Jr	100
2	Emerson Fittipaldi	183	8	Arie Luyendyk	90
3	Paul Tracy	157	9	Scott Goodyear	86
4	Bobby Rahal	133	10	Robby Gordon	84
5	Raul Boesel	132			
6	Mario Andretti	117			

1994

AUSTRALIAN FAI INDY CAR GRAND PRIX

20 March 1994. Surfers Paradise. 55 laps of a 2.794-mile circuit = 153.670 miles. PPG Indycar World Series round 1

1 Michael Andretti	Reynard 94I-Ford	55	1h53m52.770
2 Emerson Fittipaldi	Penske PC23-Ilmor	55	1h53m54.096
3 Mario Andretti	Lola T94/00-Ford	55	1h54m00.650
4 Jimmy Vasser	Reynard 94I-Ford	55	1h54m34.577
5 Stefan Johansson	Penske PC22-Ilmor	55	1h55m01.217
6 Mauricio Gugelmin	Reynard 94I-Ford	55	1h55m22.328

Winner's average speed: 80.965 mph. Pole position: Nigel Mansell (Lola T94/00-Ford), 1m34.877. Fastest lap: Mansell, 1m37.487

SLICK 50 200

10 April 1994. Phoenix. 200 laps of a 1.000-mile circuit = 200.000 miles. PPG Indycar World Series round 2

1 Emerson Fittipaldi	Penske PC23-Ilmor	200	1h51m41.615
2 Al Unser Jr	Penske PC23-Ilmor	200	1h51m55.097
3 Nigel Mansell	Lola T94/00-Ford	199	
4 Stefan Johansson	Penske PC22-Ilmor	197	
5 Jimmy Vasser	Reynard 94I-Ford	197	
6 Michael Groff	Lola T94/00-Honda	196	

Winner's average speed: 107.437 mph. Pole position: Paul Tracy (Penske PC23-Ilmor), 20.424s. Fastest lap: Fittipaldi, 21.530s

TOYOTA GRAND PRIX OF LONG BEACH

17 April 1994. Long Beach. 105 laps of a 1.586-mile circuit = 166.530 miles. PPG Indycar World Series round 3

1 Al Unser Jr	Penske PC23-Ilmor	105	1h40m53.582
2 Nigel Mansell	Lola T94/00-Ford	105	1h41m32.689
3 Robby Gordon	Lola T94/00-Ford	105	1h41m39.854
4 Raul Boesel	Lola T94/00-Ford	104	
5 Mario Andretti	Lola T94/00-Ford	104	
6 Michael Andretti	Reynard 94I-Ford	104	

Winner's average speed: 99.034 mph. Pole position: Paul Tracy (Penske PC23-Ilmor), 52.780s. Fastest lap: Tracy, 53.562s

INDIANAPOLIS 500

29 May 1994. Indianapolis. 200 laps of a 2.500-mile circuit = 500.000 miles. PPG Indycar World Series round 4

1 Al Unser Jr	Penske PC23-Mercedes-Benz	200	3h06m29.006
2 Jacques Villeneuve	Reynard 94I-Ford	200	3h06m37.606
3 Bobby Rahal	Penske PC22-Ilmor	199	

4 Jimmy Vasser	Reynard 94I-Ford	199	
5 Robby Gordon	Lola T94/00-Ford	199	
6 Michael Andretti	Reynard 94I-Ford	198	

Winner's average speed: 160.872 mph. Pole position: Unser Jr, 228.011 mph. Fastest lap: Emerson Fittipaldi (Penske PC23-Mercedes-Benz), 40.783s

MILLER GENUINE DRAFT 200

5 June 1994. Milwaukee. 192 laps of a 1.032-mile circuit = 198.144 miles. PPG Indycar World Series round 5

1 Al Unser Jr	Penske PC23-Ilmor	192	1h36m57.964
2 Emerson Fittipaldi	Penske PC23-Ilmor	192	1h36m59.458
3 Paul Tracy	Penske PC23-Ilmor	190	
4 Michael Andretti	Reynard 94I-Ford	189	
5 Nigel Mansell	Lola T94/00-Ford	189	
6 Robby Gordon	Lola T94/00-Ford	189	

Winner's average speed: 122.606 mph. Pole position: Raul Boesel (Lola T94/00-Ford), 22.310s. Fastest lap: Unser Jr, 24.584s

ITT AUTOMOTIVE DETROIT GRAND PRIX

12 June 1994. Belle Isle. 77 laps of a 2.100-mile circuit = 161.700 miles. PPG Indycar World Series round 6

1 Paul Tracy	Penske PC23-Ilmor	77	1h52m29.642
2 Emerson Fittipaldi	Penske PC23-Ilmor	77	1h52m38.891
3 Robby Gordon	Lola T94/00-Ford	77	1h52m39.929
4 Teo Fabi	Reynard 94I-Ilmor	77	1h52m54.175
5 Michael Andretti	Reynard 94I-Ford	77	1h52m56.035
6 Bobby Rahal	Lola T94/00-Honda	77	1h52m56.783

Winner's average speed: 86.245 mph. Pole position: Nigel Mansell (Lola T94/00-Ford), 1m09.582

BUDWEISER GI JOE'S 200

26 June 1994. Portland. 102 laps of a 1.967-mile circuit = 200.634 miles. PPG Indycar World Series round 7

1 Al Unser Jr	Penske PC23-Ilmor	102	1h50m43.706
2 Emerson Fittipaldi	Penske PC23-Ilmor	102	1h50m45.536
3 Paul Tracy	Penske PC23-Ilmor	102	1h51m16.162
4 Robby Gordon	Lola T94/00-Ford	102	1h51m40.032
5 Nigel Mansell	Lola T94/00-Ford	102	1h51m40.062
6 Jacques Villeneuve	Reynard 94I-Ford	101	

Winner's average speed: 108.717 mph. Pole position: Unser Jr, 1m00.071. Fastest lap: Unser Jr, 1m01.106

BUDWEISER CLEVELAND GRAND PRIX

10 July 1994. Cleveland. 85 laps of a 2.106-mile circuit = 179.010 miles. PPG Indycar World Series round 8

1 Al Unser Jr	Penske PC23-Ilmor	85	1h27m32.000
2 Nigel Mansell	Lola T94/00-Ford	85	1h27m54.950
3 Paul Tracy	Penske PC23-Ilmor	85	
4 Jacques Villeneuve	Reynard 94I-Ford	85	
5 Stefan Johansson	Penske PC22-Ilmor	84	
6 Raul Boesel	Lola T94/00-Ford	84	

Winner's average speed: 122.703 mph. Pole position: Unser Jr, 59.232s

MOLSON INDY TORONTO

17 July 1994. Toronto. 98 laps of a 1.784-mile circuit = 174.832 miles. PPG Indycar World Series round 9

1 Michael Andretti	Reynard 94I-Ford	98	1h48m15.978
2 Bobby Rahal	Lola T94/00-Honda	98	1h48m22.779
3 Emerson Fittipaldi	Penske PC23-Ilmor	98	1h48m23.527
4 Mario Andretti	Lola T94/00-Ford	98	1h49m18.393
5 Paul Tracy	Penske PC23-Ilmor	97	
6 Robby Gordon	Reynard 94I-Ford	97	

Winner's average speed: 96.890 mph. Pole position: Gordon, 58.154s. Fastest lap: Michael Andretti, 59.153s

MARLBORO 500

31 July 1994. Michigan. 250 laps of a 2.000-mile circuit = 500.000 miles. PPG Indycar World Series round 10

1 Scott Goodyear	Lola T94/00-Ford	250	3h07m44.099
2 Arie Luyendyk	Lola T94/00-Ilmor	249	
3 Dominic Dobson	Lola T94/00-Ford	248	
4 Teo Fabi	Reynard 94I-Ilmor	246	
5 Mark Smith	Lola T94/00-Ford	240	
6 Hiro Matsushita	Lola T94/00-Ford	239	

Winner's average speed: 159.800 mph. Pole position: Nigel Mansell (Lola T94/00-Ford), 30.804s. Fastest lap: Al Unser Jr (Penske PC23-Ilmor), 31.414s

MILLER GENUINE DRAFT 200

14 August 1994. Mid-Ohio. 83 laps of a 2.258-mile circuit = 187.414 miles. PPG Indycar World Series round 11

1 Al Unser Jr	Penske PC23-Ilmor	83	1h40m59.436
2 Paul Tracy	Penske PC23-Ilmor	83	1h41m01.072
3 Emerson Fittipaldi	Penske PC23-Ilmor	83	1h41m35.611
4 Robby Gordon	Lola T94/00-Ford	82	
5 Michael Andretti	Reynard 94I-Ford	82	
6 Adrian Fernandez	Reynard 94I-Ilmor	82	

Winner's average speed: 111.345 mph. Pole position: Unser Jr, 1m07.773. Fastest lap: Unser Jr, 1m08.805

SLICK 50 200

21 August 1994. New Hampshire. 200 laps of a 1.058-mile circuit = 211.600 miles. PPG Indycar World Series round 12

1 Al Unser Jr	Penske PC23-Ilmor	200	1h43m31.594
2 Paul Tracy	Penske PC23-Ilmor	200	1h43m32.485
3 Emerson Fittipaldi	Penske PC23-Ilmor	200	1h43m33.344
4 Raul Boesel	Lola T94/00-Ford	198	
5 Michael Andretti	Reynard 94I-Ford	198	
6 Dominic Dobson	Lola T94/00-Ford	197	

Winner's average speed: 122.635 mph. Pole position: Fittipaldi, 21.753s. Fastest lap: Fittipaldi, 23.157s

MOLSON INDY VANCOUVER

4 September 1994. Vancouver. 102 laps of a 1.653-mile circuit = 168.606 miles. PPG Indycar World Series round 13

1 Al Unser Jr	Penske PC23-Ilmor	102	1h53m27.345
2 Robby Gordon	Lola T94/00-Ford	102	1h53m29.584
3 Michael Andretti	Reynard 94I-Ford	102	1h53m34.428
4 Scott Goodyear	Lola T94/00-Ford	102	1h53m39.797
5 Mauricio Gugelmin	Reynard 94I-Ford	102	1h53m40.161
6 Arie Luyendyk	Lola T94/00-Ilmor	102	1h53m42.198

Winner's average speed: 89.166 mph. Pole position: Gordon, 54.570s. Fastest lap: Gordon, 55.786s

TEXACO/HAVOLINE 200

11 September 1994. Elkhart Lake. 50 laps of a 4.048-mile circuit = 202.400 miles. PPG Indycar World Series round 14

1 Jacques Villeneuve	Reynard 94I-Ford	50	1h42m37.930
2 Al Unser Jr	Penske PC23-Ilmor	50	1h42m38.539
3 Emerson Fittipaldi	Penske PC23-Ilmor	50	1h42m40.543
4 Teo Fabi	Reynard 94I-Ilmor	50	1h43m01.809
5 Adrian Fernandez	Reynard 94I-Ilmor	50	1h43m05.553
6 Raul Boesel	Lola T94/00-Ford	50	1h43m09.966

Winner's average speed: 118.325 mph. Pole position: Paul Tracy (Penske PC23-Ilmor), 1m45.416. Fastest lap: Nigel Mansell (Lola T94/00-Ford), 1m48.004

BOSCH SPARK PLUG GRAND PRIX

18 September 1994. Nazareth. 200 laps of a 0.946-mile circuit = 189.200 miles. PPG Indycar World Series round 15

1 Paul Tracy	Penske PC23-Ilmor	200	1h31m30.292
2 Al Unser Jr	Penske PC23-Ilmor	200	1h31m38.751
3 Emerson Fittipaldi	Penske PC23-Ilmor	200	1h31m44.451
4 Raul Boesel	Lola T94/00-Ford	196	
5 Stefan Johansson	Penske PC22-Ilmor	195	
6 Teo Fabi	Reynard 94I-Ilmor	194	

Winner's average speed: 124.059 mph. Pole position: Fittipaldi, 19.397s. Fastest lap: Fittipaldi, 20.578s

BANK OF AMERICA 300 KMS/TOYOTA MONTEREY GRAND PRIX

10 October 1994. Laguna Seca. 84 laps of a 2.214-mile circuit = 185.976 miles. PPG Indycar World Series round 16

1 Paul Tracy	Penske PC23-Ilmor	84	2h00m00.763
2 Raul Boesel	Lola T94/00-Ford	84	2h00m22.179
3 Jacques Villeneuve	Reynard 94I-Ford	84	2h00m23.248
4 Emerson Fittipaldi	Penske PC23-Ilmor	84	2h00m26.353
5 Teo Fabi	Reynard 94I-Ilmor	84	2h00m27.040
6 Arie Luyendyk	Lola T94/00-Ilmor	84	2h00m35.851

Winner's average speed: 92.978 mph. Pole position: Tracy, 1m10.058. Fastest lap: Tracy, 1m12.959

1994 FINAL CHAMPIONSHIP POSITIONS

1	Al Unser Jr	225	7	Raul Boesel	90
2	Emerson Fittipaldi	178	8	Nigel Mansell	88
3	Paul Tracy	152	9	Teo Fabi	79
4	Michael Andretti	118	10	Bobby Rahal	59
5	Robby Gordon	104			
6	Jacques Villeneuve	94			

1995

MARLBORO GRAND PRIX OF MIAMI

5 March 1995. Bicentennial Park, Miami. 90 laps of a 1.873-mile circuit = 168.570 miles. PPG Indycar World Series round 1

1 Jacques Villeneuve	Reynard 95I-Ford	90	1h59m16.863
2 Mauricio Gugelmin	Reynard 95I-Ford	90	1h59m17.885
3 Bobby Rahal	Lola T95/00-Mercedes-Benz	90	1h59m18.214
4 Scott Pruett	Lola T95/00-Ford	90	1h59m18.893
5 Christian Fittipaldi	Reynard 95I-Ford	90	1h59m21.945
6 Raul Boesel	Lola T95/00-Mercedes-Benz	90	1h59m22.093

Winner's average speed: 84.793 mph. Pole position: Michael Andretti (Lola T95/00-Ford), 1m03.254. Fastest lap: Pruett, 1m05.892

INDY CAR AUSTRALIA

19 March 1995. Surfers Paradise. 65 laps of a 2.795-mile circuit = 181.675 miles. PPG Indycar World Series round 2

1 Paul Tracy	Lola T95/00-Ford	65	1h58m26.054
2 Bobby Rahal	Lola T95/00-Mercedes-Benz	65	1h58m33.037
3 Scott Pruett	Lola T95/00-Ford	65	1h58m37.760
4 Mauricio Gugelmin	Reynard 95I-Ford	65	1h58m39.601
5 Danny Sullivan	Reynard 95I-Ford	65	1h58m45.188
6 Al Unser Jr	Penske PC24-Mercedes-Benz	65	1h59m01.331

Winner's average speed: 92.038 mph. Pole position: Michael Andretti (Lola T95/00-Ford), 1m36.770. Fastest lap: Andretti, 1m37.564

SLICK 50 200

2 April 1995. Phoenix. 200 laps of a 1.000-mile circuit = 200.000 miles. PPG Indycar World Series round 3

1 Robby Gordon	Reynard 95I-Ford	200	1h29m33.930
2 Michael Andretti	Lola T95/00-Ford	200	1h29m34.719
3 Emerson Fittipaldi	Penske PC24-Mercedes-Benz	200	1h29m38.878
4 Paul Tracy	Lola T95/00-Ford	200	1h29m42.776
5 Jacques Villeneuve	Reynard 95I-Ford	200	1h29m43.706
6 Raul Boesel	Lola T95/00-Mercedes-Benz	198	

Winner's average speed: 133.980 mph. Pole position: Bryan Herta (Reynard 95I-Ford), 19.785s. Fastest lap: E Fittipaldi, 21.240s

TOYOTA GRAND PRIX OF LONG BEACH

9 April 1995. Long Beach. 105 laps of a 1.586-mile circuit = 166.530 miles. PPG Indycar World Series round 4

1	Al Unser Jr	Penske PC24-Mercedes-Benz	105	1h49m32.667
2	Scott Pruett	Lola T95/00-Ford	105	1h49m55.792
3	Teo Fabi	Reynard 95I-Ford	105	1h50m08.660
4	Eddie Cheever	Lola T95/00-Ford	104	out of fuel
5	Mauricio Gugelmin	Reynard 95I-Ford	104	
6	Stefan Johansson	Penske PC23-Mercedes-Benz	104	

Winner's average speed: 91.212 mph. Pole position: Michael Andretti (Lola T95/00-Ford), 52.482s. Fastest lap: Andretti, 53.595s

BOSCH SPARK PLUG GRAND PRIX

23 April 1995. Nazareth. 200 laps of a 0.946-mile circuit = 189.200 miles. PPG Indycar World Series round 5

1	Emerson Fittipaldi	Penske PC24-Mercedes-Benz	200	1h31m23.410
2	Jacques Villeneuve	Reynard 95I-Ford	200	1h31m23.718
3	Stefan Johansson	Penske PC23-Mercedes-Benz	200	1h31m34.079
4	Robby Gordon	Reynard 95I-Ford	200	1h31m39.172
5	Eddie Cheever	Lola T95/00-Ford	199	out of fuel
6	Bobby Rahal	Lola T95/00-Mercedes-Benz	199	

Winner's average speed: 124.215 mph. Pole position: Gordon, 19.206s. Fastest lap: E Fittipaldi, 20.294s

INDIANAPOLIS 500

28 May 1995. Indianapolis. 200 laps of a 2.500-mile circuit = 500.000 miles. PPG Indycar World Series round 6

1*	Jacques Villeneuve	Reynard 95I-Ford	200	3h15m17.561
2	Christian Fittipaldi	Reynard 95I-Ford	200	3h15m20.042
3	Bobby Rahal	Lola T95/00-Mercedes-Benz	200	3h15m20.527
4	Eliseo Salazar	Lola T95/00-Ford	200	3h15m22.329
5	Robby Gordon	Reynard 95I-Ford	200	3h15m32.466
6	Mauricio Gugelmin	Reynard 95I-Ford	200	3h15m34.638

*includes 2-lap penalty for passing the pace car. Scott Goodyear (Reynard 95I-Honda), finished first on the road, but penalised for ignoring black flag. Winner's average speed: 153.616 mph. Pole position: Scott Brayton (Lola T95/00-Buick/Menard), 231.604s. Fastest lap: Scott Goodyear (Reynard 95I-Honda), 40.177s

MILLER GENUINE DRAFT 200

4 June 1995. Milwaukee. 200 laps of a 1.032-mile circuit = 206.400 miles. PPG Indycar World Series round 7

1	Paul Tracy	Lola T95/00-Ford	200	1h27m23.853
2	Al Unser Jr	Penske PC24-Mercedes-Benz	200	1h27m24.699
3	Michael Andretti	Lola T95/00-Ford	199	
4	Teo Fabi	Reynard 95I-Ford	198	
5	Robby Gordon	Reynard 95I-Ford	197	
6	Jacques Villeneuve	Reynard 95I-Ford	197	

Winner's average speed: 141.697 mph. Pole position: Fabi, 22.160s. Fastest lap: Fabi, 23.601s

ITT AUTOMOTIVE DETROIT GRAND PRIX

11 June 1995. Belle Isle. 77 laps of a 2.100-mile circuit = 161.700 miles. PPG Indycar World Series round 8

1	Robby Gordon	Reynard 95I-Ford	77	1h56m11.607
2	Jimmy Vasser	Reynard 95I-Ford	77	1h56m11.952
3	Scott Pruett	Lola T95/00-Ford	77	1h56m12.387
4	Michael Andretti	Lola T95/00-Ford	77	1h56m12.662
5	Al Unser Jr	Penske PC24-Mercedes-Benz	77	1h56m15.633
6	Adrian Fernandez	Lola T95/00-Mercedes-Benz	77	1h56m18.866

Winner's average speed: 83.499 mph. Pole position: Gordon, 1m09.795. Fastest lap: Andretti, 1m12.339

BUDWEISER GI JOE'S 200

25 June 1995. Portland. 102 laps of a 1.967-mile circuit = 200.634 miles. PPG Indycar World Series round 9

1	Al Unser Jr	Penske PC24-Mercedes-Benz	102	1h54m49.410

2	Jimmy Vasser	Reynard 95I-Ford	102	1h55m17.971
3	Bobby Rahal	Lola T95/00-Mercedes-Benz	102	1h55m19.229
4	Michael Andretti	Lola T95/00-Ford	102	1h55m30.433
5	Raul Boesel	Lola T95/00-Mercedes-Benz	102	1h55m32.071
6	Stefan Johansson	Penske PC23-Mercedes-Benz	101	accident

Winner's average speed: 104.840 mph. Pole position: Jacques Villeneuve (Reynard 95I-Ford), 59.687s. Fastest lap: Unser, 1m01.466

TEXACO/HAVOLINE 200

9 July 1995. Elkhart Lake. 50 laps of a 4.048-mile circuit = 202.400 miles. PPG Indycar World Series round 10

1	Jacques Villeneuve	Reynard 95I-Ford	50	1h55m29.659
2	Paul Tracy	Lola T95/00-Ford	50	1h55m30.625
3	Jimmy Vasser	Reynard 95I-Ford	50	1h55m32.038
4	Andre Ribeiro	Reynard 95I-Honda	50	1h55m32.956
5	Bobby Rahal	Lola T95/00-Mercedes-Benz	50	1h55m33.151
6	Adrian Fernandez	Lola T95/00-Mercedes-Benz	50	1h55m34.951

Winner's average speed: 105.148 mph. Pole position: Villeneuve, 1m41.261. Fastest lap: Villeneuve, 1m45.684

MOLSON INDY TORONTO

16 July 1995. Toronto. 98 laps of a 1.784-mile circuit = 174.832 miles. PPG Indycar World Series round 11

1	Michael Andretti	Lola T95/00-Ford	98	1h50m25.202
2	Bobby Rahal	Lola T95/00-Mercedes-Benz	98	1h50m25.627
3	Jacques Villeneuve	Reynard 95I-Ford	98	1h50m58.015
4	Teo Fabi	Reynard 95I-Ford	98	1h50m58.543
5	Robby Gordon	Reynard 95I-Ford	98	1h50m59.893
6	Raul Boesel	Lola T95/00-Mercedes-Benz	98	1h51m03.646

Winner's average speed: 95 mph. Pole position: Villeneuve, 58.046s. Fastest lap: Rahal, 58.830s

MEDIC DRUG GRAND PRIX OF CLEVELAND

23 July 1995. Cleveland. 90 laps of a 2.106-mile circuit = 189.540 miles. PPG Indycar World Series round 12

1	Jacques Villeneuve	Reynard 95I-Ford	90	1h38m19.151
2	Bryan Herta	Reynard 95I-Ford	90	1h38m20.308
3	Jimmy Vasser	Reynard 95I-Ford	90	1h38m22.723
4	Bobby Rahal	Lola T95/00-Mercedes-Benz	90	1h38m23.028
5	Danny Sullivan	Reynard 95I-Ford	90	1h38m28.475
6	Robby Gordon	Reynard 95I-Ford	90	1h38m38.050

Winner's average speed: 115.668 mph. Pole position: Gil de Ferran (Reynard 95I-Mercedes-Benz), 57.815s

MARLBORO 500

30 July 1995. Michigan. 250 laps of a 2.000-mile circuit = 500.000 miles. PPG Indycar World Series round 13

1	Scott Pruett	Lola T95/00-Ford	250	3h07m52.826
2	Al Unser Jr	Penske PC24-Mercedes-Benz	250	3h07m52.882
3	Adrian Fernandez	Lola T95/00-Mercedes-Benz	249	
4	Teo Fabi	Reynard 95I-Ford	247	
5	Emerson Fittipaldi	Penske PC24-Mercedes-Benz	245	
6	Stefan Johansson	Penske PC23-Mercedes-Benz	244	

Winner's average speed: 159.676 mph. Pole position: Parker Johnstone (Reynard 95I-Honda), 31.242s. Fastest lap: Johnstone, 31.080s

MILLER GENUINE DRAFT 200

13 August 1995. Mid-Ohio. 83 laps of a 2.258-mile circuit = 187.414 miles. PPG Indycar World Series round 14

1	Al Unser Jr	Penske PC24-Mercedes-Benz	83	1h44m04.774
2	Paul Tracy	Lola T95/00-Ford	83	1h44m46.811
3	Jacques Villeneuve	Reynard 95I-Ford	83	1h44m54.299
4	Adrian Fernandez	Lola T95/00-Mercedes-Benz	83	1h44m55.552
5	Bryan Herta	Reynard 95I-Ford	83	1h44m58.655
6	Mauricio Gugelmin	Reynard 95I-Ford	83	1h44m59.528

Winner's average speed: 108.041 mph. Pole position: Villeneuve, 1m06.836. Fastest lap: Unser, 1m09.947

NEW ENGLAND 200

20 August 1995. New Hampshire. 200 laps of a 1.058-mile circuit = 211.600 miles. PPG Indycar World Series round 15

1 Andre Ribeiro	Reynard 95I-Honda	200	1h34m36.192
2 Michael Andretti	Lola T95/00-Ford	200	1h34m50.674
3 Al Unser Jr	Penske PC24-Mercedes-Benz	199	
4 Jacques Villeneuve	Reynard 95I-Ford	199	
5 Emerson Fittipaldi	Penske PC24-Mercedes-Benz	199	
6 Jimmy Vasser	Reynard 95I-Ford	198	

Winner's average speed: 134.203 mph. Pole position: Ribeiro, 21.466s. Fastest lap: Teo Fabi (Reynard 95I-Ford), 22.968s

MOLSON INDY VANCOUVER

3 September 1995. Vancouver. 100 laps of a 1.703-mile circuit = 170.300 miles. PPG Indycar World Series round 16

1 Al Unser Jr	Penske PC24-Mercedes-Benz	100	1h46m54.900
2 Gil de Ferran	Reynard 95I-Mercedes-Benz	100	1h47m09.013
3 Robby Gordon	Reynard 95I-Ford	100	1h47m21.007
4 Stefan Johansson	Penske PC23-Mercedes-Benz	100	1h47m21.423
5 Bobby Rahal	Lola T95/00-Mercedes-Benz	100	1h47m21.524
6 Scott Pruett	Lola T95/00-Ford	100	1h47m24.373

Winner's average speed: 95.571 mph. Pole position: Jacques Villeneuve (Reynard 95I-Ford), 55.226s. Fastest lap: Rahal, 56.906s

TOYOTA GRAND PRIX OF MONTEREY

10 September 1995. Laguna Seca. 84 laps of a 2.214-mile circuit = 185.976 miles. PPG Indycar World Series round 17

1 Gil de Ferran	Reynard 95I-Mercedes-Benz	84	1h53m17.579
2 Paul Tracy	Lola T95/00-Ford	84	1h53m25.538
3 Mauricio Gugelmin	Reynard 95I-Ford	84	1h53m25.910
4 Michael Andretti	Lola T95/00-Ford	84	1h53m26.613
5 Scott Pruett	Lola T95/00-Ford	84	1h53m40.241
6 Al Unser Jr	Penske PC24-Mercedes-Benz	84	1h53m41.518

Winner's average speed: 98.493 mph. Pole position: Jacques Villeneuve (Reynard 95I-Ford), 1m09.625. Fastest lap: de Ferran, 1m13.705

1995 FINAL CHAMPIONSHIP POSITIONS

1	Jacques Villeneuve	172	7	Scott Pruett	112
2	Al Unser Jr	161	8	Jimmy Vasser	92
3	Bobby Rahal	128	9	Teo Fabi	83
4	Michael Andretti	123	10	Mauricio Gugelmin	80
5	Robby Gordon	121			
6	Paul Tracy	115			

1996

MARLBORO GRAND PRIX OF MIAMI

3 March 1996. Homestead. 133 laps of a 1.527-mile circuit = 203.091 miles. PPG Indycar World Series round 1

1 Jimmy Vasser	Reynard 96I-Honda	133	1h51m23.100
2 Gil de Ferran	Reynard 96I-Honda	133	1h51m26.256
3 Robby Gordon	Reynard 96I-Ford	133	1h51m26.840
4 Scott Pruett	Lola T96/00-Ford	133	1h51m26.844
5 Bobby Rahal	Reynard 96I-Mercedes-Benz	133	1h51m27.468
6 Christian Fittipaldi	Lola T96/00-Ford	133	1h51m39.764

Winner's average speed: 109.399 mph. Pole position: Paul Tracy (Penske PC25-Mercedes-Benz), 27.681s. Fastest lap: Greg Moore (Reynard 96I-Mercedes-Benz), 28.385s

RIO 400

17 March 1996. Rio de Janeiro. 133 laps of a 1.864-mile circuit = 247.912 miles. PPG Indycar World Series round 2

1 Andre Ribeiro	Lola T96/00-Honda	133	2h06m08.100
2 Al Unser Jr	Penske PC25-Mercedes-Benz	133	2h06m10.241
3 Scott Pruett	Lola T96/00-Ford	133	2h06m10.832
4 Alessandro Zanardi	Reynard 96I-Honda	133	2h06m10.867
5 Christian Fittipaldi	Lola T96/00-Ford	133	2h06m11.640
6 Bobby Rahal	Reynard 96I-Mercedes-Benz	133	2h06m12.151

Winner's average speed: 117.927 mph. Pole position: Zanardi, 40.162s. Fastest lap: Gil de Ferran (Reynard 96I-Honda), 40.120s

BARTERCARD INDYCAR AUSTRALIA

31 March 1996. Surfers Paradise. 65 laps of a 2.795-mile circuit = 181.675 miles. PPG Indycar World Series round 3

1 Jimmy Vasser	Reynard 96I-Honda	65	2h00m46.856
2 Scott Pruett	Lola T96/00-Ford	65	2h00m54.605
3 Greg Moore	Reynard 96I-Mercedes-Benz	65	2h00m59.172
4 Mauricio Gugelmin	Reynard 96I-Ford	65	2h01m07.074
5 Christian Fittipaldi	Lola T96/00-Ford	65	2h01m13.706
6 Stefan Johansson	Reynard 96I-Mercedes-Benz	65	2h01m31.081

Winner's average speed: 90.250 mph. Pole position: Vasser, 1m35.265. Fastest lap: Vasser, 1m37.854

TOYOTA GRAND PRIX OF LONG BEACH

14 April 1996. Long Beach. 105 laps of a 1.586-mile circuit = 166.530 miles. PPG Indycar World Series round 4

1 Jimmy Vasser	Reynard 96I-Honda	105	1h44m02.363
2 Parker Johnstone	Reynard 96I-Honda	105	1h44m05.911
3 Al Unser Jr	Penske PC25-Mercedes-Benz	105	1h44m06.772
4 Paul Tracy	Penske PC25-Mercedes-Benz	105	1h44m07.363
5 Gil de Ferran	Reynard 96I-Honda	105	1h44m34.436
6 Adrian Fernandez	Lola T96/00-Honda	105	1h44m38.685

Winner's average speed: 96.039 mph. Pole position: de Ferran, 52.208s. Fastest lap: Tracy, 53.482s

BOSCH SPARK PLUG GRAND PRIX

28 April 1996. Nazareth. 200 laps of a 0.946-mile circuit = 189.200 miles. PPG Indycar World Series round 5

1 Michael Andretti	Lola T96/00-Ford	200	1h25m08.074
2 Greg Moore	Reynard 96I-Mercedes-Benz	200	1h25m20.288
3 Al Unser Jr	Penske PC25-Mercedes-Benz	200	1h25m23.118
4 Emerson Fittipaldi	Penske PC25-Mercedes-Benz	200	1h25m23.218
5 Paul Tracy	Penske PC25-Mercedes-Benz	199	
6 Bobby Rahal	Reynard 96I-Mercedes-Benz	199	

Winner's average speed: 133.342 mph. Pole position: Tracy, 18.874s. Fastest lap: E Fittipaldi, 20.388s

US 500

26 May 1996. Michigan. 250 laps of a 2.000-mile circuit = 500.000 miles. PPG Indycar World Series round 6

1 Jimmy Vasser	Reynard 96I-Honda	250	3h11m48.712
2 Mauricio Gugelmin	Reynard 96I-Ford	250	3h11m59.707
3 Roberto Moreno	Lola T96/00-Ford	249	
4 Andre Ribeiro	Lola T96/00-Honda	249	
5 Mark Blundell	Reynard 96I-Ford	249	
6 Eddie Lawson	Lola T96/00-Mercedes-Benz	249	

Winner's average speed: 156.403 mph. Pole position: Vasser, 31.031s. Fastest lap: Alessandro Zanardi (Reynard 96I-Honda), 30.836s

MILLER 200

2 June 1996. Milwaukee. 200 laps of a 1.032-mile circuit = 206.400 miles. PPG Indycar World Series round 7

1 Michael Andretti	Lola T96/00-Ford	200	1h33m32.649
2 Al Unser Jr	Penske PC25-Mercedes-Benz	200	1h33m32.795
3 Paul Tracy	Penske PC25-Mercedes-Benz	200	1h33m33.589
4 Emerson Fittipaldi	Penske PC25-Mercedes-Benz	200	1h33m34.100
5 Greg Moore	Reynard 96I-Mercedes-Benz	200	1h33m57.229
6 Christian Fittipaldi	Lola T96/00-Ford	199	

Winner's average speed: 132.387 mph. Pole position: Tracy, 20.448s. Fastest lap: Andretti, 22.093s

ITT AUTOMOTIVE DETROIT GRAND PRIX

9 June 1996. Belle Isle. 72 laps of a 2.100-mile circuit = 151.200 miles. PPG Indycar World Series round 8

1	Michael Andretti	Lola T96/00-Ford	72	2h00m45.451
2	Christian Fittipaldi	Lola T96/00-Ford	72	2h00m46.860
3	Gil de Ferran	Reynard 96I-Honda	72	2h00m49.733
4	Adrian Fernandez	Lola T96/00-Honda	72	2h00m52.879
5	Mark Blundell	Reynard 96I-Ford	72	2h00m54.658
6	Eddie Lawson	Lola T96/00-Mercedes-Benz	72	2h00m55.081

Winner's average speed: 75.126 mph. Pole position: Scott Pruett (Lola T96/00-Ford), 1m11.802. Fastest lap: C Fittipaldi, 1m14.103

BUDWEISER GI JOE'S 200

23 June 1996. Portland. 98 laps of a 1.967-mile circuit = 192.766 miles. PPG Indycar World Series round 9

1	Alessandro Zanardi	Reynard 96I-Honda	98	1h50m25.401
2	Gil de Ferran	Reynard 96I-Honda	98	1h50m34.538
3	Christian Fittipaldi	Lola T96/00-Ford	98	1h50m37.073
4	Al Unser Jr	Penske PC25-Mercedes-Benz	98	1h50m40.306
5	Parker Johnstone	Reynard 96I-Honda	98	1h50m43.658
6	Bobby Rahal	Reynard 96I-Mercedes-Benz	98	1h50m59.518

Winner's average speed: 104.742 mph. Pole position: Zanardi, 59.893s. Fastest lap: Zanardi, 1m02.572

MEDIC DRUG GRAND PRIX OF CLEVELAND

30 June 1996. Cleveland. 90 laps of a 2.106-mile circuit = 189.540 miles. PPG Indycar World Series round 10

1	Gil de Ferran	Reynard 96I-Honda	90	1h35m39.326
2	Alessandro Zanardi	Reynard 96I-Honda	90	1h35m40.359
3	Greg Moore	Reynard 96I-Mercedes-Benz	90	1h35m55.729
4	Al Unser Jr	Penske PC25-Mercedes-Benz	90	1h36m07.595
5	Bryan Herta	Reynard 96I-Mercedes-Benz	90	1h36m14.636
6	Adrian Fernandez	Lola T96/00-Honda	90	1h36m25.197

Winner's average speed: 118.889 mph. Pole position: Jimmy Vasser (Reynard 96I-Honda), 58.336s

MOLSON INDY TORONTO

14 July 1996. Toronto. 93 laps of a 1.784-mile circuit = 165.912 miles. PPG Indycar World Series round 11

1	Adrian Fernandez	Lola T96/00-Honda	93	1h41m59.809
2	Alessandro Zanardi	Reynard 96I-Honda	93	1h42m01.760
3	Bobby Rahal	Reynard 96I-Mercedes-Benz	93	1h42m03.379
4	Greg Moore	Reynard 96I-Mercedes-Benz	93	1h42m04.135
5	Paul Tracy	Penske PC25-Mercedes-Benz	93	1h42m04.880
6	Bryan Herta	Reynard 96I-Mercedes-Benz	93	1h42m05.498

Winner's average speed: 97.598 mph. Pole position: Andre Ribeiro (Lola T96/00-Honda), 58.060s. Fastest lap: Zanardi, 59.510s

MARLBORO 500

28 July 1996. Michigan. 250 laps of a 2.000-mile circuit = 500.000 miles. PPG Indycar World Series round 12

1	Andre Ribeiro	Lola T96/00-Honda	250	3h16m33.425
2	Bryan Herta	Reynard 96I-Mercedes-Benz	250	3h16m34.803
3	Mauricio Gugelmin	Reynard 96I-Ford	250	3h16m35.717
4	Al Unser Jr	Penske PC25-Mercedes-Benz	249	
5	Stefan Johansson	Reynard 96I-Mercedes-Benz	248	
6	Mark Blundell	Reynard 96I-Ford	248	

Winner's average speed: 152.627 mph. Pole position: Jimmy Vasser (Reynard 96I-Honda), 30.682s. Fastest lap: Adrian Fernandez (Lola T96/00-Honda), 30.767s

MILLER 200

11 August 1996. Mid-Ohio. 83 laps of a 2.258-mile circuit = 187.414 miles. PPG Indycar World Series round 13

1	Alessandro Zanardi	Reynard 96I-Honda	83	1h46m49.448
2	Jimmy Vasser	Reynard 96I-Honda	83	1h46m51.362
3	Michael Andretti	Lola T96/00-Ford	83	1h46m52.853
4	Bryan Herta	Reynard 96I-Mercedes-Benz	83	1h46m53.964
5	Bobby Rahal	Reynard 96I-Mercedes-Benz	83	1h46m55.093
6	Adrian Fernandez	Lola T96/00-Honda	83	1h46m58.284

Winner's average speed: 105.265 mph. Pole position: Zanardi, 1m06.339. Fastest lap: Zanardi, 1m08.607

TEXACO/HAVOLINE 200

18 August 1996. Elkhart Lake. 50 laps of a 4.048-mile circuit = 202.400 miles. PPG Indycar World Series round 14

1	Michael Andretti	Lola T96/00-Ford	50	1h56m33.859
2	Bobby Rahal	Reynard 96I-Mercedes-Benz	50	1h56m34.400
3	Alessandro Zanardi	Reynard 96I-Honda	50	1h56m39.234
4	Stefan Johansson	Reynard 96I-Mercedes-Benz	50	1h56m40.890
5	Bryan Herta	Reynard 96I-Mercedes-Benz	50	1h56m42.339
6	Jimmy Vasser	Reynard 96I-Honda	50	1h56m53.525

Winner's average speed: 104.183 mph. Pole position: Zanardi, 1m41.998. Fastest lap: Paul Tracy (Penske PC25-Mercedes-Benz), 1m43.408

MOLSON INDY VANCOUVER

1 September 1996. Vancouver. 100 laps of a 1.703-mile circuit = 170.300 miles. PPG Indycar World Series round 15

1	Michael Andretti	Lola T96/00-Ford	100	1h48m16.253
2	Bobby Rahal	Reynard 96I-Mercedes-Benz	100	1h48m18.158
3	Christian Fittipaldi	Lola T96/00-Ford	100	1h48m23.341
4	Gil de Ferran	Reynard 96I-Honda	100	1h48m26.548
5	Al Unser Jr	Penske PC25-Mercedes-Benz	100	1h48m27.773
6	Bryan Herta	Reynard 96I-Mercedes-Benz	100	1h48m38.347

Winner's average speed: 94.374 mph. Pole position: Alessandro Zanardi (Reynard 96I-Honda), 53.980s. Fastest lap: Zanardi, 55.867s

TOYOTA GRAND PRIX OF MONTEREY

8 September 1996. Laguna Seca. 83 laps of a 2.238-mile circuit = 185.754 miles. PPG Indycar World Series round 16

1	Alessandro Zanardi	Reynard 96I-Honda	83	1h48m32.157
2	Bryan Herta	Reynard 96I-Mercedes-Benz	83	1h48m33.569
3	Scott Pruett	Lola T96/00-Ford	83	1h48m47.911
4	Jimmy Vasser	Reynard 96I-Honda	83	1h48m48.247
5	Mauricio Gugelmin	Reynard 96I-Ford	83	1h48m49.937
6	Greg Moore	Reynard 96I-Mercedes-Benz	83	1h48m50.307

Winner's average speed: 102.687 mph. Pole position: Zanardi, 1m08.004. Fastest lap: Zanardi, 1m10.148

1996 FINAL CHAMPIONSHIP POSITIONS

1	Jimmy Vasser	154		8	Bryan Herta	86
2=	Michael Andretti	132		9	Greg Moore	84
	Alessandro Zanardi	132		10	Scott Pruett	82
4	Al Unser jr	125				
5	Christian Fittipaldi	110				
6	Gil de Ferran	104				
7	Bobby Rahal	102				

1997

MARLBORO GRAND PRIX OF MIAMI

2 March 1997. Homestead. 147 laps of a 1.502-mile circuit = 220.794 miles. PPG CART World Series round 1

1	Michael Andretti	Swift 007i-Ford	147	1h38m45.666
2	Paul Tracy	Penske PC26-Mercedes-Benz	147	1h38m49.067
3	Jimmy Vasser	Reynard 97I-Honda	147	1h38m55.250
4	Greg Moore	Reynard 97I-Mercedes-Benz	147	1h38m57.246
5	Scott Pruett	Reynard 97I-Ford	147	1h39m17.613
6	Mauricio Gugelmin	Reynard 97I-Mercedes-Benz	147	1h39m29.485

Winner's average speed: 134.138 mph. Pole position: Alessandro Zanardi (Reynard 97I-Honda), 28.000s. Fastest lap: Andretti, 29.697s

SUNBELT INDYCARNIVAL AUSTRALIA

6 April 1997. Surfers Paradise. 57 laps of a 2.795-mile circuit = 159.315 miles. PPG CART World Series round 2

1 Scott Pruett	Reynard 97I-Ford	57	2h01m04.678
2 Greg Moore	Reynard 97I-Mercedes-Benz	57	2h01m05.362
3 Michael Andretti	Swift 007i-Ford	57	2h01m15.939
4 Alessandro Zanardi	Reynard 97I-Honda	57	2h01m19.505
5 Gil de Ferran	Reynard 97I-Honda	57	2h01m20.268
6 Andre Ribeiro	Lola T97/00-Honda	57	2h01m21.488

Winner's average speed: 78.948 mph. Pole position: Zanardi, 1m35.940s. Fastest lap: Zanardi, 1m38.026

TOYOTA GRAND PRIX OF LONG BEACH

13 April 1997. Long Beach. 105 laps of a 1.586-mile circuit = 166.530 miles. PPG CART World Series round 3

1 Alessandro Zanardi	Reynard 97I-Honda	105	1h46m17.792
2 Mauricio Gugelmin	Reynard 97I-Mercedes-Benz	105	1h46m21.612
3 Scott Pruett	Reynard 97I-Ford	105	1h46m33.251
4 Al Unser Jr	Penske PC26-Mercedes-Benz	105	1h46m38.320
5 Parker Johnstone	Reynard 97I-Honda	105	1h46m38.693
6 Bryan Herta	Reynard 97I-Ford	105	1h46m41.881

Winner's average speed: 93.999 mph. Pole position: Gil de Ferran (Reynard 97I-Honda), 51.293s. Fastest lap: Zanardi, 52.895s

BOSCH SPARK PLUG GRAND PRIX

27 April 1997. Nazareth. 225 laps of a 0.946-mile circuit = 212.850 miles. PPG CART World Series round 4

1 Paul Tracy	Penske PC26-Mercedes-Benz	225	1h53m31.337
2 Michael Andretti	Swift 007i-Ford	225	1h53m31.864
3 Al Unser Jr	Penske PC26-Mercedes-Benz	225	1h53m32.587
4 Gil de Ferran	Reynard 97I-Honda	225	1h53m36.090
5 Jimmy Vasser	Reynard 97I-Honda	225	1h53m37.429
6 Bobby Rahal	Reynard 97I-Ford	224	

Winner's average speed: 112.498 mph. Pole position: Tracy, 18.831s. Fastest lap: Tracy, 19.987s

HOLLYWOOD RIO 400

11 May 1997. Rio de Janeiro. 133 laps of a 1.864-mile circuit = 247.912 miles. PPG CART World Series round 5

1 Paul Tracy	Penske PC26-Mercedes-Benz	133	2h10m47.996
2 Greg Moore	Reynard 97I-Mercedes-Benz	133	2h10m49.801
3 Scott Pruett	Reynard 97I-Ford	133	2h10m50.249
4 Alessandro Zanardi	Reynard 97I-Honda	133	2h10m51.088
5 Raul Boesel	Reynard 97I-Ford	133	2h10m54.351
6 Bryan Herta	Reynard 97I-Ford	133	2h10m54.513

Winner's average speed: 113.721 mph. Pole position: Mauricio Gugelmin (Reynard 97I-Mercedes-Benz), 39.034s. Fastest lap: Gil de Ferran (Reynard 97I-Honda), 39.898s

MOTOROLA 300

24 May 1997. St Louis. 236 laps of a 1.270-mile circuit = 299.720 miles. PPG CART World Series round 6

1 Paul Tracy	Penske PC26-Mercedes-Benz	236	2h37m54.496
2 Patrick Carpentier	Reynard 97I-Mercedes-Benz	236	2h37m56.887
3 Gil de Ferran	Reynard 97I-Honda	236	2h37m59.812
4 Alessandro Zanardi	Reynard 97I-Honda	236	2h38m00.628
5 Jimmy Vasser	Reynard 97I-Honda	236	2h38m06.394
6 Mauricio Gugelmin	Reynard 97I-Mercedes-Benz	236	2h38m06.906

Winner's average speed: 113.884 mph. Pole position: Raul Boesel (Reynard 97I-Ford), 24.324s. Fastest lap: Dario Franchitti (Reynard 97I-Mercedes-Benz), 25.312s

MILLER 200

1 June 1997. Milwaukee. 200 laps of a 1.032-mile circuit = 206.400 miles. PPG CART World Series round 7

1 Greg Moore	Reynard 97I-Mercedes-Benz	200	1h43m32.873
2 Michael Andretti	Swift 007i-Ford	200	1h43m33.221
3 Jimmy Vasser	Reynard 97I-Honda	200	1h43m43.739
4 Raul Boesel	Reynard 97I-Ford	200	1h43m45.394
5 Mauricio Gugelmin	Reynard 97I-Mercedes-Benz	200	1h43m46.453
6 Paul Tracy	Penske PC26-Mercedes-Benz	200	1h43m48.459

Winner's average speed: 119.597 mph. Pole position: Tracy, 20.160s. Fastest lap: Tracy, 21.728s

ITT AUTOMOTIVE DETROIT GRAND PRIX

8 June 1997. Belle Isle. 77 laps of a 2.100-mile circuit = 161.700 miles. PPG CART World Series round 8

1 Greg Moore	Reynard 97I-Mercedes-Benz	77	1h52m45.143
2 Michael Andretti	Swift 007i-Ford	77	1h52m46.961
3 Gil de Ferran	Reynard 97I-Honda	77	1h52m47.083
4 Jimmy Vasser	Reynard 97I-Honda	77	1h52m47.238
5 Roberto Moreno	Swift 007i-Ford	77	1h52m48.870
6 Raul Boesel	Reynard 97I-Ford	77	1h52m49.507

Winner's average speed: 86.047 mph. Pole position: de Ferran, 1m09.052. Fastest lap: Dario Franchitti (Reynard 97I-Mercedes-Benz), 1m11.461

BUDWEISER GI JOE'S 200

22 June 1997. Portland. 78 laps of a 1.967-mile circuit = 153.426 miles. PPG CART World Series round 9

1 Mark Blundell	Reynard 97I-Mercedes-Benz	78	2h00m12.982
2 Gil de Ferran	Reynard 97I-Honda	78	2h00m13.009
3 Raul Boesel	Reynard 97I-Ford	78	2h00m13.037
4 Christian Fittipaldi	Swift 007i-Ford	78	2h00m14.051
5 Greg Moore	Reynard 97I-Mercedes-Benz	78	2h00m14.088
6 Mauricio Gugelmin	Reynard 97I-Mercedes-Benz	78	2h00m16.021

Winner's average speed: 76.575 mph. Pole position: Scott Pruett (Reynard 97I-Ford), 59.383s. Fastest lap: Boesel, 1m03.122

MEDIC DRUG GRAND PRIX OF CLEVELAND

13 July 1997. Cleveland. 90 laps of a 2.106-mile circuit = 189.540 miles. PPG CART World Series round 10

1 Alessandro Zanardi	Reynard 97I-Honda	90	1h41m40.661
2 Gil de Ferran	Reynard 97I-Honda	90	1h41m41.942
3 Bryan Herta	Reynard 97I-Ford	90	1h41m58.626
4 Al Unser Jr	Penske PC26-Mercedes-Benz	90	1h42m05.176
5 Bobby Rahal	Reynard 97I-Ford	90	1h42m08.080
6 Christian Fittipaldi	Swift 007i-Ford	90	1h42m15.453

Winner's average speed: 111.848 mph. Pole position: Zanardi, 56.984s. Fastest lap: Zanardi, 58.666s

MOLSON INDY TORONTO

20 July 1997. Toronto. 95 laps of a 1.721-mile circuit = 163.495 miles. PPG CART World Series round 11

1 Mark Blundell	Reynard 97I-Mercedes-Benz	95	1h45m43.936
2 Alessandro Zanardi	Reynard 97I-Honda	95	1h45m44.595
3 Andre Ribeiro	Reynard 97I-Honda	95	1h45m55.810
4 Michael Andretti	Swift 007i-Ford	95	1h45m57.033
5 Scott Pruett	Reynard 97I-Ford	95	1h46m09.872
6 Mauricio Gugelmin	Reynard 97I-Mercedes-Benz	95	1h46m10.367

Winner's average speed: 92.779 mph. Pole position: Dario Franchitti (Reynard 97I-Mercedes-Benz), 58.618s. Fastest lap: Blundell, 59.185s

US 500

27 July 1997. Michigan. 250 laps of a 2.000-mile circuit = 500.000 miles. PPG CART World Series round 12

1 Alessandro Zanardi	Reynard 97I-Honda	250	2h59m35.579
2 Mark Blundell	Reynard 97I-Mercedes-Benz	250	3h00m07.316
3 Gil de Ferran	Reynard 97I-Honda	249	
4 Paul Tracy	Penske PC26-Mercedes-Benz	249	
5 Bryan Herta	Reynard 97I-Ford	248	

6 Mauricio Gugelmin   Reynard 97I-Mercedes-Benz   242
Winner's average speed: 167.044 mph. Pole position: Scott Pruett
(Reynard 97I-Ford), 30.788s. Fastest lap: Gugelmin, 30.957s

MILLER 200

10 August 1997. Mid-Ohio. 83 laps of a 2.258-mile circuit = 187.414 miles. PPG CART World Series round 13

1 Alessandro Zanardi	Reynard 97I-Honda	83	1h41m16.682
2 Greg Moore	Reynard 97I-Mercedes-Benz	83	1h41m21.553
3 Bobby Rahal	Reynard 97I-Ford	83	1h41m23.320
4 Raul Boesel	Reynard 97I-Ford	83	1h41m29.719
5 Jimmy Vasser	Reynard 97I-Honda	83	1h41m31.887
6 Gil de Ferran	Reynard 97I-Honda	83	1h41m32.633

Winner's average speed: 111.029 mph. Pole position: Bryan Herta
(Reynard 97I-Ford), 1m06.277. Fastest lap: Zanardi, 1m07.735

TEXACO/HAVOLINE 200

17 August 1997. Elkhart Lake. 50 laps of a 4.048-mile circuit = 202.400 miles. PPG CART World Series round 14

1 Alessandro Zanardi	Reynard 97I-Honda	50	1h57m54.544
2 Mauricio Gugelmin	Reynard 97I-Mercedes-Benz	50	1h58m00.692
3 Gil de Ferran	Reynard 97I-Honda	50	1h58m05.292
4 Christian Fittipaldi	Swift 007i-Ford	50	1h58m06.373
5 Scott Pruett	Reynard 97I-Ford	50	1h58m07.573
6 Bobby Rahal	Reynard 97I-Ford	50	1h58m09.273

Winner's average speed: 102.995 mph. Pole position: Gugelmin,
1m42.379. Fastest lap: Zanardi, 1m43.672

MOLSON INDY VANCOUVER

31 August 1997. Vancouver. 100 laps of a 1.703-mile circuit = 170.300 miles. PPG CART World Series round 15

1 Mauricio Gugelmin	Reynard 97I-Mercedes-Benz	100	1h47m17.995
2 Jimmy Vasser	Reynard 97I-Honda	100	1h47m20.867
3 Gil de Ferran	Reynard 97I-Honda	100	1h47m21.768
4 Alessandro Zanardi	Reynard 97I-Honda	100	1h47m25.733
5 Al Unser Jr	Penske PC26-Mercedes-Benz	100	1h47m34.433
6 Raul Boesel	Reynard 97I-Ford	100	1h47m41.155

Winner's average speed: 95.228 mph. Pole position: Zanardi, 54.025s.
Fastest lap: Zanardi, 55.136s

TOYOTA GRAND PRIX OF MONTEREY

7 September 1997. Laguna Seca. 83 laps of a 2.238-mile circuit = 185.754 miles. PPG CART World Series round 16

1 Jimmy Vasser	Reynard 97I-Honda	83	1h41m38.813
2 Mark Blundell	Reynard 97I-Mercedes-Benz	83	1h41m39.356
3 Alessandro Zanardi	Reynard 97I-Honda	83	1h41m50.141
4 Andre Ribeiro	Reynard 97I-Honda	83	1h42m01.504
5 Gil de Ferran	Reynard 97I-Honda	83	1h42m08.749
6 Bryan Herta	Reynard 97I-Ford	83	1h42m32.993

Winner's average speed: 109.647 mph. Pole position: Herta, 1m07.895.
Fastest lap: Blundell, 1m10.960

MARLBORO 500

28 September 1997. California Speedway. 250 laps of a 2.029-mile circuit = 507.250 miles. PPG CART World Series round 17

1 Mark Blundell	Reynard 97I-Mercedes-Benz	250	3h02m42.620
2 Jimmy Vasser	Reynard 97I-Honda	250	3h02m43.467
3 Adrian Fernandez	Lola T97/00-Honda	249	
4 Mauricio Gugelmin	Reynard 97I-Mercedes-Benz	249	
5 Bobby Rahal	Reynard 97I-Ford	249	
6 Gil de Ferran	Reynard 97I-Honda	249	

Winner's average speed: 166.575 mph. Pole position: Gugelmin, 30.316s.
Fastest lap: Greg Moore (Reynard 97I-Mercedes-Benz), 30.900s

1997 FINAL CHAMPIONSHIP POSITIONS

1	Alessandro Zanardi	195	7	Greg Moore	111
2	Gil de Ferran	162	8	Michael Andretti	108
3	Jimmy Vasser	144	9	Scott Pruett	102
4	Mauricio Gugelmin	132	10	Raul Boesel	91
5	Paul Tracy	121			
6	Mark Blundell	115			

1998

MARLBORO GRAND PRIX OF MIAMI

15 March 1998. Homestead. 150 laps of a 1.502-mile circuit = 225.300 miles. FedEx Championship Series round 1

1 Michael Andretti	Swift 009c-Ford	150	1h33m39.268
2 Greg Moore	Reynard 98I-Mercedes-Benz	150	1h33m39.343
3 Alessandro Zanardi	Reynard 98I-Honda	150	1h33m40.186
4 Christian Fittipaldi	Swift 009c-Ford	150	1h33m42.627
5 Scott Pruett	Reynard 98I-Ford	150	1h33m44.525
6 Adrian Fernandez	Reynard 98I-Ford	150	1h33m45.194

Winner's average speed: 144.339 mph. Pole position: Moore, 24.856s.
Fastest lap: Moore, time n/a

BUDWEISER 500

28 March 1998. Motegi. 201 laps of a 1.549-mile circuit = 311.349 miles. FedEx Championship Series round 2

1 Adrian Fernandez	Reynard 98I-Ford	201	1h57m12.016
2 Al Unser Jr	Penske PC27-Mercedes-Benz	201	1h57m13.102
3 Gil de Ferran	Reynard 98I-Honda	201	1h57m17.404
4 Greg Moore	Reynard 98I-Mercedes-Benz	201	1h57m19.939
5 Paul Tracy	Reynard 98I-Honda	201	1h57m20.166
6 Tony Kanaan	Reynard 98I-Honda	200	

Winner's average speed: 159.393 mph. Pole position: Jimmy Vasser
(Reynard 98I-Honda), 25.584s. Fastest lap: Vasser, 25.997s

TOYOTA GRAND PRIX OF LONG BEACH

5 April 1998. Long Beach. 105 laps of a 1.586-mile circuit = 166.530 miles. FedEx Championship Series round 3

1 Alessandro Zanardi	Reynard 98I-Honda	105	1h51m29.113
2 Dario Franchitti	Reynard 98I-Honda	105	1h51m32.030
3 Bryan Herta	Reynard 98I-Ford	105	1h51m33.449
4 Adrian Fernandez	Reynard 97I-Honda	105	1h51m34.998
5 Tony Kanaan	Reynard 98I-Honda	105	1h51m45.018
6 Greg Moore	Reynard 98I-Mercedes-Benz	105	1h51m48.470

Winner's average speed: 89.624 mph. Pole position: Herta, 50.945s.
Fastest lap: Bobby Rahal (Reynard 98I-Ford), 51.333s

BOSCH SPARK PLUG GRAND PRIX

27 April 1998. Nazareth. 225 laps of a 0.946-mile circuit = 212.850 miles. FedEx Championship Series round 4

1 Jimmy Vasser	Reynard 98I-Honda	225	1h57m20.307
2 Alessandro Zanardi	Reynard 98I-Honda	225	1h57m21.707
3 Greg Moore	Reynard 98I-Mercedes-Benz	225	1h57m23.917
4 Gil de Ferran	Reynard 98I-Honda	225	1h57m28.323
5 Paul Tracy	Reynard 98I-Honda	225	1h57m28.605
6 Bobby Rahal	Reynard 98I-Ford	225	1h57m29.925

Winner's average speed: 108.839 mph. Pole position: Patrick Carpentier
(Reynard 98I-Mercedes-Benz), 18.419s. Fastest lap: Moore, 19.514s

HOLLYWOOD RIO 400

10 May 1998. Rio de Janeiro. 133 laps of a 1.864-mile circuit = 247.912 miles. FedEx Championship Series round 5

1 Greg Moore	Reynard 98I-Mercedes-Benz	133	1h52m14.135
2 Alessandro Zanardi	Reynard 98I-Honda	133	1h52m14.562
3 Adrian Fernandez	Reynard 97I-Ford	133	1h52m18.974
4 Bryan Herta	Reynard 98I-Ford	133	1h52m27.086

5 Michael Andretti   Swift 009c-Ford   133   1h52m28.459
6 Jimmy Vasser   Reynard 98I-Honda   133   1h52m29.386
Winner's average speed: 132.531 mph. Pole position: Dario Franchitti
(Reynard 98I-Honda), 39.005s. Fastest lap: Zanardi, 39.328s

MOTOROLA 300

**23 May 1998. St Louis. 236 laps of a 1.270-mile circuit = 299.720 miles.
FedEx Championship Series round 6**

1 Alessandro Zanardi	Reynard 98I-Honda	236	2h23m02.140
2 Michael Andretti	Swift 009c-Ford	236	2h23m02.713
3 Greg Moore	Reynard 98I-Mercedes-Benz	236	2h23m03.666
4 Jimmy Vasser	Reynard 98I-Honda	236	2h23m20.014
5 Scott Pruett	Reynard 98I-Ford	236	2h23m20.451
6 Gil de Ferran	Reynard 98I-Honda	236	2h23m20.863

Winner's average speed: 125.725 mph. Pole position: Moore, 25.757s.
Fastest lap: Vasser, 26.567s

MILLER LITE 200

**31 May 1998. Milwaukee. 200 laps of a 1.032-mile circuit = 206.400 miles.
FedEx Championship Series round 7**

1 Jimmy Vasser	Reynard 98I-Honda	200	1h34m17.011
2 Helio Castro-Neves	Reynard 98I-Mercedes-Benz	200	1h34m24.684
3 Al Unser Jr	Penske PC27-Mercedes-Benz	200	1h34m24.717
4 Dario Franchitti	Reynard 98I-Honda	200	1h34m28.302
5 Bobby Rahal	Reynard 97I-Ford	200	1h34m42.190
6 Richie Hearn	Swift 009c-Ford	199	

Winner's average speed: 131.349 mph. Pole position: Patrick Carpentier
(Reynard 98I-Mercedes-Benz), 20.028s. Fastest lap: Scott Pruett (Reynard
97I-Ford), 21.519s

ITT AUTOMOTIVE DETROIT GRAND PRIX

**7 June 1998. Belle Isle. 72 laps of a 2.346-mile circuit = 168.912 miles.
FedEx Championship Series round 8**

1 Alessandro Zanardi	Reynard 98I-Honda	72	1h41m17.673
2 Adrian Fernandez	Reynard 97I-Ford	72	1h41m24.297
3 Gil de Ferran	Reynard 98I-Honda	72	1h41m25.184
4 Dario Franchitti	Reynard 98I-Honda	72	1h41m26.020
5 Greg Moore	Reynard 98I-Mercedes-Benz	72	1h41m27.457
6 Jimmy Vasser	Reynard 98I-Honda	72	1h41m28.081

Winner's average speed: 100.052 mph. Pole position: Moore, 1m13.530.
Fastest lap: Zanardi, 1m16.280

BUDWEISER GI JOE'S 200

**21 June 1998. Portland. 98 laps of a 1.967-mile circuit = 192.766 miles.
FedEx Championship Series round 9**

1 Alessandro Zanardi	Reynard 98I-Honda	98	1h54m06.822
2 Scott Pruett	Reynard 98I-Ford	98	1h54m13.661
3 Bryan Herta	Reynard 98I-Ford	98	1h54m13.931
4 Tony Kanaan	Reynard 98I-Honda	98	1h54m19.730
5 Al Unser Jr	Penske PC27-Mercedes-Benz	98	1h54m20.998
6 Bobby Rahal	Reynard 97I-Ford	98	1h54m25.212

Winner's average speed: 101.355 mph. Pole position: Herta, 58.358s.
Fastest lap: Patrick Carpentier (Reynard 98I-Mercedes-Benz), 1m00.880

MEDIC DRUG GRAND PRIX OF CLEVELAND

**12 July 1998. Cleveland. 100 laps of a 2.106-mile circuit = 210.600 miles.
FedEx Championship Series round 10**

1 Alessandro Zanardi	Reynard 98I-Honda	100	1h52m22.282
2 Michael Andretti	Swift 009c-Ford	100	1h52m30.704
3 Dario Franchitti	Reynard 98I-Honda	100	1h52m31.183
4 Scott Pruett	Reynard 97I-Ford	100	1h52m40.666
5 Adrian Fernandez	Reynard 98I-Ford	100	1h52m50.351
6 Gil de Ferran	Reynard 98I-Honda	100	1h52m50.890

Winner's average speed: 112.449 mph. Pole position: Jimmy Vasser
(Reynard 98I-Honda), 56.417s. Fastest lap: Bryan Herta (Reynard 98I-
Ford), 58.817s

MOLSON INDY TORONTO

**19 July 1998. Toronto. 95 laps of a 1.721-mile circuit = 163.495 miles.
FedEx Championship Series round 11**

1 Alessandro Zanardi	Reynard 98I-Honda	95	1h52m24.080
2 Michael Andretti	Swift 009c-Ford	95	1h52m26.001
3 Jimmy Vasser	Reynard 98I-Honda	95	1h52m30.782
4 Bobby Rahal	Reynard 98I-Ford	95	1h52m32.158
5 Bryan Herta	Reynard 98I-Ford	95	1h52m37.064
6 Scott Pruett	Reynard 97I-Ford	95	1h52m38.687

Winner's average speed: 87.274 mph. Pole position: Dario Franchitti
(Reynard 98I-Honda), 58.694s. Fastest lap: Christian Fittipaldi (Swift 009c-
Ford), 59.824s

US 500

**26 July 1998. Michigan. 250 laps of a 2.000-mile circuit = 500.000 miles.
FedEx Championship Series round 12**

1 Greg Moore	Reynard 98I-Mercedes-Benz	250	3h00m48.785
2 Jimmy Vasser	Reynard 98I-Honda	250	3h00m49.044
3 Alessandro Zanardi	Reynard 98I-Honda	250	3h00m49.052
4 Scott Pruett	Reynard 98I-Ford	250	3h00m49.303
5 Richie Hearn	Swift 009c-Ford	250	3h00m50.141
6 Michael Andretti	Swift 009c-Ford	250	3h00m50.352

Winner's average speed: 165.917 mph. Pole position: Adrian Fernandez
(Reynard 97I-Ford), 31.370s. Fastest lap: Patrick Carpentier (Reynard 98I-
Mercedes-Benz) and Pruett, both 31.508s

MILLER LITE 200

**9 August 1998. Mid-Ohio. 83 laps of a 2.258-mile circuit = 187.414 miles.
FedEx Championship Series round 13**

1 Adrian Fernandez	Reynard 98I-Ford	83	1h53m39.270
2 Scott Pruett	Reynard 98I-Ford	83	1h53m39.517
3 Bobby Rahal	Reynard 97I-Ford	83	1h53m41.687
4 Mauricio Gugelmin	Reynard 98I-Mercedes-Benz	83	1h53m48.076
5 Paul Tracy	Reynard 98I-Honda	83	1h53m49.253
6 Al Unser Jr	Penske PC27-Mercedes-Benz	83	1h53m52.561

Winner's average speed: 98.939 mph. Pole position: Dario Franchitti
(Reynard 98I-Honda), 1m05.679. Fastest lap: Greg Moore (Reynard 98I-
Mercedes-Benz), 1m08.287

TEXACO/HAVOLINE 200

**16 August 1998. Elkhart Lake. 50 laps of a 4.048-mile circuit = 202.400
miles. FedEx Championship Series round 14**

1 Dario Franchitti	Reynard 98I-Honda	50	1h35m30.767
2 Alessandro Zanardi	Reynard 98I-Honda	50	1h35m37.869
3 Christian Fittipaldi	Swift 009c-Ford	50	1h36m14.689
4 Tony Kanaan	Reynard 98I-Honda	50	1h36m16.901
5 Adrian Fernandez	Reynard 98I-Ford	50	1h36m17.864
6 Paul Tracy	Reynard 98I-Honda	50	1h36m22.770

Winner's average speed: 127.145 mph. Pole position: Michael Andretti
(Swift 009c-Ford), 1m39.988. Fastest lap: Zanardi, 1m41.874

MOLSON INDY VANCOUVER

**6 September 1998. Vancouver. 86 laps of a 1.802-mile circuit = 154.972
miles. FedEx Championship Series round 15**

1 Dario Franchitti	Reynard 98I-Honda	86	2h00m37.871
2 Michael Andretti	Swift 009c-Ford	86	2h00m41.308
3 Scott Pruett	Reynard 97I-Ford	86	2h00m42.616
4 Alessandro Zanardi	Reynard 98I-Honda	86	2h00m42.873
5 Al Unser Jr	Penske PC27-Mercedes-Benz	86	2h00m51.703
6 Mauricio Gugelmin	Reynard 98I-Mercedes-Benz	86	2h00m52.804

Winner's average speed: 77.081 mph. Pole position: Franchitti, 1m04.130.
Fastest lap: Helio Castro-Neves (Reynard 98I-Mercedes-Benz), 1m06.939

HONDA GRAND PRIX OF MONTEREY

**13 September 1998. Laguna Seca. 83 laps of a 2.238-mile circuit =
185.754 miles. FedEx Championship Series round 16**

1 Bryan Herta	Reynard 98I-Ford	83	1h55m13.472

2 Alessandro Zanardi	Reynard 98I-Honda	83	1h55m13.815
3 Tony Kanaan	Reynard 98I-Honda	83	1h55m17.251
4 Dario Franchitti	Reynard 98I-Honda	83	1h55m17.874
5 Jimmy Vasser	Reynard 98I-Honda	83	1h55m20.646
6 Al Unser Jr	Penske PC27-Mercedes-Benz	83	1h55m21.335

Winner's average speed: 96.726 mph. Pole position: Herta, 1m08.146. Fastest lap: Kanaan, 1m10.824

TEXACO GRAND PRIX OF HOUSTON

4 October 1998. Houston. 70 laps of a 1.527-mile circuit = 106.890 miles. FedEx Championship Series round 17

1 Dario Franchitti	Reynard 98I-Honda	70	1h36m30.979
2 Alessandro Zanardi	Reynard 98I-Honda	70	1h36m31.625
3 Tony Kanaan	Reynard 98I-Honda	70	1h36m36.771
4 Jimmy Vasser	Reynard 98I-Honda	70	1h36m39.321
5 Massimiliano Papis	Reynard 98I-Toyota	70	1h36m42.149
6 Adrian Fernandez	Reynard 98I-Ford	70	1h36m44.404

Winner's average speed: 66.449 mph. Pole position: Greg Moore (Reynard 98I-Mercedes-Benz), 59.508s. Fastest lap: Zanardi, 1m02.797

HONDA INDY

18 October 1998. Surfers Paradise. 62 laps of a 2.795-mile circuit = 173.290 miles. FedEx Championship Series round 18

1 Alessandro Zanardi	Reynard 98I-Honda	62	2h01m51.170
2 Dario Franchitti	Reynard 98I-Honda	62	2h01m51.492
3 Christian Fittipaldi	Swift 009c-Ford	62	2h01m52.199
4 Scott Pruett	Reynard 97I-Ford	62	2h01m57.558
5 JJ Lehto	Reynard 98I-Mercedes-Benz	62	2h02m01.962
6 Adrian Fernandez	Reynard 98I-Ford	62	2h02m02.323

Winner's average speed: 85.328 mph. Pole position: Franchitti, 1m32.288. Fastest lap: Zanardi, 1m33.780

MARLBORO 500

1 November 1998. California Speedway. 250 laps of a 2.029-mile circuit = 507.250 miles. FedEx Championship Series round 19

1 Jimmy Vasser	Reynard 98I-Honda	250	3h17m54.369
2 Greg Moore	Reynard 98I-Mercedes-Benz	250	3h17m54.729
3 Alessandro Zanardi	Reynard 98I-Honda	250	3h17m55.486
4 Adrian Fernandez	Reynard 98I-Ford	250	3h17m55.506
5 Mauricio Gugelmin	Reynard 98I-Mercedes-Benz	250	3h17m55.533
6 Mark Blundell	Reynard 98I-Mercedes-Benz	250	3h17m55.832

Winner's average speed: 153.785 mph. Pole position: Scott Pruett (Reynard 97I-Ford), 31.249s. Fastest lap: Moore, 31.119s

1998 FINAL CHAMPIONSHIP POSITIONS

1	Alessandro Zanardi	285	7	Michael Andretti	112
2	Jimmy Vasser	169	8	Bryan Herta	97
3	Dario Franchitti	160	9	Tony Kanaan	92
4	Adrian Fernandez	154	10	Bobby Rahal	82
5	Greg Moore	140			
6	Scott Pruett	121			

1999

MARLBORO GRAND PRIX OF MIAMI

21 March 1999. Homestead. 150 laps of a 1.502-mile circuit = 225.300 miles. FedEx CART Championship Series round 1

1 Greg Moore	Reynard 99I-Mercedes-Benz	150	1h38m54.535
2 Michael Andretti	Swift 010c-Ford	150	1h38m55.645
3 Dario Franchitti	Reynard 99I-Honda	150	1h38m56.681
4 Jimmy Vasser	Reynard 99I-Honda	150	1h39m03.713
5 Massimiliano Papis	Reynard 99I-Ford	150	1h39m15.946
6 Gil de Ferran	Reynard 99I-Honda	150	1h39m16.235

Winner's average speed: 136.671 mph. Pole position: Moore, 24.886s. Fastest lap: Franchitti, 26.825s

FIRESTONE FIREHAWK 500

10 April 1999. Motegi. 201 laps of a 1.549-mile circuit = 311.349 miles. FedEx CART Championship Series round 2

1 Adrian Fernandez	Reynard 97I-Ford	201	1h46m01.463
2 Gil de Ferran	Reynard 99I-Honda	201	1h46m07.810
3 Christian Fittipaldi	Swift 010c-Ford	201	1h46m09.132
4 Greg Moore	Reynard 99I-Mercedes-Benz	201	1h46m39.490
5 Michael Andretti	Swift 010c-Ford	200	
6 Tony Kanaan	Reynard 99I-Honda	200	

Winner's average speed: 176.195 mph. Pole position: de Ferran, 25.463s. Fastest lap: Helio Castro-Neves (Lola B99/00-Mercedes-Benz), 25.830s

TOYOTA GRAND PRIX OF LONG BEACH

18 April 1999. Long Beach. 85 laps of a 1.824-mile circuit = 155.040 miles. FedEx CART Championship Series round 3

1 Juan Pablo Montoya	Reynard 99I-Honda	85	1h45m48.688
2 Dario Franchitti	Reynard 99I-Honda	85	1h45m51.493
3 Bryan Herta	Reynard 99I-Ford	85	1h45m55.691
4 Adrian Fernandez	Swift 010c-Ford	85	1h45m57.298
5 Christian Fittipaldi	Swift 010c-Ford	85	1h45m57.519
6 Gil de Ferran	Reynard 99I-Honda	85	1h46m02.254

Winner's average speed: 87.915 mph. Pole position: Tony Kanaan (Reynard 99I-Honda), 1m01.109. Fastest lap: Montoya, 1m02.779

BOSCH SPARK PLUG GRAND PRIX

2 May 1999. Nazareth. 225 laps of a 0.946-mile circuit = 212.850 miles. FedEx CART Championship Series round 4

1 Juan Pablo Montoya	Reynard 99I-Honda	225	1h46m13.527
2 PJ Jones	Swift 010c-Ford	225	1h46m18.630
3 Paul Tracy	Reynard 99I-Honda	225	1h46m19.407
4 Cristiano da Matta	Reynard 99I-Toyota	225	1h46m19.832
5 Adrian Fernandez	Reynard 97I-Ford	225	1h46m29.928
6 Michael Andretti	Swift 010c-Ford	225	1h46m30.246

Winner's average speed: 120.225 mph. Pole position: Montoya, 19.600s. Fastest lap: Helio Castro-Neves (Lola B99/00-Mercedes-Benz), 21.106s

GP TELEMAR RIO 200

15 May 1999. Rio de Janeiro. 108 laps of a 1.864-mile circuit = 201.312 miles. FedEx CART Championship Series round 5

1 Juan Pablo Montoya	Reynard 99I-Honda	108	1h36m32.233
2 Dario Franchitti	Reynard 99I-Honda	108	1h36m33.969
3 Christian Fittipaldi	Swift 010c-Ford	108	1h36m36.187
4 Massimiliano Papis	Reynard 99I-Ford	108	1h36m37.163
5 Tony Kanaan	Reynard 99I-Honda	108	1h36m39.269
6 Patrick Carpentier	Reynard 99I-Mercedes-Benz	108	1h36m39.851

Winner's average speed: 125.120 mph. Pole position: Fittipaldi, 38.565s. Fastest lap: Montoya, 38.891s

MOTOROLA 300

29 May 1999. St Louis. 236 laps of a 1.270-mile circuit = 299.720 miles. FedEx CART Championship Series round 6

1 Michael Andretti	Swift 010c-Ford	236	2h25m35.829
2 Helio Castro-Neves	Lola B99/00-Mercedes-Benz	236	2h25m36.158
3 Dario Franchitti	Reynard 99I-Honda	236	2h25m36.876
4 Roberto Moreno	Reynard 99I-Mercedes-Benz	236	2h25m41.564
5 Massimiliano Papis	Reynard 99I-Ford	236	2h25m46.806
6 Greg Moore	Reynard 99I-Mercedes-Benz	236	2h25m47.032

Winner's average speed: 123.513 mph. Pole position: Juan Pablo Montoya (Reynard 99I-Honda), 25.014s. Fastest lap: Castro-Neves, 26.180s

MILLER LITE 225

6 June 1999. Milwaukee. 225 laps of a 1.032-mile circuit = 232.200 miles. FedEx CART Championship Series round 7

1 Paul Tracy	Reynard 99I-Honda	225	1h48m49.169

2 Greg Moore	Reynard 99I-Mercedes-Benz	225	1h48m55.049
3 Gil de Ferran	Reynard 99I-Honda	225	1h48m55.625
4 Jimmy Vasser	Reynard 99I-Honda	225	1h48m57.106
5 Adrian Fernandez	Reynard 97I-Ford	225	1h48m59.098
6 Christian Fittipaldi	Swift 010c-Ford	225	1h49m00.420

Winner's average speed: 128.029 mph. Pole position: Helio Castro-Neves (Lola B99/00-Mercedes-Benz), 21.931s. Fastest lap: Castro-Neves, 23.517s

BUDWEISER GI JOE'S 200

20 June 1999. Portland. 98 laps of a 1.969-mile circuit = 192.962 miles. FedEx CART Championship Series round 8

1 Gil de Ferran	Reynard 99I-Honda	98	1h47m44.560
2 Juan Pablo Montoya	Reynard 99I-Honda	98	1h47m48.953
3 Dario Franchitti	Reynard 99I-Honda	98	1h47m49.556
4 Adrian Fernandez	Reynard 99I-Ford	98	1h47m58.128
5 Paul Tracy	Reynard 99I-Honda	98	1h48m04.853
6 Bryan Herta	Reynard 99I-Ford	98	1h48m12.491

Winner's average speed: 107.457 mph. Pole position: Montoya, 58.193s. Fastest lap: Michael Andretti (Swift 010c-Ford), 59.749s

MEDIC DRUG GRAND PRIX OF CLEVELAND

27 June 1999. Cleveland. 90 laps of a 2.106-mile circuit = 189.540 miles. FedEx CART Championship Series round 9

1 Juan Pablo Montoya	Reynard 99I-Honda	90	2h01m04.277
2 Gil de Ferran	Reynard 99I-Honda	90	2h01m14.881
3 Michael Andretti	Swift 010c-Ford	90	2h01m16.974
4 Paul Tracy	Reynard 99I-Honda	90	2h01m22.126
5 Al Unser Jr	Lola B99/00-Mercedes-Benz	90	2h01m23.486
6 Bryan Herta	Reynard 99I-Ford	90	2h01m24.031

Winner's average speed: 93.931 mph. Pole position: Montoya, 56.813s. Fastest lap: de Ferran, 58.790s

TEXACO/HAVOLINE 200

11 July 1999. Elkhart Lake. 55 laps of a 4.048-mile circuit = 222.640 miles. FedEx CART Championship Series round 10

1 Christian Fittipaldi	Swift 010c-Ford	55	1h37m00.799
2 Michael Andretti	Swift 010c-Ford	55	1h37m01.859
3 Adrian Fernandez	Reynard 99I-Ford	55	1h37m18.226
4 Greg Moore	Reynard 99I-Mercedes-Benz	55	1h37m20.196
5 Massimiliano Papis	Reynard 99I-Ford	55	1h37m35.292
6 Tony Kanaan	Reynard 99I-Honda	55	1h37m59.233

Winner's average speed: 137.697 mph. Pole position: Andretti, 1m40.206. Fastest lap: Helio Castro-Neves (Lola B99/00-Mercedes-Benz), 1m42.108

MOLSON INDY TORONTO

18 July 1999. Toronto. 95 laps of a 1.755-mile circuit = 166.725 miles. FedEx CART Championship Series round 11

1 Dario Franchitti	Reynard 99I-Honda	95	1h56m27.550
2 Paul Tracy	Reynard 99I-Honda	95	1h56m30.174
3 Christian Fittipaldi	Swift 010c-Ford	95	1h56m34.537
4 Roberto Moreno	Reynard 99I-Mercedes-Benz	95	1h56m38.285
5 Massimiliano Papis	Reynard 99I-Ford	95	1h56m43.030
6 Adrian Fernandez	Reynard 97I-Ford	95	1h56m50.453

Winner's average speed: 85.897 mph. Pole position: Gil de Ferran (Reynard 99I-Honda), 57.143s. Fastest lap: Franchitti, 59.361s

US 500

25 July 1999. Michigan. 250 laps of a 2.000-mile circuit = 500.000 miles. FedEx CART Championship Series round 12

1 Tony Kanaan	Reynard 99I-Honda	250	2h41m12.362
2 Juan Pablo Montoya	Reynard 99I-Honda	250	2h41m12.394
3 Paul Tracy	Reynard 99I-Honda	250	2h41m20.815
4 Michael Andretti	Swift 010c-Ford	250	2h41m20.868
5 Dario Franchitti	Reynard 99I-Honda	250	2h41m21.499
6 Adrian Fernandez	Reynard 97I-Ford	250	2h41m21.883

Winner's average speed: 186.097 mph. Pole position: Jimmy Vasser (Reynard 99I-Honda), 31.358s. Fastest lap: Vasser, 31.778s

TENNECO AUTOMOTIVE GRAND PRIX OF DETROIT

8 August 1999. Belle Isle. 71 laps of a 2.346-mile circuit = 166.566 miles. FedEx CART Championship Series round 13

1 Dario Franchitti	Reynard 99I-Honda	71	2h02m24.662
2 Paul Tracy	Reynard 99I-Honda	71	2h02m24.797
3 Greg Moore	Reynard 99I-Mercedes-Benz	71	2h02m25.192
4 Michael Andretti	Swift 010c-Ford	71	2h02m26.133
5 Jimmy Vasser	Reynard 99I-Honda	71	2h02m27.256
6 Tony Kanaan	Reynard 99I-Honda	71	2h02m28.314

Winner's average speed: 81.643 mph. Pole position: Juan Pablo Montoya (Reynard 99I-Honda), 1m13.585. Fastest lap: Montoya, 1m15.701

MILLER LITE 200

15 August 1999. Mid-Ohio. 83 laps of a 2.258-mile circuit = 187.414 miles. FedEx CART Championship Series round 14

1 Juan Pablo Montoya	Reynard 99I-Honda	83	1h42m03.808
2 Paul Tracy	Reynard 99I-Honda	83	1h42m14.735
3 Dario Franchitti	Reynard 99I-Honda	83	1h42m16.121
4 Jimmy Vasser	Reynard 99I-Honda	83	1h42m18.536
5 Massimiliano Papis	Reynard 99I-Ford	83	1h42m23.707
6 Gil de Ferran	Reynard 99I-Honda	83	1h42m27.490

Winner's average speed: 110.175 mph. Pole position: Franchitti, 1m05.347. Fastest lap: Montoya, 1m06.788

TARGET GRAND PRIX OF CHICAGO

22 August 1999. Chicago. 225 laps of a 1.029-mile circuit = 231.525 miles. FedEx CART Championship Series round 15

1 Juan Pablo Montoya	Reynard 99I-Honda	225	1h53m38.704
2 Dario Franchitti	Reynard 99I-Honda	225	1h53m39.487
3 Jimmy Vasser	Reynard 99I-Honda	225	1h53m54.483
4 Massimiliano Papis	Reynard 99I-Ford	225	1h53m54.659
5 Helio Castro-Neves	Lola B99/00-Mercedes-Benz	225	1h53m55.039
6 Patrick Carpentier	Reynard 99I-Mercedes-Benz	225	1h54m00.055

Winner's average speed: 122.236 mph. Pole position: Papis, 22.788s. Fastest lap: Roberto Moreno (Swift 010c-Ford), 23.687s

MOLSON INDY VANCOUVER

5 September 1999. Vancouver. 74 laps of a 1.781-mile circuit = 131.794 miles. FedEx CART Championship Series round 16

1 Juan Pablo Montoya	Reynard 99I-Honda	74	2h01m08.183
2 Patrick Carpentier	Reynard 99I-Mercedes-Benz	74	2h01m15.768
3 Jimmy Vasser	Reynard 99I-Honda	74	2h01m16.147
4 Mauricio Gugelmin	Reynard 99I-Mercedes-Benz	74	2h01m21.226
5 Cristiano da Matta	Reynard 99I-Toyota	74	2h01m22.184
6 Richie Hearn	Reynard 99I-Toyota	74	2h01m22.475

Winner's average speed: 65.279 mph. Pole position: Montoya, 1m00.641. Fastest lap: Montoya, 1m11.441

HONDA GRAND PRIX OF MONTEREY

12 September 1999. Laguna Seca. 83 laps of a 2.238-mile circuit = 185.754 miles. FedEx CART Championship Series round 17

1 Bryan Herta	Reynard 99I-Ford	83	1h49m20.898
2 Roberto Moreno	Swift 010c-Ford	83	1h49m22.723
3 Massimiliano Papis	Reynard 99I-Ford	83	1h49m24.516
4 Paul Tracy	Reynard 99I-Honda	83	1h49m28.942
5 Adrian Fernandez	Reynard 99I-Ford	83	1h49m36.639
6 Gil de Ferran	Reynard 99I-Honda	83	1h49m37.387

Winner's average speed: 101.924 mph. Pole position: Herta, 1m08.334. Fastest lap: Tony Kanaan (Reynard 99I-Honda), 1m10.662

TEXACO GRAND PRIX OF HOUSTON

26 September 1999. Houston. 100 laps of a 1.527-mile circuit = 152.700 miles. FedEx CART Championship Series round 18

1 Paul Tracy	Reynard 99I-Honda	100	1h55m31.263
2 Dario Franchitti	Reynard 99I-Honda	100	1h55m44.996
3 Michael Andretti	Swift 010c-Ford	100	1h55m57.124

4 Massimiliano Papis	Reynard 99I-Ford	100	1h55m58.795
5 Bryan Herta	Reynard 99I-Ford	100	1h56m12.201
6 Mauricio Gugelmin	Reynard 99I-Mercedes-Benz	100	1h56m15.426

Winner's average speed: 79.310 mph. Pole position: Juan Pablo Montoya (Reynard 99I-Honda), 58.699s. Fastest lap: Montoya, 1m01.018

HONDA INDY 300

17 October 1999. Surfers Paradise. 65 laps of a 2.795-mile circuit = 181.675 miles. FedEx CART Championship Series round 19

1 Dario Franchitti	Reynard 99I-Honda	65	1h58m40.726
2 Massimiliano Papis	Reynard 99I-Ford	65	1h58m43.335
3 Adrian Fernandez	Reynard 99I-Ford	65	1h58m48.171
4 Bryan Herta	Reynard 99I-Ford	65	1h58m51.119
5 Michael Andretti	Swift 010c-Ford	65	1h58m51.911
6 Tony Kanaan	Reynard 99I-Honda	65	1h58m52.085

Winner's average speed: 91.849 mph. Pole position: Franchitti, 1m31.703. Fastest lap: Papis, 1m34.516

MARLBORO 500

31 October 1999. California Speedway. 250 laps of a 2.029-mile circuit = 507.250 miles. FedEx CART Championship Series round 20

1 Adrian Fernandez	Reynard 97I-Ford	250	2h57m17.542
2 Massimiliano Papis	Reynard 99I-Ford	250	2h57m25.176
3 Christian Fittipaldi	Swift 010c-Ford	250	2h57m26.385
4 Juan Pablo Montoya	Reynard 99I-Honda	250	2h57m31.858
5 Jimmy Vasser	Reynard 99I-Ford	250	2h57m38.248
6 Mauricio Gugelmin	Reynard 99I-Mercedes-Benz	250	2h58m01.738

Winner's average speed: 171.666 mph. Pole position: Scott Pruett (Reynard 99I-Toyota), 31.030s. Fastest lap: Fittipaldi, 31.732s

1999 FINAL CHAMPIONSHIP POSITIONS

1*Juan Pablo Montoya	212	8 Gil de Ferran	108
2 Dario Franchitti	212	9 Jimmy Vasser	104
3 Paul Tracy	161	10 Greg Moore	97
4 Michael Andretti	151	*Awarded championship due to
5 Massimiliano Papis	150	greater number of race wins
6 Adrian Fernandez	140	
7 Christian Fittipaldi	121	

2000

MARLBORO GRAND PRIX OF MIAMI

26 March 2000. Homestead. 150 laps of a 1.502-mile circuit = 225.300 miles. FedEx Championship Series round 1

1 Massimiliano Papis	Reynard 2KI-Ford	150	1h22m01.975
2 Roberto Moreno	Reynard 2KI-Ford	150	1h22m02.595
3 Paul Tracy	Reynard 2KI-Honda	150	1h22m05.810
4 Jimmy Vasser	Lola B2K/00-Toyota	150	1h22m06.429
5 Patrick Carpentier	Reynard 2KI-Ford	150	1h22m06.806
6 Gil de Ferran	Reynard 2KI-Honda	150	1h22m14.394

Winner's average speed: 164.788 mph. Pole position: de Ferran, 25.942s. Fastest lap: Juan Pablo Montoya (Lola B2K/00-Toyota), 27.826s

TOYOTA GRAND PRIX OF LONG BEACH

16 April 2000. Long Beach. 82 laps of a 1.968-mile circuit = 161.376 miles. FedEx Championship Series round 2

1 Paul Tracy	Reynard 2KI-Honda	82	1h57m11.132
2 Helio Castro-Neves	Reynard 2KI-Honda	82	1h57m14.323
3 Jimmy Vasser	Lola B2K/00-Toyota	82	1h57m14.430
4 Alexandre Tagliani	Reynard 2KI-Ford	82	1h57m14.916
5 Bryan Herta	Reynard 2KI-Honda	82	1h57m15.340
6 Oriol Servia	Reynard 2KI-Toyota	82	1h57m16.272

Winner's average speed: 82.626 mph. Pole position: Gil de Ferran (Reynard 2KI-Honda), 1m07.494. Fastest lap: de Ferran, 1m09.602

RIO 200

30 April 2000. Rio de Janeiro. 108 laps of a 1.864-mile circuit = 201.312 miles. FedEx Championship Series round 3

1 Adrian Fernandez	Reynard 2KI-Ford	108	1h37m12.490
2 Jimmy Vasser	Lola B2K/00-Toyota	108	1h37m13.421
3 Paul Tracy	Reynard 2KI-Honda	108	1h37m13.828
4 Cristiano da Matta	Reynard 2KI-Toyota	108	1h37m14.071
5 Christian Fittipaldi	Lola B2K/00-Ford	108	1h37m14.846
6 Roberto Moreno	Reynard 2KI-Ford	108	1h37m15.268

Winner's average speed: 124.256 mph. Pole position: Alexandre Tagliani (Reynard 2KI-Ford), 38.587s. Fastest lap: Tagliani, 39.445s

FIRESTONE FIREHAWK 500

14 May 2000. Motegi. 201 laps of a 1.549-mile circuit = 311.349 miles. Race scheduled for 13 May but postponed due to rain. FedEx Championship Series round 4

1 Michael Andretti	Lola B2K/00-Ford	201	1h58m52.201
2 Dario Franchitti	Reynard 2KI-Honda	201	1h58m52.747
3 Roberto Moreno	Reynard 2KI-Ford	201	1h58m55.026
4 Cristiano da Matta	Reynard 2KI-Toyota	201	1h58m55.743
5 Kenny Brack	Reynard 2KI-Ford	201	1h58m56.126
6 Paul Tracy	Reynard 2KI-Honda	201	1h58m56.459

Winner's average speed: 157.154 mph. Pole position: Juan Pablo Montoya (Lola B2K/00-Toyota), 26.237s. Fastest lap: Montoya, 26.812s

BOSCH SPARK PLUG GRAND PRIX

27 May 2000. Nazareth. 225 laps of a 0.946-mile circuit = 212.850 miles. Race scheduled for 9 April but postponed due to snow. FedEx Championship Series round 5

1 Gil de Ferran	Reynard 2KI-Honda	225	2h06m10.334
2 Mauricio Gugelmin	Reynard 2KI-Mercedes-Benz	225	2h06m11.149
3 Kenny Brack	Reynard 2KI-Ford	225	2h06m12.214
4 Juan Pablo Montoya	Lola B2K/00-Toyota	225	2h06m12.442
5 Adrian Fernandez	Reynard 2KI-Ford	225	2h06m15.052
6 Michael Andretti	Lola B2K/00-Ford	225	2h06m15.911

Winner's average speed: 101.219 mph. Pole position: Montoya, 19.255s. Fastest lap: Helio Castro-Neves (Reynard 2KI-Honda), 20.600s

MILLER LITE 225

6 June 2000. Milwaukee. 225 laps of a 1.032-mile circuit = 232.200 miles. Race scheduled for 5 June but postponed due to rain. FedEx Championship Series round 6

1 Juan Pablo Montoya	Lola B2K/00-Toyota	225	1h37m38.526
2 Michael Andretti	Lola B2K/00-Ford	225	1h37m39.541
3 Patrick Carpentier	Reynard 2KI-Ford	225	1h37m46.983
4 Kenny Brack	Reynard 2KI-Ford	225	1h37m53.128
5 Roberto Moreno	Reynard 2KI-Ford	225	1h37m53.685
6 Dario Franchitti	Reynard 2KI-Honda	225	1h37m54.159

Winner's average speed: 142.684 mph. Pole position: Montoya, 20.899s. Fastest lap: Montoya, 22.345s

TENNECO AUTOMOTIVE GRAND PRIX OF DETROIT

18 June 2000. Belle Isle. 84 laps of a 2.346-mile circuit = 197.064 miles. FedEx Championship Series round 7

1 Helio Castro-Neves	Reynard 2KI-Honda	84	2h01m23.607
2 Massimiliano Papis	Reynard 2KI-Ford	84	2h01m28.022
3 Oriol Servia	Reynard 2KI-Toyota	84	2h01m34.072
4 Dario Franchitti	Reynard 2KI-Honda	84	2h01m37.244
5 Patrick Carpentier	Reynard 2KI-Ford	84	2h01m48.920
6 Alexandre Tagliani	Reynard 2KI-Ford	84	2h01m50.009

Winner's average speed: 97.401 mph. Pole position: Juan Pablo Montoya (Lola B2K/00-Toyota), 1m13.056. Fastest lap: Castro-Neves, 1m15.805

FREIGHTLINER GI JOE'S 200

25 June 2000. Portland. 112 laps of a 1.969-mile circuit = 220.528 miles. FedEx Championship Series round 8

1 Gil de Ferran	Reynard 2KI-Honda	112	2h00m46.002
2 Roberto Moreno	Reynard 2KI-Ford	112	2h00m49.250

3 Christian Fittipaldi	Lola B2K/00-Ford	112	2h00m55.607
4 Michael Andretti	Lola B2K/00-Ford	112	2h01m15.733
5 Cristiano da Matta	Reynard 2KI-Toyota	112	2h01m16.072
6 Kenny Brack	Reynard 2KI-Ford	112	2h01m16.592

Winner's average speed: 109.564 mph. Pole position: Helio Castro-Neves (Reynard 2KI-Honda), 57.738s. Fastest lap: Brack, 1m00.345

MARCONI GRAND PRIX OF CLEVELAND

2 July 2000. Cleveland. 100 laps of a 2.106-mile circuit = 210.600 miles. FedEx Championship Series round 9

1 Roberto Moreno	Reynard 2KI-Ford	100	1h52m12.092
2 Kenny Brack	Reynard 2KI-Ford	100	1h52m12.918
3 Cristiano da Matta	Reynard 2KI-Toyota	100	1h52m14.059
4 Michael Andretti	Lola B2K/00-Ford	100	1h52m19.654
5 Patrick Carpentier	Reynard 2KI-Ford	100	1h52m20.445
6 Juan Pablo Montoya	Lola B2K/00-Toyota	100	1h52m22.365

Winner's average speed: 112.619 mph. Pole position: Moreno, 57.436s. Fastest lap: Montoya, 59.625s

MOLSON INDY TORONTO

16 July 2000. Toronto. 112 laps of a 1.755-mile circuit = 196.560 miles. FedEx Championship Series round 10

1 Michael Andretti	Lola B2K/00-Ford	112	2h00m02.313
2 Adrian Fernandez	Reynard 2KI-Ford	112	2h00m08.840
3 Paul Tracy	Reynard 2KI-Honda	112	2h00m11.431
4 Cristiano da Matta	Reynard 2KI-Toyota	112	2h00m17.283
5 Alexandre Tagliani	Reynard 2KI-Ford	112	2h00m23.935
6 Gil de Ferran	Reynard 2KI-Honda	112	2h00m26.663

Winner's average speed: 98.248 mph. Pole position: Helio Castro-Neves (Reynard 2KI-Honda), 57.200s. Fastest lap: Andretti, 1m00.045

MICHIGAN 500

23 July 2000. Michigan. 250 laps of a 2.000-mile circuit = 500.000 miles. FedEx Championship Series round 11

1 Juan Pablo Montoya	Lola B2K/00-Toyota	250	2h48m49.790
2 Michael Andretti	Lola B2K/00-Ford	250	2h48m49.830
3 Dario Franchitti	Reynard 2KI-Honda	250	2h48m51.411
4 Patrick Carpentier	Reynard 2KI-Ford	250	2h48m51.895
5 Helio Castro-Neves	Reynard 2KI-Honda	250	2h48m52.920
6 Adrian Fernandez	Reynard 2KI-Ford	250	2h48m53.633

Winner's average speed: 177.694 mph. Pole position: Paul Tracy (Reynard 2KI-Honda), 30.645s. Fastest lap: Montoya, 31.162s

TARGET GRAND PRIX OF CHICAGO

30 July 2000. Chicago. 225 laps of a 1.029-mile circuit = 231.525 miles. FedEx Championship Series round 12

1 Cristiano da Matta	Reynard 2KI-Toyota	225	2h01m23.727
2 Michael Andretti	Lola B2K/00-Ford	225	2h01m25.417
3 Gil de Ferran	Reynard 2KI-Honda	225	2h01m26.246
4 Kenny Brack	Reynard 2KI-Ford	225	2h01m26.511
5 Adrian Fernandez	Reynard 2KI-Ford	225	2h01m38.413
6 Roberto Moreno	Reynard 2KI-Ford	225	2h01m39.276

Winner's average speed: 114.432 mph. Pole position: Juan Pablo Montoya (Lola B2K/00-Toyota), 22.107s. Fastest lap: Fernandez, 23.714s

MILLER LITE 200

13 August 2000. Mid-Ohio. 83 laps of a 2.258-mile circuit = 187.414 miles. FedEx Championship Series round 13

1 Helio Castro-Neves	Reynard 2KI-Honda	83	1h44m59.019
2 Gil de Ferran	Reynard 2KI-Honda	83	1h45m03.444
3 Christian Fittipaldi	Lola B2K/00-Ford	83	1h45m04.931
4 Massimiliano Papis	Reynard 2KI-Ford	83	1h45m07.106
5 Kenny Brack	Reynard 2KI-Ford	83	1h45m07.880
6 Adrian Fernandez	Reynard 2KI-Ford	83	1h45m08.613

Winner's average speed: 107.110 mph. Pole position: de Ferran, 1m05.347. Fastest lap: Dario Franchitti (Reynard 2KI-Honda), 1m08.162

MOTOROLA 220

20 August 2000. Elkhart Lake. 55 laps of a 4.048-mile circuit = 222.640 miles. FedEx Championship Series round 14

1 Paul Tracy	Reynard 2KI-Honda	55	1h37m53.681
2 Adrian Fernandez	Reynard 2KI-Ford	55	1h38m01.131
3 Kenny Brack	Reynard 2KI-Ford	55	1h38m02.517
4 Roberto Moreno	Reynard 2KI-Ford	55	1h38m17.260
5 Jimmy Vasser	Lola B2K/00-Toyota	55	1h38m27.630
6 Memo Gidley	Reynard 2KI-Toyota	55	1h39m28.245

Winner's average speed: 136.457 mph. Pole position: Dario Franchitti (Reynard 2KI-Honda), 1m39.866. Fastest lap: Tracy, 1m42.334

MOLSON INDY VANCOUVER

3 September 2000. Vancouver. 90 laps of a 1.781-mile circuit = 160.290 miles. FedEx Championship Series round 15

1 Paul Tracy	Reynard 2KI-Honda	90	1h53m06.024
2 Dario Franchitti	Reynard 2KI-Honda	90	1h53m06.408
3 Adrian Fernandez	Reynard 2KI-Ford	90	1h53m25.055
4 Christian Fittipaldi	Lola B2K/00-Ford	90	1h53m25.638
5 Gil de Ferran	Reynard 2KI-Honda	90	1h53m26.137
6 Jimmy Vasser	Lola B2K/00-Toyota	90	1h53m26.583

Winner's average speed: 85.034 mph. Pole position: Franchitti, 1m00.405. Fastest lap: Juan Pablo Montoya (Lola B2K/00-Toyota), 1m01.538

HONDA GRAND PRIX OF MONTEREY

10 September 2000. Laguna Seca. 83 laps of a 2.238-mile circuit = 185.754 miles. FedEx Championship Series round 16

1 Helio Castro-Neves	Reynard 2KI-Honda	83	1h46m11.800
2 Gil de Ferran	Reynard 2KI-Honda	83	1h46m12.754
3 Dario Franchitti	Reynard 2KI-Honda	83	1h46m14.442
4 Bryan Herta	Reynard 2KI-Ford	83	1h46m16.219
5 Kenny Brack	Reynard 2KI-Ford	83	1h46m16.958
6 Juan Pablo Montoya	Lola B2K/00-Toyota	83	1h46m19.101

Winner's average speed: 104.949 mph. Pole position: Castro-Neves, 1m07.722. Fastest lap: de Ferran, 1m11.034

MOTOROLA 300

17 September 2000. St Louis. 236 laps of a 1.270-mile circuit = 299.720 miles. FedEx Championship Series round 17

1 Juan Pablo Montoya	Lola B2K/00-Toyota	236	1h55m38.003
2 Patrick Carpentier	Reynard 2KI-Ford	236	1h55m49.807
3 Roberto Moreno	Reynard 2KI-Ford	235	
4 Cristiano da Matta	Reynard 2KI-Toyota	235	
5 Oriol Servia	Reynard 2KI-Toyota	235	
6 Massimiliano Papis	Reynard 2KI-Ford	235	

Winner's average speed: 155.519 mph. Pole position: Montoya, 25.353s. Fastest lap: Carpentier, 26.770s

TEXACO/HAVOLINE GRAND PRIX OF HOUSTON

1 October 2000. Houston. 100 laps of a 1.527-mile circuit = 152.700 miles. FedEx Championship Series round 18

1 Jimmy Vasser	Lola B2K/00-Toyota	100	1h59m02.370
2 Juan Pablo Montoya	Lola B2K/00-Toyota	100	1h59m04.284
3 Gil de Ferran	Reynard 2KI-Honda	100	1h59m04.687
4 Paul Tracy	Reynard 2KI-Honda	100	1h59m05.099
5 Helio Castro-Neves	Reynard 2KI-Honda	100	1h59m10.709
6 Christian Fittipaldi	Lola B2K/00-Ford	100	1h59m17.689

Winner's average speed: 76.966 mph. Pole position: de Ferran, 58.757s. Fastest lap: Michael Andretti (Lola B2K/00-Ford), 1m00.219

HONDA INDY 300

15 October 2000. Surfers Paradise. 59 laps of a 2.795-mile circuit = 164.905 miles. FedEx Championship Series round 19

1 Adrian Fernandez	Reynard 2KI-Ford	59	2h01m14.605
2 Kenny Brack	Reynard 2KI-Ford	59	2h01m14.929
3 Jimmy Vasser	Lola B2K/00-Toyota	59	2h01m18.664
4 Cristiano da Matta	Reynard 2KI-Toyota	59	2h01m19.418

5	Patrick Carpentier	Reynard 2KI-Ford	59	2h01m19.836
6	Helio Castro-Neves	Reynard 2KI-Honda	59	2h01m24.945

Winner's average speed: 81.607 mph. Pole position: Juan Pablo Montoya (Lola B2K/00-Toyota), 1m31.722. Fastest lap: Vasser, 1m34.959

MARLBORO 500

29-30 October 2000. California Speedway. 250 laps of a 2.029-mile circuit = 507.250 miles. Race started on 29 October but stopped due to rain, restarted on the following day. FedEx Championship Series round 20

1	Christian Fittipaldi	Lola B2K/00-Ford	250	3h38m04.376
2	Roberto Moreno	Reynard 2KI-Ford	250	3h38m04.570
3	Gil de Ferran	Reynard 2KI-Ford	250	3h38m04.902
4	Casey Mears	Reynard 2KI-Ford	250	3h38m05.097
5	Adrian Fernandez	Reynard 2KI-Ford	250	3h38m05.521
6	Alexandre Tagliani	Reynard 2KI-Ford	248	accident

Winner's average speed: 139.563 mph. Pole position: de Ferran, 30.255s. Fastest lap: Helio Castro-Neves (Reynard 2KI-Honda), 31.414s

2000 FINAL CHAMPIONSHIP POSITIONS

1	Gil de Ferran	168	8	Michael Andretti	127
2	Adrian Fernandez	158	9	Juan Pablo Montoya	126
3	Roberto Moreno	147	10	Cristiano da Matta	112
4	Kenny Brack	135			
5	Paul Tracy	134			
6	Jimmy Vasser	131			
7	Helio Castro-Neves	129			

2001

TECATE TELMEX GRAND PRIX OF MONTERREY

11 April 2001. Fundidora Park. 78 laps of a 2.104-mile circuit = 164.112 miles. FedEx Championship Series round 1

1	Cristiano da Matta	Lola B01/00-Toyota	78	2h00m44.850
2	Gil de Ferran	Reynard 01I-Honda	78	2h00m46.832
3	Paul Tracy	Reynard 01I-Honda	78	2h00m47.652
4	Michael Andretti	Reynard 01I-Honda	78	2h00m49.781
5	Kenny Brack	Lola B01/00-Ford	78	2h00m50.261
6	Jimmy Vasser	Reynard 01I-Toyota	78	2h00m50.560

Winner's average speed: 81.548 mph. Pole position: Brack, 1m15.244. Fastest Lap: Dario Franchitti (Reynard 01I-Honda), 1m15.403

TOYOTA GRAND PRIX OF LONG BEACH

18 April 2001. Long Beach. 82 laps of a 1.968-mile circuit = 161.376 miles. FedEx Championship Series round 2

1	Helio Castro-Neves	Reynard 01I-Honda	82	1h52m17.779
2	Cristiano da Matta	Lola B01/00-Toyota	82	1h52m18.313
3	Gil de Ferran	Reynard 01I-Honda	82	1h52m19.566
4	Paul Tracy	Reynard 01I-Honda	82	1h52m20.214
5	Jimmy Vasser	Reynard 01I-Toyota	82	1h52m21.121
6	Dario Franchitti	Reynard 01I-Honda	82	1h52m22.634

Winner's average speed: 86.223 mph. Pole position: Castro-Neves, 1m08.556. Fastest Lap: Castro-Neves, 1m08.992

TEXAS 600

29 April 2001. Texas Motor Speedway. Race cancelled after qualifying due to driver discomfort on tight oval. FedEx Championship Series round 3

NO RACE
Pole position: Kenny Brack (Lola B01/00-Ford), 22.854s

LEHIGH VALLEY GRAND PRIX

6 May 2001. Nazareth. 225 laps of a 0.946-mile circuit = 212.850 miles. FedEx Championship Series round 4

1	Scott Dixon	Reynard 01I-Toyota	225	1h51m12.419

2	Kenny Brack	Lola B01/00-Ford	225	1h51m12.785
3	Paul Tracy	Reynard 01I-Honda	225	1h51m13.763
4	Jimmy Vasser	Reynard 01I-Toyota	225	1h51m14.163
5	Christian Fittipaldi	Lola B01/00-Toyota	225	1h51m16.644
6	Michael Andretti	Reynard 01I-Honda	225	1h51m18.820

Winner's average speed: 114.840 mph. Pole position: Bruno Junqueira (Lola B01/00-Toyota), 19.700s. Fastest Lap: Tony Kanaan (Reynard 01I-Honda), 21.170s

FIRESTONE FIREHAWK 500

19 May 2001. Motegi. 201 laps of a 1.549-mile circuit = 311.349 miles. FedEx Championship Series round 5

1	Kenny Brack	Lola B01/00-Ford	201	1h44m48.888
2	Helio Castro-Neves	Reynard 01I-Honda	201	1h44m52.538
3	Tony Kanaan	Reynard 01I-Honda	200	
4	Christian Fittipaldi	Lola B01/00-Toyota	200	
5	Jimmy Vasser	Reynard 01I-Toyota	200	
6	Massimiliano Papis	Lola B01/00-Ford	200	

Winner's average speed: 178.228 mph. Pole position: Castro-Neves, 25.849s. Fastest Lap: Alessandro Zanardi (Reynard 01I-Honda), 26.715s

MILLER LITE 225

3 June 2001. Milwaukee. 225 laps of a 1.032-mile circuit = 232.200 miles. FedEx Championship Series round 6

1	Kenny Brack	Lola B01/00-Ford	225	1h54m08.097
2	Michael Andretti	Reynard 01I-Honda	225	1h54m09.404
3	Scott Dixon	Reynard 01I-Toyota	225	1h54m11.098
4	Bruno Junqueira	Lola B01/00-Toyota	225	1h54m14.811
5	Adrian Fernandez	Reynard 01I-Honda	225	1h54m17.799
6	Tony Kanaan	Reynard 01I-Honda	225	1h54m18.388

Winner's average speed: 122.066 mph. Pole position: Brack - qualifying cancelled due to rain, race started in championship order. Fastest Lap: Dario Franchitti (Reynard 01I-Honda), 23.277s

TENNECO AUTOMOTIVE GRAND PRIX OF DETROIT

17 June 2001. Belle Isle. 72 laps of a 2.346-mile circuit = 168.912 miles. FedEx Championship Series round 7

1	Helio Castro-Neves	Reynard 01I-Honda	72	1h53m51.815
2	Dario Franchitti	Reynard 01I-Honda	72	1h53m52.512
3	Roberto Moreno	Reynard 01I-Toyota	72	1h53m54.706
4	Michael Andretti	Reynard 01I-Honda	72	1h53m55.201
5	Christian Fittipaldi	Lola B01/00-Toyota	72	1h54m05.280
6	Gil de Ferran	Reynard 01I-Honda	72	1h54m06.392

Winner's average speed: 89.008 mph. Pole position: Castro-Neves, 1m13.499. Fastest Lap: Andretti, 1m16.010

FREIGHTLINER GI JOE'S 200

24 June 2001. Portland. 76 laps of a 1.969-mile circuit = 149.644 miles. FedEx Championship Series round 8

1	Massimiliano Papis	Lola B01/00-Ford	76	2h00m20.836
2	Roberto Moreno	Reynard 01I-Toyota	76	2h00m22.308
3	Christian Fittipaldi	Lola B01/00-Toyota	76	2h00m24.448
4	Max Wilson	Lola B01/00-Ford	76	2h00m32.312
5	Patrick Carpentier	Reynard 01I-Ford	76	2h00m32.875
6	Dario Franchitti	Reynard 01I-Honda	76	2h00m33.407

Winner's average speed: 74.606 mph. Pole position: Papis, 57.785s. Fastest Lap: Papis, 1m12.611

MACONI GRAND PRIX OF CLEVELAND

1 July 2001. Cleveland. 100 laps of a 2.106-mile circuit = 210.600 miles. FedEx Championship Series round 9

1	Dario Franchitti	Reynard 01I-Honda	100	1h47m04.723
2	Memo Gidley	Lola B01/00-Toyota	100	1h47m05.028
3	Bryan Herta	Reynard 01I-Ford	100	1h47m12.620
4	Gil de Ferran	Reynard 01I-Honda	100	1h47m16.793
5	Jimmy Vasser	Reynard 01I-Toyota	100	1h47m26.021
6	Kenny Brack	Lola B01/00-Ford	100	1h47m26.784

Winner's average speed: 118.007 mph. Pole position: Mauricio Gugelmin

(Reynard 01I-Toyota), 57.356s. Fastest Lap: Roberto Moreno (Reynard 01I-Toyota), 58.779

MOLSON INDY TORONTO

15 July 2001. Toronto. 95 laps of a 1.755-mile circuit = 166.725 miles. FedEx Championship Series round 10

1 Michael Andretti	Reynard 01I-Honda	95	1h59m58.904
2 Alexandre Tagliani	Reynard 01I-Ford	95	2h00m01.645
3 Adrian Fernandez	Reynard 01I-Honda	95	2h00m03.299
4 Alessandro Zanardi	Reynard 01I-Honda	95	2h00m03.805
5 Scott Dixon	Reynard 01I-Toyota	95	2h00m04.508
6 Paul Tracy	Reynard 01I-Honda	95	2h00m05.797

Winner's average speed: 83.375 mph. Pole position: Gil de Ferran (Reynard 01I-Honda), 57.703s. Fastest Lap: Helio Castro-Neves (Reynard 01I-Honda), 59.028s

HARRAH'S 500

22 July 2001. Michigan. 250 laps of a 2.000-mile circuit = 500.000 miles. FedEx Championship Series round 11

1 Patrick Carpentier	Reynard 01I-Ford	250	2h54m55.757
2 Dario Franchitti	Reynard 01I-Honda	250	2h54m56.000
3 Michel Jourdain Jr	Lola B01/00-Ford	250	2h54m56.000
4 Cristiano da Matta	Lola B01/00-Toyota	250	2h54m56.202
5 Bryan Herta	Reynard 01I-Ford	250	2h54m56.273
6 Alexandre Tagliani	Reynard 01I-Ford	249	

Winner's average speed: 171.498 mph. Pole position: Kenny Brack (Lola B01/00-Ford), 31.330s - qualifying cancelled due to rain, decided by earlier practice session. Fastest Lap: Carpentier, 32.547s

TARGET GRAND PRIX OF CHICAGO

29 July 2001. Chicago. 225 laps of a 1.029-mile circuit = 231.525 miles. FedEx Championship Series round 12

1 Kenny Brack	Lola B01/00-Ford	225	1h45m12.835
2 Patrick Carpentier	Lola B01/00-Ford	225	1h45m17.315
3 Gil de Ferran	Reynard 01I-Honda	225	1h45m18.025
4 Scott Dixon	Reynard 01I-Toyota	225	1h45m18.398
5 Memo Gidley	Lola B01/00-Toyota	225	1h45m22.486
6 Alexandre Tagliani	Reynard 01I-Ford	225	1h45m25.872

Winner's average speed: 132.031 mph. Pole position: Tony Kanaan (Reynard 01I-Honda), 23.145s. Fastest Lap: Brack, 24.687s

MILLER LITE 200

12 August 2001. Mid-Ohio. 83 laps of a 2.258-mile circuit = 187.414 miles. FedEx Championship Series round 13

1 Helio Castro-Neves	Reynard 01I-Honda	83	1h44m54.931
2 Gil de Ferran	Reynard 01I-Honda	83	1h44m56.499
3 Patrick Carpentier	Reynard 01I-Ford	83	1h44m57.479
4 Paul Tracy	Reynard 01I-Honda	83	1h45m00.257
5 Tony Kanaan	Reynard 01I-Honda	83	1h45m01.086
6 Roberto Moreno	Reynard 01I-Toyota	83	1h45m01.634

Winner's average speed: 107.180 mph. Pole position: de Ferran, 1m05.442. Fastest Lap: Castro-Neves, 1m07.669

MOTOROLA 220

19 August 2001. Elkhart Lake. 45 laps of a 4.048-mile circuit = 182.160 miles. FedEx Championship Series round 14

1 Bruno Junqueira	Lola B01/00-Toyota	45	2h00m28.453
2 Michael Andretti	Reynard 01I-Honda	45	2h00m31.140
3 Adrian Fernandez	Reynard 01I-Honda	45	2h00m28.453
4 Scott Dixon	Reynard 01I-Toyota	45	2h00m52.875
5 Gil de Ferran	Reynard 01I-Honda	45	2h00m43.537
6 Cristiano da Matta	Lola B01/00-Toyota	45	2h00m44.387

Winner's average speed: 90.721 mph. Pole position: Kenny Brack (Lola B01/00-Ford), 2m03.531. Fastest Lap: Junqueira, 1m43.606

MOLSON INDY VANCOUVER

2 September 2001. Vancouver. 98 laps of a 1.781-mile circuit = 174.538 miles. FedEx Championship Series round 15

1 Roberto Moreno	Reynard 01I-Toyota	98	2h10m01.276
2 Gil de Ferran	Reynard 01I-Honda	98	2h10m05.963
3 Michael Andretti	Reynard 01I-Honda	98	2h10m08.247
4 Tony Kanaan	Reynard 01I-Honda	98	2h10m11.775
5 Oriol Servia	Lola B01/00-Ford	98	2h10m14.773
6 Michel Jourdain Jr	Lola B01/00-Ford	98	2h10m15.126

Winner's average speed: 80.543 mph. Pole position: Alexandre Tagliani (Reynard 01I-Ford), 1m00.872. Fastest Lap: Helio Castro-Neves (Reynard 01I-Honda), 1m01.545

AMERICAN MEMORIAL 500

15 September 2001. Lausitzring. 154 laps of a 2.023-mile circuit = 311.542 miles. FedEx Championship Series round 16

1 Kenny Brack	Lola B01/00-Ford	154	2h00m20.940
2 Massimiliano Papis	Lola B01/00-Ford	154	2h00m21.094
3 Patrick Carpentier	Reynard 01I-Ford	154	2h00m23.744
4 Michael Andretti	Reynard 01I-Honda	154	2h00m25.639
5 Oriol Servia	Lola B01/00-Ford	154	2h00m26.165
6 Toranosuke Takagi	Reynard 01I-Toyota	154	2h00m27.350

Winner's average speed: 155.319 mph. Pole position: Gil de Ferran (Reynard 01I-Honda) - qualifying cancelled due to rain, started in championship order. Fastest Lap: Tony Kanaan (Reynard 01I-Honda), 34.747s

ROCKINGHAM 500

22 September 2001. Rockingham. 140 laps of a 1.479-mile circuit = 207.060 miles. FedEx Championship Series round 17

1 Gil de Ferran	Reynard 01I-Honda	140	1h20m59.050
2 Kenny Brack	Lola B01/00-Ford	140	1h20m59.684
3 Cristiano da Matta	Lola B01/00-Toyota	140	1h21m13.713
4*Helio Castro-Neves	Reynard 01I-Honda	140	1h21m15.385
5 Michael Andretti	Reynard 01I-Honda	140	1h21m16.106
6 Paul Tracy	Reynard 01I-Honda	140	1h21m17.969

*Castro-Neves penalised 1 position. Winner's average speed: 153.408 mph. Pole position: Brack - qualifying cancelled due to damp track, started in championship order. Fastest Lap: Patrick Carpentier (Reynard 01I-Ford), 25.251s

TEXACO/HAVOLINE GRAND PRIX OF HOUSTON

7 October 2001. Houston. 100 laps of a 1.527-mile circuit = 152.700 miles. FedEx Championship Series round 18

1 Gil de Ferran	Reynard 01I-Honda	100	1h54m42.315
2 Dario Franchitti	Reynard 01I-Honda	100	1h54m45.766
3 Memo Gidley	Lola B01/00-Toyota	100	1h55m01.183
4 Toranosuke Takagi	Reynard 01I-Toyota	100	1h55m03.230
5 Helio Castro-Neves	Reynard 01I-Honda	100	1h55m04.006
6 Cristiano da Matta	Lola B01/00-Toyota	100	1h55m05.438

Winner's average speed: 79.874 mph. Pole position: de Ferran, 59.421s. Fastest Lap: Jimmy Vasser (Reynard 01I-Toyota), 1m00.928

HONDA GRAND PRIX OF MONTEREY

14 October 2001. Laguna Seca. 76 laps of a 2.238-mile circuit = 170.088 miles. FedEx Championship Series round 19

1 Massimiliano Papis	Lola B01/00-Ford	76	2h00m10.589
2 Memo Gidley	Lola B01/00-Toyota	76	2h00m11.383
3 Gil de Ferran	Reynard 01I-Honda	76	2h00m12.027
4 Scott Dixon	Reynard 01I-Toyota	76	2h00m12.390
5 Jimmy Vasser	Reynard 01I-Toyota	76	2h00m13.058
6 Helio Castro-Neves	Reynard 01I-Honda	76	2h00m15.022

Winner's average speed: 84.919 mph. Pole position: de Ferran, 1m08.596. Fastest Lap: Castro-Neves, 1m11.500

HONDA INDY 300

28 October 2001. Surfers Paradise. 65 laps of a 2.795-mile circuit = 181.675 miles. FedEx Championship Series round 20

1 Cristiano da Matta	Lola B01/00-Toyota	65	1h51m47.260
2 Michael Andretti	Reynard 01I-Honda	65	1h51m53.046
3 Alexandre Tagliani	Reynard 01I-Ford	65	1h51m54.786
4 Gil de Ferran	Reynard 01I-Honda	65	1h52m08.196

| 5 | Kenny Brack | Lola B01/00-Ford | 65 | 1h52m09.834 |
| 6 | Jimmy Vasser | Reynard 01I-Toyota | 65 | 1h52m11.966 |

Winner's average speed: 97.511 mph. Pole position: Roberto Moreno (Reynard 01I-Toyota), 1m32.095. Fastest Lap: Vasser, 1m34.113

MARLBORO 500

4 November 2001. California Speedway. 220 laps of a 2.029-mile circuit = 446.380 miles. FedEx Championship Series round 21

1	Cristiano da Matta	Lola B01/00-Toyota	220	2h59m39.716
2	Massimiliano Papis	Lola B01/00-Ford	220	2h59m39.839
3	Alexandre Tagliani	Reynard 01I-Ford	220	2h59m40.208
4	Bruno Junqueira	Lola B01/00-Toyota	220	2h59m40.638
5	Tony Kanaan	Reynard 01I-Honda	220	2h59m40.902
6	Gil de Ferran	Reynard 01I-Honda	220	2h59m42.847

Winner's average speed: 149.073 mph. Pole position: Tagliani, 31.935s. Fastest Lap: Papis, 32.347

2001 FINAL CHAMPIONSHIP POSITIONS

1	Gil de Ferran	199	7	Dario Franchitti	105
2	Kenny Brack	163	8	Scott Dixon	98
3	Michael Andretti	147	9	Tony Kanaan	93
4	Helio Castro-Neves	141	10	Patrick Carpentier	91
5	Cristiano da Matta	140			
6	Massimiliano Papis	107			

2002

TECATE/TELMEX GRAND PRIX OF MONTERREY

10 March 2002. Fundidora Park. 85 laps of a 2.104-mile circuit = 178.840 miles. FedEx Championship Series round 1

1	Cristiano da Matta	Lola B2/00-Toyota	85	1h58m30.642
2	Dario Franchitti	Reynard 02I-Honda	85	1h58m32.321
3	Christian Fittipaldi	Lola B2/00-Toyota	85	1h58m33.886
4	Michel Jourdain Jr	Lola B2/00-Ford	85	1h58m34.427
5	Alexandre Tagliani	Reynard 02I-Ford	85	1h58m37.903
6	Scott Dixon	Lola B2/00-Toyota	85	1h58m40.069

Winner's average speed: 90.544 mph. Pole position: Adrian Fernandez (Lola B2/00-Honda), 1m18.929. Fastest Lap: da Matta, 1m15.386

TOYOTA GRAND PRIX OF LONG BEACH

14 April 2002. Long Beach. 90 laps of a 1.968-mile circuit = 177.120 miles. FedEx Championship Series round 2

1	Michael Andretti	Reynard 02I-Honda	90	2h02m14.542
2	Jimmy Vasser	Lola B2/00-Ford	90	2h02m15.008
3	Massimiliano Papis	Lola B2/00-Ford	90	2h02m19.240
4	Kenny Brack	Lola B2/00-Toyota	90	2h02m19.792
5	Michel Jourdain Jr	Lola B2/00-Ford	90	2h02m22.030
6	Toranosuke Takagi	Reynard 02I-Toyota	90	2h02m22.872

Winner's average speed: 86.935 mph. Pole position: Vasser, 1m07.742. Fastest Lap: Bruno Junqueira (Lola B2/00-Toyota), 1m08.981

BRIDGESTONE POTENZA 500

27 April 2002. Motegi. 201 laps of a 1.549-mile circuit = 311.349 miles. FedEx Championship Series round 3

1	Bruno Junqueira	Lola B2/00-Toyota	201	2h00m05.882
2	Alexandre Tagliani	Reynard 02I-Ford	201	2h00m18.164
3	Dario Franchitti	Reynard 02I-Honda	200	
4	Patrick Carpentier	Reynard 02I-Ford	199	
5	Michel Jourdain Jr	Lola B2/00-Ford	199	
6	Oriol Servia	Lola B2/00-Toyota	199	

Winner's average speed: 155.547 mph. Pole position: Junqueira, 25.907s. Fastest Lap: Tony Kanaan (Lola B2/00-Honda), 26.425s

MILLER LITE 250

2 June 2002. Milwaukee. 250 laps of a 1.032-mile circuit = 258.000 miles. FedEx Championship Series round 4

1	Paul Tracy	Lola B2/00-Honda	250	1h59m27.602
2	Adrian Fernandez	Lola B2/00-Honda	250	1h59m28.240
3	Massimiliano Papis	Lola B2/00-Ford	250	1h59m29.321
4	Christian Fittipaldi	Lola B2/00-Toyota	250	1h59m35.962
5	Michel Jourdain Jr	Lola B2/00-Toyota	250	1h59m45.618
6	Scott Dixon	Lola B2/00-Toyota	250	1h59m45.830

Winner's average speed: 129.583 mph. Pole position: Fernandez, 22.176s. Fastest Lap: Kenny Brack (Lola B2/00-Toyota), 22.998s

BRIDGESTONE GRAND PRIX OF MONTEREY

9 June 2002. Laguna Seca. 87 laps of a 2.238-mile circuit = 194.706 miles. FedEx Championship Series round 5

1	Cristiano da Matta	Lola B2/00-Toyota	87	1h55m28.745
2	Christian Fittipaldi	Lola B2/00-Toyota	87	1h55m47.832
3	Kenny Brack	Lola B2/00-Toyota	87	1h55m48.155
4	Bruno Junqueira	Lola B2/00-Toyota	87	1h56m03.000
5	Patrick Carpentier	Reynard 02I-Ford	87	1h56m03.840
6	Scott Dixon	Lola B2/00-Toyota	87	1h56m40.701

Winner's average speed: 101.164 mph. Pole position: da Matta, 1m09.473. Fastest Lap: da Matta, 1m11.369

GI JOE'S 200

16 June 2002. Portland. 110 laps of a 1.969-mile circuit = 216.590 miles. FedEx Championship Series round 6

1	Cristiano da Matta	Lola B2/00-Toyota	110	2h03m19.113
2	Bruno Junqueira	Lola B2/00-Toyota	110	2h03m19.738
3	Dario Franchitti	Lola B2/00-Honda	110	2h03m26.874
4	Townsend Bell	Reynard 02I-Toyota	110	2h03m27.568
5	Patrick Carpentier	Reynard 02I-Ford	110	2h03m40.588
6	Michel Jourdain Jr	Lola B2/00-Ford	110	2h03m54.104

Winner's average speed: 105.381 mph. Pole position: da Matta, 58.679s. Fastest Lap: Junqueira, 1m00.801

CART GRAND PRIX OF CHICAGO

30 June 2002. Chicago. 250 laps of a 1.029-mile circuit = 257.250 miles. FedEx Championship Series round 7

1	Cristiano da Matta	Lola B2/00-Toyota	250	2h07m00.698
2	Bruno Junqueira	Lola B2/00-Toyota	250	2h07m01.337
3	Dario Franchitti	Lola B2/00-Honda	250	2h07m04.142
4	Toranosuke Takagi	Reynard 02I-Toyota	250	2h07m12.690
5	Shinji Nakano	Lola B2/00-Honda	250	2h07m13.156
6	Scott Dixon	Lola B2/00-Toyota	250	2h07m13.668

Winner's average speed: 121.524 mph. Pole position: Franchitti, 23.428s. Fastest Lap: Paul Tracy (Lola B2/00-Honda), 24.192s

MOLSON INDY TORONTO

7 July 2002. Toronto. 112 laps of a 1.755-mile circuit = 196.560 miles. FedEx Championship Series round 8

1	Cristiano da Matta	Lola B2/00-Toyota	112	2h06m19.372
2	Kenny Brack	Lola B2/00-Toyota	112	2h06m23.770
3	Christian Fittipaldi	Lola B2/00-Toyota	112	2h06m30.729
4	Shinji Nakano	Lola B2/00-Honda	112	2h06m31.847
5	Scott Dixon	Lola B2/00-Toyota	112	2h06m33.474
6	Jimmy Vasser	Lola B2/00-Ford	112	2h06m43.314

Winner's average speed: 93.361 mph. Pole position: da Matta, 58.135s. Fastest Lap: da Matta, 58.806s

MARCONI GRAND PRIX OF CLEVELAND

14 July 2002. Cleveland. 115 laps of a 2.106-mile circuit = 242.190 miles. FedEx Championship Series round 9

1	Patrick Carpentier	Reynard 02I-Ford	115	2h00m05.785
2	Michael Andretti	Lola B2/00-Honda	115	2h00m22.844
3	Paul Tracy	Lola B2/00-Honda	115	2h00m34.080
4	Kenny Brack	Lola B2/00-Toyota	115	2h00m38.311
5	Alexandre Tagliani	Reynard 02I-Ford	115	2h00m42.937
6	Jimmy Vasser	Lola B2/00-Ford	115	2h00m56.389

Winner's average speed: 120.998 mph. Pole position: Cristiano da Matta (Lola B2/00-Toyota), 57.040s. Fastest Lap: Tracy, 58.473s

CART

MOLSON INDY VANCOUVER

28 July 2002. Vancouver. 100 laps of a 1.781-mile circuit = 178.100 miles. FedEx Championship Series round 10

1	Dario Franchitti	Lola B2/00-Honda	100	2h16m05.063
2	Paul Tracy	Lola B2/00-Honda	100	2h16m06.302
3	Tony Kanaan	Lola B2/00-Honda	100	2h16m07.423
4	Michel Jourdain Jr	Lola B2/00-Ford	100	2h16m07.772
5	Patrick Carpentier	Reynard 02I-Ford	100	2h16m08.382
6	Michael Andretti	Lola B2/00-Honda	94	

Winner's average speed: 78.525 mph. Pole position: Cristiano da Matta (Lola B2/00-Toyota), 1m00.339. Fastest Lap: da Matta, 1m01.633

CART GRAND PRIX OF MID-OHIO

11 August 2002. Mid-Ohio. 92 laps of a 2.258-mile circuit = 207.736 miles. FedEx Championship Series round 11

1	Patrick Carpentier	Reynard 02I-Ford	92	1h56m17.573
2	Christian Fittipaldi	Lola B2/00-Toyota	92	1h56m20.786
3	Michael Andretti	Lola B2/00-Honda	92	1h56m22.306
4	Bruno Junqueira	Lola B2/00-Toyota	92	1h56m23.306
5	Scott Dixon	Lola B2/00-Toyota	92	1h56m26.159
6	Kenny Brack	Lola B2/00-Toyota	92	1h56m33.086

Winner's average speed: 107.179 mph. Pole position: Carpentier, 1m06.128. Fastest Lap: Cristiano da Matta (Lola B2/00-Toyota), 1m07.966

MOTOROLA 220

18 August 2002. Elkhart Lake. 60 laps of a 4.048-mile circuit = 242.880 miles. FedEx Championship Series round 12

1	Cristiano da Matta	Lola B2/00-Toyota	60	1h56m43.030
2	Alexandre Tagliani	Reynard 02I-Ford	60	1h56m43.835
3	Bruno Junqueira	Lola B2/00-Toyota	60	1h56m44.560
4	Tony Kanaan	Lola B2/00-Honda	60	1h56m50.177
5	Jimmy Vasser	Lola B2/00-Ford	60	1h56m54.519
6	Christian Fittipaldi	Lola B2/00-Toyota	60	1h56m55.421

Winner's average speed: 124.856 mph. Pole position: Junqueira, 1m42.151. Fastest Lap: Junqueira, 1m43.792

MOLSON INDY MONTREAL

25 August 2002. Montreal. 80 laps of a 2.703-mile circuit = 216.240 miles. FedEx Championship Series round 13

1	Dario Franchitti	Lola B2/00-Honda	80	1h59m40.938
2	Cristiano da Matta	Lola B2/00-Toyota	80	1h59m43.526
3	Tony Kanaan	Lola B2/00-Honda	80	1h59m45.550
4	Paul Tracy	Lola B2/00-Honda	80	1h59m47.204
5	Jimmy Vasser	Lola B2/00-Ford	80	1h59m47.746
6	Michel Jourdain Jr	Lola B2/00-Ford	80	1h59m49.042

Winner's average speed: 108.407 mph. Pole position: da Matta, 1m18.959. Fastest Lap: Franchitti, 1m20.238

SHELL GRAND PRIX OF DENVER

1 September 2002. Denver. 100 laps of a 1.647-mile circuit = 164.700 miles. FedEx Championship Series round 14

1	Bruno Junqueira	Lola B2/00-Toyota	100	1h49m22.547
2	Scott Dixon	Lola B2/00-Toyota	100	1h49m22.829
3	Cristiano da Matta	Lola B2/00-Toyota	100	1h49m30.738
4	Adrian Fernandez	Lola B2/00-Honda	100	1h49m34.458
5	Christian Fittipaldi	Lola B2/00-Toyota	100	1h49m35.109
6	Tony Kanaan	Lola B2/00-Honda	100	1h49m35.835

Winner's average speed: 90.349 mph. Pole position: Junqueira, 1m01.703. Fastest Lap: Kenny Brack (Lola B2/00-Toyota), 1m01.648

SURE FOR MEN ROCKINGHAM 500

14 September 2002. Rockingham. 211 laps of a 1.479-mile circuit = 312.069 miles. FedEx Championship Series round 15

1	Dario Franchitti	Lola B2/00-Honda	211	1h58m44.754
2	Cristiano da Matta	Lola B2/00-Toyota	211	1h58m45.740
3	Patrick Carpentier	Reynard 02I-Ford	211	1h58m47.539
4	Oriol Servia	Reynard 02I-Toyota	211	1h58m48.511
5	Bruno Junqueira	Lola B2/00-Toyota	211	1h58m49.035
6	Toranosuke Takagi	Reynard 02I-Toyota	211	1h58m49.532

Winner's average speed: 157.682 mph. Pole position: Kenny Brack (Lola B2/00-Toyota), 24.908s. Fastest Lap: Jimmy Vasser (Lola B2/00-Ford), 25.217s

GRAND PRIX AMERICAS

6 October 2002. Bayfront Park, Miami. 105 laps of a 1.387-mile circuit = 145.635 miles. FedEx Championship Series round 16

1	Cristiano da Matta	Lola B2/00-Toyota	105	2h07m09.003
2	Christian Fittipaldi	Lola B2/00-Toyota	105	2h07m09.737
3	Jimmy Vasser	Lola B2/00-Ford	105	2h07m10.346
4	Alexandre Tagliani	Reynard 02I-Ford	105	2h07m11.600
5	Bruno Junqueira	Lola B2/00-Toyota	105	2h07m24.551
6	Michel Jourdain Jr	Lola B2/00-Toyota	104	

Winner's average speed: 68.723 mph. Pole position: Tony Kanaan (Lola B2/00-Honda), 1m01.264. Fastest Lap: Fittipaldi, 1m02.906

HONDA INDY 300

27 October 2002. Surfers Paradise. 40 laps of a 2.795-mile circuit = 111.800 miles. Race rescheduled for 70 laps but stopped due to rain. FedEx Championship Series round 17

1	Mario Dominguez	Lola B2/00-Ford	40	2h00m06.524
2	Patrick Carpentier	Reynard 02I-Ford	40	2h00m08.701
3	Paul Tracy	Lola B2/00-Honda	40	2h00m09.073
4	Kenny Brack	Lola B2/00-Toyota	40	2h00m09.271
5	Tony Kanaan	Lola B2/00-Honda	40	2h00m11.318
6	Alexandre Tagliani	Reynard 02I-Ford	40	2h00m14.352

Winner's average speed: 55.849 mph. Pole position: Cristiano da Matta (Lola B2/00-Toyota), 1m30.204. Fastest Lap: da Matta, 1m56.457

THE 500

3 November 2002. California Speedway. 250 laps of a 2.029-mile circuit = 507.250 miles. FedEx Championship Series round 18

1	Jimmy Vasser	Lola B2/00-Ford	250	2h33m42.977
2	Michael Andretti	Lola B2/00-Honda	250	2h33m43.377
3	Patrick Carpentier	Reynard 02I-Ford	250	2h33m44.771
4	Tony Kanaan	Lola B2/00-Honda	250	2h33m45.479
5	Oriol Servia	Reynard 02I-Toyota	249	
6	Scott Dixon	Lola B2/00-Toyota	249	

Winner's average speed: 197.995 mph. Pole position: Kanaan, 31.483s. Fastest Lap: Servia, 31.469s

GRAN PREMIO TELMEX/GIGANTE DE MEXICO

17 November 2002. Mexico City. 73 laps of a 2.786-mile circuit = 203.378 miles. FedEx Championship Series round 19

1	Kenny Brack	Lola B2/00-Toyota	73	1h56m48.475
2	Cristiano da Matta	Lola B2/00-Toyota	73	1h56m52.462
3	Bruno Junqueira	Lola B2/00-Toyota	73	1h56m53.548
4	Patrick Carpentier	Reynard 02I-Ford	73	1h56m59.317
5	Dario Franchitti	Lola B2/00-Honda	73	1h57m01.023
6	Toranosuke Takagi	Reynard 02I-Toyota	73	1h57m05.237

Winner's average speed: 104.468 mph. Pole position: Junqueira, 1m25.941. Fastest Lap: Shinji Nakano (Lola B2/00-Honda), 1m27.248

2002 FINAL CHAMPIONSHIP POSITIONS

1	Cristiano da Matta	237	7	Kenny Brack	114
2	Bruno Junqueira	164	8	Alexandre Tagliani	111
3	Patrick Carpentier	157	9	Michael Andretti	110
4	Dario Franchitti	148	10	Michel Jourdain jr	105
5	Christian Fittipaldi	122			
6	Jimmy Vasser	114			

Top: 1997 Two-time Champion Alessandro Zanardi at Laguna Seca's Corkscrew turn. **Bottom: 1988** Father and son champions Michael and Mario Andretti.

Drivers' Records

STARTS

Michael Andretti	309	Gary Bettenhausen	45	Bill Whittington	15
Al Unser jr	273	Parker Johnstone	45	Max Wilson	15
Bobby Rahal	264	Steve Chassey	44	Wally Dallenbach	14
Mario Andretti	208	Ed Pimm	42	Al Holbert	14
Emerson Fittipaldi	195	John Jones	41	Steve Krisiloff	14
Paul Tracy	191	Marco Greco	40	John Mahler	14
Jimmy Vasser	186	Juan Pablo Montoya	40	Jon Beekhuis	13
Rick Mears	179	Gualter Salles	40	Stan Fox	13
Raul Boesel	172	Scott Dixon	39	Greg Leffler	13
Danny Sullivan	170	Bruno Junqueira	39	Jim McElreath	13
Adrian Fernandez	161	Toranosuke Takagi	39	Bill Vukovich Jr	13
Scott Brayton	147	Mike Mosley	37	Robbie Buhl	12
Mauricio Gugelmin	147	Juan Manuel Fangio II	36	Larry Dickson	12
Scott Pruett	145	Memo Gidley	36	Sheldon Kinser	12
Arie Luyendyk	142	Bobby Unser	36	Tero Palmroth	12
Christian Fittipaldi	134	Jacques Villeneuve	36	Roger Rager	12
Gil de Ferran	129	Dennis Vitolo	36	George Snider	12
Tom Sneva	127	Herm Johnson	35	Townsend Bell	11
Bryan Herta	120	Alex Barron	34	Bruno Giacomelli	11
Michel Jourdain Jr	120	Dale Coyne	34	Olivier Grouillard	11
Teo Fabi	118	Pete Halsmer	33	Jeff Krosnoff	11
Roberto Guerrero	118	Dennis Firestone	32	Eddie Lawson	11
Pancho Carter	116	Jacques Villeneuve	32	Bob Lazier	11
Kevin Cogan	116	Luiz Garcia Jr	31	Jan Magnussen	11
Hiro Matsushita	116	Spike Gehlhausen	31	Andrea Montermini	11
Dario Franchitti	114	Nigel Mansell	31	Jerry Sneva	11
Al Unser	113	Ludwig Heimrath Jr	30	Lyn St James	11
Patrick Carpentier	108	Jerry Karl	30	Desire Wilson	11
Robby Gordon	108	Roger Mears	29	Phil Caliva	10
Johnny Rutherford	107	Arnd Meier	29	Chet Fillip	10
Massimiliano Papis	106	John Paul Jr	29	Jan Lammers	10
Roberto Moreno	101	Chip Ganassi	27	Salt Walther	10
Scott Goodyear	97	Alessandro Zampedri	27	Michael Chandler	9
Tony Bettenhausen Jr	96	Dick Ferguson	26	Billy Engelhart	9
Tony Kanaan	93	Ted Prappas	26	Tom Frantz	9
Josele Garza	88	Mark Smith	26	Michael Greenfield	9
Geoff Brabham	86	Tom Bagley	25	Naoki Hattori	9
AJ Foyt Jr	85	Fabrizio Barbazza	25	Lee Kunzman	9
Eddie Cheever	82	Ross Bentley	25	Rick Miaskiewicz	9
Mark Blundell	81	Johnny Parsons Jr	25	Don Whittington	9
Randy Lewis	81	Bill Tempero	25	Norberto Fontana	8
Helio Castro-Neves	79	Eric Bachelart	24	Takuya Kurosawa	8
Cristiano da Matta	79	Guido Dacco	23	Tim Richmond	8
Dick Simon	78	Phil Krueger	23	Rich Vogler	8
John Andretti	73	Rocky Moran	23	David Kudrave	7
Stefan Johansson	73	Tarso Marques	22	Steve Saleen	7
Gordon Johncock	73	Jeff Andretti	21	Gordon Smiley	7
Howdy Holmes	72	Dean Hall	21	Bill Vukovich III	7
Greg Moore	72	Eliseo Salazar	20	Fulvio Ballabio	6
Andre Ribeiro	68	Brian Till	20	Pat Bedard	6
Derek Daly	66	Tom Bigelow	19	Tom Gloy	6
Alessandro Zanardi	66	Mario Dominguez	19	Shigeaki Hattori	6
Kenny Brack	59	Chris Kneifel	19	Cliff Hucul	6
Richie Hearn	59	JJ Lehto	19	Al Loquasto	6
Alexandre Tagliani	59	Vern Schuppan	19	John Martin	6
PJ Jones	58	Jim Crawford	18	Chip Mead	6
Bill Alsup	56	Christian Danner	18	Nicolas Minassian	6
Shinji Nakano	56	Bernard Jourdain	18	John Morton	6
Dominic Dobson	55	Randy Lanier	18	Rick Muther	6
Buddy Lazier	55	Jeff MacPherson	18	Ian Ashley	5
Michael Groff	54	Joe Saldana	18	Claude Bourbonnais	5
Oriol Servia	53	Scott Sharp	18	Franck Freon	5
Danny Ongais	52	Carlos Guerrero	17	Hurley Haywood	5
Jeff Wood	49	Scott Atchison	16	Casey Mears	5
Didier Theys	47	Larry Cannon	16	Hector Rebaque	5
Willy T Ribbs	46	Davy Jones	16	Larry Rice	5

Records

STARTS (cont.)

Chip Robinson	5	Steve Bren	2	Andre Lotterer	1
Vinicio Salmi	5	Gregor Foitek	2	Harry MacDonald	1
Domenico Schiattarella	5	Robbie Groff	2	Darren Manning	1
Johnny Unser	5	Ken Hamilton	2	Roger McCluskey	1
Brian Bonner	4	Ken Johnson	2	Jerry Miller	1
Jim Buick	4	Michel Jourdain	2	Daniel Muniz	1
Ross Cheever	4	Tom Klausler	2	Drake Olson	1
Wally Dallenbach Jr	4	Michael Krumm	2	Tom Phillips	1
Ross Davis	4	Giovanni Lavaggi	2	Teddy Pilette	1
Mark Dismore	4	Graham McRae	2	Nelson Piquet	1
Corrado Fabi	4	Mike Thackwell	2	Eldon Rasmussen	1
Jean-Pierre Frey	4	John Wood	2	Gonzalo Rodriguez	1
Paul Jasper	4	Kenneth Acheson	1	Jose Romero	1
Mike Nish	4	Mauro Baldi	1	Franco Scapini	1
John Richards	4	Juan Carlos Bolanos	1	Bill Scott	1
Michael Roe	4	Jason Bright	1	Chico Serra	1
Vincenzo Sospiri	4	Andrea Chiesa	1	Ron Shuman	1
Phil Threshie	4	Chuck Ciprich	1	Jan Sneva	1
Fredrik Ekblom	3	Luis Diaz	1	Joseph Sposato	1
Bob Frey	3	Cor Euser	1	Hubert Stromberger	1
Jim Hickman	3	Philippe Gache	1	Tony de Tommaso	1
Rupert Keegan	3	Bertrand Gachot	1	Bob Ward	1
Peter Kuhn	3	Stephan Gregoire	1	Frank Weiss	1
Enrique Mansilla	3	Janet Guthrie	1	**Note:** A driver is credited as starting a
Jovy Marcelo	3	Bob Harkey	1	race if they take the rolling start, or subse-
Nicola Marozzo	3	Scott Harrington	1	quently makes a delayed start from the
Hideshi Matsuda	3	Billie Harvey	1	pits. If a driver retires before the green flag
Charles Nearburg	3	Doug Heveron	1	they are deemed not to have started. Some
Sammy Swindell	3	Jeff Heywood	1	official records have credited such non-
James Weaver	3	Jay Hill	1	starters as having taken the green flag,
Gary Brabham	2	Alan Jones	1	leading to some inconsistencies in records
Darin Brassfield	2	Jorge Koechlin	1	

YOUNGEST DRIVERS TO START A CART RACE

19 years 224 days	Michel Jourdain Jr	1996 Long Beach
20 years 132 days	Al Unser Jr	1982 Riverside
20 years 262 days	Scott Dixon	2001 Monterrey
20 years 316 days	Greg Moore	1996 Homestead
21 years 2 days	Andre Lotterer	2002 Mexico City

OLDEST DRIVERS TO START A CART RACE

57 years 129 days	AJ Foyt Jr	1992 Indianapolis 500
55 years 292 days	Gordon Johncock	1992 Indianapolis 500
55 years 177 days	Jim McElreath	1983 Pocono 500
55 years 4 days	Dick Simon	1988 Nazareth
54 years 225 days	Mario Andretti	1994 Laguna Seca

WINS

Michael Andretti	42	Gil de Ferran	7	Robby Gordon	2
Al Unser Jr	31	Helio Castro-Neves	6	Roberto Guerrero	2
Rick Mears	26	Kenny Brack	5	Bryan Herta	2
Bobby Rahal	24	Teo Fabi	5	Roberto Moreno	2
Emerson Fittipaldi	22	Gordon Johncock	5	Scott Pruett	2
Mario Andretti	19	Nigel Mansell	5	John Andretti	1
Paul Tracy	19	Greg Moore	5	Pancho Carter	1
Danny Sullivan	17	Jacques Villeneuve	5	Kevin Cogan	1
Alessandro Zanardi	15	Al Unser	4	Scott Dixon	1
Cristiano da Matta	11	Mark Blundell	3	Mario Dominguez	1
Dario Franchitti	10	Patrick Carpentier	3	Mauricio Gugelmin	1
Juan Pablo Montoya	10	Bruno Junqueira	3	Tony Kanaan	1
Johnny Rutherford	10	Arie Luyendyk	3	Mike Mosley	1
Tom Sneva	10	Massimiliano Papis	3	John Paul Jr	1
Bobby Unser	10	Andre Ribeiro	3	Hector Rebaque	1
Jimmy Vasser	10	Christian Fittipaldi	2	Jacques Villeneuve Sr	1
Adrian Fernandez	7	Scott Goodyear	2		

CART

YOUNGEST DRIVERS TO WIN A CART RACE

20 years 287 days	Scott Dixon	2001 Nazareth
22 years 41 days	Greg Moore	1997 Milwaukee
22 years 60 days	Al Unser Jr	1984 Portland
23 years 148 days	John Paul Jr	1983 Michigan 500
23 years 155 days	Jacques Villeneuve	1994 Elkhart Lake

OLDEST DRIVERS TO WIN A CART RACE

53 years 36 days	Mario Andretti	1993 Phoenix
48 years 143 days	Johnny Rutherford	1986 Michigan 500
48 years 132 days	Emerson Fittipaldi	1995 Nazareth
47 years 360 days	Al Unser Sr	1987 Indianapolis 500
46 years 253 days	Gordon Johncock	1983 Atlanta

POLE POSITIONS

Rick Mears	39	Helio Castro-Neves	7	Adrian Fernandez	3
Michael Andretti	32	Bryan Herta	7	Alexandre Tagliani	3
Mario Andretti	29	Cristiano da Matta	7	Kevin Cogan	2
Danny Sullivan	19	Al Unser Jr	7	Scott Goodyear	2
Emerson Fittipaldi	17	Roberto Guerrero	6	Roberto Moreno	2
Bobby Rahal	17	Jacques Villeneuve	6	Massimiliano Papis	2
Gil de Ferran	16	Gordon Johncock	5	Andre Ribeiro	2
Juan Pablo Montoya	14	Bruno Junqueira	5	Geoff Brabham	1
Bobby Unser	14	Greg Moore	5	Scott Brayton	1
Paul Tracy	13	Scott Pruett	5	Pancho Carter	1
Dario Franchitti	11	Robby Gordon	4	Christian Fittipaldi	1
Teo Fabi	10	Mauricio Gugelmin	4	Parker Johnstone	1
Nigel Mansell	10	Tony Kanaan	4	Arie Luyendyk	1
Alessandro Zanardi	10	Tom Sneva	4	John Paul Jr	1
Johnny Rutherford	8	Al Unser	4	Jacques Villeneuve Sr	1
Jimmy Vasser	8	Raul Boesel	3		
Kenny Brack	7	Patrick Carpentier	3		

LAPS IN THE LEAD

Michael Andretti	6590	Jacques Villeneuve	302	Pete Halsmer	15
Rick Mears	3281	Alexandre Tagliani	298	Salt Walther	13
Al Unser Jr	3134	Patrick Carpentier	272	Casey Mears	12
Bobby Rahal	3105	Roberto Moreno	265	Larry Dickson	10
Mario Andretti	3069	Kevin Cogan	241	Shinji Nakano	10
Paul Tracy	2727	Christian Fittipaldi	238	Jim Crawford	8
Emerson Fittipaldi	2625	Bruno Junqueira	233	Don Whittington	8
Juan Pablo Montoya	1774	Scott Goodyear	226	John Andretti	7
Alessandro Zanardi	1467	Pancho Carter	223	Takuya Kurosawa	7
Danny Sullivan	1459	Scott Pruett	152	Bill Alsup	6
Tom Sneva	1426	Memo Gidley	148	Tony Bettenhausen Jr	6
Gil de Ferran	1283	Mark Blundell	141	Derek Daly	6
Al Unser	1264	Robby Gordon	138	Stefan Johansson	6
Bobby Unser	1209	Mike Mosley	117	JJ Lehto	6
Kenny Brack	1040	AJ Foyt Jr	110	Mario Dominguez	5
Johnny Rutherford	1022	John Paul Jr	109	Jan Lammers	5
Helio Castro-Neves	946	Parker Johnstone	87	Toranosuke Takagi	4
Jimmy Vasser	938	Scott Dixon	74	Bruno Giacomelli	3
Dario Franchitti	917	Jacques Villeneuve	64	Jan Magnussen	3
Cristiano da Matta	847	Eddie Cheever	52	Sheldon Kinser	2
Teo Fabi	775	Howdy Holmes	51	Arnd Meier	2
Nigel Mansell	706	Josele Garza	49	Roger Rager	2
Gordon Johncock	640	Richie Hearn	49	Stephan Gregoire	1
Massimiliano Papis	597	Danny Ongais	40	Michael Groff	1
Greg Moore	568	Geoff Brabham	36	Randy Lanier	1
Roberto Guerrero	524	Michel Jourdain Jr	35	Ed Pimm	1
Adrian Fernandez	466	Lee Kunzman	30	Hector Rebaque	1
Andre Ribeiro	466	Scott Brayton	24	Tim Richmond	1
Tony Kanaan	418	Max Wilson	23	Gualter Salles	1
Bryan Herta	403	Alex Barron	22	George Snider	1
Mauricio Gugelmin	400	Rocky Moran	21		
Arie Luyendyk	368	Darren Manning	18		
Raul Boesel	322	Oriol Servia	17		

MILES IN THE LEAD

Michael Andretti	11200	Arie Luyendyk	600	Pete Halsmer	37
Mario Andretti	5874	Roberto Moreno	537	Oriol Servia	37
Rick Mears	5840	Alexandre Tagliani	528	Darren Manning	27
Al Unser Jr	5583	Patrick Carpentier	525	Casey Mears	24
Bobby Rahal	5211	Christian Fittipaldi	512	Jim Crawford	20
Emerson Fittipaldi	5041	Raul Boesel	505	Salt Walther	20
Paul Tracy	4144	Kevin Cogan	486	John Andretti	18
Danny Sullivan	2965	Bruno Junqueira	449	Stefan Johansson	17
Alessandro Zanardi	2942	Scott Goodyear	429	Don Whittington	16
Juan Pablo Montoya	2677	Pancho Carter	362	Larry Dickson	15
Bobby Unser	2378	Scott Pruett	323	Takuya Kurosawa	14
Gil de Ferran	2277	Mark Blundell	303	Mario Dominguez	13
Al Unser	2262	Memo Gidley	294	Tony Bettenhausen Jr	12
Tom Sneva	1998	AJ Foyt Jr	254	JJ Lehto	12
Helio Castro-Neves	1826	Robby Gordon	226	Bill Alsup	11
Johnny Rutherford	1809	John Paul Jr	197	Shinji Nakano	10
Dario Franchitti	1711	Mike Mosley	174	Jan Lammers	9
Jimmy Vasser	1645	Parker Johnstone	174	Jan Magnussen	8
Cristiano da Matta	1604	Jacques Villeneuve	113	Toranosuke Takagi	8
Kenny Brack	1561	Josele Garza	106	Derek Daly	6
Teo Fabi	1444	Geoff Brabham	99	Arnd Meier	6
Nigel Mansell	1159	Scott Dixon	96	Bruno Giacomelli	5
Massimiliano Papis	1144	Richie Hearn	76	Sheldon Kinser	5
Gordon Johncock	968	Michel Jourdain Jr	73	Roger Rager	5
Greg Moore	928	Rocky Moran	71	Hector Rebaque	4
Andre Ribeiro	842	Eddie Cheever	66	Stephan Gregoire	3
Mauricio Gugelmin	842	Howdy Holmes	57	Tim Richmond	3
Adrian Fernandez	802	Lee Kunzman	54	George Snider	3
Roberto Guerrero	801	Danny Ongais	49	Randy Lanier	2
Bryan Herta	786	Max Wilson	48	Gualter Salles	2
Jacques Villeneuve	689	Alex Barron	42	Michael Groff	1
Tony Kanaan	627	Scott Brayton	38	Ed Pimm	1

Manufacturers' Records

STARTS

Lola	350	Galmer	19	Shierson	3
Penske	270	Phoenix	19	Coyote	2
Reynard	164	Primus	18	Manta	2
March	140	King	12	McElreath	2
Eagle	139	Vollstedt	12	Schkee	2
Swift	72	Coyne	8	Spyder	2
Wildcat	60	Rahal-Hogan	7	Antares	1
McLaren	38	Orbitor	6	Armstrong	1
Watson	37	Argo	5	Finley	1
Chaparral	36	Bear	5	Ligier	1
Longhorn	35	Theodore	5	Porsche	1
Truesports	33	IAM	4	Riley	1
Lightning	31	Rattlesnake	4		
Parnelli	21	Spirit (USA)	4		

WINS

Lola	123	Wildcat	3
Reynard	94	Galmer	2
Penske	86	McLaren	2
March	60	Eagle	1
Chaparral	7	Phoenix	1
Swift	4		

POLE POSITIONS

Lola	115	Wildcat	3
Reynard	101	Longhorn	2
Penske	97	McLaren	2
March	52	Eagle	1
Chaparral	6	Galmer	1
Swift	3	Phoenix	1

Engine Records

STARTS

Cosworth	211	Judd	72
Ford	196	Porsche	47
Chevrolet	193	Alfa Romeo	43
Honda	186	Offenhauser	38
Toyota	131	Ilmor	19
Mercedes-Benz	110	Pontiac	16
Buick		AMC	1
(including Buick/Menard)	86		

WINS

Cosworth	119	Mercedes-Benz	19
Chevrolet	87	Ilmor	11
Honda	65	Judd	1
Ford	59	Porsche	1
Toyota	21		

POLE POSITIONS

Cosworth	112	Mercedes-Benz	19
Chevrolet	82	Ilmor	9
Ford	68	Porsche	3
Honda	65	Buick	
Toyota	23	(including Buick/Menard)	3

2000 Gil de Ferran receives the Vanderbilt Cup for winning the 2000 Championship.

Indy Racing League

2002 Sam Hornish Jr leads at the start of the first race of the season at Homestead, Miami.

INDY RACING LEAGUE

year	driver	nat	team	car
1996 (tied)	Buzz Calkins	USA	Bradley Motorsports	Reynard 95I-Ford
	Scott Sharp	USA	AJ Foyt Racing	Lola T95/00-Ford/Lola T94/00-Ford
1996/97	Tony Stewart	USA	Team Menard	G-Force GF01-Aurora
1998	Kenny Brack	S	AJ Foyt Racing	Dallara IR7-Aurora
1999	Greg Ray	USA	Team Menard	Dallara IR7-Aurora
2000	Buddy Lazier	USA	Hemelgarn Racing	Riley & Scott MkVII-Aurora/Dallara IR0-Aurora
2001	Sam Hornish Jr	USA	Panther Racing	Dallara IR0-Aurora
2002	Sam Hornish Jr	USA	Panther Racing	Dallara IR0-Chevrolet

1996

DISNEY WORLD INDY 200

27 January 1996. Disney World. 200 laps of a 1.000-mile circuit = 200.000 miles. Indy Racing League round 1

1	Buzz Calkins	Reynard 95I-Ford	200	1h33m30.748
2	Tony Stewart	Lola T95/00-Buick/Menard	200	1h33m31.614
3	Robbie Buhl	Reynard 94I-Ford	198	
4	Michele Alboreto	Lola T95/00-Ford	198	
5	Roberto Guerrero	Reynard 94I-Ford	197	
6	Michael Groff	Lola T95/00-Ford	195	

Winner's average speed: 128.325 mph. Pole position: Buddy Lazier (Lola T95/00-Ford), 181.388 mph

JIMMY BRYAN 200

24 March 1996. Phoenix. 200 laps of a 1.000-mile circuit = 200.000 miles. Indy Racing League round 2

1	Arie Luyendyk	Reynard 95I-Ford	200	1h42m13.610
2	Scott Sharp	Lola T94/00-Ford	200	
3	Michael Groff	Lola T94/00-Ford	199	
4	Richie Hearn	Reynard 95I-Ford	198	
5	Johnny O'Connell	Reynard 95I-Ford	197	
6	Buzz Calkins	Reynard 95I-Ford	193	

Winner's average speed: 117.386 mph. Pole position: Luyendyk, 183.599 mph

INDIANAPOLIS 500

26 May 1996. Indianapolis. 200 laps of a 2.500-mile circuit = 500.000 miles. Indy Racing League round 3

1	Buddy Lazier	Reynard 95I-Ford	200	3h22m45.753	
2	Davy Jones	Lola T95/00-Mercedes-Benz	200	3h22m46.448	
3	Richie Hearn	Reynard 95I-Ford	200		
4	Alessandro Zampedri	Reynard 95I-Ford	200		
5	Roberto Guerrero	Reynard 95I-Ford	198		accident
6	Eliseo Salazar	Lola T95/00-Ford	197		accident

Winner's average speed: 147.956 mph. Pole position: Tony Stewart (Lola T95/00-Buick/Menard), 233.100 mph - Scott Brayton (Lola T95/00-Buick/Menard) had qualified on pole at 233.718 mph but subsequently suffered a fatal accident

1996 FINAL CHAMPIONSHIP POSITIONS

1=	Buzz Calkins	246		7	Arie Luyendyk	225
	Scott Sharp	246		8	Tony Stewart	204
3	Robbie Buhl	240		9=	Davey Hamilton	192
4=	Roberto Guerrero	237			Johnny O'Connell	192
	Richie Hearn	237				
6	Michael Groff	228				

1996/97

NEW ENGLAND 200

18 August 1996. New Hampshire. 200 laps of a 1.058-mile circuit = 211.600 miles. Indy Racing League round 1

1	Scott Sharp	Lola T95/00-Ford	200	1h36m57.910
2	Buzz Calkins	Reynard 95I-Ford	200	1h37m18.390
3	Michele Alboreto	Reynard 95I-Ford	200	1h37m18.640
4	Michael Groff	Reynard 95I-Ford	199	
5	Davey Hamilton	Lola T95/00-Ford	196	
6	Roberto Guerrero	Reynard 95I-Ford	196	

Winner's average speed: 130.934 mph. Pole position: Richie Hearn (Reynard 95I-Ford), 175.367 mph. Fastest Lap: Tony Stewart (Lola T95/00-Buick/Menard), 43.26s

LAS VEGAS 500 KMS

15 September 1996. Las Vegas Speedway. 200 laps of a 1.500-mile circuit = 300.000 miles. Indy Racing League round 2

1	Richie Hearn	Reynard 95I-Ford	200	2h36m17.360
2	Michel Jourdain jr	Lola T94/00-Ford	200	
3	Michael Groff	Reynard 95I-Ford	199	
4	Roberto Guerrero	Reynard 94I-Ford	198	
5	Michele Alboreto	Reynard 95I-Ford	197	
6	Buzz Calkins	Reynard 95I-Ford	197	

Winner's average speed: 115.171 mph. Pole position: Arie Luyendyk (Reynard 95I-Ford), 226.491 mph

INDY 200

25 January 1997. Disney World. 149 laps of a 1.000-mile circuit = 149.000 miles. Indy Racing League round 3

1	Eddie Cheever	G-Force GF01-Aurora	149	1h06m43.150
2	Michael Groff	G-Force GF01-Infiniti	149	
3	Scott Goodyear	G-Force GF01-Aurora	149	
4	Scott Sharp	Dallara IR7-Aurora	149	
5	Buddy Lazier	Dallara IR7-Infiniti	149	
6	Jim Guthrie	Dallara IR7-Aurora	148	

Winner's average speed: 133.994 mph. Pole position: Tony Stewart (G-Force GF01-Aurora), 166.013 mph. Fastest Lap: Stewart, 22.58s

PHOENIX 200

23 March 1997. Phoenix. 200 laps of a 1.000-mile circuit = 200.000 miles. Indy Racing League round 4

1	Jim Guthrie	Dallara IR7-Aurora	200	2h14m32.670
2	Tony Stewart	G-Force GF01-Aurora	200	2h14m33.470
3	Davey Hamilton	G-Force GF01-Aurora	200	
4	Marco Greco	Dallara IR7-Aurora	199	
5	Stephan Gregoire	G-Force GF01-Aurora	199	
6	Michael Groff	G-Force GF01-Infiniti	195	

Winner's average speed: 89.190 mph. Pole position: Stewart, 169.484 mph

INDIANAPOLIS 500

26-27 May 1997. Indianapolis. 200 laps of a 2.500-mile circuit = 500.000 miles. Race stopped after 15 laps due to rain, restarted over remaining 185 laps. Indy Racing League round 5

1 Arie Luyendyk	G-Force GF01-Aurora	200	3h25m43.388	
2 Scott Goodyear	G-Force GF01-Aurora	200	3h25m43.958	
3 Jeff Ward	G-Force GF01-Aurora	200		
4 Buddy Lazier	Dallara IR7-Aurora	200		
5 Tony Stewart	G-Force GF01-Aurora	200		
6 Davey Hamilton	G-Force GF01-Aurora	199		

Winner's average speed: 145.827 mph. Pole position: Luyendyk, 218.263 mph. Fastest Lap: Stewart, 41.738s

TEXAS 500 KMS

7 June 1997. Texas Motor Speedway. 208 laps of a 1.455-mile circuit = 302.640 miles. Indy Racing League round 6

1 Arie Luyendyk	G-Force GF01-Aurora	208	2h19m48.170	
2 Billy Boat	G-Force GF01-Aurora	207		
3 Davey Hamilton	G-Force GF01-Aurora	207		
4 Scott Goodyear	G-Force GF01-Aurora	207		
5 Tony Stewart	G-Force GF01-Aurora	206		engine
6 Eddie Cheever	G-Force GF01-Aurora	206		

Winner's average speed: 129.886 mph. Pole position: Stewart, 167.133 mph

PIKES PEAK 200

29 June 1997. Pikes Peak. 200 laps of a 1.000-mile circuit = 200.000 miles. Indy Racing League round 7

1 Tony Stewart	G-Force GF01-Aurora	200	1h59m50.000
2 Stephan Gregoire	G-Force GF01-Aurora	200	1h59m50.220
3 Davey Hamilton	G-Force GF01-Aurora	200	
4 Eddie Cheever	G-Force GF01-Aurora	200	
5 Buzz Calkins	G-Force GF01-Aurora	200	
6 Vincenzo Sospiri	Dallara IR7-Aurora	200	

Winner's average speed: 100.139 mph. Pole position: Scott Sharp (Dallara IR7-Aurora), 176.117 mph

CHARLOTTE 500 KMS

26 July 1997. Charlotte. 208 laps of a 1.500-mile circuit = 312.000 miles. Indy Racing League round 8

1 Buddy Lazier	Dallara IR7-Aurora	208	1h55m29.000
2 Billy Boat	G-Force GF01-Aurora	208	
3 Scott Goodyear	G-Force GF01-Aurora	207	
4 Affonso Giaffone	Dallara IR7-Aurora	206	
5 Kenny Brack	G-Force GF01-Aurora	206	
6 Eddie Cheever	G-Force GF01-Aurora	206	

Winner's average speed: 162.101 mph. Pole position: Tony Stewart (G-Force GF01-Aurora), 217.164 mph

NEW ENGLAND 200

17 August 1997. New Hampshire. 200 laps of a 1.058-mile circuit = 211.600 miles. Indy Racing League round 9

1 Robbie Buhl	G-Force GF01-Aurora	200	1h26m50.574
2 Vincenzo Sospiri	Dallara IR7-Aurora	200	1h26m50.630
3 Arie Luyendyk	G-Force GF01-Aurora	200	
4 Eliseo Salazar	Dallara IR7-Aurora	200	
5 Kenny Brack	G-Force GF01-Aurora	200	
6 Roberto Guerrero	Dallara IR7-Aurora	200	

Winner's average speed: 146.195 mph. Pole position: Marco Greco (G-Force GF01-Aurora), 160.594 mph

LAS VEGAS 500 KMS

11 October 1997. Las Vegas Speedway. 208 laps of a 1.500-mile circuit = 312.000 miles. Indy Racing League round 10

1 Eliseo Salazar	Dallara IR7-Aurora	208	2h11m07.915
2 Scott Goodyear	G-Force GF01-Aurora	208	2h11m09.115
3 Robbie Buhl	G-Force GF01-Aurora	208	
4 Jim Guthrie	Dallara IR7-Aurora	208	
5 Mark Dismore	Dallara IR7-Aurora	208	
6 Jimmy Kite	Dallara IR7-Aurora	208	

Winner's average speed: 142.757 mph. Pole position: Billy Boat (Dallara IR7-Aurora), 201.568 mph

1996/97 FINAL CHAMPIONSHIP POSITIONS

1 Tony Stewart	278		7 Roberto Guerrero	221	
2 Davey Hamilton	272		8 Buddy Lazier	209	
3= Eddie Cheever	230		9 Eliseo Salazar	208	
Marco Greco	230		10 Buzz Calkins	204	
5 Scott Goodyear	226				
6 Arie Luyendyk	223				

1998

INDY 200

24 January 1998. Disney World. 200 laps of a 1.000-mile circuit = 200.000 miles. Pep Boys Indy Racing League round 1

1 Tony Stewart	G-Force GF01-Aurora	200	2h06m07.000
2 Jeff Ward	G-Force GF01-Aurora	200	2h06m15.579
3 Davey Hamilton	G-Force GF01-Aurora	200	
4 Stephan Gregoire	G-Force GF01-Aurora	200	
5 Mark Dismore	Dallara IR7-Aurora	199	
6 Scott Sharp	Dallara IR7-Aurora	198	

Winner's average speed: 95.150 mph. Pole position: Stewart - qualifying cancelled due to rain, positions decided by 96-97 championship positions. Fastest Lap: Kenny Brack (Dallara IR7-Aurora), 21.83s

DURA-LUBE 200

22 March 1998. Phoenix. 200 laps of a 1.000-mile circuit = 200.000 miles. Pep Boys Indy Racing League round 2

1 Scott Sharp	Dallara IR7-Aurora	200	2h02m18.735
2 Tony Stewart	G-Force GF01-Aurora	200	2h02m21.101
3 Billy Boat	Dallara IR7-Aurora	200	2h02m22.020
4 Stephan Gregoire	G-Force GF01-Aurora	199	
5 Jeff Ward	G-Force GF01-Aurora	199	
6 Scott Goodyear	G-Force GF01-Aurora	199	

Winner's average speed: 98.110 mph. Pole position: Ward, 20.839s. Fastest Lap: Stewart, 163.666 mph

INDIANAPOLIS 500

24 May 1998. Indianapolis. 200 laps of a 2.500-mile circuit = 500.000 miles. Pep Boys Indy Racing League round 3

1 Eddie Cheever	Dallara IR7-Aurora	200	3h26m40.524
2 Buddy Lazier	Dallara IR7-Aurora	200	3h26m43.715
3 Steve Knapp	G-Force GF01-Aurora	200	
4 Davey Hamilton	G-Force GF01-Aurora	199	
5 Robby Unser	Dallara IR7-Aurora	198	
6 Kenny Brack	Dallara IR7-Aurora	198	

Winner's average speed: 145.155 mph. Pole position: Billy Boat (Dallara IR7-Aurora), 223.503 mph. Fastest Lap: Tony Stewart (Dallara IR7-Aurora), 41.91s

TRUE VALUE 500

6 June 1998. Texas Motor Speedway. 208 laps of a 1.455-mile circuit = 302.640 miles. Pep Boys Indy Racing League round 4

1 Billy Boat	Dallara IR7-Aurora	208	2h08m45.543
2 Greg Ray	Dallara IR7-Aurora	208	2h08m46.471
3 Kenny Brack	Dallara IR7-Aurora	208	
4 Scott Goodyear	G-Force GF01-Aurora	208	
5 Scott Sharp	Dallara IR7-Aurora	208	
6 Robbie Buhl	Dallara IR7-Aurora	207	

Winner's average speed: 141.026 mph. Pole position: Tony Stewart (Dallara IR7-Aurora), 24.059s mph. Fastest Lap: Stewart, 228.012 mph

NEW HAMPSHIRE 200

28 June 1998. New Hampshire. 200 laps of a 1.058-mile circuit = 211.600 miles. Pep Boys Indy Racing League round 5

1 Tony Stewart	Dallara IR7-Aurora	200	1h51m30.262

2	Scott Goodyear	G-Force GF01-Aurora	200	1h51m32.050
3	Scott Sharp	Dallara IR7-Aurora	200	
4	Davey Hamilton	G-Force GF01-Aurora	200	
5	Arie Luyendyk	G-Force GF01-Aurora	199	
6	Eliseo Salazar	Riley & Scott MkV-Aurora	199	

Winner's average speed: 113.861 mph. Pole position: Billy Boat (Dallara IR7-Aurora), 23.490s. Fastest Lap: Hamilton, 158.252 mph

PEP BOYS 400 KMS

19 July 1998. Dover Downs. 248 laps of a 1.000-mile circuit = 248.000 miles. Pep Boys Indy Racing League round 6

1	Scott Sharp	Dallara IR7-Aurora	248	2h29m49.262
2	Buddy Lazier	Dallara IR7-Aurora	248	2h29m49.951
3	Marco Greco	G-Force GF01-Aurora	246	
4	Davey Hamilton	G-Force GF01-Aurora	246	
5	Stephan Gregoire	G-Force GF01-Aurora	244	
6	Scott Goodyear	G-Force GF01-Aurora	242	

Winner's average speed: 99.318 mph. Pole position: Stewart, 19.438s. Fastest Lap: Ray, 183.468 mph

VISIONAIRE 500

25 July 1998. Charlotte. 208 laps of a 1.500-mile circuit = 312.000 miles. Pep Boys Indy Racing League round 7

1	Kenny Brack	Dallara IR7-Aurora	208	1h58m10.555
2	Jeff Ward	G-Force GF01-Aurora	208	1h58m16.157
3	Scott Goodyear	G-Force GF01-Aurora	208	
4	Arie Luyendyk	G-Force GF01-Aurora	206	
5	Marco Greco	G-Force GF01-Aurora	205	
6	John Paul Jr	G-Force GF01-Aurora	203	

Winner's average speed: 158.408 mph. Pole position: Stewart, 24.490s. Fastest Lap: Brack, 218.314 mph

RADISSON 200

16 August 1998. Pikes Peak. 200 laps of a 1.000-mile circuit = 200.000 miles. Pep Boys Indy Racing League round 8

1	Kenny Brack	Dallara IR7-Aurora	200	1h29m52.649
2	Robbie Buhl	Dallara IR7-Aurora	200	1h30m00.191
3	Tony Stewart	Dallara IR7-Aurora	200	
4	Stephan Gregoire	G-Force GF01-Aurora	199	
5	Davey Hamilton	G-Force GF01-Aurora	199	
6	Marco Greco	G-Force GF01-Aurora	199	

Winner's average speed: 133.515 mph. Pole position: Billy Boat (Dallara IR7-Aurora), 20.160s. Fastest Lap: Jeff Ward (G-Force GF01-Aurora), 170.020 mph

ATLANTA 500 CLASSIC

29 August 1998. Atlanta. 208 laps of a 1.540-mile circuit = 320.320 miles. Pep Boys Indy Racing League round 9

1	Kenny Brack	Dallara IR7-Aurora	208	2h17m15.289
2	Davey Hamilton	Dallara IR7-Aurora	208	2h17m16.233
3	Eddie Cheever	Dallara IR7-Aurora	208	
4	Scott Goodyear	G-Force GF01-Aurora	208	
5	Tony Stewart	Dallara IR7-Aurora	208	
6	Jeff Ward	G-Force GF01-Aurora	208	

Winner's average speed: 140.026 mph. Pole position: Billy Boat (Dallara IR7-Aurora), 24.734s. Fastest Lap: Boat, 224.163 mph

LONE STAR 500

20 September 1998. Texas Motor Speedway. 208 laps of a 1.455-mile circuit = 302.640 miles. Pep Boys Indy Racing League round 10

1	John Paul Jr	G-Force GF01-Aurora	208	2h21m53.557
2	Robby Unser	G-Force GF01-Aurora	208	2h21m55.134
3	Jeff Ward	G-Force GF01-Aurora	208	
4	Roberto Guerrero	G-Force GF01-Infiniti	208	
5	Kenny Brack	Dallara IR7-Aurora	207	
6	Buddy Lazier	Dallara IR7-Aurora	206	

Winner's average speed: 127.973 mph. Pole position: Billy Boat (Dallara IR7-Aurora), 23.896s. Fastest Lap: Ward, 224.243 mph

LAS VEGAS 500 KMS

11 October 1998. Las Vegas Speedway. 208 laps of a 1.500-mile circuit = 312.000 miles. Pep Boys Indy Racing League round 11

1	Arie Luyendyk	G-Force GF01-Aurora	208	2h18m19.202
2	Sam Schmidt	Dallara IR7-Aurora	208	2h18m20.128
3	Buddy Lazier	Dallara IR7-Aurora	208	
4	John Paul Jr	G-Force GF01-Aurora	208	
5	Eddie Cheever	Dallara IR7-Aurora	207	
6	Brian Tyler	Dallara IR7-Aurora	207	

Winner's average speed: 135.338 mph. Pole position: Billy Boat (Dallara IR7-Aurora), 25.167s. Fastest Lap: Luyendyk, 206.367 mph

1998 FINAL CHAMPIONSHIP POSITIONS

1	Kenny Brack	332	7	Scott Goodyear	244
2	Davey Hamilton	292	8	Arie Luyendyk	227
3	Tony Stewart	289	9	Eddie Cheever	222
4	Scott Sharp	272	10	Marco Greco	219
5	Buddy Lazier	262			
6	Jeff Ward	252			

1999

TRANSWORLD DIVERSIFIED SERVICES INDY 200

24 January 1999. Disney World. 200 laps of a 1.000-mile circuit = 200.000 miles. Pep Boys Indy Racing League round 1

1	Eddie Cheever	Dallara IR7-Aurora	200	1h41m14.800
2	Scott Goodyear	G-Force GF01-Aurora	200	1h41m19.950
3	Jeff Ward	G-Force GF01-Aurora	200	
4	Scott Sharp	Dallara IR7-Aurora	200	
5	Raul Boesel	G-Force GF01-Aurora	199	
6	Mark Dismore	Dallara IR7-Aurora	199	

Winner's average speed: 118.522 mph. Pole position: Sharp, 21.007s. Fastest Lap: Sharp, 21.671s

MCI WORLDCOM 200

28 March 1999. Phoenix. 200 laps of a 1.000-mile circuit = 200.000 miles. Pep Boys Indy Racing League round 2

1	Scott Goodyear	G-Force GF01-Aurora	200	1h56m40.052
2	Jeff Ward	Dallara IR7-Aurora	200	1h56m44.790
3	Robbie Buhl	Dallara IR7-Infiniti	200	
4	Billy Boat	Dallara IR7-Aurora	200	
5	Scott Harrington	Dallara IR7-Infiniti	200	
6	Roberto Moreno	G-Force GF01-Aurora	199	

Winner's average speed: 102.856 mph. Pole position: Greg Ray (Dallara IR7-Aurora), 20.323s. Fastest Lap: Goodyear, 21.489s

VISIONAIRE 500

1 May 1999. Charlotte. Race abandoned due to spectator fatalities. Pep Boys Indy Racing League round 3

NO RESULT DECLARED
Pole position: Greg Ray (Dallara IR7-Aurora)

INDIANAPOLIS 500

30 May 1999. Indianapolis. 200 laps of a 2.500-mile circuit = 500.000 miles. Pep Boys Indy Racing League round 4

1	Kenny Brack	Dallara IR7-Aurora	200	3h15m51.182
2	Jeff Ward	Dallara IR7-Aurora	200	3h15m57.744
3	Billy Boat	Dallara IR7-Aurora	200	
4	Robby Gordon	Dallara IR7-Aurora	200	
5	Robby McGehee	Dallara IR7-Aurora	199	
6	Robbie Buhl	Dallara IR7-Aurora	199	

Winner's average speed: 153.176 mph. Pole position: Arie Luyendyk (G-Force GF01-Aurora), 225.179mph. Fastest Lap: Greg Ray (Dallara IR7-Aurora), 41.118s

LONGHORN 500

12 June 1999. Texas Motor Speedway. 208 laps of a 1.455-mile circuit = 302.640 miles. Pep Boys Indy Racing League round 5

1	Scott Goodyear	G-Force GF01-Aurora	208	2h00m06.816
2	Greg Ray	Dallara IR7-Aurora	208	2h00m07.710
3	Sam Schmidt	Dallara IR7-Aurora	208	
4	Stephan Gregoire	G-Force GF01-Aurora	208	
5	Eliseo Salazar	G-Force GF01-Aurora	206	
6	Robby Unser	Dallara IR7-Aurora	206	

Winner's average speed: 151.177 mph. Pole position: Mark Dismore (Dallara IR7-Aurora), 24.332s. Fastest Lap: Schmidt, 24.294s

RADISSON 200

27 June 1999. Pikes Peak. 200 laps of a 1.000-mile circuit = 200.000 miles. Pep Boys Indy Racing League round 6

1	Greg Ray	Dallara IR7-Aurora	200	1h29m28.676
2	Sam Schmidt	G-Force GF01-Aurora	200	1h29m28.796
3	Davey Hamilton	Dallara IR7-Aurora	200	
4	Eddie Cheever	Dallara IR7-Infiniti	200	
5	Buddy Lazier	Dallara IR7-Aurora	200	
6	Robby Unser	Dallara IR7-Aurora	199	

Winner's average speed: 134.111 mph. Pole position: Ray, 20.454s. Fastest Lap: Mark Dismore (Dallara IR7-Aurora), 20.454s

KOBALT MECHANICS TOOLS 500

17 July 1999. Atlanta. 208 laps of a 1.540-mile circuit = 320.320 miles. Pep Boys Indy Racing League round 7

1	Scott Sharp	Dallara IR7-Aurora	208	2h12m15.235
2	Robby Unser	Dallara IR7-Aurora	208	2h12m15.398
3	Kenny Brack	Dallara IR7-Aurora	208	
4	Eliseo Salazar	G-Force GF01-Aurora	208	
5	Buzz Calkins	G-Force GF01-Aurora	208	
6	Eddie Cheever	Dallara IR7-Infiniti	207	

Winner's average speed: 145.320 mph. Pole position: Billy Boat (Dallara IR7-Aurora), 25.087s. Fastest Lap: Jaques Lazier (G-Force GF01-Aurora), 25.10bs

MBNA MID-ATLANTIC 200

1 August 1999. Dover Downs. 200 laps of a 1.000-mile circuit = 200.000 miles. Pep Boys Indy Racing League round 8

1	Greg Ray	Dallara IR7-Aurora	200	1h45m01.503
2	Buddy Lazier	Dallara IR7-Aurora	200	1h45m02.234
3	Kenny Brack	Dallara IR7-Aurora	200	
4	Billy Boat	Dallara IR7-Aurora	200	
5	Sam Schmidt	G-Force GF01-Aurora	200	
6	Scott Harrington	Dallara IR7-Aurora	199	

Winner's average speed: 114.258 mph. Pole position: Mark Dismore (Dallara IR7-Aurora), 19.711s. Fastest Lap: Dismore, 19.745s

COLORADO 200

29 August 1999. Pikes Peak. 200 laps of a 1.000-mile circuit = 200.000 miles. Pep Boys Indy Racing League round 9

1	Greg Ray	Dallara IR7-Aurora	200	1h28m35.633
2	Davey Hamilton	Dallara IR7-Aurora	200	1h28m36.078
3	Mark Dismore	Dallara IR7-Aurora	200	
4	Buddy Lazier	Dallara IR7-Aurora	200	
5	Sam Schmidt	G-Force GF01-Aurora	199	
6	Scott Harrington	Dallara IR7-Aurora	199	

Winner's average speed: 135.450 mph. Pole position: Ray, 20.424s. Fastest Lap: B Lazier, 20.920s

LAS VEGAS 500 KMS

26 September 1999. Las Vegas Speedway. 208 laps of a 1.500-mile circuit = 312.000 miles. Pep Boys Indy Racing League round 10

1	Sam Schmidt	G-Force GF01-Aurora	208	2h29m50.204
2	Kenny Brack	G-Force GF01-Aurora	208	2h29m50.821
3	Robbie Buhl	Dallara IR7-Aurora	208	
4	Scott Sharp	Dallara IR7-Aurora	208	
5	Buzz Calkins	G-Force GF01-Aurora	207	
6	Robby McGehee	Dallara IR7-Aurora	207	

Winner's average speed: 124.936 mph. Pole position: Schmidt, 25.780s. Fastest Lap: Tyce Carlson (Dallara IR7-Aurora), 26.322s

MALL.COM 500

17 October 1999. Texas Motor Speedway. 208 laps of a 1.455-mile circuit = 302.640 miles. Pep Boys Indy Racing League round 11

1	Mark Dismore	Dallara IR7-Aurora	208	2h14m15.722
2	Davey Hamilton	Dallara IR7-Aurora	207	
3	Greg Ray	Dallara IR7-Aurora	207	
4	Eddie Cheever	Dallara IR7-Infiniti	207	
5	John Hollansworth Jr	Dallara IR7-Aurora	206	
6	Scott Harrington	Dallara IR7-Aurora	206	

Winner's average speed: 135.246 mph. Pole position: Ray, 24.238s. Fastest Lap: Scott Goodyear (G-Force GF01-Aurora), 24.074s

1999 FINAL CHAMPIONSHIP POSITIONS

1	Greg Ray	293	7	Eddie Cheever	222
2	Kenny Brack	256	8	Scott Sharp	220
3	Mark Dismore	240	9	Scott Goodyear	217
4	Davey Hamilton	237	10	Robby Unser	209
5	Sam Schmidt	233			
6	Buddy Lazier	224			

2000

DELPHI INDY 200

29 January 2000. Disney World. 200 laps of a 1.000-mile circuit = 200.000 miles. Indy Racing Northern Light Series round 1

1	Robbie Buhl	G-Force GF05-Aurora	200	1h57m18.676
2	Buddy Lazier	Riley & Scott MkVII-Aurora	200	1h57m21.841
3	Eddie Cheever	Riley & Scott MkVII-Infiniti	200	1h57m22.300
4	Scott Goodyear	Dallara IR0-Aurora	200	1h57m22.662
5	Eliseo Salazar	G-Force GF05-Aurora	200	1h57m25.666
6	Donnie Beechler	Dallara IR0-Aurora	200	1h57m32.892

Winner's average speed: 102.292 mph. Pole position: Greg Ray (Dallara IR0-Aurora) - qualifying cancelled due to rain, started in order of 1999 car owner points. Fastest Lap: Mark Dismore (Dallara IR0-Aurora), 22.205s

MCI WORLDCOM 200

19 March 2000. Phoenix. 200 laps of a 1.000-mile circuit = 200.000 miles. Indy Racing Northern Light Series round 2

1	Buddy Lazier	Riley & Scott MkVII-Aurora	200	1h47m11.029
2	Scott Goodyear	Dallara IR0-Aurora	200	1h47m15.220
3	Donnie Beechler	Dallara IR0-Aurora	200	
4	Eliseo Salazar	G-Force GF05-Aurora	200	
5	Scott Sharp	Dallara IR0-Aurora	200	
6	Billy Boat	Dallara IR0-Aurora	200	

Winner's average speed: 111.957 mph. Pole position: Greg Ray (Dallara IR0-Aurora), 20.389s. Fastest Lap: Tyce Carlson (Dallara IR0-Aurora), 21.847s

LAS VEGAS 500 KMS

22 April 2000. Las Vegas Speedway. 208 laps of a 1.500-mile circuit = 312.000 miles. Indy Racing Northern Light Series round 3

1	Al Unser Jr	G-Force GF05-Aurora	208	2h16m57.045
2	Mark Dismore	Dallara IR0-Aurora	208	2h17m09.576
3	Sam Hornish Jr	G-Force GF05-Aurora	207	
4	Jeret Schroeder	Dallara IR0-Aurora	207	
5	Robbie Buhl	G-Force GF05-Aurora	207	
6	Robby McGehee	G-Force GF05-Aurora	206	

Winner's average speed: 136.691 mph. Pole position: Dismore, 25.899s. Fastest Lap: Dismore, 26.390s

INDIANAPOLIS 500

28 May 2000. Indianapolis. 200 laps of a 2.500-mile circuit = 500.000 miles. Indy Racing Northern Light Series round 4

1	Juan Pablo Montoya	G-Force GF05-Aurora	200	2h58m59.431
2	Buddy Lazier	Dallara IR0-Aurora	200	2h59m06.615
3	Eliseo Salazar	G-Force GF05-Aurora	200	2h59m15.133
4	Jeff Ward	G-Force GF05-Aurora	200	2h59m17.844
5	Eddie Cheever	Dallara IR0-Infiniti	200	2h59m18.157
6	Robby Gordon	Dallara IR0-Aurora	200	2h59m18.505

Winner's average speed: 167.607 mph. Pole position: Greg Ray (Dallara IR0-Aurora), 223.471 mph. Fastest Lap: Lazier, 41.191s

CASINO MAGIC 500

11 June 2000. Texas Motor Speedway. 208 laps of a 1.455-mile circuit = 302.640 miles. Indy Racing Northern Light Series round 5

1	Scott Sharp	Dallara IR0-Aurora	208	1h47m19.835
2	Robby McGehee	G-Force GF05-Aurora	208	1h47m19.894
3	Al Unser Jr	G-Force GF05-Aurora	208	
4	Buzz Calkins	Dallara IR0-Aurora	208	
5	Scott Goodyear	Dallara IR0-Aurora	208	
6	Mark Dismore	Dallara IR0-Aurora	208	

Winner's average speed: 169.182 mph. Pole position: Buddy Lazier (Dallara IR0-Aurora) - qualifying cancelled due to rain, started in championship order. Fastest Lap: Eddie Cheever (Dallara IR0-Infiniti), 24.596s

RADISSON 200

18 June 2000. Pikes Peak. 200 laps of a 1.000-mile circuit = 200.000 miles. Indy Racing Northern Light Series round 6

1	Eddie Cheever	Dallara IR0-Infiniti	200	1h28m44.257
2	Airton Dare	G-Force GF05-Aurora	200	
3	Scott Sharp	Dallara IR0-Aurora	200	
4	Mark Dismore	Dallara IR0-Aurora	199	
5	Donnie Beechler	Dallara IR0-Aurora	198	accident
6	Eliseo Salazar	G-Force GF05-Aurora	198	

Winner's average speed: 135.230 mph. Pole position: Greg Ray (Dallara IR0-Aurora), 20.014s. Fastest Lap: Buzz Calkins (Dallara IR0-Aurora), 21.540s

MIDAS 500 CLASSIC

15 July 2000. Atlanta. 208 laps of a 1.540-mile circuit = 320.320 miles. Indy Racing Northern Light Series round 7

1	Greg Ray	Dallara IR0-Aurora	208	2h02m01.882
2	Buddy Lazier	Dallara IR0-Aurora	208	2h02m04.936
3	Al Unser Jr	G-Force GF05-Aurora	208	
4	Robby McGehee	G-Force GF05-Aurora	208	
5	Donnie Beechler	Dallara IR0-Aurora	207	
6	Robbie Buhl	G-Force GF05-Infiniti	207	

Winner's average speed: 157.494 mph. Pole position: Ray, 24.988s. Fastest Lap: Beechler, 25.160s

BELTERRA RESORT 300

27 August 2000. Kentucky. 200 laps of a 1.500-mile circuit = 300.000 miles. Indy Racing Northern Light Series round 8

1	Buddy Lazier	Dallara IR0-Aurora	200	1h49m21.309
2	Scott Goodyear	Dallara IR0-Aurora	200	1h49m23.188
3	Sarah Fisher	Dallara IR0-Aurora	200	1h49m29.058
4	Eddie Cheever	Dallara IR0-Infiniti	200	1h49m44.358
5	Stephan Gregoire	G-Force GF05-Aurora	199	
6	Jeff Ward	G-Force GF05-Aurora	199	

Winner's average speed: 164.601 mph. Pole position: Goodyear, 24.636s. Fastest Lap: Lazier, 24.721s

EXCITE 500

15 October 2000. Texas Motor Speedway. 208 laps of a 1.455-mile circuit = 302.640 miles. Indy Racing Northern Light Series round 9

1	Scott Goodyear	Dallara IR0-Aurora	208	1h43m35.926
2	Eddie Cheever	Dallara IR0-Infiniti	208	1h43m36.066
3	Billy Boat	Dallara IR0-Aurora	208	1h43m36.171
4	Buddy Lazier	Dallara IR0-Aurora	208	1h43m36.627
5	Eliseo Salazar	G-Force GF05-Aurora	207	
6	Donnie Beechler	Dallara IR0-Aurora	207	

Winner's average speed: 24.323s. Pole position: Greg Ray (Dallara IR0-Aurora), 24.323s. Fastest Lap: Jaques Lazier (G-Force GF05-Aurora), 24.227s

2000 FINAL CHAMPIONSHIP POSITIONS

1	Buddy Lazier	290		7	Scott Sharp	196
2	Scott Goodyear	272		8	Robbie Buhl	190
3	Eddie Cheever	257		9	Al Unser Jr	188
4	Eliseo Salazar	210		10	Billy Boat	181
5=	Mark Dismore	202				
	Donnie Beechler	202				

2001

PENNZOIL COPPER WORLD INDY 200

18 March 2001. Phoenix. 200 laps of a 1.000-mile circuit = 200.000 miles. Indy Racing Northern Light Series round 1

1	Sam Hornish Jr	Dallara IR0-Aurora	200	1h35m56.710
2	Eliseo Salazar	Dallara IR0-Aurora	200	1h35m58.090
3	Buddy Lazier	Dallara IR0-Aurora	200	1h35m58.610
4	Scott Sharp	Dallara IR0-Aurora	200	1h36m01.560
5	Billy Boat	Dallara IR0-Aurora	200	1h36m13.460
6	Felipe Giaffone	G-Force GF05-Aurora	199	

Winner's average speed: 125.071 mph. Pole position: Greg Ray (Dallara IR0-Aurora), 177.663 mph. Fastest Lap: Sharp, 21.744s

INFINITI GRAND PRIX OF MIAMI

8 April 2001. Homestead. 200 laps of a 1.502-mile circuit = 300.400 miles. Indy Racing Northern Light Series round 2

1	Sam Hornish Jr	Dallara IR0-Aurora	200	2h01m12.336
2	Sarah Fisher	Dallara IR0-Aurora	200	2h01m14.206
3	Eliseo Salazar	Dallara IR0-Aurora	200	2h01m19.545
4	Felipe Giaffone	G-Force GF05-Aurora	199	
5	Jeff Ward	G-Force GF05-Aurora	199	
6	Al Unser Jr	G-Force GF05-Aurora	199	

Winner's average speed: 148.706 mph. Pole position: Ward, 201.551 mph. Fastest Lap: Hornish, 27.5582s

ATLANTA 500 KMS

28 April 2001. Atlanta. 200 laps of a 1.540-mile circuit = 308.000 miles. Indy Racing Northern Light Series round 3

1	Greg Ray	Dallara IR0-Aurora	200	2h14m40.989
2	Scott Sharp	Dallara IR0-Aurora	200	2h15m00.846
3	Buzz Calkins	Dallara IR0-Aurora	200	2h15m05.879
4	Sam Hornish Jr	Dallara IR0-Aurora	199	
5	Eliseo Salazar	Dallara IR0-Aurora	199	
6	Buddy Lazier	Dallara IR0-Aurora	199	

Winner's average speed: 137.211 mph. Pole position: Ray, 218.265 mph. Fastest Lap: Ray, 25.0331s

INDIANAPOLIS 500

27 May 2001. Indianapolis. 200 laps of a 2.500-mile circuit = 500.000 miles. Indy Racing Northern Light Series round 4

1	Helio Castro-Neves	Dallara IR0-Aurora	200	3h31m54.180
2	Gil de Ferran	Dallara IR0-Aurora	200	3h31m55.917
3	Michael Andretti	Dallara IR0-Aurora	200	3h31m59.916
4	Jimmy Vasser	G-Force GF05-Aurora	200	
5	Bruno Junqueira	G-Force GF05-Aurora	200	
6	Tony Stewart	G-Force GF05-Aurora	200	

Winner's average speed: 141.574 mph. Pole position: Scott Sharp (Dallara IR0-Aurora), 226.037 mph. Fastest Lap: Sam Hornish Jr (Dallara IR0-Aurora), 40.9407s

CASINO MAGIC 500

9 June 2001. Texas Motor Speedway. 200 laps of a 1.455-mile circuit = 291.000 miles. Indy Racing Northern Light Series round 5

1	Scott Sharp	Dallara IR0-Aurora	200	1h55m43.578
2	Sam Hornish Jr	Dallara IR0-Aurora	200	1h55m44.291
3	Felipe Giaffone	G-Force GF05-Aurora	200	1h55m45.940
4	Buddy Lazier	Dallara IR0-Aurora	200	1h55m47.209
5	Donnie Beechler	Dallara IR0-Aurora	200	1h55m47.773
6	Billy Boat	Dallara IR0-Aurora	200	1h55m48.488

Winner's average speed: 150.873 mph. Pole position: Mark Dismore (Dallara IR0-Aurora), 215.508 mph. Fastest Lap: Eddie Cheever (Dallara IR0-Infiniti), 23.951s

RADISSON INDY 200

17 June 2001. Pikes Peak. 200 laps of a 1.000-mile circuit = 200.000 miles. Indy Racing Northern Light Series round 6

1	Buddy Lazier	Dallara IR0-Aurora	200	1h23m55.426
2	Sam Hornish Jr	Dallara IR0-Aurora	200	1h24m05.534
3	Robbie Buhl	G-Force GF05-Infiniti	200	
4	Billy Boat	Dallara IR0-Aurora	200	
5	Airton Dare	G-Force GF05-Aurora	198	
6	Eddie Cheever	Dallara IR0-Infiniti	198	

Winner's average speed: 142.987 mph. Pole position: Greg Ray (Dallara IR0-Aurora), 176.585 mph. Fastest Lap: Boat, 21.4866s

SUN TRUST INDY CHALLENGE

30 June 2001. Richmond. 250 laps of a .750-mile circuit = 187.500 miles. Indy Racing Northern Light Series round 7

1	Buddy Lazier	Dallara IR0-Aurora	250	1h55m27.730
2	Sam Hornish Jr	Dallara IR0-Aurora	250	1h55m32.613
3	Al Unser Jr	G-Force GF05-Aurora	250	
4	Didier Andre	G-Force GF05-Aurora	250	
5	Scott Sharp	Dallara IR0-Aurora	249	
6	Mark Dismore	Dallara IR0-Aurora	249	

Winner's average speed: 97.435 mph. Pole position: Jaques Lazier (Dallara IR0-Aurora), 160.417 mph. Fastest Lap: B Lazier, 17.4311s

AMERISTAR CASINO INDY 200

8 July 2001. Kansas City. 200 laps of a 1.500-mile circuit = 300.000 miles. Indy Racing Northern Light Series round 8

1	Eddie Cheever	Dallara IR0-Infiniti	200	2h02m29.203
2	Sam Hornish Jr	Dallara IR0-Aurora	200	2h02m29.401
3	Donnie Beechler	Dallara IR0-Aurora	200	
4	Felipe Giaffone	G-Force GF05-Aurora	200	
5	Buddy Lazier	Dallara IR0-Aurora	200	
6	Airton Dare	G-Force GF05-Aurora	200	

Winner's average speed: 146.955 mph. Pole position: Scott Sharp (Dallara IR0-Aurora), 216.175 mph. Fastest Lap: Mark Dismore (Dallara IR0-Aurora), 25.1763s

HURRAH'S INDY 200

21 July 2001. Nashville. 200 laps of a 1.330-mile circuit = 266.000 miles. Indy Racing Northern Light Series round 9

1	Buddy Lazier	Dallara IR0-Aurora	200	1h47m43.682
2	Billy Boat	Dallara IR0-Aurora	200	1h47m54.312
3	Jaques Lazier	Dallara IR0-Aurora	199	accident
4	Robby McGehee	Dallara IR0-Aurora	199	
5	Scott Sharp	Dallara IR0-Aurora	199	
6	Sam Hornish Jr	Dallara IR0-Aurora	198	

Winner's average speed: 148.151 mph. Pole position: Greg Ray (Dallara IR0-Aurora), 199.922 mph. Fastest Lap: B Lazier, 23.4987s

BELTERRA RESORT INDY 300

12 August 2001. Kentucky. 200 laps of a 1.500-mile circuit = 300.000 miles. Indy Racing Northern Light Series round 10

1	Buddy Lazier	Dallara IR0-Aurora	200	1h42m54.593
2	Scott Sharp	Dallara IR0-Aurora	200	1h42m56.175
3	Sam Hornish Jr	Dallara IR0-Aurora	200	

4	Al Unser Jr	G-Force GF05-Aurora	200	
5	Donnie Beechler	Dallara IR0-Aurora	200	
6	Billy Boat	Dallara IR0-Aurora	200	

Winner's average speed: 174.910 mph. Pole position: Sharp, 214.598 mph. Fastest Lap: Mark Dismore (Dallara IR0-Aurora), 25.2181s

GATEWAY INDY 250

26 August 2001. St Louis. 200 laps of a 1.270-mile circuit = 254.000 miles. Indy Racing Northern Light Series round 11

1	Al Unser Jr	G-Force GF05-Aurora	200	1h49m59.268
2	Mark Dismore	Dallara IR0-Aurora	200	1h50m00.452
3	Sam Hornish Jr	Dallara IR0-Aurora	200	
4	Eddie Cheever	Dallara IR0-Infiniti	200	
5	Robbie Buhl	G-Force GF05-Infiniti	199	
6	Billy Boat	Dallara IR0-Aurora	199	

Winner's average speed: 138.561 mph. Pole position: Hornish - qualifying cancelled due to rain, started in championship order. Fastest Lap: Buhl, 27.0291s

DELPHI INDY 300

2 September 2001. Chicagoland. 200 laps of a 1.500-mile circuit = 300.000 miles. Indy Racing Northern Light Series round 12

1	Jaques Lazier	Dallara IR0-Aurora	200	1h45m57.403
2	Sam Hornish Jr	Dallara IR0-Aurora	200	1h45m58.864
3	Eddie Cheever	Dallara IR0-Infiniti	200	
4	Jeff Ward	G-Force GF05-Aurora	200	
5	Donnie Beechler	Dallara IR0-Aurora	200	
6	Richie Hearn	Dallara IR0-Aurora	199	

Winner's average speed: 169.881 mph. Pole position: J Lazier, 221.740 mph. Fastest Lap: Robbie Buhl (G-Force GF05-Infiniti), 24.6334s

CHEVY 500

6 October 2001. Texas Motor Speedway. 200 laps of a 1.455-mile circuit = 291.000 miles. Indy Racing Northern Light Series round 13

1	Sam Hornish Jr	Dallara IR0-Aurora	200	1h43m36.376
2	Scott Sharp	Dallara IR0-Aurora	200	1h43m36.395
3	Robbie Buhl	G-Force GF05-Infiniti	200	1h43m36.844
4	Eliseo Salazar	Dallara IR0-Aurora	200	
5	Rick Treadway	G-Force GF05-Aurora	200	
6	Al Unser Jr	G-Force GF05-Aurora	200	

Winner's average speed: 168.523 mph. Pole position: Hornish - qualifying cancelled due to rain, started in championship order. Fastest Lap: Felipe Giaffone (G-Force GF05-Aurora), 23.6436s

2001 FINAL CHAMPIONSHIP POSITIONS

1	Sam Hornish Jr	503	7	Al Unser Jr	287
2	Buddy Lazier	398	8	Eddie Cheever	261
3	Scott Sharp	355	9	Buzz Calkins	242
4	Billy Boat	313	10	Airton Dare	239
5	Eliseo Salazar	308			
6	Felipe Giaffone	304			

2002

NEXTEL 250/MIAMI GRAND PRIX

2 March 2002. Homestead. 200 laps of a 1.502-mile circuit = 300.400 miles. Indy Racing League round 1

1	Sam Hornish Jr	Dallara IR0-Chevrolet	200	2h08m16.443
2	Gil de Ferran	Dallara IR0-Chevrolet	200	2h08m21.198
3	Helio Castro-Neves	Dallara IR0-Chevrolet	200	2h08m23.202
4	Jeff Ward	G-Force GF05-Chevrolet	199	
5	Eliseo Salazar	Dallara IR0-Chevrolet	199	
6	Tomas Scheckter	Dallara IR0-Infiniti	198	

Winner's average speed: 140.512 mph. Pole position: Hornish, 26.6162s. Fastest Lap: Ward, 27.6849s

2002 The Indy Racing League featured a wheel-to-wheel dice for the title between Sam Hornish Jr and Helio Castro-Neves.

BOMBARDIER ATV COPPER WORLD INDY 200

17 March 2002. Phoenix. 200 laps of a 1.000-mile circuit = 200.000 miles. Indy Racing Series round 2

1 Helio Castro-Neves	Dallara IR0-Chevrolet	200	1h43m00.028
2 Gil de Ferran	Dallara IR0-Chevrolet	200	1h43m02.170
3 Sam Hornish Jr	Dallara IR0-Chevrolet	200	
4 Eliseo Salazar	Dallara IR0-Chevrolet	200	
5 Al Unser Jr	Dallara IR0-Chevrolet	200	
6 Jaques Lazier	Dallara IR0-Chevrolet	200	

Winner's average speed: 116.504 mph. Pole position: Castro-Neves, 20.0124s. Fastest Lap: Robbie Buhl (G-Force GF05-Infiniti), 21.1003s

YAMAHA INDY 400

24 March 2002. California Speedway. 200 laps of a 2.029-mile circuit = 405.800 miles. Indy Racing Series round 3

1 Sam Hornish Jr	Dallara IR0-Chevrolet	200	2h13m49.211
2 Jaques Lazier	Dallara IR0-Chevrolet	200	2h13m49.239
3 Laurent Redon	Dallara IR0-Infiniti	200	
4 Gil de Ferran	Dallara IR0-Chevrolet	200	
5 Helio Castro-Neves	Dallara IR0-Chevrolet	200	
6 Felipe Giaffone	G-Force GF05-Chevrolet	200	

Winner's average speed: 181.946 mph. Pole position: Eddie Cheever (Dallara IR0-Infiniti), 32.5171s. Fastest Lap: Tomas Scheckter (Dallara IR0-Infiniti), 32.3509s

FIRESTONE INDY 225

21 April 2002. Nazareth. 225 laps of a.946-mile circuit = 212.850 miles. Indy Racing Series round 4

1 Scott Sharp	Dallara IR0-Chevrolet	225	2h14m35.002
2 Felipe Giaffone	G-Force GF05-Chevrolet	225	2h14m35.499
3 Gil de Ferran	Dallara IR0-Chevrolet	225	2h14m36.782
4 Sarah Fisher	G-Force GF05-Infiniti	225	2h14m43.624
5 Helio Castro-Neves	Dallara IR0-Chevrolet	225	2h14m47.950
6 Alex Barron	Dallara IR0-Chevrolet	225	2h14m48.195

Winner's average speed: 94.893 mph. Pole position: de Ferran, 19.482s. Fastest Lap: Tomas Scheckter (Dallara IR0-Infiniti), 20.1313s

INDIANAPOLIS 500

26 May 2002. Indianapolis. 200 laps of a 2.500-mile circuit = 500.000 miles. Indy Racing Series round 5

1 Helio Castro-Neves	Dallara IR0-Chevrolet	200	3h00m10.871
2 Paul Tracy	Dallara IR0-Chevrolet	200	3h00m10.909
3 Felipe Giaffone	G-Force GF05-Chevrolet	200	3h00m11.000
4 Alex Barron	Dallara IR0-Chevrolet	200	3h00m12.275
5 Eddie Cheever	Dallara IR0-Infiniti	200	3h00m13.326
6 Richie Hearn	Dallara IR0-Chevrolet	200	3h00m14.074

Winner's average speed: 166.499 mph. Pole position: Bruno Junqueira (G-Force GF05-Chevrolet), 231.342 mph. Fastest Lap: Tomas Scheckter (Dallara IR0-Infiniti), 39.7353s

BOOMTOWN 500

8 June 2002. Texas Motor Speedway. 200 laps of a 1.455-mile circuit = 291.000 miles. Indy Racing Series round 6

1 Jeff Ward	G-Force GF05-Chevrolet	200	1h45m49.708
2 Al Unser Jr	Dallara IR0-Chevrolet	200	1h45m49.719
3 Airton Dare	Dallara IR0-Chevrolet	200	1h45m49.767
4 Helio Castro-Neves	Dallara IR0-Chevrolet	200	1h45m50.332
5 Felipe Giaffone	G-Force GF05-Chevrolet	200	1h45m52.775
6 Shigeaki Hattori	Dallara IR0-Infiniti	200	1h45m54.751

Winner's average speed: 164.984 mph. Pole position: Tomas Scheckter (Dallara IR0-Infiniti), 23.7933s. Fastest Lap: Eddie Cheever (Dallara IR0-Infiniti), 23.7608s

RADISSON INDY 225

16 June 2002. Pikes Peak. 225 laps of a 1.000-mile circuit = 225.000 miles. Indy Racing Series round 7

1 Gil de Ferran	Dallara IR0-Chevrolet	225	1h51m08.609
2 Helio Castro-Neves	Dallara IR0-Chevrolet	225	1h51m10.048
3 Sam Hornish Jr	Dallara IR0-Chevrolet	225	
4 Felipe Giaffone	G-Force GF05-Chevrolet	225	
5 Scott Sharp	Dallara IR0-Chevrolet	225	
6 Al Unser Jr	Dallara IR0-Chevrolet	225	

Winner's average speed: 121.465 mph. Pole position: de Ferran, 20.2249s. Fastest Lap: Giaffone, 20.8305s

SUN TRUST INDY CHALLENGE

29 June 2002. Richmond. 250 laps of a.750-mile circuit = 187.500 miles. Indy Racing Series round 8

1 Sam Hornish Jr	Dallara IR0-Chevrolet	250	1h53m29.636
2 Gil de Ferran	Dallara IR0-Chevrolet	250	1h53m31.468
3 Felipe Giaffone	G-Force GF05-Chevrolet	250	1h53m31.833
4 Tomas Scheckter	Dallara IR0-Infiniti	250	1h53m31.879
5 Al Unser Jr	Dallara IR0-Chevrolet	250	1h53m32.496
6 Airton Dare	Dallara IR0-Chevrolet	250	1h53m32.820

Winner's average speed: 99.124 mph. Pole position: de Ferran, 16.0043s. Fastest Lap: Buddy Lazier (Dallara IR0-Chevrolet), 17.0358s

AMERISTAR CASINO INDY 200

7 July 2002. Kansas City. 200 laps of a 1.520-mile circuit = 304.000 miles. Indy Racing Series round 9

1 Airton Dare	Dallara IR0-Chevrolet	200	1h42m10.179
2 Sam Hornish Jr	Dallara IR0-Chevrolet	200	1h42m10.353
3 Helio Castro-Neves	Dallara IR0-Chevrolet	200	1h42m11.192
4 Felipe Giaffone	G-Force GF05-Chevrolet	200	1h42m11.652
5 Gil de Ferran	Dallara IR0-Chevrolet	200	1h42m11.756
6 Scott Sharp	Dallara IR0-Chevrolet	200	1h42m12.550

Winner's average speed: 178.527 mph. Pole position: Tomas Scheckter (Dallara IR0-Infiniti), 25.0381s. Fastest Lap: Scheckter, 24.8472s

FIRESTONE INDY 200

20 July 2002. Nashville. 200 laps of a 1.330-mile circuit = 266.000 miles. Indy Racing Series round 10

1 Alex Barron	Dallara IR0-Chevrolet	200	2h01m52.679
2 Gil de Ferran	Dallara IR0-Chevrolet	200	2h01m53.103
3 Sam Hornish Jr	Dallara IR0-Chevrolet	200	2h01m55.337
4 Richie Hearn	Dallara IR0-Chevrolet	200	2h01m55.930
5 Raul Boesel	Dallara IR0-Infiniti	200	2h01m56.665
6 Eddie Cheever	Dallara IR0-Infiniti	200	2h01m57.850

Winner's average speed: 130.951 mph. Pole position: Billy Boat (Dallara IR0-Chevrolet), 22.9666s. Fastest Lap: Tomas Scheckter (Dallara IR0-Infiniti), 23.1495s

MICHIGAN INDY 400

28 July 2002. Michigan. 200 laps of a 2.000-mile circuit = 400.000 miles. Indy Racing Series round 11

1 Tomas Scheckter	Dallara IR0-Infiniti	200	2h14m02.712
2 Buddy Rice	Dallara IR0-Infiniti	200	2h14m04.416

3	Felipe Giaffone	G-Force GF05-Chevrolet	200	2h14m04.451
4	Tony Renna	Dallara IR0-Chevrolet	200	2h14m04.552
5	Gil de Ferran	Dallara IR0-Chevrolet	200	2h14m05.010
6	Helio Castro-Neves	Dallara IR0-Chevrolet	200	2h14m05.258

Winner's average speed: 179.044 mph. Pole position: Scheckter, 32.4518s. Fastest Lap: Scheckter, 32.5672s

BELTERRA CASINO INDY 300

11 August 2002. Kentucky. 200 laps of a 1.500-mile circuit = 300.000 miles. Indy Racing Series round 12

1	Felipe Giaffone	G-Force GF05-Chevrolet	200	1h59m10.524
2	Sam Hornish Jr	Dallara IR0-Chevrolet	200	1h59m10.618
3	Buddy Lazier	Dallara IR0-Chevrolet	200	
4	Scott Sharp	Dallara IR0-Chevrolet	200	
5	Helio Castro-Neves	Dallara IR0-Chevrolet	200	
6	Al Unser Jr	Dallara IR0-Chevrolet	200	

Winner's average speed: 151.038 mph. Pole position: Sarah Fisher (G-Force GF05-Infiniti), 24.0661s. Fastest Lap: Tomas Scheckter (Dallara IR0-Infiniti), 24.0967s

GATEWAY INDY 250

25 August 2002. St Louis. 200 laps of a 1.270-mile circuit = 254.000 miles. Indy Racing Series round 13

1	Gil de Ferran	Dallara IR0-Chevrolet	200	1h44m22.574
2	Helio Castro-Neves	Dallara IR0-Chevrolet	200	1h44m24.676
3	Alex Barron	Dallara IR0-Chevrolet	200	
4	Buddy Rice	Dallara IR0-Infiniti	200	
5	Sam Hornish Jr	Dallara IR0-Chevrolet	200	
6	Robbie Buhl	G-Force GF05-Infiniti	200	

Winner's average speed: 146.010 mph. Pole position: de Ferran, 25.6967s. Fastest Lap: Hornish, 26.6455s

DELPHI INDY 300

8 September 2002. Chicagoland. 200 laps of a 1.500-mile circuit = 300.000 miles. Indy Racing Series round 14

1	Sam Hornish Jr	Dallara IR0-Chevrolet	200	2h04m39.535
2	Al Unser Jr	Dallara IR0-Chevrolet	200	2h04m39.538
3	Buddy Lazier	Dallara IR0-Chevrolet	200	2h04m39.595
4	Helio Castro-Neves	Dallara IR0-Chevrolet	200	2h04m39.643
5	Eddie Cheever	Dallara IR0-Infiniti	200	2h04m39.694
6	Felipe Giaffone	G-Force GF05-Chevrolet	200	2h04m40.059

Winner's average speed: 144.394 mph. Pole position: Hornish, 24.5528s. Fastest Lap: Buddy Rice (Dallara IR0-Infiniti), 24.4216s

CHEVY 500

15 September 2002. Texas Motor Speedway. 200 laps of a 1.455-mile circuit = 291.000 miles. Indy Racing Series round 15

1	Sam Hornish Jr	Dallara IR0-Chevrolet	200	1h46m28.561
2	Helio Castro-Neves	Dallara IR0-Chevrolet	200	1h46m28.571
3	Vitor Meira	Dallara IR0-Chevrolet	200	1h46m28.671
4	Scott Sharp	Dallara IR0-Chevrolet	200	1h46m28.825
5	Alex Barron	Dallara IR0-Chevrolet	200	1h46m28.924
6	Buddy Rice	Dallara IR0-Infiniti	200	1h46m30.463

Winner's average speed: 163.981 mph. Pole position: Meira, 23.6378s. Fastest Lap: Rice, 23.5415s

2002 FINAL CHAMPIONSHIP POSITIONS

1	Sam Hornish Jr	531	7	Al Unser jr	311
2	Helio Castro-Neves	511	8	Buddy Lazier	305
3	Gil de Ferran	443	9	Airton Dare	304
4	Felipe Giaffone	432	10	Eddie Cheever	280
5	Alex Barron	366			
6	Scott Sharp	332			

Drivers' Records

STARTS

Eddie Cheever	70	Tony Stewart	26	Rick Treadway	11
Buddy Lazier	70	Roberto Guerrero	25	Brian Tyler	10
Scott Sharp	66	John Paul Jr	24	Affonso Giaffone	9
Billy Boat	62	Marco Greco	23	Ronnie Johncox	8
Jeff Ward	60	Shigeaki Hattori	22	JJ Yeley	8
Robbie Buhl	59	Jimmy Kite	22	Robbie Groff	7
Mark Dismore	58	Dr Jack Miller	22	Andy Michner	7
Greg Ray	54	Robby Unser	21	Doug Didero	6
Buzz Calkins	53	Jeret Schroeder	20	Robby Gordon	6
Eliseo Salazar	53	Richie Hearn	18	Anthony Lazzaro	6
Davey Hamilton	48	Helio Castro-Neves	17	Hideki Noda	6
Stephan Gregoire	45	Laurent Redon	17	Tony Renna	6
Scott Goodyear	39	Stan Wattles	17	Vincenzo Sospiri	6
Airton Dare	37	Alex Barron	16	Fermin Velez	6
Donnie Beechler	36	Gil de Ferran	16	Michele Alboreto	5
Sam Hornish Jr	36	Billy Roe	16	Paul Durant	5
Robby McGehee	36	Jim Guthrie	15	Buddy Rice	5
Al Unser Jr	35	George Mack	15	Lyn St James	5
Sarah Fisher	32	Johnny Unser	15	Brandon Erwin	4
Kenny Brack	29	Scott Harrington	13	Vitor Meira	4
Tyce Carlson	29	Jon Herb	13	Johnny O'Connell	4
Jaques Lazier	28	Steve Knapp	13	Johnny Parsons Jr	4
Arie Luyendyk	28	Didier Andre	12	Stevie Reeves	4
Raul Boesel	27	Michael Groff	12	Jimmy Vasser	4
Felipe Giaffone	27	John Hollansworth Jr	12	John de Vries	4
Sam Schmidt	27	Tomas Scheckter	12	Niclas Jonsson	3

Indy Racing League

STARTS (cont.)

Michel Jourdain Jr	3	Danny Ongais	2	Allen May	1
David Kudrave	3	Massimiliano Papis	2	Nicolas Minassian	1
Will Langhorne	3	Bobby Regester	2	Juan Pablo Montoya	1
Jason Leffler	3	Dan Wheldon	2	Zak Morioka	1
Casey Mears	3	Cory Witherill	2	Willy T Ribbs	1
Chris Menninga	3	Claude Bourbonnais	1	Gualter Salles	1
Brad Murphey	3	Juan Carlos Carbonell	1	Mark Shank	1
Dave Steele	3	Wim Eyckmans	1	Paul Tracy	1
Alessandro Zampedri	3	Dario Franchitti	1	Dennis Vitolo	1
Michael Andretti	2	Racin Gardner	1		
Scott Brayton	2	Memo Gidley	1		
Joe Gosek	2	Andy Hillenburg	1		
Jack Hewitt	2	Davy Jones	1		
Bruno Junqueira	2	Tony Kanaan	1		
Hideshi Matsuda	2	Steve Kinser	1		
Roberto Moreno	2	Cory Kruseman	1		

Note: A driver is credited as starting a race if they take the rolling start, or subsequently makes a delayed start from the pits. If a driver retires before the green flag they are deemed not to have started.

YOUNGEST DRIVERS TO START AN IRL RACE

19 years 13 days	Sarah Fisher	1999 Texas
19 years 203 days	Michel Jourdain Jr	1996 Phoenix
20 years 210 days	Sam Hornish Jr	2000 Disney World
21 years 132 days	Jimmy Kite	1997 Pikes Peak
21 years 163 days	Tomas Scheckter	2002 Homestead

OLDEST DRIVERS TO START AN IRL RACE

54 years 250 days	Danny Ongais	1997 Disney World
53 years 76 days	Lyn St James	2000 Indianapolis 500
52 years 20 days	Johnny Parsons Jr	1996 Las Vegas
48 years 311 days	Arie Luyendyk	2002 Michigan
47 years 306 days	Eliseo Salazar	2002 Texas race 2

WINS

Sam Hornish Jr	8	Robbie Buhl	2	Richie Hearn	1
Buddy Lazier	8	Gil de Ferran	2	Jaques Lazier	1
Scott Sharp	7	Al Unser Jr	2	Juan Pablo Montoya	1
Eddie Cheever	5	Alex Barron	1	John Paul Jr	1
Greg Ray	5	Billy Boat	1	Eliseo Salazar	1
Kenny Brack	4	Buzz Calkins	1	Tomas Scheckter	1
Arie Luyendyk	4	Airton Dare	1	Sam Schmidt	1
Helio Castro-Neves	3	Mark Dismore	1	Jeff Ward	1
Scott Goodyear	3	Felipe Giaffone	1		
Tony Stewart	3	Jim Guthrie	1		

YOUNGEST DRIVERS TO WIN AN IRL RACE

21 years 259 days	Sam Hornish Jr	2001 Phoenix
21 years 309 days	Tomas Scheckter	2002 Michigan
24 years 147 days	Airton Dare	2002 Kansas City
24 years 250 days	Juan Pablo Montoya	2000 Indianapolis 500
24 years 270 days	Buzz Calkins	1996 Disney World

OLDEST DRIVERS TO WIN AN IRL RACE

45 years 20 days	Arie Luyendyk	1998 Las Vegas
43 years 178 days	Eddie Cheever	2001 Kansas City
43 years 5 days	Mark Dismore	1999 Texas
42 years 331 days	Eliseo Salazar	1997 Las Vegas
40 years 248 days	Jeff Ward	2002 Texas

POLE POSITIONS

Greg Ray	14	Buddy Lazier	2	Richie Hearn	1
Billy Boat	9	Jaques Lazier	2	Bruno Junqueira	1
Tony Stewart	8	Jeff Ward	2	Vitor Meira	1
Scott Sharp	5	Scott Brayton	1	Sam Schmidt	1
Mark Dismore	4	Helio Castro-Neves	1		
Gil de Ferran	4	Eddie Cheever	1		
Sam Hornish Jr	4	Sarah Fisher	1	Includes poles awarded on championship
Arie Luyendyk	4	Scott Goodyear	1	position if qualifying was cancelled
Tomas Scheckter	3	Marco Greco	1		

LAPS IN THE LEAD

Tony Stewart	1515	Felipe Giaffone	184	Airton Dare	37
Sam Hornish Jr	1456	Juan Pablo Montoya	167	Marco Greco	37
Greg Ray	1188	Buzz Calkins	148	Buddy Rice	37
Buddy Lazier	1024	Robby Gordon	110	Bruno Junqueira	32
Scott Sharp	940	Richie Hearn	103	Shigeaki Hattori	28
Scott Goodyear	653	Roberto Guerrero	101	Jimmy Kite	27
Gil de Ferran	631	John Paul Jr	101	Tony Kanaan	23
Eddie Cheever	611	Stephan Gregoire	89	Alessandro Zampedri	20
Jeff Ward	519	Jim Guthrie	89	Michael Andretti	16
Al Unser Jr	496	Davey Hamilton	76	Will Langhorne	9
Mark Dismore	483	Robby McGehee	73	Andy Michner	9
Tomas Scheckter	443	Affonso Giaffone	63	Vitor Meira	8
Kenny Brack	436	Raul Boesel	59	Jimmy Vasser	5
Arie Luyendyk	427	Alex Barron	49	Tyce Carlson	4
Helio Castro-Neves	407	Donnie Beechler	48	Robbie Groff	3
Billy Boat	324	Davy Jones	46	Johnny O'Connell	3
Robbie Buhl	285	Robby Unser	45	Stan Wattles	2
Eliseo Salazar	232	Sarah Fisher	39	Scott Harrington	1
Jaques Lazier	226	Laurent Redon	39	Vincenzo Sospiri	1
Sam Schmidt	208	Tony Renna	38		

MILES IN THE LEAD

Sam Hornish Jr	1990	Felipe Giaffone	299	Tony Kanaan	58
Tony Stewart	1861	Sam Schmidt	248	Airton Dare	54
Greg Ray	1674	Robby Gordon	215	Tony Renna	53
Buddy Lazier	1312	Roberto Guerrero	195	Alessandro Zampedri	50
Scott Sharp	1137	John Paul Jr	189	Shigeaki Hattori	41
Eddie Cheever	901	Buzz Calkins	154	Marco Greco	41
Scott Goodyear	861	Richie Hearn	148	Jimmy Kite	41
Tomas Scheckter	823	Davy Jones	115	Michael Andretti	40
Jeff Ward	752	Jim Guthrie	96	Laurent Redon	29
Kenny Brack	711	Robby McGehee	94	Will Langhorne	14
Arie Luyendyk	700	Davey Hamilton	94	Andy Michner	13
Gil de Ferran	686	Stephan Gregoire	94	Jimmy Vasser	13
Mark Dismore	660	Affonso Giaffone	88	Vitor Meira	12
Al Unser Jr	658	Bruno Junqueira	80	Tyce Carlson	5
Helio Castro-Neves	605	Raul Boesel	73	Johnny O'Connell	5
Billy Boat	461	Alex Barron	72	Robbie Groff	4
Juan Pablo Montoya	418	Robby Unser	66	Stan Wattles	2
Jaques Lazier	362	Donnie Beechler	65	Vincenzo Sospiri	1
Robbie Buhl	358	Buddy Rice	63	Scott Harrington	1
Eliseo Salazar	307	Sarah Fisher	61		

Manufacturers' Records

STARTS

Dallara	66
G-Force	66
Riley & Scott	23
Lola	5
Reynard	5

WINS

Dallara	48
G-Force	17
Reynard	4
Lola	1
Riley & Scott	1

POLE POSITIONS

Dallara	52
G-Force	14
Reynard	3
Lola	2

Engine Records

STARTS	
Nissan (Infiniti)	65
Oldsmobile (Aurora)	51
Chevrolet	15
Buick (including Buick/Menard)	5
Ford	5
Mercedes-Benz	1

WINS	
Oldsmobile (Aurora)	49
Chevrolet	14
Ford	5
Nissan (Infiniti)	3

POLE POSITIONS	
Oldsmobile (Aurora)	51
Chevrolet	10
Nissan (Infiniti)	5
Ford	4
Buick/Menard	1

Clockwise from top left 2002 Sam Hornish celebrates a second successive title win. **2002** Frantic pit activity during a yellow flag period at Texas. **2001** Polesitter Scott Sharp spins out of the Indy 500 at the start.

NASCAR

2000 The 2000 NASCAR Winston Cup field line up at Daytona.

NASCAR Winston Cup

The NASCAR Winston Cup is the strongest series in North America. It boasts fields of over 40 closely-matched stock cars, with full grandstands at the 36 championship races held each year. With cars from Chevrolet, Pontiac, Ford and Dodge, and a cast of almost exclusively homegrown driving talent, NASCAR is the most American of racing categories. Events are held at state-of-the-art speedways, with the races at Watkins Glen and Sears Point the only road courses on the calendar.

The Winston Cup grew out of the Grand National championship, which had been organised for "strictly stock" cars by Bill France and the National Association for Stock Car Auto Racing since 1949. When NASCAR secured sponsorship from the RJ Reynolds Tobacco Company in 1972, the top category was renamed the Winston Cup after the cigarette brand. At that time a streamlined calendar that essentially halved the num-ber of events was introduced. It concentrated on the major races and allowed all drivers to compete in every event. In previous years clashing race dates had made this impossible.

The 1972 changes launched NASCAR's "Modern Era", as the organisation worked to overtake open-wheel racing as the continent's most thriving motor-sport series.

Key to NASCAR's growth was the live television cover-age of races. The first race covered live on network tele-vision was the centrepiece Daytona 500 in 1979. It ended with race leaders Cale Yarborough and Donnie Allison clashing on the last lap to hand victory to Richard Petty, the championship's most successful driver. As the cars came to rest a fight broke out between Yarborough and Allison, who was joined by brother Bobby, live on CBS Television – a perfect way to gain vital column inches and launch NASCAR into the mainstream of American sports.

NASCAR CHAMPIONS

year	driver	nat	team	car
1949	Red Byron	USA	Parks Novelty	Oldsmobile
1950	Bill Rexford	USA	Julian Buesink	Oldsmobile
1951	Herb Thomas	USA	Thomas/Sandford Motors/Fabulous	Plymouth/Oldsmobile/Hudson Hornet
1952	Tim Flock	USA	Ted Chester	Hudson Hornet
1953	Herb Thomas	USA	Fabulous	Hudson Hornet
1954	Lee Petty	USA	Petty Engineering	Dodge/Chrysler
1955	Tim Flock	USA	Mercury Outboards/Westmoreland	Chrysler/Chevrolet
1956	Buck Baker	USA	Satcher Motors/Kiekhaefer	Ford/Chrsyler/Dodge
1957	Buck Baker	USA	Hugh Babb/Buck Baker	Chevrolet
1958	Lee Petty	USA	Petty Engineering	Oldsmobile
1959	Lee Petty	USA	Petty Engineering	Oldsmobile/Plymouth
1960	Rex White	USA	Piedmont/Friendly	Ford/Chevrolet
1961	Ned Jarrett	USA	Courtesy/BG Holloway	Ford/Chevrolet
1962	Joe Weatherly	USA	Bud Moore	Pontiac
1963	Joe Weatherly	USA	Bud Moore*	Pontiac/Chrysler/Plymouth/ Dodge/Mercury
1964	Richard Petty	USA	Petty Engineering	Plymouth
1965	Ned Jarrett	USA	Bondy Long	Ford
1966	David Pearson	USA	Cotton Owens	Dodge
1967	Richard Petty	USA	Petty Enterprises	Plymouth
1968	David Pearson	USA	Holman-Moody	Ford
1969	David Pearson	USA	Holman-Moody	Ford
1970	Bobby Isaac	USA	K&K Insurance	Dodge Daytona
1971	Richard Petty	USA	Petty Enterprises	Plymouth
1972	Richard Petty	USA	Petty Enterprises	Plymouth/Dodge
1973	Benny Parsons	USA	LG de Witt	Chevrolet
1974	Richard Petty	USA	Petty Enterprises	Dodge
1975	Richard Petty	USA	Petty Enterprises	Dodge
1976	Cale Yarborough	USA	Junior Johnson	Chevrolet
1977	Cale Yarborough	USA	Junior Johnson	Chevrolet
1978	Cale Yarborough	USA	Junior Johnson	Oldsmobile
1979	Richard Petty	USA	Petty Enterprises	Chevrolet
1980	Dale Earnhardt	USA	Osterlund Racing	Chevrolet
1981	Darrell Waltrip	USA	Junior Johnson	Buick
1982	Darrell Waltrip	USA	Junior Johnson	Buick
1983	Bobby Allison	USA	Di Gard Racing	Buick
1984	Terry Labonte	USA	Billy Hagan	Chevrolet
1985	Darrell Waltrip	USA	Junior Johnson	Chevrolet
1986	Dale Earnhardt	USA	Richard Childress Racing	Chevrolet
1987	Dale Earnhardt	USA	Richard Childress Racing	Chevrolet
1988	Bill Elliott	USA	Elliott Brothers	Ford
1989	Rusty Wallace	USA	Raymond Beadle	Pontiac
1990	Dale Earnhardt	USA	Richard Childress Racing	Chevrolet
1991	Dale Earnhardt	USA	Richard Childress Racing	Chevrolet
1992	Alan Kulwicki	USA	Alan Kulwicki	Ford
1993	Dale Earnhardt	USA	Richard Childress Racing	Chevrolet
1994	Dale Earnhardt	USA	Richard Childress Racing	Chevrolet

NASCAR CHAMPIONS (cont.)

1995	Jeff Gordon	USA	Hendrick Motorsports	Chevrolet
1996	Terry Labonte	USA	Hendrick Motorsports	Chevrolet
1997	Jeff Gordon	USA	Hendrick Motorsports	Chevrolet
1998	Jeff Gordon	USA	Hendrick Motorsports	Chevrolet
1999	Dale Jarrett	USA	Robert Yates	Ford
2000	Bobby Labonte	USA	Joe Gibbs Racing	Pontiac
2001	Jeff Gordon	USA	Hendrick Motorsports	Chevrolet
2002	Tony Stewart	USA	Joe Gibbs Racing	Pontiac

*Weatherly drove the majority of the 1963 season for Bud Moore in a Pontiac and then a Mercury. However, Moore did not enter all of the races and Weatherly also drove Pontiacs for Fred Harb, Pete Stewart, Cliff Stewart, Worth McMillion, a Chrysler for Major Melton, a Plymouth for Petty Engineering and a Dodge for Wade Younts on his way to the NASCAR Championship!

Race Winners (Modern Era)

1972

date	race	driver	nat	car	mph
23.01.72	Winston Western 500 (Riverside)	Richard Petty	USA	Plymouth	104.017
20.02.72	Daytona 500 (Daytona)	AJ Foyt Jr	USA	Mercury	161.551
27.02.72	Richmond 500 (Richmond)	Richard Petty	USA	Plymouth	76.626
05.03.72	Miller High Life 500 (Ontario)	AJ Foyt Jr	USA	Mercury	127.083
12.03.72	Carolina 500 (N Carolina)	Bobby Isaac	USA	Dodge	110.037
26.03.72	Atlanta 500 (Atlanta)	Bobby Allison	USA	Chevrolet	128.214
09.04.72	Southeastern 500 (Bristol)	Bobby Allison	USA	Chevrolet	93.893
16.04.72	Rebel 400 (Darlington)	David Pearson	USA	Mercury	124.426
23.04.72	Gwyn Staley Memorial (N Wilkesboro)	Richard Petty	USA	Plymouth	86.547
30.04.72	Virginia 500 (Martinsville)	Richard Petty	USA	Plymouth	72.719
07.05.72	Winston 500 (Talladega)	David Pearson	USA	Mercury	134.400
28.05.72	World 600 (Charlotte)	Buddy Baker	USA	Dodge	142.255
04.06.72	Mason-Dixon 500 (Dover Downs)	Bobby Allison	USA	Chevrolet	118.663
11.06.72	Motor State 400 (Michigan)	David Pearson	USA	Mercury	146.640
18.06.72	Golden State 400 (Riverside)	Ray Elder	USA	Dodge	98.761
25.06.72	Lone Star 500 (Texas World Speedway)	Richard Petty	USA	Plymouth	144.185
04.07.72	Firecracker 400 (Daytona)	David Pearson	USA	Mercury	160.813
09.07.72	Volunteer 500 (Bristol)	Bobby Allison	USA	Chevrolet	106.269
16.07.72	Northern 300 (Trenton)	Bobby Allison	USA	Chevrolet	101.304
23.07.72	Dixie 500 (Atlanta)	Bobby Allison	USA	Chevrolet	131.874
06.08.72	Talladega 500 (Talladega)	James Hylton	USA	Mercury	148.428
20.08.72	Yankee 400 (Michigan)	David Pearson	USA	Mercury	134.441
27.08.72	Nashville 420 (Nashville)	Bobby Allison	USA	Chevrolet	92.578
04.09.72	Southern 500 (Darlington)	Bobby Allison	USA	Chevrolet	128.124
10.09.72	Capital City 500 (Richmond)	Richard Petty	USA	Plymouth	75.899
17.09.72	Delaware 500 (Dover Downs)	David Pearson	USA	Mercury	120.506
24.09.72	Old Dominion 500 (Martinsville)	Richard Petty	USA	Plymouth	70.123
01.10.72	Wilkes 400 (N Wilkesboro)	Richard Petty	USA	Plymouth	95.816
08.10.72	National 500 (Charlotte)	Bobby Allison	USA	Chevrolet	133.235
22.10.72	American 500 (N Carolina)	Bobby Allison	USA	Chevrolet	118.282
12.11.72	Texas 500 (Texas World Speedway)	Buddy Baker	USA	Dodge	147.059

1973

date	race	driver	nat	car	mph
21.01.73	Winston Western 500 (Riverside)	Mark Donohue	USA	Matador	104.055
18.02.73	Daytona 500 (Daytona)	Richard Petty	USA	Dodge	157.205
25.02.73	Richmond 500 (Richmond)	Richard Petty	USA	Dodge	74.764
18.03.73	Carolina 500 (N Carolina)	David Pearson	USA	Mercury	118.656
25.03.73	Southeastern 500 (Bristol)	Cale Yarborough	USA	Chevrolet	89.975
01.04.73	Atlanta 500 (Atlanta)	David Pearson	USA	Mercury	139.403
08.04.73	Gwyn Staley Memorial (N Wilkesboro)	Richard Petty	USA	Dodge	97.224
15.04.73	Rebel 500 (Darlington)	David Pearson	USA	Mercury	123.158
29.04.73	Virginia 500 (Martinsville)	David Pearson	USA	Mercury	70.310
06.05.73	Winston 500 (Talladega)	David Pearson	USA	Mercury	131.957
12.05.73	Music City 420 (Nashville)	Cale Yarborough	USA	Chevrolet	97.023
27.05.73	World 600 (Charlotte)	Buddy Baker	USA	Dodge	134.890
03.06.73	Mason-Dixon 500 (Dover Downs)	David Pearson	USA	Mercury	119.745
10.06.73	Alamo 500 (Texas World Speedway)	Richard Petty	USA	Dodge	145.114

date	race	driver	nat	car	mph
17.06.73	Tuborg 400 (Riverside)	Bobby Allison	USA	Chevrolet	100.215
24.06.73	Motor State 400 (Michigan)	David Pearson	USA	Mercury	153.485
04.07.73	Firecracker 400 (Daytona)	David Pearson	USA	Mercury	158.468
08.07.73	Volunteer 500 (Bristol)	Benny Parsons/			
		John A Utsman	USA	Chevrolet	92.392
22.07.73	Dixie 500 (Atlanta)	David Pearson	USA	Mercury	130.221
12.08.73	Talladega 500 (Talladega)	Dick Brooks	USA	Plymouth	145.454
25.08.73	Nashville 420 (Nashville)	Buddy Baker	USA	Dodge	89.294
03.09.73	Southern 500 (Darlington)	Cale Yarborough	USA	Chevrolet	134.033
09.09.73	Capital City 500 (Richmond)	Richard Petty	USA	Dodge	64.197
16.09.73	Delaware 500 (Dover Downs)	David Pearson	USA	Mercury	112.853
23.09.73	Wilkes 400 (N Wilkesboro)	Bobby Allison	USA	Chevrolet	95.198
30.09.73	Old Dominion 500 (Martinsville)	Richard Petty	USA	Dodge	66.195
07.10.73	National 500 (Charlotte)	Cale Yarborough	USA	Chevrolet	145.241
21.10.73	American 500 (N Carolina)	David Pearson	USA	Mercury	117.756

1974

date	race	driver	nat	car	mph
20.01.74	Winston Western 500 (Riverside)	Cale Yarborough	USA	Chevrolet	101.140
17.02.74	Daytona 500 (Daytona)	Richard Petty	USA	Dodge	140.894
24.02.74	Richmond 500 (Richmond)	Bobby Allison	USA	Chevrolet	80.392
03.03.74	Carolina 500 (N Carolina)	Richard Petty	USA	Dodge	121.310
17.03.74	Southeastern 500 (Bristol)	Cale Yarborough	USA	Chevrolet	64.582
24.03.74	Atlanta 500 (Atlanta)	Cale Yarborough	USA	Chevrolet	149.991
07.04.74	Rebel 500 (Darlington)	David Pearson	USA	Mercury	117.544
21.04.74	Gwyn Staley Memorial (N Wilkesboro)	Richard Petty	USA	Dodge	96.200
28.04.74	Virginia 500 (Martinsville)	Cale Yarborough	USA	Chevrolet	70.070
05.05.74	Winston 500 (Talladega)	David Pearson	USA	Mercury	130.348
11.05.74	Music City USA 420 (Nashville)	Richard Petty	USA	Dodge	76.690
19.05.74	Mason-Dixon 500 (Dover Downs)	Cale Yarborough	USA	Chevrolet	115.057
26.05.74	World 600 (Charlotte)	David Pearson	USA	Mercury	135.935
09.06.74	Tuborg 400 (Riverside)	Cale Yarborough	USA	Chevrolet	102.489
16.06.74	Motor State 400 (Michigan)	Richard Petty	USA	Dodge	127.987
04.07.74	Firecracker 400 (Daytona)	David Pearson	USA	Mercury	138.302
14.07.74	Volunteer 500 (Bristol)	Cale Yarborough	USA	Chevrolet	75.430
20.07.74	Nashville 420 (Nashville)	Cale Yarborough	USA	Chevrolet	78.772
28.07.74	Dixie 500 (Atlanta)	Richard Petty	USA	Dodge	134.610
04.08.74	Purolator 500 (Pocono)	Richard Petty	USA	Dodge	115.593
11.08.74	Talladega 500 (Talladega)	Richard Petty	USA	Dodge	148.637
25.08.74	Yankee 400 (Michigan)	David Pearson	USA	Mercury	133.050
02.09.74	Southern 500 (Darlington)	Cale Yarborough	USA	Chevrolet	111.076
08.09.74	Capital City 500 (Richmond)	Richard Petty	USA	Dodge	64.430
15.09.74	Delaware 500 (Dover Downs)	Richard Petty	USA	Dodge	113.644
22.09.74	Wilkes 400 (N Wilkesboro)	Cale Yarborough	USA	Chevrolet	80.783
29.09.74	Old Dominion 500 (Martinsville)	Earl Ross	CDN	Chevrolet	66.289
06.10.74	National 500 (Charlotte)	David Pearson	USA	Mercury	119.912
20.10.74	American 500 (N Carolina)	David Pearson	USA	Mercury	118.499
24.11.74	Los Angeles Times 500 (Ontario)	Bobby Allison	USA	Matador	134.963

1975 "The King" Richard Petty won the banking at the Daytona 500.

1975

date	race	driver	nat	car	mph
19.01.75	Winston Western 500 (Riverside)	Bobby Allison	USA	Matador	98.632
16.02.75	Daytona 500 (Daytona)	Benny Parsons	USA	Chevrolet	153.649
23.02.75	Richmond 500 (Richmond)	Richard Petty	USA	Dodge	74.914
02.03.75	Carolina 500 (N Carolina)	Cale Yarborough	USA	Chevrolet	117.594
16.03.75	Southeastern 500 (Bristol)	Richard Petty	USA	Dodge	97.569
23.03.75	Atlanta 500 (Atlanta)	Richard Petty	USA	Dodge	133.659
06.04.75	Gwyn Staley Memorial (N Wilkesboro)	Richard Petty	USA	Dodge	90.009
13.04.75	Rebel 500 (Darlington)	Bobby Allison	USA	Matador	117.643
27.04.75	Virginia 500 (Martinsville)	Richard Petty	USA	Dodge	69.439
04.05.75	Winston 500 (Talladega)	Buddy Baker	USA	Ford	144.962
10.05.75	Music City USA 420 (Nashville)	Darrell Waltrip	USA	Chevrolet	94.017
18.05.75	Mason-Dixon 500 (Dover Downs)	David Pearson	USA	Mercury	100.829
25.05.75	World 600 (Charlotte)	Richard Petty	USA	Dodge	145.337
08.06.75	Tuborg 400 (Riverside)	Richard Petty	USA	Dodge	101.029
15.06.75	Motor Safe 400 (Michigan)	David Pearson	USA	Mercury	131.399
04.07.75	Firecracker 400 (Daytona)	Richard Petty	USA	Dodge	158.381
20.07.75	Nashville 420 (Nashville)	Cale Yarborough	USA	Chevrolet	89.792
03.08.75	Purolator 500 (Pocono)	David Pearson	USA	Mercury	143.426
17.08.75	Talladega 500 (Talladega)	Buddy Baker	USA	Ford	130.892
24.08.75	Champion Spark Plug 400 (Michigan)	Richard Petty	USA	Dodge	107.583
01.09.75	Southern 500 (Darlington)	Bobby Allison	USA	Matador	116.828
14.09.75	Delaware 500 (Dover Downs)	Richard Petty	USA	Dodge	111.372
21.09.75	Wilkes 400 (N Wilkesboro)	Richard Petty	USA	Dodge	88.986
28.09.75	Old Dominion 500 (Martinsville)	Dave Marcis	USA	Dodge	75.944
05.10.75	National 500 (Charlotte)	Richard Petty	USA	Dodge	132.209
12.10.75	Capital City 500 (Richmond)	Darrell Waltrip	USA	Chevrolet	81.887
19.10.75	American 500 (N Carolina)	Cale Yarborough	USA	Chevrolet	120.135
02.11.75	Volunteer 500 (Bristol)	Richard Petty	USA	Dodge	97.017
09.11.75	Dixie 500 (Atlanta)	Buddy Baker	USA	Ford	130.990
23.11.75	Los Angeles Times 500 (Ontario)	Buddy Baker	USA	Ford	140.713

1976

date	race	driver	nat	car	mph
18.01.76	Winston Western 500 (Riverside)	David Pearson	USA	Mercury	99.180
15.02.76	Daytona 500 (Daytona)	David Pearson	USA	Mercury	152.181
29.02.76	Carolina 500 (N Carolina)	Richard Petty	USA	Dodge	113.662
07.03.76	Richmond 400 (Richmond)	Dave Marcis	USA	Dodge	72.779
14.03.76	Southeastern 400 (Bristol)	Cale Yarborough	USA	Chevrolet	87.978
21.03.76	Atlanta 500 (Atlanta)	David Pearson	USA	Mercury	128.959
04.04.76	Gwyn Staley Memorial (N Wilkesboro)	Cale Yarborough	USA	Chevrolet	96.858
11.04.76	Rebel 500 (Darlington)	David Pearson	USA	Mercury	122.974
25.04.76	Virginia 500 (Martinsville)	Darrell Waltrip	USA	Chevrolet	71.820
02.05.76	Winston 500 (Talladega)	Buddy Baker	USA	Ford	169.887
08.05.76	Music City USA 420 (Nashville)	Cale Yarborough	USA	Chevrolet	84.512
16.05.76	Mason-Dixon 500 (Dover Downs)	Benny Parsons	USA	Chevrolet	115.436
30.05.76	World 600 (Charlotte)	David Pearson	USA	Mercury	137.352
13.06.76	Riverside 400 (Riverside)	David Pearson	USA	Mercury	106.279
20.06.76	Cam 2 Motor Oil 400 (Michigan)	David Pearson	USA	Mercury	141.149
04.07.76	Firecracker 400 (Daytona)	Cale Yarborough	USA	Chevrolet	160.966
17.07.76	Nashville 420 (Nashville)	Benny Parsons	USA	Chevrolet	86.908
01.08.76	Purolator 500 (Pocono)	Richard Petty	USA	Dodge	115.875
08.08.76	Talladega 500 (Talladega)	Dave Marcis	USA	Dodge	157.547
22.08.76	Champion Spark Plug 400 (Michigan)	David Pearson	USA	Mercury	140.078
29.08.76	Volunteer 400 (Bristol)	Cale Yarborough	USA	Chevrolet	99.176
06.09.76	Southern 500 (Darlington)	David Pearson	USA	Mercury	120.534
12.09.76	Capital City 400 (Richmond)	Cale Yarborough	USA	Chevrolet	77.993
19.09.76	Delaware 500 (Dover Downs)	Cale Yarborough	USA	Chevrolet	115.741
26.09.76	Old Dominion 500 (Martinsville)	Cale Yarborough	USA	Chevrolet	75.433
03.10.76	Wilkes 400 (N Wilkesboro)	Cale Yarborough	USA	Chevrolet	96.380
10.10.76	National 500 (Charlotte)	Donnie Allison	USA	Chevrolet	141.226
24.10.76	American 500 (N Carolina)	Richard Petty	USA	Dodge	117.725
07.11.76	Dixie 500 (Atlanta)	Dave Marcis	USA	Dodge	127.396
21.11.76	Los Angeles Times 500 (Ontario)	David Pearson	USA	Mercury	137.101

1977

date	race	driver	nat	car	mph
16.01.77	Winston Western 500 (Riverside)	David Pearson	USA	Mercury	107.039
20.02.77	Daytona 500 (Daytona)	Cale Yarborough	USA	Chevrolet	153.218
27.02.77	Richmond 400 (Richmond)	Cale Yarborough	USA	Chevrolet	73.084
13.03.77	Carolina 500 (N Carolina)	Richard Petty	USA	Dodge	97.865
20.03.77	Atlanta 500 (Atlanta)	Richard Petty	USA	Dodge	144.109
27.03.77	Gwyn Staley Memorial (N Wilkesboro)	Cale Yarborough	USA	Chevrolet	88.950
03.04.77	Rebel 500 (Darlington)	Darrell Waltrip	USA	Chevrolet	128.930
17.04.77	Southeastern 500 (Bristol)	Cale Yarborough	USA	Chevrolet	100.989
24.04.77	Virginia 500 (Martinsville)	Cale Yarborough	USA	Chevrolet	77.471
01.05.77	Winston 500 (Talladega)	Darrell Waltrip	USA	Chevrolet	164.877
07.05.77	Music City USA 420 (Nashville)	Benny Parsons	USA	Chevrolet	87.490
15.05.77	Mason-Dixon 500 (Dover Downs)	Cale Yarborough	USA	Chevrolet	123.237
29.05.77	World 600 (Charlotte)	Richard Petty	USA	Dodge	137.676
12.06.77	NAPA 400 (Riverside)	Richard Petty	USA	Dodge	105.021
19.06.77	Cam 2 Motor Oil 400 (Michigan)	Cale Yarborough	USA	Chevrolet	135.034
04.07.77	Firecracker 400 (Daytona)	Richard Petty	USA	Dodge	142.716
16.07.77	Nashville 420 (Nashville)	Darrell Waltrip	USA	Chevrolet	78.986
31.07.77	Coca-Cola 500 (Pocono)	Benny Parsons	USA	Chevrolet	128.379
07.08.77	Talladega 500 (Talladega)	Donnie Allison/ Darrell Waltrip	USA	Chevrolet	162.525
22.08.77	Champion Spark Plug 400 (Michigan)	Darrell Waltrip	USA	Chevrolet	137.944
28.08.77	Volunteer 400 (Bristol)	Cale Yarborough	USA	Chevrolet	79.726
05.09.77	Southern 500 (Darlington)	David Pearson	USA	Mercury	106.740
11.09.77	Capital City 400 (Richmond)	Neil Bonnett	USA	Dodge	80.645
18.09.77	Delaware 500 (Dover Downs)	Benny Parsons	USA	Chevrolet	114.708
25.09.77	Old Dominion 500 (Martinsville)	Cale Yarborough	USA	Chevrolet	73.509
02.10.77	Wilkes 400 (N Wilkesboro)	Darrell Waltrip	USA	Chevrolet	86.714
09.10.77	NAPA National 500 (Charlotte)	Benny Parsons	USA	Chevrolet	142.780
23.10.77	American 500 (N Carolina)	Donnie Allison	USA	Chevrolet	113.590
06.11.77	Dixie 500 (Atlanta)	Darrell Waltrip	USA	Chevrolet	110.052
20.11.77	Los Angeles Times 500 (Ontario)	Neil Bonnett	USA	Dodge	128.297

1978

19.02.78	Daytona 500 (Daytona)	Bobby Allison	USA	Ford	159.730
26.02.78	Richmond 400 (Richmond)	Benny Parsons	USA	Chevrolet	80.305
05.03.78	Carolina 500 (N Carolina)	David Pearson	USA	Mercury	116.688
19.03.78	Atlanta 500 (Atlanta)	Bobby Allison	USA	Ford	142.520
02.04.78	Southeastern 500 (Bristol)	Darrell Waltrip	USA	Chevrolet	92.401
09.04.78	Rebel 500 (Darlington)	Benny Parsons	USA	Chevrolet	127.545
16.04.78	Gwyn Staley Memorial (N Wilkesboro)	Darrell Waltrip	USA	Chevrolet	92.346
23.04.78	Virginia 500 (Martinsville)	Darrell Waltrip	USA	Chevrolet	78.119
14.05.78	Winston 500 (Talladega)	Cale Yarborough	USA	Oldsmobile	159.699
21.05.78	Mason-Dixon 500 (Dover Downs)	David Pearson	USA	Mercury	114.664
28.05.78	World 600 (Charlotte)	Darrell Waltrip	USA	Chevrolet	138.355
03.06.78	Music City USA 420 (Nashville)	Cale Yarborough	USA	Oldsmobile	87.541
11.06.78	NAPA 400 (Riverside)	Benny Parsons	USA	Chevrolet	104.312
18.06.78	Gabriel 400 (Michigan)	Cale Yarborough	USA	Oldsmobile	149.564
04.07.78	Firecracker 400 (Daytona)	David Pearson	USA	Mercury	154.341
15.07.78	Nashville 420 (Nashville)	Cale Yarborough	USA	Oldsmobile	88.924
30.07.78	Coca-Cola 500 (Pocono)	Darrell Waltrip	USA	Chevrolet	142.540
06.08.78	Talladega 500 (Talladega)	Lennie Pond	USA	Oldsmobile	174.734
20.08.78	Champion Spark Plug 400 (Michigan)	David Pearson	USA	Mercury	129.566
26.08.78	Volunteer 500 (Bristol)	Cale Yarborough	USA	Oldsmobile	78.000
04.09.78	Southern 500 (Darlington)	Cale Yarborough	USA	Oldsmobile	116.692
10.09.78	Capital City 400 (Richmond)	Darrell Waltrip	USA	Chevrolet	79.649
17.09.78	Delaware 500 (Dover Downs)	Bobby Allison	USA	Ford	119.363
24.09.78	Old Dominion 500 (Martinsville)	Cale Yarborough	USA	Oldsmobile	79.336
01.10.78	Wilkes 400 (N Wilkesboro)	Cale Yarborough	USA	Oldsmobile	91.855
08.10.78	NAPA National 500 (Charlotte)	Bobby Allison	USA	Ford	141.826
22.10.78	American 500 (N Carolina)	Cale Yarborough	USA	Oldsmobile	117.288
05.11.78	Dixie 500 (Atlanta)	Donnie Allison	USA	Chevrolet	124.432
19.11.78	Los Angeles Times 500 (Ontario)	Bobby Allison	USA	Ford	144.416

1979

date	race	driver	nat	car	mph
14.01.79	Winston Western 500 (Riverside)	Darrell Waltrip	USA	Chevrolet	107.820
18.02.79	Daytona 500 (Daytona)	Richard Petty	USA	Oldsmobile	143.977
04.03.79	Carolina 500 (N Carolina)	Bobby Allison	USA	Ford	121.792
11.03.79	Richmond 400 (Richmond)	Cale Yarborough	USA	Oldsmobile	83.617
18.03.79	Atlanta 500 (Atlanta)	Buddy Baker	USA	Oldsmobile	135.055
25.03.79	Northwestern Bank 400 (N Wilkesboro)	Bobby Allison	USA	Ford	88.400
01.04.79	Southeastern 500 (Bristol)	Dale Earnhardt	USA	Chevrolet	91.033
08.04.79	CRC Chemicals Rebel 500 (Darlington)	Darrell Waltrip	USA	Chevrolet	121.787
22.04.79	Virginia 500 (Martinsville)	Richard Petty	USA	Chevrolet	76.707
20.05.79	Mason-Dixon 500 (Dover Downs)	Neil Bonnett	USA	Mercury	111.269
27.05.79	World 600 (Charlotte)	Darrell Waltrip	USA	Chevrolet	136.674
03.06.79	Texas 400 (Texas World Speedway)	Darrell Waltrip	USA	Chevrolet	156.199
10.06.79	NAPA Riverside 400 (Riverside)	Bobby Allison	USA	Ford	103.732
17.06.79	Gabriel 400 (Michigan)	Buddy Baker	USA	Chevrolet	135.798
04.07.79	Firecracker 400 (Daytona)	Neil Bonnett	USA	Mercury	172.890
14.07.79	Busch Nashville 420 (Nashville)	Darrell Waltrip	USA	Chevrolet	92.227
30.07.79	Coca-Cola 500 (Pocono)	Cale Yarborough	USA	Chevrolet	115.207
05.08.79	Talladega 500 (Talladega)	Darrell Waltrip	USA	Chevrolet	161.229
19.08.79	Champion Spark Plug 400 (Michigan)	Richard Petty	USA	Chevrolet	130.376
25.08.79	Volunteer 500 (Bristol)	Darrell Waltrip	USA	Chevrolet	91.493
03.09.79	Southern 500 (Darlington)	David Pearson	USA	Chevrolet	126.260
09.09.79	Capital City 400 (Richmond)	Bobby Allison	USA	Ford	80.603
16.09.79	CRC Chemicals 500 (Dover Downs)	Richard Petty	USA	Chevrolet	114.366
23.09.79	Old Dominion 500 (Martinsville)	Buddy Baker	USA	Chevrolet	75.262
07.10.79	NAPA National 500 (Charlotte)	Cale Yarborough	USA	Chevrolet	134.266
14.10.79	Holly Farms 400 (N Carolina)	Benny Parsons	USA	Chevrolet	91.454
21.10.79	American 500 (N Carolina)	Richard Petty	USA	Chevrolet	108.356
04.11.79	Dixie 500 (Atlanta)	Neil Bonnett	USA	Mercury	140.120
18.11.79	Los Angeles Times 500 (Ontario)	Benny Parsons	USA	Chevrolet	132.822

1980

date	race	driver	nat	car	mph
13.01.80	Winston Western 500 (Riverside)	Darrell Waltrip	USA	Chevrolet	94.974
17.02.80	Daytona 500 (Daytona)	Buddy Baker	USA	Oldsmobile	177.602
24.02.80	Richmond 400 (Richmond)	Darrell Waltrip	USA	Chevrolet	67.703
09.03.80	Carolina 500 (N Carolina)	Cale Yarborough	USA	Oldsmobile	108.735
16.03.80	Atlanta 500 (Atlanta)	Dale Earnhardt	USA	Chevrolet	134.600
30.03.80	Valleydale Southeastern 500 (Bristol)	Dale Earnhardt	USA	Chevrolet	96.978
13.04.80	CRC Chemicals Rebel 500 (Darlington)	David Pearson	USA	Chevrolet	107.710
20.04.80	Northwestern Bank 400 (N Wilkesboro)	Richard Petty	USA	Chevrolet	95.501
27.04.80	Virginia 500 (Martinsville)	Darrell Waltrip	USA	Chevrolet	69.180
04.05.80	Winston 500 (Talladega)	Buddy Baker	USA	Oldsmobile	170.482
10.05.80	Music City 420 (Nashville)	Richard Petty	USA	Chevrolet	89.471
18.05.80	Mason-Dixon 500 (Dover Downs)	Bobby Allison	USA	Ford	113.866
25.05.80	World 600 (Charlotte)	Benny Parsons	USA	Chevrolet	119.265
01.06.80	NASCAR 400 (Texas World Speedway)	Cale Yarborough	USA	Chevrolet	159.046
08.06.80	Warner W Hodgdon 400 (Riverside)	Darrell Waltrip	USA	Chevrolet	101.846
15.06.80	Gabriel 400 (Michigan)	Benny Parsons	USA	Chevrolet	131.808
04.07.80	Firecracker 400 (Daytona)	Bobby Allison	USA	Mercury	173.473
12.07.80	Busch Nashville 420 (Nashville)	Dale Earnhardt	USA	Chevrolet	93.821
27.07.80	Coca-Cola 500 (Pocono)	Neil Bonnett	USA	Mercury	124.395
03.08.80	Talladega 500 (Talladega)	Neil Bonnett	USA	Mercury	166.894
17.08.80	Champion Spark Plug 400 (Michigan)	Cale Yarborough	USA	Chevrolet	145.352
23.08.80	Busch Volunteer 500 (Bristol)	Cale Yarborough	USA	Chevrolet	86.973
01.09.80	Southern 500 (Darlington)	Terry Labonte	USA	Chevrolet	115.210
07.09.80	Capital City 400 (Richmond)	Bobby Allison	USA	Ford	79.722
14.09.80	CRC Chemicals 500 (Dover Downs)	Darrell Waltrip	USA	Chevrolet	116.024
21.09.80	Holly Farms 400 (N Wilkesboro)	Bobby Allison	USA	Ford	75.510
28.09.80	Old Dominion 500 (Martinsville)	Dale Earnhardt	USA	Chevrolet	69.787
05.10.80	National 500 (Charlotte)	Dale Earnhardt	USA	Chevrolet	135.243
19.10.80	American 500 (N Carolina)	Cale Yarborough	USA	Chevrolet	114.159
02.11.80	Atlanta Journal 500 (Atlanta)	Cale Yarborough	USA	Chevrolet	131.190
15.11.80	Los Angeles Times 500 (Ontario)	Benny Parsons	USA	Chevrolet	129.441

1981

date	race	driver	nat	car	mph
11.01.81	Winston Western 500 (Riverside)	Bobby Allison	USA	Chevrolet	95.297
15.02.81	Daytona 500 (Daytona)	Richard Petty	USA	Buick	169.651
22.02.81	Richmond 400 (Richmond)	Darrell Waltrip	USA	Buick	76.570
01.03.81	Carolina 500 (N Carolina)	Darrell Waltrip	USA	Buick	114.594
15.03.81	Coca-Cola 500 (Atlanta)	Cale Yarborough	USA	Buick	133.619
29.03.81	Valleydale 500 (Bristol)	Darrell Waltrip	USA	Buick	89.530
05.04.81	Northwestern Bank 400 (N Wilkesboro)	Richard Petty	USA	Buick	85.381
12.04.81	CRC Chemicals Rebel 500 (Darlington)	Darrell Waltrip	USA	Buick	126.703
26.04.81	Virginia 500 (Martinsville)	Morgan Shepherd	USA	Pontiac	75.083
03.05.81	Winston 500 (Talladega)	Bobby Allison	USA	Buick	149.377
09.05.81	Melling Tool 420 (Nashville)	Benny Parsons	USA	Ford	89.917
17.05.81	Mason-Dixon 500 (Dover Downs)	Jody Ridley	USA	Ford	116.595
24.05.81	World 600 (Charlotte)	Bobby Allison	USA	Buick	129.326
07.06.81	Budweiser 400 (Texas World Speedway)	Benny Parsons	USA	Ford	132.475
14.06.81	Warner W Hodgdon 400 (Riverside)	Darrell Waltrip	USA	Buick	93.630
21.06.81	Gabriel 400 (Michigan)	Bobby Allison	USA	Buick	130.589
04.07.81	Firecracker 400 (Daytona)	Cale Yarborough	USA	Buick	142.405
11.07.81	Busch Nashville 420 (Nashville)	Darrell Waltrip	USA	Buick	90.052
26.07.81	Mountain Dew 500 (Pocono)	Darrell Waltrip	USA	Buick	119.111
02.08.81	Talladega 500 (Talladega)	Ron Bouchard	USA	Buick	156.765
16.08.81	Champion Spark Plug 400 (Michigan)	Richard Petty	USA	Buick	123.457
22.08.81	Busch 500 (Bristol)	Darrell Waltrip	USA	Buick	84.723
07.09.81	Southern 500 (Darlington)	Neil Bonnett	USA	Ford	126.410
13.09.81	Wrangler Sanfor-Set 400 (Richmond)	Benny Parsons	USA	Ford	69.998
20.09.81	CRC Chemicals 500 (Dover Downs)	Neil Bonnett	USA	Ford	120.000
27.09.81	Old Dominion 500 (Martinsville)	Darrell Waltrip	USA	Buick	70.149
04.10.81	Holly Farms 400 (N Wilkesboro)	Darrell Waltrip	USA	Buick	93.091
11.10.81	National 500 (Charlotte)	Darrell Waltrip	USA	Buick	117.483
01.11.81	American 500 (N Carolina)	Darrell Waltrip	USA	Buick	107.400
08.11.81	Atlanta Journal 500 (Atlanta)	Neil Bonnett	USA	Ford	130.391
22.11.81	Winston Western 500 (Riverside)	Bobby Allison	USA	Buick	95.289

1982

date	race	driver	nat	car	mph
14.02.82	Daytona 500 (Daytona)	Bobby Allison	USA	Buick	153.991
21.02.82	Richmond 400 (Richmond)	Dave Marcis	USA	Chevrolet	72.915
14.03.82	Valleydale 500 (Bristol)	Darrell Waltrip	USA	Buick	94.133
21.03.82	Coca-Cola 500 (Atlanta)	Darrell Waltrip	USA	Buick	124.824
28.03.82	Warner W Hodgdon Carolina 500 (N Carolina)	Cale Yarborough	USA	Buick	123.318
04.04.82	CRC Chemicals Rebel 500 (Darlington)	Dale Earnhardt	USA	Chevrolet	123.554
18.04.82	Northwestern Bank 400 (N Wilkesboro)	Darrell Waltrip	USA	Buick	97.646
25.04.82	Virginia National Bank 500 (Martinsville)	Harry Gant	USA	Buick	75.137
02.05.82	Winston 500 (Talladega)	Darrell Waltrip	USA	Buick	156.833
08.05.82	Cracker Barrel Country Store 420 (Nashville)	Darrell Waltrip	USA	Buick	83.502
16.05.82	Mason-Dixon 500 (Dover Downs)	Bobby Allison	USA	Chevrolet	120.136
30.05.82	World 600 (Charlotte)	Neil Bonnett	USA	Ford	130.058
06.06.82	Van Scoy Diamond Mine 500 (Pocono)	Bobby Allison	USA	Buick	113.579
13.06.82	Budweiser 400 (Riverside)	Tim Richmond	USA	Buick	103.816
20.06.82	Gabriel 400 (Michigan)	Cale Yarborough	USA	Buick	118.101
04.07.82	Firecracker 400 (Daytona)	Bobby Allison	USA	Buick	163.099
10.07.82	Busch Nashville 420 (Nashville)	Darrell Waltrip	USA	Buick	86.524
25.07.82	Mountain Dew 500 (Pocono)	Bobby Allison	USA	Buick	115.496
01.08.82	Talladega 500 (Talladega)	Darrell Waltrip	USA	Buick	168.157
22.08.82	Champion Spark Plug 400 (Michigan)	Bobby Allison	USA	Buick	144.680
28.08.82	Busch 500 (Bristol)	Darrell Waltrip	USA	Buick	94.318
06.09.82	Southern 500 (Darlington)	Cale Yarborough	USA	Buick	115.246
12.09.82	Wrangler Sanfor-Set 400 (Richmond)	Bobby Allison	USA	Chevrolet	82.801
19.09.82	CRC Chemicals 500 (Dover Downs)	Darrell Waltrip	USA	Buick	107.639
03.10.82	Holly Farms 400 (N Wilkesboro)	Darrell Waltrip	USA	Buick	98.071
10.10.82	National 500 (Charlotte)	Harry Gant	USA	Buick	137.208
17.10.82	Old Dominion 500 (Martinsville)	Darrell Waltrip	USA	Buick	71.376
31.10.82	Warner W Hodgdon American 500 (N Carolina)	Darrell Waltrip	USA	Buick	115.122
07.11.82	Atlanta Journal 500 (Atlanta)	Bobby Allison	USA	Buick	130.885
21.11.82	Winston Western 500 (Riverside)	Tim Richmond	USA	Buick	99.823

1983

date	race	driver	nat	car	mph
20.02.83	Daytona 500 (Daytona)	Cale Yarborough	USA	Pontiac	155.979
27.02.83	Richmond 400 (Richmond)	Bobby Allison	USA	Chevrolet	79.438
13.03.83	Warner W Hodgdon Carolina 500 (N Carolina)	Richard Petty	USA	Pontiac	113.077
27.03.83	Coca-Cola 500 (Atlanta)	Cale Yarborough	USA	Chevrolet	124.055
10.04.83	Transouth 500 (Darlington)	Harry Gant	USA	Buick	130.732
17.04.83	Northwestern Bank 400 (N Wilkesboro)	Darrell Waltrip	USA	Chevrolet	91.436
24.04.83	Virginia National Bank 500 (Martinsville)	Darrell Waltrip	USA	Chevrolet	66.517
01.05.83	Winston 500 (Talladega)	Richard Petty	USA	Pontiac	153.937
07.05.83	Marty Robbins 420 (Nashville)	Darrell Waltrip	USA	Chevrolet	70.717
15.05.83	Mason-Dixon 500 (Dover Downs)	Bobby Allison	USA	Buick	114.847
21.05.83	Valleydale 500 (Bristol)	Darrell Waltrip	USA	Chevrolet	93.445
29.05.83	World 600 (Charlotte)	Neil Bonnett	USA	Chevrolet	140.707
05.06.83	Budweiser 400 (Riverside)	Ricky Rudd	USA	Chevrolet	88.063
12.06.83	Van Scoy Diamond Mine 500 (Pocono)	Bobby Allison	USA	Buick	128.636
19.06.83	Gabriel 400 (Michigan)	Cale Yarborough	USA	Chevrolet	138.728
04.07.83	Firecracker 400 (Daytona)	Buddy Baker	USA	Ford	167.442
16.07.83	Busch Nashville 420 (Nashville)	Dale Earnhardt	USA	Ford	85.726
24.07.83	Like Cola 500 (Pocono)	Tim Richmond	USA	Pontiac	114.818
31.07.83	Talladega 500 (Talladega)	Dale Earnhardt	USA	Ford	170.611
21.08.83	Champion Spark Plug 400 (Michigan)	Cale Yarborough	USA	Chevrolet	147.511
27.08.83	Busch 500 (Bristol)	Darrell Waltrip	USA	Buick	89.430
05.09.83	Southern 500 (Darlington)	Bobby Allison	USA	Buick	123.343
11.09.83	Wrangler Sanfor-Set 400 (Richmond)	Bobby Allison	USA	Buick	79.738
18.09.83	Budweiser 500 (Dover Downs)	Bobby Allison	USA	Buick	115.942
25.09.83	Goody's 500 (Martinsville)	Ricky Rudd	USA	Chevrolet	76.134
02.10.83	Holly Farms 400 (N Wilkesboro)	Darrell Waltrip	USA	Chevrolet	100.716
09.10.83	Miller High Life 500 (Charlotte)	Richard Petty	USA	Pontiac	139.998
30.10.83	Warner W Hodgdon American 500 (N Carolina)	Terry Labonte	USA	Chevrolet	119.324
06.11.83	Atlanta Journal 500 (Atlanta)	Neil Bonnett	USA	Chevrolet	137.641
20.11.83	Winston Western 500 (Riverside)	Bill Elliott	USA	Ford	95.859

1984

date	race	driver	nat	car	mph
08.01.84	Northwestern Bank 400 (N Wilkesboro)	Tim Richmond	USA	Pontiac	97.837
19.02.84	Daytona 500 (Daytona)	Cale Yarborough	USA	Chevrolet	150.994
26.02.84	Miller High Life 400 (Richmond)	Ricky Rudd	USA	Ford	100.435
04.03.84	Warner W Hodgdon Carolina 500 (N Carolina)	Bobby Allison	USA	Buick	123.082
18.03.84	Coca-Cola 500 (Atlanta)	Benny Parsons	USA	Chevrolet	144.945
01.04.84	Valleydale 500 (Bristol)	Darrell Waltrip	USA	Chevrolet	93.967
15.04.84	Transouth 500 (Darlington)	Darrell Waltrip	USA	Chevrolet	116.466
29.04.84	Sovran Bank 500 (Martinsville)	Geoff Bodine	USA	Chevrolet	73.265
06.05.84	Winston 500 (Talladega)	Cale Yarborough	USA	Chevrolet	172.988
12.05.84	Coors 420 (Nashville)	Darrell Waltrip	USA	Chevrolet	85.702
20.05.84	Budweiser 500 (Dover Downs)	Richard Petty	USA	Pontiac	118.718
27.05.84	World 600 (Charlotte)	Bobby Allison	USA	Buick	129.233
03.06.84	Budweiser 400 (Riverside)	Terry Labonte	USA	Chevrolet	102.910
10.06.84	Van Scoy Diamond Mine 500 (Pocono)	Cale Yarborough	USA	Chevrolet	138.164
17.06.84	Miller High Life 400 (Michigan)	Bill Elliott	USA	Ford	134.705
04.07.84	Pepsi Firecracker 400 (Daytona)	Richard Petty	USA	Pontiac	171.449
14.07.84	Pepsi 420 (Nashville)	Geoff Bodine	USA	Chevrolet	80.908
22.07.84	Like Cola 500 (Pocono)	Harry Gant	USA	Chevrolet	121.286
29.07.84	Talladega 500 (Talladega)	Dale Earnhardt	USA	Chevrolet	156.221
12.08.84	Champion Spark Plug 400 (Michigan)	Darrell Waltrip	USA	Chevrolet	153.863
25.08.84	Busch 500 (Bristol)	Terry Labonte	USA	Chevrolet	85.363
02.09.84	Southern 500 (Darlington)	Harry Gant	USA	Chevrolet	128.526
09.09.84	Wrangler Sanfor-Set 400 (Richmond)	Darrell Waltrip	USA	Chevrolet	74.780
16.09.84	Delaware 500 (Dover Downs)	Harry Gant	USA	Chevrolet	111.857
23.09.84	Goody's 500 (Martinsville)	Darrell Waltrip	USA	Chevrolet	75.533
07.10.84	Miller High Life 500 (Charlotte)	Bill Elliott	USA	Ford	146.861
14.10.84	Holly Farms 400 (N Wilkesboro)	Darrell Waltrip	USA	Chevrolet	90.525
21.10.84	Warner W Hodgdon American 500 (N Carolina)	Bill Elliott	USA	Ford	112.617
11.11.84	Atlanta Journal 500 (Atlanta)	Dale Earnhardt	USA	Chevrolet	134.610
18.11.84	Winston Western 500 (Riverside)	Geoff Bodine	USA	Chevrolet	98.448

1985

date	race	driver	nat	car	mph
17.02.85	Daytona 500 (Daytona)	Bill Elliott	USA	Ford	172.265
24.02.85	Miller High Life 400 (Richmond)	Dale Earnhardt	USA	Chevrolet	67.945
03.03.85	Carolina 500 (N Carolina)	Neil Bonnett	USA	Chevrolet	114.953
17.03.85	Coca-Cola 500 (Atlanta)	Bill Elliott	USA	Ford	140.273
06.04.85	Valleydale 500 (Bristol)	Dale Earnhardt	USA	Chevrolet	81.707
14.04.85	Transouth 500 (Darlington)	Bill Elliott	USA	Ford	126.313
21.04.85	Northwestern Bank 400 (N Wilkesboro)	Neil Bonnett	USA	Chevrolet	93.818
28.04.85	Sovran Bank 500 (Martinsville)	Harry Gant	USA	Chevrolet	80.469
05.05.85	Winston 500 (Talladega)	Bill Elliott	USA	Ford	186.288
19.05.85	Budweiser 500 (Dover Downs)	Bill Elliott	USA	Ford	123.094
26.05.85	Coca-Cola World 600 (Charlotte)	Darrell Waltrip	USA	Chevrolet	141.807
02.06.85	Budweiser 400 (Riverside)	Terry Labonte	USA	Chevrolet	104.276
09.06.85	Van Scoy Diamond Mine 500 (Pocono)	Bill Elliott	USA	Ford	139.018
16.06.85	Miller 400 (Michigan)	Bill Elliott	USA	Ford	144.753
04.07.85	Pepsi Firecracker 400 (Daytona)	Greg Sacks	USA	Chevrolet	158.730
21.07.85	Summer 500 (Pocono)	Bill Elliott	USA	Ford	134.008
28.07.85	Talladega 500 (Talladega)	Cale Yarborough	USA	Ford	148.772
11.08.85	Champion Spark Plug 400 (Michigan)	Bill Elliott	USA	Ford	137.431
24.08.85	Busch 500 (Bristol)	Dale Earnhardt	USA	Chevrolet	76.974
01.09.85	Southern 500 (Darlington)	Bill Elliott	USA	Ford	121.271
08.09.85	Wrangler Sanfor-Set 400 (Richmond)	Darrell Waltrip	USA	Chevrolet	72.711
15.09.85	Delaware 500 (Dover Downs)	Harry Gant	USA	Chevrolet	120.788
22.09.85	Goody's 500 (Martinsville)	Dale Earnhardt	USA	Chevrolet	70.694
29.09.85	Holly Farms 400 (N Wilkesboro)	Harry Gant	USA	Chevrolet	95.097
06.10.85	Miller High Life 500 (Charlotte)	Cale Yarborough	USA	Ford	136.761
20.10.85	Nationwise 500 (N Carolina)	Darrell Waltrip	USA	Chevrolet	118.352
03.11.85	Atlanta Journal 500 (Atlanta)	Bill Elliott	USA	Ford	139.597
17.11.85	Winston Western 500 (Riverside)	Ricky Rudd	USA	Ford	105.065

1986

16.02.86	Daytona 500 (Daytona)	Geoff Bodine	USA	Chevrolet	148.124
23.02.86	Miller High Life 400 (Richmond)	Kyle Petty	USA	Ford	71.121
02.03.86	Goodwrench 500 (N Carolina)	Terry Labonte	USA	Oldsmobile	120.489
16.03.86	Motorcraft 500 (Atlanta)	Morgan Shepherd	USA	Buick	132.136
06.04.86	Valleydale 500 (Bristol)	Rusty Wallace	USA	Pontiac	89.714
13.04.86	Transouth 500 (Darlington)	Dale Earnhardt	USA	Chevrolet	128.994
20.04.86	First Union 400 (N Wilkesboro)	Dale Earnhardt	USA	Chevrolet	88.409
27.04.86	Sovran Bank 500 (Martinsville)	Ricky Rudd	USA	Ford	76.882
04.05.86	Winston 500 (Talladega)	Bobby Allison	USA	Buick	157.699
18.05.86	Budweiser 500 (Dover Downs)	Geoff Bodine	USA	Chevrolet	115.009
25.05.86	Coca-Cola 600 (Charlotte)	Dale Earnhardt	USA	Chevrolet	140.406
01.06.86	Budweiser 400 (Riverside)	Darrell Waltrip	USA	Chevrolet	105.083
08.06.86	Miller High Life 500 (Pocono)	Tim Richmond	USA	Chevrolet	113.279
15.06.86	Miller American 400 (Michigan)	Bill Elliott	USA	Ford	138.448
04.07.86	Firecracker 400 (Daytona)	Tim Richmond	USA	Chevrolet	131.916
20.07.86	Summer 500 (Pocono)	Tim Richmond	USA	Chevrolet	139.636
27.07.86	Talladega 500 (Talladega)	Bobby Hillin Jr	USA	Buick	151.552
10.08.86	The Budweiser at The Glen (Watkins Glen)	Tim Richmond	USA	Chevrolet	98.630
17.08.86	Champion Spark Plug 400 (Michigan)	Bill Elliott	USA	Ford	135.237
23.08.86	Busch 500 (Bristol)	Darrell Waltrip	USA	Chevrolet	86.942
31.08.86	Southern 500 (Darlington)	Tim Richmond	USA	Chevrolet	120.922
07.09.86	Wrangler Jeans Indigo 400 (Richmond)	Tim Richmond	USA	Chevrolet	70.162
14.09.86	Delaware 500 (Dover Downs)	Ricky Rudd	USA	Ford	114.329
21.09.86	Goody's 500 (Martinsville)	Rusty Wallace	USA	Pontiac	73.214
28.09.86	Holly Farms 400 (N Wilkesboro)	Darrell Waltrip	USA	Chevrolet	95.612
05.10.86	Oakwood Homes 500 (Charlotte)	Dale Earnhardt	USA	Chevrolet	132.403
19.10.86	Nationwise 500 (N Carolina)	Neil Bonnett	USA	Chevrolet	126.381
02.11.86	Atlanta Journal 500 (Atlanta)	Dale Earnhardt	USA	Chevrolet	153.317
16.11.86	Winston Western 500 (Riverside)	Tim Richmond	USA	Chevrolet	101.246

1987

15.02.87	Daytona 500 (Daytona)	Bill Elliott	USA	Ford	176.263
01.03.87	Goodwrench 500 (N Carolina)	Dale Earnhardt	USA	Chevrolet	117.556
08.03.87	Miller High Life 400 (Richmond)	Dale Earnhardt	USA	Chevrolet	81.521

date	race	driver	nat	car	mph
15.03.87	Motorcraft Quality Parts 500 (Atlanta)	Ricky Rudd	USA	Ford	133.699
29.03.87	Transouth 500 (Darlington)	Dale Earnhardt	USA	Chevrolet	122.539
05.04.87	First Union 400 (N Wilkesboro)	Dale Earnhardt	USA	Chevrolet	94.103
12.04.87	Valleydale Meats 500 (Bristol)	Dale Earnhardt	USA	Chevrolet	75.621
26.04.87	Sovran Bank 500 (Martinsville)	Dale Earnhardt	USA	Chevrolet	72.808
03.05.87	Winston 500 (Talladega)	Davey Allison	USA	Ford	154.228
24.05.87	Coca-Cola 600 (Charlotte)	Kyle Petty	USA	Ford	131.483
31.05.87	Budweiser 500 (Dover Downs)	Davey Allison	USA	Ford	112.959
14.06.87	Miller High Life 500 (Pocono)	Tim Richmond	USA	Chevrolet	121.976
21.06.87	Budweiser 400 (Riverside)	Tim Richmond	USA	Chevrolet	102.183
28.06.87	Miller American 400 (Michigan)	Dale Earnhardt	USA	Chevrolet	148.454
04.07.87	Pepsi Firecracker 400 (Daytona)	Bobby Allison	USA	Buick	161.074
19.07.87	Summer 500 (Pocono)	Dale Earnhardt	USA	Chevrolet	121.745
26.07.87	Talladega 500 (Talladega)	Bill Elliott	USA	Ford	171.293
10.08.87	The Budweiser at The Glen (Watkins Glen)	Rusty Wallace	USA	Pontiac	90.672
16.08.87	Champion Spark Plug 400 (Michigan)	Bill Elliott	USA	Ford	138.648
22.08.87	Busch 500 (Bristol)	Dale Earnhardt	USA	Chevrolet	90.373
06.09.87	Southern 500 (Darlington)	Dale Earnhardt	USA	Chevrolet	115.520
13.09.87	Wrangler Jeans Indigo 400 (Richmond)	Dale Earnhardt	USA	Chevrolet	70.721
20.09.87	Delaware 500 (Dover Downs)	Ricky Rudd	USA	Ford	124.706
27.09.87	Goody's 500 (Martinsville)	Darrell Waltrip	USA	Chevrolet	76.410
04.10.87	Holly Farms 400 (N Carolina)	Terry Labonte	USA	Chevrolet	96.061
11.10.87	Oakwood Homes 500 (Charlotte)	Bill Elliott	USA	Ford	128.443
25.10.87	AC Delco 500 (N Carolina)	Bill Elliott	USA	Ford	118.258
08.11.87	Winston Western 500 (Riverside)	Rusty Wallace	USA	Pontiac	98.035
22.11.87	Atlanta Journal 500 (Atlanta)	Bill Elliott	USA	Ford	139.047

1988

date	race	driver	nat	car	mph
14.02.88	Daytona 500 (Daytona)	Bobby Allison	USA	Buick	137.531
21.02.88	Pontiac Excitement 400 (Richmond)	Neil Bonnett	USA	Pontiac	66.401
06.03.88	Goodwrench 500 (N Carolina)	Neil Bonnett	USA	Pontiac	120.159
20.03.88	Motorcraft Quality Parts 500 (Atlanta)	Dale Earnhardt	USA	Chevrolet	137.588
27.03.88	Transouth 500 (Darlington)	Lake Speed	USA	Oldsmobile	131.284
10.04.88	Valleydale Meats 500 (Bristol)	Bill Elliott	USA	Ford	83.115
17.04.88	First Union 400 (N Wilkesboro)	Terry Labonte	USA	Chevrolet	99.075
24.04.88	Pannill Sweatshirts 500 (Martinsville)	Dale Earnhardt	USA	Chevrolet	74.740
01.05.88	Winston 500 (Talladega)	Phil Parsons	USA	Oldsmobile	156.547
29.05.88	Coca-Cola 600 (Charlotte)	Darrell Waltrip	USA	Chevrolet	124.460
05.06.88	Budweiser 500 (Dover Downs)	Bill Elliott	USA	Ford	118.726
12.06.88	Budweiser 400 (Riverside)	Rusty Wallace	USA	Pontiac	91.592
19.06.88	Miller High Life 500 (Pocono)	Geoff Bodine	USA	Chevrolet	125.865
26.06.88	Miller High Life 400 (Michigan)	Rusty Wallace	USA	Pontiac	153.551
02.07.88	Pepsi Firecracker 400 (Daytona)	Bill Elliott	USA	Ford	163.302
24.07.88	AC Spark Plug 500 (Pocono)	Bill Elliott	USA	Ford	122.867
31.07.88	Diehard 500 (Talladega)	Ken Schrader	USA	Chevrolet	154.505
14.08.88	The Budweiser at The Glen (Watkins Glen)	Ricky Rudd	USA	Buick	74.089
21.08.88	Champion Spark Plug 400 (Michigan)	Davey Allison	USA	Ford	156.863
27.08.88	Busch 500 (Bristol)	Dale Earnhardt	USA	Chevrolet	78.775
04.09.88	Southern 500 (Darlington)	Bill Elliott	USA	Ford	128.297
11.09.88	Miller High Life 400 (Richmond)	Davey Allison	USA	Ford	95.770
18.09.88	Delaware 500 (Dover Downs)	Bill Elliott	USA	Ford	109.349
25.09.88	Goody's 500 (Martinsville)	Darrell Waltrip	USA	Chevrolet	74.988
09.10.88	Oakwood Homes 500 (Charlotte)	Rusty Wallace	USA	Pontiac	130.677
16.10.88	Holly Farms 400 (N Wilkesboro)	Rusty Wallace	USA	Pontiac	94.192
23.10.88	AC Delco 500 (N Carolina)	Rusty Wallace	USA	Pontiac	111.557
06.11.88	Checker 500 (Phoenix)	Alan Kulwicki	USA	Ford	90.457
20.11.88	Atlanta Journal 500 (Atlanta)	Rusty Wallace	USA	Pontiac	129.024

1989

date	race	driver	nat	car	mph
19.02.89	Daytona 500 (Daytona)	Darrell Waltrip	USA	Chevrolet	148.466
05.03.89	Goodwrench 500 (N Carolina)	Rusty Wallace	USA	Pontiac	115.122
19.03.89	Motorcraft Quality Parts 500 (Atlanta)	Darrell Waltrip	USA	Chevrolet	139.684
26.03.89	Pontiac Excitement 400 (Richmond)	Rusty Wallace	USA	Pontiac	89.619
02.04.89	Transouth 500 (Darlington)	Harry Gant	USA	Oldsmobile	115.475
09.04.89	Valleydale Meats 500 (Bristol)	Rusty Wallace	USA	Pontiac	76.034
16.04.89	First Union 400 (N Wilkesboro)	Dale Earnhardt	USA	Chevrolet	89.937

date	race	driver	nat	car	mph
23.04.89	Pannill Sweatshirts 500 (Martinsville)	Darrell Waltrip	USA	Chevrolet	79.025
07.05.89	Winston 500 (Talladega)	Davey Allison	USA	Ford	155.869
28.05.89	Coca-Cola 600 (Charlotte)	Darrell Waltrip	USA	Chevrolet	144.077
04.06.89	Budweiser 500 (Dover Downs)	Dale Earnhardt	USA	Chevrolet	121.671
11.06.89	Banquet Frozen Foods 300 (Sears Point)	Ricky Rudd	USA	Buick	76.179
18.06.89	Miller High Life 500 (Pocono)	Terry Labonte	USA	Ford	131.320
25.06.89	Miller High Life 400 (Michigan)	Bill Elliott	USA	Ford	139.023
01.07.89	Pepsi 400 (Daytona)	Davey Allison	USA	Ford	132.207
23.07.89	AC Spark Plug 500 (Pocono)	Bill Elliott	USA	Ford	117.847
30.07.89	Diehard 500 (Talladega)	Terry Labonte	USA	Ford	157.354
13.08.89	The Budweiser at The Glen (Watkins Glen)	Rusty Wallace	USA	Pontiac	89.242
20.08.89	Champion Spark Plug 400 (Michigan)	Rusty Wallace	USA	Pontiac	157.705
26.08.89	Busch 500 (Bristol)	Darrell Waltrip	USA	Chevrolet	86.792
03.09.89	Heinz Southern 500 (Darlington)	Dale Earnhardt	USA	Chevrolet	135.462
10.09.89	Miller High Life 400 (Richmond)	Rusty Wallace	USA	Pontiac	88.380
17.09.89	Peak Performance 500 (Dover Downs)	Dale Earnhardt	USA	Chevrolet	122.909
24.09.89	Goody's 500 (Martinsville)	Darrell Waltrip	USA	Chevrolet	76.509
08.10.89	All-Pro Auto Parts 500 (Charlotte)	Ken Schrader	USA	Chevrolet	149.863
15.10.89	Holly Farms 400 (N Wilkesboro)	Geoff Bodine	USA	Chevrolet	90.289
22.10.89	AC Delco 500 (N Carolina)	Mark Martin	USA	Ford	114.079
05.11.89	Autoworks 500 (Phoenix)	Bill Elliott	USA	Ford	105.683
19.11.89	Atlanta Journal 500 (Atlanta)	Dale Earnhardt	USA	Chevrolet	140.229

1990

date	race	driver	nat	car	mph
18.02.90	Daytona 500 (Daytona)	Derrike Cope	USA	Chevrolet	165.761
25.02.90	Pontiac Excitement 400 (Richmond)	Mark Martin	USA	Ford	92.166
04.03.90	Goodwrench 500 (N Carolina)	Kyle Petty	USA	Pontiac	122.864
18.03.90	Motorcraft Quality Parts 500 (Atlanta)	Dale Earnhardt	USA	Chevrolet	157.123
01.04.90	Transouth 500 (Darlington)	Dale Earnhardt	USA	Chevrolet	124.073
08.04.90	Valleydale Meats 500 (Bristol)	Davey Allison	USA	Ford	87.258
22.04.90	First Union 400 (N Wilkesboro)	Brett Bodine	USA	Buick	83.908
29.04.90	Hanes Activewear 500 (Martinsville)	Geoff Bodine	USA	Ford	77.423
06.05.90	Winston 500 (Talladega)	Dale Earnhardt	USA	Chevrolet	159.572
27.05.90	Coca-Cola 600 (Charlotte)	Rusty Wallace	USA	Pontiac	137.650
03.06.90	Budweiser 500 (Dover Downs)	Derrike Cope	USA	Chevrolet	123.958
10.06.90	Banquet Frozen Foods 300 (Sears Point)	Rusty Wallace	USA	Pontiac	69.327
17.06.90	Miller Genuine Draft 500 (Pocono)	Harry Gant	USA	Oldsmobile	120.765
24.06.90	Miller Genuine Draft 400 (Michigan)	Dale Earnhardt	USA	Chevrolet	150.219
07.07.90	Pepsi 400 (Daytona)	Dale Earnhardt	USA	Chevrolet	160.894
19.07.90	Diehard 500 (Talladega)	Dale Earnhardt	USA	Chevrolet	174.430
22.07.90	AC Spark Plug 500 (Pocono)	Geoff Bodine	USA	Ford	124.069
12.08.90	The Budweiser at The Glen (Watkins Glen)	Ricky Rudd	USA	Chevrolet	92.452
19.08.90	Champion Spark Plug 400 (Michigan)	Mark Martin	USA	Ford	138.822
25.08.90	Busch 500 (Bristol)	Ernie Irvan	USA	Chevrolet	91.782
02.09.90	Heinz Southern 500 (Darlington)	Dale Earnhardt	USA	Chevrolet	123.141
09.09.90	Miller Genuine Draft 400 (Richmond)	Dale Earnhardt	USA	Chevrolet	95.567
16.09.90	Peak Anti-Freeze 500 (Dover Downs)	Bill Elliott	USA	Ford	126.050
23.09.90	Goody's 500 (Martinsville)	Geoff Bodine	USA	Ford	76.386
30.09.90	Tyson Holly Farms 400 (N Wilkesboro)	Mark Martin	USA	Ford	93.818
07.10.90	Mello Yello 500 (Charlotte)	Davey Allison	USA	Ford	137.428
21.10.90	AC Delco 500 (N Carolina)	Alan Kulwicki	USA	Ford	126.452
04.11.90	Checker 500 (Phoenix)	Dale Earnhardt	USA	Chevrolet	96.786
18.11.90	Atlanta Journal 500 (Atlanta)	Morgan Shepherd	USA	Ford	140.911

1991

date	race	driver	nat	car	mph
17.02.91	Daytona 500 by STP (Daytona)	Ernie Irvan	USA	Chevrolet	148.148
24.02.91	Pontiac Excitement 400 (Richmond)	Dale Earnhardt	USA	Chevrolet	105.361
03.03.91	Goodwrench 500 (N Carolina)	Kyle Petty	USA	Pontiac	124.083
17.03.91	Motorcraft Quality Parts 500 (Atlanta)	Ken Schrader	USA	Chevrolet	140.470
07.04.91	Transouth 500 (Darlington)	Ricky Rudd	USA	Chevrolet	135.594
14.04.91	Valleydale Meats 500 (Bristol)	Rusty Wallace	USA	Pontiac	67.672
21.04.91	First Union 400 (N Wilkesboro)	Darrell Waltrip	USA	Chevrolet	79.604
28.04.91	Hanes Activewear 500 (Martinsville)	Dale Earnhardt	USA	Chevrolet	75.139
06.05.91	Winston 500 (Talladega)	Harry Gant	USA	Oldsmobile	165.620
26.05.91	Coca-Cola 600 (Charlotte)	Davey Allison	USA	Ford	138.951
02.06.91	Budweiser 500 (Dover Downs)	Ken Schrader	USA	Chevrolet	120.152

date	race	driver	nat	car	mph
09.06.91	Banquet Frozen Foods 300 (Sears Point)	Davey Allison	USA	Ford	73.057
16.06.91	Champion Spark Plug 500 (Pocono)	Darrell Waltrip	USA	Chevrolet	122.666
23.06.91	Miller Genuine Draft 400 (Michigan)	Davey Allison	USA	Ford	160.912
06.07.91	Pepsi 400 (Daytona)	Bill Elliott	USA	Ford	159.116
21.07.91	Miller Genuine Draft 500 (Pocono)	Rusty Wallace	USA	Pontiac	115.459
28.07.91	Diehard 500 (Talladega)	Dale Earnhardt	USA	Chevrolet	147.383
11.08.91	The Budweiser at The Glen (Watkins Glen)	Ernie Irvan	USA	Chevrolet	98.977
18.08.91	Champion Spark Plug 400 (Michigan)	Dale Jarrett	USA	Ford	139.887
24.08.91	Bud 500 (Bristol)	Alan Kulwicki	USA	Ford	82.028
01.09.91	Heinz Southern 500 (Darlington)	Harry Gant	USA	Oldsmobile	133.508
07.09.91	Miller Genuine Draft 400 (Richmond)	Harry Gant	USA	Oldsmobile	101.361
15.09.91	Peak Anti-Freeze 500 (Dover Downs)	Harry Gant	USA	Oldsmobile	110.179
22.09.91	Goody's 500 (Martinsville)	Harry Gant	USA	Oldsmobile	74.535
29.09.91	Tyson Holly Farms 400 (N Wilkesboro)	Dale Earnhardt	USA	Chevrolet	94.113
06.10.91	Mello Yello 500 (Charlotte)	Geoff Bodine	USA	Ford	138.984
20.10.91	AC Delco 500 (N Carolina)	Davey Allison	USA	Ford	127.292
03.11.91	Pyroil 500 (Phoenix)	Davey Allison	USA	Ford	95.746
17.11.91	Hardee's 500 (Atlanta)	Mark Martin	USA	Ford	137.968

1992

date	race	driver	nat	car	mph
16.02.92	Daytona 500 by STP (Daytona)	Davey Allison	USA	Ford	160.256
01.03.92	Goodwrench 500 (N Carolina)	Bill Elliott	USA	Ford	126.125
08.03.92	Pontiac Excitement 400 (Richmond)	Bill Elliott	USA	Ford	104.378
15.03.92	Motorcraft Quality Parts 500 (Atlanta)	Bill Elliott	USA	Ford	147.746
29.03.92	Transouth 500 (Darlington)	Bill Elliott	USA	Ford	139.364
05.04.92	Food City 500 (Bristol)	Alan Kulwicki	USA	Ford	86.316
12.04.92	First Union 400 (N Wilkesboro)	Davey Allison	USA	Ford	90.653
26.04.92	Hanes Activewear 500 (Martinsville)	Mark Martin	USA	Ford	78.087
03.05.92	Winston 500 (Talladega)	Davey Allison	USA	Ford	167.609
24.05.92	Coca-Cola 600 (Charlotte)	Dale Earnhardt	USA	Chevrolet	132.980
31.05.92	Budweiser 500 (Dover Downs)	Harry Gant	USA	Oldsmobile	109.456
07.06.92	Save Mart Supermarkets 300 (Sears Point)	Ernie Irvan	USA	Chevrolet	81.509
14.06.92	Champion Spark Plug 500 (Pocono)	Alan Kulwicki	USA	Ford	144.023
21.06.92	Miller Genuine Draft 400 (Michigan)	Davey Allison	USA	Ford	152.672
04.07.92	Pepsi 400 (Daytona)	Ernie Irvan	USA	Chevrolet	170.475
19.07.92	Miller Genuine Draft 500 (Pocono)	Darrell Waltrip	USA	Chevrolet	134.058
26.07.92	Diehard 500 (Talladega)	Ernie Irvan	USA	Chevrolet	176.309
09.08.92	The Budweiser at The Glen (Watkins Glen)	Kyle Petty	USA	Pontiac	85.967
16.08.92	Champion Spark Plug 400 (Michigan)	Harry Gant	USA	Oldsmobile	143.056
29.08.92	Bud 500 (Bristol)	Darrell Waltrip	USA	Chevrolet	91.198
06.09.92	Mountain Dew Southern 500 (Darlington)	Darrell Waltrip	USA	Chevrolet	129.114
12.09.92	Miller Genuine Draft 400 (Richmond)	Rusty Wallace	USA	Pontiac	104.661
20.09.92	Peak Anti-Freeze 500 (Dover Downs)	Ricky Rudd	USA	Chevrolet	115.289
27.09.92	Goody's 500 (Martinsville)	Geoff Bodine	USA	Ford	75.424
05.10.92	Tyson Holly Farms 400 (N Wilkesboro)	Geoff Bodine	USA	Ford	107.360
11.10.92	Mello Yello 500 (Charlotte)	Mark Martin	USA	Ford	153.537
25.10.92	AC Delco 500 (N Carolina)	Kyle Petty	USA	Pontiac	130.748
01.11.92	Pyroil 500 (Phoenix)	Davey Allison	USA	Ford	103.885
15.11.92	Hooter's 500 (Atlanta)	Bill Elliott	USA	Ford	133.520

1993

date	race	driver	nat	car	mph
14.02.93	Daytona 500 by STP (Daytona)	Dale Jarrett	USA	Chevrolet	154.972
28.02.93	Goodwrench 500 (N Carolina)	Rusty Wallace	USA	Pontiac	124.486
07.03.93	Pontiac Excitement 400 (Richmond)	Davey Allison	USA	Ford	107.709
20.03.93	Motorcraft 500 (Atlanta)	Morgan Shepherd	USA	Ford	151.712
28.03.93	Transouth Financial 500 (Darlington)	Dale Earnhardt	USA	Chevrolet	140.898
04.04.93	Food City 500 (Bristol)	Rusty Wallace	USA	Pontiac	84.730
18.04.93	First Union 400 (N Wilkesboro)	Rusty Wallace	USA	Pontiac	92.602
25.04.93	Hanes 500 (Martinsville)	Rusty Wallace	USA	Pontiac	79.476
02.05.93	Winston 500 (Talladega)	Ernie Irvan	USA	Chevrolet	155.412
16.05.93	Save Mart Supermarkets 300 (Sears Point)	Geoff Bodine	USA	Ford	77.105
30.05.93	Coca-Cola 600 (Charlotte)	Dale Earnhardt	USA	Chevrolet	145.504
07.06.93	Budweiser 500 (Dover Downs)	Dale Earnhardt	USA	Chevrolet	105.597
13.06.93	Champion Spark Plug 500 (Pocono)	Kyle Petty	USA	Pontiac	138.005
20.06.93	Miller Genuine Draft 400 (Michigan)	Ricky Rudd	USA	Chevrolet	148.484
03.07.93	Pepsi 400 (Daytona)	Dale Earnhardt	USA	Chevrolet	151.755

date	race	driver	nat	car	mph
11.07.93	Slick 50 300 (New Hampshire)	Rusty Wallace	USA	Pontiac	105.947
18.07.93	Miller Genuine Draft 500 (Pocono)	Dale Earnhardt	USA	Chevrolet	133.343
25.07.93	Diehard 500 (Talladega)	Dale Earnhardt	USA	Chevrolet	153.858
08.08.93	The Budweiser at The Glen (Watkins Glen)	Mark Martin	USA	Ford	84.910
15.08.93	Champion Spark Plug 400 (Michigan)	Mark Martin	USA	Ford	144.564
28.08.93	Bud 500 (Bristol)	Mark Martin	USA	Ford	88.172
05.09.93	Mountain Dew Southern 500 (Darlington)	Mark Martin	USA	Ford	137.932
11.09.93	Miller Genuine Draft 400 (Richmond)	Rusty Wallace	USA	Pontiac	99.917
19.09.93	Splitfire Spark Plug 500 (Dover Downs)	Rusty Wallace	USA	Pontiac	100.334
26.09.93	Goody's 500 (Martinsville)	Ernie Irvan	USA	Ford	74.102
03.10.93	Tyson Holly Farms 400 (N Wilkesboro)	Rusty Wallace	USA	Pontiac	96.920
10.10.93	Mello Yello 500 (Charlotte)	Ernie Irvan	USA	Ford	154.537
24.10.93	AC Delco 500 (N Carolina)	Rusty Wallace	USA	Pontiac	114.036
31.10.93	Slick 50 500 (Phoenix)	Mark Martin	USA	Ford	100.375
14.11.93	Hooter's 500 (Atlanta)	Rusty Wallace	USA	Pontiac	125.221

1994

date	race	driver	nat	car	mph
20.02.94	Daytona 500 (Daytona)	Sterling Marlin	USA	Chevrolet	156.931
27.02.94	Goodwrench 500 (N Carolina)	Rusty Wallace	USA	Ford	125.239
06.03.94	Pontiac Excitement 400 (Richmond)	Ernie Irvan	USA	Ford	98.334
13.03.94	Purolator 500 (Atlanta)	Ernie Irvan	USA	Ford	146.136
27.03.94	Transouth Financial 500 (Darlington)	Dale Earnhardt	USA	Chevrolet	132.432
10.04.94	Food City 500 (Bristol)	Dale Earnhardt	USA	Chevrolet	89.647
17.04.94	First Union 400 (N Wilkesboro)	Terry Labonte	USA	Chevrolet	95.816
24.04.94	Hanes 500 (Martinsville)	Rusty Wallace	USA	Ford	76.707
01.05.94	Winston Select 500 (Talladega)	Dale Earnhardt	USA	Chevrolet	157.478
15.05.94	Save Mart Supermarkets 300 (Sears Point)	Ernie Irvan	USA	Ford	77.550
29.05.94	Coca-Cola 600 (Charlotte)	Jeff Gordon	USA	Chevrolet	139.445
05.06.94	Budweiser 500 (Dover Downs)	Rusty Wallace	USA	Ford	102.529
12.06.94	UAW-GM Teamwork 500 (Pocono)	Rusty Wallace	USA	Ford	128.801
19.06.94	Miller Genuine Draft 400 (Michigan)	Rusty Wallace	USA	Ford	125.022
02.07.94	Pepsi 400 (Daytona)	Jimmy Spencer	USA	Ford	155.558
10.07.94	Slick 50 300 (New Hampshire)	Ricky Rudd	USA	Ford	87.599
17.07.94	Miller Genuine Draft 500 (Pocono)	Geoff Bodine	USA	Ford	136.075
24.07.94	Diehard 500 (Talladega)	Jimmy Spencer	USA	Ford	163.217
06.08.94	Brickyard 400 (Indianapolis)	Jeff Gordon	USA	Chevrolet	131.977
14.08.94	The Budweiser at The Glen (Watkins Glen)	Mark Martin	USA	Ford	93.905
21.08.94	GM Goodwrench Dealer 400 (Michigan)	Geoff Bodine	USA	Ford	139.914
27.08.94	Goody's 500 (Bristol)	Rusty Wallace	USA	Ford	91.363
04.09.94	Mountain Dew Southern 500 (Darlington)	Bill Elliott	USA	Ford	127.952
10.09.94	Miller Genuine Draft 400 (Richmond)	Terry Labonte	USA	Chevrolet	104.056
18.09.94	Splitfire Spark Plug 500 (Dover Downs)	Rusty Wallace	USA	Ford	112.556
25.09.94	Goody's 500 (Martinsville)	Rusty Wallace	USA	Ford	77.139
02.10.94	Tyson Holly Farms 400 (N Wilkesboro)	Geoff Bodine	USA	Ford	98.522

1995 Dale Earnhardt's Chevrolet Monte Carlo receives service at Rockingham, North Carlolina.

date	race	driver	nat	car	mph
09.10.94	Mello Yello 500 (Charlotte)	Dale Jarrett	USA	Chevrolet	145.922
23.10.94	AC Delco 500 (N Carolina)	Dale Earnhardt	USA	Chevrolet	125.878
30.10.94	Slick 50 500 (Phoenix)	Terry Labonte	USA	Chevrolet	107.463
13.11.94	Hooter's 500 (Atlanta)	Mark Martin	USA	Ford	148.983

1995

date	race	driver	nat	car	mph
19.02.95	Daytona 500 (Daytona)	Sterling Marlin	USA	Chevrolet	141.710
26.02.95	Goodwrench 500 (N Carolina)	Jeff Gordon	USA	Chevrolet	125.483
05.03.95	Pontiac Excitement 400 (Richmond)	Terry Labonte	USA	Chevrolet	106.425
12.03.95	Purolator 500 (Atlanta)	Jeff Gordon	USA	Chevrolet	150.115
26.03.95	Transouth Financial 400 (Darlington)	Sterling Marlin	USA	Chevrolet	111.392
02.04.95	Food City 500 (Bristol)	Jeff Gordon	USA	Chevrolet	92.011
09.04.95	First Union 400 (N Wilkesboro)	Dale Earnhardt	USA	Chevrolet	102.424
23.04.95	Hanes 500 (Martinsville)	Rusty Wallace	USA	Ford	72.145
30.04.95	Winston Select 500 (Talladega)	Mark Martin	USA	Ford	178.902
07.05.95	Save Mart Supermarkets 300 (Sears Point)	Dale Earnhardt	USA	Chevrolet	70.765
28.05.95	Coca-Cola 600 (Charlotte)	Bobby Labonte	USA	Chevrolet	151.952
04.06.95	Miller Genuine Draft 500 (Dover Downs)	Kyle Petty	USA	Pontiac	119.880
11.06.95	UAW-GM Teamwork 500 (Pocono)	Terry Labonte	USA	Chevrolet	137.720
18.06.95	Miller Genuine Draft 400 (Michigan)	Bobby Labonte	USA	Chevrolet	134.103
01.07.95	Pepsi 400 (Daytona)	Jeff Gordon	USA	Chevrolet	166.976
09.07.95	Slick 50 300 (New Hampshire)	Jeff Gordon	USA	Chevrolet	107.029
16.07.95	Miller Genuine Draft 500 (Pocono)	Dale Jarrett	USA	Ford	134.038
23.07.95	Diehard 500 (Talladega)	Sterling Marlin	USA	Chevrolet	173.188
05.08.95	Brickyard 400 (Indianapolis)	Dale Earnhardt	USA	Chevrolet	155.206
13.08.95	The Budweiser at The Glen (Watkins Glen)	Mark Martin	USA	Ford	100.467
20.08.95	GM Goodwrench Dealer 400 (Michigan)	Bobby Labonte	USA	Chevrolet	157.739
26.08.95	Goody's 500 (Bristol)	Terry Labonte	USA	Chevrolet	81.979
03.09.95	Mountain Dew Southern 500 (Darlington)	Jeff Gordon	USA	Chevrolet	121.231
09.09.95	Miller Genuine Draft 400 (Richmond)	Rusty Wallace	USA	Ford	104.459
17.09.95	MBNA 500 (Dover Downs)	Jeff Gordon	USA	Chevrolet	124.740
24.09.95	Goody's 500 (Martinsville)	Dale Earnhardt	USA	Chevrolet	73.946
01.10.95	Tyson Holly Farms 400 (N Wilkesboro)	Mark Martin	USA	Ford	102.998
08.10.95	UAW-GM 500 (Charlotte)	Mark Martin	USA	Ford	145.358
22.10.95	AC Delco 400 (N Carolina)	Ward Burton	USA	Chevrolet	114.778
29.10.95	Slick 50 500 (Phoenix)	Ricky Rudd	USA	Ford	102.128
12.11.95	NAPA 500 (Atlanta)	Dale Earnhardt	USA	Chevrolet	163.633

1996

date	race	driver	nat	car	mph
18.02.96	Daytona 500 (Daytona)	Dale Jarrett	USA	Ford	154.308
25.02.96	Goodwrench Service 400 (N Carolina)	Dale Earnhardt	USA	Chevrolet	113.959
03.03.96	Pontiac Excitement 400 (Richmond)	Jeff Gordon	USA	Chevrolet	102.750
10.03.96	Purolator 500 (Atlanta)	Dale Earnhardt	USA	Chevrolet	161.298
24.03.96	Transouth Financial 400 (Darlington)	Jeff Gordon	USA	Chevrolet	124.793
31.03.96	Food City 500 (Bristol)	Jeff Gordon	USA	Chevrolet	91.308
14.04.96	First Union 400 (N Wilkesboro)	Terry Labonte	USA	Chevrolet	96.370
21.04.96	Goody's Headache Powder 500 (Martinsville)	Rusty Wallace	USA	Ford	81.410
28.04.96	Winston Select 500 (Talladega)	Sterling Marlin	USA	Chevrolet	149.999
05.05.96	Save Mart Supermarkets 300 (Sears Point)	Rusty Wallace	USA	Ford	77.765
26.05.96	Coca-Cola 600 (Charlotte)	Dale Jarrett	USA	Ford	147.581
02.06.96	Miller Genuine Draft 500 (Dover Downs)	Jeff Gordon	USA	Chevrolet	122.741
16.06.96	UAW-GM Teamwork 500 (Pocono)	Jeff Gordon	USA	Chevrolet	139.104
23.06.96	Miller Genuine Draft 400 (Michigan)	Rusty Wallace	USA	Ford	166.224
06.07.96	Pepsi 400 (Daytona)	Sterling Marlin	USA	Chevrolet	161.602
14.07.96	Jiffy Lube 300 (New Hampshire)	Ernie Irvan	USA	Ford	98.930
21.07.96	Miller Genuine Draft 500 (Pocono)	Rusty Wallace	USA	Ford	144.893
28.07.96	Diehard 500 (Talladega)	Jeff Gordon	USA	Chevrolet	133.388
03.08.96	Brickyard 400 (Indianapolis)	Dale Jarrett	USA	Ford	139.508
11.08.96	The Budweiser at The Glen (Watkins Glen)	Geoff Bodine	USA	Ford	92.485
18.08.96	GM Goodwrench Service Dealer 400 (Michigan)	Dale Jarrett	USA	Ford	139.792
24.08.96	Goody's Headache Powder 500 (Bristol)	Rusty Wallace	USA	Ford	91.267
01.09.96	Mountain Dew Southern 500 (Darlington)	Jeff Gordon	USA	Chevrolet	135.757
07.09.96	Miller Genuine Draft 400 (Richmond)	Ernie Irvan	USA	Ford	105.469
15.09.96	MBNA 500 (Dover Downs)	Jeff Gordon	USA	Chevrolet	105.646
22.09.96	Hanes 500 (Martinsville)	Jeff Gordon	USA	Chevrolet	82.230
29.09.96	Tyson Holly Farms 400 (N Wilkesboro)	Jeff Gordon	USA	Chevrolet	96.837
06.10.96	UAW-GM Quality 500 (Charlotte)	Terry Labonte	USA	Chevrolet	143.143

date	race	driver	nat	car	mph
20.10.96	AC Delco 400 (N Carolina)	Ricky Rudd	USA	Ford	122.320
27.10.96	Dura-Lube 500 (Phoenix)	Bobby Hamilton	USA	Pontiac	109.709
10.11.96	NAPA 500 (Atlanta)	Bobby Labonte	USA	Chevrolet	136.636

1997

date	race	driver	nat	car	mph
16.02.97	Daytona 500 (Daytona)	Jeff Gordon	USA	Chevrolet	148.295
23.02.97	Goodwrench Service 400 (N Carolina)	Jeff Gordon	USA	Chevrolet	121.371
02.03.97	Pontiac Excitement 400 (Richmond)	Rusty Wallace	USA	Ford	108.499
09.03.97	Primestar 500 (Atlanta)	Dale Jarrett	USA	Ford	132.731
23.03.97	Transouth Financial 400 (Darlington)	Dale Jarrett	USA	Ford	121.162
06.04.97	Interstate Batteries 500 (Texas Motor Speedway)	Jeff Burton	USA	Ford	121.358
13.04.97	Food City 500 (Bristol)	Jeff Gordon	USA	Chevrolet	75.035
20.04.97	Goody's Headache Powder 500 (Martinsville)	Jeff Gordon	USA	Chevrolet	70.347
04.05.97	Save Mart Supermarkets 300 (Sears Point)	Mark Martin	USA	Ford	75.878
10.05.97	Winston 500 (Talladega)	Mark Martin	USA	Ford	188.354
25.05.97	Coca-Cola 600 (Charlotte)	Jeff Gordon	USA	Chevrolet	136.745
01.06.97	Miller 500 (Dover Downs)	Ricky Rudd	USA	Ford	114.635
08.06.97	Pocono 500 (Pocono)	Jeff Gordon	USA	Chevrolet	139.828
15.06.97	Miller 400 (Michigan)	Ernie Irvan	USA	Ford	153.338
22.06.97	California 500 (California Speedway)	Jeff Gordon	USA	Chevrolet	155.012
05.07.97	Pepsi 400 (Daytona)	John Andretti	USA	Ford	157.791
13.07.97	Jiffy Lube 300 (New Hampshire)	Jeff Burton	USA	Ford	117.134
20.07.97	Pennsylvania 500 (Pocono)	Dale Jarrett	USA	Ford	142.068
03.08.97	Brickyard 400 (Indianapolis)	Ricky Rudd	USA	Ford	130.814
10.08.97	The Budweiser at The Glen (Watkins Glen)	Jeff Gordon	USA	Chevrolet	91.443
17.08.97	ITW De Vilbiss 400 (Michigan)	Mark Martin	USA	Ford	126.883
23.08.97	Goody's Headache Powder 500 (Bristol)	Dale Jarrett	USA	Ford	80.010
31.08.97	Mountain Dew Southern 500 (Darlington)	Jeff Gordon	USA	Chevrolet	121.149
06.09.97	Exide NASCAR Select Batteries 400 (Richmond)	Dale Jarrett	USA	Ford	109.047
14.09.97	CMT 300 (New Hampshire)	Jeff Gordon	USA	Chevrolet	100.364
21.09.97	MBNA 400 (Dover Downs)	Mark Martin	USA	Ford	132.719
29.09.97	Hanes 500 (Martinsville)	Jeff Burton	USA	Ford	0.000
05.10.97	UAW-GM Quality 500 (Charlotte)	Dale Jarrett	USA	Ford	144.323
12.10.97	Sears Diehard 500 (Talladega)	Terry Labonte	USA	Chevrolet	156.601
27.10.97	AC Delco 400 (N Carolina)	Bobby Hamilton	USA	Pontiac	121.730
02.11.97	Dura-Lube 500 (Phoenix)	Dale Jarrett	USA	Ford	110.824
16.11.97	NAPA 500 (Atlanta)	Bobby Labonte	USA	Pontiac	159.904

1998

date	race	driver	nat	car	mph
15.02.98	Daytona 500 (Daytona)	Dale Earnhardt	USA	Chevrolet	172.712
22.02.98	GM Goodwrench Service Plus 400 (N Carolina)	Jeff Gordon	USA	Chevrolet	117.065
01.03.98	Las Vegas 400 (Las Vegas Speedway)	Mark Martin	USA	Ford	146.554
09.03.98	Primestar 500 (Atlanta)	Bobby Labonte	USA	Pontiac	139.501
22.03.98	Transouth Financial 400 (Darlington)	Dale Jarrett	USA	Ford	127.962
29.03.98	Food City 500 (Bristol)	Jeff Gordon	USA	Chevrolet	82.850
05.04.98	Texas 500 (Texas Motor Speedway)	Mark Martin	USA	Ford	132.668
20.04.98	Goody's Headache Powder 500 (Martinsville)	Bobby Hamilton	USA	Chevrolet	70.709
25.04.98	Diehard 500 (Talladega)	Bobby Labonte	USA	Pontiac	142.428
03.05.98	California 500 (California Speedway)	Mark Martin	USA	Ford	140.220
24.05.98	Coca-Cola 600 (Charlotte)	Jeff Gordon	USA	Chevrolet	136.424
31.05.98	MBNA Platinum 400 (Dover Downs)	Dale Jarrett	USA	Ford	119.522
06.06.98	Pontiac Excitement 400 (Richmond)	Terry Labonte	USA	Chevrolet	97.044
14.06.98	Miller Lite 400 (Michigan)	Mark Martin	USA	Ford	158.695
21.06.98	Pocono 500 (Pocono)	Jeremy Mayfield	USA	Ford	117.809
28.06.98	Save Mart/Kragen 350 (Sears Point)	Jeff Gordon	USA	Chevrolet	72.387
12.07.98	Jiffy Lube 300 (New Hampshire)	Jeff Burton	USA	Ford	102.996
26.07.98	Pennsylvania 500 (Pocono)	Jeff Gordon	USA	Chevrolet	134.660
01.08.98	Brickyard 400 (Indianapolis)	Jeff Gordon	USA	Chevrolet	126.772
09.08.98	The Budweiser at The Glen (Watkins Glen)	Jeff Gordon	USA	Chevrolet	94.620
16.08.98	Pepsi 400 (Michigan)	Jeff Gordon	USA	Chevrolet	151.995
22.08.98	Goody's Headache Powder 500 (Bristol)	Mark Martin	USA	Ford	86.949
30.08.98	Farm Aid On CMT 300 (New Hampshire)	Jeff Gordon	USA	Chevrolet	112.078
06.09.98	Pepsi Southern 500 (Darlington)	Jeff Gordon	USA	Chevrolet	139.031
13.09.98	Exide NASCAR Select Batteries 400 (Richmond)	Jeff Burton	USA	Ford	91.985
20.09.98	MBNA Gold 400 (Dover Downs)	Mark Martin	USA	Ford	113.834

date	race	driver	nat	car	mph
27.09.98	NAPA Autocare 500 (Martinsville)	Ricky Rudd	USA	Ford	73.350
04.10.98	UAW-GM Quality 500 (Charlotte)	Mark Martin	USA	Ford	123.188
11.10.98	Winston 500 (Talladega)	Dale Jarrett	USA	Ford	159.318
17.10.98	Pepsi 400 (Daytona)	Jeff Gordon	USA	Chevrolet	144.549
25.10.98	Dura-Lube 500 (Phoenix)	Rusty Wallace	USA	Ford	108.211
01.11.98	AC Delco 400 (N Carolina)	Jeff Gordon	USA	Chevrolet	128.423
08.11.98	NAPA 500 (Atlanta)	Jeff Gordon	USA	Chevrolet	113.572

1999

date	race	driver	nat	car	mph
14.02.99	Daytona 500 (Daytona)	Jeff Gordon	USA	Chevrolet	161.551
21.02.99	Dura-Lube/Big Kmart 400 (N Carolina)	Mark Martin	USA	Ford	120.750
07.03.99	Las Vegas 400 (Las Vegas Speedway)	Jeff Burton	USA	Ford	137.537
14.03.99	Cracker Barrel 500 (Atlanta)	Jeff Gordon	USA	Chevrolet	143.284
21.03.99	Transouth Financial 400 (Darlington)	Jeff Burton	USA	Ford	121.294
28.03.99	Primestar 500 (Texas Motor Speedway)	Terry Labonte	USA	Chevrolet	139.948
11.04.99	Food City 500 (Bristol)	Rusty Wallace	USA	Ford	93.363
18.04.99	Goody's Body Pain 500 (Martinsville)	John Andretti	USA	Pontiac	75.653
25.04.99	Diehard 500 (Talladega)	Dale Earnhardt	USA	Chevrolet	163.395
02.05.99	California 500 (California Speedway)	Jeff Gordon	USA	Chevrolet	157.370
15.05.99	Pontiac Excitement 400 (Richmond)	Dale Jarrett	USA	Ford	100.102
30.05.99	Coca-Cola 600 (Charlotte)	Jeff Burton	USA	Ford	151.367
06.06.99	MBNA Platinum 400 (Dover Downs)	Bobby Labonte	USA	Pontiac	120.603
13.06.99	Kmart 400 (Michigan)	Dale Jarrett	USA	Ford	173.997
20.06.99	Pocono 500 (Pocono)	Bobby Labonte	USA	Pontiac	118.898
27.06.99	Save Mart/Kragen 350 (Sears Point)	Jeff Gordon	USA	Chevrolet	70.378
03.07.99	Pepsi 400 (Daytona)	Dale Jarrett	USA	Ford	169.213
11.07.99	Jiffy Lube 300 (New Hampshire)	Jeff Burton	USA	Ford	101.876
25.07.99	Pennsylvania 500 (Pocono)	Bobby Labonte	USA	Pontiac	116.982
07.08.99	Brickyard 400 (Indianapolis)	Dale Jarrett	USA	Ford	148.194
15.08.99	Frontier at The Glen (Watkins Glen)	Jeff Gordon	USA	Chevrolet	87.866
22.08.99	Pepsi 400 (Michigan)	Bobby Labonte	USA	Pontiac	144.332
28.08.99	Goody's Headache Powder 500 (Bristol)	Dale Earnhardt	USA	Chevrolet	91.276
05.09.99	Pepsi Southern 500 (Darlington)	Jeff Burton	USA	Ford	107.816
11.09.99	Exide NASCAR Select Batteries 400 (Richmond)	Tony Stewart	USA	Pontiac	104.006
19.09.99	Dura-Lube/Kmart 300 (New Hampshire)	Joe Nemechek	USA	Chevrolet	100.673
26.09.99	MBNA Gold 400 (Dover Downs)	Mark Martin	USA	Ford	127.434
03.10.99	NAPA Autocare 500 (Martinsville)	Jeff Gordon	USA	Chevrolet	72.347
10.10.99	UAW-GM Quality 500 (Charlotte)	Jeff Gordon	USA	Chevrolet	160.306
17.10.99	Winston 500 (Talladega)	Dale Earnhardt	USA	Chevrolet	166.632
24.10.99	Pop Secret Microwave Popcorn 400 (N Carolina)	Jeff Burton	USA	Ford	131.103
07.11.99	Checker Autoparts/Dura-Lube 500 (Phoenix)	Tony Stewart	USA	Pontiac	118.132
14.11.99	Pennzoil 400 (Homestead)	Tony Stewart	USA	Pontiac	140.522
21.11.99	NAPA 500 (Atlanta)	Bobby Labonte	USA	Pontiac	137.932

2000

date	race	driver	nat	car	mph
20.02.00	Daytona 500 (Daytona)	Dale Jarrett	USA	Ford	155.669
27.02.00	Dura Lube/Kmart 400 (N Carolina)	Bobby Labonte	USA	Pontiac	127.875
05.03.00	Carsdirect.com 400 (Las Vegas Speedway)	Jeff Burton	USA	Ford	119.982
12.03.00	Cracker Barrel Old Country Store 500 (Atlanta)	Dale Earnhardt	USA	Chevrolet	131.759
19.03.00	Mall.com 400 (Darlington)	Ward Burton	USA	Pontiac	128.076
26.03.00	Food City 500 (Bristol)	Rusty Wallace	USA	Ford	88.018
02.04.00	Directv 500 (Texas Motor Speedway)	Dale Earnhardt Jr	USA	Chevrolet	127.217
09.04.00	Goody's Body Pain 500 (Martinsville)	Mark Martin	USA	Ford	71.161
16.04.00	Diehard 500 (Talladega)	Jeff Gordon	USA	Chevrolet	161.157
30.04.00	NAPA Auto Parts 500 (California Speedway)	Jeremy Mayfield	USA	Ford	149.378
06.05.00	Pontiac Excitement 400 (Richmond)	Dale Earnhardt Jr	USA	Chevrolet	99.374
28.05.00	Coca-Cola 600 (Charlotte)	Matt Kenseth	USA	Ford	142.640
04.06.00	MBNA Platinum 400 (Dover Downs)	Tony Stewart	USA	Pontiac	109.514
11.06.00	Kmart 400 (Michigan)	Tony Stewart	USA	Pontiac	143.926
18.06.00	Pocono 500 (Pocono)	Jeremy Mayfield	USA	Ford	139.741
25.06.00	Save Mart/Kragen 350 (Sears Point)	Jeff Gordon	USA	Chevrolet	78.789
01.07.00	Pepsi 400 (Daytona)	Jeff Burton	USA	Ford	148.576
09.07.00	Thatlook.com 300 (New Hampshire)	Tony Stewart	USA	Pontiac	103.145
23.07.00	Pennsylvania 500 (Pocono)	Rusty Wallace	USA	Ford	130.662
05.08.00	Brickyard 400 (Indianapolis)	Bobby Labonte	USA	Pontiac	155.912
13.08.00	Global Crossing: The Glen (Watkins Glen)	Steve Park	USA	Chevrolet	91.485

2001 Jeff Gordon won the NASCAR Winston Cup for Rick Hendricks and Chevrolet for a fourth time in 2001.

date	race	driver	nat	car	mph
20.08.00	Pepsi 400 (Michigan)	Rusty Wallace	USA	Ford	132.597
26.08.00	Goracing.com 500 (Bristol)	Rusty Wallace	USA	Ford	85.394
03.09.00	Pepsi Southern 500 (Darlington)	Bobby Labonte	USA	Pontiac	108.253
09.09.00	Chevrolet 400 (Richmond)	Jeff Gordon	USA	Chevrolet	99.871
17.09.00	Dura-Lube 300 (New Hampshire)	Jeff Burton	USA	Ford	102.003
24.09.00	MBNA.com 400 (Dover Downs)	Tony Stewart	USA	Pontiac	115.191
01.10.00	NAPA Autocare 500 (Martinsville)	Tony Stewart	USA	Pontiac	73.859
08.10.00	UAW-GM Quality 500 (Charlotte)	Bobby Labonte	USA	Pontiac	133.630
15.10.00	Winston 500 (Talladega)	Dale Earnhardt	USA	Chevrolet	165.681
22.10.00	Pop Secret Microwave Popcorn 400 (N Carolina)	Dale Jarrett	USA	Ford	110.418
05.11.00	Checker Auto Parts/Dura-Lube 500 (Phoenix)	Jeff Burton	USA	Ford	105.041
12.11.00	Pennzoil 400 (Homestead)	Tony Stewart	USA	Pontiac	127.650
20.11.00	NAPA 500 (Atlanta)	Jerry Nadeau	USA	Chevrolet	141.340

2001

date	race	driver	nat	car	mph
18.02.01	Daytona 500 (Daytona)	Michael Waltrip	USA	Chevrolet	161.783
25.02.01	Dura Lube 400 (North Carolina)	Steve Park	USA	Chevrolet	111.877
04.03.01	UAW-DaimlerChrysler 400 (Las Vegas Speedway)	Jeff Gordon	USA	Chevrolet	135.546
18.03.01	Carolina Dodge Dealers 400 (Darlington)	Dale Jarrett	USA	Ford	126.557
25.03.01	Food City 500 (Bristol)	Elliott Sadler	USA	Ford	86.949
01.04.01	Harrah's 500 (Texas Motor Speedway)	Dale Jarrett	USA	Ford	137.549
08.04.01	Virginia 500 (Martinsville)	Dale Jarrett	USA	Ford	70.799
11.04.01	Cracker Barrel 500 (Atlanta)	Kevin Harvick	USA	Chevrolet	143.273
22.04.01	Talladega 500 (Talladega)	Bobby Hamilton	USA	Chevrolet	184.003
29.04.01	NAPA Auto Parts 500 (California Speedway)	Rusty Wallace	USA	Ford	143.118
05.05.01	Pontiac Excitement 400 (Richmond)	Tony Stewart	USA	Pontiac	95.872
27.05.01	Coca-Cola 600 (Charlotte)	Jeff Burton	USA	Ford	138.107
03.06.01	MBNA Platinum 400 (Dover Downs)	Jeff Gordon	USA	Chevrolet	120.361
10.06.01	Kmart 400 (Michigan)	Jeff Gordon	USA	Chevrolet	134.203
17.06.01	Pocono 500 (Pocono)	Ricky Rudd	USA	Ford	183.786
24.06.01	Dodge/Save Mart 350 (Sears Point)	Tony Stewart	USA	Pontiac	73.954
07.07.01	Pepsi 400 (Daytona)	Dale Earnhardt Jr	USA	Chevrolet	157.601
15.07.01	Tropicana 400 (Chicagoland)	Kevin Harvick	USA	Chevrolet	121.200
22.07.01	New England 300 (New Hampshire)	Dale Jarrett	USA	Ford	102.131
29.07.01	Pennsylvania 500 (Pocono)	Bobby Labonte	USA	Pontiac	134.590
05.08.01	Brickyard 400 (Indianapolis)	Jeff Gordon	USA	Chevrolet	130.790
12.08.01	Global Crossing: The Glen (Watkins Glen)	Jeff Gordon	USA	Chevrolet	89.226
19.08.01	Pepsi 400 (Michigan)	Sterling Marlin	USA	Dodge	173.473
25.08.01	Sharpie 500 (Bristol)	Tony Stewart	USA	Pontiac	85.106
02.09.01	Mountain Dew Southern 500 (Darlington)	Ward Burton	USA	Dodge	122.773
08.09.01	Chevrolet 400 (Richmond)	Ricky Rudd	USA	Ford	95.146

date	race	driver	nat	car	mph
23.09.01	MBNA Cal Ripken Jr 400 (Dover Downs)	Dale Earnhardt Jr	USA	Chevrolet	101.559
30.09.01	Protection One 400 (Kansas City)	Jeff Gordon	USA	Chevrolet	110.576
07.10.01	UAW-GM Quality 500 (Charlotte)	Sterling Marlin	USA	Dodge	139.006
15.10.01	Old Dominion 500 (Martinsville)	Ricky Craven	USA	Ford	75.750
21.10.01	EA Sports 500 (Talladega)	Dale Earnhardt Jr	USA	Chevrolet	164.185
28.10.01	Checker Auto Parts 500 (Phoenix)	Jeff Burton	USA	Ford	102.613
04.11.01	Pop Secret Microwave Popcorn 400 (N Carolina)	Joe Nemechek	USA	Chevrolet	128.941
11.11.01	Pennzoil Freedom 400 (Homestead)	Bill Elliott	USA	Dodge	117.605
18.11.01	NAPA 500 (Atlanta)	Bobby Labonte	USA	Pontiac	151.756
23.11.01	New Hampshire 300 (New Hampshire)	Robby Gordon	USA	Chevrolet	103.594

2002

date	race	driver	nat	car	mph
17.02.02	Daytona 500 (Daytona)	Ward Burton	USA	Dodge	142.971
24.02.02	Subway 400 (North Carolina)	Matt Kenseth	USA	Ford	115.478
03.03.02	UAW-DaimlerChrysler 400 (Las Vegas Speedway)	Sterling Marlin	USA	Dodge	136.754
10.03.02	MBNA America 500 (Atlanta)	Tony Stewart	USA	Pontiac	148.443
17.03.02	Carolina Dodge Dealers 400 (Darlington)	Sterling Marlin	USA	Dodge	126.070
24.03.02	Food City 500 (Bristol)	Kurt Busch	USA	Ford	82.281
08.04.02	Samsung/RadioShack 500 (Texas Motor Speedway)	Matt Kenseth	USA	Ford	138.180
14.04.02	Virginia 500 (Martinsville)	Bobby Labonte	USA	Pontiac	73.951
21.04.02	Aaron's 500 (Talladega)	Dale Earnhardt Jr	USA	Chevrolet	159.022
28.04.02	NAPA Auto Parts 500 (California Speedway)	Jimmie Johnson	USA	Chevrolet	150.088
05.05.02	Pontiac Excitement 400 (Richmond)	Tony Stewart	USA	Pontiac	86.824
26.05.02	Coca-Cola 600 (Charlotte)	Mark Martin	USA	Ford	137.729
02.06.02	MBNA Platinum 400 (Dover Downs)	Jimmie Johnson	USA	Chevrolet	117.551
09.06.02	Pocono 500 (Pocono)	Dale Jarrett	USA	Ford	143.426
16.06.02	Sirius Satellite Radio 400 (Michigan)	Matt Kenseth	USA	Ford	154.822
23.06.02	Dodge/Save Mart 350 (Sears Point)	Ricky Rudd	USA	Ford	79.338
06.07.02	Pepsi 400 (Daytona)	Michael Waltrip	USA	Chevrolet	135.952
14.07.02	Tropicana 400 (Chicagoland)	Kevin Harvick	USA	Chevrolet	136.832
21.07.02	New England 300 (New Hampshire)	Ward Burton	USA	Dodge	92.342
28.07.02	Pennsylvania 500 (Pocono)	Bill Elliott	USA	Dodge	125.809
04.08.02	Brickyard 400 (Indianapolis)	Bill Elliott	USA	Dodge	125.033
11.08.02	Sirius Satellite Radio at The Glen (Watkins Glen)	Tony Stewart	USA	Pontiac	82.342
18.08.02	Pepsi 400 (Michigan)	Dale Jarrett	USA	Ford	140.556
24.08.02	Sharpie 500 (Bristol)	Jeff Gordon	USA	Chevrolet	77.097
01.09.02	Mountain Dew Southern 500 (Darlington)	Jeff Gordon	USA	Chevrolet	118.617
07.09.02	Chevrolet Monte Carlo 400 (Richmond)	Matt Kenseth	USA	Ford	94.787
15.09.02	New Hampshire 300 (New Hampshire)	Ryan Newman	USA	Ford	105.081
22.09.02	MBNA All-American Heroes 400 (Dover Downs)	Jimmie Johnson	USA	Chevrolet	120.805
29.09.02	Protection One 400 (Kansas City)	Jeff Gordon	USA	Chevrolet	120.986
06.10.02	EA Sports Thunder 500 (Talladega)	Dale Earnhardt Jr	USA	Chevrolet	183.665
13.10.02	UAW-GM Quality 500 (Charlotte)	Jamie McMurray	USA	Dodge	141.481
20.10.02	Old Dominion 500 (Martinsville)	Kurt Busch	USA	Ford	74.651
27.10.02	NAPA 500 (Atlanta)	Kurt Busch	USA	Ford	127.519
03.11.02	Pop Secret Microwave Popcorn 400 (North Carolina)	Johnny Benson	USA	Pontiac	128.526
10.11.02	Checker Auto Parts 500 (Phoenix)	Matt Kenseth	USA	Ford	113.857
17.11.02	Ford 400 (Homestead)	Kurt Busch	USA	Ford	116.617

2001 James Thompson's Honda Accord leads the field at Jarama.

Tasman Cup

During the sixties the Tasman Cup was a healthy winter series held jointly by the Australian and New Zealand motorsport authorities. By adopting the 2.5-litre Formula 1 rules of 1954-60, the organisers attracted works teams such as Cooper, Ferrari, BRM and Lotus, who ran old Grand Prix engines in new chassis.

Drivers of the calibre of Graham Hill, Jackie Stewart, Jim Clark and Jochen Rindt were pitted against locals Jack Brabham, Chris Amon and Bruce McLaren, making the series a winter World Championship. During these years Clark won the title three times, a record matched by New Zealander Graham McRae after organisers switched to Formula 5000 rules.

But as the Grand Prix World Championship was expanded, F5000 failed to attract the European teams and the popularity of the Tasman Cup waned. Finally, in 1976 the series was abandoned in favour of separate championships in each country – the Gold Star in Australia and International Series in New Zealand.

TASMAN CUP CHAMPIONS

year	driver	nat	team	car
1964	Bruce McLaren	NZ	Bruce McLaren Motor Racing	Cooper T70-Climax
1965	Jim Clark	GB	Team Lotus	Lotus 32B-Climax
1966	Jackie Stewart	GB	Owen Racing Organisation	BRM P261
1967	Jim Clark	GB	Team Lotus	Lotus 33-Climax
1968	Jim Clark	GB	Team Lotus	Lotus 49T-Ford
1969	Chris Amon	NZ	Scuderia Ferrari	Ferrari 246T
1970	Graeme Lawrence	NZ	Graeme Lawrence	Ferrari 246T
1971	Graham McRae	NZ	Graham McRae	McLaren M10B-Chevrolet
1972	Graham McRae	NZ	Graham McRae	McRae GM1-Chevrolet
1973	Graham McRae	NZ	Graham McRae	McRae GM1-Chevrolet
1974	Peter Gethin	GB	Team VDS	Chevron B24-Chevrolet
1975	Warwick Brown	AUS	Pat Burke Racing	Lola T332-Chevrolet

1964-69 for 2500cc single-seaters, 1970-75 F5000

Race Winners

1964

date	race	driver	nat	car	mph
04.01.64	Levin	Denny Hulme	NZ	Brabham BT7A-Climax	73.370
11.01.64	New Zealand GP (Pukekohe)	Bruce McLaren	NZ	Cooper T70-Climax	87.846
18.01.64	Lady Wigram Trophy (Wigram)	Bruce McLaren	NZ	Cooper T70-Climax	94.130
25.01.64	Teretonga Park	Bruce McLaren	NZ	Cooper T70-Climax	77.040
09.02.64	Australian GP (Sandown Park)	Jack Brabham	AUS	Brabham BT7A-Climax	96.809
16.02.64	Warwick Farm	Jack Brabham	AUS	Brabham BT7A-Climax	82.370
23.02.64	Lakeside	Jack Brabham	AUS	Brabham BT7A-Climax	88.960
29.02.64	Longford	Graham Hill	GB	Brabham BT4-Climax	111.700

1965

date	race	driver	nat	car	mph
09.01.65	New Zealand GP (Pukekohe)	Graham Hill	GB	Brabham BT11A-Climax	89.512
16.01.65	Levin	Jim Clark	GB	Lotus 32B-Climax	77.180
23.01.65	Lady Wigram Trophy (Wigram)	Jim Clark	GB	Lotus 32B-Climax	95.159
30.01.65	Teretonga Park	Jim Clark	GB	Lotus 32B-Climax	84.950
14.02.65	Warwick Farm	Jim Clark	GB	Lotus 32B-Climax	84.440
21.02.65	Sandown Park	Jack Brabham	AUS	Brabham BT11A-Climax	101.180
01.03.65	Australian GP (Longford)	Bruce McLaren	NZ	Cooper T79-Climax	114.740

1966

date	race	driver	nat	car	mph
08.01.66	New Zealand GP (Pukekohe)	Graham Hill	GB	BRM P261	83.010
15.01.66	Levin	Richard Attwood	GB	BRM P261	86.897
22.01.66	Lady Wigram Trophy (Wigram)	Jackie Stewart	GB	BRM P261	95.269
29.01.66	Teretonga Park	Jackie Stewart	GB	BRM P261	90.088
13.02.66	Warwick Farm	Jim Clark	GB	Lotus 39-Climax	85.491
20.02.66	Australian GP (Lakeside)	Graham Hill	GB	BRM P261	94.838
27.02.66	Sandown Park	Jackie Stewart	GB	BRM P261	100.950
07.03.66	Longford	Jackie Stewart	GB	BRM P261	115.855

Other Major Championships

1967

date	race	driver	nat	car	mph
07.01.67	New Zealand GP (Pukekohe)	Jackie Stewart	GB	BRM P261	100.971
14.01.67	Levin	Jim Clark	GB	Lotus 33-Climax	88.482
21.01.67	Lady Wigram Trophy (Wigram)	Jim Clark	GB	Lotus 33-Climax	97.046
28.01.67	Teretonga Park	Jim Clark	GB	Lotus 33-Climax	88.947
12.02.67	Lakeside	Jim Clark	GB	Lotus 33-Climax	97.478
19.02.67	Australian GP (Warwick Farm)	Jackie Stewart	GB	BRM P261	87.677
26.02.67	Sandown Park	Jim Clark	GB	Lotus 33-Climax	101.724
05.03.67	Longford	Jack Brabham	AUS	Brabham BT23A-Repco	114.936

1968

date	race	driver	nat	car	mph
06.01.68	New Zealand GP (Pukekohe)	Chris Amon	NZ	Ferrari 246T	102.638
13.01.68	Levin	Chris Amon	NZ	Ferrari 246T	89.520
20.01.68	Lady Wigram Trophy (Wigram)	Jim Clark	GB	Lotus 49T-Ford	102.602
27.01.68	Teretonga Park	Bruce McLaren	NZ	BRM P126	84.441
11.02.68	Surfers Paradise	Jim Clark	GB	Lotus 49T-Ford	98.796
18.02.68	Warwick Farm	Jim Clark	GB	Lotus 49T-Ford	88.963
20.02.68	Australian GP (Sandown Park)	Jim Clark	GB	Lotus 49T-Ford	101.572
04.03.68	Longford	Piers Courage	GB	McLaren M4A-Cosworth	96.909

1969

date	race	driver	nat	car	mph
04.01.69	New Zealand GP (Pukekohe)	Chris Amon	NZ	Ferrari 246T	105.139
11.01.69	Levin	Chris Amon	NZ	Ferrari 246T	90.455
18.01.69	Lady Wigram Trophy (Wigram)	Jochen Rindt	A	Lotus 49B-Ford	103.102
25.01.69	Teretonga Park	Piers Courage	GB	Brabham BT24-Ford	97.313
02.02.69	Australian GP (Lakeside)	Chris Amon	NZ	Ferrari 246T	100.144
09.02.69	Warwick Farm	Jochen Rindt	A	Lotus 49B-Ford	77.672
16.02.69	Sandown Park	Chris Amon	NZ	Ferrari 246T	105.784

1970

date	race	driver	nat	car	mph
03.01.70	Levin	Graeme Lawrence	NZ	Ferrari 246T	90.305
10.01.70	New Zealand GP (Pukekohe)	Frank Matich	AUS	McLaren M10A-Chevrolet	103.810
17.01.70	Lady Wigram Trophy (Wigram)	Frank Matich	AUS	McLaren M10A-Chevrolet	101.363
24.01.70	Teretonga Park	Graham McRae	NZ	McLaren M10A-Chevrolet	94.504
07.02.70	Surfers Paradise	Graham McRae	NZ	McLaren M10A-Chevrolet	100.709
14.02.70	Warwick Farm	Kevin Bartlett	AUS	Mildren-Waggott	90.973
21.02.70	Sandown Park	Niel Allen	AUS	McLaren M10B-Chevrolet	102.706

1971

date	race	driver	nat	car	mph
02.01.71	Levin	Graham McRae	NZ	McLaren M10B-Chevrolet	89.786
09.01.71	New Zealand GP (Pukekohe)	Niel Allen	AUS	McLaren M10B-Chevrolet	107.883
16.01.71	Lady Wigram Trophy (Wigram)	Graham McRae	NZ	McLaren M10B-Chevrolet	104.937
24.01.71	Teretonga Park	Niel Allen	AUS	McLaren M10B-Chevrolet	97.765
14.02.71	Warwick Farm	Frank Gardner	AUS	Lola T192-Chevrolet	93.030
21.02.71	Sandown Park	Graham McRae	NZ	McLaren M10B-Chevrolet	107.140
28.02.71	Surfers Paradise	Frank Matich	AUS	McLaren M10B-Holden	102.961

1972

date	race	driver	nat	car	mph
08.01.72	New Zealand GP (Pukekohe)	Frank Gardner	AUS	Lola T300-Chevrolet	106.329
15.01.72	Levin	Graham McRae	NZ	McRae GM1-Chevrolet	93.381
22.01.72	Lady Wigram Trophy (Wigram)	Graham McRae	NZ	McRae GM1-Chevrolet	112.920
30.01.72	Teretonga Park	Kevin Bartlett	AUS	McLaren M10B-Chevrolet	87.941
06.02.72	Surfers Paradise	Graham McRae	NZ	McRae GM1-Chevrolet	102.389
13.02.72	Warwick Farm	Frank Matich	AUS	Matich A50-Holden/Repco	93.606
20.02.72	Australian GP (Sandown Park)	Graham McRae	NZ	McRae GM1-Chevrolet	109.447
27.02.72	Adelaide	David Hobbs	GB	McLaren M18B-Chevrolet	100.519

1973

date	race	driver	nat	car	mph
06.01.73	New Zealand GP (Pukekohe)	John McCormack	AUS	Elfin MR5-Holden/Repco	89.960
13.01.73	Levin	Graham McRae	NZ	McRae GM1-Chevrolet	96.200
20.01.73	Lady Wigram Trophy (Wigram)	Graham McRae	NZ	McRae GM1-Chevrolet	114.274
28.01.73	Teretonga Park	Alan Rollinson	GB	McRae GM1-Chevrolet	80.830
04.02.73	Surfers Paradise	Frank Matich	AUS	Matich A50-Holden/Repco	102.243
11.02.73	Warwick Farm	Steve Thompson	GB	Chevron B24-Chevrolet	81.453
18.02.73	Sandown Park	Graham McRae	NZ	McRae GM1-Chevrolet	108.366
25.02.73	Adelaide	John McCormack	AUS	Elfin MR5-Holden/Repco	104.564

1974

date	race	driver	nat	car	mph
05.01.74	Levin	Johnnie Walker	AUS	Lola T330-Holden/Repco	94.020
12.01.74	Pukekohe	Peter Gethin	GB	Chevron B24-Chevrolet	97.461
19.01.74	New Zealand GP* (Wigram)	John McCormack	AUS	Elfin MR5-Holden/Repco	114.419
26.01.74	Teretonga Park	Max Stewart	AUS	Lola T330-Chevrolet	104.104
03.02.74	Oran Park	Max Stewart	AUS	Lola T330-Chevrolet	109.995
10.02.74	Surfers Paradise	Teddy Pilette	B	Chevron B24-Chevrolet	104.278
17.02.74	Sandown Park	Peter Gethin	GB	Chevron B24-Chevrolet	110.698
24.02.74	Adelaide	Warwick Brown	AUS	Lola T332-Chevrolet	102.978

*incorporating the Lady Wigram Trophy

1975

date	race	driver	nat	car	mph
05.01.75	Levin	Graeme Lawrence	NZ	Lola T332-Chevrolet	96.112
12.01.75	New Zealand GP (Pukekohe)	Warwick Brown	AUS	Lola T332-Chevrolet	87.137
19.01.75	Lady Wigram Trophy (Wigram)	Graham McRae	NZ	McRae GM2-Chevrolet	115.021
26.01.75	Teretonga Park	Chris Amon	NZ	Talon MR1-Chevrolet	98.770
02.02.75	Oran Park	Warwick Brown	AUS	Lola T332-Chevrolet	97.983
09.02.75	Surfers Paradise	Johnnie Walker	AUS	Lola T330/332-Holden/Repco	103.719
16.02.75	Adelaide	Graeme Lawrence	NZ	Lola T332-Chevrolet	106.912
23.02.75	Sandown Park	John Goss	AUS	Matich A53-Holden/Repco	110.108

1969 Graham Hill battles Piers Courage and Jochen Rindt for fourth postition in the Tasman Cup race at Lakeside.

Can-Am Challenge

The Canadian-American Challenge was a road racing championship for Group 7 sports-racing cars established in September 1966. Large capacity stock-block engines powered these spectacular cars with Chevrolet the most popular supplier.

After John Surtees won the inaugural series in a Lola, McLaren Cars dominated, winning 23 consecutive races between 1968-70. George Follmer's Porsche 917 eventually challenged McLaren's reign in 1972. After two more seasons the series was cancelled in favour of a North American Formula 5000 Championship.

When the F5000 Championship was abandoned Can-Am was reinstated for the 1977 season with rules that led to sports cars based on F5000 chassis and engines. The Carl Haas team initially dominated the new era but in the mid-eighties Can-Am slipped into obscurity, and was cancelled again after the 1986 season.

Until its final seasons the Can-Am Challenge had been a spectacular series, attracting the World's best drivers to race on North America's finest road courses. Over the years six F1 World Champions (John Surtees, Denny Hulme, Phil Hill, Jackie Stewart, Alan Jones and Keke Rosberg) all won races.

CAN-AM CHALLENGE CUP CHAMPIONS

year	driver	nat	team	car-engine
1966	John Surtees	GB	Team Surtees	Lola T70-Chevrolet
1967	Bruce McLaren	NZ	Bruce McLaren Motor Racing	McLaren M6A-Chevrolet
1968	Denny Hulme	NZ	Bruce McLaren Motor Racing	McLaren M8A-Chevrolet
1969	Bruce McLaren	NZ	Bruce McLaren Motor Racing	McLaren M8B-Chevrolet
1970	Denny Hulme	NZ	Bruce McLaren Motor Racing	McLaren M8D-Chevrolet
1971	Peter Revson	USA	Bruce McLaren Motor Racing	McLaren M8F-Chevrolet
1972	George Follmer	USA	Penske Racing	Porsche 917/10
1973	Mark Donohue	USA	Penske Racing	Porsche 917/30
1974	Jackie Oliver	GB	Shadow Racing Team	Shadow DN4A-Chevrolet
1977	Patrick Tambay	F	Haas-Hall Racing	Lola T333CS-Chevrolet
1978	Alan Jones	AUS	Haas-Hall Racing	Lola T333CS-Chevrolet
1979	Jacky Ickx	B	Carl Haas Racing	Lola T333CS-Chevrolet
1980	Patrick Tambay	F	Carl Haas Racing	Lola T530-Chevrolet
1981	Geoff Brabham	AUS	Team VDS	Lola T530-Chevrolet/VDS 001-Chevrolet
1982	Al Unser jr	USA	Galles Racing	Frissbee GR3-Chevrolet
1983	Jacques Villeneuve	CDN	Canadian Tire	Frissbee GR3-Chevrolet
1984	Michael Roe	IRL	Don Walker	VDS 002-Chevrolet/VDS 004-Chevrolet
1985	Rick Miaskiewicz	USA	Mosquitto Autosport	Frissbee GR3-Chevrolet
1986	Horst Kroll	USA	Kroll Racing	Frissbee KR3-Chevrolet

Race Winners

1966

date	race	driver	nat	car	mph
11.09.66	Ste Jovite	John Surtees	GB	Lola T70-Chevrolet	96.680
18.09.66	Bridgehampton	Dan Gurney	USA	Lola T70-Ford	105.580
24.09.66	Canadian GP (Mosport Park)	Mark Donohue	USA	Lola T70-Chevrolet	101.870
16.10.66	Laguna Seca	Phil Hill	USA	Chaparral 2F-Chevrolet	98.040
30.10.66	Riverside	John Surtees	GB	Lola T70-Chevrolet	106.860
13.11.66	Stardust, Las Vegas	John Surtees	GB	Lola T70-Chevrolet	109.250

1967

date	race	driver	nat	car	mph
03.09.67	Elkhart Lake	Denny Hulme	NZ	McLaren M6A-Chevrolet	104.455
17.09.67	Bridgehampton	Denny Hulme	NZ	McLaren M6A-Chevrolet	109.130
23.09.67	Mosport Park	Denny Hulme	NZ	McLaren M6A-Chevrolet	105.930
15.10.67	Laguna Seca	Bruce McLaren	NZ	McLaren M6A-Chevrolet	101.613
29.10.67	Riverside	Bruce McLaren	NZ	McLaren M6A-Chevrolet	114.406
12.11.67	Stardust, Las Vegas	John Surtees	GB	Lola T70-Chevrolet	112.410

1968

date	race	driver	nat	car	mph
01.09.68	Elkhart Lake	Denny Hulme	NZ	McLaren M8A-Chevrolet	94.540
15.09.68	Bridgehampton	Mark Donohue	USA	McLaren M6B-Chevrolet	111.320
29.09.68	Edmonton	Denny Hulme	NZ	McLaren M8A-Chevrolet	102.900
13.10.68	Laguna Seca	John Cannon	CDN	McLaren M1B-Chevrolet	85.600
27.10.68	Riverside	Bruce McLaren	NZ	McLaren M8A-Chevrolet	114.460
10.11.68	Stardust, Las Vegas	Denny Hulme	NZ	McLaren M8A-Chevrolet	113.100

1969

date	race	driver	nat	car	mph
01.06.69	Mosport Park	Bruce McLaren	NZ	McLaren M8B-Chevrolet	105.901
15.06.69	Ste Jovite	Denny Hulme	NZ	McLaren M8B-Chevrolet	97.550
13.07.69	Watkins Glen	Bruce McLaren	NZ	McLaren M8B-Chevrolet	125.990
27.07.69	Edmonton	Denny Hulme	NZ	McLaren M8B-Chevrolet	104.350
17.08.69	Mid-Ohio	Denny Hulme	NZ	McLaren M8B-Chevrolet	94.212
31.08.69	Elkhart Lake	Bruce McLaren	NZ	McLaren M8B-Chevrolet	107.479
14.09.69	Bridgehampton	Denny Hulme	NZ	McLaren M8B-Chevrolet	113.723
21.09.69	Michigan	Bruce McLaren	NZ	McLaren M8B-Chevrolet	108.100
11.10.69	Laguna Seca	Bruce McLaren	NZ	McLaren M8B-Chevrolet	105.830
25.10.69	Riverside	Denny Hulme	NZ	McLaren M8B-Chevrolet	121.059
08.11.69	Texas World Speedway	Bruce McLaren	NZ	McLaren M8B-Chevrolet	109.087

1970

date	race	driver	nat	car	mph
14.06.70	Mosport Park	Dan Gurney	USA	McLaren M8D-Chevrolet	110.214
28.06.70	Ste Jovite	Dan Gurney	USA	McLaren M8D-Chevrolet	97.950
12.07.70	Watkins Glen	Denny Hulme	NZ	McLaren M8D-Chevrolet	118.560
26.07.70	Edmonton	Denny Hulme	NZ	McLaren M8D-Chevrolet	106.400
23.08.70	Mid-Ohio	Denny Hulme	NZ	McLaren M8D-Chevrolet	95.163
30.08.70	Elkhart Lake	Peter Gethin	GB	McLaren M8D-Chevrolet	105.016
13.09.70	Road Atlanta	Tony Dean	GB	Porsche 908	103.450
27.09.70	Brainerd	Denny Hulme	NZ	McLaren M8D-Chevrolet	117.570
18.10.70	Laguna Seca	Denny Hulme	NZ	McLaren M8D-Chevrolet	106.071
01.11.70	Riverside	Denny Hulme	NZ	McLaren M8D-Chevrolet	120.284

1971

date	race	driver	nat	car	mph
13.06.71	Mosport Park	Denny Hulme	NZ	McLaren M8F-Chevrolet	109.330
27.06.71	Ste Jovite	Jackie Stewart	GB	Lola T260-Chevrolet	100.950
11.07.71	Road Atlanta	Peter Revson	USA	McLaren M8F-Chevrolet	111.170
25.07.71	Watkins Glen	Peter Revson	USA	McLaren M8F-Chevrolet	128.503
22.08.71	Mid-Ohio	Jackie Stewart	GB	Lola T260-Chevrolet	95.777
29.08.71	Elkhart Lake	Peter Revson	USA	McLaren M8F-Chevrolet	109.010
12.09.71	Brainerd	Peter Revson	USA	McLaren M8F-Chevrolet	119.137
26.09.71	Edmonton	Denny Hulme	NZ	McLaren M8F-Chevrolet	94.922
17.10.71	Laguna Seca	Peter Revson	USA	McLaren M8F-Chevrolet	109.210
31.10.71	Riverside	Denny Hulme	NZ	McLaren M8F-Chevrolet	123.727

1972

date	race	driver	nat	car	mph
11.06.72	Mosport Park	Denny Hulme	NZ	McLaren M20-Chevrolet	110.660
09.07.72	Road Atlanta	George Follmer	USA	Porsche 917/10	113.960
23.07.72	Watkins Glen	Denny Hulme	NZ	McLaren M20-Chevrolet	114.440

1968 Bruce McLaren in his McLaren M8A-Chevrolet winning at Riverside.

date	race	driver	nat	car	mph
06.08.72	Mid-Ohio	George Follmer	USA	Porsche 917/10	92.876
27.08.72	Elkhart Lake	George Follmer	USA	Porsche 917/10	110.426
17.09.72	Brainerd	Francois Cevert	F	McLaren M8F-Chevrolet	118.065
01.10.72	Edmonton	Mark Donohue	USA	Porsche 917/10	109.870
15.10.72	Laguna Seca	George Follmer	USA	Porsche 917/10	108.790
29.10.72	Riverside	George Follmer	USA	Porsche 917/10	122.585

1973

10.06.73	Mosport Park	Charlie Kemp	USA	Porsche 917/10	108.645
08.07.73	Road Atlanta	George Follmer	USA	Porsche 917/10	117.050
21.07.73	Watkins Glen	Mark Donohue	USA	Porsche 917/30	117.757
12.08.73	Mid-Ohio	Mark Donohue	USA	Porsche 917/30	101.409
26.08.73	Elkhart Lake	Mark Donohue	USA	Porsche 917/30	114.021
16.09.73	Edmonton	Mark Donohue	USA	Porsche 917/30	110.870
14.10.73	Laguna Seca	Mark Donohue	USA	Porsche 917/30	102.200
28.10.73	Riverside	Mark Donohue	USA	Porsche 917/30	120.310

1974

16.06.74	Mosport Park	Jackie Oliver	GB	Shadow DN4A-Chevrolet	111.990
30.06.74	Road Atlanta	Jackie Oliver	GB	Shadow DN4A-Chevrolet	110.880
14.07.74	Watkins Glen	Jackie Oliver	GB	Shadow DN4A-Chevrolet	116.780
11.08.74	Mid-Ohio	Jackie Oliver	GB	Shadow DN4A-Chevrolet	102.085
25.08.74	Elkhart Lake	Scooter Patrick	USA	McLaren M20-Chevrolet	109.744

1975-76
NO SERIES

1977

12.06.77	Ste Jovite	Tom Klausler	USA	Schkee DB1-Chevrolet	85.137
26.06.77	Laguna Seca	Don Breidenbach	USA	Lola T333CS-Chevrolet	106.991
10.07.77	Watkins Glen	Patrick Tambay	F	Lola T333CS-Chevrolet	110.891
24.07.77	Elkhart Lake	Peter Gethin	GB	Lola T333CS-Chevrolet	105.263
07.08.77	Mid-Ohio	Patrick Tambay	F	Lola T333CS-Chevrolet	98.462
21.08.77	Mosport Park	Patrick Tambay	F	Lola T333CS-Chevrolet	111.819
04.09.77	Trois Rivieres	Patrick Tambay	F	Lola T333CS-Chevrolet	86.191
25.09.77	Sears Point	Patrick Tambay	F	Lola T333CS-Chevrolet	94.088
16.10.77	Riverside	Patrick Tambay	F	Lola T333CS-Chevrolet	116.880

1978

14.05.78	Road Atlanta	Alan Jones	AUS	Lola T333CS-Chevrolet	117.356
27.05.78	Charlotte	Elliott Forbes-Robinson	USA	Spyder NF10-Chevrolet	112.149
11.06.78	Mid-Ohio	Alan Jones	AUS	Lola T333CS-Chevrolet	99.320
25.06.78	Ste Jovite	George Follmer	USA	Prophet-Chevrolet	88.495
09.07.78	Watkins Glen	Warwick Brown	AUS	Lola T333CS-Chevrolet	111.379
23.07.78	Elkhart Lake	Alan Jones	AUS	Lola T333CS-Chevrolet	111.691
20.08.78	Mosport Park	Alan Jones	AUS	Lola T333CS-Chevrolet	115.374
04.09.78	Trois Rivieres	Elliott Forbes-Robinson	USA	Spyder NF10-Chevrolet	82.182
08.10.78	Laguna Seca	Al Holbert	USA	Lola T333CS-Chevrolet	112.595
15.10.78	Riverside	Alan Jones	AUS	Lola T333CS-Chevrolet	116.288

1979

06.05.79	Road Atlanta	Keke Rosberg	SF	Spyder NF11-Chevrolet	116.966
19.05.79	Charlotte	Jacky Ickx	B	Lola T333CS-Chevrolet	104.639
03.06.79	Mosport Park	Jacky Ickx	B	Lola T333CS-Chevrolet	113.673

date	race	driver	nat	car	mph
10.06.79	Mid-Ohio	Alan Jones	AUS	Lola T333CS-Chevrolet	100.138
08.07.79	Watkins Glen	Keke Rosberg	SF	Spyder NF11-Chevrolet	114.580
22.07.79	Elkhart Lake	Jacky Ickx	B	Lola T333CS-Chevrolet	112.959
19.08.79	Brainerd	Jacky Ickx	B	Lola T333CS-Chevrolet	117.088
02.09.79	Trois Rivieres	Elliott Forbes-Robinson	USA	Spyder NF11-Chevrolet	85.320
14.10.79	Laguna Seca	Bobby Rahal	USA	Prophet-Chevrolet	113.211
28.10.79	Riverside	Jacky Ickx	B	Lola T333CS-Chevrolet	119.784

1980

date	race	driver	nat	car	mph
25.05.80	Sears Point	Patrick Tambay	F	Lola T530-Chevrolet	101.090
08.06.80	Mid-Ohio	Patrick Tambay	F	Lola T530-Chevrolet	99.954
22.06.80	Mosport Park	Patrick Tambay	F	Lola T530-Chevrolet	115.145
05.07.80	Watkins Glen	Patrick Tambay	F	Lola T530-Chevrolet	108.190
20.07.80	Elkhart Lake	Al Holbert	USA	CAC 1-Chevrolet	108.498
10.08.80	Brainerd	Patrick Tambay	F	Lola T530-Chevrolet	117.201
24.08.80	Trois Rivieres	Patrick Tambay	F	Lola T530-Chevrolet	84.676
31.08.80	Road Atlanta	Geoff Brabham	AUS	Lola T530-Chevrolet	n/a
19.10.80	Laguna Seca	Al Unser	USA	Frissbee-Chevrolet	108.728
26.10.80	Riverside	Al Holbert	USA	CAC 1-Chevrolet	118.940

1981

date	race	driver	nat	car	mph
14.06.81	Mosport Park	Teo Fabi	I	March 817-Chevrolet	115.526
28.06.81	Mid-Ohio	Teo Fabi	I	March 817-Chevrolet	100.418
11.07.81	Watkins Glen	Al Holbert	USA	CAC 2-Chevrolet	112.050
26.07.81	Elkhart Lake	Geoff Brabham	AUS	Lola T530-Chevrolet	115.169
16.08.81	Edmonton	Geoff Brabham	AUS	VDS 001-Chevrolet	106.176
06.09.81	Trois Rivieres	Al Holbert	USA	CAC 2-Chevrolet	82.440
13.09.81	Mosport Park	Teo Fabi	I	March 817-Chevrolet	117.279
04.10.81	Riverside	Al Holbert	USA	CAC 2-Chevrolet	119.319
12.10.81	Laguna Seca	Teo Fabi	I	March 817-Chevrolet	115.895
16.10.81	Caesars Palace, Las Vegas	Danny Sullivan	USA	Frissbee GR2-Chevrolet	93.958

1982

date	race	driver	nat	car	mph
23.05.82	Road Atlanta	Al Unser Jr	USA	Frissbee GR3-Chevrolet	99.711
06.06.82	Mosport Park	Al Unser Jr	USA	Frissbee GR3-Chevrolet	110.350
27.06.82	Mid-Ohio	Al Holbert	USA	VDS 001-Chevrolet	102.230
25.07.82	Elkhart Lake	Al Holbert	USA	VDS 001-Chevrolet	114.819
05.09.82	Trois Rivieres	Al Holbert	USA	VDS 001-Chevrolet	82.728
12.09.82	Mosport Park	Al Unser Jr	USA	Frissbee GR3-Chevrolet	116.658
26.09.82	Caesars Palace, Las Vegas	Danny Sullivan	USA	March 827-Chevrolet	91.230
03.10.82	Riverside	Al Holbert	USA	VDS 001-Chevrolet	120.805
10.10.82	Laguna Seca	Al Unser Jr	USA	Frissbee GR3-Chevrolet	114.151

1983

date	race	driver	nat	car	mph
05.06.83	Mosport Park	Jacques Villeneuve	CDN	Frissbee GR3-Chevrolet	111.780
03.07.83	Lime Rock	Jim Crawford	GB	Ensign RK180B-Ford	107.448
18.07.83	Elkhart Lake	John Fitzpatrick	GB	Porsche 956	108.580
04.09.83	Trois Rivieres	Jacques Villeneuve	CDN	Frissbee GR3-Chevrolet	87.244
11.09.83	Mosport Park	Jim Crawford	GB	Ensign RK180B-Ford	116.310
09.10.83	Sears Point	Jacques Villeneuve	CDN	Frissbee GR3-Chevrolet	101.770

1984

date	race	driver	nat	car	mph
10.06.84	Mosport Park	Michael Roe	IRL	VDS 002-Chevrolet	95.740
07.07.84	Fair Park, Dallas	Michael Roe	IRL	VDS 002-Chevrolet	67.982
22.07.84	Brainerd	Michael Roe	IRL	VDS 002-Chevrolet	118.208
04.08.84	Lime Rock	Michael Roe	IRL	VDS 002-Chevrolet	107.790
19.08.84	Road Atlanta	Jim Crawford	GB	March 847-Chevrolet	109.352
02.09.84	Trois Rivieres	Jim Crawford	GB	March 847-Chevrolet	85.831

date	race	driver	nat	car	mph
09.09.84	Mosport Park	Michael Roe	IRL	VDS 002-Chevrolet	113.750
30.09.84	Sears Point	Michael Roe	IRL	VDS 002-Chevrolet	99.540
07.10.84	Riverside	Michael Roe	IRL	VDS 002-Chevrolet	119.687
28.10.84	Green Valley	Jim Crawford	GB	March 847-Chevrolet	93.710

1985

date	race	driver	nat	car	mph
02.06.85	Mosport Park	Horst Kroll	USA	Frissbee KR3-Chevrolet	95.720
06.07.85	Lime Rock	Bruce MacInnes	USA	Lola-Chevrolet	90.602
06.07.85	Lime Rock	Rick Miaskiewicz	USA	Frissbee KR3-Chevrolet	n/a
15.09.85	Mosport Park	Rick Miaskiewicz	USA	Frissbee KR3-Chevrolet	103.808
13.10.85	St Louis	Rick Miaskiewicz	USA	Frissbee KR3-Chevrolet	n/a
03.11.85	St Petersburg	Lou Sell	USA	March 832-BMW	81.227

1986

date	race	driver	nat	car	mph
01.06.86	Mosport Park	Horst Kroll	USA	Frissbee KR3-Chevrolet	98.380
05.07.86	Summit Point	Bill Tempero	USA	March 84C-Chevrolet	88.151
03.08.86	St Louis	Lou Sell	USA	March 832-Chevrolet	87.634
14.09.86	Mosport Park	Paul Tracy	CDN	Frissbee KR3-Chevrolet	110.175

BMW M1 Procar Series

This short-lived series was run by BMW Motorsport in 1979-80 to promote its spectacular M1 sports car. Races normally supported Grands Prix, with the top five Formula 1 drivers in qualifying invited to take part in the works cars. Competitors included cars entered by teams of the calibre of Sauber, Project 4

(whose owner Ron Dennis would soon buy McLaren), Schnitzer and Eggenberger.

Initial teething problems were sorted out and Procar quickly developed into a popular and entertaining diversion from the business of Grand Prix racing. In 1980 *Autosport* described the championship as "quite simply the greatest one-make series to date," but BMW decided not organise a third edition.

BMW M1 PROCAR CHAMPIONS

year	driver	nat	team	car
1979	Niki Lauda	A	Project 4 Racing	BMW M1
1980	Nelson Piquet	BR	BMW Motorsport	BMW M1

Race Winners

1979

date	race	driver	nat	team	mph
12.05.79	Zolder	Elio de Angelis	I	BMW Italia	94.020
26.05.79	Monte Carlo	Niki Lauda	A	Project 4 Racing	71.046
30.06.79	Dijon-Prenois	Nelson Piquet	BR	BMW Motorsport	n/a
13.07.79	Silverstone	Niki Lauda	A	Project 4 Racing	115.450
28.07.79	Hockenheim	Niki Lauda	A	Project 4 Racing	n/a
11.08.79	Osterreichring	Jacques Laffite	F	BMW Motorsport	114.842
25.08.79	Zandvoort	Hans-Joachim Stuck	D	Manfred Cassani	99.497
08.09.79	Monza	Hans-Joachim Stuck	D	Manfred Cassani	112.902

1980

date	race	driver	nat	team	mph
26.04.80	Donington Park	Jan Lammers	NL	BMW Nederland	94.440
11.05.80	Avus	Manfred Schurti	FL	Manfred Cassani	132.730
17.05.80	Monte Carlo	Hans-Joachim Stuck	D	Project 4 Racing	69.350
22.06.80	Norisring	Hans-Joachim Stuck	D	Project 4 Racing	95.065
12.07.80	Brands Hatch	Carlos Reutemann	RA	BMW Motorsport	102.700
09.08.80	Hockenheim	Didier Pironi	F	BMW Motorsport	113.910
16.08.80	Osterreichring	Nelson Piquet	BR	BMW Motorsport	114.036
31.08.80	Zandvoort	Nelson Piquet	BR	BMW Motorsport	96.853
13.09.80	Imola	Nelson Piquet	BR	BMW Motorsport	96.505

FIA Touring Car Championships

WORLD TOURING CAR CHAMPIONSHIP

year	driver	nat	team	car	team
1987	Roberto Ravaglia	I	Schnitzer	BMW M3	Ford/Texaco

EUROPEAN TOURING CAR CHAMPIONSHIP

year	class	driver	nat	team	car
1963		Peter Nocker	D	Peter Lindner/Peter Nocker	Jaguar MkII 3.8
1964		Warwick Banks	GB	Tyrrell Racing Organisation	Austin Mini Cooper S
1965	over 1600cc	Jacky Ickx	B	Jacky Ickx	Ford Mustang
	1600cc	Sir John Whitmore	GB	Alan Mann Racing	Lotus Cortina
	1000cc	Ed Swart	NL	Abarth	Fiat Abarth 1000TC Berlina
1966	over 1600cc	Hubert Hahne	D	BMW Deutschland	BMW 2000Ti
	1600cc	Andrea de Adamich	I	Autodelta	Alfa Romeo Giulia GTA
	1000cc	Giancarlo Baghetti	I	Abarth	Fiat Abarth 1000TC Berlina
1967	over 1600cc	Karl von Wendt	D	Karl von Wendt	Porsche 911
	1600cc	Andrea de Adamich	I	Autodelta	Alfa Romeo Giulia GTA
	1000cc	Willi Kauhsen	D	Abarth	Fiat Abarth 1000TC Berlina
1968	over 1600cc	Dieter Quester	A	BMW Deutschland	BMW 2002
	1600cc	John Rhodes	GB	Cooper Car Company	BMC Mini Cooper S
	1000cc	John Handley	GB	British Vita	Morris Mini Cooper
1969	over 1600cc	Dieter Quester	A	BMW Deutschland	BMW 2002Ti
	1600cc	Spartico Dini	I	Autodelta	Alfa Romeo GTA Junior
	1000cc	"Pam"	I	Scuderia Mirabelle	Fiat Abarth 1000TCR
1970	Overall	Toine Hezemans	NL	Autodelta	Alfa Romeo GTAm
	over 1600cc	Toine Hezemans	NL	Autodelta	Alfa Romeo GTAm
	1600cc	Carlo Truci	I	Carlo Truci	Alfa Romeo GTA Junior
	1000cc	Johann Abt	D	Abt Tuning	Fiat Abarth 1000
1971	over 2000cc	Dieter Glemser	D	Ford Deutschland	Ford Capri RS
	2000cc	Toine Hezemans	NL	Autodelta	Alfa Romeo GTAm
	1300cc	Gianluigi Picchi	I	Autodelta	Alfa Romeo GTA Junior
1972		Jochen Mass	D	Ford Deutschland	Ford Capri RS2600
1973		Toine Hezemans	NL	BMW Motorsport	BMW 3.0 CSL
1974		Hans Heyer	D	Ford Deutschland	Ford Capri RS/Ford Escort RS
1975		Siegfried Muller/Alain Peltier	D/B	Faltz-Alpina	BMW 3.0 CSL
1976		Pierre Dieudonne/Jean Xhenceval	B	Luigi Racing	BMW 3.0 CSL
1977		Dieter Quester	A	Alpina	BMW 3.0 CSL
1978		Umberto Grano	I	Luigi Racing	BMW 3.0 CSL
1979		Carlo Facetti/Martino Finotto	I	Jolly Club	BMW 3.0 CSL
1980		Helmut Kelleners/ Siegfried Muller Jr	D	Eggenberger Motorsport	BMW 320i
1981		Umberto Grano/Helmut Kelleners	I/D	Eggenberger Motorsport	BMW 635 CSi
1982		Umberto Grano/Helmut Kelleners	I/D	Eggenberger Motorsport	BMW 528i
1983		Dieter Quester	A	Schnitzer	BMW 635 CSi
1984		Tom Walkinshaw	GB	Tom Walkinshaw Racing	Jaguar XJS
1985		Gianfranco Brancatelli/ Thomas Lindstrom	I/S	Eggenberger Motorsport	Volvo 240 turbo
1986		Roberto Ravaglia	I	Schnitzer	BMW 635 CSi
1987		Winni Vogt	D	Linder	BMW M3
1988		Roberto Ravaglia	I	Schnitzer	BMW M3
2000		Fabrizio Giovanardi	I	Nordauto Engineering	Alfa Romeo 156 TS
2001	TC	Fabrizio Giovanardi	I	Nordauto Engineering	Alfa Romeo 156 TS
	Production	Peter Kox	NL	Ravaglia Motorsport	BMW 320i
2002		Fabrizio Giovanardi	I	Nordauto Engineering	Alfa Romeo 156 GTA
1989-99	no series				

MANUFACTURERS

year	class	constructor	year	class	constructor
1963-64	NO SERIES		1973	over 2000cc	BMW
1965	over 1600cc	Ford		2000cc	Ford
	1600cc	Ford	1974		Ford
	1000cc	Fiat Abarth	1975		BMW
1966	over 1600cc	BMW	1976		BMW
	1600cc	Alfa Romeo	1977		BMW
	1000cc	Fiat Abarth	1978		BMW
1967	over 1600cc	Porsche	1979		BMW
	1600cc	Alfa Romeo	1980		Audi
	1000cc	Fiat Abarth	1981		Skoda
1968	over 1600cc	BMW	1982		Alfa Romeo
	1600cc	BMC	1983		Alfa Romeo
	1000cc	BMC	1984		Alfa Romeo
1969	over 1600cc	BMW	1985		Alfa Romeo
	1600cc	Alfa Romeo	1986		Toyota
	1000cc	Fiat Abarth	1987	Entrants	Linder Motorsport
1970		BMW	1988	Entrants	Eggenberger Motorsport
1971	over 2000cc	Ford	2000	Entrants	Nordauto Engineering
	2000cc	Alfa Romeo	2001	Entrants	Nordauto Engineering
	1300cc	Alfa Romeo	2002		Alfa Romeo
1972		Alfa Romeo	1989-99	no series	

Touring Car World Cup

The World Cup was a one-off event to decide the Touring Car World champion. First held at Monza in 1993, it attracted an impressive field of the year's best from around Europe. It was run to the FIA's new 2-litre rules (thus excluding cars eligible for the 2.5-litre German series) and the event was repeated in 1994 at Donington Park, where a single race replaced the two heats used the previous year. Both occasions were dominated by Paul Radisich's British championship Ford Mondeo. The final event was held in 1995 at Paul Ricard, where Frank Biela won for Audi.

1993 FINAL CHAMPIONSHIP POSITIONS

Drivers			Nations		
1	Paul Radisich	80	1	Italy	86*
2	Nicola Larini	54	2	France	86
3	Philippe Gache	33	3	New Zealand	80
4	Alain Cudini	30	4	Germany	64
5	Alex Burgstaller	30	5	Belgium	28
6	John Cleland	24	6	Great Britain	15
7	Christophe Bouchut	23	7	Venezuela	8
8	Yannick Dalmas	20	8	Australia	7
9	Eric van de Poele	19	*won on tie-back		
10	Jean-Pierre Malcher	18			

1993

FIA WORLD CUP RACE 1

17 October 1993. Monza. 15 laps of a 3.6039-mile circuit = 54.059 miles

1 Paul Radisich	Ford Mondeo Si	15	32m17.790
2 Alain Cudini	Opel Vectra	15	32m19.307
3 Nicola Larini	Alfa Romeo 155	15	32m21.397
4 John Cleland	Vauxhall Cavalier 16V	15	32m21.508
5 Alessandro Nannini	Alfa Romeo 155	15	32m23.469
6 Yannick Dalmas	Peugeot 405 Mi16	15	32m34.295

Winner's average speed: 100.430 mph. Pole position: Radisich, 1m54.520. Fastest lap: Cleland, 2m03.887

FIA WORLD CUP RACE 2

17 October 1993. Monza. 15 laps of a 3.6039-mile circuit = 54.059 miles

1 Paul Radisich	Ford Mondeo Si	15	34m52.203
2 Nicola Larini	Alfa Romeo 155	15	34m53.065
3 Philippe Gache	Alfa Romeo 155	15	34m54.345
4 Alex Burgstaller	BMW 318i	15	34m57.094
5*Eric van de Poele	Nissan Primera eGT	15	34m57.822
6 Emanuele Pirro	BMW 318i	15	34m58.444

*including 2 second penalty for jumping the re-start after safety car.
Winner's average speed: 93.018 mph. Pole position: Radisich, based on race 1 results. Fastest lap: van de Poele, 1m58.080

1994

FIA WORLD CUP

16 October 1994. Donington Park. 25 laps of a 2.500-mile circuit = 62.500 miles

1 Paul Radisich	Ford Mondeo Ghia	25	41m56.73
2 Steve Soper	BMW 318iS	25	41m58.65
3 Joachim Winkelhock	BMW 318iS	25	42m03.84
4 Gabriele Tarquini	Alfa Romeo 155 Silverstone	25	42m04.69
5 Hans-Joachim Stuck	Audi 80 Competition	25	42m26.23
6 Johnny Cecotto	BMW 318iS	25	42m27.95

Winner's average speed: 89.400 mph. Pole position: Radisich, 1m38.09. Fastest lap: Radisich, 1m39.60

1994 FINAL CHAMPIONSHIP POSITIONS

Drivers			
		4=	Audi	16
1	Paul Radisich		Toyota	16
2	Steve Soper	6	Peugeot	6
3	Joachim Winkelhock	7	Nissan	2
4	Gabriele Tarquini	8	General Motors	1
5	Hans-Joachim Stuck			
6	Johnny Cecotto	**Nations**		
		1	Germany	53
Manufacturers		2	Great Britain	44
1	BMW	54	3	Italy	31
2	Ford	48	4	Spain	12
3	Alfa Romeo	20		

1995

FIA WORLD CUP RACE 1

15 October 1995. Paul Ricard. 26 laps of a 2.353-mile circuit = 61.178 miles

1	Frank Biela	Audi A4 Quattro	26	39m02.263
2	Steve Soper	BMW 318i	26	39m07.174
3	Yvan Muller	BMW 318i	26	39m16.472
4	Johnny Cecotto	BMW 318i	26	39m19.928
5	Hans-Joachim Stuck	Audi A4 Quattro	26	39m20.331
6	Kelvin Burt	Ford Mondeo Ghia	26	39m27.397

Winner's average speed: 94.361mph. Pole position: Pirro, 1m27.478.
Fastest lap: Soper, 1m28.698

FIA WORLD CUP RACE 1

15 October 1995. Paul Ricard. 26 26 laps of a 2.353-mile circuit = 61.178 miles

1	Emanuele Pirro	Audi A4 Quattro	26	39m11.167
2	Frank Biela	Audi A4 Quattro	26	39m13.378
3	Steve Soper	BMW 318i	26	39m14.737
4	Yvan Muller	BMW 318i	26	39m17.721
5	Alain Menu	Renault Laguna	26	39m24.461
6	Johnny Cecotto	BMW 318i	26	39m27.572

Winner's average speed: 94.004mph. Pole position: Pirro, 1m27.319.
Fastest lap: Pirro, 1m29.172

1995 FINAL CHAMPIONSHIP POSITIONS

Drivers			Manufacturers		
1	Frank Biela	70	1	Audi	126
2=	Emanuele Pirro	54	2	BMW	98
	Steve Soper	54	3	Honda	44
4	Yvan Muller	44	4	Ford	36
5	Johnny Cecotto	35	5	Renault	23
6	Kelvin Burt	23	6	General Motors	16
7=	Klaus Niedzwiedz	22	7	Volvo	15
	Armin Hahne	22	8	Alfa Romeo	10
9=	Alain Menu	16	9	Nissan	8
	Hans-Joachim Stuck	16			
			Nations		
			1	Germany	117
			2	Great Britain	99
			3	Italy	77

Various Other Major Championships

EUROPEAN 2-LITRE CHAMPIONSHIP OF MAKES

This series ended in 1975 when ten of the twelve qualifying races were cancelled due to financial problems. In the remaining events Chris Skeaping, driving a March 75S-Ford amassed the most points, but was not crowned champion.

year	formula	driver	nat	car
1970	Group 6	Jo Bonnier	S	Lola T210-Ford
	Group 5	Ed Swart	NL	Fiat Abarth 2000S
	Group 4	Kurt Simonsen	S	Porsche 911S
1971		Helmut Marko	A	Lola T212-Ford
1972		Arturo Merzario	I	Osella Abarth 2000P
1973		Chris Craft	GB	Lola T292-Ford
1974		Alain Serpaggi	F	Alpine A441-Renault
1975	series abandoned			

EUROPEAN CHAMPIONSHIP FOR GRAND TOURING CARS

year	driver	nat	car
1972*	John Fitzpatrick	GB	Porsche 911S
1973	Claude Ballot-Lena/		
	Clemens Schickentanz	F/D	Porsche 911 Carrera RSR
1974	John Fitzpatrick	GB	Porsche 911 Carrera RSR
1975	Hartwig Bertrams	D	Porsche
1976	Toine Hezemans	NL	Porsche 934

*European Trophy

EUROPEAN SPORTS CAR CHAMPIONSHIP

year	formula	driver	nat	car
1977	Class 1	Reinhold Joest	D	Porsche 908/3
	Class 2	"Gimax"	I	Osella PA6-BMW

EUROPEAN ENDURANCE CHAMPIONSHIP

year	driver	nat	team	car
1983	Bob Wollek	F	Joest Racing	Porsche 956

EUROPEAN LE MANS SERIES

year	driver	nat	team	car
2001	Stefan Johansson	S	Arena Motorsport	Audi R8

PORSCHE SUPERCUP

year	driver	nat	car
1993	Altfrid Heger	D	Porsche Carrera 2
1994	Uwe Alzen	D	Porsche 911 Carrera 3.8
1995	Jean-Pierre Malcher	F	Porsche 911 Carrera 3.8
1996	Emmanuel Collard	F	Porsche 911 Carrera 3.8
1997	Patrick Huisman	NL	Porsche 911 Carrera 3.8
1998	Patrick Huisman	NL	Porsche 911 Carrera GT3
1999	Patrick Huisman	NL	Porsche 911 Carrera GT3
2000	Patrick Huisman	NL	Porsche 911 Carrera GT3
2001	Jorg Bergmeister	D	Porsche 911 Carrera GT3
2002	Stephane Ortelli	F	Porsche 911 Carrera GT3

RENAULT CLIO CUP

(formerly Renault Europa Cup)

year	driver	nat	car
1981	Wolfgang Schultz	D	Renault 5 turbo
1982	Joel Gouhier	F	Renault 5 turbo
1983	Jan Lammers	NL	Renault 5 turbo
1984	Jan Lammers	NL	Renault 5 turbo
1985	Oscar Larrauri	RA	Renault Alpine V6 turbo
1986	Massimo Sigala	I	Renault Alpine V6 turbo
1987	Massimo Sigala	I	Renault Alpine V6 turbo
1988	Massimo Sigala	I	Renault Alpine V6 turbo
1989	Massimo Sigala	I	Renault 21 turbo
1990	Massimo Sigala	I	Renault 21 turbo
1992	Bernard Castagne	F	Renault Clio 16v
1993	Salvatore Pirro	I	Renault Clio 16v

year	driver	nat	car
1994	Bernard Castagne	F	Renault Clio 16v
1995	Marcel Klaey	CH	Renault Clio 16v
1996	Franck Lagorce	F	Renault Sport Spider
1997	Tommy Rustad	N	Renault Sport Spider
1998	Andrea Bellichi	I	Renault Sport Spider
1999	Jerome Policand	F	Renault Sport Clio
2000	Luca Rangoni	I	Renault Sport Clio
2001	Luca Rangoni	I	Renault Sport Clio
2002	Luca Rangoni	I	Renault Sport Clio

1991 no series

INTERNATIONAL TOURING CAR CHAMPIONSHIP
see page 623

ASIA-PACIFIC TOURING CAR CHAMPIONSHIP

year	driver	nat	team	car
1994	Joachim Winkelhock	D	Schnitzer	BMW 318i
1995	Championship cancelled due to a lack of entries			

ASIAN TOURING CAR CHALLENGE

(formerly South East Asian Championship 1996-99)

year	driver	nat	team	car
1996	Kasikam Suphot	T	Opel Team Thailand	Opel Vectra 16v
1997	Charles Kwan	HK	EKS Motorsport	BMW 320i
1998	Charles Kwan	HK	EKS Motorsport	BMW 320i
1999	Charles Kwan	HK	EKS Motorsport	BMW 320i
2000	Henry Lee jr	HK	WK Longman Racing	Peugeot 306 GTi
2001	Charoensukawattana Nattavude	T	WK Longman Racing	Peugeot 306 GTi
2002	Toni Ruokonen	SF	WK Longman Racing	Peugeot 306 GTi

SOUTH AMERICAN TOURING CAR CHAMPIONSHIP

(Copa de las Naciones Super Turismo)

year	driver	nat	team	car
1997	Oscar Larrauri	RA	ProAs Team	BMW 318i
1998	Oscar Larrauri	RA	ProAs Team	BMW 320i
1999	Carlos Bueno/ Emiliano Spataro	BR/RA	EF Racing	Peugeot 406
2000	Oscar Larrauri	RA	Quadrifoglio Corse	Alfa Romeo 156
2001	Championship cancelled due to lack of television coverage			

EUROPEAN FORMULA RENAULT CHAMPIONSHIP

year	driver	nat	car
1972	Alain Cudini	F	Alpine-Renault
1973	Rene Arnoux	F	Martini MK11-Renault
1974	Didier Pironi	F	Martini MK14-Renault
1975	Rene Arnoux	F	Martini MK15-Renault
1976	Didier Pironi	F	Martini MK18-Renault
1977	Alain Prost	F	Martini MK20-Renault
1993	Olivier Couvreur	F	Alpa FR93-Renault
1994	James Matthews	GB	Van Diemen FR94-Renault
1995	Cyrille Sauvage	F	Mygale FR95-Renault
1996	Enrique Bernoldi	BR	Tatuus RC96-Renault
1997	Jeffrey van Hooydonk	B	Tatuus RC97-Renault
1998	Bruno Besson	F	Tatuus RC98-Renault
1999	Gianmaria Bruni	I	Tatuus RC98-Renault
2000	Felipe Massa	BR	Tatuus 2000-Renault
2001	Augusto Farfus Jr	BR	Tatuus 2000-Renault
2002	Eric Salignon	F	Tatuus 2000-Renault

1978-92 no series

EFDA FORMULA FORD 2000 EUROSERIES

year	driver	nat	car
1979	Adrian Reynard	GB	Reynard 79SF-Ford
1980	Fred Krab	NL	Delta T79/80-Ford
1981	Tommy Byrne	IRL	Van Diemen RF81-Ford
1982	Ayrton Senna	BR	Van Diemen RF82-Ford
1983	Russell Spence	GB	Reynard 83SF-Ford

year	driver	nat	car
1984	Mauricio Gugelmin	BR	Reynard 84SF-Ford
1985	Bertrand Fabi	CDN	Reynard 84SF-Ford
1986	Mark Blundell	GB	Reynard 86SF-Ford
1987	JJ Lehto	SF	Reynard 87SF-Ford

EFDA FORMULA OPEL EUROPEAN UNION SERIES

(formerly GM-Lotus Euroseries)

year	driver	nat	team	car
1988	Mika Hakkinen	SF	Dragon Motorsport	GM-Lotus
1989	Peter Kox	NL	Opel Dealer Team Holland	GM-Lotus
1990	Rubens Barrichello	BR	Draco Racing	GM-Lotus
1991	Pedro Lamy	P	Draco Racing	GM-Lotus
1992	Gareth Rees	GB	David Sears Motorsport	GM-Lotus
1993	Patrick Crinelli	I	Draco Racing	GM-Lotus
1994	Marco Campos	BR	Draco Racing	Formula Opel
1995	Jason Watt	DK	Opel Dealer Team Holland	Formula Opel
1996	Bas Leinders	B	Van Amersfoort Racing	Formula Opel
1997	Marcelo Battistuzzi	BR	Vergani Racing	Formula Opel
1998	Etienne van der Linde	ZA	AR Motorsport	Formula Opel
1999	Tomas Scheckter	ZA	AR Motorsport	Formula Opel

FORMULA CHRYSLER EUROSERIES

year	driver	nat	car
2001	Ricardo van der Ende	NL	Reynard-Chrysler

CODASUR FORMULA TWO CHAMPIONSHIP

year	driver	nat	team	car
1983	Guillermo Maldonado	RA	Maldonado	Berta-Volkswagen
1984	Guillermo Maldonado	RA	Maldonado	Berta-Volkswagen
1985	Guillermo Maldonado	RA	Maldonado	Berta-Volkswagen
1986	Guillermo Maldonado	RA	Maldonado	Berta-Volkswagen

SUDAM FORMULA THREE CHAMPIONSHIP

year	driver	nat	team	car
1987	Leonel Friedrich	BR	INI Competicion	Berta Mk3-Volkswagen
1988	Juan Carlos Giacchino	RA	Sommi-Zanon	Dallara 387-Alfa Romeo/ Dallara 388-Alfa Romeo
1989	Gabriel Furlan	RA	Sommi-Zanon	Dallara 388-AlfaRomeo
1990	Christian Fittipaldi	BR	Fittipaldi	Reynard 883-AlfaRomeo
1991	Affonso Giaffone	BR	INI Competicion	Ralt RT32-Volkswagen/ Ralt RT33-Volkswagen
1992	Marcos Gueiros	BR	Cesario Formula	Ralt RT33-Mugen
1993	Fernando Croceri	RA	Cesario Formula	Ralt RT33-Mugen
1994	Gabriel Furlan	RA	GF Motorsport	Dallara 390-Fiat
1995	Ricardo Zonta	BR	Cesario Formula	Dallara 394-Mugen
1996	Gabriel Furlan	RA	GF Motorsport	Dallara 394-Fiat
1997	Bruno Junqueira	RA	Opel PropCar	Dallara 394-Opel
1998	Gabriel Furlan	RA	GF Motorsport	Dallara 394-Mitsubishi
1999	Hoover Orsi	BR	Cesario Formula	Dallara 394-Mugen
2000	Vitor Meira	BR	Amir Nasr Racing	Dallara 300-Mugen
2001	Juliano Moro	BR	Amir Nasr Racing	Dallara 300-Mugen
2002	Nelson Angelo Piquet	BR	Piquet Sports	Dallara 301-Mugen

ASIAN FORMULA THREE CHAMPIONSHIP

year	driver	nat	car
2002	Mark Goddard	GB	Dallara 398-Toyota

Racing Around the World

Racing Around the World

The following pages are a guide to the circuits, races and championships around the world. Details of national champions for F3 and Touring Car and above are listed, as are the winners of national Grands Prix and other major events such as Bathurst, Spa 24 hours, Mille Miglia and Targa Florio.

The history of all circuits to have held a round of the F1 World Championship, World Sports Cars, CART World Series, Indy Racing League, European F2, F3 or F3000 and all current NASCAR venues are included with major race winners, circuit changes and lap record holders.

1953 Alberto Ascari leads the first World Championship race in Argentina.

ARGENTINA

TURISMO COMPETICION 2000
(TC2000 Argentinian Touring Car Championship)

year	driver	nat	team	car
1980	Jorge del Rio	RA	Pianetto Competicion	Dodge/ Volkswagen
1981	Jorge del Rio	RA	Pianetto Competicion	Volkswagen
1982	Jorge del Rio	RA	Pianetto Competicion	Volkswagen
1983	Luis di Palma	RA	Di Palma Competicion	Volkswagen
1984	Mario Gayraud	RA	Herceg Competicion	Ford Taunus
1985	Ruben Daray	RA	Akel Competicion	Ford Sierra XR4
1986	Juan Maria Traverso	RA	Berta Sport	Renault Fuego
1987	Silvio Oltra	RA	Benavidez Competicion	Renault Fuego
1988	Juan Maria Traverso	RA	Berta Sport	Renault Fuego
1989	Miguel Angel Guerra	RA	Berta Sport	Renault Fuego
1990	Juan Maria Traverso	RA	Berta Sport	Renault Fuego
1991	Juan Maria Traverso	RA	Berta Sport	Renault Fuego
1992	Juan Maria Traverso	RA	Berta Sport	Renault Fuego
1993	Juan Maria Traverso	RA	Berta Sport	Renault Fuego
1994	Guillermo Maldonado	RA	VW Motorsport	Volkswagen Golf
1995	Juan Maria Traverso	RA	Peugeot Sport	Peugeot 405
1996	Ernesto Bessone	RA	Esso Competicion	Ford Escort Ghia-Audi
1997	Henry Martin	RA	Berta Sport	Ford Escort Zetec
1998	Omar Martinez	RA	Honda Team Pro Racing	Honda Civic 4P
1999	Juan Manuel Silva	RA	Honda Team Pro Racing	Honda Civic 4P
2000	Daniel Cingolani	RA	Berta Sport	Ford Escort Zetec
2001	Gabriel Ponce de Leon	RA	Berta Sport	Ford Escort Zetec
2002	Norberto Fontana	RA	TTA	Toyota Corolla

TEMPORADA CHAMPIONSHIPS

year	formula	driver	nat	team	car
1964	F2	Silvio Moser	CH	Silvio Moser	Brabham BT10-Ford
1966	F3	Charles Crichton-Stuart	GB	Stirling Moss ART	Brabham BT10-Ford
1967	F3	Jean-Pierre Beltoise	F	Matra Sports	Matra MS5-Ford
1968	F2	Andrea de Adamich	I	Scuderia Ferrari	Ferrari Dino 166

Major International Races

ARGENTINIAN GRAND PRIX

year	formula	circuit	winner	nat	car	mph
1953	F2 W	Buenos Aires	Alberto Ascari	I	Ferrari 500	78.135
1954	F1 W	Buenos Aires	Juan Manuel Fangio	RA	Maserati 250F	70.137
1955	F1 W	Buenos Aires	Juan Manuel Fangio	RA	Mercedes-Benz W196	77.515
1956	F1 W	Buenos Aires	Luigi Musso/Juan Manuel Fangio	I/RA	Lancia-Ferrari D50	79.385
1957	F1 W	Buenos Aires	Juan Manuel Fangio	RA	Maserati 250F	80.616
1958	F1 W	Buenos Aires	Stirling Moss	GB	Cooper T43-Climax	83.610
1960	F1 W	Buenos Aires	Bruce McLaren	NZ	Cooper T45-Climax	84.664
1971	F1	Buenos Aires	Chris Amon	NZ	Matra-Simca MS120	97.209

ARGENTINIAN GRAND PRIX (cont.)

year	formula	circuit	winner	nat	car	mph
1972	F1 W	Buenos Aires	Jackie Stewart	GB	Tyrrell 003-Ford	100.443
1973	F1 W	Buenos Aires	Emerson Fittipaldi	BR	Lotus 72D-Ford	102.964
1974	F1 W	Buenos Aires	Denny Hulme	NZ	McLaren M23-Ford	116.740
1975	F1 W	Buenos Aires	Emerson Fittipaldi	BR	McLaren M23-Ford	118.613
1977	F1 W	Buenos Aires	Jody Scheckter	ZA	Wolf WR1-Ford	117.727
1978	F1 W	Buenos Aires	Mario Andretti	USA	Lotus 78-Ford	119.208
1979	F1 W	Buenos Aires	Jacques Laffite	F	Ligier JS11-Ford	122.792
1980	F1 W	Buenos Aires	Alan Jones	AUS	Williams FW07-Ford	114.061
1981	F1 W	Buenos Aires	Nelson Piquet	BR	Brabham BT49C-Ford	124.751
1995	F1 W	Buenos Aires	Damon Hill	GB	Williams FW17-Renault	100.902
1996	F1 W	Buenos Aires	Damon Hill	GB	Williams FW18-Renault	99.427
1997	F1 W	Buenos Aires	Jacques Villeneuve	CDN	Williams FW19-Renault	101.995
1998	F1 W	Buenos Aires	Michael Schumacher	D	Ferrari F300	105.213

Major Championships

Sud-Am F3 Championship see page 560
Codusur F2 Championship see page 560

Circuits and other Races

BUENOS AIRES

Autodromo Oscar Alfredo Galvez

The October 17 Autodrome (celebrating the date of President Peron's accession to power) was built within the city limits and opened on March 9, 1952. It boasted twelve circuit variations; not content with these, sports car races combined parts of the Autodrome and the public roads outside. Boosted by Juan Manuel Fangio's successes in Europe, the circuit hosted the first World Championship Grand Prix outside of Europe in 1953. The race was marred, however, when Giuseppe Farina crashed into the crowd, claiming the lives of nine spectators. The end of Peron's era in power in Argentina prompted the circuit to be renamed after local driver Oscar Galvez. In the seventies, after more than a decade without international racing, Buenos Aires became a mainstay of the F1 and Sports Car World Championship calendars. But further political upheaval and the 1982 Falklands War again drove international racing away until 1995, when the Grand Prix returned to the overly tight Circuit Number 6. After four years the race finally slipped from the roster of championship events.

BUENOS AIRES NO. 6

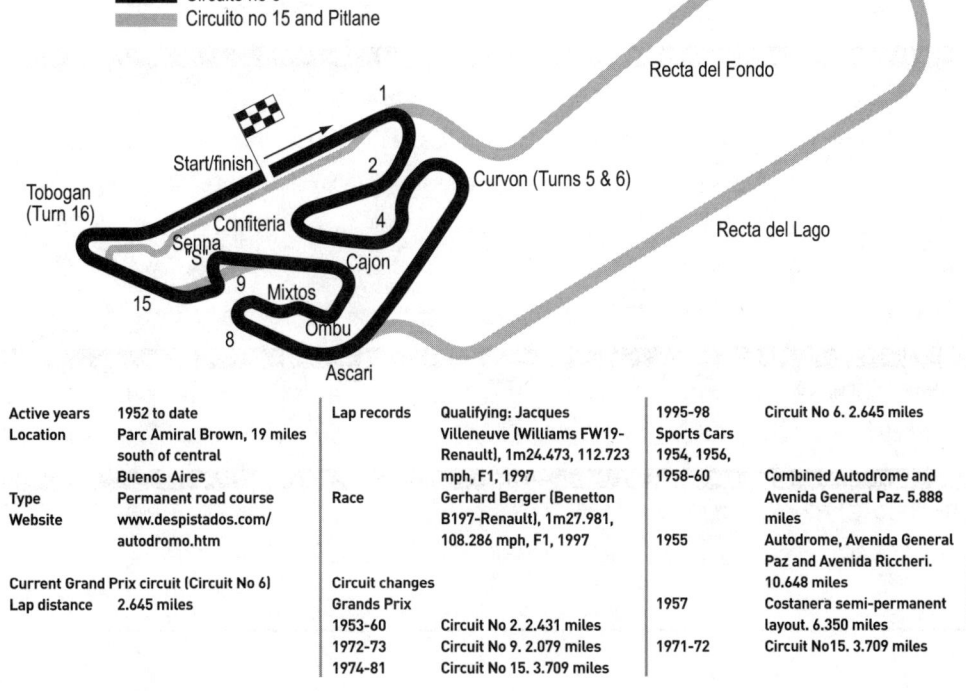

Active years	1952 to date	Lap records	Qualifying: Jacques	1995-98	Circuit No 6. 2.645 miles
Location	Parc Amiral Brown, 19 miles south of central Buenos Aires		Villeneuve (Williams FW19-Renault), 1m24.473, 112.723 mph, F1, 1997	Sports Cars 1954, 1956, 1958-60	Combined Autodrome and Avenida General Paz. 5.888
Type	Permanent road course	Race	Gerhard Berger (Benetton		miles
Website	www.despistados.com/ autodromo.htm		B197-Renault), 1m27.981, 108.286 mph, F1, 1997	1955	Autodrome, Avenida General Paz and Avenida Riccheri. 10.648 miles
Current Grand Prix circuit (Circuit No 6)		Circuit changes			
Lap distance	2.645 miles	Grands Prix		1957	Costanera semi-permanent
		1953-60	Circuit No 2. 2.431 miles		layout. 6.350 miles
		1972-73	Circuit No 9. 2.079 miles	1971-72	Circuit No15. 3.709 miles
		1974-81	Circuit No 15. 3.709 miles		

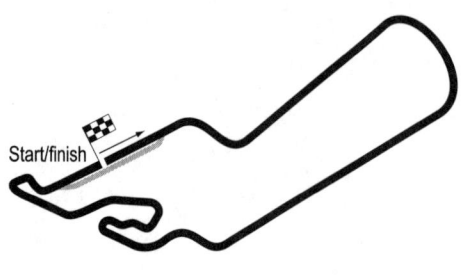

CIRCUIT No 15

CIRCUIT No 9

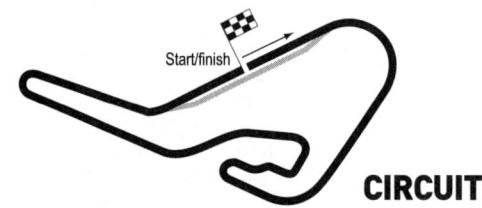

CIRCUIT No 2

Argentinian Grand Prix see above

BUENOS AIRES CITY GRAND PRIX

year	formula	winner	nat	car	mph
1953	FL	Giuseppe Farina	I	Ferrari	72.450
1954	FL	Maurice Trintignant	F	Ferrari	71.930
1955	FL	Juan Manuel Fangio	RA	Mercedes-Benz W196	73.320
1956*	F1	Juan Manuel Fangio	RA	Lancia-Ferrari D50	83.090
1957	F1	Juan Manuel Fangio	RA	Maserati 250F	71.669
1958	FL	Juan Manuel Fangio	RA	Maserati 250F	66.310
1960#	FL	Maurice Trintignant	F	Cooper-Climax	76.120

At Buenos Aires except *at Mendoza and #at Cordoba

BUENOS AIRES 1000 KMS/WORLD SPORTS CAR RACE

year	formula	winner	nat	car	mph
1954	SC W	Giuseppe Farina/Umberto Maglioli	I	Ferrari 375MM	93.221
1955	SC W	Enrique Saenz Valiente/Jose Maria Ibanez	RA	Ferrari 375 Plus	92.975
1956	SC W	Stirling Moss/Carlos Menditeguy	GB/RA	Maserati 300S	96.143
1957	SC W	Masten Gregory/Cesare Perdisa/Eugenio Castellotti/Luigi Musso	USA/I/I/I	Ferrari 290MM	99.984
1958	SC W	Peter Collins/Phil Hill	GB/USA	Ferrari 250TR	98.600
1960	SC W	Phil Hill/Cliff Allison	USA/GB	Ferrari 250TR	99.311
1970	SC	Jean-Pierre Beltoise/Henri Pescarolo	F	Matra MS30/650	110.950
1971	SC W	Jo Siffert/Derek Bell	CH/GB	Porsche 917K	112.148
1972	SC W	Ronnie Peterson/Tim Schenken	S/AUS	Ferrari 312P	108.063

TEMPORADA FORMULA 2 RACE

year	formula	winner	nat	car	mph
1978	F2	Ingo Hoffmann	BR	March 782-BMW	101.807

INVITATION FORMULA 3000 RACE

year	formula	winner	nat	car	mph
1992	F3000	Andrea Montermini	I	Reynard 91D-Cosworth	105.752

AUSTRALIA
Major Championships

AUSTRALIAN GT NATIONS' CUP

year	driver	nat	car
2000	Jim Richards	NZ	Porsche 911 GT3
2001	Jim Richards	NZ	Porsche 911 GT3
2002	Jim Richards	NZ	Porsche 911 GT3

AUSTRALIAN SUPERCAR V8 TOURING CAR CHAMPIONSHIP

year	driver	nat	car
1960*	David McKay	AUS	Jaguar 3.4
1961*	Bill Pitt	AUS	Jaguar 3.4
1962*	Bob Jane	AUS	Jaguar 3.8 MkII
1963*	Bob Jane	AUS	Jaguar 4.1 MkII
1964*	Ian Geoghegan	AUS	Ford Cortina GT
1965*	Norm Beechey	AUS	Ford Mustang
1966*	Ian Geoghegan	AUS	Ford Mustang
1967*	Ian Geoghegan	AUS	Ford Mustang
1968*	Ian Geoghegan	AUS	Ford Mustang
1969	Ian Geoghegan	AUS	Ford Mustang
1970	Norm Beechey	AUS	Holden Monaro 350GTS
1971	Bob Jane	AUS	Chevrolet Camaro
1972	Bob Jane	AUS	Chevrolet Camaro
1973	Allan Moffat	AUS	Ford Falcon GTHO
1974	Peter Brock	AUS	Holden Torana XU1
1975	Colin Bond	AUS	Holden Torana L34
1976	Allan Moffat	AUS	Ford Falcon GT
1977	Allan Moffat	AUS	Ford Falcon XCGT
1978	Peter Brock	AUS	Holden Torana A9X
1979	Rob Morris	AUS	Holden Torana A9X
1980	Peter Brock	AUS	Holden Commodore VB
1981	Dick Johnson	AUS	Ford Falcon XD
1982	Dick Johnson	AUS	Ford Falcon XD
1983	Allan Moffat	AUS	Mazda RX-7
1984	Dick Johnson	AUS	Ford Falcon XE
1985	Jim Richards	NZ	BMW 635 CSi
1986	Robbie Francevic	AUS	Volvo 240T
1987	Jim Richards	NZ	BMW M3
1988	Dick Johnson	AUS	Ford Sierra RS500
1989	Dick Johnson	AUS	Ford Sierra RS500
1990	Jim Richards	NZ	Nissan Skyline GT-R
1991	Jim Richards	NZ	Nissan Skyline GT-R
1992	Mark Skaife	AUS	Nissan Skyline GT-R
1993	Glenn Seton	AUS	Ford Falcon EB
1994	Mark Skaife	AUS	Holden Commodore VP
1995	John Bowe	AUS	Ford Falcon EF
1996	Craig Lowndes	AUS	Holden Commodore VR
1997	Glenn Seton	AUS	Ford Falcon EL
1998	Craig Lowndes	AUS	Holden Commodore VS/VT
1999	Craig Lowndes	AUS	Holden Commodore VS/VT
2000	Mark Skaife	AUS	Holden Commodore VT
2001	Mark Skaife	AUS	Holden Commodore VX
2002	Mark Skaife	AUS	Holden Commodore VX

*championship decided by a one-off race

AUSTRALIAN SUPER TOURING CAR CHAMPIONSHIP

year	driver	nat	team	car
1994	Tony Longhurst	AUS	Team Logano	BMW 318i
1995	Paul Morris	AUS	BMW Racing	BMW 318i
1996	Brad Jones	AUS	Audi Sport Australia	A4 Quattro
1997	Paul Morris	AUS	BMW Motorsport	BMW 320i
1998	Brad Jones	AUS	Audi Sport Australia	A4 Quattro
1999	Paul Morris	AUS	Nemo Racing	BMW 320i
2000	Paul Morris	AUS	Nemo Racing	BMW 320i

AUSTRALIAN FORMULA HOLDEN CHAMPIONSHIP
(formerly Gold Star, F5000 and Formula Pacific)

year	formula	driver	nat	car
1957	FL	Lex Davison	AUS	Ferrari 625
1958	FL	Stan Jones	AUS	Maserati 250F
1959	FL	Len Lukey	AUS	Cooper T45-Climax
1960	FL	Alex Mildren	AUS	Cooper T51-Maserati
1961	FL	Bill Patterson	AUS	Cooper T51-Climax
1962	FL	Bib Stillwell	AUS	Cooper T55-Climax
1963	FL	Bib Stillwell	AUS	Brabham-Climax
1964	2.5l	Bib Stillwell	AUS	Brabham-Climax
1965	2.5l	Bib Stillwell	AUS	Brabham-Climax
1966	2.5l	Spencer Martin	AUS	Brabham-Climax
1967	2.5l	Spencer Martin	AUS	Brabham BT11-Climax
1968	2.5l	Kevin Bartlett	AUS	Brabham BT23D-Alfa Romeo
1969	2.5l	Kevin Bartlett	AUS	Mildren-Alfa Romeo
1970	F5000	Leo Geoghegan	AUS	Lotus 59B-Waggott
1971	F5000	Max Stewart	AUS	Mildren-Waggott
1972	F5000	Frank Matich	AUS	Matich A50-Repco
1973	F5000	John McCormack	AUS	Elfin MR5-Repco
1974	F5000	Max Stewart	AUS	Lola T330-Chevrolet
1975	F5000	John McCormack	AUS	Elfin MR6-Chevrolet
1976	F5000	John Leffler	AUS	Lola T400-Chevrolet
1977	F5000	John McCormack	AUS	McLaren M23-Chevrolet
1978	F5000	Graham McRae	AUS	McRae GM3-Chevrolet
1979	F5000	Johnnie Walker	AUS	Lola T332-Chevrolet
1980	F5000	Alfredo Costanzo	AUS	Lola T430-Chevrolet
1981	F5000	Alfredo Costanzo	AUS	McLaren M26-Ford
1982	Pacific	Alfredo Costanzo	AUS	Tiga FA81-Ford
1983	Pacific	Alfredo Costanzo	AUS	Tiga FA81-Ford
1984	Pacific	John Bowe	AUS	Ralt RT4-Ford
1985	Pacific	John Bowe	AUS	Ralt RT4-Ford
1986	Pacific	Graham Watson	AUS	Ralt RT4-Ford
1987*	Pacific	David Brabham	AUS	Ralt RT30-Ford
1988	Pacific	Rohan Onslow	AUS	Cheetah Mk8-Ford
1989	Holden	Rohan Onslow	AUS	Ralt RT20-Holden
1990	Holden	Simon Kane	AUS	Ralt RT21-Holden
1991	Holden	Mark Skaife	AUS	SPA 003-Holden
1992	Holden	Mark Skaife	AUS	SPA 003-Holden
1993	Holden	Mark Skaife	AUS	Lola T91/50-Holden
1994	Holden	Paul Stokell	AUS	Reynard 91D-Holden
1995	Holden	Paul Stokell	AUS	Reynard 91D-Holden
1996	Holden	Paul Stokell	AUS	Reynard 91D-Holden
1997	Holden	Jason Bright	AUS	Reynard 91D-Holden
1998	Holden	Scott Dixon	NZ	Reynard 92D-Holden
1999	Holden	Simon Wills	NZ	Reynard 94D-Holden
2000	Holden	Simon Wills	NZ	Reynard 94D-Holden
2001	Holden	Rick Kelly	AUS	Reynard 94D-Holden
2002	Holden	Will Power	AUS	Reynard 95D-Holden

*Championship decided by a one-off race
that supported the Australian GP

AUSTRALIAN FORMULA 3 CHAMPIONSHIP

year	driver	nat	car
1997	Wayne Ford	AUS	Ralt RT34
1998	David Bruce	AUS	Reynard 893
1999	Paul Stephenson	AUS	Dallara 395/6-Toyota
2000	Paul Stephenson	AUS	Dallara 395/6-Toyota
2001	Peter Hackett	AUS	Dallara 398-Alfa Romeo
2002	James Manderson	AUS	Dallara 301-Opel

Racing Around the World

AUSTRALIAN GRAND PRIX

year	formula	circuit	winner	nat	car	mph
1928	(h)	Phillip Island	Arthur Waite	GB	Austin 7	58.500
1929	(h)	Phillip Island	Arthur Terdich	AUS	Bugatti T37A	62.202
1930	(h)	Phillip Island	Bill Thompson	AUS	Bugatti T37A	65.000
1931	(h)	Phillip Island	Carl Junker	AUS	Bugatti T39	69.152
1932	(h)	Phillip Island	Bill Thompson	AUS	Bugatti T37A	75.476
1933	(h)	Phillip Island	Bill Thompson	AUS	Riley 9 "Brooklands"	63.940
1934	(h)	Phillip Island	Bob Lea-Wright	AUS	Singer Nine Le Mans	62.914
1935	(h)	Phillip Island	Les Murphy	AUS	MG P-type	66.259
1937	(h)	Victor Harbour	Les Murphy	AUS	MG P-type	68.352
1938	(h)	Bathurst	Peter Whitehead	GB	ERA B-type	55.744
1939	(h)	Lobethal	Allan Tomlinson	AUS	MG TA	79.421
1947	(h)	Bathurst	Bill Murray	AUS	MG TC	59.589
1948	(h)	Point Cook	Frank Pratt	AUS	BMW 328 "Touring"	64.432
1949	FL	Leyburn	John Crouch	AUS	Delahaye 135	82.526
1950	FL	Nuriootpa	Doug Whiteford	AUS	Ford Special	105.144
1951	FL	Narrogin	Warwick Pratley	AUS	G Reed Special-Ford	63.839
1952	FL	Bathurst	Doug Whiteford	AUS	Lago-Talbot T26C	75.042
1953	FL	Albert Park	Doug Whiteford	AUS	Lago-Talbot T26C	82.854
1954	FL	Southport	Lex Davison	AUS	HWM-Jaguar	88.123
1955	FL	Port Wakefield	Jack Brabham	AUS	Cooper T40-Bristol	71.939
1956	FL	Albert Park	Stirling Moss	GB	Maserati 250F	95.996
1957	FL	Caversham	Lex Davison/Bill Patterson	AUS	Ferrari 625	74.286
1958	FL	Bathurst	Lex Davison	AUS	Ferrari 625	81.764
1959	FL	Longford	Stan Jones	AUS	Maserati 250F	188.206
1960	FL	Lowood	Alec Mildren	AUS	Cooper T51-Maserati	94.481
1961	FL	Mallala	Lex Davison	AUS	Cooper T51-Climax	70.773
1962	FL	Caversham	Bruce McLaren	NZ	Cooper T62-Climax	90.425
1963	FL	Warwick Farm	Jack Brabham	AUS	Brabham BT4-Climax	79.341
1964	2.5l	Sandown Park	Jack Brabham	AUS	Brabham BT7A-Climax	96.809
1965	2.5l	Longford	Bruce McLaren	NZ	Cooper T79-Climax	114.740
1966	2.5l	Lakeside	Graham Hill	GB	BRM P261	94.838
1967	2.5l	Warwick Farm	Jackie Stewart	GB	BRM P261	87.677
1968	2.5l	Sandown Park	Jim Clark	GB	Lotus 49T-Ford	101.572
1969	2.5l	Lakeside	Chris Amon	NZ	Ferrari 246	100.144
1970	F5000	Warwick Farm	Frank Matich	AUS	McLaren M10B-Holden	94.001
1971	F5000	Warwick Farm	Frank Matich	AUS	Matich A50-Holden/Repco	93.234
1972	F5000	Sandown Park	Graham McRae	NZ	McRae GM1-Chevrolet	109.447
1973	F5000	Sandown Park	Graham McRae	NZ	McRae GM2-Chevrolet	103.922
1974	F5000	Oran Park	Max Stewart	AUS	Lola T330-Chevrolet	86.285
1975	F5000	Surfers Paradise	Max Stewart	AUS	Lola T400-Chevrolet	89.124
1976	F5000	Sandown Park	John Goss	AUS	Matich A53-Holden/Repco	111.723
1977	F5000	Oran Park	Warwick Brown	AUS	Lola T430-Chevrolet	86.029
1978	F5000	Sandown Park	Graham McRae	NZ	McRae GM3-Chevrolet	107.505
1979	F5000	Wanneroo Park	John Walker	AUS	Lola T332-Chevrolet	95.839
1980	F1/F5000	Calder	Alan Jones	AUS	Williams FW07-Ford	94.569
1981	Pacific	Calder	Roberto Moreno	BR	Ralt RT4-Ford	88.687
1982	Pacific	Calder	Alain Prost	F	Ralt RT4-Ford	89.139
1983	Pacific	Calder	Roberto Moreno	BR	Ralt RT4-Ford	88.992
1984	Pacific	Calder	Roberto Moreno	BR	Ralt RT4-Ford	84.678
1985	F1 W	Adelaide	Keke Rosberg	SF	Williams FW10-Honda	95.689
1986	F1 W	Adelaide	Alain Prost	F	McLaren MP4/2C-TAG Porsche	100.991
1987	F1 W	Adelaide	Gerhard Berger	A	Ferrari F187	102.246
1988	F1 W	Adelaide	Alain Prost	F	McLaren MP4/4-Honda	101.967
1989	F1 W	Adelaide	Thierry Boutsen	B	Williams FW13-Renault	81.947
1990	F1 W	Adelaide	Nelson Piquet	BR	Benetton B190-Ford	103.938
1991	F1 W	Adelaide	Ayrton Senna	BR	McLaren MP4/6-Honda	80.201
1992	F1 W	Adelaide	Gerhard Berger	A	McLaren MP4/7A-Honda	106.689
1993	F1 W	Adelaide	Ayrton Senna	BR	McLaren MP4/8-Ford	107.530
1994	F1 W	Adelaide	Nigel Mansell	GB	Williams FW16B-Renault	105.754
1995	F1 W	Adelaide	Damon Hill	GB	Williams FW17B-Renault	104.392
1996	F1 W	Albert Park	Damon Hill	GB	Williams FW18-Renault	123.507
1997	F1 W	Albert Park	David Coulthard	GB	McLaren MP4/12-Mercedes-Benz	126.733
1998	F1 W	Albert Park	Mika Hakkinen	SF	McLaren MP4/13-Mercedes-Benz	124.954
1999	F1 W	Albert Park	Eddie Irvine	GB	Ferrari F399	118.585
2000	F1 W	Albert Park	Michael Schumacher	D	Ferrari F1-2000	121.943
2001	F1 W	Albert Park	Michael Schumacher	D	Ferrari F2001	116.481
2002	F1 W	Albert Park	Michael Schumacher	D	Ferrari F2001	119.927

Circuits and Other Races

ADELAIDE

Adelaide was hailed as the best temporary road course in the world when it opened in 1985. The Grand Prix held there revelled in an end-of-season party atmosphere and was universally popular. Its organisers were shocked, however, when Melbourne snatched the right to stage the event starting in 1996. But a shorter 2-mile circuit reopened in 1999 for historic races and the national staple of touring car events. The original GP circuit was restored for the unique Race of a Thousand Years held for American Le Mans Series sports cars. The race started on 31st December 2000, and finished on the first day of the New Year. It was here that Allan McNish was confirmed as 2000 ALMS champion.

Adelaide's start-line and pits are set in the Victoria Park racecourse, with the remainder of the lap made up of the surrounding streets, including the fast Dequetteville Terrace (known as Brabham Straight on raceday), where Nigel Mansell suffered his Championship-losing puncture in 1986.

Active years	1985-95, 1999 to date
Location	Victoria Park horse racetrack, 4 miles east of central Adelaide
Type	Temporary street circuit
Website	www.clipsal500.com.au
Lap distance	2.347 miles
Lap records	Qualifying: Ayrton Senna (McLaren MP4/8-Ford), 1m13.371, 115.157 mph, F1, 1993
	Race: Damon Hill (Williams FW15C-Renault), 1m15.381, 112.087 mph, F1, 1993

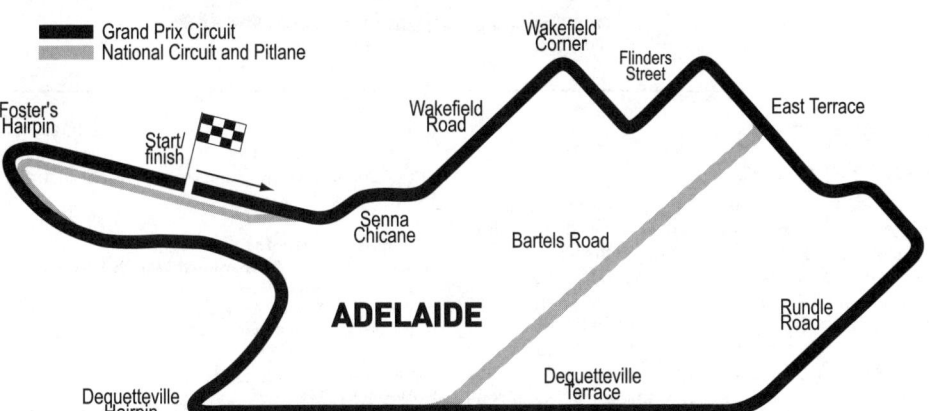

Australian Grand Prix see above

RACE OF A THOUSAND YEARS						
year	formula	winner	nat	car		mph
2000/01	SC	Rinaldo Capello/Allan McNish	I/GB	Audi R8		92.164

ALBERT PARK
Melbourne

Melbourne has been established as the opening Grand Prix of the season since supremo Ron Walker won the race from Adelaide in 1996. If Adelaide was popular, Melbourne has proved even more so. A party atmosphere and early season optimism combines with an excellent temporary circuit around the lake in Albert Park. First suggested in 1934, the circuit hosted the Australian GP twice in the fifties. Unlike other such venues it is fast and wide, allowing for good racing, and it is only a short tram ride from downtown Melbourne. It was here that Jacques Villeneuve almost won on his GP debut in 1996, and David Coulthard controversially ceded victory to McLaren teammate Mika Hakkinen in 1998. Tragedy struck Melbourne in 2001 when debris from Villeneuve's somersaulting car killed marshal Graham Beveridge.

Active years	1953-59, 1996 to date
Location	Albert Park, 1.5 miles south of central Melbourne
Type	Temporary road course
Website	www.grandprix.com.au

Current Circuit

Lap distance	3.295 miles
Lap records	Qualifying: Rubens Barrichello (Ferrari F2001), 1m25.843, 138.183 mph, F1, 2002
	Race: Michael Schumacher (Ferrari F2001), 1m28.214, 134.469 mph, F1, 2001

Circuit changes

1953-59	Anti-clockwise. 3.125 miles
1996 to date	Direction reversed, new pit section, final corner bypassed and three further modifications. Current circuit

Australian Grand Prix see above

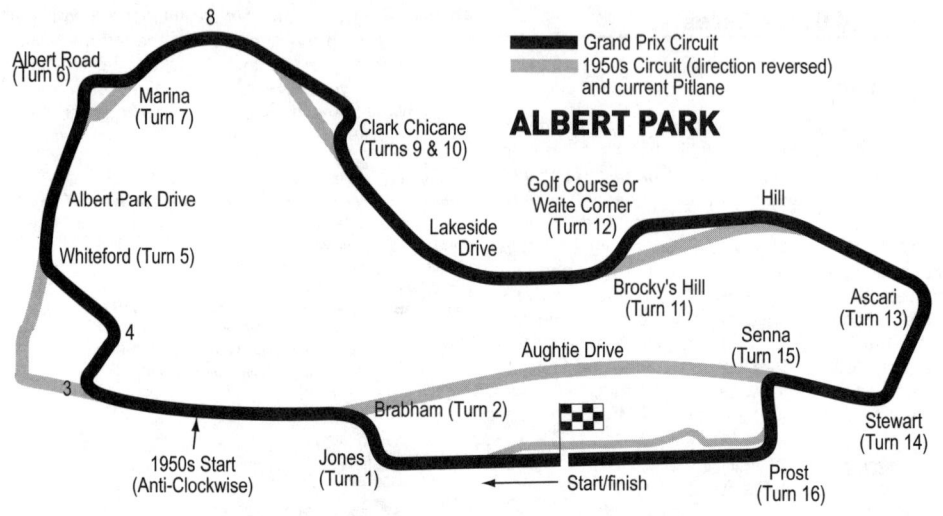

Grand Prix Circuit

1950s Circuit (direction reversed) and current Pitlane

ALBERT PARK

8

Albert Road (Turn 6)

Marina (Turn 7)

Clark Chicane (Turns 9 & 10)

Albert Park Drive

Lakeside Drive

Golf Course or Waite Corner (Turn 12)

Hill

Whiteford (Turn 5)

4

Brocky's Hill (Turn 11)

Ascari (Turn 13)

Senna (Turn 15)

Aughtie Drive

3

Brabham (Turn 2)

Stewart (Turn 14)

1950s Start (Anti-Clockwise)

Jones (Turn 1)

Start/finish

Prost (Turn 16)

BATHURST
Mount Panorama

The arrival of the Armstrong 500 from Phillip Island in 1963 established Bathurst as one of the most picturesque and demanding road courses in the world. Mount Panorama is a true drivers' challenge, with sheer drops, the daunting Skyline section and mile-long Conrod Straight. The Armstrong developed into Bathurst's annual touring car classic, known simply in Australia as "The Great Race". Traditionally a battle between Australian Holdens and Fords, the race has attracted strong European participation, which culminated in its inclusion in the one-off World Touring Car Championship. Although a chicane (Caltex Chase) was introduced to slow cars on the Conrod Straight, it is now taken flat-out. The dangers of this corner were highlighted by the death of privateer Don Watson during practice for the 1994 race. When the Bathurst 1000 adopted 2-litre Super Touring Car rules in 1997, a rival race for traditional Australian V8 Supercars was organised to compete with

it. This only served to confuse and dilute interest in one of the world's great races. In 2001, however, with support of the Super Touring category waning in Australia, only the V8 Supercar event was held.

Active years	**1938 to date**
Location	**Mount Panorama, near Bathurst, 130 miles west of Sydney**
Type	**Permanent road course**
Website	**www.v8supercar1000.com**

Current circuit

Lap distance	**3.862 miles**
Lap record	Qualifying: John Bowe (Ford Holden AU), 2m08.3873, 108.291 mph, V8 Touring Cars, 2002
	Race: Brad Jones (Ford Holden AU), 2m09.5705, 107.302 mph, V8 Touring Cars, 2002

Circuit changes

1938-86	3.835 miles (circuit re-measured in 1973, previously believed to be 3.875 miles)
1987 to date	Caltex Chase built in the middle of Conrod Straight. Current circuit

Australian Grand Prix see above

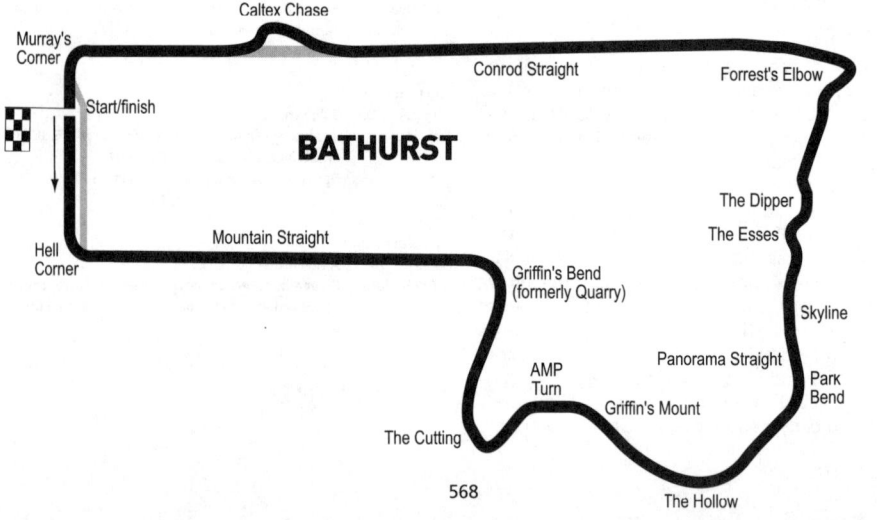

Murray's Corner

Caltex Chase

Conrod Straight

Forrest's Elbow

Start/finish

BATHURST

The Dipper

The Esses

Hell Corner

Mountain Straight

Griffin's Bend (formerly Quarry)

Skyline

AMP Turn

Panorama Straight

Park Bend

Griffin's Mount

The Cutting

The Hollow

BATHURST 1000

year	formula	winner	nat	car	mph
1963	TC	Harry Firth/Bob Jane	AUS	Ford Cortina GT	64.689
1964	TC	Bob Jane/George Reynolds	AUS	Ford Cortina GT	n/a
1965	TC	Barry Seton/Midge Bosworth	AUS	Ford Cortina GT500	69.204
1966	TC	Rauno Aaltonen/Bob Holden	SF/AUS	Morris Cooper S	70.049
1967	TC	Harry Firth/Fred Gibson	AUS	Ford Falcon XR GT	72.808
1968	TC	Bruce McPhee/Barry Mulholland	AUS	Holden Monaro GTS 327	74.793
1969	TC	Colin Bond/Tony Roberts	AUS	Holden Monaro GTS 350	77.023
1970	TC	Allan Moffat	AUS	Ford Falcon XW GTHO	76.755
1971	TC	Allan Moffat	AUS	Ford Falcon XY GTHO	81.728
1972	TC	Peter Brock	AUS	Holden Torana LJ XU1	83.521
1973	TC	Allan Moffat/Ian Geoghegan	AUS	Ford Falcon XA GT	85.220
1974	TC	John Goss/Kevin Bartlett	AUS	Ford Falcon XA GT	79.510
1975	TC	Peter Brock/Brian Sampson	AUS	Holden Torana L34	87.186
1976	TC	Bob Morris/John Fitzpatrick	AUS/GB	Holden Torana L34	87.796
1977	TC	Allan Moffat/Jacky Ickx	AUS/B	Ford Falcon XC	89.486
1978	TC	Peter Brock/Jim Richards	AUS/NZ	Holden Torana A9X	92.403
1979	TC	Peter Brock/Jim Richards	AUS/NZ	Holden Torana A9X	94.175
1980	TC	Peter Brock/Jim Richards	AUS/NZ	Holden Commodore VC	91.955
1981	TC	Dick Johnson/John French	AUS	Ford Falcon XD	93.957
1982	TC	Peter Brock/Larry Perkins	AUS	Holden Commodore VH	95.666
1983	TC	Peter Brock/Larry Perkins/John Harvey	AUS	Holden Commodore VH	96.535
1984	TC	Peter Brock/Larry Perkins	AUS	Holden Commodore VK	97.872
1985	TC	John Goss/Armin Hahne	AUS/D	Jaguar XJ-S	93.415
1986	TC	Allan Grice/Graeme Bailey	AUS	Holden Commodore VK	96.024
1987	TC	Peter Brock/David Parsons/Peter McLeod	AUS	Holden Commodore VL	86.935
1988	TC	Tony Longhurst/Tomas Mezera	AUS	Ford Sierra RS500 Cosworth	88.369
1989	TC	Dick Johnson/John Bowe	AUS	Ford Sierra RS500 Cosworth	95.441
1990	TC	Allan Grice/Win Percy	AUS/GB	Holden Commodore VL	n/a
1991	TC	Jim Richards/Mark Skaife	NZ/AUS	Nissan Skyline GT-R	98.371
1992	TC	Jim Richards/Mark Skaife	NZ/AUS	Nissan Skyline GT-R	n/a
1993	TC	Larry Perkins/Gregg Hansford	AUS	Holden Commodore VP	95.877
1994	TC	Dick Johnson/John Bowe	AUS	Ford Falcon EB	88.037
1995	TC	Larry Perkins/Russell Ingall	AUS	Holden Commodore VR	98.004
1996	TC	Craig Lowndes/Greg Murphy	AUS/NZ	Holden Commodore VR	86.990
1997	TC	Larry Perkins/Russell Ingall	AUS	Holden Commodore VR	n/a
1998	TC	Jason Bright/Steven Richards	AUS/NZ	Ford Falcon EL	92.510
1999	TC	Greg Murphy/Steven Richards	NZ	Holden Commodore VT	89.137
2000	TC	Jason Bargwanna/Garth Tander	AUS	Holden Commodore VT	84.092
2001	TC	Mark Skaife/Tony Longhurst	AUS	Holden Commodore VT	90.869
2002	TC	Mark Skaife/Jim Richards	AUS	Holden Commodore VX	89.105

SUPER TOURING CAR RACE

year	formula	winner	nat	car	mph
1997	TC	Geoff Brabham/Craig Baird	AUS/NZ	BMW 320i	92.959
1998	TC	Jim Richards/Rickard Rydell	AUS/S	Volvo S40	90.049
1999*	TC	Paul Morris	AUS	BMW 320i	65.830

*Bathurst 500. Note: Officially the Bathurst 1000 was changed to 2-litre Super Touring Car rules in 1997 but it reverted to traditional V8 Supercars in 1999

SANDOWN PARK

Sandown Park shares its facilities and a 10,000-seater grandstand with horseracing just as Aintree once did in England. Formerly a mainstay of the Tasman Cup, the infield section was added in 1984 to comply with FIA circuit length regulations and a round of the World Sports Car Championship was held. The exercise was repeated four years later, but Sandown has now returned to being a national circuit using the old the 1.9-mile old layout.

Active years	1962 to date
Location	Springvale, 16 miles south-east of Melbourne
Type	Permanent road course
Website	www.sandownraceway.com.au

International circuit

Lap distance	2.425 miles
Lap records	Qualifying: Jean-Louis Schlesser (Sauber C9/88-Mercedes-Benz), 1m28.62, 98.511 mph, Group C Sports Cars, 1988
	Race: Jean-Louis Schlesser (Sauber C9/88-Mercedes-Benz), 1m33.58, 92.712 mph, Group C Sports Cars, 1988

Circuit changes

1962-83	Current national circuit. 1.929 miles
1984 to date	Infield loop built. Current international circuit

Australian Grand Prix see above

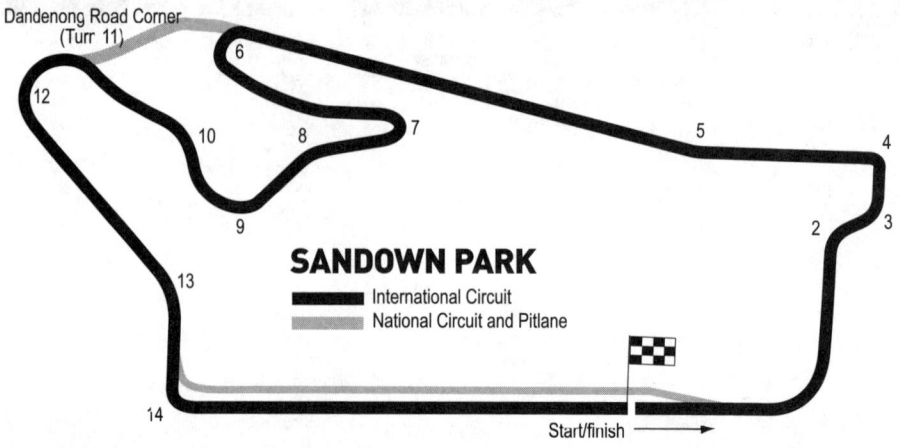

WORLD SPORTS CAR RACE						
year	formula	winner	nat	car		mph
1984	SC W	Stefan Bellof/Derek Bell	D/GB	Porsche 956		82.912
1988	SC W	Jean-Louis Schlesser/Jochen Mass	F/D	Sauber C9/88-Mercedes-Benz		89.698

SURFER'S PARADISE

Surfer's is a fast temporary road course adjacent to Queensland's Gold Coast, which holds the once-controversial Australian Champcar race. Its arrival saw CART running outside the Americas for the first time, incurring the FIA's wrath and prompting a retrospective ruling (now recinded) from Paris that the championship could only expand further on ovals. The circuit is essentially a series of long straights interrupted by chicanes; the close proximity of concrete barriers has led to many incidents, including the 1997 crash in which Christian Fittipaldi broke his leg. The 2002 race was blighted by torrential rain that resulted in a terrifying accident at the start and bizarre victory for the slowest competitor.

Active years	1991 to date
Location	Central Surfer's Paradise on Australia's Gold Coast, 60 miles south of Brisbane
Type	Temporary street circuit
Website	www.indy.com.au

Current circuit

Lap distance	2.795 miles
Lap records	Qualifying: Cristiano da Matta (Lola B2/00-Toyota), 1m30.204, 111.547 mph, CART, 2002
	Race: Alessandro Zanardi (Reynard 98I-Honda), 1m33.780, 107.294 mph, CART, 1998

Circuit changes

1991-94	2.794 miles
1995 to date	Chicane on Main Beach Parade modified. Current circuit (remeasured in 1996, previously believed to be 2.804 miles)

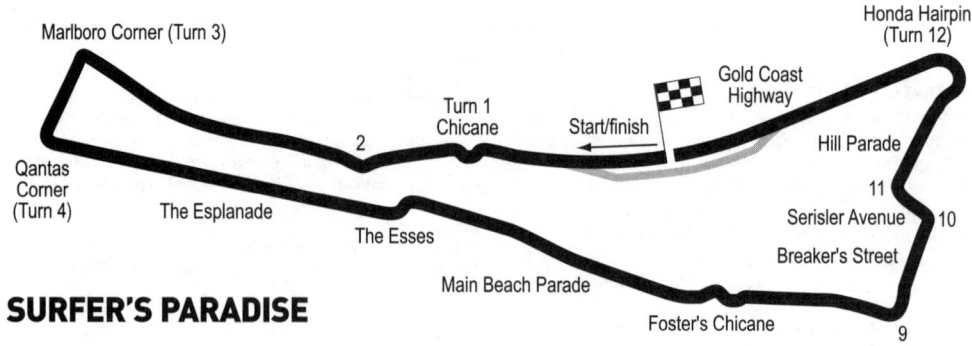

SURFER'S PARADISE

GOLD COAST CHAMPCAR GRAND PRIX

year	formula	winner	nat	car	mph
1991	CART	John Andretti	USA	Lola T91/00-Chevrolet	81.953
1992	CART	Emerson Fittipaldi	BR	Penske PC21-Chevrolet	77.561
1993	CART	Nigel Mansell	GB	Lola T93/00-Ford	97.284
1994	CART	Michael Andretti	USA	Reynard 94I-Ford	80.994
1995	CART	Paul Tracy	CDN	Lola T95/00-Ford	92.038
1996	CART	Jimmy Vasser	USA	Reynard 96I-Honda	90.250
1997	CART	Scott Pruett	USA	Reynard 97I-Ford	78.948
1998	CART	Alessandro Zanardi	I	Reynard 98I-Honda	85.328
1999	CART	Dario Franchitti	GB	Reynard 99I-Honda	91.849
2000	CART	Adrian Fernandez	MEX	Reynard 2KI-Ford	81.607
2001	CART	Cristiano da Matta	BR	Lola B01/00-Toyota	97.511
2002	CART	Mario Dominguez	MEX	Lola B2/00-Ford	55.849

AUSTRIA
Major Championships

AUSTRIAN FORMULA 3 CHAMPIONSHIP

year	driver	nat	team	car
1988	Karl Wendlinger	A	Kraft Walzen Team	Ralt RT32-Alfa Romeo
1989	Josef Neuhauser	A	MSC Aschau	Reynard 873-Volkswagen
1990	Josef Neuhauser	A	MSC Aschau	Reynard 893-Volkswagen
1991	Josef Neuhauser	A	Monninghoff Sport	Reynard 903-Volkswagen
1992	Peter Wieser	A	Peter Wieser/RSM Marko	Eufra 390-Volkswagen/Reynard 923-Alfa Romeo
1993	Alexander Wurz	A	RSM Marko	Dallara 393-Fiat
1994	Josef Neuhauser	A	Achleitner Motorsport	Ralt RT36-Volkswagen
1995	Josef Neuhauser	A	Achleitner Motorsport	Dallara 394-Opel
1996	Josef Neuhauser	A	Achleitner Motorsport	Dallara 394-Opel
1997	Josef Neuhauser	A	Achleitner Motorsport	Dallara 394-Opel
1998	Andre Fibier	D	Franz Woss Racing	Dallara 395-Opel
1999	Andre Fibier	D	Franz Woss Racing	Dallara 397-Opel
2000	Fulvio Cavicchi	I	Azeta Sava Olimpija	Dallara 397-Opel
2001	Jaroslav Kostelecky	CS	Czech National Racing	Dallara 399-Opel
2002	Jaroslav Kostelecky	CS	KFR Team F3	Dallara 300-Opel

Major International Races

AUSTRIAN GRAND PRIX

year	formula	circuit	winner	nat	car	mph
1963	F1	Zeltweg	Jack Brabham	AUS	Brabham BT3-Climax	96.350
1964	F1 W	Zeltweg	Lorenzo Bandini	I	Ferrari Dino 156	99.161
1965	SC	Zeltweg	Jochen Rindt	A	Ferrari 250LM	97.130
1966	SC	Zeltweg	Gerhard Mitter/Hans Herrmann	D	Porsche 906 Carrera 6	99.680
1967	SC	Zeltweg	Paul Hawkins	AUS	Ford GT40	95.290
1968	SC W	Zeltweg	Jo Siffert	CH	Porsche 908/8	106.831
1969	SC W	Osterreichring	Jo Siffert/Kurt Ahrens Jr	CH/D	Porsche 917	115.769
1970	F1 W	Osterreichring	Jacky Ickx	B	Ferrari 312B	129.269
1971	F1 W	Osterreichring	Jo Siffert	CH	BRM P160	131.645
1972	F1 W	Osterreichring	Emerson Fittipaldi	BR	Lotus 72D-Ford	133.298
1973	F1 W	Osterreichring	Ronnie Peterson	S	Lotus 72D-Ford	133.995
1974	F1 W	Osterreichring	Carlos Reutemann	RA	Brabham BT44-Ford	134.097
1975	F1 W	Osterreichring	Vittorio Brambilla	I	March 751-Ford	110.295
1976	F1 W	Osterreichring	John Watson	GB	Penske PC4-Ford	132.000
1977	F1 W	Osterreichring	Alan Jones	AUS	Shadow DN8A-Ford	122.972
1978	F1 W	Osterreichring	Ronnie Peterson	S	Lotus 79-Ford	118.016
1979	F1 W	Osterreichring	Alan Jones	AUS	Williams FW07-Ford	136.501
1980	F1 W	Osterreichring	Jean-Pierre Jabouille	F	Renault RE20	138.671
1981	F1 W	Osterreichring	Jacques Laffite	F	Ligier JS17-Matra	134.013
1982	F1 W	Osterreichring	Elio de Angelis	I	Lotus 91-Ford	138.064
1983	F1 W	Osterreichring	Alain Prost	F	Renault RE40	138.866
1984	F1 W	Osterreichring	Niki Lauda	A	McLaren MP4/2-TAG Porsche	139.108
1985	F1 W	Osterreichring	Alain Prost	F	McLaren MP4/2B-TAG Porsche	143.612
1986	F1 W	Osterreichring	Alain Prost	F	McLaren MP4/2C-TAG Porsche	141.554

AUSTRIAN GRAND PRIX (cont.)

year	formula	circuit	winner	nat	car	mph
1987	F1 W	Osterreichring	Nigel Mansell	GB	Williams FW11B-Honda	146.277
1997	F1 W	A1 Ring	Jacques Villeneuve	CDN	Williams FW19-Renault	130.523
1998	F1 W	A1 Ring	Mika Hakkinen	SF	McLaren MP4/13-Mercedes-Benz	126.014
1999	F1 W	A1 Ring	Eddie Irvine	GB	Ferrari F399	129.625
2000	F1 W	A1 Ring	Mika Hakkinen	SF	McLaren MP4/15-Mercedes-Benz	129.542
2001	F1 W	A1 Ring	David Coulthard	GB	McLaren MP4/16-Mercedes-Benz	130.277
2002	F1 W	A1 Ring	Michael Schumacher	D	Ferrari F2002	121.819

Circuits and Other Races

A1 RING

(formerly known as the Osterreichring)

The purists may compare the A1 Ring unfavourably with the Osterreichring it has replaced, but the Austrian Grand Prix often provides close racing, passing and drama. The original circuit was built in 1969 in the spectacular mountains above the unpopular Zeltweg airfield circuit. It was a magnificent collection of fast corners and steep elevation changes. The Bosch Kurve, 180 degrees and no run-off, was awesome. A chicane was built at the first corner following Mark Donohue's fatal accident in 1975, but that was the only slow corner. But when the 1987 Grand Prix was stopped twice by start-line accidents, the Osterreichring was removed from the calendar. The Grand Prix returned ten years later on a new circuit with a new name—the A1 Ring after Austria's leading mobile phone provider. Although the new circuit will always suffer in comparison with the Osterreichring, the stop-go nature of the A1 Ring always produces excitement.

Active years	1969 to date
Location	2 miles north of Zeltweg, 44 miles north-west of Graz, 125 miles south-east of Salzburg
Type	Permanent road course
Website	www.a1ring.at

Current circuit

Lap distance	2.684 miles
Lap records	Qualifying: Rubens Barrichello (Ferrari F2002), 1m08.082, 141.923 mph, F1, 2002
	Race: Michael Schumacher (Ferrari F2002), 1m09.298, 139.433 mph, F1, 2002

Circuit changes

1969-75	3.673 miles
1976	Hella Licht-kurve tightened. 3.672 miles
1977-96	Chicane installed at Hella Licht. 3.692 miles
1996 to date	New circuit built using the infield, main and back straights. Current circuit

Austrian Grand Prix see above

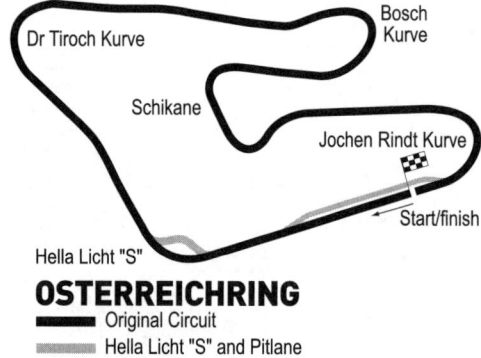

OSTERREICHRING

■■■ Original Circuit
▒▒▒ Hella Licht "S" and Pitlane

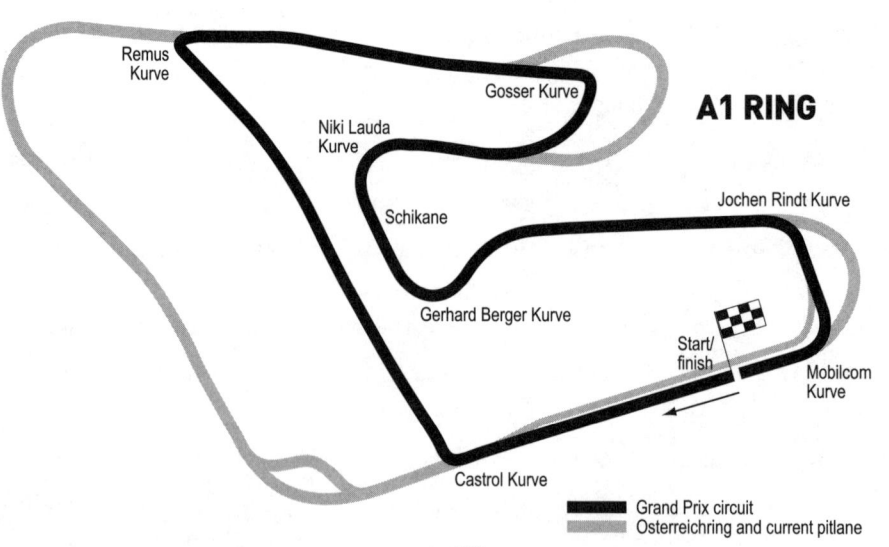

A1 RING

■■■ Grand Prix circuit
▒▒▒ Osterreichring and current pitlane

JOCHEN RINDT TROPHY

year	formula	winner	nat	car	mph
1972	F2 E	Emerson Fittipaldi	BR	Lotus 69-Ford	126.161

EUROPEAN FORMULA 3 RACE

year	formula	winner	nat	car	mph
1977	F3 E	Anders Olofsson	S	Ralt RT1-Toyota	106.234
1978	F3 E	Anders Olofsson	S	Ralt RT1-Toyota	113.861
1979	F3 E	Alain Prost	F	Martini MK27-Renault	116.432
1980	F3 E	Michele Alboreto	I	March 803-Alfa Romeo	116.658
1981	F3 E	Mauro Baldi	I	March 813-Alfa Romeo	119.129
1982	F3 E	Emanuele Pirro	I	Euroracing 101-Alfa Romeo	118.335
1983	F3 E	Tommy Byrne	IRL	Ralt RT3/83-Toyota	119.329
1984	F3 E	Gerhard Berger	A	Ralt RT3/84-Alfa Romeo	120.560

INTERNATIONAL FORMULA 3000 RACE

year	formula	winner	nat	car	mph
1985	F3000 INT	Ivan Capelli	I	March 85B-Cosworth	127.322
1986	F3000 INT	Ivan Capelli	I	March 86B-Cosworth	128.107
1997	F3000 INT	Juan Pablo Montoya	CO	Lola T96/50-Zytek	106.380
1998	F3000 INT	Soheil Ayari	F	Lola T96/50-Zytek	108.764
1999	F3000 INT	Nick Heidfeld	D	Lola B99/50-Zytek	113.927
2000	F3000 INT	Nicolas Minassian	F	Lola B99/50-Zytek	109.325
2001	F3000 INT	Justin Wilson	GB	Lola B99/50-Zytek	108.492
2002	F3000 INT	Tomas Enge	CS	Lola B2/50-Zytek	115.269

WORLD SPORTS CAR RACE (ALSO SEE AUSTRIAN GP)

year	formula	winner	nat	car	mph
1970	SC W	Jo Siffert/Brian Redman	CH/GB	Porsche 917	121.608
1971	SC W	Pedro Rodriguez/Richard Attwood	MEX/GB	Porsche 917K	123.063
1972	SC W	Jacky Ickx/Brian Redman	B/GB	Ferrari 312P	125.396
1973	SC W	Henri Pescarolo/Gerard Larrousse	F	Matra-Simca MS670	129.652
1974	SC W	Henri Pescarolo/Gerard Larrousse	F	Matra-Simca MS670C	128.595
1975	SC W	Henri Pescarolo/Derek Bell	F/GB	Alfa Romeo T33TT/12	105.652
1976	SC W	Dieter Quester/Gunnar Nilsson	A/S	BMW 3.0 CSL	114.388

FIA GT RACE

year	formula	winner	nat	car	mph
1997	GT FIA	Klaus Ludwig/Bernd Maylander/			
		Bernd Schneider	D	Mercedes-Benz CLK-GTR	107.614
1998	GT FIA	Klaus Ludwig/Ricardo Zonta	D/BR	Mercedes-Benz CLK-LM	111.471
2000	GT FIA	Tom Coronel/Mike Hezemans	NL	Chrysler Viper GTS-R	101.233
2001	GT FIA	Peter Kox/Rickard Rydell	S	Ferrari 550M	102.792

SALZBURGRING

Nestled in a beautiful valley above the famed Austrian city, the Salzburgring is surrounded by wooded hillsides that form natural grandstands. Formula 2 and European Touring Cars visited regularly in the seventies, and it was home to Austria's motorcycle Grand Prix until 1995. Today, however, it is rarely used by international categories, concentrating instead on national events. Two fast sections are joined by slow turns at each end, although these straights are now broken up by two chicanes.

Active years 1969 to date
Location 10 miles east of Salzburg, 100 miles south-east of Munich

Type Permanent road course
Website www.salzburgring.com

Current circuit
Lap distance 2.643 miles
Lap records* Qualifying: Vittorio Brambilla (Alfa Romeo T33SC/12), 1m12.65, 130.572 mph, Sports Cars, 1977
Race: Vittorio Brambilla (Alfa Romeo T33SC/12), 1m12.45, 130.435 mph, Sports Cars, 1977

*set on the 1976 layout before the chicane was built at first corner; lap record for current circuit not available.

Circuit changes
1969-75 2.633 miles
1976-79 Chicane built before last corner. 2.635 miles
1980 to date Chicane built at first corner. Current circuit

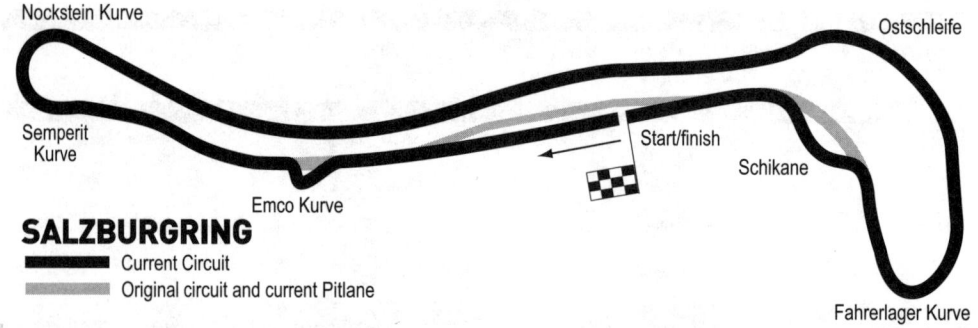

SALZBURGRING

▬▬▬▬ Current Circuit

▬▬▬▬ Original circuit and current Pitlane

EUROPEAN FORMULA 2 RACE

year	formula	winner	nat	car	mph
1970	F2	Jacky Ickx	B	BMW F270	124.580
1972	F2 E	Mike Hailwood	GB	Surtees TS10-Ford	128.912
1973	F2 E	Vittorio Brambilla	I	March 732-BMW	132.117
1974	F2 E	Jacques Laffite	F	March 742-BMW	130.454
1975	F2 E	Jean-Pierre Jabouille	F	Elf 2J-BMW	130.874
1976	F2 E	Michel Leclere	F	Elf 2J-Renault	122.596

WORLD SPORTS CAR RACE

year	formula	winner	nat	car	mph
1976	SC WSC	Jochen Mass	D	Porsche 936	125.163
1977	SC WSC	Vittorio Brambilla	I	Alfa Romeo T33SC/12	126.557
1978	SC E	Reinhold Joest	D	Porsche 908/3 Spyder	119.096

TULLN-LANGENLEBARN

Tulln was an operational airfield a mile from the River Danube that held a European F2 race for the first five years of the championship. Facilities were rudimentary, with straw bales marking the course. Local hero Jochen Rindt obliged the crowds by winning the first three races, and Ronnie Peterson's victory in the circuit's final race came as many others spun out in the heavy rain.

Active years	**1967-71**
Location	**20 miles west of Vienna**
Type	**Temporary road course**
Lap distance	**1.780 miles**
Lap records	**Qualifying: Ronnie Peterson (March 712M-Ford), 1m00.48, 105.952 mph, F2, 1971**
	Race: Francois Cevert (Tecno TF70-Ford), 1m01.6, 104.026 mph, F2, 1970

FLUGPLATZRENNEN/EUROPEAN FORMULA 2 RACE

year	formula	winner	nat	car	mph
1967	F2 E	Jochen Rindt	A	Brabham BT23-Ford	97.552
1968	F2 E	Jochen Rindt	A	Brabham BT23C-Ford	99.137
1969	F2 E	Jochen Rindt	A	Lotus 59B-Ford	101.899
1970	F2 E	Jacky Ickx	B	BMW F270	101.351
1971	F2 E	Ronnie Peterson	S	March 712M-Ford	88.434

ZELTWEG

Although Zeltweg held Austria's first F1 World Championship Grand Prix in 1964, the event proved unpopular and was not repeated there. The course was a dull, bumpy temporary circuit on an army airfield, with a concrete surface that caused a high rate of attrition. Lorenzo Bandini survived to record his only victory. The Austrian GP switched to sports cars before the new Osterreichring was built to replace Zeltweg in 1969.

Active years	1958-69
Location	44 miles north-west of Graz, 125 miles south-east of Salzburg
Type	Temporary road course
Lap distance	1.988 miles
Lap records	Qualifying: Jo Siffert (Porsche 908/8), 1m04.86, 110.343 mph, Sports Cars, 1968
	Race: Jo Siffert (Porsche 908/8), 1m04.82, 110.412 mph, Sports Cars, 1968

Austrian Grand Prix see above

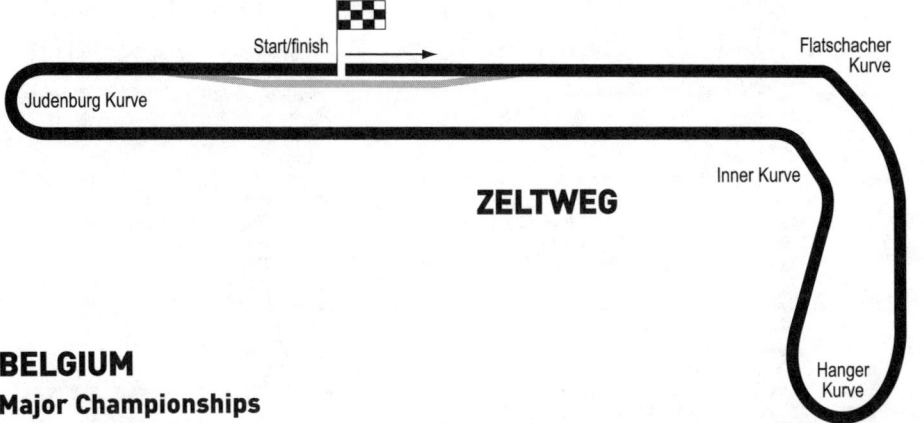

BELGIUM
Major Championships

BELGIAN PROCAR CHAMPIONSHIP (FORMERLY THE BELGIAN TOURING CAR CHAMPIONSHIP)

year	driver	nat	team	car
1989	Jean-Michel Martin	B	Volkswagen-Audi Club	Audi 200 turbo
1990	Jean-Michel Martin	B	BMW Fina Bastos Team	BMW M3
1991	Philippe Verellen	B	Volkswagen-Audi Club	Audi V8 Quattro
1992	Pierre-Alain Thibaut	B	Volkswagen-Audi Club	Audi V8 Quattro
1993	Philippe Verellen	B	Toyota Team Belgium	Toyota Carina
1994	Thierry Tassin	B	BMW Fina Bastos Team/Warthofer	BMW 318i
1995	Thierry Tassin	B	BMW Fina Bastos Team/Warthofer	BMW 318i
1996	Jean-Francois Hemroulle	B	Volkswagen-Audi Club	Audi A4 Quattro
1997	Didier de Radigues	B	BMW Fina Bastos Team/Warthofer	BMW 320i
1998	Sebastien Ugeux	B	Peugeot Belgique/Kronos	Peugeot 306 GTi
1999	Frederic Bouvy	B	Peugeot Belgium-Luxembourg/Kronos	Peugeot 306 GTi
2000	Sebastien Ugeux	B	LO Racing	Alfa Romeo 156
2001	Vincent Radermecker	B	East Belgian Racing Team	Opel Astra
2002	Nicolas Stelandre	B	Verbist	Ford Mondeo

BELGIAN BELCAR GT CHAMPIONSHIP (FORMERLY THE CARGLASS CUP)

year	category	driver	nat	team	car
1990	GT	Dumortier/Dumortier/de Rosee	B	-	Volvo 240 turbo
1991	GT	Erik Bruynoghe/Meirschaut/Guy Verheyen	B	-	Peugeot 309 turbo
1992	GT	Daniel Hubert/Patrick Hubert/Mondron	B	-	BMW 335i
1993	GT	Wuydts/Eliano/Koentges	B	-	Honda Civic
1994	GT	Albert Vanierschot/Paul Kumpen/Georges Cremer	B	-	Porsche Carrera
1995	GT	Albert Vanierschot/Paul Kumpen/Georges Cremer	B	Peka	Porsche 993
1996	GT	Daniel Hubert/Patrick Hubert/Marc Duez	B	-	BMW M3
1997	GT	Fons Taels/Vincent Dupont/Georges Cremer	B	-	Porsche 993
1998	GT	Patrick Huisman/Duncan Huisman	NL	Van de Venne Geert	Porsche 993
	TC	Jean-Francois Hemroulle/Tim Verbergt	B	Volkswagen-Audi Club	Audi A4 Quattro
1999	GT	Anthony Kumpen/Stephan Cohen	B	Cooltech	Porsche 993 turbo
	TC	Jean-Francois Hemroulle/Tim Verbergt	B	Volkswagen-Audi Club	Audi A4 Quattro
2000	GT	Bert Longin/Albert Vanierschot	B	AD Racing	Porsche 993 Bi-turbo
	TC	Erik Bruynoghe/Bas Leinders	B	Belien BMW	BMW Z3 GT
2001	GT	Patrick Schreurs/Kurt Thiers	B	GLPK Racing	Porsche 996 Bi-turbo
	TC	Pertti Kuismanen/Karl Hasenbichler	SF/A	Kuismanen Racing	Audi 80 Competition
2002	GT	Bert Longin/Anthony Kumpen	B	GLPK Racing	Chrysler Viper GTS-R
	TC	Peter Beckers/Serge Cassiers/Eric Roelands	B	Motorsport Service & Engineering	BMW M3

Major International Races

BELGIAN GRAND PRIX

year	formula	circuit	winner	nat	car	mph
1925	GP	Spa-Francorchamps	Antonio Ascari	I	Alfa Romeo P2	74.859
1930	GP	Spa-Francorchamps	Louis Chiron	MC	Bugatti T35C	71.834
1931	GP	Spa-Francorchamps	"W Williams"/Caberto Conelli	GB/I	Bugatti T51	81.277
1933	GP	Spa-Francorchamps	Tazio Nuvolari	I	Maserati 8CM	88.956
1934	GP	Spa-Francorchamps	Rene Dreyfus	F	Bugatti T59	87.414
1935	GP	Spa-Francorchamps	Rudolf Caracciola	D	Mercedes-Benz W25B	98.441
1937	GP	Spa-Francorchamps	Rudolf Hasse	D	Auto Union C	104.426
1939	GP	Spa-Francorchamps	Hermann Lang	D	Mercedes-Benz W163	92.250
1947	F1	Spa-Francorchamps	Jean-Pierre Wimille	F	Alfa Romeo 158	95.860
1949	F1	Spa-Francorchamps	Louis Rosier	F	Lago-Talbot T26C	97.422
1950	F1 W	Spa-Francorchamps	Juan Manuel Fangio	RA	Alfa Romeo 158	110.046
1951	F1 W	Spa-Francorchamps	Giuseppe Farina	I	Alfa Romeo 159	114.326
1952	F2 W	Spa-Francorchamps	Alberto Ascari	I	Ferrari 500	103.127
1953	F2 W	Spa-Francorchamps	Alberto Ascari	I	Ferrari 500	112.470
1954	F1 W	Spa-Francorchamps	Juan Manuel Fangio	RA	Maserati 250F	115.064
1955	F1 W	Spa-Francorchamps	Juan Manuel Fangio	RA	Mercedes-Benz W196	118.833
1956	F1 W	Spa-Francorchamps	Peter Collins	GB	Lancia-Ferrari D50	118.445
1958	F1 W	Spa-Francorchamps	Tony Brooks	GB	Vanwall VW5	129.920
1960	F1 W	Spa-Francorchamps	Jack Brabham	AUS	Cooper T53-Climax	133.622
1961	F1 W	Spa-Francorchamps	Phil Hill	USA	Ferrari Dino 156	128.144
1962	F1 W	Spa-Francorchamps	Jim Clark	GB	Lotus 25-Climax	131.891
1963	F1 W	Spa-Francorchamps	Jim Clark	GB	Lotus 25-Climax	113.815
1964	F1 W	Spa-Francorchamps	Jim Clark	GB	Lotus 25-Climax	132.790
1965	F1 W	Spa-Francorchamps	Jim Clark	GB	Lotus 33-Climax	117.155
1966	F1 W	Spa-Francorchamps	John Surtees	GB	Ferrari 312	113.930
1967	F1 W	Spa-Francorchamps	Dan Gurney	USA	Eagle AAR104-Weslake	145.982
1968	F1 W	Spa-Francorchamps	Bruce McLaren	NZ	McLaren M7A-Ford	147.133
1970	F1 W	Spa-Francorchamps	Pedro Rodriguez	MEX	BRM P153	149.936
1972	F1 W	Nivelles	Emerson Fittipaldi	BR	Lotus 72D-Ford	113.353
1973	F1 W	Zolder	Jackie Stewart	GB	Tyrrell 006-Ford	107.728
1974	F1 W	Nivelles	Emerson Fittipaldi	BR	McLaren M23-Ford	113.102
1975	F1 W	Zolder	Niki Lauda	A	Ferrari 312T	107.042
1976	F1 W	Zolder	Niki Lauda	A	Ferrari 312T2	108.095
1977	F1 W	Zolder	Gunnar Nilsson	S	Lotus 78-Ford	96.630
1978	F1 W	Zolder	Mario Andretti	USA	Lotus 79-Ford	111.364
1979	F1 W	Zolder	Jody Scheckter	ZA	Ferrari 312T4	111.225
1980	F1 W	Zolder	Didier Pironi	F	Ligier JS11/15-Ford	115.812
1981	F1 W	Zolder	Carlos Reutemann	RA	Williams FW07C-Ford	112.111
1982	F1 W	Zolder	John Watson	GB	McLaren MP4/1B-Ford	116.213
1983	F1 W	Spa-Francorchamps	Alain Prost	F	Renault RE40	119.136
1984	F1 W	Zolder	Michele Alboreto	I	Ferrari 126C4	115.209
1985	F1 W	Spa-Francorchamps	Ayrton Senna	BR	Lotus 97T-Renault	118.096
1986	F1 W	Spa-Francorchamps	Nigel Mansell	GB	Williams FW11-Honda	126.470
1987	F1 W	Spa-Francorchamps	Alain Prost	F	McLaren MP4/3-TAG Porsche	127.794
1988	F1 W	Spa-Francorchamps	Ayrton Senna	BR	McLaren MP4/4-Honda	126.407
1989	F1 W	Spa-Francorchamps	Ayrton Senna	BR	McLaren MP4/5-Honda	112.818
1990	F1 W	Spa-Francorchamps	Ayrton Senna	BR	McLaren MP4/5B-Honda	131.553
1991	F1 W	Spa-Francorchamps	Ayrton Senna	BR	McLaren MP4/6-Honda	130.405
1992	F1 W	Spa-Francorchamps	Michael Schumacher	D	Benetton B192-Ford	118.360
1993	F1 W	Spa-Francorchamps	Damon Hill	GB	Williams FW15C-Renault	134.662
1994	F1 W	Spa-Francorchamps	Damon Hill	GB	Williams FW16B-Renault	129.344
1995	F1 W	Spa-Francorchamps	Michael Schumacher	D	Benetton B195-Renault	118.066
1996	F1 W	Spa-Francorchamps	Michael Schumacher	D	Ferrari F310	129.499
1997	F1 W	Spa-Francorchamps	Michael Schumacher	D	Ferrari F310B	121.867
1998	F1 W	Spa-Francorchamps	Damon Hill	GB	Jordan 198-Mugen	110.112
1999	F1 W	Spa-Francorchamps	David Coulthard	GB	McLaren MP4/14-Mercedes-Benz	133.328
2000	F1 W	Spa-Francorchamps	Mika Hakkinen	SF	McLaren MP4/15-Mercedes-Benz	129.514
2001	F1 W	Spa-Francorchamps	Michael Schumacher	D	Ferrari F2001	137.341
2002	F1 W	Spa-Francorchamps	Michael Schumacher	D	Ferrari F2002	140.075

Circuits and Other Races

BASTOGNE

The Circuit des Ardennes was the first major race held on a closed course instead of running from city to city. It also began a tradition of racing in the area that continues today at Spa-Francorchamps. Pierre de Crawhez

originally suggested the event, and won the second race to be staged the following year. The 1904 race, on an extended circuit, produced the closest finish when George Heath defeated Georges Teste by just one minute.

Active years	**1902-07**
Location	**Ardennes region of Belgium**
Type	**Temporary road course**
Lap distance	**1902-03, 1906-07: 53.5 miles. 1904-05: 73.48 miles**

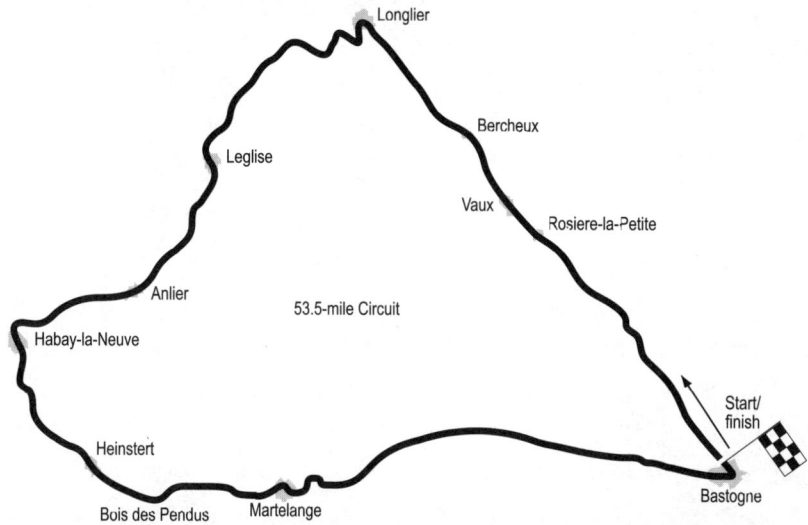

ARDENNES CIRCUIT					
year	formula	winner	nat	car	mph
1902	GP	Charles Jarrott	GB	Panhard 70	54.459
1903	GP	Pierre de Crawhez	B	Panhard 70	54.696
1904	GP	George Heath	USA	Panhard 70	56.405
1905	GP	Victor Hemery	F	Darracq	61.483
1906	GP	Arthur Duray	F	Lorraine-Dietrich	66.351
1907	Kaiserpreis	Lord Brabazon of Tara	GB	Minerva	60.067
	GP	Pierre de Caters	B	Mercedes	57.739

CHIMAY

Chimay is the home of the Grand Prix des Frontieres, named for its proximity to the French border. The fast temporary road course to the north of town became outdated and dangerous during the sixties, and closed in

1973. A shortened and slower version opened in 1986, and now holds Belgian national events.

Active years	**1926-73, 1986 to date**
Location	**South of Charleroi, near French border**
Type	**Temporary road course**

Lap distance	**2.806 miles**
Lap record	**Race: Thierry Tassin (Honda Accord), 1m52.049, 90.154 mph, Touring Cars, 1997**

Circuit changes	
1926-91	**6.754 miles**
1992 to date	**Abbreviated circuit opened. Current circuit**

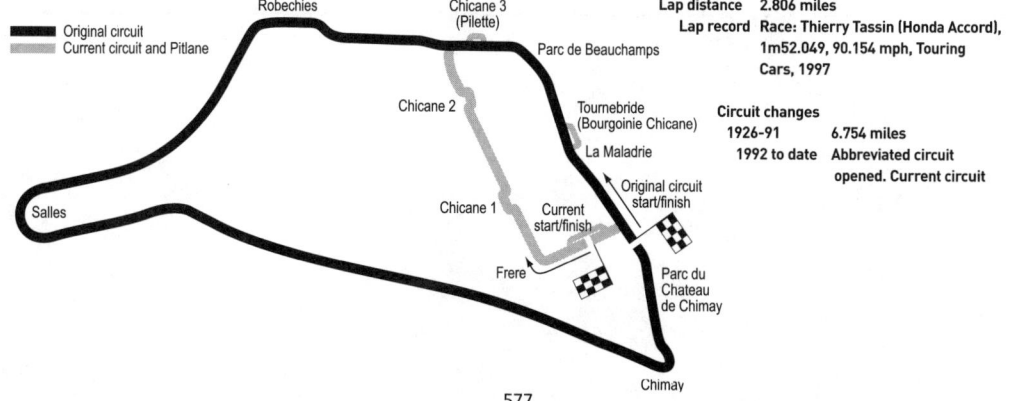

FRONTIERS GRAND PRIX

year	formula	winner	nat	car	mph
1926	Cyc	Roger Pierard	B	Salmson GS	61.602
1927	2000cc	Freddy Charlier	B	Bugatti T35	73.056
1928	V	Yves Giraud-Cabantous	F	Salmson GS	67.176
1929	GP	Goffredo Zehender	I	Alfa Romeo 6C-1750	68.578
1930	SC	Willy Longueville	B	Bugatti T35B	69.119
1931	FL	Arthur Legat	B	Bugatti T37A	70.840
1932	GP	Arthur Legat	B	Bugatti T37A	72.972
1933	GP	Willy Longueville	B	Bugatti T35B	75.479
1934	GP	Willy Longueville	B	Bugatti T35B	73.266
1935	GP	Rudolf Steinweg	D	Bugatti T51A	78.269
1936	SC	Eddie Hertzberger	NL	MG K3 Magnette	74.699
1937	FL	Hans Ruesch	CH	Alfa Romeo 8C-35	81.340
1938	FL	Maurice Trintignant	F	Bugatti T51	80.190
1939	GP	Maurice Trintignant	F	Bugatti T51	80.370
1946	FL	Leslie Brooke	GB	ERA B-type	75.000
1947	FL	"B Bira"	SM	Maserati 4CL	82.130
1948	SC	Guy Mairesse	F	Delahaye 135S	79.400
1949	F1	Guy Mairesse	F	Lago-Talbot T26C	86.420
1950	F2	Johnny Claes	B	HWM 50-Alta	84.845
1951	F2	Johnny Claes	B	Gordini 15	82.450
1952	F2	Paul Frere	B	HWM 51/52-Alta	90.236
1953	F2	Maurice Trintignant	F	Gordini 16	94.251
1954	F1	"B Bira"	SM	Maserati 250F	98.539
1955	SC	Benoit Musy	CH	Maserati A6GCS	94.970
1956	SC	Benoit Musy	CH	Maserati 300S	102.820
1957	SC	Franco Bordoni	I	Maserati 200S	99.440
1958	SC	Brian Naylor	GB	JBW-Maserati	93.430
1959	SC	Mike Taylor	GB	Lotus 15-Climax	105.560
1960	F2	Jackie Lewis	GB	Cooper T45-Climax	117.102
1961	FJ	John Love	RSR	Cooper-BMC	103.114
1962	FJ	Jose Rosinski	F	Cooper-Ford	102.870
1963	FJ	Jacques Maglia	F	Lotus-Ford	110.400
1965	F3	John Cardwell	GB	Brabham-Ford	110.605
1966	F3	Martin Davies	AUS	Brabham BT10-Ford	111.390
1967	F3	Peter Westbury	GB	Brabham BT21-Ford	111.990
1968	F3	Peter Westbury	GB	Brabham BT21-Ford	113.698
1969	F3	Jean Blanc	CH	Tecno 69-Ford	113.434
1970	F3	David Purley	GB	Brabham BT28-Ford	113.670
1971	F3	David Purley	GB	Brabham BT28-Ford	108.702
1972	F3	David Purley	GB	Ensign F371-Ford	122.311
1973	TC	Pierre-Yves Bertinchamps	B	Plymouth Hemicuda	109.086
1986	Prod	Bernard Carlier	B	Mitsubishi Starion	108.297
1987	Prod	Philip Verellen	B	Ford Cosworth	101.326
1988	Prod	Thierry Tassin	B	Ford Sierra	110.133
1996	TC	Jean-Francois Hemroulle	B	Audi A4 Quattro	88.371
1997	TC	Thierry Tassin	B	Honda Accord	85.180
1998	TC	Vincent Radermecker	B	Peugeot 306GTi	80.934
2000	Radical	Greaves/Michael Vergers	GB/NL	Radical	77.392
2001	TC	Vincent Radermecker/Bert Longin	B	Opel Astra	n/a

NIVELLES-BAULERS

A safe but bland circuit built near Brussels. When Spa fell from favour in the early seventies Nivelles held the Belgian Grand Prix twice, won on both occasions by Emerson Fittipaldi. But the teams hated the new track and the championship did not return

again. Nivelles went bankrupt and was sold in October 1977, closing soon after.

Active years	1971-78
Location	20 miles south of Brussels
Type	Permanent road course
Lap distance	2.314 miles
Lap records	Qualifying: Clay Regazzoni (Ferrari 312B3), 1m09.82, 119.313 mph, F1, 1974
	Race: Denny Hulme (McLaren M23-Ford), 1m11.31, 116.820 mph, F1, 1974

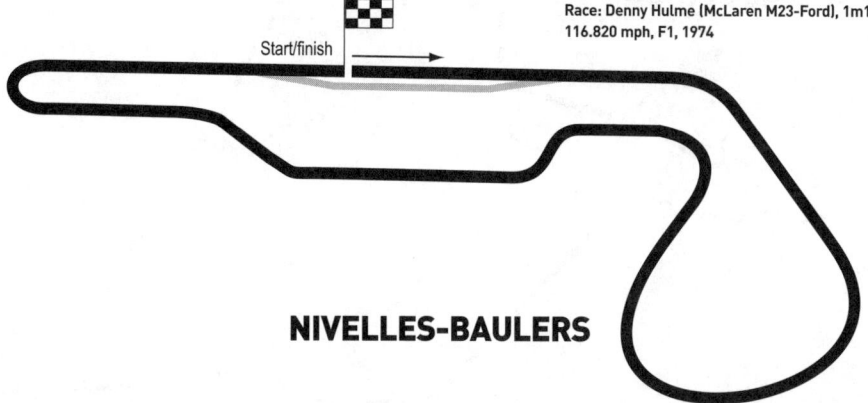

Start/finish

NIVELLES-BAULERS

Belgian Grand Prix see above

year	formula	winner	nat	car	mph
1973	F2 E	Jean-Pierre Jarier	F	March 732-BMW	110.197

SPA-FRANCORCHAMPS

Spa-Francorchamps remains the most challenging circuit in Europe, but the Belgian government's new tobacco laws have jeopardised its Grand Prix future. A race circuit had been suggested at Spa as early as 1895, but did not become a reality until 1924 when Jules de Thier designed a course in 1924. The original Spa used the narrow public roads from La Source, through Malmedy, onto the Masta straight, before passing between the houses at the fearsome Masta Kink. A hairpin at Stavelot led to an equally fast return leg to complete the lap.

When the circuit was shortened for the 1979 24-hour race, there were worries that Spa would be a shadow of its former self. But the new section was designed to match the character of the original. The old course, from the start at La Source through Eau Rouge and up the hill to Les Combes remains. A new link road was built across the valley to rejoin the old circuit on the blast back to La Source.

Eau Rouge has been considered by many to be the most demanding corner in Grand Prix racing. The weather at Spa is notoriously fickle, often raining at one corner while dry at another. The safety issues raised by all of these factors led to the closing of the old circuit in the early seventies. More recently, Luciano Burti's violent accident in 2001 was a reminder of the dangers of any fast road course.

Active years	1924 to date
Location	30 miles south-east of Liege, 30 miles south of Maastricht, 30 miles south-west of Aachen
Website	www.spa-francorchamps.be
Type	Permanent road course

Current circuit

Lap distance	4.316 miles
Lap records	Qualifying: Michael Schumacher (Ferrari F2002), 1m43.726, 149.795 mph, F1, 2002
	Race: Michael Schumacher (Ferrari F2002), 1m47.176, 144.973 mph, F1, 2002

Circuit changes

1924-33	9.236 miles
1934-38	Malmedy right-hander eased. 9.290 miles
1939-56	The Ancienne Douanne hairpin bypassed. 9.060 miles
1956-57	Stavelot Corner modified. 8.768 miles
1958-74	Some corners gradually eased. 8.755 miles.
1974-78	Chicane built before Malmedy for the 1974 Sports Car race. 8.755 miles
1979	New circuit built using the section from Blanchimont-La Source-Les Combes on the old track with a new link road. 4.317 miles
1980-83	"Bus Stop" chicane built. 4.312 miles (remeasured in 1986, previously thought to be 4.3179 miles)
1984-93	Grand Prix start moved to before La Source. 4.312 miles
1994	Chicane built at Eau Rouge for the Grand Prix and F3000 races. 4.350 miles
1995-2001	Eau Rouge Chicane removed and corner reprofiled. 4.329 miles
2002 to date	Exit of Bus Stop chicane and entry to pitlane modified. Current circuit

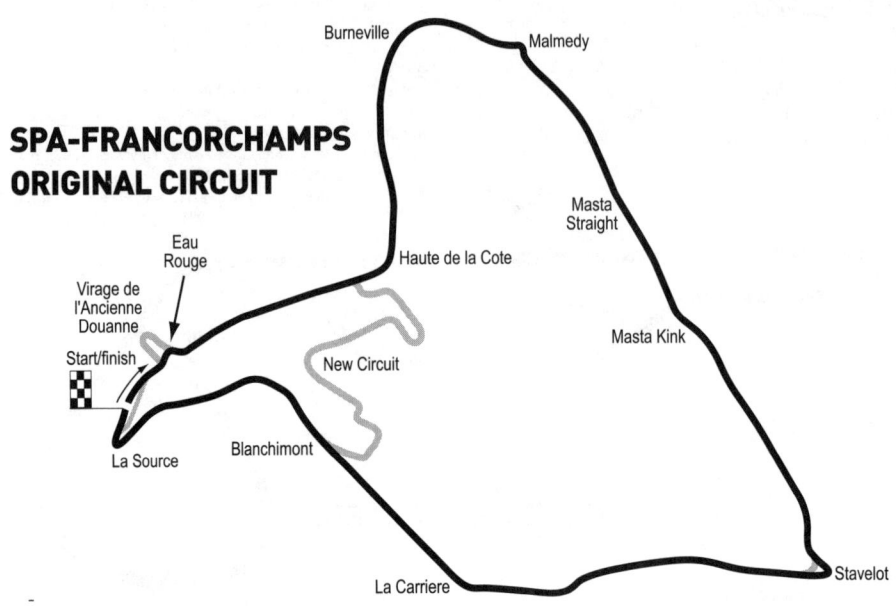

SPA-FRANCORCHAMPS ORIGINAL CIRCUIT

Burneville
Malmedy
Eau Rouge
Virage de l'Ancienne Douanne
Masta Straight
Start/finish
Haute de la Cote
New Circuit
Masta Kink
La Source
Blanchimont
La Carriere
Stavelot

CURRENT GRAND PRIX CIRCUIT

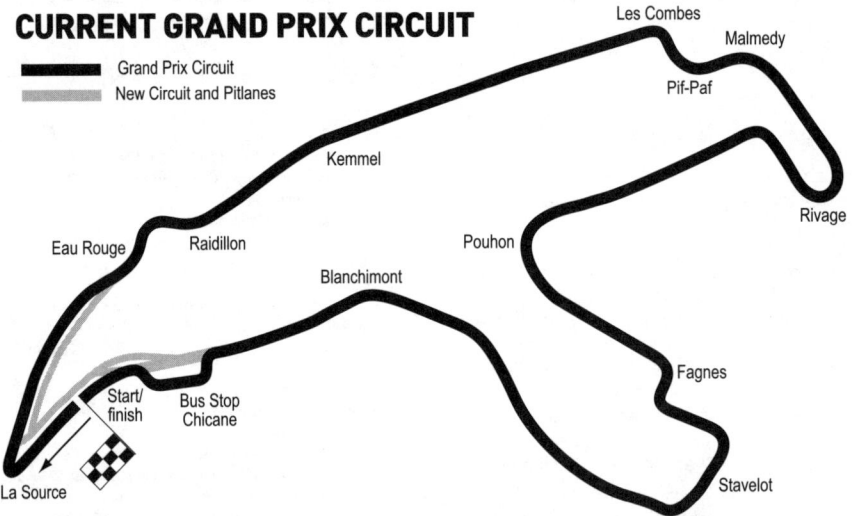

| | Grand Prix Circuit |
| | New Circuit and Pitlanes |

Les Combes
Malmedy
Pif-Paf
Kemmel
Rivage
Eau Rouge
Raidillon
Pouhon
Blanchimont
Fagnes
Start/finish
Bus Stop Chicane
La Source
Stavelot

Belgian Grand Prix see above

SPA 24 HOURS					
year	formula	winner	nat	car	mph
1924	TC	Henri Springuel/Becquet	F	Bignan	48.700
1925	TC	Andre Lagache/Rene Leonard	F	Chenard-Walcker	56.670
1926	TC	Andre Boillot/Louis Rigal	F	Peugeot	59.500
1927	TC	Robert Senechal/Nicolas Caerels	F/B	Excelsior	57.120
1928	TC	Boris Ivanowski/Attilio Marinoni	F/I	Alfa Romeo	63.800
1929	TC	Robert Benoist/Attilio Marinoni	F/I	Alfa Romeo	63.020
1930	TC	Attilio Marinoni/Pietro Ghersi	I	Alfa Romeo	68.500
1931	TC	Prince Dmitri Djordjadze/Goffredo Zehender	R/I	Mercedes-Benz	65.800
1932	TC	Antonio Brivio/Eugenio Siena	I	Alfa Romeo	72.600
1933	TC	Louis Chiron/Luigi Chinetti	MC/I	Alfa Romeo	72.660

SPA 24 HOURS (cont.)

year	formula	winner	nat	car	mph
1934*	TC	Jean Desvignes/Norbert Mahe	F	Bugatti	72.460
1936	TC	Francesco Severi/Raymond Sommer	I/F	Alfa Romeo	77.670
1938	TC	Carlo Pintacuda/Francesco Severi	I	Alfa Romeo	77.570
1948	SC	St John Horsfall/Leslie Johnson	GB	Aston Martin	72.070
1949	SC	Luigi Chinetti/Jean Lucas	I/F	Ferrari	78.700
1953	SC W	Giuseppe Farina/Mike Hawthorn	I/GB	Ferrari 340MM	95.052
1964	TC	Robert Crevits/Gustave Gosselin	B	Mercedes-Benz 300SE	102.440
1965	TC	Pascal Ickx/Gerard Langlois van Ophem	B	BMW 1800TISA	98.710
1966	TC	Jacky Ickx/Hubert Hahne	B/D	BMW 2000TI	104.710
1967	TC	Jean-Pierre Gaban/"Pedro"	B	Porsche 911	104.920
1968	TC	Erwin Kremer/Willi Kauhsen/Helmut Kelleners	D	Porsche 911	103.680
1969	TC	Guy Chasseuil/Claude Ballot-Lena	F	Porsche 911	110.610
1970	TC	Gunther Huber/Helmut Kelleners	A/D	BMW 2800CS	110.010
1971	TC	Dieter Glemser/Alex Soler-Roig	D/E	Ford Capri RS	113.521
1972	TC	Jochen Mass/Hans-Joachim Stuck	D	Ford Capri RS2600	116.467
1973	TC	Toine Hezemans/Dieter Quester	NL/A	BMW 3.0 CSL	114.516
1974	TC	Jean Xhenceval/Alain Peltier/Pierre Dieudonne	B	BMW 3.0 CSL	102.376
1975	TC	Pierre Dieudonne/Jean Xhenceval/Hugues de Fierlandt	B	BMW 3.0 CSL	110.018
1976	TC	Jean-Marie Detrin/Nino Demuth/"Chavan"	F/D/B	BMW 3.0 CSL	105.840
1977	TC	Eddy Joosen/Jean-Claude Andruet	B/F	BMW 530i	105.730
1978	TC	Gordon Spice/Teddy Pilette	GB/B	Ford Capri	111.732
1979	TC	Jean-Michel Martin/Philippe Martin	B	Ford Capri	79.846
1980	TC	Jean-Michel Martin/Philippe Martin	B	Ford Capri	76.437
1981	TC W+	Pierre Dieudonne/Tom Walkinshaw	B/GB	Mazda RX-7	82.308
1982	TC	Hans Heyer/Armin Hahne/Eddy Joosen	D/D/B	BMW 528i	81.270
1983	TC	Thierry Tassin/Hans Heyer/Armin Hahne	B/D/D	BMW 635 CSi	86.293
1984	TC	Tom Walkinshaw/Hans Heyer/Win Percy	GB/D/GB	Jaguar XJ-S	81.456
1985	TC	Roberto Ravaglia/Gerhard Berger/Marc Surer	I/A/CH	BMW 635 CSi	89.807
1986	TC	Dieter Quester/Thierry Tassin/Altfrid Heger	A/B/D	BMW 635 CSi	89.738
1987	TC	Jean-Michel Martin/Eric van de Poele/Didier Theys	B	BMW M3	86.330
1988	TC	Altfrid Heger/Dieter Quester/Roberto Ravaglia	D/A/I	BMW M3	91.299
1989	TC	Gianfranco Brancatelli/Bernd Schneider/Win Percy	I/D/GB	Ford Sierra RS500	86.454
1990	TC	Fabien Giroix/Johnny Cecotto/Markus Oestreich	F/YV/D	BMW M3	93.390
1991	TC	Anders Olofsson/David Brabham/Naoki Hattori	S/AUS/J	Nissan Skyline GT-R	92.870
1992	TC	Steve Soper/Jean-Michel Martin/Christian Danner	GB/B/D	BMW M3	92.550
1993#	TC	Christian Fittipaldi/Jean-Pierre Jarier/Uwe Alzen	BR/F/D	Porsche RSR	89.900
1994	TC	Roberto Ravaglia/Thierry Tassin/Alex Burgstaller	I/B/D	BMW 318i	93.870
1995	TC	Peter Kox/Steve Soper/Joachim Winkelhock	NL/GB/D	BMW 320i	93.540
1996	TC	Jorg Muller/Thierry Tassin/Alex Burgstaller	D/B/D	BMW 320i	90.700
1997	TC	Didier de Radigues/Marc Duez/Eric Helary	B/B/F	BMW 318i	87.153
1998	TC	Alain Cudini/Marc Duez/Eric van de Poele	F/B/B	BMW 320i	86.588
1999	TC	Frederic Bouvy/Emmanuel Collard/Anthony Beltoise	B/F/F	Peugeot 306 GTi	88.550
2000	TC	Frederic Bouvy/Didier Defourny/Kurt Mollekens	B	Peugeot 306 GTi	86.140
2001	GT FIA	Christophe Bouchut/Jean-Philippe Belloc/Marc Duez	F/F/B	Chrysler Viper GTS-R	95.054
2002	GT FIA	Christophe Bouchut/Sebastien Bourdais/ David Terrien/Vincent Vosse	F/F/F/B	Chrysler Viper GTS-R	94.446

*10 hours, #15 hours, +a round of the World Sports Car Championship

EUROPEAN FORMULA 2 RACE

year	formula	winner	nat	car	mph
1981	F2 E	Geoff Lees	GB	Ralt RH6/81-Honda	111.323
1982	F2 E	Thierry Boutsen	B	Spirit 201-Honda	102.557

EUROPEAN FORMULA 3000 RACE

year	formula	winner	nat	car	mph
1985	F3000 INT	Mike Thackwell	NZ	Ralt RB20-Cosworth	104.434
1986	F3000 INT	Philippe Alliot	F	March 86B-Cosworth	116.889
1987	F3000 INT	Michel Trolle	F	Lola T87/50-Cosworth	106.393
1989	F3000 INT	Jean Alesi	F	Reynard 89D-Mugen	115.570
1991	F3000 INT	Emanuele Naspetti	I	Reynard 91D-Cosworth	118.785
1992	F3000 INT	Andrea Montermini	I	Reynard 92D-Cosworth	120.200
1993	F3000 INT	Olivier Panis	F	Reynard 93D-Cosworth	121.101
1994	F3000 INT	Jules Boullion	F	Reynard 94D-Cosworth	98.456
1995	F3000 INT	Vincenzo Sospiri	I	Reynard 95D-Cosworth	123.145
1996	F3000 INT	Jorg Muller	D	Lola T96/50-Zytek	118.035
1997	F3000 INT	Jason Watt	DK	Lola T96/50-Zytek	115.321
1998	F3000 INT	Gonzalo Rodriguez	ROU	Lola T96/50-Zytek	119.231
1999	F3000 INT	Jason Watt	DK	Lola B99/50-Zytek	105.357
2000	F3000 INT	Fernando Alonso	E	Lola B99/50-Zytek	114.452
2001	F3000 INT	Ricardo Sperafico	BR	Lola B99/50-Zytek	110.282
2002	F3000 INT	Giorgio Pantano	I	Lola B2/50-Zytek	120.932

SPA GRAND PRIX

year	formula	winner	nat	car	mph
1954	SC	Davids	NL	Jaguar XK120C	95.390
1955	SC	Paul Frere	B	Aston Martin DB3S	107.800
1956	SC	Ninian Sanderson	GB	Jaguar D-type	109.640
1957	SC	Tony Brooks	GB	Aston Martin	103.950
1958	SC	Masten Gregory	USA	Lister-Jaguar	121.230
1959	SC	Carel Godin de Beaufort	NL	Porsche RSK	110.799
1960	SC	Paul Frere	B	Porsche	97.450
1961	GT	Willy Mairesse	B	Ferrari	121.000
1962	GT	Edgar Berney	CH	Ferrari	108.740
1963	GT	Willy Mairesse	B	Ferrari 250GTO	119.260
1964	GT W*	Michael Parkes	GB	Ferrari 250GTO	124.427
1965	GT W*	Willy Mairesse	B	Ferrari 250LM	126.359

*a round of the World Sports Car Championship

WORLD SPORTS CAR RACE/SPA 1000 KMS

year	formula	winner	nat	car	mph
1966	SC W	Michael Parkes/Ludovico Scarfiotti	GB/I	Ferrari 330P3	131.693
1967	SC W	Jacky Ickx/Dick Thompson	B/USA	Mirage Mk1-Ford	120.481
1968	SC W	Jacky Ickx/Brian Redman	B/GB	Ford GT40	120.516
1969	SC W	Jo Siffert/Brian Redman	CH/GB	Porsche 908/8	141.196
1970	SC W	Jo Siffert/Brian Redman	CH/GB	Porsche 917	149.409
1971	SC W	Pedro Rodriguez/Jackie Oliver	MEX/GB	Porsche 917K	154.759
1972	SC W	Brian Redman/Arturo Merzario	GB/I	Ferrari 312P	145.042
1973	SC W	Derek Bell/Mike Hailwood	GB	Mirage M6-Ford	151.885
1974	SC W	Jacky Ickx/Jean-Pierre Jarier	B/F	Matra-Simca MS670C	147.950
1975	SC W	Henri Pescarolo/Derek Bell	F/GB	Alfa Romeo T33TT/12	133.324
1982	SC W	Jacky Ickx/Jochen Mass	B/D	Porsche 956	102.244
1983	SC W	Jacky Ickx/Jochen Mass	B/D	Porsche 956	108.274
1984	SC W	Stefan Bellof/Derek Bell	D/GB	Porsche 956	105.599
1985	SC W	Bob Wollek/Mauro Baldi/Riccardo Patrese	F/I/I	Lancia LC2	105.220
1986	SC W	Thierry Boutsen/Frank Jelinski	B/D	Porsche 962C	111.833
1987	SC W	Martin Brundle/Johnny Dumfries/Raul Boesel	GB/GB/BR	Jaguar XJR-8	101.974
1988	SC W	Mauro Baldi/Stefan Johansson	I/S	Sauber C9/88-Mercedes-Benz	101.607
1989	SC W	Mauro Baldi/Kenneth Acheson	I/GB	Sauber C9/88-Mercedes-Benz	113.706
1990	SC W	Jochen Mass/Karl Wendlinger	D/A	Mercedes-Benz C11	111.165

FIA GT RACE

year	formula	winner	nat	car	mph
1994	GT FIA	Michel Ferte/Michel Neugarten	F/B	Venturi 600LM	94.454
1996	GT FIA	Thierry Boutsen/Hans-Joachim Stuck	B/D	Porsche 911 GT1	107.336
1997	GT FIA	JJ Lehto/Steve Soper	SF/GB	McLaren F1 GTR-BMW	108.443
2001	GT FIA*	Jean-Philippe Belloc/Christophe Bouchut/Marc Duez	F/F/B	Chrysler Viper GTS-R	95.054
2002	GT FIA*	Christophe Bouchut/Sebastien Bourdais/David Terrien/Vincent Vosse	F/F/F/B	Chrysler Viper GTS-R	94.446

*Spa 24 hours

ZOLDER

Zolder will always be remembered as the circuit at which Gilles Villeneuve died during qualifying for the 1982 Belgian Grand Prix. A memorial stands above the pits as a constant reminder. Even before 1982 it was an unloved venue – narrow, rough, hard on brakes and littered with chicanes. Zolder was renovated in 1986, adding another chicane at the point where Villeneuve crashed. The FIA GT and Euro (formerly Italian) F3000 Championships are among the international series still visiting the track.

Active years 1965 to date
Location 6 miles north-west of Hasselt, 35 miles east of Brussels, 40 miles south-east of Antwerp

Type Permanent road course
Website www.circuit-zolder.be

Current circuit
Lap distance 2.606 miles
Lap record Race: Thomas Biagi (Lola T96/50-Zytek), 1m25.919, 109.192 mph, F3000, 2001

Circuit changes
1965-72 2.601 miles
1973-74 Chicane built behind the pits. 2.622 miles
1975-85 Jack Ickx-bocht tightened. 2.648 miles
1986-95 First corner eased, Villeneuve chicane built at Terlamenbocht, 2.606 miles
1996 to date Chicane, Villeneuve and Ickx corners reprofiled. Current circuit

ZOLDER

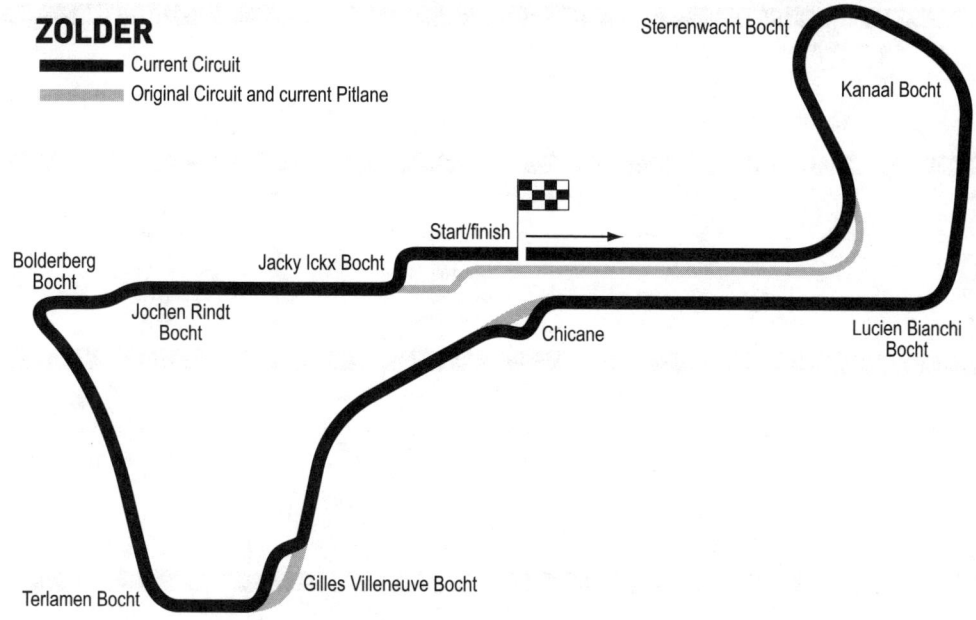

Belgian Grand Prix see above

EUROPEAN FORMULA 3 RACE

year	formula	winner	nat	car	mph
1977	F3 E	Piercarlo Ghinzani	I	March 773-Toyota	93.748
1978	F3 E	Teo Fabi	I	March 783-Toyota	78.357
1979	F3 E	Alain Prost	F	Martini MK27-Renault	98.906
1980	F3 E	Thierry Boutsen	B	Martini MK31-Toyota	95.201
	F3 E	Philippe Streiff	F	Martini MK31-Toyota	100.839
1981	F3 E	Mauro Baldi	I	March 813-Alfa Romeo	102.901
1982	F3 E	Oscar Larrauri	RA	Euroracing 101-Alfa Romeo	101.655
1983	F3 E	Emanuele Pirro	I	Ralt RT3/83-Alfa Romeo	102.348
1984	F3 E	John Nielsen	DK	Ralt RT3/84-Volkswagen	102.885

EUROPEAN FORMULA 2 RACE

year	formula	winner	nat	car	mph
1975	F2 E	Michel Leclere	F	March 752-BMW	104.784
1980	F2 E	Huub Rothengatter	NL	Toleman TG280-Hart	107.725
1983	F2 E	Jonathan Palmer	GB	Ralt RH6/83-Honda	110.399

INTERNATIONAL FORMULA 3000 RACE

year	formula	winner	nat	car	mph
1988	F3000 INT	Olivier Grouillard	F	Lola T88/50-Cosworth	104.234

FIA GT RACE

year	formula	winner	nat	car	mph
1999	GT FIA	Olivier Beretta/Karl Wendlinger	MC/A	Chrysler Viper GTS-R	91.932
2000	GT FIA	Julian Bailey/Jamie Campbell-Walter	GB	Lister Storm GT	93.131
2001	GT FIA	Jean-Philippe Belloc/Christophe Bouchut	F	Chrysler Viper GTS-R	82.246

BRAZIL
Major Championships

TEMPORADA GT TROPHY

year	driver	nat	team	car
1996	Nelson Piquet/Johnny Cecotto	BR/YV	Bigazzi	McLaren F1-GTR-BMW

TORNEIO FORMULA 2 CHAMPIONSHIP

Brazil's equivalent to the Argentinian Temporada

year	driver	nat	team	car
1971	Emerson Fittipaldi	BR	Team Bardahl	Lotus 69-Ford
1972	Emerson Fittipaldi	BR	Team Lotus	Lotus 69-Ford

BRAZILIAN FORMULA 3 CHAMPIONSHIP

year	driver	nat	team	car
1989	Christian Fittipaldi	BR	Fittipaldi	Reynard 883-Alfa Romeo
1990	Osvaldo Negri Jr	BR	Dacar	Ralt RT32-Volkswagen
1991	Marcos Gueiros	BR	Cesario Formula	Ralt RT32-Mugen
1992	Marcos Gueiros	BR	Cesario Formula	Ralt RT33-Mugen
1993	Fernando Croceri	RA	Cesario Formula	Ralt RT34-Mugen
1994	Cristiano da Matta	BR	Cesario Formula	Dallara 394-Mugen

BRAZILIAN TOURING CAR CHAMPIONSHIP

year	driver	nat	car
1988	Andreas Mattheis	BR	Volkswagen Passat 1.6 turbo
1989	Gunnar Volmer/Antonio da Matta	BR	Volkswagen Passat 1.6
1990	Andreas Mattheis/Ricardo Cosac	BR	Volkswagen Passat 1.6
1991	Paulo Gomes/Claudio Girotto	BR	Volkswagen Passat Voyage 1.6
1992	Andreas Mattheis/Paulo Judice	BR	Ford Escort 1.6
1993	Andreas Mattheis/Paulo Judice	BR	Ford Escort 1.8
1994	Egon Herzfeld/Vicente Daudt	BR	Ford Escort 1.

BRAZILIAN STOCK CAR CHAMPIONSHIP

year	driver	nat	car
1979	Paulo Gomes	BR	Chevrolet Opala
1980	Ingo Hoffmann	BR	Chevrolet Opala
1981	Affonso Giaffone Sr	BR	Chevrolet Opala
1982	"Alencar Jr"	BR	Chevrolet Opala
1983	Paulo Gomes	BR	Chevrolet Opala
1984	Paulo Gomes	BR	Chevrolet Opala
1985	Ingo Hoffmann	BR	Chevrolet Opala
1986	Marcos Gracia	BR	Chevrolet Opala
1987	Jose "Zeca" Giaffone	BR	Chevrolet Opala
1988	Fabio Sotto Mayor	BR	Chevrolet Opala
1989	Ingo Hoffmann	BR	Chevrolet Opala
1990	Ingo Hoffmann	BR	Chevrolet Opala
1991	Ingo Hoffmann/Angelo Giombelli	BR	Chevrolet Opala
1992	Ingo Hoffmann/Angelo Giombelli	BR	Chevrolet Opala
1993	Ingo Hoffmann/Angelo Giombelli	BR	Chevrolet Opala
1994	Ingo Hoffmann	BR	Chevrolet Omega
1995	Paulo Gomes	BR	Chevrolet Omega
1996	Ingo Hoffmann	BR	Chevrolet Omega
1997	Ingo Hoffmann	BR	Chevrolet Omega
1998	Ingo Hoffmann	BR	Chevrolet Omega
1999	Chico Serra	BR	Chevrolet Omega
2000	Chico Serra	BR	Fernandez-Chevrolet
2001	Chico Serra	BR	Fernandez-Chevrolet
2002	Ingo Hoffmann	BR	Fernandez-Chevrolet

Major International Races

BRAZILIAN GRAND PRIX

year	formula	circuit	winner	nat	car	mph
1972	F1	Interlagos	Carlos Reutemann	RA	Brabham BT34-Ford	112.882
1973	F1 W	Interlagos	Emerson Fittipaldi	BR	Lotus 72D-Ford	114.219
1974	F1 W	Interlagos	Emerson Fittipaldi	BR	McLaren M23-Ford	112.226
1975	F1 W	Interlagos	Carlos Pace	BR	Brabham BT44B-Ford	113.390
1976	F1 W	Interlagos	Niki Lauda	A	Ferrari 312T	112.751
1977	F1 W	Interlagos	Carlos Reutemann	RA	Ferrari 312T2	112.913
1978	F1 W	Rio de Janeiro	Carlos Reutemann	RA	Ferrari 312T2	107.423
1979	F1 W	Interlagos	Jacques Laffite	F	Ligier JS11-Ford	118.514
1980	F1 W	Interlagos	Rene Arnoux	F	Renault RE20	117.406
1981	F1 W	Rio de Janeiro	Carlos Reutemann	RA	Williams FW07C-Ford	96.589
1982	F1 W	Rio de Janeiro	Alain Prost	F	Renault RE30B	113.018
1983	F1 W	Rio de Janeiro	Nelson Piquet	BR	Brabham BT52-BMW	108.944

BRAZILIAN GRAND PRIX (cont.)

year	forumula	circuit	winner	nat	car	mph
1984	F1 W	Rio de Janeiro	Alain Prost	F	McLaren MP4/2-TAG Porsche	111.540
1985	F1 W	Rio de Janeiro	Alain Prost	F	McLaren MP4/2B-TAG Porsche	112.793
1986	F1 W	Rio de Janeiro	Nelson Piquet	BR	Williams FW11-Honda	114.937
1987	F1 W	Rio de Janeiro	Alain Prost	F	McLaren MP4/3-TAG Porsche	114.696
1988	F1 W	Rio de Janeiro	Alain Prost	F	McLaren MP4/4-Honda	117.086
1989	F1 W	Rio de Janeiro	Nigel Mansell	GB	Ferrari 640	115.592
1990	F1 W	Interlagos	Alain Prost	F	Ferrari 641	117.577
1991	F1 W	Interlagos	Ayrton Senna	BR	McLaren MP4/6-Honda	116.246
1992	F1 W	Interlagos	Nigel Mansell	GB	Williams FW14B-Renault	118.172
1993	F1 W	Interlagos	Ayrton Senna	BR	McLaren MP4/8-Ford	102.883
1994	F1 W	Interlagos	Michael Schumacher	D	Benetton B194-Ford	127.694
1995	F1 W	Interlagos	Michael Schumacher	D	Benetton B195-Renault	115.263
1996	F1 W	Interlagos	Damon Hill	GB	Williams FW18-Renault	103.396
1997	F1 W	Interlagos	Jacques Villeneuve	CDN	Williams FW19-Renault	119.870
1998	F1 W	Interlagos	Mika Hakkinen	SF	McLaren MP4/13-Mercedes-Benz	118.538
1999	F1 W	Interlagos	Mika Hakkinen	SF	McLaren MP4/14-Mercedes-Benz	117.490
2000	F1 W	Interlagos	Michael Schumacher	D	Ferrari F1-2000	124.049
2001	F1 W	Interlagos	David Coulthard	GB	McLaren MP4/16-Mercedes-Benz	114.746
2002	F1 W	Interlagos	Michael Schumacher	D	Ferrari F2002	123.860

Circuits and Other Races

BRASILIA
Circuito Nelson Piquet

A modern racing facility built at a reputed cost of $3.5 million and opened in 1974. The inaugural non-championship Presidenta Medici GP attracted a crowd of 85,000, but sadly this proved to be one of the few international races held there. The three-time World Champion Nelson Piquet has been retained as President with the goal of bringing international racing back to the capital. Brasilia hosted a round of the one-off Temporada GT series in 1996, but the venue is more normally used for South American championship races.

Active years	1974 to date
Location	North-east of downtown Brasilia
Type	Permanent road course
Lap distance	3.402 miles
Lap record	Race: Ricardo Sperafico (Dallara 394-Mugen), 1m47.651, 113.768 mph, F3, 1999

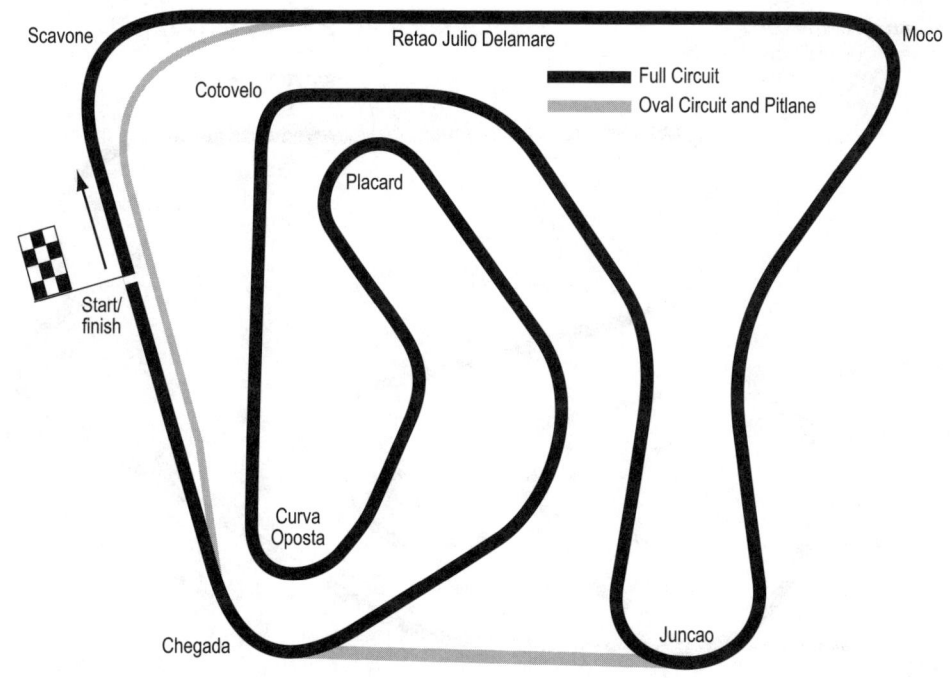

INTERLAGOS

Autodromo Jose Carlos Pace

Opened in 1940, Interlagos was a magnificent facility, with a first corner as testing as any in Grand Prix racing. The track followed a tortuous course, winding back on itself in a natural bowl among the smog-filled suburbs of Sao Paulo. When the Brazilian Grand Prix returned in 1990, it was held on a reduced but still demanding configuration. The new Senna "S" had replaced the first corner, and two more link roads had reduced the length from 4.946 to 2.687 miles. This was Ayrton Senna country, and when he spun out of the 1994 race the disappointed crowd filed home. Rubens Barrichello, who grew up within sight of the circuit, has attempted to fill the void left by Senna's death, qualifying on the front row in 1996 and leading convincingly in 1999.

Active years	1940 to date
Location	9 miles south of Sao Paulo
Type	Permanent road course
Website	www.ainterlagos.com

Current circuit	
Lap distance	2.667 miles
Lap records	Qualifying: Juan Pablo Montoya (Williams FW24-BMW), 1m13.114, 131.319 mph, F1, 2002
	Race: Michael Schumacher (Ferrari F1-2000), 1m14.755, 128.436 mph, F1, 2000

Circuit changes

1940-79	4.946 miles
1980-89	First corner tightened. 4.893 miles
1990 to date	New circuit built using sections of the old circuit. Current circuit

ORIGINAL CIRCUIT

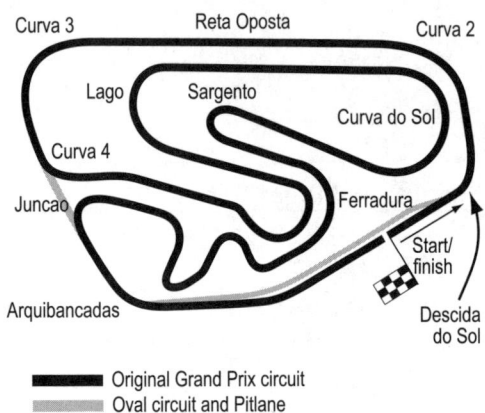

Original Grand Prix circuit
Oval circuit and Pitlane

GRAND PRIX CIRCUIT

Grand Prix circuit
Original circuit and Pitlane

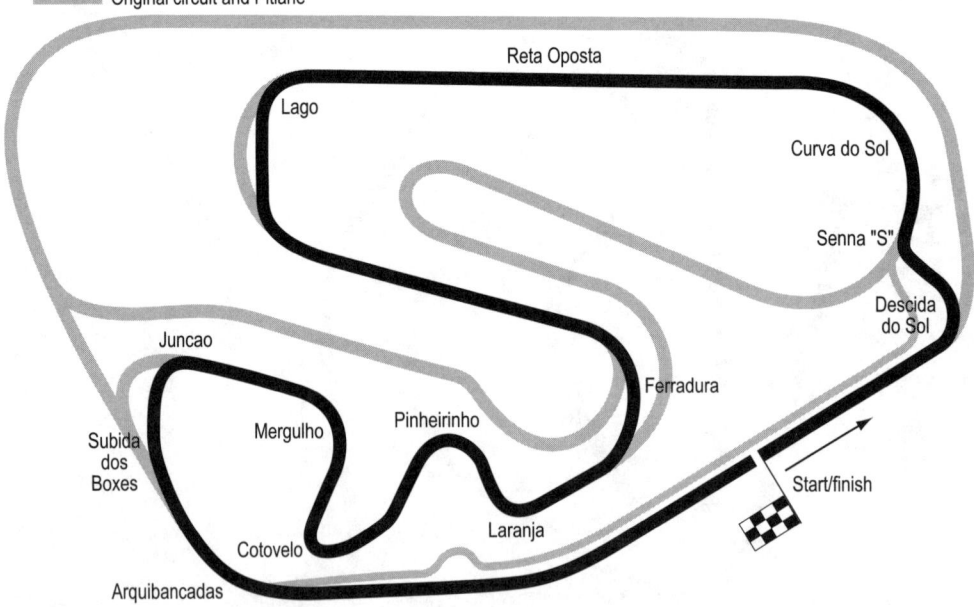

Brazilian Grand Prix see above

TORNEIO FORMULA 2 RACES					
year	formula	winner	nat	car	mph
1971	F2	Emerson Fittipaldi	BR	Lotus 69-Ford	108.100
	F2	Emerson Fittipaldi	BR	Lotus 69-Ford	105.934
1972	F2	Emerson Fittipaldi	BR	Lotus 69-Ford	109.729
	F2	Carlos Pace	BR	Surtees TS15-Ford	111.274
	F2	Mike Hailwood	GB	Surtees TS10-Ford	110.684

INTERNATIONAL FORMULA 3000 RACE					
year	formula	winner	nat	car	mph
2001	F3000 INT	Justin Wilson	GB	Lola B99/50-Zytek	104.086
2002	F3000 INT	Rodrigo Sperafico	BR	Lola B2/50-Zytek	104.866

RIO DE JANEIRO

Jacarepagua

Built on a reclaimed marsh adjacent to the Lagao de Jacarepagua, Rio's circuit is as uninspiring as Interlagos is demanding. The Grand Prix circuit is flat, with constant radius corners and a long back straight. Races were normally run in stifling heat and humidity. But Alain Prost must have enjoyed it, winning half of the ten Brazilian Grands Prix held here before the race returned to Interlagos. In 1996 Emerson Fittipaldi helped negotiate a round of the CART Champcar World Series on the "modified oval" that bears his name. Despite the number of Brazilians in the series, a dispute over money forced the late cancellation of the 2001 race, and Rio's international future is uncertain.

Active years	1977 to date
Location	20 miles west of central Rio de Janeiro
Type	Permanent road course

Grand Prix circuit (Autodromo Nelson Piquet)
Lap distance   3.126 miles
Lap records   Qualifying: Ayrton Senna (McLaren MP4/5-Honda), 1m25.302, 131.927 mph, F1, 1989
Race: Riccardo Patrese (Williams FW12C-Renault), 1m32.507, 121.652 mph, F1, 1989

Oval (Emerson Fittipaldi Speedway)
Lap distance   1.864 miles
Lap records   Qualifying: Christian Fittipaldi (Swift 010i-Ford), 38.565s, 174.002 mph, CART, 1999
Race: Juan Pablo Montoya (Reynard 99I-Honda), 38.891s, 172.545 mph, CART, 1999

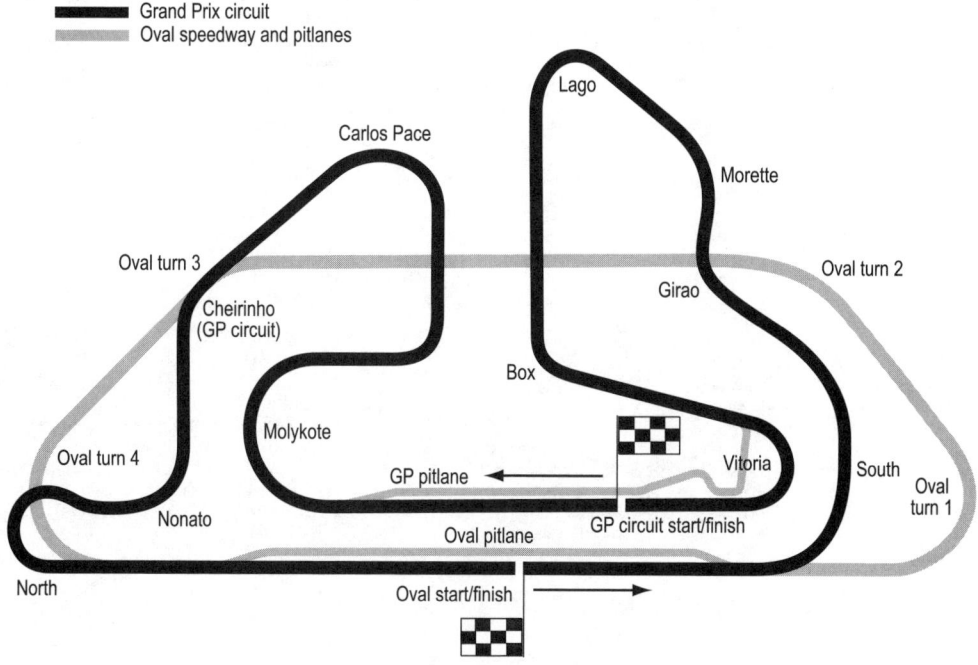

Grand Prix circuit
Oval speedway and pitlanes

Brazilian Grand Prix see above

CHAMPCAR RACE

year	formula	winner	nat	car	mph
1996	CART	Andre Ribeiro	BR	Lola T96/00-Honda	117.927
1997	CART	Paul Tracy	CDN	Penske PC26-Mercedes-Benz	113.721
1998	CART	Greg Moore	CDN	Reynard 98I-Mercedes-Benz	132.531
1999	CART	Juan Pablo Montoya	CO	Reynard 99I-Honda	125.120
2000	CART	Adrian Fernandez	MEX	Reynard 2KI-Ford	124.256

CANADA
Major Championships

Can-Am Challenge see page 552
Formula Atlantic see United States

Major International Races

CANADIAN GRAND PRIX

year	formula	circuit	winner	nat	car	mph
1961	SC	Mosport Park	Pete Ryan	CDN	Lotus 19-Climax	88.380
1962	SC	Mosport Park	Masten Gregory	USA	Lotus 19-Climax	88.520
1963	SC	Mosport Park	Pedro Rodriguez	MEX	Ferrari 250P	91.550
1964	SC	Mosport Park	Pedro Rodriguez	MEX	Ferrari 330P	94.360
1965	SC	Mosport Park	Jim Hall	USA	Chaparral 2B-Chevrolet	93.780
1966	Can-Am	Mosport Park	Mark Donohue	USA	Lola T70-Chevrolet	101.870
1967	F1 W	Mosport Park	Jack Brabham	AUS	Brabham BT24-Repco	82.647
1968	F1 W	St Jovite	Denny Hulme	NZ	McLaren M7A-Ford	97.223
1969	F1 W	Mosport Park	Jacky Ickx	B	Brabham BT26-Ford	111.185
1970	F1 W	St Jovite	Jacky Ickx	B	Ferrari 312B	101.269
1971	F1 W	Mosport Park	Jackie Stewart	GB	Tyrrell 003-Ford	81.956
1972	F1 W	Mosport Park	Jackie Stewart	GB	Tyrrell 005-Ford	114.282
1973	F1 W	Mosport Park	Peter Revson	USA	McLaren M23-Ford	99.130
1974	F1 W	Mosport Park	Emerson Fittipaldi	BR	McLaren M23-Ford	117.520
1976	F1 W	Mosport Park	James Hunt	GB	McLaren M23-Ford	117.843
1977	F1 W	Mosport Park	Jody Scheckter	ZA	Wolf WR1-Ford	118.032
1978	F1 W	Montreal	Gilles Villeneuve	CDN	Ferrari 312T3	99.671
1979	F1 W	Montreal	Alan Jones	AUS	Williams FW07-Ford	105.577
1980	F1 W	Montreal	Alan Jones	AUS	Williams FW07B-Ford	107.794
1981	F1 W	Montreal	Jacques Laffite	F	Ligier JS17-Matra	85.301
1982	F1 W	Montreal	Nelson Piquet	BR	Brabham BT50-BMW	107.895
1983	F1 W	Montreal	Rene Arnoux	F	Ferrari 126C2B	106.035
1984	F1 W	Montreal	Nelson Piquet	BR	Brabham BT53-BMW	108.162
1985	F1 W	Montreal	Michele Alboreto	I	Ferrari 156/85	108.535
1986	F1 W	Montreal	Nigel Mansell	GB	Williams FW11-Honda	110.734
1988	F1 W	Montreal	Ayrton Senna	BR	McLaren MP4/4-Honda	113.192
1989	F1 W	Montreal	Thierry Boutsen	B	Williams FW12C-Renault	93.030
1990	F1 W	Montreal	Ayrton Senna	BR	McLaren MP4/5B-Honda	111.304
1991	F1 W	Montreal	Nelson Piquet	BR	Benetton B191-Ford	115.291
1992	F1 W	Montreal	Gerhard Berger	A	McLaren MP4/7A-Honda	117.332
1993	F1 W	Montreal	Alain Prost	F	Williams FW15C-Renault	117.867
1994	F1 W	Montreal	Michael Schumacher	D	Benetton B194-Ford	109.509
1995	F1 W	Montreal	Jean Alesi	F	Ferrari 412T2	107.465
1996	F1 W	Montreal	Damon Hill	GB	Williams FW18-Renault	118.393
1997	F1 W	Montreal	Michael Schumacher	D	Ferrari F310B	114.580
1998	F1 W	Montreal	Michael Schumacher	D	Ferrari F300	112.649
1999	F1 W	Montreal	Mika Hakkinen	SF	McLaren MP4/14-Mercedes-Benz	111.940
2000	F1 W	Montreal	Michael Schumacher	D	Ferrari F1-2000	112.371
2001	F1 W	Montreal	Ralf Schumacher	D	Williams FW23-BMW	120.312
2002	F1 W	Montreal	Michael Schumacher	D	Ferrari F2002	121.286

Circuits and Other Races

MONTREAL
Circuit Gilles Villeneuve

In 1978, with Quebec's Gilles Villeneuve becoming a major star, and safety concerns over Mosport Park increasing, a new circuit on Montreal's man-made Ile de Notre Dame was prepared in record time for the Canadian GP. Villeneuve provided the perfect start by winning his first Grand Prix at the inaugural race, and the circuit was later renamed in his honour after he died at Zolder in 1982. Sadly, that year's Canadian GP was also marred by tragedy, when Ricardo Paletti was killed in a horrific start-line accident. In 1995 Jean Alesi scored his only win here in the number 27 Ferrari made famous by Villeneuve. In recent years the exit to the final corner has seen Michael Schumacher, Jacques Villeneuve and others crash into the so-called champions wall. Montreal also hosted a sports car race in 1990 and Dario Franchitti won the first Champcar race held here in 2002.

Active years	1978 to date
Location	Ile de Notre Dame in the St Lawrence Seaway, eastern Montreal
Type	Temporary road course
Website	www.grandprix.ca

Current circuit

Lap distance	2.703 miles
Lap records	Qualifying: Juan Pablo Montoya (Williams FW24-BMW), 1m12.836, 133.599 mph, F1, 2002
	Race: Juan Pablo Montoya (Williams FW24-BMW), 1m15.960, 128.104 mph, F1, 2002

Circuit changes

1978	2.796 miles
1979-87	Chicane after the start and pit lane modified. 2.740 miles
1988-90	New pits and start-line moved. 2.728 miles
1991-93	Pit lane entrance modified. 2.753 miles
1994-95	Chicane built on old pit-lane before Esses. 2.765 miles
1996-2001	Chicane on old pit lane bypassed. 2.747 miles
2002 to date	Increased run-off areas created at first corner and final hairpin by re-profiling corners. Current circuit

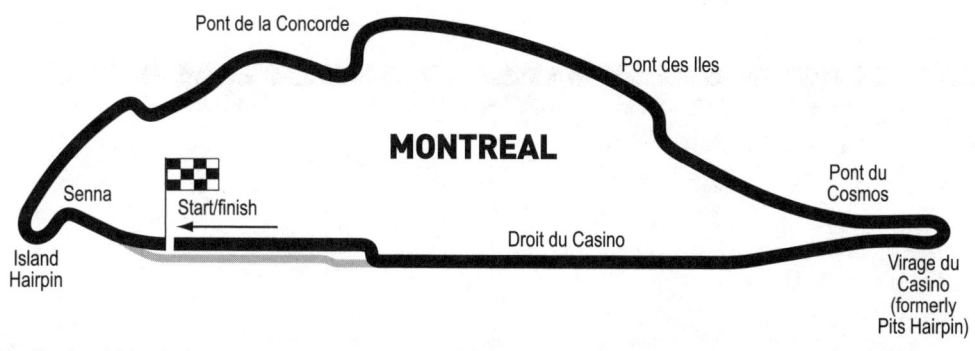

Canadian Grand Prix see above

WORLD SPORTS CAR RACE						
year	formula	winner	nat	car		mph
1990	SC W	Mauro Baldi/Jean-Louis Schlesser	I/F	Mercedes-Benz C11		95.363

MOLSON INDY MONTREAL						
year	formula	winner	nat	car		mph
2002	CART	Dario Franchitti	GB	Lola B2/00-Honda		108.407

MOSPORT PARK

Mosport Park is a beautiful and sweeping circuit that held the first international race in Canada when Stirling Moss won the 1961 Player's 200. It was always renowned as a driver's circuit, although changeable weather marred many a race. By the late seventies the circuit's lack of run-off areas made its safety questionable, and the Canadian Grand Prix moved to Montreal. The World Sports Cars Championship also left after Manfred Winkelhock was killed in 1985. Although international racing returned with the American Le Mans Series after Don Panoz bought the circuit in 1998, safety remains an issue at Mosport. The death of Mike Gagliardo in the 2001 Trans-Am race illustrates why organisers are currently increasing run-off areas and improving safety features.

Active years	1961 to date
Location	8 miles north of Bowmanville, Ontario, 45 miles east of Toronto
Type	Permanent road course
Website	www.mosport.com
Lap distance	2.459 miles
Lap record	Qualifying: Frank Biela (Audi R8), 1m07.169, 131.793 mph, ALMS Sports Cars, 2002
	Race: Tom Kristensen (Audi R8), 1m08.444, 129.338 mph, ALMS Sports Cars, 2002

MOSPORT PARK

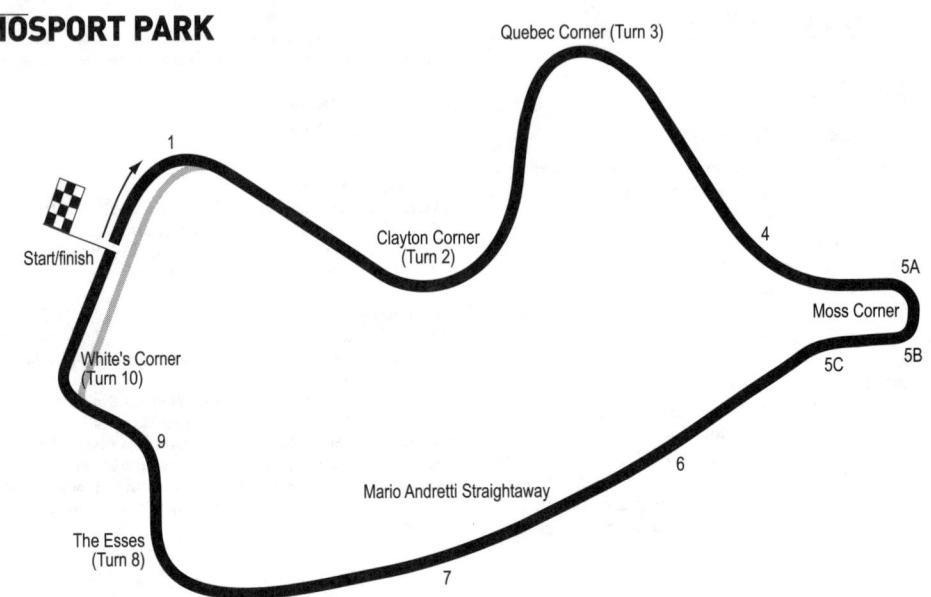

Quebec Corner (Turn 3)

1

Start/finish

Clayton Corner
(Turn 2)

4

5A

Moss Corner

5B

White's Corner
(Turn 10)

5C

9

6

Mario Andretti Straightaway

The Esses
(Turn 8)

7

Canadian Grand Prix see above

PLAYER'S 200/CAN-AM RACE

year	formula	winner	nat	car	mph
1961	SC	Stirling Moss	GB	Lotus	86.740
1962	SC	Masten Gregory	USA	Lotus	90.270
1963	SC	Chuck Daigh	USA	Lotus 19-Climax	90.930
1964	SC	Bruce McLaren	NZ	Cooper-Oldsmobile	92.510
1965	SC	John Surtees	GB	Lola T70-Chevrolet	96.515
1966	Can-Am	Bruce McLaren	NZ	McLaren Elva-Oldsmobile	101.870
1967	Can-Am	Denny Hulme	NZ	McLaren M6A-Chevrolet	105.926
1969	Can-Am	Bruce McLaren	NZ	McLaren M8B-Chevrolet	105.901
1970	Can-Am	Dan Gurney	USA	McLaren M8D-Chevrolet	110.214
1971	Can-Am	Denny Hulme	NZ	McLaren M8F-Chevrolet	109.330
1972	Can-Am	Denny Hulme	NZ	McLaren M20-Chevrolet	110.660
1973	Can-Am	Charlie Kemp	USA	Porsche 917/10	108.645
1974	Can-Am	Jackie Oliver	GB	Shadow DN4A-Chevrolet	111.990
1976	SC W	Jackie Oliver	GB	Shadow DN4A-Chevrolet	111.393
1977	Can-Am	Patrick Tambay	F	Lola T333CS-Chevrolet	111.819
1978	Can-Am	Alan Jones	AUS	Lola T333CS-Chevrolet	115.374
1979	Can-Am	Jacky Ickx	B	Lola T333CS-Chevrolet	113.673
1980	Can-Am	Patrick Tambay	F	Lola T530-Chevrolet	115.145
1981	Can-Am	Teo Fabi	I	March 817-Chevrolet	115.526
	Can-Am	Teo Fabi	I	March 817-Chevrolet	117.279
1982	Can-Am	Al Unser jr	USA	Frissbee GR3-Chevrolet	110.350
	Can-Am	Al Unser jr	USA	Frissbee GR3-Chevrolet	116.658
1983	Can-Am	Jacques Villeneuve	CDN	Frissbee GR3-Chevrolet	111.780
1983	Can-Am	Jim Crawford	GB	Ensign RK180B-Ford	116.310
1984	Can-Am	Michael Roe	IRL	VDS 002-Chevrolet	95.740
	Can-Am	Michael Roe	IRL	VDS 002-Chevrolet	113.750
1985	Can-Am	Horst Kroll	USA	Frissbee KR3-Chevrolet	95.720
	Can-Am	Rick Miaskiewicz	USA	Frissbee KR3-Chevrolet	103.808
1986	Can-Am	Horst Kroll	USA	Frissbee KR3-Chevrolet	98.380
	Can-Am	Paul Tracy	CDN	Frissbee KR3-Chevrolet	110.175

CHAMPCAR RACE

year	formula	winner	nat	car	mph
1967	USAC	Bobby Unser	USA	Eagle 67-Ford	99.609
	USAC	Bobby Unser	USA	Eagle 67-Ford	n/a
1968	USAC	Dan Gurney	USA	Eagle 68-Ford/Weslake	103.993
	USAC	Dan Gurney	USA	Eagle 68-Ford/Weslake	106.784
1977	USAC	AJ Foyt jr	USA	Coyote-Foyt/Ford	90.723
1978	USAC	Danny Ongais	USA	Parnelli VPJ6B-Cosworth	87.164

WORLD SPORTS CAR RACE

year	formula	winner	nat	car	mph
1976	SC W	Jackie Oliver	GB	Shadow DN4A-Chevrolet	111.393
1977	SC W	Ludwig Heimrath/Paul Miller	CDN/USA	Porsche 934	98.365
1980	SC W	John Fitzpatrick/Brian Redman	GB	Porsche 935-K3	100.354
1981	SC W	Rolf Stommelen/Harald Grohs	D	Porsche 935	93.665
1984	SC W	Jacky Ickx/Jochen Mass	B/D	Porsche 956	103.489
1985	SC W	Derek Bell/Hans-Joachim Stuck	GB/D	Porsche 962C	104.941

SANAIR SUPERSPEEDWAY

Sanair is a strange short tri-oval, which briefly held a round of the Champcar World Series at the behest of the Molson brewery. Rick Mears severely injured his legs here when he crashed during the inaugural 1984 race. Although the circuit was smooth, it was far too tight for Champcars, and Molson switched its sponsorship from Sanair to a new race in Toronto. Now the drag strip is used more often, and Sanair hosts snowmobile races in the winter.

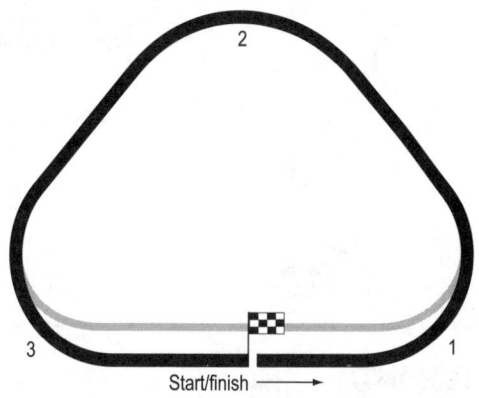

Active years	1984 to date
Location	St Pie, 40 miles east of Montreal
Type	Paved oval
Website	www.sanairracing.com
Lap distance	0.826 miles
Lap record	Qualifying: Rick Mears (Penske PC15-Chevrolet), 20.074s, 148.132 mph, CART, 1986

CHAMPCAR RACE

year	formula	winner	nat	car	mph
1984	CART	Danny Sullivan	USA	Lola T800-Cosworth	111.707
1985	CART	Johnny Rutherford	USA	March 85C-Cosworth	89.996
1986	CART	Bobby Rahal	USA	March 86C-Cosworth	103.157

ST JOVITE

Mont Tremblant

Like Mosport Park, with which it shared the Canadian Grand Prix, St Jovite is a picturesque, undulating road course without a straight worthy of the name. The highlight is Namerow Corner, where cars enter steeply uphill and exit downhill. But the circuit was narrow and bumpy, and when the drivers complained after the 1970 Grand Prix the race did not return. St Jovite was recently bought by clothing magnate Lawrence Stroll, and planned renovations include a new chicane at Turn 2 and a new section replacing Turn 6. The circuit will also be repaved and widened to 11 meters. The lap records established at the final Grand Prix in 1970 were only beaten in autumn 2001, when the United States F3 Championship visited.

Active years	1964-70, 1975 to date
Location	Lake Moore, Quebec, 70 miles north-west of Montreal
Type	Permanent road course
Website	www.lecircuit.com

Current circuit

Lap distance	2.650 miles
Lap record	Qualifying: John C Antonino (Dallara 301-Volkswagen), 1m29.089, 107.084 mph, F3, 2001
	Race: Luciano Gomide (Dallara 300-Volkswagen), 1m29.719, 106.332 mph, F3, 2001

Circuit changes

1964-65	1.5 miles
1966 to date	South Loop built. Current circuit

Canadian Grand Prix see above

CHAMPCAR RACE

year	formula	winner	nat	car	mph
1967	USAC	Mario Andretti	USA	Brawner/Hawk-Ford	87.151
	USAC	Mario Andretti	USA	Brawner/Hawk-Ford	92.401
1968	USAC	Mario Andretti	USA	Brawner/Hawk-Ford	96.492
	USAC	Mario Andretti	USA	Brawner/Hawk-Ford	90.022

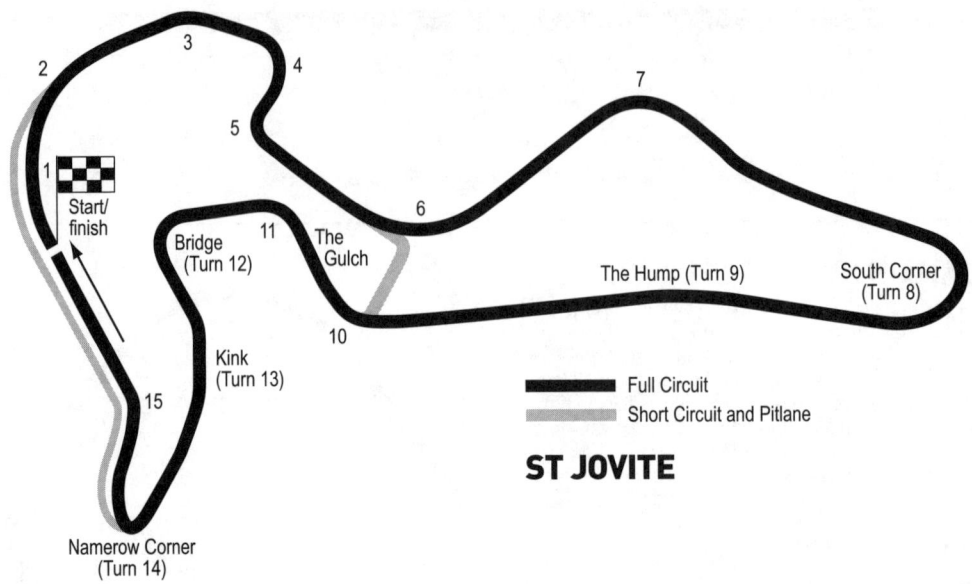

Bridge
(Turn 12)

The
Gulch

The Hump (Turn 9)

South Corner
(Turn 8)

Start/
finish

Kink
(Turn 13)

Namerow Corner
(Turn 14)

Full Circuit
Short Circuit and Pitlane

ST JOVITE

TORONTO

Exhibition Place

Run under the impressive gateway landmark in Exhibition Place, Toronto is a fast circuit that now rivals Long Beach as North America's best street race. Laid out in the grounds of the Canadian National Exhibition, it is a cross between a street circuit and demanding road course – combining the best of both types of venue. Michael Andretti scored his record seventh Toronto victory in the 2001 race.

Active years	1986 to date
Location	Exhibition Place, 1 mile east of downtown Toronto
Type	Temporary road course
Website	www.molsonindy.com
Lap distance	1.755 miles
Lap records	Qualifying: Gil de Ferran (Reynard 99I-Honda), 57.143s, 110.565 mph, CART, 1999
	Race: Cristiano da Matta (Lola B2/00-Toyota), 58.806s, 107.438 mph, CART, 2002

Circuit changes	
1986-96	1.784 miles
1997-98	Final two turns modified. 1.721 miles
1999 to date	Current circuit

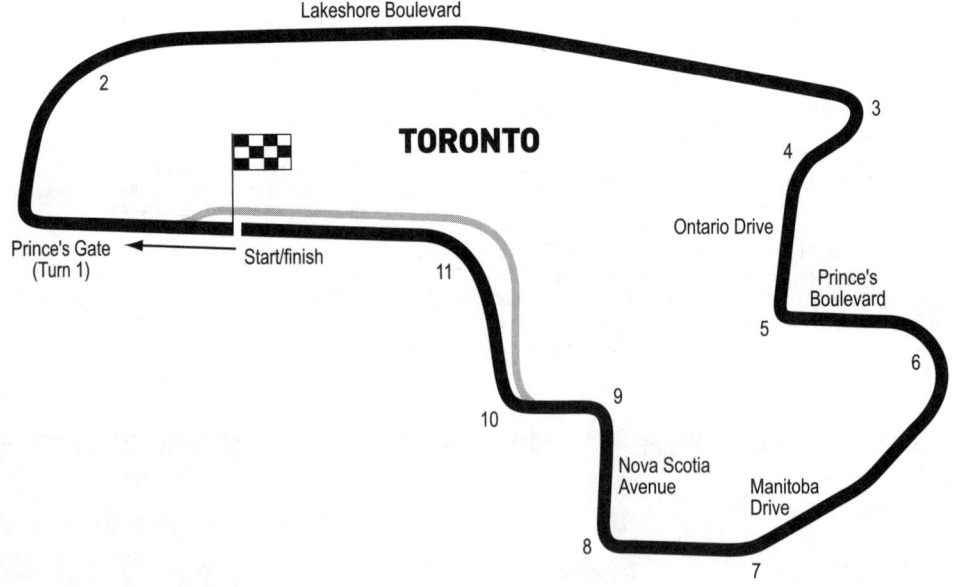

Lakeshore Boulevard

TORONTO

Prince's Gate
(Turn 1)

Start/finish

Ontario Drive

Prince's
Boulevard

Nova Scotia
Avenue

Manitoba
Drive

MOLSON INDY TORONTO

year	formula	winner	nat	car	mph
1986	CART	Bobby Rahal	USA	March 86C-Cosworth	87.414
1987	CART	Emerson Fittipaldi	BR	March 87C-Chevrolet	95.991
1988	CART	Al Unser jr	USA	March 88C-Chevrolet	91.994
1989	CART	Michael Andretti	USA	Lola T89/00-Chevrolet	90.901
1990	CART	Al Unser jr	USA	Lola T90/00-Chevrolet	74.127
1991	CART	Michael Andretti	USA	Lola T91/00-Chevrolet	99.143
1992	CART	Michael Andretti	USA	Lola T92/00-Ford	97.898
1993	CART	Paul Tracy	CDN	Penske PC22-Chevrolet	96.510
1994	CART	Michael Andretti	USA	Reynard 94I-Ford	96.673
1995	CART	Michael Andretti	USA	Lola T95/00-Ford	95.000
1996	CART	Adrian Fernandez	MEX	Lola T96/00-Honda	97.598
1997	CART	Mark Blundell	GB	Reynard 97I-Mercedes-Benz	92.779
1998	CART	Alessandro Zanardi	I	Reynard 98I-Honda	87.274
1999	CART	Dario Franchitti	GB	Reynard 99I-Honda	85.897
2000	CART	Michael Andretti	USA	Lola B2K/00-Ford	98.248
2001	CART	Michael Andretti	USA	Reynard 01I-Honda	83.375
2002	CART	Cristiano da Matta	BR	Lola B2/00-Toyota	93.361

VANCOUVER

After the success of Molson's Toronto race, the brewing giant sponsored a second street race in the vibrant city of Vancouver, British Colombia. The tight nine-turn circuit promoted close-contact racing and many resulting accidents. It was not popular with drivers, who complained about the lack of passing opportunities. A new layout around False Creek was introduced in 1998, using only the pit straight of the old layout.

Active years 1990 to date
Location Adjacent to False Creek in downtown Vancouver's waterfront
Type Temporary street circuit
Website www.molsonindy.com

Current circuit
Lap distance 1.781 miles
Lap records Qualifying: Cristiano da Matta (Lola B2/00-Toyota), 1m00.339, 106.259 mph, CART, 2002
Race: Juan Pablo Montoya (Lola B2K/00-Toyota), 1m01.538, 104.189 mph, CART, 2000

Circuit changes
1990-92	1.648 miles
1993	Turn 1 modified and final two corners combined as a hairpin. 1.677 miles
1994-97	Final hairpin tightened. 1.703 miles
1998	New Concord Pacific Place layout using Expo Boulevard section of old circuit. 1.802 miles
1999 to date	Chicane on Quebec street bypassed. Current circuit

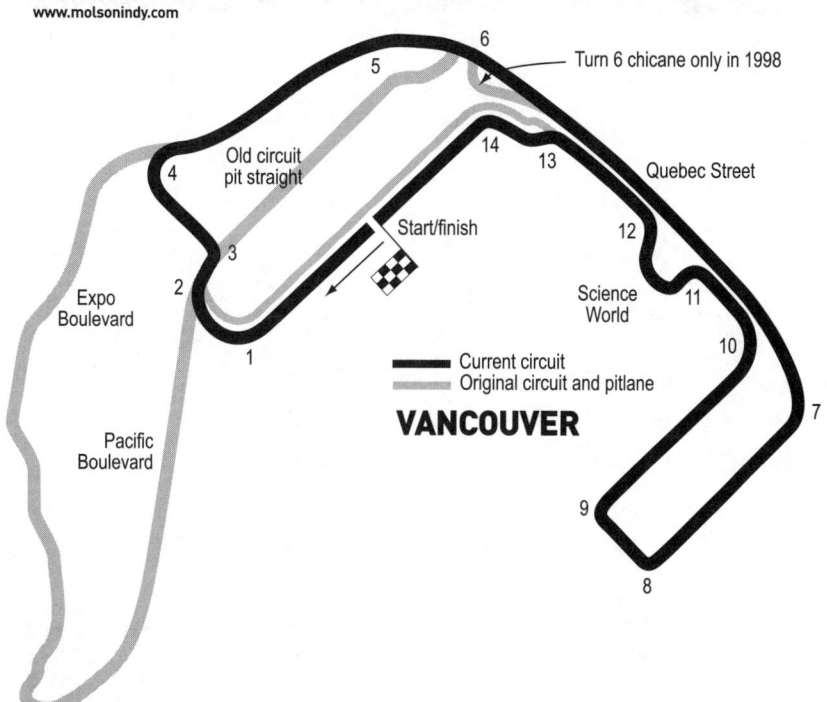

VANCOUVER

MOLSON INDY VANCOUVER

year	formula	winner	nat	car	mph
1990	CART	Al Unser jr	USA	Lola T90/00-Chevrolet	77.345
1991	CART	Michael Andretti	USA	Lola T91/00-Chevrolet	93.888
1992	CART	Michael Andretti	USA	Lola T92/00-Ford	98.796
1993	CART	Al Unser jr	USA	Lola T93/00-Chevrolet	91.794
1994	CART	Al Unser jr	USA	Penske PC23-Ilmor	88.896
1995	CART	Al Unser jr	USA	Penske PC24-Mercedes-Benz	95.571
1996	CART	Michael Andretti	USA	Lola T96/00-Ford	94.374
1997	CART	Mauricio Gugelmin	BR	Reynard 97I-Mercedes-Benz	95.228
1998	CART	Dario Franchitti	GB	Reynard 98I-Honda	77.081
1999	CART	Juan Pablo Montoya	CO	Reynard 99I-Honda	65.279
2000	CART	Paul Tracy	CDN	Reynard 2KI-Honda	85.034
2001	CART	Roberto Moreno	BR	Reynard 01I-Toyota	80.543
2002	CART	Dario Franchitti	GB	Lola B2/00-Honda	78.525

CHINA

Circuits and Races

GUIA CIRCUIT

Macau

The annual Macau Grand Prix in November has replaced the Monaco Grand Prix support race as the most important Formula 3 race of the year. Ever since Ayrton Senna won the first F3 race in 1983 it has been the unofficial World Cup for the category, pitching the best European runners against their Japanese counterparts. Despite changes in Macau's landscape and the return to Chinese rule in 1999, the circuit has remained remarkably unaffected. Statue Corner at the start of the lap is a tight right-hander that has often been the scene of a pile up. It follows a fast main stretch (which used to pass between the sea and a reservoir) and leads onto the twisting, narrow return leg. When Michael Schumacher clashed with Mika Hakkinen late in the 1990 Macau GP it hinted at F1 battles to come.

Active years	1954 to date
Location	45 miles west of Hong Kong
Type	Temporary street circuit
Website	www.macau.grandprix.gov.mo
Lap distance	3.801 miles
Lap record	Qualifying: Bjorn Wirdheim (Dallara 301-Opel), 2m11.983, 103.677 mph, F3, 2001
	Race: Derek Hayes (Dallara 300-Mugen), 2m12.921, 102.945 mph, F3, 2001

MACAU GRAND PRIX

year	formula	winner	nat	car	mph
1954	SC	Eddie Carvalho	HK	Triumph TR2	47.802
1955	SC	Robert Ritchie	HK	Austin Healey 100	58.002
1956	SC	Doug Steane	HK	Mercedes-Benz 190SL	54.147
1957	SC	Arthur Pateman	GB	Mercedes-Benz 300SL	59.605
1958	SC	Chan Lye Choon	SGP	Aston Martin DB3S	61.921
1959	SC	Ron Hardwick	HK	Jaguar XKSS	58.882
1960	SC	Martin Redfern	HK	Jaguar XKSS	65.973
1961	FL	Peter Heath	T	Lotus 15-Climax	65.270
1962	FL	Dodgie Laurel	RP	Lotus 22-Ford	66.178
1963	FL	Dodgie Laurel	RP	Lotus 22-Ford	68.000
1964	FL	Albert Poon	PRC	Lotus 23-Ford	70.629
1965	FL	John MacDonald	HK	Lotus 18-Ford	67.183
1966	FL	Mauro Bianchi	B	Alpine T66-Renault	71.126
1967	FL	Tony Maw	MAL	Lotus 20B-Ford	65.645
1968	FL	Jan Bussell	SGP	Brabham BT23C-Ford	72.697
1969	FL	Kevin Bartlett	AUS	Mildren-Waggott	83.781
1970	FL	Dieter Quester	A	BMW F270	81.424
1971	FL	Jan Bussell	SGP	McLaren M4C	73.684
1972	FL	John MacDonald	HK	Brabham BT36	85.420
1973	FL	John MacDonald	HK	Brabham BT40	86.400
1974	Pacific	Vern Schuppan	AUS	March 72B-Ford	81.693
1975	Pacific	John MacDonald	HK	Ralt RT1-Ford	86.948
1976	Pacific	Vern Schuppan	AUS	Ralt RT1-Ford	92.228
1977	Pacific	Riccardo Patrese	I	Chevron B40-Ford	91.004
1978	Pacific	Riccardo Patrese	I	Chevron B42-Ford	93.368
1979	Pacific	Geoff Lees	GB	Ralt RT1-Ford	95.083
1980	Pacific	Geoff Lees	GB	Ralt RT1-Ford	95.557
1981	Pacific	Bob Earl	USA	Hayashi 220P-Toyota	93.578
1982	Pacific	Roberto Moreno	BR	Ralt RT4-Ford	92.902

Canada-China

MACAU GRAND PRIX (cont.)

year	formula	winner	nat	car	mph
1983	F3	Ayrton Senna	BR	Ralt RT3/83-Toyota	95.579
1984	F3	John Nielsen	DK	Ralt RT3/84-Volkswagen	94.446
1985	F3	Mauricio Gugelmin	BR	Ralt RT30-Volkswagen	94.320
1986	F3	Andy Wallace	GB	Reynard 863-Volkswagen	94.328
1987	F3	Martin Donnelly	GB	Ralt RT31-Toyota	93.922
1988	F3	Enrico Bertaggia	I	Dallara 388-Alfa Romeo	94.726
1989	F3	David Brabham	AUS	Ralt RT33-Volkswagen	96.617
1990	F3	Michael Schumacher	D	Reynard 903-Volkswagen	95.765
1991	F3	David Coulthard	GB	Ralt RT35-Mugen	96.572
1992	F3	Rickard Rydell	S	TOM's 032F-Toyota	96.498
1993	F3	Jorg Muller	D	Dallara 393-Fiat	97.770
1994	F3	Sascha Maassen	D	Dallara 394-Opel	93.208
1995	F3	Ralf Schumacher	D	Dallara 395-Opel	97.469
1996	F3	Ralph Firman jr	GB	Dallara 396-Mugen	97.359
1997	F3	Soheil Ayari	F	Dallara 396-Opel	88.764
1998	F3	Peter Dumbreck	GB	Dallara 398-Toyota	94.360
1999	F3	Darren Manning	GB	Dallara 399-Toyota	100.755
2000	F3	Andre Couto	P	Dallara 399-Opel	85.960
2001	F3	Takuma Sato	J	Dallara 301-Mugen	87.262
2002	F3	Tristan Gommendy	F	Dallara 302-Renault	86.928

MACAU

GUIA RACE

year	formula	winner	nat	car	mph
1972	TC	John MacDonald	HK	Austin Cooper	63.196
1973	TC	Peter Chow	HK	Toyota Celica	64.388
1974	TC	Nobuhide Tachi	J	Toyota Celica	71.936
1975	TC	Nobuhide Tachi	J	Toyota Celica	74.941
1976	TC	Herb Adamczyk	HK	Porsche 911 Carrera RS	75.520
1977	TC	Peter Chow	HK	Toyota Celica	76.650
1978	TC	Peter Chow	HK	Toyota Celica	80.207
1979	TC	Herb Adamczyk	HK	Porsche 911 Carrera RSR	83.319
1980	TC	Hans-Joachim Stuck	D	BMW 320i Turbo	84.233
1981	TC	Manfred Winkelhock	D	BMW 320i Turbo	85.547
1982	TC	Helmet Greiner	HK	Porsche 911 Carrera RSR	83.447
1983	TC	Hans-Joachim Stuck	D	BMW 635 CSi	79.695
1984	TC	Tom Walkinshaw	GB	Jaguar XJ-S	85.662
1985	TC	Gianfranco Brancatelli	I	Volvo 240T	83.400
1986	TC	Johnny Cecotto	YV	Volvo 240T	83.239
1987	TC	Roberto Ravaglia	I	BMW M3	78.397
1988	TC	Altfrid Heger	D	BMW M3	83.369
1989	TC	Tim Harvey	GB	Ford Sierra RS500 Cosworth	84.200
1990	TC	Masahiro Hasemi	J	Nissan BNR 32	85.982
1991	TC	Emanuele Pirro	I	BMW M3	88.561
1992	TC	Emanuele Pirro	I	BMW M3	89.319
1993	TC	Charles Kwan	HK	BMW M3	86.930

GUIA RACE (cont.)

year	formula	driver	nat	car	mph
1994	TC	Joachim Winkelhock	D	BMW 318i	81.759
1995	TC	Kelvin Burt	GB	Toyota Corona EXiV	89.183
1996	TC	Frank Biela	D	Audi A4 Quattro	86.250
1997	TC	Steve Soper	GB	BMW 320i	78.439
1998	TC	Joachim Winkelhock	D	BMW 320i	89.401
1999	TC	Michael Bartels	D	Audi A4 Quattro	89.270
2000	TC	Patrick Huisman	NL	BMW 320i	78.233
2001	TC	Duncan Huisman	NL	BMW 320i	78.301
2002	TC	Duncan Huisman	NL	BMW 320i	73.625

ZHUHAI

The first permanent racing facility to be built on mainland China was nominated as the reserve race for the 1998 F1 season, but the the organisers were unable to raise the finance necessary to bring the facilty up to F1 standard. Now the announcement of the Chinese Grand Prix at Shanghai in 2004 has ended plans to bring Grand Prix racing to the circuit. Zhuhai was opened in 1996 outside the town that had previously held a GT race on a 2.61-mile temporary street circuit.

Active years	1996 to date
Location	6 miles north-east of central Zhuhai, 9 miles north-east of Macau, 36 miles west of Hong Kong
Type	Permanent road course
Website	www.zic.com.cn
Lap distance	2.680 miles
Lap record	Qualifying: Ralf Kelleners (Porsche 911 GT1), 1m30.401, 106.725 mph, GT, 1996
	Race: Yannick Dalmas (Porsche 911 GT1), 1m31.749, 105.157 mph, GT, 1996

FIA GT RACE

year	formula	winner	nat	car	mph
1994	GT	Jean-Pierre Jarier/Jacques Laffite/Bob Wollek	F	Porsche 911 turbo SLM	80.219
1995	GT INT	Olivier Grouillard/Andy Wallace	F/GB	McLaren F1 GTR-BMW	82.870
1996	GT INT	Emmanuel Collard/Ralf Kelleners	F/D	Porsche 911 GT1	99.541
1997	GT	John Greasley/Geoff Lister/Magnus Wallinder	GB/GB/S	Porsche 911 GT1	88.410
1999	GT INT	Olivier Beretta/Karl Wendlinger	MC/A	Chrysler Viper GTS-R	93.344

CURACAO
Circuits and Races

WILLEMSTAD

The first Formula 3000 race outside Europe was held on a bumpy street circuit around downtown Willemstad. Although a non-championship event the Curacao Grand Prix attracted a full F3000 field. The race was hailed a success by press and public alike but it was not repeated when the organisers, who had commissioned the Sports Car Club of America to run the event, realised that there was no possibility of holding a full Grand Prix.

Active years	1985
Location	Downtown Willemstad, Curacao
Type	Temporary street circuit
Lap distance	2.206 miles
Lap records	Qualifying: Mike Thackwell (Ralt RB20-Cosworth), 1m41.895, 77.939 mph, F3000, 1985
	Race: John Nielsen (Ralt RB20-Cosworth), 1m44.725, 75.833 mph, F3000, 1985

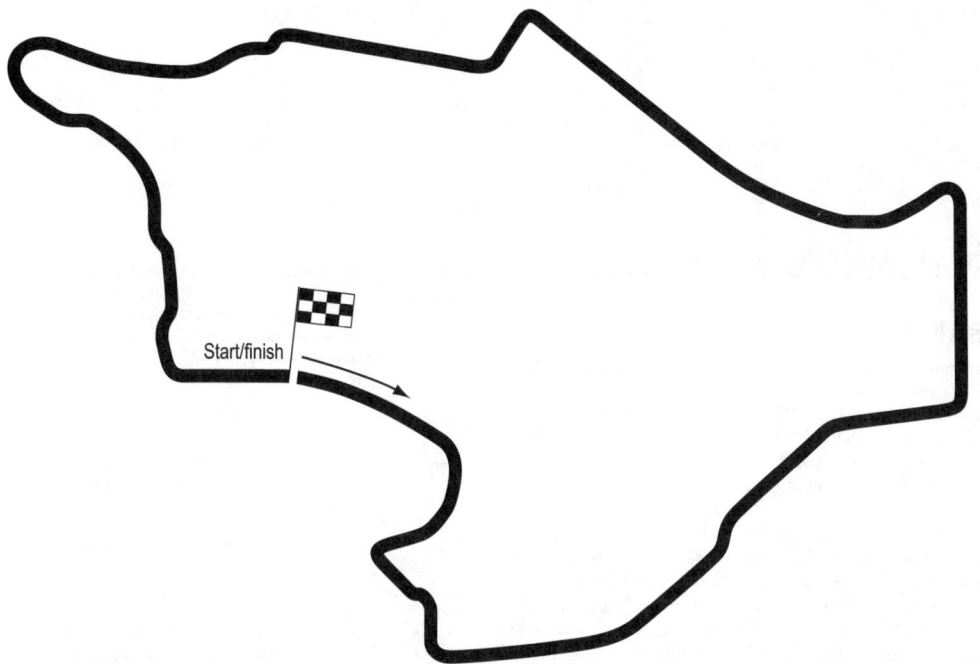

Start/finish

CURACAO GRAND PRIX

year	formula	winner	nat	car	mph
1985	F3000	John Nielsen	DK	Ralt RB20-Cosworth	75.640

CZECH REPUBLIC

Major Championships

CZECH TOURING CAR CHAMPIONSHIP

year	driver	nat	team	car
1993	Vaclav Bervid	CS	Bervid Sport Styling	BMW M3
1994	Vaclav Bervid	CS	Bervid Sport Styling	BMW 318i
1995	Josef Kopecky	CS	Ford Rasino Brno	Ford Mondeo Ghia

FIA CENTRAL EUROPEAN SUPER TOURING CHAMPIONSHIP

year	driver	nat	team	car
1996	Vaclav Bervid	CS	Team Bervid	BMW 318i
1997	Jozef Venc	CS	Czech NT Audi Kaucuk ISR	Audi A4 Quattro
1998	Jozef Venc	CS	Czech NT Mobil-Charouz Racing	Audi A4 Quattro

CZECH FORMULA 3 CHAMPIONSHIP

year	driver	nat	team	car
1995	Tomas Karhenek	CS	TKF Racing	Dallara 393-Opel
1996	Helmut Kopp	A	Shannon Racing Team	Dallara 394-Opel
1997	Leos Propkopec	CS	Leos Propkopec	Dallara 397-Fiat

Major International Races

CZECH GRAND PRIX (known as Masaryk GP 1930-37)

year	formula	circuit	winner	nat	car	mph
1930	GP	Brno	Hermann zu Leiningen/			
			Heinrich-Joachim von Morgen	D	Bugatti T35B	62.781
1931	GP	Brno	Louis Chiron	MC	Bugatti T51	73.262
1932	GP	Brno	Louis Chiron	MC	Bugatti T51	66.564
1933	GP	Brno	Louis Chiron	MC	Alfa Romeo Tipo-B "P3"	63.611
1934	GP	Brno	Hans Stuck	D	Auto Union A	79.118
1935	GP	Brno	Bernd Rosemeyer	D	Auto Union B	82.396
1937	GP	Brno	Rudolf Caracciola	D	Mercedes-Benz W125	86.041
1949	F1	Brno	Peter Whitehead	GB	Ferrari 125	78.680
1950	F1	Brno	Vaclav Hovorka	CS	Maserati	n/a

Circuits and Other Races

BRNO

A daunting road circuit with echoes from a previous era, Brno was still visited by the European Touring Car Championship up to 1986. A new circuit was built in 1987 in an attempt to lure modern Grand Prix racing to the Czech Republic. But with F1 looking outside Europe for new events, this now appears to be a forlorn hope. The original venue was 18 miles of dusty, narrow roads southwest of the town, and was the longest circuit in use when it opened in 1930. Bernd Rosemeyer scored his first Grand Prix win here in 1935 but Hitler's occupation of Czechoslovakia ended racing in 1937. A reduced 11-mile circuit opened in 1949; omitting the challenging Ostrovacice section. 200,000 spectators saw Peter Whitehead's victory in the Czech GP of that year. Vaclav Hovorka's Maserati scored a home victory in 1950, but racing did not return until 1962, when a Formula Junior race was held. The old pits and barriers still exist, providing a reminder of the past age. Although the new circuit cannot compare to the original, the new track is demanding and a good example of a modern facility.

Active years	1930-86 (road course), 1987 to date (Automotodrom)
Location	Kyvalka, 10 miles north-east of Brno, 80 miles north of Vienna, 120 miles south-east of Prague
Type	Temporary road course (1930-86); Permanent road course (Automotodrom)
Website	www.automotodrombrno.cz

Current circuit	
Lap distance	3.357 miles
Lap record	Qualifying: Jean-Louis Schlesser (Sauber C9/88-Mercedes-Benz), 1m46.44, 113.371 mph, Group C Sports Cars, 1988
	Race: Mauro Baldi (Sauber C9/88-Mercedes-Benz), 1m49.77, 110.096 mph, Group C Sports Cars, 1988

Circuit changes	
1930-37	Anti-clockwise. 18.109 miles
1949-63	Connecting road from Zebetin to Popuvky built. Direction of racing changed to clockwise. 11.061 miles
1964-74	Link road bypassed Zebetin. 8.663 miles
1975-86	Another new road linked the start to Kohoutovice. 6.789 miles
1987 to date	New Automotodrom built. Current circuit

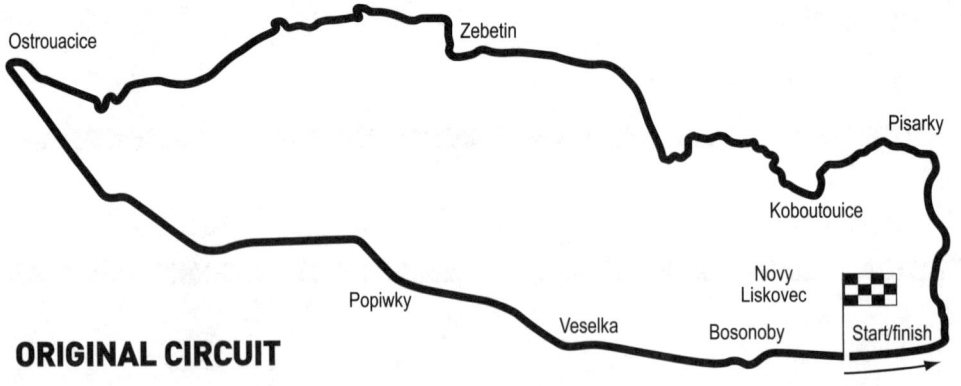

ORIGINAL CIRCUIT

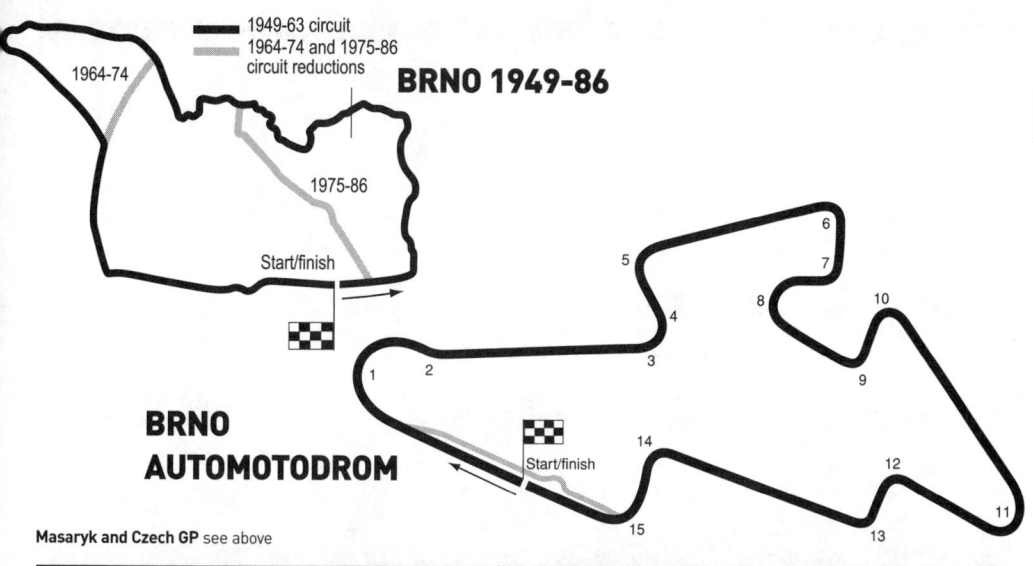

1949-63 circuit
1964-74 and 1975-86
circuit reductions

BRNO 1949-86

1964-74

1975-86

Start/finish

BRNO AUTOMOTODROM

Start/finish

Masaryk and Czech GP see above

WORLD SPORTS CAR RACE					
year	formula	winner	nat	car	mph
1988	SC W	Jean-Louis Schlesser/Jochen Mass	F/D	Sauber C9/88-Mercedes-Benz	106.532

FIA GT RACE					
year	formula	winner	nat	car	mph
2000	GT FIA	David Hart/Mike Hezemans	NL	Chrysler Viper GTS-R	82.785
2001	GT FIA	Jean-Philippe Belloc/Christophe Bouchut	F	Chrysler Viper GTS-R	86.018
2002	GT FIA	Jamie Campbell-Walter/Nicolaus Springer	GB/D	Lister Storm GT	94.315

DENMARK

Major Championships

DANISH TOURING CAR CHAMPIONSHIP				
year	driver	nat	team	car
1999	Jesper Sylvest	DK	Sylvest Racing Team	Peugeot 306 GTi
2000	Michael Carlsen	DK	Peugeot Sport Team	Peugeot 306 GTi
2001	Michael Carlsen	DK	Peugeot Sport Team	Peugeot 306 GTi
2002	Jason Watt	DK	Peugeot Sport Team	Peugeot 307 GTi

DANISH FORMULA 3 CHAMPIONSHIP					
year		driver	nat	team	car
1949		Kaj Hansen	DK	Kaj Hansen	Cooper T7-JAP
1950		Robert Nelleman	DK	Robert Nelleman	Silver Bird-JAP
1951		Robert Nelleman	DK	Robert Nelleman	Silver Bird-JAP
1953		Robert Nelleman	DK	Robert Nelleman	Silver Bird-JAP
1954		Robert Nelleman	DK	Robert Nelleman	Cooper-JAP
1955		Robert Nelleman	DK	Robert Nelleman	Silver Bird-JAP
1956		Poul Rasmussen	DK	Poul Rasmussen	Cooper T36-Norton
1957		Gunnar Henriksen	DK	Gunnar Henriksen	Cooper T36-Norton
1958		Poul Rasmussen	DK	Poul Rasmussen	Cooper T42-Norton
1959		Poul Rasmussen	DK	Poul Rasmussen	Cooper T42-Norton
1960	500cc	Robert Nelleman	DK	Robert Nelleman	Silver Bird-JAP
	Junior	Joerges Bagger	DK	Joerges Bagger	Lola Mk2-Ford
1961	500cc	Poul Anderssen	DK	Poul Anderssen	Cooper T42-Norton
	Junior	Joerges Bagger	DK	Joerges Bagger	Lola Mk2-Ford
1962	500c	Jens Winther	DK	Jens Winther	Cooper T42-Norton
	Junior	Hartvig Conradsen	DK	Hartvig Conradsen	Cooper T59-BMC
1963	500cc	Robert Nelleman	DK	Robert Nelleman	Cooper-JAP
	Junior	Jens-Christian Legath	DK	Jens-Christian Legath	Lotus 22-Ford

DANISH FORMULA 3 CHAMPIONSHIP (cont.)

year		driver	nat	team	car
1964	500cc	Robert Nelleman	DK	Robert Nelleman	Cooper-JAP
	Junior	Hartvig Conradsen	DK	Hartvig Conradsen	Cooper T72-BMC
1965	500cc	Robert Nelleman	DK	Robert Nelleman	Cooper-JAP
	Junior	Jorgen Ellekaer	DK	Jorgen Ellekaer	Brabham BT15-Ford
1966		Ole Vejlund	DK	Ole Vejlund	Brabham BT18-Ford
1976		Jac Nelleman	DK	Texaco Racing	Van Diemen 376-Ford
1977		Jac Nelleman	DK	Texaco Racing	Chevron B38-Toyota
1952, 1967-75 no series					

EUROPEAN GRAND PRIX

A courtesy title awarded annually by the FIA to Europe's World Championship races in rotation. The honour of being the European Grand Prix was of little importance, however, until 1983. Since then the race has been a Grand Prix in its own right on twelve occasions.

EUROPEAN GRAND PRIX

year	formula	circuit	winner	nat	car	mph
1923*	GP	Monza	Carlo Salamano	I	Fiat 805	91.037
1924*	GP	Lyon	Giuseppe Campari	I	Alfa Romeo P2	70.957
1925*	GP	Spa-Francorchamps	Antonio Ascari	I	Alfa Romeo P2	74.859
1926*	GP	Lasarte	Jules Goux	F	Bugatti T39A	72.301
1927*	GP	Monza	Robert Benoist	F	Delage 15S8	108.072
1928*	GP	Monza	Louis Chiron	MC	Bugatti T35C	99.361
1930*	GP	Spa-Francorchamps	Louis Chiron	MC	Bugatti T35C	71.834
1947*	F1	Spa-Francorchamps	Jean-Pierre Wimille	F	Alfa Romeo 158	95.860
1948*	F1	Bremgarten	Carlo Felice Trossi	I	Alfa Romeo 158	91.020
1949*	F1	Monza	Alberto Ascari	I	Ferrari 125	105.046
1950*	F1 W	Silverstone	Giuseppe Farina	I	Alfa Romeo 158	90.950
1951*	F1 W	Reims	Luigi Fagioli/Juan Manuel Fangio	I/RA	Alfa Romeo 159	110.962
1952*	F2 W	Spa-Francorchamps	Alberto Ascari	I	Ferrari 500	103.127
1954*	F1 W	Nurburgring	Juan Manuel Fangio	RA	Mercedes-Benz W196	82.832
1955*	F1 W	Monte Carlo	Maurice Trintignant	F	Ferrari 625 (555)	65.805
1956*	F1 W	Monza	Stirling Moss	GB	Maserati 250F	129.733
1957*	F1 W	Aintree	Tony Brooks/Stirling Moss	GB	Vanwall VW4	86.803
1958*	F1 W	Spa-Francorchamps	Tony Brooks	GB	Vanwall VW5	129.920
1959*	F1 W	Reims	Tony Brooks	GB	Ferrari Dino 246	128.136
1960*	F1 W	Monza	Phil Hill	USA	Ferrari Dino 246	132.063
1961*	F1 W	Nurburgring	Stirling Moss	GB	Lotus 18/21-Climax	92.255
1962*	F1 W	Zandvoort	Graham Hill	GB	BRM P57	95.425
1963*	F1 W	Monaco	Graham Hill	GB	BRM P57	72.447
1965*	F1 W	Spa-Francorchamps	Jim Clark	GB	Lotus 33-Climax	117.155
1967*	F1 W	Monza	John Surtees	GB	Honda RA300	140.509
1972*	F1 W	Brands Hatch	Emerson Fittipaldi	BR	Lotus 72D-Ford	112.058
1973*	F1 W	Zolder	Jackie Stewart	GB	Tyrrell 006-Ford	107.728
1974*	F1 W	Nurburgring	Clay Regazzoni	CH	Ferrari 312B3	117.330
1975*	F1 W	Osterreichring	Vittorio Brambilla	I	March 751-Ford	110.295
1976*	F1 W	Zandvoort	James Hunt	GB	McLaren M23-Ford	112.684
1977*	F1 W	Silverstone	James Hunt	GB	McLaren M26-Ford	130.357
1983	F1 W	Brands Hatch	Nelson Piquet	BR	Brabham BT52B-BMW	123.165
1984	F1 W	Nurburgring	Alain Prost	F	McLaren MP4/2-TAG Porsche	119.138
1985	F1 W	Brands Hatch	Nigel Mansell	GB	Williams FW10-Honda	126.507
1993	F1 W	Donington Park	Ayrton Senna	BR	McLaren MP4/8-Ford	102.910
1994	F1 W	Jerez	Michael Schumacher	D	Benetton B194-Ford	113.387
1995	F1 W	Nurburgring	Michael Schumacher	D	Benetton B195-Renault	113.824
1996	F1 W	Nurburgring	Jacques Villeneuve	CDN	Williams FW18-Renault	121.794
1997	F1 W	Jerez	Mika Hakkinen	SF	McLaren MP4/12-Mercedes-Benz	115.127
1999	F1 W	Nurburgring	Johnny Herbert	GB	Stewart SF3-Ford	110.012
2000	F1 W	Nurburgring	Michael Schumacher	D	Ferrari F1-2000	111.569
2001	F1 W	Nurburgring	Michael Schumacher	D	Ferrari F2001	126.857
2002	F1 W	Nurburgring	Rubens Barrichello	BR	Ferrari F2002	120.954

*run concurrently with the national Grand Prix

FINLAND
Major Championships

FINNISH TOURING CAR CHAMPIONSHIP				
year	driver	nat	team	car
1996	Toni Ruokonen	SF	Rasmus Speed	Honda Civic Vtec
1997	Heikki Salmenautio	SF	OS Motorsport	BMW 320i
1998	Arto Salmenautio	SF	OS Motorsport	BMW 320i
1999	Olli Haapalainen	SF	Lehtonen Motorsport	Volkswagen Golf GTi
2000	Olli Haapalainen	SF	Lehtonen Motorsport	Volkswagen Golf GTi
2001	Olli Haapalainen	SF	Lehtonen Motorsport	Volkswagen Golf GTi
2002	Olli Haapalainen	SF	Lehtonen Motorsport	Volkswagen Golf GTi

FINNISH FORMULA 3 CHAMPIONSHIP				
year	driver	nat	team	car
2000	Marko Nevalainen	SF	Motor Up Racing Team	Dallara 397-Opel
2001	Jari Koivisto	SF	Jari Koivisto Racing	Dallara 393-Opel
2002	Jussi Pinomaki	SF	Niinivirta Motorsport	Dallara 397-Mugen

Circuits and Races

HELSINKI

Finland's capital hosted a street race for three years, starting with Class C International Touring Cars in 1995 before switching to FIA GT and F3000 for its final year. Organised by former Trans-Am driver Robert Lappalainen, the inaugural "Thunder in the Streets" race drew 110,000 spectators. The circuit was set on the harbourfront immediately east of downtown Helsinki and lined with concrete barriers; the original circuit ran under a flyover and past a power station. Two chicanes were later inserted to reduce speeds. The one-off FIA GT was organised immediately prior to the Le Mans 24 hours, and was blighted when 12 teams missed the event to concentrate on the Sarthe classic. Lappalainen looked at running a Touring Car World Challenge in 1998, but the event was shelved when support was not forthcoming.

Active years	1995-97
Location	Central Helsinki
Type	Temporary street circuit
Lap distance	1.976 miles
Lap records	Qualifying: Juan Pablo Montoya (Lola T96/50-Zytek), 1m23.968, 84.718 mph, F3000, 1997
	Race: Juan Pablo Montoya (Lola T96/50-Zytek), 1m25.466, 83.229 mph, F3000, 1997

Circuit changes	
1995	2.051 miles
1996-97	Start moved, circuit modified. 1.976 miles

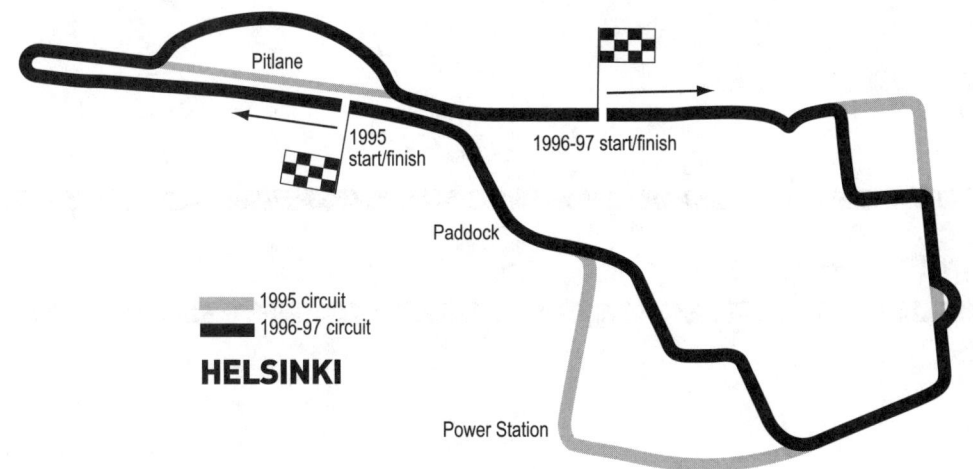

Pitlane

1995 start/finish

1996-97 start/finish

Paddock

1995 circuit
1996-97 circuit

HELSINKI

Power Station

THUNDER IN THE STREETS

year	formula	winner	nat	car	mph
1995	TC	Christian Danner	D	Alfa Romeo 155 V6 TI	72.860
	TC	Nicola Larini	I	Alfa Romeo 155 V6 TI	70.710
1996	TC	Hans-Joachim Stuck	D	Opel Calibra V6	81.170
	TC	Hans-Joachim Stuck	D	Opel Calibra V6	82.160
1997	GT FIA	JJ Lehto/Steve Soper	SF/GB	McLaren F1 GTR-BMW	74.211

INTERNATIONAL FORMULA 3000 RACE

year	formula	winner	nat	car	mph
1997	F3000 INT	Soheil Ayari	F	Lola T96/50-Zytek	78.199

FRANCE

Major Championships

FRENCH SUPERTOURISM CHAMPIONSHIP

year	driver	nat	team	car
1976	Jean-Pierre Beltoise	F	Jean-Pierre Beltoise	BMW 3.0 CSL
1977	Jean-Pierre Beltoise	F	Jean-Pierre Beltoise	BMW 530 IUS
1978	Lucien Guitteny	F	Lucien Guitteny	Ford Capri RS
1979	Dany Snobeck	F	Snobeck Racing	Ford Capri RS
1980	Dany Snobeck	F	Snobeck Racing	Ford Escort RS2000
1981	Jean-Pierre Malcher	F	Garage du Bac	BMW 320i
1982	Rene Metge	F	Tom Walkinshaw Racing	Rover 3500 Vitesse
1983	Alain Cudini	F	Snobeck Racing	Alfa Romeo GTV6
1984	Dany Snobeck	F	Snobeck Racing	Alfa Romeo GTV6
1985	Jean-Louis Schlesser	F	Marlboro Racing	Rover 3500 Vitesse
1986	Xavier Lapeyre	F	ROC Competition	Audi 200 Quattro
1987	Erik Comas	F	Sonica	Renault 5 Maxi-turbo
1988	Jean Ragnotti	F	Sonica	Renault 21 turbo 4x4
1989	Jean-Pierre Malcher	F	Pelras Competition	BMW M3
1990	Jean-Pierre Malcher	F	Pelras Competition	BMW M3
1991	Xavier Lapeyre	F	ROC Competition	Audi 80 Quattro
1992	Marc Sourd	F	ROC Competition	Audi 80 Quattro
1993	Frank Biela	D	ROC Competition	Audi 80 Quattro
1994	Laurent Aiello	F	Peugeot Sport	Peugeot 405 Mi16
1995	Yvan Muller	F	ORECA	BMW 318i
1996	Eric Cayrolle	F	Eric Cayrolle/Fenjoux	BMW 318i
1997	Eric Cayrolle	F	Eric Cayrolle/Fenjoux	BMW 318i
1998	Eric Cayrolle	F	SDA Sport/Fenjoux	BMW 320i
1999	William David	F	Gemo Sport	Peugeot 406
2000	William David	F	Gemo Sport	Peugeot 406
2001	Jean-Philippe Dayraut	F	Pelras Competition	BMW M3 Coupe
2002	Soheil Ayari	F	Solution-F	Peugeot 406

FRENCH GROUP A CHAMPIONSHIP

year	driver	nat	team	car
1987	Fabien Giroix	F	Garage du Bac	BMW M3
1988	Jean-Pierre Malcher	F	Pelras Competition	BMW M3

FRENCH FORMULA 3 CHAMPIONSHIP (INCLUDING FORMULA JUNIOR)

year	driver	nat	team	car
1960*	Jacques Cales	F	Scuderia Madunina	Stanguellini-Fiat
1962*	Jo Schlesser	F	Jo Schlesser	Brabham BT2-Ford
1963*	Jo Schlesser	F	Ford France	Brabham BT2-Ford/Brabham BT6-Ford
1964	Henry Grandsire	F	Automobiles Alpine	Alpine T64-Renault
1965	Jean-Pierre Beltoise	F	Matra Sports	Matra MS1-Ford
1966	Johnny Servoz-Gavin	F	Matra Sports	Matra MS5-Ford
1967	Henri Pescarolo	F	Matra Sports	Matra MS5-Ford
1968	Francois Cevert	F	Volant Shell	Tecno 68-Ford
1969	Francois Mazet	F	Lotus Components	Tecno 69-Ford/Lotus 59-Ford
1970	Jean-Pierre Jaussaud	F	Ecurie Winfield	Tecno 69-Ford/Martini MW5-Ford
1971	Patrick Depailler	F	Automobiles Alpine	Alpine A360-Renault

FRENCH FORMULA 3 CHAMPIONSHIP (INCLUDING FORMULA JUNIOR) (cont.)

year	driver	nat	team	car
1972	Michel Leclere	F	Automobiles Alpine	Alpine A364-Renault
1973	Jacques Laffite	F	Automobiles Martini	Martini MK12-Ford
1978	Alain Prost	F	Automobiles Martini	Martini MK21B-Renault
	Jean-Louis Schlesser	F	Jean-Louis Schlesser	Chevron B38-Toyota
1979	Alain Prost	F	Automobiles Martini	Martini MK27-Renault
1980	Alain Ferte	F	Automobiles Martini	Martini MK27/31-Renault
1981	Philippe Streiff	F	Ecurie Motul Nogaro	Martini MK34-Alfa Romeo
1982	Pierre Petit	F	Dave Price Racing	Ralt RT3-Toyota/Ralt RT3-Volkswagen
1983	Michel Ferte	F	ORECA	Martini MK39-Alfa Romeo
1984	Olivier Grouillard	F	ORECA	Martini MK42-Alfa Romeo
1985	Pierre-Henri Raphanel	F	ORECA	Martini MK45-Alfa Romeo
1986	Yannick Dalmas	F	ORECA	Martini MK49-Volkswagen
1987	Jean Alesi	F	ORECA	Martini MK49/52-Alfa Romeo/Dallara 387-Alfa Romeo
1988	Erik Comas	F	ORECA	Dallara 388-Alfa Romeo
1989	Jean-Marc Gounon	F	ORECA	Reynard 893-Alfa Romeo
1990	Eric Helary	F	Formula Project	Reynard 903-Mugen/Ralt RT34-Mugen
1991	Christophe Bouchut	F	Graff Racing	Ralt RT33-Volkswagen
1992	Franck Lagorce	F	Promatecme	Dallara 392-Opel
1993	Didier Cottaz	F	Formula Project	Dallara 393-Fiat
1994	Jean-Philippe Belloc	F	Ecurie Winfield	Dallara 393-Fiat
1995	Laurent Redon	F	Ecurie Winfield	Dallara 394-Fiat
1996	Soheil Ayari	F	Graff Racing	Dallara 396-Opel
1997	Patrice Gay	F	Graff Racing	Dallara 396-Opel
1998	David Saelens	B	ASM Formule 3	Dallara 396-Renault
1999	Sebastien Bourdais	F	La Filiere	Martini MK79-Opel
2000	Jonathan Cochet	F	Signature Competition	Dallara 399-Renault
2001	Ryo Fukuda	J	Saulnier Racing	Dallara 399-Renault
2002	Tristan Gommendy	F	ASM Formule 3	Dallara 302-Renault

*Formula Junior. 1974-77 no series

FRENCH FORMULA 2 CHAMPIONSHIP

year	driver	nat	team	car
1964	Jack Brabham	AUS	Brabham Racing Organisation	Brabham BT10-Ford
1965*	Jim Clark	GB	Ron Harris Team Lotus	Lotus 35-Ford
1966	Jack Brabham	AUS	Brabham Racing Organisation	Brabham BT18-Honda/Brabham BT21-Honda
1967	Jochen Rindt	A	Winkelmann Racing	Brabham BT23-Ford
1968	Jackie Stewart	GB	Matra International	Matra MS7-Ford

*Officially a team championship but Clark scored all his team's points

FRENCH FORMULA RENAULT CHAMPIONSHIP

year	driver	nat	car
1968	Jean Max	F	Grac MT5-Renault
1969	Denis Dayan	F	Grac MT5-Renault
1970	Francois Lacarrau	F	Martini MK4-Renault
1971	Michel Leclere	F	Alpine-Renault
1972	Jacques Laffite	F	Martini MK8-Renault
1975	Christian Debias	F	Martini MK15R-Renault
1976	Alain Prost	F	Martini MK17-Renault
1977	Joel Gouhier	F	Martini MK20-Renault
1978	Philippe Alliot	F	Martini MK24-Renault
1979	Alain Ferte	F	Martini MK26-Renault
1980	Denis Morin	F	Martini MK30-Renault
1981	Philippe Renault	F	Martini MK33-Renault
1982	Gilles Lempereur	F	Martini MK36-Renault
1983	Jean-Pierre Hoursourigaray	F	Martini MK38-Renault
1984	Yannick Dalmas	F	Martini MK41-Renault
1985	Eric Bernard	F	Martini MK44-Renault
1986	Erik Comas	F	Martini MK48-Renault
1987	Claude Degremont	F	Martini MK51-Renault
1988	Ludovic Faure	F	Martini MK54-Renault
1989	Olivier Panis	F	Martini MK57-Renault
1990	Emmanuel Collard	F	Martini MK59-Renault
1991	Olivier Couvreur	F	Alpa FR91-Renault
1992	Jean-Philippe Belloc	F	Martini MK63-Renault
1993	David Dussau	F	Martini MK65-Renault
1994	Stephane Sarrazin	F	Martini MK65-Renault
1995	Cyrille Sauvage	F	Mygale FR95-Renault
1996	Sebastien Enjolras	F	Martini-Renault
1997	Jonathan Cochet	F	Martini-Renault

FRENCH FORMULA RENAULT CHAMPIONSHIP (cont.)

year	driver	nat	car
1998	Matt Davies	GB	Mygale FR98-Renault
1999	Lucas Lasserre	F	Tatuus RC99 -Renault
2000	Renaud Derlot	F	Tatuus 2000-Renault
2001	Eric Salignon	F	Tatuus 2000-Renault
2002	Alexandre Premat	F	Tatuus 2000-Renault

1973-74 no French series

PEUGEOT 905 SPYDER CUP

Ran 1992-94 to promote Peugeot with an open-cockpit 905 shape mandatory. Chassis design was open to choice and Martini and WR leading constructors.

year	driver	nat	car
1992	Eric Helary	F	Martini-Peugeot
1993	Eric Helary	F	Martini-Peugeot
1994	William David	F	Martini-Peugeot

FRENCH GT CHAMPIONSHIP

year	driver	nat	car
1997	Patrice Goueslard	F	Porsche 911 GT2
1998	Jean-Pierre Jarier	F	Porsche 911 GT2
1999	Jean-Pierre Jarier	F	Porsche 911 GT2
2000	Dominique Dupuy/Francois Fiat	F	Chrysler Viper GTS-R
2001	Dominique Dupuy/Francois Fiat	F	Chrysler Viper GTS-R
2002	Philippe Soulan/Patrice Goueslard	F	Porsche 911 GT2

Major International Races

FRENCH GRAND PRIX

year	formula	circuit	winner	nat	car	mph
1906	GP	Le Mans	Ferenc Szisz	H	Renault AK	62.887
1907	GP	Dieppe	Felice Nazzaro	I	Fiat	70.604
1908	GP	Dieppe	Christian Lautenschlager	D	Mercedes	69.045
1912	GP	Dieppe	Georges Boillot	F	Peugeot L76	68.502
1913	GP	Amiens	Georges Boillot	F	Peugeot EX3	72.141
1914	GP	Lyon	Christian Lautenschlager	D	Mercedes GP	65.504
1921	GP	Le Mans	Jimmy Murphy	USA	Duesenberg	78.105
1922	GP	Strasbourg	Felice Nazzaro	I	Fiat 804	79.198
1923	GP	Tours	Henry Segrave	GB	Sunbeam	75.325
1924	GP	Lyon	Giuseppe Campari	I	Alfa Romeo P2	70.957
1925	GP	Montlhery	Robert Benoist/Albert Divo	F	Delage 2LCV	69.726
1926	GP	Miramas	Jules Goux	F	Bugatti T39A	66.882
1927	GP	Montlhery	Robert Benoist	F	Delage 15S8	78.299
1928	SC (h)	St Gaudens	"W Williams"	GB	Bugatti T35C	65.639
1929	GP	Le Mans	"W Williams"	GB	Bugatti T35B	82.557
1930	FL	Pau	Philippe Etancelin	F	Bugatti T35C	90.566
1931	GP	Montlhery	Achille Varzi/Louis Chiron	I/MC	Bugatti T51	78.447
1932	GP	Reims	Tazio Nuvolari	I	Alfa Romeo Tipo-B "P3"	89.350
1933	GP	Montlhery	Giuseppe Campari	I	Maserati 8C-3000	81.487
1934	GP	Montlhery	Louis Chiron	MC	Alfa Romeo Tipo-B "P3"	85.023
1935	GP	Montlhery	Rudolf Caracciola	D	Mercedes-Benz W25B	77.377
1936	SC	Montlhery	Jean-Pierre Wimille/Raymond Sommer	F	Bugatti T57G	77.849
1937	SC	Montlhery	Louis Chiron	MC	Talbot T150C	82.444
1938	GP	Reims	Manfred von Brauchitsch	D	Mercedes-Benz W154	100.990
1939	GP	Reims	Hermann Muller	D	Auto Union D	105.239
1947	F1	Lyon	Louis Chiron	MC	Lago-Talbot	77.389
1948	F1	Reims	Jean-Pierre Wimille	F	Alfa Romeo 158	102.951
1949	SC	St Gaudens	Charles Pozzi	F	Delahaye	88.137
1950	F1 W	Reims	Juan Manuel Fangio	RA	Alfa Romeo 158	104.829
1951	F1 W	Reims	Luigi Fagioli/Juan Manuel Fangio	I/RA	Alfa Romeo 159	110.962
1952	F2 W	Rouen-les-Essarts	Alberto Ascari	I	Ferrari 500	80.281
1953	F2 W	Reims	Mike Hawthorn	GB	Ferrari 500	113.646
1954	F1 W	Reims	Juan Manuel Fangio	RA	Mercedes-Benz W196	116.613
1956	F1 W	Reims	Peter Collins	GB	Lancia-Ferrari D50	122.964
1957	F1 W	Rouen-les-Essarts	Juan Manuel Fangio	RA	Maserati 250F	100.016
1958	F1 W	Reims	Mike Hawthorn	GB	Ferrari Dino 246	126.148
1959	F1 W	Reims	Tony Brooks	GB	Ferrari Dino 246	128.136
1960	F1 W	Reims	Jack Brabham	AUS	Cooper T53-Climax	132.530
1961	F1 W	Reims	Giancarlo Baghetti	I	Ferrari Dino 156	120.510
1962	F1 W	Rouen-les-Essarts	Dan Gurney	USA	Porsche 804	103.225

France

FRENCH GRAND PRIX (cont.)

year	formula	circuit	winner	nat	car	mph
1963	F1 W	Reims	Jim Clark	GB	Lotus 25-Climax	126.005
1964	F1 W	Rouen-les-Essarts	Dan Gurney	USA	Brabham BT7-Climax	108.766
1965	F1 W	Clermont-Ferrand	Jim Clark	GB	Lotus 25-Climax	89.216
1966	F1 W	Reims	Jack Brabham	AUS	Brabham BT19-Repco	137.655
1967	F1 W	Le Mans-Bugatti	Jack Brabham	AUS	Brabham BT24-Repco	98.912
1968	F1 W	Rouen-les-Essarts	Jacky Ickx	B	Ferrari 312	100.452
1969	F1 W	Clermont-Ferrand	Jackie Stewart	GB	Matra MS80-Ford	97.709
1970	F1 W	Clermont-Ferrand	Jochen Rindt	A	Lotus 72-Ford	98.417
1971	F1 W	Paul Ricard	Jackie Stewart	GB	Tyrrell 003-Ford	111.655
1972	F1 W	Clermont-Ferrand	Jackie Stewart	GB	Tyrrell 003-Ford	101.563
1973	F1 W	Paul Ricard	Ronnie Peterson	S	Lotus 72D-Ford	115.112
1974	F1 W	Dijon-Prenois	Ronnie Peterson	S	Lotus 72E-Ford	119.770
1975	F1 W	Paul Ricard	Niki Lauda	A	Ferrari 312T	116.598
1976	F1 W	Paul Ricard	James Hunt	GB	McLaren M23-Ford	115.833
1977	F1 W	Dijon-Prenois	Mario Andretti	USA	Lotus 78-Ford	113.705
1978	F1 W	Paul Ricard	Mario Andretti	USA	Lotus 79-Ford	118.306
1979	F1 W	Dijon-Prenois	Jean-Pierre Jabouille	F	Renault RE10	118.867
1980	F1 W	Paul Ricard	Alan Jones	AUS	Williams FW07B-Ford	126.143
1981	F1 W	Dijon-Prenois	Alain Prost	F	Renault RE30	118.294
1982	F1 W	Paul Ricard	Rene Arnoux	F	Renault RE30B	125.023
1983	F1 W	Paul Ricard	Alain Prost	F	Renault RE40	124.124
1984	F1 W	Dijon-Prenois	Niki Lauda	A	McLaren MP4/2-TAG Porsche	122.711
1985	F1 W	Paul Ricard	Nelson Piquet	BR	Brabham BT54-BMW	125.092
1986	F1 W	Paul Ricard	Nigel Mansell	GB	Williams FW11-Honda	116.842
1987	F1 W	Paul Ricard	Nigel Mansell	GB	Williams FW11B-Honda	117.152
1988	F1 W	Paul Ricard	Alain Prost	F	McLaren MP4/4-Honda	116.482
1989	F1 W	Paul Ricard	Alain Prost	F	McLaren MP4/5-Honda	115.455
1990	F1 W	Paul Ricard	Alain Prost	F	Ferrari 641/2	121.626
1991	F1 W	Magny-Cours	Nigel Mansell	GB	Williams FW14-Renault	116.992
1992	F1 W	Magny-Cours	Nigel Mansell	GB	Williams FW14B-Renault	111.409
1993	F1 W	Magny-Cours	Alain Prost	F	Williams FW15C-Renault	115.726
1994	F1 W	Magny-Cours	Michael Schumacher	D	Benetton B194-Ford	115.717
1995	F1 W	Magny-Cours	Michael Schumacher	D	Benetton B195-Renault	115.859
1996	F1 W	Magny-Cours	Damon Hill	GB	Williams FW18-Renault	118.254
1997	F1 W	Magny-Cours	Michael Schumacher	D	Ferrari F310B	115.428
1998	F1 W	Magny-Cours	Michael Schumacher	D	Ferrari F300	118.740
1999	F1 W	Magny-Cours	Heinz-Harald Frentzen	D	Jordan 199-Mugen	96.356
2000	F1 W	Magny-Cours	David Coulthard	GB	McLaren MP4/15-Mercedes-Benz	116.310
2001	F1 W	Magny-Cours	Michael Schumacher	D	Ferrari F2001	121.900
2002	F1 W	Magny-Cours	Michael Schumacher	D	Ferrari F2002	123.792

Officially known as Grand Prix de l'Automobile Club de France until 1967

PARIS RACES

The ACF retrospectively awarded the GP de l'Automobile Club de France title to these Paris city-to-city races of 1895-1903

year	formula	circuit	winner	nat	car	mph
1895	-	Paris-Bordeaux-Paris	Emile Levassor	F	Panhard	15.000
1896	-	Paris-Marseille-Paris	Emile Mayade	F	Panhard	15.690
1898	-	Paris-Amsterdam-Paris	Fernand Charron	F	Panhard	26.880
1899	-	Tour de France	Rene de Knyff	F	Panhard	30.180
1900	-	Paris-Toulouse-Paris	Alfred Levegh	F	Mors	40.180
1901	-	Paris-Berlin	Henri Fournier	F	Mors	44.180
1902	-	Paris-Vienna	Marcel Renault	F	Renault	38.960
1903	-	Paris-Madrid*	Fernand Gabriel	F	Mors	65.240

*stopped at Bordeaux

GRAND PRIX DE FRANCE

year	formula	circuit	winner	nat	car	mph
1911	FL	Le Mans	Victor Hemery	F	Fiat	56.710
1912	3 litre	Le Mans	Paolo Zuccarelli	I	Lion-Peugeot	64.870
1913	GP	Le Mans	Paul Bablot	F	Delage Y	77.339
1934	GP	Montlhery	Benoit Falchetto	F	Maserati 8CM	86.930
1935	GP	Montlhery	Raymond Sommer	F	Alfa Romeo Tipo-B "P3"	90.320
1949	F1	Reims	Louis Chiron	MC	Lago-Talbot T26C	99.951

Various races carried the title Grand Prix de France prior to 1968, all organised by clubs that wanted to rival the GP de l'ACF. However, apart from the 1949 race (which was a true F1 Grand Prix while the ACF event was for Sports Cars) the GP de France was always of secondary importance. The Grand Prix de France title was also used to describe a series of F2 races in 1952.

Circuits and Other Races

ALBI

Racing started near Albi on the tree-lined Circuit des Planques by the river Tarn in 1933. Unusually, the pits and start-line were on the shortest of straights, before the road twisted through St Antoine, dipping and climbing to St Juery. There the cars slowed for an extreme hairpin before negotiating a railway level crossing and a hump leading onto two flat and fast legs that completed the lap. Shortened in 1954, it was closed on safety grounds in 1960. The Grand Prix d'Albi resumed two years later at an Aerodrome on the western outskirts of town, which was flat and featureless in comparison with the previous circuit. First events were for Formula Junior and its replacement F3. There were some rumours of the French GP coming to Albi in 1970, but having briefly run an F2 race, the circuit has since returned to the French Super Touring Car and F3 Championships for its annual highlight.

Active years	1933-53 (Circuit des Planques), 1954-60 (Circuit Raymond Sommer), 1962 to date (Aerodrome)
Location	Western suburbs of Albi, 47 miles north-east of Toulouse
Type	Temporary road course (Circuit des Planques and Circuit Raymond Sommer); Permanent road course (Aerodrome)
Website	www.circuit-albi.com

Current circuit

Lap distance	2.207 miles
Lap record	Qualifying: Tiago Monteiro (Dallara 399-Renault), 1m08.413, 116.109 mph, F3, 2000
	Race: Tiago Monteiro (Dallara 399-Renault), 1m09.087, 114.976 mph, F3, 2000

Circuit changes

1933	Original Circuit des Planques. 5.733 miles		
1934-39	Hairpin near Albi bypassed. 5.537 miles		2.259 miles
1946-53	Pits and grandstands built. Minor modifications to circuit. 5.531 miles	1981-87	Virage de l'Aerodrome modified. 2.203 miles
		1988-93	Chicane du Sequestre introduced, Courbe Armand Brouzes and Virage du Parc modified. 2.197 miles
1954-60	Circuit Raymond Sommer. Shorter and updated version of the Circuit des Planques. 1.859 miles		
1962-80	Aerodrome. Original configuration without the chicane.	1994 to date	Further modifications to Virage du Parc. Current circuit

ORIGINAL CIRCUIT

St Juery
Level crossing
Pratviel
La Renaudie
Montplaisir
D69
D100
St Antoine
Circuit Raymond Sommer
N99
Pitlane
1933 start (hairpin only used in 1933)
Start/finish
Les Planques

1934-53 Circuit des Planques
1933 Les Planques hairpin and 1954-60 Circuit Raymond Sommer

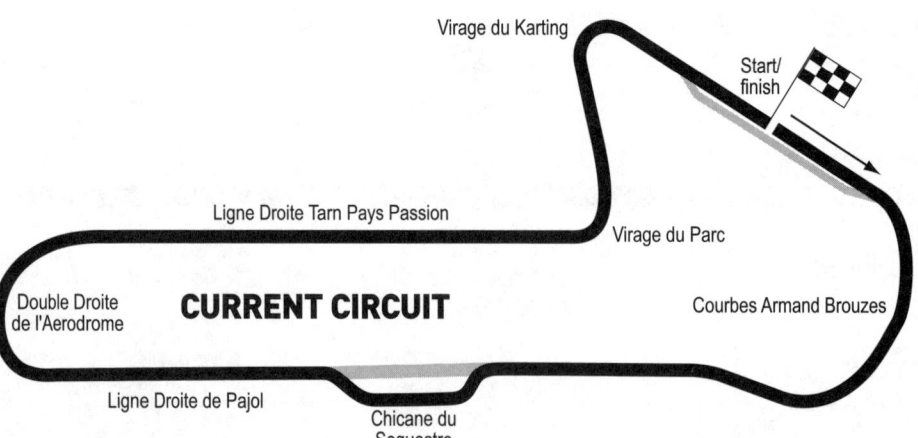

CURRENT CIRCUIT

Virage du Karting
Start/finish
Ligne Droite Tarn Pays Passion
Virage du Parc
Double Droite de l'Aerodrome
Courbes Armand Brouzes
Ligne Droite de Pajol
Chicane du Sequestre

ALBI GRAND PRIX

year	formula	winner	nat	car	mph
1933	V	Pierre Veyron	F	Bugatti T51A	79.517
1934	V	Pierre Veyron	F	Bugatti T51A	80.138
1935	V	Pierre Veyron	F	Bugatti T51A	85.774
1936	V	"B Bira"	SM	ERA B-type	92.069
1937	V	Raymond Mays/Humphrey Cook	GB	ERA C-type	90.422
1938	V	Luigi Villoresi	I	Maserati 6CM	90.165
1939	V	Johnnie Wakefield	GB	Maserati 4CL	93.912
1946	GP	Tazio Nuvolari	I	Maserati 4CL	91.737
1947	F1	Louis Rosier	F	Lago-Talbot T26C	88.607
1948	F1	Luigi Villoresi	I	Maserati 4CLT/48	99.882
1949	F1	Juan Manuel Fangio	RA	Maserati 4CLT/48	98.420
1950	F1	Louis Rosier	F	Lago-Talbot T26C	99.725
1951	F1	Maurice Trintignant	F	Simca-Gordini 15	101.299
1952	F1	Louis Rosier	F	Ferrari 375	101.972
1953	F1	Louis Rosier	F	Ferrari 375	105.514
1954	SC	Roberto Mieres	RA	DB	66.333
1955	F1	Andre Simon	F	Maserati 250F	81.690
1959	FJ	Colin Davis	GB	Taraschi	78.577
1960	FJ	Henry Taylor	GB	Cooper-BMC	80.395
1962	FJ	Peter Arundell	GB	Lotus 22-Ford	93.820
1963	FJ	Peter Arundell	GB	Lotus 27-Ford	96.500
1964	F2	Jack Brabham	AUS	Brabham BT10-Ford	95.716
1965	F2	Jim Clark	GB	Lotus 35-Ford	99.986
1966	F2	Jack Brabham	AUS	Brabham BT21-Honda	100.607
1967	F2	Jackie Stewart	GB	Matra MS7-Ford	109.178
1968	F2	Henri Pescarolo	F	Matra MS7-Ford	109.677
1969	F2	Graham Hill	GB	Lotus 59B-Ford	108.982
1970	F3	Jean-Pierre Jarier	F	Tecno 70-Ford	88.178
1971	F2 E	Emerson Fittipaldi	BR	Lotus 69-Ford	102.843
1972	F2 E	Jean-Pierre Jaussaud	F	Brabham BT38-Ford	105.902
1973	F2 E	Vittorio Brambilla	I	March 732-BMW	108.059
1974	Renault	Marc Sourd	F	Martini MK14-Renault	100.519
1975	Renault	Rene Arnoux	F	Martini MK15-Renault	107.498
1976	Renault	Didier Pironi	F	Martini MK18-Renault	107.007
1977	Renault	Alain Prost	F	Martini MK20-Renault	106.567
1978	Renault	Philippe Alliot	F	Martini MK20-Renault	102.533
1979	F3	Alain Prost	F	Martini MK27-Renault	110.353
1980*	F3	Philippe Streiff	F	Martini MK31-Toyota	90.309
1981	F3	Philippe Alliot	F	Martini MK34-Alfa Romeo	111.004
1982	F3	Francois Hesnault	F	Ralt RT3-Alfa Romeo	112.134
1983	F3	Francois Hesnault	F	Ralt RT3-Volkswagen	112.389
1984	F3	Cathy Muller	F	Ralt RT3-Alfa Romeo	112.309
1985	F3	Paul Belmondo	F	Reynard 853-Volkswagen	109.650
1986	F3	Jean Alesi	F	Dallara 386-Alfa Romeo	111.363
1987	TC	Xavier Lapeyre	F	Audi 200 Quattro	104.428
1988	F3	Eric Cheli	F	Dallara 388-Alfa Romeo	108.173
1989	F3	Eric Helary	F	Reynard 893-Alfa Romeo	108.642
1990	F3	Ludovic Faure	F	Dallara 390-Volkswagen	108.847
1991	F3	Olivier Panis	F	Ralt RT35-Alfa Romeo	110.439
1992	F3	Stephan Gregoire	F	Dallara 392-Alfa Romeo	111.268
1993	F3	Christophe Tinseau	F	Dallara 393-Opel	113.113
1994	F3	Christophe Tinseau	F	Dallara 394-Opel	110.897
1995	F3	Laurent Redon	F	Dallara 394-Fiat	110.746
1996	F3	Soheil Ayari	F	Dallara 396-Opel	109.474
1997	F3	David Saelens	B	Dallara 396-Opel	111.519
1998	F3	David Saelens	B	Dallara 396-Renault	110.698
1999	F3	Tiago Monteiro	P	Dallara 399-Renault	110.997
2000	F3	Tiago Monteiro	P	Dallara 399-Renault	108.427
2001	F3	Tiago Monteiro	P	Dallara 399-Renault	81.915
2002	F3	Tristan Gommendy	F	Dallara 302-Renault	112.863

At Albi except *at Nogaro

CLERMONT-FERRAND
Circuit Louis Rosier/Circuit de Montagne d'Auvergne/Charade

The Automobile Club de France had designed a 30-mile permanent road course at Puy de Dome near Clermont-Ferrand in 1908. Although the project was stillborn, a Grand Prix circuit with over 50 corners was opened in the beautiful surroundings of Clermont-Ferrand fifty years later. The Circuit Louis Rosier, now known as Charade, held the French Grand Prix on four occasions. It twists and undulates around two extinct volcanoes with no real straight apart from at the start. The old venue closed in 1988 and was replaced by a shortened circuit that hosted national events. Charade closed temporarily in 2000 to refurbish the pit complex.

Active years	1958-99, 2001 to date
Location	3 miles west of Clermont-Ferrand, 95 miles from Nevers, 110 miles west of Lyon, 115 miles east of Limoges
Type	Temporary road course
Website	www.charade.fr

Current circuit

Lap distance	2.470 miles
Lap record	Qualifying: David Saelens (Dallara 396-Renault), 1m42.722, 86.562 mph, F3, 1998
	Race: Sebastien Bourdais (Martini MK79-Opel), 1m43.827, 85.641 mph, F3, 1999

Circuit changes

1958-88	Grand Prix circuit. 5.005 miles
1989 to date	Shortened circuit opened using pit area. Current circuit

French Grand Prix see above

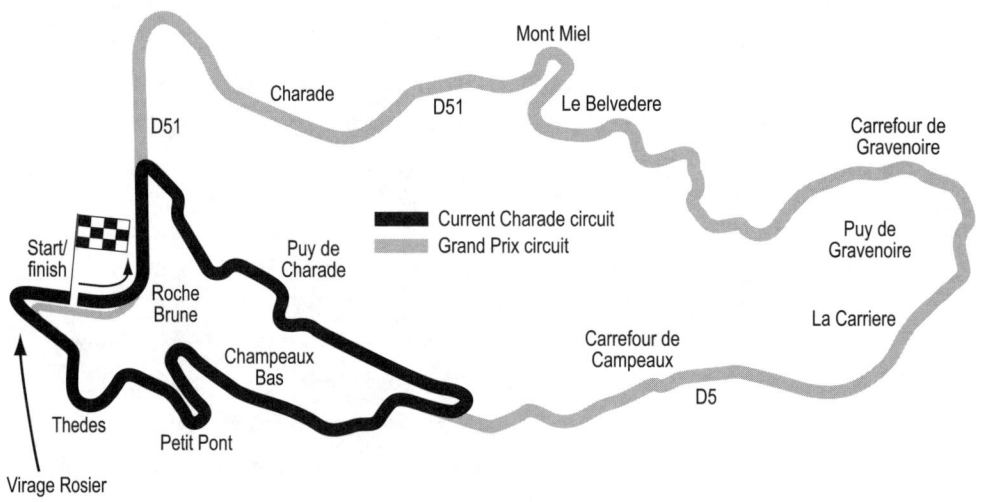

CROIX-EN-TERNOIS

Croix is a tight and twisting circuit south of Calais that hosted European Formula 3 Championship rounds in the seventies and eighties. It has been used by Formula 1 teams for testing prior to Monaco because of its succession of slow corners. But the track is basic and lacks the facilities needed in a modern venue. The circuit was sold in 2000 and plans for an extension are being considered.

Active years	1973 to date
Location	2 miles west of St Pol-sur-Ternoise, 20 miles west of Arras
Type	Permanent road course
Website	www.circuitdecroix.com
Lap distance	1.181 miles
Lap record	Qualifying: Tiago Monteiro (Dallara 399-Renault), 49.643s, 85.615 mph, F3, 2001
	Race: Tiago Monteiro (Dallara 399-Renault), 50.184s, 84.692 mph, F3, 2001

EUROPEAN F3 RACE						
year	formula	winner	nat	car		mph
1976	F3 E	Conny Andersson	S	March 763-Toyota		76.756
1977	F3 E	Derek Daly	IRL	Chevron B38-Toyota		77.363
1981	F3 E	Mauro Baldi	I	March 813-Alfa Romeo		77.980
1983	F3 E	Pierluigi Martini	I	Ralt RT3/83-Alfa Romeo		79.694

France

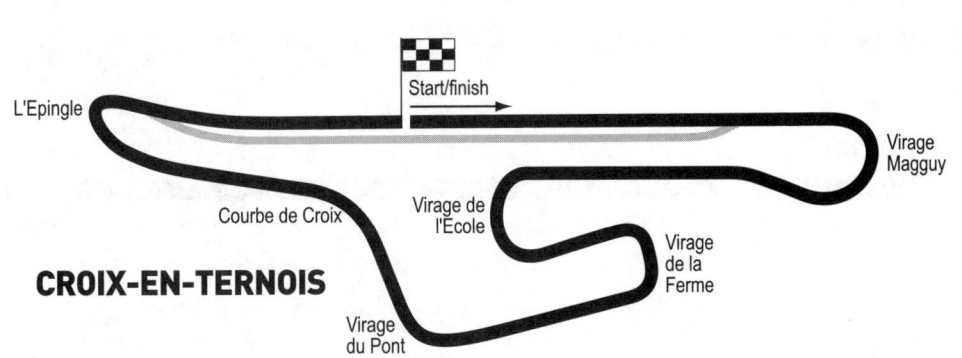

L'Epingle

Start/finish

Virage
Magguy

Courbe de Croix

Virage de
l'École

Virage
de la
Ferme

CROIX-EN-TERNOIS

Virage
du Pont

DIJON-PRENOIS

Dijon-Prenois was the third circuit to have been used in the area when it opened in 1972. Picturesque and demanding in places, it was eventually too short to continue as a top international venue. Although it was extended in 1976, Dijon eventually lost the Grand Prix to Circuit Paul Ricard. Many memorable races were held at Dijon, including first Grand Prix victories for Jabouille and Renault (1979), Prost (1981) and Rosberg (1982 Swiss GP). And it will always be remembered as the scene of GP racing's greatest modern day dice, when Rene Arnoux and Gilles Villeneuve fought to finish second in the 1979 French Grand Prix. They repeatedly swapped positions in the closing laps, banging wheels on and off the track. That was viewed as irresponsible to some, but exhilarating to most. International racing did return intermittently in the form of FIA GT Championship in the nineties, but Dijon is no longer at the forefront of French racing.

Active years	1972 to date
Location	10 miles north-west of Dijon, 185 miles east of Paris
Type	Permanent road course
Website	www.circuit-dijon-prenois.com

Current circuit

Lap distance	2.361 miles
Lap records	Qualifying: Alain Prost (Renault RE30B), 1m01.380, 138.475 mph, F1, 1982
	Race: Alain Prost (McLaren MP4/2-TAG Porsche), 1m05.257, 130.248 mph, F1, 1984

Circuit changes

1972-76	2.044 miles
1977 to date	Parabolique extension built. Current circuit

French Grand Prix see above

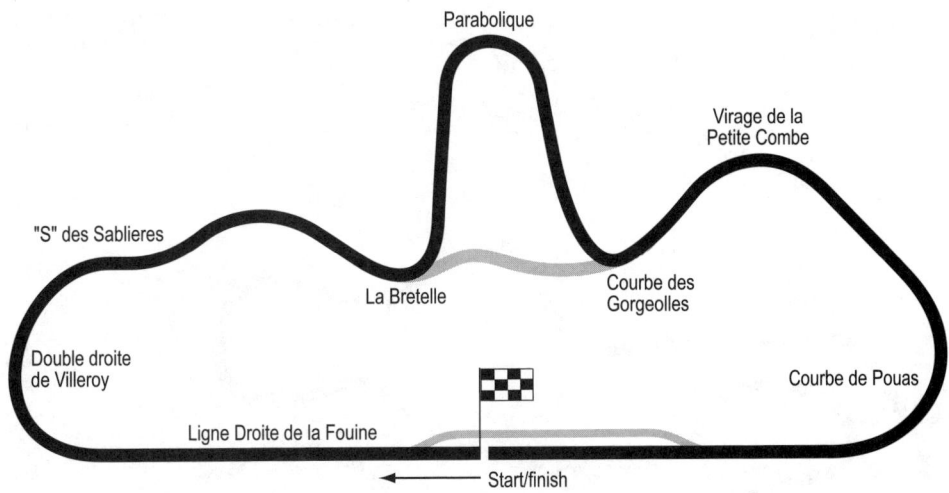

Parabolique

Virage de la
Petite Combe

"S" des Sablieres

La Bretelle

Courbe des
Gorgeolles

Double droite
de Villeroy

Courbe de Pouas

Ligne Droite de la Fouine

Start/finish

DIJON-PRENOIS

SWISS GRAND PRIX (also see Switzerland)

year	formula	winner	nat	car	mph
1975	F1	Clay Regazzoni	CH	Ferrari 312T	79.867
1982	F1 W	Keke Rosberg	SF	Williams FW08-Ford	122.272

INTERNATIONAL FORMULA 3000 RACE

year	formula	winner	nat	car	mph
1985	F3000 INT	Christian Danner	D	March 85B-Cosworth	113.079
1988	F3000 INT	Martin Donnelly	GB	Reynard 88D-Cosworth	117.776
1989	F3000 INT	Erik Comas	F	Lola T89/50-Mugen	117.470

EUROPEAN FORMULA 3 RACE

year	formula	winner	nat	car	mph
1978	F3 E	Teo Fabi	I	March 783-Toyota	103.986

WORLD SPORTS CAR RACE

year	formula	winner	nat	car	mph
1973	SC W	Henri Pescarolo/Gerard Larrousse	F	Matra-Simca MS670	114.350
1975	SC W	Arturo Merzario/Jacques Laffite	I/F	Alfa Romeo T33TT/12	112.333
1976	SC W	Jacky Ickx/Jochen Mass	B/D	Porsche 935	105.607
	SC WSC	Jacky Ickx/Jochen Mass	B/D	Porsche 936	115.499
1977	SC WSC	Arturo Merzario/Jean-Pierre Jarier	I/F	Alfa Romeo T33SC/12	102.570
1978	SC W	Bob Wollek/Henri Pescarolo	F	Porsche 935	99.367
1979	SC W	Reinhold Joest/Volkert Merl/Mario Ketterer	D/D/CH	Porsche 908/4	100.327
1980	SC W	Henri Pescarolo/Jurgen Barth	F/D	Porsche 935	96.009
1989	SC W	Bob Wollek/Frank Jelinski	F/D	Porsche 962C	110.805
1990	SC W	Jean-Louis Schlesser/Mauro Baldi	F/I	Mercedes-Benz C11	113.107

FIA GT RACE

year	formula	winner	nat	car	mph
1994	GT	Michel Ferte/Michel Neugarten	F	Venturi 600LM	96.257
1998	GT FIA	Klaus Ludwig/Ricardo Zonta	D/BR	Mercedes-Benz CLK-LM	112.451

LA CHATRE

La Chatre was a regular venue for the European F3 Championship during the eighties. It is a short, part-temporary, part permanent circuit without pits, and the paddock is in the town square a mile away! Only eighteen cars were permitted to start due to the short circuit length. A 0.684-mile version is now used for the racing school.

Active years	1961 to date
Location	8 miles south-west of Chateauroux, 180 miles south of Paris
Type	Temporary road course
Lap distance	1.445 miles
Lap record	Race: Alain Ferte (Martini MK37-Alfa Romeo), 1m03.33, 82.141 mph, F3, 1982

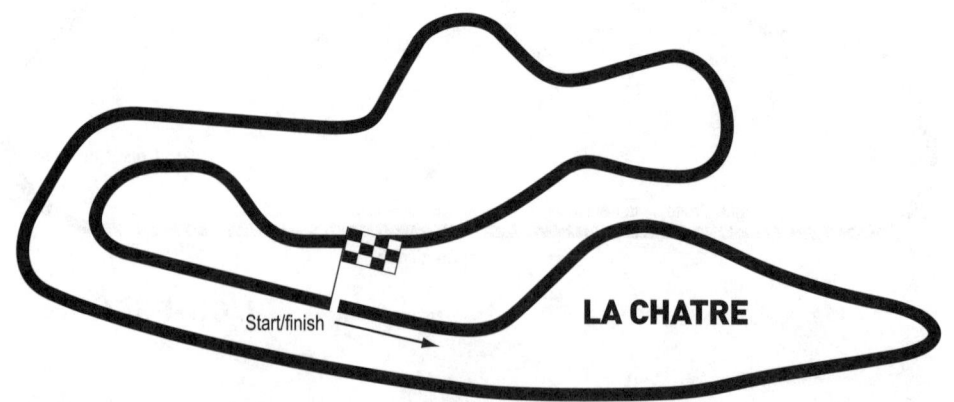

Start/finish

LA CHATRE

LE MANS

24 heures du Mans

The Le Mans 24 hours vies with the Monaco Grand Prix and Indianapolis 500 as the world's most famous automobile race. Le Mans is also one of the last remaining old-fashioned road courses, using public roads that are normally open to general traffic. The area around the town has been instrumental in the growth of the sport and it held the first Grand Prix in 1906. The current circuit was first used for the 1921 French Grand Prix, and the original unpaved roads were soon laid with tarmac. The 1955 24-hour race was marred by the worst disaster in motor racing history when the Mercedes of "Pierre Levegh" (real name: Pierre Bouillon) crashed into the crowd opposite the pits, killing the driver and over 80 spectators. The recriminations were felt throughout the world, with racing suspended in France and banned permanently by Swiss authorities. In the nineties, safety concerns resulted in the 3-mile Mulsanne Straight being interrupted by two chicanes. A new section approaching the Esses was used in 2002—the first major modification in a decade. Even with these changes, the lure of Le Mans remains as strong as ever to drivers, spectators and manufacturers alike.

Active years 1921 to date
Location 3 miles south of Le Mans, 130 miles south-west of Paris

Type Temporary road course with some permanent sections
Website www.lemans.org

Current circuit
Lap distance 8.451 miles
Lap record Qualifying: Rinaldo Capello (Audi R8), 3m29.905, 144.939 mph, Sports Cars, 2002
Race: Tom Kristensen (Audi R8), 3m33.483, 142.511 mph, Sports Cars, 2002

Circuit changes
1921-28 Original circuit with western hairpin at Pontlieue. 10.726 miles
1929-31 Western end of circuit shortened with the "Rue du Circuit" link road for safety reasons. 10.153 miles
1932-55 The current track from the pits straight to Tertre Rouge built. The Dunlop Bridge installed after the first corner. 8.378 miles
1956-67 Following the 1955 disaster the pits straight was widened and the Dunlop Corner eased. 8.365 miles
1968-71 Ford chicane built before the start-line. 8.369 miles
1972-78 Old Maison Blanche bypassed with a new section from Arnage to the Ford chicane. 8.476 miles
1979-85 Tertre Rouge tightened to accommodate new ring road built around the town. 8.467 miles
1986 A new Mulsanne Corner built to avoid newly built roundabout. 8.406 miles
1987-89 Chicane built at Dunlop Corner. 8.410 miles
1990 2 chicanes built on the Mulsanne straight. 8.450 miles
1991-2001 Arnage and Indianapolis modified, some corners re-profiled. Mulsanne crest eased in 2001
2002 to date Section between Dunlop Chicane and Esses modified. Current circuit

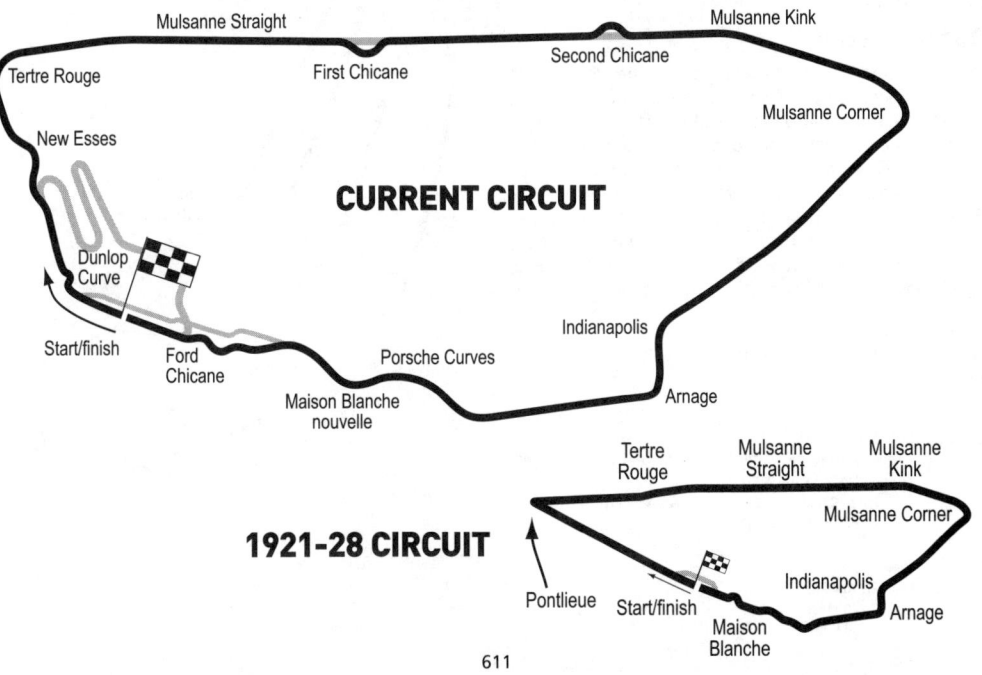

CURRENT CIRCUIT

Mulsanne Straight · Mulsanne Kink · First Chicane · Second Chicane · Tertre Rouge · Mulsanne Corner · New Esses · Dunlop Curve · Start/finish · Ford Chicane · Porsche Curves · Indianapolis · Maison Blanche nouvelle · Arnage

1921-28 CIRCUIT

Tertre Rouge · Mulsanne Straight · Mulsanne Kink · Mulsanne Corner · Pontlieue · Start/finish · Maison Blanche · Indianapolis · Arnage

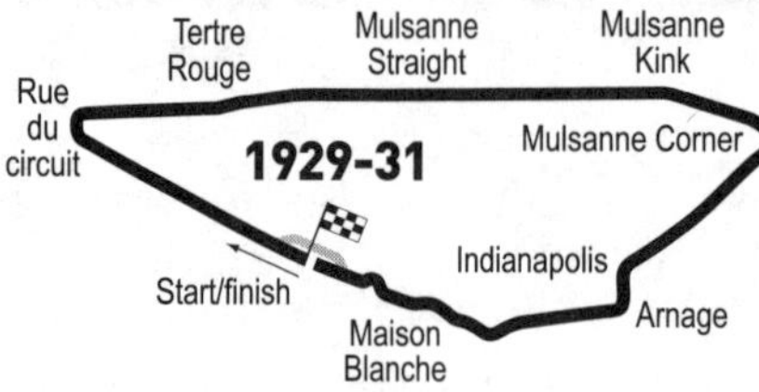

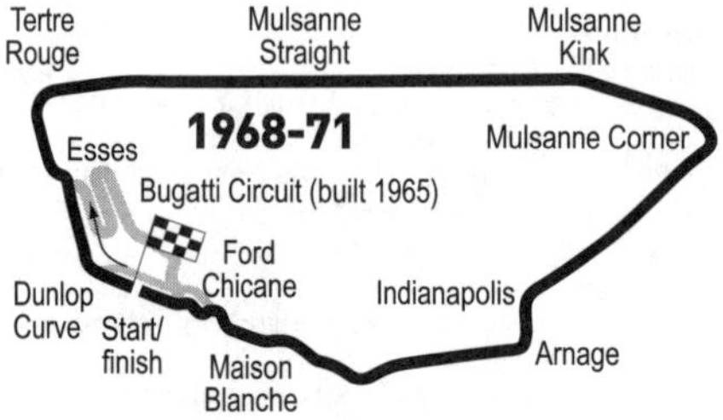

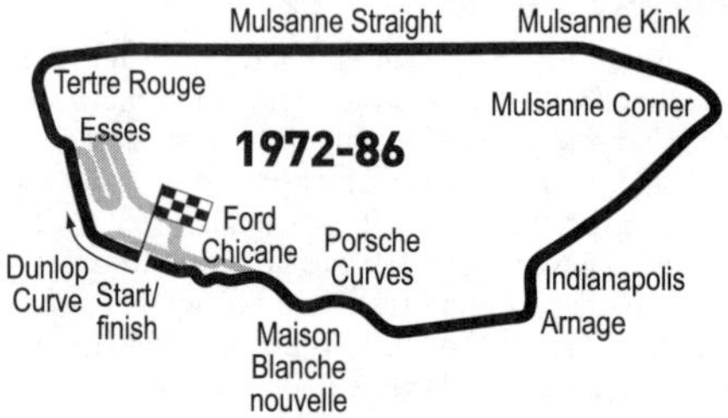

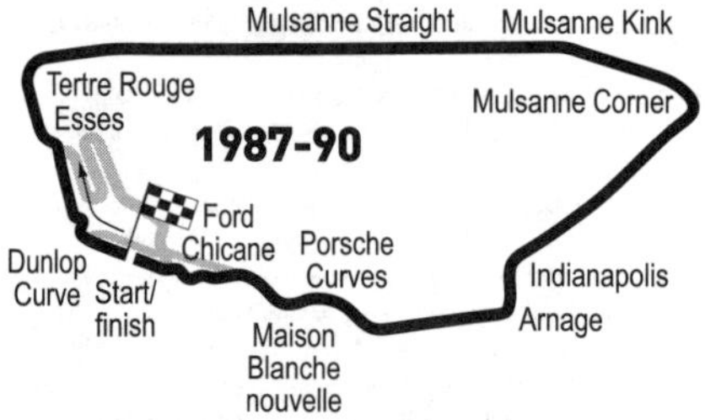

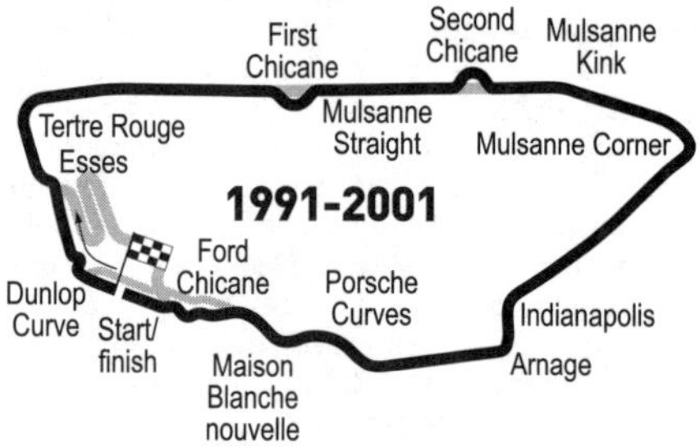

1929-31

Rue du circuit · Tertre Rouge · Mulsanne Straight · Mulsanne Kink · Mulsanne Corner · Indianapolis · Arnage · Maison Blanche · Start/finish

1932-67

Tertre Rouge · Mulsanne Straight · Mulsanne Kink · Esses · Mulsanne Corner · Indianapolis · Arnage · Maison Blanche · Start/finish

1968-71

Tertre Rouge · Mulsanne Straight · Mulsanne Kink · Esses · Mulsanne Corner · Bugatti Circuit (built 1965) · Ford Chicane · Indianapolis · Arnage · Dunlop Curve · Start/finish · Maison Blanche

1972-86

Mulsanne Straight · Mulsanne Kink · Tertre Rouge · Esses · Mulsanne Corner · Ford Chicane · Porsche Curves · Indianapolis · Dunlop Curve · Start/finish · Arnage · Maison Blanche nouvelle

1987-90

Mulsanne Straight · Mulsanne Kink · Tertre Rouge · Esses · Mulsanne Corner · Ford Chicane · Porsche Curves · Indianapolis · Dunlop Curve · Start/finish · Arnage · Maison Blanche nouvelle

1991-2001

First Chicane · Second Chicane · Mulsanne Kink · Mulsanne Straight · Tertre Rouge · Esses · Mulsanne Corner · Ford Chicane · Porsche Curves · Indianapolis · Dunlop Curve · Start/finish · Arnage · Maison Blanche nouvelle

French Grand Prix see above
Grand Prix de France see above
Le Mans 24 hours see page 356

LE MANS
Bugatti Circuit

Charles Deutsch, who divided his time between being chief engineer for the French Department of Bridges and Roads and being a partner in the Deutsch-Bonnet racing car constructor, designed the Bugatti circuit in 1965. It incorporates the main straight from the Circuit des 24 heures with a tight section behind the pits. The Bugatti circuit held the 1967 French Grand Prix, but since then it has not been regularly used for international events. One exception was the FIA F3000 race, which was held here from 1986-91.

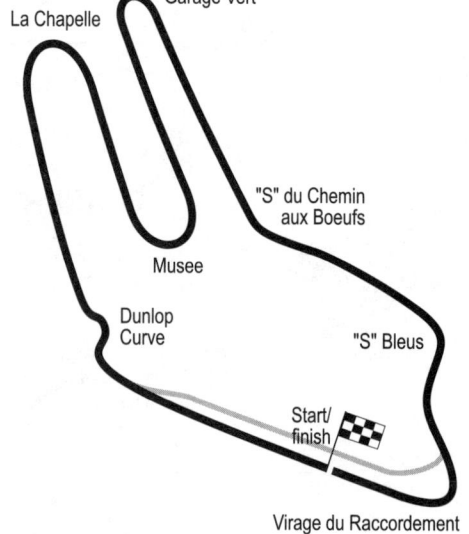

La Chapelle · Garage Vert · "S" du Chemin aux Boeufs · Musee · Dunlop Curve · "S" Bleus · Start/finish · Virage du Raccordement

Active years	1965 to date
Type	Permanent road course
Website	www.lemans.org

Current Circuit

Lap distance	2.655 miles
Lap record	Qualifying: Olivier Pla (Dallara 302-Renault), 1m32.900, 102.885 m ph, F3, 2002
	Race: Renaud Derlot (Dallara 302-Renault), 1m34.506, 98.960 mph, F3, 2002

Circuit changes

1965-66	2.710 miles
1967-76	2.748 miles
1979-88	2.635 miles
1989-90	2.750 miles
1991-2001	2.753 miles
2002 to date	Section between Dunlop Chicane and Esses modified. Current circuit

INTERNATIONAL FORMULA 3000 RACE

year	formula	winner	nat	car	mph
1986	F3000 INT	Emanuele Pirro	I	March 86B-Cosworth	105.240
1987	F3000 INT	Luis Perez Sala	E	Lola T87/50-Cosworth	102.044
1988	F3000 INT	Olivier Grouillard	F	Lola T88/50-Cosworth	102.842
1989	F3000 INT	Erik Comas	F	Lola T89/50-Mugen	104.718
1990	F3000 INT	Erik Comas	F	Lola T90/50-Mugen	103.565
1991	F3000 INT	Antonio Tamburini	I	Reynard 91D-Mugen	88.316

MAGNY-COURS

Circuit de Nevers

The Circuit Jean Behra, as it was known, was a second-division, slightly run-down national track that was also home to the Martini racing car constructor when political pressure was exercised on its behalf in the eighties. President Mitterand, so long a supporter of French racing in general and the Ligier team in particular, supported a plan to move the French Grand Prix to the Nevers region. A major redevelopment of Magny-Cours was completed in time for the 1991 race, and the renamed Circuit de Nevers had the smoothest track surface on the calendar. But after the fast open layout of Circuit Paul Ricard, the new circuit was somewhat tight and uninspiring in comparison. Magny-Cours also held the last Group C Sports Car race in history in 1992.

Active years	1961 to date
Location	7 miles south of Nevers, 155 miles south of Paris
Type	Permanent road course
Website	www.magny-cours.com

Current circuit

Lap distance	2.641 miles
Lap records	Qualifying: Juan Pablo Montoya (Williams FW24-BMW), 1m11.985, 132.078 mph, F1, 2002
	Race: David Coulthard (McLaren MP4/17-Mercedes-Benz), 1m15.045, 126.692 mph, F1, 2002

Circuit changes

1961-70	1.243 miles
1971-88	Extended to Adelaide hairpin. 2.391 miles
1989-91	Circuit rebuilt, start moved to current location. 2.654 miles
1992 to date	Chicane after Adelaide Hairpin bypassed. Pit lane exit modified in 2001. Current circuit

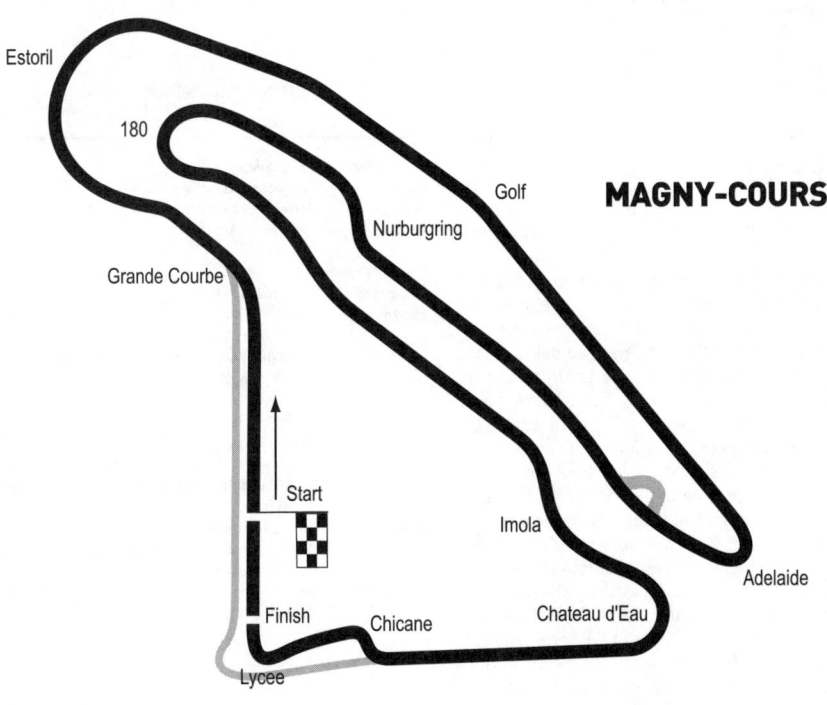

MAGNY-COURS

French Grand Prix see above

NON CHAMPIONSHIP FORMULA 2 RACE

year	formula	winner	nat	car	mph
1975	F2	Jean-Pierre Jabouille	F	Elf 2J-BMW	102.947

INTERNATIONAL FORMULA 3000 RACE

year	formula	winner	nat	car	mph
1992	F3000 INT	Jean-Marc Gounon	F	Lola T92/50-Cosworth	109.172
1993	F3000 INT	Franck Lagorce	F	Reynard 93D-Cosworth	96.293
1994	F3000 INT	Jules Boullion	F	Reynard 94D-Cosworth	107.600
1995	F3000 INT	Kenny Brack	S	Reynard 95D-Judd	107.946
1996	F3000 INT	Marc Goossens	B	Lola T96/50-Zytek	105.250
1999	F3000 INT	Nick Heidfeld	D	Lola B99/50-Zytek	90.342
2000	F3000 INT	Nicolas Minassian	F	Lola B99/50-Zytek	102.511
2001	F3000 INT	Mark Webber	AUS	Lola B99/50-Zytek	104.359
2002	F3000 INT	Tomas Enge	CS	Lola B2/50-Zytek	100.897

EUROPEAN FORMULA 3 RACE

year	formula	winner	nat	car	mph
1978	F3 E	Jan Lammers	NL	Ralt RT1-Toyota	98.401
1979	F3 E	Alain Prost	F	Martini MK27-Renault	98.542
1980	F3 E	Thierry Boutsen	B	Martini MK31-Toyota	98.781
1981	F3 E	Philippe Alliot	F	Martini MK34-Alfa Romeo	101.259
1982	F3 E	Alain Ferte	F	Martini MK37-Alfa Romeo	101.525
1983	F3 E	John Nielsen	DK	Ralt RT3/83-Volkswagen	97.829
1984	F3 E	Ivan Capelli	I	Martini MK42-Alfa Romeo	102.472

WORLD SPORTS CAR RACE

year	formula	winner	nat	car	mph
1991	SC W	Yannick Dalmas/Keke Rosberg	F/SF	Peugeot 905B	106.064
1992	SC W	Philippe Alliot/Mauro Baldi	F/I	Peugeot 905B	113.787

FIA GT RACE

year	formula	winner	nat	car	mph
2000	GT FIA	Julian Bailey/Jamie Campbell-Walter	GB	Lister Storm GT	93.106
2001	GT FIA	Jamie Campbell-Walter/Tom Coronel	GB/NL	Lister Storm GT	94.064
2002	GT FIA	Jamie Campbell-Walter/Nicolaus Springer	GB/D	Lister Storm GT	95.067

MONTLHERY

Designed by Raymond Jamin and built in 1924 as a 33-degree banked oval, the road course was completed a year later in time to hold the French Grand Prix. Although Antonio Ascari was tragically killed during that race, Montlhery had already become France's leading Grand Prix circuit. In 1934, Louis Chiron scored an unexpected victory for Alfa Romeo against the debut of the much-vaunted Mercedes-Benz and Auto Union teams, but the tide was clearly turning in Germany's favour. Rather than suffer the inevitable German wins, the organisers turned to sports cars for the French Grand Prix in 1936-37. It was not a popular move and Montlhery lost the 1938 race to Reims, never to regain it. After the war organisers introduced the Paris 1000 kms sports car race, but an accident in 1964 left two drivers and three officials dead. The circuit fell into decline and closed in 1973. After a lengthy absence from international motor racing, the Paris 1000 kms was revived in 1994 as part of the new FIA GT series, but the course proved too bumpy and Montlhery dropped once more from the international calendar a year later.

Active years	1924 to date
Location	16 miles south-west of Paris
Type	Permanent road course and paved oval
Website	montlhery.com

Current circuit

Lap distance	2.116 miles
Lap record	Qualifying: Michel Ferte (Venturi 600LM), 1m20.43, 94.711 mph, GT, 1994
	Race: Bob Wollek (Porsche 911 Bi-turbo), 1m21.99, 92.909 mph, GT, 1995

Circuit changes (for International events)

1924	Oval. 1.55 miles
1925-50	Full Grand Prix circuit. 3 chicanes were introduced for 1935 Grand Prix but official circuit length remained unaltered. 7.767 miles
1948-50	Road circuit. 4.700 miles
1950-52	Combined road and track circuit. 3.900 miles
1956-73	Paris 1000 kms circuit. 4.837 miles
1982 to date	Circuit using banked course with short road course. Current circuit

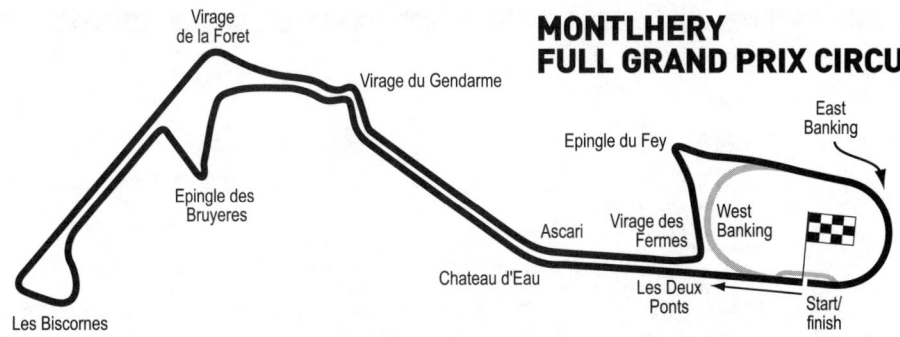

MONTLHERY
FULL GRAND PRIX CIRCUIT

Virage de la Foret

Virage du Gendarme

Epingle des Bruyeres

Les Biscornes

Epingle du Fey

East Banking

Ascari

Virage des Fermes

West Banking

Chateau d'Eau

Les Deux Ponts

Start/finish

French Grand Prix see above

PARIS 1000 KMS					
year	formula	winner	nat	car	mph
1956	SC	Jean Behra/Louis Rosier	F	Maserati 300S	93.357
1960	GT	Olivier Gendebien/Lucien Bianchi	B	Ferrari 250GT	91.441
1961	GT	Ricardo Rodriguez/Pedro Rodriguez	MEX	Ferrari 250GT	95.448
1962	GT	Ricardo Rodriguez/Pedro Rodriguez	MEX	Ferrari 250GTO	98.015
1964	SC W	Graham Hill/Jo Bonnier	GB/S	Ferrari 330P	95.291
1966	SC	Michael Parkes/David Piper	GB	Ferrari 250LM	95.880
1967	SC	Jacky Ickx/Paul Hawkins	B/AUS	Mirage Mk1-Ford	85.217
1968	SC	Hans Herrmann/Rolf Stommelen	D	Porsche 908	100.242
1969	SC	Jean-Pierre Beltoise/Henri Pescarolo	F	Matra MS650	105.454
1970	SC	Jack Brabham/Francois Cevert	AUS/F	Matra-Simca MS660	106.729
1971	SC	Derek Bell/Gijs van Lennep	GB/NL	Porsche 917	99.000
1972*	SC	Gerard Larrousse/Jean-Pierre Beltoise	F	Lola T282-Ford	102.645
1994	GT FIA	Henri Pescarolo/Jean-Claude Basso	F	Venturi 600LM	81.710
1995	GT FIA	Detlef Hubner/Stefan Oberndorfer	D	Porsche 911 GT2	83.799
At Montlhery except at *Rouen-les-Essarts					

NOGARO

Circuit Paul Armagnac

The Circuit Paul Armagnac is set on the northern edge of Nogaro, a small, sleepy town in the brandy region south of Bordeaux. It combines a tight complex around the pits (which formed the original circuit) and two long straights, one of which runs parallel to an airfield runway. In the late nineties the Grand Prix de Nogaro was a round of the FIA Formula 3000 Championship, but in 1994 this race was cancelled and replaced by Formula Renault and later a GT race. The temperate climate, fine food and beautiful countryside have made Nogaro a popular winter testing venue.

Active years	1960 to date
Location	Northern suburbs of Nogaro, 40 miles north-east of Pau, 75 miles west of Toulouse, 90 miles south-east of Bordeaux
Type	Permanent road course
Website	www.circuit-nogaro.com

Current circuit	
Lap distance	2.259 miles
Lap record	Qualifying: Franck Lagorce (Reynard 93D-Cosworth), 1m17.342, 105.149 mph, F3000, 1993
	Race: Alessandro Zanardi (Reynard 91D-Mugen), 1m20.16, 101.453 mph, F3000, 1991

Circuit changes	
1960-72	1.089 miles
1973-88	Extended to the Epingle de Caupenne. 1.939 miles
1989 to date	A complex added after the Courbe de Caupenne. Current circuit

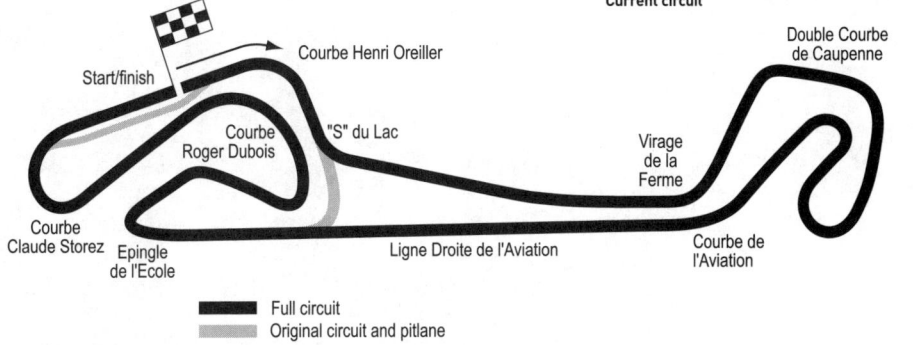

Start/finish

Courbe Henri Oreiller

Courbe Roger Dubois

"S" du Lac

Double Courbe de Caupenne

Virage de la Ferme

Courbe Claude Storez

Epingle de l'Ecole

Ligne Droite de l'Aviation

Courbe de l'Aviation

▬▬▬ Full circuit
▬▬▬ Original circuit and pitlane

NOGARO GRAND PRIX

year	formula	winner	nat	car	mph
1960	FJ	Basini	F	Raineri	52.512
1961	FJ	John Love	RSR	Cooper	58.416
1962	FJ	Jo Schlesser	F	Brabham-Ford	61.722
1963	FJ	Jean Vinatier	F	Lotus-Ford	59.261
1964	F3	Pierre Ryser	CH	Cooper-Ford	57.959
1965	F3	Trevor Blokdyk	ZA	Brabham-Ford	67.176
1966	F3	Jean-Pierre Jaussaud	F	Matra MS5-Ford	66.200
1967	F3	Henri Pescarolo	F	Matra MS5-Ford	66.068
1968	F3	Francois Cevert	F	Tecno 68-Ford	68.814
1969	F3	Francois Mazet	F	Tecno 69-Ford	69.019
1970	F3	Jean-Pierre Jaussaud	F	Martini MW5-Ford	71.040
1971	F3	Jean-Pierre Jabouille	F	Alpine-Ford	73.462
1972	SC	Jean-Pierre Beltoise	F	Chevron	73.461
1973	SC	Gerard Larrousse	F	Lola-BMW	83.887
1974	F2	Patrick Tambay	F	Elf 2/A367-BMW	92.672
1975	F2 E	Patrick Tambay	F	March 752-BMW	93.666
1976	F2 E	Patrick Tambay	F	Martini MK19-Renault	94.273
1977	F2 E	Rene Arnoux	F	Martini MK22-Renault	93.695
1978	F2 E	Bruno Giacomelli	I	March 782-BMW	95.476
1979	F1/F2	Emilio de Villota	E	Lotus 78-Ford	95.663
1980	F3	Philippe Streiff	F	Martini MK31-Toyota	90.309
1981	F3	Philippe Streiff	F	Martini MK34-Alfa Romeo	90.743
1982	F3 E	James Weaver	GB	Ralt RT3/82-Toyota	91.950
1983	F3 E	Pierluigi Martini	I	Ralt RT3/83-Alfa Romeo	91.849
1984	F3 E	John Nielsen	DK	Ralt RT3/84-Volkswagen	94.408
1985	TC E	Tom Walkinshaw/Win Percy	GB	Rover Vitesse	78.868
1986	TC E	Roberto Ravaglia/Gerhard Berger	I/A	BMW 635 CSi	81.481
1987	TC E	Fabien Giroix/Jean-Pierre Jaussaud	F	BMW M3	81.278
1988	TC E	Klaus Ludwig/Klaus Niedzwiedz	D	Ford Sierra RS500	83.094
1989	TC	Jean Ragnotti/Jean-Louis Bousquet	F	Renault 21 turbo	82.218
1990	F3000 INT	Eric van de Poele	B	Reynard 90D-Cosworth	92.647
1991	F3000 INT	Christian Fittipaldi	BR	Reynard 91D-Mugen	100.149
1992	F3000 INT	Luca Badoer	I	Reynard 92D-Cosworth	99.841
1993	F3000 INT	Franck Lagorce	F	Reynard 93D-Cosworth	99.737
1994	Renault	Stephane Sarrazin	F	Martini MK65-Renault	86.686
1995	GT FIA	Olivier Grouillard/Andy Wallace	F/GB	McLaren F1 GTR-BMW	84.526
1996	GT FIA	Ray Bellm/James Weaver	GB	McLaren F1 GTR-BMW	86.772
1997	GT	Patrice Goueslard/Jean-Luc Chereau/			
		Jack Laconte	F	Porsche 911 GT2	82.100
1998	GT	n/a			
1999*	GT	Michel Nourry/Patrick Herbert	F	Porsche 911 GT2	82.067
	GT	Lucien Guitteny/Jean-Pierre Jarier	F	Porsche 911 GT2	82.547
2000*	GT	Dominique Dupuy/Francois Fiat	F	Chrysler Viper GTS-R	80.272
	GT	Patrick Bornhauser/Olivier Thevenin	F	VBM 4000 GTC	82.599
2001	GT	Patrice Goueslard/Philippe Soulan	F	Porsche 911 GT2	81.820
2002*	GT	Patrice Goueslard/Philippe Soulan	F	Porsche 911 GT2	85.775
	GT	Patrice Goueslard/Philippe Soulan	F	Porsche 911 GT2	84.352

*Two heats, no overall winner

PAU

The 1901 GP de Pau was the first race on record to carry the title "Grand Prix". In 1930, the French GP was held on a 10-mile circuit outside of the picturesque Pyrenees town, and three years later, in the February snow, a street circuit was introduced in the city for the second Grand Prix de Pau. This layout has been used, almost uninterruptedly and unchanged ever since. After the Station hairpin, overlooked by a steep hill that acts as spectator bank, the road climbs to the narrow Pont Oscar. Another hairpin, almost too tight for modern racing cars, follows and leads to the challenging Parc Beaumont section. After the Monument Foch the track winds its way to another hairpin and back to the start-line to complete the lap. The organisers have held an increasingly popular invitation F3 race since F3000 moved to Monte Carlo in 1999.

Active years	**1933 to date**
Location	**125 miles south of Bordeaux, 125 miles west of Toulouse**
Type	**Temporary street circuit**
Lap distance	**1.715 miles**
Lap record	**Qualifying: Andrea Montermini (Reynard 92D-Judd), 1m08.60, 90.000 mph, F3000, 1992**
	Race: Emanuele Naspetti (Reynard 92D-Cosworth), 1m09.82, 88.428 mph, F3000, 1992

French Grand Prix see above

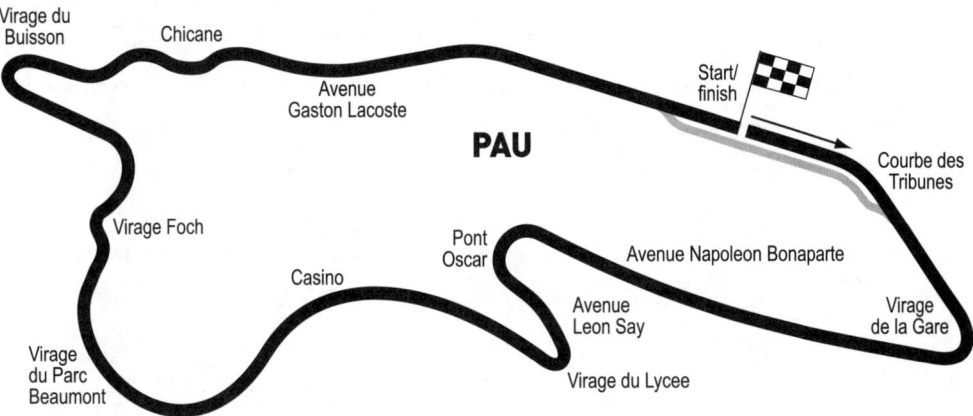

PAU GRAND PRIX

year	formula	winner	nat	car	mph
1901	FL	Maurice Farman	F	Panhard 24CV	46.986
1933	GP	Marcel Lehoux	DZ	Bugatti T51	47.280
1935	GP	Tazio Nuvolari	I	Alfa Romeo Tipo-B "P3"	51.993
1936	GP	Philippe Etancelin	F	Maserati V8RI	50.829
1937	SC	Jean-Pierre Wimille	F	Bugatti T59S	51.051
1938	GP	Rene Dreyfus	F	Delahaye 145	54.449
1939	GP	Hermann Lang	D	Mercedes-Benz W163	54.903
1947	F1	Nello Pagani	I	Maserati 4CL	51.798
1948	F1	Nello Pagani	I	Maserati 4CL	53.015
1949	F1	Juan Manuel Fangio	RA	Maserati 4CLT/48	52.598
1950	F1	Juan Manuel Fangio	RA	Maserati 4CLT/48	58.245
1951	F1	Luigi Villoresi	I	Ferrari 375	57.264
1952	F2	Alberto Ascari	I	Ferrari 500	56.595
1953	F2	Alberto Ascari	I	Ferrari 500	60.597
1954	F1	Jean Behra	F	Gordini 16	62.299
1955	F1	Jean Behra	F	Maserati 250F	62.138
1957	F1	Jean Behra	F	Maserati 250F	62.804
1958	F2	Maurice Trintignant	F	Cooper T43-Climax	59.359
1959	F2	Maurice Trintignant	F	Cooper T51-Climax	57.336
1960	F2	Jack Brabham	AUS	Cooper T45-Climax	63.929
1961	F1	Jim Clark	GB	Lotus 18-Climax	63.517
1962	F1	Maurice Trintignant	F	Lotus 18/21-Climax	64.477
1963	F1	Jim Clark	GB	Lotus 25-Climax	61.619
1964	F2	Jim Clark	GB	Lotus 32-Ford	61.990
1965	F2	Jim Clark	GB	Lotus 35-Ford	57.390
1966	F2	Jack Brabham	AUS	Brabham BT18-Honda	68.420
1967	F2	Jochen Rindt	A	Brabham BT23-Ford	75.085

PAU GRAND PRIX (cont.)

year	formula	winner	nat	car	mph
1968	F2	Jackie Stewart	GB	Matra MS7-Ford	74.928
1969	F2	Jochen Rindt	A	Lotus 59B-Ford	76.497
1970	F2	Jochen Rindt	A	Lotus 69-Ford	76.930
1971	F2	Reine Wisell	S	Lotus 69-Ford	77.125
1972	F2 E	Peter Gethin	GB	Chevron B20-Ford	76.889
1973	F2 E	Francois Cevert	F	Elf 2/A367-Ford	79.302
1974	F2 E	Patrick Depailler	F	March 742-BMW	67.367
1975	F2 E	Jacques Laffite	F	Martini MK16-BMW	81.491
1976	F2 E	Rene Arnoux	F	Martini MK19-Renault	81.478
1977	F2 E	Rene Arnoux	F	Martini MK22-Renault	81.083
1978	F2 E	Bruno Giacomelli	I	March 782-BMW	80.602
1979	F2 E	Eddie Cheever	USA	Osella FA2/79-BMW	65.601
1980	F2 E	Richard Dallest	F	AGS JH17-BMW	79.861
1981	F2 E	Geoff Lees	GB	Ralt RH6/81-Honda	80.570
1982	F2 E	Johnny Cecotto	YV	March 822-BMW	82.546
1983	F2 E	Jo Gartner	A	Spirit 201-BMW	71.329
1984	F2 E	Mike Thackwell	NZ	Ralt RH6/84-Honda	83.778
1985	F3000 INT	Christian Danner	D	March 85B-Cosworth	81.886
1986	F3000 INT	Mike Thackwell	NZ	Ralt RT20-Honda	82.276
1987	F3000 INT	Yannick Dalmas	F	March 87B-Cosworth	82.099
1988	F3000 INT	Roberto Moreno	BR	Reynard 88D-Cosworth	83.218
1989	F3000 INT	Jean Alesi	F	Reynard 89D-Mugen	83.371
1990	F3000 INT	Eric van de Poele	B	Reynard 90D-Cosworth	84.212
1991	F3000 INT	Jean-Marc Gounon	F	Ralt RT23-Cosworth	85.630
1992	F3000 INT	Emanuele Naspetti	I	Reynard 92D-Cosworth	86.502
1993	F3000 INT	Pedro Lamy	P	Reynard 92D-Cosworth	86.219
1994	F3000 INT	Gil de Ferran	BR	Reynard 94D-Judd	85.295
1995	F3000 INT	Vincenzo Sospiri	I	Reynard 95D-Cosworth	85.358
1996	F3000 INT	Jorg Muller	D	Lola T96/50-Zytek	83.322
1997	F3000 INT	Juan Pablo Montoya	CO	Lola T96/50-Zytek	83.219
1998	F3000 INT	Juan Pablo Montoya	CO	Lola T96/50-Zytek	82.833
1999	F3	Benoit Treluyer	F	Dallara 399-Renault	83.320
2000	F3	Jonathan Cochet	F	Dallara 399-Renault	83.600
2001	F3	Anthony Davidson	GB	Dallara 301-Mugen	86.688
2002	F3	Renaud Derlot	F	Dallara 302-Renault	79.565

PAUL RICARD

Le Castellet

Built with generous finance from pastis tycoon Paul Ricard, this flat, dusty circuit in southern France was an impressive venue with great facilities when it opened in 1970. The mile-long Mistral straight dominates the full circuit and is followed by the dauntingly fast Signes corner. Though initially heralded as very safe, the Grand Prix stopped using the full circuit after Elio de Angelis was killed while testing in 1986. Political pressure in France led to the Grand Prix moving to Magny-Cours in 1991. Bernie Ecclestone bought the circuit in 1998, and the circuit has been rebuilt as the ultimate Formula 1 test circuit.

Active years	1970 to date
Location	20 miles north-west of Toulon, 35 miles east of Marseille, 110 miles west of Nice
Type	Permanent road course

Full circuit

Active years	Used for Grands Prix from 1970-85. Reintroduced for 1994 International GT race
Lap distance	3.610 miles
Lap records	Qualifying: Keke Rosberg (Williams FW10-Honda), 1m32.462, 140.556 mph, F1, 1985
	Race: Keke Rosberg (Williams FW10-Honda), 1m39.914, 130.072 mph, F1, 1985

Short Grand Prix circuit

Active years	Used for Grands Prix from 1986-90
Lap distance	2.353 miles
Lap records	Qualifying: Nigel Mansell (Ferrari 642), 1m04.402, 131.530 mph, F1, 1990
	Race: Nigel Mansell (Ferrari 642), 1m08.012, 125.410 mph, F1, 1990

French Grand Prix see above

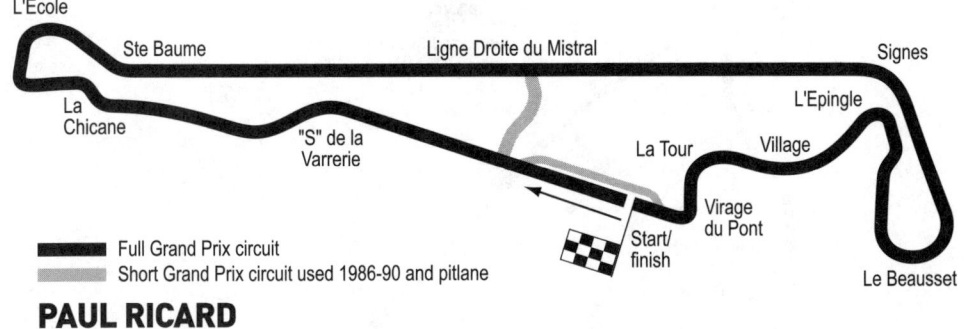

France

L'Ecole
Ste Baume
Ligne Droite du Mistral
Signes
La Chicane
"S" de la Varrerie
L'Epingle
La Tour
Village
Virage du Pont
Start/finish
Le Beausset

■ Full Grand Prix circuit
Short Grand Prix circuit used 1986-90 and pitlane

PAUL RICARD

EUROPEAN FORMULA 3 RACE

year	formula	winner	nat	car	mph
1977	F3 E	Beppe Gabbiani	I	Chevron B38-Toyota	91.573
1985*	F3 E	Alex Caffi	I	Dallara 385-Alfa Romeo	93.629

*European F3 Cup

WORLD SPORTS CAR RACE

year	formula	winner	nat	car	mph
1974	SC W	Jean-Pierre Beltoise/Jean-Pierre Jarier	F	Matra-Simca MS670C	112.200
1977	SC WSC	Arturo Merzario/Jean-Pierre Jarier	I/F	Alfa Romeo T33SC/12	89.801

INTERNATIONAL GT RACE

year	formula	winner	nat	car	mph
1994	GT INT	Bob Wollek/Jean-Pierre Jarier/			
		Jesus Pareja	F/F/E	Porsche 911 turbo SLM	102.224
1995	GT INT	Ray Bellm/Maurizio Sandro Sala	GB/BR	McLaren F1 GTR-BMW	101.560
1996	GT INT	Ray Bellm/James Weaver	GB	McLaren F1 GTR-BMW	108.349
1998	GT	Maxwell Beaverbrook/Geoff Lister/			
		Barrie Williams	GB	Porsche 911 GT2 Evo	93.260

REIMS

A spectacular, triangular road course using public roads, races at Reims were often decided by frequent slipstreaming battles. The circuit was also very fast, and the quest for greater speed led the organisers to cut down trees and demolish houses to ease the corners. New sections of permanent circuit were also built. Run by the flamboyant Raymond "Toto" Roche for the Automobile Club de Champagne, Reims was the dominant French circuit during the sixties. During this period an international 12-hour sports car race was also run at the French GP meeting. But financial and political problems forced Reims to close in 1970, although the old, decaying pits can still be seen.

Active years	1925-70
Location	West of Reims at the villages of Thillois and Gueux
Type	Temporary road course

Final circuit

Lap distance	5.187 miles
Lap record	Qualifying: Lorenzo Bandini (Ferrari 312), 2m07.8, 146.113 mph, F1, 1966
	Race: Lorenzo Bandini (Ferrari 312), 2m11.3, 142.218 mph, F1, 1966

Circuit changes

1925-51	Reims-Gueux. 4.865 miles
1952	Gueux village bypassed by linking the finishing straight with the Virage de la Hovette. 4.472 miles
1953-70	Link road extended to join the Soissons-Reims public road at the new Virage de Muizon. Final circuit

French Grand Prix see above

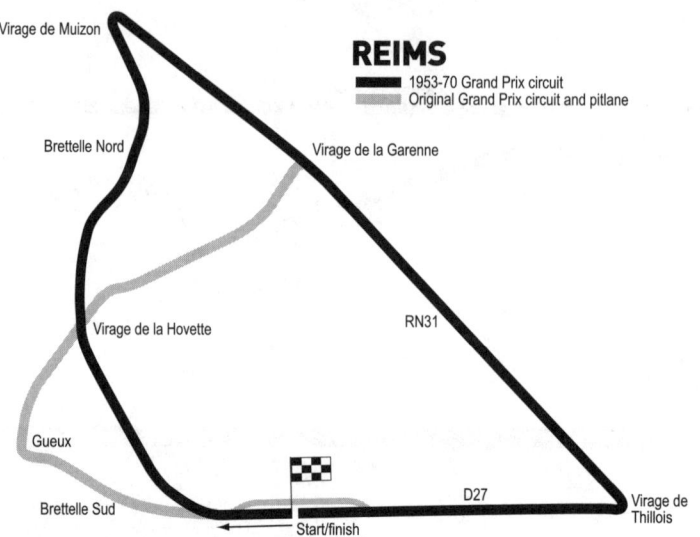

REIMS

■ 1953-70 Grand Prix circuit
■ Original Grand Prix circuit and pitlane

Virage de Muizon
Brettelle Nord
Virage de la Garenne
Virage de la Hovette
RN31
Gueux
Brettelle Sud
D27
Virage de Thillois
Start/finish

French Grand Prix see above
Grand Prix de France see above

MARNE GRAND PRIX

year	formula	winner	nat	car	mph
1925	FL	Pierre Clause	F	Bignan	63.611
1926	FL	Francois Lescot	F	Bugatti T35	68.451
1927	FL	Philippe Etancelin	F	Bugatti T35B	70.603
1928	GP	Louis Chiron	MC	Bugatti T35B	80.580
1929	GP	Philippe Etancelin	F	Bugatti T35C	83.607
1930	GP	Rene Dreyfus	F	Bugatti T35B	85.967
1931	GP	Marcel Lehoux	DZ	Bugatti T51	86.909
1933	GP	Philippe Etancelin	F	Alfa Romeo 8C "Monza"	88.180
1934	GP	Louis Chiron	MC	Alfa Romeo Tipo-B "P3"	79.257
1935	GP	Rene Dreyfus	F	Alfa Romeo Tipo-B "P3"	82.552
1936	SC	Jean-Pierre Wimille	F	Bugatti T57G	87.140
1937	SC	Jean-Pierre Wimille	F	Bugatti T57G	90.120
1947	F1	Christian Kautz	CH	Maserati 4CL	95.800

REIMS GRAND PRIX

year	formula	winner	nat	car	mph
1952	F2	Jean Behra	F	Gordini 16	105.837
1957	F1	Luigi Musso	I	Lancia-Ferrari D50	124.046
1962	F1	Bruce McLaren	NZ	Cooper T60-Climax	126.290
1964	F2	Alan Rees	GB	Brabham BT10-Ford	118.990
1965	F2	Jochen Rindt	A	Brabham BT16-Ford	121.920
1966	F2	Jack Brabham	AUS	Brabham BT18-Honda	122.430
1967	F2	Jochen Rindt	A	Brabham BT23-Ford	134.065
1968	F2	Jackie Stewart	GB	Matra MS7-Ford	129.167
1969	F2	Francois Cevert	F	Tecno 69-Ford	136.514

REIMS 12 HOURS

year	formula	winner	nat	car	mph
1953	SC	Peter Whitehead/Stirling Moss	GB	Jaguar	105.520
1954	SC	Peter Whitehead/Ken Wharton	GB	Jaguar	104.540
1956	SC	Duncan Hamilton/Ivor Bueb	GB	Jaguar	111.010
1957	GT	Paul Frere/Olivier Gendebien	B	Ferrari	104.020
1958	GT	Paul Frere/Olivier Gendebien	B	Ferrari	106.050
1964	SC W	Graham Hill/Jo Bonnier	GB/S	Ferrari 250LM	126.649
1965	SC W	Pedro Rodriguez/Jean Guichet	MEX/F	Ferrari 365P2	122.759
1967	SC	Jo Schlesser/Guy Ligier	F	Ford GT40 Mk2	127.294

ROUEN-LES-ESSARTS

Set in attractive woodland south of the city, this was one of Europe's finest circuits. The Automobile Club de Normand opened Rouen in 1950, and modernised it just two years later with new pits, grandstand and wider track. The sharp descent to the cobbled Nouveau Monde hairpin was breathtaking and the return, uphill leg required a strong engine. But the course was also very dangerous: Jo Schlesser was killed during the 1968 French GP, two died in an F3 race in 1970, and Gerry Birrell perished during the 1973 F2 race. A chicane was built in 1973 to slow the cars on the approach to the hairpin.

Active years	1950-93
Location	8 miles south-west of Rouen

Type	Temporary road course

Final circuit

Lap distance	3.444 miles
Lap record	Qualifying: Eddie Cheever (Ralt RT1-BMW), 1m45.7, 117.298 mph, F2, 1977
	Race: Ingo Hoffmann (March 782-BMW), 1m46.31, 116.625 mph, F2, 1978

Circuit changes

1950-54	3.169 miles
1955-70	Extended. 4.065 miles
1971	Chicanes built at Virage Gresil and Virage de la Scierie. Circuit length unchanged
1972	New pits and a new section built due to the opening of a motorway over the previous circuit. 3.444 miles.
1973	Temporary chicane built at Virage des Six Freres. Circuit length unchanged
1974-93	Permanent chicane built. Final circuit

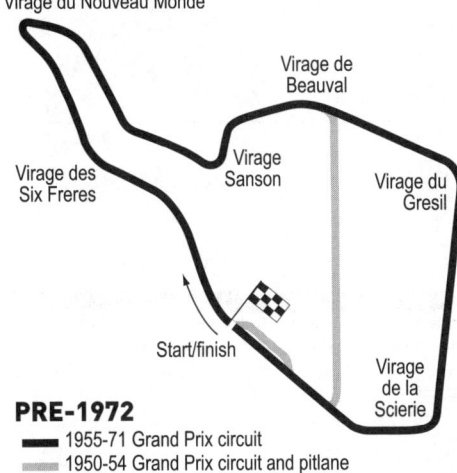

PRE-1972

■ 1955-71 Grand Prix circuit
■ 1950-54 Grand Prix circuit and pitlane

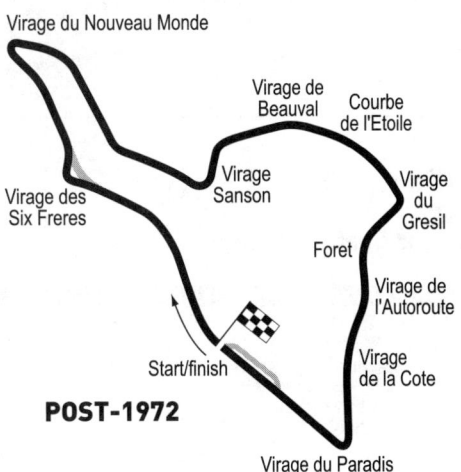

POST-1972

French Grand Prix see above
Paris 1000 kms see Montlhery

ROUEN-LES-ESSARTS GRAND PRIX

year	formula	winner	nat	car	mph
1951	F2	Giannino Marzotto	I	Ferrari 166/F2	75.315
1952*	F2 W	Alberto Ascari	I	Ferrari 500	80.281
1953	F1	Giuseppe Farina	I	Ferrari 500	84.446
1954	F1	Maurice Trintignant	F	Ferrari 625	81.892
1956	SC	Eugenio Castellotti	I	Ferrari	103.380
1957*	F1 W	Juan Manuel Fangio	RA	Maserati 250F	100.016
1958	SC	Jean Behra	F	Porsche	89.520
1959	F2	Stirling Moss	GB	Cooper T45-Borgward	96.899
1960	SC	Jack Fairman	GB	Aston Martin	88.350
1961	SC	Lucky Casner	USA	Maserati	92.250
1962*	F1 W	Dan Gurney	USA	Porsche 804	103.225
1963	FJ	Paul Hawkins	AUS	Brabham-Ford	98.980
1964*	F1 W	Dan Gurney	USA	Brabham BT7-Climax	108.766
1965	F2	Jim Clark	GB	Lotus 35-Ford	103.400
1966	F2	Denny Hulme	NZ	Brabham BT18-Honda	105.290
1967	F2	Jochen Rindt	A	Brabham BT23-Ford	116.760
1968*	F1 W	Jacky Ickx	B	Ferrari 312	100.452
1969	F3	Jean-Pierre Jaussaud	F	Tecno 69-Ford	102.878
1970	F2 E	Jo Siffert	CH	BMW F270	118.617
1971	F2 E	Ronnie Peterson	S	March 712M-Ford	109.657

ROUEN-LES-ESSARTS GRAND PRIX (cont.)

year	formula	winner	nat	car	mph
1972	F2 E	Emerson Fittipaldi	BR	Lotus 69-Ford	114.096
1973	F2 E	Jean-Pierre Jarier	F	March 732-BMW	110.022
1974	F2	Hans-Joachim Stuck	D	March 742-BMW	96.699
1975	F2 E	Michel Leclere	F	March 752-BMW	112.445
1976	F2 E	Maurizio Flammini	I	March 762-BMW	112.196
1977	F2 E	Eddie Cheever	USA	Ralt RT1-BMW	114.460
1978	F2 E	Bruno Giacomelli	I	March 782-BMW	114.265
1980	F3	Alain Ferte	F	Martini MK27-Renault	102.520
1982	F3	Pierre Petit	F	Ralt RT3/82-Volkswagen	104.400
1983	F3	Michel Ferte	F	Martini MK39-Alfa Romeo	105.810
1984	F3	Frederic Delavallade	F	Martini MK42-Alfa Romeo	106.560
1985	F3	Yannick Dalmas	F	Martini MK45-Alfa Romeo	95.570
1986	F3	Frederic Delavallade	F	Ralt RT30-Volkswagen	108.150
1987	F3	Jean Alesi	F	Dallara 387-Alfa Romeo	104.220
1988	F3	Eric Cheli	F	Dallara 388-Alfa Romeo	108.990
1989	F3	Jean-Marc Gounon	F	Reynard 893-Alfa Romeo	109.210
1990	F3	Eric Helary	F	Reynard 903-Mugen	108.860
1991	F3	Christophe Bouchut	F	Ralt RT33-Volkswagen	105.203
1992	F3	Stephane Gregoire	F	Dallara 392-Alfa Romeo	109.585
1993	F3	Guillaume Gomez	F	Dallara 393-Fiat	110.513

*French Grand Prix

GERMANY

Major Championships

GERMAN RACING CHAMPIONSHIP/GERMAN SUPERCUP

Originally introduced for Group 2-4 Touring Cars, the Deutsche Rennsportmeisterschaft switched to Group 5 Sports Cars in 1977 (briefly threatening to overshadow the World title). After a poor final year in 1985 the Group C-based Supercup replaced it for four years.

year	driver	nat	team	car
1972	Hans-Joachim Stuck	D	Ford Deutschland	Ford Capri RS
1973	Dieter Glemser	D	Zakspeed Racing	Ford Escort
1974	Dieter Glemser	D	Zakspeed Racing	Ford Escort
1975	Hans Heyer	D	Zakspeed Racing	Ford Escort
1976	Hans Heyer	D	Zakspeed Racing	Ford Escort
1977	Rolf Stommelen	D	Georg Loos	Porsche 935
1978	Harald Ertl	A	Schnitzer	BMW 320i turbo
1979	Klaus Ludwig	D	Porsche Kremer Racing	Porsche 935-K3
1980	Hans Heyer	A	Lancia Corse	Lancia Beta Monte Carlo
1981	Klaus Ludwig	D	Zakspeed Racing	Ford Capri
1982	Bob Wollek	F	Joest Racing	Porsche 936C
1983	Bob Wollek	F	Joest Racing	Porsche 956
1984	Stefan Bellof	D	Brun Motorsport	Porsche 956B
1985	Jochen Mass	D	Joest Racing	Porsche 956
1986	Hans-Joachim Stuck	D	Porsche System Engineering	Porsche 962C
1987	Hans-Joachim Stuck	D	Porsche System Engineering	Porsche 962C
1988	Jean-Louis Schlesser	F	Team Sauber Mercedes	Sauber C9/88-Mercedes-Benz
1989	Bob Wollek	F	Joest Racing	Porsche 962C

ADAC GT CUP

year	driver	nat	car
1993	Johnny Cecotto	YV	BMW M3 GTR
1994	Ralf Kelleners	D	Porsche Carrera RSR
1995	Uwe Alzen	D	Porsche 911 GT2
1996	Marc Simon	D	BMW M3 GTR
1997	Jorg Breuer	D	Ford Escort Cosworth

INTERSERIE

Inaugurated in 1970 as Europe's answer to Can-Am, Interserie has remained a mainly German affair and became a club event in 1999.

year	driver	nat	car
1970	Jurgen Neuhaus	D	Porsche 910
1971	Leo Kinnunen	SF	Porsche 917S

INTERSERIE (cont.)

year	driver	nat	car
1972	Leo Kinnunen	SF	Porsche 917/10
1973	Leo Kinnunen	SF	Porsche 917/10K turbo
1974	Herbert Muller	CH	Porsche 917/20K turbo/Porsche 917/30 turbo
1975	Herbert Muller	CH	Porsche 917/20K/Porsche 908/3 Spyder
1976	Herbert Muller	CH	Sauber C5-BMW
1977	Helmut Bross	D	Lola T294-BMW
1978	Reinhold Joest	D	Porsche 908/3 turbo
1979	Kurt Lotterschmid	D	Toj C205-BMW
1980	Kurt Lotterschmid	D	Toj C205-BMW
1981	Roland Binder	D	Lola T296-BMW
1982	Roland Binder	D	Lola T296-BMW
1983	Walter Lechner	A	March 821-Ford Can-Am
1984	Klaus Niedzwiedz	D	Ford Zakspeed C1/8
1985	Roland Binder	D	Persy 85/01-BMW Can-Am
1986	"John Winter"	D	Porsche 956
1987	Walter Lechner	A	Porsche 962C
1988	Jochen Dauer	D	Porsche 962C
1989	Walter Lechner	A	Porsche 962C
1990	Bernd Schneider	D	Porsche 962-K6
1991	Bernd Schneider	D	Porsche 962C
1992	Manuel Reuter	D	Kremer CK7-Porsche/Porsche 962-K6
1993	Giovanni Lavaggi	I	Kremer CK7-Porsche
1994	Johan Rajamaki	S	Footwork FA12-Judd Can-Am
1995	Heinz Becker	D	Minardi M190-Ford Can-Am
1996	Robbie Stirling	CDN	Lola T92/10-Judd/Argo JM19C-Judd
1997	Josef Neuhauser	A	Lola-Judd Can-Am
1998	Josef Neuhauser	A	Reynard-Judd Can-Am
1999	Heinz Becker	D	Minardi 190-Hart
2000	Josef Neuhauser	A	Minardi 190-Ford
2001	Josef Neuhauser	A	Minardi 190-Ford
2002	Rolf-Torsten Dietrich	A	Opel-Lotus

INTERNATIONAL TOURING CAR CHAMPIONSHIP

year	driver	nat	team	car
1995	Bernd Schneider	D	AMG Motorenbau	Mercedes-Benz C Class
1996	Manuel Reuter	D	Joest Racing	Opel Calibra V6

GERMAN TOURING CAR CHAMPIONSHIP (DTM)

year	driver	nat	team	car
1984	Volker Strycek	D	Team Gubin	BMW 635 CSi
1985	Per Stureson	S	IPS	Volvo 240 turbo
1986	Kurt Thiim	DK	Team Nickel	Rover 3500 Vitesse
1987	Eric van de Poele	B	Zakspeed Racing	BMW M3
1988	Klaus Ludwig	D	Team Grab	Ford Sierra RS500
1989	Roberto Ravaglia	I	Schnitzer	BMW M3
1990	Hans-Joachim Stuck	D	Schmidt Motor Sport	Audi V8 Quattro
1991	Frank Biela	D	Audi Zentrum Reutlingen	Audi V8 Quattro
1992	Klaus Ludwig	D	AMG Motorenbau	Mercedes-Benz 190E Evo2
1993	Nicola Larini	I	Alfa Corse	Alfa Romeo 155 V6 Ti
1994	Klaus Ludwig	D	AMG Motorenbau	Mercedes-Benz C Class
1995	Bernd Schneider	D	AMG Motorenbau	Mercedes-Benz C Class
1996	Manuel Reuter	D	Joest Team Opel	Opel Calibra V6
2000	Bernd Schneider	D	AMG Motorenbau	Mercedes-Benz CLK-DTM
2001	Bernd Schneider	D	AMG Motorenbau	Mercedes-Benz CLK-DTM
2002	Laurent Aiello	F	Abt Sportsline	Audi TT-R

1997-99 no series

GERMAN SUPER TOURING CAR CHAMPIONSHIP

year	driver	nat	team	car
1994	Johnny Cecotto	YV	Team Warthofer	BMW 318i
1995	Joachim Winkelhock	D	Schnitzer	BMW 318i
1996	Emanuele Pirro	I	ROC Competition	Audi A4 Quattro
1997	Laurent Aiello	F	ORECA	Peugeot 406
1998	Johnny Cecotto	YV	Schnitzer	BMW 320i
1999	Uwe Alzen	D	Holzer Team Opel	Opel Vectra

GERMAN V8-STAR SILHOUETTE CHAMPIONSHIP

year	driver	nat	team	car
2001	Johnny Cecotto	YV	Irmscher Motorsport	Opel Astra
2002	Johnny Cecotto	YV	Irmscher Motorsport	Opel Astra

GERMAN FORMULA 3 CHAMPIONSHIP (INCLUDING FORMULA JUNIOR)

year	driver	nat	team	car
1950	Toni Krauzer	D	Toni Krauzer	Cooper-JAP
1951	Walter Kornossa	D	Walter Kornossa	Scampolo 502-BMW
1952	Hellmut Deutz	D	Hellmut Deutz	Scampolo 501-DKW/Scampolo 502-Norton
1953	Adolf Lang	D	Adolf Lang	Cooper-JAP
1960*	Gerhard Mitter	D	Autohaus Mitter	Lotus 18-DKW
1961*	Kurt Ahrens Jr	D	Kurt Ahrens jr	Cooper-Ford
1963*	Kurt Ahrens Jr	D	Kurt Ahrens jr	Cooper T67-Ford
1975	Ernst Maring	D	Maring Motorsport	Maco 375-Ford/Maco 375-Toyota
1976	Bertram Schafer	D	Klaus Zimmermann Racing	Ralt RT1-BMW/Ralt RT1-Toyota
1977	Peter Scharmann	A	Team Jorg Obermoser	Toj F302-BMW/Toj F302-Toyota
1978	Bertram Schafer	D	Klaus Zimmermann Racing	Ralt RT1-BMW/Ralt RT1-Toyota
1979	Michael Korten	D	Korten Motorsport	March 793-Toyota
1980	Frank Jelinski	D	Bertram Schafer Racing	Ralt RT3-Toyota
1981	Frank Jelinski	D	Bertram Schafer Racing	Ralt RT3-Toyota
1982	John Nielsen	DK	Bertram Schafer Racing	Ralt RT3-Volkswagen
1983	Franz Konrad	A	Konrad Racing	Anson SA4-Toyota/Anson SA4-Alfa Romeo
1984	Kurt Thiim	DK	Malte Bongers Racing	Ralt RT3-Alfa Romeo
1985	Volker Weidler	D	Josef Kaufmann Racing	Martini MK45-Volkswagen
1986	Kris Nissen	DK	Bertram Schafer Racing	Ralt RT30-Volkswagen
1987	Bernd Schneider	D	Schubel Rennsport	Dallara 387-Volkswagen
1988	Joachim Winkelhock	D	WTS Racing	Reynard 883-Volkswagen
1989	Karl Wendlinger	A	RSM Marko	Ralt RT33-Alfa Romeo
1990	Michael Schumacher	D	WTS Racing	Reynard 903-Volkswagen
1991	Tom Kristensen	DK	Bertram Schafer Racing	Ralt RT35-Volkswagen
1992	Pedro Lamy	P	WTS Racing	Reynard 923-Opel
1993	Jos Verstappen	NL	WTS Racing	Dallara 393-Opel
1994	Jorg Muller	D	RSM Marko	Dallara 394-Fiat
1995	Norberto Fontana	RA	KMS Motorsport	Dallara 395-Opel
1996	Jarno Trulli	I	KMS Motorsport	Dallara 396-Opel
1997	Nick Heidfeld	D	Bertram Schafer Racing	Dallara 397-Opel
1998	Bas Leinders	B	Van Amersfoort Racing	Dallara 397-Opel/Dallara 398-Opel
1999	Christijan Albers	NL	Bertram Schafer Racing	Dallara 399-Opel
2000	Giorgio Pantano	I	KMS Motorsport	Dallara 300-Opel
2001	Toshihiro Kaneishi	J	Bertram Schafer Racing	Dallara 300-Opel
2002	Gary Paffett	GB	Team Rosberg Engineering	Dallara 302-Opel

*Formula Junior. 1960, 1961 and 1963 were unofficial championships. 1954-59, 1962, 1964-74 no series

POLIFAC FORMULA 3 CHAMPIONSHIP

year	driver	nat	team	car
1974	Giorgio Francia	I	Scuderia Mirabella MM	March 743-Toyota

EAST GERMAN FORMULA 3 CHAMPIONSHIP

year	driver	nat	team	car
1950	Richard Weiser	DDR	Richard Weiser	Weiser-BMW
1951	Daniel Zimmermann	DDR	Daniel Zimmermann	Zimmermann Eigenbau
1952	Willy Lehmann	DDR	Willy Lehmann	Lehmann-BMW
1953	Willy Lehmann	DDR	Willy Lehmann	Lehmann-BMW/Scampolo 502-BMW
1954	Willy Lehmann	DDR	Willy Lehmann	Scampolo 502-BMW
1955	Willy Lehmann	DDR	Willy Lehmann	Scampolo 502-BMW
1956	Willy Lehmann	DDR	Willy Lehmann	Scampolo 502-BMW

Major International Races

GERMAN GRAND PRIX

year	formula	circuit	winner	nat	car	mph
1926	SC	Avus	Rudolf Caracciola	D	Mercedes	83.719
1927	SC	Nurburgring	Otto Merz	D	Mercedes-Benz S	63.313
1928	SC	Nurburgring	Rudolf Caracciola/Christian Werner	D	Mercedes-Benz SS	64.429
1929	SC	Nurburgring	Louis Chiron	MC	Bugatti T35C	66.297
1931	GP	Nurburgring	Rudolf Caracciola	D	Mercedes-Benz SSKL	67.227
1932	GP	Nurburgring	Rudolf Caracciola	D	Alfa Romeo Tipo-B "P3"	73.946
1934	GP	Nurburgring	Hans Stuck	D	Auto Union A	76.353
1935	GP	Nurburgring	Tazio Nuvolari	I	Alfa Romeo Tipo-B "P3"	75.384
1936	GP	Nurburgring	Bernd Rosemeyer	D	Auto Union C	81.783

Germany

GERMAN GRAND PRIX (cont.)

year	formula	circuit	winner	nat	car	mph
1937	GP	Nurburgring	Rudolf Caracciola	D	Mercedes-Benz W125	82.745
1938	GP	Nurburgring	Dick Seaman	GB	Mercedes-Benz W154	80.685
1939	GP	Nurburgring	Rudolf Caracciola	D	Mercedes-Benz W163	75.194
1950	F2	Nurburgring	Alberto Ascari	I	Ferrari 166/F2	77.710
1951	F1 W	Nurburgring	Alberto Ascari	I	Ferrari 375	83.723
1952	F2 W	Nurburgring	Alberto Ascari	I	Ferrari 500	82.162
1953	F2 W	Nurburgring	Giuseppe Farina	I	Ferrari 500	83.876
1954	F1 W	Nurburgring	Juan Manuel Fangio	RA	Mercedes-Benz W196	82.832
1956	F1 W	Nurburgring	Juan Manuel Fangio	RA	Lancia-Ferrari D50	85.496
1957	F1 W	Nurburgring	Juan Manuel Fangio	RA	Maserati 250F	88.780
1958	F1 W	Nurburgring	Tony Brooks	GB	Vanwall VW4	90.268
1959	F1 W	Avus	Tony Brooks	GB	Ferrari Dino 246	143.331
1960	F2	Nurburgring	Jo Bonnier	S	Porsche 718	80.232
1961	F1 W	Nurburgring	Stirling Moss	GB	Lotus 18/21-Climax	92.255
1962	F1 W	Nurburgring	Graham Hill	GB	BRM P57	80.314
1963	F1 W	Nurburgring	John Surtees	GB	Ferrari Dino 156	95.785
1964	F1 W	Nurburgring	John Surtees	GB	Ferrari 158	96.535
1965	F1 W	Nurburgring	Jim Clark	GB	Lotus 33-Climax	99.710
1966	F1 W	Nurburgring	Jack Brabham	AUS	Brabham BT19-Repco	86.707
1967	F1 W	Nurburgring	Denny Hulme	NZ	Brabham BT24-Repco	101.408
1968	F1 W	Nurburgring	Jackie Stewart	GB	Matra MS10-Ford	85.714
1969	F1 W	Nurburgring	Jacky Ickx	B	Brabham BT26-Ford	108.428
1970	F1 W	Hockenheim	Jochen Rindt	A	Lotus 72-Ford	124.082
1971	F1 W	Nurburgring	Jackie Stewart	GB	Tyrrell 003-Ford	114.451
1972	F1 W	Nurburgring	Jacky Ickx	B	Ferrari 312B2	116.616
1973	F1 W	Nurburgring	Jackie Stewart	GB	Tyrrell 006-Ford	116.793
1974	F1 W	Nurburgring	Clay Regazzoni	CH	Ferrari 312B3	117.330
1975	F1 W	Nurburgring	Carlos Reutemann	RA	Brabham BT44B-Ford	117.734
1976	F1 W	Nurburgring	James Hunt	GB	McLaren M23-Ford	117.182
1977	F1 W	Hockenheim	Niki Lauda	A	Ferrari 312T2	129.589
1978	F1 W	Hockenheim	Mario Andretti	USA	Lotus 79-Ford	129.425
1979	F1 W	Hockenheim	Alan Jones	AUS	Williams FW07-Ford	134.309
1980	F1 W	Hockenheim	Jacques Laffite	F	Ligier JS11/15-Ford	137.252
1981	F1 W	Hockenheim	Nelson Piquet	BR	Brabham BT49C-Ford	132.570
1982	F1 W	Hockenheim	Patrick Tambay	F	Ferrari 126C2	130.448
1983	F1 W	Hockenheim	Rene Arnoux	F	Ferrari 126C3	130.819
1984	F1 W	Hockenheim	Alain Prost	F	McLaren MP4/2-TAG Porsche	131.613
1985	F1 W	Nurburgring	Michele Alboreto	I	Ferrari 156/85	118.762
1986	F1 W	Hockenheim	Nelson Piquet	BR	Williams FW11-Honda	135.751
1987	F1 W	Hockenheim	Nelson Piquet	BR	Williams FW11B-Honda	136.951
1988	F1 W	Hockenheim	Ayrton Senna	BR	McLaren MP4/4-Honda	120.021
1989	F1 W	Hockenheim	Ayrton Senna	BR	McLaren MP4/5-Honda	139.543
1990	F1 W	Hockenheim	Ayrton Senna	BR	McLaren MP4/5B-Honda	141.270
1991	F1 W	Hockenheim	Nigel Mansell	GB	Williams FW14-Renault	143.565
1992	F1 W	Hockenheim	Nigel Mansell	GB	Williams FW14B-Renault	145.909
1993	F1 W	Hockenheim	Alain Prost	F	Williams FW15C-Renault	145.327
1994	F1 W	Hockenheim	Gerhard Berger	A	Ferrari 412T1B	137.906
1995	F1 W	Hockenheim	Michael Schumacher	D	Benetton B195-Renault	138.005
1996	F1 W	Hockenheim	Damon Hill	GB	Williams FW18-Renault	140.049
1997	F1 W	Hockenheim	Gerhard Berger	A	Benetton B197-Renault	141.328
1998	F1 W	Hockenheim	Mika Hakkinen	SF	McLaren MP4/13-Mercedes-Benz	141.650
1999	F1 W	Hockenheim	Eddie Irvine	GB	Ferrari F399	139.617
2000	F1 W	Hockenheim	Rubens Barrichello	BR	Ferrari F1-2000	133.748
2001	F1 W	Hockenheim	Ralf Schumacher	D	Williams FW23-BMW	146.176
2002	F1 W	Hockenheim	Michael Schumacher	D	Ferrari F2002	130.023

GERMAN GRAND PRIX FORMULA 2 CLASS

year	formula	circuit	winner	nat	car	mph
1931	Cyc	Nurburgring	Dudley Froy	GB	Riley 9	58.030
1932	V	Nurburgring	Henri Tauber	D	Alfa Romeo 6C-1500	66.360
1957	F2	Nurburgring	Edgar Barth	DDR	Porsche 550RS	82.418
1958	F2	Nurburgring	Bruce McLaren	NZ	Cooper T45-Climax	86.332
1966	F2	Nurburgring	Jean-Pierre Beltoise	F	Matra MS5-Ford	80.055
1967	F2	Nurburgring	Jackie Oliver	GB	Lotus 48-Cosworth	96.683
1969	F2	Nurburgring	Henri Pescarolo	F	Matra MS7-Cosworth	100.915

Circuits and Other Races

AVUS
Automobil Verkehrs und Ubungs Strasse

The layout for the circuit in the Grunewald district of Berlin was simple: two straights joined by a slightly banked corner at Charlottenburg and a hairpin six miles south at Nikolasse. Average lap speeds at AVUS were boosted to over 170 mph when the awesome 43-degree banked North Curve (or "Wall of Death") was built in 1937. At the end of the war the southern end ran into the Soviet zone, so a new South curve was built cutting the circuit in half. The German GP was held twice at AVUS, with Rudolf Caracciola's private Mercedes winning the inaugural event in 1926 and

Tony Brooks succeeding in 1959. Both were also tragic affairs: in 1926 Adolf Rosenberger crashed into a scoring hut killing the three occupants, and Jean Behra died in a sports car race supporting the 1959 race. The North Curve was dismantled in 1967, but a further shortened AVUS continued to hold national events until it finally closed in May 1998.

Active years	1921-98
Location	South-western suburbs of Berlin
Type	Temporary road course with one permanent banked turn (1937-67)

Circuit changes	
1921-36	12.160 miles
1937-39	North curve banking built. 11.987 miles
1951-67	New South Curve built as half the circuit was in Soviet held territory. 5.157 miles
1968-88	North Curve banking dismantled. 5.039 miles
1989-91	3.032 miles
1992-98	1.640 miles

German Grand Prix see above

AVUSRENNEN					
year	formula	winner	nat	car	mph
1931	FL	Rudolf Caracciola	D	Mercedes-Benz SSKL	115.047
1932	FL	Manfred von Brauchitsch	D	Mercedes-Benz SSKL	120.431
1933	FL	Achille Varzi	I	Bugatti T54	128.140
1934	FL	Guy Moll	DZ	Alfa Romeo Tipo-B "P3"	127.182
1935	FL	Luigi Fagioli	I	Mercedes-Benz W25B	148.232
1937	FL	Hermann Lang	D	Mercedes-Benz W125 streamlined	162.063
1951	F2	Paul Greifzu	DDR	BMW Eigenbau	112.582
1952	F2	Rudolf Fischer	CH	Ferrari 500	115.922
1953	F2	Jacques Swaters	B	Ferrari 500	118.907
1954	SC	Richard von Frankenberg	D	Porsche	120.200
1962	GT	Edgar Berney	CH	Ferrari	126.450
1963	GT	Peter Nocker	D	Jaguar 3.8	131.050
1966	SC	Udo Schutz	D	Porsche Carrera 6	142.795
1967	SC	Gunther Klass	D	Porsche Carrera 6	n/a
1976	F3	Conny Andersson	S	March 763-Toyota	n/a
1978	SC	Toine Hezemans	D	Porsche 935	n/a
1980	Procar	Manfred Schurti	FL	BMW M1	132.310
1983	SC	Bob Wollek	F	Porsche 956	144.480
1984	TC	Olaf Manthey	D	Rover Vitesse	113.014
1985	TC	Klaus Niedzwiedz	D	Ford Sierra XR4Ti	117.207
1986	TC	Volker Weidler	D	Mercedes-Benz 190E	116.960
1987	TC	Frank Biela	D	Ford Sierra XR4Ti	119.697
1988*	TC	Johnny Cecotto	YV	Mercedes-Benz 190E	122.115
	TC	Johnny Cecotto	YV	Mercedes-Benz 190E	122.488
1989*	TC	Roberto Ravaglia	I	BMW M3	111.155
	TC	Klaus Niedzwiedz	D	Ford Sierra Cosworth	111.102
1990*	TC	Hans-Joachim Stuck	D	Audi V8 Quattro	112.593
	TC	Hans-Joachim Stuck	D	Audi V8 Quattro	114.165
1991*	TC	Hans-Joachim Stuck	D	Audi V8 Quattro	118.305
	TC	Frank Biela	D	Audi V8 Quattro	118.429

AVUSRENNEN

year	formula	winner	nat	car	mph
1992*	TC	Steve Soper	GB	BMW M3	101.713
	TC	Bernd Schneider	D	Mercedes-Benz 190E	102.363
1993*	TC	Roland Asch	D	Mercedes-Benz 190E	94.821
	TC	Roland Asch	D	Mercedes-Benz 190E	102.387
1994*	TC	Stefano Modena	I	Alfa Romeo 155 V6 Ti	97.153
	TC	Stefano Modena	I	Alfa Romeo 155 V6 Ti	96.935
1995*	TC	Kurt Thiim	DK	Mercedes-Benz C Class	108.085
	TC	Kurt Thiim	DK	Mercedes-Benz C Class	68.576
1996*	TC	Armin Hahne	D	Honda Accord	96.830
	TC	Emanuele Pirro	I	Audi A4	96.740
1998#	Prod	Stefan Kissling	D	Opel Calibra 16v	85.293
	Prod	Stefan Kissling	D	Opel Calibra 16v	86.027

From 1988 two races with no overall winner; *German and International Touring Cars, #German Touring Car Challenge. Note: incomplete list of results

HOCKENHEIM

On 7 April 1968, in an accident that may never be fully explained, Jim Clark died during the Formula 2 Deutschland Trophae race at Hockenheim. Although the circuit has held the German Grand Prix since 1977, it is still Clark's death for which it is best known. The circuit originally stretched from the edge of Hockenheim town to the Ost Curve. When the Autobahn was built in 1966 the circuit was reduced in length and redesigned by John Hugenholtz, who introduced a tight stadium section around the pits. Hockenheim first held the Grand Prix in 1970 while the Nurburgring was being modernised. Chicanes were built on the two main straights for that race, and after Patrick Depailler died in testing in 1980, a third chicane was installed at the demanding Ost Curve. Visibility is appalling in the wet, a contributing factor to the accident that ended Didier Pironi's career in 1982. Hockenheim's lap was among Formula 1's longest and most unique, but a new section linking the first and third chicanes and bypassing the Ost Curve was built for the 2002 Grand Prix. As a result, drivers lost the flat-out full-throttle blast through the forests that had given Hockenheim its character.

Active years	1929 to date
Location	15 miles south of Heidelberg, 55 miles south of Frankfurt, 85 miles north-west Stuttgart
Type	Permanent road course
Website	www.hockenheimring.de

Current circuit

Lap distance	2.842 miles
Lap records	Qualifying: Michael Schumacher (Ferrari F2002), 1m14.389, 137.537 mph, F1, 2002
	Race: Michael Schumacher (Ferrari F2002), 1m16.462, 133.808 mph, F1, 2002

Circuit changes

1929-65	4.779 miles
1966-70	Western section replaced by new pit straight and stadium complex. 4.206 miles
1970-81	Chicanes inserted on the two main straights, first used 1970 German GP. 4.219 miles
1982-91	First chicane reconstructed and Ost Curve chicane built. 4.227 miles
1992-93	Ost Curve chicane tightened. 4.234 miles
1994-2001	Chicanes reprofiled. 4.239 miles
2002 to date	Ost Curve bypassed by new section between old first and third chicanes. Current circuit

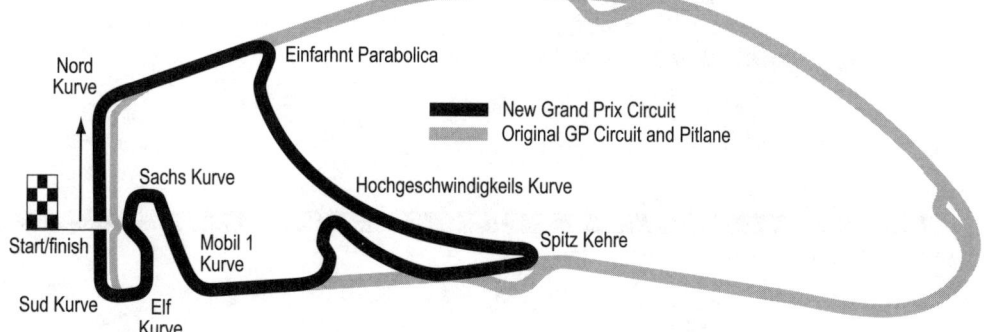

HOCKENHEIM GRAND PRIX CIRCUIT

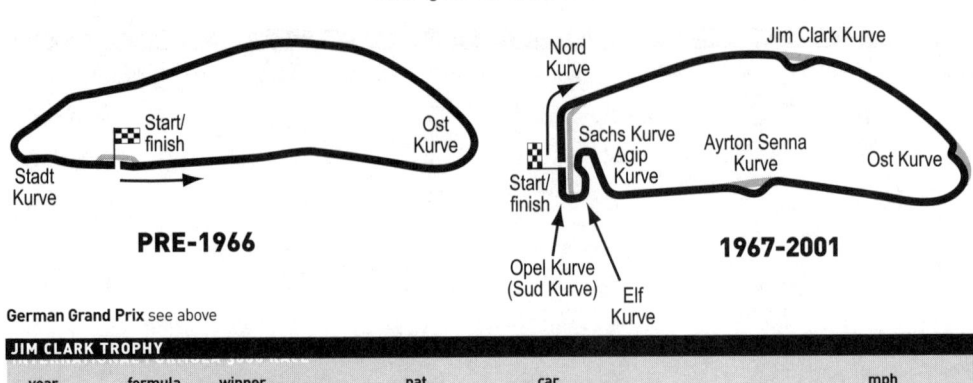

PRE-1966

1967-2001

German Grand Prix see above

JIM CLARK TROPHY

year	formula	winner	nat	car	mph
1969	F2 E	Jean-Pierre Beltoise	F	Matra MS7-Ford	123.615
1970	F2 E	Clay Regazzoni	CH	Tecno 70-Ford	123.070
1971	F2 E	Francois Cevert	F	Tecno 71-Ford	116.168
1972	F2 E	Jean-Pierre Jaussaud	F	Brabham BT38-Ford	118.562
1973	F2 E	Jean-Pierre Jarier	F	March 732-BMW	122.809
1974	F2 E	Hans-Joachim Stuck	D	March 742-BMW	124.060
1975	F2 E	Gerard Larrousse	F	Elf 2/A367-BMW	122.047
1976	F2 E	Hans-Joachim Stuck	D	March 762-BMW	123.845
1977	F2 E	Jochen Mass	D	March 772P-BMW	124.485
1978	F2 E	Bruno Giacomelli	I	March 782-BMW	125.993
1979	F2 E	Keke Rosberg	SF	March 792-BMW	125.859
1980	F2 E	Teo Fabi	I	March 802-BMW	125.448
1981	F2 E	Stefan Johansson	S	Toleman T850-Hart	125.591
1982	F2 E	Stefan Bellof	D	Maurer MM82-BMW	120.565
1983	F2 E	Jonathan Palmer	GB	Ralt RH6/83-Honda	121.795
1984	F2 E	Roberto Moreno	BR	Ralt RH6/84-Honda	123.163

JOCHEN RINDT TROPHY

year	formula	winner	nat	car	mph
1971	F1	Jacky Ickx	B	Ferrari 312B	126.218
1972	F2 E	Emerson Fittipaldi	BR	Lotus 69-Ford	103.107
1973	F2 E	Jochen Mass	D	Surtees TS15-Ford	122.966
1974	F2 E	Jean-Pierre Jabouille	F	Elf 2/A367-BMW	123.514
1975	F2 E	Jacques Laffite	F	Martini MK16-BMW	122.211

OTHER EUROPEAN FORMULA 2 RACES

year	formula	winner	nat	car	mph
1967	F2 E	Frank Gardner	AUS	Brabham BT23-Ford	122.366
1968	F2 E	Jean-Pierre Beltoise	F	Matra MS7-Ford	117.612
	F2 E	Tino Brambilla	I	Ferrari Dino 166	123.240
1970	F2 E	Dieter Quester	A	BMW F270	115.348
1972	F2 E	Tim Schenken	AUS	Brabham BT38-Ford	120.224
1974	F2 E	Patrick Depailler	F	March 742-BMW	121.352
1976	F2 E	Hans-Joachim Stuck	D	March 762-BMW	124.301
	F2 E	Jean-Pierre Jabouille	F	Elf 2J-Renault	122.663
1978	F2 E	Bruno Giacomelli	I	March 782-BMW	125.809
1979	F2 E	Stephen South	GB	March 792-BMW	125.096
1980	F2 E	Teo Fabi	I	March 802-BMW	127.239
1982	F2 E	Corrado Fabi	I	March 822-BMW	120.537
1984	F2 E	Pascal Fabre	F	March 842-BMW	121.958

INTERNATIONAL FORMULA 3000 RACE

year	formula	winner	nat	car	mph
1990	F3000 INT	Eddie Irvine	GB	Reynard 90D-Mugen	126.277
1991	F3000 INT	Emanuele Naspetti	I	Reynard 91D-Cosworth	128.311
1992	F3000 INT	Luca Badoer	I	Reynard 92D-Cosworth	130.630
1993	F3000 INT	Olivier Panis	F	Reynard 93D-Cosworth	129.473
1994	F3000 INT	Franck Lagorce	F	Reynard 94D-Cosworth	126.770
1995	F3000 INT	Marc Goossens	B	Lola T95/50-Cosworth	127.012
1996	F3000 INT	Kenny Brack	S	Lola T96/50-Zytek	122.971
	F3000 INT	Christophe Tinseau	F	Lola T96/50-Zytek	124.162

INTERNATIONAL FORMULA 3000 RACE (cont.)

year	formula	winner	nat	car	mph
1997	F3000 INT	Ricardo Zonta	BR	Lola T96/50-Zytek	122.138
1998	F3000 INT	Nick Heidfeld	D	Lola T96/50-Zytek	108.067
1999	F3000 INT	Bruno Junqueira	BR	Lola B99/50-Zytek	128.635
2000	F3000 INT	Tomas Enge	CS	Lola B99/50-Zytek	105.348
2001	F3000 INT	Antonio Pizzonia	BR	Lola B99/50-Zytek	124.920
2002	F3000 INT	Giorgio Pantano	I	Lola B2/50-Zytek	112.514

WORLD SPORTS CAR RACE

year	formula	winner	nat	car	mph
1977	SC W	Bob Wollek/John Fitzpatrick	F/GB	Porsche 935	116.023
1985	SC W	Derek Bell/Hans-Joachim Stuck	GB/D	Porsche 956C	115.328

FIA GT RACE

year	formula	winner	nat	car	mph
1997	GT FIA	JJ Lehto/Steve Soper	SF/GB	McLaren F1 GTR-BMW	119.135
1998	GT FIA	Bernd Schneider/Mark Webber	D/AUS	Mercedes-Benz CLK-LM	122.852
1999	GT FIA	Jean-Philippe Belloc/Dominique Dupuy	F	Chrysler Viper GTS-R	87.709

KASSEL-CALDEN

Kassel-Calden was a simple, uninspiring airfield circuit in Northern Germany which used to host a round of the European F3 Championship. After the championship was abandoned in 1982 it was no longer used for inter-national events.

Active years   1974-82
Location   75 miles south of Hannover
Type   Temporary road course

Lap distance   1.609 miles
Lap record   Race: Oscar Larrauri (Euroracing 101-Alfa Romeo), 1m03.87, 90.691 mph, F3, 1982

Circuit changes
1976-80   1.644 miles
1981-82   Final circuit

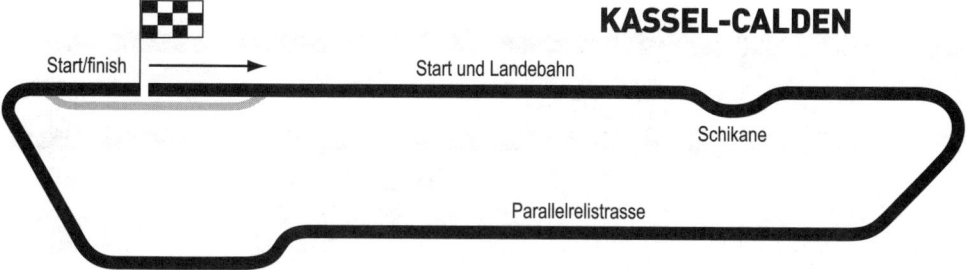

KASSEL-CALDEN

Start/finish — Start und Landebahn — Schikane — Parallelrelistrasse

EUROPEAN FORMULA 3 RACE

year	formula	winner	nat	car	mph
1976	F3 E	Riccardo Patrese	I	Chevron B34-Toyota	n/a
1977	F3 E	Nelson Piquet	BR	Ralt RT1-Toyota	101.603
1978	F3 E	Anders Olofsson	S	Ralt RT1-Toyota	102.505
1979	F3 E	Michael Korten	D	March 793-Toyota	101.264
1980	F3 E	Michele Alboreto	I	March 803B-Alfa Romeo	104.960
1982	F3 E	Emanuele Pirro	I	Euroracing 101-Alfa Romeo	87.381

LAUSITZ

Eurospeedway

The new Lausitzring in eastern Germany was the first banked oval opened in Europe since the twenties. The circuit's first race, a German Touring Car Championship event scheduled for 3 September 2000, was cancelled due to rain. Worse, the circuit's short history has already been racked by tragedy. Michele Alboreto was killed while testing for the 2001 Le Mans 24 hours, and a marshal died in an event one week later. In September 2001, Europe's first CART race was marred by Alex Zanardi's horrific accident and serious injuries. However, the low-banked tri-oval is a magnificent facility, and an impressive 87,000-crowd watched the inaugural Champcar race.

Active years	2000 to date
Location	Klettwitz, 40 miles north of Dresden, 80 miles south of Berlin
Type	Paved oval
Website	www.eurospeedway.de

Oval circuit

Lap distance	2.023 miles
Lap records	Qualifying: not held
	Race: Tony Kanaan (Reynard 01I-Honda), 34.747s, 209.596 mph, CART, 2001

Road circuit

Lap distance	2.796 miles
Lap record	Qualifying: Bernd Schneider (Mercedes-Benz CLK-DTM), 1m42.072, 94.204 mph, DTM Touring Cars, 2000
	Race: Julian Bailey (Lister Storm GT), 1m43.830, 96.943 mph, GT, 2000

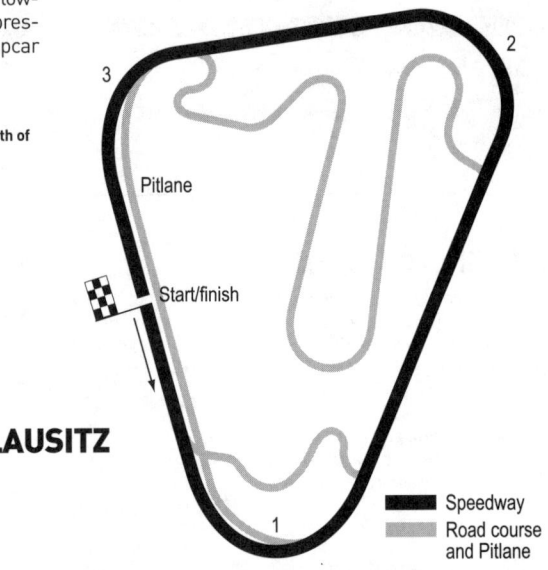

LAUSITZ

Speedway

Road course and Pitlane

AMERICAN MEMORIAL 500 CHAMPCAR RACE					
year	formula	winner	nat	car	mph
2001	CART	Kenny Brack	S	Lola B01/00-Ford	155.319

FIA GT RACE					
year	formula	winner	nat	car	mph
2000	GT FIA	Hubert Haupt/Wolfgang Kaufmann	D	Porsche 911 GT2	73.149

NORISRING

The Norisring is a simple temporary circuit on the grounds of Adolf Hitler's Nuremberg rallies of the thirties. The track passes either side of the imposing concrete grandstands, which hold 40,000 spectators. The Norisring takes its name from the ancient word for Nuremberg (Noris) to avoid confusion with the more famous Nurburgring. A 200-mile race with healthy prize money has been held here since 1967. It was made famous as a round of the German Racing Championship and is now part of the Touring Car series.

Active years	1947 to date
Location	Nuremberg stadium, south-western suburbs of Nuremberg, 105 miles north of Munich, 150 miles south-east of Frankfurt
Type	Temporary road course
Website	www.norisring.de
Lap distance	1.429 miles
Lap record	Qualifying: Hans-Joachim Stuck (Porsche 962C), 46.54s, 110.549 mph, Group C Sports Cars, 1986
	Race: Jean-Louis Schlesser (Sauber C9/88-Mercedes-Benz), 47.790s, 107.646 mph, Group C Sports Cars, 1988

Germany

Circuit changes

1947   Circuit laid out around the stadium. Track turned 90-degree right after the start with three 90-degree left-hand corners taking it back onto the current circuit behind the Steintribune. 1.243 miles

1948-49   New circuit for motorcycle races in front of the Steintribune. Featured a crossover and a new hairpin on Beuthnerstrasse. 2.486 miles

1950-59, 1961-65, 1967 and 1969-71   Return leg of the circuit rerouted behind the Steintribune to a new hairpin. 2.299 miles

1960, 1966 and 1968   Circuit shortened by bypassing Beuthnerstrasse and introducing a 180-degree corner after the start. 1.007 miles

1972 to date   Hairpin on Beuthnerstrasse moved to its current position. Current circuit

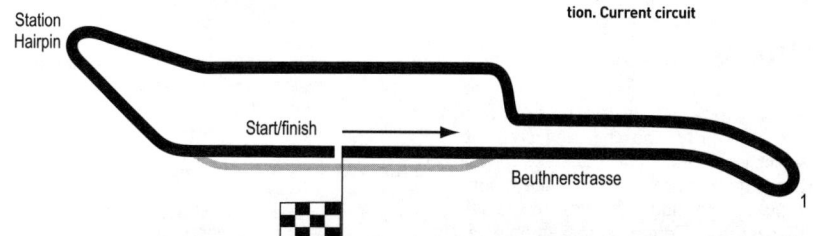

Station Hairpin — Start/finish — Beuthnerstrasse — 1

NORISRING 200 MILES

year	formula	winner	nat	car	mph
1967	SC	Frank Gardner	AUS	Lola T70 Mk2-Chevrolet	101.475
1968	SC	David Piper	GB	Ferrari P4	106.146
1969	SC	Brian Redman	GB	Lola T70 Mk3B-Chevrolet	110.990
1970	SC	Jurgen Neuhaus	D	Porsche 917	111.300
1971	SC	Chris Craft	GB	McLaren M8E-Chevrolet	114.291
1972	SC	Leo Kinnunen	SF	Porsche 917/10T	94.936
1973	SC	Leo Kinnunen	SF	Porsche 917/10T	93.231
1974	SC	Hans-Joachim Stuck	D	BMW 3.0 CSL	88.560
1975	SC	Toine Hezemans	NL	Porsche Carrera RSR	89.144
1976	SC	Bob Wollek	F	Porsche 934	89.338
1977	SC	Manfred Schurti	FL	Porsche 935	94.832
1978	SC	Bob Wollek	F	Porsche 935	95.496
1979	SC	Rolf Stommelen	D	Porsche 935	90.612
1980	SC	John Fitzpatrick	GB	Porsche 935	86.290
1981	SC	Bob Wollek	F	Porsche 935-K4	93.200
1982	SC	Jochen Mass	D	Porsche 956	94.850
1983	SC	Stefan Bellof	D	Porsche 956	103.246
1984	SC	Manfred Winkelhock	D	Porsche 956B	100.990
1985	SC	Klaus Ludwig	D	Porsche 956B	102.440
1986	SC W	Klaus Ludwig	D	Porsche 956	101.087
1987	SC W	Mauro Baldi/Jonathan Palmer	I/GB	Porsche 962GTi	101.831
1988	SC	Jean-Louis Schlesser	F	Sauber C9/88-Mercedes-Benz	102.610
1989	SC	Frank Jelinski	D	Porsche 962C	100.040
1990*	TC	Hans-Joachim Stuck	D	Audi V8 Quattro	87.562
	TC	Roberto Ravaglia	I	BMW M3	91.117
1991*	TC	Kurt Thiim	DK	Mercedes-Benz 190E	93.632
	TC	Hans-Joachim Stuck	D	Audi V8 Quattro	93.440
1992*	TC	Joachim Winkelhock	D	BMW M3	94.219
	TC	Steve Soper	GB	BMW M3	94.453
1993*	TC	Nicola Larini	I	Alfa Romeo 155 V6 TI	94.514
	TC	Nicola Larini	I	Alfa Romeo 155 V6 TI	95.170
1994*	TC	Nicola Larini	I	Alfa Romeo 155 V6 TI	96.590
	TC	Kris Nissen	DK	Alfa Romeo 155 V6 TI	96.770
1995*	TC	Christian Danner	D	Alfa Romeo 155 V6 TI	93.390
	TC	Bernd Schneider	D	Mercedes-Benz C Class	99.760
1996*	TC	Klaus Ludwig	D	Opel Calibra V6	101.830
	TC	Klaus Ludwig	D	Opel Calibra V6	103.333
1997#	TC	Joachim Winkelhock	D	BMW 320i	92.694
	TC	Joachim Winkelhock	D	BMW 320i	84.156
1998#	TC	Jorg van Ommen	D	Peugeot 406	89.070
	TC	Laurent Aiello	F	Peugeot 406	93.160
1999#	TC	Uwe Alzen	D	Opel Vectra	91.580
	TC	Manuel Reuter	D	Opel Vectra	86.640
2000#	TC	Joachim Winkelhock	D	Opel Astra V8 Coupe	97.520
	TC	Bernd Schneider	D	Mercedes-Benz CLK-DTM	92.920
2001#	TC	Bernd Schneider	D	Mercedes-Benz CLK-DTM	99.999
	TC	Uwe Alzen	D	Mercedes-Benz CLK-DTM	99.470
2002	TC	Laurent Aiello	F	Audi TT-R	100.380

*1988-96 German and International Touring Car races had two heats with no aggregate winner, #1997-2001 - two rounds of the German Super Touring Championship with no aggregate winner, 2002 main race winner recorded above

NURBURGRING

The old 'Ring is the greatest road racing circuit in the world. 14 miles and 176 corners, it is a never-ending succession of evocative turns and changing gradient. After the start, which is dominated by a castle overlooking Nurburg village, the cars race out into the mountains, to Flugplatz, Adenau Bridge, Karussel, Wippermann, Pflanzgarten, Tiergarten and so on. Over the years the 'Ring's organisers have tried to keep it up-to-date, resurfacing the track in 1957 and completely rebuilding large parts in 1970. But after Niki Lauda's near fatal accident in 1976 the CSI ruled that the circuit was no longer safe for F1. Instead, government investment helped build a modern Grand Prix track at the old start/finish area. The result was an uninspiring "designed-by-computer" venue that suffers in comparison with the original. The old pits were replaced with a new complex and a modern hotel now overlooks the start-line. The circuit length was increased by the introduction of a new infield loop after Turn 1 in 2002. Thankfully for enthusiasts, the old circuit, or Nordschleife, is still used for the 24-hour race.

Active years	1926 to date
Location	35 miles north-west of Koblenz, 44 miles south of Bonn, 55 miles south-west of Cologne
Type	Permanent road course
Website	www.nuerburgring.de

Current circuit (New Grand Prix circuit)

Lap distance	3.196 miles
Lap records	Qualifying: Juan Pablo Montoya (Williams FW24-BMW), 1m29.906, 127.974 mph, F1, 2002
	Race: Michael Schumacher (Ferrari F2002), 1m32.226, 124.755 mph, F1, 2002

Original circuits

Total	17.563 miles
Nordschleife	14.167 miles
Sudschleife	4.814 miles

Nordschleife/Grand Prix circuit changes

1926-66	14.167 miles
1967-82	Circuit resurfaced, some bumps eased in 1970. 14.189 miles
1983	Pit straight bypassed while new Grand Prix circuit was being built. 12.944 miles
1984-94	New Grand Prix circuit built. 2.822 miles
1995-2001	Veedol Chicane tightened. 2.831 miles
2002 to date	New infield section built after Turn 1. Current circuit

CURRENT GRAND PRIX CIRCUIT

1984-2001 GRAND PRIX CIRCUIT

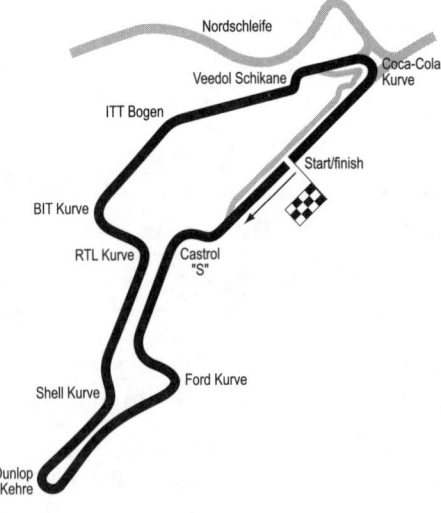

Germany

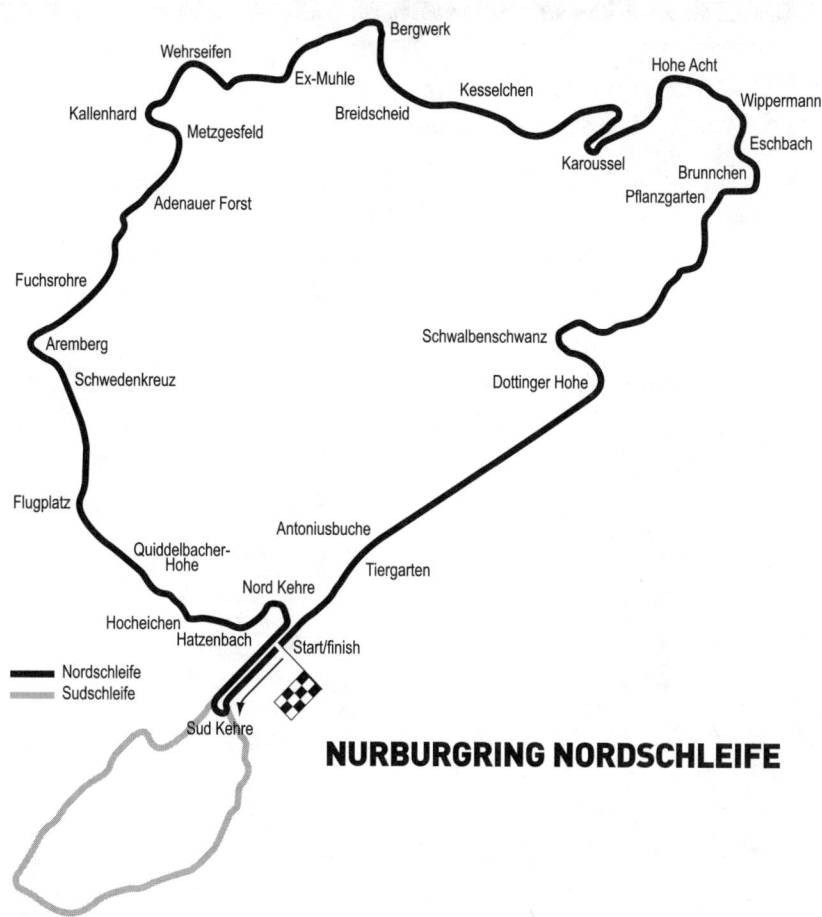

Wehrseifen
Bergwerk
Ex-Muhle
Hohe Acht
Kallenhard
Metzgesfeld
Breidscheid
Kesselchen
Wippermann
Eschbach
Karoussel
Brunnchen
Adenauer Forst
Pflanzgarten
Fuchsrohre
Aremberg
Schwalbenschwanz
Schwedenkreuz
Dottinger Hohe
Flugplatz
Antoniusbuche
Quiddelbacher-Hohe
Tiergarten
Nord Kehre
Hocheichen
Start/finish
Hatzenbach

■ Nordschleife
■ Sudschleife

Sud Kehre

NURBURGRING NORDSCHLEIFE

German Grand Prix see above
European Grand Prix see page 600

LUXEMBOURG GRAND PRIX

year	formula	winner	nat	car	mph
1997	F1 W	Jacques Villeneuve	CDN	Williams FW19-Renault	124.427
1998	F1 W	Mika Hakkinen	SF	McLaren MP4/13-Mercedes-Benz	123.372

EIFELRENNEN

year	formula	winner	nat	car	mph
1927	SC	Rudolf Caracciola	D	Mercedes-Benz S	59.960
1928	SC	Otto Spandel	D	Steyr	54.490
1929	SC	W Bartsch	D	Amilcar	45.130
1930	GP	Heinrich-Joachim von Morgen	D	Bugatti T35B	67.233
1931	GP	Rudolf Caracciola	D	Mercedes-Benz SSK	67.649
1932	GP	Rudolf Caracciola	D	Alfa Romeo 8C "Monza"	70.681
1933	GP	Tazio Nuvolari	I	Alfa Romeo 8C "Monza"	70.450
1934	GP	Manfred von Brauchitsch	D	Mercedes-Benz W25A	76.070
1935	GP	Rudolf Caracciola	D	Mercedes-Benz W25B	73.027
1936	GP	Bernd Rosemeyer	D	Auto Union C	72.846
1937	GP	Bernd Rosemeyer	D	Auto Union C	83.183
1939	GP	Hermann Lang	D	Mercedes-Benz W163	84.201
1949	SC	Karl Kling	D	Veritas	69.960
1950	F2	Fritz Riess	D	AFM 3-BMW	73.685
1951	F2	Paul Pietsch	D	Veritas Meteor	71.463

EIFELRENNEN (cont.)

year	formula	winner	nat	car	mph
1952	F2	Rudolf Fischer	CH	Ferrari 500	77.303
1953	F2	Emanuel de Graffenried	CH	Maserati A6GCM	70.388
1954	SC	Gunther Bechem	D	Borgward	73.360
1955	SC	Juan Manuel Fangio	RA	Mercedes-Benz	81.080
1956	GT	W Shock	D	Mercedes-Benz	76.080
1957	GT	Heine Walter	CH	Porsche	75.280
1958	GT	Wolfgang Seidel	D	Ferrari	74.630
1959	FJ	Wolfgang von Trips	D	Stanguellini-Fiat	77.670
1960	FJ	Dennis Taylor	GB	Lola Mk2-Ford	70.030
1961	FJ	Jo Siffert	CH	Lotus 20-Ford	75.250
1962	FJ	Peter Warr	GB	Lotus 22-Ford	85.560
1963	FJ	Gerhard Mitter	D	Lotus-DKW	77.550
1964	F2	Jim Clark	GB	Lotus 32-Ford	91.100
1965	F2	Paul Hawkins	AUS	Alexis Mk6-Ford	79.390
1966	F2	Jochen Rindt	A	Brabham BT18-Ford	78.700
1967	F2 E	Jochen Rindt	A	Brabham BT23-Ford	90.476
1968	F2	Chris Irwin	GB	Lola T100-Ford	101.783
1969	F2 E	Jackie Stewart	GB	Matra MS7-Ford	104.237
1970	F2	Jochen Rindt	A	Lotus 69-Ford	101.348
1971	F2 E	Francois Cevert	F	Tecno 71-Ford	105.994
1972	F2	Jochen Mass	D	March 722-Ford	106.298
1973	F2 E	Reine Wisell	S	GRD 273-Ford	93.163
1975	F2 E	Jacques Laffite	F	Martini MK16-BMW	112.015
1976	F2	Freddy Kottulinsky	S	Ralt RT1-BMW	110.550
1977	F2 E	Jochen Mass	D	March 772P-BMW	114.899
1978	F2 E	Alex Ribeiro	BR	March 782-Hart	115.098
1979	F2 E	Marc Surer	CH	March 792-BMW	105.279
1980	F2 E	Teo Fabi	I	March 802-BMW	112.443
1981	F2 E	Thierry Boutsen	B	March 812-BMW	117.738
1982	F2 E	Thierry Boutsen	B	Spirit 201-Honda	117.836
1983	F2 E	Beppe Gabbiani	I	March 832-BMW	118.926
1985	F3000 INT	CANCELLED - SNOW			
1986	TC	Volker Weidler	D	Mercedes-Benz 190E	88.093
1987	TC	Manuel Reuter	D	Ford Sierra XR4Ti	89.553
1988*	TC	Kurt Thiim	DK	BMW M3	91.229
	TC	Dany Snobeck	F	Mercedes-Benz 190E	91.554
1989*	TC	Steve Soper	GB	BMW M3	88.094
	TC	Steve Soper	GB	BMW M3	88.528
1990*	TC	Steve Soper	GB	BMW M3	93.914
	TC	Steve Soper	GB	BMW M3	94.314
1991*	TC	Klaus Ludwig	D	Mercedes-Benz 190E	97.298
	TC	Klaus Ludwig	D	Mercedes-Benz 190E	97.300
1992*	TC	Frank Biela	D	Audi V8 Quattro	88.903
	TC	Roland Asch	D	Mercedes-Benz 190E	97.708
1993*	TC	Nicola Larini	I	Alfa Romeo 155 V6 TI	98.724
	TC	Klaus Ludwig	D	Mercedes-Benz 190E	98.701
1994*	TC	Klaus Ludwig	D	Mercedes-Benz C Class	89.510
	TC	Nicola Larini	I	Alfa Romeo 155 V6 TI	88.370
1995*	TC	Bernd Schneider	D	Mercedes-Benz C Class	80.515
	TC	Kurt Thiim	DK	Mercedes-Benz C Class	80.048
1996*	TC	Jorg van Ommen	D	Mercedes-Benz C Class	100.439
	TC	Manuel Reuter	D	Opel Calibra V6	99.645
1997*	TC	Laurent Aiello	F	Peugeot 406	96.044
	TC	Laurent Aiello	F	Peugeot 406	97.243
1998*	TC	Roland Asch	D	Nissan Primera GT	96.087
	TC	Johnny Cecotto	YV	BMW 320i	95.944
1999*	TC	Manuel Reuter	D	Opel Vectra 16V	88.319
	TC	Tom Kristensen	DK	Honda Accord Ei	96.037
2000*	TC	Bernd Schneider	D	Mercedes-Benz CLK-DTM	89.511
	TC	Bernd Schneider	D	Mercedes-Benz CLK-DTM	89.460
2001*	TC	Laurent Aiello	F	Audi TT-R	92.950
	TC	Laurent Aiello	F	Audi TT-R	101.333
2002	TC	Uwe Alzen	D	Mercedes-Benz CLK-DTM	91.784

*1988-2001 German and International Touring Car races had two heats with no aggregate winner, 2002 main race winner recorded above

Germany

INTERNATIONAL F3000 RACE

year	formula	winner	nat	car	mph
1985*	F3000 INT		CANCELLED - SNOW		
1992	F3000 INT	Luca Badoer	I	Reynard 92D-Cosworth	115.142
1993	F3000 INT	Olivier Panis	F	Reynard 93D-Cosworth	113.945
1996	F3000 INT	Kenny Brack	S	Lola T96/50-Zytek	108.882
1997	F3000 INT	Ricardo Zonta	BR	Lola T96/50-Zytek	85.404
1998	F3000 INT	Gonzalo Rodriguez	ROU	Lola T96/50-Zytek	105.259
1999	F3000 INT	Jason Watt	DK	Lola B99/50-Zytek	109.836
2000	F3000 INT	Bruno Junqueira	BR	Lola B99/50-Zytek	90.855
2001	F3000 INT	Tomas Enge	CS	Lola B99/50-Zytek	110.248
2002	F3000 INT	Sebastien Bourdais	F	Lola B2/50-Zytek	104.746

*Eifelrennen

NURBURGRING 1000 KMS/WORLD SPORTS CAR RACE

year	formula	winner	nat	car	mph
1953	SC W	Alberto Ascari/Giuseppe Farina	I	Ferrari 340MM	74.692
1956	SC W	Stirling Moss/Jean Behra/Harry Schell/			
		Piero Taruffi	GB/F/USA/I	Maserati 300S	80.621
1957	SC W	Tony Brooks/Noel Cunningham-Reid	GB	Aston Martin DBR1/300	82.447
1958	SC W	Stirling Moss/Jack Brabham	GB/AUS	Aston Martin DBR1/300	84.322
1959	SC W	Stirling Moss/Jack Fairman	GB	Aston Martin DBR1/300	82.508
1960	SC W	Stirling Moss/Dan Gurney	GB/USA	Maserati T61	82.805
1961	SC W	Masten Gregory/Lucky Casner	USA	Maserati T61	79.297
1962	SC W	Olivier Gendebien/Phil Hill	B/USA	Ferrari Dino 246SP	82.661
1963	SC W	John Surtees/Willy Mairesse	GB/B	Ferrari 250P	82.689
1964	SC W	Ludovico Scarfiotti/Nino Vaccarella	I	Ferrari 275P	87.293
1965	SC W	John Surtees/Ludovico Scarfiotti	GB/I	Ferrari 275P2	90.539
1966	SC W	Phil Hill/Jo Bonnier	USA/S	Chaparral 2D-Chevrolet	89.306
1967	SC W	Udo Schutz/Joe Buzzetta	D/USA	Porsche 910/6	90.434
1968	SC W	Jo Siffert/Vic Elford	CH/GB	Porsche 908/8	95.048
1969	SC W	Jo Siffert/Brian Redman	CH/GB	Porsche 908/8	100.957
1970	SC W	Vic Elford/Kurt Ahrens jr	GB/D	Porsche 908/3	102.528
1971	SC W	Vic Elford/Gerard Larrousse	GB/F	Porsche 908/3	106.471
1972	SC W	Ronnie Peterson/Tim Schenken	S/AUS	Ferrari 312P	103.572
1973	SC W	Jacky Ickx/Brian Redman	B/GB	Ferrari 312P	111.190
1974	SC W	Jean-Pierre Beltoise/Jean-Pierre Jarier	F	Matra-Simca MS670C	113.557
1975	SC W	Arturo Merzario/Jacques Laffite	I/F	Alfa Romeo T33TT/12	109.775
1976	SC W	Dieter Quester/Albrecht Krebs	A/D	BMW 3.0 CSL	100.448
1977	SC W	Toine Hezemans/Tim Schenken/			
		Rolf Stommelen	NL/AUS/D	Porsche 935	104.486
1978	SC W	Klaus Ludwig/Hans Heyer/Toine Hezemans	D/D/NL	Porsche 935	105.288
1979	SC W	Manfred Schurti/John Fitzpatrick/			
		Bob Wollek	FL/GB/F	Porsche 935	104.755
1980	SC W	Rolf Stommelen/Jurgen Barth	D	Porsche 908/3	106.341
1981	SC W	Hans-Joachim Stuck/Nelson Piquet	D/BR	BMW M1	105.758
1982	SC W	Riccardo Patrese/Michele Alboreto/Teo Fabi	I	Lancia LC1	105.762
1983	SC W	Jochen Mass/Jacky Ickx	D/B	Porsche 956	104.637
1984	SC W	Stefan Bellof/Derek Bell	D/GB	Porsche 956	97.163
1986	SC W	Mike Thackwell/Henri Pescarolo	NZ/F	Sauber C8-Mercedes-Benz	92.080
1987	SC W	Eddie Cheever/Raul Boesel	USA/BR	Jaguar XJR-8	105.145
1988	SC W	Jean-Louis Schlesser/Jochen Mass	F/D	Sauber C9/88-Mercedes-Benz	95.929
1989	SC W	Jean-Louis Schlesser/Jochen Mass	F/D	Sauber C9/88-Mercedes-Benz	107.316
1990	SC W	Mauro Baldi/Jean-Louis Schlesser	I/F	Mercedes-Benz C11	112.692
1991	SC W	David Brabham/Derek Warwick	AUS/GB	Jaguar XJR-14	111.950

300 KM SPORTS CAR RACE

year	formula	winner	nat	car	mph
1976	SC W	Reinhold Joest	D	Porsche 908/3	89.818
1978	SC E	Giorgio Francia	I	Osella PA6-BMW	107.684

FIA GT RACE

year	formula	winner	nat	car	mph
1995	GT FIA	Ray Bellm/Maurizio Sandro Sala	GB/BR	McLaren F1 GTR-BMW	93.959
1996	GT FIA	Thomas Bscher/Peter Kox	D/NL	McLaren F1 GTR-BMW	97.507
1997	GT FIA	Klaus Ludwig/Bernd Schneider	D	Mercedes-Benz CLK-GTR	103.956
2001	GT FIA	Jamie Campbell-Walter/Mike Jordan	GB	Lister Storm GT	91.368

NURBURGRING 24 HOURS

year	formula	winner	nat	car	mph
1970	TC	Hans-Joachim Stuck/Clemens Schickentanz	D	BMW 2002TI	n/a
1971	TC	Prince von Hohenzollern/Gerhold Pankl	D/A	BMW 2002TI Alpina	73.324
1972	TC	Helmut Kelleners/Gerhold Pankl	D/A	BMW Alpina	n/a
1973	TC	Niki Lauda/Hans-Peter Joisten	A/D	BMW CSL Alpina	n/a
1976	TC	Karl-Heinz Quirin/Hubert Hechler/Fritz Muller	D	Porsche Carrera	n/a
1977	TC	Fritz Muller/Hubert Hechler	D	Porsche Carrera	n/a
1978	TC	Fritz Muller/Hubert Hechler/Franz Geschwendtner	D	Porsche Carrera	n/a
1979	TC	Herbert Kummle/Karl Mauer/Winni Vogt	D	Ford Escort	n/a
1980	TC	Dieter Selzer/Wolfgang Wolf/Mattias Schneider	D	Ford Escort RS	n/a
1981	TC	Helmut Doring/Dieter Gartmann/Fritz Muller	D	Ford Capri	n/a
1982	TC	Dieter Gartmann/Klaus Ludwig/Klaus Niedzwiedz	D	Ford Capri	n/a
1984	TC	Axel Felder/Franz-Josef Brohling/Peter Oberndorfer	D	BMW 635	n/a
1985	TC	Axel Felder/Jurgen Hamelmann/Robert Walterscheid-Muller	D	BMW 635	n/a
1986	TC	Markus Oestreich/Otto Rensing/Winni Vogt	D	BMW 325i	83.330
1987	TC	Klaus Ludwig/Klaus Niedzwiedz/Steve Soper	D/D/GB	Ford Sierra Cosworth	n/a
1988	TC	Edgar Doren/Gerhard Holup/Peter Faubel	D	Porsche Carrera	n/a
1989	TC	Emanuele Pirro/Roberto Ravaglia/Fabien Giroix	I/I/F	BMW M3	94.216
1990	TC	Altfrid Heger/Joachim Winkelhock/Frank Schmickler	D	BMW M3	n/a
1991	TC	Kris Nissen/Joachim Winkelhock/Armin Hahne	DK/D/D	BMW M3	n/a
1992	TC	Johnny Cecotto/Christian Danner/Marc Duez/			
		Jean-Michel Martin	YV/D/B/B	BMW M3	63.830
1993	TC	Antonio de Azevedo/Franz Konrad/Oernulf Wirdheim/			
		Frank Katthofer	BR/A/S/D	Porsche Carrera	84.280
1994	TC	Fred Rosterg/Frank Katthofer/Karl-Heinz Wlazik	D	BMW M3	77.591
1995	TC	Roberto Ravaglia/Marc Duez/Alexander Burgstaller	I/B/D	BMW 320i	85.125
1996	TC	Johannes Schied/Sabine Reck/Hans Widmann	D	BMW M3	88.090
1997	TC	Johannes Schied/Sabine Reck/Hans-Jurgen Tiemann/			
		Peter Zakowski	D	BMW M3	n/a
1998	TC	Marc Duez/Hans-Joachim Stuck/Christian Menzel/			
		Andy Bovensiepen	B/D/D/D	BMW 320i diesel	89.997
1999	GT/TC	Han-Jurgen Tiemann/Klaus Ludwig/Peter Zakowski/			
		Marc Duez	D/D/D/B	Chrysler Viper GTS-R	93.820
2000	GT/TC	Bernd Maylander/Michael Bartels/Uwe Alzen/Altfrid Heger	D	Porsche 996 GT3-R	n/a
2001	GT/TC	Peter Zakowski/Michael Bartels/Pedro Lamy	D/D/P	Chrysler Viper GTS-R	n/a
2002	GT/TC	Peter Zakowski/Pedro Lamy/Robert Lechner	D/P/A	Chrysler Viper GTS-R	n/a

EUROPEAN FORMULA 3 RACE

year	formula	winner	nat	car	mph
1975	F3 E	Freddy Kottulinsky	S	Modus M1-BMW	104.260
1976	F3 E	Conny Andersson	S	March 753-Toyota	101.282
1977	F3 E	Piercarlo Ghinzani	I	March 773-Toyota	88.897
1978	F3 E	Anders Olofsson	S	Ralt RT1-Toyota	106.484
	F3 E	Patrick Gaillard	F	Chevron B43-Toyota	107.655
1980	F3 E	Thierry Boutsen	B	Martini MK31-Toyota	105.972
1981	F3 E	Oscar Larrauri	RA	March 813-Toyota	94.370
1982	F3 E	Oscar Larrauri	RA	Euroracing 101-Alfa Romeo	98.467
1984	F3 E	Johnny Dumfries	GB	Ralt RT3/83-Volkswagen	103.697
1987*	F3 E	Roland Ratzenberger	A	Ralt RT31-Volkswagen	87.972
	F3 E	Victor Rosso	RA	Ralt RT31-Volkswagen	98.496
1988#	F3 E	Joachim Winkelhock	D	Reynard 883-Volkswagen	86.239

*EFDA Euroseries races. #European F3 Cup

OSCHERSLEBEN

For a country so rich in motor racing history Germany has surprisingly few permanent circuits. In 1997, when Oschersleben opened in the remote countryside of the former East Germany it was only the third such venue, joining the Grand Prix circuits at the Nurburgring and Hockenheim. Although the circuit was only expected to hold events below F3 when it opened, it has gone on to host both FIA F3000 and GT events. Oschersleben may be flat and uninspring, but it does offer state-of-the-art testing facilities, including a sprinkler system that can be used to simulate wet racing conditions.

Active years	1997 to date
Location	20 miles south-west of Magdeburg, 75 miles south-east of Hannover, 120 miles west of Berlin
Type	Permanent road course
Website	www.motopark.de
Lap distance	2.279 miles
Lap record	Qualifying: Juan Pablo Montoya (Lola T96/50-Zytek), 1m18.475, 104.548 mph, F3000, 1998
	Race: Uwe Alzen (Porsche 911 GT1-98), 1m20.206, 102.272 mph, GT, 1998

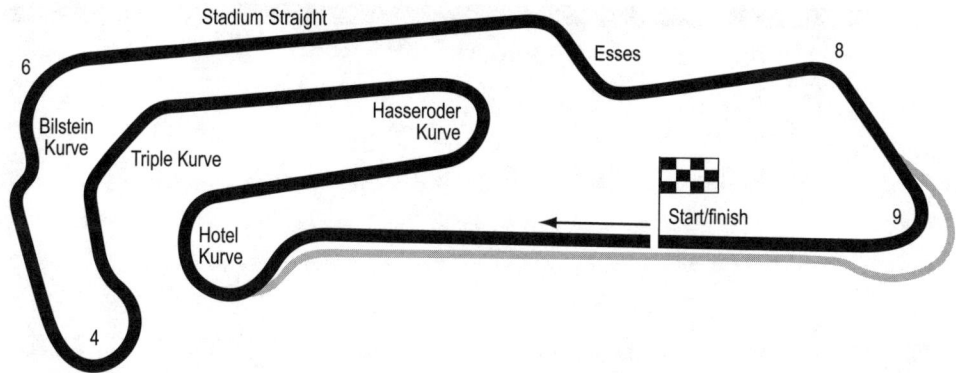

INTERNATIONAL FORMULA 3000 RACE					
year	formula	winner	nat	car	mph
1998	F3000 INT	Stephane Sarrazin	F	Lola T96/50-Zytek	90.222

FIA GT RACE					
year	formula	winner	nat	car	mph
1998	GT FIA	Klaus Ludwig/Ricardo Zonta	D/BR	Mercedes-Benz CLK-GTR	96.388
1999	GT FIA	Olivier Beretta/Karl Wendlinger	MC/A	Chrysler Viper GTS-R	88.818
2002	GT FIA	Jean-Denis Deletraz/Andrea Piccini	CH/I	Ferrari 550M	91.028

SOLITUDE

A narrow temporary circuit set in the wooded country-side near Stuttgart that briefly held an important non-championship F1 race. Used mainly for motorcycles, a Grand Prix for cars was run sporadically. The Mercedes-Benz GP team occasionally used the circuit for testing in the thirties, especially before races at the Nurburgring, which the Solitude circuit resembled. When the circuit closed in 1965 the Solitude Grand Prix was revived on two occasions at Hockenheim.

Active years	1922-65
Location	Near Stuttgart
Type	Permanent road course
Lap distance	7.089 miles
Lap record	Qualifying: Jim Clark (Lotus 33-Climax), 3m49.6, 111.152 mph, F1, 1964
	Race: Jim Clark (Lotus 25-Climax), 3m49.1, 111.567 mph, F1, 1963

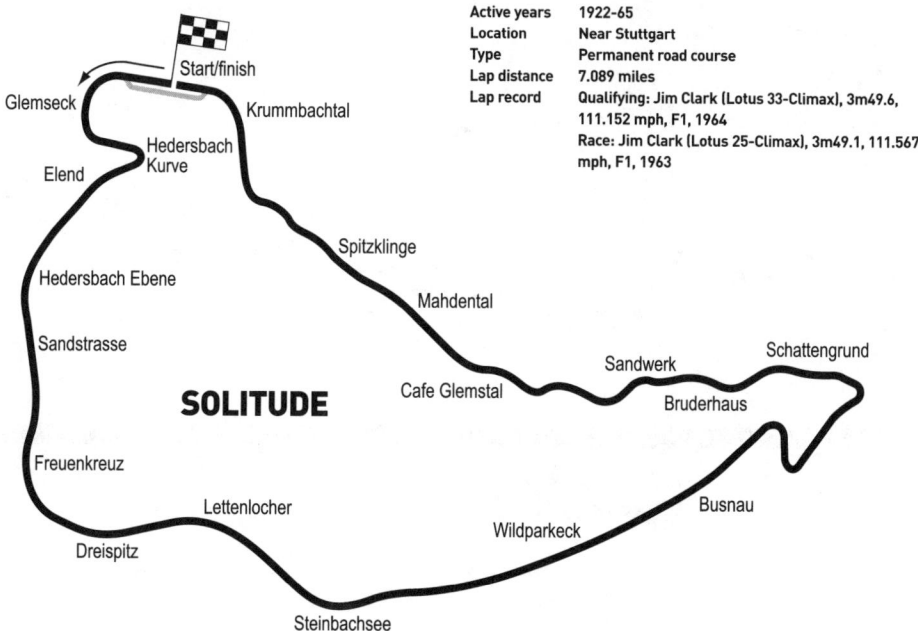

SOLITUDE GRAND PRIX

year	formula	winner	nat	car	mph
1925	FL	Otto Merz	D	Mercedes	58.470
1926	FL	Otto Merz	D	Mercedes	57.290
1927	FL	August Momberger	D	Bugatti	63.070
1950	F2	Karl Kling	D	Veritas	80.840
1956	SC	Hans Herrmann	D	Porsche	92.020
1959	FJ	Michel May	CH	Stangellini-Fiat	85.940
1960	F2	Wolfgang von Trips	D	Ferrari Dino 156	102.190
1961	F1	Innes Ireland	GB	Lotus 21-Climax	105.202
1962	F1	Dan Gurney	USA	Porsche 804	100.677
1963	F1	Jack Brabham	AUS	Brabham BT3-Climax	106.213
1964	F1	Jim Clark	GB	Lotus 33-Climax	91.435
1965	F1	Chris Amon	NZ	Lola T60-Ford	104.080
1968*	SC	David Piper	GB	Ferrari P3/4	126.266
1969*	SC	Hans Herrmann	D	Lola T70 Mk3B-Chevrolet	128.950

*held at Hockenheim

TAUNUS

In 1907, the Kaiserpreis was a one-off event for modified 8-litre touring cars organised at Taunus to compete with the French Grand Prix. The huge field of 92 cars made qualifying heats necessary, but the event was not repeated. The circuit was also used as part of the 1904 Gordon Bennett Trophy course.

Active years	1907
Location	Open roads from Homburg to Weilburg
Type	Temporary road course
Lap distance	73.150 miles
Lap record	Race: Vincenzo Lancia (Fiat), 1h21m55.6, 53.572 mph, Kaiserpreis class, 1907

KAISERPREIS

year	formula	winner	nat	car	mph
1907	Kaiserpreis	Felice Nazzaro	I	Fiat	52.489

GREAT BRITAIN

Major Championships

BRITISH GT CHAMPIONSHIP

year	series sponsor	driver	nat	car
1993		John Greasley	GB	Porsche 935-K3
1994		Thorkild Thyrring	DK	Lotus Esprit S300
1995		Chris Hodgetts	GB	Marcos LM600-Chevrolet
1996	Privilege Insurance	David Warnock/Rob Schirle	GB	Marcos LM600-Chevrolet
1997	Privilege Insurance	Steve O'Rourke/Tim Sugden	GB	Porsche 911 GT2
1998	Privilege Insurance	Kurt Luby/Richard Dean	GB	Chrysler Viper GTS-R
1999	Privilege Insurance	Julian Bailey/Jamie Campbell-Walter	GB	Lister Storm GT
2000	Privilege Insurance	Calum Lockie	GB	Marcos Mantara LM600
2001	Privilege Insurance	Mike Jordan/David Warnock	GB	Lister Storm GT
2002		Tomas Erdos/Ian McKellar	BR/GB	Saleen S7R-Ford

BRITISH TOURING CAR CHAMPIONSHIP

year	series sponsor	driver	nat	team	car
1958		Jack Sears	GB	Jack Sears	Austin A105 Westminster
1959		Jeff Uren	GB	Jeff Uren	Ford Zephyr
1960		Doc Shepherd	GB	Don Moore	Austin A40
1961		Sir John Whitmore	GB	Cooper Car Company	Mini Cooper
1962		John Love	RSR	Vita	Mini Cooper
1963		Jack Sears	GB	Wilment	Ford Galaxie/Lotus Cortina
1964		Jim Clark	GB	Team Lotus	Lotus Cortina
1965		Roy Pierpoint	GB	Roy Pierpoint	Ford Mustang
1966		John Fitzpatrick	GB	Broadspeed	Ford Anglia
1967		Frank Gardner	AUS	Alan Mann Racing	Ford Falcon
1968		Frank Gardner	AUS	Alan Mann Racing	Ford Escort/Ford Cortina
1969		Alec Poole	IRL	Equipe Arden	Mini Cooper S
1970		Bill McGovern	GB	George Bevan	Sunbeam Imp
1971		Bill McGovern	GB	George Bevan	Sunbeam Imp
1972	Wiggins Teape	Bill McGovern	GB	George Bevan	Sunbeam Imp
1973		Frank Gardner	AUS	SCA European Road Services	Chevrolet Camaro
1974	Castrol	Bernard Unett	GB	Chrysler Dealer Team	Hillman Avenger
1975	Southern Organs	Andy Rouse	GB	Broadspeed	Triumph Dolomite Sprint
1976	Keith Prowse	Bernard Unett	GB	Chrysler Dealer Team	Chrysler Avenger GT
1977	Tricentrol	Bernard Unett	GB	Chrysler Dealer Team	Chrysler Avenger GT
1978	Tricentrol	Richard Longman	GB	Richard Longman	Mini 1275GT
1979	Tricentrol	Richard Longman	GB	Richard Longman	Mini 1275GT
1980	Tricentrol	Win Percy	GB	Tom Walkinshaw Racing	Mazda RX7
1981	Tricentrol	Win Percy	GB	Tom Walkinshaw Racing	Mazda RX7
1982	Tricentrol	Win Percy	GB	Toyota GB	Toyota Corolla
1983	Trimoco	Andy Rouse	GB	Andy Rouse Engineering	Alfa Romeo GTV6
1984	Trimoco	Andy Rouse	GB	Andy Rouse Engineering	Rover 3500 Vitesse
1985	Trimoco	Andy Rouse	GB	Andy Rouse Engineering	Ford Sierra 2.3 turbo
1986		Chris Hodgetts	GB	Toyota GB	Toyota Celica GT
1987	Dunlop	Chris Hodgetts	GB	Toyota GB	Toyota Corolla GT
1988	Dunlop	Frank Sytner	GB	Prodrive	BMW M3
1989	Esso	John Cleland	GB	Vauxhall Dealer Sport	Vauxhall Astra GTE 16v
1990	Esso	Robb Gravett	GB	Trakstar	Ford Sierra RS500
1991	Esso	Will Hoy	GB	Vic Lee Motorsport	BMW M3
1992	Esso	Tim Harvey	GB	Vic Lee Motorsport	BMW 318i
1993	Auto Trader	Joachim Winkelhock	D	Schnitzer	BMW 318i
1994	Auto Trader	Gabriele Tarquini	I	Alfa Corse	Alfa Romeo 155 TS
1995	Auto Trader	John Cleland	GB	Vauxhall Sport	Vauxhall Cavalier 16v
1996	Auto Trader	Frank Biela	D	Audi Sport UK	Audi A4 Quattro
1997	Auto Trader	Alain Menu	CH	Williams Renault Dealer Racing	Renault Laguna
1998	Auto Trader	Rickard Rydell	S	Tom Walkinshaw Racing	Volvo S40
1999	Auto Trader	Laurent Aiello	F	Nissan Racing/Ray Mallock Ltd	Nissan Primera GT
2000	Auto Trader	Alain Menu	CH	Ford Team Mondeo	Ford Mondeo Zetec
2001	theAA.com	Jason Plato	GB	Triple Eight Race Engineering	Vauxhall Astra Coupe
2002	Green Flag	James Thompson	GB	Triple Eight Race Engineering	Vauxhall Astra Coupe

Racing Around the World

BRITISH AND EUROPEAN FORMULA 5000 CHAMPIONSHIP

year	series sponsor	driver	nat	team	car
1969	Guards	Peter Gethin	GB	Church Farm Racing	McLaren M10A-Chevrolet
1970	Guards	Peter Gethin	GB	Church Farm Racing	McLaren M10B-Chevrolet
1971	Rothmans	Frank Gardner	AUS	Speed International	Lola T192-Chevrolet/ Lola T300-Chevrolet
1972	Rothmans	Gijs van Lennep	NL	Speed International	Surtees TS11-Chevrolet
1973	Rothmans	Teddy Pilette	B	Team VDS	Chevron B24-Chevrolet
1974	Rothmans	Bob Evans	GB	McKechnie	Lola T332-Chevrolet
1975	ShellSport	Teddy Pilette	B	Team VDS	Lola T400-Chevrolet

BRITISH GROUP 8 CHAMPIONSHIP

year	series sponsor	driver	nat	team	car
1976	ShellSport	David Purley	GB	Lec Refridgeration	Chevron B30-Ford
1977	ShellSport	Tony Trimmer	GB	Melchester Racing	Surtees TS19-Ford

BRITISH FORMULA 1 CHAMPIONSHIP

year	series sponsor	driver	nat	team	car
1969	VAT 69	Jackie Stewart	GB	Matra International	Matra MS80-Ford
1978	Aurora AFX	Tony Trimmer	GB	Melchester Racing	McLaren M23-Ford/ McLaren M25-Ford
1979	Aurora AFX	Rupert Keegan	GB	Charles Clowes Racing	Arrows A1-Ford
1980	Aurora AFX	Emilio de Villota	E	RAM Racing	Williams FW07-Ford/ Williams FW07B-Ford
1982		Jim Crawford	GB	AMCO Racing	Ensign N180B-Ford

1970-77, 1981 no series

BRITISH FORMULA 2 CHAMPIONSHIP

year	series sponsor	driver	nat	team	car
1957	Autocar	Tony Marsh	GB	Tony Marsh	Cooper T43-Climax
1958	Autocar	Jack Brabham	AUS	Cooper Car Company	Cooper T45-Climax
1959	Autocar	Stirling Moss	GB	RRC Walker Racing Team	Cooper T43-Borgward
1960	Autocar	Jackie Lewis	GB	H&L Motors/Alan Brown	Cooper T45-Climax
1964	Autocar	Mike Spence	GB	Ron Harris Team Lotus	Lotus 32-Ford
1965	Autocar	Jim Clark	GB	Ron Harris Team Lotus	Lotus 35-Ford
1966	Autocar	Jack Brabham	AUS	Brabham Racing Organisation	Brabham BT18-Honda/ Brabham BT21-Honda
1967	Autocar	Alan Rees	GB	Winkelmann Racing	Brabham BT23-Ford
	British	Jochen Rindt	A	Winkelmann Racing	Brabham BT23-Ford
1972	John Player	Niki Lauda	A	March Engineering	March 722-Ford

1961-63, 1969-71 no series

BRITISH FORMULA 3000 CHAMPIONSHIP

year	series sponsor	driver	nat	team	car
1989		Gary Brabham	AUS	Bromley Motorsport	Reynard 88D-Cosworth
1990		Pedro Chaves	P	Mansell Madgwick Motorsport	Reynard 90D-Cosworth
1991		Paul Warwick*	GB	Mansell Madgwick Motorsport	Reynard 90D-Cosworth
1992	Halfords	Yvan Muller	F	Omegaland	Reynard 91D-Cosworth
1993	Halfords	Philippe Adams	B	Madgwick International/Argo Racing	Reynard 92D Cosworth/ Reynard 91D-Cosworth
1994	Venson	Jose Luis di Palma	RA	Madgwick International	Reynard 92D-Cosworth
1996	Venson	Gareth Rees	GB	Super Nova Racing	Reynard 95D-Cosworth

Officially known as F2 from 1992-97. *Warwick won the championship posthumously, having died in an accident at Oulton Park. 1995 cancelled and 1997 abandoned both due to lack of entries

BRITISH FORMULA 3 CHAMPIONSHIP (INCLUDING FORMULA JUNIOR)

year	series sponsor	driver	nat	team	car
1951	Autosport	Eric Brandon	GB	Ecurie Richmond	Cooper T15-Norton
1952	Autosport	Don Parker	GB	Don Parker	Kieft C52-Norton
1953	Autosport	Don Parker	GB	Don Parker	Kieft C53-Norton
1954	BRSCC National	Les Leston	GB	Les Leston	Cooper T31-Norton
1955	BRSCC National	Jim Russell	GB	Cooper Car Company	Cooper T37-Norton
1956	BRSCC National	Jim Russell	GB	Cooper Car Company	Cooper T42-Norton
1957	BRSCC National	Jim Russell	GB	Cooper Car Company	Cooper T43-Norton
1958	BRSCC National	Trevor Taylor	GB	Trevor Taylor	Cooper T43-Norton
1959	BRSCC National*	Don Parker	GB	Don Parker	Cooper T43-Norton
1960	BRSCC National*	Jack Pitcher	GB	Jack Pitcher	Alexis 2-BMC
	John Davy*	Jim Clark	GB	Team Lotus	Lotus 18-Ford
	Motor Racing*	Jim Clark/ Trevor Taylor (tied)	GB	Team Lotus	Lotus 18-Ford

640

Great Britain

BRITISH FORMULA 3 CHAMPIONSHIP (INCLUDING FORMULA JUNIOR) (cont.)

year	series sponsor	driver	nat	team	car
1961	BRSCC National*	Mike Ledbrook	GB	Ron Harris	Lotus 20-Ford
	John Davy*	Bill Moss	GB	Chequered Flag Racing	Gemini Mk3A-Ford/
					Lotus 18-Ford
	Motor Racing*	Trevor Taylor	GB	Team Lotus	Lotus 20-Ford
1962	John Davy*	John Flemming	GB	Ron Harris	Lola Mk5-Ford
1963	Express & Star*	Peter Arundell	GB	Ron Harris Team Lotus	Lotus 27-Ford
1964	Express & Star	Jackie Stewart	GB	Tyrrell Racing	Cooper T72-BMC
	BRSCC	Rod Banting	GB	Rod Banting	Lotus 31-BMC
1965	BRSCC	Tony Dean	GB	Tony Dean	Brabham BT15-Ford
1966	Les Leston	Harry Stiller	GB	Motor Racing Stables	Brabham BT16-Ford/
					Brabham BT18-Ford
1967	Les Leston	Harry Stiller	GB	Motor Racing Stables	Brabham BT18-Ford/
					Brabham BT21-Ford
1968	Lombank	Tim Schenken	AUS	Sports Motors	Chevron B9-Ford/
					Titan Mk3-Ford/
					Brabham BT21X-Ford
1969	Lombank	Emerson Fittipaldi	BR	Jim Russell Racing	Lotus 59-Ford
1970	Forward Trust	Carlos Pace	BR	Jim Russell Racing	Lotus 59-Ford
	Lombank	Dave Walker	AUS	Team Lotus	Lotus 59-Ford
	Shell	Tony Trimmer	GB	Race Cars International	Lotus 59-Ford/
					Brabham BT28-Ford
1971	Lombank	Roger Williamson	GB	Wheatcroft Racing	March 713M-Ford
	Shell/Motor Sport	Dave Walker	AUS	Team Lotus	Lotus 69-Ford
1972	Forward Trust	Roger Williamson	GB	Wheatcroft Racing	GRD 372-Ford/March 723-Ford
	Lombard	Rikky von Opel	FL	Team Ensign	Ensign F372-Ford
	Shell/Motor Sport	Roger Williamson	GB	Wheatcroft Racing	GRD 372-Ford/March 723-Ford
1973	Forward Trust	Ian Taylor	GB	Chris Andrews	March 733-Ford
	Lombard	Tony Brise	GB	Team Kent Messanger	GRD 372-Ford/GRD 373-Ford/
					March 733-Ford
	John Player	Tony Brise	GB	Team Kent Messanger	GRD 373-Ford/March 733-Ford
1974	Forward Trust	Brian Henton	GB	March Engineering	March 743-Ford/
					March 743-Toyota
	Lombard	Brian Henton	GB	March Engineering	March 743-Ford/
					March 743-Toyota
1975	BP	Gunnar Nilsson	S	March Engineering	March 753-Toyota
1976	ShellSport	Bruno Giacomelli	I	March Engineering	March 763-Toyota
	BP	Rupert Keegan	GB	British Air Ferries	March 743-Toyota/
					Chevron B34-Toyota
1977	Vandervell	Stephen South	GB	Team BP	March 763-Toyota/
					March 773-Toyota
	BP	Derek Daly	IRL	Derek McMahon Racing	Chevron B38-Toyota
1978	Vandervell	Derek Warwick	GB	Warwick Trailers	Ralt RT1-Toyota
	BP	Nelson Piquet	BR	Greg Siddle	Ralt RT1-Toyota
1979	Vandervell	Chico Serra	BR	Project 4 Racing	March 793-Toyota
1980	Vandervell	Stefan Johansson	S	Project 4 Racing	March 803-Toyota/
					March 803B-Toyota/
					Ralt RT3-Toyota
1981	Marlboro	Jonathan Palmer	GB	West Surrey Racing	Ralt RT3-Toyota
1982	Marlboro	Tommy Byrne	IRL	Murray Taylor Racing	Ralt RT3/81-Toyota/
					Ralt RT3/82-Toyota
1983	Marlboro	Ayrton Senna	BR	West Surrey Racing	Ralt RT3/83-Toyota
1984	Marlboro	Johnny Dumfries	GB	Dave Price Racing	Ralt RT3/83-Volkswagen
1985	Marlboro	Mauricio Gugelmin	BR	West Surrey Racing	Ralt RT30-Volkswagen
1986	Lucas	Andy Wallace	GB	Madgwick Motorsport	Reynard 863-Volkswagen
1987	Lucas	Johnny Herbert	GB	Eddie Jordan Racing	Reynard 873-Volkswagen
1988	Lucas	JJ Lehto	SF	Pacific Racing	Reynard 883-Toyota
1989	Lucas	David Brabham	AUS	Bowman Racing	Ralt RT33-Volkswagen
1990		Mika Hakkinen	SF	West Surrey Racing	Ralt RT34-Mugen
1991		Rubens Barrichello	BR	West Surrey Racing	Ralt RT35-Mugen
1992		Gil de Ferran	BR	Paul Stewart Racing	Reynard 923-Mugen
1993		Kelvin Burt	GB	Paul Stewart Racing	Reynard 933-Mugen/
					Dallara 393-Mugen
1994		Jan Magnussen	DK	Paul Stewart Racing	Dallara 394-Mugen
1995		Oliver Gavin	GB	Edenbridge Racing	Dallara 395-Vauxhall
1996		Ralph Firman Jr	GB	Paul Stewart Racing	Dallara 396-Mugen
1997	Autosport	Jonny Kane	GB	Paul Stewart Racing	Dallara 397-Mugen
1998	Autosport	Mario Haberfeld	BR	Paul Stewart Racing	Dallara 398-Mugen
1999	Autosport	Marc Hynes	GB	Manor Motorsport	Dallara 399-Mugen
2000	Green Flag	Antonio Pizzonia	BR	Manor Motorsport	Dallara 300-Mugen
2001	Green Flag	Takuma Sato	J	Carlin Motorsport	Dallara 301-Mugen
2002	Green Flag	Robbie Kerr	GB	Alan Docking Racing	Dallara 302-Mugen

*Formula Junior

BRITISH FORMULA ATLANTIC CHAMPIONSHIP

year	series sponsor	driver	nat	car
1971	Yellow Pages	Vern Schuppan	AUS	Palliser WDB4-Ford
1972	Yellow Pages	Bill Gubelmann	USA	March 72B-Ford
1973	Yellow Pages	Colin Vandervell	GB	March 73B-Ford
	BP	John Nicholson	NZ	Lyncar 005-Ford
1974	John Player	John Nicholson	NZ	Lyncar 005-Ford
	Southern Organs	Jim Crawford	GB	March 73B-Ford/March 74B-Ford
1975	John Player	Tony Brise	GB	Modus M1-Ford
	Southern Organs	Ted Wentz	USA	Lola T360-Ford
1976	Indylantic	Ted Wentz	USA	Lola T460-Ford
1979	Hitachi	Ray Mallock	GB	Ralt RT1-Ford/Ralt RT4-Ford
1980	Hitachi	David Leslie	GB	Ralt RT4-Ford
1981		Ray Mallock	GB	Ralt RT4-Ford
1982		Alo Lawler	IRL	Ralt RT4-Ford
1983		Alo Lawler	IRL	Ralt RT4-Ford
1977-78 no series				

ASCAR CHAMPIONSHIP

year	driver	nat	team	car
2001	John Mickel	GB	Torquespeed	Chevrolet Monte Carlo
2002	Nicolas Minassian	F	Ray Mallock Ltd	Chevrolet Monte Carlo

Major International Races

BRITISH GRAND PRIX

year	formula	circuit	winner	nat	car	mph
1926*	GP	Brooklands	Robert Senechal/Louis Wagner	F	Delage 15S8	71.661
1927*	GP	Brooklands	Robert Benoist	F	Delage 15S8	85.586
1935#	GP	Donington Park	Richard Shuttleworth	GB	Alfa Romeo Tipo-B "P3"	63.928
1936#	GP	Donington Park	Hans Ruesch/Dick Seaman	CH/GB	Alfa Romeo Tipo-C "8C-35"	69.187
1937#	GP	Donington Park	Bernd Rosemeyer	D	Auto Union C	82.856
1938#	GP	Donington Park	Tazio Nuvolari	I	Auto Union D	80.486
1948	F1	Silverstone	Luigi Villoresi	I	Maserati 4CLT/48	72.270
1949	F1	Silverstone	Emanuel de Graffenried	CH	Maserati 4CLT/48	77.307
1950	F1 W	Silverstone	Giuseppe Farina	I	Alfa Romeo 158	90.950
1951	F1 W	Silverstone	Jose Froilan Gonzalez	RA	Ferrari 375	96.107
1952	F2 W	Silverstone	Alberto Ascari	I	Ferrari 500	90.921
1953	F2 W	Silverstone	Alberto Ascari	I	Ferrari 500	92.975
1954	F1 W	Silverstone	Jose Froilan Gonzalez	RA	Ferrari 625 (555)	89.687
1955	F1 W	Aintree	Stirling Moss	GB	Mercedes-Benz W196	86.468
1956	F1 W	Silverstone	Juan Manuel Fangio	RA	Lancia-Ferrari D50	98.661
1957	F1 W	Aintree	Tony Brooks/Stirling Moss	GB	Vanwall VW4	86.803
1958	F1 W	Silverstone	Peter Collins	GB	Ferrari Dino 246	102.049
1959	F1 W	Aintree	Jack Brabham	AUS	Cooper T51-Climax	89.884
1960	F1 W	Silverstone	Jack Brabham	AUS	Cooper T53-Climax	108.695
1961	F1 W	Aintree	Wolfgang von Trips	D	Ferrari Dino 156	83.907
1962	F1 W	Aintree	Jim Clark	GB	Lotus 25-Climax	92.247
1963	F1 W	Silverstone	Jim Clark	GB	Lotus 25-Climax	107.341
1964	F1 W	Brands Hatch	Jim Clark	GB	Lotus 25-Climax	94.141
1965	F1 W	Silverstone	Jim Clark	GB	Lotus 33-Climax	112.017
1966	F1 W	Brands Hatch	Jack Brabham	AUS	Brabham BT19-Repco	95.479
1967	F1 W	Silverstone	Jim Clark	GB	Lotus 49-Ford	117.642
1968	F1 W	Brands Hatch	Jo Siffert	CH	Lotus 49B-Ford	104.831
1969	F1 W	Silverstone	Jackie Stewart	GB	Matra MS80-Ford	127.254
1970	F1 W	Brands Hatch	Jochen Rindt	A	Lotus 72-Ford	108.687
1971	F1 W	Silverstone	Jackie Stewart	GB	Tyrrell 003-Ford	130.480
1972	F1 W	Brands Hatch	Emerson Fittipaldi	BR	Lotus 72D-Ford	112.058
1973	F1 W	Silverstone	Peter Revson	USA	McLaren M23-Ford	131.752
1974	F1 W	Brands Hatch	Jody Scheckter	ZA	Tyrrell 007-Ford	115.735
1975	F1 W	Silverstone	Emerson Fittipaldi	BR	McLaren M23-Ford	120.019
1976	F1 W	Brands Hatch	Niki Lauda	A	Ferrari 312T2	114.236
1977	F1 W	Silverstone	James Hunt	GB	McLaren M26-Ford	130.357
1978	F1 W	Brands Hatch	Carlos Reutemann	RA	Ferrari 312T3	116.607
1979	F1 W	Silverstone	Clay Regazzoni	CH	Williams FW07-Ford	138.799
1980	F1 W	Brands Hatch	Alan Jones	AUS	Williams FW07B-Ford	125.690
1981	F1 W	Silverstone	John Watson	GB	McLaren MP4/1-Ford	137.638
1982	F1 W	Brands Hatch	Niki Lauda	A	McLaren MP4/1B-Ford	124.713

BRITISH GRAND PRIX (cont.)

year	formula	circuit	winner	nat	car	mph
1983	F1 W	Silverstone	Alain Prost	F	Renault RE40	139.218
1984	F1 W	Brands Hatch	Niki Lauda	A	McLaren MP4/2-TAG Porsche	124.436
1985	F1 W	Silverstone	Alain Prost	F	McLaren MP4/2B-TAG Porsche	146.274
1986	F1 W	Brands Hatch	Nigel Mansell	GB	Williams FW11-Honda	129.756
1987	F1 W	Silverstone	Nigel Mansell	GB	Williams FW11B-Honda	146.208
1988	F1 W	Silverstone	Ayrton Senna	BR	McLaren MP4/4-Honda	124.142
1989	F1 W	Silverstone	Alain Prost	F	McLaren MP4/5-Honda	143.645
1990	F1 W	Silverstone	Alain Prost	F	Ferrari 641/2	145.204
1991	F1 W	Silverstone	Nigel Mansell	GB	Williams FW14-Renault	131.227
1992	F1 W	Silverstone	Nigel Mansell	GB	Williams FW14B-Renault	134.098
1993	F1 W	Silverstone	Alain Prost	F	Williams FW15C-Renault	134.223
1994	F1 W	Silverstone	Damon Hill	GB	Williams FW16-Renault	128.314
1995	F1 W	Silverstone	Johnny Herbert	GB	Benetton B195-Renault	124.212
1996	F1 W	Silverstone	Jacques Villeneuve	CDN	Williams FW18-Renault	124.027
1997	F1 W	Silverstone	Jacques Villeneuve	CDN	Williams FW19-Renault	128.445
1998	F1 W	Silverstone	Michael Schumacher	D	Ferrari F300	107.421
1999	F1 W	Silverstone	David Coulthard	GB	McLaren MP4/14-Mercedes-Benz	124.304
2000	F1 W	Silverstone	David Coulthard	GB	McLaren MP4/15-Mercedes-Benz	129.435
2001	F1 W	Silverstone	Mika Hakkinen	SF	McLaren MP4/16-Mercedes-Benz	134.385
2002	F1 W	Silverstone	Michael Schumacher	D	Ferrari F2002	125.323

*also known as English GP. #Donington GP

TOURIST TROPHY

year	formula	circuit	winner	nat	car	mph
1905	TC	Isle of Man	John Napier	GB	Arrol-Johnston	33.960
1906	TC	Isle of Man	Charles Rolls	GB	Rolls-Royce 20hp	39.400
1907	TC	Isle of Man	Ernest Courtis	GB	Rover 20hp	28.800
1908	FL	Isle of Man	W Watson	GB	Napier-Hutton	50.300
1914	FL	Isle of Man	Kenelm Lee Guinness	GB	Sunbeam	56.440
1922	FL	Isle of Man	Jean Chassagne	F	Sunbeam	55.782
1928	SC (h)	Ards	Kaye Don	GB	Lea-Francis	64.060
1929	SC (h)	Ards	Rudolf Caracciola	D	Mercedes-Benz SS	72.820
1930	SC (h)	Ards	Tazio Nuvolari	I	Alfa Romeo 6C	70.880
1931	SC (h)	Ards	Norman Black	GB	MG Midget C-type	67.900
1932	SC (h)	Ards	CR Whitcroft	GB	Riley 9	74.230
1933	SC (h)	Ards	Tazio Nuvolari	I	MG Magnette K3	78.650
1934	SC (h)	Ards	Charles Dodson	GB	MG Magnette NE	74.650
1935	SC (h)	Ards	Fred Dixon	GB	Riley 1.5	76.900
1936	SC (h)	Ards	Fred Dixon/Charles Dodson	GB	Riley 1.5	78.010
1937	SC (h)	Donington Park	Gianfranco Comotti	I	Talbot-Darracq	68.700
1938	SC (h)	Donington Park	Louis Gerard	F	Delage	67.610
1950	SC (h)	Dundrod	Stirling Moss	GB	Jaguar XK120	75.150
1951	SC (h)	Dundrod	Stirling Moss	GB	Jaguar XK120C	83.550
1953	SC (h) W	Dundrod	Peter Collins/Pat Griffith	GB	Aston Martin DB3S	81.710
1954*	SC (h) W	Dundrod	Paul Armagnac/Gerard Laureau	F	DB-Panhard	68.750
1955	SC W	Dundrod	Stirling Moss/John Fitch	GB/USA	Mercedes-Benz 300SLR	88.323
1958	SC W	Goodwood	Stirling Moss/Tony Brooks	GB	Aston Martin DBR1/300	88.328
1959	SC W	Goodwood	Carroll Shelby/Jack Fairman/ Stirling Moss	USA/GB/GB	Aston Martin DBR1/300	89.406
1960	GT	Goodwood	Stirling Moss	GB	Ferrari 250GT	85.580
1961	GT	Goodwood	Stirling Moss	GB	Ferrari 250GT	86.620
1962	GT	Goodwood	Innes Ireland	GB	Ferrari 250GTO	94.050
1963	GT	Goodwood	Graham Hill	GB	Ferrari 250GTO	95.140
1964	SC/GT W	Goodwood	Graham Hill	GB	Ferrari 330P	97.132
1965	SC/GT W	Oulton Park	Denny Hulme	NZ	Brabham BT8-Climax	94.069
1966	SC	Oulton Park	Denny Hulme	NZ	Lola T70 Mk2-Chevrolet	95.170
1967	TC	Oulton Park	Andrea de Adamich	I	Alfa Romeo Giulia GTA	80.650
1968	SC	Oulton Park	Denny Hulme	NZ	Lola T70 Mk3-Chevrolet	99.060
1969	SC	Oulton Park	Trevor Taylor	GB	Lola T70 Mk3B-Chevrolet	96.800
1970	TC	Silverstone	Brian Muir	AUS	Chevrolet Camaro Z28	99.940
1972	TC	Silverstone	Jochen Mass/Dieter Glemser	D	Ford Capri RS2600	106.530
1973	TC	Silverstone	Derek Bell/Harald Ertl	GB/A	BMW 3.0 CSL	108.783
1974	TC	Silverstone	Stuart Graham	GB	Chevrolet Camaro Z28	96.710
1975	TC	Silverstone	Stuart Graham	GB	Chevrolet Camaro Z28	97.710
1976	TC	Silverstone	Jean Xhenceval/Pierre Dieudonne/ Hughes de Fierlandt	B	BMW 3.0 CSL	101.361
1977	TC	Silverstone	Dieter Quester/Tom Walkinshaw	A/GB	BMW 3.0 CSL	105.496

TOURIST TROPHY (cont)

year	formula	circuit	winner	nat	car	mph
1978	TC	Silverstone	Raijmond van Hove/Eddy Joosen	B	BMW 3.0 CSL	102.084
1979	TC	Silverstone	Martino Finotto/Carlo Facetti	I	BMW 3.0 CSL	103.980
1980	TC	Silverstone	Umberto Grano/Harald Neger/			
			Heribert Werginz	I/A/A	BMW 635 CSi	102.190
1981	TC	Silverstone	Tom Walkinshaw/Chuck Nicholson	GB	Mazda RX7	103.130
1982	TC	Silverstone	Tom Walkinshaw/Chuck Nicholson	GB	Jaguar XJ-S	100.490
1983	TC	Silverstone	Rene Metge/Steve Soper	F/GB	Rover Vitesse	99.317
1984	TC	Silverstone	Helmut Kelleners/			
			Gianfranco Brancatelli	D/I	BMW 635 CSi	92.980
1985	TC	Silverstone	Tom Walkinshaw/Win Percy	GB	Rover Vitesse	103.880
1986	TC	Silverstone	Denny Hulme/Jeff Allam	NZ/GB	Rover Vitesse	103.457
1987	TC	Silverstone	Enzo Calderari/Fabio Mancini	CH/I	BMW M3	100.847
1988	TC	Silverstone	Andy Rouse/Alain Ferte	GB/F	Ford Sierra RS500	103.935
1994#	TC W	Donington Park	Paul Radisich	NZ	Ford Mondeo Ghia	89.400
1996	TC	Donington Park	Alain Menu	CH	Renault Laguna	90.770
1997	TC	Donington Park	Alain Menu	CH	Renault Laguna	97.367
1998	SC INT	Donington Park	Emmanuel Collard/Vincenzo Sospiri	F/I	Ferrari 333SP	97.760
1999	SC INT	Donington Park	Eric Bernard/Jean-Marc Gounon	F	Lola B98/10-Judd	98.947
2000	SC INT	Donington Park	Christian Pescatori/David Terrien	I/F	Ferrari 333SP	94.881
2001	SC INT	Donington Park	Ben Collins/Werner Lupberger	GB/ZA	Ascari A410-Judd	98.085

*World Championship points awarded for overall result, which was won by Mike Hawthorn/Maurice Trintignant (Ferrari 750). #The Tourist Trophy was awarded to the winner of the 1994 FIA Touring Car World Cup

BRITISH EMPIRE TROPHY

year	formula	circuit	winner	nat	car	mph
1932	FL	Brooklands	John Cobb	GB	Delage V12/LSR	126.360
1933	FL	Brooklands	Stanislav Czaykowski	PL	Bugatti T54	123.554
1934	FL (h)	Brooklands	George Eyson	GB	MG Magnette K3	80.010
1935	FL (h)	Brooklands	Fred Dixon	GB	Riley 6	75.470
1936	FL (h)	Donington Park	Dick Seaman	GB	Maserati 8CM	66.300
1937	FL (h)	Donington Park	Raymond Mays	GB	ERA C-type	62.960
1938	FL (h)	Donington Park	Charles Dodson	GB	Austin	69.620
1939	FL (h)	Donington Park	Tony Rolt	GB	ERA B-type	75.910
1947	F1	Douglas	Bob Gerard	GB	ERA B-type	68.020
1948	F1	Douglas	Geoffrey Ansell	GB	ERA B-type	67.710
1949	F1	Douglas	Bob Gerard	GB	ERA B-type	71.060
1950	F1	Douglas	Bob Gerard	GB	ERA B-type	70.050
1951	SC (h)	Douglas	Stirling Moss	GB	Frazer-Nash LM	67.270
1952	SC (h)	Douglas	Pat Griffith	GB	Lester-MG	64.200
1953	SC (h)	Douglas	Reg Parnell	GB	Aston Martin DB3S	73.960
1954	SC (h)	Oulton Park	Alan Brown	GB	Cooper T22-Bristol	70.560
1955	SC (h)	Oulton Park	Archie Scott-Brown	GB	Lister-Bristol	73.520
1956	SC (h)	Oulton Park	Stirling Moss	GB	Cooper T39-Climax	83.720
1957	SC	Oulton Park	Archie Scott-Brown	GB	Lister-Jaguar	84.210
1958	SC	Oulton Park	Stirling Moss	GB	Aston Martin DBR2/390	87.450
1959	F2	Oulton Park	Jim Russell	GB	Cooper T45-Climax	76.932
1960	FJ	Silverstone	Henry Taylor	GB	Lotus 18-Ford	80.780
1961	IC	Silverstone	Stirling Moss	GB	Cooper T53-Climax	104.580
1970	F3	Oulton Park	Bev Bond	GB	Lotus 59A-Ford	96.580
1971	F3	Oulton Park	Dave Walker	AUS	Lotus 69-Ford	96.730
1972	Hist	Silverstone	Willie Green	GB	Maserati T61	*
1973	Hist	Silverstone	Neil Corner	GB	Maserati 250F/	
					Aston Martin DNR4/300	*
1974	Hist	Silverstone	John Harper	GB	Lister-Jaguar	*
1977	Hist	Donington Park	Neil Corner	GB	BRM P25	84.080
1978	Hist	Donington Park	Neil Corner	GB	BRM P25	82.530
1990	SC W	Silverstone	Martin Brundle/Alain Ferte	GB/F	Jaguar XJR-11	128.830
1991	SC W	Silverstone	Derek Warwick/Teo Fabi	GB/I	Jaguar XJR-14	122.037
1992	SC W	Silverstone	Derek Warwick/Yannick Dalmas	GB/F	Peugeot 905B	122.651
1995	GT FIA	Silverstone	Olivier Grouillard/Andy Wallace	F/GB	McLaren F1 GTR-BMW	79.967
1996	GT FIA	Silverstone	Olivier Grouillard/Andy Wallace	F/GB	McLaren F1 GTR-BMW	98.270
1997	GT FIA	Silverstone	Peter Kox/Roberto Ravaglia	NL/I	McLaren F1 GTR-BMW	83.176
1998	GT FIA	Silverstone	Bernd Schneider/Mark Webber	D/AUS	Mercedes-Benz CLK-GTR	107.647
1999	GT FIA	Silverstone	Olivier Beretta/Karl Wendlinger	MC/A	Chrysler Viper GTS-R	96.306
2000	GT FIA	Silverstone	Julian Bailey/Jamie Campbell-Walter	GB	Lister Storm GT	99.282
2001	GT FIA	Silverstone	Jean-Philippe Belloc/			
			Christophe Bouchut	F	Chrysler Viper GTS-R	98.669
2002	GT FIA	Silverstone	Fabio Babini/Marc Duez	I/B	Chrysler Viper GTS-R	100.997

*Historic Racing and Sports Car championship held at Silverstone

Circuits and Other Races

AINTREE

Aintree was a flat and largely featureless circuit built outside the Grand National racecourse, scene of Britain's greatest horse race. Except for the difficult Melling Crossing, Aintree's corners were slow and unchallenging. But its spectator facilities, accommodating up to 140,000 people, were unrivalled by other British circuits, and within a year of opening in 1954 Aintree held the British GP. Aintree hosted that race on five occasions before the International circuit was closed in 1964. Stirling Moss starred here, scoring his first Grand Prix win in 1955, and two years later sharing

Vanwall's first Championship victory with Tony Brooks. After 1964 the short circuit remained for 18 years, but today Aintree's fame is once again restricted to horse racing.

Active years	1954-82
Location	5 miles north of Liverpool
Type	Permanent road course

Grand Prix circuit

Active years	1954-64
Lap distance	3.000 miles
Lap record	Qualifying: Jim Clark (Lotus 25-Climax), 1m53.6, 95.071 mph, F1, 1962
	Race: Jim Clark (Lotus 25-Climax), 1m55.0, 93.913 mph, F1, 1962

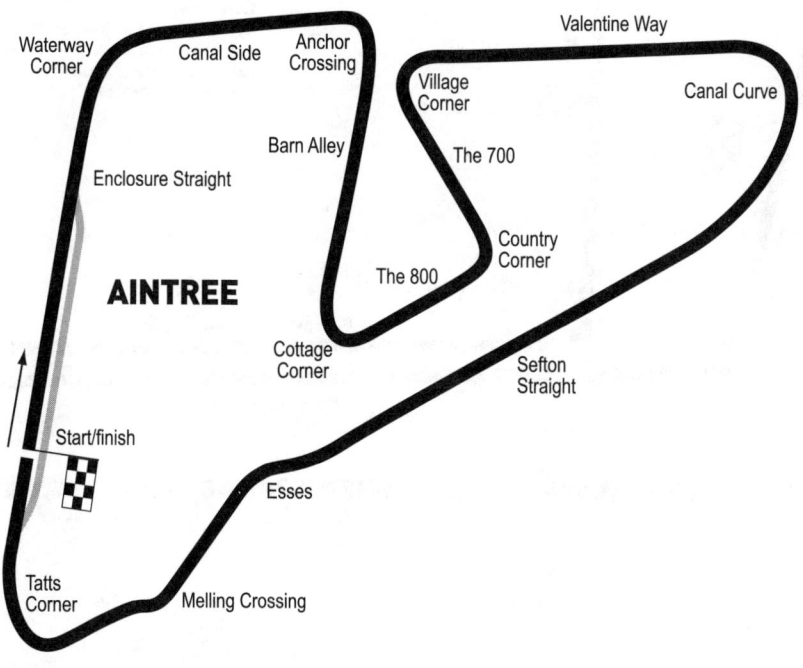

British Grand Prix see above

AINTREE 200

year	formula	winner	nat	car	mph
1954	FL	Stirling Moss	GB	Maserati 250F	85.435
1956	F1	Stirling Moss	GB	Maserati 250F	84.273
1958	F1/F2	Stirling Moss	GB	Cooper T45-Climax	85.664
1959	F1/F2	Jean Behra	F	Ferrari Dino 246	88.763
1960	F2	Stirling Moss	GB	Porsche 718	88.410
1961	F1	Jack Brabham	AUS	Cooper T55-Climax	78.066
1962	F1	Jim Clark	GB	Lotus 24-Climax	92.653
1963	F1	Graham Hill	GB	BRM P57	94.392
1964	F1	Jack Brabham	AUS	Brabham BT7-Climax	93.457

BIRMINGHAM

Britain's first street race took fifteen years to plan, but lasted just five. Racing had been banned on the open roads of mainland Britain until parliament passed the Birmingham Road Race Bill in 1985. A round of the FIA Formula 3000 series was secured, and the event generated a unique atmosphere of noise, accidents, unglamorous surroundings and sometimes-chaotic race schedules. But for all its shortcomings, Birmingham was one of the great British race experiences. The circuit was quick, with average speeds of over 100 mph in dry conditions. The dual carriageway to and from Halfords Corner, a roundabout-turned-hairpin with a pronounced bump on entry, was the quickest part of the track. The pits were placed by the start in the forecourt of Bristol Street Motors, and the paddock was in a multi-story car park! The first Birmingham Super Prix was marred by torrential rain. A year later Stefano Modena won conclusively, although the star was Roberto Moreno, who finished second from the back of the grid. Plans to lengthen the circuit in 1991 to comply with FIA demands were shelved as the much-publicised event slipped quietly from the racing calendar.

Active years	1986-90
Location	Birmingham city centre
Type	Temporary street circuit
Lap distance	2.470 miles
Lap records	Qualifying: Jean Alesi (Reynard 89D-Mugen), 1m20.66, 110.241 mph, F3000, 1989
	Race: Roberto Moreno (Ralt RT21-Honda), 1m22.91, 107.249 mph, F3000, 1987

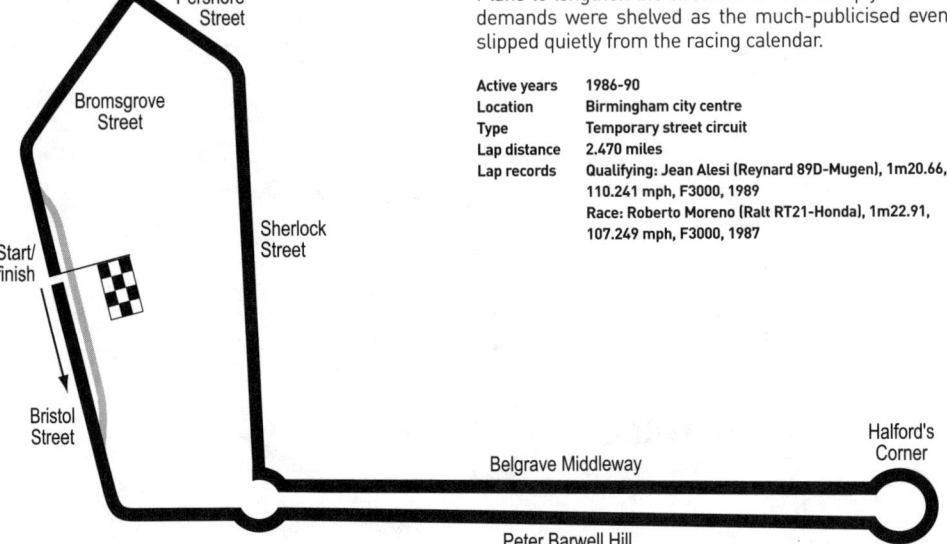

BIRMINGHAM SUPER PRIX						
year	formula	winner	nat	car		mph
1986	F3000 INT	Luis Perez Sala	E	Ralt RT20-Cosworth		59.872
1987	F3000 INT	Stefano Modena	I	March 87B-Cosworth		105.353
1988	F3000 INT	Roberto Moreno	BR	Reynard 88D-Cosworth		105.630
1989	F3000 INT	Jean Alesi	F	Reynard 89D-Mugen		105.243
1990	F3000 INT	Eric van de Poele	B	Reynard 90D-Cosworth		105.291

BRANDS HATCH

Brands Hatch was the home of 500cc Formula 3 racing when it opened for cars on 16 April 1950. By 1964 the circuit had been extended and the direction of racing reversed, changes that allowed it to become a full Grand Prix venue. Jim Clark scored a convincing home win in the first British GP held there. Brands Hatch then alternated with Silverstone, holding 14 Grands Prix (twelve British and two European) before Silverstone won an exclusive contract to stage the British GP starting in 1987. Although the Kent venue eventually won its own exclusive contract to hold the Grand Prix beginning in 2002, new owners Octagon Motorsports eventually decided it would be cheaper to lease Silverstone rather than upgrade Brands to F1 standard. The full circuit at Brands Hatch is one of the most demanding in the world, and the Indy circuit offers fans some of best viewing possible. But the short run-off areas have made safety an issue, one illustrated by serious accidents to Johnny Herbert and Michel Trolle during the 1988 Formula 3000 meeting.

Active years	1950 to date
Location	Near Farningham, 20 miles south-east of London
Type	Permanent road course
Website	www.brands-hatch.co.uk

Current Grand Prix circuit
Lap distance	2.6228 miles
Lap record	Qualifying: James Courtney (Dallara 302-Mugen),

1m18.313, 120.569 mph, F3, 2002
Race: Takuma Sato (Dallara 301-Mugen), 1m18.372,
120.478 mph, F3, 2001

1960-75	Grand Prix circuit opened. 2.650 miles
1976-87	Paddock Hill Bend and Bottom Straight modified. 2.6136 miles
1988-98	Chicane built at Dingle Dell. 2.6002 miles
1999 to date	Graham Hill Bend re-profiled. Current circuit

Grand Prix circuit changes

| 1950-53 | Original Indy circuit. 1.000 mile |
| 1954-59 | Track widened, Druids Hill Bend added, direction of racing now reversed to clockwise. 1.240 miles |

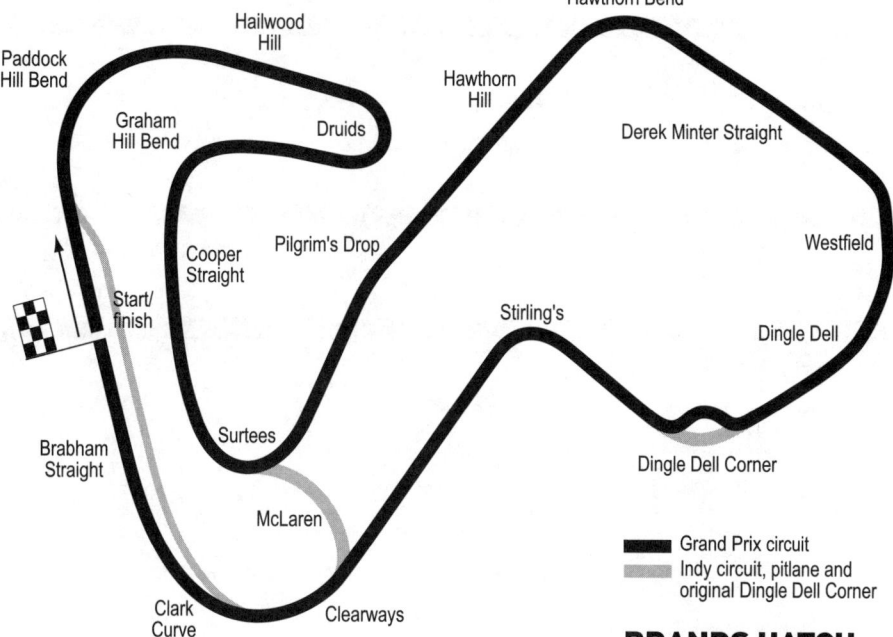

BRANDS HATCH

British Grand Prix see above
European Grand Prix see above

RACE OF CHAMPIONS

year	formula	winner	nat	car	mph
1965	F1	Mike Spence	GB	Lotus 33-Climax	96.583
1967	F1	Dan Gurney	USA	Eagle AAR102-Weslake	98.589
1968	F1	Bruce McLaren	NZ	McLaren M7A-Ford	100.773
1969	F1	Jackie Stewart	GB	Matra MS80-Ford	108.646
1970	F1	Jackie Stewart	GB	March 701-Ford	109.108
1971	F1	Clay Regazzoni	CH	Ferrari 312B2	108.041
1972	F1/F5000	Emerson Fittipaldi	BR	Lotus 72D-Ford	112.215
1973	F1/F5000	Peter Gethin	GB	Chevron B24-Chevrolet	110.837
1974	F1/F5000	Jacky Ickx	B	Lotus 72D-Ford	99.958
1975	F1/F5000	Tom Pryce	GB	Shadow DN5A-Ford	113.792
1976	F1	James Hunt	GB	McLaren M23-Ford	108.111
1977	F1	James Hunt	GB	McLaren M23-Ford	116.363
1979	F1	Gilles Villeneuve	CDN	Ferrari 312T3	117.718
1983	F1	Keke Rosberg	SF	Williams FW08C-Ford	117.787

ROTHMANS WORLD CHAMPIONSHIP VICTORY RACE

year	formula	winner	nat	car	mph
1971	F1/F5000	Peter Gethin	GB	BRM P160	111.822

JOHN PLAYER CHALLENGE TROPHY

year	formula	winner	nat	car	mph
1972	F1/F5000	Jean-Pierre Beltoise	F	BRM P180	106.360

ROTHMANS £50,000

year	formula	winner	nat	car	mph
1972	Various	Emerson Fittipaldi	BR	Lotus 72D-Ford	109.836

EUROPEAN FORMULA 2 RACE

year	formula	winner	nat	car	mph
1967	F2 E	Jochen Rindt	A	Brabham BT23-Ford	101.376
1984	F2 E	Philippe Streiff	F	AGS JH19C-BMW	106.524

INTERNATIONAL FORMULA 3000 RACE

year	formula	winner	nat	car	mph
1987	F3000 INT	Julian Bailey	GB	Lola T87/50-Cosworth	119.270
1988	F3000 INT	Martin Donnelly	GB	Reynard 88D-Cosworth	120.813
1989	F3000 INT	Martin Donnelly	GB	Reynard 89D-Mugen	120.662
1990	F3000 INT	Allan McNish	GB	Lola T90/50-Mugen	108.277
1991	F3000 INT	Emanuele Naspetti	I	Reynard 91D-Cosworth	123.905

DAILY MAIL INDY TROPHY

year	formula	winner	nat	car	mph
1978	USAC	Rick Mears	USA	Penske PC6-Cosworth	95.789

WORLD SPORTS CAR RACE

year	formula	winner	nat	car	mph
1967	SC W	Mike Spence/Phil Hill	GB/USA	Chaparral 2F-Chevrolet	93.080
1968	SC W	Jacky Ickx/Brian Redman	B/GB	Ford GT40	95.959
1969	SC W	Jo Siffert/Brian Redman	CH/GB	Porsche 908/8	100.219
1970	SC W	Pedro Rodriguez/Leo Kinnunen	MEX/SF	Porsche 917	92.147
1971	SC W	Andrea de Adamich/Henri Pescarolo	I/F	Alfa Romeo T33/3	97.169
1972	SC W	Jacky Ickx/Mario Andretti	B/USA	Ferrari 312P	105.118
1974	SC W	Jean-Pierre Beltoise/Jean-Pierre Jarier	F	Matra-Simca MS670C	107.510
1977	SC W	Jacky Ickx/Jochen Mass	B/D	Porsche 935	98.181
1979	SC W	Reinhold Joest/Volkert Merl	D	Porsche 908/4	100.605
1980	SC W	Riccardo Patrese/Walter Rohrl	I/D	Lancia Beta Monte Carlo	99.383
1981	SC W	Guy Edwards/Emilio de Villota	GB/E	Lola T600-Ford	99.917
1982	SC W	Jacky Ickx/Derek Bell	B/GB	Porsche 956	98.763
1983	SC E	Derek Warwick/John Fitzpatrick	GB	Porsche 956	100.771
1984	SC W	Jonathan Palmer/Jan Lammers	GB/NL	Porsche 956	109.202
1985	SC W	Derek Bell/Hans-Joachim Stuck	GB/D	Porsche 962C	111.598
1986	SC W	Bob Wollek/Mauro Baldi	F/I	Porsche 956GTi	104.621
1987	SC W	Raul Boesel/John Nielsen	BR/DK	Jaguar XJR-8	111.807
1988	SC W	John Nielsen/Martin Brundle/Andy Wallace	DK/GB/GB	Jaguar XJR-9	112.311
1989	SC W	Mauro Baldi/Kenneth Acheson	I/GB	Sauber C9/88-Mercedes-Benz	111.003

FIA GT RACE

year	formula	winner	nat	car	mph
1996	GT FIA	Thierry Boutsen/Hans-Joachim Stuck	B/D	Porsche 911 GT1	107.593

CELLNET SUPER PRIX

year	formula	winner	nat	car	mph
1986	F3	Andy Wallace	GB	Reynard 863-Volkswagen	92.489
1987	F3	Johnny Herbert	GB	Reynard 873-Volkswagen	90.416
1988	F3	Gary Brabham	AUS	Ralt RT32-Volkswagen	87.400
1989	F3	Mika Hakkinen	SF	Ralt RT33-Mugen	98.316

BROOKLANDS

Brooklands became Europe's first permanent circuit when it opened on 17 July 1907. As Grand Prix racing began to capture the imagination on the continent, Brooklands held Britain's first GP events in 1926 and 1927. The liberal use of straw bales made various circuit layouts possible around the starting straight and test hill. A permanent Grand Prix circuit named after Sir Malcolm Campbell was introduced in 1937, although by then Donington Park was already playing host to the continental teams. High speeds and a society atmosphere became central to Brooklands folklore. In 1935, the fastest lap of the outer circuit was run at over 143 mph by John Cobb's Napier-Railton — on a day when the track was not completely dry! Brooklands closed for World War II, never to reopen. Part of the Members Banking remains, overlooking the clubhouse and paddock sheds which now house a museum. The remainder of the track has been redeveloped as business parks and retail shopping, with access to a supermarket car park now cutting through the Byfleet Banking.

Active years	1907-39
Location	Weybridge, 20 miles south of London
Type	Paved oval
Website	www.brooklands.org.uk

Banked Outer Circuit

Lap distance	2.767 miles
Lap record	John Cobb (Napier-Railton), 1m09.44, 143.451 mph, over 8000cc, 1935

Mountain Circuit

Lap distance	1.170 miles
Lap record	Raymond Mays (ERA D-type), 49.96s, 84.31 mph, 1500cc Voiturette, 1936

Campbell Circuit

Lap distance	2.267 miles
Lap record	Raymond Mays (ERA D-type), 1m44.91, 77.79 mph, 2000cc, 1939

British Grand Prix see above
British Empire Trophy see above

Grand Prix Circuit

Lap distance	2.616 miles
Lap record	Henry Segrave (Talbot 700), 1m49.5, 80.006 mph, GP, 1926

BROOKLANDS

Railway Straight
Temporary Chicances
Byfleet Banking
Start/finish
Members Banking
Vickers

━━━ Grand Prix circuit
━━━ Outer circuit and Pitlane

CRYSTAL PALACE

Crystal Palace was a twisting road course in its original form. But when it reopened after the war the RAC ruled that the sinuous infield was too tight, so it was bypassed, making the course essentially an oval with kinks. The proximity of houses meant that the Palace could only hold a limited number of races each year, and eventually noise and safety concerns forced the Greater London Council to close Crystal Palace in 1972. That year's final visit of the European F2 Championship resulted in a win for Jody Scheckter in the unique McLaren M21.

Active years	1937-72
Location	Anerley Hill, Sydenham, South London
Type	Permanent road course

Circuit changes

1937-39	2.000 miles
1953-72	Infield section bypassed by new link road from Park to Stadium Curve. 1.390 miles

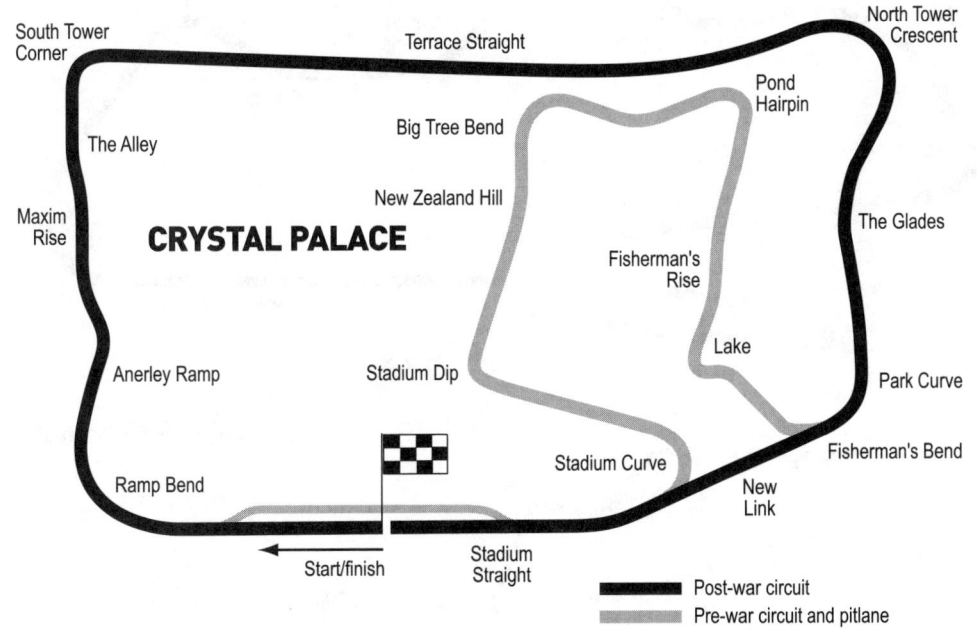

South Tower Corner · Terrace Straight · North Tower Crescent · Pond Hairpin · The Alley · Big Tree Bend · New Zealand Hill · The Glades · Maxim Rise · **CRYSTAL PALACE** · Fisherman's Rise · Anerley Ramp · Stadium Dip · Lake · Park Curve · Ramp Bend · Stadium Curve · Fisherman's Bend · New Link · Start/finish · Stadium Straight

━━━ Post-war circuit
▬▬▬ Pre-war circuit and pitlane

EUROPEAN FORMULA 2 RACES

year	formula	winner	nat	car	mph
1967	F2	Jacky Ickx	B	Matra MS5-Ford	93.420
1968	F2 E	Jochen Rindt	A	Brabham BT23C-Ford	93.692
1970	F2	Jackie Stewart	GB	Brabham BT30-Ford	99.440
1971	F2 E	Emerson Fittipaldi	BR	Lotus 69-Ford	99.168
1972	F2 E	Jody Scheckter	ZA	McLaren M21-Ford	100.385

DONINGTON PARK

Donington Park opened as a motorcycle circuit in 1931 under the direction of local garage owner and competitor Fred Craner. Car racing followed two years later, and in 1935 the circuit hosted its first Grand Prix. It was an expanded club race at first, but for 1937 the all-conquering German teams entered with Bernd Rosemeyer scoring the last win of his meteoric career. Both Auto Union and Mercedes-Benz returned in 1938 despite the Munich crisis, with Tazio Nuvolari again winning for Auto Union. Like Brooklands in the south, Donington remained closed after the war. But Tom Wheatcroft bought the land in 1971, and successfully reopened the venue six years later. He also built a museum to house the largest collection of single-seater racing cars in the world. Since 1977 Donington has held European Touring Cars, Formulae 2, 3000 and 3, the Motorcycle Grand Prix and finally a full F1 World Championship Grand Prix in 1993. In an event dogged by heavy rain, Ayrton Senna's opening lap (in which he passed four cars to take the lead) is now as legendary as Donington's Mercedes/Auto Union battles 50 years earlier.

Active years	1931-39, 1977 to date
Location	8 miles south of Derby, 35 miles north-east of Birmingham
Type	Permanent road course
Website	www.donington.co.uk

Current circuit

Lap distance	2.500 miles
Lap records	Qualifying: Alain Prost (Williams FW15C-Renault), 1m10.458, 127.736 mph, F1, 1993
	Race: Ayrton Senna (McLaren MP4/8-Ford), 1m18.029, 115.331 mph, F1, 1993 (set on a lap through the pit-lane)

Circuit changes

1931-33	2.190 miles
1934-36	Track extended to a hairpin beyond Redgate. 2.550 miles
1937-39	Old Melbourne Corner added. 3.125 miles
1977-95	New circuit built on sight of pre-war venue. 1.9573 miles
1985 to date	New Melbourne Hairpin opened. Current circuit (old circuit used as Club circuit)

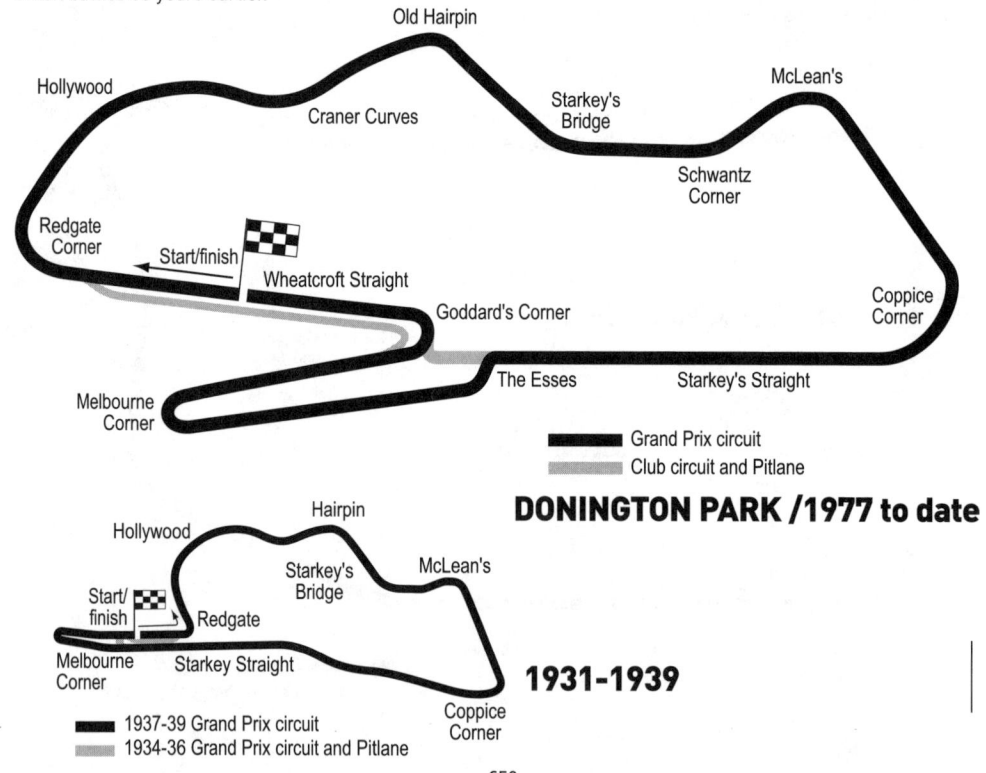

Grand Prix circuit
Club circuit and Pitlane

DONINGTON PARK /1977 to date

1931-1939

1937-39 Grand Prix circuit
1934-36 Grand Prix circuit and Pitlane

European Grand Prix see above
British Empire Trophy see above

DONINGTON GRAND PRIX

year	formula	winner	nat	car	mph
1935	GP	Richard Shuttleworth	GB	Alfa Romeo Tipo-B "P3"	63.928
1936	GP	Hans Ruesch/Dick Seaman	CH/GB	Alfa Romeo Tipo C "8C-35"	69.187
1937	GP	Bernd Rosemeyer	D	Auto Union C	82.856
1938	GP	Tazio Nuvolari	I	Auto Union D	80.486

EUROPEAN FORMULA 2 RACE

year	formula	winner	nat	car	mph
1977	F2 E	Bruno Giacomelli	I	March 782/772P-BMW	105.039
1978	F2 E	Keke Rosberg	SF	Chevron B42-Hart	104.555
1979	F2 E	Derek Daly	IRL	March 792-BMW	106.188
1981	F2 E	Geoff Lees	GB	Ralt RH6/81-Honda	106.998
1982	F2 E	Corrado Fabi	I	March 822-BMW	108.593
1983	F2 E	Jonathan Palmer	GB	Ralt RH6/83-Honda	107.249
1984	F2 E	Roberto Moreno	BR	Ralt RH6/84-Honda	107.404

INTERNATIONAL FORMULA 3000 RACE

year	formula	winner	nat	car	mph
1985	F3000 INT	Christian Danner	D	March 85B-Cosworth	101.185
1987	F3000 INT	Luis Perez Sala	E	Lola T87/50-Cosworth	103.772
1990	F3000 INT	Erik Comas	F	Lola T90/50-Mugen	103.798
1993	F3000 INT	Olivier Beretta	MC	Reynard 93D-Cosworth	109.485

EUROPEAN FORMULA 3 RACE

year	formula	winner	nat	car	mph
1977	F3 E	Brett Riley	NZ	March 773-Toyota	98.142
1978	F3 E	Derek Warwick	GB	Ralt RT1-Toyota	99.330
1979	F3 E	Brett Riley	NZ	March 783/793-Triumph	80.856
1981	F3 E	Mike White	ZA	March 813-Alfa Romeo	100.797
1982	F3 E	James Weaver	GB	Ralt RT3/81-Toyota	100.903
1983	F3 E	Martin Brundle	GB	Ralt RT3/83-Toyota	93.242
1984	F3 E	Johnny Dumfries	GB	Ralt RT3/83-Volkswagen	85.842

WORLD SPORTS CAR RACE

year	formula	winner	nat	car	mph
1989	SC W	Jochen Mass/Jean-Louis Schlesser	D/F	Sauber C9/88-Mercedes-Benz	101.210
1990	SC W	Jean-Louis Schlesser/Mauro Baldi	F/I	Mercedes-Benz C11	103.638
1992	SC W	Mauro Baldi/Philippe Alliot	I/F	Peugeot 905B	107.719

FIA GT RACE

year	formula	winner	nat	car	mph
1995	GT FIA	Thomas Bscher/John Nielsen	D/DK	McLaren F1 GTR-BMW	90.816
1997	GT FIA	Bernd Schneider/Alexander Wurz	D/A	Mercedes-Benz CLK-GTR	99.363
1998	GT FIA	Bernd Schneider/Mark Webber	D/AUS	Mercedes-Benz CLK-LM	101.345
1999	GT FIA	Olivier Beretta/Karl Wendlinger	MC/A	Chrysler Viper GTS-R	91.969
2002	GT FIA	Mike Hezemans/Anthony Kumpen	NL/B	Chrysler Viper GTS-R	93.975

DUNDROD

The Dundrod road course in Northern Ireland was the finest and most demanding British circuit of the fifties. It had everything from a tight hairpin to numerous fast corners. But the earth banks that lined the circuit meant that many of the corners were blind to approaching drivers and allowed no room for error. The circuit also suffered from bad weather and the financial problems of its promoters, the Ulster Automobile Club. Dundrod was always dangerous, and closed after three drivers lost their lives during the 1955 Tourist Trophy.

Active years	1950-55
Location	9 miles north-west of Belfast, Northern Ireland
Type	Temporary road course
Lap distance	7.416 miles
Lap record	Qualifying: Stirling Moss (Mercedes-Benz 300SLR), 4m48.0, 92.700 mph, Sports Cars, 1955
	Race: Mike Hawthorn (Jaguar D-type), 4m42.0, 94.672 mph, Sports Cars, 1955

Tourist Trophy see above

ULSTER TROPHY					
year	formula	winner	nat	car	mph
1950	F1	Peter Whitehead	GB	Ferrari 125	84.326
1951	F1	Giuseppe Farina	I	Alfa Romeo 159	91.456
1952	F1	Piero Taruffi	I	Ferrari 375	81.432
1953	F2	Mike Hawthorn	GB	Ferrari 500	86.488
1955	FL	Desmond Titterington	GB	Jaguar D-type	89.860

GOODWOOD

In 1946, Australian Tony Gaze suggested to the Duke of Richmond and Gordon that the Westhampnett airfield near Chichester, from which Gaze had flown his Hurricane during the war, would be ideal for motor racing. Two years later Goodwood Motor Circuit opened for its first race, replacing Brooklands as the home of the BARC. With some of the Surrey circuit's atmosphere, Goodwood was more like a road course than an airfield venue, and the traditional Easter Monday meeting became the annual highlight. But the Duke closed the circuit in 1966 due to safety concerns, although it continued to be used for testing. Goodwood was the site of Stirling Moss's career-ending crash in 1962, as well as the testing crash that killed Bruce McLaren in 1970. In 1998, five years after launching a popular historic hillclimb in the grounds of nearby Goodwood House, the Earl of March reopened the circuit for the historic Revival meeting. The event has proved an unreserved success, as past heroes mix with current stars in a paddock that resembles a television period drama.

Goodwood's outright race lap record of 1m20.4 (jointly held by Jim Clark and Jackie Stewart since the last F1 race in 1965) only fell when the Revival hosted 3-litre F1 cars for the first time in 1999.

Active years	**1948-66, 1998 to date**
Location	**2 miles north of Chichester, 30 miles west of Brighton, 60 miles south of London**
Type	**Permanent road course**
Website	**www.goodwood.co.uk**

Current circuit	
Lap distance	**2.400 miles**
Lap record	**Qualifying: Jackie Stewart (BRM P261), 1m19.8, 108.271 mph, F1, 1965**
	Race: Geoff Farmer (Lotus 49-Ford), 1m20.096, 107.879 mph, Historic F1, 1999

Circuit changes	
1948-51	**2.380 miles**
1952-66,	
1998 to date	**Chicane inserted at Paddock on 14 April 1952. Current circuit**

Great Britain

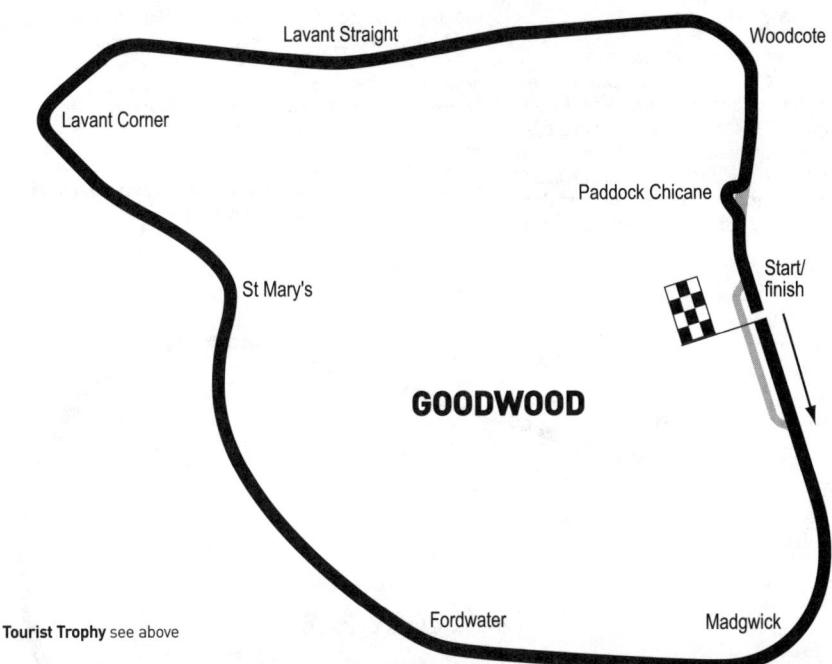

Lavant Straight
Woodcote
Lavant Corner
Paddock Chicane
St Mary's
Start/finish
GOODWOOD
Fordwater
Madgwick

Tourist Trophy see above

GLOVER TROPHY

year	formula	winner	nat	car	mph
1953	FL	Ken Wharton	GB	BRM P15	90.470
1954	FL	Ken Wharton	GB	BRM P15	86.400
1955	F1	Roy Salvadori	GB	Maserati 250F	89.247
1956	F1	Stirling Moss	GB	Maserati 250F	94.349
1957	F1	Stuart Lewis-Evans	GB	Connaught B-Alta	90.655
1958	F1	Mike Hawthorn	GB	Ferrari Dino 246	94.885
1959	F1	Stirling Moss	GB	Cooper T51-Climax	90.314
1960	F1	Innes Ireland	GB	Lotus 18-Climax	100.387
1961	F1	John Surtees	GB	Cooper T53-Climax	95.747
1962	F1	Graham Hill	GB	BRM P57	102.648
1963	F1	Innes Ireland	GB	Lotus 24-BRM	102.439

OTHER FORMULA 1 RACES

year	formula	winner	nat	car	mph
1949	F1	Reg Parnell	GB	Maserati 4CLT/48	86.430
	F1	Reg Parnell	GB	Maserati 4CLT/48	82.890
1950	F1	Reg Parnell	GB	Maserati 4CLT/48	77.609
	F1	Reg Parnell	GB	BRM P15	81.704
1951	F1	"B Bira"	SM	Maserati 4CLT/48	86.838
	F1	Giuseppe Farina	I	Alfa Romeo 159	95.115
1952	F1	Jose Froilan Gonzalez	RA	Ferrari 375	88.238
1954	F1	Reg Parnell	GB	Ferrari 625	88.758
	F1	Reg Parnell	GB	Ferrari 625	87.591
	F1	Stirling Moss	GB	Maserati 250F	91.489
1962	F1	Bruce McLaren	NZ	Cooper T55-Climax	99.050
1964	F1	Jim Clark	GB	Lotus 25-Climax	104.909
1965	F1	Jim Clark	GB	Lotus 25-Climax	105.067

BARC 9 HOURS

year	formula	winner	nat	car	mph
1952	SC	Peter Collins/Pat Griffith	GB	Aston Martin DB3	75.420
1953	SC	Reg Parnell/Eric Thompson	GB	Aston Martin DB3S	78.940
1955	SC	Peter Walker/Dennis Poore	GB	Aston Martin DB3S	82.240

MALLORY PARK

Mallory Park is a club circuit built in 1956 around a lake on the site of a former grass-track. It has suffered from the proximity of Donington, and its future was threatened during the eighties. The major race to have been held here was the 2000 Guineas, a non-championship F1 race that in 1962 that attracted the likes of Jim Clark, Graham Hill, Jack Brabham and eventual winner John Surtees. The European F2 Championship opened at Mallory in 1972 and 1973, but the circuit was too short to hold international events in the modern era.

Active years	1956 to date
Location	Near Hinckley, 8 miles south-west of Leicester
Type	Permanent road course
Website	www.mallorypark.co.uk
Lap distance	1.350 miles
Lap record	Race: Johan Rajamaki (Footwork FA13-Judd), 38.23s, 127.126 mph, Historic F1, 1997

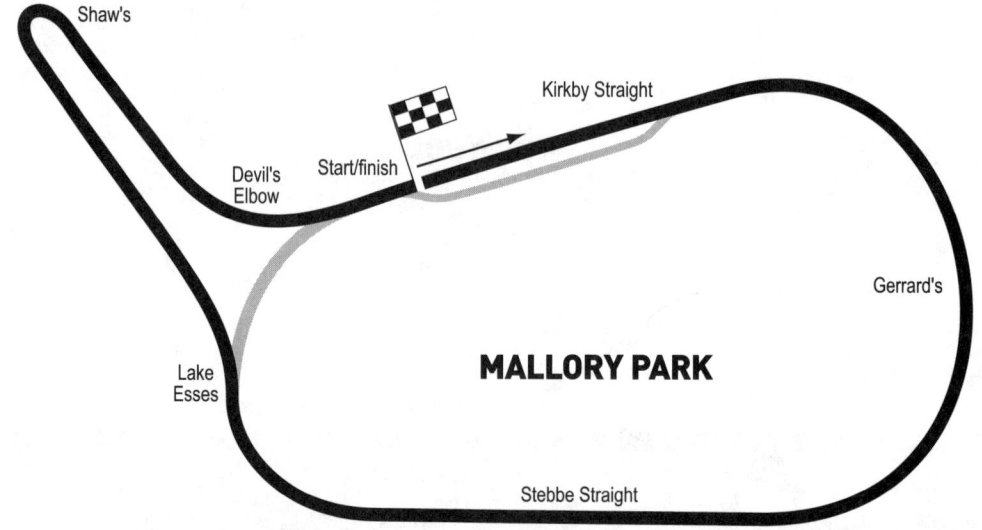

INTERNATIONAL 2000 GUINEAS					
year	formula	winner	nat	car	mph
1962	F1	John Surtees	GB	Lola Mk4-Climax	93.375

EUROPEAN FORMULA 2 RACE					
year	formula	winner	nat	car	mph
1972	F2 E	Dave Morgan	GB	Brabham BT35-Ford	108.657
1973	F2 E	Jean-Pierre Jarier	F	March 732-BMW	112.245

OULTON PARK

Oulton Park is one of Britain's most challenging circuits. Though too narrow to be considered for more international events, most national series visit annually. The traditional Gold Cup meeting started in 1954, a year after the circuit had opened. Once a major non-championship F1 race, by the eighties the Gold Cup suffered without a suitable category to promote. It was a round of the British Touring Car and later GT championships, before becoming a major historic meeting in 2002. Originally configured as a square, Oulton was soon extended with a hairpin next to the lake. Various alterations to this section followed until it was bypassed in 1975. The hairpin was reopened in 1989, but further modifications were necessary following Paul Warwick's fatal accident at the fast Knickerbrook corner in 1991.

Active years	1953 to date
Location	Near Tarporley, 10 miles south of Chester, 35 miles south-east of Liverpool
Type	Permanent road course
Website	www.octagonmotorsports.com

Current circuit	
Lap distance	2.776 miles
Lap record	Race: Gareth Rees (Reynard 95D-Cosworth), 1m24.68, 118.016 mph, British F2 (F3000), 1996

Circuit changes	
1953	1.504 miles
1954	Extended to lower lake in April. 2.230 miles
1954-75	Esso bend added to extension in August. 2.761 miles
1975-83	Link road from Cascades to Knickerbrook built, long circuit retained for bike races. 1.654 miles
1984-86	Long circuit refurbished and reopened. 2.356 miles
1987-91	Lakeside loop reopened. 2.769 miles
1992 to date	Chicane built at Knickerbrook. Current circuit

Great Britain

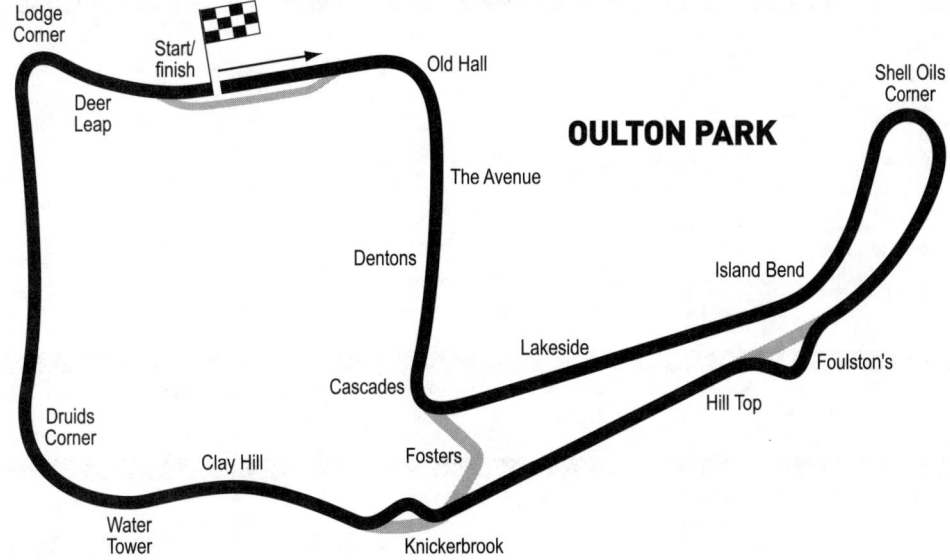

Oulton Park circuit map with labels: Lodge Corner, Deer Leap, Start/finish, Old Hall, Shell Oils Corner, The Avenue, Dentons, Island Bend, Lakeside, Foulston's, Cascades, Hill Top, Druids Corner, Fosters, Clay Hill, Water Tower, Knickerbrook. OULTON PARK.

Tourist Trophy see above
British Empire Trophy see above

INTERNATIONAL GOLD CUP

year	formula	winner	nat	car	mph
1954	F1	Stirling Moss	GB	Maserati 250F	83.468
1955	F1	Stirling Moss	GB	Maserati 250F	85.941
1956	F2/SC	Roy Salvadori	GB	Cooper T41-Climax	83.843
1957	F2	Jack Brabham	AUS	Cooper T43-Climax	84.963
1958	SC	Roy Salvadori	GB	Lotus 15-Climax	84.990
1959	F1	Stirling Moss	GB	Cooper T51-Climax	96.294
1960	F1	Stirling Moss	GB	Lotus 18-Climax	93.858
1961	F1	Stirling Moss	GB	Ferguson P99-Climax	88.828
1962	F1	Jim Clark	GB	Lotus 25-Climax	97.702
1963	F1	Jim Clark	GB	Lotus 25-Climax	98.337
1964	F2	Jack Brabham	AUS	Brabham BT10-Ford	95.500
1965	F2	John Surtees	GB	Lola T60-Ford	96.400
1966	F1	Jack Brabham	AUS	Brabham BT19-Repco	100.041
1967	F1/F2	Jack Brabham	AUS	Brabham BT24-Repco	106.319
1968	F1	Jackie Stewart	GB	Matra MS10-Ford	109.256
1969	F1/F5000	Jacky Ickx	B	Brabham BT26A-Ford	109.570
1970	F1/F5000	John Surtees	GB	Surtees TS7-Ford	110.803
1971	F1/F5000	John Surtees	GB	Surtees TS9-Ford	114.955
1972	F1/F5000	Denny Hulme	NZ	McLaren M19A-Ford	115.725
1973	F5000	Peter Gethin	GB	Chevron B24-Chevrolet	114.443
1974	F5000	Ian Ashley	GB	Lola T330-Chevrolet	114.639
1975	F5000	David Purley	GB	Chevron B30-Ford	93.055
1976	F1/F5000	Guy Edwards	GB	Brabham BT42/44B-Ford	105.603
1977	G8	Derek Bell	GB	Penske PC3-Ford	103.953
1978	F1/F2	Tony Trimmer	GB	McLaren M25-Ford	106.381
1979	F1/F2	David Kennedy	IRL	Wolf WR4-Ford	106.627
1980	F1/F2	Guy Edwards	GB	Arrows A1-Ford	107.796
1981	Hist	John Surtees	GB	Maserati 250F	67.200
1982	F1	Tony Trimmer	GB	Fittipaldi F8-Ford	104.283
1983	Thunder	Richard Budge/Vin Malkie	GB	Chevron B19-Ford	91.900
1984	Thunder	Peter Lovett/Ian Taylor	GB	Lola T594C-Mazda	101.490
1985	Thunder	Tim Lee Davey/Neil Crang	GB/AUS	Tiga GC84-Ford	103.020
1986	Thunder	John Foulston/John Brindley	GB	Lola T530-Chevrolet	103.510
1987	Thunder	John Foulston/John Brindley	GB	Lola T530-Chevrolet	103.950
1988	F3	Gary Brabham	AUS	Ralt RT32-Volkswagen	108.990
1989	F3000	Paulo Carcasci	BR	Reynard 88D-Cosworth	105.537
1990	F3000	Richard Dean	GB	Reynard 90D-Mugen	122.290

INTERNATIONAL GOLD CUP (cont.)

year	formula	winner	nat	car	mph
1991	F3000	Paul Warwick*	GB	Reynard 90D-Cosworth	121.995
1992	F3000	Yvan Muller	F	Reynard 91D-Cosworth	107.144
1993	TC	Joachim Winkelhock	D	BMW 318i	93.620
1994	TC	Joachim Winkelhock	D	BMW 318i	94.600
1995	TC	Alain Menu	CH	Renault Laguna	95.880
1996	TC	Rickard Rydell	S	Volvo 850	96.530
1997	TC	Alain Menu	CH	Renault Laguna	97.700
1998	GT	Steve O'Rourke/Tim Sugden	GB	McLaren F1 GTR-BMW	101.181
1999	GT	Julian Bailey/Jamie Campbell-Walter	GB	Lister Storm GTL	104.523
2000	GT	Tim Harvey/Mike Youles	GB	Porsche 911 GT2	96.784
2001	GT	Tim Harvey/Rob Wilson	GB/NZ	Chrysler Viper GTS-R	97.447
2002	Historic	Flavien Marcais	F	BRM P180	94.928

*Race stopped when Warwick suffered a fatal accident while leading, he was awarded victory posthumously

OULTON PARK INTERNATIONAL TROPHY

year	formula	winner	nat	car	mph
1971	F1	Pedro Rodriguez	MEX	BRM P160	115.128

SPRING TROPHY

year	formula	winner	nat	car	mph
1967	F1	Jack Brabham	AUS	Brabham BT20-Repco	104.944

ROCKINGHAM
Corby

The Rockingham Motor Speedway was an audacious attempt to bring American oval racing to Britain. It was built at a reputed cost of over £50m on site of a former steelworks in Corby, Northamptonshire. The inaugural Rockingham 500 in 2001 featured a magnificent late-race dice in the fading autumn light between winner Gil de Ferran and Kenny Brack but the event was marred by organisational shortcomings, a barely-finished facility, and worse, water seeping onto the track from below. These problems were rectified for the 2002 race but only a disappointing crowd saw Dario Franchitti's home victory and the event has been replaced on the 2003 CART calendar. Rockingham may have a five-year contract with CART, but the long-term future of this exciting addition to the British racing calendar is in doubt.

Active years 2001 to date
Location: Rockingham, Northamptonshire, 2 miles north-east of Corby
Type Paved oval
Website www.rockingham.co.uk
Lap distance 1.479 miles

Lap records Qualifying: Kenny Brack (Lola B2/00-Toyota), 24.908s, 213.765 mph, CART, 2002
Race: Jimmy Vasser (Lola B2/00-Ford), 25.217s, 211.144 mph, CART, 2002

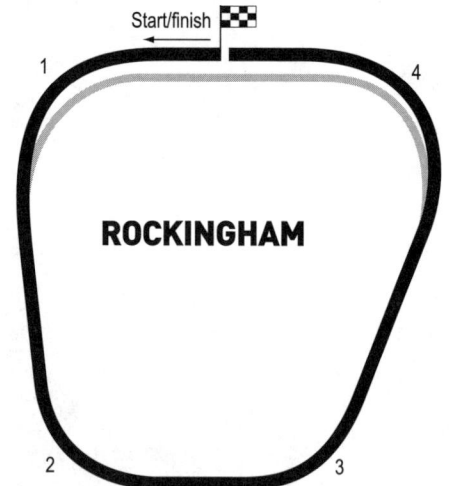

CHAMPCAR RACE

year	formula	winner	nat	car	mph
2001	CART	Gil de Ferran	BR	Reynard 01I-Honda	153.408
2002	CART	Dario Franchitti	GB	Lola B2/00-Honda	157.682

SILVERSTONE

Though built around a bleak WWII airfield, within three years of peace Silverstone was the new home of the British Grand Prix. Two years later, in the presence of King George IV, it held the first round of the new World Championship, in which Giuseppe Farina led an Alfa Romeo clean sweep of the podium positions. The perimeter circuit was an unbroken succession of quick corners until Jody Scheckter triggered a seven-car pile-up at Woodcote in 1973, and a chicane was built there for the next British GP. Eventually, a complex of corners was built ahead of Woodcote as part of a major refurbishment in 1991. When JJ Lehto and Pedro Lamy crashed during testing in 1994 further alterations were made to improve safety. After many years of sharing the British Grand Prix with Aintree and then Brands Hatch, in 1987 Silverstone became the race's sole venue. Although Brands Hatch secured an exclusive contract to stage the race starting in 2002, that circuit's owners eventually decided to lease Silverstone instead of upgrading their own circuit. But after a disastrous 2000 British GP, in which heavy traffic and waterlogged car parks marred the meeting, the FIA has demanded improved access and spectator facilities if the race is to continue at Silverstone.

Active years	1948 to date
Location	16 miles south-west of Northampton, 41 miles north-east of Oxford
Type	Permanent road course
Website	www.silverstone-circuit.co.uk

Current circuit

Lap distance	3.194 miles
Lap record	Qualifying: Juan Pablo Montoya (Williams FW24-BMW), 1m18.998, 145.554 mph, F1, 2002
	Race: Rubens Barrichello (Ferrari F2002), 1m23.083, 138.397 mph, F1, 2002

Grand Prix Circuit changes

1948	Using perimeter road and runways. Pits situated before Woodcote. 3.664 miles
1949	Perimeter road only with straw bale chicane at Club. 3.000 miles
1950-51	Perimeter road only. 2.8886 miles
1952-75	Circuit length officially revised. Pits moved to between Woodcote and Copse. 2.927 miles
1975-86	Woodcote chicane built in April. 2.932 miles
1987-90	Chicane removed, new complex built before Woodcote. 2.969 miles
1991-94	New sections built at Becketts, Vale and infield from Woodcote. 3.247 miles
1994-95	New sections at Copse, Stowe, Vale, Abbey and Brooklands. 3.210 miles
1996	Stowe modified. 3.152 miles
1997 to date	Copse and Priory eased. Current circuit

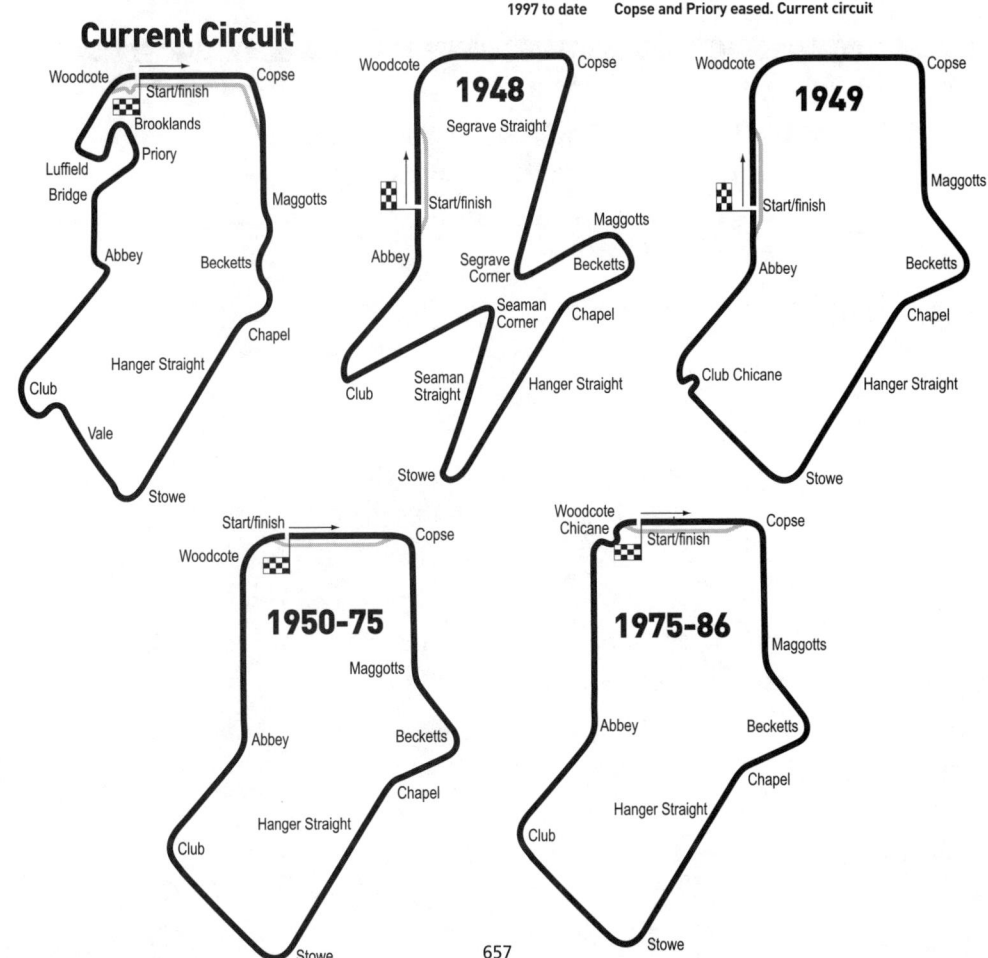

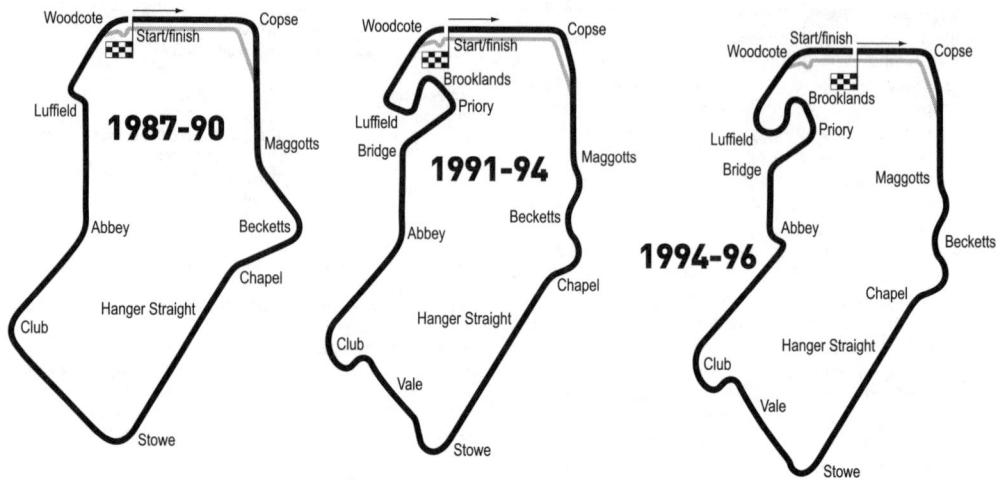

British Grand Prix see above
Tourist Trophy see above
British Empire Trophy see above

INTERNATIONAL TROPHY

year	formula	winner	nat	car	mph
1949	F1	Alberto Ascari	I	Ferrari 125	89.580
1950	F1	Giuseppe Farina	I	Alfa Romeo 158	90.157
1951*	F1	Reg Parnell	GB	Ferrari 375	61.899
1952	F2	Lance Macklin	GB	HWM 52-Alta	85.410
1953	F2	Mike Hawthorn	GB	Ferrari 500	92.293
1954	F1	Jose Froilan Gonzalez	RA	Ferrari 553 Squalo	92.780
1955	F1	Peter Collins	GB	Maserati 250F	95.938
1956	F1	Stirling Moss	GB	Vanwall VW2	100.466
1957	F1/F2	Jean Behra	F	BRM P25	99.946
1958	F1/F2	Peter Collins	GB	Ferrari Dino 246	101.817
1959	F1/F2	Jack Brabham	AUS	Cooper T51-Climax	102.730
1960	F1/F2	Innes Ireland	GB	Lotus 18-Climax	108.831
1961	IC	Stirling Moss	GB	Cooper T53-Climax	87.040
1962	F1	Graham Hill	GB	BRM P57	99.730
1963	F1	Jim Clark	GB	Lotus 25-Climax	108.125
1964	F1	Jack Brabham	AUS	Brabham BT7-Climax	110.355
1965	F1	Jackie Stewart	GB	BRM P261	111.664
1966	F1	Jack Brabham	AUS	Brabham BT19-Repco	116.063
1967	F1	Michael Parkes	GB	Ferrari 312	114.650
1968	F1	Denny Hulme	NZ	McLaren M7A-Ford	122.176
1969	F1	Jack Brabham	AUS	Brabham BT26A-Ford	107.002
1970	F1/F5000	Chris Amon	NZ	March 701-Ford	124.186
1971	F1/F5000	Graham Hill	GB	Brabham BT34-Ford	128.527
1972	F1/F5000	Emerson Fittipaldi	BR	Lotus 72D-Ford	131.806
1973	F1/F5000	Jackie Stewart	GB	Tyrrell 006-Ford	132.827
1974	F1/F5000	James Hunt	GB	Hesketh 308-Ford	133.577
1975	F1	Niki Lauda	A	Ferrari 312T	134.335
1976	F1	James Hunt	GB	McLaren M23-Ford	132.579
1977	F2 E	Rene Arnoux	F	Martini MK22-Renault	125.736
1978	F1	Keke Rosberg	SF	Theodore TR1-Ford	96.637
1979	F2 E	Eddie Cheever	USA	Osella FA2/79-BMW	114.033
1980	F1/F2	Eliseo Salazar	RCH	Williams FW07-Ford	133.887
1981	F2 E	Mike Thackwell	NZ	Ralt RH6/81-Honda	115.246
1982	F2 E	Stefan Bellof	D	Maurer MM82-BMW	115.066
1983	F2 E	Beppe Gabbiani	I	March 832-BMW	120.683
1984	F2 E	Mike Thackwell	NZ	Ralt RH6/84-Honda	135.393
1985	F3000 INT	Mike Thackwell	NZ	Ralt RB20-Cosworth	114.363
1986	F3000 INT	Pascal Fabre	F	Lola T86/50-Cosworth	118.711

INTERNATIONAL TROPHY (cont.)

year	formula	winner	nat	car	mph
1987	F3000 INT	Mauricio Gugelmin	BR	Ralt RT21-Honda	130.989
1988	F3000 INT	Roberto Moreno	BR	Reynard 88D-Cosworth	132.273
1989	F3000 INT	Thomas Danielsson	S	Reynard 89D-Cosworth	131.523
1990	F3000 INT	Allan McNish	GB	Lola T90/50-Mugen	134.293
1992	F3000 INT	Jordi Gene	E	Reynard 92D-Mugen	121.439
1993	F3000 INT	Gil de Ferran	BR	Reynard 93D-Cosworth	119.465
1994	F3000 INT	Franck Lagorce	F	Reynard 94D-Cosworth	119.509
1995	F3000 INT	Ricardo Rosset	BR	Reynard 95D-Cosworth	112.925
1996	F3000 INT	Kenny Brack	S	Lola T96/50-Zytek	109.162
1997	F3000 INT	Tom Kristensen	DK	Lola T96/50-Zytek	94.197
1998	F3000 INT	Juan Pablo Montoya	CO	Lola T96/50-Zytek	109.277
1999	F3000 INT	Nicolas Minassian	F	Lola B99/50-Zytek	113.042
2000	F3000 INT	Mark Webber	AUS	Lola B99/50-Zytek	93.025
2001	F3000 INT	Sebastien Bourdais	F	Lola B99/50-Zytek	112.861
2002	F3000 INT	Tomas Enge	CS	Lola B2/50-Zytek	115.547

*race abandoned due to heavy rain after 7 laps

OTHER EUROPEAN F2 RACES

year	formula	winner	nat	car	mph
1967	F2 E	Jochen Rindt	A	Brabham BT23-Ford	116.659
1975	F2 E	Michel Leclere	F	March 752-BMW	123.726
1980	F2 E	Derek Warwick	GB	Toleman TG280-Hart	130.597

EUROPEAN F3 RACE

year	formula	winner	nat	car	mph
1980	F3 E	Mike White	ZA	March 803B-Toyota	119.763
1981	F3 E	Roberto Moreno	BR	Ralt RT3/81-Toyota	122.634
1982	F3 E	Emanuele Pirro	I	Euroracing 101-Alfa Romeo	121.741
1983	F3 E	Martin Brundle	GB	Ralt RT3/83-Toyota	122.400
1984	F3 E	Johnny Dumfries	GB	Ralt RT3/83-Volkswagen	124.430
1987*	F3 E	Steve Kempton	GB	Reynard 873-Alfa Romeo	117.541

*European F3 Cup

DAILY EXPRESS INDY SILVERSTONE

year	formula	winner	nat	car	mph
1978	USAC	AJ Foyt jr	USA	Coyote-Foyt/Ford	104.361

WORLD SPORTS CAR RACE

year	formula	winner	nat	car	mph
1976	SC W	John Fitzpatrick/Tom Walkinshaw	GB	BMW 3.0 CSL	106.041
1977	SC W	Jacky Ickx/Jochen Mass	B/D	Porsche 935	112.393
1978	SC W	Jacky Ickx/Jochen Mass	B/D	Porsche 935	114.837
1979	SC W	John Fitzpatrick/Bob Wollek/Hans Heyer	GB/F/D	Porsche 935	111.416
1980	SC W	Alain de Cadenet/Desire Wilson	GB/ZA	De Cadenet LM-Ford	114.348
1981	SC W	Dieter Schornstein/Harald Grohs/Walter Rohrl	D	Porsche 935	100.177
1982	SC W	Riccardo Patrese/Michele Alboreto	I	Lancia LC1	117.196
1983	SC W	Derek Bell/Stefan Bellof	GB/D	Porsche 956	123.202
1984	SC W	Jacky Ickx/Jochen Mass	B/D	Porsche 956	122.137
1985	SC W	Jacky Ickx/Jochen Mass	D/B	Porsche 962C	126.831
1986	SC W	Derek Warwick/Eddie Cheever	GB/USA	Jaguar XJR-6	129.083
1987	SC W	Eddie Cheever/Raul Boesel	USA/BR	Jaguar XJR-8	123.421
1988	SC W	Eddie Cheever/Martin Brundle	USA/GB	Jaguar XJR-9	128.639
1990*	SC W	Martin Brundle/Alain Ferte	GB/F	Jaguar XJR-11	128.830
1991*	SC W	Derek Warwick/Teo Fabi	GB/I	Jaguar XJR-14	122.037
1992*	SC W	Derek Warwick/Yannick Dalmas	GB/F	Peugeot 905B	122.651

*British Empire Trophy - also see above

SNETTERTON

Snetterton is a national venue on the site of another World War II airfield. From 1980 to 1994 the biggest event was the Willhire 24-hour race for production saloon cars. It was also the venue for the first round of the new European Formula 2 Championship in 1967, but today a British Touring Car race is the annual highlight.

Active years	1951 to date
Location	10 miles south-east of Thetford, 22 miles south of Norwich
Type	Permanent road course
Website	www.octagonmotorsports.com

Current circuit

Lap distance	1.952 miles
Lap record	Race: Nigel Greensall (Tyrrell 022-Ford), 58.97s, 119.160 mph, Historic F1, 1997

Circuit changes

1951-64	2.710 miles
1965-73	Russell Bend introduction before the pits. Officially lap distance remained 2.710 miles
1974-89	New short circuit opened. 1.917 miles
1990-96	Russell Bend re-profiled. 1.949 miles
1997 to date	Russell Bend eased, track resurfaced. Current circuit

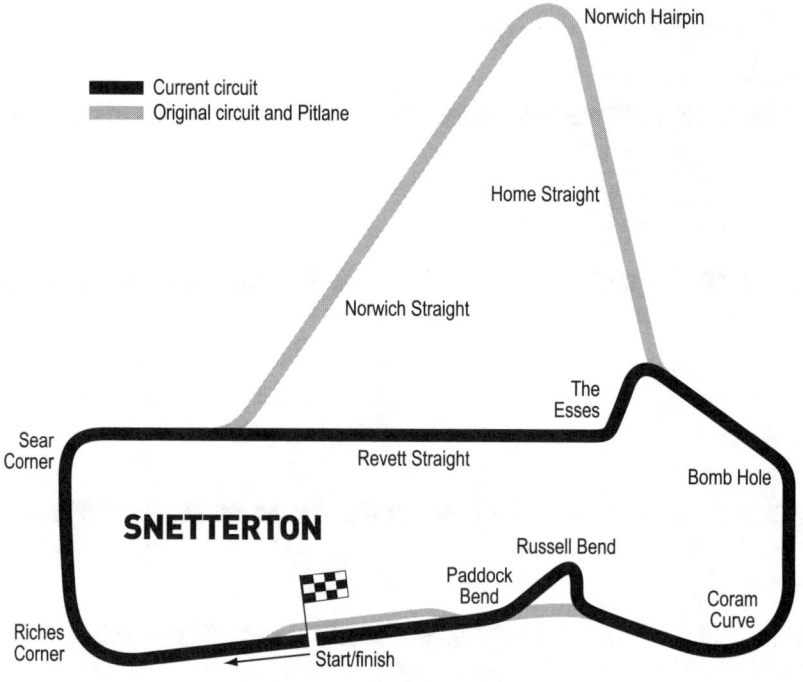

Current circuit
Original circuit and Pitlane

Norwich Hairpin

Home Straight

Norwich Straight

The Esses

Sear Corner

Revett Straight

Bomb Hole

SNETTERTON

Russell Bend

Paddock Bend

Coram Curve

Riches Corner

Start/finish

GUARDS 100 EUROPEAN FORMULA 2 RACE					
year	formula	winner	nat	car	mph
1967	F2 E	Jochen Rindt	A	Brabham BT23-Ford	108.987

THRUXTON

Thruxton was originally a motorcycle circuit which also held a few car meetings in 1953 and 1954. It was chosen as the new home of the BARC after Goodwood closed in 1966, and a refurbished venue opened in March 1968. The highlight of the Thruxton racing calendar was the Easter Monday Formula 2 race, which was named after three-time race winner Jochen Rindt following his death at Monza in 1970. Unfortunately, the rising cost of attracting the new Formula 3000 killed the event after the 1985 race. The Rindt trophy was revived for a historic

F2 race as part of Thruxton's twenty-fifth anniversary celebrations in 1993. The festivities also saw Damon Hill set an unofficial lap record of 57.6s during a demonstration run in his F1 Williams FW15C-Renault. The circuit was resurfaced in 2000, easing some of the most pronounced bumps on the fast backstretch.

Active years	1950-65 (motorbikes plus a few car meetings), 1968 to date
Location	5 miles west of Andover, Hampshire, 16 miles north-east of Salisbury
Type	Permanent road course
Website	www.barc.net

Great Britain

Current circuit
Lap distance 2.356 miles
Lap record Race: Earl Goddard (Reynard 95D-Cosworth), 1m01.96, 136.888 mph, Boss Formula (F3000), 2000

Circuit changes
1950-52 1.890 miles
1953-65 Using runways. 2.757 miles
1966-67 Not used
1968 to date Reopened using perimeter road only. Resurfaced in 2000. Current circuit

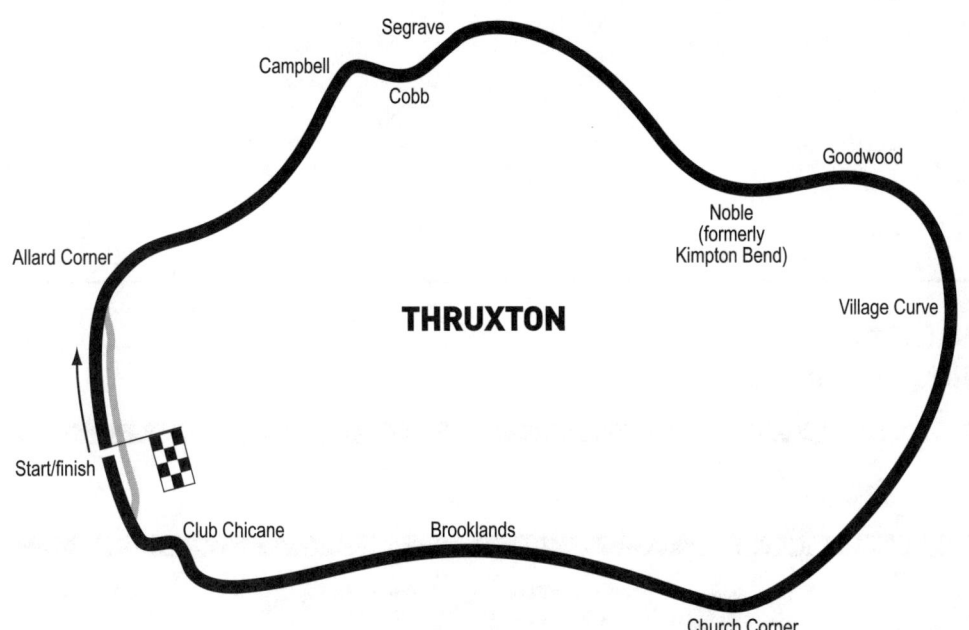

THRUXTON

Segrave
Campbell
Cobb
Goodwood
Noble
(formerly
Kimpton Bend)
Allard Corner
Village Curve
Start/finish
Club Chicane
Brooklands
Church Corner

EUROPEAN FORMULA 2 RACE (PRIOR TO JOCHEN RINDT TROPHY)

year	formula	winner	nat	car	mph
1968	F2 E	Jochen Rindt	A	Brabham BT23C-Ford	109.424
1969	F2 E	Jochen Rindt	A	Lotus 59B-Ford	112.649
1970	F2 E	Jochen Rindt	A	Lotus 69-Ford	112.729

JOCHEN RINDT TROPHY

year	formula	winner	nat	car	mph
1971	F2 E	Graham Hill	GB	Brabham BT36-Ford	112.901
1972	F2 E	Ronnie Peterson	S	March 722-Ford	117.169
1973	F2 E	Henri Pescarolo	F	Motul M1-Ford	114.449
1975	F2 E	Jacques Laffite	F	Martini MK16-BMW	115.980
1976	F2 E	Maurizio Flammini	I	March 762-BMW	116.287
1977	F2 E	Brian Henton	GB	Boxer PR276-Hart	117.817
1978	F2 E	Bruno Giacomelli	I	March 782-BMW	117.392
1979	F2 E	Rad Dougall	ZA	March 782-Hart	121.156
1980	F2 E	Brian Henton	GB	Toleman TG280-Hart	121.148
1981	F2 E	Roberto Guerrero	USA	Maurer MM81-BMW	121.405
1982	F2 E	Johnny Cecotto	YV	March 822-BMW	121.823
1983	F2 E	Beppe Gabbiani	I	March 832-BMW	121.669
1984	F2 E	Mike Thackwell	NZ	Ralt RH6/84-Honda	123.026
1985	F3000 INT	Emanuele Pirro	I	March 85B-Cosworth	117.413
1993	Hist F2	Marc Surer	CH	March 792-BMW	112.220

GREECE
Major Championships

GREEK FORMULA 3 CHAMPIONSHIP

year	driver	nat	team	car
1990	"Ninos"	GR	"Ninos"	Ralt RT3-Alfa Romeo
1991	Konstantin Kyritsis	GR	ABM	Reynard 873-Volkswagen
1992	Konstantin Kyritsis	GR	ABM	Reynard 903-Toyota
1993	Panayotis Fabiatos	GR	Panayotis Fabiatos	Reynard 883-Volkswagen
1994	Emmanuel Moschus	GR	ADM Competition	Dallara 392-Alfa Romeo
1995	Nikolas Nikolouzos	GR	Prema Powerteam	Dallara 392-Fiat
1996	Andreas Halkiopoulos	GR	BVM Racing	Ralt RT36-Mugen
1997	George Magliveras	GR	Eko Racing Team	Ralt RT35-Alfa Romeo
1998	Nikolas Nikolouzos	GR	Karting Racing Centre	Dallara 396-Alfa Romeo
1999	Vassilis Papafilipou	GR	BVM Racing	Dallara 396-Mugen
2000	Vassilis Papafilipou	GR	BVM Racing	Dallara 396-Mugen

HOLLAND
Major Championships

DUTCH SUPERCAR GT CHALLENGE

year	driver	nat	car
2002	Cor Euser/ Pieter van Soelen	NL	Marcos Mantis

DUTCH TOURING CAR CHAMPIONSHIP

year	driver	nat	team	car
1996	Frans Verschuur	NL	Renault Nederland	Renault Megane
1997	Duncan Huisman	NL	H&P Panorama Team	BMW 320i
1998	Donald Molenaar	NL	Renault Nederland	Renault Megane
1999	Cor Euser	NL	Carly Motors	BMW 320i
2000	Duncan Huisman	NL	Carly Motors	BMW 320i
2001	Sandor van Es	NL	Carly Motors	BMW 320i
2002	Duncan Huisman	NL	Carly Motors	BMW 320i

Major International Races

DUTCH GRAND PRIX

year	formula	circuit	winner	nat	car	mph
1950	F1	Zandvoort	Louis Rosier	F	Lago-Talbot T26C-DA	76.616
1951	F1	Zandvoort	Louis Rosier	F	Lago-Talbot T26C-DA	78.445
1952	F2 W	Zandvoort	Alberto Ascari	I	Ferrari 500	81.089
1953	F2 W	Zandvoort	Alberto Ascari	I	Ferrari 500	81.033
1955	F1 W	Zandvoort	Juan Manuel Fangio	RA	Mercedes-Benz W196	89.623
1958	F1 W	Zandvoort	Stirling Moss	GB	Vanwall VW10	93.915
1959	F1 W	Zandvoort	Jo Bonnier	S	BRM P25 (59)	93.446
1960	F1 W	Zandvoort	Jack Brabham	AUS	Cooper T53-Climax	96.254
1961	F1 W	Zandvoort	Wolfgang von Trips	D	Ferrari Dino 156	96.190
1962	F1 W	Zandvoort	Graham Hill	GB	BRM P57	95.425
1963	F1 W	Zandvoort	Jim Clark	GB	Lotus 25-Climax	97.522
1964	F1 W	Zandvoort	Jim Clark	GB	Lotus 25-Climax	98.001
1965	F1 W	Zandvoort	Jim Clark	GB	Lotus 33-Climax	100.851
1966	F1 W	Zandvoort	Jack Brabham	AUS	Brabham BT19-Repco	100.091
1967	F1 W	Zandvoort	Jim Clark	GB	Lotus 49-Ford	104.392
1968	F1 W	Zandvoort	Jackie Stewart	GB	Matra MS10-Ford	84.645
1969	F1 W	Zandvoort	Jackie Stewart	GB	Matra MS80-Ford	111.025
1970	F1 W	Zandvoort	Jochen Rindt	A	Lotus 72-Ford	112.930
1971	F1 W	Zandvoort	Jacky Ickx	B	Ferrari 312B2	94.047
1973	F1 W	Zandvoort	Jackie Stewart	GB	Tyrrell 006-Ford	114.349
1974	F1 W	Zandvoort	Niki Lauda	A	Ferrari 312B3	114.722
1975	F1 W	Zandvoort	James Hunt	GB	Hesketh 308-Ford	110.484
1976	F1 W	Zandvoort	James Hunt	GB	McLaren M23-Ford	112.684

DUTCH GRAND PRIX (cont.)

year	formula	circuit	winner	nat	car	mph
1977	F1 W	Zandvoort	Niki Lauda	A	Ferrari 312T2	116.120
1978	F1 W	Zandvoort	Mario Andretti	USA	Lotus 79-Ford	116.918
1979	F1 W	Zandvoort	Alan Jones	AUS	Williams FW07-Ford	116.619
1980	F1 W	Zandvoort	Nelson Piquet	BR	Brabham BT49-Ford	116.190
1981	F1 W	Zandvoort	Alain Prost	F	Renault RE30	113.709
1982	F1 W	Zandvoort	Didier Pironi	F	Ferrari 126C2	116.399
1983	F1 W	Zandvoort	Rene Arnoux	F	Ferrari 126C3	115.639
1984	F1 W	Zandvoort	Alain Prost	F	McLaren MP4/2-TAG Porsche	115.604
1985	F1 W	Zandvoort	Niki Lauda	A	McLaren MP4/2B-TAG Porsche	119.977

Circuits and Other Races

ZANDVOORT

Holland's only motor racing circuit was a regular highlight on the Grand Prix calendar until 1985. Designer John Hugenholtz used communications roads adjacent to the North Sea coast left by the departing German army after World War II. The combination of a fast final corner onto the long pits straight before the famous 180-degree Tarzan corner produced great racing with plenty of overtaking and great racing. Sand dunes act as natural grandstands around the circuit. Zandvoort struggled after the end of the Dutch GP. In 1988 it was taken over by the town council after falling into bankruptcy. Dutch noise pollution laws also led to alterations, including a man-made sand dune built between the town and a new, shorter circuit in 1989. The layout was extended ten years later, taking Zandvoort back to F1 length while retaining the character of the original course. Although there is sporadic talk of the Grand Prix returning, it seems unlikely as the series seeks expansion outside Europe. Today the annual highlight is the Marlboro Masters, which has replaced the Monaco support race as Europe's most prestigious F3 event. Luca

Badoer set a new unofficial lap record of 1m21.568 in the Ferrari F1-2000 during a 2001 demonstration.

Active years	1948 to date
Location	Northern suburbs of Zandvoort, 8 miles west of Haarlem, 15 miles west of Amsterdam
Type	Permanent road course
Website	www.circuit-zandvoort.nl

Current Circuit

Lap distance	2.672 miles
Lap records	Qualifying: Jonathan Cochet (Dallara 399-Renault), 1m33.192, 103.219 mph, F3, 2000
	Race: Bruce Jouanny (Dallara 302-Mugen), 1m34.533, 101.755 mph, F3, 2002

Circuit changes

1948-72	Grand Prix circuit designed using communications roads from German World War II defences. 2.605 miles
1973-78	A new right-left corner before Pulleveld. 2.626 miles
1979	"Scheckter" chicane built after Scheivak. Circuit length unchanged
1980-88	Permanent Marlboro chicane built to replace "Scheckter" chicane. 2.642 miles
1989-98	New shorter circuit opened using pit straight, Tarzan and Hunserug. 1.569 miles
1999 to date	Extension built using old Schleivak. Current circuit

ORIGINAL GRAND PRIX CIRCUIT

Dutch Grand Prix see above

CURRENT CIRCUIT

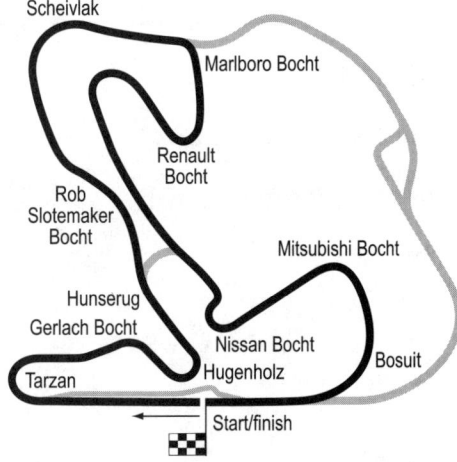

ZANDVOORT GRAND PRIX

year	formula	winner	nat	car	mph
1948	FL	"B Bira"	SM	Maserati 4CL	73.250
1949	F1	Luigi Villoresi	I	Ferrari 125	77.120

EUROPEAN FORMULA 2 RACE

year	formula	winner	nat	car	mph
1967	F2 E	Jacky Ickx	B	Matra MS5-Ford	104.852
1968	F2 E	Jean-Pierre Beltoise	F	Matra MS7-Ford	105.794
1979	F2 E	Eddie Cheever	USA	Osella FA2/79-BMW	113.139
1980	F2 E	Richard Dallest	F	AGS JH17-BMW	93.993

INTERNATIONAL FORMULA 3000 RACE

year	formula	winner	nat	car	mph
1985	F3000 INT	Christian Danner	D	March 85B-Cosworth	101.026

EUROPEAN FORMULA 3 RACE

year	formula	winner	nat	car	mph
1976	F3 E	Riccardo Patrese	I	Chevron B34-Toyota	102.642
1977	F3 E	Anders Olofsson	S	Ralt RT1-Toyota	103.263
1978	F3 E	Jan Lammers	NL	Ralt RT1-Toyota	104.335
1979	F3 E	Alain Prost	F	Martini MK27-Renault	104.428
1980	F3 E	Mauro Baldi	I	Martini MK31-Toyota	100.396
1981	F3 E	Mauro Baldi	I	March 813-Alfa Romeo	102.672
1982	F3 E	Oscar Larrauri	RA	Euroracing 101-Alfa Romeo	102.130
1983	F3 E	John Nielsen	DK	Ralt RT3/83-Volkswagen	101.668

MARLBORO MASTERS OF FORMULA 3

year	formula	winner	nat	car	mph
1991	F3	David Coulthard	GB	Ralt RT35-Mugen	88.182
1992	F3	Pedro Lamy	P	Reynard 923-Opel	90.145
1993	F3	Jos Verstappen	NL	Dallara 393-Opel	90.900
1994	F3	Gareth Rees	GB	Dallara 394-Mugen	77.212
1995	F3	Norberto Fontana	RA	Dallara 395-Opel	86.585
1996	F3	Kurt Mollekens	B	Dallara 396-Mugen	82.709
1997	F3	Tom Coronel	NL	Dallara 397-Toyota	83.771
1998	F3	David Saelens	B	Dallara 396-Renault	87.286
1999	F3	Marc Hynes	GB	Dallara 399-Mugen	99.515
2000	F3	Jonathan Cochet	F	Dallara 399-Renault	91.860
2001	F3	Takuma Sato	J	Dallara 301-Mugen	100.697
2002	F3	Fabio Carbone	BR	Dallara 302-Renault	100.881

HUNGARY

Major International Races

HUNGARIAN GRAND PRIX

year	formula	circuit	winner	nat	car	mph
1936	GP	Nepliget Park	Tazio Nuvolari	I	Alfa Romeo Tipo-C "8C-35"	69.373
1986	F1 W	Hungaroring	Nelson Piquet	BR	Williams FW11-Honda	94.320
1987	F1 W	Hungaroring	Nelson Piquet	BR	Williams FW11B-Honda	95.211
1988	F1 W	Hungaroring	Ayrton Senna	BR	McLaren MP4/4-Honda	96.554
1989	F1 W	Hungaroring	Nigel Mansell	GB	Ferrari 640	103.908
1990	F1 W	Hungaroring	Thierry Boutsen	B	Williams FW13B-Renault	104.035
1991	F1 W	Hungaroring	Ayrton Senna	BR	McLaren MP4/6-Honda	104.318
1992	F1 W	Hungaroring	Ayrton Senna	BR	McLaren MP4/7A-Honda	107.157
1993	F1 W	Hungaroring	Damon Hill	GB	Williams FW15C-Renault	105.831
1994	F1 W	Hungaroring	Michael Schumacher	D	Benetton B194-Ford	105.444
1995	F1 W	Hungaroring	Damon Hill	GB	Williams FW17-Renault	107.012
1996	F1 W	Hungaroring	Jacques Villeneuve	CDN	Williams FW18-Renault	107.081

HUNGARIAN GRAND PRIX (cont.)

year	formula	circuit	winner	nat	car	mph
1997	F1 W	Hungaroring	Jacques Villeneuve	CDN	Williams FW19-Renault	107.654
1998	F1 W	Hungaroring	Michael Schumacher	D	Ferrari F300	108.022
1999	F1 W	Hungaroring	Mika Hakkinen	SF	McLaren MP4/14-Mercedes-Benz	107.041
2000	F1 W	Hungaroring	Mika Hakkinen	SF	McLaren MP4/15-Mercedes-Benz	107.880
2001	F1 W	Hungaroring	Michael Schumacher	D	Ferrari F2001	111.839
2002	F1 W	Hungaroring	Rubens Barrichello	BR	Ferrari F2002	111.851

Circuits

HUNGARORING

In 1986 the Hungaroring attracted an estimated crowd of 200,000 for the first Grand Prix behind the Iron Curtain. Unfortunately the circuit offers precious few overtaking opportunities, and resembles a street circuit more than a purpose-built facility. Under the circumstances, Nigel Mansell's 1989 victory from twelfth on the grid was especially impressive. In contrast, Thierry Boutsen held off a train of quicker cars for the entire race to win for Williams a year later. It was here that Mansell won the World Championship in 1992, and Michael Schumacher clinched a fourth title in 2001.

Active years	1986 to date
Location	Mogyorod, 12 miles north-east of Budapest
Type	Permanent road course
Website	www.hungaroring.hu

Current circuit

Lap distance	2.465 miles
Lap record	Qualifying: Rubens Barrichello (Ferrari F2002), 1m13.333, 121.010 mph, F1, 2002
	Race: Michael Schumacher (Ferrari F2002), 1m16.207, 116.446 mph, F1, 2002

Circuit changes

1986-88	2.494 miles
1989 to date	Original diversion bypassed by straight. Current circuit

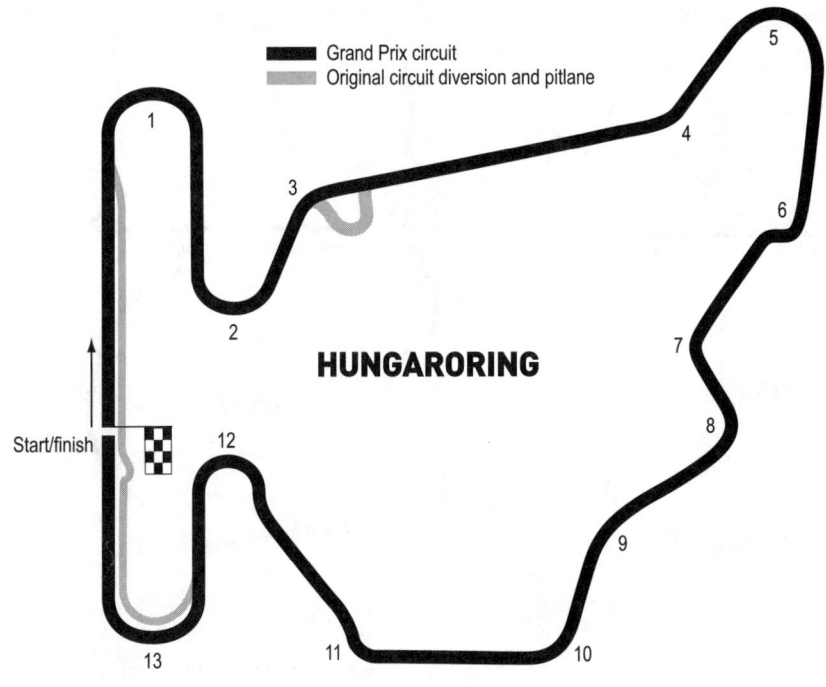

Grand Prix circuit
Original circuit diversion and pitlane

Start/finish

HUNGARORING

Hungarian Grand Prix see above

INTERNATIONAL FORMULA 3000 RACE					
year	formula	winner	nat	car	mph
1998	F3000 INT	Nick Heidfeld	D	Lola T96/50-Zytek	95.842
1999	F3000 INT	Stephane Sarrazin	F	Lola B99/50-Zytek	96.463
2000	F3000 INT	Bruno Junqueira	BR	Lola B99/50-Zytek	94.365
2001	F3000 INT	Justin Wilson	GB	Lola B99/50-Zytek	96.895
2002	F3000 INT	Enrico Toccacelo	I	Lola B2/50-Zytek	94.568

FIA GT RACE					
year	formula	winner	nat	car	mph
1998	GT FIA	Bernd Schneider/Mark Webber	D/AUS	Mercedes-Benz CLK-LM	92.600
1999	GT FIA	Jean-Philippe Belloc/Dominique Dupuy	F	Chrysler Viper GTS-R	84.623
2000	GT FIA	Boris Derichebourg/Vincent Vosse	F/B	Chrysler Viper GTS-R	84.615
2001	GT FIA	Jeroen Bleekemolen/Mike Hezemans	NL	Chrysler Viper GTS-R	83.207

NEPLIGET PARK

Budapest

The first Hungarian Grand Prix was held in Budapest's Nepliget Park in 1936 when Tazio Nuvolari held off the all-conquering German teams in his underpowered Alfa Romeo. Racing returned to Hungary in the early sixties at Ferhegy airfield before Formula 3 and European Touring Cars used a modified circuit in Nepliget Park.

Active years	1936-72
Location	Nepliget Park, central Budapest
Type	Temporary road course
Circuits	
1936	3.100 miles
1945-72	3.290 miles

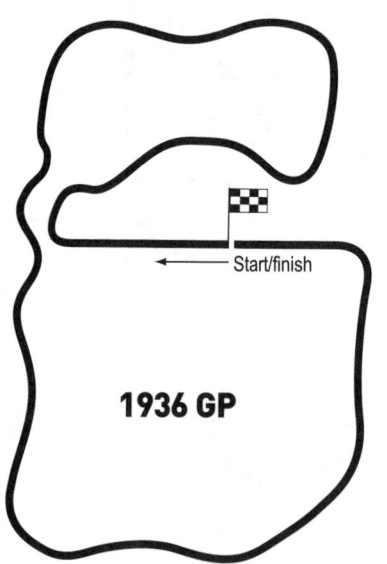

Start/finish

1936 GP

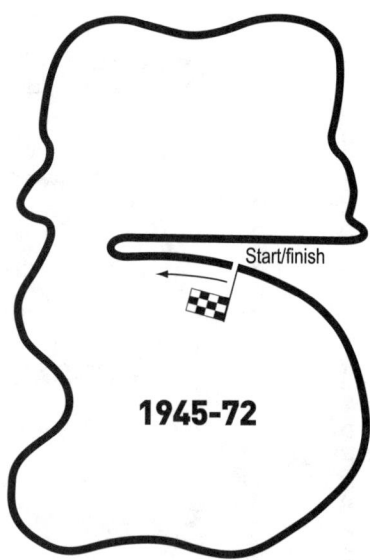

Start/finish

1945-72

Hungarian Grand Prix see above

ITALY
Major Championships

ITALIAN SUPERTURISMO CHAMPIONSHIP

year	driver	nat	team	car
1987	Michele di Gioia	I	Michele di Gioia	BMW M3
1988	Gianfranco Brancatelli	I	Jolly Club	Alfa Romeo 75 turbo
1989	Johnny Cecotto	YV	Schnitzer	BMW M3
1990	Roberto Ravaglia	I	Schnitzer	BMW M3
1991	Roberto Ravaglia	I	CiBiEmme Engineering	BMW M3
1992	Nicola Larini	I	Alfa Corse	Alfa Romeo 155 GTA
1993	Roberto Ravaglia	I	CiBiEmme Engineering	BMW 318i
1994	Emanuele Pirro	I	Audi Sport Italia	Audi 80 Quattro
1995	Emanuele Pirro	I	Audi Sport Italia	Audi A4
1996	Rinaldo Capello	I	Audi Sport Italia	Audi A4
1997	Emanuele Naspetti	I	BMW Italia	BMW 320i
1998	Fabrizio Giovanardi	I	Nordauto Engineering	Alfa Romeo 156 TS
1999	Fabrizio Giovanardi	I	Nordauto Engineering	Alfa Romeo 156 TS

EURO FORMULA 3000 CHAMPIONSHIP (FORMERLY ITALIAN F3000 1999-2000)

year	driver	nat	team	car
1999	Giorgio Vinella	I	Team Martello	Lola T96/50-Zytek
2000	Ricardo Sperafico	BR	Team ADM	Lola T96/50-Zytek
2001	Felipe Massa	BR	Draco Engineering	Lola T96/50-Zytek
2002	Jaime Melo Jr	BR	Great Wall Racing	Lola T99/50-Zytek

ITALIAN FORMULA 3 CHAMPIONSHIP (INCLUDING FORMULA JUNIOR)

year	driver	nat	team	car
1958*	Roberto Lippi	I	Scuderia Bardahl	Stanguellini-Fiat
1959*	Raffaele Cammarota	I	Scuderia Bardahl	Stanguellini-Fiat
1960*	Renato Pirocchi	I	Scuderia Pescara	Stanguellini-Fiat
1961*	"Geki" Russo	I	Scuderia Madunina	Stanguellini-Fiat/Lotus 18-Ford
1962*	"Geki" Russo	I	Scuderia Madunina	Lotus 18-Ford/Lotus 20-Ford/de Sanctis-Ford
1963*	"Geki" Russo	I	Scuderia Madunina	de Sanctis-Ford
1964	"Geki" Russo	I	Scuderia Sorocaima	de Sanctis-Ford
1965	Andrea de Adamich	I	Jolly Club	Lola T5A-Ford/Brabham BT15-Ford
1966	Tino Brambilla	I	Scuderia Madunina	Brabham BT16-Ford
1968	Franco Bernabei	I	Franco Bernabei	Tecno 68-Ford
1969	Gianluigi Picchi	I	Tecno Racing Team	Tecno 69-Ford
1970	Giovanni Salvati	I	Giovanni Salvati	Tecno 70-Ford
1971	Giancarlo Naddeo	I	Giancarlo Naddeo	Tecno 69-Ford
1972	Vittorio Brambilla	I	Team Brambilla	Birel 72-Alfa Romeo/Brabham BT35-Ford
1973	Carlo Giorgio	I	Trivellato Racing	Ensign 373-Ford/March 733-Ford
1974	Alberto Colombo	I	Scuderia del Lario	GRD 374-Ford/March 743-Toyota
1975	Luciano Pavesi	I	Scuderia ala d'Oro	Brabham BT41-Toyota/March 753-Toyota
1976	Riccardo Patrese	I	Trivellato Racing	Chevron B34-Toyota
1977	Elio de Angelis	I	Trivellato Racing	Chevron B38-Toyota/Ralt RT1-Toyota
1978	Siegfried Stohr	I	Trivellato Racing	Chevron B43-Toyota
1979	Piercarlo Ghinzani	I	Euroracing	March 793-Alfa Romeo
1980	Guido Pardini	I	Ferdinando Ravarotto	Dallara 380-Toyota
1981	Eddy Bianchi	I	Team del Porto	Martini MK34-Toyota/Martini MK34-Alfa Romeo
1982	Enzo Coloni	I	Enzo Coloni Racing	March 813-Alfa Romeo/Ralt RT3-Alfa Romeo
1983	Ivan Capelli	I	Enzo Coloni Racing	Ralt RT3-Alfa Romeo
1984	Alessandro Santin	I	Enzo Coloni Racing	Ralt RT3-Alfa Romeo
1985	Franco Forini	CH	Forti Corse	Dallara 385-Volkswagen
1986	Nicola Larini	I	Enzo Coloni Racing	Dallara 386-Alfa Romeo
1987	Enrico Bertaggia	I	Forti Corse	Dallara 387-Alfa Romeo
1988	Emanuele Naspetti	I	Forti Corse	Dallara 388-Alfa Romeo
1989	Gianni Morbidelli	I	Forti Corse	Dallara 389-Alfa Romeo
1990	Roberto Colciago	I	Prema Powerteam	Reynard 903-Alfa Romeo
1991	Giambattista Busi	I	Piemme Motors	Dallara 391-Volkswagen
1992	Massimiliano Angelelli	I	RC Motorsport	Dallara 392-Opel
1993	Christian Pescatori	I	Supercars	Dallara 393-Fiat
1994	Giancarlo Fisichella	I	RC Motorsport	Dallara 394-Opel
1995	Luca Rangoni	I	EF Project	Dallara 395-Fiat
1996	Andrea Boldrini	I	RC Motorsport	Dallara 395/96-Opel
1997	Oliver Martini	I	RC Motorsport	Dallara 396-Opel/Dallara 397-Opel
1998	Donny Crevels	NL	Prema Powerteam	Dallara 397-Opel/Dallara 398-Opel
1999	Peter Sundberg	S	Prema Powerteam	Dallara 399-Opel

ITALIAN FORMULA 3 CHAMPIONSHIP (INCLUDING FORMULA JUNIOR) (cont.)

year	driver	nat	team	car
2000	Davide Uboldi	I	Uboldi Corse	Dallara 399-Fiat
2001	Lorenzo del Gallo	I	PMS	Dallara 300-Fiat
2002	Milos Pavlovic	YU	Target Racing	Dallara 302-Opel

*Formula Junior

ITALIAN SUPERCAR GT CHAMPIONSHIP

year	driver	nat	car
1992	Rosario Parasiliti	I	Ferrari F40
1993	Marco Brand	I	Ferrari F40
1994	Vittorio Colombo	I	Ferrari F40
1996	Antonio de Castro	I	Porsche 911 Carrera RSR
1997	Antonio de Castro	I	Porsche 911 Carrera RSR
1998	Luca Cattaneo	I	Porsche 911 Carrera RSR
1999	Mario Spagnoli	I	Porsche 966 GT3 Cup
2000	Massimo Pasini	I	Porsche 3.3 turbo
2001	Mario Spagnoli	I	Porsche 996

ITALIAN PROTOTYPE CHAMPIONSHIP

An open cockpit sports car series introduced in 1988 using 2.5-litre 6-cylinder Alfa Romeo engines.

year	driver	nat	car
1988	Stefano Sanesi	I	Lucchini SN88-Alfa Romeo
1989	Stefano Sanesi	I	Lucchini SN89-Alfa Romeo
1990	Stefano Sanesi	I	Lucchini SP90-Alfa Romeo
1991	Giorgio Francia	I	Osella PA16-Alfa Romeo
1992	Fabio Mancini	I	Osella PA16-Alfa Romeo
1993	Ermanno Martinello	I	Lucchini P3-Alfa Romeo
1994	Ermanno Martinello	I	Lucchini P3-Alfa Romeo
1995	Massimo Saccomanno	I	Lucchini P3-Alfa Romeo
1996	Stefano Sanesi	I	Lucchini P3-Alfa Romeo
1997	Stefano Sanesi	I	Lucchini P3-Alfa Romeo
1998	Filippo Francioni	I	Lucchini P3-Alfa Romeo

Major International Races

ITALIAN GRAND PRIX

year	formula	circuit	winner	nat	car	mph
1921	GP	Brescia	Jules Goux	F	Ballot 3L	89.937
1922	GP	Monza	Pietro Bordino	I	Fiat 804	86.905
1923	GP	Monza	Carlo Salamano	I	Fiat 805	91.037
1924	GP	Monza	Antonio Ascari	I	Alfa Romeo P2	98.738
1925	GP	Monza	Gastone Brilli-Peri	I	Alfa Romeo P2	94.823
1926	GP	Monza	"Sabipa"	F	Bugatti T39A	85.880
1927	GP	Monza	Robert Benoist	F	Delage 15S8	108.072
1928	GP	Monza	Louis Chiron	MC	Bugatti T35C	99.361
1931	FL	Monza	Giuseppe Campari/Tazio Nuvolari	I	Alfa Romeo 8C "Monza"	96.317
1932	FL	Monza	Tazio Nuvolari/Giuseppe Campari	I	Alfa Romeo Tipo-B "P3"	103.152
1933	FL	Monza	Luigi Fagioli	I	Alfa Romeo Tipo-B "P3"	108.584
1934	GP	Monza	Rudolf Caracciola/Luigi Fagioli	D/I	Mercedes-Benz W25A	65.513
1935	GP	Monza	Hans Stuck	D	Auto Union B	85.949
1936	GP	Monza	Bernd Rosemeyer	D	Auto Union C	83.532
1937	GP	Livorno	Rudolf Caracciola	D	Mercedes-Benz W125	78.954
1938	GP	Monza	Tazio Nuvolari	I	Auto Union D	96.870
1947	F1	Milan	Carlo Felice Trossi	I	Alfa Romeo 158	70.346
1948	F1	Turin	Jean-Pierre Wimille	F	Alfa Romeo 158	70.317
1949	F1	Monza	Alberto Ascari	I	Ferrari 125	105.046
1950	F1 W	Monza	Giuseppe Farina	I	Alfa Romeo 159	109.709
1951	F1 W	Monza	Alberto Ascari	I	Ferrari 375	115.533
1952	F2 W	Monza	Alberto Ascari	I	Ferrari 500	110.049
1953	F2 W	Monza	Juan Manuel Fangio	RA	Maserati A6SSG	110.694
1954	F1 W	Monza	Juan Manuel Fangio	RA	Mercedes-Benz W196	111.992
1955	F1 W	Monza	Juan Manuel Fangio	RA	Mercedes-Benz W196	128.494
1956	F1 W	Monza	Stirling Moss	GB	Maserati 250F	129.733
1957	F1 W	Monza	Stirling Moss	GB	Vanwall VW5	120.279

ITALIAN GRAND PRIX (cont.)

year	formula	circuit	winner	nat	car	mph
1958	F1 W	Monza	Tony Brooks	GB	Vanwall VW5	121.220
1959	F1 W	Monza	Stirling Moss	GB	Cooper T51-Climax	124.388
1960	F1 W	Monza	Phil Hill	USA	Ferrari Dino 246	132.063
1961	F1 W	Monza	Phil Hill	USA	Ferrari Dino 156	130.107
1962	F1 W	Monza	Graham Hill	GB	BRM P57	123.620
1963	F1 W	Monza	Jim Clark	GB	Lotus 25-Climax	127.743
1964	F1 W	Monza	John Surtees	GB	Ferrari 158	127.779
1965	F1 W	Monza	Jackie Stewart	GB	BRM P261	130.468
1966	F1 W	Monza	Ludovico Scarfiotti	I	Ferrari 312	135.928
1967	F1 W	Monza	John Surtees	GB	Honda RA300	140.509
1968	F1 W	Monza	Denny Hulme	NZ	McLaren M7A-Ford	145.420
1969	F1 W	Monza	Jackie Stewart	GB	Matra MS80-Ford	146.972
1970	F1 W	Monza	Clay Regazzoni	CH	Ferrari 312B	147.081
1971	F1 W	Monza	Peter Gethin	GB	BRM P160	150.759
1972	F1 W	Monza	Emerson Fittipaldi	BR	Lotus 72D-Ford	131.599
1973	F1 W	Monza	Ronnie Peterson	S	Lotus 72D-Ford	132.616
1974	F1 W	Monza	Ronnie Peterson	S	Lotus 72E-Ford	135.117
1975	F1 W	Monza	Clay Regazzoni	CH	Ferrari 312T	135.498
1976	F1 W	Monza	Ronnie Peterson	S	March 761-Ford	124.117
1977	F1 W	Monza	Mario Andretti	USA	Lotus 78-Ford	128.010
1978	F1 W	Monza	Niki Lauda	A	Brabham BT46-Alfa Romeo	128.949
1979	F1 W	Monza	Jody Scheckter	ZA	Ferrari 312T4	131.844
1980	F1 W	Imola	Nelson Piquet	BR	Brabham BT49-Ford	114.906
1981	F1 W	Monza	Alain Prost	F	Renault RE30	129.893
1982	F1 W	Monza	Rene Arnoux	F	Renault RE30B	136.411
1983	F1 W	Monza	Nelson Piquet	BR	Brabham BT52B-BMW	135.177
1984	F1 W	Monza	Niki Lauda	A	McLaren MP4/2-TAG Porsche	137.019
1985	F1 W	Monza	Alain Prost	F	McLaren MP4/2B-TAG Porsche	141.400
1986	F1 W	Monza	Nelson Piquet	BR	Williams FW11-Honda	141.903
1987	F1 W	Monza	Nelson Piquet	BR	Williams FW11B-Honda	144.551
1988	F1 W	Monza	Gerhard Berger	A	Ferrari F187/88C	141.998
1989	F1 W	Monza	Alain Prost	F	McLaren MP4/5-Honda	144.230
1990	F1 W	Monza	Ayrton Senna	BR	McLaren MP4/5B-Honda	146.995
1991	F1 W	Monza	Nigel Mansell	GB	Williams FW14-Renault	147.107
1992	F1 W	Monza	Ayrton Senna	BR	McLaren MP4/7A-Honda	146.448
1993	F1 W	Monza	Damon Hill	GB	Williams FW15C-Renault	148.595
1994	F1 W	Monza	Damon Hill	GB	Williams FW16B-Renault	147.702
1995	F1 W	Monza	Johnny Herbert	GB	Benetton B195-Renault	146.057
1996	F1 W	Monza	Michael Schumacher	D	Ferrari F310	146.671
1997	F1 W	Monza	David Coulthard	GB	McLaren MP4/12-Mercedes-Benz	147.908
1998	F1 W	Monza	Michael Schumacher	D	Ferrari F300	147.747
1999	F1 W	Monza	Heinz-Harald Frentzen	D	Jordan 199-Mugen	142.238
2000	F1 W	Monza	Michael Schumacher	D	Ferrari F1-2000	130.067
2001	F1 W	Monza	Juan Pablo Montoya	CO	Williams FW23-BMW	148.683
2002	F1 W	Monza	Rubens Barrichello	BR	Ferrari F2002	149.933

MILLE MIGLIA

year	formula	circuit	winner	nat	car	mph
1927	SC	Brescia-Rome-Brescia	Ferdinando Minoia/Giuseppe Morandi	I	OM	48.270
1928	SC	Brescia-Rome-Brescia	Giuseppe Campari/Giulio Ramponi	I	Alfa Romeo 1500S	52.580
1929	SC	Brescia-Rome-Brescia	Giuseppe Campari/Giulio Ramponi	I	Alfa Romeo 1750S	56.050
1930	SC	Brescia-Rome-Brescia	Tazio Nuvolari/Giovanni-Battista Guidotti	I	Alfa Romeo 1750S	62.780
1931	SC	Brescia-Rome-Brescia	Rudolf Caracciola/Wilhelm Sebastian	D	Mercedes-Benz SSKL	63.210
1932	SC	Brescia-Rome-Brescia	Baconin Borzacchini/Amedeo Bignami	I	Alfa Romeo 8C "Monza"	68.670
1933	SC	Brescia-Rome-Brescia	Tazio Nuvolari/Decimo Compagnoni	I	Alfa Romeo 8C "Monza"	67.850
1934	SC	Brescia-Rome-Brescia	Achille Varzi/Amedeo Bignami	I	Alfa Romeo 8C "Monza"	71.440
1935	SC	Brescia-Rome-Brescia	Carlo Pintacuda/Alessandro della Stufa	I	Alfa Romeo Tipo-B "P3"	71.720
1936	SC	Brescia-Rome-Brescia	Antonio Brivio/Carlo Ongaro	I	Alfa Romeo 2900A	76.010
1937	SC	Brescia-Rome-Brescia	Carlo Pintacuda/Paride Mambelli	I	Alfa Romeo 2900A	71.710
1938	SC	Brescia-Rome-Brescia	Clemente Biondetti/Aldo Stefani	I	Alfa Romeo 2900A	84.610
1940	SC	Brescia	Huschke von Hanstein/Walter Baumer	D	BMW 328	104.200
1947	SC	Brescia-Rome-Brescia	Clemente Biondetti/Emilio Romano	I	Alfa Romeo 2900B	70.140
1948	SC	Brescia-Rome-Brescia	Clemente Biondetti/Giuseppe Navone	I	Ferrari 166S	75.453
1949	SC	Brescia-Rome-Brescia	Clemente Biondetti/Ettore Salani	I	Ferrari 166MM	82.109
1950	SC	Brescia-Rome-Brescia	Giannino Marzotto/Marco Crosara	I	Ferrari 195S	77.000

MILLE MIGLIA (cont.)

year	formula	circuit	winner	nat	car	mph
1951	SC	Brescia-Rome-Brescia	Luigi Villoresi/P Cassani	I	Ferrari	76.130
1952	SC	Brescia-Rome-Brescia	Giovanni Bracco/Alfonso Rolfo	I	Ferrari 225S	80.360
1953	SC W	Brescia-Rome-Brescia	Giannino Marzotto/Marco Crosara	I	Ferrari 340MM	88.450
1954	SC W	Brescia-Rome-Brescia	Alberto Ascari	I	Lancia D24	87.267
1955	SC W	Brescia-Rome-Brescia	Stirling Moss/Denis Jenkinson	GB	Mercedes-Benz 300SLR	98.519
1956	SC W	Brescia-Rome-Brescia	Eugenio Castellotti	I	Ferrari 290MM	85.891
1957	SC W	Brescia-Rome-Brescia	Piero Taruffi	I	Ferrari 315S	95.383
1958	Reg	Brescia	Luigi Taramazzo/Gerino Gerini	I	Ferrari	Regularity test
1959	Reg	Brescia	Carlo Abate/Gianni Balzarini	I	Ferrari	Regularity test
1961	Reg	Brescia	Gunnar Andersson/Carl Lohmander	S	Ferrari 250GT	Regularity test

TARGA FLORIO

year	formula	circuit	winner	nat	car	mph
1906	TC	Madonie	Alessandro Cagno	I	Itala	29.031
1907	GP	Madonie	Felice Nazzaro	I	Fiat 60HP	33.450
1908	GP	Madonie	Vincenzo Trucco	I	Isotta-Fraschini	35.457
1909	GP	Madonie	Francesco Ciuppa	I	SPA	33.972
1910	GP	Madonie	Tullio Cariolato	I	Franco	29.380
1911	GP	Madonie	Ernesto Ceirano	I	SCAT	29.081
1912	FL	Madonie	Cyril Snipe/Pedrini	GB/I	SCAT	27.620
1913	FL	Madonie	Felice Nazzaro	I	Nazzaro	33.780
1914	FL	Madonie	Ernesto Ceirano	I	SCAT	36.080
1919	FL	Madonie	Andre Boillot	F	Peugeot EX5	34.194
1920	FL	Madonie	Guido Meregalli	I	Nazzaro GP	31.743
1921	FL	Madonie	Giulio Masetti	I	Fiat 451	36.187
1922	FL	Madonie	Giulio Masetti	I	Mercedes GP/14	39.204
1923	FL	Madonie	Ugo Sivocci	I	Alfa Romeo RLTF	36.772
1924	FL	Madonie	Christian Werner	D	Mercedes PP	41.023
1925	FL	Madonie	Meo Costantini	F	Bugatti T35	44.497
1926	FL	Madonie	Meo Costantini	F	Bugatti T35T	45.679
1927	FL	Madonie	Emilio Materassi	I	Bugatti T35C	44.159
1928	GP	Madonie	Albert Divo	F	Bugatti T35B	45.659
1929	GP	Madonie	Albert Divo	F	Bugatti T35C	46.210
1930	GP	Madonie	Achille Varzi	I	Alfa Romeo P2	48.481
1931	GP	Madonie	Tazio Nuvolari	I	Alfa Romeo 8C "Monza"	41.065
1932	GP	Madonie	Tazio Nuvolari	I	Alfa Romeo 8C "Monza"	49.272
1933	GP	Madonie	Antonio Brivio	I	Alfa Romeo 8C "Monza"	47.558
1934	GP	Madonie	Achille Varzi	I	Alfa Romeo Tipo-B "P3"	43.013
1935	GP	Madonie	Antonio Brivio	I	Alfa Romeo Tipo-B "P3"	49.181
1936	SC	Madonie	Costantino Magistri	I	Lancia	41.690
1937	V	Palermo	Guilio Severi	I	Maserati 6CM	66.920
1938	V	Palermo	Giovanni Rocco	I	Maserati 6CM	71.020
1939	V	Palermo	Luigi Villoresi	I	Maserati 6CM	84.780
1940	V	Palermo	Luigi Villoresi	I	Maserati 4CL	88.718
1948	SC	Madonie	Clemente Biondetti/Igor Troubetskoy	I	Ferrari	55.008
1949	SC	Madonie	Clemente Biondetti/Aldo Benedetti	I	Ferrari	50.639
1950	SC	Madonie	Mario Bornigia/Giancarlo Bornigia	I	Alfa Romeo	53.870
1951	SC	Madonie	Franco Cortese	I	Frazer-Nash	45.570
1952	SC	Madonie	Felice Bonetto	I	Lancia	49.700
1953	SC	Madonie	Umberto Maglioli	I	Lancia	50.100
1954	SC	Madonie	Piero Taruffi	I	Lancia	55.850
1955	SC W	Madonie	Stirling Moss/Peter Collins	GB	Mercedes-Benz 300SLR	59.833
1956	SC	Madonie	Umberto Maglioli/ Huschke von Hanstein	I/D	Porsche	56.370
1957	Reg	Madonie	Fabio Colonna	I	Fiat	Regularity test
1958	SC W	Madonie	Luigi Musso/Olivier Gendebien	I/B	Ferrari 250TR	58.907
1959	SC W	Madonie	Edgar Barth/Wolfgang Seidel	DDR/D	Porsche 718 RSK	56.737
1960	SC W	Madonie	Jo Bonnier/Hans Herrmann/ Graham Hill	S/D/GB	Porsche RS60	59.239
1961	SC W	Madonie	Wolfgang von Trips/Olivier Gendebien	D/B	Ferrari Dino 246SP	64.271
1962	SC W	Madonie	Willy Mairesse/Ricardo Rodriguez/ Olivier Gendebien	B/MEX/B	Ferrari Dino 246SP	63.468
1963	SC W	Madonie	Jo Bonnier/Carlo Abate	S/I	Porsche RS62	64.566
1964	SC W	Madonie	Antonio Pucci/Colin Davis	I/GB	Porsche 904GTS	62.297
1965	SC W	Madonie	Nino Vaccarella/Lorenzo Bandini	I	Ferrari 275P2	63.730
1966	SC W	Madonie	Willy Mairesse/Herbert Muller	B/CH	Porsche 906 Carrera 6	61.492
1967	SC W	Madonie	Paul Hawkins/Rolf Stommelen	AUS/D	Porsche 910/8	67.613
1968	SC W	Madonie	Vic Elford/Umberto Maglioli	GB/I	Porsche 907/8	69.042
1969	SC W	Madonie	Gerhard Mitter/Udo Schutz	D	Porsche 908/8	72.991

year	formula	circuit	winner	nat	car	mph
			TARGA FLORIO (cont.)			
1970	SC W	Madonie	Jo Siffert/Brian Redman	CH/GB	Porsche 908/3	74.659
1971	SC W	Madonie	Nino Vaccarella/Toine Hezemans	I/NL	Alfa Romeo T33/3	74.608
1972	SC W	Madonie	Arturo Merzario/Sandro Munari	I	Ferrari 312P	76.142
1973	SC W	Madonie	Gijs van Lennep/Herbert Muller	NL/CH	Porsche 911 Carrera RSR	71.266
1974	SC	Madonie	Gerard Larrousse/Ballestrieri	F/I	Lancia Stratos	n/a
1975	SC	Madonie	Nino Vaccarella/Arturo Merzario	I	Alfa Romeo	n/a
1976	SC	Madonie	"Amphicar"/Armando Floridia	I	Osella	n/a
1977	SC	Madonie	Raffaele Restivo/"Apache"	I	Chevron	n/a

Circuits and Other Races

ENNA-PERGUSA

This high-speed slipstreaming circuit is built around Lake Pergusa in an arid and stifling bowl in central Sicily. On the original layout drivers would only really brake for the first corner, but since the mid-seventies it has been interrupted by three chicanes, the first of which is almost certain to cause a shunt on the opening lap. The Mediterranean Grand Prix began as a non-championship F1 race in 1962, and two years later Jo Siffert won the first of two successive victories, narrowly beating Jim Clark on both occasions. The race was a permanent fixture on the F3000 calendar until the FIA decided the series should exclusively support Formula 1. Enna has also been threatened by environmental pressure, as it is just two miles from an area of natural interest. A swarm of baby frogs was killed during practice for the 1996 F3000 race and two years later environmentalists threatened to disrupt the event until a compromise was reached just ten days before it was due to be held. Despite Enna's distance from the heart of Europe the FIA GT, European Touring Car and Euro 3000 championships all visited in 2002.

Active years	1961 to date
Location	3 miles south of Enna in central Sicily
Type	Permanent road course

Current circuit	
Lap distance	3.076 miles
Lap record	Qualifying: Franck Lagorce (Reynard 94D-Cosworth), 1m24.159, 131.579 mph, F3000, 1994
	Race: Christian Pescatori (Reynard 93D-Cosworth), 1m25.157, 130.038 mph, F3000, 1994

Circuit changes	
1961-69	Original circuit, no chicanes. 2.983 miles
1970	Variante Prosperina inserted immediately after the old start, pits moved to current location. 3.010 miles
1971-75	Second chicane built. 3.011 miles
1975 to date	Variante Vivalo built at first corner, used for 1975 F2 race (but not sports cars). Current circuit

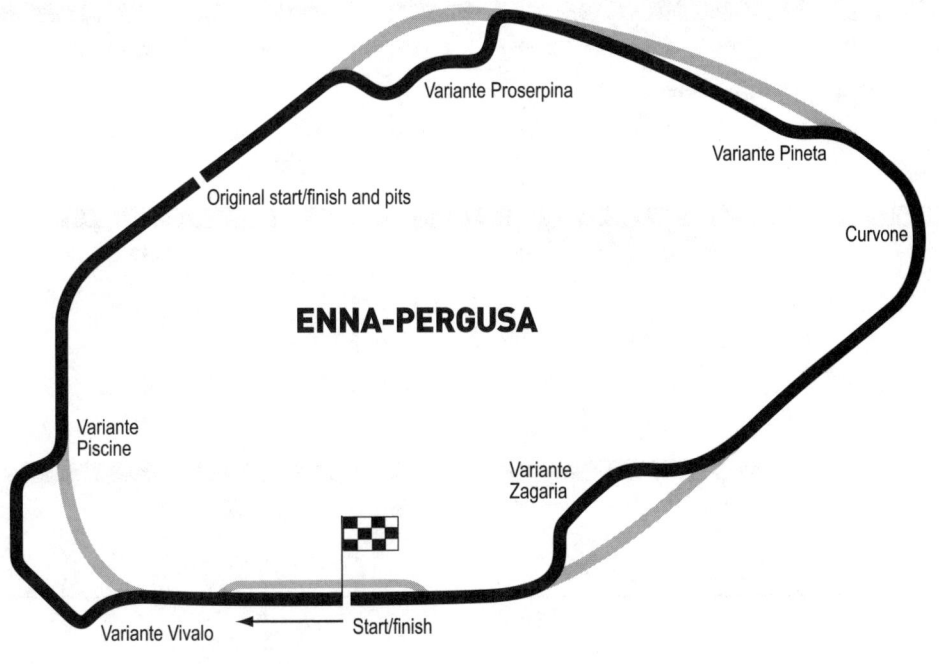

ENNA-PERGUSA

Variante Proserpina

Variante Pineta

Original start/finish and pits

Curvone

Variante Piscine

Variante Zagaria

Start/finish

Variante Vivalo

MEDITERRANEAN GRAND PRIX

year	formula	winner	nat	car	mph
1962	F1	Lorenzo Bandini	I	Ferrari 156	128.892
1963	F1	John Surtees	GB	Ferrari 156	137.653
1964	F1	Jo Siffert	CH	Brabham BT11-BRM	137.698
1965	F1	Jo Siffert	CH	Brabham BT11-BRM	139.308
1966	F3	Jonathan Williams	GB	de Sanctis-Ford	n/a
1967	F2 E	Jackie Stewart	GB	Matra MS7-Ford	142.727
1968	F2 E	Jochen Rindt	A	Brabham BT23C-Ford	142.780
1969	F2 E	Piers Courage	GB	Brabham BT30-Ford	142.327
1970	F2 E	Clay Regazzoni	CH	Tecno 70-Ford	127.157
1972	F2 E	Henri Pescarolo	F	Brabham BT38-Ford	123.819
1973	F2 E	Jean-Pierre Jarier	F	March 732-BMW	129.207
1974	F2 E	Hans-Joachim Stuck	D	March 742-BMW	128.231
1975	F2 E	Jacques Laffite	F	Martini MK16-BMW	110.767
1976	F2 E	Rene Arnoux	F	Martini MK19-Renault	115.092
1977	F2 E	Keke Rosberg	SF	Chevron B40-Hart	114.991
1978	F2 E	Bruno Giacomelli	I	March 782-BMW	118.062
1979	F2 E	Eje Elgh	S	March 792-BMW	116.895
1980	F2 E	Siegfried Stohr	I	Toleman TG280-Hart	117.532
1981	F2 E	Thierry Boutsen	B	March 812-BMW	118.369
1982	F2 E	Thierry Boutsen	B	Spirit 201-Honda	119.725
1983	F2 E	Jonathan Palmer	GB	Ralt RH6/83-Honda	118.327
1984	F2 E	Mike Thackwell	NZ	Ralt RH6/84-Honda	120.505
1985	F3000 INT	Mike Thackwell	NZ	Ralt RB20-Cosworth	119.103
1986	F3000 INT	Luis Perez Sala	E	Ralt RT20-Cosworth	119.627
1987	F3000 INT	Roberto Moreno	BR	Ralt RT21-Honda	119.797
1988	F3000 INT	Pierluigi Martini	I	March 88B-Judd	121.198
1989	F3000 INT	Andrea Chiesa	CH	Reynard 89D-Cosworth	122.187
1990	F3000 INT	Gianni Morbidelli	I	Lola T90/50-Cosworth	119.815
1991	F3000 INT	Emanuele Naspetti	I	Reynard 91D-Cosworth	123.926
1992	F3000 INT	Luca Badoer	I	Reynard 92D-Cosworth	126.521
1993	F3000 INT	David Coulthard	GB	Reynard 93D-Cosworth	126.946
1994	F3000 INT	Gil de Ferran	BR	Reynard 94D-Judd	131.153
1995	F3000 INT	Ricardo Rosset	BR	Reynard 95D-Cosworth	118.580
1996	F3000 INT	Marc Goossens	B	Lola T96/50-Zytek	116.137
1997	F3000 INT	Jamie Davies	GB	Lola T96/50-Zytek	116.765
1998	F3000 INT	Juan Pablo Montoya	CO	Lola T96/50-Zytek	117.331

EUROPEAN FORMULA 3 RACE

year	formula	winner	nat	car	mph
1976	F3 E	Riccardo Patrese	I	Chevron B34-Toyota	101.092
1977	F3 E	Oscar Pedersoli	I	Ralt RT1-Toyota	107.930
1978	F3 E	Michael Bleekemolen	NL	Chevron B43-Toyota	109.640
1979	F3 E	Piercarlo Ghinzani	I	March 793-Alfa Romeo	105.790
1982	F3 E	Oscar Larrauri	RA	Euroracing 101-Alfa Romeo	111.011
1984	F3 E	Ivan Capelli	I	Martini MK42-Alfa Romeo	112.675

WORLD SPORTS CAR RACE

year	formula	winner	nat	car	mph
1975	SC W	Arturo Merzario/Jochen Mass	I/D	Alfa Romeo T33TT/12	122.440
1976	SC WSC	Jochen Mass/Rolf Stommelen	D	Porsche 936	105.869
1977	SC WSC	Arturo Merzario	I	Alfa Romeo T33SC/12	103.878
1978	SC E	Giorgio Francia/"Gimax"	I	Osella PA6-BMW	105.687
1979	SC W	Lella Lombardi/			
		Enrico Grimaldi	I	Osella PA7-BMW	98.908
1981	SC W	Guy Edwards/			
		Emilio de Villota	GB/E	Lola T600-Ford	103.310

FIA GT RACE

year	formula	winner	nat	car	mph
2002	GT FIA	Jamie Campbell-Walter/			
		Nicolaus Springer	GB/D	Lister Storm GT	103.422

IMOLA
Autodromo Enzo e Dino Ferrari

Imola is an early-season F1 highlight, but since a tragic weekend in 1994 it is best remembered for the deaths of Roland Ratzenberger and Ayrton Senna. It survived the disaster with extensive modifications, particularly to the ultra-quick Tamburello corner where Senna crashed. But Formula 1's desire to expand outside Europe has cast new doubt over Imola's future as a Grand Prix circuit. Set in the undulating Castellaccio Park outside Imola, the circuit is a fast succession of demanding corners broken up by a series of chicanes. It did not reach the forefront of International motor racing until it was refurbished in the early seventies. Imola held a non-championship F1 race in 1979 and was chosen to hold the 1980 Italian Grand Prix following Ronnie Peterson's fatal accident at Monza in 1978. Although Monza was back in favour within 12 months, Imola was awarded the San Marino Grand Prix – a title of convenience referring to the principality fifty miles away – and it has held the race ever since.

Active years 1952 to date
Location Southern suburbs of Imola, 20 miles south-east of Bologna

Type Permanent road course
Website www.autodromoimola.com

Current circuit
Lap distance 3.064 miles
Lap record Qualifying: Michael Schumacher (Ferrari F2002), 1m21.091, 136.025 mph, F1, 2002
Race: Rubens Barrichello (Ferrari F2002), 1m24.170, 131.049 mph, F1, 2002

Circuit changes
1952-73 No chicanes. 3.118 miles
1973 Varianta Bassa built in September. 3.183 miles
1974-79 Variante Alta built. 3.144 miles
1980-94 Chicane built at Acqua Minerale. 3.132 miles
1995 to date Chicanes built at Tamburello and Villeneuve, Piratella tightened, Acqua Minerale chicane bypassed and corner reprofiled, Variante Bassa straightened. Current circuit

Italian Grand Prix see above

SAN MARINO GRAND PRIX (also see Misano)

year	formula	winner	nat	car	mph
1981	F1 W	Nelson Piquet	BR	Brabham BT49C-Ford	101.214
1982	F1 W	Didier Pironi	F	Ferrari 126C2	116.662
1983	F1 W	Patrick Tambay	F	Ferrari 126C2B	115.201
1984	F1 W	Alain Prost	F	McLaren MP4/2-TAG Porsche	116.366
1985	F1 W	Elio de Angelis	I	Lotus 97T-Renault	119.189
1986	F1 W	Alain Prost	F	McLaren MP4/2C-TAG Porsche	121.929
1987	F1 W	Nigel Mansell	GB	Williams FW11B-Honda	121.303
1988	F1 W	Ayrton Senna	BR	McLaren MP4/4-Honda	121.647
1989	F1 W	Ayrton Senna	BR	McLaren MP4/5-Honda	125.490
1990	F1 W	Riccardo Patrese	I	Williams FW13B-Renault	126.073
1991	F1 W	Ayrton Senna	BR	McLaren MP4/6-Honda	120.353
1992	F1 W	Nigel Mansell	GB	Williams FW14B-Renault	127.142
1993	F1 W	Alain Prost	F	Williams FW15C-Renault	122.810

SAN MARINO GRAND PRIX (cont.)

year	formula	winner	nat	car	mph
1994	F1 W	Michael Schumacher	D	Benetton B194-Ford	123.188
1995	F1 W	Damon Hill	GB	Williams FW17-Renault	113.873
1996	F1 W	Damon Hill	GB	Williams FW18-Renault	121.358
1997	F1 W	Heinz-Harald Frentzen	D	Williams FW19-Renault	125.238
1998	F1 W	David Coulthard	GB	McLaren MP4/13-Mercedes-Benz	120.730
1999	F1 W	Michael Schumacher	D	Ferrari F399	121.584
2000	F1 W	Michael Schumacher	D	Ferrari F1-2000	124.348
2001	F1 W	Ralf Schumacher	D	Williams FW23-BMW	125.603
2002	F1 W	Michael Schumacher	D	Ferrari F2002	127.810

IMOLA GRAND PRIX

year	formula	winner	nat	car	mph
1954	-	Umberto Maglioli	I	Ferrari	87.053
1955	SC	Cesare Perdisa	I	Maserati	87.861
1956	SC	Eugenio Castellotti	I	OSCA	87.562
1963	F1	Jim Clark	GB	Lotus 25-Climax	99.380

DINO FERRARI GRAND PRIX

year	formula	winner	nat	car	mph
1979	F1	Niki Lauda	A	Brabham BT48-Alfa Romeo	118.026

EUROPEAN FORMULA 3 RACE

year	formula	winner	nat	car	mph
1977	F3 E	Piercarlo Ghinzani	I	March 773-Toyota	101.789
1978	F3 E	Patrick Gaillard	F	Chevron B43-Toyota	103.190
1981	F3 E	Mauro Baldi	I	March 813-Alfa Romeo	101.749
1983	F3 E	Pierluigi Martini	I	Ralt RT3/83-Alfa Romeo	103.857
1986*	F3 E	Stefano Modena	I	Reynard 863-Alfa Romeo	85.602

*European F3 Cup

EUROPEAN FORMULA 2 RACE

year	formula	winner	nat	car	mph
1970	F2 E	Clay Regazzoni	CH	Tecno 70-Ford	115.331
1971	F2	Carlos Pace	BR	March 712M-Ford	115.040
1972	F2 E	John Surtees	GB	Surtees TS10-Ford	118.866

INTERNATIONAL FORMULA 3000 RACE

year	formula	winner	nat	car	mph
1986	F3000 INT	Pierluigi Martini	I	Ralt RT20-Cosworth	111.365
1987	F3000 INT	Stefano Modena	I	March 87B-Cosworth	113.507
1998	F3000 INT	Jason Watt	DK	Lola T96/50-Zytek	100.745
1999	F3000 INT	Nick Heidfeld	D	Lola B99/50-Zytek	107.992
2000	F3000 INT	Nicolas Minassian	F	Lola B99/50-Zytek	108.595
2001	F3000 INT	Mark Webber	AUS	Lola B99/50-Zytek	100.401
2002	F3000 INT	Sebastien Bourdais	F	Lola B2/50-Zytek	110.337

WORLD SPORTS CAR RACE

year	formula	winner	nat	car	mph
1974	SC W	Henri Pescarolo/Gerard Larrousse	F	Matra-Simca MS670C	99.975
1976	SC W	Jacky Ickx/Jochen Mass	B/D	Porsche 936	104.820
1977	SC W	Vittorio Brambilla	I	Alfa Romeo T33SC/12	105.121
1983	SC	Teo Fabi/Hans Heyer	I/D	Lancia LC2/83	99.639
1984	SC W	Stefan Bellof/Hans-Joachim Stuck	D	Porsche 956B	105.359

MISANO
Autodromo Santamonica

Set just inland from Rimini, the Autodromo Santamonica is the only privately owned circuit in Italy. It is a flat, counter-clockwise circuit that was a regular for Formula 2 until that series ended. Closer to San Marino than Imola, it held an F3 San Marino GP before Imola's World Championship event started. Misano now hosts national saloon car and Formula 3 rounds as well as Superbikes and Truck racing.

Active years	1972 to date
Location	12 miles south of Rimini
Type	Permanent road course
Website	www.misanocircuit.com
Lap distance	2.522 miles
Lap record	Race: Marco Apicella (Lola T96/50-Zytek), 1m24.971, 106.883 mph, F3000, 1999

Circuit changes

1972-92	2.167 miles
1993 to date	Curva del Rio extension built. Current circuit

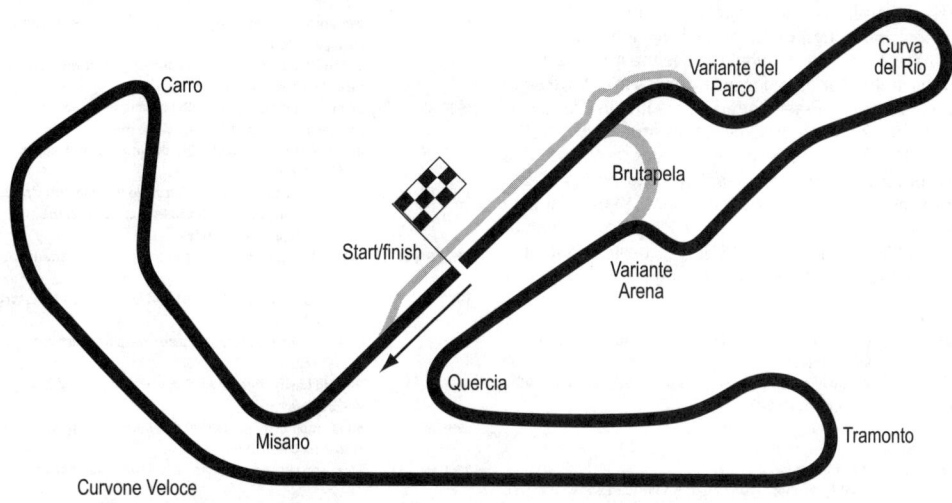

ADRIATIC GRAND PRIX/EUROPEAN FORMULA 2 RACE

year	formula	winner	nat	car	mph
1973	F2	Wilson Fittipaldi	BR	Brabham BT40-Ford	102.021
1975	F2	Maurizio Flammini	I	March 742-BMW	94.675
1976	F2	Hans-Joachim Stuck	D	March 762-BMW	104.742
1977	F2 E	Lamberto Leoni	I	Chevron B40-Ferrari	105.784
1978	F2 E	Bruno Giacomelli	I	March 782-BMW	105.777
1979	F2 E	Brian Henton	GB	Ralt RT2-Hart	104.738
1980	F2 E	Andrea de Cesaris	I	March 802-BMW	107.371
1981	F2 E	Michele Alboreto	I	Minardi FLY281-BMW	108.256
1982	F2 E	Corrado Fabi	I	March 822-BMW	99.480
1983	F2 E	Jonathan Palmer	GB	Ralt RH6/83-Honda	108.305
1984	F2 E	Mike Thackwell	NZ	Ralt RH6/84-Honda	110.474

EUROPEAN FORMULA 3 RACE

year	formula	winner	nat	car	mph
1980	F3 E	Mauro Baldi	I	Martini MK31-Toyota	100.742
1981	F3 E	Mauro Baldi	I	March 813-Alfa Romeo	87.162
1983	F3 E	Tommy Byrne	IRL	Ralt RT3/83-Toyota	101.984
1989*	F3 E	Gianni Morbidelli	I	Dallara 389-Alfa Romeo	104.265

*European F3 Cup

SAN MARINO F3 GRAND PRIX also see Imola

year	formula	winner	nat	car	mph
1978	F3	Teo Fabi	I	March 783-Toyota	100.920
1979	F3	Michele Alboreto	I	March 793-Toyota	96.650

WORLD SPORTS CAR RACE						
year	formula	winner	nat	car		mph
1978	SC W	Bob Wollek/Henri Pescarolo	F	Porsche 935		94.018

MONZA

Opened on 28 August 1922, the Autodromo Nazionale is among the most evocative and historic venues still in use. Set in a park in Monza, just north of Milan, it offered a fast, slipstreaming road course (now interrupted with chicanes) and a bumpy banked oval which has long been disused. Monza attracts what may be the most passionate fans in the world, and over the years they have seen some great races. Peter Gethin's 1971 Italian Grand Prix win was not only the quickest of all time, but also the closest. Similar slipstreaming classics resulted in a group of cars finishing as one both in 1967 and 1969. But Monza has also suffered more accidents than most venues; from Emilio Materassi and twenty-seven spectators in 1928 to marshal Paolo Ghislimberti in 2000, the list of fatalities is long and depressing.

Active years 1922 to date
Location On the northern outskirts of Monza, 10 miles north-west of Milan
Type Permanent road course and paved oval (now disused)
Website www.monzanet.it

Current circuit
Lap distance 3.599 miles
Lap records Qualifying: Juan Pablo Montoya (Williams FW24-BMW), 1m20.264, 161.423 mph, F1, 2002

Race: Rubens Barrichello (Ferrari F2002), 1m23.657, 154.876 mph, F1, 2002

Circuit changes
1922-33 Full Grand Prix circuit including both banked corners. 6.214 miles
1934 Temporary circuit using South banking and start/finish straight. 2.690 miles
1935-37 Grand Prix circuit and South banking used with temporary chicanes. 4.320 miles
1938-49 Grand Prix circuit and South banking used with a chicane only on the banking. 4.350 miles
1950-54 Grand Prix circuit used, without banking or chicanes. 3.915 miles
1955-56, 60-61 Parabolica built to replace Curva de Vedano, full circuit used incorporating the Grand Prix circuit and the banked circuit. 6.2137 miles
1957-59, 62-71 Grand Prix circuit used, without banking or chicanes. 3.573 miles
1972-75 Chicanes built after the start and at the Variante Ascari. 3.588 miles
1976-94 First chicane modified, Variante della Roggia built. 3.6039 miles
1994-95 Second Lesmo tightened, Curva Grande reprofiled. 3.625 miles
1996-99 Minor modifications to first and second (Roggia) chicanes. 3.585 miles
2000 to date First and second chicanes redesigned. Current circuit

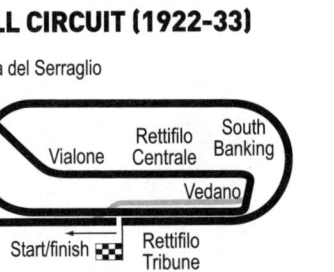

FULL CIRCUIT (1922-33)

Lesmo
Curva del Serraglio
Roggia
North Banking
Vialone
Rettifilo Centrale
South Banking
Vedano
Curva Grande
Start/finish
Rettifilo Tribune

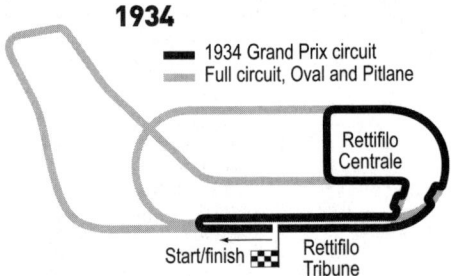

1934

■ 1934 Grand Prix circuit
■ Full circuit, Oval and Pitlane

Rettifilo Centrale
Start/finish
Rettifilo Tribune

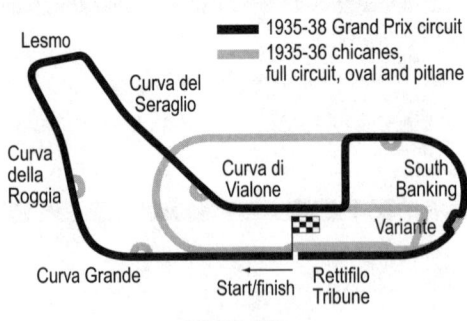

Lesmo
Curva del Serraglio
Curva della Roggia
Curva di Vialone
South Banking
Variante
Curva Grande
Start/finish
Rettifilo Tribune

■ 1935-38 Grand Prix circuit
■ 1935-36 chicanes, full circuit, oval and pitlane

1935-38

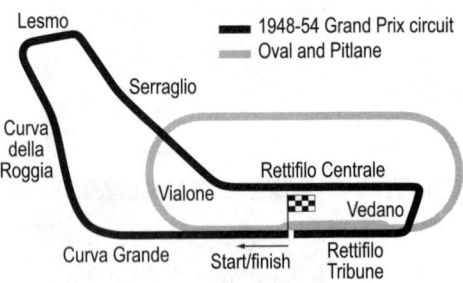

Lesmo
Serraglio
Curva della Roggia
Vialone
Rettifilo Centrale
Vedano
Curva Grande
Start/finish
Rettifilo Tribune

■ 1948-54 Grand Prix circuit
■ Oval and Pitlane

1948-54

1955-61 COMBINED

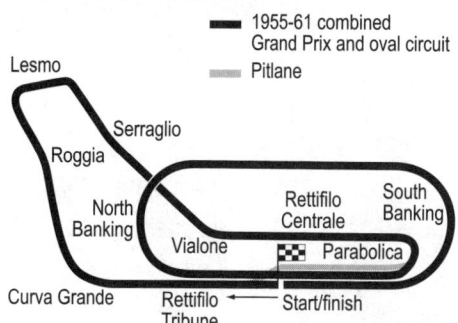

1957-71 GP CIRCUIT

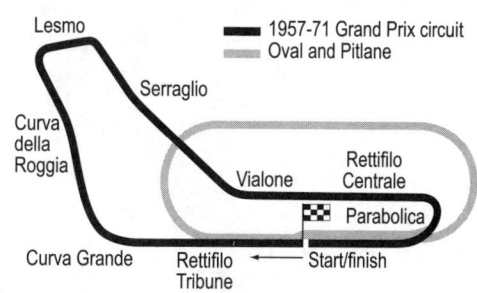

1972-99

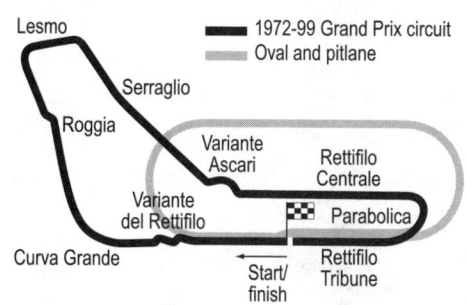

CURRENT GP CIRCUIT

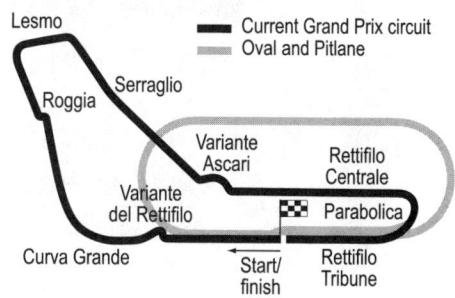

Italian Grand Prix see above

MONZA GRAND PRIX

year	formula	winner	nat	car	mph
1927	(h)	Zampieri	I	Amilcar	82.220
1929	GP	Achille Varzi	I	Alfa Romeo P2	116.647
1930	GP	Achille Varzi	I	Maserati 26M	93.477
1931	GP	Luigi Fagioli	I	Maserati 26M	96.618
1932	GP	Rudolf Caracciola	D	Alfa Romeo Tipo-B "P3"	110.871
1933	GP	Marcel Lehoux	DZ	Bugatti T51	110.368

AUTODROME GRAND PRIX

A non-championship race in which Fangio crashed, breaking his neck in 1952.

year	formula	winner	nat	car	mph
1948	F1	Jean-Pierre Wimille	F	Alfa Romeo 158	110.062
1949	F2	Juan Manuel Fangio	RA	Ferrari 166C	99.510
1950	F2	Luigi Villoresi	I	Ferrari 166/F2	101.540
1951	F2	Alberto Ascari	I	Ferrari 166/F2	101.830
1952	F2	Giuseppe Farina	I	Ferrari 500	109.480
1953	SC	Luigi Villoresi	I	Ferrari 250MM	109.280

MONZA GRAND PRIX FORMULA 2 RACE

year	formula	winner	nat	car	mph
1980	F2	Derek Warwick	GB	Toleman TG280B-Hart	123.967

MONZA LOTTERY GRAND PRIX

year	formula	winner	nat	car	mph
1959	GT	Alfonso Thiele	USA	Ferrari 250GT	97.840
1960	FJ	Colin Davis	GB	OSCA-Fiat	104.660
1961	FJ	Tony Maggs	ZA	Cooper-BMC	106.300
1962	FJ	Peter Arundell	GB	Lotus 22-Ford	113.460
1963	FJ	Jacques Maglia	F	Lotus 27-Ford	113.750
1964	F3	Geki Russo	I	de Sanctis-Ford	99.696
1965	F3	Picko Troberg	S	Brabham-Ford	114.200
1966	F3	Jonathan Williams	GB	de Sanctis-Ford	114.280
1967	F3	Jonathan Williams	GB	de Sanctis-Ford	88.968
1968	F2	Jonathan Williams	GB	Brabham BT23C-Ford	130.078
1969	F2	Robin Widdows	GB	Brabham BT23C-Ford	133.869
1970	F5000	Mike Walker	GB	McLaren M10B-Chevrolet	140.343
1971	F2	Dieter Quester	A	March 712M-BMW	135.550
1972	F2	Graham Hill	GB	Brabham BT38-Ford	137.181
1973	F2 E	Roger Williamson	GB	March 732-BMW	124.110
1974	F3	Alessandro Pesenti-Rossi	I	GRD 374-Ford	113.760
1975	F3 E	Larry Perkins	AUS	Ralt RT1-Ford	116.799
1976	F3 E	Riccardo Patrese	I	Chevron B34-Toyota	112.524
1977	F3 E	Elio de Angelis	I	Ralt RT1-Toyota	113.476
1978	F3 E	Jan Lammers	NL	Ralt RT1-Toyota	94.510
1979	F3 E	Mike Thackwell	NZ	March 793-Toyota	114.082
1980	F3 E	Michele Alboreto	I	March 803-Alfa Romeo	113.443
1981	F3	Eddy Bianchi	I	Martini MK34-Alfa Romeo	97.213
1982	F3 E	Oscar Larrauri	RA	Euroracing 101-Alfa Romeo	115.625
1983	F3 E	John Nielsen	DK	Ralt RT3/83-Volkswagen	116.290
1984	F3 E	Gerhard Berger	A	Ralt RT3/84-Alfa Romeo	115.723
1985	F3	Franco Forini	CH	Dallara 385-Volkswagen	117.080
1986	F3	Nicola Larini	I	Dallara 386-Alfa Romeo	115.740
1987	F3	Enrico Bertaggia	I	Dallara 387-Alfa Romeo	116.280
1988	F3	Rinaldo Capello	I	Dallara 388-Alfa Romeo	116.170
1989	F3	Gianni Morbidelli	I	Dallara 389-Alfa Romeo	118.270
1990	F3	Mauro Martini	I	Dallara 390-Alfa Romeo	116.880
1991	F3	Luca Badoer	I	Dallara 391-Alfa Romeo	120.821
1992	F3	Vincenzo Sospiri	I	Dallara 392-Mugen	119.057
1993	F3	Giancarlo Fisichella	I	Dallara 393-Fiat	119.018
1994*	F3	Luca Rangoni	I	Dallara 393-Fiat	119.850
	F3	Luca Riccitelli	I	Dallara 393-Fiat	120.170
1995*	F3	Andrea Boldrini	I	Dallara 395-Fiat	119.002
	F3	Andrea Boldrini	I	Dallara 395-Fiat	118.611
1996	F3	Andrea Boldrini	I	Dallara 396-Opel	117.895
1997	F3	Niki Cadei	I	Dallara 396-Fiat	115.045
1998	F3	Maurizio Mediani	I	Dallara 396-Alfa Romeo	120.716
1999*	F3	Peter Sundberg	S	Dallara 399-Opel	121.127
	F3	Peter Sundberg	S	Dallara 399-Opel	120.688
2000	F3	Valerio Scassellati	I	Dallara 300-Opel	118.028
2001	F3000	Felipe Massa	BR	Lola T96/50-Zytek	121.853
2002	F3000	Romain Dumas	F	Lola T99/50-Zytek	121.669

1980 race was originally to be a British F1 Championship event but not enough entries were received. *Run as two heats without an aggregate winner

RACE OF TWO WORLDS/MONZA 500

year	formula	winner	nat	car	mph
1957	USAC/SC	Jimmy Bryan	USA	Kuzma-Offenhauser	160.060
1958	USAC/SC	Jim Rathmann	USA	Watson-Offenhauser	166.720

INTERNATIONAL FORMULA 3000 RACE

year	formula	winner	nat	car	mph
1988	F3000 INT	Roberto Moreno	BR	Reynard 88D-Cosworth	129.717
1990	F3000 INT	Erik Comas	F	Lola T90/50-Mugen	132.902
2001	F3000 INT	Giorgio Pantano	I	Lola B99/50-Zytek	117.847
2002	F3000 INT	Bjorn Wirdheim	S	Lola B2/50-Zytek	124.879

FILIPPO CARACCIOLO TROPHY/MONZA 1000 KMS

year	formula	winner	nat	car	mph
1965	SC W	Michael Parkes/Jean Guichet	GB/F	Ferrari 275P2	125.897
1966	SC W	John Surtees/Michael Parkes	GB	Ferrari 330P3	102.089
1967	SC W	Chris Amon/Lorenzo Bandini	NZ/I	Ferrari 330P4	121.158
1968	SC W	Paul Hawkins/David Hobbs	AUS/GB	Ford GT40	117.219
1969	SC W	Jo Siffert/Brian Redman	CH/GB	Porsche 908/8	126.945
1970	SC W	Pedro Rodriguez/Leo Kinnunen	MEX/SF	Porsche 917	144.566
1971	SC W	Pedro Rodriguez/Jackie Oliver	MEX/GB	Porsche 917K	147.387
1972	SC W	Jacky Ickx/Clay Regazzoni	B/CH	Ferrari 312P	105.944
1973	SC W	Jacky Ickx/Brian Redman	B/GB	Ferrari 312P	150.671
1974	SC W	Arturo Merzario/Mario Andretti	I/USA	Alfa Romeo T33TT/12	130.896
1975	SC W	Arturo Merzario/Jacques Laffite	I/F	Alfa Romeo T33TT/12	132.341
1976	SC W	Jacky Ickx/Jochen Mass	B/D	Porsche 936	136.610
1977	SC W	Vittorio Brambilla	I	Alfa Romeo T33SC/12	114.803
1978	SC E	Reinhold Joest	D	Porsche 908/3	106.865
1979	SC	Renzo Zorzi/Marco Capoferri	I	Lola T286-Ford	107.674
1980	SC W	Alain de Cadenet/Desire Wilson	GB/ZA	De Cadenet LM-Ford	109.570
1981	SC W	Edgar Doren/Jurgen Laessig/Gerhard Holup	D	Porsche 935	94.989
1982	SC W	Henri Pescarolo/Giorgio Francia/			
		Jean Rondeau	F/I/F	Rondeau M382C-Ford	112.023
1983	SC W	Bob Wollek/Thierry Boutsen	F/B	Porsche 956	119.855
1984	SC W	Derek Bell/Stefan Bellof	GB/D	Porsche 956	122.146
1985	SC W	Manfred Winkelhock/Marc Surer	D/CH	Porsche 962C	121.951
1986	SC W	Hans-Joachim Stuck/Derek Bell	D/GB	Porsche 962C	125.357
1987	SC W	Jan Lammers/John Watson	NL/GB	Jaguar XJR-8	123.085
1988	SC W	Martin Brundle/Eddie Cheever	GB/USA	Jaguar XJR-9	128.012
1990	SC W	Mauro Baldi/Jean-Louis Schlesser	I/F	Mercedes-Benz C11	130.816
1991	SC W	Martin Brundle/Derek Warwick	GB	Jaguar XJR-14	129.003
1992	SC W	Geoff Lees/Hitoshi Ogawa	GB/J	Toyota TS010	137.607
1997	SC/GT	Thomas Bscher/John Nielsen	D/DK	Kremer K8-Porsche	112.158
1998	SC/GT	Geoff Lees/Thomas Bscher	GB/D	McLaren F1 GTR-BMW	121.510
1999*	SC FIA	Emmanuel Collard/Vincenzo Sospiri	F/I	Ferrari 333SP	123.726
2000*	SC FIA	Mauro Baldi/Gary Formato	I/ZA	Riley & Scott MkIII-Judd	115.138
2001#	SC FIA	Giovanni Lavaggi/Christian Vann	I/GB	Ferrari 333SP-Judd	117.818

*500km, #380km

FIA GT RACE

year	formula	winner	nat	car	mph
1995	GT INT	Thomas Bscher/John Nielsen	D/DK	McLaren F1 GTR-BMW	111.925
1996	GT INT	Thomas Bscher/John Nielsen	D/DK	McLaren F1 GTR-BMW	113.705
1999	GT INT	Olivier Beretta/Karl Wendlinger	MC/A	Chrysler Viper GTS-R	115.377
2000	GT INT	David Hart/Mike Hezemans	NL	Chrysler Viper GTS-R	114.499
2001	GT INT	Jamie Campbell-Walter/Tom Coronel	GB/NL	Lister Storm GT	114.625

MUGELLO

Autodromo Mugello

This area of Tuscany had a long racing history before the modern circuit was opened. The Mille Miglia passed through here on open roads that included the famed Futa Pass, and these roads were also used for the 41.135-mile Circuit of Mugello, a sports car race that ran from 1920 to 1969. Five years after the final event a modern circuit was built in a valley near Barberino di Mugello at the southwestern end of the course. The Autodromo Mugello is a spectacular F1-standard facility, but it is underused for cars now that F3000 and Sports Cars no longer visit. It does currently hold the motorcycle Grand Prix and has often been used for F1 testing since Ferrari acquired it in 1988.

Active years	1974 to date
Location	14 miles north of Florence, 50 miles south of Bologna, 80 miles north-east of Pisa
Type	Permanent road course
Website	www.mugellocircuit.it
Lap distance	3.259 miles
Lap record	Qualifying: Alessandro Zanardi (Reynard 91D-Mugen), 1m35.096, 123.375 mph, F3000, 1991
	Race: Alessandro Zanardi (Reynard 91D-Mugen), 1m38.367, 119.274 mph, F3000, 1991

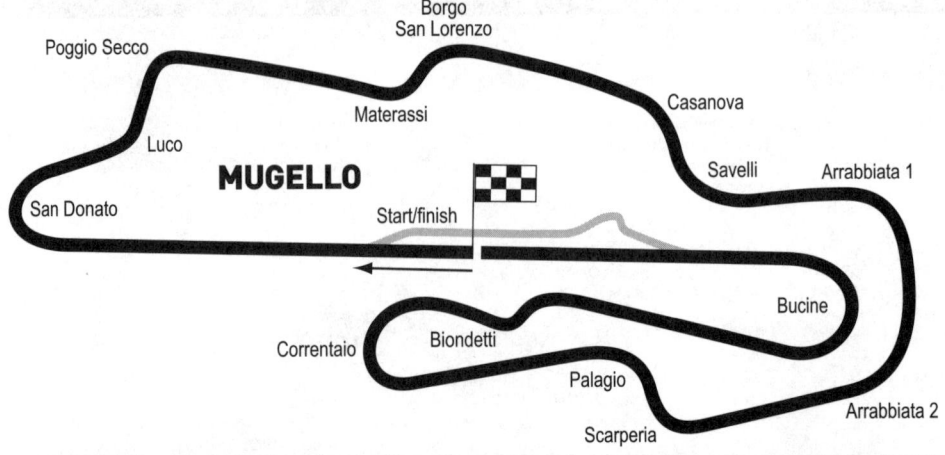

MUGELLO CIRCUIT

year	formula	winner	nat	car	mph
1920	FL	Giuseppe Campari	I	Alfa Romeo 40/60	37.621
1921	FL	Giuseppe Campari	I	Alfa Romeo 40/60	38.696
1922	FL	Alfieri Maserati	I	Isotta-Fraschini	41.750
1923	FL	Gastone Brilli-Peri	I	Steyr VI Klausen	41.423
1924	FL	Giuseppe Morandi	I	OM 665	40.627
1925	FL	Emilio Materassi	I	Itala Special 4.7	43.259
1926#	FL	Emilio Materassi	I	Itala Special 4.7	73.013
1928	GP	Emilio Materassi	I	Talbot T700	43.968
1929	GP	Gastone Brilli-Peri	I	Talbot T700	44.525
1955*	SC	Umberto Maglioli	I	Ferrari	66.650
1964	GT	Gianni Bulgari	I	Porsche 904	65.650
1965	GT	Antonio Nicodemi/Mario Casoni	I	Ferrari 250LM	66.020
1966	SC	Gerhard Koch/Jochen Neerpasch	D	Porsche 906 Carrera 6	66.717
1967	SC	Gerhard Mitter/Udo Schutz	D	Porsche 910/8	76.241
1968	SC	Lucien Bianchi/Nino Vaccarella/Nanni Galli	B/I/I	Alfa Romeo T33	75.154
1969	SC	Arturo Merzario	I	Abarth 2000	77.647

*officially known as Targa Mugello. On the Circuit of Mugello except #at Cascine

MUGELLO GRAND PRIX

year	formula	winner	nat	car	mph
1974	F2 E	Patrick Depailler	F	March 742-BMW	105.386
1975	F2 E	Maurizio Flammini	I	March 742-BMW	103.530
1976	F2 E	Jean-Pierre Jabouille	F	Elf 2J-Renault	105.790
1977	F2 E	Bruno Giacomelli	I	March 772P-BMW	107.203
1978	F2 E	Derek Daly	IRL	Chevron B42-Hart	108.545
1979	F2 E	Brian Henton	GB	Ralt RT2-Hart	108.375
1980	F2 E	Brian Henton	GB	Toleman TG280B-Hart	108.955
1981	F2 E	Corrado Fabi	I	March 812-BMW	108.994
1982	F2 E	Corrado Fabi	I	March 822-BMW	110.169
1983	F2 E	Jonathan Palmer	GB	Ralt RH6/83-Honda	109.542
1984	F2 E	Mike Thackwell	NZ	Ralt RH6/84-Honda	111.512
1986	F3000 INT	Pierluigi Martini	I	Ralt RT20-Cosworth	104.940
1991	F3000 INT	Alessandro Zanardi	I	Reynard 91D-Mugen	117.684
1996	F3000 INT	Ricardo Zonta	BR	Lola T96/50-Zytek	113.031
1997	F3000 INT	Ricardo Zonta	BR	Lola T96/50-Zytek	113.259

EUROPEAN FORMULA 3 RACE

year	formula	winner	nat	car	mph
1980	F3 E	Corrado Fabi	I	March 803-Alfa Romeo	101.170
1981	F3 E	Emanuele Pirro	I	Martini MK34-Toyota	102.792
1982	F3 E	Oscar Larrauri	RA	Euroracing 101-Alfa Romeo	102.980
1984	F3 E	Ivan Capelli	I	Martini MK42-Alfa Romeo	104.569

WORLD SPORTS CAR RACE

year	formula	winner	nat	car	mph
1975	SC W	Gerard Larrousse/Jean-Pierre Jabouille	F	Alpine A442-Renault	101.993
1976	SC W	Jacky Ickx/Jochen Mass	B/D	Porsche 935	94.277
1977	SC W	Rolf Stommelen/Manfred Schurti	D/FL	Porsche 935	87.399
1978	SC W	Toine Hezemans/John Fitzpatrick/Hans Heyer	NL/GB/D	Porsche 935	95.116
1979	SC W	John Fitzpatrick/Manfred Schurti/Bob Wollek	GB/FL/F	Porsche 935	85.450
1980	SC W	Riccardo Patrese/Eddie Cheever	I/USA	Lancia Beta Monte Carlo	95.840
1981	SC W	Lella Lombardi/Giorgio Francia	I	Osella PA9-BMW	96.031
1982	SC W	Michele Alboreto/Piercarlo Ghinzani	I	Lancia LC1	98.630
1983	SC	Bob Wollek/Stefan Johansson	F/S	Porsche 956	101.571
1985	SC W	Jacky Ickx/Jochen Mass	B/D	Porsche 956C	103.239

FIA GT RACE

year	formula	winner	nat	car	mph
1997	GT FIA	JJ Lehto/Steve Soper	SF/GB	McLaren F1 GTR-BMW	106.570

PESCARA

Pescara was a magnificent road course, the longest ever to hold a World Championship Formula 1 race. It featured two 4-mile straights, with the opening 8 miles of the lap climbing and twisting through the villages inland from the town. The return leg includes "the flying kilometre" where top speeds were measured; it was here that Guy Moll was killed in 1934. Pescara came complete with level crossings and barely guarded corners. Cancellation of races in 1957 elevated the Pescara GP to World Championship status, which was won by Stirling Moss' Vanwall. When it closed in the early sixties, the circuit and its facilities had changed little in the forty years since Enzo Ferrari's inaugural victory.

Active years	1924–61
Location	The Abruzzi region on Italy's Adriatic coast
Type	Temporary road course
Lap distance	16.032 miles
Lap record	Qualifying: Juan Manuel Fangio (Maserati 250F), 9m44.6, 98.726 mph, F1, 1957
	Race: Stirling Moss (Vanwall VW5), 9m44.6, 98.726 mph, F1, 1957

Circuit changes

1924–33	15.894 miles
1934–61	Chicane built before the pits. 16.032 miles

COPPA ACERBO/PESCARA GRAND PRIX

year	formula	winner	nat	car	mph
1924	FL	Enzo Ferrari	I	Alfa Romeo RL	65.055
1925	FL	Guido Ginaldi	I	Alfa Romeo RL	58.073
1926	FL	Luigi Spinozzi	I	Bugatti T35	63.007
1927	FL	Giuseppe Campari	I	Alfa Romeo P2	64.961
1928	GP	Giuseppe Campari	I	Alfa Romeo P2	68.453
1930	GP	Achille Varzi	I	Maserati 26M	75.604
1931	GP	Giuseppe Campari	I	Alfa Romeo Tipo-A	81.912
1932	GP	Tazio Nuvolari	I	Alfa Romeo Tipo-B "P3"	87.148
1933	GP	Luigi Fagioli	I	Alfa Romeo Tipo-B "P3"	88.601
1934	GP	Luigi Fagioli	I	Mercedes-Benz W25A	80.513
1935	GP	Achille Varzi	I	Auto Union B	85.979
1936	GP	Bernd Rosemeyer	D	Auto Union C	86.483
1937	GP	Bernd Rosemeyer	D	Auto Union C	87.621
1938	GP	Rudolf Caracciola	D	Mercedes-Benz W154	83.754
1939	V	Clemente Biondetti	I	Alfa Romeo 158	83.310
1947	SC	Vincenzo Auricchio	I	Stanguellini-Fiat	72.190
1948	SC	Alberto Ascari/Giovanni Bracco	I	Maserati	83.260
1949	SC	Franco Rol	I	Alfa Romeo	75.200
1950	F1	Juan Manuel Fangio	RA	Alfa Romeo 158	84.168
1951	F1	Jose Froilan Gonzalez	RA	Ferrari 375	85.506
1952	SC	Giovanni Bracco/Paolo Marzotto	I	Ferrari 340MM	79.730
1953	SC	Mike Hawthorn/Umberto Maglioli	GB/I	Ferrari 375MM	79.830
1954	F1	Luigi Musso	I	Maserati 250F	87.493
1956	SC	Robert Manzon	F	Gordini	82.880
1957	F1 W	Stirling Moss	GB	Vanwall VW5	96.525
1960	FJ	Denny Hulme	NZ	Cooper-BMC	84.110
1961*	SC W	Lorenzo Bandini/Giorgio Scarlatti	I	Ferrari 250TR	88.176

*Pescara 4 hours. Known as Coppa Acerbo before World War II

VALLELUNGA

Originally a tiny oval, Vallelunga was extended with a loop through a newly blasted cutting in 1967 and further modernised in 1971. The highlight was the Rome Grand Prix, which eventually became a F2 and then F3000 round. But the circuit fell into dispute with the FIA and slipped from the calendar in the nineties. Vallelunga returned to the international scene with a round of the European Le Mans Series in 2001, but the race attracted a small field of cars and few spectators.

Active years 1961 to date
Location North of Campagnano di Roma, 20 miles north of Rome

Type Permanent road course
Website www.vallelunga.it

Current circuit
Lap distance 1.988 miles
Lap record Qualifying: Christian Fittipaldi (Reynard 91D-Mugen), 1m03.236, 113.176 mph, F3000, 1991
Race: Alessandro Zanardi (Reynard 91D-Mugen), 1m04.939, 110.208 mph, F3000, 1991

Circuit changes
1961-66 Oval. 1.102 miles
1967 to date Extension to Curva Cimini and infield built. Circuit also refurbished in 1971. Current circuit

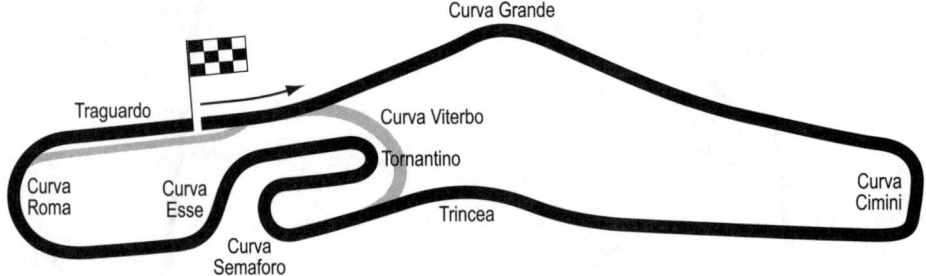

Italy

ROME GRAND PRIX

year	formula	winner	nat	car	mph
1925*	FL	Carlo Masetti	I	Bugatti T35	60.594
1926#	FL	Aymo Maggi	I	Bugatti T35	61.648
1927	FL	Tazio Nuvolari	I	Bugatti T35	68.840
1928~	GP	Louis Chiron	MC	Bugatti T35C	78.274
1929~	GP	Achille Varzi	I	Alfa Romeo P2	79.402
1930~	GP	Luigi Arcangeli	I	Maserati 26M	83.135
1931^	GP	Ernesto Maserati	I	Maserati V4	91.393
1932^	GP	Luigi Fagioli	I	Maserati V5	95.203
1947→	F1	Franco Cortese	I	Ferrari 125	54.990
1949→	F2	Luigi Villoresi	I	Ferrari 166/F2	62.550
1950→	F2	Alberto Ascari	I	Ferrari 166/F2	62.320
1951→	F2	Mario Raffaeli	I	Ferrari 166/F2	61.200
1954+	F1	Onofre Marimon	RA	Maserati 250F	106.198
1956+	SC	Jean Behra	F	Maserati 300S	103.170
1963	F1	Bob Anderson	RSR	Lola Mk4-Climax	77.874
1964	F2	Jo Schlesser	F	Brabham BT10-Ford	85.370
1965	F2	Richard Attwood	GB	Lola T60-Ford	81.790
1966	F3	Tino Brambilla	I	Brabham BT16-Ford	79.930
1967	F2 E	Jacky Ickx	B	Matra MS7-Ford	88.945
1968	F2 E	Tino Brambilla	I	Ferrari Dino 166	92.604
1969	F2 E	Johnny Servoz-Gavin	F	Matra MS7-Ford	92.894
1971	F2 E	Ronnie Peterson	S	March 712M-Ford	97.330
1973	F2 E	Jacques Coulon	F	March 732-BMW	98.617
1974	F2 E	Patrick Depailler	F	March 742-BMW	100.829
1975	F2 E	Vittorio Brambilla	I	March 752-BMW	96.925
1976	F2 E	Jean-Pierre Jabouille	F	Elf 2J-Renault	99.334
1977	F2 E	Bruno Giacomelli	I	March 772P-BMW	100.748
1978	F2 E	Derek Daly	IRL	Chevron B42-Hart	100.426
1979	F2 E	Marc Surer	CH	March 792-BMW	101.241
1980	F2 E	Brian Henton	GB	Toleman TG280-Hart	102.103
1981	F2 E	Eje Elgh	S	Maurer MM81-BMW	101.990
1982	F2 E	Corrado Fabi	I	March 822-BMW	102.343
1983	F2 E	Beppe Gabbiani	I	March 832-BMW	103.385
1984	F2 E	Mike Thackwell	NZ	Ralt RH6/84-Honda	102.029
1985	F3000 INT	Emanuele Pirro	I	March 85B-Cosworth	103.036
1986	F3000 INT	Ivan Capelli	I	March 86B-Cosworth	102.601
1987	F3000 INT	Stefano Modena	I	March 87B-Cosworth	103.791
1988	F3000 INT	Gregor Foitek	CH	Lola T88/50-Cosworth	101.782
1989	F3000 INT	Fabrizio Giovanardi	I	Leyton March 89B-Judd	104.541
1991	F3000 INT	Alessandro Zanardi	I	Reynard 91D-Mugen	108.295

At Vallelunga except at *Monte Mario, #Valle Guila, Parioli, ~Tre Fontana, ^Littorio, →Terme di Caracalla, +Castel Fusano

MANDUNINA GRAND PRIX

year	formula	winner	nat	car	mph
1971	F2 E	Mike Beuttler	GB	March 712M-Ford	97.136

COPPA ITALIA

year	formula	winner	nat	car	mph
1961	F1	Giancarlo Baghetti	I	Porsche 718	65.145

ITALIAN REPUBLIC GRAND PRIX

year	formula	winner	nat	car	mph
1972	F1	Emerson Fittipaldi	BR	Lotus 72D-Ford	97.839

EUROPEAN FORMULA 3 RACE

year	formula	winner	nat	car	mph
1976	F3 E	Gianfranco Brancatelli	I	March 763-Toyota	93.691
1977	F3 E	Oscar Pedersoli	I	Ralt RT1-Toyota	94.230
1978	F3 E	Teo Fabi	I	March 783-Toyota	95.659
1979	F3 E	Piercarlo Ghinzani	I	March 793-Alfa Romeo	95.095
1981	F3 E	Mauro Baldi	I	March 813-Alfa Romeo	n/a
1983	F3 E	Emanuele Pirro	I	Ralt RT3/83-Alfa Romeo	96.920

WORLD SPORTS CAR RACE

year	formula	winner	nat	car	mph
1973	SC W	Henri Pescarolo/Gerard Larrousse/			
		Francois Cevert	F	Matra-Simca MS670	96.087
1976	SC W	Jacky Ickx/Jochen Mass	B/D	Porsche 935	89.129
1977	SC WSC	Vittorio Brambilla	I	Alfa Romeo T33SC/12	95.402
	SC W	Luigi Moreschi/"Dino"	I	Porsche 935	82.475
1978	SC	Reinhold Joest/Mario Casoni	D/I	Porsche 908/3	92.568
	SC W	Bob Wollek/Henri Pescarolo	F	Porsche 935	88.219
1979	SC W	Lella Lombardi/Giorgio Francia	I	Osella PA7-BMW	87.742
1980	SC W	Giorgio Francia/Roberto Marazzi	I	Osella PA8-BMW	89.487

FIA GT RACE

year	formula	winner	nat	car	mph
1994	GT FIA	Luciano della Noce/Anders Olofsson	I/S	Ferrari F40	88.050

JAPAN

Major Championships

ALL-JAPAN FORMULA NIPPON CHAMPIONSHIP (FORMERLY FORMULA 2000, FORMULA 2 AND FORMULA 3000)

year	formula	driver	nat	team	car
1973	F2000	Motoharu Kurosawa	J	Heroes Racing	March 722-BMW
1974	F2000	Noritake Takahara	J	Takahara Racing	March 742-BMW
1975	F2000	Kazuyoshi Hoshino	J	Heroes Racing	March 742-BMW
1976	F2000	Noritake Takahara	J	Takahara Racing	Nova 512-BMW
1977	F2000	Kazuyoshi Hoshino	J	Heroes Racing	Nova 512B-BMW/Nova 532P-BMW
1978	F2	Kazuyoshi Hoshino	J	Heroes Racing	Nova 532-BMW/Nova 522-BMW
1979	F2	Keiji Matsumoto	J	Le Mans Company	March 782-BMW/March 792-BMW
1980	F2	Masahiro Hasemi	J	Nova Engineering	March 802-BMW
1981	F2	Satoru Nakajima	J	I&I	Ralt RH6/80-Honda/March 812-Honda
1982	F2	Satoru Nakajima	J	Team Ikuzawa	March 812-Honda/March 822-Honda
1983	F2	Geoff Lees	GB	Team Ikuzawa	Spirit 201-Honda/March 832-Honda
1984	F2	Satoru Nakajima	J	Heroes Racing	March 842-Honda
1985	F2	Satoru Nakajima	J	Heroes Racing	March 85J-Honda
1986	F2	Satoru Nakajima	J	Heroes Racing	March 86J-Honda
1987	F3000	Kazuyoshi Hoshino	J	Leyton House	March 87B-Honda/Lola T87/50-Honda
1988	F3000	Aguri Suzuki	J	Footwork Formula	Mooncraft 030-Yamaha/
					March 87B-Yamaha/Reynard 88D-Yamaha
1989	F3000	Hitoshi Ogawa	J	Stellar International	Lola T88/50-Mugen/Lola T89/50-Mugen
1990	F3000	Kazuyoshi Hoshino	J	Heroes Racing	Lola T90/50-Mugen
1991	F3000	Ukyo Katayama	J	Heroes Racing	Lola T91/50-Cosworth/
					Lola T90/50-Cosworth
1992	F3000	Mauro Martini	I	Nova Engineering	Lola T92/50-Mugen
1993	F3000	Kazuyoshi Hoshino	J	Hoshino Racing Team	Lola T92/50-Cosworth
1994	F3000	Marco Apicella	I	Dome	Dome MF104-Mugen
1995	F3000	Toshio Suzuki	J	Hoshino Racing Team	Lola T94/50-Mugen
1996	Nippon	Ralf Schumacher	D	Le Mans Company	Reynard 96D-Mugen
1997	Nippon	Pedro de la Rosa	E	Nova Engineering	Lola T97/51-Mugen
1998	Nippon	Satoshi Motoyama	J	Le Mans Company	Reynard 97D-Mugen
1999	Nippon	Tom Coronel	NL	Nakajima Racing	Reynard 99L-Mugen
2000	Nippon	Toranosuke Takagi	J	Nakajima Racing	Reynard 2KL-Mugen
2001	Nippon	Satoshi Motoyama	J	Hoshino Racing Team	Reynard 01L-Mugen
2002	Nippon	Ralph Firman Jr	GB	Nakajima Racing	Reynard 01L-Mugen

ALL-JAPAN SPORTS-PROTOTYPE CHAMPIONSHIP

year	driver	nat	team	car
1983	Vern Schuppan/Naohiro Fujita	AUS/J	Trust Racing	Porsche 956
1984	Naoki Nagasaka/Keiichi Suzuki	J	Auto Beaurex	Lotec M1C-BMW
1985	Kunimitsu Takahashi/Kenji Takahashi	J	Alpha Racing Team	Porsche 962C
1986	Kunimitsu Takahashi/Kenji Takahashi	J	Alpha Racing Team	Porsche 962C
1987	Kunimitsu Takahashi/Kenneth Acheson	J/GB	Alpha Racing Team	Porsche 962C
1988	Stanley Dickens/Hideki Okada	S/J	From A Racing	Porsche 962C
1989	Kunimitsu Takahashi/Stanley Dickens	J/S	Alpha Racing Team	Porsche 962C
1990	Masahiro Hasemi/Anders Olofsson	J/S	NISMO	Nissan R90CP
1991	Kazuyoshi Hoshino/Toshio Suzuki	J	NISMO	Nissan R91CP
1992	Kazuyoshi Hoshino/Toshio Suzuki	J	NISMO	Nissan R92CP

Championship officially decided by the driver who leads the greatest distance in the winning car – both drivers are included, the first of which was official champion

ALL-JAPAN GT CHAMPIONSHIP

year	driver	nat	team	car
1993	Masahiko Kageyama	J	NISMO	Nissan Skyline GT-R
1994	Masahiko Kageyama	J	NISMO	Nissan Skyline GT-R
1995	Masahiko Kageyama	J	NISMO	Nissan Skyline GT-R
1996	David Brabham/John Nielsen	AUS/DK	Lark	McLaren F1-GTR-BMW
1997	Pedro de la Rosa/Michael Krumm	E/D	TOM's	Toyota Supra
1998	Erik Comas/Masami Kageyama	F/J	NISMO	Nissan Skyline GT-R
1999	Erik Comas	F	NISMO	Nissan Skyline GT-R
2000	Ryo Michigami	J	Dome Project	Mugen Honda NSX
2001	Hironori Takeuchi/Yuji Tachikawa	J	Cerumo	Toyota Supra
2002	Juichi Wakisaka/Akira Iida	J	Toyota Team Le Mans	Toyota Supra

ALL-JAPAN TOURING CAR CHAMPIONSHIP

year	driver	nat	team	car
1985	Naoki Nagasaka/Kazuo Mogi	J	Auto Beaureaux	BMW 635CSi
1986	Aguri Suzuki/Takao Wada	J	NISMO	Nissan Skyline RS
1987	Naoki Nagasaki	J	Object T	Ford Sierra RS/Ford Sierra RS500
1988	Hisashi Yokoshima	J	Object T	Ford Sierra RS500
1989	Masahiro Hasemi/Anders Olofsson	J/S	Hasemi Motorsport	Nissan Skyline GT-R
1990	Kazuyoshi Hoshino/Toshio Suzuki	J	NISMO	Nissan Skyline GT-R
1991	Masahiro Hasemi/Anders Olofsson	J/S	Hasemi Motorsport	Nissan Skyline GT-R
1992	Hideo Fukuyama/Masahiro Hasemi	J	NISMO	Nissan Skyline GT-R
1993	Masahiko Kageyama	J	Hoshino Racing	Nissan Skyline GT-R
1994	Masanori Sekiya	J	TOM's	Toyota Corona E
1995	Steve Soper	GB	Schnitzer	BMW 318i
1996	Naoki Hattori	J	JACCS Mooncraft	Honda Accord
1997	Osamu Nakako	J	Team Mugen Honda	Honda Accord
1998	Masanori Sekiya	J	TOM's	Toyota Chaser

ALL-JAPAN F3 CHAMPIONSHIP

year	driver	nat	team	car
1979	Toshio Suzuki	J	Heroes Racing	Ralt RT1-Toyota
1980	Shuroko Sasaki	J	Shuroko Sasaki	March 793-Toyota/March 803-Toyota
1981	Osamu Nakako	J	Hayashi Racing	Hayashi 320-Toyota
1982	Kengo Nakamoto	J	Hayashi Racing	Ralt RT3-Toyota
1983	Yoshimasa Fujiwara	J	Umeda Racing	Ralt RT3-Toyota
1984	Shuji Hyoudo	J	Hayashi Racing	Hayashi 322-Toyota
1985	Kohji Satoh	J	Le Garage Cox	Ralt RT30-Volkswagen
1986	Akio Morimoto	J	Le Mans Company	Ralt RT30-Toyota
1987	Ross Cheever	USA	Funaki Racing Team	Reynard 873-Toyota
1988	Akihiko Nakaya	J	Le Garage Cox	Ralt RT32-Mugen
1989	Masahiko Kageyama	J	Leyton House	Ralt RT33-Mugen
1990	Naoki Hattori	J	Le Garage Cox	Ralt RT34-Mugen
1991	Paulo Carcasci	BR	TOM's	TOM's 031F-Toyota
1992	Anthony Reid	GB	Tomei Sport	Ralt RT35-Mugen
1993	Tom Kristensen	DK	TOM's	TOM's 033F-Toyota
1994	Michael Krumm	D	TOM's	TOM's 034F-Toyota
1995	Pedro de la Rosa	E	TOM's	Dallara 395-Toyota
1996	Juichi Wakisaka	J	Anabuki	Dallara 396-Mugen
1997	Tom Coronel	NL	TOM's	Dallara 397-Toyota
1998	Peter Dumbreck	GB	TOM's	Dallara 398-Toyota
1999	Darren Manning	GB	TOM's	Dallara 399-Toyota
2000	Sebastien Philippe	F	Dome Project	Dallara 300-Mugen
2001	Benoit Treluyer	F	Dome Project	Dallara 301-Mugen
2002	Takashi Kogure	J	Dome Project	Dallara 302-Mugen

Major International Races

JAPANESE GRAND PRIX

year	formula	circuit	winner	nat	car	mph
1976	F1 W	Fuji	Mario Andretti	USA	Lotus 77-Ford	114.111
1977	F1 W	Fuji	James Hunt	GB	McLaren M26-Ford	129.167
1987	F1 W	Suzuka	Gerhard Berger	A	Ferrari F187	119.842
1988	F1 W	Suzuka	Ayrton Senna	BR	McLaren MP4/4-Honda	119.241
1989	F1 W	Suzuka	Alessandro Nannini	I	Benetton B189-Ford	121.744
1990	F1 W	Suzuka	Nelson Piquet	BR	Benetton B190-Ford	122.375
1991	F1 W	Suzuka	Gerhard Berger	A	McLaren MP4/6-Honda	125.609
1992	F1 W	Suzuka	Riccardo Patrese	I	Williams FW14B-Renault	124.286
1993	F1 W	Suzuka	Ayrton Senna	BR	McLaren MP4/8-Ford	115.248
1994	F1 W	Suzuka	Damon Hill	GB	Williams FW16B-Renault	94.250
1995	F1 W	Suzuka	Michael Schumacher	D	Benetton B195-Renault	119.510
1996	F1 W	Suzuka	Damon Hill	GB	Williams FW18-Renault	122.726
1997	F1 W	Suzuka	Michael Schumacher	D	Ferrari F310B	128.925
1998	F1 W	Suzuka	Mika Hakkinen	SF	McLaren MP4/13-Mercedes-Benz	127.512
1999	F1 W	Suzuka	Mika Hakkinen	SF	McLaren MP4/14-Mercedes-Benz	126.799
2000	F1 W	Suzuka	Michael Schumacher	D	Ferrari F1-2000	128.805
2001	F1 W	Suzuka	Michael Schumacher	D	Ferrari F2001	132.241
2002	F1 W	Suzuka	Michael Schumacher	D	Ferrari F2002	132.215

Circuits and other Races

AUTOPOLIS

Nippon Autopolis

An ultra-modern facility built to attract Grand Prix racing to the remote mountain region of Kyushu on Japan's southern island. Nippon Autopolis made it as far as a provisional slot on the F1 calendar, but bankruptcy ended its hopes of holding the Asian Grand Prix. Once hailed as the epitome of a modern, state-of-the art facility, the circuit faded from the international scene after just one World Sports Car race.

Active years	1992 to date
Location	19 miles north-east of Kumamoto, 50 miles south-east of Fukuoka
Type	Permanent road course
Website	www.autopolis.jp
Lap distance	2.904 miles
Lap record	Qualifying: Teo Fabi (Jaguar XJR14), 1m27.188, 119.907 mph, Group C Sports Cars, 1991
	Race: Yannick Dalmas (Peugeot 905B), 1m30.615, 115.372 mph, Group C Sports Cars, 1991

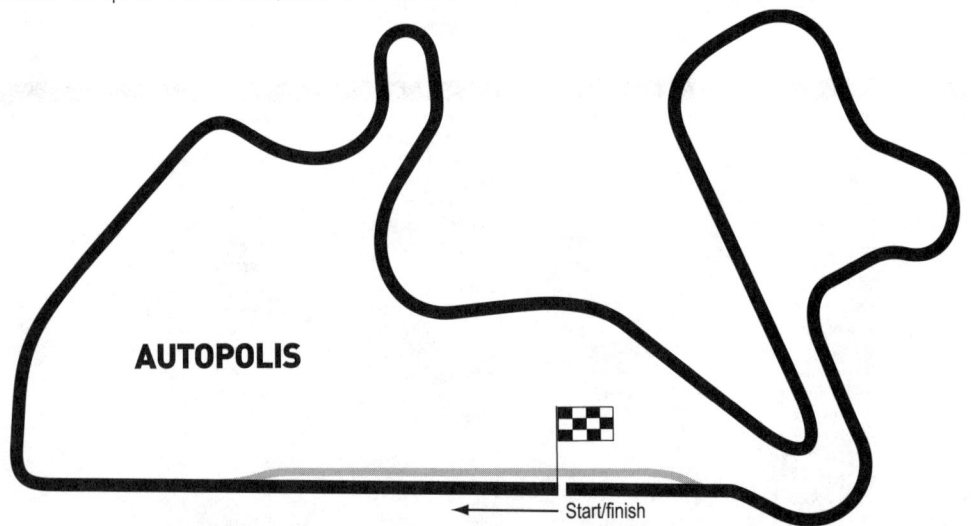

AUTOPOLIS

Start/finish

WORLD SPORTS CAR RACE						
year	formula	winner		nat	car	mph
1991	SC W	Michael Schumacher/Karl Wendlinger		D/A	Mercedes-Benz C291	110.525

FUJI

Built in the shadow of Mount Fuji, plans for this circuit originally called for an American-style 2.5-mile superspeedway with 30-degree banking and a road course. But the money ran out before both ends of banking could be built, leaving a 6 km-road course with a fearsome banked curve at one end. In 1974, the organisers changed the direction of the circuit to clockwise and added a new downhill right-hand first corner that bypassed the banking. In 1976 Fuji held a round of the F1 World Championship in which James Hunt struggled through the rain to win the Championship. A year later, Gilles Villeneuve's Ferrari somersaulted into a prohibited area killing a marshal and the spectator he was trying to move. After that the Grand Prix did not return, and Fuji has settled for a Group C World Sports Car race held in the eighties. It was a mainstay of the Japanese

national series before closing at the end of the 2002 season for refurbishment.

Active years	1965-2002
Location	7.5 miles north of Gotemba, 40 miles north-west of Yokohama, 62 miles west of Tokyo
Type	Permanent road course
Website	www.fisco-jp.com

Current circuit

Lap distance	2.734 miles
Lap record	Race: Naoki Hattori (Reynard 01L-Mugen), 1m17.728, 126.626 mph, Formula Nippon, 2002

Circuit changes

1965-73	Original circuit with banking at one end. 3.728 miles
1974-85	Banking bypassed. 2.709 miles
1986-92	Dunlop Chicane built at the last corner. 2.759 miles
1993 to date	Suntory Chicane built after first corner. Current circuit

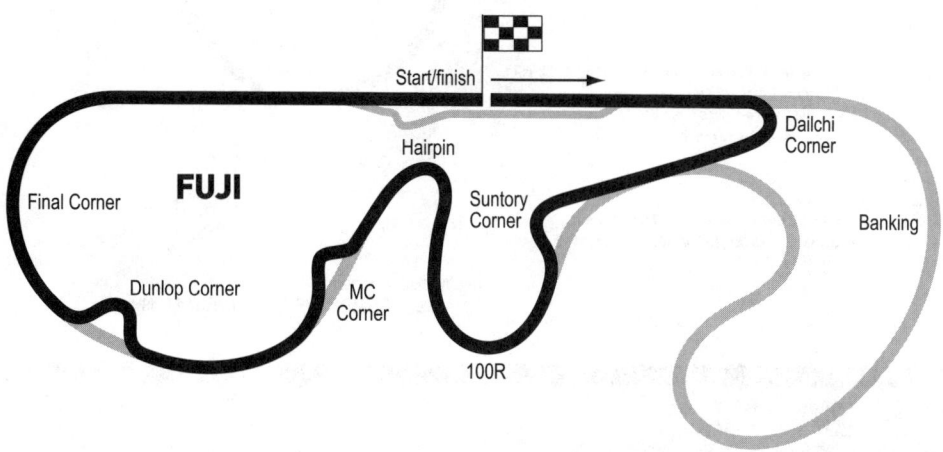

Japanese Grand Prix see above

EURO-MACAU-FUJI FORMULA 3 CHALLENGE

year	formula	driver	nat	car	mph
1990	F3	Michael Schumacher	D	Reynard 903-Volkswagen	95.810
1991	F3	Jordi Gene	E	Ralt RT35-Mugen	110.859
1992	F3	Roberto Colciago	I	Dallara 392-Opel	110.155
1993	F3	Tom Kristensen	DK	TOM's 033F-Toyota	111.320

WORLD SPORTS CAR RACE

year	formula	driver	nat	car	mph
1982	SC W	Jacky Ickx/Jochen Mass	B/D	Porsche 956	115.567
1983	SC W	Derek Bell/Stefan Bellof	GB/D	Porsche 956	122.988
1984	SC W	Stefan Bellof/John Watson	D/GB	Porsche 956	112.603
1985	SC W	Kazuyoshi Hoshino/ Keiji Matsumoto*/Akira Hagiwara*	J	March 85G-Nissan	84.125
1986	SC W	Paolo Barilla/Piercarlo Ghinzani	I	Porsche 956	112.803
1987	SC W	Jan Lammers/			
		John Watson	NL/GB	Jaguar XJR-8	109.478
1988	SC W	Martin Brundle/			
		Eddie Cheever	GB/USA	Jaguar XJR-9	113.755
*Race stopped before Matsumoto and Hagiwara had driven					

MOTEGI
Twin-Ring Motegi

With Honda's increasing involvement in Champcar races during the nineties, the corporation decided to build a new oval to bring American racing to Japan. The Twin-Ring Motegi is a magnificent facility that boasts both a banked oval and a road course, both of which have separate pit lanes. Ironically, despite hosting five Champcar races to date, Honda has yet to win at its home speedway, and with the company now switching to the Indy Racing League the 2003 race will also be for these cars.

Active years	1997 to date
Location	20 miles north-west of Mito City, 22 miles east of Utsunomiya City, 56 miles north-east of Tokyo
Type	Paved oval and permanent road course
Website	www.twinring.jp

Oval circuit

Lap distance	1.549 miles
Lap records	Qualifying: Gil de Ferran (Reynard 99I-Honda), 25.463s, 219.002 mph, CART, 1999
	Race: Helio Castro-Neves (Lola B99/00-Mercedes-Benz), 25.830s, 215.889 mph, CART, 1999

Road course

Lap distance	2.849 miles
Lap record	Race: Pedro de la Rosa (Lola T97/51-Mugen), 1m33.436, 109.769 mph, Formula Nippon, 1997

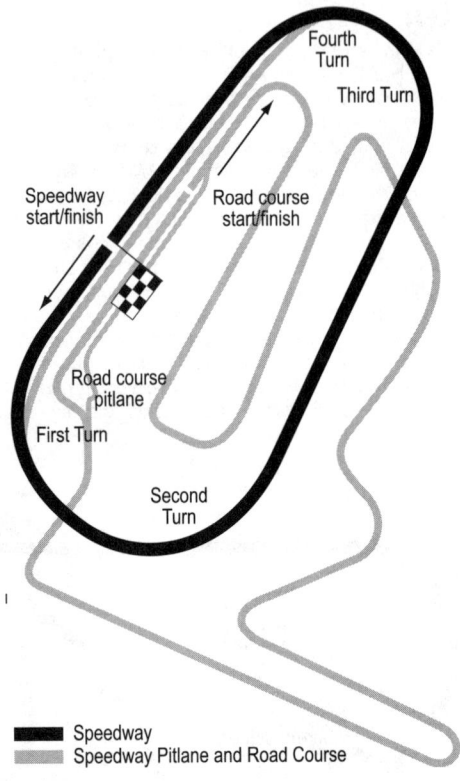

Speedway start/finish

Road course start/finish

Fourth Turn

Third Turn

Road course pitlane

First Turn

Second Turn

■■■ Speedway
■■■ Speedway Pitlane and Road Course

CHAMPCAR RACE					
year	formula	winner	nat	car	mph
1998	CART	Adrian Fernandez	MEX	Reynard 98I-Ford	159.393
1999	CART	Adrian Fernandez	MEX	Reynard 97I-Ford	176.195
2000	CART	Michael Andretti	USA	Lola B2K/00-Ford	157.154
2001	CART	Kenny Brack	S	Lola B01/00-Ford	178.228
2002	CART	Bruno Junqueira	BR	Lola B2/00-Toyota	155.547

SUZUKA

Set in an amusement park, Suzuka's figure-of-eight layout is unique in F1. Since hosting the Japanese Grand Prix in 1987, it has been widely recognised as one of the sport's finest circuits, rivalled only by Spa as the greatest test for today's GP drivers. Originally designed by John Hugenholtz as a test circuit for Honda (which still owns the facility), Suzuka was the scene of championship showdowns between Ayrton Senna and Alain Prost in 1989 and 1990, when the bitter rivals collided. Damon Hill and Mika Hakkinen have both secured world titles here, and Michael Schumacher clinched Ferrari's first drivers' crown in 21 years at Suzuka in 2000.

Active years	1962 to date
Location	30 miles south-west of Nagoya, 93 miles east of Osaka
Type	Permanent road course
Website	www.suzukacircuit.co.jp

Current circuit

Lap distance	3.617 miles
Lap records	Qualifying: Michael Schumacher (Ferrari F2002), 1m31.317, 142.594 mph, F1, 2002
	Race: Michael Schumacher (Ferrari F2002), 1m36.125, 135.462 mph, F1, 2002

Circuit changes

1962-82	3.731 miles
1983-86	Chicane inserted before the start. 3.694 miles
1987-2001	Some corners reprofiled. 3.641 miles
2002 to date	S Curve modified. Current circuit

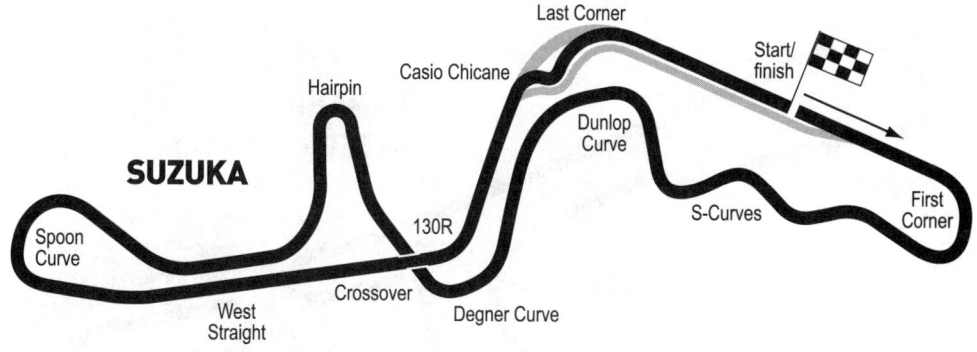

SUZUKA

Last Corner

Casio Chicane

Hairpin

Start/finish

Dunlop Curve

130R

S-Curves

First Corner

Spoon Curve

Crossover

West Straight

Degner Curve

Japanese Grand Prix see above

WORLD SPORTS CAR RACE

year	formula	winner	nat	car	mph
1989	SC W	Jean-Louis Schlesser/Mauro Baldi	F/I	Sauber C9/88-Mercedes-Benz	106.015
1990	SC W	Jean-Louis Schlesser/Mauro Baldi	F/I	Sauber C9/88-Mercedes-Benz	109.392
1991	SC W	Mauro Baldi/Philippe Alliot	I/F	Peugeot 905	111.468
1992	SC W	Derek Warwick/Yannick Dalmas	GB/F	Peugeot 905B	113.147

INTERNATIONAL GT 1000 KMS RACE

year	formula	winner	nat	car	mph
1994	GT	Jean-Pierre Jarier/Bob Wollek/Jesus Pareja	F/F/E	Porsche 911 RSR	91.886
1995	GT	Ray Bellm/Maurizio Sandro Sala/Masanori Sekiya	GB/BR/J	McLaren F1 GTR-BMW	93.777
1996	GT	Ray Bellm/JJ Lehto/James Weaver	GB/SF/GB	McLaren F1 GTR-BMW	98.616
1997	GT	Alessandro Nannini/Bernd Schneider/Marcel Tiemann	I/D/D	Mercedes-Benz CLK-GTR	103.908
1998	GT	Bernd Schneider/Mark Webber	D/AUS	Mercedes-Benz CLK-LM	107.664
1999	GT	Osamu Nakako/Ryo Michigami/Katsutomo Kaneishi	J	Honda NSX-GT	98.885
2000	GT	Juichi Wakisaka/Katsutomo Kaneishi/Daisuke Ito	J	Honda NSX-GT	99.675
2001	GT	Hironori Takeuchi/Yuji Tachikawa/			
		Shigekazu Wakisaka	J	Toyota Supra	101.649
2002	GT	Juichi Wakisaka/Akira Iida/			
		Shigekazu Wakisaka	J	Toyota Supra	101.353

TANAKA INTERNATIONAL

Aida

Tanaka International (TI) was designed as an exclusive club where Japan's elite could drive Grand Prix cars. In 1994 and 1995 it held Japan's second Formula 1 race, the Pacific Grand Prix. Although the circuit's location is inaccessible, the race was a success, with nearly 100,000 spectators attending the inaugural event. The track itself is tight and narrow, and after Michael Schumacher had won his second race in as many years the circuit returned to concentrating on local events.

Active years	1992 to date
Location	Aida village, 40 miles south-east of Okayama on Honshu Island.
Type	Permanent road course
Website	www.ti-circuit.co.jp
Lap distance	2.314 miles
Lap records	Qualifying: Ayrton Senna (Williams FW16-Renault), 1m10.218, 118.636 mph, F1, 1994
	Race: Michael Schumacher (Benetton B194-Ford), 1m14.023, 112.538 mph, F1, 1994

PACIFIC GRAND PRIX

year	formula	winner	nat	car	mph
1994	F1 W	Michael Schumacher	D	Benetton B194-Ford	108.685
1995	F1 W	Michael Schumacher	D	Benetton B195-Renault	105.885

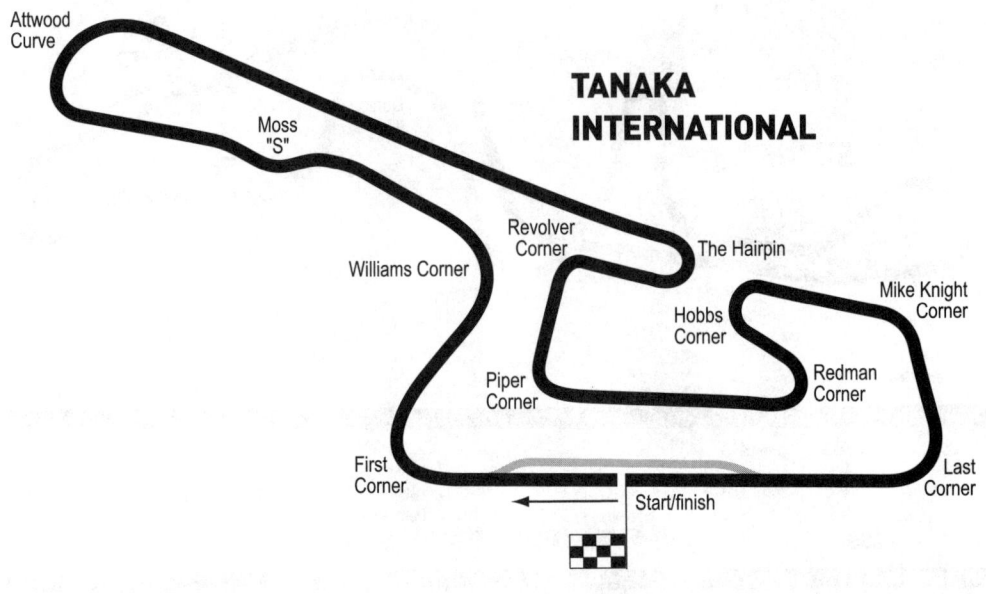

LIBYA
Circuits and Races

MELLAHA

Mellaha was an ultra-fast blast around a salt lake that developed into one of the classic races of the thirties. It had started in 1925 on 40 miles of open roads to the east of Tripoli. The introduction of a lottery made it one of the richest races in the world. The first Mellaha race, held in 1933 north of the original course, produced perhaps the most public example of race fixing in the sport's history. The top drivers conspired with a lottery ticket holder to ensure that Achille Varzi won the race and then divided the prize money among themselves. Unhappy with the German domination of Grand Prix racing, the Italian organisers switched to the Alfa- and Maserati-dominated voiturette category for the 1939 race. Mercedes-Benz responded by building two W165 voiturettes in absolute secrecy — and finished first and second!

Active years	1933-40
Location	10 miles east of Tripoli
Type	Permanent road course
Lap distance	8.165 miles
Lap record	Qualifying: Hans Stuck (Auto Union C), 3m19.90, 147.044 mph, GP, 1937
	Race: Hans Stuck (Auto Union C), 3m25.73, 142.877 mph, GP, 1937

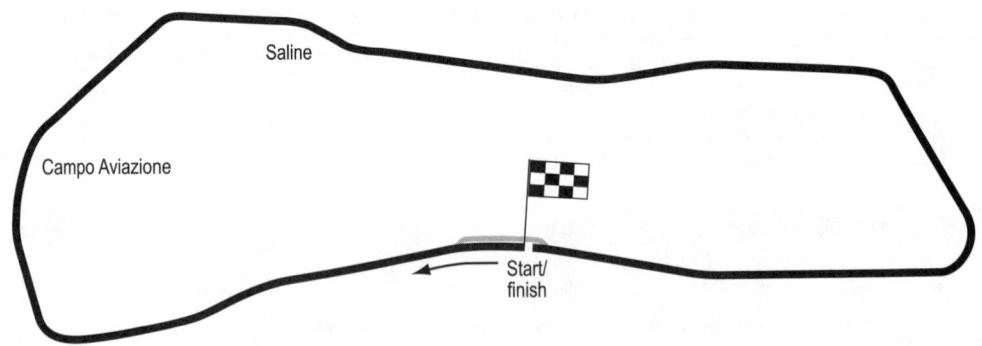

TRIPOLI GRAND PRIX

year	formula	winner	nat	car	mph
1925*	FL	Renato Balestrero	I	OM 665	58.718
1926*	FL	Francois Eysermann	F	Bugatti T35	68.092
1927*	FL	Emilio Materassi	I	Bugatti T35C	82.071
1928*	GP	Tazio Nuvolari	I	Bugatti T35C	77.982
1929*	GP	Gastone Brilli-Peri	I	Talbot T700	83.243
1930*	GP	Baconin Borzacchini	I	Maserati V4	91.063
1933	GP	Achille Varzi	I	Bugatti T51	105.086
1934	GP	Achille Varzi	I	Alfa Romeo Tipo-B "P3"	116.024
1935	GP	Rudolf Caracciola	D	Mercedes-Benz W25B	123.406
1936	GP	Achille Varzi	I	Auto Union C	129.412
1937	GP	Hermann Lang	D	Mercedes-Benz W125	132.440
1938	GP	Hermann Lang	D	Mercedes-Benz W154	127.840
1939	V	Hermann Lang	D	Mercedes-Benz W165	123.291
1940	V	Giuseppe Farina	I	Alfa Romeo 158	128.611

At Mellaha except *at Tripoli

MALAYSIA
Major International Races

MALAYSIAN GRAND PRIX

year	formula	circuit	winner	nat	car	mph
1999	F1 W	Sepang	Eddie Irvine	GB	Ferrari F399	116.263
2000	F1 W	Sepang	Michael Schumacher	D	Ferrari F1-2000	117.157
2001	F1 W	Sepang	Michael Schumacher	D	Ferrari F2001	102.577
2002	F1 W	Sepang	Ralf Schumacher	D	Williams FW24-BMW	122.823

Circuits and Races

SEPANG

Grand Prix racing's newest circuit, Sepang has set the standards to which other venues must aspire. The unique double-sided grandstands, complete with imposing Canopy Tower give it a unique and ultra-modern look. The track is wide, and long straights followed by tight hairpins help promote overtaking. And with an international airport adjacent to the complex, accessibility could not be better for the Formula 1 entourage. But excessively hot and humid conditions prevail and high-ticket prices have kept crowds to a minimum. A plan to run Formula 1's first floodlit night race to boost interest and improve television schedules in Europe was abandoned due to logistical problems and safety fears.

Active years	1999 to date
Location	Kuala Lumpur International Airport, 30 miles south of Kuala Lumpur
Type	Permanent road course
Website	www.malaysiangp.com.my
Lap distance	3.444 miles

Lap records: Qualifying: Michael Schumacher (Ferrari F2001), 1m35.220, 130.208 mph, F1, 2001
Race: Juan Pablo Montoya (Williams FW24-BMW), 1m38.049, 126.451 mph, F1, 2002

Malaysian Grand Prix see above

SHAH ALAM
Batu Tiga/Selangor

This circuit was originally known as Batu Tiga, and is sometimes referred to as Selangor in deference to the palace that overlooks it. The Selangor 800 sports car race was the only World Championship race to have been held in Malaysia until the opening of Sepang. It was run at the start of the monsoon season, and after only 3,000 spectators paid to watch the exercise was not repeated. The circuit was closed in 1977 after an accident claimed the lives of six children. It reopened after a £100,000 refit with better protection for spectators.

Active years	1968 to date
Location	13 miles east of Kuala Lumpur
Type	Permanent road course
Website	www.btsc.com.my

Current circuit

Lap distance	2.295 miles
Lap record	Qualifying: Jochen Mass (Porsche 962C), 1m21.33, 101.586 mph, Group C Sports Car, 1985
	Race: Jochen Mass (Porsche 962C), 1m24.52, 97.752 mph, Group C Sports Car, 1985

Circuit changes

1968-84	2.100 miles
1985 to date	Turn 11 built. Current circuit

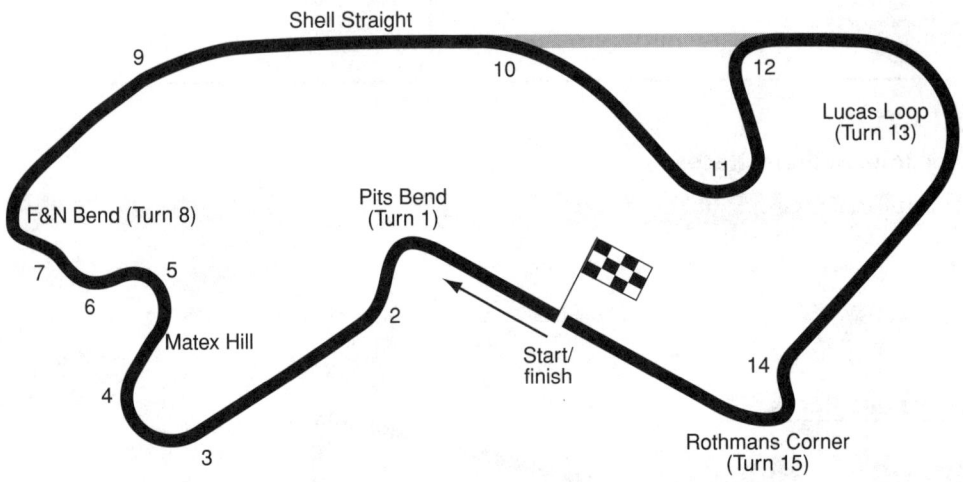

SELANGOR WORLD SPORTS CAR RACE

year	formula	winner	nat	car	mph
1985	SC W	Jochen Mass/Jacky Ickx	D/B	Porsche 962C	89.988

MEXICO
Major Championships

MARLBORO CUP FORMULA K CHAMPIONSHIP

year	driver	nat	car
1984	Enrique Contreras	MEX	Enco-Chrysler
1985	Gilberto Jimenez	MEX	CDD Lider-Chrysler
1986	Gilberto Jimenez	MEX	CDD Lider-Chrsyler
1987	Gerardo Martinez	MEX	Martiga R1FH87-Chrysler
1988	Oscar Manautou	MEX	Martiga R1FH88-Chrysler
1989	Gerardo Martinez	MEX	Martiga R1FH89-Chrysler

MEXICAN FORMULA 2 CHAMPIONSHIP

New championship using Formula Atlantic chassis and 2.2-litre Chrysler engines which replaced Formula K. A new Chrysler Neon engine introduced in 1996 but the series was replaced after 1997

year	driver	nat	car
1990	Enrique Contreras	MEX	March 90A-Chrysler
1991	Carlos Guerrero	MEX	March 90A-Chrysler
1992	Carlos Guerrero	MEX	March 90A-Chrysler
1993	Allen Berg	CDN	Ralt RT40-Chrysler

MEXICAN FORMULA 2 CHAMPIONSHIP (cont.)

year	driver	nat	car
1994	Fernando Plata	MEX	Ralt RT40-Chrysler
1995	Jimmy Morales	MEX	Ralt RT40-Chrysler
1996	David Martinez	MEX	Ralt RT40-Chrysler
1997	Ricardo Perez de Lara	MEX	Ralt RT40-Chrysler

MEXICAN FORMULA 3000 CHAMPIONSHIP

Replaced Formula 2 as Mexico's top series. Identical F3000 Lola chassis equipped with the 2.2-litre Chrysler engine previously used in F2

year	driver	nat	car
1996	Jaime Cordero	MEX	Lola T93/50-Chysler
1997	Jimmy Morales	MEX	Lola T93/50-Chysler

MEXICAN INDY LIGHTS CHAMPIONSHIP (ALSO KNOWN AS FORMULA DE LAS AMERICAS CHAMPIONSHIP)

The Latest attempt as Mexico's top formula with identical Chevy V8 powered Lola Indy Lights T93/20 chassis

year	driver	nat	team	car
1998	Osvaldo Negri jr	BR	Ferrara-Jiminez	Lola T93/20-Chevrolet
1999	Waldemar Coronas	RA	Carusi	Lola T93/20-Chevrolet
2000	Waldemar Coronas	RA	Carusi	Lola T93/20-Chevrolet
2001	Allen Berg	CDN	Scuadra Berg	Lola T93/20-Chevrolet

MEXICAN FORMULA 3 CHAMPIONSHIP (ALSO KNOWN AS LATIN AMERICAN F3 CHAMPIONSHIP)

year	driver	nat	team	car
1990	Carlos Guerrero	MEX	Dasatec	Reynard 903-Alfa Romeo
1991	Adrian Fernandez	MEX	Lozana Racing	Reynard 903-Volkswagen
1992	Cesar Jimenez	MEX	Cesar Tiberio Jimenez	Reynard 903-Alfa Romeo
1993	Carlos Guerrero	MEX	Team GO	Reynard 903-Alfa Romeo/ Reynard 933-Alfa Romeo
1994	Carlos Guerrero	MEX	Team GO	Reynard 933-Alfa Romeo
1995	Derek Higgins	IRL	Team GO	Reynard 933-Alfa Romeo
1996	Rod McLeod	GB	Team GO	Reynard 933-Alfa Romeo
1997	Derek Higgins	IRL	Team GO	Reynard 933-Alfa Romeo
1998	Carlos Perea	MEX	Inverlat Perea Racing	Reynard 933-Volkswagen
1999	Eduardo Oliveira	MEX	El Conejo Bus Line	Reynard 933-Volkswagen
2000	Jose Antonio Ramos	MEX	El Universal Ramos Racing	Reynard 933-Volkswagen
2001	Gilberto Jimenez jr	MEX	Carusi	Reynard 933-Volkswagen
2002	Guillermo Zapata	MEX	Guillermo Zapata	Reynard 933-Volkswagen

Major International Races

MEXICAN GRAND PRIX

year	formula	circuit	winner	nat	car	mph
1962	F1	Mexico City	Jim Clark/Trevor Taylor	GB	Lotus 25-Climax	90.314
1963	F1 W	Mexico City	Jim Clark	GB	Lotus 25-Climax	93.305
1964	F1 W	Mexico City	Dan Gurney	USA	Brabham BT7-Climax	93.326
1965	F1 W	Mexico City	Richie Ginther	USA	Honda RA272	94.272
1966	F1 W	Mexico City	John Surtees	GB	Cooper T81-Maserati	95.722
1967	F1 W	Mexico City	Jim Clark	GB	Lotus 49-Ford	101.418
1968	F1 W	Mexico City	Graham Hill	GB	Lotus 49B-Ford	103.804
1969	F1 W	Mexico City	Denny Hulme	NZ	McLaren M7A-Ford	106.156
1970	F1 W	Mexico City	Jacky Ickx	B	Ferrari 312B	106.786
1986	F1 W	Mexico City	Gerhard Berger	A	Benetton B186-BMW	120.111
1987	F1 W	Mexico City	Nigel Mansell	GB	Williams FW11B-Honda	120.176
1988	F1 W	Mexico City	Alain Prost	F	McLaren MP4/4-Honda	122.343
1989	F1 W	Mexico City	Ayrton Senna	BR	McLaren MP4/5-Honda	119.263
1990	F1 W	Mexico City	Alain Prost	F	Ferrari 641/2	122.819
1991	F1 W	Mexico City	Riccardo Patrese	I	Williams FW14-Renault	122.877
1992	F1 W	Mexico City	Nigel Mansell	GB	Williams FW14B-Renault	123.759
2002	CART	Mexico City	Kenny Brack	S	Lola B2/00-Toyota	104.468

CARRERA PANAMERICANA

year	formula	winner	nat	car	mph
1950	Production	Hershel McGriff/Ray Elliott	USA	Oldsmobile	77.430
1951	SC	Piero Taruffi/Luigi Chinetti	I	Ferrari Vignale	88.070
1952	SC	Karl Kling/Hans Klenk	D	Mercedes-Benz	102.590
1953	SC W	Juan Manuel Fangio/Gino Bronzoni	RA/I	Lancia Sport V6	105.150
1954	SC W	Umberto Maglioli	I	Ferrari 375 Plus	107.930

Circuits and Other Races

FUNDIDORA PARK

Monterrey

The popularity of Champcar racing in Mexico was vividly illustrated in 2001 by the enthusiasm for a new race in Monterrey's Fundidora Park. The Jerry Forsythe and Pat Patrick-inspired circuit is laid out in the shadow of a dilapidated 100-year-old steel works, and is a difficult mixture of turns. Flat and wide, the track offers good good views for spectators and plenty of passing opportunities for drivers. The circuit is the first phase of a new sports complex that will feature a baseball stadium and entertainment complex in the park.

Active years	2001 to date
Location	Fundidora Park, 1.5 miles east of downtown Monterrey
Type	Temporary road course
Website	www.monterreygp.com
Lap distance	2.104 miles
Lap records	Qualifying: Kenny Brack (Lola B01/00-Ford), 1m15.244, 100.665 mph, CART, 2001
	Race: Cristiano da Matta (Lola B2/00-Toyota), 1m15.386, 100.475 mph, CART, 2002

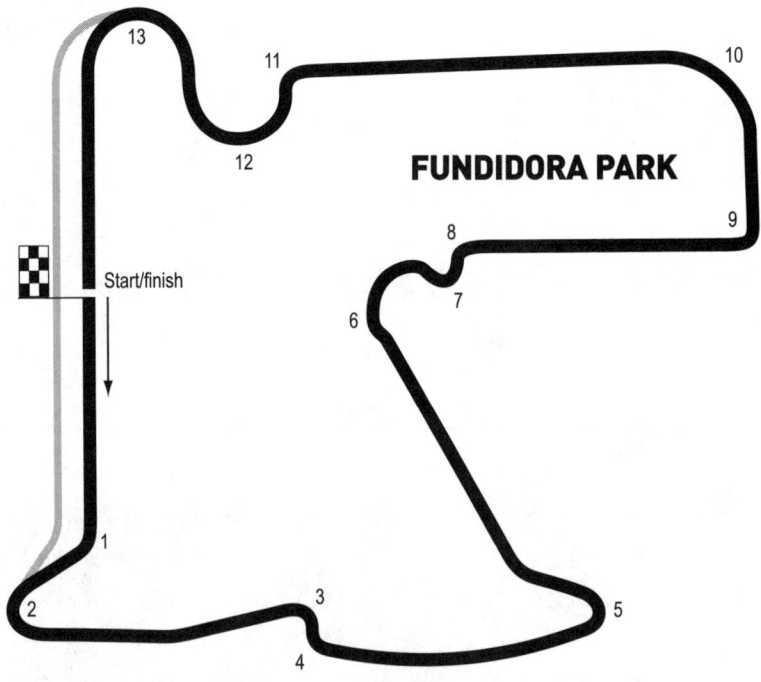

CHAMPCAR RACE

year	formula	winner	nat	car	mph
2001	CART	Cristiano da Matta	BR	Lola B01/00-Toyota	81.548
2002	CART	Cristiano da Matta	BR	Lola B2/00-Toyota	90.544

MEXICO CITY

Autodromo Hermanos Rodriguez

Located 6000 ft above sea level, Mexico's Grand Prix circuit has had a chequered history of tragedy and drama. The first Mexican GP in 1962 was marred by the death in practice of local hero, Ricardo Rodriguez. Two years later John Surtees clinched a dramatic last lap World Championship victory here. Grand Prix racing abandoned Mexico after the 1970 race, when the already notorious crowd degenerated into chaos. The track's final corner was a fearsome 180-degree slightly banked Peraltada, although it was modified after Senna crashed there in 1991. The circuit closed in 1999 amid rumours of property development on the site. But it reopened for the final round of the 2002 CART Championship with a new complex through the Baseball stadium that had been built on the Peraltada. Huge crowds confirmed a once-again promising future for Mexico's traditional home of motor racing.

Active years	1962-99, 2002 to date
Location	East of downtown Mexico City
Type	Permanent road course
Website	www.telmexgigantegranpremiomexico.com
Lap distance	2.786 miles
Lap records	Qualifying: Bruno Junqueira (Lola B2/00-Toyota), 1m25.941, 116.703 mph, CART, 2002
	Race: Shinji Nakano (Lola B2/00-Honda), 1m27.248, 114.955 mph, CART, 2002

Grand Prix circuit changes

1962-85	3.107 miles
1986-99	New esses built at the end of the main straight. 2.747 miles
2002 to date	New section built on the first half of the final corner. Current circuit

Original Champcar circuit

Active years	1980-81
Lap distance	2.479 miles
Lap record	Qualifying: Bobby Unser (Penske PC9B-Cosworth), 1m11.538, 124.751 mph, CART, 1981

Mexican Grand Prix see above

CHAMPCAR RACE

year	formula	winner	nat	car	mph
1980	CART	Rick Mears	USA	Penske PC9-Cosworth	116.329
1981	CART	Rick Mears	USA	Penske PC9B-Cosworth	103.487
2002*	CART	Kenny Brack	S	Lola B2/00-Toyota	104.468

*Mexican Grand Prix

WORLD SPORTS CAR RACE

year	formula	winner	nat	car	mph
1989	SC W	Jean-Louis Schlesser/Jochen Mass	F/D	Sauber C9/88-Mercedes-Benz	104.877
1990	SC W	Jochen Mass/Michael Schumacher	D	Mercedes-Benz C11	107.000
1991	SC W	Keke Rosberg/Yannick Dalmas	SF/F	Peugeot 905B	108.093

MONACO

Circuits and Races

MONTE CARLO

Monte Carlo has been a highlight of the Grand Prix calendar since the enigmatic "W Williams" won the first race here in 1929. Much of the original round-the-houses circuit inspired by local cigarette manufacturer Antony Nogues remains the same today. A chicane has been added at Ste Devote, the swimming pool section was built on reclaimed land and the road now continues to a hairpin at La Rascasse. A hotel (originally called Loews and now Grand) has been built over the tunnel. Although today's Grand Prix cars are barely able to overtake at Monte Carlo, the anachronistic "race of a thousand corners" remains the glamour event of the year. Over the years two drivers have crashed into the harbour: Alberto Ascari in 1955 and Paul Hawkins ten years later. Both men escaped without injury. But Monte Carlo

did prove fatal for Luigi Fagioli in 1952 and Lorenzo Bandini in 1967.

Active years	1929 to date
Location	Central Monte Carlo, 11 miles east of Nice
Type	Temporary street circuit
Website	www.acm.mc

Current circuit

Lap distance	2.092 miles
Lap record	Qualifying: Juan Pablo Montoya (Williams FW24-BMW), 1m16.676, 98.221 mph, F1, 2002
	Race: Rubens Barrichello (Ferrari F2002), 1m18.023, 96.526 mph, F1, 2002

Circuit changes

1929-54	Original circuit (cobbles and tramlines removed in 1932). 1.976 miles
1955-72	Chicane repositioned. 1.954 miles
1973-75	Loews (now Grand) Hotel built over tunnel, swimming pool section built and La Rascasse added. 2.037 miles
1976-85	Ste Devote and La Rascasse modified. 2.058 miles
1986-96	New chicane built. 2.068 miles
1997 to date	Entry to the swimming pool section modified. Current circuit

MONACO GRAND PRIX

year	formula	winner	nat	car	mph
1929	GP	"W Williams"	GB	Bugatti T35B	50.198
1930	GP	Rene Dreyfus	F	Bugatti T35B	53.637
1931	GP	Louis Chiron	MC	Bugatti T51	54.099
1932	GP	Tazio Nuvolari	I	Alfa Romeo 8C "Monza"	55.814
1933	GP	Achille Varzi	I	Bugatti T51	57.048
1934	GP	Guy Moll	DZ	Alfa Romeo Tipo-B "P3"	56.051
1935	GP	Luigi Fagioli	I	Mercedes-Benz W25B	58.166
1936	GP	Rudolf Caracciola	D	Mercedes-Benz W25C	51.696
1937	GP	Manfred von Brauchitsch	D	Mercedes-Benz W125	63.266
1948	F1	Giuseppe Farina	I	Maserati 4CLT	59.744
1950	F1 W	Juan Manuel Fangio	RA	Alfa Romeo 158	61.331
1952	SC	Vittorio Marzotto	I	Ferrari 225MM	58.200
1955	F1 W	Maurice Trintignant	F	Ferrari 625	65.805
1956	F1 W	Stirling Moss	GB	Maserati 250F	64.936
1957	F1 W	Juan Manuel Fangio	RA	Maserati 250F	64.718
1958	F1 W	Maurice Trintignant	F	Cooper T45-Climax	67.979
1959	F1 W	Jack Brabham	AUS	Cooper T51-Climax	66.669
1960	F1 W	Stirling Moss	GB	Lotus 18-Climax	67.473
1961	F1 W	Stirling Moss	GB	Lotus 18-Climax	70.697
1962	F1 W	Bruce McLaren	NZ	Cooper T60-Climax	70.417
1963	F1 W	Graham Hill	GB	BRM P57	72.447
1964	F1 W	Graham Hill	GB	BRM P261	72.673
1965	F1 W	Graham Hill	GB	BRM P261	74.363
1966	F1 W	Jackie Stewart	GB	BRM P261	76.539
1967	F1 W	Denny Hulme	NZ	Brabham BT20-Repco	75.848
1968	F1 W	Graham Hill	GB	Lotus 49B-Ford	77.811
1969	F1 W	Graham Hill	GB	Lotus 49B-Ford	80.171
1970	F1 W	Jochen Rindt	A	Lotus 49C-Ford	81.836
1971	F1 W	Jackie Stewart	GB	Tyrrell 003-Ford	83.478
1972	F1 W	Jean-Pierre Beltoise	F	BRM P160B	63.842
1973	F1 W	Jackie Stewart	GB	Tyrrell 006-Ford	80.969
1974	F1 W	Ronnie Peterson	S	Lotus 72E-Ford	80.747
1975	F1 W	Niki Lauda	A	Ferrari 312T	75.534
1976	F1 W	Niki Lauda	A	Ferrari 312T2	80.357
1977	F1 W	Jody Scheckter	ZA	Wolf WR1-Ford	79.611
1978	F1 W	Patrick Depailler	F	Tyrrell 008-Ford	80.360
1979	F1 W	Jody Scheckter	ZA	Ferrari 312T4	81.339
1980	F1 W	Carlos Reutemann	RA	Williams FW07B-Ford	81.200
1981	F1 W	Gilles Villeneuve	CDN	Ferrari 126CK	82.040
1982	F1 W	Riccardo Patrese	I	Brabham BT49D-Ford	82.185

MONACO GRAND PRIX (cont.)

year	formula	winner	nat	car	mph
1983	F1 W	Keke Rosberg	SF	Williams FW08C-Ford	80.460
1984	F1 W	Alain Prost	F	McLaren MP4/2-TAG Porsche	62.620
1985	F1 W	Alain Prost	F	McLaren MP4/2B-TAG Porsche	86.020
1986	F1 W	Alain Prost	F	McLaren MP4/2C-TAG Porsche	83.661
1987	F1 W	Ayrton Senna	BR	Lotus 99T-Honda	82.088
1988	F1 W	Alain Prost	F	McLaren MP4/4-Honda	82.519
1989	F1 W	Ayrton Senna	BR	McLaren MP4/5-Honda	84.137
1990	F1 W	Ayrton Senna	BR	McLaren MP4/5B-Honda	85.813
1991	F1 W	Ayrton Senna	BR	McLaren MP4/6-Honda	85.619
1992	F1 W	Ayrton Senna	BR	McLaren MP4/7A-Honda	87.200
1993	F1 W	Ayrton Senna	BR	McLaren MP4/8-Ford	86.272
1994	F1 W	Michael Schumacher	D	Benetton B194-Ford	88.046
1995	F1 W	Michael Schumacher	D	Benetton B195-Renault	85.506
1996	F1 W	Olivier Panis	F	Ligier JS43-Mugen	77.062
1997	F1 W	Michael Schumacher	D	Ferrari F310B	64.801
1998	F1 W	Mika Hakkinen	SF	McLaren MP4/13-Mercedes-Benz	87.892
1999	F1 W	Michael Schumacher	D	Ferrari F399	89.387
2000	F1 W	David Coulthard	GB	McLaren MP4/15-Mercedes-Benz	89.436
2001	F1 W	Michael Schumacher	D	Ferrari F2001	91.180
2002	F1 W	David Coulthard	GB	McLaren MP4/17-Mercedes-Benz	92.669

RAINIER CUP

year	formula	winner	nat	car	mph
1936	V	"B Bira"	SM	ERA B-type	52.990
1937	SC	Laury Schell	F	Delahaye 145	51.320

PRIX DE MONTE CARLO

year	formula	winner	nat	car	mph
1950	F3	Stirling Moss	GB	Cooper IV-JAP	55.680
1952	SC	Robert Manzon	F	Gordini	57.120

MONACO FORMULA 3 GRAND PRIX

year	formula	winner	nat	car	mph
1959	FJ	Michel May	CH	Stanguellini-Fiat	60.620
1960	FJ	Henry Taylor	GB	Cooper T52-BMC	64.660
1961	FJ	Peter Arundell	GB	Lotus 20-Ford	64.810
1962	FJ	Peter Arundell	GB	Lotus 22-Ford	67.460
1963	FJ	Richard Attwood	GB	Lola Mk5A-Ford	69.280
1964	F3	Jackie Stewart	GB	Cooper T72-BMC	65.940
1965	F3	Peter Revson	USA	Lotus 35-Ford	67.039
1966	F3	Jean-Pierre Beltoise	F	Matra MS5-Ford	70.600
1967	F3	Henri Pescarolo	F	Matra MS6-Ford	70.938
1968	F3	Jean-Pierre Jaussaud	F	Tecno 68-Ford	71.576
1969	F3	Ronnie Peterson	S	Tecno 69-Ford	74.719
1970	F3	Tony Trimmer	GB	Brabham BT28-Ford	74.030
1971	F3	Dave Walker	AUS	Lotus 69-Ford	71.650
1972	F3	Patrick Depailler	F	Alpine A367-Renault	60.926
1973	F3	Jacques Laffite	F	Martini MK12-Ford	74.446
1974	F3	Tom Pryce	GB	March 743-Ford	76.097
1975	F3 E	Renzo Zorzi	I	GRD 374-Lancia	75.515
1976	F3	Bruno Giacomelli	I	March 763-Toyota	74.841
1977	F3	Didier Pironi	F	Martini MK21-Toyota	74.451
1978	F3	Elio de Angelis	I	Chevron B38-Toyota	74.974
1979	F3	Alain Prost	F	Martini MK27-Renault	75.718
1980	F3	Mauro Baldi	I	Martini MK31-Toyota	74.707
1981	F3	Alain Ferte	F	Martini MK34-Alfa Romeo	77.246
1982	F3	Alain Ferte	F	Martini MK37-Alfa Romeo	77.483
1983	F3	Michel Ferte	F	Martini MK39-Alfa Romeo	77.353
1984	F3	Ivan Capelli	I	Martini MK42-Alfa Romeo	77.351
1985	F3	Pierre-Henri Raphanel	F	Martini MK45-Alfa Romeo	77.090
1986	F3	Yannick Dalmas	F	Martini MK49-Volkswagen	75.921
1987	F3	Didier Artzet	F	Ralt RT30-Volkswagen	75.313
1988	F3	Enrico Bertaggia	I	Dallara 388-Alfa Romeo	73.304

MONACO FORMULA 3 GRAND PRIX (cont.)

year	formula	winner	nat	car	mph
1989	F3	Antonio Tamburini	I	Reynard 893-Alfa Romeo	74.668
1990	F3	Laurent Aiello	F	Dallara 390-Volkswagen	57.470
1991	F3	Jorg Muller	D	Reynard 913-Volkswagen	75.449
1992	F3	Marco Werner	D	Ralt RT36-Opel	75.554
1993	F3	Gianantonio Pacchioni	I	Dallara 393-Fiat	76.352
1994	F3	Giancarlo Fisichella	I	Dallara 394-Opel	76.156
1995	F3	Gianantonio Pacchioni	I	Dallara 395-Fiat	76.496
1996	F3	Marcel Tiemann	D	Dallara 396-Opel	76.384
1997	F3	Nick Heidfeld	D	Dallara 397-Opel	80.190

MONACO FORMULA 3000 GRAND PRIX

year	formula	winner	nat	car	mph
1998	F3000 INT	Nick Heidfeld	D	Lola T96/50-Zytek	80.376
1999	F3000 INT	Gonzalo Rodriguez	ROU	Lola B99/50-Zytek	80.085
2000	F3000 INT	Bruno Junqueira	BR	Lola B99/50-Zytek	79.297
2001	F3000 INT	Mark Webber	AUS	Lola B99/50-Zytek	77.005
2002	F3000 INT	Sebastien Bourdais	F	Lola B2/50-Zytek	83.463

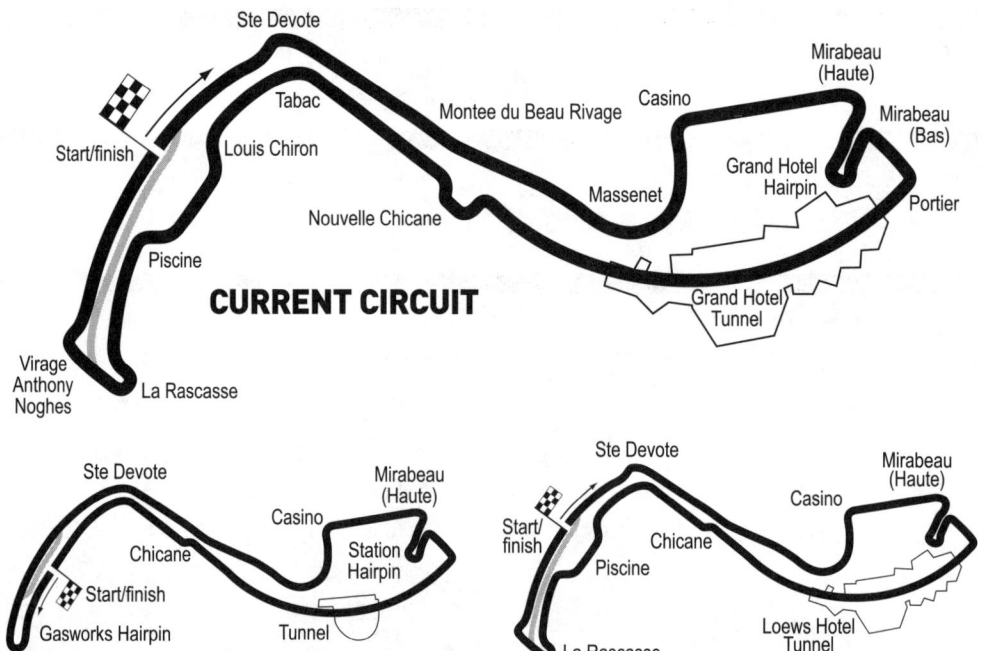

MOROCCO
Major International Races

MOROCCAN GRAND PRIX						
year	formula	circuit	winner	nat	car	mph
1925	TC	Casablanca	de Vaugelas	-	Delage	59.220
1926	TC	Casablanca	E Meyer	-	Bugatti	63.750
1927	TC	Casablanca	G Rost	-	Georges Irat	77.050
1928	TC	Casablanca	E Meyer	-	Bugatti	91.780
1930	SC(h)	Casablanca	C Benitah	-	Amilcar	69.800
1934	GP	Anfa	Louis Chiron	MC	Alfa Romeo Tipo-B "P3"	81.094
1957	F1	Ain Diab	Jean Behra	F	Maserati 250F	112.652
1958	F1 W	Ain Diab	Stirling Moss	GB	Vanwall VW5	116.227

MOROCCAN GRAND PRIX FORMULA 2 CLASS						
year	formula	circuit	winner	nat	car	mph
1958	F2	Ain Diab	Jack Brabham	AUS	Cooper T45-Climax	105.057

Circuits and Other Races

AIN DIAB
Casablanca

As a French colony, it is not surprising that Morocco had held a Grand Prix before World War II. The event returned in 1957 on a new circuit near Casablanca when racing in Europe was threatened by the Suez crisis. In six weeks, and with the blessing of King Mohammed V, the Royal Automobile Club of Morocco designed a course using the public roads of Casablanca's Ain-Diab suburb, the desert road towards Azemmour and the coast road through the Sidi Abderhaman forest. The first race was a non-championship affair, but the 1958

Moroccan Grand Prix was the site of the championship showdown between Mike Hawthorn and Stirling Moss. Moss won the race, but Hawthorn was crowned Britain's first World Champion.

Active years	1957-58
Location	Ain-Diab suburb of Casablanca
Type	Temporary road course
Lap distance	4.724 miles
Lap record	Qualifying: Mike Hawthorn (Ferrari Dino 246), 2m23.1, 118.843 mph, F1, 1958
	Race: Stirling Moss (Vanwall VW5), 2m22.5, 119.343 mph, F1, 1958

Moroccan Grand Prix see above

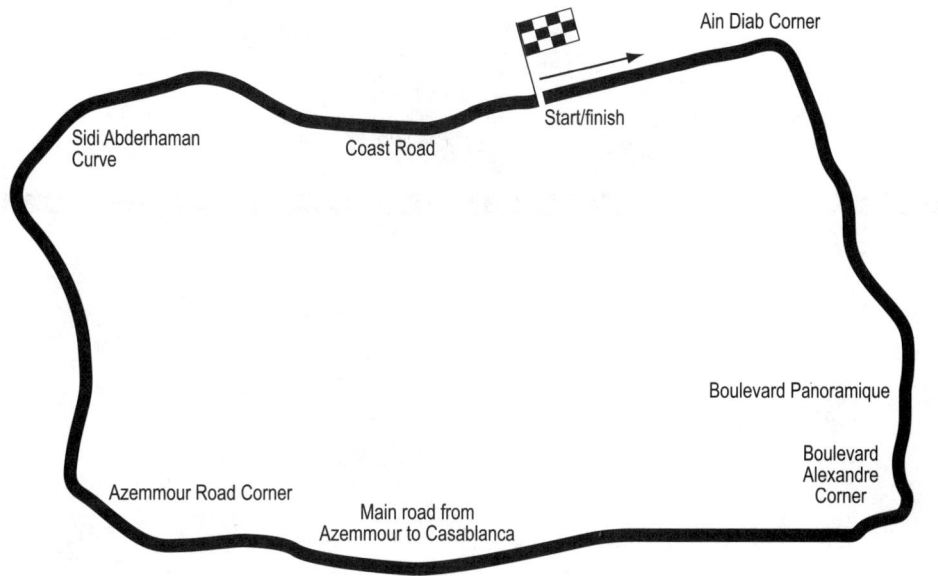

699

NEW ZEALAND
Major Championships

NEW ZEALAND GOLD STAR CHAMPIONSHIP

Although the Gold Star was replaced as New Zealand's premier single-seater series by the International Championship in 1976, since 1999 it has been revived as the Tasman Cup. At times the Gold Star and International Championship were one and the same. Both Formula Pacific and F5000 were eligible in 1977, with F5000 cars competing under a handicap system until enough Pacific cars were available. Although Ken Smith won every race, he still lost the series to McMillan as a result of this unusual scoring system!

year	driver	nat	car
1957	Ross Jensen	NZ	Ferrari 750 Monza/Austin-Healey
1958	Ross Jensen	NZ	Maserati 250F
1959	Bruce McLaren	NZ	Cooper T45-Climax
1960	Syd Jensen	NZ	Cooper T45-Climax
1961	Denny Hulme	NZ	Cooper T51-Climax
1962	Pat Hoare	NZ	Ferrari 256
1963	Angus Hyslop	NZ	Cooper T45-Climax
1964	Jim Palmer	NZ	Cooper T45-Climax
1965	Jim Palmer	NZ	Brabham BT7A-Climax
1966	Jim Palmer	NZ	Lotus 32B-Climax
1967	Roly Levis	NZ	Brabham BT18-Ford
1968	Jim Palmer	NZ	McLaren M4A-Cosworth
1969	Roly Levis	NZ	Brabham BT23-Cosworth
1970	Graham McRae	NZ	Begg FM2-Chevrolet/McLaren M10A-Chevrolet
1971	Graeme Lawrence	NZ	Ferrari Dino 246T/Brabham BT29-Cosworth
1972	David Oxton	NZ	Begg FM4-Chevrolet
1973	David Oxton	NZ	Begg FM5-Chevrolet
1974	David Oxton	NZ	Begg FM5-Chevrolet
1975	Graeme Lawrence	NZ	Lola T332-Chevrolet
1976	Ken Smith	NZ	Lola T332-Chevrolet
1977	Dave McMillan	NZ	Ralt RT1-Ford
1978	RP Stone	NZ	Cuda-Ford
1979	Dave McMillan	NZ	Ralt RT1-Ford
1980	Dave McMillan	NZ	Ralt RT1-Ford
1981	Dave Oxton	NZ	Ralt RT4-Ford
1982	Dave Oxton	NZ	Ralt RT4-Ford
1984	Ken Smith	NZ	Ralt RT4-Ford
1985	Ken Smith	NZ	Ralt RT4-Ford
1987	Ken Smith	NZ	Ralt RT4-Ford
1988	Paul Radisich	NZ	Ralt RT4-Ford
1989	Dean Hall	USA	Swift DB4-Ford
1990	Ken Smith	NZ	Swift DB4-Ford
1991	Craig Baird	NZ	Swift DB4-Toyota
1992	Craig Baird	NZ	Reynard 92H-Toyota
1993	Craig Baird	NZ	Reynard 92H-Toyota
1994	Greg Murphy	NZ	Reynard 92D-Holden
1995	Greg Murphy	NZ	Reynard 92D-Holden
1999	Simon Wills	NZ	Reynard 94D-Holden
2000	Simon Wills	NZ	Reynard 94D-Holden
2001	Andrew Booth	NZ	Reynard 94D-Holden
2002	Fabian Coulthard	NZ	Stealth RF94-Ford

1983, 1986, 1996-98

NEW ZEALAND INTERNATIONAL CHAMPIONSHIP

year	formula	driver	nat	car
1976	2.0l/F5000	Ken Smith	NZ	Lola T332-Chevrolet
1977	Pacific	Keke Rosberg	SF	Chevron B34-Ford
1978	Pacific	Keke Rosberg	SF	Chevron B39-Ford
1979	Pacific	Teo Fabi	I	March 78/79B-Ford
1980	Pacific	Dave McMillan	NZ	Ralt RT1-Ford
1981	Pacific	Dave Oxton	NZ	Ralt RT4-Ford
1982	Pacific	Roberto Moreno	BR	Ralt RT4-Ford
1983	Pacific	Allen Berg	CDN	Ralt RT4-Ford
1984	Pacific	Ken Smith	NZ	Ralt RT4-Ford
1985	Pacific	Ross Cheever	USA	Ralt RT4-Ford
1986	Pacific	Jeff MacPherson	USA	Ralt RT4-Ford
1987	Pacific	Mike Thackwell	NZ	Ralt RT4-Ford
1988	Pacific	Paul Radisich	NZ	Ralt RT4-Ford

NEW ZEALAND INTERNATIONAL CHAMPIONSHIP (cont.)

year	formula	driver	nat	car
1989	Pacific	Dean Hall	USA	Swift DB4-Ford
1990	Pacific	Ken Smith	NZ	Swift DB4-Ford
1991	Pacific	Craig Baird	NZ	Swift DB4-Toyota
1992	Pacific	Craig Baird	NZ	Reynard 92H-Toyota
1993	Pacific/Brabham	Craig Baird	NZ	Reynard 92H-Toyota
1994	Brabham	Paul Stokell	AUS	Reynard 90D-Holden
1995	Brabham	Greg Murphy	NZ	Reynard 92D-Holden

NEW ZEALAND TOURING CAR CHAMPIONSHIP

year	driver	nat	car
1984	G Sprague	NZ	Ford Falcon XD
1985	Kent Baigent	NZ	BMW 635 CSi
1986	Graeme Bowkett	NZ	Holden Commodore
1987	G McIntyre	NZ	BMW 635 CSi
1988	T Crowe	NZ	BMW M3
1989	Robbie Francevic	AUS	Ford Sierra Cosworth RS500
1990	Robbie Francevic	AUS	Ford Sierra Cosworth RS500
1991	Brett Riley	NZ	BMW M3
1992	G Crosby	NZ	Ford Sierra Cosworth
1993	E Lamont	NZ	Holden Commodore
1994	Craig Baird	NZ	BMW 320i
1995	Craig Baird	NZ	BMW 320i
1996	Craig Baird	NZ	BMW 320i
1997	Craig Baird	NZ	BMW 320i
1998	Brett Riley	NZ	BMW 320i
1999	Jason Richards	NZ	BMW 320i
2000	Jason Richards	NZ	BMW 320i
2001	Jason Richards	NZ	Nissan Primera
2002	Barrie Tomlinson	NZ	Toyota Altezza

NEW ZEALAND TRANZ-AM CHAMPIONSHIP

year	driver	nat	car
1997	Ashley Stichbury	NZ	Ford Mustang
1999	Shane Drake	NZ	Chevrolet Camaro
2000	Craig Baird	NZ	Chevrolet Camaro
2001	Ashley Stichbury	NZ	Chevrolet Corvette
2002	Paul Pedersen	NZ	Chevrolet Camaro

1998 no series

Major International Races

NEW ZEALAND GRAND PRIX

year	formula	circuit	winner	nat	car	mph
1950	FL	Ohakea	John McMillan	NZ	Jackson-Ford	63.809
1951	FL	Ohakea	George Smith	NZ	GeeCeeEss-Mercury	66.403
1954	FL	Ardmore	Stan Jones	AUS	Maybach Mk1	72.500
1955	FL	Ardmore	"B Bira"	SM	Maserati 250F	78.750
1956	FL	Ardmore	Stirling Moss	GB	Maserati 250F	78.900
1957	FL	Ardmore	Reg Parnell	GB	Ferrari 555	76.940
1958	FL	Ardmore	Jack Brabham	AUS	Cooper T43-Climax	79.360
1959	FL	Ardmore	Stirling Moss	GB	Cooper T45-Climax	82.800
1960	FL	Ardmore	Jack Brabham	AUS	Cooper T51-Climax	86.600
1961	FL	Ardmore	Jack Brabham	AUS	Cooper T53-Climax	87.800
1962	FL	Ardmore	Stirling Moss	GB	Lotus 21-Climax	72.300
1963	FL	Pukekohe	John Surtees	GB	Lola Mk4-Climax	85.410
1964	FL	Pukekohe	Bruce McLaren	NZ	Cooper T70-Climax	87.846
1965	FL	Pukekohe	Graham Hill	GB	Brabham BT11A-Climax	89.512
1966	2.5l	Pukekohe	Graham Hill	GB	BRM P261	83.010
1967	2.5l	Pukekohe	Jackie Stewart	GB	BRM P261	100.971
1968	2.5l	Pukekohe	Chris Amon	NZ	Ferrari 246T	102.638
1969	2.5l	Pukekohe	Chris Amon	NZ	Ferrari 246T	105.139
1970	F5000	Pukekohe	Frank Matich	AUS	McLaren M10A-Chevrolet	103.810
1971	F5000	Pukekohe	Niel Allen	AUS	McLaren M10B-Chevrolet	107.883
1972	F5000	Pukekohe	Frank Gardner	AUS	Lola T300-Chevrolet	106.329
1973	F5000	Pukekohe	John McCormack	AUS	Elfin MR5-Holden/Repco	89.960
1974*	F5000	Wigram	John McCormack	AUS	Elfin MR5-Holden/Repco	114.419
1975	F5000	Pukekohe	Warwick Brown	AUS	Lola T332-Chevrolet	87.137
1976	F5000	Pukekohe	Ken Smith	NZ	Lola T332-Chevrolet	98.688

NEW ZEALAND GRAND PRIX (cont.)

year	formula	circuit	winner	nat	car	mph
1977	Pacific	Pukekohe	Keke Rosberg	SF	Chevron B34-Ford	94.010
1978	Pacific	Pukekohe	Keke Rosberg	SF	Chevron B39-Ford	97.111
1979	Pacific	Pukekohe	Teo Fabi	I	March 78/79B-Ford	n/a
1980	Pacific	Pukekohe	Steve Millen	NZ	Ralt RT1-Ford	98.920
1981	Pacific	Pukekohe	Dave McMillan	NZ	Ralt RT1-Ford	104.600
1982	Pacific	Pukekohe	Roberto Moreno	BR	Ralt RT4-Ford	107.184
1983	Pacific	Pukekohe	Dave Oxton	NZ	Ralt RT4-Ford	107.005
1984#	Pacific	Pukekohe	Davy Jones	USA	Ralt RT4-Ford	100.080
1984#	Pacific	Pukekohe	Ross Cheever	USA	Ralt RT4-Ford	91.530
1986	Pacific	Pukekohe	Ross Cheever	USA	Ralt RT4-Ford	n/a
1987	Pacific	Pukekohe	Davy Jones	USA	Ralt RT4-Ford	107.190
1988	Pacific	Pukekohe	Paul Radisich	NZ	Ralt RT4-Ford	n/a
1989	Pacific	Pukekohe	Dean Hall	USA	Swift DB4-Ford	106.213
1990	Pacific	Pukekohe	Ken Smith	NZ	Swift DB4-Ford	106.390
1991	Pacific	Pukekohe	Craig Baird	NZ	Swift DB4-Toyota	106.470
1992	Pacific	Manfeild	Craig Baird	NZ	Reynard 92H-Toyota	106.836
1993	Pacific	Manfeild	Craig Baird	NZ	Reynard 92H-Toyota	104.420
1994	Brabham	Manfeild	Greg Murphy	NZ	Reynard 90D-Holden	n/a
1995	Brabham	Manfeild	Brady Kennett	NZ	Reynard 91D-Holden	n/a
1999	Holden	Ruapuna	Simon Wills	NZ	Reynard 94D-Holden	n/a
2000	Holden	Ruapuna	Simon Wills	NZ	Reynard 94D-Holden	n/a
2001	Holden	Pukekohe	Andrew Booth	NZ	Reynard 94D-Holden	n/a
2002	FF1600	Teretonga	Fabian Coulthard	NZ	Stealth RF94-Ford	n/a

*Run concurrently with the Lady Wigram Trophy. #Two races in 1984, first in January, second in December. 1952-53, 1985 and 1996-98 no race

Circuits and other Races

PUKEKOHE

A flat circuit built around a horse racecourse, Pukekohe Park Raceway was the home of the New Zealand Grand Prix until 1991, when it moved to Manfeild. The race returned to Pukekohe in 2000, and an Australian V8 Supercar round was held a year later. The hairpin that follows the long back straight is the trickiest point on the circuit, while spectator banks give excellent viewing near the start-line.

Active years	1963 to date
Location	25 miles south of Auckland
Type	Permanent road course
Lap distance	1.752 miles
Lap record	Race: Greg Murphy (Reynard 90D-Holden), 54.74s, 115.222 mph, Formula Holden, 1994

Circuit changes

1963-66	2.175 miles
1967 to date	Loop after first corner bypassed. Current circuit

New Zealand Grand Prix see above

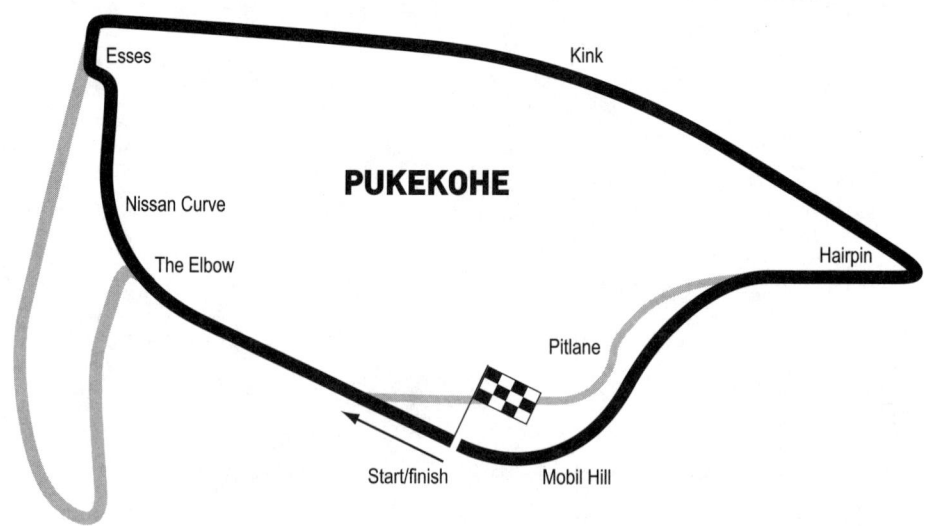

NORWAY
Major Championships

NORWEGIAN FORMULA 3 CHAMPIONSHIP				
year	driver	nat	team	car
1999	Ole Martin Lindum	N	Franz Woss Racing	Dallara 394-Opel
2000	Marko Nevalainen	SF	Motor Up Racing Team	Dallara 397-Opel

Major International Races

NORWEGIAN GRAND PRIX							
year	formula	circuit	winner	nat	car		mph
1934	GP	Mjosa	Per-Viktor Widengren	S	Alfa Romeo 8C "Monza"		70.215
1935	GP	Lake Bogstad	Per-Viktor Widengren	S	Alfa Romeo 8C "Monza"		111.600
1936	GP	Gjerstadsjon	Eugen Bjornstad	N	Alfa Romeo 8C "Monza"		64.539

POLAND
Major Championships

POLISH FORMULA 3 CHAMPIONSHIP				
year	driver	nat	team	car
1995	Jaroslaw Wierczuk	PL	GPF Motorsport	Dallara 393-Fiat

Circuits and Races

LWOW

Poland's only international race was organised on the narrow and dangerous streets of Lwow by the Malopolski Klub Automobilowy. The many sharp corners caused frequent accidents and kept average speeds down to 50mph. A circuit now operates at Poznan but international racing has not visited since the thirties.

Active years	1930-33
Location	Central Lwow
Type	Temporary street circuit
Lap distance	1.865 miles
Lap record	Race: Rudolf Caracciola (Alfa Romeo 8C "Monza"), 2m02.8, 54.672 mph, GP, 1932

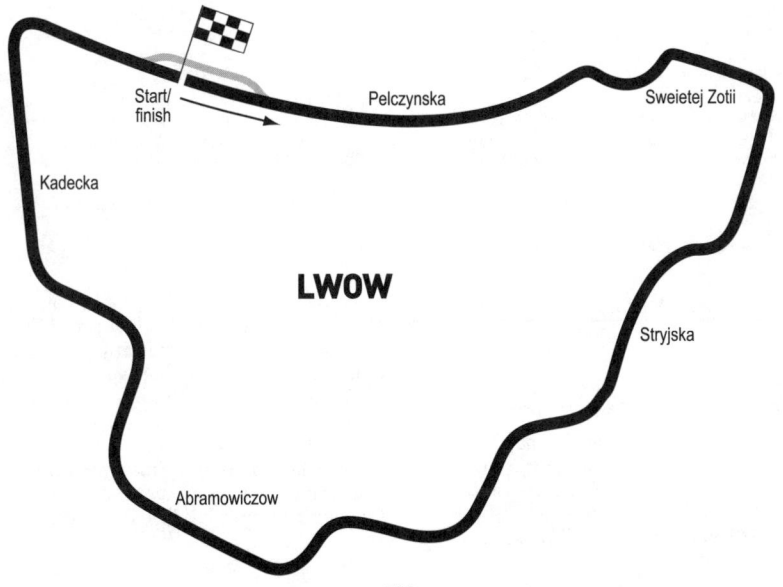

LWOW GRAND PRIX

year	formula	winner	nat	car	mph
1930	FL	Henryk Liefeld	PL	Austro-Daimler	50.530
1931	GP	Hans Stuck	D	Mercedes-Benz SSK	48.308
1932	GP	Rudolf Caracciola	D	Alfa Romeo 8C "Monza"	53.221
1933	GP	Eugen Bjornstad	N	Alfa Romeo 8C "Monza"	51.123

PORTUGAL
Major Championships

PORTUGUESE TOURING CAR CHAMPIONSHIP

year	driver	nat	car
1992	Hernani Castro Lopo	P	Honda Civic VTi
1993	Ni Amorim	P	Opel Astra GSi
1994	Pedro Faria	P	Toyota Carina

Major International Races

PORTUGUESE GRAND PRIX

year	formula	circuit	winner	nat	car	mph
1951	SC	Oporto	Casimiro de Oliveira	P	Ferrari 260MM Vignale	78.210
1952	SC	Oporto	Eugenio Castellotti	I	Ferrari	85.710
1953	SC	Oporto	N Pinto Nogueira	P	Ferrari	85.380
1954	SC	Monsanto	Jose Froilan Gonzalez	RA	Ferrari	82.770
1955	SC	Oporto	Jean Behra	F	Maserati 300S	91.650
1957	SC	Monsanto	Juan Manuel Fangio	RA	Maserati	86.890
1958	F1 W	Oporto	Stirling Moss	GB	Vanwall VW10	105.041
1959	F1 W	Monsanto	Stirling Moss	GB	Cooper T51-Climax	95.310
1960	F1 W	Oporto	Jack Brabham	AUS	Cooper T53-Climax	109.279
1965	F3	Cascais	Rod Banting	GB	Cooper-Ford	n/a
1966	F3	Cascais	Jorg Dubler	CH	Brabham-Ford	n/a
1967	F3	Montes Claros	Carlos Gaspar	P	Brabham BT21-Ford	n/a
1968	SC	Montes Claros	Carlos Gaspar	P	Ford GT40	n/a
1969	SC	Montes Claros	Manuel Pinto	P	Porsche Carrera 6	n/a
1984	F1 W	Estoril	Alain Prost	F	McLaren MP4/2-TAG Porsche	112.184
1985	F1 W	Estoril	Ayrton Senna	BR	Lotus 97T-Renault	90.200
1986	F1 W	Estoril	Nigel Mansell	GB	Williams FW11-Honda	116.598
1987	F1 W	Estoril	Alain Prost	F	McLaren MP4/3-TAG Porsche	116.959
1988	F1 W	Estoril	Alain Prost	F	McLaren MP4/4-Honda	116.219
1989	F1 W	Estoril	Gerhard Berger	A	Ferrari 640	118.943
1990	F1 W	Estoril	Nigel Mansell	GB	Ferrari 641/2	120.377
1991	F1 W	Estoril	Riccardo Patrese	I	Williams FW14-Renault	120.315
1992	F1 W	Estoril	Nigel Mansell	GB	Williams FW14B-Renault	121.493
1993	F1 W	Estoril	Michael Schumacher	D	Benetton B193B-Ford	124.119
1994	F1 W	Estoril	Damon Hill	GB	Williams FW16B-Renault	114.069
1995	F1 W	Estoril	David Coulthard	GB	Williams FW17-Renault	113.286
1996	F1 W	Estoril	Jacques Villeneuve	CDN	Williams FW18-Renault	113.345

Note: incomplete list of results

Circuits and Other Races

ESTORIL
Autodromo Fernanda Pires da Silva

The need for a replacement race for the final Grand Prix of 1984 gave Estoril the opportunity to join the World Championship. Estoril opened in 1972 but fell into disrepair in the late 1970s. The 1984 race saw the closest-ever finish to the Championship as Niki Lauda edged out McLaren teammate Alain Prost by half a point for the title. Ayrton Senna won his first Grand Prix at Estoril a year later, delivering a masterly performance in atrocious conditions. Prost had an eventful race here in 1993, securing his fourth world crown and announcing his retirement within a 24-hour period. A new hairpin was built to slow cars at Turn 9 in the aftermath of the 1994 Imola tragedy. The climate has made Estoril a popular winter testing venue and rumours suggest a Champcar race may be held in the future.

Active years 1972 to date
Location 4 miles north of Estoril, 20 miles west of Lisbon
Type Permanent road course
Website www.fpak.pt

Current circuit
Lap distance 2.599 miles
Lap record Qualifying: Olivier Beretta (Dallara LMP-Judd), 1m29.401, 104.666 mph, Sports Cars, 2002

Race: Olivier Beretta (Dallara LMP-Judd), 1m31.442, 102.321 mph, Sports Cars, 2002

Circuit changes
1972-93 2.703 miles
1994-99 A new hairpin was constructed at Turn 9. 2.709 miles
2000 to date First two corners tightened. Parabolica moved towards pit complex to allow greater run-off area. Current circuit

ESTORIL

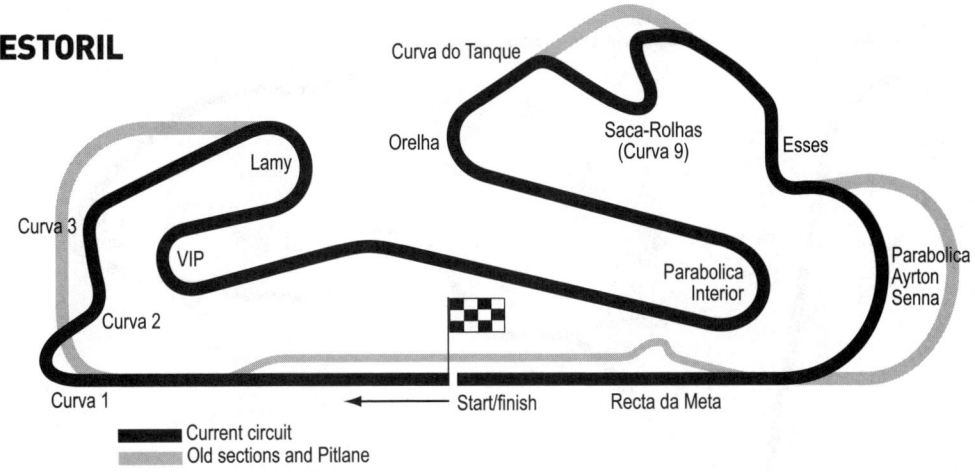

Portuguese Grand Prix see above

EUROPEAN FORMULA 2 RACE

year	formula	winner	nat	car	mph
1973	F2	Jean-Pierre Jarier	F	March 732-BMW	99.748
1975	F2 E	Jacques Laffite	F	Martini MK16-BMW	85.271
1976	F2 E	Rene Arnoux	F	Martini MK19-Renault	100.947
1977	F2 E	Didier Pironi	F	Martini MK22-Renault	102.015

INTERNATIONAL FORMULA 3000 RACE

year	formula	winner	nat	car	mph
1985	F3000 INT	John Nielsen	DK	Ralt RB20-Cosworth	104.790
1994	F3000 INT	Jules Boullion	F	Reynard 94D-Cosworth	104.879
1995	F3000 INT	Tarso Marques	BR	Reynard 95D-Cosworth	104.098
1996	F3000 INT	Ricardo Zonta	BR	Lola T96/50-Zytek	99.799

WORLD SPORTS CAR RACE

year	formula	winner	nat	car	mph
1977	SC WSC	Arturo Merzario	I	Alfa Romeo T33SC/12	95.625

FIA GT RACE

year	formula	winner	nat	car	mph
2000	GT FIA	Julian Bailey/			
		Jamie Campbell-Walter	GB	Lister Storm GT	65.876
2001	GT FIA	Jeroen Bleekemolen/			
		Mike Hezemans	NL	Chrysler Viper GTS-R	77.471
2002	GT FIA	Jean-Denis Deletraz/			
		Andrea Piccini	CH/I	Ferrari 550M	86.312

705

MONSANTO

Scene of the Portuguese Sports Car Grand Prix twice in the fifties, Monsanto also held an F1 World Championship event in 1959. It was set in a park in the hills north of Lisbon and the main straight was part of the road to Estoril.

Active years   1953-59
Location   North of Lisbon

Type	Temporary road course
Lap distance	3.380 miles
Lap record	Qualifying: Stirling Moss (Cooper T51-Climax), 2m02.89, 99.015 mph, F1, 1959
	Race: Stirling Moss (Cooper T51-Climax), 2m05.07, 97.290 mph, F1, 1959

Circuit changes	
1953-57	3.500 miles
1958-59	3.380 miles

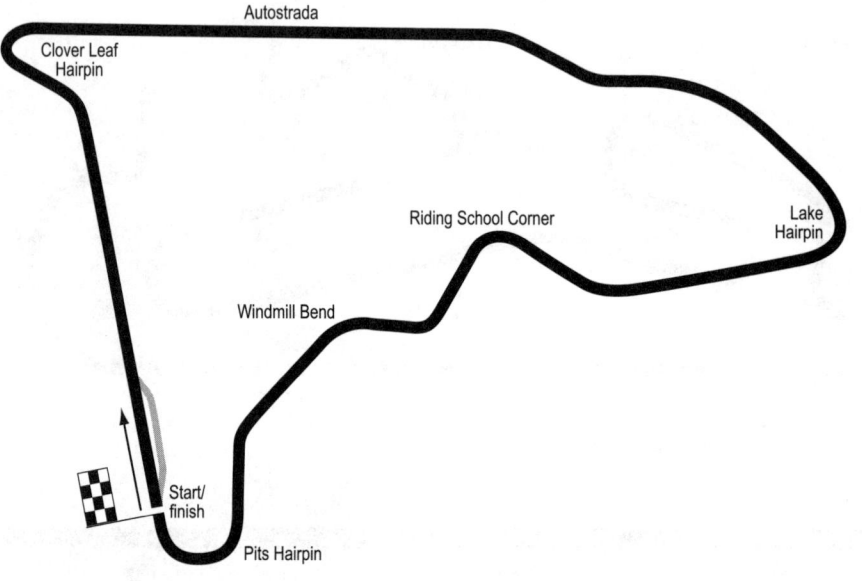

Portuguese Grand Prix see above

OPORTO

This was a temporary circuit on the outskirts of Oporto that hosted a sports car race in the early fifties before being included in the F1 World Championship. The round-the-houses circuit consisted of a mixture of fast and slow corners, tramlines and cobbles, and even passed a fish-drying factory at the conclusion of the lap. Safety concerns forced it to close in 1960.

Active years   1950-60
Location   Northern Portugal at the mouth of the River Douro

Type	Temporary street circuit
Lap distance	4.603 miles
Lap record	Qualifying: John Surtees (Lotus 18-Climax), 2m25.56, 113.842 mph, F1, 1960
	Race: John Surtees (Lotus 18-Climax), 2m27.53, 112.322 mph, F1, 1960

Portuguese Grand Prix see above

RUSSIA
Major Championships

RUSSIAN TOURING CAR CHAMPIONSHIP

year	driver	nat	team	car
1999	Alexandr Sukhov	R	MTS-AC Racing	BMW 320i
2000	Mikhail Ukhov	R	MTS-AC Racing	BMW 320i
2001	Alexandr Lvov	R	-	Opel Astra OPC
2002	Gregory Komarov	R	-	BMW 320i

RUSSIAN FORMULA 3 CHAMPIONSHIP

year	driver	nat	car
1997	Alberto Pedemonte	I	Dallara 397-Fiat
1998	Alberto Pedemonte	I	Dallara 398-Renault
1999	Alberto Pedemonte	I	Dallara 398-Renault
2000	Alberto Pedemonte	I	Dallara 399-Renault
2001	Maurizio Mediani	I	Dallara 399-Fiat
2002	Andrea Belicchi	I	Dallara 399-Renault

SOUTH AFRICA
Major Championships

SOUTH AFRICAN DRIVERS CHAMPIONSHIP

year	driver	nat	car
1953	Doug Duff	ZA	Riley
1954	Bill Jennings	ZA	Riley
1955	Frank Brodie	ZA	MG
1956	Bill Jennings	ZA	Riley
1957	Bill Jennings	ZA	Riley
1958	Ian Fraser-Jones	ZA	Porsche RS
1959	Ian Fraser-Jones	ZA	Porsche RS
1960	Syd van der Vyver	ZA	Cooper-Alfa Romeo
1961	Syd van der Vyver	ZA	Lotus 18-Alfa Romeo
1962	Ernest Pieterse	ZA	Heron-Alfa Romeo/Lotus 20-Climax
1963	Neville Lederle	ZA	Lotus 20-Climax
1964	John Love	RSR	Cooper T55-Climax
1965	John Love	RSR	Cooper T55-Climax
1966	John Love	RSR	Cooper T79-Climax
1967	John Love	RSR	Cooper T79-Climax/Brabham BT20-Repco
1968	John Love	RSR	Brabham BT20-Repco/Lotus 49-Ford
1969	John Love	RSR	Lotus 49B-Ford
1970	Dave Charlton	ZA	Lotus 49C-Ford
1971	Dave Charlton	ZA	Lotus 49C-Ford
1972	Dave Charlton	ZA	Lotus 72D-Ford
1973	Dave Charlton	ZA	Lotus 72D-Ford
1974	Dave Charlton	ZA	McLaren M23-Ford
1975	Dave Charlton	ZA	McLaren M23-Ford
1976	Ian Scheckter	ZA	March 76B-Ford
1977	Ian Scheckter	ZA	March 77B-Ford
1978	Ian Scheckter	ZA	March 78B-Ford
1979	Ian Scheckter	ZA	March 79B-Mazda
1980	Tony Martin	ZA	Chevron B31-Mazda
1981	Bernard Tilanus	ZA	March 77B-Mazda/March 792-Mazda
1982	Graham Duxbury	ZA	March 822-Mazda
1983	Ian Scheckter	ZA	March 832-Mazda

SOUTH AFRICAN DRIVERS CHAMPIONSHIP (cont.)

year	driver	nat	car
1984	Ian Scheckter	ZA	March 832-Mazda
1985	Trevor van Rooyen	ZA	Maurer MM83-Mazda
1986	Wayne Taylor	ZA	Ralt RT4-Mazda
1990	Anthony Taylor	ZA	DAW Mk1-Volkswagen
1991	Mike Briggs	ZA	Swift-Volkswagen
1992	Shaun van der Linde	ZA	Swift-Volkswagen
1993	Duncan Vos	ZA	Swift-Volkswagen
1995	Etienne van der Linde	ZA	Ray-Volkswagen
1996	Morne Jurgens	ZA	Swift-Volkswagen
1997	Johan Smith	ZA	Swift-Volkswagen
1998	Johan Smith	ZA	Swift SC92
2002	Johan Fourie	ZA	Opel Astra

Formula 1 1962-75, Formula Atlantic 1976-86, Formula GTi 1990-93 and 1995-97, Formula 2000 Pro-Series 1998, 1987-89, 1994 and 1999-2001 no series

SOUTH AFRICAN TOURING CAR CHAMPIONSHIP

year	driver	nat	team	car
1992	Deon Joubert	ZA	BMW Motorsport SA	BMW 535i
1993	Mike Briggs	ZA	Opel Racing/Duxbury	Opel Astra GSi
1994	Shaun van der Linde	ZA	BMW Motorsport SA	BMW 318i
1995	Mike Briggs	ZA	Opel Racing/Duxbury	Opel Vectra
1996	Terry Moss	ZA	Audi Sport/Engen	Audi A4 Quattro
1997	Giniel de Villiers	ZA	Nissan Motorsport	Nissan Primera GT
1998	Giniel de Villiers	ZA	Nissan Motorsport	Nissan Primera GT
1999	Giniel de Villiers	ZA	Nissan Motorsport	Nissan Primera GT
2000	Giniel de Villiers	ZA	Nissan Motorsport	Nissan Primera GT

2001 to date no series

SOUTH AFRICAN SPRINGBOK SPORTS CAR CHAMPIONSHIP

year	driver	nat	car
1970	Brian Redman	GB	Chevron B16-Ford
1971	John Love	RSR	Lola T212
1972	Gerry Birrell	GB	Chevron B23

SOUTH AFRICAN V8 STOCK CAR CHAMPIONSHIP

year	driver	nat	car
2001	Sarel van der Merwe	ZA	Ford Mustang
2002	Sarel van der Merwe	ZA	Ford Mustang

Major International Races

SOUTH AFRICAN GRAND PRIX

year	formula	circuit	winner	nat	car	mph
1934	(h)	East London	Whitney Straight	USA	Maserati 8CM	95.680
1936	(h)	East London	Mario Massacurati	I	Bugatti T35B	87.430
1937	(h)	East London	Pat Fairfield	ZA	ERA A-type	89.170
1938	(h)	East London	Buller Meyer	ZA	Riley	86.530
1939	V	East London	Luigi Villoresi	I	Maserati 4CM	99.670
1960*	FL	East London	Paul Frere	B	Cooper T45-Climax	84.880
1960#	FL	East London	Stirling Moss	GB	Porsche 718	89.240
1961	F1	East London	Jim Clark	GB	Lotus 21-Climax	92.200
1962	F1 W	East London	Graham Hill	GB	BRM P57	93.594
1963	F1 W	East London	Jim Clark	GB	Lotus 25-Climax	95.116
1965	F1 W	East London	Jim Clark	GB	Lotus 33-Climax	98.004
1966	F1	East London	Mike Spence	GB	Lotus 33-Climax	97.750
1967	F1 W	Kyalami	Pedro Rodriguez	MEX	Cooper T81-Maserati	97.095
1968	F1 W	Kyalami	Jim Clark	GB	Lotus 49-Ford	107.422
1969	F1 W	Kyalami	Jackie Stewart	GB	Matra MS10-Ford	110.617
1970	F1 W	Kyalami	Jack Brabham	AUS	Brabham BT33-Ford	111.703
1971	F1 W	Kyalami	Mario Andretti	USA	Ferrari 312B	112.341
1972	F1 W	Kyalami	Denny Hulme	NZ	McLaren M19A-Ford	114.224
1973	F1 W	Kyalami	Jackie Stewart	GB	Tyrrell 006-Ford	117.140
1974	F1 W	Kyalami	Carlos Reutemann	RA	Brabham BT44-Ford	116.222
1975	F1 W	Kyalami	Jody Scheckter	ZA	Tyrrell 007-Ford	115.548
1976	F1 W	Kyalami	Niki Lauda	A	Ferrari 312T	116.649
1977	F1 W	Kyalami	Niki Lauda	A	Ferrari 312T2	116.589
1978	F1 W	Kyalami	Ronnie Peterson	S	Lotus 78-Ford	116.699
1979	F1 W	Kyalami	Gilles Villeneuve	CDN	Ferrari 312T4	117.192
1980	F1 W	Kyalami	Rene Arnoux	F	Renault RE20	123.189
1981	F1	Kyalami	Carlos Reutemann	RA	Williams FW07B-Ford	112.306
1982	F1 W	Kyalami	Alain Prost	F	Renault RE30B	127.860

year	formula	circuit	winner	nat	car	mph
1983	F1 W	Kyalami	Riccardo Patrese	I	Brabham BT52B-BMW	126.096
1984	F1 W	Kyalami	Niki Lauda	A	McLaren MP4/2-TAG Porsche	128.369
1985	F1 W	Kyalami	Nigel Mansell	GB	Williams FW10-Honda	129.835
1992	F1 W	Kyalami	Nigel Mansell	GB	Williams FW14B-Renault	118.230
1993	F1 W	Kyalami	Alain Prost	F	Williams FW15C-Renault	115.840

SOUTH AFRICAN GRAND PRIX (cont.)

*run 1 January, #run 27 December

Circuits and Other Races

EAST LONDON

A new Grand Prix circuit was opened in the countryside between East London and the Indian Ocean in July 1959 using part of the 1936-39 Prince George circuit. The Mercedes and Auto Union teams had raced here in 1937, although the organisers' decision to run a handicap race ensured a local win. East London was the scene of the title decider in 1962 between Graham Hill and Jim Clark. Clark led convincingly before suffering an engine failure that handed his rival the title. Later, however, the

Scotsman won three F1 GPs at East London including victories in his 1963 and 1965 championship seasons. The South African GP became a non-championship affair in 1966, and the race moved to Kyalami a year later.

Active years	1959 to date
Location	East London, adjacent to the Indian Ocean
Type	Permanent road course
Website	www.mercedes-benz-circuit.co.za
Lap distance	2.436 miles
Lap record	Qualifying: John Love (Lotus 49-Ford), 1m23.0, 105.658 mph, F1, 1969
	Race: John Love (Lotus 49-Ford), 1m22.4, 106.428 mph, F1, 1969

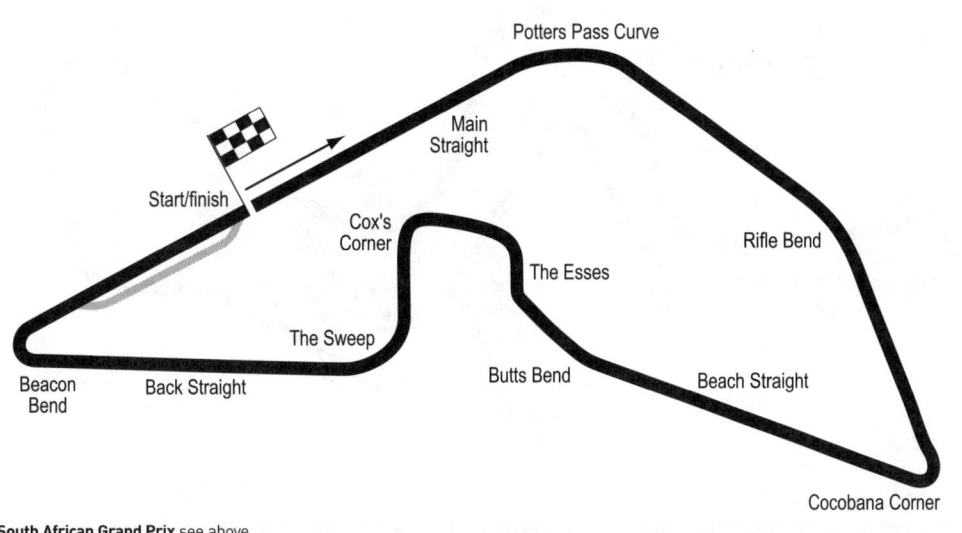

South African Grand Prix see above

KYALAMI

Kyalami first staged the South African Grand Prix in 1967 and has been the home of the sport in South Africa ever since. It was originally a superb circuit with a long main straight cresting the brow of a hill opposite the pits before descending to the demanding first corner at Crowthorne. Curiously, while other sports severed links with South Africa during apartheid, the Grand Prix remained until some teams boycotted the 1985 race. When the race returned in 1992 as apartheid was ending Kyalami had been completely rebuilt using part of

the existing track. The new version offered improved facilities but lacked the splendour of the old circuit. Since overtaking was now almost impossible, processional races became the rule at Kyalami, with qualifying even more important than at many other circuits. The race only returned once more, but Kyalami has survived continual financial and political problems. However, as ever the future of the circuit is in doubt as plans to sell half of the land for industrial redevelopment are being discussed and, if accepted, would likely end the possibility of International racing returning to South Africa.

Active years	1961 to date
Location	16 miles north of Johannesburg, 18 miles south of Pretoria
Type	Permanent road course
Website	www.aakyalami.co.za

Current circuit	
Lap distance	2.652 miles
Lap records	Race: Mauro Baldi (Ferrari 333SP), 1m34.776, 100.735 mph, Sports Cars, 1998

Circuit changes

1961-67	2.544 miles
1968-86	Widened and resurfaced. 2.550 miles
1987-91	New circuit built using sections of the old circuit. 2.300 miles
1992-96	Track extended to Gestetner Corner, new pits built. 2.648 miles
1997 to date	Chicane built. Current circuit

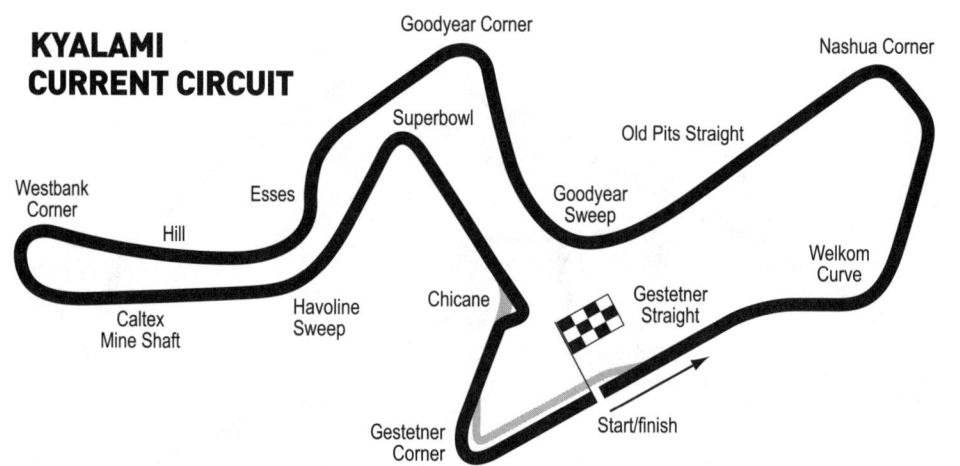

1961-86

Crowthorn Corner
The Kink
Start/finish
Barbeque Bend
Clubhouse
Jukskei Sweep
The Esses
Leeukop Bend
Sunset Bend

1987-91

Yellow Pages Corner
Panasonic Corner
Esses Hill
Sunset
Start/finish
Westbank Corner
Welkom Curve
Continental

■ 1987-91 circuit
▨ Original Grand Prix circuit and 1987-91 pitlane

KYALAMI CURRENT CIRCUIT

Goodyear Corner
Nashua Corner
Superbowl
Old Pits Straight
Westbank Corner
Esses
Goodyear Sweep
Hill
Welkom Curve
Caltex Mine Shaft
Havoline Sweep
Chicane
Gestetner Straight
Start/finish
Gestetner Corner

South African Grand Prix see above

INVITATION FORMULA 3000 RACE

year	formula	winner	nat	car	mph
1995	F3000	Jan Lammers	NL	Reynard 94D-Cosworth	92.570

RAND 9 HOURS

year	formula	winner	nat	car	mph
1958*	SC	Ian Fraser-Jones/Tony Fergusson	ZA	Porsche Speedster	62.330
1959*	SC	Hugh Carrington/Chris Fergusson	ZA	Dart-Climax	63.670
1960*	SC	John Love/Dawie Gous	RSR/ZA	Porsche RS Spyder	68.340
1961*	SC	Dawie Gous/John Love	ZA/RSR	Porsche RS Spyder	74.740
1962	SC	David Piper/Bruce Johnstone	GB/ZA	Ferrari GTB	76.840
1963	GT	David Piper/Tony Maggs	GB/ZA	Ferrari GTO	82.760
1964	SC	David Piper/Tony Maggs	GB/ZA	Ferrari 250LM	84.885
1965	SC	David Piper/Richard Attwood	GB	Ferrari 365P2	85.661
1966	SC	David Piper/Richard Attwood	GB	Ferrari 365 P2/3	82.260
1967	SC	Jacky Ickx/Brian Redman	B/GB	Mirage-Ford	96.900

RAND 9 HOURS (cont.)

year	formula	winner	nat	car	mph
1968	SC	Jacky Ickx/David Hobbs	B/GB	Mirage-Ford	88.900
1969	SC	David Piper/Richard Attwood	GB	Porsche 917	92.366
1970	SC	Jacky Ickx/Ignazio Giunti	B/I	Ferrari 512S	104.833
1971	SC	Clay Regazzoni/Brian Redman	CH/GB	Ferrari 312P	100.580
1972	SC	Arturo Merzario/Clay Regazzoni	I/CH	Ferrari 312P	103.275
1973	SC	Reinhold Joest/Herbert Muller	D/CH	Porsche 908/3	102.007
1974#	SC W	Henri Pescarolo/Gerard Larrousse	F	Matra-Simca MS670C	99.875

At Kyalami except *at Grand Central, Johannesburg. #Reduced to a 6 hour race due to the oil crisis

KYALAMI 1000 KMS/WORLD SPORTS CAR RACE

year	formula	winner	nat	car	mph
1975	SC/GT	Hans Heyer/Paul Hennige/Jochen Mass	D/-/D	Ford Escort RS	n/a
1976	SC	Gunnar Nilsson/Jody Scheckter/			
		Harald Grohs	S/ZA/D	BMW 3.0 CSL	93.150
1977	SC	Hans Heyer/Jody Scheckter	D/ZA	Ford Escort RS	98.154
1978	SC	Brian Cooke/Phil Adams	-	Datsun 140Z	n/a
1979	SC	Helmut Kelleners/Eddie Keizan	D/ZA	BMW M1	n/a
1981	SC	Jochen Mass/Reinhold Joest	D	Porsche 908	103.240
1982	SC	Jacky Ickx/Jochen Mass	B/D	Porsche 956	107.307
1983	SC W	Derek Bell/Stefan Bellof	GB/D	Porsche 956	108.490
1984	SC W	Riccardo Patrese/Alessandro Nannini	I	Lancia LC2	110.374
1986	SC	Piercarlo Ghinzani	I	Porsche 956	120.660
1987	SC	Jochen Mass	D	Porsche 962C	115.250

SOUTH KOREA

Circuits and Races

CHANGWON

Changwon is a semi-permanent circuit that holds South Korea's only international race, an end-of-season F3 invitational the week after Macau. It is a combination of public streets and permanent hairpins through a series of sports stadia northeast of central Changwon City. The

Korean Super Prix is now established as the second part of the F3 double-header after Macau.

Active years	1999 to date
Location	2 miles north-east of downtown Changwon City in south-eastern South Korea
Type	Temporary street circuit
Website	www.f3korea.net
Lap distance	1.892 miles
Lap records	Qualifying: Jonathan Cochet (Dallara 399-Renault), 1m10.332, 96.844 mph, F3, 2001
	Race: Gianmaria Bruni (Dallara 300-Mugen), 1m11.277, 95.559 mph, F3, 2000

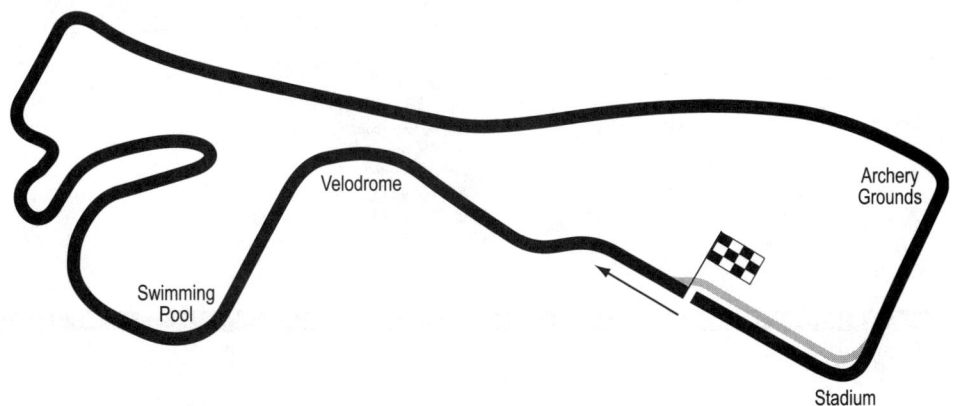

KOREAN SUPER PRIX

year	formula	winner	nat	car	mph
1999	F3	Darren Manning	GB	Dallara 399-Toyota	80.684
2000	F3	Narain Karthikeyan	IND	Dallara 300-Mugen	94.251
2001	F3	Jonathan Cochet	F	Dallara 399-Renault	94.069
2002	F3	Olivier Pla	F	Dallara 302-Renault	87.666

SPAIN
Major Championships

SPANISH SUPER NISSAN V6 WORLD SERIES

year	driver	nat	team	car
2002	Ricardo Zonta	BR	Gabord Competicion	Dallara SN01-Nissan

SPANISH FORMULA NISSAN 2000 CHAMPIONSHIP

year	driver	nat	car
1998	Marc Gene	E	Coloni CN1/C-Nissan
1999	Fernando Alonso	E	Coloni CN1/C-Nissan
2000	Antonio Garcia	E	Coloni CN1/C-Nissan
2001	Franck Montagny	F	Coloni CN1/C-Nissan
2002	Santiago Porteiro	E	Coloni CN1/C-Nissan

SPANISH GT CHAMPIONSHIP

year	driver	nat	car
1999	Tom Puig	E	Venturi 400GT
2000	Miguel de Castro/Balba Camino	E	Marcos
2001	Alberto Castello/Carlos Palau	E	Saleen S7R-Ford
2002	Pedro Chaves/Miguel Ramos	P	Saleen S7R-Ford

SPANISH TOURING CAR CHAMPIONSHIP (CAMPEONATO DE ESPANA TURISMOS SERIES)

year	driver	nat	car
1969	Jorge de Bagration	E	BMW 2002Ti
1970	Jorge Babler	E	BMW 2002Ti
1971	Alex Soler-Roig	E	Ford Capri RS2600
1972	Alex Soler-Roig	E	Ford Capri RS2600
1973	Jorge de Bagration	E	Ford Capri RS2600
1974	Francisco Torredemer	E	Ford Capri RS2600
1975	Jose Jaime Sanz de Madrid	E	Ford Escort RS
1976	Manuel Juncosa	E	Chrysler 180
1977	Juan Carlos Onoro	E	Chrysler 180
1978	Hansi Babler	E	SEAT 124
1979	Salvador Canellas	E	SEAT 124
1980	Carlos Martinez Penacoba	E	Ford Escort
1981	Santi Martin-Cantero	E	SEAT 131
1982	Jorge de Bagration	E	Lancia Stratos
1983	Emilio de Villota	E	Ford Capri RS3000
1984	Francisco Romero	E	Volkswagen Golf GTi
1985	Francisco Romero	E	Volkswagen Golf GTi
1986	"Correcaminos"	E	Renault 11 turbo
1987	Luis Miguel Arias	E	Volkswagen Golf GTi
1988	Luis Villamil	E	Alfa Romeo 33/Alfa Romeo 75
1989	Luis Lopez de la Camara	E	Ford Sierra Cosworth
1990	Jose Angel Sasiambarrena	E	Ford Sierra Cosworth
1991	Luis Perez Sala	E	Alfa Romeo 75 America
1992	Juan Ignacio Villacieros	E	BMW M3
1993	Luis Perez Sala	E	Nissan Skyline GT-R
1994	Adrian Campos	E	Alfa Romeo 155 TS
1995	Luis Villamil	E	Alfa Romeo 155 TS
1996	Jordi Gene	E	Audi A4 Quattro
1997	Fabrizio Giovanardi	I	Alfa Romeo 155 TS
1998	Alfredo Mostajo	E	Citroen ZX Kit-Car

SPANISH FORMULA 3 CHAMPIONSHIP

year	driver	nat	team	car
2001	Anders Vilarino	E	Racing Engineering	Dallara 301-Toyota
2002	Marcel Costa	E	EV Racing	Dallara 300-Toyota

Major International Races

SPANISH GRAND PRIX

year	formula	circuit	winner	nat	car	mph
1913	TC	Guadarrama	Carlo de Salamanca	E	Rolls-Royce	54.000
1923	GP	Sitges	Albert Divo	F	Sunbeam	96.962
1926	FL	Lasarte	Meo Costantini	F	Bugatti T35	78.829
1927	GP	Lasarte	Robert Benoist	F	Delage 15S8	82.524
1928	SC (h)	Lasarte	Louis Chiron	MC	Bugatti	68.456
1929	GP	Lasarte	Louis Chiron	MC	Bugatti T35B	74.124
1930	GP	Lasarte	Achille Varzi	I	Maserati 26M	88.990
1933	GP	Lasarte	Louis Chiron	MC	Alfa Romeo Tipo-B "P3"	85.954
1934	GP	Lasarte	Luigi Fagioli	I	Mercedes-Benz W25A	99.413
1935	GP	Lasarte	Rudolf Caracciola	D	Mercedes-Benz W25B	104.491
1951	F1 W	Pedralbes	Juan Manuel Fangio	RA	Alfa Romeo 159	98.771
1954	F1 W	Pedralbes	Mike Hawthorn	GB	Ferrari 553 Squalo	97.452
1967	F1/F2	Jarama	Jim Clark	GB	Lotus 49-Ford	83.595
1968	F1 W	Jarama	Graham Hill	GB	Lotus 49-Ford	84.407
1969	F1 W	Montjuich Park	Jackie Stewart	GB	Matra MS80-Ford	92.893
1970	F1 W	Jarama	Jackie Stewart	GB	March 701-Ford	87.220
1971	F1 W	Montjuich Park	Jackie Stewart	GB	Tyrrell 003-Ford	97.174
1972	F1 W	Jarama	Emerson Fittipaldi	BR	Lotus 72D-Ford	92.355
1973	F1 W	Montjuich Park	Emerson Fittipaldi	BR	Lotus 72D-Ford	97.843
1974	F1 W	Jarama	Niki Lauda	A	Ferrari 312B3	88.484
1975	F1 W	Montjuich Park	Jochen Mass	D	McLaren M23-Ford	95.529
1976	F1 W	Jarama	James Hunt	GB	McLaren M23-Ford	93.016
1977	F1 W	Jarama	Mario Andretti	USA	Lotus 78-Ford	92.537
1978	F1 W	Jarama	Mario Andretti	USA	Lotus 79-Ford	93.524
1979	F1 W	Jarama	Patrick Depailler	F	Ligier JS11-Ford	95.963
1980	F1	Jarama	Alan Jones	AUS	Williams FW07B-Ford	98.358
1981	F1 W	Jarama	Gilles Villeneuve	CDN	Ferrari 126CK	95.267
1986	F1 W	Jerez	Ayrton Senna	BR	Lotus 98T-Renault	104.069
1987	F1 W	Jerez	Nigel Mansell	GB	Williams FW11B-Honda	103.673
1988	F1 W	Jerez	Alain Prost	F	McLaren MP4/4-Honda	104.131
1989	F1 W	Jerez	Ayrton Senna	BR	McLaren MP4/5-Honda	106.485
1990	F1 W	Jerez	Alain Prost	F	Ferrari 641/2	106.268
1991	F1 W	Catalunya	Nigel Mansell	GB	Williams FW14-Renault	116.563
1992	F1 W	Catalunya	Nigel Mansell	GB	Williams FW14B-Renault	99.019
1993	F1 W	Catalunya	Alain Prost	F	Williams FW15C-Renault	124.418
1994	F1 W	Catalunya	Damon Hill	GB	Williams FW16-Renault	119.533
1995	F1 W	Catalunya	Michael Schumacher	D	Benetton B195-Renault	121.413
1996	F1 W	Catalunya	Michael Schumacher	D	Ferrari F310	95.594
1997	F1 W	Catalunya	Jacques Villeneuve	CDN	Williams FW19-Renault	124.485
1998	F1 W	Catalunya	Mika Hakkinen	SF	McLaren MP4/13-Mercedes-Benz	122.340
1999	F1 W	Catalunya	Mika Hakkinen	SF	McLaren MP4/14-Mercedes-Benz	121.560
2000	F1 W	Catalunya	Mika Hakkinen	SF	McLaren MP4/15-Mercedes-Benz	121.954
2001	F1 W	Catalunya	Michael Schumacher	D	Ferrari F2001	125.795
2002	F1 W	Catalunya	Michael Schumacher	D	Ferrari F2002	126.567

PENYA RHIN GRAND PRIX

year	formula	circuit	winner	nat	car	mph
1921	V	Villafranca	Pierre de Vizcaya	E	Bugatti T22	53.136
1922	V	Villafranca	Kenelm Lee Guinness	GB	Talbot-Darracq 56	65.251
1923	V	Villafranca	Albert Divo	F	Talbot T70	67.503
1933	GP	Montjuich Park	Juan Zanelli	RCH	Alfa Romeo 8C "Monza"	59.098
1934	GP	Montjuich Park	Achille Varzi	I	Alfa Romeo Tipo-B "P3"	64.633
1935	GP	Montjuich Park	Luigi Fagioli	I	Mercedes-Benz W25B	66.997
1936	GP	Montjuich Park	Tazio Nuvolari	I	Alfa Romeo Tipo-C "8C-35"	69.297
1946	GP	Pedralbes	Giorgio Pelassa	E	Maserati 4CL	80.250
1948	F1	Pedralbes	Luigi Villoresi	I	Maserati 4CLT/48	89.440
1950	F1	Montjuich Park	Alberto Ascari	I	Ferrari 375	56.409

Circuits and Other Races

ALBACETE

Albacete is a narrow and twisting modern circuit set on the flat countryside outside the quiet Spanish town. Overtaking proved near impossible when the International Formula 3000 championship visited in 1992, and major international categories have not returned. The tight confines are better suited to bikes (more popular in Spain), although the circuit is occasionally used as a winter testing venue.

Active years	1990 to date
Location	3 miles east of Albacete, 100 miles north-west of Alicante
Type	Permanent road course
Website	www.circuitoalbacete.com
Lap distance	2.236 miles
Lap record	Qualifying: Luca Badoer (Reynard 92D-Cosworth), 1m18.54, 102.491 mph, F3000, 1992
	Race: Jean-Christophe Ravier (Dallara SN01-Nissan), 1m20.423, 100.091 mph, Super Nissan, 2002

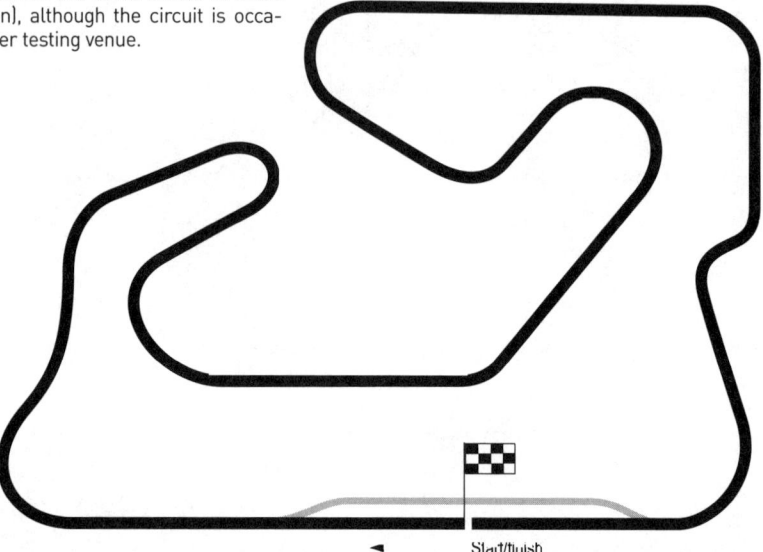

Start/finish

INTERNATIONAL FORMULA 3000 RACE						
year	formula	winner	nat	car		mph
1992	F3000 INT	Andrea Montermini	I	Reynard 92D-Cosworth		94.873

CATALUNYA

Barcelona

The Circuito de Catalunya at Montmelo is Barcelona's fourth Grand Prix circuit after Villafranca, Pedralbes and Montjuich Park. It was built at great expense to hold the 1991 Spanish Grand Prix in the backlash surrounding Martin Donnelly's near-fatal accident at Jerez a year earlier. The inaugural race featured Ayrton Senna and Nigel Mansell going wheel to wheel along the long main straight as they battled for the World Championship. The Nissan corner was slowed by a temporary tyre chicane in the 1994 race as Formula 1 struggled to address safety concerns, and has since been bypassed. Mika Hakkinen won three straight races here from 1998-2000, and Michael Schumacher is now a four-time winner.

Active years	1991 to date
Location	Montmelo, 15 miles north of Barcelona
Type	Permanent road course
Website	www.circuitcat.com
Current circuit	
Lap distance	2.937 miles
Lap records	Qualifying: Michael Schumacher (Ferrari F2002), 1m16.364, 138.458 mph, F1, 2002
	Race: Michael Schumacher (Ferrari F2001), 1m20.355, 131.581 mph, F1, 2002
Circuit changes	
1991-93	2.9497 miles
1994	Temporary tyre chicane inserted before Nissan. 2.9497 miles
1995 to date	The back straight built to bypass Nissan esses. Current circuit

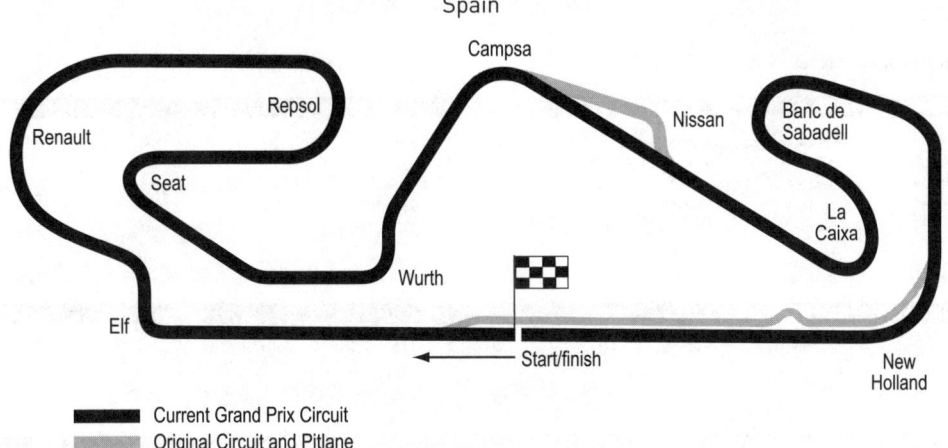

Spain

Current Grand Prix Circuit
Original Circuit and Pitlane

Spanish Grand Prix see above

INTERNATIONAL FORMULA 3000 RACE					
year	formula	winner	nat	car	mph
1992	F3000 INT	Andrea Montermini	I	Reynard 92D-Judd	113.836
1994	F3000 INT	Massimiliano Papis	I	Reynard 94D-Judd	110.462
1995	F3000 INT	Vincenzo Sospiri	I	Reynard 95D-Cosworth	113.209
1998	F3000 INT	Juan Pablo Montoya	CO	Lola T96/50-Zytek	106.456
1999	F3000 INT	Nick Heidfeld	D	Lola B99/50-Zytek	105.805
2000	F3000 INT	Bruno Junqueira	BR	Lola B99/50-Zytek	107.888
2001	F3000 INT	Tomas Enge	CS	Lola B99/50-Zytek	108.427
2002	F3000 INT	Giorgio Pantano	I	Lola B2/50-Zytek	108.982

JARAMA

In 1967 John Hugenholtz, the creator of both Zandvoort and Suzuka, was hired by the Real Automovil Club de Espana to design a new circuit at Jarama, site of one of the fiercest battles of the Spanish Civil War. It was the first purpose-built autodrome in Europe, and its layout of slow corners and a long straight now seems ahead of its time. Gilles Villeneuve, whose turbocharged Ferrari was all power and no handling, held off a queue of four cars here in 1981 to record an unlikely final victory. Jarama was extended after it lost the Grand Prix a year later, but international racing returned in 1994 with a round of the new GT series.

Current circuit
Lap distance   2.393 miles
Lap record   Qualifying: Ricardo Zonta (Dallara SN01-Nissan), 1m22.128, 104.895 mph, Super Nissan, 2002
              Race: Ricardo Zonta (Dallara SN01-Nissan), 1m23.530, 103.135 mph, Super Nissan, 2002

Circuit changes
1967-90   2.1154 miles
1991 to date   Extension built to Portago. Current circuit

Active years   **1967 to date**
Location   **18 miles north of Madrid**
Type   **Permanent road course**
Website   **www.race.es**

Current Circuit
Original Circuit and Pitlane

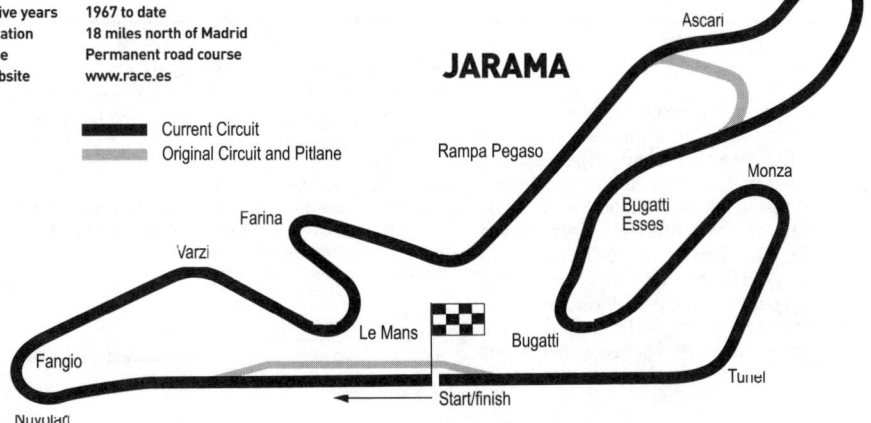

Spanish Grand Prix see above

MADRID GRAND PRIX

year	formula	winner	nat	car	mph
1967	F2 E	Jim Clark	GB	Lotus 48-Ford	81.661
1968	F2 E	Jean-Pierre Beltoise	F	Matra MS7-Ford	84.464
1969	F1/F5000	Keith Holland	GB	Lola T142-Chevrolet*	79.956
1971	F2 E	Emerson Fittipaldi	BR	Lotus 69-Ford	84.885

*F5000 car

OTHER EUROPEAN FORMULA 2 RACES

year	formula	winner	nat	car	mph
1969	F2 E	Jackie Stewart	GB	Matra MS7-Ford	84.983
1983	F2 E	Mike Thackwell	NZ	Ralt RH6/83-Honda	92.857

INTERNATIONAL FORMULA 3000 RACE

year	formula	winner	nat	car	mph
1986	F3000 INT	Pierluigi Martini	I	Ralt RT20-Cosworth	94.268
1987	F3000 INT	Yannick Dalmas	F	March 87B-Cosworth	92.884

EUROPEAN FORMULA 3 RACE

year	formula	winner	nat	car	mph
1977	F3 E	Nelson Piquet	BR	Ralt RT1-Toyota	85.291
1978	F3 E	Alain Prost	F	Martini MK21B-Renault	86.456
1979	F3 E	Alain Prost	F	Martini MK27-Renault	86.280
1980	F3 E	Mauro Baldi	I	Martini MK31-Toyota	88.399
1981	F3 E	Alain Ferte	F	Martini MK34-Alfa Romeo	89.297
1982	F3 E	James Weaver	GB	Ralt RT3/82-Toyota	89.057
1983	F3 E	Pierluigi Martini	I	Ralt RT3/83-Alfa Romeo	89.404
1984	F3 E	Johnny Dumfries	GB	Ralt RT3/83-Volkswagen	90.527

WORLD SPORTS CAR RACE

year	formula	winner	nat	car	mph
1987	SC W	Jan Lammers/John Watson	NL/GB	Jaguar XJR-8	92.269
1988	SC W	Eddie Cheever/Martin Brundle	USA/GB	Jaguar XJR-9	92.180
1989	SC W	Jochen Mass/Jean-Louis Schlesser	D/F	Sauber C9/88-Mercedes-Benz	89.239

FIA GT RACE

year	formula	winner	nat	car	mph
1994	GT FIA	Jesus Pareja/Jean-Pierre Jarier/Dominique Dupuy	E/F/F	Porsche 911 turbo SLM	83.178
1995	GT FIA	Ray Bellm/Maurizio Sandro Sala	GB/BR	McLaren F1 GTR-BMW	85.212
1996	GT FIA	Ray Bellm/James Weaver	GB	McLaren F1 GTR-BMW	87.410
1998	GT E	Thomas Bscher/Geoff Lees	D/GB	McLaren F1 GTR-BMW	87.740
2001	GT FIA	Alain Menu/Rickard Rydell	CH/S	Ferrari 550M	87.979
2002	GT FIA	Jean-Denis Deletraz/Andrea Piccini	CH/I	Ferrari 550M	88.895

JEREZ

Built near the sherry town of Jerez de la Frontera to host the 1986 Spanish Grand Prix, Jerez is a slow circuit with excellent facilities. But it was too far from Spain's major cities to attract more than a sprinkling of spectators. The most demanding section was behind the paddock, with two fast right-handers and little run-off area. It was here that Martin Donnelly crashed in qualifying for the 1990 race, prompting the Grand Prix circus to move to a new home near Barcelona. By the time Jerez hosted the 1994 European GP a new chicane had been built at the site of Donnelly's accident. In 1997 Michael Schumacher and Jacques Villeneuve clashed at Jerez in a race that left the Canadian with his first world title and Schumacher excluded from the championship for deliberately colliding with his rival.

Active years	1986 to date
Location	6 miles north-east of Jerez de la Frontera, 22 miles north-east of Cadiz, 50 miles south of Seville
Type	Permanent road course
Website	www.circuitodejerez.com

Current circuit

Lap distance	2.752 miles
Lap records	Qualifying: Jacques Villeneuve (Williams FW19-

Renault), Michael Schumacher (Ferrari F310B) and
Heinz-Harald Frentzen (Williams FW19-Renault), all
1m21.072, 122.202 mph, F1, 1997
Race: Heinz-Harald Frentzen (Williams FW19-Renault),
1m23.135, 119.145 mph, F1, 1997

Circuit changes
1986-91   2.6209 miles
1992-93   Curva Sito Pons and back straight built. 2.748 miles
1994 to date   Ayrton Senna chicane built. Current circuit

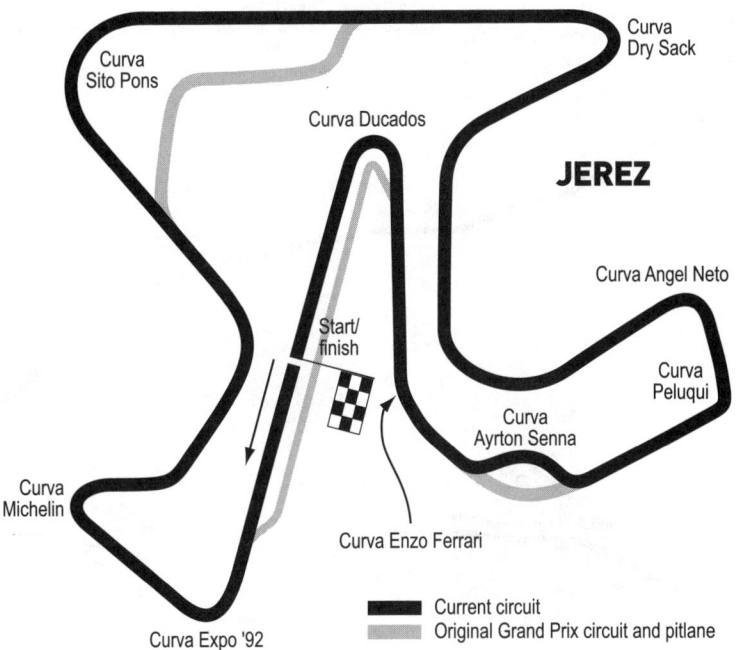

Curva Sito Pons

Curva Dry Sack

Curva Ducados

JEREZ

Curva Angel Neto

Start/finish

Curva Peluqui

Curva Ayrton Senna

Curva Michelin

Curva Enzo Ferrari

Curva Expo '92

Current circuit
Original Grand Prix circuit and pitlane

Spanish Grand Prix see above
European Grand Prix see above

INTERNATIONAL FORMULA 3000 RACE

year	formula	winner	nat	car	mph
1988	F3000 INT	Johnny Herbert	GB	Reynard 88D-Cosworth	95.572
1989	F3000 INT	Eric Bernard	F	Lola T89/50-Mugen	96.186
1990	F3000 INT	Erik Comas	F	Lola T90/50-Mugen	96.627
1991	F3000 INT	Christian Fittipaldi	BR	Reynard 91D-Mugen	96.448
1997	F3000 INT	Juan Pablo Montoya	CO	Lola T96/50-Zytek	98.463

WORLD SPORTS CAR RACE

year	formula	winner	nat	car	mph
1986	SC W	Oscar Larrauri/Jesus Pareja	RA/E	Porsche 962C	91.508
1987	SC W	Eddie Cheever/Raul Boesel	USA/BR	Jaguar XJR-8	91.847
1988	SC W	Jean-Louis Schlesser/Mauro Baldi/Jochen Mass	F/I/D	Sauber C9/88-Mercedes-Benz	93.941

FIA GT RACE

year	formula	winner	nat	car	mph
1995	GT FIA	Ray Bellm/Maurizio Sandro Sala	GB/BR	McLaren F1 GTR-BMW	84.537

LASARTE

Lasarte was a long, demanding pre-war road course in the tradition of Nurburgring, Spa and Brno. Set on undulating, tree-lined public roads it was the home of Grand Prix racing in Spain from its opening in 1923 until 1935. A dual carriageway has now been built on part of the road from Lasarte to Andoain where the track originally ran between the River Oria and a cliff. The next section to Urnieta and Hernani remains largely unchanged. The counter-clockwise circuit was also known as San Sebastian after the port to the north.

Active years	1923-35
Location	South of San Sebastian in northern Spain, south west of the French border
Type	Temporary road course
Lap distance	11.029 miles
Lap record	Race: Achille Varzi (Auto Union B), 5m58, 110.906 mph, GP, 1935

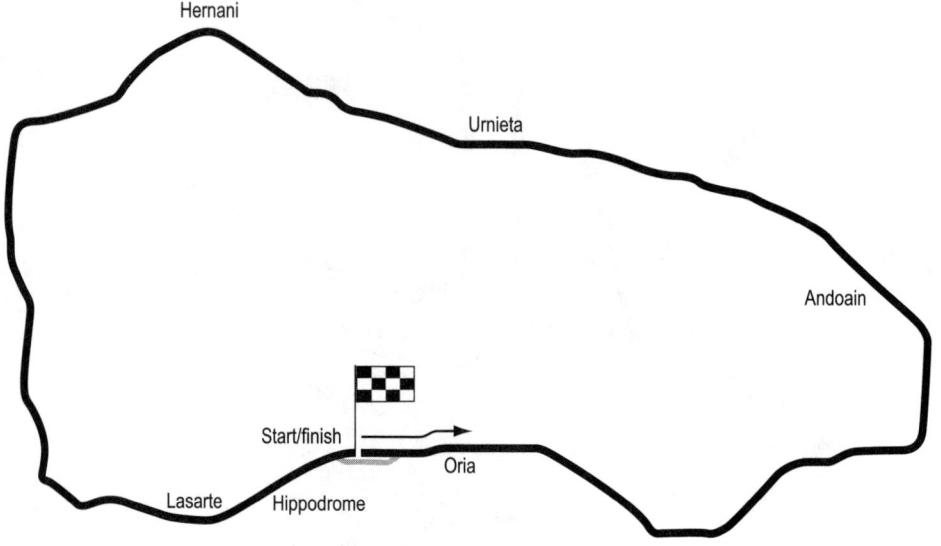

Spanish Grand Prix see above
European Grand Prix see above

SAN SEBASTIAN GRAND PRIX

year	formula	winner	nat	car	mph
1923	GP	Albert Guyot	F	Rolland Pilain	57.851
1924	GP	Henry Segrave	GB	Sunbeam	64.101
1925	GP	Albert Divo/Andre Morel	F	Delage 2LCV	76.720
1926*	GP	Jules Goux	F	Bugatti T39A	70.530
1927	FL	Emilio Materassi	I	Bugatti T35C	80.663
1928	GP	Louis Chiron	MC	Bugatti T35C	82.588

*European Grand Prix

MONTJUICH PARK

Barcelona

When the Penya Rhin Grand Prix was revived for Grand Prix cars in 1933 it took place on a temporary course in Barcelona's undulating Montjuich Park. The circuit was not used immediately after the war, but when Jarama was built outside Madrid in 1966 Montjuich was hastily recommissioned so that Barcelona could share the Grand Prix with its rival city. The layout remained essentially unaltered until the tragic 1975 Grand Prix when Rolf Stommelen, leading a race for the first time, crashed into the crowd killing four spectators. The accident spelled the end of one of the most picturesque and demanding street circuits to grace the F1 World Championship.

Active years	1933-75
Location	Montjuich Park in central Barcelona, near Plaza de Espana
Type	Temporary street circuit
Lap distance	2.355 miles
Lap record	Qualifying: Ronnie Peterson (Lotus 72E-Ford), 1m21.8, 103.643 mph, 101.169 mph, F1, 1973
	Race: Ronnie Peterson (Lotus 72E-Ford), 1m23.8, 101.169 mph, F1, 1973

Spain

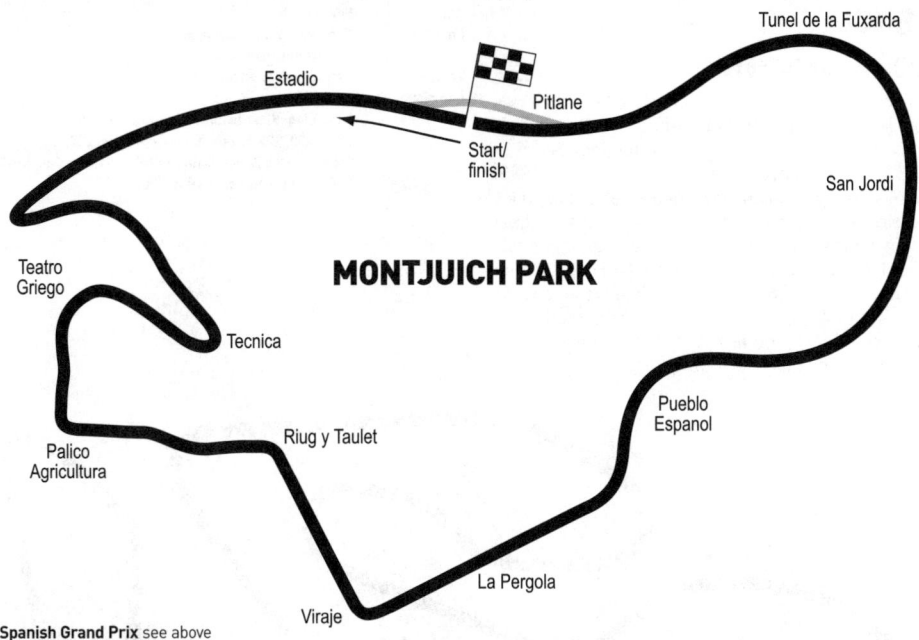

Spanish Grand Prix see above
Penya Rhin Grand Prix see above

PEDRALBES

Barcelona

An unusually fast "round-the-houses" circuit with wide straights and fast, open corners. Pedralbes held the final Grand Prix of 1951 when a poor tyre choice by Ferrari handed Juan Manuel Fangio his first championship. The race returned three years later with Mike Hawthorn scoring his second victory.

Active years	**1946-55**
Location	**Western suburbs of Barcelona**
Type	**Temporary street circuit**

Circuit changes
1946-50	**2.774 miles**
1951	**Extended to Calle de Numancia. 3.925 miles**
1954-55	**Some corners re-profiled. 3.936 miles**

Spanish Grand Prix see above

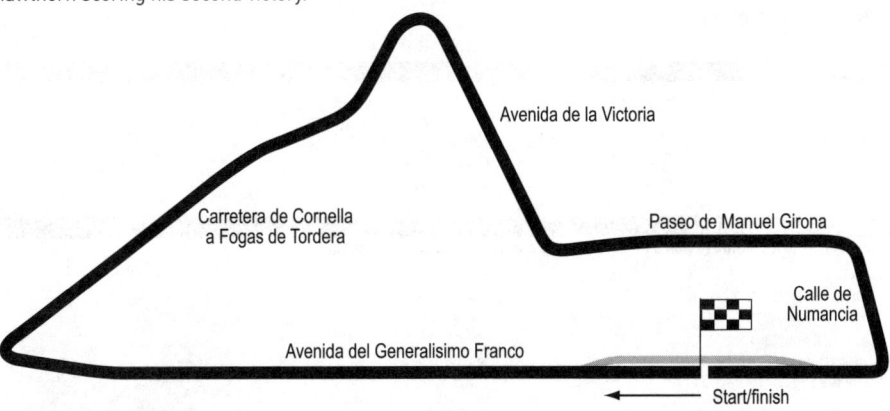

VALENCIA

Circuito Ricardo Tormo

Like Albacete, Valencia is more suited to bikes, but it has also proved a popular testing venue for Grand Prix teams. Olivier Panis set an unofficial testing record of 1m13.530 for McLaren-Mercedes here in 1999. Although some car races have been held, the 500cc motorcycle Grand Prix has been Valencia's biggest event. It is another tight and flat complex that, unusually for Europe, runs counter-clockwise. Much of the circuit can be seen from the ample grandstands, and facilities are state-of-the-art. The venue is named after Ricardo Tormo Blaya, the first local to win a bike World Championship who died from cancer in 1998.

Active years	1999 to date
Location	20 miles west of Valencia
Type	Permanent road course
Website	www.circuitvalencia.com
Lap distance	2.489 miles
Lap record	Qualifying: Ricardo Zonta (Dallara SN01-Nissan), 1m23.200, 107.697 mph, Super Nissan, 2002
	Race: Ricardo Zonta (Dallara SN01-Nissan), 1m23.570, 107.221 mph, Super Nissan, 2002

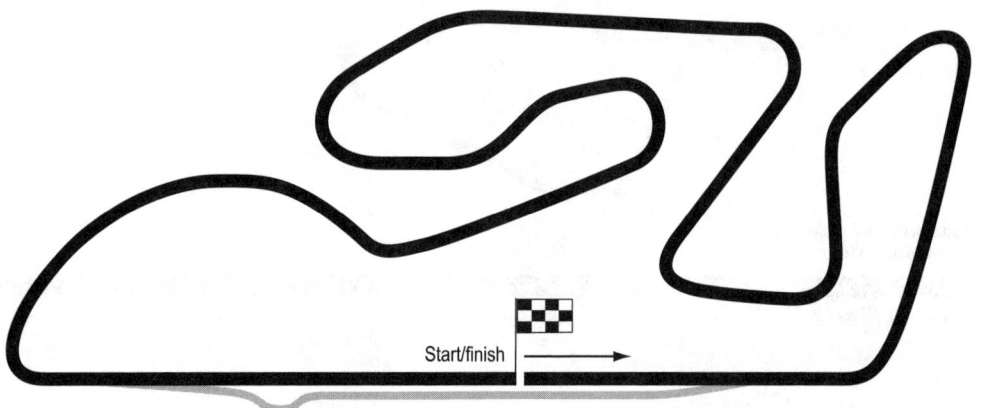

Start/finish

FIA GT RACE

year	formula	winner	nat	car	mph
2000	GT FIA	Julian Bailey/Jamie Campbell-Walter	GB	Lister Storm GT	90.336

SWEDEN
Major Championships

SWEDISH GTR CHAMPIONSHIP

year	driver	nat	car
1999	Lennart Pehrsson	S	Porsche 933 GT2
2000	Henrik Roos	S	Chrysler Viper GTS-R
2001	Henrik Roos	S	Chrysler Viper GTS-R
2002	Magnus Wallinder/Henrik Roos	S	Chrysler Viper GTS-R

NORDIC TOURING CAR CHAMPIONSHIP
Replaced the Swedish series as the region's leading Touring Car Championship until 1995

year	driver	nat	car
1991	Mika Hakkinen	SF	BMW M3
1992	Kris Nissen	DK	BMW M3
1993	Peggan Andersson	S	BMW M3
1994	Slim Borgudd	S	Mazda Xedos 6
1995	Peggan Andersson	S	BMW 318i

SWEDISH TOURING CAR CHAMPIONSHIP

year	driver	nat	car
1984	Anders Dahlgren	S	-
1985	Anders Berggren	S	-
1986	Stig Gruen	S	-
1987	Peggan Andersson	S	-
1988	Lennart Bohlin	S	-
1989	Peggan Andersson	S	-
1990	Stig Blomqvist	S	-
1991	Peggan Andersson	S	BMW M3
1992	Peggan Andersson	S	BMW M3
1993	Peggan Andersson	S	BMW M3
1994	Slim Borgudd	S	Mazda Xedos 6
1995	Georg Bakajev	S	BMW M3-Volvo
1996	Jan Nilsson	S	Volvo 850 GLT
1997	Jan Nilsson	S	Volvo 850 GLT
1998	Fredrik Ekblom	S	BMW 320i
1999	Mattias Ekstrom	S	Audi A4 Quattro
2000	Tommy Rustad	N	Nissan Primera GT
2001	Roberto Colciago	I	Audi A4 Quattro
2002	Roberto Colciago	I	Audi A4 Quattro

NORDIC FORMULA 3 CHAMPIONSHIP

year	driver	nat	team	car
1984	Hasse Thaung	S	The Swedish Lions	Ralt RT3-Alfa Romeo
1985	Steven Andskar	S	The Swedish Lions	Ralt RT30-Volkswagen
1992	Peter Aslund	S	Claes Rothstein Motorsport	Ralt RT35-Volkswagen
1993	Magnus Wallinder	S	Team Itchi Ban	Ralt RT35-Volkswagen/ Reynard 913-Mugen
1994	Magnus Wallinder	S	Magnus Wallinder	Reynard 913-Mugen
1995	Toni Teittinen	SF	Toni Team	Reynard 913-Mugen
1996	Pontus Morth	S	Claes Rothstein Motorsport	Ralt RT35-Volkswagen
1997	Niclas Karlsson	S	Franz Woss Racing	Dallara 394-Fiat
1998	Jimmy Bohlin	S	Jimmy Bohlin	Dallara 394-Opel
1999	Thed Bjork	S	Monica Strath Motorsport	Dallara 394-Opel
2000	Mikael Karlsson	S	Monica Strath Motorsport	Dallara 394-Mugen
2001	Sanna Pinola	SF	JP Vasainen Group	Dallara 394-Opel

1986-91 no series

SWEDISH FORMULA 3 CHAMPIONSHIP (INCLUDING FORMULA JUNIOR)

year	driver	nat	team	car
1961*	Yngve Rosqvist	S	Lotus Racing Team	Lotus 18-Ford
1962*	Yngve Rosqvist	S	Rosqvist Racing Team	Cooper T59-BMC
1963*	Gunnar Karlsson	S	Gunnar Karlsson	Lotus 22-Ford
1964	Sven Mattsson	S	SMK Stockholm	Lotus 22-Ford
1965	Picko Troberg	S	Picko Troberg	Brabham BT15-Ford
1966	Freddy Kottulinsky	S	Fredy Kottulinsky	Lotus 35-Ford
1967	Reine Wisell	S	Team Baltzar Racing	Brabham BT18-Ford
1968	Ronnie Peterson	S	Ronnie Peterson	Tecno 68-Ford
1969	Ronnie Peterson	S	Ronnie Peterson	Tecno 69-Ford
1970	Torsten Palm	S	Picko Troberg	Brabham BT28-Ford
1971	Torsten Palm	S	Torsten Palm Racing	Brabham BT28-Ford/Brabham BT35-Ford
1972	Conny Andersson	S	Conny Andersson	Brabham BT35-Ford/Brabham BT38-Ford
1973	Hakan Dahlqvist	S	Karlssons Klister	Merlyn 22-Ford
1974	Conny Andersson	S	Gekas Klader Racing	March 743-Toyota
1975	Conny Ljungfeldt	S	Rotel Racing	March 743-Toyota
1976	Conny Ljungfeldt	S	Rotel Racing	Viking TH1A-Toyota
1977	Anders Olofsson	S	Fuss O Kram Jeans Racing	Ralt RT1-Toyota
1978	Anders Olofsson	S	Strike Up Racing Team	Ralt RT1-Toyota
1979	Slim Borgudd	S	Strike Ten Racing	Ralt RT1-Toyota
1980	Thorbjorn Carlsson	S	Thorbjorn Carlsson	Ralt RT1-Toyota
1981	Bengt Tragardh	S	Top Print	March 803B-Toyota
1982	Thorbjorn Carlsson	S	Thorbjorn Carlsson	Ralt RT3-Volkswagen
1983	Leo Andersson	S	Sunsett Liftar	Ralt RT3-Toyota
1984	Leif Lindstrom	S	Leif Lindstrom	Ralt RT3-Toyota
1985	Thomas Danielsson	S	Picko Troberg	Reynard 853-SAAB/ Reynard 853-Volkswagen
1986	Niclas Schonstrom	S	Picko Troberg	Reynard 863-Volkswagen/ Ralt RT3-Volkswagen
1987	Micke Johansson	S	Tommy Jagervall Racing	Ralt RT31-Alfa Romeo
1988	Micke Johansson	S	Tommy Jagervall Racing	Ralt RT31-Alfa Romeo

SWEDISH FORMULA 3 CHAMPIONSHIP (INCLUDING FORMULA JUNIOR) (cont.)

year	driver	nat	team	car
1989	Jan Nilsson	S	G-Son Racing	Reynard 883-Volkswagen
1990	Niclas Jonsson	S	Team Itchi Ban	Reynard 903-Mugen
1991	Niclas Jonsson	S	Team Itchi Ban	Reynard 913-Mugen
1992	Peter Aslund	S	Claes Rothstein Motorsport	Ralt RT35-Volkswagen
1993	Magnus Wallinder	S	Team Itchi Ban	Ralt RT35-Volkswagen/ Reynard 913-Mugen
1997	Ulf Johansson	S	Ulf Johansson	Dallara 394-Opel
1998	Jimmy Bohlin	S	Bohlin Racing	Dallara 394-Opel
1999	Thed Bjork	S	Monica Strath Motorsport	Dallara 394-Opel
2000	Mikael Karlsson	S	Monica Strath Motorsport	Dallara 394-Mugen

*Formula Junior. 1994-96, 2001 to date no series

Major International Races

SWEDISH GRAND PRIX

year	formula	circuit	winner	nat	car	mph
1955	SC	Kristianstad	Juan Manuel Fangio	RA	Mercedes-Benz	99.720
1956	SC W	Kristianstad	Maurice Trintignant/Phil Hill	F/USA	Ferrari 290MM	94.692
1957	SC W	Kristianstad	Jean Behra/Stirling Moss	F/GB	Maserati 450S	97.889
1973	F1 W	Anderstorp	Denny Hulme	NZ	McLaren M23-Ford	102.645
1974	F1 W	Anderstorp	Jody Scheckter	ZA	Tyrrell 007-Ford	101.125
1975	F1 W	Anderstorp	Niki Lauda	A	Ferrari 312T	100.462
1976	F1 W	Anderstorp	Jody Scheckter	ZA	Tyrrell P34-Ford	100.912
1977	F1 W	Anderstorp	Jacques Laffite	F	Ligier JS7-Matra	100.884
1978	F1 W	Anderstorp	Niki Lauda	A	Brabham BT46B-Alfa Romeo	104.158

Circuits and Other Races

ANDERSTORP

Scandinavian Raceway

Built on a marsh in the expanse of central Sweden, Anderstorp came to prominence in the early seventies during the Swedish motor racing boom inspired by Ronnie Peterson. Ironically, Peterson never won his home GP, although he came close in the 1973 race before a deflating tyre delayed him in the closing laps. The long backstretch (which is also a runway) and the slightly banked corners made Anderstorp a course requiring set-up compromises and often produced surprising results. The six-wheel Tyrrell and the infamous Brabham "fan-car" won their only Grand Prix wins here, while Jacques Laffite scored the first victory for himself and Ligier at Anderstorp in 1977. When both Peterson and his heir apparent, Gunnar Nilsson, died during 1978, the Swedish Grand Prix was lost. The European Touring Car and FIA GT Championships both visited in 2002.

Active years	1968 to date
Location	4 miles east of Gislaved, 100 miles south-east of Gothenburg
Type	Permanent road course

Current circuit	
Lap distance	2.505 miles
Lap records	Qualifying: Mario Andretti (Lotus 78-Ford), 1m22.058, 109.898 mph, F1, 1978
	Race: Niki Lauda (Brabham BT46B-Alfa Romeo), 1m24.836, 106.299 mph, F1, 1978

Circuit changes	
1968-77	2.497 miles
1978 to date	Chicane built at the end of the main straight. Current circuit

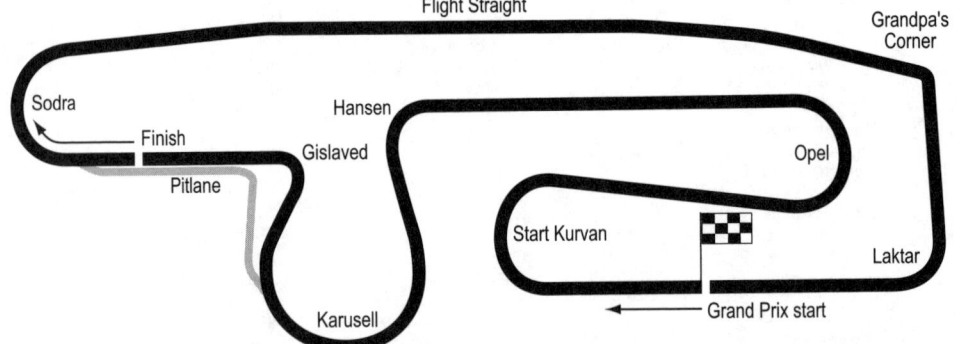

722

Swedish Grand Prix see above

EUROPEAN FORMULA 3 RACE

year	formula	winner	nat	car	mph
1975	F3 E	Conny Andersson	S	March 753-Toyota	92.390

FIA GT RACE

year	formula	winner	nat	car	mph
1995	GT FIA	Michel Ferte/Olivier Thevenin	F	Ferrari F40	91.656
1996	GT FIA	Luciano della Noce/Anders Olofsson	I/S	Ferrari F40 GT-E	94.382
2002	GT FIA	Jean-Denis Deletraz/Andrea Piccini	CH/I	Ferrari 550M	69.645

KARLSKOGA

Karlskoga was Ronnie Peterson's home circuit. It is a flat succession of straights and hairpins that provides good viewing. The 1970 Kannonloppet was marred by an accident in which five spectators were killed, forcing the circuit to close for two years.

Active years	1955-70, 1972 to date
Location	44 miles east of Karland, 155 miles west of Stockholm
Type	Permanent road course
Website	www.karlskogamotorstadion.com
Lap distance	1.864 miles
Lap record	Qualifying: Patrick Depailler (March 742-BMW), 1m11.2, 94.248 mph, F2, 1974
	Race: Patrick Depailler (March 742-BMW), 1m12.1, 93.071 mph, F2, 1974

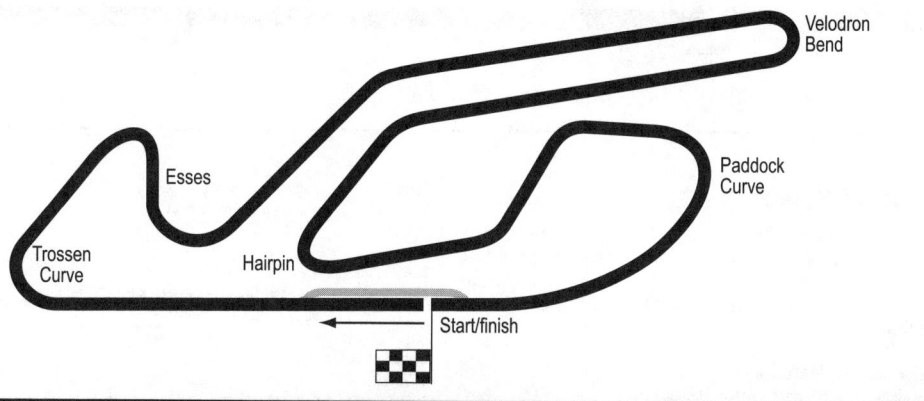

KANNONLOPPET

year	formula	winner	nat	car	mph
1955	SC	Gunnar Carlsson	S	Ferrari	n/a
1956	SC	Gunnar Carlsson	S	Ferrari	n/a
1957	SC	Peter Ashdown	GB	Lotus	n/a
1958	SC	Stirling Moss	GB	Maserati	n/a
1959	SC	Stirling Moss	GB	Cooper	67.700
1960	SC	Stirling Moss	GB	Lotus	67.870
1961	F1	Stirling Moss	GB	Lotus 18/21-Climax	72.498
1962	F1	Masten Gregory	USA	Lotus 24-BRM	78.292
1963	F1	Jim Clark	GB	Lotus 25-Climax	69.417
1964	F2	Jack Brabham	AUS	Brabham-Ford	76.294
1965	F2	Jack Brabham	AUS	Brabham-Ford	78.484
1966	F2	Jack Brabham	AUS	Brabham BT21-Honda	76.320
1967	F2	Jackie Stewart	GB	Matra MS7-Ford	86.010
1968	SC	David Piper	GB	Ferrari P4	n/a
1969	F3	Ronnie Peterson	S	Tecno 69-Ford	82.166
1970	SC	Chris Craft	GB	McLaren M8C-Ford	83.660
1973	F2 E	Jean-Pierre Jarier	F	March 732-BMW	90.620
1974	F2 E	Ronnie Peterson	S	March 742-BMW	91.621
1977	F3	Anders Olofsson	S	Ralt RT1-Toyota	85.830
1978	F3 E	Jan Lammers	NL	Ralt RT1-Toyota	86.959
1980	F3	Thorbjorn Carlsson	S	Ralt RT1-Toyota	n/a
1981	F3	Thorbjorn Carlsson	S	Ralt RT3-Toyota	86.437
1982	F3	Thorbjorn Carlsson	S	Ralt RT3-Toyota	84.075
1983	F3	Mats Karlsson	S	TMS 833-Toyota	n/a
1985	F3	Joackim Lindstrom	S	Ralt RT30-Toyota	86.379

Note: Incomplete list of results

KINNEKULLE

Kinnekulle was built in an old quarry on the edge of Lake Vanern set in a spectacular valley. It held a round of the European F2 Championship in 1973.

Active years	1969 to date
Location	20 miles south-west of Lidkoping
Type	Permanent road course
Lap distance	1.286 miles
Lap record	Race: Niclas Jonsson (Reynard 903-Mugen), 47.41s, 97.651 mph, F3, 1993

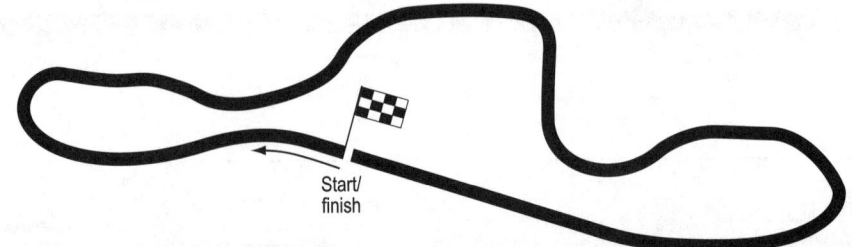

Start/finish

SWEDISH GOLD CUP

year	formula	winner	nat	car	mph
1971	F2	Ronnie Peterson	S	March 712M-Ford	92.581
1973	F2 E	Jochen Mass	D	Surtees TS15-Ford	91.651

EUROPEAN FORMULA 3 RACE

year	formula	winner	nat	car	mph
1979	F3 E	Richard Dallest	F	Martini MK27-Toyota	88.822

KNUTSTORP

Knutstorp is a short circuit that for a time was Sweden's only international venue, regularly holding European Formula 3 races. The Swedish Touring Car Championship remains a highlight of the circuit's calendar.

Active years	1970 to date
Location	45 miles north of Malmo

Type	Permanent road course
Website	www.motorevents.com

Current circuit	
Lap distance	1.292 miles
Lap record	Race: Niclas Jonsson (Reynard 903-Mugen), 55.854s, 83.274 mph, F3, 1990

Circuit changes	
1970-79	1.367 miles
1980 to date	Current circuit

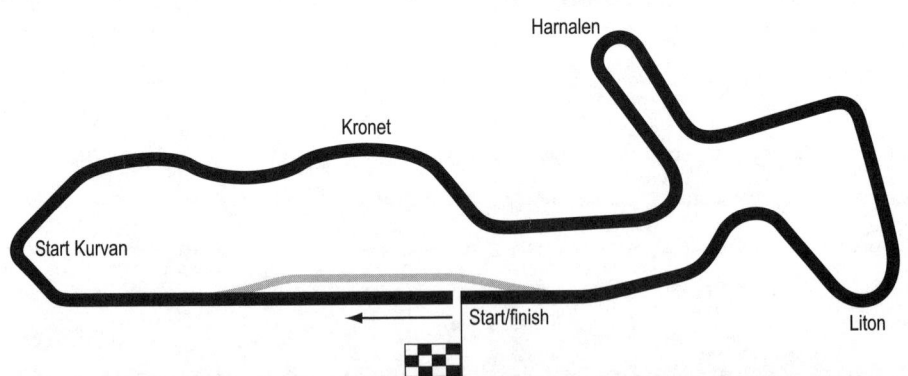

Harnalen

Kronet

Start Kurvan

Start/finish

Liton

EUROPEAN FORMULA 3 RACE

year	formula	winner	nat	car	mph
1976	F3 E	Conny Andersson	S	March 763-Toyota	78.517
1977	F3 E	Anders Olofsson	S	Ralt RT1-Toyota	79.956
1978	F3 E	Anders Olofsson	S	Ralt RT1-Toyota	79.498
1979	F3 E	Alain Prost	F	Martini MK27-Renault	80.125
1980	F3 E	Corrado Fabi	I	March 803-Alfa Romeo	77.576

EUROPEAN FORMULA 3 RACE (cont.)

year	formula	driver	nat	car	mph
1981	F3 E	Mauro Baldi	I	March 813-Alfa Romeo	80.037
1982	F3 E	Oscar Larrauri	RA	Euroracing 101-Alfa Romeo	80.131
1983	F3 E	John Nielsen	DK	Ralt RT3/83-Volkswagen	80.671
1984	F3 E	Claudio Langes	I	Ralt RT3/84-Toyota	80.082
1987*	F3 E	Peter Zakowski	D	Ralt RT31-Volkswagen	75.322
	F3 E	Dave Coyne	GB	Reynard 873-Volkswagen	68.916

*EFDA Euroseries F3 race

KRISTIANSTAD

The first Swedish Grand Prix, a non-championship sports car race, was held in 1955 on the closed public roads through the countryside north of Kristianstad. The event became a round of the World Championship in 1956 and 1957.

Active years	**1955-57**
Location	**Northern suburbs of Kristianstad, 390 miles from Stockholm**
Type	**Temporary road course**
Lap distance	**4.062 miles**
Lap record	**Qualifying: Jean Behra (Maserati 450S), 2m22.5, 102.619 mph, Sports Cars, 1957**
	Race: Jean Behra (Maserati 450S), 2m20.9, 103.784 mph, Sports Cars, 1957

Swedish Grand Prix see above

MANTORP PARK

Built with financing from BP Sweden, Mantorp Park includes three different circuits and a drag strip. The European Formula 2 Championship visited from 1971 (when Peterson won) until 1973, and again in 1981 and 1982. Swedish star Stefan Johansson scored a popular victory in the penultimate race. Mantorp Park has now returned to being a national venue.

Active years	**1969 to date**
Location	**10 miles west of Linkoping**
Type	**Permanent road course**
Website	**www.motorevents.com**

Current circuit	
Lap distance	**1.942 miles**
Lap record	**Qualifying: Corrado Fabi (March 822-BMW), 1m09.40, 100.738 mph, F2, 1982**
	Race: Johnny Cecotto (March 812-BMW), 1m11.69, 97.520 mph, F2, 1981

Circuit changes	
1969-80	**Circuit No3. 2.543 miles**
1981 to date	**Circuit No2. Current circuit**

EUROPEAN FORMULA 2 RACE

year	formula	winner	nat	car	mph
1970	F2	Francois Cevert	F	Tecno 70-Ford	103.515
1971	F2 E	Ronnie Peterson	S	March 712M-Ford	103.506
1972	F2 E	Mike Hailwood	GB	Surtees TS10-Ford	103.784
1973	F2 E	Jean-Pierre Jarier	F	March 732-BMW	107.616
1981	F2 E	Stefan Johansson	S	Toleman TG280B-Hart	94.499
1982	F2 E	Johnny Cecotto	YV	March 822-BMW	96.514

EUROPEAN FORMULA 3 RACE

year	formula	winner	nat	car	mph
1976	F3 E	Gianfranco Brancatelli	I	March 763-Toyota	101.219

SWITZERLAND

With motor racing banned in Switzerland since the Le Mans catastrophe of 1955, the country's F3 and Touring Car championships are a collection of hillclimbs and races held in Italy, France and Germany. These are the least competitive series in Europe.

Major Championships

SWISS TOURING CAR CHAMPIONSHIP

year	driver	nat	team	car
1993	Bernard Thuner	CH	Wira Peugeot	Peugeot 405 Mi16
1994	Bernard Thuner	CH	Wira Peugeot	Peugeot 405 Mi16
1995	Rolf Kuhn	CH	Wira Peugeot	Peugeot 405 Mi16
1996	"Nikko"	CH	Bemani Motorenbau	Toyota Carina E-GT
1997	Johnny Hauser	CH	Wittwer Motorsport	Peugeot 405 Mi16
1998	Carlo Lusser	CH	Bemani Motorenbau	Toyota Carina E-GT

SWISS FORMULA 3 CHAMPIONSHIP

year	driver	nat	team	car
1978	Patrick Studer	CH	Formel Rennsport Club	Chevron B42-Toyota
1979	Beat Blatter	CH	Sauber Racing	Lola T670-Toyota
1980	Jakob Bordoli	CH	Jakob Bordoli	Ralt RT1-Toyota
1981	Marcel Wettstein	CH	Squadra Caposcarico	Ralt RT1-Toyota
1982	Jo Zeller	CH	Formel Rennsport Club	Ralt RT3-Toyota
1983	Hans-Peter Kaufmann	CH	Formel Rennsport Club	Ralt RT3-Alfa Romeo
1984	Jo Zeller	CH	Formel Rennsport Club	Ralt RT3-Toyota
1985	Jakob Bordoli	CH	Scuderia Calanda	Ralt RT3-Toyota
1986	Gregor Foitek	CH	Squadra Foitek	Dallara 386-Volkswagen
1987	Jakob Bordoli	CH	Formel Rennsport Club	Martini MK45-Volkswagen
1988	Jakob Bordoli	CH	Formel Rennsport Club	Martini MK52-Volkswagen
1989	Jacques Isler	CH	Squadra Foitek	Dallara 388-Alfa Romeo
1990	Jo Zeller	CH	Jo Zeller Racing	Ralt RT34-Alfa Romeo
1991	Jo Zeller	CH	Jo Zeller Racing	Ralt RT34-Alfa Romeo
1992	Jo Zeller	CH	Jo Zeller Racing	Ralt RT35-Alfa Romeo
1993	Rudi Schurter	CH	KMS Motorsport	Dallara 393-Opel
1994	Rudi Schurter	CH	KMS Motorsport	Dallara 393-Opel
1995	Jo Zeller	CH	Jo Zeller Racing	Dallara 393-Fiat
1996	Norbert Zehnder	CH	KMS Motorsport	Dallara 394-Opel
1997	Norbert Zehnder	CH	KMS Motorsport	Dallara 394-Opel
1998	Jo Zeller	CH	Jo Zeller Racing	Dallara 394-Opel
1999	Jo Zeller	CH	Jo Zeller Racing	Dallara 396-Opel
2000	Jo Zeller	CH	Jo Zeller Racing	Dallara 399-Opel
2001	Jo Zeller	CH	Jo Zeller Racing	Dallara 399-Opel
2002	Jo Zeller	CH	Jo Zeller Racing	Dallara 301-Opel

Major International Races

SWISS GRAND PRIX						
year	formula	circuit	winner	nat	car	mph
1934	GP	Bremgarten	Hans Stuck	D	Auto Union A	87.176
1935	GP	Bremgarten	Rudolf Caracciola	D	Mercedes-Benz W25B	89.964
1936	GP	Bremgarten	Bernd Rosemeyer	D	Auto Union C	100.519
1937	GP	Bremgarten	Rudolf Caracciola	D	Mercedes-Benz W125	98.594
1938	GP	Bremgarten	Rudolf Caracciola	D	Mercedes-Benz W154	89.213
1939	GP	Bremgarten	Hermann Lang	D	Mercedes-Benz W163	96.036
1947	F1	Bremgarten	Jean-Pierre Wimille	F	Alfa Romeo 158	95.632
1948	F1	Bremgarten	Carlo Felice Trossi	I	Alfa Romeo 158	91.020
1949	F1	Bremgarten	Alberto Ascari	I	Ferrari 125	90.927
1950	F1 W	Bremgarten	Giuseppe Farina	I	Alfa Romeo 158	92.766
1951	F1 W	Bremgarten	Juan Manuel Fangio	RA	Alfa Romeo 159	89.140
1952	F2 W	Bremgarten	Piero Taruffi	I	Ferrari 500	92.586
1953	F2 W	Bremgarten	Alberto Ascari	I	Ferrari 500	97.171
1954	F1 W	Bremgarten	Juan Manuel Fangio	RA	Mercedes-Benz W196	99.211
1975	F1	Dijon-Prenois (F)	Clay Regazzoni	CH	Ferrari 312T	79.867
1982	F1 W	Dijon-Prenois (F)	Keke Rosberg	SF	Williams FW08-Ford	122.272

BREMGARTEN

Bremgarten was a succession of quick corners without a straight worthy of the name set in the forests between the north-western outskirts of Bern and the River Wohlensee. It had the reputation of being dangerous, and the trees overhanging the circuit made it particularly hazardous in the wet. Bremgarten asked for a special combination of skill and bravery and only the best were quick. Opened in 1931 for motorbikes, the first Swiss GP was held in 1934. Racing continued until the sport was banned in Switzerland in aftermath of the Le Mans disaster of 1955. There were a number of serious acci-dents, and Bremgarten has had more than its share of fatalities, from Hugh Hamilton in the first Swiss Grand Prix to those of Achille Varzi and Christan Kautz in the 1948 event.

Active years	1931-54
Location	North-west suburbs of Bern
Type	Permanent road course
Lap distance	4.524 miles
Lap records	Qualifying: Rudolf Caracciola (Mercedes-Benz W125), 2m32.0, 107.147 mph, GP, 1937
	Race: Bernd Rosemeyer (Auto Union C-typ), 2m34.5, 105.414 mph, GP, 1936

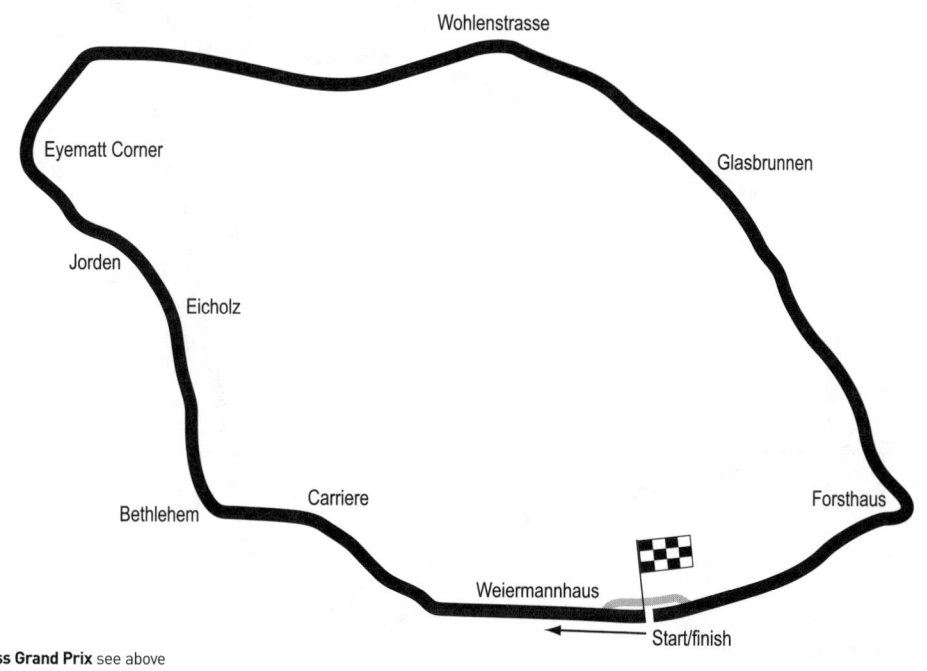

Swiss Grand Prix see above

TUNISIA
Major International Races

	TUNIS GRAND PRIX						
year	formula	circuit	winner	nat	car	mph
1928	GP	Bardo	Marcel Lehoux	DZ	Bugatti T35C	75.194
1929	GP	Bardo	Gastone Brilli-Peri	I	Alfa Romeo P2	83.387
1931	GP	Carthage	Achille Varzi	I	Bugatti T51	86.189
1932	GP	Carthage	Achille Varzi	I	Bugatti T51	90.249
1933	GP	Carthage	Tazio Nuvolari	I	Alfa Romeo 8C "Monza"	83.811
1935	FL	Carthage	Achille Varzi	I	Auto Union B	100.824
1936	FL	Carthage	Rudolf Caracciola	D	Mercedes-Benz W25C	99.619
1937	SC	Carthage	Raymond Sommer	F	Talbot	92.650
1955	SC	Belvedere	Luigi Piotti	I	Ferrari	71.7300

Circuits and other Races

CARTHAGE

During the thirties, the Tunis Grand Prix was the second important race in the French colony after Tripoli. It was held on the flat temporary circuit outside Carthage. A chicane immediately before the start line was removed for the 1935 race, creating a 2.25-mile straight made dangerous by strong crosswinds. After driver protests the chicane was again used for the race a year later. Achille Varzi escaped injury after his car was blown off the circuit in 1936, the last race featuring the top GP teams before the French switched all races to sports cars in 1937.

Active years 1931-37
Location Adjacent to Lac de Tunis, outside Carthage
Type Temporary road course
Lap distance 7.829 miles
Lap record Qualifying: Achille Varzi (Auto Union B), 4m24.8, 106.437 mph, Grand Prix, 1935
Race: Achille Varzi (Auto Union B), 4m28.8, 104.853 mph, Grand Prix, 1935

Circuit changes
1931-34, 36-37 Chicane before the start. 7.900 miles
1935 Chicane removed. 7.829 miles

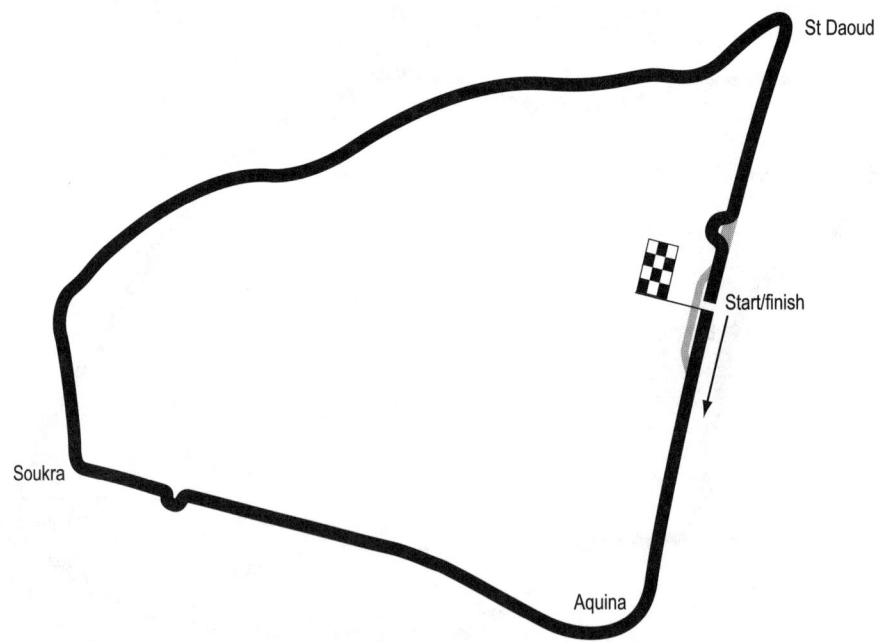

St Daoud

Start/finish

Soukra

Aquina

Tunis Grand Prix see above

UNITED STATES Of AMERICA
Major Championships

IMSA GTP CHAMPIONSHIP (INCLUDING WORLD SPORTS CARS)
(known as IMSA World Sports Car Championship 1994-97 and Professional Sports Car Championship 1998)

year	driver	nat	car
1971	Peter Gregg/Hurley Haywood	USA	Porsche 914/6
1972	Hurley Haywood	USA	Porsche 911S
1973	Peter Gregg	USA	Porsche Carrera
1974	Peter Gregg	USA	Porsche Carrera
1975	Peter Gregg	USA	Porsche Carrera
1976	Al Holbert	USA	Porsche Carrera/Chevrolet Monza GT
1977	Al Holbert	USA	Chevrolet Monza GT
1978	Peter Gregg	USA	Porsche 935
1979	Peter Gregg	USA	Porsche 935
1980	John Fitzpatrick	GB	Porsche 935
1981	Brian Redman	GB	Porsche 935/Lola T600-Chevrolet
1982	John Paul Jr	USA	Lola T600-Chevrolet/Porsche 935
1983	Al Holbert	USA	March 83G-Porsche/March 83G-Chevrolet/Porsche 935
1984	Randy Lanier	USA	March 83G-Chevrolet/March 84G-Chevrolet
1985	Al Holbert	USA	Porsche 962
1986	Al Holbert	USA	Porsche 962
1987	Chip Robinson	USA	Porsche 962
1988	Geoff Brabham	AUS	Nissan GTP ZX-T
1989	Geoff Brabham	AUS	Nissan GTP ZX-T
1990	Geoff Brabham	AUS	Nissan GTP ZX-T/Nissan NPT-90
1991	Geoff Brabham	AUS	Nissan R90C/Nissan NPT-90/Nissan NPT-91
1992	Juan Manuel Fangio II	RA	Eagle MkIII-Toyota
1993	Juan Manuel Fangio II	RA	Eagle MkIII-Toyota
1994*	Wayne Taylor	ZA	Kudzu DG-3-Mazda/Kudza DG3-Buick
1995*	Fermin Velez	E	Ferrari 333SP
1996*	Wayne Taylor	ZA	Riley & Scott MkIII-Oldsmobile
1997*	Butch Leitzinger	USA	Riley & Scott MkIII-Ford
1998*	Butch Leitzinger	USA	Riley & Scott MkIII-Ford

*World Sports Cars

IMSA LIGHTS

year	driver	nat	car
1985	Jim Downing	USA	Argo JM16B-Mazda
1986	Jim Downing	USA	Argo JM19-Mazda
1987	Jim Downing	USA	Argo JM19B-Mazda
1988	Tom Hessert	USA	Tiga GT286-Buick/Tiga GT286-Chevrolet/Tiga GT288-Buick
1989	Scott Schubot	USA	Spice SE88P-Buick
1990	Tomas Lopez	MEX	Spice SE90P-Buick
1991	Parker Johnstone	USA	Spice SE90P-Acura
1992	Parker Johnstone	USA	Spice SE91P-Acura
1993	Parker Johnstone	USA	Spice SE92P-Acura

OTHER IMSA CATEGORIES

	GTO		GTU		GTS	
year	driver	nat	driver	nat	driver	nat
1971	David Heinz	USA	-		-	
1972	Phil Currin	USA	Hurley Haywood	USA	-	
1973	-		Bob Bergstrom	USA	-	
1974	-		Walt Maas	USA	-	
1975	-		Bob Sharp	USA	-	
1976	-		Brad Frisselle	USA	-	
1977	-		Walt Maas	USA	-	
1978	David Cowart	USA	David White	USA	-	
1979	Howard Meister	USA	Don Devendorf	USA	-	
1980	Luis Mendez	USA	Walt Bohren	USA	-	
1981	David Cowart	USA	Lee Mueller	USA	-	
1982	Don Devendorf	USA	Jim Downing	USA	-	
1983	Wayne Baker	USA	Roger Mandeville	USA	-	
1984	Roger Mandeville	USA	Jack Baldwin	USA	-	
1985	John Jones	CDN	Jack Baldwin	USA	-	
1986	Scott Pruett	USA	Tom Kendall	USA	-	
1987	Chris Cord	USA	Tom Kendall	USA	-	
1988	Scott Pruett	USA	Tom Kendall	USA	-	

	GTO		GTU		GTS	
year	driver	nat	driver	nat	driver	nat
1989	Pete Halsmer	USA	Bob Leitzinger	USA	-	
1990	Dorsey Schroeder	USA	Lance Stewart	USA	-	
1991	Pete Halsmer	USA	John Fergus	USA	-	
1992	Irv Hoerr	USA	David Loring	USA	Steve Millen	NZ
1993	Charles Morgan	USA	Butch Leitzinger	USA	Tom Kendall	USA
1994	Joe Pezza	USA	Jim Pace	USA	Steve Millen	NZ
1995	-		-		Irv Hoerr	USA
1996	-		-		Irv Hoerr	USA
1997	-		-		Andy Pilgrim	GB
1998	-		-		Andy Wallace/ David Brabham	GB/AUS

AMERICAN LE MANS SERIES – PROTOTYPE CLASS

year	driver	nat	team	car
1999	Elliott Forbes-Robinson	USA	Rob Dyson Racing	Riley & Scott MkIII-Ford
2000	Allan McNish	GB	Joest Team Audi Sport	Audi R8
2001	Emanuele Pirro	I	Joest Team Audi Sport	Audi R8
2002	Tom Kristensen	DK	Joest Team Audi Sport	Audi R8

OTHER ALMS CATEGORIES

	LMP675		GTS		GT	
year	driver	nat	driver	nat	driver	nat
1999	-		Olivier Beretta	MC	Cort Wagner	USA
2000	-		Olivier Beretta	MC	Dirk Muller	D
2001	Didier de Radigues	B	Terry Borcheller	USA	Jorg Muller	D
2002	Jon Field	USA	Ron Fellows	CDN	Lucas Luhr	D

European Le Mans Series see page 559

GRAND-AMERICAN ROAD RACING CHAMPIONSHIP (FORMERLY UNITED STATES ROAD RACING CHAMPIONSHIP 1998-99)

year	driver	nat	team	car
1998	James Weaver	GB	Rob Dyson Racing	Riley & Scott MkIII-Ford
1999	Elliott Forbes-Robinson	USA	Rob Dyson Racing	Riley & Scott MkIII-Ford
2000	James Weaver	GB	Rob Dyson Racing	Riley & Scott MkIII-Ford
2001	James Weaver	GB	Rob Dyson Racing	Riley & Scott MkIII-Ford
2002	Didier Theys	B	Doran Lista Racing	Dallara LMP-Judd

INDY LIGHTS (FORMERLY KNOWN AS AMERICAN RACING SERIES 1986-90)

year	series sponsor	driver	nat	team	car
1986		Fabrizio Barbazza	I	Arciero Racing	Wildcat 86A-Buick
1987		Didier Theys	B	TrueSports	Wildcat 86A-Buick
1988	HFC	Jon Beekhuis	USA	PIG Racing	Wildcat 86A-Buick
1989	HFC	Michael Groff	USA	Leading Edge Motorsports	Wildcat 86A-Buick
1990	HFC	Paul Tracy	CDN	Landford Racing	Wildcat 86A-Buick
1991	Firestone	Eric Bachelart	B	Landford Racing	Wildcat 86A-Buick
1992	Firestone	Robbie Buhl	USA	Leading Edge Motorsports	Wildcat 86A-Buick
1993	Firestone	Bryan Herta	USA	Tasman Motorsports	Lola T93/20-Buick
1994	Firestone	Steve Robertson	GB	Tasman Motorsports	Lola T93/20-Buick
1995	Firestone	Greg Moore	CDN	Player's Forsythe Racing	Lola T93/20-Buick
1996	Firestone	David Empringham	CDN	Player's Forsythe Racing	Lola T93/20-Buick
1997	Firestone	Tony Kanaan	BR	Tasman Motorsports	Lola T97/20-Buick
1998	Dayton	Cristiano da Matta	BR	Tasman Motorsports	Lola T97/20-Buick
1999	Dayton	Oriol Servia	E	Dorricott-Mears Racing	Lola T97/20-Buick
2000	Dayton	Scott Dixon	NZ	PacWest Racing Group	Lola T97/20-Dayton
2001	Dayton	Townsend Bell	USA	Dorricott Racing	Lola T97/20-Dayton

2002 no series

IMSA BARBER-DODGE PRO-SERIES (FORMERLY BARBER-SAAB 1986-94)

year	driver	nat	car
1986	Willy Lewis	USA	Mondiale Barber-SAAB
1987	Ken Murillo	USA	Mondiale Barber-SAAB
1988	Bruce Feldman	USA	Mondiale Barber-SAAB
1989	Robbie Buhl	USA	Mondiale Barber-SAAB
1990	Rob Wilson	NZ	Mondiale Barber-SAAB
1991	Bryan Herta	USA	Mondiale Barber-SAAB
1992	Robert Amren	S	Mondiale Barber-SAAB
1993	Kenny Brack	S	Mondiale Barber-SAAB
1994	Diego Guzman	CO	Mondiale Barber-SAAB
1995	Jaki Scheckter	ZA	Mondiale Barber-Dodge
1996	Fredrik Larsson	S	Mondiale Barber-Dodge

IMSA BARBER-DODGE PRO-SERIES (FORMERLY BARBER-SAAB 1986-94) (cont.)

year	driver	nat	car
1997	Derek Hill	USA	Mondiale Barber-Dodge
1998	Jeff Simmons	USA	Reynard Barber-Dodge
1999	Jeff Simmons	USA	Reynard Barber-Dodge
2000	Nilton Rossoni	BR	Reynard Barber-Dodge
2001	Nicolas Rondet	F	Reynard Barber-Dodge
2002	AJ Allmendinger	USA	Reynard Barber-Dodge

INTERNATIONAL RACE OF CHAMPIONS (IROC)

year	driver	nat	car
1974	Mark Donohue	USA	Porsche Carrera RSR
1975	Bobby Unser	USA	Chevrolet Camaro
1976	AJ Foyt Jr	USA	Chevrolet Camaro
1977	AJ Foyt Jr	USA	Chevrolet Camaro
1978	Al Unser	USA	Chevrolet Camaro
1979	Mario Andretti	USA	Chevrolet Camaro
1980	Bobby Allison	USA	Chevrolet Camaro
1984	Cale Yarborough	USA	Chevrolet Camaro
1985	Harry Gant	USA	Chevrolet Camaro
1986	Al Unser Jr	USA	Chevrolet Camaro
1987	Geoff Bodine	USA	Chevrolet Camaro
1988	Al Unser Jr	USA	Chevrolet Camaro
1989	Terry Labonte	USA	Chevrolet Camaro
1990	Dale Earnhardt	USA	Dodge Daytona
1991	Rusty Wallace	USA	Dodge Daytona
1992	Ricky Rudd	USA	Dodge Daytona
1993	Davey Allison*	USA	Dodge Daytona
1994	Mark Martin	USA	Dodge Avenger
1995	Dale Earnhardt	USA	Dodge Avenger
1996	Mark Martin	USA	Pontiac Firebird
1997	Mark Martin	USA	Pontiac Firebird
1998	Mark Martin	USA	Pontiac Firebird
1999	Dale Earnhardt	USA	Pontiac Firebird
2000	Dale Earnhardt	USA	Pontiac Firebird
2001	Bobby Labonte	USA	Pontiac Firebird
2002	Kevin Harvick	USA	Pontiac Firebird

*Allison won the series posthumously, having been killed in a helicopter accident. Terry Labonte replaced him for the final race.

NORTH AMERICAN FORMULA 5000 CHAMPIONSHIP
(formerly known as Formula A 1967-71)

year	driver	nat	car
1967	Gus Hutchison	USA	Lotus 41-Chevrolet
1968	Lou Sell	USA	Eagle-Chevrolet
1969	Tony Adamowicz	USA	Eagle-Chevrolet
1970	John Cannon	CDN	McLaren M10B-Chevrolet
1971	David Hobbs	GB	McLaren M10B-Chevrolet
1972	Graham McRae	NZ	McRae GM1-Chevrolet
1973	Jody Scheckter	ZA	Trojan T101-Chevrolet/ Lola T330-Chevrolet
1974	Brian Redman	GB	Lola T332-Chevrolet
1975	Brian Redman	GB	Lola T332-Chevrolet/ Lola T400-Chevrolet
1976	Brian Redman	GB	Lola T332C-Chevrolet

NORTH AMERICAN TOYOTA ATLANTIC CHAMPIONSHIP

year	division	driver	nat	car	year	division	driver	nat	car
1974		Bill Brack	CDN	Lotus 59-Ford/ Lotus 69-Ford	1988	Eastern	Steve Shelton	USA	Swift DB4-Ford
						Western	Dean Hall	USA	Swift DB4-Ford
1975		Bill Brack	CDN	Chevron B29-Ford	1989	Eastern	Jacko Cunningham	USA	Swift DB4-Ford
1976		Gilles Villeneuve	CDN	March 76B-Ford		Western	Hiro Matsushita	J	Swift DB4-Ford/ Swift DB4-Toyota
1977		Gilles Villeneuve	CDN	March 77B-Ford					
1978		Howdy Holmes	USA	March 78B-Ford	1990	Eastern	Brian Till	USA	Swift DB4-Toyota
1979		Tom Gloy	USA	Ralt RT1-Ford		Western	Mark Dismore	USA	Swift DB4-Toyota
1980		Jacques Villeneuve	CDN	March 80A-Ford	1991		Jovy Marcelo	RP	Swift DB4-Toyota
1981		Jacques Villeneuve	CDN	March 81A-Ford	1992		Chris Smith	USA	Swift DB4-Toyota
1982		Dave McMillen	NZ	Ralt RT4-Ford	1993		David Empringham	CDN	Ralt RT40-Toyota
1983		Michael Andretti	USA	Ralt RT4-Ford	1994		David Empringham	CDN	Ralt RT41-Toyota
1984		Dan Marvin	USA	Ralt RT4-Ford	1995		Richie Hearn	USA	Ralt RT41-Toyota
1985	Eastern	Michael Angus	USA	Ralt RT4-Ford	1996		Patrick Carpentier	CDN	Ralt RT41-Toyota
	Western	Jeff Wood	USA	Ralt RT4-Ford	1997		Alex Barron	USA	Ralt RT41-Toyota
1986	Eastern	Scott Goodyear	CDN	Ralt RT4-Ford	1998		Len Bentham	USA	Swift 008a-Toyota
	Western	Ted Prappas	USA	Ralt RT4-Ford	1999		Anthony Lazzaro	USA	Swift 008a-Toyota
1987	Eastern	Calvin Fish	GB	Ralt RT4-Ford	2000		Buddy Rice	USA	Swift 008a-Toyota
	Western	Johnny O'Connell	USA	Ralt RT4-Ford	2001		Hoover Orsi	BR	Swift 008a-Toyota
					2002		Jon Fogarty	USA	Swift 008a-Toyota

SCCA SUPER VEE CHAMPIONSHIP

year	driver	nat	car
1971	Bill Scott	USA	Royale-Volkswagen
1972	Bill Scott	USA	Royale-Volkswagen
1973	Bertil Roos	S	Tui BH3-Volkswagen
1974	Elliott Forbes-Robinson	USA	Lola T320-Volkswagen
1975	Eddie Miller	USA	Lola T324-Volkswagen
1976	Tom Bagley	USA	Zink Z11-Volkswagen
1977	Bob Lazier	USA	Lola T324-Volkswagen
1978	Bill Alsup	USA	Argo JM2-Volkswagen
1979	Geoff Brabham	AUS	Ralt RT1-Volkswagen
1980	Peter Kuhn	USA	Ralt RT1-Volkswagen/ Ralt RT5-Volkswagen
1981	Al Unser Jr	USA	Ralt RT5-Volkswagen
1982	Michael Andretti	USA	Ralt RT5-Volkswagen
1983	Ed Pimm	USA	Ralt RT5-Volkswagen/ Anson SA4-Volkswagen
1984	Arie Luyendyk	NL	Ralt RT5-Volkswagen
1985	Ken Johnson	USA	Ralt RT5-Volkswagen
1986	Didier Theys	B	Martini MK47-Volkswagen/ Martini MK50-Volkswagen
1987	Scott Atchison	USA	Ralt RT5-Volkswagen
1988	Ken Murillo	USA	Ralt RT5-Volkswagen
1989	Mark Smith	USA	Ralt RT5-Volkswagen
1990	Stuart Crow	USA	Ralt RT5-Volkswagen

INFINITI PRO-SERIES

year	driver	nat	car
2002	AJ Foyt IV	USA	Dallara-Infiniti

TRANS-AM CHAMPIONSHIP

DRIVERS CHAMPIONSHIP

MANUFACTURERS

year	class	driver	nat	car	constructor
1966		Horst Kwech/Gaston Andrey	AUS/CH	Alfa Romeo GTA	Ford
1967		Jerry Titus	USA	Ford Mustang	Ford
1968		Mark Donohue	USA	Chevrolet Camaro	Chevrolet
1969		Mark Donohue	USA	Chevrolet Camaro	Chevrolet
1970		Parnelli Jones	USA	Ford Mustang	Ford
1971		Mark Donohue	USA	AMC Javelin	American Motors
1972		George Follmer	USA	AMC Javelin	American Motors
1973		Peter Gregg	USA	Porsche 911 Carrera RS	Chevrolet
1974		Peter Gregg	USA	Porsche 911 Carrera RS	Porsche
1975		John Greenwood	USA	Chevrolet Corvette	Chevrolet
1976	Overall	George Follmer	USA	Porsche 934 turbo	Porsche
	Class 1	George Follmer	USA	Porsche 934 turbo	
	Class 2	Jocko Maggiacomo	USA	AMC Javelin	
1977	Class 1	Bob Tullius	USA	Jaguar XJS	Porsche
	Class 2	Ludwig Heimrath	CDN	Porsche 934	Porsche
1978	Class 1	Bob Tullius	USA	Jaguar XJS	Jaguar
	Class 2	Greg Pickett	USA	Chevrolet Corvette	Chevrolet
1979	Class 1	Gene Bothello	USA	Chevrolet Corvette	Chevrolet
	Class 2	John Paul	USA	Porsche 935	Porsche
1980		John Bauer	USA	Porsche 911SC	Chevrolet
1981		Eppie Wietzes	CDN	Chevrolet Corvette	Chevrolet
1982		Elliott Forbes-Robinson	USA	Pontiac Trans-Am	Pontiac
1983		David Hobbs	GB	Chevrolet Camaro	Chevrolet
1984		Tom Gloy	USA	Lincoln-Mercury Capri RS	Lincoln-Mercury
1985		Wally Dallenbach Jr	USA	Lincoln-Mercury Capri RS	Lincoln-Mercury
1986		Wally Dallenbach Jr	USA	Chevrolet Camaro	Lincoln-Mercury
1987		Scott Pruett	USA	Lincoln-Mercury Merkur XR4Ti	Lincoln-Mercury
1988		Hurley Haywood	USA	Audi Quattro 200	Audi
1989		Dorsey Schroeder	USA	Ford Mustang	Ford
1990		Tom Kendall	USA	Chevrolet Beretta	Chevrolet
1991		Scott Sharp	USA	Chevrolet Camaro	Chevrolet
1992		Jack Baldwin	USA	Chevrolet Camaro Z28	Chevrolet
1993		Scott Sharp	USA	Chevrolet Camaro Z28	Chevrolet
1994		Scott Pruett	USA	Chevrolet Camaro Z28	Chevrolet
1995		Tom Kendall	USA	Ford Mustang Cobra	Chevrolet
1996		Tom Kendall	USA	Ford Mustang Cobra	Ford
1997		Tom Kendall	USA	Ford Mustang Cobra	Ford
1998		Paul Gentilozzi	USA	Chevrolet Corvette	Chevrolet
1999		Paul Gentilozzi	USA	Ford Mustang Cobra	Ford
2000		Brian Simo	USA	Qvale de Tomaso Mangusta	Chevrolet
2001		Paul Gentilozzi	USA	Jaguar XKR	Jaguar
2002		Boris Said III	USA	Panoz Esparante/Ford Mustang	Panoz

NORTH AMERICAN TOURING CAR CHAMPIONSHIP

year	driver	nat	team	car
1996	Randy Pobst	USA	TC Kline Racing	Honda Accord
1997	David Donohue	USA	PacWest Touring Car Group	Dodge Stratus

UNITED STATES FORMULA 3 CHAMPIONSHIP

year	driver	nat	team	car
2000	Stuart Crow	USA	Dave McMillan Racing	Ralt F3/2000-Volkswagen
2001	Luciano Gomide	BR	Eurointernational	Dallara 300-Volkswagen

Major International Races

AMERICAN GRAND PRIZE

year	formula	circuit	winner	nat	car	mph
1908	GP	Savannah	Louis Wagner	F	Fiat	65.111
1910	GP	Savannah	David Bruce-Brown	USA	Benz	70.554
1911	AAA	Savannah	David Bruce-Brown	USA	Fiat S74	74.458
1912	GP	Milwaukee	Caleb Bragg	USA	Fiat S74	68.396
1914	AAA	Santa Monica	Eddie Pullen	USA	Mercer	77.324
1915	AAA	San Francisco	Dario Resta	I	Peugeot EX3	56.000
1916	AAA	Santa Monica	Howdy Wilcox/Johnny Aitken	USA	Peugeot EX5	85.723

UNITED STATES GRAND PRIX (also see Detroit and Dallas)

year	formula	circuit	winner	nat	car	mph
1958	SC	Riverside	Chuck Daigh	USA	Scarab	88.800
1959	F1 W	Sebring	Bruce McLaren	NZ	Cooper T45-Climax	98.827
1960	F1 W	Riverside	Stirling Moss	GB	Lotus 18-Climax	98.996
1961	F1 W	Watkins Glen	Innes Ireland	GB	Lotus 21-Climax	105.410
1962	F1 W	Watkins Glen	Jim Clark	GB	Lotus 25-Climax	110.835
1963	F1 W	Watkins Glen	Graham Hill	GB	BRM P57	111.288
1964	F1 W	Watkins Glen	Graham Hill	GB	BRM P261	113.515
1965	F1 W	Watkins Glen	Graham Hill	GB	BRM P261	110.312
1966	F1 W	Watkins Glen	Jim Clark	GB	Lotus 43-BRM	117.438
1967	F1 W	Watkins Glen	Jim Clark	GB	Lotus 49-Ford	123.584
1968	F1 W	Watkins Glen	Jackie Stewart	GB	Matra MS10-Ford	127.604
1969	F1 W	Watkins Glen	Jochen Rindt	A	Lotus 49B-Ford	129.108
1970	F1 W	Watkins Glen	Emerson Fittipaldi	BR	Lotus 72-Ford	129.549
1971	F1 W	Watkins Glen	Francois Cevert	F	Tyrrell 002-Ford	115.096
1972	F1 W	Watkins Glen	Jackie Stewart	GB	Tyrrell 005-Ford	117.483
1973	F1 W	Watkins Glen	Ronnie Peterson	S	Lotus 72D-Ford	118.055
1974	F1 W	Watkins Glen	Carlos Reutemann	RA	Brabham BT44-Ford	119.120
1975	F1 W	Watkins Glen	Niki Lauda	A	Ferrari 312T	116.098
1976	F1 W	Watkins Glen	James Hunt	GB	McLaren M23-Ford	116.427
1977	F1 W	Watkins Glen	James Hunt	GB	McLaren M26-Ford	100.978
1978	F1 W	Watkins Glen	Carlos Reutemann	RA	Ferrari 312T3	118.581
1979	F1 W	Watkins Glen	Gilles Villeneuve	CDN	Ferrari 312T4	106.456
1980	F1 W	Watkins Glen	Alan Jones	AUS	Williams FW07B-Ford	126.369
1989	F1 W	Phoenix	Alain Prost	F	McLaren MP4/5-Honda	87.370
1990	F1 W	Phoenix	Ayrton Senna	BR	McLaren MP4/5B-Honda	90.586
1991	F1 W	Phoenix	Ayrton Senna	BR	McLaren MP4/6-Honda	93.018
2000	F1 W	Indianapolis	Michael Schumacher	D	Ferrari F1-2000	118.310
2001	F1 W	Indianapolis	Mika Hakkinen	SF	McLaren MP4/16-Mercedes-Benz	123.160
2002	F1 W	Indianapolis	Rubens Barrichello	BR	Ferrari F2002	125.298

VANDERBILT CUP

year	formula	circuit	driver	nat	car	mph
1904	GP	Long Island	George Heath	USA	Panhard 70	52.223
1905	GP	Long Island	Victor Hemery	F	Darracq 80hp	61.492
1906	GP	Long Island	Louis Wagner	F	Darracq 120hp	61.434
1908	GP	Long Island	George Robertson	USA	Locomobile	64.380
1909	AAA	Long Island	Harry Grant	USA	Alco	62.796
1910	AAA	Long Island	Harry Grant	USA	Alco	65.181
1911	AAA	Savannah	Ralph Mulford	USA	Lozier	74.076
1912	AAA	Milwaukee	Ralph de Palma	USA	Mercedes	68.980
1914	AAA	Santa Monica	Ralph de Palma	USA	Mercedes	75.500
1915	AAA	San Francisco	Dario Resta	I	Peugeot EX3	66.400
1916	AAA	Santa Monica	Dario Resta	I	Peugeot	87.155
1936*	AAA	Roosevelt Raceway	Tazio Nuvolari	I	Alfa Romeo 12C-36	65.503
1937*	AAA	Roosevelt Raceway	Bernd Rosemeyer	D	Auto Union C	82.234

WK Vanderbilt Cup except *George Vanderbilt Cup. Note: A replica of the WK Vanderbilt Cup was awarded to the winner of the US 500 from 1996-99 and to the CART champion since 2000

MARLBORO CHALLENGE

year	formula	circuit	driver	nat	car	mph
1987	CART	Tamiami Park	Bobby Rahal	USA	Lola T87/00-Cosworth	108.782
1988	CART	Tamiami Park	Michael Andretti	USA	Lola T88/00-Cosworth	91.989
1989	CART	Laguna Seca	Al Unser Jr	USA	Lola T89/00-Chevrolet	105.580
1990	CART	Nazareth	Rick Mears	USA	Penske PC19-Chevrolet	153.484
1991	CART	Laguna Seca	Michael Andretti	USA	Lola T91/00-Chevrolet	105.455
1992	CART	Nazareth	Emerson Fittipaldi	BR	Penske PC21-Chevrolet	156.127

Circuits and Other Races

ATLANTA
Atlanta Motor Speedway

Built in 1960 just outside Georgia's state capital, Atlanta is a high-banked (24-degree) superspeedway with the best viewing on the current NASCAR calendar. Winston Cup races in March and November are the highlights of Atlanta's year. Richard Petty made his final appearance here at the end of the 1992 season. Owner Bruton Smith rebuilt the facility in 1997, adding a dogleg at the start line to match his other speedways at Charlotte and Texas. Champcars visited Atlanta in the sixties and late seventies, and a round of the Indy Racing League was held on four occasions.

Active years	1960 to date
Location	East of Hampton, 30 miles south of Atlanta, Georgia
Type	Paved oval
Website	www.atlantamotorspeedway.com

Current circuit

Lap distance	1.540 miles
Lap records	Qualifying: Billy Boat (Dallara IR7-Aurora), 24.734s, 224.145 mph, IRL, 1998
	Race: Billy Boat (Dallara IR7-Aurora), 24.732s, 224.163 mph, IRL, 1998

Circuit changes

1960-96	1.522 miles
1997 to date	New dogleg start/finish built, with new pit lane and pits built on old back straight. Current circuit

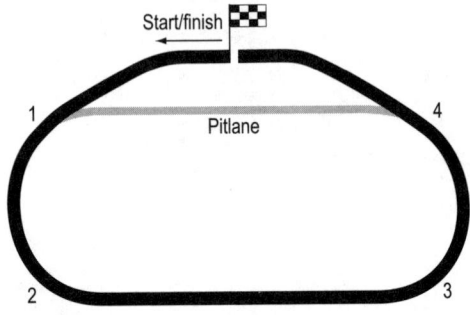

INDY/CHAMPCAR RACE

year	formula	winner	nat	car	mph
1965	USAC	Johnny Rutherford	USA	Watson-Ford	143.807
1966	USAC	Mario Andretti	USA	Brawner/Brabham-Ford	141.362
1978	USAC	Rick Mears	USA	Penske PC6-Cosworth	143.286
1979	CART	Johnny Rutherford	USA	McLaren M24B-Cosworth	157.758
	CART	Johnny Rutherford	USA	McLaren M24B-Cosworth	163.976
	CART	Rick Mears	USA	Penske PC7-Cosworth	182.094
1981	CART	Rick Mears	USA	Penske PC9B-Cosworth	147.224
	CART	Rick Mears	USA	Penske PC9B-Cosworth	167.196
1982	CART	Rick Mears	USA	Penske PC10-Cosworth	164.750
1983	CART	Gordon Johncock	USA	Wildcat Mk9C-Cosworth	146.133
1998	IRL	Kenny Brack	S	Dallara IR7-Aurora	140.026
1999	IRL	Scott Sharp	USA	Dallara IR7-Aurora	145.320
2000	IRL	Greg Ray	USA	Dallara IR0-Aurora	157.494
2001	IRL	Greg Ray	USA	Dallara IR0-Aurora	137.211

NASCAR RACE (SINCE 1990)

year	formula	winner	nat	car	mph
1990	NASCAR	Dale Earnhardt	USA	Chevrolet Lumina	157.123
	NASCAR	Morgan Shepherd	USA	Ford Thunderbird	140.911
1991	NASCAR	Ken Schrader	USA	Chevrolet Lumina	140.470
	NASCAR	Mark Martin	USA	Ford Thunderbird	137.968
1992	NASCAR	Bill Elliott	USA	Ford Thunderbird	147.746
	NASCAR	Bill Elliott	USA	Ford Thunderbird	133.520
1993	NASCAR	Morgan Shepherd	USA	Ford Thunderbird	151.712
	NASCAR	Rusty Wallace	USA	Pontiac Grand Prix	125.221
1994	NASCAR	Ernie Irvan	USA	Ford Thunderbird	146.136
	NASCAR	Mark Martin	USA	Ford Thunderbird	148.983
1995	NASCAR	Jeff Gordon	USA	Chevrolet Monte Carlo	150.115
	NASCAR	Dale Earnhardt	USA	Chevrolet Monte Carlo	163.633
1996	NASCAR	Dale Earnhardt	USA	Chevrolet Monte Carlo	161.298
	NASCAR	Bobby Labonte	USA	Chevrolet Monte Carlo	136.636
1997	NASCAR	Dale Jarrett	USA	Ford Thunderbird	132.731
	NASCAR	Bobby Labonte	USA	Pontiac Grand Prix	159.904
1998	NASCAR	Bobby Labonte	USA	Pontiac Grand Prix	139.501
	NASCAR	Jeff Gordon	USA	Chevrolet Monte Carlo	113.572
1999	NASCAR	Jeff Gordon	USA	Chevrolet Monte Carlo	143.284
	NASCAR	Bobby Labonte	USA	Pontiac Grand Prix	137.932
2000	NASCAR	Dale Earnhardt	USA	Chevrolet Monte Carlo	131.759
	NASCAR	Jerry Nadeau	USA	Chevrolet Monte Carlo	141.340

		NASCAR RACE (SINCE 1990) (cont.)				
year	formula	winner	nat	car		mph
2001	NASCAR	Kevin Harvick	USA	Chevrolet Monte Carlo		143.273
	NASCAR	Bobby Labonte	USA	Pontiac Grand Prix		151.756
2002	NASCAR	Tony Stewart	USA	Pontiac Grand Prix		148.443
	NASCAR	Kurt Busch	USA	Ford Taurus		127.519

BRISTOL

Not only is Tennessee's Bristol Motor Speedway among the shortest circuits on the NASCAR calendar, it also boasts the steepest banking at 36 degrees. Over 100,000 spectators cram into the facility, especially for the flood-lit August night race. With mountains on either side,

Bristol is nicknamed "Thunder Valley", although one peak has now been flattened as new owner Bruton Smith brought the circuit up –to date.

Location	5 miles south of Bristol, Tennessee, 200 south-west of Cincinnati
Active years	1961 to date
Type	Paved oval
Website	www.bristolmotorspeedway.com

Current circuit	
Lap distance	0.533 miles
Lap records	Qualifying: Steve Park (Chevrolet Monte Carlo), 15.184s, 126.370 mph, NASCAR, 2000

Circuit changes	
1961-69	1.500 miles with 22 degree banking
1969 to date	Reshaped and banking raised to 36 degree. Current circuit

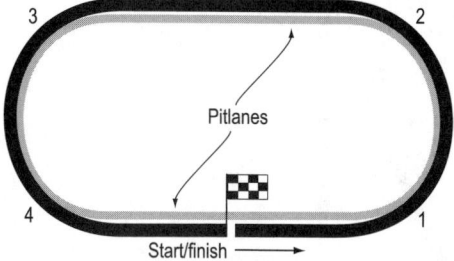

		NASCAR RACE (SINCE 1990)				
year	formula	winner	nat	car		mph
1990	NASCAR	Davey Allison	USA	Ford Thunderbird		87.258
	NASCAR	Ernie Irvan	USA	Chevrolet Lumina		91.782
1991	NASCAR	Rusty Wallace	USA	Pontiac Grand Prix		67.672
	NASCAR	Alan Kulwicki	USA	Ford Thunderbird		82.028
1992	NASCAR	Alan Kulwicki	USA	Ford Thunderbird		86.316
	NASCAR	Darrell Waltrip	USA	Chevrolet Lumina		91.198
1993	NASCAR	Rusty Wallace	USA	Pontiac Grand Prix		84.730
	NASCAR	Mark Martin	USA	Ford Thunderbird		88.172
1994	NASCAR	Dale Earnhardt	USA	Chevrolet Lumina		89.647
	NASCAR	Rusty Wallace	USA	Ford Thunderbird		91.363
1995	NASCAR	Jeff Gordon	USA	Chevrolet Monte Carlo		92.011
	NASCAR	Terry Labonte	USA	Chevrolet Monte Carlo		81.979
1996	NASCAR	Jeff Gordon	USA	Chevrolet Monte Carlo		91.308
	NASCAR	Rusty Wallace	USA	Ford Thunderbird		91.267
1997	NASCAR	Jeff Gordon	USA	Chevrolet Monte Carlo		75.035
	NASCAR	Dale Jarrett	USA	Ford Thunderbird		80.010
1998	NASCAR	Jeff Gordon	USA	Chevrolet Monte Carlo		82.850
	NASCAR	Mark Martin	USA	Ford Taurus		86.949
1999	NASCAR	Rusty Wallace	USA	Ford Taurus		93.363
	NASCAR	Dale Earnhardt	USA	Chevrolet Monte Carlo		91.276
2000	NASCAR	Rusty Wallace	USA	Ford Taurus		88.018
	NASCAR	Rusty Wallace	USA	Ford Taurus		85.394
2001	NASCAR	Elliott Sadler	USA	Ford Taurus		86.949
	NASCAR	Tony Stewart	USA	Pontiac Grand Prix		85.106
2002	NASCAR	Kurt Busch	USA	Ford Taurus		82.281
	NASCAR	Jeff Gordon	USA	Chevrolet Monte Carlo		77.097

CAESARS PALACE

Las Vegas

The makeshift road course at Caesars Palace Hotel and Casino in Las Vegas epitomised the madness that afflicted Formula 1 in the United States during the eighties. Constructed in the hotel's parking lot, the course was over two miles of racing circuit bordered by concrete barriers – no visual landmarks and no atmos-

phere, just the new show in town. The organisers hired Long Beach promoter Chris Pook and used taxi drivers to bed in the new tarmac. The general reaction was that it was better than expected, but Formula 1 lasted just two years at the site. During this time Caesars Palace staged the final race of the championship, and both Nelson Piquet (1981) and Keke Rosberg (1982) claimed world titles here. The circuit began hosting Champcars on a modified oval the following season before that series too moved on after two races.

Active years   1981–84
Location   The car park of Caesars Palace Hotel in downtown Las
  Vegas
Type   Temporary road course

Grand Prix circuit (1981–82)
Lap distance   2.268 miles
Lap records   Qualifying: Alain Prost (Renault RE30B), 1m16.356,
  106.931 mph, F1, 1982

Race: Michele Alboreto (Tyrrell 011-Ford), 1m19.639,
  102.523 mph, F1, 1982

Champcar circuit (1983–84)
Lap distance   1.125 miles
Lap record   Qualifying: Danny Sullivan (Lola T800-Cosworth)
  39.952s, 101.372 mph, CART, 1984

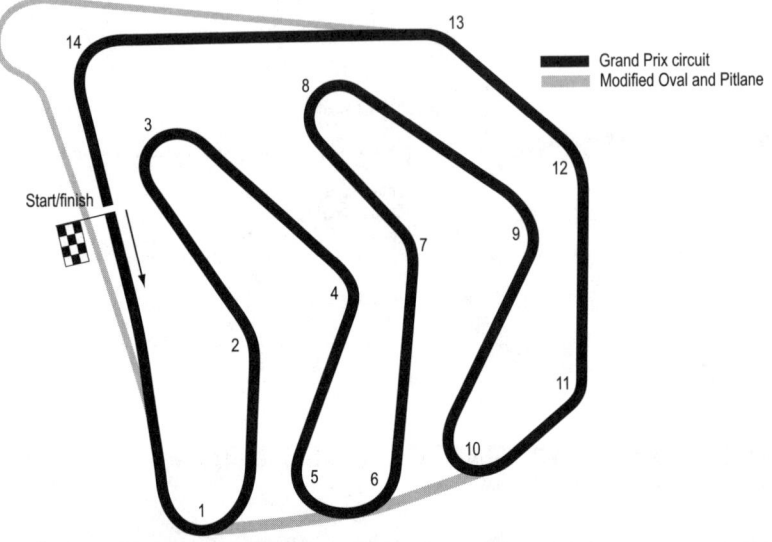

Grand Prix circuit
Modified Oval and Pitlane

Start/finish

LAS VEGAS GRAND PRIX					
year	formula	winner	nat	car	mph
1981	F1 W	Alan Jones	AUS	Williams FW07C-Ford	97.992
1982	F1 W	Michele Alboreto	I	Tyrrell 011-Ford	100.110
1983	CART	Mario Andretti	USA	Lola T700-Cosworth	87.192
1984	CART	Tom Sneva	USA	March 84C-Cosworth	93.702

CALIFORNIA SPEEDWAY

Fontana

California Speedway was built by Roger Penske's speedway corporation on the site of the disused Kaiser steelworks in Fontana at an estimated cost of $110m. The concrete water tower on the infield is the only reminder of the former site, which was so bleak that it served as the set for futuristic films such as Terminator 2, Robocop and Independence Day. The circuit is a near-copy of the Michigan Speedway that Penske also owned, but the shallower 14-degree turns have resulted in world record speeds – witness Gil de Ferran's 2000 pole position and the average speed of the 2002 CART race. The backstretch is also raised to provide a better view for the 86,439 spectators. The 1999 Champcar race was marred by the tragic death of emerging Canadian star Greg Moore. Penske sold his speedways to the International Speedway Corporation in 1999.

Active years   1997 to date
Location   Fontana, California, 40 miles east of Los Angeles
Type   Paved oval
Website   www.californiaspeedway.com
Lap distance   2.029 miles
Lap records   Qualifying: Gil de Ferran (Reynard 2KI-Honda), 30.255s,
  241.428 mph, CART, 2000 (world record speed for a
  closed lap)
  Race: Greg Moore (Reynard 97I-Mercedes-Benz),
  30.900s, 236.389 mph, CART, 1997

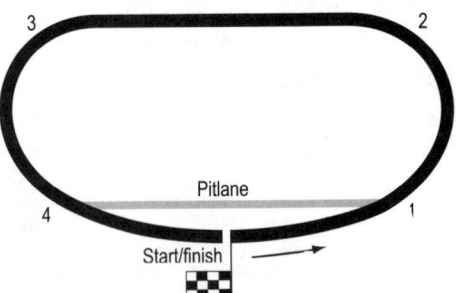

Pitlane

Start/finish

CHAMPCAR RACE

year	formula	winner	nat	car	mph
1997	CART	Mark Blundell	GB	Reynard 97I-Mercedes-Benz	166.575
1998	CART	Jimmy Vasser	USA	Reynard 98I-Honda	153.785
1999	CART	Adrian Fernandez	MEX	Reynard 97I-Ford	171.666
2000	CART	Christian Fittipaldi	BR	Lola B2K/00-Ford	139.563
2001	CART	Cristiano da Matta	BR	Lola B01/00-Toyota	169.401
2002	CART	Jimmy Vasser	USA	Lola B2/00-Ford	197.995*

*Fastest race in history

INDYCAR RACE

year	formula	winner	nat	car	mph
2002	IRL	Sam Hornish Jr	USA	Dallara IR0-Chevrolet	181.946

NASCAR RACE

year	formula	winner	nat	car	mph
1997	NASCAR	Jeff Gordon	USA	Chevrolet Monte Carlo	155.012
1998	NASCAR	Mark Martin	USA	Ford Taurus	140.220
1999	NASCAR	Jeff Gordon	USA	Chevrolet Monte Carlo	157.370
2000	NASCAR	Jeremy Mayfield	USA	Ford Taurus	149.378
2001	NASCAR	Rusty Wallace	USA	Ford Taurus	143.118
2002	NASCAR	Jimmie Johnson	USA	Chevrolet Monte Carlo	150.088

CHARLOTTE

Lowe's Motor Speedway

The crown jewel of Bruton Smith's speedway empire since 1976, Charlotte is also the centre of the NASCAR racing industry. It is a superb high-banked 24-degree superspeedway, which hosts the World 600 (now sponsored by Coca-Cola) on the same weekend as the Indianapolis 500. The crowd for that race is the third largest single-day sporting attendance in America. Facilities have been continually updated (including new floodlights to allow night racing), making Charlotte arguably the finest circuit of its type in the world. The Indy Racing League visited until the 1999 race was abandoned after three spectators were killed by debris from an accident. Although the track was renamed Lowe's in deference to a new sponsor, it is still universally known as Charlotte.

Active years	1959 to date
Location	Concord, 12 miles north of Charlotte, North Carolina
Type	Paved oval
Website	www.lowesmotorspeedway.com
Lap distance	1.500 miles
Lap records	Qualifying: Tony Stewart (Dallara IR7-Aurora), 24.490s, 220.498 mph, IRL, 1998
	Race: Kenny Brack (Dallara IR7-Aurora), 24.735s, 218.314 mph, IRL, 1998

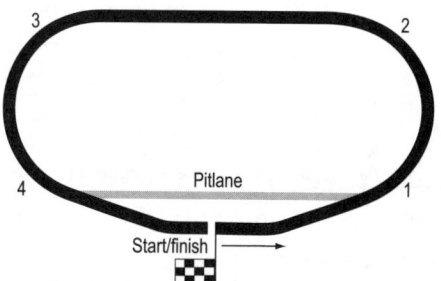

COCA COLA/WORLD 600

year	formula	winner	nat	car	mph
1960	NASCAR	Joe Lee Johnson	USA	Chevrolet	107.735
1961	NASCAR	David Pearson	USA	Pontiac	111.633
1962	NASCAR	Nelson Stacey	USA	Ford	125.552
1963	NASCAR	Fred Lorenzen	USA	Ford	132.418
1964	NASCAR	Jim Paschal	USA	Plymouth	125.772
1965	NASCAR	Fred Lorenzen	USA	Ford	121.772
1966	NASCAR	Marvin Panch	USA	Plymouth	135.042
1967	NASCAR	Jim Paschal	USA	Plymouth	135.832
1968	NASCAR	Buddy Baker	USA	Dodge	104.207
1969	NASCAR	Lee Roy Yarborough	USA	Mercury	134.361
1970	NASCAR	Donnie Allison	USA	Ford	129.680
1971	NASCAR	Bobby Allison	USA	Mercury	140.442
1972	NASCAR	Buddy Baker	USA	Dodge	142.255
1973	NASCAR	Buddy Baker	USA	Dodge	134.890
1974	NASCAR	David Pearson	USA	Mercury	135.720
1975	NASCAR	Richard Petty	USA	Dodge	145.327
1976	NASCAR	David Pearson	USA	Mercury	137.352
1977	NASCAR	Richard Petty	USA	Dodge	137.676
1978	NASCAR	Darrell Waltrip	USA	Chevrolet	138.355

COCA COLA/WORLD 600 (cont.)

year	formula	winner	nat	car	mph
1979	NASCAR	Darrell Waltrip	USA	Chevrolet	136.674
1980	NASCAR	Benny Parsons	USA	Chevrolet	119.265
1981	NASCAR	Bobby Allison	USA	Buick	129.326
1982	NASCAR	Neil Bonnett	USA	Ford	130.058
1983	NASCAR	Neil Bonnett	USA	Chevrolet	140.707
1984	NASCAR	Bobby Allison	USA	Buick	129.233
1985	NASCAR	Darrell Waltrip	USA	Chevrolet	141.807
1986	NASCAR	Dale Earnhardt	USA	Chevrolet	140.406
1987	NASCAR	Kyle Petty	USA	Ford	131.483
1988	NASCAR	Darrell Waltrip	USA	Chevrolet	124.460
1989	NASCAR	Darrell Waltrip	USA	Chevrolet	144.077
1990	NASCAR	Rusty Wallace	USA	Pontiac Grand Prix	137.650
1991	NASCAR	Davey Allison	USA	Ford Thunderbird	138.951
1992	NASCAR	Dale Earnhardt	USA	Chevrolet Lumina	132.980
1993	NASCAR	Dale Earnhardt	USA	Chevrolet Lumina	145.504
1994	NASCAR	Jeff Gordon	USA	Chevrolet Lumina	139.445
1995	NASCAR	Bobby Labonte	USA	Chevrolet Monte Carlo	151.952
1996	NASCAR	Dale Jarrett	USA	Ford Thunderbird	147.581
1997	NASCAR	Jeff Gordon	USA	Chevrolet Monte Carlo	136.745
1998	NASCAR	Jeff Gordon	USA	Chevrolet Monte Carlo	136.424
1999	NASCAR	Jeff Burton	USA	Ford Taurus	151.367
2000	NASCAR	Matt Kenseth	USA	Ford Taurus	142.640
2001	NASCAR	Jeff Burton	USA	Ford Taurus	138.107
2002	NASCAR	Mark Martin	USA	Ford Taurus	137.729

AUTUMN NASCAR RACE (SINCE 1990)

year	formula	winner	nat	car	mph
1990	NASCAR	Davey Allison	USA	Ford Thunderbird	137.428
1991	NASCAR	Geoff Bodine	USA	Ford Thunderbird	138.984
1992	NASCAR	Mark Martin	USA	Ford Thunderbird	153.537
1993	NASCAR	Ernie Irvan	USA	Ford Thunderbird	154.537
1994	NASCAR	Dale Jarrett	USA	Chevrolet Lumina	145.922
1995	NASCAR	Mark Martin	USA	Ford Thunderbird	145.358
1996	NASCAR	Terry Labonte	USA	Chevrolet Monte Carlo	143.143
1997	NASCAR	Dale Jarrett	USA	Ford Thunderbird	144.323
1998	NASCAR	Mark Martin	USA	Ford Taurus	123.188
1999	NASCAR	Jeff Gordon	USA	Chevrolet Monte Carlo	160.306
2000	NASCAR	Bobby Labonte	USA	Pontiac Grand Prix	133.630
2001	NASCAR	Sterling Marlin	USA	Dodge Intrepid	139.006
2002	NASCAR	Jamie McMurray	USA	Dodge Intrepid	141.481

INDYCAR RACE

year	formula	winner	nat	car	mph
1997	IRL	Buddy Lazier	USA	Dallara IR7-Aurora	162.101
1998	IRL	Kenny Brack	S	Dallara IR7-Aurora	158.408
1999	IRL	no result declared due to spectator fatalities			

CHICAGO

Cicero

The recent growth of oval racing in North America is on display in the Chicago area, where two speedways have been built in the last four years. Chip Ganassi opened his 67,000 capacity 1-mile speedway in Cicero two years ahead of a new rival in Joliet (see Chicagoland). Built around an active horse track, the circuit is very wide with shallow six-degree banking. However, the long-term viability of the venue was in doubt in 2002 when the Champcar race could only go ahead when CART took over as promoters and has lost its place on the 2003 schedule.

Active years   **1999 to date**

Location	Sportsman's Park, Cicero, Illinois, 7 miles west of downtown Chicago
Type	Paved oval
Website	www.chicagomotorspeedway.com
Lap distance	1.029 miles
Lap records	Qualifying: Juan Pablo Montoya (Reynard 2KI-Toyota), 22.107s, 167.567 mph, CART, 2000
	Race: Roberto Moreno (Swift 010c-Ford), 23.687s, 156.390 mph, CART, 1999

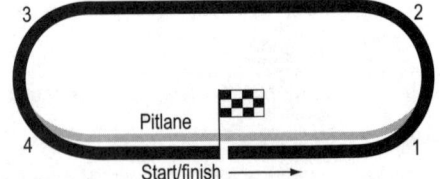

CHAMPCAR RACE

year	formula	winner	nat	car	mph
1999	CART	Juan Pablo Montoya	CO	Reynard 99I-Honda	122.236
2000	CART	Cristiano da Matta	BR	Reynard 2KI-Toyota	114.432
2001	CART	Kenny Brack	S	Lola B01/00-Ford	132.031
2002	CART	Cristiano da Matta	BR	Lola B2/00-Toyota	121.524

CHICAGOLAND
Joliet

Chicagoland was built southwest of Chicago by the combined might of the Indianapolis Motor Speedway and the International Speedway Corporation. In addition to the tri-oval it features a drag strip and a dirt oval, and every need of the 75,000 spectators is catered to. The inaugural 2001 season saw races for both the NASCAR Winston Cup and Indy Racing League. The turns are banked at 18 degrees, with 11 degrees in the front stretch.

Lap records Qualifying: Sam Hornish Jr (Dallara IR0-Chevrolet), 24.5528s, 219.934 mph, IRL, 2002
Race: Buddy Rice (Dallara IR0-Infiniti), 24.4216s, 221.118 mph, IRL, 2002

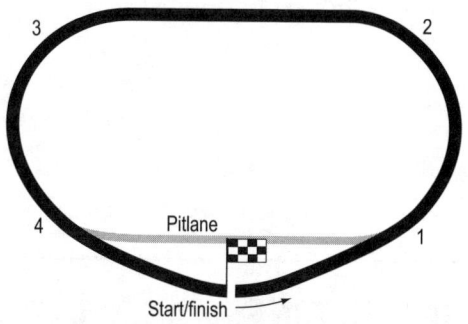

Active years	**2001 to date**
Location	**Joliet, Illinois, 30 miles south-west of Chicago**
Type	**Paved oval**
Website	**www.chicagolandspeedway.com**
Lap distance	**1.500 miles**

INDYCAR RACE

year	formula	winner	nat	car	mph
2001	IRL	Jaques Lazier	USA	Dallara IR0-Aurora	169.881
2002	IRL	Sam Hornish Jr	USA	Dallara IR0-Chevrolet	144.394

NASCAR RACE

year	formula	winner	nat	car	mph
2001	NASCAR	Kevin Harvick	USA	Chevrolet Monte Carlo	121.200
2002	NASCAR	Kevin Harvick	USA	Chevrolet Monte Carlo	136.832

CLEVELAND
Burke Lakefront Airport

Champcars have visited Cleveland's still-operational Burke Lakefront Airport on the shores of Lake Erie since 1982. Although an unattractive venue and unpopular with the drivers, the wide, bumpy runways allow numerous lines to be taken into the corners, producing surprisingly good racing with plenty of overtaking. Because it is so flat, spectators can see almost the entire track from the grandstands.

Active years	**1982 to date**
Location	**Burke Lakefront Airport, 1-mile north-east of downtown Cleveland**
Type	**Temporary road course**
Website	**www.imgmotorsports.com**

Current circuit
Lap distance	**2.106 miles (remeasured in 1997, previously believed to be 2.369 miles)**
Lap records	**Qualifying: Jimmy Vasser (Reynard 98I-Honda), 56.417s, 134.385 mph, CART, 1998** **Race: Alessandro Zanardi (Reynard 97I-Honda), 58.666s, 129.233 mph, CART, 1997**

Circuit changes
1982-89	**2.485 miles**
1990 to date	**New first corner bypassed left/right kink after the pits. Current circuit**

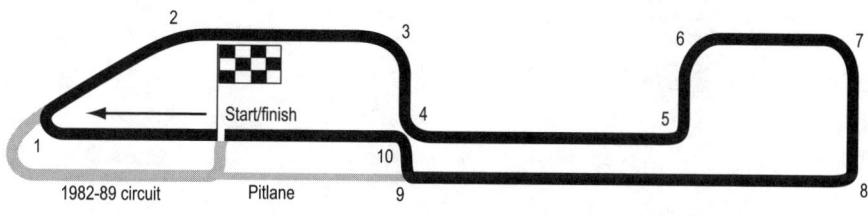

Current circuit
1982-89 Circuit and Pitlane

CLEVELAND GRAND PRIX

year	formula	winner	nat	car	mph
1982	CART	Bobby Rahal	USA	March 82C-Cosworth	101.438
1983	CART	Al Unser	USA	Penske PC11-Cosworth	108.421
1984	CART	Danny Sullivan	USA	Lola T800-Cosworth	118.974
1985	CART	Al Unser Jr	USA	Lola T900-Cosworth	124.331
1986	CART	Danny Sullivan	USA	March 86C-Cosworth	127.362
1987	CART	Emerson Fittipaldi	BR	March 87C-Chevrolet	128.703
1988	CART	Mario Andretti	USA	Lola T88/00-Chevrolet	124.546
1989	CART	Emerson Fittipaldi	BR	Penske PC18-Chevrolet	128.330
1990	CART	Danny Sullivan	USA	Penske PC19-Chevrolet	112.483
1991	CART	Michael Andretti	USA	Lola T91/00-Chevrolet	117.530
1992	CART	Emerson Fittipaldi	BR	Penske PC21-Chevrolet	133.292
1993	CART	Paul Tracy	CDN	Penske PC22-Chevrolet	127.913
1994	CART	Al Unser Jr	USA	Penske PC23-Ilmor	138.026
1995	CART	Jacques Villeneuve	CDN	Reynard 95I-Ford	115.668
1996	CART	Gil de Ferran	BR	Reynard 96I-Honda	118.889
1997	CART	Alessandro Zanardi	I	Reynard 97I-Honda	111.848
1998	CART	Alessandro Zanardi	I	Reynard 98I-Honda	112.449
1999	CART	Juan Pablo Montoya	CO	Reynard 99I-Honda	93.931
2000	CART	Roberto Moreno	BR	Reynard 2KI-Ford	112.619
2001	CART	Dario Franchitti	GB	Reynard 01I-Honda	118.007
2002	CART	Patrick Carpentier	CDN	Reynard 02I-Ford	120.998

DARLINGTON

Inspired by a visit to the Indianapolis 500, local peanut farmer Harold Brasington built a speedway in his hometown and instituted a new Labour Day tradition, the NASCAR Southern 500. The first race on the odd, egg-shaped facility attracted a field of 75 cars, and was won by Johnny Mantz in a Plymouth. A difficult circuit to master, Darlington has seen many a driver end his day in the wall. The banking is different at both ends of the speedway, making car set-up particularly difficult. Turns 1 and 2 are 25 degrees, while 3 and 4 are two degrees shallower, and each end has a different radius. Modernisation during the nineties led to the start being moved to allow the space for larger 65,000-capacity grandstands.

Circuit changes
1950-52	1.250 miles
1953-97	Extended. 1.366 miles (original thought to be 1.375 miles but remeasured in 1970)
1998 to date	Front and back straights switched. Current circuit

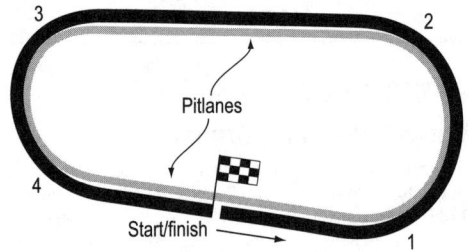

Active years	1950 to date
Location	2 miles west of Darlington, South Carolina
Type	Paved oval
Website	www.darlingtonraceway.com
Lap distance	1.366 miles
Lap records	Qualifying: Ward Burton (Pontiac Grand Prix), 28.295s, 173.797 mph, NASCAR, 1996

TRANSOUTH 500 NASCAR RACE (SINCE 1990)

year	formula	winner	nat	car	mph
1990	NASCAR	Dale Earnhardt	USA	Chevrolet Lumina	124.073
1991	NASCAR	Ricky Rudd	USA	Chevrolet Lumina	135.594
1992	NASCAR	Bill Elliott	USA	Ford Thunderbird	139.364
1993	NASCAR	Dale Earnhardt	USA	Chevrolet Lumina	140.898
1994	NASCAR	Dale Earnhardt	USA	Chevrolet Lumina	132.432
1995	NASCAR	Sterling Marlin	USA	Chevrolet Monte Carlo	111.392
1996	NASCAR	Jeff Gordon	USA	Chevrolet Monte Carlo	124.793
1997	NASCAR	Dale Jarrett	USA	Ford Thunderbird	121.162
1998	NASCAR	Dale Jarrett	USA	Ford Taurus	127.962
1999	NASCAR	Jeff Burton	USA	Ford Taurus	121.294
2000	NASCAR	Ward Burton	USA	Pontiac Grand Prix	128.076
2001	NASCAR	Dale Jarrett	USA	Ford Taurus	126.557
2002	NASCAR	Sterling Marlin	USA	Dodge Intrepid	126.070

SOUTHERN 500 NASCAR RACE (SINCE 1990)

year	formula	winner	nat	car	mph
1990	NASCAR	Dale Earnhardt	USA	Chevrolet Lumina	123.141
1991	NASCAR	Harry Gant	USA	Oldsmobile Cutlass	133.508
1992	NASCAR	Darrell Waltrip	USA	Chevrolet Lumina	129.114
1993	NASCAR	Mark Martin	USA	Ford Thunderbird	137.932
1994	NASCAR	Bill Elliott	USA	Ford Thunderbird	127.952
1995	NASCAR	Jeff Gordon	USA	Chevrolet Monte Carlo	121.231
1996	NASCAR	Jeff Gordon	USA	Chevrolet Monte Carlo	135.757
1997	NASCAR	Jeff Gordon	USA	Chevrolet Monte Carlo	121.149
1998	NASCAR	Jeff Gordon	USA	Chevrolet Monte Carlo	139.031
1999	NASCAR	Jeff Burton	USA	Ford Taurus	107.816
2000	NASCAR	Bobby Labonte	USA	Pontiac Grand Prix	108.253
2001	NASCAR	Ward Burton	USA	Dodge Intrepid	122.773
2002	NASCAR	Jeff Gordon	USA	Chevrolet Monte Carlo	118.617

DAYTONA

The self-styled "World Center of Racing", Daytona Beach is the spiritual home of NASCAR, as well as the organisation's headquarters. The season-opening Daytona 500 has been NASCAR's most prestigious event since the speedway opened in 1959. Lee Petty's Oldsmobile won the first race in a photo finish that took three days to decide, and the tradition of close racing at Daytona continues to this day. In 1979, a fight broke out between Cale Yarborough and Donnie Allison, after they crashed while leading on the last lap of the Daytona 500. For today's fans, however, Daytona will be forever associated with the shocking loss of NASCAR stalwart Dale Earnhardt, who was killed in the closing laps of the 2001 race. In addition to stock car racing, Daytona also features a road course used for a 24-hour sports car race since 1966. Excavating the dirt required to build the imposing 31-degree banking left an area that has since become Lake Lloyd, a 44-acre body of water located in the infield.

Active years 1959 to date
Location 4 miles west of Daytona Beach, Florida, 45 miles north-east of Orlando, 90 miles south-east of Jacksonville
Type Paved oval and permanent road course
Websites www.daytonausa.com and www.daytonaintlspeedway.com

Oval circuit
Active years 1959 to date

Lap distance 2.500 miles
Lap record Qualifying: Bill Elliott (Ford Thunderbird), 42.783s, 210.364 mph, NASCAR, 1987

Road Course
Active years 1964 to date
Lap distance 3.560 miles
Lap records Qualifying: Juan Manuel Fangio II (Eagle MkIII-Toyota), 1m35.86, 133.695 mph, IMSA Sports Cars, 1992
Race: Massimiliano Papis (Ferrari 333SP), 1m40.545, 127.465 mph, Sports Cars, 1998

Road course circuit changes
1966-74 3.810 miles
1975-84 Chicane inserted by Lake Lloyd before Turn 3. 3.870 miles
1985 to date current circuit

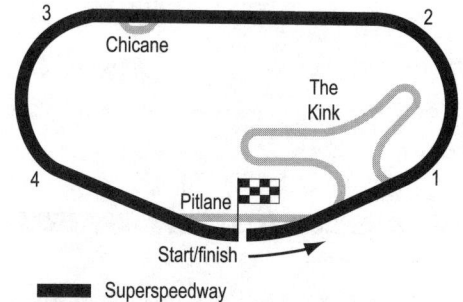

DAYTONA 24 HOURS

year	formula	winner	nat	car	mph
1966	SC W	Ken Miles/Lloyd Ruby	USA	Ford GT40 Mk2	107.388
1967	SC W	Lorenzo Bandini/Chris Amon	I/NZ	Ferrari 330P4	105.681
1968	SC W	Vic Elford/Jochen Neerpasch/Rolf Stommelen/			
		Jo Siffert/Hans Herrmann	GB/D/D/CH/D	Porsche 907/8	106.697
1969	SC W	Mark Donohue/Chuck Parsons	USA	Lola T70 Mk3B-Chevrolet	99.267
1970	SC W	Pedro Rodriguez/Leo Kinnunen	MEX/SF	Porsche 917	114.866
1971	SC W	Pedro Rodriguez/Jackie Oliver	MEX/GB	Porsche 917K	109.203
1972*	SC W	Jacky Ickx/Mario Andretti	B/USA	Ferrari 312P	122.643
1973	SC W	Peter Gregg/Hurley Haywood	USA	Porsche 911 Carrera RS	106.274
1975	SC W	Peter Gregg/Hurley Haywood	USA	Porsche 911 Carrera RS	109.440
1976	SC	Peter Gregg/Brian Redman/			
		John Fitzpatrick	USA/GB/GB	BMW 3.0 CSL	104.042
1977	SC W	John Graves/Hurley Haywood/			
		Dave Helmick	USA	Porsche 911 Carrera RSR	108.801
1978	SC W	Rolf Stommelen/Toine Hezemans/			
		Peter Gregg	D/NL/USA	Porsche 935	108.743

DAYTONA 24 HOURS (cont.)

year	formula	winner	nat	car	mph
1979	SC W	Danny Ongais/Hurley Haywood/Ted Field	USA	Porsche 935	109.409
1980	SC W	Rolf Stommelen/Reinhold Joest/Volkert Merl	D	Porsche 935	114.303
1981	SC W	Bob Garretson/Bobby Rahal/ Brian Redman	USA/USA/GB	Porsche 935	113.153
1982	SC	John Paul/John Paul Jr/ Rolf Stommelen	USA/USA/D	Porsche 935	114.794
1983	SC	Preston Henn/Bob Wollek/ Claude Ballot-Lena/AJ Foyt Jr	USA/F/F/USA	Porsche 935	98.781
1984	SC	Sarel van der Merwe/Tony Martin/ Graham Duxbury	ZA	March 83G-Porsche	103.119
1985	SC	AJ Foyt Jr/Bob Wollek/Al Unser/ Thierry Boutsen	USA/F/USA/B	Porsche 962	104.162
1986	SC	Al Holbert/Derek Bell/Al Unser Jr	USA/GB/USA	Porsche 962	105.484
1987	SC	Chip Robinson/Derek Bell/Al Unser Jr/ Al Holbert	USA/GB/USA/USA	Porsche 962	111.599
1988	SC	Martin Brundle/John Nielsen/ Raul Boesel/Jan Lammers	GB/DK/BR/NL	Jaguar XJR-9	107.943
1989	SC	John Andretti/Derek Bell/Bob Wollek	USA/GB/F	Porsche 962	92.009
1990	SC	Davy Jones/Jan Lammers/ Andy Wallace	USA/NL/GB	Jaguar XJR-12	112.857
1991	SC	"John Winter"/Frank Jelinski/Henri Pescarolo/ Hurley Haywood/Bob Wollek	D/D/F/USA/F	Porsche 962	106.633
1992	SC	Masahiro Hasemi/Kazuyoshi Hoshino/ Toshio Suzuki	J	Nissan R91CP	112.897
1993	SC	PJ Jones/Mark Dismore/Rocky Moran	USA	Eagle Mk3-Toyota	103.504
1994	SC	Scott Pruett/Paul Gentilozzi/ Butch Leitzinger/Steve Millen	USA/USA/USA/NZ	Nissan 300ZX	104.800
1995	SC	Christophe Bouchut/Jurgen Laessig/ Giovanni Lavaggi/Marco Werner	F/D/I/D	Kremer K8-Porsche	102.350
1996	SC	Wayne Taylor/Scott Sharp/Jim Pace	ZA/USA/USA	Riley & Scott MkIII-Oldsmobile	103.310
1997	SC	Elliott Forbes-Robinson/Rob Dyson/ James Weaver/Butch Leitzinger/Andy Wallace/ John Paul jr/John Schneider	USA/USA/GB/USA/ GB/USA/USA	Riley & Scott MkIII-Oldsmobile	102.292
1998	SC	Gianpiero Moretti/Didier Theys/ Arie Luyendyk/Mauro Baldi	I/B/NL/I	Ferrari 333SP	105.450
1999	SC	Andy Wallace/Elliott Forbes-Robinson/ Butch Leitzinger	GB/USA/USA	Riley & Scott MkIII-Ford	104.940
2000	SC	Olivier Beretta/Karl Wendlinger/ Dominique Dupuy	MC/A/F	Chrysler Viper GTS-R	107.245
2001	SC	Ron Fellows/Chris Kneifel/Franck Freon/ Johnny O'Connell	CDN/USA/F/USA	Chevrolet Corvette CR-5	97.304
2002	SC	Didier Theys/Fredy Lienhard/ Massimiliano Papis/Mauro Baldi	B/CH/I/I	Dallara LMP-Judd	106.142

*6 hour race

OTHER WORLD SPORTS CAR RACES

year	formula	winner	nat	car	mph
1964	SC W	Phil Hill/Pedro Rodriguez	USA/MEX	Ferrari 250GTO	98.303
1965	SC W	Ken Miles/Lloyd Ruby	USA	Ford GT40	100.050
1981	SC W	Roger Manderville/Amos Johnson	USA	Mazda RX-7	97.146

DAYTONA 500

year	formula	winner	nat	car	mph
1959	NASCAR	Lee Petty	USA	Oldsmobile	135.521
1960	NASCAR	Junior Johnson	USA	Chevrolet	124.740
1961	NASCAR	Marvin Panch	USA	Pontiac	149.601
1962	NASCAR	"Fireball" Roberts	USA	Pontiac	152.529
1963	NASCAR	Tiny Lund	USA	Ford	151.566
1964	NASCAR	Richard Petty	USA	Plymouth	154.334
1965	NASCAR	Fred Lorenzen	USA	Ford	141.539
1966	NASCAR	Richard Petty	USA	Plymouth	160.627
1967	NASCAR	Mario Andretti	USA	Ford	146.926
1968	NASCAR	Cale Yarborough	USA	Mercury	143.251
1969	NASCAR	Lee Roy Yarborough	USA	Ford	157.950
1970	NASCAR	Pete Hamilton	USA	Plymouth	149.601
1971	NASCAR	Richard Petty	USA	Plymouth	144.462
1972	NASCAR	AJ Foyt Jr	USA	Mercury	161.551
1973	NASCAR	Richard Petty	USA	Dodge	157.205
1974	NASCAR	Richard Petty	USA	Dodge	140.894

DAYTONA 500 (cont.)

year	formula	winner	nat	car	mph
1975	NASCAR	Benny Parsons	USA	Chevrolet	153.649
1976	NASCAR	David Pearson	USA	Mercury	152.181
1977	NASCAR	Cale Yarborough	USA	Chevrolet	153.218
1978	NASCAR	Bobby Allison	USA	Ford	159.730
1979	NASCAR	Richard Petty	USA	Oldsmobile	143.977
1980	NASCAR	Buddy Baker	USA	Oldsmobile	177.602
1981	NASCAR	Richard Petty	USA	Buick	169.651
1982	NASCAR	Bobby Allison	USA	Buick	153.991
1983	NASCAR	Cale Yarborough	USA	Pontiac	155.979
1984	NASCAR	Cale Yarborough	USA	Chevrolet	150.994
1985	NASCAR	Bill Elliott	USA	Ford	172.265
1986	NASCAR	Geoff Bodine	USA	Chevrolet	148.124
1987	NASCAR	Bill Elliott	USA	Ford	176.263
1988	NASCAR	Bobby Allison	USA	Buick	137.531
1989	NASCAR	Darrell Waltrip	USA	Chevrolet	148.466
1990	NASCAR	Derrike Cope	USA	Chevrolet Lumina	165.761
1991	NASCAR	Ernie Irvan	USA	Chevrolet Lumina	148.148
1992	NASCAR	Davey Allison	USA	Ford Thunderbird	160.256
1993	NASCAR	Dale Jarrett	USA	Chevrolet Lumina	154.972
1994	NASCAR	Sterling Marlin	USA	Chevrolet Lumina	156.931
1995	NASCAR	Sterling Marlin	USA	Chevrolet Monte Carlo	141.710
1996	NASCAR	Dale Jarrett	USA	Ford Thunderbird	154.308
1997	NASCAR	Jeff Gordon	USA	Chevrolet Monte Carlo	148.295
1998	NASCAR	Dale Earnhardt	USA	Chevrolet Monte Carlo	172.712
1999	NASCAR	Jeff Gordon	USA	Chevrolet Monte Carlo	161.551
2000	NASCAR	Dale Jarrett	USA	Ford Taurus	155.669
2001	NASCAR	Michael Waltrip	USA	Chevrolet Monte Carlo	161.783
2002	NASCAR	Ward Burton	USA	Dodge Intrepid	142.971

PEPSI/FIRECRACKER 400 NASCAR RACE (SINCE 1990)

year	formula	winner	nat	car	mph
1990	NASCAR	Dale Earnhardt	USA	Chevrolet Lumina	160.894
1991	NASCAR	Bill Elliott	USA	Ford Thunderbird	159.116
1992	NASCAR	Ernie Irvan	USA	Chevrolet Lumina	170.475
1993	NASCAR	Dale Earnhardt	USA	Chevrolet Lumina	151.755
1994	NASCAR	Jimmy Spencer	USA	Ford Thunderbird	155.558
1995	NASCAR	Jeff Gordon	USA	Chevrolet Monte Carlo	166.976
1996	NASCAR	Sterling Marlin	USA	Chevrolet Monte Carlo	161.602
1997	NASCAR	John Andretti	USA	Ford Thunderbird	157.791
1998	NASCAR	Jeff Gordon	USA	Chevrolet Monte Carlo	144.549
1999	NASCAR	Dale Jarrett	USA	Ford Taurus	169.213
2000	NASCAR	Jeff Burton	USA	Ford Taurus	148.576
2001	NASCAR	Dale Earnhardt Jr	USA	Chevrolet Monte Carlo	157.601
2002	NASCAR	Michael Waltrip	USA	Chevrolet Monte Carlo	135.952

CHAMPCAR RACE

year	formula	winner	nat	car	mph
1959	USAC	Jim Rathmann	USA	Watson-Offenhauser	170.261

DENVER

1990-91 circuit

Denver, Colorado held two Champcar races in the early nineties on a tight street circuit, both won by Al Unser jr in front of capacity 55,000 crowds. The high altitude of the city posed particular problems for the teams, especially for cooling and brakes. The layout with the pits on a corner was unique.

Active years	1990-91
Location	Central Denver, Colorado
Type	Temporary street circuit
Lap distance	1.900 miles
Lap record	Qualifying: Michael Andretti (Lola T91/00-Chevrolet), 1m25.896, 79.631 mph, CART, 1991

DENVER
1990-91

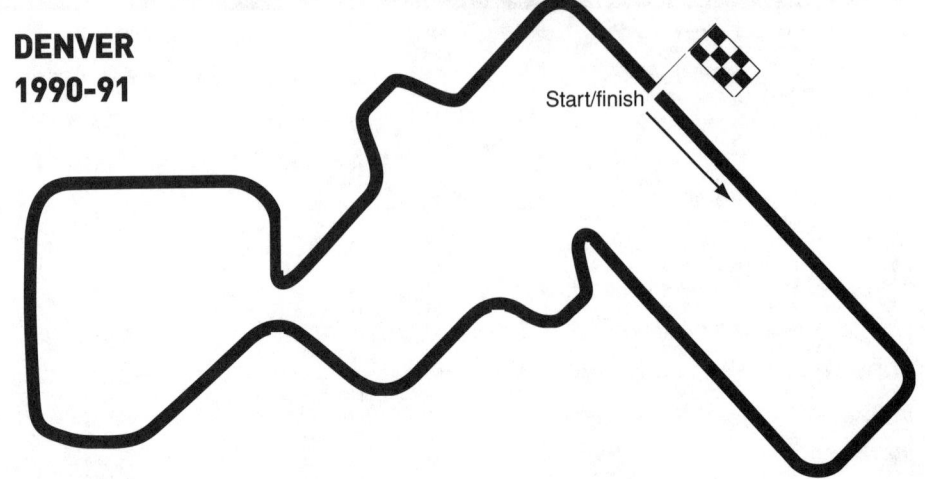

Start/finish

DENVER

Pepsi Center Expo Circuit

CART's desire to hold events in North America's leading cities took the series back to Denver in 2002. It returned on a new temporary circuit around the Pepsi Center Expo. The mixture of tarmac and concrete surface was universally critcised as too bumpy and lacking in grip, and the circuit will be repaved in time for the 2003 race. The turn 5 hairpin is among the widest sections of any temporary course in the world.

Active years	2002 to date
Location	Pepsi Center Expo, Denver, Colorado
Type	Temporary street circuit
Website	www.grandprixofdenver.com
Lap distance	1.647 miles
Lap record	Qualifying: Bruno Junqueira (Lola B2/00-Toyota), 1m01.703, 96.093 mph, CART, 2002
	Race: Kenny Brack (Lola B2/00-Toyota), 1m01.648, 96.179 mph, CART, 2002

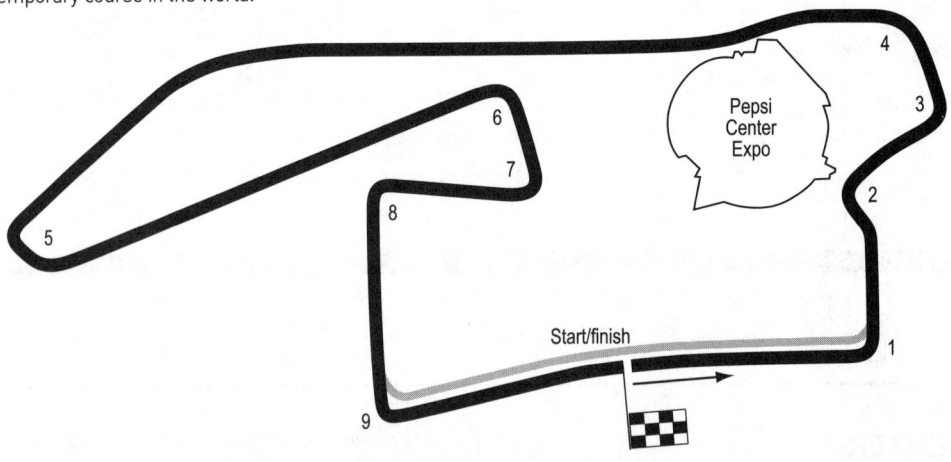

Pepsi Center Expo

Start/finish

DENVER CHAMPCAR GRAND PRIX					
year	formula	winner	nat	car	mph
1990	CART	Al Unser Jr	USA	Lola T90/00-Chevrolet	71.243
1991	CART	Al Unser Jr	USA	Lola T91/00-Chevrolet	68.141
2002	CART	Bruno Junqueira	BR	Lola B2/00-Toyota	90.349

DETROIT

City Centre Street Circuit

The growth of F1 in the United States resulted in a third American Grand Prix for the 1982 season. But the temporary circuit around the Detroit's Renaissance Center was an unloved and bumpy succession of 90-degree corners. Ayrton Senna was the acknowledged master of the Formula 1 event, but spiralling costs forced the organisers to switch to Champcars in 1989. A new circuit on Belle Isle replaced the street circuit three years later.

Active years	1982-91
Location	Central Detroit

Type	Temporary street circuit
Lap distance	2.500 miles
Lap records	Qualifying: Ayrton Senna (Lotus 99T-Honda), 1m40.464, 89.584 mph, F1, 1987
	Race: Ayrton Senna (Lotus 98T-Renault), 1m38.301, 91.556 mph, F1, 1986

Circuit changes	
1982	2.493 miles
1983-91	Original Turn 5 bypassed. Final circuit

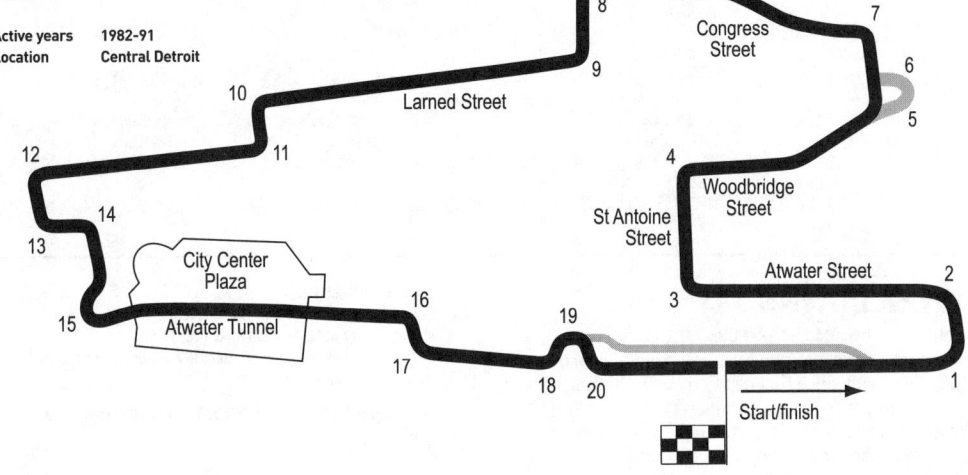

DETROIT

Belle Isle

In addition to hosting the Detroit Grand Prix since it moved from downtown in 1992, Bell Isle marked the start of CART's mid-season run of road courses before being dropped from the calendar in 2002. It is a 14-turn temporary road course in parkland on an island on the Detroit River. The combination of tarmac and concrete surface is bumpy. The extension opened in 1998 improved overtaking opportunities, but passing remained difficult.

Active years	1992-2001
Location	Belle Isle, in the Detroit River, 3 miles east of downtown Detroit
Type	Temporary road course
Website	www.imgmotorsports.com

Final circuit	
Lap distance	2.346 miles
Lap record	Qualifying: Juan Pablo Montoya (Reynard 2KI-Toyota), 1m13.056, 115.605 mph, CART, 2000
	Race: Juan Pablo Montoya (Reynard 99I-Honda), 1m15.701, 111.566 mph, CART, 1999

Circuit changes	
1992-97	2.100 miles
1998-2001	Track extended to Turns 3 and 4 before rejoining original layout at new Turn 5. Final circuit

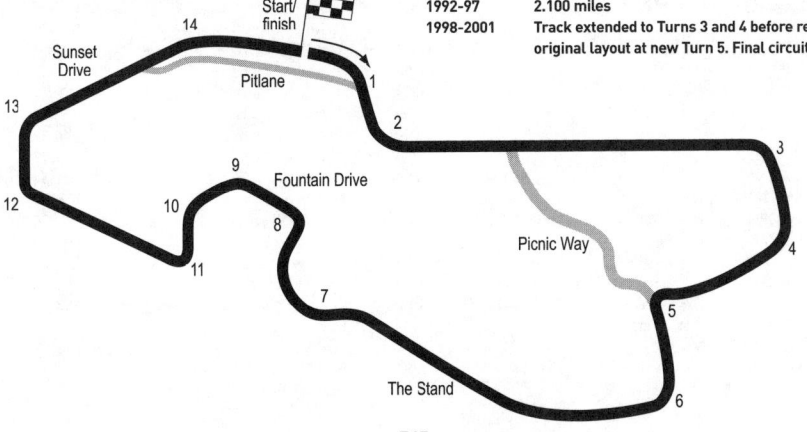

DETROIT GRAND PRIX

year	formula	winner	nat	car	mph
1982	F1 W	John Watson	GB	McLaren MP4/1B-Ford	78.140
1983	F1 W	Michele Alboreto	I	Tyrrell 011-Ford	81.158
1984	F1 W	Nelson Piquet	BR	Brabham BT53-BMW	81.679
1985	F1 W	Keke Rosberg	SF	Williams FW10-Honda	81.702
1986	F1 W	Ayrton Senna	BR	Lotus 98T-Renault	84.971
1987	F1 W	Ayrton Senna	BR	Lotus 99T-Honda	85.697
1988	F1 W	Ayrton Senna	BR	McLaren MP4/4-Honda	82.221
1989	CART	Emerson Fittipaldi	BR	Penske PC18-Chevrolet	76.112
1990	CART	Michael Andretti	USA	Lola T90/00-Chevrolet	84.902
1991	CART	Emerson Fittipaldi	BR	Penske PC20-Chevrolet	78.824
1992	CART	Bobby Rahal	USA	Lola T92/00-Chevrolet	81.989
1993	CART	Danny Sullivan	USA	Lola T93/00-Chevrolet	83.116
1994	CART	Paul Tracy	CDN	Penske PC23-Ilmor	86.245
1995	CART	Robby Gordon	USA	Reynard 95I-Ford	83.499
1996	CART	Michael Andretti	USA	Lola T96/00-Ford	75.126
1997	CART	Greg Moore	CDN	Reynard 97I-Mercedes-Benz	86.047
1998	CART	Alessandro Zanardi	I	Reynard 98I-Honda	100.052
1999	CART	Dario Franchitti	GB	Reynard 99I-Honda	81.643
2000	CART	Helio Castro-Neves	BR	Reynard 2KI-Honda	97.401
2001	CART	Helio Castro-Neves	BR	Reynard 01I-Honda	103.842

1982-91 Detroit city centre 1992 to date at Belle Isle

DOVER DOWNS

Known as the "Monster Mile," the 24-degree Dover Downs International Speedway has been a fixture on the NASCAR circuit since Richard Petty won the first race in 1969. Champcars also raced here that year (with Art Pollard winning for Andy Granatelli), but it wasn't until the birth of the Indy Racing League that open-wheelers returned. The narrow exit from the corners often causes multi-car accidents, frequently at the exit of Turn 2. The circuit was repaved with concrete in 1995, and like Chicago it also features an active horse racetrack.

Active years 1969 to date
Location 1 mile north of Dover, Delaware
Type Paved oval
Website www.doverspeedway.com

Lap distance 1.000 miles
Lap records Qualifying: Tony Stewart (G-Force GF01-Aurora), 19.438s, 185.205 mph, IRL, 1998
Race: Greg Ray (Dallara IR7-Aurora), 19.622s, 183.468 mph, IRL, 1998

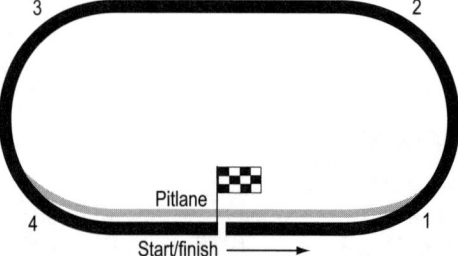

INDYCAR RACE

year	formula	winner	nat	car	mph
1998	IRL	Scott Sharp	USA	Dallara IR7-Aurora	99.318
1999	IRL	Greg Ray	USA	Dallara IR7-Aurora	114.258

NASCAR RACE (SINCE 1990)

year	formula	winner	nat	car	mph
1990	NASCAR	Derrike Cope	USA	Chevrolet Lumina	123.958
	NASCAR	Bill Elliott	USA	Ford Thunderbird	126.050
1991	NASCAR	Ken Schrader	USA	Chevrolet Lumina	120.152
	NASCAR	Harry Gant	USA	Oldsmobile Cutlass	110.179
1992	NASCAR	Harry Gant	USA	Oldsmobile Cutlass	109.456
	NASCAR	Ricky Rudd	USA	Chevrolet Lumina	115.289
1993	NASCAR	Dale Earnhardt	USA	Chevrolet Lumina	105.597
	NASCAR	Rusty Wallace	USA	Pontiac Grand Prix	100.334
1994	NASCAR	Rusty Wallace	USA	Ford Thunderbird	102.529
	NASCAR	Rusty Wallace	USA	Ford Thunderbird	112.556
1995	NASCAR	Kyle Petty	USA	Pontiac Grand Prix	119.880
	NASCAR	Jeff Gordon	USA	Chevrolet Monte Carlo	124.740
1996	NASCAR	Jeff Gordon	USA	Chevrolet Monte Carlo	122.741
	NASCAR	Jeff Gordon	USA	Chevrolet Monte Carlo	105.646
1997	NASCAR	Ricky Rudd	USA	Ford Thunderbird	114.635
	NASCAR	Mark Martin	USA	Ford Thunderbird	132.719
1998	NASCAR	Dale Jarrett	USA	Ford Taurus	119.522
	NASCAR	Mark Martin	USA	Ford Taurus	113.834

NASCAR RACE (SINCE 1990) (cont.)

year	formula	winner	nat	car	mph
1999	NASCAR	Bobby Labonte	USA	Pontiac Grand Prix	120.603
	NASCAR	Mark Martin	USA	Ford Taurus	127.434
2000	NASCAR	Tony Stewart	USA	Pontiac Grand Prix	109.514
	NASCAR	Tony Stewart	USA	Pontiac Grand Prix	115.191
2001	NASCAR	Jeff Gordon	USA	Chevrolet Monte Carlo	120.361
	NASCAR	Dale Earnhardt Jr	USA	Chevrolet Monte Carlo	101.559
2002	NASCAR	Jimmie Johnson	USA	Chevrolet Monte Carlo	117.551
	NASCAR	Jimmie Johnson	USA	Chevrolet Monte Carlo	120.805

ELKHART LAKE

Road America

A 5.3-mile road course around Elkhart Lake was used between 1950-53, but when racing was outlawed on public roads in Wisconsin local businessmen built the new Road America circuit in the hills two miles east of the Lake. It is the most picturesque and challenging road course in the United States, but suffers from changeable weather. The 2001 CART race was red flagged after accidents were caused by a virtual river running across the track. Some of the series' more surprising results have occurred at Road America, among them Hector Rebaque's victory at the inaugural event and Jacques Villeneuve senior (Gilles' brother) triumph four years later. His nephew, Jacques junior, convincingly scored his first CART victory here in 1994.

Active years	1955 to date
Location	1.5 miles south-east of Elkhart Lake, 60 miles north of Milwaukee
Type	Permanent road course
Website	www.roadamerica.com
Lap distance	4.048 miles
Lap records	Qualifying: Dario Franchitti (Reynard 2KI-Honda), 1m39.886, 145.894 mph, CART, 2000
	Race: Alessandro Zanardi (Reynard 98I-Honda), 1m41.874, 143.047 mph, CART, 1998

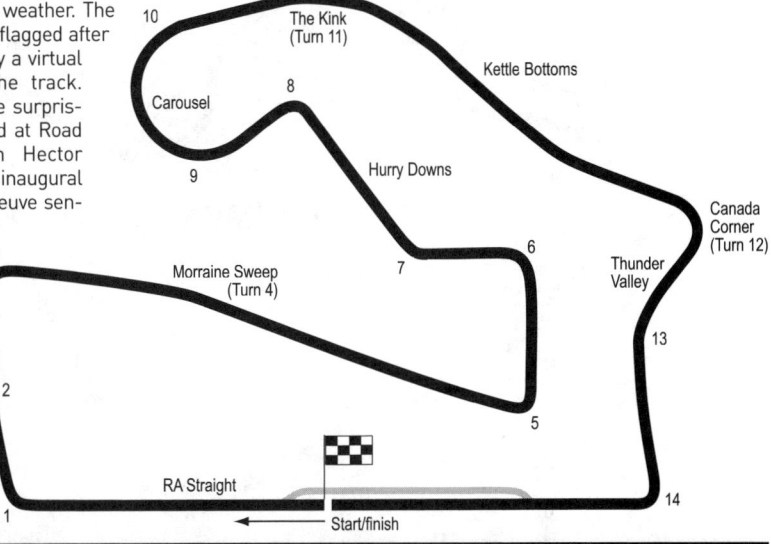

ROAD AMERICA CHAMPCAR RACE

year	formula	winner	nat	car	mph
1982	CART	Hector Rebaque	MEX	March 82C-Cosworth	109.156
1983	CART	Mario Andretti	USA	Lola T700-Cosworth	99.410
1984	CART	Mario Andretti	USA	Lola T800-Cosworth	116.347
1985	CART	Jacques Villeneuve Sr	CDN	March 85C-Cosworth	114.066
1986	CART	Emerson Fittipaldi	BR	March 86C-Cosworth	81.833
1987	CART	Mario Andretti	USA	Lola T87/00-Chevrolet	120.155
1988	CART	Emerson Fittipaldi	BR	Lola T87/00-Chevrolet	122.215
1989	CART	Danny Sullivan	USA	Penske PC18-Chevrolet	122.803
1990	CART	Michael Andretti	USA	Lola T90/00-Chevrolet	106.192
1991	CART	Michael Andretti	USA	Lola T91/00-Chevrolet	126.205
1992	CART	Emerson Fittipaldi	BR	Penske PC21-Chevrolet	110.656
1993	CART	Paul Tracy	CDN	Penske PC22-Chevrolet	118.408
1994	CART	Jacques Villeneuve	CDN	Reynard 94I-Ford	114.634
1995	CART	Jacques Villeneuve	CDN	Reynard 95I-Ford	105.148
1996	CART	Michael Andretti	USA	Lola T96/00-Ford	104.183
1997	CART	Alessandro Zanardi	I	Reynard 97I-Honda	102.995
1998	CART	Dario Franchitti	GB	Reynard 98I-Honda	127.145
1999	CART	Christian Fittipaldi	BR	Swift 010c-Ford	137.697
2000	CART	Paul Tracy	CDN	Reynard 2KI-Honda	136.457
2001	CART	Bruno Junqueira	BR	Lola B01/00-Toyota	90.721
2002	CART	Cristiano da Matta	BR	Lola B2/00-Toyota	124.856

ROAD AMERICA WORLD SPORTS CAR RACE					
year	formula	winner	nat	car	mph
1981	SC W	Rolf Stommelen/Harald Grohs	D	Porsche 935	105.415

FAIR PARK
Dallas

This was a one-off event held in 100-degree heat in July 1984. Although the track surface disintegrated as the weekend progressed, the Grand Prix was an exciting affair, with Keke Rosberg eventually scoring his only win of the year. Nigel Mansell had qualified on pole but ended the race in a state of collapse after trying to push his broken Lotus across the finish line. It is also notable as the only race in which Osella scored points.

Active years	1984 (used once)
Location	Fair Park, Dallas
Type	Temporary street circuit
Lap distance	2.424 miles
Lap records	Qualifying: Nigel Mansell (Lotus 95T-Renault), 1m37.041, 89.925 mph, F1, 1984
	Race: Niki Lauda (McLaren MP4/2-TAG Porsche), 1m45.353, 82.830 mph, F1, 1984

DALLAS GRAND PRIX					
year	formula	winner	nat	car	mph
1984	F1 W	Keke Rosberg	SF	Williams FW09-Honda	80.283

HOUSTON

Just as a race in the Motor City (Detroit) seems logical, so a race around the streets of America's petrol capitol was inevitable. The race was instigated in 1998 by Champcar team owner Carl Haas, and was sponsored by his long-time backers Texaco/Havoline. Former Newman-Haas driver Mario Andretti advised on track layout. Although the long back straight makes it easier to pass, the circuit has a proliferation of second-gear 90-degree corners. Dario Franchitti survived a downpour to win the inaugural race. The race was not held in 2002 as the area is being redeveloped although there are plans for it to return to the CART World Series at a future date.

Active years	1998-2001
Location	1 mile east of downtown Houston
Type	Temporary street circuit
Website	www.texacogp.com
Lap distance	1.527 miles
Lap records	Qualifying: Juan Pablo Montoya (Reynard 99I-Honda), 58.699s, 93.651 mph, CART, 1999
	Race: Michael Andretti (Lola B2K/01-Ford), 1m00.219, 91.287 mph, CART, 2000

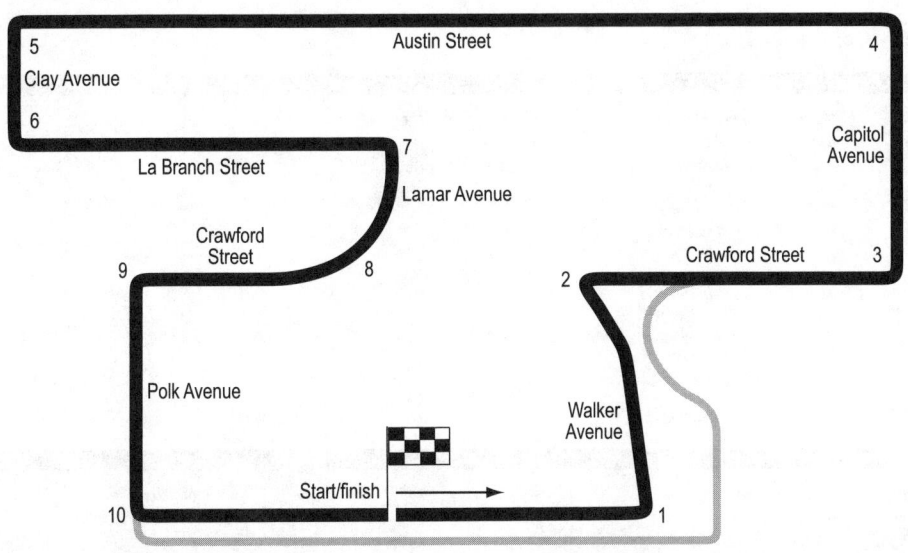

5

Clay Avenue

6

La Branch Street

7

Lamar Avenue

Crawford
Street

9   8

Polk Avenue

Start/finish →

10   1

4

Capitol
Avenue

Crawford Street   3

2

Walker
Avenue

CHAMPCAR RACE					
year	formula	winner	nat	car	mph
1998	CART	Dario Franchitti	GB	Reynard 98I-Honda	66.449
1999	CART	Paul Tracy	CDN	Reynard 99I-Honda	79.310
2000	CART	Jimmy Vasser	USA	Lola B2K/00-Toyota	76.966
2001	CART	Gil de Ferran	BR	Reynard 01I-Honda	79.874

INDIANAPOLIS MOTOR SPEEDWAY

From 1916 to 1994 the Indianapolis Motor Speedway was used for just one race, albeit one that could lay claim to being the greatest motorsports event in the world. Today, just seven years later, IMS President Tony George has added NASCAR's Brickyard 400 and the F1 United States GP to the Indianapolis 500, creating a calendar unrivalled by any other venue. The Indy 500 attracts the world's largest one-day sporting crowd; the NASCAR race has been an immense commercial success, and F1's return to the States in 2000 marked the promising beginning of a long contract. George also organises the Indy Racing League, which has competed with CART in open-wheel racing since 1996 and boasts the 500 as its centrepiece event. While the schism in open-wheel racing may have tarnished George's crown jewel at first, the leading CART teams are beginning to return and win at Indy, and the IRL itself is gathering momentum.

Indy's nickname, "The Brickyard", dates back to the speedway's construction in 1909, when founder Carl Fisher decided to pave his new circuit with 3.2 million bricks. The track was soon paved, but a "yard of bricks" remains at the start-line. The quintessentially American race has always attracted overseas interest. Frenchman Jules Goux, aided by a bottle or two of fine champagne, won the third Indy 500, while Jim Clark and Graham Hill both won in the sixties. More recently, Holland's Arie Luyendyk scored his first Champcar win here in 1990.

But even with this diversity, they say there are really only two types of Indianapolis drivers – those who have hit the wall, and those who are going to hit the wall.

On the Grand Prix circuit, drivers stay on full throttle through the banked final corner (Turn 1 on the oval) and along the front stretch for up to 25 seconds — the longest such opportunity on the entire F1 calendar. They then enter a tight series of corners behind the pits that wind through the golf course and back to the oval on the South Shute.

Active years	1909 to date
Location	Speedway, Indiana, 6 miles west of downtown Indianapolis
Type	Paved oval and permanent road course
Website	www.indy500.com

Oval circuit

Lap distance	2.500 miles
Lap records	Qualifying: Arie Luyendyk (Reynard 95I-Ford), 37.895s, 237.498 mph, IRL, 1996
	Race: Michael Andretti (Lola T90/00-Ford), 39.281s, 229.120 mph, CART, 1992

Grand Prix circuit

Active years	2000 to date
Lap distance	2.607 miles
Lap records	Qualifying: Michael Schumacher (Ferrari F2002), 1m10.790, 132.579 mph, F1, 2002
	Race: Rubens Barrichello (Ferrari F2002) 1m12.738, 129.027 mph, F1, 2002

Indianapolis 500 see page 434
United States Grand Prix see above

OTHER CHAMPCAR RACES

year	formula	winner	nat	car	mph
1909	AAA	Bob Burman	USA	Buick	53.772
	AAA	Louis Strang	USA	Buick	64.739
	AAA	Leigh Lynch	USA	Jackson	57.983
1910	AAA	Tom Kincaid	USA	National	71.669
	AAA	Ray Harroun	USA	Marmon	72.058
	AAA	Ray Harroun	USA	Marmon	70.551
	AAA	Bob Burman	USA	Marquette-Buick	74.447
	AAA	Joe Dawson	USA	Marmon	73.468
	AAA	Eddie Hearne	USA	Benz	75.030
	AAA	Howdy Wilcox	USA	National	72.238
	AAA	Eddie Hearne	USA	Benz	78.851
	AAA	Johnny Aitken	USA	National	71.466
1916	AAA	Johnny Aitken	USA	Peugeot	89.440

BRICKYARD 400

year	formula	winner	nat	car	mph
1994	NASCAR	Jeff Gordon	USA	Chevrolet Lumina	131.977
1995	NASCAR	Dale Earnhardt	USA	Chevrolet Monte Carlo	155.206
1996	NASCAR	Dale Jarrett	USA	Ford Thunderbird	139.508
1997	NASCAR	Ricky Rudd	USA	Ford Thunderbird	130.814
1998	NASCAR	Jeff Gordon	USA	Chevrolet Monte Carlo	126.772
1999	NASCAR	Dale Jarrett	USA	Ford Taurus	148.194
2000	NASCAR	Bobby Labonte	USA	Pontiac Grand Prix	155.912
2001	NASCAR	Jeff Gordon	USA	Chevrolet Monte Carlo	130.790
2002	NASCAR	Bill Elliott	USA	Dodge Intrepid	125.033

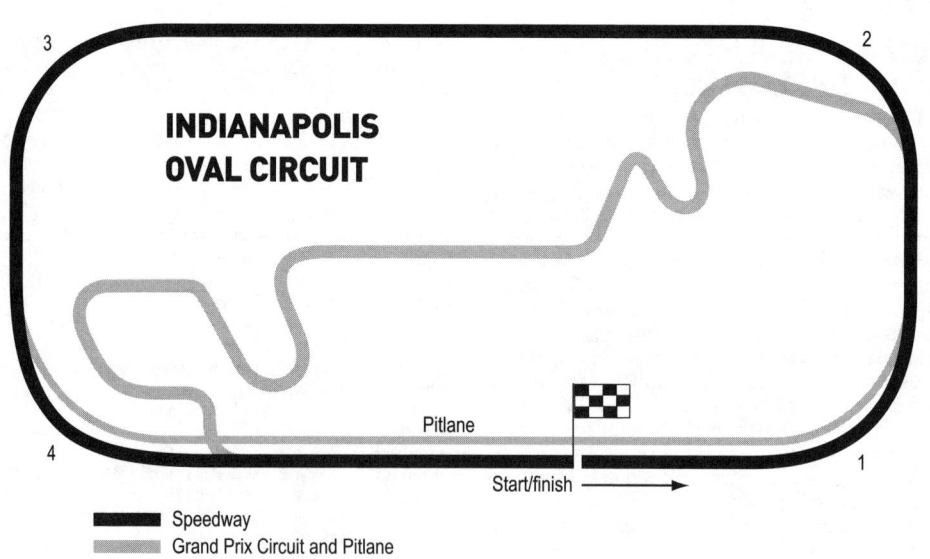

INDIANAPOLIS OVAL CIRCUIT

Pitlane

Start/finish

Speedway
Grand Prix Circuit and Pitlane

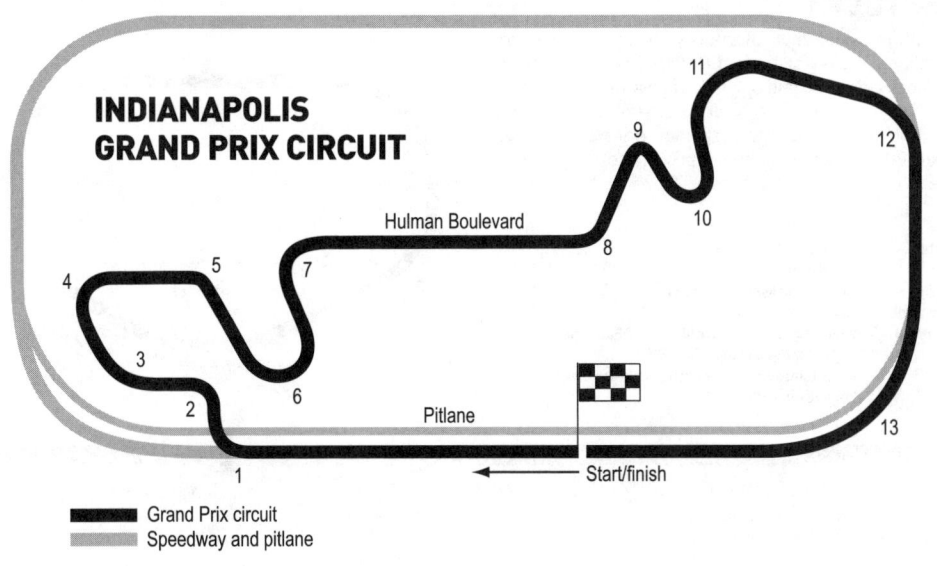

INDIANAPOLIS GRAND PRIX CIRCUIT

Hulman Boulevard

Pitlane

← Start/finish

▬▬▬ Grand Prix circuit
▬▬▬ Speedway and pitlane

KANSAS CITY

With 75,000 seats, the newly opened Kansas Speedway is the state's largest tourist attraction. A sister-track to Chicagoland, the 15-degree banked tri-oval held both NASCAR Winston Cup and Indy Racing League races in its first season.

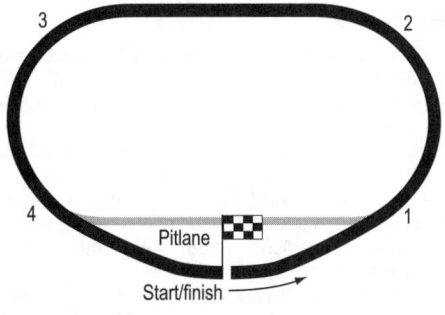

Pitlane

Start/finish →

Active years	**2001 to date**
Location	**15 miles west of Kansas City**
Type	**Paved oval**
Website	**www.kansasspeedway.com**
Lap distance	**1.520 miles**
Lap record	**Qualifying: Scott Sharp (Dallara IR0-Aurora), 24.980s, 219.058 mph, IRL, 2001**
	Race: Tomas Scheckter (Dallara IR0-Infiniti), 24.8472s, 220.226 mph, IRL, 2002

INDYCAR RACE					
year	formula	winner	nat	car	mph
2001	IRL	Eddie Cheever	USA	Dallara IR0-Infiniti	146.955
2002	IRL	Airton Dare	BR	Dallara IR0-Chevrolet	178.527

NASCAR RACE					
year	formula	winner	nat	car	mph
2001	NASCAR	Jeff Gordon	USA	Chevrolet Monte Carlo	110.576
2002	NASCAR	Jeff Gordon	USA	Chevrolet Monte Carlo	120.986

KENTUCKY

Opened in June, 2000, Kentucky's tri-oval is the first permanent racing facility in the state. It was designed by Bill Moss (who also laid out Talladega and the Las Vegas Speedway) and features 14-degree banked curves. The Indy Racing League is the leading series to visit, with Sarah Fisher becoming the first woman to qualify on pole for a major US race here in 2002.

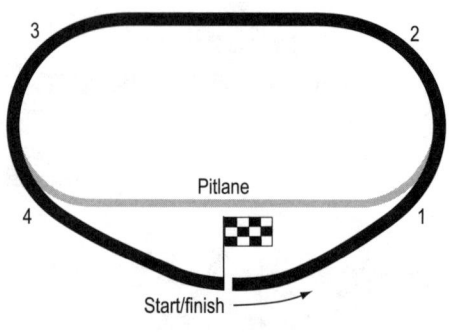

Active years	2000 to date
Location	Sparta, Kentucky
Type	Paved oval
Website	www.kentuckyspeedway.com
Lap distance	1.500 miles
Lap record	Qualifying: Sarah Fisher (G-Force GF05-Infiniti), 24.0661s, 224.383 mph, IRL, 2002
	Race: Tomas Scheckter (Dallara IR0-Infiniti), 24.0967s, 224.098 mph, IRL, 2002

INDYCAR RACE

year	formula	winner	nat	car	mph
2000	IRL	Buddy Lazier	USA	Dallara IR0-Aurora	164.601
2001	IRL	Buddy Lazier	USA	Dallara IR0-Aurora	174.910
2002	IRL	Felipe Giaffone	BR	G-Force GF05-Chevrolet	151.038

LAGUNA SECA

Monterey

Laguna Seca is built in the hills of California's Monterey peninsula at the US Army base of Fort Ord. Laguna is great for spectators and a true challenge to drivers, with its striking elevation change and the aptly named Corkscrew – the plunging left-right esses at the top of the course. In 1988 a new section was opened across the infield lake after Turn 2, now a downhill hairpin. Bobby Rahal was almost unbeatable here early in his CART career. But Gonzalo Rodriguez's fatal accident at the Corkscrew while practicing for the 1999 Champcar race highlighted the constant need to improve safety in the sport.

Active years	1957 to date
Location	10 miles east of Monterey, 120 miles south of San Francisco
Type	Permanent road course
Website	www.laguna-seca.com
Current circuit	
Lap distance	2.238 miles
Lap records	Qualifying: Helio Castro-Neves (Reynard 2KI-Honda), 1m07.722, 118.969 mph, CART, 2000
	Race: Alessandro Zanardi (Reynard 96I-Honda), 1m10.148, 114.854 mph, CART, 1996
Circuit changes	
1958-87	1.900 miles
1988-95	Infield section built from Turn 2 to Turn 5. 2.214 miles
1996 to date	Circuit repaved, Turns 10 and 11 re-profiled to improve entry to the pit lane. Current circuit

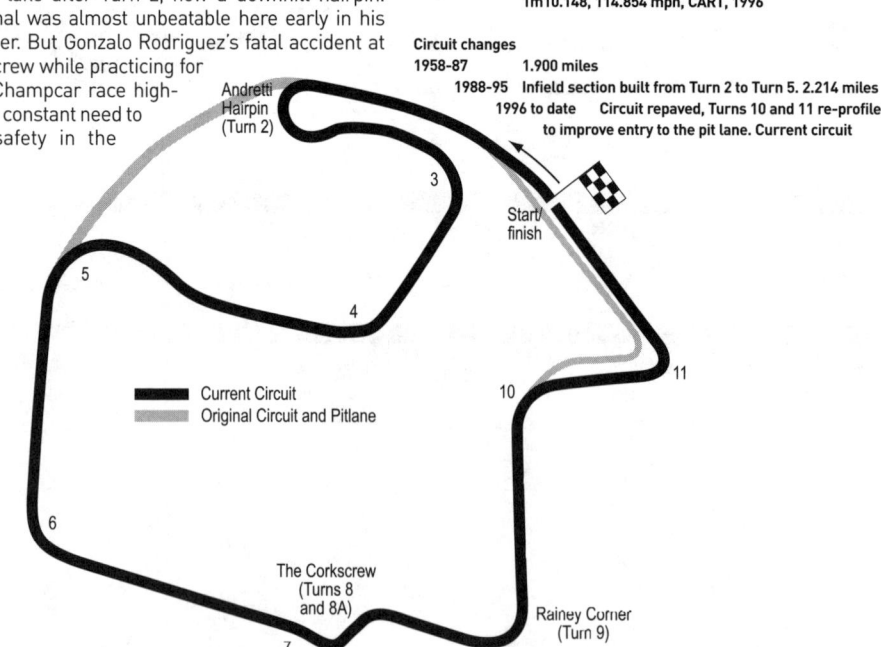

Current Circuit
Original Circuit and Pitlane

Andretti Hairpin (Turn 2)

The Corkscrew (Turns 8 and 8A)

Rainey Corner (Turn 9)

MONTEREY GRAND PRIX

year	formula	winner	nat	car	mph
1964	SC	Roger Penske	USA	Chaparral-Chevrolet	93.850
1965	SC	Walt Hansgen	USA	Lola T70-Chevrolet	97.310
1966	Can-Am	Phil Hill	USA	Chaparral 2E-Chevrolet	98.040
1967	Can-Am	Bruce McLaren	NZ	McLaren M6A-Chevrolet	101.613
1968	Can-Am	John Cannon	CDN	McLaren M1B-Oldsmobile	85.600
1969	Can-Am	Bruce McLaren	NZ	McLaren M8B-Chevrolet	105.830
1970	Can-Am	Denny Hulme	NZ	McLaren M8D-Chevrolet	106.071
1971	Can-Am	Peter Revson	USA	McLaren M8F-Chevrolet	109.210
1972	Can-Am	George Follmer	USA	Porsche 917/10	108.794
1973	F5000	Jody Scheckter	ZA	Trojan T101-Chevrolet	111.620
1974	F5000	Brian Redman	GB	Lola T332-Chevrolet	112.418
1975	F5000	Mario Andretti	USA	Lola T332-Chevrolet	114.167
1976	SC	Jim Busby	USA	Porsche 911 Carrera RSR	93.961
1977	SC	David Hobbs	GB	BMW 320i turbo	98.533
1978	Can-Am	Al Holbert	USA	Lola T333CS-Chevrolet	112.595
1979	Can-Am	Bobby Rahal	USA	Prophet/Lola-Chevrolet	113.211
1980	Can-Am	Al Unser	USA	Frissbee-Chevrolet	108.728
1981	Can-Am	Teo Fabi	I	March 817-Chevrolet	115.895
1982	Can-Am	Al Unser jr	USA	Frissbee-Chevrolet	114.151
1983	CART	Teo Fabi	I	March 83C-Cosworth	106.943
1984	CART	Bobby Rahal	USA	March 84C-Cosworth	119.105
1985	CART	Bobby Rahal	USA	March 85C-Cosworth	112.923
1986	CART	Bobby Rahal	USA	March 86C-Cosworth	119.693
1987	CART	Bobby Rahal	USA	Lola T87/00-Cosworth	118.879
1988	CART	Danny Sullivan	USA	Penske PC17-Chevrolet	94.090
1989	CART	Rick Mears	USA	Penske PC18-Chevrolet	94.174
1990	CART	Danny Sullivan	USA	Penske PC19-Chevrolet	103.556
1991	CART	Michael Andretti	USA	Lola T91/00-Chevrolet	103.604
1992	CART	Michael Andretti	USA	Lola T92/00-Ford	99.996
1993	CART	Paul Tracy	CDN	Penske PC22-Chevrolet	106.303
1994	CART	Paul Tracy	CDN	Penske PC23-Ilmor	92.978
1995	CART	Gil de Ferran	BR	Reynard 95I-Mercedes-Benz	98.493
1996	CART	Alessandro Zanardi	I	Reynard 96I-Honda	102.687
1997	CART	Jimmy Vasser	USA	Reynard 97I-Honda	109.647
1998	CART	Bryan Herta	USA	Reynard 98I-Ford	96.726
1999	CART	Bryan Herta	USA	Reynard 99I-Ford	101.924
2000	CART	Helio Castro-Neves	BR	Reynard 2KI-Honda	104.949
2001	CART	Massimiliano Papis	I	Lola B01/00-Ford	84.919
2002	CART	Cristiano da Matta	BR	Lola B2/00-Toyota	101.164

FIA GT RACE

year	formula	winner	nat	car	mph
1997	GT FIA	Klaus Ludwig/Bernd Schneider	D	Mercedes-Benz CLK-GTR	96.560
1998	GT FIA	Klaus Ludwig/Ricardo Zonta	D/BR	Mercedes-Benz CLK-LM	98.683

LAS VEGAS SPEEDWAY

Bruton Smith's speedway corporation built this facility to reflect the opulence of the nearby gambling mecca. Dubbed "The Race Track for the Next Century," Las Vegas features every conceivable type of track, from the 12-degree banked oval to a BMX course. The oval seats 102,000 spectators. The 2.5-mile road course has hosted American Le Mans Series races, albeit without the crowds attracted to NASCAR's annual visit.

Active years	1996 to date
Location	8 miles north of downtown Las Vegas
Type	Paved oval and permanent road course
Website	www.lvms.com
Lap distance	1.500 miles
Lap records	Qualifying: Arie Luyendyk (Reynard 95I-Ford), 23.842 s, 226.491 mph, IRL, 1996

Race: Arie Luyendyk (G-Force GF01-Aurora), 26.167s, 206.367 mph, IRL, 1998

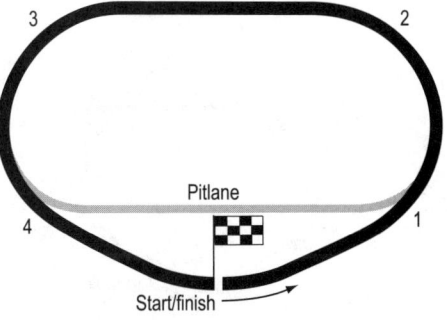

INDYCAR RACE

year	formula	winner	nat	car	mph
1996	IRL	Richie Hearn	USA	Reynard 95I-Ford	115.171
1997	IRL	Eliseo Salazar	RCH	Dallara IR7-Aurora	142.774
1998	IRL	Arie Luyendyk	NL	G-Force GF01-Aurora	135.338
1999	IRL	Sam Schmidt	USA	G-Force GF01-Aurora	124.936
2000	IRL	Al Unser jr	USA	G-Force GF05-Aurora	136.691

NASCAR RACE

year	formula	winner	nat	car	mph
1998	NASCAR	Mark Martin	USA	Ford Taurus	146.554
1999	NASCAR	Jeff Burton	USA	Ford Taurus	137.537
2000	NASCAR	Jeff Burton	USA	Ford Taurus	119.982
2001	NASCAR	Jeff Gordon	USA	Chevrolet Monte Carlo	135.546
2002	NASCAR	Sterling Marlin	USA	Dodge Intrepid	136.754

LONG BEACH

Once-seedy Long Beach has become a thriving, modern town since racing started here in 1975. After a trial Formula 5000 event, promoter Chris Pook attracted the F1 World Championship to the United States Grand Prix West (a cumbersome title that was soon dropped). Clay Regazzoni walked away with the first victory, but would be badly injured at Long Beach four years later. Since becoming a Champcar venue in 1984, Long Beach has been dominated by the Andretti family and Al Unser Jr, whose five wins include four consecutive victories. It was appropriate that Michael Andretti scored his final Champcar win here in 2002. City redevelopment has gradually shortened the course, so that it is now essentially two parallel straights joined by a succession of tight and twisting corners at each end. Long Beach remains a crowd-puller, and it is significant that the popularity of Grand Prix racing in North America began to fade when the race was lost to Champcars.

Active years	1975 to date
Location	Downtown Long Beach, 15 miles south of Los Angeles
Type	Temporary street circuit

Website	www.longbeachgp.com

Current circuit

Lap distance	1.968 miles
Lap record	Qualifying: Gil de Ferran (Reynard 2KI-Honda), 1m07.494, 104.969 mph, CART, 2000
	Race: Bruno Junqueira (Lola B2/00-Toyota), 1m08.981, 102.707 mph, CART, 2002

Circuit changes

1975-81	2.020 miles
1982	West Hairpin at the end of Shoreline Drive bypassed and a kink introduced on Shoreline Drive at Linden Avenue. 2.130 miles
1983	Original start straight (Ocean Boulevard) replaced by a complex through the Hyatt Hotel garage and a straight on Seaside Way, run to east hairpin shortened, start moved to Shoreline. 2.035 miles
1984-91	East Hairpin on Shoreline Drive moved away from Ocean Boulevard. 1.670 miles
1992-98	Hyatt Hotel underpass bypassed extended the straight on Seaside Way. 1.586 miles
1999	New section from Turns 1-6 at the end of Shoreline Drive. 1.824 miles
2000 to date	Turn 6 moved to Pine Avenue. Current circuit

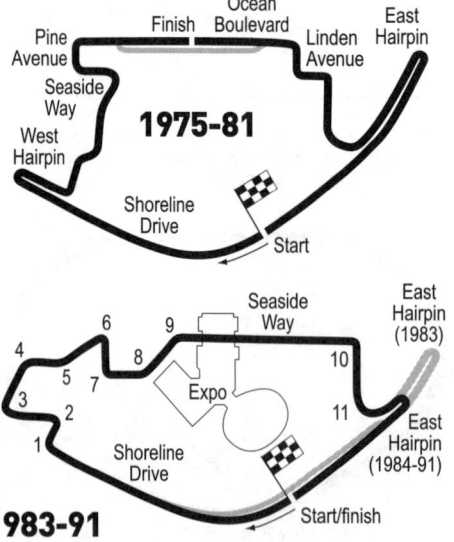

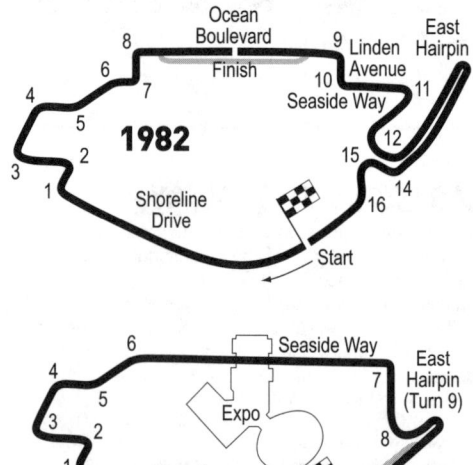

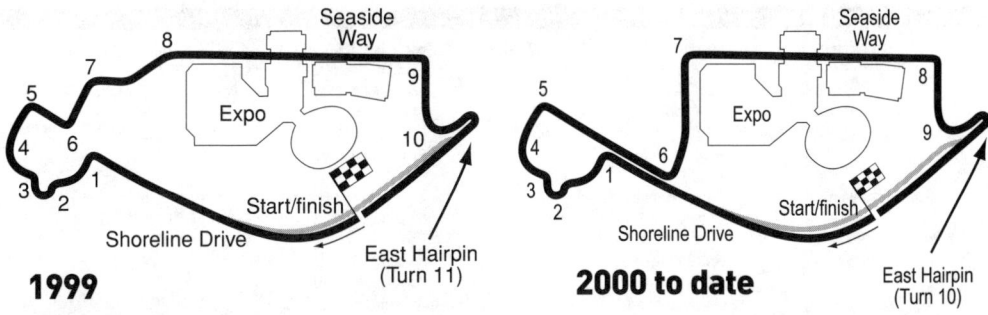

1999

Seaside Way

Expo

Start/finish

Shoreline Drive

East Hairpin
(Turn 11)

2000 to date

Seaside Way

Expo

Start/finish

Shoreline Drive

East Hairpin
(Turn 10)

LONG BEACH GRAND PRIX

year	formula	winner	nat	car	mph
1975	F5000	Brian Redman	GB	Lola T332-Chevrolet	86.324
1976	F1 W	Clay Regazzoni	CH	Ferrari 312T	85.572
1977	F1 W	Mario Andretti	USA	Lotus 78-Ford	86.889
1978	F1 W	Carlos Reutemann	RA	Ferrari 312T3	87.096
1979	F1 W	Gilles Villeneuve	CDN	Ferrari 312T4	88.356
1980	F1 W	Nelson Piquet	BR	Brabham BT49-Ford	88.448
1981	F1 W	Alan Jones	AUS	Williams FW07C-Ford	88.144
1982	F1 W	Niki Lauda	A	McLaren MP4/1B-Ford	81.479
1983	F1 W	John Watson	GB	McLaren MP4/1C-Ford	80.625
1984	CART	Mario Andretti	USA	Lola T800-Cosworth	82.894
1985	CART	Mario Andretti	USA	Lola T900-Cosworth	87.694
1986	CART	Michael Andretti	USA	March 86C-Cosworth	80.965
1987	CART	Mario Andretti	USA	Lola T87/00-Chevrolet	85.333
1988	CART	Al Unser Jr	USA	March 88C-Chevrolet	83.655
1989	CART	Al Unser Jr	USA	Lola T89/00-Chevrolet	85.503
1990	CART	Al Unser Jr	USA	Lola T90/00-Chevrolet	84.227
1991	CART	Al Unser Jr	USA	Lola T91/00-Chevrolet	81.195
1992	CART	Danny Sullivan	USA	Galmer G92-Chevrolet	91.945
1993	CART	Paul Tracy	CDN	Penske PC22-Chevrolet	93.089
1994	CART	Al Unser Jr	USA	Penske PC23-Ilmor	99.283
1995	CART	Al Unser Jr	USA	Penske PC24-Mercedes-Benz	91.212
1996	CART	Jimmy Vasser	USA	Reynard 96I-Honda	96.039
1997	CART	Alessandro Zanardi	I	Reynard 97I-Honda	93.999
1998	CART	Alessandro Zanardi	I	Reynard 98I-Honda	89.624
1999	CART	Juan Pablo Montoya	CO	Reynard 99I-Honda	87.915
2000	CART	Paul Tracy	CDN	Reynard 2KI-Honda	82.626
2001	CART	Helio Castro-Neves	BR	Reynard 01I-Honda	86.223
2002	CART	Michael Andretti	USA	Reynard 02I-Honda	86.935

MARTINSVILLE

Situated near the Virginia/North Carolina border, Martinsville is the shortest speedway currently on the NASCAR Winston Cup calendar. It is also one of the oldest, pre-dating the championship by two years. The turns are almost as tight as hairpins, albeit banked at 12 degrees. Drivers must negotiate a tricky change of surface between the straights and the concrete corners, and conserving brakes is essential. Recent modernisation has raised the grandstand capacity to 91,000.

Active years	1947 to date
Location	2 miles south of Martinsville, Virginia
Type	Paved oval
Website	www.martinsvillespeedway.com
Lap distance	0.526 miles
Lap records	Qualifying: Tony Stewart (Pontiac Grand Prix), 19.855s, 95.371 mph, NASCAR, 2000

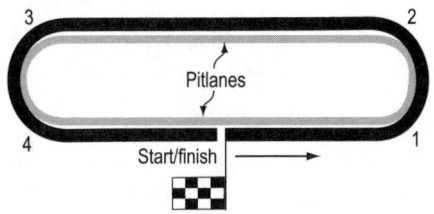

Pitlanes

Start/finish

NASCAR RACE (SINCE 1990)

year	formula	winner	nat	car	mph
1990	NASCAR	Geoff Bodine	USA	Ford Thunderbird	77.423
	NASCAR	Geoff Bodine	USA	Ford Thunderbird	76.386
1991	NASCAR	Dale Earnhardt	USA	Chevrolet Lumina	75.139
	NASCAR	Harry Gant	USA	Oldsmobile Cutlass	74.535
1992	NASCAR	Mark Martin	USA	Ford Thunderbird	78.087
	NASCAR	Geoff Bodine	USA	Ford Thunderbird	75.424
1993	NASCAR	Rusty Wallace	USA	Pontiac Grand Prix	79.476
	NASCAR	Ernie Irvan	USA	Ford Thunderbird	74.102
1994	NASCAR	Rusty Wallace	USA	Ford Thunderbird	76.707
	NASCAR	Rusty Wallace	USA	Ford Thunderbird	77.139
1995	NASCAR	Rusty Wallace	USA	Ford Thunderbird	72.145
	NASCAR	Dale Earnhardt	USA	Chevrolet Monte Carlo	73.946
1996	NASCAR	Rusty Wallace	USA	Ford Thunderbird	81.410
	NASCAR	Jeff Gordon	USA	Chevrolet Monte Carlo	82.230
1997	NASCAR	Jeff Gordon	USA	Chevrolet Monte Carlo	70.347
	NASCAR	Jeff Burton	USA	Ford Thunderbird	70.312
1998	NASCAR	Bobby Hamilton	USA	Chevrolet Monte Carlo	70.709
	NASCAR	Ricky Rudd	USA	Ford Taurus	73.350
1999	NASCAR	John Andretti	USA	Pontiac Grand Prix	75.653
	NASCAR	Jeff Gordon	USA	Chevrolet Monte Carlo	72.347
2000	NASCAR	Mark Martin	USA	Ford Taurus	71.161
	NASCAR	Tony Stewart	USA	Pontiac Grand Prix	73.859
2001	NASCAR	Dale Jarrett	USA	Ford Taurus	70.799
	NASCAR	Ricky Craven	USA	Ford Taurus	75.750
2002	NASCAR	Bobby Labonte	USA	Pontiac Grand Prix	73.951
	NASCAR	Kurt Busch	USA	Ford Taurus	74.651

MEADOWLANDS

During the eighties Formula 1 and then Champcars searched for a venue in the New York City area. Although suggestions ranged from Central Park to Flushing Meadow, a temporary circuit on the grounds of the Meadowlands Sports Arena was an unsatisfactory compromise. Despite being close to downtown Manhattan the race never attracted a substantial crowd, and the circuit was unpopular with almost everybody. A change to a "modified" oval failed to save the race from disappearing from the calendar in 1992.

Active years	1984-91
Location	Meadowlands Sports Arena, East Rutherford, New Jersey
Type	Temporary road course

Street circuit (1984-87)
Lap distance   1.682 miles
Lap record   Qualifying: Michael Andretti (March 86C-Cosworth), 1m00.535, 100.028 mph, CART, 1986

"Modified oval" (1988-91)
Lap distance   1.217 miles
Lap record   Qualifying: Emerson Fittipaldi (Penske PC18-Chevrolet), 37.219s, 117.714 mph, CART, 1989

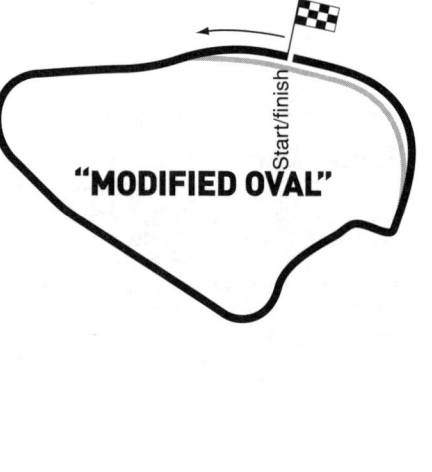

"MODIFIED OVAL"

STREET CIRCUIT

CHAMPCAR RACE					
year	formula	winner	nat	car	mph
1984	CART	Mario Andretti	USA	Lola T800-Cosworth	80.742
1985	CART	Al Unser jr	USA	Lola T900-Cosworth	90.167
1986	CART	Danny Sullivan	USA	March 86C-Cosworth	92.340
1987	CART	Bobby Rahal	USA	Lola T87/00-Cosworth	86.032
1988	CART	Al Unser jr	USA	March 88C-Chevrolet	99.352
1989	CART	Bobby Rahal	USA	Lola T89/00-Cosworth DFS	81.863
1990	CART	Michael Andretti	USA	Lola T90/00-Chevrolet	97.291
1991	CART	Bobby Rahal	USA	Lola T91/00-Chevrolet	95.551

MIAMI

Bayfront Park

Racing returned to downtown Miami in 2002 for the inaugural Grand Prix Americas—a weekend that combined both the CART Championship and American Le Mans Series. The circuit is layed out in the Port of Miami's Bayfront Park, just south of the original Bicentennial Park street circuit (see below). In keeping with other new temporary venues the track is short, overly tight and slippery. But 85,000 enthusiatic spectators saw Cristiano da Matta clinch the CART title and Emanuele Pirro and Frank Biela score another emphatic ALMS win for Audi.

Active years	**2002 to date**
Location	**Bayfront Park, Downtown Miami**
Type	**Temporary street circuit**
Website	**www.miamirace.com**
Lap distance	**1.387 miles**
Lap records	**Qualifying: Tony Kanaan (Lola B2/00-Honda), 1m01.264, 81.503 mph, CART, 2002** **Race: Christian Fittipaldi (Lola B2/00-Toyota), 1m02.906, 79.376 mph, CART, 2002**

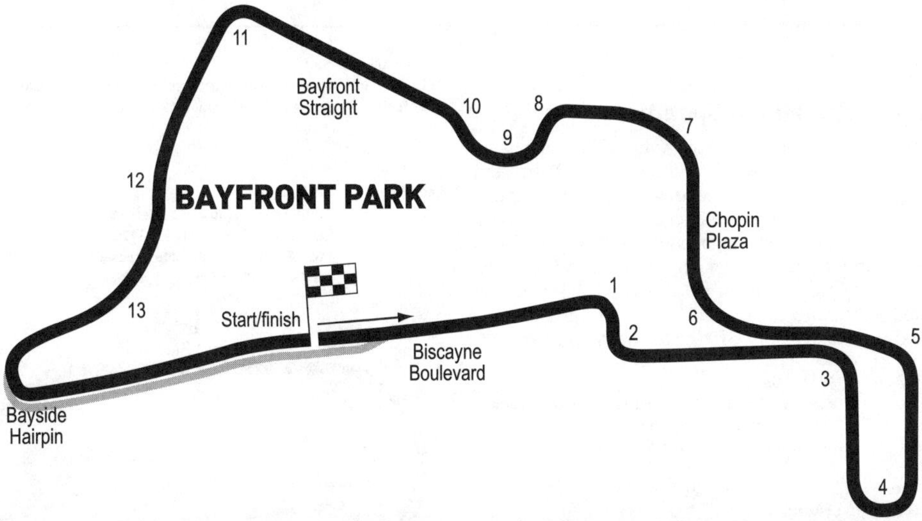

GRAND PRIX OF THE AMERICAS					
year	formula	winner	nat	car	mph
2002	CART	Cristiano da Matta	BR	Lola B2/00-Toyota	68.723

MIAMI

Bicentennial Park

From 1983 to 1993 the Miami Grand Prix was an early season highlight of the IMSA GTP Championship. The street race switched to the Trans-Am series in 1994 and then to Champcars a year later, the last event before moving to the new Homestead oval. The direction of the circuit was changed for this final race to avoid the normal Turn 1 bottleneck. However the Homestead oval failed to match the locals' enthusiam for racing downtown and a new street race has been introduced in nearby Bayfront Park.

Active years	**1983-95**
Location	**Bicentennial Park, Downtown Miami**
Type	**Temporary street circuit**
Lap distance	**1.873 miles**
Lap records	**Qualifying: Michael Andretti (Lola T95/00-Ford), 1m03.254, 106.599 mph, CART, 1995**

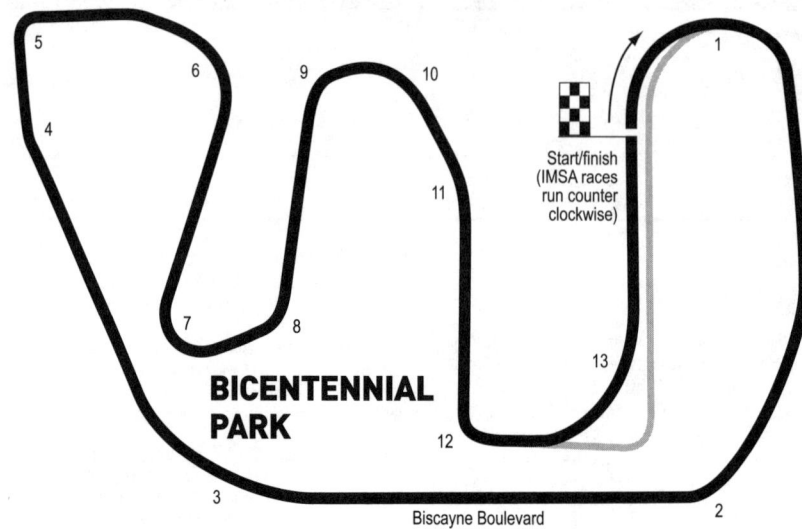

MIAMI

Homestead-Miami Speedway

Ralph Sanchez opened his new oval in 1995 in the wake of Hurricane Andrew, which had devastated the Miami area. The ultra-modern speedway's grounds include 680 palm trees, and offer superb facilties for drivers, teams and nearly 72,000 spectators. When CART failed to draw the anticipated attendance Homestead switched to the Indy Racing League in 2001.The track has also hosted a NASCAR race since 1999, and the 2.21-mile road course held an FIA GT race for two years.

Active years	1995 to date
Location	Downtown Homestead, 25 miles south-west of Miami
Type	Paved oval and permanent road course
Website	www.homesteadmiamispeedway.com

Oval circuit

Lap distance	1.502 miles
Lap records	Qualifying: Greg Moore (Reynard 98I-Mercedes-Benz), 24.856s, 217.541 mph, CART, 1998
	Race: Dario Franchitti (Reynard 99I-Honda), 26.825s, 201.576 mph, CART, 1999

Oval circuit changes

1995-96	Quad-oval with four distinct corners. 1.527 miles
1997 to date	Banked corners remodelled. Track widened. Current circuit

Road Course

Lap distance	2.210 miles
Lap record	Qualifying: Ricardo Zonta (Mercedes-Benz CLK-LM) 1m14.298, 107.082 mph, GT, 1998
	Race: Bernd Schneider (Mercedes-Benz CLK-LM) 1m16.495, 103.988 mph, GT, 1998

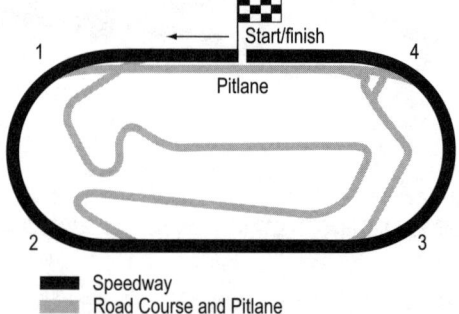

Speedway
Road Course and Pitlane

FIA GT RACE					
year	formula	winner	nat	car	mph
1998	GT FIA	Klaus Ludwig/Ricardo Zonta	D/BR	Mercedes-Benz CLK-LM	94.022
1999	GT FIA	Paul Belmondo/Emmanuel Clerico	F	Chrysler Viper GTS-R	89.121

MIAMI GRAND PRIX

year	formula	winner	nat	car	mph
1983	SC	Al Holbert	USA	March-Chevrolet	55.417
1984	SC	Brian Redman/Doc Bundy	GB/USA	Jaguar XJR-5	72.623
1985	SC	Al Holbert/Derek Bell	USA/GB	Porsche 962	68.342
1986	SC	Bob Wollek/Paolo Barilla	F/I	Porsche 962	79.309
1987	SC	Geoff Brabham/Elliott Forbes-Robinson	AUS/USA	Nissan GTP ZX-T	82.927
1988	SC	Price Cobb/James Weaver	USA/GB	Porsche 962	77.203
1989	SC	Geoff Brabham/Chip Robinson	AUS/USA	Nissan GTP ZX-T	81.358
1990	SC	Geoff Brabham/Chip Robinson/ Bob Earl	AUS/USA/USA	Nissan GTP ZX-T	82.426
1991	SC	Raul Boesel	BR	Jaguar XJR-10	84.470
1992	SC	Geoff Brabham	AUS	Nissan NPT92	92.040
1993	SC	Juan Manuel Fangio II	RA	Eagle Mk3-Toyota	88.632
1994	Trans-Am	Tom Kendall	USA	Ford Mustang	68.760
1995	CART	Jacques Villeneuve	CDN	Reynard 95I-Ford	84.793
1996	CART	Jimmy Vasser	USA	Reynard 96I-Honda	109.399
1997	CART	Michael Andretti	USA	Swift 007i-Ford	134.138
1998	CART	Michael Andretti	USA	Swift 009c-Ford	144.339
1999	CART	Greg Moore	CDN	Reynard 99I-Mercedes-Benz	136.671
2000	CART	Massimiliano Papis	I	Reynard 2KI-Ford	164.788
2001	IRL	Sam Hornish Jr	USA	Dallara IR0-Aurora	148.706
2002	IRL	Sam Hornish Jr	USA	Dallara IR0-Chevrolet	140.512

Miami Bicentenial Park 1983-95; Homestead 1996 to date

NASCAR RACE

year	formula	winner	nat	car	mph
1999	NASCAR	Tony Stewart	USA	Pontiac Grand Prix	140.522
2000	NASCAR	Tony Stewart	USA	Pontiac Grand Prix	127.650
2001	NASCAR	Bill Elliott	USA	Dodge Intrepid	117.605
2002	NASCAR	Kurt Busch	USA	Ford Taurus	116.617

MIAMI

Tamiami Park

Ralph Sanchez's previous attempt to establish Champcar racing in Miami was on a temporary road course laid out in the suburban Tamiami Park. It had none of the character of the spring IMSA race downtown and floundered after just four years. The 1986 Marlboro Challenge, however, was a titanic duel between Al Unser Jr and Michael Andretti, who won after Unser crashed while trying to pass in the race's penultimate lap.

Active years	1985-88
Location	Tamiami Park, suburbs of Miami
Type	Temporary road course
Lap distance	1.784 miles
Lap record	Qualifying: Danny Sullivan (Penske PC17-Chevrolet), 55.062s, 116.639 mph, CART, 1988

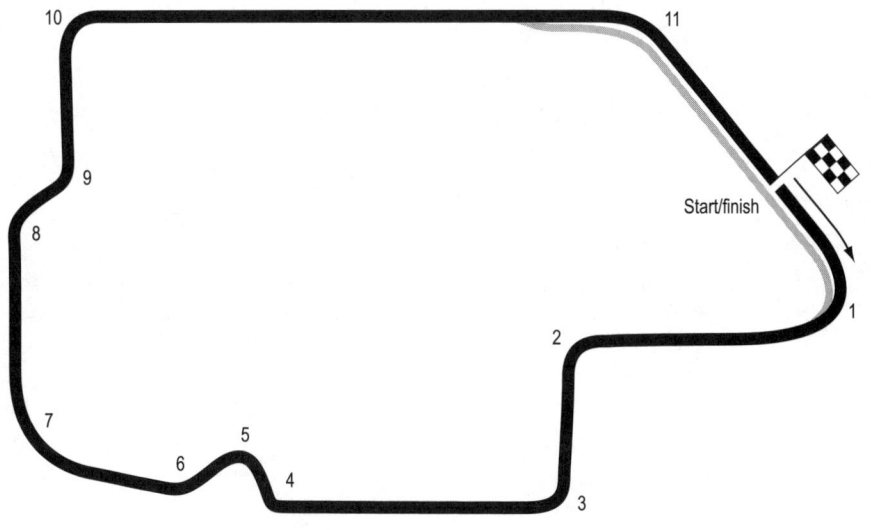

Marlboro Challenge see above

TAMIAMI PARK CHAMPCAR RACE

year	formula	winner	nat	car	mph
1985	CART	Danny Sullivan	USA	March 85C-Cosworth	95.915
1986	CART	Al Unser Jr	USA	Lola T86/00-Cosworth	106.322
1987	CART	Michael Andretti	USA	March 87C-Cosworth	94.873
1988	CART	Al Unser Jr	USA	March 88C-Chevrolet	101.471

MICHIGAN

One of America's great superspeedways, Michigan was the fastest circuit in the world until California Speedway opened in 1997. Designed by Charlie Moneypenny (who also created Daytona), Michigan boasts 18-degree banking, and the 125,971 capacity crowd can see the entire circuit from the grandstands. Its highlights included a 500-mile Champcar race and two NASCAR events. But after many years as a CART venue, Michigan switched to the Indy Racing League in 2002. Over the years Michigan has earned a reputation for broken cars and crashes. The worst accident in CART history happened at Michigan in 1998, when a wheel from a crashed car bounced into the crowd and killed three spectators. Stirling Moss was the Director of Road Racing when MIS opened, but the 3.31-mile Grand Prix course closed after two years when management decided to concentrate on staging oval races.

Active years 1968 to date
Location Irish Hills, Michigan, 18 miles south of Jackson, 67 miles south-west of Detroit

Type Paved oval
Website www.mispeedway.com
Lap distance 2.000 miles
Lap records Qualifying: Paul Tracy (Reynard 2KI-Honda), 30.645s, 234.949 mph, CART, 2000
Race: Adrian Fernandez (Lola T96/00-Honda), 30.767s, 234.019 mph, CART, 1996

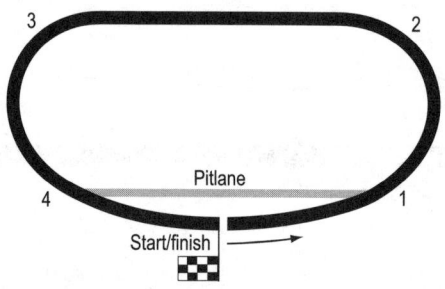

MICHIGAN 500 CHAMPCAR RACE (INCLUDING US 500)

year	formula	winner	nat	car	mph
1981	CART	Pancho Carter	USA	Penske PC7-Cosworth	132.890
1982	CART	Gordon Johncock	USA	Wildcat Mk8B-Cosworth	153.925
1983	CART	John Paul Jr	USA	Penske PC10-Cosworth	134.862
1984	CART	Mario Andretti	USA	Lola T800-Cosworth	133.482
1985	CART	Emerson Fittipaldi	BR	March 85C-Cosworth	128.220
1986	CART	Johnny Rutherford	USA	March 86C-Cosworth	137.140
1987	CART	Michael Andretti	USA	March 87C-Cosworth	171.493
1988	CART	Danny Sullivan	USA	Penske PC17-Chevrolet	180.654
1989	CART	Michael Andretti	USA	Lola T89/00-Chevrolet	160.210
1990	CART	Al Unser Jr	USA	Lola T90/00-Chevrolet	189.727
1991	CART	Rick Mears	USA	Penske PC20-Chevrolet	167.230
1992	CART	Scott Goodyear	CDN	Lola T92/00-Chevrolet	177.625
1993	CART	Nigel Mansell	GB	Lola T93/00-Ford	188.203
1994	CART	Scott Goodyear	CDN	Lola T94/00-Ford	159.800
1995	CART	Scott Pruett	USA	Lola T95/00-Ford	159.676
1996	CART	Andre Ribeiro	BR	Lola T96/00-Honda	152.627
	CART*	Jimmy Vasser	USA	Reynard 96I-Honda	156.403
1997	CART*	Alessandro Zanardi	I	Reynard 97I-Honda	167.044
1998	CART*	Greg Moore	CDN	Reynard 98I-Mercedes-Benz	165.917
1999	CART*	Tony Kanaan	BR	Reynard 99I-Honda	186.097
2000	CART*	Juan Pablo Montoya	CO	Lola B2K/00-Toyota	177.694
2001	CART	Patrick Carpentier	CDN	Reynard 01I-Ford	171.498
*US 500					

OTHER INDY/CHAMPCAR RACES

year	formula	winner	nat	car	mph
1968	USAC	Ronnie Bucknum	USA	Eagle 68-Drake/Offenhauser	161.812
1970	USAC	Gary Bettenhausen	USA	Gerhardt-Drake/Offenhauser	140.625
1971	USAC	Mark Donohue	USA	McLaren M16A-Drake/Offenhauser	146.074
1972	USAC	Joe Leonard	USA	Parnelli-Offenhauser	139.316
1973	USAC	Roger McCluskey	USA	McLaren M16B-Offenhauser	161.146
	USAC	Bill Vukovich Jr	USA	Eagle 73-Offenhauser	134.026
	USAC	Johnny Rutherford	USA	McLaren M16C-Offenhauser	157.243
1974	USAC	Bobby Unser	USA	Eagle 74-Offenhauser	141.717
	USAC	Al Unser	USA	Eagle 74-Offenhauser	142.141
1975	USAC	AJ Foyt Jr	USA	Coyote-Foyt/Ford	158.907
	USAC	Tom Sneva	USA	McLaren M16C-Offenhauser	176.160
1976	USAC	Gordon Johncock	USA	Wildcat-DGS/Offenhauser	165.033
	USAC	AJ Foyt Jr	USA	Coyote-Foyt/Ford	164.068
1977	USAC	Danny Ongais	USA	Parnelli VPJ6B-Cosworth	149.152
	USAC	Gordon Johncock	USA	Wildcat-DGS/Offenhauser	175.250
1978	USAC	Johnny Rutherford	USA	McLaren M24B-Cosworth	159.941
	USAC	Danny Ongais	USA	Parnelli VPJ6B-Cosworth	146.246
1979	CART	Gordon Johncock	USA	Penske PC6-Cosworth	170.976
	CART	Bobby Unser	USA	Penske PC7-Cosworth	155.342
	CART	Bobby Unser	USA	Penske PC7-Cosworth	175.211
1980	CART	Johnny Rutherford	USA	Chaparral 2K-Cosworth	148.515
	CART	Mario Andretti	USA	Penske PC9-Cosworth	167.494
1981	CART	Rick Mears	USA	Penske PC9B-Cosworth	125.957
1982	CART	Bobby Rahal	USA	March 82C-Cosworth	140.515
1983	CART	Rick Mears	USA	Penske PC10B-Cosworth	182.325
1984	CART	Mario Andretti	USA	Lola T800-Cosworth	168.523
1985	CART	Bobby Rahal	USA	March 85C-Cosworth	163.657
1986	CART	Bobby Rahal	USA	March 86C-Cosworth	181.701
2002	IRL	Tomas Scheckter	ZA	Dallara IR0-Infiniti	179.044

NASCAR RACE (SINCE 1990)

year	formula	winner	nat	car	mph
1990	NASCAR	Dale Earnhardt	USA	Chevrolet Lumina	150.219
	NASCAR	Mark Martin	USA	Ford Thunderbird	138.822
1991	NASCAR	Davey Allison	USA	Ford Thunderbird	160.912
	NASCAR	Dale Jarrett	USA	Ford Thunderbird	139.887
1992	NASCAR	Davey Allison	USA	Ford Thunderbird	152.672
	NASCAR	Harry Gant	USA	Oldsmobile Cutlass	143.056
1993	NASCAR	Ricky Rudd	USA	Chevrolet Lumina	148.484
	NASCAR	Mark Martin	USA	Ford Thunderbird	144.564
1994	NASCAR	Rusty Wallace	USA	Ford Thunderbird	125.022
	NASCAR	Geoff Bodine	USA	Ford Thunderbird	139.914
1995	NASCAR	Bobby Labonte	USA	Chevrolet Monte Carlo	134.103
	NASCAR	Bobby Labonte	USA	Chevrolet Monte Carlo	157.739
1996	NASCAR	Rusty Wallace	USA	Ford Thunderbird	166.224
	NASCAR	Dale Jarrett	USA	Ford Thunderbird	139.792
1997	NASCAR	Ernie Irvan	USA	Ford Thunderbird	153.338
	NASCAR	Mark Martin	USA	Ford Thunderbird	126.883
1998	NASCAR	Mark Martin	USA	Ford Taurus	158.695
	NASCAR	Jeff Gordon	USA	Chevrolet Monte Carlo	151.995
1999	NASCAR	Dale Jarrett	USA	Ford Taurus	173.997
	NASCAR	Bobby Labonte	USA	Pontiac Grand Prix	144.332
2000	NASCAR	Tony Stewart	USA	Pontiac Grand Prix	143.926
	NASCAR	Rusty Wallace	USA	Ford Taurus	132.597
2001	NASCAR	Jeff Gordon	USA	Chevrolet Monte Carlo	134.203
	NASCAR	Sterling Marlin	USA	Dodge Intrepid	173.473
2002	NASCAR	Matt Kenseth	USA	Ford Taurus	154.822
	NASCAR	Dale Jarrett	USA	Ford Taurus	140.556

MID-OHIO

The Mid-Ohio Sports Car Course is a pristine and demanding road circuit set in undulating countryside near Lexington, Ohio. It suffers from being too narrow but has been a regular autumn Champcar fixture since the late Jim Trueman (owner of the championship-winning Truesports team) bought it in the early eighties. Teo Fabi scored Porsche's only CART win here in 1989. Michael Andretti barrel-rolled into Turn 4 in 1998, and Adrian Fernandez also crashed here in 2001, hitting the barriers with almost unabated speed. Both men were lucky to escape injury.

Active years	1962 to date
Location	7 miles south-west of Mansfield, 60 miles north of Columbus, 75 miles south of Cleveland
Type	Permanent road course
Website	www.midohio.com

Current circuit	
Lap distance	2.258 miles
Lap records	Qualifying: Dario Franchitti (Reynard 99I-Honda), 1m05.347, 124.395 mph, CART, 1999 and Gil de Ferran (Reynard 2KI-Honda), 1m05.347, 124.395 mph, CART, 2000

Race: Juan Pablo Montoya (Reynard 99I-Honda), 1m06.788, 121.711 mph, CART, 1999

Circuit changes	
1962-89	2.400 miles
1990 to date	Chicane before the Keyhole bypassed. Current circuit

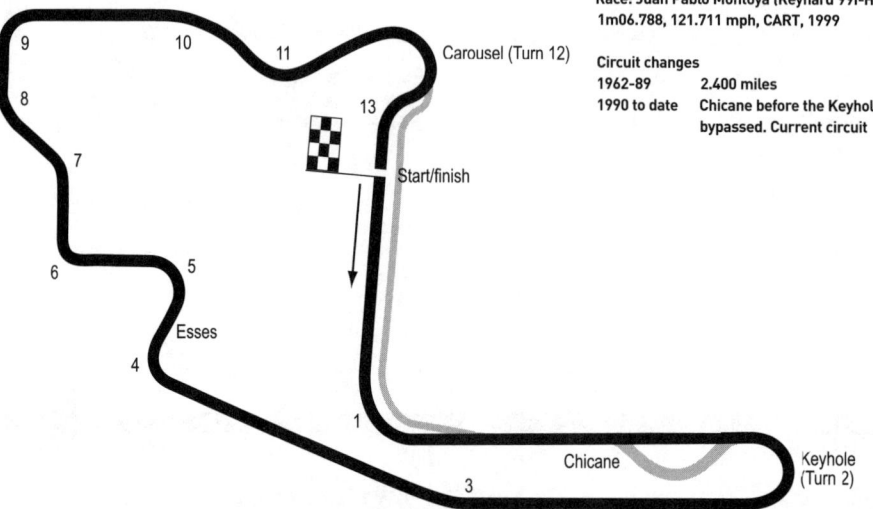

CHAMPCAR RACE

year	formula	winner	nat	car	mph
1980	CART	Johnny Rutherford	USA	Chaparral 2K-Cosworth	86.601
1983	CART	Teo Fabi	I	March 83C-Cosworth	99.297
1984	CART	Mario Andretti	USA	Lola T800-Cosworth	100.939
1985	CART	Bobby Rahal	USA	March 85C-Cosworth	107.628
1986	CART	Bobby Rahal	USA	March 86C-Cosworth	103.998
1987	CART	Roberto Guerrero	USA	March 87C-Cosworth	108.021
1988	CART	Emerson Fittipaldi	BR	Lola T87/00-Chevrolet	90.062
1989	CART	Teo Fabi	I	March 89P-Porsche	105.395
1990	CART	Michael Andretti	USA	Lola T90/00-Chevrolet	86.160
1991	CART	Michael Andretti	USA	Lola T91/00-Chevrolet	100.265
1992	CART	Emerson Fittipaldi	BR	Penske PC21-Chevrolet	107.864
1993	CART	Emerson Fittipaldi	BR	Penske PC22-Chevrolet	102.704
1994	CART	Al Unser Jr	USA	Penske PC23-Ilmor	109.079
1995	CART	Al Unser Jr	USA	Penske PC24-Mercedes-Benz	108.041
1996	CART	Alessandro Zanardi	I	Reynard 96I-Honda	105.265
1997	CART	Alessandro Zanardi	I	Reynard 97I-Honda	111.029
1998	CART	Adrian Fernandez	MEX	Reynard 98I-Ford	98.939
1999	CART	Juan Pablo Montoya	CO	Reynard 99I-Honda	110.175
2000	CART	Helio Castro-Neves	BR	Reynard 2KI-Honda	107.110
2001	CART	Helio Castro-Neves	BR	Reynard 01I-Honda	107.180
2002	CART	Patrick Carpentier	CDN	Reynard 02I-Ford	107.179

MILWAUKEE
Wisconsin State Fair Park

The oldest permanent racing circuit in the world, Milwaukee held its first race on 11 September 1903, four years before Brooklands opened. Set in the heart of America's brewery town, the Wisconsin State Fair Park is a lightly banked (9 degrees), bumpy, short oval. Its race is traditionally held the week after Indy, giving the event an after-party feel. The track was was paved following the August 1953 event, and both Jim Clark (1963) and Nigel Mansell (1993) scored their first oval wins here.

Active years	1903 to date
Location	West Allis, 6 miles west of downtown Milwaukee
Type	Paved oval

Website	www.milwaukeemile.com
Lap distance	1.032 miles
Lap records	Qualifying: Patrick Carpentier (Reynard 98I-Mercedes-Benz), 20.028s, 185.500 mph, CART, 1998
	Race: Scott Pruett (Reynard 97I-Ford), 21.519s, 172.647 mph, CART, 1998

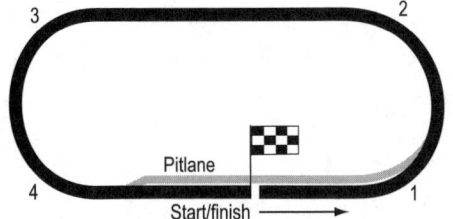

CHAMPCAR RACES

year	formula	winner	nat	car	mph
1912	AAA	Ralph de Palma	USA	Mercedes	68.962
	AAA	Bill Endicott	USA	Mason	55.699
	AAA	Mortimer Roberts	USA	Mason	58.799
1939	AAA	Babe Stapp	USA	Stevens-Miller	83.663
1941	AAA	Rex Mays	USA	Stevens-Winfield	82.248
1946	AAA	Rex Mays	USA	Stevens-Winfield	84.814
1947	AAA	Bill Holland	USA	Wetteroth-Offenhauser	87.280
	AAA	Charles van Acker	USA	Stevens-Offenhauser	85.960
	AAA	Ted Horn	USA	Horn-Offenhauser	84.336
1948	AAA	Emil Andres	USA	Kurtis-Offenhauser	85.320
	AAA	Johnny Mantz	USA	Kurtis-Offenhauser	85.327
	AAA	Myron Fohr	USA	Marchese-Offenhauser	86.734
	AAA	Tony Bettenhausen	USA	Marchese-Offenhauser	86.734
1949	AAA	Myron Fohr	USA	Marchese-Offenhauser	83.615
	AAA	Johnnie Parsons	USA	Kurtis-Offenhauser	85.817
1950	AAA	Tony Bettenhausen	USA	Wetteroth-Offenhauser	85.027
	AAA	Walt Faulkner	USA	Kurtis KK2000-Offenhauser	87.315
1951	AAA	Tony Bettenhausen	USA	Kurtis-Offenhauser	90.041
	AAA	Walt Faulkner	USA	Kuzma-Offenhauser	91.342
1952	AAA	Mike Nazaruk	USA	Kurtis-Offenhauser	92.255
	AAA	Chuck Stevenson	USA	Kurtis KK4000-Offenhauser	81.392
1953	AAA	Jack McGrath	USA	Kurtis KK4000-Offenhauser	93.634
	AAA	Chuck Stevenson	USA	Kuzma-Offenhauser	89.580
1954	AAA	Chuck Stevenson	USA	Kuzma-Offenhauser	97.527
	AAA	Manuel Ayulo	USA	Kuzma-Offenhauser	96.261
1955	USAC	Johnny Thomson	USA	Kuzma-Offenhauser	98.844
	USAC	Pat Flaherty	USA	Kurtis KK500B-Offenhauser	95.033
1956	USAC	Pat Flaherty	USA	Watson-Offenhauser	98.847
	USAC	Jimmy Bryan	USA	Kuzma-Offenhauser	92.733
1957	USAC	Rodger Ward	USA	Lesovsky-Offenhauser	97.789
	USAC	Jim Rathmann	USA	Epperly-Offenhauser	98.134
1958	USAC	Art Bisch	USA	Kuzma-Offenhauser	94.013
	USAC	Rodger Ward	USA	Lesovsky-Offenhauser	97.809
1959	USAC	Johnny Thomson	USA	Lesovsky-Offenhauser	98.609
	USAC	Rodger Ward	USA	Watson-Offenhauser	96.317
1960	USAC	Rodger Ward	USA	Watson-Offenhauser	99.465
	USAC	Len Sutton	USA	Watson-Offenhauser	100.131
1961	USAC	Rodger Ward	USA	Watson-Offenhauser	103.860
	USAC	Lloyd Ruby	USA	Watson-Offenhauser	101.638
1962	USAC	AJ Foyt Jr	USA	Watson Trevis-Offenhauser	100.860
	USAC	Rodger Ward	USA	Watson-Offenhauser	100.015
1963	USAC	Rodger Ward	USA	Watson-Offenhauser	100.585
	USAC	Jim Clark	GB	Lotus 29-Ford	104.452
1964	USAC	AJ Foyt Jr	USA	Watson-Offenhauser	100.346
	USAC	Parnelli Jones	USA	Lotus 34-Ford	104.751
1965	USAC	Parnelli Jones	USA	Kuzma/Lotus 34-Offenhauser	101.747
	USAC	Joe Leonard	USA	Hallibrand-Ford	97.277
	USAC	Gordon Johncock	USA	Gerhardt-Offenhauser	100.453

Racing Around the World

year	formula	winner	nat	car	mph
1966	USAC	Mario Andretti	USA	Brawner/Brabham-Ford	95.655
	USAC	Mario Andretti	USA	Brawner/Brabham-Ford	104.060
1967	USAC	Gordon Johncock	USA	Gerhardt-Ford	98.643
	USAC	Mario Andretti	USA	Brawner/Hawk-Ford	105.386
1968	USAC	Lloyd Ruby	USA	Mongoose-Drake/Offenhauser	100.739
	USAC	Lloyd Ruby	USA	Mongoose-Drake/Offenhauser	108.735
1969	USAC	Art Pollard	USA	Gerhardt-Drake/Offenhauser	112.156
	USAC	Al Unser	USA	Lola T152-Ford	106.758
1970	USAC	Joe Leonard	USA	Colt 70-Ford	108.299
	USAC	Al Unser	USA	Colt 70-Ford	114.304
1971	USAC	Al Unser	USA	Colt 71-Ford	114.912
	USAC	Bobby Unser	USA	Eagle 71-Drake/Offenhauser	109.384
1972	USAC	Bobby Unser	USA	Eagle 72-Offenhauser	109.131
	USAC	Joe Leonard	USA	Parnelli-Offenhauser	111.652
1973	USAC	Bobby Unser	USA	Eagle 73-Offenhauser	113.957
	USAC	Wally Dallenbach	USA	Eagle 73-Offenhauser	108.320
1974	USAC	Johnny Rutherford	USA	McLaren M16C/D-Offenhauser	110.226
	USAC	Gordon Johncock	USA	Eagle 74-Offenhauser	118.752
1975	USAC	AJ Foyt Jr	USA	Coyote-Foyt/Ford	114.042
	USAC	Mike Mosley	USA	Eagle 75-Offenhauser	114.393
1976	USAC	Mike Mosley	USA	Eagle 76-Offenhauser	121.557
	USAC	Al Unser	USA	Parnelli VPJ6B-Cosworth	121.907
1977	USAC	Johnny Rutherford	USA	McLaren M24-Cosworth	92.962
	USAC	Johnny Rutherford	USA	McLaren M24-Cosworth	103.798
1978	USAC	Rick Mears	USA	Penske PC6-Cosworth	120.677
	USAC	Danny Ongais	USA	Parnelli VPJ6B-Cosworth	108.385
1979	USAC	AJ Foyt Jr	USA	Parnelli VPJ6C-Cosworth	108.955
	USAC	Roger McCluskey	USA	Lola T500B-Cosworth	117.135
1980	CART	Bobby Unser	USA	Penske PC9-Cosworth	112.773
	CART	Johnny Rutherford	USA	Chaparral 2K-Cosworth	105.063
1981	CART	Mike Mosley	USA	Eagle 81-Chevrolet	113.839
	CART	Tom Sneva	USA	March 81C-Cosworth	118.013
1982	CART	Gordon Johncock	USA	Wildcat Mk8B-Cosworth	126.978
	CART	Tom Sneva	USA	March 82C-Cosworth	109.132
1983	CART	Tom Sneva	USA	March 83C-Cosworth	116.104
1984	CART	Tom Sneva	USA	March 84C-Cosworth	118.030
1985	CART	Mario Andretti	USA	Lola T900-Cosworth	124.162
1986	CART	Michael Andretti	USA	March 86C-Cosworth	116.788
1987	CART	Michael Andretti	USA	March 87C-Cosworth	111.853
1988	CART	Rick Mears	USA	Penske PC17-Chevrolet	122.819
1989	CART	Rick Mears	USA	Penske PC18-Chevrolet	130.160
1990	CART	Al Unser Jr	USA	Lola T90/00-Chevrolet	133.670
1991	CART	Michael Andretti	USA	Lola T91/00-Chevrolet	134.557
1992	CART	Michael Andretti	USA	Lola T92/00-Ford	138.031
1993	CART	Nigel Mansell	GB	Lola T93/00-Ford	110.970
1994	CART	Al Unser Jr	USA	Penske PC23-Ilmor	118.804
1995	CART	Paul Tracy	CDN	Lola T95/00-Ford	141.697
1996	CART	Michael Andretti	USA	Lola T96/00-Ford	132.387
1997	CART	Greg Moore	CDN	Reynard 97I-Mercedes-Benz	119.597
1998	CART	Jimmy Vasser	USA	Reynard 98I-Honda	131.349
1999	CART	Paul Tracy	CDN	Reynard 99I-Honda	128.029
2000	CART	Juan Pablo Montoya	CO	Lola B2K/00-Toyota	142.684
2001	CART	Kenny Brack	S	Lola B01/00-Ford	122.066
2002	CART	Paul Tracy	CDN	Lola B2/00-Honda	129.583

NASHVILLE

Nashville Superspeedway was the third concrete oval in the United States when it was opened in 2001, joining Bristol and its owner Dover Downs in rejecting the more normal tarmac surface. Buddy Lazier won the first Indy Racing League event held under lights on the D-shaped 14-degree banked oval. These floodlights incorporate mirrors to reduce glare and simulate daylight during a night race. Future plans for Nashville call for a 1.8-mile road course and increasing capacity from the 25,000 permanent seats now available.

Active years	2001 to date
Location	East of Nashville, Tennessee
Type	Paved oval
Website	www.nashvillesuperspeedway.com
Lap distance	1.330 miles

Lap records	Qualifying: Billy Boat (Dallara IR0-Chevrolet), 22.9666s, 208.477 mph, IRL, 2002
	Race: Tomas Scheckter (Dallara IR0-Infiniti), 23.1495s, 206.830 mph, IRL, 2002

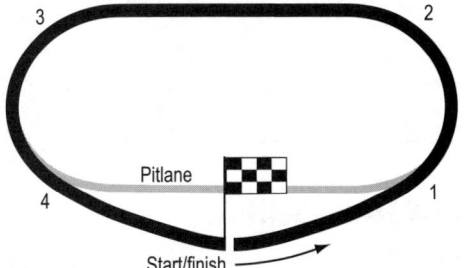

INDYCAR RACE

year	formula	winner	nat	car	mph
2001	IRL	Buddy Lazier	USA	Dallara IR0-Aurora	148.151
2002	IRL	Alex Barron	USA	Dallara IR0-Chevrolet	130.951

NAZARETH
Pennsylvania International Raceway

In its orginal incarnation as a 1.125-mile dirt oval, two Champcar races were held at Nazareth in the sixties. Roger Penske later bought the site, paved it and opened a shortened track in 1987. Fittingly, hometown-boy Michael Andretti won the inaugural race. Nazareth is an odd tri-oval that also includes some elevation change. Although officially one mile, it is in fact 0.946 miles long— a miscalculation which resulted in fast official speeds before it was remeasured. Scott Dixon became the youngest winner of an international single-seater race here in 2001. After fifteen years with CART, Nazareth switched to the rival Indy Racing League in 2002.

Active years	1968 to date
Location	Southern suburbs of Nazareth, 6 miles north of Bethlehem, Pennsylvania
Type	Paved oval
Websites	www.nazarethspeedway.com and www.iscmotorsports.com

Lap distance	0.946 miles
Lap records	Qualifying: Patrick Carpentier (Reynard 98I-Mercedes-Benz), 18.419s, 184.896 mph, CART, 1998
	Race: Greg Moore (Reynard 98I-Mercedes-Benz), 19.514s, 174.523 mph, CART, 1998

Circuit changes	
1968-84	Dirt oval. 1.125 miles
1987 to date	Redesigned and paved. Current circuit

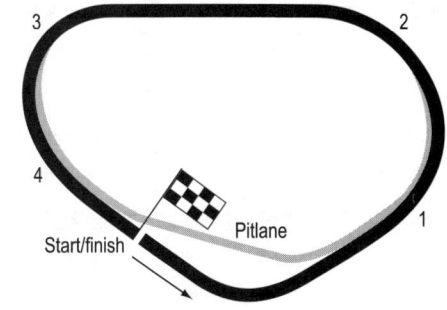

Marlboro Challenge see above

INDY/CHAMPCAR RACE

year	formula	winner	nat	car	mph
1968	USAC	Al Unser	USA	Ward-Offenhauser	99.558
1969	USAC	Mario Andretti	USA	Kuzma-Offenhauser	105.851
1987	CART	Michael Andretti	USA	March 87C-Cosworth	128.971
1988	CART	Danny Sullivan	USA	Penske PC17-Chevrolet	148.526
1989	CART	Emerson Fittipaldi	BR	Penske PC18-Chevrolet	134.759
1990	CART	Emerson Fittipaldi	BR	Penske PC19-Chevrolet	112.700
1991	CART	Arie Luyendyk	NL	Lola T91/00-Chevrolet	131.310
1992	CART	Bobby Rahal	USA	Lola T92/00-Chevrolet	128.848
1993	CART	Nigel Mansell	GB	Lola T93/00-Ford	158.686
1994	CART	Paul Tracy	CDN	Penske PC23-Ilmor	131.141
1995	CART	Emerson Fittipaldi	BR	Penske PC24-Mercedes-Benz	124.215

INDY/CHAMPCAR RACE (cont.)

year	formula	winner	nat	car	mph
1996	CART	Michael Andretti	USA	Lola T96/00-Ford	133.342
1997	CART	Paul Tracy	CDN	Penske PC26-Mercedes-Benz	112.498
1998	CART	Jimmy Vasser	USA	Reynard 98I-Honda	108.839
1999	CART	Juan Pablo Montoya	CO	Reynard 99I-Honda	120.225
2000	CART	Gil de Ferran	BR	Reynard 2KI-Honda	101.219
2001	CART	Scott Dixon	NZ	Reynard 01I-Toyota	114.840
2002	IRL	Scott Sharp	USA	Dallara IR0-Chevrolet	94.893

NEW HAMPSHIRE

Loudon

After a succession of temporary street circuits joined the CART calendar during the eighties, the short oval at Loudon, New Hampshire was a refreshing addition to the series. Bob Bahre's new speedway was built on the site of Bryar Motorsports Park, which had held events in the sixties and seventies. It is just over a mile long with 12-degree banking and features state-of-the-art facilities. The 1993 CART race saw Nigel Mansell win a mighty contest with Paul Tracy by less than half a second. After four years Loudon moved to the Indy Racing League but this too ended in 1998. Two NASCAR Winston Cup events are now the season highlights for the circuit.

Location   Loudon, New Hampshire, 70 miles north of Boston

Active years	1992 to date
Type	Paved oval
Website	www.nhis.com
Lap distance	1.058 miles
Lap records	Qualifying: Andre Ribeiro (Reynard 95I-Honda), 21.466s, 177.436 mph, CART, 1995
	Race: Teo Fabi (Reynard 95I-Ford), 22.968s, 165.831 mph, CART, 1995

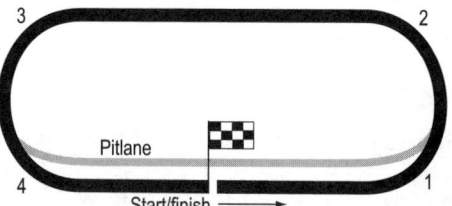

NEW ENGLAND 200 INDY/CHAMPCAR RACE

year	formula	winner	nat	car	mph
1992	CART	Bobby Rahal	USA	Lola T92/00-Chevrolet	133.621
1993	CART	Nigel Mansell	GB	Lola T93/00-Ford	130.148
1994	CART	Al Unser Jr	USA	Penske PC23-Ilmor	122.635
1995	CART	Andre Ribeiro	BR	Reynard 95I-Honda	134.203
1996	IRL	Scott Sharp	USA	Lola T95/00-Ford	130.934
1997	IRL	Robbie Buhl	USA	G-Force GF01-Aurora	146.195
1998	IRL	Tony Stewart	USA	Dallara IR7-Aurora	113.861

NASCAR RACE

year	formula	winner	nat	car	mph
1993	NASCAR	Rusty Wallace	USA	Pontiac Grand Prix	105.947
1994	NASCAR	Ricky Rudd	USA	Ford Thunderbird	87.599
1995	NASCAR	Jeff Gordon	USA	Chevrolet Monte Carlo	107.029
1996	NASCAR	Ernie Irvan	USA	Ford Thunderbird	98.930
1997	NASCAR	Jeff Burton	USA	Ford Thunderbird	117.134
	NASCAR	Jeff Gordon	USA	Chevrolet Monte Carlo	100.364
1998	NASCAR	Jeff Burton	USA	Ford Taurus	102.996
	NASCAR	Jeff Gordon	USA	Chevrolet Monte Carlo	112.078
1999	NASCAR	Jeff Burton	USA	Ford Taurus	101.876
	NASCAR	Joe Nemechek	USA	Chevrolet Monte Carlo	100.673
2000	NASCAR	Tony Stewart	USA	Pontiac Grand Prix	103.145
	NASCAR	Jeff Burton	USA	Ford Taurus	102.003
2001	NASCAR	Dale Jarrett	USA	Ford Taurus	102.131
	NASCAR	Robby Gordon	USA	Chevrolet Monte Carlo	103.594
2002	NASCAR	Ward Burton	USA	Dodge Intrepid	92.342
	NASCAR	Ryan Newman	USA	Ford Taurus	105.081

NORTH CAROLINA MOTOR SPEEDWAY

Rockingham

Type	Paved oval
Website	www.northcarolinaspeedway.com
Lap distance	1.017 miles
Lap records	Qualifying: Rusty Wallace (Ford Taurus), 23.167s, 158.035 mph, NASCAR, 2000

As other circuits have modernised in recent years the North Carolina Motor Speedway has remained relatively unchanged. The speedway has held NASCAR races every year since it opened in 1965. The uneven configuration of the turns (which are banked 22 degrees and 25 degrees) makes good car set-up difficult to achieve, and the track is particularly hard on brakes and tyres.

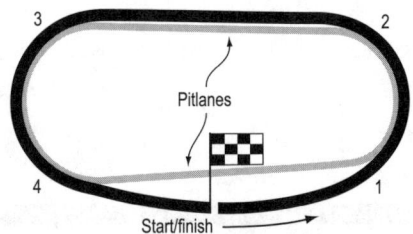

Location	Sand Hills, 10 miles east of Rockingham, North Carolina
Active years	1965 to date

NASCAR RACE (SINCE 1990)

year	formula	winner	nat	car	mph
1990	NASCAR	Kyle Petty	USA	Pontiac Grand Prix	122.864
	NASCAR	Alan Kulwicki	USA	Ford Thunderbird	126.452
1991	NASCAR	Kyle Petty	USA	Pontiac Grand Prix	124.083
	NASCAR	Davey Allison	USA	Ford Thunderbird	127.292
1992	NASCAR	Bill Elliott	USA	Ford Thunderbird	126.125
	NASCAR	Kyle Petty	USA	Pontiac Grand Prix	130.748
1993	NASCAR	Rusty Wallace	USA	Pontiac Grand Prix	124.486
	NASCAR	Rusty Wallace	USA	Pontiac Grand Prix	114.036
1994	NASCAR	Rusty Wallace	USA	Ford Thunderbird	125.239
	NASCAR	Dale Earnhardt	USA	Chevrolet Lumina	125.878
1995	NASCAR	Jeff Gordon	USA	Chevrolet Monte Carlo	125.483
	NASCAR	Ward Burton	USA	Chevrolet Monte Carlo	114.778
1996	NASCAR	Dale Earnhardt	USA	Chevrolet Monte Carlo	113.959
	NASCAR	Ricky Rudd	USA	Ford Thunderbird	122.320
1997	NASCAR	Jeff Gordon	USA	Chevrolet Monte Carlo	121.371
	NASCAR	Bobby Hamilton	USA	Pontiac Grand Prix	121.730
1998	NASCAR	Jeff Gordon	USA	Chevrolet Monte Carlo	117.065
	NASCAR	Jeff Gordon	USA	Chevrolet Monte Carlo	128.423
1999	NASCAR	Mark Martin	USA	Ford Taurus	120.750
	NASCAR	Jeff Burton	USA	Ford Taurus	131.103
2000	NASCAR	Bobby Labonte	USA	Pontiac Grand Prix	127.875
	NASCAR	Dale Jarrett	USA	Ford Taurus	110.418
2001	NASCAR	Steve Park	USA	Chevrolet Monte Carlo	111.877
	NASCAR	Joe Nemechek	USA	Chevrolet Monte Carlo	128.941
2002	NASCAR	Matt Kenseth	USA	Ford Taurus	115.478
	NASCAR	Johnny Benson	USA	Pontiac Grand Prix	128.526

ONTARIO MOTOR SPEEDWAY

Built near Los Angeles in 1970 at a reported cost of US$25.5m, it is ironic that Ontario Motor Speedway should close due to lack of funding. The inaugural event on 6 September 1970 was the F1 versus F5000 Questor Grand Prix won by Mario Andretti's Ferrari on the road course. A full F1 World Championship race was scheduled in 1972 but was subsequently cancelled. After that, racing at Ontario was concentrated on the Superspeedway, whose nine-degree turns made it quicker than Indy. The California 500 was part of the Champcar National Championship for the decade Ontario remained in operation, and a capacity crowd of 180,000 watched the first full 500-mile Champcar race held outside Indiana.

Lap record	Qualifying: Rick Mears (Penske PC7-Cosworth), 44.325s, 203.046 mph, CART, 1979

Grand Prix Circuit

Lap distance	3.194 miles
Lap record	Qualifying: Jackie Stewart (Tyrrell 001-Ford), 1m41.227, 113.590 mph, F1, 1971
	Race: Pedro Rodriguez (BRM P160), 1m42.777, 111.852 mph, F1, 1971

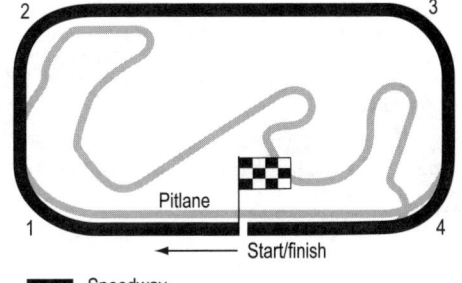

Speedway
Road Course and Pitlane

Active years	1970-81
Location	40 miles east of Los Angeles
Type	Paved oval and permanent road course

Oval	
Lap distance	2.500 miles

767

CALIFORNIA 500

year	formula	winner	nat	car	mph
1970	USAC	Jim McElreath	USA	Coyote-Ford	160.106
1971	USAC	Joe Leonard	USA	Colt 71-Ford	152.355
1972	USAC	Roger McCluskey	USA	McLaren M16B-Offenhauser	148.995
1973	USAC	Wally Dallenbach	USA	Eagle 73-Offenhauser	157.660
1974	USAC	Bobby Unser	USA	Eagle 74-Offenhauser	157.017
1975	USAC	AJ Foyt Jr	USA	Coyote-Foyt/Ford	154.344
1976	USAC	Bobby Unser	USA	Eagle 76-Offenhauser	143.246
1977	USAC	Al Unser	USA	Parnelli VPJ6B-Cosworth	152.074
1978	USAC	Al Unser	USA	Lola T500-Cosworth	145.158
1979	CART	Bobby Unser	USA	Penske PC7-Cosworth	146.795
1980	CART	Bobby Unser	USA	Penske PC9-Cosworth	156.372

CALIFORNIA 500 QUALIFYING RACES

year	formula	winner	nat	car	mph
1973	USAC	Wally Dallenbach	USA	Eagle 73-Offenhauser	179.919
	USAC	Johnny Rutherford	USA	McLaren M16C-Offenhauser	164.162
1974	USAC	AJ Foyt Jr	USA	Coyote-Foyt/Ford	176.873
	USAC	Johnny Rutherford	USA	McLaren M16C/D-Offenhauser	172.673
1975	USAC	AJ Foyt Jr	USA	Coyote-Foyt/Ford	177.085
	USAC	Wally Dallenbach	USA	Eagle 75-Offenhauser	150.305

OTHER CHAMPCAR RACES

year	formula	winner	nat	car	mph
1977	USAC	AJ Foyt Jr	USA	Coyote-Foyt/Ford	154.073
1978	USAC	Danny Ongais	USA	Parnelli VPJ6B-Cosworth	162.810
1979	USAC	AJ Foyt Jr	USA	Parnelli VPJ6C-Cosworth	154.279
1980	CART	Johnny Rutherford	USA	Chaparral 2K-Cosworth	162.016

QUESTOR GRAND PRIX

year	formula	winner	nat	car	mph
1971	F1/F5000	Mario Andretti	USA	Ferrari 312B	109.692

PHOENIX INTERNATIONAL RACEWAY

Nigel Mansell's practice accident for the 1993 CART race once again proved that PIR is not a place for the faint-hearted. It was traditionally the first oval of the CART Champcar and more recently Indy Racing League seasons, and is often used for pre-season testing. Banked at 11-degrees in Turns 1 and 2, and nine-degrees in 3 and 4, Phoenix has an awkward dogleg on the backstretch. Drivers are flat-out except for touching the brakes entering Turn 1. Lap times had dipped under 20 seconds before the race switched from CART to IRL, so running in traffic is guaranteed throughout the race. Phoenix was built to replace the Arizona State Fairgrounds dirt oval, which had held races from 1910 until a crash-filled 1962 event.

Active years	1964 to date
Location	15 miles south-west of downtown Phoenix, Arizona
Type	Paved oval
Website	www.phoenixinternationalraceway.com

Lap distance	1.000 miles
Lap records	Qualifying: Arie Luyendyk (Reynard 95I-Ford), 19.608s, 183.599 mph, IRL, 1996
	Race: Robbie Buhl (G-Force GF05-Infiniti), 21.1003s, 170.616 mph, IRL, 2002

United States of America

year	formula	winner	nat	car	mph
1915*	AAA	Earl Cooper	USA	Stutz	64.390
1950*	AAA	Jimmy Davies	USA	Ewing-Offenhauser	78.020
1951*	AAA	Johnnie Parsons	USA	Kurtis KK4000-Offenhauser	84.626
1952*	AAA	Johnnie Parsons	USA	Kurtis KK4000-Offenhauser	85.878
1953*	AAA	Tony Bettenhausen	USA	Kurtis-Offenhauser	83.916
1954*	AAA	Jimmy Bryan	USA	Kuzma-Offenhauser	84.524
1955*	USAC	Jimmy Bryan	USA	Kuzma-Offenhauser	83.862
1956*	USAC	George Amick	USA	Lesovsky-Offenhauser	91.826
1957*	USAC	Jimmy Bryan	USA	Kuzma-Offenhauser	86.001
1958*	USAC	Jud Larson	USA	Lesovsky-Offenhauser	92.738
1959*	USAC	Tony Bettenhausen	USA	Kuzma-Offenhauser	88.458
1960*	USAC	AJ Foyt Jr	USA	Meskowski-Offenhauser	89.078
1961*	USAC	Parnelli Jones	USA	Kuzma-Offenhauser	n/a
1962*	USAC	Bobby Marshman	USA	Meskowski-Offenhauser	92.122
1963*	USAC	Rodger Ward	USA	Watson-Offenhauser	85.026
1964	USAC	AJ Foyt Jr	USA	Watson-Offenhauser	107.536
	USAC	Lloyd Ruby	USA	Halibrand-Offenhauser	107.736
1965	USAC	Don Branson	USA	Watson-Offenhauser	106.456
	USAC	AJ Foyt Jr	USA	Bignotti/Lotus 34-Ford	99.986
1966	USAC	Jim McElreath	USA	Brabham-Ford	98.819
	USAC	Mario Andretti	USA	Brawner/Brabham-Ford	104.686
1967	USAC	Lloyd Ruby	USA	Mongoose-Drake/Offenhauser	86.295
	USAC	Mario Andretti	USA	Brawner/Hawk-Ford	109.872
1968	USAC	Bobby Unser	USA	Eagle 68-Drake/Offenhauser	100.938
	USAC	Gary Bettenhausen	USA	Gerhardt-Drake/Offenhauser	104.972
1969	USAC	George Follmer	USA	Gilbert-Chevrolet	109.866
	USAC	Al Unser	USA	Lola T152-Ford	110.109
1970	USAC	Al Unser	USA	Colt 70-Ford	n/a
	USAC	Swede Savage	USA	Eagle 70-Ford	116.807
1971	USAC	Al Unser	USA	Colt 71-Ford	111.565
	USAC	AJ Foyt Jr	USA	Coyote-Ford	110.701
1972	USAC	Bobby Unser	USA	Eagle 72-Offenhauser	102.825
	USAC	Bobby Unser	USA	Eagle 72-Offenhauser	127.618
1973	USAC	Gordon Johncock	USA	Eagle 73-Offenhauser	115.015
1974	USAC	Mike Mosley	USA	Eagle 74-Offenhauser	116.681
	USAC	Gordon Johncock	USA	Eagle 74-Offenhauser	124.202
1975	USAC	Johnny Rutherford	USA	McLaren M16D-Offenhauser	110.971
	USAC	AJ Foyt Jr	USA	Coyote-Foyt/Ford	111.055
1976	USAC	Bobby Unser	USA	Eagle 76-Offenhauser	107.918
	USAC	Al Unser	USA	Parnelli VPJ6B-Cosworth	107.695
1977	USAC	Johnny Rutherford	USA	McLaren M24-Cosworth	111.395
	USAC	Gordon Johncock	USA	Wildcat-DGS/Offenhauser	108.596
1978	USAC	Gordon Johncock	USA	Wildcat-DGS/Offenhauser	116.757
	USAC	Johnny Rutherford	USA	McLaren M24B-Cosworth	120.974
1979	CART	Gordon Johncock	USA	Penske PC6-Cosworth	119.389
	CART	Al Unser	USA	Chaparral 2K-Cosworth	123.203
1980	CART	Tom Sneva	USA	Phoenix-Cosworth	99.926
1981	CART	Johnny Rutherford	USA	Chaparral 2K-Cosworth	116.681
	CART	Tom Sneva	USA	March 81C-Cosworth	112.266
1982	CART	Rick Mears	USA	Penske PC10-Cosworth	118.727
	CART	Tom Sneva	USA	March 82C-Cosworth	110.997
1983	CART	Teo Fabi	I	March 83C-Cosworth	126.671
1984	CART	Tom Sneva	USA	March 84C-Cosworth	120.551
	CART	Bobby Rahal	USA	March 84C-Cosworth	98.048
1985	CART	Al Unser	USA	March 85C-Cosworth	120.644
1986	CART	Kevin Cogan	USA	March 86C-Cosworth	120.346
	CART	Michael Andretti	USA	March 86C-Cosworth	134.676
1987	CART	Roberto Guerrero	USA	March 87C-Cosworth	138.020
1988	CART	Mario Andretti	USA	Lola T88/00-Chevrolet	121.993
1989	CART	Rick Mears	USA	Penske PC18-Chevrolet	126.112
1990	CART	Rick Mears	USA	Penske PC19-Chevrolet	126.291
1991	CART	Arie Luyendyk	NL	Lola T91/00-Chevrolet	129.988
1992	CART	Bobby Rahal	USA	Lola T92/00-Chevrolet	130.526
1993	CART	Mario Andretti	USA	Lola T93/00-Ford	123.847
1994	CART	Emerson Fittipaldi	BR	Penske PC23-Ilmor	107.437
1995	CART	Robby Gordon	USA	Reynard 95I-Ford	133.980
1996	IRL	Arie Luyendyk	NL	Reynard 95I-Ford	117.386
1997	IRL	Jim Guthrie	USA	Dallara IR7-Aurora	89.190

INDY/CHAMPCAR RACE (cont.)

year	formula	winner	nat	car	mph
1998	IRL	Scott Sharp	USA	Dallara IR7-Aurora	98.110
1999	IRL	Scott Goodyear	CDN	G-Force GF01-Aurora	102.856
2000	IRL	Buddy Lazier	USA	Riley & Scott MkVII-Aurora	111.957
2001	IRL	Sam Hornish jr	USA	Dallara IR0-Aurora	125.071
2002	IRL	Helio Castro-Neves	BR	Dallara IR0-Chevrolet	116.504

At Phoenix International Raceway except *at Arizona State Fairgrounds

NASCAR RACE (SINCE 1990)

year	formula	winner	nat	car	mph
1990	NASCAR	Dale Earnhardt	USA	Chevrolet Lumina	96.786
1991	NASCAR	Davey Allison	USA	Ford Thunderbird	95.746
1992	NASCAR	Davey Allison	USA	Ford Thunderbird	103.885
1993	NASCAR	Mark Martin	USA	Ford Thunderbird	100.375
1994	NASCAR	Terry Labonte	USA	Chevrolet Lumina	107.463
1995	NASCAR	Ricky Rudd	USA	Ford Thunderbird	102.128
1996	NASCAR	Bobby Hamilton	USA	Pontiac Grand Prix	109.709
1997	NASCAR	Dale Jarrett	USA	Ford Thunderbird	110.824
1998	NASCAR	Rusty Wallace	USA	Ford Taurus	108.211
1999	NASCAR	Tony Stewart	USA	Pontiac Grand Prix	118.132
2000	NASCAR	Jeff Burton	USA	Ford Taurus	105.041
2001	NASCAR	Jeff Burton	USA	Ford Taurus	102.613
2002	NASCAR	Matt Kenseth	USA	Ford Taurus	113.857

PHOENIX GRAND PRIX CIRCUIT

Phoenix was the last city in North American to hold the F1 United States Grand Prix before the race returned to Indianapolis. The inaugural race was held in the mid-summer desert heat before switching to a more temperate spring date. The wide circuit featured a memorable battle for the lead between Ayrton Senna and Jean Alesi in 1990. But Grand Prix racing was never a hit in Phoenix, and when a local ostrich race drew a bigger crowd the event was cancelled!

Active years 1989-91
Location Central Phoenix
Type Temporary street circuit

Inaugural Grand Prix Circuit (1989-90)
Lap distance 2.360 miles
Lap records Qualifying: Gerhard Berger (McLaren MP4/5B-Honda), 1m28.664, 95.823 mph, F1, 1990
Race: Gerhard Berger (McLaren MP4/5B-Honda), 1m31.050, 93.312 mph, F1, 1990

Final Grand Prix Circuit (1991)
Lap distance 2.312 miles
Lap records Qualifying: Ayrton Senna (McLaren-Honda), 1m21.434, 102.208 mph, F1, 1991
Race: Jean Alesi (Ferrari 642), 1m26.758, 95.936 mph, F1, 1991

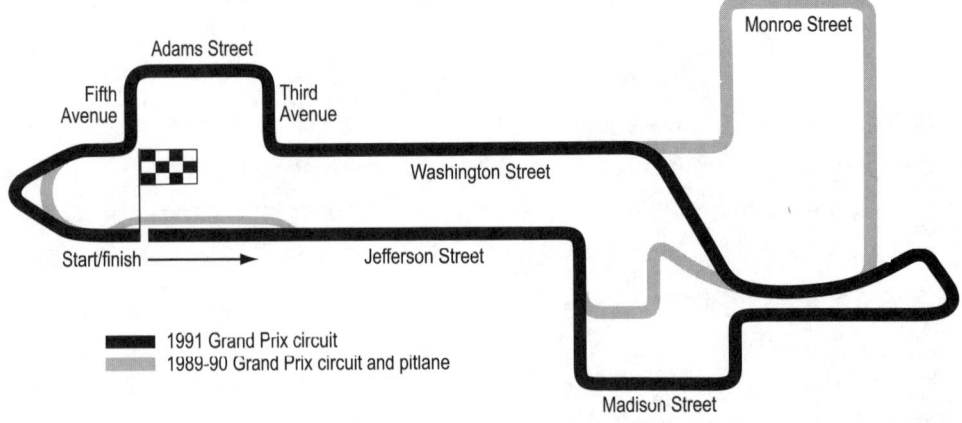

Monroe Street
Adams Street
Fifth Avenue
Third Avenue
Washington Street
Start/finish
Jefferson Street
Madison Street

■■■ 1991 Grand Prix circuit
▓▓▓ 1989-90 Grand Prix circuit and pitlane

United States Grand Prix see above

PIKES PEAK INTERNATIONAL RACEWAY

Pikes Peak has long been associated with motor racing through its renowned 12-mile hillclimb. Located on the site of a former horse racetrack, Colorado's first permanent speedway has held a round of the Indy Racing League since opening in 1997. A smooth, wide tri-oval with 10-degree banked turns, Pike's Peak was the quickest circuit on the IRL calendar until Michigan switched over from CART in 2002. The Rocky Mountains form a majestic background for the 42,787 grandstand seats.

Active years	1997 to date
Location	Fountain, Colorado, 10 miles south of Colorado Springs, 75 miles south of Denver
Type	Paved oval
Website	www.ppir.com
Lap distance	1.000 miles

Lap records — Qualifying: Greg Ray (Dallara IR7-Aurora), 20.014s, 179.874 mph, IRL, 2000
Race: Jeff Ward (G-Force GF01-Aurora), 21.174s, 170.020 mph, IRL, 1998

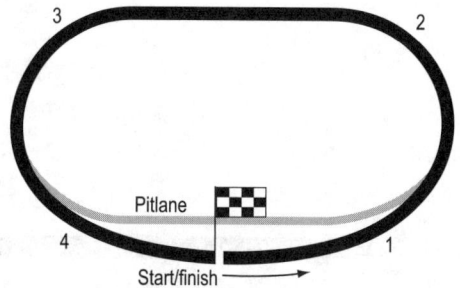

INDYCAR RACE

year	formula	winner	nat	car	mph
1997	IRL	Tony Stewart	USA	G-Force GF01-Aurora	100.139
1998	IRL	Kenny Brack	S	Dallara IR7-Aurora	133.515
1999	IRL	Greg Ray	USA	Dallara IR7-Aurora	134.111
	IRL	Greg Ray	USA	Dallara IR7-Aurora	135.450
2000	IRL	Eddie Cheever	USA	Dallara IR0-Infiniti	135.230
2001	IRL	Buddy Lazier	USA	Dallara IR0- Aurora	142.987
2002	IRL	Gil de Ferran	BR	Dallara IR0-Chevrolet	121.465

POCONO

Set deep in the Pennsylvania countryside, Pocono is unique among America's superspeedways. Like Daytona, it is a tri-oval, but all three corners are different. Turn 1 is banked at 14 degrees, compared to eight degrees for the narrow and challenging Turn 2, and just six degrees for Turn 3. The front straight is the also longest on the NASCAR calendar. Champcars regularly visited Pocono for two decades, but the track proved too bumpy for top-line open-wheel racing and the series moved elsewhere.

Active years	1968 to date
Location	30 miles north of Scranton, 100 miles north of Philadelphia, 100 miles west of New York City
Type	Paved oval
Website	www.poconoraceway.com

Current circuit

Lap distance	2.500 miles
Lap record	Qualifying: Emerson Fittipaldi (Penske PC18-Chevrolet), 42.510s, 211.715 mph, CART, 1989

Circuit changes

1968-70	Oval. 0.750 miles
1971 to date	Circuit rebuilt. Current circuit

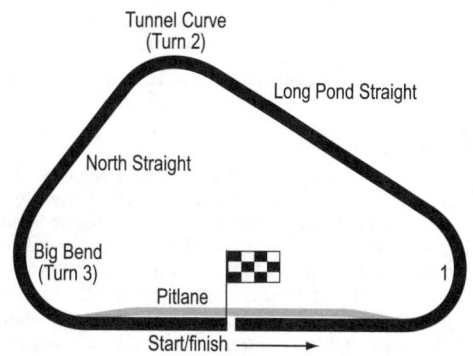

POCONO 500 CHAMPCAR RACE

year	formula	winner	nat	car	mph
1971	USAC	Mark Donohue	USA	McLaren M16A-Drake/Offenhauser	138.650
1972	USAC	Joe Leonard	USA	Parnelli-Offenhauser	154.781
1973	USAC	AJ Foyt jr	USA	Coyote-Foyt/Ford	144.948
1974	USAC	Johnny Rutherford	USA	McLaren M16C/D-Offenhauser	156.701

POCONO 500 CHAMPCAR RACE (cont.)

year	fomula	winner	nat	car	mph
1975	USAC	AJ Foyt Jr	USA	Coyote-Foyt/Ford	140.712
1976	USAC	Al Unser	USA	Parnelli VPJ6B-Cosworth	143.622
1977	USAC	Tom Sneva	USA	McLaren M24-Cosworth	152.131
1978	USAC	Al Unser	USA	Lola T500-Cosworth	142.261
1979	USAC	AJ Foyt Jr	USA	Parnelli VPJ6C-Cosworth	134.995
1980	CART	Bobby Unser	USA	Penske PC9-Cosworth	151.454
1981	CART	AJ Foyt Jr	USA	March 81C-Cosworth	137.196
1982	CART	Rick Mears	USA	Penske PC10-Cosworth	145.879
1983	CART	Teo Fabi	I	March 83C-Cosworth	134.852
1984	CART	Danny Sullivan	USA	Lola T800-Cosworth	137.303
1985	CART	Rick Mears	USA	March 85C-Cosworth	151.676
1986	CART	Mario Andretti	USA	Lola T86/00-Cosworth	152.107
1987	CART	Rick Mears	USA	March 86C-Chevrolet	156.373
1988	CART	Bobby Rahal	USA	Lola T88/00-Judd	133.713
1989	CART	Danny Sullivan	USA	Penske PC18-Chevrolet	170.720

NASCAR RACE (SINCE 1990)

year	formula	winner	nat	car	mph
1990	NASCAR	Harry Gant	USA	Oldsmobile Cutlass	120.765
	NASCAR	Geoff Bodine	USA	Ford Thunderbird	124.069
1991	NASCAR	Darrell Waltrip	USA	Chevrolet Lumina	122.666
	NASCAR	Rusty Wallace	USA	Pontiac Grand Prix	115.459
1992	NASCAR	Alan Kulwicki	USA	Ford Thunderbird	144.023
	NASCAR	Darrell Waltrip	USA	Chevrolet Lumina	134.058
1993	NASCAR	Kyle Petty	USA	Pontiac Grand Prix	138.005
	NASCAR	Dale Earnhardt	USA	Chevrolet Lumina	133.343
1994	NASCAR	Rusty Wallace	USA	Ford Thunderbird	128.801
	NASCAR	Geoff Bodine	USA	Ford Thunderbird	136.075
1995	NASCAR	Terry Labonte	USA	Chevrolet Monte Carlo	137.720
	NASCAR	Dale Jarrett	USA	Ford Thunderbird	134.038
1996	NASCAR	Jeff Gordon	USA	Chevrolet Monte Carlo	139.104
	NASCAR	Rusty Wallace	USA	Ford Thunderbird	144.893
1997	NASCAR	Jeff Gordon	USA	Chevrolet Monte Carlo	139.828
	NASCAR	Dale Jarrett	USA	Ford Thunderbird	142.068
1998	NASCAR	Jeremy Mayfield	USA	Ford Taurus	117.809
	NASCAR	Jeff Gordon	USA	Chevrolet Monte Carlo	134.660
1999	NASCAR	Bobby Labonte	USA	Pontiac Grand Prix	118.898
	NASCAR	Bobby Labonte	USA	Pontiac Grand Prix	116.982
2000	NASCAR	Jeremy Mayfield	USA	Ford Taurus	139.741
	NASCAR	Rusty Wallace	USA	Ford Taurus	130.662
2001	NASCAR	Ricky Rudd	USA	Ford Taurus	183.786
	NASCAR	Bobby Labonte	USA	Pontiac Grand Prix	134.590
2002	NASCAR	Dale Jarrett	USA	Ford Taurus	143.426
	NASCAR	Bill Elliott	USA	Dodge Intrepid	125.809

PORTLAND

Champcars have been visiting America's Pacific north-west region since 1984. The circuit is built on the site of Vanport, once Oregon's second-largest city before flooding led to its destruction in 1948. The Festival Curves are a difficult combination of tarmac and concrete and are often the scene of an accident at the start. The race forms part of Portland's annual Rose Festival, attracting many locals, but few visitors due to Portland's inaccessibility. The 1986 event witnessed the closest finish to a CART race since 1923, when Mario Andretti celebrated Father's Day by edging out his son Michael by just 0.07 seconds! Mark Blundell's last-lap victory in 1997 was even closer – beating Gil de Ferran by 0.027s and setting another new championship record.

Active years	1961 to date
Location	West Delta Park, 7 miles north of downtown Portland, Oregon
Type	Permanent road course
Website	www.globaleventsgrouppdx.com

Current circuit

Lap distance	1.969 miles
Lap records	Qualifying: Helio Castro-Neves (Reynard 2KI-Honda), 57.738s, 122.644 mph, CART, 2000
	Race: Michael Andretti (Swift 010c-Ford), 59.749s, 118.516 mph, CART, 1999

Circuit changes

1961-90	1.915 miles
1991	Chicane built at the site of the Festival Curves. 1.922 miles
1992-98	Festival Curves built. 1.967 miles (remeasured in 1997, previously believed to be 1.950 miles)
1999 to date	Current circuit

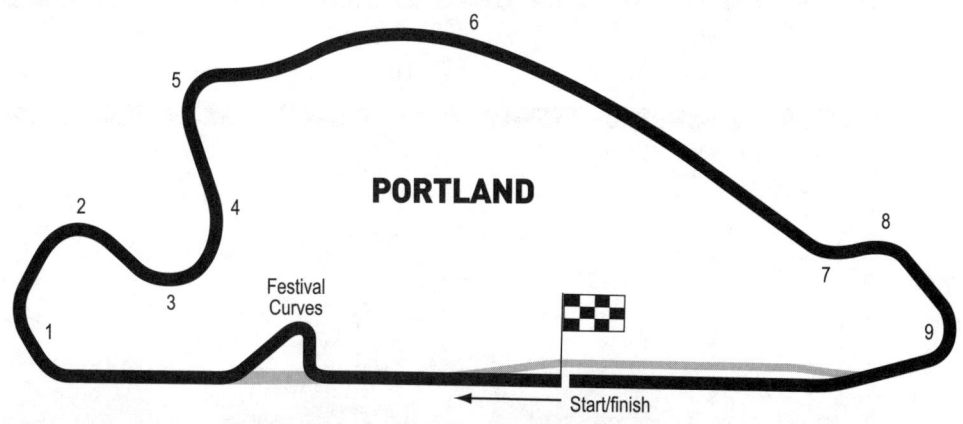

PORTLAND

5

6

2

4

Festival
Curves

3

1

8

7

9

Start/finish

CHAMPCAR RACE					
year	formula	winner	nat	car	mph
1984	CART	Al Unser Jr	USA	March 84C-Cosworth	105.478
1985	CART	Mario Andretti	USA	Lola T900-Cosworth	107.083
1986	CART	Mario Andretti	USA	Lola T86/00-Cosworth	107.760
1987	CART	Bobby Rahal	USA	Lola T87/00-Cosworth	108.591
1988	CART	Danny Sullivan	USA	Penske PC17-Chevrolet	101.881
1989	CART	Emerson Fittipaldi	BR	Penske PC18-Chevrolet	103.605
1990	CART	Michael Andretti	USA	Lola T90/00-Chevrolet	110.269
1991	CART	Michael Andretti	USA	Lola T91/00-Chevrolet	115.208
1992	CART	Michael Andretti	USA	Lola T92/00-Ford	105.219
1993	CART	Emerson Fittipaldi	BR	Penske PC22-Chevrolet	96.312
1994	CART	Al Unser Jr	USA	Penske PC23-Ilmor	108.371
1995	CART	Al Unser Jr	USA	Penske PC24-Mercedes-Benz	104.840
1996	CART	Alessandro Zanardi	I	Reynard 96I-Honda	104.742
1997	CART	Mark Blundell	GB	Reynard 97I-Mercedes-Benz	76.575
1998	CART	Alessandro Zanardi	I	Reynard 98I-Honda	101.355
1999	CART	Gil de Ferran	BR	Reynard 99I-Honda	107.457
2000	CART	Gil de Ferran	BR	Reynard 2KI-Honda	109.564
2001	CART	Massimiliano Papis	I	Lola B01/00-Ford	74.606
2002	CART	Cristiano da Matta	BR	Lola B2/00-Toyota	105.381

RICHMOND

Racing on the site of the Richmond International Raceway started in 1946 when Ted Horn's Champcar won on the dirt of Richmond Fairgrounds. Despite being paved in 1968 Richmond remained a low-key venue until owner Paul Sawyer refurbished it for the autumn NASCAR race in 1988. It reopened as a 0.75 miles D-shaped modern speedway, with 14 degree banked turns and grandstands for 94,030 spectators. The IRL event and one of the two NASCAR races are held under floodlights.

Active years	1946 to date
Location	Henrico County, Virginia, 5 miles north of downtown Richmond
Type	Paved oval
Website	www.rir.com

Current circuit
Lap distance   0.750 miles

Lap records   Qualifying: Gil de Ferran (Dallara IR0-Chevrolet), 16.0043s, 168.706 mph, IRL, 2002
Race: Buddy Lazier (Dallara IR0-Chevrolet), 17.0358s, 158.492 mph, IRL, 2002

Circuit changes

1946-68	Dirt oval. 0.500 miles
1968-88 September	Paved. 0.542 miles
1988 to date	Extended for autumn race. Current circuit

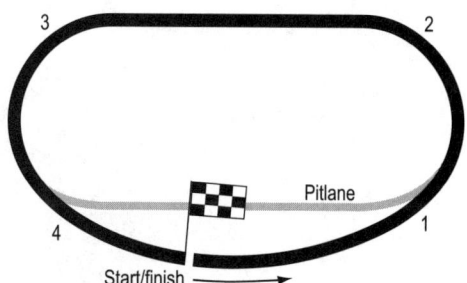

3

2

Pitlane

4

1

Start/finish

INDYCAR RACE

year	formula	winner	nat	car	mph
2001	IRL	Buddy Lazier	USA	Dallara IR0-Aurora	97.435
2002	IRL	Sam Hornish Jr	USA	Dallara IR0-Chevrolet	99.124

NASCAR RACE (SINCE 1990)

year	formula	winner	nat	car	mph
1990	NASCAR	Mark Martin	USA	Ford Thunderbird	92.166
	NASCAR	Dale Earnhardt	USA	Chevrolet Lumina	95.567
1991	NASCAR	Dale Earnhardt	USA	Chevrolet Lumina	105.361
	NASCAR	Harry Gant	USA	Oldsmobile Cutlass	101.361
1992	NASCAR	Bill Elliott	USA	Ford Thunderbird	104.378
	NASCAR	Rusty Wallace	USA	Pontiac Grand Prix	104.661
1993	NASCAR	Davey Allison	USA	Ford Thunderbird	107.709
	NASCAR	Rusty Wallace	USA	Pontiac Grand Prix	99.917
1994	NASCAR	Ernie Irvan	USA	Ford Thunderbird	98.334
	NASCAR	Terry Labonte	USA	Chevrolet Lumina	104.056
1995	NASCAR	Terry Labonte	USA	Chevrolet Monte Carlo	106.425
	NASCAR	Rusty Wallace	USA	Ford Thunderbird	104.459
1996	NASCAR	Jeff Gordon	USA	Chevrolet Monte Carlo	102.750
	NASCAR	Ernie Irvan	USA	Ford Thunderbird	105.469
1997	NASCAR	Rusty Wallace	USA	Ford Thunderbird	108.499
	NASCAR	Dale Jarrett	USA	Ford Thunderbird	109.047
1998	NASCAR	Terry Labonte	USA	Chevrolet Monte Carlo	97.044
	NASCAR	Jeff Burton	USA	Ford Taurus	91.985
1999	NASCAR	Dale Jarrett	USA	Ford Taurus	100.102
	NASCAR	Tony Stewart	USA	Pontiac Grand Prix	104.006
2000	NASCAR	Dale Earnhardt Jr	USA	Chevrolet Monte Carlo	99.374
	NASCAR	Jeff Gordon	USA	Chevrolet Monte Carlo	99.871
2001	NASCAR	Tony Stewart	USA	Pontiac Grand Prix	95.872
	NASCAR	Ricky Rudd	USA	Ford Taurus	95.146
2002	NASCAR	Tony Stewart	USA	Pontiac Grand Prix	86.824
	NASCAR	Matt Kenseth	USA	Ford Taurus	94.787

RIVERSIDE

Set in the desert near the San Bernardino Mountains, Riverside succumbed to the urban sprawl of Los Angeles and closed in 1988. It held the first United States GP, a sports car race in 1958 and hosted a full World Championship Grand Prix two years later. The three layouts were challenging, the uphill esses in particular. Dan Gurney excelled here, winning the early season NASCAR race five times and the Champcar event twice.

Active years	1957-88
Location	East of Los Angeles
Type	Permanent road course

Circuits

Sports Car Long Course	3.250 miles
Stock Car Course	2.620 miles
Sports Car Short Course	2.547 miles

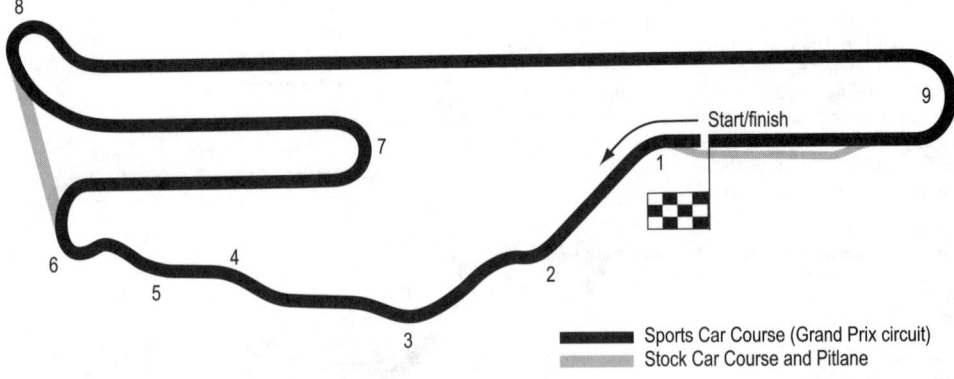

Start/finish

Sports Car Course (Grand Prix circuit)
Stock Car Course and Pitlane

United States Grand Prix see above

CHAMPCAR RACE					
year	formula	winner	nat	car	mph
1967	USAC	Dan Gurney	USA	Eagle 67-Ford/Weslake	107.995
1968	USAC	Dan Gurney	USA	Eagle 68-Ford/Weslake	112.548
1969	USAC	Mario Andretti	USA	Brawner/Hawk-Ford	107.786
1981	CART	Rick Mears	USA	Penske PC9B-Cosworth	113.176
1982	CART	Rick Mears	USA	Penske PC10-Cosworth	111.783
1983	CART	Bobby Rahal	USA	March 83C-Cosworth	111.956

WORLD SPORTS CAR RACE					
year	formula	winner	nat	car	mph
1981	SC W	John Fitzpatrick/Jim Busby	USA	Porsche 935-K3	107.563

ROAD ATLANTA

Road Atlanta is a testing, undulating road course built in the heart of NASCAR country. It was a mainstay of North American road racing (hosting Trans-Am, Can-Am, F5000 and IMSA among others) since opening on 13 September 1970. An annual highlight from 1970-95 was the weeklong SCCA run-offs, an end-of-season festival for amateur championships from across the land. But the circuit fell into decline and disrepair in the nineties, and filed for bankruptcy in 1993. Although Road Atlanta continued to operate under new owners, it was not until entrepreneur Don Panoz acquired it in December 1996 that a programme of modernisation restored it to the forefront of American sports car racing. Uniquely, Road Atlanta now features pit lanes on either side of the starting straight to accommodate more competitors. Panoz also inaugurated the 1000-mile Petit Le Mans race in 1998 as the centrepiece of his new championship, the American Le Mans Series. The event is now firmly established as the late-season highlight of the sports car year.

Active years	1970 to date
Location	2 miles west of Braselton, 10 miles south of Gainesville, north-east of Atlanta, Georgia
Type	Permanent road course
Website	www.roadatlanta.com
Lap distance	2.540 miles
Lap record	Qualifying: Allan McNish (Audi R8), 1m10.379, 129.925 mph, ALMS Sports Cars, 2000
	Race: Allan McNish (Audi R8), 1m11.782, 127.386 mph, ALMS Sports Cars, 2000

ROAD ATLANTA

PETIT LE MANS					
year	formula	winner	nat	car	mph
1998	SC	Eric van de Poele/Wayne Taylor/Emmanuel Collard	B/ZA/F	Ferrari 333SP	102.068
1999	SC	David Brabham/Eric Bernard/Andy Wallace	AUS/F/GB	Panoz LMP Roadster S	111.914
2000	SC	Allan McNish/Rinaldo Capello/Michele Alboreto	GB/I/I	Audi R8	109.437
2001	SC	Frank Biela/Emanuele Pirro	D/I	Audi R8	108.004
2002	SC	Rinaldo Capello/Tom Kristensen	I/DK	Audi R8	105.777

SEARS POINT

Infineon Raceway

When Riverside closed in 1988 Sears Point replaced it as NASCAR's annual California road race. As only one of two road races on the NASCAR calendar many drivers find it hard to adapt, but Jeff Gordon won three races in a row from 1998-2000, his adaptability confirmed by a similar run at the other road course, Watkins Glen from 1997-99. Sears Point was built in 1968, but closed within two years. However, it soon reopened to house the Bob Bondurant racing school. Long Beach promoter Chris Pook bought it in 1980 and repaved the track five years later, before selling it to Bruton Smith in 1996. Technology company Infineon officially bought the naming rights to the circuit in 2002.

Active years 1968 to date
Location 10 miles south of Sonoma, California, 40 miles north-east of San Francisco
Type Permanent road course
Website www.infineonraceway.com

Current circuit
Lap distance 1.949 miles
Lap records Qualifying: Rusty Wallace (Ford Taurus), 1m10.652, 99.309 mph, NASCAR, 2000

Circuit Changes
1968-97 2.523 miles
1998 to date The Chute used to shorten the circuit for NASCAR. Current circuit

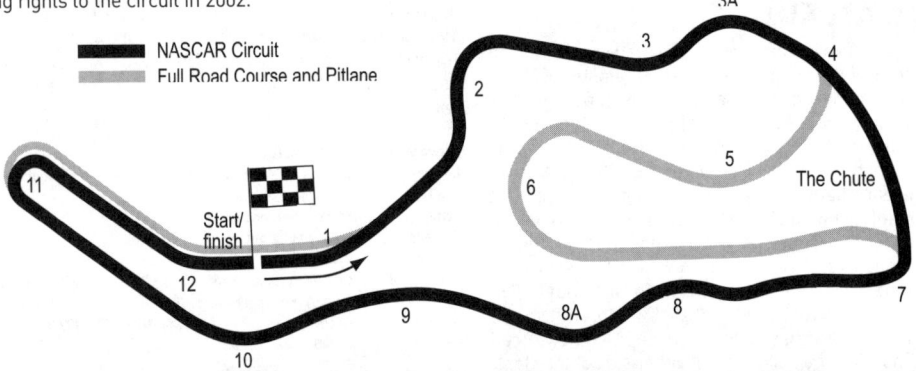

NASCAR Circuit
Full Road Course and Pitlane

NASCAR RACE (SINCE 1990)					
year	formula	winner	nat	car	mph
1990	NASCAR	Rusty Wallace	USA	Pontiac Grand Prix	69.327
1991	NASCAR	Davey Allison	USA	Ford Thunderbird	73.057
1992	NASCAR	Ernie Irvan	USA	Chevrolet Lumina	81.509
1993	NASCAR	Geoff Bodine	USA	Ford Thunderbird	77.105
1994	NASCAR	Ernie Irvan	USA	Ford Thunderbird	77.550
1995	NASCAR	Dale Earnhardt	USA	Chevrolet Monte Carlo	70.765
1996	NASCAR	Rusty Wallace	USA	Ford Thunderbird	77.765
1997	NASCAR	Mark Martin	USA	Ford Thunderbird	75.878
1998	NASCAR	Jeff Gordon	USA	Chevrolet Monte Carlo	72.387
1999	NASCAR	Jeff Gordon	USA	Chevrolet Monte Carlo	70.378
2000	NASCAR	Jeff Gordon	USA	Chevrolet Monte Carlo	78.789
2001	NASCAR	Tony Stewart	USA	Pontiac Grand Prix	73.954
2002	NASCAR	Ricky Rudd	USA	Ford Taurus	79.338

SEBRING

Sebring has been one of the most famous names in American racing ever since the concrete runways of this World War II airfield were first used in 1950. Within two years the first of the now traditional 12-hour races was held. The first World Championship United States GP was also held here in 1959. Although it was the only time GP racing would visit Sebring, it was a memorable race, as Bruce McLaren became the youngest GP winner to date and teammate Jack Brabham pushed his car across the line to clinch his first Championship. The formerly abrasive surface was repaved with tarmac in 1991, and new owner Don Panoz is committed to further modernisation. A new pit complex, hospitality units and a hotel by the Hairpin were opened in 1999.

Active years 1950 to date
Location 6 miles south-east of Sebring, Florida, 79 miles south of Orlando, 92 miles south-east of Tampa
Type Permanent road course
Website www.sebringraceway.com

Current circuit
Lap distance 3.700 miles
Lap record Qualifying: Frank Biela (Audi R8), 1m48.029, 123.300 mph, ALMS Sports Cars, 2002
Race: Tom Kristensen (Audi R8), 1m48.418, 122.858 mph, ALMS Sports Cars, 2002

Circuit changes
1950-51 3.500 miles
1952-66 Classic layout introduced using two concrete airport runways. 5.200 miles
1967-82 Chicane built at Webster Turn. 5.200 miles

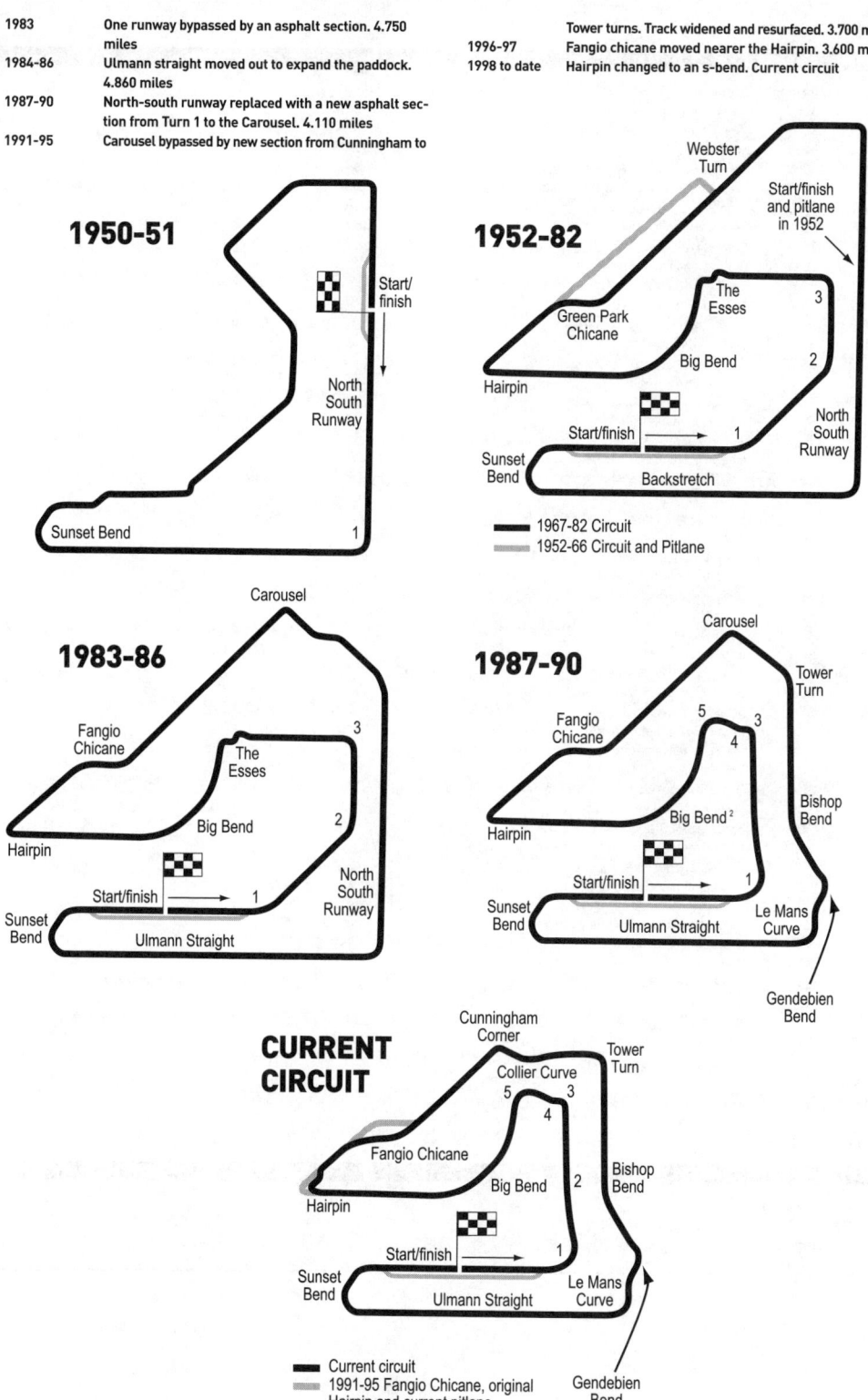

1983	One runway bypassed by an asphalt section. 4.750 miles
1984–86	Ulmann straight moved out to expand the paddock. 4.860 miles
1987–90	North-south runway replaced with a new asphalt section from Turn 1 to the Carousel. 4.110 miles
1991–95	Carousel bypassed by new section from Cunningham to

1996–97	Tower turns. Track widened and resurfaced. 3.700 miles
	Fangio chicane moved nearer the Hairpin. 3.600 miles
1998 to date	Hairpin changed to an s-bend. Current circuit

1950-51

Start/finish

North South Runway

Sunset Bend

1

1952-82

Webster Turn

Start/finish and pitlane in 1952

Green Park Chicane

The Esses

3

Big Bend

2

Hairpin

North South Runway

Sunset Bend

Start/finish

1

Backstretch

■ 1967-82 Circuit
■ 1952-66 Circuit and Pitlane

1983-86

Carousel

Fangio Chicane

The Esses

3

Big Bend

2

Hairpin

North South Runway

Sunset Bend

Start/finish

1

Ulmann Straight

1987-90

Carousel

Tower Turn

Fangio Chicane

5

3

4

Bishop Bend

Big Bend 2

Hairpin

Sunset Bend

Start/finish

1

Ulmann Straight

Le Mans Curve

Gendebien Bend

CURRENT CIRCUIT

Cunningham Corner

Tower Turn

Collier Curve

5

3

Fangio Chicane

4

Bishop Bend

Big Bend

2

Hairpin

1

Sunset Bend

Start/finish

Le Mans Curve

Ulmann Straight

Gendebien Bend

■ Current circuit
■ 1991-95 Fangio Chicane, original Hairpin and current pitlane

Racing Around the World

United States Grand Prix see above

SEBRING 12 HOURS

year	formula	winner	nat	car	mph
1952	SC	Harry Gray/Larry Kulok	USA	Frazer-Nash	62.830
1953	SC W	John Fitch/Phil Walters	USA	Cunningham C4R-Chrysler	74.961
1954	SC W	Stirling Moss/Bill Lloyd	GB/USA	OSCA MT4	72.370
1955	SC W	Mike Hawthorn/Phil Walters	GB/USA	Jaguar D-type	78.860
1956	SC W	Juan Manuel Fangio/Eugenio Castellotti	RA/I	Ferrari 860 Monza	84.067
1957	SC W	Juan Manuel Fangio/Jean Behra	RA/F	Maserati 450S	85.360
1958	SC W	Peter Collins/Phil Hill	GB/USA	Ferrari 250TR	86.501
1959	SC W	Dan Gurney/Chuck Daigh/Phil Hill/Olivier Gendebien	USA/USA/USA/B	Ferrari 250TR	81.467
1960	SC W	Olivier Gendebien/Hans Herrmann	B/D	Porsche 718 RSK	84.928
1961	SC W	Phil Hill/Olivier Gendebien	USA/B	Ferrari 250TR	90.700
1962	SC W	Jo Bonnier/Lucien Bianchi	S/B	Ferrari 250TR	89.142
1963	SC W	John Surtees/Ludovico Scarfiotti	GB/I	Ferrari 250P	90.390
1964	SC W	Michael Parkes/Umberto Maglioli	GB/I	Ferrari 275P	92.363
1965	SC W	Jim Hall/Hap Sharp	USA	Chaparral 2D-Chevrolet	84.720
1966	SC W	Lloyd Ruby/Ken Miles	USA	Ford GTX1	98.626
1967	SC W	Mario Andretti/Bruce McLaren	USA/NZ	Ford GT40 Mk4	102.901
1968	SC W	Hans Herrmann/Jo Siffert	D/CH	Porsche 907/8	102.512
1969	SC W	Jacky Ickx/Jackie Oliver	B/GB	Ford GT40	103.363
1970	SC W	Ignazio Giunti/Nino Vaccarella/Mario Andretti	I/I/USA	Ferrari 512S	107.290
1971	SC W	Vic Elford/Gerard Larrousse	GB/F	Porsche 917K	112.501
1972	SC W	Jacky Ickx/Mario Andretti	B/USA	Ferrari 312P	111.511
1973	SC	Peter Gregg/Hurley Haywood/Dave Helmick	USA	Porsche Carrera	97.854
1975	SC	Brian Redman/Allan Moffat/Sam Posey/			
		Hans-Joachim Stuck	GB/AUS/USA/D	BMW 3.0 CSL	102.640
1976	SC	Al Holbert/Michael Keyser	USA	Porsche 911 Carrera RSR	99.667
1977	SC	George Dyer/Brad Frisselle	USA	Porsche 911 Carrera RSR	101.322
1978	SC	Brian Redman/Charles Mendez/			
		Bob Garretson	GB/USA/USA	Porsche 935	103.978
1979	SC	Bob Akin/Rob McFarlin/Roy Woods	USA	Porsche 935	103.466
1980	SC	Dick Barbour/John Fitzpatrick	USA/GB	Porsche 935	109.520
1981	SC W	Bruce Leven/Hurley Haywood/Al Holbert	USA	Porsche 935	106.044
1982	SC	John Paul/John Paul Jr	USA	Porsche 935	105.401
1983	SC	Wayne Baker/Jim Mullen/Kees Nierop	USA/USA/CDN	Porsche 934	91.273
1984	SC	Maurizio de Narvaez/Hans Heyer/Stefan Johansson	CO/D/S	Porsche 935	106.364
1985	SC	Bob Wollek/AJ Foyt Jr	F/USA	Porsche 962	113.787
1986	SC	Bob Akin/Hans-Joachim Stuck/Jo Gartner	USA/D/A	Porsche 962	115.852
1987	SC	Jochen Mass/Bobby Rahal	D/USA	Porsche 962	101.859
1988	SC	Klaus Ludwig/Hans-Joachim Stuck	D	Porsche 962	108.782
1989	SC	Geoff Brabham/Chip Robinson/Arie Luyendyk	AUS/USA/NL	Nissan GTP ZX-T	112.742
1990	SC	Derek Daly/Bob Earl	IRL/USA	Nissan GTP ZX-T	102.993
1991	SC	Geoff Brabham/Derek Daly/Gary Brabham	AUS/IRL/AUS	Nissan NPT90	91.626
1992	SC	Juan Manuel Fangio II/Andy Wallace	RA/GB	Eagle Mk3-Toyota	110.724
1993	SC	Juan Manuel Fangio II/Andy Wallace	RA/GB	Eagle Mk3-Toyota	70.699
1994	SC	Steve Millen/Johnny O'Connell/John Morton	NZ/USA/USA	Nissan 300ZX	100.634
1995	SC	Andy Evans/Eric van de Poele/Fermin Velez	USA/B/E	Ferrari 333SP	80.167
1996	SC	Jim Pace/Eric van de Poele/Wayne Taylor	USA/B/ZA	Riley & Scott MkIII-Oldsmobile	100.167
1997	SC	Yannick Dalmas/Stefan Johansson/			
		Andy Evans/Fermin Velez	F/S/USA/E	Ferrari 333SP	84.286
1998	SC	Gianpiero Moretti/Didier Theys/Mauro Baldi	I/B/I	Ferrari 333SP	98.310
1999	SC	JJ Lehto/Tom Kristensen/Jorg Muller	SF/DK/D	BMW V12 LMR	96.391
2000	SC	Frank Biela/Tom Kristensen/Emanuele Pirro	D/DK/I	Audi R8	110.692
2001	SC	Rinaldo Capello/Michele Alboreto/Laurent Aiello	I/I/F	Audi R8	113.983
2002	SC	Rinaldo Capello/Johnny Herbert/Christian Pescatori	I/GB/I	Audi R8	105.507

FIA GT RACE

year	formula	winner	nat	car	mph
1997	GT FIA	Klaus Ludwig/Bernd Schneider	D	Mercedes-Benz CLK-GTR	83.851

ST LOUIS

Gateway International Raceway

A modern oval opened on 24 May 1997 on the site of a former drag strip and road course. The circuit was masterminded by Long Beach promoter Chris Pook and is owned by Dover Downs Speedway. Turns 1 and 2 are banked at nine-degrees and are tighter than the 11-degree Turns 3 and 4. After holding four CART races Gateway joined the oval-only Indy Racing League in 2001.

Active years	1997 to date
Location	Madison, Illinois, 5 miles east of downtown St Louis
Type	Paved oval
Website	www.gatewayraceway.com

Lap distance	1.270 miles
Lap records	Qualifying: Raul Boesel (Reynard 97I-Ford) 24.324s, 187.963 mph, CART, 1997
	Race: Dario Franchitti (Reynard 97I-Mercedes-Benz), 25.312s, 180.626 mph, CART, 1997

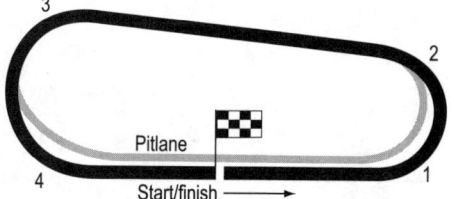

INDY/CHAMPCAR RACE

year	formula	winner	nat	car	mph
1997	CART	Paul Tracy	CDN	Penske PC26-Mercedes-Benz	113.884
1998	CART	Alessandro Zanardi	I	Reynard 98I-Honda	125.725
1999	CART	Michael Andretti	USA	Swift 010c-Ford	123.513
2000	CART	Juan Pablo Montoya	CO	Lola B2K/00-Toyota	155.519
2001	IRL	Al Unser Jr	USA	G-Force GF05-Aurora	138.561
2002	IRL	Gil de Ferran	BR	Dallara IR0-Chevrolet	146.010

TALLADEGA

Talladega, or the Alabama International Motor Speedway as it was originally known, is the longest oval on the NASCAR calendar, and it remains one of the fastest. Its debut race was marred by a mass boycott by drivers who thought it too bumpy and dangerous. Several spectators were injured in 1987 when Bobby Allison's car flew into the fence. Organisers immediately moved to slow the cars by introducing aerodynamic restrictions, so Bill Elliott's lap record is unlikely ever to be challenged. Tragedy struck Talladega away from the racetrack when Davey Allison was killed here in a helicopter accident in 1993.

Active years	1969 to date
Location	40 miles east of Birmingham, Alabama, 90 miles west of Atlanta, Georgia

Type	Paved oval
Website	www.talladegasuperspeedway.com
Lap distance	2.660 miles
Lap records	Qualifying: Bill Elliott (Ford Thunderbird), 44.998s, 212.809 mph, NASCAR, 1987

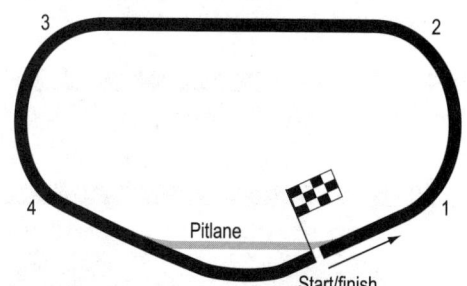

NASCAR RACE (SINCE 1990)

year	formula	winner	nat	car	mph
1990	NASCAR	Dale Earnhardt	USA	Chevrolet Lumina	159.572
	NASCAR	Dale Earnhardt	USA	Chevrolet Lumina	174.430
1991	NASCAR	Harry Gant	USA	Oldsmobile Cutlass	165.620
	NASCAR	Dale Earnhardt	USA	Chevrolet Lumina	147.383
1992	NASCAR	Davey Allison	USA	Ford Thunderbird	167.609
	NASCAR	Ernie Irvan	USA	Chevrolet Lumina	176.309
1993	NASCAR	Ernie Irvan	USA	Chevrolet Lumina	155.412
	NASCAR	Dale Earnhardt	USA	Chevrolet Lumina	153.858
1994	NASCAR	Dale Earnhardt	USA	Chevrolet Lumina	157.478
	NASCAR	Jimmy Spencer	USA	Ford Thunderbird	163.217
1995	NASCAR	Mark Martin	USA	Ford Thunderbird	178.902
	NASCAR	Sterling Marlin	USA	Chevrolet Monte Carlo	173.188
1996	NASCAR	Sterling Marlin	USA	Chevrolet Monte Carlo	149.999
	NASCAR	Jeff Gordon	USA	Chevrolet Monte Carlo	133.388

NASCAR RACE (SINCE 1990) (cont.)

year	formula	winner	nat	car	mph
1997	NASCAR	Mark Martin	USA	Ford Thunderbird	188.354
	NASCAR	Terry Labonte	USA	Chevrolet Monte Carlo	156.601
1998	NASCAR	Bobby Labonte	USA	Pontiac Grand Prix	142.428
	NASCAR	Dale Jarrett	USA	Ford Taurus	159.318
1999	NASCAR	Dale Earnhardt	USA	Chevrolet Monte Carlo	163.395
	NASCAR	Dale Earnhardt	USA	Chevrolet Monte Carlo	166.632
2000	NASCAR	Jeff Gordon	USA	Chevrolet Monte Carlo	161.157
	NASCAR	Dale Earnhardt	USA	Chevrolet Monte Carlo	165.681
2001	NASCAR	Bobby Hamilton	USA	Chevrolet Monte Carlo	184.003
	NASCAR	Dale Earnhardt Jr	USA	Chevrolet Monte Carlo	164.185
2002	NASCAR	Dale Earnhardt Jr	USA	Chevrolet Monte Carlo	159.022
	NASCAR	Dale Earnhardt Jr	USA	Chevrolet Monte Carlo	183.665

TEXAS MOTOR SPEEDWAY

When Bruton Smith's new D-shaped tri-oval at Fort Worth opened on 6 April 1997 its high 24-degree banking and narrow track immediately caused controversy. Many NASCAR drivers were unhappy about the numerous accidents in that race. Worse was to come when the CART Champcar Series made its first scheduled visit in 2001. Drivers suffered dizziness and blackouts due to high centrifugal forces generated by excessive speeds at such a tight facility. The race was cancelled after qualifying, infuriating fans as well as the race's promotor. Although CART will not return to the track, the Indy Racing League has run here since 1997. The opening race featured a pit-lane scuffle involving AJ Foyt, and the winner was not declared for 24 hours. The 154,861-grandstand capacity makes the Texas Motor Speedway the second largest sporting venue in the country. It has no connection to the similarly named Texas World Speedway, which was active in the seventies.

Active years	1997 to date
Location	20 miles north of Fort Worth, Texas
Type	Paved oval
Website	www.texasmotorspeedway.com
Lap distance	1.455 miles
Lap records	Qualifying: Kenny Brack (Lola B01/00-Ford), 22.854s, 229.195 mph, CART, 2001
	Race: Tony Stewart (G-Force GF01-Aurora), 22.972s, 228.012 mph, IRL, 1998

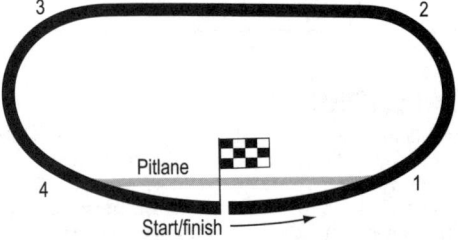

CHAMPCAR RACE

year	formula	winner	nat	car	mph
2001	CART	RACE CANCELLED AFTER QUALIFYING			

INDYCAR RACE

year	formula	winner	nat	car	mph
1997	IRL	Arie Luyendyk	NL	G-Force GF01-Aurora	129.886
1998	IRL	Billy Boat	USA	Dallara IR7-Aurora	141.026
	IRL	John Paul Jr	USA	G-Force GF01-Aurora	127.973
1999	IRL	Scott Goodyear	CDN	G-Force GF01-Aurora	151.177
	IRL	Mark Dismore	USA	Dallara IR7-Aurora	135.246
2000	IRL	Scott Sharp	USA	Dallara IR0-Aurora	169.182
	IRL	Scott Goodyear	CDN	Dallara IR0-Aurora	175.276
2001	IRL	Scott Sharp	USA	Dallara IR0-Aurora	150.873
	IRL	Sam Hornish Jr	USA	Dallara IR0-Aurora	168.523
2002	IRL	Jeff Ward	USA	G-Force GF05-Chevrolet	164.984
	IRL	Sam Hornish Jr	USA	Dallara IR0-Chevrolet	163.981

NASCAR RACE

year	formula	winner	nat	car	mph
1997	NASCAR	Jeff Burton	USA	Ford Thunderbird	121.358
1998	NASCAR	Mark Martin	USA	Ford Taurus	132.668
1999	NASCAR	Terry Labonte	USA	Chevrolet Monte Carlo	139.948
2000	NASCAR	Dale Earnhardt Jr	USA	Chevrolet Monte Carlo	127.217
2001	NASCAR	Dale Jarrett	USA	Ford Taurus	137.549
2002	NASCAR	Matt Kenseth	USA	Ford Taurus	138.180

TRENTON

New Jersey State Fairgrounds

Built immediately after World War II on the sight of a 0.5-mile dirt oval (which had been used as early as 1914) the New Jersey State Fairgrounds was a mainstay of Champcar racing until 1979. Paved for its second race in 1957, it was a lightly banked oval. Trenton was always well attended and traditionally held two races, one in the spring and one in the autumn.

Circuits

1946-56	Dirt. 1 mile	
1957-68	Paved. 1 mile	
1969-80	Extended. 1.5 miles	

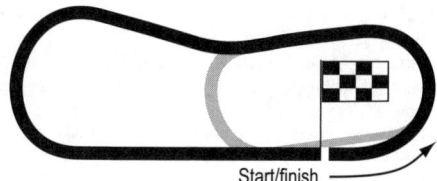

Start/finish

Active years	1946-80
Location	Trenton, New Jersey
Type	Dirt/paved oval

 1969-80 oval
1946-68 oval and final pitlane

CHAMPCAR RACE

year	formula	winner	nat	car	mph
1949	AAA	Myron Fohr	USA	Marchese-Offenhauser	75.765
1957	USAC	Pat O'Connor	USA	Kuzma-Offenhauser	100.279
1958	USAC	Len Sutton	USA	Kuzma-Offenhauser	95.527
	USAC	Rodger Ward	USA	Lesovsky-Offenhauser	99.368
1959	USAC	Tony Bettenhausen	USA	Kuzma-Offenhauser	91.161
	USAC	Eddie Sachs	USA	Meskowski-Offenhauser	97.398
1960	USAC	Rodger Ward	USA	Watson-Offenhauser	95.486
	USAC	Eddie Sachs	USA	Kuzma-Offenhauser	99.223
1961	USAC	Eddie Sachs	USA	Kuzma-Offenhauser	98.680
	USAC	Eddie Sachs	USA	Kuzma-Offenhauser	101.013
1962	USAC	AJ Foyt jr	USA	Meskowski-Offenhauser	101.102
	USAC	Rodger Ward	USA	Watson-Offenhauser	100.977
	USAC	Don Branson	USA	Watson-Offenhauser	102.529
1963	USAC	AJ Foyt Jr	USA	Meskowski-Offenhauser	102.492
	USAC	AJ Foyt Jr	USA	Watson Trevis-Offenhauser	100.403
	USAC	AJ Foyt Jr	USA	Watson Trevis-Offenhauser	101.358
1964	USAC	AJ Foyt Jr	USA	Watson-Offenhauser	104.530
	USAC	AJ Foyt Jr	USA	Watson-Offenhauser	105.590
	USAC	Parnelli Jones	USA	Lotus 34-Ford	96.415
1965	USAC	Jim McElreath	USA	Brabham-Offenhauser	97.186
	USAC	AJ Foyt Jr	USA	Bignotti/Lotus 34-Ford	98.361
	USAC	AJ Foyt Jr	USA	Bignotti/Lotus 34-Ford	99.953
1966	USAC	Rodger Ward	USA	Lola T90-Drake/Offenhauser	99.905
	USAC	Mario Andretti	USA	Brawner/Brabham-Ford	105.127
1967	USAC	Mario Andretti	USA	Brawner/Hawk-Ford	109.838
	USAC	AJ Foyt Jr	USA	Coyote-Ford	92.223
1968	USAC	Bobby Unser	USA	Eagle 68-Drake/Offenhauser	103.397
	USAC	Mario Andretti	USA	Brawner-Drake/Offenhauser	104.543
1969	USAC	Mario Andretti	USA	Brawner/Hawk-Ford	139.591
	USAC	Mario Andretti	USA	Brawner-Ford	134.382
1970	USAC	Lloyd Ruby	USA	Mongoose-Drake/Offenhauser	135.967
	USAC	Al Unser	USA	Colt 70-Ford	137.639
1971	USAC	Mike Mosley	USA	Eagle 71-Ford	132.562
	USAC	Bobby Unser	USA	Eagle 71-Drake/Offenhauser	140.778
1972	USAC	Gary Bettenhausen	USA	McLaren M16B-Offenhauser	145.642
	USAC	Bobby Unser	USA	Eagle 72-Offenhauser	143.880
1973	USAC	AJ Foyt Jr	USA	Coyote-Foyt/Ford	138.359
	USAC	Mario Andretti	USA	Parnelli-Offenhauser	149.626
	USAC	Gordon Johncock	USA	Eagle 73-Offenhauser	135.025
1974	USAC	Bobby Unser	USA	Eagle 74-Offenhauser	128.708
	USAC	AJ Foyt Jr	USA	Coyote-Foyt/Ford	135.372
	USAC	Bobby Unser	USA	Eagle 74-Offenhauser	156.069
1975	USAC	AJ Foyt Jr	USA	Coyote-Foyt/Ford	154.646
	USAC	Gordon Johncock	USA	Wildcat-Offenhauser	123.511
1976	USAC	Johnny Rutherford	USA	McLaren M16E-Offenhauser	147.499
	USAC	Gordon Johncock	USA	Wildcat-DGS/Offenhauser	135.929
1977	USAC	Wally Dallenbach	USA	Wildcat-DGS/Offenhauser	151.288
1978	USAC	Gordon Johncock	USA	Wildcat-DGS/Offenhauser	130.988
	USAC	Mario Andretti	USA	Penske PC6-Cosworth	120.080
1979	CART	Bobby Unser	USA	Penske PC7-Cosworth	121.003
	CART	Bobby Unser	USA	Penske PC7-Cosworth	147.915
	CART	Rick Mears	USA	Penske PC7-Cosworth	129.808

WALT DISNEY WORLD

Built in late 1995 by the Indianapolis Motor Speedway at the southern end of the parking lot for Florida's Walt Disney World. The tri-oval shape of the track was dictated by the space available. Each corner is different, making optimum car set-up difficult to achieve. Opened on 28 November 1995, the Disney World track held the first ever Indy Racing League race in January 1996, but has since dropped from the calendar.

Active years	1995-2000
Location	Southern end of the Magic Kingdom theme park, 10 miles south-west of Orlando, Florida
Type	Paved oval
Lap distance	1.000 miles
Lap records	Qualifying: Buddy Lazier (Lola T95/00-Ford), 19.847s, 181.388 mph, IRL, 1996
	Race: Scott Sharp (Dallara IR7-Aurora), 21.670s, 166.129 mph, IRL, 1999

INDYCAR RACE

year	formula	winner	nat	car	mph
1996	IRL	Buzz Calkins	USA	Reynard 95I-Ford	128.325
1997	IRL	Eddie Cheever	USA	G-Force GF01-Aurora	133.994
1998	IRL	Tony Stewart	USA	G-Force GF01-Aurora	95.150
1999	IRL	Eddie Cheever	USA	Dallara IR7-Aurora	118.522
2000	IRL	Robbie Buhl	USA	G-Force GF05-Aurora	102.292

WATKINS GLEN

The current Bill Milliken-designed road course is the third circuit to have been used in this area of New York State. The first 6.6-mile temporary road course was founded by Cameron Argetsinger and opened on 2 October 1948. It was used until fatal accidents in two successive years forced it to close. A transitional 4.6-mile circuit in the hills was used from 1953 until the permanent venue on a hilltop near Watkins Glen village was opened in 1956. The Glen became the home of Grand Prix racing in the United States in 1961, but it fell into disrepair after the race moved to the unsatisfactory street circuits of Detroit and Phoenix. New management has refurbished the Glen, and it is thriving once more as one of NASCAR's two road courses.

Active years	1956 to date
Location	5 miles south-west of Watkins Glen, New York State, 80 miles south-west of Syracuse, 260 miles north-west of New York City
Type	Permanent road course
Website	www.theglen.com

Current NASCAR circuit

Lap distance	2.454 miles
Lap records	Qualifying: Dale Jarrett (Ford Taurus), 1m11.884, 122.698 mph, NASCAR, 2001

NASCAR Circuit changes

1986-91	2.428 miles
1992 to date	Chicane built before Turn 5. Current circuit

Grand Prix circuit

Lap distance	3.377 miles
Lap records	Qualifying: Bruno Giacomelli (Alfa Romeo 179B), 1m33.291, 130.315 mph, F1, 1980
	Race: Alan Jones (Williams FW07B-Ford), 1m34.068, 129.238 mph, F1, 1980

Grand Prix Circuit changes

1956-70	2.350 miles
1971	Widened, new straight before "The 90". Used for 1971 Sports Car race. 2.430 miles
1971-74	Grand Prix extension opened. 3.377 miles
1975 to date	Chicane inserted. Current circuit

United States Grand Prix see above

CHAMPCAR RACE

year	formula	winner	nat	car	mph
1979	CART	Bobby Unser	USA	Penske PC7-Cosworth	121.012
1980	CART	Bobby Unser	USA	Penske PC9-Cosworth	99.500
1981	CART	Rick Mears	USA	Penske PC9B-Cosworth	108.273

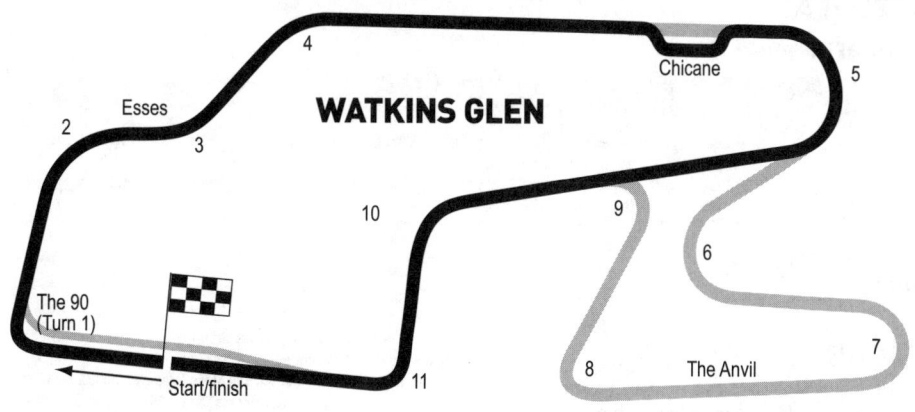

WATKINS GLEN

▬▬▬ NASCAR Circuit and Original Grand Prix circuit (omitting chicane)
▬▬▬ Long Grand Prix Circuit and Pitlane

WORLD SPORTS CAR RACE

year	formula	winner	nat	car	mph
1968	SC W	Jacky Ickx/Lucien Bianchi	B	Ford GT40	111.873
1969	SC W	Jo Siffert/Brian Redman	CH/GB	Porsche 908/8	113.607
1970	SC W	Pedro Rodriguez/Leo Kinnunen	MEX/SF	Porsche 917	120.368
1971	SC W	Andrea de Adamich/Ronnie Peterson	I/S	Alfa Romeo T33/3	112.864
1972	SC W	Jacky Ickx/Mario Andretti	B/USA	Ferrari 312P	109.392
1973	SC W	Henri Pescarolo/Gerard Larrousse	F	Matra-Simca MS670	111.895
1974	SC W	Jean-Pierre Beltoise/Jean-Pierre Jarier	F	Matra-Simca MS670C	108.157
1975	SC W	Henri Pescarolo/Derek Bell	F/GB	Alfa Romeo T33TT/12	85.220
1976	SC W	Rolf Stommelen/Manfred Schurti	D/FL	Porsche 935	97.804
1977	SC W	Jacky Ickx/Jochen Mass	B/D	Porsche 935	96.847
1978	SC W	Toine Hezemans/John Fitzpatrick/Peter Gregg	NL/GB/USA	Porsche 935	81.738
1979	SC W	Don Whittington/Klaus Ludwig/Bill Whittington	USA/D/USA	Porsche 935	98.449
1980	SC W	Riccardo Patrese/Hans Heyer	I/D	Lancia Beta Monte Carlo	77.747
1981	SC W	Riccardo Patrese/Michele Alboreto	I	Lancia Beta Monte Carlo	92.240

FIA GT RACE

year	formula	winner	nat	car	mph
1999	GT FIA	Jean-Philippe Belloc/David Donohue	F/USA	Chrysler Viper GTS-R	107.714

NASCAR RACE

year	formula	winner	nat	car	mph
1986	NASCAR	Tim Richmond	USA	Chevrolet	90.463
1987	NASCAR	Rusty Wallace	USA	Pontiac	90.682
1988	NASCAR	Ricky Rudd	USA	Buick	74.096
1989	NASCAR	Rusty Wallace	USA	Pontiac	87.242
1990	NASCAR	Ricky Rudd	USA	Chevrolet Lumina	97.452
1991	NASCAR	Ernie Irvan	USA	Chevrolet Lumina	98.977
1992	NASCAR	Kyle Petty	USA	Pontiac Grand Prix	85.967
1993	NASCAR	Mark Martin	USA	Ford Thunderbird	84.910
1994	NASCAR	Mark Martin	USA	Ford Thunderbird	93.905
1995	NASCAR	Mark Martin	USA	Ford Thunderbird	100.467
1996	NASCAR	Geoff Bodine	USA	Ford Thunderbird	92.485
1997	NASCAR	Jeff Gordon	USA	Chevrolet Monte Carlo	91.443
1998	NASCAR	Jeff Gordon	USA	Chevrolet Monte Carlo	94.620
1999	NASCAR	Jeff Gordon	USA	Chevrolet Monte Carlo	87.866
2000	NASCAR	Steve Park	USA	Chevrolet Monte Carlo	91.485
2001	NASCAR	Jeff Gordon	USA	Chevrolet Monte Carlo	89.226
2002	NASCAR	Tony Stewart	USA	Pontiac Grand Prix	82.342

VENEZUELA

Major International Races

VENEZUELAN GRAND PRIX						
year	formula	circuit	winner	nat	car	mph
1955	SC	Caracas	Juan Manuel Fangio	RA	Maserati 300S	81.710
1956	SC	Caracas	Stirling Moss	GB	Maserati 300S	84.250
1957	SC W	Caracas	Peter Collins/Phil Hill	GB/USA	Ferrari 412	95.864

Circuits

CARACAS

An international sports car race had been held at Caracas for two years before the event obtained World Championship status in 1957. The course was described as "very tricky" by understated contemporary reports and the drivers association protested to the FIA that it was too dangerous to hold such an event. It did proceed as planned, with one serious accident, but was not repeated.

Active years	**1955-57**
Location	**Central Caracas**
Type	**Temporary street circuit**
Lap distance	**6.170 miles**
Lap records	**Qualifying: Stirling Moss (Maserati 300S), 3m41.4, 100.325 mph, Sports Cars, 1957**
	Race: Stirling Moss (Maserati 300S), 3m38.4, 101.703 mph, Sports Cars, 1957

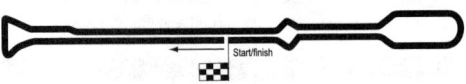

Venezuelan Grand Prix see above

YUGOSLAVIA

Circuits and Races

KALEMAGDAN PARK

Belgrade

The only Yugoslavian Grand Prix was held on a cobbled street circuit in Belgrade on the day that England declared war on Germany in 1939. The circuit was uninspiring and only five cars started. It proved to be Tazio Nuvolari's final GP victory but needless-to-say events elsewhere overshadowed the race!

Active years	**1939 (used once)**
Location	**Kalemagdan Park, central Belgrade**
Type	**Temporary street circuit**
Lap distance	**1.734 miles**
Lap records	**Qualifying: Manfred von Brauchitsch (Mercedes-Benz W163), 1m14.2, 84.129 mph, GP, 1939**
	Race: Hermann Muller (Auto Union D), 1m14.0, 84.357 mph, GP, 1939

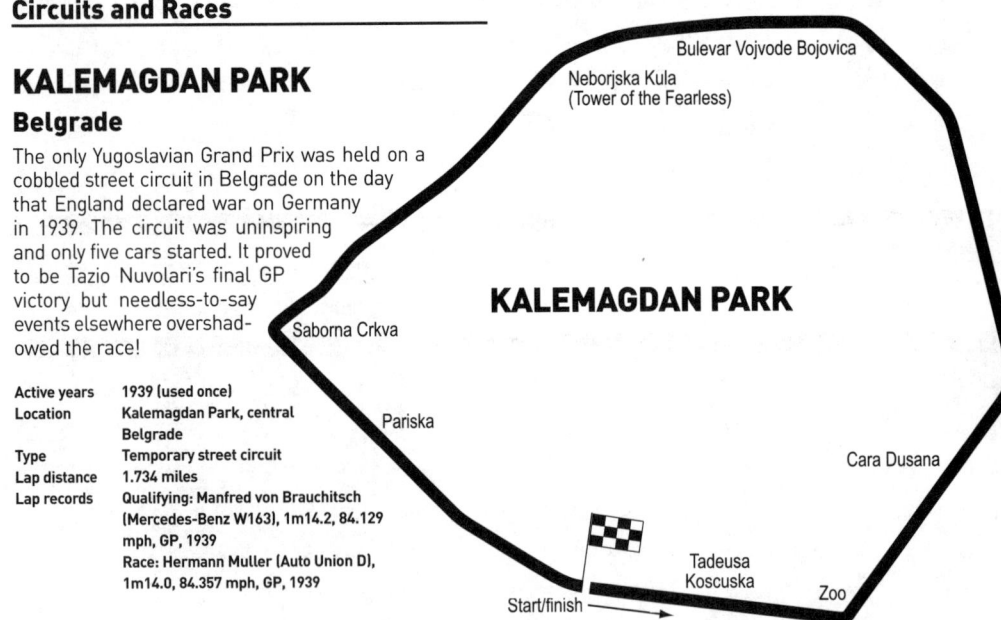

YUGOSLAV GRAND PRIX					
year	formula	winner	nat	car	mph
1939	GP	Tazio Nuvolari	I	Auto Union D	81.201

Drivers A-Z

1930 Tazio Nuvolari celebrates victory in the Tourist Trophy accompanied by Achille Varzi and Giuseppe Campari.

DRIVERS A-Z

The following pages are an index of international racing drivers who have achieved any of the following:

— Raced in World Championship Grands Prix, or attempted to qualify for an event.

— Won a pre-1950 national Grand Prix, or a World Sports Car Championship, FIA GT, Sports-Racing World Championship, IndyCar (AAA, USAC, CART or IRL), NASCAR, Tasman Cup, or European F3 race.

— Scored points in a European F2 or FIA F3000 Championship race.

— Won an important international event, such as non-championship national GPs, Daytona 24 Hours, Sebring 12 Hours, Bathurst, Spa 24 Hours, or Tourist Trophy.

— Won a national championship of F3 or higher, or a national Touring Car Championship overall (class wins not recorded).

Extensive summaries are given for the results achieved in all the above categories for all drivers who have qualified in any one of the above. Points totals are published for series that have had consistent scoring systems (F1, F2 and F3000) which allow comparison. The total number of fastest laps is given for each series/race where known but it should be noted that US championships such as CART and IRL have only recently started publishing details so these records are incomplete. Details of World Sports Car Championship careers are only included when a driver has finished in the top 6 in a race; with over 10,000 drivers having competed it would be impossible to do otherwise. The total for Pre-1950 Grands Prix are for the races detailed in the chapter on Early Grand Prix racing from 1900-49.

Every care has been taken to publish driver's dates of birth and, where relevant, death but on occasion it has proved impossible to find the information. In some instances different sources record conflicting biographical information, in which case I have published what I consider to be the most likely.

Note: number in brackets is occasions on which a driver did not qualify or start for a major single-seater championship event.

A

Rauno Aaltonen
SF. Born: 17.1.1938, Turku

formula	years	starts (DNS)	wins	2nd	3rd	4th	5th	6th	PP	FL	points
Le Mans	1965	1	-	-	-	-	-	-	-	-	

Major win: 1966 Bathurst

Carlo Abate
I. Born: 10.7.1932, Turin

formula	years	starts (DNS)	wins	2nd	3rd	4th	5th	6th	PP	FL	points
Le Mans	1961-63	3	-	-	-	-	-	-	-	-	
SC W	1957-64		1	-	1	1	1	-	-	-	

Win: 1963 Targa Florio
Other Major Win: 1959 Mille Miglia (regularity test)

George Abecassis
GB. Born: 21.3.1913, Chertsey, Surrey. Died: 18.12.1991, Ibstone, Buckinghamshire

formula	years	starts (DNS)	wins	2nd	3rd	4th	5th	6th	PP	FL	points
F1 W	1951-52	2	-	-	-	-	-	-	-	-	0

Best result: no finishes. Best qualifying: 10th. Team: HWM

formula	years	starts (DNS)	wins	2nd	3rd	4th	5th	6th	PP	FL	points
GP Pre-50	1948-49	3	-	-	-	-	-	-			
Le Mans	1950-53	3	-	-	-	2	-	-			
SC W	1953-55		-	1	-	1	-	-			

Johann Abt
D
1970 European Touring Car Champion (1000cc class)

Kenneth Acheson
GB. Born: 27.11.1957, Cookstown, Northern Ireland
1987 Japanese Sports-Prototype Champion (with Kunimitsu Takahashi)

formula	years	starts (DNS)	wins	2nd	3rd	4th	5th	6th	PP	FL	points
F1 W	1983-85	3 (7)	-	-	-	-	-	-	-	-	0

Best result: 12th. Best qualifying: 23rd. Team: RAM

| Le Mans | 1989-95 | 6 | - | 2 | 1 | - | - | - | | | |
| SC W | 1985-92 | | 2 | 4 | 3 | 2 | 3 | - | - | - | |

Wins: 1989 Brands Hatch, Spa. Best championship: 1989, 4th

| F2 E | 1981-83 | 29 | - | 2 | 1 | 1 | 1 | 2 | - | 1 | 23 |

Best championship: 1982, 7th

| F3000 INT | 1986 | 1 | | | | | | | | | 0 |
| CART | 1984 | 1 | | | | | | | | | |

Charles van Acker
USA. Born: 14.3.1912, Brussels (B). Died: 31.5.1998, South Bend, Indiana

formula	years	starts (DNS)	wins	2nd	3rd	4th	5th	6th	PP	FL	points
Indy 500	1947-49	3	-	-	-	-	-	-			

Champcar Win: 1 – 1947 Milwaukee race 2

Herb Adamczyk
HK
Major wins: 1976 and 1979 Macau Guia race

Andrea de Adamich
I. Born: 3.10.1941, Trieste
1966 and 1967 European Touring Car Champion (1600cc class), 1968 Temporada F2 Champion, 1965 Italian F3 Champion

formula	years	starts (DNS)	wins	2nd	3rd	4th	5th	6th	PP	FL	points
F1 W	1968-73	30 (6)	-	-	-	2	-	-	-	-	6

Best championship: 1973, 15th. Best result: 4th. Best qualifying: 7th. Teams: Ferrari, McLaren, March, Surtees, Brabham

| Le Mans | 1970-72 | | - | - | 1 | - | - | - | | | |
| SC W | 1964-74 | | 2 | 3 | 9 | 4 | 3 | - | - | - | |

Wins: 1971 Brands Hatch, Watkins Glen

| F2 E | 1967-73 | 11 (1) | - | 1 | - | 1 | - | - | - | - | 10 |

Best championship: 1968, 10th
Other Major Win: 1967 Tourist Trophy (Oulton)

Tony Adamowicz
USA. Born: 2.5.1941, Torrance, California
1969 North American Formula A (F5000) Champion

formula	years	starts (DNS)	wins	2nd	3rd	4th	5th	6th	PP	FL	points
Le Mans	1970-84	4	-	-	-	1	-	-			
SC W	1968-89		-	2	1	1	1	-	-	-	

Nick Adams
GB. Born: 7.8.1948, Braunton, Devon
1989 World Group C2 Sports Car Champion (with Fermin Velez)

formula	years	starts (DNS)	wins	2nd	3rd	4th	5th	6th	PP	FL	points
Le Mans	1985-95	9	-	-	-	-	-	-			
SC W	1985-92		-	-	-	-	1	-	-	-	

Philippe Adams
B. Born: 19.11.1969, Mouscron, Hainaut
1993 British F2 Champion

formula	years	starts (DNS)	wins	2nd	3rd	4th	5th	6th	PP	FL	points
F1 W	1994	2	-	-	-	-	-	-	-	-	0

Best result: 16th. Best qualifying: 25th. Team: Lotus

A

Walt Ader

USA. Born: 15.12.1913, Long Valley, New Jersey. Died: 25.11.1982, Califon, New Jersey

formula	years	starts (DNS)	wins	2nd	3rd	4th	5th	6th	PP	FL	points
Indy 500	1950	1	-	-	-	-	-	-	-	-	

Champcar Win: 1 – 1947 Atlanta

Kurt Adolff

D. Born: 5.11.1921, Stuttgart

formula	years	starts (DNS)	wins	2nd	3rd	4th	5th	6th	PP	FL	points
F1 W	1953	1	-	-	-	-	-	-	-	-	0

Best result: no finishes. Best qualifying: 27th. Team: Ecurie Espadon

Fred "Doc" Agabashian

USA. Born: 21.8.1913, Modesto, California. Died: 13.10.1989, Alamo, California

formula	years	starts (DNS)	wins	2nd	3rd	4th	5th	6th	PP	FL	points
Indy 500	1947-57	11	-	-	-	1	-	1	1	-	

Champcar win: 1 – 1949 Sacramento

Rui Aguas

P. Born: 29.2.1972, Mozambique

formula	years	starts (DNS)	wins	2nd	3rd	4th	5th	6th	PP	FL	points
F3000 INT	1997-98	16	-	-	1	2	-	-	1		7

Best championship: 1997, 10th

Karl Heinrich "Kurt" Ahrens Jr

D. Born: 19.4.1940, Braunschweig, near Hannover
1961 and 1963 German Formula Junior Champion

formula	years	starts (DNS)	wins	2nd	3rd	4th	5th	6th	PP	FL	points
F1 W	1966-69	4	-	-	-	-	-	-	-	-	0

Best result: 12th. Best qualifying: 17th. Teams: Caltex, Ron Harris, Brabham, driver

formula	years	starts (DNS)	wins	2nd	3rd	4th	5th	6th	PP	FL	points
Le Mans	1969-70	2	-	-	-	-	-	1	-		
SC W	1962-75	2	2	4	-	-	1	1	-		

Wins: 1969 Austrian GP, 1970 Nurburgring

formula	years	starts (DNS)	wins	2nd	3rd	4th	5th	6th	PP	FL	points
F2 E	1968-69	12	-	-	1	2	1	-	-	-	19

Best championship: 1968, 6th

Laurent Aiello

F. Born: 23.5.1969, Fontenay-aux-Roses
1994 French Touring Car Champion, 1997 German Super Touring Car Champion, 1999 British Touring Car Champion, 2002 German Touring Car Champion

formula	years	starts (DNS)	wins	2nd	3rd	4th	5th	6th	PP	FL	points
Le Mans	1998-2001	4	1	2	-	1	-	-	-	1	

Win: 1998 Le Mans 24 hrs

formula	years	starts (DNS)	wins	2nd	3rd	4th	5th	6th	PP	FL	points
F3000 INT	1991-92	19 (1)	-	-	1	-	1	1	1	-	7

Best championship: 1992, 13th

Other major wins: 1990 Monaco F3, 2001 Sebring 12 hrs

Johnny Aitken

USA. Born: 3.5.1885, Indianapolis, Indiana. Died: 15.10.1918, influenza

formula	years	starts (DNS)	wins	2nd	3rd	4th	5th	6th	PP	FL	points
GP Pre-50	1916	1	1	-	-	-	-	-	-	-	

Win: 1916 American GP

formula	years	starts (DNS)	wins	2nd	3rd	4th	5th	6th	PP	FL	points
Indy 500	1911-16	3	-	-	1	1	-	-	1	-	

Champcar wins: 7 – 1910 Atlanta race 4, Indianapolis race 9, 1916 Cincinnati, Indianapolis race 2, Sheepshead race 2, Sheepshead race 3, American GP

Bob Akin

USA. Born: 6.3.1936, North Tarrytown, New York State. Died: 30.4.2002, following an accident at Road Atlanta

formula	years	starts (DNS)	wins	2nd	3rd	4th	5th	6th	PP	FL	points
Le Mans	1978-84	6	-	-	-	1	-	-	-		
SC W	1978-87		-	1	1	1	-	4	-	-	

Best championship: 1981, 8th

Major wins: 1979 and 1986 Sebring 12 hrs

Christijan Albers

NL. Born: 16.4.1979, Eindhoven
1999 German F3 Champion

formula	years	starts (DNS)	wins	2nd	3rd	4th	5th	6th	PP	FL	points
F3000 INT	2000	9 (1)	-	-	-	-	-	-	-	-	0

Michele Alboreto

I. Born: 23.12.1956, Milan. Died: 25.4.2001, Lausitzring, sports car testing
1980 European F3 Champion

formula	years	starts (DNS)	wins	2nd	3rd	4th	5th	6th	PP	FL	points
F1 W	1981-94	194 (21)	5	9	9	10	8	6	2	5	186.5

Wins: 1982 Las Vegas GP, 1983 Detroit GP, 1984 Belgian GP, 1985 Canadian GP, German GP. Best championship: 1985, 2nd. Best qualifying: 1st. Teams: Tyrrell, Ferrari, Larrousse, Arrows, Footwork, Scuderia Italia, Minardi

formula	years	starts (DNS)	wins	2nd	3rd	4th	5th	6th	PP	FL	points
Le Mans	1981-2000	8	1	-	1	1	-	-	1	-	

Win: 1997 Le Mans 24 hrs

formula	years	starts (DNS)	wins	2nd	3rd	4th	5th	6th	PP	FL	points
SC W	1980-92		4	3	-	1	-	-	1	2	

Wins: 1981 Watkins Glen, 1982 Silverstone, Nurburgring, Mugello. Best championship: 1982, 5th

formula	years	starts (DNS)	wins	2nd	3rd	4th	5th	6th	PP	FL	points
F2 E	1981	10	1	-	1	-	-	-	1	1	13

Win: 1981 Misano. Best championship: 1981, 8th

formula	years	starts (DNS)	wins	2nd	3rd	4th	5th	6th	PP	FL	points
Indy 500	1996	1	-	-	-	-	-	-	-	-	
IRL	1996	5	-	-	1	1	-	-	-		

F3 E wins: 4 – 1980 Osterreichring, La Chatre, Monza, Kassel-Calden

Other major wins: 2000 Petit LeMans, 2001 Sebring 12 hrs

"Alencar Jr"

BR. Born: 19.4.1954
1982 Brazilian Stock Car Champion

Giovanni "Jean" Alesi

F. Born: 11.6.1964, Montfavet, near Avignon
1989 FIA F3000 Champion,
1987 French F3 Champion

formula	years	starts (DNS)	wins	2nd	3rd	4th	5th	6th	PP	FL	points
F1 W	1989-2001	201 (1)	1	16	15	11	15	12	2	4	241

Win: 1995 Canadian GP. Best championship: 1997, 3rd. Best qualifying: 1st. Teams: Tyrrell, Ferrari, Benetton, Sauber, Prost, Jordan

formula	years	starts (DNS)	wins	2nd	3rd	4th	5th	6th	PP	FL	points
Le Mans	1989	1	-	-	-	-	-	-	-	-	
F3000 INT	1988-89	20	3	2	-	1	3	2	2	1	50

Wins: 1989 Pau, Birmingham, Spa. Best championship: 1989, 1st

Jeff Allam

GB. Born: 19.12.1954, Epsom, Surrey

formula	years	starts (DNS)	wins	2nd	3rd	4th	5th	6th	PP	FL	points
Le Mans	1982-83	2	-	-	-	-	-	-	-	-	
SC W	1979-83		-	-	-	1	-	-	-		

Major win: 1986 Tourist Trophy (Silverstone)

Johnny Allen

USA. Born: 17.9.1934
NASCAR wins: 1

Niel Allen

AUS
Tasman wins: 3 – 1970 Sandown Park, 1971 New Zealand GP, Teretonga

Tom Alley

USA. Born: 1890, Metamora, Indiana. Died: 26.3.1953, Indianapolis, Indiana

formula	years	starts (DNS)	wins	2nd	3rd	4th	5th	6th	PP	FL	points
GP Pre-50	1915	1	-	-	-	-	-	-	-	-	
Indy 500	1913-22	7	-	-	-	-	1	-	-	-	

Champcar wins: 2 – 1914 Minneapolis, 1917 Chicago race 4

Philippe Alliot

F. Born: 27.7.1954, Voves, Eure-et-Loir
1978 French Formula Renault Champion

formula	years	starts (DNS)	wins	2nd	3rd	4th	5th	6th	PP	FL	points
F1 W	1984-94	109 (7)	-	-	-	-	1	5	-	-	7

Best championship: 1987, 16th. Best qualifying: 5th. Teams: RAM, Ligier, Larrousse, McLaren

| Le Mans | 1981-96 | 9 | - | - | 3 | - | - | 3 | - | | |
| SC W | 1980-92 | | 3 | 2 | 3 | 1 | - | 1 | 5 | 3 | |

Wins: 1991 Suzuka, 1992 Donington, Magny-Cours. Best championships: 1991 and 1992, 3rd

| F2 E | 1983 | 10 (1) | - | - | - | - | 2 | - | 1 | 1 | 4 |
| F3000 INT | 1985-86 | 7 | 1 | - | - | - | - | 1 | 1 | - | 10 |

Win: 1986 Spa. Best championship: 1986, 9th

F3 E wins: 3 – 1981 Magny-Cours, La Chatre, 1982 La Chatre

Bobby Allison

USA. Born: 3.12.1937, Miami, Florida
1983 NASCAR Champion, 1980 IROC Champion

formula	years	starts (DNS)	wins	2nd	3rd	4th	5th	6th	PP	FL	points
Indy 500	1973-75	2	-	-	-	-	-	-	-	-	-

NASCAR wins: 84 (54 in Modern era) including 1978, 1982, 1988 Daytona 500, 1981, 1984 World 600

Cliff Allison

GB. Born: 8.2.1932, Brough, Westmorland

formula	years	starts (DNS)	wins	2nd	3rd	4th	5th	6th	PP	FL	points
F1 W	1958-61	16 (2)	-	1	-	1	2	2	-	-	11

Best championship: 1960, 12th. Best qualifying: 5th. Teams: Lotus, Ferrari, BRP

| Le Mans | 1956-61 | 5 | - | - | - | - | - | - | - | | |
| SC W | 1955-61 | | 1 | 1 | 2 | - | 1 | 1 | - | | |

Win: 1960 Buenos Aires

Davey Allison

USA. Born: 25.2.1961, Hollywood, near Miami, Florida. Died: 13.7.1993, Talladega, helicopter accident
1993 IROC Champion

NASCAR wins: 19 (all Modern era) including 1992 Daytona 500, 1991 World 600

Donnie Allison

USA. Born: 7.9.1939, Miami, Florida

formula	years	starts (DNS)	wins	2nd	3rd	4th	5th	6th	PP	FL	points
Indy 500	1970-71	2	-	-	-	1	-	1	-		

NASCAR wins: 10 (4 in Modern era)

AJ Allmendinger

USA. Born: 16.12.1981
2002 Barber-Dodge Champion

Fernando Alonso

E. Born: 29.7.1981, Oviedo
1999 Spanish Formula Nissan Champion

formula	years	starts (DNS)	wins	2nd	3rd	4th	5th	6th	PP	FL	points
F1 W	2001	17	-	-	-	-	-	-	-	-	0

Best result: 10th. Best qualifying: 17th. Team: Minardi

| F3000 INT | 2000 | 9 (1) | 1 | 1 | - | - | 1 | 1 | 2 | | 17 |

Win: 2000 Spa. Best championship: 2000, 4th

Bill Alsup

USA. Born: 15.7.1938, Honolulu, Hawaii
1978 SCCA Super Vee champion

formula	years	starts (DNS)	wins	2nd	3rd	4th	5th	6th	PP	FL	points
Indy 500	1981	1	-	-	-	-	-	-	-	-	-
CART	1979-84	56 (6)	-	-	3	3	3	1	-	-	

Best championship: 1981, 2nd

Uwe Alzen

D. Born: 18.8.1967, Kirchen
1994 Porsche Supercup Champion, 1995 German GT Champion, 1999 German Super Touring Car Champion

formula	years	starts (DNS)	wins	2nd	3rd	4th	5th	6th	PP	FL	points
Le Mans	1998-99	2	-	1	-	-	-	-	-	-	-

Major win: 1993 Spa 24 hrs

Giovanna Amati

I. Born: 20.7.1962, Rome

formula	years	starts (DNS)	wins	2nd	3rd	4th	5th	6th	PP	FL	points
F1 W	1992	0 (3)	-	-	-	-	-	-	-	-	0

Best result: no starts. Best qualifying: 30th. Team: Brabham

| F3000 INT | 1987-91 | 14 (18) | - | - | - | - | - | - | - | - | 0 |

Bill Amick

USA. Born: 16.11.1925

NASCAR win: 1

George Amick

USA. Born: 24.10.1924, Vernonia, Oregon. Died: 4.4.1959, Daytona, Champcar race

formula	years	starts (DNS)	wins	2nd	3rd	4th	5th	6th	PP	FL	points
Indy 500	1958	1	-	1	-	-	-	-	-	-	

Champcar wins: 3 – 1956 Langhorne, Phoenix, 1957 Atlanta

Chris Amon

NZ. Born: 20.7.1943, Bulls
1969 Tasman Champion

formula	years	starts (DNS)	wins	2nd	3rd	4th	5th	6th	PP	FL	points
F1 W	1963-76	96 (12)	-	3	8	4	7	7	5	3	83

Best championship: 1967, 4th. Best qualifying: 1st. Teams: Reg Parnell, Ian Raby, Cooper, Amon, Ferrari, March, Matra, Tecno, Tyrrell, BRM, Ensign, Williams

| Le Mans | 1964-73 | 8 | 1 | - | - | - | - | - | - | | |

Win: 1966 Le Mans 24 hrs

| SC W | 1964-73 | | 3 | 3 | 1 | 2 | 3 | - | 2 | 2 | |

Wins: 1966 Le Mans 24 hrs, 1967 Daytona 24 hrs, Monza

| F2 E | 1968-70 | 3 | - | - | - | - | 1 | - | - | | 0 |

Non-championship F1 wins: 1970 International Trophy (Silverstone), 1971 Argentinian GP

Tasman wins: 7 – 1968 New Zealand GP, Levin, 1969 New Zealand GP, Levin, Australian GP, Sandown Park, 1975 Teretonga

Ni Amorim

P. Born: 1.3.1962, Porto
1993 Portuguese Touring Car Champion

formula	years	starts (DNS)	wins	2nd	3rd	4th	5th	6th	PP	FL	points
Le Mans	1998-2001	4	-	-	-	-	-	-	-	-	-

"Amphicar" (Eugenio Renna)

I

formula	years	starts (DNS)	wins	2nd	3rd	4th	5th	6th	PP	FL	points
SC W	1967-80		-	1	-	1	3	2	-	-	

Major win: 1976 Targa Florio

Robert Amren

S. Born: 19.12.1968
1992 Barber-SAAB Champion

Bob Anderson

RSR/GB. Born: 19.5.1931, Hendon, London (GB). Died: 14.8.1967, Northampton, following a testing accident at Silverstone

formula	years	starts (DNS)	wins	2nd	3rd	4th	5th	6th	PP	FL	points
F1 W	1963-67	25 (4)	-	-	1	-	1	2	-	-	8

Best championship: 1964, 11th. Best qualifying: 7th. Teams: DW Racing Enterprises, driver

Non-championship F1 wins: 1963 Rome GP (Vallelunga), 1966 Rhodesian GP (Kumalo)

Gil Anderson

USA. Born: 1880, Norway. Died: 26.7.1935

formula	years	starts (DNS)	wins	2nd	3rd	4th	5th	6th	PP	FL	points
GP Pre-50	1912-15	23	-	-	1	1	1	-	-		
Indy 500	1911-16	6	-	-	1	-	1	-			

Champcar wins: 3 – 1913 Elgin race 2, 1915 Elgin race 2, Sheepshead race 1

Poul Anderssen
DK
1961 Danish 500cc Champion

Conny Andersson
S. Born: 28.12.1939, Alingas, near Gothenburg
1972 and 1974 Swedish F3 Champion

formula	years	starts (DNS)	wins	2nd	3rd	4th	5th	6th	PP	FL	points
F1 W	1976-77	1 (4)	-	-	-	-	-	-	-	-	0

Best result: no finishes. Best qualifying: 26th. Teams: Surtees, Stanley BRM
F3 E wins: 5 – 1975 Anderstorp, 1976 Nurburgring, Avus, Croix-en-Ternois, Knutstorp

Gunnar Andersson
S. Born: 1927, Ragard
Major win: 1961 Mille Miglia (regularity test)

Leo Andersson
S. Born: 20.5.1955
1983 Swedish F3 Champion

Per-Gunnar "Peggan" Andersson
S. Born: 15.8.1957, Falkenberg
1993 and 1995 Nordic Touring Car Champion, 1987, 1989, 1991, 1992 and 1993 Swedish Touring Car Champion

Emil Andres
USA. Born: 22.2.1911, Chicago, Illinois. Died: 20.7.1999, after falling at home

formula	years	starts (DNS)	wins	2nd	3rd	4th	5th	6th	PP	FL	points
Indy 500	1936-49	10	-	-	-	1	-	-	-	-	

Champcar win: 1 – 1948 Milwaukee race 1

John Andretti
USA. Born: 12.3.1963, Bethlehem, Pennsylvania

formula	years	starts (DNS)	wins	2nd	3rd	4th	5th	6th	PP	FL	points
Le Mans	1988	1	-	-	-	-	-	1	-	-	
SC W	1988-93		-	-	-	-	-	1	-	-	
Indy 500	1988-94	7	-	-	-	1	-	1	-	-	
CART	1987-94	73	1	1	-	2	8	8	-	-	

Win: 1991 Surfers Paradise. Best championships: 1991 and 1992, 8th
NASCAR wins: 2 (both Modern era)
Other Major win: 1989 Daytona 24 hrs

Mario Andretti
USA. Born: 28.2.1940, Montona, near Trieste (I)
1978 F1 World Champion, 1965, 1966 and 1969 Champcar Champion, 1984 CART Champion, 1979 IROC Champion

formula	years	starts (DNS)	wins	2nd	3rd	4th	5th	6th	PP	FL	points
F1 W	1968-82	128 (3)	12	2	5	7	7	5	18	10	180

Wins: 1971 South African GP, 1976 Long Beach GP, 1977 Long Beach GP, French GP, Italian GP, 1978 Argentinian GP, Belgian GP, Spanish GP, French GP, German GP, Dutch GP. Best championship: 1978, 1st. Best qualifying: 1st. Teams: Lotus, STP, Ferrari, Parnelli, Alfa Romeo, Williams

Le Mans	1966-2000	8	-	1	-	-	1	-	1
SC W	1965-92		7	2	3	1	-	2	6	1

Wins: 1967 Sebring 12 hrs, 1970 Sebring 12 hrs, 1972 Daytona, Sebring 12 hrs, Brands Hatch, Watkins Glen, 1974 Monza

Indy 500	1965-94	29	1	2	1	1	1	3	-

Win: 1969 Indianapolis 500
Pre-CART Champcar wins: 33 – 1965 Indianapolis Raceway Park, 1966 Milwaukee race 1, Langhorne 1, Atlanta, Indianapolis Raceway Park, Milwaukee race 2, Indiana State Fairgrounds, Trenton race 2, Phoenix race 2, 1967 Trenton race 1, Indianapolis Raceway Park, Langhorne race 2, St Jovite race 1, St Jovite race 2, Milwaukee race 2, Indiana State Fairgrounds, Phoenix race 2, 1968 St Jovite race 1, St Jovite race 2, Du Quoin, Trenton race 2, 1969 Hanford, Indianapolis 500, Pikes Peak, Nazareth, Trenton race 1, Springfield, Trenton race 2, Seattle race 1, Riverside, 1970 Castle Rock, 1973 Trenton race 2, 1978 Trenton

formula	years	starts (DNS)	wins	2nd	3rd	4th	5th	6th	PP	FL	points
CART	1979-94	208 (1)	19	23	21	15	18	6	29	-	

Wins: 1980 Michigan, 1983 Elkhart Lake, Las Vegas, 1984 Long Beach, Meadowlands, Michigan 500, Elkhart Lake, Mid-Ohio, Michigan, 1985 Long Beach, Milwaukee, Portland, 1986 Portland, Pocono 500, 1987 Long Beach, Elkhart Lake, 1988 Phoenix, Cleveland, 1993 Phoenix. Best championship: 1984, 1st.
Non-championship F1 win: 1971 Questor GP
NASCAR wins: 1 – 1967 Daytona 500

Michael Andretti
USA. Born: 5.10.1962, Bethlehem, Pennsylvania
1991 CART Champion, 1983 North American Formula Atlantic Champion, 1982 SCCA Super Vee Champion

formula	years	starts (DNS)	wins	2nd	3rd	4th	5th	6th	PP	FL	points
F1 W	1993	13	-	-	1	-	1	1	-	-	7

Best championship: 1993, 11th. Best qualifying: 5th. Team: McLaren

Le Mans	1983-97	3	-	-	1	-	1	-	-
SC W	1983-92		-	1	-	-	1	-	-
Indy 500	1984-2002	13	-	1	1	1	1	2	-	1
CART	1983-2002	309 (1)	42	34	22	22	16	13	32	13

Wins: 1986 Long Beach, Milwaukee, Phoenix, 1987 Milwaukee, Michigan 500, Nazareth, Miami, 1989 Toronto, Michigan 500, 1990 Detroit, Portland, Meadowlands, Mid-Ohio, Elkhart Lake, 1991 Milwaukee, Portland, Cleveland, Toronto, Vancouver, Mid-Ohio, Elkhart Lake, Laguna Seca, 1992 Portland, Milwaukee, Toronto, Vancouver, Laguna Seca, 1994 Surfers Paradise, Toronto, 1995 Toronto, 1996 Nazareth, Milwaukee, Detroit, Elkhart Lake, Vancouver, 1997 Miami, 1998 Miami, 1999 St Louis, 2000 Motegi, Toronto, 2001 Toronto, 2002 Long Beach. Best championship: 1991, 1st

IRL	2001-02	2	-	-	1	-	-	-	-

Keith Andrews
USA. Born: 15.6.1920, Denver, Colorado. Died: 15.5.1957, Indianapolis, practice

formula	years	starts (DNS)	wins	2nd	3rd	4th	5th	6th	PP	FL	points
Indy 500	1955-56	2	-	-	-	-	-	-	-	-	

Champcar win: 1 – 1954 Pikes Peak

Gaston Andrey
CH. Born: 8.8.1926
1966 Trans-Am Champion (with Horst Kwech)

Jean-Claude Andruet
F. Born: 13.8.1940, Montreuil, Pas de Calais

formula	years	starts (DNS)	wins	2nd	3rd	4th	5th	6th	PP	FL	points
Le Mans	1967-89	19	-	-	-	-	2	-	-	
SC W	1967-89		-	2	-	3	-	-	-	

Major win: 1977 Spa 24 hrs

Steven Andskar
S. Born: 30.10.1964, Stockholm
1985 Nordic F3 Champion

formula	years	starts (DNS)	wins	2nd	3rd	4th	5th	6th	PP	FL	points
Le Mans	1989-94	6	-	-	1	1	1	-	-	
SC W	1989-92		-	1	-	3	1	-	-	
F3000 INT	1986-88	9 (8)	-	-	-	-	-	-	-	0

Massimiliano "Max" Angelelli
I. Born: 15.12.1966, Bologna
1992 Italian F3 Champion

formula	years	starts (DNS)	wins	2nd	3rd	4th	5th	6th	PP	FL	points
Le Mans	1999-2002	4	-	-	-	-	-	-	-	
F3000 INT	1991	1	-	-	-	-	-	-	-	0

Elio de Angelis
I. Born: 26.3.1958, Rome. Died: 15.5.1986,
Marseille Hospital, following a testing accident at
Paul Ricard on the previous day
1977 Italian F3 Champion

formula	years	starts (DNS)	wins	2nd	3rd	4th	5th	6th	PP	FL	points
F1 W	1979-86	108 (1)	2	2	5	11	17	6	3	-	122

Wins: 1982 Austrian GP, 1985 San Marino GP. Best championship: 1984, 3rd.
Best qualifying: 1st. Teams: Shadow, Lotus, Brabham

formula	years	starts (DNS)	wins	2nd	3rd	4th	5th	6th	PP	FL	points
F2 E	1977-78	13 (1)	-	-	1	-	-	-	-	-	4

Best championship: 1978, 14th
F3 E win: 1 – 1977 Monza
Other Major win: 1978 Monaco F3

Michael Angus
USA
1985 North American Formula Atlantic (Eastern) Champion

"Apache"
I
Major win: 1977 Targa Florio

Marco Apicella
I. Born: 7.10.1965, Bologna
1994 Japanese F3000 Champion

formula	years	starts (DNS)	wins	2nd	3rd	4th	5th	6th	PP	FL	points
F1 W	1993	1	-	-	-	-	-	-	-	-	0

Best result: no finishes. Best qualifying: 23rd. Team: Jordan

| Le Mans | 1995-99 | 2 | - | - | - | - | - | - | - | - | |
| F3000 INT | 1987-99 | 52 (2) | - | 7 | 3 | 3 | 4 | 1 | 2 | 6 | 71 |

Best championship: 1989, 4th

Luis Miguel Arias
E
1987 Spanish Touring Car Champion

Paul Armagnac
F. Born: 1924. Died: 20.10.1962, Montlhery, Paris 1000 kms practice

formula	years	starts	wins	2nd	3rd	4th	5th	6th	PP	FL	points
Le Mans	1955-62	8	-	-	-	-	-	-	-	-	

Major win: 1954 Tourist Trophy handicap

Billy Arnold
USA. Born: 16.12.1905, Chicago, Illinois. Died: 10.11.1976, Oklahoma City
1930 Champcar Champion

formula	years	starts (DNS)	wins	2nd	3rd	4th	5th	6th	PP	FL	points
Indy 500	1928-32	5	1	-	-	-	-	-	1	-	

Win: 1930 Indianapolis 500
Champcar wins: 3 – 1930 Indianapolis 500, Altoona race 1, Altoona race 2

Charles Arnold
USA. Born: n/a. Died: 19??

formula	years	starts (DNS)	wins	2nd	3rd	4th	5th	6th	PP	FL	points
Indy 500	1912	1	-	-	-	-	-	-	-	-	

Champcar win: 1 – 1909 Portland race 2

Rene Arnoux
F. Born: 4.7.1948, Pontcharra, near Grenoble
1977 European F2 Champion, 1973 and 1975
European Formula Renault Champion

formula	years	starts (DNS)	wins	2nd	3rd	4th	5th	6th	PP	FL	points
F1 W	1978-89	149 (15)	7	9	7	8	5	18	12	181	

Wins: 1980 Brazilian GP, South African GP, 1982 French GP, Italian GP, 1983
Canadian GP, German GP, Dutch GP. Best championship: 1983, 3rd. Best qualifying: 1st. Teams: Martini, Surtees, Renault, Ferrari, Ligier

| Le Mans | 1977-95 | 3 | - | - | - | - | - | - | - | - | |

formula	years	starts (DNS)	wins	2nd	3rd	4th	5th	6th	PP	FL	points
F2 E	1974-77	26	6	5	1	1	2	1	2	6	104

Wins: 1976 Pau, Enna, Estoril, 1977 Silverstone, Pau, Nogaro. Best championship: 1977, 1st

Didier Artzet
F. Born: 10.2.1963, Nice

formula	years	starts (DNS)	wins	2nd	3rd	4th	5th	6th	PP	FL	points
Le Mans	1989-92	2	-	-	-	-	-	-	-	-	
F3000 INT	1988-90	11 (3)	-	-	1	-	-	-	-	-	4

Best championship: 1990, 15th
Major win: 1987 Monaco F3

Peter Arundell
GB. Born: 8.11.1933, Ilford, Essex
1963 British Formula Junior Champion

formula	years	starts (DNS)	wins	2nd	3rd	4th	5th	6th	PP	FL	points
F1 W	1963-66	11 (2)	-	-	2	1	-	1	-	-	12

Best championship: 1964, 8th. Best qualifying: 4th. Team: Lotus
Major wins: 1961 and 1962 Monaco Formula Junior

Alberto Ascari
I. Born: 13.7.1918, Milan. Died: 26.5.1955,
Monza, testing
1952 and 1953 World Champion

formula	years	starts (DNS)	wins	2nd	3rd	4th	5th	6th	PP	FL	points
F1 W	1950-55	31 (1)	13	4	-	2	1	1	14	13	140.64

Wins: 1951 German GP, Italian GP, 1952 Belgian GP, French GP, British GP,
German GP, Dutch GP, Italian GP, 1953 Argentinian GP, Dutch GP, Belgian GP,
British GP, Swiss GP. Best championships: 1952 and 1953, 1st. Best qualifying:
1st. Teams: Ferrari, Maserati, Lancia

| GP Pre-50 | 1947-49 | 10 | | 2 | 1 | 2 | 1 | 3 | - | 1 | 2 |

Wins: 1949 Swiss GP, Italian GP

| Le Mans | 1952-53 | 2 | - | - | - | - | - | - | 1 | 2 | |
| SC W | 1953-54 | 2 | - | - | - | - | - | - | 2 | 2 | |

Wins: 1953 Nurburgring, 1954 Mille Miglia

| Indy 500 | 1952 | 1 | - | - | - | - | - | - | - | - | |

Non-championship F1 wins: 1950 Penya Rhin, 1951 San Remo, 1955 Valentino,
Naples
Other major wins: 1948 Pescara GP, 1949 International Trophy (Silverstone),
1950 German GP

Antonio Ascari
I. Born: 15.9.1888, Moratica di Bonferraro, Sorga. Died: 26.7.1925,
Montlhery, French GP

formula	years	starts (DNS)	wins	2nd	3rd	4th	5th	6th	PP	FL	points
GP Pre-50	1923-25	4 (1)	2	-	-	-	-	-	1	2	

Wins: 1924 Italian GP, 1925 Belgian GP

Peter Ashdown
GB. Born: 16.10.1934, Danbury, Essex

formula	years	starts (DNS)	wins	2nd	3rd	4th	5th	6th	PP	FL	points
F1 W	1959	1	-	-	-	-	-	-	-	-	0

Best result: 12th. Best qualifying: 23rd. Team: Alan Brown

| Le Mans | 1960 | 1 | - | - | - | - | - | - | - | - | |
| SC W | 1957-62 | | - | - | - | - | - | - | 1 | - | |

Ian Ashley
GB. Born: 26.10.1947, Wuppertal (D)

formula	years	starts (DNS)	wins	2nd	3rd	4th	5th	6th	PP	FL	points
F1 W	1974-77	4 (7)	-	-	-	-	-	-	-	-	0

Best result: 17th. Best qualifying: 20th. Teams: Token, Chequered Flag Racing,
Williams, Stanley BRM, Hesketh

| F2 E | 1976 | 0 (1) | - | - | - | - | - | - | - | - | 0 |
| CART | 1985-87 | 5 | - | - | - | - | - | - | - | - | |

Gerry Ashmore
GB. Born: 25.7.1936, West Bromwich, Staffordshire

formula	years	starts (DNS)	wins	2nd	3rd	4th	5th	6th	PP	FL	points
F1 W	1961-62	3 (1)	-	-	-	-	-	-	-	-	0

Best result: 16th. Best qualifying: 24th. Team: driver

Peter Aslund
S. Born: 22.11.1967, Karlstad
1992 Nordic F3 Champion, 1992 Swedish F3 Champion

Bill Aston
GB. Born: 29.3.1900, Stafford. Died: 4.3.1974, Lingfield, Surrey

formula	years	starts (DNS)	wins	2nd	3rd	4th	5th	6th	PP	FL	points
F1 W	1952	1 (2)	-	-	-	-	-	-	-	-	0

Best result: no finishes. Best qualifying: 30th. Team: driver

Scott Atchison
USA. Born: 16.7.1962, Bakersfield, California
1987 SCCA Super Vee Champion

formula	years	starts (DNS)	wins	2nd	3rd	4th	5th	6th	PP	FL	points
CART	1988-89	16 (2)	-	-	-	-	-	-	-	-	

Dick Atkins
USA. Born: 16.7.1938, Oakland, California. Died: 13.11.1966, from injuries inflicted during the Gardena sprint car race on the previous day

Champcar win: 1 – 1966 Sacramento

Richard "Dickie" Attwood
GB. Born: 4.4.1940, Wolverhampton, Staffordshire

formula	years	starts (DNS)	wins	2nd	3rd	4th	5th	6th	PP	FL	points
F1 W	1964-69	17 (1)	-	1	-	1	-	2	-	1	11

Best championships: 1968 and 1969, 13th. Best qualifying: 6th. Teams: BRM, Reg Parnell, Cooper, Lotus, Williams

Le Mans	1963-84	9	1	1	-	-	-	-			

Win: 1970 Le Mans 24 hrs

SC W	1962-84		2	4	5	3	1	3	-	-	

Wins: 1970 Le Mans 24 hrs, 1971 Osterreichring

F2 E	1968-70	2	-	-	1	-	-	-	-	1	4

Best championship: 1968, 12th

Tasman win: 1 – 1966 Levin

Other Major win: 1963 Monaco Formula Junior

Vincenzo Auricchio
I

Major win: 1947 Pescara GP

Soheil Ayari
F. Born: 5.4.1970, Aix-les-Bains
2002 French Touring Car Champion, 1996 French F3 Champion

formula	years	starts (DNS)	wins	2nd	3rd	4th	5th	6th	PP	FL	points
Le Mans	1997-99	2	-	-	-	-	-	-			
F3000 INT	1997-2000	40 (2)	2	1	2	3	1	3	1	3	48

Wins: 1997 Helsinki, 1998 A1 Ring. Best championship: 1998, 5th

Other Major win: 1997 Macau

Manuel Ayulo
USA. Born: 20.10.1921, Los Angeles, California. Died: 16.5.1955, Indianapolis, practice

formula	years	starts (DNS)	wins	2nd	3rd	4th	5th	6th	PP	FL	points
Indy 500	1949-54	6	-	-	1	-	-	-			

Champcar wins: 2 – 1954 Darlington, Milwaukee race 2

B

Fabio Babini
I. Born: 3.11.1969, Faenza

GT FIA win: 1 – 2002 Silverstone

Hansi Babler
E
1978 Spanish Touring Car Champion

Jorge Babler
E
1970 Spanish Touring Car Champion

Paul Bablot
F. Born: 20.11.1873, Boulogne-sur-Seine. Died: 23.12.1932, Marseille

formula	years	starts (DNS)	wins	2nd	3rd	4th	5th	6th	PP	FL	points
GP Pre-50	1907-14	6		1	-	-	1	-	-	-	1

Win: 1913 Unofficial French GP

Indy 500	1919	1	-	-	-	-	-	-			

Eric Bachelart
B. Born: 28.2.1961, Charleroi
1991 CART Indy Lights Champion

formula	years	starts (DNS)	wins	2nd	3rd	4th	5th	6th	PP	FL	points
Le Mans	1993-96	2	-	-	-	-	-	-			
F3000 INT	1988	0 (2)	-	-	-	-	-	-	-	-	0
Indy 500	1992-95	2	-	-	-	-	-	-			
CART	1992-95	24 (2)	-	-	-	-	-	-			

Luca Badoer
I. Born: 25.1.1971, Montebelluna, near Treviso
1992 FIA F3000 Champion

formula	years	starts (DNS)	wins	2nd	3rd	4th	5th	6th	PP	FL	points
F1 W	1993-99	49 (8)	-	-	-	-	-	-	-	-	0

Best result: 7th. Best qualifying: 12th. Teams: Scuderia Italia, Minardi, Forti

F3000 INT	1992	10	4	1	-	-	1	2	5	3	46

Wins: 1992 Enna, Hockenheim, Nurburgring, Nogaro. Best championship: 1992, 1st

Joerges Bagger
DK
1960 and 1961 Danish Formula Junior Champion

Giancarlo Baghetti
I. Born: 25.12.1934, Milan. Died: 27.11.1995, Milan, cancer
1966 European Touring Car Champion (1000cc class)

formula	years	starts (DNS)	wins	2nd	3rd	4th	5th	6th	PP	FL	points
F1 W	1961-67	21	1	-	-	1	1	-	-	1	14

Win: 1961 French GP. Best championship: 1961, 9th. Best qualifying: 6th. Teams: FISA, Scuderia Sant Ambroeus, Ferrari, ATS, Scuderia Centro Sud, Brabham, Reg Parnell, Lotus

Le Mans	1961-68	6	-	-	-	-	-	-			
SC W	1961-68		-	3	-	-	1	1	1	-	

Non-championship F1 wins: 1961 Syracuse, Naples, Vallelunga

Tom Bagley
USA. Born: 3.12.1939
1976 SCCA Super Vee Champion

formula	years	starts (DNS)	wins	2nd	3rd	4th	5th	6th	PP	FL	points
F2 E	1975	0 (1)	-	-	-	-	-	-	-	-	0
Indy 500	1978-80	3	-	-	-	-	-	-			
CART	1979-83	25 (1)	-	-	-	2	2	4	-	-	

Best championship: 1979, 8th

Principe Jorge de Bagration
E. Born: 22.2.1944, Rome (I)
1969, 1973 and 1982 Spanish Touring Car Champion

formula	years	starts (DNS)	wins	2nd	3rd	4th	5th	6th	PP	FL	points
Le Mans	1972-73	2	-	-	-	-	-	-			
SC W	1972-73		-	-	-	-	-	1	-	-	
F2 E	1968	1 (2)	-	-	-	-	-	1	-	-	2

Best championship: 1968, 7th

Kent Baigent
NZ. Born: 18.5.1948
1985 New Zealand Touring Car Champion

Graeme Bailey
AUS. Born: 11.7.1943

Major win: 1986 Bathurst

Julian Bailey

GB. Born: 9.10.1961, Woolwich, London
2000 FIA GT Champion (with Jamie Campbell-Walter), 1999 British GT Champion (with Campbell-Walter)

formula	years	starts (DNS)	wins	2nd	3rd	4th	5th	6th	PP	FL	points
F1 W	1988-91	7 (13)	-	-	-	-	1	-	-		1

Best championship: 1991, 18th. Best qualifying: 21st. Teams: Tyrrell, Lotus

| Le Mans | 1989-2002 | 5 | - | - | - | - | - | - | | | |
| SC W | 1989-92 | | - | 2 | 4 | - | - | 1 | - | 1 | |

Best championship: 1990, 9th
GT FIA wins: 5 – 2000 Valencia, Estoril, Silverstone, Zolder, Magny-Cours

| F3000 INT | 1987 | 7 | 1 | - | - | 1 | - | 1 | - | - | 13 |

Win: 1987 Brands Hatch. Best championship: 1987, 7th

Craig Baird

NZ. Born: 22.7.1970
2000 New Zealand Tranz-Am Champion, 1994, 1995, 1996 and 1997 New Zealand Touring Car Champion, 1991, 1992 and 1993 New Zealand Gold Star Champion, 1991 and 1992 New Zealand Formula Pacific Champion, 1993 New Zealand Formula Brabham Champion
Major wins: 1991, 1992 and 1993 New Zealand GP, 1997 Bathurst 2-litre

Georg Bakajev

S
1995 Swedish Touring Car Champion

Elzie "Buck" Baker

USA. Born: 4.3.1919, Hartville, South Carolina. Died: 15.4.2002
1956 and 1957 NASCAR Champion
NASCAR wins: 46

Elzie "Buddy" Baker Jr

USA. Born: 25.1.1941, Florence, South Carolina
NASCAR wins: 19 (15 in Modern era) including 1980 Daytona 500, 1972, 1973 World 600

Wayne Baker

USA. Born: 18.12.1941
1983 IMSA GTO Champion
Major win: 1983 Sebring 12 hrs

Mauro Baldi

I. Born: 31.1.1954, Reggio Emilia
1990 World Sports Car Champion (with Jean-Louis Schlesser), 1981 European F3 Champion

formula	years	starts (DNS)	wins	2nd	3rd	4th	5th	6th	PP	FL	points
F1 W	1982-85	36 (5)	-	-	-	1	3	-	-		5

Best championship: 1983, 16th. Best qualifying: 7th. Teams: Arrows, Alfa Romeo, Spirit

| Le Mans | 1984-2000 | 12 | 1 | 1 | 2 | - | - | - | - | | |

Win: 1994 Le Mans 24 hrs

| SC W | 1982-92 | 17 | 9 | 8 | 6 | 2 | 1 | 12 | 10 | | |

Wins: 1985 Spa, 1986 Brands Hatch, 1987 Norisring, 1988 Jerez, Spa, 1989 Suzuka, Brands Hatch, Spa, 1990 Suzuka, Monza, Dijon, Nurburgring, Donington, Montreal, 1991 Suzuka, 1992 Donington, Magny-Cours. Best championship: 1990, 1st

| CART | 1994 | 1 | - | - | - | - | - | - | - | | |

F3 E wins: 11 – 1980 Zandvoort, Misano, Jarama, 1981 Vallelunga, Osterreichring, Zolder, Zandvoort, Croix-en-Ternois, Misano, Knutstorp, Imola
SRWC wins: 3 – 1999 Spa, 2000 Monza, Elkhart Lake
Other major wins: 1980 Monaco F3, 1998 and 2002 Daytona 24 hrs, 1998 Sebring 12 hrs

Jack Baldwin

USA. Born: 31.5.1948
1992 Trans-Am Champion, 1984 and 1985 IMSA GTU Champion

Renato Balestrero

I. Born: 1898, Lucca, near Pisa. Died: 18.2.1948, near Turin, road accident

formula	years	starts (DNS)	wins	2nd	3rd	4th	5th	6th	PP	FL	points
GP Pre-50	1931-47	11 (1)	-	-	-	-	-	-	2	-	

Major win: 1925 Tripoli

Bobby Ball

USA. Born: 26.8.1925, Phoenix, Arizona. Died: 27.2.1954, Phoenix, Arizona, after failing to regain consciousness after an accident at Gardena on 4.1.1953

formula	years	starts (DNS)	wins	2nd	3rd	4th	5th	6th	PP	FL	points
Indy 500	1951-52	2	-	-	-	-	1	-	-		

Champcar win: 1 – 1952 San Jose

Fulvio Maria Ballabio

I. Born: 8.10.1954, Milan

formula	years	starts (DNS)	wins	2nd	3rd	4th	5th	6th	PP	FL	points
Le Mans	1986	1	-	-	-	1	-	-			
SC W	1983-92		-	-	2	1	-	-			

Best championship: 1986, 12th

| F2 E | 1983 | 11 (1) | - | - | - | 1 | 1 | - | - | | 3 |

Best championship: 1983, 17th

| F3000 INT | 1985-86 | 1 (1) | - | - | - | - | - | - | | | 0 |
| CART | 1987-90 | 6 (2) | - | - | - | - | - | - | | | |

Ballestrieri

I
Major win: 1974 Targa Florio

Claude Ballot-Lena

F. Born: 4.8.1936, Paris. Died: 6.12.1999
1973 European GT Champion (with Clemens Schickentanz)

formula	years	starts (DNS)	wins	2nd	3rd	4th	5th	6th	PP	FL	points
Le Mans	1966-89	23	-	-	1	2	3	-	-		
SC W	1963-90		-	1	-	5	3	-	-		

Major wins: 1969 Spa 24 hrs, 1983 Daytona 24 hrs

Earl "Bomber" Balmer

USA. Born: 13.12.1933
NASCAR wins: 1

Marcel Balsa

F. Born: 1.1.1909, St Frion. Died: 11.8.1984, Maisons Alfort, Val de Marne

formula	years	starts (DNS)	wins	2nd	3rd	4th	5th	6th	PP	FL	points
F1 W	1952	1	-	-	-	-	-	-	-		0

Best result: no finishes. Best qualifying: no times set. Team: driver

Gianni Balzarini

I

formula	years	starts (DNS)	wins	2nd	3rd	4th	5th	6th	PP	FL	points
Le Mans	1962	1	-	-	-	-	-	-			
SC W	1953-64		-	1	-	-	-	-			

Major win: 1959 Mille Miglia (regularity test)

Lorenzo Bandini

I. Born: 21.12.1935, Barce, Cyrenaica Province (LT). Died: 10.5.1967, Monaco GP

formula	years	starts (DNS)	wins	2nd	3rd	4th	5th	6th	PP	FL	points
F1 W	1961-67	42	1	2	5	2	4	3	1	2	58

Win: 1964 Austrian GP. Best championship: 1964, 4th. Best qualifying: 1st. Teams: Scuderia Centro Sud, Ferrari

| Le Mans | 1962-66 | 5 | 1 | - | 1 | - | - | - | | | |

Win: 1963 Le Mans 24 hrs

| SC W | 1960-67 | | 5 | 5 | 3 | 1 | 1 | - | - | 1 | |

Wins: 1961 Pescara, 1963 Le Mans 24 hrs, 1965 Targa Florio, 1967 Daytona 24 hrs, Monza
Non-championship F1 win: 1962 Mediterranean GP (Enna)

Henry Banks

USA. Born: 14.6.1913, London (GB). Died: 18.12.1994, Indianapolis, Indiana
1950 Champcar Champion

formula	years	starts (DNS)	wins	2nd	3rd	4th	5th	6th	PP	FL	points
Indy 500	1937-52	9	-	-	-	-	-	1	-	-	

Champcar win: 1 – 1950 Detroit

Warwick Banks
GB. Born: 12.7.1939
1964 European Touring Car Champion

Rod Banting
GB. Born: 31.5.1941
1964 BRSCC British F3 Champion
Major win: 1965 Portuguese GP

Fabrizio Barbazza
I. Born: 2.4.1963, Monza
1986 American Racing Series Champion

formula	years	starts (DNS)	wins	2nd	3rd	4th	5th	6th	PP	FL	points
F1 W	1991-93	8 (12)	-	-	-	-	2	-	-	-	2

Best championship: 1993, 17th. Best qualifying: 20th. Teams: AGS, Minardi

formula	years	starts (DNS)	wins	2nd	3rd	4th	5th	6th	PP	FL	points
F3000 INT	1987-91	14 (4)	-	-	-	1	-	-	-	-	3

Best championship: 1990, 16th

formula	years	starts (DNS)	wins	2nd	3rd	4th	5th	6th	PP	FL	points
Indy 500	1987	1	-	-	-	-	-	-			
CART	1987-92	25 (1)	-	-	1	1	-	1	-	-	

John Barber
GB. Born: 22.7.1929, Marlow, Buckinghamshire

formula	years	starts (DNS)	wins	2nd	3rd	4th	5th	6th	PP	FL	points
F1 W	1953	1	-	-	-	-	-	-	-	-	0

Best result: 8th. Best qualifying: 16th. Team: Cooper

John "Skip" Barber
USA. Born: 16.11.1936, Philadelphia, Pennsylvania

formula	years	starts (DNS)	wins	2nd	3rd	4th	5th	6th	PP	FL	points
F1 W	1971-72	5 (1)	-	-	-	-	-	-	-	-	0

Best result: 16th. Best qualifying: 20th. Team: Gene Mason

Dick Barbour
USA

formula	years	starts (DNS)	wins	2nd	3rd	4th	5th	6th	PP	FL	points
Le Mans	1978-80	3	-	1	-	2	-	-			
SC W	1977-80		-	5	-	1	1	-			

Major win: 1980 Sebring 12 hrs

Patrick Bardinon
F

formula	years	starts (DNS)	wins	2nd	3rd	4th	5th	6th	PP	FL	points
Le Mans	1979	1	-	-	-	-	-	-			
F2 E	1977	2	-	-	-	-	-	-	-	-	1

Best championship: 1977, 20th. Best result: 7th

Jason Bargwanna
AUS. Born: 26.4.1972, Sydney, New South Wales
Major win: 2000 Bathurst

Paolo Barilla
I. Born: 20.4.1961, Milan

formula	years	starts (DNS)	wins	2nd	3rd	4th	5th	6th	PP	FL	points
F1 W	1989-90	9 (6)	-	-	-	-	-	-	-	-	0

Best result: 11th. Best qualifying: 14th. Team: Minardi

formula	years	starts (DNS)	wins	2nd	3rd	4th	5th	6th	PP	FL	points
Le Mans	1983-89	6	1	-	-	-	-	-			

Win: 1985 Le Mans 24 hrs

formula	years	starts (DNS)	wins	2nd	3rd	4th	5th	6th	PP	FL	points
SC W	1983-91		2	1	5	2	1	4	-	-	

Wins: 1985 Le Mans 24 hrs, 1986 Fuji. Best championship: 1985, 7th

formula	years	starts (DNS)	wins	2nd	3rd	4th	5th	6th	PP	FL	points
F2 E	1981-83	15 (1)	-	-	-	-	-	-	-	-	0
F3000 INT	1986-88	18 (4)	-	-	-	1	-	-	-	-	3

Best championship: 1988, 17th

Woolf "Babe" Barnato
GB. Born: 27.9.1895, London. Died: 27.7.1948, London, operation

formula	years	starts (DNS)	wins	2nd	3rd	4th	5th	6th	PP	FL	points
Le Mans	1928-30	3	3	-	-	-	-	-			

Wins: 1928, 1929 and 1930 Le Mans 24 hrs

Rubens Barrichello
BR. Born: 23.5.1972, Sao Paulo
1991 British F3 Champion, 1990 European GM-Lotus Champion

formula	years	starts (DNS)	wins	2nd	3rd	4th	5th	6th	PP	FL	points
F1 W	1993-2002	162 (3)	5	16	14	14	12	4	6	8	272

Win: 2000 German GP, 2002 European GP, Hungarian GP, Italian GP, United States GP. Best championship: 2002, 2nd. Best qualifying: 1st. Teams: Jordan, Stewart, Ferrari

formula	years	starts (DNS)	wins	2nd	3rd	4th	5th	6th	PP	FL	points
F3000 INT	1992	10	-	2	2	-	2	3	-	2	27

Best championship: 1992, 3rd

Alex Barron
USA. Born: 6.11.1970, San Diego, California
1997 North American Toyota Atlantic Champion

formula	years	starts (DNS)	wins	2nd	3rd	4th	5th	6th	PP	FL	points
Indy 500	2002	1	-	-	-	1	-	-			
CART	1998-2001	34 (2)	-	-	-	-	-	-			
IRL	2001-02	16	1	-	1	1	1	-			

Win: 2002 Nashville. Best championship: 2002, 5th

Michael Bartels
D. Born: 8.3.1968, Plettenberg

formula	years	starts (DNS)	wins	2nd	3rd	4th	5th	6th	PP	FL	points
F1 W	1991	0 (4)	-	-	-	-	-	-	-	-	0

Best result: no starts. Best qualifying: 28th. Team: Lotus

formula	years	starts (DNS)	wins	2nd	3rd	4th	5th	6th	PP	FL	points
F3000 INT	1990-93	31 (1)	-	3	2	1	-	1	1	1	30

Best championship: 1992, 4th
Major win: 1999 Macau Guia race

Edgar Barth
DDR. Born: 26.1.1917, Herold-Erzegeberge. Died: 20.5.1965, Ludwigsburg, near Stuttgart, cancer

formula	years	starts (DNS)	wins	2nd	3rd	4th	5th	6th	PP	FL	points
F1 W	1953-64	5	-	-	-	-	-	-	-	-	0

Best result: 7th. Best qualifying: 12th. Teams: EMW, Porsche, Rob Walker

formula	years	starts (DNS)	wins	2nd	3rd	4th	5th	6th	PP	FL	points
Le Mans	1957-64	8	-	-	-	1	-	-			
SC W	1956-64		1	1	3	4	5	4	-	-	

Win: 1959 Targa Florio

Jurgen Barth
D. Born: 10.12.1947, Thoum

formula	years	starts (DNS)	wins	2nd	3rd	4th	5th	6th	PP	FL	points
Le Mans	1971-93	12	1	1	1	1	-	1	-	-	

Win: 1977 Le Mans 24 hrs

formula	years	starts (DNS)	wins	2nd	3rd	4th	5th	6th	PP	FL	points
SC W	1971-92		2	2	3	8	5	4	-	-	

Wins: 1980 Nurburgring, Dijon

Kevin Bartlett
AUS. Born: 25.5.1940
1968 and 1969 Australian Gold Star Champion
Tasman wins: 2 – 1970 Warwick Farm, 1972 Teretonga
Other major wins: 1969 Macau, 1974 Bathurst

Giorgio Bassi
I. Born: 20.1.1934, Milan

formula	years	starts (DNS)	wins	2nd	3rd	4th	5th	6th	PP	FL	points
F1 W	1965	1	-	-	-	-	-	-	-	-	0

Best result: no finishes. Best qualifying: 22nd. Team: Scuderia Centro Sud

Jean-Claude Basso
F. Born: 10.8.1949, Bournel
GT FIA win: 1 – 1994 Montlhery

Norman Batten
USA. Born: Brooklyn, New York. Died: 12.11.1928, lost at sea aboard the SS Vestris

formula	years	starts (DNS)	wins	2nd	3rd	4th	5th	6th	PP	FL	points
Indy 500	1925-28	4	1	-	-	-	1	-	-		

Win: 1925 Indianapolis 500
Champcar wins: 2 – 1925 Indianapolis 500, 1926 Atlantic City race 3

Marcelo Battistuzzi
BR. Born: 20.7.1976, Sao Paulo
1997 European Formula Opel Champion

formula	years	starts (DNS)	wins	2nd	3rd	4th	5th	6th	PP	FL	points
F3000 INT	1998-99	14 (4)	-	-	-	-	1	-	-		1

Best championship: 1998, 24th

Erwin Bauer
D. Born: 17.7.1912, Stuttgart. Died: 3.6.1958, Cologne, following accident during the post-finish lap of the Nurburgring 1000 kms

formula	years	starts (DNS)	wins	2nd	3rd	4th	5th	6th	PP	FL	points
F1 W	1953	1	-	-	-	-	-	-	-	-	0

Best result: no finishes. Best qualifying: 33rd. Team: driver

Le Mans	1957	1	-	-	-	-	-	-	-		

John Bauer
USA. Born: 14.9.1949
1980 Trans-Am Champion

formula	years	starts (DNS)	wins	2nd	3rd	4th	5th	6th	PP	FL	points
SC W	1976-87		-	-	-	1	-	-	-		

Walter Baumer
D. Born: 17.10.1908, Bunde, Westphalia. Died: 29.6.1941, Bunde, road accident

formula	years	starts (DNS)	wins	2nd	3rd	4th	5th	6th	PP	FL	points
GP Pre-50	1938-39	4	-	-	-	-	-	-	-		

Major win: 1940 Mille Miglia

Zsolt Baumgartner
H. Born: 1.1.1981, Debrecen

formula	years	starts (DNS)	wins	2nd	3rd	4th	5th	6th	PP	FL	points
F3000 INT	2001-02	19	-	-	-	-	-	1	-	-	1

Best championship: 2002, 15th

Astrubel Bayardo
ROU. Born: 26.12.1922, Pan de Azucar

formula	years	starts (DNS)	wins	2nd	3rd	4th	5th	6th	PP	FL	points
F1 W	1959	0 (1)	-	-	-	-	-	-	-	-	0

Best result: no starts. Best qualifying: no times set. Team: Scuderia Centro Sud

Elie Bayol
F. Born: 28.2.1914, Marseille. Died: 25.5.1995, La Ciotat

formula	years	starts (DNS)	wins	2nd	3rd	4th	5th	6th	PP	FL	points
F1 W	1952-56	7 (1)	-	-	-	-	1	1	-	-	2

Best championship: 1954, 18th. Best qualifying: 10th. Teams: driver, Gordini

Le Mans	1950-54	5	-	-	-	-	-	-	-		
SC W	1953-56		-	-	-	-	1	-	-		

Johnny Beauchamp
USA. Born: 23.3.1923. Died: 17.4.1981
NASCAR wins: 2

Count Carel Godin de Beaufort
NL. Born: 10.4.1934, Maarsbergen Castle. Died: 3.8.1964, Dusseldorf, following an accident during German GP practice at the Nurburgring

formula	years	starts (DNS)	wins	2nd	3rd	4th	5th	6th	PP	FL	points
F1 W	1957-64	28 (3)	-	-	-	-	4	-	-		4

Best championship: 1963, 14th. Best qualifying: 8th. Teams: Ecurie Maarsbergen, Scuderia Ugolini

Le Mans	1957-63	7	-	-	-	-	1	-	-		
SC W	1956-64		-	-	-	-	1	1	-	-	

Don Beauman
GB. Born: 26.7.1928, Farnborough, Hampshire. Died: 9.7.1955, Rathnew, County Wicklow, Republic of Ireland, Leinster Trophy

formula	years	starts (DNS)	wins	2nd	3rd	4th	5th	6th	PP	FL	points
F1 W	1954	1	-	-	-	-	-	-	-	-	0

Best result: 11th. Best qualifying: 17th. Team: Sir Jeremy Boles

Le Mans	1955	1									

Gunther Bechem
D. Born: 21.12.1921, Hagen. Also raced as "Bernd Nacke"

formula	years	starts (DNS)	wins	2nd	3rd	4th	5th	6th	PP	FL	points
F1 W	1952-53	2	-	-	-	-	-	-	-	-	0

Best result: no finishes. Best qualifying: 30th. Team: driver

Heinz Becker (Karl-Heinz Becker)
D
1995 and 1999 Interserie Champion

formula	years	starts (DNS)	wins	2nd	3rd	4th	5th	6th	PP	FL	points
SC W	1964-87		-	-	-	-	-	1	-	-	

Peter Beckers
B
2002 Belgian Belcar Touring Car Champion (with Serge Cassiers and Eric Roelands)

Becquet
F
Major win: 1924 Spa 24 hrs

Norm Beechey
AUS
1965 and 1970 Australian Touring Car Champion

Jon Beekhuis
USA. Born: 31.3.1960, Zurich (CH)
1988 American Racing Series Champion

formula	years	starts (DNS)	wins	2nd	3rd	4th	5th	6th	PP	FL	points
CART	1989-92	13 (2)	-	-	-	-	-	-	-		

Jean Behra
F. Born: 16.2.1921, Nice. Died: 1.8.1959, Avus, sports car race

formula	years	starts (DNS)	wins	2nd	3rd	4th	5th	6th	PP	FL	points
F1 W	1952-59	52 (1)	-	2	7	2	4	6	-	1	51.14

Best championship: 1956, 4th. Best qualifying: 2nd. Teams: Gordini, Maserati, Ken Kavanagh, BRM, Ferrari, driver

Le Mans	1950-59	9	-	-	1	-	-	-	-	1
SC W	1953-59		3	3	4	1	1	-	3	4

Wins: 1956 Nurburgring, 1957 Sebring 12 hrs, Swedish GP
Non-championship F1 wins: 1954 Pau, Cadours, 1955 Pau, Bordeaux, 1957 Pau, Caen, International Trophy (Silverstone), Modena, Moroccan GP, 1959 Aintree
Other Major win: 1955 Portuguese GP

Andrea Belicchi
I. Born: 18.12.1976, Parma
1998 European Renault Spider Cup Champion, 2002 Russian F3 Champion

Derek Bell
GB. Born: 31.10.1941, Pinner, Middlesex
1985 (with Hans-Joachim Stuck) and 1986 World Sports Car Champion

formula	years	starts (DNS)	wins	2nd	3rd	4th	5th	6th	PP	FL	points
F1 W	1968-74	9 (7)	-	-	-	-	-	1	-	-	1

Best championship: 1970, 22nd. Best qualifying: 8th. Teams: Ferrari, McLaren, Tom Wheatcroft, Surtees, Tecno

formula	years	starts (DNS)	wins	2nd	3rd	4th	5th	6th	PP	FL	points
Le Mans	1970-96	26		5	2	2	2	1	2	-	-

Wins: 1975, 1981, 1982, 1986 and 1987 Le Mans 24 hrs

formula	years	starts (DNS)	wins	2nd	3rd	4th	5th	6th	PP	FL	points
SC W	1970-92		21	20	13	14	6	1	5	3	

Wins: 1971 Buenos Aires, 1973 Spa, 1975 Spa, Osterreichring, Watkins Glen, 1981 Le Mans 24 hrs, 1982 Le Mans 24 hrs, Brands Hatch, 1983 Silverstone, Fuji, Kyalami, 1984 Monza, Nurburgring, Spa, Sandown Park, 1985 Hockenheim, Mosport Park, Brands Hatch, 1986 Monza, Le Mans 24 hrs, 1987 Le Mans 24 hrs. Best championships: 1985 and 1986, 1st

formula	years	starts (DNS)	wins	2nd	3rd	4th	5th	6th	PP	FL	points
F2 E	1968-84	32 (1)	1	-	7	4	2	2	2		83

Win: 1970 Montjuich Park. Best championship: 1970, 2nd
Other major wins: 1973 Tourist Trophy (Silverstone), 1986, 1987 and 1989 Daytona 24 hrs

Justin Bell
GB. Born: 23.2.1968, Rustington, Sussex
1997 FIA GT2 class Champion

formula	years	starts (DNS)	wins	2nd	3rd	4th	5th	6th	PP	FL	points
Le Mans	1992-2000	8	-	-	1	-	-	-			

Townsend Bell
USA. Born: 19.4.1975, San Francisco, California
2001 CART Indy Lights Champion

formula	years	starts (DNS)	wins	2nd	3rd	4th	5th	6th	PP	FL	points
CART	2001-02	11	-	-	-	1	-	-	-		

Ray Bellm
GB. Born: 20.5.1950, New Malden, Surrey
1986 and 1988 World Group C2 Sports Car Champion (both with Gordon Spice), 1996 FIA GT Champion (with James Weaver), 1996 European GT Champion (with Weaver)

formula	years	starts (DNS)	wins	2nd	3rd	4th	5th	6th	PP	FL	points
Le Mans	1984-97	9	-	-	-	1	-	-			
SC W	1984-92		-	-	-	1	3	1	-		

Best championship: 1988, 12th
GT FIA wins: 9 – 1995 Jerez, Paul Ricard, Jarama, Nurburgring, Suzuka, 1996 Paul Ricard, Jarama, Suzuka, Nogaro

Jean-Philippe Belloc
F. Born: 24.4.1970, Montauban, near Toulouse
2001 FIA GT Champion (with Christophe Bouchut), 1994 French F3 Champion, 1992 French Formula Renault Champion

formula	years	starts (DNS)	wins	2nd	3rd	4th	5th	6th	PP	FL	points
Le Mans	1997-2002	6	-	-	-	-	-	-			

GT FIA wins: 7 – 1999 Hockenheim, Hungaroring, Watkins Glen, 2001 Brno, Silverstone, Zolder, Spa 24 hrs

formula	years	starts (DNS)	wins	2nd	3rd	4th	5th	6th	PP	FL	points
F3000 INT	1995-97	22	-	-	1	-	1	-	-		6

Best championship: 1995, 10th

Stefan Bellof
D. Born: 20.11.1957, Giessen, near Frankfurt-am-Main. Died: 1.9.1985, Spa 1000 kms
1984 World Sports Car Champion, 1984 German Racing Champion

formula	years	starts (DNS)	wins	2nd	3rd	4th	5th	6th	PP	FL	points
F1 W	1984-85	20 (2)	-	-	-	1	-	1	-	-		4

Best championship: 1985, 15th. Best qualifying: 16th. Team: Tyrrell

formula	years	starts (DNS)	wins	2nd	3rd	4th	5th	6th	PP	FL	points
Le Mans	1983	1	-	-	-	-	-	-			
SC W	1982-85		9	1	1	1	1	-	9	9	

Wins: 1983 Silverstone, Fuji, Kyalami, 1984 Monza, Nurburgring, Spa, Imola, Fuji, Sandown Park. Best championship: 1984, 1st

formula	years	starts (DNS)	wins	2nd	3rd	4th	5th	6th	PP	FL	points
F2 E	1982-83	21 (2)	2	2	1	2	1	2	6		42

Wins: 1982 Silverstone, Hockenheim race 1. Best championship: 1982, 4th

Paul Belmondo
F. Born: 23.4.1963, Boulogne-Billancourt, Paris

formula	years	starts (DNS)	wins	2nd	3rd	4th	5th	6th	PP	FL	points
F1 W	1992-94	7 (20)	-	-	-	-	-	-			0

Best result: 9th. Best qualifying: 17th. Teams: March, Pacific

formula	years	starts (DNS)	wins	2nd	3rd	4th	5th	6th	PP	FL	points
Le Mans	1985-99	8	-	-	-	-	-	-			
SC W	1984-92		-	-	-	-	1	-			

GT FIA win: 1 – 1999 Homestead

formula	years	starts (DNS)	wins	2nd	3rd	4th	5th	6th	PP	FL	points
F3000 INT	1987-91	45 (8)	-	-	-	1	1	-			3

Best championship: 1987, 18th

Tom Belso
DK. Born: 27.8.1942, Copenhagen

formula	years	starts (DNS)	wins	2nd	3rd	4th	5th	6th	PP	FL	points
F1 W	1973-74	2 (3)	-	-	-	-	-	-			0

Best result: 8th. Best qualifying: 21st. Team: Williams

formula	years	starts (DNS)	wins	2nd	3rd	4th	5th	6th	PP	FL	points
F2 E	1972	6 (4)	-	-	1	1	-	-	-		5

Best championship: 1972, 17th

Anthony Beltoise
F. Born: 27.7.1971, Neuilly-sur-Seine, near Paris

formula	years	starts (DNS)	wins	2nd	3rd	4th	5th	6th	PP	FL	points
Le Mans	2000-01	2	-	-	-	-	-	-			
F3000 INT	1997	7	-	-	-	-	-	-			0

Major win: 1999 Spa 24 hrs

Jean-Pierre Beltoise
F. Born: 26.4.1937, Boulogne-Billancourt, Paris
1968 European F2 Champion, 1967 Temporada F3 Champion, 1976 and 1977 French Touring Car Champion, 1965 French F3 Champion

formula	years	starts (DNS)	wins	2nd	3rd	4th	5th	6th	PP	FL	points
F1 W	1966-74	86 (2)	1	3	4	3	10	5	-	4		77

Win: 1972 Monaco GP. Best championship: 1969, 5th. Best qualifying: 2nd.
Teams: Matra, Tyrrell, BRM

formula	years	starts (DNS)	wins	2nd	3rd	4th	5th	6th	PP	FL	points
Le Mans	1963-79	14	-	-	-	1	-	-			
SC W	1963-79		4	2	2	2	1	-	3	2	

Wins: 1974 Nurburgring, Watkins Glen, Paul Ricard, Brands Hatch

formula	years	starts (DNS)	wins	2nd	3rd	4th	5th	6th	PP	FL	points
F2 E	1967-75	36 (5)	4	5	4	3	-	1	6	5		75

Wins: 1968 Hockenheim race 1, Jarama, Zandvoort, 1969 Hockenheim. Best championship: 1968, 1st
F1 ZA win: 1 – 1968 Killarney. Non-championship F1 win: 1972 John Player Challenge (Brands Hatch)
Other Major win: 1966 Monaco F3

Aldo Benedetti
I
Major win: 1949 Targa Florio

Dr Joseph Dudley "JD" Benjafield
GB. Born: 6.8.1887, North London. Died: 20.1.1957

formula	years	starts (DNS)	wins	2nd	3rd	4th	5th	6th	PP	FL	points
Le Mans	1925-35	7	1	-	1	-	-	-			

Win: 1927 Le Mans 24 hrs

Robert Benoist
F. Born: 20.3.1895, Auffargis. Died: 12.9.1944, Buchenwald Prisoner of War camp, executed

formula	years	starts (DNS)	wins	2nd	3rd	4th	5th	6th	PP	FL	points
GP Pre-50	1924-36	20 (1)	5	2	3	2	1	1	3		

Wins: 1925 French GP, 1927 French GP, Spanish GP, Italian GP, British GP

formula	years	starts (DNS)	wins	2nd	3rd	4th	5th	6th	PP	FL	points
Le Mans	1928-37	3	1	-	-	-	1	-			

Win: 1937 Le Mans 24 hrs
Other Major win: 1929 Spa 24 hrs

Johnny Benson
USA. Born: 27.6.1963, Grand Rapids, Michigan
NASCAR wins: 1 (in Modern era)

Len Bentham
USA
1998 North American Toyota Atlantic Champion

Olivier Beretta
MC. Born: 23.11.1969, Monte Carlo
1999 FIA GT Champion (with Karl Wendlinger), 1998 FIA GT2 class Champion (with Pedro Lamy), 1999 and 2000 American Le Mans Series GTS Champion

formula	years	starts (DNS)	wins	2nd	3rd	4th	5th	6th	PP	FL	points
F1 W	1994	9 (1)	-	-	-	-	-	-	-	-	0

Best result: 7th. Best qualifying: 17th. Team: Larrousse

| Le Mans | 1996-2002 | 7 | - | - | 1 | 1 | - | - | | | |

GT FIA wins: 5 – 1999 Monza, Silverstone, Zolder, Oschersleben, Donington
SRWC win: 1 – 2002 Estoril

| F3000 INT | 1992-93 | 19 | | 1 | - | 3 | 1 | - | 1 | - | 20 |

Win: 1993 Donington. Best championship: 1993, 6th
Other Major win: 2000 Daytona 24 hrs

Allen Berg
CDN. Born: 1.8.1961, Calgary, Alberta
1983 New Zealand Formula Pacific Champion, 1993 Mexican F2 Champion, 2001 Mexican Indy Lights Champion

formula	years	starts (DNS)	wins	2nd	3rd	4th	5th	6th	PP	FL	points
F1 W	1986	9	-	-	-	-	-	-	-	-	0

Best result: 12th. Best qualifying: 25th. Team: Osella

| Le Mans | 1990 | 1 | | | | | | | | | |

Erwin Bergdoll
USA. Born: 1891. Died: 21.3.1965

formula	years	starts (DNS)	wins	2nd	3rd	4th	5th	6th	PP	FL	points
GP Pre-50	1911-12	2	-	1	-	-	-	-			

Champcar win: 1 – 1911 Philadelphia race 1

Georges Berger
B. Born: 14.9.1918, Brussels. Died: 23.8.1967, Nurburgring

formula	years	starts (DNS)	wins	2nd	3rd	4th	5th	6th	PP	FL	points
F1 W	1953-54	2	-	-	-	-	-	-	-	-	0

Best result: no finishes. Best qualifying: 20th. Teams: driver, Gordini

| Le Mans | 1958-62 | 3 | | | | | | | | | |

Gerhard Berger
A. Born: 27.8.1959, Worgl, near Innsbruck

formula	years	starts (DNS)	wins	2nd	3rd	4th	5th	6th	PP	FL	points
F1 W	1984-97	210	10	17	21	26	8	13	12	21	385

Wins: 1986 Mexican GP, 1987 Japanese GP, Australian GP, 1988 Italian GP, 1989 Portuguese GP, 1991 Japanese GP, 1992 Canadian GP, Australian GP, 1994 German GP, 1997 German GP. Best championships: 1988, 1990 and 1994, 3rd. Best qualifying: 1st. Teams: ATS, Arrows, Benetton, Ferrari, McLaren

| SC W | 1985 | | - | - | - | - | 1 | - | - | | |

F3 E wins: 2 – 1984 Osterreichring, Monza
Other Major win: 1985 Spa 24 hrs

Anders Berggren
S
1985 Swedish Tourish Car Champion

Jorg Bergmeister
D. Born: 13.2.1976, Leverkusen
2001 Porsche Supercup Champion

formula	years	starts (DNS)	wins	2nd	3rd	4th	5th	6th	PP	FL	points
Le Mans	2002	1	-	-	-	-	-	-			

Bob Bergstrom
USA
1973 IMSA GTU Champion

Franco Bernabei
I. Born: 1940, Rome
1968 Italian F3 Champion

formula	years	starts (DNS)	wins	2nd	3rd	4th	5th	6th	PP	FL	points
SC W	1965-77		-	-	-	-	1	-	-		
F2 E	1969	1	-	-	-	1	-	-	-		2

Best championship: 1969, 15th

Eric Bernard
F. Born: 24.8.1964, Istres
1985 French Formula Renault Champion

formula	years	starts (DNS)	wins	2nd	3rd	4th	5th	6th	PP	FL	points
F1 W	1989-94	45 (2)	-	1	1	-	3	-	-	-	10

Best championship: 1990, 13th. Best qualifying: 8th. Teams: Larrousse, Ligier, Lotus

| Le Mans | 1995-2002 | 8 | | | | | | | | | |

SRWC wins: 3 – 1999 Donington, Nurburgring, Kyalami

| F3000 INT | 1988-89 | 19 (1) | 1 | 2 | 1 | 4 | - | 1 | 3 | 3 | 38 |

Win: 1989 Jerez. Best championship: 1989, 3rd
Other Major win: 1999 Petit LeMans

Enrique Bernoldi
BR. Born: 19.10.1978, Curitiba
1996 European Formula Renault Champion

formula	years	starts (DNS)	wins	2nd	3rd	4th	5th	6th	PP	FL	points
F1 W	2001-02	28 (2)	-	-	-	-	-	-	-	-	0

Best result: 8th. Best qualifying: 12th. Team: Arrows

| F3000 INT | 1999-2000 | 18 (2) | - | - | - | 1 | 1 | 2 | 1 | - | 7 |

Best championship: 2000, 15th

Enrico Bertaggia
I. Born: 19.9.1964, Noale, near Venice
1987 Italian F3 Champion

formula	years	starts (DNS)	wins	2nd	3rd	4th	5th	6th	PP	FL	points
F1 W	1989-92	0 (8)	-	-	-	-	-	-	-	-	0

Best result: no starts. Best qualifying: 37th. Teams: Coloni, Andrea Moda

| Le Mans | 1995 | 1 | | | | | | | | | |
| F3000 INT | 1988-93 | 10 (12) | - | - | - | - | 1 | - | - | - | 2 |

Best championship: 1993, 17th
Major wins: 1988 Monaco F3, 1988 Macau

Hartwig Bertrams
D
1975 European GT Champion

formula	years	starts (DNS)	wins	2nd	3rd	4th	5th	6th	PP	FL	points
Le Mans	1975-76	2	-	-	-	-	-	-			
SC W	1974-76		-	-	-	1	2	1	-	-	

Vaclav Bervid
CS. Born: 5.1.1973, Prague
1993 and 1994 Czech Touring Car Champion, 1996 Central European Touring Car Champion

Bruno Besson
F. Born: 26.9.1979
1998 European Formula Renault Champion

Ernesto Bessone
RA. Born: 3.4.1958, Buenos Aires
1996 TC2000 Argentinian Touring Car Champion

Gary Bettenhausen
USA. Born: 18.11.1941, Tinley Park, near Chicago, Illinois

formula	years	starts (DNS)	wins	2nd	3rd	4th	5th	6th	PP	FL	points
Indy 500	1968-93	21	-	-	1	-	2	-	-		

Pre-CART Champcar wins: 4 – 1968 Phoenix race 2, 1970 Michigan, 1972 Trenton race 1, 1973 Texas

| CART | 1979-96 | 45 (8) | - | - | 2 | - | 1 | 2 | - | - | |

Best championship: 1980, 9th

Melvin "Tony" Bettenhausen

USA. Born: 12.9.1916, Tinley Park, near Chicago, Illinois. Died: 12.5.1961, Indianapolis 500, practice
1951 and 1958 Champcar Champion

formula	years	starts (DNS)	wins	2nd	3rd	4th	5th	6th	PP	FL	points
Indy 500	1946-60	14	-	-	1	-	2	1	-	-	1

Champcar wins: 22 – 1946 Goshen, 1947 Goshen, Springfield, 1948 Milwaukee race 3, 1949 Du Quoin, Detroit, 1950 Milwaukee race 1, Springfield race 2, Bay Meadows, 1951 Milwaukee race 1, Langhorne, Springfield race 1, Du Quoin race 1, Du Quoin race 2, Syracuse, Denver, San Jose, 1953 Syracuse, Phoenix, 1956 Syracuse, 1959 Trenton race 1, Phoenix

Mike Beuttler

GB. Born: 13.8.1940, Cairo (ET). Died: 29.12.1988, San Francisco, California (USA)

formula	years	starts (DNS)	wins	2nd	3rd	4th	5th	6th	PP	FL	points
F1 W	1971-73	28 (1)	-	-	-	-	-	-	-	-	0

Best result: 7th. Best qualifying: 11th. Teams: Clarke-Mordaundt-Guthrie-Durlacher, March

| F2 E | 1971-73 | 18 (8) | 1 | 1 | 1 | 4 | - | - | - | 1 | 39 |

Win: 1971 Vallelunga race 2. Best Championships: 1971 and 1973, 7th

Thomas Biagi

I. Born: 7.5.1976, Bologna

formula	years	starts (DNS)	wins	2nd	3rd	4th	5th	6th	PP	FL	points
F3000 INT	1995-99	21 (10)	-	-	-	1	1	2	-	-	7

Best championship: 1996, 12th

Eddy Bianchi

I
1981 Italian F3 Champion

formula	years	starts (DNS)	wins	2nd	3rd	4th	5th	6th	PP	FL	points
F2 E	1982	3	-	-	-	-	-	-	-	-	0

Luciano "Lucien" Bianchi

B. Born: 10.11.1934, Milan (I). Died: 30.3.1969, Le Mans, testing

formula	years	starts (DNS)	wins	2nd	3rd	4th	5th	6th	PP	FL	points
F1 W	1959-68	17 (2)	-	-	1	-	-	2	-	-	6

Best championship: 17th. Best qualifying: 12th. Teams: ENB, Fred Tuck, BRP, Reg Parnell, Scuderia Centro Sud, Cooper

| Le Mans | 1956-68 | 13 | 1 | - | - | - | 1 | - | - | |
| SC W | 1956-69 | | 3 | 1 | 2 | 2 | 2 | 1 | - | |

Win: 1968 Le Mans 24 hrs
Wins: 1962 Sebring 12 hrs, 1968 Watkins Glen, Le Mans 24 hrs

Mauro Bianchi

B. Born: 1938

formula	years	starts (DNS)	wins	2nd	3rd	4th	5th	6th	PP	FL	points
Le Mans	1962-68	6	-	-	-	-	-	-	-	-	

Major win: 1966 Macau

Gino Bianco

BR. Born: 22.7.1916, Milan (I). Died: 17.1.1983

formula	years	starts (DNS)	wins	2nd	3rd	4th	5th	6th	PP	FL	points
F1 W	1952	4	-	-	-	-	-	-	-	-	0

Best result: 18th. Best qualifying: 12th. Team: Bandeirantes

Frank Biela

D. Born: 2.8.1964, Neuss, near Dusseldorf
1995 Touring Car World Cup winner, 1991 German Touring Car Champion, 1993 French Touring Car Champion, 1996 British Touring Car Champion

formula	years	starts (DNS)	wins	2nd	3rd	4th	5th	6th	PP	FL	points
Le Mans	1999-2002	4	3	-	1	-	-	-	-	-	

Wins: 2000, 2001 and 2002 Le Mans 24 hrs
Other major wins: 1996 Macau Guia race, 2000 Sebring 12 hrs, 2001 Petit LeMans

Charles Bigelow

USA. Born: c1873. Died: 19??

formula	years	starts (DNS)	wins	2nd	3rd	4th	5th	6th	PP	FL	points
Indy 500	1911	1	-	-	-	-	-	-	-	-	

Champcar win: 1 – 1911 Oakland race 1

Amedeo Bignami

I
Major wins: 1932 and 1934 Mille Miglia

Rolf Biland

CH

formula	years	starts (DNS)	wins	2nd	3rd	4th	5th	6th	PP	FL	points
SC W	1977-83		-	-	-	-	-	1	-	-	
F2 E	1983-84	7	-	-	-	-	-	1	-	-	1

Best championship: 1983, 20th

Hans Binder

A. Born: 12.6.1948, Zell-am-Ziller, near Innsbruck

formula	years	starts (DNS)	wins	2nd	3rd	4th	5th	6th	PP	FL	points
F1 W	1976-78	13 (2)	-	-	-	-	-	-	-	-	0

Best result: 8th. Best qualifying: 18th. Teams: Ensign, Williams, Surtees, ATS

| F2 E | 1974-76 | 23 (2) | - | 1 | - | 4 | 1 | - | - | - | 21 |

Best championship: 1976, 7th

Roland Binder

D
1981, 1982 and 1985 Interserie Champion

formula	years	starts (DNS)	wins	2nd	3rd	4th	5th	6th	PP	FL	points
F2 E	1970-77	21 (16)	-	-	-	1	-	1	-	-	5

Best championship: 1973, 19th

Clemente Biondetti

I. Born: 18.8.1898, Budduso, Sardinia. Died: 24.2.1955, Florence, cancer

formula	years	starts (DNS)	wins	2nd	3rd	4th	5th	6th	PP	FL	points
F1 W	1950	1	-	-	-	-	-	-	-	-	0

Best result: no finishes. Best qualifying: 25th. Team: driver

GP Pre-50	1930-49	15	-	-	1	1	-	-	-	-	
Le Mans	1938-53	3	-	-	-	-	-	-	-	-	
SC W	1953-54		-	-	-	1	-	-	-	-	

Major wins: 1938, 1947, 1948 and 1949 Mille Miglia, 1939 Coppa Acerbo (Pescara), 1948 and 1949 Targa Florio

"B Bira"
(Prince Birabongse Bhanudej Bhanubandh)

SM. Born: 15.7.1914, Bangkok. Died: 23.12.1985, Baron's Court, London (GB)

formula	years	starts (DNS)	wins	2nd	3rd	4th	5th	6th	PP	FL	points
F1 W	1950-54	19	-	-	-	2	1	1	-	-	8

Best championship: 1950, 8th. Best qualifying: 5th. Teams: Enrico Plate, driver, Gordini, Connaught, Milano, Maserati

| GP Pre-50 | 1935-49 | 15 (2) | - | 1 | 1 | - | 4 | 1 | 1 | 2 | |
| Le Mans | 1939-54 | 2 | - | - | - | - | - | - | - | - | |

Non-championship F1 wins: 1951 Goodwood, 1954 Frontiers GP (Chimay)
Other major wins: 1936 Monaco Rainier Cup, 1948 Zandvoort GP, 1955 New Zealand GP

Pablo Birger

RA. Born: 6.1.1924, Buenos Aires. Died: 9.3.1966, Buenos Aires

formula	years	starts (DNS)	wins	2nd	3rd	4th	5th	6th	PP	FL	points
F1 W	1953-55	2	-	-	-	-	-	-	-	-	0

Best result: no finishes. Best qualifying: 9th. Team: Gordini

Sir Henry "Tim" Birkin

GB. Born: 26.7.1896, Nottingham. Died: 22.6.1933, London, after burning his arm at the Tripoli GP

formula	years	starts (DNS)	wins	2nd	3rd	4th	5th	6th	PP	FL	points
GP Pre-50	1928-33	6 (1)	-	1	-	2	-	-	-	-	
Le Mans	1928-32	5	2	-	-	-	1	-	-	3	

Wins: 1929 and 1931 Le Mans 24 hrs

Gerry Birrell

GB. Born: 30.7.1944, Glasgow. Died: 23.6.1973, Rouen, F2 practice
1972 South African Springbok Sports Car Champion

formula	years	starts (DNS)	wins	2nd	3rd	4th	5th	6th	PP	FL	points
Le Mans	1972-73	2	-	-	-	-	-	-	-	-	
SC W	1973		-	-	-	-	-	1	-	-	
F2 E	1970-73		-	-	1	1	3	-	-	-	11

Best championship: 1971, 11th

Art Bisch
USA. Born: 10.11.1926, Mesa, Arizona. Died: 4.7.1958, Champcar race, Lakewood Speedway, Atlanta, Georgia

formula	years	starts (DNS)	wins	2nd	3rd	4th	5th	6th	PP	FL	points
Indy 500	1958	1	-	-	-	-	-	-	-	-	

Champcar win: 1 – 1958 Milwaukee race 1

Thed Bjork
S. Born: 14.12.1980, Orebro
2001 Sports Racing SRL class Champion (with Larry Oberto), 1999 Nordic F3 Champion, 1999 Swedish F3 Champion

formula	years	starts (DNS)	wins	2nd	3rd	4th	5th	6th	PP	FL	points
Le Mans	2002	1	-	-	-	-	-	-	-	-	
F3000 INT	2002	4 (1)	-	-	-	-	-	-	-	-	0

Eugen Bjornstad
N. Born: n/a. Died: 1993

formula	years	starts (DNS)	wins	2nd	3rd	4th	5th	6th	PP	FL	points
GP Pre-50	1934	1 (1)	-	-	-	-	-	-	-	-	

Major win: 1936 Norwegian GP

Norman Black
GB

formula	years	starts (DNS)	wins	2nd	3rd	4th	5th	6th	PP	FL	points
Le Mans	1932-37	5	-	-	-	-	-	-	-	-	

Major win: 1931 Tourist Trophy (Ards)

Bill Blair
USA. Born: 14.7.1911, High Point, North Carolina. Died: 2.11.1995

NASCAR wins: 3

Harry Blanchard
USA. Born: 30.6.1931, Burlington, Vermont. Died: 31.1.1960, Buenos Aires 1000 kms

formula	years	starts (DNS)	wins	2nd	3rd	4th	5th	6th	PP	FL	points
F1 W	1959	1	-	-	-	-	-	-	-	-	0

Best result: 7th. Best qualifying: 16th. Team: driver

Beat Blatter
CH
1979 Swiss F3 Champion

Jeroen Bleekemolen
NL. Born: 23.10.1981, Heemstede

GT FIA wins: 2 – 2001 Hungaroring, Estoril

Michael Bleekemolen
NL. Born: 2.10.1949, Amsterdam

formula	years	starts (DNS)	wins	2nd	3rd	4th	5th	6th	PP	FL	points
F1 W	1977-78	1 (4)	-	-	-	-	-	-	-	-	0

Best result: no finishes. Best qualifying: 25th. Teams: RAM, ATS

| F2 E | 1978 | 2 (1) | - | - | - | - | - | - | - | - | 0 |

F3 E win: 1 – 1978 Enna

Robert Bloch
F

formula	years	starts (DNS)	wins	2nd	3rd	4th	5th	6th	PP	FL	points
Le Mans	1923-28	5	1	1	-	-	-	-	-	-	

Win: 1926 Le Mans 24 hrs

Trevor Blokdyk
ZA. Born: 30.11.1935, Krugersdorp, Transvaal. Died: 19.3.1995, Hekpoort, near Krugersdorp, Transvaal, heart attack

formula	years	starts (DNS)	wins	2nd	3rd	4th	5th	6th	PP	FL	points
F1 W	1963-65	1 (1)	-	-	-	-	-	-	-	-	0

Best result: 12th. Best qualifying: 19th. Teams: Scuderia Lupini, driver

Stig Blomqvist
S. Born: 29.7.1946, Lindesberg
1990 Swedish Touring Car Champion

Mark Blundell
GB. Born: 8.4.1966, Barnet, Hertfordshire
1986 European FF2000 Champion

formula	years	starts (DNS)	wins	2nd	3rd	4th	5th	6th	PP	FL	points
F1 W	1991-95	61 (2)	-	-	3	2	6	2	-	-	32

Best championships: 1993 and 1995, 10th. Best qualifying: 4th. Teams: Brabham, Ligier, Tyrrell, McLaren

| Le Mans | 1989-2002 | 6 | | 1 | - | - | 1 | - | - | 1 | - | |

Win: 1992 Le Mans 24 hrs

| SC W | 1989-92 | | | 1 | 2 | 3 | - | 1 | 1 | - | |

Win: 1992 Le Mans 24 hrs. Best championship: 1990, 10th

| F3000 INT | 1987-89 | 28 (3) | - | 3 | 2 | - | 2 | 4 | - | 1 | 31 |

Best championship: 1988, 6th

| CART | 1996-2000 | 81 | 3 | 2 | - | - | 2 | 2 | - | 2 | |

Wins: 1997 Portland, Toronto, California Speedway. Best championship: 1997, 6th

Billy Boat
USA. Born: 2.2.1966, Phoenix, Arizona

formula	years	starts (DNS)	wins	2nd	3rd	4th	5th	6th	PP	FL	points
Indy 500	1997-2002	6	-	-	1	-	-	1	-	
IRL	1997-2002	62	1	3	3	3	1	4	9	2	

Win: 1998 Texas. Best championship: 2001, 4th

Brett Bodine
USA. Born: 11.1.1959, Elmira, New York State

NASCAR wins: 1 (in Modern era)

Geoff Bodine
USA. Born: 18.4.1949, Elmira, New York State
1987 IROC Champion

NASCAR wins: 18 (all Modern era) including 1986 Daytona 500

Raul Boesel
BR. Born: 4.12.1957, Curitiba
1987 World Sports Car Champion

formula	years	starts (DNS)	wins	2nd	3rd	4th	5th	6th	PP	FL	points
F1 W	1982-83	23 (7)	-	-	-	-	-	-	-	-	0

Best result: 7th. Best qualifying: 17th. Teams: March, Ligier

| Le Mans | 1987-91 | 3 | | - | 1 | - | - | 1 | - | - | |
| SC W | 1982-92 | | | 5 | 2 | 1 | 1 | 1 | - | - | |

Wins: 1987 Jerez, Silverstone, Brands Hatch, Nurburgring, Spa. Best championship: 1987, 1st

| Indy 500 | 1985-2002 | 13 | | - | - | 1 | 1 | - | - | - | |
| CART | 1985-99 | 172 (1) | - | 5 | 3 | 12 | 8 | 17 | 3 | 2 | |

Best championship: 1993, 5th

| IRL | 1998-2002 | 27 (1) | - | - | - | - | 2 | - | - | - | |

Other Major win: 1988 Daytona 24 hrs

Jimmy Bohlin
S. Born: 31.7.1969
1998 Nordic F3 Champion, 1998 Swedish F3 Champion

Lennart Bohlin
S. Born: 19.9.1943
1988 Swedish Touring Car Champion

Walt Bohren
USA. Born: 4.2.1948
1980 IMSA GTU Champion

formula	years	starts (DNS)	wins	2nd	3rd	4th	5th	6th	PP	FL	points
Le Mans	1984	1	-	-	-	-	-	-	-	-	
SC W	1978-92			-	-	-	-	1	-	-	

Andre Boillot
F. Born: 1891. Died: 1932, La Chatre, testing. Also known as "Dribus"

formula	years	starts (DNS)	wins	2nd	3rd	4th	5th	6th	PP	FL	points
GP Pre-50	1921-31	3		-	1	-	-	1	1	-	
Le Mans	1926	1	-	-	-	-	-	-	-	-	
Indy 500	1919-21	3	-	-	-	-	-	-	-	-	

Major win: 1919 Targa Florio, 1926 Spa 24 hrs

Georges Boillot

F. Born: 1885. Died: 21.4.1916, Verdun, shot down while fighting for the French Air Service (death reported on this day but may have died earlier)

formula	years	starts (DNS)	wins	2nd	3rd	4th	5th	6th	PP	FL	points
GP Pre-50	1912-14	3	2	-	-	-	-	-	-	-	

Wins: 1912 French GP, 1913 French GP

Indy 500	1914	1	-	-	-	-	-	-	-	-	

Andrea Boldrini

I. Born: 10.7.1971, Milan
1996 Italian F3 Champion

formula	years	starts (DNS)	wins	2nd	3rd	4th	5th	6th	PP	FL	points
F3000 INT	1999	1 (3)	-	-	-	-	-	-	-	-	0

Colin Bond

AUS. Born: 15.8.1941
1975 Australian Touring Car Champion

formula	years	starts (DNS)	wins	2nd	3rd	4th	5th	6th	PP	FL	points
SC W	1984		-	-	-	-	-	1	-	-	

Major win: 1969 Bathurst

Bob Bondurant

USA. Born: 27.4.1933, Evanston, Illinois

formula	years	starts (DNS)	wins	2nd	3rd	4th	5th	6th	PP	FL	points
F1 W	1965-66	9	-	-	-	1	-	-	-	-	3

Best championship: 1966, 14th. Best qualifying: 11th. Teams: Ferrari, Reg Parnell, Chamaco, Bernard White, Eagle

Le Mans	1964-67	4		-	-	1	-	-	-		
SC W	1964-81		-	-	1	3	3	-	-	-	

Felice Bonetto

I. Born: 9.6.1903, Manerbio, near Brescia. Died: 21.11.1953, Silao, near Leon, Carrera Panamericana

formula	years	starts (DNS)	wins	2nd	3rd	4th	5th	6th	PP	FL	points
F1 W	1950-53	15 (2)	-	-	2	3	3	1	-	-	17.5

Best championship: 1951, 8th. Best qualifying: 2nd. Teams: Milano, Alfa Romeo, Maserati

GP Pre-50	1949	1		-	-	-	-	-			
Le Mans	1952-53	2		-	-	-	-	-			
SC W	1953		-	1	-	-	-	-			

Major win: 1952 Targa Florio

Neil Bonnett

USA. Born: 30.7.1946. Died: 11.2.1994, Daytona 500, practice
NASCAR wins: 18 (all Modern era) including 1982, 1983 World 600

Joakim "Jo" Bonnier

S. Born: 31.1.1930, Stockholm. Died: 11.6.1972, Le Mans 24 hrs
1970 European 2-litre Sports Car Champion (Group 6 class)

formula	years	starts (DNS)	wins	2nd	3rd	4th	5th	6th	PP	FL	points
F1 W	1956-71	104 (4)	1	-	-	1	10	8	1	-	39

Win: 1959 Dutch GP. Best championship: 1959, 8th. Best qualifying: 1st. Teams: Maserati, Scuderia Centro Sud, driver, Giorgio Scarlatti, BRM, Porsche, Rob Walker, Anglo-Suisse

Le Mans	1957-72	13	-	1	-	-	-	-			
SC W	1955-72		6	5	6	1	2	4	5	2	

Wins: 1960 Targa Florio, 1962 Sebring 12 hrs, 1963 Targa Florio, 1964 Reims, Montlhery, 1966 Nurburgring

F2 E	1971	1	-	-	-	-	-	-	-	-	0

Other Major win: 1960 German GP

Roberto Bonomi

RA. Born: 30.9.1919, Buenos Aires

formula	years	starts (DNS)	wins	2nd	3rd	4th	5th	6th	PP	FL	points
F1 W	1960	1	-	-	-	-	-	-	-	-	0

Best result: 11th. Best qualifying: 17th. Team: Scuderia Centro Sud

SC W	1954-60		-	-	-	1	-	-			

Andrew Booth

NZ. Born: 2.6.1974, Auckland
2001 New Zealand Gold Star Champion
Major win: 2001 New Zealand GP

Terry Borcheller

USA. Born: 22.3.1966, Hialeah, Florida
2001 American Le Mans Series GTS Champion

formula	years	starts (DNS)	wins	2nd	3rd	4th	5th	6th	PP	FL	points
Le Mans	2001	1	-	-	-	-	-	-			

Pietro Bordino

I. Born: 22.11.1887, Turin. Died: 16.4.1928, Alessandria, practice

formula	years	starts (DNS)	wins	2nd	3rd	4th	5th	6th	PP	FL	points
GP Pre-50	1921-24	6	1	-	1	-	1	-	-	-	5

Win: 1922 Italian GP

Indy 500	1925	1	-	-	-	-	-	-	-	-	

Champcar wins: 2 – 1922 Beverly Hills race 2, Cotati race 1

Jakob Bordoli

CH
1980, 1985, 1987 and 1988 Swiss F3 Champion

Tommy "Slim" Borgudd

S. Born: 25.11.1946, Borgholm, Oland Island, near Kalmar
1994 Nordic Touring Car Champion, 1994 Swedish Touring Car Champion, 1979 Swedish F3 Champion

formula	years	starts (DNS)	wins	2nd	3rd	4th	5th	6th	PP	FL	points
F1 W	1981-82	10 (5)	-	-	-	-	-	1	-	-	1

Best championship: 1981, 18th. Best qualifying: 20th. Teams: ATS, Tyrrell

F3000 INT	1985	3 (1)	-	-	-	-	-	-	-	-	0

Giancarlo Bornigia

I
Major win: 1950 Targa Florio

Mario Bornigia

I
Major win: 1950 Targa Florio

Baconin Borzacchini

I. Born: 28.9.1898, Terni, near Rome. Died: 10.9.1933, Monza GP

formula	years	starts (DNS)	wins	2nd	3rd	4th	5th	6th	PP	FL	points
GP Pre-50	1928-33	16 (1)	-	5	3	-	-	-	2	-	
Indy 500	1930	1	-	-	-	-	-	-			

Major win: 1930 Tripoli, 1932 Mille Miglia

Midge Bosworth

AUS
Major win: 1965 Bathurst

Luki Botha

ZA. Born: 16.1.1930, Pretoria

formula	years	starts (DNS)	wins	2nd	3rd	4th	5th	6th	PP	FL	points
F1 W	1967	1	-	-	-	-	-	-	-	-	0

Best result: no finishes. Best qualifying: 17th. Team: driver

Gene Bothello

USA
1979 Trans-Am Class 1 Champion

Ron Bouchard

USA. Born: 23.11.1948
NASCAR wins: 1 (in Modern era)

Christophe Bouchut

F. Born: 24.9.1966, Voiron
2001 (with Jean-Philippe Belloc) and 2002 FIA GT Champion, 2000 FIA N-GT class Champion (with Patrice Goueslard), 1991 French F3 Champion

formula	years	starts (DNS)	wins	2nd	3rd	4th	5th	6th	PP	FL	points
Le Mans	1993-2002	10	1	-	-	-	-	1	-	-	

Win: 1993 Le Mans 24 hrs

formula	years	starts (DNS)	wins	2nd	3rd	4th	5th	6th	PP	FL	points
SC W	1992	-	1	-	-	-	-	-	-	-	-

Best championship: 1992, 16th. GT FIA wins: 5 – 2001 Brno, Silverstone, Zolder, Spa 24 hrs, 2002 Spa 24 hrs

formula	years	starts (DNS)	wins	2nd	3rd	4th	5th	6th	PP	FL	points
F3000 INT	1995	7	-	1	-	-	-	-	-	-	6

Best championship: 1995, 10th

Other Major win: 1995 Daytona 24 hrs

Jean-Christophe "Jules" Boullion
F. Born: 27.12.1969, St Brieuc, Brittany
1994 FIA F3000 Champion

formula	years	starts (DNS)	wins	2nd	3rd	4th	5th	6th	PP	FL	points
F1 W	1995	11	-	-	-	-	1	1	-	-	3

Best championship: 1995, 16th. Best qualifying: 13th. Team: Sauber

Le Mans	1994-2002	6	-	-	-	-	-	-			

SRWC wins: 3 – 2001 Magny-Cours, 2002 Barcelona, Spa

F3000 INT	1993-94	17	3	3	-	1	-	-	-	2	48

Wins: 1994 Spa, Estoril, Magny-Cours. Best championship: 1994, 1st

Sebastien Bourdais
F. Born: 28.2.1979, Le Mans
2002 FIA F3000 Champion, 1999 French F3 Champion

formula	years	starts (DNS)	wins	2nd	3rd	4th	5th	6th	PP	FL	points
Le Mans	1999-2002	4	-	-	-	-	-	-			

GT FIA win: 1 – 2002 Spa 24 hrs. SRWC wins: 2 – 2002 Barcelona, Spa

F3000 INT	2000-02	33 (1)	4	4	4	3	-	2	8	4	91

Win: 2001 Silverstone, 2002 Imola, Monte Carlo, Nurburgring. Best championship: 2002, 1st

Claude Bourgoignie
B

formula	years	starts (DNS)	wins	2nd	3rd	4th	5th	6th	PP	FL	points
Le Mans	1969-85	5	-	-	-	1	-	-	-		
SC W	1969-85		-	-	-	1	-	-	1	1	
F2 E	1972-75	19 (6)	-	1	1	1	-	1	-	-	16

Best championship: 1975, 7th

Thierry Boutsen
B. Born: 13.7.1957, Brussels

formula	years	starts (DNS)	wins	2nd	3rd	4th	5th	6th	PP	FL	points
F1 W	1983-93	163 (1)	3	2	10	8	11	7	1	1	132

Wins: 1989 Canadian GP, Australian GP, 1990 Hungarian GP. Best championship: 1988, 4th. Best qualifying: 1st. Teams: Arrows, Benetton, Williams, Ligier, Jordan

Le Mans	1981-99	10	-	2	1	-	-	1		1	
SC W	1979-92	2	1	4	1	1	3	1			

Wins: 1983 Monza, 1986 Spa. Best championship: 1983, 6th. GT FIA wins: 2 – 1996 Brands Hatch, Spa

F2 E	1981-82	25	5	4	2	3	-	2	8	2	88

Wins: 1981 Nurburgring, Enna, 1982 Nurburgring, Spa, Enna. Best championship: 1981, 2nd

F3 E wins: 3 – 1980 Nurburgring, Zolder, Magny-Cours

Other Major win: 1985 Daytona 24 hrs

Frederic Bouvy
B. Born: 6.6.1966, Brussels
1999 Belgian Procar Touring Car Champion
Major wins: 1999 and 2000 Spa 24 hrs

John Bowe
AUS. Born: 16.4.1954
1995 Australian Touring Car Champion, 1984 and 1985 Australian Formula Pacific Champion
Major wins: 1989 and 1994 Bathurst

Graeme Bowkett
NZ. Born: 29.6.1951
1986 New Zealand Touring Car Champion

Joe Boyer
USA. Born: 12.5.1890, Detroit, Michigan. Died: 2.9.1924, Altoona, Pennsylvania, from injuries inflicted the previous day

formula	years	starts (DNS)	wins	2nd	3rd	4th	5th	6th	PP	FL	points
GP Pre-50	1921	1	-	-	-	-	-	-	-	-	-
Indy 500	1919-24	5	1	-	-	-	-	1	-	-	

Win: 1924 Indianapolis 500

Champcar wins: 3 – 1919 Uniontown race 7, Cincinnati, 1924 Indianapolis 500

Lord Brabazon of Tara (John Moore-Brabazon)
GB. Born: 8.2.1884, Kent. Died: 17.5.1964, Chertsey, Surrey

formula	years	starts (DNS)	wins	2nd	3rd	4th	5th	6th	PP	FL	points
GP Pre-50	1908	1	-	-	-	-	-	-	-	-	-

Major win: 1907 Ardennes Circuit (Kaiserpreis class)

David Brabham
AUS. Born: 5.9.1965, Wimbledon, London (GB)
1998 IMSA GT Champion (with Andy Wallace), 1996 Japanese GT Champion (with John Nielsen), 1989 British F3 Champion, 1987 Australian Formula Pacific Champion

formula	years	starts (DNS)	wins	2nd	3rd	4th	5th	6th	PP	FL	points
F1 W	1990-94	24 (6)	-	-	-	-	-	-	-	-	0

Best result: 10th. Best qualifying: 21st. Teams: Brabham, Simtek

Le Mans	1992-2002	9	-	-	-	-	-	1	-	-	
SC W	1991-92		1	2	3	1	1	-	-		

Win: 1991 Nurburgring. Best championship: 1992, 10th

F3000 INT	1991	4	-	-	-	-	-	-	-	-	0

Other major wins: 1989 Macau, 1991 Spa 24 hrs, 1999 Petit LeMans

Gary Brabham
AUS. Born: 29.3.1961, Wimbledon, London (GB)
1989 British F3000 Champion

formula	years	starts (DNS)	wins	2nd	3rd	4th	5th	6th	PP	FL	points
F1 W	1990	0 (2)	-	-	-	-	-	-	-	-	0

Best result: no starts. Best qualifying: 34th. Team: Life

Le Mans	1989	1	-	-	-	-	-	-	-		
F3000 INT	1989-90	15 (3)	-	-	2	-	1	-	-		10

Best championship: 1990, 11th

CART	1993-94	2	-	-	-	-	-	-	-	-	

Major wins: 1988 Cellnet Superprix (Brands Hatch), 1991 Sebring 12 hrs

Geoff Brabham
AUS. Born: 20.3.1952, Sydney, New South Wales
1981 Can-Am Champion, 1988, 1989, 1990 and 1991 IMSA GTP Champion, 1979 SCCA Super Vee Champion

formula	years	starts (DNS)	wins	2nd	3rd	4th	5th	6th	PP	FL	points
Le Mans	1989-93	3	1	-	-	-	-	-	-		

Win: 1993 Le Mans 24 hrs

SC W	1987-92		-	-	-	-	1	-	-		
Indy 500	1981-93	10	-	-	-	1	1	-	-	-	
CART	1981-93	86 (1)	-	5	4	5	5	3	1	-	

Best championships: 1982, 1984 and 1987, 8th

Other major wins: 1989 and 1991 Sebring 12 hrs, 1997 Bathurst 2-litre

Sir Jack Brabham
AUS. Born: 2.4.1926, Hurstville, near Sydney, New South Wales
1959, 1960 and 1966 F1 World Champion, 1958 and 1966 British F2 Champion, 1964 and 1966 French F2 Champion

formula	years	starts (DNS)	wins	2nd	3rd	4th	5th	6th	PP	FL	points
F1 W	1955-70	126 (2)	14	10	7	13	5	7	13	12	261

Wins: 1959 Monaco GP, British GP, 1960 Dutch GP, Belgian GP, French GP, British GP, Portuguese GP, 1966 French GP, British GP, Dutch GP, German GP, 1967 French GP, Canadian GP, 1970 South African GP. Best championships: 1959, 1960 and 1966, 1st. Best qualifying: 1st. Teams: Cooper, driver, Rob Walker, Brabham

Le Mans	1957-70	3	-	-	-	-	-	-	-		
SC W	1957-84		1	1	-	-	1	-	-	-	

Win: 1958 Nurburgring

formula	years	starts (DNS)	wins	2nd	3rd	4th	5th	6th	PP	FL	points
F2 E	1967-70	8	–	2	–	1	–	1	–	–	0
Indy 500	1961-70	4	–	–	–	–	–	–	–	–	

Non-championship F1 wins: 1959 International Trophy (Silverstone), 1960 Brands Hatch, 1961 Snetterton, Brussels, Aintree, 1962 Danish GP, 1963 Solitude, Austrian GP, 1964 Aintree, International Trophy (Silverstone), 1965 Rand GP (Kyalami), 1966 International Trophy (Silverstone), Oulton Park Gold Cup, 1967 Oulton Spring Trophy, Oulton Park Gold Cup, 1969 International Trophy (Silverstone)

Tasman wins: 2 – 1964 Australian GP, 1967 Longford

Other major wins: 1955 and 1963 Australian GP, 1958, 1960 and 1961 New Zealand GP

Giovanni Bracco

I. Born: 6.6.1908, Biella. Died: 6.8.1968

formula	years	starts (DNS)	wins	2nd	3rd	4th	5th	6th	PP	FL	points
GP Pre-50	1947	1	–	–	–	–	–	–	–	–	–
Le Mans	1951	1	–	–	–	–	–	–	–	–	–

Major wins: 1948 and 1952 Pescara GP, 1952 Mille Miglia

Bill Brack

CDN. Born: 26.12.1935, Toronto, Ontario

1974 and 1975 North American Formula Atlantic Champion

formula	years	starts (DNS)	wins	2nd	3rd	4th	5th	6th	PP	FL	points
F1 W	1968-72	3	–	–	–	–	–	–	–	–	0

Best result: no finishes. Best qualifying: 18th. Teams: Lotus, BRM

Kenny Brack

S. Born: 21.3.1966, Arvika

1998 Indy Racing League Champion, 1993 Barber-SAAB Champion

formula	years	starts (DNS)	wins	2nd	3rd	4th	5th	6th	PP	FL	points
F3000 INT	1994-96	25 (1)	4	3	4	1	2	1	5	3	78

Wins: 1995 Magny-Cours, 1996 Nurburgring, Hockenheim, Silverstone. Best championship: 1996, 2nd

formula	years	starts (DNS)	wins	2nd	3rd	4th	5th	6th	PP	FL	points
Indy 500	1997-2002	4	1	–	–	–	–	–	–	1	–

Win: 1999 Indianapolis 500

formula	years	starts (DNS)	wins	2nd	3rd	4th	5th	6th	PP	FL	points
CART	2000-02	59 (1)	5	5	3	5	5	3	7	3	

Wins: 2001 Motegi, Milwaukee, Chicago, Lausitzring, 2002 Mexico City. Best championship: 2001, 2nd

formula	years	starts (DNS)	wins	2nd	3rd	4th	5th	6th	PP	FL	points
IRL	1997-2002	29	4	1	3	–	3	1	–	2	

Wins: 1998 Charlotte, Pikes Peak, Atlanta, 1999 Indianapolis 500. Best championship: 1998, 1st

Caleb Bragg

USA. Born: 1888, Cincinnati, Ohio. Died: 24.10.1943

formula	years	starts (DNS)	wins	2nd	3rd	4th	5th	6th	PP	FL	points
GP Pre-50	1911-15	3	1	–	–	1	–	–	–	–	–

Win: 1912 American GP

formula	years	starts (DNS)	wins	2nd	3rd	4th	5th	6th	PP	FL	points
Indy 500	1911-14	4	–	1	–	–	–	–	–	1	–

Ernesto "Tino" Brambilla

I. Born: 31.1.1934, Monza, near Milan

1966 Italian F3 Champion

formula	years	starts (DNS)	wins	2nd	3rd	4th	5th	6th	PP	FL	points
F1 W	1963-69	0 (2)	–	–	–	–	–	–	–	–	0

Best result: no starts. Best qualifying: 15th. Teams: Scuderia Centro Sud, Ferrari

formula	years	starts (DNS)	wins	2nd	3rd	4th	5th	6th	PP	FL	points
F2 E	1968-73	30 (5)	2	–	1	–	–	4	1	2	38

Wins: 1968 Hockenheim race 2, Vallelunga. Best championship: 1968, 2nd

Vittorio Brambilla

I. Born: 11.11.1937, Monza, near Milan. Died: 26.5.2001, Brianza, heart attack

1972 Italian F3 Champion

formula	years	starts (DNS)	wins	2nd	3rd	4th	5th	6th	PP	FL	points
F1 W	1974-80	74 (5)	1	–	–	1	2	5	1	1	15.5

Win: 1975 Austrian GP. Best championship: 1975, 11th. Best qualifying: 1st. Teams: March, Surtees, Alfa Romeo

formula	years	starts (DNS)	wins	2nd	3rd	4th	5th	6th	PP	FL	points
SC W	1974-80	4	3	–	–	1	–	–	–	9	7

Wins: 1977 Monza, Vallelunga, Imola, Salzburgring

formula	years	starts (DNS)	wins	2nd	3rd	4th	5th	6th	PP	FL	points
F2 E	1970-77	32 (3)	3	2	1	1	2	2	2	1	58

Wins: 1973 Salzburgring, Albi, 1975 Vallelunga. Best championship: 1973, 4th

Antonio Branca

CH. Born: 15.9.1916, Sion. Died: 10.5.1985, Sierre

formula	years	starts (DNS)	wins	2nd	3rd	4th	5th	6th	PP	FL	points
F1 W	1950-51	3	–	–	–	–	–	–	–	–	0

Best result: 10th. Best qualifying: 13th. Teams: Scuderia Varzi, driver

formula	years	starts (DNS)	wins	2nd	3rd	4th	5th	6th	PP	FL	points
GP Pre-50	1949	1	–	–	–	–	–	–	–	–	–

Gianfranco Brancatelli

I. Born: 18.1.1950, Turin

1985 European Touring Car Champion (with Thomas Lindstrom), 1988 Italian Touring Car Champion

formula	years	starts (DNS)	wins	2nd	3rd	4th	5th	6th	PP	FL	points
F1 W	1979	0 (3)	–	–	–	–	–	–	–	–	0

Best result: no starts. Best qualifying: 25th. Teams: Kauhsen, Merzario

formula	years	starts (DNS)	wins	2nd	3rd	4th	5th	6th	PP	FL	points
Le Mans	1979-90	5	–	1	–	–	–	–	–	–	–
SC W	1979-2		–	–	–	2	2	3	–	–	

Best championship: 1990, 17th

formula	years	starts (DNS)	wins	2nd	3rd	4th	5th	6th	PP	FL	points
F2 E	1976-79	14 (5)	–	–	–	1	–	–	–	–	3

Best championship: 1977, 17th

F3 E wins: 2 – 1976 Mantorp Park, Vallelunga

Other major wins: 1984 Tourist Trophy (Silverstone), 1985 Macau Guia race, 1989 Spa 24 hrs

Marco Brand

I. Born: 31.1.1957, Milan

1993 Italian Supercar GT Champion

formula	years	starts (DNS)	wins	2nd	3rd	4th	5th	6th	PP	FL	points
Le Mans	1991-92	2	–	–	–	–	–	–	–	–	–
F2 E	1981	1 (1)	–	–	–	–	–	–	–	–	–

Eric Brandon

GB. Born: 18.7.1920, East London. Died: 8.8.1982, Gosport, Hampshire

1951 British F3 Champion

formula	years	starts (DNS)	wins	2nd	3rd	4th	5th	6th	PP	FL	points
F1 W	1952-54	5	–	–	–	–	–	–	–	–	0

Best result: 8th. Best qualifying: 12th. Team: Ecurie Richmond

Don Branson

USA. Born: 2.6.1920, Rantoul, Illinois. Died: 12.11.1966, Ascot, California

formula	years	starts (DNS)	wins	2nd	3rd	4th	5th	6th	PP	FL	points
Indy 500	1959-66	8	–	–	–	1	1	–	–	–	–

Champcar wins: 6 – 1962 Langhorne race 2, Trenton race 3, 1965 Phoenix race 1, Du Quoin, Sacramento, 1966 Springfield

Manfred von Brauchitsch

D. Born: 15.8.1905, Hamburg. Died: 5.2.2003, Stuttgart

formula	years	starts (DNS)	wins	2nd	3rd	4th	5th	6th	PP	FL	points
GP Pre-50	1931-39	32 (1)	–	2	6	6	–	2	–	5	3

Wins: 1937 Monaco GP, 1938 French GP

Other major wins: 1932 Avus, 1934 Eifelrennen (Nurburgring)

Jorg Breuer

D

1997 German GT Champion

Richard Brickhouse

USA. Born: Rocky Point, North Carolina

NASCAR wins: 1

Tommy Bridger

GB. Born: 24.6.1934, Welwyn, Hertfordshire. Died: 30.7.1991, Aboyne, Aberdeenshire

formula	years	starts (DNS)	wins	2nd	3rd	4th	5th	6th	PP	FL	points
F1 W	1958	1	–	–	–	–	–	–	–	–	0

Best result: no finishes. Best qualifying: no times set. Team: BRP

formula	years	starts (DNS)	wins	2nd	3rd	4th	5th	6th	PP	FL	points
Le Mans	1958	1	–	–	–	–	–	–	–	–	–

Mike Briggs
ZA. Born: 24.7.1966, Port Elizabeth
1993 and 1995 South African Touring Car Champion, 1991 South African Formula GTi Champion

Jason Bright
AUS. Born: 7.3.1973, Moe, Victoria
1997 Australian Formula Holden Champion

formula	years	starts (DNS)	wins	2nd	3rd	4th	5th	6th	PP	FL	points
CART	2000	1	-	-	-	-	-	-	-	-	-

Major win: 1998 Bathurst

Gastone Brilli-Peri
I. Born: 24.3.1893, Montevarchi, near Florence. Died: 22.3.1930, Mellaha, Tripoli GP practice

formula	years	starts (DNS)	wins	2nd	3rd	4th	5th	6th	PP	FL	points
GP Pre-50	1925-29	6	1	-	-	2	-	-	-	-	

Win: 1925 Italian GP
Other major wins: 1929 Tripoli, 1929 Tunis

Tony Brise
GB. Born: 28.3.1952, Dartford, Kent. Died: 29.11.1975, Arkley, near Barnet, Hertfordshire, aircraft accident with Graham Hill Racing
1975 John Player British Formula Atlantic Champion, 1973 Lombard and John Player British F3 Champion

formula	years	starts (DNS)	wins	2nd	3rd	4th	5th	6th	PP	FL	points
F1 W	1975	10	-	-	-	-	-	1	-	-	1

Best championship: 1975, 19th. Best qualifying: 6th. Teams: Williams, Hill

Chris Bristow
GB. Born: 2.12.1937, Lambeth, London. Died: 19.6.1960, Spa, Belgian GP

formula	years	starts (DNS)	wins	2nd	3rd	4th	5th	6th	PP	FL	points
F1 W	1959-60	4	-	-	-	-	-	-	-	-	0

Best result: 10th. Best qualifying: 4th. Team: BRP

Antonio Brivio (Conte Sforza)
I. Born: 27.12.1905, Biella. Died: 1995

formula	years	starts (DNS)	wins	2nd	3rd	4th	5th	6th	PP	FL	points
GP Pre-50	1928-37	15 (1)	-	1	2	2	2	1	1	1	

Major wins: 1932 Spa 24 hrs, 1933 and 1935 Targa Florio, 1936 Mille Miglia

Peter Brock
AUS. Born: 17.8.1945, Hurstbridge
1974, 1978 and 1980 Australian Touring Car Champion

formula	years	starts (DNS)	wins	2nd	3rd	4th	5th	6th	PP	FL	points
Le Mans	1976-84	2	-	-	-	-	-	-	-	-	-

Major wins: 1972, 1975, 1978, 1979, 1980, 1982, 1983, 1984 and 1987 Bathurst

Frank Brodie
ZA
1955 South African Drivers' Champion

Peter Broeker
CDN. Born: 15.5.1929, Ontario. Died: 1980

formula	years	starts (DNS)	wins	2nd	3rd	4th	5th	6th	PP	FL	points
F1 W	1963	1	-	-	-	-	-	-	-	-	0

Best result: 7th. Best qualifying: 21st. Team: Stebro

Gino Bronzoni
I

formula	years	starts (DNS)	wins	2nd	3rd	4th	5th	6th	PP	FL	points
SC W	1953	1	-	-	-	-	-	-	-	-	

Win: 1953 Carrera Panamericana

Dick Brooks
USA. Born: 14.4.1942

formula	years	starts (DNS)	wins	2nd	3rd	4th	5th	6th	PP	FL	points
Le Mans	1976-82	2	-	-	-	-	-	-	-	-	-

NASCAR wins: 1 (in Modern era)

Tony Brooks
GB. Born: 25.2.1932, Dukinfield, Cheshire

formula	years	starts (DNS)	wins	2nd	3rd	4th	5th	6th	PP	FL	points
F1 W	1956-61	38 (1)	6	2	2	1	3	-	3	3	75

Wins: 1957 British GP, 1958 Belgian GP, German GP, Italian GP, 1959 French GP, German GP. Best championship: 1959, 2nd. Best qualifying: 1st. Teams: BRM, Vanwall, Ferrari, BRP

formula	years	starts (DNS)	wins	2nd	3rd	4th	5th	6th	PP	FL	points
Le Mans	1955-58	4	-	-	-	-	-	-	-	-	-
SC W	1954-59	2	-	2	-	2	-	-	1		

Wins: 1957 Nurburgring, 1958 Tourist Trophy (Goodwood)
Non-championship F1 win: 1955 Syracuse

Helmut Bross
D. Born: 5.5.1939
1977 Interserie Champion

formula	years	starts (DNS)	wins	2nd	3rd	4th	5th	6th	PP	FL	points
SC W	1974-81		-	-	1	-	-	1	-	-	
F2 E	1976-80	6 (3)	-	-	-	-	-	-	-	-	0

Alan Brown
GB. Born: 20.11.1919, Malton, Yorkshire

formula	years	starts (DNS)	wins	2nd	3rd	4th	5th	6th	PP	FL	points
F1 W	1952-54	8 (1)	-	-	-	1	1	-	-		2

Best championship: 1952, 16th. Best qualifying: 9th. Teams: Ecurie Richmond, Cooper, RJ Chase, Equipe Anglaise

Walt Brown
USA. Born: 30.12.1911, Springfield, New York State. Died: 29.7.1951, Williams Grove, Pennsylvania

formula	years	starts (DNS)	wins	2nd	3rd	4th	5th	6th	PP	FL	points
Indy 500	1947-51	4	-	-	-	-	-	-	-	-	-

Champcar win: 1 – 1948 Langhorne

Warwick Brown
AUS. Born: 24.12.1949, Sydney, New South Wales
1975 Tasman Champion

formula	years	starts (DNS)	wins	2nd	3rd	4th	5th	6th	PP	FL	points
F1 W	1976	1	-	-	-	-	-	-	-	-	0

Best result: 14th. Best qualifying: 23rd. Team: Williams
Tasman wins: 3 – 1974 Adelaide, 1975 New Zealand GP, Oran Park
Other Major win: 1977 Australian GP

David Bruce
AUS
1998 Australian F3 Champion

David Bruce-Brown
USA. Born: 1887. Died: 1.10.1912, Milwaukee, American GP practice

formula	years	starts (DNS)	wins	2nd	3rd	4th	5th	6th	PP	FL	points
GP Pre-50	1910-12	3 (1)	2	-	-	-	-	-	-	-	1

Wins: 1910 American GP, 1911 American GP

formula	years	starts (DNS)	wins	2nd	3rd	4th	5th	6th	PP	FL	points
Indy 500	1911-12	2	-	-	1	-	-	-	-	-	

Champcar win: 1 – 1911 American GP

Adolf Brudes von Breslau
D. Born: 15.10.1899, Wrozlau (PL). Died: 5.11.1986, Bremen

formula	years	starts (DNS)	wins	2nd	3rd	4th	5th	6th	PP	FL	points
F1 W	1952	1	-	-	-	-	-	-	-	-	0

Best result: no finishes. Best qualifying: no times set. Team: driver

formula	years	starts (DNS)	wins	2nd	3rd	4th	5th	6th	PP	FL	points
Le Mans	1953	1	-	-	-	-	-	-	-	-	-
SC W	1953-54		-	-	1	-	-	-	-		

Martin Brundle
GB. Born: 1.6.1959, King's Lynn, Norfolk
1988 World Sports Car Champion

formula	years	starts (DNS)	wins	2nd	3rd	4th	5th	6th	PP	FL	points
F1 W	1984-96	158 (7)	-	2	7	8	12	10	-	-	98

Best championship: 1992, 6th. Best qualifying: 3rd. Teams: Tyrrell, Zakspeed, Williams, Brabham, Benetton, Ligier, McLaren, Jordan

| Le Mans | 1987-2001 | 7 | 1 | - | - | - | - | - | 1 | 1 | |

Win: 1990 Le Mans 24 hrs

| SC W | 1985-92 | | 8 | 4 | 5 | - | 2 | - | 1 | | 3 |

Wins: 1987 Spa, 1988 Jarama, Monza, Silverstone, Brands Hatch, Fuji, 1990 Silverstone, 1991 Monza. Best championship: 1988, 1st

F3 E wins: 2 – 1983 Silverstone, Donington

Other Major win: 1988 Daytona 24 hrs

Gianmaria Bruni

I. Born: 30.5.1981, Rome
1999 European Formula Renault Champion

Erik Bruynoghe

B. Born: 5.7.1967
1991 Belgian Belcar GT Champion (with Meirschaut and Guy Verheyen), 2000 Belgian Belcar Touring Car Champion (with Bas Leinders)

Jimmy Bryan

USA. Born: 28.1.1927, Phoenix, Arizona. Died: 19.6.1960, Langhorne, Pennsylvania
1954, 1956 and 1957 Champcar Champion

formula	years	starts (DNS)	wins	2nd	3rd	4th	5th	6th	PP	FL	points
Indy 500	1952-60	9	1	1	1	-	-	1	-	-	

Win: 1958 Indianapolis 500

Champcar wins: 19 – 1953 Sacramento, 1954 Langhorne, Indiana State Fairgrounds, Sacramento, Phoenix, Las Vegas, 1955 Langhorne, Springfield, Du Quoin, Indiana State Fairgrounds, Sacramento, Phoenix, 1956 Springfield, Milwaukee race 2, Du Quoin, Indiana State Fairgrounds, 1957 Detroit, Phoenix, 1958 Indianapolis 500

Other Major win: 1957 Race of Two Worlds (Monza)

Lilian Bryner

CH. Born: 21.4.1959, Milan (I)
1995 FIA GT2 class Champion (with Enzo Calderari)

formula	years	starts (DNS)	wins	2nd	3rd	4th	5th	6th	PP	FL	points
Le Mans	1993-97	4	-								

Thomas Bscher

D. Born: 2.4.1952, Cologne
1995 FIA GT Champion (with John Nielsen), 1995 (with Nielsen) and 1998 (with Geoff Lees) European GT Champion

formula	years	starts (DNS)	wins	2nd	3rd	4th	5th	6th	PP	FL	points
Le Mans	1994-2000	6	-	-	-	1	1	-	-	-	

GT FIA wins: 4 – 1995 Monza, Donington, 1996 Monza, Nurburgring

Clemar Bucci

RA. Born: 4.9.1920, Zenon Pereyra, Santa Fe

formula	years	starts (DNS)	wins	2nd	3rd	4th	5th	6th	PP	FL	points
F1 W	1954-55	5	-	-	-	-	-	-	-	-	0

Best result: no finishes. Best qualifying: 10th. Teams: Gordini, Maserati

| GP Pre-50 | 1948 | 1 (1) | - | - | - | - | - | - | - | - | |

Dave Buck

USA. Born: n/a. Died: 26.8.1911, Elgin road race
Champcar win: 1 – 1910 Elgin race 1

Ronnie Bucknum

USA. Born: 5.4.1936, Alhambra, California. Died: 25.4.1992, San Luis Obispo, California, diabetes complications

formula	years	starts (DNS)	wins	2nd	3rd	4th	5th	6th	PP	FL	points
F1 W	1964-66	11	-	-	-	-	1	-	-	-	2

Best championship: 1965, 14th. Best qualifying: 6th. Team: Honda

Le Mans	1965-70	4	-	-	1	1	-	-	-	
SC W	1963-83		-	1	1	2	1	-	-	-
Indy 500	1968-70	3	-	-	-	-	-	-	-	

Champcar win: 1 – 1968 Michigan

Ivor Bueb

GB. Born: 6.6.1923, Dulwich, London. Died: 1.8.1959, Clermont-Ferrand, after an accident in the Auvergne F2 Race

formula	years	starts (DNS)	wins	2nd	3rd	4th	5th	6th	PP	FL	points
F1 W	1957-59	5 (1)	-	-	-	-	-	-	-	-	0

Best result: 8th. Best qualifying: 16th. Team: Connaught, Gilby, Bernie Ecclestone, Ecurie Demi Litre, BRP

| Le Mans | 1955-59 | 5 | 2 | - | - | - | - | - | 1 | - | - |

Wins: 1955 and 1957 Le Mans 24 hrs

| SC W | 1955-59 | | 2 | - | 1 | - | - | - | - | - | |

Wins: 1955 Le Mans 24 hrs, 1957 Le Mans 24 hrs

Carlos "Caca" Bueno

BR. Born: 24.7.1976, Rio de Janeiro
1999 South American Touring Car Champion (with Emiliano Spataro)

Luiz-Pereira Bueno

BR. Born: 16.1.1937, Sao Paulo

formula	years	starts (DNS)	wins	2nd	3rd	4th	5th	6th	PP	FL	points
F1 W	1973	1	-	-	-	-	-	-	-	-	0

Best result: 12th. Best qualifying: 20th. Team: Surtees

Giuseppe Bugatti

I. Born: 1.3.1965, Brescia

formula	years	starts (DNS)	wins	2nd	3rd	4th	5th	6th	PP	FL	points
F3000 INT	1991-93	23 (2)	-	-	1	-	2	-	-	-	8

Best championship: 1991, 11th

Robbie Buhl

USA. Born: 2.9.1963, Detroit, Michigan
1992 CART Indy Lights Champion, 1989 Barber-SAAB Champion

formula	years	starts (DNS)	wins	2nd	3rd	4th	5th	6th	PP	FL	points
Indy 500	1996-2002	7	-	-	-	-	-	-	1	-	-
CART	1993-94	12 (1)	-	-	-	-	-	-	1	-	-
IRL	1996-2002	59 (1)	2	1	6	-	2	4	-	3	

Wins: 1997 New Hampshire, 2000 Disney World. Best championship: 1996, 3rd

Bob Burdick

USA
NASCAR wins: 1

Ian Burgess

GB. Born: 6.7.1930, London

formula	years	starts (DNS)	wins	2nd	3rd	4th	5th	6th	PP	FL	points
F1 W	1958-63	16 (4)	-	-	-	-	-	-	1	-	-	0

Best qualifying: 13th. Teams: Cooper, High Efficiency, Scuderia Centro Sud, Camoradi, Anglo-American, Scirocco Powell

Alex Burgstaller

D. Born: 26.8.1969, Munich
Major wins: 1994 and 1996 Spa 24 hrs

Marvin Burke

USA
NASCAR wins: 1

Bob Burman

USA. Born: 23.4.1884, Imlay City, Michigan. Died: 8.4.1916, Corona, California

formula	years	starts (DNS)	wins	2nd	3rd	4th	5th	6th	PP	FL	points
GP Pre-50	1908-12	4	-	-	1	-	-	-	-	-	
Indy 500	1911-15	5	-	-	1	-	-	-	-	-	

Champcar wins: 6 – 1909 Indianapolis race 1, Lowell race 1, 1910 Indianapolis race 4, 1914 Kalamazoo, 1915 Oklahoma City, Burlington

Kelvin Burt

GB. Born: 7.9.1967, Birmingham
1993 British F3 Champion
Major win: 1995 Macau Guia race

Luciano Burti

BR. Born: 5.3.1975, Sao Paulo

formula	years	starts (DNS)	wins	2nd	3rd	4th	5th	6th	PP	FL	points
F1 W	2000-01	15	-	-	-	-	-	-	-	-	0

Best result: 8th. Best qualifying: 14th. Teams: Jaguar, Prost

Jeff Burton

USA. Born: 29.6.1967, South Boston, Virginia

NASCAR wins: 17 (all Modern era) including 1999, 2001 World 600

Ward Burton

USA. Born: 25.10.1961, Danville, Virginia

NASCAR wins: 5 (all Modern era) including 2002 Daytona 500

Jim Busby

USA. Born: 14.6.1942

formula	years	starts (DNS)	wins	2nd	3rd	4th	5th	6th	PP	FL	points
Le Mans	1978-84	3	-	-	-	-	-	1	-	-	
SC W	1973-87		1	-	-	1	-	2	-	-	

Win: 1981 Riverside

Kurt Busch

USA. Born: 4.8.1978, Las Vegas, Nevada

NASCAR wins: 4 (all modern era)

Giambattista Busi

I. Born: 21.4.1968, Bergamo
1991 Italian F3 Champion

formula	years	starts (DNS)	wins	2nd	3rd	4th	5th	6th	PP	FL	points
F3000 INT	1992	7 (1)	-	-	-	-	-	-	-	-	0

Jan Bussell

SGP

Major wins: 1968 and 1971 Macau

Roberto Bussinello

I. Born: 4.10.1927, Pistoia. Died: 24.8.1999, Vicenza

formula	years	starts (DNS)	wins	2nd	3rd	4th	5th	6th	PP	FL	points
F1 W	1961-65	2 (1)	-	-	-	-	-	-	-	-	0

Best result: 13th. Best qualifying: 21st. Teams: de Tomaso, Scuderia Centro Sud

Le Mans	1964-65	2									
SC W	1963-67			-	-	1	-	1	-	-	

Jenson Button

GB. Born: 19.1.1980, Frome, Somerset

formula	years	starts (DNS)	wins	2nd	3rd	4th	5th	6th	PP	FL	points
F1 W	2000-02	51	-	-	-	3	8	3	-	-	28

Best championship: 2002, 7th. Best qualifying: 3rd. Teams: Williams, Benetton, Renault

Joe Buzzetta

USA. Born: 1937, Brooklyn, New York

formula	years	starts (DNS)	wins	2nd	3rd	4th	5th	6th	PP	FL	points
Le Mans	1967-68	2	-	-	-	-	-	-	-	-	
SC W	1961-69		1	-	3	2	-	1	-	-	

Win: 1967 Nurburgring

Tommy Byrne

IRL. Born: 6.5.1958, Drogheda, County Louth
1982 British F3 Champion, 1981 European FF2000 Champion

formula	years	starts (DNS)	wins	2nd	3rd	4th	5th	6th	PP	FL	points
F1 W	1982	2 (3)	-	-	-	-	-	-	-	-	0

Best result: no finishes. Best qualifying: 26th. Team: Theodore

F3000 INT	1986	1	-	-	-	-	-	-	-	-	0

F3 E wins: 2 – 1983 Osterreichring, Misano

Robert "Red" Byron

USA. Born: 12.3.1915, Boulder, Colorado. Died: 11.11.1960, Chicago, Illinois
1949 NASCAR Champion

NASCAR wins: 2

C

Giulio Cabianca

I. Born: 19.2.1923, Verona. Died: 15.6.1961, Modena

formula	years	starts (DNS)	wins	2nd	3rd	4th	5th	6th	PP	FL	points
F1 W	1958-60	3 (1)	-	-	-	1	-	-	-	-	3

Best championship: 1960, 19th. Best qualifying: 4th. Teams: OSCA, Joakim Bonnier, Ottorino Volonterio, Eugenio Castellotti

Le Mans	1955-59	2		-	-	-	-	-	-	-	
SC W	1953-61			-	-	1	1	-	-	-	

Mario Araujo de Cabral

P. Born: 15.1.1934, Cedofeita, near Porto. Also known as "Nicha"

formula	years	starts (DNS)	wins	2nd	3rd	4th	5th	6th	PP	FL	points
F1 W	1959-64	4 (1)	-	-	-	-	-	-	-	-	0

Best result: 10th. Best qualifying: 14th. Teams: Scuderia Centro Sud, Alf Francis

Le Mans	1972	1									

Phil Cade

USA. Born: 12.7.1916, Charles City, Iowa. Died: 28.8.2001, Winchester, Massachusetts

formula	years	starts (DNS)	wins	2nd	3rd	4th	5th	6th	PP	FL	points
F1 W	1959	0 (1)	-	-	-	-	-	-	-	-	0

Best result: no starts. Best qualifying: 18th. Team: driver

Alain de Cadenet

GB. Born: 27.11.1945

formula	years	starts (DNS)	wins	2nd	3rd	4th	5th	6th	PP	FL	points
Le Mans	1971-86	15	-	-	1	-	1	-	-	-	
SC W	1969-86		2	1	2	-	2	1	-	-	

Wins: 1980 Monza, Silverstone

Nicolas Caerels

B

formula	years	starts (DNS)	wins	2nd	3rd	4th	5th	6th	PP	FL	points
Le Mans	1923	1	-	-	-	1	-	-	-	-	

Major win: 1927 Spa 24 hrs

Alex Caffi

I. Born: 18.3.1964, Rovato, Brescia
1985 European F3 Cup winner

formula	years	starts (DNS)	wins	2nd	3rd	4th	5th	6th	PP	FL	points
F1 W	1986-92	56 (21)	-	-	-	1	1	1	-	-	6

Best championships: 1989 and 1990, 16th. Best qualifying: 3rd. Teams: Osella, Scuderia Italia, Arrows, Footwork, Andrea Moda

Le Mans	1999	1	-	-	-	-	1	-	-	-	
SC W	1992		-	-	-	1	1	-	-	-	

Best championship: 1992, 20th

Alessandro Cagno

I. Born: 2.5.1883, Turin. Died: 23.12.1971

formula	years	starts (DNS)	wins	2nd	3rd	4th	5th	6th	PP	FL	points
GP Pre-50	1904-14	6	-	-	1	-	-	-	-	-	

Major win: 1906 Targa Florio

Enzo Calderari

CH. Born: 18.4.1952, Bienne
1995 FIA GT2 class Champion (with Lilian Bryner)

formula	years	starts (DNS)	wins	2nd	3rd	4th	5th	6th	PP	FL	points
Le Mans	1985-97	5	-	-	-	-	-	-	-	-	
SC W	1977-92		-	-	1	-	-	1	-	-	

Major win: 1987 Tourist Trophy (Silverstone)

Jacques Cales

F

1960 French Formula Junior Champion

Bradley "Buzz" Calkins

USA. Born: 2.5.1971, Denver, Colorado
1996 Indy Racing League Champion (tied with Scott Sharp)

formula	years	starts (DNS)	wins	2nd	3rd	4th	5th	6th	PP	FL	points
Indy 500	1996-2001	6	-	-	-	-	-	-	-	-	
IRL	1996-2001	53	1	1	1	1	3	2	-	1	

Win: 1996 Disney World. Best championship: 1996, 1st

Joel Camathias
CH. Born: 9.2.1981, Lugano

formula	years	starts (DNS)	wins	2nd	3rd	4th	5th	6th	PP	FL	points
F3000 INT	2001	12	-	-	-	-	1	-	-	-	2

Best championship: 2001, 16th

Balba Camino
E
2000 Spanish GT Champion (with Miguel Angel de Castro)

Raffaele Cammarota
I
1959 Italian Formula Junior Champion

formula	years	starts (DNS)	wins	2nd	3rd	4th	5th	6th	PP	FL	points
Le Mans	1961	1	-	-	-	-	-	-			

Giuseppe Campari
I. Born: 8.6.1892, Fanfullo, Lodi, near Milan. Died: 10.9.1933, Monza GP

formula	years	starts (DNS)	wins	2nd	3rd	4th	5th	6th	PP	FL	points
GP Pre-50	1923-33	13 (2)	3	4	1	1	-	-	1	2	

Wins: 1924 French GP, 1931 Italian GP, 1933 French GP
Other major wins: 1927, 1928 and 1931 Coppa Acerbo (Pescara), 1928 and 1929 Mille Miglia

Sir Malcolm Campbell
GB. Born: 11.3.1885, Chislehurst, Kent. Died: 31.12.1948, Reigate, Surrey

formula	years	starts (DNS)	wins	2nd	3rd	4th	5th	6th	PP	FL	points
GP Pre-50	1926-27	2	-	1	-	-	-	-			

John Campbell-Jones
GB. Born: 21.1.1930, Epsom, Surrey

formula	years	starts (DNS)	wins	2nd	3rd	4th	5th	6th	PP	FL	points
F1 W	1962-63	2	-	-	-	-	-	-	-	-	0

Best result: 11th. Best qualifying: 19th. Teams: Emeryson, Tim Parnell

Jamie Campbell-Walter
GB. Born: 19.12.1972, Oban, Scotland
2000 FIA GT Champion (with Julian Bailey), 1999 British GT Champion (with Bailey)

GT FIA wins: 11 – 2000 Valencia, Estoril, Silverstone, Zolder, Magny-Cours, 2001 Monza, Magny-Cours, Nurburgring, 2002 Magny-Cours, Brno, Enna

Adrian Campos
E. Born: 17.6.1960, Alcira, near Valencia
1994 Spanish Touring Car Champion

formula	years	starts (DNS)	wins	2nd	3rd	4th	5th	6th	PP	FL	points
F1 W	1987-88	17 (4)	-	-	-	-	-	-	-	-	0

Best result: 14th. Best qualifying: 16th. Team: Minardi

formula	years	starts (DNS)	wins	2nd	3rd	4th	5th	6th	PP	FL	points
Le Mans	1997	1	-	-	-	-	-	-			
F3000 INT	1986	5 (4)	-	-	-	-	-	-	-	-	0

Marco Campos
BR. Born: 24.2.1976, Curitiba. Died: 17.10.1995, Paris, following an accident during Magny-Cours F3000 race on 15.10.95
1994 European Formula Opel Champion

formula	years	starts (DNS)	wins	2nd	3rd	4th	5th	6th	PP	FL	points
F3000 INT	1995	8	-	-	-	1	-	-	-	-	3

Best championship: 1995, 13th

Salvador Canellas
E
1979 Spanish Touring Car Champion

John Cannon
CDN. Born: 21.6.1937, London (GB). Died: 18.10.1999, Quemado, New Mexico, airplane accident
1970 North American Formula A (F5000) Champion

formula	years	starts (DNS)	wins	2nd	3rd	4th	5th	6th	PP	FL	points
F1 W	1971	1	-	-	-	-	-	-	-	-	0

Best result: 14th. Best qualifying: 26th. Team: BRM

formula	years	starts (DNS)	wins	2nd	3rd	4th	5th	6th	PP	FL	points
SC W	1963-77		-	-	-	-	1	-	-	-	
F2 E	1971	6 (2)	-	-	-	1	-	-	-	-	4

Best championship: 1971, 16th

William "Shorty" Cantlon
USA. Born: 1904, Paris, Illinois. Died: 30.5.1947, Indianapolis 500

formula	years	starts (DNS)	wins	2nd	3rd	4th	5th	6th	PP	FL	points
Indy 500	1928-47	12	-	1	-	-	1	-	1	-	

Champcar wins: 4 – 1930 Akron, 1931 Altoona race 3, Altoona race 4, 1934 Syracuse

Heitel Cantoni
ROU. Born: 4.10.1896, Montevideo. Died: ??.6.1997, Montevideo

formula	years	starts (DNS)	wins	2nd	3rd	4th	5th	6th	PP	FL	points
F1 W	1952	3	-	-	-	-	-	-	-	-	0

Best result: 11th. Best qualifying: 23rd. Team: Bandeirantes

Ivan Capelli
I. Born: 24.5.1963, Milan
1986 FIA F3000 Champion, 1984 European F3 Champion, 1983 Italian F3 Champion

formula	years	starts (DNS)	wins	2nd	3rd	4th	5th	6th	PP	FL	points
F1 W	1985-93	93 (5)	-	2	1	1	4	4	-	-	31

Best championship: 1988, 7th. Best qualifying: 3rd. Teams: Tyrrell, AGS, March, Leyton House, Ferrari, Jordan

formula	years	starts (DNS)	wins	2nd	3rd	4th	5th	6th	PP	FL	points
Le Mans	1995	1	-	-	-	-	-	-			
F3000 INT	1985-86	17 (2)	3	1	3	2	-	-	3	2	51

Wins: 1985 Osterreichring, 1986 Vallelunga, Osterreichring. Best championship: 1986, 1st
F3 E wins: 4 – 1984 Magny-Cours, La Chatre, Enna, Mugello
Other Major win: 1984 Monaco F3

Rinaldo Capello
I. Born: 17.6.1964, Asti, near Turin
1996 Italian Touring Car Champion

formula	years	starts (DNS)	wins	2nd	3rd	4th	5th	6th	PP	FL	points
Le Mans	1998-2002	5	-	2	1	1	-	-	2	-	

Major wins: 2000 and 2002 Petit LeMans, 2001 and 2002 Sebring 12 hrs

Rudolf Caracciola
D. Born: 30.1.1901, Remagen, near Bonn. Died: 28.9.1959, Lugano (CH), cancer
1935, 1937 and 1938 European Grand Prix Champion

formula	years	starts (DNS)	wins	2nd	3rd	4th	5th	6th	PP	FL	points
GP Pre-50	1926-39	46 (2)	16	6	6	-	1	-	8	7	

Wins: 1926 German GP, 1928 German GP, 1931 German GP, 1932 German GP, 1934 Italian GP, 1935 French GP, Belgian GP, Swiss GP, Spanish GP, 1936 Monaco GP, 1937 German GP, Swiss GP, Italian GP, Masaryk GP, 1938 Swiss GP, 1939 German GP

formula	years	starts (DNS)	wins	2nd	3rd	4th	5th	6th	PP	FL	points
Le Mans	1930	1	-	-	-	-	-	-			

Other major wins: 1927, 1931, 1932 and 1935 Eifelrennen (Nurburgring), 1929 Tourist Trophy (Ards), 1931 Avus, 1931 Mille Miglia, 1932 Monza GP, 1935 Tripoli, 1936 Tunis, 1938 Coppa Acerbo (Pescara)

Fabio Carbone
BR. Born: 4.9.1980, Sao Paulo
Major win: 2002 Marlboro Masters (Zandvoort)

Paulo Carcasci
BR. Born: 7.1.1964
1991 Japanese F3 Champion

formula	years	starts (DNS)	wins	2nd	3rd	4th	5th	6th	PP	FL	points
F3000 INT	1994	1	-	-	-	-	-	-	-	-	0

Bob Carey
USA. Born: 28.9.1904, Anderson, Indiana. Died: 16.4.1933, Ascot
1932 Champcar Champion

formula	years	starts (DNS)	wins	2nd	3rd	4th	5th	6th	PP	FL	points
Indy 500	1932	1	-	-	-	1	-	-			

Champcar wins: 2 – 1932 Detroit race 1, Syracuse

Piero Carini
I. Born: 6.3.1921, Sondrio, near Genoa. Died: 30.5.1957, Forez 6 hrs, St Etienne, France

formula	years	starts (DNS)	wins	2nd	3rd	4th	5th	6th	PP	FL	points
F1 W	1952-53	3	-	-	-	-	-	-	-	-	0

Best result: no finishes. Best qualifying: 19th. Teams: Marzotto, Ferrari

| GP Pre-50 | 1949 | 1 | - | - | - | - | - | - | - | - | |
| Le Mans | 1953 | 1 | - | - | - | - | - | - | - | - | |

Tullio Cariolato
I

Major win: 1910 Targa Florio

Michael Carlsen
DK. Born: 8.11.1963, Slagenrup

2000 and 2001 Danish Touring Car Champion

Willie Carlson
USA. Born: 1884. Died: 4.7.1915, Tacoma, Washington

formula	years	starts (DNS)	wins	2nd	3rd	4th	5th	6th	PP	FL	points
GP Pre-50	1915	1	-	-	-	-	-	-	-	-	
Indy 500	1914-15	2	-	-	-	-	-	-	-	-	

Champcar win: 1 – 1913 San Diego race 2

Thorbjorn Carlsson
S. Born: 4.12.1949

1980 and 1982 Swedish F3 Champion

Patrick Carpentier
CDN. Born: 13.8.1971, Ville Lasalle, Quebec

1996 North American Toyota Atlantic Champion

formula	years	starts (DNS)	wins	2nd	3rd	4th	5th	6th	PP	FL	points
CART	1997-2002	108 (2)	3	5	5	3	8	2	3	5	

Wins: 2001 Michigan 500, 2002 Cleveland, Mid-Ohio. Best championship: 2002, 3rd

Duane "Pancho" Carter Jr
USA. Born: 11.6.1950, Racine, Wisconsin

formula	years	starts (DNS)	wins	2nd	3rd	4th	5th	6th	PP	FL	points
Indy 500	1974-91	17	-	-	1	1	1	1	1	-	
CART	1979-92	116 (1)	1	1	3	1	4	10	1	-	

Win: 1981 Michigan 500. Best championship: 1981, 3rd

Eddie Carvalho
HK

Major win: 1954 Macau

Lloyd "Lucky" Casner
USA. Born: 1916, Miami, Florida. Died: 10.4.1965, Le Mans, testing

formula	years	starts (DNS)	wins	2nd	3rd	4th	5th	6th	PP	FL	points
Le Mans	1960-63	2	-	-	-	-	-	-	-	-	
SC W	1959-64		1	-	-	-	-	-	-	-	

Win: 1961 Nurburgring

P Cassani
I

Major win: 1951 Mille Miglia

Serge Cassiers
B

2002 Belgian Belcar Touring Car Champion (with Peter Beckers and Eric Roelands)

Bernard Castagne
F. Born: 27.4.1958

1992 and 1994 European Renault Clio Cup Champion

Jean-Claude de Castelli
F. Born: 24.12.1969

1998 Sports Racing SR2 class Champion

Alberto Castello
E

2001 Spanish GT Champion (with Carlos Palau)

Roberto del Castello
I. Born: 13.9.1957, Roccasaso

formula	years	starts (DNS)	wins	2nd	3rd	4th	5th	6th	PP	FL	points
F2 E	1981-84	33 (4)	-	-	1	1	-	1	-	-	8

Best championship: 1983, 12th

| F3000 INT | 1985 | 3 | - | - | - | - | - | - | - | - | 0 |

Eugenio Castellotti
I. Born: 10.10.1930, Lodi, near Milan. Died: 14.3.1957, Modena, testing

formula	years	starts (DNS)	wins	2nd	3rd	4th	5th	6th	PP	FL	points
F1 W	1955-57	14	-	2	1	1	1	1	1	-	19.5

Best championship: 1955, 3rd. Best qualifying: 1st. Teams: Lancia, Ferrari

| Le Mans | 1955 | 1 | - | - | - | - | - | - | 1 | - | |
| SC W | 1953-57 | | 3 | 1 | 4 | - | 1 | 1 | - | | |

Wins: 1956 Sebring 12 hrs, Mille Miglia, 1957 Buenos Aires
Other Major win: 1952 Portuguese GP

Antonio de Castro
I

1996 and 1997 Italian Supercar GT Champion

formula	years	starts (DNS)	wins	2nd	3rd	4th	5th	6th	PP	FL	points
SC W	1970-77		-	-	-	1	-	-	-	-	

Hernani Castro Lopo
P

1992 Portuguese Touring Car Champion

Miguel Angel de Castro
E. Born: 5.6.1970, Avila

2000 Spanish GT Champion (with Balba Camino)

formula	years	starts (DNS)	wins	2nd	3rd	4th	5th	6th	PP	FL	points
Le Mans	1995	1	-	-	-	-	-	-	-	-	
F3000 INT	1997	0 (1)	-	-	-	-	-	-	-	-	0

Helio Castro-Neves (Helio Castroneves)
BR. Born: 10.5.1975, Sao Paulo

formula	years	starts (DNS)	wins	2nd	3rd	4th	5th	6th	PP	FL	points
Indy 500	2001-02	2	2	-	-	-	-	-	-	-	

Wins: 2001 and 2002 Indianapolis 500

| CART | 1998-2001 | 79 (1) | 6 | 4 | - | 1 | 4 | 2 | 7 | 14 | |

Wins: 2000 Detroit, Mid-Ohio, Laguna Seca, 2001 Long Beach, Detroit, Mid-Ohio. Best championship: 2001, 4th

| IRL | 2001-02 | 17 | - | 3 | 3 | 2 | 2 | 3 | 1 | - | |

Wins: 2001 Indianapolis 500, 2002 Phoenix, Indianapolis 500. Best championship: 2002, 2nd

Pierre de Caters
B. Born: 1875. Died: 1944

formula	years	starts (DNS)	wins	2nd	3rd	4th	5th	6th	PP	FL	points
GP Pre-50	1903-06	4	-	-	-	1	-	-	-	-	

Major win: 1907 Ardennes Circuit (GP class)

Luca Cattaneo
I

1998 Italian Supercar GT Champion

Fulvio Cavicchi
I. Born: 14.1.1980

2000 Austrian F3 Champion

Eric Cayrolle
F. Born: 27.8.1962, Pau

1996, 1997 and 1998 French Touring Car Champion

Robert la Caze
MA. Born: 26.2.1917, Paris (F)

formula	years	starts (DNS)	wins	2nd	3rd	4th	5th	6th	PP	FL	points
F1 W	1958	1	-	-	-	-	-	-	-	-	0

Best result: no finishes. Best qualifying: no times set. Team: driver

| Le Mans | 1957-60 | 3 | - | - | - | - | - | - | | | |

Johnny Cecotto

YV. Born: 25.1.1956, Caracas

1996 Temporada GT Champion (with Nelson Piquet), 1993 German GT Champion, 1989 Italian Touring Car Champion, 1994 and 1998 German Super Touring Car Champion, 2001 and 2002 German V8-Star Champion

formula	years	starts (DNS)	wins	2nd	3rd	4th	5th	6th	PP	FL	points
F1 W	1983-84	18 (5)	-	-	-	-	-	1	-	-	1

Best championship: 1983, 19th. Best qualifying: 15th.

Teams: Theodore, Toleman

| Le Mans | 1981-98 | 3 | | - | - | - | - | - | - | | | |
| F2 E | 1980-82 | 27 (1) | 3 | 3 | 3 | 1 | - | 4 | - | 2 | 64 |

Wins: 1982 Thruxton, Pau, Mantorp Park. Best championship: 1982, 2nd
Other major wins: 1986 Macau Guia race, 1990 Spa 24 hrs

Ernesto Ceirano

I

Major wins: 1911 and 1914 Targa Florio

Andrea de Cesaris

I. Born: 31.5.1959, Rome

formula	years	starts (DNS)	wins	2nd	3rd	4th	5th	6th	PP	FL	points
F1 W	1980-94	208 (6)	-	2	3	7	4	6	1	1	59

Best championship: 1983, 8th. Best qualifying: 1st. Teams: Alfa Romeo, McLaren, Ligier, Minardi, Brabham, Rial, Scuderia Italia, Jordan, Tyrrell, Sauber

| SC W | 1980-89 | | - | 2 | 1 | - | - | 2 | 2 | | |
| F2 E | 1979-80 | 12 | 1 | 2 | 1 | - | 1 | 2 | 1 | - | 29 |

Win: 1980 Misano. Best championship: 1980, 5th

Francois Cevert

F. Born: 25.2.1944, Paris. Died: 6.10.1973, Watkins Glen, US GP practice

1968 French F3 Champion

formula	years	starts (DNS)	wins	2nd	3rd	4th	5th	6th	PP	FL	points
F1 W	1969-73	47 (1)	1	10	2	2	2	2	-	2	89

Win: 1971 United States GP. Best championship: 1971, 3rd. Best qualifying: 2nd. Teams: Tecno, Tyrrell

| Le Mans | 1970-73 | 3 | | - | 1 | - | - | - | 1 | 1 | |
| SC W | 1970-73 | | 1 | 2 | 1 | - | - | 7 | 6 | | |

Win: 1973 Vallelunga

| F2 E | 1969-73 | 27 (2) | 3 | 1 | 2 | 1 | 2 | 1 | 3 | | 52 |

Wins: 1971 Hockenheim, Nurburgring, 1973 Pau. Best championship: 1969, 3rd

Eugene Chaboud

F. Born: 12.4.1907, Lyon. Died: 28.12.1983, Montfermeil, Paris

formula	years	starts (DNS)	wins	2nd	3rd	4th	5th	6th	PP	FL	points
F1 W	1950-51	3	-	-	-	-	1	-	-	-	1

Best championship: 1950, 20th. Best qualifying: 10th. Teams: Lutetia, Philippe Etancelin, driver

| GP Pre-50 | 1937-49 | 12 | - | 1 | - | 2 | - | | |
| Le Mans | 1937-52 | 6 | 1 | - | - | - | - | | |

Win: 1938 Le Mans 24 hrs

Alain de Chagny
(Alain Carpentier, Comte de Chagny)

B. Born: 5.2.1922, Brussels. Died: 5.8.1994, Etterbeek

formula	years	starts (DNS)	wins	2nd	3rd	4th	5th	6th	PP	FL	points
F1 W	1959	0 (1)	-	-	-	-	-	-	-	-	0

Best result: no starts. Best qualifying: 20th. Team: ENB

| Le Mans | 1956-59 | 4 | - | - | - | - | 1 | - | |
| SC W | 1956-59 | | - | - | - | 1 | 1 | - | |

Jay Chamberlain

USA. Born: 29.12.1925, Los Angeles, California. Died: 1.8.2001, Tucson, Arizona

formula	years	starts (DNS)	wins	2nd	3rd	4th	5th	6th	PP	FL	points
F1 W	1962	1 (2)	-	-	-	-	-	-	-	-	0

Best result: 15th. Best qualifying: 20th. Team: Excelsior

| Le Mans | 1957-58 | 2 | - | - | - | - | - | - | |

Chan Lye Choon

SGP

Major win: 1958 Macau

Colin Chapman

GB. Born: 19.5.1928, Richmond, Surrey. Died: 16.12.1982, East Carleton, Norfolk

formula	years	starts (DNS)	wins	2nd	3rd	4th	5th	6th	PP	FL	points
F1 W	1956	0 (1)	-	-	-	-	-	-	-	-	0

Best result: no starts. Best qualifying: 5th (time set by Harry Schell). Team: Vanwall

| Le Mans | 1955-56 | 2 | - | - | - | - | - | - | |
| SC W | 1954-58 | | - | - | - | - | - | 1 | - |

Dave Charlton

ZA. Born: 27.10.1936, Brotton, near Redcar, Yorkshire (GB)

1970, 1971, 1972, 1973, 1974 and 1975 South African F1 Champion

formula	years	starts (DNS)	wins	2nd	3rd	4th	5th	6th	PP	FL	points
F1 W	1965-75	11 (3)	-	-	-	-	-	-	-	-	0

Best result: 12th. Best qualifying: 8th. Teams: Tomahawk, Scuderia Scribante, Brabham, Lotus

F1 ZA wins: 49 – 1966 Kumalo, Mozambique, Kyalami, 1967 Kyalami (x2), 1968 Kyalami, 1969 Rhodesian GP, 1970 Kyalami (x3), Pietermaritzburg (x2), Mozambique, Killarney, Rhodesian GP, Welkom, 1971 Kyalami (x4), Pietermaritzburg, Bulawayo, Welkom, 1972 Killarney (x2), Peitermaritzburg, Bulawayo, Kyalami (x3), Welkom, 1973 Killarney (x2), Kyalami (x4), Welkom, Pietermaritzburg (x2), Rhodesian GP, 1974 Pietermaritzburg, Killarney, Kyalami (x2), Brandkop, Bulawayo, 1975 Killarney, Pietermaritzburg

Fernand Charron

F. Born: 1866. Died: 13.8.1928

formula	years	starts (DNS)	wins	2nd	3rd	4th	5th	6th	PP	FL	points
GP Pre-50	1900-01	2	1	-	-	-	-	-	

Win: 1900 Gordon Bennett Trophy
City-to-city wins: 1898 Paris-Amsterdam-Paris, 1899 Paris-Bordeaux

Jean Chassagne

F. Born: 26.7.1881, La Croisille-sur-Briance, Limoges. Died: 13.4.1947, La Croisille-sur-Briance, Limoges

formula	years	starts (DNS)	wins	2nd	3rd	4th	5th	6th	PP	FL	points
GP Pre-50	1913-29	9	-	1	1	-	-	1	-	-	
Le Mans	1925-30	6	-	1	-	1	1	-	-	
Indy 500	1914-21	4	-	-	-	-	-	1	-	

Major win: 1922 Tourist Trophy (Isle of Man)

Guy Chasseuil

F. Born: 26.1.1942

formula	years	starts (DNS)	wins	2nd	3rd	4th	5th	6th	PP	FL	points
Le Mans	1968-81	12	-	1	-	-	1	-	-	
SC W	1968-81		-	-	-	1	2	-	-	

Major win: 1969 Spa 24 hrs

"Pierre Chauvet" (Fritz Glatz)

A. Born: 21.7.1943, Vienna. Died: 14.7.2002, Most, EuroBross historic F1 race. Also known as "Umberto Calvo"

formula	years	starts (DNS)	wins	2nd	3rd	4th	5th	6th	PP	FL	points
F2 E	1981-84	30 (1)	-	-	-	-	-	1	-	-	1

Best championship: 1984, 15th

| F3000 INT | 1985-88 | 12 (6) | - | - | - | - | - | - | - | - | 0 |

"Chavan"

B

Major win: 1976 Spa 24 hrs

Pedro Chaves

P. Born: 27.2.1965, Porto
1990 British F3000 Champion, 2002 Spanish GT Champion (with Miguel Ramos)

formula	years	starts (DNS)	wins	2nd	3rd	4th	5th	6th	PP	FL	points
F1 W	1991	0 (14)	-	-	-	-	-	-	-	-	0

Best result: no starts. Best qualifying: 32nd. Team: Coloni

formula	years	starts (DNS)	wins	2nd	3rd	4th	5th	6th	PP	FL	points
Le Mans	2002	1	-	-	-	-	-	-	-	-	
F3000 INT	1989-92	18 (6)	-	-	-	1	-	-	-	-	3

Best championship: 1990, 16th

Eddie Cheever

USA. Born: 10.1.1958, Phoenix, Arizona

formula	years	starts (DNS)	wins	2nd	3rd	4th	5th	6th	PP	FL	points
F1 W	1978-89	132 (11)	-	2	7	5	4	7	-	-	70

Best championship: 1983, 6th. Best qualifying: 2nd. Teams: Theodore, Hesketh, Osella, Tyrrell, Ligier, Renault, Alfa Romeo, Haas Lola, Arrows

formula	years	starts (DNS)	wins	2nd	3rd	4th	5th	6th	PP	FL	points
Le Mans	1981-87	3	-	-	-	-	1	-	-	-	
SC W	1977-92		9	5	6	2	3	2	1	2	

Wins: 1980 Mugello, 1986 Silverstone, 1987 Jerez, Silverstone, Nurburgring, 1988 Jarama, Monza, Silverstone, Fuji. Best championships: 1987 and 1988, 4th

formula	years	starts (DNS)	wins	2nd	3rd	4th	5th	6th	PP	FL	points
F2 E	1976-79	46 (1)	4	5	4	2	5	2	2	4	106

Wins: 1977 Rouen, 1979 Silverstone, Pau, Zandvoort. Best championship: 1977, 2nd

formula	years	starts (DNS)	wins	2nd	3rd	4th	5th	6th	PP	FL	points
Indy 500	1990-2002	13	1	-	-	1	2	-	-	1	

Win: 1998 Indianapolis 500

formula	years	starts (DNS)	wins	2nd	3rd	4th	5th	6th	PP	FL	points
CART	1986-95	82 (1)	-	1	3	7	3	4	-	-	

Best championships: 1990, 1991 and 1992, 9th

formula	years	starts (DNS)	wins	2nd	3rd	4th	5th	6th	PP	FL	points
IRL	1996-2002	70	5	1	3	5	4	5	1	4	

Wins: 1997 Disney World, 1998 Indianapolis 500, 1999 Disney World, 2000 Pikes Peak, 2001 Kansas City. Best championships: 1996/97 and 2000, 3rd

Ross Cheever

USA. Born: 12.4.1964, Rome (I)
1985 New Zealand Formula Pacific Champion, 1987 Japanese F3 Champion

formula	years	starts (DNS)	wins	2nd	3rd	4th	5th	6th	PP	FL	points
Le Mans	1989	1	-	-	-	-	-	-	-	-	
F3000 INT	1986	0 (1)	-	-	-	-	-	-	-	-	0
CART	1992	4 (1)	-	-	-	-	-	-	-	-	

Major wins: 1984 (December) and 1986 New Zealand GP

Gaston Chevrolet

USA. Born: 26.10.1892, Beaune, Burgundy (F). Died: 25.11.1920, Beverly Hills, California
1920 Champcar Champion

formula	years	starts (DNS)	wins	2nd	3rd	4th	5th	6th	PP	FL	points
Indy 500	1919-20	2	1	-	-	-	-	-	-	-	

Win: 1920 Indianapolis 500
Champcar wins: 4 – 1919 Sheepshead race 4, Uniontown race 7, Sheepshead race 5, 1920 Indianapolis 500

Louis Chevrolet

USA. Born: 25.12.1878, La Chaux de Fond (CH). Died: 6.6.1941, Detroit, Michigan

formula	years	starts (DNS)	wins	2nd	3rd	4th	5th	6th	PP	FL	points
GP Pre-50	1910	1	-	-	-	-	-	-	-	-	
Indy 500	1915-20	4	-	-	-	-	-	-	-	-	

Champcar wins: 10 – 1909 Crown Point race 2, Lowell race 3, Riverhead race 4, 1917 Cincinnati, Chicago race 3, Sheepshead Bay, Ascot race 2, 1918 Uniontown race 4, Uniontown race 6, 1919 Tacoma

Andrea Chiesa

CH. Born: 6.5.1964, Milan (I)

formula	years	starts (DNS)	wins	2nd	3rd	4th	5th	6th	PP	FL	points
F1 W	1992	3 (7)	-	-	-	-	-	-	-	-	0

Best result: no finishes. Best qualifying: 20th. Team: Fondmetal

formula	years	starts (DNS)	wins	2nd	3rd	4th	5th	6th	PP	FL	points
F3000 INT	1988-91	36 (4)	1	3	-	-	3	1	-	-	34

Win: 1989 Enna. Best championship: 1989, 6th

formula	years	starts (DNS)	wins	2nd	3rd	4th	5th	6th	PP	FL	points
CART	1993	1	-	-	-	-	-	-	-	-	

Ettore Chimeri

YV. Born: 4.6.1921, Lodi (I). Died: 27.2.1960, Cuban sports car GP, practice

formula	years	starts (DNS)	wins	2nd	3rd	4th	5th	6th	PP	FL	points
F1 W	1960	1	-	-	-	-	-	-	-	-	0

Best result: no finishes. Best qualifying: 21st. Team: Escuderia Sorocaima

formula	years	starts (DNS)	wins	2nd	3rd	4th	5th	6th	PP	FL	points
SC W	1957		-	-	-	-	-	1	-	-	

Luigi Chinetti

I (emigrated to USA). Born: 17.7.1906, Milan. Died: 17.8.1994, Connecticut

formula	years	starts (DNS)	wins	2nd	3rd	4th	5th	6th	PP	FL	points
GP Pre-50	1936-49	4	-	-	-	-	-	-	-	-	
Le Mans	1932-53	12	3	1	-	-	-	-	-	-	

Wins: 1932, 1934 and 1949 Le Mans 24 hrs

formula	years	starts (DNS)	wins	2nd	3rd	4th	5th	6th	PP	FL	points
SC W	1953-54		-	-	-	-	-	1	-	-	

Other major wins: 1933 and 1949 Spa 24 hrs, 1951 Carrera Panamericana

Louis Chiron

MC. Born: 3.8.1899, Monte Carlo. Died: 22.6.1979, Monte Carlo

formula	years	starts (DNS)	wins	2nd	3rd	4th	5th	6th	PP	FL	points
F1 W	1950-56	15 (3)	-	-	1	-	2	-	-	-	4

Best championship: 1950, 9th. Best qualifying: 8th. Teams: Maserati, Enrico Plate, Louis Rosier, Ecurie France, driver, Lancia, Scuderia Centro Sud

formula	years	starts (DNS)	wins	2nd	3rd	4th	5th	6th	PP	FL	points
GP Pre-50	1927-49	60	16	4	3	5	3	2	4	8	

Wins: 1928 San Sebastian GP, Spanish GP, Italian GP, 1929 German GP, Spanish GP, 1930 Belgian GP, 1931 Monaco GP, French GP, Masaryk GP, 1932 Masaryk GP, 1933 Masaryk GP, Spanish GP, 1934 French GP, 1937 French GP, 1947 French GP, 1949 Unofficial French GP

formula	years	starts (DNS)	wins	2nd	3rd	4th	5th	6th	PP	FL	points
Le Mans	1928-53	9	-	-	-	-	-	-	-	-	
Indy 500	1929	1	-	-	-	-	-	-	-	-	

Other major wins: 1933 Spa 24 hrs, 1934 Moroccan GP

Peter Chow

HK
Major wins: 1973, 1977 and 1978 Macau Guia race

Daniel Cingolani

RA. Born: 25.5.1961, Buenos Aires
2000 TC2000 Argentinian Touring Car Champion

Sandro Cinotti

I

formula	years	starts (DNS)	wins	2nd	3rd	4th	5th	6th	PP	FL	points
F2 E	1975-78	17 (3)	-	-	-	1	-	-	-	-	2

Best championship: 1975, 25th

Francesco Ciuppa

I
Major win: 1909 Targa Florio

Johnny Claes

B. Born: 11.8.1916, Fulham, London (GB). Died: 3.2.1956, Brussels, tuberculosis

formula	years	starts (DNS)	wins	2nd	3rd	4th	5th	6th	PP	FL	points
F1 W	1950-55	23 (2)	-	-	-	-	-	-	-	-	0

Best result: 7th. Best qualifying: 10th. Teams: Ecurie Belge, driver, Gordini, HWM, Vickomtesse de Walckiers, Maserati, Stirling Moss, ENB

formula	years	starts (DNS)	wins	2nd	3rd	4th	5th	6th	PP	FL	points
GP Pre-50	1949	6	-	-	-	-	-	1	1	-	
Le Mans	1951-55	3	-	-	1	-	-	-	-	-	
SC W	1954-55		-	-	1	-	-	-	-	-	

Jim Clark

GB. Born: 4.3.1936, Kilmany, Fifeshire. Died: 7.4.1968, Hockenheim, F2 race
1963 and 1965 F1 World Champion, 1965, 1967 and 1968 Tasman Champion, 1965 British F2 Champion, 1965 French F2 Champion, 1964 British Touring Car Champion, 1960 John Davy (solo) and Motor Racing (tied with Trevor Taylor) British Formula Junior Champion

formula	years	starts (DNS)	wins	2nd	3rd	4th	5th	6th	PP	FL	points
F1 W	1960-68	72 (1)	25	1	6	4	3	1	33	28	274

Wins: 1962 Belgian GP, British GP, United States GP, 1963 Belgian GP, Dutch GP, French GP, British GP, Italian GP, Mexican GP, South African GP, 1964 Dutch GP, Belgian GP, British GP, 1965 South African GP, Belgian GP, French GP, British GP, Dutch GP, German GP, 1966 United States GP, 1967 Dutch GP, British GP, United States GP, Mexican GP, 1968 South African GP. Best championships: 1963 and 1965, 1st. Best qualifying: 1st. Team: Lotus

Le Mans	1959-61	3	-	-	1	-	-	-	-		
SC W	1959-65		-	1	-	-	-	-	-		
F2 E	1967-68	5	1	-	-	-	-	1	2		0

Win: 1967 Jarama

Indy 500	1963-67	5	1	2	-	-	-	-	1	1	

Win: 1965 Indianapolis 500
Champcar wins: 2 – 1963 Milwaukee race 2, 1965 Indianapolis 500
Non-championship F1 wins: 1961 Pau, Rand GP (Kyalami), Natal GP, South African GP, 1962 Snetterton, Aintree, Oulton Park Gold Cup, Mexican GP, Rand GP (Kyalami), 1963 Pau, Imola, International Trophy (Silverstone), Karlskoga, Oulton Park Gold Cup, 1964 Goodwood, Solitude, 1965 Syracuse, Goodwood, 1967 Spanish GP
Tasman wins: 10 – 1966 Warwick Farm, 1967 Levin, Lady Wigram Trophy, Teretonga, Lakeside, Sandown Park, 1968 Lady Wigram Trophy, Surfers Paradise, Warwick Farm, Australian GP

John Cleland

GB. Born: 15.7.1952, Wishaw, Scotland
1989 and 1995 British Touring Car Champion

Frank Clement

GB. Born: 1886. Died: 15.2.1970, Northumberland

formula	years	starts (DNS)	wins	2nd	3rd	4th	5th	6th	PP	FL	points
Le Mans	1923-30	8	1	1	-	2	-	-	-		2

Win: 1924 Le Mans 24 hrs

Emmanuel Clerico

F. Born: 30.12.1969, Paris

formula	years	starts (DNS)	wins	2nd	3rd	4th	5th	6th	PP	FL	points
Le Mans	1995-2002	6	-	-	-	1	-	-	-		
F3000 INT	1994-97	17	-	1	-	2	1	1	3		15

GT FIA win: 1 – 1999 Homestead
Best championship: 1995, 5th

June Cleveland

USA
NASCAR wins: 1

Price Cobb

USA. Born: 10.12.1954, Dallas, Texas

formula	years	starts (DNS)	wins	2nd	3rd	4th	5th	6th	PP	FL	points
Le Mans	1986-97	7	1	-	-	-	-	-	-		

Win: 1990 Le Mans 24 hrs

SC W	1986-92		-	1	-	-	-	-	-		

Jonathan Cochet

F. Born: 4.1.1976, Alencon
2000 French F3 Champion, 1997 French Formula Renault Champion

formula	years	starts (DNS)	wins	2nd	3rd	4th	5th	6th	PP	FL	points
Le Mans	2001-02	2	-	-	-	-	-	-	-		
F3000 INT	2001	4	-	-	-	-	-	-	-		0

Major wins: 2000 Pau, 2000 Marlboro Masters (Zandvoort), 2001 Korea F3

Kevin Cogan

USA. Born: 31.3.1956, Culver City, California

formula	years	starts (DNS)	wins	2nd	3rd	4th	5th	6th	PP	FL	points
F1 W	1980-81	0 (2)	-	-	-	-	-	-	-	-	0

Best result: no starts. Best qualifying: 25th. Teams: RAM, Tyrrell

Le Mans	1988	1	-	-	-	1	-	-	-		
SC W	1988-90		-	-	-	1	-	-	-		
Indy 500	1981-93	12	-	1	-	1	1	-	-		
CART	1981-93	116 (1)	1	4	2	7	7	2	2	-	

Win: 1986 Phoenix. Best championships: 1982 and 1986, 6th

Stephan Cohen

B
1999 Belgian Belcar GT Champion (with Anthony Kumpen)

Roberto Colciago

I. Born: 4.4.1968, Saronno, near Milan
2001 and 2002 Swedish Touring Car Champion, 1990 Italian F3 Champion

formula	years	starts (DNS)	wins	2nd	3rd	4th	5th	6th	PP	FL	points
F3000 INT	1991	8 (2)	-	-	-	-	-	-	-	-	0

Neil Cole

USA
NASCAR wins: 1

Emmanuel Collard

F. Born: 3.4.1971, Arpajon, near Paris
1998 and 1999 Sports Racing World Champion (with Vincenzo Sospiri), 1996 Porsche Supercup Champion, 1990 French Formula Renault Champion

formula	years	starts (DNS)	wins	2nd	3rd	4th	5th	6th	PP	FL	points
Le Mans	1995-2002	8									

GT FIA win: 1 – 1996 Zhuhai. SRWC wins: 8 – 1998 Brno, Misano, Donington, Anderstorp, Nurburgring, Le Mans, 1999 Barcelona, Monza

F3000 INT	1991-93	20 (1)	-	-	2	3	-	-	1	-	17

Best championship: 1992, 8th
Other major wins: 1998 Petit LeMans, 1999 Spa 24 hrs

Ben Collins

GB. Born: 13.2.1975, Bristol

formula	years	starts (DNS)	wins	2nd	3rd	4th	5th	6th	PP	FL	points
Le Mans	2001-02	2	-	-	-	-	-	-	-		

SRWC win: 1 – 2001 Donington

Peter Collins

GB. Born: 6.11.1931, Kidderminster, Worcestershire. Died: 3.8.1958, Bonn, following an accident during the German GP at the Nurburgring

formula	years	starts (DNS)	wins	2nd	3rd	4th	5th	6th	PP	FL	points
F1 W	1952-58	32 (3)	3	3	3	1	1	2	-	-	47

Wins: 1956 Belgian GP, French GP, 1958 British GP. Best championship: 1956, 3rd. Best qualifying: 2nd. Teams: HWM, GA Vandervell, BRM, Maserati, Ferrari

Le Mans	1952-58	7	-	2	-	-	-	-	-		
SC W	1953-58		-	5	6	3	1	1	1	-	3

Wins: 1953 Tourist Trophy (Dundrod), 1955 Targa Florio, 1957 Venezuelan GP, 1958 Buenos Aires, Sebring 12 hrs
Non-championship F1 wins: 1955 International Trophy (Silverstone), 1957 Syracuse, Naples, 1958 International Trophy (Silverstone)

Bernard Collomb

F. Born: 7.10.1930, Annecy

formula	years	starts (DNS)	wins	2nd	3rd	4th	5th	6th	PP	FL	points
F1 W	1961-64	4 (2)	-	-	-	-	-	-	-	-	0

Best result: 10th. Best qualifying: 17th. Team: driver

Le Mans	1968	1									

Alberto Colombo

I. Born: 23.2.1946, Varedo, near Milan
1974 Italian F3 Champion

formula	years	starts (DNS)	wins	2nd	3rd	4th	5th	6th	PP	FL	points
F1 W	1978	0 (3)	-	-	-	-	-	-	-	-	0

Best result: no starts. Best qualifying: 28th. Teams: ATS, Merzario

formula	years	starts (DNS)	wins	2nd	3rd	4th	5th	6th	PP	FL	points
F2 E	1973-80	74 (1)	-	-	3	5	5	9	-	1	48

Best championship: 1977, 7th

Vittorio Colombo
I
1994 Italian Supercar GT Champion

Enzo Coloni
I. Born: 17.10.1946
1982 Italian F3 Champion

formula	years	starts (DNS)	wins	2nd	3rd	4th	5th	6th	PP	FL	points
SC W	1979		-	1	-	-	-	-	1	-	
F2 E	1980-83	2	-	-	-	-	-	-	-	-	0

Fabio Colonna
I
Major win: 1957 Targa Florio (regularity test)

Erik Comas
F. Born: 28.9.1963, Romans, near Valence
1990 FIA F3000 Champion, 1998 (with Masami Kageyama) and 1999 (solo) Japanese GT Champion, 1987 French Touring Car Champion, 1988 French F3 Champion, 1986 French Formula Renault Champion

formula	years	starts (DNS)	wins	2nd	3rd	4th	5th	6th	PP	FL	points
F1 W	1991-94	59 (4)	-	-	-	1	5	-	-		7

Best championship: 1992, 11th. Best qualifying: 7th. Teams: Ligier, Larrousse

Le Mans	1995-2002	6				1	1	-			
F3000 INT	1989-90	20 (1)	6	4	1	2	1	-	5	4	90

Wins: 1989 Le Mans, Dijon, 1990 Donington, Jerez, Monza, Le Mans. Best championship: 1990, 1st

Fred Comer
USA. Born: 1896, Topeka, Kansas. Died: 12.10.1928, Salem, New Hampshire

formula	years	starts (DNS)	wins	2nd	3rd	4th	5th	6th	PP	FL	points
Indy 500	1924-28	4	-	-	-	1	-	1	-	-	

Champcar win: 1 – 1926 Atlantic City race 4

Gianfranco Comotti
I. Born: 24.7.1906, Brescia. Died: 10.5.1963, Bergamo

formula	years	starts (DNS)	wins	2nd	3rd	4th	5th	6th	PP	FL	points
F1 W	1950-52	2	-	-	-	-	-	-	-	-	0

Best result: 12th. Best qualifying: 18th. Teams: Milano, Marzotto

GP Pre-50	1928-48	11 (1)	-	1	1	1	-	2	-	-	
Le Mans	1938	1	-	-	-	-	-	-	-	-	

Major win: 1937 Tourist Trophy (Donington)

Decimo Compagnoni
I
Major win: 1933 Mille Miglia

Caberto Conelli (Conte di Properi)
I

formula	years	starts (DNS)	wins	2nd	3rd	4th	5th	6th	PP	FL	points
GP Pre-50	1925-31	7	1	1	1	-	-	-	-	-	

Win: 1931 Belgian GP

Le Mans	1931	1	-	-	-	-	-	-	-	-	

George Connor
USA. Born: 16.8.1908, Rialto, California. Died: 28.3.2001, Hesperia, California

formula	years	starts (DNS)	wins	2nd	3rd	4th	5th	6th	PP	FL	points
Indy 500	1935-52	14	-	-	1	-	-	-	-	-	

Champcar win: 1 – 1946 Atlanta

Hartvig Conradsen
DK
1962 and 1964 Danish Formula Junior Champion

George Constantine
USA. Born: 22.2.1918, Southbridge, Massachusetts. Died: 7.1.1968, New York City

formula	years	starts (DNS)	wins	2nd	3rd	4th	5th	6th	PP	FL	points
F1 W	1959	1	-	-	-	-	-	-	-	-	0

Best result: no finishes. Best qualifying: 15th. Team: Mike Taylor

SC W	1958-62		-	-	-	-	-	-	1	-	

Enrique Contreras
MEX. Born: 21.5.1962
1984 Mexican Formula K Champion, 1990 Mexican F2 Champion

Jim Cook
USA
NASCAR wins: 1

Earl Cooper
USA. Born: 1886, Nebraska. Died: 23.10.1965, Atwater, California

formula	years	starts (DNS)	wins	2nd	3rd	4th	5th	6th	PP	FL	points
GP Pre-50	1914-27	4	-	1	1	-	-	-	-	-	
Indy 500	1913-26	8	-	1	1	2	-	-	1	-	

Champcar wins: 21 – 1912 Tacoma race 2, 1913 Tacoma race 1, Tacoma race 2, Santa Monica, Corona race 1, Corona race 2, 1914 Tacoma race 2, 1915 San Diego, Elgin race 1, Minneapolis, Phoenix, San Francisco race 2, 1917 Ascot, Chicago race 1, Minneapolis race 1, Tacoma, 1921 Fresno race 2, 1924 Fresno, 1925 Charlotte race 1, 1926 Salem race 2, Charlotte race 2

Derrike Cope
USA. Born: 3.11.1958, San Diego, California
NASCAR wins: 2 (both Modern era) including 1990 Daytona 500

Chris Cord
USA. Born: 15.7.1940
1987 IMSA GTO Champion

formula	years	starts (DNS)	wins	2nd	3rd	4th	5th	6th	PP	FL	points
Le Mans	1978	1	-	-	-	-	-	-	1	-	
SC W	1976-92		-	-	1	-	1	-	-	-	

Jaime Cordero
MEX
1996 Mexican F3000 Champion

John Cordts
CDN. Born: 23.7.1935, Huntsville

formula	years	starts (DNS)	wins	2nd	3rd	4th	5th	6th	PP	FL	points
F1 W	1969	1	-	-	-	-	-	-	-	-	0

Best result: no finishes. Best qualifying: 19th. Team: Paul Seitz

Waldemar Coronas
RA. Born: 9.12.1976, Lezama
1999 and 2000 Mexican Indy Lights Champion

Tom Coronel
NL. Born: 5.4.1972, Maarden
1999 Japanese Formula Nippon Champion, 1997 Japanese F3 Champion

formula	years	starts (DNS)	wins	2nd	3rd	4th	5th	6th	PP	FL	points
Le Mans	1999-2002	4	-	-	-	-	-	-	-	-	

GT FIA wins: 3 – 2000 A1 Ring, 2001 Monza, Magny-Cours
Other Major win: 1997 Marlboro Masters (Zandvoort)

"Correcaminos"
E
1986 Spanish Touring Car Champion

Franco Cortese
I. Born: 10.2.1903, Oggebbio, near Turin. Died: 13.11.1986

formula	years	starts (DNS)	wins	2nd	3rd	4th	5th	6th	PP	FL	points
GP Pre-50	1937-49	4	-	-	1	-	-	-	-	-	
Le Mans	1932-33	2	-	1	-	-	-	-	-	-	

Major win: 1951 Targa Florio

Enzo Corti

I

formula	years	starts (DNS)	wins	2nd	3rd	4th	5th	6th	PP	FL	points
F2 E	1968-70	8 (2)	-	-	-	-	-	-	-	-	2

Best championship: 1969, 15th. Best result: 9th

Lora L "Slim" Corum

USA. Born: 8.1.1899, Jonesville, Indiana. Died: 7.3.1949, Indianapolis, Indiana

formula	years	starts (DNS)	wins	2nd	3rd	4th	5th	6th	PP	FL	points
Indy 500	1922-33	10	1	-	-	-	2	-	-	-	

Win: 1924 Indianapolis 500

Champcar win: 1 – 1924 Indianapolis 500

Ricardo Cosac

BR

1990 Brazilian Touring Car Champion (with Andreas Mattheis)

Marcel Costa

E. Born: 4.11.1978, Guardiola de Bergueda

2002 Spanish F3 Champion

Bartholomeo "Meo" Costantini

F. Born: 1889, Vittorio Veneto, near Venice. Died: 1940, Milan

formula	years	starts (DNS)	wins	2nd	3rd	4th	5th	6th	PP	FL	points
GP Pre-50	1914-26	10	1	2	2	1	-	-	-	-	4

Win: 1926 Spanish GP

Other major wins: 1925 and 1926 Targa Florio

Alfredo Costanzo

AUS. Born: 3.1.1943

1980 and 1981 Australian F5000 Champion, 1982 and 1983 Australian Formula Pacific Champion

Didier Cottaz

F. Born: 23.5.1967, Bourgoin-Jallieu, near Lyon

1993 French F3 Champion

formula	years	starts (DNS)	wins	2nd	3rd	4th	5th	6th	PP	FL	points
Le Mans	1996-2002	7	-	-	-	1	-	-	-	-	

SRWC win: 1 – 1997 Jarama

formula	years	starts (DNS)	wins	2nd	3rd	4th	5th	6th	PP	FL	points
F3000 INT	1994-95	16	-	1	1	-	1	2	-	-	14

Best championship: 1994, 5th

Pedro Couceiro

P. Born: 23.3.1970, Lobito (ANG)

formula	years	starts (DNS)	wins	2nd	3rd	4th	5th	6th	PP	FL	points
F3000 INT	1996-97	18 (1)	-	1	-	-	1	-	-	-	8

Best championship: 1997, 11th

Jacques Coulon

F. Born: 15.1.1942

formula	years	starts (DNS)	wins	2nd	3rd	4th	5th	6th	PP	FL	points
F2 E	1973-74	22 (3)	1	-	3	3	1	1	-	1	38

Win: 1973 Vallelunga. Best championship: 1973, 5th

formula	years	starts (DNS)	wins	2nd	3rd	4th	5th	6th	PP	FL	points
Le Mans	1977-79	2	-	-	-	-	-	-	-	-	

David Coulthard

GB. Born: 27.3.1971, Twynholm, Kirkcudbright

formula	years	starts (DNS)	wins	2nd	3rd	4th	5th	6th	PP	FL	points
F1 W	1994-2002	141	12	25	20	7	11	7	12	18	400

Wins: 1995 Portuguese GP, 1997 Australian GP, Italian GP, 1998 San Marino GP, 1999 British GP, Belgian GP, 2000 British GP, Monaco GP, French GP, 2001 Brazilian GP, Austrian GP, 2002 Monaco GP. Best championship: 2001, 2nd.

Best qualifying: 1st. Teams: Williams, McLaren

formula	years	starts (DNS)	wins	2nd	3rd	4th	5th	6th	PP	FL	points
Le Mans	1993	1	-	-	-	-	-	-	-	-	
F3000 INT	1992-94	20	1	3	3	1	-	-	-	3	42

Win: 1993 Enna. Best championship: 1993, 7th

Other major wins: 1991 Marlboro Masters (Zandvoort), 1991 Macau

Fabian Coulthard

NZ. Born: 28.7.1982, Burnley (GB)

2002 New Zealand Gold Star Champion

Major win: 2002 New Zealand GP

Piers Courage

GB. Born: 27.5.1942, Colchester, Essex. Died: 21.6.1970, Zandvoort, Dutch GP

formula	years	starts (DNS)	wins	2nd	3rd	4th	5th	6th	PP	FL	points
F1 W	1966-70	28 (2)	-	2	-	1	2	1	-	-	20

Best championship: 1969, 8th. Best qualifying: 4th. Teams: Ron Harris, Reg Parnell, Williams

formula	years	starts (DNS)	wins	2nd	3rd	4th	5th	6th	PP	FL	points
Le Mans	1966-70	4	-	-	-	1	-	-	-	-	
SC W	1966-70		-	-	-	1	-	-	-	-	
F2 E	1967-69	21 (1)	1	2	4	-	1	-	-	-	37

Win: 1969 Enna. Best championship: 1967, 4th

Tasman wins: 2 – 1968 Longford, 1969 Teretonga

Gerard de Courcelles

F. Born: n/a. Died: 1927

formula	years	starts (DNS)	wins	2nd	3rd	4th	5th	6th	PP	FL	points
Le Mans	1923-26	4	1	1	1	-	-	-	-	1	

Win: 1925 Le Mans 24 hrs

Ernest Courtis

GB

Major win: 1907 Tourist Trophy (Isle of Man)

Andre Couto

P. Born: 14.12.1976, Lisbon

formula	years	starts (DNS)	wins	2nd	3rd	4th	5th	6th	PP	FL	points
F3000 INT	1998-2000	30 (2)	-	-	2	-	3	1	-	-	15

Best championship: 1998, 11th

Major win: 2000 Macau

Olivier Couvreur

F. Born: 23.5.1970, Bondy

1993 European Formula Renault Champion, 1991 French Formula Renault Champion

formula	years	starts (DNS)	wins	2nd	3rd	4th	5th	6th	PP	FL	points
Le Mans	1994	1	-	-	-	-	-	-	-	-	

Howard Covey

USA

Champcar win: 1 – 1909 Portland race 1

David Cowart

USA

1978 and 1981 IMSA GTO Champion

formula	years	starts (DNS)	wins	2nd	3rd	4th	5th	6th	PP	FL	points
Le Mans	1982	1	-	-	-	-	-	-	-	-	
SC W	1976-89		-	-	-	-	1	-	-	-	

Dave Coyne

GB. Born: 31.3.1958

1987 EFDA Euroseries F3 Champion

formula	years	starts (DNS)	wins	2nd	3rd	4th	5th	6th	PP	FL	points
F3000 INT	1991	1	-	-	-	-	-	-	-	-	0

F3 E win: 1 – 1987 Knutstorp EFDA

Chris Craft

GB. Born: 17.11.1939, Porthleven, Cornwall

1973 European 2-litre Sports Car Champion

formula	years	starts (DNS)	wins	2nd	3rd	4th	5th	6th	PP	FL	points
F1 W	1971	1 (1)	-	-	-	-	-	-	-	-	0

Best result: no finishes. Best qualifying: 25th. Teams: Alain de Cadenet, Brabham

formula	years	starts (DNS)	wins	2nd	3rd	4th	5th	6th	PP	FL	points
Le Mans	1971-84	14	-	-	1	1	1	-	-	1	
SC W	1969-84		-	-	1	2	-	-	-	-	

formula	years	starts (DNS)	wins	2nd	3rd	4th	5th	6th	PP	FL	points
F2 E	1971	1 (1)	-	-	-	-	-	-	-	-	0

Ricky Craven

USA. Born: 24.5.1966, Bangor, Maine
NASCAR win: 1 (in Modern era)

Jim Crawford

GB. Born: 13.2.1948, Dunfermline, Fifeshire. Died: 6.8.2002, Terre Verde, Florida (USA)
1982 British F1 Champion, 1974 Southern Organs British Formula Atlantic Champion

formula	years	starts (DNS)	wins	2nd	3rd	4th	5th	6th	PP	FL	points
F1 W	1975	2	-	-	-	-	-	-	-	-	0

Best result: 13th. Best qualifying: 25th. Team: Lotus

F2 E	1975-81	14	-	-	-	1	-	1	-	-	4

Best championship: 1981, 16th

Indy 500	1985-93	8	-	-	-	-	-	1	-	-	
CART	1984-93	18 (1)	-	-	-	2	-	1	-	-	

F1 GB wins: 1980 Oulton Park (in F2 car), 1982 Brands Hatch, Thruxton, Donington

Pierre de Crawhez

B

formula	years	starts (DNS)	wins	2nd	3rd	4th	5th	6th	PP	FL	points
GP Pre-50	1904	1	-	-	-	-	-	-			

Major win: 1903 Ardennes Circuit

Georges Cremer

B
1994 and 1995 (both with Albert Vanierschot and Paul Kumpen) and 1997 (with Fons Taels and Vincent Dupont) Belgian Belcar GT Champion

Alberto Crespo

RA. Born: 16.1.1920, Buenos Aires. Died: 14.8.1991, Buenos Aires

formula	years	starts (DNS)	wins	2nd	3rd	4th	5th	6th	PP	FL	points
F1 W	1952	0 (1)	-	-	-	-	-	-	-	-	0

Best result: no starts. Best qualifying: 26th. Team: Enrico Plate

Antonio Creus

E. Born: 28.10.1919, Madrid. Died: 19.2.1966, Madrid

formula	years	starts (DNS)	wins	2nd	3rd	4th	5th	6th	PP	FL	points
F1 W	1960	1	-	-	-	-	-	-	-	-	0

Best result: no finishes. Best qualifying: 22nd. Team: driver

Donny Crevels

NL. Born: 6.2.1974, Amsterdam
1998 Italian F3 Champion

formula	years	starts (DNS)	wins	2nd	3rd	4th	5th	6th	PP	FL	points
Le Mans	2001	1	-	-	-	-	-	-			

Robert Crevits

B
Major win: 1964 Spa 24 hrs

Charles Crichton-Stuart

GB. Born: 10.3.1939, London. Died: 2.7.2001, Philippines, heart attack
1966 Temporada F3 Champion

Patrick Crinelli

I. Born: 5.8.1971, Rome
1993 European GM-Lotus Champion

formula	years	starts (DNS)	wins	2nd	3rd	4th	5th	6th	PP	FL	points
F3000 INT	1994	2	-	-	-	-	-	-	-	-	0

Fernando Croceri

RA. Born: 6.1.1960, Buenos Aires
1993 Sud-Am F3 Champion, 1993 Brazilian F3 Champion

formula	years	starts (DNS)	wins	2nd	3rd	4th	5th	6th	PP	FL	points
F3000 INT	1988	0 (5)	-	-	-	-	-	-	-	-	0

Tony Crook

GB. Born: 16.2.1920, Manchester

formula	years	starts (DNS)	wins	2nd	3rd	4th	5th	6th	PP	FL	points
F1 W	1952-53	2	-	-	-	-	-	-	-	-	0

Best result: 21st. Best qualifying: 25th. Team: driver

Marco Crosara

I

formula	years	starts (DNS)	wins	2nd	3rd	4th	5th	6th	PP	FL	points
SC W	1953	1	-	-	-	-	-	-			

Win: 1953 Mille Miglia
Other Major win: 1950 Mille Miglia

G Crosby

NZ
1992 New Zealand Touring Car Champion

Geoffrey Crossley

GB. Born: 11.5.1921, Baslow, Derbyshire. Died: 7.1.2002, Oxfordshire

formula	years	starts (DNS)	wins	2nd	3rd	4th	5th	6th	PP	FL	points
F1 W	1950	2	-	-	-	-	-	-	-	-	0

Best result: 9th. Best qualifying: 12th. Team: driver

GP Pre-50	1949	1	-	-	-	-	-	-			

John Crouch

AUS
Major win: 1949 Australian GP

Stuart Crow

USA. Born: 21.8.1959
1990 SCCA Super Vee Champion, 2000 United States F3 Champion

T Crowe

NZ
1988 New Zealand Touring Car Champion

Alain Cudini

F. Born: 19.4.1946, Colombes, Paris
1983 French Touring Car Champion, 1972 European Formula Renault Champion

formula	years	starts (DNS)	wins	2nd	3rd	4th	5th	6th	PP	FL	points
Le Mans	1972-96	13	-	-	-	-	1	2	-	-	
SC W	1972-92		-	-	-	-	1	1	-	-	
F2 E	1974	3	-	-	-	-	1	-	-		2

Best championship: 1974, 16th
Major win: 1998 Spa 24 hrs

Bill Cummings

USA. Born: 11.11.1906, Indianapolis, Indiana. Died: 8.2.1939, Indianapolis, Indiana, road accident
1934 Champcar Champion

formula	years	starts (DNS)	wins	2nd	3rd	4th	5th	6th	PP	FL	points
Indy 500	1930-38	9	1	-	1	-	1	1	2	-	

Win: 1934 Indianapolis 500
Champcar wins: 6 – 1930 Langhorne, Syracuse, 1932 Oakland, 1933 Detroit, 1933 Syracuse, 1934 Indianapolis 500

Jacko Cunningham

USA
1989 North American Formula Atlantic (Eastern) Champion

Noel Cunningham-Reid

GB

formula	years	starts (DNS)	wins	2nd	3rd	4th	5th	6th	PP	FL	points
Le Mans	1957	1	-	-	-	-	-	-			
SC W	1957		1	-	-	-	-	-			

Win: 1957 Nurburgring

Phil Currin

USA
1972 IMSA GTO Champion

formula	years	starts (DNS)	wins	2nd	3rd	4th	5th	6th	PP	FL	points
SC W	1972-87		-	-	-	1	-	-	-	-	

D

Guido Dacco

I. Born: 10.9.1942, Limbiate, near Milan

formula	years	starts (DNS)	wins	2nd	3rd	4th	5th	6th	PP	FL	points
Le Mans	1984-85	2	-	-	-	-	-	-			
SC W	1982-92		-	-	1	-	-	-			
F2 E	1980-84	48 (4)	-	-	1	1	1	-	-		6

Best championship: 1983, 12th

F3000 INT	1985-87	12 (11)	-	-	2	2	-	-			6

Best championship: 1985, 13th

CART	1989-92	23 (2)	-	-	-	-	-	-			

Anders Dahlgren

S
1984 Swedish Tourish Car Champion

Hakan Dahlqvist

S. Born: 1947
1973 Swedish F3 Champion

formula	years	starts (DNS)	wins	2nd	3rd	4th	5th	6th	PP	FL	points
F2 E	1973	1	-	-	-	1	-	-	-		3

Best championship: 1973, 26th

Charles "Chuck" Daigh

USA. Born: 29.11.1923, Long Beach, California

formula	years	starts (DNS)	wins	2nd	3rd	4th	5th	6th	PP	FL	points
F1 W	1960	3 (3)	-	-	-	-	-	-	-	-	0

Best result: 10th. Best qualifying: 16th. Teams: Lance Reventlow, Cooper

Le Mans	1960	1	-	-	-	-	-	-			
SC W	1955-62		1	-	-	-	-	1			

Win: 1959 Sebring 12 hrs

Other Major win: 1958 United States GP

Patrick Dal Bo

F. Born: 1945

formula	years	starts (DNS)	wins	2nd	3rd	4th	5th	6th	PP	FL	points
Le Mans	1973	1	-	-	-	-	-	-			
F2 E	1969-73	13 (17)	-	-	-	1	-	-	-		7

Best championship: 1972, 15th

Wally Dallenbach

USA. Born: 12.12.1936, East Brunswick, New Jersey

formula	years	starts (DNS)	wins	2nd	3rd	4th	5th	6th	PP	FL	points
Indy 500	1967-79	13	-	-	-	2	1	-	-	1	

Pre-CART Champcar wins: 5 – 1973 Milwaukee, California 500 qualifying race 1, California 500, 1975 California 500 qualifying race 2, 1977 Trenton

CART	1979	14	-	1	-	3	1	1	-		

Best championship: 1979, 9th

Wally Dallenbach Jr

USA. Born: 23.5.1963, Basalt, Colorado
1985 and 1986 Trans-Am Champion

formula	years	starts (DNS)	wins	2nd	3rd	4th	5th	6th	PP	FL	points
CART	1987-90	4	-	-	-	-	-	-	-	-	

Richard Dallest

F. Born: 15.2.1951

formula	years	starts (DNS)	wins	2nd	3rd	4th	5th	6th	PP	FL	points
F2 E	1978-83	35 (5)	2	-	-	1	3	1	2	-	28

Wins: 1980 Pau, Zandvoort. Best championship: 1980, 6th

F3000 INT	1986	3 (1)	-	-	-	1	-	-	-		3

Best championship: 1986, 17th

F3 E win: 1 – 1979 Kinnekulle

Yannick Dalmas

F. Born: 28.7.1961, Le Beausset, near Toulon
1992 World Sports Car Champion (with Derek Warwick), 1986 French F3 Champion, 1984 French Formula Renault Champion

formula	years	starts (DNS)	wins	2nd	3rd	4th	5th	6th	PP	FL	points
F1 W	1987-94	23 (27)	-	-	-	-	1*	-	-	-	0

***Dalmas was not eligible for points as his car was not entered in the Championship in 1987. Best qualifying: 15th. Teams: Larrousse, AGS**

Le Mans	1991-2002	12	4	1	1	-	-	-			

Wins: 1992, 1994, 1995 and 1999 Le Mans 24 hrs

SC W	1991-92		5	2	-	1	-	2	2		

Wins: 1991 Magny-Cours, Mexico City, 1992 Silverstone, Le Mans 24 hrs, Suzuka. Best championship: 1992, 1st

F3000 INT	1986-87	11	2	-	-	1	-	1	3		20

Wins: 1987 Pau, Jarama. Best championship: 1987, 5th

Other major wins: 1986 Monaco F3, 1997 Sebring 12 hrs

Derek Daly

IRL. Born: 11.3.1953, Dundrum, Dublin
1977 BP British F3 Champion

formula	years	starts (DNS)	wins	2nd	3rd	4th	5th	6th	PP	FL	points
F1 W	1978-82	49 (15)	-	-	-	2	3	3	-	-	15

Best championship: 1980, 10th. Best qualifying: 7th. Teams: Hesketh, Ensign, Tyrrell, March, Theodore, Williams

Le Mans	1988-90	3	-	-	-	1	-	-			
SC W	1982-92		-	-	-	1	-	-			
F2 E	1977-83	23	3	4	2	-	1	1	2	5	62

Wins: 1978 Mugello, Vallelunga, 1979 Donington. Best championships: 1978 and 1979, 3rd

Indy 500	1983-89	6	-	-	-	-	-	-	-	-	
CART	1982-89	66	-	-	1	2	2	4	-	-	

Best championship: 1988, 9th

F3 E win: 1 – 1977 Croix-en-Ternois

Other major wins: 1990 and 1991 Sebring 12 hrs

Lloyd Dane

USA. Born: 8.9.1925, Eldon
NASCAR wins: 4

Thomas Danielsson

S. Born: 4.12.1964, Kungsbacka, near Gothenburg
1985 Swedish F3 Champion

formula	years	starts (DNS)	wins	2nd	3rd	4th	5th	6th	PP	FL	points
Le Mans	1990-91	2	-	-	-	-	-	-			
F3000 INT	1988-89	14 (1)	1	-	1	-	-	1	-	-	14

Win: 1989 Silverstone. Best championship: 1989, 7th

Christian Danner

D. Born: 4.4.1958, Munich
1985 FIA F3000 Champion

formula	years	starts (DNS)	wins	2nd	3rd	4th	5th	6th	PP	FL	points
F1 W	1985-89	36 (11)	-	-	-	1	1	-	-	-	4

Best championship: 1986, 18th. Best qualifying: 16th. Teams: Zakspeed, Osella, Arrows, Rial

Le Mans	1981-86	3	-	-	-	-	-	-			
SC W	1981-86		-	-	-	1	-	-			
F2 E	1980-84	47 (2)	-	2	5	4	3	3	2	2	53

Best championships: 1983 and 1984, 5th

F3000 INT	1985	11	4	-	3	1	-	1	2	4	52

Wins: 1985 Pau, Dijon, Zandvoort, Donington. Best championship: 1985, 1st

CART	1992-97	18	-	-	-	-	-	-	-	-	

Other Major win: 1992 Spa 24 hrs

Jorge Daponte

RA. Born: 5.6.1923, Buenos Aires. Died: 9.3.1963, Buenos Aires

formula	years	starts (DNS)	wins	2nd	3rd	4th	5th	6th	PP	FL	points
F1 W	1954	2	-	-	-	-	-	-	-	-	0

Best result: 11th. Best qualifying: 17th. Team: driver

Ruben Daray

RA
1985 TC2000 Argentinian Touring Car Champion

Airton Dare

BR. Born: 9.2.1978, Bauru

formula	years	starts (DNS)	wins	2nd	3rd	4th	5th	6th	PP	FL	points
Indy 500	2000-02	3	-	-	-	-	-	-	-	-	
IRL	2000-02	37	1	1	1	-	1	2	-	-	

Win: 2002 Kansas City. Best championship: 2002, 9th

Vicente Daudt

BR
1994 Brazilian Touring Car Champion (with Egon Herzfeld)

Jochen Dauer

D. Born: 10.1.1952, Nuremberg
1988 Interserie Champion

formula	years	starts (DNS)	wins	2nd	3rd	4th	5th	6th	PP	FL	points
F2 E	1979-81	5 (1)	-	-	-	1	-	-	-	-	2

Best championship: 1980, 15th

William David

F. Born: 21.2.1969, Pau
1999 and 2000 French Touring Car Champion, 1994 Peugeot 905 Spyder
Cup Champion

formula	years	starts (DNS)	wins	2nd	3rd	4th	5th	6th	PP	FL	points
Le Mans	1995-96	2	-	-	-	-	-	-	1	1	

Anthony Davidson

GB. Born: 18.4.1979, Hemel Hempstead

formula	years	starts (DNS)	wins	2nd	3rd	4th	5th	6th	PP	FL	points
F1 W	2002	2	-	-	-	-	-	-	-	-	0

Best result: no finishes. Best qualifying: 20th. Team: Minardi
Major win: 2001 Pau

Jamie Davies

GB. Born: 16.2.1974, Yeovil

formula	years	starts (DNS)	wins	2nd	3rd	4th	5th	6th	PP	FL	points
Le Mans	1998-2001	2	-	-	-	-	-	-	-	-	
F3000 INT	1997-2000	32 (3)	1	1	5	-	-	1	1	1	37

Win: 1997 Enna. Best championship: 1997, 4th

Jimmy Davies

USA. Born: 8.8.1929, Glendale, California. Died: 11.6.1966, Chicago, Illinois
from injuries inflicted in a Midget race on 3.6.1966

formula	years	starts (DNS)	wins	2nd	3rd	4th	5th	6th	PP	FL	points
Indy 500	1950-55	5	-	-	1	-	-	-	-	-	

Champcar wins: 3 – 1949 Del Mar, 1950 Phoenix, 1954 Springfield

Matt Davies

GB. Born: 28.12.1976
1998 French Formula Renault Champion

Colin Davis

GB. Born: 29.7.1933, London

formula	years	starts (DNS)	wins	2nd	3rd	4th	5th	6th	PP	FL	points
F1 W	1959	2	-	-	-	-	-	-	-	-	0

Best result: 11th. Best qualifying: 17th. Team: Scuderia Centro Sud

Le Mans	1958-66	7	-	-	-	1	-	-	-	-	
SC W	1958-67		1	1	1	2	1	1	-	1	

Win: 1964 Targa Florio

Floyd Davis

USA. Born: 9.3.1905, Oakford, Illinois. Died: 31.5.1977, Indianapolis,
Indiana

formula	years	starts (DNS)	wins	2nd	3rd	4th	5th	6th	PP	FL	points
Indy 500	1937-41	4	1	-	-	-	-	-	-	-	

Win: 1941 Indianapolis 500
Champcar win: 1 – 1941 Indianapolis 500

SCH "Sammy" Davis

GB. Born: 9.1.1887, London. Died: 9.1.1981, Guildford, heart attack

formula	years	starts (DNS)	wins	2nd	3rd	4th	5th	6th	PP	FL	points
GP Pre-50	1927	1	-	-	-	-	-	-	-	-	
Le Mans	1925-33	6	1	1	-	-	-	-	-	-	

Win: 1927 Le Mans 24 hrs

Lex Davison

AUS. Born: 12.2.1923, Moonee Ponds, Melbourne. Died: 20.2.1965,
Sandown Park, Australian GP practice
1957 Australian Gold Star Champion

formula	years	starts (DNS)	wins	2nd	3rd	4th	5th	6th	PP	FL	points
Le Mans	1961	1	-	-	-	-	-	-	-	-	

Major wins: 1954, 1957, 1958 and 1961 Australian GP

Joe Dawson

USA. Born: 17.7.1889, Indianapolis, Indiana. Died: 17.6.1946, Pennsylvania

formula	years	starts (DNS)	wins	2nd	3rd	4th	5th	6th	PP	FL	points
GP Pre-50	1910	1	-	-	-	-	-	1	-	-	
Indy 500	1911-14	3	1	-	-	-	1	-	-	-	

Win: 1912 Indianapolis 500
Champcar wins: 2 – 1910 Indianapolis race 5, 1912 Indianapolis 500

Denis Dayan

F
1969 French Formula Renault Champion

formula	years	starts (DNS)	wins	2nd	3rd	4th	5th	6th	PP	FL	points
Le Mans	1967	1	-	-	-	-	-	-	-	-	

Jean-Philippe Dayraut

F. Born: 14.4.1969, Toulouse
2001 French Touring Car Champion

formula	years	starts (DNS)	wins	2nd	3rd	4th	5th	6th	PP	FL	points
Le Mans	2001	1	-	-	-	-	-	-	-	-	

Richard Dean

GB. Born: 7.10.1965, Leeds, Yorkshire
1998 British GT Champion (with Kurt Luby)

formula	years	starts (DNS)	wins	2nd	3rd	4th	5th	6th	PP	FL	points
F3000 INT	1990-92	6	-	-	-	1	-	-	-	-	2

Best championship: 1990, 19th

Tony Dean

GB. Born: 23.7.1930
1965 British F3 Champion

formula	years	starts (DNS)	wins	2nd	3rd	4th	5th	6th	PP	FL	points
SC W	1967-72		-	-	-	1	-	-	-	-	

Christian Debias

F. Born: 12.10.1946
1975 French Formula Renault Champion

formula	years	starts (DNS)	wins	2nd	3rd	4th	5th	6th	PP	FL	points
Le Mans	1978-80	2	-	-	-	-	-	-	-	-	

Didier Defourny

B. Born: 18.6.1966, Liege
Major win: 2000 Spa 24 hrs

Claude Degremont

F. Born: 10.11.1960
1987 French Formula Renault Champion

Jean-Denis Deletraz

CH. Born: 1.10.1963, Geneva

formula	years	starts (DNS)	wins	2nd	3rd	4th	5th	6th	PP	FL	points
F1 W	1994-95	3	-	-	-	-	-	-	-	-	0

Best result: 15th. Best qualifying: 24th. Teams: Larrousse, Pacific

Le Mans	1995-2002	5	-	-	-	-	2	-	-	-	

GT FIA wins: 4 – 2002 Jarama, Anderstorp, Oschersleben, Estoril

F3000 INT	1988-91	20 (8)	-	-	2	-	-	-	-	-	8

Best championship: 1988, 13th

Nino Demuth
L
Major win: 1976 Spa 24 hrs

Patrick Depailler
F. Born: 9.8.1944, Clermont-Ferrand. Died:
1.8.1980, Hockenheim, testing
1974 European F2 Champion, 1971 French F3
Champion

formula	years	starts (DNS)	wins	2nd	3rd	4th	5th	6th	PP	FL	points
F1 W	1972-80	95	2	10	7	6	6	5	1	4	141

Wins: 1978 Monaco GP, 1979 Spanish GP. Best championship: 1976, 4th. Best qualifying: 1st. Teams: Tyrrell, Ligier, Alfa Romeo

Le Mans	1967-78	8	-	-	-	-	-	-	-	-	
SC W	1967-78		-	1	1	1	-	1	2	-	
F2 E	1970-75	37 (5)	4	9	2	2	1	1	8	7	119

Wins: 1974 Pau, Mugello, Hockenheim race 3, Vallelunga. Best championship: 1974, 1st
Other Major win: 1972 Monaco F3

Boris Derichebourg
F. Born: 16.3.1978, Enghien-les-Bains

formula	years	starts (DNS)	wins	2nd	3rd	4th	5th	6th	PP	FL	points
Le Mans	2000-02	3									

GT FIA win: 1 – 2000 Hungaroring

F3000 INT	1997-99	23 (1)	-	-	2	-	-	1	-	-	9

Best championship: 1998, 12th

Renaud Derlot
F. Born: 4.3.1979, Aubervilliers
2000 French Formula Renault Champion
Major win: 2002 Pau

Jean Desvignes
F

formula	years	starts (DNS)	wins	2nd	3rd	4th	5th	6th	PP	FL	points
Le Mans	1934-35	2	-	-	-	-	1	-	-	-	

Major win: 1934 Spa 24 hrs

Jean-Marie Detrin
B

formula	years	starts (DNS)	wins	2nd	3rd	4th	5th	6th	PP	FL	points
Le Mans	1976-77	2	-	-	-	-	-	-	-	-	

Major win: 1976 Spa 24 hrs

Willi Deutsch
D

formula	years	starts (DNS)	wins	2nd	3rd	4th	5th	6th	PP	FL	points
F2 E	1971-77	23 (3)	-	-	-	1	-	-	-	-	4

Best championship: 1976, 12th

Hellmut Deutz
D
1952 German F3 Champion

Don Devendorf
USA
1982 IMSA GTO Champion, 1979 IMSA GTU Champion

Stanley Dickens
S. Born: 7.5.1952, Farila
1988 (with Hideki Okada) and 1989 (with Kunimitsu Takahashi) Japanese Sports-Prototype Champion

formula	years	starts (DNS)	wins	2nd	3rd	4th	5th	6th	PP	FL	points
Le Mans	1986-96	7	1	-	1	-	-	-	-	-	

Win: 1989 Le Mans 24 hrs

SC W	1984-92		-	1	2	3	2	1	-	-	

Best championship: 1988, 15th

F2 E	1981-82	2	-	-	-	-	-	-	-	-	0

Darel "Yancy" Dieringer
USA. Born: 1.6.1926, Indianapolis, Indiana. Died: 28.10.1989
NASCAR wins: 6

Rolf-Torsten Dietrich
A
2002 Interserie Champion

Pierre Dieudonne
B. Born: 24.3.1947, Brussels
1976 European Touring Car Champion (with Jean Xhenceval)

formula	years	starts (DNS)	wins	2nd	3rd	4th	5th	6th	PP	FL	points
Le Mans	1977-91	11	-	-	-	-	-	1	-	-	
SC W	1977-91		1	-	-	-	-	1	-	-	

Win: 1981 Spa 24 hrs

F2 E	1980	1	-	-	-	-	-	-	-	-	0

Other major wins: 1974 and 1975 Spa 24 hrs, 1976 Tourist Trophy (Silverstone)

Bert Dingley
USA. Born: 21.8.1885, Oakdale, California. Died: 7.4.1966, Indianapolis, Indiana

formula	years	starts (DNS)	wins	2nd	3rd	4th	5th	6th	PP	FL	points
GP Pre-50	1905	1	-	-	-	-	-	-	-	-	
Indy 500	1912	1	-	-	-	-	-	-	-	-	

Champcar wins: 3 – 1909 Portland race 3, Santa Monica race 2, 1911 Oakland race 3

Spartico Dini
I. Born: 1943, Greve, Chianti, Florence
1969 European Touring Car Champion (1600cc class)

formula	years	starts (DNS)	wins	2nd	3rd	4th	5th	6th	PP	FL	points
Le Mans	1966-80	6	-	-	-	-	1	-	-	-	
SC W	1964-81		-	-	2	-	1	-	-	-	
F2 E	1973	2	-	-	-	-	-	-	-	-	0

Pedro Diniz
BR. Born: 22.5.1970, Sao Paulo

formula	years	starts (DNS)	wins	2nd	3rd	4th	5th	6th	PP	FL	points
F1 W	1995-2000	98 (1)	-	-	-	2	6	-	-	-	10

Best championships: 1998 and 1999, 13th. Best qualifying: 8th. Teams: Forti, Ligier, Arrows, Sauber

F3000 INT	1993-94	16 (1)	-	-	-	1	-	-	-	-	3

Best championship: 1994, 12th

"Dino" (Antonio Ferrari)
I

formula	years	starts (DNS)	wins	2nd	3rd	4th	5th	6th	PP	FL	points
SC W	1977-78		1	-	-	-	-	-	-	-	

Win: 1977 Vallelunga

Carlyle "Duke" Dinsmore
USA. Born: 10.4.1913, Williamstown, West Virginia. Died: 12.10.1985, Daytona Beach, Florida

formula	years	starts (DNS)	wins	2nd	3rd	4th	5th	6th	PP	FL	points
Indy 500	1946-56	7	-	-	-	-	-	-	-	-	

Champcar win: 1 – 1950 Sacramento

Count Jules de Dion
F
City-to-city win: 1894 Paris-Rouen

Lou Disbrow
USA. Born: 1877. Died: 9.7.1939, Philadelphia, Pennsylvania

formula	years	starts (DNS)	wins	2nd	3rd	4th	5th	6th	PP	FL	points
GP Pre-50	1910-15	3	-	-	-	-	2	-	-	-	
Indy 500	1911-14	4	-	-	-	-	-	-	-	-	

Champcar wins: 4 – 1911 Jacksonville, Philadelphia race 3, 1913 Galveston race 1, Galveston race 3

Mark Dismore
USA. Born: 12.10.1956, Greenfield, Indiana

1990 North American Toyota Atlantic (Western) Champion

formula	years	starts (DNS)	wins	2nd	3rd	4th	5th	6th	PP	FL	points
Le Mans	1996	1	-	-	-	-	-	-	-	-	-
Indy 500	1996-2002	7	-	-	-	-	-	-	-	-	-
CART	1989-91	4	-	-	-	-	-	-	-	-	-
IRL	1996-2002	58	1	2	1	1	2	3	4	6	

Win: 1999 Texas. Best championship: 1999, 3rd

Other Major win: 1993 Daytona 24 hrs

Albert Divo

F. Born: 1895, Paris. Died: ??.11.1966, Paris

formula	years	starts (DNS)	wins	2nd	3rd	4th	5th	6th	PP	FL	points
GP Pre-50	1923-37	22	3	2	4	2	-	1	-	1	

Wins: 1923 Spanish GP, 1925 French GP, San Sebastian GP

| Le Mans | 1931-38 | 2 | - | - | - | - | - | - | - | - | - |

Other major wins: 1928 and 1929 Targa Florio

Fred Dixon

GB. Born: 21.4.1892, Stockton-on-Tees, Yorkshire. Died: 4.11.1956, Reigate, Surrey

formula	years	starts (DNS)	wins	2nd	3rd	4th	5th	6th	PP	FL	points
Le Mans	1934-35	2	-	-	1	-	-	-	-	-	-

Major wins: 1935 and 1936 Tourist Trophy (Ards)

Scott Dixon

NZ. Born: 22.7.1980, Auckland
2000 CART Indy Lights Champion, 1998 Australian Formula Holden Champion

formula	years	starts (DNS)	wins	2nd	3rd	4th	5th	6th	PP	FL	points
CART	2001-02	39 (1)	1	1	1	3	3	5	-	-	

Win: 2001 Nazareth. Best championship: 2001, 8th

Prince Dmitri Djordjadze

R

Major win: 1931 Spa 24 hrs

Frank Dochnal

USA. Born: 8.10.1920, Missouri

formula	years	starts (DNS)	wins	2nd	3rd	4th	5th	6th	PP	FL	points
F1 W	1963	0 (1)	-	-	-	-	-	-	-	-	0

Best result: no starts. Best qualifying: no times set. Team: driver

Charles Dodson

GB. Born: 6.12.1901. Died: 1983, motorcycle accident

formula	years	starts (DNS)	wins	2nd	3rd	4th	5th	6th	PP	FL	points
Le Mans	1935-37	2	-	-	-	-	-	-	-	-	-

Major wins: 1934 and 1936 Tourist Trophy (Ards)

Jose Dolhem

F. Born: 26.4.1944, Paris. Died: 16.4.1988, near St Etienne, light plane accident

formula	years	starts (DNS)	wins	2nd	3rd	4th	5th	6th	PP	FL	points
F1 W	1974	1 (2)	-	-	-	-	-	-	-	-	0

Best result: no finishes. Best qualifying: 26th. Team: Surtees

| Le Mans | 1973-78 | 3 | - | - | - | 1 | - | - | - | - | - |
| F2 E | 1971-79 | 26 (5) | - | - | 1 | - | - | - | - | 1 | 6 |

Best championship: 1974, 14th

Mario Dominguez

MEX. Born: 1.12.1975, Mexico City

formula	years	starts (DNS)	wins	2nd	3rd	4th	5th	6th	PP	FL	points
CART	2002	19	1	-	-	-	-	-	-	-	

Win: 2002 Surfers Paradise

Kaye Don

GB. Born: 1891, Dublin (IRL). Died: 29.8.1981

formula	years	starts (DNS)	wins	2nd	3rd	4th	5th	6th	PP	FL	points
GP Pre-50	1936	1	-	-	-	-	-	-	-	-	-

Major win: 1928 Tourist Trophy (Ards)

Martin Donnelly

GB. Born: 26.3.1964, Belfast, Northern Ireland

formula	years	starts (DNS)	wins	2nd	3rd	4th	5th	6th	PP	FL	points
F1 W	1989-90	13 (2)	-	-	-	-	-	-	-	-	0

Best result: 7th. Best qualifying: 11th. Teams: Arrows, Lotus

| Le Mans | 1989-90 | 2 | - | - | - | - | - | - | - | - | - |
| F3000 INT | 1988-89 | 15 | 3 | 2 | 1 | - | - | - | 2 | 3 | 43 |

Wins: 1988 Brands Hatch, Dijon, 1989 Brands Hatch. Best championship: 1988, 3rd

Other Major win: 1987 Macau

David Donohue

USA. Born: 5.1.1967, Malvern
1997 North American Touring Car Champion

formula	years	starts (DNS)	wins	2nd	3rd	4th	5th	6th	PP	FL	points
Le Mans	1998-2002	4	-	-	-	-	-	-	-	-	-

GT FIA win: 1 – 1999 Watkins Glen

Mark Donohue

USA. Born: 18.3.1937, Summit, New Jersey. Died: 19.8.1975, Graz, following an accident during the warm-up for the Austrian GP at the Osterreichring on 17.8.1975
1973 Can-Am Champion, 1968, 1969 and 1971 Trans-Am Champion, 1974 IROC Champion

formula	years	starts (DNS)	wins	2nd	3rd	4th	5th	6th	PP	FL	points
F1 W	1971-75	14 (2)	-	-	1	-	2	-	-	-	8

Best championship: 1975, 15th. Best qualifying: 8th. Team: Penske

| Le Mans | 1966-71 | 3 | - | - | - | 1 | - | - | - | - | - |
| SC W | 1962-73 | | 1 | 1 | 3 | 1 | - | 2 | 3 | 1 | |

Win: 1969 Daytona 24 hrs

| Indy 500 | 1969-73 | 5 | - | 1 | 1 | - | - | - | - | - | - |

Win: 1972 Indianapolis 500

Champcar wins: 3 – 1971 Pocono 500, Michigan, 1972 Indianapolis 500

NASCAR wins: 1 (in Modern era)

Other Major win: 1966 Canadian GP

Edgar Doren

D. Born: 6.10.1942, Wuppertal

formula	years	starts (DNS)	wins	2nd	3rd	4th	5th	6th	PP	FL	points
Le Mans	1978-85	6	-	-	-	-	-	-	-	-	-
SC W	1975-92		1	1	2	5	2	1	-	1	

Win: 1981 Monza. Best championship: 1981, 7th

Rad Dougall

ZA. Born: 7.9.1951, Johannesburg

formula	years	starts (DNS)	wins	2nd	3rd	4th	5th	6th	PP	FL	points
Le Mans	1978	1	-	-	-	-	-	-	-	-	-
F2 E	1978-80	24 (3)	1	1	1	-	1	3	1	-	24

Win: 1979 Thruxton. Best championship: 1979, 5th

Jim Downing

USA. Born: 4.1.1942, Atlanta, Georgia
1985, 1986 and 1987 IMSA Lights Champion, 1982 IMSA GTU Champion

formula	years	starts (DNS)	wins	2nd	3rd	4th	5th	6th	PP	FL	points
Le Mans	1995-2002	4	-	-	-	-	-	-	-	-	-
SC W	1978-92		-	1	-	-	-	1	-	1	

Ken Downing

GB. Born: 5.12.1917, Chesterton, Staffordshire

formula	years	starts (DNS)	wins	2nd	3rd	4th	5th	6th	PP	FL	points
F1 W	1952	2	-	-	-	-	-	-	-	-	0

Best result: 9th. Best qualifying: 5th. Teams: Connaught, driver

Bob Drake

USA. Born: 14.12.1919, San Francisco, California. Died: 18.4.1990, Woodland Hills, California

formula	years	starts (DNS)	wins	2nd	3rd	4th	5th	6th	PP	FL	points
F1 W	1960	1	-	-	-	-	-	-	-	-	0

Best result: 13th. Best qualifying: 22nd. Team: Joe Lubin

Shane Drake
NZ
1999 New Zealand Tranz-Am Champion

Rene Dreyfus
F. Born: 6.5.1905, Nice. Died: 16.8.1993, New York City

formula	years	starts (DNS)	wins	2nd	3rd	4th	5th	6th	PP	FL	points
GP Pre-50	1929-39	34	2	2	4	6	4	1	1	2	

Wins: 1930 Monaco GP, 1934 Belgian GP

Le Mans	1937-52	3	-	-	1	-	-	-	-	-	
Indy 500	1940	1	-	-	-	-	-	-	-	-	

Ernest "Paddy" Driver
ZA. Born: 13.5.1934, Johannesburg

formula	years	starts (DNS)	wins	2nd	3rd	4th	5th	6th	PP	FL	points
F1 W	1963-74	1 (1)	-	-	-	-	-	-	-	-	0

Best result: no finishes. Best qualifying: 21st. Teams: Selby, Team Gunston

Piero Drogo
YV. Born: 8.8.1926, Vignale, Monferrato. Died: 28.4.1973, Bologna

formula	years	starts (DNS)	wins	2nd	3rd	4th	5th	6th	PP	FL	points
F1 W	1960	1	-	-	-	-	-	-	-	-	0

Best result: 8th. Best qualifying: 15th. Team: Scuderia Colonia

Le Mans	1958	1	-	-	-	-	-	-	-	-	
SC W	1957-59	-	-	-	1	1	-	-	-	-	

Bernard de Dryver
B. Born: 19.9.1952, Brussels

formula	years	starts (DNS)	wins	2nd	3rd	4th	5th	6th	PP	FL	points
F1 W	1977	0 (1)	-	-	-	-	-	-	-	-	0

Best result: no starts. Best qualifying: 31st. Team: British F1 Racing

Le Mans	1979-92	10	-	1	-	-	-	-	-	-	
SC W	1979-92	-	-	1	-	-	-	-	-	-	
F2 E	1975-79	28 (16)	-	-	-	1	2	-	-	-	4

Best championship: 1977, 20th

F3000 INT	1988	0 (1)	-	-	-	-	-	-	-	-	0

Jorg Dubler
CH. Born: 13.4.1941

formula	years	starts (DNS)	wins	2nd	3rd	4th	5th	6th	PP	FL	points
F2 E	1971-74	2 (6)	-	-	-	-	-	-	-	-	0

Major win: 1966 Portuguese GP

Marc Duez
B. Born: 18.4.1957, Verviers, near Spa
1996 Belgian Belcar GT Champion (with Daniel and Patrick Hubert)

formula	years	starts (DNS)	wins	2nd	3rd	4th	5th	6th	PP	FL	points
Le Mans	1983-2002	12	-	-	-	-	-	-	-	-	
SC W	1979-92	-	-	-	-	2	1	-	-		

GT FIA wins: 1 – 2001 Spa 24 hrs, 2002 Silverstone
Other major wins: 1997 and 1998 Spa 24 hrs

Doug Duff
ZA
1953 South African Drivers' Champion

John Duff
GB. Born: ??.1.1895. Died: ??.1.1958, Epping Forest, horse riding

formula	years	starts (DNS)	wins	2nd	3rd	4th	5th	6th	PP	FL	points
Le Mans	1923-25	3	1	-	-	1	-	-	-	-	

Win: 1924 Le Mans 24 hrs

Indy 500	1926	1	-	-	-	-	-	-	-	-	

Peter Dumbreck
GB. Born: 13.10.1973, Kirkaldy
1998 Japanese F3 Champion

formula	years	starts (DNS)	wins	2nd	3rd	4th	5th	6th	PP	FL	points
Le Mans	1999	1	-	-	-	-	-	-	-	-	

Major win: 1998 Macau

Johnny Dumfries
(John Crichton-Stuart, Earl of Dumfries)
GB. Born: 26.4.1958, Rothesay, Isle of Bute
1984 British F3 Champion

formula	years	starts (DNS)	wins	2nd	3rd	4th	5th	6th	PP	FL	points
F1 W	1986	15 (1)	-	-	-	1	1	-	-	-	3

Best championship: 1986, 13th. Best qualifying: 8th. Team: Lotus

Le Mans	1987-91	5	1	-	-	-	-	-	-	1	

Win: 1988 Le Mans 24 hrs

SC W	1984-91		2	2	1	2	-	-	-	1	

Wins: 1987 Spa, 1988 Le Mans 24 hrs. Best championship: 1988, 14th

F3000 INT	1985-88	8	-	-	-	-	1	-	-	-	1

Best championship: 1985, 16th

F3 E wins: 4 – 1984 Donington, Silverstone, Nurburgring, Jarama

Dumortier
B
1990 Belgian Belcar GT Champion (with Dumortier and de Rosee)

Dumortier
B
1990 Belgian Belcar GT Champion (with Dumortier and de Rosee)

Vincent Dupont
B. Born: 23.10.1960
1997 Belgian Belcar GT Champion (with Fons Taels and Georges Cremer)

Dominique Dupuy
F. Born: 26.8.1957, Ars
2000 and 2001 French GT Champion (with Francois Fiat)

formula	years	starts (DNS)	wins	2nd	3rd	4th	5th	6th	PP	FL	points
Le Mans	1993-2000	7	-	-	-	-	-	-	-	-	

GT FIA wins: 3 – 1994 Jarama, 1999 Hockenheim, Hungaroring
Other Major win: 2000 Daytona 24 hrs

Cliff Durant
USA. Born: 26.11.1890. Died: 30.10.1937

formula	years	starts (DNS)	wins	2nd	3rd	4th	5th	6th	PP	FL	points
GP Pre-50	1915-16	2	-	-	-	-	-	-	-	-	
Indy 500	1919-28	6	-	-	-	-	-	-	-	-	

Champcar wins: 3 – 1918 Tacoma race 1, Tacoma race 2, 1919 Santa Monica

Arthur Duray
F. Born: 1881, New York City (USA). Died: 1954

formula	years	starts (DNS)	wins	2nd	3rd	4th	5th	6th	PP	FL	points
GP Pre-50	1905-30	11	-	-	-	1	1	1	-	1	
Le Mans	1924-28	4	-	-	-	-	-	-	-	-	
Indy 500	1914	1	-	1	-	-	-	-	-	-	

Major win: 1906 Ardennes Circuit

"Leon Duray" (George Stewart)
USA. Born: 30.4.1894, Cleveland, Ohio. Died: 12.5.1956

formula	years	starts (DNS)	wins	2nd	3rd	4th	5th	6th	PP	FL	points
Le Mans	1934	1	-	-	-	-	-	-	-	-	
Indy 500	1922-31	8	-	-	-	-	-	-	2	2	-

Champcar wins: 4 – 1926 Salem race 4, Charlotte race 9, 1927 Culver City, 1928 Salem race 1

Piero Dusio
I. Born: 13.10.1899, Scurzolengo d'Asti. Died: 7.11.1975, Buenos Aires

formula	years	starts (DNS)	wins	2nd	3rd	4th	5th	6th	PP	FL	points
F1 W	1952	0 (1)	-	-	-	-	-	-	-	-	0

Best result: no starts. Best qualifying: no times set. Team: driver

GP Pre-50	1935-36	2	-	-	-	-	-	1	-	-	

David Dussau
F. Born: 8.7.1971, Pau
1993 French Formula Renault Champion

formula	years	starts (DNS)	wins	2nd	3rd	4th	5th	6th	PP	FL	points
F3000 INT	1996	2	-	-	-	-	-	-	-	-	0

Graham Duxbury

ZA. Born: 1.12.1955
1982 South African Formula Atlantic Champion

formula	years	starts (DNS)	wins	2nd	3rd	4th	5th	6th	PP	FL	points
Le Mans	1985-87	2	-	-	-	-	-	-	-	-	
SC W	1983-88		-	-	-	-	-	1	-	-	

Major win: 1984 Daytona 24 hrs

George Dyer

USA

formula	years	starts (DNS)	wins	2nd	3rd	4th	5th	6th	PP	FL	points
SC W	1975-77		-	-	-	2	-	-	-	-	

Major win: 1977 Sebring 12 hrs

Rob Dyson

USA. Born: 21.6.1946

formula	years	starts (DNS)	wins	2nd	3rd	4th	5th	6th	PP	FL	points
Le Mans	1986	1	-	-	-	-	-	-	-	-	

Major win: 1997 Daytona 24 hrs

E

Bob Earl

USA. Born: 13.1.1950, Great Bend, Kansas

formula	years	starts (DNS)	wins	2nd	3rd	4th	5th	6th	PP	FL	points
Le Mans	1990	1	-	-	-	-	-	-	-	-	

Major wins: 1981 Macau, 1990 Sebring 12 hrs

Dale Earnhardt Sr

USA. Born: 29.4.1951, Kannapolis, North Carolina.
Died: 18.2.2001, Daytona 500
1980, 1986, 1987, 1990, 1991, 1993 and 1994
NASCAR Champion, 1990, 1995, 1999 and 2000
IROC Champion
**NASCAR wins: 76 (all Modern era) including 1998
Daytona 500, 1986, 1992, 1993 World 600**

Dale Earnhardt Jr

USA. Born: 10.10.1974, Kannapolis, North Carolina
NASCAR wins: 7 (all Modern era)

George Eaton

CDN. Born: 12.11.1945, Toronto, Ontario

formula	years	starts (DNS)	wins	2nd	3rd	4th	5th	6th	PP	FL	points
F1 W	1969-71	11 (2)	-	-	-	-	-	-	-	-	0

Best result: 10th. Best qualifying: 9th. Team: BRM

Le Mans	1971	1	-	-	-	-	-	-	-	-	

Bernie Ecclestone

GB. Born: 28.10.1930, St Peter's, Suffolk

formula	years	starts (DNS)	wins	2nd	3rd	4th	5th	6th	PP	FL	points
F1 W	1958	0 (1)	-	-	-	-	-	-	-	-	0

Best result: no starts. Best qualifying: 21st. Team: driver

Selwyn Edge

GB. Born: 29.3.1868, Sydney, New South Wales (AUS). Died: 12.2.1940,
Eastbourne, falling from a hotel window

formula	years	starts (DNS)	wins	2nd	3rd	4th	5th	6th	PP	FL	points
GP Pre-50	1901-04	3 (1)	1	-	-	-	-	-	-	-	

Win: 1902 Gordon Bennett Trophy

Guy Edwards

GB. Born: 30.12.1942, Macclesfield, Cheshire

formula	years	starts (DNS)	wins	2nd	3rd	4th	5th	6th	PP	FL	points
F1 W	1974-77	11 (5)	-	-	-	-	-	-	-	-	0

Best result: 7th. Best qualifying: 14th. Teams: Hill, Hesketh, Stanley BRM

Le Mans	1971-85	9	-	-	1	1	-	-	-	-	
SC W	1966-85	2	-	2	2	1	1	-	-		

Wins: 1981 Enna, Brands Hatch

formula	years	starts (DNS)	wins	2nd	3rd	4th	5th	6th	PP	FL	points
F2 E	1977	1 (1)	-	-	-	-	-	-	-	-	0

F1 GB wins: 1978 Oulton Park, Thruxton, 1979 Race of Champions British F1
class (Brands Hatch), 1980 Oulton Park Gold Cup, Snetterton

Bruno Eichmann

CH. Born: 13.5.1952, Rogwill
1996 FIA GT2 class Champion (with Gerd Ruch)

formula	years	starts (DNS)	wins	2nd	3rd	4th	5th	6th	PP	FL	points
Le Mans	1996-97	2	-	-	-	-	-	-	-	-	
F2 E	1980-82	2	-	-	-	-	-	-	-	-	0

Fredrik Ekblom

S. Born: 6.10.1970, Kumla, near Orebro
1998 Swedish Touring Car Champion

formula	years	starts (DNS)	wins	2nd	3rd	4th	5th	6th	PP	FL	points
Le Mans	1997-99	3	-	-	-	-	-	-	-	-	
CART	1994-96	3	-	-	-	-	-	-	-	-	

Mattias Ekstrom

S. Born: 14.7.1978, Falun
1999 Swedish Touring Car Champion

Ray Elder

USA. Born: 19.8.1942
NASCAR wins: 2 (1 in Modern era)

Vic Elford

GB. Born: 10.6.1935, Peckham, London

formula	years	starts (DNS)	wins	2nd	3rd	4th	5th	6th	PP	FL	points
F1 W	1968-71	13	-	-	-	1	2	1	-	-	8

Best championship: 1969, 13th. Best qualifying: 5th. Teams: Cooper, Antique
Automobiles, BRM

Le Mans	1967-83	9	-	-	-	-	-	1	-	2	
SC W	1964-84		6	5	7	5	-	1	4	8	

Wins: 1968 Daytona 24 hrs, Targa Florio, Nurburgring, 1970 Nurburgring, 1971
Sebring 12 hrs, Nurburgring

F2 E	1972	1	-	-	-	1	-	-	-	-	3

Best championship: 1972, 24th

Eje Elgh

S. Born: 15.6.1953, Karlskoga

formula	years	starts (DNS)	wins	2nd	3rd	4th	5th	6th	PP	FL	points
Le Mans	1982-93	10	-	-	-	-	-	1	-	-	
F2 E	1977-82	40 (4)	2	2	2	2	3	3	1	-	53

Wins: 1979 Enna, 1981 Vallelunga. Best championship: 1981, 4th

Eliano

B
1993 Belgian Belcar GT Champion (with Wuydts and Koentges)

Jorgen Ellekaer

DK
1965 Danish Formula Junior Champion

Bill Elliott

USA. Born: 8.10.1955, Cumming, Georgia
1988 NASCAR Champion
NASCAR wins: 43 (all Modern era) including 1985, 1987 Daytona 500

Frank Elliott

USA. Born: Lathrop, Missouri. Died: 1957

formula	years	starts (DNS)	wins	2nd	3rd	4th	5th	6th	PP	FL	points
Indy 500	1916-27	7	-	-	-	-	-	2	-	-	

Champcar wins: 5 – 1917 Uniontown race 2, 1922 Beverly Hills race 5, Cotati
race 3, Cotati race 4, 1925 Culver City race 2

Ray Elliott
USA. Born: 12.9.1921
Major win: 1950 Carrera Panamericana

Paul Emery
GB. Born: 12.11.1916, Chiswick, London. Died: 3.2.1993, Epsom, Surrey

formula	years	starts (DNS)	wins	2nd	3rd	4th	5th	6th	PP	FL	points
F1 W	1956-58	1 (1)	-	-	-	-	-	-	-	-	0

Best result: no finishes. Best qualifying: 23rd. Teams: Emeryson, Bernie Ecclestone

David Empringham
CDN. Born: 28.12.1963
1996 CART Indy Lights Champion, 1993 and 1994 North American Toyota Atlantic Champion

Ricardo van der Ende
NL. Born: 13.7.1979
2001 European Formula Chrysler Champion

Bill Endicott
USA. Born: c1880. Died: 1945

formula	years	starts (DNS)	wins	2nd	3rd	4th	5th	6th	PP	FL	points
Indy 500	1911-13	3	-	-	-	-	1	-	-	-	

Champcar wins: 3 – 1910 Atlanta race 2, Long Island race 1, 1912 Milwaukee race 2

Tomas Enge
CS. Born: 11.9.1976, Liberec

formula	years	starts (DNS)	wins	2nd	3rd	4th	5th	6th	PP	FL	points
F1 W	2001	3	-	-	-	-	-	-	-	-	0

Best result: 12th. Best qualifying: 19th. Team: Prost

Le Mans	2002	1	-	-	-	-	-	-	-	-	
F3000 INT	1998-2002	45 (3)	6	3	4	2	4	3	8	7	111

Wins: 2000 Hockenheim, 2001 Barcelona, Nurburgring, 2002 A1 Ring, Silverstone, Magny-Cours. Best championship: 2001, 2nd

Paul England
AUS. Born: 28.3.1929, Melbourne, Victoria

formula	years	starts (DNS)	wins	2nd	3rd	4th	5th	6th	PP	FL	points
F1 W	1957	1	-	-	-	-	-	-	-	-	0

Best result: no finishes. Best qualifying: no times set. Team: Ridgeway Managements

Sebastien Enjolras
F. Born: 4.4.1976, Seclin. Died: 3.5.1997, Le Mans, testing
1996 French Formula Renault Champion

formula	years	starts (DNS)	wins	2nd	3rd	4th	5th	6th	PP	FL	points
Le Mans	1996	1	-	-	-	-	-	-	-	-	

Thomas Erdos
BR. Born: 30.10.1965, Rio de Janeiro
2002 British GT Champion (with Ian McKellar Jr)

formula	years	starts (DNS)	wins	2nd	3rd	4th	5th	6th	PP	FL	points
Le Mans	1995-99	4	-	-	-	-	-	-	-	-	

Harald Ertl
A. Born: 31.8.1948, Mannheim (D). Died: 7.4.1982, near Giessen (D), aircraft accident
1978 German Racing Champion

formula	years	starts (DNS)	wins	2nd	3rd	4th	5th	6th	PP	FL	points
F1 W	1975-80	19 (9)	-	-	-	-	-	-	-	-	0

Best result: 7th. Best qualifying: 17th. Teams: driver, Hesketh, Sachs Sporting, ATS

F2 E	1974-78	24 (1)	-	-	1	-	-	1	-	-	6

Best championship: 1976, 15th
Major win: 1973 Tourist Trophy (Silverstone)

Sandor van Es
NL. Born: 19.8.1970, Deventer
2001 Dutch Touring Car Champion

Nasif Estefano
RA. Born: 18.11.1932, Concepcion, Tucuman. Died: 21.10.1973, Aimogasta

formula	years	starts (DNS)	wins	2nd	3rd	4th	5th	6th	PP	FL	points
F1 W	1960-63	1 (2)	-	-	-	-	-	-	-	-	0

Best result: 14th. Best qualifying: 20th. Teams: Camoradi, de Tomaso

SC W	1964-71		-	-	-	-	1	-	-	-	

Philippe Etancelin
F. Born: 28.12.1896, Rouen. Died: 13.10.1981, Neuilly-sur-Seine, near Paris

formula	years	starts (DNS)	wins	2nd	3rd	4th	5th	6th	PP	FL	points
F1 W	1950-52	12	-	-	-	2	-	-	-	-	3

Best championship: 1950, 12th. Best qualifying: 4th. Teams: driver, Talbot, Bandeirantes

GP Pre-50	1929-49	33	1	3	-	3	1	2	1	-	

Win: 1930 French GP

Le Mans	1934-38	2	1	-	-	-	-	-	-	-	1

Win: 1934 Le Mans 24 hrs

Joe Eubanks
USA
NASCAR wins: 1

Cor Euser
NL. Born: 25.4.1957, Rotterdam
2002 Dutch GT Champion (with Pieter van Soelen), 1999 Dutch Touring Car Champion

formula	years	starts (DNS)	wins	2nd	3rd	4th	5th	6th	PP	FL	points
Le Mans	1991-97	6	-	-	-	-	-	-	-	-	
SC W	1990-92		-	-	1	4	1	1	-	-	

Best championship: 1991, 5th

F3000 INT	1986-89	17 (5)	-	-	-	-	1	-	-	-	2

Best championship: 1988, 19th

CART	1991	1									

Andy Evans
USA. Born: 27.6.1951, Pomona, California

formula	years	starts (DNS)	wins	2nd	3rd	4th	5th	6th	PP	FL	points
Le Mans	1993-97	4	-	-	-	-	-	-	-	-	

Major wins: 1995 and 1997 Sebring 12 hrs

Bob Evans
GB. Born: 11.6.1947, Waddington, Lincolnshire
1974 British F5000 Champion

formula	years	starts (DNS)	wins	2nd	3rd	4th	5th	6th	PP	FL	points
F1 W	1975-76	10 (2)	-	-	-	-	-	-	-	-	0

Best result: 9th. Best qualifying: 20th. Teams: Stanley BRM, Lotus, RAM

Le Mans	1978-82	4	-	-	-	-	-	-	-	-	
F2 E	1977	2	-	-	-	-	-	-	-	-	0

F1 GB win: 1978 Zandvoort

Gary Evans
GB. Born: 21.10.1960, Harpenden

formula	years	starts (DNS)	wins	2nd	3rd	4th	5th	6th	PP	FL	points
F3000 INT	1986-89	30 (13)	-	-	-	-	1	1	-	-	2.5

Best championship: 1989, 17th

Wim Eyckmans
B. Born: 23.3.1973, Heretals

formula	years	starts (DNS)	wins	2nd	3rd	4th	5th	6th	PP	FL	points
F3000 INT	1994-95	10	-	-	-	-	-	1	-	-	1

Best championship: 1994, 17th

Indy 500	1999	1	-	-	-	-	-	-	-	-	
IRL	1999	1	-	-	-	-	-	-	-	-	

Francois Eysermann
F
Major win: 1926 Tripoli

F

Bertrand Fabi
CDN. Born: 21.6.1961, Sherbrooke. Died: 22.2.1986, Chichester, following an accident testing at Goodwood on 21.2.86
1985 European FF2000 Champion

Corrado Fabi
I. Born: 12.4.1961, Milan
1982 European F2 Champion

formula	years	starts (DNS)	wins	2nd	3rd	4th	5th	6th	PP	FL	points
F1 W	1983-84	12 (6)	-	-	-	-	-	-	-	-	0

Best result: 7th. Best qualifying: 11th. Teams: Osella, Brabham

| SC W | 1982 | 1 | - | 1 | - | - | - | - | | | |

Best championship: 1982, 19th

| F2 E | 1981-82 | 25 | 6 | 2 | 3 | 2 | 1 | - | 4 | 5 | 86 |

Wins: 1981 Mugello, 1982 Mugello, Vallelunga, Hockenheim race 2, Donington, Misano. Best championship: 1982, 1st

| F3000 INT | 1987 | 1 (1) | - | - | - | - | - | - | - | - | 0 |
| CART | 1984 | 4 | - | - | - | - | 1 | - | | | |

F3 E wins: 2 – 1980 Mugello, Knutstorp

Teodorico "Teo" Fabi
I. Born: 9.3.1955, Milan
1991 World Sports Car Champion, 1979 New Zealand Formula Pacific Champion

formula	years	starts (DNS)	wins	2nd	3rd	4th	5th	6th	PP	FL	points
F1 W	1982-87	64 (7)	-	-	2	2	4	1	3	2	23

Best championship: 1987, 9th. Best qualifying: 1st. Teams: Toleman, Brabham, Benetton

| Le Mans | 1980-93 | 6 | - | 1 | 1 | - | - | - | | | |
| SC W | 1981-92 | | 2 | 4 | 4 | 1 | - | 4 | 2 | | |

Wins: 1982 Nurburgring, 1991 Silverstone. Best championship: 1991, 1st

| F2 E | 1979-80 | 24 | 3 | 1 | 2 | 3 | - | 1 | 2 | 2 | 51 |

Wins: 1980 Hockenheim race 1, Nurburgring, Hockenheim race 2. Best championship: 1980, 3rd

| Indy 500 | 1983-95 | 8 | - | - | - | - | - | - | 1 | 1 | |
| CART | 1983-96 | 118 | 5 | 3 | 6 | 14 | 2 | 4 | 10 | 3 | |

Wins: 1983 Pocono 500, Mid-Ohio, Laguna Seca, Phoenix, 1989 Mid-Ohio. Best championship: 1983, 2nd

F3 E wins: 3 – 1978 Zolder, Dijon, Vallelunga
Other Major win: 1979 New Zealand GP

Panayotis Fabiatos
GR
1993 Greek F3 Champion

Pascal Fabre
F. Born: 9.1.1960, Lyon

formula	years	starts (DNS)	wins	2nd	3rd	4th	5th	6th	PP	FL	points
F1 W	1987	11 (3)	-	-	-	-	-	-	-	-	0

Best result: 9th. Best qualifying: 22nd. Team: AGS

Le Mans	1983-2001	10	-	-	-	-	1	-			
SC W	1983-92		-	-	-	-	1	-			
F2 E	1982-84	19 (1)	1	-	1	-	2	1	-	-	18

Win: 1984 Hockenheim race 2. Best championship: 1984, 8th

| F3000 INT | 1985-86 | 10 | - | 1 | 1 | 1 | - | - | 1 | 1 | 15.5 |

Win: 1986 Silverstone. Best championship: 1986, 7th

Carlo Facetti
I. Born: 26.6.1935, Cormano, Milan
1979 European Touring Car Champion (with Martino Finotto)

formula	years	starts (DNS)	wins	2nd	3rd	4th	5th	6th	PP	FL	points
F1 W	1974	0 (1)	-	-	-	-	-	-	-	-	0

Best result: no starts. Best qualifying: 27th. Team: Scuderia Finotto

Le Mans	1968-84	8	-	-	-	-	1	-			
SC W	1961-86		-	4	5	2	6	2	3	3	
F2 E	1968-69	2 (1)	-	-	-	-	-	-	-	-	0

Major win: 1979 Tourist Trophy (Silverstone)

Luigi Fagioli
I. Born: 9.6.1898, Osimo, near Ancona. Died: 20.6.1952, Monaco, sports car GP practice

formula	years	starts (DNS)	wins	2nd	3rd	4th	5th	6th	PP	FL	points
F1 W	1950-51	7	1	4	1	-	-	-	-	-	32

Win: 1951 French GP. Best championship: 1950, 3rd. Best qualifying: 2nd. Team: Alfa Romeo

| GP Pre-50 | 1930-48 | 30 | 4 | 10 | 1 | 2 | 2 | 2 | 2 | 6 | |

Wins: 1933 Italian GP, 1934 Italian GP, Spanish GP, 1935 Monaco GP
Other major wins: 1931 Monza GP, 1933 and 1934 Coppa Acerbo (Pescara), 1935 Avus

Pat Fairfield
ZA. Born: 26.11.1907, Liverpool (GB). Died: 21.6.1937, Le Mans, injuries inflicted in the 24 hour race

formula	years	starts (DNS)	wins	2nd	3rd	4th	5th	6th	PP	FL	points
GP Pre-50	1935	1	-	-	-	-	-	1	-	-	
Le Mans	1937	1	-	-	-	-	-	-	-	-	

Major win: 1937 South African GP

Jack Fairman
GB. Born: 15.3.1913, Smallfield, Surrey. Died: 7.2.2002, Rugby, Warwickshire

formula	years	starts (DNS)	wins	2nd	3rd	4th	5th	6th	PP	FL	points
F1 W	1953-61	12 (1)	-	-	-	1	1	-	-	-	5

Best championship: 1956, 10th. Best qualifying: 11th. Teams: HWM, Connaught, BRM, Bernie Ecclestone, Cooper, High Efficiency, Rob Walker, Fred Tuck

| Le Mans | 1949-62 | 12 | - | - | - | - | - | - | | | |
| SC W | 1953-64 | | - | 2 | - | - | - | - | | | |

Wins: 1959 Nurburgring, Tourist Trophy (Goodwood)

Benoit Falchetto
F. Born: Nice

formula	years	starts (DNS)	wins	2nd	3rd	4th	5th	6th	PP	FL	points
GP Pre-50	1933-47	4	-	-	-	-	-	-	-	-	

Major win: 1934 Unofficial French GP

Juan Manuel Fangio
RA. Born: 24.6.1911, Balcarce, near Buenos Aires. Died: 17.7.1995, Balcarce, near Buenos Aires
1951, 1954, 1955, 1956 and 1957 F1 World Champion

formula	years	starts (DNS)	wins	2nd	3rd	4th	5th	6th	PP	FL	points
F1 W	1950-58	51	24	10	1	6	-	-	29	23	278.64

Wins: 1950 Monaco GP, Belgian GP, French GP, 1951 Swiss GP, French GP, Spanish GP, 1954 French GP, German GP, Swiss GP, Italian GP, 1955 Argentinian GP, Belgian GP, Dutch GP, Italian GP, 1956 Argentinian GP, British GP, German GP, 1957 Argentinian GP, Monaco GP, French GP, German GP. Best championships: 1951, 1954, 1955, 1956 and 1957, 1st. Teams: Alfa Romeo, Maserati, Daimler-Benz, Ferrari, Sud Americana, driver

GP Pre-50	1948-49	3	-	-	-	-	-	-			
Le Mans	1950-57	5	-	-	-	-	-	-	1	-	
SC W	1953-58		3	6	-	1	1	-	8	1	

Wins: 1953 Carrera Panamericana, 1956 Sebring 12 hrs, 1957 Sebring 12 hrs
Non-championship F1 wins: 1949 Pau, 1950 Pau, San Remo, Nations GP, Pescara, 1951 Bari, 1956 Buenos Aires, Syracuse, 1957 Buenos Aires
Other major wins: 1955 Swedish GP, 1955 Venezuelan GP, 1957 Portuguese GP

Juan Manuel Fangio II
RA. Born: 19.9.1956, Balcarce, near Buenos Aires
1992 and 1993 IMSA GTP Champion

formula	years	starts (DNS)	wins	2nd	3rd	4th	5th	6th	PP	FL	points
Le Mans	1993	1	-	-	-	-	-	-			

formula	years	starts (DNS)	wins	2nd	3rd	4th	5th	6th	PP	FL	points
F3000 INT	1985	7	-	-	-	-	-	1	-	-	1

Best championship: 1985, 16th

| CART | 1995-97 | 36 (1) | - | - | - | - | - | - | - | - | |

Major wins: 1992 and 1993 Sebring 12 hrs

Augusto Farfus Jr
BR. Born: 3.9.1983, Parana
2001 European Formula Renault Champion

Pedro Leite Faria
P. Born: 10.9.1964, Porto
1994 Portuguese Touring Car Champion

Giuseppe Farina
I. Born: 30.10.1906, Turin. Died: 30.6.1966, Chambery, Aiguebelle (F), road accident
1950 F1 World Champion

formula	years	starts (DNS)	wins	2nd	3rd	4th	5th	6th	PP	FL	points
F1 W	1950-55	33 (1)	5	9	6	3	2	1	5	5	127.33

Wins: 1950 British GP, Swiss GP, Italian GP, 1951 Belgian GP, 1953 German GP.
Best championship: 1950, 1st. Best qualifying: 1st. Teams: Alfa Romeo, Ferrari

| GP Pre-50 | 1935-49 | 23 (2) | 1 | 1 | - | - | 2 | 2 | 3 | 3 | |

Win: 1948 Monaco GP

| Le Mans | 1953 | 1 | - | - | - | - | - | - | - | - | |
| SC W | 1953-54 | | 3 | - | - | - | - | - | 2 | | |

Wins: 1953 Spa 24 hrs, Nurburgring, 1954 Buenos Aires
Non-championship F1 wins: 1948 Geneva, 1950 Bari, International Trophy (Silverstone), 1951 Paris, Dundrod, Goodwood, 1952 Monza Autodrome GP, 1953 Rouen, 1954 Syracuse
Other Major win: 1940 Tripoli

Maurice Farman
F. Born: 21.3.1877, Paris. Died: 25.2.1964, Paris
Major win: 1901 Pau (first race with title Grand Prix)

Walt Faulkner
USA. Born: 6.2.1918, Tell, Texas. Died: 22.4.1956, Vallejo, California

formula	years	starts (DNS)	wins	2nd	3rd	4th	5th	6th	PP	FL	points
Indy 500	1950-55	5	-	-	-	-	1	-	1	-	

Champcar wins: 3 – 1950 Milwaukee race 2, 1951 Darlington, Milwaukee race 2

Ludovic Faure
F. Born: 23.5.1966
1988 French Formula Renault Champion

Philippe Favre
CH. Born: 11.12.1961, Geneva

formula	years	starts (DNS)	wins	2nd	3rd	4th	5th	6th	PP	FL	points
Le Mans	1994-95	2	-	-	-	-	-	-	-	-	
F3000 INT	1989-90	10 (2)	-	1	-	-	-	1	1		6

Best championship: 1989, 13th

Bruce Feldman
USA. Born: 5.3.19??
1988 Barber-SAAB Champion

Ron Fellows
CDN. Born: 28.9.1959, Windsor, Ontario
2002 American Le Mans Series GTS class Champion

formula	years	starts (DNS)	wins	2nd	3rd	4th	5th	6th	PP	FL	points
Le Mans	2000-02	3	-	-	-	-	-	-	-	-	

Major win: 2001 Daytona 24 hrs

Harlan Fengler
USA. Born: 1.3.1903, Chicago, Illinois. Died: 26.3.1981, New Lebanon, Ohio

formula	years	starts (DNS)	wins	2nd	3rd	4th	5th	6th	PP	FL	points
Indy 500	1923	1	-	-	-	-	-	-	-	-	

Champcar wins: 2 – 1923 Kansas City race 2, 1924 Beverly Hills

John Fergus
USA. Born: 21.3.1952, Powell
1991 IMSA GTU Champion

formula	years	starts (DNS)	wins	2nd	3rd	4th	5th	6th	PP	FL	points
Le Mans	2002	1	-	-	-	-	-	-	-	-	

WE Ferguson
USA
Champcar win: 1 – 1913 Galveston race 2

William Ferguson
ZA. Born: 6.3.1940, Johannesburg

formula	years	starts (DNS)	wins	2nd	3rd	4th	5th	6th	PP	FL	points
F1 W	1972	0 (1)	-	-	-	-	-	-	-	-	0

Best result: no starts. Best qualifying: 27th. Team: Team Gunston

Adrian Fernandez
MEX. Born: 20.4.1965, Mexico City
1991 Mexican F3 Champion

formula	years	starts (DNS)	wins	2nd	3rd	4th	5th	6th	PP	FL	points
Indy 500	1994-95	2	-	-	-	-	-	-	-	-	
CART	1993-2002	161 (4)	7	4	8	7	10	13	3	2	

Wins: 1996 Toronto, 1998 Motegi, Mid-Ohio, 1999 Motegi, California Speedway, 2000 Rio de Janeiro, Surfers Paradise. Best championship: 2000, 2nd

Gil de Ferran
BR. Born: 11.11.1967, Paris (F)
2000 and 2001 CART Champion, 1992 British F3 Champion

formula	years	starts (DNS)	wins	2nd	3rd	4th	5th	6th	PP	FL	points
F3000 INT	1993-94	17		3	2	2	-	1	-	2	1	49

Wins: 1993 Silverstone, 1994 Pau, Enna. Best championship: 1994, 3rd

| Indy 500 | 1995-2002 | 3 | - | 1 | - | - | - | - | - | - | |
| CART | 1995-2001 | 129 (1) | 7 | 12 | 15 | 5 | 5 | 12 | 16 | 6 | |

Wins: 1995 Laguna Seca, 1996 Cleveland, 1999 Portland, 2000 Nazareth, Portland, 2001 Rockingham, Houston. Best championships: 2000 and 2001, 1st

| IRL | 2001-02 | 16 | | 2 | 5 | 1 | 1 | 2 | - | 4 | - |

Wins: 2002 Pikes Peak, St Louis. Best championship: 2002, 3rd

Enzo Ferrari
I. Born: 18.2.1898, Modena. Died: 14.8.1988, Modena

formula	years	starts (DNS)	wins	2nd	3rd	4th	5th	6th	PP	FL	points
GP Pre-50	1924-30	0 (2)	-	-	-	-	-	-	-	-	

Major win: 1924 Coppa Acerbo (Pescara)

Alain Ferte
F. Born: 8.10.1955, Falaise
1980 French F3 Champion, 1979 French Formula Renault Champion

formula	years	starts (DNS)	wins	2nd	3rd	4th	5th	6th	PP	FL	points
Le Mans	1983-97	12	-	-	-	-	-	-	1	1	
SC W	1981-92		1	-	2	-	2	-	-	-	

Win: 1990 Silverstone. Best championship: 1990, 12th

| F2 E | 1982-84 | 10 | - | - | - | - | 3 | - | - | - | 6 |

Best championship: 1983, 12th

| F3000 INT | 1985-89 | 25 | - | 1 | 1 | 1 | 1 | 2 | - | - | 17 |

Best championship: 1985, 9th
F3 E wins: 2 – 1981 Jarama, 1982 Magny-Cours
Other major wins: 1981 and 1982 Monaco F3, 1988 Tourist Trophy (Silverstone)

Michel Ferte
F. Born: 8.12.1958, Falaise
1983 French F3 Champion

formula	years	starts (DNS)	wins	2nd	3rd	4th	5th	6th	PP	FL	points
Le Mans	1983-99	12	-	1	-	-	-	-	-	-	
SC W	1983-92		-	1	-	-	-	-	-	-	

GT FIA wins: 3 – 1994 Dijon, Spa, 1995 Anderstorp

| F2 E | 1983-84 | 14 (1) | - | 2 | 3 | 1 | 1 | 1 | 1 | - | 30 |

Best championship: 1984, 3rd

| F3000 INT | 1985-89 | 35 (2) | - | 3 | 6 | 1 | 1 | 2 | 2 | 2 | 47 |

Best championship: 1985, 5th
Other Major win: 1983 Monaco F3

Ira Fetterman
USA. Born: n/a. Died: 19??

formula	years	starts (DNS)	wins	2nd	3rd	4th	5th	6th	PP	FL	points
Indy 500	1922	1	-	-	-	-	-	-	-	-	

Champcar wins: 2 – 1919 Uniontown race 4, 1921 Uniontown race 2

Francois Fiat
F

2000 and 2001 French GT Champion (with Dominique Dupuy)

Andre Fibier
D. Born: 4.7.1973, Hamburg

1998 and 1999 Austrian F3 Champion

Jon Field
USA. Born: 18.9.1955, La Rue, Ohio

2002 American Le Mans Series LMP675 class Champion

Ted Field
USA

formula	years	starts (DNS)	wins	2nd	3rd	4th	5th	6th	PP	FL	points
Le Mans	1979-82	4	-	-	-	-	-	-	-	-	
SC W	1977-83		1	1	3	1	1	-	-	-	

Win: 1979 Daytona 24 hrs

Hugues de Fierlandt
B

formula	years	starts (DNS)	wins	2nd	3rd	4th	5th	6th	PP	FL	points
Le Mans	1970-76	7	-	-	-	-	1	-	-	-	
SC W	1967-76		-	1	-	1	2	1	-	-	

Major wins: 1975 Spa 24 hrs, 1976 Tourist Trophy (Silverstone)

Lou Figaro
USA. Born: n/a. Died: 1954, North Wilkesboro

NASCAR wins: 1

Maria Teresa de Filippis
I. Born: 11.11.1926, Campania, Naples

formula	years	starts (DNS)	wins	2nd	3rd	4th	5th	6th	PP	FL	points
F1 W	1958-59	3 (2)	-	-	-	-	-	-	-	-	0

Best result: 10th. Best qualifying: 15th. Teams: driver, Scuderia Centro Sud, Porsche

Bob Finney
USA

Champcar win: 1 – 1955 Pikes Peak

Martino Finotto
I. Born: 11.11.1933

1979 European Touring Car Champion (with Carlo Facetti)

formula	years	starts (DNS)	wins	2nd	3rd	4th	5th	6th	PP	FL	points
Le Mans	1974-85	6	-	-	-	-	-	-	-	-	
SC W	1973-92		-	2	1	2	2	5	1	-	

Major win: 1979 Tourist Trophy (Silverstone)

Ralph Firman Jr
GB. Born: 20.5.1975, Norwich

2002 Japanese Formula Nippon Champion, 1996 British F3 Champion

Major win: 1996 Macau

Harry Firth
AUS

Major wins: 1963 and 1967 Bathurst

Ludwig Fischer
D. Born: 17.12.1915, Straubing. Died: 8.3.1991, Bad Reichenhall

formula	years	starts (DNS)	wins	2nd	3rd	4th	5th	6th	PP	FL	points
F1 W	1952	0 (1)	-	-	-	-	-	-	-	-	0

Best result: no starts. Best qualifying: no times set. Team: driver

Rudolf Fischer
CH. Born: 19.4.1912, Stuttgart (D). Died: 30.12.1976, Lucerne

formula	years	starts (DNS)	wins	2nd	3rd	4th	5th	6th	PP	FL	points
F1 W	1951-52	7 (1)	-	1	1	-	1	-	1	-	10

Best championship: 1952, 4th. Best qualifying: 5th. Team: Ecurie Espadon

GP Pre-50	1949	1	-	-	-	-	-	-	-	-	

Calvin Fish
GB. Born: 22.7.1961, Norwich

1987 North American Formula Atlantic (Eastern) Champion

Mike Fisher
USA. Born: 13.3.1943, Hollywood, California

formula	years	starts (DNS)	wins	2nd	3rd	4th	5th	6th	PP	FL	points
F1 W	1967	2	-	-	-	-	-	-	-	-	0

Best result: 11th. Best qualifying: 18th. Team: driver

Giancarlo Fisichella
I. Born: 14.1.1973, Rome

1994 Italian F3 Champion

formula	years	starts (DNS)	wins	2nd	3rd	4th	5th	6th	PP	FL	points
F1 W	1996-2002	107 (1)	-	5	4	5	8	5	1	1	82

Best championship: 2000, 6th. Best qualifying: 1st. Teams: Minardi, Jordan, Benetton

Major win: 1994 Monaco F3

John Fitch
USA. Born: 4.8.1917, Indianapolis, Indiana

formula	years	starts (DNS)	wins	2nd	3rd	4th	5th	6th	PP	FL	points
F1 W	1953-55	2	-	-	-	-	-	-	-	-	0

Best result: 9th. Best qualifying: 20th. Teams: HWM, Stirling Moss

Le Mans	1951-60	6	-	-	1	-	-	-	-	-	
SC W	1953-66		2	-	1	1	2	-	-	-	

Wins: 1953 Sebring 12 hrs, 1955 Tourist Trophy (Dundrod)

Christian Fittipaldi
BR. Born: 18.1.1971, Sao Paulo

1991 FIA F3000 Champion, 1990 Sud-Am F3 Champion, 1989 Brazilian F3 Champion

formula	years	starts (DNS)	wins	2nd	3rd	4th	5th	6th	PP	FL	points
F1 W	1992-94	40 (3)	-	-	-	3	1	1	-	-	12

Best championship: 1993, 13th. Best qualifying: 6th. Teams: Minardi, Arrows

F3000 INT	1991	10	2	3	2	1	-	4	1		47

Wins: 1991 Jerez, Nogaro. Best championship: 1991, 1st

Indy 500	1995	1	-	1	-	-	-	-	-	-	
CART	1995-2002	134 (4)	2	5	13	6	8	6	1	4	

Wins: 1999 Elkhart Lake, 2000 California Speedway. Best championships: 1996 and 2002, 5th

Other Major win: 1993 Spa 24 hrs

Emerson Fittipaldi
BR. Born: 12.12.1946, Sao Paulo

1972 and 1974 F1 World Champion, 1989 CART Champion, 1971 and 1972 Torneio F2 Champion, 1969 British F3 Champion

formula	years	starts (DNS)	wins	2nd	3rd	4th	5th	6th	PP	FL	points
F1 W	1970-80	144 (5)	14	13	8	9	5	8	6	6	281

Wins: 1970 United States GP, 1972 Spanish GP, Belgian GP, British GP, Austrian GP, Italian GP, 1973 Argentinian GP, Brazilian GP, Spanish GP, 1974 Brazilian GP, Belgian GP, Canadian GP, 1975 Argentinian GP, British GP. Best championships: 1972 and 1974, 1st. Best qualifying: 1st. Teams: Lotus, McLaren, Fittipaldi

F2 E	1970-73	19 (1)	6	2	2	1	2	-	6	5	25

Wins: 1971 Jarama, Crystal Palace, Albi, 1972 Thruxton, Rouen, Hockenheim race 2. Best championship: 1970, 3rd

Indy 500	1984-94	11	2	1	1	-	-	-	1	4	

Wins: 1989 and 1993 Indianapolis 500

CART	1984-96	195 (2)	22	21	22	8	11	6	17	12	

Wins: 1985 Michigan 500, 1986 Elkhart Lake, 1987 Cleveland, Toronto, 1988 Mid-Ohio, Elkhart Lake, 1989 Indianapolis 500, Detroit, Portland, Cleveland,

Nazareth, 1990 Nazareth, 1991 Detroit, 1992 Surfers Paradise, Cleveland, Elkhart Lake, Mid-Ohio, 1993 Indianapolis 500, Portland, Mid-Ohio, 1994 Phoenix, 1995 Nazareth. Best championship: 1989, 1st
Non-championship F1 wins: 1972 Race of Champions (Brands Hatch), International Trophy (Silverstone), Italian Republic GP (Vallelunga), Rothmans £50,000 (Brands Hatch), 1974 Presidenta Medici GP (Brasilia)

Wilson Fittipaldi
BR. Born: 25.12.1943, Sao Paulo

formula	years	starts (DNS)	wins	2nd	3rd	4th	5th	6th	PP	FL	points
F1 W	1972-75	35 (3)	-	-	-	-	1	1	-	-	3

Best championship: 1973, 15th. Best qualifying: 9th. Teams: Brabham, Fittipaldi

| F2 E | 1971-73 | 26 (5) | - | - | - | 5 | 2 | 2 | - | - | 32 |

Best championship: 1971, 6th

Theo Fitzau
D. Born: 10.2.1923. Died: 18.3.1982, Gross Gerau

formula	years	starts (DNS)	wins	2nd	3rd	4th	5th	6th	PP	FL	points
F1 W	1953	1	-	-	-	-	-	-	-	-	0

Best result: no finishes. Best qualifying: 21st. Team: Helmut Niedermayr

John Fitzpatrick
GB. Born: 9.6.1943, Birmingham
1980 IMSA GTP Champion, 1972 and 1974 European GT Champion, 1966 British Touring Car Champion

formula	years	starts (DNS)	wins	2nd	3rd	4th	5th	6th	PP	FL	points
Le Mans	1972-83	10	-	-	-	1	3	-	-	-	
SC W	1964-83		9	6	4	4	5	7	4	5	

Wins: 1976 Silverstone, 1977 Hockenheim, 1978 Mugello, Watkins Glen, 1979 Mugello, Silverstone, Nurburgring, 1980 Mosport Park, 1981 Riverside. Best championship: 1982, 12th
Other major wins: 1976 Daytona 24 hrs, 1976 Bathurst, 1980 Sebring 12 hrs

Pat Flaherty
USA. Born: 6.1.1926, Glendale, California. Died: 9.4.2002, Oxnard, California

formula	years	starts (DNS)	wins	2nd	3rd	4th	5th	6th	PP	FL	points
Indy 500	1950-59	6	1	-	-	-	-	-	1	-	

Win: 1956 Indianapolis 500
Champcar wins: 3 – 1955 Milwaukee race 2, 1956 Indianapolis 500, Milwaukee race 1

Maurizio Flammini
I. Born: 29.12.1949, Rome

formula	years	starts (DNS)	wins	2nd	3rd	4th	5th	6th	PP	FL	points
Le Mans	1981	1	-	-	-	-	-	-	-	-	
SC W	1979-81		-	-	-	-	-	-	-	1	
F2 E	1974-80	36 (2)	3	1	4	-	1	2	2	-	54

Wins: 1975 Mugello, 1976 Thruxton, Rouen. Best championships: 1975 and 1976, 6th

Jack Fleming
USA
Champcar win: 1 – 1909 San Leandro

John Flemming
GB
1962 British Formula Junior Champion

Johannes "Jan" Flinterman
NL. Born: 2.10.1919, Den Haag. Died: 26.12.1992, Leiden

formula	years	starts (DNS)	wins	2nd	3rd	4th	5th	6th	PP	FL	points
F1 W	1952	1	-	-	-	-	-	-	-	-	0

Best result: 9th. Best qualifying: 15th. Team: Bandeirantes

Bob Flock
USA. Born: 16.4.1918. Died: 16.5.1964
NASCAR wins: 4

Truman "Fonty" Flock
USA. Born: 21.3.1921, Fort Payne, Alabama. Died: 15.7.1972, Atlanta
NASCAR wins: 19

Julius "Tim" Flock
USA. Born: 11.5.1924, Fort Payne, Alabama. Died: 1.4.1998
1952 and 1955 NASCAR Champion
NASCAR wins: 40

Ron Flockhart
GB. Born: 16.6.1923, Edinburgh. Died: 12.4.1962, Dandenong Ranges, near Melbourne (AUS), aircraft accident

formula	years	starts (DNS)	wins	2nd	3rd	4th	5th	6th	PP	FL	points
F1 W	1954-60	13 (1)	-	-	1	-	-	2	-	-	5

Best championship: 1956, 11th. Best qualifying: 8th. Teams: "B Bira", BRM, Connaught, Rob Walker, Lotus, Cooper

| Le Mans | 1955-61 | 6 | 2 | - | - | - | - | - | | | |

Wins: 1956 and 1957 Le Mans 24 hrs

| SC W | 1955-61 | | 1 | - | - | - | - | - | | | |

Win: 1957 Le Mans 24 hrs
Non-championship F1 win: 1959 Snetterton

Jimmy Florian
USA
NASCAR wins: 1

Armando Floridia
I

formula	years	starts (DNS)	wins	2nd	3rd	4th	5th	6th	PP	FL	points
SC W	1967-77		-	-	-	1	1	1	-	-	

Major win: 1976 Targa Florio

Jon Fogarty
USA. Born: 25.5.1975, Palo Alto
2002 North American Toyota Atlantic Champion

Myron Fohr
USA. Born: 17.6.1912, Milwaukee, Wisconsin. Died: 14.1.1994, Milwaukee, Wisconsin

formula	years	starts (DNS)	wins	2nd	3rd	4th	5th	6th	PP	FL	points
Indy 500	1949-50	2	-	-	-	1	-	-	-	-	

Champcar wins: 4 – 1948 Milwaukee race 3, Springfield, 1949 Milwaukee race 1, Trenton

Gregor Foitek
CH. Born: 27.3.1965, Zurich
1986 Swiss F3 Champion

formula	years	starts (DNS)	wins	2nd	3rd	4th	5th	6th	PP	FL	points
F1 W	1989-90	7 (15)	-	-	-	-	-	-	-	-	0

Best result: 7th. Best qualifying: 20th. Teams: EuroBrun, Rial, Brabham, Onyx

| Le Mans | 1991 | 1 | - | - | - | - | - | - | - | - | |
| F3000 INT | 1986-88 | 18 (4) | 1 | - | - | 2 | - | - | 1 | - | 15 |

Win: 1988 Vallelunga. Best championship: 1988, 7th

| CART | 1992 | 2 | - | - | - | - | - | - | - | - | |

George Follmer
USA. Born: 27.1.1934, Phoenix, Arizona
1972 Can-Am Champion, 1972 and 1976 Trans-Am Champion

formula	years	starts (DNS)	wins	2nd	3rd	4th	5th	6th	PP	FL	points
F1 W	1973	12 (1)	-	-	1	-	-	1	-	-	5

Best championship: 1973, 13th. Best qualifying: 11th. Team: Shadow

Le Mans	1966-86	2	-	-	1	-	-	-	-	-	
SC W	1966-86		-	2	1	-	-	2	-	-	
Indy 500	1969-71	3	-	-	-	-	-	-	-	-	

Champcar win: 1 – 1969 Phoenix race 1

Norberto Fontana
RA. Born: 20.1.1975, Arrecifes
1995 German F3 Champion

formula	years	starts (DNS)	wins	2nd	3rd	4th	5th	6th	PP	FL	points
F1 W	1997	4	-	-	-	-	-	-	-	-	0

Best result: 9th. Best qualifying: 18th. Team: Sauber

formula	years	starts (DNS)	wins	2nd	3rd	4th	5th	6th	PP	FL	points
F3000 INT	1996-2001	14	-	-	-	2	-	-	-		4

Best championship: 1999, 13th

| CART | 2000 | 8 (1) | - | - | - | - | - | - | - | | |

Major win: 1995 Marlboro Masters (Zandvoort)

Luis Fontes
BR. Born: 1914. Died: ??.10.1940, Wales, airplane accident serving with the RAF

formula	years	starts (DNS)	wins	2nd	3rd	4th	5th	6th	PP	FL	points
Le Mans	1935	1	1	-	-	-	-	-	-	-	

Win: 1935 Le Mans 24 hrs

Elliott Forbes-Robinson
USA. Born: 31.10.1943, San Francisco, California
1999 American Le Mans Series Champion, 1999 US Grand-Am Champion, 1982 Trans-Am Champion, 1974 SCCA Super Vee Champion

formula	years	starts (DNS)	wins	2nd	3rd	4th	5th	6th	PP	FL	points
Le Mans	1971-89	2	-	-	-	-	-	-	-	-	
SC W	1971-92		-	-	-	2	1	-	-	-	

Major wins: 1997 and 1999 Daytona 24 hrs

Wayne Ford
AUS
1997 Australian F3 Champion

Franco Forini
CH. Born: 22.9.1958, Muralto, near Locarno
1985 Italian F3 Champion

formula	years	starts (DNS)	wins	2nd	3rd	4th	5th	6th	PP	FL	points
F1 W	1987	2 (1)	-	-	-	-	-	-	-	-	0

Best result: no finishes. Best qualifying: 26th. Team: Osella

| F3000 INT | 1986 | 2 (4) | - | - | - | - | - | 1 | - | - | 1 |

Best championship: 1986, 21st

Garry Formato
ZA. Born: 19.11.1974, Johannesburg

formula	years	starts (DNS)	wins	2nd	3rd	4th	5th	6th	PP	FL	points
Le Mans	1999-2001	3	-	-	-	-	-	-	-	-	

SRWC wins: 3 - 1998 Kyalami, 2000 Monza, Kyalami

| F3000 INT | 1995 | 8 | - | - | - | - | - | - | - | - | 0 |

Philip Fotheringham-Parker
GB. Born: 22.9.1907, Beckenham, Kent. Died: 15.10.1981, Beckley, near Rye, East Sussex

formula	years	starts (DNS)	wins	2nd	3rd	4th	5th	6th	PP	FL	points
F1 W	1951	1	-	-	-	-	-	-	-	-	0

Best result: no finishes. Best qualifying: 16th. Team: driver

| GP Pre-50 | 1949 | 1 | - | - | - | - | - | - | - | - | |
| Le Mans | 1953 | 1 | - | - | - | - | - | - | - | - | |

Non-championship F1 win: 1951 Scottish GP (Winfield)

Johan Fourie
ZA
2002 South African Drivers Champion

Henri Fournier
F. Born: 1871, Le Mans. Died: 18.12.1919, Paris

formula	years	starts (DNS)	wins	2nd	3rd	4th	5th	6th	PP	FL	points
GP Pre-50	1902-08	3	-	-	-	-	-	-			

City-to-city wins: 1901 Paris-Bordeaux, Paris-Berlin

Anthony Joseph "AJ" Foyt Jr
USA. Born: 16.1.1935, Houston, Texas
1960, 1961, 1963, 1964, 1967, 1975 and 1979 (USAC) Champcar Champion, 1976 and 1977 IROC Champion

formula	years	starts (DNS)	wins	2nd	3rd	4th	5th	6th	PP	FL	points
Le Mans	1967	1	1	-	-	-	-	-	-		

Win: 1967 Le Mans 24 hrs

formula	years	starts (DNS)	wins	2nd	3rd	4th	5th	6th	PP	FL	points
SC W	1962-88	1	1	-	-	-	-	-	-		

Win: 1967 Le Mans 24 hrs

Pre-CART Champcar wins: 67 (66 plus 1 non-championship USAC race in 1981) – 1960 Du Quoin, Indiana State Fairgrounds, Sacramento, Phoenix, 1961 Indianapolis 500, Langhorne, Du Quoin, Indiana State Fairgrounds, 1962 Trenton race 1, Milwaukee race 1, Langhorne race 1, Sacramento, 1963 Trenton race 1, Langhorne, Trenton race 2, Du Quoin, Trenton race 3, 1964 Phoenix race 1, Trenton race 1, Indianapolis 500, Milwaukee race 1, Langhorne, Trenton race 2, Springfield, Du Quoin, Indiana State Fairgrounds, Sacramento, 1965 Trenton race 2, Springfield, Indiana State Fairgrounds, Trenton race 3, Phoenix race 2, 1967 Indianapolis 500, Springfield, Du Quoin, Trenton race 2, Sacramento, 1968 Castle Rock, Indiana State Fairgrounds, Sacramento, Hanford race 2, 1969 Indiana State Fairgrounds, 1971 Phoenix race 2, 1973 Trenton race 1, Pocono 500, 1974 California 500 qualifying race 1, Trenton race 2, 1975 California 500 qualifying race 1, California 500, Trenton, Milwaukee, Pocono 500, Michigan, Phoenix, 1976 Texas, Michigan, 1977 Ontario, Indianapolis 500, Mosport Park, 1978 Texas, Silverstone, 1979 Ontario, Texas, Milwaukee, Pocono 500, Texas, 1981 Pocono 500 (non-championship)

formula	years	starts (DNS)	wins	2nd	3rd	4th	5th	6th	PP	FL	points
CART	1979-92	85 (5)	-	2	-	2	3	4	-	-	
Indy 500	1958-92	35	4	2	3	-	1	2	4	2	

Wins: 1961, 1964, 1967 and 1977 Indianapolis 500
NASCAR wins: 7 (2 in Modern era) including 1972 Daytona 500
Other major wins: 1983 and 1985 Daytona 24 hrs, 1985 Sebring 12 hrs

AJ Foyt IV
USA. Born: 25.5.1984, Hockley, Texas
2002 Infiniti Pro Series Champion

Fred Frame
USA. Born: 3.6.1894, Exeter, New Hampshire. Died: 25.4.1962, Hayward, California

formula	years	starts (DNS)	wins	2nd	3rd	4th	5th	6th	PP	FL	points
Indy 500	1927-37	9	1	1	-	-	-	-	-	-	

Win: 1932 Indianapolis 500
Champcar win: 1 – 1932 Indianapolis 500

Robbie Francevic
AUS. Born: 18.9.1941, Auckland (NZ)
1986 Australian Touring Car Champion, 1989 and 1990 New Zealand Touring Car Champion

Dario Franchitti
GB. Born: 19.5.1973, Edinburgh

formula	years	starts (DNS)	wins	2nd	3rd	4th	5th	6th	PP	FL	points
Indy 500	2002	1	-	-	-	-	-	-	-	-	
CART	1997-2002	114 (1)	10	12	10	4	2	3	11	8	

Wins: 1998 Elkhart Lake, Vancouver, Houston, 1999 Toronto, Detroit, Surfers Paradise, 2001 Cleveland, 2002 Vancouver, Montreal, Rockingham. Best championship: 1999, 2nd

| IRL | 2002 | 1 | - | - | - | - | - | - | - | - | |

Giorgio Francia
I. Born: 8.11.1947, San Giorgio di Piano, Bologna
1974 Polifac F3 Champion, 1991 Italian Prototype Champion

formula	years	starts (DNS)	wins	2nd	3rd	4th	5th	6th	PP	FL	points
F1 W	1977-81	0 (2)	-	-	-	-	-	-	-	-	0

Best result: no starts. Best qualifying: 30th. Teams: Brabham, Osella

| SC W | 1974-84 | | 4 | 4 | 4 | 4 | 1 | 2 | 3 | - | |

Wins: 1979 Vallelunga, 1980 Vallelunga, 1981 Mugello, 1982 Monza. Best championship: 1981, 4th

| F2 E | 1975-76 | 21 (3) | - | - | - | 2 | 4 | 1 | - | 1 | 17 |

Best championship: 1975, 7th

Filippo Francioni
I
1998 Italian Prototype Champion
SRWC win: 1 – 2000 Spa

Claudio Francisci
I

formula	years	starts (DNS)	wins	2nd	3rd	4th	5th	6th	PP	FL	points
SC W	1972-80			-	-	1	-	1	-		
F2 E	1969-73	11 (6)	-	-	-	-	1	-	-	-	4

Best championship: 1972, 19th

Larry Frank
USA. Born: 29.4.1931, Mountain City, Tennessee
NASCAR wins: 1

Ian Fraser-Jones
ZA
1958 and 1959 South African Drivers' Champion

John French
AUS. Born: 1931, Mille Miglia, Queensland
Major win: 1981 Bathurst

Heinz-Harald Frentzen
D. Born: 18.5.1967, Monchengladbach

formula	years	starts (DNS)	wins	2nd	3rd	4th	5th	6th	PP	FL	points
F1 W	1994-2002	141 (4)	3	3	11	12	9	15	2	6	161

Wins: 1997 San Marino GP, 1999 French GP, Italian GP. Best championship: 1997, 2nd. Best qualifying: 1st. Teams: Sauber, Williams, Jordan, Prost, Arrows

formula	years	starts (DNS)	wins	2nd	3rd	4th	5th	6th	PP	FL	points
Le Mans	1992	1		-	-	-	-	-	-	-	
SC W	1990-92		-	1	-	1	-	-	-	-	

Best championship: 1992, 15th

formula	years	starts (DNS)	wins	2nd	3rd	4th	5th	6th	PP	FL	points
F3000 INT	1990-91	19 (2)	-	-	-	-	3	2	-	-	8

Best championship: 1991, 14th

Franck Freon
F. Born: 16.3.1962, Paris

formula	years	starts (DNS)	wins	2nd	3rd	4th	5th	6th	PP	FL	points
Le Mans	1994-2002	9		-	-	-	-	-	-	-	
F3000 INT	1990	3 (4)	-	-	-	1	-	-	-	-	2

Best championship: 1990, 19th

formula	years	starts (DNS)	wins	2nd	3rd	4th	5th	6th	PP	FL	points
CART	1994-95	5 (3)	-								

Major win: 2001 Daytona 24 hrs

Paul Frere
B. Born: 30.1.1917, Le Havre (F)

formula	years	starts (DNS)	wins	2nd	3rd	4th	5th	6th	PP	FL	points
F1 W	1952-56	11	-	1	-	1	1	-	-	-	11

Best championship: 1956, 7th. Best qualifying: 6th. Teams: HWM, Ecurie Belge, Gordini, Ferrari

formula	years	starts (DNS)	wins	2nd	3rd	4th	5th	6th	PP	FL	points
Le Mans	1953-60	8	1	2	-	2	-	-	-	-	

Win: 1960 Le Mans 24 hrs

formula	years	starts (DNS)	wins	2nd	3rd	4th	5th	6th	PP	FL	points
SC W	1953-66		1	2	-	3	-	-	-	-	

Win: 1960 Le Mans 24 hrs

Other Major win: 1960 (January) South African GP

Leonel Friedrich
BR. Born: 17.12.1948
1987 Sud-Am F3 Champion

Patrick Friesacher
A. Born: 26.9.1980, Wolfsberg

formula	years	starts (DNS)	wins	2nd	3rd	4th	5th	6th	PP	FL	points
F3000 INT	2001-02	24	-	1	-	3	3	1	-	-	22

Best championship: 2002, 9th

Brad Frisselle
USA
1976 IMSA GTU Champion

formula	years	starts (DNS)	wins	2nd	3rd	4th	5th	6th	PP	FL	points
Le Mans	1978	1	-	-	-	-	-	-	-	-	
SC W	1977-80			-	-	1	-	-	-		

Major win: 1977 Sebring 12 hrs

Joe Fry
GB. Born: 26.10.1915, Chipping Sodbury, Gloucestershire. Died: 29.7.1950, Blandford Camp, Dorset

formula	years	starts (DNS)	wins	2nd	3rd	4th	5th	6th	PP	FL	points
F1 W	1950	1	-	-	-	-	-	-	-	-	0

Best result: 10th. Best qualifying: 20th. Team: driver

Naohiro Fujita
J
1983 Japanese Sports-Prototype Champion (with Vern Schuppan)

formula	years	starts (DNS)	wins	2nd	3rd	4th	5th	6th	PP	FL	points
SC W	1982-83		-	-	1	-	-	-	-	-	

Yoshimasa Fujiwara
J
1983 Japanese F3 Champion

Ryo Fukuda
J. Born: 26.6.1979, Fukuoka
2001 French F3 Champion

formula	years	starts (DNS)	wins	2nd	3rd	4th	5th	6th	PP	FL	points
Le Mans	2002	1	-	-	-	-	-	-	-	-	

Hideo Fukuyama
J. Born: 13.8.1955, Mie
1992 Japanese Touring Car Champion (with Masahiro Hasemi)

formula	years	starts (DNS)	wins	2nd	3rd	4th	5th	6th	PP	FL	points
Le Mans	1988-2001	4	-	-	-	-	-	-	-	-	

Gabriel Furlan
RA. Born: 13.10.1964, Buenos Aires
1989, 1994, 1996 and 1998 Sud-Am F3 Champion

formula	years	starts (DNS)	wins	2nd	3rd	4th	5th	6th	PP	FL	points
F3000 INT	1991	9 (1)	-	-	-	-	-	1	-	-	1

Best championship: 1991, 19th

Hiroshi Fushida
J. Born: 10.3.1946, Kyoto

formula	years	starts (DNS)	wins	2nd	3rd	4th	5th	6th	PP	FL	points
F1 W	1975	0 (2)	-	-	-	-	-	-	-	-	0

Best result: no starts. Best qualifying: 25th. Team: Maki

formula	years	starts (DNS)	wins	2nd	3rd	4th	5th	6th	PP	FL	points
Le Mans	1973-81	3	-	-	-	-	-	-	-	-	

G

Jean-Pierre Gaban
B

formula	years	starts (DNS)	wins	2nd	3rd	4th	5th	6th	PP	FL	points
Le Mans	1968-71	4	-	-	-	-	-	-	-	-	

Major win: 1967 Spa 24 hrs

Giuseppe "Beppe" Gabbiani
I. Born: 2.1.1957, Piacenza

formula	years	starts (DNS)	wins	2nd	3rd	4th	5th	6th	PP	FL	points
F1 W	1978-81	3 (14)	-	-	-	-	-	-	-	-	0

Best result: no finishes. Best qualifying: 20th. Teams: Surtees, Osella

formula	years	starts (DNS)	wins	2nd	3rd	4th	5th	6th	PP	FL	points
Le Mans	1981-86	3	-	-	-	-	-	-	-	-	
F2 E	1978-84	50 (6)	4	3	4	4	2	1	1	2	87

Wins: 1983 Silverstone, Thruxton, Nurburgring, Vallelunga. Best championship: 1983, 3rd

formula	years	starts (DNS)	wins	2nd	3rd	4th	5th	6th	PP	FL	points
F3000 INT	1986-87	2 (1)	-	-	-	-	-	-	-	-	0

F3 E win: 1 – 1977 Paul Ricard

Fernand Gabriel
F. Born: n/a. Died: 1943, Paris, RAF air raid

formula	years	starts (DNS)	wins	2nd	3rd	4th	5th	6th	PP	FL	points
GP Pre-50	1903-14	8	-	-	-	2	-	-	-	-	1

City-to-city win: 1903 Paris-Madrid (stopped at Bordeaux)

| Le Mans | 1924-28 | 5 | - | - | - | - | - | - | - | - | |

Philippe Gache
F. Born: 31.5.1962, Avignon

formula	years	starts (DNS)	wins	2nd	3rd	4th	5th	6th	PP	FL	points
Le Mans	1987-2002	9	-	-	-	-	-	-	-	-	
F3000 INT	1989-91	24 (3)	-	-	-	-	1	-	-	1	2

Best championship: 1991, 16th

| Indy 500 | 1992 | 1 | - | - | - | - | - | - | - | - | |
| CART | 1992 | 1 | - | - | - | - | - | - | - | - | |

Bertrand Gachot
B/F (dual nationality). Born: 23.12.1962, Luxembourg

formula	years	starts (DNS)	wins	2nd	3rd	4th	5th	6th	PP	FL	points
F1 W	1989-95	47 (37)	-	-	-	-	1	3	-	1	5

Best championship: 1991, 12th. Best qualifying: 10th. Teams: Onyx, Rial, Coloni, Jordan, Larrousse, Pacific

| Le Mans | 1990-97 | 6 | 1 | - | 1 | - | - | - | - | - | |

Win: 1991 Le Mans 24 hrs

| SC W | 1989-92 | | 1 | - | 1 | - | - | - | - | - | |

Win: 1991 Le Mans 24 hrs

| F3000 INT | 1988 | 11 | - | 2 | - | 2 | 1 | 1 | 1 | - | 21 |

Best championship: 1988, 5th

| CART | 1993 | 1 | - | - | - | - | - | - | - | - | |

Patrick Gaillard
F. Born: 12.2.1952, Paris

formula	years	starts (DNS)	wins	2nd	3rd	4th	5th	6th	PP	FL	points
F1 W	1979	2 (3)	-	-	-	-	-	-	-	-	0

Best result: 13th. Best qualifying: 23rd. Team: Ensign

| Le Mans | 1980-85 | 4 | - | - | - | - | - | - | - | - | |
| F2 E | 1979-81 | 8 | - | - | - | 1 | 1 | - | - | - | 5 |

Best championship: 1979, 15th

F3 E wins: 2 – 1978 Imola, Nurburgring

Divina Galica
GB. Born: 13.8.1946, Bushey Heath, Hertfordshire

formula	years	starts (DNS)	wins	2nd	3rd	4th	5th	6th	PP	FL	points
F1 W	1976-78	0 (3)	-	-	-	-	-	-	-	-	0

Best result: no starts. Best qualifying: 27th. Teams: Whiting, Hesketh

| F2 E | 1977-80 | 6 (1) | - | - | - | - | - | - | - | - | 0 |

Giovanni "Nanni" Galli
I. Born: 2.10.1940, Bologna

formula	years	starts (DNS)	wins	2nd	3rd	4th	5th	6th	PP	FL	points
F1 W	1970-73	17 (3)	-	-	-	-	-	-	-	-	

Best result: 9th. Best qualifying: 15th. Teams: McLaren, March, Tecno, Ferrari, Williams

Le Mans	1968-72	4	-	-	-	1	-	-	-	-	
SC W	1963-74		-	3	2	2	3	1	-	-	
F2 E	1967-71	12	-	-	-	-	-	1	-	-	8

Best championship: 1969, 7th

Lorenzo del Gallo
I. Born: 6.12.1974, Cortona
2001 Italian F3 Champion

Oscar Galvez
RA. Born: 17.8.1913, Buenos Aires. Died: 16.12.1989, Buenos Aires

formula	years	starts (DNS)	wins	2nd	3rd	4th	5th	6th	PP	FL	points
F1 W	1953	1	-	-	-	-	1	-	-	-	2

Best championship: 1953, 13th. Best qualifying: 9th. Team: Maserati

Fred Gamble
USA. Born: 17.3.1932, Pittsburg, Pennsylvania

formula	years	starts (DNS)	wins	2nd	3rd	4th	5th	6th	PP	FL	points
F1 W	1960	1	-	-	-	-	-	-	-	-	0

Best result: 10th. Best qualifying: 14th. Team: Camoradi

| Le Mans | 1960 | 1 | - | - | - | - | - | - | - | - | |

Howden Ganley
NZ. Born: 24.12.1941, Hamilton

formula	years	starts (DNS)	wins	2nd	3rd	4th	5th	6th	PP	FL	points
F1 W	1971-74	35 (6)	-	-	-	2	1	2	-	-	10

Best championship: 1972, 12th. Best qualifying: 4th. Teams: BRM, Williams, March, Maki

| Le Mans | 1972-76 | 4 | - | 1 | - | - | - | - | - | - | |
| SC W | 1968-76 | | - | 3 | - | 1 | 1 | - | - | - | |

Harry Gant
USA. Born: 10.1.1940, Taylorsville, North Carolina
1985 IROC Champion

NASCAR wins: 18 (all Modern era)

Antonio Garcia
E. Born: 5.6.1980, Madrid
2000 Spanish Formula Nissan Champion

formula	years	starts (DNS)	wins	2nd	3rd	4th	5th	6th	PP	FL	points
F3000 INT	2001	7	-	-	-	-	-	-	-	-	0

Frank Gardner
AUS. Born: 1.10.1930, Sydney, New South Wales
1967, 1968 and 1973 British Touring Car Champion, 1971 British F5000 Champion

formula	years	starts (DNS)	wins	2nd	3rd	4th	5th	6th	PP	FL	points
F1 W	1964-68	8 (1)	-	-	-	-	-	-	-	-	

Best result: 8th. Best qualifying: 11th. Teams: John Willment, Bernard White

Le Mans	1962-69	5	-	-	-	-	-	-	-	-	
SC W	1962-69		-	1	-	1	-	1	-		
F2 E	1967-68	11 (1)	1	-	1	3	-	1	-	-	35

Win: 1967 Hockenheim. Best championship: 1967, 2nd

Tasman wins: 2 – 1971 Warwick Farm, 1972 New Zealand GP

Bob Garretson
USA. Born: c1933
1981 World Sports Car Champion

formula	years	starts (DNS)	wins	2nd	3rd	4th	5th	6th	PP	FL	points
Le Mans	1978-82	5	-	-	-	-	-	1	-	-	
SC W	1978-83		1	1	1	2	-	1	-	-	

Win: 1981 Daytona 24 hrs. Best championship: 1981, 1st

Other Major win: 1978 Sebring 12 hrs

Jo Gartner
A. Born: 4.1.1954, Vienna. Died: 1.6.1986, Le Mans 24 hrs

formula	years	starts (DNS)	wins	2nd	3rd	4th	5th	6th	PP	FL	points
F1 W	1984	8	-	-	-	1*	-	-	-	-	0

*Gartner was not eligible for points as his car was not entered in the Championship in 1984. Best qualifying: 22nd. Team: Osella

Le Mans	1985-86	2	-	-	-	1	-	-	-	-	
SC W	1985-86		-	-	1	1	-	-	-	-	
F2 E	1980-84	36 (1)	1	-	1	1	2	-	-	16	

Win: 1983 Pau. Best championship: 1983, 6th

Other Major win: 1986 Sebring 12 hrs

Carlos Gaspar
P
Major wins: 1967 and 1968 Portuguese GP

Oliver Gavin
GB. Born: 29.9.1972, Huntingdon
1995 British F3 Champion

formula	years	starts (DNS)	wins	2nd	3rd	4th	5th	6th	PP	FL	points
Le Mans	2001-02	2	-	-	-	-	-	-	-	-	
F3000 INT	1994-99	9 (8)	-	-	-	1	-	-	-	-	3

Best championship: 1999, 16th

Patrice Gay
F. Born: 14.11.1973, Bourges
1997 French F3 Champion

formula	years	starts (DNS)	wins	2nd	3rd	4th	5th	6th	PP	FL	points
Le Mans	1998-99	2	-	-	-	-	-	-	-	-	

Peter Gaydon
GB. Born: 6.5.1941

formula	years	starts (DNS)	wins	2nd	3rd	4th	5th	6th	PP	FL	points
F2 E	1967-70	3 (1)	-	-	-	-	-	-	-	-	1

Best championship: 1970, 18th. Best result: 7th

Mario Gayraud
RA
1984 TC2000 Argentinian Touring Car Champion

Tony Gaze
AUS. Born: 3.2.1920, Melbourne, Victoria

formula	years	starts (DNS)	wins	2nd	3rd	4th	5th	6th	PP	FL	points
F1 W	1952	3 (1)	-	-	-	-	-	-	-	-	0

Best result: 15th. Best qualifying: 16th. Team: driver

Le Mans	1956	1	-	-	-	-	-	-			
SC W	1953-56		-	-	-	1	-	-			

Frank Gelnaw
USA

Champcar win: 1 – 1910 Long Island race 2

Olivier Gendebien
B. Born: 12.1.1924, Brussels. Died: 2.10.1998, Tarascon (F)

formula	years	starts (DNS)	wins	2nd	3rd	4th	5th	6th	PP	FL	points
F1 W	1956-61	14 (1)	-	1	1	2	1	2	-	-	18

Best championship: 1960, 6th. Best qualifying: 3rd. Teams: Ferrari, BRP, ENB

Le Mans	1955-62	8	4	-	1	-	1	-			
SC W	1953-62	11	7	6	1	2	-	-			

Wins: 1958, 1960, 1961 and 1962 Le Mans 24 hrs

Wins: 1958 Targa Florio, Le Mans 24 hrs, 1959 Sebring 12 hrs, 1960 Sebring 12 hrs, Le Mans 24 hrs, 1961 Sebring 12 hrs, Targa Florio, Le Mans 24 hrs, 1962 Targa Florio, Nurburgring, Le Mans 24 hrs

Jordi Gene
E. Born: 5.12.1970, Sabadell, Barcelona
1996 Spanish Touring Car Champion

formula	years	starts (DNS)	wins	2nd	3rd	4th	5th	6th	PP	FL	points
Le Mans	2000-02	3	-	-	-	-	1	-			
F3000 INT	1992-93	19	1	1	1	1	1	-	1	-	24

Win: 1992 Silverstone. Best championship: 1992, 5th

Marc Gene
E. Born: 29.3.1974, Sabadell, Barcelona
1998 Spanish Formula Nissan Champion

formula	years	starts (DNS)	wins	2nd	3rd	4th	5th	6th	PP	FL	points
F1 W	1999-2000	33	-	-	-	-	-	1	-	-	1

Best championship: 1999, 17th. Best qualifying: 15th. Team: Minardi

F3000 INT	1997	4 (2)	-	-	-	-	-	-	-	1	0

Paul Gentilozzi
USA. Born: 6.2.1950, Detroit, Michigan
1998, 1999 and 2001 Trans-Am Champion

formula	years	starts (DNS)	wins	2nd	3rd	4th	5th	6th	PP	FL	points
Le Mans	1994	1	-	-	-	-	-	-			

Major win: 1994 Daytona 24 hrs

Ian Geoghegan
AUS
1964, 1966, 1967, 1968 and 1969 Australian Touring Car Champion
Major win: 1973 Bathurst

Leo Geoghegan
AUS

1970 Australian F5000 Champion

Elmer George
USA. Born: 5.7.1928, Hockerville, Oklahoma. Died: 30.5.1976, Terre Haute, Indiana

formula	years	starts (DNS)	wins	2nd	3rd	4th	5th	6th	PP	FL	points
Indy 500	1962-63	2	-	-	-	-	-	-			

Champcar win: 1 – 1957 Syracuse

Bob Gerard
GB. Born: 19.1.1914, Leicester. Died: 26.1.1990, South Croxton, Leicestershire

formula	years	starts (DNS)	wins	2nd	3rd	4th	5th	6th	PP	FL	points
F1 W	1950-57	8	-	-	-	-	3	-	-	0

Best qualifying: 10th. Team: driver

GP Pre-50	1947-49	3 (1)	-	1	1	1	-	-			
Le Mans	1953	1	-	-	-	-	-	-			

Non-championship F1 wins: 1950 British Empire Trophy (Douglas), 1955 Charterhall

Louis Gerard
F. Born: 16.4.1899, Arres. Died: 10.5.2000

formula	years	starts (DNS)	wins	2nd	3rd	4th	5th	6th	PP	FL	points
GP Pre-50	1939	1	-	-	-	-	1	-			
Le Mans	1937-49	4	-	1	-	2	-	-			

Major win: 1938 Tourist Trophy (Donington)

Gerino Gerini
I. Born: 10.8.1928, Rome

formula	years	starts (DNS)	wins	2nd	3rd	4th	5th	6th	PP	FL	points
F1 W	1956-58	6 (1)	-	-	-	1	-	-	-	1.5

Best championship: 1956, 25th. Best qualifying: 15th. Teams: Maserati, Guastalla, Scuderia Centro Sud
Major win: 1958 Mille Miglia (regularity test)

Peter Gethin
GB. Born: 21.2.1940, Ewell, Surrey
1974 Tasman Champion, 1969 and 1970 British F5000 Champion

formula	years	starts (DNS)	wins	2nd	3rd	4th	5th	6th	PP	FL	points
F1 W	1970-74	30 (1)	1	-	-	-	2	-	-	11

Win: 1971 Italian GP. Best championship: 1971, 9th. Best qualifying: 5th. Teams: McLaren, BRM, Hill

SC W	1964-74		-	-	-	1	-	-			
F2 E	1967-73	21 (4)	1	1	1	-	1	-	3	3	22

Win: 1972 Pau. Best championship: 1972, 9th
Non-championship F1 wins: 1971 World Championship Victory Race (Brands Hatch), 1973 Race of Champions (Brands Hatch)
Tasman wins: 2 – 1974 Pukekohe, Sandown Park

Pietro Ghersi
I. Born: 1899, Liguria. Died: 1972

formula	years	starts (DNS)	wins	2nd	3rd	4th	5th	6th	PP	FL	points
GP Pre-50	1931-38	10	-	-	-	-	1	-	-	

Major win: 1930 Spa 24 hrs

Piercarlo Ghinzani
I. Born: 16.1.1952, Riviera d'Adda, Bergamo
1977 European F3 Champion, 1979 Italian F3 Champion

formula	years	starts (DNS)	wins	2nd	3rd	4th	5th	6th	PP	FL	points
F1 W	1981-89	76 (35)	-	-	-	-	1	-	-	-	2

Best championship: 1984, 19th. Best qualifying: 13th. Teams: Osella, Toleman, Ligier, Zakspeed

Le Mans	1980-83	4	-	-	-	-	-	-			
SC W	1976-87		2	-	-	1	2	2	1	1	

Wins: 1982 Mugello, 1986 Fuji. Best championship: 1982, 16th

F2 E	1977-78	13	-	-	-	1	-	-	-	3

Best championship: 1978, 16th
F3 E wins: 5 – 1977 Nurburgring, Zolder, Imola, 1979 Vallelunga, Enna

Juan Carlos Giacchino
RA. Born: 7.12.1958
1988 Sud-Am F3 Champion

Bruno Giacomelli
I. Born: 10.9.1952, Borgo Poncarale, Brescia
1978 European F2 Champion, 1976 Shell British F3 Champion

formula	years	starts (DNS)	wins	2nd	3rd	4th	5th	6th	PP	FL	points
F1 W	1977-90	69 (14)	-	-	1	1	3	1	1	-	14

Best championship: 1981, 15th. Best qualifying: 1st. Teams: McLaren, Alfa Romeo, Toleman, Life

Le Mans	1988-90	3	-	-	-	-	-	-			
SC W	1979-92		-	-	1	1	1	1	-	-	

Best championship: 1990, 17th

F2 E	1977-78	25	11	1	1	1	-	1	11	9	114

Wins: 1977 Vallelunga, Mugello, Donington, 1978 Thruxton, Hockenheim race 1, Pau, Rouen, Nogaro, Enna, Misano, Hockenheim race 2. Best championship: 1978, 1st

CART	1984-85	11 (1)	-	-	-	-	1	2	-	-	

Other Major win: 1976 Monaco F3

Affonso Giaffone Neto
BR. Born: 6.4.1968, Santos
1991 Sud-Am F3 Champion

formula	years	starts (DNS)	wins	2nd	3rd	4th	5th	6th	PP	FL	points
Indy 500	1997	1	-	-	-	-	-	-			
IRL	1996-2001	9	-	-	-	1	-	-			

Affonso Giaffone Sr
BR
1981 Brazilian Stock Car Champion

Felipe Giaffone
BR. Born: 22.1.1975, Sao Paulo

formula	years	starts (DNS)	wins	2nd	3rd	4th	5th	6th	PP	FL	points
Indy 500	2001-02	2	-	-	1	-	-	-			
IRL	2001-02	27	1	1	4	4	1	3	-	2	

Win: 2002 Kentucky. Best championship: 2002, 4th

Jose "Zeca" Giaffone
BR
1987 Brazilian Stock Car Champion

"Gianfranco" (Gianfranco Trombetti)
I

formula	years	starts (DNS)	wins	2nd	3rd	4th	5th	6th	PP	FL	points
SC W	1974-77		-	-	1	-	-	1	-	-	
F2 E	1975-81	27 (10)	-	-	1	-	-	1	-	-	5

Best championship: 1975, 19th

Dick Gibson
GB. Born: 16.4.1918, Bourne, Lincolnshire

formula	years	starts (DNS)	wins	2nd	3rd	4th	5th	6th	PP	FL	points
F1 W	1957-58	2	-	-	-	-	-	-	-	-	0

Best result: no finishes. Best qualifying: no times set. Team: driver

Fred Gibson
AUS
Major win: 1967 Bathurst

Andrea Gilardi
I. Born: 18.5.1969, Alessandria

formula	years	starts (DNS)	wins	2nd	3rd	4th	5th	6th	PP	FL	points
F3000 INT	1993	4	-	-	-	-	-	2	-	-	2

Best championship: 1993, 17th

Andrew Gilbert-Scott
GB. Born: 11.6.1958, Cookham Dene, Berkshire

formula	years	starts (DNS)	wins	2nd	3rd	4th	5th	6th	PP	FL	points
Le Mans	1989-97	2	-	-	-	1	-	-			
F3000 INT	1986-91	20 (5)	-	-	1	-	-	-			4

Best championship: 1989, 15th

"Gimax" (Carlo Franchi)
I. Born: 1.1.1938, Barbaiana di Lainate, Milan
1977 European Sports Car Champion (class 2)

formula	years	starts (DNS)	wins	2nd	3rd	4th	5th	6th	PP	FL	points
F1 W	1978	0 (1)	-	-	-	-	-	-	-	-	0

Best result: no starts. Best qualifying: 28th. Team: Surtees

SC W	1974-84		-	-	4	-	1	-	-	-	
F2 E	1975-78	2 (5)	-	-	-	-	-	-	-	-	0

Guido Ginaldi
I
Major win: 1925 Coppa Acerbo (Pescara)

Richie Ginther
USA. Born: 5.8.1930, Hollywood, California. Died: 20.9.1989, Touzac le Roucou, near Bordeaux (F)

formula	years	starts (DNS)	wins	2nd	3rd	4th	5th	6th	PP	FL	points
F1 W	1960-67	52 (2)	1	8	5	6	4	4	-	3	107

Win: 1965 Mexican GP. Best championship: 1963, 2nd. Best qualifying: 2nd. Teams: Ferrari, Lance Reventlow, BRM, Honda, Cooper, Eagle

Le Mans	1957-66	7	-	-	-	-	-	1	-		
SC W	1954-67		-	3	3	-	1	1	1	1	

Michele di Gioia
I
1987 Italian Touring Car Champion

formula	years	starts (DNS)	wins	2nd	3rd	4th	5th	6th	PP	FL	points
SC W	1976-78		-	-	-	-	1	1	-	-	

Angelo Giombelli
BR
1991, 1992 and 1993 Brazilian Stock Car Champion (with Ingo Hoffmann)

Carlo Giorgio
I
1973 Italian F3 Champion

formula	years	starts (DNS)	wins	2nd	3rd	4th	5th	6th	PP	FL	points
F2 E	1974-79	14 (14)	-	-	-	1	-	-	-	-	3

Best championship: 1975, 22nd

Fabrizio Giovanardi
I. Born: 14.12.1966, Sassuolo
2000, 2001 and 2002 European Touring Car Champion, 1997 Spanish Touring Car Champion, 1998 and 1999 Italian Touring Car Champion

formula	years	starts (DNS)	wins	2nd	3rd	4th	5th	6th	PP	FL	points
F3000 INT	1989-91	25 (6)	1	1	-	1	2	3	-	-	25

Win: 1989 Vallelunga. Best championships: 1989 and 1990, 10th

Leonce Girardot
F. Born: 1864. Died: 1922

formula	years	starts (DNS)	wins	2nd	3rd	4th	5th	6th	PP	FL	points
GP Pre-50	1900-02	3	1	1	-	-	-	-			

Win: 1901 Gordon Bennett Trophy

Yves Giraud-Cabantous
F. Born: 8.10.1904, St Gaudens. Died: 31.3.1973, Paris

formula	years	starts (DNS)	wins	2nd	3rd	4th	5th	6th	PP	FL	points
F1 W	1950-53	13	-	-	-	1	1	-	-	-	5

Best championship: 1950, 12th. Best qualifying: 5th. Teams: Talbot, driver, HWM

GP Pre-50	1947-49	9	-	-	-	-	-	1	-	-	
Le Mans	1931-55	10	-	1	-	-	-	-			

Fabien Giroix
F. Born: 17.9.1960, St Maur
1987 French Group A Touring Car Champion

formula	years	starts (DNS)	wins	2nd	3rd	4th	5th	6th	PP	FL	points
Le Mans	1995-96	2	-	-	-	-	1	-	-	-	
F3000 INT	1988	5	-	-	-	1	-	-	-	-	3

Best championship: 1988, 17th
Major win: 1990 Spa 24 hrs

Claudio Girotto
BR
1991 Brazilian Touring Car Champion (with Paulo Gomes)

Ignazio Giunti
I. Born: 30.8.1941, Rome. Died: 10.1.1971, Buenos Aires 1000 kms

formula	years	starts (DNS)	wins	2nd	3rd	4th	5th	6th	PP	FL	points
F1 W	1970	4	-	-	-	1	-	-	-	-	3

Best championship: 1970, 17th. Best qualifying: 5th. Team: Ferrari

Le Mans	1966-70	3	-	-	-	1	-				
SC W	1963-71		1	2	2	2	1	-			

Win: 1970 Sebring 12 hrs

Jimmy Gleason
USA. Born: c1898, Philadelphia, Pennsylvania. Died: 12.9.1931, Syracuse

formula	years	starts (DNS)	wins	2nd	3rd	4th	5th	6th	PP	FL	points
Indy 500	1925-31	5	-	-	1	-	-	1	-		

Champcar win: 1 – 1931 Altoona race 2

Dieter Glemser
D
1971 European Touring Car Champion (over 2000cc class), 1973 and 1974 German Racing Champion

formula	years	starts (DNS)	wins	2nd	3rd	4th	5th	6th	PP	FL	points
Le Mans	1965-73	3	-	-	-	-	-	-			

Major wins: 1971 Spa 24 hrs, 1972 Tourist Trophy (Silverstone)

Helmut Glockler
D. Born: 13.1.1909, Frankfurt. Died: 18.12.1993, Frankfurt

formula	years	starts (DNS)	wins	2nd	3rd	4th	5th	6th	PP	FL	points
F1 W	1953	0 (1)	-	-	-	-	-	-	-	-	0

Best result: no starts. Best qualifying: no times set. Team: Equipe Anglaise

Le Mans	1953-56	4	-	-	-	-	1	-			
SC W	1953-57		-	-	-	-	1	-			

Charlie Glotzbach
USA. Born: 19.6.1938
NASCAR wins: 4

Tom Gloy
USA. Born: 11.6.1947
1984 Trans-Am Champion, 1979 North American Formula Atlantic Champion

formula	years	starts (DNS)	wins	2nd	3rd	4th	5th	6th	PP	FL	points
SC W	1973-88		-	-	-	1	-	-			
F2 E	1980	2	-	-	-	-	-	-			0
Indy 500	1984	1	-	-	-	-	-	-			
CART	1980-84	6	-	-	-	-	1	1	-		

Mark Goddard
GB. Born: 27.8.1958
2002 Asian F3 Champion

Francesco "Chico" Godia-Sales
E. Born: 21.3.1921, Barcelona. Died: 28.11.1990, Barcelona

formula	years	starts (DNS)	wins	2nd	3rd	4th	5th	6th	PP	FL	points
F1 W	1951-58	13 (1)	-	-	-	2	-	1	-	-	6

Best championship: 1956, 7th. Best qualifying: 9th. Teams: Milano, Maserati, driver

GP Pre-50	1948	0 (1)	-	-	-	-	-	-			
Le Mans	1949-58	2	-	-	-	1	-	-			
SC W	1956-58		-	-	-	-	1	-			
F2 E	1967	0 (1)	-	-	-	-	-	-			0

Christian Goethals
B. Born: 4.8.1928, Heule

formula	years	starts (DNS)	wins	2nd	3rd	4th	5th	6th	PP	FL	points
F1 W	1958	1	-	-	-	-	-	-	-	-	0

Best result: no finishes. Best qualifying: no times set. Team: Eperon d'Or

SC W	1959-60		-	-	-	-	1	-			

Paul Goldsmith
USA. Born: 2.10.1927, Parkersburg, West Virginia

formula	years	starts (DNS)	wins	2nd	3rd	4th	5th	6th	PP	FL	points
Indy 500	1958-63	6	-	-	1	-	1	-			

NASCAR wins: 9

Fabrizio Gollin
I. Born: 28.3.1975, Camposampiero, Padua

formula	years	starts (DNS)	wins	2nd	3rd	4th	5th	6th	PP	FL	points
F3000 INT	1996-2001	48 (10)	-	1	-	-	1	2	-	-	10

Best championship: 2000, 10th

Paulo Gomes
BR
1991 Brazilian Touring Car Champion (with Claudio Girotto), 1979, 1983, 1984 and 1995 Brazilian Stock Car Champion

formula	years	starts (DNS)	wins	2nd	3rd	4th	5th	6th	PP	FL	points
Le Mans	1978	1	-	-	-	-	-	-			

Guillaume Gomez
F. Born: 25.7.1969, Orleans

formula	years	starts (DNS)	wins	2nd	3rd	4th	5th	6th	PP	FL	points
Le Mans	2002	1	-	-	-	-	-	-			
F3000 INT	1994-96	22 (3)	-	-	4	1	-	1	2	2	20

Best championship: 1994, 7th

Luciano Gomide
BR. Born: 31.10.1975, Rio de Janeiro
2001 United States F3 Champion

Tristan Gommendy
F. Born: 4.1.1979, Chesnay
2002 French F3 Champion
Major win: 2002 Macau

Jose Froilan Gonzalez
RA. Born: 5.10.1922, Arrecifes, Buenos Aires

formula	years	starts (DNS)	wins	2nd	3rd	4th	5th	6th	PP	FL	points
F1 W	1950-60	26	2	7	6	2	1	-	3	6	77.64

Wins: 1951 British GP, 1954 British GP. Best championship: 1954, 2nd. Best qualifying: 1st. Teams: Scuderia Varzi, driver, Ferrari, Maserati, Vanwall

Le Mans	1950-54	4	1	-	-	-	-	-			1

Win: 1954 Le Mans 24 hrs

SC W	1953-60		1	-	1	-	-	-			2

Win: 1954 Le Mans 24 hrs
Non-championship F1 wins: 1951 Pescara, 1952 Goodwood, 1954 Bordeaux, International Trophy (Silverstone), Bari
Other Major win: 1954 Portuguese GP

Oscar Gonzalez
ROU. Born: 10.11.1923, Montevideo. Died: 1999

formula	years	starts (DNS)	wins	2nd	3rd	4th	5th	6th	PP	FL	points
F1 W	1956	1	-	-	-	-	-	1	-	-	0

Best qualifying: no times set. Team: Alberto Uria

Scott Goodyear
CDN. Born: 20.12.1959, Toronto, Ontario
1986 North American Formula Atlantic (Eastern) Champion

formula	years	starts (DNS)	wins	2nd	3rd	4th	5th	6th	PP	FL	points
Le Mans	1987-96	2	-	-	-	1	-	-			
Indy 500	1990-2001	11	-	2	-	-	-	-			1
CART	1987-96	97 (1)	2	2	4	3	1	2	1		

Wins: 1992 Michigan 500, 1994 Michigan 500. Best championship: 1992, 5th

IRL	1997-2001	39	3	6	3	4	1	2	1	2	

Wins: 1999 Phoenix, Texas, 2000 Texas. Best championship: 2000, 2nd

Marc Goossens
B. Born: 30.11.1969, Lommel

formula	years	starts (DNS)	wins	2nd	3rd	4th	5th	6th	PP	FL	points
Le Mans	1996-2002	7	-	-	-	1	-	-			
F3000 INT	1994-2001	39 (4)	3	3	1	2	3	2	1		63

Wins: 1995 Hockenheim, 1996 Enna, Magny-Cours. Best championships: 1995 and 1996, 3rd

Aldo Gordini
F. Born: 20.5.1921, Bologna (I). Died: 28.1.1995, Paris

formula	years	starts (DNS)	wins	2nd	3rd	4th	5th	6th	PP	FL	points
F1 W	1951	1	-	-	-	-	-	-	-	-	0

Best result: no finishes. Best qualifying: 17th. Team: Gordini

GP Pre-50	1949	1	-	-	-	-	-	-			
Le Mans	1950-51	2	-	-	-	-	-	-			

Jeff Gordon
USA. Born: 4.8.1971, Vallejo, California
1995, 1997, 1998 and 2001 NASCAR Champion

NASCAR wins: 61 (all Modern era) including 1997, 1999 Daytona 500, 1994, 1997, 1998 World 600

Robby Gordon
USA. Born: 2.1.1969, Bellflower, California

formula	years	starts (DNS)	wins	2nd	3rd	4th	5th	6th	PP	FL	points
Indy 500	1993-2002	8	-	-	-	1	2	1	-	-	
CART	1992-99	108 (1)	2	2	5	4	5	5	4	1	
IRL	1996-2002	6	-	-	-	1	-	1	-	-	

Wins: 1995 Phoenix, Detroit. Best championships: 1994 and 1995, 5th

NASCAR wins: 1 (in Modern era)

John Goss
AUS. Born: 2.5.1943

formula	years	starts (DNS)	wins	2nd	3rd	4th	5th	6th	PP	FL	points
Le Mans	1976	1	-	-	-	-	-	-			

Tasman win: 1 – 1975 Sandown Park

Other major wins: 1974 and 1985 Bathurst, 1976 Australian GP

Gustave Gosselin
B

formula	years	starts (DNS)	wins	2nd	3rd	4th	5th	6th	PP	FL	points
Le Mans	1965-71	5	-	1	-	-	-	-			
SC W	1959-71		-	1	-	-	2	-			

Major win: 1964 Spa 24 hrs

Mike Goth
USA

formula	years	starts (DNS)	wins	2nd	3rd	4th	5th	6th	PP	FL	points
F2 E	1970	2	-	-	-	-	-	1	-	-	2

Best championship: 1970, 16th

Patrice Goueslard
F. Born: 26.11.1965, Caen
2000 FIA N-GT class Champion (with Christophe Bouchut), 1997 (solo) and 2002 (with Philippe Soulan) French GT Champion

formula	years	starts (DNS)	wins	2nd	3rd	4th	5th	6th	PP	FL	points
Le Mans	1994-2002	8	-	-	-	-	1	-	-		

Joel Gouhier
F. Born: 22.10.1949, Nogent-le-Rotrou
1982 Renault Europa Cup Champion, 1977 French Formula Renault Champion

formula	years	starts (DNS)	wins	2nd	3rd	4th	5th	6th	PP	FL	points
Le Mans	1983-94	6	-	1	-	-	-	-			
SC W	1983-92		-	1	-	-	-	-			

Horace Gould
GB. Born: 20.9.1921, Southmead, Bristol. Died: 4.11.1968, Southmead, Bristol

formula	years	starts (DNS)	wins	2nd	3rd	4th	5th	6th	PP	FL	points
F1 W	1954-60	14 (3)	-	-	-	-	1	-	-	-	2

Best result: 1956, 19th. Best qualifying: 10th. Teams: driver, Maserati, Scuderia Centro Sud

SC W	1953-57		-	-	-	-	1	-	-	-	

Non-championship F1 wins: 1954 Castle Combe, 1956 Aintree

Jean-Marc Gounon
F. Born: 1.1.1963, Aubenas
1989 French F3 Champion

formula	years	starts (DNS)	wins	2nd	3rd	4th	5th	6th	PP	FL	points
F1 W	1993-94	9	-	-	-	-	-	-	-	-	0

Best result: 9th. Best qualifying: 22nd. Teams: Minardi, Simtek

Le Mans	1995-2000	5	-	1	-	-	-	-			

SRWC wins: 5 – 1999 Donington, Brno, Nurburgring, Kyalami, 2001 Spa

F3000 INT	1990-92	29 (2)	2	1	1	3	1	4	-	1	43

Wins: 1991 Pau, 1992 Magny-Cours. Best championships: 1991 and 1992, 6th

Jules Goux
F. Born: 6.3.1885, Paris. Died: 6.3.1965, Mirmande

formula	years	starts (DNS)	wins	2nd	3rd	4th	5th	6th	PP	FL	points
GP Pre-50	1912-26	16	3	2	1	1	2	-	-	1	

Wins: 1921 Italian GP, 1926 French GP, European GP

Indy 500	1913-22	5	1	-	1	1	-	-			

Win: 1913 Indianapolis 500

Champcar win: 1 – 1913 Indianapolis 500

Marcos Gracia
BR
1986 Brazilian Stock Car Champion

Baron Emanuel "Toulo" de Graffenried
CH. Born: 18.5.1914, Paris (F)

formula	years	starts (DNS)	wins	2nd	3rd	4th	5th	6th	PP	FL	points
F1 W	1950-56	22 (2)	-	-	-	1	3	4	-	-	9

Best championship: 1953, 7th. Best qualifying: 5th. Teams: Enrico Plate, Alfa Romeo, driver, Scuderia Centro Sud

GP Pre-50	1938-49	15 (2)	1	-	1	1	-	-	-	1	

Win: 1949 British GP

Stuart Graham
GB. Born: 9.1.1942, West Kirby, Cheshire
Major wins: 1974 and 1975 Tourist Trophy

Henry Grandsire
F. Born: 1936
1964 French F3 Champion

formula	years	starts (DNS)	wins	2nd	3rd	4th	5th	6th	PP	FL	points
Le Mans	1964-69	6	-	-	-	-	-	-			

Umberto Grano
I. Born: 13.4.1940
1978 (solo), 1981 and 1982 (both with Helmut Kelleners) European Touring Car Champion

formula	years	starts (DNS)	wins	2nd	3rd	4th	5th	6th	PP	FL	points
SC W	1968-82		-	-	1	1	-	1	-	-	

Major win: 1980 Tourist Trophy (Silverstone)

Harry Grant
USA. Born: 10.7.1877, Cambridge, Massachusetts. Died: 8.10.1915, Sheepshead Bay, New York State from injuries inflicted on 28.9.1915

formula	years	starts (DNS)	wins	2nd	3rd	4th	5th	6th	PP	FL	points
GP Pre-50	1910-15	2	-	-	-	-	-	-			
Indy 500	1911-15	4	-	-	-	-	-	-			

Champcar wins: 2 – 1909 WK Vanderbilt Cup, 1910 WK Vanderbilt Cup

Danny Graves
USA
NASCAR wins: 1

John Graves
USA

formula	years	starts (DNS)	wins	2nd	3rd	4th	5th	6th	PP	FL	points
SC W	1974-77		1	-	-	-	-	2	-	-	

Win: 1977 Daytona 24 hrs

Robb Gravett
GB. Born: 2.5.1956, London
1990 British Touring Car Champion

Eddie Gray
USA

NASCAR wins: 4

Harry Gray
USA

formula	years	starts (DNS)	wins	2nd	3rd	4th	5th	6th	PP	FL	points
SC W	1953-54		-	-	-	1	-	-	-	-	

Major win: 1952 Sebring 12 hrs

John Greasley
GB
1993 British GT Champion

Keith Greene
GB. Born: 5.1.1938, Leytonstone, London

formula	years	starts (DNS)	wins	2nd	3rd	4th	5th	6th	PP	FL	points
F1 W	1959-62	3 (2)	-	-	-	-	-	-	-	-	0

Best result: 15th. Best qualifying: 19th. Team: Gilby

Le Mans	1959	1	-	-	-	-	-	-	-	-	

John Greenwood
USA
1975 Trans-Am Champion

formula	years	starts (DNS)	wins	2nd	3rd	4th	5th	6th	PP	FL	points
Le Mans	1972-76	3	-	-	-	-	-	-	-	-	
SC W	1970-77		-	-	-	-	-	1	1		

Peter Gregg
USA. Born: 4.5.1940, New York City. Died: 15.12.1980, Jacksonville, suicide
1971 (with Hurley Haywood), 1973, 1974, 1975, 1978 and 1979 (all solo)
IMSA GTP Champion, 1973 and 1974 Trans-Am Champion

formula	years	starts (DNS)	wins	2nd	3rd	4th	5th	6th	PP	FL	points
Le Mans	1966-79	6	-	-	2	-	-	-	-	-	
SC W	1964-80		4	-	1	1	1	1	-	1	

Wins: 1973 Daytona 24 hrs, 1975 Daytona 24 hrs, 1978 Daytona 24 hrs, Watkins Glen

Other major wins: 1973 Sebring 12 hrs, 1976 Daytona 24 hrs

Masten Gregory
USA. Born: 29.2.1932, Kansas City, Missouri. Died: 8.11.1985, Porto Ecole, near Rome (I)

formula	years	starts (DNS)	wins	2nd	3rd	4th	5th	6th	PP	FL	points
F1 W	1957-65	38 (5)	-	1	2	3*	-	2	-	-	21

***Includes one shared drive for which no points were awarded. Best championship: 1957, 6th. Best qualifying: 3rd. Teams: Scuderia Centro Sud, Horace Gould, Temple Buell, Cooper, Camoradi, BRP, Tim Parnell, Reg Parnell**

Le Mans	1955-72	16	1	-	-	1	2	-	1		

Win: 1965 Le Mans 24 hrs

SC W	1953-72		3	1	1	2	3	2	1	1	

Wins: 1957 Buenos Aires, 1961 Nurburgring, 1965 Le Mans 24 hrs

Indy 500	1965	1	-	-	-	-	-	-	-	-	

Non-championship F1 win: 1962 Karlskoga

Other Major win: 1962 Canadian GP

Helmet Greiner
HK

Major win: 1982 Macau Guia race

Allan Grice
AUS. Born: 21.10.1942

formula	years	starts (DNS)	wins	2nd	3rd	4th	5th	6th	PP	FL	points
Le Mans	1984-88	2	-	-	-	-	-	-	-	-	

Major wins: 1986 and 1990 Bathurst

Pat Griffith
GB. Born: 26.4.1925, Weybridge, Surrey. Died: 28.1.1980

formula	years	starts (DNS)	wins	2nd	3rd	4th	5th	6th	PP	FL	points
Le Mans	1952	1	-	-	-	-	-	-	-	-	
SC W	1953-64		1	-	1	-	-	-	-	-	

Win: 1953 Tourist Trophy

Georges Grignard
F. Born: 25.7.1905, Villeneuve St George, Paris. Died: 7.12.1977, Port Marly, Yvelines

formula	years	starts (DNS)	wins	2nd	3rd	4th	5th	6th	PP	FL	points
F1 W	1951	1	-	-	-	-	-	-	-	-	0

Best result: no finishes. Best qualifying: 16th. Team: driver

GP Pre-50	1949	3	-	-	-	-	-	-	-	-	
Le Mans	1949-53	2	-	-	-	-	1	-	-	-	

Non-championship F1 win: 1950 Paris

Bobby Grim
USA. Born: 4.9.1924, Coal City, Indiana. Died: 14.6.1995, Indianapolis, Indiana

formula	years	starts (DNS)	wins	2nd	3rd	4th	5th	6th	PP	FL	points
Indy 500	1959-68	9	-	-	-	-	-	-	-	-	

Champcar win: 1 – 1960 Syracuse

Enrico Grimaldi
I

formula	years	starts (DNS)	wins	2nd	3rd	4th	5th	6th	PP	FL	points
SC W	1976-79		1	-	-	-	-	-	-	-	

Win: 1979 Florio Cup

Michael Groff
USA. Born: 16.11.1961, Van Nuys, California
1989 American Racing Series Champion

formula	years	starts (DNS)	wins	2nd	3rd	4th	5th	6th	PP	FL	points
Indy 500	1991-98	5	-	-	-	-	-	-	-	-	
CART	1990-96	54 (4)	-	-	-	-	-	1	-	-	
IRL	1996-98	12	-	1	2	1	-	2	-	-	

Best championship: 1996, 6th

Harald Grohs
D. Born: 28.1.1944, Essen

formula	years	starts (DNS)	wins	2nd	3rd	4th	5th	6th	PP	FL	points
Le Mans	1976-90	10	-	-	-	-	-	-	-	-	
SC W	1976-92		3	1	2	8	3	2	-	1	

Wins: 1981 Silverstone, Mosport Park, Elkhart Lake. Best championship: 1981, 2nd

F2 E	1980	1	-	-	-	-	-	-	-	-	0

Olivier Grouillard
F. Born: 2.9.1958, Fenouillet, Toulouse
1984 French F3 Champion

formula	years	starts (DNS)	wins	2nd	3rd	4th	5th	6th	PP	FL	points
F1 W	1989-92	41 (21)	-	-	-	-	-	-	1	-	1

Best championship: 1989, 26th. Best qualifying: 8th. Teams: Ligier, Osella, Fondmetal, AGS, Tyrrell

Le Mans	1990-2000	7	-	-	-	1	1	1	-	-	

GT FIA wins: 4 – 1995 Silverstone, Nogaro, Zhuhai, 1996 Silverstone

F3000 INT	1985-88	32 (2)	2	1	2	4	1	3	3	2	49

Wins: 1988 Le Mans, Zolder. Best championship: 1988, 2nd

CART	1993	11 (2)	-	-	-	-	-	-	-	-	

Stig Gruen
S
1986 Swedish Touring Car Champion

Brian Gubby
GB. Born: 17.4.1934, Epsom, Surrey

formula	years	starts (DNS)	wins	2nd	3rd	4th	5th	6th	PP	FL	points
F1 W	1965	0 (1)	-	-	-	-	-	-	-	-	0

Best result: no starts. Best qualifying: 24th. Team: driver

Bill Gubelmann
USA
1972 British Formula Atlantic Champion

formula	years	starts (DNS)	wins	2nd	3rd	4th	5th	6th	PP	FL	points
F2 E	1973-76	22 (4)	-	-	-	1	1	-	-		6

Best championship: 1973, 13th

Marcos Gueiros
BR. Born: 16.1.1970
1992 Sud-Am F3 Champion, 1991 and 1992 Brazilian F3 Champion

formula	years	starts (DNS)	wins	2nd	3rd	4th	5th	6th	PP	FL	points
F3000 INT	1995-96	18	-	1	2	2	1	-	-	-	22

Best championship: 1996, 5th

Andre Guelfi
F. Born: 6.5.1919, Mazagan (MA)

formula	years	starts (DNS)	wins	2nd	3rd	4th	5th	6th	PP	FL	points
F1 W	1958	1	-	-	-	-	-	-	-	-	0

Best result: no finishes. Best qualifying: no times set. Team: driver

formula	years	starts (DNS)	wins	2nd	3rd	4th	5th	6th
Le Mans	1950-58	7	-	-	-	-	1	-
SC W	1953-58		-	-	-	1	-	

Miguel Angel Guerra
RA. Born: 31.8.1953, Buenos Aires
1989 TC2000 Argentinian Touring Car Champion

formula	years	starts (DNS)	wins	2nd	3rd	4th	5th	6th	PP	FL	points
F1 W	1981	1 (3)	-	-	-	-	-	-	-	-	0

Best result: no finishes. Best qualifying: 22nd. Team: Osella

formula	years	starts (DNS)	wins	2nd	3rd	4th	5th	6th	PP	FL	points
F2 E	1978-81	30 (2)	-	-	1	2	3	2	-	-	18

Best championship: 1979, 8th

Carlos Guerrero
MEX. Born: 20.11.1957
1991 and 1992 Mexican Formula K Champion, 1990, 1993 and 1994 Mexican F3 Champion

formula	years	starts (DNS)	wins	2nd	3rd	4th	5th	6th
Indy 500	1995	1	-	-	-	-	-	
CART	1995-96	17	-	-	-	-	-	

Roberto Guerrero
CO (emigrated to USA). Born: 16.11.1958, Medellin

formula	years	starts (DNS)	wins	2nd	3rd	4th	5th	6th	PP	FL	points
F1 W	1982-83	21 (8)	-	-	-	-	-	-	-	-	0

Best result: 8th. Best qualifying: 11th. Teams: Ensign, Theodore

formula	years	starts (DNS)	wins	2nd	3rd	4th	5th	6th	PP	FL	points
F2 E	1981	12	1	-	-	2	-	1	-	-	16

Win: 1981 Thruxton. Best championship: 1981, 7th

formula	years	starts (DNS)	wins	2nd	3rd	4th	5th	6th	PP	FL
Indy 500	1984-99	14	-	2	1	1	1	-	-	1
CART	1984-95	118 (4)	2	5	3	6	6	3	6	1

Wins: 1987 Phoenix, Mid-Ohio. Best championship: 1987, 4th

formula	years	starts (DNS)	wins	2nd	3rd	4th	5th	6th	PP
IRL	1996-2001	25 (1)	-	-	2	2	2	-	-

Best championship: 1996, 4th

Mauricio Gugelmin
BR. Born: 20.4.1963, Joinville
1985 British F3 Champion, 1984 European FF2000 Champion

formula	years	starts (DNS)	wins	2nd	3rd	4th	5th	6th	PP	FL	points
F1 W	1988-92	74 (6)	-	-	1	1	1	1	-	1	10

Best championship: 1988, 13th. Best qualifying: 5th. Teams: March, Leyton House, Jordan

formula	years	starts (DNS)	wins	2nd	3rd	4th	5th	6th	PP	FL	points
F3000 INT	1986-87	20 (2)	1	2	2	1	-	1	2	-	33

Win: 1987 Silverstone. Best championship: 1987, 4th

formula	years	starts (DNS)	wins	2nd	3rd	4th	5th	6th	PP	FL
Indy 500	1994-95	2	-	-	-	-	-			
CART	1993-2001	147 (1)	1	5	2	5	5	11	4	1

Win: 1997 Vancouver. Best championship: 1997, 4th
Other Major win: 1985 Macau

Jean Guichet
F. Born: 1927, Marseille

formula	years	starts (DNS)	wins	2nd	3rd	4th	5th	6th	PP	FL	points
Le Mans	1956-75	13	1	1	1	-	1	-	-		
SC W	1956-75		3	6	2	-	1	1	-	-	

Win: 1964 Le Mans 24 hrs
Wins: 1964 Le Mans 24 hrs, 1965 Monza, Reims

Giovanni-Battista Guidotti
I. Born: 1902, Bellagio, Lake Como. Died: 2.7.1994

formula	years	starts (DNS)	wins	2nd	3rd	4th	5th	6th
GP Pre-50	1937-47	2	-	-	1	-	-	-
Le Mans	1932-37	2	-	1	-	-	-	

Major win: 1930 Mille Miglia

Kenelm Lee "Bill" Guinness
GB. Born: 1887. Died: 1937, Surrey

formula	years	starts (DNS)	wins	2nd	3rd	4th	5th	6th
GP Pre-50	1913-24	7	-	-	-	1	-	-

Major win: 1914 Tourist Trophy

Lucien Guitteny
F. Born: 17.6.1944, Angers
1978 French Touring Car Champion

formula	years	starts (DNS)	wins	2nd	3rd	4th	5th	6th
Le Mans	1973-83	7	-	-	-	-	-	-

Sten Gunnarsson
S

formula	years	starts (DNS)	wins	2nd	3rd	4th	5th	6th	PP	FL	points
F2 E	1971-73	10 (2)	-	-	-	1	-	-	-	-	5

Best championship: 1973, 19th

Dan Gurney
USA. Born: 13.4.1931, Port Jefferson, New York State

formula	years	starts (DNS)	wins	2nd	3rd	4th	5th	6th	PP	FL	points
F1 W	1959-70	86 (1)	4	8	7	2	5	5	3	6	133

Wins: 1962 French GP, 1964 French GP, Mexican GP, 1967 Belgian GP. Best championship: 1961, 3rd. Best qualifying: 1st. Teams: Ferrari, BRM, Porsche, Wolfgang Seidel, Brabham, Eagle, McLaren

formula	years	starts (DNS)	wins	2nd	3rd	4th	5th	6th	PP	FL
Le Mans	1958-67	10	1	-	-	1	-	-	3	1
SC W	1958-70		3	2	1	2	2	-	5	4

Win: 1967 Le Mans 24 hrs
Wins: 1959 Sebring 12 hrs, 1960 Nurburgring, 1967 Le Mans 24 hrs

formula	years	starts (DNS)	wins	2nd	3rd	4th	5th	6th
Indy 500	1962-70	9	-	2	1	-	-	-

Champcar wins: 7 – 1967 Riverside, 1968 Mosport Park race 1, Mosport Park race 2, Riverside, 1969 Indianapolis Raceway Park race 1, Brainerd race 2, 1970 Sears Point
Non-championship F1 wins: 1962 Solitude, 1967 Race of Champions (Brands Hatch)
NASCAR wins: 5

Jim Guthrie
USA. Born: 13.9.1961, Gadsden, Alabama

formula	years	starts (DNS)	wins	2nd	3rd	4th	5th	6th	PP	FL	points
Indy 500	1996-98	3	-	-	-	-	-	-			
IRL	1996-98	15	1	-	-	1	-	1	-	-	

Win: 1997 Phoenix

Malcolm Guthrie
GB

formula	years	starts (DNS)	wins	2nd	3rd	4th	5th	6th	PP	FL	points
F2 E	1969-70	7 (3)	-	-	-	-	-	-	-	-	2

Best championship: 1969, 15th. Best result: 8th

Albert Guyot
F. Born: 1882, Orleans. Died: 24.3.1947

formula	years	starts (DNS)	wins	2nd	3rd	4th	5th	6th	PP	FL	points
GP Pre-50	1912-25	9	-	-	1	-	1	1	-	-	
Indy 500	1913-26	5	-	-	1	2	-	1	-	-	

Major win: 1923 San Sebastian GP

Diego Guzman
CO
1994 Barber-SAAB Champion

H

Olli Haapalainen
SF. Born: 27.11.1969, Helsinki
1999, 2000, 2001 and 2002 Finnish Touring Car Champion

Mario Haberfeld
BR. Born: 25.1.1976, Sao Paulo
1998 British F3 Champion

formula	years	starts (DNS)	wins	2nd	3rd	4th	5th	6th	PP	FL	points
F3000 INT	1999-2002	36 (6)	-	1	1	2	2	1	-	1	21

Best championship: 2002, 7th

Peter Hackett
AUS. Born: 17.9.1975, Sydney, New South Wales
2001 Australian F3 Champion

Royce Hagerty
USA
NASCAR wins: 1

Akira Hagiwara
J

formula	years	starts (DNS)	wins	2nd	3rd	4th	5th	6th	PP	FL	points
SC W	1983-85	1	-	-	-	-	-	-	-	-	

Win: 1985 Fuji (had not driven car when the race was stopped due to rain)

Armin Hahne
D. Born: 10.9.1955, Moers

formula	years	starts (DNS)	wins	2nd	3rd	4th	5th	6th	PP	FL	points
Le Mans	1986-97	6	-	-	-	-	1	-	-	-	
SC W	1977-92		-	-	-	-	-	1	-	-	
F2 E	1979	1 (5)	-	-	-	-	-	-	-	-	0

Major wins: 1982 and 1983 Spa 24 hrs, 1985 Bathurst

Hubert Hahne
D. Born: 28.3.1935, Moers
1966 European Touring Car Champion (over 1600cc class)

formula	years	starts (DNS)	wins	2nd	3rd	4th	5th	6th	PP	FL	points
F1 W	1966-70	3 (2)	-	-	-	-	-	-	-	-	0

Best result: 10th. Best qualifying: 14th. Teams: Tyrrell, BMW, driver

F2 E	1967-70	13 (5)	-	1	-	3	1	-	-	-	38

Best championship: 1969, 2nd
Major win: 1966 Spa 24 hrs

Mike Hailwood
GB. Born: 2.4.1940, Great Milton, Oxfordshire. Died: 23.3.1981, Portway Hospital, Birmingham, following a road accident
1972 European F2 Champion

formula	years	starts (DNS)	wins	2nd	3rd	4th	5th	6th	PP	FL	points
F1 W	1963-74	50	-	1	1	5	1	2	-	1	29

Best championship: 1972, 8th. Best qualifying: 4th. Teams: Reg Parnell, Surtees, McLaren

Le Mans	1969-74	4	-	-	1	1	-	-	-	-	
SC W	1968-74		1	2	1	4	3	-	-	1	

Win: 1973 Spa

F2 E	1972-73	16 (2)	2	5	-	-	2	-	2	2	55

Wins: 1972 Mantorp Park, Salzburgring. Best championship: 1972, 1st

Mika Hakkinen
SF. Born: 28.9.1968, Helsinki
1998 and 1999 F1 World Champion, 1990 British F3 Champion, 1988 European GM-Lotus Champion, 1991 Nordic Touring Car Champion

formula	years	starts (DNS)	wins	2nd	3rd	4th	5th	6th	PP	FL	points
F1 W	1991-2001	161 (4)	20	14	17	13	10	9	26	25	420

Wins: 1997 European GP, 1998 Australian GP, Brazilian GP, Spanish GP, Monaco GP, Austrian GP, German GP, Luxembourg GP, Japanese GP, 1999 Brazilian GP, Spanish GP, Canadian GP, Hungarian GP, Japanese GP, 2000 Spanish GP, Austrian GP, Hungarian GP, Belgian GP, 2001 British GP, United States GP. Best championships: 1998 and 1999, 1st. Best qualifying: 1st.
Teams: Lotus, McLaren
Other Major win: 1989 Cellnet Superprix (Brands Hatch)

Bruce Halford
GB. Born: 18.5.1931, Hampton-in-Arden, Warwickshire. Died: 2.12.2001, Churston Ferriers, Brixham

formula	years	starts (DNS)	wins	2nd	3rd	4th	5th	6th	PP	FL	points
F1 W	1956-60	8 (1)	-	-	-	-	-	-	-	-	0

Best result: 8th. Best qualifying: 11th. Teams: driver, John Fisher, High Efficiency, BRP

Le Mans	1957-61	5	-	-	-	-	-	-	-	-	

Andreas Halkiopoulos
GR
1996 Greek F3 Champion

Dean Hall
USA. Born: 11.11.1957, Palo Alto, California
1988 North American Formula Atlantic (Western) Champion, 1989 New Zealand Gold Star Champion, 1989 New Zealand Formula Pacific Champion

formula	years	starts (DNS)	wins	2nd	3rd	4th	5th	6th	PP	FL	points
Indy 500	1990	1	-	-	-	-	-	-	-	-	
CART	1990-95	21	-	-	-	-	-	-	-	-	

Major win: 1989 New Zealand GP

Jim Hall
USA. Born: 23.7.1935, Abilene, Texas

formula	years	starts (DNS)	wins	2nd	3rd	4th	5th	6th	PP	FL	points
F1 W	1960-63	11 (1)	-	-	-	1	1	-	-	3

Best championship: 1963, 12th. Best qualifying: 12th. Teams: driver, BRP

Le Mans	1963	1	-	-	-	-	-	-	-	-	
SC W	1959-67		1	-	-	-	2	1	1	

Win: 1965 Sebring 12 hrs
Other Major win: 1965 Canadian GP

Pete Halsmer
USA. Born: 3.3.1944, Lafayette, Indiana
1989 and 1991 IMSA GTO Champion

formula	years	starts (DNS)	wins	2nd	3rd	4th	5th	6th	PP	FL	points
Indy 500	1981-82	2	-	-	-	-	-	-	-	-	
CART	1980-85	33 (3)	-	1	-	1	1	1	-	-	

Bobby Hamilton
USA. Born: 29.5.1957, Nashville, Tennessee
NASCAR wins: 4 (all Modern era)

Duncan Hamilton
GB. Born: 30.4.1920, Cork (IRL). Died: 13.5.1994, Sherbourne, Dorset

formula	years	starts (DNS)	wins	2nd	3rd	4th	5th	6th	PP	FL	points
F1 W	1951-53	5	-	-	-	-	-	-	-	-	0

Best result: 7th. Best qualifying: 10th. Teams: driver, HWM

GP Pre-50	1948-49	2	-	-	-	-	-	-	-	-	
Le Mans	1950-58	9	1	1	-	1	-	2	-	-	

Win: 1953 Le Mans 24 hrs

SC W	1953-58		1	1	1	-	2	-		

Win: 1953 Le Mans 24 hrs

Pete Hamilton
USA. Born: 20.7.1942
NASCAR wins: 4

George Hammond
USA
Champcar win: 1 – 1952 Pikes Peak

David Hampshire
GB. Born: 29.12.1917, Mickleover, Derbyshire. Died: 25.8.1990, Newton Solney, Derbyshire

formula	years	starts (DNS)	wins	2nd	3rd	4th	5th	6th	PP	FL	points
F1 W	1950	2	-	-	-	-	-	-	-	-	0

Best result: 9th. Best qualifying: 16th. Team: Scuderia Ambrosiana

GP Pre-50	1948-49	2	-	-	-	1	-	-	-	-	
Le Mans	1951	1	-	-	-	-	-	-	-	-	

Non-championship F1 win: 1950 Gamston

John Handley
GB
1968 European Touring Car Champion (1000cc class)

Sam Hanks
USA. Born: 13.7.1914, Columbus, Ohio. Died: 27.6.1994, Pacific Palisades, California
1953 Champcar Champion

formula	years	starts (DNS)	wins	2nd	3rd	4th	5th	6th	PP	FL	points
Indy 500	1940-57	12	1	1	2	-	1	-	-	-	

Win: 1957 Indianapolis 500
Champcar wins: 4 – 1953 Springfield race 2, Du Quoin, 1954 Du Quoin, 1957 Indianapolis 500

Kaj Hansen
DK
1949 Danish F3 Champion

Mel Hansen
USA. Born: 1912, Redfield, South Dakota. Died: 5.6.1963, California

formula	years	starts (DNS)	wins	2nd	3rd	4th	5th	6th	PP	FL	points
Indy 500	1939-49	7	-	-	-	-	-	-	-	-	

Champcar wins: 2 – 1948 Atlanta, 1949 Springfield race 1

Gregg Hansford
AUS. Born: 8.4.1952. Died: 5.3.1995, Phillip Island
Major win: 1993 Bathurst

Walt Hansgen
USA. Born: 28.10.1919, Westfield, New Jersey. Died: 7.4.1966, Orleans (F), following an accident at Le Mans

formula	years	starts (DNS)	wins	2nd	3rd	4th	5th	6th	PP	FL	points
F1 W	1961-64	2	-	-	-	-	1	-	-	-	2

Best championship: 1964, 16th. Best qualifying: 14th. Teams: Momo Corporation, Lotus

Le Mans	1959-63	5	-	-	-	-	-	-	-	-	
SC W	1953-66	-	1	2	-	1	-	-	1		
Indy 500	1964-65	2	-	-	-	-	-	-	-	-	

Harris Hanshue
USA
Champcar win: 1 – 1909 Santa Monica race 1

Fritz Huschke von Hanstein
D. Born: 3.1.1911, Halle. Died: 5.3.1996

formula	years	starts (DNS)	wins	2nd	3rd	4th	5th	6th	PP	FL	points
Le Mans	1937-52	2	-	-	-	-	-	-	-	-	
SC W	1955-61	-	-	1	-	1	1	-	-		

Major wins: 1940 Mille Miglia, 1956 Targa Florio

Ron Hardwick
HK
Major win: 1959 Macau

Mike Harris
RSR. Born: 25.5.1939, Mufulira (ZAM)

formula	years	starts (DNS)	wins	2nd	3rd	4th	5th	6th	PP	FL	points
F1 W	1962	1	-	-	-	-	-	-	-	-	0

Best result: no finishes. Best qualifying: 15th. Team: driver

Cuth Harrison
GB. Born: 6.7.1906, Ecclesall, Sheffield. Died: 21.1.1981, Sheffield

formula	years	starts (DNS)	wins	2nd	3rd	4th	5th	6th	PP	FL	points
F1 W	1950	3	-	-	-	-	-	-	-	-	0

Best result: 7th. Best qualifying: 13th. Team: driver

GP Pre-50	1947-49	5	-	-	-	1	-	1	-	-	

Ray Harroun
USA. Born: 12.1.1879, Spartansburg, Pennsylvania. Died: 19.1.1968, Anderson, Indiana

formula	years	starts (DNS)	wins	2nd	3rd	4th	5th	6th	PP	FL	points
GP Pre-50	1910	1	-	-	-	-	-	-	1	-	
Indy 500	1911	1	1	-	-	-	-	-	-	-	

Win: 1911 Indianapolis 500
Champcar wins: 4 – 1910 Atlanta race 1, Indianapolis race 2, Indianapolis race 3, 1911 Indianapolis 500

Brian Hart
GB. Born: 7.9.1936, Enfield, Middlesex

formula	years	starts (DNS)	wins	2nd	3rd	4th	5th	6th	PP	FL	points
F1 W	1967	1	-	-	-	-	-	-	-	-	0

Best result: no finishes. Best qualifying: no times set. Team: Ron Harris

F2 E	1967-71	16 (3)	-	1	-	-	2	-	1		13

Best championship: 1967, 10th

David Hart
NL. Born: 9.8.1957, Rotterdam

formula	years	starts (DNS)	wins	2nd	3rd	4th	5th	6th	PP	FL	points
Le Mans	2000	1									

GT FIA wins: 2 – 2000 Monza, Brno

Harry Hartz
USA. Born: 24.12.1896, Pomona, California. Died: 26.9.1974, Indianapolis, Indiana
1926 Champcar Champion

formula	years	starts (DNS)	wins	2nd	3rd	4th	5th	6th	PP	FL	points
Indy 500	1922-27	6	-	3	2	-	-	-	-	-	

Champcar wins: 7 – 1922 San Carlos, 1923 Fresno race 2, 1926 Atlantic City race 1, Atlantic City race 2, Atlantic City race 5, Salem race 5, Charlotte race 8

John Harvey
AUS. Born: 21.2.1938
Major win: 1983 Bathurst

Tim Harvey
GB. Born: 20.11.1961, Farnborough
1992 British Touring Car Champion

formula	years	starts (DNS)	wins	2nd	3rd	4th	5th	6th	PP	FL	points
Le Mans	1988-91	4	-	-	-	-	-	-	-	-	
SC W	1988-91	-	-	1	1	-	-	-	-		

Best championship: 1990, 15th
Major win: 1989 Macau Guia race

Kevin Harvick
USA. Born: 8.12.1975, Bakersfield, California
2002 IROC Champion
NASCAR wins: 3 (in Modern era)

Masahiro Hasemi
J. Born: 13.11.1945, Tokyo
1980 Japanese F2 Champion, 1990 Japanese Sports-Prototype Champion (with Anders Olofsson), 1989, 1991 (both with Olofsson) and 1992 (with Hideo Fukuyama) Japanese Touring Car Champion

formula	years	starts (DNS)	wins	2nd	3rd	4th	5th	6th	PP	FL	points
F1 W	1976	1	-	-	-	-	-	-	-	1	0

Best result: 11th. Best qualifying: 10th. Team: Kojima

formula	years	starts (DNS)	wins	2nd	3rd	4th	5th	6th	PP	FL	points
Le Mans	1986-96	5	-	-	-	-	1	-	-	-	
SC W	1981-92		-	-	1	-	1	-	-	-	

Best championship: 1990, 20th
Major wins: 1990 Macau Guia race, 1992 Daytona 24 hrs

Karl Hasenbichler
A
2001 Belgian Belcar Touring Car Champion (with Pertti Kuismanen)

Rudolf Hasse
D. Born: 30.5.1906, Sassonia. Died: 12.8.1942, in action on Germany's Eastern Front

formula	years	starts (DNS)	wins	2nd	3rd	4th	5th	6th	PP	FL	points
GP Pre-50	1936-39	14 (2)	1	1	-	1	3	-	-		

Win: 1937 Belgian GP

Naoki Hattori
J. Born: 13.6.1966, Tokyo
1996 Japanese Touring Car Champion, 1990 Japanese F3 Champion

formula	years	starts (DNS)	wins	2nd	3rd	4th	5th	6th	PP	FL	points
F1 W	1991	0 (2)	-	-	-	-	-	-	-	-	0

Best result: no starts. Best qualifying: 31st. Team: Andrea Moda

formula	years	starts (DNS)	wins	2nd	3rd	4th	5th	6th	PP	FL	points
Le Mans	1995	1									
F3000 INT	1995	2									0
CART	1999	9									

Major win: 1991 Spa 24 hrs

Hubert Haupt
D. Born: 30.4.1969, Munich

formula	years	starts (DNS)	wins	2nd	3rd	4th	5th	6th	PP	FL	points
Le Mans	1999	1									

GT FIA win: 1 – 2000 Lausitzring

Johnny Hauser
CH. Born: 16.8.1971
1997 Swiss Touring Car Champion

Paul Hawkins
AUS. Born: 12.10.1937, Melbourne, Victoria. Died: 26.5.1969, Oulton Park, Tourist Trophy practice

formula	years	starts (DNS)	wins	2nd	3rd	4th	5th	6th	PP	FL	points
F1 W	1965	3	-	-	-	-	-	-	-	-	0

Best result: 9th. Best qualifying: 14th. Teams: John Willment, DW Racing Enterprises

formula	years	starts (DNS)	wins	2nd	3rd	4th	5th	6th	PP	FL	points
Le Mans	1961-68	5									
SC W	1960-69		2	2	2	4	-	2	1	-	

Wins: 1967 Targa Florio, 1968 Monza
Other Major win: 1967 Austrian GP

Mike Hawthorn
GB. Born: 10.4.1929, Mexborough, Yorkshire. Died: 22.1.1959, near Guildford, road accident
1958 F1 World Champion

formula	years	starts (DNS)	wins	2nd	3rd	4th	5th	6th	PP	FL	points
F1 W	1952-58	45 (2)	3	9	6	7	2	3	4	6	127.64

Wins: 1953 French GP, 1954 Spanish GP, 1958 French GP. Best championship: 1958, 1st. Best qualifying: 1st. Teams: LD Hawthorn, AHM Bryde, Ferrari, Vanwall, BRM, Maserati

formula	years	starts (DNS)	wins	2nd	3rd	4th	5th	6th	PP	FL	points
Le Mans	1953-58	5	1	-	-	-	-	-	1	1	4

Win: 1955 Le Mans 24 hrs

formula	years	starts (DNS)	wins	2nd	3rd	4th	5th	6th	PP	FL	points
SC W	1953-58		4	2	4	1	-	-	4	6	

Wins: 1953 Spa 24 hrs, 1954 Tourist Trophy scratch, 1955 Sebring 12 hrs, Le Mans 24 hrs
Non-championship F1 wins: 1955 Crystal Palace, 1958 Goodwood
Other major wins: 1953 International Trophy (Silverstone), 1953 Pescara

Boy Hayje
NL. Born: 3.5.1949, Amsterdam

formula	years	starts (DNS)	wins	2nd	3rd	4th	5th	6th	PP	FL	points
F1 W	1976-77	3 (4)	-	-	-	-	-	-	-	-	0

Best result: 15th. Best qualifying: 21st. Teams: Hexagon, RAM

formula	years	starts (DNS)	wins	2nd	3rd	4th	5th	6th	PP	FL	points
Le Mans	1984	1									
F2 E	1978-79	8 (2)	-	-	-	-	-	-	-	-	0

Hurley Haywood
USA. Born: 4.5.1948, Chicago, Illinois
1971 (with Peter Gregg) and 1972 (solo) IMSA GTP Champion, 1972 IMSA GTU Champion, 1988 Trans-Am Champion

formula	years	starts (DNS)	wins	2nd	3rd	4th	5th	6th	PP	FL	points
Le Mans	1977-94	14	3	-	2	-	-	-	-	1	

Wins: 1977, 1983 and 1994 Le Mans 24 hrs

formula	years	starts (DNS)	wins	2nd	3rd	4th	5th	6th	PP	FL	points
SC W	1969-92		6	-	4	1	3	-	-	1	

Wins: 1973 Daytona 24 hrs, 1975 Daytona 24 hrs, 1977 Daytona 24 hrs, 1979 Daytona 24 hrs, 1981 Sebring 12 hrs, 1983 Le Mans 24 hrs. Best championship: 1981, 10th

formula	years	starts (DNS)	wins	2nd	3rd	4th	5th	6th	PP	FL	points
Indy 500	1980	1									
CART	1979-82	5 (2)									

Other major wins: 1973 Sebring 12 hrs, 1991 Daytona 24 hrs

Richie Hearn
USA. Born: 4.1.1971, Glendale, California
1995 North American Toyota Atlantic Champion

formula	years	starts (DNS)	wins	2nd	3rd	4th	5th	6th	PP	FL	points
Indy 500	1996-2002	3	-	-	1	-	1	-	-		
CART	1996-99	59	-	-	-	1	2	-	-		
IRL	1996-2002	18	1	-	1	2	-	2	1	-	

Win: 1996 Las Vegas. Best championship: 1996, 4th

Eddie Hearne
USA. Born: 1.3.1887, Kansas City, Kansas. Died: 9.2.1955, Los Angeles, California
1923 Champcar Champion

formula	years	starts (DNS)	wins	2nd	3rd	4th	5th	6th	PP	FL	points
GP Pre-50	1911-15	2	-	1	-	-					
Indy 500	1911-27	11	-	1	1	1	-	1	-	-	

Champcar wins: 11 – 1910 Indianapolis race 6, Indianapolis race 8, 1911 Cincinnati race 2, 1917 Uniontown race 3, Ascot race 3, 1918 Uniontown race 3, Tacoma race 3, 1921 Cotati race 1, Beverly Hills race 11, 1923 Kansas City race 1, Altoona

George Heath
USA. Born: Long Island, New York State

formula	years	starts (DNS)	wins	2nd	3rd	4th	5th	6th	PP	FL	points
GP Pre-50	1906-08	3	-	-	-	-	1	-	-		

Major wins: 1904 Ardennes Circuit, 1904 WK Vanderbilt Cup

Peter Heath
T
Major win: 1961 Macau

Willi Heeks
D. Born: 13.2.1922, Moorlage. Died: 13.8.1996, Bocholt

formula	years	starts (DNS)	wins	2nd	3rd	4th	5th	6th	PP	FL	points
F1 W	1952-53	2	-	-	-	-	-	-	-	-	0

Best result: no finishes. Best qualifying: 18th. Team: driver

Altfrid Heger
D. Born: 24.1.1958, Essen
1993 Porsche Supercup Champion

formula	years	starts (DNS)	wins	2nd	3rd	4th	5th	6th	PP	FL	points
Le Mans	1984-85	2									
F3000 INT	1986-87	7 (7)	-	-	-	-	-	-	-	-	0

Major wins: 1986 and 1988 Spa 24 hrs, 1988 Macau Guia race

Nick Heidfeld
D. Born: 10.5.1977, Monchengladbach
1999 FIA F3000 Champion, 1997 German F3 Champion

formula	years	starts (DNS)	wins	2nd	3rd	4th	5th	6th	PP	FL	points
F1 W	2000-02	50 (1)	-	-	1	2	1	7	-	-	19

Best championship: 2001, 8th. Best qualifying: 5th. Teams: Prost, Sauber

Le Mans	1999	1	-	-	-	-	-	-	-	-	
F3000 INT	1998-99	22	7	5	2	3	-	-	5	9	117

Wins: 1998 Monaco, Hockenheim, Hungaroring, 1999 Imola, Barcelona, Magny-Cours, A1 Ring. Best championship: 1999, 1st

Other Major win: 1997 Monaco F3

Ludwig Heimrath

CDN. Born: 11.8.1934

1977 Trans-Am Class 2 Champion

formula	years	starts (DNS)	wins	2nd	3rd	4th	5th	6th	PP	FL	points
SC W	1961-85		1	-	-	2	-	-	-	-	

Win: 1977 Mosport Park

David Heinz

USA

1971 IMSA GTO Champion

formula	years	starts (DNS)	wins	2nd	3rd	4th	5th	6th	PP	FL	points
Le Mans	1972-74	2	-	-	-	-	-	1	-	-	
SC W	1968-87		-	-	1	1	-	2	-	-	

Eric Helary

F. Born: 10.8.1966, Paris

1990 French F3 Champion, 1992 and 1993 Peugeot 905 Spyder Cup Champion

formula	years	starts (DNS)	wins	2nd	3rd	4th	5th	6th	PP	FL	points
Le Mans	1993-2002	7	1	1	1	-	-	-	-	-	

Win: 1993 Le Mans 24 hrs

SC W	1992		-	1	-	-	-	-	-	-	

Best championship: 1992, 16th

F3000 INT	1991-92	9	-	-	1	1	1	-	-	-	9

Best championship: 1991, 8th

Other Major win: 1997 Spa 24 hrs

Theo Helfrich

D. Born: 13.5.1913, Frankfurt-am-Main. Died: 29.4.1978, Ludwigshafen

formula	years	starts (DNS)	wins	2nd	3rd	4th	5th	6th	PP	FL	points
F1 W	1952-54	3	-	-	-	-	-	-	-	-	0

Best result: 12th. Best qualifying: 21st. Teams: driver, Hans Klenk

Le Mans	1952	1	-	1	-	-	-	-	-	-	

Dave Helmick

USA

formula	years	starts (DNS)	wins	2nd	3rd	4th	5th	6th	PP	FL	points
SC W	1972-77		1	-	-	-	-	2	-	-	

Win: 1977 Daytona 24 hrs

Other Major win: 1973 Sebring 12 hrs

Victor Hemery

F. Born: 18.11.1876, Sille-le-Gullaume, Sarthe. Died: 8.9.1950, Le Mans, suicide

formula	years	starts (DNS)	wins	2nd	3rd	4th	5th	6th	PP	FL	points
GP Pre-50	1906-23	9	-	3	-	-	-	-	-	1	

Major wins: 1905 Ardennes Circuit, 1905 WK Vanderbilt Cup, 1911 Unofficial French GP

Jean-Francois Hemroulle

B. Born: 12.7.1969, Mol

1996 Belgian Procar Touring Car Champion, 1998 and 1999 Belgian Belcar Touring Car Champion (both with Tim Verbergt)

Pete Henderson

USA. Born: Fernie, British Colombia (CDN). Died: 19??

formula	years	starts (DNS)	wins	2nd	3rd	4th	5th	6th	PP	FL	points
Indy 500	1916-20	2	-	-	-	-	-	1	-	-	

Champcar win: 1 – 1917 Chicago race 6

Preston Henn

USA

formula	years	starts (DNS)	wins	2nd	3rd	4th	5th	6th	PP	FL	points
Le Mans	1979-84	5	-	1	-	-	-	-	-	-	
SC W	1977-86		-	1	1	1	1	-	-	-	

Major win: 1983 Daytona 24 hrs

Gunnar Henriksen

DK

1957 Danish F3 Champion

Brian Henton

GB. Born: 19.9.1946, Derby

1980 European F2 Champion, 1974 Forward Trust and Lombard British F3 Champion

formula	years	starts (DNS)	wins	2nd	3rd	4th	5th	6th	PP	FL	points
F1 W	1975-82	19 (18)	-	-	-	-	-	-	-	1	0

Best result: 7th. Best qualifying: 11th. Teams: Lotus, March, British F1 Racing, Boro, Toleman, Arrows, Tyrrell

F2 E	1974-80	49 (2)	6	6	4	2	3	2	8	12	123

Wins: 1977 Thruxton, 1979 Mugello, Misano, 1980 Thruxton, Vallelunga, Mugello. Best championship: 1980, 1st

Johnny Herbert

GB. Born: 25.6.1964, Brentwood, Essex

1987 British F3 Champion

formula	years	starts (DNS)	wins	2nd	3rd	4th	5th	6th	PP	FL	points
F1 W	1989-2000	162 (3)	3	1	3	11	6	5	-	-	98

Wins: 1995 British GP, Italian GP, 1999 European GP. Best championship: 1995, 4th. Best qualifying: 4th. Teams: Benetton, Tyrrell, Lotus, Ligier, Sauber, Stewart, Jaguar

Le Mans	1990-2002	5	1	1	-	1	-	-	-	-	

Win: 1991 Le Mans 24 hrs

SC W	1988-92		1	1	-	1	-	-	-	-	

Win: 1991 Le Mans 24 hrs. Best championship: 1992, 9th

F3000 INT	1988	6	1	-	1	-	-	-	2	1	13

Win: 1988 Jerez. Best championship: 1988, 8th

F3 E win: 1 – 1987 Cellnet Superprix (Brands Hatch)

Other Major win: 2002 Sebring 12 hrs

Don Herr

USA. Born: 30.8.1889, Salunga, Pennsylvania. Died: 21.6.1953, Indianapolis, Indiana

formula	years	starts (DNS)	wins	2nd	3rd	4th	5th	6th	PP	FL	points
Indy 500	1912-13	2	1	-	-	-	-	-	-	-	

Win: 1912 Indianapolis 500

Champcar wins: 2 – 1911 Elgin race 2, 1912 Indianapolis 500

Harvey Herrick

USA

Champcar wins: 2 – 1911 Bakersfield, Santa Monica race 4

Hans Herrmann

D. Born: 23.2.1928, Stuttgart

formula	years	starts (DNS)	wins	2nd	3rd	4th	5th	6th	PP	FL	points
F1 W	1953-69	18 (2)	-	-	1	2	-	1	-	1	10

Best championship: 1954, 6th. Best qualifying: 4th. Teams: Hans Klenk, Mercedes-Benz, Maserati, Scuderia Centro Sud, Joakim Bonnier, BRP, Porsche, Ecurie Maarsbergen, Roy Winkelmann

Le Mans	1953-70	14	1	1	1	-	2	-	-	-	

Win: 1970 Le Mans 24 hrs

SC W	1953-70		5	8	8	9	3	10	1	-	

Wins: 1960 Sebring 12 hrs, Targa Florio, 1968 Daytona 24 hrs, Sebring 12 hrs, 1970 Le Mans 24 hrs

Other Major win: 1966 Austrian GP

Bryan Herta

USA. Born: 23.5.1970, Warren, Michigan

1993 CART Indy Lights Champion, 1991 Barber-SAAB Champion

formula	years	starts (DNS)	wins	2nd	3rd	4th	5th	6th	PP	FL	points
Le Mans	2002	1	-	-	-	-	-	-	-	-	
Indy 500	1994-95	2	-	-	-	-	-	-	-	-	
CART	1994-2001	120 (2)	2	3	5	4	8	7	7	1	

Wins: 1998 Laguna Seca, 1999 Laguna Seca. Best championships: 1996 and 1998, 8th

Egon Herzfield
BR
1994 Brazilian Touring Car Champion (with Vicente Daudt)

Francois Hesnault
F. Born: 30.12.1956, Neuilly-sur-Seine, near Paris

formula	years	starts (DNS)	wins	2nd	3rd	4th	5th	6th	PP	FL	points
F1 W	1984-85	19 (2)	-	-	-	-	-	-	-	-	0

Best result: 7th. Best qualifying: 13th. Teams: Ligier, Brabham, Renault

Le Mans	1982-83	2	-	-	-	-	-	-			

Tom Hessert
USA. Born: 1.4.1951
1988 IMSA Lights Champion

formula	years	starts (DNS)	wins	2nd	3rd	4th	5th	6th	PP	FL	points
Le Mans	1987	1	-	-	-	-	-	-			

Hans Heyer
D. Born: 16.3.1943, Monchengladbach
1974 European Touring Car Champion, 1975, 1976 and 1980 German Racing Champion

formula	years	starts (DNS)	wins	2nd	3rd	4th	5th	6th	PP	FL	points
F1 W	1977	1	-	-	-	-	-	-	-	-	0

Best result: no finishes. Best qualifying: 27th. Team: ATS

Le Mans	1972-86	12	-	-	-	-	-	-			
SC W	1972-86		4	5	3	4	2	1	-	-	

Wins: 1978 Mugello, Nurburgring, 1979 Silverstone, 1980 Watkins Glen. Best championship: 1983, 12th

F2 E	1976	1 (1)	-	-	-	-	-	-			1

Best championship: 1976, 17th

Other major wins: 1982, 1983 and 1984 Spa 24 hrs, 1984 Sebring 12 hrs

Mike Hezemans
NL. Born: 25.7.1969, Eindhoven

formula	years	starts (DNS)	wins	2nd	3rd	4th	5th	6th	PP	FL	points
Le Mans	1997-2002	3	-	-	-	-	-	-			

GT FIA wins: 6 – 2000 Monza, A1 Ring, Brno, 2001 Hungaroring, Estoril, 2002 Donington

Toine Hezemans
NL. Born: 14.4.1943, Eindhoven
1970 (overall and over 1600cc class), 1971 (2000cc class) and 1973 European Touring Car Champion, 1976 European GT Champion

formula	years	starts (DNS)	wins	2nd	3rd	4th	5th	6th	PP	FL	points
Le Mans	1970-78	6	-	-	-	-	1	-			
SC W	1967-78		6	6	5	1	5	1	2	2	

Wins: 1971 Targa Florio, 1977 Nurburgring, 1978 Daytona 24 hrs, Mugello, Nurburgring, Watkins Glen

F2 E	1968	0 (1)	-	-	-	-	-	-	-	-	0

Other Major win: 1973 Spa 24 hrs

Derek Higgins
IRL. Born: 12.6.1964, Dublin
1995 and 1997 Mexican F3 Champion

Bennett Hill
USA. Born: 31.5.1893, New York City. Died: 9.12.1977, Los Angeles, California

formula	years	starts (DNS)	wins	2nd	3rd	4th	5th	6th	PP	FL	points
Indy 500	1920-33	8	-	1	-	1	-	-			

Champcar wins: 6 – 1922 Fresno race 2, 1923 Beverly Hills race 2, 1924 Culver City, 1926 Culver City, Fresno race 1, Salem race 3

Damon Hill
GB. Born: 17.9.1960, Hampstead, London
1996 F1 World Champion

formula	years	starts (DNS)	wins	2nd	3rd	4th	5th	6th	PP	FL	points
F1 W	1992-99	115 (7)	22	15	5	7	2	5	20	19	360

Wins: 1993 Hungarian GP, Belgian GP, Italian GP, 1994 Spanish GP, British GP, Belgian GP, Italian GP, Portuguese GP, Japanese GP, 1995 Argentinian GP, San Marino GP, Hungarian GP, Australian GP, 1996 Australian GP, Brazilian GP, Argentinian GP, San Marino GP, Canadian GP, French GP, German GP, Japanese GP, 1998 Belgian GP. Best championship: 1996, 1st. Best qualifying: 1st. Teams: Brabham, Williams, Arrows, Jordan

Le Mans	1989	1	-	-	-	-	-	-			
F3000 INT	1988-91	27 (2)	-	1	1	2	-	1	3	2	17

Best championship: 1991, 7th

Derek Hill
USA. Born: 28.3.1975, Santa Monica, California
1997 Barber-Dodge Champion

formula	years	starts (DNS)	wins	2nd	3rd	4th	5th	6th	PP	FL	points
F3000 INT	2001-02	19	-	-	-	-	-	-	-	-	0

George Hill
USA. Born: n/a. Died: 19??

formula	years	starts (DNS)	wins	2nd	3rd	4th	5th	6th	PP	FL	points
Indy 500	1915	1	-	-	-	-	-	-			

Champcar win: 1 – 1913 San Diego race 1

Graham Hill
GB. Born: 15.2.1929, Hampstead, London. Died: 29.11.1975, Arkley, near Barnet, Hertfordshire, aircraft accident with Graham Hill Racing
1962 and 1968 F1 World Champion

formula	years	starts (DNS)	wins	2nd	3rd	4th	5th	6th	PP	FL	points
F1 W	1958-75	176 (3)	14	15	7	9	7	9	13	10	289

Wins: 1962 Dutch GP, German GP, Italian GP, South African GP, 1963 Monaco GP, United States GP, 1964 Monaco GP, United States GP, 1965 Monaco GP, United States GP, 1968 Spanish GP, Monaco GP, Mexican GP, 1969 Monaco GP. Best championships: 1962 and 1968, 1st. Best qualifying: 1st. Teams: Lotus, BRM, Rob Walker, Brabham, Hill

Le Mans	1958-72	10	-	1	1	-	-	-			

Win: 1972 Le Mans 24 hrs

SC W	1958-73		4	1	3	1	1	-	1	1	

Wins: 1964 Reims, Tourist Trophy (Goodwood), Montlhery, 1972 Le Mans 24 hrs

F2 E	1967-72	29 (3)	1	2	2	1	4	2	1	3	0

Win: 1971 Thruxton

Indy 500	1966-68	3	1	-	-	-	-	-			

Win: 1966 Indianapolis 500

Champcar win: 1 – 1966 Indianapolis 500

Non-championship F1 wins: 1962 Goodwood, International Trophy (Silverstone), 1963 Snetterton, Aintree, 1964 Rand GP (Kyalami), 1971 International Trophy (Silverstone)

Tasman wins: 2 – 1966 New Zealand GP, Australian GP

Other major wins: 1963 Tourist Trophy (Goodwood), 1965 New Zealand GP

Phil Hill
USA. Born: 20.4.1927, Miami, Florida
1961 F1 World Champion

formula	years	starts (DNS)	wins	2nd	3rd	4th	5th	6th	PP	FL	points
F1 W	1958-66	48 (3)	3	5	8	2	-	3	6	6	98

Wins: 1960 Italian GP, 1961 Belgian GP, Italian GP. **Best championship:** 1961, 1st. **Best qualifying:** 1st. **Teams:** Joakim Bonnier, Ferrari, BRP, ATS, Ecurie Filipinetti, Cooper, driver, Eagle

Le Mans	1953-67	14	3	-	-	2					3

Wins: 1958, 1961 and 1962 Le Mans 24 hrs

SC W	1953-67	14	7	3	2	-	1			7	8

Wins: 1956 Swedish GP, 1957 Venezuelan GP, 1958 Buenos Aires, Sebring 12 hrs, Le Mans 24 hrs, 1959 Sebring 12 hrs, 1960 Buenos Aires, 1961 Sebring 12 hrs, Le Mans 24 hrs, 1962 Nurburgring, Le Mans 24 hrs, 1964 Daytona, 1966 Nurburgring, 1967 Brands Hatch

Val Hillebrand
B. Born: 22.6.1981, Wickede (D)
2002 Sports Racing World Champion (with Jan Lammers)

formula	years	starts (DNS)	wins	2nd	3rd	4th	5th	6th	PP	FL	points
Le Mans	2001-02	2									

SRWC wins: 4 – 2001 Nurburgring, 2002 Brno, Magny-Cours, Dijon

Bobby Hillin Jr
USA. Born: 5.6.1964, Midland, Texas
NASCAR wins: 1 (in Modern era)

John Hindmarsh
GB. Born: c1908. Died: 6.9.1938, St George's Hill, Weybridge, Surrey during Hurricane test flight

formula	years	starts (DNS)	wins	2nd	3rd	4th	5th	6th	PP	FL	points
Le Mans	1930-37	5	1	-	1	-	-				

Win: 1935 Le Mans 24 hrs

Peter Hirt
CH. Born: 30.3.1910, Lenzburg. Died: 28.6.1992, Zurich

formula	years	starts (DNS)	wins	2nd	3rd	4th	5th	6th	PP	FL	points
F1 W	1951-53	5	-	-	-	-	-	-	-	-	0

Best result: 7th. **Best qualifying:** 16th. **Team:** Ecurie Espadon

Pat Hoare
NZ
1962 New Zealand Gold Star Champion

David Hobbs
GB. Born: 9.6.1939, Leamington Spa, Warwickshire
1971 North American Formula A (F5000) Champion, 1983 Trans-Am Champion

formula	years	starts (DNS)	wins	2nd	3rd	4th	5th	6th	PP	FL	points
F1 W	1967-74	7	-	-	-	-	-	-	-	-	0

Best result: 7th. **Best qualifying:** 12th. **Teams:** Bernard White, Lola, Honda, Penske, McLaren

Le Mans	1962-89	20	-	-	2	2	1	-	-		
SC W	1961-90		1	5	7	5	5	5	-	-	

Win: 1968 Monza. **Best championship:** 1984, 8th

F2 E	1968	2	-	-	-	-	1	-	-		2

Best championship: 1968, 17th

Indy 500	1971-76	4	-	-	-	1	-	-			

Tasman win: 1 – 1972 Adelaide

Chris Hodgetts
GB. Born: 6.12.1950, Tanworth-in-Arden, Worcestershire
1995 British GT Champion, 1986 and 1987 British Touring Car Champion

formula	years	starts (DNS)	wins	2nd	3rd	4th	5th	6th	PP	FL	points
Le Mans	1988-95	4									

Irv Hoerr
USA. Born: 14.11.1946
1992 IMSA GTO Champion, 1995 and 1996 IMSA GT Champion

formula	years	starts (DNS)	wins	2nd	3rd	4th	5th	6th	PP	FL	points
SC W	1978-92		-	-	-	-	-	-	-	1	-

Ingo Hoffmann
BR. Born: 18.2.1953, Sao Paulo
1980, 1985, 1989, 1990 (all solo), 1991, 1992, 1993 (with Angelo Giombelli), 1994, 1996, 1997, 1998 and 2002 (all solo) Brazilian Stock Car Champion

formula	years	starts (DNS)	wins	2nd	3rd	4th	5th	6th	PP	FL	points
F1 W	1976-77	3 (3)	-	-	-	-	-	-	-	-	0

Best result: 7th. **Best qualifying:** 19th. **Team:** Fittipaldi

F2 E	1976-78	32 (3)	-	-	3	4	3	2	-	2	34

Best championship: 1978, 6th

Al Holbert
USA. Born: 11.11.1946, Abington, Pennsylvania. Died: 30.9.1988, Columbus, Ohio, aircraft accident
1976, 1977, 1983, 1985 and 1986 IMSA GTP Champion

formula	years	starts (DNS)	wins	2nd	3rd	4th	5th	6th	PP	FL	points
Le Mans	1977-87	7	3	-	1	-	-	-			

Wins: 1983, 1986 and 1987 Le Mans 24 hrs

SC W	1972-88		4	1	1	-	2	-	-		

Wins: 1981 Sebring 12 hrs, 1983 Le Mans 24 hrs, 1986 Le Mans 24 hrs, 1987 Le Mans 24 hrs. **Best championship:** 1983, 16th

Indy 500	1984	1	-	-	-	1	-	-			
CART	1984-87	14 (1)	-	-	1	1	-	-			

Other major wins: 1976 Sebring 12 hrs, 1986 and 1987 Daytona 24 hrs

Bob Holden
AUS. Born: 1.12.1932, Notting Hill, Victoria
Major win: 1966 Bathurst

Bill Holland
USA. Born: 18.12.1907, Philadelphia, Pennsylvania. Died: 20.5.1984, Tuscon, Arizona

formula	years	starts (DNS)	wins	2nd	3rd	4th	5th	6th	PP	FL	points
Indy 500	1947-53	5	1	3	-	-	-	-			

Win: 1949 Indianapolis 500
Champcar wins: 3 – 1947 Milwaukee race 1, Langhorne, 1949 Indianapolis 500

Keith Holland
GB. Born: 6.12.1935
Non-championship F1 win: 1969 Madrid GP (in F5000 car)

Howdy Holmes
USA. Born: 14.12.1947, Ann Arbor, Michigan
1978 North American Formula Atlantic Champion

formula	years	starts (DNS)	wins	2nd	3rd	4th	5th	6th	PP	FL	points
F2 E	1976	1	-	-	-	-	-	-	-	-	0
Indy 500	1979-88	6	-	-	-	1	-	-			
CART	1979-88	72 (3)	-	1	-	1	2	2	-	-	

Jeffrey van Hooydonk
B. Born: 1.10.1977, Antwerp
1997 European Formula Renault Champion

formula	years	starts (DNS)	wins	2nd	3rd	4th	5th	6th	PP	FL	points
Le Mans	2000	1									
F3000 INT	1999-2000	17 (3)	-	-	2	-	-	1	-		6

Best championship: 1999, 16th

Theodore "Ted" Horn
USA. Born: 27.2.1910, Cincinnati. Died: 10.10.1948, Du Quoin
1946, 1947 and 1948 Champcar Champion

formula	years	starts (DNS)	wins	2nd	3rd	4th	5th	6th	PP	FL	points
Indy 500	1935-48	10	-	1	4	4	-	1	-		

Champcar wins: 5 – 1947 Bainbridge, Milwaukee race 3, Dallas, 1948 Dallas, Springfield

Christian Horner
GB. Born: 16.11.1973, Leamington Spa, Warwickshire

formula	years	starts (DNS)	wins	2nd	3rd	4th	5th	6th	PP	FL	points
F3000 INT	1997-98	14 (5)	-	-	-	-	1	-	1		

Best championship: 1997, 21st

Sam Hornish Jr
USA. Born: 2.7.1979, Bryan, Ohio
2001 and 2002 Indy Racing League Champion

formula	years	starts (DNS)	wins	2nd	3rd	4th	5th	6th	PP	FL	points
Indy 500	2000-02	3	-	-	-	1					

formula	years	starts (DNS)	wins	2nd	3rd	4th	5th	6th	PP	FL	points
IRL	2000-02	36	8	7	6	1	1	1	4		3

Wins: 2001 Phoenix, Miami, Texas, 2002 Miami, California Speedway, Richmond, Chicagoland, Texas race 2. Best championships: 2001 and 2002, 1st

St John Horsfall

GB. Born: 1910, Norfolk. Died: 20.8.1949, Silverstone, International Trophy
Major win: 1948 Spa 24 hrs

Kazuyoshi Hoshino

J. Born: 1.7.1947, Shizuoka Prefecture, Tokyo
1975 and 1977 Japanese F2000 Champion, 1978 Japanese F2 Champion, 1987, 1990 and 1993 Japanese F3000 Champion, 1991 and 1992 Japanese Sports-Prototype Champion (with Toshio Suzuki), 1990 Japanese Touring Car Champion (with Suzuki)

formula	years	starts (DNS)	wins	2nd	3rd	4th	5th	6th	PP	FL	points
F1 W	1976-77	2	-	-	-	-	-	-	-	-	0

Best result: 11th. Best qualifying: 11th. Team: Heros

Le Mans	1986-98	9	-	-	1	-	1	-	-		
SC W	1983-92		1	-	-	1	-	-			

Win: 1985 Fuji

F2 E	1978-83	3	-	-	-	1	-	-	-		3

Best championship: 1983, 16th
Other Major win: 1992 Daytona 24 hrs

Markus Hotz

CH

formula	years	starts (DNS)	wins	2nd	3rd	4th	5th	6th	PP	FL	points
SC W	1976-78		-	-	2	-	1	-	-		
F2 E	1975-78	6 (2)	-	-	-	1	-	-			1

Best championship: 1976, 17th

Jean-Pierre Hoursourigaray

F
1983 French Formula Renault Champion

Raijmond van Hove

B
Major win: 1978 Tourist Trophy (Silverstone)

Vaclav Hovorka

CS
Major win: 1950 Czech GP

Earl Howe (Edward Richard Assheton)

GB. Born: 1.5.1884. Died: 26.7.1964

formula	years	starts (DNS)	wins	2nd	3rd	4th	5th	6th	PP	FL	points
GP Pre-50	1931-37	17	-	1	-	1	-	-	1	-	
Le Mans	1929-35	6	1	-	-	-	1	-	-		1

Win: 1931 Le Mans 24 hrs

Will Hoy

GB. Born: 2.4.1953, Royston. Died 19.12.2002, cancer
1991 British Touring Car Champion

formula	years	starts (DNS)	wins	2nd	3rd	4th	5th	6th	PP	FL	points
Le Mans	1985-91	5	-	-	-	-	-	-	-		
SC W	1985-92		-	-	1	-	1	-	-		

Best championship: 1992, 12th

Gunther Huber

A

formula	years	starts (DNS)	wins	2nd	3rd	4th	5th	6th	PP	FL	points
Le Mans	1971	1	-	-	-	-	-	-	-		
F2 E	1968-69	2	-	-	-	-	-	-	-		0

Major win: 1970 Spa 24 hrs

Daniel Hubert

B. Born: 1.2.1960
1992 (with Patrick Hubert and Mondron) and 1996 (with Patrick Hubert and Marc Duez) Belgian Belcar GT Champion

formula	years	starts (DNS)	wins	2nd	3rd	4th	5th	6th	PP	FL	points
Le Mans	1985	1	-	-	-	-	-	-	-		

Patrick Hubert

B. Born: 27.4.1962
1992 (with Daniel Hubert and Mondron) and 1996 (with Daniel Hubert and Marc Duez) Belgian Belcar GT Champion

Detlef Hubner

D
GT FIA win: 1 – 1995 Montlhery

Hughie Hughes

GB. Born: c1886, London. Died: 2.12.1916, Uniontown, Pennsylvania

formula	years	starts (DNS)	wins	2nd	3rd	4th	5th	6th	PP	FL	points
GP Pre-50	1912-15	2	-	-	1	-	-				
Indy 500	1911-15	4	-	-	1	-	-				

Champcar race: 4 – 1911 Elgin race 1, Philadelphia race 4, 1912 Elgin race 1, 1914 Tacoma race 1

Ed Hugus

USA

formula	years	starts (DNS)	wins	2nd	3rd	4th	5th	6th	PP	FL	points
Le Mans	1956-65	10	1	-	-	-	-				

Win: 1965 Le Mans 24 hrs

SC W	1956-69		1	-	1	-	-				

Win: 1965 Le Mans 24 hrs

Duncan Huisman

NL. Born: 11.11.1971, Doornspijk
1998 Belgian Belcar GT Champion (with Patrick Huisman), 1997, 2000 and 2002 Dutch Touring Car Champion
Major wins: 2001 and 2002 Macau Guia race

Patrick Huisman

NL. Born: 23.8.1966, Den Haag
1997, 1998, 1999 and 2000 Porsche Supercup Champion, 1998 Belgian Belcar GT Champion (with Duncan Huisman)

formula	years	starts (DNS)	wins	2nd	3rd	4th	5th	6th	PP	FL	points
Le Mans	1994-2000	4	-	-	-	-	-	-	-		

Major win: 2000 Macau Guia race

Denis "Denny" Hulme

NZ. Born: 18.6.1936, Te Puke. Died: 4.10.1992, Bathurst, heart attack during race
1967 F1 World Champion, 1968 and 1970 Can-Am Champion, 1961 New Zealand Gold Star Champion

formula	years	starts (DNS)	wins	2nd	3rd	4th	5th	6th	PP	FL	points
F1 W	1965-74	112	8	9	16	11	8	9	1	9	248

Wins: 1967 Monaco GP, 1968 Italian GP, Canadian GP, 1969 Mexican GP, 1972 South African GP, 1973 Swedish GP, 1974 Argentinian GP.
Best championship: 1967, 1st. Best qualifying: 1st. Teams: Brabham, McLaren

Le Mans	1961-67	3	-	1	-	-	-	-			1
SC W	1961-70		1	2	-	1	-	-		1	2

Win: 1965 Tourist Trophy (Oulton)

F2 E	1967	2	-	-	-	1	-	-	-		0
Indy 500	1967-71	4	-	-	2	-	-				

Non-championship F1 wins: 1968 International Trophy (Silverstone), 1972 Oulton Park Gold Cup
Other major wins: 1960 Pescara, 1966, 1968 (both at Oulton) and 1986 (at Silverstone) Tourist Trophy

James Hunt

GB. Born: 29.8.1947, Belmont, Surrey. Died: 15.6.1993, Wimbledon, heart attack
1976 F1 World Champion

formula	years	starts (DNS)	wins	2nd	3rd	4th	5th	6th	PP	FL	points
F1 W	1973-79	92 (1)	10	6	7	7	2	3	14	8	179

Wins: 1975 Dutch GP, 1976 Spanish GP, French GP, German GP, Dutch GP,

Canadian GP, United States GP, 1977 British GP, United States GP, Japanese GP. Best championship: 1976, 1st. Best qualifying: 1st. Teams: Hesketh, McLaren, Wolf

formula	years	starts (DNS)	wins	2nd	3rd	4th	5th	6th	PP	FL	points
SC W	1974						1				
F2 E	1972-73	6 (2)					1				5

Best championship: 1972, 17th
Non-championship F1 wins: 1974 and 1976 International Trophy (Silverstone), 1976 and 1977 Race of Champions (Brands Hatch)

Jim Hurtubise

USA. Born: 5.12.1932, North Tonawanda, New York State. Died: 6.1.1989, Port Arthur, Texas, heart attack

formula	years	starts (DNS)	wins	2nd	3rd	4th	5th	6th	PP	FL	points
Indy 500	1960-74	10									

Champcar wins: 4 – 1959 Sacramento, 1960 Langhorne, 1961 Springfield, 1962 Springfield
NASCAR wins: 1

Dick Hutcherson

USA. Born: 30.11.1931, Iowa

formula	years	starts (DNS)	wins	2nd	3rd	4th	5th	6th	PP	FL	points
Le Mans	1966-76	2			1						
SC W	1966-76				1						

NASCAR wins: 14

Augustus "Gus" Hutchison

USA. Born: 26.4.1937, Atlanta, Georgia
1967 North American Formula A (F5000) Champion

formula	years	starts (DNS)	wins	2nd	3rd	4th	5th	6th	PP	FL	points
F1 W	1970	1									0

Best result: no finishes. Best qualifying: 22nd. Team: driver

James Hylton

USA. Born: 26.8.1935
NASCAR wins: 2 (1 in Modern era)

Marc Hynes

GB. Born: 26.2.1978, Guildford
1999 British F3 Champion

formula	years	starts (DNS)	wins	2nd	3rd	4th	5th	6th	PP	FL	points
F3000 INT	2000	2 (1)									0

Major win: 1999 Marlboro Masters (Zandvoort)

Shuji Hyoudo

J. Born: 28.12.1960
1984 Japanese F3 Champion

Angus Hyslop

NZ
1963 New Zealand Gold Star Champion

formula	years	starts (DNS)	wins	2nd	3rd	4th	5th	6th	PP	FL	points
Le Mans	1961	1									

Mario Hytten

CH. Born: 20.4.1957, Stockholm (S)

formula	years	starts (DNS)	wins	2nd	3rd	4th	5th	6th	PP	FL	points
SC W	1980-90						1				
Le Mans	1985	1					1				
F3000 INT	1985-88	21 (6)		1			1				8

Best championship: 1985, 10th

I

Jose Maria Ibanez

RA. Born: 1.2.1921

formula	years	starts (DNS)	wins	2nd	3rd	4th	5th	6th	PP	FL	points
SC W	1954-55		1								

Win: 1955 Buenos Aires

Jacques-Bernard "Jacky" Ickx

B. Born: 1.1.1945, Ixelles, Brussels
1982 and 1983 World Sports Car Champion, 1967 European F2 Champion, 1965 European Touring Car Champion (over 1600cc), 1979 Can-Am Champion

formula	years	starts (DNS)	wins	2nd	3rd	4th	5th	6th	PP	FL	points
F1 W	1966-79	116 (6)	8	7	10	4	7	4	13	14	181

Wins: 1968 French GP, 1969 German GP, Canadian GP, 1970 Austrian GP, Canadian GP, Mexican GP, 1971 Dutch GP, 1972 German GP. Best championships: 1969 and 1970, 2nd. Best qualifying: 1st. Teams: Tyrrell, Cooper, Ferrari, Brabham, McLaren, Williams, Lotus, Ensign, Ligier

formula	years	starts (DNS)	wins	2nd	3rd	4th	5th	6th	PP	FL	points
Le Mans	1966-85	15		6	3				5	4	

Wins: 1969, 1975, 1976, 1977, 1981 and 1982 Le Mans 24 hrs

formula	years	starts (DNS)	wins	2nd	3rd	4th	5th	6th	PP	FL	points
SC W	1963-85		37	22	8	1	2	1	19	25	

Wins: 1967 Spa, 1968 Brands Hatch, Spa, Watkins Glen, 1969 Sebring 12 hrs, Le Mans 24 hrs, 1972 Daytona, Sebring 12 hrs, Brands Hatch, Monza, Osterreichring, Watkins Glen, 1973 Monza, Nurburgring, 1974 Spa, 1976 Mugello, Vallelunga, Monza, Imola, Dijon, Dijon, 1977 Silverstone, Watkins Glen, Brands Hatch, 1978 Silverstone, 1981 Le Mans 24 hrs, 1982 Le Mans 24 hrs, Spa, Fuji, Brands Hatch, 1983 Nurburgring, Spa, 1984 Silverstone, Mosport Park, 1985 Mugello, Silverstone, Shah Alam. Best championships: 1982 and 1983, 1st

formula	years	starts (DNS)	wins	2nd	3rd	4th	5th	6th	PP	FL	points
F2 E	1967-70	16 (1)	3		3	1	2	2	3	4	45

Wins: 1967 Zandvoort, Vallelunga, 1970 Tulln. Best championship: 1967, 1st
Non-championship F1 wins: 1969 Oulton Park Gold Cup, 1971 Jochen Rindt Trophy (Hockenheim), 1974 Race of Champions (Brands Hatch)
Other major wins: 1966 Spa 24 hrs, 1977 Bathurst

Pascal Ickx

B
Major win: 1965 Spa 24 hrs

Jesus Iglesias

RA. Born: 22.2.1922, Pergamino, near Buenos Aires

formula	years	starts (DNS)	wins	2nd	3rd	4th	5th	6th	PP	FL	points
F1 W	1955	1									0

Best result: no finishes. Best qualifying: 17th. Team: Gordini

Akira Iida

J. Born: 18.12.1969, Kanagawa
2002 Japanese GT Champion (with Juichi Wakisaka)

formula	years	starts (DNS)	wins	2nd	3rd	4th	5th	6th	PP	FL	points
Le Mans	1994-2002	5									
F3000 INT	1996	10									0

Tetsu Ikuzawa

J. Born: 21.8.1942

formula	years	starts (DNS)	wins	2nd	3rd	4th	5th	6th	PP	FL	points
Le Mans	1973-81	3									
SC W	1967-80							1			
F2 E	1970-73	24 (5)		1							9

Best championship: 1970, 6th

Russell Ingall

AUS. Born: 1.7.1965
Major wins: 1995 and 1997 Bathurst

Takachino "Taki" Inoue

J. Born: 5.9.1963, Kobe

formula	years	starts (DNS)	wins	2nd	3rd	4th	5th	6th	PP	FL	points
F1 W	1994-95	18									0

Best result: 8th. Best qualifying: 18th. Teams: Simtek, Arrows

formula	years	starts (DNS)	wins	2nd	3rd	4th	5th	6th	PP	FL	points
F3000 INT	1994	8									0

Innes Ireland
GB. Born: 12.6.1930, Mytholmroyd, Yorkshire.
Died: 22.10.1993, Reading, cancer

formula	years	starts (DNS)	wins	2nd	3rd	4th	5th	6th	PP	FL	points
F1 W	1959-66	50 (3)	1	2	1	4	4	2	-	1	47

Win: 1961 United States GP. Best championship: 1960, 4th. Best qualifying:
2nd. Teams: Lotus, BRP, Reg Parnell, Bernard White

Le Mans	1958-66	7	-	-	-	-	1	-	-		
SC W	1957-84		-	-	-	2	4	-	-		

Non-championship F1 wins: 1960 Goodwood, International Trophy
(Silverstone), Snetterton, 1961 Solitude, Zeltweg, 1962 Crystal Palace, 1963
Goodwood, 1964 Snetterton

Other Major win: 1962 Tourist Trophy (Goodwood)

Ernie Irvan
USA. Born: 13.1.1959, Salinas, California

NASCAR wins: 15 (all Modern era) including 1991 Daytona 500

Eddie Irvine
GB. Born: 10.11.1965, Conlig, County Down,
Northern Ireland

formula	years	starts (DNS)	wins	2nd	3rd	4th	5th	6th	PP	FL	points
F1 W	1993-2002	146 (2)	4	6	16	10	7	7	-	1	191

Wins: 1999 Australian GP, Austrian GP, German GP, Malaysian GP. Best championship: 1999, 2nd. Best qualifying: 2nd. Teams: Jordan, Ferrari, Jaguar

Le Mans	1992-94	3	-	1	-	1	-	-	-		
F3000 INT	1989-90	19 (2)	1	1	3	3	-	2	1	-	38

Win: 1990 Hockenheim. Best championship: 1990, 3rd

Chris Irwin
GB. Born: 27.6.1942, Wandsworth, London

formula	years	starts (DNS)	wins	2nd	3rd	4th	5th	6th	PP	FL	points
F1 W	1966-67	10	-	-	-	1	-	-	-		2

Best championship: 1967, 16th. Best qualifying: 9th. Teams: Brabham, Reg
Parnell

Le Mans	1967	1	-	-	-	-	-	-	-		
F2 E	1967-68	10 (1)	-	-	1	-	-	1	-		15

Best championship: 1967, 6th

Bobby Isaac
USA. Born: 1.8.1932. Died: 14.8.1977, North Carolina, collapsed after a
race

1970 NASCAR Champion

NASCAR wins: 37 (1 in Modern era)

Jacques Isler
CH. Born: 14.8.1950, Zurich

1989 Swiss F3 Champion

Boris Ivanowski
F. Born: Russia

formula	years	starts (DNS)	wins	2nd	3rd	4th	5th	6th	PP	FL	points
GP Pre-50	1931	3 (1)	-	-	-	-	2	-	-	-	
Le Mans	1931	1	-	1	-	-	-	-	-	1	

Major win: 1928 Spa 24 hrs

J

Jean-Pierre Jabouille
F. Born: 1.10.1942, Paris
1976 European F2 Champion

formula	years	starts (DNS)	wins	2nd	3rd	4th	5th	6th	PP	FL	points
F1 W	1974-81	49 (7)	2	-	-	1	-	-	6	-	21

Wins: 1979 French GP, 1980 Austrian GP. Best championship: 1980, 8th. Best
qualifying: 1st. Teams: Williams, Surtees, Tyrrell, Renault, Ligier

Le Mans	1968-93	13	-	-	4	1	1	-	2	2	
SC W	1966-92		1	-	5	1	-	1	1	1	

Win: 1975 Mugello

F2 E	1968-76	49 (11)	5	4	4	4	2	1	6	7	109

Wins: 1974 Hockenheim race 2, 1975 Salzburgring, 1976 Vallelunga, Mugello,
Hockenheim race 3. Best championship: 1976, 1st

John James
GB. Born: 10.5.1914, Packwood, Warwickshire

formula	years	starts (DNS)	wins	2nd	3rd	4th	5th	6th	PP	FL	points
F1 W	1951	1	-	-	-	-	-	-	-	-	0

Best result: no finishes. Best qualifying: 17th. Team: driver

Paul Jamin
F

City-to-city win: 1897 Paris-Dieppe

Bob Jane
AUS

1962, 1963, 1971 and 1972 Australian Touring Car Champion

Major wins: 1963 and 1964 Bathurst

Jaroslav Janis
CS. Born: 8.7.1983, Olomovc

formula	years	starts (DNS)	wins	2nd	3rd	4th	5th	6th	PP	FL	points
F3000 INT	2001	1	-	-	-	-	-	-	-	-	0

Jean-Pierre Jarier
F. Born: 10.7.1946, Charenton-le-Pont, near Paris
1973 European F2 Champion, 1998 and 1999 French GT Champion

formula	years	starts (DNS)	wins	2nd	3rd	4th	5th	6th	PP	FL	points
F1 W	1971-83	133 (10)	-	-	3	2	6	3	3	3	31.5

Best championships: 1979 and 1980, 10th. Best qualifying: 1st. Teams: Hubert
Hahne, March, Shadow, ATS, Ligier, Lotus, Tyrrell, Osella

Le Mans	1972-99	15	-	1	-	1	-	-	1	-	1
SC W	1972-92		7	2	3	1	-	3	2	6	

Wins: 1974 Spa, Nurburgring, Watkins Glen, Paul Ricard, Brands Hatch, 1977
Dijon, Paul Ricard. GT FIA wins: 4 – 1994 Paul Ricard, Jarama, Suzuka, Zhuhai

F2 E	1971-78	26 (2)	7	2	3	1	-	-	4	4	88

Wins: 1973 Mallory Park, Hockenheim race 1, Nivelles, Rouen, Mantorp Park,
Karlskoga, Enna. Best championship: 1973, 1st

Other Major win: 1993 Spa 24 hrs

Dale Jarrett
USA. Born: 26.11.1956, Conover, North Carolina
1999 NASCAR Champion

NASCAR wins: 30 (all Modern era) including 1993, 1996, 2000 Daytona 500,
1996 World 600

Ned Jarrett
USA. Born: 12.10.1932, Newton, North Carolina
1961 and 1965 NASCAR Champion

NASCAR wins: 50

Charles Jarrott
GB. Born: 1877. Died: 1944

formula	years	starts (DNS)	wins	2nd	3rd	4th	5th	6th	PP	FL	points
GP Pre-50	1903-04	2	-	-	-	-	-	-	-	-	

Major win: 1902 Ardennes Circuit

Jean-Pierre Jaussaud
F. Born: 3.6.1937
1970 French F3 Champion

formula	years	starts (DNS)	wins	2nd	3rd	4th	5th	6th	PP	FL	points
Le Mans	1966-83	13	2	-	2	-	-	-	-	-	

Wins: 1978 and 1980 Le Mans 24 hrs

SC W	1966-87		1	-	2	-	-	-	-	-	

Win: 1980 Le Mans 24 hrs

F2 E	1967-78	42 (6)	2	1	1	4	1	6	1	2	62

Wins: 1972 Hockenheim race 1, Albi. Best championship: 1972, 2nd

Other Major win: 1968 Monaco F3

Frank Jelinski
D. Born: 23.5.1958, Bad Munder, Hannover
1980 and 1981 German F3 Champion

formula	years	starts (DNS)	wins	2nd	3rd	4th	5th	6th	PP	FL	points
Le Mans	1983-95	11	-	-	1	1	-	-	-	-	
SC W	1982-92		2	4	6	6	5	6	1	-	

Wins: 1986 Spa, 1989 Dijon. Best championship: 1986, 4th

F2 E	1982-83	17	-	-	-	1	2	1	-	-	8

Best championship: 1982, 12th

Other Major win: 1991 Daytona 24 hrs

Camille Jenatzy
B. Born: 4.11.1868, Brussels. Died: 7.10.1913, shot accidently during wild boar hunt

formula	years	starts (DNS)	wins	2nd	3rd	4th	5th	6th	PP	FL	points
GP Pre-50	1900-08	7	1	1	-	-	-	-	-	-	

Win: 1903 Gordon Bennett Trophy

John Jenkins
USA. Born: c1888, Cardiff, Wales (GB). Died: 1948, Brownsville, Texas

formula	years	starts (DNS)	wins	2nd	3rd	4th	5th	6th	PP	FL	points
Indy 500	1911-13	3	-	-	-	-	-	-	-	-	

Champcar win: 1 – 1911 Cincinnati race 1

Denis Jenkinson
GB. Born: 11.12.1920, London. Died: 29.11.1996, London

formula	years	starts (DNS)	wins	2nd	3rd	4th	5th	6th	PP	FL	points
SC W	1955		1	-	-	-	-	-	-	-	

Win: 1955 Mille Miglia

Bill Jennings
ZA
1954, 1956 and 1957 South African Drivers' Champion

Ross Jensen
NZ. Born: 7.7.1925
1957 and 1958 New Zealand Gold Star Champion

Syd Jensen
NZ
1960 New Zealand Gold Star Champion

Cesar Jimenez
MEX. Born: 4.7.1969
1992 Mexican F3 Champion

Gilberto Jimenez
MEX. Born: 24.4.1958
1985 and 1986 Mexican Formula K Champion

Gilberto Jimenez Jr
MEX
2001 Mexican F3 Champion

George Joermann
USA

Champcar win: 1 – 1912 Santa Monica race 1

Reinhold Joest
D. Born: 24.4.1937, Oberabtsteinach
1977 European Sports Car Champion (class 1), 1978 Interserie Champion

formula	years	starts (DNS)	wins	2nd	3rd	4th	5th	6th	PP	FL	points
Le Mans	1969-81	9	-	1	2	1	-	1	-	-	
SC W	1964-81		4	7	7	6	5	4	3	1	

Wins: 1976 Nurburgring, 1979 Dijon, Brands Hatch, 1980 Daytona 24 hrs

F2 E	1976	1 (1)	-	-	-	-	-	-	-	-	0

Mikael "Micke" Johansson
S. Born: 18.5.1962
1987 and 1988 Swedish F3 Champion

Stefan Johansson
S. Born: 8.9.1956, Vaxjo
2001 European Le Mans Series Champion, 1980 British F3 Champion

formula	years	starts (DNS)	wins	2nd	3rd	4th	5th	6th	PP	FL	points
F1 W	1980-91	79 (24)	-	4	8	7	4	3	-	-	88

Best championship: 1986, 5th. Best qualifying: 2nd. Teams: Shadow, Spirit, Tyrrell, Toleman, Ferrari, McLaren, Ligier, Onyx, AGS, Footwork

Le Mans	1983-2001	10	1	-	-	-	1	2	-	-	

Win: 1997 Le Mans 24 hrs

SC W	1982-92		1	3	-	1	1	2	-	-	

Win: 1988 Spa. Best championship: 1983, 11th. SRWC win: 1 – 1997 Donington

F2 E	1979-82	26 (1)	2	1	1	4	-	2	5	-	42

Wins: 1981 Hockenheim, Mantorp Park. Best championship: 1981, 3rd

Indy 500	1993-95	3	-	-	-	-	-	-	-	-	
CART	1992-96	73 (1)	-	-	4	4	4	6	-	-	

Other major wins: 1984 and 1997 Sebring 12 hrs

Ulf Johansson
S. Born: 1.7.1964
1997 Swedish F3 Champion

Gordon Johncock
USA. Born: 5.8.1936, Hastings, Michigan
1976 Champcar Champion

formula	years	starts (DNS)	wins	2nd	3rd	4th	5th	6th	PP	FL	points
Indy 500	1965-92	24	2	-	2	3	1	2	-	4	

Wins: 1973 and 1982 Indianapolis 500

Pre-CART Champcar wins: 20 (19 plus 1 non-championship USAC race in 1982) – 1965 Milwaukee race 3, 1967 Milwaukee race 1, Hanford, 1968 Hanford race 1, Langhorne race 1, 1969 Castle Rock, Brainerd race 1, 1973 Indianapolis 500, Trenton, Phoenix, 1974 Milwaukee race 2, Phoenix, 1975 Trenton, 1976 Michigan, Trenton, 1977 Michigan, Phoenix, 1978 Phoenix, Trenton, 1982 Indianapolis 500 (non-championship)

CART	1979-92	73 (4)	5	4	6	7	5	8	5	1	

Wins: 1979 Phoenix, Michigan race 1, 1982 Milwaukee, Michigan 500, 1983 Atlanta. Best championship: 1979, 3rd

Bobby Johns
USA. Born: 22.5.1934

formula	years	starts (DNS)	wins	2nd	3rd	4th	5th	6th	PP	FL	points
Indy 500	1965-69	2	-	-	-	-	-	-	-	-	

NASCAR wins: 2

Amos Johnson
USA. Born: 9.4.1941

formula	years	starts (DNS)	wins	2nd	3rd	4th	5th	6th	PP	FL	points
SC W	1970-92		1	-	-	-	-	-	-	-	

Win: 1981 Daytona. Best championship: 1981, 16th

Dick Johnson
AUS. Born: 26.4.1945
1981, 1982, 1984, 1988 and 1989 Australian Touring Car Champion
Major wins: 1981, 1989 and 1994 Bathurst

Joe Lee Johnson
USA. Born: 9.11.1929, Cowpens, South Carolina
NASCAR wins: 2 including 1960 World 600

Robert "Junior" Johnson
USA. Born: 28.6.1931
NASCAR wins: 50 including 1960 Daytona 500

Ken Johnson
USA. Born: 28.11.1962
1985 SCCA Super Vee champion

formula	years	starts (DNS)	wins	2nd	3rd	4th	5th	6th	PP	FL	points
F3000 INT	1986	3 (2)	-	-	-	-	-	-	-	-	0
CART	1988-89	2	-	-	-	-	-	-	-	-	

Jimmie Johnson
USA. Born: 17.9.1975, El Cajon, California
NASCAR wins: 3 (all modern era)

Leslie Johnson
GB. Born: 22.3.1912, Walthamstow, London. Died: 8.6.1959, Withington, Gloucestershire, heart attack

formula	years	starts (DNS)	wins	2nd	3rd	4th	5th	6th	PP	FL	points
F1 W	1950	1	-	-	-	-	-	-	-	-	0

Best result: no finishes. Best qualifying: 12th. Team: ERA

GP Pre-50	1947-48	2 (1)	-	-	-	-	-	-	-	-	
Le Mans	1949-53	5	-	-	1	-	-	-	-	-	

Major win: 1948 Spa 24 hrs

Van Johnson
USA. Born: 4.2.1927, Greely, California. Died: 19.7.1959, Williams Grove, Pennsylvania
Champcar win: 1 – 1959 Langhorne

Bruce Johnstone
ZA. Born: 30.1.1937, Durban

formula	years	starts (DNS)	wins	2nd	3rd	4th	5th	6th	PP	FL	points
F1 W	1962	1	-	-	-	-	-	-	-	-	0

Best result: 9th. Best qualifying: no times set. Team: driver

Parker Johnstone
USA. Born: 27.5.1961, Fort Benning, Georgia
1991, 1992 and 1993 IMSA Lights Champion

formula	years	starts (DNS)	wins	2nd	3rd	4th	5th	6th	PP	FL	points
CART	1994-97	45 (1)	-	1	-	-	2	-	1	1	

Alan Jones
AUS. Born: 2.11.1946, Melbourne, Victoria
1980 F1 World Champion, 1978 Can-Am Champion

formula	years	starts (DNS)	wins	2nd	3rd	4th	5th	6th	PP	FL	points
F1 W	1975-86	116 (1)	12	7	5	8	5	2	6	13	206

Wins: 1977 Austrian GP, 1979 German GP, Austrian GP, Dutch GP, Canadian GP, 1980 Argentinian GP, French GP, British GP, Canadian GP, United States GP, 1981 Long Beach GP, Las Vegas GP. Best championship: 1980, 1st. Best qualifying: 1st. Teams: Harry Stiller, Hill, Surtees, Shadow, Williams, Arrows, Haas Lola

Le Mans	1984-87	2	-	-	-	-	-	1	-	-	
SC W	1975-87		-	-	-	1	1	-	-	-	
F2 E	1977	1	-	-	-	-	-	-	-	-	0
CART	1985	1	-	-	1	-	-	-	-	-	

Non-championship F1 win: 1980 Spanish GP
Other Major win: 1980 Australian GP

Brad Jones
AUS. Born: 2.4.1960, Albury, New South Wales
1996 and 1998 Australian Super Touring Car Champion

Davy Jones
USA. Born: 1.6.1964, Chicago, Illinois

formula	years	starts (DNS)	wins	2nd	3rd	4th	5th	6th	PP	FL	points
Le Mans	1988-96	5	1	1	-	-	-	-	-	-	

Win: 1996 Le Mans 24 hrs

SC W	1988-92		-	1	1	-	-	-	-	-	

Best championship: 1990, 20th

Indy 500	1987-96	5	-	-	-	-	-	-	-	-	
CART	1987-96	16 (1)	-	-	-	-	-	-	-	-	
IRL	1996	1	-	1	-	-	-	-	-	-	

Other major wins: 1984 (January) and 1987 New Zealand GP, 1990 Daytona 24 hrs

John Jones
CDN. Born: 19.10.1965, Thunder Bay, Ontario
1985 IMSA GTO Champion

formula	years	starts (DNS)	wins	2nd	3rd	4th	5th	6th	PP	FL	points
F3000 INT	1986-90	28 (5)	-	1	1	1	1	1	-	16	

Best championship: 1987, 11th

Indy 500	1989	1	-	-	-	-	-	-	-	-	
CART	1988-92	41	-	-	-	-	-	-	-	-	

Best championship: 1988, 10th

PJ Jones
USA. Born: 23.4.1969, Torrance, California

formula	years	starts (DNS)	wins	2nd	3rd	4th	5th	6th	PP	FL	points
CART	1996-99	58	-	1	-	-	-	-	-	-	

Major win: 1993 Daytona 24 hrs

Parnelli Jones
USA. Born: 12.8.1933, Texarkana, Arkansas
1970 Trans-Am Champion

formula	years	starts (DNS)	wins	2nd	3rd	4th	5th	6th	PP	FL	points
Indy 500	1961-67	7	1	1	-	-	1	2	2		

Win: 1963 Indianapolis 500
Champcar wins: 6 – 1961 Phoenix, 1962 Indiana State Fairgrounds, 1963 Indianapolis 500, 1964 Milwaukee race 2, Trenton race 3, 1965 Milwaukee race 1
NASCAR wins: 4

Stan Jones
AUS
1958 Australian Gold Star Champion
Major wins: 1954 New Zealand GP, 1959 Australian GP

Tom Jones
USA. Born: 26.4.1943, Dallas, Texas

formula	years	starts (DNS)	wins	2nd	3rd	4th	5th	6th	PP	FL	points
F1 W	1967	0 (1)	-	-	-	-	-	-	-	-	0

Best result: no starts. Best qualifying: 19th. Team: driver

Niclas Jonsson
S. Born: 4.8.1967, Bankeryd
1990 and 1991 Swedish F3 Champion

formula	years	starts (DNS)	wins	2nd	3rd	4th	5th	6th	PP	FL	points
IRL	1999-2000	3 (1)	-	-	-	-	-	-	-	-	

Eddy Joosen
B

formula	years	starts (DNS)	wins	2nd	3rd	4th	5th	6th	PP	FL	points
Le Mans	1977	1	-	-	-	-	-	-	-	-	
SC W	1977-81		-	1	1	-	-	-	-	-	

Major wins: 1977 and 1982 Spa 24 hrs, 1978 Tourist Trophy (Silverstone)

Mike Jordan
GB. Born: 17.2.1958
2001 British GT Champion (with David Warnock)
GT FIA win: 1 – 2001 Nurburgring

Deon Joubert
ZA. Born: 18.4.1965, Cape Town
1992 South African Touring Car Champion

Juan Jover

E. Born: 23.11.1903, Barcelona. Died: 28.6.1960, Sitges

formula	years	starts (DNS)	wins	2nd	3rd	4th	5th	6th	PP	FL	points
F1 W	1951	0 (1)	-	-	-	-	-	-	-	-	0

Best result: no starts. Best qualifying: 18th. Team: Milano

GP Pre-50	1948	0 (1)	-	-	-	-	-	-	-	-	
Le Mans	1949	1	-	1	-	-	-	-			

Paulo Judice

BR

1992 and 1993 Brazilian Touring Car Champion (with Andreas Mattheis)

Elton Julian

USA. Born: 16.8.1974, Canary Isles (E)

formula	years	starts (DNS)	wins	2nd	3rd	4th	5th	6th	PP	FL	points
F3000 INT	1994-96	12 (1)	-	-	-	-	1	-	-	-	2

Best championship: 1996, 13th

Manuel Juncosa

E

1976 Spanish Touring Car Champion

Carl Junker

AUS

Major win: 1931 Australian GP

Bruno Junqueira

BR. Born: 4.11.1976, Belo Horizonte

2000 FIA F3000 Champion, 1997 Sud-Am F3 Champion

formula	years	starts (DNS)	wins	2nd	3rd	4th	5th	6th	PP	FL	points
F3000 INT	1998-2000	31 (1)	5	2	-	1	2	2	3	1	71

Wins: 1999 Hockenheim, 2000 Barcelona, Nurburgring, Monaco, Hungaroring.

Best championship: 2000, 1st

Indy 500	2001-02	2	-	-	-	-	1	-	1	-	
CART	2001-02	39 (1)	3	2	2	4	2	-	5	4	

Wins: 2001 Elkhart Lake, 2002 Motegi, Denver. Best championship: 2002, 2nd

IRL	2001-02	2	-	-	-	-	1	-	1	-	

Morne Jurgens

ZA

1996 South African Formula GTi Champion

K

Masahiko Kageyama

J. Born: 8.8.1963, Kanagawa

1993, 1994 and 1995 Japanese GT Champion, 1993 Japanese Touring Car Champion, 1989 Japanese F3 Champion

formula	years	starts (DNS)	wins	2nd	3rd	4th	5th	6th	PP	FL	points
Le Mans	1995-2000	5	-	-	1	-	-	1	-	-	

Masemi Kageyama

J. Born: 2.5.1967, Kanagawa

1998 Japanese GT Champion (with Erik Comas)

formula	years	starts (DNS)	wins	2nd	3rd	4th	5th	6th	PP	FL	points
Le Mans	1996-2000	3	-	-	-	-	-	1	-	-	

Tomas Kaiser

S. Born: 2.11.1956, Saelen

formula	years	starts (DNS)	wins	2nd	3rd	4th	5th	6th	PP	FL	points
F2 E	1982-84	21 (2)	-	-	-	1	-	-	-	-	3

Best championship: 1984, 11th

F3000 INT	1985-87	27 (3)	-	-	-	2	1	-	-	-	7

Best championship: 1986, 13th

Tony Kanaan

BR. Born: 31.12.1974, Salvador, Bahia

1997 CART Indy Lights Champion

formula	years	starts (DNS)	wins	2nd	3rd	4th	5th	6th	PP	FL	points
Indy 500	2002	1	-	-	-	-	-	-	-	-	
CART	1998-2002	93 (3)	1	-	5	5	5	7	4	5	

Win: 1999 US 500 (Michigan). Best championships: 1998 and 2001, 9th

IRL	2002	1	-	-	-	-	-	-	-	-	

Jonny Kane

GB. Born: 14.5.1973, Comber, Northern Ireland

1997 British F3 Champion

formula	years	starts (DNS)	wins	2nd	3rd	4th	5th	6th	PP	FL	points
Le Mans	2001-02	2	-	-	-	-	-	-	-	-	
F3000 INT	1998	4	-	-	-	-	-	-	-	-	0

Simon Kane

AUS. Born: 9.10.1967

1990 Australian Formula Holden Champion

formula	years	starts (DNS)	wins	2nd	3rd	4th	5th	6th	PP	FL	points
F3000 INT	1991	0 (2)	-	-	-	-	-	-	-	-	0

Toshihiro Kaneishi

J. Born: 19.12.1978, Osaka

2001 German F3 Champion

Oswald Karch

D. Born: 6.3.1917, Ludwigshafen

formula	years	starts (DNS)	wins	2nd	3rd	4th	5th	6th	PP	FL	points
F1 W	1953	1	-	-	-	-	-	-	-	-	0

Best result: no finishes. Best qualifying: 34th. Team: driver

Tomas Karhenek

CS

1995 Czech F3 Champion

Gunnar Karlsson

S

1963 Swedish Formula Junior Champion

Mikael Karlsson

S. Born: 25.5.1972

2000 Nordic F3 Champion, 2000 Swedish F3 Champion

Niclas Karlsson

S. Born: 24.1.1974

1997 Nordic F3 Champion

Narain Karthikeyan

IND. Born: 14.1.1976, Chennai

Major win: 2000 Korea F3

Ukyo Katayama

J. Born: 29.5.1963, Tokyo

1991 Japanese F3000 Champion

formula	years	starts (DNS)	wins	2nd	3rd	4th	5th	6th	PP	FL	points
F1 W	1992-97	95 (2)	-	-	-	-	2	1	-	-	5

Best championship: 1994, 17th. Best qualifying: 5th. Teams: Larrousse, Tyrrell, Minardi

Le Mans	1988-2002	5	-	1	-	-	-	-	-	1	
F3000 INT	1989	2 (2)	-	-	-	-	-	-	-	-	0

Hiroki Katoh

J. Born: 23.2.1968, Kanagawa

formula	years	starts (DNS)	wins	2nd	3rd	4th	5th	6th	PP	FL	points
Le Mans	1999-2002	4	-	-	-	-	1	-	-	-	

SRWC wins: 2 – 2001 Brno, Mondello Park

Hans-Peter Kaufmann

CH. Born: 4.9.1953

1983 Swiss F3 Champion

formula	years	starts (DNS)	wins	2nd	3rd	4th	5th	6th	PP	FL	points
SC W	1987		-	-	-	-	-	1	-	-	

Wolfgang Kaufmann
D. Born: 24.1.1964, Dernbach, Friburg

formula	years	starts (DNS)	wins	2nd	3rd	4th	5th	6th	PP	FL	points
Le Mans	1995-2000	3	-	-	-	-	-	-	-	-	

GT FIA win: 1 – 2000 Lausitzring

Willi Kauhsen
D

1967 European Touring Car Champion (1000cc class)

formula	years	starts (DNS)	wins	2nd	3rd	4th	5th	6th	PP	FL	points
Le Mans	1969-71	3	-	1	-	-	-	-	-	-	
SC W	1965-74		-	1	-	2	3	4	-	-	

Major win: 1968 Spa 24 hrs

Christian Kautz
CH. Born: 23.11.1913. Died: 4.7.1948, Bremgarten, Swiss GP

formula	years	starts (DNS)	wins	2nd	3rd	4th	5th	6th	PP	FL	points
GP Pre-50	1936-48	13 (2)	-	-	1	1	-	2	-	-	

Kamrick "Ken" Kavanagh
AUS. Born: 12.12.1923, Melbourne, Victoria

formula	years	starts (DNS)	wins	2nd	3rd	4th	5th	6th	PP	FL	points
F1 W	1958	0 (2)	-	-	-	-	-	-	-	-	0

Best result: no starts. Best qualifying: 19th. Team: driver

Hiroshi Kazato
J. Born: 13.3.1949. Died: 1974

formula	years	starts (DNS)	wins	2nd	3rd	4th	5th	6th	PP	FL	points
F2 E	1972-73	21 (5)	-	-	-	-	2	1	-	-	7

Best championship: 1973, 21st

Ray Keech
USA. Born: 1.5.1900, Coatesville, Pennsylvania. Died: 15.6.1929, Altoona, Pennsylvania, racing

formula	years	starts (DNS)	wins	2nd	3rd	4th	5th	6th	PP	FL	points
Indy 500	1928-29	2	1	-	1	-	-	-	-	-	

Win: 1929 Indianapolis 500

Champcar wins: 4 – 1928 Detroit, Salem race 2, Syracuse, 1929 Indianapolis 500

Rupert Keegan
GB. Born: 26.2.1955, Westcliff-on-Sea, Essex

1979 British F1 Champion, 1976 BP British F3 Champion

formula	years	starts (DNS)	wins	2nd	3rd	4th	5th	6th	PP	FL	points
F1 W	1977-82	25 (12)	-	-	-	-	-	-	-	-	0

Best result: 7th. Best qualifying: 13th. Teams: Hesketh, Surtees, RAM, March

Le Mans	1982-95	4	-	-	-	-	1	-	-	-	
SC W	1974-92		-	1	2	-	1	-	-	-	

Best championship: 1984, 12th

F2 E	1976-79	2	-	-	-	-	-	-	-	-	0
CART	1985	3	-	-	-	-	-	-	-	-	

F1 GB wins: 1979 Mallory Park, Snetterton, Donington, Snetterton, Thruxton

Bruce Keen
USA. Born: n/a. Died: 13.10.1964, Indianapolis, Indiana

Champcar win: 1 – 1911 Santa Monica race 1

Eddie Keizan
ZA. Born: 12.9.1944, Johannesburg

formula	years	starts (DNS)	wins	2nd	3rd	4th	5th	6th	PP	FL	points
F1 W	1973-75	3	-	-	-	-	-	-	-	-	0

Best result: 13th. Best qualifying: 22nd. Teams: Alex Blignaut, Team Gunston

F1 ZA wins: 1972 Welkom, 1973 Bulawayo

Helmut Kelleners
D. Born: 29.12.1938

1980 (with Siegfried Muller jr), 1981 and 1982 (both with Umberto Grano) European Touring Car Champion

formula	years	starts (DNS)	wins	2nd	3rd	4th	5th	6th	PP	FL	points
Le Mans	1969-80	3	-	-	-	-	-	1	-	-	
SC W	1963-82		-	2	3	1	3	-	-		

Major wins: 1968 and 1970 Spa 24 hrs, 1984 Tourist Trophy (Silverstone)

Ralf Kelleners
D. Born: 18.5.1968, Dinslaken

1994 German GT Champion

formula	years	starts (DNS)	wins	2nd	3rd	4th	5th	6th	PP	FL	points
Le Mans	1996-2001	6	-	-	-	-	-	-	-	-	

GT FIA win: 1 – 1996 Zhuhai. SRWC win: 1 – 2000 Kyalami

Al Keller
USA. Born: 11.4.1920, Alexandria Bay, New York State. Died: 19.11.1961, Phoenix, Arizona

formula	years	starts (DNS)	wins	2nd	3rd	4th	5th	6th	PP	FL	points
Indy 500	1955-61	6	-	-	-	-	1	-	-	-	

NASCAR wins: 1

Joe Kelly
IRL. Born: 13.3.1913, Dublin. Died: 28.11.1993, Neston, Cheshire

formula	years	starts (DNS)	wins	2nd	3rd	4th	5th	6th	PP	FL	points
F1 W	1950-51	2	-	-	-	-	-	-	-	-	0

Best result: no finishes. Best qualifying: 18th. Team: driver

Rick Kelly
AUS. Born: 17.1.1983, Mildura, Victoria

2001 Australian Formula Holden Champion

Steve Kempton
GB. Born: 8.2.1960, Nottingham

1987 European F3 Cup winner

formula	years	starts (DNS)	wins	2nd	3rd	4th	5th	6th	PP	FL	points
Le Mans	1984	1	-	-	-	-	-	-	-	-	
F3000 INT	1988	1 (2)	-	-	-	-	-	-	-	-	0

Tom Kendall
USA. Born: 17.10.1966

1990, 1995, 1996 and 1997 Trans-Am Champion, 1986, 1987 and 1988 IMSA GTU Champion, 1993 IMSA GTS Champion

formula	years	starts (DNS)	wins	2nd	3rd	4th	5th	6th	PP	FL	points
Le Mans	2000	1	-	-	-	-	-	-	-	-	

David Kennedy
IRL. Born: 15.1.1953, Sligo

formula	years	starts (DNS)	wins	2nd	3rd	4th	5th	6th	PP	FL	points
F1 W	1980	0 (7)	-	-	-	-	-	-	-	-	0

Best result: no starts. Best qualifying: 25th. Team: Shadow

Le Mans	1983-91	9	-	-	-	-	1	-	-	-	
SC W	1981-92		-	-	-	1	2	-	-	-	

Best championship: 1991, 19th

F1 GB wins: 1978 Snetterton, 1979 Zolder, Oulton Park Gold Cup, Mallory Park

Brady Kennett
NZ

Major win: 1995 New Zealand GP

Matt Kenseth
USA. Born: 10.3.1972, Madison, Wisconsin

NASCAR wins: 6 (in Modern era) – including 2000 World 600

Robbie Kerr
GB. Born: 26.9.1979

2002 British F3 Champion

Loris Kessel
CH. Born: 1.4.1950, Lugano

formula	years	starts (DNS)	wins	2nd	3rd	4th	5th	6th	PP	FL	points
F1 W	1976-77	3 (4)	-	-	-	-	-	-	-	-	0

Best result: 12th. Best qualifying: 23rd. Teams: RAM, Jolly Club

Le Mans	1993	1	-	-	-	-	-	-	-	-	
F2 E	1974-81	15 (2)	-	-	-	2	-	-	-	-	7

Best championship: 1975, 16th

Bruce Kessler
USA. Born: 23.3.1936, Seattle, Washington State

formula	years	starts (DNS)	wins	2nd	3rd	4th	5th	6th	PP	FL	points
F1 W	1958	0 (1)	-	-	-	-	-	-	-	-	0

Best result: no starts. Best qualifying: 21st. Team: Bernie Ecclestone

Le Mans	1958	1	-	-	-	-	-	-			
SC W	1956-58		-	-	-	-	1	-	-		

Mario Ketterer
CH

formula	years	starts (DNS)	wins	2nd	3rd	4th	5th	6th	PP	FL	points
Le Mans	1980	1	-	-	-	-	-	-			
SC W	1979-84		1	-	1	1	-	-	-		

Win: 1979 Dijon

Michael Keyser
USA

formula	years	starts (DNS)	wins	2nd	3rd	4th	5th	6th	PP	FL	points
Le Mans	1972-76	3	-	-	-	-	-	-			
SC W	1971-80		-	1	-	-	-	-			

Major win: 1976 Sebring 12 hrs

Glen Kidston
GB. Born: 23.1.1899, London. Died: 5.5.1931, Van Reenan, Drakensberg Mountains (ZA), aircraft accident

formula	years	starts (DNS)	wins	2nd	3rd	4th	5th	6th	PP	FL	points
Le Mans	1929-30	2	1	1	-	-	-	-			

Win: 1930 Le Mans 24 hrs

John Kieper
USA

NASCAR wins: 1

Nicolas Kiesa
DK. Born: 3.3.1978, Copenhagen

formula	years	starts (DNS)	wins	2nd	3rd	4th	5th	6th	PP	FL	points
F3000 INT	2002	12	-	-	-	-	1	1	-	-	3

Best championship: 2002, 12th

Tom Kincaid
USA. Born: n/a. Died: 6.7.1910, Indianapolis, testing

Champcar wins: 2 – 1910 Atlanta race 4, Indianapolis race 1

Leo Kinnunen
SF. Born: 5.8.1943, Tampere
1971, 1972 and 1973 Interserie Champion

formula	years	starts (DNS)	wins	2nd	3rd	4th	5th	6th	PP	FL	points
F1 W	1974	1 (5)	-	-	-	-	-	-	-	-	0

Best result: no finishes. Best qualifying: 26th. Team: AAW

Le Mans	1970-76	2	-	-	-	-	-	-			
SC W	1970-77		4	2	4	2	-	-	-	2	

Wins: 1970 Daytona 24 hrs, Brands Hatch, Monza, Watkins Glen

Harold Kite
USA

NASCAR wins: 1

Marcel Klaey
CH
1995 European Renault Clio Cup Champion

Art Klein
USA. Born: 1889, Cleveland, Ohio. Died: 19??

formula	years	starts (DNS)	wins	2nd	3rd	4th	5th	6th	PP	FL	points
GP Pre-50	1915	1	-	-	-	-	-	-			
Indy 500	1914-22	5	-	-	-	-	-	-			

Champcar win: 1 – 1920 Beverly Hills race 2

Hans Klenk
D. Born: 28.10.1919, Kunzelsau

formula	years	starts (DNS)	wins	2nd	3rd	4th	5th	6th	PP	FL	points
F1 W	1952	1	-	-	-	-	-	-	-	-	0

Best result: no finishes. Best qualifying: no times set. Team: driver

Le Mans	1952										

Major win: 1952 Carrera Panamericana

Piet de Klerk
ZA. Born: 16.3.1936, Pilgrim's Rest, Transvaal

formula	years	starts (DNS)	wins	2nd	3rd	4th	5th	6th	PP	FL	points
F1 W	1963-70	4	-	-	-	-	-	-	-	-	0

Best result: 10th. Best qualifying: 16th. Teams: Otelle Nucci, Jack Holme, Team Gunston

Le Mans	1966-67	2	-	-	-	-	1	-			
SC W	1966-67		-	-	-	-	1	-			

F1 ZA win: 1970 Kyalami

Karl Kling
D. Born: 16.9.1910, Giessen. Died: 19.3.2003

formula	years	starts (DNS)	wins	2nd	3rd	4th	5th	6th	PP	FL	points
F1 W	1954-55	11	-	1	1	2	1	-	-	1	17

Best championship: 1954, 5th. Best qualifying: 2nd. Team: Mercedes-Benz

Le Mans	1952-55	3	-	-	-	-	-	-			
SC W	1953-55		-	2	1	-	-	-			

Non-championship F1 win: 1954 Berlin GP (Avus)
Other Major win: 1952 Carrera Panamericana

Ernst Klodwig
DDR. Born: 23.5.1903, Aschersleben. Died: 15.4.1973, Hamburg

formula	years	starts (DNS)	wins	2nd	3rd	4th	5th	6th	PP	FL	points
F1 W	1952-53	2	-	-	-	-	-	-	-	-	0

Best result: 15th. Best qualifying: 32nd. Team: driver

Chris Kneifel
USA. Born: 23.4.1961, Chicago, Illinois

formula	years	starts (DNS)	wins	2nd	3rd	4th	5th	6th	PP	FL	points
Le Mans	2000	1	-	-	-	-	-	-			
Indy 500	1983-84	2	-	-	-	-	-	-			
CART	1982-84	19 (3)	-	-	-	-	-	-			

Major win: 2001 Daytona 24 hrs

William Knipper
USA. Born: n/a. Died: 19??

formula	years	starts (DNS)	wins	2nd	3rd	4th	5th	6th	PP	FL	points
Indy 500	1911-14	4	-	-	-	1	-	1	-	-	

Champcar win: 1 – 1909 Lowell race 2

Rene de Knyff
F. Born: 1864, Belgium. Died: 1954

formula	years	starts (DNS)	wins	2nd	3rd	4th	5th	6th	PP	FL	points
GP Pre-50	1900-03	3	-	1	-	-	-	-			

City-to-city win: 1899 Tour de France Automobile

Koentges
B
1993 Belgian Belcar GT Champion (with Wuydts and Eliano)

Takashi Kogure
J. Born: 1.8.1980, Kangawa
2002 Japanese F3 Champion

Helmuth Koinigg
A. Born: 3.11.1948, Vienna. Died: 6.10.1974, Watkins Glen, United States GP

formula	years	starts (DNS)	wins	2nd	3rd	4th	5th	6th	PP	FL	points
F1 W	1974	2 (1)	-	-	-	-	-	-	-	-	0

Best result: 10th. Best qualifying: 22nd. Teams: Scuderia Finotto, Surtees

Le Mans	1973-74	2	-	-	-	-	-	-			
F2 E	1974	1	-	-	-	-	-	-			0

Jari Koivisto
SF. Born: 3.10.1968
2001 Finnish F3 Champion

Kristian Kolby

DK. Born: 9.10.1978, Ringkobing

formula	years	starts (DNS)	wins	2nd	3rd	4th	5th	6th	PP	FL	points
Le Mans	2000	1	-	-	-	-	-	-	-	-	
F3000 INT	2000-02	9 (4)	-	-	-	-	1	-	-	-	2

Best championship: 2000, 23rd

Gregory Komarov

R. Born: 27.10.1963, Kursk
2002 Russian Touring Car Champion

Franz Konrad

A. Born: 8.6.1951, Graz
1983 German F3 Champion

formula	years	starts (DNS)	wins	2nd	3rd	4th	5th	6th	PP	FL	points
Le Mans	1978-2002	16	-	1	-	1	1	-	-	-	
SC W	1977-92		-	2	2	4	3	4	-	-	
F2 E	1980-82	6 (1)	-	-	-	-	-	-	-	-	0

Josef Kopecky

CS
1995 Czech Touring Car Champion

Helmut Kopp

A
1996 Czech F3 Champion

Walter Kornossa

D
1951 German F3 Champion

Michael Korten

D
1979 German F3 Champion

formula	years	starts (DNS)	wins	2nd	3rd	4th	5th	6th	PP	FL	points
Le Mans	1980	1	-	-	-	-	-	-	-	-	
F2 E	1978-80	2 (2)	-	-	-	-	-	-	-	-	0

F3 E win: 1 – 1979 Kassel-Calden

Jaroslav Kostelecky

CS
2001 and 2002 Austrian F3 Champion

Freddy Kottulinsky

S
1966 Swedish F3 Champion

formula	years	starts (DNS)	wins	2nd	3rd	4th	5th	6th	PP	FL	points
SC W	1972-81		-	-	2	-	1	-	-	-	
F2 E	1975-77	21 (3)	-	-	-	-	-	-	-	-	1

Best championship: 1976, 17th
F3 E win: 1 – 1975 Nurburgring

Peter Kox

NL. Born: 23.2.1964, Eindhoven
2001 European Super Production Champion, 1989 European GM-Lotus Champion

formula	years	starts (DNS)	wins	2nd	3rd	4th	5th	6th	PP	FL	points
Le Mans	1996-2002	5	-	-	1	1	-	-	-	-	
F3000 INT	1988	1	-	-	-	-	-	-	-	-	0

GT FIA wins: 3 – 1996 Nurburgring, 1997 Silverstone, 2001 A1 Ring
Other Major win: 1995 Spa 24 hrs

Mikko Kozarowitsky

SF. Born: 17.5.1948, Helsinki

formula	years	starts (DNS)	wins	2nd	3rd	4th	5th	6th	PP	FL	points
F1 W	1977	0 (2)	-	-	-	-	-	-	-	-	0

Best result: no starts. Best qualifying: 31st. Team: RAM

F2 E	1976	4 (2)	-	-	-	-	-	-	-	-	0

Fred Krab

NL
1980 European FF2000 Champion

Willi Krakau

D. Born: 4.12.1911, Schonebeck-Felgeleben. Died: 26.4.1995, Peine

formula	years	starts (DNS)	wins	2nd	3rd	4th	5th	6th	PP	FL	points
F1 W	1952	0 (1)	-	-	-	-	-	-	-	-	0

Best result: no starts. Best qualifying: no times set. Team: driver

Rudolf Krause

DDR. Born: 30.3.1907, Ober-Reichenbach. Died: 11.4.1987, Reichenbach

formula	years	starts (DNS)	wins	2nd	3rd	4th	5th	6th	PP	FL	points
F1 W	1952-53	2	-	-	-	-	-	-	-	-	0

Best result: 14th. Best qualifying: 26th. Teams: driver, Dora Greifzu

Toni Krauzer

D
1950 German F3 Champion

Albrecht Krebs

D

formula	years	starts (DNS)	wins	2nd	3rd	4th	5th	6th	PP	FL	points
Le Mans	1976	1	-	-	-	-	-	-	-	-	
SC W	1973-80		1	-	1	-	-	1	-	-	

Win: 1976 Nurburgring

Erwin Kremer

D. Born: 26.6.1937

formula	years	starts (DNS)	wins	2nd	3rd	4th	5th	6th	PP	FL	points
Le Mans	1970-74	5	-	-	-	-	-	-	-	-	
SC W	1969-74		-	-	-	-	-	1	-	-	

Major win: 1968 Spa 24 hrs

Tom Kristensen

DK. Born: 7.7.1967, Hobro
2002 American Le Mans Series Champion, 1991 German F3 Champion, 1993 Japanese F3 Champion

formula	years	starts (DNS)	wins	2nd	3rd	4th	5th	6th	PP	FL	points
Le Mans	1997-2002	6	4	-	-	-	-	-	-	-	2

Wins: 1997, 2000, 2001 and 2002 Le Mans 24 hrs

F3000 INT	1996-97	16 (1)	1	2	2	2	1	4	2		37

Win: 1997 Silverstone. Best championships: 1996 and 1997, 6th
Other major wins: 1999 and 2000 Sebring 12 hrs, 2002 Petit LeMans

Horst Kroll

USA. Born: 16.5.1936, Germany
1986 Can-Am Champion

Michael Krumm

D. Born: 19.3.1970, Reutlingen
1997 Japanese GT Champion (with Pedro de la Rosa), 1994 Japanese F3 Champion

formula	years	starts (DNS)	wins	2nd	3rd	4th	5th	6th	PP	FL	points
Le Mans	1998-2002	3	-	-	1	-	1	-	-	-	
CART	2001	2	-	-	-	-	-	-	-	-	

Peter Kuhn

USA
1980 SCCA Super Vee Champion

formula	years	starts (DNS)	wins	2nd	3rd	4th	5th	6th	PP	FL	points
CART	1984	3 (1)	-	-	-	-	-	-	-	-	

Rolf Kuhn

CH
1995 Swiss Touring Car Champion

Kurt Kuhnke

D. Born: 30.4.1910, Stellin. Died: 8.2.1969, Brunswick

formula	years	starts (DNS)	wins	2nd	3rd	4th	5th	6th	PP	FL	points
F1 W	1963	0 (1)	-	-	-	-	-	-	-	-	0

Best result: no starts. Best qualifying: 26th. Team: driver

Pertti Kuismanen

SF
2001 Belgian Belcar Touring Car Champion (with Karl Hasenbichler)

Larry Kulok
USA
Major win: 1952 Sebring 12 hrs

Alan Kulwicki
USA. Born: 14.12.1954, Greenfield, Wisconsin. Died: 1.4.1993, Tennesee, aircraft accident
1992 NASCAR Champion
NASCAR wins: 5 (all Modern era)

Anthony Kumpen
B. Born: 3.10.1978, Hasselt
1999 (with Stephan Cohen) and 2002 (with Bert Longin) Belgian Belcar GT Champion

formula	years	starts (DNS)	wins	2nd	3rd	4th	5th	6th	PP	FL	points
Le Mans	2001-02	2	-	-	-	-	-	-	-	-	

GT FIA win: 1 – 2002 Donington

Paul Kumpen
B
1994 and 1995 Belgian Belcar GT Champion (both with Albert Vanierschot and Georges Cremer)

Motoharu Kurosawa
J. Born: 1942
1973 Japanese F2000 Champion

formula	years	starts (DNS)	wins	2nd	3rd	4th	5th	6th	PP	FL	points
F2 E	1973	2	-	-	-	-	-	-	-	-	0

Masami Kuwashima
J. Born: 14.9.1950, Kumagaya

formula	years	starts (DNS)	wins	2nd	3rd	4th	5th	6th	PP	FL	points
F1 W	1976	0 (1)	-	-	-	-	-	-	-	-	0

Best result: no starts. Best qualifying: 26th. Team: Williams

F2 E	1974-75	12	-	-	-	1	-	-	-	-	4

Best championship: 1974, 14th

Charles Kwan
HK
1997, 1998 and 1999 Asian Touring Car Champion
Major win: 1993 Macau Guia race

Horst Kwech
AUS
1966 Trans-Am Champion (with Gaston Andrey)

Konstantin Kyritsis
GR
1991 and 1992 Greek F3 Champion

L

Bobby Labonte
USA. Born: 8.5.1964, Corpus Christi, Texas
2000 NASCAR Champion, 2001 IROC Champion
NASCAR wins: 19 (all Modern era) including 1995 World 600

Terry Labonte
USA. Born: 16.11.1956, Corpus Christi, Texas
1984 and 1996 NASCAR Champion, 1989 IROC Champion
NASCAR wins: 21 (all Modern era)

Francois Lacarrau
F
1970 French Formula Renault Champion

formula	years	starts (DNS)	wins	2nd	3rd	4th	5th	6th	PP	FL	points
Le Mans	1968	1	-	-	-	-	-	-	-	-	

Jurgen Laessig
D. Born: 25.2.1943, Tuttlingen

formula	years	starts (DNS)	wins	2nd	3rd	4th	5th	6th	PP	FL	points
Le Mans	1981-97	16	-	1	-	-	1	1	-	-	
SC W	1976-92		1	1	-	6	6	3	-	-	

Win: 1981 Monza. Best championship: 1983, 8th
Other Major win: 1995 Daytona 24 hrs

Jacques Laffite
F. Born: 21.11.1943, Paris
1975 European F2 Champion, 1973 French F3 Champion, 1972 French Formula Renault Champion

formula	years	starts (DNS)	wins	2nd	3rd	4th	5th	6th	PP	FL	points
F1 W	1974-86	176 (4)	6	10	16	7	9	11	7	6	228

Wins: 1977 Swedish GP, 1979 Argentinian GP, Brazilian GP, 1980 German GP, 1981 Austrian GP, Canadian GP. Best championships: 1979, 1980 and 1981, 4th.
Best qualifying: 1st. Teams: Williams, Ligier

Le Mans	1972-96	9	-	-	-	-	-	-	-	-	
SC W	1972-92		3	1	-	-	-	-	-	-	

Wins: 1975 Dijon, Monza, Nurburgring. GT FIA win: 1 – 1994 Zhuhai

F2 E	1974-78	32	7	5	2	-	-	6	6		91

Wins: 1974 Salzburgring, 1975 Estoril, Thruxton, Nurburgring, Pau, Hockenheim race 2, Enna. Best championship: 1975, 1st
Other Major win: 1973 Monaco F3

Andre Lagache
F

formula	years	starts (DNS)	wins	2nd	3rd	4th	5th	6th	PP	FL	points
Le Mans	1923-25	3	1	-	-	-	-	-	-	2	

Win: 1923 Le Mans 24 hrs
Other Major win: 1925 Spa 24 hrs

Franck Lagorce
F. Born: 1.9.1968, L'Hay-les-Roses, near Paris
1996 European Renault Spider Champion, 1992 French F3 Champion

formula	years	starts (DNS)	wins	2nd	3rd	4th	5th	6th	PP	FL	points
F1 W	1994	2	-	-	-	-	-	-	-	-	0

Best result: 11th. Best qualifying: 20th. Team: Ligier

Le Mans	1994-2002	9	-	-	-	-	1	-	-	-	
F3000 INT	1993-94	16 (1)	4	2	-	1	2	-	5	4	55

Wins: 1993 Magny-Cours, Nogaro, 1994 Silverstone, Hockenheim. Best championship: 1994, 2nd

Chris Lambert
GB. Born: c1944. Died: 28.7.1968, Zandvoort F2 race

formula	years	starts (DNS)	wins	2nd	3rd	4th	5th	6th	PP	FL	points
F2 E	1967-68	9	-	-	-	1	-	-	-	-	3

Best championship: 1968, 15th

Jan Lammers
NL. Born: 2.6.1956, Zandvoort
2002 Sports Racing World Champion (with Val Hillebrand), 1978 European F3 Champion, 1983 and 1984 Renault Europa Cup Champion

formula	years	starts (DNS)	wins	2nd	3rd	4th	5th	6th	PP	FL	points
F1 W	1979-92	23 (18)	-	-	-	-	-	-	-	-	0

Best result: 9th. Best qualifying: 4th. Teams: Shadow, ATS, Ensign, Theodore, March

Le Mans	1983-2002	15	1	1	-	1	1	1	-	1	
SC W	1979-92		5	10	7	5	7	2	2	5	

Wins: 1984 Brands Hatch, 1987 Jarama, Monza, Fuji, 1988 Le Mans 24 hrs.
Best championship: 1987, 2nd. SRWC wins: 4 – 2001 Nurburgring, 2002 Brno, Magny-Cours, Dijon

F2 E	1980	1	-	-	-	-	-	-	-	-	0
F3000 INT	1986-95	10	-	-	-	-	1	-	-	-	3

Best championship: 1993, 15th

CART	1985-86	10	-	-	-	-	-	1	-	-	

F3 E wins: 4 – 1978 Zandvoort, Monza, Magny-Cours, Karlskoga
Other major wins: 1988 and 1990 Daytona 24 hrs, 1995 Kyalami F3000

E Lamont

NZ
1993 New Zealand Touring Car Champion

Pedro Lamy

P. Born: 20.3.1972, Aldeia Galega
1998 FIA GT2 class Champion (with Olivier Beretta), 1992 German F3
Champion, 1991 European GM-Lotus Champion

formula	years	starts (DNS)	wins	2nd	3rd	4th	5th	6th	PP	FL	points
F1 W	1993-96	32	-	-	-	-	-	1	-	-	1

Best championship: 1995, 17th. Best qualifying: 14th. Teams: Lotus, Minardi

| Le Mans | 1997-2002 | 5 | - | - | - | 1 | 2 | - | - | |
| F3000 INT | 1993 | 8 (1) | 1 | 2 | 1 | 2 | - | - | 2 | 2 | 31 |

Win: 1993 Pau. Best championship: 1993, 2nd

Other Major win: 1992 Marlboro Masters (Zandvoort)

Angelo Lancellotti

I. Born: 14.10.1977, Gardone Val Trompia
1999 Sports Racing SR2 class Champion

Francesco "Chico" Landi

BR. Born: 14.7.1907, Sao Paulo. Died: 7.6.1989, Sao Paulo

formula	years	starts (DNS)	wins	2nd	3rd	4th	5th	6th	PP	FL	points
F1 W	1951-56	6	-	-	1	-	-	-	-	-	1.5

Best championship: 1956, 25th. Best qualifying: 11th. Teams: Ferrari, Bandeirantes, driver, Milano, Maserati

Adolf Lang

D. Born: 4.5.1913, Ebelsbach
1953 German F3 Champion

Hermann Lang

D. Born: 6.4.1909, Bad Cannstatt, near Stuttgart. Died: 19.10.1987, Bad Cannstatt, near Stuttgart
1939 European Grand Prix Champion (see page 274)

formula	years	starts (DNS)	wins	2nd	3rd	4th	5th	6th	PP	FL	points
F1 W	1953-54	2	-	-	-	1	-	-	-	2

Best championship: 1953, 13th. Best qualifying: 11th. Teams: Maserati, Mercedes-Benz

| GP Pre-50 | 1935-39 | 21 | 2 | 4 | 2 | 1 | - | 1 | 6 | 7 |

Wins: 1939 Belgian GP, Swiss GP

| Le Mans | 1952 | 1 | 1 | - | - | - | - | - | |

Win: 1952 Le Mans 24 hrs

Other major wins: 1937, 1938 and 1939 Tripoli, 1937 Avus, 1939 Pau, 1939 Eifelrennen (Nurburgring)

Claudio Langes

I. Born: 20.7.1960, Brescia

formula	years	starts (DNS)	wins	2nd	3rd	4th	5th	6th	PP	FL	points
F1 W	1990	0 (14)	-	-	-	-	-	-	-	-	0

Best result: no starts. Best qualifying: 32nd. Team: EuroBrun

| F3000 INT | 1985-89 | 33 (1) | - | 1 | - | 1 | 2 | 2 | - | - | 15 |

Best championship: 1989, 12th

F3 E win: 1 – 1984 Knutstorp

Elmo Langley

USA. Born: 22.8.1929. Died: 21.11.1996
NASCAR wins: 2

Gerald Langlois van Ophem

B

formula	years	starts (DNS)	wins	2nd	3rd	4th	5th	6th	PP	FL	points
Le Mans	1963-65	3	-	1	-	-	-	-	
SC W	1961-66		-	1	-	1	2	1	-	-	

Major win: 1965 Spa 24 hrs

Randy Lanier

USA. Born: 22.9.1954
1984 IMSA GTP Champion

formula	years	starts (DNS)	wins	2nd	3rd	4th	5th	6th	PP	FL	points
Le Mans	1982	1	-	-	-	-	-	-	
Indy 500	1986	1	-	-	-	-	-	-	

formula	years	starts (DNS)	wins	2nd	3rd	4th	5th	6th	PP	FL	points
CART	1985-86	18	-	-	-	-	1	-	-	

Xavier Lapeyre

F. Born: 13.4.1942
1986 and 1991 French Touring Car Champion

formula	years	starts (DNS)	wins	2nd	3rd	4th	5th	6th	PP	FL	points
Le Mans	1974-91	13	-	-	-	-	-	-	
SC W	1974-91		-	-	-	1	-	-	
F2 E	1975-77	13 (13)	-	-	-	-	-	-	0

Nicola Larini

I. Born: 19.3.1964, Lido di Camaiore
1992 Italian Touring Car Champion, 1993 German Touring Car Champion, 1986 Italian F3 Champion

formula	years	starts (DNS)	wins	2nd	3rd	4th	5th	6th	PP	FL	points
F1 W	1987-97	49 (26)	-	1	-	-	1	-	-	7

Best championship: 1994, 14th. Best qualifying: 6th. Teams: Coloni, Osella, Ligier, Lamborghini, Ferrari, Sauber

| F3000 INT | 1986-87 | 5 | - | - | - | - | - | - | 0 |

Oscar "Poppy" Larrauri

RA. Born: 19.8.1954, Rosario
1982 European F3 Champion, 1985 Renault Europa Cup Champion, 1997, 1998 and 2000 South American Touring Car Champion

formula	years	starts (DNS)	wins	2nd	3rd	4th	5th	6th	PP	FL	points
F1 W	1988-89	7 (14)	-	-	-	-	-	-	0

Best result: 13th. Best qualifying: 18th. Team: EuroBrun

| Le Mans | 1983-94 | 9 | - | 1 | - | - | - | - | |
| SC W | 1983-92 | | 1 | 4 | 5 | 5 | 7 | 7 | 1 | 1 | |

Win: 1986 Jerez. Best championship: 1986, 6th

| F2 E | 1983 | 3 (1) | - | - | - | - | - | - | 0 |

F3 E wins: 8 – 1981 Nurburgring, 1982 Mugello, Nurburgring, Zolder, Zandvoort, Monza, Enna, Knutstorp

Alberto Rodriguez Larreta

RA. Born: 14.1.1934, Buenos Aires. Died: 11.3.1977, Buenos Aires

formula	years	starts (DNS)	wins	2nd	3rd	4th	5th	6th	PP	FL	points
F1 W	1960	1	-	-	-	-	-	-	0

Best result: 9th. Best qualifying: 15th. Team: Lotus

Gerard Larrousse

F. Born: 23.5.1940, Lyon

formula	years	starts (DNS)	wins	2nd	3rd	4th	5th	6th	PP	FL	points
F1 W	1974	1 (1)	-	-	-	-	-	-	0

Best result: no finishes. Best qualifying: 28th. Team: Scuderia Finotto

| Le Mans | 1967-74 | 8 | 2 | 2 | - | - | - | 1 | - | |
| SC W | 1967-75 | | 12 | 4 | 5 | 1 | 4 | 3 | 5 | 5 | |

Wins: 1971 Sebring 12 hrs, Nurburgring, 1973 Vallelunga, Dijon, Le Mans 24 hrs, Osterreichring, Watkins Glen, 1974 Imola, Le Mans 24 hrs, Osterreichring, Kyalami, 1975 Mugello

| F2 E | 1975 | 10 (1) | 1 | 2 | - | 1 | - | 1 | - | 1 | 26 |

Win: 1975 Hockenheim race 1. Best championship: 1975, 4th

Other Major win: 1974 Targa Florio

Jud Larson

USA. Born: 21.1.1923, Grand Prairie, Missouri. Died: 11.6.1966, Reading, Pennsylvania

formula	years	starts (DNS)	wins	2nd	3rd	4th	5th	6th	PP	FL	points
Indy 500	1958-59	2	-	-	-	-	-	-	

Champcar wins: 5 – 1956 Sacramento, 1957 Du Quoin, Indiana State Fairground, 1958 Atlanta, Phoenix

Fredrik Larsson

S
1996 Barber-Dodge Champion

Lucas Lasserre

F. Born: 1978, Pau
1999 French Formula Renault Champion

Andreas-Nikolaus "Niki" Lauda
A. Born: 22.2.1949, Vienna
1975, 1977 and 1984 F1 World Champion, 1972
British F2 Champion, 1979 BMW M1 Procar
Champion

formula	years	starts (DNS)	wins	2nd	3rd	4th	5th	6th	PP	FL	points
F1 W	1971-85	171 (6)	25	20	9	7	7	5	24	24	420.5

Wins: 1974 Spanish GP, Dutch GP, 1975 Monaco GP, Belgian GP, Swedish GP, French GP, United States GP, 1976 Brazilian GP, Belgian GP, Monaco GP, British GP, 1977 South African GP, German GP, Dutch GP, 1978 Swedish GP, Italian GP, 1982 Long Beach GP, British GP, 1984 South African GP, French GP, British GP, Austrian GP, Italian GP, 1985 Dutch GP. Best championships: 1975, 1977 and 1984, 1st. Best qualifying: 1st. Teams: March, BRM, Ferrari, Brabham, McLaren

formula	years	starts (DNS)	wins	2nd	3rd	4th	5th	6th	PP	FL	points
SC W	1969-74						1				
F2 E	1971-72	20 (2)		1	2	1		2	2		33

Best championship: 1972, 5th
Non-championship F1 wins: 1975 International Trophy (Silverstone), 1979 Dino Ferrari GP (Imola)

Gerard Laureau
F

formula	years	starts	wins	2nd	3rd	4th	5th	6th	PP	FL	points
Le Mans	1955-64	10									

Major win: 1954 Tourist Trophy handicap

Arsenio "Dodgie" Laurel
RP. Born: n/a. Died: 19.11.1967, Macau GP

Major wins: 1962 and 1963 Macau

Roger Laurent
B. Born: 21.2.1913, Liege. Died: 6.2.1997, Uccle

formula	years	starts (DNS)	wins	2nd	3rd	4th	5th	6th	PP	FL	points
F1 W	1952	2							1		0

Best qualifying: 20th. Teams: HWM, Ecurie Francorchamps

formula	years	starts	wins	2nd	3rd	4th	5th	6th	PP	FL	points
Le Mans	1953-54	2				1					
SC W	1953-54					1					

Non-championship F1 win: 1952 Helsinki

Christian Lautenschlager
D. Born: 13.4.1877, Magstadt. Died: 1.4.1954, Stuttgart

formula	years	starts (DNS)	wins	2nd	3rd	4th	5th	6th	PP	FL	points
GP Pre-50	1908-14	3	2					1			

Wins: 1908 French GP, 1914 French GP

formula	years	starts	wins	2nd	3rd	4th	5th	6th	PP	FL	points
Indy 500	1923	1									

Giovanni Lavaggi
I. Born: 18.2.1958, Augusta, Sicily
1993 Interserie Champion

formula	years	starts (DNS)	wins	2nd	3rd	4th	5th	6th	PP	FL	points
F1 W	1995-96	7 (3)									0

Best result: 10th. Best qualifying: 20th. Teams: Pacific, Minardi

formula	years	starts	wins	2nd	3rd	4th	5th	6th	PP	FL	points
Le Mans	1989-2000	5									
SC W	1987-92				1						

SRWC wins: 2 - 1999 Magny-Cours, 2001 Monza

formula	years	starts (DNS)	wins	2nd	3rd	4th	5th	6th	PP	FL	points
F3000 INT	1991	2 (8)									0
CART	1994	2 (2)									

Other Major win: 1995 Daytona 24 hrs

Alo Lawler
IRL
1982 and 1983 British Formula Atlantic Champion

formula	years	starts (DNS)	wins	2nd	3rd	4th	5th	6th	PP	FL	points
F2 E	1977	0 (2)									0

Chris Lawrence
GB. Born: 27.7.1933, Ealing, London

formula	years	starts (DNS)	wins	2nd	3rd	4th	5th	6th	PP	FL	points
F1 W	1966	2									0

Best result: 11th. Best qualifying: 18th. Team: JA Pearce

formula	years	starts (DNS)	wins	2nd	3rd	4th	5th	6th	PP	FL	points
Le Mans	1962-68	5									

Graeme Lawrence
NZ. Born: 25.12.1940
1970 Tasman Champion, 1971 and 1975 New Zealand Gold Star Champion

formula	years	starts (DNS)	wins	2nd	3rd	4th	5th	6th	PP	FL	points
F2 E	1968	2 (1)									0

Tasman wins: 3 - 1970 Levin, 1975 Levin, Adelaide

Bob Lazier
USA. Born: 22.12.1938
1977 SCCA Super Vee Champion

formula	years	starts (DNS)	wins	2nd	3rd	4th	5th	6th	PP	FL	points
Indy 500	1981	1									
CART	1981	11			2	1					

Best championship: 1981, 9th

Jaques Lazier
USA. Born: 25.1.1971, Vail, Colorado

formula	years	starts (DNS)	wins	2nd	3rd	4th	5th	6th	PP	FL	points
Indy 500	2000-01	2									
IRL	1999-2002	28 (1)	1	1	1			1	2	2	

Win: 2001 Chicagoland

Robert "Buddy" Lazier
USA. Born: 31.10.1967, Loveland Pass, Colorado
2000 Indy Racing League Champion

formula	years	starts (DNS)	wins	2nd	3rd	4th	5th	6th	PP	FL	points
Indy 500	1991-2002	10	1	2		1				1	

Win: 1996 Indianapolis 500

formula	years	starts (DNS)	wins	2nd	3rd	4th	5th	6th	PP	FL	points
CART	1989-95	55 (15)									
IRL	1996-2002	70	8	6	4	4	3	2	2	5	

Wins: 1996 Indianapolis 500, 1997 Charlotte, 2000 Phoenix, Kentucky, 2001 Pikes Peak, Richmond, Nashville, Kentucky. Best championship: 2000, 1st

Anthony Lazzaro
USA. Born: 23.8.1963, Charleston, South Carolina
1999 North American Toyota Atlantic Champion

formula	years	starts (DNS)	wins	2nd	3rd	4th	5th	6th	PP	FL	points
IRL	2001-02	6 (1)									

Bob Lea-Wright
AUS

Major wins: 1934 Australian GP

Nicolas Leboissetier
F. Born: 5.6.1971

formula	years	starts (DNS)	wins	2nd	3rd	4th	5th	6th	PP	FL	points
Le Mans	1996	1									
F3000 INT	1993-94	9				1					3

Best championship: 1993, 15th

Walter Lechner
A. Born: 4.8.1949, Vienna
1983, 1987 and 1989 Interserie Champion

formula	years	starts (DNS)	wins	2nd	3rd	4th	5th	6th	PP	FL	points
Le Mans	1988-89	2									
SC W	1983-89									1	

Michel Leclere
F. Born: 18.3.1946, Mantes-la-Jolie, near Paris
1972 French F3 Champion, 1971 French Formula Renault Champion

formula	years	starts (DNS)	wins	2nd	3rd	4th	5th	6th	PP	FL	points
F1 W	1975-76	7 (1)									0

Best result: 10th. Best qualifying: 18th. Teams: Tyrrell, Williams

formula	years	starts (DNS)	wins	2nd	3rd	4th	5th	6th	PP	FL	points
Le Mans	1974-79	4									
F2 E	1973-79	43 (6)	4	3	2	2	3	1	5	3	81

Wins: 1975 Rouen, Silverstone, Zolder, 1976 Salzburgring. Best championship: 1975, 2nd

Mike Ledbrook
GB
1961 BRSCC National Formula Junior Champion

Neville Lederle
ZA. Born: 25.9.1938, Theunissen, Winburg
1963 South African F1 Champion

formula	years	starts (DNS)	wins	2nd	3rd	4th	5th	6th	PP	FL	points
F1 W	1962-65	1 (1)	-	-	-	-	-	1	-	-	1

Best championship: 1962, 18th. Best qualifying: 10th. Teams: driver, Scuderia Scribante

Kenelm Lee Guinness see Guinness

Henry Lee Jr
HK. Born: 18.3.1958, Hong Kong
2000 Asian Touring Car Champion

Geoff Lees
GB. Born: 1.5.1951, Atherstone, Warwickshire
1981 European F2 Champion, 1998 European GT Champion (with Thomas Bscher), 1983 Japanese F2 Champion

formula	years	starts (DNS)	wins	2nd	3rd	4th	5th	6th	PP	FL	points
F1 W	1978-82	5 (7)	-	-	-	-	-	-	-	-	0

Best result: 7th. Best qualifying: 16th. Teams: Mario Deliotti, Tyrrell, Shadow, Ensign, RAM, Theodore, Lotus

Le Mans	1982-2000	14	-	-	-	-	1	-			
SC W	1982-92		1	1	2	2	1	2	1		

Win: 1992 Monza. Best championship: 1992, 5th

F2 E	1978-81	17 (1)	3	3	-	1	3	1	1	5	55

Wins: 1981 Pau, Spa, Donington. Best championship: 1981, 1st
F1 GB win: 1 – 1978 Mallory Park
Other major wins: 1979 and 1980 Macau

John Leffler
AUS
1976 Australian F5000 Champion

Arthur Legat
B. Born: 1.11.1898, Haine St Paul. Died: 23.2.1960, Haine St Pierre

formula	years	starts (DNS)	wins	2nd	3rd	4th	5th	6th	PP	FL	points
F1 W	1952-53	2	-	-	-	-	-	-	-	-	0

Best result: 13th. Best qualifying: 19th. Team: driver

Jens-Christian Legath
DK
1963 Danish Formula Junior Champion

Willy Lehmann
DDR
1952, 1953, 1954, 1955 and 1956 East German F3 Champion

Marcel Lehoux
DZ/F (dual nationality). Born: 3.4.1888, Blois (F). Died: 19.7.1936, Deauville GP

formula	years	starts (DNS)	wins	2nd	3rd	4th	5th	6th	PP	FL	points
GP Pre-50	1925-36	28 (1)	-	-	3	3	-	1	2	-	

Major wins: 1928 Tunis, 1933 Monza GP

JJ Lehto (Jyrki Jarvilehto)
SF. Born: 31.1.1966, Espoo
1988 British F3 Champion, 1987 European FF2000 Champion

formula	years	starts (DNS)	wins	2nd	3rd	4th	5th	6th	PP	FL	points
F1 W	1989-94	62 (8)	-	-	1	1	1	1	-	-	10

Best championship: 1991, 12th. Best qualifying: 4th. Teams: Onyx, Scuderia Italia, Sauber, Benetton

Le Mans	1990-2002	7	1	-	-	-	-	-			

Win: 1995 Le Mans 24 hrs
GT FIA wins: 5 – 1996 Suzuka, 1997 Hockenheim, Helsinki, Spa, Mugello

F3000 INT	1989	9	-	-	1	1	1	-	-		6

Best championship: 1989, 13th

formula	years	starts (DNS)	wins	2nd	3rd	4th	5th	6th	PP	FL	points
CART	1998	19	-	-	-	-	1	-	-	-	

Other Major win: 1999 Sebring 12 hrs

Bas Leinders
B. Born: 16.7.1975, Bree
1996 European Formula Opel Champion, 2000 Belgian Belcar Touring Car Champion (with Erik Bruynoghe), 1998 German F3 Champion

formula	years	starts (DNS)	wins	2nd	3rd	4th	5th	6th	PP	FL	points
F3000 INT	1998-2001	28 (5)	-	2	-	1	-	3	-	-	18

Best championship: 2001, 7th

Prinz Hermann zu Leiningen
D. Born: 4.1.1901, Amorbach. Died: 29.3.1971, Amorbach

formula	years	starts (DNS)	wins	2nd	3rd	4th	5th	6th	PP	FL	points
GP Pre-50	1930-34	7 (1)	1	1	-	2	1	-	-	-	

Win: 1930 Masaryk GP

Bob Leitzinger
USA
1989 IMSA GTU Champion

Butch Leitzinger
USA. Born: 28.2.1969, Homestead
1997 and 1998 IMSA WSC Champion, 1993 IMSA GTU Champion

Le Mans	1997-2002	5	-	-	1	1	-	-			

Major wins: 1994, 1997 and 1999 Daytona 24 hrs

Patrick Lemarie
F. Born: 6.2.1968, Paris

formula	years	starts (DNS)	wins	2nd	3rd	4th	5th	6th	PP	FL	points
Le Mans	2000-01	2	-	-	-	-	-	-			
F3000 INT	1996-97	16 (1)	-	-	-	1	1	1	-	-	6

Best championships: 1996 and 1997, 13th

Gilles Lempereur
F. Born: 1.3.1959, Orleans
1982 French Formula Renault Champion

formula	years	starts (DNS)	wins	2nd	3rd	4th	5th	6th	PP	FL	points
Le Mans	1987	1	-	-	-	-	-	-			
F3000 INT	1987	1 (1)	-	-	-	-	-	-	-	-	0

Gijs van Lennep
NL. Born: 16.3.1942, Bloemendaal
1972 British F5000 Champion

formula	years	starts (DNS)	wins	2nd	3rd	4th	5th	6th	PP	FL	points
F1 W	1971-75	8 (2)	-	-	-	-	-	2	-	-	2

Best championships: 1973 and 1975, 19th. Best qualifying: 20th. Teams: Stichting Autoraces, Surtees, Williams, Ensign

Le Mans	1970-76	7	2	1	-	1	1	-	-		1

Wins: 1971 and 1976 Le Mans 24 hrs

SC W	1966-76		2	4	3	5	6	2	-		1

Wins: 1971 Le Mans 24 hrs, 1973 Targa Florio

F2 E	1967	1	-	-	-	-	-	-	-	-	0

Joe Leonard
USA. Born: 4.8.1934, San Diego, California
1971 and 1972 Champcar Champion

Indy 500	1965-73	9	-	-	2	-	-	1	1	1	

Champcar wins: 6 – 1965 Milwaukee race 2, 1970 Milwaukee race 1, 1971 California 500, 1972 Michigan, Pocono 500, Milwaukee race 2

Rene Leonard
F

Le Mans	1923-25	3	1	-	-	-	-	-			

Win: 1923 Le Mans 24 hrs
Other Major win: 1925 Spa 24 hrs

Lamberto Leoni

I. Born: 24.5.1953, Argenta, Ferrara

formula	years	starts (DNS)	wins	2nd	3rd	4th	5th	6th	PP	FL	points
F1 W	1977-78	1 (4)	-	-	-	-	-	-	-	-	0

Best result: no finishes. Best qualifying: 17th. Teams: Surtees, Ensign

Le Mans	1988	1	-	-	-	-	-	-	-	-	
F2 E	1975-84	28 (4)	1	-	1	-	-	1	1	-	14

Win: 1977 Misano. Best championship: 1977, 11th.

F3000 INT	1985-87	27 (2)	-	-	2	3	1	1	-	1	20

Best championship: 1987, 8th

John Lepp

GB

formula	years	starts (DNS)	wins	2nd	3rd	4th	5th	6th	PP	FL	points
SC W	1968-76		-	-	-	1	1	-	-	-	
F2 E	1973	1	-	-	-	-	1	-	-	-	3

Best championship: 1973, 26th

Frank Lescault

USA

Champcar win: 1 – 1909 Riverhead race 2

David Leslie

GB. Born: 9.11.1953, Dumfries

1980 British Formula Atlantic Champion

formula	years	starts (DNS)	wins	2nd	3rd	4th	5th	6th	PP	FL	points
Le Mans	1984-95	10	-	-	-	-	-	-	-	-	
SC W	1984-92		-	-	1	1	3	-	-		

Best championship: 1987, 12th

Les Leston

GB. Born: 16.12.1920, Nottingham

1954 British F3 Champion

formula	years	starts (DNS)	wins	2nd	3rd	4th	5th	6th	PP	FL	points
F1 W	1956-57	2 (1)	-	-	-	-	-	-	-	-	0

Best result: no finishes. Best qualifying: 12th. Teams: Connaught, Cooper, BRM

Le Mans	1955-61	4	-	-	-	-	-	-	-	-	
SC W	1957-62		-	-	-	-	-	1	-	-	

Danny Letner

USA

NASCAR wins: 2

Emile Levassor

F. Born: 1844. Died: 14.4.1897

City-to-city win: 1895 Paris-Bordeaux-Paris

"Alfred Levegh" (Alfred Velghe)

F. Born: n/a. Died: 1904

formula	years	starts (DNS)	wins	2nd	3rd	4th	5th	6th	PP	FL	points
GP Pre-50	1901	1	-	-	-	-	-	-	-	-	

City-to-city win: 1900 Paris-Toulouse-Paris

"Pierre Levegh" (Pierre Bouillon)

F. Born: 22.12.1905, Paris. Died: 11.6.1955, Le Mans 24 hrs

formula	years	starts (DNS)	wins	2nd	3rd	4th	5th	6th	PP	FL	points
F1 W	1950-51	6	-	-	-	-	-	-	-	-	0

Best result: 7th. Best qualifying: 9th. Team: driver

GP Pre-50	1947-49	8	-	-	-	1	-	-	-	-	
Le Mans	1938-55	7	-	-	-	1	-	-	-	-	

Bruce Leven

USA. Born: 27.9.1945

formula	years	starts (DNS)	wins	2nd	3rd	4th	5th	6th	PP	FL	points
SC W	1978-89		1	-	-	-	1	-	-	-	

Win: 1981 Sebring 12 hrs

Roly Levis

NZ

1967 and 1969 New Zealand Gold Star Champion

Dave Lewis

USA. Born: 11.5.1881. Died: 13.5.1928, Los Angeles, California

formula	years	starts (DNS)	wins	2nd	3rd	4th	5th	6th	PP	FL	points
GP Pre-50	1914	1	-	-	-	-	-	-	-	-	
Indy 500	1916-27	6	-	-	-	-	-	-	-	-	

Champcar wins: 5 – 1919 Uniontown race 3, 1926 Altoona race 1, Charlotte race 3, Charlotte race 7, 1927 Atlantic City

Jackie Lewis

GB. Born: 1.11.1936, Stroud, Gloucestershire

1960 British F2 Champion

formula	years	starts (DNS)	wins	2nd	3rd	4th	5th	6th	PP	FL	points
F1 W	1961-62	9 (1)	-	-	-	1	-	-	-	-	3

Best championship: 1961, 13th. Best qualifying: 13th. Teams: H&L, Ecurie Galloise

Paul Lewis

USA

NASCAR wins: 1

Willy Lewis

USA

1986 Barber-SAAB Champion

Stuart Lewis-Evans

GB. Born: 20.4.1930, Luton, Bedfordshire. Died: 25.10.1958, East Grinstead, following an accident at the Moroccan GP

formula	years	starts (DNS)	wins	2nd	3rd	4th	5th	6th	PP	FL	points
F1 W	1957-58	14	-	-	2	2	1	-	2	-	16

Best championship: 1958, 9th. Best qualifying: 1st. Teams: Connaught, Vanwall

Le Mans	1957-58	2	-	-	-	-	1	-	-	-	
SC W	1957-58		-	-	1	1	-	-	-	-	

Non-championship F1 win: 1957 Goodwood

Fredy Lienhard

CH. Born: 14.9.1947, Dergersteim

formula	years	starts (DNS)	wins	2nd	3rd	4th	5th	6th	PP	FL	points
F2 E	1976-83	3 (2)	-	-	-	-	-	1	-	-	1

Best championship: 1983, 20th

SRWC wins: 3 – 1997 Zolder, 1998 Paul Ricard, 2000 Elkhart Lake

Other Major win: 2002 Daytona 24 hrs

Guy Ligier

F. Born: 12.7.1930, Vichy

formula	years	starts (DNS)	wins	2nd	3rd	4th	5th	6th	PP	FL	points
F1 W	1966-67	12 (1)	-	-	-	-	-	1	-	-	1

Best championship: 1967, 19th. Best qualifying: 11th. Teams: driver, Brabham

Le Mans	1964-73	8	-	-	-	-	-	-	-	-	
SC W	1964-73		-	-	-	1	2	-	-	-	
F2 E	1968	3 (1)	-	-	-	-	-	-	-	-	0

Etienne van der Linde

ZA. Born: 25.2.1978, Johannesburg

1998 European Formula Opel Champion, 1995 South African Formula GTi Champion

Shaun van der Linde

ZA. Born: 9.9.1970, Johannesburg

1994 South African Touring Car Champion, 1992 South African Formula GTi Champion

Dick Linder

USA. Born: n/a. Died: 1959, Trenton

NASCAR wins: 3

Werner Lindermann

D

formula	years	starts (DNS)	wins	2nd	3rd	4th	5th	6th	PP	FL	points
F2 E	1968-70	7 (2)	-	-	-	-	-	-	-	-	2

Best championship: 1969, 15th. Best result: 9th

Leif Lindstrom
S
1984 Swedish F3 Champion

Thomas Lindstrom
S
1985 European Touring Car Champion (with Gianfranco Brancatelli)

Ole Martin Lindum
N. Born: 22.2.1954
1999 Norwegian F3 Champion

Roberto Lippi
I. Born: 17.10.1926, Rome
1958 Italian Formula Junior Champion

formula	years	starts (DNS)	wins	2nd	3rd	4th	5th	6th	PP	FL	points
F1 W	1961-63	1 (2)	-	-	-	-	-	-	-	-	0

Best result: no finishes. Best qualifying: 28th. Team: Scuderia Settecolli

| Le Mans | 1957 | 1 | - | - | - | - | - | - | | | |

Al Livingstone
USA. Born: n/a. Died: 1.10.1910, Atlanta, Georgia, practice

Champcar win: 1 – 1910 Elgin race 2

Conny Ljungfeldt
S
1975 and 1976 Swedish F3 Champion

Bill Lloyd
USA. Born: 12.7.1923, New York

formula	years	starts (DNS)	wins	2nd	3rd	4th	5th	6th	PP	FL	points
SC W	1953-58		1	-	-	-	1	-	-	-	

Win: 1954 Sebring 12 hrs

Frank Lockhart
USA. Born: 8.3.1903, Dayton, Ohio. Died: 25.4.1928, Daytona Beach, Florida

formula	years	starts (DNS)	wins	2nd	3rd	4th	5th	6th	PP	FL	points
Indy 500	1926-27	2	1	-	-	-	-	-	1	-	

Win: 1926 Indianapolis 500

Champcar wins: 10 – 1926 Indianapolis 500, Charlotte race 4, Charlotte race 5, Altoona race 2, Fresno race 2, Charlotte race 6, 1927 Altoona race 2, Charlotte race 1, Salem race 2, Salem race 3

Calum Lockie
GB. Born: 23.7.1964
2000 British GT Champion

Andries "Dries" van der Lof
NL. Born: 23.8.1919, Emmen. Died: 24.5.1990, Enschede

formula	years	starts (DNS)	wins	2nd	3rd	4th	5th	6th	PP	FL	points
F1 W	1952	1	-	-	-	-	-	-	-	-	0

Best result: no finishes. Best qualifying: 14th. Team: HWM

Carl Lohmander
S

Major win: 1961 Mille Miglia (regularity test)

Lella Lombardi
I. Born: 26.3.1941, Frugarolo, near Alessandria. Died: 3.3.1992, Milan, cancer

formula	years	starts (DNS)	wins	2nd	3rd	4th	5th	6th	PP	FL	points
F1 W	1974-76	12 (5)	-	-	-	-	-	1	-	-	0.5

Best championship: 1975, 21st. Best qualifying: 22nd. Teams: John Goldie, March, Williams, RAM

| Le Mans | 1975-80 | 4 | - | - | - | - | - | - | | | |
| SC W | 1975-81 | | 3 | 2 | 1 | 4 | 2 | 1 | - | 1 | |

Wins: 1979 Florio Cup (Enna), Vallelunga, 1981 Mugello. Best championship: 1981, 4th

Tony Longhurst
AUS. Born: 1.10.1957, Sydney, New South Wales
1994 Australian Super Touring Car Champion

Major wins: 1988 and 2001 Bathurst

Bert Longin
B. Born: 26.10.1965
2000 (with Albert Vanierschot) and 2002 (with Anthony Kumpen) Belgian Belcar GT Champion

Richard Longman
GB
1978 and 1979 British Touring Car Champion

Ernst Loof
D. Born: 4.7.1907, Neindorf. Died: 3.3.1956, Bonn, brain tumour

formula	years	starts (DNS)	wins	2nd	3rd	4th	5th	6th	PP	FL	points
F1 W	1953	1	-	-	-	-	-	-	-	-	0

Best result: no finishes. Best qualifying: 31st. Team: driver

Tomas Lopez
MEX
1990 IMSA Lights Champion

formula	years	starts (DNS)	wins	2nd	3rd	4th	5th	6th	PP	FL	points
Le Mans	1991	1	-	-	-	-	-	-			

Luis Lopez de la Camara
E
1989 Spanish Touring Car Champion

Fred Lorenzen
USA. Born: 30.12.1934, Elmhurst, Illinois

NASCAR wins: 26

David Loring
USA. Born: 15.10.1950
1992 IMSA GTU Champion

Kurt Lotterschmid
D
1979 and 1980 Interserie Champion

formula	years	starts (DNS)	wins	2nd	3rd	4th	5th	6th	PP	FL	points
F2 E	1978	0 (1)	-	-	-	-	-	-	-	-	0

Henri Louveau
F. Born: 25.1.1910, Suresnes, near Paris. Died: 7.1.1991, Orleans

formula	years	starts (DNS)	wins	2nd	3rd	4th	5th	6th	PP	FL	points
F1 W	1950-51	2	-	-	-	-	-	-	-	-	0

Best result: no finishes. Best qualifying: 11th. Team: Louis Rosier

| GP Pre-50 | 1947-49 | 7 | - | 1 | - | - | 2 | 1 | 1 | - | |
| Le Mans | 1939-50 | 3 | - | 1 | - | - | - | - | | | |

John Love
RSR. Born: 7.12.1924, Bulawayo
1962 British Touring Car Champion, 1964, 1965, 1966, 1967, 1968 and 1969 South African F1 Champion, 1971 South African Springbok Sports Car Champion

formula	years	starts (DNS)	wins	2nd	3rd	4th	5th	6th	PP	FL	points
F1 W	1962-72	9 (1)	-	1	-	-	-	-	-	-	6

Best championship: 1967, 11th. Best qualifying: 5th. Teams: driver, Cooper, Team Gunston

F1 ZA wins: 35 – 1966 Killarney, Kyalami (x3), Pietermaritzburg (x3), 1967 Killarney (x2), Pietermaritzburg (x3), Kumalo, Mozambique, Rhodesian GP, 1968 Kyalami (x3), Pietermaritzburg, East London, Rhodesian GP, 1969 Kyalami (x2), Kumalo, East London, Mozambique, Killarney, 1970 Killarney, Bulawayo, 1971 Welkom, Mozambique, Killarney, Rhodesian GP, 1972 Pietermaritzburg, Rhodesian GP

Gerard "Pete" Lovely
USA. Born: 11.4.1926, Livingston, Montana

formula	years	starts (DNS)	wins	2nd	3rd	4th	5th	6th	PP	FL	points
F1 W	1959-71	7 (4)	-	-	-	-	-	-	-	-	0

Best result: 7th. Best qualifying: 16th. Teams: Lotus, Fred Armbruster, driver

| Le Mans | 1958 | 1 | - | - | - | - | - | - | - | - | |
| SC W | 1956-61 | | - | - | 1 | - | - | - | - | - | |

Craig Lowndes
AUS. Born: 21.6.1974, Melbourne
1996, 1998 and 1999 Australian Touring Car Champion

formula	years	starts (DNS)	wins	2nd	3rd	4th	5th	6th	PP	FL	points
F3000 INT	1997	10	-	-	-	1	-	-	-	-	3

Best championship: 1997, 17th

Major win: 1996 Bathurst

Roger Loyer
F. Born: 5.8.1907, Paris. Died: 24.3.1988, Boulogne-Billancourt, Paris

formula	years	starts (DNS)	wins	2nd	3rd	4th	5th	6th	PP	FL	points
F1 W	1954	1	-	-	-	-	-	-	-	-	0

Best result: no finishes. Best qualifying: 15th. Team: Gordini

| GP Pre-50 | 1947 | 0 (1) | - | - | - | - | - | - | - | - | |
| Le Mans | 1938-53 | 5 | - | - | - | - | - | - | - | - | |

Kurt Luby
GB. Born: 6.3.1963
1998 British GT Champion (with Richard Dean)

Jean Lucas
F. Born: 25.4.1917, Le Mans

formula	years	starts (DNS)	wins	2nd	3rd	4th	5th	6th	PP	FL	points
F1 W	1955	1	-	-	-	-	-	-	-	-	0

Best result: no finishes. Best qualifying: 22nd. Team: Gordini

| Le Mans | 1949-57 | 8 | - | - | 1 | - | - | - | - | - | |
| SC W | 1953-59 | | - | - | 1 | - | - | - | - | - | |

Major win: 1949 Spa 24 hrs

"Jean Lucienbonnet" (Jean Bonnet)
F. Born: 7.1.1923, Nice. Died: 19.8.1962, Enna, Sicily, Formula Junior race

formula	years	starts (DNS)	wins	2nd	3rd	4th	5th	6th	PP	FL	points
F1 W	1959	0 (1)	-	-	-	-	-	-	-	-	0

Best result: no starts. Best qualifying: 23rd. Team: driver

| Le Mans | 1958 | 1 | - | - | - | - | - | - | - | - | |

Klaus Ludwig
D. Born: 5.10.1949, Roisdorf, Bonn
1998 FIA GT Champion (with Ricardo Zonta), 1979 and 1981 German Racing Champion, 1988, 1992 and 1994 German Touring Car Champion

formula	years	starts (DNS)	wins	2nd	3rd	4th	5th	6th	PP	FL	points
Le Mans	1977-98	10	3	1	-	-	-	1	-	1	

Wins: 1979, 1984 and 1985 Le Mans 24 hrs

| SC W | 1973-92 | | 6 | 7 | 4 | 2 | 4 | 2 | 1 | 4 | |

Wins: 1978 Nurburgring, 1979 Le Mans 24 hrs, Watkins Glen, 1984 Le Mans 24 hrs, 1985 Le Mans 24 hrs, 1986 Norisring. Best championship: 1985, 5th. GT FIA wins: 9 – 1997 Nurburgring, A1 Ring, Sebring, Laguna Seca, 1998 Oschersleben, Dijon, A1 Ring, Homestead, Laguna Seca

| F2 E | 1976-77 | 14 | - | - | - | - | - | 1 | - | - | 4 |

Best championship: 1976, 12th

Other Major win: 1988 Sebring 12 hrs

Lucas Luhr
D. Born: 22.7.1979, Koblenz
2002 American Le Mans Series GT class Champion

formula	years	starts (DNS)	wins	2nd	3rd	4th	5th	6th	PP	FL	points
Le Mans	2000-02	2	-	-	-	-	-	-	-	-	

Len Lukey
AUS
1959 Australian Gold Star Champion

DeWayne "Tiny" Lund
USA. Born: 3.3.1936, Harlan, Iowa. Died: 17.8.1975, Talladega
NASCAR wins: 2

Erik Lundgren
S

formula	years	starts (DNS)	wins	2nd	3rd	4th	5th	6th	PP	FL	points
SC W	1956-57		-	-	-	1	-	-	-	-	

Non-championship F1 wins: 1953 Skarpnack

Brett Lunger
USA. Born: 14.11.1945, Wilmington, Delaware

formula	years	starts (DNS)	wins	2nd	3rd	4th	5th	6th	PP	FL	points
F1 W	1975-78	34 (9)	-	-	-	-	-	-	-	-	0

Best result: 7th. Best qualifying: 13th. Teams: Hesketh, Surtees, BS Fabrications, Ensign

| SC W | 1974-80 | | - | 1 | - | 1 | - | - | - | - | |
| F2 E | 1972-73 | 9 (6) | - | - | - | 1 | - | - | - | - | 4 |

Best championship: 1972, 24th

Werner Lupberger
ZA. Born: 15.12.1975, Pretoria

formula	years	starts (DNS)	wins	2nd	3rd	4th	5th	6th	PP	FL	points
Le Mans	2001-02	2	-	-	-	-	-	-	-	-	

SRWC win: 1 – 2001 Donington

| F3000 INT | 1997-98 | 20 (1) | - | - | - | 1 | - | 1 | - | - | 4 |

Best championship: 1997, 17th

Carlo Lusser
CH
1998 Swiss Touring Car Champion

Arie Luyendyk
NL. Born: 21.9.1953, Sommelsdyk
1984 SCCA Super Vee Champion

formula	years	starts (DNS)	wins	2nd	3rd	4th	5th	6th	PP	FL	points
Le Mans	1989	1	-	-	-	-	-	-	-	-	
F2 E	1979	1	-	-	-	-	-	-	-	-	0
Indy 500	1985-2002	17	2	1	1	-	-	-	3	2	

Wins: 1990 and 1997 Indianapolis 500

| CART | 1984-97 | 142 (3) | 3 | 4 | 6 | 6 | 9 | 14 | 1 | 2 | |

Wins: 1990 Indianapolis 500, 1991 Phoenix, Nazareth. Best championship: 1991, 6th

| IRL | 1996-2002 | 28 | 4 | - | 1 | 1 | 1 | - | 4 | 1 | |

Wins: 1996 Phoenix, 1997 Indianapolis 500, Texas, 1998 Las Vegas. Best championship: 1996/97, 6th

Other major wins: 1989 Sebring 12 hrs, 1998 Daytona 24 hrs

Alexandr Lvov
R
2001 Russian Touring Car Champion

Leigh Lynch
USA
Champcar win: 1 – 1909 Indianapolis race 3

Herb Lytle
USA. Born: c1877. Died: 1933

formula	years	starts (DNS)	wins	2nd	3rd	4th	5th	6th	PP	FL	points
GP Pre-50	1905	1	-	-	-	-	-	-	-	-	
Indy 500	1911	1	-	-	-	-	-	-	-	-	

Champcar win: 1 – 1910 Atlanta race 3

M

Walt Maas
USA
1974 and 1977 IMSA GTU Champion

Sascha Maassen
D. Born: 28.9.1969, Aachen

formula	years	starts (DNS)	wins	2nd	3rd	4th	5th	6th	PP	FL	points
Le Mans	2000-02	3	-	-	-	-	-	-	-	-	

Major win: 1994 Macau

John MacDonald
HK. Born: 1936, Worcester (GB)
Major wins: 1965, 1972, 1973 and 1975 Macau, 1972 Macau Guia race

Mike MacDowel
GB. Born: 13.9.1932, Great Yarmouth, Norfolk

formula	years	starts (DNS)	wins	2nd	3rd	4th	5th	6th	PP	FL	points
F1 W	1957	1	-	-	-	-	-	-	-	-	0

Best result: 7th. Best qualifying: 15th. Team: Cooper

Herbert MacKay-Fraser
USA. Born: 23.6.1927, Pernambuco (BR). Died: 14.7.1957, Reims, F2 race

formula	years	starts (DNS)	wins	2nd	3rd	4th	5th	6th	PP	FL	points
F1 W	1957	1	-	-	-	-	-	-	-	-	0

Best result: no finishes. Best qualifying: 12th. Team: BRM

Le Mans	1956-57	2	-	-	-	-	-	-			

Jeff MacPherson
USA. Born: 9.6.1956, Santa Ana, California
1986 New Zealand Formula Pacific Champion

formula	years	starts (DNS)	wins	2nd	3rd	4th	5th	6th	PP	FL	points
F3000 INT	1986	4 (3)	-	-	-	-	-	-	-	-	0
Indy 500	1987	1	-	-	-	-	-	-			
CART	1986-87	18 (1)	-	-	-	-	-	-			

Lance Macklin
GB. Born: 2.9.1919, Kensington, London. Died: 29.8.2002, Bethersden, Kent

formula	years	starts (DNS)	wins	2nd	3rd	4th	5th	6th	PP	FL	points
F1 W	1952-55	13 (2)	-	-	-	-	-	-	-	-	0

Best result: 8th. Best qualifying: 9th. Teams: HWM, Stirling Moss

Le Mans	1950-55	6	-	-	1	-	1	-			
SC W	1953-56		-	-	1	-	1	-			

Major win: 1952 International Trophy (Silverstone)

Damien Magee
GB. Born: 17.11.1945, Belfast, Northern Ireland

formula	years	starts (DNS)	wins	2nd	3rd	4th	5th	6th	PP	FL	points
F1 W	1975-76	1 (1)	-	-	-	-	-	-	-	-	0

Best result: 14th. Best qualifying: 22nd. Teams: Williams, RAM

Jocko Maggiacomo
USA
1976 Trans-Am Class 2 Champion

Tony Maggs
ZA. Born: 9.2.1937, Pretoria

formula	years	starts (DNS)	wins	2nd	3rd	4th	5th	6th	PP	FL	points
F1 W	1961-65	25 (2)	-	2	1	1	2	3	-	-	26

Best championship: 1962, 7th. Best qualifying: 4th. Teams: Louise Bryden-Brown, Cooper, Scuderia Centro Sud, Reg Parnell

Le Mans	1961-64	3	-	-	-	-	1	-			
SC W	1961-65		-	-	1	3	-	1	-		

Costantino Magistri
I
Major win: 1936 Targa Florio

Umberto Maglioli
I. Born: 5.6.1928, Bioglio, Vercelli. Died: 6.2.1999, Monza

formula	years	starts (DNS)	wins	2nd	3rd	4th	5th	6th	PP	FL	points
F1 W	1953-57	10	-	-	2	-	1	-	-	-	3.33

Best championship: 1954, 18th. Best qualifying: 7th. Teams: Ferrari, Scuderia Guastalla, Maserati, Porsche

Le Mans	1953-68	11	-	-	1	-	-	-			
SC W	1953-70		4	1	4	3	5	2	2	-	

Wins: 1954 Buenos Aires, Carrera Panamericana, 1964 Sebring 12 hrs, 1968 Targa Florio
Other major wins: 1953 and 1956 Targa Florio, 1953 Pescara

George Magliveras
GR
1997 Greek F3 Champion

Jan Magnussen
DK. Born: 4.7.1973, Roskilde
1994 British F3 Champion

formula	years	starts (DNS)	wins	2nd	3rd	4th	5th	6th	PP	FL	points
F1 W	1995-98	25	-	-	-	-	-	1	-	1	1

Best championship: 1998, 15th. Best qualifying: 6th. Teams: McLaren, Stewart

Le Mans	1999-2002	4	-	-	-	-	-	-			
CART	1996-99	11	-	-	-	-	-	-			

Norbert Mahe
F

formula	years	starts (DNS)	wins	2nd	3rd	4th	5th	6th	PP	FL	points
Le Mans	1934-53	7	-	-	-	-	-	-			

Major win: 1934 Spa 24 hrs

Guy Mairesse
F. Born: 10.8.1910, La Capelle, L'Aisne. Died: 24.4.1954, Montlhery, Paris Cup practice

formula	years	starts (DNS)	wins	2nd	3rd	4th	5th	6th	PP	FL	points
F1 W	1950-51	3	-	-	-	-	-	-	-	-	0

Best result: 9th. Best qualifying: 11th. Teams: driver, Ecurie Belgique

GP Pre-50	1949	2	-	-	-	-	-	-			
Le Mans	1949-53	5	-	2	-	-	-	-			

Willy Mairesse
B. Born: 1.10.1928, Mommignies. Died: 2.9.1969, Ostend, suicide

formula	years	starts (DNS)	wins	2nd	3rd	4th	5th	6th	PP	FL	points
F1 W	1960-63	12	-	-	1	1	-	-	-	-	7

Best championship: 1962, 14th. Best qualifying: 3rd. Teams: Ferrari, ENB, Lotus

Le Mans	1958-68	8	-	1	2	-	-	-			
SC W	1957-68		4	5	5	1	1	-	-	1	

Wins: 1962 Targa Florio, 1963 Nurburgring, 1965 Spa, 1966 Targa Florio
Non-championship F1 wins: 1962 Brussels, Naples

Jean-Pierre Malcher
F. Born: 19.2.1950, Paris
1995 Porsche Supercup Champion, 1981, 1989 and 1990 French Touring Car Champion, 1988 French Group A Touring Car Champion

formula	years	starts (DNS)	wins	2nd	3rd	4th	5th	6th	PP	FL	points
Le Mans	1979	1	-	-	-	-	-	-			

Guillermo Maldonado
RA. Born: 29.10.1952
1983, 1984, 1985 and 1986 Codasur F2 Champion, 1994 TC2000 Argentinian Touring Car Champion

Ray Mallock
GB. Born: 12.4.1951
1979 and 1981 British Formula Atlantic Champion

formula	years	starts (DNS)	wins	2nd	3rd	4th	5th	6th	PP	FL	points
Le Mans	1979-89	8	-	-	-	-	-	-			
SC W	1977-89		-	-	1	2	3	-	-		

Best championship: 1987, 12th

F2 E	1975-82	17 (8)	-	1	-	-	1	-	-		7

Best championship: 1977, 12th

Paride Mambelli
I
Major win: 1937 Mille Miglia

Oscar Manautou
MEX. Born: 9.9.1956
1988 Mexican Formula K Champion

Fabio Mancini
I. Born: 6.8.1958, Florence
1992 Italian Prototype Champion

formula	years	starts (DNS)	wins	2nd	3rd	4th	5th	6th	PP	FL	points
Le Mans	1994-95	2	-	-	-	-	-	-			
F3000 INT	1988	0 (2)	-	-	-	-	-	-	-	-	0

Major win: 1987 Tourist Trophy (Silverstone)

Roger Mandeville

USA. Born: 22.9.1941
1984 IMSA GTO Champion, 1983 IMSA GTU Champion

formula	years	starts (DNS)	wins	2nd	3rd	4th	5th	6th	PP	FL	points
SC W	1973-92	1	-	-	-	-	1	-	-		

Win: 1981 Daytona. Best championship: 1981, 16th

James Manderson

AUS. Born: 19.1.1981
2002 Australian F3 Champion

Darren Manning

GB. Born: 30.4.1975, Knaresborough, Yorkshire
1999 Japanese F3 Champion

formula	years	starts (DNS)	wins	2nd	3rd	4th	5th	6th	PP	FL	points
F3000 INT	2000-01	22	-	2	1	-	1	1	1	1	19

Best championship: 2000, 8th

| CART | 2002 | 1 | - | - | - | - | - | - | - | - | |

Major wins: 1999 Macau, 1999 Korea F3

Nigel Mansell

GB. Born: 8.8.1953, Baughton, Warwickshire
1992 F1 World Champion, 1993 CART Champion

formula	years	starts (DNS)	wins	2nd	3rd	4th	5th	6th	PP	FL	points
F1 W	1980-95	187 (4)	31	17	11	8	6	9	32	29	482

Wins: 1985 European GP, South African GP, 1986 Belgian GP, Canadian GP, French GP, British GP, Portuguese GP, 1987 San Marino GP, French GP, British GP, Austrian GP, Mexican GP, 1989 Brazilian GP, Hungarian GP, 1990 Portuguese GP, 1991 French GP, British GP, German GP, Italian GP, Spanish GP, 1992 South African GP, Mexican GP, Brazilian GP, Spanish GP, San Marino GP, French GP, British GP, German GP, Portuguese GP, 1994 Australian GP. Best championship: 1992, 1st. Best qualifying: 1st. Teams: Lotus, Williams, Ferrari, McLaren

| F2 E | 1978-80 | 4 (1) | - | 1 | - | - | 1 | - | - | - | 8 |

Best championship: 1980, 12th

| Indy 500 | 1993-94 | 2 | - | - | 1 | - | - | - | - | - | |
| CART | 1993-94 | 31 (1) | 5 | 4 | 4 | - | 2 | 1 | 10 | 3 | |

Wins: 1993 Surfers Paradise, Milwaukee, Michigan 500, New Hampshire, Nazareth. Best championship: 1993, 1st

Enrique Mansilla

RA

formula	years	starts (DNS)	wins	2nd	3rd	4th	5th	6th	PP	FL	points
F2 E	1983	9 (1)	-	-	-	-	-	2	-	-	2

Best championship: 1983, 19th

| CART | 1985 | 3 | - | - | - | - | - | - | - | - | |

Gaudenzio Mantova

I

formula	years	starts (DNS)	wins	2nd	3rd	4th	5th	6th	PP	FL	points
F2 E	1976-78	10 (3)	-	-	-	-	2	-	-	-	4

Best championship: 1977, 14th

Sergio Mantovani

I. Born: 22.5.1929, Cusano Milianino, Milan. Died: 23.2.2001, Milan

formula	years	starts (DNS)	wins	2nd	3rd	4th	5th	6th	PP	FL	points
F1 W	1953-55	7 (1)	-	-	-	-	2	-	-	-	4

Best championship: 1954, 15th. Best qualifying: 9th. Team: Maserati

| SC W | 1953-57 | | - | - | - | - | 1 | - | - | - | |

Johnny Mantz

USA. Born: 18.9.1918, Hebron, Indiana. Died: 25.10.1972, Ojai, California, road accident

formula	years	starts (DNS)	wins	2nd	3rd	4th	5th	6th	PP	FL	points
Indy 500	1948-53	3	-	-	-	-	-	-	-	-	

Champcar win: 1 – 1948 Milwaukee race 2
NASCAR wins: 1

Robert Manzon

F. Born: 12.4.1917, Marseille

formula	years	starts (DNS)	wins	2nd	3rd	4th	5th	6th	PP	FL	points
F1 W	1950-56	28 (1)	-	-	2	2	1	-	-	-	16

Best championship: 1952, 6th. Best qualifying: 3rd. Teams: Gordini, Louis Rosier, Ferrari

GP Pre-50	1948-49	3	-	-	-	-	-	-	-	-	
Le Mans	1950-56	6	-	-	-	-	-	-	-	-	
SC W	1953-56		-	-	2	-	-	-	-	1	

Non-championship F1 win: 1956 Naples
Other major wins: 1952 Prix de Monaco, 1956 Pescara

Roberto Marazzi

I

formula	years	starts (DNS)	wins	2nd	3rd	4th	5th	6th	PP	FL	points
Le Mans	1984	1	-	-	-	-	-	-	-	-	
SC W	1975-84		1	-	-	-	-	-	-	-	

Win: 1980 Vallelunga

| F2 E | 1976-78 | 16 (5) | - | - | - | 2 | - | - | - | - | 6 |

Best championship: 1976, 10th

Jovy Marcelo

RP. Born: 21.7.1965. Died: 15.5.1992, Indianapolis, practice
1991 North American Toyota Atlantic Champion

formula	years	starts (DNS)	wins	2nd	3rd	4th	5th	6th	PP	FL	points
CART	1992	3	-	-	-	-	-	-	-	-	

Dave Marcis

USA. Born: 1.3.1941, Wausau, Wisconsin
NASCAR wins: 5 (all Modern era)

Onofre Marimon

RA. Born: 19.12.1923, Buenos Aires. Died: 31.7.1954, Nurburgring, German GP practice

formula	years	starts (DNS)	wins	2nd	3rd	4th	5th	6th	PP	FL	points
F1 W	1951-54	11 (1)	-	-	2	-	-	-	-	1	8.14

Best championship: 1953, 11th. Best qualifying: 4th. Teams: Milano, Maserati

| Le Mans | 1951-53 | 2 | - | - | - | - | - | - | - | - | |

Non-championship F1 win: 1954 Rome GP (Castel Fusano)

Ernst Maring

D. Born: 31.3.1936, Braunschweig
1975 German F3 Champion

formula	years	starts (DNS)	wins	2nd	3rd	4th	5th	6th	PP	FL	points
F2 E	1971	0 (1)	-	-	-	-	-	-	-	-	0

Attilio Marinoni

I. Born: 1886, Lodi. Died: 18.6.1942, testing on a public road

formula	years	starts (DNS)	wins	2nd	3rd	4th	5th	6th	PP	FL	points
GP Pre-50	1932-37	5	-	-	1	2	-	1	-	-	
Le Mans	1931-32	2	-	-	-	-	-	-	-	-	

Major wins: 1928, 1929 and 1930 Spa 24 hrs

Helmut Marko

A. Born: 27.4.1943, Graz
1971 European 2-litre Sports Car Champion

formula	years	starts (DNS)	wins	2nd	3rd	4th	5th	6th	PP	FL	points
F1 W	1971-72	9 (1)	-	-	-	-	-	-	-	-	0

Best result: 8th. Best qualifying: 6th. Teams: Joakim Bonnier, BRM

| Le Mans | 1970-72 | 3 | 1 | - | 1 | - | - | - | - | - | |

Win: 1971 Le Mans 24 hrs

| SC W | 1968-72 | | 1 | 2 | 4 | 1 | 1 | 1 | - | 1 | |

Win: 1971 Le Mans 24 hrs

| F2 E | 1971 | 4 | - | - | - | - | - | - | - | - | 1 |

Best championship: 1971, 20th

Sterling Marlin

USA. Born: 30.6.1957, Franklin, Tennessee
NASCAR wins: 10 (all Modern era) including 1994, 1995 Daytona 500

Tarso Marques

BR. Born: 19.1.1976, Curitiba

formula	years	starts (DNS)	wins	2nd	3rd	4th	5th	6th	PP	FL	points
F1 W	1996-2001	24 (2)	-	-	-	-	-	-	-	-	0

Best result: 9th. Best qualifying: 14th. Team: Minardi

F3000 INT	1994-95	15 (1)	1	-	1	1	1	-	2	3	18

Win: 1995 Estoril. Best championship: 1995, 5th

CART	1999-2000	22	-	-	-	-	-	-	-	-	-

Leslie Marr
GB. Born: 14.8.1922, Durham

formula	years	starts (DNS)	wins	2nd	3rd	4th	5th	6th	PP	FL	points
F1 W	1954-55	2	-	-	-	-	-	-	-	-	0

Best result: 13th. Best qualifying: 19th. Team: driver

Non-championship F1 win: 1955 Davidstow

Tony Marsh
GB. Born: 20.7.1931, Stourbridge, Warwickshire

1957 British F2 Champion

formula	years	starts (DNS)	wins	2nd	3rd	4th	5th	6th	PP	FL	points
F1 W	1957-61	4 (1)	-	-	-	-	-	-	-	-	0

Best result: 15th. Best qualifying: 20th. Teams: Ridgeway Managements, driver

Le Mans	1960	1	-	-	-	-	-	-	-	-	-

Non-championship F1 win: 1961 Brands Hatch

Bobby Marshman
USA. Born: 24.9.1936, Norristown, Pennsylvania. Died: 4.12.1964, Phoenix, Arizona, from injuries inflicted testing on 27.11.1964

formula	years	starts (DNS)	wins	2nd	3rd	4th	5th	6th	PP	FL	points
Indy 500	1961-64	4	-	-	-	-	1	-	-	1	

Champcar win: 1 – 1962 Phoenix

Eugene Martin
F. Born: 24.3.1915, Suresnes, near Paris

formula	years	starts (DNS)	wins	2nd	3rd	4th	5th	6th	PP	FL	points
F1 W	1950	2	-	-	-	-	-	-	-	-	0

Best result: no finishes. Best qualifying: 7th. Team: Talbot

Le Mans	1952-53	2	-	-	-	-	-	-	-	-	-

Henry Martin
RA. Born: 25.7.1965, San Juan

1997 TC2000 Argentinian Touring Car Champion

Jean-Michel Martin
B. Born: 19.6.1953

1989 and 1990 Belgian Procar Touring Car Champion

formula	years	starts (DNS)	wins	2nd	3rd	4th	5th	6th	PP	FL	points
Le Mans	1980-86	7	-	-	1	-	-	-	-	-	
SC W	1979-92		-	2	1	-	-	-	-	-	

Best championship: 1982, 12th

Major wins: 1979, 1980, 1987 and 1992 Spa 24 hrs

Mark Martin
USA. Born: 9.1.1959, Batesville, Arkansas

1994, 1996, 1997 and 1998 IROC Champion

NASCAR wins: 33 (all Modern era) including 2002 World 600

Philippe Martin
B. Born: 26.1.1955

formula	years	starts (DNS)	wins	2nd	3rd	4th	5th	6th	PP	FL	points
Le Mans	1980-85	6	-	-	1	-	-	-	-	-	
SC W	1979-85		-	2	1	1	-	-	-	-	

Best championship: 1982, 12th

Major wins: 1979 and 1980 Spa 24 hrs

Spencer Martin
AUS

1966 and 1967 Australian Gold Star Champion

Tony Martin
ZA

1980 South African Formula Atlantic Champion

formula	years	starts (DNS)	wins	2nd	3rd	4th	5th	6th	PP	FL	points
SC W	1974-85		-	-	-	-	-	1	-	-	

Major win: 1984 Daytona 24 hrs

Santi Martin-Cantero
E

1981 Spanish Touring Car Champion

Ermanno Martinello
I. Born: 26.6.1956, Padua

1993 and 1994 Italian Prototype Champion

David Martinez
MEX. Born: 8.12.1981, Monterrey

1996 Mexican F2 Champion

Gerardo Martinez
MEX. Born: 10.10.1947

1987 and 1989 Mexican Formula K Champion

Omar "Guri" Martinez
RA. Born: 1.1.1966, Rosario del Taia

1998 TC2000 Argentinian Touring Car Champion

Giancarlo Martini
I. Born: 16.8.1947, Lavezzola

formula	years	starts (DNS)	wins	2nd	3rd	4th	5th	6th	PP	FL	points
F2 E	1974-79	41 (2)	-	-	2	-	4	3	-	-	22

Best championship: 1976, 7th

F1 GB win: 1978 Donington

Mauro Martini
I. Born: 17.5.1964, Alfonsine

1992 Japanese F3000 Champion

formula	years	starts (DNS)	wins	2nd	3rd	4th	5th	6th	PP	FL	points
Le Mans	1991-96	5	-	1	-	-	1	-	-	-	
SC W	1991-92		-	-	-	1	-	-	-	-	
F3000 INT	1989	3 (1)	-	-	-	-	-	-	-	-	0

Oliver Martini
I. Born: 12.12.1971, Bologna

1997 Italian F3 Champion

formula	years	starts (DNS)	wins	2nd	3rd	4th	5th	6th	PP	FL	points
F3000 INT	1998-99	14 (7)	-	-	-	-	1	1	-	-	3

Best championship: 1998, 14th

Pierluigi Martini
I. Born: 23.4.1961, Lugo di Romagna, near Ravenna

1983 European F3 Champion

formula	years	starts (DNS)	wins	2nd	3rd	4th	5th	6th	PP	FL	points
F1 W	1984-95	118 (6)	-	-	-	2	4	4	-	-	18

Best championship: 1991, 11th. Best qualifying: 2nd. Teams: Toleman, Minardi, Scuderia Italia

Le Mans	1984-99	5	1	-	-	-	-	1	-	-	

Win: 1999 Le Mans 24 hrs

SC W	1984-92		-	-	-	-	1	-	-	-	

SRWC win: 1 – 1997 Donington

F2 E	1983	1	-	1	-	-	-	-	-	-	6

Best championship: 1983, 10th

F3000 INT	1986-88	31 (1)	4	4	2	-	1	-	2	2	67

Wins: 1986 Imola, Mugello, Jarama, 1988 Enna. Best championship: 1986, 2nd

F3 E wins: 4 – 1983 Nogaro, Jarama, Imola, Croix-en-Ternois

Dan Marvin
USA. Born: 13.8.1952

1984 North American Formula Atlantic Champion

Giannino Marzotto
I. Born: 13.4.1928

formula	years	starts (DNS)	wins	2nd	3rd	4th	5th	6th	PP	FL	points
Le Mans	1953	1	-	-	-	-	1	-	-	-	
SC W	1953-54		1	-	-	-	1	-	-	-	

Win: 1953 Mille Miglia

Other major win: 1950 Mille Miglia

Paolo Marzotto
I. Born: 1930

formula	years	starts (DNS)	wins	2nd	3rd	4th	5th	6th	PP	FL	points
Le Mans	1953-55	3	-	-	-	-	1	-	-	-	
SC W	1953-55		-	-	-	-	1	-	-	-	

Major win: 1952 Pescara

Vittorio Marzotto
I. Born: 1932

formula	years	starts (DNS)	wins	2nd	3rd	4th	5th	6th	PP	FL	points
SC W	1954		-	1	-	-	-	-	-	-	

Major win: 1952 Monaco GP

Giulio Masetti
I. Born: 1895, Florence. Died: 25.4.1926, Madonie Circuit, Targa Florio

formula	years	starts (DNS)	wins	2nd	3rd	4th	5th	6th	PP	FL	points
GP Pre-50	1922-25	5	-	-	1	-	-	-	-	-	

Major wins: 1921 and 1922 Targa Florio

Jochen Mass
D. Born: 30.9.1946, Dorfen, near Munich
1972 European Touring Car Champion, 1985 German Racing Champion

formula	years	starts (DNS)	wins	2nd	3rd	4th	5th	6th	PP	FL	points
F1 W	1973-82	105 (9)	1	1	6	7	4	9	-	2	71

Win: 1975 Spanish GP. Best championship: 1977, 6th. Best qualifying: 4th.
Teams: Surtees, McLaren, ATS, Arrows, March

Le Mans	1972-95	11	1	1	-	-	-	1	1	

Win: 1989 Le Mans 24 hrs

SC W	1972-92		32	21	8	4	4	3	14	12	

Wins: 1975 Florio Cup (Enna), 1976 Mugello, Vallelunga, Monza, Imola, Florio Cup (Enna), Dijon (x2), Salzburgring, 1977 Silverstone, Watkins Glen, Brands Hatch, 1978 Silverstone, 1982 Spa, Fuji, 1983 Nurburgring, Spa, 1984 Silverstone, Mosport Park, 1985 Mugello, Silverstone, Shah Alam, 1988 Jerez, Brno, Nurburgring, Sandown Park, 1989 Jarama, Nurburgring, Donington, Mexico City, 1990 Spa, Mexico City. Best championships: 1984 and 1989, 2nd

F2 E	1972-78	24 (1)	4	3	1	-	-	2	3	4	43

Wins: 1973 Kinnekulle, Hockenheim race 2, 1977 Hockenheim, Nurburgring. Best championship: 1973, 2nd
Other major wins: 1972 Spa 24 hrs, 1972 Tourist Trophy (Silverstone), 1987 Sebring 12 hrs

Felipe Massa
BR. Born: 25.4.1981, Sao Paulo
2001 Euro F3000 Champion, 2000 European Formula Renault Champion

formula	years	starts (DNS)	wins	2nd	3rd	4th	5th	6th	PP	FL	points
F1 W	2002	16	-	-	-	-	1	2	-	-	4

Best championship: 2002, 12th. Best qualifying: 7th. Team: Sauber

Mario Massacurati
I

Major win: 1936 South African GP

Emilio Materassi
I. Born: 1889, Florence. Died: 9.9.1928, Monza, Italian GP

formula	years	starts (DNS)	wins	2nd	3rd	4th	5th	6th	PP	FL	points
GP Pre-50	1925-28	5	-	-	-	1	-	2	-	-	

Major wins: 1927 Tripoli, 1927 Targa Florio, 1927 San Sebastian GP

Frank Matich
AUS. Born: 1935, Sydney, New South Wales
1972 Australian F5000 Champion
Tasman wins: 5 – 1970 New Zealand GP, Lady Wigram Trophy, 1971 Surfers Paradise, 1972 Warwick Farm, 1973 Surfers Paradise
Other major wins: 1970 and 1971 Australian GP

Joe Matson
USA. Born: n/a. Died: 19??

formula	years	starts (DNS)	wins	2nd	3rd	4th	5th	6th	PP	FL	points
Indy 500	1912	1	-	-	-	-	-	-	-	-	

Champcar win: 1 – 1909 Crown Point race 1

Keiji Matsumoto
J. Born: 26.12.1949, Kyoto
1979 Japanese F2 Champion

formula	years	starts (DNS)	wins	2nd	3rd	4th	5th	6th	PP	FL	points
Le Mans	1986-87	2	-	-	-	-	-	-	-	-	
SC W	1982-87		1	-	-	-	-	-	-	-	

Win: 1985 Fuji (had not driven car when the race was stopped due to rain)

F2 E	1981	1	-	-	-	-	-	-	-	-	0

Hiroyuki "Hiro" Matsushita
J. Born: 14.3.1961, Kobe
1989 North American Formula Atlantic (Western) Champion

formula	years	starts (DNS)	wins	2nd	3rd	4th	5th	6th	PP	FL	points
Le Mans	1999	1	-	-	-	-	-	-	-	-	
Indy 500	1991-95	4	-	-	-	-	-	-	-	-	
CART	1990-98	116 (6)	-	-	-	-	-	1	-	-	

Antonio da Matta
BR
1989 Brazilian Touring Car Champion (with Gunnar Volmer)

Cristiano da Matta
BR. Born: 19.9.1973, Belo Horizonte
2002 CART Champion, 1998 CART Indy Lights Champion, 1994 Brazilian F3 Champion

formula	years	starts (DNS)	wins	2nd	3rd	4th	5th	6th	PP	FL	points
F3000 INT	1996	10	-	-	-	1	2	-	-	-	7

Best championship: 1996, 8th

CART	1999-2002	79 (1)	11	4	3	7	2	2	7	6	

Wins: 2000 Chicago, 2001 Monterrey, Surfers Paradise, California Speedway, 2002 Monterrey, Laguna Seca, Portland, Chicago, Toronto, Elkhart Lake, Miami. Best championship: 2002, 1st

Andreas Mattheis
BR
1988 (solo), 1990 (with Ricardo Cosac), 1992 and 1993 (both with Paulo Judice) Brazilian Touring Car Champion

James Matthews
GB
1994 European Formula Renault Champion

Sven Mattsson
S
1964 Swedish F3 Champion

Ricardo Mauricio
BR. Born: 7.1.1979, Sao Paulo

formula	years	starts (DNS)	wins	2nd	3rd	4th	5th	6th	PP	FL	points
F3000 INT	1999-2002	37 (3)	-	1	3	1	2	3	-	-	28

Best championship: 2001, 8th

Tony Maw
MAL
Major win: 1967 Macau

Jean Max
F. Born: 27.7.1943, Marseille
1968 French Formula Renault Champion

formula	years	starts (DNS)	wins	2nd	3rd	4th	5th	6th	PP	FL	points
F1 W	1971	1	-	-	-	-	-	-	-	-	0

Best result: no finishes. Best qualifying: 23rd. Team: Williams

Le Mans	1968	1	-	-	-	-	-	-	-	-	
F2 E	1970-72	2 (2)	-	-	-	-	-	-	-	-	0

Michel May

CH. Born: 18.8.1934, Stuttgart (D)

formula	years	starts (DNS)	wins	2nd	3rd	4th	5th	6th	PP	FL	points
F1 W	1961	2 (1)	-	-	-	-	-	-	-	-	0

Best result: 11th. Best qualifying: 14th. Team: Scuderia Colonia

Major win: 1959 Monaco Formula Junior

Emile Mayade

F. Born: n/a. Died: 17.9.1898, Chevanceaux

City-to-city win: 1896 Paris-Marseille-Paris

Timmy Mayer

USA. Born: 22.2.1938, Dalton, Pennsylvania. Died: 28.2.1964, Longford, Tasmania

formula	years	starts (DNS)	wins	2nd	3rd	4th	5th	6th	PP	FL	points
F1 W	1962	1	-	-	-	-	-	-	-	-	0

Best result: no finishes. Best qualifying: 12th. Team: Cooper

Jeremy Mayfield

USA. Born: 27.5.1969, Owensboro, Kentucky

NASCAR wins: 3 (all Modern era)

Bernd Maylander

D. Born: 29.5.1971, Waiblingen

formula	years	starts (DNS)	wins	2nd	3rd	4th	5th	6th	PP	FL	points
Le Mans	1999	1	-	-	-	-	-	-	-	-	

GT FIA win: 1 – 1997 A1 Ring

Rex Mays

USA. Born: 10.3.1913, Colton, California. Died: 6.11.1949, Del Mar, California

1940 and 1941 Champcar Champion

formula	years	starts (DNS)	wins	2nd	3rd	4th	5th	6th	PP	FL	points
Indy 500	1934-49	12	-	2	-	-	-	1	4	-	

Champcar wins: 8 – 1936 Goshen, 1940 Springfield, Syracuse, 1941 Milwaukee, Syracuse, 1946 Langhorne, Indiana State Fairgrounds, Milwaukee

Francois Mazet

F. Born: 26.2.1943, Paris

1969 French F3 Champion

formula	years	starts (DNS)	wins	2nd	3rd	4th	5th	6th	PP	FL	points
F1 W	1971	1	-	-	-	-	-	-	-	-	0

Best result: 13th. Best qualifying: 24th. Team: Jo Siffert

F2 E	1970-71	7 (2)	-	-	-	-	-	-	-	-	0

Gaston Mazzacane

RA. Born: 8.5.1975, La Plata

formula	years	starts (DNS)	wins	2nd	3rd	4th	5th	6th	PP	FL	points
F1 W	2000-01	21	-	-	-	-	-	-	-	-	0

Best result: 8th. Best qualifying: 19th. Teams: Minardi, Prost

F3000 INT	1996-99	29 (4)	-	-	-	-	2	-	-	-	2

Best championship: 1998, 21st

SRWC win: 1 – 1999 Magny-Cours

Kenneth McAlpine

GB. Born: 21.9.1920, Chobham, Surrey

formula	years	starts (DNS)	wins	2nd	3rd	4th	5th	6th	PP	FL	points
F1 W	1952-55	7	-	-	-	-	-	-	-	-	0

Best result: 13th. Best qualifying: 13th. Team: Connaught

Le Mans	1955	1	-	-	-	-	-	-	-	-	

Perry McCarthy

GB. Born: 3.3.1962, Stepney, London

formula	years	starts (DNS)	wins	2nd	3rd	4th	5th	6th	PP	FL	points
F1 W	1992	0 (10)	-	-	-	-	-	-	-	-	0

Best result: no starts. Best qualifying: 29th. Team: Andrea Moda

Le Mans	1996-2002	4	-	-	-	-	-	-	-	-	
F3000 INT	1988-89	5 (2)	-	-	-	-	-	-	-	-	0

Roger McCluskey

USA. Born: 24.8.1930, San Antonio, Texas. Died: 29.8.1993, Indianapolis, Indiana

1973 Champcar Champion

Dave McConnell

CDN

formula	years	starts (DNS)	wins	2nd	3rd	4th	5th	6th	PP	FL	points
Le Mans	1967	1	-	-	-	-	-	-	-	-	
Indy 500	1961-79	18	-	-	1	-	1	-	-		2

Pre-CART Champcar wins: 5 – 1966 Langhorne race 2, 1968 Springfield, 1972 California 500, 1973 Michigan, 1979 Milwaukee

CART	1979	1	-	-	-	-	-	-	-	-	

Dave McConnell

CDN

formula	years	starts (DNS)	wins	2nd	3rd	4th	5th	6th	PP	FL	points
F2 E	1973	3 (1)	-	-	1	-	-	-	-	-	6

Best championship: 1973, 13th

John McCormack

AUS

1973, 1975 and 1977 Australian F5000 Champion

Tasman wins: 3 – 1973 New Zealand GP, Adelaide, 1974 New Zealand GP

Robert McDonough

USA. Born: 1900, Altoona, Pennsylvania. Died: 10.12.1945, Columbus, Ohio

formula	years	starts (DNS)	wins	2nd	3rd	4th	5th	6th	PP	FL	points
Indy 500	1924-32	7	-	-	-	-	-	1	-	-	

Champcar wins: 2 – 1925 Altoona race 2, Laurel race 2

Jim McElreath

USA. Born: 18.2.1928, Arlington, Dallas, Texas

formula	years	starts (DNS)	wins	2nd	3rd	4th	5th	6th	PP	FL	points
Indy 500	1962-80	15	-	-	1	-	2	3	-	-	

Pre-CART Champcar wins: 5 – 1965 Trenton race 1, Langhorne race 1, Langhorne race 2, 1966 Phoenix race 1, 1970 California 500

CART	1979-84	13 (4)	-	-	-	-	-	1	-	-	

Rob McFarlin

USA

formula	years	starts (DNS)	wins	2nd	3rd	4th	5th	6th	PP	FL	points
Le Mans	1979	1	-	-	-	-	-	-	-	-	
SC W	1978-84		-	-	2	-	-	-	-	-	

Major win: 1979 Sebring 12 hrs

Kevin McGarrity

GB. Born: 3.8.1973, Belfast, Northern Ireland

formula	years	starts (DNS)	wins	2nd	3rd	4th	5th	6th	PP	FL	points
Le Mans	2001-02	2	-	-	-	-	-	-	-	-	
F3000 INT	1998-2000	22 (6)	-	1	-	2	-	-	-	-	12

Best championship: 1999, 10th

Bill McGovern

GB. Born: 2.1.1937

1970, 1971 and 1972 British Touring Car Champion

Jack McGrath

USA. Born: 8.10.1919, Los Angeles, California. Died: 6.11.1955, Phoenix, Arizona

formula	years	starts (DNS)	wins	2nd	3rd	4th	5th	6th	PP	FL	points
Indy 500	1948-55	8	-	-	2	-	1	-	1	1	

Champcar wins: 4 – 1950 Langhorne, Syracuse, 1952 Syracuse, 1953 Milwaukee race 1

Hershel McGriff

USA. Born: 14.12.1927

formula	years	starts (DNS)	wins	2nd	3rd	4th	5th	6th	PP	FL	points
Le Mans	1976-82	2	-	-	-	-	-	-	-	-	

NASCAR wins: 4

Other major win: 1950 Carrera Panamericana

Brian McGuire

AUS. Born: 13.12.1945, Melbourne, Victoria. Died: 29.8.1977, Brands Hatch

formula	years	starts (DNS)	wins	2nd	3rd	4th	5th	6th	PP	FL	points
F1 W	1977	0 (1)	-	-	-	-	-	-	-	-	0

Best result: no starts. Best qualifying: 35th. Team: driver

G McIntyre

NZ
1987 New Zealand Touring Car Champion

David McKay

AUS
1960 Australian Touring Car Champion

Ian McKellar Jr

GB. Born: 11.2.1978, London
2002 British GT Champion (with Thomas Erdos)

formula	years	starts (DNS)	wins	2nd	3rd	4th	5th	6th	PP	FL	points
Le Mans	2001-02	2	-	-	-	-	-	-			

Bruce McLaren

NZ. Born: 30.8.1937, Auckland. Died: 2.6.1970,
Goodwood, testing
1964 Tasman Champion, 1967 and 1969 Can-Am
Champion, 1959 New Zealand Gold Star Champion

formula	years	starts (DNS)	wins	2nd	3rd	4th	5th	6th	PP	FL	points
F1 W	1958-70	100 (4)	4	11	12	7	11	5	-	3	196.5

Wins: 1959 United States GP, 1960 Argentinian GP, 1962 Monaco GP, 1968 Belgian GP. Best championship: 1960, 2nd. Best qualifying: 2nd. Teams: Cooper, McLaren, Eagle

Le Mans	1959-67	8		1	-	-	1	-	-	1	-

Win: 1966 Le Mans 24 hrs

SC W	1958-68			2	1	2	2	2	-	2	3

Wins: 1966 Le Mans 24 hrs, 1967 Sebring 12 hrs

F2 E	1967	3		-	-	-	1	1	1	-	-	0

Non-championship F1 wins: 1962 Goodwood, Reims, 1968 Race of Champions (Brands Hatch)
Tasman wins: 2 – 1965 Australian GP, 1968 Teretonga
Other major wins: 1962 Australian GP, 1964 New Zealand GP

Peter McLeod

AUS. Born: 6.5.1948, Newcastle, New South Wales
Major win: 1987 Bathurst

Rod McLeod

GB
1996 Mexican F3 Champion

John McMillan

NZ
Major win: 1950 New Zealand GP

Dave McMillen

NZ. Born: 5.5.1944
1977, 1979 and 1980 New Zealand Gold Star Champion, 1980 New Zealand Formula Pacific Champion, 1982 North American Formula Atlantic Champion
Major win: 1981 New Zealand GP

Eaton McMillian

USA
Champcar win: 1 – 1909 Denver

Jamie McMurray

USA. Born: 3.6.1976
NASCAR wins: 1 (in Modern era)

John McNicol

ZA
F1 ZA wins: 3 – 1969 Pietermaritzburg, Kyalami, 1973 Welkom

Allan McNish

GB. Born: 29.12.1969, Dumfries
2000 American Le Mans Series Champion

formula	years	starts (DNS)	wins	2nd	3rd	4th	5th	6th	PP	FL	points
F1 W	2002	16 (1)	-	-	-	-	-	-	-	-	0

Best result: 7th. Best qualifying: 10th. Team: Toyota

Le Mans	1997-2000	4		1	1	-	-	-	1	1	

Win: 1998 Le Mans 24 hrs

F3000 INT	1989-95	36 (2)		2	2	2	-	3	3	3	1	47

Wins: 1990 Silverstone, Brands Hatch. Best championship: 1990, 4th
Other major win: 2000 Petit LeMans

Bruce McPhee

AUS
Major win: 1968 Bathurst

Sam McQuagg

USA. Born: 11.11.1935, Columbus, Georgia
NASCAR wins: 1

Steve McQueen

USA. Born: 24.3.1930, Beech Grove, Indiana. Died: 7.11.1980, Juarez, Mexico, cancer

formula	years	starts (DNS)	wins	2nd	3rd	4th	5th	6th	PP	FL	points
SC W	1962-70		-	1	-	-	-	-	-	-	

Graham McRae

NZ. Born: 5.3.1940, Wellington
1971, 1972 and 1973 Tasman Champion, 1970 New Zealand Gold Star Champion, 1972 North American F5000 Champion, 1978 Australian F5000 Champion

formula	years	starts (DNS)	wins	2nd	3rd	4th	5th	6th	PP	FL	points
F1 W	1973	1	-	-	-	-	-	-	-	-	0

Best result: no finishes. Best qualifying: 28th. Team: Williams

F2 E	1969	2	-	-	-	-	-	-	-	-	0
Indy 500	1973	1									
CART	1984-87	2 (1)									

Tasman wins: 13 – 1970 Teretonga, Surfers Paradise, 1971 Levin, Lady Wigram Trophy, Sandown Park, 1972 Levin, Lady Wigram Trophy, Surfers Paradise, Australian GP, 1973 Levin, Lady Wigram Trophy, Sandown Park, 1975 Lady Wigram Trophy
Other major wins: 1973 and 1978 Australian GP

Rick Mears

USA. Born: 3.12.1951, Wichita, Kansas
1979, 1981 and 1982 CART Champion

formula	years	starts (DNS)	wins	2nd	3rd	4th	5th	6th	PP	FL	points
SC W	1979-81			-	-	2	-	1	-	-	
Indy 500	1978-92	15		4	1	2	-	2	-	6	1

Wins: 1979, 1984, 1988 and 1991 Indianapolis 500
Pre-CART Champcar wins: 3 – 1978 Milwaukee, Atlanta, Brands Hatch

CART	1979-92	179 (1)	26	18	24	15	18	8	39	2	

Wins: 1979 Indianapolis 500, Trenton race 3, Atlanta, 1980 Mexico City, 1981 Atlanta race 1, Atlanta race 2, Riverside, Michigan, Watkins Glen, Mexico City, 1982 Phoenix, Atlanta, Pocono 500, Riverside, 1983 Michigan, 1984 Indianapolis 500, 1985 Pocono 500, 1987 Pocono 500, 1988 Indianapolis 500, Milwaukee, 1989 Phoenix, Milwaukee, Laguna Seca, 1990 Phoenix, 1991 Indianapolis 500, Michigan 500. Best championships: 1979, 1981 and 1982, 1st

Maurizio Mediani

I
2001 Russian F3 Champion

Vitor Meira

BR. Born: 27.3.1977, Brasilia
2000 Sud-Am F3 Champion

formula	years	starts (DNS)	wins	2nd	3rd	4th	5th	6th	PP	FL	points
IRL	2002	4	-	-	1	-	-	-	1	-	

Meirschaut

B
1991 Belgian Belcar GT Champion (with Erik Bruynoghe and Guy Verheyen)

Howard Meister

USA
1979 IMSA GTO Champion

formula	years	starts (DNS)	wins	2nd	3rd	4th	5th	6th	PP	FL	points
SC W	1977-84		-	-	1	-	1	-	-		

Jaime Melo Jr

BR. Born: 24.4.1980, Cascavel
2002 Euro F3000 Champion

formula	years	starts (DNS)	wins	2nd	3rd	4th	5th	6th	PP	FL	points
F3000 INT	2000-01	17 (2)	-	1	-	1	2	1	1		14

Best championship: 2000, 11th

Charles Mendez

USA

formula	years	starts (DNS)	wins	2nd	3rd	4th	5th	6th	PP	FL	points
Le Mans	1980-81	2	-	-	-	-	-	-	-		
SC W	1976-92		-	-	-	-	1	-	-		

Major win: 1978 Sebring 12 hrs

Luis Mendez

USA
1980 IMSA GTO Champion

Carlos Menditeguy

RA. Born: 10.8.1915, Buenos Aires. Died: 28.4.1973

formula	years	starts (DNS)	wins	2nd	3rd	4th	5th	6th	PP	FL	points
F1 W	1953-60	10 (1)	-	-	1	1	1	-	-		9

Best championship: 1957, 14th. Best qualifying: 6th. Teams: Gordini, Onofre Marimon, Maserati, Scuderia Sud Americana, Scuderia Centro Sud

SC W	1954-57		1	1	-	-	-	-	-		

Win: 1956 Buenos Aires

Alain Menu

CH. Born: 9.8.1963, Geneva
1997 and 2000 British Touring Car Champion

formula	years	starts (DNS)	wins	2nd	3rd	4th	5th	6th	PP	FL	points
Le Mans	2002	1	-	-	-	-	-	-	-		
F3000 INT	1990-91	6 (1)	-	-	-	-	2	-	-		2

Best championship: 1991, 16th

GT FIA win: 1 – 2001 Jarama

Other major wins: 1996 and 1997 Tourist Trophy (Donington)

Guido Meregalli

I. Born: 1894. Died: 1959

formula	years	starts (DNS)	wins	2nd	3rd	4th	5th	6th	PP	FL	points
GP Pre-50	1922	1									

Major win: 1920 Targa Florio

Harry Merkel

D

formula	years	starts (DNS)	wins	2nd	3rd	4th	5th	6th	PP	FL	points
F1 W	1952	0 (1)	-	-	-	-	-	-	-		0

Best result: no starts. Best qualifying: no times set. Team: Willi Krakau

Volkert Merl

D

formula	years	starts (DNS)	wins	2nd	3rd	4th	5th	6th	PP	FL	points
Le Mans	1980-84	3	-	-	-	1	1	-	-		
SC W	1977-84		3	1	1	3	4	4	-	-	

Wins: 1979 Dijon, Brands Hatch, 1980 Daytona 24 hrs. Best championship: 1982, 19th

Sarel van der Merwe

ZA. Born: 5.12.1946, Port Elizabeth
2001 South African V8 Stock Car Champion

formula	years	starts (DNS)	wins	2nd	3rd	4th	5th	6th	PP	FL	points
Le Mans	1984-90	7	-	-	1	-	1	-	-		
SC W	1983-90		-	-	1	1	1	1	-	-	

Major win: 1984 Daytona 24 hrs

Charles Merz

USA. Born: 6.7.1888, Indianapolis, Indiana. Died: 8.7.1952, Indianapolis, Indiana

formula	years	starts (DNS)	wins	2nd	3rd	4th	5th	6th	PP	FL	points
Indy 500	1911-16	4	-	-	1	1	-	-	-		

Champcar wins: 3 – 1911 Oakland race 2, Santa Monica race 2, 1912 Elgin race 2

Otto Merz

D. Born: 1889, Bad Cannstadt, near Stuttgart. Died: 19.5.1933, Avusrennen

formula	years	starts (DNS)	wins	2nd	3rd	4th	5th	6th	PP	FL	points
GP Pre-50	1927-31	4		1	1	-	-	1	-	-	

Win: 1927 German GP

Arturo Merzario

I. Born: 11.3.1943, Civenna, near Como
1972 European 2-litre Sports Car Champion

formula	years	starts (DNS)	wins	2nd	3rd	4th	5th	6th	PP	FL	points
F1 W	1972-79	57 (29)	-	-	-	3	-	2	-	-	11

Best championship: 1973, 12th. Best qualifying: 3rd. Teams: Ferrari, Williams, Fittipaldi, March, Merzario, Shadow

Le Mans	1970-73	2	-	1	-	-	-	1	-		
SC W	1963-92		11	10	2	6	2	1	8	6	

Wins: 1972 Spa, Targa Florio, 1974 Monza, 1975 Dijon, Monza, Florio Cup (Enna), Nurburgring, 1977 Dijon, Florio Cup (Enna), Estoril, Paul Ricard

F2 E	1971-81	17 (7)	-	-	-	1	1	-	-		0

Other major win: 1975 Targa Florio

Rene Metge

F. Born: 23.10.1941, Montrouge
1982 French Touring Car Champion

formula	years	starts (DNS)	wins	2nd	3rd	4th	5th	6th	PP	FL	points
Le Mans	1977-87	6	-	-	-	-	1	-	-		
SC W	1977-87		-	-	-	1	-	-	-		

Major win: 1983 Tourist Trophy (Silverstone)

Buller Meyer

ZA. Born: 1899. Died: 1958
Major win: 1938 South African GP

Louis Meyer

USA. Born: 21.7.1904, Yonkers, New York. Died: 7.10.1995, Las Vegas, Nevada
1928, 1929 and 1933 Champcar Champion

formula	years	starts (DNS)	wins	2nd	3rd	4th	5th	6th	PP	FL	points
Indy 500	1927-39	13	3	1	-	3	-	-	-		

Wins: 1928, 1933 and 1936 Indianapolis 500

Champcar wins: 8 – 1928 Indianapolis 500, Altoona, 1929 Altoona race 1, Altoona race 2, 1931 Detroit, 1933 Indianapolis 500, 1935 Altoona, 1936 Indianapolis 500

Tomas Mezera

AUS. Born: 5.11.1958

formula	years	starts (DNS)	wins	2nd	3rd	4th	5th	6th	PP	FL	points
Le Mans	1990	1	-	-	-	-	-	-	-		

Major win: 1988 Bathurst

Rick Miaskiewicz

USA. Born: 22.3.1953
1985 Can-Am Champion

formula	years	starts (DNS)	wins	2nd	3rd	4th	5th	6th	PP	FL	points
CART	1986-87	9 (2)	-	-	-	-	-	-	-		

Ryo Michigami

J. Born: 1.3.1973, Nara
2000 Japanese GT Champion

John Mickel

GB. Born: 28.1.1971
2001 ASCAR Champion

Roberto Mieres

RA. Born: 3.12.1924, Mar del Plata

formula	years	starts (DNS)	wins	2nd	3rd	4th	5th	6th	PP	FL	points
F1 W	1953-55	17	-	-	-	3	2	2	-	1	13

Best championships: 1954 and 1955, 8th. Best qualifying: 6th. Teams: Gordini, driver, Maserati

Le Mans	1953-55	2	-	-	-	-	-	-	-	-	
SC W	1953-60		-	-	-	1	1	-	-	-	

Francois Migault

F. Born: 4.12.1944, Le Mans

formula	years	starts (DNS)	wins	2nd	3rd	4th	5th	6th	PP	FL	points
F1 W	1972-75	13 (3)	-	-	-	-	-	-	-	-	0

Best result: 14th. Best qualifying: 14th. Teams: Connew, BRM, Hill, Williams

Le Mans	1972-2002	24	-	2	1	2	-	-	-	-	
SC W	1972-92		-	2	2	-	1	4	-	-	
F2 E	1971-76	10 (3)	-	-	-	1	1	1	-	-	8

Best championship: 1971, 11th

Alec Mildren

AUS
1960 Australian Gold Star Champion
Major win: 1960 Australian GP

John Miles

GB. Born: 14.6.1943, Islington, London

formula	years	starts (DNS)	wins	2nd	3rd	4th	5th	6th	PP	FL	points
F1 W	1969-70	12 (3)	-	-	-	-	1	-	-	-	2

Best championship: 1970, 19th. Best qualifying: 7th. Team: Lotus

F2 E	1969-70	2 (2)	-	-	1	-	-	-	-	-	4

Best championship: 1969, 11th

Ken Miles

USA. Born: 1.11.1918, Sutton Coldfield (GB). Died: 17.8.1966, Riverside

formula	years	starts (DNS)	wins	2nd	3rd	4th	5th	6th	PP	FL	points
Le Mans	1955-66	3	-	1	-	-	-	-	-	-	
SC W	1955-66		3	2	1	-	-	-	1	-	

Wins: 1965 Daytona, 1966 Daytona 24 hrs, Sebring 12 hrs

Andre Milhoux

B. Born: 9.12.1928, Bressoux

formula	years	starts (DNS)	wins	2nd	3rd	4th	5th	6th	PP	FL	points
F1 W	1956	1	-	-	-	-	-	-	-	-	0

Best result: no finishes. Best qualifying: no times set. Team: Gordini

Le Mans	1956	1	-	-	-	-	-	-	-	-	

Steve Millen

NZ. Born: 17.2.1953, Auckland
1992 and 1994 IMSA GTS Champion

formula	years	starts (DNS)	wins	2nd	3rd	4th	5th	6th	PP	FL	points
Le Mans	1990-94	2	-	-	-	-	1	-	-	1	

Major wins: 1980 New Zealand GP, 1994 Daytona 24 hrs, 1994 Sebring 12 hrs

Eddie Miller

USA
1975 SCCA Super Vee Champion

Paul Miller

USA

formula	years	starts (DNS)	wins	2nd	3rd	4th	5th	6th	PP	FL	points
Le Mans	1980-82	3	-	-	-	-	-	-	-	-	
SC W	1973-88		1	-	-	-	-	1	-	-	

Win: 1977 Mosport Park

Tommy Milton

USA. Born: 14.11.1893, St Paul, Minnesota. Died: 11.7.1962, Mount Clemens, Missouri
1921 Champcar Champion

formula	years	starts (DNS)	wins	2nd	3rd	4th	5th	6th	PP	FL	points
GP Pre-50	1925	1									
Indy 500	1919-27	8	2	-	1	-	1	-	1	-	

Wins: 1921 and 1923 Indianapolis 500
Champcar wins: 23 – 1917 Providence race 2, Providence race 3, 1918 Uniontown race 1, 1919 Uniontown race 1, Sheepshead race 1, Uniontown race 2, Uniontown race 6, Elgin, 1920 Beverly Hills race 4, Uniontown race 1, Tacoma, Uniontown race 2, 1921 Beverly Hills race 4, Indianapolis 500, Tacoma, 1922 Beverly Hills race 1, Beverly Hills race 3, Beverly Hills race 6, Kansas City, 1923 Indianapolis 500, 1924 Charlotte, 1925 Culver City race 1, Charlotte race 2

Nicolas Minassian

F. Born: 28.2.1973, Marseille
2002 ASCAR Champion

formula	years	starts (DNS)	wins	2nd	3rd	4th	5th	6th	PP	FL	points
Le Mans	1994-2002	3	-	-	-	-	-	1	-	-	
SRWC win: 1 – 2002 Estoril											
F3000 INT	1998-2000	31	4	1	3	2	3	-	1	-	70

Wins: 1999 Silverstone, 2000 Imola, Magny-Cours, A1 Ring. Best championship: 2000, 2nd

Indy 500	2001	1									
CART	2001	6 (1)									
IRL	2001	1									

Ferdinando "Nando" Minoia

I. Born: 2.6.1884, Milan. Died: 28.6.1940

formula	years	starts (DNS)	wins	2nd	3rd	4th	5th	6th	PP	FL	points
GP Pre-50	1908-31	11	-	1	1	4	1	1	3	1	
Le Mans	1925-32	3	-	-	-	-	-	1			

Major win: 1927 Mille Miglia

Gerhard Mitter

D. Born: 30.8.1935, Schonlinde, Sudetenland. Died: 1.8.1969, Nurburgring, German GP practice
1960 German Formula Junior Champion

formula	years	starts (DNS)	wins	2nd	3rd	4th	5th	6th	PP	FL	points
F1 W	1963-69	5 (2)	-	-	-	-	-	-	-	-	3

Best championship: 1963, 12th. Best qualifying: 12th. Teams: Ecurie Maarsbergen, Lotus, Ron Harris, driver, BMW

Le Mans	1964-69	5	-	-	-	-	-	-	-	-	
SC W	1960-69		1	3	3	3	1	1	-	1	

Win: 1969 Targa Florio

F2 E	1967-69	3	-	-	-	-	-	-	-	-	2

Best championship: 1967, 15th
Other major win: 1966 Austrian GP

Stefano Modena

I. Born: 12.5.1963, San Prospero, Modena
1987 FIA F3000 Champion, 1986 European F3 Cup winner

formula	years	starts (DNS)	wins	2nd	3rd	4th	5th	6th	PP	FL	points
F1 W	1987-92	70 (11)	-	1	1	1	1	2	-	-	17

Best championship: 1991, 8th. Best qualifying: 2nd. Teams: Brabham, EuroBrun, Tyrrell, Jordan

F3000 INT	1987	11	3	1	-	2	-	2	-	1	41

Wins: 1987 Vallelunga, Birmingham, Imola. Best championship: 1987, 1st

Allan Moffat

AUS. Born: 10.11.1939, Saskatoon, Saskatchewan (CDN)
1973, 1976, 1977 and 1983 Australian Touring Car Champion

formula	years	starts (DNS)	wins	2nd	3rd	4th	5th	6th	PP	FL	points
Le Mans	1980-82	2	-	-	-	-	-	-	-	-	

Major wins: 1970, 1971, 1973 and 1977 Bathurst, 1975 Sebring 12 hrs

Kazuo Mogi

J. Born: 2.2.1953
1985 Japanese Touring Car Champion (with Naoki Nagasaka)

formula	years	starts (DNS)	wins	2nd	3rd	4th	5th	6th	PP	FL	points
SC W	1984-90		-	-	-	-	1	1	-	-	

Donald Molenaar

NL. Born: 28.5.1971, Soest
1998 Dutch Touring Car Champion

Guy Moll

DZ. Born: 28.5.1910, Rivet. Died: 15.8.1934, Pescara, Coppa Acerbo

formula	years	starts (DNS)	wins	2nd	3rd	4th	5th	6th	PP	FL	points
GP Pre-50	1933-34	7	1	-	1	-	1	-	-	-	

Win: 1934 Monaco GP

| Le Mans | 1933 | 1 | - | - | - | - | - | - | - | - | |

Other major win: 1934 Avus

Kurt Mollekens

B. Born: 8.3.1973, Bonheiden

formula	years	starts (DNS)	wins	2nd	3rd	4th	5th	6th	PP	FL	points
F3000 INT	1997-98	18 (3)	-	2	-	1	3	1	-	-	22

Best championship: 1998, 6th

Major wins: 1996 Marlboro Masters (Zandvoort), 2000 Spa 24 hrs

Emanuele Moncini

I

SRWC win: 1 – 1999 Enna

Mondron

B

1992 Belgian Belcar GT Champion (with Daniel and Patrick Hubert)

Franck Montagny

F. Born: 5.1.1978, Feurs, Loire

2001 Spanish Formula Nissan Champion

formula	years	starts (DNS)	wins	2nd	3rd	4th	5th	6th	PP	FL	points
Le Mans	1998-2002	5	-	-	-	-	1	-	-		
F3000 INT	1999-2000	20	-	1	1	-	4	-	-		11

Best championship: 1999, 10th

Tiago Monteiro

P. Born: 24.7.1976, Porto

formula	years	starts (DNS)	wins	2nd	3rd	4th	5th	6th	PP	FL	points
F3000 INT	2002	12	-	-	-	-	1	-	-	-	2

Best championship: 2002, 13th

Andrea Montermini

I. Born: 30.5.1964, Sassuolo, Modena

formula	years	starts (DNS)	wins	2nd	3rd	4th	5th	6th	PP	FL	points
F1 W	1994-96	20 (9)	-	-	-	-	-	-	-	-	0

Best result: 8th. Best qualifying: 20th. Teams: Simtek, Pacific, Forti

| Le Mans | 1998-99 | 2 | - | - | - | - | 2 | - | | | |
| F3000 INT | 1990-92 | 31 | 3 | 1 | 4 | 2 | - | - | 5 | 4 | 55 |

Wins: 1992 Barcelona, Spa, Albacete. Best championship: 1992, 2nd

| CART | 1993-99 | 11 (1) | - | - | - | 1 | - | - | - | - | |

Other major win: 1992 Buenos Aires F3000

Robin Montgomerie-Charrington

USA. Born: 22.6.1915, London (GB)

formula	years	starts (DNS)	wins	2nd	3rd	4th	5th	6th	PP	FL	points
F1 W	1952	1	-	-	-	-	-	-	-	-	0

Best result: no finishes. Best qualifying: 15th. Team: Bill Aston

Juan Pablo Montoya

CO. Born: 20.9.1975, Bogota

1999 CART Champion, 1998 FIA F3000 Champion

formula	years	starts (DNS)	wins	2nd	3rd	4th	5th	6th	PP	FL	points
F1 W	2001-02	34	1	7	3	5	1	-	10	6	81

Win: 2001 Italian GP. Best championship: 2002, 4th. Best qualifying: 1st. Team: Williams

| F3000 INT | 1997-98 | 22 | 7 | 2 | 4 | 1 | 1 | 1 | 10 | 8 | 102.5 |

Wins: 1997 Pau, A1 Ring, Jerez, 1998 Barcelona, Silverstone, Pau, Enna. Best championship: 1998, 1st

| Indy 500 | 2000 | 1 | 1 | - | - | - | - | - | - | - | |

Win: 2000 Indianapolis 500

| CART | 1999-2000 | 40 | 10 | 3 | - | 2 | - | 2 | 14 | 12 | |

Wins: 1999 Long Beach, Nazareth, Rio de Janeiro, Cleveland, Mid-Ohio, Chicago, Vancouver, 2000 Milwaukee, US 500 (Michigan), St Louis. Best championship: 1999, 1st

formula	years	starts (DNS)	wins	2nd	3rd	4th	5th	6th	PP	FL	points
IRL	2000	1	1	-	-	-	-	-	-	-	

Win: 2000 Indianapolis 500

Ralph Moody

USA. Born: 10.9.1917

NASCAR wins: 5

Greg Moore

CDN. Born: 22.4.1975, New Westminster, British Columbia. Died: 31.10.1999, Marlboro 500 Champcar race, California Speedway

1995 CART Indy Lights Champion

formula	years	starts (DNS)	wins	2nd	3rd	4th	5th	6th	PP	FL	points
CART	1996-99	72	5	7	5	5	3	3	5	6	

Wins: 1997 Milwaukee, Detroit, 1998 Rio de Janeiro, US 500 (Michigan), 1999 Miami. Best championship: 1998, 5th

Lloyd Moore

USA

NASCAR wins: 1

Lou Moore

USA. Born: 12.9.1904, Hinton, Oklahoma. Died: 25.3.1956, Lakewood Park, Atlanta, heart attack

formula	years	starts (DNS)	wins	2nd	3rd	4th	5th	6th	PP	FL	points
Indy 500	1928-36	9	-	1	2	-	-	-	1	-	

Champcar wins: 2 – 1931 Altoona race 1, Syracuse

Jimmy Morales

MEX

1995 Mexican F2 Champion, 1997 Mexican F3000 Champion

Rocky Moran

USA. Born: 3.2.1950, Pasadena, California

formula	years	starts (DNS)	wins	2nd	3rd	4th	5th	6th	PP	FL	points
Indy 500	1988-90	3	-	-	-	-	-	-	-	-	
CART	1981-90	23 (5)	-	-	-	-	-	2	-	-	

Major win: 1993 Daytona 24 hrs

Giuseppe Morandi

I. Born: 1894. Died: 1.11.1977

formula	years	starts (DNS)	wins	2nd	3rd	4th	5th	6th	PP	FL	points
GP Pre-50	1927	1	-	1	-	-	-	-	-	-	

Major win: 1927 Mille Miglia

Gianni Morbidelli

I. Born: 13.1.1968, Pesaro, near Rimini

1989 European F3 Cup winner, 1989 Italian F3 Champion

formula	years	starts (DNS)	wins	2nd	3rd	4th	5th	6th	PP	FL	points
F1 W	1990-97	67 (3)	-	-	1	-	1	3	-	-	8.5

Best championship: 1995, 14th. Best qualifying: 6th. Teams: Scuderia Italia, Minardi, Ferrari, Arrows, Sauber

| F3000 INT | 1990 | 11 | 1 | - | 2 | 1 | - | - | 1 | - | 20 |

Win: 1990 Enna. Best championship: 1990, 7th

Andre Morel

F. Born: 1884. Died: 1961

formula	years	starts (DNS)	wins	2nd	3rd	4th	5th	6th	PP	FL	points
GP Pre-50	1923-36	9	1	-	2	1	-	-	-	-	

Win: 1925 San Sebastian GP

| Le Mans | 1924-52 | 8 | - | - | 1 | - | - | - | - | - | |

Dino Morelli

GB. Born: 6.6.1973, Ballymoney, Northern Ireland

formula	years	starts (DNS)	wins	2nd	3rd	4th	5th	6th	PP	FL	points
F3000 INT	1995-2001	17 (2)	-	-	1	-	1	-	-	-	6

Best championship: 1997, 11th

Roberto Moreno

BR. Born: 11.2.1959, Rio de Janeiro
1988 FIA F3000 Champion, 1982 New Zealand Formula Pacific Champion

formula	years	starts (DNS)	wins	2nd	3rd	4th	5th	6th	PP	FL	points
F1 W	1982-95	42 (34)	-	1	-	2	1	1	-	1	15

Best championships: 1990 and 1991, 10th. Best qualifying: 5th. Teams: Lotus, AGS, Coloni, EuroBrun, Benetton, Jordan, Minardi, Andrea Moda, Forti

Le Mans	1984	1	-	-	-	-	-	-	-	-	
F2 E	1984	11	2	3	2	-	-	3	2		44

Wins: 1984 Hockenheim race 1, Donington. Best championship: 1982, 2nd

F3000 INT	1985-88	27	5	1	3	2	4	1	7	4	76

Wins: 1987 Enna, 1988 Pau, Silverstone, Monza, Birmingham. Best championship: 1988, 1st

Indy 500	1986-99	2	-	-	-	-	-	-	-	-	
CART	1985-2001	101 (2)	2	5	4	3	3	6	2	2	

Wins: 2000 Cleveland, 2001 Vancouver. Best championship: 2000, 3rd

IRL	1999	2	-	-	-	-	1	-	-	-	

F3 E win: 1 – 1981 Silverstone
Other major wins: 1981, 1983 and 1984 Australian GP, 1982 New Zealand GP, 1982 Macau

Luigi Moreschi

I

formula	years	starts (DNS)	wins	2nd	3rd	4th	5th	6th	PP	FL	points
SC W	1970-83		1	-	2	2	3	2	-	-	

Win: 1977 Vallelunga. Best championship: 1982, 17th

Gianpiero Moretti

I. Born: 20.3.1940, Milan

formula	years	starts (DNS)	wins	2nd	3rd	4th	5th	6th	PP	FL	points
Le Mans	1970-98	4	-	-	-	-	-	1	-		
SC W	1961-92		-	-	-	-	2	2	-	-	

Major wins: 1998 Daytona 24 hrs, 1998 Sebring 12 hrs

Charles Morgan

USA. Born: 4.2.1943
1993 IMSA GTO Champion

Dave Morgan

GB. Born: 7.8.1944, Shepton Mallet, Somerset

formula	years	starts (DNS)	wins	2nd	3rd	4th	5th	6th	PP	FL	points
F1 W	1975	1	-	-	-	-	-	-	-	-	0

Best result: no finishes. Best qualifying: 23rd. Team: Surtees

SC W	1975		-	-	-	-	1	-	-	-	
F2 E	1972-73	18 (4)	1	-	1	3	1	1	-	-	31

Win: 1972 Mallory Park. Best championship: 1972, 6th

Heinrich-Joachim von Morgen

D. Born: 1902, Berlin. Died: 28.5.1932, Nurburgring, Eifelrennen practice

formula	years	starts (DNS)	wins	2nd	3rd	4th	5th	6th	PP	FL	points
GP Pre-50	1928-31	6	1	-	1	-	-	-	-	-	

Win: 1930 Masaryk GP
Other major win: 1930 Eifelrennen (Nurburgring)

Akio Morimoto

J. Born: 24.9.1960, Hyogo
1986 Japanese F3 Champion

formula	years	starts (DNS)	wins	2nd	3rd	4th	5th	6th	PP	FL	points
Le Mans	1986-89	3	-	-	-	-	-	-	-	-	
SC W	1984-89		-	1	-	-	-	-	-	-	

Denis Morin

F. Born: 6.9.1956, Elbeuf
1980 French Formula Renault Champion

formula	years	starts (DNS)	wins	2nd	3rd	4th	5th	6th	PP	FL	points
Le Mans	1979-94	8	-	-	-	-	-	-	-	-	

Juliano Moro

BR. Born: 13.9.1977, Palmas
2001 Sud-Am F3 Champion

Paul Morris

AUS. Born: 22.12.1967, Morwell
1995, 1997, 1999 and 2000 Australian Super Touring Car Champion
Major win: 1999 Bathurst 2-litre

Rob Morris

AUS. Born: 4.10.1948
1979 Australian Touring Car Champion
Major win: 1976 Bathurst

Pontus Morth

S. Born: 16.1.1977, Karstadt
1996 Nordic F3 Champion

John Morton

USA. Born: 17.2.1942, Chicago, Illinois

formula	years	starts (DNS)	wins	2nd	3rd	4th	5th	6th	PP	FL	points
Le Mans	1979-98	9	-	-	1	-	1	-	-	-	
SC W	1964-92		-	1	1	-	-	2	-	-	
CART	1984-90	6 (3)	-	-	-	-	-	-	-	-	

Major win: 1994 Sebring 12 hrs

Emmanuel Moschus

GR
1994 Greek F3 Champion

Silvio Moser

CH. Born: 24.4.1941, Zurich. Died: 26.5.1974, Locarno, following accident during the Monza 1000 kms
1964 Temporada F2 Champion

formula	years	starts (DNS)	wins	2nd	3rd	4th	5th	6th	PP	FL	points
F1 W	1966-71	12 (8)	-	-	-	-	1	1	-	-	3

Best championship: 1969, 16th. Best qualifying: 13th. Teams: Martinelli-Sonvico, Charles Vogele, driver, Jolly Club

SC W	1963-74		-	-	-	-	1	-	-	-	
F2 E	1968-73	28 (4)	-	-	-	1	-	1	-	-	7

Best championship: 1968, 15th

Max Mosley

GB. Born: 13.4.1940

formula	years	starts (DNS)	wins	2nd	3rd	4th	5th	6th	PP	FL	points
F2 E	1968-69	5 (2)	-	-	-	-	-	-	-	-	0

Mike Mosley

USA. Born: 13.12.1944, Oklahoma City. Died: 3.3.1984, Fallbrook, California

formula	years	starts (DNS)	wins	2nd	3rd	4th	5th	6th	PP	FL	points
Indy 500	1968-83	15	-	-	1	-	-	-	-	1	

Pre-CART Champcar wins: 4 – 1971 Trenton race 1, 1974 Phoenix, 1975 Milwaukee, 1976 Milwaukee

CART	1979-83	37 (1)	1	1	1	2	1	1	-	1	

Win: 1981 Milwaukee race 1. Best championship: 1979, 10th

Bill Moss

GB. Born: 4.9.1933, Luton, Bedfordshire
1961 John Davy British Formula Junior Champion

formula	years	starts (DNS)	wins	2nd	3rd	4th	5th	6th	PP	FL	points
F1 W	1959	0 (1)	-	-	-	-	-	-	-	-	0

Best result: no finishes. Best qualifying: no times set. Team: United Racing Stable

Sir Stirling Moss

GB. Born: 17.9.1929, West Kensington, London
1959 British F2 Champion

formula	years	starts (DNS)	wins	2nd	3rd	4th	5th	6th	PP	FL	points
F1 W	1951-61	66 (1)	16	5	3	3	2	1	16	19	186.64

Wins: 1955 British GP, 1956 Monaco GP, Italian GP, 1957 British GP, Pescara,

GP, Italian GP, 1958 Argentinian GP, Dutch GP, Portuguese GP, Moroccan GP, 1959 Portuguese GP, Italian GP, 1960 Monaco GP, United States GP, 1961 Monaco GP, German GP. Best championships: 1955, 1956, 1957 and 1958, 2nd. Best qualifying: 1st. Teams: HWM, ERA, Connaught, Cooper, AE Moss, Maserati, Daimler-Benz, Vanwall, Rob Walker, BRP

formula	years	starts (DNS)	wins	2nd	3rd	4th	5th	6th	PP	FL	points
Le Mans	1951-61	10	-	2	-	-	-	-	1	1	
SC W	1953-62		12	3	3	-	1	1	7	11	

Wins: 1954 Sebring 12 hrs, 1955 Mille Miglia, Tourist Trophy (Dundrod), Targa Florio, 1956 Buenos Aires, Nurburgring, 1957 Swedish GP, 1958 Nurburgring, Tourist Trophy (Goodwood), 1959 Nurburgring, Tourist Trophy (Goodwood), 1960 Nurburgring

Non-championship F1 wins: 1954 Oulton Park Gold Cup, Goodwood, Aintree, 1955 Oulton Park Gold Cup, 1956 Goodwood, Aintree, International Trophy (Silverstone), 1958 Aintree, Caen, 1959 Goodwood, Oulton Park Gold Cup, 1960 Oulton Park Gold Cup, 1961 Vienna, Brands Hatch, Karlskoga, Danish GP, Modena, Oulton Park Gold Cup

Other major wins: 1950 Prix de Monaco, 1950, 1951 (both at Dundrod), 1960 and 1961 (both Goodwood) Tourist Trophy, 1956 Australian GP, 1956, 1959 and 1962 New Zealand GP, 1956 Venezuelan GP, 1960 (December) South African GP, 1961 International Trophy (Silverstone)

Terry Moss
ZA. Born: 16.8.1957, Port Elizabeth
1996 South African Touring Car Champion

Alfredo Mostajo
E
1998 Spanish Touring Car Champion

Satoshi Motoyama
J. Born: 4.3.1971, Tokyo
1998 and 2001 Japanese Formula Nippon Champion

formula	years	starts (DNS)	wins	2nd	3rd	4th	5th	6th	PP	FL	points
Le Mans	1998-99	2	-	-	-	-	-	-	-	-	

Lee Mueller
USA
1981 IMSA GTU Champion

formula	years	starts (DNS)	wins	2nd	3rd	4th	5th	6th	PP	FL	points
SC W	1976-86		-	-	-	-	-	-	-	-	

Best championship: 1981, 14th

Brian Muir
AUS. Born: n/a. Died: 11.9.1983, collapsed driving home from Silverstone after the Tourist Trophy

formula	years	starts (DNS)	wins	2nd	3rd	4th	5th	6th	PP	FL	points
Le Mans	1966-76	4	-	-	-	-	-	-	-	-	

Major win: 1970 Tourist Trophy (Silverstone)

Ralph Mulford
USA. Born: 28.12.1884. Died: 23.10.1973

formula	years	starts (DNS)	wins	2nd	3rd	4th	5th	6th	PP	FL	points
GP Pre-50	1908-12	3 (1)	-	-	-	1	-	-	-	-	
Indy 500	1911-22	10	-	1	1	-	-	-	-	-	

Champcar wins: 17 – 1910 Elgin race 3, 1911 Philadelphia race 2, WK Vanderbilt Cup, 1912 Brighton Beach, 1913 Columbus, 1914 Galveston race 1, Galveston race 2, Galveston race 3, Galesburg, 1915 Des Moines, 1917 Omaha, Providence race 1, Chicago race 5, 1918 Uniontown race 5, Uniontown race 7, 1919 Sheepshead race 2

Barry Mulholland
AUS
Major win: 1968 Bathurst

Jim Mullen
USA

formula	years	starts (DNS)	wins	2nd	3rd	4th	5th	6th	PP	FL	points
Le Mans	1984	1	-	-	-	-	-	-	-	-	

Major win: 1983 Sebring 12 hrs

Alex Muller
D. Born: 20.1.1979, Emmerich

formula	years	starts (DNS)	wins	2nd	3rd	4th	5th	6th	PP	FL	points
F3000 INT	1998-2002	21 (4)	-	-	-	1	-	-	-	-	2

Best championship: 1998, 21st

Dirk Muller
D. Born: 18.11.1975, Burbach
2000 American Le Mans Series GT Champion

formula	years	starts (DNS)	wins	2nd	3rd	4th	5th	6th	PP	FL	points
Le Mans	1999-2000	2	-	-	-	-	-	-	-	-	

Herbert Muller
CH. Born: 11.5.1940, Reinach. Died: 24.5.1981, Nurburgring 1000 kms
1974, 1975 and 1976 Interserie Champion

formula	years	starts (DNS)	wins	2nd	3rd	4th	5th	6th	PP	FL	points
Le Mans	1964-79	13	-	2	-	2	-	-	-	-	
SC W	1961-81		2	4	4	6	7	5	-	1	
F2 E	1975	3	-	-	-	-	-	-	-	-	0

Wins: 1966 Targa Florio, 1973 Targa Florio

Hermann Muller
D. Born: 21.11.1909, Bielefeld. Died: 30.12.1975, Ingolstadt
1939 European Grand Prix Champion (see page 274)

formula	years	starts (DNS)	wins	2nd	3rd	4th	5th	6th	PP	FL	points
GP Pre-50	1937-39	14 (1)	1	1	2	4	1	-	-	1	

Win: 1939 French GP

Jorg Muller
D. Born: 3.9.1969, Kerkrade (NL)
1996 FIA F3000 Champion, 1994 German F3 Champion, 2001 American Le Mans Series GT Champion

formula	years	starts (DNS)	wins	2nd	3rd	4th	5th	6th	PP	FL	points
Le Mans	1997-99	3	-	1	-	-	-	-	-	-	
F3000 INT	1996	10	2	5	1	-	-	2	4		52

Wins: 1996 Pau, Spa. Best championship: 1996, 1st
Other major wins: 1991 Monaco F3, 1993 Macau, 1996 Spa 24 hrs, 1999 Sebring 12 hrs

Siegfried "Sigi" Muller
D
1975 European Touring Car Champion (with Alain Peltier)

formula	years	starts (DNS)	wins	2nd	3rd	4th	5th	6th	PP	FL	points
SC W	1975-77		-	-	1	-	-	-	-	-	

Siegfried "Sigi" Muller Jr
D
1980 European Touring Car Champion (with Helmut Kelleners)

formula	years	starts (DNS)	wins	2nd	3rd	4th	5th	6th	PP	FL	points
Le Mans	1982	1	-	-	-	-	-	-	-	-	
SC W	1981-82		-	-	-	-	1	-	-	-	

Yvan Muller
F. Born: 16.8.1969, Altkirch
1995 French Touring Car Champion, 1992 British F2 Champion

formula	years	starts (DNS)	wins	2nd	3rd	4th	5th	6th	PP	FL	points
Le Mans	1993-96	2	-	-	-	-	-	-	-	-	
F3000 INT	1993	9	-	-	-	-	1	-	-	-	2

Best championship: 1993, 17th

Sandro Munari
I. Born: 27.3.1940, Cavarzere, Venice

formula	years	starts (DNS)	wins	2nd	3rd	4th	5th	6th	PP	FL	points
SC W	1966-92		1	1	-	1	-	-	-	-	

Win: 1972 Targa Florio

Gino Munaron
I. Born: 2.4.1928, Turin

formula	years	starts (DNS)	wins	2nd	3rd	4th	5th	6th	PP	FL	points
F1 W	1960	4	-	-	-	-	-	-	-	-	0

Best result: 13th. Best qualifying: 8th. Teams: driver, Eugenio Castellotti

Le Mans	1959-60	2	-	-	-	-	1	-	-	-	

formula	years	starts (DNS)	wins	2nd	3rd	4th	5th	6th	PP	FL	points
SC W	1955-61		-	-	-	-	2	2	-	-	

"Frank Mundy" (Frank Menendez)
USA. Born: 18.6.1918, Atlanta, Georgia
NASCAR wins: 3

Ken Murillo
USA
1988 SCCA Super Vee Champion, 1987 Barber-SAAB Champion

Greg Murphy
NZ. Born: 23.8.1972, Hastings, New Zealand
1994 and 1995 New Zealand Gold Star Champion, 1995 New Zealand
Formula Brabham Champion

formula	years	starts (DNS)	wins	2nd	3rd	4th	5th	6th	PP	FL	points
Le Mans	1996	1									

Major wins: 1994 New Zealand GP, 1996 and 1999 Bathurst

Jimmy Murphy
USA. Born: 12.9.1894, San Francisco, California. Died: 15.9.1924, Syracuse
1922 and 1924 Champcar Champion

formula	years	starts (DNS)	wins	2nd	3rd	4th	5th	6th	PP	FL	points
GP Pre-50	1921-23	2	1	-	1	-	-	-		1	

Win: 1921 French GP

Indy 500	1920-24	5	1	-	2	2	-	-	2	-	

Win: 1922 Indianapolis 500

Champcar wins: 19 – 1920 Beverly Hills race 1, Beverly Hills race 3, Fresno,
1921 Beverly Hills race 3, Beverly Hills race 9, Beverly Hills race 10, San
Carlos, 1922 Beverly Hills race 4, Fresno race 1, Cotati race 2, Indianapolis
500, Uniontown, Tacoma, Beverly Hills race 7, 1923 Beverly Hills race 1,
Fresno race 1, 1924 Altoona race 1, Kansas City, Altoona race 2

Les Murphy
AUS
Major wins: 1935 and 1937 Australian GP

Bill Murray
AUS
Major win: 1947 Australian GP

David Murray
GB. Born: 28.12.1909, Edinburgh. Died: 5.4.1973, Las Palmas, Canary
Islands (E), road accident

formula	years	starts (DNS)	wins	2nd	3rd	4th	5th	6th	PP	FL	points
F1 W	1950-52	4 (1)	-	-	-	-	-	-	-	-	0

**Best result: no finishes. Best qualifying: 15th. Teams: Scuderia Ambrosiana,
Ecurie Ecosse**

GP Pre-50	1949	4	-	-	-	-	-	-			
Le Mans	1937	1	-	-	-	-	-	-			

Luigi Musso
I. Born: 29.7.1924, Rome. Died: 6.7.1958, Reims,
French GP

formula	years	starts (DNS)	wins	2nd	3rd	4th	5th	6th	PP	FL	points
F1 W	1953-58	24 (1)	1	5	1	1	1	-	-	1	44

**Win: 1956 Argentinian GP. Best championship: 1957, 3rd. Best qualifying: 2nd.
Teams: Maserati, Ferrari**

Le Mans	1955-57	2	-	-	-	-	-	-			
SC W	1953-58		2	4	2	2	3	1	-	-	

Wins: 1957 Buenos Aires, 1958 Targa Florio
Non-championship F1 wins: 1954 Pescara, 1957 Reims, 1958 Syracuse

Billy Myers
USA. Born: n/a. Died: 12.4.1958, Winston-Salem NASCAR
NASCAR wins: 2

N

"Bernd Nacke" see Gunther Bechem

Giancarlo Naddeo
I
1971 Italian F3 Champion

formula	years	starts (DNS)	wins	2nd	3rd	4th	5th	6th	PP	FL	points
F2 E	1978	0 (5)	-	-	-	-	-	-	-	-	0

Jerry Nadeau
USA. Born: 9.9.1970, Danbury, Connecticut
NASCAR wins: 1 (in Modern era)

Naoki Nagasaka
J. Born: 24.4.1953, Aichi
1984 Japanese Sports-Prototype Champion (with Keiichi Suzuki), 1985
(with Kazuo Mogi) and 1987 (solo) Japanese Touring Car Champion

formula	years	starts (DNS)	wins	2nd	3rd	4th	5th	6th	PP	FL	points
Le Mans	1990-93	3	-	-	-	-	1	-	-	-	
SC W	1982-92		-	-	-	2	-	1	-	-	

Satoru Nakajima
J. Born: 23.2.1953, Okazaki City
1981, 1982, 1984, 1985 and 1986 Japanese F2 Champion

formula	years	starts (DNS)	wins	2nd	3rd	4th	5th	6th	PP	FL	points
F1 W	1987-91	74 (6)	-	-	-	2	2	6	-	1	16

Best championship: 1987, 11th. Best qualifying: 6th. Teams: Lotus, Tyrrell

Le Mans	1985-86	2	-	-	-	-	-	-			
SC W	1984-86		-	1	-	-	-	-			
F2 E	1982	5	-	1	-	-	-	-			6

Best championship: 1982, 13th

F3000 INT	1986	7	-	-	-	1	2	-	-	-	7

Best championship: 1986, 10th

Osamu Nakako
J. Born: 20.8.1954
1997 Japanese Touring Car Champion, 1981 Japanese F3 Champion

formula	years	starts (DNS)	wins	2nd	3rd	4th	5th	6th	PP	FL	points
SC W	1982-87		-	1	-	-	-	-	-	-	

Kengo Nakamoto
J
1982 Japanese F3 Champion

Shinji Nakano
J. Born: 4.4.1971, Osaka

formula	years	starts (DNS)	wins	2nd	3rd	4th	5th	6th	PP	FL	points
F1 W	1997-98	33	-	-	-	-	2	-	-	2	

Best championship: 1997, 16th. Best qualifying: 12th. Teams: Prost, Minardi

CART	2000-02	56 (1)	-	-	-	1	1	-	-	1	

Akihiko Nakaya
J. Born: 3.11.1957, Tokyo
1988 Japanese F3 Champion

formula	years	starts (DNS)	wins	2nd	3rd	4th	5th	6th	PP	FL	points
Le Mans	1989-99	3	-	-	-	-	-	-			

Alessandro Nannini
I. Born: 7.7.1959, Siena

formula	years	starts (DNS)	wins	2nd	3rd	4th	5th	6th	PP	FL	points
F1 W	1986-90	76 (2)	1	2	6	4	2	4	-	2	65

**Win: 1989 Japanese GP. Best championship: 1989, 6th. Best qualifying: 3rd.
Teams: Minardi, Benetton**

Le Mans	1983-85	3	-	-	-	-	-	1	-	1	
SC W	1982-92		1	3	3	2	-	1	-	3	

Win: 1984 Kyalami. Best championship: 1985, 8th. GT FIA win: 1 – 1997 Suzuka

formula	years	starts (DNS)	wins	2nd	3rd	4th	5th	6th	PP	FL	points
F2 E	1982-84	35 (1)	-	2	1	2	3	-	-	1	28

Best championship: 1983, 7th

John Napier
GB
Major win: 1905 Tourist Trophy

Maurizio de Narvaez
CO. Born: 18.5.1941

formula	years	starts (DNS)	wins	2nd	3rd	4th	5th	6th	PP	FL	points
Le Mans	1981-85	4	-	-	-	1	-	-			
SC W	1975-86		-	-	-	1	-	1	-	-	

Major win: 1984 Sebring 12 hrs

Emanuele Naspetti
I. Born: 24.2.1968, Ancona
1997 Italian Touring Car Champion, 1988 Italian F3 Champion

formula	years	starts (DNS)	wins	2nd	3rd	4th	5th	6th	PP	FL	points
F1 W	1992-93	6	-	-	-	-	-	-	-	-	0

Best result: 11th. Best qualifying: 21st. Teams: March, Jordan

Le Mans	2000	1	-	-	-	-	-	-			
F3000 INT	1989-92	31 (4)	5	1	-	1	1	3	2	4	59

Wins: 1991 Enna, Hockenheim, Brands Hatch, Spa, 1992 Pau. Best championship: 1991, 3rd

Massimo Natili
I. Born: 28.7.1935, Ronciglione, Viterbo

formula	years	starts (DNS)	wins	2nd	3rd	4th	5th	6th	PP	FL	points
F1 W	1961	1	-	-	-	-	-	-	-	-	0

Best result: no finishes. Best qualifying: 28th. Team: Scuderia Centro Sud

Le Mans	1966	1									

Charoensukawattana Nattavude
T. Born: 4.9.1963
2001 Asian Touring Car Champion

Giuseppe Navone
I

formula	years	starts (DNS)	wins	2nd	3rd	4th	5th	6th	PP	FL	points
Le Mans	1951	1	-	-	-	-	-	-			

Major win: 1948 Mille Miglia

Brian Naylor
GB. Born: 24.3.1923, Salford, near Manchester. Died: 8.8.1989, Marbella (E)

formula	years	starts (DNS)	wins	2nd	3rd	4th	5th	6th	PP	FL	points
F1 W	1957-61	7 (1)	-	-	-	-	-	-	-	-	0

Best result: 13th. Best qualifying: 7th. Teams: driver, JBW

Le Mans	1958-59	2	-	-	-	-	-	-			

Mike Nazaruk
USA. Born: 2.10.1921, Newark, New Jersey. Died: 1.5.1955, Langhorne, Pennsylvania

formula	years	starts (DNS)	wins	2nd	3rd	4th	5th	6th	PP	FL	points
Indy 500	1951-54	3	-	1	-	-	1	-	-	-	

Champcar win: 1 – 1952 Milwaukee race 1

Felice Nazzaro
I. Born: 1880, Turin. Died: 21.3.1940, Turin

formula	years	starts (DNS)	wins	2nd	3rd	4th	5th	6th	PP	FL	points
GP Pre-50	1905-24	12	2	4	1	-	-	1		1	1

Wins: 1907 French GP, 1922 French GP
Other major wins: 1907 Kaiserpreis, 1907 and 1913 Targa Florio

Piero Necchi
I. Born: 26.12.1951, Alessandria

formula	years	starts (DNS)	wins	2nd	3rd	4th	5th	6th	PP	FL	points
F2 E	1978-82	31 (7)	-	1	3	1	1	-	-	1	23

Best championship: 1978, 6th

Timothy "Tiff" Needell
GB. Born: 29.10.1951, Havant, Hampshire

formula	years	starts (DNS)	wins	2nd	3rd	4th	5th	6th	PP	FL	points
F1 W	1980	1 (1)	-	-	-	-	-	-	-	-	0

Best result: no finishes. Best qualifying: 23rd. Team: Ensign

Le Mans	1981-97	14	-	-	1	-	-	-			
SC W	1981-92		-	-	1	1	1	1	-	-	
F2 E	1977-81	4	-	-	-	-	-	-	-	-	0

Jochen Neerpasch
D. Born: 1939, Krefeld

formula	years	starts (DNS)	wins	2nd	3rd	4th	5th	6th	PP	FL	points
Le Mans	1964-68	5	-	-	1	-	1	-			
SC W	1962-68		1	2	4	3	-	1	-	-	

Win: 1968 Daytona 24 hrs

Harald Neger
A
Major win: 1980 Tourist Trophy

Osvaldo Negri Jr
BR. Born: 29.5.1964
1998 Mexican Indy Lights Champion, 1990 Brazilian F3 Champion

Jac Nelleman
DK. Born: 19.4.1944, Copenhagen
1976 and 1977 Danish F3 Champion

formula	years	starts (DNS)	wins	2nd	3rd	4th	5th	6th	PP	FL	points
F1 W	1976	0 (1)	-	-	-	-	-	-	-	-	0

Best result: no starts. Best qualifying: 27th. Team: RAM

Robert Nelleman
DK
1950, 1951, 1953, 1954 and 1955 Danish F3 Champion, 1960, 1963, 1964 and 1965 Danish 500cc Champion

Joe Nemechek
USA. Born: 26.9.1963, Naples, Florida
NASCAR wins: 2 (in Modern era)

Michel Neugarten
B. Born: 10.4.1955, Uccle

formula	years	starts (DNS)	wins	2nd	3rd	4th	5th	6th	PP	FL	points
Le Mans	1993-2002	8	-	-	-	-	-	-			

GT FIA wins: 2 – 1994 Dijon, Spa

Jurgen Neuhaus
D
1970 Interserie Champion

Josef Neuhauser
A. Born: 3.1.1959
1989, 1990, 1991, 1994, 1995, 1996 and 1997 Austrian F3 Champion, 1997, 1998, 2000 and 2001 Interserie Champion

Marko Nevalainen
SF. Born: 11.1.1977
2000 Norwegian F3 Champion, 2000 Finnish F3 Champion

Patrick Neve
B. Born: 13.10.1949, Liege

formula	years	starts (DNS)	wins	2nd	3rd	4th	5th	6th	PP	FL	points
F1 W	1976-77	10 (3)	-	-	-	-	-	-	-	-	0

Best result: 7th. Best qualifying: 19th. Teams: RAM, Ensign, Williams

Le Mans	1980-82	2	-	-	-	-	-	-			

formula	years	starts (DNS)	wins	2nd	3rd	4th	5th	6th	PP	FL	points
SC W	1978-82					1					
F2 E	1975-83	8 (1)			1					1	4

Best championship: 1977, 14th

Paul Newman
USA. Born: 26.1.1925, Shaker Heights, Ohio

formula	years	starts (DNS)	wins	2nd	3rd	4th	5th	6th	PP	FL	points
Le Mans	1979	1		1							
SC W	1977-92			2			1				

Ryan Newman
USA. Born: 8.12.1977, South Bend, Indiana

NASCAR wins: 1 (in Modern era)

Rob Nguyen
AUS. Born: 16.8.1980

formula	years	starts (DNS)	wins	2nd	3rd	4th	5th	6th	PP	FL	points
F3000 INT	2002	12				1					2

Best championship: 2002, 13th

Chuck Nicholson (Charles Nickerson)
GB

formula	years	starts (DNS)	wins	2nd	3rd	4th	5th	6th	PP	FL	points
Le Mans	1982	1									
SC W	1981-82						1				

Major wins: 1981 and 1982 Tourist Trophy (Silverstone)

John Nicholson
NZ. Born: 6.10.1941, Auckland
1973 BP and 1974 John Player British Formula Atlantic Champion

formula	years	starts (DNS)	wins	2nd	3rd	4th	5th	6th	PP	FL	points
F1 W	1974-75	1 (1)									0

Best result: 17th. Best qualifying: 26th. Team: Lyncar

formula	years	starts (DNS)	wins	2nd	3rd	4th	5th	6th	PP	FL	points
Le Mans	1974	1									
F2 E	1976	1 (5)									0

Helmut Niedermayr
D. Born: 29.11.1915, Munich. Died: 3.4.1985, Virgin Islands

formula	years	starts (DNS)	wins	2nd	3rd	4th	5th	6th	PP	FL	points
F1 W	1952	1									0

Best result: no finishes. Best qualifying: no times set. Team: driver

formula	years	starts (DNS)	wins	2nd	3rd	4th	5th	6th	PP	FL	points
Le Mans	1952	1		1							

Klaus Niedzwiedz
D. Born: 24.2.1951, Dortmund
1984 Interserie Champion

formula	years	starts (DNS)	wins	2nd	3rd	4th	5th	6th	PP	FL	points
Le Mans	1981-82	2									
SC W	1979-86			1		1					1

Best championship: 1986, 20th

John Nielsen
DK. Born: 7.2.1956, Varde
1995 FIA GT Champion (with Thomas Bscher), 1995 European GT Champion (with Bscher), 1996 Japanese GT Champion (with David Brabham), 1982 German F3 Champion

formula	years	starts (DNS)	wins	2nd	3rd	4th	5th	6th	PP	FL	points
Le Mans	1986-2001	14	1			2	1				

Win: 1990 Le Mans 24 hrs

formula	years	starts (DNS)	wins	2nd	3rd	4th	5th	6th	PP	FL	points
SC W	1985-92		2	3	1	2	2	1			

Wins: 1987 Brands Hatch, 1988 Brands Hatch. Best championship: 1988, 11th. GT FIA wins: 3 – 1995 Monza, Donington, 1996 Monza. SRWC wins: 2 – 2001 Brno, Mondello Park

formula	years	starts (DNS)	wins	2nd	3rd	4th	5th	6th	PP	FL	points
F2 E	1981	1 (1)									0
F3000 INT	1985-86	22	1	5	2	1	1	1	2	3	51

Win: 1985 Estoril. Best championship: 1985, 4th

F3 E wins: 6 – 1983 Magny-Cours, Monza, Zandvoort, Knutstorp, 1984 Zolder, Nogaro

Other major wins: 1984 Macau, 1985 Curacao F3000, 1988 Daytona 24 hrs

Ambrausus "Brausch" Niemann
ZA. Born: 7.1.1939, Durban

formula	years	starts (DNS)	wins	2nd	3rd	4th	5th	6th	PP	FL	points
F1 W	1963-65	1 (1)									0

Best result: 14th. Best qualifying: 15th. Team: Ted Lanfear

Kees Nierop
CDN. Born: 16.3.1958

formula	years	starts (DNS)	wins	2nd	3rd	4th	5th	6th	PP	FL	points
Le Mans	1987	1									
SC W	1979-87							1			

Major win: 1983 Sebring 12 hrs

"Nikko"
CH
1996 Swiss Touring Car Champion

Nikolas Nikolouzos
GR
1995 and 1998 Greek F3 Champion

Joe Nikrent
USA. Born: n/a. Died: 19??

formula	years	starts (DNS)	wins	2nd	3rd	4th	5th	6th	PP	FL	points
Indy 500	1913	1									

Champcar win: 1 – 1909 Los Angeles-Phoenix

Louis Nikrent
USA

formula	years	starts (DNS)	wins	2nd	3rd	4th	5th	6th	PP	FL	points
GP Pre-50	1915	1									

Champcar win: 1 – 1911 Santa Monica race 3

Gunnar Nilsson
S. Born: 20.11.1948, Helsingborg. Died: 20.10.1978, Charring Cross Hospital, Hammersmith, London, cancer
1975 British F3 Champion

formula	years	starts (DNS)	wins	2nd	3rd	4th	5th	6th	PP	FL	points
F1 W	1976-77	31 (1)	1		3	1	3	1		1	31

Win: 1977 Belgian GP. Best championship: 1977, 8th. Best qualifying: 3rd. Team: Lotus

formula	years	starts (DNS)	wins	2nd	3rd	4th	5th	6th	PP	FL	points
SC W	1976		1								

Win: 1976 Osterreichring

formula	years	starts (DNS)	wins	2nd	3rd	4th	5th	6th	PP	FL	points
F2 E	1973-74	3				1					6

Best championship: 1973, 13th

Jan "Flash" Nilsson
S. Born: 15.12.1960, Karlstad
1996 and 1997 Swedish Touring Car Champion, 1989 Swedish F3 Champion

"Ninos"
GR
1990 Greek F3 Champion

Kris Nissen
DK. Born: 20.7.1960, Arnum
1986 German F3 Champion, 1992 Nordic Touring Car Champion

formula	years	starts (DNS)	wins	2nd	3rd	4th	5th	6th	PP	FL	points
Le Mans	1987-88	2									
SC W	1986-92			1		1	2	1			

Best championship: 1987, 18th

formula	years	starts (DNS)	wins	2nd	3rd	4th	5th	6th	PP	FL	points
F3000 INT	1987	0 (1)									0

Luciano della Noce
I. Born: 5.8.1940, Rome

formula	years	starts (DNS)	wins	2nd	3rd	4th	5th	6th	PP	FL	points
Le Mans	1994-96	3									

GT FIA wins: 2 – 1994 Vallelunga, 1996 Anderstorp

Peter Nocker

D
1963 European Touring Car Champion

formula	years	starts (DNS)	wins	2nd	3rd	4th	5th	6th	PP	FL	points
Le Mans	1964-65	2	-	-	-	-	1	-	-	-	
SC W	1956-68		-	-	-	1	1	1	-	-	

Hideki Noda

J. Born: 7.3.1969, Osaka

formula	years	starts (DNS)	wins	2nd	3rd	4th	5th	6th	PP	FL	points
F1 W	1994	3	-	-	-	-	-	-	-	-	0

Best result: no finishes. Best qualifying: 23rd. Team: Larrousse

formula	years	starts (DNS)	wins	2nd	3rd	4th	5th	6th	PP	FL	points
F3000 INT	1992-94	24 (2)	-	-	1	-	1	-	-	-	6

Best championship: 1994, 9th

formula	years	starts (DNS)	wins	2nd	3rd	4th	5th	6th	PP	FL	points
IRL	2002	6									

Bill Norton

USA
NASCAR wins: 1

Buddy Norton

USA
NASCAR wins: 1

Rodney Nuckey

GB. Born: 26.6.1929, Muswell Hill, London. Died: 29.6.2000, Manila (RP)

formula	years	starts (DNS)	wins	2nd	3rd	4th	5th	6th	PP	FL	points
F1 W	1953	1	-	-	-	-	-	-	-	-	0

Best result: 11th. Best qualifying: 20th. Team: driver
Non-championship F1 win: 1953 Helsinki

Tazio Nuvolari

I. Born: 16.11.1892, Casteldario, near Mantua. Died: 11.8.1953, Mantua

formula	years	starts (DNS)	wins	2nd	3rd	4th	5th	6th	PP	FL	points
GP Pre-50	1928-48	53	10	7	5	5	6	-	2	9	

Wins: 1931 Italian GP, 1932 Monaco GP, Italian GP, French GP, 1933 Belgian GP, 1935 German GP, 1936 Hungarian GP, 1938 Italian GP, Donington GP, 1939 Yugoslavian GP

formula	years	starts (DNS)	wins	2nd	3rd	4th	5th	6th	PP	FL	points
Le Mans	1933	1	1	-	-	-	-	-	-	-	

Win: 1933 Le Mans 24 hrs
Champcar win: 1 – 1936 George Vanderbilt Cup
Other major wins: 1928 Tripoli, 1930 and 1933 Mille Miglia, 1930 and 1933 Tourist Trophy (Ards), 1931 and 1932 Targa Florio, 1932 Coppa Acerbo (Pescara), 1933 Tunis, 1933 Eifelrennen (Nurburgring)

O

Robert O'Brien

USA. Born: 30.3.1922. Died: 30.5.1997

formula	years	starts (DNS)	wins	2nd	3rd	4th	5th	6th	PP	FL	points
F1 W	1952	1	-	-	-	-	-	-	-	-	0

Best result: 14th. Best qualifying: 22nd. Team: driver

Johnny O'Connell

USA. Born: 24.7.1962, Poughkeepsie, New York State
1987 North American Formula Atlantic (Western) Champion

formula	years	starts (DNS)	wins	2nd	3rd	4th	5th	6th	PP	FL	points
Le Mans	1994-2002	6	-	-	-	2	-	-	-		
Indy 500	1996	1	-	-	-	-	-	-	-		
IRL	1996-97	4 (1)	-	-	-	1	-	-	-		

Best championship: 1996, 9th
Major wins: 1994 Sebring 12 hrs, 2001 Daytona 24 hrs

Pat O'Connor

USA. Born: 9.10.1928, North Vernon, Indiana. Died: 30.5.1958, Indianapolis 500

formula	years	starts (DNS)	wins	2nd	3rd	4th	5th	6th	PP	FL	points
Indy 500	1954-58	5	-	-	-	-	-	-	1	-	

Champcar wins: 2 – 1956 Darlington, 1957 Trenton

Eddie O'Donnell

USA. Born: Whitewater, Wisconsin. Died: 26.11.1920, Beverly Hills, California, from injuries inflicted the previous day

formula	years	starts (DNS)	wins	2nd	3rd	4th	5th	6th	PP	FL	points
GP Pre-50	1915	1	-	-	-	-	-	-	-	-	
Indy 500	1915-20	3	-	-	-	1	-	-	-	-	

Champcar wins: 3 – 1915 Glendale, Ascot, Galesburg

Steve O'Rourke

GB. Born: 1.10.1940, London
1997 British GT Champion (with Tim Sudgen)

formula	years	starts (DNS)	wins	2nd	3rd	4th	5th	6th	PP	FL	points
Le Mans	1979-98	8	-	-	-	1	-	-	-	-	
SC W	1979-92		-	1	-	-	-	-	-	-	

Stefan Oberndorfer

D. Born: 3.8.1959, Munich
GT FIA win: 1 – 1995 Montlhery

Larry Oberto

USA. Born: 13.2.1962
2001 Sports Racing SRL class Champion (with Thed Bjork)

Markus Oestreich

D. Born: 3.7.1963, Fulda

formula	years	starts (DNS)	wins	2nd	3rd	4th	5th	6th	PP	FL	points
F3000 INT	1988	0 (2)	-	-	-	-	-	-	-	-	0

Major win: 1990 Spa 24 hrs

Eric Offenstadt

F. Born: 1939

formula	years	starts (DNS)	wins	2nd	3rd	4th	5th	6th	PP	FL	points
F2 E	1967-69	4 (2)	-	-	-	-	1	-	-	-	2

Best championship: 1968, 17th

Hitoshi Ogawa

J. Born: 15.2.1956, Tokyo. Died: 24.5.1992, Suzuka F3000 race
1989 Japanese F3000 Champion

formula	years	starts (DNS)	wins	2nd	3rd	4th	5th	6th	PP	FL	points
Le Mans	1988-90	3	-	-	-	-	-	1	-	-	
SC W	1985-92		1	-	-	1	1	1	-	-	

Win: 1992 Monza. Best championship: 1992, 11th

Hideki Okada

J. Born: 28.11.1958, Okayama
1988 Japanese Sports-Prototype Champion (with Stanley Dickens)

formula	years	starts (DNS)	wins	2nd	3rd	4th	5th	6th	PP	FL	points
Le Mans	1987-95	6	-	-	-	-	-	-	-	-	
SC W	1982-92		-	-	-	1	-	-	1	-	

Bernd "Barney" Oldfield

USA. Born: 3.6.1878, Monticello, Toledo, Ohio. Died: 4.10.1946, Beverly Hills, California

formula	years	starts (DNS)	wins	2nd	3rd	4th	5th	6th	PP	FL	points
GP Pre-50	1912-15	3	-	-	-	1	-	-	-	-	
Indy 500	1914-16	2	-	-	-	2	-	-	-	-	

Champcar wins: 2 – 1915 Venice, Tucson

Casimiro de Oliveira

P
Major win: 1951 Portuguese GP

Eduardo Oliveira

MEX
1999 Mexican F3 Champion

Jackie Oliver

GB. Born: 14.8.1942, Chadwell Heath, Romford, Essex
1974 Can-Am Champion

formula	years	starts (DNS)	wins	2nd	3rd	4th	5th	6th	PP	FL	points
F1 W	1967-77	50 (2)	-	-	2	-	2	1	-	1	13

Best championship: 1968, 13th. Best qualifying: 2nd. Teams: Lotus, BRM, McLaren, Shadow

| Le Mans | 1968-71 | 3 | - | 1 | - | - | - | - | - | - | 1 |

Win: 1969 Le Mans 24 hrs

| SC W | 1967-76 | | 6 | 1 | - | - | 1 | - | - | 1 | 2 |

Wins: 1969 Sebring 12 hrs, Le Mans 24 hrs, 1971 Daytona 24 hrs, Monza, Spa, 1976 Mosport Park

| F2 E | 1967-68 | 11 (2) | - | - | - | 3 | 1 | 1 | - | - | 17 |

Best championship: 1968, 5th

Anders Olofsson

S. Born: 31.3.1952, Argelholm
1990 Japanese Sports-Prototype Champion (with Masahiro Hasemi), 1989 and 1991 Japanese Touring Car Champion (with Hasemi), 1977 and 1978 Swedish F3 Champion

formula	years	starts (DNS)	wins	2nd	3rd	4th	5th	6th	PP	FL	points
Le Mans	1987-97	9	-	1	-	-	-	-	-	-	
SC W	1978-92		-	-	1	-	-	1	-	-	

Best championship: 1990, 20th. GT FIA wins: 2 – 1994 Vallelunga, 1996 Anderstorp

| F2 E | 1979-81 | 3 | - | - | - | - | - | - | - | - | 0 |

F3 E wins: 7 – 1977 Zandvoort, Osterreichring, Knutstorp, 1978 Nurburgring, Osterreichring, Knutstorp, Kassel-Calden
Other major win: 1991 Spa 24 hrs

Silvio Oltra

RA
1987 TC2000 Argentinian Touring Car Champion

Danny Ongais

USA. Born: 21.5.1942, Honolulu, Hawaii

formula	years	starts (DNS)	wins	2nd	3rd	4th	5th	6th	PP	FL	points
F1 W	1977-78	4 (2)	-	-	-	-	-	-	-	-	0

Best result: 7th. Best qualifying: 21st. Teams: Interscope, Ensign

| Le Mans | 1980-88 | 3 | - | - | - | - | - | - | - | - | |
| SC W | 1971-88 | | 1 | - | 2 | 1 | 1 | - | 1 | 2 | |

Win: 1979 Daytona 24 hrs

| Indy 500 | 1977-96 | 11 | - | - | - | 1 | - | - | - | - | |

Pre-CART Champcar wins: 6 – 1977 Michigan, 1978 Ontario, Texas, Mosport Park, Milwaukee, Michigan

| CART | 1979-87 | 52 (4) | - | - | 2 | 2 | 4 | 4 | - | - | |

Best championship: 1979, 6th

| IRL | 1996-97 | 2 | - | - | - | - | - | - | - | - | |

Carlo Ongaro

I
Major win: 1936 Mille Miglia

Juan Carlos Onoro

E
1977 Spanish Touring Car Champion

Rohan Onslow

AUS
1988 Australian Formula Pacific Champion, 1989 Australian Formula Holden Champion

Rikky von Opel

FL. Born: 14.10.1947, New York City (USA)
1972 Lombard British F3 Champion

formula	years	starts (DNS)	wins	2nd	3rd	4th	5th	6th	PP	FL	points
F1 W	1973-74	10 (4)	-	-	-	-	-	-	-	-	0

Best result: 9th. Best qualifying: 14th. Teams: Ensign, Brabham

Karl Oppitzhauser

A

formula	years	starts (DNS)	wins	2nd	3rd	4th	5th	6th	PP	FL	points
F1 W	1976	0 (1)	-	-	-	-	-	-	-	-	0

Best result: no starts. Best qualifying: not allowed to qualify. Team: Sports Cars of Austria

Frederico "Fritz" d'Orey

BR. Born: 25.3.1938, Sao Paulo. Died: 1961

formula	years	starts (DNS)	wins	2nd	3rd	4th	5th	6th	PP	FL	points
F1 W	1959	3	-	-	-	-	-	-	-	-	0

Best result: 10th. Best qualifying: 17th. Teams: Scuderia Centro Sud, Camoradi USA

| SC W | 1960 | | - | - | - | - | 1 | - | - | - | |

Hoover Orsi

BR. Born: 16.5.1978, Campo Grande
1999 Sud-Am F3 Champion, 2001 North American Toyota Atlantic Champion

Stephane Ortelli

F. Born: 30.3.1970, Hyeres
2002 FIA GT N-GT class Champion, 2002 Porsche Supercup Champion

formula	years	starts (DNS)	wins	2nd	3rd	4th	5th	6th	PP	FL	points
Le Mans	1995-2002	8	1	1	-	-	-	-	-	-	

Win: 1998 Le Mans 24 hrs

Arthur Owen

GB. Born: 23.3.1915, London

formula	years	starts (DNS)	wins	2nd	3rd	4th	5th	6th	PP	FL	points
F1 W	1960	1	-	-	-	-	-	-	-	-	0

Best result: no finishes. Best qualifying: 11th. Team: driver

Peter Owen

GB. Born: 17.10.1946, Beverley, Yorkshire
2000 Sports Racing SRL class Champion (with Mark Smithson)

Everett "Cotton" Owens

USA. Born: 21.5.1924
NASCAR wins: 9

Dave Oxton

NZ. Born: 1946
1972, 1973, 1974, 1981 and 1982 New Zealand Gold Star Champion, 1981 New Zealand Formula Pacific Champion
Major win: 1983 New Zealand GP

P

Gianantonio Pacchioni

I. Born: 23.12.1969
Major wins: 1993 and 1995 Monaco F3

Carlos Pace

BR. Born: 6.10.1944, Sao Paulo. Died: 18.3.1977, Mairipora, near Sao Paulo, aircraft accident
1970 Forward Trust British F3 Champion

formula	years	starts (DNS)	wins	2nd	3rd	4th	5th	6th	PP	FL	points
F1 W	1972-77	72 (1)	1	3	2	5	3	2	1	5	58

Win: 1975 Brazilian GP. Best championship: 1975, 6th. Best qualifying: 1st.
Teams: Williams, Surtees, John Goldie, Brabham

Le Mans	1973	1	-	1	-	-	-	-	-	-	
SC W	1972-73		-	3	2	3	-	1	-	-	
F2 E	1971-73	13 (2)	-	1	-	1	-	-	1	1	7

Best championship: 1972, 15th

Jim Pace

USA. Born: 1.2.1961, Monticello

1994 IMSA GTU Champion

formula	years	starts (DNS)	wins	2nd	3rd	4th	5th	6th	PP	FL	points
Le Mans	1996	1	-	-	-	-	-	-	-	-	

Major wins: 1996 Daytona 24 hrs, 1996 Sebring 12 hrs

Jim Packard
USA. Born: 23.7.1931, Hendersonville, North Carolina. Died: 1.10.1960, Fairfield, Illinois
Champcar wins: 1 – 1960 Springfield

Gary Paffett
GB. Born: 24.3.1981, Bromley
2002 German F3 Champion

Eddie Pagan
USA. Born: 1.8.1918, Midland, Texas. Died: 1.8.1984, Harrisburg, North Carolina
NASCAR wins: 4

Cirillo "Nello" Pagani
I. Born: 11.10.1911, Milan

formula	years	starts (DNS)	wins	2nd	3rd	4th	5th	6th	PP	FL	points
F1 W	1950	1	-	-	-	-	-	-	-	-	0

Best result: 7th. Best qualifying: 15th. Team: Scuderia Varzi

| GP Pre-50 | 1947-49 | 5 (1) | - | - | - | - | - | - | - | - | |

Non-championship F1 wins: 1947 Pau, 1948 Pau

Carlos Palau
E. Born: 4.3.1959, Ripolo, Barcelona
2001 Spanish GT Champion (with Alberto Castello)

formula	years	starts (DNS)	wins	2nd	3rd	4th	5th	6th	PP	FL	points
Le Mans	1994-97	3	-	-	-	-	-	-	-	-	

Ricardo Paletti
I. Born: 15.6.1958, Milan. Died: 13.6.1982, Montreal, Canadian GP

formula	years	starts (DNS)	wins	2nd	3rd	4th	5th	6th	PP	FL	points
F1 W	1982	2 (6)	-	-	-	-	-	-	-	-	0

Best result: no finishes. Best qualifying: 13th. Team: Osella

| F2 E | 1979-81 | 17 | - | 2 | - | - | - | 1 | - | 1 | 13 |

Best championship: 1981, 8th

Torsten Palm
S. Born: 23.7.1947, Kristinehamn
1970 and 1971 Swedish F3 Champion

formula	years	starts (DNS)	wins	2nd	3rd	4th	5th	6th	PP	FL	points
F1 W	1975	1 (1)	-	-	-	-	-	-	-	-	0

Best result: 10th. Best qualifying: 21st. Team: Hesketh

| F2 E | 1973-74 | 7 | - | 1 | - | 1 | - | 1 | - | 1 | 6 |

Best championship: 1974, 16th

Jose Luis di Palma
RA. Born: 31.3.1966
1994 British F2 Champion

Luis di Palma
RA. Born: 1945. Died: 1.10.2000, helicopter accident
1983 TC2000 Argentinian Touring Car Champion

formula	years	starts (DNS)	wins	2nd	3rd	4th	5th	6th	PP	FL	points
Le Mans	1973	1	-	-	-	-	-	-	-	-	

Ralph de Palma
USA. Born: 19.12.1882, Troia, Foggia (I). Died: 31.3.1956, Pasadena, California

formula	years	starts (DNS)	wins	2nd	3rd	4th	5th	6th	PP	FL	points
GP Pre-50	1908-21	10	-	1	1	1	1	-	1	1	
Indy 500	1911-25	10	1	1	-	1	1	2	2	-	

Win: 1915 Indianapolis 500
Champcar wins: 24 – 1909 Riverhead race 1, 1912 Santa Monica race 2, Elgin race 3, Elgin race 4, WK Vanderbilt Cup, 1913 Elgin race 1, 1914 WK Vanderbilt Cup, Elgin race 1, Elgin race 2, 1915 Indianapolis 500, Kalamazoo, 1916 Des

Moines, Minneapolis, 1917 Chicago race 2, 1918 Chicago race 1, Chicago race 2, Sheepshead race 1, Sheepshead race 2, Sheepshead race 3, 1919 Sheepshead race 3, 1920 Elgin, 1921 Beverly Hills race 1, Beverly Hills race 5, Beverly Hills race 6

Jim Palmer
NZ
1964, 1965, 1966 and 1968 New Zealand Gold Star Champion

Jonathan Palmer
GB. Born: 7.11.1956, Lewisham, London
1983 European F2 Champion, 1981 British F3 Champion

formula	years	starts (DNS)	wins	2nd	3rd	4th	5th	6th	PP	FL	points
F1 W	1983-89	83 (5)	-	-	-	1	4	3	-	1	14

Best championship: 1987, 11th. Best qualifying: 9th. Teams: Williams, RAM, Zakspeed, Tyrrell

| Le Mans | 1983-91 | 5 | - | 1 | - | - | - | - | - | - | |
| SC W | 1982-91 | | 2 | 2 | 2 | 2 | 8 | - | 1 | 3 | |

Wins: 1984 Brands Hatch, 1987 Norisring. Best championship: 1984, 6th

| F2 E | 1982-83 | 23 (1) | 6 | 1 | 4 | 1 | 2 | 2 | 5 | 3 | 85 |

Wins: 1983 Hockenheim, Donington, Misano, Enna, Zolder, Mugello. Best championship: 1983, 1st

"Pam" (Marsilio Pasotti)
I
1969 European Touring Car Champion (1000cc class)

formula	years	starts (DNS)	wins	2nd	3rd	4th	5th	6th	PP	FL	points
Le Mans	1973	1	-	-	-	-	-	-	-	-	
SC W	1962-74		-	-	-	1	1	-	-	-	

Marvin Panch
USA. Born: 28.5.1926, Menominee, Wisconsin
NASCAR wins: 17 including 1961 Daytona 500

Olivier Panis
F. Born: 2.9.1966, Lyon
1993 FIA F3000 Champion, 1989 French Formula Renault Champion

formula	years	starts (DNS)	wins	2nd	3rd	4th	5th	6th	PP	FL	points
F1 W	1994-2002	125	1	3	1	4	6	8	-	-	64

Win: 1996 Monaco GP. Best championship: 1995, 8th. Best qualifying: 3rd. Teams: Ligier, Prost, BAR

| F3000 INT | 1992-93 | 18 (1) | 3 | 1 | 2 | - | - | 1 | 2 | 2 | 42 |

Wins: 1993 Hockenheim, Nurburgring, Spa. Best championship: 1993, 1st

Giorgio Pantano
I. Born: 4.2.1979, Conselve, Padua
2000 German F3 Champion

formula	years	starts (DNS)	wins	2nd	3rd	4th	5th	6th	PP	FL	points
F3000 INT	2001-02	24	4	1	3	2	1	-	1	5	66

Wins: 2001 Monza, 2002 Barcelona, Hockenheim, Spa. Best championship: 2002, 2nd

Jean-Pierre Paoli
F. Born: 3.5.1940

formula	years	starts (DNS)	wins	2nd	3rd	4th	5th	6th	PP	FL	points
Le Mans	1973-74	2	-	-	-	-	-	-	-	-	
F2 E	1974	6	-	1	-	-	-	-	-		6

Best championship: 1974, 11th

Peter de Paolo
USA. Born: 6.4.1898, Philadelphia, Pennsylvania. Died: 26.11.1980, Costa Mesa, California
1925 and 1927 Champcar Champion

formula	years	starts (DNS)	wins	2nd	3rd	4th	5th	6th	PP	FL	points
GP Pre-50	1925	1	-	-	-	-	1	-	-		
Indy 500	1922-30	7	1	-	1	-	1	2	-	-	

Win: 1925 Indianapolis 500
Champcar wins: 10 – 1925 Fresno, Indianapolis 500, Altoona race 1, Laurel

race 1, Salem, 1926 Miami, Salem race 1, 1927 Altoona race 1, Salem race 1, Charlotte race 2

Vassilis Papafilipou
GR
1999 and 2000 Greek F3 Champion

Massimiliano "Max" Papis
I. Born: 3.10.1969, Como

formula	years	starts (DNS)	wins	2nd	3rd	4th	5th	6th	PP	FL	points
F1 W	1995	7	-	-	-	-	-	-	-	-	0

Best result: 7th. Best qualifying: 15th. Team: Arrows

| Le Mans | 1997 | 1 | | | | - | 1 | - | - | | |
| F3000 INT | 1993-94 | 17 | 1 | - | - | 2 | 1 | 2 | 1 | - | 19 |

Win: 1994 Barcelona. Best championship: 1993, 10th

| Indy 500 | 2002 | 1 | | | | - | - | - | | | |
| CART | 1996-2002 | 106 (1) | 3 | 5 | 3 | 4 | 6 | 2 | 2 | 3 | |

Wins: 2000 Miami, 2001 Portland, Laguna Seca. Best championship: 1999, 5th

| IRL | 2002 | 2 | - | - | - | - | - | - | - | - | |

Other major win: 2002 Daytona 24 hrs

Rosario Parasiliti
I
1992 Italian Supercar GT Champion

Guido Pardini
I
1980 Italian F3 Champion

formula	years	starts (DNS)	wins	2nd	3rd	4th	5th	6th	PP	FL	points
F2 E	1977-81	11 (1)	-	-	-	-	-	-	-	-	0

Jim Pardue
USA. Born: 1932. Died: ??.9.1964, Charlotte, testing
NASCAR wins: 2

Jesus Pareja
E. Born: 6.3.1955, Madrid

formula	years	starts (DNS)	wins	2nd	3rd	4th	5th	6th	PP	FL	points
Le Mans	1985-97	13		-	1	-	-	-	-		
SC W	1984-92		1	1	2	2	3	3	-	-	

Win: 1986 Jerez. Best championship: 1986, 6th. GT FIA wins: 3 – 1994 Paul Ricard, Jarama, Suzuka

Steve Park
USA. Born: 23.8.1967, Islip, New York State
NASCAR wins: 2 (in Modern era)

Don Parker
GB. Born: 11.11.1908, Ramsgate. Died: 26.5.1997
1952 and 1953 British F3 Champion, 1959 British Formula Junior Champion

Michael Parkes
GB. Born: 24.9.1931, Richmond, Surrey. Died: 28.8.1977, Turin, road accident

formula	years	starts (DNS)	wins	2nd	3rd	4th	5th	6th	PP	FL	points
F1 W	1959-67	6 (1)	-	2	-	1	-	1	-	1	14

Best championship: 1966, 8th. Best qualifying: 1st. Teams: David Fry, Ferrari

| Le Mans | 1960-72 | 11 | | - | 2 | 1 | - | - | | | |
| SC W | 1960-72 | | 5 | 8 | 2 | 2 | 2 | 2 | 5 | 3 | |

Wins: 1964 Sebring 12 hrs, Spa, 1965 Monza, 1966 Monza, Spa
Non-championship F1 wins: 1967 International Trophy (Silverstone), Syracuse

Reg Parnell
GB. Born: 2.7.1911, Derby. Died: 7.1.1964, Derby, after a medical operation

formula	years	starts (DNS)	wins	2nd	3rd	4th	5th	6th	PP	FL	points
F1 W	1950-54	6 (1)	-	-	1	1	1	-	-	-	9

Best championship: 1950, 9th. Best qualifying: 4th. Teams: Alfa Romeo, Scuderia Ambrosiana, GA Vandervell, BRM, AHM Bryde

GP Pre-50	1936-49	11	-	-	-	-	1	-	-	-	
Le Mans	1950-56	7	-	-	-	-	1	-	-	-	
SC W	1953-59		-	2	-	-	1	-	-	-	

Non-championship F1 wins: 1950 Goodwood (x2), 1951 International Trophy (Silverstone), 1954 Goodwood, 1954 Goodwood, Crystal Palace (x2), Snetterton
Other major win: 1957 New Zealand GP

RHH "Tim" Parnell
GB. Born: 25.6.1932, Derby

formula	years	starts (DNS)	wins	2nd	3rd	4th	5th	6th	PP	FL	points
F1 W	1959-63	2 (2)	-	-	-	-	-	-	-	-	0

Best result: 10th. Best qualifying: 25th. Teams: Reg Parnell, driver

Benny Parsons
USA. Born: 12.7.1941
1973 NASCAR Champion
NASCAR wins: 21 (20 in Modern era) including 1975 Daytona 500, 1980 World 600

Chuck Parsons
USA. Born: 6.2.1924, Bruin, Kentucky

formula	years	starts (DNS)	wins	2nd	3rd	4th	5th	6th	PP	FL	points
Le Mans	1967-70	2									
SC W	1964-71		1	-	-	-	1	-			

Win: 1969 Daytona 24 hrs

David Parsons
AUS. Born: 17.5.1959, Devonport, Tasmania
Major win: 1987 Bathurst

Johnnie Parsons
USA. Born: 4.7.1918, Los Angeles, California. Died: 8.9.1984, Van Nuys, California
1949 Champcar Champion

formula	years	starts (DNS)	wins	2nd	3rd	4th	5th	6th	PP	FL	points
Indy 500	1949-58	10		1	1	-	1	-	-	1	

Win: 1950 Indianapolis 500
Champcar wins: 11 – 1948 Du Quoin, 1949 Dallas, Milwaukee race 2, Syracuse, Springfield race 2, Langhorne, 1950 Indianapolis 500, Darlington, 1951 Phoenix, Bay Meadows, 1952 Phoenix

Phil Parsons
USA. Born: 21.6.1957, Detroit, Michigan
NASCAR wins: 1 (in Modern era)

Jim Paschal
USA. Born: 5.12.1926, High Point, North Carolina
NASCAR wins: 25

Massimo Pasini
I
2000 Italian Supercar GT Champion

Dick Passwater
USA
NASCAR wins: 1

Arthur Pateman
GB
Major win: 1957 Macau

Riccardo Patrese
I. Born: 17.4.1954, Padua
1976 European F3 Champion, 1976 Italian F3 Champion

formula	years	starts (DNS)	wins	2nd	3rd	4th	5th	6th	PP	FL	points
F1 W	1977-93	256 (1)	6	17	14	8	15	13	8	15	281

Wins: 1982 Monaco GP, 1983 South African GP, 1990 San Marino GP, 1991 Mexican GP, Portuguese GP, 1992 Japanese GP. Best championship: 1992, 2nd. Best qualifying: 1st. Teams: Shadow, Arrows, Brabham, Alfa Romeo,

Williams, Benetton

formula	years	starts (DNS)	wins	2nd	3rd	4th	5th	6th	PP	FL	points
Le Mans	1981-97	3	-	-	-	-	-	-	-	-	
SC W	1979-92		8	4	5	3	1	-	10	6	

Wins: 1980 Brands Hatch, Mugello, Watkins Glen, 1981 Watkins Glen, 1982 Silverstone, Nurburgring, 1984 Kyalami, 1985 Spa. Best championship: 1982, 2nd

formula	years	starts (DNS)	wins	2nd	3rd	4th	5th	6th	PP	FL	points
F2 E	1977-78	14	-	3	2	-	1	2	2	2	32

Best championship: 1977, 4th

F3 E wins: 4 – 1976 Zandvoort, Enna, Monza, Kassel-Calden

Other major wins: 1977 and 1978 Macau

Cyrus Patschke
USA. Born: n/a. Died: 19??

formula	years	starts (DNS)	wins	2nd	3rd	4th	5th	6th	PP	FL	points
GP Pre-50	1911	1	-	-	-	-	-	-	-	-	
Indy 500	1911	1	1	-	-	-	1	-	-	-	

Win: 1911 Indianapolis 500

Champcar win: 1 – 1911 Indianapolis 500

Bill Patterson
AUS
1961 Australian Gold Star Champion
Major win: 1957 Australian GP

John Paul Sr
USA
1979 Trans-Am Class 2 Champion

formula	years	starts (DNS)	wins	2nd	3rd	4th	5th	6th	PP	FL	points
Le Mans	1978-82	3	-	-	-	-	1	-	-	-	
SC W	1969-83		-	3	1	1	1	-	-	-	

Major wins: 1982 Daytona 24 hrs, 1982 Sebring 12 hrs

John Paul Jr
USA. Born: 19.2.1960, Muncie, Indiana
1982 IMSA GTP Champion

formula	years	starts (DNS)	wins	2nd	3rd	4th	5th	6th	PP	FL	points
Le Mans	1980-95	3	-	1	-	-	-	-	-	-	
SC W	1980-92		-	3	1	-	-	1	1	4	
Indy 500	1985-98	7	-	-	-	-	-	-	-	-	
CART	1982-94	29 (3)	1	1	3	-	1	1	1	-	

Win: 1983 Michigan 500. Best championship: 1983, 8th

formula	years	starts (DNS)	wins	2nd	3rd	4th	5th	6th	PP	FL	points
IRL	1996-99	24 (1)	1	-	1	-	1	-	-		

Win: 1998 Texas

Other major wins: 1982 and 1997 Daytona 24 hrs, 1982 Sebring 12 hrs

Luciano Pavesi
I
1975 Italian F3 Champion

formula	years	starts (DNS)	wins	2nd	3rd	4th	5th	6th	PP	FL	points
F2 E	1976-78	6 (2)	-	-	-	-	1	-	-		1

Best championship: 1977, 20th

Milos Pavlovic
YU. Born: 8.12.1980, Belgrade
2002 Italian F3 Champion

David Pearson
USA. Born: 22.12.1934, Woodruff, Carolina
1966, 1968 and 1969 NASCAR Champion
NASCAR wins: 105 (45 in Modern era) including 1976 Daytona 500, 1961, 1974, 1976 World 600

Al Pease
CDN. Born: 15.10.1921, Darlington, Yorkshire (GB)

formula	years	starts (DNS)	wins	2nd	3rd	4th	5th	6th	PP	FL	points
F1 W	1967-69	2 (1)	-	-	-	-	-	-	-	-	0

Best result: no finishes. Best qualifying: 16th. Teams: driver, John Maryon

Alberto Pedemonte
I. Born: 14.8.1974
1997, 1998, 1999 and 2000 Russian F3 Champion

Paul Pedersen
NZ
2002 New Zealand TranzAm Champion

Oscar Pedersoli
I. Born: 3.4.1951

formula	years	starts (DNS)	wins	2nd	3rd	4th	5th	6th	PP	FL	points
F2 E	1979-82	25 (2)	-	-	-	-	1	2	-	-	4

Best championship: 1980, 14th

formula	years	starts (DNS)	wins	2nd	3rd	4th	5th	6th	PP	FL	points
F3000 INT	1986	0 (1)	-	-	-	-	-	-	-	-	0

F3 E wins: 2 – 1977 Enna, Vallelunga

Pedrini
I
Major win: 1912 Targa Florio

"Pedro"
B
Major win: 1967 Spa 24 hrs

Lennart Pehrsson
S
1999 Swedish GTR Champion

Alain Peltier
B
1975 European Touring Car Champion (with Siegfried Muller)

formula	years	starts (DNS)	wins	2nd	3rd	4th	5th	6th	PP	FL	points
Le Mans	1976	1	-	-	-	-	-	-	-	-	
SC W	1972-81		-	-	1	-	-	-	-	-	
F2 E	1975	1	-	-	-	-	-	-	-	-	0

Major win: 1974 Spa 24 hrs

Carlos Martinez Penacoba
E
1980 Spanish Touring Car Champion

Roger Penske
USA. Born: 20.2.1937, Shaker Heights, Ohio

formula	years	starts (DNS)	wins	2nd	3rd	4th	5th	6th	PP	FL	points
F1 W	1961-62	2	-	-	-	-	-	-	-	-	0

Best result: 8th. Best qualifying: 13th. Teams: John M Wyatt III, Penske

formula	years	starts (DNS)	wins	2nd	3rd	4th	5th	6th	PP	FL	points
Le Mans	1963	1	-	-	-	-	-	-	-	-	
SC W	1961-64		-	-	-	1	2	-	-	-	

Win Percy
GB. Born: 28.9.1943, Tolpuddle, Dorset
1980, 1981 and 1982 British Touring Car Champion

formula	years	starts (DNS)	wins	2nd	3rd	4th	5th	6th	PP	FL	points
Le Mans	1981-95	6	-	-	-	-	-	-	-	-	
SC W	1977-92		-	-	-	-	1	-	-	-	

Major wins: 1984 and 1989 Spa 24 hrs, 1985 Tourist Trophy (Silverstone), 1990 Bathurst

Cesare Perdisa
I. Born: 21.10.1932, Bologna. Died: 10.5.1998, Bologna

formula	years	starts (DNS)	wins	2nd	3rd	4th	5th	6th	PP	FL	points
F1 W	1955-57	7 (1)	-	-	2	-	1	1	-	-	5

Best championship: 1956, 15th. Best qualifying: 6th. Teams: Maserati, Ferrari

formula	years	starts (DNS)	wins	2nd	3rd	4th	5th	6th	PP	FL	points
Le Mans	1955	1	-	-	-	-	-	-	-	-	
SC W	1954-56		-	-	1	1	-	-	-	-	

Carlos Perea
MEX
1998 Mexican F3 Champion

Ricardo Perez de Lara

MEX
1997 Mexican F2 Champion

Larry Perkins

AUS. Born: 18.3.1950, Murrayville, Victoria
1975 European F3 Champion

formula	years	starts (DNS)	wins	2nd	3rd	4th	5th	6th	PP	FL	points
F1 W	1974-77	11 (4)	-	-	-	-	-	-	-	-	0

Best result: 8th. Best qualifying: 13th. Teams: Amon, Boro, Brabham, Stanley BRM, Surtees

Le Mans	1978-88	3	-	-	-	1	-	-			
SC W	1978-88		-	-	-	1	-	-			
F2 E	1978	1	-	-	-	-	-	-			0

F3 E win: 1 – 1975 Monza
Other major wins: 1982, 1983, 1984, 1993, 1995 and 1997 Bathurst

Terry Perkins

AUS
F3 E win: 1 – 1975 Danish GP

Piergiuseppe Peroni

I. Born: 19.4.1954, Milan
2002 Sports Racing SRL class Champion (with Mirko Savoldi)

Xavier Perrot

CH. Born: 1.2.1942, Zurich

formula	years	starts (DNS)	wins	2nd	3rd	4th	5th	6th	PP	FL	points
F1 W	1969	1	-	-	-	-	-	-	-	-	0

Best result: no finishes. Best qualifying: no times set. Team: Squadra Tartaruga

F2 E	1968-72	20 (1)	-	-	-	1	1	1	-	-	11

Best championships: 1969 and 1972, 13th

Henri Pescarolo

F. Born: 25.9.1942, Montfermeil, Paris
1967 French F3 Champion

formula	years	starts (DNS)	wins	2nd	3rd	4th	5th	6th	PP	FL	points
F1 W	1968-76	57 (8)	-	-	1	1	1	3	-	1	12

Best championship: 1970, 12th. Best qualifying: 5th. Teams: Matra, Williams, March, BRM, Surtees, BS Fabrications

Le Mans	1966-99	33	4	-	-	-	2	1	-		
SC W	1966-92		21	11	10	6	3	4	2	1	

Wins: 1972, 1973, 1974 and 1984 Le Mans 24 hrs
Wins: 1971 Brands Hatch, 1972 Le Mans 24 hrs, 1973 Vallelunga, Dijon, Le Mans 24 hrs, Osterreichring, Watkins Glen, 1974 Imola, Le Mans 24 hrs, Osterreichring, Kyalami, 1975 Spa, Osterreichring, Watkins Glen, 1978 Dijon, Misano, Vallelunga, 1980 Dijon, 1982 Monza, 1984 Le Mans 24 hrs, 1986 Nurburgring. Best championship: 1984, 4th. GT FIA win: 1 – 1994 Montlhery

F2 E	1967-73	30 (5)	2	4	2	3	3	-	4	1	50

Wins: 1972 Enna, 1973 Thruxton. Best championship: 1968, 2nd
Other major wins: 1967 Monaco F3, 1991 Daytona 24 hrs

Christian Pescatori

I. Born: 1.12.1971, Brescia
2000 Sports Racing World Champion (with David Terrien), 2001 FIA N-GT class Champion (with Terrien), 1993 Italian F3 Champion

formula	years	starts (DNS)	wins	2nd	3rd	4th	5th	6th	PP	FL	points
Le Mans	1997-2002	4	-	2	-	-	-	-			

SRWC wins: 7 – 1999 Enna, 2000 Barcelona, Brno, Donington, Nurburgring, Magny-Cours, 2001 Barcelona

F3000 INT	1994-96	26	-	-	1	1	1	4	-	1	13

Best championship: 1995, 9th
Other major win: 2002 Sebring 12 hrs

Alessandro Pesenti-Rossi

I. Born: 31.8.1942, Bergamo

formula	years	starts (DNS)	wins	2nd	3rd	4th	5th	6th	PP	FL	points
F1 W	1976	3 (1)	-	-	-	-	-	-	-	-	0

Best result: 11th. Best qualifying: 21st. Team: Scuderia Rondini

F2 E	1974-78	20 (3)	-	1	-	5	2	2	-	1	30

Best championships: 1975 and 1977, 9th

Philipp Peter

A/CH (dual nationality). Born: 6.4.1969, Vienna

formula	years	starts (DNS)	wins	2nd	3rd	4th	5th	6th	PP	FL	points
Le Mans	2002	1	-	-	1	-	-	-			

Josef Peters

D. Born: 16.9.1914, Dusseldorf. Died: 24.4.2001, Dusseldorf

formula	years	starts (DNS)	wins	2nd	3rd	4th	5th	6th	PP	FL	points
F1 W	1952	1	-	-	-	-	-	-	-	-	0

Best result: no finishes. Best qualifying: no times set. Team: driver

SC W	1953		-	-	-	-	1	-	-		

Ronnie Peterson

S. Born: 14.2.1944, Orebro. Died: 11.9.1978, Milan, following Italian GP accident
1971 European F2 Champion, 1968 and 1969 Swedish F3 Champion

formula	years	starts (DNS)	wins	2nd	3rd	4th	5th	6th	PP	FL	points
F1 W	1970-78	123	10	10	6	5	7	4	14	9	206

Wins: 1973 French GP, Austrian GP, Italian GP, United States GP, 1974 Monaco GP, French GP, Italian GP, 1976 Italian GP, 1978 South African GP, Austrian GP.
Best championships: 1971 and 1978, 2nd. Best qualifying: 1st. Teams: Antique Automobiles, March, Lotus, Tyrrell

Le Mans	1970	1	-	-	-	-	-	-			
SC W	1970-78		3	4	2	1	1	1	4	2	

Wins: 1971 Watkins Glen, 1972 Buenos Aires, Nurburgring

F2 E	1970-76	30 (2)	6	4	1	2	2	7	7		68

Wins: 1971 Rouen, Mantorp Park, Tulln, Vallelunga race 1, 1972 Thruxton, 1974 Karlskoga. Best championship: 1971, 1st
Other major win: 1969 Monaco F3

Kelly Petillo

USA. Born: 5.12.1903, Philadelphia, Pennsylvania. Died: 30.6.1970, California
1935 Champcar Champion

formula	years	starts (DNS)	wins	2nd	3rd	4th	5th	6th	PP	FL	points
Indy 500	1932-41	10	1	-	1	-	-	-	1	-	

Win: 1935 Indianapolis 500
Champcar wins: 4 – 1934 Los Angeles, 1935 Indianapolis 500, St Paul, Langhorne

Pierre Petit

F. Born: 27.9.1957, Gueret
1982 French F3 Champion

formula	years	starts (DNS)	wins	2nd	3rd	4th	5th	6th	PP	FL	points
Le Mans	1992-96	4	-	-	-	-	-	-			
F2 E	1983-84	21 (1)	-	-	1	1	1	1	-	-	10

Best championship: 1984, 9th

Kyle Petty

USA. Born: 2.6.1960, Randleman, North Carolina
NASCAR wins: 8 (all Modern era) including 1987 World 600

Lee Petty

USA. Born: 14.3.1914, Randleman, North Carolina. Died: 5.4.2000, Greensboro, North Carolina
1954, 1958 and 1959 NASCAR Champion
NASCAR wins: 54 including 1959 Daytona 500

Richard Petty

USA. Born: 2.7.1937, Level Cross, North Carolina
1964, 1967, 1971, 1972, 1974, 1975 and 1979 NASCAR Champion
NASCAR wins: 200 (60 in Modern era) including 1973, 1974, 1979, 1981 Daytona 500, 1975, 1977 World 600

Joe Pezza
USA
1994 IMSA GTO Champion

Sebastien Philippe
F. Born: 8.2.1975, Villeurbanne
2000 Japanese F3 Champion

Alfredo Pian
RA. Born: 21.10.1912, Santa Fe. Died: 25.7.1990, Santa Fe

formula	years	starts (DNS)	wins	2nd	3rd	4th	5th	6th	PP	FL	points
F1 W	1950	0 (1)	-	-	-	-	-	-	-	-	0

Best result: no starts. Best qualifying: no times set. Team: Scuderia Varzi

Paolo delle Piane
I. Born: 1.5.1964, Bologna

formula	years	starts (DNS)	wins	2nd	3rd	4th	5th	6th	PP	FL	points
F3000 INT	1990-94	36 (7)	-	-	-	-	1	-	-	-	2

Best championship: 1993, 17th

Francois Picard
F. Born: 26.4.1921, Villefranche-sur-Saone. Died: 29.4.1996, Monte Carlo

formula	years	starts (DNS)	wins	2nd	3rd	4th	5th	6th	PP	FL	points
F1 W	1958	1	-	-	-	-	-	-	-	-	0

Best result: no finishes. Best qualifying: no times set. Team: Rob Walker

Le Mans	1952-58	4	-	-	-	-	-	-	-	-	

Gianluigi Picchi
I
1971 European Touring Car Champion (1300cc class), 1969 Italian F3 Champion

formula	years	starts (DNS)	wins	2nd	3rd	4th	5th	6th	PP	FL	points
SC W	1976-77		-	-	-	-	1	-	-	-	
F2 E	1971	1 (1)	-	-	-	-	-	-	-	-	0

Andrea Piccini
I. Born: 12.12.1978, Sansepolcro

formula	years	starts (DNS)	wins	2nd	3rd	4th	5th	6th	PP	FL	points
F3000 INT	1999-2001	27 (5)	-	-	-	1	1	1	-	-	6

Best championships: 1999 and 2001, 18th

GT FIA wins: 4 – 2002 Jarama, Anderstorp, Oschersleben, Estoril

Greg Pickett
USA. Born: 8.1.1947
1978 Trans-Am Class 2 Champion

Roy Pierpoint
GB
1965 British Touring Car Champion

formula	years	starts (DNS)	wins	2nd	3rd	4th	5th	6th	PP	FL	points
SC W	1967-69		-	-	-	1	-	-	-	-	

Ernest Pieterse
ZA. Born: 4.7.1938, Parows-Bellville
1962 South African F1 Champion

formula	years	starts (DNS)	wins	2nd	3rd	4th	5th	6th	PP	FL	points
F1 W	1962-65	2 (1)	-	-	-	-	-	-	-	-	0

Best result: 10th. Best qualifying: 12th. Teams: driver, Lawson Organisation

Paul Pietsch
D. Born: 20.6.1911, Freiburg-im-Breisgau

formula	years	starts (DNS)	wins	2nd	3rd	4th	5th	6th	PP	FL	points
F1 W	1950-52	3	-	-	-	-	-	-	-	-	0

Best result: no finishes. Best qualifying: 7th. Teams: driver, Alfa Romeo

GP Pre-50	1932-39	12 (3)	-	-	2	-	-	1	-	-	

Andre Pilette
B. Born: 6.10.1918, Paris (F). Died: 27.12.1993, Etterbeek

formula	years	starts (DNS)	wins	2nd	3rd	4th	5th	6th	PP	FL	points
F1 W	1951-64	9 (5)	-	-	-	-	1	3	-	-	2

Best championship: 1954, 18th. Best qualifying: 8th. Teams: Ecurie Belgique,

Ecurie Belge, Gordini, Ferrari, ENB, driver, Scirocco

formula	years	starts (DNS)	wins	2nd	3rd	4th	5th	6th	PP	FL	points
Le Mans	1954-61	4	-	-	1	-	1	-	1	-	-
SC W	1953-61		-	-	1	-	1	-	-	-	

Theodore "Teddy" Pilette
B. Born: 26.7.1942, Brussels
1973 and 1975 British F5000 Champion

formula	years	starts (DNS)	wins	2nd	3rd	4th	5th	6th	PP	FL	points
F1 W	1974-77	1 (3)	-	-	-	-	-	-	-	-	0

Best result: 17th. Best qualifying: 27th. Teams: Brabham, Stanley BRM

Le Mans	1968-87	8	-	-	-	-	-	-	-	-	
SC W	1963-87		-	-	-	1	1	2	-	-	
CART	1981	1	-	-	-	-	-	-	-	-	

Tasman win: 1 – 1974 Surfers Paradise

Other major win: 1978 Spa 24 hrs

Andy Pilgrim
USA. Born: 18.8.1956, Nottingham (GB)
1997 IMSA GT Champion

formula	years	starts (DNS)	wins	2nd	3rd	4th	5th	6th	PP	FL	points
Le Mans	1996-2002	5	-	-	-	-	-	-	-	-	

Ed Pimm
USA. Born: 3.5.1956
1983 SCCA Super Vee Champion

formula	years	starts (DNS)	wins	2nd	3rd	4th	5th	6th	PP	FL	points
Indy 500	1985-87	3	-	-	-	-	-	-	-	-	
CART	1984-88	42 (4)	-	-	1	-	1	1	-	-	

Sanna Pinola
SF. Born: 8.10.1975
2001 Nordic F3 Champion

Jussi Pinomaki
SF
2002 Finnish F3 Champion

Carlo Maria Pintacuda
I. Born: 1900. Died: 1972, Milan

formula	years	starts (DNS)	wins	2nd	3rd	4th	5th	6th	PP	FL	points
GP Pre-50	1936-37	2	-	-	-	-	1	-	-	-	

Major wins: 1935 and 1937 Mille Miglia, 1938 Spa 24 hrs

Manuel Pinto
P

Major win: 1969 Portuguese GP

N Pinto Nogueira
P

Major win: 1953 Portuguese GP

Luigi Piotti
I. Born: 27.10.1913, Milan. Died: 19.4.1971, Godiasco

formula	years	starts (DNS)	wins	2nd	3rd	4th	5th	6th	PP	FL	points
F1 W	1955-58	6 (3)	-	-	-	-	1	-	-	-	0

Best qualifying: 12th. Teams: driver, Maserati, OSCA

SC W	1953-58		-	-	-	1	-	-	-	-	

Major win: 1955 Tunis

David Piper
GB. Born: 2.12.1930, Edgware, Middlesex

formula	years	starts (DNS)	wins	2nd	3rd	4th	5th	6th	PP	FL	points
F1 W	1959-60	2 (1)	-	-	-	-	-	-	-	-	0

Best result: 12th. Best qualifying: 21st. Teams: Dorchester, Robert Bodle

Le Mans	1963-70	8	-	-	-	-	-	1	-	-	
SC W	1957-70		-	-	4	2	4	1	2	-	-

Nelson Piquet (Nelson Souto Maior)

BR. Born: 17.8.1952, Rio de Janeiro
1981, 1983 and 1987 F1 World Champion, 1980
BMW M1 Procar Champion, 1996 Temporada GT
Champion (with Johnny Cecotto), 1978 BP British
F3 Champion

formula	years	starts (DNS)	wins	2nd	3rd	4th	5th	6th	PP	FL	points
F1 W	1978-91	204 (3)	23	20	17	18	15	7	24	23	485.5

Wins: 1980 Long Beach GP, Dutch GP, Italian GP, 1981 Argentinian GP, San
Marino GP, German GP, 1982 Canadian GP, 1983 Brazilian GP, Italian GP,
European GP, 1984 Canadian GP, Detroit GP, 1985 French GP, 1986 Brazilian
GP, German GP, Hungarian GP, Italian GP, 1987 German GP, Hungarian GP,
Italian GP, 1990 Japanese GP, Australian GP, 1991 Canadian GP. **Best champi-
onships:** 1981, 1983 and 1987, 1st. **Best qualifying:** 1st. **Teams:** Ensign, BS
Fabrications, Brabham, Williams, Lotus, Benetton

Le Mans	1996-97	2	-	-	-	-	-	-			
SC W	1980-92		1	-	1	-	-	-			

Win: 1981 Nurburgring

Indy 500	1993	1	-	-	-	-	-	-			
CART	1993	1	-	-	-	-	-	-			

F3 E wins: 2 – 1977 Kassel-Calden, Jarama

Nelson Angelo Piquet

BR. Born: 25.7.1985
2002 Sud-Am F3 Champion

Renato Pirocchi

I. Born: 23.6.1933, Notaresco, Teramo
1960 Italian Formula Junior Champion

formula	years	starts (DNS)	wins	2nd	3rd	4th	5th	6th	PP	FL	points
F1 W	1961	1	-	-	-	-	-	-	-	-	0

Best result: 12th. **Best qualifying:** 29th. **Team:** Pescara Racing Club

Didier Pironi

F. Born: 26.3.1952, Villecresnes, near Paris. Died:
23.8.1987, Isle of Wight (GB), powerboat accident
1974 and 1976 European Formula Renault
Champion

formula	years	starts (DNS)	wins	2nd	3rd	4th	5th	6th	PP	FL	points
F1 W	1978-82	70 (2)	3	3	7	3	6	7	4	5	101

Wins: 1980 Belgian GP, 1982 San Marino GP, Dutch GP. **Best championship:**
1982, 2nd. **Best qualifying:** 1st. **Teams:** Tyrrell, Ligier, Ferrari

Le Mans	1976-80	4	1	-	-	-	-	-			

Win: 1978 Le Mans 24 hrs

SC W	1976-80		-	-	-	-	1	-			
F2 E	1977	13	1	2	2	2	1	-	1	1	38

Win: 1977 Estoril. **Best championship:** 1977, 3rd

Other major win: 1977 Monaco F3

Emanuele Pirro

I. Born: 12.1.1962, Rome
2001 American Le Mans Series Champion, 1994 and 1995 Italian Touring
Car Champion, 1996 German Super Touring Car Champion

formula	years	starts (DNS)	wins	2nd	3rd	4th	5th	6th	PP	FL	points
F1 W	1989-91	37 (3)	-	-	-	1	1	-	-		3

Best championship: 1991, 18th. **Best qualifying:** 7th. **Teams:** Benetton,
Scuderia Italia

Le Mans	1981-2002	6	3	-	1	-	-	-			

Wins: 2000, 2001 and 2002 Le Mans 24 hrs

SC W	1981-92		-	1	-	1	-	-			
F2 E	1984	11	-	1	-	3	-	3	-	-	18

Best championship: 1984, 6th

F3000 INT	1985-86	22	3	5	1	2	1	1	4	3	67

Wins: 1985 Thruxton, Vallelunga, 1986 Le Mans. **Best championships:** 1985
and 1986, 3rd
F3 E wins: 6 – 1981 Mugello, 1982 Osterreichring, Silverstone, Kassel-Calden,
1983 Vallelunga, Zolder
Other major wins: 1991 and 1992 Macau Guia race, 2000 Sebring 12 hrs,
2001 Petit LeMans

Salvatori Pirro

I. Born: 12.12.1962, Naples
1994 European Renault Clio Cup Champion

Tom Pistone

USA. Born: 17.3.1929
NASCAR wins: 2

Jack Pitcher

GB
1960 BRSCC National Formula Junior Champion

Bill Pitt

AUS
1961 Australian Touring Car Champion

Antonio Pizzonia

BR. Born: 11.9.1980, Manaus
2000 British F3 Champion

formula	years	starts (DNS)	wins	2nd	3rd	4th	5th	6th	PP	FL	points
F3000 INT	2001-02	24	1	-	2	6	1	2	1	2	40

Win: 2001 Hockenheim. **Best championship:** 2001, 6th

Olivier Pla

F. Born: 22.10.1981, Toulouse
Major win: 2002 Korea F3

Fernando Plata

MEX. Born: 28.9.1962, Guadalajara
1994 Mexican F2 Champion

formula	years	starts (DNS)	wins	2nd	3rd	4th	5th	6th	PP	FL	points
F3000 INT	1991	0 (5)	-	-	-	-	-	-	-	-	0

Jason Plato

GB. Born: 14.10.1967, Oxford
2001 British Touring Car Champion

Randy Pobst

USA. Born: 26.6.1957, Dayton, Ohio
1996 North American Touring Car Champion

Eric van de Poele

B. Born: 30.9.1961, Verviers, near Spa
1987 German Touring Car Champion

formula	years	starts (DNS)	wins	2nd	3rd	4th	5th	6th	PP	FL	points
F1 W	1991-92	5 (24)	-	-	-	-	-	-	-	-	0

Best result: 9th. **Best qualifying:** 15th. **Teams:** Lamborghini, Brabham,
Fondmetal

Le Mans	1992-2002	8	-	-	1	1	-	-	-	1	
SC W	1990-92		-	-	-	1	1	-			
F3000 INT	1989-90	21	3	1	1	2	2	2	-	-	49

Wins: 1990 Pau, Birmingham, Nogaro. **Best championship:** 1990, 2nd
Other major wins: 1987 and 1998 Spa 24 hrs, 1995 and 1996 Sebring 12 hrs,
1998 Petit LeMans

Jerome Policand

CH. Born: 1.10.1964, Geneva (CH)
1999 European Renault Clio Cup Champion

formula	years	starts (DNS)	wins	2nd	3rd	4th	5th	6th	PP	FL	points
Le Mans	1996-2002	7	-	-	1	-	-	-			

SRWC wins: 2 – 1997 Jarama, 1998 Kyalami

F3000 INT	1992-95	34	-	-	1	1	1	2	-	-	11

Best championship: 1993, 11th

Art Pollard

USA. Born: 5.5.1927, Dragon, Utah. Died: 12.5.1973, Indianapolis 500,
practice

formula	years	starts (DNS)	wins	2nd	3rd	4th	5th	6th	PP	FL	points
Indy 500	1967-71	5	-	-	-	-	-	-			

Champcar wins: 2 – 1969 Milwaukee race 1, Dover Downs

Jacques "Jacky" Pollet

F. Born: 28.7.1922, Roubiax. Died: 16.8.1997, Paris

formula	years	starts (DNS)	wins	2nd	3rd	4th	5th	6th	PP	FL	points
F1 W	1954-55	5	-	-	-	-	-	-	-	-	0

Best result: 7th. Best qualifying: 12th. Team: Gordini

Le Mans	1954-55	2	-	-	-	-	-	1	-	-	
SC W	1954-56		-	-	-	-	-	1	-	-	

John Pollock

IRL

formula	years	starts (DNS)	wins	2nd	3rd	4th	5th	6th	PP	FL	points
F2 E	1969	2	-	-	-	-	-	1	-	-	1

Best championship: 1969, 19th

Bernardos "Ben" Pon

NL. Born: 9.12.1936, Leiden

formula	years	starts (DNS)	wins	2nd	3rd	4th	5th	6th	PP	FL	points
F1 W	1962		-	-	-	-	-	-	-	-	0

Best result: no finishes. Best qualifying: 18th. Team: Ecurie Maarsbergen

Le Mans	1961-67	6	-	-	2	2	-	1	-	-	
SC W	1961-68		-	-	2	2	-	1	-	-	

Gabriel Ponce de Leon

RA. Born: 24.3.1979, Junin, Buenos Aires
2001 TC2000 Argentinian Touring Car Champion

Lennie Pond

USA. Born: 11.8.1940, Petersburg, Virginia
NASCAR wins: 1 (in Modern era)

Alec Poole

IRL
1969 British Touring Car Champion

formula	years	starts (DNS)	wins	2nd	3rd	4th	5th	6th	PP	FL	points
Le Mans	1968-76	2	-	-	-	-	-	-	-	-	
SC W	1966-79		-	-	1	-	-	-	-	-	

Albert Poon

PRC
Major wins: 1964 Macau

Dennis Poore

GB. Born: 19.8.1916, West London. Died: 12.2.1987, Kensington, London

formula	years	starts (DNS)	wins	2nd	3rd	4th	5th	6th	PP	FL	points
F1 W	1952	2	-	-	1	-	-	-	-	-	3

Best championship: 1952, 13th. Best qualifying: 8th. Team: Connaught

Le Mans	1952-55	4	-	-	-	-	-	-	-	-	
SC W	1953-55		-	-	1	-	-	-	-	-	

Alfonso de Portago
(Alfonso Cabeza de Vaca, Marquis de Portago)

E. Born: 11.10.1928, London (GB). Died: 12.5.1957, between Goito and Guidizzolo, Mille Miglia

formula	years	starts (DNS)	wins	2nd	3rd	4th	5th	6th	PP	FL	points
F1 W	1956-57	5	-	1	-	1	-	-	-	-	4

Best championship: 1956, 15th. Best qualifying: 9th. Team: Ferrari

Le Mans	1954-56	2	-	-	-	-	-	-	-	-	
SC W	1954-57		-	1	3	-	-	-	-	-	

Santiago Porteiro

E. Born: 12.12.1979, Madrid
2002 Spanish Formula Nissan Champion

Marvin Porter

USA
NASCAR wins: 2

Sam Posey

USA. Born: 26.5.1944, New York City

formula	years	starts (DNS)	wins	2nd	3rd	4th	5th	6th	PP	FL	points
F1 W	1971-72	2	-	-	-	-	-	-	-	-	0

Best result: 12th. Best qualifying: 18th. Teams: Surtees, ChampCarr

Le Mans	1966-78	10	-	-	1	1	-	1	-	-	
SC W	1966-81		-	2	1	2	-	2	-	-	
Indy 500	1972	1	-	-	-	-	-	1	-	-	

Major win: 1975 Sebring 12 hrs

Will Power

AUS. Born: 1.3.1979
2002 Australian Formula Holden Champion

Carlo "Charles" Pozzi

F. Born: 27.8.1909, Paris. Died: 28.2.2001, Levallois-Perret

formula	years	starts (DNS)	wins	2nd	3rd	4th	5th	6th	PP	FL	points
F1 W	1950	1	-	-	-	-	-	1	-	-	0

Best qualifying: 16th. Team: driver

GP Pre-50	1947-49	5 (1)	1	-	-	-	1	-	-	-	
Le Mans	1949-53	4	-	-	-	-	-	-	-	-	

Win: 1949 French GP

Theodore "Ted" Prappas

USA. Born: 14.11.1955, Santa Monica, California
1986 North American Formula Atlantic (Western) Champion

formula	years	starts (DNS)	wins	2nd	3rd	4th	5th	6th	PP	FL	points
Indy 500	1992	1	-	-	-	-	-	-	-	-	
CART	1991-92	26	-	-	-	-	-	1	-	-	

Warwick Pratley

AUS
Major win: 1951 Australian GP

Frank Pratt

AUS
Major win: 1948 Australian GP

Alexandre Premat

F. Born: 5.4.1982, Juvisy-sur-Orge
2002 French Formula Renault Champion

Jacobus "Jackie" Pretorius

ZA. Born: 22.11.1934, Potchefstroom, Transvaal

formula	years	starts (DNS)	wins	2nd	3rd	4th	5th	6th	PP	FL	points
F1 W	1965-73	3 (1)	-	-	-	-	-	-	-	-	0

Best result: no finishes. Best qualifying: 20th. Teams: driver, Team Pretoria, Team Gunston, Williams

F1 ZA wins: 1968 Mozambique, Killarney, 1969 Kyalami, 1971 Killarney, Pietermaritzburg

Ernesto Prinoth

I. Born: 15.4.1923, Ortisei, Bolzano. Died: 26.11.1981, Innsbruck (A)

formula	years	starts (DNS)	wins	2nd	3rd	4th	5th	6th	PP	FL	points
F1 W	1962	0 (1)	-	-	-	-	-	-	-	-	0

Best result: no starts. Best qualifying: 27th. Team: Jolly Club

David Prophet

GB. Born: 9.10.1937, Hong Kong. Died: 29.3.1981, Silverstone

formula	years	starts (DNS)	wins	2nd	3rd	4th	5th	6th	PP	FL	points
F1 W	1963-65	2	-	-	-	-	-	-	-	-	0

Best result: 14th. Best qualifying: 14th. Team: driver

Leos Propkopec

CS
1997 Czech F3 Champion

Alain Prost
F. Born: 24.2.1955, Lorette, St Chamond
1985, 1986, 1989 and 1993 F1 World Champion,
1979 European F3 Champion, 1978 (with Jean-Louis Schlesser) and 1979 French F3 Champion,
1977 European Formula Renault Champion, 1976
French Formula Renault Champion

formula	years	starts (DNS)	wins	2nd	3rd	4th	5th	6th	PP	FL	points
F1 W	1980-93	199 (3)	51	35	20	10	5	7	33	41	798.5

Wins: 1981 French GP, Dutch GP, Italian GP, 1982 South African GP, Brazilian GP, 1983 French GP, Belgian GP, British GP, Austrian GP, 1984 Brazilian GP, San Marino GP, Monaco GP, German GP, Dutch GP, European GP, Portuguese GP, 1985 Brazilian GP, Monaco GP, British GP, Austrian GP, Italian GP, 1986 San Marino GP, Monaco GP, Austrian GP, Australian GP, 1987 Brazilian GP, Belgian GP, Portuguese GP, 1988 Brazilian GP, Monaco GP, Mexican GP, French GP, Portuguese GP, Spanish GP, Australian GP, 1989 United States GP, French GP, British GP, Italian GP, 1990 Brazilian GP, Mexican GP, French GP, British GP, Spanish GP, 1993 South African GP, San Marino GP, Spanish GP, Canadian GP, French GP, British GP, German GP. Best championships: 1985, 1986, 1989 and 1993, 1st. Best qualifying: 1st. Teams: McLaren, Renault, Ferrari, Williams

formula	years	starts (DNS)	wins	2nd	3rd	4th	5th	6th	PP	FL	points
F2 E	1977-78	3	-	-	-	-	-	-	-	-	0

F3 E wins: 7 – 1978 Jarama, 1979 Osterreichring, Zolder, Magny-Cours, Zandvoort, Knutstorp, Jarama
Other major wins: 1979 Monaco F3, 1982 Australian GP

Stephane Proulx
CDN. Born: 12.12.1965, Ste Adele, Quebec. Died: 21.11.1993, Ste Adele, Quebec, AIDS

formula	years	starts (DNS)	wins	2nd	3rd	4th	5th	6th	PP	FL	points
F3000 INT	1989-90	20 (1)	-	-	-	-	1	-	1	-	2

Best championship: 1989, 17th

Scott Pruett
USA. Born: 24.3.1960, Sacramento, California
1987 and 1994 Trans-Am Champion, 1986 and 1988 IMSA GTO Champion

formula	years	starts (DNS)	wins	2nd	3rd	4th	5th	6th	PP	FL	points
Le Mans	2001	1	-	-	-	-	-	-	-	-	
Indy 500	1989-95	4	-	-	-	-	-	-	-	-	
CART	1988-99	145 (2)	2	5	8	9	12	6	5	4	

Wins: 1995 Michigan 500, 1997 Surfers Paradise. Best championship: 1998, 6th
Other major win: 1994 Daytona 24 hrs

Tom Pryce
GB. Born: 11.6.1949, Ruthin, Denbighshire. Died: 5.3.1977, Kyalami, South African GP

formula	years	starts (DNS)	wins	2nd	3rd	4th	5th	6th	PP	FL	points
F1 W	1974-77	42	-	-	2	3	-	4	1	-	19

Best championship: 1975, 10th. Best qualifying: 1st. Teams: Token, Shadow

formula	years	starts (DNS)	wins	2nd	3rd	4th	5th	6th	PP	FL	points
F2 E	1973-76	14	-	1	1	1	2	-	1	-	20

Best championship: 1974, 9th
Non-championship F1 win: 1975 Race of Champions (Brands Hatch)
Other major win: 1974 Monaco F3

Antonio Pucci
I. Born: 1923, Palermo, Sicily

formula	years	starts (DNS)	wins	2nd	3rd	4th	5th	6th	PP	FL	points
SC W	1955-66		1	-	2	-	2	2	-	-	

Win: 1964 Targa Florio

Tom Puig
E
1999 Spanish GT Champion

Eddie Pullen
USA. Born: 1888. Died: 19??

formula	years	starts (DNS)	wins	2nd	3rd	4th	5th	6th	PP	FL	points
GP Pre-50	1914-16	3	1	-	-	-	-	-	-	-	

Win: 1914 American GP

formula	years	starts (DNS)	wins	2nd	3rd	4th	5th	6th	PP	FL	points
Indy 500	1914-21	2	-	-	-	-	-	-	-	-	

Champcar wins: 5 – 1912 Tacoma race 1, 1914 American GP, Corona, 1915 Tacoma race 2, 1921 Beverly Hills race 7

David Purley
GB. Born: 26.1.1945, Bognor Regis, West Sussex. Died: 2.7.1985, Bognor Regis, aircraft accident
1976 British Group 8 (F5000) Champion

formula	years	starts (DNS)	wins	2nd	3rd	4th	5th	6th	PP	FL	points
F1 W	1973-77	7 (4)	-	-	-	-	-	-	-	-	0

Best result: 9th. Best qualifying: 16th. Teams: Lec, Token

formula	years	starts (DNS)	wins	2nd	3rd	4th	5th	6th	PP	FL	points
F2 E	1972-75	18 (3)	-	2	1	-	-	-	-	-	17

Best championship: 1974, 5th

Clive Puzey
RSR. Born: 11.7.1941, Bulawayo

formula	years	starts (DNS)	wins	2nd	3rd	4th	5th	6th	PP	FL	points
F1 W	1965	0 (1)	-	-	-	-	-	-	-	-	0

Best result: no starts. Best qualifying: no times set. Team: driver

Q

Dieter Quester
A. Born: 30.5.1939, Vienna
1968 (over 1600cc class), 1969 (over 1600cc class), 1977 and 1983 European Touring Car Champion

formula	years	starts (DNS)	wins	2nd	3rd	4th	5th	6th	PP	FL	points
F1 W	1969-74	1 (1)	-	-	-	-	-	-	-	-	0

Best result: 9th. Best qualifying: 25th. Teams: BMW, Surtees

formula	years	starts (DNS)	wins	2nd	3rd	4th	5th	6th	PP	FL	points
Le Mans	1973-86	8	-	-	-	-	-	-	-	-	
SC W	1967-92		2	-	3	1	2	2	-	-	

Wins: 1976 Nurburgring, Osterreichring

formula	years	starts (DNS)	wins	2nd	3rd	4th	5th	6th	PP	FL	points
F2 E	1969-74	25 (2)	1	4	1	-	1	-	-	3	45

Win: 1970 Hockenheim race 2. Best championship: 1971, 3rd
Other major wins: 1970 Macau, 1973, 1986 and 1988 Spa 24 hrs, 1977 Tourist Trophy (Silverstone)

R

Ian Raby
GB. Born: 22.9.1921, London. Died: 7.11.1967, Zandvoort F2 race

formula	years	starts (DNS)	wins	2nd	3rd	4th	5th	6th	PP	FL	points
F1 W	1963-65	3 (4)	-	-	-	-	-	-	-	-	0

Best result: 11th. Best qualifying: 17th. Team: driver

formula	years	starts (DNS)	wins	2nd	3rd	4th	5th	6th	PP	FL	points
Le Mans	1957	1	-	-	-	-	-	-	-	-	
F2 E	1967	7	-	-	-	-	1	-	-	-	7

Best championship: 1967, 12th

Vincent Radermecker
B. Born: 5.7.1967, Liege
2001 Belgian Procar Touring Car Champion

Didier de Radigues
B. Born: 27.3.1958, Louvain
1997 Belgian Procar Touring Car Champion, 2001 American Le Mans Series LMP675 Champion

formula	years	starts (DNS)	wins	2nd	3rd	4th	5th	6th	PP	FL	points
Le Mans	1998-2002	5	-	-	-	-	-	-	-	-	

Major win: 1997 Spa 24 hrs

Paul Radisich
NZ. Born: 9.10.1962, Auckland
1993 and 1994 Touring Car World Cup winner, 1988 New Zealand Gold Star Champion, 1988 New Zealand Formula Pacific Champion
Major wins: 1988 New Zealand GP, 1994 Tourist Trophy (Donington)

Jean Ragnotti
F. Born: 29.8.1945, Carpentras
1988 French Touring Car Champion

formula	years	starts (DNS)	wins	2nd	3rd	4th	5th	6th	PP	FL	points
Le Mans	1975-82	7	-	-	-	2	1	-	1	1	
SC W	1972-82		-	-	-	-	1	-	1	1	

Bobby Rahal
USA. Born: 10.1.1953, Medina, Ohio
1986, 1987 and 1992 CART Champion

formula	years	starts (DNS)	wins	2nd	3rd	4th	5th	6th	PP	FL	points
F1 W	1978	2	-	-	-	-	-	-	-	-	0

Best result: 12th. Best qualifying: 20th. Team: Wolf

| Le Mans | 1980-82 | 2 | - | - | - | - | - | - | - | - | |
| SC W | 1976-87 | | 1 | 1 | 1 | - | 1 | 2 | 1 | - | |

Win: 1981 Daytona 24 hrs. Best championship: 1981, 6th

| F2 E | 1979 | 11 | - | - | 2 | 1 | 2 | - | - | | 10 |

Best championship: 1979, 11th

| Indy 500 | 1982-95 | 13 | 1 | 1 | 2 | - | 1 | 1 | - | 1 | |

Win: 1986 Indianapolis 500

| CART | 1982-98 | 264 (1) | 24 | 37 | 27 | 13 | 18 | 21 | 17 | 4 | |

Wins: 1982 Cleveland, Michigan, 1983 Riverside, 1984 Phoenix, Laguna Seca, 1985 Mid-Ohio, Michigan, Laguna Seca, 1986 Indianapolis 500, Toronto, Mid-Ohio, Sanair, Michigan, Laguna Seca, 1987 Portland, Meadowlands, Laguna Seca, 1988 Pocono 500, 1989 Meadowlands, 1991 Meadowlands, 1992 Phoenix, Detroit, New Hampshire, Nazareth. Best championships: 1986, 1987 and 1992, 1st

Other major win: 1987 Sebring 12 hrs

Kimi Raikkonen
SF. Born: 17.10.1979, Espoo

formula	years	starts (DNS)	wins	2nd	3rd	4th	5th	6th	PP	FL	points
F1 W	2001-02	34	-	1	3	4	1	1	-	1	33

Best championship: 2002, 6th. Best qualifying: 2nd. Team: Sauber, McLaren

Johan Rajamaki
S. Born: 30.10.1957
1994 Interserie Champion

Jose Antonio Ramos
MEX
2000 Mexican F3 Champion

Miguel Ramos
P. Born: 26.9.1971, Porto
2002 Spanish GT Champion (with Pedro Chaves)

formula	years	starts (DNS)	wins	2nd	3rd	4th	5th	6th	PP	FL	points
Le Mans	2002	1	-	-	-	-	-	-	-	-	

Giulio Ramponi
I. Born: n/a. Died: 1987

formula	years	starts (DNS)	wins	2nd	3rd	4th	5th	6th	PP	FL	points
Le Mans	1930	1	-	-	-	-	-	-	-	-	

Major wins: 1928 and 1929 Mille Miglia

Luca Rangoni
I. Born: 23.9.1968, Bologna
2000, 2001 and 2002 European Renault Clio Champion, 1995 Italian F3 Champion

formula	years	starts (DNS)	wins	2nd	3rd	4th	5th	6th	PP	FL	points
F3000 INT	1996	1	-	-	-	-	-	1	-		1

Best championship: 1996, 17th

Pierre-Henri Raphanel
F. Born: 27.5.1961, Algiers (DZ)
1985 French F3 Champion

formula	years	starts (DNS)	wins	2nd	3rd	4th	5th	6th	PP	FL	points
F1 W	1988-89	1 (16)	-	-	-	-	-	-	-	-	0

Best result: no finishes. Best qualifying: 18th. Teams: Larrousse, Coloni, Rial

| Le Mans | 1986-2000 | 14 | - | 2 | 1 | - | 2 | - | - | - | |
| SC W | 1986-92 | | - | 1 | 1 | - | - | - | - | - | |

Best championship: 1992, 16th

formula	years	starts (DNS)	wins	2nd	3rd	4th	5th	6th	PP	FL	points
F3000 INT	1986-88	32 (1)	-	-	3	1	1	3	1	-	20

Best championship: 1986, 12th
Major win: 1985 Monaco F3

Poul Rasmussen
DK
1956, 1958 and 1959 Danish F3 Champion

James "Dick" Rathmann
USA. Born: 6.1.1926, Los Angeles, California. Died: 1.2.2000, Melbourne, Florida

formula	years	starts (DNS)	wins	2nd	3rd	4th	5th	6th	PP	FL	points
Indy 500	1950-64	9	-	-	-	-	1	-	1	-	

NASCAR wins: 13

Richard "Jim" Rathmann
USA. Born: 16.7.1928, Los Angeles, California

formula	years	starts (DNS)	wins	2nd	3rd	4th	5th	6th	PP	FL	points
Indy 500	1949-63	14	1	3	-	-	1	-	-	2	

Win: 1960 Indianapolis 500
Champcar wins: 3 – 1957 Milwaukee race 2, 1959 Daytona, 1960 Indianapolis 500
Other major win: 1958 Race of Two Worlds (Monza)

Roland Ratzenberger
A. Born: 4.7.1962, Salzburg. Died: 30.4.1994, Bologna Hospital following a qualifying accident at the San Marino GP

formula	years	starts (DNS)	wins	2nd	3rd	4th	5th	6th	PP	FL	points
F1 W	1994	1 (2)	-	-	-	-	-	-	-	-	0

Best result: 11th. Best qualifying: 26th. Team: Simtek

| Le Mans | 1989-93 | 5 | - | - | - | 1 | - | - | - | - | |
| SC W | 1989-92 | | - | - | - | 1 | - | - | - | - | |

F3 E win: 1 – 1987 Nurburgring EFDA

Roberto Ravaglia
I. Born: 26.5.1957, Mestra
1987 World Touring Car Champion, 1986 and 1988 European Touring Car Champion, 1989 German Touring Car Champion, 1990, 1991 and 1993 Italian Touring Car Champion

formula	years	starts (DNS)	wins	2nd	3rd	4th	5th	6th	PP	FL	points
Le Mans	1990-97	2	-	-	1	-	-	-	-	-	

GT FIA win: 1 – 1997 Silverstone
F3 E win: 1 – 1983 La Chatre
Other major wins: 1985, 1988 and 1994 Spa 24 hrs, 1987 Macau Guia race

Greg Ray
USA. Born: 3.8.1966, Dallas, Texas
1999 Indy Racing League Champion

formula	years	starts (DNS)	wins	2nd	3rd	4th	5th	6th	PP	FL	points
Indy 500	1997-2002	6	-	-	-	-	-	-	1	1	
IRL	1997-2002	54 (1)	5	2	1	-	-	-	14	3	

Wins: 1999 Pikes Peak, Dover Downs, Pikes Peak, 2000 Atlanta, 2001 Atlanta.
Best championship: 1999, 1st

Hector Rebaque
MEX. Born: 5.2.1956, Mexico City

formula	years	starts (DNS)	wins	2nd	3rd	4th	5th	6th	PP	FL	points
F1 W	1977-81	41 (17)	-	-	-	3	1	2	-	-	13

Best championship: 1981, 9th. Best qualifying: 6th. Teams: Hesketh, Rebaque, Brabham

| Le Mans | 1974 | 1 | - | - | - | - | - | - | - | - | |
| F2 E | 1975 | 5 (1) | - | - | - | 1 | - | - | - | - | 3 |

Best championship: 1975, 22nd

| Indy 500 | 1982 | 1 | - | - | - | - | - | - | - | - | |
| CART | 1982 | 5 (1) | 1 | - | - | - | - | - | - | - | |

Win: 1982 Elkhart Lake

Martin Redfern
HK
Major wins: 1960 Macau

Brian Redman

GB. Born: 9.3.1937, Colne, Lanceshire
1974, 1975 and 1976 North American F5000 Champion, 1981 IMSA GTP
Champion, 1970 South African Springbok Sports Car Champion

formula	years	starts (DNS)	wins	2nd	3rd	4th	5th	6th	PP	FL	points
F1 W	1967-74	12 (4)	-	-	1	-	2	-	-	-	8

Best championship: 1972, 12th. Best qualifying: 10th. Teams: David Bridges,
Cooper, Rob Walker, Williams, Surtees, McLaren, BRM, Shadow

Le Mans	1967-89	14	-	-	-	-	2	-			
SC W	1966-92		17	8	7	4	2	3	-	2	

Wins: 1968 Brands Hatch, Spa, 1969 Brands Hatch, Monza, Spa, Nurburgring,
Watkins Glen, 1970 Daytona 24 hrs, Targa Florio, Spa, Osterreichring, 1972
Spa, Osterreichring, 1973 Monza, Nurburgring, 1980 Mosport Park, 1981
Daytona 24 hrs. Best championship: 1981, 9th

F2 E	1967-68	5	-	1	-	1	1	-	-		17

Other major wins: 1975 and 1978 Sebring 12 hrs, 1975 Long Beach GP, 1976
Daytona 24 hrs

Laurent Redon

F. Born: 5.8.1973, St Chamond
1995 French F3 Champion

formula	years	starts (DNS)	wins	2nd	3rd	4th	5th	6th	PP	FL	points
Le Mans	2001	1	-	-	-	-	-	-			

SRWC wins: 2 – 1999 Spa, 2001 Magny-Cours

F3000 INT	1996-97	20	-	-	1	3	1	2	-		17

Best championship: 1996, 7th

Indy 500	2002	1	-	-	-	-	-	-			
IRL	2001-02	17	-	-	1	-	-	-			

Jim Reed

USA. Born: 21.2.1926
NASCAR wins: 7

Alan Rees

GB. Born: 12.1.1938, Langstone, Monmouthshire
1967 Autocar F2 Champion

formula	years	starts (DNS)	wins	2nd	3rd	4th	5th	6th	PP	FL	points
F1 W	1966-67	3	-	-	-	-	-	-	-	-	0

Best result: 9th. Best qualifying: 15th. Teams: Roy Winkelmann, Cooper

Le Mans	1966	1	-	-	-	-	-	-			
F2 E	1967-68	12 (1)	-	1	1	-	1	1	-	-	24

Best championship: 1967, 5th

Gareth Rees

GB. Born: 12.3.1969, London
1996 British F2 Champion, 1992 European GM-Lotus Champion

formula	years	starts (DNS)	wins	2nd	3rd	4th	5th	6th	PP	FL	points
F3000 INT	1995-98	25 (1)	-	-	1	3	-	1	-	-	14

Best championship: 1998, 8th
Major win: 1994 Marlboro Masters (Zandvoort)

Gianclaudio "Clay" Regazzoni

CH. Born: 5.9.1939, Mendrisio, near Lugano
1970 European F2 Champion

formula	years	starts (DNS)	wins	2nd	3rd	4th	5th	6th	PP	FL	points
F1 W	1970-80	132 (7)	5	13	10	8	9	7	5	15	212

Wins: 1970 Italian GP, 1974 German GP, 1975 Italian GP, 1976 Long Beach GP,
1979 British GP. Best championship: 1974, 2nd. Best qualifying: 1st. Teams:
Ferrari, BRM, Ensign, Shadow, Williams

Le Mans	1970	1	-	-	-	-	-	-			
SC W	1970-73		1	3	-	1	1	-	2	2	

Win: 1972 Monza

F2 E	1968-79	25 (1)	3	2	1	2	1	1	4	1	62

Wins: 1970 Hockenheim race 1, Enna, Imola. Best championship: 1970, 1st

Indy 500	1977	1	-	-	-	-	-	-			

Non-championship F1 wins: 1971 Race of Champions (Brands Hatch), 1975
Swiss GP (Dijon)

Anthony Reid

GB. Born: 17.5.1959, Glasgow
1992 Japanese F3 Champion

formula	years	starts (DNS)	wins	2nd	3rd	4th	5th	6th	PP	FL	points
Le Mans	1990-2002	5	-	-	1	-	-	-			
SC W	1990-92		-	-	-	-	-	-			

Tommy Reid

IRL. Born: 1934

formula	years	starts (DNS)	wins	2nd	3rd	4th	5th	6th	PP	FL	points
F2 E	1969-71	3 (1)	-	-	-	-	-	-	-	-	1

Best championship: 1970, 18th. Best result: 9th

Marcel Renault

F. Born: 1872. Died: 26.5.1903, Paris-Madrid city-to-city race
City-to-city win: 1902 Paris-Vienna

Philippe Renault

F. Born: 28.6.1959
1981 French Formula Renault Champion

formula	years	starts (DNS)	wins	2nd	3rd	4th	5th	6th	PP	FL	points
Le Mans	1984	1	-	-	-	-	-	-			

Dario Resta

I. Born: 1884, Milan. Died: 3.9.1924, Brooklands
(GB)
1916 Champcar Champion

formula	years	starts (DNS)	wins	2nd	3rd	4th	5th	6th	PP	FL	points
GP Pre-50	1908-24	8	1	-	-	1	1	1	-	-	

Win: 1915 American GP

Indy 500	1915-23	3	1	1	-	-	-	-			

Win: 1916 Indianapolis 500
Champcar wins: 10 – 1915 American GP, WK Vanderbilt Cup, Chicago race 1,
Chicago race 2, Sheepshead race 2, 1916 Indianapolis 500, Chicago race 1,
Omaha, Chicago race 2, WK Vanderbilt Cup

Raffaele Restivo

I
Major win: 1977 Targa Florio

Carlos Reutemann

RA. Born: 12.4.1942, Santa Fe

formula	years	starts (DNS)	wins	2nd	3rd	4th	5th	6th	PP	FL	points
F1 W	1972-82	146	12	13	20	11	3	7	6	5	310

Wins: 1974 South African GP, Austrian GP, United States GP, 1975 German GP,
1977 South African GP, 1978 Brazilian GP, Long Beach GP, British GP, United States
GP, 1980 Monaco GP, 1981 Brazilian GP, Belgian GP. Best championship: 1981,
2nd. Best qualifying: 1st. Teams: Brabham, Ferrari, Lotus, Williams

Le Mans	1973	1	-	-	-	-	-	-			
SC W	1971-74		-	4	-	-	-	-			
F2 E	1970-72	28 (1)	-	1	9	-	2	3	1	1	67

Best championship: 1971, 2nd
Non-championship F1 wins: 1972 Brazilian GP, 1981 South African GP

Manuel Reuter

D. Born: 6.12.1961, Mainz
1996 International Touring Car Champion, 1996 German Touring Car
Champion, 1992 Interserie Champion

formula	years	starts (DNS)	wins	2nd	3rd	4th	5th	6th	PP	FL	points
Le Mans	1988-96	7	2	-	-	-	-	-			

Wins: 1989 and 1996 Le Mans 24 hrs

SC W	1987-92		-	-	3	2	2	3	-	-	

Best championship: 1991, 9th

R

Lance Reventlow
USA. Born: 24.2.1936, London (GB). Died: 24.7.1972, Colorado, aircraft accident

formula	years	starts (DNS)	wins	2nd	3rd	4th	5th	6th	PP	FL	points
F1 W	1960	1 (3)	-	-	-	-	-	-	-	-	0

Best result: no finishes. Best qualifying: 16th. Teams: driver, Cooper

| SC W | 1957-59 | | - | - | - | - | 1 | - | - | | |

Peter Revson
USA. Born: 27.2.1939, New York City. Died: 22.3.1974, Kyalami, testing
1971 Can-Am Champion

formula	years	starts (DNS)	wins	2nd	3rd	4th	5th	6th	PP	FL	points
F1 W	1964-74	30 (2)	2	2	4	3	3	-	1	-	61

Wins: 1973 British GP, Canadian GP. Best championships: 1972 and 1973, 5th. Best qualifying: 1st. Teams: driver, Reg Parnell, Tyrrell, McLaren, Shadow

Le Mans	1965-66	2	-	-	-	-	-	-			
SC W	1965-72		-	1	3	-	-	-			
Indy 500	1969-73	5	-	1	-	-	1	-	1	-	

Champcar win: 1 – 1969 Indianapolis Raceway Park race 2
Other major win: 1965 Monaco F3

Bill Rexford
USA. Born: 14.3.1927. Died: 18.4.1994
1950 NASCAR Champion
NASCAR wins: 1

Adrian Reynard
GB. Born: 23.3.1951
1979 European FF2000 Champion

George Reynolds
AUS
Major win: 1964 Bathurst

John Rhodes
GB. Born: 18.8.1927, Wolverhampton, Staffordshire
1968 European Touring Car Champion (1600cc class)

formula	years	starts (DNS)	wins	2nd	3rd	4th	5th	6th	PP	FL	points
F1 W	1965	1	-	-	-	-	-	-	-	-	0

Best result: no finishes. Best qualifying: 21st. Team: Bob Gerard

| Le Mans | 1965-66 | 2 | - | - | - | - | - | - | | | |

Alex Dias Ribeiro
BR. Born: 7.11.1948, Belo Horizonte

formula	years	starts (DNS)	wins	2nd	3rd	4th	5th	6th	PP	FL	points
F1 W	1976-79	10 (10)	-	-	-	-	-	-	-	-	0

Best result: 8th. Best qualifying: 17th. Teams: Hesketh, March, Fittipaldi

| F2 E | 1975-78 | 28 (1) | 1 | 2 | 3 | 1 | 2 | 2 | 2 | - | 46 |

Win: 1978 Nurburgring. Best championship: 1976, 5th

Andre Ribeiro
BR. Born: 18.1.1966, Sao Paulo

formula	years	starts (DNS)	wins	2nd	3rd	4th	5th	6th	PP	FL	points
Indy 500	1995	1	-	-	-	-	-	-			
CART	1995-98	68 (1)	3	-	1	3	-	1	2	-	

Wins: 1995 New Hampshire, 1996 Rio de Janeiro, Michigan 500

Buddy Rice
USA. Born: 31.1.1976, Phoenix, Arizona
2000 North American Toyota Atlantic Champion

formula	years	starts (DNS)	wins	2nd	3rd	4th	5th	6th	PP	FL	points
IRL	2002	5	-	1	-	1	-	1	-	2	

Jason Richards
NZ. Born: 10.4.1976, Nelson
1999, 2000 and 2001 New Zealand Touring Car Champion

Jim Richards
NZ. Born: 2.9.1947
1985, 1987, 1990 and 1991 Australia Touring Car Champion, 2000, 2001 and 2002 Australian GT Champion
Major wins: 1978, 1979, 1980, 1991, 1992 and 2002 Bathurst, 1998 Bathurst 2-litre

Steven Richards
NZ. Born: 11.7.1972, Auckland
Major wins: 1998 and 1999 Bathurst

Ken Richardson
GB. Born: 21.8.1911, Bourne, Lincolnshire. Died: 27.6.1997, Bourne, Lincolnshire

formula	years	starts (DNS)	wins	2nd	3rd	4th	5th	6th	PP	FL	points
F1 W	1951	0 (1)	-	-	-	-	-	-	-	-	0

Best result: no starts. Best qualifying: 10th. Team: BRM

| GP Pre-50 | 1949 | 1 | - | - | - | - | - | - | | | |
| Le Mans | 1955 | 1 | - | - | - | - | - | - | | | |

Tim Richmond
USA. Born: 7.6.1955, Ohio. Died: 9.8.1989, West Palm Beach, Florida, AIDS

formula	years	starts (DNS)	wins	2nd	3rd	4th	5th	6th	PP	FL	points
Indy 500	1980-81	2	-	-	-	-	-	-			
CART	1979-80	8 (2)	-	-	-	-	-	-			

NASCAR wins: 13 (all Modern era)

Eddie Rickenbacher
USA. Born: 8.10.1890, Columbus, Ohio. Died: 23.7.1973, Zurich (CH)

formula	years	starts (DNS)	wins	2nd	3rd	4th	5th	6th	PP	FL	points
GP Pre-50	1914-16	3	-	-	-	-	1	-	-		
Indy 500	1911-16	5	-	-	-	1	-	-			

Champcar wins: 7 – 1914 Sioux City, 1915 Sioux City, Omaha, Providence, 1916 Sheepshead race 1, Tacoma, Ascot

Jody Ridley
USA. Born: c1943
NASCAR wins: 1 (in Modern era)

Kurt Rieder
A

formula	years	starts (DNS)	wins	2nd	3rd	4th	5th	6th	PP	FL	points
F2 E	1973-74	1 (1)	-	-	-	-	-	-	-	-	1

Best championship: 1973, 31st. Best result: 7th

Fritz Riess
D. Born: 11.7.1922, Nuremburg. Died: 15.5.1991, Samedan (CH)

formula	years	starts (DNS)	wins	2nd	3rd	4th	5th	6th	PP	FL	points
F1 W	1952	1	-	-	-	-	-	-	-	-	0

Best result: 7th. Best qualifying: no times set. Team: driver

| Le Mans | 1952-53 | 2 | 1 | - | - | - | - | - | | | |

Win: 1952 Le Mans 24 hrs

Louis Rigal
F. Born: 1887. Died: 1974

formula	years	starts (DNS)	wins	2nd	3rd	4th	5th	6th	PP	FL	points
GP Pre-50	1928-31	3	-	-	-	-	-	-			
Le Mans	1924-38	7	-	-	-	-	-	-			

Major win: 1926 Spa 24 hrs

Brett Riley
NZ. Born: 30.7.1953
1991 and 1998 New Zealand Touring Car Champion
F3 E wins: 1977 Donington, 1979 Donington

Jochen Rindt
A. Born: 18.4.1942, Mainz-am-Rhein (D). Died: 5.9.1970, Monza, Italian GP practice
1970 F1 World Champion, 1967 British F2 Champion, 1967 French F2 Champion

formula	years	starts (DNS)	wins	2nd	3rd	4th	5th	6th	PP	FL	points
F1 W	1964-70	60 (2)	6	3	4	6	1	1	10	3	109

Wins: 1969 United States GP, 1970 Monaco GP, Dutch GP, French GP, British GP, German GP. Best championship: 1970, 1st. Best qualifying: 1st. Teams: Rob Walker, Cooper, Brabham, Lotus

Le Mans	1964-67	4		1	-	-	-	-	-	-

Win: 1965 Le Mans 24 hrs

SC W	1964-67		1	-	2	-	-	-	-	-

Win: 1965 Le Mans 24 hrs

F2 E	1967-70	19		12	1	-	-	-	10	11	0

Wins: 1967 Snetterton, Silverstone, Nurburgring, Tulln, Brands Hatch, 1968 Thruxton, Crystal Palace, Tulln, Enna, 1969 Thruxton, Tulln, 1970 Thruxton

Indy 500	1967-68	2	-	-	-	-	-	-	-	-

Tasman wins: 2 – 1969 Lady Wigram Trophy, Warwick Farm
Other major win: 1965 Austrian GP

Jorge del Rio
RA
1980, 1981 and 1982 TC2000 Argentinian Touring Car Champion

John Riseley-Prichard
GB. Born: 17.1.1924, Hereford. Died: 8.7.1993, Bangkok (T)

formula	years	starts (DNS)	wins	2nd	3rd	4th	5th	6th	PP	FL	points
F1 W	1954	1	-	-	-	-	-	-	-	-	0

Best result: no finishes. Best qualifying: 21st. Team: Rob Walker

Le Mans	1955	1	-	-	-	-	-	-	-	-

Non-championship F1 win: 1954 Davidstow

Robert Ritchie
HK
Major wins: 1955 Macau

Giovanni de Riu
I. Born: 10.3.1924, Macomer, Nuoro

formula	years	starts (DNS)	wins	2nd	3rd	4th	5th	6th	PP	FL	points
F1 W	1954	0 (1)	-	-	-	-	-	-	-	-	0

Best result: no starts. Best qualifying: 21st. Team: driver

Richard Robarts
GB. Born: 22.9.1944, Bicknacre, Essex

formula	years	starts (DNS)	wins	2nd	3rd	4th	5th	6th	PP	FL	points
F1 W	1974	3 (1)	-	-	-	-	-	-	-	-	0

Best result: 15th. Best qualifying: 22nd. Teams: Brabham, Williams

F2 E	1976	3 (5)	-	-	-	-	-	-	-	-	0

Edward "Fireball" Roberts
USA. Born: 20.1.1929, Daytona Beach, Florida. Died: 2.7.1964, Charlotte Hospital, following an accident during the World 600 on 24.5.64

formula	years	starts (DNS)	wins	2nd	3rd	4th	5th	6th	PP	FL	points
Le Mans	1962	1	-	-	-	-	-	1	-
SC W	1962-63		-	-	-	-	-	1	-

NASCAR wins: 32

Floyd Roberts
USA. Born: 12.2.1904, Jamestown, North Dakota. Died: 30.5.1939, Indianapolis 500
1938 Champcar Champion

formula	years	starts (DNS)	wins	2nd	3rd	4th	5th	6th	PP	FL	points
Indy 500	1935-39	5	1	-	-	1	-	-	1	-

Win: 1938 Indianapolis 500
Champcar win: 1 – 1938 Indianapolis 500

Mortimer Roberts
USA
Champcar win: 1 – 1912 Milwaukee race 3

Tony Roberts
AUS
Major win: 1969 Bathurst

George Robertson
USA. Born: 1884, New York City. Died: 3.7.1955
Champcar wins: 2 – 1909 Lowell race 4, Philadelphia
Other major win: 1908 WK Vanderbilt Cup

Steve Robertson
GB. Born: 4.7.1965, Hackney, London
1994 CART Indy Lights Champion

formula	years	starts (DNS)	wins	2nd	3rd	4th	5th	6th	PP	FL	points
F3000 INT	1992	7 (2)	-	-	-	-	-	-	-	-	0

Brian Robinson
GB

formula	years	starts (DNS)	wins	2nd	3rd	4th	5th	6th	PP	FL	points
Le Mans	1972-84	2	-	-	-	-	-	-	-	-
F2 E	1973-81	2 (2)	-	-	-	-	-	1	-	-	1

Best championship: 1981, 19th

Chip Robinson
USA. Born: 29.3.1954
1987 IMSA GTP Champion

formula	years	starts (DNS)	wins	2nd	3rd	4th	5th	6th	PP	FL	points
Le Mans	1985-90	4	-	-	-	-	-	-	-	-
CART	1986-87	5	-	-	-	-	-	1	-	-

Major wins: 1987 Daytona 24 hrs, 1989 Sebring 12 hrs

Philip Robinson
GB

formula	years	starts (DNS)	wins	2nd	3rd	4th	5th	6th	PP	FL	points
F2 E	1967	4 (1)	-	-	-	-	-	-	-	-	2

Best championship: 1967, 15th. Best result: 11th

George Robson
USA. Born: 24.2.1909, Newcastle-upon-Tyne (GB). Died: 2.9.1946, Lakewood Park, Atlanta

formula	years	starts (DNS)	wins	2nd	3rd	4th	5th	6th	PP	FL	points
Indy 500	1939-46	4	1	-	-	-	-	-	-	-

Win: 1946 Indianapolis 500
Champcar win: 1 – 1946 Indianapolis 500

Giovanni Rocco
I

formula	years	starts (DNS)	wins	2nd	3rd	4th	5th	6th	PP	FL	points
GP Pre-50	1939	1	-	-	-	-	-	-	-	-

Major win: 1938 Targa Florio

Gonzalo Rodriguez
ROU. Born: 22.1.1972, Montevideo. Died: 11.9.1999, Laguna Seca, CART practice

formula	years	starts (DNS)	wins	2nd	3rd	4th	5th	6th	PP	FL	points
F3000 INT	1997-99	27 (2)	3	3	1	2	1	1	-	4	60.5

Wins: 1998 Spa, Nurburgring, 1999 Monaco. Best championships: 1998 and 1999, 3rd

CART	1999	1 (1)	-	-	-	-	-	-	-	-

Pedro Rodriguez
MEX. Born: 18.1.1940, Mexico City. Died: 11.7.1971, Norisring sports car race

formula	years	starts (DNS)	wins	2nd	3rd	4th	5th	6th	PP	FL	points
F1 W	1963-71	55	2	3	2	4	4	7	-	1	71

Wins: 1967 South African GP, 1970 Belgian GP. Best championships: 1967 and 1968, 6th. Best qualifying: 2nd. Teams: Lotus, Ferrari, Ron Harris, Cooper, BRM, Reg Parnell

Le Mans	1958-71	14		1	-	-	-	-	2	-

Win: 1968 Le Mans 24 hrs

SC W	1958-71		11	6	4	5	1	-	7	7

Wins: 1964 Daytona, 1965 Reims, 1968 Le Mans 24 hrs, 1970 Daytona 24 hrs,

Brands Hatch, Monza, Watkins Glen, 1971 Daytona 24 hrs, Monza, Spa, Osterreichring

formula	years	starts (DNS)	wins	2nd	3rd	4th	5th	6th	PP	FL	points
F2 E	1967-68	5	-	-	-	-	-	-	-	-	0

Non-championship F1 win: 1971 Oulton Park International Trophy
Other major wins: 1963 and 1964 Canadian GP

Ricardo Rodriguez
MEX. Born: 14.2.1942, Mexico City. Died: 1.11.1962, Mexico City, Mexican GP practice

formula	years	starts (DNS)	wins	2nd	3rd	4th	5th	6th	PP	FL	points
F1 W	1961-62	5 (1)	-	-	-	1	-	1	-	-	4

Best championship: 1962, 12th. Best qualifying: 2nd. Team: Ferrari

| Le Mans | 1959-62 | 4 | - | 1 | - | - | - | - | - | 1 |
| SC W | 1959-62 | | 1 | 2 | 1 | - | - | - | - | 1 |

Win: 1962 Targa Florio

Michael Roe
IRL. Born: 8.8.1955
1984 Can-Am Champion

formula	years	starts (DNS)	wins	2nd	3rd	4th	5th	6th	PP	FL	points
Le Mans	1989-90	2	-	-	-	-	-	-	-	-	
SC W	1984-90		-	-	-	-	1	-	-	
CART	1985	4 (1)	-	-	-	-	-	-	-	-	

Eric Roelands
B
2002 Belgian Belcar Touring Car Champion (with Peter Beckers and Serge Cassiers)

Al Rogers
USA
Champcar wins: 4 – 1948 Pikes Peak, 1949 Pikes Peak, 1950 Pikes Peak, 1951 Pikes Peak

Walter Rohrl
D. Born: 7.3.1947, Regensburg

formula	years	starts (DNS)	wins	2nd	3rd	4th	5th	6th	PP	FL	points
Le Mans	1981-93	2	-	-	-	-	-	-	-	-	
SC W	1979-92		2	1	1	2	1	-	-	-	

Wins: 1980 Brands Hatch, 1981 Silverstone

Franco Rol
I. Born: 5.6.1908, Turin. Died: 18.6.1977, Rapallo

formula	years	starts (DNS)	wins	2nd	3rd	4th	5th	6th	PP	FL	points
F1 W	1950-52	5	-	-	-	-	-	-	-	-	0

Best result: 9th. Best qualifying: 7th. Teams: Maserati, OSCA

| GP Pre-50 | 1949 | 1 | - | - | - | - | - | - | - | - |

Major win: 1949 Pescara

Alfonso Rolfo
I
Major win: 1952 Mille Miglia

Lloyd "Shorty" Rollins
USA. Born: 3.4.1929
NASCAR wins: 1

Alan Rollinson
GB. Born: 15.5.1943, Walsall, Staffordshire

formula	years	starts (DNS)	wins	2nd	3rd	4th	5th	6th	PP	FL	points
F1 W	1965	0 (1)	-	-	-	-	-	-	-	-	0

Best result: no starts. Best qualifying: 23rd. Team: Bob Gerard

| F2 E | 1967-71 | 10 | - | - | - | - | - | 1 | - | 5 |

Tasman win: 1 – 1973 Teretonga

Charles Stewart "CS" Rolls
GB. Born: 28.8.1877, London. Died: 12.7.1910, Bournemouth, Hampshire

formula	years	starts (DNS)	wins	2nd	3rd	4th	5th	6th	PP	FL	points
GP Pre-50	1905	1	-	-	-	-	-	-	-	-	

Major win: 1906 Tourist Trophy (Isle of Man)

Tony Rolt
GB. Born: 16.10.1918, Bordon, Hampshire

formula	years	starts (DNS)	wins	2nd	3rd	4th	5th	6th	PP	FL	points
F1 W	1950-55	3	-	-	-	-	-	-	-	-	0

Best result: no finishes. Best qualifying: 10th. Teams: Peter Walker, Rob Walker

| GP Pre-50 | 1939-49 | 2 (1) | - | - | - | - | - | - | - | - |
| Le Mans | 1949-55 | 7 | 1 | 1 | - | 1 | - | 1 | - | - |

Win: 1953 Le Mans 24 hrs

| SC W | 1953-55 | | 1 | 1 | - | - | - | - | - | - |

Win: 1953 Le Mans 24 hrs

Emilio Romano
I

formula	years	starts (DNS)	wins	2nd	3rd	4th	5th	6th	PP	FL	points
GP Pre-50	1938-39	1 (1)	-	-	-	-	-	-	-	-	

Major win: 1947 Mille Miglia

Francesco "Paco" Romero
E
1984 and 1985 Spanish Touring Car Champion

formula	years	starts (DNS)	wins	2nd	3rd	4th	5th	6th	PP	FL	points
Le Mans	1986	1	-	-	-	-	-	-	-	-	

Salvatore Ronca
I
SRWC win: 1 – 2000 Spa

Jean Rondeau
F. Born: 1946, Le Mans

formula	years	starts (DNS)	wins	2nd	3rd	4th	5th	6th	PP	FL	points
Le Mans	1972-85	13	1	1	-	1	-	-	-	-	

Win: 1980 Le Mans 24 hrs

| SC W | 1972-85 | | 2 | 1 | - | - | - | - | - | - |

Wins: 1980 Le Mans 24 hrs, 1982 Monza

Nicolas Rondet
F. Born: 9.3.1970, Melle
2001 Barber-Dodge Champion

Bertil Roos
S. Born: 12.10.1943, Gothenburg
1973 SCCA Super Vee Champion

formula	years	starts (DNS)	wins	2nd	3rd	4th	5th	6th	PP	FL	points
F1 W	1974	1	-	-	-	-	-	-	-	-	0

Best result: no finishes. Best qualifying: 23rd. Team: Shadow

| F2 E | 1973-74 | 5 | - | - | - | - | - | 1 | - | - | 2 |

Best championship: 1974, 22nd

Henrik Roos
S. Born: c1963
2000, 2001 (both solo) and 2002 (with Magnus Wallinder) Swedish GTR Champion

Basil van Rooyen
ZA. Born: 19.4.1939, Johannesburg

formula	years	starts (DNS)	wins	2nd	3rd	4th	5th	6th	PP	FL	points
F1 W	1968-69	2	-	-	-	-	-	-	-	-	0

Best result: no finishes. Best qualifying: 9th. Teams: John Love, Lawson Organisation
F1 ZA wins: 1968 Kumalo, Pietermaritzburg, 1969 Killarney, Pietermaritzburg

Trevor van Rooyen
ZA. Born: Johannesburg
1985 South African Formula Atlantic Champion

Jim Roper
USA. Born: 13.8.1916
NASCAR wins: 1

Pedro de la Rosa
E. Born: 24.2.1971, Barcelona
1997 Japanese Formula Nippon Champion, 1997 Japanese GT Champion
(with Michael Krumm), 1995 Japanese F3 Champion

formula	years	starts (DNS)	wins	2nd	3rd	4th	5th	6th	PP	FL	points
F1 W	1999-2002	63	-	-	-	1	4	-	-	-	6

Best championship: 2000, 15th. Best qualifying: 5th. Teams: Arrows, Jaguar

Kejio "Keke" Rosberg
SF. Born: 6.12.1948, Stockholm (S)
1982 F1 World Champion, 1977 and 1978 New
Zealand Formula Pacific Champion

formula	years	starts (DNS)	wins	2nd	3rd	4th	5th	6th	PP	FL	points
F1 W	1978-86	114 (14)	5	8	4	11	9	1	5	3	159.5

Wins: 1982 Swiss GP, 1983 Monaco GP, 1984 Dallas GP, 1985 Detroit GP,
Australian GP. Best championship: 1982, 1st. Best qualifying: 1st. Teams:
Theodore, ATS, Wolf, Fittipaldi, Williams, McLaren

Le Mans	1991	1	-	-	-	-	-	-			
SC W	1983-91	2	-	1	-	-	-	-			

Wins: 1991 Magny-Cours, Mexico City. Best championship: 1991, 13th

F2 E	1976-79	28 (3)	3	2	1	2	1	-	2	1	55

Wins: 1977 Enna, 1978 Donington, 1979 Hockenheim race 1. Best championship: 1978, 5th

Non-championship F1 wins: 1978 International Trophy (Silverstone), 1983
Race of Champions (Brands Hatch)
Other major wins: 1977 and 1978 New Zealand GP

Mauri Rose
USA. Born: 26.5.1906, Columbus, Ohio. Died: 1.1.1981, Royal Oak,
Michigan
1936 Champcar Champion

formula	years	starts (DNS)	wins	2nd	3rd	4th	5th	6th	PP	FL	points
Indy 500	1933-51	15	3	1	2	1	-	-	1	-	

Wins: 1941, 1947 and 1948 Indianapolis 500
Champcar wins: 6 – 1932 Detroit race 2, 1936 Syracuse, 1939 Syracuse, 1941
Indianapolis 500, 1947 Indianapolis 500, 1948 Indianapolis 500

de Rosee
B
1990 Belgian Belcar GT Champion (with Dumortier and Dumortier)

Bernd Rosemeyer
D. Born: 14.10.1909, Lingen. Died: 28.1.1938,
Frankfurt-Darmstadt autobahn, record attempt
1936 European Grand Prix Champion

formula	years	starts (DNS)	wins	2nd	3rd	4th	5th	6th	PP	FL	points
GP Pre-50	1935-37	17	5	1	5	2	3	-	3	6	

Wins: 1935 Masaryk GP, 1936 German GP, Swiss GP, Italian GP, 1937
Donington GP
Champcar win: 1 – 1937 George Vanderbilt Cup
Other major wins: 1936 and 1937 Eifelrennen (Nurburgring), 1936 and 1937
Coppa Acerbo (Pescara)

Jean-Louis Rosier (Louis Jean Rosier)
F. Born: 1925

formula	years	starts (DNS)	wins	2nd	3rd	4th	5th	6th	PP	FL	points
Le Mans	1949-54	5	1	-	-	-	-	-			

Win: 1950 Le Mans 24 hrs

Louis Rosier
F. Born: 5.11.1905, Chapdes Beaufort. Died: 29.10.1956, Neuilly-sur-Seine,
3 weeks after an accident during the Salon de Paris Cup at Montlhery

formula	years	starts (DNS)	wins	2nd	3rd	4th	5th	6th	PP	FL	points
F1 W	1950-56	38	-	-	2	2	2	2	-	-	18

Best championship: 1950, 4th. Best qualifying: 6th. Teams: driver, Talbot,

---

Charles Pozzi, Maserati

formula	years	starts (DNS)	wins	2nd	3rd	4th	5th	6th	PP	FL	points
GP Pre-50	1947-49	15		1	-	1	3	-	4	-	-

Win: 1949 Belgian GP

Le Mans	1938-56	8		1	-	-	-	1			

Win: 1950 Le Mans 24 hrs

SC W	1953-56		-	-	-	1	-	-			

Non-championship F1 wins: 1950 Albi, Dutch GP, 1951 Bordeaux, Dutch GP,
1952 Albi, 1953 Albi

Yngve Rosqvist
S
1961 and 1962 Swedish Formula Junior Champion

Earl Ross
CDN. Born: 4.9.1941
NASCAR wins: 1 (in Modern era)

Ricardo Rosset
BR. Born: 27.7.1968, Sao Paulo

formula	years	starts (DNS)	wins	2nd	3rd	4th	5th	6th	PP	FL	points
F1 W	1996-98	27 (7)	-	-	-	-	-	-	-	-	0

Best result: 8th. Best qualifying: 17th. Teams: Arrows, Lola, Tyrrell

F3000 INT	1995	8		2	1	-	1	1	-	1	2	29

Wins: 1995 Silverstone, Enna. Best championship: 1995, 2nd

Carlo Rossi
I

formula	years	starts (DNS)	wins	2nd	3rd	4th	5th	6th	PP	FL	points
F2 E	1980-82	21 (2)	-	-	-	1	1	1	-	-	6

Best championship: 1981, 13th

Andre Rossignol
F

formula	years	starts (DNS)	wins	2nd	3rd	4th	5th	6th	PP	FL	points
Le Mans	1923-28	5	2	-	2	-	-	-			

Wins: 1925 and 1926 Le Mans 24 hrs

Victor Rosso
RA. Born: 16.10.1960
F3 E win: 1 – 1987 Nurburgring EFDA

Nilton Rossoni
BR. Born: 22.4.1981, Curitiba
2000 Barber-Dodge Champion

John Rostek
USA
NASCAR wins: 1

Hubertus "Huub" Rothengatter
NL. Born: 8.10.1954, Bussum, near Hilversum

formula	years	starts (DNS)	wins	2nd	3rd	4th	5th	6th	PP	FL	points
F1 W	1984-86	25 (5)	-	-	-	-	-	-	-	-	0

Best result: 7th. Best qualifying: 21st. Teams: Spirit, Osella, Zakspeed

F2 E	1979-81	28 (1)	1	1	-	2	3	3	-	-	30

Win: 1980 Zolder. Best championship: 1980, 7th

Andy Rouse
GB. Born: 2.12.1947, Dymock, Gloucestershire
1975, 1983, 1984 and 1985 British Touring Car Champion

formula	years	starts (DNS)	wins	2nd	3rd	4th	5th	6th	PP	FL	points
Le Mans	1980-82	3	-	-	-	-	-	-			

Major win: 1988 Tourist Trophy (Silverstone)

Hans Royer
A

formula	years	starts (DNS)	wins	2nd	3rd	4th	5th	6th	PP	FL	points
F2 E	1977	3	-	-	-	-	-	1	-	-	1

Best championship: 1977, 20th

R-S

Bernard Rubin
GB

formula	years	starts (DNS)	wins	2nd	3rd	4th	5th	6th	PP	FL	points
Le Mans	1928-29	2	1	-	-	-	-	-	-	-	

Win: 1928 Le Mans 24 hrs

Lloyd Ruby
USA. Born: 12.1.1928, Wichita Falls, Texas

formula	years	starts (DNS)	wins	2nd	3rd	4th	5th	6th	PP	FL	points
F1 W	1961	1	-	-	-	-	-	-	-	-	0

Best result: no finishes. Best qualifying: 19th. Team: J Frank Harrison

Le Mans	1967	1	-	-	-	-	-	-	-	-	
SC W	1957-68	3	1	-	-	-	-	-	-	-	

Wins: 1965 Daytona, 1966 Daytona 24 hrs, Sebring 12 hrs

Indy 500	1960-77	18	-	-	1	-	1	1	-	1	

Champcar wins: 7 – 1961 Milwaukee race 2, 1964 Phoenix race 2, 1967 Phoenix race 1, Langhorne race 1, 1968 Milwaukee race 1, Milwaukee race 2, 1970 Trenton race 1

Gerd Ruch
D. Born: 21.11.1953, Bad Hersfeld
1996 FIA GT2 class Champion (with Bruno Eichmann)

Grover Ruckstell
USA

formula	years	starts (DNS)	wins	2nd	3rd	4th	5th	6th	PP	FL	points
GP Pre-50	1915-16	2	-	-	-	-	-	-	-	1	

Champcar win: 1 – 1915 Tacoma race 1

Jean-Claude Rudaz
CH. Born: 7.7.1943, Sion

formula	years	starts (DNS)	wins	2nd	3rd	4th	5th	6th	PP	FL	points
F1 W	1964	0 (1)	-	-	-	-	-	-	-	-	0

Best result: no starts. Best qualifying: 20th. Team: Fabre Urbain

Le Mans	1964	1	-	-	-	-	-	-	-	-	

Ricky Rudd
USA. Born: 12.9.1956, Chesapeake, Virginia
1992 IROC Champion
NASCAR wins: 23 (all Modern era)

Carlos Ruesch
RA. Born: 20.10.1943

formula	years	starts (DNS)	wins	2nd	3rd	4th	5th	6th	PP	FL	points
F2 E	1971-72	17 (6)	-	-	1	1	1	-	-		14

Best championship: 1972, 11th

Hans Ruesch
CH. Born: 1913, Zurich

formula	years	starts (DNS)	wins	2nd	3rd	4th	5th	6th	PP	FL	points
GP Pre-50	1934-37	7 (4)	1	-	-	-	-	-	-	-	

Win: 1936 Donington GP

Other major win: 1937 Bucharest GP

Toni Ruokonen
SF. Born: 15.8.1973, Espoo
1996 Finnish Touring Car Champion, 2002 Asian Touring Car Champion

Jim Russell
GB. Born: 28.5.1920, Downham Market, Norfolk
1955, 1956 and 1957 British F3 Champion

formula	years	starts (DNS)	wins	2nd	3rd	4th	5th	6th	PP	FL	points
Le Mans	1957-59	2	-	-	-	-	-	-	-	-	

Giacomo "Geki" Russo
I. Born: 23.10.1937, Milan. Died: 18.6.1967, Caserta, near Naples
1961, 1962 and 1963 Italian Formula Junior Champion, 1964 Italian F3 Champion

formula	years	starts (DNS)	wins	2nd	3rd	4th	5th	6th	PP	FL	points
F1 W	1964-66	2 (1)	-	-	-	-	-	-	-	-	0

Best result: 9th. Best qualifying: 20th. Teams: Rob Walker, Lotus

Le Mans	1965	1	-	-	-	-	-	-	-	-	

Paul Russo
USA. Born: 10.4.1914, Kenosha, Wisconsin. Died: 13.2.1976, Daytona Beach, Florida

formula	years	starts (DNS)	wins	2nd	3rd	4th	5th	6th	PP	FL	points
Indy 500	1940-62	15	-	1	-	2	-	-	1		

Champcar wins: 2 – 1950 Springfield race 1, 1951 Detroit

Tommy Rustad
N. Born: 3.9.1968, Oslo
1997 European Renault Spider Cup Champion, 2000 Swedish Touring Car Champion

Johnny Rutherford
USA. Born: 12.3.1938, Coffeyville, Kansas
1980 CART Champion

formula	years	starts (DNS)	wins	2nd	3rd	4th	5th	6th	PP	FL	points
SC W	1973-81		-	1	1	1	-	-	-	-	
Indy 500	1963-88	24	3	1	-	-	1	3	1		

Wins: 1974, 1976 and 1980 Indianapolis 500
Pre-CART Champcar wins: 17 – 1965 Atlanta, 1973 California 500 qualifying race 2, Michigan race 2, 1974 California 500 qualifying race 2, Indianapolis 500, Milwaukee race 1, Pocono 500, 1975 Phoenix, 1976 Trenton, Indianapolis 500, Texas, 1977 Phoenix, Milwaukee, Texas, Milwaukee, 1978 Michigan, Phoenix

CART	1979-92	107 (6)	-	10	5	5	7	4	3	8	1

Wins: 1979 Atlanta race 1, Atlanta race 2, 1980 Ontario, Indianapolis 500, Mid-Ohio, Michigan, Milwaukee, 1981 Phoenix, 1985 Sanair, 1986 Michigan 500.
Best championship: 1980, 1st
NASCAR wins: 1

Troy Ruttman
USA. Born: 11.3.1930, Mooreland, Oklahoma. Died: 19.5.1997, Lake Havasu City, Arizona, cancer

formula	years	starts (DNS)	wins	2nd	3rd	4th	5th	6th	PP	FL	points
F1 W	1958	1 (1)	-	-	-	-	-	-	-	-	0

Best championship: 1952, 7th (due to result at Indy 500, did not race in a GP that year). Best result: 10th. Best qualifying: 18th. Team: Scuderia Centro Sud

Indy 500	1949-64	12	1	-	-	1	-	-	1		

Win: 1952 Indianapolis 500
Champcar wins: 2 – 1952 Indianapolis 500, Raleigh

Peter Ryan
CDN. Born: 10.6.1940, Philadelphia, Pennsylvania (USA). Died: 2.7.1962, Paris (F)

formula	years	starts (DNS)	wins	2nd	3rd	4th	5th	6th	PP	FL	points
F1 W	1961	1	-	-	-	-	-	-	-	-	0

Best result: 9th. Best qualifying: 13th. Team: J Wheeler Autosport

Le Mans	1962	1	-	-	-	-	-	-	-	-	

Major win: 1961 Canadian GP

Rickard Rydell
S. Born: 22.9.1967, Stockholm
1998 British Touring Car Champion

formula	years	starts (DNS)	wins	2nd	3rd	4th	5th	6th	PP	FL	points
Le Mans	1990-2002	2	-	-	-	-	-	-	-	-	

GT FIA wins: 2 – 2001 A1 Ring, Jarama

F3000 INT	1989	1	-	-	-	-	-	-	-	-	0

Other major wins: 1992 Macau, 1998 Bathurst 2-litre

S

"Sabipa" (Louis Charavel)
F. Born: 1890. Died: 19??

formula	years	starts (DNS)	wins	2nd	3rd	4th	5th	6th	PP	FL	points
GP Pre-50	1926-30	3	1	-	-	-	-	-	-	-	

Win: 1926 Italian GP

Le Mans	1928-33	3	-	-	-	1	-	-	-	-	

Massimo Saccomanno
I. Born: 14.5.1964
1995 Italian Prototype Champion

Eddie Sachs
USA. Born: 28.5.1927, Allentown, Pennsylvania. Died: 30.5.1964, Indianapolis 500

formula	years	starts (DNS)	wins	2nd	3rd	4th	5th	6th	PP	FL	points
Indy 500	1957-64	8	-	1	1	-	-	2	-		

Champcar wins: 8 – 1956 Atlanta, 1958 Langhorne, Indiana State Fairgrounds, 1959 Syracuse, Trenton race 2, 1960 Trenton race 2, 1961 Trenton race 1, Trenton race 2

Greg Sacks
USA. Born: 3.11.1952, Mattituck, New York State
NASCAR wins: 1 (in Modern era)

Elliott Sadler
USA. Born: 30.4.1975, Emporia, Virginia
NASCAR wins: 1 (in Modern era)

David Saelens
B. Born: 2.7.1975, Ypres
1998 French F3 Champion

formula	years	starts (DNS)	wins	2nd	3rd	4th	5th	6th	PP	FL	points
F3000 INT	1999-2002	30 (6)	-	-	4	3	4	-	2	-	33

Best championship: 2000, 6th
Major win: 1998 Marlboro Masters (Zandvoort)

Enrique Saenz Valiente
RA. Born: 8.3.1917. Died: 1956, Cordoba, light aircraft accident

formula	years	starts (DNS)	wins	2nd	3rd	4th	5th	6th	PP	FL	points
SC W	1955-56		1	-	-	-	-	-	1	-	

Win: 1955 Buenos Aires

Boris "Bob" Said
USA. Born: 5.5.1932, New York City. Died: 24.3.2002, Los Angeles, California

formula	years	starts (DNS)	wins	2nd	3rd	4th	5th	6th	PP	FL	points
F1 W	1959	1	-	-	-	-	-	-	-	-	0

Best result: no finishes. Best qualifying: 13th. Team: Connaught

Boris Said III
USA. Born: 18.9.1962, Stamford, Connecticut
2002 North American Trans-Am Champion

Luis Perez Sala
E. Born: 15.5.1959, Barcelona
1991 and 1993 Spanish Touring Car Champion

formula	years	starts (DNS)	wins	2nd	3rd	4th	5th	6th	PP	FL	points
F1 W	1988-89	26 (6)	-	-	-	-	-	1	-	-	1
F3000 INT	1986-87	21 (1)	4	1	1	2	5	-	2	2	57.5

Best championship: 1989, 26th. Best qualifying: 9th. Team: Minardi
Wins: 1986 Enna, Birmingham, 1987 Donington, Le Mans. Best championship: 1987, 2nd

Carlo de Salamanca
E
Major win: 1913 Spanish Touring Car GP

Carlo Salamano
I. Born: 1890. Died: 19.1.1969

formula	years	starts (DNS)	wins	2nd	3rd	4th	5th	6th	PP	FL	points
GP Pre-50	1923	2	1	-	-	-	-	-	-	-	

Win: 1923 Italian GP

Ettore Salani
I
Major win: 1949 Mille Miglia

Eliseo Salazar
RCH. Born: 14.11.1954, Santiago

formula	years	starts (DNS)	wins	2nd	3rd	4th	5th	6th	PP	FL	points
F1 W	1981-83	24 (13)	-	-	-	-	1	1	-	-	3

Best championship: 1981, 18th. Best qualifying: 12th. Teams: March, Ensign, ATS, RAM

Le Mans	1982-97	6	-	-	-	-	-	-	-	-	
SC W	1982-92		-	-	-	-	1	-	-	-	
F3000 INT	1986-87	14 (6)	-	-	-	1	-	-	1		1.5

Best championship: 1986, 19th

Indy 500	1995-2001	6	-	-	1	1	-	1	-	-	
CART	1995-96	20 (1)	-	-	-	-	-	-	-	-	
IRL	1996-2002	53 (1)	1	1	2	5	5	3	-	-	

Win: 1997 Las Vegas. Best championship: 2000, 4th
F1 GB wins: 1980 International Trophy (Silverstone), Thruxton (x2)

Leon Sales
USA
NASCAR wins: 1

Eric Salignon
F. Born: 22.7.1982, Carpentras
2002 European Formula Renault Champion, 2001 French Formula Renault Champion

Bob Salisbury
GB

formula	years	starts (DNS)	wins	2nd	3rd	4th	5th	6th	PP	FL	points
F2 E	1973-73	4 (1)	-	-	-	-	-	-	-	-	1

Best championship: 1973, 31st. Best result: 7th

Arto Salmenautio
SF. Born: 9.6.1964, Espoo
1998 Finnish Touring Car Champion

Heikki Salmenautio
SF
1997 Finnish Touring Car Champion

Mika Salo
SF. Born: 30.11.1966, Helsinki

formula	years	starts (DNS)	wins	2nd	3rd	4th	5th	6th	PP	FL	points
F1 W	1994-2002	110 (1)	-	1	1	1	7	6	-	-	33

Best championships: 1999 and 2000, 10th. Best qualifying: 4th. Teams: Lotus, Tyrrell, Arrows, BAR, Ferrari, Sauber, Toyota

Roy Salvadori
GB. Born: 12.5.1922, Dovercourt, Essex

formula	years	starts (DNS)	wins	2nd	3rd	4th	5th	6th	PP	FL	points
F1 W	1952-62	47 (3)	-	1	1	1	2	5	-	-	19

Best championship: 1958, 4th. Best qualifying: 2nd. Teams: G Caprara, Connaught, Gilby, BRM, Vanwall, Cooper, High Efficiency, Aston Martin, Reg Parnell

GP Pre-50	1948-49	2	-	-	-	-	-	-	-	-	
Le Mans	1953-63	11	1	-	1	1	-	-	-	-	

Win: 1959 Le Mans 24 hrs

SC W	1953-64		1	2	1	2	-	1	-	-	

Win: 1959 Le Mans 24 hrs
Non-championship F1 wins: 1954 Snetterton, 1955 Goodwood, Snetterton, Aintree, 1956 Snetterton, 1961 Crystal Palace

Giovanni Salvati
I. Born: 1943, Naples. Died: 21.11.1971, Porto Alegre (BR), F2 race
1970 Italian F3 Champion

formula	years	starts (DNS)	wins	2nd	3rd	4th	5th	6th	PP	FL	points
F2 E	1970-71	5 (1)	-	-	-	-	-	-	-	-	0

Brian Sampson
AUS
Major win: 1975 Bathurst

Ninian Sanderson
GB. Born: 14.5.1925. Died: 1.10.1985, Glasgow, cancer

formula	years	starts (DNS)	wins	2nd	3rd	4th	5th	6th	PP	FL	points
Le Mans	1955-63	9		1	1	-	-	-	-	-	

Win: 1956 Le Mans 24 hrs

SC W	1953-63		-	1	-	2	-	-	-	-	

Maurizio Sandro Sala
BR. Born: 27.8.1958, Sao Paulo

formula	years	starts (DNS)	wins	2nd	3rd	4th	5th	6th	PP	FL	points
Le Mans	1989-96	6	-	-	-	2	-	1	-	-	
SC W	1987-92		-	1	-	1	2	3	-	-	

Best championship: 1992, 8th. GT FIA wins: 5 – 1995 Jerez, Paul Ricard, Jarama, Nurburgring, Suzuka

F3000 INT	1988	1	-	-	-	-	-	-	-	-	0

Consalvo Sanesi
I. Born: 28.3.1911, Tarranuova Bracciolini. Died: 28.7.1998, Milan

formula	years	starts (DNS)	wins	2nd	3rd	4th	5th	6th	PP	FL	points
F1 W	1950-51	5	-	-	-	1	-	1	-	-	3

Best championship: 1951, 12th. Best qualifying: 4th. Team: Alfa Romeo

GP Pre-50	1947-48	6	-	1	1	1	1	-	1	-	
Le Mans	1953	1	-	-	-	-	-	-	-	-	

Stefano Sanesi
I
1988, 1989, 1990, 1996 and 1997 Italian Prototype Champion

Alessandro Santin
I. Born: 6.10.1958
1984 Italian F3 Champion

formula	years	starts (DNS)	wins	2nd	3rd	4th	5th	6th	PP	FL	points
F3000 INT	1985-88	20 (1)	-	-	-	-	-	2	-	-	1.5

Best championship: 1986, 19th

Jose Jaime Sanz de Madrid
E
1975 Spanish Touring Car Champion

Roscoe Sarles
USA. Born: 1891, New Albany, Indiana. Died: 17.9.1922, Kansas City

formula	years	starts (DNS)	wins	2nd	3rd	4th	5th	6th	PP	FL	points
Indy 500	1919-22	4	-	1	-	-	-	-	-	-	

Champcar wins: 6 – 1919 Ascot, Uniontown race 5, 1920 Beverly Hills race 5, 1921 Beverly Hills race 2, Uniontown race 1, Cotati race 2

Stephane Sarrazin
F. Born: 2.11.1974, Barjac, Ales
1994 French Formula Renault Champion

formula	years	starts (DNS)	wins	2nd	3rd	4th	5th	6th	PP	FL	points
F1 W	1999	1	-	-	-	-	-	-	-	-	0

Best result: no finishes. Best qualifying: 18th. Team: Minardi

Le Mans	2001-02	2	-	-	-	-	-	1	-	-	
F3000 INT	1998-2001	29	2	1	2	2	3	2	1	3	48

Wins: 1998 Oschersleben, 1999 Hungaroring. Best championship: 1999, 4th

Shuroko Sasaki
J
1980 Japanese F3 Champion

Jose Angel Sasiambarrena
E
1990 Spanish Touring Car Champion

Takuma Sato
J. Born: 28.1.1977, Tokyo
2001 British F3 Champion

formula	years	starts (DNS)	wins	2nd	3rd	4th	5th	6th	PP	FL	points
F1 W	2002	17	-	-	-	-	-	1	-	-	2

Best championship: 2002, 15th. Best qualifying: 7th. Team: Jordan
Major wins: 2001 Marlboro Masters (Zandvoort), Macau

Kohji Satoh
J. Born: 3.2.1955, Nagoya
1985 Japanese F3 Champion

Cyrille Sauvage
F. Born: 16.1.1973
1995 European Formula Renault Champion, 1995 French Formula Renault Champion

formula	years	starts (DNS)	wins	2nd	3rd	4th	5th	6th	PP	FL	points
F3000 INT	1996-99	33 (2)	-	-	-	1	2	1	-	-	8

Best championship: 1997, 13th

David "Swede" Savage
USA. Born: 26.8.1946, San Bernadino, California. Died: 2.7.1973, Indianapolis, Indiana, from injuries inflicted on 30.5.1973 during the Indianapolis 500

formula	years	starts (DNS)	wins	2nd	3rd	4th	5th	6th	PP	FL	points
Indy 500	1972-73	2	-	-	-	-	-	-	-	-	

Champcar win: 1 – 1970 Phoenix race 2

Mirko Savoldi
I. Born: 5.12.1966
2002 Sports Racing SRL class Champion (with Piergiuseppe Peroni)

Ludovico Scarfiotti
I. Born: 18.10.1933, Turin. Died: 8.6.1968, Rossfeld, hillclimb

formula	years	starts (DNS)	wins	2nd	3rd	4th	5th	6th	PP	FL	points
F1 W	1963-68	10 (2)	1	-	2	-	2	-	1		17

Win: 1966 Italian GP. Best championship: 1966, 10th. Best qualifying: 2nd. Teams: Ferrari, Eagle, Cooper

Le Mans	1960-67	8		1	1	-	-	-	-	-	

Win: 1963 Le Mans 24 hrs

SC W	1956-68			5	8	1	1	3	-	-	

Wins: 1963 Sebring 12 hrs, Le Mans 24 hrs, 1964 Nurburgring, 1965 Nurburgring, 1966 Spa
Non-championship F1 win: 1967 Syracuse

Giorgio Scarlatti
I. Born: 2.10.1921, Rome. Died: 26.7.1990, Rome

formula	years	starts (DNS)	wins	2nd	3rd	4th	5th	6th	PP	FL	points
F1 W	1956-61	12 (3)	-	-	-	-	1	1	-	-	1

Best championship: 1957, 20th. Best qualifying: 5th. Teams: driver, Scuderia Centro Sud, Maserati, Scuderia Ugolini, Cooper, Eugenio Castellotti, Scuderia Serenissima

Le Mans	1957-62	4	-	-	-	-	-	-	-	-	
SC W	1954-63		1	1	1	2	1	1	-	-	

Win: 1961 Pescara

Bertram Schafer
D. Born: 18.3.1946
1976 and 1978 German F3 Champion

formula	years	starts (DNS)	wins	2nd	3rd	4th	5th	6th	PP	FL	points
F2 E	1976	0 (2)	-	-	-	-	-	-	-	-	0

Peter Scharmann
A
1977 German F3 Champion

formula	years	starts (DNS)	wins	2nd	3rd	4th	5th	6th	PP	FL	points
F2 E	1978	5 (1)	-	-	-	-	-	-	-	-	0

Ian Scheckter
ZA. Born: 22.8.1947, East London, near Durban
1976, 1977, 1978, 1979, 1983 and 1984 South African Formula Atlantic Champion

formula	years	starts (DNS)	wins	2nd	3rd	4th	5th	6th	PP	FL	points
F1 W	1974-77	18 (2)	-	-	-	-	-	-	-	-	0

Best result: 10th. Best qualifying: 16th. Teams: Team Gunston, Hesketh,

Lexington Racing, Williams, March

F1 ZA wins: 11 – 1974 Pietermaritzburg, Killarney, Rhodesian GP, Kyalami, Welkom, 1975 Welkom, Pietermaritzburg, Brandkop, Kyalami (x3)

Jaki Scheckter
ZA. Born: 14.7.1974
1995 Barber-Dodge Champion

Jody Scheckter
ZA. Born: 29.1.1950, East London, near Durban
1979 F1 World Champion, 1973 North American
F5000 Champion

formula	years	starts (DNS)	wins	2nd	3rd	4th	5th	6th	PP	FL	points
F1 W	1972-80	112 (1)	10	14	9	9	7	4	3	5	255

Wins: 1974 Swedish GP, British GP, 1975 South African GP, 1976 Swedish GP, 1977 Argentinian GP, Monaco GP, Canadian GP, 1979 Belgian GP, Monaco GP, Italian GP. Best championship: 1979, 1st. Best qualifying: 1st. Teams: McLaren, Tyrrell, Wolf, Ferrari

formula	years	starts (DNS)	wins	2nd	3rd	4th	5th	6th	PP	FL	points
SC W	1974-76								1	1	1
F2 E	1972-73	10 (2)	1	-	-	1	-	1	-	1	15

Win: 1972 Crystal Palace. Best championship: 1972, 8th

Tomas Scheckter
ZA. Born: 21.9.1980, Monte Carlo (MC)
1999 European Formula Opel Champion

formula	years	starts (DNS)	wins	2nd	3rd	4th	5th	6th	PP	FL	points
F3000 INT	2000-01	4 (1)	-	1	-	-	-	-	-	-	6

Best championship: 2000, 11th

formula	years	starts (DNS)	wins	2nd	3rd	4th	5th	6th	PP	FL	points
Indy 500	2002	1							-	1	
IRL	2002	12	1	-	-	1	-	1	3	7	

Win: 2002 Michigan

Harry Schell
USA. Born: 29.6.1921, Paris (F). Died: 13.5.1960, Silverstone, testing

formula	years	starts (DNS)	wins	2nd	3rd	4th	5th	6th	PP	FL	points
F1 W	1950-60	56	-	1	1	3	7	4	-	-	32

Best championship: 1958, 5th. Best qualifying: 2nd. Teams: Horschell Racing Corporation, Ecurie Bleue, Enrico Plate, Gordini, driver, Maserati, Ferrari, Vanwall, Scuderia Centro Sud, Joakim Bonnier, BRM

formula	years	starts (DNS)	wins	2nd	3rd	4th	5th	6th	PP	FL	points
GP Pre-50	1947-49	2 (1)	-	-	-	-	-	-	-	-	
Le Mans	1953-57	3	-	-	-	-	-	1	-	-	
SC W	1953-58		1	3	2	-	2	1	-	-	

Win: 1956 Nurburgring
Non-championship F1 wins: 1955 Snetterton, Castle Combe, 1956 Caen

Laury Schell
F. Born: n/a. Died: ??.11.1939

formula	years	starts (DNS)	wins	2nd	3rd	4th	5th	6th	PP	FL	points
GP Pre-50	1936-37	3	-	-	-	1	-	-	-	-	
Le Mans	1937	1	-	-	-	-	-	-	-	-	

Major win: 1937 Monaco Rainier Cup

Tim Schenken
AUS. Born: 26.9.1943, Gordon, Sydney, New South Wales
1968 British F3 Champion

formula	years	starts (DNS)	wins	2nd	3rd	4th	5th	6th	PP	FL	points
F1 W	1970-74	34 (2)	-	-	1	-	1	1	-	-	7

Best championship: 1971, 14th. Best qualifying: 5th. Teams: Williams, Brabham, Surtees, Trojan, Lotus

formula	years	starts (DNS)	wins	2nd	3rd	4th	5th	6th	PP	FL	points
Le Mans	1973-77	4	-	-	-	-	-	-	-	-	
SC W	1970-77		3	8	2	-	-	2	1	2	

Wins: 1972 Buenos Aires, Nurburgring, 1977 Nurburgring

formula	years	starts (DNS)	wins	2nd	3rd	4th	5th	6th	PP	FL	points
F2 E	1970-75	36 (1)	4	2	4	3	2	3	4	-	4	33

Wins: 1972 Hockenheim, 1973 Norisring. Best championship: 1971, 4th

Albert Scherrer
CH. Born: 28.2.1908. Died: 5.7.1986

formula	years	starts (DNS)	wins	2nd	3rd	4th	5th	6th	PP	FL	points
F1 W	1953	1	-	-	-	-	-	-	-	-	0

Best result: 8th. Best qualifying: 18th. Team: HWM

Domenico "Mimmo" Schiattarella
I. Born: 17.11.1967, Milan

formula	years	starts (DNS)	wins	2nd	3rd	4th	5th	6th	PP	FL	points
F1 W	1994-95	7	-	-	-	-	-	-	-	-	0

Best result: 9th. Best qualifying: 20th. Team: Simtek

formula	years	starts (DNS)	wins	2nd	3rd	4th	5th	6th	PP	FL	points
Le Mans	1999-2000	2	-	-	-	-	1	-	-	-	
CART	1994-98	5	-	-	-	-	-	-	-	-	

Clemens Schickentanz
D
1973 European GT Champion (with Claude Ballot-Lena)

formula	years	starts (DNS)	wins	2nd	3rd	4th	5th	6th	PP	FL	points
Le Mans	1973-83	5	-	-	-	1	-	-	-	-	
SC W	1970-84		-	-	1	2	2	3	-	-	

Best championship: 1983, 15th

Heinz Schiller
CH. Born: 25.1.1930, Frauenfeld

formula	years	starts (DNS)	wins	2nd	3rd	4th	5th	6th	PP	FL	points
F1 W	1962	1	-	-	-	-	-	-	-	-	0

Best result: no finishes. Best qualifying: 20th. Team: Ecurie Filipinetti

formula	years	starts (DNS)	wins	2nd	3rd	4th	5th	6th	PP	FL	points
Le Mans	1962-64	3	-	-	-	-	-	-	-	-	

Bill Schindler
USA. Born: 6.3.1909, Ellenville, New York State. Died: 20.9.1952, Allentown, Pennsylvania

formula	years	starts (DNS)	wins	2nd	3rd	4th	5th	6th	PP	FL	points
Indy 500	1950-52	3	-	-	-	-	-	-	-	-	

Champcar win: 1 – 1952 Springfield

Robert Schirle
GB. Born: 31.3.1967, Tamworth
1996 British GT Champion (with David Warnock)

formula	years	starts (DNS)	wins	2nd	3rd	4th	5th	6th	PP	FL	points
Le Mans	1997-98	2	-	-	-	-	-	-	-	-	

Jean-Louis Schlesser
F. Born: 12.9.1948, Nancy
1989 (solo) and 1990 (with Mauro Baldi) World Sports Car Champion, 1985 French Touring Car Champion, 1978 French F3 Champion (with Alain Prost), 1988 German Racing Champion

formula	years	starts (DNS)	wins	2nd	3rd	4th	5th	6th	PP	FL	points
F1 W	1983-88	1 (1)	-	-	-	-	-	-	-	-	0

Best result: 11th. Best qualifying: 22nd. Teams: RAM, Williams

formula	years	starts (DNS)	wins	2nd	3rd	4th	5th	6th	PP	FL	points
Le Mans	1981-91	7	-	1	-	1	-	1	-		
SC W	1977-91		15	6	5	2	3	-	11	10	

Wins: 1988 Jerez, Brno, Nurburgring, Sandown Park, 1989 Suzuka, Jarama, Nurburgring, Donington, Mexico City, 1990 Suzuka, Monza, Dijon, Nurburgring, Donington, Montreal. Best championships: 1989 and 1990, 1st

formula	years	starts (DNS)	wins	2nd	3rd	4th	5th	6th	PP	FL	points
F2 E	1982	8	-	-	-	-	-	-	-	-	0

Joseph "Jo" Schlesser
F. Born: 18.5.1928, Lionville, Madagascar. Died: 7.7.1968, Rouen, French GP
1962 and 1963 French Formula Junior Champion

formula	years	starts (DNS)	wins	2nd	3rd	4th	5th	6th	PP	FL	points
F1 W	1966-68	3	-	-	-	-	-	-	-	-	0

Best result: no finishes. Best qualifying: 17th. Teams: Matra, Ford France, Honda

formula	years	starts (DNS)	wins	2nd	3rd	4th	5th	6th	PP	FL	points
Le Mans	1957-67	7	-	-	-	-	-	-	-	-	
SC W	1957-68		-	3	1	1	2	2	-	1	
F2 E	1967-68	7	-	-	1	1	1	1	-	-	18

Best championship: 1967, 8th

Sam Schmidt
USA. Born: 15.8.1964, Lincoln, Nebraska

formula	years	starts (DNS)	wins	2nd	3rd	4th	5th	6th	PP	FL	points
Indy 500	1997-99	3	-	-	-	-	-	-	-	-	
IRL	1997-99	27	1	2	1	-	2	-	1	1	

Win: 1999 Las Vegas. Best championship: 1999, 5th

Fredy Schnarwiler
CH

formula	years	starts (DNS)	wins	2nd	3rd	4th	5th	6th	PP	FL	points
F2 E	1980-82	22 (1)	-	-	-	-	1	-	-		1

Best championship: 1980, 16th

Bernd Schneider
D. Born: 20.7.1964, St Ingbert
1997 FIA GT Champion, 1995 International Touring Car Champion, 1995, 2000 and 2001 German Touring Car Champion, 1987 German F3 Champion, 1990 and 1991 Interserie Champion

formula	years	starts (DNS)	wins	2nd	3rd	4th	5th	6th	PP	FL	points
F1 W	1988-90	9 (25)	-	-	-	-	-	-	-	-	0

Best result: 12th. Best qualifying: 15th. Teams: Zakspeed, Arrows

Le Mans	1991-99	3	-	-	-	-	-	1	-		
SC W	1990-92		-	1	1	1	-	-			

GT FIA wins: 11 – 1997 Nurburgring, A1 Ring, Suzuka, Donington, Sebring, Laguna Seca, 1998 Silverstone, Hockenheim, Hungaroring, Suzuka, Donington
Other major win: 1989 Spa 24 hrs

Frankie Schneider
USA. Born: 8.11.1926, Maplewood, New Jersey
NASCAR wins: 1

John Schneider
USA
Major win: 1997 Daytona 24 hrs

Louis Schneider
USA. Born: 19.12.1901, Indianapolis, Indiana. Died: 22.9.1942, Indianapolis, Indiana
1931 Champcar Champion

formula	years	starts (DNS)	wins	2nd	3rd	4th	5th	6th	PP	FL	points
Indy 500	1927-33	6	1	1	1	-	-	-	-	-	

Win: 1931 Indianapolis 500
Champcar win: 1 – 1931 Indianapolis 500

Rudolf Schoeller
CH. Born: 27.4.1902, Duren (D). Died: 7.3.1978, Grabs

formula	years	starts (DNS)	wins	2nd	3rd	4th	5th	6th	PP	FL	points
F1 W	1952	1	-	-	-	-	-	-	-	-	0

Best result: no finishes. Best qualifying: no times set. Team: Ecurie Espadon

Niclas Schonstrom
S. Born: 27.5.1966
1986 Swedish F3 Champion

Dieter Schornstein
D. Born: 28.6.1940, Aachen

formula	years	starts (DNS)	wins	2nd	3rd	4th	5th	6th	PP	FL	points
Le Mans	1978-84	5	-	-	-	-	1	-	-	-	
SC W	1976-84		1	-	2	5	5	-	-		

Win: 1981 Silverstone. Best championship: 1984, 14th

Ken Schrader
USA. Born: 29.5.1955, St Louis, Missouri
NASCAR wins: 4 (all Modern era)

Patrick Schreurs
B
2001 Belgian Belcar GT Champion (with Kurt Thiers)

Dorsey Schroeder
USA. Born: 5.2.1953, St Louis
1989 Trans-Am Champion, 1990 IMSA GTO Champion

Rob Schroeder
USA. Born: 11.5.1926, El Dorado, Arizona

formula	years	starts (DNS)	wins	2nd	3rd	4th	5th	6th	PP	FL	points
F1 W	1962	1	-	-	-	-	-	-	-	-	0

Best result: 10th. Best qualifying: 17th. Team: John Mecom

Scott Schubot
USA. Born: 25.2.1955
1989 IMSA Lights Champion

Wolfgang Schultz
D
1981 Renault Europa Cup Champion

Michael Schumacher
D. Born: 3.1.1969, Hurth-Hermuhlheim
1994, 1995, 2000, 2001 and 2002 F1 World Champion, 1990 German F3 Champion

formula	years	starts (DNS)	wins	2nd	3rd	4th	5th	6th	PP	FL	points
F1 W	1991-2002	178 (1)	64	34	16	7	6	4	50	51	945

Wins: 1992 Belgian GP, 1993 Portuguese GP, 1994 Brazilian GP, Pacific GP, San Marino GP, Monaco GP, Canadian GP, French GP, Hungarian GP, European GP, 1995 Brazilian GP, Spanish GP, Monaco GP, French GP, German GP, Belgian GP, European GP, Pacific GP, Japanese GP, 1996 Spanish GP, Belgian GP, Italian GP, 1997 Monaco GP, Canadian GP, French GP, Belgian GP, Japanese GP, 1998 Argentinian GP, Canadian GP, French GP, British GP, Hungarian GP, Italian GP, 1999 San Marino GP, Monaco GP, 2000 Australian GP, Brazilian GP, San Marino GP, European GP, Canadian GP, Italian GP, United States GP, Japanese GP, Malaysian GP, 2001 Australian GP, Malaysian GP, Spanish GP, Monaco GP, European GP, French GP, Hungarian GP, Belgian GP, Japanese GP, 2002 Australian GP, Brazilian GP, San Marino GP, Spanish GP, Austrian GP, Canadian GP, British GP, French GP, German GP, Belgian GP, Japanese GP. Best championships: 1994, 1995, 2000, 2001 and 2002, 1st. Best qualifying: 1st. Teams: Jordan, Benetton, Ferrari

Le Mans	1991	1	-	-	-	-	1	-	1		
SC W	1990-91		2	3	-	-	1	-	-	3	

Wins: 1990 Mexico City, 1991 Autopolis. Best championship: 1990, 5th
Other major win: 1990 Macau

Ralf Schumacher
D. Born: 30.6.1975, Hurth-Hermuhlheim
1996 Japanese Formula Nippon Champion

formula	years	starts (DNS)	wins	2nd	3rd	4th	5th	6th	PP	FL	points
F1 W	1997-2002	100	4	4	12	11	14	4	1	6	177

Wins: 2001 San Marino GP, Canadian GP, German GP, 2002 Malaysian GP. Best championship: 2001 and 2002, 4th. Best qualifying: 1st. Teams: Jordan, Williams
Other major win: 1995 Macau

Vern Schuppan
AUS. Born: 19.3.1943, Booleroo Whyalla, South Australia
1983 Japanese Sports-Prototype Champion (with Naohiro Fujita), 1971 British Formula Atlantic Champion

formula	years	starts (DNS)	wins	2nd	3rd	4th	5th	6th	PP	FL	points
F1 W	1972-77	9 (4)	-	-	-	-	-	-	-	-	0

Best result: 7th. Best qualifying: 14th. Teams: BRM, Ensign, Hill, Surtees

Le Mans	1973-89	15	1	2	1	-	1	1	-	-	

Win: 1983 Le Mans 24 hrs

SC W	1973-90		1	3	3	2	4	4	-	-	

Win: 1983 Le Mans 24 hrs. Best championship: 1982, 9th

F2 E	1972-73	2	-	-	-	-	-	-	-	-	0
Indy 500	1976-81	3	-	-	1	-	-	-	-	-	
CART	1979-82	19 (3)	-	-	-	-	2	-	-	-	

Best championship: 1980, 10th
Other major wins: 1974 and 1976 Macau

Rudi Schurter
CH. Born: 22.3.1952
1993 and 1994 Swiss F3 Champion

Manfred Schurti

FL

formula	years	starts (DNS)	wins	2nd	3rd	4th	5th	6th	PP	FL	points
Le Mans	1974-82	9	-	-	-	1	1	1	-	-	
SC W	1973-82		4	6	1	-	2	3	1	-	

Wins: 1976 Watkins Glen, 1977 Mugello, 1979 Mugello, Nurburgring

formula	years	starts (DNS)	wins	2nd	3rd	4th	5th	6th	PP	FL	points
F2 E	1973-76	4 (3)	-	-	-	-	-	-	-	-	0

Udo Schutz

D. Born: 1936

formula	years	starts (DNS)	wins	2nd	3rd	4th	5th	6th	PP	FL	points
Le Mans	1966-69	3	-	-	-	-	-	1	-	-	
SC W	1964-69		2	-	1	-	2	1	-	-	

Wins: 1967 Nurburgring, 1969 Targa Florio

Dominik Schwager

D. Born: 18.9.1976, Munich

formula	years	starts (DNS)	wins	2nd	3rd	4th	5th	6th	PP	FL	points
F3000 INT	1998	11 (1)	-	-	-	1	-	-	-	-	3

Best championship: 1998, 14th

Adolfo Schwelm Cruz

RA. Born: 28.6.1923, Buenos Aires

formula	years	starts (DNS)	wins	2nd	3rd	4th	5th	6th	PP	FL	points
F1 W	1953	1	-	-	-	-	-	-	-	-	0

Best result: no finishes. Best qualifying: 13th. Team: Cooper

Bill Scott

USA. Born: 10.10.1948

1971 and 1972 SCCA Super Vee Champion

formula	years	starts (DNS)	wins	2nd	3rd	4th	5th	6th	PP	FL	points
Indy 500	1976	1	-	-	-	-	-	-	-	-	
CART	1979	1	-	-	-	-	-	-	-	-	

Dave Scott

GB. Born: 14.5.1962, Petersfield

formula	years	starts (DNS)	wins	2nd	3rd	4th	5th	6th	PP	FL	points
F2 E	1983	10 (2)	-	-	-	-	1	1	1	-	3

Best championship: 1983, 17th

formula	years	starts (DNS)	wins	2nd	3rd	4th	5th	6th	PP	FL	points
F3000 INT	1986	0 (1)	-	-	-	-	-	-	-	-	0

Richard Scott

GB. Born: 8.11.1946, Aberdeen

formula	years	starts (DNS)	wins	2nd	3rd	4th	5th	6th	PP	FL	points
F2 E	1970-73	15 (10)	-	-	-	-	-	-	-	-	2

Best championship: 1973, 29th. Best result: 7th

Wendell Scott

USA. Born: 29.8.1921. Died: 23.12.1990

NASCAR wins: 1

Archie Scott-Brown

GB. Born: 13.5.1927, Paisley, Renfrewshire. Died: 19.5.1958, Spa, Belgian Sports Car GP

formula	years	starts (DNS)	wins	2nd	3rd	4th	5th	6th	PP	FL	points
F1 W	1956	1	-	-	-	-	-	-	-	-	0

Best result: no finishes. Best qualifying: 10th. Team: Connaught

Non-championship F1 win: 1956 Brands Hatch

Piero Scotti

I. Born: 11.11.1909, Florence. Died: 14.2.1976, Samedan (CH)

formula	years	starts (DNS)	wins	2nd	3rd	4th	5th	6th	PP	FL	points
F1 W	1956	1	-	-	-	-	-	-	-	-	0

Best result: no finishes. Best qualifying: 12th. Team: driver

Dick Seaman

GB. Born: 4.2.1913, Aldingbourne, near Chichester, Sussex. Died: 25.6.1939, Spa, Belgian GP

formula	years	starts (DNS)	wins	2nd	3rd	4th	5th	6th	PP	FL	points
GP Pre-50	1936-39	12	2	1	1	2	-	-	1	2	

Wins: 1936 Donington GP, 1938 German GP

Jack Sears

GB. Born: 16.2.1930, Northampton

1958 and 1963 British Touring Car Champion

formula	years	starts (DNS)	wins	2nd	3rd	4th	5th	6th	PP	FL	points
Le Mans	1960-65	4	-	-	-	-	1	-	-	-	
SC W	1960-65		-	1	1	-	-	-	-	-	

Wilhelm Sebastian

D. Born: 1903. Died: 1978

formula	years	starts (DNS)	wins	2nd	3rd	4th	5th	6th	PP	FL	points
GP Pre-50	1934	2	-	-	-	-	-	-	-	-	

Major win: 1931 Mille Miglia

Arthur See

USA

Champcar win: 1 – 1909 Riverhead race 5

Sir Henry Segrave

GB. Born: 22.9.1896, Baltimore (USA). Died: 13.6.1930, Lake Windermere, record attempt

formula	years	starts (DNS)	wins	2nd	3rd	4th	5th	6th	PP	FL	points
GP Pre-50	1921-26	8	2	-	-	1	-	1	2	
Le Mans	1925	1	-	-	-	-	-	-	-	-	

Wins: 1923 French GP, 1924 San Sebastian GP

Wolfgang Seidel

D. Born: 4.7.1926, Dusseldorf. Died: 1.3.1987, Munich

formula	years	starts (DNS)	wins	2nd	3rd	4th	5th	6th	PP	FL	points
F1 W	1953-62	10 (2)	-	-	-	-	-	-	-	-	0

Best result: 9th. Best qualifying: 13th. Teams: driver, Scuderia Centro Sud, Rob Walker, Scuderia Colonia, Ecurie Maarsbergen

formula	years	starts (DNS)	wins	2nd	3rd	4th	5th	6th	PP	FL	points
Le Mans	1955-60	5	-	-	-	-	1	-	-	-	
SC W	1953-62		1	-	2	-	4	-	-	-	

Win: 1959 Targa Florio

Gunther Seiffert

D

formula	years	starts (DNS)	wins	2nd	3rd	4th	5th	6th	PP	FL	points
F1 W	1962	0 (1)	-	-	-	-	-	-	-	-	0

Best result: no starts. Best qualifying: 30th. Team: driver

Masanori Sekiya

J. Born: 27.11.1949, Shizuoka

1994 and 1998 Japanese Touring Car Champion

formula	years	starts (DNS)	wins	2nd	3rd	4th	5th	6th	PP	FL	points
Le Mans	1985-97	11	1	1	-	1	-	1	-	1	

Win: 1995 Le Mans 24 hrs

formula	years	starts (DNS)	wins	2nd	3rd	4th	5th	6th	PP	FL	points
SC W	1982-92		-	1	1	-	-	1	-	-	

GT FIA win: 1 – 1995 Suzuka

Lou Sell

USA

1968 North American Formula A (F5000) Champion

formula	years	starts (DNS)	wins	2nd	3rd	4th	5th	6th	PP	FL	points
SC W	1969		-	-	-	-	-	1	-	-	

Peter Selsdon
(Patrick Mitchell-Thompson, Lord Selsdon)

GB. Born: 1913. Died: ??.2.1963

formula	years	starts (DNS)	wins	2nd	3rd	4th	5th	6th	PP	FL	points
GP Pre-50	1947-48	1 (1)	-	-	-	-	-	-	-	-	
Le Mans	1935-50	4	1	-	1	-	-	-	-	-	

Win: 1949 Le Mans 24 hrs

Robert Senechal

F. Born: 1892. Died: 1985

formula	years	starts (DNS)	wins	2nd	3rd	4th	5th	6th	PP	FL	points
GP Pre-50	1926-31	7	1	1	-	-	2	1	-	-	

Win: 1926 British GP

formula	years	starts (DNS)	wins	2nd	3rd	4th	5th	6th	PP	FL	points
Le Mans	1924-25	2	-	-	-	-	-	-	-	-	

Other major win: 1927 Spa 24 hrs

Ayrton Senna (Ayrton da Silva)

BR. Born: 21.3.1960, Sao Paulo. Died: 1.5.1994, Bologna Hospital, following an accident during the San Marino GP at Imola
1988, 1990 and 1991 F1 World Champion, 1983 British F3 Champion, 1982 European FF2000 Champion

formula	years	starts (DNS)	wins	2nd	3rd	4th	5th	6th	PP	FL	points
F1 W	1984-94	161 (1)	41	23	16	7	6	3	65	19	614

Wins: 1985 Portuguese GP, Belgian GP, 1986 Spanish GP, Detroit GP, 1987 Monaco GP, Detroit GP, 1988 San Marino GP, Canadian GP, Detroit GP, British GP, German GP, Hungarian GP, Belgian GP, Japanese GP, 1989 San Marino GP, Monaco GP, Mexican GP, German GP, Belgian GP, Spanish GP, 1990 United States GP, Monaco GP, Canadian GP, German GP, Italian GP, 1991 United States GP, Brazilian GP, San Marino GP, Monaco GP, Hungarian GP, Belgian GP, Australian GP, 1992 Monaco GP, Hungarian GP, Italian GP, 1993 Brazilian GP, European GP, Monaco GP, Japanese GP, Australian GP. Best championships: 1988, 1990 and 1991, 1st. Best qualifying: 1st. Teams: Toleman, Lotus, McLaren, Williams
Other major win: 1983 Macau

Teodoro "Dorino" Serafini

I. Born: 22.7.1909, Pesaro. Died: 5.7.2000, Bologna

formula	years	starts (DNS)	wins	2nd	3rd	4th	5th	6th	PP	FL	points
F1 W	1950	1	-	1	-	-	-	-	-	-	3

Best championship: 1950, 12th. Best qualifying: 6th. Team: Ferrari

Le Mans	1950	1	-	-	-	-	-	-			

Gabriele Serblin

I

formula	years	starts (DNS)	wins	2nd	3rd	4th	5th	6th	PP	FL	points
F2 E	1973-75	25 (1)	-	-	3	1	2	-	-	-	21

Best championship: 1975, 10th

Alain Serpaggi

F. Born: 19.9.1938
1974 European 2-litre Sports Car Champion

formula	years	starts (DNS)	wins	2nd	3rd	4th	5th	6th	PP	FL	points
Le Mans	1968-89	5	-	-	-	-	-	-			
F2 E	1974	6 (1)	-	-	-	-	-	-	-	-	0

Francesco "Chico" Serra

BR. Born: 3.2.1957, Sao Paulo
1999, 2000 and 2001 Brazilian Stock Car Champion, 1979 British F3 Champion

formula	years	starts (DNS)	wins	2nd	3rd	4th	5th	6th	PP	FL	points
F1 W	1981-83	18 (15)	-	-	-	-	-	1	-	-	1

Best championship: 1982, 26th. Best qualifying: 15th. Teams: Fittipaldi, Arrows

F2 E	1980	12	-	-	3	-	-	-			9

Best championship: 1980, 10th

CART	1985	1	-	-	-	-	-	-			

Doug Serrurier

ZA. Born: 9.12.1920, Germiston, Transvaal

formula	years	starts (DNS)	wins	2nd	3rd	4th	5th	6th	PP	FL	points
F1 W	1962-65	2 (1)	-	-	-	-	-	-	-	-	0

Best result: 11th. Best qualifying: 14th. Team: Otelle Nucci

Oriol Servia

E. Born: 13.7.1974, Pals, Catalunya
1999 CART Indy Lights Champion

formula	years	starts (DNS)	wins	2nd	3rd	4th	5th	6th	PP	FL	points
CART	2000-02	53 (1)	-	-	1	1	4	2	-	1	

Georges-Francois "Johnny" Servoz-Gavin

F. Born: 18.1.1942, Grenoble
1969 European F2 Champion, 1966 French F3 Champion

formula	years	starts (DNS)	wins	2nd	3rd	4th	5th	6th	PP	FL	points
F1 W	1967-70	12 (1)	-	1	-	-	1	1	-	-	9

Best championship: 1968, 13th. Best qualifying: 2nd. Teams: Matra, Tyrrell, Cooper

formula	years	starts (DNS)	wins	2nd	3rd	4th	5th	6th	PP	FL	points
Le Mans	1966-69	4									
SC W	1966-70		-	-	-	1	1	1	-	-	
F2 E	1967-69	13	1	1	1	1	3	2	1	1	55

Win: 1969 Vallelunga. Best championship: 1969, 1st

Barry Seton

AUS. Born: 5.10.1936
Major win: 1965 Bathurst

Glenn Seton

AUS. Born: 5.5.1965
1993 and 1997 Australian Touring Car Champion

Tony Settember

USA. Born: 10.7.1926, California

formula	years	starts (DNS)	wins	2nd	3rd	4th	5th	6th	PP	FL	points
F1 W	1962-63	6 (1)	-	-	-	-	-	-	-	-	0

Best result: 8th. Best qualifying: 18th. Teams: Emeryson, Scirocco Powell

Le Mans	1962	1	-	-	-	-	-	-			

Francesco Severi

I

formula	years	starts (DNS)	wins	2nd	3rd	4th	5th	6th	PP	FL	points
GP Pre-50	1936-37	2	-	-	-	-	-	-			

Major wins: 1936 and 1938 Spa 24 hrs

Guilio Severi

I
Major win: 1937 Targa Florio

Philip "Red" Shafer

USA. Born: 13.11.1896. Died: 29.1.1971, Des Moines, Iowa

formula	years	starts (DNS)	wins	2nd	3rd	4th	5th	6th	PP	FL	points
GP Pre-50	1931	1	-	-	-	-	-	-			
Indy 500	1922-34	10	-	-	1	-	-	-			

Champcar win: 1 – 1924 Syracuse

Bob Sharp

USA
1975 IMSA GTU Champion

James "Hap" Sharp

USA. Born: 1.1.1928, Tulsa, Oklahoma. Died: 11.5.1992, San Martin de los Andes (RA), suicide

formula	years	starts (DNS)	wins	2nd	3rd	4th	5th	6th	PP	FL	points
F1 W	1961-64	6	-	-	-	-	-	-	-	-	0

Best result: 7th. Best qualifying: 15th. Teams: driver, Reg Parnell, Rob Walker

SC W	1959-68		1	-	-	1	-	2	-	-	

Win: 1965 Sebring 12 hrs

Scott Sharp

USA. Born: 14.2.1968, East Norwalk, Connecticut
1996 Indy Racing League Champion (tied with Buzz Calkins), 1991 and 1993 Trans-Am Champion

formula	years	starts (DNS)	wins	2nd	3rd	4th	5th	6th	PP	FL	points
Le Mans	1996	1	-	-	-	-	-	-			
Indy 500	1994-2002	8	-	-	-	-	-	1	-		
CART	1993-95	18	-	-	-	2	-	-			
IRL	1996-2002	66 (1)	7	4	2	6	5	2	5	2	

Wins: 1996 New Hampshire, 1998 Phoenix, Dover Downs, 1999 Atlanta, 2000 Texas, 2001 Texas, 2002 Nazareth. Best championship: 1996, 1st
Other major win: 1996 Daytona 24 hrs

William Sharp

USA
Champcar win: 1 – 1909 Riverhead race 3

Wilbur Shaw

USA. Born: 13.10.1902, Shelbyville, Indiana. Died: 30.10.1954, Decatur, Indiana, aircraft accident

1937 and 1939 Champcar Champion

formula	years	starts (DNS)	wins	2nd	3rd	4th	5th	6th	PP	FL	points
Indy 500	1927-41	14		3	3	1	2	-	1	-	-

Wins: 1937, 1939 and 1940 Indianapolis 500

Champcar wins: 8 – 1929 Toledo, Cleveland, Syracuse, 1930 Detroit, Bridgeville, 1937 Indianapolis 500, 1939 Indianapolis 500, 1940 Indianapolis 500

Brian Shawe-Taylor
GB. Born: 28.1.1915, Dublin (IRL). Died: 1.5.1999, Dowdeswell

formula	years	starts (DNS)	wins	2nd	3rd	4th	5th	6th	PP	FL	points
F1 W	1950-51	2		-	-	-	-	-	-	-	0

Best result: 8th. Best qualifying: 12th. Teams: Joe Fry, driver

GP Pre-50	1949	1		-	-	-	-	-	-	-	
Le Mans	1951	1		-	-	-	1	-	-	-	

Carroll Shelby
USA. Born: 11.1.1923, Leesburg, Texas

formula	years	starts (DNS)	wins	2nd	3rd	4th	5th	6th	PP	FL	points
F1 W	1958-59	8		-	-	-	1*	-	-	-	0

*Shared car, no points awarded. Best qualifying: 6th. Teams: Scuderia Centro Sud, Temple Buell, Aston Martin

Le Mans	1954-59	2		1	-	-	-	-	-	-	

Win: 1959 Le Mans 24 hrs

SC W	1954-60			2	1	1	1	-	-	-	

Wins: 1959 Le Mans 24 hrs, Tourist Trophy (Goodwood)

Tony Shelly
NZ. Born: 2.2.1937, Wellington. Died: 4.10.1998, Taupo

formula	years	starts (DNS)	wins	2nd	3rd	4th	5th	6th	PP	FL	points
F1 W	1962	1 (2)		-	-	-	-	-	-	-	0

Best result: no finishes. Best qualifying: 18th. Teams: John Dalton, Wolfgang Seidel

Steve Shelton
USA. Born: 16.5.1949
1988 North American Formula Atlantic (Eastern) Champion

George "Doc" Shepherd
GB. Born: n/a. Died: 1986
1960 British Touring Car Champion

Morgan Shepherd
USA. Born: 12.10.1941, Ferguson, North Carolina
NASCAR wins: 4 (all Modern era)

Buddy Shurman
USA
NASCAR wins: 1

Richard Shuttleworth
GB. Born: 16.7.1909, Old Warden, Biggleswade, Bedfordshire. Died: 2.8.1940, RAF night air mission

formula	years	starts (DNS)	wins	2nd	3rd	4th	5th	6th	PP	FL	points
GP Pre-50	1935	1		1	-	-	-	-	-	-	

Win: 1935 Donington GP

Eugenio Siena
I. Born: n/a. Died: 15.5.1938, Tripoli GP

formula	years	starts (DNS)	wins	2nd	3rd	4th	5th	6th	PP	FL	points
GP Pre-50	1932-37	8 (1)		-	-	-	2	-	-	-	

Major win: 1932 Spa 24 hrs

Joseph "Jo" Siffert
CH. Born: 7.7.1936, Fribourg, near Berne. Died: 24.10.1971, Brands Hatch, Rothmans F1 victory race

formula	years	starts (DNS)	wins	2nd	3rd	4th	5th	6th	PP	FL	points
F1 W	1962-71	96 (4)	2	2	2	7	2	5	2	4	68

Wins: 1968 British GP, 1971 Austrian GP. Best championship: 1971, 4th. Best qualifying: 1st. Teams: Ecurie Filipinetti, driver, Rob Walker, March, BRM

Le Mans	1965-71	7		-	-	1	1	-	-	-	
SC W	1961-71		14	8	2	4	4	3	13	8	

Wins: 1968 Daytona 24 hrs, Sebring 12 hrs, Nurburgring, Austrian GP, 1969 Brands Hatch, Monza, Spa, Nurburgring, Watkins Glen, Austrian GP, 1970 Targa Florio, Spa, Osterreichring, 1971 Buenos Aires

F2 E	1967-71	15 (1)	1	2	-	-	-	1	-		0

Win: 1970 Rouen
Non-championship F1 wins: 1963 Syracuse, 1964 Enna, 1965 Enna

Massimo Sigala
I. Born: 7.1.1951, Milan
1986, 1987, 1988, 1989 and 1990 Renault Europa Cup Champion

formula	years	starts (DNS)	wins	2nd	3rd	4th	5th	6th	PP	FL	points
Le Mans	1983-95	7		-	-	-	-	-	-	-	
SC W	1983-95		-	1	2	1	4	5	-	-	

Best championship: 1984, 19th

Juan Manuel "Pato" Silva
RA. Born: 12.10.1972, Resistencia
1999 TC2000 Argentinian Touring Car Champion

Hermano da Silva Ramos
BR. Born: 7.12.1925, Paris (F)

formula	years	starts (DNS)	wins	2nd	3rd	4th	5th	6th	PP	FL	points
F1 W	1955-56	7		-	-	-	1	-	-	-	2

Best championship: 1956, 19th. Best qualifying: 14th. Team: Gordini

Le Mans	1954-59	4		-	-	-	-	-	-	-	

Jeff Simmons
USA. Born: 5.8.1976, Hartford, Connecticut
1998 and 1999 Barber-Dodge Champion

Brian Simo
USA. Born: 1.10.1959
2000 Trans-Am Champion

Andre Simon
F. Born: 5.1.1920, Paris

formula	years	starts (DNS)	wins	2nd	3rd	4th	5th	6th	PP	FL	points
F1 W	1951-57	11 (1)		-	-	-	-	2	-	-	0

Best qualifying: 4th. Teams: Gordini, Ferrari, Mercedes-Benz, Maserati, driver, Scuderia Centro Sud, Ottorino Volonterio

Le Mans	1949-64	12		-	-	-	1	-	1		
SC W	1954-65		-	-	1	-	-	-	-	-	

Non-championship F1 win: 1955 Albi

Marc Simon
D. Born: 17.1.1973, Wiesbaden
1996 German GT Champion

Fabrizio de Simone
I. Born: 30.3.1971, Rome

formula	years	starts (DNS)	wins	2nd	3rd	4th	5th	6th	PP	FL	points
F3000 INT	1994-95	16		-	1	-	1	1	-	-	9

Best championship: 1994, 8th

Giampiero Simoni
I. Born: 12.9.1969, Milan

formula	years	starts (DNS)	wins	2nd	3rd	4th	5th	6th	PP	FL	points
F3000 INT	1992-93	14		-	-	-	-	2	-	-	2

Best championship: 1992, 17th

Kurt Simonsen
S
1970 European 2-litre Sports Car Champion (Group 4 class)

formula	years	starts (DNS)	wins	2nd	3rd	4th	5th	6th	PP	FL	points
SC W	1962-84		-	-	1	-	1	-	-	-	

Ugo Sivocci

I. Born: 1885, Milan. Died: 8.9.1923, Monza, Italian GP practice

formula	years	starts (DNS)	wins	2nd	3rd	4th	5th	6th	PP	FL	points
GP Pre-50	1921-23	2	-	-	-	-	-	-	-	-	

Major win: 1923 Targa Florio

Mark Skaife

AUS. Born: 4.4.1966, Gosford, New South Wales
1992, 1994, 2000, 2001 and 2002 Australian Touring Car Champion, 1991, 1992 and 1993 Australian Formula Holden Champion

formula	years	starts (DNS)	wins	2nd	3rd	4th	5th	6th	PP	FL	points
Le Mans	1997	1	-	-	-	-	-	-	-	-	
F3000 INT	1992	2	-	-	-	-	-	-	-	-	0

Major wins: 1991, 1992, 2001 and 2002 Bathurst

Gordon Smiley

USA. Born: 20.4.1949. Died: 15.5.1982, Indianapolis 500, qualifying

formula	years	starts (DNS)	wins	2nd	3rd	4th	5th	6th	PP	FL	points
Indy 500	1980-81	2	-	-	-	-	-	-	-	-	
CART	1980-82	7 (1)	-	-	-	-	-	1	-	-	

F1 GB win: 1979 Silverstone

Chris Smith

USA. Born: 4.9.1966
1992 North American Toyota Atlantic Champion

George Smith

NZ

Major win: 1951 New Zealand GP

Jack Smith

USA. Born: 24.5.1924

NASCAR wins: 21

Johan Smith

ZA
1997 South African Formula GTi Champion, 1998 South African Pro-Series Champion

Ken Smith

NZ. Born: 11.8.1941
1976, 1984, 1985, 1987 and 1990 New Zealand Gold Star Champion, 1976 New Zealand International Champion, 1984 and 1990 New Zealand Formula Pacific Champion

Major wins: 1976 and 1990 New Zealand GP

Mark Smith

USA. Born: 10.4.1967, McMinnville, Oregon
1989 SCCA Super Vee Champion

formula	years	starts (DNS)	wins	2nd	3rd	4th	5th	6th	PP	FL	points
CART	1993-94	26 (3)	-	-	-	-	1	-	-	-	

Mark Smithson

GB. Born: 31.8.1960, Hull
2000 Sports Racing SRL class Champion (with Peter Owen)

formula	years	starts (DNS)	wins	2nd	3rd	4th	5th	6th	PP	FL	points
Le Mans	2002	1	-	-	-	-	-	-	-	-	

Tom Sneva

USA. Born: 1.6.1948, Spokane, Washington
1977 and 1978 Champcar Champion

formula	years	starts (DNS)	wins	2nd	3rd	4th	5th	6th	PP	FL	points
Indy 500	1974-92	17	1	3	-	1	-	1	3	-	

Win: 1983 Indianapolis 500
Pre-CART Champcar wins: 3 – 1975 Michigan, 1977 Texas, Pocono 500

formula	years	starts (DNS)	wins	2nd	3rd	4th	5th	6th	PP	FL	points
CART	1979-92	127 (3)	10	10	8	9	8	7	4	-	

Wins: 1980 Phoenix, 1981 Milwaukee race 2, Phoenix, 1982 Milwaukee, Phoenix, 1983 Indianapolis 500, Milwaukee, 1984 Phoenix, Milwaukee, Las Vegas. Best championship: 1984, 2nd

Cyril Snipe

GB

Major win: 1912 Targa Florio

Dany Snobeck

F. Born: 2.5.1946
1979, 1980 and 1984 French Touring Car Champion

formula	years	starts (DNS)	wins	2nd	3rd	4th	5th	6th	PP	FL	points
Le Mans	1977-83	4	-	-	-	-	1	-	-	-	
SC W	1977-83		-	-	-	-	1	-	-	-	

Jimmy Snyder

USA. Born: 1907, Chicago, Illinois. Died: 29.6.1939, Cohokia, Illinois

formula	years	starts (DNS)	wins	2nd	3rd	4th	5th	6th	PP	FL	points
Indy 500	1935-39	5	-	1	-	-	-	-	1	-	

Champcar win: 1 – 1938 Syracuse

John Soares Jr

USA

NASCAR wins: 1

Pieter van Soelen

NL. Born: 25.1.1964
2002 Dutch GT Champion (with Cor Euser)

Moises Solana

MEX. Born: 26.12.1935, Mexico City. Died: 27.7.1969, near Mexico City, Valle de Bravo hillclimb

formula	years	starts (DNS)	wins	2nd	3rd	4th	5th	6th	PP	FL	points
F1 W	1963-68	8	-	-	-	-	-	-	-	-	0

Best result: 10th. Best qualifying: 7th. Teams: Scuderia Centro Sud, Lotus, Cooper

formula	years	starts (DNS)	wins	2nd	3rd	4th	5th	6th	PP	FL	points
F2 E	1967	1	-	-	-	-	-	-	-	-	0

Alejandro "Alex" Soler-Roig

E. Born: 29.10.1932, Barcelona
1971 and 1972 Spanish Touring Car Champion

formula	years	starts (DNS)	wins	2nd	3rd	4th	5th	6th	PP	FL	points
F1 W	1970-72	6 (4)	-	-	-	-	-	-	-	-	0

Best result: no finishes. Best qualifying: 17th. Teams: Garvey, Lotus, March, BRM

formula	years	starts (DNS)	wins	2nd	3rd	4th	5th	6th	PP	FL	points
Le Mans	1968-72	2	-	-	-	-	-	-	-	-	
SC W	1967-72		-	-	-	1	-	-	-	-	
F2 E	1968-70	3 (1)	-	-	-	-	-	-	-	-	0

Major win: 1971 Spa 24 hrs

Raymond Sommer

F. Born: 31.8.1906, Paris. Died: 10.9.1950, Cadours, Haute Garonne GP

formula	years	starts (DNS)	wins	2nd	3rd	4th	5th	6th	PP	FL	points
F1 W	1950	5	-	-	-	1	-	-	-	-	3

Best championship: 1950, 12th. Best qualifying: 5th. Teams: driver, Talbot

formula	years	starts (DNS)	wins	2nd	3rd	4th	5th	6th	PP	FL	points
GP Pre-50	1933-49	34	1	-	3	3	5	2	2	1	

Win: 1936 French GP

formula	years	starts (DNS)	wins	2nd	3rd	4th	5th	6th	PP	FL	points
Le Mans	1931-50	9	2	-	-	-	-	-	-	-	2

Wins: 1932 and 1933 Le Mans 24 hrs
Other major wins: 1935 Unofficial French GP, 1936 Spa 24 hrs, 1937 Tunis

Steve Soper

GB. Born: 27.9.1951, Greenford, London
1995 Japanese Touring Car Champion

formula	years	starts (DNS)	wins	2nd	3rd	4th	5th	6th	PP	FL	points
Le Mans	1983-99	5	-	-	-	-	1	-	-	-	

GT FIA wins: 4 – 1997 Hockenheim, Helsinki, Spa, Mugello
Other major wins: 1983 Tourist Trophy (Silverstone), 1992 and 1995 Spa 24 hrs, 1997 Macau Guia race

Gober Sosebee

USA

NASCAR wins: 2

Vincenzo Sospiri
I. Born: 7.10.1966, Forli
1995 FIA F3000 Champion, 1998 and 1999 Sports Racing World Champion (with Emmanuel Collard)

formula	years	starts (DNS)	wins	2nd	3rd	4th	5th	6th	PP	FL	points
F1 W	1997	0 (2)	-	-	-	-	-	-	-	-	0

Best result: no starts. Best qualifying: 23rd. Team: Lola

| Le Mans | 1998-99 | 2 | - | - | - | - | - | - | - | - | |

SRWC wins: 8 – 1998 Brno, Misano, Donington, Anderstorp, Nurburgring, Le Mans, 1999 Barcelona, Monza

| F3000 INT | 1990-95 | 35 (2) | 3 | 6 | 2 | 4 | 3 | 2 | - | 1 | 91 |

Wins: 1995 Barcelona, Pau, Spa. Best championship: 1995, 1st

Indy 500	1997	1	-	-	-	-	-	-	-	-	
CART	1998	4	-	-	-	-	-	-	-	-	
IRL	1997	6	-	1	-	-	-	1	-	-	

Fabio Sotto Mayor
BR
1988 Brazilian Stock Car Champion

George Souders
USA. Born: 11.9.1900, Lafayette, Indiana. Died: 26.7.1976, Lafayette, Indiana

formula	years	starts (DNS)	wins	2nd	3rd	4th	5th	6th	PP	FL	points
GP Pre-50	1927	1	-	-	-	-	-	-	-	-	
Indy 500	1927-28	2	1	-	1	-	-	-	-	-	

Win: 1927 Indianapolis 500
Champcar win: 1 – 1927 Indianapolis 500

Philippe Soulan
F
2002 French GT Champion (with Patrice Goueslard)

Marc Sourd
F. Born: 27.4.1946, Lyon
1992 French Touring Car Champion

formula	years	starts (DNS)	wins	2nd	3rd	4th	5th	6th	PP	FL	points
Le Mans	1977-95	5	-	-	-	-	-	-	-	-	
F2 E	1977-78	3	-	-	-	-	-	-	-	-	0

Stephen South
GB. Born: 19.2.1952, Harrow, Middlesex
1977 Vandervell British F3 Champion

formula	years	starts (DNS)	wins	2nd	3rd	4th	5th	6th	PP	FL	points
F1 W	1980	0 (1)	-	-	-	-	-	-	-	-	0

Best result: no starts. Best qualifying: 27th. Team: McLaren

| F2 E | 1978-79 | 14 | 1 | - | 2 | 1 | 1 | - | 2 | 2 | 22 |

Win: 1979 Hockenheim race 2. Best championship: 1979, 5th

Mario Spagnoli
I
1999 and 2001 Italian Supercar GT Champion

"Mike Sparken" (Michel Poberejsky)
F. Born: 16.6.1930, Neuilly-sur-Seine, near Paris

formula	years	starts (DNS)	wins	2nd	3rd	4th	5th	6th	PP	FL	points
F1 W	1955	1	-	-	-	-	-	-	-	-	0

Best result: 7th. Best qualifying: 23rd. Team: Gordini

| Le Mans | 1955 | 1 | - | - | - | - | - | - | - | - | |

Emiliano Spataro
RA. Born: 25.5.1976, Lanus, Buenos Aires
1999 South American Touring Car Champion (with Carlos Bueno)

formula	years	starts (DNS)	wins	2nd	3rd	4th	5th	6th	PP	FL	points
F3000 INT	1997	6 (2)	-	-	-	-	-	-	-	-	0

Lake Speed
USA. Born: 17.1.1948, Jackson, Missouri
NASCAR wins: 1 (in Modern era)

Mike Spence
GB. Born: 30.12.1936, Croydon, Surrey. Died: 7.5.1968, Indianapolis 500, practice

1964 British F2 Champion

formula	years	starts (DNS)	wins	2nd	3rd	4th	5th	6th	PP	FL	points
F1 W	1963-68	36 (1)	-	-	1	3	6	2	-	-	27

Best championship: 1965, 8th. Best qualifying: 4th. Teams: Lotus, Reg Parnell, BRM

| Le Mans | 1967 | 1 | - | - | - | - | - | - | - | - | |
| SC W | 1966-68 | | 1 | - | - | - | - | 1 | 2 | | |

Win: 1967 Brands Hatch

| F2 E | 1967 | 1 | - | - | - | - | - | - | - | - | 0 |

Non-championship F1 wins: 1965 Race of Champions (Brands Hatch), 1966 South African GP

Russell Spence
GB. Born: 3.1.1960, Bradford, Yorkshire
1983 European FF2000 Champion

formula	years	starts (DNS)	wins	2nd	3rd	4th	5th	6th	PP	FL	points
F3000 INT	1986-88	26 (7)	-	1	1	-	-	1	-	-	10.5

Best championship: 1987, 10th

Jimmy Spencer
USA. Born: 15.2.1957, Berwick, Pennsylvania
NASCAR wins: 2 (all Modern era)

Ricardo Sperafico
BR. Born: 23.7.1979, Toledo, Parana
2000 Italian F3000 Champion

formula	years	starts (DNS)	wins	2nd	3rd	4th	5th	6th	PP	FL	points
F3000 INT	2001-02	24	1	1	5	1	3	1	2	2	46

Win: 2001 Spa. Best championship: 2001 and 2002, 5th

Rodrigo Sperafico
BR. Born: 23.7.1979, Toledo, Parana

formula	years	starts (DNS)	wins	2nd	3rd	4th	5th	6th	PP	FL	points
F3000 INT	2001-02	21	1	1	1	-	-	-	-	-	20

Win: 2002 Interlagos. Best championship: 2002, 6th

Gordon Spice
GB. Born: 18.4.1940, London
1985, 1986 (with Ray Bellm), 1987 (with Fermin Velez) and 1988 (with Ray Bellm) World Group C2 Sports Car Champion

formula	years	starts (DNS)	wins	2nd	3rd	4th	5th	6th	PP	FL	points
Le Mans	1964-89	12	-	-	2	-	-	1	-	-	
SC W	1969-89		-	-	2	2	5	3	-	-	

Best championship: 1987, 10th
Major win: 1978 Spa 24 hrs

Luigi Spinozzi
I
Major win: 1926 Coppa Acerbo (Pescara)

G Sprague
NZ
1984 New Zealand Touring Car Champion

Nicolas Springer
D. Born: 16.9.1962, Zurich (CH)
GT FIA wins: 3 – 2002 Magny-Cours, Brno, Enna

Henri Springuel
F

formula	years	starts (DNS)	wins	2nd	3rd	4th	5th	6th	PP	FL	points
Le Mans	1924-25	2	-	-	-	-	-	-	-	-	

Major win: 1924 Spa 24 hrs

Alan Stacey
GB. Born: 29.8.1933, Broomfield, Essex. Died: 19.6.1960, Spa, Belgian GP

formula	years	starts (DNS)	wins	2nd	3rd	4th	5th	6th	PP	FL	points
F1 W	1958-60	7	-	-	-	-	-	-	-	-	0

Best result: 8th. Best qualifying: 8th. Team: Lotus

| Le Mans | 1958-59 | 2 | - | - | - | - | - | - | - | - | |

Nelson Stacy
USA. Born: 28.12.1921, Ohio. Died: 14.5.1986
NASCAR wins: 4

Gwyn Staley
USA
NASCAR wins: 3

Egbert "Babe" Stapp
USA. Born: 26.2.1904, San Antonio, Texas. Died: 17.9.1980, Indianapolis, Indiana

formula	years	starts (DNS)	wins	2nd	3rd	4th	5th	6th	PP	FL	points
GP Pre-50	1930	1	-	-	-	-	-	-			
Indy 500	1927-40	13	-	-	-	1	1	1	-	-	

Champcar wins: 2 – 1927 Charlotte race 3, 1939 Milwaukee

Gaetano Starrabba (Prince di Giardinelli)
I. Born: 3.12.1932, Palermo, Sicily

formula	years	starts (DNS)	wins	2nd	3rd	4th	5th	6th	PP	FL	points
F1 W	1961	1	-	-	-	-	-	-	-	-	0

Best result: no finishes. Best qualifying: 30th. Team: driver

Doug Steane
HK
Major win: 1956 Macau

Aldo Stefani
I
Major win: 1938 Mille Miglia

Nicolas Stelandre
B. Born: 27.3.1978, Mouscron
2002 Belgian Procar Champion

Paul Stephenson
AUS. Born: 17.3.1977, Melbourne
1999 and 2000 Australian F3 Champion

Charles "Chuck" Stevenson
USA. Born: 15.10.1919, Sidney, Montana. Died: 21.8.1995, Benson, Arizona
1952 Champcar Champion

formula	years	starts (DNS)	wins	2nd	3rd	4th	5th	6th	PP	FL	points
Indy 500	1951-65	9	-	-	-	-	-	1	-	-	

Champcar wins: 4 – 1952 Milwaukee race 2, Du Quoin, 1953 Milwaukee race 2, 1954 Milwaukee race 1
NASCAR wins: 1

Ian Stewart
GB. Born: 15.7.1929, Edinburgh

formula	years	starts (DNS)	wins	2nd	3rd	4th	5th	6th	PP	FL	points
F1 W	1953	1	-	-	-	-	-	-	-	-	0

Best result: no finishes. Best qualifying: 20th. Team: Ecurie Ecosse

	years	starts (DNS)	wins	2nd	3rd	4th	5th	6th	PP	FL	points
Le Mans	1952-53	2	-	-	-	1	-	-			
SC W	1953-54		-	1	-	1	-	-			

Sir Jackie Stewart
GB. Born: 11.6.1939, Milton, Dumbartonshire
1969, 1971 and 1973 F1 World Champion, 1969 British F1 Champion, 1966 Tasman Champion, 1968 French F2 Champion, 1964 Express & Star British F3 Champion

formula	years	starts (DNS)	wins	2nd	3rd	4th	5th	6th	PP	FL	points
F1 W	1965-73	99 (1)	27	11	5	6	5	3	17	15	360

Wins: 1965 Italian GP, 1966 Monaco GP, 1968 Dutch GP, German GP, United States GP, 1969 South African GP, Spanish GP, Dutch GP, French GP, British GP, Italian GP, 1970 Spanish GP, 1971 Spanish GP, Monaco GP, French GP, British GP, German GP, Canadian GP, 1972 Argentinian GP, French GP, Canadian GP, United States GP, 1973 South African GP, Belgian GP, Monaco

GP, Dutch GP, German GP. Best championships: 1969, 1971 and 1973, 1st. Best qualifying: 1st. Teams: BRM, Tyrrell

formula	years	starts (DNS)	wins	2nd	3rd	4th	5th	6th	PP	FL	points
Le Mans	1965	1		-	-	-	-	-			
SC W	1964-67		-	1	-	-	-	1			
F2 E	1967-70	10 (1)	3	5	-	-	1	-	2	2	0

Wins: 1967 Enna, 1969 Nurburgring, Jarama

	years	starts (DNS)	wins	2nd	3rd	4th	5th	6th	PP	FL	points
Indy 500	1966-67	2		-	-	-	1	-	-		

Non-championship F1 wins: 1965 and 1973 International Trophy (Silverstone), 1968 Oulton Park Gold Cup, 1969 and 1970 Race of Champions (Brands Hatch)
Tasman wins: 6 – 1966 Lady Wigram Trophy, Teretonga, Sandown Park, Longford, 1967 New Zealand GP, Australian GP
Other major win: 1964 Monaco F3

Jimmy Stewart
GB. Born: 6.3.1931, Bowling, Dumbartonshire

formula	years	starts (DNS)	wins	2nd	3rd	4th	5th	6th	PP	FL	points
F1 W	1953	1	-	-	-	-	-	-	-	-	0

Best result: no finishes. Best qualifying: 15th. Team: Ecurie Ecosse

	years	starts (DNS)	wins	2nd	3rd	4th	5th	6th	PP	FL	points
Le Mans	1954	1		-	-	-	-	-			
SC W	1953		-	-	-	-	1	-			

Lance Stewart
USA
1990 IMSA GTU Champion

Max Stewart
AUS. Born: n/a. Died: 1977
1971 and 1974 Australian F5000 Champion
Tasman wins: 2 – 1974 Teretonga, Oran Park
Other major wins: 1974 and 1975 Australian GP

Paul Stewart
GB. Born: 29.10.1965, Geneva (CH)

formula	years	starts (DNS)	wins	2nd	3rd	4th	5th	6th	PP	FL	points
F3000 INT	1991-93	26 (3)	-	-	1	1	2	2	-	-	13

Best championship: 1993, 9th

Tony Stewart
USA. Born: 20.5.1971, Columbus, Indiana
1996/97 Indy Racing League Champion, 2002 NASCAR Champion

formula	years	starts (DNS)	wins	2nd	3rd	4th	5th	6th	PP	FL	points
Indy 500	1996-2001	5	-	-	-	1	1	-	2		
IRL	1996-2001	26	3	3	1	-	3	1	8	6	

Wins: 1997 Pikes Peak, 1998 Disney World, New Hampshire. Best championship: 1996/97, 1st
NASCAR wins: 15 (all Modern era)

Ashley Stichbury
NZ. Born: 1971. Died: 17.5.2002, brain haemorrhage
1997 and 2001 New Zealand Tranz-Am Champion

Harry Stiller
GB. Born: 28.5.1938
1966 and 1967 British F3 Champion

formula	years	starts (DNS)	wins	2nd	3rd	4th	5th	6th	PP	FL	points
F2 E	1967-68	2	-	-	-	-	-	-	-	-	0

Bib Stillwell
AUS
1962, 1963, 1964 and 1965 Australian Gold Star Champion

formula	years	starts (DNS)	wins	2nd	3rd	4th	5th	6th	PP	FL	points
Le Mans	1961	1	-	-	-	-	-	-			

Robbie Stirling
CDN. Born: 7.9.1960, Toronto, Ontario
1996 Interserie Champion

formula	years	starts (DNS)	wins	2nd	3rd	4th	5th	6th	PP	FL	points
Le Mans	1989-91	3	-	-	-	-	-	-			
F3000 INT	1994	1	-	-	-	-	-	-	-	-	0

Siegfried Stohr

I. Born: 10.10.1952, Rimini
1978 Italian F3 Champion

formula	years	starts (DNS)	wins	2nd	3rd	4th	5th	6th	PP	FL	points
F1 W	1981	9 (4)	-	-	-	-	-	-	-	-	0

Best result: 7th. Best qualifying: 13th. Team: Arrows

F2 E	1979-82	23	1	3	2	2	2	1	1	-	46

Win: 1980 Enna. Best championship: 1980, 4th

Paul Stokell

AUS. Born: 3.8.1970
1994, 1995 and 1996 Australian Formula Holden Champion, 1994 New Zealand Formula Brabham Champion

Rolf Stommelen

D. Born: 11.7.1943, Siegen. Died: 24.4.1983, Riverside 6 hrs
1977 German Racing Champion

formula	years	starts (DNS)	wins	2nd	3rd	4th	5th	6th	PP	FL	points
F1 W	1969-78	54 (9)	-	-	1	-	4	2	-	-	14

Best championship: 1970, 11th. Best qualifying: 7th. Teams: Roy Winkelmann, Brabham, Surtees, Eifelland, Hill, Hesketh, Arrows

Le Mans	1965-82	13	-	1	1	1	-	1	1	1	
SC W	1965-83		11	12	10	3	4	4	8	10	

Wins: 1967 Targa Florio, 1968 Daytona 24 hrs, 1976 Florio Cup (Enna), Watkins Glen, 1977 Mugello, Nurburgring, 1978 Daytona 24 hrs, 1980 Daytona 24 hrs, Nurburgring, 1981 Mosport Park, Elkhart Lake. Best championship: 1982, 9th

F2 E	1970-76	12 (2)	-	-	-	-	1	2	-	-	0

Other major win: 1982 Daytona 24 hrs

RP Stone

NZ
1978 New Zealand Gold Star Champion

Whitney Straight

GB (emigrated from the USA). Born: 6.11.1912, New York City (USA). Died: 5.4.1979, England

formula	years	starts (DNS)	wins	2nd	3rd	4th	5th	6th	PP	FL	points
GP Pre-50	1933-34	3	-	-	-	-	-	-	-	-	

Major win: 1934 South African GP

Louis Strang

USA. Born: Amsterdam, New York State. Died: 20.7.1911, Blue River, Wisconsin, reliability run

formula	years	starts (DNS)	wins	2nd	3rd	4th	5th	6th	PP	FL	points
GP Pre-50	1908	2	-	-	-	-	-	1	-	-	
Indy 500	1911	1	-	-	-	-	-	1	-		

Champcar win: 1 – 1909 Indianapolis race 2

Philippe Streiff

F. Born: 26.6.1955, La Tronche, near Grenoble
1981 French F3 Champion

formula	years	starts (DNS)	wins	2nd	3rd	4th	5th	6th	PP	FL	points
F1 W	1984-88	53 (1)	-	-	1	1	1	2	-	-	11

Best championship: 1986, 13th. Best qualifying: 5th. Teams: Renault, Ligier, Tyrrell, AGS

Le Mans	1978-84	4	-	1	1	-	-	-	-		
SC W	1978-88		-	1	1	1	-	-	-		
F2 E	1982-84	36	1	5	4	3	5	-	-	-	74

Win: 1984 Brands Hatch. Best championships: 1983 and 1984, 4th

F3000 INT	1985	11	-	-	1	-	4	-	-	-	12

Best championship: 1985, 8th

F3 E win: 1 – 1980 Zolder

Volker Strycek

D. Born: 13.10.1957
1984 German Touring Car Champion

Hartwell "Stubby" Stubblefield

USA. Born: 1908. Died: 21.5.1935, Indianapolis 500, practice

formula	years	starts (DNS)	wins	2nd	3rd	4th	5th	6th	PP	FL	points
Indy 500	1930-34	5	-	-	-	-	1	-	-	-	

Champcar win: 1 – 1932 Roby

Hans Stuck

D. Born: 27.12.1900, Warsaw (PL). Died: 8.2.1978, Grainau

formula	years	starts (DNS)	wins	2nd	3rd	4th	5th	6th	PP	FL	points
F1 W	1952-53	3 (1)	-	-	-	-	-	-	-	-	0

Best result: 14th. Best qualifying: 14th. Teams: AFM, Ecurie Espadon, driver

GP Pre-50	1927-39	32 (2)		4	5	3	4	1	2	2	5

Wins: 1934 German GP, Swiss GP, Masaryk GP, 1935 Italian GP
Other major win: 1939 Bucharest GP

Hans-Joachim Stuck

D. Born: 1.1.1951, Grainau
1985 World Sports Car Champion (with Derek Bell), 1972, 1986 and 1987 German Racing Champion, 1990 German Touring Car Champion

formula	years	starts (DNS)	wins	2nd	3rd	4th	5th	6th	PP	FL	points
F1 W	1974-79	74 (7)	-	-	2	3	5	2	-	-	29

Best championship: 1977, 11th. Best qualifying: 2nd. Teams: March, Brabham, Shadow, ATS

Le Mans	1972-98	18		2	2	3	1	-	1	2	1

Wins: 1986 and 1987 Le Mans 24 hrs

SC W	1970-92		8	9	8	3	2	2	10	4	

Wins: 1981 Nurburgring, 1984 Imola, 1985 Hockenheim, Mosport Park, Brands Hatch, 1986 Monza, Le Mans 24 hrs, 1987 Le Mans 24 hrs. Best championship: 1985, 1st. GT FIA wins: 2 – 1996 Brands Hatch, Spa

F2 E	1971-79	25		5	3	1	-	-	-	7	5	43

Wins: 1974 Montjuich Park, Hockenheim race 1, Enna, 1976 Hockenheim race 1, Hockenheim race 2. Best championship: 1974, 2nd
Other major wins: 1972 Spa 24 hrs, 1975, 1986 and 1988 Sebring 12 hrs, 1980 and 1983 Macau Guia race

Patrick Studer

CH
1978 Swiss F3 Champion

formula	years	starts (DNS)	wins	2nd	3rd	4th	5th	6th	PP	FL	points
F2 E	1980	3	-	-	-	-	-	-	-	-	0

Alessandro della Stufa

I
Major win: 1935 Mille Miglia

Otto Stuppacher

A. Born: 3.3.1947, Vienna. Died: 15.8.2001, Vienna

formula	years	starts (DNS)	wins	2nd	3rd	4th	5th	6th	PP	FL	points
F1 W	1976	0 (4)	-	-	-	-	-	-	-	-	0

Best result: no starts. Best qualifying: 26th. Team: OASC

Le Mans	1972	1									

Per Stureson

S. Born: 22.3.1948
1985 German Touring Car Champion

Tim Sugden

GB. Born: 26.4.1964, Bradford, Yorkshire
1997 British GT Champion (with Steve O'Rourke)

formula	years	starts (DNS)	wins	2nd	3rd	4th	5th	6th	PP	FL	points
Le Mans	1998	1	-	-	-	1	-	-			

Alexandr Sukhov

R
1999 Russian Touring Car Champion

Danny Sullivan
USA. Born: 9.3.1950, Louisville, Kentucky
1988 CART Champion

formula	years	starts (DNS)	wins	2nd	3rd	4th	5th	6th	PP	FL	points
F1 W	1983	15	-	-	-	-	1	-	-	-	2

Best championship: 1983, 17th. Best qualifying: 9th. Team: Tyrrell

Le Mans	1988-96	3	-	-	1	-	-	-			
F2 E	1976-77	5 (3)	-	-	-	1	-	-	-		2

Best championship: 1977, 18th

Indy 500	1982-95	12	1	-	-	-	1	-	-		

Win: 1985 Indianapolis 500

CART	1982-95	170	17	11	12	10	14	4	19	-	

Wins: 1984 Cleveland, Pocono 500, Sanair, 1985 Indianapolis 500, Miami, 1986 Meadowlands, Cleveland, 1988 Portland, Michigan 500, Nazareth, Laguna Seca, 1989 Pocono 500, Elkhart Lake, 1990 Cleveland, Laguna Seca, 1992 Long Beach, 1993 Detroit. Best championship: 1988, 1st

Peter Sundberg
S. Born: 10.5.1976, Marbella (E)
1999 Italian F3 Champion

Kasikam Suphot
T
1996 Asian Touring Car Champion

Marc Surer
CH. Born: 18.9.1951, Aresdorf
1979 European F2 Champion

formula	years	starts (DNS)	wins	2nd	3rd	4th	5th	6th	PP	FL	points
F1 W	1979-86	81 (7)	-	-	2	2	7	-	1		17

Best championship: 1985, 13th. Best qualifying: 5th. Teams: Ensign, ATS, Theodore, Arrows, Brabham

Le Mans	1978-82	3	-	-	-	-	-	-			
SC W	1977-85		1	1	2	2	2	1	1	-	

Win: 1985 Monza. Best championship: 1985, 9th

F2 E	1976-81	33 (2)	2	7	6	2	2	-	3	3	94

Wins: 1979 Nurburgring, Vallelunga. Best championship: 1979, 1st
Other major win: 1985 Spa 24 hrs

John Surtees
GB. Born: 11.2.1934, Tatsfield, Surrey
1964 F1 World Champion, 1966 Can-Am Champion

formula	years	starts (DNS)	wins	2nd	3rd	4th	5th	6th	PP	FL	points
F1 W	1960-72	111 (2)	6	10	8	5	8	3	8	11	180

Wins: 1963 German GP, 1964 German GP, Italian GP, 1966 Belgian GP, Mexican GP, 1967 Italian GP. Best championship: 1964, 1st. Best qualifying: 1st. Teams: Lotus, Reg Parnell, Ferrari, Cooper, Honda, BRM, Surtees

Le Mans	1963-67	4	-	-	1	-	-	1	1		
SC W	1962-70		4	4	4	-	-	9	10		

Wins: 1963 Sebring 12 hrs, Nurburgring, 1965 Nurburgring, 1966 Monza

F2 E	1967-72	5 (3)	1	1	1	-	-	-			0

Win: 1972 Imola
Non-championship F1 wins: 1961 Goodwood, 1962 Mallory Park, 1963 Enna, Rand GP (Kyalami), 1964 Syracuse, 1966 Syracuse, 1970 Oulton Park Gold Cup, 1971 Oulton Park Gold Cup
Other major win: 1963 New Zealand GP

Andy Sutcliffe
GB. Born: 9.5.1947, Mildenhall, Suffolk

formula	years	starts (DNS)	wins	2nd	3rd	4th	5th	6th	PP	FL	points
F1 W	1977	0 (1)	-	-	-	-	-	-	-	-	0

Best result: no starts. Best qualifying: 32nd. Team: RAM

F2 E	1973-77	7 (1)	-	-	1	-	1	1	-		7

Best championship: 1974, 10th

Len Sutton
USA. Born: 9.8.1925, Aims, Oregon

formula	years	starts (DNS)	wins	2nd	3rd	4th	5th	6th	PP	FL	points
Indy 500	1958-65	7	-	1	-	-	-	-	-	-	

Champcar wins: 3 – 1958 Trenton race 1, 1959 Springfield, 1960 Milwaukee race 2

Aguri Suzuki
J. Born: 8.9.1960, Tokyo
1988 Japanese F3000 Champion, 1986 Japanese Touring Car Champion (with Takao Wada)

formula	years	starts (DNS)	wins	2nd	3rd	4th	5th	6th	PP	FL	points
F1 W	1988-95	64 (24)	-	-	1	-	-	-	-	-	8

Best championship: 1990, 10th. Best qualifying: 6th. Teams: Larrousse, Zakspeed, Footwork, Jordan, Ligier

Le Mans	1986-98	7	-	-	1	-	-	-			
SC W	1982-92		-	-	-	-	1	-			
F3000 INT	1988	2 (1)	-	-	-	-	-	-	-	-	0

Keiichi Suzuki
J. Born: 21.3.1949, Kanagawa
1984 Japanese Sports-Prototype Champion (with Naoki Nagasaka)

formula	years	starts (DNS)	wins	2nd	3rd	4th	5th	6th	PP	FL	points
Le Mans	1989	1	-	-	-	-	-	-			
SC W	1982-92		-	-	-	-	-	3	-	-	

Toshio Suzuki
J. Born: 10.3.1955, Saitama
1995 Japanese F3000 Champion, 1991 and 1992 Japanese Sports-Prototype Champion (with Kazuyoshi Hoshino), 1990 Japanese Touring Car Champion (with Hoshino), 1979 Japanese F3 Champion

formula	years	starts (DNS)	wins	2nd	3rd	4th	5th	6th	PP	FL	points
F1 W	1993	2	-	-	-	-	-	-	-	-	0

Best result: 12th. Best qualifying: 23rd. Team: Larrousse

Le Mans	1985-2000	12	-	1	-	1	1	1	-	-	
SC W	1984-92		-	-	-	1	-	-			

Major win: 1992 Daytona 24 hrs

Ed Swart
NL
1965 European Touring Car Champion (1000cc class), 1970 European 2-litre Sports Car Champion (Group 5 class)

Jacques Swaters
B. Born: 30.10.1926, Woluwe St Lambert, Brussels

formula	years	starts (DNS)	wins	2nd	3rd	4th	5th	6th	PP	FL	points
F1 W	1951-54	7 (1)	-	-	-	-	-	-	-	-	0

Best result: 7th. Best qualifying: 13th. Teams: Ecurie Belgique, Ecurie Francorchamps

Le Mans	1954-57	4	-	-	1	2	-	-			
SC W	1953-57		-	-	1	1	-	-			

Bob Sweikert
USA. Born: 20.5.1926, Los Angeles, California. Died: 17.6.1956, Salem, Indiana
1955 Champcar Champion

formula	years	starts (DNS)	wins	2nd	3rd	4th	5th	6th	PP	FL	points
SC W	1956		-	1	-	-	-	-			
Indy 500	1952-56	5	1	-	-	-	1	-			

Win: 1955 Indianapolis 500
Champcar wins: 4 – 1953 Indiana State Fairgrounds, 1954 Syracuse, 1955 Indianapolis 500, Syracuse

Jesper Sylvest
DK. Born: 3.3.1963, Odense
1999 Danish Touring Car Champion

Frank Sytner
GB. Born: 29.6.1944, Liverpool
1988 British Touring Car Champion

Ferenc Szisz
H. Born: 21.9.1873. Died: 21.2.1944, Auffargis, Seine-sur-Oise (F)

formula	years	starts (DNS)	wins	2nd	3rd	4th	5th	6th	PP	FL	points
GP Pre-50	1906-14	5		1	1	-	-	-	-	-	

Win: 1906 French GP

T

Nobuhide Tachi
J. Born: 23.3.1947

formula	years	starts (DNS)	wins	2nd	3rd	4th	5th	6th	PP	FL	points
SC W	1980-82		-	-	-	1	-	-		

Major wins: 1974 and 1975 Macau Guia race

Yuji Tachikawa
J. Born: 5.7.1975, Kanagawa
2001 Japanese GT Champion (with Hironori Takeuchi)

Fons Taels
B. Born: 23.3.1952
1997 Belgian Belcar GT Champion (with Vincent Dupont and Georges Cremer)

Toranosuke "Tora" Takagi
J. Born: 12.2.1974, Shizuoka
2000 Japanese Formula Nippon Champion

formula	years	starts (DNS)	wins	2nd	3rd	4th	5th	6th	PP	FL	points
F1 W	1998-99	32	-	-	-	-	-	-	-	-	0

Best result: 7th. Best qualifying: 13th. Teams: Tyrrell, Arrows

CART	2001-02	39 (1)	-	-	-	2	-	4	-	-	

Noritake Takahara
J. Born: 6.6.1951, Tokyo
1974 and 1976 Japanese F2000 Champion

formula	years	starts (DNS)	wins	2nd	3rd	4th	5th	6th	PP	FL	points
F1 W	1976-77	2	-	-	-	-	-	-	-	-	0

Best result: 9th. Best qualifying: 19th. Teams: Surtees, Kojima

Kenji Takahashi
J. Born: 18.5.1946
1985 and 1986 Japanese Sports-Prototype Champion (with Kunimitsu Takahashi)

formula	years	starts (DNS)	wins	2nd	3rd	4th	5th	6th	PP	FL	points
Le Mans	1987	1	-	-	-	-	-	-		
SC W	1983-90		-	-	-	-	1	-	-	

Kunimitsu Takahashi
J. Born: 29.1.1940, Tokyo
1985, 1986 (both with Kenji Takahashi), 1987 (with Kenneth Acheson) and 1989 (with Staley Dickens) Japanese Sports-Prototype Champion

formula	years	starts (DNS)	wins	2nd	3rd	4th	5th	6th	PP	FL	points
F1 W	1977	1	-	-	-	-	-	-	-	-	0

Best result: 9th. Best qualifying: 22nd. Team: Meiritsu Racing Team

Le Mans	1986-96	8	-	-	-	-	-	-		
SC W	1983-92		-	-	-	-	1	1	-	-	

Hironori Takeuchi
J. Born: 22.12.1964, Kanagawa
2001 Japanese GT Champion (with Yuji Tachikawa)

Patrick Tambay
F. Born: 25.6.1949, Paris
1977 and 1980 Can-Am Champion

formula	years	starts (DNS)	wins	2nd	3rd	4th	5th	6th	PP	FL	points
F1 W	1977-86	114 (10)	2	4	5	6	8	7	5	2	103

Wins: 1982 German GP, 1983 San Marino GP. Best championship: 1983, 4th. Best qualifying: 1st. Teams: Surtees, Theodore, McLaren, Ligier, Arrows,

Ferrari, Renault, Haas Lola

formula	years	starts (DNS)	wins	2nd	3rd	4th	5th	6th	PP	FL	points
Le Mans	1976-89	4	-	-	-	1	-	-		
SC W	1976-92		-	1	-	-	1	1	-	-	

Best championship: 1989, 8th

F2 E	1974-78	39	2	5	5	4	1	1	6	1	86

Wins: 1975 Nogaro, 1976 Nogaro. Best championship: 1975, 2nd

Antonio Tamburini
I. Born: 15.9.1966, Arezza

formula	years	starts (DNS)	wins	2nd	3rd	4th	5th	6th	PP	FL	points
F3000 INT	1990-93	23 (1)	1	-	1	4	1	1	-	1	28

Win: 1991 Le Mans. Best championship: 1991, 4th
Other major win: 1989 Monaco F3

Garth Tander
AUS. Born: 31.3.1977, Perth
Major win: 2000 Bathurst

Luigi Taramazzo
I. Born: 5.5.1932, Ceva

formula	years	starts (DNS)	wins	2nd	3rd	4th	5th	6th	PP	FL	points
SC W	1955-72		-	-	-	-	1	-	-	

Major win: 1958 Mille Miglia (regularity test)

Gabriele Tarquini
I. Born: 2.3.1962, Guilianova Lido, near Pescara
1994 British Touring Car Champion

formula	years	starts (DNS)	wins	2nd	3rd	4th	5th	6th	PP	FL	points
F1 W	1987-95	38 (40)	-	-	-	-	-	1	-	-	1

Best championship: 1989, 26th. Best qualifying: 11th. Teams: Osella, Coloni, AGS, Fondmetal, Tyrrell

Le Mans	1985	1	-	-	-	-	-	-		
F3000 INT	1985-87	31 (1)	-	1	3	3	3	-	-	1	33

Best championship: 1985, 6th

Piero Taruffi
I. Born: 12.10.1906, Albano Laziale, Rome. Died: 12.1.1988, Rome

formula	years	starts (DNS)	wins	2nd	3rd	4th	5th	6th	PP	FL	points
F1 W	1950-56	18	1	3	1	2	2	1	-	1	41

Win: 1952 Swiss GP. Best championship: 1952, 3rd. Best qualifying: 2nd.
Teams: Alfa Romeo, Ferrari, Mercedes-Benz, Maserati, Vanwall

GP Pre-50	1933-49	13	-	-	-	-	1	2	-	-	
Le Mans	1953	1	-	-	-	-	-	-		
SC W	1953-57		2	2	-	-	2	1	-	-	

Wins: 1956 Nurburgring, 1957 Mille Miglia
Non-championship F1 win: 1952 Dundrod
Other major wins: 1951 Carrera Panamericana, 1954 Targa Florio

Thierry Tassin
B. Born: 11.1.1959, Brussels
1994 and 1995 Belgian Procar Touring Car Champion

formula	years	starts (DNS)	wins	2nd	3rd	4th	5th	6th	PP	FL	points
F2 E	1982-84	25 (1)	-	1	-	5	3	3	1	-	30

Best championship: 1984, 8th

F3000 INT	1985-87	10	-	-	-	-	-	1	-	1	1

Best championship: 1985, 16th
Major wins: 1983, 1986, 1994 and 1996 Spa 24 hrs

Anthony Taylor
ZA. Born: 27.9.1973, Krugersdorp
1990 South African Formula GTi Champion

Henry Taylor
GB. Born: 16.12.1932, Shefford, Bedfordshire

formula	years	starts (DNS)	wins	2nd	3rd	4th	5th	6th	PP	FL	points
F1 W	1959-61	8 (2)	-	-	-	1	-	-	-	-	3

Best championship: 1960, 19th. Best qualifying: 13th. Teams: Reg Parnell, BRP

Le Mans	1960	1	-	-	-	-	-	-		

Major win: 1960 Monaco Formula Junior

Ian Taylor
GB. Born: 28.1.1947. Died: 7.6.1992, Spa-Francorchamps
1973 Forward Trust British F3 Champion

John Taylor
GB. Born: 23.3.1933, Leicester. Died: 6.9.1966, Koblenz Hospital, following an accident at the German GP on 7.8.1966

formula	years	starts (DNS)	wins	2nd	3rd	4th	5th	6th	PP	FL	points
F1 W	1964-66	5	-	-	-	-	-	1	-	-	1

Best championship: 1966, 17th. Best qualifying: 16th. Teams: Bob Gerard, David Bridges

formula	years	starts (DNS)	wins	2nd	3rd	4th	5th	6th	PP	FL	points
SC W	1966		-	-	-	-	-	1	-	-	

Mike Taylor
GB. Born: 24.4.1934, London

formula	years	starts (DNS)	wins	2nd	3rd	4th	5th	6th	PP	FL	points
F1 W	1959-60	1 (1)	-	-	-	-	-	-	-	-	0

Best result: no finishes. Best qualifying: 19th. Teams: Alan Brown, Taylor-Crawley

formula	years	starts (DNS)	wins	2nd	3rd	4th	5th	6th	PP	FL	points
Le Mans	1958-59	2	-	-	-	-	-	-	-	-	

Trevor Taylor
GB. Born: 26.12.1936, Gleadless, Sheffield, Yorkshire
1958 British F3 Champion, 1960 (tied with Jim Clark) and 1961 Motor Racing British Formula Junior Champion

formula	years	starts (DNS)	wins	2nd	3rd	4th	5th	6th	PP	FL	points
F1 W	1959-66	27 (2)	-	1	-	-	-	2	-	-	8

Best championship: 1962, 10th. Best qualifying: 3rd. Teams: Ace Garage, Lotus, BRP, Shannon

formula	years	starts (DNS)	wins	2nd	3rd	4th	5th	6th	PP	FL	points
Le Mans	1961	1	-	-	-	-	-	-	-	-	
F2 E	1967	2	-	-	-	-	-	-	-	-	0

Non-championship F1 wins: 1962 Cape GP (Killarney), Mexican GP, Natal GP
Other major win: 1969 Tourist Trophy (Oulton)

Wayne Taylor
ZA. Born: 14.7.1960, Port Elizabeth
1994 and 1996 IMSA WSC Champion, 1986 South African Formula Atlantic Champion

formula	years	starts (DNS)	wins	2nd	3rd	4th	5th	6th	PP	FL	points
Le Mans	1987-2002	13	-	-	-	1	-	-	-	-	
SC W	1983-92		-	-	-	2	1	3	-	-	
F3000 INT	1986	0 (1)	-	-	-	-	-	-	-	-	0

Major wins: 1996 Daytona 24 hrs, 1996 Sebring 12 hrs, 1998 Petit LeMans

William Taylor
USA. Born: 1888. Died: 1918, in combat

formula	years	starts (DNS)	wins	2nd	3rd	4th	5th	6th	PP	FL	points
GP Pre-50	1914-15	2	-	-	1	-	-	-	-	-	

Champcar win: 1 – 1917 Uniontown race 1

Marshall Teague
USA. Born: 25.5.1921, Daytona Beach, Florida. Died: 11.2.1959, Daytona 500, practice

formula	years	starts (DNS)	wins	2nd	3rd	4th	5th	6th	PP	FL	points
Indy 500	1953-57	3	-	-	-	-	-	-	-	-	

NASCAR wins: 7

Toni Teittinen
SF. Born: 26.10.1973
1995 Nordic F3 Champion

Arthur Terdich
AUS
Major win: 1929 Australian GP

Max de Terra
CH. Born: 6.10.1918, Zurich. Died: 29.12.1982, Zollikon

formula	years	starts (DNS)	wins	2nd	3rd	4th	5th	6th	PP	FL	points
F1 W	1952-53	2	-	-	-	-	-	-	-	-	0

Best result: 9th. Best qualifying: 19th. Teams: Alfred Dattner, Ecurie Espadon

David Terrien
F. Born: 27.10.1976, Nantes
2000 Sports Racing World Champion (with Christian Pescatori), 2001 FIA N-GT class Champion (with Pescatori)

formula	years	starts (DNS)	wins	2nd	3rd	4th	5th	6th	PP	FL	points
Le Mans	1999-2001	3									

GT FIA win: 1 – 2002 Spa 24 hrs. SRWC wins: 5 – 2000 Barcelona, Brno, Donington, Nurburgring, Magny-Cours

formula	years	starts (DNS)	wins	2nd	3rd	4th	5th	6th	PP	FL	points
F3000 INT	1999	6 (4)	-	-	-	-	-	-	-	-	0

Andre Testut
MC. Born: 13.4.1926, Lyon (F)

formula	years	starts (DNS)	wins	2nd	3rd	4th	5th	6th	PP	FL	points
F1 W	1958-59	0 (2)	-	-	-	-	-	-	-	-	0

Best result: no starts. Best qualifying: 24th. Teams: driver, Monte Carlo Auto Sport

formula	years	starts (DNS)	wins	2nd	3rd	4th	5th	6th	PP	FL	points
Le Mans	1959	1									

Teddy Tetzlaff
USA. Born: 1887. Died: 8.12.1929, Artesia, California

formula	years	starts (DNS)	wins	2nd	3rd	4th	5th	6th	PP	FL	points
GP Pre-50	1912-14	2	-	-	-	-	-	-	-	-	2
Indy 500	1911-14	4	-	1	-	-	-	-	-	-	

Champcar wins: 3 – 1912 Santa Monica race 3, Tacoma race 3, Tacoma race 4

Mike Thackwell
NZ. Born: 30.3.1961, Auckland
1984 European F2 Champion, 1987 New Zealand Formula Pacific Champion

formula	years	starts (DNS)	wins	2nd	3rd	4th	5th	6th	PP	FL	points
F1 W	1980-84	2 (3)	-	-	-	-	-	-	-	-	0

Best result: no finishes. Best qualifying: 24th. Teams: Arrows, Tyrrell, RAM

formula	years	starts (DNS)	wins	2nd	3rd	4th	5th	6th	PP	FL	points
Le Mans	1985-87	3	-	-	-	-	-	-	-	-	
SC W	1984-87		1	1	2	-	2	2	1	1	

Win: 1986 Nurburgring. Best championship: 1985, 11th

formula	years	starts (DNS)	wins	2nd	3rd	4th	5th	6th	PP	FL	points
F2 E	1980-84	52	9	6	8	3	2	2	9	15	164

Wins: 1981 Silverstone, 1983 Jarama, 1984 Silverstone, Thruxton, Vallelunga, Mugello, Pau, Misano, Enna. Best championship: 1984, 1st

formula	years	starts (DNS)	wins	2nd	3rd	4th	5th	6th	PP	FL	points
F3000 INT	1985-88	16	4	3	-	1	-	-	5	4	55.5

Wins: 1985 Silverstone, Spa, Enna, 1986 Pau. Best championship: 1985, 2nd

formula	years	starts (DNS)	wins	2nd	3rd	4th	5th	6th	PP	FL	points
CART	1984	2									

F3 E win: 1 – 1979 Monza

Hasse Thaung
S. Born: 17.9.1958
1984 Nordic F3 Champion

Leon Thery
F. Born: 1878. Died: 1909, tuberculosis

formula	years	starts (DNS)	wins	2nd	3rd	4th	5th	6th	PP	FL	points
GP Pre-50	1904-08	3	2	-	-	-	-	-	-	1	

Wins: 1904 Gordon Bennett Trophy, 1905 Gordon Bennett Trophy

Olivier Thevenin
F. Born: 25.2.1968, Orleans

formula	years	starts (DNS)	wins	2nd	3rd	4th	5th	6th	PP	FL	points
Le Mans	1995-2002	6	-	-	-	-	-	-	-	-	

GT FIA win: 1 – 1995 Anderstorp

Didier Theys
B. Born: 19.10.1956, Nivelles
1987 American Racing Series Champion, 1986 SCCA Super Vee Champion, 2002 US Grand-Am Champion

formula	years	starts (DNS)	wins	2nd	3rd	4th	5th	6th	PP	FL	points
Le Mans	1982-2002	13	-	-	1	-	1	1	-	-	
SC W	1979-92		-	-	-	-	-	-	-	-	

SRWC wins: 3 – 1997 Zolder, 1998 Paul Ricard, 2000 Elkhart Lake

formula	years	starts (DNS)	wins	2nd	3rd	4th	5th	6th	PP	FL	points
F2 E	1983-84	8	-	-	-	-	-	3	-	-	3

Best championship: 1984, 11th

formula	years	starts (DNS)	wins	2nd	3rd	4th	5th	6th	PP	FL	points
Indy 500	1989-93	3	-	-	-	-	-	-	-	-	
CART	1987-93	47 (1)	-	-	1	-	-	-	-	-	

Other major wins: 1987 Spa 24 hrs, 1998 and 2002 Daytona 24 hrs, 1998 Sebring 12 hrs

Pierre-Alain Thibaut

B
1992 Belgian Procar Touring Car Champion

Alfonso Thiele

USA. Born: 5.4.1922, Arizona. Died: 1986

formula	years	starts (DNS)	wins	2nd	3rd	4th	5th	6th	PP	FL	points
F1 W	1960	1	-	-	-	-	-	-	-	-	0

Best result: no finishes. Best qualifying: 9th. Team: Scuderia Centro Sud

| SC W | 1953-64 | | - | - | - | 1 | - | - | | | |

Kurt Thiers

B
2001 Belgian Belcar GT Champion (with Patrick Schreurs)

Kurt Thiim

DK. Born: 3.8.1958, Vojens
1986 German Touring Car Champion, 1984 German F3 Champion

formula	years	starts (DNS)	wins	2nd	3rd	4th	5th	6th	PP	FL	points
Le Mans	1991	1	-	-	-	-	-	-			

Herb Thomas

USA. Born: 6.4.1923, Barbeque Township, Harnett County, North Carolina. Died: 9.8.2000
1951 and 1953 NASCAR Champion

NASCAR wins: 49

Joe Thomas

USA. Born: Seattle, Washington. Died: 28.12.1965

formula	years	starts (DNS)	wins	2nd	3rd	4th	5th	6th	PP	FL	points
Indy 500	1920-22	3	-	-	-	-	-	-			

Champcar wins: 2 – 1921 Beverly Hills race 8, Fresno race 1

Rene Thomas

F. Born: 7.3.1886, Perigueux. Died: 23.9.1975, Columbes

formula	years	starts (DNS)	wins	2nd	3rd	4th	5th	6th	PP	FL	points
GP Pre-50	1912-25	9	-	-	1	-	-	1	2	-	
Indy 500	1914-21	4	1	1	-	-	-	-	1	-	

Win: 1914 Indianapolis 500
Champcar win: 1 – 1914 Indianapolis 500

Bill Thompson

AUS
Major wins: 1930, 1932 and 1933 Australian GP

Eric Thompson

GB. Born: 4.11.1919, Surbiton, Surrey

formula	years	starts (DNS)	wins	2nd	3rd	4th	5th	6th	PP	FL	points
F1 W	1952	1	-	-	-	-	1	-	-	-	2

Best championship: 1952, 16th. Best qualifying: 9th. Team: Connaught

| Le Mans | 1949-55 | 7 | | - | - | 1 | - | - | | | |
| SC W | 1953-55 | | | - | 1 | - | - | - | | | |

James Thompson

GB. Born: 26.4.1974, York
2002 British Touring Car Champion

Richard Thompson

USA

formula	years	starts (DNS)	wins	2nd	3rd	4th	5th	6th	PP	FL	points
Le Mans	1960-68	6	-	-	-	1	-	-			
SC W	1955-68		1	-	1	1	-	1	-	-	

Win: 1967 Spa

Alfred "Speedy" Thompson

USA. Born: 3.4.1926, Union County, North Carolina. Died: 2.4.1972, Mecklenburg

NASCAR wins: 19

Steve Thompson

GB
Tasman win: 1 – 1973 Warwick Farm

Tommy Thompson

USA
NASCAR wins: 2

Johnny Thomson

USA. Born: 9.4.1922, Lowell, Massachusetts. Died: 24.9.1960, Allentown, Pennsylvania

formula	years	starts (DNS)	wins	2nd	3rd	4th	5th	6th	PP	FL	points
Indy 500	1953-60	8		-	1	1	1	-	1	1	

Champcar wins: 7 – 1955 Milwaukee race 1, 1957 Langhorne, 1958 Springfield, Du Quoin, Syracuse, Sacramento, 1959 Milwaukee race 1

Leslie Thorne

GB. Born: 23.6.1916, Greenock, Renfrewshire. Died: 13.7.1993, Troon, Ayrshire

formula	years	starts (DNS)	wins	2nd	3rd	4th	5th	6th	PP	FL	points
F1 W	1954	1	-	-	-	-	-	-	-	-	0

Best result: 14th. Best qualifying: 23rd. Team: Ecurie Ecosse

Bernard Thuner

CH. Born: 29.11.1960, Signy
1993 and 1994 Swiss Touring Car Champion

formula	years	starts (DNS)	wins	2nd	3rd	4th	5th	6th	PP	FL	points
Le Mans	1989-95	4	-	-	-	-	-	-			
SC W	1989-92		-	-	1	-	-	-			

Thorkyld Thyrring

DK. Born: 24.10.1950, Copenhagen
1994 British GT Champion

formula	years	starts (DNS)	wins	2nd	3rd	4th	5th	6th	PP	FL	points
Le Mans	1986-95	7	-	-	-	-	-	-			
SC W	1985-92		-	-	-	1	3	1	-	-	

Best championship: 1988, 16th

Oliver Tichy

A. Born: 6.5.1975

formula	years	starts (DNS)	wins	2nd	3rd	4th	5th	6th	PP	FL	points
F3000 INT	1996-98	24 (1)	-	2	1	-	1	1	-	-	19

Best championship: 1997, 7th

Marcel Tiemann

D. Born: 19.3.1974, Hamburg
GT FIA win: 1 – 1997 Suzuka
Other major win: 1996 Monaco F3

Bernard Tilanus

ZA
1981 South African Formula Atlantic Champion

Brian Till

USA. Born: 26.3.1960, Houston, Texas
1990 North American Toyota Atlantic (Eastern) Champion

formula	years	starts (DNS)	wins	2nd	3rd	4th	5th	6th	PP	FL	points
Indy 500	1994	1	-	-	-	-	-	-			
CART	1992-95	20	-	-	-	-	-	-			

Bud Tingelstad

USA. Born: 4.4.1928, Frazee, Minnesota. Died: 30.7.1981, Indianapolis, Indiana

formula	years	starts (DNS)	wins	2nd	3rd	4th	5th	6th	PP	FL	points
Indy 500	1960-71	10	-	-	-	-	-	-	1	-	

Champcar win: 1 – 1966 Du Quoin

Sam Tingle

RSR. Born: 24.8.1921, Manchester (GB)

formula	years	starts (DNS)	wins	2nd	3rd	4th	5th	6th	PP	FL	points
F1 W	1963-69	5	-	-	-	-	-	-	-	-	0

Best result: 8th. Best qualifying: 14th. Teams: driver, Team Gunston
F1 ZA wins: 1966 East London, Killarney, 1967 Killarney

Christophe Tinseau

F. Born: 18.12.1969, Nouan-le-Fuzelier, near Orleans

formula	years	starts (DNS)	wins	2nd	3rd	4th	5th	6th	PP	FL	points
Le Mans	1998-2002	5	-	-	-	-	-	-	-	-	

SRWC win: 1 – 1999 Brno

formula	years	starts (DNS)	wins	2nd	3rd	4th	5th	6th	PP	FL	points
F3000 INT	1995-96	18	1	-	1	1	-	3	-	-	19

Win: 1996 Hockenheim. Best championship: 1996, 6th

Desmond Titterington

GB. Born: 1.5.1928, Cultra, County Down, Northern Ireland. Died: 13.4.2002, Belfast

formula	years	starts (DNS)	wins	2nd	3rd	4th	5th	6th	PP	FL	points
F1 W	1956	1	-	-	-	-	-	-	-	-	0

Best result: no finishes. Best qualifying: 11th. Team: Connaught

formula	years	starts (DNS)	wins	2nd	3rd	4th	5th	6th	PP	FL	points
Le Mans	1956	1	-	-	-	-	-	-	-	-	
SC W	1953-56		-	-	1	1	-	-	-	-	

Jerry Titus

USA. Born: 24.10.1928, Johnson City, New York State. Died: 5.8.1970, Milwaukee, following an accident at Elkhart Lake in July
1967 Trans-Am Champion

formula	years	starts (DNS)	wins	2nd	3rd	4th	5th	6th	PP	FL	points
SC W	1963-69		-	-	1	1	1	-	-	-	

Enrico Toccacelo

I. Born: 14.2.1978, Rome

formula	years	starts (DNS)	wins	2nd	3rd	4th	5th	6th	PP	FL	points
F3000 INT	2001-02	16	1	-	-	-	4	-	-		14

Win: 2002 Hungaroring. Best championship: 2002, 9th

Alejandro de Tomaso

RA. Born: 10.7.1928, Buenos Aires

formula	years	starts (DNS)	wins	2nd	3rd	4th	5th	6th	PP	FL	points
F1 W	1957-59	2	-	-	-	-	-	-	-	-	0

Best result: 9th. Best qualifying: 12th. Teams: Scuderia Centro Sud, OSCA

formula	years	starts (DNS)	wins	2nd	3rd	4th	5th	6th	PP	FL	points
Le Mans	1958-59	2	-	-	-	-	-	-	-	-	
SC W	1955-59		-	-	-	1	-	1	-	-	

Allan Tomlinson

AUS

Major win: 1939 Australian GP

Barrie Tomlinson

NZ. Born: 3.5.1959, Kaitala
2002 New Zealand Touring Car Champion

Charles de Tornaco

B. Born: 7.6.1927, Brussels. Died: 18.9.1953, Modena GP, practice

formula	years	starts (DNS)	wins	2nd	3rd	4th	5th	6th	PP	FL	points
F1 W	1952-53	2 (2)	-	-	-	-	-	-	-	-	0

Best result: 7th. Best qualifying: 13th. Team: Ecurie Francorchamps

formula	years	starts (DNS)	wins	2nd	3rd	4th	5th	6th	PP	FL	points
Le Mans	1953	1	-	-	-	-	-	-	-	-	

Francisco "Paco" Torredemer

E
1974 Spanish Touring Car Champion

formula	years	starts (DNS)	wins	2nd	3rd	4th	5th	6th	PP	FL	points
Le Mans	1972-74	3	-	-	-	-	-	1	-	-	
SC W	1972-74		-	-	-	-	-	1	-	-	

Paul Tracy

CDN. Born: 17.12.1968, Scarborough, Ontario
1990 American Racing Series Champion

formula	years	starts (DNS)	wins	2nd	3rd	4th	5th	6th	PP	FL	points
Indy 500	1992-2002	5	-	1	-	-	-	-	-	-	
CART	1991-2002	191 (3)	19	13	16	10	7	5	13	10	

Wins: 1993 Long Beach, Cleveland, Toronto, Elkhart Lake, Laguna Seca, 1994 Detroit, Nazareth, Laguna Seca, 1995 Surfers Paradise, Milwaukee, 1997 Nazareth, Rio de Janeiro, St Louis, 1999 Milwaukee, Houston, 2000 Long Beach, Elkhart Lake, Vancouver, 2002 Milwaukee. Best championships: 1993, 1994 and 1999, 3rd

formula	years	starts (DNS)	wins	2nd	3rd	4th	5th	6th	PP	FL	points
IRL	2002	1	-	1	-	-	-	-	-	-	

Bengt Tragardh

S
1981 Swedish F3 Champion

Juan Maria Traverso

RA. Born: 28.12.1950, Ramallo, Buenos Aires
1986, 1988, 1990, 1991, 1992, 1993 and 1995 TC2000 Argentinian Touring Car Champion

formula	years	starts (DNS)	wins	2nd	3rd	4th	5th	6th	PP	FL	points
F2 E	1979	11	-	-	-	1	-	-	-	-	3

Best championship: 1979, 18th

Benoit Treluyer

F. Born: 7.12.1976, Elene, Orne
2001 Japanese F3 Champion

formula	years	starts (DNS)	wins	2nd	3rd	4th	5th	6th	PP	FL	points
Le Mans	2002	1	-	-	-	-	-	-	-	-	

Major win: 1999 Pau

Jean Tremoulet

F. Born: 1909. Died: 13.10.1944, Sagelat, motorcycle accident while on a mission for the French resistance

formula	years	starts (DNS)	wins	2nd	3rd	4th	5th	6th	PP	FL	points
GP Pre-50	1937	1	-	-	-	-	-	-	1	-	
Le Mans	1937-39	3	1	-	-	-	-	-	-	-	

Win: 1938 Le Mans 24 hrs

Tony Trimmer

GB. Born: 24.1.1943, Maidenhead, Berkshire
1977 and 1978 British F1 Champion, 1970 Shell British F3 Champion

formula	years	starts (DNS)	wins	2nd	3rd	4th	5th	6th	PP	FL	points
F1 W	1975-78	0 (6)	-	-	-	-	-	-	-	-	0

Best result: no starts. Best qualifying: 26th. Teams: Maki, Melchester Racing

formula	years	starts (DNS)	wins	2nd	3rd	4th	5th	6th	PP	FL	points
Le Mans	1979-81	2									
F2 E	1978	0 (1)	-	-	-	-	-	-	-	-	0

F1 GB wins: 1978 Oulton Park Gold Cup, Brands Hatch, Snetterton, Thruxton, Brands Hatch, 1982 Oulton Park Gold Cup
Other major win: 1970 Monaco F3

Maurice Trintignant

F. Born: 30.10.1917, Ste Cecile-les-Vignes

formula	years	starts (DNS)	wins	2nd	3rd	4th	5th	6th	PP	FL	points
F1 W	1950-64	82 (2)	2	3	5	4	8	3	-	1	72.33

Wins: 1955 Monaco GP, 1958 Monaco GP. Best championships: 1954 and 1955, 4th. Best qualifying: 3rd. Teams: Gordini, Louis Rosier, Ferrari, Vanwall, Bugatti, Rob Walker, Scuderia Centro Sud, BRM, Aston Martin, Scuderia Serenissima, Reg Parnell, driver

formula	years	starts (DNS)	wins	2nd	3rd	4th	5th	6th	PP	FL	points
GP Pre-50	1947-49	5	-	-	-	1	1	-	-	-	
Le Mans	1950-65	15	1	1	1	-	-	-	1	-	

Win: 1954 Le Mans 24 hrs

formula	years	starts (DNS)	wins	2nd	3rd	4th	5th	6th	PP	FL	points
SC W	1953-65		3	1	1	4	-	2	-	-	

Wins: 1954 Le Mans 24 hrs, Tourist Trophy scratch, 1956 Swedish GP
Non-championship F1 wins: 1951 Albi, 1954 Rouen, Caen, 1962 Pau

Count Wolfgang von Trips

D. Born: 4.5.1928, Horrem, near Cologne. Died: 10.9.1961, Monza, Italian GP

formula	years	starts (DNS)	wins	2nd	3rd	4th	5th	6th	PP	FL	points
F1 W	1956-61	27 (2)	2	2	2	3	4	3	1	-	56

Wins: 1961 Dutch GP, British GP. Best championship: 1961, 2nd. Best qualifying: 1st. Teams: Ferrari, Porsche, Scuderia Centro Sud

formula	years	starts (DNS)	wins	2nd	3rd	4th	5th	6th	PP	FL	points
Le Mans	1956-61	5	-	-	-	-	-	1	-	-	
SC W	1955-61		1	7	7	1	-	1	2	1	

Win: 1961 Targa Florio

Per-Olof "Picko" Troberg

S. Born: 1.1.1938, Sundsvall
1965 Swedish F3 Champion

formula	years	starts (DNS)	wins	2nd	3rd	4th	5th	6th	PP	FL	points
F2 E	1968	0 (1)	-	-	-	-	-	-	-	-	0

Michel Trolle
F. Born: 23.6.1959, Lens

formula	years	starts (DNS)	wins	2nd	3rd	4th	5th	6th	PP	FL	points
Le Mans	1986-91	5	-	-	-	-	-	-	-	-	
F3000 INT	1987-88	17 (1)	1	1	3	-	1	1	-	2	25.5

Win: 1987 Spa. Best championship: 1987, 6th

Count Carlo Felice Trossi
I. Born: 27.4.1908, Biella. Died: 9.5.1949, Milan, cancer

formula	years	starts (DNS)	wins	2nd	3rd	4th	5th	6th	PP	FL	points
GP Pre-50	1933-48	17 (1)	2	-	4	1	1	-	1	2	

Win: 1947 Italian GP, 1948 Swiss GP

Igor Troubetskoy
I. Also raced as "Prince Igor"

formula	years	starts (DNS)	wins	2nd	3rd	4th	5th	6th	PP	FL	points
GP Pre-50	1948	2	-	-	-	-	-	-	-	-	

Major win: 1948 Targa Florio

Vincenzo Trucco
I. Born: n/a. Died: 19??

formula	years	starts (DNS)	wins	2nd	3rd	4th	5th	6th	PP	FL	points
Indy 500	1913	1	-	-	-	-	-	-	-	-	

Major win: 1908 Targa Florio

Carlo Truci
I

1970 European Touring Car Champion (1600cc class)

Duilio Truffo
I

formula	years	starts (DNS)	wins	2nd	3rd	4th	5th	6th	PP	FL	points
Le Mans	1981	1	-	-	-	-	-	-	-	-	
SC W	1972-83		-	-	-	1	1	-	-	-	
F2 E	1974-75	17 (1)	-	-	-	4	3	1	1		12

Best championship: 1975, 10th

Jarno Trulli
I. Born: 13.7.1974, Pescara

1996 German F3 Champion

formula	years	starts (DNS)	wins	2nd	3rd	4th	5th	6th	PP	FL	points
F1 W	1997-2002	95 (2)	-	1	-	6	4	6	-	-	38

Best championship: 2001, 7th. Best qualifying: 2nd. Teams: Minardi, Prost, Jordan, Renault

Esteban Tuero
RA. Born: 22.4.1978, Buenos Aires

formula	years	starts (DNS)	wins	2nd	3rd	4th	5th	6th	PP	FL	points
F1 W	1998	16	-	-	-	-	-	-	-	-	0

Best result: 8th. Best qualifying: 17th. Team: Minardi

F3000 INT	1996	6	-	-	-	-	-	-	-	-	0

Bob Tullius
USA. Born: 7.12.1936, Rochester, New York State

1977 and 1978 Trans-Am Class 1 Champion

formula	years	starts (DNS)	wins	2nd	3rd	4th	5th	6th	PP	FL	points
Le Mans	1964-85	4	-	-	-	-	-	-	-	-	
SC W	1963-88		-	1	-	1	-	-	-	-	

Guy Tunmer
ZA. Born: 1.12.1948, Ficksburg, Transvaal. Died: 22.6.1999, Sandton, near Johannesburg, road accident injuries

formula	years	starts (DNS)	wins	2nd	3rd	4th	5th	6th	PP	FL	points
F1 W	1975	1	-	-	-	-	-	-	-	-	0

Best result: 11th. Best qualifying: 25th. Team: Team Gunston

SC W	1974-75		-	-	-	1	-	-	-	-	

F1 ZA win: 1975 Killarney

Cosimo Turizio
I

formula	years	starts (DNS)	wins	2nd	3rd	4th	5th	6th	PP	FL	points
F2 E	1973-76	13 (5)	-	-	-	-	1	-	-		1

Best championship: 1974, 22nd

Curtis Turner
USA. Born: 12.4.1924, Floyd, Virginia. Died: 4.10.1970, Punxsutawney, Pennsylvania, aircraft accident

NASCAR wins: 17

U

Davide Uboldi
I. Born: 5.4.1973, Saronno

2000 Italian F3 Champion

Sebastien Ugeux
B. Born: 29.9.1970, Lasne

1998 and 2000 Belgian Procar Touring Car Champion

Mikhail Ukhov
R. Born: 22.7.1958, Moscow

2000 Russian Touring Car Champion

Anton "Toni" Ulmen
D. Born: 25.1.1906, Dusseldorf. Died: 4.11.1976, Dusseldorf

formula	years	starts (DNS)	wins	2nd	3rd	4th	5th	6th	PP	FL	points
F1 W	1952	2	-	-	-	-	-	-	-	-	0

Best result: no finishes. Best qualifying: 16th. Team: driver

SC W	1953		-	-	1	-	-	-	-	-	

Bernard Unett
GB. Born: c1936. Died: ??.1.2000, cancer

1974, 1976 and 1977 British Touring Car Champion

Al Unser Sr
USA. Born: 29.5.1939, Albuquerque, New Mexico

1970 Champcar Champion, 1983 and 1985 CART Champion, 1978 IROC Champion

formula	years	starts (DNS)	wins	2nd	3rd	4th	5th	6th	PP	FL	points
Indy 500	1965-93	27	4	3	4	1	1	-	1	-	

Wins: 1970, 1971, 1978 and 1987 Indianapolis 500

Pre-CART Champcar wins: 35 – 1965 Pikes Peak, 1968 Nazareth, Indianapolis Raceway Park race 1, Indianapolis Raceway Park race 2, Langhorne race 2, Langhorne race 3, 1969 Milwaukee race 2, Du Quoin, Sacramento, Seattle race 2, Phoenix race 2, 1970 Phoenix race 1, Indianapolis 500, Indianapolis Raceway Park, Springfield, Milwaukee race 2, Du Quoin, Indiana State Fairgrounds, Sedalia, Trenton race 2, Sacramento, 1971 Rafaela race 1, Rafaela race 2, Phoenix race 1, Indianapolis 500, Milwaukee race 1, 1973 Texas, 1974 Michigan, 1976 Pocono 500, Milwaukee, Phoenix, 1977 California 500, 1978 Indianapolis 500, Pocono 500, California 500

CART	1979-93	113 (2)	4	10	13	10	9	4	4	-	

Wins: 1979 Phoenix, 1983 Cleveland, 1985 Phoenix, 1987 Indianapolis 500.

Best championships: 1983 and 1985, 1st

Other major win: 1985 Daytona 24 hrs

Al Unser Jr
USA. Born: 19.4.1962, Albuquerque, New Mexico

1990 and 1994 CART Champion, 1982 Can-Am Champion, 1986 and 1988 IROC Champion, 1981 SCCA Super Vee Champion

formula	years	starts (DNS)	wins	2nd	3rd	4th	5th	6th	PP	FL	points
Indy 500	1983-2002	15	2	1	-	3	1	-	1	-	

Wins: 1992 and 1994 Indianapolis 500

CART	1982-99	273 (2)	31	28	21	30	17	13	7	6	

Wins: 1984 Portland, 1985 Meadowlands, Cleveland, 1986 Miami, 1988 Long Beach, Toronto, Meadowlands, Miami, 1989 Long Beach, 1990 Long Beach,

Milwaukee, Toronto, Michigan 500, Denver, Vancouver, 1991 Long Beach, Denver, 1992 Indianapolis 500, 1993 Vancouver, 1994 Long Beach, Indianapolis 500, Milwaukee, Portland, Cleveland, Mid-Ohio, New Hampshire, Vancouver, 1995 Long Beach, Portland, Mid-Ohio, Vancouver. Best championships: 1990 and 1994, 1st

formula	years	starts (DNS)	wins	2nd	3rd	4th	5th	6th	PP	FL	points
IRL	2000-02	35	2	2	3	1	2	4	-	-	

Wins: 2000 Las Vegas, 2001 St Louis. Best championships: 2001 and 2002, 7th
Other major wins: 1986 and 1987 Daytona 24 hrs

Bobby Unser
USA. Born: 20.2.1934, Colorado Springs, Colorado
1968 and 1974 Champcar Champion, 1975 IROC Champion

formula	years	starts (DNS)	wins	2nd	3rd	4th	5th	6th	PP	FL	points
F1 W	1968	1 (1)	-	-	-	-	-	-	-	-	0

Best result: no finishes. Best qualifying: 19th. Team: BRM

| Indy 500 | 1963-81 | 19 | 3 | 1 | 1 | - | 1 | 1 | 2 | - | |

Wins: 1968, 1975 and 1981 Indianapolis 500
Pre-CART Champcar wins: 25 (24 plus 1 non-championship USAC race in 1981)
– 1966 Pikes Peak, 1967 Mosport Park race 1, Mosport Park race 2, 1968 Stardust, Phoenix race 1, Trenton race 1, Indianapolis 500, Pikes Peak, 1969 Langhorne, 1970 Langhorne, 1971 Milwaukee race 2, Trenton race 2, 1972 Phoenix race 1, Milwaukee race 1, Trenton race 2, Phoenix race 2, 1973 Milwaukee, 1974 California 500, Trenton race 1, Michigan, Trenton race 3, 1975 Indianapolis 500, 1976 Phoenix, California 500, 1981 Indianapolis 500 (non-championship)

| CART | 1979-81 | 36 (1) | 10 | 7 | 3 | 1 | 2 | 1 | 14 | - | |

Wins: 1979 Trenton race 1, Trenton race 2, Michigan race 2, Watkins Glen, California 500, Michigan race 3, 1980 Milwaukee, Pocono 500, Watkins Glen, California 500. Best championship: 1979 and 1980, 2nd

Louis Unser
USA
Champcar wins: 2 – 1947 Pikes Peak, 1953 Pikes Peak

Jeff Uren
GB. Born: 17.10.1925
1959 British Touring Car Champion

Alberto Uria
ROU. Born: 11.7.1924, Montevideo. Died: 4.12.1988, Montevideo

formula	years	starts (DNS)	wins	2nd	3rd	4th	5th	6th	PP	FL	points
F1 W	1955-56	2	-	-	-	-	1	-	-	-	0

Best qualifying: 21st. Team: driver

John A Utsman
USA
NASCAR wins: 1 (in Modern era)

V

Nino Vaccarella
I. Born: 4.3.1933, Palermo, Sicily

formula	years	starts (DNS)	wins	2nd	3rd	4th	5th	6th	PP	FL	points
F1 W	1961-65	4 (1)	-	-	-	-	-	-	-	-	0

Best result: 9th. Best qualifying: 14th. Team: Scuderia Serenissima, Scuderia Venezia, Ferrari

| Le Mans | 1961-72 | 11 | 1 | - | 1 | 1 | - | - | | |

Win: 1964 Le Mans 24 hrs

| SC W | 1958-72 | | 5 | 4 | 5 | 5 | 5 | - | 3 | 1 | |

Wins: 1964 Nurburgring, Le Mans 24 hrs, 1965 Targa Florio, 1970 Sebring 12 hrs, 1971 Targa Florio
Other major win: 1975 Targa Florio

Ira Vail
USA. Born: 22.11.1893, Montreal (CDN). Died: 21.4.1979, Daytona Beach, Florida

formula	years	starts (DNS)	wins	2nd	3rd	4th	5th	6th	PP	FL	points
GP Pre-50	1916	1	-	-	-	-	-	-		
Indy 500	1919-27	7	-	-	-	-	-	-		

Champcar win: 1 – 1917 Minneapolis race 2

Colin Vandervell
GB
1973 Yellow Pages British Formula Atlantic Champion

formula	years	starts (DNS)	wins	2nd	3rd	4th	5th	6th	PP	FL	points
F2 E	1973	9 (1)	-	1	-	-	1	1	-	-	12

Best championship: 1973, 9th

Wes Vandervoort
USA
Champcar win: 1 – 1967 Pikes Peak

Albert Vanierschot
B
1994, 1995 (both with Paul Kumpen and Georges Cremer) and 2000 (with Bert Longin) Belgian Belcar GT Champion

Christian Vann
GB. Born: 5.8.1974, Birmingham

formula	years	starts (DNS)	wins	2nd	3rd	4th	5th	6th	PP	FL	points
Le Mans	1999	1	-	-	-	-	-	-		

SRWC win: 1 – 2001 Monza

Achille Varzi
I. Born: 8.8.1904, Galliante, near Milan. Died: 30.6.1948, Bremgarten, Swiss GP practice

formula	years	starts (DNS)	wins	2nd	3rd	4th	5th	6th	PP	FL	points
GP Pre-50	1928-48	39 (2)	5	8	3	3	3	2	3	7	

Wins: 1929 Monza GP, 1930 Monza GP, Spanish GP, 1931 French GP, 1933 Monaco GP

| Le Mans | 1931 | 1 | - | - | - | - | - | - | | |

Other major wins: 1930 and 1934 Targa Florio, 1930 and 1935 Coppa Acerbo (Pescara), 1931, 1932 and 1935 Tunis, 1933, 1934 and 1936 Tripoli, 1933 Avus, 1934 Mille Miglia

Jimmy Vasser
USA. Born: 20.11.1965, Canoga Park, California
1996 CART Champion

formula	years	starts (DNS)	wins	2nd	3rd	4th	5th	6th	PP	FL	points
Indy 500	1992-2002	7	-	-	2	-	-	-		
CART	1992-2002	186 (2)	10	8	11	11	14	9	8	8	

Wins: 1996 Miami, Surfers Paradise, Long Beach, US 500 (Michigan), 1997 Laguna Seca, 1998 Nazareth, Milwaukee, California Speedway, 2000 Houston, 2002 California Speedway (fastest race of all time). Best championship: 1996, 1st

| IRL | 2000-02 | 4 | - | - | - | 1 | - | - | | |

Ole Vejlund
DK
1966 Danish F3 Champion

Fermin Velez
E. Born: 3.4.1959, Barcelona
1987 (with Gordon Spice) and 1989 (with Nick Adams) World Group C2 Sports Car Champion, 1995 IMSA WSC Champion

formula	years	starts (DNS)	wins	2nd	3rd	4th	5th	6th	PP	FL	points
Le Mans	1986-98	6	-	-	-	1	-	1	-		
SC W	1986-92		-	-	2	3	1	2	-	-	

Best championship: 1987, 10th

F3000 INT	1988	4 (4)	-	-	-	-	-	-	-	-	0
Indy 500	1996-97	2	-	-	-	-	-	-		
IRL	1996-97	6	-	-	-	-	-	-		

Major wins: 1995 and 1997 Sebring 12 hrs

Jozef Venc

CS. Born: 6.5.1966, Havlickuv
1997 and 1998 Central European Touring Car Champion

Tim Verbergt

B
1998 and 1999 Belgian Belcar Touring Car Champion (both with Jean-Francois Hemroulle)

Philippe Verellen

B. Born: 25.5.1962, Anvers
1991 and 1993 Belgian Procar Touring Car Champion

formula	years	starts (DNS)	wins	2nd	3rd	4th	5th	6th	PP	FL	points
Le Mans	1993-2000	2	-	-	-	-	-	-	-	-	

Guy Verheyen

B. Born: 6.12.1967
1991 Belgian Belcar GT Champion (with Erik Bruynoghe and Meirschaut)

Frans Verschuur

NL. Born: 15.1.1954, Nijmegen
1996 Dutch Touring Car Champion

Jos Verstappen

NL. Born: 4.3.1972, Montfort (F)
1993 German F3 Champion

formula	years	starts (DNS)	wins	2nd	3rd	4th	5th	6th	PP	FL	points
F1 W	1994-2001	91	-	-	2	1	2	2	-	-	17

Best championship: 1994, 10th. Best qualifying: 6th. Teams: Benetton, Simtek, Arrows, Tyrrell, Stewart
Major win: 1993 Marlboro Masters (Zandvoort)

Pierre Veyron

F. Born: 1903, Lozere. Died: 3.10.1970, Cap d'Eze

formula	years	starts (DNS)	wins	2nd	3rd	4th	5th	6th	PP	FL	points
GP Pre-50	1934-48	3	-	-	-	-	-	1	-	-	
Le Mans	1934-53	9	1	-	-	-	-	-	-	-	

Win: 1939 Le Mans 24 hrs

Anders Vilarino Jr

E. Born: 6.12.1979
2001 Spanish F3 Champion

Juan Ignacio Villacieros

E
1992 Spanish Touring Car Champion

Luis Villamil

E. Born: 21.6.1955, Madrid
1988 and 1995 Spanish Touring Car Champion

Gilles Villeneuve

CDN. Born: 18.1.1950, St Jean-sur-Richelieu, Quebec. Died: 8.5.1982, Leuvern Hospital, following accident during practice for Belgian GP at Zolder
1976 and 1977 North American Formula Atlantic Champion

formula	years	starts (DNS)	wins	2nd	3rd	4th	5th	6th	PP	FL	points
F1 W	1977-82	67 (1)	6	5	2	2	3	3	2	8	107

Wins: 1978 Canadian GP, 1979 South African GP, Long Beach GP, United States GP, 1981 Monaco GP, Spanish GP. Best championship: 1979, 2nd. Best qualifying: 1st. Teams: McLaren, Ferrari

SC W	1977		-	1	-	-	-	-	-	-	
F2 E	1976	1	-	-	-	-	-	-	-	-	0

Non-championship F1 win: 1979 Race of Champions (Brands Hatch)

Jacques Villeneuve Sr

CDN. Born: 4.11.1953, St Jean-sur-Richelieu, Quebec
1983 Can-Am Champion, 1980 and 1981 North American Formula Atlantic Champion

formula	years	starts (DNS)	wins	2nd	3rd	4th	5th	6th	PP	FL	points
F1 W	1981-83	0 (3)	-	-	-	-	-	-	-	-	0

Best result: no starts. Best qualifying: 27th. Teams: Arrows, RAM

Le Mans	1983	1	-	-	-	-	-	-	-	-	
F3000 INT	1987	0 (1)	-	-	-	-	-	-	-	-	0
Indy 500	1986	1	-	-	-	-	-	-	-	-	
CART	1982-92	36 (1)	1	-	1	1	2	3	1	-	

Win: 1985 Elkhart Lake. Best championship: 1985, 8th

Jacques Villeneuve Jr

CDN. Born: 9.4.1971, St Jean-sur-Richelieu, Quebec
1997 F1 World Champion, 1995 CART Champion

formula	years	starts (DNS)	wins	2nd	3rd	4th	5th	6th	PP	FL	points
F1 W	1996-2002	116	11	5	7	9	6	6	13	9	213

Wins: 1996 European GP, British GP, Hungarian GP, Portuguese GP, 1997 Brazilian GP, Argentinian GP, Spanish GP, British GP, Hungarian GP, Austrian GP, Luxembourg GP. Best championship: 1997, 1st. Best qualifying: 1st. Teams: Williams, BAR

Indy 500	1994-95	2	-	1	1	-	-	-	-	-	

Win: 1995 Indianapolis 500

CART	1994-95	32 (1)	5	2	3	2	1	2	6	1	

Wins: 1994 Elkhart Lake, 1995 Miami, Indianapolis 500, Elkhart Lake, Cleveland. Best championship: 1995, 1st

Giniel de Villiers

ZA. Born: 25.3.1972, Robertson
1997, 1998, 1999 and 2000 South African Touring Car Champion

Luigi Villoresi

I. Born: 16.5.1909, Milan. Died: 24.8.1997, Modena

formula	years	starts (DNS)	wins	2nd	3rd	4th	5th	6th	PP	FL	points
F1 W	1950-56	31 (3)	-	2	6	2	3	4	-	1	49

Best championships: 1951 and 1953, 5th. Best qualifying: 2nd. Teams: Ferrari, Maserati, Lancia, Scuderia Centro Sud, Luigi Piotti

GP Pre-50	1938-49	16	1	3	1	-	1	1	3	2	

Win: 1948 British GP

Le Mans	1952-53	2	-	-	-	-	-	-	-	-	
Indy 500	1946	1	-	-	-	-	-	-	-	-	

Non-championship F1 wins: 1951 Syracuse, Pau, 1952 Valentino, Boreham Other major wins: 1939 and 1940 Targa Florio, 1939 South African GP, 1949 Zandvoort GP, 1951 Mille Miglia

Emilio de Villota

E. Born: 26.7.1946, Madrid
1980 British F1 Champion, 1983 Spanish Touring Car Champion

formula	years	starts (DNS)	wins	2nd	3rd	4th	5th	6th	PP	FL	points
F1 W	1976-82	2 (13)	-	-	-	-	-	-	-	-	0

Best result: 13th. Best qualifying: 23rd. Teams: RAM, driver, Onyx

Le Mans	1981-86	3	-	-	-	1	-	-	-	-	
SC W	1981-92		2	-	1	1	1	-	-	1	

Wins: 1981 Enna, Brands Hatch. Best championship: 1986, 14th

F2 E	1983	2	-	-	-	-	-	-	-	-	0

F1 GB wins: 1979 Thruxton, Zandvoort, Oulton Park, Nogaro, 1980 Mallory Park, Monza, Mallory Park, Brands Hatch, Silverstone

Giorgio Vinella

I. Born: 22.8.1973, Putignano, Bari
1999 Italian F3000 Champion

formula	years	starts (DNS)	wins	2nd	3rd	4th	5th	6th	PP	FL	points
F3000 INT	1998	7 (4)	-	-	-	-	-	-	-	-	0

Alfonso de Vinuesa

E. Born: 30.12.1960, Madrid

formula	years	starts (DNS)	wins	2nd	3rd	4th	5th	6th	PP	FL	points
F3000 INT	1986-88	5 (9)	-	-	-	-	-	1	-	-	1

Best championship: 1987, 19th

Winni Vogt
D
1987 European Touring Car Champion

Gunnar Volmer
BR
1989 Brazilian Touring Car Champion (with Antonio da Matta)

Ottorino Volonterio
CH. Born: 7.12.1917, Orselina

formula	years	starts (DNS)	wins	2nd	3rd	4th	5th	6th	PP	FL	points
F1 W	1954-57	3	-	-	-	-	-	-	-	-	0

Best result: 11th. Best qualifying: 20th. Teams: Emanuel de Graffenried, driver

Joseph Vonlanthen
CH. Born: 31.5.1942, St Ursen

formula	years	starts (DNS)	wins	2nd	3rd	4th	5th	6th	PP	FL	points
F1 W	1975	1	-	-	-	-	-	-	-	-	0

Best result: no finishes. Best qualifying: 29th. Team: Williams

| F2 E | 1973-76 | 26 (6) | - | 1 | 1 | - | - | - | - | - | 10 |

Best championship: 1975, 17th

Earl de Vore
USA. Born: n/a. Died: 12.11.1928, lost at sea aboard the SS Vestris

formula	years	starts (DNS)	wins	2nd	3rd	4th	5th	6th	PP	FL	points
Indy 500	1925-28	3	-	1	-	-	-	-	-	-	

Champcar win: 1 – 1926 Charlotte race 1

Duncan Vos
ZA. Born: 30.11.1960, Johannesburg
1993 South African Formula GTi Champion

Vincent Vosse
B. Born: 5.1.1972, Verviers, near Spa

formula	years	starts (DNS)	wins	2nd	3rd	4th	5th	6th	PP	FL	points
Le Mans	1999-2002	3	-	-	-	-	-	-	-	-	

GT FIA wins: 2 – 2000 Hungaroring, 2002 Spa 24 hrs

Bill Vukovich (William Vucerovich)
USA. Born: 13.12.1918, Alameda, California. Died: 30.5.1955, Indianapolis 500

formula	years	starts (DNS)	wins	2nd	3rd	4th	5th	6th	PP	FL	points
Indy 500	1951-55	5	2	-	-	-	-	-	1	3	

Wins: 1953 and 1954 Indianapolis 500

Champcar wins: 4 – 1952 Detroit, Denver, 1953 Indianapolis 500, 1954 Indianapolis 500

Bill Vukovich Jr
USA. Born: 29.3.1944, Fresno, California

formula	years	starts (DNS)	wins	2nd	3rd	4th	5th	6th	PP	FL	points
Indy 500	1968-80	12	-	1	1	-	1	1	-	-	

Pre-CART Champcar win: 1 – 1973 Michigan race 1

| CART | 1979-82 | 13 (1) | - | - | - | - | - | - | - | - | |

Syd van der Vyver
ZA
1960 and 1961 South African Drivers' Champion

W

Fred Wacker
USA. Born: 10.7.1918, Chicago, Illinois. Died: 16.6.1998, Lake Buff, Illinois

formula	years	starts (DNS)	wins	2nd	3rd	4th	5th	6th	PP	FL	points
F1 W	1953-54	3 (2)	-	-	-	-	-	1	-	-	0

Best qualifying: 15th. Team: Gordini

| Le Mans | 1951-53 | 2 | - | - | - | - | - | - | - | - | |

Takao Wada
J. Born: 24.6.1953, Tokyo
1986 Japanese Touring Car Champion (with Aguri Suzuki)

formula	years	starts (DNS)	wins	2nd	3rd	4th	5th	6th	PP	FL	points
Le Mans	1986-90	5	-	-	-	-	-	-	-	-	
SC W	1983-92		-	-	-	-	1	-	1	-	

Billy Wade
USA. Born: c1930, Texas. Born: 5.1.1965, Daytona, testing
NASCAR wins: 4

Cort Wagner
USA. Born: 28.1.1966, Los Angeles, California
1999 American Le Mans Series GT Champion

formula	years	starts (DNS)	wins	2nd	3rd	4th	5th	6th	PP	FL	points
Le Mans	2000-02	3	-	-	-	-	-	-	-	-	

Louis Wagner
F. Born: 5.2.1882, Pre-St-Gervais. Died: 13.3.1960, Montlhery

formula	years	starts (DNS)	wins	2nd	3rd	4th	5th	6th	PP	FL	points
GP Pre-50	1906-27	18	-	2	4	2	2	-	-	1	

Wins: 1908 American GP, 1926 British GP

| Le Mans | 1925-26 | 2 | - | - | - | - | 1 | - | - | - | |
| Indy 500 | 1919 | 1 | - | - | - | - | - | - | - | - | |

Other major win: 1906 WK Vanderbilt Cup

Arthur Waite
GB
Major win: 1928 Australian GP

Juichi Wakisaka
J. Born: 29.7.1972, Nara
2002 Japanese GT Champion (with Akira Iida), 1996 Japanese F3 Champion

Fabrice Walfrisch
F. Born: 22.2.1970, Paris

formula	years	starts (DNS)	wins	2nd	3rd	4th	5th	6th	PP	FL	points
F3000 INT	1998-2000	25 (5)	-	-	1	-	-	1	-	4	

Best championship: 1999, 13th

Alistair Walker
GB

formula	years	starts (DNS)	wins	2nd	3rd	4th	5th	6th	PP	FL	points
Le Mans	1970	1	-	-	-	-	1	-	-	-	
SC W	1970		-	-	-	-	1	-	-	-	
F2 E	1968-71	11 (6)	-	-	-	-	1	-	-	6	

Best championship: 1970, 11th

Dave Walker
AUS. Born: 10.6.1941, Sydney, New South Wales
1970 Lombank and 1971 Shell British F3 Champion

formula	years	starts (DNS)	wins	2nd	3rd	4th	5th	6th	PP	FL	points
F1 W	1971-72	11	-	-	-	-	-	-	-	-	0

Best result: 9th. Best qualifying: 12th. Team: Lotus

| F2 E | 1973-74 | 2 (1) | - | - | - | - | - | - | - | - | 0 |

Major win: 1971 Monaco F3

Johnnie Walker
AUS
1979 Australian F5000 Champion
Tasman wins: 2 – 1974 Levin, 1975 Surfers Paradise
Other major win: 1979 Australian GP

Mike Walker
GB. Born: 18.12.1945, Birmingham

formula	years	starts (DNS)	wins	2nd	3rd	4th	5th	6th	PP	FL	points
F2 E	1967-68	2 (2)	-	-	-	-	-	-	-	-	0

Peter Walker

GB. Born: 7.10.1912, Leeds, Yorkshire. Died: 1.3.1984, Newtown, Worcestershire

formula	years	starts (DNS)	wins	2nd	3rd	4th	5th	6th	PP	FL	points
F1 W	1950-55	4	-	-	-	-	-	-	-	-	0

Best result: 7th. Best qualifying: 10th. Teams: driver, BRM, Stirling Moss, Rob Walker

GP Pre-50	1936-49	3	-	-	1	-	-	-	-	-	
Le Mans	1951-56	6	1	1	-	-	-	-	-	-	

Win: 1951 Le Mans 24 hrs

SC W	1953-56		-	1	1	1	-	-	-	-	1

Tom Walkinshaw

GB. Born: 14.8.1946, Mauldslie, Scotland
1984 European Touring Car Champion

formula	years	starts (DNS)	wins	2nd	3rd	4th	5th	6th	PP	FL	points
Le Mans	1976-82	5	-	-	-	-	-	-	-	-	
SC W	1976-82		2	1	-	1	-	1	-	-	

Wins: 1976 Silverstone, 1981 Spa 24 hrs

F2 E	1971-73	2 (3)	-	-	-	-	-	-	-	-	0

Other major wins: 1977, 1981, 1982 and 1985 Tourist Trophy (Silverstone), 1984 Spa 24 hrs, 1984 Macau Guia race

Andy Wallace

GB. Born: 19.2.1961, Oxford
1998 IMSA GT Champion (with David Brabham), 1986 British F3 Champion

formula	years	starts (DNS)	wins	2nd	3rd	4th	5th	6th	PP	FL	points
Le Mans	1988-2002	14	1	1	2	2	-	1	-	-	

Win: 1988 Le Mans 24 hrs

SC W	1985-92		2	3	1	5	3	2	-	-	

Wins: 1988 Le Mans 24 hrs, Brands Hatch. Best championship: 1990, 4th. GT FIA wins: 4 – 1995 Silverstone, Nogaro, Zhuhai, 1996 Silverstone. SRWC win: 1 – 2000 Daytona

F3000 INT	1987-88	18 (2)	-	-	-	1	1	1	-	-	4.5

Best championship: 1987, 16th

Other major wins: 1986 Cellnet Superprix (Brands Hatch), 1986 Macau, 1990, 1997 and 1999 Daytona 24 hrs, 1992 and 1993 Sebring 12 hrs, 1999 Petit LeMans

Russell "Rusty" Wallace

USA. Born: 14.8.1956, Fenton, Missouri
1989 NASCAR Champion, 1991 IROC Champion

NASCAR wins: 54 (all Modern era) including 1990 World 600

Lee Wallard

USA. Born: 8.9.1911, Schenectady, New York State. Died: 28.11.1963, St Petersburg, Florida

formula	years	starts (DNS)	wins	2nd	3rd	4th	5th	6th	PP	FL	points
Indy 500	1948-51	4	1	-	-	-	-	1	-	1	

Win: 1951 Indianapolis 500

Champcar wins: 2 – 1948 Du Quoin, 1951 Indianapolis 500

Magnus Wallinder

S. Born: 29.5.1968
2002 Swedish GTR Champion (with Henrik Roos), 1993 and 1994 Nordic F3 Champion, 1993 Swedish F3 Champion

Heini Walter

CH. Born: 28.7.1927, Ruti

formula	years	starts (DNS)	wins	2nd	3rd	4th	5th	6th	PP	FL	points
F1 W	1962	1	-	-	-	-	-	-	-	-	0

Best result: 14th. Best qualifying: 14th. Team: Ecurie Filipinetti

SC W	1956-67		-	-	-	-	2	-	-	-	

Phil "Tappett" Walters

USA. Born: 1917, New York City

formula	years	starts (DNS)	wins	2nd	3rd	4th	5th	6th	PP	FL	points
Le Mans	1950-55	6	-	-	1	-	-	-	-	-	
SC W	1953-55		2	-	1	-	-	1	-		

Wins: 1953 Sebring 12 hrs, 1955 Sebring 12 hrs

Darrell Waltrip

USA. Born: 5.2.1947, Owensboro, Kentucky
1981, 1982 and 1985 NASCAR Champion

NASCAR wins: 85 (all Modern era) including 1989 Daytona 500, 1978, 1979, 1985 and 1988 World 600

Michael Waltrip

USA. Born: 30.4.1963, Owensboro, Kentucky

NASCAR wins: 1 (in Modern era) – 2001 Daytona 500

Jeff Ward

USA. Born: 22.6.1961, Glasgow (GB)

formula	years	starts (DNS)	wins	2nd	3rd	4th	5th	6th	PP	FL	points
Indy 500	1997-2002	6	-	1	1	1	-	-	-	-	
CART	1995	0 (1)	-	-	-	-	-	-	-	-	
IRL	1997-2002	60	1	4	3	3	2	2	2	3	

Win: Texas race 1

Rodger Ward

USA. Born: 10.1.1921, Beloit, Kansas
1959 and 1962 Champcar Champion

formula	years	starts (DNS)	wins	2nd	3rd	4th	5th	6th	PP	FL	points
F1 W	1959-63	2	-	-	-	-	-	-	-	-	0

Best championship: 1959, 10th (due to result at Indy 500, did finish only GP that year). Best result: no finishes. Best qualifying: 17th. Teams: Leader Card Racers, Reg Parnell

Indy 500	1951-66	15	2	2	1	1	-	-	-	-	

Wins: 1959 and 1962 Indianapolis 500

Champcar wins: 26 – 1953 Springfield race 1, Detroit, 1957 Milwaukee race 1, Springfield, Sacramento, 1958 Milwaukee race 2, Trenton race 2, 1959 Indianapolis 500, Milwaukee race 2, Du Quoin, Indiana State Fairgrounds, 1960 Trenton race 1, Milwaukee race 1, 1961 Milwaukee race 1, Syracuse, Sacramento, 1962 Indianapolis 500, Trenton race 2, Milwaukee race 2, Syracuse, 1963 Milwaukee race 1, Springfield, Indiana State Fairgrounds, Sacramento, Phoenix, 1966 Trenton race 1

David Warnock

GB. Born: 1.2.1962, Mulfulira (ZAM)
1996 (with Rob Schirle) and 2001 (with Mike Jordan) British GT Champion

formula	years	starts (DNS)	wins	2nd	3rd	4th	5th	6th	PP	FL	points
Le Mans	1997-2002	4	-	-	-	-	-	-	-	-	

Derek Warwick

GB. Born: 27.8.1954, Alresford, Hampshire
1992 World Sports Car Champion (with Yannick Dalmas), 1978 Vandervell British F3 Champion

formula	years	starts (DNS)	wins	2nd	3rd	4th	5th	6th	PP	FL	points
F1 W	1981-93	146 (16)	-	2	2	8	9	9	-	2	71

Best championships: 1984 and 1988, 7th. Best qualifying: 3rd. Teams: Toleman, Renault, Brabham, Arrows, Lotus, Footwork

Le Mans	1983-96	5	1	-	-	1	-	-	-	-	

Win: 1992 Le Mans 24 hrs

SC W	1983-92		7	4	3	2	2	1	3	2	

Wins: 1986 Silverstone, 1991 Monza, Silverstone, Nurburgring, 1992 Silverstone, Le Mans 24 hrs, Suzuka. Best championship: 1992, 1st

F2 E	1979-80	22 (1)	1	3	3	1	1	-	4	1	44

Win: 1980 Silverstone. Best championship: 1980, 2nd

F3 E win: 1 – 1978 Donington

Other major wins: 1980 Monza F2

Paul Warwick

GB. Born: 29.1.1969, Alresford, Hampshire. Died: 21.7.1991, Oulton Park, Gold Cup
1991 British F3000 Champion

formula	years	starts (DNS)	wins	2nd	3rd	4th	5th	6th	PP	FL	points
F3000 INT	1990	3 (1)	-	-	-	-	-	-	-	-	0

Graham Watson

AUS. Born: 13.1.1948, Palmerston (NZ)
1986 Australian Formula Pacific Champion

John Watson

GB. Born: 4.5.1946, Belfast, Northern Ireland

formula	years	starts (DNS)	wins	2nd	3rd	4th	5th	6th	PP	FL	points
F1 W	1973-85	152 (2)	5	6	9	9	7	11	2	5	169

Wins: 1976 Austrian GP, 1981 British GP, 1982 Belgian GP, Detroit GP, 1983 Long Beach GP. Best championship: 1982, 2nd. Best qualifying: 1st. Teams: Brabham, John Goldie, Surtees, Lotus, Penske, McLaren

Le Mans	1973-90	7	-	-	-	-	-	-	-	-	
SC W	1972-90		4	3	2	1	1	1	-	-	

Wins: 1984 Fuji, 1987 Jarama, Monza, Fuji. Best championship: 1987, 2nd

F2 E	1969-74	23 (5)	-	1	1	-	3	1	-	-	19

Best championship: 1974, 11th

Stephen Watson

ZA. Born: 18.2.1973, Durban

formula	years	starts (DNS)	wins	2nd	3rd	4th	5th	6th	PP	FL	points
F3000 INT	1995-97	27 (1)	-	-	-	-	-	2	-	-	2

Best championship: 1997, 20th

W Watson

GB

formula	years	starts (DNS)	wins	2nd	3rd	4th	5th	6th	PP	FL	points
GP Pre-50	1912-14	2	-	-	-	-	-	-	-	-	

Major win: 1908 Tourist Trophy (Isle of Man)

Jason Watt

DK. Born: 24.2.1970, Frederiksberg
1995 European Formula Opel Champion, 2002 Danish Touring Car Champion

formula	years	starts (DNS)	wins	2nd	3rd	4th	5th	6th	PP	FL	points
F3000 INT	1997-99	31 (1)	4	5	2	3	-	1	3	-	85

Wins: 1997 Spa, 1998 Imola, 1999 Spa, Nurburgring. Best championship: 1999, 2nd

Art Watts

USA

NASCAR wins: 1

Joe Weatherly

USA. Born: 29.5.1922, Oak Grove, Virginia. Died: 19.1.1964, Riverside, Motor Trend 500
1962 and 1963 NASCAR Champion

NASCAR wins: 24

James Weaver

GB. Born: 4.3.1955, London
1996 FIA GT Champion (with Ray Bellm), 1996 European GT Champion (with Bellm), 1998, 2000 and 2001 US Grand-Am Champion

formula	years	starts (DNS)	wins	2nd	3rd	4th	5th	6th	PP	FL	points
Le Mans	1983-99	12	-	1	-	-	-	-	-	-	
SC W	1983-92		-	1	2	3	1	-	-	-	

Best championship: 1985, 19th. GT Fia wins: 4 – 1996 Paul Ricard, Jarama, Suzuka, Nogaro. SRWC win: 1 – 2000 Daytona

F3000 INT	1985-88	4 (2)	-	-	-	-	-	-	-	-	0
CART	1989	3	-	-	-	-	-	-	-	-	

F3 E wins: 3 – 1982 Donington, Nogaro, Jarama
Other major win: 1997 Daytona 24 hrs

Mark Webber

AUS. Born: 27.8.1976, Queanbeyan, New South Wales

formula	years	starts (DNS)	wins	2nd	3rd	4th	5th	6th	PP	FL	points
F1 W	2002	16 (1)	-	-	-	-	1	-	-	-	2

Best championship: 2002, 15th. Best qualifying: 18th. Team: Minardi

Le Mans	1998	1	-	-	-	-	-	-	-	-	

GT FIA wins: 5 – 1998 Silverstone, Hockenheim, Hungaroring, Suzuka, Donington

formula	years	starts (DNS)	wins	2nd	3rd	4th	5th	6th	PP	FL	points
F3000 INT	2000-01	22	4	1	2	2	-	-	2	5	60

Wins: 2000 Silverstone, 2001 Imola, Monaco, Magny-Cours. Best championship: 2001, 2nd

Volker Weidler

D. Born: 18.3.1962, Weinheim, near Mannheim
1985 German F3 Champion

formula	years	starts (DNS)	wins	2nd	3rd	4th	5th	6th	PP	FL	points
F1 W	1989	0 (10)	-	-	-	-	-	-	-	-	0

Best result: no starts. Best qualifying: 30th. Team: Rial

Le Mans	1987-92	5		1	-	-	1	-	-	-	

Win: 1991 Le Mans 24 hrs

SC W	1985-92			1	1	-	3	1	3	-	-

Win: 1991 Le Mans 24 hrs. Best championship: 1991, 16th

F3000 INT	1986-88	14 (4)	-	-	-	1	-	2	-	-	5

Best championship: 1988, 15th

Danny Weinberg

USA

NASCAR wins: 1

Richard Weiser

DDR
1950 East German F3 Champion

Bob Welborn

USA. Born: 5.5.1928, High Point, North Carolina. Died: 1997

NASCAR wins: 7

Karl Wendlinger

A. Born: 20.12.1968, Kufstein, Tirol
1999 FIA GT Champion (with Olivier Beretta), 1988 Austrian F3 Champion, 1989 German F3 Champion

formula	years	starts (DNS)	wins	2nd	3rd	4th	5th	6th	PP	FL	points
F1 W	1991-95	41 (1)	-	-	-	3	1	3	-	-	14

Best championship: 1993, 11th. Best qualifying: 5th. Teams: Leyton House, March, Sauber

Le Mans	1991-2001	8		-	-	1	1	1	-	-	
SC W	1990-92			2	3	-	-	1	-	-	

Wins: 1990 Spa, 1991 Autopolis. Best championship: 1990, 5th. GT FIA wins: 5 – 1999 Monza, Silverstone, Zolder, Oschersleben, Donington

F3000 INT	1990-91	11 (3)	-	-	1	-	2	-	-	-	8

Best championship: 1991, 11th
Other major win: 2000 Daytona 24 hrs

Karl von Wendt

D
1967 European Touring Car Champion (over 1600cc class)

formula	years	starts (DNS)	wins	2nd	3rd	4th	5th	6th	PP	FL	points
Le Mans	1968	1	-	-	-	-	-	-	-	-	
SC W	1965-70		-	-	-	1	2	1	-	-	

Ted Wentz

USA. Born: 7.11.1946, Pennsylvania
1975 Southern Organs and 1976 British Formula Atlantic Champion

formula	years	starts (DNS)	wins	2nd	3rd	4th	5th	6th	PP	FL	points
F2 E	1975-76	3	-	-	-	-	-	-	-	-	0

Heribert Werginz

A

Major win: 1980 Tourist Trophy (Silverstone)

Christian Werner

D. Born: 19.5.1892, Stuttgart. Died: 17.6.1932, Bad Cannstatt, near Stuttgart

formula	years	starts (DNS)	wins	2nd	3rd	4th	5th	6th	PP	FL	points
GP Pre-50	1904-28	5	1	1	1	-	1	-	-	1	

Win: 1928 German GP

Le Mans	1930	1	-	-	-	-	-	-	-	-	
Indy 500	1923	1	-	-	-	-	-	-	-	-	

Other major win: 1924 Targa Florio

Marco Werner

D. Born: 27.4.1966, Dortmund

formula	years	starts (DNS)	wins	2nd	3rd	4th	5th	6th	PP	FL	points
Le Mans	2002	1	-	-	1	-	-	-	-	-	

Major wins: 1992 Monaco F3, 1995 Daytona 24 hrs

Peter Westbury

GB. Born: 26.5.1938, Roehampton, London

formula	years	starts (DNS)	wins	2nd	3rd	4th	5th	6th	PP	FL	points
F1 W	1969-70	1 (1)	-	-	-	-	-	-	-	-	0

Best result: no finishes. Best qualifying: 25th. Teams: Felday Engineering, BRM

Le Mans	1972	1	-	-	-	-	-	-	-	-	
SC W	1964-72		-	-	-	-	1	-	-	-	
F2 E	1969-72	27 (3)	-	1	-	2	-	-	-	-	23

Best championship: 1969, 5th

Marcel Wettstein

CH

1981 Swiss F3 Champion

Ken Wharton

GB. Born: 21.3.1916, Smethwick, Worcestershire. Died: 12.1.1957, Ardmore (NZ)

formula	years	starts (DNS)	wins	2nd	3rd	4th	5th	6th	PP	FL	points
F1 W	1952-55	15 (1)	-	-	-	1	-	1	-	-	3

Best championship: 1952, 13th. Best qualifying: 7th. Teams: Scuderia Franera, driver, Cooper, BRM, Vanwall

Le Mans	1953-56	3	-	-	-	-	-	-	-	-	
SC W	1953-55		-	-	-	2	-	-			

CR Whitcroft

GB

Major win: 1932 Tourist Trophy (Ards)

Dave White

USA

1978 IMSA GTU Champion

Jack White

USA

NASCAR wins: 1

Mike White

ZA. Born: 2.7.1954

F3 E wins: 2 – 1980 Silverstone, 1981 Donington

Rex White

USA. Born: 17.8.1929

1960 NASCAR Champion

NASCAR wins: 26

Ted Whiteaway

GB. Born: 1.11.1928, Feltham, Middlesex

formula	years	starts (DNS)	wins	2nd	3rd	4th	5th	6th	PP	FL	points
F1 W	1955	0 (1)	-	-	-	-	-	-	-	-	0

Best result: no starts. Best qualifying: 22nd. Team: driver

Le Mans	1959	1	-	-	-	-	-	-	-	-	

Doug Whiteford

AUS

Major wins: 1950, 1952 and 1953 Australian GP

Graham Whitehead

GB. Born: 15.4.1922, Harrogate, Yorkshire. Died: 15.1.1981, Lower Basildon, Berkshire

formula	years	starts (DNS)	wins	2nd	3rd	4th	5th	6th	PP	FL	points
F1 W	1952	1	-	-	-	-	-	-	-	-	0

Best result: 12th. Best qualifying: 12th. Team: Peter Whitehead

Le Mans	1953-60	7	-	1	-	-	-	-	-	-	
SC W	1953-60		-	1	-	1	-	1	-	-	

Peter Whitehead

GB. Born: 12.11.1914, Menston, Yorkshire. Died: 20.9.1958, Lasalle, near Nimes, Tour de France Automobile

formula	years	starts (DNS)	wins	2nd	3rd	4th	5th	6th	PP	FL	points
F1 W	1950-54	10 (2)	-	-	1	-	-	-	-	-	4

Best championship: 1950, 9th. Best qualifying: 8th. Teams: driver, Graham Whitehead, GA Vandervell, Atlantic Stable

GP Pre-50	1936-49	10		1	-	2	1	-	-	1

Win: 1949 Czech GP

Le Mans	1950-58	8		1	1	-	1	-	-	-

Win: 1951 Le Mans 24 hrs

SC W	1953-58		-	1	-	1	-	2	-	-

Non-championship F1 wins: 1950 Jersey, Dundrod

Other major win: 1938 Australian GP

Bill Whitehouse

GB. Born: 1.4.1909, London. Died: 14.7.1957, Reims, F2 race

formula	years	starts (DNS)	wins	2nd	3rd	4th	5th	6th	PP	FL	points
F1 W	1954	1	-	-	-	-	-	-	-	-	0

Best result: no finishes. Best qualifying: 19th. Team: driver

Sir John Whitmore

GB. Born: 16.10.1937, near Grays, Essex

1965 European Touring Car Champion (1600cc class), 1961 British Touring Car Champion

formula	years	starts (DNS)	wins	2nd	3rd	4th	5th	6th	PP	FL	points
Le Mans	1959-66	5	-	-	-	-	-	-	-	-	
SC W	1959-66		-	2	-	1	-	-	-	-	

Bill Whittington

USA. Born: 11.9.1949, Lubbock, Texas

formula	years	starts (DNS)	wins	2nd	3rd	4th	5th	6th	PP	FL	points
Le Mans	1978-82	4	1	-	-	-	-	-	-	-	

Win: 1979 Le Mans 24 hrs

SC W	1978-85		2	-	2	1	-	-	1	2

Wins: 1979 Le Mans 24 hrs, Watkins Glen. Best championship: 1981, 16th

Indy 500	1980-85	5	-	-	-	-	-	-	-	-	
CART	1979-85	15 (3)	-	-	-	-	-	1	-	-	

Don Whittington

USA. Born: 23.1.1946, Lubbock, Texas

formula	years	starts (DNS)	wins	2nd	3rd	4th	5th	6th	PP	FL	points
Le Mans	1978-81	4	1	-	-	-	-	-	-	-	

Win: 1979 Le Mans 24 hrs

SC W	1978-85		2	-	1	-	1	-	-	

Wins: 1979 Le Mans 24 hrs, Watkins Glen

Indy 500	1980-85	5	-	-	-	-	1	-	-	-	
CART	1979-85	9 (1)	-	-	-	-	-	-	-	-	

Robin Widdows

GB. Born: 27.5.1942, Cowley, near Uxbridge, Middlesex

formula	years	starts (DNS)	wins	2nd	3rd	4th	5th	6th	PP	FL	points
F1 W	1968	1	-	-	-	-	-	-	-	-	0

Best result: no finishes. Best qualifying: 18th. Team: Cooper

Le Mans	1969	1	-	-	-	-	-	-	-	-	
F2 E	1967-70	20 (3)	-	-	-	4	-	1	-	-	22

Best championship: 1970, 6th

Per-Viktor Widengren

S

Major wins: 1934 and 1935 Norwegian GP

Jaroslaw Wierczuk

PL. Born: 6.1.1977, Warsaw

1995 Polish F3 Champion

Peter Wieser

A. Born: 20.9.1966

1992 Austrian F3 Champion

Eppie Wietzes

CDN. Born: 28.5.1938, Assen (NL)

1981 Trans-Am Champion

formula	years	starts (DNS)	wins	2nd	3rd	4th	5th	6th	PP	FL	points
F1 W	1967-74	2	-	-	-	-	-	-	-	-	0

Best result: no finishes. Best qualifying: 17th. Teams: Lotus, Team Canada F1

| SC W | 1966-87 | | - | 1 | - | - | - | - | | | |

Howdy Wilcox

USA. Born: 24.6.1889, Crawfordsville, Indiana. Died: 4.9.1923, Altoona, Pennsylvania

formula	years	starts (DNS)	wins	2nd	3rd	4th	5th	6th	PP	FL	points
GP Pre-50	1915-16	2		1	1	-	-	-			

Win: 1916 American GP

| Indy 500 | 1911-23 | 11 | | 2 | - | - | - | 1 | 1 | - | |

Wins: 1919 and 1923 Indianapolis 500

Champcar wins: 4 – 1910 Indianapolis race 7, 1916 American GP, 1919 Indianapolis 500, 1923 Indianapolis 500

Mike Wilds

GB. Born: 7.1.1946, Chiswick, London

formula	years	starts (DNS)	wins	2nd	3rd	4th	5th	6th	PP	FL	points
F1 W	1974-76	3 (5)	-	-	-	-	-	-	-	-	0

Best result: no finishes. Best qualifying: 22nd. Teams: Dempster International, Ensign, Stanley BRM, Team PR Reilly

| Le Mans | 1981-88 | 7 | | - | - | - | - | - | | | |
| SC W | 1980-88 | | | - | - | - | 1 | - | | | |

Chris Williams

GB. Born: 1939, India. Died: 26.3.1969, Silverstone, testing

formula	years	starts (DNS)	wins	2nd	3rd	4th	5th	6th	PP	FL	points
F2 E	1968	2	-	-	-	-	1	-	-	-	2

Best championship: 1968, 17th

Jonathan Williams

GB. Born: 26.10.1942, Cairo (ET)

formula	years	starts (DNS)	wins	2nd	3rd	4th	5th	6th	PP	FL	points
F1 W	1967	1	-	-	-	-	-	-	-	-	0

Best result: 8th. Best qualifying: 16th. Team: Ferrari

Le Mans	1968-70	2		-	-	-	-	-			
SC W	1963-71			-	-	1	-	1	-		
F2 E	1968-69	3		-	-	-	-	-			0

"W Williams" (William Grover-Williams)

GB. Born: 16.1.1903, Montrouge, near Paris (F). Died: 18.3.1945, Paris, shot by Gestapo having been arrested on 2.8.1943

formula	years	starts (DNS)	wins	2nd	3rd	4th	5th	6th	PP	FL	points
GP Pre-50	1926-36	21 (1)	4	-	-	1	-	3	1	4	

Wins: 1928 French GP, 1929 Monaco GP, French GP, 1931 Belgian GP

Roger Williamson

GB. Born: 4.2.1948, Leicester. Died: 29.7.1973, Zandvoort, Dutch GP 1971 Lombark, 1972 Forward Trust and Shell British F3 Champion

formula	years	starts (DNS)	wins	2nd	3rd	4th	5th	6th	PP	FL	points
F1 W	1973	2	-	-	-	-	-	-	-	-	0

Best result: no finishes. Best qualifying: 18th. Team: March

| F2 E | 1972-73 | 9 (2) | 1 | - | - | - | - | - | 1 | 1 | 11 |

Win: 1973 Monza. Best championship: 1973, 10th

Simon Wills

NZ. Born: 3.10.1976, Auckland
1999 and 2000 Australian Formula Holden Champion, 1999 and 2000 New Zealand Gold Star Champion

Major wins: 1999 and 2000 New Zealand GP

Desire Wilson

ZA. Born: 26.11.1953, Johannesburg

formula	years	starts (DNS)	wins	2nd	3rd	4th	5th	6th	PP	FL	points
F1 W	1980	0 (1)	-	-	-	-	-	-	-	-	0

Best result: no starts. Best qualifying: 27th. Team: RAM

| Le Mans | 1982-91 | 3 | | - | - | - | - | - | | | |
| SC W | 1980-92 | | | 2 | - | 1 | 2 | - | | | |

Wins: 1980 Monza, Silverstone

| CART | 1983-86 | 11 (1) | | - | - | - | - | - | | | |

F1 GB win: 1980 Brands Hatch (only woman to win an F1 race)

Justin Wilson

GB. Born: 31.7.1978, Sheffield, Yorkshire
2001 FIA F3000 Champion

formula	years	starts (DNS)	wins	2nd	3rd	4th	5th	6th	PP	FL	points
F3000 INT	1999-2001	32	3	7	2	-	3	3	2	1	89

Wins: 2001 Interlagos, A1 Ring, Hungaroring. Best championship: 2001, 1st

Max Wilson

BR. Born: 22.8.1972, Hamburg (D)

formula	years	starts (DNS)	wins	2nd	3rd	4th	5th	6th	PP	FL	points
F3000 INT	1997-99	30 (1)	-	4	3	1	2	1	2	-	43

Best championship: 1997, 5th

| CART | 2001 | 15 (2) | - | - | - | 1 | - | - | - | - | |

Rob Wilson

NZ. Born: 6.9.1952
1990 Barber-SAAB Champion

Vic Wilson

GB. Born: 14.4.1931, Drypool, Kingston-upon-Hull. Died: 2002, Boca Raton, Florida (USA)

formula	years	starts (DNS)	wins	2nd	3rd	4th	5th	6th	PP	FL	points
F1 W	1960-66	1 (1)	-	-	-	-	-	-	-	-	0

Best result: no finishes. Best qualifying: 16th. Teams: Equipe Prideaux, Chamaco

Jean-Pierre Wimille

F. Born: 26.2.1908, Paris. Died: 28.1.1949, Buenos Aires GP practice

formula	years	starts (DNS)	wins	2nd	3rd	4th	5th	6th	PP	FL	points
GP Pre-50	1930-48	31	5	1	1	2	1	2	6	5	

Wins: 1936 French GP, 1947 Swiss GP, Belgian GP, 1948 French GP, Italian GP

| Le Mans | 1937-39 | 2 | 2 | - | - | - | - | - | | | 1 |

Wins: 1937 and 1939 Le Mans 24 hrs

Non-championship F1 win: 1948 Monza Autodrome GP

John Wingfield

GB. Born: c1943, Windsor. Died: 12.9.1976, Thruxton

formula	years	starts (DNS)	wins	2nd	3rd	4th	5th	6th	PP	FL	points
Le Mans	1968	1		-	-	-	-	-			
F2 E	1970-75	14 (7)		-	-	-	1	-	-	-	1

Best championship: 1972, 28th

Joachim Winkelhock

D. Born: 24.10.1960, Waiblingen, near Stuttgart
1994 Asia-Pacific Touring Car Champion, 1993 British Touring Car Champion, 1995 German Super Touring Car Champion, 1988 European F3 Cup winner, 1988 German F3 Champion

formula	years	starts (DNS)	wins	2nd	3rd	4th	5th	6th	PP	FL	points
F1 W	1989	0 (7)	-	-	-	-	-	-	-	-	0

Best result: no starts. Best qualifying: 35th. Team: AGS

| Le Mans | 1998-99 | 2 | 1 | - | - | - | - | - | | | |

Win: 1999 Le Mans 24 hrs

Other major wins: 1994 and 1998 Macau Guia race, 1995 Spa 24 hrs

Manfred Winkelhock

D. Born: 6.10.1951, Waiblingen, near Stuttgart. Died: 12.8.1985, Toronto hospital, following an accident during Mosport Park 1000 kms the previous day

formula	years	starts (DNS)	wins	2nd	3rd	4th	5th	6th	PP	FL	points
F1 W	1980-85	47 (9)	-	-	-	-	1	-	-	-	2

Best championship: 1982, 22nd. Best qualifying: 5th. Teams: Arrows, ATS, Brabham, RAM

| Le Mans | 1979-82 | 3 | | - | - | - | - | 1 | - | | |
| SC W | 1977-85 | | 1 | 1 | 1 | 1 | 4 | 1 | 2 | 1 | |

Win: 1985 Monza. Best championship: 1985, 9th

| F2 E | 1978-81 | 30 | - | 1 | 4 | 1 | 3 | - | 1 | 1 | 31 |

Best championship: 1978, 8th

Other major win: 1981 Macau Guia race

Billy Winn
USA. Born: c1905, Kansas City, Kansas. Died: 20.8.1938, Springfield, Illinois

formula	years	starts (DNS)	wins	2nd	3rd	4th	5th	6th	PP	FL	points
Indy 500	1931-38	8	-	-	-	-	-	1	-	-	

Champcar wins: 4 – 1934 Springfield, 1935 Springfield, Syracuse, 1937 Syracuse

"John Winter" (Louis Krages)
D. Born: 2.8.1949, Bremen. Died: 11.1.2001, Atlanta, Georgia, suicide
1986 Interserie Champion

formula	years	starts (DNS)	wins	2nd	3rd	4th	5th	6th	PP	FL	points
Le Mans	1978-93	10	1	-	1	1	-	-			

Win: 1985 Le Mans 24 hrs

SC W	1978-92		1	-	4	5	9	4	-	-	

Win: 1985 Le Mans 24 hrs. Best championship: 1988, 7th
Other major win: 1991 Daytona 24 hrs

Jens Winther
DK
1962 Danish 500cc Champion

formula	years	starts (DNS)	wins	2nd	3rd	4th	5th	6th	PP	FL	points
Le Mans	1983-86	4	-	-	-	-	-	-			

Bjorn Wirdheim
S. Born: 4.4.1980, Lund

formula	years	starts (DNS)	wins	2nd	3rd	4th	5th	6th	PP	FL	points
F3000 INT	2002	12	1	2	-	1	1	2	1	-	29

Win: 2002 Monza. Best championship: 2002, 4th

Reine Wisell
S. Born: 30.9.1941, Motala, near Linkoping
1967 Swedish F3 Champion

formula	years	starts (DNS)	wins	2nd	3rd	4th	5th	6th	PP	FL	points
F1 W	1970-74	22 (1)	-	-	1	2	1	1	-	-	13

Best championship: 1971, 9th. Best qualifying: 6th. Teams: Lotus, BRM, Pierre Robert, Clarke-Mordaunt-Guthrie-Durlacher, March

Le Mans	1969-74	4	-	-	-	-	-	-			
SC W	1969-81		-	-	1	1	4	-	1		
F2 E	1970-74	20 (2)	1	-	-	-	-	1	-	-	0

Win: 1973 Nurburgring

Spencer Wishart
USA. Born: 3.12.1889. Died: 22.8.1914, Elgin, Illinois

formula	years	starts (DNS)	wins	2nd	3rd	4th	5th	6th	PP	FL	points
GP Pre-50	1911-14	3	-	-	-	-	-	-			
Indy 500	1911-14	4	-	1	-	1	-	-			

Champcar win: 1 – 1912 Columbus

Bob Wollek
F. Born: 4.11.1943, Strasbourg. Died: 15.3.2001, Sebring, road accident
1983 European Endurance Champion, 1982, 1983 and 1989 German Racing Champion

formula	years	starts (DNS)	wins	2nd	3rd	4th	5th	6th	PP	FL	points
Le Mans	1968-2000	30	-	4	2	1	-	3	3	-	
SC W	1968-92		11	14	12	9	9	10	6	3	

Wins: 1977 Hockenheim, 1978 Dijon, Misano, Vallelunga, 1979 Mugello, Silverstone, Nurburgring, 1983 Monza, 1985 Spa, 1986 Brands Hatch, 1989 Dijon. Best championships: 1983 and 1985, 5th. GT FIA wins: 3 – 1994 Paul Ricard, Suzuka, Zhuhai

F2 E	1971-73	25 (5)	-	2	2	-	3	3	-	-	45

Best championship: 1973, 6th
Other major wins: 1983, 1985, 1989 and 1991 Daytona 24 hrs, 1985 Sebring 12 hrs

Glen Wood
USA. Born: 18.7.1925
NASCAR wins: 4

Jeff Wood
USA. Born: 20.1.1957, Wichita, Kansas
1985 North American Formula Atlantic (Western) Champion

formula	years	starts (DNS)	wins	2nd	3rd	4th	5th	6th	PP	FL	points
CART	1983-95	49 (16)									

Cliff Woodbury
USA. Born: 8.7.1894, Chicago, Illinois. Died: 13.11.1984, Alton, Illinois

formula	years	starts (DNS)	wins	2nd	3rd	4th	5th	6th	PP	FL	points
Indy 500	1926-29	4	-	-	1	-	1	-	1	-	

Champcar wins: 2 – 1928 Salem race 3, 1929 Detroit

Roy Woods
USA

formula	years	starts (DNS)	wins	2nd	3rd	4th	5th	6th	PP	FL	points
Le Mans	1979	1	-	-	-	-	-	-			
SC W	1977-81		-	1	1	1	-	-			

Major win: 1979 Sebring 12 hrs

Roelof Wunderink
NL. Born: 12.12.1948, Eindhoven

formula	years	starts (DNS)	wins	2nd	3rd	4th	5th	6th	PP	FL	points
F1 W	1975	3 (3)	-	-	-	-	-	-	-	-	0

Best result: no finishes. Best qualifying: 19th. Team: Ensign

Alexander Wurz
A. Born: 15.2.1974, Waithafen
1993 Austrian F3 Champion

formula	years	starts (DNS)	wins	2nd	3rd	4th	5th	6th	PP	FL	points
F1 W	1997-2000	52	-	1	5	3	1	-	1	-	26

Best championship: 1998, 7th. Best qualifying: 5th. Team: Benetton

Le Mans	1996	1	1	-	-	-	-	-			

Win: 1996 Le Mans 24 hrs
GT FIA win: 1 – 1997 Donington

Wuydts
B
1993 Belgian Belcar GT Champion (with Eliano and Koentges)

X

Jean Xhenceval
B
1976 European Touring Car Champion (with Pierre Dieudonne)

formula	years	starts (DNS)	wins	2nd	3rd	4th	5th	6th	PP	FL	points
Le Mans	1977-81	3	-	-	-	-	-	-			
SC W	1972-81		-	-	-	1	-	-			

Major wins: 1974 and 1975 Spa 24 hrs, 1976 Tourist Trophy (Silverstone)

Y

Caleb "Cale" Yarborough
USA. Born: 27.3.1939, Florence, South Carolina
1976, 1977 and 1978 NASCAR Champion, 1984 IROC Champion

formula	years	starts (DNS)	wins	2nd	3rd	4th	5th	6th	PP	FL	points
Le Mans	1981	1	-	-	-	-	-	-			
Indy 500	1966-72	4	-	-	-	-	-	-			

NASCAR wins: 83 (67 in Modern era) including 1977, 1983, 1984 Daytona 500

Lee Roy Yarbrough
USA. Born: 17.9.1938, Jacksonville, Florida. Died: 7.12.1984

formula	years	starts (DNS)	wins	2nd	3rd	4th	5th	6th	PP	FL	points
Indy 500	1967-70	3	-	-	-	-	-	-			

NASCAR wins: 14

Hisashi Yokoshima
J. Born: 28.12.1957, Ibaragi, Tokyo
1988 Japanese Touring Car Champion

formula	years	starts (DNS)	wins	2nd	3rd	4th	5th	6th	PP	FL	points
Le Mans	1991	1									

Alex Yoong
MAL. Born: 20.7.1976, Kuala Lumpur

formula	years	starts (DNS)	wins	2nd	3rd	4th	5th	6th	PP	FL	points
F1 W	2001-02	14 (4)	–	–	–	–	–	–	–	–	0

Best result: 7th. Best qualifying: 19th. Team: Minardi

| F3000 INT | 1999 | 2 (3) | – | – | – | – | – | – | – | – | 0 |

Z

Marco Zadra
I. Born: 27.6.1978, Milan
2001 Sports Racing World Champion
SRWC wins: 2 – 2001 Barcelona, Spa

Peter Zakowski
D. Born: 13.5.1966, Burgbrohl

formula	years	starts (DNS)	wins	2nd	3rd	4th	5th	6th	PP	FL	points
F3000 INT	1991	2 (1)	–	–	–	–	–	–	–	–	0

F3 E win: 1 – 1987 Knutstorp EFDA

Alessandro Zampedri
I. Born: 3.10.1969, Brescia

formula	years	starts (DNS)	wins	2nd	3rd	4th	5th	6th	PP	FL	points
F3000 INT	1992-93	18 (1)	–	–	1	–	2	–	–	–	8

Best championship: 1993, 11th

Indy 500	1995-97	3	–	–	–	1	–	–			
CART	1994-95	27 (1)	–	–	–	1	–	–			
IRL	1996-97	3	–	–	–	1	–	–			

Zampieri
I
Major win: 1927 Monza GP

Alessandro "Alex" Zanardi
I. Born: 23.10.1966, Bologna
1997 and 1998 CART Champion, 1990 European F3
Cup winner

formula	years	starts (DNS)	wins	2nd	3rd	4th	5th	6th	PP	FL	points
F1 W	1991-99	41 (3)	–	–	–	–	–	1	–	–	1

Best championship: 1993, 20th. Best qualifying: 4th. Teams: Jordan, Minardi, Lotus, Williams

| F3000 INT | 1989-91 | 11 | 2 | 4 | – | – | – | 3 | 3 | | 42 |

Wins: 1991 Vallelunga, Mugello. Best championship: 1991, 2nd

| CART | 1996-2001 | 66 (2) | 15 | 8 | 5 | 7 | – | 10 | | | 18 |

Wins: 1996 Portland, Mid-Ohio, Laguna Seca, 1997 Long Beach, Cleveland, US 500 (Michigan), Mid-Ohio, Elkhart Lake, 1998 Long Beach, St Louis, Detroit, Portland, Cleveland, Toronto, Surfers Paradise. Best championships: 1997 and 1998, 1st

Guillermo Zapata
MEX
2002 Mexican F3 Champion

Emilio Zapico
E. Born: 21.5.1944, Leon. Died: 6.8.1996, Huete, road accident

formula	years	starts (DNS)	wins	2nd	3rd	4th	5th	6th	PP	FL	points
F1 W	1976	0 (1)	–	–	–	–	–	–	–	–	0

Best result: no starts. Best qualifying: 27th. Team: Williams

Goffredo Zehender
I. Born: 1901, Reggio di Calabria. Died: 7.1.1958

formula	years	starts (DNS)	wins	2nd	3rd	4th	5th	6th	PP	FL	points
GP Pre-50	1928-38	24	–	–	3	2	4	3	–	–	
Le Mans	1928-56	3	–	–	–	–	–	–	–	–	

Major win: 1931 Spa 24 hrs

Norbert Zehnder
CH
1996 and 1997 Swiss F3 Champion

Jo Zeller
CH. Born: 17.7.1955
1982, 1984, 1990, 1991, 1992, 1995, 1998, 1999, 2000, 2001 and 2002 Swiss F3 Champion

Len Zengel
USA. Born: 1887, Ohio. Died: 24.9.1963, Bryn Mawr, Pennsylvania

formula	years	starts (DNS)	wins	2nd	3rd	4th	5th	6th	PP	FL	points
GP Pre-50	1908	1	–	–	–	–	–	–	–	–	
Indy 500	1911-12	2	–	–	–	–	–	1	–	–	

Champcar win: 1 – 1911 Elgin race 3

Emanuel Zervakis
USA. Born: 23.1.1930
NASCAR wins: 2

Daniel Zimmermann
DDR
1951 East German F3 Champion

Vittorio Zoboli
I. Born: 24.6.1968, Bologna

formula	years	starts (DNS)	wins	2nd	3rd	4th	5th	6th	PP	FL	points
F3000 INT	1990-93	17 (6)	–	–	–	1	–	–	–	–	3

Best championship: 1992, 13th

Ricardo Zonta
BR. Born: 23.3.1976, Curitiba
1997 FIA F3000 Champion, 1998 FIA GT Champion (with Klaus Ludwig), 2002 Dallara Nissan World Series Champion, 1995 Sud-Am F3 Champion

formula	years	starts (DNS)	wins	2nd	3rd	4th	5th	6th	PP	FL	points
F1 W	1999-2001	31 (1)	–	–	–	3	–	–	–	–	3

Best championship: 2000, 14th. Best qualifying: 6th. Teams: BAR, Jordan

| Le Mans | 1998 | 1 | – | – | – | – | – | – | – | – | |

GT FIA wins: 5 – 1998 Oschersleben, Dijon, A1 Ring, Homestead, Laguna Seca

| F3000 INT | 1996-97 | 20 | 5 | 2 | 2 | – | 1 | 1 | 5 | 6 | 66 |

Wins: 1996 Estoril, Mugello, 1997 Nurburgring, Hockenheim, Mugello. Best championship: 1997, 1st

Renzo Zorzi
I. Born: 12.12.1946, Ziano di Fiemme, near Turin

formula	years	starts (DNS)	wins	2nd	3rd	4th	5th	6th	PP	FL	points
F1 W	1975-77	7	–	–	–	–	–	1	–	–	1

Best championship: 1977, 19th. Best qualifying: 17th. Teams: Williams, Shadow

| SC W | 1974-85 | | – | – | – | – | 1 | 1 | 1 | 1 | |

F3 E win: 1 – 1975 Monaco F3

Paolo Zuccarelli
I. Born: 1886. Died: 19.6.1913, Amiens, French GP practice

formula	years	starts (DNS)	wins	2nd	3rd	4th	5th	6th	PP	FL	points
GP Pre-50	1912	1	–	–	–	–	–	–	–	–	
Indy 500	1913	1	–	–	–	–	–	–	–	–	

Major win: 1912 Unofficial French GP

Ricardo Zunino
RA. Born: 13.4.1949, Buenos Aires

formula	years	starts (DNS)	wins	2nd	3rd	4th	5th	6th	PP	FL	points
F1 W	1979-81	10 (1)	–	–	–	–	–	–	–	–	0

Best result: 7th. Best qualifying: 9th. Teams: Brabham, Tyrrell

| F2 E | 1977-79 | 26 (2) | – | – | – | – | 3 | 2 | – | – | 9 |

Best championship: 1978, 11th
F1 ZA win: 1979 Brands Hatch

WITHDRAWN